The United States
of America

MAINE

★ Augusta

Burlington
Montpelier • Portland
VT. N.H.
★ Concord
NEW ★ Manchester
YORK ★ Boston
MASS. ★ Providence
Albany ★ Hartford ★
CONN. R.I.

Lake Superior

Lake
of the
Woods

WISCONSIN
MICHIGAN

Lake Huron

Lake Michigan

★ St. Paul
...polis
★

Milwaukee ●
Lansing ●
Madison ★
Detroit ●

Chicago ●
Lake Ontario

Buffalo ●

Lake Erie

Cleveland ●

PENNSYLVANIA

New York ●

★ Trenton
Harrisburg ● Philadelphia
Pittsburgh ● NEW JERSEY
Wheeling ● Baltimore ● Dover
OHIO DELAWARE
Columbus ● Annapolis ★
Washington, D.C. MARYLAND

INDIANA
Indianapolis ★

Des Moines ★

ILLINOIS
Springfield ★
Cincinnati ●

WEST
VIRGINIA

...nsas City ●
Jefferson ★
City
St. Louis ●

Frankfort ★
Louisville ●
KENTUCKY

Charleston ●
Richmond ★
VIRGINIA
Norfolk ●

Chesapeake Bay

MISSOURI

ATLANTIC
OCEAN

Winston-Salem ●
Raleigh ★
Knoxville ●
Nashville ★
NORTH CAROLINA
Charlotte ●

ARKANSAS

Memphis ●
Chattanooga ●
SOUTH CAROLINA
Columbia ★
Little Rock ●
Atlanta ★
Charleston ●

Birmingham ●
MISSISSIPPI
ALABAMA
GEORGIA

Shreveport ●
Jackson ★
Montgomery ★

LOUISIANA
Mobile ●
Tallahassee ★
Jacksonville ●

Baton Rouge ★
New Orleans ●

FLORIDA

GULF OF MEXICO

Orlando ●
Tampa ●

Miami ●

BAHAMAS

Key West ●

CUBA

DOMINICAN
REPUBLIC

HAITI

APPALACHIAN MOUNTAINS

St. Lawrence R.

Connecticut R.

Hudson R.

Delaware R.

Mississippi R.

Cumberland R.

Tennessee R.

Land Elevation

Feet		Meters
10,000		3,000
5,000		1,500
2,000		600
1,000		300
500		150
0		0
Below Sea Level		Below Sea Level

ATLANTIC OCEAN
San Juan
VIRGIN ISLANDS
PUERTO RICO

| 0 | 50 | 100 Miles |
| 0 | 50 | 100 Kilometers |

| 0 | 200 | 400 Miles |
| 0 | 200 | 400 Kilometers |

Albers Equal-Area Projection

The Enduring Vision

A History of the American People   Fifth Edition

Paul S. Boyer
University of Wisconsin

Clifford E. Clark, Jr.
Carleton College

Joseph F. Kett
University of Virginia

Neal Salisbury
Smith College

Harvard Sitkoff
University of New Hampshire

Nancy Woloch
Barnard College

Houghton Mifflin Company   Boston   New York

Publisher: Charles Hartford
Editor-in-Chief: Jean Woy
Sponsoring Editor: Mary Dougherty
Senior Development Editor: Jennifer Sutherland
Editorial Associate: Noria Morales
Senior Project Editor: Bob Greiner
Editorial Assistant: Wendy Thayer
Senior Production/Design Coordinator: Jodi O'Rourke
Manufacturing Manager: Florence Cadran
Senior Marketing Manager: Sandra McGuire

Cover art: Thomas Moran (1837–1926), *The Grand Canyon of the Yellowstone,* 1872. Oil on canvas, 84 × 144 1/4 in. (231.0 × 266.3 cm). Lent by the Department of the Interior Museum. Smithsonian American Art Museum, Washington, DC, U.S.A.

Photo credit: Smithsonian American Art Museum, Washington, DC/Art Resource, NY.

Printed in the U.S.A.

Library of Congress Catalog Number: 2002109369

ISBN: 0-618-28064-2

123456789-VH-06 05 04 03

Brief Contents

Contents

18 The Rise of Industrial America, 1865–1900   543

19 Immigration, Urbanization, and Everyday Life, 1860–1900   575

20 Politics and Expansion in an Industrializing Age, 1877–1900   609

21 The Progressive Era, 1900–1917 641

22 Global Involvements and World War I, 1902–1920 677

Appendix 993

Additional Bibliography B-1

Photograph Credits C-1

Index I-1

Special Features

Maps

Figures

Tables

Preface

Much has changed in America and the world since we first began planning *The Enduring Vision* more than a decade ago. Some of these developments have been welcome and positive; others have been troubling and unsettling. In this new Fifth Edition, we fully document the scope of these changes, for good or ill. But we have also taken care to stress the continuities that can provide assurance and inspire hope in troubled times.

Although the United States of today is profoundly different from the nation of even a few decades ago, the determination to live up to the values that give meaning to America—among them freedom, social justice, tolerance for diversity, and equality of opportunity—remains a strong and vibrant force in our life as a people. Our desire to convey the strength of this enduring vision in a world of change has guided our efforts throughout the writing of this book.

For the Fifth Edition we have built on the underlying strategy that has guided us from the beginning. We want our version of U.S. history to be not only comprehensive and illuminating, but also lively, readable, and true to the actual lives of many earlier generations of Americans. We have maintained a clear political and chronological framework into which we integrate the best recent scholarship in all areas of American history. Our particular interest in social and cultural history, which looms large in the courses we ourselves teach at our various colleges and universities, has been a shaping force in *The Enduring Vision* from the outset, and it remains strongly evident in this Fifth Edition. This edition expands and integrates coverage of the historical experience of women, African-Americans, Hispanic Americans, Asian Americans, and American Indians—in short, of men and women of all regions, ethnic groups, and social classes who make up the American mosaic.

Organization

In a few key instances we have reorganized the chapter sequence so the narrative flows more smoothly and to assure full coverage of recent events. Two chapters on the late-nineteenth-century era, "The Transformation of Urban America" and "Daily Life, Popular Culture, and the Arts, 1860–1900," have been combined into one: Chapter 19, "Immigration, Urbanization, and Everyday Life, 1860–1900." Similarly, the two chapters on the 1930s have been consolidated into one taut chapter, Chapter 24, "The Great Depression and the New Deal, 1929–1939." This allows us to convey more directly how the economic crisis and the reform energies of the 1930s played out not only in Washington, D.C., but across American society and culture as a whole.

We also decided to shift some material among chapters to promote clarity and coherence. We moved the discussion of early twentieth-century foreign relations, including the Open Door notes to China and the building of the Panama Canal, into Chapter 22, "Global Involvements and World War I, 1902–1920," allowing us to trace America's expanding world role in those crucial years. Similarly, the diplomacy of the 1930s, which as the decade wore on focused heavily on the deepening foreign menace in Europe and Asia, formerly included in the chapter on the Great Depression and the New Deal, is now covered at the beginning of Chapter 25, "Americans and a World in Crisis, 1933–1945," which also deals with World War II.

Having restructured and tightened our treatment of earlier time periods, we were able to add a new concluding chapter, so that we now devote three full chapters to the eventful contemporary era, from Richard Nixon's resignation in 1974 to the present—a period of nearly thirty years. The energy crises of the 1970s, the ferment and controversies of the Reagan years, the end of the Cold War, new patterns of immigration, the economic transformation associated with the rise of the service economy and the revolution in information processing, the roller-coaster economy of the late 1990s and beyond, the deadly attack on America in September 2001, and even the corporate scandals and stock-market collapse of 2002 are now treated in full analytic detail.

New Interpretations, Expanded Coverage

The changes we have made in this latest edition of *The Enduring Vision* extend beyond simply a new chapter arrangement. In our planning we carefully assessed the coverage, interpretations, and analytic framework of the entire book, to be sure that it continues to incorporate the latest scholarship. We have been especially attentive to new work in social and cultural history, building on a strength of the book that instructors have long recognized.

As in earlier editions, our extensive coverage of environmental history, the land, and the West is fully integrated into the narrative, and treated analytically, not simply mechanically "tacked on" to a traditional account. We have incorporated the best of the new political history, stressing the social and economic issues at stake in politics, rather than simply recounting election results and party battles. We give close attention to America's emergence as a world power and the evolution of the nation's global role over time.

Building on a theme we have stressed from the beginning, this edition of *The Enduring Vision* pays even closer attention to the crucial role of science and technology in American history. From the hunting implements of the Paleo-Indians to the key inventions and manufacturing innovations of the industrial age and today's breakthroughs in information processing and genetic engineering, the applications of science and technology are central throughout the text. In addition, we have created a new feature, "Technology and Culture," to highlight key innovations in each stage of American history (see "Special Features" section, below).

Continuing one of the distinctive strengths of *The Enduring Vision*, we have also expanded coverage of the vital areas of medicine and disease. From the devastating epidemics brought by the first European explorers and settlers and the appalling health conditions of the industrial city to the rise of the public-health movement, the controversies over health-care financing, the AIDS crisis, bioethics debates, and much else, this central and growing area of research receives the attention it deserves in *The Enduring Vision*.

Revisions and Innovations in Each Chapter

A chapter-by-chapter glimpse of some of the changes in this edition highlights the depth of effort that went into its preparation.

Chapter 1 incorporates the latest archaeological findings relating to the earliest Native American peoples while a new section on Mesoamerica and South America places the discussion of North American Indians in a broader hemispheric perspective. Chapter 2 focuses more sharply on the emerging Atlantic world and offers revised discussions of West African and European societies and the Spanish invasions of Mexico and New Mexico.

Chapter 3 features a reorganized, more concise section on New England, a revised discussion of slavery and race in the Chesapeake, and an expanded treatment of the Pueblo Revolt. In Chapter 4 new material appears on patterns of consumption in colonial America and on slavery and African-American life, along with material from other chapters on the Tuscarora, Yamasee, and King George's Wars. A new section, "Public Life in British America" combines discussions of colonial politics, the Enlightenment, and the Great Awakening.

Chapter 5 has new material on the ideological underpinnings of colonial resistance to British rule and a discussion of African-Americans in the mid-eighteenth century, while Chapter 6 includes revised discussions of Native Americans and of state constitutions. In Chapter 7 we offer revised and expanded discussions of African-Americans and of white women, formerly discussed in Chapter 6.

In Chapter 8, we have added material on the Thomas Jefferson and Sally Hemings relationship and a greatly expanded discussion of Tecumseh and his reaction to the 1809 Treaty of Fort Wayne. In keeping with recent scholarship, Chapter 9 includes more on rural capitalism and how industrialization evolved out of a crisis in the New England countryside, as well as economic developments in the South. A section on northern free blacks and the A.M.E. church has been added as well.

To further the chronological flow of the work, the discussion of the Mormons in Chapter 10 ends with Joseph Smith's death in 1844, leaving the story of the great trek to Deseret for Chapter 13. In Chapter 11 we provide more attention to the development in the 1830s and 1840s of machine tools and the two industries that immediately benefited from them, the manufacture of guns and sewing machines. Chapter 13, which now starts with the Mormon trek, includes enhanced coverage of the Gold Rush.

Chapters 14, 15, and 16, on the Civil War and Reconstruction eras, include a new segment on the lives of Civil War soldiers, an expanded discussion of the experiences of Confederate women, new material on the start of woman-suffrage organizations during Reconstruction, and expanded treatment of postwar changes in plantation labor.

Chapter 17 incorporates new scholarship on the connections between western expansionism, Native Americans, and the environment in the trans-Mississippi West. In Chapter 18, on late-nineteenth-century industrialization, we have added a new section on the role of small manufacturers such as the furniture makers of Grand Rapids, Michigan, who could adapt quickly to new tastes and social trends.

Chapter 19, a melding of two chapters from the fourth edition, shows how industrialization, urbanization, and immigration transformed everyday life, sharpened racial and ethnic divisions, and made Americans more conscious of social class. Chapter 20 incorporates the latest scholarship on industrialization's impact on politics and foreign policy as well as new material on women's influence on the political ideology of the era. In Chapter 21, on the Progressive Era, we offer more coverage of urban popular culture; the woman-suffrage movement in the West; and the public-health aspects of Progressive reform, including more on the birth-control movement. Chapter 22 explores in greater analytic depth America's growing world role in the early twentieth century and World War I homefront developments, including the devastating influenza pandemic of 1918. The treatment of the 1920s in Chapter 23 offers more on the burgeoning consumer culture, including the importance of air conditioning, the growth of the cosmetics industry, the implications of the automobile for women, and the environmental impact of tourism. Republican domestic policy, the Immigration Act of 1924, the experience of Hispanic newcomers, and the larger impact of the terrible Mississippi River flood of 1927 all receive expanded coverage.

Chapter 24, on the 1930s, offers a newly integrated, single-chapter interpretive treatment of American life in the era of the Depression and New Deal. The Depression's human toll, with specific examples and quotations from ordinary Americans, is vividly evoked. The environmental consequences of New Deal public-works programs, particularly the great dams built in the West, are fully explored.

We have reorganized Chapter 25 to include the events of the 1930s leading up to World War II, as well to expand the treatment of the Holocaust and American minorities during wartime. Chapter 26 includes a new section on the GI Bill of Rights, while Chapter 27 enlarges the discussions of the postwar development of the West and of political conservatism, and adds new sections on TV culture, rock-and-roll, Native Americans, and Latinos and Latinas.

A restructured Chapter 28 now treats the key developments of the struggle for black equality and the Vietnam War in separate, comprehensive narratives. In this chapter we have also expanded the discussion of the women's movement and added sections on Asian Americans, Hispanic Americans, and Native Americans. Chapter 29 greatly expands the discussion of the Youth Movement and adds new sections on Kent State-Jackson State, the legacy of student activism, hippies and drugs, the musical revolution, and gay liberation—all topics of great interest to today's students.

Chapters 30 and 31 now cover the period from Nixon's resignation through the era of Bill Clinton's first term. Chapter 30 offers expanded treatment of popular culture in the 1970s and 1980s; the environmental history of the period, including the Alaska Lands Bill and the Love Canal crisis; the shift of the South into the Republican camp; and the Democratic party's move to the center. In Chapter 31 we analyze the Welfare Reform Act of 1996 and other important measures; draw on the 2000 Census to explore the social trends of the 1990s and beyond, including new immigration patterns, developments in rural America, and the experience of Hispanic-Americans, Asian-Americans, and other groups; and offer an interpretive perspective on the popular culture and religious trends of the contemporary era.

The final chapter, 32, presents an integrated narrative and preliminary assessment of recent events: the scandals and impeachment crisis of Clinton's second term, the "new economy," the speculative bubble of the later 1990s, the disputed 2000 presidential election, the domestic and international policies of the George W. Bush administration, the attack of September 11, 2001, and its aftermath, the worsening Mideast crisis, the scandals that gripped corporate America in late 2001 and 2002, and the 2002 midterm election.

Special Features

To underscore the centrality of technological change throughout American history, we have added a major new feature to the Fifth Edition. Seventeen "Technology and Culture" essays describe key innovations and their impact on American society and culture. In Chapter 8, for example, the "Mapping America" feature explains the importance of surveying techniques and cartography in mapping the vast lands of the new nation. The feature in Chapter 22 examines the development of sound-recording technology and explores the way it influenced the popular-music industry and helped build homefront morale during World War I. All the essays include focus questions at the end. (A full list of the Technology and Culture essays appears on p. xxi.)

The new Technology and Culture essays alternate with the popular "A Place in Time" feature found in earlier editions. We have added two new "Places in Time": one in Chapter 10 on the Shaker village at Alfred, Maine, and one in Chapter 17 on the Phoenix, New Mexico, Indian school.

Visual Resources and Aids to the Student

Complementing the innovations in content is a fresh new design, giving the Fifth Edition a strikingly contemporary look. The authors have selected scores of new photographs and other illustrations, many in color and many enlarged in size, not only to add visual appeal but to further the book's instructional value.

To help students gain an immediate sense of the chapter structure, a chapter outline has been added on the first page of each chapter. The focus questions are highlighted, further helping students grasp each chapter's key themes. For readers wishing to investigate a topic of interest on-line, an annotated listing of relevant websites appears in the "For Future Reference" section at the end of each chapter. The Chronologies now appear at the end of each chapter, alongside the Conclusions, to facilitate review.

A firm grasp of geography is central to an understanding of history, and we have given careful attention to the map program of the Fifth Edition. We have included seventeen new maps, including maps showing possible migration routes of the first Americans, nineteenth-century religious and utopian settlements, early industrialization, county-by-county settlement patterns of immigrants in 1910, the Interstate highway system, and present-day federal land ownership in the West. We have added fifteen new charts and graphs as well, illustrating important social developments such as changing patterns of work and major sources of immigration.

Supplementary Resources

In addition to the main text, *The Enduring Vision* offers instructors and students a wide array of ancillary resources. They have been developed with the diverse needs of today's students and instructors in mind, with comprehensive print and non-print resources available.

For Students:

- **Enduring Vision Student Website** has been redesigned and expanded for the Fifth Edition. On the interactive site, students will find ACE self-assessment quizzes, collapsible outlines, vocabulary flashcards, and skill-building activities centered on a map or figure from the textbook. In addition, a selection of the book's Places in Time and Technology and Culture features are posted on the site, along with questions to consider. Students can respond to the questions by emailing their instructor.

- **American Ethnic Identities Online Activities** is an exciting new addition to the Houghton Mifflin website, by Susan Oliver of Cerritos College. A.E.I. is a series of free-standing historical activities, to which students and instructors have access to from their respective *Enduring Vision* websites. Ranging from the "Making of British America" to "Cesar Chavez," these five-step interactive activities encourage the student to think about history within different ethnic themes, including African-American, American Indian, Latin American, Asian American, and Euro American. By asking the students to act as historians, integrating web-based resources with more traditional research, they take history "out of the book," which has more personal meaning for an increasingly diverse student body.

- *The Enduring Vision* @ history CD-ROM for students presents approximately 1,000 primary sources—text, audio, video, and animations—that cover the span of American history and include sources on political, social, economic, diplomatic, environmental, and cultural history. Half of these sources include suggested activities to be used for discussion or assignments, as well as a notepad with which a student may record questions or comments on particular sources. The contents of the CD-ROM have been selected and the activities prepared by Paula Petrik of the University of Maine and Kelly Woestman of Pittsburg State University.

- **The Student Guide with Map Exercises,** by Barbara Blumberg, offers students chapter outlines and summaries, vocabulary words and their definitions, identification suggestions, map exercises, skill-building activities, various historical sources for further research, and multiple-choice, short-answer, and essay questions, in two easy-to-carry volumes.

For Instructors:

- **The Enduring Vision Instructor Website** offers the *Instructor's Guide* by Penelope Harper and Robert Grant, an online manual summarizing chapter themes, offering lecture suggestions, teaching ideas and activities, as well as a guideline to teaching with *Enduring Voices* document sets. Instructors may also create exams from the online *Test Item File*, and presentations with online powerpoint slides.

- **American Ethnic Identities Online Activities,** by Susan Oliver, may be customized so the instructor may assign activities or steps to students, and receive completed assignments via email.

- **Classprep with HM Testing CD-ROM** is a comprehensive teaching tool, offering testing, lecture, and course planning resources. A computerized test bank is available complete with search functions. Now, instructors may design tests thematically, by entering keywords to bring up certain questions. Also available is the Instructor's Guide, Powerpoint Slides, and HM ImageBank, a selection of images from the book with additional pedagogy from the authors. These may be used in powerpoint slides to stimulate class discussion or to enhance a class presentation in an innovative way.

- *The Enduring Vision @history CD-ROM* for instructors includes everything on the student version plus additional notes suggesting ways to use a particular source with students. For instructors who want to create multimedia lectures and use these sources as presentation material, there are instructor notes as well as activity questions to pose to the student.

- **Test Item File,** by Kenneth Blume, is the complete testing resource for the book in print format, with multiple-choice, map exercises, and essay questions.

- *Enduring Voices* **Document Sets,** by Penelope Harper and James Lorence, is a two-volume reader organized to follow the chapter sequence of *The Enduring Vision* and presents discrete sets of primary sources, with each set built around a problem closely related to a major theme in the corresponding textbook chapter.

- **The Houghton Mifflin U.S. History Transparency Set** offers approximately 135 full-color maps and graphs.

Acknowledgments

In undertaking this major revision of our textbook, we have drawn on our own scholarly work and teaching experience (see "About the Authors"). We have also kept abreast of the most innovative and pathbreaking new work of historical interpretation, as reported by our U.S. history colleagues in their books, articles in historical journals, and papers at scholarly meetings. We list much of this new work in the annotated "For Further Research" sections at the close of each chapter, and in the Additional Bibliography at the end of the book.

We have also benefited from the comments and suggestions of instructors who have adopted *The Enduring Vision*; from students who have written or e-mailed us about specific details; and from the following scholars and teachers who offered systematic evaluations of specific chapters. Their perceptive comments have been most helpful in the revision process.

Elisabeth Ansnes, *San Jose State University*

Richard Aquila, *Ball State University*

Robert Becker, *Louisiana State University*

Bruce A. Castleman, *San Diego State University*

Jonathan Chu, *University of Massachusetts Boston*

Roger P. Davis, *University of Nebraska at Kearney*

Michael B. Dougan, *Arkansas State University*

Patience Essah, *Auburn University*

John M. Glen, *Ball State University*

Penelope Harper, *Louisiana State University*

Ari Kelman, *University of Denver*

Carolyn Lawes, *Old Dominion University*

Glenn Linden, *Southern Methodist University*

Ronald Rainger, *Texas Tech University*

Hal Rothman, *University of Nevada, Las Vegas*

Michael Steiner, *Northwest Missouri State University*

Robert Stinson, *Moravian College*

Richard Straw, *Radford University*

Tamara Thornton, *SUNY Buffalo*

Karin Wulf, *American University*

In addition, Clifford Clark would like to thank Colleen McFarland, reference librarian at Carleton College.

Finally, we would be sadly remiss if we failed to mention the skilled professionals at Houghton Mifflin Company whose expertise and enthusiastic commitment to this new Fifth Edition guided us through every stage of the process and helped sustain our own determination to make this the best book we could possibly write. Our warmest thanks, then, go to Jean Woy, Editor-in-chief for History, Political Science, and Economics, who offered shrewd suggestions and kept us focused on the big picture; sponsoring editor Mary Dougherty, who played a key role as we initially planned this new edition and continued to offer support and wise advice at every stage; Jennifer Sutherland, senior developmental editor, who with great skill and unfailing calm and good nature pushed us to do the tough work of rethinking each chapter and making every paragraph and every sentence models of clarity; Bob Greiner, senior project editor, who saw the work through the crucial production stages with

careful attention to detail and supportive good humor; Henry Rachlin, the senior designer responsible for the book's stunning visual appearance; Sandra McGuire, senior marketing manager, an enthusiastic supporter of *The Enduring Vision* from the beginning and one of its most able and effective advocates; the gifted editorial associate Noria Morales, who provided invaluable help in many ways, including supervising the supplements program, and who played a particularly important role at several crucial stages of the project; Wendy Thayer, editorial assistant, who provided support at every stage during production; and finally, Jodi O'Rourke and Florence Cadran, who supervised the quality while maintaining the schedule throughout. Pembroke Herbert and Sandi Rygiel of Picture Research Consultants & Archives brought their creative skills to bear in seeking out fresh and powerful photographic images for the work.

Paul S. Boyer
Clifford E. Clark, Jr.
Joseph F. Kett
Neal Salisbury
Harvard Sitkoff
Nancy Woloch

About the Authors

Paul S. Boyer, Merle Curti Professor of History emeritus at the University of Wisconsin, Madison, earned his Ph.D. from Harvard University. An editor of *Notable American Women, 1607–1950* (1971), he also coauthored *Salem Possessed: The Social Origins of Witchcraft* (1974), for which, with Stephen Nissenbaum, he received the John H. Dunning Prize of the American Historical Association. His other works include *Urban Masses and Moral Order in America, 1820–1920* (1978), *By the Bomb's Early Light: American Thought and Culture at the Dawn of the Atomic Age* (1985), *When Time Shall Be No More: Prophecy Belief in Modern American Culture* (1992), and *Promises to Keep: The United States since World War II*, 2nd ed. (1999). He is also editor-in-chief of the *Oxford Companion to United States History* (2001). His articles and essays have appeared in the *American Quarterly, New Republic,* and other journals. He has been a visiting professor at the University of California, Los Angeles, Northwestern University, and the College of William and Mary.

Clifford E. Clark, Jr., M.A. and A.D. Hulings Professor of American Studies and professor of history at Carleton College, earned his Ph.D. from Harvard University. He has served as both the chair of the History Department and director of the American Studies program at Carleton. Clark is the author of *Henry Ward Beecher: Spokesman for a Middle-Class America* (1978), *The American Family Home, 1800–1960* (1986), *The Intellectual and Cultural History of Anglo-America since 1789* in the *General History of the Americas,* and, with Carol Zellie, *Northfield: The History and Architecture of a Community* (1997). He also has edited and contributed to *Minnesota in a Century of Change: The State and Its People since 1900* (1989). A past member of the Council of the American Studies Association, Clark is active in the fields of material culture studies and historic preservation, and he serves on the Northfield, Minnesota, Historical Preservation Commission.

Joseph F. Kett, Commonwealth Professor of History at the University of Virginia, received his Ph.D. from Harvard University. His works include *The Formation of the American Medical Profession: The Role of Institutions, 1780–1860* (1968), *Rites of Passage: Adolescence in America, 1790–Present* (1977), *The Pursuit of Knowledge under Difficulties: From Self-Improvement to Adult Education in America, 1750–1990* (1994), and *The New Dictionary of Cultural Literacy* (2002), of which he is coauthor. A former History Department chair at Virginia, he also has partici-pated on the Panel on Youth of the President's Science Advisory Committee, has served on the Board of Editors of the *History of Education Quarterly,* and is a past member of the Council of the American Studies Association.

Neal Salisbury, professor of history at Smith College, received his Ph.D. from the University of California, Los Angeles. He is the author of *Manitou and Providence: Indians, Europeans, and the Making of New England, 1500–1643* (1982), editor of *The Sovereignty and Goodness of God,* by Mary Rowlandson (1997), and coeditor, with Philip J. Deloria, of *The Companion to American Indian History* (2002). He also has contributed numerous articles to journals and edited collections. Formerly chair of the History Department at Smith, he is active in the fields of colonial and Native American history, has served as president of the American Society for Ethnohistory, and coedits a book series, *Cambridge Studies in North American Indian History.*

Harvard Sitkoff, professor of history at the University of New Hampshire, earned his Ph.D. from Columbia University. He is the author of *A New Deal for Blacks* (1978), *The Struggle for Black Equality, 1954–1992* (1992), and *Postwar America: A Student Companion* (2000); coauthor of the National Park Service's *Racial Desegregation in Public Education in the United States* (2000) and *The World War II Homefront* (2003); and editor of *Fifty Years Later: The New Deal Reevaluated* (1984), *A History of Our Time*, 6th ed. (2002), and *Perspectives on Modern America: Making Sense of the Twentieth Century* (2001). His articles have appeared in the *American Quarterly, Journal of American History,* and *Journal of Southern History,* among others. A frequent lecturer at universities abroad, he has been awarded the Fulbright Commission's John Adams Professorship of American Civilization in the Netherlands and the Mary Ball Washington Professorship of American History in Ireland.

Nancy Woloch received her Ph.D. from Indiana University. She is the author of *Women and the American Experience* (1984, 1994, 1996, 2000, 2002), editor of *Early American Women: A Documentary History, 1600–1900* (1992, 1997, 2002), and coauthor, with Walter LaFeber and Richard Polenberg, of *The American Century: A History of the United States since the 1890s* (1986, 1992, 1998). She is also the author of *Muller v. Oregon: A Brief History with Documents* (1996). She teaches American history and American Studies at Barnard College, Columbia University.

Enduring Vision, Enduring Land

This is the story of America and of a vision that Americans have shared. One part of that vision was of the American land. For the Native Americans who spread over the land thousands of years ago, for the Europeans who began to arrive in the sixteenth century, and for the later immigrants who poured in by the tens of millions from all parts of the world, North America was a haven for new beginnings. If life was hard elsewhere, it would be better here. Once here, the immigrants continued to be lured by the land. If times were tough in the East, they would be better in the West. New Englanders migrated to Ohio; Ohioans migrated to Kansas; Kansans migrated to California. For Africans the migration to America was forced and brutal. But after the Civil War, newly freed African Americans embraced the vision and dreamed of traveling to a Promised Land of new opportunities. Interviewed in 1938, a former Texas slave recalled a popular verse that he and other blacks had sung when emancipated:

> I got my ticket,
> Leaving the thicket,
> And I'm a-heading for the Golden Shore!

For most of America's history, its peoples have celebrated the land—its beauty, its diversity, and its ability to provide sustenance and even wealth to those who tapped its resources. But within this shared vision were deep-seated tensions. Even Native Americans, who regarded the land and other natural phenomena as spiritual forces to be feared and respected, some-times depleted the resources on which they depended. Europeans and their

◀ **Snake Meridian, Chuck Forsman (1997)**
Human as well as non-human forces have molded even the most rugged American landscapes.

PROLOGUE OUTLINE

An Ancient Heritage

The Continent and Its Regions

A Legacy and a Challenge

descendants considered "nature" an alien force to be conquered and were even less restrained. The very abundance of America's natural resources led them to think of these resources as infinitely available and exploitable. In moving from one place to another, some sought to escape starvation or oppression, while others pursued wealth despite the environmental consequences. Regardless of their motives, migrants often left behind a land bereft of wild animals, its fertility depleted by intensive farming, its waters dammed and polluted or dried up altogether. If the land today remains part of some Americans' vision, it is only because they realize its vulnerability, rather than its immunity, to permanent destruction at the hands of people and their technology.

The vision of America has always included not only a love of the land but also a commitment to human freedom. To be sure, Americans' commitment to freedom has often been inconsistent. The Puritans who sought freedom of worship for themselves denied it to others. Southern whites who cheered the Declaration of Independence lived by the labor of enslaved blacks. The freedom afforded generations of westward-moving settlers came at the expense of Native Americans and their ways of life. Many a wealthy employer has conveniently forgotten that economic exploitation can extinguish freedom as effectively as political tyranny or military force. Through most of our history, girls and women—half the population—have been relegated to second-class status. Yet the battered vision has endured, prodding a sometimes reluctant nation to confront and explore its full meaning.

Freedom can be an empty and cheerless thing unless one is also part of a social group. Depicting the emotions of a nineteenth-century Norwegian immigrant farmwoman on the Great Plains, novelist O. E. Rölvaag captured this feeling of social isolation:

> A sense of desolation so profound settled upon her that she seemed unable to think at all. . . . She threw herself back in the grass and looked up into the heavens. But darkness and infinitude lay there, also—the sense of utter desolation still remained. . . . Suddenly, for the first time, she realized the full extent of her loneliness. . . .

In order to avoid or modify the most extreme forms of individual freedom, the vision for most Americans has also been one of community. Puritan leader John Winthrop, addressing a group of fellow immigrants aboard the *Arbella* on the way to America in 1630, eloquently summed up this dimension of the vision: "We must delight in each other, make others' conditions our own, rejoice together, mourn together, labor and suffer together: always having before our eyes our commission and community . . . as members of the same body."

The family, the town, the neighborhood, the church, the ethnic group, and the nation itself have been ways by which Americans have joined others as "members of the same body," reconciling their individual needs and desires with those of the group or community. Community is not just a high-sounding abstraction; it has political implications. If Americans are not only a fragmented collection of self-absorbed individuals but also a people, what obligations do they owe one another? What limitations on their freedom are they willing to accept in order to be part of a social group? In struggling with tough questions like these, they have further defined their vision of America.

Finally, this vision is one of renewal and new beginnings. The story of America is part of the human story, and thus it has dark and shameful passages as well as bright moments of achievement. Arrogance, injustice, callous blindness to suffering, and national self-delusion have all figured in American history. But balancing the times when the American people have lost their way are the moments when they found their bearings and returned to the hard task of defining what their society at its best might truly be.

The American vision, then, is not one of a foreordained national destiny unfolding effortlessly but rather of Americans' laborious, often frustrating struggle to define what their common life as a people should be. For all the failures and the wrong turns, it remains a vision rooted in hope, not despair. In 1980 Jesse de la Cruz, a Mexican-American woman who fought for years to improve conditions for California's migrant workers, summed up the philosophy that kept her going: "Is America progressing toward the better? . . . We're the ones that are gonna do it. We have to keep on struggling. . . . With us, there's a saying: La esperanza muere al último. Hope dies last. You can't lose hope. If you lose hope, that's losing everything."

No sentiment could better sum up the enduring vision of American history.

AN ANCIENT HERITAGE

"The land was ours before we were the land's." So begins "The Gift Outright," which poet Robert Frost read at President John F. Kennedy's inauguration in 1961. Frost's poem meditates on the interrelatedness of history, geography, and human consciousness. At first, wrote Frost, American settlers merely possessed the land; but then, in a subtle spiritual process, they became possessed by it. Only by entering into this deep relationship with the

land did their identity as a people fully take shape. Frost's poem speaks of the encounter of English colonists with a strange new continent of mystery and promise; but the land Europeans called the "New World" was in fact the homeland of Native American peoples whose ancestors had been "possessed by" the land for at least fifteen thousand years.

Frost does remind us, however, that to comprehend America's human past, we first must know the American land itself. The patterns of weather; the undulations of valley, plain, and mountain; the shifting mosaic of sand, soil, and rock; the intricate network of rivers, streams, and lakes—these have profoundly influenced U.S. history. North America's fundamental physical characteristics have shaped human events from the earliest migrations from Asia to the later cycles of agricultural and industrial development, the rise of cities, the course of politics, and even the basic themes of American literature, art, and music. Geology, geography, and environment are among the fundamental building blocks of human history.

Geologists trace the oldest known rocks on the continent back some 3 billion years when a single landmass, which they call Pangaea, encompassed Earth's dry surfaces (see Map P.1). The earliest life forms appeared about 500 million years ago, marking the transition from the earliest geologic era, the Precambrian, to the Paleozoic ("ancient life") era. Halfway between that remote age and the present, forests covered much of what would eventually be the United States. From this organic matter, America's enormous coal reserves would be created, the largest yet discovered in the entire world. Around 180 million years ago, during the Mesozoic ("middle life") era—the age of the dinosaurs—Pangaea began to break apart in a gradual process known as continental drift. Initially, North America and Eurasia formed one continent while South America, Africa, Antarctica, and Australia constituted a second. But as the process continued, the continents we know today slowly formed.

So enormous a gulf of time separates the origins of North America from the beginning of its human history that, if those 180 million years were compressed into the space of a single twenty-four-hour day, everything that has happened since the Indians' ancestors arrived would flash by in the last half-second before midnight, and America's history since Columbus would occupy about five-thousandths of a second.

Over millions of years after Pangaea's breakup, violent movements of Earth's crust thrust up the Pacific Coastal, Sierra Nevada, and Cascade ranges in what later became western North America. Active Pacific-rim

180 million years ago

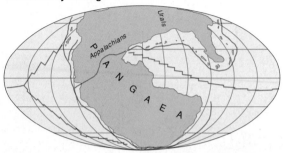

125 million years ago

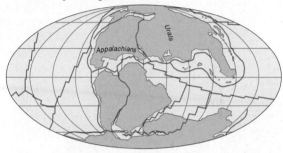

55 million years ago

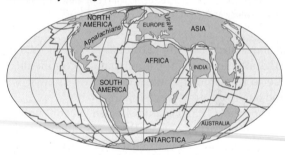

Today

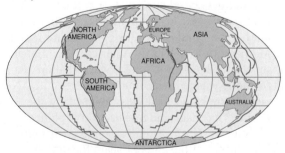

MAP P.1
Formation of the Continents
After the breakup of the supercontinent of Pangaea, drifting landmasses gradually formed today's continents.

Earthquake Damage, Los Angeles, 1994
Earthquakes forcefully remind us of the limits that Earth imposes on human ingenuity and technology.

volcanoes and powerful earthquakes all over the continent dramatically demonstrate that the continents continue to drift and that the world as we know it is not static but in a state of steady change.

The most cataclysmic known event in North American history occurred about 65 million years ago when a giant asteroid crashed into the Caribbean Sea off the coast of Mexico's Yucatán Peninsula. More than six miles in diameter and traveling fifteen miles per second, the asteroid generated such heat that it killed off most plants and animals, including dinosaurs, between the equator and the Arctic Circle, bringing an abrupt end to the Mesozoic era in North America. The meteorite's impact also reshaped the land. A vast, shallow sea that had formerly washed over much of west-central North America disappeared and was replaced by the Rocky Mountains. The decay and fossilization of plant and animal life created North America's once great petroleum deposits. It took thousands of years for new species to repopulate what was now a hot, tropical continent.

Cooling temperatures eventually brought further changes to North America, beginning about 33 million years ago. Then, about 2.8 million years ago, North and South America joined at the Isthmus of Panama, enabling hundreds of species on each continent to move into the other. As a result, opossums, porcupines, anteaters, and armadillos, among other species, found places for themselves in North America.

Between 2 million and twelve thousand years ago, as cooling continued, four periods of Arctic glacial expansion left a tremendous imprint on the land. The Ice Age staggers the imagination. During periods of maximum expansion, a carpet of ice as thick as thirteen thousand feet extended over most of Canada and crept southward into what is now New England, New York State, and much of the Midwest.

Like the slow but relentless shaping of the planet itself, the origins of the human species extend back to the mists of prehistoric time. Beginning at least two and half million years ago, ancestors of modern humans evolved in Africa. Beginning about one hundred thousand years ago, modern humans migrated throughout the Eastern Hemisphere. Between 33,000 and 15,000 B.C., small, mobile communities traveled by sea and land from Asia to Alaska, becoming the first Americans (see Chapter 1).

THE CONTINENT AND ITS REGIONS

As the glacial ice melted, raising the world's oceans to their present levels, North America slowly warmed. The ensuing differences in climate, physical features, soils and minerals, and organic life were the basis of America's geographic diversity (see Maps P.2, P.3, and P.4). As each region's human inhabitants utilized available resources, geographic diversity contributed to a diversity of regional cultures, first among American Indians and then among the immigrant peoples who spread across America after 1492. Taken together, the variety of these resources would also contribute to the rise to wealth and global preeminence of the United States.

The West

With its extreme climate and profuse wildlife, Alaska recalls the land that North America's earliest peoples encountered. Alaska's far north resembles a world from which ice caps have just retreated—a treeless tundra of grasses, lichens, and stunted shrubs. This region, the Arctic, appears as a stark wilderness in winter and is reborn in fleeting summers of colorful flowers and returning birds. In contrast, the subarctic of central Alaska is a heavily forested country known as taiga. Here rises North America's highest peak, 20,320-foot Mt. McKinley. Average temperatures in the subarctic range

Douglas Firs, Washington State
The impact of clear-cutting timber to meet worldwide demand for wood is made vividly clear in this photograph.

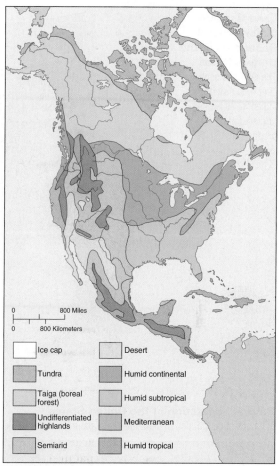

Ice cap	Desert
Tundra	Humid continental
Taiga (boreal forest)	Humid subtropical
Undifferentiated highlands	Mediterranean
Semiarid	Humid tropical

MAP P.2
North American Climatic Regions
America's variety of mostly temperate climates is key to its environmental and economic diversity.

from the fifties above zero Fahrenheit in summer to well below zero in the long, dark winters, and the soil is permanently frozen except during summer surface thaws and where, ominously, global warming has had an effect.

The Pacific coastal region is in some ways a world apart. Vegetation and animal life, isolated from the rest of the continent by mountains and deserts, include many species unfamiliar farther east. Warm, wet westerly winds blowing off the Pacific create a climate more uniformly temperate than anywhere else in North America. From Anchorage and the Alaska panhandle to south of San Francisco Bay, winters are cool, humid, and foggy, and the coast's dense forest cover includes the largest living organisms on Earth, the giant redwood trees. Along the southern California coast, winds and currents generate a warmer, Mediterranean climate, and vegetation includes a heavy growth of shrubs and short trees, scattered stands of oak, and grasses able to endure prolonged seasonal drought.

To the east of the coastal region, the rugged Sierra Nevada, Cascade, and coastal ranges stretch the length of Washington, Oregon, and California. Their majestic peaks trap abundant Pacific Ocean moisture that is carried eastward by gigantic clockwise air currents. Between the ranges nestle flat, fertile valleys— California's Central Valley (formed by the San Joaquin and Sacramento Rivers), Oregon's Willamette Valley, and

the Puget Sound region in Washington—that have been major agricultural centers in recent times.

Still farther east lies the Great Basin, encompassing Nevada, western Utah, southern Idaho, and eastern Oregon. The few streams here have no outlet to the ocean. An inland sea holding glacial meltwater, a remnant of which survives in Utah's Great Salt Lake, once covered much of the Great Basin (see Map P.5). Today, however, the Great Basin is dry and severely eroded, a cold desert rich in minerals and imposing in its austere grandeur and lonely emptiness. North of the basin, the Columbia and Snake Rivers, which drain the plateau country of Idaho and eastern Washington and Oregon, provide plentiful water for farming.

Western North America's "backbone" is the Rocky Mountains. The Rockies form part of the immense mountain system that reaches from Alaska to the Andes

MAP P.3
Land Use and Major Mineral Resources in the United States

The land has been central to America's industrial as well as agricultural productivity.

Dominant Land Use

- Farming and dairying
- Range livestock
- Forests
- Nonagricultural land
- Industrial regions

Major Mineral Occurrences

- **Ag** Silver
- **Au** Gold
- **C** Coal
- **Cu** Copper
- **P** Petroleum
- **G** Natural gas

MAP P.4
Natural Vegetation of the United States

The current distribution of plant life came about only after the last Ice Age ended, c. 10,000 B.C., and Earth's climate warmed.

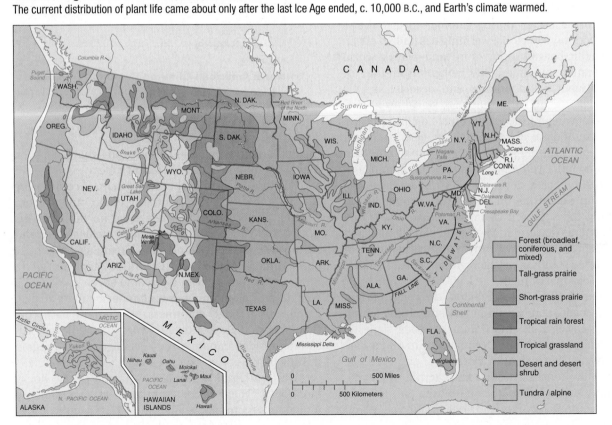

- Forest (broadleaf, coniferous, and mixed)
- Tall-grass prairie
- Short-grass prairie
- Tropical rain forest
- Tropical grassland
- Desert and desert shrub
- Tundra / alpine

0   500 Miles
0   500 Kilometers

of South America. Elevations in the Rockies rise from a mile above sea level in Denver, Colorado, at their foot to permanently snowcapped peaks more than fourteen thousand feet above sea level. Beyond the front range of the Rockies lies the Continental Divide, the watershed separating the rivers flowing eastward into the Atlantic from those draining westward into the Pacific. The climate and vegetation of the Rocky Mountain high country resemble that of the Arctic and subarctic regions.

Arizona, southern Utah, western New Mexico, and southeastern California form America's southwestern desert. The climate is arid, searingly hot on summer days and cold on winter nights. Adapted to stringent environmental conditions, many plants and animals that thrive here could not survive elsewhere. Dust storms, cloudbursts, and flash floods have everywhere carved, abraded, and twisted the rocky landscape. Works of fantastic geological sculpture appear on the most monumental scale in the Grand Canyon, where the Colorado River has been cutting down to Precambrian bedrock for 20 million years. In the face of such tremendous natural forces, human activity might well seem paltry and transitory. Yet it was in the Southwest that Native Americans cultivated the first crops in what is now the continental United States.

The Heartland

North America's heartland comprises the area extending eastward from the Rockies to the Appalachians. This vast region forms one of the world's largest drainage systems. From it the Great Lakes empty into the North Atlantic through the St. Lawrence River, and the Mississippi-Missouri-Ohio river network flows southward into the Gulf of Mexico. By facilitating the transportation of peoples and goods, the heartland's network of waterways have supported commerce and communication among

MAP P.5 Lakes and Marshes in the Great Basin During the Last Ice Age
The Great Basin's extensive lakes and marshes during the last Ice Age contrast starkly with the diminished amount of surface water in the region today.

peoples for centuries—before the arrival of Europeans as well as since.

The Mississippi—the "Father of Waters" to nearby Native Americans, and one of the world's longest rivers—carries a prodigious volume of water and silt. It has changed course many times. Southward from its junction with the Ohio River, the Mississippi meanders constantly, depositing rich sediments throughout its

Mississippi River Flood, 1993, at Davenport, Iowa
The river's most severe floods disrupt human routines in cities as well as in the countryside.

broad, ancient floodplain. It has carried so much silt over the millennia that in its lower stretches, the river flows above the surrounding valley, which it periodically floods when its high banks (levees) are breached. Over millions of years, such riverborne sediment covered what was once the westward extension of the Appalachians in northern Mississippi and eastern Arkansas. Only the Ozark Plateau and Ouachita Mountains remain exposed, forming the hill country of southern Missouri, north-central Arkansas, and eastern Oklahoma.

Below New Orleans the Mississippi empties into the Gulf of Mexico through an enormous delta with an intricate network of grassy swamps known as bayous. The Mississippi Delta offers rich farm soil capable of supporting a large population. Swarming with waterfowl, insects, alligators, and marine plants and animals, this environment has nurtured a distinctive way of life for the Indian, white, and black peoples who have inhabited it.

North of the Ohio and Missouri Rivers, themselves products of glacial runoff, Ice Age glaciation molded the American heartland. Because the local terrain was generally flat prior to glaciation, the ice sheets distributed glacial debris quite evenly. Spread even farther by wind and rivers, this fine-ground glacial dust slowly created the fertile farm soil of the Midwest. Glaciers also dug out the five Great Lakes (Superior, Huron, Michigan,

Tennessee Strip Mining
The impact of human hands is dramatically apparent in this Appalachian hill country scene.

Ontario, and Erie), collectively the world's largest body of fresh water. Water flowing from Lake Erie to the lower elevation of Lake Ontario created Niagara Falls, a testimony like the Grand Canyon to the way that water can shape a beautiful landscape.

Most of the heartland's eastern and northern sectors were once heavily forested. To the west thick, tallgrass prairie covered Illinois, parts of adjoining states, and much of the Missouri River basin and the middle Arkansas River basin (Oklahoma and central Texas). Beyond the Missouri the prairie gave way to short-grass steppe—the Great Plains, cold in winter, blazing hot in summer, and often dry. The great distances that separate the heartland's prairies and Great Plains from the moderating effects of the oceans continue to make this region's annual temperature range the most extreme in North America. As one moves westward, elevations rise gradually; trees grow only along streambeds; long droughts alternate with violent thunderstorms and tornadoes; and water and wood are ever scarcer.

Now much of this forested, grassy world is forever altered. The heartland has become open farming country. Gone are the flocks of migratory birds that once darkened the daytime skies of the plains; gone are the free-roaming bison. Forests now only fringe the heartland: in the lake country of northern Minnesota and Wisconsin, on Michigan's upper peninsula, and across the hilly uplands of the Appalachians, southern Indiana, and the Ozarks. The settlers who displaced the region's Indian inhabitants have done most of the plowing of prairie grass and felling of trees since the early nineteenth century. Destruction of the forest and grassy cover has made the heartland both a "breadbasket" for the world market and, during intervals of drought, a bleak "dust bowl."

The Atlantic Seaboard

The eastern edge of the heartland is formed by the ancient Appalachian Mountain chain, which over the course of 210 million years has been ground down to gentle ridges paralleling one another southwest to northeast. Between the ridges lie fertile valleys such as Virginia's Shenandoah. The Appalachian hill country's wealth is in thick timber and mineral beds—particularly the Paleozoic coal deposits—whose heavy exploitation since the nineteenth century has accelerated destructive soil erosion in this softly beautiful, mountainous land.

Descending gently from the Appalachians' eastern slope is the Piedmont region. In this broad, rolling upland extending from Alabama to Maryland, the rich, red soil has been ravaged in modern times by excessive

cotton and tobacco cultivation. The Piedmont's modern piney-woods cover constitutes "secondary growth," replacing the sturdy hardwood trees that Native Americans and pioneering whites and blacks once knew. The northward extension of the Piedmont from Pennsylvania to New England has more broadleaf vegetation and a harsher winter climate, and was shaped by glacial activity. The terrain in upstate New York and New England comprises hills contoured by advancing and retreating ice, and numerous lakes scoured out by glaciers. Belts of rocky debris remain, and in many places granite boulders shoulder their way up through the soil. Though picturesque, the land is the despair of anyone who has tried to plow it.

From southeastern Massachusetts and Rhode Island to south-central Alabama runs the fall line, at which rivers fall quickly to near sea level as they pass from the hard rock of the upland interior to the softer sediment of the coastal plain. Over time in many of the rivers, the abrupt fall has made rapids that block navigation upstream from the coast.

The character of the Atlantic coastal plain varies strikingly from south to north. At the tip of the Florida peninsula in the extreme south, the climate and vegetation are subtropical. The southern coastal lands running north from Florida to Chesapeake Bay and the mouth of the Delaware River compose the tidewater region. This is a wide, rather flat lowland, heavily wooded with a mixture of broadleaf and coniferous forests, ribboned with numerous small rivers, occasionally swampy, and often miserably hot and humid in summer. North of Delaware Bay, the coastal lowlands narrow and flatten to form the

New Jersey pine barrens, Long Island, and Cape Cod—all created by the deposit of glacial debris. Here the climate is noticeably milder than in the interior. North of Massachusetts Bay, the land back of the immediate shoreline becomes increasingly mountainous.

Many large rivers drain into the Atlantic—the St. Lawrence, flowing out of the Great Lakes northeastward through eastern Canada; the Connecticut in New England; the Hudson, Delaware, Susquehanna, and Potomac in what are now the Middle Atlantic states; the Savannah in the South. Most of these originally carried glacial meltwater. The Susquehanna and the Potomac filled in the broad, shallow Chesapeake Bay, teeming with marine life and offering numerous anchorages for oceangoing ships.

North America's true eastern edge is not the coastline but the offshore continental shelf, whose relatively shallow waters extend as far as 250 miles into the Atlantic before plunging deeply. Along the rocky Canadian and Maine coasts, where at the end of the Ice Age the rising ocean half-covered glaciated mountains and valleys, oceangoing craft may find numerous small anchorages. South of Massachusetts Bay, the Atlantic shore and the Gulf of Mexico coastline form a shoreline of sandy beaches and long barrier islands paralleling the mainland. Tropical storms boiling up from the open seas regularly lash North America's Atlantic shores, and at all times brisk winds make coastal navigation treacherous.

Crossing the Atlantic east to west can daunt even skilled mariners, particularly those battling against powerful winds by sail. Here, on one of the world's stormiest seas, the mighty Gulf Stream current sweeps

Fisherman, Gloucester, Massachusetts
The depletion of fish in the North Atlantic and elsewhere is dooming not just an occupation but a deep-seated way of life.

from southwest to northeast. Winds off the North American mainland also trend steadily eastward, and dangerous icebergs floating south from Greenland's waters threaten every ship. Little wonder that in 1620 the Mayflower Pilgrims' first impulse on landing was to sink to their knees and thank God for having transported them safely across "the vast and furious ocean." Many a vessel went to the bottom.

For millions, the Atlantic coastal region of North America offered a welcome. Ancient Indian hunters and more recent European colonists alike found its climate and its abundance of food sources alluring. Offshore, well within their reach, lay such productive fishing grounds as the Grand Banks, off Newfoundland, and Cape Cod's coastal bays, where cool-water upwellings on the continental shelf had lured swarms of fish and crustaceans. "The abundance of sea-fish are almost beyond believing," wrote a breathless English settler in 1630, "and sure I should scarce have believed it, except I had seen it with my own eyes."

acceleration of population growth, intensive agriculture, industrialization, urbanization, and hunger for material goods—processes that are exhausting resources and polluting the environment at levels that endanger human health and well-being.

In searching for ways to avoid environmental catastrophe, Americans would do well to recall the Native American legacy. Although Indians often wasted, and occasionally exhausted, a region's resources to their detriment, their practices generally encouraged the renewal of plants, animals, and soil over time. Underlying these practices were Indians' beliefs that they were spiritually related to the land and all living beings that shared it. In recapturing a sense that the life-sustaining bounty and soul-sustaining beauty of the land is itself of inestimable value, not merely a means to the end of material growth, future American generations could reestablish a sense of continuity with their Native American precursors. Thereby they could truly be possessed by the land instead of simply being its possessors.

A LEGACY AND A CHALLENGE

North America's fertile soil, extensive forests, and rich mineral resources long nourished visions of limitless natural abundance that would yield limitless wealth to its human inhabitants. Such visions have contributed to the

Abandoned "Rust Belt" Factory
The American landscape is littered with reminders that large-scale factory production has ended or been diminished in many industries.

CHRONOLOGY	
3,000,000,000 B.P. (before present)	Formation of oldest known rocks in Pangaea landmass.
500,000,000 B.P.	Precambrian era ends; Paleozoic era begins.
	Earliest forms of animal life appear.
225,000,000 B.P.	Paleozoic era ends; Mesozoic era begins.
210,000,000 B.P.	Appalachian Mountains emerge.
180,000,000 B.P.	Pangaea begins to break up.
65,000,000 B.P.	Asteroid strikes Earth in Caribbean Sea.
	Mesozoic era ends; Cenozoic era begins.
	Rocky Mountains form.
20,000,000 B.P.	Grand Canyon begins to form.
2,800,000 B.P.	North and South America join at Isthmus of Panama.
2,500,000 B.P.	Earliest humans appear in Africa.
2,000,000 B.P.	Ice Age begins.
100,000 B.P.	Modern humans begin to spread throughout Eastern Hemisphere.
33,000–15,000 B.C.	Earliest Native Americans arrive in Western Hemisphere.
c. 13,000 B.C.	Native Americans established throughout Western Hemisphere.
c. 10,000 B.C.	Ice Age ends.

The Enduring Vision

CHAPTER 1

Native Peoples of America, to 1500

Hiawatha was in the depths of despair. For years his people, a group of five Native American nations known as the Iroquois, had engaged in a seemingly endless cycle of violence and revenge. Iroquois families, villages, and nations fought one another, and neighboring Indians attacked relentlessly. When Hiawatha tried to restore peace within his own Onondaga nation, an evil sorcerer caused the deaths of his seven beloved daughters. Grief-stricken, Hiawatha wandered alone into the forest. After several days, he experienced a series of visions. First he saw a flock of wild ducks fly up from the lake, taking the water with them. Hiawatha walked onto the dry lakebed, gathering the beautiful purple-and-white shells that lay there. He saw the shells, called wampum, as symbolic "words" of condolence that, when properly strung into belts and ceremonially presented, would soothe anyone's grief, no matter how deep. Then he met a holy man named Deganawidah (the Peacemaker), who presented him with several wampum belts and spoke the appropriate words—one to dry his weeping eyes, another to open his ears to words of peace and reason, and a third to clear his throat so that he himself could once again speak peacefully and reasonably. Deganawidah and Hiawatha took the wampum to the five Iroquois nations. To each they introduced the ritual of condolence as a new message of peace. The Iroquois subsequently submerged their differences and created a council of chiefs

◀ **Anasazi Wicker Basket with Turquoise Mosaic**
Anasazi artisans in the Southwest crafted fine objects like this basket from the tenth through mid-twelfth centuries (*Pueblo Bonito, Chaco Canyon*).

CHAPTER OUTLINE

The First Americans,
c. 13,000–2500 B.C.

Cultural Diversity,
ca. 2500 B.C.–A.D. 1500

North American Peoples on the Eve
of European Contact

and a confederacy based on the condolence ritual. Thus was born the powerful League of the Iroquois.

Although the story of Hiawatha and Deganawidah was retold by speakers through the generations but not written down until the late nineteenth century, it depicts a concrete event in American history. Archaeological findings corroborate the sequence of bloody warfare followed by peace, and date the league's origins at about A.D. 1400. Visionary Indian prophets continued to emerge among the Iroquois and other Native American peoples during the centuries after 1492. As with all of American history before Europeans brought their system of writing, archaeological evidence, oral traditions, and cultural patterns—examined critically—are our principal sources of evidence.

The founding of the League of the Iroquois represents one moment in a long history that began more than ten thousand years before Christopher Columbus reached America in 1492. It is also an example of the remarkable cultural diversity that had come to characterize the Western Hemisphere's indigenous peoples. Adapting to varied and changing environments, some Native Americans lived in small, mobile bands of hunter-gatherers. Others resided in seasonal or permanent villages where they grew crops, fished for salmon, or processed acorns. Still others lived in larger towns or even in cities. While the smallest bands were relatively egalitarian, in most societies leaders came from prominent families. In the largest societies, hereditary chiefs, kings, and emperors ruled far-flung peoples.

Underlying their diversity, Native Americans had much in common. First, they identified themselves primarily as members of multigenerational families rather than as individuals or (except in the very largest societies) subjects of governments. Second, most emphasized reciprocity and mutual obligation rather then coercion as means of maintaining harmony within and between communities. Third, they perceived the entire universe, including nature, as sacred. These core values arrived with the earliest Americans and persisted beyond the invasions of Europeans and their sharply contrasting ideas. Throughout their long history, Native Americans reinforced their commonalties through exchanges of material goods, new technologies, and religious ideas.

This chapter will focus on three major questions:

■ What factors prompted the transition from Paleo-Indian to Archaic ways of life among the earliest Americans?

■ How did the varied environments of the Western Hemisphere shape the emergence of a wide diversity of Native American cultures?

■ What common values and practices did Native Americans share, despite their vast diversity?

THE FIRST AMERICANS, C. 13,000–2500 B.C.

Precisely how and when the vast Western Hemisphere was first settled remains uncertain. Many Indians believe that their ancestors originated in the Americas, but most scientific theories point to the arrival of peoples from northeastern Asia during the last Ice Age (c. 33,000–10,500 B.C.), when land linked Siberia and Alaska. Thereafter, as the Ice Age waned and Earth's climate warmed, Native Americans (like their contemporaries in the Eastern Hemisphere) adapted to environments ranging from frigid to tropical. Though divided into small, widely scattered groups, they interacted through trade and travel. Over several thousand years, Indians learned from one another and developed ways of life that had much in common despite their diverse linguistic, ethnic, and historical backgrounds.

Peopling New Worlds

Among several theories of the peopling of America, two predominate (see Map 1.1). One theory holds that Siberian hunters, pursuing game animals, crossed the expanse of land linking Asia with North America during the last Ice Age, arriving only around 10,500 B.C. According to this theory, the hunters made their way through a glacial corridor, dispersing themselves over much of the Western Hemisphere. There they discovered a hunter's paradise in which megafauna—giant mammoths, mastodons, horses, camels, bison, caribou, and moose—roamed, innocent of the ways of human predators. A second theory, based on recent archaeological finds, suggests that the first humans arrived much earlier by boat, following the then-continuous coast to Alaska and progressing southward. At various points along the way, groups stopped and either settled nearby or traveled inland to establish new homes. Coastal sites as far south as Monte Verde, in Chile, reveal evidence from about 10,500 B.C. of peoples who fed on marine life, birds, small mammals, and wild plants, as well as on the occasional mastodon. Most archaeologists and other scientists now conclude that the earliest Americans

arrived in multiple migrations by both these routes. In light of the most recent discoveries, it is probable that Americans had arrived by 13,000 B.C., if not earlier.

Most Native Americans are descended from the earliest migrants, but the ancestors of some came later, also from northeastern Asia. Peoples speaking a language known as Athapaskan settled in Alaska and northwestern Canada in about 7000 B.C. Some Athapaskan speakers later migrated to the Southwest to form the Apaches and Navajos. After 3000 B.C., non-Indian Eskimos, or Inuits, and Aleuts began crossing the Bering Sea from Siberia to Alaska.

MAP 1.1
The Peopling of the Americas
Scientists postulate two probable routes by which the earliest peoples reached America. By 9500 B.C., they had settled throughout the Western Hemisphere.

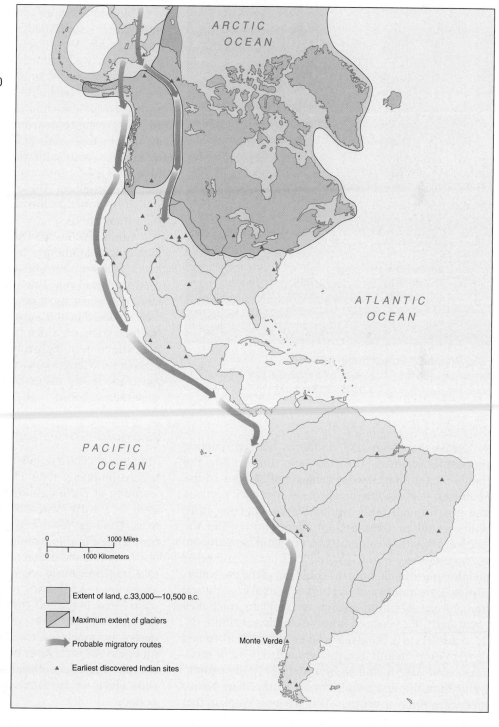

"Sky Woman," Ernest Smith (1936)
A visual depiction of the Iroquois people's account of their origins, in which a woman fell from the sky to a watery world.

Native American oral traditions offer conflicting support for scientists' theories, depending on how the traditions are interpreted. Pueblos and Navajos in the Southwest tell how their forebears experienced perilous journeys through other worlds before emerging from underground in their present homelands, while the Iroquois trace their ancestry to a pregnant woman who fell from the "sky world." Among the Iroquois and other peoples, the original humans could not settle the water-covered planet until a diving bird or animal brought soil from the ocean bottom, creating an island on which they could walk. The Haida of British Columbia attribute rising seawaters to a "flood tide woman" whose work forced them to move inland to higher ground. Still other traditions recall large mammals, monsters, or "hairy people" with whom the first people shared Earth. Many Native Americans today insist that such accounts confirm that

their ancestors originated in the Western Hemisphere. However, other Indians note that the stories do not specify a place of origin and may well reflect the experiences of their ancestors as they journeyed from Asia, across water, ice, and unknown lands, and encountered large mammals before settling in their new homes. If not taken literally, they maintain, the traditions reinforce rather than contradict scientists' theories.

Paleo-Indians, as archaeologists call the earliest Americans, established the foundations of Native American life. Most Paleo-Indians appear to have traveled within well-defined hunting territories in bands consisting of several families and totaling about fifteen to fifty people. Men hunted, while women prepared food and cared for the children. Bands left their territories when traveling to quarries to obtain favored materials for making tools and spear points. There they encountered other bands, with whose members they exchanged ideas and goods, intermarried, and participated in religious ceremonies. These encounters enabled Paleo-Indians to develop a broad cultural life that transcended their small bands.

Around 9000 B.C. many species of megafauna, including mammoths, mastodons, horses, and giant bison, suddenly became extinct. Although scholars formerly believed that Paleo-Indian hunters killed off the large mammals, most now maintain that the mammals were doomed by the warming climate, which disrupted the food chain on which they depended. In other words, the extinction of big-game mammals was part of environmental changes associated with the end of the Ice Age. Among the major beneficiaries of these changes were human beings.

Archaic Societies

After about 8000 B.C., peoples throughout the Americas began modifying their Paleo-Indian ways of life. The warming of Earth's atmosphere continued until about 4000 B.C., with far-reaching global effects. Sea levels rose, flooding low-lying coastal areas, while glacial runoff filled interior waterways. As the glaciers receded northward, so did the arctic and subarctic environments that had previously extended into what are now the lower forty-eight states of the United States. Treeless plains and evergreen forests gave way to deciduous forests in the East, grassland prairies on the Plains, and desert in much of the West. Grasslands in South America's Amazon River basin were replaced by a tropical rain forest. The immense range of flora and fauna with which we are familiar today emerged during this period.

Archaic peoples, as archeologists term Native Americans who flourished in these new environments, lived off the wider varieties of smaller mammals, fish, and wild plants that were now available. Using the resources of their environments more efficiently, communities required less land area and supported larger populations. Even peoples in the most extreme environments, such as deserts and the Arctic, while still traveling in small bands, now hunted smaller game and gathered wild plants. Indians in more temperate regions made even more drastic changes, with some residing in year-round villages. From about 3900 to 2800 B.C., for example, the 100 to 150 residents of a community near Kampsville, Illinois, obtained ample supplies of fish, mussels, deer and other mammals, birds, nuts, and seeds without leaving home.

Over time, Archaic Americans sharpened some distinctions between women's and men's roles. Men took responsibility for fishing as well as hunting, while women procured wild plant products. Gender roles are apparent in burials at Indian Knoll, in Kentucky, where tools relating to hunting, fishing, woodworking, and leatherworking were usually buried with men and those relating to cracking nuts and grinding seeds with women. Yet gender-specific distinctions did not apply to all activities, for objects used by religious healers were distributed equally between male and female graves.

Archaic Indians—women in most North American societies—honed their skills at harvesting wild plants. Through generations of close observation, they determined how to weed, prune, irrigate, transplant, burn, and otherwise manipulate their environments to favor plants that provided food and medicine. They also developed specialized tools for digging and grinding as well as more effective methods of drying and storing seeds. By 5000 B.C.—well before farming reached Europe—some Native American farmers were planting selected seeds for future harvesting.

The most sophisticated early plant cultivators lived in Mesoamerica (Mexico and Central America), particularly in the highland valleys of Tehuacan and Tamaulipas. Indians there cultivated squash, gourds, beans, chili peppers, and several species of fruits before 3000 B.C. At around this time, Tehuacan farmers began experimenting with a lowlands plant called teosinte. Some teosinte seeds grew in the mountain valleys, while others failed to grow. The successful seeds eventually evolved into a distinct but related species, called maize or corn. The earliest ears of maize were about the size of an adult human finger—much smaller than the corn we know today.

Maize agriculture quickly spread from Tehuacan. By 2500 B.C., Indians were growing it elsewhere in Mexico and Central America, in the Amazon River basin, and as far north as what is now New Mexico. Although maize itself was not yet grown elsewhere in North America, Indians cultivated squash and gourds in Missouri and Kentucky. Similarly, maize did not reach South America for several more centuries, but Andean peoples already cultivated potatoes; Amazonians grew manioc, a starchy root crop; and Pacific coastal dwellers harvested squash, beans, and peppers.

For a thousand years after plants were first domesticated, crops made up only a small part of Native Americans' diets. Meat, fish, and wild plants still predominated. Farming developed over many centuries before becoming any society's primary source of food.

CULTURAL DIVERSITY, C. 2500 B.C.–A.D. 1500

After about 2500 B.C., many Native Americans moved beyond the ways of their Archaic forebears. The most far-reaching transformation occurred among peoples whose cultivated crops were their primary sources of food. Farming in some of these societies was so intensive that it radically changed the environment. Some nonfarming as well as farming societies transformed trade networks into extensive religious and political systems linking several—sometimes dozens of—local communities. Some of these groupings evolved into formal confederacies and even hierarchical states. In environments where food sources were few and widely scattered, mobile bands survived by hunting, fishing, and gathering.

Mesoamerica and South America

As Mesoamerican farmers developed their methods, the quantity and quality of their crops increased. Annual production tripled at Tehuacan and Tamaulipas from 2500 to 2000 B.C., and selective breeding of maize resulted in larger ears. Farmers also planted beans alongside maize. The beans eaten released an amino acid, lysine, in the maize that further heightened its nutritional value. Higher yields and improved nutrition led some societies to center their lives around farming. Over the next eight centuries, maize-based farming societies spread throughout Mesoamerica.

After 2000 B.C., some Mesoamerican farming societies produced crop surpluses that they traded to less-populous, nonfarming neighbors. Expanding their trade contacts, a few of these societies established formal

exchange networks that enabled them to enjoy more wealth and power than their partners. After 1200 B.C., a few communities, such as those of the Olmecs in Mesoamerica (see Map 1.2) and Chavín de Huántar in the Andes (see Map 1.3), developed into large urban centers, subordinating smaller neighbors. Unlike earlier egalitarian societies, Indian cities were highly unequal, with thousands of residents dominated by a few wealthy elites and with hereditary rulers claiming kinship with religious deities. Laborers built elaborate religious temples and palaces, including the earliest pyramids in the Americas, and artisans created statues of the rulers and the gods.

Although the hereditary rulers exercised absolute power, their realms were limited to a few closely clustered communities. Anthropologists term such political societies chiefdoms, as opposed to states in which centralized, hierarchical power and institutions extend across broad spans of territory. Chiefdoms eventually emerged over much of the Americas, from the Miss-

issippi valley to the Amazon valley and the Andes Mountains. A few states arose in Mesoamerica after A.D. 1 and in South America after A.D. 500. Although men ruled most chiefdoms and states, women served as chiefs in some Andean societies until the Spanish arrived.

From capital cities with thousands of inhabitants, states centered at Monte Albán and Teotihuacán in Mesoamerica (see Map 1.2) and at Wari in the Andes (see Map 1.3) drafted soldiers and waged bloody wars of conquest. Bureaucrats administered state territories, collected taxes, and managed huge public works projects. Priests conducted ceremonies in enormous temples and presided over religious hierarchies extending throughout the states. The capital of the largest early state, Teotihuacán, was situated about fifty miles northeast of modern Mexico City and numbered about a hundred thousand people at the height of its power between the second and seventh centuries A.D. At its center was a complex of pyramids, the largest of which, the Sun

MAP 1.2

Major Mesoamerican Cultures, c. 1000 B.C..–A.D.1519

The Aztecs consolidated earlier Mesoamerican cultural traditions. They were still expanding when invaded by Spain in 1519.

Pyramid, was about 1 million cubic meters in volume. Teotihuacán dominated the peoples of the valley of Mexico, and its trade networks extended over much of modern-day Mexico. Although Teotihuacán declined in the eighth century, it exercised enormous influence on the religion, government, and culture of its neighbors.

Teotihuacán's greatest influence was on the Maya, whose kingdom-states flourished from southern Mexico to Honduras between the seventh and fifteenth centuries. The Maya moved far beyond their predecessors in developing a calendar, a numerical system (which included the concept of zero), and a system of phonetic, hieroglyphic writing. Mayan scribes produced thousands of codices (singular, codex) in the form of pieces of bark paper glued into long, folded strips. The codices and other books recorded religious ceremonies, historical traditions, and astronomical observations.

Other powerful states flourished in Mesoamerica and South America until the fifteenth century, when two mighty empires arose to challenge them. The first was the empire of the Aztecs (known at the time as the Mexica), who had migrated from the north during the thirteenth century and settled on the shore of Lake Texcoco as subjects of the local inhabitants. Overthrowing their rulers in 1428, the Aztecs went on to conquer other cities around the lake and extended their domain to the Gulf Coast (see Map 1.2). The Aztec expansion took a bloody turn in the 1450s during a four-year drought, which the Aztecs interpreted as a sign that the gods, like themselves, were hungry. Aztec priests maintained that the only way to satisfy the gods was to serve them human blood and hearts. From then on, conquering Aztec warriors sought captives for sacrifice in order, as they believed, to nourish the gods.

A massive temple complex at the capital of Tenochtitlan formed the sacred center of the Aztec empire. The Great Temple consisted of two joined pyramids and was surrounded by several smaller pyramids and other buildings. Aztec culture reflected both Mesoamerican tradition and the multicultural character of the state. Most of the more than two hundred deities they honored originated with earlier and contemporary societies, including those they had subjugated. They based their system of writing on the one developed centuries before at Teotihuacán and their calendar on that of the Maya.

To support the nearly two hundred thousand people residing in and around Tenochtitlan, the Aztecs maximized their production of food. They drained swampy areas and added rich soil from the lake bottom to the *chinampas* (artificial islands) that formed. The highly fertile *chinampas* enabled Aztec farmers to supply the

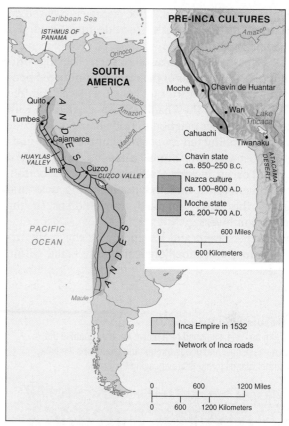

MAP 1.3

Major Andean Cultures, 900 B.C.–A.D.1432
Despite the challenges posed by the rugged Andes Mountains, native peoples there developed several complex societies and cultures, culminating in the Inca Empire.

Sun Pyramid, Teotihuacán
Built over several centuries, this pyramid remained the largest structure in the Americas until after the Spanish arrived.

urban population with food. Aztec engineers devised an elaborate irrigation system to provide fresh water for both people and crops.

The Aztecs collected taxes from subjects living within about a hundred miles of the capital. Conquered peoples farther away paid tribute, which replaced the free exchanges of goods they had formerly carried on with the Aztecs and other neighbors. Trade beyond the Aztec domain was conducted by *pochteca*, professional merchants who traveled in armed caravans. The *pochteca* sought salt, cacao, jewelry, feathers, jaguar pelts, cotton, and precious stones and metals, including gold and turquoise, the latter obtained from Indians in the American Southwest.

The Aztecs were still expanding in the early sixteenth century, but rebellions constantly flared within their realm. They had surrounded and weakened, but not subjugated, one neighboring rival, while another blocked their westward expansion. Might the Aztecs have expanded still farther? We will never know because, seemingly from out of nowhere, Spanish *conquistadores* arrived in 1519 to alter forever the course of Meso-american history (see Chapter 2).

Meanwhile, another empire had arisen far to the south. From their sumptuous capital at Cuzco, the Inca people conquered and subordinated societies over much of the Andes and adjacent regions after 1438. One key to the Incas' expansion was their ability to produce and distribute a wide range of surplus crops, including maize, beans, potatoes, and meats. They constructed terraced irrigation systems for watering crops on uneven terrain, perfected freeze-drying and other preservation techniques, built vast storehouses, and constructed a vast network of roads and bridges. The Inca were still expanding when they were violently crushed in the sixteenth century by another, even more far-flung empire, the Spanish.

The Southwest

The Southwest (including the modern American Southwest and most of northern Mexico) is a uniformly arid region with a variety of landscapes. Waters from rugged mountains and forested plateaus follow ancient channels through vast expanses of desert on their way to the gulfs of Mexico and California. The amount of water has fluctuated over time, depending on climatic conditions, but securing water has always been a challenge for southwestern peoples. Nevertheless, some of them augmented their supplies of water and became farmers.

Maize reached the Southwest via Mesoamerican trade links by about 2500 B.C. Yet full-time farming began only after 400 B.C., when the introduction of a more drought-resistant strain enabled some farmers to move from the highlands to drier lowlands. In the centuries that followed, southwestern populations rose, and Indian cultures were transformed. The two most influential new cultural traditions were the Hohokam and the Anasazi.

The Hohokam emerged during the third century B.C., when ancestors of the Pima and Tohono O'odham Indians began farming in the Gila and Salt River valleys of southern Arizona. Hohokam peoples built irrigation canals that enabled them to harvest two crops a year, an unprecedented feat in the arid environment. To construct and maintain their canals, the Hohokam organized large, coordinated work forces. They built perma-

Inca Suspension Bridge
Bridges like this one, sketched by a native Andean, enabled the Incas to move people and goods through the mountains. An Inca administrator stands to the left, overseeing the bridge.

nent towns, usually consisting of several hundred people. Although many towns remained independent, others joined confederations in which several towns were linked by canals. The central village in each confederation coordinated labor, trade, religion, and political life for all member communities.

Although a local creation, Hohokam culture drew extensively on Mesoamerican materials and ideas. From about the sixth century A.D., the large villages had ball courts and platform mounds similar to those in Mesoamerica at the time. Mesoamerican influence was also apparent in the creations of Hohokam artists, who worked in clay, stone, turquoise, and shell. Archaeologists have uncovered rubber balls, macaw feathers, cottonseeds, and copper bells from Mesoamerica at Hohokam sites.

The culture of the Anasazi, a Navajo term meaning ancient ones, originated during the first century B.C.. in the Four Corners area where Arizona, New Mexico, Colorado, and Utah meet. By around A.D. 700, the Anasazi people were harvesting crops, living in permanent villages, and making pottery. Thereafter, they expanded over a wide area and became the most powerful people in the Southwest.

One of the distinguishing characteristics of Anasazi culture was its architecture. Anasazi villages consisted of extensive complexes of attached apartments and storage rooms, along with kivas, partly underground structures in which men conducted religious ceremonies. To this day, Anasazi-style apartments and kivas are central features of Pueblo Indian architecture in the Southwest.

The height of Anasazi culture occurred between about 900 and 1150, during an unusually wet period in the Southwest. In Chaco Canyon, a cluster of twelve large towns forged a powerful confederation numbering about fifteen thousand people. A system of roads radiated from the canyon to satellite towns as far as sixty-five miles away. The roads were perfectly straight; their builders even carved out stairs or footholds on the sides of steep cliffs rather than go around them. By controlling rainwater runoff through small dams and terraces, the towns fed themselves as well as the satellites. The largest of the towns, Pueblo Bonito, had about twelve hundred inhabitants and was the home of two Great Kivas, each about fifty feet in diameter. People traveled over the roads from the satellites to Chaco Canyon's large kivas for religious ceremonies. The canyon was also a major trade center, importing and exporting a wide range of materials from and to Mesoamerica, the Great Plains, the Mississippi valley, and California.

The classic Anasazi culture, as manifested at Chaco Canyon, Mesa Verde in southwestern Colorado, and other sites, came to an end in the twelfth and thirteenth centuries. Although other factors contributed, the overriding cause of the Anasazi demise was drought. As has often happened in human history, an era of especially

Pueblo Bonito, Chaco Canyon, New Mexico
Pueblo Bonito illustrates the richness and grand scale of Anasazi architecture.

abundant rainfall, which the Anasazi thought would last forever, abruptly ended. Without enough water, the highly concentrated inhabitants abandoned the great Anasazi centers, dispersing to form new, smaller pueblos. Their descendants would encounter Spanish colonizers three centuries later (see Chapter 2). Other concentrated communities, including the Hohokam, also dispersed when drought came. With farming peoples now clustered in the few areas with enough water, the drier lands of the Southwest attracted the nonfarming Apaches and Navajos, whose arrival at the end of the fourteenth century ended their long migration from the far north (mentioned above).

The Eastern Woodlands

In contrast to the Southwest, the Eastern Woodlands—the vast expanse stretching from the Mississippi valley to the Atlantic Ocean—had abundant water. Water and deciduous forests provided Woodlands Indians with a rich variety of food sources, while the region's extensive river systems facilitated long-distance communication and travel. As a result, many eastern Indians established populous villages and complex confederations well before adopting full-time, maize-based farming.

By 1200 B.C., about five thousand people lived at Poverty Point on the lower Mississippi River. The town featured earthworks consisting of two large mounds and six concentric embankments, the outermost of which spanned more than half a mile in diameter. During the spring and autumn equinoxes, a person standing on the larger mound could watch the sun rise directly over the village center. As in some Mesoamerican societies at the time, solar observations were the basis for religious beliefs and a calendar.

Poverty Point was the center of a much larger political and economic unit. The settlement imported large quantities of quartz, copper, obsidian, crystal, and other sacred materials from long distances for redistribution to nearby communities. These communities almost certainly supplied some of the labor for the earthworks. Poverty Point's general design and organization indicate Olmec influence from Mesoamerica (see above). Poverty Point flourished for about three centuries and then declined, for reasons unknown. Nevertheless, it foreshadowed later developments in the Eastern Woodlands.

A different kind of mound-building culture, called Adena, emerged in the Ohio valley around 400 B.C. Adena villages were smaller than Poverty Point, rarely exceeding four hundred inhabitants. But Adena people spread over a wide area and built hundreds of mounds, most of them containing graves. The treatment of Adena dead varied according to social or political status. Some corpses were cremated; others were placed in round clay basins; and still others were given elaborate tombs.

After 100 B.C. Adena culture evolved into a more complex and widespread culture known as Hopewell, which spread from the Ohio valley to the Illinois River valley. Some Hopewell centers contained two or three dozen mounds within enclosures of several square miles. The variety and quantity of goods buried with

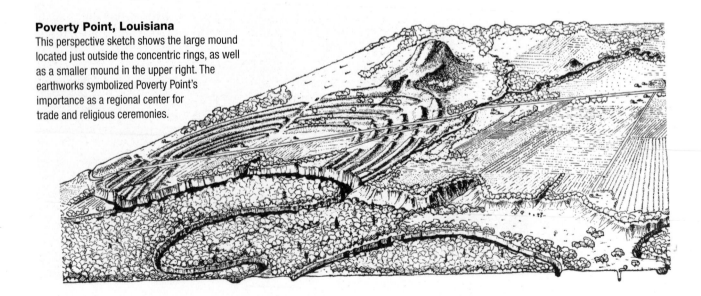

Poverty Point, Louisiana
This perspective sketch shows the large mound located just outside the concentric rings, as well as a smaller mound in the upper right. The earthworks symbolized Poverty Point's importance as a regional center for trade and religious ceremonies.

Hopewell Mounds, Mound City, Ohio
Many Hopewell earthworks that served as temples remain visible today in the Ohio valley.

members of the elite were also greater. Hopewell elites were buried with thousands of freshwater pearls or copper ornaments or with sheets of mica, quartz, or other sacred substances. Hopewell artisans fashioned fine ornaments and jewelry, which their owners wore in life and took to their graves. The raw materials for these objects originated in locales throughout America east of the Rockies. Through far-flung trade networks, Hopewell religious and technological influence spread to communities as far away as Wisconsin, Missouri, Florida, and New York. Although the great Hopewell centers were abandoned by about 600 (for reasons that are unclear), they had an enormous influence on subsequent developments in eastern North America.

The peoples of Poverty Point and the Adena and Hopewell cultures did little farming. Indian women in Kentucky and Missouri had cultivated small amounts of squash as early as 2500 B.C., and maize first appeared east of the Mississippi by 300 B.C.. But agriculture did not become a dietary mainstay for Woodlands people until between the seventh and twelfth centuries A.D., as women moved beyond gathering and minor cultivating activities to become the major producers of food.

The first full-time farmers in the East lived on the floodplains of the Mississippi River and its major tributaries. Beginning around A.D. 700, they developed a new culture, called Mississippian. The volume of Mississippian craft production and long-distance trade dwarfed that of the Adena and Hopewell peoples. As in Mesoamerica, Mississippian centers, numbering hundreds or even thousands of people, arose around open plazas. Large platform mounds adjoined the plazas, topped by sumptuous religious temples and the residences of chiefs and other elites. Religious ceremonies focused on the worship of the sun as the source of agricultural fertility. The people considered chiefs to be related to the sun. When a chief died, his wives and servants were killed so that they could accompany him in the afterlife. Largely in connection with their religious and funeral rituals, Mississippian artists produced highly sophisticated work in clay, stone, shell, copper, wood, and other materials.

After A.D. 900, Mississippian centers formed extensive networks based on river-borne trade and shared religious beliefs, each dominated by a single metropolis. The most powerful such system centered around Cahokia located near modern St. Louis (see A Place in Time: Cahokia in 1200).

For about two and a half centuries, Cahokia reigned supreme in the Mississippi valley. After A.D. 1200, however, Cahokia and other valley centers experienced shortages of food and other resources. As in the Southwest, densely concentrated societies had taxed a fragile environment with a fluctuating climate. One result was competition for suddenly scarce resources, which led to debilitating warfare and the undermining of Cahokia and

Between the tenth and thirteenth centuries, a city of about twenty thousand people flourished near the confluence of the Mississippi and Missouri Rivers. Called Cahokia, it filled more than 6 square miles and contained more than 120 earthworks. At its center, a four-terraced structure called Monk's Mound covered 15 acres (more than the Great Pyramids of Egypt) and rose a hundred feet at its highest point. Surrounding the city, a 125-square-mile metropolitan area encompassed ten large towns and more than fifty farming villages. In addition, Cahokia dominated a vast network of commercial and political alliances extending over much of the American heartland.

Cahokia's beginnings lay in the seventh century A.D., as Native Americans in the East were shifting to farming as their primary means of procuring food. In search of better soil, several small villages moved to the low flood-plain extending eastward from the Mississippi around what is now the Illinois side of greater St. Louis. Around A.D. 900, these villages began their transformation into a city with the construction of several mounds. Two centuries later, a stockade enclosed Monk's Mound and numerous other public structures, and most of the city's residents lived outside the walled precincts.

Cahokia was ideally situated for preeminence in mid-America. Its fertile land yielded surplus agricultural crops, which the women harvested, and the river provided rich supplies of fish and mussels. Game and wild plants abounded in nearby uplands. The city had ready access not only to the Mississippi and Missouri Rivers but also to the Ohio and Illinois Rivers, where Adena and Hopewell peoples had previously developed extensive trade networks based on shared religious beliefs. Cahokia and other Mississippian societies drew on Hopewell beliefs and new ideas from Mexico as they erected even more complex political, economic, and

religious institutions. By the twelfth century, some scholars believe, Cahokia was the capital of a potential nation-state.

Archaeology provides evidence of what Cahokians made and left in the ground as well as clues to their social structure, trade networks, and beliefs. Work gangs collected soil for the mounds with shovels made of wood and stone and carried the dirt in baskets to construction sites, often more than half a mile away. Much of the work force for this backbreaking labor undoubtedly was drawn from neighboring towns, which also contributed agricultural surpluses to feed specialized artisans and elites in the city. The artisans produced pottery, shell beads, copper ornaments, clothing, stone tools, and a range of other goods. Indians brought the raw materials for these objects from locations throughout eastern and central North America as tribute—payment by societies subordinated by Cahokia—or in return for the finished

Cahokia Woman Grinding Food
This five-inch-tall figurine, carved from bauxite stone around 1200, depicted a woman using a mortar and pestle to prepare food, probably corn.

Cahokia Mounds
This contemporary painting conveys Cahokia's grand scale. Not until the late eighteenth century did another North American city (Philadelphia) surpass the population of Cahokia, c. 1200.

products. The coordination of labor, trade, and other activities also required a sizable class of managers or overseers. Atop all these were the political and religious leaders, whose overpowering roles are confirmed by eighteenth-century French accounts of a similar society among the Natchez Indians near Louisiana.

Archaeologists also find evidence of social ranking at Cahokia in the treatment of the dead. Most people were buried in mass graves outside the city, but more prestigious commoners were placed in ridge-top mounds, and those of highest status in conical mounds. In the most remarkable mound, a man was laid out on a platform of twenty thousand beads made from shells originating in the Gulf of Mexico. He was surrounded by bushels of mica from the Appalachians, a sheet of rolled copper from Lake Superior, and quivers of arrows from communities throughout the Mississippi valley. This extraordinary man did not go to his grave alone. An adjacent pit contained the bodies of fifty young females in their late teens and early twenties; another held the remains of four men whose heads and hands were cut off; and a third included three men and three women. French witnesses describe how, when a Natchez ruler died, his wife, servants, guards, and others personally attached to him were killed so that they could accompany him in the afterlife. The people called this ruler the Great Sun to denote his position as an earthly representative of the sun, the central focus of Mississippian religion. This burial and others at Cahokia appear to be based on similar beliefs.

By 1200 Cahokia had reached its peak. During the century that followed, it declined in size and power, while other centers in the Southeast and Midwest surpassed it. Although the causes of this decline are not certain, the archaeological evidence provides clues. First, neighboring communities were straining to produce enough crops to feed themselves and the many Cahokians who did not grow their own food. Second, the city's demands for fuel and construction materials were seriously reducing the supply of wood in and around Cahokia. This depletion of the forests also deprived residents of the animals and wild plants on which they depended for food. Third, the strengthening of the stockade surrounding central Cahokia suggests that the elites were facing a military challenge from inside or outside the city, or both. Finally, the trade networks that formerly brought tribute to Cahokia and carried away the city's finished products had collapsed. Taken together, these trends indicate that a combination of environmental factors and resistance to centralized authority probably led to Cahokia's downfall. By the time the French explorer La Salle passed through in 1682 (see Chapter 3), Cahokia was a small village of Illinois Indians who, like other native peoples of the region, had abandoned Mississippian religious and political systems for the autonomous villages of their ancestors.

its allies . The survivors fled to the surrounding prairies and, in some cases, westward to the lower valleys of the Plains. By the fifteenth century, their descendants were living in villages linked by reciprocity rather than coercion. Mississippian chiefdoms and temple mound centers persisted in the Southeast, where Spanish explorers would later encounter them (see Chapter 2).

Despite Cahokia's decline, Mississippian culture profoundly affected Native Americans in the Eastern Woodlands. Mississippians spread new strains of maize and beans, along with techniques and tools for cultivating these crops, enabling women to weave agriculture into the fabric of village life. Only in some northerly areas was the growing season usually too short for maize (which required 120 frost-free days) to be a reliable crop.

Woodland peoples' slash-and-burn method of land management was environmentally sound and economically productive. Indian men systematically burned hardwood forests, eliminating the underbrush and forming open, parklike expanses. Although they occasionally lost control of a fire, so that it burned beyond their hunting territory, the damage was not lasting. Burned-over tracts favored the growth of grass and berry bushes that attracted a profusion of deer and other game. They then cleared fields so that women could plant corn, beans, and pumpkins in soil enriched by ash. After several years of abundant harvests, yields declined, and the Indians moved to another site to repeat the process. Ground cover eventually reclaimed the abandoned clearing, restoring fertility naturally, and the Indians could return.

Haida Grease Dish, c. 1700
Northwest Coast artists crafted even the most seemingly mundane objects with an eye for beauty and form.

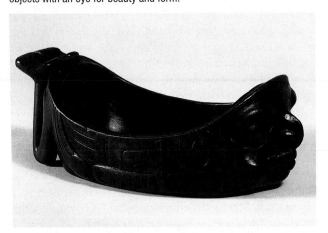

Nonfarming Societies

Outside the Southwest and the Eastern Woodlands, farming north of Mesoamerica was either impossible because of inhospitable environments or impractical because native peoples could obtain enough food from wild sources with less work. On the Northwest coast, from the Alaskan panhandle to northern California, and in the Columbia Plateau, Indians devoted brief periods of each year to catching salmon and other spawning fish. After drying the fish, they stored it in quantities sufficient to last the year. As a result, their seasonal movements gave way to a settled lifestyle in permanent villages. For example, the Makah Indians of Ozette, on Washington's Olympic Peninsula, pursued fish and sea mammals, including whales, while procuring shellfish, salmon and other river fish, land mammals, and wild plants.

By A.D. 1, most Northwest Coast villages numbered several hundred people who lived in multifamily houses built of cedar planks. Trade and warfare with interior groups strengthened the wealth and power of chiefs and other elites. Leading families displayed their power in elaborate totem poles depicting their descent from spiritual figures, and in potlatches—ceremonies in which they gave away or destroyed their material wealth. From the time of the earliest contacts, Europeans were amazed by the artistic and architectural achievements of the Northwest Coast Indians. "What must astonish most," wrote a French explorer in 1791, "is to see painting everywhere, everywhere sculpture, among a nation of hunters."

At about the same time, Native Americans on the coast and in the valleys of what is now California were clustering in villages of about a hundred people to coordinate the processing of acorns. After gathering millions of acorns from California's extensive oak groves each fall, the Indians ground them into meal, leached them of their bitter tannic acid, and then roasted, boiled, or baked the nuts prior to eating or storing them. Facing intense competition for acorns, California Indians combined their villages into chiefdoms and defended their territories. Chiefs conducted trade, diplomacy, war, and religious ceremonies. Along with other wild species, acorns enabled the Indians of California to prosper. As a Spanish friar arriving in California from Mexico in 1770 wrote, "This land exceeds all the preceding territory in fertility and abundance of things necessary for sustenance."

Between the Eastern Woodlands and the Pacific coast, the Plains and deserts remained too dry to sup-

port large human settlements. Dividing the region are the Rocky Mountains, to the east of which lie the grasslands of the Great Plains, while to the west are several deserts of varying elevations that ecologists call the Great Basin. Except in the Southwest, Native Americans in this region remained in mobile hunting-gathering bands.

Plains Indian hunters pursued a variety of game animals, including antelope, deer, elk, and bear, but their favorite prey was buffalo, or bison, a smaller relative of the giant bison that had flourished before the arrival of humans. Buffalo provided Plains Indians with meat and with hides, from which they made clothing, bedding, portable houses (tipis), kettles, shields, and other items. They made tools from buffalo bones and containers and arrowheads from buffalo horns, and they used most other buffalo parts as well. Limited to travel by foot, Plains hunters stampeded herds of bison into small box canyons, easily killing the trapped animals, or over cliffs. Dozens, or occasionally hundreds, of buffalo would be killed. Since a single buffalo could provide two hundred to four hundred pounds of meat and a band had no means of preserving and storing most of it, the latter practice was especially wasteful. On the other hand, humans were so few in number that they had no significant impact on the bison population before the arrival of Europeans. There are no reliable estimates of the number of buffalo then roaming the Plains, but the earliest European observers were flabbergasted. One Spanish colonist, for example, witnessed a "multitude so great that it might be considered a falsehood by one who had not seen them."

During and after the Mississippian era, groups of Eastern Woodlands Indians migrated to the lower river valleys of the Plains, where over time the rainfall had increased enough to support cultivated plants. In contrast to Native Americans already living on the Plains, such as the Blackfeet and the Crow, farming newcomers like the Mandans and Pawnees built year-round villages and permanent earth lodges. But they also hunted buffalo and other animals. (Many of the Plains Indians familiar today, such as the Sioux and Comanche, moved to the region only after Europeans had begun colonizing North America [see Chapter 4].)

As Indians elsewhere increased their food production, the Great Basin grew warmer and dryer, further limiting already scarce sources of foods. Ducks and other waterfowl on which Native Americans formerly feasted disappeared as marshlands dried up after 1200 B.C., and the number of buffalo and other game animals also dwindled. Great Basin Indians countered these

Chumash Baskets
California Indians, including the Chumash, gathered, prepared, and stored acorns and other foods in baskets crafted by specialized weavers.

trends by relying more heavily on piñon nuts, which they harvested, stored, and ate in winter camps. Hunting improved after about A.D. 500, when Indians in the region adopted the bow and arrow.

In western Alaska, where the first Americans had appeared thousands of years earlier, Eskimos and Aleuts, carrying highly sophisticated tools and weapons from their Siberian homeland, arrived after 3000 B.C. Combining ivory, bone, and other materials, they fashioned harpoons and spears for the pursuit of sea mammals and—in the case of the Eskimos—caribou. Through continued contacts with Siberia, the Eskimos introduced the bow and arrow in North America. As they perfected their ways of living in the cold tundra environment, many Eskimos spread westward across upper Canada and to Greenland.

Long before the arrival of Columbus, some Eskimos and Indians made contact with Europeans and used some of their material goods. From about A.D. 1, Eskimos in western Alaska acquired European-made iron tools by way of Russia and Siberia. However, the tools were too few in number to affect Eskimo culture in any substantial way. Contacts between Native Americans and Europeans were more direct and sustained after about 980, when Norse expansionists from Scandinavia colonized parts of Greenland. The Greenland Norse hunted furs, obtained timber, and traded with Eskimo people on the eastern Canadian mainland. They also made several attempts,

beginning in about 1000, to colonize Vinland, as they called Newfoundland. The Vinland Norse initially exchanged metal goods for ivory with the local Beothuk Indians, but peaceful trade gave way to hostile encounters. Within a century, Beothuk resistance led the Norse to withdraw from Vinland. As a Norse leader, dying after losing a battle with some natives, put it, "There is fat around my belly! We have won a fine and fruitful country, but will hardly be allowed to enjoy it." Although some Norse remained in Greenland as late as the 1480s, it was other Europeans who would enjoy, at the expense of native peoples, the fruits of a "New World."

Although the peoples of the Western and Eastern Hemispheres developed entirely apart from one another, their histories are in many ways comparable. Yet environmental and other limitations prevented some features of Eurasian and African cultures from arising in the Americas. Most fundamental was the unavailability of animals that could have been domesticated (other than llamas in the Andes and dogs). Lacking cattle, sheep, and hogs, Native Americans relied on wild meat instead of producing their own. Without horses, they had no incentive to develop the wheel (although the Maya made children's toys with wheels). There is no telling how American history might have unfolded in the absence of the European invasions that began in 1492.

NORTH AMERICAN PEOPLES ON THE EVE OF EUROPEAN CONTACT

By A.D. 1500, native peoples had transformed the Americas into a dazzling array of cultures and societies (see Map 1.4). The Western Hemisphere numbered about 75 million people, most thickly clustered in urbanized areas of Mesoamerica and South America. But North America was no empty wasteland. Between 7 million and 10 million Indians lived north of Mesoamerica. They were unevenly distributed. As they had for thousands of years, small, mobile hunting bands peopled the Arctic, Subarctic, Great Basin, and much of the Plains. More sedentary societies based on fishing or gathering predominated along the Pacific coast, while village-based agriculture was typical in the Eastern Woodlands and the river valleys of the Southwest and Plains. Mississippian urban centers still prevailed in areas of the Southeast. All these peoples grouped themselves in several hundred

nations and tribes, and spoke hundreds of languages and dialects.

Despite the vast differences among Native Americans, much bound them together. Rooted in common practices, Indian societies were based on kinship, the norms of reciprocity, and communal use and control of resources. Trade facilitated the exchange not only of goods but also of technologies and ideas. Thus, the bow and arrow, ceramic pottery, and certain religious values and practices characterized Indians everywhere.

Kinship and Gender

Like their Archaic forebears, Indian peoples north of the Mesoamerican states were bound together primarily by kinship. Ties among biological relatives created complex patterns of social obligation and interdependence, even in societies that did not expect spouses to be married forever. Customs regulating marriage varied considerably, but strict rules always prevailed. In most cultures, young people married in their teens, after winning social acceptance as adults and, generally, after a period of sexual experimentation. Sometimes male leaders took more than one wife, but nuclear families (a husband, a wife, and their biological children) never stood alone. Instead, they lived with one of the parents' relatives in what social scientists call extended families.

In some Native American societies, such as the Iroquois, the extended families of women took precedence over those of men. Upon marriage, a new husband moved in with his wife's extended family. The primary male authority figure in a child's life was the mother's oldest brother, not the father. In many respects, a husband and father was simply a guest of his wife's family. Other Indian societies recognized men's extended families as primary, and still others did not distinguish sharply between the status of female and male family lines.

Kinship was also the basis for armed conflict. Indian societies typically considered homicide a matter to be resolved by the extended families of the victim and the perpetrator. If the perpetrator's family offered a gift that the victim's family considered appropriate, the question was settled; if not, political leaders attempted to resolve the dispute. Otherwise, the victim's family members and their supporters might seek to avenge the killing by armed retaliation. Such feuds could escalate into wars between communities. The potential for war rose when densely populated societies competed for scarce resources, as on the Northwest and California coasts,

and when centralized Mississippian societies used coercion to dominate trade networks. Yet Native American warfare generally remained minimal, with rivals seeking to humiliate one another and seize captives rather than inflict massive casualties or conquer land. A New England officer, writing in the seventeenth century, described a battle between two Indian groups as "more for pastime than to conquer and subdue enemies." He concluded that "they might fight seven years and not kill seven men."

MAP 1.4

Locations of Selected Native American Peoples, A.D. 1500

Today's Indian nations were well established in homelands across the continent when Europeans first arrived. Many would combine with others or move in later centuries, either voluntarily or because they were forced.

Guale Indians Planting Crops, 1564
A French explorer sketched this scene on the Florida coast in which men are breaking up the soil while women sow corn, bean, and squash seeds.

Women did most of the cultivating in farming societies except in the Southwest (where women and men shared the responsibility). With women producing the greater share of the food supply, some societies accorded them more power than did Europeans. Among the Iroquois, for example, women collectively owned the fields, distributed food, and played a decisive role in selecting chiefs. In New England, women often served as sachems, or political leaders.

Spiritual and Social Values

Native American religions revolved around the conviction that all nature was alive, pulsating with spiritual power—*manitou* in the Algonquian languages, *orenda* in the Iroquoian, and *wakan* in the Siouan. A mysterious, awe-inspiring force that could affect human life for both good and evil, such power united all nature in an unbroken web. *Manitou* encompassed "every thing which they cannot comprehend," reported Rhode Island's Roger Williams. Native Americans endeavored to conciliate the spiritual forces in their world—living

things, rocks and water, sun and moon, even ghosts and witches. For example, Indian hunters prayed to the spirits of the animals they killed, thanking them for the gift of food.

Indians had several ways of gaining access to spiritual power. One was through dreams. Most Native Americans took very seriously the visions that came to them in sleep. Some also sought power through difficult physical ordeals. Young men in many societies gained recognition as adults through a vision quest—a solitary venture that entailed fasting and awaiting the appearance of a spirit who would endow them with special powers and sometimes, as in Hiawatha's case, entrust them with a message of import for their people. Girls underwent rituals at the onset of menstruation to initiate them into the spiritual world from which female reproductive power flowed. Entire communities often practiced collective power-seeking rituals such as the Sun Dance, performed by Indians of the Plains and Great Basin.

Native Americans who had gained special religious powers assisted others in communicating with unseen

spirits. These medicine men and women were healers who used both medicinal plants and magical chants to cure illnesses. They also served as spiritual advisers and leaders, interpreting dreams, guiding vision quests, and conducting ceremonies. Chiefs claiming kinship with spiritual forces had to maintain respectful relations with these religious leaders to support their claims.

Native American societies demanded a strong degree of cooperation. From early childhood, Indians in most cultures learned to be accommodating and reserved—slow to reveal their own feelings until they could sense the feelings of others. Using physical punishment sparingly, if at all, Indians punished children psychologically, by public shaming. Communities sought unity through consensus rather than tolerating lasting divisions. Political leaders articulated slowly emerging agreements in dramatic oratory. The English colonizer John Smith noted that the most effective Native American leaders spoke "with vehemency and so great passions that they sweat till they drop and are so out of breath they scarce can speak."

Native Americans reinforced cooperation with a strong sense of order. Custom, the demands of social conformity, and the rigors of nature strictly regulated life and people's everyday affairs. Exacting familial or community revenge was a ritualized way of restoring order that had broken down. On the other hand, the failure of measures to restore order could bring the fearful consequences experienced by Hiawatha's Iroquois—blind hatred, unending violence, and the most dreaded of evils, witchcraft. In fearing witchcraft, Native Americans resembled the Europeans and Africans they would encounter after 1492.

The principle of reciprocity, perfected in Archaic times, remained strong among Native Americans. Reciprocity involved mutual give-and-take, but its aim was not to ensure equality. Instead, societies based on reciprocity tried to maintain equilibrium and interdependence between individuals of unequal power and prestige. Even in the most complex societies, chiefs coordinated families' uses of land and other resources, but never awarded these outright.

Most Indian leaders' authority depended on the obligations they bestowed rather than on coercion. By distributing gifts, they obligated members of the community to support them and to accept their authority, however limited. The same principle applied to relations between societies. Powerful communities distributed gifts to weaker neighbors who reciprocated with tribute in the form of material goods and submission. A French observer in early-seventeenth-century Canada clearly understood: "For the savages have that noble quality, that they give liberally, casting at the feet of him whom they will honor the present that they give him. But it is with hope to receive some reciprocal kindness, which is a kind of contract, which we call . . . 'I give thee, to the end thou shouldst give me.' "

CONCLUSION

When Europeans "discovered" America in 1492, they did not, as they thought, enter a static world of simple savages. For thousands of years, Native Americans had tapped the secrets of the land, sustaining themselves and flourishing in almost every environment. Native Americans transformed the landscape, as evidenced by their hunting camps, communities, and cornfields. But Indians never viewed these accomplishments as evidence of their ability to conquer nature. Rather, they saw themselves as participants in a natural and spiritual order that pervaded the universe, and their attitudes, as expressed in their religious practices, were gratitude and concern lest they violate that order.

These beliefs did not necessarily make all Native Americans careful conservationists. Plains hunters often killed more animals than they could eat; and eastern Indians sometimes burned more land than intended. But the effect of such acts were limited; Indians did not repeat them often enough to eliminate entire species. However, some Indians' actions were more consequential. The decline of the great Anasazi and Mississippian centers resulted from excessive demands placed on their environments by large concentrations of people.

After 1500, a new attitude toward the land made itself felt in North America. "A people come from under the world, to take their world from them"—thus a Mannahoac Indian characterized the English who invaded his homeland to found Virginia. Certain that God had given Christians dominion over nature, European newcomers claimed vast expanses of territory for their crowned heads. They divided much of the land into plots, each to be owned by an individual or family and to be valued according to the wealth it produced. Over the ensuing centuries, they ignored and even belittled Native American strategies that allowed natural resources to renew themselves. The modern society that has arisen on the Indians' ancient continent bears little resemblance to the world that Native Americans once knew.

CHRONOLOGY 13,000 B.C.–A.D. 1500

c. 13,000 B.C.	People present in America.
c. 10,500–9000 B.C.	Paleo-Indians established throughout Western Hemisphere.
c. 9000 B.C.	Extinction of big-game mammals.
c. 8000 B.C.	Earliest Archaic societies.
c. 7000 B.C.	Athapaskan-speaking peoples enter North America.
c. 5000 B.C.	First domesticated plants grown.
c. 3000 B.C.	First maize grown in Mesoamerica.
c. 3000–2000 B.C.	Eskimo and Aleut peoples enter North America from Siberia.
c. 2500 B.C.	Archaic societies begin giving way to a more diverse range of cultures. First maize grown in North America.
c. 1200 B.C.	First chiefdoms emerge.
c. 1200–900 B.C.	Poverty Point flourishes in Louisiana.
c. 400–100 B.C.	Adena culture flourishes in Ohio valley.
c. 250 B.C.	Hohokam culture begins in Southwest.
c. 100 B.C.	Anasazi culture begins in Southwest.
c. 100 B.C.–A.D. 600	Hopewell culture thrives in Midwest.
c. A.D. 1	Rise of chiefdoms on Northwest Coast and in California.
c. 100–700	Teotihuacán flourishes in Mesoamerica.
c. 600–1400	Mayan kingdoms flourish.
c. 700	Mississippian culture begins. Anasazi expansion begins.
c. 900	Urban center arises at Cahokia.
c. 980	Norse arrive in Greenland.
c. 1000–1100	Norse attempt to colonize Vinland (Newfoundland).
c. 1200	Anasazi and Hohokam peoples disperse in Southwest.
c. 1200–1400	Cahokia declines and inhabitants disperse.
c. 1400	League of the Iroquois formed.
1428	Rise of Aztec Empire.
1438	Rise of Inca Empire.
1492	Christopher Columbus reaches Western Hemisphere.

FOR FURTHER REFERENCE

READINGS

The Cambridge History of the Native Peoples of the Americas (3 vols., 1996–2000). Volumes on North America, Mesoamerica, and South America, each containing authoritative essays by archaeologists and historians covering the entire expanse of Native American history.

Cheryl Claassen and Rosemary A. Joyce, eds., *Women in Prehistory: North America and Mesoamerica* (1997). Fourteen essays draw on and examine archaeological evidence of women's roles and gender identity in a range of Native American societies.

Thomas D. Dillehay, *The Settlement of the Americas: A New Prehistory* (2000). An excellent critical review of current scholarly debates on the earliest Americans.

Brian Fagan, *Ancient North America: The Archaeology of a Continent* (2000). A comprehensive introduction to the continent's history before Europeans' arrival.

William W. Fitzhugh and Elisabeth I. Ward, eds., *Vikings: The North Atlantic Saga* (2000). Thirty-one essays, along with hundreds of illustrations, cover virtually everything scholars now know about Norse colonization in the North Atlantic.

Alvin M. Josephy, Jr., *America in 1492: The World of the Indian Peoples Before the Arrival of Columbus* (1992). Highly readable regional and thematic essays on life in the Western Hemisphere on the eve of European contact.

Shepard Krech III, *The Ecological Indian: Myth and History* (1999). A controversial, well-informed critique of the idea that Native Americans invariably lived in harmony with nature before Europeans arrived.

Lynda Norene Shaffer, *Native Americans Before 1492: The Moundbuilding Centers of the Eastern Woodlands* (1992). A thoughtful, readable interpretation of eastern moundbuilders from Poverty Point to the Mississippians.

William C. Sturtevant, gen. ed., *Handbook of North American Indians* (20 vols. projected, 1978–). A reference work, still in progress, providing basic information on the history and culture of Native American societies, as well as surveys of regional archaeology and essays on topics of special interest.

Lawrence E. Sullivan, ed., *Native American Religions: North America* (1989). Essays focusing on religious life and expression throughout the continent.

WEBSITES

American Indian History and Related Issues
http://www.csulb.edu/projects/ais/index.html#north
(American Indian Studies Program, California State
University, Long Beach) Provides links to hundreds of
sites relating to Native Americans before and after 1492.

Cahokia Mounds State Historic Site
http://medinfo.wustl.edu/~mckinney/cahokia/cahokia.html
(Cahokia Mounds State Historic Site, Collinsville, IL)
An introduction to archaeology at Cahokia, with visitor
information about the site of North America's earliest
metropolis.

Mashantucket Pequot Museum and Research Center
http://www.mashantucket.com/index1.html
(Mashantucket Pequot Museum and Research Center,
Mashantucket, CT) Includes discussion of the museum's
ongoing archaeological research, an introduction to its
collection of more than two thousand objects, and an
online information resources catalog. Emphasis on
northeastern Native Americans, especially in New
England.

Sipapu: The Anasazi Emergence into the Cyber World
http://sipapu.gsu.edu/
(John Kantner, Department of Anthropology and
Geography, Georgia State University, Atlanta) An excellent site that enables visitors to explore Anasazi structures as well as learn about the history of a major southwestern culture.

The Rise of the Atlantic World, 1400–1625

At ten o'clock on a moonlit night the tense crew spotted a glimmering light. At two the next morning came the shout, "Land! Land!" At daybreak they entered a shallow lagoon. The captain, Christopher Columbus, rowed ashore, the royal flag fluttering in the breeze. "And, all having rendered thanks to the Lord, kneeling on the ground, embracing it with tears of joy for the immeasurable mercy of having reached it, [he] rose and gave this island the name San Salvador." The date was October 12, 1492. The place was a tiny tropical island less than four hundred miles southeast of present-day Florida.

Other than his crew, the only witnesses to Columbus's landing were some Taíno Indians who watched from a distance as he claimed for Spain the island that they called Guanahaní. Soon curiosity overcame their fears. Gesturing and smiling, the Taínos walked down to the beach, where the new-comers quickly noticed the cigars they offered and the gold pendants in their noses.

The voyagers learned to savor the islanders' tobacco and trade for golden ornaments. Columbus was sure that he had reached Asia—the Indies. Two months later, bringing with him some "Indians" and various souvenirs, he sailed home to tell of "a land to be desired and, once seen, never to be left."

◀ **Bartholomew Gosnold Trading with Wampanoag Indians at Martha's Vineyard (1602), by Theodore de Bry, 1634.**
By exchanging of material goods and hospitality, Native Americans and Europeans transformed the Atlantic Ocean from a barrier to a bridge between Earth's two hemispheres.

CHAPTER OUTLINE

African and European Peoples

Europe and the Atlantic World, 1440–1600

Footholds in North America, 1512–1625

Columbus' achievement marked not only Europe's discovery of America but also a critical step in the formation of an Atlantic world. After 1492 peoples from Europe, Africa, and North and South America became intertwined in colonial societies, obligatory and forced labor relations, trade networks, religious missions, and wars. Traveling freely or as captives, they left familiar settings for new worlds in which their customary ways of thinking and acting were repeatedly challenged. Adding to the challenges were the far-reaching environmental effects of sudden, unprecedented interactions not only of humans but also of animals, plants, and germs. Significantly shaping this Columbian exchange, as these environmental consequences are often termed, were the efforts of several European nations to increase their wealth and power through the control of the land and labor of non-Europeans they considered less than civilized.

In much of what is now Latin America, the coming of Europeans quickly turned into conquest. In the future United States and Canada, European mastery would come more slowly. More than a hundred years would pass before truly self-sustaining colonies were established. Nevertheless, from the moment of Columbus's landing on October 12, 1492, the American continents became the stage for the encounter of Native American, European, and African peoples in the emergent Atlantic world.

This chapter will focus on four major questions:

■ How did trade and political centralization transform West Africa before the advent of the Atlantic slave trade?

■ How did European monarchs use commerce and religion to advance their nations' fortunes?

■ What role did the Columbian exchange play in the formation of an Atlantic world?

■ Why did Indians in North America sometimes welcome and other times resist European traders and colonizers?

AFRICAN AND EUROPEAN PEOPLES

Even before the Atlantic world emerged in the fifteenth and sixteenth centuries, and continuing thereafter, each continent bordering the Atlantic Ocean was undergoing change. In the Americas, some societies rose, others fell, and still others adapted to new circumstances (see

Chapter 1). Both West Africa and western Europe were also being transformed. In Africa, the growth of long-distance trade enabled some empires and kingdoms to flourish at their rivals' expense. A market economy was emerging alongside older social and religious customs. Meanwhile, in Europe, ambitious monarchs joined forces with profit-minded merchants to propel the territorial expansion of some nation-states. At the same time, an intellectual Renaissance was underway, and profound divisions among Roman Catholics were leading to a religious Reformation.

Mediterranean Crossroads

One of the most vibrant areas in the Eastern Hemisphere was the Mediterranean Sea. Here African, Asian, and European peoples had interacted in both peace and war since ancient times. By 1400 hundreds of small ships were crossing the sea annually, unloading luxury goods from one part of the world and loading others for the next leg of their journeys. West African gold enriched Turkish sultans; European guns strengthened North African armies; and Indian spices stimulated Italian palates. In Africa and Asia many of these goods moved to and from the Mediterranean by caravans that traveled thousands of miles. Merchant ships linked East and South Asia with the Arabian peninsula and East Africa, and others connected northern and southern Europe. But before the fifteenth century, intercontinental travel and trade were unknown on the Atlantic Ocean.

Mediterranean commerce was closely intertwined with religion and politics. From the seventh to the fourteenth centuries, Islam spread, often by conquest, to Southeast Asia, West Africa, and much of southern Europe. During the same period, Roman Catholic rulers introduced Christianity to new areas of central and northern Europe. Political leaders sought to capture some of the wealth being generated by commerce, while merchants valued the security afforded by close ties with strong rulers. Above all, each of the two religions provided a common faith and identity to peoples spread over vast distances, reinforcing the political and economic links being forged between them.

Religion did not always divide people along political or economic lines. Christian and Muslim rulers on the Mediterranean frequently signed treaties with one another in order to secure commercial ties and protect against piracy. Christians, Jews, and Muslims, especially merchants, often traveled and lived in lands where they were in the minority. In the fourteenth century, for example, Morocco was Muslim-dominated but welcomed and tolerated Jews as well as Christians. In several

parts of the Mediterranean world, Muslim, Jewish, and Christian scholars read and commented on one another's work, a collaboration that led to Europe's Renaissance (see below).

But other Christians and Muslims regarded one another as enemies. Since the eleventh century, European Christians had conducted numerous Crusades against Islamic "infidels" in Europe and the Middle East, and some Muslim leaders waged *jihad* (holy war) against Christians. While the Islamic Ottoman Empire conquered Christian strongholds in the eastern Mediterranean, the Christian monarchies of Portugal, Castile, and Aragón undertook a "reconquest" of the Iberian peninsula by expelling non-Christians. Portugal was entirely Christian by 1250. In 1492 Castile and Aragón drove the last Muslim rulers from Spain and decreed that all remaining Jews convert to Catholicism. Such Jews were called *conversos*.

West Africa and Its Peoples

Before the advent of Atlantic travel, the broad belt of grassland, or savanna, separating the Sahara Desert from the forests to the south was a major arena of long-distance trade and of rivalries among states for control of that trade. The trans-Saharan caravan trade stimulated the rise of grassland kingdoms and empires whose size and wealth rivaled any in Europe at the time. The richest grassland states were in West Africa, with its ample stores of gold. During the fifteenth century, the empire of Mali was the leading power in the West African savanna (see Map 2.1). Its Muslim rulers had access to a network of wealthy Muslim rulers and merchants in North Africa and the Middle East. Mali imported salt from the Sahara as well as brass, copper, cloth, spices, manufactured goods, and Arabian horses. Mali's best-known city, Timbuktu, was widely recognized for its intellectual and academic vitality and for its beautiful mosque, designed and built by a Spanish Muslim architect.

Early in the fifteenth century, divisions within Mali's royal family severely weakened the empire, leading several territories to secede. A successor empire, Songhai, flourished briefly and forcibly united most of the seceded territory. But by the sixteenth century, most of Mali and Songhai had been absorbed by Morocco to the north.

Immediately south of the grassland empires lay a region of small states and chiefdoms. In Senegambia at Africa's westernmost bulge, several Islamic states took root. Infestation by the tsetse fly, the carrier of sleeping sickness, kept livestock-herding peoples out of Guinea's

coastal forests, but many small states arose here, too. Among these was Benin, where artisans had been fashioning magnificent metalwork for centuries.

Still farther south, along the coast and inland on the Congo River, a welter of chiefdoms gave rise to four major kingdoms by the fifteenth century. Their kings were chiefs who, after defeating neighboring chiefdoms, installed their own kin as local rulers of the newly conquered territories. Of these kingdoms, Kongo was the most powerful and highly centralized.

With gold having recently been made the standard for nearly all European currencies, demand for the precious metal rose. During the fifteenth century, this demand brought thousands of newcomers from the savanna and Central Africa to the region later known as Africa's Gold Coast. New states emerged to take advantage of the opportunities afforded by exporting gold, though none was as extensive or powerful as Mali at its height. Similarly eager to capitalize on its neighbor's resources were the Portuguese, who in the mid-fifteenth century used new maritime techniques to sail along

Mali Horseman, c. 13th-14th century
This terra-cotta figure originated in Mali, one of several powerful empires in West Africa before the arrival of Europeans.

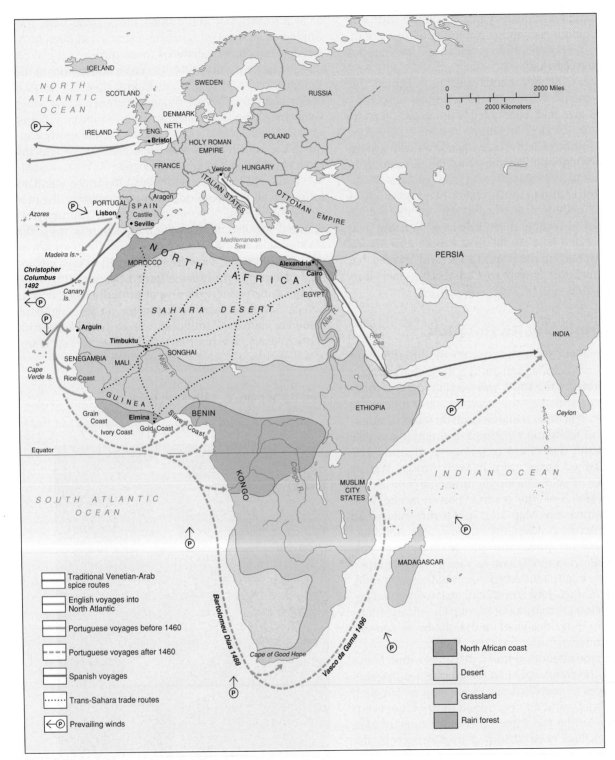

MAP 2.1

Europe, Africa, and Southwestern Asia in 1500

During the fifteenth century, Portugal led the way in integrating Europe with Africa in a new Atlantic world.
Several voyages near the end of the century extended Europe's reach to India and the Americas.

West Africa's coast in search of gold and slaves (see below).

West African political leaders differed sharply in the amounts and kinds of political power they wielded. Some kings and emperors enjoyed semigodlike status, which they only thinly disguised if they adopted Islam. Rulers of smaller kingdoms depended largely on their ability to persuade, to conform to prevailing customs, and to satisfy their people when redistributing wealth.

In West Africa, the cohesiveness of kinship groups knitted society together. As did Native Americans, Africans lived within a network of interlocking mutual obligations to kinfolk (see Chapter 1). Not just parents but also aunts, uncles, distant cousins, and persons sharing clan ties formed an African's kin group and claimed his or her first loyalty. Africans held their grandparents in high esteem and accorded village or clan elders great deference. In centuries to come, the tradition of strong extended families would help enslaved Africans in the Americas endure the forced breakup of nuclear families by sale.

West Africans viewed marriage as a way for extended families to forge alliances for mutual benefit. A prospective husband made a payment to his bride's kin before marriage. He was not "buying" a wife; in effect, he was posting bond for good behavior and acknowledging the relative prestige of his own and his bride's kin groups. West African wives generally maintained lifelong links with their own kin groups, and in many societies children traced descent through the mother's, not the father's, bloodline. All this buttressed women's status.

A driving force behind marriage in West Africa was the region's high mortality rate from frequent famines and tropical disease epidemics. The shortage of people placed a high premium on the production of children. Children represented the labor force of the future who, within a few years, would contribute to a family's wealth by increasing its food production and the amount of land it could cultivate. Men of means frequently married more than one wife in order to produce children more frequently, and women generally married soon after reaching puberty.

West Africans depended on farming by both men and women for most of their food. The abundance of land relative to population enabled African farmers— like many Native Americans and unlike Europeans—to shift their fields periodically and thereby maintain high soil quality. Before planting new fields, men felled the trees and burned off the wild vegetation. After several years of intensive cultivation, largely by women, farmers shifted to a new location. After a few years, while the soil

of the recently used fields was being replenished, they returned to repeat the cycle. In the coastal rain forests West Africans grew such crops as yams, sugar cane, bananas, and eggplant, among other foods, as well as cotton for weaving cloth. On the grasslands the staff of life was grain—millet, sorghum, and rice—supplemented by cattle raising and fishing.

By the fifteenth century the market economy, stimulated by long-distance trade, extended to many small families. Farmers traded surplus crops at local marketplaces for other food or cloth. Artisans wove cotton or raffia palm leaves, made clothing and jewelry, and crafted tools and religious objects of iron and wood. While gold was the preferred currency among wealthy rulers and merchants, cowry shells served as the medium of exchange for most people.

Religion permeated African life. Like Native Americans and Europeans, Africans believed that another world lay beyond the one people perceived through their five senses. This other world was only rarely glimpsed by living persons other than priests, but the souls of most people passed there at death. Deities spoke to mortals through priests, dreams, religious "speaking shrines," and magical charms. More than most religious traditions, those of West Africa emphasized the importance of continuous revelations as foundations of spiritual truth. Such an emphasis on revelations originating from multiple sources precluded the development of fixed dogma and institutional hierarchies as found in Islam and in medieval Christianity (see below). Also like Native Americans and Europeans, Africans explained misfortunes in terms of witchcraft. But African religion differed from other traditions in its emphasis on ancestor worship, in which departed forebears were venerated as spiritual guardians.

Africa's magnificent artistic traditions were also steeped in religion. The ivory, cast iron, and wood sculptures of West Africa (whose bold designs would influence twentieth-century western art) were used in ceremonies reenacting creation myths and honoring spirits. A strong moralistic streak ran through African folk tales. Storytellers transmitted these tales in dramatic public presentations with ritual masks, dance, and music of a highly complex rhythmic structure, which is now appreciated as one of the foundations of jazz.

Among Africans, Islam appealed primarily to merchants trading with North Africa and the Middle East and to kings and emperors eager to consolidate their power. Some Muslim rulers, however, modified Islam, retaining elements of traditional religion as a concession to popular opinion. By the fifteenth century, Islam had

only begun to affect the daily lives of some cultivators and artisans in the savanna. Similarly, the impact of Christianity, introduced by the Portuguese, remained limited until the nineteenth century.

European Culture and Society

When Columbus landed on San Salvador in 1492, western Europe was undergoing a mighty cultural revival known as the Renaissance. Intellectuals and poets believed that their age marked a return to the ideals of ancient Greek and Roman civilization. European scholars had recently discovered scores of forgotten ancient texts in philosophy, science, medicine, geography, and other subjects. Western Europeans came across these texts, and a rich tradition of commentary on them, in the writings of Muslim, Eastern Orthodox, and Jewish scholars. Armed with the new learning, Renaissance scholars strove to reconcile ancient philosophy with Christian faith, to explore the mysteries of nature, to map the world, and to explain the motions of the heavens.

The Woman Spinning by Geertruyd Roghman (c. 1650) (detail)

In early modern Europe, mothers introduced their daughters to spinning at an early age. Roghmann, one of the few female engravers of her time, specialized in depicting the daily lives of women.

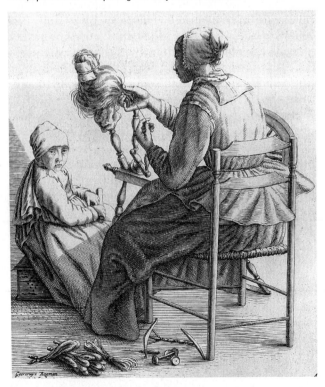

The Renaissance was also an era of intense artistic creativity. After a century-long economic recession, money had accumulated by 1500 to pay for magnificent architecture, and wealthy patrons—especially in several Italian city-states—commissioned master painters and sculptors to create works glowing with idealized human beauty. Europeans celebrated these artistic achievements, along with those of writers, philosophers, scientists, and explorers, as the height of civilization to which all other cultures ought to aspire.

But European society was quivering with tension. The era's artistic and intellectual creativity was partly inspired by intense social and spiritual stress as Renaissance Europeans groped for stability by glorifying order, hierarchy, and beauty. A concern for power and rank ("degree") dominated European life between the fifteenth and seventeenth centuries. Writing near the end of the Renaissance, William Shakespeare (1564–1616), expressed these values with eloquence:

> The heavens themselves, the planets and this
> center [earth]
> Observe degree, priority, and place. . .
> Take but degree away, untune that string,
> And hark, what discord follows!

Gender, wealth, inherited position, and political power affected every European's status, and few lived outside the reach of some political authority's taxes and laws. But this order was shaky. Conflicts between states, between religions, and between social classes constantly threatened the balance.

At the heart of these conflicts lay deep-seated forces of change. By the end of the fifteenth century, strong national monarchs in France and England had unified their realms and reduced the ability of both the Catholic Church and the nobility to dictate national policy. On the Iberian Peninsula, King Ferdinand of Aragón had married Queen Isabella of Castile in 1479 to create the Spanish monarchy. The new nation's crowning achievement came in 1492, not with Columbus' "discovery," the full significance of which was not immediately appreciated, but with the final "reconquest" of the peninsula (discussed above).

Most Europeans, about 75 percent of them, were peasants. Peasants ranged from a few prosperous families with large holdings to landless laborers who barely scraped by on odd jobs. Taxes, rents, and other dues to landlords and Catholic Church officials were burdensome, and poor harvests or war drove even well-to-do peasants to starvation. Not surprisingly, peasant revolts were frequent, but the authorities mercilessly suppressed such uprisings.

Conditions among European peasants were made worse by a sharp rise in population, from about 55 million in 1450 to almost 100 million by 1600, while agricultural yields remained pitifully low. Families in many areas cooperated in plowing, sowing, and harvesting as well as in grazing their livestock on fallow fields and jointly owned "commons." But with new land at a premium, landlords, especially the English gentry, wanted to "enclose" the commons—that is, convert the land to private property. Peasants who had no written title to their land were especially vulnerable, although some small landowners (called "yeomen" in England) with secure titles kept their land, and a few even profited by enclosure.

The environmental effects of land scarcity and population growth further exacerbated peasants' circumstances. Beginning at the end of the sixteenth century, lower-than-average temperatures marked a "Little Ice Age" that lasted for two centuries. During this time, many European crops were less abundant or failed to grow. Hunger and malnutrition were widespread, and full-scale famine struck in some areas. Another consequence of population growth was deforestation resulting from increased human demand for wood to use as fuel and building materials. Deforestation also deprived peasants of wild foods and game (whose food sources disappeared with deforestation), accelerating the exodus of rural Europeans to towns and cities.

European towns were numerous but small, typically with several thousand inhabitants each. A great metropolis like London, whose population ballooned from fifty-five thousand in 1550 to two hundred thousand in 1600, was quite exceptional. But all towns were dirty and disease-ridden, and townspeople lived close-packed with their neighbors.

Unappealing as sixteenth-century towns might seem today, many men and women of the time preferred them to the villages and tiny farms they left behind. Immigration from the countryside—rather than an excess of urban births over deaths—accounted for towns' expansion. Most people who flocked into towns remained at the bottom of the social order as servants or laborers and could not accumulate enough money to marry and live independently.

The consequences of rapid population growth were particularly acute in England, where the number of people doubled from about 2.5 million in 1500 to 5 million in 1620. As throughout western Europe, prices rose while wages fell during the sixteenth and early seventeenth centuries (see Figure 2.1), widening the gap between rich and poor. Although English entrepreneurs expanded textile production by assembling spinners

and weavers in household workshops, the workers were competing for fewer jobs in the face of growing competition that was diminishing European markets for English cloth. Enclosures severely aggravated unemployment, forcing large numbers of people to wander the country in search of work. To the upper and middle classes, these poor vagabonds seemed to threaten law and order. To control them, Parliament passed Poor Laws that ordered vagrants whipped and sent home, but most offenders only moved on to other towns.

As in America and Africa, traditional society in Europe rested on maintaining long-term, reciprocal relationships. European reciprocity required the upper classes to act with self-restraint and dignity, and the lower classes to show deference to their "betters." It also demanded strict economic regulation to ensure that no purchaser paid more than a "just price"—one that permitted a seller a "reasonable" profit but that barred him from taking advantage of buyers' and borrowers' misfortunes to make "excessive" profits.

Yet for several centuries Europeans had been compromising the ideals of traditional economic behavior. "In the Name of God and of Profit," thirteenth-century Italian merchants had written on their ledgers. By the sixteenth century, nothing could stop the charging of

FIGURE 2.1

Decline in Real Wages in England, 1500-1700

This index measures the drop in purchasing power due to inflation and declining wages. It indicates that by around 1630, living standards for English workers had declined by about two-thirds since the base year, 1500.

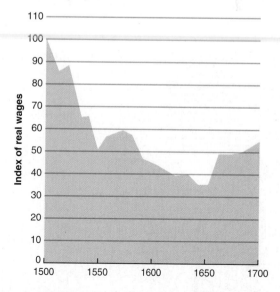

Source: E.H. Phelps Brown and S. V. Hopkins, "Builders' Wage-Rates, Prices and Population: Some Further Evidence," *Economica*, XXVI (1959): 18–38; adapted from D.C. North and R. P. Thomas, The Rise of the Western World: A New Economic History (Cambridge: Cambridge University Press, 1973), 111.

interest on borrowed money or sellers' price increases in response to demand. New forms of business organization slowly spread in the commercial world—especially the impersonal joint-stock company with many investors, the ancestor of the modern corporation. Demand rose for capital investment, and so did the supply of accumulated wealth. A new economic outlook gradually took form that justified the unimpeded acquisition of wealth and insisted that individuals owed one another nothing but the money necessary to settle their transactions. This new outlook, the central value system of capitalism or the "market economy," opposed traditional demands for the strict regulation of economic activity to ensure social reciprocity and maintain "just prices."

Sixteenth- and seventeenth-century Europeans therefore held conflicting attitudes toward economic enterprise and social change, and their ambivalence remained unresolved. A restless desire for fresh opportunity kept European life simmering with competitive tension. But those who prospered still sought the security and prestige provided by high social status, whereas the poor longed for the age-old values that would restrain irresponsible greed.

Perhaps the most sensitive barometer of social change was the family. Throughout Europe the typical household consisted of a small nuclear family—two parents and several children—in which the husband and father functioned as a head whose authority was not to be questioned. The role of the wife and mother was to bear and rear children as well as assist her husband in providing for the family's subsistence. Children were regarded as potential laborers who would assist in these tasks until they left home to start their own families. The household, then, was not only a family of intimately related people but also the principal economic unit in European society. Peasants on their tiny farms, artisans and merchants in their shops, and even nobles in their castles all lived and worked in households. People who did not live with their own families resided as dependents in the households of others as servants, apprentices, or relatives. Europeans regarded those who lived outside family-based households with extreme suspicion, often accusing them of crime or even witchcraft.

In a common cliché of the age, the nuclear family was a "little commonwealth." A father's authority over his family was supposed to mirror God's rule over Creation and the king's over his subjects. Even grown sons and daughters regularly knelt for their father's blessing. The ideal, according to a German writer, was that "wives should obey their husbands and not seek to dominate them; they must manage the home efficiently. Husbands . . . should treat their wives with consideration and occasionally close an eye to their faults." In practice, the father's sovereignty often had to make room for the wife's responsibility in managing family affairs and helping to run the farm or the workshop. Repeated male complaints, such as that of an English author in 1622 about wives "who think themselves every way as good as their husbands, and no way inferior to them," suggest that male domination had its limits.

There Is No Greater Treasure Here on Earth Than an Obedient Wife Who Desires Honor (Erhard Schön, 1533)
This German woodcut satirizes domineering wives and submissive husbands for subverting conventional gender roles. The people following behind the wagon criticize the couple. The woodcut's title also asserts conventional norms regarding gender roles in marriage.

Religious Upheavals

Christianity, to which most sixteenth-century Europeans adhered, taught that Jesus Christ, God's Son, had redeemed sinners by suffering crucifixion and rising from the dead. Equally vivid was Christians' belief in the devil, Satan, whom God had hurled from heaven soon after the Creation and who ceaselessly lured people to damnation by tempting them to do evil. The non-Christian minority encompassed scattered Jewish communities plus Muslims in southern Europe. But all Europe's population—Christians, Jews, and Muslims—worshiped a single supreme being, based on the God of the Hebrew Bible.

Although Christianity had spread throughout Europe by the sixteenth century, older, non-Christian beliefs persisted. Many Europeans feared witches and thought that individuals could manipulate nature by invoking unseen spiritual powers—that is, by magic. Others looked to astrology, insisting that a person's fate depended on the conjunction of various planets and stars. Such beliefs in spiritual forces not originating with a supreme deity resembled those of Native Americans and Africans.

The Catholic Church, based in Rome, taught that Christ's sacrifice was repeated every time a priest said Mass, and that divine grace flowed to sinners through the sacraments that priests alone could administer—above all, baptism, confession, and the Eucharist (communion). The Church was a huge network of clergymen and religious orders, male and female, set apart from laypeople by the fact that its members did not marry. At the top was the pope, the "vicar [representative] of Christ."

The papacy wielded awesome spiritual power. Fifteenth- and early-sixteenth-century popes dispensed extra blessings, or "indulgences," to repentant sinners in return for such "good works" as donating money to the Church. Indulgences promised time off from future punishment in purgatory, where the dead atoned for sins they had already confessed and been forgiven. (Hell, from which there was no escape, awaited those who died unforgiven.) Given people's anxieties about sinful behavior, indulgences were enormously popular. The jingle of one successful indulgence seller in early sixteenth-century Germany promised that

As soon as the coin in the cash box rings,
The soul from purgatory's fire springs.

The sale of indulgences provoked charges that the materialism and corruption infecting economic life had spread to the Church. In 1517 a German monk, Martin Luther (1483–1546), attacked the practice. When the papacy tried to silence him, Luther broadened his criticism to encompass the Mass, purgatory, priests, and the pope. After Luther refused to recant, the Roman Church excommunicated him. Luther's revolt initiated what became known as the Protestant Reformation, which changed Christianity forever. (The word *Protestant* comes from the *protest* of Luther's princely supporters against the anti-Lutheran policies of Holy Roman Emperor Charles V.)

To Luther, indulgence selling and similar examples of clerical corruption were evil not just because they bilked people. The Church, he charged, gave people false confidence that they could earn salvation simply by doing good works. His own agonizing search for salvation had convinced Luther that God bestowed salvation not on the basis of worldly deeds, but solely to reward a believer's faith. "I did not love a just and angry God, but rather hated and murmured against him," recalled Luther, "until I saw the connection between the justice of God and the [New Testament] statement that 'the just shall live [be saved] by faith.' . . . Thereupon I felt myself to be reborn and to have gone through open doors into paradise." Luther's spiritual struggle and experience of being "reborn" constituted a classic conversion experience—the heart of Protestant Christianity.

Other Protestant reformers followed Luther in breaking from Catholicism, but they challenged his interpretation of Christianity. Whereas Luther stressed faith in Christ as the key to salvation, French theologian John Calvin (1509–1564) insisted on the stark doctrine of predestination. Calvin asserted that an omnipotent God predestined most sinful humans to hell, saving only a few in order to demonstrate his power and grace. It was only these few, called the "elect" or the "godly," who would have a true conversion experience. At this moment, said Calvin, a person confronted the horrifying truth of his or her unworthiness and felt God's transcending power. A good Christian, in Calvin's view, would never be absolutely certain that he or she was saved and could do nothing to affect the outcome. But good Christians would be pious and avoid sin because they knew that godly behavior was a sign (not a cause and not a guarantee) of salvation.

Calvinists and Lutherans, as the followers of the two Reformation leaders came to be called, were equally horrified by more radical Protestants such as the Anabaptists, who appealed strongly to women and common people with their criticisms of the rich and powerful and sought to restrict baptism to "converted" adults. Judging the Anabaptists a threat to the social order, governments and mainstream churches persecuted them.

Saint Teresa of Avila
One of the leading Catholic reformers, Saint Teresa was a nun whose exemplary life and forceful views helped reshape the Roman church in the face of defections to Protestantism.

But Protestants also shared much common ground. For one thing, they denied that God had endowed priests with special powers. The church, Luther claimed, was a "priesthood of all believers." Protestant reformers insisted that laypeople take responsibility for their own spiritual and moral conditions. Accordingly, they placed a high value on reading. Protestants demanded that the Bible be translated from Latin into spoken languages so that believers could read it for themselves instead of relying on priests for knowledge of its contents. The new faith was spread by the newly invented printing press. Wherever Protestantism became established, basic education and religious indoctrination followed. Finally, Protestantism represented a yearning in many people for the simplicity and purity of the ancient Christian church. More forcefully than Catholicism, it condemned the replacement of traditional reciprocity by marketplace values. Protestantism's greatest appeal was to all those—ordinary individuals, merchants, and aristocrats alike—who brooded over their chances for salvation and valued the steady performance of duty.

In the face of the Protestant challenge, Rome was far from idle. Reformers like Teresa of Avila (1515–1582), a Spanish nun from a *converso* (converted Jewish) family, urged members of Catholic holy orders to repudiate corruption and to lead the Church's renewal by living piously and austerely. Another reformer, Ignatius Loyola (1491–1556), founded a militant religious order, the Jesuits, whose members would distinguish themselves for centuries as royal advisers and missionaries. The high point of Catholic reform came during the Council of Trent (1545–1563), convened by the pope. The council defended Catholic teachings and denounced those of the Protestants. But it also reformed Church administration in order to combat corruption and encourage wide public participation in religious observances. This Catholic revival, the Counter-Reformation, brought the modern Roman Catholic Church into existence.

The Protestant Reformation changed the religious map of much of Europe (see Map 2.2). Lutheranism became the state religion in the Scandinavian countries, and Calvinism made significant inroads in France, the Netherlands (ruled by Spain), and England, where it competed with Catholicism and with the moderately reformed Church of England. The tiny states comprising the modern nations of Germany and Switzerland were divided among Catholics, Lutherans, and Calvinists.

The Reformation in England, 1533–1625

England's Reformation began not with the writings of a theologian or with cries of the people, but with the actions of a king and Parliament. King Henry VIII (ruled 1509–1547) wanted a male heir, but his queen, Catherine of Aragón, failed to bear a son. Frustrated and determined, Henry asked the pope to annul his marriage. Equally determined, the pope refused. Henry then persuaded Parliament to pass a series of acts in 1533–1534 dissolving his marriage and proclaiming him supreme head of the Church of England (or Anglican Church). The move justified Henry's wholesale seizure of Catholic Church properties as means of consolidating royal power.

Religion remained a source of conflict in England for more than a century after Henry's break with Rome. Under Edward VI (ruled 1547–1553), the church veered sharply toward Protestantism; then Mary I (ruled 1553–1558) tried to restore Catholicism, in part by burning several hundred Protestants at the stake.

The reign of Elizabeth I (ruled 1558–1603) marked a crucial watershed. After the reign of "Bloody Mary," most English people were ready to become Protestant; *how* Protestant was the divisive question. Militant Calvinists, now called Puritans, demanded a wholesale purification of the Church of England from "popish [Catholic] abuses." They affirmed salvation by predestination, denied Christ's presence in the Eucharist, and believed that a

learned sermon was the heart of true worship. They wished to free each congregation and its minister from outside interference by Anglican bishops and encouraged lay members (nonclergy) to participate in church affairs. Above all, Puritans insisted that membership in a true Christian church be reserved exclusively for those who had had a conversion experience. In this respect, they repudiated the Catholic and Anglican churches, both of which extended membership to anyone who had been baptized. Nevertheless, some Puritans, hoping to reform the Church of England from within, declined to break openly with it. Others, called Separatists, insisted that a "pure" church had to avoid all contact with Anglican "pollution."

The severe self-discipline and moral uprightness of Puritans appealed to only a few among the titled nobility and the poor. Puritanism's primary appeal was instead to the small but growing number of people in the "middling" ranks of English society—landowning gentry, yeoman farmers, merchants, shopkeepers, artisans, and university-educated clergymen and intellectuals. Self-discipline had become central to both the secular and spiritual dimensions of these people's lives. From their ranks, and particularly from among farmers, artisans, and clergymen, would later come the settlers of New England (see Chapter 3).

Elizabeth distrusted Puritan militancy; but, after 1570 when the pope declared her a heretic and urged Catholics to overthrow her, she regarded English Catholics as even more dangerous. Thereafter, she courted influential Puritans and embraced militant anti-Catholicism.

Under Elizabeth, most Puritans came to expect that they would eventually transform the Church of England into independent congregations of "saints." But her successor, James I (ruled 1603–1625), the founder of England's Stuart dynasty, bitterly opposed Puritan efforts to eliminate the office of bishop. He made clear that he saw Puritan attacks on bishops as a direct threat to the throne when he snapped, "No bishop, no king." Although James insisted on outward conformity to Anglican practice, he quietly tolerated Calvinists within the Church of England who did not dissent loudly.

EUROPE AND THE ATLANTIC WORLD, 1440–1600

At the beginning of the fifteenth century, European wealth was concentrated in Mediterranean city-states such as Florence and Venice. Over the next two centuries, much of this wealth shifted from the Mediterranean to

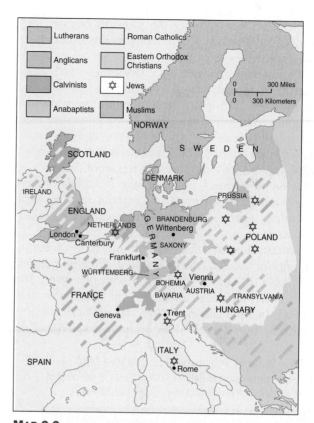

MAP 2.2

Major Religions in Europe, c. 1560

By 1560 some European lands were solidly Catholic, Lutheran, or Calvinist, but others remained bitterly divided for another century or more.

the Atlantic, where the monarchs of several nation-states were consolidating their power over vast territories in Europe and the Americas. Although England and France were also active, the first of the emerging new Atlantic powers were Portugal and Spain. Situated on the Iberian Peninsula where the Mediterranean and Atlantic come together, Portugal and Spain led a new European imperialism across the oceans of the world. Two prominent outcomes of this new imperialism were a trans-Atlantic slave trade and the colonization of new lands, especially in the Americas. Out of the new imperialism and the multiple intercontinental encounters that resulted arose a new Atlantic world.

Portugal and the Atlantic, 1440–1600

Portugal led the shift from a Mediterranean to an Atlantic world. While European merchants had long traded with Asia and Africa by way of the Mediterranean (see above), some recognized that they could increase their profits by establishing direct contacts with sources

of prized imports. During the fifteenth century, tiny Portugal led the way in overcoming impediments to long-distance oceanic travel.

Important changes in maritime technology occurred in the early fifteenth century. Shipbuilders and mariners along Europe's stormy Atlantic coast added the triangular Arab sail to the heavy cargo ships they used for voyaging between England and the Mediterranean. They created a more maneuverable vessel, the caravel, which sailed more easily against the wind. Sailors also mastered the compass and astrolabe, by which they got their bearings on the open sea. Without this maritime revolution, European exploration would have been impossible.

Renaissance scholars' search for more accurate readings of ancient texts enabled fifteenth-century Europeans to look at their world with new eyes. The great ancient Greek authority on geography was Ptolemy, but Renaissance cartographers corrected his data when they tried to draw accurate maps based on

recent European and Arabic observations. Thus, Renaissance "new learning" helped sharpen Europeans' geographic sense.

Led by Prince Henry "the Navigator" (1394–1460), Portugal was the first nation to capitalize on these developments. Henry gained the support of merchants seeking to circumvent Moroccan control of the African-European gold trade and of religious zealots eager to confront Muslim power. He hoped to find a sea route to Asia that would enable Portugal to bypass Mediterranean traders in tapping the markets of that continent as well. Henry encouraged Portuguese seamen to pilot the new caravels far down the African coast, searching for weak spots in Muslim defenses and for opportunities to trade profitably. By the time of his death, the Portuguese operated a successful gold-making factory at Arguin and had established trade ties south of the Sahara. In 1488 Bartolomeu Días reached the Cape of Good Hope at Africa's southern tip. A decade later Vasco da Gama led a Portuguese fleet around the Cape of Good Hope and on to India (see Map 2.1).

Ultimately the Portuguese failed to destroy older Euro-Asian commercial links, although they remained an imperial presence in the Indian Ocean and present-day Indonesia. Meanwhile, they had brought Europeans face-to-face with black Africans and an already flourishing slave trade.

The "New Slavery" and Racism

Slavery was well established in fifteenth-century Africa. The institution took two basic forms. Many Africans were enslaved because of indebtedness. Their debts were purchased by kings and emperors who made them servants or by families seeking additional laborers. They or their children were either absorbed into their new families over time or released from bondage when their debts were considered paid off through their work. But a long-distance commercial trade in slaves also flourished. For several centuries, Middle Eastern and North African traders had furnished local rulers with a range of fine, imported products in exchange for black laborers. Some of these slaves had been debtors, while others were captured in raids and wars.

One fifteenth-century Italian who witnessed Portuguese and Muslim slave trading noted that the Arabs "have many Berber horses, which they trade, and take to the Land of the Blacks, exchanging them with the rulers for slaves. Ten or fifteen slaves are given for one of these horses, according to their quality." Portuguese traders quickly realized how lucrative the trade in slaves

African View of Portuguese, c. 1650-1700
A carver in the kingdom of Benin, on Africa's west coast, created this saltholder depicting Portuguese officials and their ship.

could be for them, too. The same Italian observer continued, "Slaves are brought to the market town of Hoden; there they are divided. . . . [Some] are taken . . . and sold to the Portuguese leaseholders [in Arguin]. As a result every year the Portuguese carry away . . . a thousand slaves."

Although in 1482 the Portuguese built an outpost, Elmina, on West Africa's Gold Coast, they primarily traded through African-controlled commercial networks. Often Portuguese merchants traded slaves and local products to other Africans for gold. The local African kingdoms were too strong for the Portuguese to attack, and African rulers traded—or chose not to trade—according to their own self-interest.

Despite preventing the Portuguese from directly colonizing them, West African societies were profoundly affected by the new Atlantic slave trade. Portuguese traders enriched favored African rulers not only with gold and other luxury products but also with guns. As a result, they exacerbated conflicts among African communities and helped redraw the political map of West Africa. In Guinea and Senegambia, where most sixteenth-century slaves came from, small kingdoms expanded to "service" the trade. Some of their rulers became comparatively rich. Farther south, the kings of Kongo used the slave trade to expand their regional power and voluntarily adopted Christianity, just as rulers farther north had converted to Islam. Kongo flourished until the late sixteenth century, when rival powers from the interior destroyed it.

Although slavery had long been practiced in many parts of the Eastern Hemisphere, there were ominous differences in the slavery that arose once the Portuguese began voyaging to West Africa. First, the unprecedented magnitude of the trade resulted in a demographic catastrophe for West Africa and its peoples. Before the Atlantic slave trade finally ended in the nineteenth century, nearly 12 million Africans would be shipped in terrible conditions across the sea. Slavery on this scale had been unknown to Europeans since the collapse of the Roman Empire. Second, African slaves were subjected to new extremes of dehumanization. In medieval Europe and in West Africa itself, most slaves had lived in their masters' households and primarily performed domestic service. Africans shipped to Arab lands endured harsher conditions, but were regarded as humans. But by 1450 the Portuguese and Spanish created large slave-labor plantations on their Atlantic and Mediterranean islands (see Technology and Culture: Sugar Production in the Americas). These plantations produced sugar for European markets, using capital supplied by Italian

Portrait of a Black Man
Although the vast majority of Africans taken from their continent went to the Americas, some went to Europe. The famed German artist, Albrecht Dürer, sketched this portrait in the early sixteenth century.

investors to buy African slaves who toiled until death. In short, Africans enslaved by Europeans were regarded as property rather than as persons of low status; as such, they were consigned to labor that was unending, exhausting, and mindless. By 1600 the "new slavery" had become a central, brutal component of the Atlantic world.

Finally, race became the ideological basis of the new slavery. Africans' blackness, along with their alien religion and customs, dehumanized them in European eyes. As their racial prejudice hardened, Europeans justified enslaving blacks as their Christian duty. From the fifteenth century onward, European Christianity made few attempts to soften slavery's rigors, and race defined a slave. Slavery became a lifelong, hereditary, and despised status.

Europeans Reach America, 1492–1541

Europeans' varying motivations for expanding their horizons converged in the fascinating, contradictory figure of Christopher Columbus (1451–1506), the son of a weaver from the Italian port of Genoa. Columbus's

Sugar Production in the Americas

Beginning with Christopher Columbus's first expedition, organisms ranging from bacteria to human beings crossed the Atlantic in both directions. This Columbian exchange had wide-ranging ecological, economic, political, and cultural consequences for the lands and peoples of the Americas, Africa, and Europe. One significant set of consequences arose from the transfer of Mediterranean sugar production to the Americas. Out of this transfer came the single-crop plantation system, based on enslaved African labor, and a new consumer product that revolutionized diets and, quite literally, taste in Europe and its colonies.

Domesticated in New Guinea before 8000 B.C., sugar cane was one of the earliest wild plants harvested by human beings. By 350 B.C. sugar was an ingredient in several dishes favored by elites in India, from where it spread to the Mediterranean world. It became a significant commodity in the Mediterranean in the eight century A.D. when expanding Arabs carried it as far west as Spain and Morocco. The Mediterranean would remain the center of sugar production for Europe over the next seven centuries.

The basic process of making sugar from the sugar cane plant changed little over time. (Sugar made from sugar beets did not become widespread until the nineteenth century.) The earliest producers discovered that one of the six species of cane, *Saccharum officinarum*, produced the most sugar in the shortest span of time. The optimal time for harvesting was when the cane had grown twelve to fifteen feet in height, with stalks about two inches thick. At this point, it was necessary to extract the juice from the plant and then the sucrose (a carbohydrate) from the juice as quickly as possible or risk spoilage. Sugar makers crushed the cane fibers in order to extract the liquid, which they then heated so that it evaporated, leaving the sucrose—or sugar—in the form of crystals or molasses, depending on its temperature.

Sugar production was central to the emerging Atlantic world during the fifteenth century, after Spanish and Portuguese planters established large sugar plantations in the Madeira, Canary, and Cape Verde islands off Africa's Atlantic coast. Initially, the islands' labor force included some free Europeans, but enslaved Africans soon predominated. The islands were the birthplace of the European colonial plantation system. Planters focused entirely on the production of a single export crop and sought to maximize profits by minimizing labor costs. Although some planters used servants, the largest-scale, most profitable plantations imported slaves and worked them as hard as possible until they died. Utilizing such methods, the island planters soon outstripped the production of older sugar makers in the

Sugar Making in the West Indies

This drawing, published in 1665, shows enslaved Africans feeding sugar cane into a three-roller mill, driven by cattle, that crushes the cane into juice. Other slaves then boil the juice.

Mediterranean. By 1500 the Spanish and Portuguese had successfully tapped new markets across Europe, especially among the wealthy classes.

On his second voyage in 1493, Columbus took a cargo of sugar from the Canaries to Hispaniola. Early efforts by Spanish colonists to produce sugar failed because they lacked efficient milling technology, because the Taíno Indians were dying so quickly from epidemic diseases, and because most colonists concentrated on mining gold. But as miners quickly exhausted Hispaniola's limited gold, the enslaved Africans brought to work in the mines became available for sugar production. In 1515 a planter named Gonzalo de Vellosa hired some experienced sugar masters from the Canaries who urged him to import a more efficient type of mill. The mill featured two vertical rollers that could be powered by either animals or water, through which laborers passed the cane in order to crush it. With generous subsidies from the Spanish crown, the combination of vertical-roll mills and slave labor led to a rapid proliferation of sugar plantations in Spain's island colonies, with some using as many as five hundred slaves. But when Spain discovered gold and silver in Mexico and the Andes, its interest in sugar declined almost as rapidly as it had arisen.

Portugal's colony of Brazil emerged as the major source of sugar in the sixteenth century. Here, too, planters established the system of large plantations and enslaved Africans. By 1526 Brazil was exporting shiploads of sugar annually, and before the end of the century it supplied most of the sugar consumed in Europe. Shortly after 1600 Brazilian planters either invented or imported a three-roller mill that increased production still further and became the Caribbean standard for several more centuries. Portugal's sugar monopoly proved short-lived. Between 1588 and 1591, English "sea dogs" captured and diverted thirty-four sugar-laden vessels during their nation's war with Spain and Portugal. In 1630 the Netherlands seized Brazil's prime sugar-producing region and increased annual production to a century-high 30,000 tons. Ten years later some Dutch sugar and slave traders, seeking to expand their activity, shared the technology of sugar production with English planters in Barbados, who were looking for a new crop following disappointing profits from tobacco and cotton. The combination of sugar and slaves took hold so quickly that, within three years, Barbados' annual output rose to 150 tons.

Sugar went on to become the economic heart of the Atlantic economy (see Chapter 3). Its price dropped so low that even many poor Europeans could afford it. As a result, sugar became central to European diets as they

Consuming Sugar in North America
The plantation system's low production costs made sugar affordable for many Europeans and colonists. In this painting, made in 1730, Susanna Truax, a New York colonist, adds sugar to her tea.

were revolutionized by the Columbian exchange. Like tobacco, coffee, and several other products of the exchange, sugar and such sugar products as rum, produced from molasses, proved habit-forming, making sugar even more attractive to profit-seeking planters and merchants.

More than any other single commodity, sugar sustained the early slave trade in the Americas, facilitating slavery's spread to tobacco, rice, indigo, and other plantation crops as well as to domestic service and other forms of labor. Competition between British and French sugar producers in the West Indies later fueled their nations' imperial rivalry (see Chapter 4) and eventually led New England's merchants to resist British imperial controls—a resistance that helped prepare the way for the American Revolution (see Chapter 5).

Focus Questions

- What was the role played by Spain's and Portugal's island colonies in revolutionizing sugar production?

- How did developments in mill technology interact with other factors to make sugar the most profitable crop produced in colonial America?

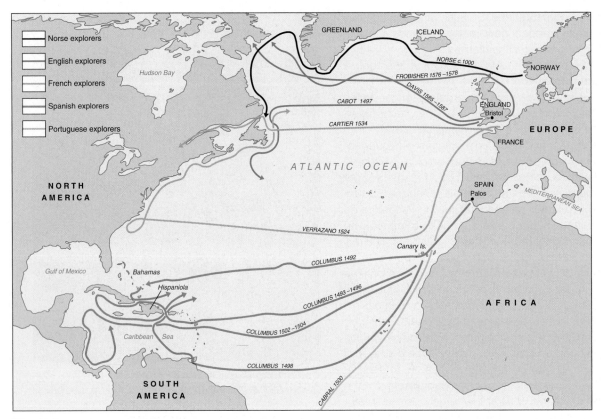

MAP 2.3
Major Transatlantic Explorations, 1000-1587
Following Columbus's 1492 voyage, Spain's rivals soon began laying claim to parts of the New World based on the voyages of Cabot for England, Cabral for Portugal, and Verrazano for France. Later English and French exploration focused on finding a passage to Asia around or through Canada.

maritime experience, self-taught geographical learning, and keen imagination led him to conclude that Asia could be reached by sailing westward across the Atlantic. By the early 1480s he was obsessed with this idea. Religious fervor led Columbus to dream of carrying Christianity around the globe and liberating Jerusalem from Muslim rule, but he also burned with ambition to win wealth and glory.

Columbus would not be the first European to venture far out into the Atlantic. Besides the early Norse (see Chapter 1), English fishermen in the North Atlantic may already have landed on the North American coast. But Columbus was unique in the persistence with which he hawked his "enterprise of the Indies" around the royal courts of western Europe. John II of Portugal showed interest until Días's discovery of the Cape of Good Hope promised a surer way to India. Finally, in 1492, hoping to break a threatened Portuguese monopoly on direct trade with Asia, Queen Isabella and King Ferdinand of Spain

accepted Columbus's offer. Picking up the westward-blowing trade winds at the Canary Islands, Columbus's three small ships reached Guanahaní within a month (see Map 2.3).

Word of Columbus's discovery caught Europeans' imaginations. To forestall competition between them as well as potential rivals, Isabella and Portugal's King John II in 1492 signed the Treaty of Tordesillas (see Map 2.4). The treaty drew a line in the mid-Atlantic dividing all future discoveries between Spain and Portugal. After Isabella sent Columbus back to explore further, he established a colony on Hispaniola, the Caribbean island today occupied by Haiti and the Dominican Republic. Columbus proved to be a poor administrator, and he was shunted aside after his last voyages (1498–1502). He died an embittered man, convinced that he had reached the threshold of Asia only to be cheated of his rightful rewards.

England's Henry VII (ruled 1485–1509) ignored the Treaty of Tordesillas and sent an Italian navigator, John

**Departure of Columbus'
Second Voyage, 1493**
Encouraged by Columbus' reports of fabulous wealth in "the Indies," Spain's King Ferdinand and Queen Isabella (standing at right) commissioned Columbus to return there with seventeen ships under his command.

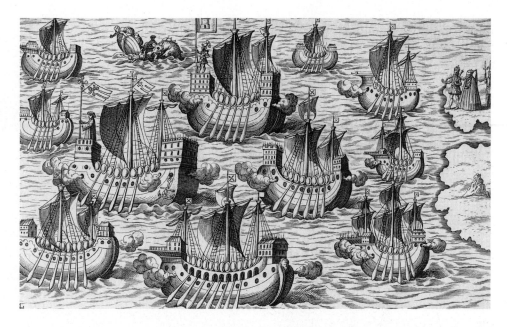

Cabot, to explore the north Atlantic in 1497. Sailing past Nova Scotia, Newfoundland, and the rich Grand Banks fisheries, Cabot claimed everything he saw and the lands beyond them for England. Like Columbus, Cabot thought that he had reached Asia.

The more Europeans explored, the more apparent it became that a vast landmass blocked the route to Asia. In 1500 the Portuguese claimed Brazil (much of which lay, unexpectedly, east of the line established in the Treaty of Tordesillas), and other voyages soon revealed a continuous coastline from the Caribbean to Brazil. In 1507 this landmass got its name when a publisher brought out a collection of voyagers' tales. One of the chroniclers was an Italian named Amerigo Vespucci. With a shrewd marketing touch, the publisher devised a catchy name for the new continent: America.

Getting past America and reaching Asia remained the early explorers' primary aim. In 1513 the Spaniard Vasco Núñez de Balboa chanced upon the Pacific Ocean when he crossed the narrow isthmus of Panama. Then in 1519 the Portuguese Ferdinand Magellan, sailing for Spain, began a voyage around the world by way of the stormy straits (later named for him) at South America's southern tip. In an incredible feat of endurance, he crossed the Pacific to the Philippines, only to die fighting with local natives. One of his five ships and fifteen emaciated sailors finally returned to Spain in 1522, the first people to have sailed around the world.

France joined the race for Asia's fabled wealth in 1524 when King Francis I (ruled 1515–1547) dispatched

MAP 2.4
The Spanish and Portuguese Empires, 1610
By 1610 Spain dominated Latin America, including Portugal's possessions. Having devoted its energies to exploiting Mexico and the Caribbean, Spain had not yet expanded into what is now the United States, aside from establishing outposts in Florida and New Mexico.

Spanish Map of the Antilles, 1519
This map offers a rare glimpse of Spain's early colonies in the West Indies. It depicts African laborers, forcibly imported to replace Native Americans lost to disease and harsh treatment.

an Italian navigator, Giovanni da Verrazano, to find a more direct "northwest passage" to the Pacific. Verrazano explored the North American coast from the Carolinas to Newfoundland. In three subsequent voyages between 1534 and 1542, the French explorer Jacques Cartier carefully probed the coasts of Newfoundland, Quebec, and Nova Scotia and sailed up the St. Lawrence River as far as present-day Montreal. Although encountering large numbers of Native Americans, Verrazano and Cartier found no gold and no northwest passage.

Spain's Conquistadors, 1492–1536

Columbus was America's first slave trader and the first Spanish conqueror, or conquistador. At his struggling colony on Hispaniola, he enslaved Native people and created *encomiendas*—grants awarding Indian land, labor, and tribute to wealthy colonists. The earliest *encomiendas* were gold mines, which produced limited profits for a few mine operators.

From the beginning, *encomiendas* harshly exploited Native Americans, who died in droves from overwork, malnutrition, and disease. Then Portuguese slavers stepped in, supplying shiploads of Africans to replace the perishing Indians. Spanish missionaries who came to Hispaniola to convert the Indians quickly sent back grim reports of Indian exploitation; King Ferdinand (who had made money by selling *encomiendas*) felt sufficiently shocked to attempt to forbid the practice. But while the missionaries deemed Native Americans potential Christians, they joined most other colonizers in condemning Africans as less than fully human and thereby beyond hope of redemption. Blacks could therefore be exploited without limit. In Cuba, Puerto Rico, and other islands, they were forced to perform back-

breaking work on Spanish sugar plantations (see Technology and Culture: Sugar Production in the Americas).

Meanwhile, Spanish settlers fanned out across the Caribbean in search of Indian slaves and gold. In 1519 a restless nobleman, Hernán Cortés (1485–1547), led six hundred troops to the Mexican coast. Destroying his boats, he enlisted the support of enemies and discontented subjects of the Aztecs (see Chapter 1) in a quest to conquer that empire. Besides military support, Cortés gained the services of Malintzin (or Malinche), later known as Doña Marina, an Aztec woman brought up among the Maya. Malintzin served as Cortés' interpreter, diplomatic broker, and mistress.

Upon reaching the Aztec capital of Tenochtitlan, the Spanish were stunned by its size and wealth. "We were amazed and said that it was like the enchantments they tell of [in stories], and some of our soldiers even asked whether the things that we saw were not a dream," recalled one soldier. Certainly, the golden gifts that the Aztec emperor, Moctezuma II (ruled 1502–1520) initially offered the invaders were no dream. "They picked up the gold and fingered it like monkeys," one Aztec recalled. "Their bodies swelled with greed, and their hunger was ravenous. They hungered like pigs for that gold."

The Spanish ignored Moctezuma's offer, raiding his palace and treasury, and melting down all the gold they could find. Despite their emperor's imprisonment, the Aztecs regrouped and drove the invaders from the city, killing three hundred Spanish and four thousand of their Indian allies before reinforcements from Cuba enabled the Spanish to prevail. The victory was also ensured by the smallpox epidemic the Spanish brought with them, the same one that was killing large numbers of Indians on Hispaniola and the other islands. Lacking any previous contact with the disease, the Aztecs' and other Indians' immune systems were ill equipped to resist it. Just when the Aztecs took back Tenochtitlan, the epidemic struck. When the Spanish finally recaptured the city, wrote one Spanish chronicler, "the streets were so filled with dead and sick people that our men walked over nothing but bodies." By striking down other Indians, friends as well as foes, the epidemic enabled the Spanish to consolidate their control over much of central Mexico. By 1521 Cortés had overthrown the Aztecs and began to build a Spanish capital, Mexico City, on the ruins of Tenochtitlan.

Over the remainder of the sixteenth century, other conquistadors and officials established a great Spanish empire stretching from New Spain (Mexico) southward to Chile (see Map 2.4). The most important of these conquests was that of the Inca empire (see Chapter 1)

Cortés and Malintzin (Doña Marina)
The Spanish conqueror and his most important Indian collaborator meet with other Native allies on their march toward the Aztec capital of Tenochtitlán.

between 1532 and 1536 by a second reckless conquistador, Francisco Pizarro (c. 1478–1541). As with the Aztecs, smallpox and native unfamiliarity with European ways and weapons enabled a small army to overpower a mighty emperor and his realm. The human cost of the Spanish conquest was enormous. Mourned a vanquished Aztec,

> Broken spears lie in the roads;
> We have torn our hair in our grief.
> The houses are roofless now. . .
> And the walls are splattered with gore. . .
> We have pounded our hands in despair
> Against the adobe walls.

When Cortés landed in 1519, central Mexico's population had been between 13 and 25 million. By 1600 it had shrunk to about seven hundred thousand. Peru and other regions experienced similar devastation. America had witnessed the greatest demographic disaster in world history.

The Columbian Exchange

The emerging Atlantic world linked not only peoples but also animals, plants, and microbes from Europe, Africa, and the Americas. After 1492 Native Americans died

above all because they lacked antibodies that could ward off European and African infections—especially deadly, highly communicable smallpox. From the first years of contact, frightful epidemics of smallpox and other unknown diseases scourged the defenseless Indian communities. In the larger West Indian islands, 95 percent of the native population perished within thirty years. "The people began to die very fast, and many in a short space," an Englishman later remarked, adding that the deaths invariably occurred after Europeans had visited an area. Whole villages perished at once, with no one left to bury the dead. Such devastation directly facilitated European colonization everywhere in the Americas, whether accompanied by a military effort or not.

The Columbian exchange—the biological encounter of the Eastern and Western Hemispheres—affected the everyday lives of peoples throughout the Atlantic world. Besides diseases, sixteenth-century Europeans introduced horses, cattle, sheep, swine, chickens, wheat and other grains, coffee, sugar cane, numerous fruits and garden vegetables, and many species of weeds, insects, and rodents to America. In the next century, enslaved Africans carried rice and yams with them across the Atlantic. The list of American gifts to Europe and Africa was equally impressive: corn, many varieties of beans, white and sweet potatoes, the tropical root crop manioc, tomatoes, squash, pumpkins, peanuts, vanilla, cacao, avocados, pineapples, chilis, tobacco, and turkeys. Often, several centuries passed before new plants became widely accepted across the ocean. For example, many Europeans initially suspected that potatoes were aphrodisiacs and that tomatoes were poisonous, and few Indians would ever grow wheat.

European weeds and domestic animals drastically altered many American environments. Especially in temperate zones, livestock devoured indigenous plants, enabling hardier European weeds to take over. As a result, wild animals that had fed on the plants stayed away, depriving Indians of a critical source of food. Free-roaming livestock, especially hogs, also invaded Native Americans' cornfields. In this way, colonists' ways of life impinged directly on those of Native peoples. Settlers' crops, intensively cultivated on lands never replenished by lying fallow, often exhausted American soil. But the worldwide exchange of food products also enriched human diets and later made enormous population growth possible.

Another dimension of the Atlantic world was the mixing of peoples. During the sixteenth century, about three hundred thousand Spaniards immigrated, 90 percent of them male. Particularly in towns, a racially blended people emerged as these men married Indian women, giving rise to the large mestizo (mixed Spanish-Indian) population of Mexico and other Latin American countries. Lesser numbers of *métis*, as the French termed people of both Indian and European descent, would appear in the French and English colonies of North America. Throughout the Americas, particularly in plantation colonies, European men fathered mulatto children with enslaved African women, and African-Indian unions occurred in most regions. Colonial societies differed significantly in their official attitudes toward the different kinds of interracial unions and in their classifications of the children who resulted.

The Americas supplied seemingly limitless wealth for Spain. Some Spaniards grew rich from West Indian sugar plantations and Mexican sheep and cattle ranches, and immense quantities of silver crossed the Atlantic after rich mines in Mexico and Peru began producing in the 1540s. Spain took in far more American silver than its economy could absorb, setting off inflation that eventually engulfed all Europe. Bent on dominating Europe, the Spanish kings needed ever more American silver to finance their wars. Several times they went bankrupt, and in the 1560s their efforts to squeeze more taxes from their subjects helped provoke the revolt of Spain's rich Netherlands provinces (see below). In the end, American wealth proved to be a mixed blessing for Spain.

FOOTHOLDS IN NORTH AMERICA, 1512–1625

Most European immigrants in the sixteenth century flocked to Mexico, the Caribbean, and points farther south. But a minority helped extend the Atlantic world to North America through exploratory voyages, fishing expeditions, trade with Native Americans, and piracy and smuggling. Except for a Spanish base at St. Augustine, Florida, the earliest attempts to plant colonies failed, generally because they were predicated on unrealistic expectations of fabulous wealth and pliant natives.

After 1600 the ravaging of Indian populations by disease and the rise of English, French, and Dutch power finally made colonization possible. By 1614 Spain, England, France, and the Netherlands had made often overlapping territorial claims and established North American footholds (see Maps 2.4 and 2.5). Within another decade, each colony developed a distinct economic orientation and its own approach to Native Americans.

Spain's Northern Frontier, 1512–1625

The Spanish had built their American empire by subduing the Aztec, Inca, and other Indian states. The dream of more such finds drew would-be conquistadors to lands north of Mexico. "As it was his object to find another treasure like that . . . of Peru," a witness wrote of one such man, Hernando de Soto, he "would not be content with good lands nor pearls."

The earliest of these invaders was Juan Ponce de León, the conqueror of Puerto Rico, who in 1512–1513 and again in 1521 trudged through Florida in search of gold and slaves. His quest ended in death in a skirmish with Native Americans. The most astonishing early expedition began in Florida in 1527. After provoking several attacks by Apalachee Indians, the three hundred explorers were separated into several parties. All were thought to have perished until eight years later, when four survivors, led by Alvar Nuñez Cabeza de Vaca and including an African slave, Estevanico, arrived in northern Mexico. Cabeza de Vaca's account of their journey from Florida through Texas and New Mexico is the most compelling European literary work on North America before permanent colonization.

Cabeza de Vaca provided direct inspiration for the two most formidable attempts at Spanish conquest. De Soto and his party in 1539–1543 blundered from Tampa Bay to the Appalachians to the southern Plains, scouring the land for gold and alienating Native people wherever they went. "Think, then," one Indian chief appealed to him vainly,

what must be the effect on me and mine, of the sight of you]and your people, whom we have at no time seen, astride the fierce brutes, your horses, entering with such speed and fury into my country, that we had no tidings of your coming—things so absolutely new, as to strike awe and terror into our hearts.

In 1540 a coalition of Native Americans gathered at the Mississippian city of Mábila to confront the invaders. Although victorious militarily, the expedition's own losses doomed the Spanish effort. Most of their

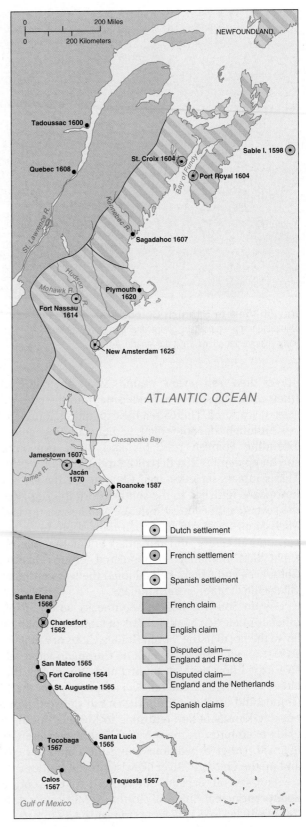

MAP 2.5

European Imperial Claims and Settlements in Eastern North America, 1565–1625

By 1625 four European nations contended for territory on North America's Atlantic coast. Except for St. Augustine, Florida, all settlements established before 1607 had been abandoned by 1625.

Navajo View of Spanish Colonizers
This pictograph—a painting or drawing on rock—was sketched in the early colonial period in Cañón del Muerto, Arizona.

horses died from arrow wounds while their livestock (their principal source of food aside from the corn they seized) scattered. Thereafter, the expedition floundered.

Although de Soto died without finding gold or extending Spanish rule, his and other expeditions spread epidemics that destroyed most of the remaining Mississippian societies (see Chapter 1). By the time Europeans returned to the southeastern interior late in the seventeenth century, only the Natchez on the lower Mississippi River still inhabited their sumptuous temple-mound center and remained under the rule of a Great Sun monarch. Depopulated groups like the Cherokees and Creeks had adopted the less-centralized village life of other eastern Indians.

As de Soto roamed the Southeast, some Spanish officials in Mexico heard rumors of fabulous wealth that lay to the north in the "Seven Golden Cities of Cíbola." In 1540–1542 Francisco Vásquez de Coronado led a massive expedition bent on finding and conquering these cities. Coronado plundered several pueblos on the Rio Grande and wandered from the Grand Canyon to present-day Kansas before returning to Mexico, finding no gold but embittering many Native Americans toward the Spanish. Other expeditions along the California coast and up the Colorado River likewise proved fruitless.

For several decades after these failed ventures, Spain's principal interest north of Mexico and the Caribbean lay in establishing strategic bases to keep out French and English intruders. In 1565 Spain established the first successful European settlement in North America, a fortress at St. Augustine, Florida. Despite attempts to strengthen Florida and to build forts linking it to Mexico, St. Augustine remained a lone military stronghold and a base for a chain of religious missions extending north to Chesapeake Bay. Rejecting missionary efforts to reorder their lives, the Guale, Powhatan, and other Indians rebelled and forced the closing of all the missions before 1600. Franciscan missionaries renewed their efforts in Florida in the early seventeenth century and secured the nominal allegiance of about sixteen thousand Guale and Timucua Indians. But epidemics in the 1610s killed about half the converts.

Meanwhile, in the 1580s, Spanish missionaries had returned to the Southwest, preaching Christianity and scouting the area's potential wealth. Encouraged by their reports, New Spain's viceroy in 1598 commissioned Juan de Oñate to lead five hundred Spaniards, mestizos, Mexican Indians, and African slaves into the upper Rio Grande Valley. They seized a pueblo of the Tewa Indians, renamed it San Juan, and proclaimed the royal colony of New Mexico.

The Spanish encountered swift resistance at the mesa-top pueblo of Ácoma in December 1598. When the Ácoma Indians refused Spanish demands for provisions for an exploring expedition, fifteen Spanish soldiers ascended the mesa to obtain the goods by force. But the natives resisted and killed most of the soldiers. Determined to make an example of Ácoma, Oñate ordered massive retaliation. In January Spanish troops captured the pueblo, killing eight hundred inhabitants in the process. Oñate forced surviving men to have one foot cut off and, along with the women and children, to be servants of the soldiers and missionaries. Two prominent leaders also had their right hands amputated.

Despite having crushed Ácoma and forced other Pueblo Indians to serve in Spanish *encomiendas*, the new colony barely survived. The Spanish government replaced Oñate in 1606 because of mismanagement and excessive brutality toward the Indians, and seriously considered withdrawing from New Mexico altogether. Franciscan missionaries, aiming to save Pueblo Indian souls, persuaded the authorities to keep New Mexico alive. By 1630 Franciscans had been dispatched to more than fifty pueblos and nominally converted up to twenty thousand Indians. But resistance was common because, as the leading Franciscan summarized it, "the main and general answer given [by the Pueblos] for not becoming Christians is that when they do, . . . they are at once compelled to pay tribute and render personal service."

New Mexico began, then, amidst uneasy tensions between colonists and natives.

France: Initial Failures and Canadian Success, 1541–1610

The voyages of Verrazano and Cartier (see above) marked the beginning of French activity in North America. France made its first colonizing attempt in 1541 when Cartier returned with ten ships carrying four hundred soldiers, three hundred sailors, and a few women to the St. Lawrence Valley. Cartier had earned Native Americans' distrust during his previous expeditions, and his construction of a fortified settlement on Stadacona Indian land (near the modern city of Quebec) removed all possibility of friendly relations. Over the next two years, the French suffered heavy casualties from Stadacona attacks and from scurvy (for which the Stadoconas could have shown them a cure) before abandoning the colony.

The failed French expedition seemed to verify the Spanish opinion, voiced by the cardinal of Seville, that "this whole coast as far [south] as Florida is utterly unproductive." The next French effort at colonization came in 1562 when French Huguenots (Calvinists) briefly established a base in what is now South Carolina. In 1564 the Huguenots founded a settlement near present-day Jacksonville, Florida. Sensing a Protestant threat to their control of the Caribbean, Spanish forces destroyed the settlement a year later, executing all 132 male defenders. These failures, along with a civil war between French Catholics and Huguenots, temporarily hindered France's colonizing efforts.

Meanwhile, French and other European fishermen were working the plenteous Grand Banks fisheries off the coast of Newfoundland. Going ashore to dry their fish, some French sailors bartered with Beothuk Indians for skins of beaver, a species almost extinct in Europe. By the late sixteenth century, as European demand for beaver hats skyrocketed, a French-dominated fur trade blossomed. Before the end of the century, French traders were returning annually to sites from Newfoundland to New England and along the lower St. Lawrence.

Unlike explorers such as de Soto and colonizers such as those at Roanoke (see below), most traders recognized the importance of reciprocity in dealing with Native Americans. Consequently, they were generally more successful. In exchange for pelts, they traded metal tools such as axes and knives, cloth, and glass beads. Seen by the Europeans as trinkets, glass beads were considered by northeastern Indians to possess spiritual

power comparable to the power of quartz, mica, and other sacred substances that they had long obtained via trade networks (see Chapter 1). By the next century, specialized factories in Europe would be producing both cloth and glass for the "Indian trade."

Seeing the lucrative Canadian trade as a source of revenue, the French government dispatched the explorer Samuel de Champlain to establish the colony of New France at Quebec in 1608. The French decided that a colony was the surest means of deterring English, Dutch, and independent French competitors. Having previously explored much of the Northeast and headed a short-lived French settlement at Acadia, Champlain was familiar with Indian politics and diplomacy in the region. Building on this understanding, he shrewdly allied with the Montagnais and Algonquins of the St. Lawrence and the Hurons of the lower Great Lakes. He agreed to help these allies defeat their enemies, the Mohawks of the Iroquois Confederacy, who sought direct access to European traders on the St. Lawrence. Champlain's new allies were equally shrewd in recognizing the advantage that French guns would give them against the usually dreaded Mohawks.

In July 1609 Champlain and two other Frenchmen accompanied sixty Montagnais and Huron warriors to Lake Champlain (which the explorer named for himself). Soon they encountered two hundred Mohawks at Point Ticonderoga near the lake's southern tip. After a night of

The Beaver as Worker and as Prey
This French engraving illustrates beavers' environmental impact and Indian methods of hunting them for commercial purposes.

mutual taunting, the two parties met on shore the following morning. As the main French-Indian column neared its opponents, Champlain stepped ahead and confronted the Mohawks' three spectacularly attired war leaders.

> When I saw them make a move to draw their bows upon us, I took aim with my arquebus [a kind of gun] and shot straight at one of the three chiefs, and with this same shot two fell to the ground, and one of their companions was wounded and died a little later. . . . As I was reloading my arquebus, one of my [French] companions fired a shot from within the woods, which astonished them again so much that, seeing their chiefs dead, they lost courage and took to flight.

The French and their allies pursued the fleeing Mohawks, killing about fifty and capturing a dozen prisoners. A few pro-French Indians suffered minor arrow wounds.

The battle of Lake Champlain marked the end of casual Indian-European encounters in the Northeast and the beginning of a deadly era of trade, diplomacy, and warfare. Through their alliance with the powerful Hurons, the French gained access to the thick beaver pelts of the Canadian interior in exchange for European goods and protection from the Iroquois. These economic and diplomatic arrangements defined the course of New France's history for the rest of the seventeenth century.

England and the Atlantic World, 1558–1603

When Elizabeth I became queen in 1558, England was a minor power; Spain and France grappled for supremacy in Europe; and Spain and Portugal garnered wealth from the Americas. Although England and Spain had been at peace, the largely Protestant English worried about Spanish interventions against Calvinists in France and the Netherlands, and about the pope's call for Elizabeth's overthrow. In securing the loyalty of England's rival Protestant movements (see above), Elizabeth shifted toward a militantly anti-Catholic foreign policy. Secretly, she stepped up her aid to the Calvinist rebels and encouraged English "sea dogs" like John Hawkins and Francis Drake—privateers who plundered Spanish ships.

The Anglo-Spanish rivalry in the Atlantic extended to Ireland after 1565, when Spain and the pope began directly aiding Irish Catholics' resistance to English rule. In a war that ground on through the 1580s, the English drove the Irish clans out of their strongholds, especially in northern Ireland, or Ulster, and established their own settlements ("plantations") of English and Scottish Protestants. The English practiced total war to break the rebellious population's spirit, inflicting starvation and mass slaughter by destroying villages in the winter.

Elizabeth's generals justified these atrocities by claiming that the Irish were "savages" and that Irish customs, religion, and method of fighting absolved the English from guilt in waging exceptionally cruel warfare. Ireland thus furnished precedents for later English tactics and rationales for crushing Native Americans.

England had two objectives in the Western Hemisphere in the 1570s. The first was to find the northwest passage to Asia and discover gold on the way; the second, in Drake's words, was to "singe the king of Spain's beard" by raiding Spanish fleets and ports from Spain to the West Indies. The search for the northwest passage only led to such embarrassments as explorer Martin Frobisher's return from the Canadian Arctic with a shipload of "fool's gold." However, privateering raids proved spectacularly successful and profitable for their financial backers, including merchants, gentry, government leaders, and Elizabeth herself. The most breathtaking enterprise was Drake's voyage around the world (1577–1580) in quest of sites for colonies. During this voyage, he sailed up the California coast and entered Drake's Bay, north of San Francisco, where he traded with Miwok Indians.

Now deadly rivals, Spain and England sought to outmaneuver one another in America. In 1572 the Spanish tried to fortify a Jesuit mission on the Chesapeake Bay. They failed, largely because Powhatan Indians resisted. After an attempt to colonize Newfoundland failed, Sir Walter Raleigh obtained a royal patent (charter) in 1584 to start an English colony farther south, closer to the Spanish—a region the English soon named Virginia in honor of their virgin queen. Raleigh dispatched Arthur Barlowe to explore the region, and Barlowe returned singing the praises of Roanoke Island, its peaceable natives, and its ideal location as a base for anti-Spanish privateers. Raleigh then persuaded Elizabeth to dispatch a colonizing expedition to Roanoke.

At first all went well. The Roanoke Indians eagerly traded and shared their corn. Given such abundance and native hospitality, the colonists wondered why they should work at all. Refusing to grow their own food, they expected the Roanokes to feed them. By the first winter, the English had outlived their welcome. Fearing that the natives were about to attack, English soldiers killed Wingina, the Roanoke leader, in June 1586. When Raleigh's friend Drake visited soon after on his way back to England, many colonists joined him.

Thereafter, the Anglo-Spanish conflict repeatedly prevented English ships from returning to Roanoke to supply those who remained. When a party finally arrived in 1590, it found only rusty armor, moldy books, and the word *CROATOAN* cut into a post. Although the stranded colonists were presumably living among the Croatoan Indians of Cape Hatteras, the exact fate of the "lost colony" remains a mystery to this day.

Roanoke's brief history underscored several stubborn realities about European expansion to North America. First, even a large-scale, well-financed colonizing effort could fail, given the settlers' lack of preparedness for the American environment. Second, colonists did not bring enough provisions for the first winter and disdained growing their own food. Although some settlers were curious and open-minded about the Indians' way of life, most assumed that Native Americans would submit to their authority and feed them while they looked for gold—a sure recipe for trouble. Third, colonizing attempts would have to be self-financing; financially strapped monarchs like Elizabeth I would not throw good money after bad. Fourth, conflict with the Spanish hung menacingly over every European attempt to gain a foothold in North America.

In 1588, while Roanoke struggled, England won a spectacular naval victory over the Armada, a huge invasion fleet sent into the English Channel by Spain's Philip II. This famous victory preserved England's independence and confirmed its status as a major power in the Atlantic.

The Beginnings of English Colonization, 1603–1625

Anglo-Spanish relations took a new turn after 1603, when Elizabeth died and her cousin, the king of Scotland, ascended the English throne as James I. The cautious, peace-loving king signed a truce with Spain in 1604. Alarmed by Dutch naval victories (see below), the Spanish now considered England the lesser danger. Consequently, Spain's new king, Philip III (ruled 1598–1621), conceded what his predecessors had always refused: a free hand to another power in part of the Americas. Spain renounced its claims to Virginia, and England could now colonize unmolested.

The question of how to finance English colonies remained. Neither the crown nor Parliament would agree to spend money on colonies, and Roanoke's failure had proved that private fortunes were inadequate to finance successful settlements. Political and financial leaders determined that joint-stock companies—business corporations that would amass capital through

sales of stock to the public—could raise enough funds for American settlement. Such stock offerings produced large sums with limited risk for each investor.

On April 10, 1606, James I granted a charter authorizing overlapping grants of land in Virginia to two separate joint-stock companies, one based in London and the other in Plymouth. The Virginia Company of Plymouth received a grant extending south from modern Maine to the Potomac River, and the Virginia Company of London's lands ran north from Cape Fear to the Hudson River. Both companies dispatched colonists in 1607.

The Virginia Company of Plymouth sent 120 men to Sagadahoc, at the mouth of the Kennebec River. Half left in 1608 after alienating nearby Abenaki Indians and enduring a hard Maine winter, and the rest went back to England a year later. Soon thereafter the company disbanded.

The Virginia Company of London barely avoided a similar failure. Its first expedition included many gentlemen who disdained work and expected riches to fall into their laps. They chose a site on the James River in May 1607 and named it Jamestown. Discipline quickly fell apart and, as at Roanoke, the colonists neglected to plant crops. When relief ships arrived in January 1608 with reinforcements, only 38 survivors remained out of 105 immigrants.

Short of workers who could farm, fish, hunt, and do carpentry, Virginia also lacked effective leadership. The council's first president hoarded supplies, and its second was lazy and indecisive. By September 1608, three councilors had died and three others had returned to England, leaving only a brash soldier of fortune, Captain John Smith.

Twenty-eight years old and of yeoman origin, Smith had experience fighting Spaniards and Turks that prepared him for assuming control in Virginia. Organizing all but the sick in work gangs, he ensured sufficient food and housing for winter. Applying lessons learned in his soldiering days, he laid down rules for maintaining sanitation and hygiene to limit disease. Above all, he brought order through military discipline. During the next winter (1608–1609), Virginia lost just a dozen men out of two hundred.

Smith also became the colony's diplomat. After Powhatan Indians captured him in late 1607, Smith displayed such courage that their *weroance* (chief), also named Powhatan, arranged an elaborate reconciliation ceremony in which his daughter Pocahontas "saved" Smith's life during a mock execution. Smith maintained satisfactory relations with the Powhatans in part through his personality, but he also employed calculated

demonstrations of English military strength to mask the settlers' actual weakness.

John Smith prevented Virginia from disintegrating as Sagadahoc had. But when he returned to England in 1609 after being wounded in a gunpowder explosion, discipline again crumbled. Expecting the Indians to provide them with corn, the colonists had not laid away sufficient food for the winter. A survivor wrote,

> So lamentable was our scarcity, that we were constrained to eat dogs, cats, rats, snakes, toadstools, horsehides, and what not; one man out of the misery endured, killing his wife powdered her up [with flour] to eat her, for which he was burned. Many besides fed on the corpses of dead men.

Of the five hundred residents at Jamestown in September 1609, about 400 died by May 1610. But an influx of new recruits, coupled with the reimposition of military rule, enabled Virginia to win the First Anglo-Powhatan War (1610–1614). The English population remained small, however, just 380 in 1616, and it had yet to produce anything of value for Virginia Company stockholders.

Tobacco emerged as Virginia's salvation. John Rolfe, an Englishman who married Pocahontas after the war, spent several years adapting a salable variety of Caribbean tobacco to conditions in Virginia. By 1619 the product commanded high prices, and that year Virginia exported large amounts to a newly emergent European market.

To attract labor and capital to its suddenly profitable venture, the Virginia Company awarded a fifty-acre "headright" for each person ("head") entering the colony, to whomever paid that person's passage. By paying the passage of prospective laborers, some enterprising planters accumulated sizable tracts of land. Thousands of young men and a few hundred women calculated that uncertainty in Virginia was preferable to continued unemployment and poverty in England. In return for their passage, they agreed to work as indentured servants for fixed terms, usually four to seven years. The Virginia Company abandoned military rule in 1619 and provided for an assembly to be elected by the "inhabitants" (apparently meaning only the planters). Although the assembly's actions were subject to the company's veto, it was the first representative legislature in North America.

By 1622 Virginia faced three serious problems. First, local officials systematically defrauded the shareholders by embezzling treasury funds, overcharging for supplies, and using company laborers to work their own tobacco fields. They profited, but the company sank deep into debt. Second, the colony's population suffered from an appallingly high death rate. The majority of fatalities stemmed from malnutrition owing to the poor diets of the servants, or from salt poisoning, typhus, or dysentery contracted when the settlers drank the salty, polluted water from the lower James River. Most of the 3,500 immigrants entering Virginia from 1618 to 1622 died within three years. Finally, relations with the Powhatans steadily worsened after Pocahontas died in England in 1617 and Powhatan died a year later. Leadership passed to Opechancanough, who at first sought to accommodate the English. But relentless English expansion led to Indian discontent and to the rise of a powerful religious leader, Nemattenew, who urged the Powhatans to resist the English to the death. After some settlers killed Nemattenew, the Indians launched a surprise attack in 1622 that killed 347 of the 1,240 colonists. With much of their livestock destroyed, spring planting prevented, and disease spreading through cramped fortresses, hundreds more colonists died in the ensuing months.

After the Virginia Company sent more men, Governor Francis Wyatt reorganized the settlers and took the offensive during the Second Anglo-Powhatan War (1622–1632). Using tactics developed during the Irish war, Wyatt inflicted widespread starvation by destroying food supplies, conducted winter campaigns to drive Indians from their homes when they would suffer most, and fought (according to John Smith) as if he had "just cause to destroy them by all means possible." By 1625 the English had effectively won the war, and the Powhatans had lost their best chance of driving out the intruders.

The clash left the Virginia Company bankrupt and James I concerned over complaints against its officers. After receiving a report critical of the company's management, James revoked its charter in 1624, and Virginia became a royal colony. Only about five hundred colonists now lived in Virginia, including a handful of Africans who had been brought in since 1619. The vast majority of this population, white as well as black, consisted of unfree laborers, and most would die early deaths (see Chapter 3). The roots from which Virginia's Anglo-American and African-American peoples later grew were fragile indeed.

New England Begins, 1614–1625

The next English colony, after Virginia, that proved permanent arose in New England. In 1614 the ever-enterprising John Smith, exploring its coast, gave New England its name. "Who," he asked, "can but approve this most excellent place, both for health and fertility?"

An admirer of Cortés, Smith planned to conquer its "goodly, strong, and well-proportioned [Indian] people" and establish a colony there. But his hopes came to nothing. As for the region's Native peoples, a terrible epidemic spread by fishermen or traders devastated coastal communities by about 90 percent in 1616–1618. Later visitors found the ground littered with the "bones and skulls" of the unburied dead and acres of overgrown cornfields.

In 1620, against this tragic backdrop, the Virginia Company of London gave a patent to some London merchants headed by Thomas Weston for a settlement. Weston sent over twenty-four families (a total of 102 people) in a small, leaky ship called the *Mayflower*. The colonists promised to send lumber, furs, and fish back to Weston in England for seven years, after which they would own the tract.

The expedition's leaders, but only half its members, were Separatist Puritans who had withdrawn from the Church of England and fled to the Netherlands to practice their religion freely. Fearing that their children were assimilating into Dutch culture, they decided to immigrate to America.

In November 1620 the *Mayflower* landed at Plymouth Bay, north of Virginia's boundary in present-day Massachusetts. Knowing that they had no legal right to be there, the expedition's leaders insisted that all the adult males in the group (including non-Separatists) sign the Mayflower Compact before they landed. By this document they constituted themselves a "civil body politic," or government, under English rule, and established the colony of New Plymouth, or Plymouth.

Weakened by their journey and unprepared for winter, half the Pilgrims, as the colonists later came to be known, died within four months of landing. Those still alive in the spring of 1621 owed much to the aid of two English-speaking Native Americans. One was Squanto, a Wampanoag Indian who had been taken to Spain as a slave in 1614 and then escaped to England. Returning home with a colonizing expedition, he learned that most of the two thousand people of his village had perished in the recent epidemic. The other friendly Indian, an Abenaki from Maine named Samoset, had experience trading with the English. To prevent the colonists from stealing the natives' food, Squanto showed them how to grow corn, using fish as fertilizer. Plymouth's first harvest was marked by a festival, "at which time . . . we exercised our arms, many of the Indians coming amongst us, . . . some 90 men, whom for three days we entertained and feasted." This festival became the basis for Thanksgiving, a holiday established in the nineteenth century.

Plymouth's relations with the Native Americans soon worsened. The alliance that Squanto and Samoset had arranged between Plymouth and the Wampanoags, headed by Massasoit, had united two weak parties. But with their firearms the colonists became the dominant partner, forcing the Wampanoags to acknowledge English sovereignty. News of the Powhatan attack in 1622 hastened the colony's militarization under the leadership of a professional soldier, Miles Standish. Standish threatened Plymouth's "allies" with the colony's monopoly of firepower. For although Massasoit remained loyal, many Wampanoags were offended by the colonists' conduct.

Relations with Native Americans also enabled Plymouth to become economically self-sufficient. After the colony turned from communal farming to individually owned plots, its more-prosperous farmers produced corn surpluses, which they traded to nonfarming Abenakis in Maine for furs. Within a decade, Plymouth had attracted several hundred colonists.

The Plymouth colonists' lasting importance was threefold. First, they constituted an outpost for Puritans dissenting from the Church of England. Second, they proved that a self-governing society consisting mostly of farm families could flourish in New England. Finally, they foreshadowed the aggressive methods that later generations of European Americans would use to gain mastery over Indians. In all three respects, Plymouth was the vanguard of a massive, voluntary migration of Puritans to New England in the 1630s (see Chapter 3).

The Enterprising Dutch, 1609–1625

Among the most fervently Calvinist regions of Europe were the Dutch-speaking provinces of the Netherlands. The provinces had come under Spanish rule during the sixteenth century, but Spain's religious intolerance and high taxes drove the Dutch to revolt beginning in 1566. Repeatedly unable to quell the revolt, Spain and the Dutch Republic agreed on a truce in 1609. By then the Netherlands was a wealthy commercial power. The Dutch built an empire stretching from Brazil to South Africa to Taiwan, and played a key role in colonizing North America.

Just as the French were routing the Mohawk Iroquois at Lake Champlain in 1609, Henry Hudson sailed up the river later named for him, traded with Native Americans, and claimed the land for the Netherlands. When Dutch traders returned the following year, some of their most eager customers were—not surprisingly—Mohawk. Having established lucrative ties with Indians on the lower Hudson River, Dutch traders

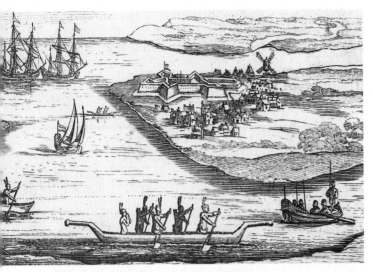

New Amsterdam
After the Dutch "purchase" of Manhattan Island, the fortified settlement of New Amsterdam grew only slowly, as this view from 1651 (the earliest known depiction) clearly shows. Except for the tip, the island remained farmland or forest. Corn brought by canoe-paddling Indians also helped feed the settlement. Note the windmill, where grain was ground.

CHRONOLOGY, 1400–1625	
c. 1400–1600	European Renaissance.
c. 1400	Mali challenged in West African grassland. Coastal West African kingdoms rise and expand.
1440	Portuguese slave trade in West Africa begins.
1488	Días reaches the Cape of Good Hope.
1492	Christian "reconquest" of Spain. Columbus lands at Guanahaní.
1517	Protestant Reformation begins in Germany.
1519–1521	Cortés leads Spanish conquest of Aztec empire.
1519–1522	Magellan's expedition circumnavigates the globe.
1532–1536	Pizarro leads Spanish conquest of Inca empire.
1534	Church of England breaks from Roman Catholic Church.
1541–1542	Cartier attempts to colonize eastern Canada.
1539–1543	De Soto attempts conquests in southeastern United States.
1540–1542	Coronado attempts conquests in southwestern United States.
1558	Elizabeth I becomes queen of England.
1565	St. Augustine founded by Spanish.
1585–1590	English colony of Roanoke established, then disappears.
1588	England defeats the Spanish Armada.
1598	Oñate founds New Mexico.
1603	James I becomes king of England.
1607	English found colonies at Jamestown and Sagadahoc.
1608	Champlain founds New France.
1609	Henry Hudson explores the Hudson River.
1610–1614	First Anglo-Powhatan War.
1614	New Netherland founded.
1619	Large exports of tobacco from Virginia begin. First Africans arrive in Virginia.
1620	Plymouth colony founded.
1622–1632	Second Anglo-Powhatan War.
1624	James I revokes Virginia Company's charter.

in 1614 built Fort Nassau near what would become Albany, and established the colony of New Netherland. In 1626 the Dutch bought an island at the mouth of the Hudson from local Indians and began a second settlement there. The Dutch named the island Manhattan and the settlement New Amsterdam.

New Netherlanders lived by the fur trade. Through the Mohawks, they relied on the Five Nations Iroquois, much as the French depended on the Hurons, as commercial clients and military allies. In the 1620s, to stimulate a flow of furs to New Netherland, Dutch traders obtained from coastal Indians large quantities of wampum—sacred shells like those used by Deganawidah and Hiawatha to convey solemn "words" of condolence in rituals (see Chapter 1)—for trade with the Iroquois. The Dutch-Iroquois and French-Huron alliances became embroiled in an ever-deepening contest to control the movement of goods between Europeans and Indians.

CONCLUSION

The sixteenth century marked the emergence of an Atlantic world linking Europe, Africa, and the Americas. Kings and emperors in West Africa were already competing ferociously for the wealth brought by long-distance trade, including trade in slaves. Western Europe halting-

ly entered a new era in which nation-states drew on Renaissance knowledge, merchants' capital, and religious zeal to advance national power and overseas expansion.

The Atlantic world brought few benefits to West Africans and Native Americans. Proclaiming that civilization and Christianity rendered them superior, Europeans denigrated Native Americans and Africans as savages whose land and labor Europeans could seize and exploit. Initial Portuguese incursions promised to expand West Africa's trade ties with Europe. But Europe's overwhelming demand for slave labor depleted the

region's population and accelerated the reshaping of trade, politics, warfare, and societies. Africa's notorious underdevelopment, which persists in our own time, had begun.

After 1492 the Atlantic world spread to the Americas. Indigenous peoples in Mexico, Peru, and elsewhere felt the terrible violence of Spanish conquest, suffering untold losses of population as well as the shattering of political, social, and religious institutions. The forced and unforced movements of people, as well as those of animals, plants, and disease-bearing germs, constituted a Columbian exchange that profoundly affected peoples and environments of both exploiters and exploited.

Native peoples north of Mexico and the Caribbean held would-be conquerors and colonizers at bay until after 1600. Depending on Europeans' dealings with them, native North Americans cooperated with Europeans who practiced reciprocity while resisting those who tried to dominate them. By 1625 Spain had advanced only as far north as seemed worthwhile to protect its prized Mexican and Caribbean conquests. Meanwhile, French, English, and Dutch colonists focused on less-spectacular resources. New France and New Netherland existed primarily to obtain furs from Indians, while the English in Virginia and Plymouth cultivated lands once belonging to Native Americans. All these colonies depended for their success on maintaining stable relations with at least some Native Americans. The transplantation of Europeans into North America was hardly a story of inevitable triumph.

FOR FURTHER REFERENCE

READINGS

Robert J. Berkhofer, Jr., *The White Man's Indian: Images of the American Indian from Columbus to the Present* (1978). A penetrating analysis of the shaping of European and American attitudes, ideologies, and policies toward Native Americans.

Nicholas Canny, ed., *The Origins of Empire (The Oxford History of the British Empire,* vol. 1; 1998). Essays by leading authorities offer a comprehensive treatment of the origins and early development of English imperialism.

Alfred W. Crosby, Jr., *Ecological Imperialism: The Biological Expansion of Europe, 900–1900* (1986). Accessible discussion of the environmental and medical history of European overseas colonization.

Philip Curtin, et al., eds., *African History: From Earliest Times to Independence,* 2nd ed. (1995). Excellent essay overviews by leading historians in the field.

Olwen Hufton, *The Prospect Before Her: A History of Women in Western Europe*, vol. I: *1500–1800* (1996). An outstanding interpretive synthesis.

D. W. Meinig, *The Shaping of America*, vol. 1: *Atlantic America, 1492–1800* (1986). A geographer's engrossing study of Europeans' encounter with North America and the rise of colonial societies.

Sidney W. Mintz, *Sweetness and Power: The Place of Sugar in Modern History* (1985). The role of sugar as crop, commodity, food, and cultural artifact.

Anthony Pagden, *Lords of All the World: Ideologies of Empire in Spain, Britain and France, c. 1500–c. 1800* (1995). A comparative discussion of imperialist thought in Europe's three most powerful overseas empires.

David B. Quinn, *North America from Earliest Discoveries to First Settlements: The Norse Voyages to 1612* (1977). A thorough, learned account of European exploration, based on a wide range of scholarship.

John Thornton, *Africa and Africans in the Making of the Atlantic World,* 2nd ed. (1998). Insightful perspectives on the role of West Africans in American colonization.

WEBSITES

Africans in America
http://www.pbs.org/wgbh/aia/part1/title.html
WGBH Educational Foundation.
An excellent site, offering a good narrative history and multiple resources and documents for further pursuing the subject. Part, 1, The Terrible Transformation, 1450–1750, is especially pertinent for this chapter.

A Biography of America, 1: New World Encounters
http://www.learner.org/biographyofamerica/prog01/index.html
Annenberg/CPB Learner.org.
A good introduction to North America before and after the arrival of Europeans, emphasizing Native Americans' experiences and Spanish and English imperialism.

Plimoth-on-Web
http://www.plimoth.org/index.html
A wealth of information on the histories of Wampanoag Indians and Pilgrim colonists in Plymouth, as well as on visiting Plimoth Plantation, the careful re-creation of Indian and English life in New England's first colony.

Texts of Imagination and Empire: The Founding of Jamestown in Its Atlantic Context
http://www.folger.edu/institute/jamestown/index_main.htm
An excellent, comprehensive introduction to the peoples and forces that shaped Virginia's early history.

CHAPTER 3

Expansion and Diversity: The Rise of Colonial America, 1625–1700

On the West Indian island of Barbados in 1692, a widowed Englishwoman named Sarah Horbin drew up a list of her relatives to see who might deserve bequests of property in case her only son—a sailor being held for ransom in a North African prison—died. Through her kinsman, John Seabury of Barbados, she had kept in contact with a dozen Seabury cousins in New England. She had also remained in touch with several Virginia relatives in the Empereur family and with a kinsman of her husband's, Andrew Rouse, who lived in Carolina.

Sarah Horbin and her far-flung clan were part of a massive migration of European women and men, predominantly English, who built new communities in North America and the Caribbean during the seventeenth century (see Map 3.1). By 1700 there were more than 250,000 people of European birth or parentage, most of them English, within the modern-day United States. They made up North America's first large wave of immigrant settlers.

In 1672 another recently widowed immigrant, Mary Johnson of Somerset County, Maryland, conducted a similar survey of her kin as she drew up a will. Each of her two sons, living nearby, had a wife and two children. Johnson's other relatives were undoubtedly as widely scattered as Horbin's, but unlike Horbin, she had no idea where they were. Mary Johnson had arrived in Virginia fifty years earlier as a slave. Although Mary's origins are

◀ **Portrait of Virginia's Governor William Berkeley, by Peter Laly**
After several decades of expansion and relative stability under Berkeley, Virginia exploded during Bacon's Rebellion (1676).

CHAPTER OUTLINE

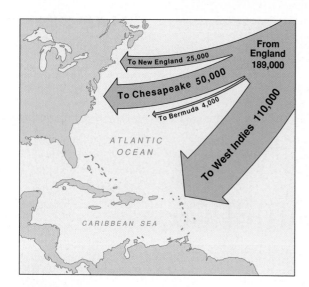

MAP 3.1
English Migration, 1610–1660
During the first phase of English transatlantic migration, the West Indies attracted more than twice as many colonists as went to the Chesapeake, and over four times as many as settled in New England.

unknown, her husband Anthony had previously been called Antonio, indicating that he had already been enslaved by the Portuguese. Soon after their marriage in 1625, the Johnsons managed to gain their freedom, as did a few dozen other enslaved Africans in Virginia's early decades. Thereafter they bought some land and even a few black slaves. Still, they faced the uncertainties confronting all small tobacco planters in the seventeenth-century Chesapeake region, besides daunting legal restrictions based on race.

Most of the Johnsons' fellow Africans were less fortunate. Whereas Europeans might at least hope to realize economic opportunity or religious freedom, most Africans and their children remained the property of others for as long as they lived. The Johnsons' grandchildren disappeared from Maryland records after the turn of the eighteenth century, most likely the victims of legislation forcing most free blacks into slavery.

The vast majority of the three hundred thousand Africans taken to the Caribbean and North America during the seventeenth century went to the sugar plantations of Sarah Horbin's neighbors in Barbados and elsewhere in the West Indies. A small but distinct minority went to the mainland plantation colonies of the Southeast, and a scattered few to other regions.

The vast migrations of Europeans and Africans were possible only because of yet another demographic upheaval, the depopulation and uprooting of Native Americans. Having begun in the sixteenth century (see Chapter 2), the process continued in the seventeenth, primarily as a result of epidemic diseases but also because of warfare and other factors arising from Europeans' occupation of Indian lands. Although many Native populations partly recovered, it is likely that about 1 million North American Indians died as a result of contact with Europeans by 1700. Sarah Horbin, Mary Johnson, and their extended families settled not in wildernesses but in lands long inhabited and worked by Native Americans.

Patterns of Indian depopulation and of European and African immigration transformed North America in the seventeenth century. From a few scattered outposts in 1625, Europeans expanded their territorial domains and built colonial societies from the St. Lawrence River to the Rio Grande. At the same time, the arrival of western Europeans and West Africans further enriched the continent's cultural diversity.

The preponderance of immigrants and capital from England ensured that nation's domination of North America's eastern coast as well as the Caribbean. Before 1700 the English would force the Dutch out of North America altogether and leave France and Spain with lands less attractive to colonists. Within England's mainland colonies, four distinct regions emerged: New England, the Chesapeake, Carolina, and the middle colonies. Several factors distinguished these regions from one another, including their physical environments, the motives of white immigrants, and the concentrations of enslaved Africans.

This chapter will focus on four major questions:

■ Why did colonial New Englanders abandon John Winthrop's vision of a "city on a hill"?

■ Why did indentured servitude give way to racial slavery in England's plantation colonies? Why were both these institutions more limited in the nonplantation colonies?

■ What were the major factors facilitating French and Spanish colonial expansion?

■ Why was England's North American empire so much larger and wealthier than those of France and Spain by 1700?

THE NEW ENGLAND WAY

One of the earliest colonial regions to prosper in North America was New England. Separatist Puritans had established Plymouth in 1620 (see Chapter 2), and a few hundred others had drifted into the region over the next decade. In 1630 a Puritan-led Great Migration to New England began (see Map 3.1). Establishing a colony based on religious ideals, this larger, more formidable group of Puritans endeavored to build America's first utopian, or ideal, society. Although internal divisions and social-economic change undermined these ideals, Puritanism gave New England a distinctive regional identity.

A City upon a Hill, 1625–1642

After Charles I (ruled 1625–1649) became England's king, Anglican authorities undertook a systematic campaign to eliminate Puritan influence within the Church of England. With the king's backing, bishops insisted that services be conducted according to the Book of Common Prayer, which prescribed rituals similar to Catholic practices. They dismissed Puritan ministers who refused to perform these "High Church" rites, and church courts fined or excommunicated Puritan laypersons.

In the face of such harassment, several Puritan merchants obtained a charter to colonize at Massachusetts Bay, north of Plymouth, in 1628. Organizing as the Massachusetts Bay Company, they took advantage of a gap in their charter and in 1629 moved the seat of their colony's government, along with four hundred colonists, to Salem, Massachusetts. Like Plymouth, Massachusetts Bay would be a Puritan-dominated, self-governing colony rather than controlled from England by stockholders, proprietors, or the crown. But unlike in Plymouth, in Massachusetts leaders were nonseparatists, advocating the reform of, rather than separation from, the Anglican church.

In 1630, the company sent out eleven ships and seven hundred passengers under Governor John Winthrop. In midvoyage Winthrop delivered an address titled "A Model of Christian Charity," spelling out the new colony's utopian goals.

Winthrop boldly announced that "we shall be as a city upon a hill, the eyes of all people are upon us." The settlers would build a godly community whose example would shame England into truly reforming the Church of England. The revival of piety would create a nation governed according to God's will.

Winthrop denounced the economic jealousy that bred class hatred. God intended that "in all times some must be rich and some poor," he asserted. The rich had an obligation to show charity and mercy toward the poor, who should accept rule by their social superiors as God's will. God expected the state to keep the greedy among the rich from exploiting the needy and to prevent the lazy among the poor from burdening their fellow citizens. In outlining a divine plan in which all people, rich and poor, served one another, Winthrop expressed a conservative European's understanding of social hierarchy (see Chapter 2) and voiced Puritans' dismay at the economic forces battering—and changing—English society.

Winthrop and his fellow immigrants reached Boston (the new capital) in June 1630, and by fall six towns had sprung up nearby. During the unusually severe first winter, 30 percent of Winthrop's party died, and another 10 percent went home in the spring. By mid-1631, however, thirteen hundred new settlers had landed, and more were on the way. The worst was over. The colony would never suffer another starving time. Like Plymouth, Massachusetts Bay primarily attracted landowning farm families of modest means, most of them receptive if not actively committed to Calvinism. These immigrants quickly established a healthier, more stable colony than did their contemporaries in Virginia. By 1642 more than fifteen thousand colonists had settled in New England.

The Pequot War, 1637

Also in contrast to Virginia, colonization in New England began with little sustained resistance from Native Americans, whose numbers were drastically reduced by the ravages of disease. After one epidemic killed about 90 percent of New England's coastal Indians (see Chapter 2), a second inflicted comparable casualties on Indians throughout the Northeast in 1633–1634. Having dwindled from twenty thousand in 1600 to a few dozen survivors by the mid-1630s, the Massachusett and Pawtucket Indians were pressed to sell most of their land to the English. During the 1640s Massachusetts Bay passed laws prohibiting them from practicing their own religion and encouraging missionaries to convert them to Christianity. Thereafter they ceded more land to the colonists and moved into "praying towns" like Natick, a reservation established by the colony. In the praying towns Puritan missionary John Eliot hoped to teach the Native Americans Christianity and English ways.

The rapid expansion of English settlement farther inland, however, aroused Indian resistance. Beginning

Attack on Mystic Fort, Pequot War
This print, published in an English participant's account of the war, shows English troops, backed by allied Indians, surrounding the Pequot village while soldiers prepare to burn it.

in 1633, settlers moved into the Connecticut River Valley and in 1635 organized the new colony of Connecticut. Friction quickly developed with the Pequot Indians, who controlled the trade in furs and wampum with New Netherland. After tensions escalated into violence, Massachusetts and Connecticut took coordinated military action in 1637. Having gained the support of the Mohegan and Narragansett Indians, they waged a ruthless campaign, using tactics similar to those devised by the English to break Irish resistance during the 1570s (see Chapter 2). In a predawn attack English troops surrounded and set fire to a Pequot village at Mystic, Connecticut, and then cut down all who tried to escape. Several hundred Pequots, mostly women and children, were killed. Although their Narragansett allies protested that "it is too furious, and slays too many men," the English found a cause for celebration in the grisly massacre. Wrote Plymouth's Governor William Bradford,

> It was a fearful sight to see them [the Pequots] thus frying in the fire and the streams of blood quenching the same, and horrible was the stink and scent thereof; but the victory seemed a sweet sacrifice, and they [the English] gave the praise to God, who had wrought so wonderfully for them, thus to enclose their enemies in their hands and give them so speedy a victory over so proud and insulting an enemy.

By late 1637 Pequot resistance was crushed, with the survivors taken by pro-English Indians as captives or by the English as slaves. The Pequots' lands were awarded to the colonists of Connecticut and another new Puritan colony, New Haven. (Connecticut absorbed New Haven in 1662.)

Dissent and Orthodoxy, 1630–1650

As members of a popular religious movement in England, Puritans had focused on their common opposition to Anglican practices. But upon arriving in New England, theological differences began to undermine the harmony Winthrop had envisioned. To ensure harmony, ministers in Massachusetts, Connecticut, and New Haven struggled to define a set of orthodox practices—the "New England Way." Other Puritans resisted their efforts.

One means of establishing orthodoxy was through education. Like most European Protestants, Puritans insisted that conversion required familiarity with the Bible and, therefore, literacy. Education, they believed, should begin in childhood and should be promoted by each colony. In 1647 Massachusetts Bay ordered every town of fifty or more households to appoint a teacher to whom all children could come for instruction, and every town of at least one hundred households to maintain a grammar school. This and similar laws in other Puritan

colonies represented New England's first steps toward public education. But none of these laws required school attendance, and boys were more likely to be taught reading and especially writing than were girls.

Because orthodoxy also required properly trained ministers, Massachusetts founded Harvard College in 1636. From 1642 to 1671 the college produced 201 graduates, including 111 ministers. As a result, New England was the only part of English America with a college-educated elite during the seventeenth century.

Puritans agreed that the church must be free of state control, and they opposed theocracy (government run by clergy). But Winthrop and other Massachusetts Bay leaders insisted that a holy commonwealth required cooperation between church and state. The colony obliged all adults to attend services and pay set rates (or tithes) to support their local churches. Massachusetts thus had a state-sponsored, or "established," church, whose relationship to civil government was symbolized by the fact that a single building—called a meetinghouse rather than a church—was used for both religious services and town business.

Roger Williams, who arrived in 1631, took a different stance. He argued that civil government should remain absolutely uninvolved with religious matters, whether blasphemy (cursing God), failure to pay tithes, refusal to attend worship, or swearing oaths on the Bible in court. Williams also opposed any kind of compulsory church service or government interference with religious practice, not because all religions deserved equal respect but because the state (a creation of sinful human beings) would corrupt the church.

Recognizing the seriousness of Williams' challenge, the colony's officials declared his opinions subversive and banished him in 1635. Williams moved south to a place that he called Providence, which he purchased from the Narragansett Indians. At Williams's invitation a steady stream of dissenters drifted to the group of settlements near Providence, which in 1647 joined to form Rhode Island colony. (Other Puritans scorned the place as "Rogues Island.") True to Williams's ideals, Rhode Island was the only New England colony to practice religious toleration. Growing slowly, the colony's four towns had eight hundred settlers by 1650.

A second major challenge to the New England Way came from Anne Hutchinson, whom Winthrop described as "a woman of haughty and fierce carriage, of a nimble wit and active spirit." The controversy surrounding Hutchinson centered on her assertion that most New England ministers implicitly endorsed the Catholic idea that one's "good works" on earth were the key to salvation thereafter (see Chapter 2). Supposedly, all Puritans

Home of Governor Theophilus Eaton of New Haven Colony, ca. 1640
A prosperous merchant as well as political leader, Eaton built a home that was far larger and more comfortable than those of most New England colonists.

agreed that "good works" were a false road to heaven, instead following John Calvin in maintaining that God had predetermined who would and would not be saved. But Hutchinson argued that ministers who scrutinized a person's outward behavior for "signs" of salvation, especially when that person was relating his or her conversion experience, were discarding God's judgment in favor of their own. Only by looking inward and ignoring such false prophets could individuals hope to find salvation. Hutchinson charged that only two of the colony's ministers had been saved; the rest lacked authority over the elect.

By casting doubt on the clergy's spiritual state, Hutchinson undermined its authority over laypersons. Critics charged that her beliefs would delude individuals into imagining that they were accountable to no one but themselves. Winthrop branded her followers Antinomians, meaning those opposed to the rule of law. Hutchinson bore the additional liability of being a woman who stepped outside her prescribed role. As one of her accusers put it, "You have stepped out of your place; you [would] have rather been a husband than a wife, a preacher than a hearer; and a magistrate than a subject."

By 1636 Massachusetts Bay had split into two camps. Hutchinson's supporters included Boston merchants (like her husband) who disliked the government's economic restrictions on their businesses, young men chafing against the rigid control of church elders, and

women impatient with their second-class status in church affairs. In 1636 the Antinomians were strong enough to have their candidate elected governor, but they suffered defeat with Winthrop's return to office in 1637.

The victorious Winthrop brought Hutchinson to trial for heresy before the Massachusetts Bay legislature (the General Court), whose members peppered her with questions. Hutchinson's knowledge of Scripture was so superior to that of her interrogators, however, that she would have been acquitted had she not claimed to be converted through a direct revelation from God. Like most Christians, Puritans believed that God had ceased to make known matters of faith by personal revelation after New Testament times. Thus Hutchinson's own words condemned her.

The General Court banished the leading Antinomians from the colony, and others voluntarily followed them to Rhode Island or New Hampshire, or back to England. The largest group, led by Hutchinson, settled in Rhode Island.

Antinomianism's defeat was followed by new restrictions on women's independence and religious expression. Increasingly, women were prohibited from assuming the kind of public religious roles claimed by Hutchinson, and were even required to relate their conversion experiences in private to their ministers rather than publicly before their congregations (see below).

The most fundamental threat to Winthrop's city upon a hill was that the people would abandon the ideal of a close-knit community to pursue self-interest. Other colonies—most pointedly, Virginia—displayed the acquisitive impulses transforming England, but in New England, as one minister put it, "religion and profit jump together." While hoping for prosperity, Puritans believed that there were limits to legitimate commercial behavior. Government leaders tried to regulate prices so that consumers would not suffer from the chronic shortage of manufactured goods that afflicted New England. In 1635, when the Massachusetts General Court forbade pricing any item more than 5 percent above its cost, Robert Keayne of Boston and other merchants objected. These men argued that they had to sell some goods at higher rates in order to offset their losses from other sales, shipwrecked cargoes, and inflation. In 1639, after selling nails at 25 percent to 33 percent above cost, Keayne was fined heavily in court and was forced to make a humiliating apology before his congregation.

Controversies like the one involving Keayne were part of a struggle for New England's soul. At stake was the Puritans' ability and desire to insulate their city upon a hill from a market economy that, they feared, would strangle the spirit of community within a harsh new world of frantic competition.

Power to the Saints, 1630–1660

Despite sharp limits on dissent, New England's religious and political institutions were based on greater popular participation than elsewhere in Europe and its colonies. Although most Puritan colonists considered themselves nominal members of the Church of England, their self-governing congregations, like those in Separatist Plymouth, ignored Anglican bishops' authority. Control of each congregation lay squarely in the hands of its male "saints," as Puritans termed those who had been saved. By majority vote these men chose their minister, elected a board of elders to handle finances, and decided who else deserved recognition as saints. Compared to Anglican parishes in England and Virginia, where a few powerful landowners selected priests (subject to a bishop's formal approval) and made other major decisions, control of New England churches was broadly based.

In its church membership requirements, New England diverged even from other Puritans' practices. English Puritans accepted as saints any who correctly professed the Calvinist faith, repented their sins, and lived free of scandal. Massachusetts Puritans, however, insisted that candidates for membership stand before their congregation and provide a convincing, soul-baring "relation," or account, of their conversion experience (see Chapter 2). Many colonists shared the reluctance of Jonathan Fairbanks, who refused for several years to give a public profession of grace before the church in Dedham, Massachusetts, until the faithful persuaded him with many "loving conferences." The conversion relation emerged as the New England Way's most vulnerable feature.

Political participation was also more broadly based in New England than elsewhere. Massachusetts did not require voters or officeholders to own property but bestowed suffrage on every adult male "saint." By 1641 about 55 percent of the colony's twenty-three hundred men could vote. By contrast, English property requirements allowed fewer than 30 percent of adult males to vote.

In 1634, after public protest that the governor and council held too much power, each town gained the option of sending two delegates to the General Court. In 1644 the General Court became a bicameral (two-chamber) lawmaking body when the towns' deputies separated from the appointed Governor's Council.

New England legislatures established a town by awarding a grant of land to several dozen landowner-saints. These men then laid out the settlement, organized its church, distributed land among themselves, and established a town meeting—a distinctly New England institution. In England and Virginia (see below), justices of the peace administered local government through county courts. By contrast, New England's county courts served strictly as courts of law, and local administration was conducted by the town meeting. Town meetings decentralized authority over political and economic decisions to a degree unknown in England and its other colonies. Each town determined its own qualifications for voting and holding office in the town meeting, although most allowed all male taxpayers (including nonsaints) to participate. The meeting could exclude anyone from settling in town, and it could grant the right of sharing in any future land distributions to newcomers, whose children would inherit this privilege.

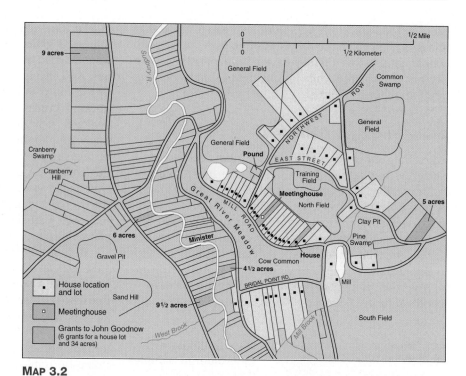

MAP 3.2

Land Divisions in Sudbury, Massachusetts, 1639-1656
Early New England towns sought to heighten communalism by clustering homes around a meetinghouse and a town commons (used for grazing). Sudbury, like many towns, followed an English practice of distributing croplands in scattered strips. John Goodnow, for example, grew crops in five fields at varying distances from his house. (Source: *Puritan Village: The Formation of a New England Town.* Copyright © 1963 by Sumner Chilton Powell and reprinted by permission of Wesleyan University Press.)

Few aspects of early New England life are more revealing than the first generation's attempt in many, but not all, towns to keep settlement tightly clustered (see Map 3.2). They did so by granting house lots near the town center and by granting families no more land than they needed to support themselves. Dedham's forty-six founders, for example, received 128,000 acres from Massachusetts Bay in 1636 yet gave themselves just 3,000 acres by 1656, or about 65 acres per family. The rest remained in trust for future generations.

With families clustered within a mile of one another, the physical settings of New England towns were conducive to traditional reciprocity. They also fostered an atmosphere of mutual watchfulness that Puritans hoped would promote godly order. For the enforcement of such order, they relied on the women of each town as well as male magistrates.

Although women's public roles had been sharply curtailed following the Antinomian crisis, women—especially female saints—remained a social force in their communities. With their husbands and older sons attending the family's fields, women remained at home in the tightly clustered neighborhoods at the center of each town. Neighboring women exchanged not only goods—say, a pound of butter for a section of spun wool—but advice and news of other neighbors as well. They also gathered at the bedside when one of them gave birth, an occasion supervised by a midwife and entirely closed to men. In these settings women confided in one another, creating a "community of women" within each town that helped enforce morals and protect the poor and vulnerable. In 1663 Mary Rolfe of Newbury, Massachusetts, was being sexually harassed by a high-ranking gentleman while her fisherman husband was at sea. Rolfe confided in her mother, who in turn consulted with a neighboring woman of influence before filing formal charges. Clearly influenced by the town's women, a male jury convicted the gentleman of attempted adultery. When a gentlewoman, Patience Dennison, charged her maidservant with repeatedly

stealing food and clothing, a fourth woman testified that the maid had given the provisions to a poor young wife, whose family was thereby saved from perishing. The servant was cleared while her mistress gained a lifelong reputation for stinginess.

New England Families

Like other Europeans of the time, Puritans believed that society's foundation rested not on the individual but rather on the "little commonwealth"—the nuclear family at the heart of every household. "Well ordered families," declared minister Cotton Mather in 1699, "naturally produce a Good Order in other Societies." In a proper family, the wife, children, and servants dutifully obeyed the household's male head. According to John Winthrop, a "true wife" thought of herself "in subjection to her husband's authority."

Mary Hollingsworth Embroidered Sampler
Many women found in embroidery a creative outlet that was compatible with their domestic duties.

Puritans defined matrimony as a contract rather than a religious sacrament, and New England couples were married by justices of the peace instead of ministers. As a civil institution, a marriage could be dissolved by the courts in cases of desertion, bigamy, adultery, or physical cruelty. By permitting divorce, the colonies diverged radically from practices in England, where Anglican authorities rarely annulled marriages and civil divorces required a special act of Parliament. Still, New Englanders saw divorce as a remedy fit only for extremely wronged spouses, such as the Plymouth woman who discovered that her husband was also married to women in Boston, Barbados, and England. Massachusetts courts allowed just twenty-seven divorces from 1639 to 1692.

Because Puritans believed that healthy families were crucial to the community's welfare, authorities intervened whenever they discovered a breakdown of household order. The courts disciplined unruly youngsters, disobedient servants, disrespectful wives, and violent or irresponsible husbands. Churches also censured, and sometimes expelled, spouses who did not maintain domestic tranquillity. Negligent parents, one minister declared, "not only wrong each other, but they provoke God by breaking his law."

New England wives enjoyed significant legal protections against spousal violence and nonsupport and also had more opportunity than other European women to escape failed marriages. But they also suffered the same legal disabilities as all Englishwomen. An English wife had no property rights independent of her husband unless he consented to a prenuptial agreement leaving her in control of property she already owned. Only if a husband had no other heirs or so stipulated in a will could a widow claim more than the third of the estate reserved by law for her lifetime use.

In contrast to England, New England benefited from a remarkably benign disease environment. Although settlements were compact, minimal travel occurred between towns, especially in the winter when people were most susceptible to infection. Furthermore, easy access to land allowed most families an adequate diet, which improved resistance to disease and lowered death rates associated with childbirth.

Consequently, New Englanders lived longer and raised larger families than almost any society in the world in the seventeenth century. Life expectancy for men reached sixty-five, and women lived nearly that long. More than 80 percent of all infants survived long enough to get married. The 58 men and women who founded Andover, Massachusetts, for example, had 247 children; by the fourth generation, the families of their

descendants numbered 2,000 (including spouses who married in from other families). The fact that most settlers came as members of family groups soon resulted in a population evenly divided between males and females. This balance permitted rapid population growth without heavy immigration.

Most colonists had little or no cash, relying instead on the labor of their large, healthy families to sustain them and secure their futures. Male household heads managed the family's crops and livestock, conducted most of its business transactions, and represented it in town government. Their wives bore, nursed, and reared their children. Women were in charge of work in the house, barn, and garden, including the making of food and clothing. Women also did charitable work and played other roles in their communities (see above).

More than in England and the other colonies, the sons of New England's founding generation depended on their parents to provide them with acreage for farming. With eventual land ownership guaranteed and few other opportunities available, sons delayed marriage and worked in their fathers' fields until finally receiving their own land. Because the average family raised three or four boys to adulthood, parents could depend on thirty to forty years of work if their sons delayed marriage beyond age twenty-five.

While daughters performed equally vital labor, their future lay with another family—the one into which they would marry. Being young, with many childbearing years ahead of them, enhanced their value to that family. Thus first-generation women, on average, were only twenty-one when they married.

Families with more sons and daughters enjoyed a labor surplus that allowed them to send their children to work as apprentices or hired hands for others. However, this system of family labor was inefficient for two reasons. First, the available supply of labor could not expand in times of great demand. Second, parents were reluctant to force their own children to work as hard as strangers. Nevertheless, family labor was the only system that most New Englanders could afford.

Saddled with the burdens of a short growing season, rocky soil salted with gravel, and (in most towns) a system of land distribution in which farmers cultivated widely scattered parcels, the colonists managed to feed large families and keep ahead of their debts, but few became wealthy from farming. Seeking greater fortunes than agriculture offered, some seventeenth-century New Englanders turned lumbering, fishing, fur trading, shipbuilding, and rum distilling into major industries. As its economy became more diversified, New England

prospered. But the colonists grew more worldly, and fewer of their children emerged as saints.

The Half-Way Covenant, 1662

As New England slowly prospered, England fell into chaos. The efforts of Charles I to impose taxes without Parliament's consent sparked a civil war in 1642. Alienated by years of religious harassment, Puritans gained control of the successful revolt and beheaded Charles in 1649. The consolidation of power by Puritan Oliver Cromwell raised New Englanders' hopes that England would finally heed their example and establish a truly reformed church. But Cromwell proved more receptive to Rhode Island's Roger Williams than to advocates of the New England Way. After Cromwell died, chaos returned to England until a provisional government "restored" the Stuart monarchy and crowned King Charles II (ruled 1660–1685). The Restoration left New England Puritans without a mission. Contrary to Winthrop's vision, "the eyes of all people" were no longer, if ever they had been, fixed on New England.

Meanwhile, a crisis over church membership also gripped New England. The first generation believed that they had accepted a holy contract, or covenant, with God, obliging them to implement godly rule and charge their descendants with its preservation. In return, God would make the city upon a hill prosper and shield it from corruption. The crisis arose because many Puritans' children were not joining the elect. By 1650, for example, fewer than half the adults in the Boston congregation were saints. The principal reason was the children's reluctance to subject themselves to public grilling on their conversion experience. Most New England children must have witnessed at least one person suffer an ordeal like Sarah Fiske's. For more than a year, Fiske answered petty charges of speaking uncharitably about her relatives—especially her husband—and then was admitted to the Wenham, Massachusetts, congregation only after publicly denouncing herself as worse "than any toad."

Because Puritan ministers baptized only babies born to saints, the unwillingness of the second generation to provide a conversion relation meant that most third-generation children would remain unbaptized. Unless a solution were found, saints' numbers would dwindle and Puritan rule would end. In 1662 a synod of clergy proposed a compromise known as the Half-Way Covenant, which would permit the children of baptized adults, including nonsaints, to receive baptism. Derisively

termed the "halfway" covenant by its opponents, the proposal would allow the founders' descendants to transmit potential church membership to their grandchildren, leaving their adult children "halfway" members who could not take communion or vote in church affairs. Congregations divided bitterly over limiting membership to pure saints or compromising purity in order to maintain Puritan power in New England. In the end, they opted for worldly power over spiritual purity.

The crisis in church membership signaled a weakening of the New England Way. Most second-generation adults remained in "halfway" status for life, and the saints became a shrinking minority as the third and fourth generations matured. Sainthood tended to flow in certain families, and by the 1700s there were more women than men among the elect. But because women could not vote in church affairs, religious authority stayed in male hands. Nevertheless, ministers publicly recognized women's role in upholding piety and the church itself.

Expansion and Native Americans, 1650–1676

As settlements grew and colonists prospered, the numbers and conditions of Native Americans in New England declined. Although Indians began to recover from the initial epidemics by midcentury, the settlers brought new diseases such as diphtheria, measles, and tuberculosis as well as new outbreaks of smallpox, which took heavy tolls. New England's Indian population fell from 125,000 in 1600 to 10,000 in 1675.

Native Americans felt the English presence in other ways. The fur trade, which initially benefited interior Natives, became a liability after midcentury. Once Indians began hunting for trade instead of just for their own subsistence needs, they quickly depleted the region's beavers and other fur-bearing animals. Because English traders shrewdly advanced trade goods on credit to Indian hunters before the hunting season, the lack of pelts pushed many Natives into debt. Traders such as John Pynchon of Springfield, Massachusetts, began taking Indian land as collateral and selling it to settlers.

Elsewhere, English townsmen, eager to expand their agricultural output and provide land for their sons, voted themselves larger amounts of land after 1660 and insisted that their scattered parcels be consolidated. For example, Dedham, Massachusetts, which distributed only three thousand acres from 1636 to 1656, allocated five times as much in the next dozen years. Rather than continue living closely together, many farmers built homes on their outlying tracts, often cutting Native settlements from one another and from hunting, gathering, and fishing areas (see Map 3.3).

English expansion put new pressures on Native peoples and the land. As early as 1642 Miantonomi, a Narragansett sachem (chief), warned neighboring Indians,

> These English having gotten our land, they with scythes cut down the grass, and with axes fell the trees; their cows and horses eat the grass, and their hogs spoil our clam banks, and we shall all be starved.

Within a generation, Miantonomi's fears were being borne out. By clearing away extensive stands of trees for fields and for use as fuel and building material, colonial farmers altered an entire ecosystem. Deer were no longer attracted, and the wild plants upon which Native Americans depended for food and medicine could not grow. The soil became drier and flooding more frequent in the face of this deforestation. The settlers also introduced domestic livestock, which, according to English custom, ranged freely. Pigs damaged Indian cornfields (until the Natives adopted the alien practice of fencing their fields) and shellfish-gathering sites. English cattle and horses quickly devoured native grasses, which the settlers then replaced with English varieties.

With their leaders powerless to halt the alarming decline of their population, land, and food sources, many Indians became demoralized. In their despair some turned to alcohol, increasingly available during the 1660s despite colonial efforts to suppress its sale to Native Americans. Interpreting the crisis as one of belief, other Natives joined those who had already converted to Christianity. By 1675 Puritan missionaries had established about thirty praying towns in eastern Massachusetts, Plymouth, and nearby islands. Supervised by missionaries, each praying town had its own Native American magistrate, usually a sachem, and many congregations had Indian preachers. Although the missionaries struggled to convert the Indians to "civilization" (meaning English culture and lifestyles) as well as Christianity, most praying Indians integrated the new faith with their native cultural identities.

Anglo-Indian conflict became acute during the 1670s because of pressures imposed on unwilling Indians to sell their land and to accept missionaries and the legal authority of colonial courts. Tension ran especially high in Plymouth colony where Metacom, or "King Philip," the son of the colony's onetime ally Massasoit, (see Chapter 2) was now the leading Wampanoag sachem. The English had engulfed the Wampanoags, persuaded many of them to renounce their loyalty to

MAP 3.3
Colonizing New England, 1620-1674
White expansion reached its maximum extent in the seventeenth century just before King Philip's War, which erupted as a result of the pressure on Indian communities. New England's territorial expansion did not resume until after 1715. (Source: Frederick Merk, *History of the Westward Movement*. Copyright © 1979 by Lois Bannister Merk. Used by permission of Alfred A Knopf, a division of Random House, Inc.)

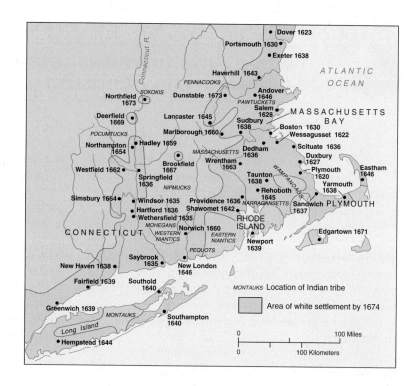

Metacom, and forced a number of humiliating concessions on the sachem.

In 1675 Plymouth hanged three Wampanoags for killing a Christian Indian and threatened to arrest Metacom. A minor incident, in which several Wampanoags were shot while burglarizing a farmhouse, ignited the conflict known as King Philip's War.

Eventually, two-thirds of the colonies' Native Americans, including some Christians, rallied around Metacom. Unlike Indians in the Pequot War, they were familiar with guns and as well armed as the colonists. Indian raiders attacked fifty-two of New England's ninety towns (entirely destroying twelve), burned twelve hundred houses, slaughtered eight thousand head of cattle, and killed twenty-five hundred colonists (5 percent).

The tide turned against Metacom in 1676 after the Mohawk Indians of New York and many Christian Indians joined the English against him. The English and their allies destroyed their enemies' food supplies and sold hundreds of captives into slavery, including Metacom's wife and child. "It must have been as bitter as death to him," wrote Puritan clergyman Cotton Mather, "to lose his wife and only son, for the Indians are marvellously fond and affectionate toward their children." About five thousand Indians starved or fell in battle, including Metacom himself, and others fled to New York and Canada.

King Philip's War reduced southern New England's Indian population by about 40 percent and eliminated

overt resistance to white expansion. It also deepened English hostility toward all Native Americans, even the Christian and other Indians who had supported the colonies. In Massachusetts ten praying towns were disbanded and Native peoples restricted to the remaining four; all Indian courts were dismantled; and English "guardians" were appointed to supervise the reservations. "There is a cloud, a dark cloud upon the work of the Gospel among the poor Indians," mourned John Eliot. In the face of poverty and discrimination, remaining Indians managed to maintain their communities and cultural identities.

Salem Witchcraft and the Demise of the New England Way, 1691–1693

Along with the relaxation of church membership requirements, social and economic changes undermined the New England Way. The dispersal of settlers away from town centers, besides pressuring Native Americans, generated friction between townspeople settled near the meetinghouse and "outlivers," whose distance from the town center limited their influence over town affairs. Moreover, the region's commercial economy was growing, especially in its port cities, and the distribution of wealth was becoming less even. These developments heightened Puritan anxieties that a small minority might be profiting at the community's expense. They also

Native American Baskets and Textiles in New England

For thousands of years before 1492, peoples of the Eastern and Western Hemispheres exchanged materials and techniques for making things with their neighbors. After Columbus broke the Atlantic barrier in 1492, they were able to broaden those exchanges across the hemispheres. Such exchanges rarely resulted in one group's wholesale adoption of another's technology. Instead, each group selected materials and techniques from the other group, incorporating what it selected into customary practices. Such was the case with Native Americans living near New England colonists in the seventeenth century.

Among the Wampanoags, Narragansetts, Mohegans, Pequots, and other Native peoples of southern New England, men and women each specialized in crafting objects for everyday use. Men made tobacco pipes from stone, ornaments from copper, and bows from wood. Women used the wild and domestic plants they harvested not only for preparing food but also to make baskets and other containers, fish traps, and mats to cover wigwams

Native American Basket, Rhode Island, 1675

This basket stands about four-and-a-half inches tall and is four inches in diameter. It is similar to baskets described by English writers in which Indians carried *yoheage*, a parched corn meal, and the shell beads known as wampum.

and line graves. English observers admired the scale and variety of women's products. One described an underground storage container that held sixty gallons of maize. Another saw baskets of "rushes; . . . others of maize husks; others of a kind of silk grass; others of a wild hemp; and some of barks of trees, . . . very neat and artificial, with the portraitures of birds, beasts, fishes, and flowers upon them in colors."

Indian women employed a variety of techniques in crafting these objects. One author told how Massachusett Indian women made mats by stitching together long strips of sedge, a marsh grass, with "needles made of the splinter bones of a cranes leg, with threads made of . . . hemp." Another described Abenaki women's "dishes . . . of birch bark sewed with threads drawn from spruce and white cedar roots, and garnished on . . . the brims with glistening quills taken from the porcupine and dyed, some black, others red." Others elaborated on the several varieties of bark and plant fibers that women interwove to make wigwams—materials that combined to ensure that a house kept its occupants warm and dry while remaining light and flexible enough to be carried from place to place.

When English colonists arrived in New England beginning in 1620, they brought the practices and products of their own textile traditions. Many colonial families raised sheep for wool while others harvested flax, a plant used to make linen. Englishwomen used spinning wheels to make woolen yarn and linen thread, and both men and women operated looms to weave yarn and thread into cloth.

Over time Native American women incorporated these English materials into their traditional baskets. A few such baskets survive today in museums. For one, the weaver used long strips of bark as the warp, or long thread, which she stitched together with two different "wefts," or "woofs," one of red and blue wool and the second probably from cornhusks (see photo). The basic technique of "twining" the warp and wefts is found in New England baskets dating to a thousand years earlier; the use of wool, however, was new. The basket came into English hands during King Philip's War (1675–1676). A Native woman whose community was at peace with

the colonists entered the English garrison town at what is now Cranston, Rhode Island, and asked a woman there for some milk. In return, the Indian woman gave her English benefactor the basket.

The story behind a second twined basket made of bark and wool has been lost. But it is clear that someone worked the wool into this basket after it was originally made. Archaeological evidence suggests that the addition of new materials to existing baskets was not exceptional. One Rhode Island site yielded seventy-three pieces of European cloth among the remains of sixty-six Indian baskets.

Besides incorporating European yarn and thread into familiar objects, Native Americans obtained finished European cloth, especially duffel, a woolen fabric that manufacturers dyed red or blue to suit Indian tastes. European traders furnished Native American customers with cloth as well as iron scissors, needles, and pins made to shape and sew it. In return, they obtained the material from which Indians made their own garments— beaver pelts. In these two-way exchanges of textiles, the English realized profits while Native Americans broadened ties of reciprocity (see Chapter 1) with the colonists.

English colonists and Indians shaped their newly acquired materials to their own tastes. The traders sold the pelts to European hatters, who cut and reworked them into beaver hats, a fashion rage in Europe. Native women used cloth in ways that were just as unfamiliar to Europeans. Mary Rowlandson, an Englishwoman captured by enemy Indians during King Philip's War, wrote a vivid description of what Americans would later call "the Indian fashion." As her captors danced during a ceremony, Rowlandson described the garb of her Narragansett "master" and Wampanoag "mistress":

> He was dressed in his holland shirt [a common
> English shirt], with great laces sewed at the tail of it.
> His garters were hung round with shillings, and he had
> girdles of wampum upon his head and shoulders. She
> had a kersey [coarse wool] coat covered with girdles
> of wampum from the loins upward. Her arms from her
> elbows to her hands were covered with bracelets.
> There were handfuls of necklaces about her neck and
> several sorts of jewels in her ears. She had fine red
> stockings and white shoes, [and] her hair [was]
> powdered and face painted red.

In combining indigenous materials in distinctive styles, the dancers—like Native basket makers and textile artisans—acknowledged the colonists' presence while resisting assimilating to English culture. They

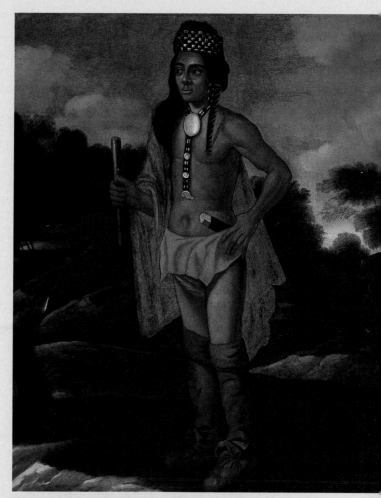

Ninigret, Eastern Niantic Sachem, c. 1684
Ninigret was a powerful sachem who traded with both English and Dutch. His outfit in this portrait artfully combines indigenous and European materials and objects in a way that is unmistakably Native American.

affirmed the new, multicultural reality of New England life but defied colonial efforts to suppress their culture and their communities. Once again technological exchange had led people to change without abandoning familiar ways of making things and expressing cultural identity.

Focus Questions

- How did Native American women in New England use English materials and techniques to modify traditional ways of making baskets and textiles during the seventeenth century?
- How did the new products Indians made reflect their attitudes about the colonists and about English culture?

65

prompted many colonists, both urban and rural, to act more competitively, aggressively, and impersonally toward one another. John Winthrop's vision of a religiously oriented community sustained by a sense of reciprocity was giving way to the materialistic, acquisitive society that the original immigrants had fled in England.

Nowhere in New England did these trends converge more forcefully than in Salem, Massachusetts, the region's second largest port. Trade made Salem prosperous but also destroyed the relatively equal society of first-generation fishermen and farmers. Salem's divisions were especially sharp in the precinct of Salem Village (now Danvers), an economically stagnant district located north of Salem Town. Residents of the village's

Images of Witchcraft
Most seventeenth-century Europeans and colonists feared that, at any time, Satan and those in his grip (witches) could attack and harm them with the power of evil.

eastern section farmed richer soils and benefited from Salem Town's commercial expansion, whereas those in the less fertile western half did not share in this prosperity and had lost the political influence that they once held in Salem.

In late 1691 several Salem Village girls encouraged an African slave woman, Tituba, to tell them their fortunes and talk about sorcery. When the girls later began behaving strangely, villagers assumed that they were victims of witchcraft. Pressed to identify their tormenters, the girls named two local white women and Tituba.

So far the incident was not unusual. Witchcraft beliefs remained strong in seventeenth-century Europe and its colonies. Witches were people (nearly always women) whose pride, envy, discontent, or greed supposedly led them to sign a pact with the devil. Thereafter they allegedly used maleficium (the devil's supernatural power of evil) to torment neighbors and others by causing illness, destroying property, or—as with the girls in Salem Village—inhabiting or "possessing" their victims' bodies and minds. Witnesses usually also claimed that witches displayed aggressive, unfeminine behavior. A disproportionate number of the 342 accused witches in New England were women who had inherited, or stood to inherit, property beyond the one-third of a husband's estate normally bequeathed to widows. In other words, most witches were assertive women who had or soon might have more economic power and independence than many men. For New Englanders, who felt the need to limit both female independence and economic individualism, witches symbolized the dangers awaiting those who disregarded such limits. In most earlier witchcraft accusations, there was only one defendant and the case never went to trial. The few exceptions to this rule were tried with little fanfare. Events in Salem Village, on the other hand, led to a colony-wide panic.

By April 1692 the girls had denounced two locally prominent women and had identified the village's former minister as a wizard (male witch). Fears of witchcraft soon overrode doubts about the girls' credibility and led local judges to sweep aside normal procedural safeguards. Specifically, the judges ignored the law's ban on "spectral evidence"—testimony that a spirit resembling the accused had been seen tormenting a victim. Thereafter, accusations multiplied until the jails overflowed with accused witches.

The pattern of hysteria in Salem Village reflected that community's internal divisions. Most charges came from the village's troubled western division, and most of those accused came from wealthier families in the eastern village or in Salem Town (see Map 3.4).

MAP 3.4
The Geography of Witchcraft: Salem Village, 1692

Geographic patterns of witchcraft testimony mirrored tensions within Salem Village. Accused witches and their defenders lived mostly in the village's eastern division or in Salem Town, whereas their accusers overwhelmingly resided in the village's western sector. (Source: Adapted from Paul Boyer and Stephen Nissenbaum. *Salem Possessed: The Social Origins of Witchcraft* (Cambridge, Mass.: Harvard University Press, 1974).)

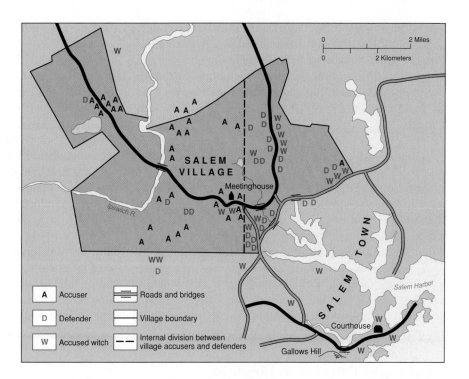

Other patterns were also apparent. Two-thirds of all "possessed" accusers were females aged eleven to twenty, and more than half had lost one or both parents in Anglo-Indian conflicts in Maine. They and other survivors had fled to Massachusetts, where most were now servants in other families' households. They most frequently named as witches middle-aged wives and widows—women who had avoided the poverty and uncertainty they themselves faced. At the same time, the "possessed" accusers gained momentary power and prominence by voicing the anxieties and hostilities of others in their community and by virtually dictating the course of events in and around Salem for several months.

The number of persons facing trial multiplied quickly. Those found guilty desperately tried to stave off death by implicating others. As the pandemonium spread beyond Salem, fear dissolved ties of friendship and family. A minister heard himself condemned by his own granddaughter. A seven-year-old girl helped send her mother to the gallows. Fifty persons saved themselves by confessing. Twenty others who refused to disgrace their own names or betray other innocents went to their graves. Shortly before she was hanged, a victim named Mary Easty begged the court to come to its senses: "I petition your honors not for my own life, for I know I must die . . . [but] if it be possible, that no more innocent blood be shed."

By late 1692 most Massachusetts ministers came to doubt that justice was being done. They objected that spectral evidence, crucial in most convictions, lacked legal credibility because the devil could manipulate it. New Englanders, concluded Increase Mather, a leading clergyman, had fallen victim to a deadly game of "blind man's buffet" set up by Satan and were "hotly and madly, mauling one another in the dark." Backed by the clergy (and alarmed by an accusation against his wife), Governor William Phips forbade further imprisonments for witchcraft in October—by which time over a hundred individuals were in jail and twice that many stood accused. Shortly thereafter he suspended all trials. Phips ended the terror in early 1693 by pardoning all those convicted or suspected of witchcraft.

The witchcraft hysteria was but an extreme expression of more widespread anxieties over social change in New England. The underlying causes of this tension were most evident in the antagonism of Salem Village's communally oriented farmers toward the competitive, individualistic, and impersonal way of life represented by Salem Town. In this clash of values, the rural villagers sought to purge their city upon a hill of its commercial witches, only to desecrate the landscape with gallows.

Recognizing the folly of hunting witches, New Englanders—especially the younger generation—concluded that Winthrop's vision belonged to the past. The generation reaching maturity after 1692 would be far

less willing to accept society's right to restrict their personal behavior and economic freedom. True to their Puritan roots, they would retain their forceful convictions and self-discipline, but they would apply them to the pursuit of material gain. Puritanism gave New England a distinctive regional identity that would endure.

CHESAPEAKE SOCIETY

As New England moved away from its roots, Virginia and its Chesapeake neighbor Maryland single-mindedly devoted themselves to the production of tobacco for export. In this pursuit, the Chesapeake was quite unlike New England, where farm families sought primarily to feed themselves. Also unlike New England, Chesapeake society was sharply divided between a few wealthy planters who dominated a majority consisting of (mostly white) indentured servants and small but growing numbers of black slaves and poor white farmers.

State and Church in Virginia

King James I disliked representative government and planned to rule Virginia through a governor of his own choosing, who would appoint and dismiss advisers to a council. But Virginians petitioned repeatedly that their elected assembly be revived. In 1628 the new king, Charles I, grudgingly relented, but only to induce the assembly to tax tobacco exports, transferring the cost of the colony's government from the crown to Virginia's planters.

After 1630 the need for additional taxes led royal governors to call regular assemblies. The small number of elected representatives, or burgesses, initially met as a single body with the council to pass laws. During the 1650s the legislature split into two chambers—the House of Burgesses and the Governor's Council, whose members held lifetime appointments.

In 1634 Virginia adopted England's county-court system for local government. Justices of the peace served as judges but also set local tax rates, paid county officials, and oversaw the construction and maintenance of roads, bridges, and public buildings. Justices and sheriffs, who administered the counties during the courts' recesses, were chosen by the governor instead of by an electorate. Everywhere south of New England, unelected county courts would become the basic unit of local government by 1710.

In contrast to Puritan New England, Virginia's established church was the Church of England. In each parish, six vestrymen—chosen from among the wealthier planters—handled all church finances, determined who was deserving of poor relief, and investigated complaints against the minister. The taxpayers, who were legally obliged to pay fixed rates to the Anglican Church, elected vestries until 1662, when the assembly made them self-perpetuating and independent of the voters.

Because few counties supported more than one parish, many residents could not conveniently attend

View of Jamestown, 1625
As Virginia's tobacco production boomed, the capital expanded beyond the fort that had originally confined it.

services. A chronic shortage of clergymen left many communities without functioning congregations. In 1662 ten ministers served Virginia's forty-five parishes. Compared to New Englanders, Chesapeake dwellers felt religion's influence lightly.

Maryland

Until 1632 successful English colonization had resulted from the ventures of joint-stock companies. Thereafter, the crown awarded portions of the Virginia Company's forfeited territory to favored English politicians. These proprietors, as they were called, assumed responsibility for peopling, governing, and defending their colonies.

In 1632 the first such grant went to Lord Baltimore (Cecilius Calvert) for a large tract of land north of the Potomac River and east of Chesapeake Bay, which he named Maryland in honor of England's Queen Henrietta Maria. Lord Baltimore also secured freedom from royal taxation, the power to appoint all sheriffs and judges, and the privilege of creating a local nobility. The only checks on the proprietor's power were the crown's control of war and trade and the requirement that an elected assembly approve all laws.

With the consent of Charles I, Lord Baltimore intended to create an overseas refuge for English Catholics, who constituted about 2 percent of England's population. Although English Catholics were rarely molested and many (like the Calverts) were very wealthy, they could not worship in public, had to pay tithes to the Anglican Church, and were barred from holding political office.

In making Maryland a Catholic haven, Baltimore had to avoid antagonizing English Protestants. He sought to accomplish this by transplanting to the Chesapeake the old English institution of the manor—an estate on which a lord could maintain private law courts and employ a Catholic priest as his chaplain. Local Catholics could then come to the manor to hear Mass and receive the sacraments privately. Baltimore adapted Virginia's headright system (see Chapter 2) by offering wealthy English Catholic aristocrats large land grants on condition that they bring settlers at their own cost. Anyone transporting five adults (a requirement raised to twenty by 1640) received a two-thousand-acre manor. Baltimore hoped that this arrangement would allow Catholics to survive and prosper in Maryland while making it unnecessary to pass any special laws alarming to Protestants.

Maryland's colonization did not proceed as Baltimore envisioned. In 1634 the first two hundred immigrants landed. Maryland was the first colony

spared a starving time, thanks to the Calvert family's careful study of Virginia's early history. The new colony's success showed that English overseas expansion had come of age. Baltimore, however, stayed in England, governing as an absentee proprietor, and few Catholics went to Maryland. From the outset, Protestants formed the majority of the population. With land prices low, they purchased their own property, thereby avoiding becoming tenants on the manors. These conditions doomed Calvert's dream of creating a manorial system of mostly Catholic lords collecting rents. By 1675 all of Maryland's sixty nonproprietary manors had evolved into plantations.

Religious tensions soon emerged. In 1642 Catholics and Protestants in the capital at St. Mary's argued over use of the city's chapel, which the two groups had shared until then. As antagonisms intensified, Baltimore drafted the Act for Religious Toleration, which the Protestant-dominated assembly passed in 1649. The toleration act made Maryland the second colony (after Rhode Island) to affirm liberty of worship. However, the act did not protect non-Christians, nor did it separate church and state, since it empowered the government to punish religious offenses such as blasphemy.

The toleration act also failed to secure religious peace. In 1654 the Protestant majority barred Catholics from voting, ousted Governor William Stone (a pro-tolerance Protestant), and repealed the toleration act. In 1655 Stone raised an army of both faiths to regain the government but was defeated at the Battle of the Severn River. The victors imprisoned Stone and hanged three Catholic leaders. Catholics in Maryland actually experienced more trouble than had their counterparts during the English Civil War, in which the victorious Puritans seldom molested them.

Maryland remained in Protestant hands until 1658. Ironically, Lord Baltimore resumed control by order of the Puritan authorities then ruling England. Even so, the Calverts would encounter continued obstacles in governing Maryland because of Protestant resistance to Catholic political influence.

Death, Gender, and Kinship

Tobacco sustained a sharp demand for labor that lured about 110,000 English to the Chesapeake from 1630 to 1700. Ninety percent of these immigrants were indentured servants and, because men were more valued as field hands than women, 80 percent of arriving servants were males. So few women initially immigrated to the Chesapeake that only a third of male colonists found brides before 1650. Male servants married late because

their indentures forbade them to wed before completing their term of labor. Their scarcity gave women a great advantage in negotiating favorable marriages. Female indentured servants often found prosperous planters to be their suitors and to buy their remaining time of service.

Death ravaged seventeenth-century Chesapeake society mercilessly and left domestic life exceptionally fragile. Before 1650 the greatest killers were diseases contracted from contaminated water: typhoid, dysen-

Blank Servant Indenture Form, 1635
The vast majority of Chesapeake colonists immigrated from England after signing contracts similar to this one.

The forme of binding a servant.

This Indenture *made the*   *day of*
in the
yeere of our Soveraigne Lord King Charles, *&c.*
betweene   *of the one*
party, and   *on the*
other party, Witnesseth, *that the said*
                    doth hereby covenant promise, and
grant, to and with the said
*his Executors and Assignes, to serve him from
the day of the date hereof, untill his first and
next arrivall in Maryland; and after for and
during the tearme of   yeeres, in such
service and imployment, as he the said*
                    *or his assignes shall there im-
ploy him, according to the custome of the Countrey
in the like kind. In consideration whereof, the said*
                    doth promise
and grant, to and with the said
                    *to pay for his passing, and to
find him with Meat, Drinke, Apparell and Lodging, with other necessaries during the said terme;
and at the end of the said terme, to give him one
whole yeeres provision of Corne, and fifty acres of
Land, according to the order of the countrey. In
witnesse whereof, the said
hath hereunto put his hand and seale, the day and
yeere above written.*

Sealed and delivered in
the presence of   H

*The usuall terme of binding a servant, is for
five yeers; but for any artificer, or one that shall
deserve more then ordinary, the Adventurer
shall doe well to shorten that time, and adde
encouragements of another nature (as he shall
see cause) rather then to want such usefull men.*

tery, and salt poisoning. After 1650 malaria became endemic as sailors and slaves arriving from Africa carried it into the marshy lowlands, where the disease was spread rapidly by mosquitoes. Life expectancy in the 1600s was about forty-eight for men and forty-four for women—slightly lower than in England and nearly twenty years lower than in New England. Servants died at horrifying rates, with perhaps 40 percent going to their graves within six years of arrival, and 70 percent by age forty-nine. Such high death rates severely crippled family life. Half of all people married in Charles County, Maryland, during the late 1600s became widows or widowers within seven years. The typical Maryland family saw half of its four children die in childhood.

Chesapeake women who lost their husbands tended to enjoy greater property rights than widows elsewhere. To ensure that their own children would inherit the family estate in the event that their widows remarried, Chesapeake men often wrote wills giving their wives perpetual and complete control of their estates. A widow in such circumstances gained economic independence yet still faced enormous pressure to marry a man who could produce income by farming her fields.

The prevalence of early death produced complex households in which stepparents might raise children with two or three different surnames. Mary Keeble of Middlesex County, Virginia, bore seven children before being widowed at age twenty-nine, whereupon she married Robert Beverley, a prominent planter. Mary died in 1678 at age forty-one after having five children by Beverley, who then married Katherine Hone, a widow with one child. Upon Beverley's death in 1687, Katherine quickly wed Christopher Robinson, who had just lost his wife and needed a mother for his four children. Christopher and Katherine's household included children named Keeble, Beverley, Hone, and Robinson. This tangled chain of six marriages among seven people eventually produced twenty-five children who lived at least part of their lives with one or more stepparents.

The combination of predominantly male immigration and devastating death rates notably retarded population growth. Although the Chesapeake had received perhaps one hundred thousand English immigrants by 1700, its white population stood at just eighty-five thousand that year. By contrast, a benign disease environment and a more balanced gender ratio among the twenty-eight thousand immigrants to New England during the 1600s allowed that region's white population to grow to ninety-one thousand by 1700.

The Chesapeake's dismal demographic history began improving in the late seventeenth century. By

then, resistance acquired from childhood immunities allowed native-born residents to survive into their fifties, or ten years longer than immigrants. As a result, more laborers now lived beyond their terms of indenture instead of dying without tasting freedom. But especially in Virginia, newly freed servants faced conditions little more promising than before.

Tobacco Shapes a Region, 1630–1670

Compared to colonists in New England's compact towns (where five hundred people often lived within a mile of the meetinghouse), Chesapeake residents had few neighbors. A typical community contained about two dozen families in an area of twenty-five square miles, or about six persons per square mile. Friendship networks seldom extended beyond a three-mile walk from one's farm and rarely included more than twenty adults. Many, if not most, Chesapeake colonists lived in a constricted world much like that of Robert Boone, a Maryland farmer. An Annapolis paper described Boone

as having died at age seventy-nine "on the same Plantation where he was born in 1680, from which he never went 30 Miles in his Life."

The isolated folk in Virginia and Maryland and in the unorganized settlements of what would become North Carolina shared a way of life shaped by one overriding fact—their future depended on the price of tobacco. Tobacco had dominated Chesapeake agriculture since 1618, when demand for the crop exploded and prices spiraled to dizzying levels. The boom ended in 1629 when prices sank a stunning 97 percent (see Figure 3.1). After stabilizing, tobacco rarely again fetched more than 10 percent of its former price.

Despite the plunge, tobacco stayed profitable as long as it sold for more than two pence per pound and was cultivated on fertile soil near navigable water. The plant grew best on level ground with good internal drainage, so-called light soil, which was usually found beside rivers. Locating a farm along Chesapeake Bay or one of its tributary rivers also minimized transportation costs by permitting tobacco to be loaded on ships at wharves near one's home. Perhaps 80 percent of early Chesapeake homes lay

FIGURE 3.1
Tobacco Prices, 1618-1710
Even after its great plunge in 1629, tobacco remained profitable until about 1660, when its price fell below the break-even point—the income needed to support a family or pay off a farm mortgage.

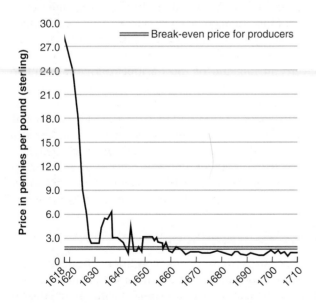

Source: Russell R. Menard, "The Chesapeake Economy, 1618–1720: An Interpretation" (unpublished paper presented at the Johns Hopkins University Seminar on the Atlantic Community, November 20, 1973) and "Farm Prices of Maryland Tobacco, 1659–1710," Maryland Historical Magazine, LVIII (Spring 1973): 85.

Tobacco Label
The slave's central role in growing tobacco and serving his white master (here enjoying a smoke) is depicted.

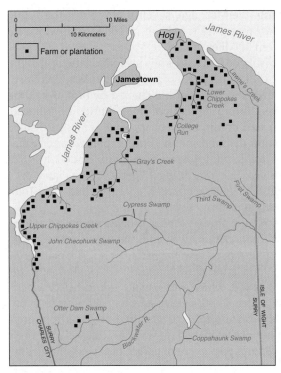

MAP 3.5
Pattern of Settlement in Surry County, Virginia, 1620–1660
In contrast to New Englanders (see Map 3.2), Chesapeake colonists spread out along the banks of rivers and creeks. (Source: Thad W. Tate and David Ammerman, eds., *The Chesapeake in the Seventeenth Century* (Chapel Hill: University of North Carolina Press, 1979). Copyright © 1979 by the University of North Carolina Press. Used by permission of the publisher.)

within a half-mile of a riverbank, and most were within just six hundred feet of the shoreline (see Map 3.5).

From such waterfront bases, wealthy planters built wharves that served not only as depots for tobacco exports but also as distribution centers for imported goods. Their control of both export and import commerce stunted the growth of towns and the emergence of a powerful merchant class. Urbanization proceeded slowly in the Chesapeake, even in a capital like Maryland's St. Mary's, which as late as 1678 was still a mere hamlet of thirty scattered houses.

Taking advantage of the headright system, a few planters built up large landholdings and grew wealthy from their servants' labor. The servants' lot was harsh. Most were poorly fed, clothed, and housed. The exploitation of labor in the Chesapeake was unequaled anywhere in the English-speaking world outside the West Indies, and the gap between rich and poor whites far exceeded that of New England.

Servants faced a bleak future when they managed to survive until their indentures ended. Having received no pay, they entered into freedom impoverished. Virginia obliged masters to provide a new suit of clothes and a year's supply of corn to a freed servant. Maryland required these items plus a hoe and an ax and gave the right to claim fifty acres—if an individual paid to have the land surveyed and deeded. Maryland's policy permitted many of its freedmen to become landowners. Two-thirds of all Chesapeake servants lived in Virginia, however, where no such entitlement existed. After 1650 large planters and English speculators monopolized most available land, making it even less affordable for freedmen.

After 1660 the possibility of upward mobility almost vanished from the Chesapeake as the price of tobacco fell far below profitable levels, to a penny a pound (see Figure 3.1). So began a depression lasting over fifty years. Large planters found ways to compensate for their tobacco losses through income from rents, trade, interest on loans, and fees earned as government officials. They also extended servants' terms as penalties for even minor infractions.

Many landowners held on by offsetting tobacco losses with small sales of corn and cattle to the West Indies. A typical family nevertheless inhabited a shack barely twenty feet by sixteen feet and owned no more property than Adam Head of Maryland possessed when he died in 1698: three mattresses without bedsteads, a chest and barrel that served as table and chair, two pots, a kettle, "a parcell of old pewter," a gun, and some books. Most tobacco farmers lacked furniture, lived on mush or stew because they had just one pot, and slept on the ground—often on a pile of rags. Having fled poverty in England or the Caribbean for the promise of a better life, they found utter destitution in the Chesapeake.

The growing number of servants who completed their indentures after 1660 fared even worse, for the depression slashed wages well below the level needed to build savings and in this way placed landownership beyond their means. Lacking capital, many freedmen worked as tenants or wage laborers on large plantations.

Bacon's Rebellion, 1675–1676

By the 1670s these bleak conditions trapped most Virginia landowners in a losing battle against poverty and left the colony's laborers and freedmen verging on despair. In addition, some wealthy planters resented their exclusion from Governor Berkeley's inner circle, whose members profited as collectors of government fees or as merchants in the colony's fur trade monopoly.

These groups focused their varied resentments against Native Americans.

Virginia had been free of serious conflict with Indians since the Third Anglo-Powhatan War (1644–1646). Resentful of tobacco planters' continued encroachments on their land, a coalition of Indians led by Opechancanough, then nearly a century old but able to direct battles from a litter, killed five hundred of the colony's eight thousand whites before being defeated. By 1653 tribes encircled by English settlement began agreeing to remain within boundaries set by the government—in effect, on reservations. White settlement then expanded north to the Potomac River, and by 1675 Virginia's four thousand Indians were greatly outnumbered by forty thousand whites.

As in New England, tensions flared between Chesapeake Natives struggling to retain land and sovereignty in the face of settlers' expansionism (see Map 3.6). The conflict also divided white society because both Governor Berkeley and Lord Baltimore, along with a few cronies, held fur-trade monopolies that profited from friendly relations with frontier Indians. As a result, settler resentments against the governor and proprietor became fused with those against Indians. In June 1675 a dispute between some Doeg Indians and a Virginia farmer escalated until a force of Virginia and Maryland militia pursuing the Doegs instead murdered fourteen friendly Susquehannocks and then assassinated the Susquehannocks' leaders during a peace conference. The violence was now unstoppable.

Tensions were especially acute in Virginia, reflecting the greater disparities among whites there. Governor Berkeley proposed defending the panic-stricken frontier with a chain of forts linked by patrols. Stung by low tobacco prices and taxes that took almost a quarter of their yearly incomes, small farmers preferred the less costly solution of waging a war of extermination. They were inspired by Nathaniel Bacon, a newly arrived, wealthy planter and Berkeley's distant relative. Defying the governor's orders, three hundred colonists elected Bacon to lead them against nearby Indians in April 1676. Bacon's expedition found only peaceful Indians but massacred them anyway.

When he returned in June 1676, Bacon sought authority to wage war "against all Indians in generall." Bacon's newfound popularity forced the governor to grant his demand. The legislature voted a program designed to appeal to both hard-pressed taxpayers and former servants desperate for land. The assembly defined as enemies any Indians who left their villages without English permission (even if they did so out of fear of attack by Bacon), and declared their lands forfeit-

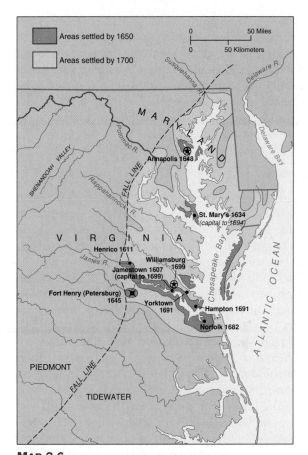

MAP 3.6
Chesapeake Expansion, 1607–1700
The Chesapeake colonies expanded slowly before midcentury. By 1700 Anglo-Indian wars, a rising English population, and an influx of enslaved Africans permitted settlers to spread throughout the tidewater.

ed. Bacon's troops were free to plunder all "enemies" of their furs, guns, wampum, and corn harvests and also to keep Indian prisoners as slaves. The assembly's incentives for enlisting were directed at land-bound buccaneers eager to get rich quickly by seizing land and enslaving any Indians who fell into their clutches.

But Berkeley soon had second thoughts about letting Bacon's thirteen hundred men continue their frontier slaughter and called them back. The rebels returned with their guns pointed toward Jamestown. Forcing Berkeley to flee across Chesapeake Bay, the rebels burned the capital, offered freedom to any Berkeley supporters' servants or slaves who joined the uprising, and looted their enemies' plantations. But at the very moment of triumph in late 1676, Bacon died of dysentery and his followers dispersed.

The tortured course of Bacon's Rebellion revealed a society under deep internal stress. It was an outburst of

long pent-up frustrations by marginal taxpayers and former servants driven to desperation by the tobacco depression, as well as by wealthier planters excluded from Berkeley's circle of favorites. Although sheer economic opportunism was one motive for the uprising, the willingness of whites to murder, enslave, and rob all Native Americans, no matter how loyal, made clear that racism also played a major role.

Slavery

Chesapeake whites drew racialized boundaries between themselves and the region's growing population of Africans. Even before Bacon's Rebellion, planters had begun to avert the potential for class conflict by substituting black slaves for white servants.

Racial slavery developed in three stages in the Chesapeake. From 1619 to 1640, Anglo-Virginians carefully distinguished between blacks and whites in official documents, but did not assume that every African sold was a slave for life. The same was true for Native Americans captured in the colony's wars. Some Africans gained their freedom, and a few, such as Anthony and Mary Johnson (see above), owned their own tobacco farms.

During the second phase, between 1640 and 1660, growing numbers of blacks and some Indians were treated as slaves for life, in contrast to white indentured servants who had fixed terms of service. Slaves' children inherited their parents' status. Evidence from this period also shows that white and black laborers often ran away or rebelled against a master together, and occasionally married one another.

Apparently in reaction to such incidents, the colonies officially recognized slavery and regulated it by law after 1660. Maryland first defined slavery as a lifelong, inheritable racial status in 1661. Virginia followed suit in 1670. This hardening of status lines did not prevent some black and white laborers from joining Bacon's Rebellion together. Indeed the last contingent of rebels to lay down their arms consisted entirely of slaves and servants. By 1705 strict legal codes defined the place of slaves in society and set standards of racial etiquette. By then free blacks like Mary Johnson's grandchildren had all but disappeared from the Chesapeake. Although this period saw racial slavery become fully legalized, many of the specific practices enacted into law had evolved into custom before 1660.

Emerging gradually in the Chesapeake, slavery was formally codified by planter elites attempting to stabilize Chesapeake society and defuse the resentment of whites. In deeming nonwhite "pagans" unfit for freedom, the elites created a common, exclusive identity for whites as free or potentially free persons.

Chesapeake planters began formulating this racial caste system before slavery itself became economically significant. As late as 1660, fewer than a thousand slaves lived in Virginia and Maryland. The number in bondage first became truly significant in the 1680s when the Chesapeake's slave population (by now almost entirely black, owing to Indian decline) almost tripled, rising from forty-five hundred to about twelve thousand. By 1700 slaves made up 22 percent of the inhabitants and over 80 percent of all unfree laborers.

Having been made possible by racism, slavery replaced indentured servitude for economic reasons. First, it became more difficult for planters to import white laborers as the seventeenth century advanced. Between 1650 and 1700, a gradual decline both in England's population growth and in its rate of unemployment led to a 50 percent rise in wages at home. Under these new circumstances, servile labor and its prospects in the Chesapeake attracted fewer immigrants. Second, before 1690 the Royal African Company, which held a monopoly on selling slaves to the English colonies, shipped nearly all its cargoes to the West Indies. During the 1690s this monopoly was broken, and rival companies began shipping large numbers of Africans directly to the Chesapeake.

The rise of a direct trade in slaves between the Chesapeake and West Africa exacerbated the growing gap between whites and blacks in another way. Until 1690 most blacks in the Chesapeake, like Mary and Anthony Johnson, had either been born, or spent many years, in West African ports or in other American colonies. As a consequence, they were familiar with Europeans and European ways and, in most cases, had learned to speak some English while laboring in the West Indies. Such familiarity had enabled some blacks to carve out space for themselves as free landowners, and had facilitated marriages and acts of resistance across racial lines among laborers. But after 1690, far larger numbers of slaves poured into Virginia and Maryland, arriving directly from the West African interior. Language and culture now became barriers rather than bridges to mutual understanding among blacks as well as between blacks and whites, reinforcing the overt racism arising among whites.

The changing composition of the white population also contributed to the emergence of racism in the Chesapeake colonies. As increasing numbers of immigrants lived long enough to marry and form their own families, the number of such families slowly rose, and the ratio of men to women became more equal, since half of all children were girls. By 1690 an almost even division existed between males and females. Thereafter,

the white population grew primarily through an excess of births over deaths rather than through immigration, so that by 1720 most Chesapeake colonists were native-born. Whites' shared attachments to the colony still further heightened their sense of a common racial identity vis-à-vis an increasingly fragmented and seemingly alien black population.

From its beginnings as a region where profits were high but life expectancy was low, the Chesapeake had transformed by 1700. As nonwhites' conditions deteriorated, Virginia and Maryland expanded their territories, and their white colonists flourished.

THE SPREAD OF SLAVERY: THE CARIBBEAN AND CAROLINA

Simultaneously with the expansion of European colonization in mainland North America, an even larger wave of settlement swept the West Indies (see Map 3.7). Between 1630 and 1642 almost 60 percent of the seventy thousand English who emigrated to the Americas went to the Caribbean. By 1660 France's West Indian colonies had a white population of seven thousand compared to just twenty-five hundred colonists in Canada. Beginning in the 1640s the English and French followed Spanish, Portuguese, and Dutch practice by using slave labor to produce sugar on large plantations. The fastest-growing and most profitable sugar plantations were those of the English.

After 1670 many English islanders moved to the Chesapeake and to Carolina, thereby introducing large-scale plantation slavery to the mainland colonies. By 1710 the population of Carolina, like that of the Caribbean colonies, was predominantly black and enslaved.

Sugar and Slaves: The West Indies

The tobacco boom that powered Virginia's economy until 1630 also led English settlers to cultivate that plant in the Caribbean. But with most colonists arriving after 1630, few realized spectacular profits. Through the 1630s

MAP 3.7
The Caribbean Colonies, 1660
By 1660 nearly every West Indian island had been colonized by Europeans and was producing sugar with slave labor.

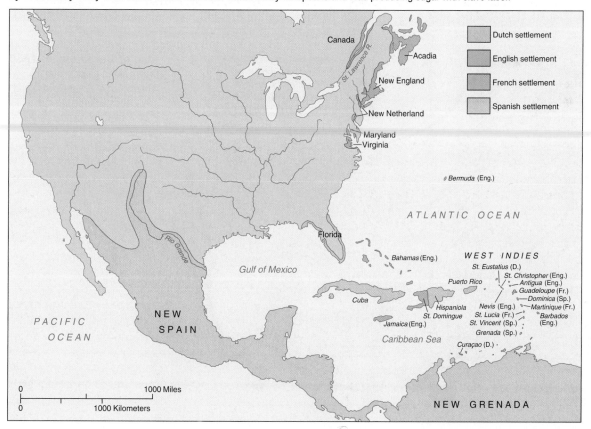

the English West Indies remained a society with a large percentage of independent landowners, an overwhelmingly white population, and a relative equality of wealth.

During the early 1640s an alternative to tobacco rapidly revolutionized the islands' economy and society. Dutch merchants familiar with Portuguese methods of sugar production in Brazil began encouraging English (and French) planters to raise and process sugar cane, which the Dutch would then market (see Technology and Culture, Chapter 2).

Because planters needed three times as many workers per acre to raise cane as tobacco, rising sugar production greatly multiplied the demand for labor. As in the Chesapeake, planters initially imported white indentured servants. After 1640, however, sugar planters increasingly purchased enslaved Africans from Dutch traders to do common fieldwork and used their indentured servants as overseers or skilled artisans.

Although slavery had died out in England after the eleventh century, English planters in the Caribbean quickly copied the example set by Spanish slaveowners. On Barbados, for example, English newcomers imposed slavery on both blacks and Indians immediately after settling the island in 1627. The Barbados government in 1636 condemned every black brought there to lifelong bondage. Planters on other English islands likewise

plunged into slave owning with gusto.

Sugar planters like Sarah Horbin's husband (see above) preferred black slaves to white servants because slaves could be driven harder and cost less to maintain. Moreover, most servants ended their indentures after four years, but slaves toiled until death. Although slaves initially cost two to four times more than servants, they proved a more economical long-term investment. In this way the profit motive and the racism that emerged with the "new slavery" (see Chapter 2) reinforced one another.

By 1670 the sugar revolution had transformed the British West Indies into a predominantly slave society. Thereafter the number of blacks shot up from approximately 40,000 to 130,000 in 1713. Meanwhile, the white population remained stable at about 33,000 because the planters' preference for slave labor greatly reduced the importation of indentured servants after 1670.

Declining demand for white labor in the West Indies diverted the flow of English immigration from the islands to mainland North America and so contributed to population growth there. Furthermore, because the expansion of West Indian sugar plantations priced land beyond the reach of most whites, perhaps thirty thousand people left the islands from 1655 to 1700. Most whites who quit the West Indies migrated to the mainland colonies, especially Carolina.

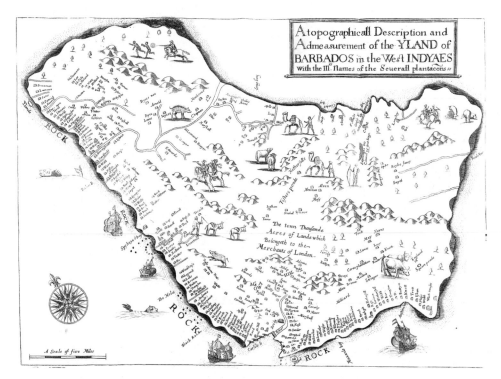

Map of Barbados, c. 1650
Drawn only a decade after the introduction of sugar planting and slave labor in Barbados, this English map shows how far the new economy and society had already spread.

Rice and Slaves: Carolina

During the 1650s settlers from New England and the English West Indies established several unauthorized outposts along the swampy coast between Virginia and Spanish Florida. After the Restoration revived England's monarchy, King Charles II bestowed this unpromising coast on several English supporters in 1663, making it the first of several Restoration colonies. The grateful proprietors named their colony Carolina in honor of Charles (*Carolus* in Latin).

Carolina grew haltingly until 1669, when one of the proprietors, Anthony Ashley Cooper, speeded up settlement by offering immigrants fifty-acre land grants for every family member, indentured servant, or slave they brought in. Cooper's action marked a turning point. In 1670 settlement of southern Carolina began when two hundred colonists landed near modern-day Charleston, "in the very chops of the Spanish." Here, the settlement they called Charles Town formed the colony's nucleus, with a bicameral legislature distinct from that of the northern district.

Cooper and his young secretary, John Locke—later acclaimed as one of the great philosophers of the age (see Chapter 4)—devised an intricate plan for Carolina's settlement and government. Their Fundamental Constitutions of Carolina attempted to ensure the colony's stability by decreeing that political power and social rank accurately reflect settlers' landed wealth. Thus they invented a three-tiered nobility that would hold two-fifths of all land, make laws through a Council of Nobles, and dispense justice through manorial law courts. Ordinary Carolinians with smaller landholdings were expected to defer to this nobility, although they would enjoy religious toleration and the benefits of English common law.

Until the 1680s most settlers were small landowners from Barbados or the mainland colonies, along with some French Huguenots. Obtaining all the land they needed, they saw little reason to obey pseudofeudal lords and all but ignored most of the plans drawn up for them across the Atlantic. Southern Carolinians raised livestock and exported deerskins and Indian slaves (see below), and colonists in northern Carolina exported tobacco, lumber, and pitch, giving local people the name "tarheels." At first these activities did not produce enough profit to warrant maintaining many slaves, so self-sufficient white families predominated in the area.

But many southern Carolinians were not content merely to eke out a marginal existence. Like colonists in the Chesapeake and Caribbean, they sought a staple crop that could make them rich. By the early eighteenth century, they found it in rice. Because rice, like sugar, enormously enriched a few men with capital to invest in costly dams, dikes, and slaves, it remade southern Carolina into a society resembling that of the West Indies. By earning annual profits of 25 percent, rice planters within a generation became the only colonial elite whose wealth rivaled that of the Caribbean sugar planters.

No matter how inhumanly they might be driven, indentured English servants simply did not survive in humid rice paddies swarming with malaria-bearing mosquitoes. The planters' solution was to import an ever-growing force of enslaved Africans who, from their masters' standpoint, possessed two major advantages. First, perhaps 15 percent of the Africans taken to Carolina had cultivated rice in their homelands in Senegambia, and their expertise was vital in teaching whites how to raise the unfamiliar crop. Second, many Africans had developed immunities to malaria and yellow fever, infectious and deadly diseases transmitted by mosquito bites, which were endemic to coastal regions of West Africa. Enslaved Africans, along with infected slave ships' crews, carried both diseases to North America. (Tragically, the antibody that helps ward off malaria also tends to produce the sickle-cell trait, a genetic condition often fatal to the children who inherit it.) These two advantages made commercial rice production possible in Carolina. Because a typical rice planter farming 130 acres needed sixty-five slaves, a great demand for black slave labor resulted. The proportion of slaves in southern Carolina's population rose from just 17 percent in 1680 to about half by 1700. Carolina was becoming the first North American colony with a black majority.

Rice thrived only within a forty-mile-wide coastal strip extending from Cape Fear to present-day Georgia. The hot, humid, marshy lowlands quickly became infested with malaria. Carolinians grimly joked that the rice belt was a paradise in spring, an inferno in summer, and a hospital in the wet, chilly fall. In the worst months, planters' families usually escaped to the relatively cool and more healthful climate of Charles Town and let overseers supervise their slaves during harvests. By 1700 southern Carolina's harsh combination of racism, exploitation, and an environment suitable for rice had already rendered it one of Britain's wealthier colonial regions.

White Carolinians' attitudes toward Native Americans likewise hardened into exploitation and violence. In the 1670s traders in southern Carolina armed nearby

Indians and encouraged them to raid Spanish missions in Florida. These allies captured unarmed Guale, Apalachee, and Timucua Indians at the missions and traded them, along with deerskins, to the Carolinians for guns and other European goods. The English then sold the enslaved Indians, mostly to planters in the West Indies but also in the mainland colonies as far north as New England. By the mid-1680s the Carolinians had extended the trade inland through alliances with the Yamasees (Guale Indians who had fled the inadequate

protection of the Spanish in Florida) and the Creeks, a powerful confederacy centered in what is now western Georgia and northern Alabama. For three decades these Indian allies of the English terrorized Catholic mission Indians in Spanish Florida with their slave raids. No statistical records of Carolina's Indian slave trade survive, but one study estimates that the number of Native Americans enslaved was in the tens of thousands. Once shipped to the West Indies, most died quickly because they lacked immunities to both European and tropical diseases.

THE MIDDLE COLONIES

Between the Chesapeake and New England, two non-English nations established colonies (see Map 3.8). New Netherland and New Sweden were small commercial outposts, although the Dutch colony eventually flourished and took over New Sweden. But England seized New Netherland from the Dutch in 1664, and by 1681 established New York, New Jersey, and Pennsylvania on the former Dutch territory. These actions together created a fourth English colonial region, the middle colonies.

Precursors: New Netherland and New Sweden

New Netherland was North America's first multiethnic colony. Barely half its colonists were Dutch; most of the rest were Germans, French, Scandinavians, and Africans, free as well as enslaved. In 1643 the population included Protestants, Catholics, Jews, and Muslims; and eighteen European and African languages were spoken. But religion counted for little (in 1642 the colony had seventeen taverns but not one place of worship), and the colonists' get-rich-quick attitude had fostered New Amsterdam's growth as a thriving port. The same attitude sapped company profits as private individuals persisted in illegally trading furs. In 1639 the company bowed to mounting pressure and legalized private fur trading.

Privatization led to a rapid influx of guns into the hands of New Netherland's Iroquois allies, giving them a distinct advantage over other Natives. As overhunting depleted local supplies of beaver skins and as smallpox epidemics took their toll, the Iroquois encroached on rival pro-French Indians in a quest for pelts and for captives who could be adopted into Iroquois families to replace the dead. Between 1648 and 1657 the Iroquois, in a series of bloody "beaver wars," dispersed the Hurons and other French allies, incorporating many members of these nations into their own ranks. Then they attacked

MAP 3.8

European Colonization in the Middle and North Atlantic, c. 1650

North of Spanish Florida, four European powers competed for territory and trade with Native Americans in the early seventeenth century. Swedish and Dutch colonization was the foundation upon which England's middle colonies were built.

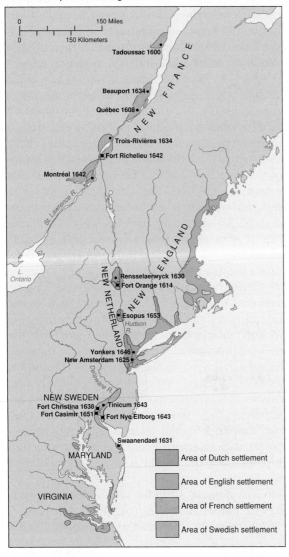

the French settlements along the St. Lawrence. "They come like foxes, they attack like lions, they disappear like birds," wrote a French Jesuit of the Iroquois.

Although the Dutch allied successfully with the inland Iroquois, their relations with nearby coastal Native Americans paralleled white-Indian relations in England's seaboard colonies. With its greedy settlers and military weakness, New Netherland had largely itself to blame. In 1643 all-out war erupted when the colony's governor ordered the massacre of previously friendly Indians who were protesting settler encroachments on Long Island. By 1645 the Dutch prevailed over these Indians and their allies only with English help and by inflicting additional atrocities. But the fighting, known as Kieft's War for the governor who ordered the massacre, helped reduce New Netherland's Indian population from sixteen hundred to seven hundred.

Another European challenger distracted the Dutch as they sought to suppress neighboring Native Americans. In 1638 Sweden had planted a small fur-trading colony in the lower Delaware Valley. Trading with the Delaware (or Lenni Lenape) and Susquehannock Indians, New Sweden diverted many furs from New Netherland. Annoyed, the Dutch colony's governor, Peter Stuyvesant, marched his militia against New Sweden in 1655. The four hundred residents of the rival colony peacefully accepted Dutch annexation.

Tiny though they were, the Dutch and Swedish colonies were historically significant. New Netherland had attained a population of nine thousand and featured a wealthy, thriving port city by the time it came under English rule in 1664. Even short-lived New Sweden left a mark—the log cabin, that durable symbol of the American frontier, which Finnish settlers in the Swedish colony first introduced to the continent. Above all, the two colonies bequeathed a social environment characterized by ethnic and religious diversity that would continue in England's middle colonies.

English Conquests: New York and New Jersey

Like Carolina, the English colonies of New York and New Jersey originated in the speculative enterprise of Restoration courtiers close to King Charles II. Here, too, upper-class proprietors hoped to create a hierarchical society in which they could profit from settlers' rents. These plans failed for the most part in New Jersey, as in Carolina. Only in New York did they achieve some success.

In 1664, waging war against the Dutch Republic, Charles II dispatched a naval force to conquer New Netherland. Weakened by additional wars with Indians as New Netherland sought to expand northward on the Hudson River, Dutch governor Peter Stuyvesant and four hundred poorly armed civilians surrendered peacefully. Nearly all the Dutch (including Stuyvesant himself) remained in the colony on generous terms.

Charles II made his brother James, Duke of York, proprietor of the new province and renamed it New York. When the duke became King James II in 1685, he proclaimed New York a royal colony. Immigration from New England, Britain, and France boosted the population from nine thousand in 1664 to twenty thousand in 1700. Just 44 percent were descended from the original New Netherlanders.

Following Dutch precedent, New York's governors rewarded their wealthiest political supporters, both Dutch and English, with large land grants. By 1703 five families held approximately 1.75 million acres (about half the area east of the Hudson River and south of Albany; see Map 3.9), which they withheld from sale in hope of creating manors with numerous rent-paying

Iroquois Funeral, c. 1720
The Iroquois traditionally buried their dead in a flexed position, along with material goods to accompany the deceased in the afterlife. They continued these practices during the colonial period as mortality rates rose dramatically.

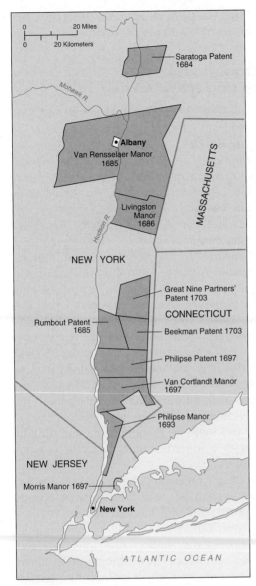

MAP 3.9

New York Manors and Land Grants

Between 1684 and 1703, English governors awarded most of the best land east of the Hudson River as manors to prominent politicians—the majority of them Dutch—whose heirs became the wealthiest elite in the rural northern colonies.

tenants. Earning an enormous income from their rents over the next half-century, the New York *patroons* (the Dutch name for manor lords) formed a landed elite second in wealth only to the Carolina rice planters.

Ambitious plans collided with American realities in New Jersey, which also was carved out of New Netherland. Immediately after the Dutch province's conquest in 1664, the Duke of York awarded New Jersey to a group of proprietors headed by William Penn, John Lord Berkeley, and Sir Philip Carteret. The area at the time was inhabited by about four thousand Delaware Indians and a few hundred Dutch and Swedes. From the beginning New Jersey's proprietors had difficulty controlling their province. By 1672 several thousand New Englanders had settled along the Atlantic shore. After the quarrelsome Puritans renounced allegiance to them, Berkeley and Carteret sold the region to a group of even more contentious religious dissenters called Quakers, who split the territory into the two colonies of West Jersey (1676) and East Jersey (1682).

The Jerseys' Quakers, Anglicans, Puritans, Scottish Presbyterians, Dutch Calvinists, and Swedish Lutherans got along poorly with one another and even worse with the proprietors. Both governments collapsed between 1698 and 1701 as mobs disrupted the courts. In 1702 the disillusioned proprietors finally surrendered their political powers to the crown, which proclaimed New Jersey a royal province.

Quaker Pennsylvania

The noblest attempt to carry out European concepts of justice and stability in founding a colony began in 1681. That year Charles II paid off a huge debt by making a supporter's son, William Penn, the proprietor of the last unallocated tract of American territory at the king's disposal. Penn (1644–1718) had two aims in developing his colony. First, he was a Quaker and wanted to launch a "holy experiment" based on the teachings of the radical English preacher George Fox. Second, "though I desire to extend religious freedom," he explained, "yet I want some recompense for my trouble."

Quakers in late-seventeenth-century England stood well beyond the fringe of respectability. Quakerism appealed strongly to men and women at the bottom of the economic ladder, and its adherents challenged the conventional foundation of the social order. George Fox, the movement's originator, had received his inspiration while wandering civil war-torn England's byways and searching for spiritual meaning among distressed common people. Tried on one occasion for blasphemy, he warned the judge to "tremble at the word of the Lord" and was ridiculed as a "quaker." Fox's followers called themselves the Society of Friends, but the name Quaker stuck. They were the most successful of the many radical religious sects born in England during the 1640s and 1650s.

The core of Fox's theology was his belief that the Holy Spirit or "Inner Light" could inspire every soul.

William Penn's Map of Philadelphia, c. 1681

Central to Penn's master plan for Philadelphia was the idea that each residence should stand in the middle of its plot, encircled by gardens and orchards.

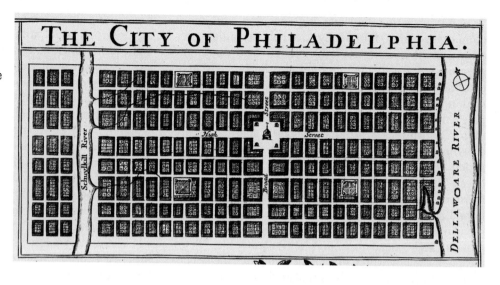

Mainstream Christians, by contrast, found any such claim of special communication with God highly suspicious, as Anne Hutchinson's banishment from Massachusetts Bay colony in 1637 revealed. Although trusting direct inspiration and disavowing the need for a clergy, Quakers also took great pains to ensure that individual opinions would not be mistaken for God's will. They felt confident that they understood the Inner Light only after having reached near-unanimous agreement through intensive and searching discussion led by "Public Friends"—ordinary laypeople. In their simple religious services ("meetings"), Quakers sat silently until the Inner Light prompted one of them to speak.

Some of the Quakers' beliefs led them to behave in ways that aroused fierce hostility for being disrespectful to authorities and their social superiors. For example, insisting that individuals deserved recognition for their spiritual state rather than their wealth or status, Quakers refused to tip their hats to their social betters. They likewise flouted convention by not using the formal pronoun "you" when speaking to members of the gentry, instead addressing everyone with the informal "thee" and "thou" as a token of equality. By wearing their hats in court, moreover, Quakers appeared to mock the state's authority; and by taking literally Scripture's ban on swearing oaths, they seemed to place themselves above the law. The Friends' refusal to bear arms appeared unpatriotic and cowardly to many. Finally, Quakers accorded women unprecedented equality. The Inner Light, Fox insisted, could "speak in the female as well as the male." Acting on these beliefs, Quakers suffered persecution and occasionally death in England, Massachusetts, and Virginia.

Not all Quakers came from the bottom of society. The movement's emphasis on quiet introspection and its refusal to adopt a formal creed also attracted some well-educated and prosperous individuals disillusioned by the quarreling of rival faiths. The possessor of a great fortune, William Penn was hardly a typical Friend, but there were significant numbers of merchants among the estimated sixty thousand Quakers in the British Isles in the early 1680s. Moreover, the industriousness that the Society of Friends encouraged in its members ensured that many humble Quakers accumulated money and property.

Much care lay behind the Quaker migration to Pennsylvania that began in 1681, and it resulted in the most successful beginning of any European colony in North America. Penn sent an advance party to the Delaware Valley, where about five thousand Delaware Indians and one thousand Swedes and Dutch already lived. After an agonizing voyage in which one-third of the passengers died, Penn arrived in 1682. Choosing a site for the capital, he named it Philadelphia—the "City of Brotherly Love." By 1687 some eight thousand settlers had joined Penn across the Atlantic. Most were Quakers from the British Isles, but they also included Presbyterians, Baptists, Anglicans, and Catholics, as well as Lutherans and radical sectarians from Germany—all attracted by Pennsylvania's religious toleration. Because most Quakers immigrated in family groups rather than as single males, a high birthrate resulted, and the population grew rapidly. In 1698 one Quaker reported that in Pennsylvania one seldom met "any young Married Woman but hath a Child in her belly, or one upon her lap."

After wavering between authoritarian and more democratic plans, Penn finally gave Pennsylvania a government with a strong executive branch (a governor and governor's council) and granted the lower legislative chamber (the assembly) only limited powers. Friends, forming the majority of the colony's population, dominated this elected assembly. Penn named Quakers and their supporters as governor, judges, and sheriffs. Hardly a democrat, he feared "the ambitions of the populace which shakes the Constitution," and he intended to check "the rabble" as much as possible. Because he also insisted on the orderly disposition of property and hoped to avoid unseemly wrangling, he carefully oversaw land sales in the colony. To prevent haphazard growth and social turmoil in Philadelphia, Penn designed the city with a grid plan, laying out the streets at right angles and reserving small areas for parks.

Unlike most seaboard colonies, Pennsylvania avoided early hostilities with Native Americans. This was partly a result of the reduced Native population in the Delaware Valley. But it was also a testament to Penn's Quaker tolerance. To the Indians Penn expressed a wish "to live together as Neighbours and Friends," and he made it the colony's policy to buy land it wanted for settlement from them.

Land was a key to Pennsylvania's early prosperity. Rich, level lands and a lengthy growing season enabled immigrants to produce bumper crops. West Indian demand for the colony's grain rose sharply and by 1700 made Philadelphia a major port.

Like other attempts to base new American societies on preconceived plans or lofty ideals, Penn's "peaceable kingdom" soon bogged down in human bickering. In 1684 the founder returned to England, and the settlers quarreled incessantly (until he returned in 1699). An opposition party attacked Penn's efforts to monopolize foreign trade and to make each landowner pay him a small annual fee. Bitter struggles between Penn's supporters in the governor's council and opponents in the assembly deadlocked the government. From 1686 to 1688, the legislature passed no laws, and the council once ordered the lower house's speaker arrested. Penn's brief return to Pennsylvania from 1699 to 1701 helped little. Just before he sailed home, he made the legislature a unicameral (one-chamber) assembly and allowed it to initiate measures.

Religious conflict shook Pennsylvania during the 1690s, when George Keith, a college-educated Public Friend, urged Quakers to adopt a formal creed and train ministers. This would have changed the democratically functioning Quaker movement—in which the humblest member had equal authority in interpreting the Inner Light—into a hierarchical church dominated by the clergy. The majority of Quakers rejected Keith's views in 1692, whereupon he joined the Church of England, taking some Quakers with him. Keith's departure began a major decline in the Quaker share of Pennsylvania's population. The proportion fell further once Quakers ceased immigrating in large numbers after 1710.

William Penn met his strongest opposition in the counties on the lower Delaware River, where the best lands had been taken up by Swedes and Dutch. In 1704 these counties became the separate colony of Delaware, but Penn continued to name their governors.

The middle colonies soon demonstrated that British America could benefit by encouraging pluralism. New York and New Jersey successfully integrated New Netherland's Swedish and Dutch population; and Pennsylvania, New Jersey, and Delaware refused to require residents to pay support for any official church. Meanwhile, England's European rivals, France and Spain, were also extending their claims in North America.

RIVALS FOR NORTH AMERICA: FRANCE AND SPAIN

In marked contrast to England's compact, densely populated settlements on the Atlantic, France and Spain established far-flung inland networks of fortified trading posts and missions. Unable to attract large numbers of colonists, they enlisted Native Americans as trading partners and military allies, and the two Catholic nations had far more success than English Protestants in converting Indians to Christianity. By 1700 French and Spanish missionaries, traders, and soldiers—and relatively few farmers and ranchers—were spreading European influence well beyond the range of England's colonies, to much of Canada and to what is now the American Midwest, Southeast, and Southwest.

England's rivals exercised varying degrees of control in developing their American colonies. France, the supreme power in late-seventeenth-century Europe, poured in state resources, whereas Spain, then in economic decline, made little attempt to influence North American affairs from Europe. In both cases, local officials and missionaries assumed the primary burden for extending imperial interests.

France Claims a Continent

After briefly losing Canada to England (1629–1632), France resumed and extended its colonization there. Paralleling the early English and Dutch colonies, a privately held company initially assumed responsibility for settling New France. The Company of New France granted extensive tracts, or *seigneuries*, to large landlords (*seigneurs*), who could either import indentured servants or rent out small tracts within their holdings to prospective farmers. Although some farmers and other colonists spread along the St. Lawrence River as far inland as Montreal (see Map 3.8), Canada's harsh winters and short growing season sharply limited their numbers.

More successful in New France were commercial traders and missionaries who spread beyond the settlements and relied on stable relations with Indians to succeed. Despite costly wars with the Iroquois, which entailed the defeat of some of France's Native American allies (see above), French-Indian trade prospered. Indeed the more lucrative opportunities offered by trade diverted many French men who had initially arrived to take up farming.

The colony also benefited from the substantial efforts of Catholic religious workers, especially Jesuit missionaries and Ursuline nuns. Given a virtual monopoly on missions to Native Americans in 1633, the Jesuits followed the fur trade into the Canadian interior. Although the missionaries often feuded with the traders, whose morality they condemned, the two groups together spread French influence westward to the Great Lakes, securing the loyalty of the region's Indians in their struggles with the Iroquois. The Ursulines ministered particularly to Native American women and girls nearer Quebec, ensuring that Catholic piety and morality directly reached all members of Indian families.

Even more forcefully than his English counterparts, France's King Louis XIV (reigned 1661–1715) sought to subordinate his American colony to the nation's interests. His principal adviser, Jean-Baptiste Colbert, was a forceful proponent of the doctrine of mercantilism (see Chapter 4), which held that colonies should provide their home country with the raw materials it lacked and with markets for its manufactured goods. In this way, the nation would not have to depend on rival countries for trade. Accordingly, Colbert and Louis hoped that New France could increase its output of furs, ship agricultural surpluses to France's new sugar-producing colonies in the West Indies, and export timber to those colonies and

for the French navy. To begin realizing these goals, they revoked the charter of the Company of New France in 1663 and placed the colony under royal direction. They then sought to stifle the Iroquois threat to New France's economy and to encourage French immigration to Canada.

For more than half a century, and especially since the "beaver wars," the Iroquois had limited New France's productivity by intercepting convoys of beaver pelts from the interior. After assuming control of the colony, the royal government sent fifteen hundred soldiers to stop Iroquois interference with the fur trade. In 1666 these troops sacked and burned four Mohawk villages that were well stocked with winter food. After the alarmed Iroquois made a peace that lasted until 1680, New France enormously expanded its North American fur exports.

Meanwhile, the French crown energetically built up the colony's population. Within a decade of the royal takeover, the number of whites rose from twenty-five hundred to eighty-five hundred. The vast majority con-

View of Quebec, 1699
New France's security was built on its rising commercial economy and its close ties to Canada's Indians.

sisted of indentured servants who were paid wages and given land after three years' work. Others were former soldiers and their officers who were given land grants and other incentives to remain in New France and farm while strengthening the colony's defenses. The officers were encouraged to marry among the "king's girls," female orphans shipped over with dowries.

The upsurge in French immigration petered out after 1673. Tales of disease and other hazards of the transatlantic voyage, of Canada's hard winters, and of wars with the "savage" Iroquois were spread by the two-thirds of French immigrants who returned to their native land over the next century. New France would grow slowly, relying on the natural increase of its small population rather than on newcomers from Europe.

Colbert had encouraged immigration in order to enhance New France's agricultural productivity. But as in earlier years, many French men who remained spurned farming in the St. Lawrence Valley, instead swarming westward in search of furs. By 1670 one-fifth of them were *voyageurs*, or *coureurs de bois*—independent traders unconstrained by government authority. Living in Indian villages and often marrying Native women, the *coureurs* built an empire for France. From Canadian and Great Lakes Indians they obtained furs in exchange for European goods, including guns to use against the Iroquois and other rivals. In their commercial interactions, the French and Indians observed Native American norms of reciprocity (see Chapter 1). Their exchanges of goods sealed bonds of friendship and alliance, which served their mutual interests in trade and in war against common enemies.

Alarmed by the rapid expansion of England's colonies and by Spanish plans to link Florida with New Mexico (see below), France boldly sought to dominate the North American heartland. As early as 1672, fur trader Louis Jolliet and Jesuit missionary Jacques Marquette became the first Europeans known to have reached the upper Mississippi River (near modern Prairie du Chien, Wisconsin); they later paddled twelve hundred miles downstream to the Mississippi's junction with the Arkansas River. Ten years later, the Sieur de La Salle, an ambitious upper-class adventurer, descended the entire Mississippi to the Gulf of Mexico. When he reached the delta, La Salle formally claimed the entire Mississippi basin—half the territory of the present-day continental United States—for Louis XIV, in whose honor he named the territory Louisiana.

Having asserted title to this vast empire, the French began settling the southern gateway into it. In 1698 the first colonizers arrived on the Gulf of Mexico coast. A

year later the French erected a fort near present-day Biloxi, Mississippi. In 1702 they occupied the former Mississippian city of Mábila, where De Soto's expedition had faltered a century and a half earlier (see Chapter 2), founding a trading post, and calling it Mobile. But Louisiana's growth would be delayed for another decade.

New Mexico: The Pueblo Revolt

Spanish colonization in North America after 1625 expanded upon the two bases established earlier in New Mexico and Florida (see Chapter 2). With few settlers, the two colonies needed ties with friendly Native Americans in order to obtain land, labor, and security. But friendly relations proved hard to come by in both locales.

From the beginning, the Spanish sought to rule New Mexico by subordinating the Pueblo Indians to their authority in several ways. First, Franciscan missionaries supervised the Indians' spiritual lives by establishing churches in most of the Indian communities (pueblos) and attempting to force the natives to attend mass and observe Catholic rituals and morality. Second, Spanish landowners were awarded *encomiendas* (see Chapter 2), which allowed them to exploit Indian labor and productivity for personal profits. Finally, the Spanish drove a wedge between the Pueblo Indians and their nonfarming trade partners, the Apaches and Navajos. By collecting corn as tribute, the Pueblo Indians could no longer trade their surplus crops with the Apaches and Navajos. Having incorporated corn into their diets, the Apaches in particular raided the pueblos as well as the Spanish for the grain. A few outlying pueblos made common cause with the Apaches, but most responded to the raids by strengthening their ties to the Spanish.

Although rebellions erupted sporadically over the first six decades of Spanish rule, most pueblos accommodated themselves to Spanish rule and Catholicism. Beginning in the 1660s, however, many Natives grew disillusioned. For several consecutive years their crops withered under the effects of sustained drought. Drought-induced starvation plus deadly epidemic diseases sent the Pueblo population plummeting from about eighty thousand in 1598 to just seventeen thousand in the 1670s. Riding horses stolen from the Spanish, Apaches inflicted more damage than ever in their raids. Reeling under the effects of these catastrophes, Christian Indians returned to traditional Pueblo beliefs and ceremonies in hopes of restoring the spiritual balance that had brought ample rainfall, good health, and peace before the Spanish arrived. Seeking to sup-

press this religious revival as "witchcraft" and "idolatry," the Franciscan missionaries entered sacred kivas (underground ceremonial centers), destroyed religious objects, and publicly whipped Native religious leaders and their followers.

Matters came to a head in 1675 when Governor Juan Francisco Treviño ordered soldiers to sack the kivas and arrest Pueblo religious leaders. Three leaders were sent to the gallows; a fourth hanged himself; and forty-three others were jailed, whipped, and sentenced to be sold as slaves. In response, armed warriors from several pueblos converged on Santa Fe and demanded the prisoners' release. With most of his soldiers off fighting the Apaches, Governor Treviño complied.

Despite this concession, there was now no cooling of Pueblo resentment against the Spanish. Pueblo leaders began gathering secretly to plan the overthrow of Spanish rule. At the head of this effort was Popé, one of those who had been arrested in 1675. Besides Popé and one El Saca, the leaders included men such as Luis Tupatú, Antonio Malacate, and others whose Christian names signified that they had once been baptized. Some were of mixed Pueblo-Spanish ancestry, and one leader, Domingo Naranjo, combined Pueblo, Mexican Indian, and African ancestors. They and many of their followers had attempted to reconcile conversion to Christianity and subjection to Spanish rule with their identities as Indians. But deteriorating conditions and the cruel intolerance of the Spanish had turned them against Catholicism.

In August 1680 Popé and his cohorts were ready to act. On the morning of August 10, some Indians from the pueblo of Taos and their Apache allies attacked the homes of the seventy Spanish colonists residing near Taos and killed all but two. Then, with Indians from neighboring pueblos, they proceeded south and joined a massive siege of New Mexico's capital, Santa Fe. Thus began the Pueblo Revolt of 1680, the most significant event in the history of the colonial Southwest.

At each pueblo, rebels destroyed the churches and religious paraphernalia and killed those missionaries who did not escape. All told, about four hundred colonists were slain. Then they "plunge[d] into the rivers and wash[ed] themselves with amole," a native root, in order to undo their baptisms. As a follower later testified, Popé also called on the Indians "to break and enlarge their cultivated fields, saying now they were as they had been in ancient times, free from the labor they had performed for the religious and the Spaniards."

The siege of Santa Fe led to the expulsion of the Spanish from New Mexico for twelve years. Only in 1692 did a new governor, Diego de Vargas, arrive to "reconquer" New Mexico. Exploiting divisions that had emerged among the Pueblos in the colonists' absence, Vargas used violence and threats of violence to reestablish Spanish rule. Even then Spain did not effectively quash Pueblo resistance until 1700, and thereafter its control of the province was more limited than before. To appease the Pueblos, on whom they depended for the colony to endure, Spanish authorities abolished the hated *encomienda*. They also ordered the Franciscans not to disturb the Pueblos in their traditional religious practices and to cease inflicting corporal punishment on the Indians.

Pueblos' suspicions of the Spanish lingered after 1700, but they did not again attempt to overthrow them. With the missions and *encomienda* less intrusive, they

Diego de Vargas
As the newly appointed governor of New Mexico, Vargas led Spain's reoccupation of New Mexico, beginning in 1692.

sustained their cultural identities within, rather than outside, the bounds of colonial rule.

Florida and Texas

The Spanish fared no better in Florida, an even older colony than New Mexico. Before 1680 the colony faced periodic rebellions from Guale, Timucua, and Apalachee Indians protesting forced labor and the religious discipline imposed by Franciscan missionaries. Beginning in the 1680s Creek and other Indian slave raiders allied to the English in Carolina added to the effects of recurrent diseases. While the Spanish, with their small numbers of soldiers and arms looked on helplessly, the invading Indians killed and captured thousands of Florida's Natives and sold them to English slave traders (see above). Even before a new round of warfare erupted in Europe at the turn of the century, Spain was ill prepared to defend its beleaguered North American colonies.

English expansion threatened Florida, while the French establishment of Louisiana defied Spain's hope of one day linking that colony with New Mexico. To counter the French, Spanish authorities in Mexico proclaimed the province of Texas (Tejas) in 1691. But no permanent Spanish settlements appeared there until 1716 (see Chapter 4).

CONCLUSION

In less than a century, from 1625 to 1700, the movements of peoples and goods, across the Atlantic and within the continent transformed the map of North America. The kin of Sarah Horbin, Mary Johnson, and others spread far and wide among colonial regions in the Americas, while emergent trade routes linked some regions to others and all of them to Europe. While strong, favorably located Indian groups like the Creek and the Iroquois used trade with colonists to enhance their economic and political standing, other Native Americans confronted colonists who sought their land, labor, or loyalty. From New England to New Mexico, such Indians either reconciled themselves to coexistence with Europeans or fled their homelands in order to avoid contact with the intruders.

Within the English colonies, four distinct regions emerged. New England's Puritanism grew less utopian and more worldly as the inhabitants gradually reconciled their religious views with the realities of a commercial economy. After beginning with a labor force consisting primarily of white indentured servants, the tobacco planters of the Chesapeake region began replacing them

with enslaved Africans. Slavery had been instituted earlier by English sugar planters in the West Indies, some of whom introduced it at the very beginning of colonization in the third North American region, Carolina. Between the Chesapeake and New England, a fourth region, the middle colonies, combined the ethnic and religious pluralism of Swedish and Dutch predecessors with the religious tolerance of the Quakers. Middle colonists embraced the market economy with far less hesitation than their Puritan neighbors in New England. While planters or merchants rose to prominence in each English region, most whites continued to live on family farms.

The English colonies were by far the most populous. By 1700 the combined number of whites and blacks in England's mainland North American colonies was about 250,000, compared with 15,000 for those of France and 4,500 for those of Spain.

With far fewer colonists, French and Spanish colonists depended more on friendly relations with Native Americans for their livelihoods and security than did the English. Most French North Americans lived in the St. Lawrence Valley, where a lively commercial-agrarian economy was emerging, though on a smaller scale than in New England and the middle colonies. Most Spanish colonists not connected to the government, military, or a missionary order were concentrated in the Rio Grande valley in New Mexico. But smaller numbers and geographic isolation precluded the Southwest's development as a major center of colonization.

By 1700 there were clear differences between the societies and economies of the three colonial powers in North America. These differences would prove decisive in shaping American history during the century that followed.

FOR FURTHER REFERENCE

READINGS

Ira Berlin, *Many Thousands Gone: The First Two Centuries of Slavery in North America* (1998). A major study comparing the experiences and cultures of three distinct cohorts of mainland slaves, from the earliest arrivals through the age of the American Revolution.

Paul Boyer and Stephen Nissenbaum, *Salem Possessed: The Social Origins of Witchcraft* (1974). A study of the witchcraft episode as the expression of social conflict in one New England community.

William Cronon, *Changes in the Land: Indians, Colonists, and the Ecology of New England* (1983). A pioneering study of the interactions of Native Americans and European settlers with the New England environment.

CHRONOLOGY, 1625–1700

1627 English establish Barbados.	**1661** Maryland defines slavery as a lifelong, inheritable racial status.
1629 Massachusetts Bay colony founded.	**1662** Half-Way Covenant debated.
1630–1642 "Great Migration" to New England.	**1664** English conquer New Netherland; establish New York and New Jersey.
1633 First English settlements in Connecticut.	
1634 Lord Baltimore establishes Maryland.	**1670** Charles Town, Carolina, founded. Virginia defines slavery as a lifelong, inheritable racial status.
1636 Roger Williams founds Providence, Rhode Island. Harvard College established.	
1637 Antinomian crisis in Massachusetts Bay. Pequot War in Connecticut.	**1675–1676** King Philip's War in New England.
1638 New Sweden established.	**1676** Bacon's Rebellion in Virginia.
1642–1648 English Civil War.	**1680** Pueblo revolt begins in New Mexico.
1643–1645 Kieft's War in New Netherland.	**1681** William Penn founds Pennsylvania.
1644–1646 Third Anglo-Powhatan War in Virginia.	**1682** La Salle claims Louisiana for France.
1648–1657 Iroquois "beaver wars."	**1690s** End of Royal African Company's monopoly on English slave trade.
1649 Maryland's Act for Religious Toleration. King Charles I beheaded. Five Nations Iroquois disperse Hurons.	**1691** Spain establishes Texas.
	1692–1700 Spain "reconquers" New Mexico.
1655 New Netherland annexes New Sweden.	**1692–1693** Salem witchcraft trials.
1660 Restoration in England; Charles II crowned king.	**1698** First French settlements in Louisiana.

James Deetz and Patricia Scott Deetz, *The Times of Their Lives: Life, Love, and Death in Plymouth Colony* (2000). An examination of everyday life in New England using archaeological and documentary evidence and offering some surprising conclusions.

Allison Games, *Migration and the Origins of the English Atlantic World* (1999). An in-depth study of English emigrants to the Chesapeake, New England, and the Caribbean in the second quarter of the seventeenth century.

Jack P. Greene, *Pursuits of Happiness: The Social Development of Early Modern British Colonies and the Formation of American Culture* (1988). A brilliant synthesis that takes a regional approach in discussing England's mainland and island colonies.

Allan Greer, *The People of New France* (1997). An excellent brief introduction to the social history of French North America.

Andrew L. Knaut, *The Pueblo Revolt of 1680: Conquest and Resistance in Seventeenth-Century New Mexico* (1995). A comprehensive, insightful account of Pueblo-Spanish relations during the seventeenth century.

Edmund S. Morgan, *American Slavery, American Freedom: The Ordeal of Colonial Virginia* (1975). A classic analysis of the origins of southern slavery and race relations.

Mary Beth Norton, *Founding Mothers and Fathers: Gendered Power and the Forming of American Society* (1996). A major study of female and male power in the seventeenth-century English colonies.

WEBSITES

From Indentured Servitude to Racial Slavery
http.www.pbs.org/wgbh/aia/part1/1narr3.html
A useful introduction to Virginia's changing labor force and the lives and legal treatment of enslaved Africans in the colony.

Salem Witch Trials Documentary Archive and Transcription Project
http://etext.lib.virginia.edu/salem/witchcraft
An excellent site featuring extensive courtroom transcripts and other documents, maps, and biographies of accusers, accused, magistrates, and other figures.

William Penn: Visionary Proprietor
http://xroads.virginia.edu.~CAP/PENN/pnhome.html
A good introduction to Penn and his Quaker idealism, emphasizing his approach to Native Americans and his design for Philadelphia.

For additional works please consult the Bibliography at the end of the book.

CHAPTER 4

The Bonds of Empire, 1660–1750

Alexander Garden, the Church of England's commissary (representative) in the southern colonies, was furious. George Whitefield, a young Anglican minister just over from England, was preaching that Garden's ministers were unsaved and were endangering their parishioners' souls. Asserting his authority, Garden summoned Whitefield to Charles Town and demanded a retraction. But Whitefield brushed off the demand, claiming that Garden "was as ignorant as the rest" of the local clergy for failing to teach the central Calvinist doctrine of salvation by predestination (see Chapter 2). Whitefield threatened to widen his attacks if Garden refused to condemn dancing and other "sinful" entertainments. Garden shot back that Whitefield would be suspended if he preached in any church in the province, to which Whitefield retorted that he would treat such an action as he would an order from the pope. The meeting ended with Garden shouting, "Get out of my house!"

Garden got Whitefield out of his house but not out of his hair. The two men continued their dispute in public. Garden accused Whitefield of jeopardizing the stability of colonial society, while Whitefield charged the Anglican clergy with abandoning piety in favor of the cold heresy of reason. An extraordinary orator, Whitefield was the first intercolonial celebrity, traveling thousands of miles to spread his critique of the established religious

Mrs. Harme Gansevoort (Magdalena Bouw) by Pieter Vanderlyn, c. 1740
This New York "lady" personified the ideal of gentility, developed in the eighteenth century as colonists consciously emulated the lifestyles of English elites.

CHAPTER OUTLINE

Rebellion and War, 1660–1713

Colonial Economies and Societies , 1660–1750

Competing for a Continent, 1713–1750

Public Life in British America, 1689–1750

order. Everywhere he went, people from all walks of life poured out by the thousands to individually experience the overwhelming power of a direct connection with God.

Whitefield represented one of two European cultural currents that crossed the Atlantic, primarily from or through Britain, during the middle decades of the eighteenth century. He was the greatest English-speaking prophet of a powerful revival of religious piety sweeping the Protestant world. The second current was the Enlightenment—a faith in reason rooted in natural science—which found its earliest and foremost American exponent in Benjamin Franklin. Franklin's emphasis on reason might seem at odds with Whitefield's conscious efforts to tap his audience's deepest emotions. But both men repudiated the self-contained hierarchical communities of the past in favor of a more dynamic society that was intercolonial and transatlantic in its orientation.

Whitefield, an Englishman in America, and Franklin, a colonist who traveled frequently to England, also signaled the close ties that increasingly bound Britain and America. Beginning with a series of Navigation Acts in the late seventeenth century, England tightened the economic bonds linking the colonies' economic fortunes with its own. Coupled with the astonishing growth of its population, slave as well as free, these policies enabled British North America to achieve a level of growth and collective prosperity unknown elsewhere in the Americas. The accelerating movement of goods and people was accompanied by the movement of news and ideas that, by 1750, made the British Empire a leading world power and distinguished its colonies sharply from their French and Spanish neighbors.

This chapter will focus on four major questions:

- How did the Glorious Revolution and its outcome shape relations between England and its North American colonies?

- What were the most important consequences of British mercantilism for the mainland colonies?

- What factors best explain the relative strengths of the British, French, and Spanish colonial empires in North America?

- What were the most significant consequences of the Enlightenment and the Great Awakening for life in the British colonies?

REBELLION AND WAR, 1660–1713

Before the Restoration (1660), England made little serious effort to weld its colonies into a coherent empire. Thereafter, English authorities undertook a concerted effort to expand overseas trade at the expense of the nation's rivals and to subordinate its colonies to English commercial interests and political authority. These efforts were modified but continued after the fall of the Stuarts in 1689 and by a succession of international wars that followed.

Royal Centralization, 1660–1688

As the sons of a king (Charles I) executed by Parliament, the Restoration monarchs disliked representative government. Charles II rarely called Parliament into session after 1674, and not at all after 1681. James II (ruled 1685–1688) hoped to reign as an "absolute" monarch like France's Louis XIV, who never faced an elected legislature. Not surprisingly, the two English kings had little sympathy for American colonial assemblies.

Royal intentions of extending direct political control to North America first became evident in New York. The proprietor, Charles II's brother James, the Duke of York, considered elected assemblies "of dangerous consequence" and forbade them to meet, except briefly between 1682 and 1686. Meanwhile, Charles appointed former army officers to about 90 percent of all gubernatorial positions, thereby compromising the time-honored English tradition of holding the military strictly accountable to civilian authority. By 1680 such "governors general" ruled 60 percent of all American colonists. James II continued this policy.

Ever resentful of outside meddling, New Englanders proved most stubborn in defending self-government and resisting crown policies. As early as 1661, the Massachusetts assembly declared its citizens exempt from all laws and royal decrees from England except for a declaration of war. The colony ignored the Navigation Acts and continued to welcome Dutch traders. Charles II responded by targeting Massachusetts for special punishment. In 1679 he carved a new royal colony, New Hampshire, out of its territory. Then in 1684 he declared Massachusetts itself a royal colony and revoked its charter, the very foundation of the Puritan city upon a hill. Puritan minister Increase Mather repudiated the King's actions, calling on colonists to resist even to the point of martyrdom.

Despite such resistance, royal centralization accelerated after James II ascended to the throne. In 1686 the new king consolidated Massachusetts, New Hampshire, Connecticut, Rhode Island, and Plymouth into a single administrative unit, the Dominion of New England, with a capital at Boston. He added New York and the Jerseys to the Dominion in 1688. With this bold stroke, all legislatures in these colonies ceased to exist, and still another former army officer, Sir Edmund Andros, became governor of the new supercolony.

Massachusetts burned with hatred for the dominion and its governor. By "Exercise of an arbitrary Government," preached Salem's minister, "ye wicked walked on Every Side & ye Vilest of men ware [sic] exalted." Andros was indeed arbitrary. He suppressed the legislature, limited towns to a single annual meeting, and strictly enforced toleration of Anglicans and the Navigation Acts. "You have no more privileges left you," Andros reportedly told a group of outraged colonists, "than not to be sold for slaves." Andros' success in gaining some local support, including his appointing some Massachusetts elites to high office, further enraged most other colonists.

Tensions also ran high in New York, where Catholics held prominent political and military posts under the Duke of York's rule. By 1688 colonists feared that these Catholic officials would betray New York to France, now England's chief imperial rival. When Andros's local deputy, Captain Francis Nicholson, allowed the harbor's forts to deteriorate and reacted skeptically to rumors that Native Americans would attack, New Yorkers suspected the worst.

The Glorious Revolution in England and America, 1688–1689

Not only colonists but also English people were alarmed by the religious, political, and diplomatic directions in which the monarchy was taking their nation. The Duke of York became a Catholic in 1676, and Charles II converted on his deathbed. Both rulers ignored Parliament and violated its laws, issuing decrees allowing Catholics to hold high office and worship openly. English Protestants' fears that they would have to accept Catholicism intensified after both kings expressed their preference for allying with France just as Louis XIV was launching new persecutions of that country's Protestant Huguenots in 1685.

The English tolerated James II's Catholicism only because the potential heirs to the throne, his daughters Mary and Anne, remained Anglican. But in 1688 James's wife bore a son who would be raised—and would eventually reign—as a Catholic. Aghast at the thought of a Catholic succeeding to the throne, some of England's political and religious leaders asked Mary and her husband, William of Orange (head of the Dutch Republic), to intervene. When William and Mary led a small Dutch Protestant army to England in November 1688, most royal troops defected to them, and James II fled to France.

This bloodless revolution of 1688, called the Glorious Revolution, created a "limited monarchy" as defined by England's Bill of Rights of 1689. The crown promised to summon Parliament annually, sign all its bills, and respect traditional civil liberties. This vindication of limited representative government burned deeply into the English political consciousness, and Anglo-Americans never forgot it. Colonists struck their own blows for liberty when Massachusetts, New York, and Maryland rose up against local representatives of the Stuart regime.

News that England's Protestant leaders had rebelled against James II electrified New Englanders. On April 18, 1689, well before confirmation of the English revolt's success, Boston's militia arrested Andros and his councilors. (The governor tried to flee in women's clothing but was caught after an alert guard spotted a "lady" in army boots.) The Massachusetts political leaders acted in the name of William and Mary, risking their necks should James return to power in England.

Although William and Mary dismantled the Dominion of New England and restored the power to elect their own governors to Connecticut and Rhode Island, they acted to retain royal authority in Massachusetts. While allowing the province to absorb Plymouth and Maine, they refused to let it regain New Hampshire. More seriously, Massachusetts' new charter of 1691 stipulated that the crown, rather than the electorate, would choose the governor. In addition, property ownership, not church membership, became the criterion for voting. Finally, the colony had to tolerate other Protestants, especially proliferating numbers of Anglicans, Baptists, and Quakers (although non-Puritans' taxes would continue to support the established Congregational church). For Puritans already demoralized by the demise of the "New England Way" (see Chapter 3), this was indeed bitter medicine.

New York's counterpart of the anti-Stuart uprising was Leisler's Rebellion. Emboldened by news of Boston's coup, the city's militia—consisting mainly of Dutch and other non-English artisans and shopkeepers—seized

Sir Edmund Andros and Boston Broadside Urging Him to Surrender, 1689
News of the Glorious Revolution in England quickly undermined Andros' authority within the Dominion of New England. Shortly after town authorities issued this public warning to Andros, Boston's militia arrested him.

the harbor's main fort on May 31, 1689. Captain Jacob Leisler of the militia took command of the colony, repaired its rundown defenses, and called elections for an assembly. When English troops arrived at New York in 1691, Leisler, fearing that their commander was loyal to James II, denied them entry to key forts. A skirmish resulted, and Leisler was arrested.

"Hott brain'd" Leisler unwittingly had set his own downfall in motion. He had jailed many elite New Yorkers for questioning his authority, only to find that his former enemies had gained the new governor's ear and persuaded him to charge Leisler with treason for firing on royal troops. In the face of popular outrage, a packed jury found Leisler and his son-in-law, Jacob Milborne, guilty. Both men went to the gallows insisting that they were dying "for the king and queen and the Protestant religion."

News of England's Glorious Revolution heartened Maryland's Protestant majority, which had long chafed under Catholic rule. Hoping to prevent a repetition of religion-tinged uprisings that had flared in 1676 and

1681, Lord Baltimore sent a messenger from England in early 1689 to command Maryland's obedience to William and Mary. But the courier died en route, leaving the colony's unknowing Protestants in fear that their Catholic proprietor was a traitor who supported James II.

John Coode and three others organized the Protestant Association to secure Maryland for William and Mary. These conspirators may have been motivated more by their exclusion from high public office than by religious zeal, for three of the four had Catholic wives. Coode's group seized the capital in July 1689, removed all Catholics from office, and requested a royal governor. They got their wish in 1691 and made the Church of England the established religion in 1692. Catholics, who composed less than one-fourth of the population, lost the right to vote and thereafter could worship only in private. Maryland stayed in royal hands until 1715, when the fourth Lord Baltimore joined the Church of England and regained his proprietorship.

The revolutionary events of 1688–1689 decisively changed the colonies' political climate by reestablishing

legislative government and ensuring religious freedom for Protestants. Dismantling the Dominion of New England and directing governors to call annual assemblies, William and Mary allowed colonial elites to reassert control over local affairs. By encouraging the assemblies to work with royal and proprietary governors, the monarchs expected colonial elites to identify their interests with those of England. A foundation was thus laid for an empire based on voluntary allegiance rather than submission to raw power imposed from faraway London. The crowning of William and Mary opened a new era in which Americans drew rising confidence from their relationship to the English throne. "As long as they reign," wrote a Bostonian who helped topple Andros, "New England is secure."

A Generation of War, 1689–1713

Ironically, the bloodless revolution of 1688 ushered in a quarter-century of warfare, convulsing both Europe and North America. In 1689 England joined a general European coalition against France's Louis XIV, who supported James II's claim to the English crown. The resulting War of the League of Augsburg (which Anglo-Americans called King William's War) was the first struggle to embroil colonists and Native Americans in European rivalries.

With the outbreak of King William's War, New Yorkers and New Englanders launched a two-pronged invasion of New France in 1690, with one prong aimed at Montreal and the other at Quebec. After both invasions failed, the war took the form of cruel but inconclusive border raids against civilians carried out by both English and French troops and their respective Indian allies.

Already weary from a new wave of wars with pro-French Indians, the Five Nations Iroquois Confederacy bore the bloodiest fighting in King William's War. Standing almost alone against their foes, the Iroquois faced overwhelming odds. Not only did their English allies fail to intercept most enemy war parties, but the French were allied with virtually all other Indians from Maine to the Great Lakes. In 1691 every Mohawk and Oneida war chief died in battle; by 1696 French armies had destroyed the villages of every Iroquois nation but the Cayugas and Oneidas.

Although King William's War ended in 1697, the Five Nations staggered until 1700 under invasions by pro-French Indians (including Iroquois who had become Catholic and moved to Canada). By then one-quarter of the Confederacy's two thousand warriors had been killed or taken prisoner or had fled to Canada. The total

Iroquois population declined 20 percent over twelve years, from eighty-six hundred to seven thousand. (By comparison, the war cost about thirteen hundred English, Dutch, and French lives.)

By 1700 the Confederacy was divided into pro-English, pro-French, and neutralist factions. Under the impact of war, the neutralists set a new direction for Iroquois diplomacy. In two separate treaties, together called the Grand Settlement of 1701, the Five Nations made peace with France and its Indian allies in exchange for access to western furs, while redefining their British alliance to exclude military cooperation. Skillful negotiations brought the exhausted Iroquois far more success than had war by allowing them to keep control of their lands, rebuild their decimated population, and gain recognition as a key to the balance of power in the Northeast.

In 1702 European war again erupted when England fought France and Spain in the War of the Spanish Succession, called Queen Anne's War by England's American colonists. This conflict reinforced Anglo-Americans' awareness of their military weakness. French and Indian raiders from Canada destroyed several towns in Massachusetts and Maine that colonists had recently established on the Indians' homelands. In the Southeast, the outbreak of Anglo-Spanish war broadened an older conflict involving the English in Carolina, the Spanish in Florida, and Native peoples in the region (see Chapter 3). The Spanish invaded Carolina and nearly took Charles Town in 1706. Enemy warships captured many English colonial vessels and landed looting parties along the Atlantic coast. Meanwhile, colonial sieges of Quebec and St. Augustine ended as expensive failures.

England's own forces had more success than those of the colonies, seizing the Hudson Bay region as well as Newfoundland and Acadia (henceforth called Nova Scotia). Although Great Britain kept these gains in the Treaty of Utrecht (1713), the French and Indian hold on the continent's interior remained unbroken.

The most important consequence of the imperial wars for Anglo-Americans was political, not military. The clashes with France reinforced their identity with post-1689 England as a bastion of Protestantism and political liberty. Recognizing their own military weakness and the extent to which the Royal Navy had protected their shipping, colonists acknowledged their dependence on the newly formed United Kingdom of Great Britain (created by the formal union of England and Scotland in 1707). As a new generation of English colonists matured, war buttressed their loyalty to the crown and reinforced their identity as Britons.

COLONIAL ECONOMIES AND SOCIETIES, 1660–1750

The achievement of peace in 1713 enabled Britain, France, and Spain to concentrate on competing economically rather than militarily. Each nation was already acting to subordinate its North American colonies to serve its larger imperial goals. Thereafter, the two principal powers, Britain and France, sought to integrate their American colonies into single imperial economies. Spain pursued a similar course but was limited in its ability to control developments north of Mexico and the Caribbean.

Mercantilist Empires in America

The imperial practices of Britain, France, and Spain were rooted in a set of political-economic assumptions known as mercantilism. The term refers to policies aimed at guaranteeing prosperity by making a nation as economically self-sufficient as possible by eliminating dependence on foreign suppliers, damaging foreign competitors' commercial interests, and increasing its net stock of gold and silver by selling more abroad than buying.

Britain's mercantilist policies were articulated above all in a series of Navigation Acts governing commerce between England and its colonies. Parliament enacted the first Navigation Act in 1651, requiring that colonial trade be carried on in English- or colonial-owned vessels in order to wrest control of that trade from Dutch merchants. After the Restoration, Parliament enacted the Navigation Acts of 1660 and 1663, barring colonial merchants from exporting such commodities as sugar and tobacco anywhere except to England, and from importing goods in non-English ships. An act in 1672 provided administrative machinery to enforce these rules. Finally, the Molasses Act of 1733 taxed all foreign molasses (produced from sugar plants and imported primarily for distilling rum) entering the mainland colonies at sixpence per gallon. This act was intended less to raise revenue than to serve as a tariff that would protect British West Indian sugar producers at the expense of their French rivals.

The Navigation Acts affected the British colonial economy in four major ways. First, they limited all imperial trade to British-owned ships whose crews were at least three-quarters British. The acts classified all colonists, including slaves (many of whom served as seamen), as British. This restriction not only contributed to Britain's rise as Europe's foremost shipping nation but also laid the foundations of an American shipbuilding industry and merchant marine. By the 1750s one-third of all "British" vessels were American-owned, mostly by merchants in New England and the middle colonies. The swift growth of this merchant marine diversified the northern colonial economy and made it more commercial. The expansion of colonial shipping also hastened urbanization by creating a need for centralized docks, warehouses, and repair shops in the colonies. By mid-century Philadelphia, New York City, Boston, and Charles Town had emerged as major transatlantic ports.

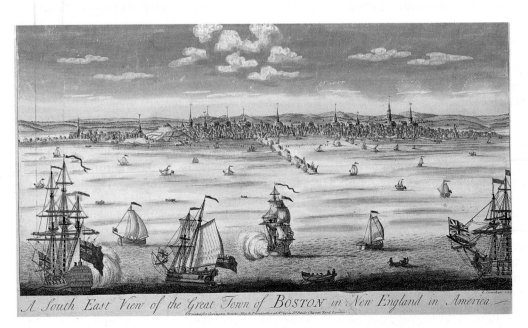

A South East View of the Great Town of BOSTON in New England in America

View of Boston, c. 1735
Maritime commerce was the principal factor in the rise of Boston, as well as New York and Philadelphia, during the eighteenth century.

The second major way in which the Navigation Acts affected the colonies lay in their barring the export of certain "enumerated goods" to foreign nations unless these items first passed through England or Scotland. The mainland colonies' major "enumerated" exports were tobacco, rice, furs, indigo (a Carolina plant that produced a blue dye), and naval stores (masts, hemp, tar, and turpentine). Parliament never restricted grain, livestock, fish, lumber, or rum, which together made up 60 percent of colonial exports. Parliament further reduced the burdens on exporters of tobacco and rice— the chief commodities affected by enumeration—with two significant concessions. First, it gave tobacco growers a monopoly over the British market by excluding foreign tobacco, even though this hurt British consumers. (Rice planters enjoyed a natural monopoly because they had no competitors.) Second, it minimized the added cost of landing tobacco and rice in Britain by refunding customs duties when those products were later shipped to other countries. With about 85 percent of all American tobacco and rice eventually being sold outside the British Empire, planters' profits were reduced by less than 3 percent.

The navigation system's third effect on the colonies was to encourage economic diversification. Parliament used British tax revenues to pay modest bounties to Americans producing such items as silk, iron, dyes, hemp, and lumber, which Britain would otherwise have had to import from other countries, and it raised the price of commercial rivals' imports by imposing protective tariffs on them. The trade laws did prohibit Anglo-Americans from competing with large-scale British manufacturing of certain products, most notably clothing. However, colonial tailors, hatters, and housewives could continue to make any item of dress in their households or small shops. Manufactured by low-paid labor, British clothing imports generally undersold whatever the colonists could have produced given their higher labor costs. The colonists were also free to produce iron, and by 1770 they had built 250 ironworks employing thirty thousand men, a work force larger than the entire population of Georgia or of any provincial city.

Finally, the Navigation Acts made the colonies a protected market for low-priced consumer goods and other exports from Britain. Steady overseas demand for colonial products spawned a prosperity that enabled white colonists to consume ever larger amounts not only of clothing but also of dishware, home furnishings, tea, and a range of other items both produced in Britain and imported by British and colonial merchants from elsewhere. Shops sprang up in cities and rural crossroads throughout the colonies, and itinerant peddlers

Tobacco Production in Virginia
Slaves performed virtually every task in the production of tobacco on plantations as well as on many smaller farms in the Chesapeake colonies.

took imported wares into more remote areas of the countryside. One such peddler arrived in Berwick, Maine, in 1721 and sold several kinds of cloth, a "pair of garters," and various "small trifles" before local authorities confiscated his goods because he had failed to purchase a license. Other traders traveled to Native American communities where they exchanged cloth and other commodities for furs. As a result of colonial consumption, the share of British exports bound for North America spurted from just 5 percent in 1700 to almost 40 percent by 1760. Mercantilism had given rise to a "consumer revolution" in British America.

Cheap imported goods enabled middle-class colonists to emulate the lifestyles of their British counterparts. One of the most popular imports was tea. Colonists desired tea not simply for its caffeine or its taste. As in Britain, "taking tea" was a social occasion that called for the fashionable (as well as heat-resistant) cups, saucers, pots, and sugar bowls produced in

Staffordshire, England. "Without too much exaggeration," writes one historian, "Staffordshire pottery might be seen as the Coca-Cola of the eighteenth century."

The economic development of the French and Spanish colonies paled beside that of British North America. Although France's most forceful proponent of mercantilism, Colbert (see Chapter 3) and his successors had great difficulty implementing mercantilist policies. New France gradually developed agricultural self-sufficiency and, in good years, exported some of its wheat to France's West Indian colonies. It also exported small amounts of fish and timber to the Caribbean and to France. The colony's chief imports were wine and brandy, its chief export, furs. Although furs were no longer very profitable by the eighteenth century, the French government maintained and even expanded the fur trade because it would need Native American military support in another war with Britain. The government actually lost money by sending large amounts of cloth, firearms, and other manufactured commodities to Indian allies in exchange for furs. Moreover, France maintained a sizable army in its Canadian colony that, like the trade with Native Americans, was a drain on the royal treasury. Meanwhile, Canada attracted little private investment from France or from within the colony. French Canadians enjoyed a comfortable if modest standard of living but lacked the private investment, extensive commercial infrastructure, vast consumer market, and manufacturing capacity of their British neighbors.

France's greatest American success was in the West Indies where French planters emulated the English by importing large numbers of enslaved Africans to produce sugar under appalling conditions. Ironically, this success was partly a result of French planters' defying mercantilist policies. In St. Domingue, Martinique, and Guadeloupe, many planters built their own sugar refineries and made molasses instead of shipping their raw sugar to refineries in France, as mercantilism prescribed. They then sold much of their molasses to merchants in Britain's mainland colonies, especially Massachusetts. France attempted to duplicate its Caribbean success in Louisiana but, like New France, Louisiana remained unprofitable.

Although Spain had squandered the wealth from gold and silver extracted by the conquistadors and early colonists (see Chapter 2), its economy and that of Latin America revived during the eighteenth century. That revival did not extend to North America, where colonists conducted little overseas commerce. Spanish traders in Texas offered horses to Louisianans in exchange for French goods. Spaniards in Florida traded with English, French, and the Indian allies of both—even for commodities as basic as food. Without the flourishing of contraband trade, Spain's colonies in North America might not have survived.

At bottom, Britain's colonies differed from those of France and Spain in their respective economies and societies. While all three nations were governed according to mercantilist principles, in France and Spain most wealth was controlled by the monarchy, the nobility, and the Catholic Church. Most private wealth was inherited and took the form of land rather than liquid assets. England, on the other hand, had become a mercantile-commercial economy, and a significant portion of the nation's wealth was in the form of capital held by merchants who reinvested it in commercial and shipping enterprises. For its part, the British government used much of its considerable income from duties, tariffs, and other taxes to enhance commerce. For example, the government strengthened Britain's powerful navy to protect the empire's trade and created the Bank of England in 1694 to ensure a stable money supply and lay the foundation for a network of lending institutions. These benefits extended not only to Britain but also to colonial entrepreneurs and consumers. Although Parliament intended the laws to benefit only Britain, the colonies' per capita income rose 0.6 percent annually from 1650 to 1770, a pace twice that of Britain.

Immigration, Population Growth, and Diversity

Britain's economic advantage over its North American rivals was reinforced by its sharp demographic edge. In 1700 approximately 250,000 non-Indians resided in English America, compared to only 15,000 French colonists and 4,500 Spanish. During the first half of the eighteenth century, all three colonial populations at least quadrupled in size—the British to 1,170,000, the French to 60,000, and the Spanish to 19,000—but this only magnified Britain's advantage.

Spanish emigrants could choose from among that nation's many Latin American colonies, most of which offered more opportunities than remote, poorly developed Florida, Texas, and New Mexico. Reports of Canada's harsh winters and Louisiana's poor economy deterred most potential French colonists. France and Spain made few attempts to attract immigrants to North America from outside their own empires. And both limited nonslave immigration to Roman Catholics, a restriction that diverted French Huguenots to the English colonies instead. The English colonies, for their part, boasted good farmlands, healthy economies, and a willingness to absorb members of most European

nationalities and Protestant denominations. While anti-Catholicism remained strong, small Jewish communities also formed in several colonial cities.

Spain regarded its northernmost colonies less as centers of population than as buffers against French and English penetration of their more valued colonies to the south. While hoping to lure civilian settlers, the Spanish relied heavily on soldiers stationed in *presidios* (forts) for defense plus missionaries who would, they hoped, settle loyal Native Americans at strategically placed missions. Most immigrants came not from Spain itself but from Mexico and other Spanish colonies.

Although boasting more people than the Spanish colonies, New France and Louisiana were comparably limited. There too the military played a strong role, while missionaries and traders worked to enhance the colony's relations with Native Americans. New France's population growth in the eighteenth century resulted largely from natural increase rather than immigration. Some rural Canadians established new settlements along the Mississippi River in Upper Louisiana, in what are now the states of Illinois and Missouri. But on the lower Mississippi, Louisiana acquired a foul reputation, and few French went there willingly. To boost its population, the government sent paupers and criminals,

recruited some German refugees, and encouraged large-scale slave imports. By 1732 two-thirds of lower Louisiana's 5,800 people were black and enslaved.

The British colonies outpaced the population growth of not only their French and Spanish rivals but of Britain itself. White women in the colonies had an average of eight children and forty-two grandchildren, compared to five children and fifteen grandchildren for women in Britain. The ratio of England's population to that of the mainland colonies plummeted from 20 to 1 in 1700 to 3 to 1 in 1775.

Although immigration contributed less to eighteenth-century population growth than did natural increase, it remained important. In the forty years after Queen Anne's War, the colonies absorbed 350,000 newcomers, 40 percent of them (140,000) African-born slaves who had survived a sea crossing of sickening brutality. All but a few enslaved immigrants departed from West African ports from Senegambia to Angola (see Map 4.1). Most planters deliberately mixed slaves who came from various regions and spoke different languages, in order to minimize the potential for collective rebellion. But some in South Carolina and Georgia expressly sought slaves from Gambia and nearby regions for their rice-growing experience.

MAP 4.1
African Origins of North American Slaves, 1690-1807
Virtually all slaves brought to English North America came from West Africa, between Senegambia and Angola. Most were captured or bought inland and marched to the coast, where they were sold to African merchants who in turn sold them to European slave traders.

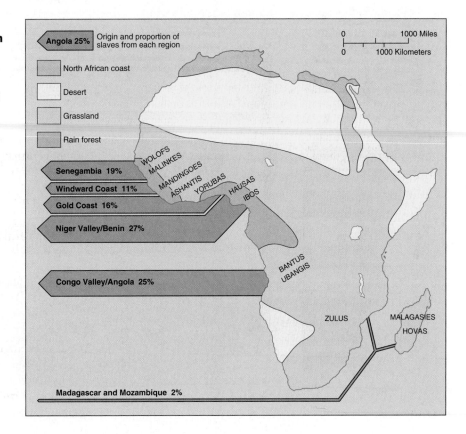

Conditions aboard slave ships were appalling by any standard. Africans were crammed into tight quarters with inadequate sanitary facilities, and many died from disease. Those who refused to eat or otherwise defied the slavers' authority were flogged. If they found the chance, a significant number of slaves hurled themselves overboard in a last, desperate act of defiance against those who would profit from their misery. A Guinea-born slave, later named Venture Smith, was one of 260 who were shipped from the Gold Coast port of Anomabu in 1735. But "smallpox...broke out on board," Smith recalled, and "when we reached [Barbados], there were found...not more than two hundred alive."

From 1713 to 1754, five times as many slaves poured onto mainland North America as in all the preceding years. The proportion of blacks in the colonies doubled, rising from 11 percent at the beginning of the century to 20 percent by midcentury. Slavery was primarily a southern institution, but 15 percent of its victims lived north of Maryland, mostly in New York and New Jersey. By 1750 every seventh New Yorker was a slave.

Because West Indian and Brazilian slave buyers outbid the mainland colonists, a mere 5 percent of enslaved Africans were transported to the present-day United States. Unable to buy as many male field hands as they wanted, masters purchased enslaved women and protected their investments by maintaining the slaves' health. These factors promoted family formation and increased life expectancy far beyond the Caribbean's low levels (see Chapter 3). By 1750 the rate of natural increase for mainland blacks almost equaled that for whites.

As the numbers of creole (American-born) slaves grew, sharp differences emerged between them and African-born blacks in the southern colonies. Unlike African-born slaves, creoles spoke a single language, English, and were familiar from birth with their environment and with the ways of their masters. These advantages translated into more autonomy for some creoles.

Architect's Plan of a Slave Ship

This plan graphically depicts the crowded, unsanitary conditions under which enslaved Africans were packed like cargo and transported across the Atlantic.

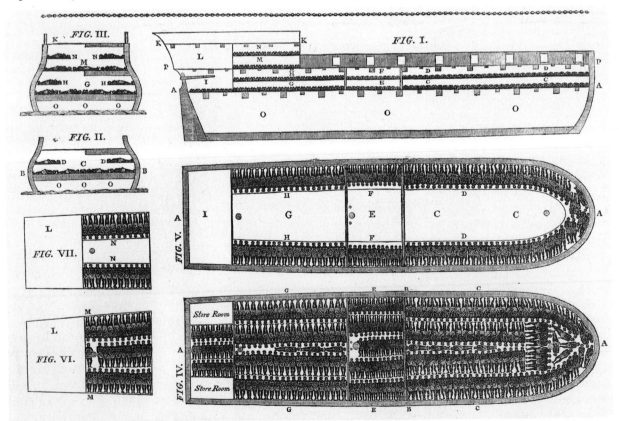

Until the 1770s, planters continued to import African-born slaves to labor in their fields, especially on more remote lands recently gained from Native Americans. But as wealthier, more long-established planters diversified economically and developed more elaborate lifestyles (see below), they diverted favored creoles toward such services as shoeing horses, repairing and driving carriages, preparing and serving meals, sewing and mending clothing, and caring for planters' children.

The approximately 210,000 whites who immigrated to the British colonies during these years included a sharply reduced share from England compared to the seventeenth century (see Figure 4.1). Whereas between 1630 and 1700 about 2,000 English settlers landed annually (constituting 90 percent of all European immigrants), after 1713 the English contribution dropped to about 500 a year. Rising employment and higher wages in eighteenth-century England made voluntary immigration to America less attractive than before. But economic hardship elsewhere in the British Isles and northern Europe supplied a steady stream of immigrants, who contributed to greater ethnic diversity among white North Americans.

One of the largest contingents was made up of 100,000 newcomers from Ireland, two-thirds of them "Scots-Irish" descendants of sixteenth-century Scottish Presbyterians who had settled in northern Ireland. After 1718 Scots-Irish fled to America to escape rack renting (frequent sharp increases in farm rents), usually moving as complete families. In contrast, 90 percent of all Catholic Irish immigrants were unmarried males who arrived as indentured servants. Rarely able to find Catholic wives, they often abandoned their faith to marry Protestant women.

Meanwhile, from German-speaking regions in central Europe came 125,000 settlers, most of them fleeing terrible economic conditions in the Rhine Valley. Wartime devastation had compounded the misery of Rhenish peasants, many of whom were squeezed onto plots of land too small to feed a family. One-third of German immigrants financed their voyage by indenturing themselves or their children as servants. Most Germans were either Lutherans or Calvinists. But a significant minority belonged to small, pacifist religious sects that desired above all to be left alone.

Overwhelmingly, the eighteenth-century immigrants were poor. Those who became indentured servants worked from one to four years for an urban or rural master. Servants could be sold or rented out, beaten, granted minimal legal protection, kept from marrying, and sexually harassed. Attempted escape usually

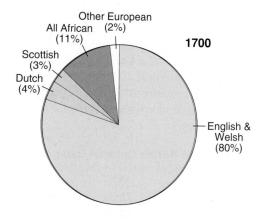

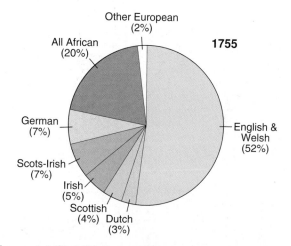

Figure 4.1 Distribution of Non-Indian Nationalities Within the British Mainland Colonies, 1700-1755
The impact of heavy immigration from 1720 to 1755 can be seen in the reduction of the English and Welsh from four-fifths of the colonial population to a slight majority; in the doubling of the African population; and in the sudden influx of Germans and Irish, who together comprised a fifth of white colonists by 1755. For a more detailed breakdown of African origins see Map 4.1.

Source: Thomas L. Purvis, "The European Ancestry of the United States Population," *William & Mary Quarterly,* LXI (1984): 85–101.

meant an extension of their service. But at the end of their terms, most managed to collect "freedom dues," which could help them marry and acquire land.

Few immigrants settled in New England, New Jersey, lower New York, and the southern tidewater, where land was most scarce and expensive. Philadelphia became immigrants' primary port of entry. So many foreigners went to Pennsylvania that by 1755 the English accounted for only one-third of that colony's population; the rest came mostly from elsewhere in the British Isles and from Germany.

Rising numbers of immigrants also traveled to the Piedmont region, stretching along the eastern slope of the Appalachians. A significant German community developed in upper New York, and thousands of other Germans as well as Scots-Irish fanned southward from Pennsylvania into western Maryland. Many more from Germany and Ireland arrived in the second-most popu-

MAP 4.2
Immigration and British Colonial Expansion, to 1755

Black majorities emerged in much of the Chesapeake tidewater and the Carolina-Georgia low country. Immigrants from Germany, Ireland, and Scotland predominated among the settlers in the piedmont. A significant Jewish population emerged in the seaports.

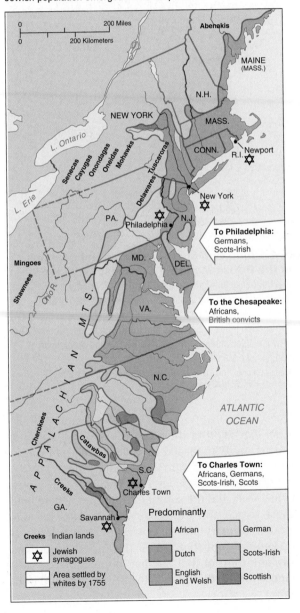

lar American gateway, Charles Town. Most moved on to the Carolina Piedmont, where they raised grain, livestock, and tobacco, generally without slaves. After 1750 both streams of immigration merged with an outpouring of Anglo-Americans from the Chesapeake in the rolling, fertile hills of western North Carolina. In 1713 few Anglo-Americans had lived more than fifty miles from the sea, but by 1750 one-third of all colonists resided in the Piedmont (see Map 4.2).

The least free of white immigrants were convict laborers. England had deported some lawbreakers to America in the seventeenth century, but between 1718 and 1783 about thirty thousand convicts arrived. A few were murderers; most were thieves; some were guilty of the most trivial offenses, like a young Londoner who "got intoxicated with liquor, and in that condition attempted to snatch a handkerchief from the body of a person in the street to him unknown." Convicts were sold as servants on arrival. Relatively few committed crimes in America, and some eventually managed to establish themselves as backcountry farmers.

Affluent English-descended colonists did not relish the influx of so many people different from themselves. "These confounded Irish will eat us all up," snorted one Bostonian. Benjamin Franklin spoke for many when he asked in a 1751 essay on population,

> Why should Pennsylvania, founded by the English, become a colony of aliens, who will shortly be so numerous as to Germanize us instead of us Anglicizing them, and will never adopt our language or customs any more than they can acquire our complexion?

In the same ungenerous spirit, Franklin objected to the slave trade because it would increase America's black population at the expense of industrious whites, and suggested that the colonists send rattlesnakes to Britain in return for its convict laborers.

Rural White Men and Women

Although the benefits of rising living standards in the British colonies were widespread, even the white population enjoyed these advantages unevenly. Except for Benjamin Franklin (who was born neither rich nor poor) and a few others, true affluence was reserved for those who inherited their wealth. For other whites, personal success was limited and came through hard work, if at all.

Because most farm families owned just enough acreage for a working farm, they could not provide all

their children with land of their own when they married. Moreover, since couples typically started having children in their mid-twenties, had their last babies sometime after forty, and lived past sixty, all but their youngest children would be approaching middle age before receiving any inheritance. Young adults rarely got more than a sixth or seventh of their parents' estate, because most families wrote wills that divided property more or less evenly among all daughters and sons. A young male had to build savings to buy farm equipment by working (from about age sixteen to twenty-three) as a field hand for his father or neighbors. Because mortgages usually required down payments of 33 percent, a young husband normally supported his growing family by renting a farm from a more prosperous landowner until his early or mid-thirties. In some areas, most notably the oldest colonized areas of New England, the continued high birthrates of rural families combined with a shortage of productive land to limit farming opportunities altogether. As a result, many young men turned elsewhere to make their livings—the frontier, the port cities, or the high seas.

Even after acquiring their own land, farmers often supplemented their incomes through seasonal or part-time work. Some learned crafts like carpentry that earned money year-round. Others trapped furs, gathered honey and beeswax, or made cider, shingles, or turpentine. Whenever possible, farmers found wintertime jobs draining meadows, clearing fields, or fencing land for wealthier neighbors.

Families worked off mortgages slowly because the long-term cash income from a farm (6 percent) about equaled the interest on borrowed money (5 to 8 percent). After making a down payment of one-third, a husband and wife generally satisfied the next third upon inheriting shares of their deceased parents' estates. They paid off the final third when their children reached their teens and the family could expand farm output with two or three full-time workers. Only by their late fifties, just as their youngest offspring got ready to leave home, did most colonial parents free themselves of debt.

In general, the more isolated a community or the less productive its farmland, the more self-sufficiency and bartering its people practiced, although only the remotest settlements were completely self-sufficient. Rural families depended heavily on wives' and daughters' making items that the family would otherwise have had to purchase. Besides cooking, cleaning, and washing, wives preserved food, boiled soap, made clothing, and tended the garden, dairy, orchard, poultry house, and pigsty. They also sold dairy products to neighbors or

A New England Woman's Cupboard
Modest prosperity enabled some married women to exercise power as consumers and even to express their individuality. Hannah Barnard, a Hadley, Massachusetts, farm woman, commissioned this cupboard for storing linens and other fine textiles, in about 1720.

merchants, spun yarn into cloth for tailors, knitted garments for sale, and even sold their own hair for wigs. A farm family's ability to feed itself and its animals was worth about half of its cash income (a luxury that few European peasants enjoyed), and women worked as much as men did in meeting this end.

Legally, however, white women in the British colonies were constrained (see Chapter 3). A woman's single most autonomous decision was her choice of a husband. Once married, she lost control of her dowry, unless she was a New Yorker subject to Dutch custom, which allowed her somewhat more authority. Women in the French and Spanish colonies retained ownership of, and often augmented, the property they brought to a marriage. Widows did control between 8 and 10 percent of all property in eighteenth-century Anglo-America, and a few—among them Eliza Pinckney of South Carolina, a prominent political figure—owned and managed large estates.

Colonial Farmers and the Environment

The rapid expansion of Britain's colonies hastened environmental change east of the Appalachians. Whereas the earliest colonists farmed land already cleared and cultivated by Native Americans, eighteenth-century settlers usually had to remove trees before beginning their plots. Despite the labor involved, farmers and planters, especially those using slave labor, preferred heavily forested areas where the soil was most fertile. New England farmers had to clear innumerable heavy rocks—debris from the last Ice Age—with which they built walls around their fields. Colonists everywhere used timber to construct their houses, barns, and fences and to provide fuel for heating and cooking. Farmers and planters also sold firewood to the inhabitants of cities and towns. Only six years after Georgia's founding, a colonist noted, there was "no more firewood in Savannah; . . . it must be bought from the plantations for which reason firewood is already right expensive."

In removing the trees (deforestation), farmers drove away bears, panthers, wild turkeys, and other forest animals while attracting grass- and seed-eating rabbits, mice, and possums. By removing protection from winds and, in summer, from the sun, deforestation also brought warmer summers and colder winters, further increasing colonists' demand for firewood. By hastening the runoff of spring waters, it led both to heavier flooding and drier streambeds in most areas and, where water could not escape, to more extensive swamps. In turn, less stable temperatures and water levels, along with impediments created by mills and by the floating of timbers downstream, rapidly reduced the number of fish in colonial waters. Writing in 1766, naturalist John Bartram noted that fish "abounded formerly when the Indians lived much on them & was very numerous," but that "now there is not the 100th or perhaps the 1000th [portion of] fish to be found."

Deforestation dried and hardened the soil, but colonists' crops had even more drastic effects. Native Americans, recognizing the soil-depleting effects of intensive cultivation, rotated their crops regularly so that fields could lie fallow (unplanted) and thereby be replenished with vital nutrients (see Chapter 1). But many colonial farmers either did not have enough land to leave some unplanted or were unwilling to sacrifice short-term profits for potential long-term benefits. As early as 1637, one New England farmer discovered that his soil "after five or six years [of planting corn] grows barren beyond belief and puts on the face of winter in the time of summer." Chesapeake planters' tobacco yields declined after only three or four years in the same plot. Like farmers elsewhere, they used animal manure to fertilize their food crops but not their tobacco, fearing that manure would spoil the taste for consumers. As Chesapeake tobacco growers moved inland to hillier areas, away from rivers and streams, they also contributed to increased soil erosion.

Confronting a more serious shortage of land and resources, Europe's well-to-do farmers were already turning their attention to conservation and "scientific" farming. But most colonists ignored such techniques, either because they could not afford to implement them or because they believed that American land, including that still held by Indians, would sustain them and future generations indefinitely.

The Urban Paradox

The cities were British North America's economic paradox. As major ports of entry and exit, they were keys to the colonies' rising prosperity; yet they held only 4 percent of the colonies' population, and a growing percentage of city-dwellers were caught in a downward spiral of declining opportunity.

As colonial prosperity reached new heights after 1740, economic success proved ever more elusive for residents of the three major seaports—Philadelphia, New York, and, especially, Boston. The cities' poor rolls bulged as poor white men, women (often widowed), and children arrived from both Europe and the colonial countryside. High population density and poor sanitation in urban locales allowed contagious diseases to run rampant, so that half of all city children died before age twenty-one and urban adults lived ten years less on average than country folk.

Even the able-bodied found cities increasingly treacherous. Early eighteenth-century urban artisans typically trained apprentices and employed them as journeymen for many years until they opened their own shops. By midcentury, however, more and more employers kept laborers only as long as business was brisk, releasing them when sales slowed. In 1751 a shrewd Benjamin Franklin recommended this practice to employers as a way to reduce labor costs. Recessions hit more frequently after 1720 and created longer spells of unemployment, making it increasingly difficult for many to afford rents, food, and firewood.

Insignificant before 1700, urban poverty became a major problem. By 1730 Boston could no longer shelter its destitute in the almshouse built in 1685. The proportion of residents considered too poor to pay taxes

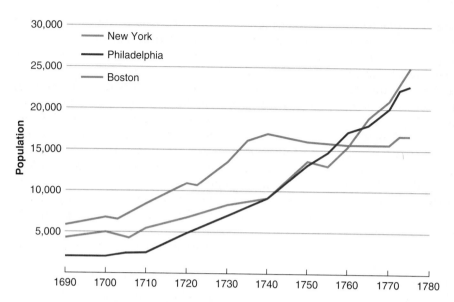

FIGURE 4.2

Populations of Boston, New York, and Philadelphia, 1690-1776

Transatlantic commerce contributed to the rapid growth of the three northern seaports. But Boston's growth leveled off in 1740 while New York and Philadelphia continued to flourish.

Source: Gary B. Nash, The Urban Crucible: Social Change, Political Consciousness, and the Origins of the American Revolution (Cambridge: Harvard University Press, 1979) p. 409.

climbed even as the total population leveled (see Figure 4.2). Not until 1736 did New York need a poorhouse (for just forty people), but by 1772, 4 percent of its residents (over eight hundred people) required public assistance to survive. The number of Philadelphia families listed as poor on tax rolls jumped from 3 percent in 1720 to 11 percent by 1760.

Wealth, on the other hand, remained highly concentrated. For example, New York's wealthiest 10 percent (mostly merchants) owned about 45 percent of the property throughout the eighteenth century. Similar patterns existed in Boston and Philadelphia. Set alongside the growth of a poor underclass in these cities, such statistics underscored the polarization of status and wealth in urban America.

Most southern cities were little more than large towns. Charles Town, however, became North America's fourth-largest city. South Carolina's capital offered gracious living to the wealthy planters who flocked from their plantations to townhouses during the months of the worst heat and insect infestation. Shanties on the city's outskirts sheltered a growing crowd of destitute whites. The colony encouraged whites to immigrate in hopes of reducing blacks' numerical preponderance, but most European newcomers could not establish farms or find any work except as ill-paid temporary laborers. Like their counterparts in northern ports, Charles Town's poor whites competed for work with urban slaves whose masters rented out their labor.

Although middle-class women in cities and large towns performed somewhat less manual drudgery than their country cousins, they nonetheless managed complex households that often included servants, slaves,

Juſt imported in Capt. *Part ilge* from LONDON and to be Sold by

Suſanna Renken,

At her Shop in Fore-Street near the Draw-Bridge, BOSTON, Viz.

EARLY Charlton, Hotſpur, Marrowfat, Golden Hotſpur, and blue Marrowfat Peas; Large Windſor, early Hotſpur, early yellow Kidney, early Spaniſh Beans:—Early *Yorkſhire*, Dutch, Batterſea, Red, and large Winter Cabbage: yellow and green Savoy; Purple and Colliflower Brocoli; white Goſs-Cabbage, Marble, white Sileſia, green Sileſia, and ſcarlet Lettice, green and yellow Hyſſop; Turkey Melons; and Winter Savory; with all ſorts of other Garden Seeds, among which are a great Variety of Flower-Seeds:—Red and white Clover, Herd Graſs and Trefoile.

Juſt Imported from LONDON, and to be Sold

By Sarah DeCoſter,

At the Sign of the Walnut-Tree in Milk-Street in *Boſton*, a little below the Rev. Dr. *Sewall's* Meeting-Houſe,

WINDSOR Beans; Early Peas of ſeveral Sorts; Early Cabbage-Seeds; and other Sorts of Garden-Seeds; too many to enumerate: All at reaſonable Rates.

Newspaper Ads

Women shopkeepers were common in the cities, especially in trades that required only a small investment. These Boston women advertised imported garden seeds.

and apprentices. While raising poultry and vegetables as well as sewing and knitting, urban wives purchased their cloth and most of their food in daily trips to public markets. Many had one or more household servants, usually young single women or widows, to help with cooking, cleaning, and laundering—tasks that required more attention than in the country because of higher urban standards of cleanliness and appearance. Wives also worked in family businesses or their own shops, which were located in owners' homes.

Less affluent wives and widows had the fewest opportunities of all. They housed boarders rather than servants, and many spun and wove cloth in their homes for local merchants. Poor widows with children looked to the community for relief. Whereas John Winthrop and other Puritan forebears had deemed it a Christian's duty to care for poor dependents (see Chapter 3), affluent Bostonians in the eighteenth century looked more warily upon the needy. Preaching in 1752, the city's leading minister, Charles Chauncy, lamented "the swarms of children, of both sexes, that are continually strolling and playing about the streets of our metropolis, clothed in rags, and brought up in idleness and ignorance." Another clergyman warned that charity for widows and their children was money "worse than lost."

Slavery's Wages

For slaves, the economic progress achieved in colonial America meant only that most masters could afford to keep them healthy. Rarely, however, did masters choose to make their human property comfortable. A visitor to a Virginia plantation from Poland (where peasants lived in dire poverty) recorded this impression of slaves' quality of life:

> We entered some Negroes huts—for their habitations cannot be called houses. They are far more miserable than the poorest of the cottages of our peasants. The husband and wife sleep on a miserable bed, the children on the floor . . . a little kitchen furniture amid this misery . . . a teakettle and cups . . . five or six hens, each with ten or fifteen chickens, walked there. That is the only pleasure allowed to the negroes.

To maintain slaves, masters normally spent just 40 percent of the amount paid for the upkeep of indentured servants. Whereas white servants ate two hundred pounds of meat yearly, black slaves consumed fifty pounds. The value of the beer and hard cider given to a typical servant alone equaled the expense of feeding and clothing the average slave. Masters usually provided adult slaves with eight quarts of corn and a pound of pork each week but expected them to grow their own vegetables, forage for wild fruits, and perhaps raise poultry.

Blacks worked for a far longer portion of their lives than whites. Slave children entered the fields as part-time helpers soon after reaching seven and began working full-time between eleven and fourteen. Whereas most white women worked in their homes, barns, and gardens, black females routinely tended tobacco or rice crops, even when pregnant, and often worked outdoors in the winter. Most slaves toiled until they died, although those who survived to their sixties rarely performed hard labor.

Africans and creoles proved resourceful at maximizing opportunities within this harsh, confining system. House slaves aggressively demanded that guests tip them for shining shoes and stabling horses. They also sought presents on holidays, as a startled New Jersey visitor to a Virginia plantation discovered early one Christmas morning when slaves demanding gifts of cash roused him from bed.

In the South Carolina and Georgia rice country, slaves working under the task system gained control of about half their waking hours. Under tasking, each slave spent some hours caring for a quarter-acre, after which his or her duties ended for the day. This system permitted a few slaves to keep hogs and sell surplus vegetables on their own. In 1728 an exceptional slave, Sampson, earned enough money in his off-hours to buy another slave, whom he then sold to his master in exchange for his own freedom.

The gang system used on tobacco plantations afforded Chesapeake slaves less free time than those in Carolina. As one white observer noted, Chesapeake blacks labored "from daylight until the dusk of evening and some part of the night, by moon or candlelight, during the winter."

Despite Carolina slaves' greater autonomy, racial tensions ran high in the colony. As long as Europeans outnumbered Africans, race relations in Carolina remained relaxed. But as a black majority emerged, whites increasingly used force and fear to control "their" blacks. For example, a 1735 law, noting that many Africans wore "clothes much above the condition of slaves," imposed a dress code limiting slaves' apparel to fabrics worth less than ten shillings per yard and even prohibited their wearing their owners' cast-off clothes. Of even greater concern were large gatherings of blacks uncontrolled by whites. In 1721 Charles Town enacted a nine P.M. curfew for blacks, while Carolina's assembly

placed all local slave patrols under the colonial militia. Slaves responded to the colony's vigilance and harsher punishments with increased instances of arson, theft, flight, and violence.

Despite these measures, South Carolina (separated from North Carolina since 1729) was rocked in 1739 by a powerful slave uprising, the Stono Rebellion. It began when twenty blacks seized guns and ammunition from a store at the Stono River Bridge, outside Charles Town. Marching under a makeshift flag and crying "Liberty!" they collected eighty men and headed south toward Spanish Florida, a well-known refuge for escapees (see A Place in Time: Mose, Florida, 1740). Along the way they burned seven plantations and killed twenty whites, but they spared a Scottish innkeeper known for being "a good Man and kind to his slaves." Within a day, mounted militia surrounded the slaves near a riverbank, cut them down mercilessly, and spiked a rebel head on every mile-post between that spot and Charles Town. Uprisings elsewhere in the colony required more than a month to suppress, with insurgents generally "put to the most cruel Death." Thereafter, whites enacted a new slave code, essentially in force until the Civil War, which kept South Carolina slaves under constant surveillance. Furthermore, it threatened masters with fines for not disciplining slaves and required legislative approval for manumission (freeing of individual slaves). The Stono Rebellion and its cruel aftermath thus reinforced South Carolina's emergence as a rigid, racist, and fear-ridden society.

Slavery and racial tensions were by no means confined to plantations. By midcentury slaves made up 20 percent of New York City's population and formed a majority in Charles Town and Savannah. Southern urban slave owners augmented their incomes by renting out the labor of their slaves, who were cheaper to employ than white workers. Slave artisans—usually creoles—worked as coopers, shipwrights, rope makers, and, in a few cases, goldsmiths and cabinetmakers. Some artisans supplemented their work as slaves by earning income of their own. Slaves in northern cities were more often unskilled. Urban slaves in both North and South typically lived apart from their masters in rented quarters alongside free blacks.

Although city life afforded slaves greater freedom of association than did plantations, urban blacks remained the property of others and chafed at racist restrictions. In 1712 rebellious slaves in New York City killed nine whites in a calculated attack. As a result, eighteen slaves were hanged or tortured to death, and six others committed suicide to avoid similar treatment. In 1741 a wave

Asante Drum
Enslaved Africans carried their cultures with them to the Americas. This drum, made from African wood, was found in Virginia.

of thefts and fires attributed to New York slaves led to similar executions of twenty-six slaves and four white accomplices, and the sale of seventy more blacks to the West Indies.

The Rise of Colonial Elites

A few colonists benefited disproportionately from the growing wealth of Britain and its colonies. Most of these elite colonists inherited their advantages at birth and augmented them by producing plantation crops, buying and selling commodities across the Atlantic or carrying them in ships, or serving as attorneys for other elite colonists. They constituted British America's upper class, or gentry. (In Britain, the gentry constituted the lesser, untitled nobility.)

A gentleman was expected by his contemporaries to behave with an appropriate degree of responsibility, to display dignity and generosity, and to be a community leader. His wife, a "lady," was to be a skillful household manager and, in the presence of men, a refined yet deferring hostess.

Before 1700 the colonies' class structure was not readily apparent because elites spent their limited

The Spanish presence in Florida was always tenuous and, after English colonists established Charles Town, Carolina, in 1670, vulnerable to outside attack. During the eighteenth century Spain retained its hold in Florida by enlisting the support of Native Americans and Africans alienated by the English. In particular, by promising freedom to slaves who fled from Carolina to Florida and converted to Catholicism, the Spanish bolstered Florida's population and defenses. The black community of Mose, established near St. Augustine in 1738, vividly demonstrated the importance of these immigrants.

Blacks had lived in Florida since the founding of St. Augustine in 1565. In 1683, after Indians armed by Carolina began attacking and capturing Florida mission Indians for sale into slavery, the Spanish colony formed a black militia unit. In 1686 fifty-three blacks and Indians conducted a counterraid into Carolina and returned with, among other prizes, thirteen of the governor's slaves. In subsequent negotiations between the two colonies, Florida's governor, Diego de Quiroga, refused English demands that he return the blacks, instead giving them paying jobs. Soon other Carolina slaves began making their way to Florida. Spain's King Charles II ruled in 1693 that all arriving slaves should be given their freedom, "so that by their example and my liberality others will do the same."

With Spain deliberately encouraging Carolina slaves to escape to Florida, the numbers continued to rise, especially during the Yamasee War (1715–1716), when the English were nearly crushed by a massive uprising of Indians. In 1726 a former South Carolina slave, Francisco Menéndez, was appointed to command a black militia unit to defend against an expected English invasion. The Spanish built a fortified village for Menéndez's men and their families in 1738 and called it Gracia Real de Santa Teresa de Mose, usually shortened to Mose, an Indian name for the location.

Mose was strategically placed just two miles north of St. Augustine, and its residents served as both sentries and a buffer for the capital. Spanish and English documents, along with recent archaeological excavations, reveal that it had sturdy earthen walls "lined round with prickly royal" (a thorny plant) and was surrounded by a moat. A stone fort was the most prominent structure inside the walls. Outside the fort the one hundred residents planted fields and gathered shellfish from the banks of a nearby saltwater stream. In a letter to the

English Map of St. Augustine and Mose, 1762
Mose is indicated as "Negroe Fort"; "Indian Town" is a settlement of pro-Spanish Indians.

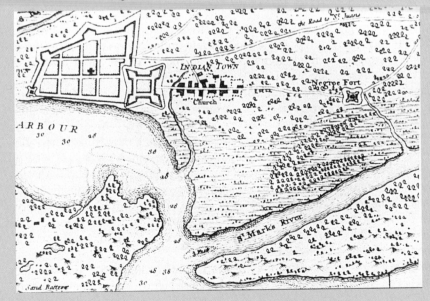

Spanish king, Florida's governor, Manuel de Montiano, praised Menéndez for having "distinguished himself in the establishment and cultivation of Mose, . . . [and] doing all he could so that the rest of his subjects, following his example, would apply themselves and learn good customs."

To its residents Mose symbolized their new status as freed men and women. Most had been born in West Africa and enslaved and carried to Carolina. After escaping, they had lived among friendly Indians who helped them make their way to the Spanish colony. Mose was their own community, their first since being taken from Africa. In agreeing to live there, they understood the price they might have to pay. Writing to the king in 1738, they declared themselves "the most cruel enemies of the English" who were ready to shed their "last drop of blood in defense of the Great Crown of Spain and the Holy Faith."

The importance of Florida's free blacks and their town was demonstrated in 1740 when, with England and Spain at war, Georgia's governor, James Oglethorpe, led colonial troops, Indian allies, and seven warships in an invasion of Florida. The English captured Mose in May after its residents had been evacuated, but Menéndez's militia and other troops recaptured the town a month later in a fierce battle that helped Oglethorpe decide to withdraw. (The British called the battle Bloody Mose.) As a result of the English destruction of the town and the Spanish crown's refusal to fund its rebuilding, Mose's residents moved into St. Augustine. For twelve years they lived among the Spanish as laborers, seamen, and hunters and in other capacities. In 1752 a new governor had Mose rebuilt and ordered the blacks to return to their former town despite their express "desire to live in complete liberty." To return to the town, which they once had cherished as a symbol of their freedom, after twelve years of assimilation in the capital city now seemed like relegation to second-class citizenship.

In 1763 Spain ceded Florida to Britain in the Treaty of Paris (see Chapter 5). Spanish authorities evacuated the people of Mose and allotted them homesteads in Matanzas, Cuba. But the meager provisions given the blacks proved inadequate, and many, including Francisco Menéndez, soon moved to Havana. In 1783 another Treaty of Paris returned Florida to Spain (see Chapter 6), and the following year, a new Florida governor resumed the policy of granting freedom to escaped slaves. Hearing the news and recalling Florida's earlier reputation, hundreds of slaves responded. But now Spain proceeded more cautiously with the slaveholders' government to Florida's north; and in 1790 U.S. Secretary of State Thomas Jefferson persuaded the Spanish to rescind the policy of granting freedom to escaped slaves. In 1819 the United States annexed Florida, and in 1845 Florida joined the Union as a slave state.

Ft. Mose Watercolor
Artist's reconstruction of Mose, based on archaeological and documentary evidence.

St. Christopher's Medal from Mose
Upon reaching Florida and freedom, Mose's formerly enslaved black residents converted to Catholicism. One convert made this medal, uncovered by archaeologists, by hand.

John Potter and His Family
The Potters of Matunuck, Rhode Island, relax at tea. In commissioning a portrait depicting themselves at leisure and attended by a black slave, the Potters proclaimed their elite status.

resources buying land, servants, and slaves instead of on luxuries. As late as 1715 a traveler noticed that one of Virginia's richest planters, Robert Beverley, owned "nothing in or about his house but just what is necessary, . . . [such as] good beds but no curtains and instead of cane chairs he hath stools made of wood."

As British mercantilist trade flourished, higher incomes enabled elite colonists to display their wealth more openly, particularly in their housing. The greater gentry—the richest 2 percent, owning about 15 percent of all property—constructed residences such as the Cornelius Low House, New Jersey's most splendid home in 1741, and the Shirley mansion in Virginia. The lesser gentry, or second wealthiest 2 to 10 percent holding about 25 percent of all property, lived in more modest dwellings such as Pennsylvania's Lincoln homestead or the wood-frame house, Whitehall in Rhode Island. In contrast, middle-class farmers commonly inhabited one-story wooden buildings with four small rooms and a loft.

Colonial gentlemen and ladies also exhibited their status by imitating the "refinement" of upper-class Europeans. They wore costly English fashions, drove carriages instead of wagons, and bought expensive chinaware, books, furniture, and musical instruments. They pursued a gracious life by studying foreign languages, learning formal dances, and cultivating polite manners. In sports men's preference shifted to horse racing (on which they bet avidly) and away from cockfighting, a less elegant diversion. A few young gentlemen even traveled abroad to get an English education. Thus, elites led colonists' growing taste for British fashions and consumer goods (see above).

Low House, New Jersey
Wealthy merchant Cornelius Low's house exemplifies the Georgian style of architecture favored by many eighteenth-century elites in British America.

COMPETING FOR A CONTINENT, 1713–1750

After a generation of war, Europe's return to peace in 1713 only heightened British, French, and Spanish imperial ambitions in North America. Europeans competed in expanding their territorial claims, intensifying both trade and warfare with Native Americans, and carving out new settlements. Native Americans welcomed some of these developments and resisted others, depending on how they expected their sovereignty and livelihoods to be affected.

France and Native Americans

A principal focus of France's imperial efforts was its new colony of Louisiana (see Chapter 3). In 1718 Louisiana officials established New Orleans, which became the colony's capital and port. Louisiana's staunchest Indian allies were the Choctaws, through whom the French hoped to counter both the rapidly expanding influence of Carolina's traders and the weakening Spanish presence in Florida. But by the 1730s inroads by the persistent Carolinians led the Choctaws to become bitterly divided into pro-English and pro-French factions.

Life was dismal in Louisiana for whites as well as blacks. A thoroughly corrupt government ran the colony. With Louisiana's sluggish export economy failing to sustain them, settlers and slaves found other means of survival. Like the Indians, they hunted, fished, gathered wild plants, and cultivated gardens. In 1727 a priest described how some whites eventually prospered: "A man with his wife or partner clears a little ground, builds himself a house on four piles, covers it with sheets of bark, and plants corn and rice for his provisions; the next year he raises a little more for food, and has also a field of tobacco; if at last he succeeds in having three or four Negroes, then he is out of difficulties."

But many red, white, and black Louisianans depended on exchanges with one another in order to stay "out of difficulties." Indians provided corn, bear oil, tallow (for candles), and above all deerskins to French merchants in return for blankets, kettles, axes, chickens, hogs, guns, and alcohol. Indians from west of the Mississippi brought horses and cattle, usually stolen from Spanish ranches in Texas. Familiar with cattle from their homelands, enslaved Africans managed many of Louisiana's herds, and some became rustlers and illicit traders of beef.

French settlements in Upper Louisiana, usually referred to as "Illinois," were somewhat better off.

Although more than a third of the colony's twenty-six hundred inhabitants were nonwhite slaves in 1752, their principal export was wheat, a more reliably profitable crop than the plantation commodities grown farther south. In exporting wheat, Illinois resembled Pennsylvania to the east; but the colony's remote location limited such exports and attracted few whites, obliging it to depend on France's Native American allies to defend it from Indian enemies.

With Canada and the Mississippi Valley secure from European rivals, France sought to counter growing British influence in the Ohio Valley. The valley was at peace after the Iroquois declared their neutrality in 1701, encouraging Indian refugees to settle there. Nations such as the Kickapoos and Mascoutens returned from the upper Great Lakes, while Shawnees arrived from the east to reoccupy older homelands. Other arrivals were newcomers, such as Delawares escaping English encroachments and Seneca Iroquois seeking new hunting territories. Hoping to secure commercial and diplomatic ties with these Natives, the French expanded their trade activities. Detroit and several other French posts ballooned into sizable villages housing Indians, French, and mixed-ancestry *métis*. But English traders were arriving with better goods at lower prices, and most Indians steered a more independent course.

Huron (Wyandotte) Woman
Her cloth dress, glass beads, and iron hoe reflect the influence of French trade on this woman and other Indians of the Great Lakes-Ohio region in the eighteenth century.

Although generally more effective in Indian diplomacy than the English, the French did not enjoy universal success. The Carolina-supported Chickasaws frequently attacked the French and their native allies on the Mississippi River. Although ultimately unsuccessful, the Mesquakie, or Fox, Indians led a prolonged effort to prevent French traders from making direct contact with Sioux Indians to the west. And the French in 1729–1730 brutally suppressed the Natchez Indians, the last practitioners of Mississippian culture, in order to gain additional plantation land. The French enslaved many Native Americans seized in these wars for labor in Louisiana, Illinois, Canada, and (in a few cases) the West Indies.

By 1744 French traders were traveling as far west as North Dakota and Colorado and were buying beaver pelts and Indian slaves on the Great Plains. At the instigation of these traders and their British competitors, trade goods, including guns, spread to Native Americans throughout central Canada and then to the Plains. Meanwhile, Indians in the Great Basin and southern Plains were acquiring horses, thousands of which had been left behind by the Spanish when they fled New Mexico during the Pueblo Revolt of 1680. Adopting the horse and gun, Indians such as the Lakota Sioux and Comanches moved to the Plains and built a new, highly mobile way of life based on the pursuit of buffalo. With this way of life, they met whites traveling westward to adopt their own new ways of life a century later (see Chapter 17). By 1750 France had an immense domain, but one that depended on often-precarious relations with Native Americans.

Native Americans and British Expansion

As in the seventeenth century, British colonial expansion was made possible by the depopulation and dislocation of Native Americans. Epidemic diseases, environmental changes, war, and political pressures on Indians to cede land and to emigrate all combined to make new lands available to white immigrants.

Conflict came early to Carolina, where a trade in Indian slaves (see Chapter 3) and imperial war had already produced violence. In 1711 Iroquoian-speaking Tuscarora Indians, provoked by whites encroaching on their land and kidnapping and enslaving some of their people, destroyed New Bern, a nearby settlement of seven hundred Swiss immigrants. To retaliate, northern Carolina enlisted the aid of southern Carolina and its well-armed Indian allies. By 1713, after about a thousand Tuscaroras (about one-fifth of the total population)

had been killed or enslaved, the nation surrendered. Most Tuscarora survivors migrated northward to what is now upstate New York and in 1722 became the sixth nation of the Iroquois Confederacy.

Having helped defeat the Tuscaroras, Carolina's Indian allies resented a growing number of abuses, including cheating, violence, and enslavement, by English traders and encroachments on their land by settlers. In 1715 the Yamasees, who were most seriously affected, led a coordinated series of attacks by Catawbas, Creeks, and other allies on English trading houses and settlements. Only by enlisting the aid of the Cherokee Indians, and allowing four hundred slaves to bear arms, did the colony crush the uprising. Yamasees not killed or captured fled to Florida or to Creek towns in the interior.

The defeat of the Yamasees left their Catawba supporters vulnerable to pressures from English on one side and Iroquois on the other. As Carolina settlers moved uncomfortably close to some Catawba villages, the inhabitants abandoned these villages and joined more remote Catawbas. Having escaped the settlers, however, the Catawbas faced rising conflict with the Iroquois. After making peace with the Indian allies of New France in 1701 (see above), the Iroquois looked south when launching raids for captives to adopt into their ranks. To counter the well-armed Iroquois, the Catawbas turned back to South Carolina. By ceding land and helping defend that colony against outside Indians, the Catawbas received guns, food, and clothing. Their relationship with the English allowed the Catawbas the security they needed to strengthen their traditional institutions. However, the growing gap in numbers between Natives and colonists, and their competition with the English for resources, limited the Catawbas' autonomy.

To the north, the Iroquois Confederacy accommodated English expansion while consolidating its own power among Native Americans. Late in the seventeenth century, the Iroquois and several colonies forged a series of treaties known as the Covenant Chain. Under these treaties the Confederacy helped the colonies subjugate Indians whose lands the English wanted. Under one such agreement, the Iroquois assisted Massachusetts in subjugating that colony's Natives following King Philip's War in New England. Under another, the Susquehannock Indians, after being crushed in Bacon's Rebellion, moved northward from Maryland to a new homeland adjacent to the Iroquois' own. By relocating non-Iroquois on their periphery as well as by inviting the Tuscaroras into their Confederacy, the Iroquois controlled a center of Native American power that was distinct from, but cooperative with, the British. At the same

Tuscarora Resistance, 1711
Defending their homeland against an influx of settlers, the Tuscaroras captured Baron Christopher von Graffenried, leader of the Swiss community at New Bern. Graffenried drew this sketch, which depicts him being held along with an English trader, John Lawson, and an African slave. Lawson was later executed.

time, the Confederacy established buffers against, and deflected, potential English expansion to their own lands.

The Covenant Chain grew more powerful with Pennsylvania's entry in 1737. With immigration and commercial success, William Penn's early idealism waned in Pennsylvania. Between 1729 and 1734 the colony coerced the Delaware Indians into selling more than fifty thousand acres. Then the colony's leaders (Penn's sons and his former secretary) produced a patently fraudulent treaty in which the Delawares allegedly had agreed in 1686 to sell their land as far westward as a man could walk in a day and a half. In 1737, Pennsylvania blazed a trail and hired three men to walk west as fast as they could. The men covered nearly sixty miles, meaning that the Delawares, in what became known as the Walking Purchase, had to hand over an additional twelve hundred square miles of land. Despite the protests of Delaware elders who had been alive in 1686 and remembered no such treaty, the Delawares were forced to move under Iroquois supervision. The proprietors then sold these lands to settlers and speculators at a large profit. Within a generation, the Delawares' former lands were among the most productive in the British Empire.

British Expansion in the South: Georgia

Britain's undertook a new expansionist thrust in 1732 when Parliament authorized a new colony, Georgia. Ignoring Spain's claims, Oglethorpe purchased the land for Georgia from Creek Indians. Although expecting Georgia to export expensive commodities like wine and silk, the colony's sponsors intended that Georgia be a refuge for bankrupt but honest debtors. Parliament even allotted funds to ensure Georgia's success, making it the only North American province besides Nova Scotia to be directly subsidized by the British government.

A tough-minded idealist, James Oglethorpe, dominated the provincial board of trustees during Georgia's first decade. Oglethorpe founded the port of entry, Savannah, in 1733, and by 1740 a small contingent of twenty-eight hundred colonists had arrived. Almost half the immigrants came from Germany, Switzerland, and Scotland, and most had their overseas passage paid by the government. A small number of Jews were among the early colonists. Along with Pennsylvania, early Georgia was the most inclusive of all the British colonies.

Oglethorpe hated slavery. "They live like cattle," he wrote to the trustees after viewing Charles Town's slave market. "If we allow slaves, we act against the very principles by which we associated together, which was to relieve the distressed." Slavery, he thought, degraded blacks, made whites lazy, and presented a terrible risk. Oglethorpe worried that wherever whites relied on a slave labor force, they courted slave revolts, which the Spanish could then exploit. But most of all, he recognized that slavery undermined the economic position of poor whites like those he sought to settle in Georgia.

At Oglethorpe's insistence, Parliament made Georgia the only colony where slavery was outlawed. Oglethorpe also pushed through a requirement that landholdings be no larger than five hundred acres. These measures were aimed at keeping rural Georgia populated by white, independent farmer-soldiers who would defend the colony and would not speculate in real estate or build up slave-labor plantations.

But Oglethorpe's well-intentioned plans failed completely. Few debtors arrived because Parliament set impossibly stringent conditions for their release from prison. Limitations on settlers' rights to sell or enlarge their holdings, as well as the ban on slavery, also discouraged immigration. Raising exotic export crops proved impractical. As in South Carolina, only rice, which required substantial capital and many cheap laborers, proved profitable. Oglethorpe struggled against economic reality for a decade and then gave up. After the trustees legalized slavery and lifted restrictions on landholdings in 1750, Georgia, like Britain's other plantation colonies, boomed.

Spain's Tenacity

While endeavoring to maintain its empire in the face of Native American, French, and British adversaries, Spain spread its language and culture over much of North America, especially in the Southwest. Seeking to repopulate New Mexico after the Pueblo Revolt, Spain awarded grants of approximately twenty-six square miles wherever ten or more families founded a town. Soldiers erected strong fortifications to protect against Indian attacks, now coming primarily from the Apaches. As in early New England towns, the settlers built homes on small lots around the church plaza, farmed separate fields nearby, grazed livestock at a distance, and shared a community wood lot and pasture.

Slave-Raiding Expedition in New Mexico

This surviving portion of a painting on buffalo hide, dating to the 1720s, depicts a Spanish soldier and allied Indians as they encounter resistance at an encampment, probably of Apaches. Women and children look on from behind a palisade surrounding the encampment.

The livestock-raising ranchos, radiating out for many miles from little clusters of houses, monopolized vast tracts along the Rio Grande and blocked further town settlement. On the ranchos, mounted cattle herders created the way of life later associated with the American cowboy, featuring lariat and roping skills, cattle drives, roundups (rodeos), and livestock branding.

By 1750 New Mexico numbered about 14,000, more than half of them Pueblo Indians. Most Pueblos now cooperated with the Spanish, and although many had converted to Catholicism, they also practiced their traditional religion. The two peoples continued to experience Apache raids, now augmented by those of armed and mounted Utes from the north and Comanches from the east. The raiders sought livestock and European goods as well as captives, often to replace those of their own people who had been enslaved by Spanish raiders and sent to mine silver in Mexico.

Spain had established Texas in order to counter growing French influence among the Comanches and other Native Americans on the southern Plains (see Chapter 3). Colonization began after 1716, when Spaniards established several outposts on the San Antonio and Guadalupe Rivers. The most prominent center was at San Antonio de Béxar, where two towns, a presidio, and a mission (later known as the Alamo) were clustered. But most Indians in Texas preferred trading with the French to farming, Christianity, and the ineffective protection of the Spanish. Lack of security also deterred Hispanic settlement, so that by 1760 only twelve hundred Spaniards faced the periodic raids by Comanches and other Indians.

Spain's position in Florida was equally precarious. After 1715 the neutrality of the Creeks enabled the Spanish to compete with the English and French in the southeastern deerskin trade, though with limited effectiveness, and to sponsor Indian counterraids into Carolina. In addition, the Spanish offered freedom to any English-owned slaves who escaped and made their way to Florida (see A Place in Time: Mose, Florida, 1740). As in Texas, Florida's relatively few colonists hampered Spain's ability to counter its chief imperial rival in the region. As early as 1700, there were already thirty-eight hundred English in recently founded Carolina, compared to just fifteen hundred Spanish in Florida. This disparity widened during the decades that followed. The Spanish saw Georgia's founding in 1733 as a bold new threat to Florida, but fought the English colony to a bloody draw when Spain and England went to war (see below).

By 1750 Spain controlled much of the Southeast and Southwest, while France exercised influence in the

Mississippi, Ohio, and Missouri River valleys, as well as around the Great Lakes and in Canada (see Map 4.3). Both empires were spread thin and depended on the goodwill or acquiescence of Native Americans. In contrast, British North America was compact, wealthy, densely populated by non-Indians, and aggressively expansionist.

The Return of War, 1739–1748

After a generation of war ended in 1713, the American colonies enjoyed a generation of peace as well as prosperity. But in 1739 British launched a war against Spain, using as a pretext Spain's cutting off the ear of a British smuggler named Jenkins. (Thus the British termed the conflict the War of Jenkins' Ear.) In 1740 James Oglethorpe led a massive British assault on Florida. Although failing to seize St. Augustine (see A Place in Time: Mose, Florida, 1740), he led 650 men in repelling 3,000 Spanish troops and refugee South Carolina slaves who counterattacked Georgia in 1742. Meanwhile 3,500

colonists joined a British assault on Cartagena, in what is now Colombia, but more than half perished due to Spain's repelling the attack and to yellow fever.

The Anglo-Spanish War quickly merged with a second one in Europe, the War of the Austrian Succession, called King George's War in British America (1740–1748). King George's War followed the pattern of earlier imperial conflicts. Few battles involved more than six hundred men, and most were attacks and counterattacks on civilians in the Northeast in which many noncombatants were killed and others captured. Most captives were New Englanders seized by French and Indians from isolated towns. Although prisoners were exchanged at the end of the war, some English captives, particularly women and children, elected to remain with the French or Indians.

King George's War produced just one major engagement. In 1745 almost four thousand New Englanders under William Pepperell of Maine besieged and, after seven weeks of intense fighting, captured the French bastion of Louisbourg, which guarded the entrance to the St. Lawrence River. After three more years

MAP 4.3

French and Spanish Occupation of North America, to 1750

While British colonists concentrated themselves on the Atlantic seaboard, the French and Spanish together established themselves thinly over two-thirds of the present-day United States.

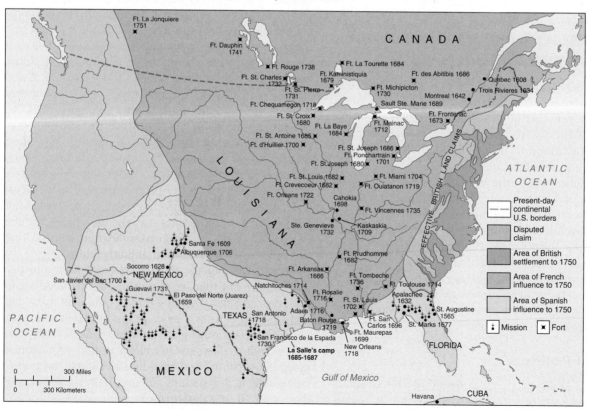

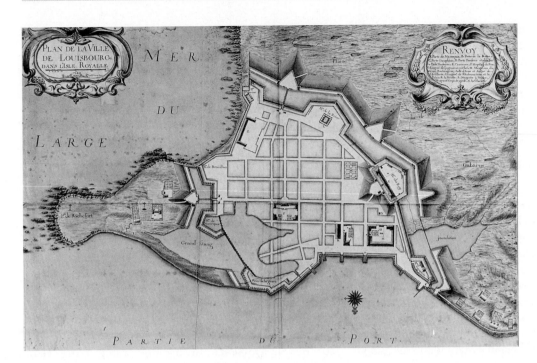

Plan of Louisbourg, 1744
Built to defend New France, Louisbourg fell to New Englanders in 1745, but was returned to France by the Treaty of Aix-la-Chapelle (1748). France would lose the fortress for good when British troops seized it in 1758 (see Chapter 5).

of inconclusive warfare, Britain signed the Treaty of Aix-la-Chapelle (1748), exchanging Louisbourg for a British outpost in India that the French had seized. The memory of how their sacrifices at Cartagena and Louis-bourg went for naught would rankle colonists thereafter.

PUBLIC LIFE IN BRITISH AMERICA, 1689–1750

During the early and middle eighteenth century, the ties linking Britain and its colonies consisted of much more than the movements of goods and peoples. England's new Bill of Rights was the foundation of government and politics in the colonies. The ideas of English thinkers initially inspired the intellectual movement known as the Enlightenment, while the English preacher George Whitefield sparked a generation of colonists to transform the practice of Protestantism in British America. While reinforcing the colonies' links with Britain, these developments were also significant because they involved many more colonists than before as active participants in politics, in intellectual discussions, and in new religious movements. Taken as a whole, this wider participation signaled the emergence of a new phenomenon in colonial life, the "public."

Colonial Politics

The most significant political result of the Glorious Revolution was the rise of colonial legislatures, or assemblies, as a major political force. Except in Connecticut and Rhode Island, the crown or a proprietor in England chose each colony's governor. Except in Massachusetts, the governor named a council, or upper house of the legislature. The assembly was the only political body subject to control by colonists rather than by English officials. Before 1689 governors and councils took the initiative in drafting laws, and the assemblies followed their lead; but thereafter the assemblies assumed a more central role in politics.

Colonial leaders argued that their legislatures should exercise the same rights as those won by Parliament in its seventeenth-century struggle with royal authority. Indeed, Anglo-Americans saw their assemblies as miniature Houses of Commons, which represented the people and defended their liberty against centralized authority, in particular by its exclusive power to originate revenue-raising measures. After Parliament won supremacy over the monarchy through the Bill of Rights in 1689, assemblymen insisted that their governors' powers were similarly limited.

The lower houses steadily asserted their prestige and authority by refusing to permit outside meddling in their proceedings, by taking firm control over taxes and budgets, and especially by keeping a tight rein on executive salaries. Although governors had considerable powers (including the right to veto acts, call and dismiss assembly sessions, and schedule elections), they were vulnerable to legislatures' financial pressure because they received no salary from British sources and relied

on the assemblies for income. This "power of the purse" sometimes enabled assemblies to force governors to sign laws opposed by the crown.

The assemblies' growing importance was reinforced by British policy. The Board of Trade, established in 1696 to monitor American developments, could have weakened the assemblies by persuading the crown to disallow objectionable colonial laws signed by the governors. But it rarely exercised this power before midcentury. The resulting political vacuum allowed the colonies to become self-governing in most respects except for trade regulation, restrictions on printing money, and declaring war. Representative government in the colonies originated and was nurtured within the protective environment of the British Empire.

The elite planters, merchants, and attorneys who monopolized colonial wealth also dominated politics. Most assemblymen ranked among the wealthiest 2 percent of colonists. To placate them, governors invariably appointed other members of the greater gentry to sit on their councils and as judges on the highest courts. Although members of the lesser gentry sat less often in the legislature, they commonly served as justices of the peace.

Outside New England (where any voter was eligible for office), legal requirements barred 80 percent of white men from running for the assembly, most often by specifying that a candidate must own a minimum of a thousand acres. (Farms then averaged 180 acres in the South and 120 acres in the middle colonies.) Even without such property qualifications (as New England showed), few ordinary colonists could have afforded to hold elective office. Assemblymen received only living expenses, which might not fully cover the cost of staying at their province's capital, much less compensate a farmer or an artisan for his absence from farm or shop for six to ten weeks a year. As a result, a few wealthy families in each colony dominated the highest political offices. Nine families, for example, provided one-third of Virginia's royal councilors after 1680. John Adams, a rising young Massachusetts politician, estimated that most towns in his colony chose their legislators from among just three or four families.

By eighteenth-century standards, the colonies set liberal qualifications for male voters, but all provinces barred women and nonwhites from voting. In seven colonies voters had to own land (usually forty to fifty acres), and the rest demanded that an elector have enough property to furnish a house and work a farm with his own tools. About 40 percent of free white men —mostly indentured servants and young men still living with parents or just beginning family life—could not meet these requirements. Still, most white males in British North America could vote by age forty, whereas two-thirds of all men in England and nine-tenths in Ireland were never eligible.

In rural areas voter participation was low unless a vital issue was at stake. The difficulties of voting limited the average rural turnout to about 45 percent (a rate of participation higher, however, than in typical U.S. elections today, apart from those for president). Most governors called elections when they saw fit, so that elections might lapse for years and suddenly be held on very short notice. Thus voters in isolated areas often had no knowledge of upcoming contests. The fact that polling took place at the county seat discouraged many electors from traveling long distances over poor roads to vote. In several colonies voters stated their choices orally and publicly, often with the candidates present. This procedure inhibited the participation of those whose views differed from those of elites. Finally, most rural elections before 1750 were uncontested. Local elites decided in advance which of them would "stand" for office. Regarding officeholding as a gentleman's public duty, they considered it demeaning to appear interested in being chosen, much less to compete or "run" for a position.

Given all these factors, many rural voters were indifferent about politics at the colony level. For example, to avoid paying legislators' expenses at the capital, many smaller Massachusetts towns refused to elect assemblymen. Thirty percent of men elected to South Carolina's assembly neglected to take their seats from 1731 to 1760, including a majority of those chosen in 1747 and 1749.

Hanover County Courthouse, Virginia

The county courthouse was the seat of local government and the center of political and social life in the Chesapeake colonies.

Despite these limitations, rural elections slowly emerged as community events in which many nonelite white men participated. In time, rural voters would follow urban colonists and express themselves more forcefully.

Meanwhile, a truly competitive political life developed in the northern seaports. Depending on their economic interests, wealthy colonists aligned themselves with or against royal and proprietary governors. To gain advantage over rivals, some factions courted artisans and small shopkeepers whose fortunes had stagnated or declined as the distribution of urban wealth tilted increasingly toward the rich. In actively courting nonelite voters, they scandalized rival elites who feared that an unleashing of popular passions could disturb the social order.

New York was the site of the bitterest factional conflicts. In one episode in 1733, Governor William Cosby suspended his principal rival, Lewis Morris, from Morris' position as chief justice after Morris ruled against the governor. To mobilize popular support for Morris, his faction established the *New-York Weekly Journal*, which repeatedly accused Cosby and his associates of rampant corruption. In 1734 the governor's supporters engineered the arrest of the *Weekly Journal's* printer, John Peter Zenger, on charges that he had seditiously libeled Cosby. Following a celebrated trial in August 1735, Zenger was acquitted.

Although it did not lead to a change in New York's libel law nor significantly enhance freedom of the press at the time, the Zenger verdict was significant for several reasons. In New York and elsewhere, it encouraged the broadening of political discussion and participation beyond a small circle of elites. Equally significant were its legal implications. Zenger's brilliant attorney, Andrew Hamilton, effectively seized on the growing colonial practice of allowing attorneys to speak directly to juries on behalf of defendants. He persuaded the jury that it alone, without the judge's advice, could reject a charge of libel "if you should be of the opinion that there is no falsehood in [Zenger's] papers." Until then, truth alone had not served as a sufficient defense against a charge of libel in British and colonial courts of law. By empowering nonelites as voters, readers, and jurors, the Morris-Cosby rivalry and the Zenger trial encouraged their participation in New York's public life.

The Enlightenment

If property and wealth were the keys to political participation and officeholding, literacy and education permitted Anglo-Americans to participate in the trans-Atlantic world of ideas and beliefs. Perhaps 90 percent of New England's adult white men and 40 percent of white women could write well enough to sign documents, thanks to the region's traditional support for primary education. Among white males elsewhere in the colonies, the literacy rate varied from about 35 percent to more than 50 percent. (In England, by contrast, no more than one-third of all males could read and write.) How readily most of these people read a book or wrote a letter was another matter.

The best-educated colonists—members of the gentry, well-to-do merchants, educated ministers, and growing numbers of self-improving artisans and farmers—embraced a wider world of ideas and information. Though costly, books, newspapers, and writing paper could open up eighteenth-century European civilization to reading men and women. A rich, exciting world it was. Scientific advances seemed to explain the laws of nature; human intelligence appeared poised to triumph over ignorance and prejudice. For those who had the time to read and think, an age of optimism and progress was dawning, an age known as the Enlightenment.

Enlightenment ideals combined confidence in human reason with skepticism toward beliefs not founded on science or strict logic. A major source of Enlightenment thought was English physicist Sir Isaac Newton (1642–1727), who in 1687 explained how gravitation ruled the universe. Newton's work captured Europe's imagination by demonstrating the harmony of natural laws and stimulated others to search for rational principles in medicine, law, psychology, and government.

Before 1750 no American more fully embodied the Enlightenment spirit than Benjamin Franklin. Born in Boston in 1706, Franklin migrated to Philadelphia at age seventeen. He brought along skill as a printer, considerable ambition, and insatiable intellectual curiosity. In moving to Philadelphia, Franklin put himself in the right place at the right time, for the city was growing much more rapidly than Boston and was attracting merchants and artisans who shared Franklin's zest for learning and new ideas. Franklin organized some of these men into a reading-discussion group called the Junto, and they helped him secure printing contracts. In 1732 he first published *Poor Richard's Almanack*, a collection of maxims and proverbs that made him famous. By age forty-two Franklin had earned enough money to retire and devote himself to science and community service.

These dual goals—science and community benefit—were intimately related in Franklin's mind, for he believed that all true science would be useful, in the sense of making everyone's life more comfortable. For example, experimenting with a kite, Franklin demon-

strated in 1752 that lightning was electricity, a discovery that led to the lightning rod.

Although some southern planters, such as Thomas Jefferson, eventually championed progress through science, the Enlightenment's earliest and primary American centers were cities, where the latest European books and ideas circulated and where gentlemen and self-improving artisans met to investigate nature and conduct experiments. Franklin organized one such group, the American Philosophical Society, in 1743 to encourage "all philosophical experiments that let light into the nature of things, tend to increase the power of man over matter, and multiply the conveniences and pleasures of life." By 1769 this society had blossomed into an intercolonial network of amateur scientists. The societies emulated the Royal Society in London, the foremost learned society in the English-speaking world. In this respect, the Enlightenment initially strengthened the ties between colonial and British elites.

Although confident that science would benefit everyone, the Enlightenment's followers envisioned progress as gradual and proceeding from the top down. They trusted reason far more than they trusted the common people, whose judgment, especially on religious matters, seemed too easily deranged.

Just as Newton inspired the scientific bent of Enlightenment intellectuals, English philosopher John Locke, in his *Essay Concerning Human Understanding* (1690), led many to embrace "reasonable" or "rational" religion. Locke contended that ideas, including religion, are not inborn but are acquired by toilsome investigation of and reflection upon experience. To most Enlightenment intellectuals, the best argument for the existence of God was the harmony and order of nature, which pointed to a rational Creator. Some individuals, including Franklin and, later, Jefferson and Thomas Paine, carried this argument a step farther by insisting that where the Bible conflicted with reason, one should follow the dictates of reason rather than the Bible. Called Deists, they concluded that God, having created a perfect universe, did not miraculously intervene in its workings but rather left it alone to operate according to natural laws.

Most colonists influenced by the Enlightenment described themselves as Christians and attended church. But they feared Christianity's excesses, particularly as indulged in by those who persecuted others in religion's name and by "enthusiasts" who emphasized emotion rather than reason in the practice of piety. Mindful of Locke's caution that no human can be absolutely certain of anything but his or her own existence, they distrusted zealots and sectarians. Typically,

Meeting of the Tuesday Club
Like Franklin's Junto and similar groups in other colonial cities, the Tuesday Club of Annapolis, Maryland, appealed to the elite white men who cultivated the literary and cultural tastes of "gentlemen."

Franklin contributed money to most of the churches in Philadelphia but thought that religion's value lay in its encouragement of virtue and morality rather than in theological hair splitting.

In 1750 the Enlightenment's greatest contributions to American life still lay in the future. A quarter-century later, Anglo-Americans drew on the Enlightenment's revolutionary ideas as they declared their independence from Britain and created the foundations of a new nation (see Chapters 5 and 6). Meanwhile, a series of religious revivals known as the Great Awakening challenged the Enlightenment's most basic assumptions.

The Great Awakening

Viewing the world as orderly and predictable, rationalists were inclined to a sense of smug self-satisfaction. Writing his will in 1750, Franklin thanked God for giving

him "such a mind, with moderate passions" and "such a competency of this world's goods as might make a reasonable mind easy." But many Americans lacked such a comfortable competency of goods and lived neither orderly nor predictable lives. For example, in 1737 and 1738 an epidemic of diphtheria, a contagious throat disease, killed every tenth child under sixteen from New Hampshire to Pennsylvania. Such an event starkly reminded colonists of the fragility of earthly life and turned their thoughts to religion.

Throughout the colonial period, religious fervor periodically quickened within a denomination or region and then receded. But in 1739 an outpouring of European Protestant revivalism spread to British North America. This "Great Awakening," as its promoters termed it, cut across lines of class, gender, and even race. Above all, the revivals represented an unleashing of anxiety and longing among ordinary people—anxiety about sin, and longing for assurances of salvation. The answers

A Satirical View of George Whitefield, 1760
Whitefield's detractors portrayed him as a charlatan and demagogue who exploited simple-minded common people.

they received were conveyed through the powerful preaching of charismatic ministers who appealed directly and brazenly to their audiences' emotions rather than to their intellects. Some revivalists were themselves intellectuals, comfortable amid the books and ideas of the Enlightenment. But for all, religion was primarily a matter of emotional commitment.

In contrast to rationalists, who stressed the potential for human betterment, revivalist ministers roused their audiences into outbursts of religious fervor by depicting the emptiness of material comfort, the utter corruption of human nature, the fury of divine wrath, and the need for immediate repentance. Although he was a brilliant thinker, well aware of contemporary philosophy and science, the Congregationalist Jonathan Edwards, who led a revival at Northampton, Massachusetts, in 1735, drove home this message with breathtaking clarity. "The God that holds you over the pit of Hell, much as one holds a spider or other loathsome insect over the fire, abhors you," Edwards intoned in one of his famous sermons, "Sinners in the Hands of an Angry God." "His wrath toward you burns like fire; He looks upon you as worthy of nothing else but to be cast into the fire."

Even before Edwards's Northampton revival, two New Jersey ministers, Presbyterian William Tennent and Theodore Frelinghuysen of the Dutch Reformed Church, had stimulated conversions in prayer meetings called Refreshings. But the event that brought these various threads of revival together was the arrival in 1739 of George Whitefield (see above). So overpowering was Whitefield that some joked that he could make crowds swoon simply by uttering "Mesopotamia." In age without microphones, crowds exceeding twenty thousand could hear his booming voice clearly, and many wept at his eloquence.

Whitefield's American tour inspired thousands to seek salvation. Most converts were young adults in their late twenties. In Connecticut alone, the number joining churches jumped from 630 in 1740 to 3,217 after Whitefield toured in 1741. Within two more years, every fifth Connecticut resident under forty-five had reportedly been saved by God's grace. Whitefield's allure was so mighty that he even awed potential critics. Hearing him preach in Philadelphia, Benjamin Franklin first vowed to contribute nothing to the collection. But so admirably did Whitefield conclude his sermon, Franklin recalled, "that I empty'd my Pocket wholly into the Collector's Dish, Gold and all."

Divisions over the revivals quickly developed in Whitefield's wake and were often exacerbated by social and economic tensions. For example, after leaving

Boston in October 1740, Whitefield invited Gilbert Tennent (William's son) to follow "in order to blow up the divine flame lately kindled there." Denouncing Boston's established clergymen as "dead Drones" and lashing out at aristocratic fashion, Tennent built a following among the city's poor and downtrodden. So did another preacher, James Davenport, who was expelled for having said that Boston's clergy were leading the people blindfolded to hell.

Exposing colonial society's divisions, Tennent and Davenport corroded support for the revivals among established ministers and officials. As Whitefield's exchange with Alexander Garden showed, the lines hardened between the revivalists, known as New Lights, and the rationalist clergy, or Old Lights, who dominated the Anglican, Presbyterian, and Congregational churches. In 1740 Gilbert Tennent published *The Danger of an Unconverted Ministry*, which hinted that most Presbyterian ministers lacked saving grace and hence were bound for hell, and urged parishioners to abandon them for the New Lights. By thus sowing the seeds of doubt about individual ministers, Tennent undermined one of the foundations of social order. For if the people could not trust their own ministers, whom would they trust?

Old Light rationalists fired back. In 1742 Charles Chauncy, Boston's leading Congregationalist, condemned the revival as an epidemic of the "enthusiasm" that enlightened intellectuals so loathed. Chauncy particularly blasted those who mistook the ravings of their overheated imaginations for the experience of divine grace. He even provided a kind of checklist for spotting enthusiasts: look for "a certain wildness" in their eyes, the "quakings and tremblings" of their limbs, and foaming at the mouth, Chauncy suggested. Put simply, the revival had unleashed "a sort of madness."

The Great Awakening opened unprecedented splits in American Protestantism. In 1741 New and Old Light Presbyterians formed rival branches that did not reunite until 1758, when the revivalists emerged victorious. The Anglicans lost many members to New Light congregations, especially Presbyterian and Baptist. Congregationalists splintered so badly that by 1760, New Lights had seceded from one-third of New England's churches and formed separate congregations.

The secession of New Lights was especially bitter in Massachusetts and Connecticut, where the Congregational church was established by law. To force New Lights into paying tithes to their former church, Old Lights repeatedly denied new churches legal status. Connecticut passed repressive laws forbidding revivalists to preach or perform marriages, and the colony expelled many New Lights from the legislature. In Connecticut's Windham County, an extra story had to be added to the jail to hold all the New Lights arrested for not paying tithes. Elisha Paine, a revivalist imprisoned there for illegal preaching, gave sermons from his cell and drew such crowds that his followers built bleachers nearby to hear him. Paine and his fellow victims generated widespread sympathy for the New Lights, who finally won control of Connecticut's assembly in 1759.

Although New Lights made steady gains until the 1770s, the Great Awakening peaked in 1742. The revival then crested everywhere but in Virginia, where its high point came after 1755 with an upsurge of conversions by Baptists, who also suffered legal harassment.

For all the commotion it raised at the time, the Great Awakening's long-term effects exceeded its immediate impact. First, the revival marked a decline in the influence of Quakers (who were not significantly affected by revivalism), Anglicans, and Congregationalists. In undermining Anglicans and Congregationalists, the Great Awakening contributed to the weakening of officially established denominations. As these churches' importance waned after 1740, the number of Presbyterians and Baptists increased.

The Great Awakening also stimulated the founding of new colleges as both Old and New Lights sought institutions free of one another's influence. In 1746 New Light Presbyterians established the College of New Jersey (Princeton). Then followed King's College (Columbia) for Anglicans in 1754, the College of Rhode Island (Brown) for Baptists in 1764, Queen's College (Rutgers) for Dutch Reformed in 1766, and Dartmouth College for Congregationalists in 1769.

The revivals were also significant because they spread beyond the ranks of white society. The emphasis on piety over intellectual learning as the key to God's grace led some Africans and Native Americans to combine aspects of their traditional cultures with Christianity. The Great Awakening marked the beginnings of black Protestantism after New Lights reached out to slaves, some of whom joined white churches and even preached at revival meetings. Meanwhile, a few New Light preachers became missionaries to Native Americans residing within the colonies. A few Christian Indians, such as Samson Occom, a Mohegan born in Connecticut, became widely known as preachers themselves. Despite these breakthroughs, blacks and Indians still faced considerable religious discrimination, even among New Lights.

The Great Awakening also added to white women's religious prominence. For several decades ministers had singled out women—who constituted the majority of church members—as embodying the Christian ideal of

Reverend Samson Occom, Mohegan Indian Preacher
Born in a wigwam in Connecticut, Occom converted to Christianity
under the influence of the Great Awakening and preached to other
Native Americans. But he grew disillusioned with the treatment of his
people by whites and, after the American Revolution, joined an exodus
of Indians from New England to upstate New York.

piety. Now some New Light churches, mostly Baptist and
Congregationalist, granted women the right to speak
and vote in church meetings. Like Anne Hutchinson a
century earlier, some women moved from leading
women's prayer and discussion groups to presiding over
meetings that included men. One such woman, Sarah
Osborn of Newport, Rhode Island, conducted "private
praying Societies Male and female" that included black
slaves in her home. In 1770 Osborn and her followers
won a bitter fight over their congregation's choice of a
new minister. While most assertive women were prevented from exercising as much power as Osborn, none
was persecuted as Hutchinson had been in Puritan New
England.

Finally the revivals had the unintended effect of
blurring denominational differences among Protestants.
Although George Whitefield was an Anglican who
defied his superior, Garden, and later helped found
Methodism, he preached with Presbyterians such as
Gilbert Tennent and Congregationalists like Jonathan
Edwards. By emphasizing the need for salvation over
doctrinal and institutional fine points, revivalism
emphasized Protestants' common experiences and promoted the coexistence of denominations.

Historians have disagreed over whether the Great
Awakening had political as well as religious effects.
Although Tennent and Davenport called the poor "God's
people" and flayed the wealthy, they never advocated a
social revolution, and the Awakening did not produce a
distinct political ideology. Yet by empowering ordinary
people to assert and act openly on beliefs that countered
those in authority, the revivals laid some of the groundwork for political revolutionaries a generation later.

CONCLUSION

By 1750 Britain's mainland colonies barely resembled
those of a century earlier. Mercantilist policies bound
the colonies to the rising prosperity of the British
Empire. A healthy environment for whites, along with a
steady supply of Native Americans' land, enabled the
population to grow and expand at an astonishing rate.
The political settlement that followed England's
Glorious Revolution provided the foundation for representative government in the colonies. Educated Anglo-
Americans joined the intellectual ferment known as the
Enlightenment. The Great Awakening, with its European
origins and its intercolonial appeal, further signaled the
colonies' emergence from provincial isolation.

The achievements of France and Spain on the North
American mainland contrasted starkly with those of
Britain. More lightly populated by Europeans, their
colonies were largely remote from the more dynamic
centers of Atlantic commerce. Despite their mercantilist
orientations, neither France nor Spain developed
colonies that substantially enriched the home country.
And neither could avoid depending militarily on Native
Americans for their colonies' survival.

For all of its evident wealth and progress, British
America was rife with tensions. In some areas, vast dis-
crepancies in the distribution of wealth and opportunities fostered a rebellious spirit among whites who were
less well off. The Enlightenment and the Great
Awakening revealed deep-seated religious and ideological divisions. Slave resistance and Anglo-Indian warfare
demonstrated the depths of racial antagonisms. The
revived imperial warfare of 1739–1748 added to the
uncertainties of colonial life.

FOR FURTHER REFERENCE

READINGS

Bernard Bailyn and Philip D. Morgan, eds., *Strangers
Within the Realm: Cultural Margins of the First British
Empire* (1991). Leading historians examine the interplay
of ethnicity and empire in North America, the
Caribbean, and the British Isles.

CHRONOLOGY, 1660–1750

1651–1733 England enacts Navigation Acts.

1660 Restoration of the English monarchy.

1686–1689 Dominion of New England.

1688–1689 Glorious Revolution in England.

1689–1691 Uprisings in Massachusetts, New York, and Maryland; royal authority established.

1689–1697 King William's War (in Europe, War of the League of Augsburg).

1690 John Locke, *Essay Concerning Human Understanding.*

1693 Spain begins offering freedom to English slaves escaping to Florida.

1701 Iroquois Confederacy's Grand Settlement with England and France.

1702–1713 Queen Anne's War (in Europe, War of the Spanish Succession).

1711 Tuscarora War in Carolina.

1715–1716 Yamasee War in Carolina.

1716 San Antonio de Béxar founded.

1718 New Orleans founded.

1729–1730 French war on Natchez Indians in Louisiana.

1733 Georgia founded.

1735 John Peter Zenger acquitted of seditious libel in New York.
Jonathan Edwards leads revival in Northampton, Massachusetts.

1737 Walking Purchase of Delaware Indian lands in Pennsylvania.

1739 Great Awakening begins with George Whitefield's arrival in British colonies. Stono Rebellion in South Carolina.

1739–1744 Anglo-Spanish War.

1743 Benjamin Franklin founds American Philosophical Society.

1744–1748 King George's War (in Europe, the War of the Austrian Succession).

1750 Slavery legalized in Georgia.

Jon Butler, *Becoming America: The Revolution Before 1776* (2000). A provocative discussion of the British colonies, arguing that they became a distinctive modern society between 1680 and 1770.

W. J. Eccles, *France in America,* rev. ed. (1991). An interpretive overview of French colonization in North America and the Caribbean by a distinguished scholar.

Ronald Hoffman et al., eds., *Through a Glass Darkly: Reflections on Personal Identity in Early America* (1997). Essays that explore issues of personal identity for individual Americans during the seventeenth and eighteenth centuries.

John J. McCusker and Russell R. Menard, *The Economy of British America, 1607–1789,* rev. ed. (1991). A comprehensive discussion of the economy, drawing on a wide range of scholarship.

James H. Merrell, *Into the Woods: Negotiators on the Pennsylvania Frontier* (1999). A brilliant, innovative study of intercultural diplomacy as practiced by Indians and colonists.

Philip D. Morgan, *Slave Counterpoint: Black Culture in the Eighteenth-Century Chesapeake and Lowcountry* (1998). The definitive study of African-American life in Britain's southern colonies.

Daniel K. Richter, *Facing East from Indian Country: A Native History of Early America* (2001). A highly original examination of colonial American history from the perspective of Native Americans.

Laurel Thatcher Ulrich, *The Age of Homespun: Objects and Stories in the Creation of an American Myth* (2001). A pathbreaking study that uses New England women's work with textiles as a window into economic, gender, and cultural history.

David J. Weber, *The Spanish Frontier in North America* (1992). A masterful synthesis of Spanish colonial history north of the Caribbean and Mexico.

WEBSITES

From Indentured Servitude to Racial Slavery
http://innercity.org/holt/slavechron.html
Part 1, 1619–1789, includes an excellent discussion of slavery and the slave trade in North America, including African contexts. Features useful maps and links to primary and secondary sources.

Historic Deerfield Collections and Research
http://www.historic-deerfield.org/collections/collections.html
View furniture, china, and other examples of elite consumption in eighteenth-century New England. Photos are accompanied by information on artisans and techniques.

Religion and the Founding of the American Republic
http://lcweb.loc.gov/exhibits/religion/rel02.html
Part 2, Religion in Eighteenth-Century America, shows the role of religion in the British colonies, examining both the revivals and the deism of Enlightenment thinkers. Includes illustrations from the period.

For additional works please consult the bibliography at the end of the book.

The BLOODY MASSACRE perpetrated in King Street BOSTON on March 5th 1770 by a party of the 29th REG.

BUTCHER'S HALL.

Engrav'd Printed & Sold by PAUL REVERE BOSTON

Unhappy Boston! see thy Sons deplore,
Thy hallow'd Walks besmear'd with guiltless Gore
While faithless P—n and his savage Bands,
With murd'rous Rancour stretch their bloody Hands;
Like fierce Barbarians grinning o'er their Prey.
Approve the Carnage, and enjoy the Day.

If scalding drops from Rage from Anguish Wrung
If speechless Sorrows lab'ring for a Tongue
Or if a weeping World can ought appease
The plaintive Ghosts of Victims such as these;
The Patriot's copious Tears for each are shed,
A glorious Tribute which embalm the Dead.

But know Fate summons to that awful
Where Justice strips the Murd'rer of his
Should venal C—ts the scandal of the
Snatch the relentless Villain from her H
Keen Execrations on this Plate inscr
Shall reach a Judge who never can be

The unhappy Sufferers were Messrs SAML GRAY SAML MAVERICK, JAMS CALDWELL, CRISPUS ATTUCKS & PAT
Killed. Six wounded; two of them (CHRIST MONK & JOHN CLARK) Mortally

Roads to Revolution, 1750–1776

On the evening of March 5, 1770, an angry crowd of poor and working-class Bostonians gathered in front of the guard post outside the Boston customs house. The crowd was protesting a British soldier's abusive treatment a few hours earlier of a Boston apprentice who was trying to collect a debt from a British officer. Suddenly, shots rang out. When the smoke had cleared, four Bostonians lay dead, and seven more were wounded, one mortally.

Among those in the crowd was an impoverished twenty-eight-year-old shoemaker named George Robert Twelves Hewes. Hewes had already witnessed, and once experienced, abuses by British troops, but the appalling violence of the "Boston Massacre," as the shooting became known, led Hewes to political activism. Four of the five who died were personal friends, and he himself received a serious blow to the shoulder from a soldier's rifle butt. Over the next several days, Hewes attended meetings and signed petitions denouncing British conduct in the shooting, and he later testified against the soldiers. Thereafter he participated prominently in such anti-British actions as the Boston Tea Party.

How was it that four thousand British troops were stationed on the streets of Boston—a city of sixteen thousand—in 1770? What had brought those troops and the city's residents to the verge of war? What led obscure, humble people like George Robert Twelves Hewes to become angry political

◀ **The Boston Massacre, 1770, Engraving by Paul Revere**
Shortly after this incident, one Bostonian observed that "unless there is some great alteration in the state of things, the era of the independence of the colonies is much nearer than I once thought it, or now wish it."

activists in an age when the lowborn were expected to defer to their social superiors? The Boston Massacre was one of a long chain of events that finally resulted in the complete rupture of Britain's relationship with its American colonies.

The conflict between Britain and the colonies erupted after 1763, when Parliament attempted to reorganize its suddenly enlarged empire by tightening control over economic and political affairs in the colonies. Long accustomed to benefiting economically from the empire while conducting provincial and local affairs on their own (see Technology and Culture), colonists were shocked by this unexpected effort to centralize decision making in London. Many colonial leaders, such as Benjamin Franklin, interpreted Britain's clampdown as calculated antagonism intended to deprive the colonists of their prosperity and their relative independence. Others, such as Massachusetts Lieutenant Governor and Chief Justice Thomas Hutchinson, stressed the importance of maintaining order and authority.

For many ordinary colonists like Hewes, however, the conflict was more than a constitutional crisis. In the port cities, crowds of poor and working people engaged in direct, often violent demonstrations against British authority. Sometimes they acted in concert with elite radicals, and other times in defiance of them. Settlers in the remote backcountry of several colonies invoked the language and ideas of urban radicals when resisting large landowners and distant colonial governments dominated by seaboard elites. These movements reflected social-economic tensions within the colonies as well as the growing defiance of elites by ordinary colonists. By the same token, the growing participation of white women in colonial resistance reflected their impatience with the restraints imposed by traditional gender norms. Nonwhite African-Americans and Native Americans had varying views, but many in each group perceived the colonists as greater threats to their liberty than Britain. Moreover, colonial protests did not arise in a vacuum but rather drew from ideas and opposition movements in Britain and elsewhere in Europe.

Taken as a whole, colonial resistance involved many kinds of people with many outlooks. It arose most immediately from a constitutional crisis within the British Empire, but it also reflected deep democratic stirrings in America and in the Atlantic world generally. These stirrings would erupt in the American Revolution in 1776, then in the French Revolution in 1789, and subsequently spread over much of Europe and the Americas.

Most colonists expressed their opposition peacefully before 1775, through such tactics as legislative resolutions and commercial boycotts, and did not foresee the revolutionary outcome of their protests. Despite eruptions of violence, relatively few Anglo-Americans and no royal officials or soldiers lost their lives during the twelve years prior to the battles at Lexington and Concord. Even after fighting broke out, some colonists agonized for more than a year about whether to sever their political relationship with England, which even native-born colonists sometimes referred to affectionately as "home." Anglo-Americans were the most reluctant of revolutionaries in 1776.

George Robert Twelves Hewes

Hewes was present at the Boston massacre and actively participated in the Boston Tea party before enlisting in the Continental Army. This portrait was painted in 1835, when he was celebrated as one of the last surviving veterans of the Revolutionary War.

This chapter focuses on four major questions:

- How and why did their joint triumph in the Seven Years' War lead to a rupture between Britain and its American colonies?

- Why did differences between British officials and colonists over revenue-raising measures lead to a more fundamental conflict over political authority within the colonies?

- How did the imperial crisis lead non-elite colonists to become politically active?

- What were the major factors leading most colonists to abandon their loyalty to Britain and instead choose national independence?

THE TRIUMPH OF THE BRITISH EMPIRE, 1750–1763

King George's War (see Chapter 4) did nothing to avert a showdown between Britain and France. After a "diplomatic revolution" in which Austria shifted its allegiance from Britain to France, Britain aligned with Prussia, and the conflict resumed. Known as the Seven Years' War (1756–1763), it would constitute a major turning point in American as well as European history.

A Fragile Peace, 1750–1754

King George's War failed to establish either Britain or France as the dominant power in North America, and each side soon began preparations for another war. Although there were many points of contention between the two powers, the Ohio valley became the tinderbox for conflict. The valley was the subject of competing claims by Virginia, Pennsylvania, France, and the Six Nations Iroquois, as well as by the Native Americans who actually lived there.

Seeking to drive traders from Virginia and Pennsylvania out of the Ohio valley, the French began building a chain of forts there in 1753. Virginia retaliated by sending a twenty-one-year-old surveyor and speculator, George Washington, to persuade or force the French to leave. But in 1754 French troops drove Washington and his militiamen back to their homes.

Sensing the need to resolve differences among themselves and to restore Native Americans' confidence in the British, delegates from seven colonies north of Virginia gathered at Albany, New York, in mid-1754 to lay plans for mutual defense. By showering the wavering Iroquois with thirty wagonloads of presents, the colonists kept them neutral for the moment. (But virtually all Indians in Ohio itself now supported the French.) The delegates then endorsed a proposal for a colonial confederation, the so-called Albany Plan of Union, largely based on the ideas of Pennsylvania's Franklin and Massachusetts's Thomas Hutchinson. The plan called for a Grand Council representing all the colonial assemblies, with a crown-appointed president general as its executive officer. The Grand Council would devise policies regarding military defense and Indian affairs, and, if necessary, it could demand funds from the colonies according to an agreed-upon formula. Although it provided a precedent for later American unity, the Albany Plan came to nothing, primarily because no colonial legislature would surrender the least control over its powers of taxation, even to fellow Americans and in the face of grave mutual danger.

The Seven Years' War in America, 1754–1760

Although France and Britain remained at peace in Europe until 1756, Washington's 1754 clash with French troops created a virtual state of war in North America. In response, the British dispatched General Edward Braddock and a thousand regular troops to North America to seize Fort Duquesne at the headwaters of the Ohio.

Stiff-necked and scornful of both colonial soldiers and Native Americans, Braddock expected his disciplined British regulars to make short work of the enemy. On July 9, 1755, about 850 French, Canadians, and Indians ambushed Braddock's force of 2,200 Britons and Virginians nine miles east of Fort Duquesne. Riddled by three hours of steady fire from an unseen foe, Braddock's

Chief Hendrick (Theyanoguin) of the Mohawk Iroquois
A lifelong ally of the British, Hendrick led a Mohawk delegation to the Albany Congress (1754).

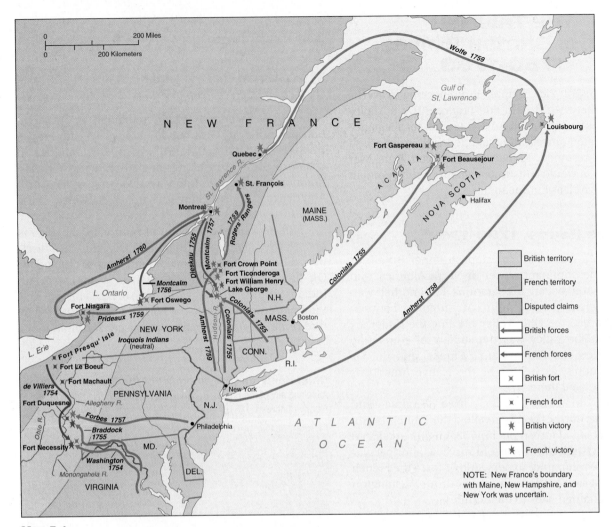

MAP 5.1
The Seven Years' War in America
After experiencing major defeats early in the war, Anglo-American forces turned the tide against the French by taking Fort Duquesne in late 1757 and Louisbourg in 1758. After Canada fell in 1760, the fighting shifted to Spain's Caribbean colonies.

troops retreated. Nine hundred regular and provincial soldiers died in Braddock's defeat, including the general himself, compared to just twenty-three on the French and Indian side.

As British colonists absorbed the shock of Braddock's disastrous loss, French-armed Shawnees, Delawares, and Mingos from the upper Ohio valley struck hard at encroaching settlers in western Pennsylvania, Maryland, and Virginia. For three years, these attacks halted English expansion and prevented the three colonies from joining the British war against France.

Confronted by the numerically superior but disorganized Anglo-Americans, the French and their Native American allies captured Fort Oswego on Lake Ontario

in 1756 and took Fort William Henry on Lake George in 1757. The French now threatened central New York and western New England. In Europe, too, the war began badly for Britain, which by 1757 seemed to be facing defeat on all fronts (see Map 5.1).

In this dark hour, two developments turned the tide for the British. First, the Iroquois and most Ohio Indians, sensing that the French were gaining too decisive an advantage, agreed at a treaty conference at Easton, Pennsylvania, in 1758 to abandon their support of the French. Their subsequent withdrawal from Fort Duquesne enabled the British to capture it and other French forts. Although some Native Americans withdrew from the fighting, others actively joined Britain's cause.

Destruction of Quebec, 1759

After the fall of Quebec to British forces, France's defeat in North America was virtually certain.

The second decisive development occurred when William Pitt took control of military affairs in the British cabinet and reversed the downward course. Imaginative and single-minded in his conception of Britain's imperial destiny, Pitt saw himself as the man of the hour. "I know," he declared, "that I can save this country and that no one else can." True to his word, Pitt reinvigorated British patriotism throughout the empire. By the war's end, he was the colonists' most popular hero, the symbol of what Americans and the English could accomplish when united.

Hard-pressed in Europe by France and its allies (which included Spain after 1761), Pitt chose not to send large numbers of additional troops to America. He believed that the key to crushing New France lay in the mobilization of colonial soldiers. To encourage the colonies to assume the military burden, he promised that if they raised the necessary men, Parliament would bear most of the cost of fighting the war.

Pitt's offer to free Anglo-Americans from the war's financial burdens generated unprecedented support. The colonies organized more than forty thousand troops in 1758–1759, far more soldiers than the crown sent to the mainland during the entire war.

The impact of Pitt's decision was immediate. Anglo-American troops under General Jeffery Amherst captured Fort Duquesne and Louisbourg by late 1758 and drove the French from northern New York the next year.

In September 1759 Quebec fell after General James Wolfe defeated the French commander-in-chief, Louis Joseph Montcalm, on the Plains of Abraham, where both commanders died in battle. French resistance ended in 1760 when Montreal surrendered.

The End of French North America, 1760–1763

Although the fall of Montreal effectively dashed its hopes in North America, the war continued in Europe and elsewhere, and France made one last desperate attempt to capture Newfoundland in June 1762. Thereafter, with defeat inevitable, France entered into negotiations with its enemies. The Seven Years' War officially ended in both America and Europe with the signing of the Treaty of Paris in 1763.

Under terms of the treaty, France gave up all its lands and claims east of the Mississippi (except New Orleans) to Britain. In return for Cuba, which a British expedition had seized in 1762, Spain ceded Florida to Britain. Neither France nor Britain wanted the other to control Louisiana, so in the Treaty of San Ildefonso (1762), France ceded the vast territory to Spain. Thus France's once mighty North American empire was reduced to a few tiny fishing islands off Newfoundland and several thriving sugar islands in the West Indies. Britain reigned supreme in eastern North America

while Spain now claimed the west below Canada (see Map 5.2).

Several thousand French colonists in an area stretching from Quebec to Illinois to Louisiana were suddenly British and Spanish subjects. The most adversely affected Franco-Americans were the Acadians, who had been nominal British subjects since England took over Acadia in 1713 and renamed it Nova Scotia. At the war's outbreak, Nova Scotia's government ordered all Acadians to swear loyalty to Britain and not to bear arms for France. After most refused to take the oath, British soldiers drove them from their homes—often with nothing more than they could carry in their arms—and burned their villages. Almost 5 percent of Canada's population was forcibly deported in this way to the British colonies, especially Maryland and Pennsylvania. But facing poverty and intense anti-French, anti-Catholic prejudice, most Acadians moved on to Louisiana. There they became known as Cajuns.

King George's War and the Seven Years' War produced an ironically mixed effect. On one hand, they fused the bonds between the British and the Anglo-Americans. Fighting side by side, shedding their blood in common cause, the British and the American colonists came to rely on each other as rarely before. But the conclusion of each war planted the seeds first of misunderstanding, then of suspicion, and finally of hostility between the two former compatriots.

IMPERIAL REVENUES AND REORGANIZATION, 1760–1766

Even as the Seven Years War wound down, tensions developed in the victorious coalition of Britons, colonists, and Native Americans. Much of the tension originated in British plans to finance its suddenly enlarged empire by means of a series of revenue measures and to enforce these and other measures directly rather than relying on local authorities. Following passage of the Stamp Act, opposition movements arose in the mainland colonies to protest not only the new measures' costs but also what many people considered a dangerous extension of Parliament's power.

The new revenue measures followed the ascension to the British throne of George III (ruled 1760–1820) at age twenty-two. Although content to reign as a constitutional monarch who cooperated with Parliament and worked through prime ministers, the new king was determined to have a strong influence on government policy. However, neither his experience, his temperament, nor his philosophy suited George III to the formidable task of building political coalitions and pursuing consistent policies. The king made frequent abrupt changes in government leadership that exacerbated relations with the colonies.

The colonists' protests reflected class and other divisions within Anglo-American society. Most elites, including members of the assemblies, expressed themselves in carefully worded arguments based on the British constitution and their colonial charters. Artisans, businessmen, and some planters used more inflammatory language and organized street demonstrations,

MAP 5.2
European Powers in North America 1763
The Treaty of Paris (1763) divided France's North American empire between Britain and Spain. Hoping to prevent unnecessary violence between whites and Indians, Britain forbade any new colonial settlements west of the Appalachians' crest in the Proclamation of 1763.

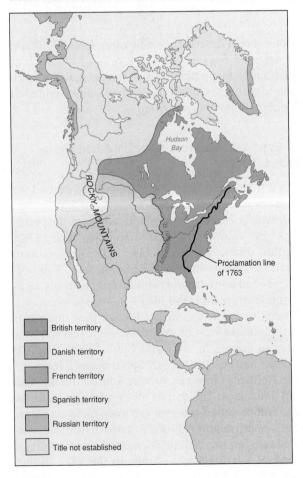

Hudson Bay

ROCKY MOUNTAINS

Mississippi R.

Proclamation line of 1763

- British territory
- Danish territory
- French territory
- Spanish territory
- Russian territory
- Title not established

appealing to the populace rather than to Parliament. Poor and working people in port cities, especially in economically strapped New England, showed a willingness to defy colonial elites as well as British authorities and even to resort to violence to make their views known.

Friction Among Allies, 1760–1763

An extraordinary coalition of Britons, colonists, and Native Americans had achieved the victory over France in North America. But the return of peace brought deep-seated tensions among these allies back to the surface.

During the war, British officers regularly complained about the quality of colonial troops, not only their inability to fight but also their tendency to return home—even in the midst of campaigns—when their terms were up or when they were not paid on time. For their part, colonial soldiers complained of British officers who, as one put it, contemptuously treated their troops "but little better than slaves."

Tensions between British officers and colonial civilians also flared, with officers complaining about colonists' unwillingness to provide food and shelter and with colonists resenting the officers' arrogant manners. One general groused that South Carolina planters were "extremely pleased to have Soldiers to protect their Plantations but will feel no inconveniences for them." Quakers in the Pennsylvania assembly, acting from pacifist convictions, refused to vote funds to support the war effort, while assemblies in New York and Massachusetts opposed the quartering of British troops on their soil as an encroachment on their English liberties. English authorities regarded such actions as affronts to the king's prerogative and as stifling Britain's efforts to defend its territories.

Pitt's promise to reimburse the colonial assemblies for their military expenses also angered many Britons, who concluded that the colonists were escaping scot-free from the war's financial burden. The colonies had already profited enormously from the war, as military contracts and spending by British troops brought an influx of British currency into the hands of farmers, artisans, and merchants. Some colonial merchants, moreover, had continued their illicit trade with the French West Indies during the conflict, not only violating the Navigation Acts but also trading with the enemy. Meanwhile, Britain's national debt nearly doubled during the war, from £72 million to over £132 million. At a time when the total debt of all the colonies collectively amounted to £2 million, the interest charges alone on the British debt came to more than £4 million a year.

George III, Studio of A. Ramsay, c. 1767
Although unsure of himself and emotionally little more than a boy upon his accession to the English throne, George III possessed a deep moral sense and a fierce determination to rule as well as to reign.

This debt was assumed by British landowners through a land tax and, increasingly, by ordinary consumers through excise duties on a wide variety of items, including beer, tea, salt, and bread.

But many colonists felt equally burdened. Those who profited during the war spent their additional income on goods imported from Britain, the annual value of which doubled during the war's brief duration. Thus, the effect of the war was to accelerate the Anglo-American "consumer revolution" in which colonists' purchases of British goods fueled Britain's economy, particularly its manufacturing sector. But when peace returned in 1760, the wartime boom in the colonies ended as abruptly as it had begun. To maintain their lifestyles, many colonists went into debt. British creditors obliged their American merchant customers by extending the usual period for remitting payments from six months to a year. Nevertheless, many recently prosperous colonists suddenly found themselves overloaded with debts and, in many cases, bankrupt. As colonial

Public Sanitation in Philadelphia

Even as the imperial crisis intruded on their lives, city-dwellers confronted long-standing problems occasioned by rapid growth. The fastest-growing city in eighteenth-century America was Philadelphia, whose population approached seventeen thousand in 1760 (see Figure 4.2 in Chapter 4). One key to Philadelphia's rise was its location as both a major Atlantic port and the gateway to Pennsylvania's farmlands and the Appalachian backcountry. Local geography also contributed to its success. Choosing a site at the confluence of the Delaware and Schuylkill Rivers, William Penn had built Philadelphia along a system of streams and the tidal cove on the Delaware into which they flowed. Philadelphians referred to the principal stream and cove together as "the Dock," for one of their principal functions. The Dock's shores were the setting for the early city's mansions and public gathering spaces. As some residents pointed out in 1700, the Dock was the city's heart and "the Inducing Reason . . . to Settle the Town where it now is."

Over time, the growth that made Philadelphia so successful rendered its environment, especially its water, dangerous to inhabitants' health. Several leading industries used water for transforming animals and grains into consumer products. Tanneries made leather by soaking cowhides several times in mixtures of water and acidic liquids, including sour milk and fermented rye, and with an alkaline solution of buttermilk and dung. Before periodically cleaning their vats, tanners dumped residues from these processes into the streets or into underground pits from which they seeped into wells and streams. Breweries and distilleries also used water-based procedures and similarly discarded their waste, while slaughterhouses put dung, grease, fat, and other unwanted by-products into streets and streams. Individual residents exacerbated the problems by tossing garbage into streets, using privies that polluted wells, and leaving animal carcasses to rot in the open air. Most of the city's sewers were open channels that frequently backed up, diverting the sewage to the streets. Buildings and other obstructions caused stagnant pools to form in streets, and when the polluted water did drain freely, it flowed into the Dock.

Almost from the city's founding, residents had complained about the stench arising from waste and stagnant water left by the tanneries and other large industries. Many attributed the city's frequent disease epidemics to these practices. In 1739 a residents' petition complained of "the great Annoyance arising from the Slaughter-Houses, Tan-yards, . . . *etc.* erected on the publick Dock, and Streets, adjacent." It called for prohibiting new tanneries and for eventually removing existing ones. Such efforts made little headway at first. Tanners, brewers, and other manufacturers were among the city's wealthiest residents and dissuaded their fellow elites from regulating their industries.

A turning point came in 1748 when, after another epidemic, the Pennsylvania Assembly appointed an ad hoc committee to recommend improvements in Philadelphia's sanitation. One member, Benjamin Franklin, was already known both for his innovative approaches to urban issues, as when he organized Philadelphia's first fire company in 1736, and for his interest in the practical applications of technology. Combining these interests, Franklin advocated applying new findings in hydrology (the study of water and its distribution) and water-pumping technology to public sanitation. Accordingly, the committee recommended building a wall to keep the high tides of the Delaware River out of the Dock, widening the stream's channel, and covering over a tributary that had become a "common sewer." The plan was innovative not only because it was based on hydrology but also because it acknowledged the need for a public approach to sanitation problems. But once again, neither the city, the colony, nor private entrepreneurs would pay for the proposal. Many elites declined to assume the sense of civic responsibility that Franklin and his fellow advocates of Enlightenment sought to inculcate.

Only in the 1760s, after both growth and pollution had accelerated, did Philadelphia begin to address the Dock's problems effectively. In 1762 the Pennsylvania Assembly appointed a board to oversee the "Pitching [sloping], Paving and Cleansing" of streets and walkways, and the design, construction, and maintenance of sewers and storm drains—all intended to prevent waste and

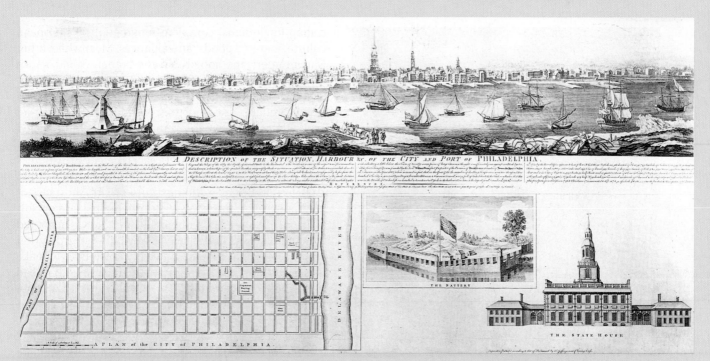

"An East Prospect of the City of Philadelphia" (1756)
The converging streams flowing into the Delaware River in the map (lower left) constitute the Dock. The engraving at the top illustrates Philadelphia's dynamism as a port city at the time of the Seven Years War.

stagnant water from accumulating on land. In the next year, residents petitioned that the Dock itself be "cleared out, planked at the bottom, and walled on each side" to maximize its flow and prevent it from flooding. The Pennsylvania Assembly responded by requiring adjoining property owners to build "a good, strong, substantial wall of good, flat stone from the bottom of the said Dock," and remove any "encroachments" that blocked drainage into or on the streams. Finally, legislators had implemented the kind of public, engineering-based solution that Franklin had advocated two decades earlier.

While some owners evaded their responsibility, others went even farther by also building an arch over the principal stretch of the Dock. Then they installed market stalls on the newly available surface. Once an open waterway used for transport and valued as a central landmark, the Dock was now a completely enclosed, engineered sewer. A new generation of entrepreneurs now dominated the neighborhood, catering to consumers who preferred a clean, attractive environment.

By 1763, however, Philadelphia's problem with sanitation had grown well beyond the Dock. Thereafter, the growing controversy over British imperial policies diverted official attention from public health problems. Yet by empowering poor and working people, that very contro-

versy encouraged some to point out that improvements at the Dock had changed nothing in their own neighborhoods. Writing in a city newspaper in 1769, "Tom Trudge" lamented the lot of "such poor fellows as I, who sup on a cup of skim milk, etc., have a parcel of half naked children about our doors, . . . whose wives must, at many seasons of the Year, wade to the knees in carrying a loaf of bread to bake, and near whose penurious doors the dung-cart never comes, nor the sound of the paver will be heard for many ages." Both public and private solutions, Trudge and others asserted, favored the wealthy and ignored the less fortunate. Environmental controversy had once again shifted with the course of politics. But the Revolution would postpone the search for solutions. Philadelphia's problems with polluted water persisted until 1799, when the city undertook construction of the United States' first municipal water system.

Focus Questions

- How did early manufacturing contribute to pollution in Philadelphia?
- How did engineering provide a successful resolution of sanitary problems at the Dock?

Indian-British Diplomacy, 1764
Throughout the colonial period, treaty councils such as this one were occasions on which Native Americans aired grievances and made or renewed alliances with European powers.

indebtedness to Britain grew, some Americans began to suspect the British of deliberately plotting to "enslave" the colonies.

Victory over the French did not end the British need for revenue, for the settlement of the war spurred new Anglo-Indian conflicts that drove the British debt even higher. With the French vanquished, Ohio and Great Lakes Indians recognized that they could no longer play the two imperial rivals off against each other. Their fears that the British would treat them as subjects rather than as allies were confirmed when General Jeffrey Amherst, Britain's commander in North America, decided to cut expenses by refusing to distribute food, ammunition (needed for hunting), and other gifts. Moreover, squatters from the colonies were moving onto Indian lands in some areas and harassing the occupants, and many Native Americans feared that the British occupation was intended to support these incursions.

As tensions mounted, a Delaware religious prophet named Neolin attracted a large intertribal following by calling for Indians' complete repudiation of European culture, material goods, and alliances. Meanwhile, other Native Americans hoped that the French would return so they could once again manipulate an imperial balance of power. Political leaders such as Pontiac, an Ottawa Indian, drew on these sentiments to forge an explicitly anti-British movement, misleadingly called "Pontiac's Rebellion." During the spring and summer of 1763, they and their followers sacked eight British forts near the Great Lakes and besieged those at Pittsburgh and Detroit. But over the next three years, shortages of food and ammunition, a smallpox epidemic at Fort Pitt (triggered when British officers deliberately distributed infected blankets at a peace parley), and a recognition that the French would not return led the Indians to make peace with Britain. Although word of the uprising spread to Native Americans in the Southeast and Mississippi valley, the effective diplomacy of British agent John Stuart prevented violence from erupting in these areas.

Despite the uprising's failure, the Native Americans had not been decisively defeated. Hoping to conciliate the Indians and end the fighting, George III issued the Proclamation of 1763 asserting direct control of land transactions, settlement, trade, and other activities of non-Indians west of the Appalachian crest (see Map 5.2). The government's goal was to restore order to the process of colonial expansion by replacing the authority of the various (and often competing) colonies with that of the crown. The proclamation recognized existing Indian land titles everywhere west of the "proclamation line" until such time as tribal governments agreed to cede their land through treaties. Although calming Indian fears, the proclamation angered the colonies by subordinating their western claims to imperial authority and by slowing expansion.

The uprising was also a factor in the British government's decision that ten thousand soldiers should remain in North America to occupy its new territories and to intimidate the Indian, French, and Spanish inhabitants. The burden of maintaining control over the western territories would reach almost a half million pounds a year, fully 6 percent of Britain's peacetime budget. Britons considered it perfectly reasonable for the colonists to help offset this expense, which the colonists, however, saw as none of their responsibility. Although the troops would help offset the colonies' unfavorable balance of payments with Britain, they appeared to many Americans as a "standing army" that in peacetime could only threaten their liberty. With the French menace to their security removed, increasing numbers of colonists saw westward expansion onto

Indian lands as a way to prosperity, and they viewed British troops enforcing the Proclamation of 1763 as hindering rather than enhancing that expansion.

The Writs of Assistance, 1760–1761

Even before the Seven Years' War ended, British authorities began attempts to halt American merchants from trading with the enemy in the French West Indies. In 1760 the royal governor of Massachusetts authorized revenue officers to employ a document called a writ of assistance to seize illegally imported goods. The writ was a general search warrant that permitted customs officials to enter any ships or buildings where smuggled goods might be hidden. Because the document required no evidence of probable cause for suspicion, many critics considered it unconstitutional. The writ of assistance also threatened the traditional respect accorded the privacy of a family's place of residence, since most merchants conducted business from their homes.

Writs of assistance proved a powerful weapon against smuggling. In quick reaction to the writs, merchants in Boston, virtually the smuggling capital of the colonies, hired lawyer James Otis to challenge the constitutionality of these warrants. Arguing his case before the Massachusetts Supreme Court in 1761, Otis proclaimed that "an act against the Constitution is void"— even one passed by Parliament. But the court, influenced by the opinion of Chief Justice Thomas Hutchinson, who noted the use of identical writs in England, ruled against the Boston merchants.

Despite losing the case, Otis expressed with absolute clarity the fundamental conception of many, both in Britain and in the colonies, of Parliament's role under the British constitution. The British constitution was not a written document but instead a collection of customs and accepted principles that guaranteed certain rights to all citizens. Most British politicians assumed that Parliament's laws were themselves part of the constitution and hence that Parliament could alter the constitution at will. Like other colonists, Otis contended that Parliament possessed no authority to violate any of the traditional "rights of Englishmen," and he asserted that there were limits "beyond which if Parliaments go, their Acts bind not."

The Sugar Act, 1764

In 1764, just three years after Otis's court challenge, Parliament passed the Sugar Act. The measure's goal was to raise revenues that would help offset Britain's military expenses in North America, and thus end Britain's long-standing policy of exempting colonial trade from revenue-raising measures. The Navigation Acts had not been designed to bring money into the British treasury but rather to benefit the imperial economy indirectly by stimulating trade and protecting English manufacturers from foreign competition. English importers paid the taxes that Parliament levied on colonial products entering Britain and passed the cost on to consumers; the taxes were not paid by American producers. So little revenue did the Navigation Acts bring in (just £1,800 in 1763) that they did not even pay for the cost of their own enforcement.

The Sugar Act amended the Molasses Act of 1733 (see Chapter 4), which amounted to a tariff on French West Indian molasses entering British North America. But colonists simply continued to import the cheaper French molasses, bribing customs officials into taking 1 1/2 pence per gallon to look the other way when it was unloaded. Aware of the widespread bribery, Parliament erroneously assumed that rum drinkers could stomach a three-pence duty per gallon.

New taxes were not the only feature of the Sugar Act that American merchants found objectionable. The act also stipulated that colonists could export lumber, iron, skins, and many other commodities to foreign countries only if the shipments first landed in Britain. Previously, American ships had taken these products directly to Dutch and German ports and returned with goods to sell to colonists. By channeling this trade through Britain, Parliament hoped that colonial shippers would purchase more imperial wares for the American market, buy fewer goods from foreign competitors, and provide jobs for Englishmen.

The Sugar Act also vastly complicated the requirements for shipping colonial goods. A captain now had to fill out a confusing series of documents to certify his trade as legal, and the absence of any of them left his entire cargo liable to seizure. The law's petty regulations made it virtually impossible for many colonial shippers to avoid committing technical violations, even if they traded in the only manner possible under local circumstances.

Finally, the Sugar Act disregarded many traditional English protections for a fair trial. First, the law allowed customs officials to transfer smuggling cases from the colonial courts, in which juries decided the outcome, to vice-admiralty courts, where a judge alone gave the verdict. Because the Sugar Act (until 1768) awarded vice-admiralty judges 5 percent of any confiscated cargo, judges had a financial incentive to find defendants

guilty. Second, until 1767 the law did not permit defendants to be tried where their offense allegedly had taken place (usually their home province) but required all cases to be heard in the vice-admiralty court at Halifax, Nova Scotia. Third, the law reversed normal courtroom procedures, which presumed innocence until guilt was proved, by requiring the defendant to disprove the prosecution's charge.

The Sugar Act was no idle threat. British Prime Minister George Grenville ordered the navy to enforce the measure, and it did so vigorously. A Boston resident complained in 1764 that "no vessel hardly comes in or goes out but they find some pretense to seize and detain her." That same year, Pennsylvania's chief justice reported that customs officers were extorting fees from small boats carrying lumber across the Delaware River to Philadelphia from New Jersey and seemed likely "to destroy this little River-trade."

Stamp Act Protest

A Boston crowd burns bundles of the special water-marked paper intended for use as stamps.

Rather than pay the three-pence tax, Americans continued smuggling molasses until 1766. Then, to discourage smuggling, Britain lowered the duty to a penny—less than the customary bribe American shippers paid to get their cargoes past inspectors. The law thereafter raised about £30,000 annually in revenue.

Opposition to the Sugar Act remained fragmented and ineffective. The law's burden fell overwhelmingly on Massachusetts, New York, and Pennsylvania; other provinces had little interest in resisting a measure that did not affect them directly. The Sugar Act's immediate effect was minor, but it heightened some colonists' awareness of the new direction of imperial policies and their implications.

The Stamp Act, 1765

The revenue raised by the Sugar Act did little to ease Britain's financial crisis. The national debt continued to rise, and the British public groaned under the weight of the second-highest tax rates in Europe. Particularly irritating to Britons was the fact that by 1765 their rates averaged 26 shillings per person, whereas the colonial tax burden varied from 1/2 to 1 1/2 shillings per inhabitant, or barely 2 to 6 percent of the British rate. Well aware of how lightly the colonists were taxed, Grenville thought that fairness demanded a larger contribution to the empire's American expenses.

To raise such revenues, Parliament passed the Stamp Act in March 1765. The law obliged colonists to purchase and use special stamped (watermarked) paper for newspapers, customs documents, various licenses, college diplomas, and legal forms used for recovering debts, buying land, and making wills. As with the Sugar Act, violators would face prosecution in vice-admiralty courts, without juries. The prime minister projected yearly revenues of £60,000 to £100,000, which would offset 12 to 20 percent of North American military expenses.

Unlike the Sugar Act, which was an external tax levied on imports as they entered the colonies, the Stamp Act was an internal tax, or a duty levied directly on property, goods, and government services in the colonies. Whereas external taxes were intended to regulate trade and fell mainly on merchants and ship captains, internal taxes were designed to raise revenue for the crown and had far wider effects. In the case of the Stamp Act, anyone who made a will, transferred property, borrowed money, or bought playing cards or newspapers would pay the tax.

To Grenville and his supporters, the new tax seemed a small price for the benefits of the empire, especially

since Britons had been paying a similar tax since 1695. Nevertheless, some in England, most notably William Pitt, objected in principle to Britain's levying an internal tax on the colonies. They emphasized that the colonists had never been subject to British revenue bills and noted that they taxed themselves through their own elected assemblies.

Grenville and his followers agreed that Parliament could not tax any British subjects unless they enjoyed representation in that body. But they contended that Americans shared the same status as the majority of British adult males who either lacked sufficient property to vote or lived in large cities that had no seats in Parliament. Such people, they maintained, were "virtually" represented in Parliament. The theory of virtual representation held that every member of Parliament stood above the narrow interests of his constituents and considered the welfare of all subjects when deciding issues. By definition, then, British subjects, including colonists, were not represented by particular individuals but by all members of Parliament.

Grenville and his supporters also denied that the colonists were entitled to any exemption from British taxation because they elected their own assemblies. These legislative bodies, they alleged, were no different from English or Scottish town councils, whose local powers to pass laws and taxes did not nullify Parliament's authority over them. Accordingly, colonial assemblies were an adaptation to unique American circumstances and possessed no more power than Parliament allowed them to exercise. But Grenville's position clashed directly with the stance of many colonists who had been arguing for several decades that their assemblies exercised legislative powers equivalent to those of the House of Commons in Great Britain (see Chapter 4).

Many colonists felt that the Stamp Act forced them either to confront the issue of parliamentary taxation head-on or to surrender any claim to meaningful rights of self-government. However much they might admire and respect Parliament, few colonists imagined that it represented them. They accepted the theory of virtual representation as valid for England and Scotland but denied that it could be extended to the colonies. Instead, they argued, they enjoyed a substantial measure of self-governance similar to that of Ireland, whose Parliament alone could tax its people but could not interfere with laws, like the Navigation Acts, passed by the British Parliament. In a speech before the Boston town meeting opposing the Sugar Act, James Otis had expressed Americans' basic argument: "that by [the British] Constitution, every man in the dominions is a free man:

that no parts of His Majesty's dominions can be taxed without consent: that every part has a right to be represented in the supreme or some subordinate legislature." In essence, the colonists assumed that the empire was a loose federation in which their legislatures possessed considerable autonomy, rather than an extended nation governed directly from London.

Resisting the Stamp Act, 1765–1766

Unlike the Sugar Act, the Stamp Act generated a political storm that rumbled through all the colonies in 1765. To many colonists Parliament's passage of the act demonstrated both its indifference to their interests and the shallowness of the theory of virtual representation. Colonial agents in London had lobbied against passage of the law, and provincial legislatures had sent petitions warning against passage. Parliament had dismissed the petitions without a hearing. Parliament "must have thought us Americans all a parcel of Apes and very tame Apes too," concluded Christopher Gadsden of South Carolina, "or they would have never ventured on such a hateful, baneful experiment."

In late May 1765, Patrick Henry, a twenty-nine-year-old Virginia lawyer and planter with a talent for fiery oratory, dramatically conveyed the rising spirit of resistance. Henry urged the Virginia House of Burgesses to adopt several strongly worded resolutions denying Parliament's power to tax the colonies. In the debate over the resolutions, Henry reportedly stated that "he did not doubt but some good American would stand up in favor of his country." Viewing such language as treasonous, the Assembly passed only the weakest four of Henry's seven resolutions. Garbled newspaper accounts of Henry's resolutions and the debates were published in other colonies, and by year's end seven other assemblies had passed resolutions against the act. As in Virginia, the resolutions were grounded in constitutional arguments and avoided Henry's inflammatory language.

Henry's words resonated more loudly outside elite political circles, particularly in Boston. There, in late summer, a group of mostly middle-class artisans and small business owners joined together as the Loyal Nine to fight the Stamp Act. They recognized that the stamp distributors, who alone could accept money for watermarked paper, were the law's weak link. If the public could pressure them into resigning before taxes became due on November 1, the Stamp Act would become inoperable.

It was no accident that Boston set the pace in opposing Parliament. A large proportion of Bostonians

lived by shipbuilding, maritime trade, and distilling, and in 1765 they were not living well. In part they could blame British policies for their misfortune. No other port suffered so much from the Sugar Act's trade restrictions. The law burdened rum producers with a heavy tax on molasses, dried up a flourishing import trade in Portuguese wines, and prohibited the direct export of many New England products to profitable overseas markets.

But Boston's misery was largely rooted in older problems. Even before the Seven Years War, its shipbuilding industry had lost significant ground to New York and Philadelphia, and the output of its rum and sugar producers had fallen by half in just a decade. British impressment (forced recruitment) of Massachusetts fishermen for naval service had undermined the fishing industry. The resulting unemployment led to increased taxes for poor-relief. The taxes, along with a shrinking number of customers, drove many marginal artisans out of business and into the ranks of the poor. Other Bostonians, while remaining employed or in business, struggled in the face of rising prices for basic necessities as well as taxes. To compound its misery, the city still struggled to recover from a great fire in 1760 that had burned 176 warehouses and left every tenth family homeless.

Widespread economic distress produced an explosive situation in Boston. Already resentful of an elite whose fortunes had risen spectacularly while their own had foundered, many blamed British officials and policies for the town's hard times. The crisis was sharpened because poor and working-class Bostonians were accustomed to forming large crowds to engage in pointed political expression. The high point of each year was November 5, Pope's Day, when thousands gathered to commemorate the failure of a Catholic plot in England in 1605 to blow up Parliament and kill King James I. On that day each year, crowds from the North End and the South End customarily burned gigantic effigies of the pope as well as of local political leaders and other elite figures, and generally satirized the behavior of the "better sort."

In the aftermath of the Stamp Act, Boston's crowds aimed their traditional forms of protest more directly and forcefully against imperial officials. The morning of August 14 found a likeness of Boston's stamp distributor, Andrew Oliver, swinging from a tree guarded by a menacing crowd. Oliver apparently did not realize that the Loyal Nine were warning him to resign immediately, so at dusk several hundred Bostonians, led by a South End shoemaker named Ebenezer MacIntosh, demolished a new building of Oliver's at the dock. Thereafter, the Loyal Nine withdrew and the crowd continued on its own. The men surged toward Oliver's house, where they beheaded his effigy and "stamped" it to pieces. The crowd then shattered the windows of his home, smashed his furniture, and even tore out the paneling. When Lieutenant Governor Hutchinson and the sheriff tried to disperse the crowd, they were driven off under a barrage of rocks. Surveying his devastated home the next morning, Oliver announced his resignation.

Bitterness against the Stamp Act unleashed spontaneous, contagious violence. Twelve days after the first Boston riot, Bostonians demolished the elegant home of Thomas Hutchinson. This attack occurred in part because smugglers held grudges against Hutchinson for certain of his decisions as chief justice and also because many financially pinched citizens saw him as a symbol of the royal policies crippling Boston's already troubled economy and their own livelihoods. In their view, wealthy officials "rioted in luxury," with homes and fancy furnishings that cost hundreds of times the annual incomes of most Boston workingmen. They were also reacting to Hutchinson's efforts to stop the destruction of his brother-in-law Andrew Oliver's house. Ironically, Hutchinson privately opposed the Stamp Act.

Meanwhile, groups similar to the Loyal Nine calling themselves Sons of Liberty were forming throughout the colonies. After the assault on Hutchinson's mansion and an even more violent incident in Newport, Rhode Island, the leaders of the Sons of Liberty sought to prevent more such outbreaks. They recognized that people in the crowds were casting aside their customary deference toward their social "superiors," a development that could broaden to include all elites if not carefully contained. Fearful of alienating wealthy opponents of the Stamp Act, the Sons of Liberty focused their actions strictly against property and invariably left avenues of escape for their victims. Especially fearful that a royal soldier or revenue officer might be shot or killed, they forbade their followers to carry weapons, even when facing armed adversaries. Realizing the value of martyrs, they resolved that the only lives lost over the issue of British taxation would come from their own ranks.

In October 1765 representatives of nine colonial assemblies met in New York City in the so-called Stamp Act Congress. The session was remarkable for the colonies' agreement on and bold articulation of the general principle that Parliament lacked authority to levy taxes outside Great Britain and to deny any person a jury trial. Only once before had a truly intercolonial meeting taken place—the Albany Congress in 1754—and its plea

for unity had fallen on deaf ears. In 1765 the colonial response was entirely different. "The Ministry never imagined we could or would so generally unite in opposition to their measures," wrote a Connecticut delegate to the congress, "nor I confess till I saw the Experiment made did I."

By late 1765 most stamp distributors had resigned or fled, and without the watermarked paper required by law, most royal customs officials and court officers were refusing to perform their duties. In response, legislators compelled the reluctant officials to resume operation by threatening to withhold their pay. At the same time, merchants obtained sailing clearances by insisting that they would sue if cargoes spoiled while delayed in port. By late December the courts and harbors of almost every colony were again functioning.

Thus colonial elites moved to keep an explosive situation from getting out of hand by taking over leadership of local Sons of Liberty groups, by coordinating protest through the Stamp Act Congress, and by having colonial legislatures restore normal business. Elite leaders feared that chaos could break out, particularly if British troops landed to enforce the Stamp Act. An influential Pennsylvanian, John Dickinson, summed up how respectable gentlemen envisioned the dire consequences of revolutionary turmoil: "a multitude of Commonwealths, Crimes, and Calamities, Centuries of mutual jealousies, Hatreds, Wars of Devastation, till at last the exhausted provinces shall sink into savagery under the yoke of some fortunate Conqueror."

To force the Stamp Act's repeal, New York's merchants agreed on October 31, 1765, to boycott all British goods, and businessmen in other cities soon followed their example. Because American colonists purchased about 40 percent of England's manufactures, this non-importation strategy put the English economy in danger of recession. The colonial boycotts consequently triggered panic within England's business community, whose members descended on Parliament to warn that continuation of the Stamp Act would stimulate a wave of bankruptcies, massive unemployment, and political unrest.

The Declaratory Act, 1766

For reasons unconnected with the Stamp Act, the Marquis of Rockingham had succeeded Grenville as prime minister in mid-1765. Rockingham hesitated to advocate repeal because the overwhelming majority within the House of Commons was outraged at colonial defiance of the law. Then in January 1766 William Pitt, a

steadfast opponent of the Stamp Act, boldly denounced all efforts to tax the colonies, declaring, "I rejoice that America has resisted." Parliamentary support for repeal thereafter grew, though only as a matter of practicality, not as a surrender of principle. In March 1766 Parliament revoked the Stamp Act, but only in conjunction with passage of the Declaratory Act, which affirmed parliamentary power to legislate for the colonies "in all cases whatsoever."

Because the Declaratory Act was written in general language, Americans interpreted its meaning to their own advantage. Most colonial political leaders recognized that the law was modeled after an earlier statute of 1719 regarding Ireland, which was considered exempt from British taxation. The measure therefore seemed no more than a parliamentary exercise in saving face to compensate for the Stamp Act's repeal, and Americans ignored it. The House of Commons, however, intended that the colonists take the Declaratory Act literally to mean that they could not claim exemption from any parliamentary statute, including a tax law. The Stamp Act crisis thus ended in a fundamental disagreement between Britain and America over the colonists' political rights.

Although the Stamp Act crisis had not resolved the underlying philosophical differences between Britain and America, most colonists eagerly put the events of 1765 behind them, and they showered both king and Parliament with loyal statements of gratitude for the Stamp Act's repeal. The Sons of Liberty disbanded. Still possessing a deep emotional loyalty to "Old England," Anglo-Americans concluded with relief that their active resistance to the law had slapped Britain's leaders back to their senses. Nevertheless, the crisis led many to ponder British policies and actions more deeply than ever before.

Ideology, Religion, and Resistance

The Stamp Act and the conflicts that arose around it revealed a chasm between England and its colonies that startled Anglo-Americans. For the first time, some colonists critically and systematically examined the imperial relationship that they previously had taken for granted and valued. In their efforts to grasp the significance of their new perceptions, a number of educated colonists turned to the works of philosophers, historians, and political writers. Many more, both educated and uneducated, looked to religion.

By the 1760s the colonists were already widely familiar with the political writings of European

Enlightenment thinkers, particularly John Locke (see Chapter 4). Locke argued that humanity originated in a state of nature in which each man enjoyed the "natural rights" of life, liberty, and property. Thereafter, groups of men entered into a "social contract" in order to form governments that would protect those individual rights. A government that encroached on natural rights, then, broke its contract with the people. In such cases, people could resist their government, although Locke cautioned against outright rebellion except in the most extreme cases. To many colonial readers, Locke's concept of natural rights appeared to justify opposition to arbitrary legislation by Parliament.

Other writers placed particular emphasis on excessive concentrations of political power as threats to the liberty of the people. Some of them balanced Locke's emphasis on the rights of individuals with an emphasis on the political community. Looking to the ancient Greeks and Romans as well as to more recent European theorists, they articulated a set of ideas termed "republican." "Republicans" especially admired the sense of civic duty that motivated citizens of the Roman republic. Like the early Romans, they maintained that a free people had to avoid moral and political corruption and practice a disinterested "public virtue," in which all citizens subordinated their personal interests to those of the polity. An elected leader of a republic, one author noted, would command obedience "more by the virtue of the people, than by the terror of his power."

Among those influenced by republican ideas were a widely read group of English political writers known as oppositionists. According to John Trenchard, Thomas Gordon, and others belonging to this group, Parliament—consisting of the freely elected representatives of the people—formed the foundation of England's unique political liberties and protected those liberties against the inherent corruption and tyranny of executive power. But since 1720, the oppositionists argued, prime ministers had exploited the treasury's vast resources to provide pensions, contracts, and profitable offices to politicians or had bought elections by bribing voters in small boroughs. Most members of Parliament, in their view, no longer represented the true interests of their constituents; rather, they had sold their souls for financial gain and joined in a "conspiracy against liberty." Often referring to themselves as the "country party," these oppositionists feared that a power-hungry "court party" of nonelected officials close to the king was using a corrupted Parliament to gain absolute power for themselves.

Influenced by such ideas, a number of colonists pointed to a diabolical conspiracy behind British policy during the Stamp Act crisis. James Otis characterized a group of pro-British Rhode Islanders as a "little, dirty, drinking, drabbing, contaminated knot of thieves, beggars, and transports . . . made up of Turks, Jews, and other infidels, with a few renegade Christians and Catholics." Joseph Warren of Massachusetts noted that the act "induced some to imagine that the minister designed by this to force the colonies into a rebellion, and from thence to take occasion to treat them with severity, and, by military power, to reduce them to servitude." Over the next decade, a proliferation of pamphlets denounced British efforts to "enslave" the colonies through excessive taxation and the imposition of officials, judges, and a standing army directed from London. In such assaults on liberty and natural rights, some Americans found principled reasons for opposing British policies and actions.

A Patriot View of British Officials, 1766
This Boston editorial cartoon depicts two British officials as enslaved to the devil.

Many colonists also followed the lead of Massachusetts assemblyman Samuel Adams, who expressed hope that America would become a "Christian Sparta." By linking Christian piety and republican ideals, Adams was combining two of colonial leaders' most potent rhetorical appeals in rallying public protest. Almost every eighteenth-century American had been steeped in Protestantism since childhood; and all whose education had gone beyond the basics had imbibed Greek and Latin learning as well as seventeenth-century English literature. All these hallowed traditions, Americans believed, confirmed the legitimacy of their cause.

Recalling in later years the inspiring debate over the Stamp Act that he had witnessed in Virginia's House of Burgesses in 1765, Thomas Jefferson said of Patrick Henry that "he appeared to me to speak as Homer wrote." Jefferson was a typical educated man of his day in revering the ancient republics of Greece and Rome for their supposedly stern, virtuous devotion to liberty. The pamphlets, speeches, and public declarations that gentlemen like Jefferson and John Dickinson wrote resounded with quotations from the ancient classics. These allusions served as constant reminders to upper-class Americans of the righteous dignity of their cause. But appeals to ordinary Americans had to draw upon deeper wellsprings of belief. Significantly, the power of Henry's oratory also reflected his ability (unique among Virginia's political leaders) to evoke the religious fervor of the Great Awakening.

Beginning with the Stamp Act protest, many Protestant clergymen mounted their pulpits and summoned their flocks to stand up for God and liberty. "A just regard to our liberties . . . is so far from being displeasing to God that it would be ingratitude to him who has given them to us to . . . tamely give them up," exhorted one New England minister. Many Anglican ministers, whose church was headed by the king, tried to stay neutral or opposed the protest; and many pacifist Quakers kept out of the fray. But to most American Protestant clergymen, memories of battling for the Lord in the old Calvinist tradition proved too powerful to resist.

Voicing such a message, clergymen exerted an enormous influence on public opinion. Far more Americans heard sermons than had access to newspapers or pamphlets, and ministers always got a respectful hearing at town meetings. Community leaders' proclamations of days of "fasting and public humiliation"—in colonial America, a familiar means of focusing public attention on an issue and invoking divine aid—inspired sermons on the theme of God's sending the people woes only to strengthen and sustain them until victory. Even Virginia gentlemen not notable for their piety felt moved by such proclamations. Moreover, protest leaders' calls for boycotting British luxuries meshed neatly with traditional pulpit warnings against frivolity and wastefulness. Few ordinary Americans escaped the unceasing public reminders that community solidarity against British tyranny and "corruption" meant rejecting sin and obeying God.

The ebbing of the Stamp Act crisis momentarily took the urgency out of such extreme views. But the alarm that Britain's actions raised in the minds of many colonists was not easily put to rest.

RESISTANCE RESUMES, 1766–1770

Although Parliament's repeal of the Stamp Act momentarily quieted colonial protests, its search for new sources of revenue soon revived them. While British leaders condemned the colonists for evading their financial responsibilities and for insubordination, growing numbers of Anglo-Americans became convinced that the Stamp Act had not been an isolated mistake but rather part of a deliberate design to undermine colonial self-governance. In this they were joined by many in Britain who questioned policies that were economically costly and actions that seemed to threaten Britons and colonists alike.

Opposing the Quartering Act, 1766–1767

In August 1766, in a move unrelated to colonial affairs, George III dismissed the Rockingham government and summoned William Pitt to form a cabinet. Opposed to taxing the colonies, Pitt might have repaired the Stamp Act's damage, for no man was more respected in America. But after Pitt's health collapsed in March 1767, effective leadership passed to his Chancellor of the Exchequer (treasurer) Charles Townshend.

Just as Townshend took office, a conflict arose with the New York legislature over the Quartering Act, enacted in 1765. This law ordered colonial legislatures to pay for certain goods needed by soldiers stationed within their respective borders. The necessary items were relatively inexpensive barracks supplies such as candles, window-panes, mattress straw, polish, and a small liquor ration.

Despite its seemingly petty stipulations, the Quartering Act aroused resentment, for it constituted an

indirect tax; that is, although it did not (like the Stamp Act) empower royal officials to collect money directly from the colonists, it obligated assemblies to raise a stated amount of revenue. Such obligations clashed with the assemblies' claimed power to initiate all revenue-raising measures. Likewise, by reinforcing the presence of a standing army, the Quartering Act further reinforced tyranny in the eyes of many colonists. The law fell lightly or not at all on most colonies; but New York, where more soldiers were stationed than in any other province, found compliance very burdensome and refused to grant any supplies.

New York's resistance to the Quartering Act produced a torrent of anti-American feeling in the House of Commons, whose members remained bitter at having had to withdraw the Stamp Act. Townshend responded by drafting the New York Suspending Act, which threatened to nullify all laws passed by the colony if the assembly refused to vote the supplies. By the time George III signed the measure, however, New York had appropriated the necessary funds.

Although New York's retreat averted further confrontation, the conflict over the Quartering Act demonstrated that British leaders would not hesitate to defend Parliament's authority through the most drastic of all steps: by interfering with American claims to self-governance.

The Townshend Duties, 1767

The new wave of parliamentary resentment toward the colonies coincided with an outpouring of British frustration over the government's failure to cut taxes from wartime levels. Dominating the House of Commons, members of the landed gentry slashed their own taxes by 25 percent in 1767. This move cost the government £500,000 and prompted Townshend to propose laws that would tax imports entering America from Britain and increase colonial customs revenue.

Townshend sought to tax the colonists by exploiting an oversight in their arguments against the Stamp Act. In confronting the Stamp Act, Americans had emphasized their opposition to internal taxes, but had said little about Parliament's right to tax imports as they entered the colonies. Townshend and other British leaders chose to interpret this silence as evidence that the colonists accepted Britain's right to tax their trade—to impose external taxes. Yet not all British politicians were so mistaken. "They will laugh at you," predicted a now wiser George Grenville, "for your distinctions about regulations of trade." Brushing aside

Grenville's warnings, Parliament passed Townshend's Revenue Act of 1767 (popularly called the Townshend duties) in June and July 1767. The new law taxed glass, paint, lead, paper, and tea imported to the colonies from England.

On the surface, Townshend's contention that the Americans would submit to this external tax on imports was convincing, for the colonists had long accepted Parliament's right to regulate their overseas trade and had in principle acknowledged taxation as a legitimate form of regulation. But Townshend's Revenue Act differed significantly from what Americans had long seen as a legitimate way of regulating trade through taxation. To the colonists, charging a duty was a lawful way for British authorities to control trade only if that duty excluded foreign goods by making them prohibitively expensive to consumers. The Revenue Act of 1767, however, set moderate rates that did not price goods out of the colonial market; clearly, its purpose was to collect money for the treasury. Thus from the colonial standpoint, Townshend's duties were taxes just like the Stamp Act duties.

Although Townshend had introduced the Revenue Act in response to the government's budgetary problems, he had an ulterior motive for establishing an American source of revenue. Traditionally, royal governors had depended on colonial legislatures to vote their salaries; for their part, the legislatures had often refused to allocate these salaries until governors signed certain bills they themselves opposed. Through the Revenue Act, Townshend hoped to establish a fund that would pay the salaries of governors and other royal officials in America, thus freeing them from the assemblies' control. In effect, by stripping the assemblies of their most potent weapon, the power of the purse, the Revenue Act threatened to tip the balance of constitutional power away from elected colonial representatives and toward nonelected royal officials.

In reality the Revenue Act would never yield anything like the income that Townshend anticipated. Of the various items taxed, only tea produced any significant revenue—£20,000 of the £37,000 that the law was expected to yield. And because the measure would serve its purpose only if British tea were affordable to colonial consumers, Townshend eliminated £60,000 worth of import fees paid on tea entering Britain from India before transshipment to America. On balance, the Revenue Act worsened the British treasury's deficit by £23,000. By 1767 Britain's financial difficulties were more an excuse for, than the driving force behind, political demands to tax the colonies. From Parliament's stand-

point, the conflict with America was becoming a test of national will over the principle of taxation.

The Colonists' Reaction, 1767–1769

Resistance to the Revenue Act remained weak until December 1767, when John Dickinson published twelve essays entitled *Letters from a Farmer in Pennsylvania*. The essays, which appeared in nearly every colonial newspaper, emphasized that although Parliament could regulate trade by voting duties capable of providing small amounts of "incidental revenue," it had no right to tax commerce for the single purpose of raising revenue. In other words, the legality of any external tax depended on its intent. No tax designed to produce revenue could be considered constitutional unless a people's elected representatives voted for it. Dickinson said nothing that others had not stated or implied during the Stamp Act crisis. Rather, his contribution lay in persuading many Americans that the arguments they had marshaled against the Stamp Act also applied to the Revenue Act.

Soon after publication of Dickinson's *Letters*, James Otis, the Boston lawyer famed for his arguments in the writs-of-assistance case, chaired a Boston town meeting that asked the Massachusetts legislature to oppose the Townshend duties. In response, the assembly called on Samuel Adams to draft a "circular letter" to every other colonial legislature in early 1768. Adams's letter forthrightly condemned both taxation without representation and the threat to self-governance posed by Parliament's making governors and other royal officials financially independent of the legislatures. But it acknowledged Parliament as the "supreme legislative Power over the whole Empire," and it advocated no illegal activities. Virginia's assembly warmly approved Adams's message and sent out a more strongly worded circular letter of its own, urging all colonies to oppose imperial policies that would "have an immediate tendency to enslave them." But most colonial legislatures reacted indifferently. In fact, resistance to the Revenue Act might have disintegrated had the British government not overreacted to the circular letters.

Parliamentary leaders regarded even the mild Massachusetts letter as "little better than an incentive to Rebellion." Disorganized by Townshend's sudden death in 1767, the king's Privy Council directed Lord Hillsborough, first appointee to the new post of secretary of state for the colonies, to express the government's displeasure. Hillsborough flatly told the Massachusetts assembly to disown its letter, forbade all colonial assemblies to endorse it, and commanded royal governors to dissolve any legislature that violated his instructions. George III later commented that he never met "a man of less judgment than Lord Hillsborough." A wiser man might have tried to divide the colonists by appealing to their sense of British patriotism, but Hillsborough had chosen to challenge their elected representatives directly, guaranteeing a unified, angry response.

To protest Hillsborough's crude bullying, many legislatures previously indifferent to the Massachusetts circular letter now adopted it enthusiastically. The Massachusetts House of Representatives voted 92 to 17 not to recall its letter. The number 92 immediately acquired symbolic significance for Americans; colonial politicians on more than one occasion drank 92 toasts in tipsy salutes to Massachusetts's action. In obedience to Hillsborough, royal governors responded by dismissing legislatures in Massachusetts and elsewhere. These moves played directly into the hands of Samuel Adams, James Otis, and John Dickinson, who wanted nothing more than to ignite widespread public opposition to the Townshend duties.

Although increasingly outraged over the Revenue Act, the colonists still needed some effective means of pressuring Parliament for its repeal. One approach, nonimportation, seemed especially promising because it offered an alternative to violence and would distress Britain's economy. In August 1768 Boston's merchants therefore adopted a nonimportation agreement, and the tactic slowly spread southward. "Save your money, and you save your country!" became the watchword of the Sons of Liberty, who began reorganizing after two years of inactivity. Not all colonists supported nonimportation, however. Its effectiveness ultimately depended on the compliance of merchants whose livelihood relied on buying and selling imports. In several major communities, including Philadelphia, Baltimore, and Charles Town, South Carolina, merchants continued buying British goods until 1769. The boycott probably kept out about 40 percent of all imports from Britain, and was even more significant in the longer run because it mobilized colonists into more actively resisting British policies.

"Wilkes and Liberty," 1768–1770

The exclusion of 40 percent of imports seriously affected many people in Britain and thus heightened pressure there, too, for repeal of the Townshend duties. Hardest hit were merchants and artisans dealing in consumer goods. Their protests formed part of a larger movement that arose during the 1760s to oppose the domestic and foreign policies of George III and a Parliament dominated

John Wilkes, by William Hogarth, 1763
A sworn enemy of Wilkes and all he stood for, Hogarth depicted the radical leader as menacing and untrustworthy.

imposing and establishing the most impolitic and unconstitutional taxations and regulations on your Majesty's colonies." They were joined by (nonvoting) weavers, coal heavers, seamen, and other workers who protested low wages and high prices that stemmed in part from government policies. All these people rallied around the cry "Wilkes and liberty!"

After he was again elected to Parliament, Wilkes was arrested. The next day, twenty to forty thousand angry "Wilkesites" massed on St. George's Fields, outside the prison where he was being held. When members of the crowd began throwing stones, soldiers and police responded with gunfire, killing eleven protesters. The "massacre of St. George's Fields" had given the movement some martyrs. Wilkes and an associate were elected to the seat twice more and were both times denied their seats by other legislators. Meanwhile, the imprisoned Wilkes was besieged by outpourings of popular support from the colonies as well as from Britain. Some Virginians sent him tobacco, and the South Carolina assembly voted to contribute £1,500 to help defray his debts. He maintained a regular correspondence with the Boston Sons of Liberty and, upon his release in April 1770, was hailed in a massive Boston celebration as "the illustrious martyr to Liberty."

Wilkes's cause sharpened the political thinking of government opponents in Britain and the colonies alike. Thousands of voters in English cities and towns signed petitions to Parliament protesting its refusal to seat Wilkes as an affront to the electorate's will. Like the colonists, they regarded the theory of "virtual representation" in Parliament as a sham. Fearing arbitrary government actions, some of them formed a Society of the Supporters of the Bill of Rights "to defend and maintain the legal, constitutional liberty of the subject." And while more "respectable" opponents of the government such as William Pitt and Edmund Burke disdained Wilkes for courting the "mob," his movement emboldened them to speak more forcefully against the government, especially on its policies toward the colonies. For the colonists themselves, Wilkes and his following made clear that Parliament and the government represented a small if powerful minority whose authority could be legitimately questioned.

Women and Colonial Resistance

The tactical value of nonimportation was not restricted to damaging Britain's economy. It also hinged on colonists convincing the British—and one another—that they were determined to sustain resistance, and on

by wealthy landowners. The leader of this movement was John Wilkes, a fiery London editor and member of Parliament who had first gained notoriety in 1763 when his newspaper regularly and irreverently denounced George III's policies. The government had finally arrested Wilkes for seditious libel, but to great popular acclaim, he had won his case in court. The government, however, had succeeded in shutting down his newspaper and in persuading members of the House of Commons to deny Wilkes his seat. After again offending the government with a publication, Wilkes had fled to Paris.

Wilkes returned to England in 1768, defying a warrant for his arrest, and again ran for Parliament. By this time, the Townshend acts and other government policies were stirring up widespread protests. Merchants and artisans in London, Bristol, and other cities demanded the dismissal of the "obnoxious" ministers who were "ruining our manufactories by invidiously

demonstrating that their cause rested on the republican foundations of moderation, morality, and self-sacrifice. In this respect, the nonimportation movement provided a unique opportunity for white women to join the defense of Anglo-American liberties.

White women's participation in public affairs had been widening slowly and unevenly in the colonies for several decades. Women far outnumbered men among white church members, especially in New England, where ministers frequently hailed them as superior to most men in piety and morality. By the 1760s, when colonial protests against British policies began, colonial women such as Sarah Osborn (see Chapter 4) had become well-known religious activists. Calling themselves the Daughters of Liberty, a contingent of upperclass female patriots had played a minor part in defeating the Stamp Act. Some had attended political rallies during the Stamp Act crisis, and many more had expressed their opposition in discussions and correspondence with family and friends.

Just two years later, women assumed an even more visible role during the Townshend crisis. To protest the Revenue Act's tax on tea, more than three hundred "mistresses of families" in Boston denounced consumption of the beverage in early 1770. In some ways, the threat of nonconsumption was even more effective than that of nonimportation, for women served and drank most of the tea consumed by colonists.

Nonconsumption agreements soon became popular and were extended to include English manufactures, especially clothing. Again women played a vital role, both because they made most decisions about consumption in colonial households and because it was they who could replace British imports with apparel of their own making. Responding to leaders' pleas that they expand domestic cloth production, women of all social ranks, even those who customarily did not weave their own fabric or sew their own clothing, organized spinning bees. These events attracted intense publicity as evidence of American determination to forego luxury and idleness for the common defense of liberty. One historian calculates that more than sixteen hundred women participated in spinning bees in New England alone from 1768 to 1770. The colonial cause, noted a New York woman, had enlisted "a fighting army of amazons . . . armed with spinning wheels."

Spinning bees not only helped undermine the notion that women had no place in public life but also endowed spinning and weaving, previously considered routine household tasks, with special political virtue. "Women might recover to this country the full and free

Mercy Otis Warren by John Singleton Copley, 1763
Essayist and playwright Mercy Otis Warren was the most prominent woman intellectual of the Revolutionary era.

enjoyment of all our rights, properties and privileges," exclaimed the Reverend John Cleaveland of Ipswich, Massachusetts, in 1769, adding that this "is more than the men have been able to do." For many colonists, such logic enlarged the arena of supposed feminine virtues from strictly religious matters to include political issues.

Spinning bees, combined with female support for boycotting tea, dramatically demonstrated that American resistance ran far deeper than the protests of a few male merchants and the largely male crowds in American seaports. Women's participation showed that colonial protests extended into the heart of many American households and congregations, and were leading to broadened popular participation in politics.

Customs "Racketeering," 1767–1768

Besides taxing colonial imports, Townshend sought to increase revenues through stricter enforcement of the Navigation Acts. While submitting the Revenue Act of 1767, he also introduced legislation creating the

American Board of Customs Commissioners. This law raised the number of port officials, funded the construction of a colonial coast guard, and provided money for secret informers. It also awarded an informer one-third of the value of all goods and ships appropriated through a conviction of smuggling. The fact that fines could be tripled under certain circumstances provided an even greater incentive to seize illegal cargoes. Smuggling cases were heard in vice-admiralty courts, moreover, where the probability of conviction was extremely high.

In the face of lax enforcement, including widespread bribery of customs officials by colonial shippers and merchants, Townshend wanted the board to bring honesty, efficiency, and more revenue to overseas customs operations. But the law quickly drew protests because of the way it was enforced and because it

John Hancock

A prominent anti-British merchant, Hancock was also a popular political leader in pre-Revolutionary Boston.

assumed those accused to be guilty until or unless they could prove otherwise.

Under the new provisions, revenue agents commonly filed charges for technical violations of the Sugar Act, even when no evidence existed of intent to conduct illegal trade. They most often exploited the provision that declared any cargo illegal unless it had been loaded or unloaded with a customs officer's written authorization. Customs commissioners also fanned angry passions by invading the traditional rights of sailors. Longstanding maritime custom allowed a ship's crew to supplement their incomes by making small sales between ports. Anything stored in a sailor's chest was considered private property that did not have to be listed as cargo on the captain's manifest. After 1767, however, revenue agents began treating such belongings as cargo, thus establishing an excuse to seize the entire ship. Under this new policy, crewmen saw their trunks ruthlessly broken open by arrogant inspectors who confiscated trading stock worth several months' wages because it was not listed on the captain's loading papers.

To merchants and seamen alike, the commissioners had embarked on a program of "customs racketeering" that constituted little more than a system of legalized piracy. The board's program fed an upsurge in popular violence. Above all, customs commissioners' use of informers provoked retaliation. In 1769 the *Pennsylvania Journal* scorned these agents as "dogs of prey, thirsting after the fortunes of worthy and wealthy men." By betraying the trust of employers, and sometimes of friends, informers aroused wild hatred in their victims and were roughly handled whenever found.

Nowhere were customs agents and informers more detested than in Boston, where in June 1768 citizens finally retaliated against their tormentors. The occasion was the seizure, on a technicality, of colonial merchant John Hancock's sloop *Liberty*. Hancock, reportedly North America's richest merchant and a leading opponent of British taxation, had become a chief target of the customs commissioners. Now they fined him £9,000, an amount almost thirteen times greater than the taxes he supposedly evaded on a shipment of Madeira wine. A crowd tried to prevent the towing of

Hancock's ship and then began assaulting customs agents. Growing to several hundred as it surged through the streets, the mob drove all revenue inspectors from Boston. The violence and distrust unleashed by the crisis over the customs commissioners foreshadowed a further darkening of relations between Britain and the colonies.

THE DEEPENING CRISIS, 1770–1774

Hancock's case forced colonists to reevaluate their former acceptance of the principle that Parliament had limited authority to pass laws for them. Previously, colonial leaders had single-mindedly denied Britain's power to tax them without considering that freedoms of equal importance might be jeopardized by other kinds of legislation. But by 1770 many argued that measures like the Sugar Act and the act creating the American Board of Customs Commissioners seriously endangered property rights and civil liberties. They expanded their opposition from a rejection of taxation without representation to a more broadly based rejection of legislation without representation. By 1774 there would emerge a new consensus that Parliament possessed no lawmaking authority over the colonies except the right to regulate imperial commerce through statutes like the old Navigation Acts.

Hancock's case provoked a very different reaction from British authorities who, responding to the violence, dispatched four thousand British troops to Boston in the summer and fall of 1768. Regarding the troops as a standing army that threatened their liberty as well as a financial burden, Bostonians resented the soldiers' presence. Violence soon escalated, intersecting with internal tensions in Anglo-American society and extending the crisis beyond the colonies' capitals and port cities.

The Boston Massacre, 1770

In the presence of so many troops, Boston took on the atmosphere of an occupied city and crackled with tension. Armed sentries and resentful civilians traded insults. The mainly Protestant townspeople found it especially galling that many soldiers were Irish Catholics. The poorly paid enlisted men, moreover, were free to seek employment following the morning muster. Often agreeing to work for less than local laborers, they generated fierce hostility in a community that was plagued by persistently high unemployment.

Poor Bostonians' deep-seated resentment against all who upheld British authority suddenly boiled over on February 22, 1770, when a customs informer shot into a crowd picketing the home of a customs-paying merchant, killing an eleven-year-old boy. While elite Bostonians had disdained the unruly exchanges between soldiers and crowds, the horror at a child's death momentarily united the community. "My Eyes never beheld such a funeral," wrote John Adams. "A vast Number of Boys walked before the Coffin, a vast Number of Women and Men after it. . . . This Shews there are many more Lives to spend if wanted in the Service of their country."

Although the army had played no part in the shooting, it became a natural target for popular frustration and rage. A week after the boy's funeral, tensions between troops and a crowd led by Crispus Attucks, a seaman of African and Native American descent, and including George Robert Twelves Hewes, erupted at the guard post protecting the customs office. When an officer tried to disperse the civilians, his men endured a steady barrage of flying objects and dares to shoot. A private finally did fire, after having been knocked down by a block of ice, and then shouted, "Fire! Fire!" to his fellow soldiers. The soldiers' volley hit eleven persons, five of whom, including Attucks, died.

The shock that followed the March 5 bloodshed marked the emotional high point of the Townshend crisis. Royal authorities in Massachusetts tried to defuse the situation by isolating all British soldiers on a fortified island in the harbor, and Governor Thomas Hutchinson promised that the soldiers who had fired would be tried. Patriot leader John Adams, an opponent of crowd actions, served as their attorney. Adams appealed to the Boston jury by claiming that the soldiers had been provoked by a "motley rabble of saucy boys, negroes and mulattoes, Irish teagues, and outlandish jack tarres," in other words, people not considered "respectable" by the city's elites and middle class. All but two of the soldiers were acquitted, and the ones found guilty suffered only a branding on their thumbs.

Burning hatreds produced by an intolerable situation underlay the Boston Massacre, as it came to be called in conscious recollection of the St. George's Fields Massacre in London two years earlier. The shooting of unarmed American civilians by British soldiers and the light punishment given the soldiers forced the colonists to confront the stark possibility that the British government was bent on coercing and suppressing them through naked force. In a play written by Mercy Otis Warren, a character predicted that soon "Murders, blood and carnage/Shall crimson all these streets" as patriots rose to defend their republican liberty against tyrannical authority.

Lord North's Partial Retreat, 1770

As the Boston Massacre raged, a new British prime minister, Lord North, quietly worked to stabilize relations between Britain and its colonies. North favored eliminating most of the Townshend duties to prevent the American commercial boycott from widening, but to underscore British authority, he insisted on retaining the tax on tea. Parliament agreed, and in April 1770, giving in for the second time in three years to colonial pressure, it repealed most of the Townshend duties.

Parliament's partial repeal produced a dilemma for American politicians. They considered it intolerable that taxes remained on tea, the most profitable item for the royal treasury. Colonial leaders were unsure whether they should press on with the nonimportation agreement until they achieved total victory, or whether it would suffice to maintain a selective boycott of tea. When the nonimportation movement collapsed in July 1770, colonists resisted external taxation by voluntary agreements not to drink British tea. Through nonconsumption they succeeded in limiting revenue from tea to about one-sixth the level originally expected. This amount was far too little to pay the salaries of royal governors as Townshend had intended. Yet colonial resistance leaders took little satisfaction in having forced Parliament to compromise. The tea duty remained a galling reminder that Parliament refused to retreat from the broadest possible interpretation of the Declaratory Act.

Meanwhile, the British government, aware of officers' excesses, took steps to rein in the powers of the American Board of Customs Commissioners. The smuggling charges against Hancock were finally dropped because the prosecution feared that Hancock would appeal a conviction to England, where honest officials would take action against the persons responsible for violating his rights.

The Committees of Correspondence, 1772–1773

In fall 1772 Lord North's ministry was preparing to implement Townshend's goal of paying the royal governors' salaries out of customs revenue. The colonists had always viewed this intention to free the governors from legislative domination as a fundamental threat to representative government. In response, Samuel Adams persuaded Boston's town meeting to request that every Massachusetts community appoint persons responsible for exchanging information and coordinating measures to defend colonial rights. Of approximately 260 towns,

about half immediately established "committees of correspondence," and most others did so within a year. The idea soon spread throughout New England.

The committees of correspondence were the colonists' first attempt to maintain close and continuing political cooperation over a wide area. By linking almost every interior community to Boston through a network of dedicated activists, the system enabled Adams to send out messages for each local committee to read at its own town meeting, which would then debate the issues and adopt a formal resolution. Involving tens of thousands of colonists to consider evidence that their rights were in danger, the system committed them to take a personal stand by voting.

Adams's most successful effort to mobilize popular sentiment came in June 1773, when he publicized certain letters of Massachusetts Governor Thomas Hutchinson that Benjamin Franklin had obtained. Massachusetts town meetings discovered through the letters that their own chief executive had advocated "an abridgement of what are called English liberties" and "a great restraint of natural liberty." The publication of the Hutchinson correspondence confirmed many colonists' suspicions of a plot to destroy basic freedoms.

In March 1773 Patrick Henry, Thomas Jefferson, and Richard Henry Lee proposed that Virginia establish colony-level committees of correspondence. Within a year every province but Pennsylvania had followed its example. By early 1774 a communications web linked colonial leaders for the first time since 1766.

In contrast to the brief, intense Stamp Act crisis, the dissatisfaction spawned by the Townshend duties and the American Board of Customs Commissioners persisted and gradually poisoned relations between Britain and the colonies. In 1765 feelings of loyalty and affection toward Britain had remained strong among Anglo-Americans, disguising the depth of their divisions. By 1773, however, colonists' allegiance to Britain was increasingly balanced by their receptivity to notions that British authority threatened liberty and virtue.

Backcountry Tensions

Although most of the conflicts between colonists and British officials took place in the eastern seaports, tensions in the West contributed to a continuing sense of crisis among Indians, settlers, and colonial authorities. These stresses were rooted in the rapid growth that had spurred the migration of people and capital to the Appalachian backcountry, where colonists and their governments sought access to Indian land.

Land pressures and the lack of adequate revenue from the colonies left the British government utterly helpless in enforcing the Proclamation of 1763. Speculators such as George Washington sought western land because "any person who . . . neglects the present opportunity of hunting out good Lands will never regain it." Settlers, traders, hunters, and thieves also trespassed on Indian land, and a growing number of instances of violence by colonists toward Indians were going unpunished. In the meantime, the British government was unable to maintain garrisons at many of its forts, to enforce violations of laws and treaties, or to provide gifts to its native allies. Under such pressure, Britain and its Six Nations Iroquois allies agreed in the Treaty of Fort Stanwix (1768) to grant land along the Ohio River that was occupied and claimed by the Shawnees, Delawares, and Cherokees to the governments of Pennsylvania and Virginia. The Shawnees now assumed leadership of the Ohio Indians who, along with the Cherokees, sensed that no policy of appeasement could stop colonial expansion.

The treaty served to heighten rather than ease western tensions, especially in the Ohio country, where settlers agitated to establish a new colony, Kentucky. Growing violence there culminated in 1774 in the unprovoked slaughter by colonists of thirteen Shawnees and Mingos, including eight members of the family of Logan, until then a moderate Mingo leader. The outraged Logan led a force of Shawnees and Mingos who retaliated by killing an equal number of white Virginians. Virginia in turn opened a campaign against the Indians known as Lord Dunmore's War (1774), for the colony's governor. The two forces met at Point Pleasant on the Virginia side of the Ohio River, where the English soundly defeated Logan's people. During the peace conference that followed, Virginia gained uncontested rights to lands south of the Ohio in exchange for its claims on the northern side. But Anglo-Indian resentments remained strong, and fighting would resume once Britain and its colonies went to war.

The Treaty of Fort Stanwix resolved the conflicting claims of Pennsylvania and Virginia in Ohio at the Indians' expense. But other western disputes led to conflict among the colonists themselves. Settlers moving west in Massachusetts in the early 1760s found their titles challenged by some of New York's powerful landlords. When two landlords threatened to evict tenants in 1766, the New Englanders joined the tenants in an armed uprising, calling themselves Sons of Liberty after the Stamp Act protesters. In 1769, in what is now Vermont, settlers from New Hampshire also came into

The Alternative of Williamsburg, by Philip Dawe, 1775
In this cartoon, armed patriots in Williamsburg, Virginia, obtain a merchant's written agreement not to import British goods. The "alternative" is the containers of tar and feathers hanging in the background.

conflict with New York. After four years of guerrilla warfare, the New Hampshire settlers, calling themselves the Green Mountain Boys, established an independent government. Unrecognized at the time, it eventually became the government of Vermont. A third group of New England settlers from Connecticut settled in the Wyoming valley of Pennsylvania, where they clashed in 1774 with Pennsylvanians claiming title to the same land.

Expansion also provoked conflicts between backcountry settlers and their colonial governments. In North Carolina a group known as the Regulators aimed to redress the grievances of westerners who, underrepresented in the colonial assembly, found themselves exploited by dishonest eastern officeholders. The Regulator movement climaxed on May 16, 1771, at the battle of Alamance Creek. Leading an army of perhaps thirteen hundred eastern militiamen, North Carolina's

royal governor defeated about twenty-five hundred Regulators in a clash that produced almost three hundred casualties. Although the Regulator uprising then disintegrated, it crippled the colony's subsequent ability to resist British authority.

An armed Regulator movement also arose in South Carolina, in this case to counter the government's unwillingness to prosecute bandits who were terrorizing settlers. But the South Carolina government did not dispatch its militia to the backcountry for fear that the colony's restive slave population might use the occasion to revolt. Instead it conceded to the principal demands of the Regulators by establishing four new judicial circuits and allowing jury trials in the newly settled areas.

Although not directly interrelated, these episodes all reflected the tensions generated by a increasing land-hungry white population and its willingness to resort to violence against Native Americans, other colonists, and British officials. As Anglo-American tensions mounted in older settled areas, the western settlers' anxious mood spread.

The Tea Act, 1773

Colonial smuggling and nonconsumption had taken a heavy toll on the British East India Company, which enjoyed a legal monopoly on the sale of tea within Britain's empire. By 1773, with tons of tea rotting in its warehouses, the company was teetering on the brink of bankruptcy. Lord North could not afford to let the company fail. Not only did it pay substantial duties on the tea it shipped to Britain, but it also provided huge indirect savings for the government by maintaining British authority in India at its own expense.

If the company could only control the colonial market, North reasoned, its chances for returning to profitability would greatly increase. Americans supposedly consumed more than a million pounds of tea each year, but by 1773 they were purchasing just one-quarter of it from the company. In May 1773, to save the beleaguered East India Company from financial ruin, Parliament passed the Tea Act, which eliminated all remaining import duties on tea entering England and thus lowered the selling price to consumers. (Ironically, the same saving could have been accomplished by repealing the Townshend tax, which would have ended colonial objections to the company's tea and produced enormous goodwill toward the British government.) To lower the price further, the Tea Act also permitted the company to sell its tea directly to consumers rather than through wholesalers. These two concessions reduced the cost of East India Company tea in the colonies well below the price of all smuggled competition. Parliament expected simple economic self-interest to overcome Anglo-American scruples about buying taxed tea.

But the Tea Act alarmed many Americans, above all because they saw in it a menace to liberty and virtue as well as to colonial representative government. By making taxed tea competitive in price with smuggled tea, the law would raise revenue, which the British government would use to pay royal governors. The law thus threatened to corrupt Americans into accepting the principle of parliamentary taxation by taking advantage of their weakness for a frivolous luxury. Quickly, therefore, the committees of correspondence decided to resist the importation of tea, though without violence and without the destruction of private property. Either by pressuring

Edenton Ladies' Tea Party

In October 1774, fifty-one women gathered at Edenton, North Carolina, and declared it their "duty" to support the boycotting of all British imports. Nevertheless, the British man who drew this cartoon chose to satirize the event as an unruly "tea party."

the company's agents to refuse acceptance or by intercepting the ships at sea and ordering them home, the committees would keep East India Company cargoes from being landed. In Philadelphia an anonymous "Committee for Tarring and Feathering" warned harbor pilots not to guide any ships carrying tea into port.

In Boston, however, this strategy failed. On November 28, 1773, the first ship came under the jurisdiction of the customhouse, where duties would have to be paid on its cargo within twenty days. Otherwise, the cargo would be seized from the captain and the tea claimed by the company's agents and placed on sale. When Samuel Adams, John Hancock, and other popular leaders repeatedly asked the customs officers to issue a special clearance for the ship's departure, they were blocked by Thomas Hutchinson's refusal to compromise.

On the evening of December 16, five thousand Bostonians gathered at Old South Church. Samuel Adams informed the citizens of Hutchinson's insistence upon landing the tea and proclaimed that "this meeting can do no more to save the country." About fifty young men, including George Robert Twelves Hewes, stepped forward and disguised themselves as Mohawk Indians—symbolizing a virtuous, proud, and assertive American identity distinct from that of corrupt Britain. Armed with "tomahawks," they headed for the wharf, followed by most of the crowd.

The disciplined band assaulted no one and damaged nothing but the hated cargo. Thousands lined the waterfront to see them heave forty-five tons of tea overboard. For almost an hour, the onlookers stood silently transfixed, as if at a religious service, while they peered through the crisp, cold air of a moonlit night. The only sounds were the steady chop of hatchets breaking open wooden chests and the soft splash of tea on the water. When Boston's "Tea Party," as it was later called, was finished, the participants left quietly, and the town lapsed into a profound hush—"never more still and calm," according to one observer.

TOWARD INDEPENDENCE, 1774–1776

The calm that followed the Boston Tea Party proved to be a calm before the storm. The incident inflamed the British government and Parliament, which now determined once and for all to quash colonial insubordination. Colonial political leaders responded with equal determination to defend self-government and liberty.

The empire and its American colonies were on a collision course, leading by spring 1775 to armed clashes. Yet even after blood was shed, colonists hesitated before declaring their complete independence from Britain. In the meantime, free and enslaved African-Americans pondered how best to realize their own freedom.

Liberty for Black Americans

Throughout the imperial crisis, African-American slaves, as a deeply alienated group within society, quickly responded to calls for liberty and equality. In 1765, when a group of blacks, inspired by the protests against the Stamp Act, had marched through Charles Town, South Carolina, shouting "Liberty!" they had faced arrest for inciting a rebellion. Thereafter, unrest among slaves—usually in the form of violence or escape—kept pace with that among white rebels. Then in 1772 a court decision in England electrified much of the black population. A Massachusetts slave, James Somerset, whose master had taken him to England, sued for his freedom. Writing for the King's Court, Lord Chief Justice William Mansfield ruled that because Parliament had never explicitly established slavery, no court could compel a slave to obey an order depriving him of his liberty.

Although the decision applied only within England, African-Americans seized upon it in a number of ways. In January 1773 some of Somerset's fellow Massachusetts blacks filed the first of three petitions to the legislature, arguing that the decision should be applied in the colony as well. In Virginia and Maryland, dozens of slaves ran away from their masters and sought passage aboard ships bound for England. As Anglo-American tensions mounted in 1774, many slaves, especially in the Chesapeake colonies, looked for war and the arrival of British troops as a means to their liberation. The young Virginia planter James Madison said that "if America and Britain come to a hostile rupture, I am afraid an insurrection among the slaves may and will be promoted" by England.

Madison's fears were borne out in 1775 when Virginia's governor, Lord Dunmore, promised freedom to any slave who enlisted in the cause of restoring royal authority. As had Florida when it provided a refuge for escaping South Carolina slaves (see Chapter 4), Dunmore appealed to slaves' longings for freedom in order to undermine a planter-dominated society. About one thousand blacks joined Dunmore before hostile patriots forced him to flee the colony. Nevertheless, Dunmore's proclamation associated British forces with

"List of Negroes that went off to Dunmore" (1775)
As this list shows, African-Americans of all ages and both genders responded to Lord Dunmore's offer to emancipate any slaves who joined the British cause.

slave liberation in the minds of both blacks and whites in the southern colonies, an association that continued during the war that followed.

The Coercive Acts

Following the Boston Tea Party, Lord North fumed that only "New England fanatics" could imagine themselves oppressed by inexpensive tea. A Welsh member of Parliament drew wild applause by declaring that "the town of Boston ought to be knocked about by the ears, and destroy'd." In vain did the great parliamentary orator Edmund Burke plead for the one action that could end the crisis. "Leave America . . . to tax herself. . . . Leave the Americans as they anciently stood." The British government, however, swiftly asserted its authority by enacting four Coercive Acts that, together with the unrelated Quebec Act, became known to many colonists as the "Intolerable Acts."

The first of the Coercive Acts, the Boston Port Bill, became law on April 1, 1774. It ordered the navy to close Boston harbor unless the Privy Council certified by June 1 that the town had arranged to pay for the ruined tea. Lord North's cabinet deliberately imposed this impossibly short deadline in order to ensure the harbor's closing, which would lead to serious economic distress.

The second Coercive Act, the Massachusetts Government Act, revoked the Massachusetts charter and restructured the government to make it less democratic. The colony's upper house would no longer be elected annually by the assembly but instead appointed for life by the crown. The governor gained absolute control over the naming of all judges and sheriffs. Jurymen, previously elected, were now appointed by sheriffs. Finally, the new charter forbade communities to hold more than one town meeting a year without the governor's permission. These changes simply brought Massachusetts into line with other royal colonies, but

the colonists interpreted them as evidence of hostility toward representative government and liberty.

The third of the new acts, the Administration of Justice Act, which some colonists cynically called the Murder Act, permitted any person charged with murder while enforcing royal authority in Massachusetts (such as the British soldiers indicted for the Boston Massacre) to be tried in England or in other colonies.

Finally, a new Quartering Act went beyond the earlier act of 1765 by allowing the governor to requisition empty private buildings for housing troops. These measures, along with the appointment of General Thomas Gage, Britain's military commander in North America, as the new governor of Massachusetts, struck New Englanders as proof of a plan to place them under a military tyranny.

Americans learned of the Quebec Act along with the previous four statutes and associated it with them. Intended to cement loyalty to Britain among conquered French-Canadian Catholics, the law established Roman Catholicism as Quebec's official religion. This provision alarmed Protestant Anglo-Americans who widely believed that Catholicism went hand in hand with despotism. Furthermore, the Quebec Act gave Canada's governors sweeping powers but established no legislature. It also permitted property disputes (but not criminal cases) to be decided by French law, which did not use juries. Additionally, the law extended Quebec's territorial claims south to the Ohio River and west to the Mississippi, a vast area populated by Native Americans and some French. Although designated off-limits by the Proclamation of 1763, several colonies continued to claim portions of the region.

The "Intolerable Acts" convinced Anglo-Americans that Britain was plotting to corrode traditional English liberties throughout North America. Rebel pamphlets fed fears that the governor of Massachusetts would starve Boston into submission and appoint corrupt sheriffs and judges to crush political dissent through rigged trials. By this reasoning, the new Quartering Act would repress any resistance by forcing troops on an unwilling population, and the "Murder Act" would encourage massacres by preventing local juries from convicting soldiers who killed civilians. Once resistance in Massachusetts had been smashed, the Quebec Act would serve as a blueprint for extinguishing representative government throughout the colonies. Parliament would revoke every colony's charter and introduce a government like Quebec's. Elected assemblies, freedom of religion for Protestants, and jury trials would all disappear.

Intended by Parliament simply to punish Massachusetts—and particularly that rotten apple in the barrel, Boston—the acts instead pushed most colonies to the brink of rebellion. Repeal of these laws became, in effect, the colonists' nonnegotiable demand. Of the twenty-seven reasons justifying the break with Britain that Americans later cited in the Declaration of Independence, six concerned these statutes.

The First Continental Congress

In response to the "Intolerable Acts," the extralegal committees of correspondence of every colony but Georgia sent delegates to a Continental Congress in Philadelphia. Among those in attendance when the Congress assembled on September 5, 1774, were many of the colonies' most prominent politicians: Samuel and John Adams of Massachusetts; John Jay of New York; Joseph Galloway and John Dickinson of Pennsylvania; and Patrick Henry, Richard Henry Lee, and George Washington of Virginia. The fifty-six delegates had come together to find a way of defending the colonies' rights in common, and in interminable dinner parties and cloakroom chatter, they took one another's measure.

The First Continental Congress opened by endorsing a set of statements of principle called the Suffolk Resolves that recently had placed Massachusetts in a state of passive rebellion. Adopted by delegates at a convention of Massachusetts towns just as the Continental Congress was getting under way, the resolves declared that the colonies owed no obedience to any of the Coercive Acts, that a provisional government should collect all taxes until the former Massachusetts charter was restored, and that defensive measures should be taken in the event of an attack by royal troops. The Continental Congress also voted to boycott all British goods after December 1 and to cease exporting almost all goods to Britain and its West Indian possessions after September 1775 unless a reconciliation had been accomplished. This agreement, the Continental Association, would be enforced by locally elected committees of "observation" or "safety," whose members in effect were usurping control of American trade from the royal customs service.

Such bold defiance was not to the liking of all delegates. Jay, Dickinson, Galloway, and other moderates who dominated the middle-colony contingent most feared the internal turmoil that would surely accompany a head-on confrontation with Britain. These "trimmers" (John Adams's scornful phrase) vainly opposed nonimportation and tried unsuccessfully to win endorsement

of Galloway's plan for a "Grand Council," an American legislature that would share the authority to tax and govern the colonies with Parliament.

Finally, however, the delegates summarized their principles and demands in a petition to the king. This document affirmed Parliament's power to regulate imperial commerce, but it argued that all previous parliamentary efforts to impose taxes, enforce laws through admiralty courts, suspend assemblies, and unilaterally revoke charters were unconstitutional. By addressing the king rather than Parliament, Congress was imploring George III to end the crisis by dismissing those ministers responsible for passing the Coercive Acts.

From Resistance to Rebellion

Most Americans hoped that their resistance would jolt Parliament into renouncing all authority over the colonies except trade regulation. But tensions between moderates and radicals ran high, and bonds between men formerly united in outlook sometimes snapped. John Adams's onetime friend Jonathan Sewall, for example, charged that the Congress had made the "breach with the parent state a thousand times more irreparable than it was before." Fearing that Congress was enthroning "their High Mightinesses, the MOB," he and like-minded Americans fell back on their loyalty to the king. Sewall's instincts, and those of other American loyalists, were correct. A revolution was indeed brewing.

To solidify their defiance, colonial resistance leaders coerced waverers and loyalists (or "Tories," as they were often called). Thus the elected committees that Congress had created to enforce the Continental Association often turned themselves into vigilantes, compelling merchants who still traded with Britain to burn their imports and make public apologies, browbeating clergymen who preached pro-British sermons, and pressuring Americans to adopt simpler diets and dress in order to relieve their dependence on British imports. Additionally, in colony after colony, the committees took on government functions by organizing volunteer military companies and extralegal legislatures. By spring 1775 colonial patriots had established provincial "congresses" that paralleled and rivaled the existing colonial assemblies headed by royal governors.

Britain answered the colonies' challenge in Massachusetts in April 1775. There as elsewhere, colonists had prepared for the worst by collecting arms and organizing extralegal militia units (locally known as minutemen) whose members could respond instantly to an emergency. The British government ordered Massachusetts' Governor Gage to quell the "rude rabble" by arresting the principal patriot leaders. On April 19, 1775, aware that most of these leaders had already fled Boston, Gage instead sent seven hundred British soldiers to seize military supplies that the colonists had stored at Concord. Two couriers, William Dawes and Paul Revere, rode out to warn nearby towns of the British troops movements and target. At Lexington about seventy minutemen confronted the soldiers. After a confused skirmish in which eight minutemen died and a single redcoat was wounded, the British pushed on to Concord. There they found few munitions but encountered a growing swarm of armed Yankees. When some minutemen mistakenly became convinced that the town was being burned, they exchanged fire with the British regulars and touched off a running battle that continued for most of the sixteen miles back to Boston. By day's end the redcoats had suffered 273 casualties, compared to only 92 for the colonists, and they had gained some respect for Yankee courage. These engagements awakened the countryside, and by the evening of April 20, some twenty thousand New Englanders were besieging the British garrison in Boston.

Three weeks later, the Second Continental Congress convened in Philadelphia. Most delegates still opposed independence and at Dickinson's urging agreed to send a "loyal message" to George III. Dickinson composed what became known as the Olive Branch Petition. Excessively polite, it nonetheless presented three demands: a cease-fire at Boston, repeal of the Coercive Acts, and negotiations to establish guarantees of American rights. Yet while pleading for peace, the delegates also passed measures that Britain could only construe as rebellious. In particular, they voted in May 1775 to establish an "American continental army" and appointed George Washington its commander.

The Olive Branch Petition reached London along with news of the Continental Army's formation and of a battle fought just outside Boston on June 17. In this engagement British troops attacked colonists entrenched on Breed's Hill and Bunker Hill. Although successfully dislodging the Americans, the British suffered 1,154 casualties out of 2,200 men, compared to a loss of 311 patriots.

After Bunker Hill many Britons wanted retaliation, not reconciliation. On August 23 George III proclaimed New England in a state of rebellion, and in October he extended that pronouncement to include all the colonies. In December Parliament likewise declared all the colonies rebellious, outlawing all British trade with them and subjecting their ships to seizure.

A View of the Town of Concord, 1775, by Ralph Earl
British troops enter Concord to search for armaments. A few hours later, hostilities with the townspeople would erupt.

Common Sense

Despite the turn of events, many colonists clung to hopes of reconciliation. Even John Adams, who believed in the inevitability of separation, described himself as "fond of reconciliation, if we could reasonably entertain Hopes of it on a constitutional basis." Like many elites, Adams recognized that a war for independence would entail arming common people, many of whom reviled all men of wealth regardless of political allegiance. Such an outcome would threaten elite rule and social order as well as British rule.

Through 1775 many colonists, not only elites, clung to the notion that evil ministers rather than the king were forcing unconstitutional measures on them and that saner heads would rise to power in Britain. On both counts they were wrong. The Americans exaggerated the influence of Pitt, Burke, Wilkes (who finally took his seat in Parliament in 1774), and their other friends in Britain.

And once George III himself declared the colonies to be in "open and avowed rebellion . . . for the purpose of establishing an independent empire," Anglo-Americans had no choice but either to submit or to acknowledge their goal of national independence.

Most colonists' sentimental attachment to the king, the last emotional barrier to their accepting independence, finally crumbled in January 1776 with the publication of Thomas Paine's *Common Sense*. A failed corset maker and schoolmaster, Paine immigrated to the colonies from England late in 1774 with a letter of introduction from Benjamin Franklin, a penchant for radical politics, and a gift for writing plain and pungent prose that anyone could understand.

Paine told Americans what they had been unable to bring themselves to say: monarchy was an institution rooted in superstition, dangerous to liberty, and inappropriate to Americans. The king was "the royal brute" and a "hardened, sullen-tempered Pharaoh." Whereas

Thomas Paine
Having arrived in the colonies less than two years earlier, Paine became a best-selling author with the publication of *Common Sense* (1776).

previous writers had maintained that certain corrupt politicians were directing an English conspiracy against American liberty, Paine argued that such a conspiracy was rooted in the very institutions of monarchy and empire. Moreover, he argued, America had no economic need for the British connection. As he put it, "The commerce by which she [America] hath enriched herself are the necessaries of life, and will always have a market while eating is the custom in Europe." In addition, he pointed out, the events of the preceding six months had made independence a reality. Finally, Paine linked America's awakening nationalism with the sense of religious mission felt by many in New England and elsewhere when he proclaimed, "We have it in our power to begin the world over again. A situation, similar to the present, hath not happened since the days of Noah until now." America, in Paine's view, would be not only a new nation but a new kind of nation, a model society founded on republican principles and unburdened by the oppressive beliefs and corrupt institutions of the European past.

Printed in both English and German, *Common Sense* sold more than one hundred thousand copies within three months, equal to one for every fourth or fifth adult male, making it the best seller in American history. Readers passed copies from hand to hand and read passages aloud in public gatherings. The *Connecticut Gazette* described Paine's pamphlet as "a landflood that sweeps all before it." *Common Sense* had dissolved lingering allegiance to George III and Great Britain, removing the last psychological barrier to American independence.

Declaring Independence

By spring 1776 Paine's pamphlet had stimulated dozens of local gatherings—artisan guilds, town meetings, county conventions, and militia musters—to pass resolutions favoring American independence. The groundswell quickly spread to the colonies' extralegal legislatures. New England was already in rebellion, and Rhode Island declared itself independent in May 1776. The middle colonies hesitated to support independence because they feared, correctly, that any war would largely be fought over control of Philadelphia and New York. Following the news in April that North Carolina's congressional delegates were authorized to vote for independence, several southern colonies pressed for separation. Virginia's legislature instructed its delegates at the Second Continental Congress to propose independence, which Richard Henry Lee did on June 7. Formally adopting Lee's resolution on July 2, Congress created the United States of America.

The task of drafting a statement to justify the colonies' separation from England fell to a committee of five, including John Adams, Benjamin Franklin, and Thomas Jefferson, with Jefferson as the principal author. Among Congress's revisions to Jefferson's first draft were its insertion of the phrase "pursuit of happiness" in place of "property" in the Declaration's most famous sentence, and its deletion of a statement blaming George III for foisting the slave trade on unwilling colonists. The Declaration of Independence (see Appendix) never mentioned Parliament by name, for Congress had moved beyond arguments over who should represent Americans within the British empire and now wanted to separate America altogether from Britain and its head of state, the king. Jefferson instead followed England's own Bill of Rights, which had sharply reduced monarchical power after the Glorious Revolution (see Chapter 4), as well as Paine, and focused on the king. He listed twenty-

seven "injuries and usurpations" committed by George III against the colonies. And he drew on a familiar line of radical thinking when he added that the king's actions had as their "direct object the establishment of an absolute tyranny over these states."

Also like Paine, Jefferson elevated the colonists' grievances from a dispute over English freedoms to a struggle of universal dimensions. In the tradition of Locke and other Enlightenment figures, Jefferson argued that the English government had violated its contract with the colonists, thereby giving them the right to replace it with a government of their own design. And his eloquent emphasis on the equality of all individuals and their natural entitlement to justice, liberty, and self-fulfillment expressed republicans' deepest longing for a government that would rest on neither legal privilege nor exploitation of the majority by the few.

Jefferson addressed the Declaration of Independence as much to Americans uncertain about the wisdom of independence as to world opinion, for even at this late date a significant minority opposed independence or hesitated to endorse it. Above all he wanted to convince his fellow citizens that social and political progress could no longer be accomplished within the British Empire. But he left unanswered just which Americans were and were not equal to one another and entitled to liberty. All the colonies endorsing the Declaration countenanced, on grounds of racial inequality, the enslavement of blacks and severe restrictions on the freedoms of those blacks who were not enslaved. Moreover, all had property qualifications that also prevented many white men from voting. The proclamation that "all men" were created equal accorded with the Anglo-American assumption that women could not and should not function politically or legally as autonomous individuals. And Jefferson's accusation that George III had unleashed "the merciless Indian savages" on innocent colonists seemed to place Native Americans outside the bounds of humanity.

Was the Declaration of Independence a statement that expressed the sentiments of all but a minority of colonists? In a very narrow sense it was, but by framing the Declaration in universal terms, Jefferson and the Continental Congress made it something much greater. The ideas motivating Jefferson and his fellow delegates had moved thousands of ordinary colonists to political action over the preceding eleven years, both on their own behalf and on behalf of the colonies in their quarrel with Britain. For better or worse, the struggle for national independence had hastened, and become intertwined

with, a quest for equality and personal independence that, for many Americans, transcended boundaries of class, race, or gender. In their reading, the Declaration never claimed that perfect justice and equal opportunity existed in the United States; rather, it challenged the Revolutionary generation and all who later inherited the nation to bring this ideal closer to reality.

CONCLUSION

In 1763 Britain and its North American colonies concluded a stunning victory over France, entirely eliminating that nation's formidable mainland American empire. Britain was indisputably the world's most powerful nation. Yet just over a decade later, the partners in victory were fighting with one another. The war had exhausted Britain's treasury and led the government to look to the colonies for help in defraying the costs of maintaining its enlarged empire. In attempting to collect more revenue and to centralize imperial authority, English officials confronted the ambitions and attitudes of Americans who felt themselves to be in every way equal to Britons.

For much of the long imperial crisis, most colonists were content to pursue the goal of reestablishing the empire as it had functioned before 1763, when colonial trade had been protected and encouraged by the Navigation Acts and when colonial assemblies had exercised exclusive power over taxation and internal legislation. But the conflict between empire and colonies quickly passed from differences over the merits of various revenue-raising measures to more fundamental issues. First, people asked, who had the authority, as the people's representatives, to levy taxes on the colonists? Failing to resolve that question to everyone's satisfaction, colonists began to debate whether Parliament had any authority at all in the colonies. Finally, Americans challenged not only British rule but the legitimacy of monarchy itself.

Americans by no means followed a single path to the point of advocating independence. Ambitious elites resented British efforts to curtail colonial autonomy as exercised almost exclusively by members of their own class in the assemblies. They and many more in the middle classes were angered by British policies that made commerce less profitable as an occupation and more costly to consumers. But others, including both western settlers and poor and working urban people like George Robert Twelves Hewes, defied conventions demanding that humble people defer to the authority of their social

CHRONOLOGY, 1750–1776

1744–1748 King George's War (in Europe, the War of
Austrian Succession, 1740–1748).

1755–1761 Seven Years' War (in Europe, 1756–1763).

1760 George III becomes king of Great Britain.
Writs of assistance.

1762 Treaty of San Ildefonso

1763–1766 Indian uprising in Ohio valley and Great Lakes.

1763 Proclamation of 1763.

1764 Sugar Act.

1765 Stamp Act followed by colonial resistance.
African-Americans demand liberty in Charles Town.
First Quartering Act.

1766 Stamp Act repealed.
Declaratory Act.

1767 Revenue Act (Townshend duties).
American Board of Customs Commissioners created.

1768 Massachusetts "circular letters."
John Hancock's ship *Liberty* seized by Boston customs
commissioner.

First Treaty of Fort Stanwix.
St. George's Fields Massacre in London.

1770 Townshend duties, except tea tax, repealed.
Boston Massacre.

1771 Battle of Alamance Creek in North Carolina.

1772–1774 Committees of Correspondence formed.

1772 Somerset decision in England.

1773 Tea Act and Boston Tea Party.

1774 Lord Dunmore's War.
Coercive Acts and Quebec Act.
First Continental Congress.

1775 Battles of Lexington and Concord.
Lord Dunmore offers freedom to Virginia slaves joining
British forces.
Olive Branch Petition.
Battles at Breed's Hill and Bunker Hill.

1776 Thomas Paine, *Common Sense.*
Declaration of Independence.

superiors. Sometimes resorting to violence, they directed their wrath toward British officials and colonial elites alike. Many African-Americans, on the other hand, considered Britain as more likely than white colonists, especially slaveholders, to liberate them. And Native Americans recognized that British authority, however limited, provided a measure of protection from land-hungry colonists.

Americans were the most reluctant of revolutionaries. Their troops had clashed with Britain's, and George III had declared them to be in rebellion, but only after Paine talked "common sense" and a grass-roots independence movement began did Congress formally proclaim American independence.

FOR FURTHER REFERENCE

READINGS

Fred Anderson, *Crucible of War: The Seven Years' War and the Fate of Empire in British North America, 1754–1766* (2000). A meticulous, but engaging study of the war as a critical turning point in the history of British North America.

Bernard Bailyn, *The Ideological Origins of the American Revolution* (1967). A probing discussion of the ideologies that shaped colonial resistance to British authority.

Linda Colley, *Britons: Forging the Nation, 1707–1837* (1992). A major study of the formation of political identity in Great Britain, providing an important perspective on relations between the empire and its North American colonies.

Edward Countryman, *The American Revolution* (1985). An outstanding introduction to the Revolution, its background, and its consequences and their effect on all Americans.

Eric Hinderaker, *Elusive Empires: Constructing Colonialism in the Ohio Valley, 1673–1800* (1997). A study of the multifaceted competition among Native Americans, Europeans, and European Americans for control of a critical American region.

Woody Holton, *Forced Founders: Indians, Debtors, Slaves, and the Making of the American Revolution* (1999). A major reinterpretation of the causes of the Revolution in one colony, emphasizing the role of internal conflicts across lines of class, race, and economic interest in propelling secession from Britain.

Pauline Maier, *American Scripture: Making the Declaration of Independence* (1997). A fine study of the immediate context in which independence was conceived and the Declaration was drafted and received.

Mary Beth Norton, *Liberty's Daughters: The Revolutionary Experience of American Women, 1750–1800* (1980). A wide-ranging discussion of the experiences and roles of women in eighteenth-century colonial society and the American Revolution.

Gordon S. Wood, *The American Revolution: A History* (2002). A concise interpretive overview of the Revolutionary-Constitutional period by one of its leading historians.

Alfred F. Young, *The Shoemaker and the Revolution: Memory and the American Revolution* (1999). A fascinating study of ordinary people's participation in the Revolution, and of how later generations of Americans interpreted and memorialized their role.

WEBSITES

All the News? The American Revolution and Maryland's Press
http:www.mdarchives.state.md.us/msa/stagser/s1259/121/5912/html/0000.html
Features articles, letters, and broadsides on the growing imperial crisis, as published in the *Maryland Gazette*.

Maps of the French and Indian War
http://www.masshist.org/maps/MapsHome/Home.htm
Fourteen original maps published in England, mostly during the Seven Years' War, showing forts, contested territories, and other sites of military interest at the time. The site permits viewers to examine the maps closely for both written and illustrative details.

Thomas Paine
http://www.ushistory.org/paine/index.htm
Includes a brief biography plus the complete texts of *Common Sense* and other major writings by Paine.

For additional works please consult the bibliography at the end of the book.

CHAPTER 6

Securing Independence, Defining Nationhood, 1776–1788

I n November 1775 General George Washington ordered Colonel Henry Knox to bring the British artillery recently captured at Fort Ticonderoga to reinforce the siege of Boston. Washington knew firsthand of the difficulties of wilderness travel, especially in the winter, and he must have wondered if this city-bred officer was up to the task. Only twenty-five years old and a Boston bookseller with little experience in the woods, Knox was nevertheless the army's senior artillerist, largely because he had read several books on the subject whenever business in his store was slow.

Knox and his men built crude sleds to haul their fifty-nine cannons through dense forest covered by two feet of snow. On good days they moved these sixty tons of artillery about seven miles. On two very bad ones, they shivered for hours in freezing water while retrieving guns that had fallen through the ice at river crossings. As their oxen grew weak from overexertion and poor feed, the men had to throw their own backs into pulling the cannons across New York's frozen landscape. On reaching the Berkshire Mountains in western Massachusetts, their pace slowed to a crawl as they trudged uphill through snow-clogged passes. Forty days and three hundred miles after leaving Ticonderoga, Knox and his exhausted New Yorkers reported to Washington in late January 1776. The Boston bookseller had more than proved himself; he had accomplished one of the Revolution's great feats of endurance.

CHAPTER OUTLINE

◀ **George Washington,** by John Trumbull, 1780
Washington posed for this portrait at the height of the Revolutionary War, accompanied by his personal servant, William Lee. Lee was a slave whom Washington had purchased in 1768.

The guns from Ticonderoga placed the outnumbered British in a hopeless position and forced them to evacuate Boston on March 17, 1776. A lifelong friendship formed between Knox and Washington. Knox served on the Virginian's staff throughout the war and accepted his request to be the nation's first secretary of war in 1789.

Friendships like the one between Washington and Knox were almost as revolutionary as the war that produced them. Colonists of different regions had few opportunities to become acquainted before 1775, and most Americans harbored regional prejudices. George Washington at first described New Englanders as "an exceeding dirty and nasty people." Yankee soldiers irritated troops from the southern colonies with smug assumptions of superiority expressed in their popular marching song "Chester," whose rousing lyrics rang out:

> Let tyrants shake their iron rods,
> And Slaver'y clank her galling chains.
> We fear them not, We trust in God,
> New England's God forever reigns.

The Revolution gave white northerners and southerners their first real chance to learn what they had in common, and they soon developed mutual admiration. George Washington, who in the war's early days dismissed New England officers as "the most indifferent kind of people I ever saw," changed his mind after meeting men like Henry Knox.

In July 1776 the thirteen colonies had declared independence out of desperation and joined together in a loosely knit confederation of states. Only as a result of the collective hardships experienced during eight years of terrible fighting did the inhabitants cease to see themselves only as military allies and begin to accept one another as fellow citizens.

Even while the war was still under way, the United States of America was formalized with the adoption of a constitution, called the Articles of Confederation. But Americans remained divided over some basic political questions relating to the distribution of power and authority. These divisions were apparent in some states' struggles to adopt constitutions and, even more forcefully, in the national contest over replacing the Articles. The ratification of a second Constitution in 1787 marked the passing of America's short-lived Confederation and a triumph for those favoring more centralization of power at the national level.

This chapter focuses on four major questions:

■ What were the most critical factors enabling the Americans to win the War of Independence with Britain?

■ What changes did the Revolution promote in relationships among Americans of different classes, races, and genders?

■ In what ways did the first state constitutions and the Articles of Confederation reflect older, pre-Revolutionary ideas about political power and authority? In what ways did they depart from older ideas?

How were the Constitution's proponents able to appeal to Americans with wide-ranging views about the balance of power between national and state governments?

THE PROSPECTS OF WAR

The Revolution was both a collective struggle that pitted the independent states against Britain and a civil war between American peoples. Americans opposed to the colonies' independence constituted one of several factors working in Britain's favor as war began. Others included Britain's larger population and its superior military resources and preparation. America, on the other hand, was located far from Britain and enjoyed the intense commitment to independence of patriots and the Continental Army, led by the formidable George Washington.

Loyalists and Other British Sympathizers

As late as January 1776, most colonists still hoped that declaring independence from Britain would not be necessary. Not surprisingly, when separation came six months later, some Americans remained unconvinced that it was justified. About 20 percent of all whites either opposed the rebellion actively or refused to support the Confederation unless threatened with fines or imprisonment. Although these internal enemies of the Revolution called themselves loyalists, they were "Tories" to their Whig foes. Whigs remarked, but only half in jest, that "a tory was a thing with a head in England, a body in America, and a neck that needed stretching."

Loyalists avowed many of the same political values as did the patriots. Like the rebels, they usually opposed Parliament's claim to tax the colonies. Many loyalists thus found themselves fighting for a cause with which they did not entirely agree, and as a result many of them would change sides during the war. Most doubtless shared the apprehension expressed in 1775 by the Reverend Jonathan Boucher, a well-known Maryland loyalist, who preached with two loaded pistols lying on his pulpit cushion: "For my part I equally dread a Victory by either side."

Loyalists disagreed, however, with the patriots' insistence that only independence could preserve the colonists' constitutional rights. The loyalists denounced separation as an illegal act certain to ignite an unnecessary war. Above all, they retained a profound reverence for the crown and believed that if they failed to defend their king, they would sacrifice their personal honor.

The mutual hatred between Whigs and Tories exceeded that of patriots and the British. Each side saw its cause as so sacred that opposition by a fellow American was an unforgivable act of betrayal. The worst atrocities committed during the war were inflicted by Americans upon each other.

The most important factor in determining loyalist strength in any area was the degree to which local Whigs exerted political authority and successfully convinced their neighbors that the king and Parliament threatened their liberty. New England town leaders, the Virginia gentry, and the rice planters of South Carolina's seacoast had vigorously pursued a program of political education and popular mobilization from 1772 to 1776. Repeatedly explaining the issues at public meetings, these elites persuaded the overwhelming majority to favor resistance. As a result, probably no more than 5 percent of whites in these areas were committed loyalists in 1776. Where leading families acted indecisively, however, their communities remained divided when the fighting began. With elites in New York and New Jersey especially reluctant to declare their allegiance to either side, the proportion of loyalists was highest there. Those two states eventually furnished about half of the twenty-one thousand Americans who fought in loyalist military units.

The next most significant factor influencing loyalist military strength was the geographic distribution of recent British immigrants, who remained closely identified with their homeland. Among these newcomers were thousands of British soldiers who had served in the Seven Years' War and stayed on in the colonies, usually

Loyalist Recruitment Broadside
Loyalists attempted to recruit troops by appealing to Americans' distaste for arbitrary government (applied in this case to the Continental Congress) as well as offering material rewards.

in New York, where they could obtain land grants of two hundred acres. An additional 125,000 English, Scots, and Irish landed from 1763 to 1775—the greatest number of Britons to arrive during any dozen years of the colonial era. In New York, Georgia, and the backcountry of North and South Carolina, where native-born Britons were heavily concentrated, the proportion of loyalists among whites probably ranged from 25 percent to 40 percent in 1776. In wartime the British army organized many Tory units comprising immigrants from the British Isles, including the Loyal Highland Emigrants, the North Carolina Highlanders, and the Volunteers of Ireland. After the war foreign-born loyalists were a majority of those compensated by the British for property losses during the Revolution—including three-quarters of all such claimants from the Carolinas and Georgia.

Canada's religious and secular elites comprised another significant white minority to hold pro-British

sympathies. After the British had conquered New France in the Seven Years' War, the Quebec Act of 1774 guaranteed Canadians religious freedom and continued partial use of French civil law, measures that reconciled Quebec's elites to British rule. But as Continental forces invaded Quebec in 1775–1776, they found widespread support among both French and English Canadians. Although British forces repulsed the invasion, many Canadians continued to hope for an American victory. But Britain's military hold on the region remained strong throughout the war.

Other North Americans supported the British cause not out of loyalty to the crown but from a perception that an independent America would pose the greater threat to their own liberty and independence. For example, recent settlers in the Ohio Valley disagreed about which course would guarantee the personal independence they valued above all (see A Place in Time: Boonesborough, Kentucky, 1778). A few German, Dutch,

Stockbridge Indian Serving With the Continental Army

Like other Native Americans in locales long dominated by whites, the Stockbridge Indians of western Massachusetts contributed substantially to the patriots' military effort.

and French religious congregations doubted that their rights would be as safe in an independent nation dominated by Anglo-Americans. Yet as in Canada, most non-British whites in the thirteen colonies supported the Revolution. The great majority of German colonists, for example, had embraced republicanism by 1776 and would overwhelmingly support the cause of American independence.

The rebels never attempted to win over three other mainland colonies—Nova Scotia and East and West Florida—whose small British populations consisted of recent immigrants and British troops. Nor was independence seriously considered in Britain's thirteen West Indian colonies, which were dominated by absentee plantation owners who lived in England and depended on selling their sugar exports in the protected British market.

The British cause would also draw significant wartime support from nonwhites. Prior to the outbreak of fighting, African-Americans made clear that they considered their own liberation from slavery a higher priority than the colonies' independence from Britain. While Virginia slaves flocked to Lord Dunmore's ranks (see Chapter 5), hundreds of South Carolina slaves had escaped and had taken refuge on British ships in Charles Town's harbor. During the war thousands of enslaved African-Americans, mostly from the southern colonies, escaped their southern owners and signed on as laborers or soldiers in the Royal Army. Among the slaveholders who saw many of his slaves escape to British protection was Thomas Jefferson. On the other hand, most African-Americans in the northern colonies calculated that supporting the rebels would hasten their own liberation.

Although Native Americans were deeply divided, most supported the British, either from the outset or after being pressured by one side or the other to abandon neutrality. Indians in contested areas recognized the danger to their homelands posed by expansion-minded Anglo-Americans. In the Ohio Country, Shawnees, Delawares, Mingos, and other Indians continued to bristle at settlers' incursions, as did the Cherokees to the south. After the uprising of 1763 (see Chapter 5), Native Americans in the Upper Great Lakes had developed good rapport with British agents in the former French forts and were solidly in the British camp.

The Six Nations Iroquois and the Creek confederacies, whose neutrality had been a source of unity and strength until the French defeat in 1760, were now divided. Creeks' allegiances reflected each village's earlier trade ties with either Britain or Spain (the latter leaned

toward the colonists' cause). Among the Six Nations, the central council fire at Onondaga, a symbol of unity since Hiawatha's time (see Chapter 1), died out. Most Iroquois followed the lead of the English-educated Mohawk chief Joseph Brant in supporting Britain. But the Oneidas and Tuscaroras, influenced by Congregationalist missionary Samuel Kirkland, actively sided with the rebels against other Iroquois.

The patriots also had other sources of Indian support. Native Americans in upper New England, easternmost Canada, and the Illinois and Wabash valleys initially took an anti-British stand because of earlier ties with the French, though many of them became alienated from the colonists during the war. In eastern areas long populated by whites, there were fewer Indians, and most of them actively and effectively supported the American war effort.

The Opposing Sides

Britain entered the war with two major advantages. First, in 1776 the 11 million inhabitants of the British Isles greatly outnumbered the 2.5 million colonists, one-third of whom were either slaves or loyalists. Second, Britain possessed the world's largest navy and one of its best professional armies. Even so, the royal military establishment grew during the war years to a degree that strained Britain's resources. The number of soldiers stationed in North America, the British Isles, and the West Indies more than doubled from 48,000 to 111,000 men. To meet its manpower needs, the British government hired 30,000 German mercenaries known as Hessians and later enlisted 21,000 loyalists.

Despite its smaller population, the new nation mobilized about 220,000 troops, compared to the 162,000 who served in the British army. But most Americans served short terms, and the new nation would have been hard-pressed had it not been for the military contributions of France and Spain in the war's later stages.

Britain's ability to crush the rebellion was further weakened by the decline in its sea power, a result of budget cuts after 1763. Midway through the war, half of the Royal Navy's ships sat in dry dock awaiting major repairs. Although the navy expanded rapidly from 18,000 to 111,000 sailors, it lost 42,000 men to desertion and 20,000 to disease or wounds. In addition, Britain's merchant marine suffered from raids by American privateers. During the war rebel privateers and the fledgling U.S. navy would capture over two thousand British merchant vessels and sixteen thousand crewmen.

Britain could ill afford these losses, for it faced a colossal task in trying to supply its troops in America. In fact, it had to import from Britain most of the food consumed by its army, a third of a ton per soldier per year. Seriously overextended, the navy barely kept the army supplied and never effectively blockaded American ports.

Mindful of the enormous strain that the war imposed, British leaders faced serious problems maintaining their people's support for the conflict. The war more than doubled the national debt, thereby adding to the burdens of a people already paying record taxes. The politically influential landed gentry could not be expected to vote against their pocketbooks forever.

The new nation faced different but no less severe wartime problems. Besides the fact that many colonists and Native Americans favored the British, the patriots faced a formidable military challenge. Although state militias sometimes performed well in hit-and-run guerrilla skirmishes, they lacked the training to fight pitched battles against professional armies like Britain's. Congress recognized that independence would never be secured if the new nation relied on guerrilla tactics, avoided major battles, and allowed the British to occupy all major population centers. Moreover, because European powers would interpret dependence on guerrilla warfare as evidence that Americans could not drive out the British army, that strategy would doom efforts by the Continental Congress to gain foreign loans, diplomatic recognition, and military allies.

The Continental Army thus had to fight in the standard European fashion. Professional eighteenth-century armies relied on expert movements of mass formations. Victory often depended on rapid maneuvers to crush an enemy's undefended flank or rear. Attackers needed exceptional skill in close-order drill in order to fall on an enemy before the enemy could re-form and return fire. Because muskets had a range of less than one hundred yards, armies in battle were never far apart. Battles usually occurred in open country with space for maneuver. The troops advanced within musket range of each other, stood upright without cover, and fired volleys at one another until one line weakened from its casualties. Discipline, training, and nerve were essential if soldiers were to stay in ranks while comrades fell beside them. The stronger side then attacked at a quick walk with bayonets drawn and drove off its opponents.

In 1775 Britain possessed a well-trained army with a strong tradition of discipline and bravery under fire. In contrast, the Continental Army had neither an inspirational heritage nor many experienced officers or

sergeants who might turn raw recruits into crack units. Consequently, the Americans experienced a succession of heartbreaking defeats in the war's early years. Yet, to win the war, the Continentals did not have to destroy the British army but only prolong the rebellion until Britain's taxpayers lost patience with the struggle. Until then, American victory would depend on the ability of one man to keep his army fighting despite defeat. That man was George Washington.

George Washington

Few generals ever looked and acted the role as much as Washington. He spoke with authority and comported himself with dignity. At six feet two inches, he stood a half-foot taller than the average man of his day. Powerfully built, athletic, and hardened by a rugged outdoor life, he was one of the war's few generals whose presence on the battlefield could inspire troops to heroism.

Washington's military experience began at age twenty-two, when he took command of a Virginia regiment raised to resist French claims. His mistakes and lost battles in the Ohio Valley (see Chapter 5) taught him lessons that he might not have learned from easy, glorious victories. He discovered the dangers of overconfidence and the need for determination in the face of defeat. He also learned much about American soldiers, especially that they performed best when led by example and treated with respect.

With Virginia's borders safe from attack in 1758, Washington resigned his commission and became a tobacco planter. He sat in the Virginia House of Burgesses, where his influence grew, not because he thrust himself into every issue but because others respected him and sought his opinion. Having emerged as an early, though not outspoken, opponent of parliamentary taxation, he also sat in the Continental Congress. In the eyes of the many who valued his advice and remembered his military experience, Washington was the logical choice to head the Continental Army.

WAR AND PEACE, 1776–1783

The Revolutionary War initially centered on the North, where each side won some important victories. Meanwhile, American forces prevailed over British troops and their Native American allies to gain control of the trans-Appalachian West. The war was decided in the South when American and French forces won a stunning

victory at Yorktown, Virginia, in 1781. In the peace treaty that followed, Britain finally acknowledged American independence.

Shifting Fortunes in the North, 1776–1778

Henry Knox's successful transport of artillery from Ticonderoga to Boston prompted the British to evacuate Boston in March 1776 and to move on to New York, which they wished to seize and use as a base for conquering New England. Under two brothers—General William Howe and Admiral Richard, Lord Howe—130 warships carrying thirty-two thousand royal troops landed near New York harbor in the summer of 1776 (see Map 6.1). Defending New York, America's second-largest city, were eighteen thousand poorly trained soldiers under George Washington.

By the end of the year, William Howe's men had killed or captured one-quarter of Washington's troops and had forced the survivors to retreat from New York across New Jersey and the Delaware River into Pennsylvania. Thomas Paine aptly described these demoralizing days as "the times that try men's souls."

With the British in striking distance of Philadelphia, Washington decided to seize the offensive before the morale of his army and country collapsed completely. On Christmas night 1776 he led his troops back into New Jersey and attacked a Hessian garrison at Trenton, where he captured 918 Germans and lost only 4 Continentals. Washington then attacked 1,200 British at Princeton on January 3, 1777, and killed or took captive one-third of them while sustaining only 40 casualties.

These American victories at Trenton and Princeton had several important consequences. At a moment when defeat seemed inevitable, they boosted civilian and military morale. In addition, they drove a wedge between New Jersey's five thousand loyalists and the British army. Washington's victories forced the British to remove virtually all their New Jersey garrisons to New York early in 1777, while Washington established winter quarters at Morristown, New Jersey, only twenty-five miles from New York City.

New Jersey loyalism never recovered from the blow it received when the British evacuated the state. The state militia disarmed known loyalists, jailed their leaders, and kept a constant watch on suspected Tories. Ironically, the British themselves contributed to the undermining of New Jersey loyalism, for prior to the Battle of Trenton, British commanders had failed to prevent an orgy of looting by their troops that victimized

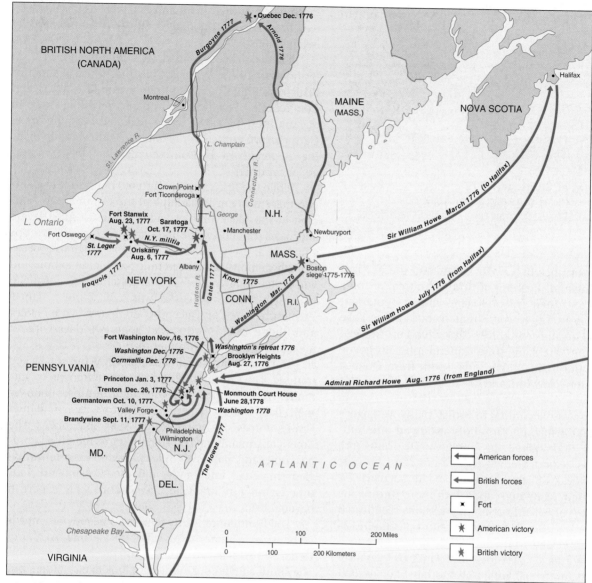

MAP 6.1
The War in the North, 1775–1778
Following the British evacuation of Boston, the war shifted to New York City, which the British held from 1776 to 1783. In 1777 Britain's success in taking Philadelphia was offset by defeat in upstate New York. The hard-fought battle of Monmouth Court House, New Jersey, ended the northern campaigns in 1778.

loyalists and Whigs equally. Surrounded by armed enemies and facing constant danger of arrest, most loyalists who remained in the state bowed to the inevitable and swore allegiance to the Continental Congress. Some even enlisted in the rebel militia.

After the battle of Princeton, the Marquis de Lafayette, a young French aristocrat, joined Washington's staff. Lafayette was twenty years old, highly idealistic, very brave, and infectiously optimistic. Given Lafayette's

close connections with the French court, his presence in America indicated that the French king, Louis XVI, might recognize American independence and perhaps declare war on Britain. Before recognizing the new nation, however, Louis wanted proof that the Americans could win a major battle, a feat they had not yet accomplished.

Louis did not have to wait long. In summer 1777 the British planned a two-pronged assault intended to crush

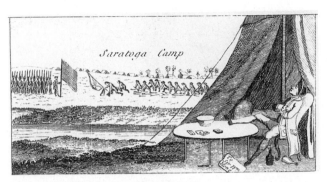

British Defeat at Saratoga, 1777
A British cartoonist expresses his disgust for Britain's surrender by depicting an abject General Burgoyne and a sleeping General Howe.

American resistance in New York State and thereby isolate New England. Pushing off from Montreal, a force of regulars and their Iroquois allies under Lieutenant Colonel Barry St. Leger would march south along Lake Ontario and invade central New York from Fort Oswego in the west. At the same time General John Burgoyne would lead the main British force south from Quebec through eastern New York and link up with St. Leger near Albany.

Nothing went according to British plans. St. Leger's force of 1,900 British and Iroquois advanced one hundred miles and halted to besiege 750 New York Continentals at Fort Stanwix. Unable to take the post after three weeks, St. Leger retreated in late August 1777.

Burgoyne's campaign appeared more promising after his force of 8,300 British and Hessians recaptured Fort Ticonderoga. But Burgoyne ran short of supplies as General Horatio Gates gathered nearly 17,000 American troops for an attack. Gates fought two indecisive battles near Saratoga in the fall, inflicting another 1,200 casualties on Burgoyne. Surrounded and hopelessly outnumbered, Burgoyne's 5,800 troops honorably laid down their arms on October 17, 1777.

The diplomatic impact of the Battle of Saratoga rivaled its military significance and would prove to be the war's turning point. The victory convinced France that the Americans could win the war. In February 1778 France formally recognized the United States. Four months later, it went to war with Britain. Spain declared war on Britain in 1779, but as an ally of France, not the United States, and the Dutch Republic joined them in the last days of 1780. Now facing a coalition of enemies, Britain had no allies.

Meanwhile, as Gates and Burgoyne maneuvered in upstate New York, Britain's General Howe landed eighteen thousand troops near Philadelphia. With Washington at their head and Lafayette at his side, sixteen thousand Continentals occupied the imperiled city in late August 1777.

The two armies collided on September 11, 1777, at Brandywine Creek, Pennsylvania. In the face of superior British discipline, most Continental units crumbled, and Congress fled Philadelphia in panic, enabling Howe to occupy the city. Howe again defeated Washington at Germantown on October 4. In one month's bloody fighting, 20 percent of the Continentals were killed, wounded, or captured.

While the British army wintered comfortably eighteen miles away in Philadelphia, the Continentals huddled in the bleak hills of Valley Forge. Despite severe shortages of food, clothing, and shelter, the troops somehow preserved a sense of humor, which they occasionally demonstrated by joining together in a thousand voices to squawk like crows watching a cornfield. Underlying these squawks was real hunger: James Varnum reported on December 20 that his Connecticut and Rhode Island troops had gone two days without meat and three days without bread.

The army slowly regained its strength but still lacked training. The Continentals had forced Burgoyne to surrender more by their overwhelming numbers than by their skill. Indeed, when Washington's men had met Howe's forces on equal terms, they lost badly. The Americans mainly lacked the ability to march as compact units and maneuver quickly. Regiments often straggled single-file into battle and then wasted precious time forming to attack, and few troops were expert in bayonet drill.

The Continental Army received a desperately needed boost in February 1778, when the German soldier of fortune Friedrich von Steuben arrived at Valley Forge. The short, squat Steuben did not look like a soldier, but this earthy German instinctively liked Americans and became immensely popular. He had a talent for motivating men (sometimes by staging humorous tantrums featuring a barrage of German, English, and French swearing); but more important, he possessed administrative genius. In a mere four months, General Steuben almost single-handedly turned the army into a formidable fighting force.

General Henry Clinton, now British commander-in-chief, evacuated Philadelphia in mid-1778 and marched to New York. The Continental Army got its first opportunity to demonstrate Steuben's training when it caught up with Clinton's rear guard at Monmouth Court House, New Jersey, on June 28, 1778. The battle raged for six hours in one-hundred-degree heat until Clinton broke off contact. Expecting to renew the fight at daybreak, the

Americans slept on their arms, but Clinton's army slipped away before then. The British would never again win easily, except when they faced more militiamen than Continentals.

The Battle of Monmouth ended the contest for the North. Clinton occupied New York, which the Royal Navy made safe from attack. Washington kept his army nearby to watch Clinton, while the Whig militia hunted down the last few Tory guerrillas and extinguished loyalism.

The War in the West, 1776–1782

A different kind of war developed west of the Appalachians and along the western borders of New York and Pennsylvania, where the fighting consisted of small-scale skirmishes rather than major battles involving thousands of troops. Native Americans and Anglo-Americans had alternately traded, negotiated, and fought in this region for several decades. But longstanding tensions between Native peoples and land-hungry settlers continued to simmer. In one sense, then, the warfare between Indians and white Americans only continued a more deeply rooted struggle. Despite its smaller scale, the war in the West was fierce, and the stakes—for the new nation, for the British, and for Indians in the region—could not have been higher.

The war in the West erupted in 1776 when Cherokees began attacking whites from North Carolina and other southern colonies who had settled in or near their homelands (see Map 6.2). After suffering heavy losses, the colonies recovered and organized retaliatory expeditions. Within a year these expeditions had burned most Cherokee towns, forcing the Cherokees to sign treaties that ceded most of their land in South Carolina and substantial tracts in North Carolina and Tennessee.

The intense fighting lasted longer in the Northwest. Largely independent of American and British coordination, Ohio Indians and white settlers fought for two years in Kentucky with neither side gaining a clear advantage (see A Place in Time: Boonesborough, Kentucky, 1778). But after British troops occupied French settlements in the area that is now Illinois and Indiana, Colonel George Rogers Clark led 175 Kentucky militiamen north of the Ohio River. After capturing and losing the French community of Vincennes on the Wabash River, Clark retook the settlement for good in February 1779. With the British unable to offer assistance, their Native American allies were vulnerable. In May, John Bowman led a second Kentucky unit in a campaign that destroyed most Shawnee villages, and in August a move northward from Pittsburgh by Daniel

Thaddeus Kosciuszko, engraving by Gabriel Fiesinger, 1798
A Polish military engineer, Kosciuszko contributed significantly to several American victories during the Revolution. After the war, he led an unsuccessful effort to overthrow Poland's king.

Brodhead inflicted similar damage on the Delawares and the Seneca Iroquois. Although these raids depleted their populations and food supplies, most Ohio Indians resisted the Americans until the war's end.

Meanwhile pro-British Iroquois, led by the gifted Mohawk leader Joseph Brant, devastated the Pennsylvania and New York frontiers in 1778. They killed 340 Pennsylvania militia at Wyoming, Pennsylvania, and probably slew an equal number in their other raids. In 1779 American General John Sullivan retaliated by invading Iroquois country with 3,700 Continental troops, along with several hundred Tuscaroras and Oneidas who had broken with the other Iroquois nations. Sullivan fought just one battle, near present-day Elmira, New York, in which his artillery routed Brant's warriors. Then he burned two dozen Indian villages and destroyed a million bushels of corn, causing most Iroquois to flee without food into Canada. Untold hundreds starved during the next winter, when more than sixty inches of snow fell.

In 1780 Brant's thousand warriors fell upon the Tuscaroras and Oneidas and then laid waste to Pennsylvania and New York for two years. But this final whirlwind of Iroquois fury masked reality: Sullivan's campaign had devastated the Iroquois, whose

Although the American Revolution was primarily a contest involving the seaboard colonies and Britain, it had another dimension in the trans-Appalachian West. There it was one in a long sequence of wars for control of the region. From 1753 to 1815 Native Americans cooperated, fought with, or tried to avoid the Spanish, French, British, and Anglo-Americans who intruded on their homelands.

Anglo-American settlers were usually the most immediate threat to Indians because the two peoples competed for the same resources needed for survival—above all, land. Yet many settlers could not count on support from eastern whites, either because they had defied eastern political authorities or because the westerners were simply too far away from the East, where the war was centered. Concerned above all with securing land and surviving, most western settlers cared little about the outcome of the Revolution, except to the extent that it might affect their own prospects. Indeed, many were prepared to make peace with Britain or even with Native Americans, with whom they were often personally if uneasily acquainted.

This was the case with Daniel Boone of Kentucky. As a young North Carolinian, Boone had hunted in the upper Ohio country, where in 1769 he was seized by Shawnees and held for two years. Undaunted, Boone attempted to lead kinfolk and neighbors into the Ohio valley in 1773 but was turned back by attacking Indians. Two years later, he was hired by land speculators to guide a road-building crew through the Cumberland Gap and founded the town of Boonesborough on the upper Kentucky River in April 1775.

Although Boonesborough officially celebrated news of America's Declaration of Independence in July 1776, townspeople were divided. Some opposed eastern patriot elites, while others wanted no contact with outside authorities and tried to remain neutral. Still others thought that American independence was the best guarantee of their personal independence. Finally, many simply followed other family members in joining either the Tories or the Whigs.

The Shawnees were likewise divided. While some remain neutral, others sided with Blackfish, a renowned war leader from Chillicothe who felt that the war would allow Shawnees to regain their former homelands south of the Ohio (ceded by the Iroquois to Britain in 1768; see Chapter 5). Other Shawnees, seeing no hope for peace, moved west.

In 1777 Blackfish led two war parties against Boonesborough and in February 1778 captured Boone

Daniel Boone Escorting Settlers Through the Cumberland Gap, 1851–52 by George Caleb Bingham
Bingham's is the best known of the many prints and paintings depicting this singular moment in colonial westward expansion.

and twenty-six other Boonesborough men. The men were publicly paraded before Chillicothe villagers seeking to adopt individuals to replace dead family members. Half the captives were taken to the British authorities in Detroit for bounties. The rest, including Boone, were adopted.

Boone was adopted by Blackfish himself to replace a son killed in an earlier raid on Boonesborough. The illustrious white captive was bathed in the river, plucked of all hair except for a scalplock that hung from the top of his head to one side, and dressed for his naming ceremony. Blackfish then welcomed his adopted son Sheltowee ("Big Turtle") into his family.

Several fellow captives feared that Boone's adoption meant he might betray them to the Shawnees or British, but he escaped in June and returned to Boonesborough. Townspeople suspected Boone's intentions but agreed to prepare for an anticipated attack by securing the stockade and expanding the food supply.

On the morning of September 7, 1778, sixty fighting men and other residents of Boonesborough watched as four hundred Shawnees plus a British unit from Detroit emerged from the woods to within rifle range of the stockade. A young African man, Pompey, captured as a boy from a Virginia plantation and now Chillicothe's English translator, stepped forward to summon Boone to come out and speak with his father Blackfish. After the two men embraced and exchanged gifts, Blackfish lamented his son's escape and hoped they could now reunite, with the townspeople surrendering and accompanying the Shawnees to Detroit. Boone agreed to consult with his men and report back the next day. Although Boone would have been willing to take his chances and surrender, the rest of the men vowed to fight to the death. Boone then said, "Well, well, I'll die with the rest."

The next day Boonesborough's leading men emerged from the stockade to invite their Shawnee counterparts to join them in an elaborate feast. They were repaying Blackfish and his people for their earlier hospitality but also wanted to show that they had enough provisions to withstand a prolonged siege. When Blackfish asked his son for Boonesborough's decision, Boone replied that the men had vowed to fight to the death. Blackfish expressed great sorrow and made another offer: the adversaries would recognize the Ohio as the boundary dividing them but allow one another to cross the river freely to hunt or visit. The townspeople asked for time to consider the offer. The next event occurred so suddenly that participants could not later recall the details.

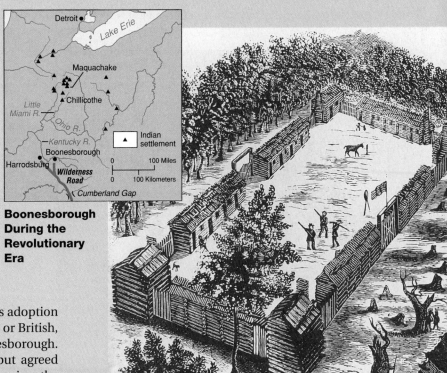

Boonesborough During the Revolutionary Era

Early Drawing of Fort Boonesborough
The townspeople of Boonesborough completed their stockade just in time to face the Shawnee-British siege of September 1778.

Declaring that peace was now at hand, Blackfish called on his leading men to embrace their Boonesborough counterparts, but the white men sensed a trap and fought their way past the approaching Shawnees and into the stockade, while riflemen on both sides unleashed hales of gunfire.

For seventeen days, the two sides fired at each other while the Shawnees tried to burn the fort and tunnel toward it. Inside, men, women, and children—free and enslaved—fired guns and prepared and distributed food. Boone's daughter, Gamma Calloway, was wounded while tending to the wounds of others. Finally, after a torrential downpour collapsed the nearly completed tunnel, the exhausted and demoralized Shawnees withdrew.

The siege of Boonesborough, like the rest of the Revolutionary War in the West, had no immediate military significance. Instead, it reflected the divided and uncertain loyalties of both Native Americans and whites in the region. The siege would later be remembered as a symbolic moment in the history of the American West, when outnumbered settlers defended their tiny world against a "savage" onslaught and made possible America's future growth and prosperity. Such remembering was partial at best, for it overlooked what settlers and Shawnees had shared and forgot that even the siege's hero was far from certain of his own loyalties at the time.

169

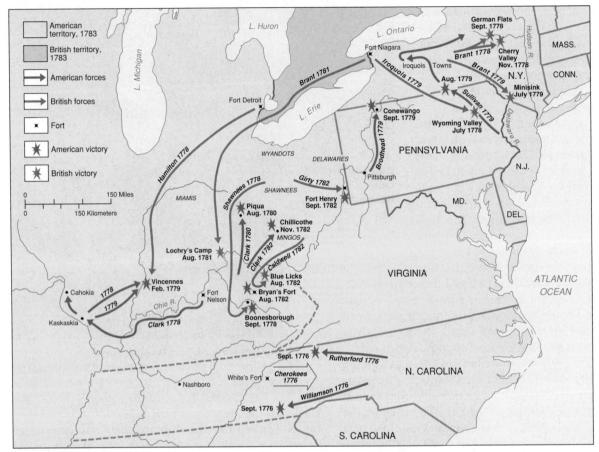

MAP 6.2
The War in the West, 1776–1782
Carolina militiamen drove attacking Cherokees far back into the Appalachians in 1776. George Rogers Clark's victory at Vincennes in 1779 gave the United States effective control of the Ohio valley. In retaliation for their raids on New York and Pennsylvania, John Sullivan inflicted widespread starvation on the Iroquois by burning their villages and winter food supplies in 1779.

population declined by about one-third during the eight-year war.

Fighting continued in the West until 1782. Despite their intensity, the western campaigns did not determine the outcome of the war itself. Nevertheless, they had a significant impact on the future shape of the United States, as discussed later.

American Victory in the South, 1778–1781

In 1778 the war's focus shifted to the South. The entry of France and Spain turned the conflict into an international war; Britain was suddenly locked in a struggle that extended from India to Gibraltar to the West Indies and the American mainland. Between 1779 and 1781, Spanish troops based in Louisiana drove the British

from West Florida, effectively preventing Britain from taking the Mississippi valley. Britain sent thousands of soldiers to Ireland and the West Indies to guard against a French invasion, thus reducing the manpower available to fight in North America. The French and Spanish navies, which together approximately equaled the British fleet, won several large battles, denied Britain control of the sea, and punctured the Royal Navy's blockade.

Nevertheless, British officials remained optimistic. By securing ports in the South, Britain would acquire the flexibility to move its forces back and forth between the West Indies and the mainland as necessity dictated. In addition, the South looked like a relatively easy target. General Henry Clinton expected that a renewed invasion there would tap a huge reservoir of loyalist support. In sum, the British plan was to seize key southern ports

MAP 6.3

The War in the South, 1778–1781

By 1780 Britain held the South's major cities, Charles Town and Savannah, but could not establish control over the backcountry because of resistance from Nathanael Greene's Continentals. By invading Virginia, Lord Cornwallis placed himself within striking distance of American and French forces, a decision that led to the British surrender at Yorktown in October 1781.

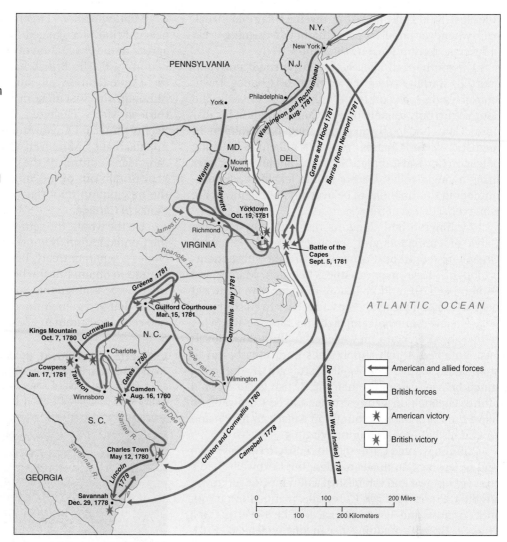

and, with the aid of loyalist militiamen, move back toward the North, pacifying one region after another.

The plan unfolded smoothly at first. In spring 1778 British troops from East Florida took control of Georgia. After a two-year delay caused by political bickering at home, Clinton sailed from New York with nine thousand troops and forced the surrender of Charles Town, South Carolina, and its thirty-four-hundred-man garrison on May 12, 1780 (see Map 6.3). However, the British quickly found that there were fewer loyalists than they had expected.

Southern loyalism had suffered several serious blows since the war began. When the Cherokees had attacked the Carolina frontier in 1776, they killed whites indiscriminately. Numerous Tories had switched sides, joining the rebel militia to defend their homes. Then, as

in Virginia earlier, the arrival of British troops sparked a mass exodus of enslaved Africans from their plantations. About one-third of Georgia's blacks and one-fourth of South Carolina's—twenty-five thousand in all—fled to British lines or to British-held Florida in quest of freedom. However, the British had no interest in emancipating slaves, and British officials made every effort to return the runaways to loyalist owners or otherwise to keep them in bondage. But plantation owners were angry about the loss of many slaves and fearful that the wholesale rupturing of their authority would lead to a black uprising. Despite British efforts to placate them, many loyalist planters and other whites abandoned the British and welcomed the rebels' return to power in 1782. Those who remained loyalists, embittered by countless instances of harsh treatment under patriot

rule, lost little time in taking revenge. Patriots struck back whenever possible, perpetuating an ongoing cycle of revenge, retribution, and retaliation.

The southern conflict was not all personal feuds and guerrilla warfare. After the capture of Charles Town, Horatio Gates took command of American forces in the South. With only a small force of Continentals at his disposal, Gates had to rely on poorly trained militiamen. In August 1780 Lord Charles Cornwallis inflicted a crushing defeat on Gates at Camden, South Carolina. Fleeing after firing a single volley, Gates's militia left his badly outnumbered Continentals to be overrun. Camden was the worst rebel defeat of the war.

Washington and Congress responded by relieving Gates of command and sending General Nathanael Greene to confront Cornwallis. Greene subsequently fought three major battles between March and September 1781, and he lost all of them. "We fight, get beat, rise, and fight again," he wrote back to Washington. Still, Greene won the campaign, for he gave the Whig militia the protection they needed to hunt down loyalists, stretched British supply lines until they began to snap, and sapped Cornwallis's strength by inflicting much heavier casualties than the British general could afford. Greene's dogged resistance forced Cornwallis to leave the Carolina backcountry in American hands and to lead his battered troops into Virginia.

Clinton wanted Cornwallis to return to Charles Town and renew his Carolina campaign; but Cornwallis had a mind of his own and established a new base at Yorktown, Virginia. From Yorktown Cornwallis planned to fan out into Virginia and Pennsylvania, but he never got the chance. Britain's undoing began on August 30, 1781, when a French fleet dropped anchor off the Virginia coast and landed troops near Yorktown. After Lafayette and a small force of Continentals joined the French, Washington moved his army south from New York to tighten the noose around Cornwallis. Trapped in Yorktown, six thousand British stood off eighty-eight hundred Americans and seventy-eight hundred French for three weeks before surrendering with military honors on October 19, 1781.

Peace at Last, 1781–1783

"Oh God!" Lord North exclaimed upon hearing of Yorktown, "It's all over." Cornwallis's surrender drained the will of England's overtaxed people to fight and forced the government to commence peace negotiations. John Adams, Benjamin Franklin, and John Jay were America's principal diplomats at the peace talks in Paris, which began in June 1782.

Military realities largely influenced the terms of the peace. Britain recognized American independence and agreed to the evacuation of all royal troops from the new nation's soil. The British had little choice but to award the Confederation all lands east of the Mississippi. Although the vast majority of Americans lived in the thirteen states clustered near the eastern seaboard, twenty thousand Anglo-Americans now lived west of the Appalachians. Moreover, Clark's victories had given Americans control of the Northwest, while Spain had kept Britain out of the Southwest. The treaty also gave the new nation important fishing rights off the Grand Banks of Canada.

On the whole, the settlement was highly favorable to the Confederation, but it left some disputes unresolved. Under a separate treaty, Britain returned East and West Florida to Spain, but the boundaries designated by this treaty were ambiguous. Spain interpreted the treaty to mean that it regained the same Florida territory that it had ceded to Britain in 1763. But Britain's treaty with the

Lafayette at Yorktown, by Jean-Baptiste Le Paon, 1783
The brilliant young French general appears here with his African-American aid, a Virginia slave named James. Among other services to Lafayette, James spied on Cornwallis before the latter's surrender.

Confederation named the thirty-first parallel as the Floridas' northern border, well south of the area claimed by Spain. Spain and the United States would dispute the northern boundary of Florida until 1795 (see below and Chapter 7).

The Peace of Paris also planted the seeds of several future disputes between Britain and the Americans. Contrary to terms in the treaty agreed to by the Americans, several state governments later refused to compensate loyalists for their property losses and erected barriers against British creditors' attempts to collect prewar debts. Ostensibly in response, Britain refused to honor treaty pledges to abandon forts in the Northwest and to return Americans' slaves under their control.

Notably missing in the Peace of Paris was any reference to Native Americans, most of whom had supported the British in order to avert the alternative—an independent American nation that would be no friend to Indian interests. In effect, the treaty left the Native peoples to deal with the Confederation on their own, without any provision for their status or treatment. Not surprisingly, many Native Americans did not acknowledge the new nation's claims to sovereignty over their territory.

The Peace of Paris ratified American independence, but winning independence had exacted a heavy price. At least 5 percent of all free males between the ages of sixteen and forty-five—white, black, and Native American—died fighting the British. Only the Civil War produced a higher ratio of casualties to the nation's population. Furthermore, the war drove perhaps one of

every six loyalists and several thousand slaves into exile in Canada, Britain, the West Indies, and West Africa. Perhaps as much as 20 percent of New York's white population fled. When the British evacuated Savannah in 1782, 15 percent of Georgia's whites accompanied them. Most whites who departed were recent British immigrants. Finally, although the war secured American independence, it did not settle two important issues: what kind of society America was to become and what sort of government the new nation would possess. But the war had a profound effect on both questions.

THE REVOLUTION AND SOCIAL CHANGE

The social tensions exposed during the imperial crises of 1765–1775 (see Chapter 5) were subsequently magnified and complicated by two factors: first, the principles articulated in the Declaration of Independence; and second, dislocations caused by the war itself. As a result, the Revolution brought significant, if limited, changes to relationships between members of different classes, races, and genders. Increasingly, political elites had to earn the respect of common whites rather than receive unquestioned deference. The Revolution dealt slavery a decisive blow in the North, greatly enlarged the numbers of free blacks, and extended important political rights to free African-Americans. Even elite white males publicly acknowledged the wartime contributions of

Surrender of the British at Yorktown
French naval power combined with American military savvy to produce the decisive defeat of the British.

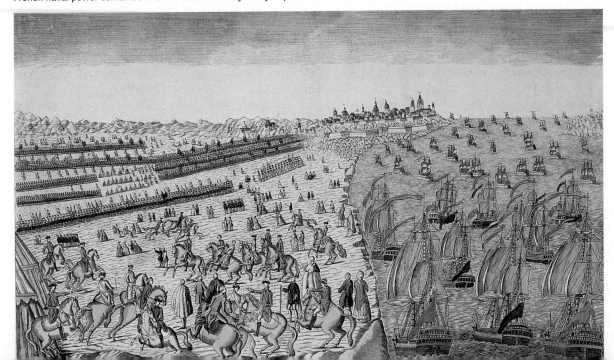

white women, implying that gender relations could become a subject of national debate. By occupying lands sought by whites, Native Americans posed the most serious challenge of all to Revolutionary notions of liberty and equality.

Egalitarianism Among White Males

For much of the eighteenth century, social relations between elites and other white colonists became more formal, distant, and restrained (see Chapter 4). Members of the colonial gentry emphasized their social position by living far beyond the means of ordinary families. By the late 1760s, however, many in the upper classes began wearing homespun rather than imported English clothes in order to win popular political approval, especially by showing their support for the colonial boycott of British goods. When Virginia planters organized minutemen companies in 1775, they put aside their expensive officer's uniforms and dressed in buckskin or homespun hunting shirts of a sort that even the poorest farmer could afford. By 1776 the anti-British movement had persuaded many elites to maintain the appearance, if not the substance, of equality with common people.

Then came war, which accelerated the erosion of class differences by forcing the gentry, who held officers' rank, to show respect to the ordinary folk serving as privates. Indeed, the soldiers demanded to be treated with consideration, especially in light of the ringing words of the Declaration of Independence, "All men are created equal." The soldiers would follow commands, but not if they were addressed as inferiors.

The best officers realized this fact immediately. Some, among them General Israel Putnam of Connecticut, went out of their way to show that they felt no superiority to their troops. While inspecting a regiment digging fortifications around Boston in 1776, Putnam saw a large stone nearby and told a noncommissioned officer to throw it onto the outer wall. The individual protested, "Sir, I am a corporal." "Oh," replied Putnam, "I ask your pardon, sir." The general then dismounted his horse and hurled the rock himself, to the immense delight of the troops working there.

Over the course of the war, common soldiers came to expect that their officers would recognize their worth as individuals. After returning to civilian life, the soldiers retained their sense of self-esteem and insisted on respectful treatment by elites. As these feelings of personal pride gradually translated into political behavior

and beliefs, many candidates took care not to scorn the common people. The war thus subtly but fundamentally democratized Americans' political assumptions.

The gentry's sense of social rank also diminished as elites met men who rose through ability rather than through advantages of wealth or family. The war produced numerous examples like James Purvis, the illiterate son of a nonslaveholding Virginia farmer, who joined the First Virginia Regiment as a private in 1775, soon rose to sergeant, and then taught himself to read and write so that he could perform an officer's duties. Captain Purvis fought through the entire war and impressed his well-born officers as "an uneducated man, but of sterling worth." As elites saw more and more men like Purvis performing responsibilities previously thought to be above their station in life, many came to recognize that a person's merit was not always related to his wealth.

Not all those who considered themselves republicans welcomed the apparent trend toward democracy. Especially among elites, many continued to insist that each social class had its own particular virtues and that a chief virtue of the lower classes was deference to those possessing the wealth and education necessary to govern. Writing to John Adams in 1778, Mercy Otis Warren observed that while "a state of war has ever been deemed unfavorable to virtue, . . . such a total change of manners in so short a period . . . was never known in the history of man. Rapacity and profusion, pride and servility, and almost every vice is contrasted in the same heart."

Nevertheless, most Revolutionary-generation Americans came to insist that virtue and sacrifice defined a citizen's worth independently of his wealth. Voters began to view members of the "natural aristocracy"— those who had demonstrated fitness for government service by personal accomplishments—as the ideal candidates for political office. This natural aristocracy had room for a few self-made men such as Benjamin Franklin, as well as for those, like Thomas Jefferson and John Hancock, who were born into wealth. Voters still elected the wealthy to office, but not if they flaunted their money or were condescending toward common people. The new emphasis on equality did not extend to propertyless males, women, and nonwhites, but it undermined the tendency to believe that wealth or distinguished family background conferred a special claim to public office.

Although many whites became more egalitarian, the Revolution left the overall distribution of wealth in the nation unchanged. Because the 3 percent of Americans

who fled abroad as loyalists represented a cross-section of society, their departure left the new nation's class structure unaltered. Loyalists' confiscated estates tended to be bought up by equally well-to-do Whig gentlemen. Overall, the American upper class seems to have owned about as much of the national wealth in 1783 as it did in 1776.

A Revolution for Black Americans

The wartime situation of African-Americans contradicted the ideals of equality and justice for which Americans were fighting. About five hundred thousand black persons—20 percent of the total population—inhabited the United States in 1776, of whom all but about twenty-five thousand lived in bondage. Even those who were free could not vote, lived under curfews and other galling restrictions, and lacked the guarantees of equal justice held by the poorest white criminal. Free blacks could expect no more than grudging toleration, and few slaves ever gained their freedom.

Although the United States was a "white man's country" in 1776, the war opened some opportunities for African-Americans. Amid the confusion of war, some slaves, among them Jehu Grant of Rhode Island, ran off and posed as free persons. Grant later recalled his excitement "when I saw liberty poles and the people all engaged for the support of freedom, and I could not but like and be pleased with such a thing."

In contrast to the twenty-five thousand who joined British forces, approximately five thousand African-Americans, most from the North, served in the Continental forces. Even though the army forbade enlistment by African-Americans in 1775, black soldiers were already fighting in units during the siege of Boston, and the ban on black enlistments started to collapse in 1777. The majority were free blacks, but some were slaves serving with their masters' consent.

For the most part, these wartime opportunities for African-American men grew out of the army's need for personnel rather than a white commitment to equal justice. In fact, until the mid-eighteenth century, few Europeans and white Americans had criticized slavery at all. Like disease and sin, slavery was considered part of the natural order. But in the decade before the Revolution, American opposition to slavery had swelled, especially as resistance leaders increasingly compared the colonies' relationship with Britain to that between slaves and a master. The first American prohibition against slave owning came from the yearly meeting of the New England Quakers in 1770. The yearly meetings of New York and Philadelphia Quakers followed suit in 1776, and by 1779 Quaker slave owners had freed 80 percent of their slaves.

Although the Quakers aimed mainly to abolish slaveholding within their own ranks, the Declaration of Independence's broad assertion of natural rights and human equality spurred a more general attack on the institution of slavery. Between 1777 and 1784 Vermont, Pennsylvania, Massachusetts, Rhode Island, and Connecticut began phasing out slavery. New York did not do so until 1799, and New Jersey until 1804. New Hampshire, unmoved by petitions like that written in 1779 by Portsmouth slaves demanding liberty "to dispose of our lives, freedom, and property," never freed its slaves; but by 1810 none remained in the state.

The Revolutionary generation, rather than immediately abolishing slavery, took steps that would weaken the institution and in this way bring about its eventual demise. Most state abolition laws provided for gradual emancipation, typically declaring all children born of a slave woman after a certain date—often July 4—free. (They still had to work, without pay, for their mother's master for up to twenty-eight years.) Furthermore, the Revolution's leaders did not press for decisive action against slavery in the South out of fear that widespread southern emancipation would either bankrupt or end the Union. They argued that the Confederation, already deeply in debt as a result of the war, could not finance immediate abolition in the South, and any attempt to do so without compensation would drive that region into secession.

Yet even in the South, where it was most firmly entrenched, slavery troubled some whites. When one of his slaves ran off to join the British and later was recaptured, James Madison of Virginia concluded that it would be hypocritical to punish the runaway "merely for coveting that liberty for which we have paid the price of so much blood." Still, Madison did not free the slave, and no state south of Pennsylvania abolished slavery. Nevertheless, all states except South Carolina and Georgia ended slave imports and all but North Carolina passed laws making it easy for masters to manumit (set free) slaves. The number of free blacks in Virginia and Maryland had risen from about four thousand in 1775 to nearly twenty-one thousand, or about 5 percent of all African-Americans there, by 1790.

These "free persons of color" faced the future as destitute, second-class citizens. Most had purchased

their freedom by spending small cash savings earned in off-hours and were past their physical prime. Once free, they found whites reluctant to hire them or to pay equal wages. Black ship carpenters in Charleston (formerly Charles Town), South Carolina, for example, earned one-third less than their white coworkers in 1783. Under such circumstances, most free blacks remained poor laborers, domestic servants, and tenant farmers.

Even with these disadvantages, some free blacks became landowners or skilled artisans, and a few gained recognition from whites. One of the best known was Benjamin Banneker of Maryland, a self-taught mathematician and astronomer. In 1789 Banneker was one of three surveyors who laid out the new national capital in Washington, D.C., and after 1791 he published a series of widely read almanacs. Sending a copy of one to Thomas Jefferson, Banneker chided the future president for holding views of black inferiority that contradicted his own words in the Declaration of Independence. Another prominent African American was the Boston poet and slave Phillis Wheatley. Several of Wheatley's poems explicitly linked the liberty sought by white Americans with a plea for the liberty of slaves, including one that was autobiographical:

> I, young in life, by seeming cruel fate
> Was snatch'd from Afric's fancy'ed happy seat:
>
> . . . . .
>
> Such, such my case. And can I then but pray
> Others may never feel tyrannic sway?

Most states granted some civil rights to free blacks during and after the Revolution. Free blacks had not participated in colonial elections, but those who were male and met the property qualification gained this privilege in several states by the 1780s. Most northern states repealed or stopped enforcing curfews and other colonial laws restricting free African-Americans' freedom of movement. These same states generally changed their laws to guarantee free blacks equal treatment in court hearings.

The Revolution neither ended slavery nor brought equality to free blacks, but it did begin a process by which slavery eventually could be extinguished. In half the nation, the end of human bondage was in sight. White southerners increasingly viewed slavery as a necessary evil—an attitude that implicitly recognized its immorality. Slavery had begun to crack, and free blacks had made some gains. But events in the 1790s would stall the move toward egalitarianism (see Chapter 7).

White Women in Wartime

"To be adept in the art of Government is a prerogative to which your sex lay almost exclusive claim," wrote Abigail Adams to her husband John in 1776. She was one of the era's shrewdest political commentators and her husband's political confidante and best friend, but she had no public role. Indeed, the assumption that women were naturally dependent—either as children subordinate to their parents or as wives to their husbands—continued to dominate discussions of the female role. Nevertheless, the circumstances of war partially relaxed gender barriers and proved significant for some white American women.

White women's support of colonial resistance before the Revolution (see Chapter 5) broadened into an even wider range of support activities during the war. Female "camp followers," many of them soldiers' wives, served military units on both sides by cooking, laundering, and nursing the wounded. A few female patriots, such as Massachusetts' Deborah Sampson, even disguised themselves as men and joined in the fighting. But most

Phillis Wheatley, African-American Poet
Though a slave, Wheatley was America's best-known poet at the time of the Revolution. Despite her fame, Wheatley died in poverty in 1784.

women remained at home, where they managed families, households, farms, and businesses on their own.

Yet even traditional roles took on new meaning in the absence of male household heads. After her civilian husband was seized by loyalists and turned over to the British on Long Island, Mary Silliman of Fairfield, Connecticut, tended to her four children (and bore a fifth), oversaw several servants and slaves, ran a commercial farm that had to be evacuated when the British attacked Fairfield, and launched repeated appeals for her husband's release. Despite often enormous struggles, such experiences boosted white women's confidence in their abilities to think and act on matters traditionally reserved for men. "I have the vanity," wrote another Connecticut woman, Mary Fish, to a female friend, "to think I have in some measure acted the *heroine* as well as my dear Husband the Hero."

As in all wars, women's public roles and visibility were heightened during the Revolution. The question was to what extent the new Republic would make these gains permanent.

Native Americans and the Revolution

For Native Americans, the consequences of the United States' triumph over Britain were even less certain. Whereas Revolutionary ideology held out at least an abstract hope for blacks, white women, and others seeking liberty and equal rights within American society, it made no provision for Indian nations that sought to maintain their political and cultural independence from Europeans and European-Americans. Moreover, in an overwhelmingly agrarian society like the United States, the Revolution's implicit promise of equal economic opportunity for all male citizens set the stage for territorial expansion beyond the areas already settled, thereby threatening Native American landholdings. Even where Indians retained land, the influx of settlers posed dangers to them in the form of deadly diseases, farming practices inimical to Indian subsistence (see Chapter 3), and alcohol. Native Americans were all the more vulnerable because, during the three decades encompassed by the Seven Years' War and the Revolution (1754–1783), the Native population east of the Mississippi had declined by about half, and many Indian communities had been uprooted.

In the face of these uncertainties, Native Americans continued their efforts to incorporate the most useful aspects of European culture into their own. From the beginning of the colonial period, Indians had selectively adopted European-made goods of cloth, metal, glass,

Woodcut from "A New Touch on the Times . . . By a Daughter of Liberty, Living in Marblehead," 1779
Americans on the home front as well as in the front lines experienced crippling wartime hardships. This illustration of a female partisan holding a musket accompanied a poem by Molly Gutridge, whose theme was women's sacrifice and suffering in a seaport economy upset by war.

and other materials into their lives. But Native Americans did not give up their older ways altogether; rather, their clothing, tools, weapons, utensils, and other material goods combined elements of the old and the new. Indians, especially those no longer resisting American expansion, also selectively participated in the American economy by occasionally working for wages or by selling food, crafts, or other products. This interweaving of the new with the traditional characterized Indian communities throughout eastern North America.

Native Americans, then, did not remain stubbornly rooted in traditional ways nor resist participation in a larger world dominated by whites. But they did insist on retaining control of their communities and their ways of life. In this spirit, the Chickasaws of the Mississippi valley addressed Congress in 1783. While asking "from

whare and whome we are to be supplied with necessaries," they also requested that the Confederation "put a stop to any encroachments on our lands, without our consent, and silence those [white] People who . . . inflame and exasperate our Young Men."

In the Revolution's aftermath, it appeared doubtful that the new nation would concede even this much to Native Americans.

FORGING NEW GOVERNMENTS, 1776–1787

Even as they joined in resisting Britain's authority, white mainland colonists differed sharply among themselves over basic questions of social and political order. Many elite republicans welcomed hierarchical rule, so long as it was not based on heredity, and feared democracy as "mob rule." Working and poor people, especially in cities, worried that propertied elites profited at their expense. Rural colonists emphasized decentralizing power and authority as much as possible. These conflicts were reflected in the independent United States' first experiments in government at the state and national levels.

From Colonies to States

The state governments that Americans constructed during the Revolution magnified the prewar struggle between more-radical democratic elements and elites who would minimize popular participation. To a significant degree, the new state constitutions retained colonial precedents that favored the wealthiest elites.

In keeping with colonial practice, eleven of the thirteen states maintained bicameral legislatures. Colonial legislatures had consisted of two houses: an elected lower chamber (or assembly) and an upper chamber (or council) appointed by the governor or chosen by the assembly (see Chapter 4). These two-part legislatures mirrored Parliament's division into the House of Commons and House of Lords, symbolizing the assumption that a government should have separate representation by the upper class and the common people.

Despite participation by people from all classes in the struggle against Britain, few questioned the longstanding practice of setting property requirements for voters and elected officials. In the prevailing view, only the ownership of property, especially land, made it possible for voters to think and act independently. Whereas tenant farmers and hired laborers might sell their votes, mindlessly follow a demagogue, or vote to avoid dis-

pleasing their landlords or employers, property holders supposedly had the financial means and the education to express their political preferences freely and responsibly. The association between property and citizenship was so deeply ingrained that even radicals such as Samuel Adams opposed allowing all males—much less women—to vote and hold office.

The notion that elected representatives should exercise independent judgment in leading the people rather than simply carry out the popular will also survived from the colonial period and limited democratization. Although Americans today take political parties for granted, the idea of parties as necessary instruments for identifying and mobilizing public opinion was alien to the eighteenth-century political temper, which equated parties with "factions"—selfish groups that advanced their own interests at the expense of liberty or the public good. Most candidates for office did not present voters with a clear choice between policies calculated to benefit rival interest groups; instead, they campaigned on the basis of their personal reputations and fitness for office. As a result, voters often did not know where office seekers stood on specific issues and hence found it hard to influence government actions.

Another colonial practice that persisted into the 1770s and 1780s was the equal (or nearly equal) division of legislative seats among all counties or towns, regardless of differences in population. Inasmuch as representation had never before been apportioned according to population, a minority of voters normally elected a majority of assemblymen. Only the most radical constitution, Pennsylvania's, sought to avoid such outcomes by attempting to ensure that election districts would be roughly equal in population. Nine of the thirteen states reduced property requirements for voting, but none abolished such qualifications entirely, and most of the reductions were modest.

Yet the holdover of certain colonial-era practices should not obscure the pathbreaking components of the state constitutions. Above all, they were written documents whose adoption usually required popular ratification and that could be changed only if voters chose to amend them. In short, Americans jettisoned the British conception of a constitution as a body of customary arrangements and practices, insisting instead that constitutions were written compacts that defined and limited the powers of rulers. Moreover, as a final check on government power, the Revolutionary constitutions spelled out citizens' fundamental rights. By 1784 all state constitutions included explicit bills of rights that outlined certain freedoms that lay beyond the control of any government.

Without intending to extend political participation, elites had found themselves pulled in a democratic direction by the logic of the imperial crisis of the 1760s and 1770s. Elite-dominated but popularly elected assemblies had led the fight against royal governors and their appointees—the executive branch of colonial governments—who had repeatedly enforced laws and policies deemed dangerous to liberty. Colonists entered the Revolution dreading executive officeholders and convinced that even elected governors could no more be trusted with power than could monarchs. Recent history seemed to confirm the message hammered home by British "country party" ideology (see Chapter 5) that those in power tended to become either corrupt or dictatorial. Consequently, Revolutionary statesmen proclaimed the need to strengthen legislatures at the governors' expense.

Accordingly, the earliest state constitutions severely limited executive power. In most states the governor became an elected official, and elections themselves occurred far more frequently. (Pennsylvania actually eliminated the office of governor altogether.) Whereas most colonial elections had been called at the governor's pleasure, after 1776 all states scheduled annual elections except South Carolina, which held them every two years. In most states the power of appointments was transferred from the governor to the legislature. Legislatures usually appointed judges and could reduce their salaries or impeach them (try them for wrongdoing). By relieving governors of most appointive powers, denying them the right to veto laws, and making them subject to impeachment, the constitutions turned governors into figureheads who simply chaired executive councils that made militia appointments and supervised financial business.

As the new state constitutions weakened the executive branch and vested more power in the legislatures, they also made the legislatures more responsive to the will of the people. Nowhere could the governor appoint the upper chamber. Eight constitutions written before 1780 allowed voters to select both houses of the legislature; one (Maryland) used a popularly chosen "electoral college" for its upper house; and the remaining "senates" were filled by vote of their assemblies. Pennsylvania and Georgia abolished the upper house and substituted a unicameral (single-chamber) legislature. American assaults on the executive branch and enhancement of legislative authority reflected bitter memories of royal governors who had acted arbitrarily to dismiss assemblies and control government through their power of appointment, and fear that republics' undoing began with executive usurpation of authority.

Despite their high regard for popularly elected legislatures, Revolutionary leaders described themselves as republicans rather than democrats. Although used interchangeably today, these words had different connotations in the eighteenth century. At worst, democracy suggested mob rule; at best, it implied the concentration of power in the hands of an uneducated multitude. In contrast, republicanism presumed that government would be entrusted to capable leaders elected for their superior talents and wisdom. For most republicans, the ideal government would delicately balance the interests of different classes to prevent any one group from gaining absolute power. Some, including John Adams, thought that a republic could include a hereditary aristocracy or even a monarchy as part of this balance, but most thought otherwise. Having blasted one king in the Declaration of Independence, most political leaders had no desire to enthrone another. Still, their rejection of hereditary aristocracy and monarchy posed a problem for republicans trying to reconcile their preference for strong, elite leadership with most Americans' pervasive distrust of executive power.

In the first flush of revolutionary enthusiasm, elites had to content themselves with state governments dominated by popularly elected legislatures. Gradually, however, wealthier landowners, bankers, merchants, and lawyers reasserted their desires for centralized authority and the political prerogatives of wealth. In Massachusetts an elite-dominated convention in 1780 pushed through a constitution stipulating stiff property qualifications for voting and holding office, state senate districts that were apportioned according to property values, and a governor with considerable powers in making appointments and vetoing legislative measures. The Massachusetts constitution signaled a general trend. Georgia and Pennsylvania substituted bicameral for unicameral legislatures by 1790. Other states raised property qualifications for members of the upper chamber in a bid to encourage the "senatorial element" and to make room for men of "Wisdom, remarkable integrity, or that Weight which arises from property."

The later state constitutions revealed a central feature of elites' thought. Gradations among social classes and restrictions on the expression of popular will troubled them far less than the prospect of tyranny by those in power. But some republican elites believed that social divisions, if deep-seated and permanent, could jeopardize liberty, and attempted to prevent such an outcome through legislation. In 1776 in Virginia, for example, Thomas Jefferson persuaded the legislature to abolish entails, legal requirements that prevented an heir and all his descendants from selling or dividing an estate.

Although entails were easy to break through special laws—Jefferson himself had escaped the constraints of one—he hoped that their elimination would strip wealthy families of the opportunity to amass land continuously and become an overbearing aristocracy. Through Jefferson's efforts, Virginia also ended primogeniture, the legal requirement that the eldest son inherit all a family's property in the absence of a will. Jefferson hoped that these laws would ensure a continuous division of wealth. By 1791 no state provided for primogeniture, and only two still allowed entails.

These years also witnessed the end of state-established churches in most of the country. The exceptions were New Hampshire, Connecticut, and Massachusetts, where the Congregational church continued to collect tithes (church taxes) from citizens not belonging to recognized Christian denominations into the nineteenth century. Wherever colonial taxpayers had supported the Church of England, independent states abolished such support by 1786. Thomas Jefferson best expressed the ideal behind disestablishment in his Statute for Religious Freedom (1786), whose preamble resounded with a defense of religious freedom at all times and places. "Truth is great," proclaimed Jefferson, "and will prevail if left to itself."

The American Revolution, wrote Thomas Paine in 1782, was intended to ring in "a new era and give a new turn to human affairs." This was an ambitious declaration and seemed to conflict with the states' retention of institutions such as state senates and property requirements for voting. But Paine's point was that all political institutions, new and old alike, now were being judged by the standard of whether they served the public good rather than the interests of the powerful few. More than any single innovation of the era, it was this new way of thinking that made American politics revolutionary.

Formalizing a Confederation, 1776–1781

As did their revolt against Britain and their early state constitutions, Americans' first national government reflected widespread fears of centralized authority and its potential for corruption. In 1776 John Dickinson, who had stayed in Congress despite having refused to sign the Declaration of Independence, drafted a proposal for a national constitution. Congress adopted a weakened version of Dickinson's proposal, called the Articles of Confederation and Perpetual Union (see Appendix), and sent it to the states for ratification in 1777.

The Articles of Confederation explicitly reserved to each state "its sovereignty, freedom and independence" and established a form of government in which Americans were citizens of their own states first and of the United States second. As John Adams later explained, the Whigs of 1776 never thought of "consolidating this vast Continent under one national Government" but instead erected "a Confederacy of States, each of which must have a separate government."

Under the Articles, the national government consisted of a single-chamber Congress, elected by the state legislatures, in which each state had one vote. Congress could request funds from the states but could enact no tax of its own without every state's approval, nor could it regulate interstate or overseas commerce. The Articles did not provide for an executive branch. Rather, congressional committees oversaw financial, diplomatic, and military affairs. Nor was there a judicial system by which the national government could compel allegiance to its laws.

By 1781 all thirteen state legislatures had ratified the Articles, and the Confederation was in place. The new nation had taken a critical step in defining the role of national sovereignty in relation to the sovereignty of the individual states. Whereas the Continental Congress had directed most of the war effort without defined powers, the nation now had a formal government. Nevertheless, many Americans' misgivings about centralized power left the Confederation severely limited in the views of more nationally minded elites.

Finance, Trade, and the Economy, 1781–1786

For proponents of a strong national government, the greatest challenge facing the Confederation was putting the nation on a sound financial footing. Winning the war had cost the nation's six hundred thousand taxpayers a staggering $160 million, a sum that exceeded by 2,400 percent the taxes raised to pay for the Seven Years' War. To finance the War for Independence, which cost far more than could be immediately collected through taxation, the government borrowed funds from abroad and printed its own paper money, called Continentals. Lack of public faith in the government destroyed 98 percent of the value of the Continentals from 1776 to 1781, an inflationary disaster that gave rise to the expression "not worth a Continental."

In 1781, seeking to overcome the national government's financial weakness, Congress appointed a wealthy, self-made Philadelphia merchant, Robert Morris, as the

nation's superintendent of finance. Morris proposed that the states authorize the collection of a national import duty of 5 percent, which would finance the congressional budget and guarantee interest payments on the war debt. Because the Articles stipulated that every state had to approve the levying of national taxes, the import duty failed to pass in 1782 when Rhode Island alone rejected it.

Meanwhile, seeing themselves as sovereign, most states had assumed some responsibility for the war debt and begun compensating veterans and creditors within their borders. But Morris and other nationally minded elites insisted that the United States needed sources of revenue independent of the states in order to establish its credit-worthiness, enabling it to attract capital, and to establish a strong national government. Hoping to panic the country into seeing things their way, Morris and New York Congressman Alexander Hamilton engineered a dangerous gamble known later as the Newburgh Conspiracy. In 1783 the two men secretly persuaded some army officers, then encamped at Newburgh, New York, to threaten a coup d'état unless the treasury obtained the taxation authority needed to raise their pay, which was months in arrears. But George Washington, learning of the conspiracy before it was carried out, ended the plot by delivering a speech that appealed to his officers' honor and left them unwilling to proceed. Although Morris may never have intended for a coup to actually occur, his willingness to take such a risk demonstrated the new nation's perilous financial straits and the vulnerability of its political institutions.

When peace came in 1783, Congress sent another tax measure to the states, but once again a single legislature, this time New York's, blocked it. From then on, the states steadily decreased their contributions to Congress. By the late 1780s, the states had fallen behind nearly 80 percent in providing the funds that Congress requested to operate the government and honor the national debt.

Nor did the Confederation succeed in prying trade concessions from Britain. Before independence, almost 60 percent of northern exports had gone to the West Indies, and New England's maritime community had employed approximately 15 percent of the region's adult males. After declaring the colonies in rebellion, Britain had virtually halted American trade with its Caribbean colonies and Great Britain itself (see Chapter 5). Because half of all American exports went to Great Britain and its colonies, these restrictions enabled British shippers to increase their share of Atlantic trade at American expense.

The decline in trade with Britain contributed substantially to an economic depression that gripped parts of the nation beginning in 1784. New Englanders were the least fortunate. A short growing season and poor soil kept yields so low, even in the best of times, that farmers barely produced enough grain for local consumption. New Englanders also faced both high taxes to repay the money borrowed to finance the Revolution and a tightening of credit that spawned countless lawsuits against debtors. Economic depression only aggravated the region's chronic overpopulation. Young New England men continued to migrate to more remote lands or to cities; their discontent and restless mobility loosened the bonds of parental authority and left many women without marriage prospects.

British restrictions against trading with the West Indies fell especially hard on New England. Resourceful captains took cargoes to the French West Indies, Scandinavia, and China. Some even smuggled foodstuffs to the British West Indies under the very nose of the Royal Navy. Nevertheless, by 1791 discriminatory British treatment had reduced the number of seamen in the Massachusetts cod and whale fisheries by 42 percent compared to the 1770s.

The mid-Atlantic states, on the other hand, were less dependent on British-controlled markets for their exports. As famine stalked Europe, farmers in Pennsylvania and New York prospered from climbing export prices—much as Thomas Paine had predicted (see Chapter 5). By 1788 the region had largely recovered from the Revolution's ravages.

Southern planters faced frustration at the failure of their principal crops, tobacco and rice, to return to prewar export levels. Whereas nearly two-thirds of American exports originated in the South in 1770, less than half were produced by southern states in 1790. In an effort to stay afloat, many Chesapeake tobacco growers shifted to wheat, and others expanded their production of hemp. But these changes had little effect on the region's exports and, because wheat and hemp required fewer laborers than tobacco, left slave owners with a large amount of underemployed, restless "human property." These factors, along with Native American and Spanish resistance to westward expansion, reinforced nagging uncertainties about the South's future.

The Confederation and the West, 1785–1787

After winning the war against Britain, one of the most formidable challenges confronting the Confederation

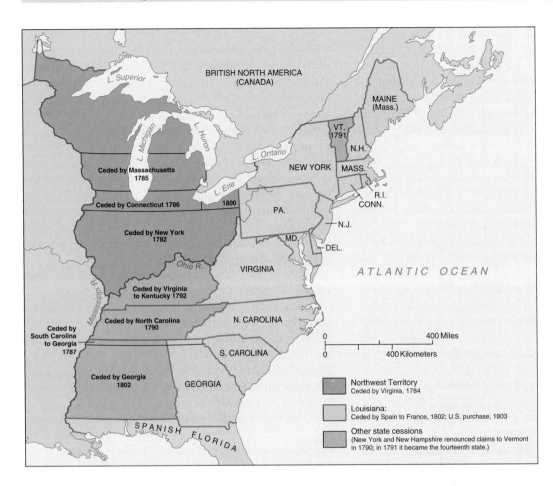

MAP 6.4
State Claims to Western Lands, and State Cessions to the Federal Government, 1782–1802
Eastern states' surrender of land claims paved the way for new state governments in the West. Georgia was the last state to cede its western lands in 1802.

was the postwar settlement and administration of western lands. White American settlers and speculators were determined to possess these lands, and Native Americans were just as determined to keep them out. At the same time, Britain and Spain supported the Indian nations in the hope of strengthening their own positions in North America.

After the states surrendered claims to more than 160 million acres north of the Ohio River, forming the Northwest Territory (see Map 6.4), Congress established uniform procedures for surveying this land in the Ordinance of 1785 (see Map 6.5). The law established a township six miles square as the basic unit of settlement. Every township would be subdivided into thirty-six sections of 640 acres each, one of which would be reserved as a source of income for schools. The Ordinance imposed an arbitrary grid of straight lines and right angles across the landscape that conformed to European-American notions of private property while utterly ignoring the land's natural features. Subsequently, in the Northwest Ordinance of 1787, Congress defined the steps for the

creation and admission of new states. This law designated the area north of the Ohio River as the Northwest Territory and provided for its later division into states. It forbade slavery while the region remained a territory, although the citizens could legalize the institution after statehood.

The Northwest Ordinance outlined three stages for admitting states into the Union. First, during the initial years of settlement, Congress would appoint a territorial governor and judges. Second, as soon as five thousand adult males lived in a territory, voters would approve a temporary constitution and elect a legislature that would pass the territory's laws. Third, when the total population reached sixty thousand, voters would ratify a state constitution, which Congress would have to approve before granting statehood.

The Ordinance of 1785 and the Northwest Ordinance had a lasting effect on later American history. Besides laying out procedures for settling and establishing governments in the Northwest, they later served as models for organizing territories farther west. The

MAP 6.5
The Northwest Territory 1785–1787

The Ordinance of 1785 provided for surveying land into townships of thirty-six sections, each supporting four families on 160-acre plots (approximately twenty-five people per square mile). In 1787 the Northwest Ordinance stipulated that states would ultimately be created in the region.

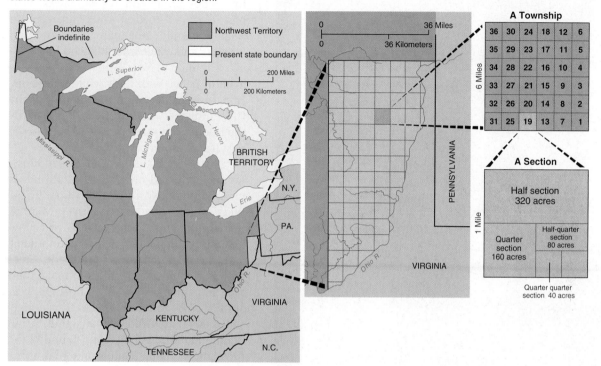

Northwest Ordinance also established a significant precedent for banning slavery from certain territories. But because Native Americans, who were determined to keep out Confederation immigrants, controlled virtually the entire region north of the Ohio River, the ordinances could not be implemented immediately.

The Northwest Territory seemed to offer enough rich land to guarantee future citizens landownership for centuries. This fact satisfied American republicans who feared that the rapidly growing white population would quickly exhaust available land east of the Appalachians and so create a large class of tenants and poor laborers who would lack the property needed to vote. By poisoning politics through class conflict, such a development would undermine the equality among whites that republicans thought essential for a healthy nation.

The realization of these republican dreams was by no means inevitable. Most "available" territory from the Appalachians to the Mississippi River belonged to those peoples whom the Declaration of Independence had condemned as "merciless Indian savages." Divided into more than eighty tribes and numbering perhaps 150,000

people in 1789, these Native Americans were struggling to preserve their own independence. At postwar treaty negotiations, they repeatedly heard Confederation commissioners scornfully declare, "You are a subdued people . . . we claim the country by conquest."

Under threats of continued warfare, some northwestern Indian leaders initially gave in. The Iroquois, who had suffered heavily during the war, lost about half their land in New York and Pennsylvania in the second Treaty of Fort Stanwix (1784). In the treaties of Fort McIntosh (1785) and Fort Finney (1786), Delaware and Shawnee leaders, respectively, were obliged to recognize American sovereignty over their lands. But most Indians reacted with outrage and repudiated these treaties on the grounds that their negotiators lacked the authority to give up territory without their nations' express approval.

Native Americans' resistance to Confederation encroachments also stemmed from their confidence that the British—still a presence in the West—would provide the arms and ammunition they needed to defy the United States. Britain had refused to abandon seven

Joseph Brant, Gilbert Stuart, 1786
The youthful Mohawk leader was a staunch ally of the British during the Revolutionary War, and thereafter resisted U.S. expansion in the Northwest.

northwestern forts within the new nation's boundaries, citing certain states' failure to compensate loyalists for confiscated property and to honor prewar debts owed by citizens. But even before Britain knew about these violations of the peace treaty, its colonial office had secretly ordered the governor of Canada to hold the forts. With Indian support, Britain hoped eventually to reclaim "Ohio country" lands that now lay within the Northwest Territory. The British strengthened their presence in the region by encouraging Canadian traders to exchange cloth, tools, and arms with Native peoples for furs.

The Mohawk Joseph Brant emerged as the initial inspiration behind Indian resistance in the Northwest. Courageous in battle, skillful in diplomacy, and highly educated (he had translated an Anglican prayer book and the Gospel of Mark into Mohawk), Brant became a minor celebrity when he visited King George in London

in 1785. At British-held Fort Detroit in 1786, he helped organize the northwestern Indians into a military alliance to exclude Confederation citizens north of the Ohio River. But Brant and his Mohawks, who had relocated beyond American reach in Canada, could not win support from Senecas and other Iroquois who had chosen to remain in New York, where they now lived in peace with their white neighbors. Nor could he count on the support of the Ohio Indians, who had been betrayed by the Iroquois on numerous occasions in the past (see Chapters 4 and 5).

Seizing on disunity within Indian ranks, Kentuckians and others organized militia raids into the Northwest Territory. These raids gradually forced the Miamis, Shawnees, and Delawares to evacuate southern Indiana and Ohio. The Indians' withdrawal northward, toward the Great Lakes, soon tempted whites to make their first settlements in what is now Ohio. In spring 1788 about fifty New Englanders sailed down the Ohio River in a bulletproof barge named *Mayflower* and founded the town of Marietta. That same year some Pennsylvanians and New Jerseyites established a second community north of the Ohio on the site of modern-day Cincinnati. By then the contest for the Ohio valley was nearing a decisive stage.

The Confederation confronted similar challenges in the Southeast, where Spain and its Indian allies took steps to prevent American settlers from occupying their lands. The Spanish found a brilliant ally in the Creek leader Alexander McGillivray. In some fraudulent treaties, two Creeks had surrendered extensive territory to Georgia that McGillivray intended to regain. Patiently holding back his followers for three years, McGillivray negotiated a secret treaty in which Spain promised weapons so that the Creeks could protect themselves "from the Bears and other fierce Animals." When the Creeks finally attacked in 1786, they shrewdly expelled only those whites occupying disputed lands and then offered Georgia a cease-fire. Eager to avoid voting taxes for a costly war, Georgia politicians let the Creeks keep the land.

Spain also sought to prevent American infiltration by denying western settlers permission to ship their crops down the Mississippi River to New Orleans.

Having negotiated a separate treaty with Britain (see above), Spain had not signed the Peace of Paris, by which Britain promised the United States export rights down the Mississippi, and in 1784 the Spanish closed New Orleans to Anglo-American commerce. To negotiate trading privileges at New Orleans, the United States sent John Jay to Spain. Jay returned in 1786 with a treaty that opened up valuable Spanish markets to eastern merchants and renounced Spanish claims to disputed southwestern lands—at the cost, however, of relinquishing American export rights through New Orleans for another twenty years. Westerners and southerners charged that this Jay-Gardoqui Treaty sacrificed their interests to benefit northern commerce, and Congress rejected it.

Toward a New Constitution, 1786–1788

After six years under the Articles of Confederation, the United States had made enormous strides in establishing itself as an independent nation. But impatience with the national government's limitations continued to grow among those seeking to establish the Republic on a more solid financial and military footing. Impatience turned to anxiety after Massachusetts farmers defied local authorities in protesting measures that would worsen their already severe economic circumstances. A national convention called to consider amendments to the Articles instead proposed a radical new frame of government, the Constitution. In 1788 the states ratified the Constitution, setting a new course for America.

Shays's Rebellion, 1786–1787

The Jay-Gardoqui Treaty revealed deep-seated tensions that lay just beneath the surface appearance of American national unity. The depression that had begun in 1784 persisted in New England, which had never recovered from the loss of its prime export market in the British West Indies. With farmers already squeezed financially, the state legislature, dominated by commercially minded elites, voted early in 1786 to pay off its Revolutionary debt in three years. This ill-considered policy necessitated a huge tax hike. Meanwhile, the state's unfavorable balance of payments with Britain had produced a shortage of specie (gold and silver coin) because British creditors refused any other currency. Fearing a flood of worthless paper notes, Massachusetts bankers and merchants insisted that they, too, be paid in specie, while the state mandated the same for payment of taxes. Lowest in this cycle of debt were thousands of small family farmers.

In contrast, the mid-Atlantic and southern states were emerging from the depression, thanks to rising tobacco and food exports to Europe. Taxpayers in these sections, moreover, were paying off war debts easily, and most were indifferent to national politics.

Despite the nation's prosperity outside New England, a growing minority of nationalists was dissatisfied

General Daniel Shays, Col. Joseph Shattuck, 1787
An anti-Shays cartoonist depicts Shays and a key supporter as bogus military officers who sought power and threatened the people's liberty.

with the Confederation. Merchants and shippers wanted a central government powerful enough to secure trading privileges for them abroad, and to ensure economic stability and America's standing in the Atlantic economy, still dominated by Britain. Land speculators and western settlers, on the other hand, preferred a government that would pursue a more activist policy against Spain, Britain, and Native Americans in the West. Meanwhile, urban artisans hoped for a stronger national government that would impose a uniformly high tariff and thereby protect them from foreign competition.

Perhaps not surprisingly, the spark that ignited this tinderbox originated in Massachusetts. The plight of that state's farmers was especially severe in the western part of the state, where agriculture was least profitable. Facing demands that they pay their debts and taxes in hard currency, which few of them had in abundance if at all, farmers held public meetings. As in similar meetings more than a decade earlier, they discussed "the Suppressing of tyrannical government;" referring this time to the Massachusetts government rather than the British. In 1786 in a move reminiscent of pre-Revolutionary backcountry dissidents (see Chapter 5), farmer and former Revolutionary War officer Daniel Shays led two thousand angry men in an attempt to shut down the courts in three western counties. The Shaysites hoped thereby to stop sheriffs' auctions for unpaid taxes and prevent foreclosures on farm mortgages. Although routed by state troops after several skirmishes, sympathizers of Shays won control of the Massachusetts legislature in 1787, cut taxes, and secured a pardon for their leader.

The Shaysites had limited objectives, were dispersed with relatively little bloodshed, and never seriously threatened anarchy. But their uprising, and similar but less militant movements in other states, became the rallying cry for advocates of a stronger central government. By threatening to seize weapons from a federal arsenal at Springfield, Massachusetts, the farmers' movement unintentionally enabled nationalists to argue that the United States had become vulnerable to "mobocracy." Writing to Henry Knox for news from Massachusetts, an anxious George Washington worried that "there are combustibles in every state, which a spark might set fire to," destroying the Republic. Meanwhile, rumors were flying that the Spanish had offered export rights at New Orleans to westerners if they would secede from the Union. Nationalists sowed fears that the United States was on the verge of coming apart.

Instead of igniting a popular uprising, as Washington feared, Shays's Rebellion sparked aggressive nationalists into pushing for a wholesale reform of the Republic's legal and institutional structure. Shortly before the outbreak of the rebellion, delegates from five states had assembled at Annapolis, Maryland. They had intended to discuss means of promoting interstate commerce but instead called for a general convention to propose amendments to the Articles of Confederation. Accepting their suggestion, Congress asked the states to appoint delegations to meet in Philadelphia.

The Philadelphia Convention, 1787

In May 1787 fifty-five delegates from every state but Rhode Island began gathering at the Pennsylvania State House in Philadelphia, later known as Independence Hall. Among them were established figures like George Washington and Benjamin Franklin, as well as talented newcomers such as Alexander Hamilton and James Madison. Most were wealthy and in their thirties or forties, and nineteen owned slaves. More than half had legal training.

The convention immediately closed its sessions to the press and the public, kept no official journal, and even appointed chaperones to accompany the aged and talkative Franklin to dinner parties lest he disclose details of what was happening. Although these measures opened the members of the convention to the charge of acting undemocratically and conspiratorially, the delegates thought secrecy essential to ensure freedom of debate without fear of criticism from home.

The delegates shared a "continental" or "nationalist" perspective, instilled through their extended involvement with the national government. Thirty-nine had sat in Congress, where they had seen the Confederation's weaknesses firsthand. In the postwar years, they had become convinced that unless the national government was freed from the control of more popularly and locally oriented state legislatures, the country would fall victim to foreign aggression or simply disintegrate.

The convention faced two basic issues. The first was whether to tinker with the Articles of Confederation, as the state legislatures had formally instructed the delegates to do, or to replace the Articles altogether with a new constitution that gave more power to the national government. The second fundamental question was how to balance the conflicting interests of large and small states. James Madison of Virginia, who had entered Congress in 1780 at twenty-nine, proposed an answer to each issue. Despite his youth and almost frail build, Madison commanded enormous respect for his

profound knowledge of history and the passionate intensity he brought to debates.

Madison's Virginia Plan, introduced in late May, boldly called for the establishment of a strong central government rather than a federation of states. Madison's blueprint gave Congress virtually unrestricted rights of legislation and taxation, the power to veto any state law, and authority to use military force against the states. As one delegate immediately saw, the Virginia Plan was designed "to abolish the State Govern[men]ts altogether." The Virginia Plan specified a bicameral legislature and fixed representation in both houses of Congress proportionally to each state's population. The voters would elect the lower house, which would then choose delegates to the upper chamber from nominations submitted by the legislatures. Both houses would jointly name the country's president and judges.

Madison's scheme aroused immediate opposition, however, especially his call for state representation according to population—a provision highly favorable to his own Virginia. On June 15 William Paterson of New Jersey offered a counterproposal, the so-called New Jersey Plan, which recommended a single-chamber congress in which each state had an equal vote, just as under the Articles.

The two plans exposed the convention's great stumbling block: the question of representation. The Virginia Plan would have given the four largest states a majority in both houses. The New Jersey Plan would have allowed the seven smallest states, which included just 25 percent of all Americans, to control Congress. By July 2 the convention had arrived "at a full stop," as one delegate put it. To end the impasse, the delegates assigned a member from each state to a "grand committee" dedicated to compromise. The panel adopted a proposal offered earlier by the Connecticut delegation: an equal vote for each state in the upper house and proportional voting in the lower house. Madison and the Virginians doggedly fought this so-called Connecticut Compromise, but they were voted down on July 17.

Despite their differences over representation, Paterson's and Madison's proposals alike would have strengthened the national government at the states' expense. No less than Madison, Paterson wished to empower Congress to raise taxes, regulate interstate commerce, and use military force against the states. The New Jersey Plan, in fact, defined congressional laws and treaties as the "supreme law of the land" and would also have established courts to force reluctant states to accept these measures. But other delegates were wary of

James Madison
Although one of the Philadelphia convention's youngest delegates, Madison of Virginia was among its most politically astute. He played a central role in the Constitution's adoption.

undermining the sovereignty of the states altogether. Out of hard bargaining emerged the Constitution's delicate balance between the desire of nearly all delegates for a stronger national government and their fear that governments tended to grow despotic.

As finally approved on September 17, 1787, the Constitution of the United States (see Appendix) was an extraordinary document, and not merely because it reconciled the conflicting interests of the large and small states. The new frame of government augmented national authority in several ways. Although it did not incorporate Madison's proposal to give Congress a veto over state laws, it vested in Congress the authority to lay and collect taxes, to regulate interstate commerce, and to conduct diplomacy. States could no longer coin money, interfere with contracts and debts, or tax interstate commerce. Following the New Jersey Plan, all acts and treaties of the United States became "the supreme law of the land." All state officials had to swear to uphold the Constitution, even against acts of their own states. The national government could use military force

against any state. These provisions added up to a complete abandonment of the principle on which the Articles of Confederation had rested: that the United States was a federation of states, with ultimate authority concentrated in their legislatures.

To allay the concerns of more moderate delegates, the Constitution's framers devised two means of restraining the power of the new central government. First, in keeping with republican political theory, they established three distinct branches—executive, legislative, and judicial—within the national government; and second, they designed a system of checks and balances to prevent any one branch from dominating the other two. The framers systematically applied to the national government the principle of a functional separation of powers, as it had been evolving in the states since about 1780. In the bicameral Congress, states' equal representation in the Senate was offset by the proportional representation, by population, in the House; and each chamber could block measures approved by the other. Furthermore, where the state constitutions had deliberately weakened the executive, the Constitution gave the president the power to veto acts of Congress; but to prevent capricious use of the veto, Congress could override the president by a two-thirds majority in each house. The president could conduct diplomacy, but only the Senate could ratify treaties. The president named his cabinet, but only with Senate approval. The president and all his appointees could be removed from office by a joint vote of Congress, but only for "high crimes," not for political disagreements.

To further ensure the independence of each branch, the Constitution provided that the members of one branch would not choose those of another, except for judges, whose independence was protected by lifetime appointment. For example, the president was to be selected by an electoral college, whose members the states would select as their legislatures saw fit. The state legislatures also elected the members of the Senate, whereas the election of delegates to the House of Representatives was achieved by direct popular vote.

In addition to checks and balances, the founders devised a system of shared power and dual lawmaking by the national and state governments—"federalism"—in order to place limits on central authority. Not only did the state legislatures have a key role in electing the president and senators, but the Constitution could be amended by the votes of three-fourths of the states. Thus, the convention departed sharply from Madison's plan to establish a "consolidated" national government entirely independent of, and superior to, the states.

A key assumption behind federalism was that the national government would limit its activities to foreign affairs, national defense, regulating interstate commerce, and coining money. Most other political matters were left to the states. Regarding slavery in particular, each state retained full authority.

The dilemma confronting the Philadelphia convention centered not on whether slavery should be allowed in the new Republic but only on the much narrower question of whether slaves could be counted as persons when it came to determining a state's representation at the national level. For most legal purposes, slaves were regarded not as persons but rather as the chattel property of their owners, meaning that they were on a par with other living property such as horses and cattle. But southern states saw their large numbers of slaves as a means of augmenting their numbers in the House of Representatives and in the electoral colleges that would elect the nation's presidents every four years. So strengthened, they could prevent northerners from ever abolishing slavery.

Representing states that had begun ending slavery, northern delegates hesitated to give southern states a political advantage by allowing them to count people who had no civil or political rights. But as property owners themselves, northern delegates were also hesitant to question southern planters' notions of property rights, no matter what form the property took. Southerners also played on northern fears of disunion. After Georgia and South Carolina threatened to secede if their demands were not met, northerners agreed to allow three-fifths of all slaves to be counted for congressional representation. "Great as the evil [of slavery] is," Madison warned, "a dismemberment of the union would be worse."

The Constitution also reinforced slavery in other ways. Most notably, it forbade citizens of any state, even those which had abolished slavery, to prevent the return of escaped slaves to another state. The Constitution limited slavery only to the extent of permitting Congress to ban the importation of slaves after 1808, and by not repudiating Congress's earlier ban on slavery in the Northwest Territory.

Although leaving much authority to the states, the Constitution established a national government clearly superior to the states in several spheres, and it utterly abandoned the notion of a federation of virtually independent states. Having thus strengthened national authority, the convention had to face the issue of ratifi-

cation. For two reasons, it seemed unwise to submit the Constitution to state legislatures for ratification. First, the framers realized that the state legislatures would reject the Constitution, which shrank their power relative to the national government. Second, most of the framers repudiated the idea—implicit in ratification by state legislatures—that the states were the foundation of the new government. The opening words of the Constitution, "We the People of the United States," underlined the delegates' conviction that the government had to be based on the consent of the American people themselves, "the fountain of all power" in Madison's words.

In the end, the Philadelphia convention provided for the Constitution's ratification by special state conventions composed of delegates elected by the voters. Approval by only nine such conventions would put the new government in operation. Because any state refusing to ratify the Constitution would remain under the Articles, the possibility existed that the country might divide into two nations.

Under the Constitution the framers expected the nation's "natural aristocracy" to continue exercising political leadership; but did they also intend to rein in the democratic currents set in motion by the Revolution? In one respect they did, by curtailing what most nationalists considered the excessive power of popularly elected state legislatures. But the Constitution made no attempt to control faction and disorder by suppressing liberty—a "remedy," wrote Madison, that would be "worse than the disease." The framers did provide for one crucial democratic element in the new government, the House of Representatives. Equally important, the Constitution recognized the American people as the ultimate source of political legitimacy. Moreover, by making the Constitution flexible and amendable (though not easily amendable) and by dividing political power among competing branches of government, the framers made it possible for the national government to be slowly democratized, in ways unforeseen in 1787, without turning into a tyranny of ideologues or temporary majorities. Madison eloquently expressed the founders' intention of controlling the dangers inherent in any society:

> If men were angels, no government would be necessary. If angels were to govern men, neither external nor internal controls on government would be necessary. In framing a government which is to be administered by men over men, the great difficulty lies in this: You must first enable the

government to control the governed; and in the next place, oblige it to control itself. A dependence on the people is no doubt the primary control on the government; but experience has taught mankind the necessity of external precautions.

The Struggle over Ratification, 1787–1788

The Constitution's supporters began the campaign for ratification without significant national support. Most Americans had expected the Philadelphia convention to offer only limited amendments to the Articles of Confederation, and therefore hesitated to endorse a radical proposal to restructure the government. Undaunted, the Constitution's friends moved decisively to marshal political support. In a clever stroke, they called themselves "Federalists," a term implying that the Constitution would more nearly balance the relationship between the national and state governments, and thereby undermined the arguments of those hostile to a centralization of national authority.

The Constitution's opponents commonly became known as "Antifederalists." This negative-sounding title probably hurt them, for it did not convey the crux of their argument against the Constitution—that it was not "federalist" at all since it failed to balance the power of the national and state governments. By augmenting national authority, Antifederalists maintained, the Constitution would ultimately doom the states.

The Antifederalist arguments reflected a deep-seated Anglo-American suspicion of concentrated power, expressed from the time of the Stamp Act crisis through the War of Independence and during the framing of the first state constitutions and the Articles of Confederation. Unquestionably, the Constitution gave the national government unprecedented authority in an age when most writers on politics taught that the primary means of preventing despotism was to restrain the power of government officials. Compared to a distant national government, Antifederalists argued, state governments were far more responsive to the popular will. True, the framers had guarded against tyranny by preserving limited state powers and devising a system of checks and balances, but no one could be certain that the untried scheme would work. To Mercy Otis Warren, the proposed government was "of such motley mixture that its enemies cannot trace a feature of Democratick or Republican extract," and one that would "have passed through the short period of its existence without

a name, had not Mr. [James] Wilson . . . suggested the happy epithet of a *Federal Republic*." For all its checks and balances, in addition, the Constitution nowhere contained ironclad guarantees that the new government would protect the liberties of individuals or the states. The absence of a bill of rights made an Antifederalist of Madison's nationalist ally and fellow Virginian George Mason, the author of the first such state bill in 1776.

Although the Antifederalists advanced some formidable arguments, they confronted a number of disadvantages in publicizing their cause. While Antifederalist ranks included prominent figures, among them Patrick Henry, Richard Henry Lee, and Mercy Otis Warren, the Federalists claimed most of the country's wealthiest and most honored men. No Antifederalist had the stature of George Washington or Benjamin Franklin. Moreover, most American newspapers were pro-Constitution and did not hesitate to bias their reporting in favor of the Federalist cause. Finally, as state and local leaders, the Antifederalists lacked their opponents' contacts and experience at the national level, acquired through service in the officer corps of the Continental Army or in Congress.

The Federalists' advantages in funds and political organizing proved decisive. The Antifederalists failed to create a sense of urgency among their supporters, assuming incorrectly that a large majority would rally to them. Only one-quarter of the voters turned out to elect delegates to the state ratifying conventions, however, and most had been mobilized by Federalists.

Federalist delegates prevailed in eight conventions between December 1787 and May 1788, in all cases except one by margins of at least two-thirds. Such lopsided votes reflected the Federalists' organizational skills and aggressiveness rather than the degree of popular support for the Constitution. Advocates of the new plan of government did indeed ram through approval in some states "before it can be digested or deliberately considered," in the words of a Pennsylvania Antifederalist. Only Rhode Island and North Carolina rejected the Constitution and thus refused to join the new United States.

But unless Virginia and New York—two of the largest states—ratified, the new government would be fatally weakened. In both states (and elsewhere) Antifederalist sentiment ran high among small farmers, who saw the Constitution as a scheme favoring city dwellers and moneyed interests (see Map 6.6). Prominent political leaders in these two states who called for refusing ratifi-

cation included New York Governor George Clinton and Virginia's Richard Henry Lee, George Mason, Patrick Henry, and future president James Monroe.

The Constitution became the law of the land on June 21, 1788, when the ninth state, New Hampshire, ratified by the close vote of 57 to 47. At that moment debate was still under way in the Virginia convention. The Federalists won crucial support from the representatives of the Allegheny counties—modern West Virginia—who wanted a strong national government capable of ending Indian raids across the Ohio River. Western Virginians' votes, combined with James Madison's logic and growing support for the Constitution among tidewater planters, proved too much for Henry's spellbinding oratory. On June 25 the Virginia delegates ratified by a narrow 53 percent majority.

The struggle was even closer and more hotly contested in New York. Antifederalists had solid control of the state convention and would probably have voted down the Constitution, but then news arrived of New Hampshire's and Virginia's ratifications. The Federalist forces, led by Alexander Hamilton and John Jay, spread rumors that if the convention voted to reject, pro-Federalist New York City and adjacent counties would secede from the state and join the Union alone, leaving upstate New York a landlocked enclave. When several Antifederalist delegates took alarm at this threat and switched sides, New York ratified on July 26 by a 30 to 27 vote.

So the Antifederalists went down in defeat, and they did not survive as a political movement. Yet they left an important legacy. At their insistence, the Virginia, New York, and Massachusetts conventions ratified the Constitution with the accompanying request that the new charter be amended to include a bill of rights protecting Americans' basic freedoms. So widespread was the public demand for a bill of rights that it became an inevitable item on the new government's agenda, even as the states were choosing members of Congress and as presidential electors were unanimously designating George Washington president of the United States.

Antifederalists' objections in New York also stimulated a response in the form of one of the great classics of political thought, *The Federalist*, a series of eighty-five newspaper essays penned by Alexander Hamilton, James Madison, and John Jay. The Federalist papers probably had little or no influence on voting in the New York State convention. Rather, their importance lay in articulating arguments for the Constitution that addressed Americans' wide-ranging concerns about the

MAP 6.6
Federalist and Antifederalist Strongholds, 1787–1790

Federalists drew their primary backing from densely populated areas along major transportation routes, where trade, mobility, and frequent contact with people in other states encouraged a nationalistic identity. Antifederalist support came from interior regions where geographic isolation bred a localistic perspective. However, some westerners, especially in Georgia and western Virginia, voted for a strong central government that would push back the Indians or the Spanish.

powers and limits of the new federal government, thereby shaping a new philosophy of government. The Constitution, insisted *The Federalist's* authors, had a twofold purpose: first, to defend the minority's rights against majority tyranny; and second, to prevent a stubborn minority from blocking well-considered measures that the majority believed necessary for the national interest. Critics, argued *The Federalist*, had no reason to fear that the Constitution would allow a single economic or regional interest to dominate. In the most profound essay in the series, *Federalist* No. 10, Madison rejected the Antifederalist argument that establishing a republic for a nation as large as the United States would unleash a chaotic contest for power and ultimately leave the majority exploited by a minority. "Extend the sphere," Madison insisted, "and . . . you make it less probable that a majority of the whole will have a common motive to invade the rights of other citizens, . . . [or will be able to] act in unison with each other." The country's very size and diversity would neutralize the attempts of factions to push unwise laws through Congress.

Madison's analysis was far too optimistic, however. As the Antifederalists predicted, the Constitution afforded enormous scope for special interests to influence the government. The great challenge for Madison's generation would be how to maintain a government that would provide equal benefits to all and at the same time accord special privileges to none.

CHRONOLOGY, 1776–1788

1776 American victory in Battle of Trenton.
Cherokees attack North Carolina frontier.

1777 British General John Burgoyne surrenders at Saratoga.
Congress approves Articles of Confederation.

1778 France formally recognizes the United States; declares war on Britain.
American victory in Battle of Monmouth Court House.
Iroquois attacks in western Pennsylvania and New York.

1779 Spain declares war on Britain.
George Rogers Clark recaptures Vincennes.
John Sullivan leads American raids in Iroquois country.

1780 British seize Charles Town.

1781 Articles of Confederation become law.
Battle of Yorktown; British General Cornwallis surrenders.

1782 Rhode Island rejects national import duty.

1783 Peace of Paris.
Newburgh Conspiracy.

1784 Spain closes New Orleans to American trade.
Economic depression begins.
Second Treaty of Fort Stanwix.

1785 Ordinance of 1785.
Treaty of Fort McIntosh.

1786 Congress rejects Jay-Gardoqui Treaty.
Treaty of Fort Finney.
Joseph Brant organizes Indian resistance to U.S. expansion.
Virginia adopts Thomas Jefferson's Statute for Religious Freedom.

1786–1787 Shays's Rebellion in Massachusetts.

1787 Northwest Ordinance.
Philadelphia Convention frames federal Constitution.

1787–1788 Alexander Hamilton, James Madison, and John Jay, *The Federalist*.

1788 Federal Constitution ratified.

CONCLUSION

The entry of North Carolina into the Union in late 1789 and of Rhode Island in May 1790 marked the final triumph of the uncertain nationalism born of the War for Independence. The devastating eight-year conflict swept up half of all men of military age and made casualties of one-fifth of these. Among whites, blacks, and Native Americans alike, the conflict was a civil war as well as a war for independence from Great Britain. The fighting also affected large numbers of civilians because it took place in America's cities, towns, and countryside, and because troops needed provisions and other forms of local support. Never before had so many Americans participated together in an event of such magnitude.

Winning the war proved to be only the first step in establishing a new American nation. Establishing new governments at the state and national levels was just as challenging, for Americans were deeply divided over how to strike a proper balance between power and liberty and between national and state sovereignty. For a decade, conflicts between competing political visions were played out in the protracted debates over several state constitutions and, most decisively, in the efforts to frame and ratify the new federal Constitution. The Constitution struck careful balances on these and many other questions and definitely limited democracy; but by locating sovereignty in the people it created a legal and institutional framework within which Americans could struggle to attain democracy. In that way its conception was a fundamental moment in the history of America's enduring vision.

FOR FURTHER REFERENCE

READINGS

Colin G. Calloway, *The American Revolution in Indian Country: Crisis and Diversity in Native American Communities* (1995). A powerful set of case studies examining eight Indian communities from Canada to Florida and showing the variety of Native American experiences during and immediately after the Revolution.

Stephen Conway, *The British Isles and the War for American Independence* (2000). A thorough study of the effect on Britain and Ireland of the war in America.

Saul Cornell, *The Other Founders: Anti-Federalism and the Dissenting Tradition in America, 1788–1828* (1999). The definitive study of opponents to ratification of the Constitution and their continuing influence on politics during the early Republic.

Elizabeth A. Fenn, *Pox Americana: The Great Smallpox Epidemic of 1775–82* (2001). A pathbreaking study arguing for the importance of smallpox in shaping the Revolutionary War as well as Native American-European conflicts across the continent.

Sylvia R. Frey, *Water from the Rock: Black Resistance in a Revolutionary Age* (1991). A major study of southern African-Americans during and after the Revolution.

Linda K. Kerber, *Women of the Republic: Intellect and Ideology in Revolutionary America* (1980). A pathbreaking discussion of women and of ideologies of gender during the Revolutionary and early republican eras.

Robert Middlekauff, *The Glorious Cause: The American Revolution, 1763–1789* (1982). A narrative of military and political developments through the ratification of the Constitution.

Jack N. Rakove, *Original Meanings: Politics and Ideas in the Making of the Constitution* (1996). A thorough study of the Constitution's framing, rooted in historical context.

Charles Royster, *A Revolutionary People at War: The Continental Army and American Character* (1980). An illuminating analysis of how Revolutionary Americans created and fought in an army.

Gordon S. Wood, *The Radicalism of the American Revolution* (1991). A sweeping interpretation of the Revolution's long-range effect on American society.

WEBSITES

Liberty! The American Revolution
http://www.pbs.org/ktca/liberty/
An elaborate site offering perspectives on major events from the Seven Years' War to the adoption of the Bill of Rights and featuring dozens of links to related sites.

A Multitude of Amendments, Alterations, and Additions
http://www.cr.nps.gov/history/inde1.htm
A part of the site for Independence National Historical Park that examines the drafting and promulgating of three major founding documents—the Declaration of Independence, the Articles of Confederation, and the Constitution.

Religion and the Founding of the American Republic
http://lcweb.loc.gov/exhibits/religion/religion.html
Based on an exhibit at the Library of Congress, this site provides many insights on the relationship between religion and the Revolution and on church-state relations under the new state and national governments.

For additional works please consult the bibliography at the end of the book.

CHAPTER 7

Launching the New Republic, 1789–1800

Early in 1789 a mysterious stranger from New Orleans named André Fagot appeared in Nashville, Tennessee. Fagot was officially there to talk business with local merchants, but in reality he was a Spanish agent sent to exploit discontent. For years, westerners had agonized over the American government's failure to win Spanish permission for them to export crops through New Orleans, without which their settlements would never flourish. Fagot made westerners a tempting offer—unrestricted export privileges at New Orleans, which promised to ensure them prosperity. But in return they would have to request that Spain annex Tennessee to its Louisiana colony.

Fagot found many local residents willing to discuss becoming Spanish subjects. One of his more enthusiastic contacts was a young lawyer recently arrived from the Carolinas. Aware that poor communities could support only poor lawyers, the Carolinian was irresistibly drawn to the plot. Learning that Spain would give valuable land grants in the lower Mississippi valley to anyone who renounced U.S. citizenship, the lawyer began visiting Louisiana regularly to investigate settling there. Fagot probably placed little reliance on this brash conspirator, who had a wild temper and a reputation for gambling and drinking, and who seemed just another western opportunist. The obscure lawyer's name was Andrew Jackson.

◀ **Judith Sargent Stevens (Murray)** by John Singleton Copley, c. 1770
Drawing on discussions then going on in Europe, Judith Sargent Murray became the foremost advocate of womens's rights at the end of the eighteenth century.

CHAPTER OUTLINE

Constitutional Government Takes Shape, 1789–1796

Hamilton and the Formulation of Federalist Policies, 1789–1994

The United States on the World Stage, 1789–1796

The Emergence of Party Politics, 1793–1800

Economic and Social Change

The fact that a future patriot and president such as Jackson was talking secession with the Spanish underscores the fragility of the United States in 1789, the year of George Washington's first inauguration. North Carolina (which controlled Tennessee territory) and Rhode Island had not yet joined the Union. Thousands of western settlers appeared to be abandoning the new government. Native Americans and their Spanish and British allies were effectively challenging the United States' claims to western territories. The development of American economic power was severely limited by foreign restrictions on U.S. exports and by the government's inability to obtain credit abroad.

During the 1790s Americans fought bitterly over the social and economic course their new nation should take, and these conflicts merged with the dissension between Americans loyal to revolutionary France and those favoring its British opponents. By 1798 voters had divided into two parties, each of which accused the other of threatening republican liberty. Only when the election of 1800 had been settled—by the narrowest of margins—could it be said that the United States had managed to avoid dissolution.

This chapter focuses on four major questions:

■ What were the principal features of Hamilton's economic program, and what were its opponents' primary objections?

■ Why was the United States at odds with Spain, Britain, and France at various times at the end of the eighteenth century?

■ What principal issues divided Federalists and Republicans in the presidential election of 1800?

■ What were the primary factors contributing to the declining status and welfare of nonwhites in the new Republic?

CONSTITUTIONAL GOVERNMENT TAKES SHAPE, 1789-1796

Traveling slowly over the nation's miserable roads, the men entrusted with launching the federal experiment began assembling in New York, the new national capital, in March 1789. Because so few members were on hand, Congress opened its session a month late. George Washington did not arrive until April 23 and took his oath of office a week later.

The slowness of these first steps disguised the seriousness of the tasks at hand. The country's elected leaders had to make far-reaching decisions on several critical questions left unresolved by the Constitution's framers. "We are in a wilderness," wrote James Madison, "without a footstep to guide us."

Defining the Presidency

No office in the new government aroused more suspicion than the presidency. Many feared that the president's powers could make him a virtual king. Public apprehension remained in check only because of George Washington's reputation for honesty. Washington tried to calm fears of unlimited executive power.

The Constitution mentioned the executive departments only in passing, required the president to obtain the Senate's "advice and consent" to his nominees to head these bureaus, and made all executive personnel liable to impeachment. Otherwise, Congress was free to determine the organization and accountability of what became known as the cabinet. The first cabinet, established by Congress, consisted of four departments, headed by the secretaries of state, treasury, and war and by the attorney general. Vice President John Adams's tie-breaking vote defeated a proposal that would have forbidden the president from dismissing cabinet officers without Senate approval. This outcome reinforced the president's authority to make and carry out policy; it also separated the powers of the executive and legislative branches beyond what the Constitution required, and so made the president a more equal partner with Congress.

President Washington proposed few laws to Congress and generally limited his public statements to matters of foreign relations and military affairs. He generally deferred to congressional decisions concerning domestic policy and cast only two vetoes during his eight-year tenure (1789–1797).

Washington tried to reassure the public that he was above favoritism and conflicts of interest. Accordingly, he strove to understand the aspirations of the two groups that dominated American society—northeastern merchants and entrepreneurs, and southern planters—and he balanced his cabinet between them. Eventually, when Secretary of State Thomas Jefferson opposed certain policies of Secretary of the Treasury Alexander Hamilton, Washington implored Jefferson not to leave his post, even though the president supported Hamilton. Like most republican elites, Washington believed that the proper role for ordinary citizens was not to set policy through elections but rather to choose

George Washington's Inaugural Journey Through Trenton, 1789
Washington received a warm welcome in Trenton, site of his first victory during the Revolutionary War.

well-educated, politically sophisticated men who would make laws in the people's best interest, though independently of direct popular influence.

The president endured rather than enjoyed the pomp of office. Suffering from a variety of ailments that grew as the years passed, Washington longed to escape the presidency and Philadelphia (the nation's capital from 1790 to 1800). Only with difficulty was he persuaded to accept reelection in 1792. He dreaded dying while in office and thus setting the precedent for a lifetime presidency. With great anxiety he realized that "the preservation of the sacred fire of liberty and the destiny of the republican model of government are . . . deeply, perhaps finally, staked on the experiment entrusted to the hands of the American people." Should he contribute to that experiment's failure, he feared, his name would live only as an "awful monument."

National Justice and the Bill of Rights

The Constitution authorized Congress to establish federal courts below the level of the Supreme Court, but it offered no guidance in structuring a judicial system. Nor did it go far in protecting citizens' individual rights. The Constitution did bar the federal government from committing such abuses as passing ex post facto laws (criminalizing previously legal actions and then punishing those who had engaged in them) and bills of attainder (proclaiming a person's guilt and stipulating punishment without a trial). Nevertheless, the absence of a comprehensive bill of rights had led several delegates at Philadelphia to refuse to sign the Constitution and had been a condition of several states' ratification of the new frame of government. The task of filling in these gaps fell to the First Congress.

In 1789 many citizens feared that the new federal courts would ride roughshod over local customs. Every state had gradually devised its own time-honored blend of judicial procedures. Any attempt to force states to abandon their legal heritages would have produced strong counterdemands that federal justice be narrowly restricted.

In passing the Judiciary Act of 1789, Congress managed to quiet popular apprehensions by establishing in each state a federal district court that operated according

to local procedures. As the Constitution stipulated, the Supreme Court exercised final jurisdiction. Congress had struck a compromise between nationalists and states' rights advocates, one that respected state traditions while offering wide access to federal justice.

Behind the movement for a bill of rights lay Americans' long-standing fear that a strong central government would lead to tyranny. Many Antifederalists believed that the best defense against tyranny would be to strengthen the powers of state governments at the expense of the federal government, but many more Americans wanted the Constitution to guarantee basic personal liberties to all American citizens. James Madison, who had been elected to the House of Representatives, played the leading role in drafting the ten amendments that became known as the Bill of Rights (see Appendix).

Madison insisted that the first eight amendments guarantee personal liberties, not strip the national government of any necessary authority. The First Amendment guaranteed the most fundamental freedoms of expression—religion, speech, press, and political activity—against federal interference. The Second Amendment ensured that "a well-regulated militia" would preserve the nations' security by guaranteeing "the right of the people to bear arms." Along with the Third Amendment, it sought to protect citizens from what eighteenth-century Britons and Americans alike considered the most sinister embodiment of tyrannical power: standing armies. The Fourth through Eighth Amendments limited the police powers of the state by guaranteeing individuals' fair treatment in legal and judicial proceedings. The Ninth and Tenth Amendments reserved to the people or to the states powers not allocated to the federal government under the Constitution, but Madison headed off proposals to limit federal power more explicitly. In general, the Bill of Rights imposed no serious check on the framers' nationalist objectives.

Once the Bill of Rights was ratified by the states in December 1791, the federal judiciary moved decisively to establish its authority. In 1793, in *Chisholm* v. *Georgia*, the Supreme Court ruled that a state could be sued in federal courts by nonresidents. But Congress decided that the Court had encroached too far on states' authority in *Chisholm*; in 1794 it voted to overturn this decision through a constitutional amendment. Ratified in 1798, the Eleventh Amendment revised Article III, Section 2, so that private citizens could no longer use federal courts to sue another state's government in civil cases. The defeat of *Chisholm* stands as one of the handful of instances in American history in which the Supreme Court was subsequently overruled by a constitutional amendment.

In endorsing the Eleventh Amendment, Congress sought to limit federal power vis-à-vis that of the states, delivering another blow to the nationalist coalition that had written the Constitution, secured its ratification, and dominated the First Congress. The catalyst of this split was Alexander Hamilton, whose bold program raised fears that federal policies could be shaped to reward special interests.

HAMILTON AND THE FORMULATION OF FEDERALIST POLICIES, 1789–1794

Washington's reluctance to become involved with pending legislation and with domestic affairs enabled his energetic secretary of the treasury, Alexander Hamilton, to set many of the administration's priorities. Hamilton quickly emerged as an imaginative and dynamic statesman with a sweeping program for strengthening the federal government and promoting economic development.

Hamilton and His Objectives

Born on the British Caribbean island of Nevis in 1755, Hamilton had sailed to New York in 1772 and entered the Continental Army in 1775. Serving on Washington's staff, the brilliant Hamilton gained extraordinary influence over Washington. Born outside the thirteen colonies, he felt little identification with his adopted state, New York, or any other American locale. His background likewise reinforced his insensitivity to Americans' concerns for liberty and fears of centralized authority.

In Hamilton's mind, the most immediate danger facing the United States concerned the possibility of war with Britain, Spain, or both. The Republic could finance a major war only by borrowing heavily, but because Congress under the Confederation had not assumed responsibility for the Revolutionary debt, the nation's credit was weakened abroad and at home.

Hamilton also feared that the Union might disintegrate because of Americans' tendency to think first of their local loyalties and interests. For him, the Constitution's adoption had been a close victory of national over state authority. Now he worried that the states might reassert power over the new government. If this happened, he doubted whether the nation could

prevent ruinous trade discrimination between states, deter foreign aggression, and avoid civil war.

Both his wartime experiences and his view of human nature forged Hamilton's political beliefs. Like many nationalists, he believed that the American people were incapable of displaying consistent self-sacrifice and virtue. Hamilton concluded that the federal government's survival depended not on building popular support but by cultivating politically influential citizens through a straightforward appeal to their financial interests. Private ambitions would then serve the national welfare.

Charming and brilliant, vain and handsome, a notorious womanizer, and thirsting for fame and power, Hamilton himself exemplified the worldly citizen whose fortunes he hoped to link to the Republic's future. But to his opponents, Hamilton embodied the dark forces luring the Republic to its doom—a man who, Jefferson wrote, believed in "the necessity of either force or corruption to govern men."

Report on the Public Credit, 1790

Dominated by nationalists, Congress directed Hamilton's Treasury Department to evaluate the status of the Revolutionary debt in 1789. Hamilton responded in January 1790 with the Report on the Public Credit, containing recommendations that would at once strengthen the country's credit, enable it to defer paying its debt, and entice wealthy investors to place their capital at its service. The report listed $54 million in U.S. debt, $42 million of which was owed to Americans, and the rest to foreigners. Hamilton estimated that on top of the national debt, the states had debts of $25 million, an amount that included several million dollars that the United States had promised to reimburse, such as Virginia's expenses in defending settlements in the Ohio valley.

Hamilton's first major recommendation was that the federal government support the national debt by "funding" it—that is, raise the $54 million needed to honor the debt by selling an equal sum in new securities. Purchasers of these securities would choose from several combinations of federal "stock" and western lands. Those who wished could retain their original bonds and earn 4 percent interest. All of the options would reduce interest payments on the debt from the full 6 percent set by the Confederation Congress. Hamilton knew that creditors would not object to this reduction because their investments would now be more valuable and more secure.

Alexander Hamilton, by John Trumbull, 1792
Hamilton's self-confident pride clearly shines through in this portrait, painted at the height of his influence in the Washington administration.

Second, the report proposed that the federal government pay off the state debts remaining from the Revolution. Such obligations would be funded along with the national debt in the manner described above.

Hamilton exhorted the government to use the money earned by selling federal lands in the West to pay off the $12 million owed to Europeans as quickly as possible. The Treasury could easily accumulate the interest owed on the remaining $42 million by collecting customs duties on imports and an excise tax (a tax on domestic products transported within a nation's borders) on whiskey. In addition, Hamilton proposed that money owed to American citizens should be made a permanent debt. That is, he urged that the government not attempt to repay the $42 million principal but instead keep paying interest to people wishing to hold bonds as

an investment. If Hamilton's recommendation were adopted, the only burden on taxpayers would be the small annual cost of interest. It would then be possible to uphold the national credit at minimal expense, without ever paying off the debt itself.

Hamilton advocated a perpetual debt as a lasting means of uniting the economic fortunes of the nation's creditors to the United States. In an age when financial investments were notoriously risky, the federal government would protect the savings of wealthy bondholders through conservative policies while offering an interest rate competitive with the Bank of England's. The guarantee of future interest payments would unite the interests of the moneyed class with those of the government. Few other investments would entail so little risk.

Hamilton's Report on the Public Credit provoked immediate controversy. Although no one in Congress doubted that its provisions would greatly enhance the country's fiscal reputation, many objected that those least deserving of reward would gain the most. The original owners of more than three-fifths of the debt certificates issued by the Continental Congress were Revolutionary patriots of modest means who had long before sold their certificates for a fraction of their promised value, usually out of dire financial necessity. Foreseeing Hamilton's intentions, wealthy speculators had bought the certificates and now stood to reap huge gains at the expense of the original owners, even collecting interest that had accrued before they purchased the certificates. "That the case of those who parted with their securities from necessity is a hard one, cannot be denied," Hamilton admitted. But making exceptions would be even worse.

To Hamilton's surprise, Madison—his longtime colleague and initially a supporter of the plan—emerged as one of the chief opponents of reimbursing current certificate holders at full face value. Sensing opposition to the plan in his home state of Virginia, Madison tried but failed to obtain compensation for original owners who had sold their certificates. Congress rejected his suggestions primarily because some members feared that they would weaken the nation's credit. Hamilton's policy generated widespread resentment because it rewarded rich profiteers while ignoring the wartime sacrifices of soldiers and other ordinary citizens.

Opposition to Hamilton's proposal that the federal government assume states' war debts also ran high. Only Massachusetts, Connecticut, and South Carolina had failed to make effective provisions for satisfying their creditors. Understandably, the issue stirred the fiercest indignation in the South, which except for South Carolina had paid off 83 percent of its debt. Madison and other southerners maintained that to allow residents of the laggard states to escape heavy taxes while others had liquidated theirs at great expense was to reward irresponsibility. South Carolina became the sole southern state that supported Hamilton's policies.

Southern hostility almost defeated assumption. In the end, however, Hamilton managed to save his proposal by exploiting the strong desire among Virginians to relocate the national capital in their region. Virginians expected that moving the capital would make their state the crossroads of the country and thus help preserve its position as the nation's largest, most influential state. In return for the northern votes necessary to transfer the capital to the Potomac River, Hamilton secured enough Virginians' support to win the battle for assumption. Yet the debate over state debts alienated many white southerners by confirming their suspicions that other regions would monopolize the benefits of a stronger union.

Congressional enactment in 1790 of the Report on the Public Credit dramatically reversed the nation's fiscal standing. Thereafter, European investors grew so enthusiastic about U.S. bonds that by 1792 some securities were selling at 10 percent above face value.

Creating a National Bank, 1790–1791

Having significantly expanded the stock of capital available for investment, Hamilton intended to direct that money toward projects that would diversify the national economy through a federally chartered bank. Accordingly, in December 1790 he presented Congress with a second message, the Report on a National Bank.

The proposed bank would raise $10 million through a public stock offering. Private investors could purchase shares by paying for three-quarters of their value in government bonds. In this way, the bank would capture a significant portion of the recently funded debt and make it available for loans; it would also receive a substantial and steady flow of interest payments from the Treasury. Anyone buying shares under these circumstances had little chance of losing money and was positioned to profit handsomely.

Hamilton argued that the Bank of the United States would cost the taxpayers nothing and greatly benefit the nation. It would provide a safe place for the federal government to deposit tax revenues, make inexpensive loans to the government when taxes fell short, and help relieve the scarcity of hard cash by issuing paper notes that would circulate as money. Furthermore, it would possess authority to regulate the business practices of

state banks. Above all, the bank would provide much needed credit to expand the economy.

Hamilton's critics denounced his proposal for a national bank, interpreting it as a dangerous scheme that would give a small, elite group special power to influence the government. These critics believed that the Bank of England had undermined the integrity of government in Britain. Shareholders of the new Bank of the United States could just as easily become the tools of unscrupulous politicians. If significant numbers in Congress owned bank stock, they would likely support the bank even at the cost of the national good. To Jefferson, the bank was "a machine for the corruption of the legislature [Congress]." John Taylor of Virginia predicted that its vast wealth would enable the bank to take over the country, which would thereafter, he quipped, be known as the United States of the Bank.

Opponents also argued that the bank was unconstitutional. In fact the Philadelphia convention had rejected a proposal giving Congress just such power. Unless Congress adhered to a "strict interpretation" of the Constitution, critics argued, the central government might oppress the states and trample individual liberties, just as Parliament had done to the colonies. Strictly limiting federal power seemed the surest way of preventing the United States from degenerating into a corrupt despotism.

Congress approved the bank by only a thin margin. Uncertain of the bank's constitutionality, Washington turned to both Jefferson and Hamilton for advice before signing the measure into law. Like many southern planters whose investments in slaves left them short of capital and often in debt, Jefferson distrusted banking. Moreover, his fear of excessively concentrated economic and political power led him to favor a "strict interpretation" of the Constitution. "To take a single step beyond the boundaries thus specifically drawn around the powers of Congress is to take possession of a boundless field of power no longer susceptible of any definition," warned Jefferson.

Hamilton fought back, urging Washington to sign the bill. Because Congress could enact all measures "necessary and proper" (Article I, Section 8), Hamilton contended that the only unconstitutional activities were those actually forbidden to the national government. In the end, the president accepted Hamilton's argument for a "loose interpretation" of the Constitution. In February 1791 the Bank of the United States obtained a charter guaranteeing its existence for twenty years. Washington's acceptance of the principle of loose interpretation was an important victory for those advocating an active,

assertive national government. But the split between Jefferson and Hamilton, and Washington's siding with the latter, signaled a deepening political divide within the administration.

Hamilton's Legacy

Hamilton's attempt to erect a base of political support by appealing to economic self-interest proved highly successful but also divisive. His arrangements for rescuing the nation's credit provided enormous gains for the speculators, merchants, and other "monied men" of the port cities who by 1790 held most of the Revolutionary debt. As holders of bank stock, these same groups had yet another reason to use their prestige on behalf of national authority. Assumption of the state debts liberated New England, New Jersey, and South Carolina taxpayers from a crushing burden. Hamilton's efforts to promote industry, commerce, and shipping struck a responsive chord among the Northeast's budding entrepreneurs.

Those attracted to Hamilton's policies called themselves Federalists, implying (incorrectly) that their opponents had formerly been Antifederalist opponents of the Constitution. In actuality, Federalists favored a highly centralized national government instead of a truly "federal" system with substantial powers left to the states. Federalists dominated public opinion in New England, New Jersey, and South Carolina and enjoyed considerable support in Pennsylvania and New York.

Hamilton's program sowed dissension in sections of the country where it offered few benefits. Resentment ran high among those who felt that the government appeared to be rewarding special interests. Southern reaction to Hamilton's program, for example, was overwhelmingly negative. Outside of Charleston, South Carolina, few southerners retained Revolutionary certificates in 1790. The Bank of the United States attracted few southern stockholders, and it allocated very little capital for loans there.

Hamilton's plans offered little to the West, where agriculture promised to be exceptionally profitable if only the right to export through New Orleans would be guaranteed. In Pennsylvania and New York, too, the uneven effect of Hamiltonian policies generated dissatisfaction. Resentment against a national economic program whose main beneficiaries seemed to be eastern "monied men" and New Englanders who refused to pay their debts gradually united westerners, southerners, and some mid-Atlantic citizens into a political coalition that challenged the Federalists and called for a return to the "true principles" of republicanism.

For many Americans, the question of manufacturing or farming was not only economic and political but also ideological and moral. As outlined in his Report on the Subject of Manufactures (1791), Hamilton admired efficiently run factories in which a few managers supervised large numbers of workers. Not only would manufacturing provide employment opportunities, promote emigration, and expand the applications of technology; it would also offer "greater scope for the talents and dispositions [of] men," afford "a more ample and various field for enterprise," and create "a more certain and steady demand for the surplus produce of the soil." Jefferson, on the other hand, idealized white, landowning family farmers as bulwarks of republican liberty and virtue. "Those who labour in the earth are the chosen people," he wrote in 1784, whereas the dependency of European factory workers "begets subservience and venality, suffocates the germ of virtue, and prepares fit tools for the designs of ambition." For Hamilton, capital, technology, and managerial discipline were the surest roads to national order and wealth. Jefferson, putting more trust in white male citizens, envisioned land as the key to prosperity and liberty for all. The argument over the relative merits of these two ideals would remain a constant in American politics and culture for at least another two centuries.

The Whiskey Rebellion, 1794

Hamilton's program not only sparked an angry debate in Congress but also helped ignite a civil insurrection called the Whiskey Rebellion. Reflecting serious regional and class tensions, this popular uprising was the young republic's first serious crisis.

To augment the national government's revenues, Hamilton had recommended an excise tax on domestically produced whiskey. He insisted that such a tax would not only distribute the expense of financing the national debt evenly but would improve Americans' morals by inducing them to drink less liquor, a contention enthusiastically endorsed by Philadelphia's College of Physicians. Though Congress complied with Hamilton's request in March 1791, many members doubted that Americans (who on average annually imbibed six gallons of hard liquor per adult) would submit tamely to sobriety. James Jackson of Georgia, for example, warned the administration that his constituents "have long been in the habit of getting drunk and that they will get drunk in defiance of a dozen colleges or all the excise duties which Congress might be weak or wicked enough to pass."

The accuracy of Jackson's prophecy became apparent in September 1791 when a crowd tarred and feathered an excise agent near Pittsburgh. Western Pennsylvanians found the new tax especially burdensome. Unable to ship their crops to world markets through New Orleans, most farmers had grown accustomed to distilling their rye or corn into alcohol, which could be carried across the Appalachians at a fraction of the price charged for bulkier grain. Hamilton's excise equaled 25 percent of whiskey's retail value, enough to wipe out a farmer's profit.

The law also stipulated that trials for evading the tax be conducted in federal courts. Any western Pennsylvanian indicted for noncompliance thus had to travel three hundred miles to Philadelphia. Not only would the accused face a jury of unsympathetic easterners, but he would also have to bear the cost of the long journey and lost earnings while at court, in addition to fines and other court penalties if found guilty. Moreover, Treasury officials rarely enforced the law rigorously outside western Pennsylvania. For all these reasons, western Pennsylvanians complained that the whiskey excise was excessively burdensome.

In a scene reminiscent of pre- and post-Revolutionary popular protests, large-scale resistance erupted in July 1794. One hundred men attacked a U.S. marshal serving sixty delinquent taxpayers with summonses to appear in court at Philadelphia. A crowd of five hundred burned the chief revenue officer's house after a shootout with federal soldiers assigned to protect him. Roving bands torched buildings, assaulted tax collectors, chased government supporters from the region, and flew a flag symbolizing an independent country that they hoped to create from six western counties.

Echoing elites' denunciations of earlier protests, Hamilton condemned the rebellion as simple lawlessness. He pointed out that Congress had reduced the tax rate per gallon in 1792 and had recently voted to allow state judges in western Pennsylvania to hear trials. Showing the same anxiety he had expressed six years earlier during Shays's Rebellion (see Chapter 6), Washington concluded that failure to respond strongly to the uprising would encourage outbreaks in other western areas where distillers were avoiding the tax.

Washington accordingly mustered nearly thirteen thousand militiamen from Pennsylvania, Maryland, Virginia, and New Jersey to march west under his command. Opposition evaporated once the troops reached the Appalachians, and the president left Hamilton in charge of making arrests. Of about 150 suspects seized, Hamilton sent twenty in irons to Philadelphia. Two men

Washington and Hamilton Confront the Whiskey Rebels, 1794
To underscore the importance of asserting federal authority, the president and treasury secretary personally led 13,000 troops to crush the Whiskey Rebellion in western Pennsylvania.

received death sentences, but Washington eventually pardoned them both, noting that one was a "simpleton" and the other "insane."

The Whiskey Rebellion set severe limits on public opposition to federal policies. In the early 1790s, many Americans—including the whiskey rebels—still assumed that it was legitimate to protest unpopular laws using the same tactics with which they had blocked parliamentary measures like the Stamp Act. Indeed, western Pennsylvanians had justified their resistance with exactly such reasoning. By firmly suppressing the first major challenge to national authority, Washington served notice that citizens who resorted to violent or other extralegal means of political action would feel the full force of federal authority. In this way, he gave voice and substance to elites' fears of "mobocracy," now resurfacing in reaction to the French Revolution (see below).

THE UNITED STATES ON THE WORLD STAGE, 1789–1796

By 1793 disagreements over foreign affairs had emerged as the primary source of friction in American public life. The political divisions created by Hamilton's financial program hardened into ideologically oriented factions that argued vehemently over whether the country's foreign policy should favor industrial and overseas mercantile interests or those of farmers, planters, small busi-

nesses, and artisans. Moreover, having ratified its Constitution in the year that the French Revolution began (1789), the new government entered the international arena as European tensions were once again exploding. The rapid spread of pro-French revolutionary ideas and organizations alarmed Europe's monarchs and aristocrats. Perceiving a threat to their social orders as well as their territorial interests, most European nations declared war on France by early 1793. For most of the next twenty-two years—until Napoleon's final defeat in 1815—Europe and the Atlantic world remained in a state of war.

While most Americans hoped that their nation could avoid this latest European conflict, the fact was that the interests and ambitions of many of their compatriots collided at critical points with those of Britain, France, and Spain. Thus, differences over foreign policy fused with differences over domestic affairs, further intensifying the partisanship of American politics.

Spanish Power in Western North America

Stimulated by its winning Louisiana from France in 1762 (see Chapter 5), Spain enjoyed a limited revival of its North American fortunes in the late eighteenth century. Influenced by the Indian policies of France and Britain, Spanish officials shifted from futilely attempting to conquer hostile Native Americans in the Southwest and southern Plains to a policy of peaceful trade. Under the

new plan, they would, as Louisiana's Governor Bernardo de Gálvez put it, provide Native Americans with the "sundry conveniences of life of whose existence they previously knew nothing, and which they now look upon as indispensable." Among the "conveniences" Gálvez had in mind were alcohol and poorly made guns, which the Indians would need to have regularly repaired by Spanish gunsmiths. By 1800 the new policy had enabled Spain to make peace with the Comanches, Utes, Navajos, and most of the Apache nations that had previously threatened their settlements in New Mexico and Texas.

These reforms were part of a larger Spanish effort to counter European rivals for North American territory and influence. The first challenge came in the north Pacific Ocean, where Spain had enjoyed an unchallenged monopoly for two centuries. Lacking any maritime rivals, Spain dispatched its "Manila galleons," which sailed north from Mexico's Pacific coast to Monterey Bay in California and then turned westward for the long voyage to Asia's shores. But in the 1740s Russian traders in Siberia crossed the Bering Sea and began brutally forcing the indigenous Aleut peoples to supply them with sea-otter pelts, spreading deadly diseases in the process. Using Aleut hunters, the Russians gradually moved farther south to expand their quest for

otterskins, eventually as far as northern California. The Russians carried the otterskins overland through Siberia to China, where they exchanged them for silk cloth, porcelain ware, and other fine objects.

By the 1770s the exploring voyages of Britain's Captain James Cook and others revealed the wealth such pelts were bringing to Russian merchants. Sensing that they could undercut the Russians, British and American maritime traders began plying northwestern coastal waters in the 1780s. Trading cloth, metal tools, and other goods to the Indians, they carried furs to Hawaii—also made known to Europeans and Americans by Cook—and traded them to China-bound merchants for Chinese goods. They then returned with these luxuries to Europe and America and sold them to affluent consumers who prized them for their exotic designs and fine craftsmanship. Thus began the "China trade," which brought tidy profits to many a Boston merchant and fueled American dreams of expanding to the Pacific.

Spain responded to these inroads by boldly expanding its empire northward from Mexico. In 1769 it established "New California" along the Pacific coast to the San Francisco Bay area (see Map 7.1). Efforts to encourage large-scale Mexican immigration to New California failed, leaving the colony to be sustained by a chain of religious missions, several presidios (forts), and a few large ranchos (ranches). Seeking support against inland adversaries, coastal Indians welcomed the Spanish at first. But the Franciscan missionaries sought to convert them to Catholicism and "civilize" them by imposing harsh disciplinary measures and putting them to work in vineyards and in other enterprises. Meanwhile, Spanish colonists' spreading of epidemic and venereal diseases among natives precipitated a decline in the Native American population from about seventy-two thousand in 1770 to about eighteen thousand by 1830.

Having strengthened its positions in Texas, New Mexico, and California, Spain attempted to befriend Indians in the area later known as Arizona. Spain hoped to dominate North America from the Pacific to Louisiana on the Gulf of Mexico. But resistance from the Hopi, Quechan (Yuma), and other Native Americans thwarted these hopes. Fortunately for Spain, Arizona had not yet attracted the interest of other outside powers.

Challenging American Expansion, 1789–1792

Between the Appalachians and the Mississippi River, Spain, Britain, the United States, and numerous Indian nations jockeyed for advantage in a region that all con-

MAP 7.1
Spanish Settlements in New California, 1784
While the United States was struggling to establish its independence, Spain was extending its empire northward along the Pacific coast.

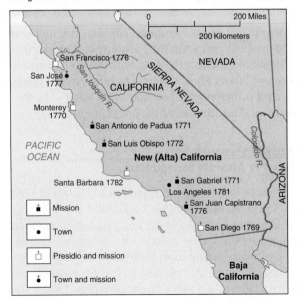

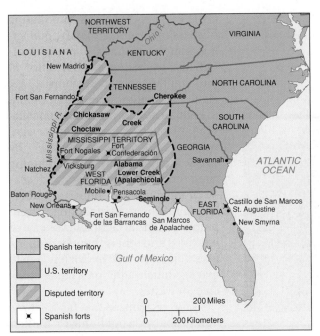

New Orleans
The French and Spanish developed this port city during the eighteenth century. By century's end many in the United States saw New Orleans as a key to their nation's future expansion and prosperity.

MAP 7.2
Disputed Territorial Claims, Spain and the United States, 1783–1796
The two nations' claims to lands east of the Mississippi and north of the thirty-first parallel were a principal point of contention until the Treaty of San Lorenzo was ratified in 1796.

sidered central to their interests and that Native Americans regarded as homelands. Unable to prevent American settlers from occupying territory it claimed in the Southeast (see Map 7.2), Spain sought to win the newcomers' allegiance by offering them citizenship. Noting that Congress seemed ready to accept the permanent closing of New Orleans in return for Spanish concessions elsewhere (see Chapter 6), many westerners began talking openly of secession. "I am decidedly of the opinion," wrote Kentucky's attorney general in 1787, "that this western country will in a few years Revolt from the Union and endeavor to erect an Independent Government." In 1788 Tennessee conspirators boldly advertised their flirtation with Spain by naming a large district along the Cumberland River after Louisiana's governor. Most westerners who accepted Spanish favors and gold meant only to pocket badly needed cash in return for vague promises of goodwill. The episode showed, however, that leading citizens were susceptible to foreign manipulation. As young Andrew Jackson concluded in 1789, making some arrangements with the Spanish seemed "the only immediate way to obtain peace with the Savage [Indians]."

Realizing that he could not quickly resolve the complex western problem, President Washington pursued a course of patient diplomacy that was intended "to preserve the country in peace if I can, and to be prepared for war if I cannot." The prospect of peace improved in 1789 when Spain unexpectedly opened New Orleans to American commerce, although exports remained subject to a 15 percent duty. Although westerners bitterly resented paying the Spanish duty on exports, secessionist sentiment gradually subsided.

Thereafter, Spanish officials continued to bribe well-known political figures in Tennessee and Kentucky, among them a former general on Washington's staff, James Wilkinson. Thomas Scott, a congressman from western Pennsylvania, meanwhile schemed with the British. Between 1791 and 1796, the federal government anxiously admitted Vermont, Kentucky, and Tennessee to the Union, partly in the hope of strengthening their residents' flickering loyalty to the United States.

Washington also tried to weaken Spanish influence by neutralizing Spain's most important ally, the Creek Indians. The Creeks numbered more than twenty thousand, including perhaps five thousand warriors, and they bore a fierce hostility toward Georgian settlers, whom they called Ecunnaunuxulgee, or "the greedy people who want our lands." In 1790 the Creek leader Alexander McGillivray signed the Treaty of New York

Creek House, 1791
By the end of the eighteenth century, most eastern Native Americans used traditional and
European ideas and materials in their everyday lives.

with the United States. The treaty permitted American settlers to remain on lands in the Georgia Piedmont fought over since 1786 (see Chapter 6), but in other respects preserved Creek territory against U.S. expansion. Washington insisted that Georgia restore to the Creeks' allies, the Chickasaws and Choctaws, the vast area along the Mississippi River known as the Yazoo Tract, which Georgia claimed and had begun selling off to white land speculators (see Chapter 8).

Washington adopted a harsher policy toward Britain's Indian allies in the Ohio valley. In 1790 his first effort to force peace through military action failed when allied Native Americans defeated General Josiah Harmar on the Maumee River. A second campaign ended in disaster in November 1791 when one thousand warriors assembled on the Wabash River killed nine hundred out of a total of fourteen hundred soldiers led by General Arthur St. Clair.

While employing military force, the Washington administration, led by Secretary of War Henry Knox, also pursued a benevolent policy similar to that proclaimed by the British in 1763 (see Chapter 5). Alarmed by the chaos in the West, where trespassers invaded Indian lands and Native peoples rejected U.S. claims to sovereignty, the government formally recognized Indian title as secure and inalienable except by the "free consent" of the Indians themselves. To reinforce this policy,

Congress enacted laws prohibiting trespassing on Indian lands, punishing crimes committed there by non-Indians, outlawing alcohol, and, in the Indian Non-Intercourse Act (1790), regulating trade. In addition, the administration sought to encourage Indians to leave off their "savage" ways and become "civilized," by which it meant above all abandoning communal landownership and seasonal migrations for hunting, gathering, and fishing. By adopting private property and an agricultural way of life, Knox and others thought, Indians would join American society while making much additional land available for whites.

Knox recognized that his "civilization" policy would have limited appeal. Although most Indians were receptive to European material goods, they were unwilling to give up their traditional ways entirely and assimilate into an alien culture. Most whites were equally averse to integrating Native Americans into their society. Accordingly, the United States continued to pressure most Native Americans to sell their lands and move farther west.

With many Indians refusing to abandon their lands and cultures, and with their having twice defeated U.S. forces in the Northwest Territory, Washington's western policy was in shambles. Matters worsened in 1792 when Spain persuaded the Creeks to renounce the Treaty of New York and resume hostilities. Ultimately, the damage done to U.S. prestige by these setbacks convinced many Americans that the combined strength of Britain, Spain, and the Native Americans could be counterbalanced only by an alliance with France.

France and Factional Politics, 1793

One of the most momentous events in history, the French Revolution began in 1789 with the meeting (for the first time in almost two centuries) of France's legislative assembly, the Estates General. Americans remained fundamentally sympathetic to the revolutionary cause as the French abolished nobles' privileges, wrote a constitution, and bravely repelled invading armies from Austria and Prussia. France became a republic early in 1793; it then proclaimed a war of all peoples against all

kings, in which it assumed the United States would eagerly enlist.

White southern slaveowners were among France's fiercest supporters. In 1793 a slave uprising in the Caribbean colony of Saint Domingue became a revolution against French rule. Thousands of terrified French planters fled to the United States, recounting how British invaders had supported the uprising. Inspired by the American and French Revolutions, blacks had fought with determination and inflicted heavy casualties on French colonists. Recalling British courting of their own slaves during the Revolution, southern whites concluded that the British had intentionally sparked the bloodbath and would do the same in the South. Anti-British hysteria even eroded South Carolina's loyalty to Federalist policies.

Many northerners, on the other hand, were more repelled by the blood being shed in revolutionary France. The revolution was an abomination—"an open hell," thundered Massachusetts' Fisher Ames, "still ringing with agonies and blasphemies, still smoking with sufferings and crimes." New England was the most militantly Protestant region, and most of its middle-class and elite citizens came to detest the French government's punishing its opponents and its substituting the adoration of Reason for the worship of God. Middle Atlantic Federalists, while perhaps less religious than New Englanders, condemned French leaders as evil radicals who incited the poor against the rich.

Northern and southern reactions to the French Revolution also diverged for economic reasons. In the North merchants' growing antagonism toward France reflected the facts that virtually all the nation's merchant marine operated from northern ports and that most of the country's foreign trade was with Great Britain. Merchants, shippers, and ordinary sailors in New England, Philadelphia, and New York feared that an alliance with France would provoke British retaliation against this valuable commerce, and they argued that the United States could win valuable concessions by demonstrating friendly intentions toward Britain. Indeed, some influential members of Parliament now seemed to favor liberalizing trade with the United States.

Southerners had no such reasons to favor Britain. Southern spokesmen viewed Americans' reliance on British commerce as a menace to national self-determination and wished to divert most U.S. trade to France. Jefferson and Madison repeatedly demanded that British imports be reduced through the imposition of steep discriminatory duties on cargoes shipped from England and Scotland in British vessels. In the heat of

Citizen Genet
By recruiting Americans to fight for France's revolutionary cause, French envoy Edmond Genet contributed to political polarization in the young Republic.

the debate, Federalist opponents of a discriminatory tariff warned that Britain, which sold more manufactured goods to the United States than to any other country, would not stand by while a weak French ally pushed it into depression. If Congress adopted this program of trade retaliation, Hamilton predicted in 1792, "there would be, in less than six months, an open war between the United States and Great Britain."

Enthusiasm for a pro-French foreign policy raged in the southern and western states, in particular after France went to war against Spain and Great Britain in 1793. Increasingly, western settlers and speculators hoped for a decisive French victory that, they reasoned, would induce Britain and Spain to cease blocking U.S. expansion. The United States could then insist on free navigation of the Mississippi, force the evacuation of British garrisons, and end both nations' support of Indian resistance.

After declaring war on Britain and Spain in 1793, France actively tried to embroil the United States in the conflict. The French dispatched Edmond Genet as minister to the United States with orders to mobilize

republican sentiment in support of France, enlist American mercenaries to conquer Spanish territories and attack British shipping, and strengthen the alliance between the two nations. Much to the French government's dislike, however, President Washington issued a proclamation of American neutrality on April 22.

Meanwhile, Citizen Genet (as he was known in French Revolutionary style) had arrived on April 8. He found no shortage of southern volunteers for his American Foreign Legion despite America's official neutrality. Making generals of George Rogers Clark of Kentucky and Elisha Clarke of Georgia, Genet directed them to seize Spanish garrisons at New Orleans and St. Augustine. Clark openly defied Washington's Neutrality Proclamation by advertising for recruits for his mission in Kentucky newspapers, and Clarke began drilling three hundred troops on the Florida border. But the French failed to provide adequate funds for either campaign. Although the American recruits were willing to fight for France, few were willing to fight for free, so both expeditions eventually disintegrated.

However, Genet did not need funds to outfit privateers, who financed themselves with captured plunder. By the summer of 1793, almost a thousand Americans were at sea in a dozen ships flying the French flag. These privateers seized more than eighty British vessels and towed them to U.S. ports, where French consuls sold the ships and cargoes at auction.

Avoiding War, 1793–1796

Even though the Washington administration swiftly closed the nation's harbors to Genet's buccaneers and requested the French ambassador's recall, his exploits provoked an Anglo-American crisis. George III's ministers decided that only a massive show of force would deter American support for France. Accordingly, on November 6, 1793, the Privy Council issued secret orders confiscating any foreign ships trading with French islands in the Caribbean. The council purposely delayed publishing these instructions until after most American ships carrying winter provisions to the Caribbean left port, so that their captains would not know that they were sailing into a war zone. The Royal Navy then seized more than 250 American vessels.

Meanwhile, the Royal Navy inflicted a second galling indignity—the impressment (forced enlistment) of crewmen on U.S. ships. Thousands of British sailors had previously fled to the U.S. merchant marine, where they hoped to find an easier life than under the tough, poorly paying British system. In late 1793 British naval officers began routinely inspecting American crews for British subjects, whom they then impressed as the king's sailors. Overzealous commanders sometimes broke royal orders by taking U.S. citizens, and in any case the British did not recognize former subjects' right to adopt American citizenship. Impressment scratched a raw nerve in most

Negotiating the Treaty of Greenville
In this detail of a contemporary painting believed to have been done by a member of General Wayne's staff, Chief Little Turtle of the Miamis speaks to Wayne, who stands with one hand behind his back.

Presidential Proclamation of a National Thanksgiving, 1795

President Washington called for a day of celebration and thankfulness for the young republic's having avoided war with Britain and suppressed the Whiskey Rebellion. One month later, news of Jay's Treaty would set off heightened political tensions.

By Authority.

By The President
OF THE UNITED STATES OF AMERICA,

A Proclamation.

WHEN we review the calamities which afflict so many other Nations, the present condition of the *United States* affords much matter of consolation and satisfaction. Our exemption hitherto from foreign war----an increasing prospect of the continuance of that exemption----the great degree of internal tranquillity we have enjoyed----the recent confirmation of that tranquillity, by the suppression of an insurrection which so wantonly threatened it----the happy course of our public affairs in general----the unexampled prosperity of all classes of our Citizens, are circumstances which peculiarly mark our situation with indications of the Divine Benificence towards us. In such a state of things it is, in an especial manner, our duty as a People, with devout reverence and affectionate gratitude, to acknowledge our many and great obligations to ALMIGHTY GOD, and to implore him to continue and confirm the blessings we experience.

Deeply penetrated with this sentiment, I GEORGE WASHINGTON, President of the United States, do recommend to all Religious Societies and Denominations, and to all Persons whomsoever within the United States, to set apart and observe *THURSDAY* the *Nineteenth* day of *February* next, as a Day of PUBLIC THANKSGIVING and PRAYER ; and on that Day to meet together, and render their sincere and hearty thanks to the Great Ruler of Nations, for the manifold and signal mercies, which distinguish our lot as a nation ; particularly for the possession of Constitutions of Government, which unite, and by their union establish liberty with order----for the preservation of our Peace foreign and domestic----for the seasonable control which has been given to a spirit of disorder, in the suppression of the late Insurrection----and generally, for the prosperous course of our affairs public and private ; and at the same time, humbly and fervently to beseech the Kind Author of these Blessings, graciously to prolong them to us----to imprint on our hearts a deep and solemn sense of our obligations to Him for them----to teach us rightly to estimate their immense value----to preserve us from the arrogance of prosperity, and from hazarding the advantages we enjoy by delusive pursuits---to dispose us to merit the continuance of his favours, by not abusing them, by our gratitude for them, and by a correspondent conduct as Citizens and as Men---to render this Country more and more a safe and propitious Asylum for the unfortunate of other Countries---to extend among us true and useful knowledge---to diffuse and establish habits of sobriety, order, morality and piety ; and finally, to impart all the blessings we possess, or ask for ourselves, to the whole Family of Mankind.

In Testimony Whereof, I have caused the SEAL *of the* UNITED STATES *of* AMERICA *to be affixed to these Presents, and signed the same with my Hand. Done at the city of* PHILADELPHIA, *the first day of* January, *one thousand seven hundred and ninety-five, and of the Independence of the United States of America the nineteenth.*

G°: WASHINGTON.

By The President---EDM: RANDOLPH.

Americans, who recognized that their government's willingness to defend its citizens from such contemptuous abuse was a critical test of national character.

Meanwhile, Britain, Spain and many Native Americans continued to challenge the United States for control of territory west of the Appalachians. During a large intertribal council in February 1794, the Shawnees and other Ohio Indians welcomed an inflammatory speech by Canada's royal governor denying U.S. claims north of the Ohio River and urging destruction of every white settlement in the Northwest. Soon British troops were building an eighth garrison on U.S. soil, Fort Miami, near present-day Toledo. Meanwhile, the Spanish encroached on territory owned by the United States by building Fort San Fernando in 1794 at what is now Memphis, Tennessee.

Hoping to halt the drift toward war, Washington launched three desperate initiatives in 1794. He authorized General Anthony Wayne to negotiate a treaty with the Shawnees and their Ohio valley allies, sent Chief Justice John Jay to Great Britain, and dispatched Thomas Pinckney to Spain.

Having twice defeated federal armies, the Indians scoffed at Washington's peace offer. "Mad Anthony" Wayne then led thirty-five hundred U.S. troops deep into Shawnee homelands, building forts and ruthlessly burning every village within his reach. On August 20, 1794, his troops routed four hundred Shawnees at the Battle of Fallen Timbers just two miles from British Fort Miami. (The British closed the fort's gates, denying entry to their fleeing allies.) Wayne's army then built an imposing stronghold to challenge British authority in the Northwest, appropriately named Fort Defiance. Indian morale plummeted, not only because of the American victory and their own losses but also because of Britain's betrayal.

In August 1795 Wayne compelled the Shawnees and eleven other tribes to sign the Treaty of Greenville, which opened most of modern-day Ohio and a portion of Indiana to white settlement and ended U.S.-Indian hos-

tilities in the region for sixteen years. But aside from the older leaders who were pressured to sign the treaty, most Shawnees knew that American designs on Indian land in the Northwest had not been satisfied and would soon resurface. Among them was a rising young warrior named Tecumseh (see Chapter 8).

Wayne's success helped John Jay win a British promise to withdraw troops from American soil. Jay also managed to gain access to West Indian markets for small American ships, but only by bargaining away other American complaints as well as U.S. rights to load cargoes of sugar, molasses, and coffee from French colonies during wartime. Aside from fellow Federalists, few Americans would interpret Jay's Treaty as preserving peace with honor.

Jay's Treaty left Britain free not only to violate American neutrality but also to ruin a profitable commerce by restricting U.S. trade with France. Opponents condemned the treaty's failure to end impressment and predicted that Great Britain would thereafter force even more Americans into the Royal Navy. Slave owners were resentful that Jay had not obtained compensation for slaves taken away by the British army during the Revolution. As the Senate ratified the treaty by just one vote in 1795, Jay nervously joked that he could find his way across the country at night by the fires of rallies burning him in effigy.

Despite its unpopularity, Jay's Treaty defused an explosive crisis with Great Britain before war became inevitable and finally ended Britain's post-Revolutionary occupation of U.S. territory. The treaty also helped stimulate an enormous expansion of American trade. Upon its ratification, British governors in the West Indies proclaimed their harbors open to U.S. ships. Other British officials permitted Americans to develop commercial ties with India, even though such trade infringed on the East India Company's monopoly. Within a few years after 1795, American exports to the British Empire shot up 300 percent.

On the heels of Jay's controversial treaty came an unqualified diplomatic triumph engineered by Thomas Pinckney. Ratified in 1796, the Treaty of San Lorenzo with Spain (also called Pinckney's Treaty) won westerners the right of unrestricted, duty-free access to world markets via the Mississippi River. Spain also promised to recognize the thirty-first parallel as the United States' southern boundary, to dismantle all fortifications on American soil, and to discourage Indian attacks against western settlers.

By 1796 the Washington administration could claim to have successfully extended American authority throughout the trans-Appalachian West, opened the Mississippi for western exports, enabled northeastern shippers to regain British markets, and kept the nation out of a dangerous European war. As the popular outcry over Jay's Treaty demonstrated, however, the nation's foreign policy left Americans much more deeply divided in 1796 than they had been in 1789.

THE EMERGENCE OF PARTY POLITICS, 1793–1800

Since the pre-Revolutionary era, many Americans (like many Britons) believed that deliberately organizing a political faction or party was a corrupt, subversive action. The Constitution's framers had neither wanted nor planned for political parties. Republican ideology assumed that factions or parties would fill Congress with politicians who would pursue selfish goals and conspire against the people's liberty. Indeed, in *Federalist* No. 10, Madison (a future partisan) had argued that the Constitution would prevent the rise of national political factions.

These ideals began to waver as controversy mounted over Federalist policies and the French Revolution. Before the end of Washington's second term, politically conscious Americans had split into two hostile parties, Federalists and Republicans, as instruments for advancing their interests, ambitions, and ideals. Thereafter, a battle raged over the very future of representative government, culminating in the election of 1800, whose outcome would determine whether the nation's political elite could accommodate demands from ordinary citizens for a more active and influential role in determining government policy.

Ideological Confrontation, 1793–1794

American attitudes about events in France prompted a polarization of American opinion along ideological and regional lines. Recalling Shays's Rebellion and the Whiskey Rebellion, Federalists trembled at the thought of guillotines and "mob rule." They also dreaded the sight of artisans in Philadelphia and New York bandying the French revolutionary slogan "Liberty, Equality, Fraternity" and admiring pro-French politicians such as Jefferson. Citizen Genet had openly encouraged opposition to the Washington administration; and, even more troubling, he had found hundreds of Americans willing to fight for France. Federalists worried that all of this was just the tip of a revolutionary iceberg.

By the mid-1790s Federalists' worst fears of public participation in politics seemed to have been confirmed. The people, they believed, were not evil-minded but simply undependable and vulnerable to rabble rousers such as Genet. As Senator George Cabot of Massachusetts put it, "the many do not think at all." For Federalists, democracy meant "government by the passions of the multitude." They consequently argued that ordinary white male property owners should not be presented with choices over policy during elections, but should vote simply on the basis of the personal merits of elite candidates. Elected officials, they maintained, should rule in the people's name but be independent of direct popular influence.

A very different perspective on government and politics surfaced, especially in urban areas of New England and the Middle Atlantic states and in the South. Republicans stressed the corruption inherent in a powerful government dominated by a highly visible few, and insisted that liberty would be safe only if power were diffused among virtuous, independent citizens. Whereas Federalists denounced self-interest as inimical to the public good, Republicans argued that self-interest could be pursued virtuously in a society in which property and other means to economic independence were widely available rather than being monopolized by a wealthy few. Jefferson, Madison, and other republicans interpreted the American and French Revolutions as opening the way to a new kind of human community in which self-interested individuals recognized their common interest in maintaining a stable society responsive to the needs of all.

A radical ideology like republicanism, with its emphasis on liberty and equality, might seem anomalous among southern slaveowners. In fact, however, such men were among its most forceful proponents. Although a few southern republicans advocated abolishing slavery gradually, most declined to trouble themselves unduly over their ownership of human beings. Although articulated in universal terms, the liberty and equality they advocated were intended for white men only. With their own labor force consisting of enslaved blacks rather than of free white wage workers, southern elites feared popular participation in politics far less than did their northern counterparts. Overlooking the possibility that their slaves understood their ideas and their debates, they maintained a confidence built on the loyalty toward them of nonelite whites.

Ambition, too, drove men like Jefferson and Madison to rouse ordinary citizens' concerns about civic affairs. The widespread awe in which Washington was held inhibited open criticism of him, his policies, and his fellow Federalists. If, however, the Federalists could be held accountable to the public, they would think twice before enacting measures opposed by the majority; or if they persisted in advocating misguided policies, they would ultimately be removed from office. Such reasoning led Jefferson, a wealthy landowner and large slaveholder, to say, "I am not among those who fear the people; they and not the rich, are our dependence for continued freedom."

Jefferson's frustration at being overruled at every turn by Hamilton and Washington finally prompted his resignation from the cabinet in 1793, and thereafter even the president could not halt the widening political split. Each side saw itself as the guardian of republican virtue and attacked the other as an illegitimate "cabal" or "faction."

Efforts to turn public opinion against the Federalists had begun as early as October 1791 with the publication of the nation's first opposition newspaper, the *National Gazette*. Then in 1793–1794, opponents of the Federalist policies began organizing Democratic (or Republican) societies. The societies formed primarily in seaboard cities but also in the rural South and West. Their memberships ranged from planters and merchants to artisans and sailors; conspicuously absent were clergymen, the poor, nonwhites, and women.

Federalists interpreted the Democratic societies' emotional appeals to ordinary people as demagoguery and denounced their followers as "democrats, mobocrats, & all other kinds of rats." They feared that the societies would grow into revolutionary organizations. During the Whiskey Rebellion, Washington publicly denounced "certain self-created societies." Although the societies did not support the rebellion, so great was the president's prestige that the societies temporarily broke up. But by attacking them, Washington had at last ended his nonpartisan stance and identified himself unmistakably with the Federalists. The censure would cost him dearly.

The Republican Party, 1794–1796

Neither Jefferson nor Madison belonged to a Democratic society. However, these private clubs helped publicize their views, and they initiated into political activity numerous voters who would later support a new Republican party.

In 1794 party development reached a decisive stage after Washington openly identified himself with Federalist policies. Calling themselves Republicans (rather

than the more radical-sounding "Democrats"), followers of Jefferson successfully attacked the Federalists' pro-British leanings in many local elections and won a slight majority in the House of Representatives. The election signaled the Republicans' transformation from a coalition of officeholders and local societies to a broad-based party capable of coordinating local political campaigns throughout the nation.

Federalists and Republicans alike used the press to mold public opinion. In the 1790s American journalism came of age as the number of newspapers multiplied from 92 to 242, mostly in New England and the Middle Atlantic states. By 1800 newspapers had perhaps 140,000 paid subscribers (about one-fifth of the eligible voters), and their secondhand readership probably exceeded 300,000. Newspapers of both camps were libelous and irresponsible. They cheapened the quality of public discussion through incessant fear-mongering and character assassination. Republicans stood accused of plotting a reign of terror and of conspiring to turn the nation over to France. Federalists were charged with favoring a hereditary aristocracy and even an American dynasty that would form when John Adams's daughter married George III. Such tactics whipped up mutual distrust and made political debate emotional and subjective. Nevertheless, newspaper warfare stimulated many citizens to become politically active.

Behind the inflammatory rhetoric, the Republicans' central charge was that the Federalists had evolved into a faction bent on enriching wealthy citizens at the taxpayers' expense. In 1794 a Republican writer claimed that Federalist policies would create "a privileged order of men . . . who shall enjoy the honors, the emoluments, and the patronage of government, without contributing a farthing to its support." While many of their claims were wildly exaggerated, the Republicans effectively identified the Federalists' fundamental assumption: that citizens' worth could be measured in terms of their money.

Washington had long dreaded the nation's growing polarization into hostile factions. Republican charges that he secretly supported alleged Federalist plots to establish a monarchy enraged the president. "By God," Jefferson reported him swearing, "he [Washington] would rather be in his grave than in his present situation . . . he had rather be on his farm than to be made emperor of the world." Lonely and surrounded by mediocre advisers after Hamilton returned to private life, Washington decided in the spring of 1796 to retire after two terms. Washington recalled Hamilton to give a sharp political twist to his Farewell Address.

The heart of Washington's message was a vigorous condemnation of political parties. Partisan alignments, he insisted, endangered the Republic's survival, especially if they became entangled in disputes over foreign policy. Washington warned that the country's safety depended on citizens' avoiding "excessive partiality for one nation and excessive dislike of another." Otherwise, "real patriots" would be overwhelmed by demagogues championing foreign causes and paid by foreign governments. Aside from scrupulously fulfilling its existing treaty obligations and maintaining its foreign commerce, the United States must avoid "political connection" with Europe and its wars. If the United States gathered its strength under "an efficient government," it could defy any foreign challenge; but if it became sucked into Europe's quarrels, violence, and corruption, the republican experiment was doomed. Washington and Hamilton had skillfully turned republicanism's fear of corruption against their Republican critics. They had also evoked a vision of an America virtuously isolated from foreign intrigue and power politics, which would remain a potent inspiration until the twentieth century.

Washington left the presidency in 1797 and died in 1799. Like many later presidents, he went out amid a barrage of criticism. As he retired, the division between Republicans and Federalists hardened into a two-party system.

The Election of 1796

With the election of 1796 approaching, the Republicans cultivated a large, loyal body of voters. Their efforts to marshal support marked the first time since the Revolution that political elites had effectively mobilized ordinary Americans to take an interest in public affairs. The Republicans' constituency included the Democratic societies, workingmen's clubs, and immigrant-aid associations.

Immigrants became prime targets for Republican recruiters. During the 1790s the United States absorbed about twenty thousand French refugees from Saint Domingue and more than sixty thousand Irish, including some who had been exiled for opposing British rule. Although potential immigrant voters were few—comprising less than 2 percent of the electorate—the Irish could make a difference in Pennsylvania and New York, where public opinion was closely divided and a few hundred immigrant voters could tip the balance toward the Republicans.

In 1796 the presidential candidates were the Federalist Vice President John Adams and the Republicans' Jefferson. Republicans expected to win as many southern electoral votes and congressional seats as the Federalists counted on in New England, New Jersey, and

South Carolina. The crucial "swing" states were Pennsylvania and New York, where the Republicans fought hard to win the large immigrant (particularly Irish) vote with their pro-French and anti-British rhetoric. In the end, the Republicans took Pennsylvania but not New York, so that Jefferson lost the presidency by just three electoral votes. The Federalists narrowly regained control of the House and maintained their firm grip on the Senate. But because the Constitution did not foresee the emergence of parties, Jefferson—as the second-highest vote-getter in the electoral college—became vice president. (This provision would later be superseded by the Twelfth Amendment; see Chapter 8).

Adams's brilliance, insight, and idealism have rarely been equaled among American presidents. But the new president was more comfortable with ideas than with people, more theoretical than practical, and rather inflexible. He inspired trust and often admiration but could not command personal loyalty. His wisdom and historical vision were drowned out in highly emotional political debate. Adams's rational, reserved personality was likewise ill suited to inspiring the electorate, and he ultimately proved unable to unify the country.

The French Crisis, 1798–1799

Adams was initially fortunate that French provocations produced a sharp backlash against the Republicans. The French interpreted Jay's Treaty as an American attempt to assist Britain in its war against France. On learning of Jefferson's defeat, France began seizing American ships carrying goods to British ports, and within a year had plundered more than three hundred vessels. The French rubbed in their contempt for the United States by directing that every American captured on a British naval ship (even those involuntarily impressed) should be hanged.

Hoping to avoid war, Adams sent a peace commission to Paris. But the French foreign minister, Charles de Talleyrand, refused to meet the delegation, instead promising through three unnamed agents ("X, Y, and Z") that talks could begin after he received $250,000 and France obtained a loan of $12 million. This barefaced demand for a bribe became known as the XYZ Affair. Americans reacted to it with outrage. "Millions for defense, not one cent for tribute" became the nation's battle cry as the 1798 congressional elections began.

The XYZ Affair discredited the Republicans' foreign policy views, but the party's leaders compounded the damage by refusing to condemn French aggression and opposing Adams's call for defensive measures. The Republicans tried to excuse French behavior, whereas the Federalists rode a wave of militant patriotism. In the 1798 elections, Jefferson's supporters were routed almost everywhere, even in the South.

Congress responded to the XYZ Affair by arming fifty-four ships to protect American commerce. During the Quasi-War—an undeclared Franco-American naval conflict in the Caribbean from 1798 to 1800—U.S. forces seized ninety-three French privateers at the loss of just one vessel. The British navy meanwhile extended the protection of its convoys to America's merchant marine. By early 1799 the French remained a nuisance but were no longer a serious threat at sea.

Meanwhile, the Federalists in Congress tripled the regular army to ten thousand men in 1798, with an automatic expansion of land forces to fifty thousand in case of war. But the risk of a land war with the French was minimal. In reality, the Federalists primarily wanted a military force ready in the event of a civil war, for the crisis had produced near-hysteria about conspiracies that were being hatched by French and Irish malcontents flooding into the United States.

The Adams administration was aware that the French legation not only engaged in espionage but was also continuing Spain's policy of undermining western citizens' loyalty to America. The government knew, for example, that in 1796 General Victor Collot had traveled from Pittsburgh to New Orleans under orders to investigate the prospects for establishing an independent pro-French nation west of the mountains, and also that he had examined strategic locations to which rebellious westerners might rally. In 1798 the State Department heard that France had created "a party of mad Americans ready to join with them at a given Signal" in the West.

The Alien and Sedition Acts, 1798

The most heated controversies of the late 1790s arose from Federalists' insistence that open war with France was likely and that stringent legislation was needed to protect national security. In 1798 the Federalist-dominated Congress accordingly passed four measures known collectively as the Alien and Sedition Acts. Adams neither requested nor particularly wanted these laws, but he deferred to Federalist congressional leaders and signed them.

The least controversial of the four laws, the Alien Enemies Act, outlined procedures for determining whether the citizens of a hostile country posed a threat to the United States as spies or saboteurs. If so, they were to be deported or jailed. The law established fundamental principles for protecting national security and respecting the rights of enemy citizens. It was to operate

only if Congress declared war and thus was not used until the War of 1812 (see Chapter 8).

Second, the Alien Friends Act, a temporary peace-time statute, authorized the president to expel any foreign residents whose activities he considered dangerous. The law did not require proof of guilt, on the assumption that spies would hide or destroy evidence of their crime. Republicans maintained that the law's real purpose was to deport prominent immigrants critical of Federalist policies.

Republicans also denounced the third law, the Naturalization Act. This measure increased the residency requirement for U.S. citizenship from five to fourteen years (the last five continuously in one state), with the purpose of reducing Irish voting.

Finally came the Sedition Act, the only one of these measures enforceable against U.S. citizens. Its alleged purpose was to distinguish between free speech and attempts at encouraging others to violate federal laws or to overthrow the government. But the act nevertheless defined criminal activity so broadly that it blurred any real distinction between sedition and legitimate political discussion. Thus it forbade an individual or group "to oppose any measure or measures of the United States"— wording that could be interpreted to ban any criticism of the party in power. Another clause made it illegal to speak, write, or print any statement about the president

that would bring him "into contempt or disrepute." Under such restrictions, for example, a newspaper editor might face imprisonment for disapproving of an action by Adams or his cabinet members. The Federalist *Gazette of the United States* expressed the twisted logic of the Sedition Act perfectly: "It is patriotism to write in favor of our government—it is sedition to write against it."

Sedition cases were heard by juries, which could decide if the defendant had really intended to stir up rebellion or was merely expressing political dissent. However one looked at it, the Sedition Act interfered with free speech. Ingeniously, the Federalists wrote the law to expire in 1801 (so that it could not be turned against them if they lost the next election) and to leave them free meanwhile to heap abuse on Vice President Jefferson.

The principal target of Federalist repression was the opposition press. Four of the five largest Republican newspapers were charged with sedition just as the election of 1800 was getting under way. The attorney general used the Alien Friends Act to threaten Irish journalist John Daly Burk with expulsion (Burk went underground instead). Scottish editor Thomas Callender was being deported when he suddenly qualified for citizenship. Unable to expel Callender, the government tried him for sedition before an all-Federalist jury, which sent him to prison for criticizing the president.

He in a trice struck Lyon thrice
Upon his head, enrag'd sir.

Who seiz'd the tongs to ease his wrongs,
And Griswold thus engag'd sir.

Congress Hall,
in Philad.ᵃ Feb. 15. 1798.
S. E. Corᵣ 6ᵗʰ & Chesnut Sᵗ.

Congressional Pugilists, 1798

A cartoonist satirizes the fiercely partisan debates in Congress surrounding the Alien and Sedition Acts.

Federalist leaders never intended to fill the jails with Republican martyrs. Rather, they hoped to use a small number of highly visible prosecutions to silence Republican journalists and candidates during the election of 1800. The attorney general charged seventeen persons with sedition and won ten convictions. Among the victims was Republican congressman Matthew Lyon of Vermont ("Ragged Matt, the democrat," to the Federalists), who spent four months in prison for publishing a blast against Adams.

Vocal criticism of Federalist repression erupted during the summer of 1798 in Virginia and Kentucky. Militia commanders in these states mustered their regiments not to drill but to hear speeches demanding that the federal government respect the Bill of Rights. Entire units then signed petitions denouncing the Alien and Sedition Acts. The symbolic implications of these protests were sobering. Young men stepped forward to sign petitions on drumheads with a pen in one hand and a gun in the other, as older officers who had fought in the Continental Army looked on approvingly. It was not hard to imagine Kentucky rifles being substituted for quill pens as the men who had joined one revolution took up arms again.

Ten years earlier, opponents of the Constitution had warned that giving the national government extensive powers would eventually endanger freedom. By 1798 their prediction seemed to have come true. Shocked Republicans realized that because the Federalists controlled all three branches of the government, neither the Bill of Rights nor the system of checks and balances protected individual liberties. In this context, they advanced the doctrine of states' rights as a means of preventing the national government from violating basic freedoms.

Madison and Jefferson anonymously wrote two manifestos on states' rights that the legislatures of Virginia and Kentucky approved in 1798. Madison's Virginia Resolutions and Jefferson's Kentucky Resolutions declared that the state legislatures had never surrendered their right to judge the constitutionality of federal actions and that they retained an authority called interposition, which enabled them to protect the liberties of their citizens. A set of Kentucky Resolutions adopted in November 1799 added that objectionable federal laws might be "nullified" by the states. The resolutions did not define the terms *interposition* and *nullification*, but their intention was to invalidate the enforcement of any federal law in a state that had deemed the law unconstitutional. Although the resolutions were intended as nonviolent protests, they challenged the jurisdiction of federal courts and could have enabled state militias to march into a federal courtroom to halt proceedings at bayonet point.

Although none of the other twelve states endorsed these resolutions (ten expressed disapproval), their passage demonstrated the great potential for disunion in the late 1790s. So did a minor insurrection called the Fries Rebellion, which broke out in 1799 when crowds of Pennsylvania German farmers released prisoners jailed for refusing to pay taxes needed to fund the national army's expansion. But the disturbance collapsed when federal troops intervened.

The nation's leaders increasingly acted as if a crisis were imminent. Vice President Jefferson hinted that events might push the southern states into secession from the Union, while President Adams hid guns in his home. After passing through Richmond and learning that state officials were purchasing thousands of muskets for the militia, an alarmed Supreme Court justice wrote in January 1799 that "the General Assembly of Virginia are pursuing steps which will lead directly to civil war." A tense atmosphere hung over the Republic as the election of 1800 neared.

The Election of 1800

In the election campaign, the two parties once again rallied around the Federalist Adams (now an incumbent) and the Republican Jefferson. That the nation survived the election of 1800 without a civil war or the disregard of voters' wishes owed much to the leadership of moderates in both parties. Thus Jefferson and Madison discouraged radical activity that might provoke intervention by the national army, while Adams rejected demands by extreme "High Federalists" that he ensure victory by deliberately sparking an insurrection or asking Congress to declare war on France.

"Nothing but an open war can save us," argued one High Federalist cabinet officer. But when Adams suddenly discovered the French willing to seek peace in 1799, he proposed a special diplomatic mission. "Surprise, indignation, grief & disgust followed each other in quick succession," said a Federalist senator on hearing the news. Adams obtained Senate approval for his envoys only by threatening to resign and so make Jefferson president. Outraged High Federalists tried unsuccessfully to dump Adams, but this ill-considered maneuver rallied most New Englanders around their stubborn, upright president.

Adams's negotiations with France did not achieve a settlement until 1801, but the expectation that normal—perhaps even friendly—relations with the French would resume prevented the Federalists from exploiting

charges of Republican sympathy for the enemy. Without the immediate threat of war, moreover, voters grew resentful that in merely two years, taxes had soared 33 percent to support an army that had done nothing except chase terrified Pennsylvania farmers. As the danger of war receded, voters gave the Federalists less credit for standing up to France and more blame for adding $10 million to the national debt.

As High Federalists spitefully withheld the backing that Adams needed to win, the Republicans redoubled their efforts to elect Jefferson. They were especially successful in mobilizing voters in Philadelphia and New York, where artisans, farmers, and some entrepreneurs were ready to forsake the Federalists, whom they saw as defenders of entrenched privilege and upstart wealth. As a result, popular interest in politics rose sharply. Voter turnout in 1800 leaped to more than double that of 1788, rising from about 15 percent to almost 40 percent; in hotly contested Pennsylvania and New York, more than half the eligible voters participated.

Playing on their opponent's reputation as a religious freethinker, the Federalists forged a case against Jefferson that came down to urging citizens to vote for "GOD—AND A RELIGIOUS PRESIDENT" or impiously declare for "JEFFERSON—AND NO GOD!!!" The ploy did not prevent thousands of pious Baptists, Methodists, and other dissenters from voting Republican. (The Federalists overlooked the fact that Adams was scarcely more conventional in his religious views than Jefferson.)

Adams lost the presidency by just 8 electoral votes out of 138. He would have won if his party had not lost control of New York's state senate, which chose the electors, after a narrow defeat in New York City. Jefferson and his running mate, New York's Aaron Burr, also carried South Carolina after their backers made lavish promises of political favors to that state's legislators.

Although Adams lost, Jefferson's election was not assured. Because all 73 Republican electors voted for both of their party's nominees, the electoral college deadlocked in a Jefferson-Burr tie. Even more seriously than in 1796, the Constitution's failure to anticipate organized, rival parties affected the outcome of the electoral college's vote. The choice of president devolved upon the House of Representatives, where thirty-five ballots over six days produced no result. Aware that Republican voters and electors wanted Jefferson to be president, the wily Burr cast about for Federalist support. But after Hamilton—Burr's bitter rival in New York politics—declared his preference for Jefferson as "by far not so dangerous a man," a Federalist representative abandoned Burr and gave Jefferson the presidency by history's narrowest margin.

ECONOMIC AND SOCIAL CHANGE

During the nation's first twelve years under the Constitution, the spread of economic production for markets, even by households, transformed the lives of many Americans. For some people the changes were for the better and for others for the worse, but for most the ultimate outcome remained uncertain in 1800. At the same time, many Americans were rethinking questions of gender and race in American society.

Households and Market Production

For centuries the backbone of European societies and their colonial offshoots had been economies in which most production took place in household settings. At the core of each household was a patriarchal family—the male head, his wife, and their unmarried children. Beyond these family members, most households included other people. Some outsiders were relatives, but most were either boarders or workers—apprentices and journeymen in artisan shops, servants and slaves in well-off urban households, and slaves, "hired hands," and tenant farmers in rural settings. (Even slaves living in separate "quarters" on large plantations labored in an enterprise centered on their owners' households.) Unlike in our modern world, before the nineteenth century nearly everyone worked at what was temporarily or permanently "home." The notion of "going to work" would have struck them as odd.

Although households varied in size and economic orientation, in the late eighteenth century the vast majority were on small farms and consisted of only an owner and his family. By 1800 such farm families typically included seven children who contributed to production. While husbands and older sons worked in fields away from the house, women, daughters, and young sons maintained the barns and gardens near the house and provided food and clothing for all family members. Women, of course, bore and reared all the children as well. As in the colonial period, most farm families produced food and other products largely for their own consumption, adding small surpluses for bartering with neighbors or local merchants.

In the aftermath of the American Revolution, households in the most heavily settled regions of the Northeast began to change. Relatively prosperous farm families, particularly in the mid-Atlantic states, increasingly directed their surplus production to meet the growing demands of urban customers for produce, meat, and dairy products (see Technology and Culture: Mid-Atlantic Daily Production in the 1790s).

Poorer farm families, especially in New England, found less lucrative ways to produce for commercial markets. Small plots of land on New England's thin, rocky soil no longer supported large families, leading young people to look beyond their immediate locales for means of support. While many young men and young couples moved west, unmarried daughters more frequently remained at home where they could help satisfy a growing demand for manufactured cloth. Before the Revolution, affluent colonists had imported cloth as well as finished clothing, but the boycott of British goods led many women to either spin their own or purchase it from other women (see Chapter 5). After the Revolution, enterprising merchants began catering to urban consumers as well as southern slaveowners seeking to clothe their slaves as cheaply as possible. Making regular circuits through rural areas, the merchants supplied cloth to mothers and daughters in farm households. A few weeks later they would return and pay the women in cash for their handiwork.

A comparable transition began in some artisans' households. The shoemakers of Lynn, Massachusetts, had expanded their production during the Revolution when filling orders from the Continental Army. After the war, some more-successful artisans began supplying leather to other shoemakers, paying them for the finished product. By 1800 these merchants were taking leather to farm families beyond Lynn in order to fill an annual demand that had risen to 400,000 from 189,000 pairs in 1789.

Numerous other enterprises likewise emerged, employing men as well as women to satisfy demands that self-contained households could never have met on their own. For example, a traveler passing through Middleborough, Massachusetts, observed,

> In the winter season, the inhabitants . . . are principally employed in making nails, of which they send large quantities to market. This business is a profitable addition to their husbandry; and fills up a part of the year, in which, otherwise, many of them would find little employment.

Behind the new industries was an ambitious, aggressive class of businessmen, most of whom had begun as merchants and now invested their profits in factories, ships, government bonds, and banks. Such entrepreneurs stimulated a flurry of innovative business ventures that pointed toward the future. The country's first private banks were founded in the 1780s in Philadelphia, Boston, and New York. Philadelphia merchants created the Pennsylvania Society for the Encouragement of Manufactures and the Useful Arts in 1787. This organiza-

Philadelphia City Directory, 1796
Like other city directories of its time, Philadelphia's listed all heads of households from the most prominent to the most humble.

tion promoted the immigration of English artisans familiar with the latest industrial technology, including Samuel Slater, a pioneer of American industrialization who helped establish a cotton-spinning mill at Pawtucket, Rhode Island, in 1790 (see Chapter 9). In 1791 investors from New York and Philadelphia, with Hamilton's enthusiastic endorsement, started the Society for the Encouragement of Useful Manufactures, which attempted to demonstrate the potential of large-scale industrial enterprises by building a factory town at Paterson, New Jersey. That same year, New York merchants and insurance underwriters organized America's first formal association for trading government bonds, out of which the New York Stock Exchange evolved.

White Women and the Republic

Along with the growing importance of women's economic roles, whites' discussions of republicanism during and after the Revolution raised larger questions of women's equality. The Revolution and the adoption of republican constitutions had not significantly affected the legal position of white women, although some states eased women's difficulties in obtaining divorces. Nor did women gain new political rights, except in New Jersey. That state's 1776 constitution, by not specifying gender and race, left a loophole that enabled white female and black property holders to vote, which many began to do. During the 1790s, New Jersey explicitly permitted otherwise qualified women to vote by adopting laws that stipulated "he or she" when referring to voters. In the hotly contested state election of 1797, women's votes nearly gave the victory to a Federalist candidate. His victorious Republican opponent, John Condict, would get his revenge in 1807 by successfully advocating a bill to disenfranchise women (along with free blacks).

Mid-Atlantic Dairy Production in the 1790s

Nine out of ten white Americans lived on farms in 1800, and virtually every farm included a dairy operation. Although the work of dairying was divided by gender, it involved men and women alike. Along with other responsibilities in the fields, men maintained and fed the farm's herd of dairy cattle. Among their many tasks in the house, yard, and outbuildings, women milked the cows and turned most of the milk into cream and butter. In dairying, as in all farm work, men and women drew on the labor of their sons and daughters, respectively, and often of live-in relatives or laborers.

At the end of the eighteenth century, a growing urban demand for dairy products spurred farmers near northeastern cities, especially Philadelphia, whose population surpassed forty-two thousand in 1790, to seek cost-effective ways to increase production. The farmers often turned to agricultural experts, whose advice their parents and grandparents had usually, and proudly, spurned. Many farm men introduced clover into the pastures they tended, following the suggestion of one author who maintained that clover "flushes [a cow] to milk." Men also recognized that while milk production was lower during winter, when most cattle remained outdoors, protecting their herds then would improve milk production year-round. Accordingly, they expanded acreage devoted to hay and built barns to shelter the cows in cold weather and to store the hay. A federal census in 1798 revealed that about half the farms in eastern Pennsylvania had barns, usually of logs or framed but occasionally of stone. After the turn of the century, men would also begin to shop for particular breeds of cattle that produced more milk for more months of each year.

Farmwomen of the period—often referred to as "dairymaids"—likewise sought to improve cows' productivity. The milking process itself changed little. Mid-Atlantic women milked an average of six animals twice a

Churning Butter

During the late eighteenth century, farmwomen shifted from the plunger churn (background) to the more efficent barrel churn in order to increase their production of butter.

day, with each "milch cow" producing about two gallons per day during the summer. Most of women's efforts to increase production had to do with making butter, the dairy product in greatest demand among urban consumers.

During the 1780s and 1790s many farmwomen moved butter making from the cellar to the springhouse, or milkhouse, a structure (originating in Continental Europe) built of logs or stone over a spring or stream. The water flowing under a springhouse was diverted to a smooth-bottomed trench. The house also featured shelves for storage and counters on which the women worked. Women carried the milk in six-gallon pails from the barn to the springhouse (typically a distance of one hundred to two hundred yards), where they poured it into shallow pans or tubs. Although most women preferred pans made of glazed earthenware, some used wooden tubs out of fears that lead in the glaze of the pans could poison their milk. The glaze in American earthenware "is pure *lead*, and consequently a strong *poison*," warned a farm advice book published in 1801. Women placed the pans or tubs in the trench, allowing the milk to cool for about a day or two until the cream rose to the top. Then they skimmed off the cream, using a paddle with holes, and placed the cream in a barrel. Once the barrel was full or the contents began to sour, it was time to churn the cream into butter.

Churning separates the fat particles in cream from the liquid encasing them, thereby allowing the fat to clump together. As eighteenth-century farmers phrased it, churning was the way "to bring the butter." Butter churns had been developed in England as early as the fifteenth century, but were used only by the most affluent farmers there and in the colonies until the late eighteenth century. These early churns were called plunger or dasher churns. Women moved the plungers up, down, and around to agitate the cream. Although taking about three hours to produce a pound or two of butter, plunger churns were adequate for supplying the family and a few local customers. But as women sought to increase production for urban markets, those who could afford it purchased barrel churns in which they turned a handle that moved a barrel of cream around an axle.

They then pressed the churned butter with their hand or a wooden utensil to remove the remaining liquid and salted it to preserve it during storage and transport to market.

The innovations undertaken by "dairymaids" and male farmers at the end of the eighteenth century appear minimal compared with those that would be undertaken during the decades that followed. But it was these small beginnings that set in motion a series of technological changes in churning and other aspects of dairy production. These changes eventually led to the point where a typical farm was, as one visitor described a Pennsylvania farm in 1867, "a butter factory rather than a farm." Central to these innovations were women, whose labor and knowledge of their craft enabled their households to change from simple subsistence farming to lucrative commercial operations.

Focus Questions:

- What conditions led mid-Atlantic farm families to strive to increase dairy production at the end of the eighteenth century?
- What were the most important technological changes enabling women to increase their production of butter?

Wooden Milk Tub for Separating Cream
Women cooled milk for one or two days in tubs like this one, then skimmed the cream that had risen to the top. This tub is fifteen inches in diameter and five inches deep (excluding handles).

In other areas of American life, social change and republican ideology together fostered more formidable challenges to traditional attitudes toward women's rights. American republicans increasingly recognized the right of a woman to choose her husband—a striking departure from the continued practice among some elites whereby fathers approved or even arranged marriages. Thus in 1790, on the occasion of his daughter Martha's marriage, Jefferson wrote to a friend that, following "the usage of my country, I scrupulously suppressed my wishes, [so] that my daughter might indulge her sentiments freely."

Outside elite circles, such independence was even more apparent. Especially in the Northeast, daughters increasingly got pregnant by prospective husbands, thus forcing their fathers to consent to their marrying in order to avoid a public scandal. In Hallowell, Maine, in May 1792, for example, Mary Brown's father objected to her marrying John Chamberlain. In December, he finally consented and the couple wed—just two days before Mary Chamberlain gave birth. By becoming pregnant, northeastern women secured economic support in a region where an exodus of young, unmarried men was leaving a growing number of women single.

White women also had fewer children overall than had their mothers and grandmothers. In Sturbridge, Massachusetts, women in the mid-eighteenth century averaged nearly nine children per marriage, compared with six in the first decade of the nineteenth century. Whereas 40 percent of Quaker women had nine or more children before 1770, only 14 percent bore that many thereafter. Such statistics testify to declining farm sizes and urbanization, both of which were incentives for having fewer children. But they also indicate that some women were finding relief from the near-constant state of pregnancy and nursing that had consumed their grandmothers.

As white women's roles expanded, so too did republican notions of male-female relations. "I object to the word 'obey' in the marriage-service," wrote a female author calling herself Matrimonial Republican, "because it is a general word, without limitations or definition. . . . The obedience between man and wife is, or ought to be mutual." Lack of mutuality was one reason for a rising number of divorce petitions from women, from fewer than fourteen per year in Connecticut before the Revolution, to forty-five in 1795.

A few women also challenged the sexual double standard that allowed men to indulge in extramarital affairs while their female partners, single or married, were condemned. Writing in 1784, an author calling herself Daphne pointed out how a woman whose illicit affair was exposed was "forever deprive[d] . . . of all that renders life valuable," while "the base [male] betrayer is suffered to triumph in the success of his unmanly arts, and to pass unpunished even by a frown." Daphne called on her "sister Americans" to "stand by and support the dignity of our own sex" by publicly condemning seducers rather than their victims.

Gradually, the subordination of women, which once was taken for granted among most whites, became the subject of debate. In "On the Equality of the Sexes" (1790), essayist and poet Judith Sargent Murray contended that the genders had equal intellectual ability and deserved equal education. "We can only reason from what we know," she wrote, "and if an opportunity of acquiring knowledge hath been denied us, the inferi-

Advocating Women's Rights, 1792

In this illustration from an American magazine for women, the "Genius of the Ladies Magazine" and the "Genius of Emulation" presents Liberty with a petition based on British feminist Mary Wollstonecraft's *Vindication of the Rights of Woman.*

FRONTISPIECE.

ority of our sex cannot fairly be deduced from there." Murray hoped that "sensible and informed" women would improve their minds rather than rush into marriage (as she had at eighteen), enabling them to instill republican ideals in their children.

Like many of her contemporaries, Murray supported "republican motherhood." Republicans emphasized the importance of educating white women in the values of liberty and independence in order to strengthen virtue in the new nation. It was the duty of women to inculcate these values in their sons as well as their daughters. Even so conservative a man as John Adams reminded his daughter that she was part of "a young generation, coming up in America . . . [and] will be responsible for a great share of the duty and opportunity of educating a rising family, from whom much will be expected." Before the 1780s only a few women had acquired an advanced education through private tutors. Thereafter, urban elites broadened such opportunities by founding numerous private schools, or academies, for girls. Massachusetts also established an important precedent in 1789 when it forbade any town to exclude girls from its elementary schools.

By itself, however, the expansion of educational opportunities for white women would have a limited effect. "I acknowledge we have an equal share of curiosity with the other sex," wrote Mercy Otis Warren to Abigail Adams, but men "have the opportunities of gratifying their inquisitive humour to the utmost, in the great school of the world, while we are confined to the narrow circle of domesticity." Although the great struggle for female political equality would not begin until the next century, republican assertions that women were intellectually and morally men's peers provoked scattered calls for political equality. In 1793 Priscilla Mason, a young woman graduating from one of the female academies, blamed "*Man*, despotic man" for shutting women out of the church, the courts, and government. In her salutatory oration, she urged that a women's senate be established by Congress to evoke "all that is human—all that is *divine* in the soul of woman." Warren and Mason had pointed out a fundamental limitation to republican egalitarianism in the America of the 1790s: while women could be virtuous wives and mothers, the world outside their homes still offered them few opportunities to apply their education.

Native Americans in the New Republic

By 1795 Native Americans in eastern North America had suffered severe losses of population, territory (see Map 7.3), and political and cultural self-determination. Thousands of deaths had resulted from battle, famine, and disease during the succession of wars since the 1740s and from poverty, losses of land, and discrimination during peacetime as well. From 1775 to 1795, the Cherokees declined from sixteen thousand to ten thousand and the Iroquois fell from about nine thousand to four thousand. During the quarter-century before 1800, Native Americans east and west of the Appalachians forfeited more land than the area inhabited by whites in 1775. Ignoring the Indian Non-Intercourse Act, eastern states seized Indian lands without congressional approval, crowding Native Americans onto tiny, widely separated reservations. Settlers, liquor dealers, and criminals trespassed on Indian lands, while government agents and missionaries pressured Native Americans to give up their communal lands and traditional cultures. Indians who sold land or worked for whites were often paid in the unfamiliar medium of cash and then found little to spend it on in their isolated communities other than alcohol.

In the face of such losses and pressures, many Native Americans became demoralized. Unable to strike back at whites, Indian men often drank heavily and inflicted violence on one another. All too typical were the tragedies that beset Mary Jemison, born a half-century earlier to white settlers but a Seneca Iroquois since her wartime capture at age ten. Jemison saw one of her sons murder his two brothers in alcohol-related episodes before meeting a similar fate himself.

Such predicaments spawned a profound social and moral crisis within tribes, like the Seneca, threatened by whites' expansion. But in 1799 a Seneca prophet, Handsome Lake, emerged and led his people in a remarkable spiritual revival. Severely ill, alcoholic, and near death, he experienced a series of visions, which Iroquois people traditionally interpreted as spiritually meaningful. As in the visions of the Iroquois prophet Hiawatha in the fourteenth century (see Chapter 1), spiritual guides instructed Handsome Lake first in his own recovery and then in the healing of his people. Invoking Iroquois religious traditions, Handsome Lake preached against alcoholism and sought to revive unity and self-confidence among the Seneca. At the same time, he welcomed Quaker missionaries and federal aid earmarked for teaching Euro-American agricultural methods to Seneca men, whose older roles as traders and warriors were no longer tenable.

The most traditional Senecas rejected the notion that Native men should work like white farmers; said one, only "squaws and hedgehogs are made to scratch the ground." But many Seneca men welcomed the

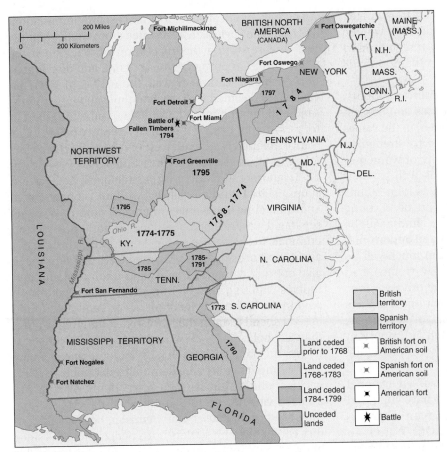

MAP 7.3

Indian Land Cessions, 1768–1799

During the last third of the eighteenth century, Native Americans were forced to give up extensive homelands throughout the eastern backcountry and farther west in the Ohio and Tennessee River valleys.

through wartime service. Ten years later 11 percent controlled their own fates (see Figure 7.1). Various state reforms meanwhile attempted to improve slaves' conditions. In 1791, for example, the North Carolina legislature declared that the former "distinction of criminality between the murder of a white person and one who is equally an human creature, but merely of a different complexion, is disgraceful to humanity" and authorized the execution of whites who murdered slaves. Although for economic as much as for humanitarian reasons, by 1794 most states had outlawed the Atlantic slave trade.

Hesitant measures to ensure free blacks' legal equality also appeared in the 1780s and early 1790s. Most states dropped restrictions on African Americans' freedom of movement and protected their property. Of the sixteen states in the Union by 1796, all but three either permitted free blacks to vote or made no specific attempt to exclude them. But by then a countertrend was reversing many of Revolutionary era advances. Before the 1790s ended, abolitionist sentiment ebbed, slavery became more entrenched, and whites resisted accepting even free blacks as fellow citizens.

Federal law led the way in restricting the rights of blacks and other nonwhites. When Congress established procedures for naturalizing aliens in 1790, it limited eligibility for U.S. citizenship to foreign whites. The federal militia law of 1792 required whites to enroll in local units but allowed states to exclude free blacks, an option that state governments increasingly chose. The navy and the marine corps forbade nonwhite enlistments in 1798. Delaware stripped free, property-owning black males of the vote in 1792, and by 1807 Maryland, Kentucky, and New Jersey had followed suit. Free black men continued to vote and to serve in some integrated militia organizations after 1800 (including in the slave states of North Carolina and Tennessee), but the number of places that treated them as the political equals of whites dropped sharply.

change. It was women who resisted most, because they stood to lose their collective ownership of farmland, their control of the food supply, and their considerable political influence. Other Senecas accused women who rejected Handsome Lake's teachings of witchcraft, and even killed a few of them. As among other Native Americans, the conflict between traditional and new ways among the Senecas was divisive and proceeded fitfully.

Redefining the Color Line

The Republic's first years marked the high tide of African-Americans' Revolutionary era success in bettering their lot. Although racism had not disappeared, Jefferson's eloquent words "all men are created equal" had stirred blacks' aspirations and awakened many whites' consciences. By 1790, 8 percent of all African-Americans enjoyed freedom —many having purchased their liberty or earned it

In the face of growing constrictions on their freedom and opportunities, free African-Americans in the North turned to one another for support. Self-help among African-Americans flowed especially through religious channels. During the 1780s two recently freed black Christians, Richard Allen and Absalom Jones, formed the Free African Society of Philadelphia, a community organization whose members pooled their scarce resources to assist one another and other blacks in need. After the white-dominated Methodist church they attended tried to restrict black worshippers to the gallery, Allen, Jones and most of the black membership withdrew and formed a separate congregation. Comparable developments unfolded in other northern communities, eventually leading to the formation of a new denomination, the African Methodist Episcopal Church (see Chapter 9).

An especially revealing indication of whites' changing racial attitudes occurred in 1793, when Congress enacted the Fugitive Slave Law. This law required judges to award possession of an escaped slave upon any formal request by a master or his representative. Accused runaways not only were denied a jury trial but also were sometimes refused permission to present evidence of their freedom. Slaves' legal status as property disqualified them from claiming these constitutional privileges, but the Fugitive Slave Law denied free blacks the legal protections that the Bill of Rights guaranteed them as citizens. Congress nevertheless passed this measure without serious opposition. The law marked a striking departure from the atmosphere of the 1780s, when state governments had moved toward granting whites and free blacks legal equality.

The slave revolution on Saint Domingue (which victorious blacks had renamed Haiti) notably undermined the American trend toward abolition and helped transform many whites' image of blacks from victims to a menacing threat. In August 1800 such fears were kindled when a slave insurrection broke out near Virginia's capital, Richmond. Amid the election campaign that year, in which Federalists and Republicans accused one another

FIGURE 7.1

Number and Percentage of Free Blacks, by State, 1800

Within a generation of the Declaration of Independence, a large free-black population emerged that included every ninth African American. In the North, only in New Jersey and New York did most blacks remain slaves. Almost half of all free blacks lived in the South. Every sixth black in Maryland was free by 1800.

State	Total Number of Free Blacks	Free Blacks as a Percentage of Total Black Population
Massachusetts	7,378	100%
Vermont	557	100%
New Hampshire	855	99%
Rhode Island	3,304	90%
Pennsylvania	14,564	89%
Connecticut	5,300	85%
Delaware	8,268	57%
New York	10,374	33%
New Jersey	4,402	26%
Maryland	19,587	16%
Virginia	20,124	6%
North Carolina	7,043	5%
South Carolina	3,185	2%
Georgia	1,019	2%
Kentucky	741	2%
Tennessee	309	2%
UNITED STATES	108,395*	11%

* Total includes figures from the District of Columbia, Mississippi Territory, and Northwest Territory. These areas are not shown on the chart.

Source: U.S. Bureau of the Census.

of endangering liberty and hinted at violence, a slave named Gabriel calculated that the split among whites afforded blacks an opportunity to gain their freedom. Having secretly assembled weapons, he and several other blacks organized a march on Richmond by more than a thousand slaves. The plot was leaked on the eve of the march. Obtaining confessions from some participants, the authorities rounded up the rest and executed thirty-five of them, including Gabriel. "I have nothing more to offer than what General Washington would have had to offer, had he been taken by the British officers and put to trial by them," said one rebel before his execution. "I have ventured my life in endeavoring to obtain the liberty of my countrymen, and I am a willing sacrifice to their cause." In the end, Gabriel's Rebellion only confirmed whites' anxieties that Haiti's revolution could be replayed on American soil.

A technological development also strengthened slavery. During the 1790s demand in the British textile industry stimulated the cultivation of cotton in coastal

Absalom Jones, by Raphael Peale, 1810
Born a slave, Jones was allowed to study and work for pay; eventually he bought his freedom. He became a businessman, a cofounder of the African Methodist Episcopal Church, and a stalwart in Philadelphia's free black community.

South Carolina and Georgia. The soil and climate were ideal for growing long-staple cotton, a variety whose fibers could be separated easily from its seed by squeezing it through rollers. In the South's upland and interior regions, however, the only cotton that would thrive was the short-staple variety, whose seed stuck so tenaciously to the fibers that rollers crushed the seeds and ruined the fibers. It was as if growers had discovered gold only to find that they could not mine it. But in 1793 a New Englander, Eli Whitney, invented a cotton gin that successfully separated the fibers of short-staple cotton from the seed. Quickly copied and improved upon by others, Whitney's invention removed a major obstacle to the spread of cotton cultivation. It gave a new lease on life to plantation slavery and undermined the doubts of those who considered slavery economically outmoded.

By 1800 free blacks had suffered noticeable erosion of their post-Revolutionary gains, and southern slaves were farther from freedom than a decade earlier. Two vignettes poignantly communicate the plight of African-Americans. By arrangement with her late husband, Martha Washington freed the family's slaves a year after George died. But many of the freed blacks remained impoverished and dependent on the Washington estate

because Virginia law prohibited the education of blacks and otherwise denied them opportunities to realize their freedom. Meanwhile, across the Potomac, enslaved blacks were performing most of the labor on the new national capital that would bear the first president's name. African-Americans were manifestly losing ground.

CONCLUSION

The survival of the United States was by no means assured during its first twelve years under the new Constitution. With the country badly divided along lines of region, economic interest, and ideology, Hamilton pushed through a series of bold innovations that strengthened the federal government by giving it responsibility for the nation's debt and for overseeing a national bank. Jefferson, Madison, and many others opposed these measures, arguing that they favored northeastern commercial interests at the expense of other Americans and that they threatened liberty with their concentration of economic and political power in relatively few hands. At the same time Spain and Britain resisted U.S. expansion west of the Appalachians, while Britain and revolutionary France each tried to coerce the young Republic into supporting it against the other. All these issues bitterly divided white elites, finally causing them to form two rival political parties—the Federalists and the Republicans. Only with the peaceful transfer of power from Federalists to Republicans in 1800 could the nation's long-term political stability be taken for granted.

Meanwhile, some whites granted limited recognition of women's independence, while most abandoned the Revolution's loftiest goals for nonwhites, placing new restrictions on free and enslaved blacks' quest for freedom and new obstacles to Native Americans' physical and cultural survival. In the face of such barriers, both peoples persisted, but they did not flourish.

FOR FURTHER REFERENCE

READINGS

Douglas R. Egerton, *Gabriel's Rebellion: The Virginia Slave Conspiracies of 1800 and 1802* (1993). A thorough, well-written narrative that presents slave resistance against the backdrop of post-Revolutionary society and politics.

Stanley Elkins and Eric McKitrick, *The Age of Federalism: The Early American Republic, 1788–1800* (1993). A magisterial account of politics and diplomacy through the election of 1800.

Joseph J. Ellis, *Founding Brothers: The Revolutionary Generation* (2000). A vivid study of the role of personalities and personal relationships among political leaders in shaping the new nation.

CHRONOLOGY, 1789–1800

1789 First Congress convenes in New York.
George Washington inaugurated as first president.
Judiciary Act.
French Revolution begins.

1790 Alexander Hamilton submits Reports on Public Credit and National Bank to Congress.
Treaty of New York.

1791 Bank of the United States established with twenty-year charter.
Vermont admitted to the Union.
Bill of Rights ratified.
Slave uprising begins in French colony of Saint Domingue.
Society for the Encouragement of Useful Manufactures founded.
Hamilton submits his Report on Manufactures to Congress.

1792 Washington reelected president.
Kentucky admitted to the Union.

1793 Fugitive Slave Law.
Chisholm v. *Georgia.*
French planters flee slaves' revolution in Saint Domingue for the United States.

France declares war on Britain and Spain.
Washington's Neutrality Proclamation.
Citizen Genet arrives in United States.
First Democratic societies established.

1794 Whiskey Rebellion in western Pennsylvania.
General Anthony Wayne's forces defeat Shawnees in the Battle of Fallen Timbers.

1795 Treaty of Greenville.
Jay's Treaty with Britain ratified.

1796 Tennessee admitted to the Union.
Treaty of San Lorenzo (Pinckney's Treaty) ratified.
Washington's Farewell Address.
John Adams elected president.

1798 XYZ Affair.
Alien and Sedition Acts.
Eleventh Amendment to the Constitution ratified.

1798–1799 Virginia and Kentucky Resolutions.

1798–1800 Quasi-War between United States and France.

1799 Fries Rebellion in Pennsylvania.

1800 Gabriel's Rebellion in Virginia.
Thomas Jefferson elected president.

Joanne B. Freeman, *Affairs of Honor: National Politics in the New Republic* (2001). An insightful discussion of politics in the 1790s and the passions that underlay them.

Ramón A. Gutiérrez and Richard J. Orsi (eds.), *Contested Eden: California and the Gold Rush* (1998). A fine collection of essays, introducing the history of the Pacific colony under Spanish and Mexican rule.

Joan M. Jensen, *Loosening the Bonds: Mid-Atlantic Farm Women, 1750–1850* (1986). A study of the interplay of women's roles and commercialization in what was then America's most dynamic agricultural region.

Gary B. Nash, *Forging Freedom: The Formation of Philadelphia's Black Community, 1720–1840* (1988). A landmark study of how North America's largest African-American community formed and survived in the face of racism and poverty.

Claudio Saunt, *A New Order of Things: Property, Power, and the Transformation of the Creek Indians, 1733–1816* (1999). A pathbreaking account of how eastern North America's most powerful Indian nation adapted to political, economic, and cultural change, and of the price its people paid for their survival.

Alan Taylor, *William Cooper's Town: Power and Persuasion on the Frontier of the Early American Republic* (1995). The compelling story of one elite Federalist's fall in the face of the Republicans' rise to power.

Laurel Thatcher Ulrich, *A Midwife's Tale: The Life of Martha Ballard, Based on Her Diary, 1785–1812* (1990). A Pulitzer Prize-winning study of a rural woman's life in northern New England.

WEBSITES

Africans in America: The Constitution and New Nation
http://www.pbs.org/wgbh/aia/part2/2narr5.html
A segment of a very informative site devoted to African-Americans from 1450 to 1865, documenting legislation and the activism of blacks, white abolitionists, and proslavery planters.

DoHistory
http://www.dohistory.org/
An outstanding website that uses the diary of midwife Martha Ballard to demonstrate how historians and students can reconstruct and interpret the history of any subject through evidence from primary sources.

The Papers of George Washington
http://gwpapers.virginia.edu/
An excellent introduction to Washington's multifaceted life and to his public and private writings.

For additional readings please consult the bibliography at the end of the book.

CHAPTER 8

Jeffersonianism and the Era of Good Feelings,

1801–1824

O n March 4, 1801, Vice President Thomas Jefferson walked from his board-ing house to the Capitol to be inaugurated as the nation's third president. His decision to walk rather than ride in a coach reflected his distaste for pomp and ceremony, which he thought had grown out of hand in the Washington and Adams administrations. The stroll was also practical, for the new capital, Washington, had scarcely any streets. Pennsylvania Avenue was no more than a path cut through swamp and woods (so dense that congress-men got lost in them) to connect the unfinished Capitol with the city's only other building of note, the president's mansion. Officials called the place "hateful," "this abode of splendid misery," a "desert city," and the "abomina-tion of desolation."

After arriving at the Capitol, Jefferson was sworn in by the new chief jus-tice, John Marshall, a John Adams appointee whom Jefferson already had begun to distrust. The absence of the outgoing president reminded everyone of the bitterness of the 1800 election, which Federalists had interpreted as a victory for the "worthless, the dishonest, the rapacious, the vile and the ungodly."

Nevertheless, in his inaugural address, Jefferson struck a conciliatory note. The will of the majority must prevail, but the minority had "their equal rights," he assured the beaten Federalists. He traced the political convulsions

Portrait of Samuel Chester Reid by John Wesley Jarvis, 1815
The proud look on this young naval officer's face, painted at the conclusion of the War of 1812, illustrates the confidence and patriotism with which Americans emerged from their first major war since Independence. But the prelude to the war had tested American unity and self-assurance, and so would its aftermath.

CHAPTER OUTLINE

The Age of Jefferson

The Gathering Storm

The War of 1812

The Awakening of American Nationalism

of the 1790s to differing responses to the French Revolution, an external event whose fury had passed, and he thereby suggested that the source of American discord was foreign and distant. What Americans needed to recognize was that they agreed on essentials, that "every difference of opinion is not a difference of principle," that "we are all republicans, we are all federalists."

Newspapers added capitals and printed the last clause as "we are all Republicans, we are all Federalists," but in Jefferson's manuscript the words appear as "republicans" and "federalists." The distinction is critical. Jefferson's point was not that the Federalist and Republican parties would merge or dissolve. Compared to President Adams, Jefferson would play a much more active role as leader of his party. Rather, Jefferson hoped that, since the vast majority of Americans accepted the federal union (federalism) and representative government (republicanism), they would develop a more harmonious spirit in politics.

Jefferson's ideals cast a lengthy shadow over the period from 1801 to 1824. His purchase in 1803 of the vast Louisiana Territory, motivated by a mixture of principle and opportunity, nearly doubled the size of the United States. His successors in the "Virginia Dynasty" of Republican presidents, James Madison and James Monroe, warmly supported his principle that governments were strong to the extent that they earned the affection of a contented people. Increasingly deserted by voters, the opposition Federalist party first disintegrated and then collapsed as a national force by 1820.

Yet the harmony for which Jefferson longed proved elusive. Contrary to Jefferson's expectation, events in Europe continued to agitate American politics. In 1807 the United States moved to end all trade with Europe to avoid being sucked into the ongoing war between Britain and France. The failure of this policy led to war with Britain in 1812.

Foreign policy was not the only source of discord. The Federalist decline opened the way for intensified factionalism in the Republican party during Jefferson's second term (1805–1809) and again during the misleadingly named Era of Good Feelings (1817–1824). Republican factionalism often grew out of conflicting assessments of Jefferson's philosophy by his followers. Some, like the eccentric John Randolph, argued that, as president, Jefferson was deserting his own principles. Other Republicans interpreted the often inept performance of the American government and army during the War of 1812 as proving the need for a stronger centralized government than Jefferson had desired. Most ominously, in 1819 and 1820 northern and southern Republicans

divided along sectional lines over the extension of slavery into Missouri, much to the dismay of Jefferson, who found nothing in the Constitution to prevent either slavery or its extension.

This chapter focuses on five major questions:

■ How did Jefferson's philosophy of government shape his policies toward public expenditures, the judiciary, and the Louisiana Purchase?

■ What divisions emerged within the Republican party during Jefferson's second term?

■ What led James Madison to abandon Jefferson's policy of "peaceable coercion" and go to war with Britain in 1812?

■ How did the War of 1812 influence American domestic politics?

■ To what extent did Jefferson's legacy persist into the Era of Good Feelings? To what extent was it discarded?

THE AGE OF JEFFERSON

Narrowly elected in 1800, Jefferson saw his popularity rise during his first term, when he moved quickly to scale down seemingly unnecessary government expenditures. Increasingly confident of popular support, he worked to loosen the Federalists' grip on appointive federal offices, especially in the judiciary. His purchase of Louisiana against Federalist opposition added to his popularity. In all of these moves, Jefferson was guided not merely by political calculation but also by his philosophy of government, eventually known as Jeffersonianism.

Jefferson and Jeffersonianism

A man of extraordinary attainments, Jefferson was fluent in French, read Latin and Greek, and studied several Native American languages. He served for more than twenty years as president of America's foremost scientific association, the American Philosophical Society. A student of architecture, he designed his own mansion in Virginia, Monticello, and spent over forty years overseeing its construction. Gadgets fascinated him. He invented a device for duplicating his letters, of which he wrote over twenty thousand, and he improved the design for a revolving book stand, which enabled him to consult up

to five books at once (by 1814 he owned seven thousand books in a host of languages). His public career was luminous: principal author of the Declaration of Independence, governor of Virginia, ambassador to France, secretary of state under Washington, and vice-president under John Adams.

Yet he was, and remains, a controversial figure. His critics, pointing to his doubts about some Christian doctrines and his early support for the French Revolution, portrayed him as an infidel and radical. During the election campaign of 1800, Federalists alleged that he kept a slave mistress. In 1802 James Callender, a former supporter furious about not receiving a government job he wanted, wrote a newspaper account in which he named Sally Hemings, a house slave at Monticello, as the mistress. Drawing on the DNA of Sally's male heirs and link-ing the timing of Jefferson's visits to Monticello with the start of Sally's pregnancies, most scholars now view it as very likely that Jefferson, a widower, was the father of at least one of her four surviving children.

Callender's story did Jefferson little damage in Virginia, not because it was discounted but because Jefferson acted according to the rules of white Virginia gentlemen by never acknowledging any of Sally's children as his own. Although he freed two of her children (the other two ran away), he never freed Sally, the daughter of Jefferson's own father-in-law and so light-skinned that she could pass for white, nor did he ever mention her in his vast correspondence. Yet the story of Sally fed the charge that Jefferson was a hypocrite, for throughout his career he condemned the very "race-mixing" to which he appears to have contributed.

Jefferson did not believe that blacks and whites could live permanently side-by-side in American society. As the black population grew, he feared a race war so vicious that it could be suppressed only by a dictator. This view was consistent with his conviction that the real threat to republics rose less from hostile neighbors than from within. He knew that the French had turned to a dictator, Napoleon Bonaparte, to save them from the chaos of their own revolution. Only by colonizing blacks in Africa, an idea embodied in the American Colonization Society (1816), could America avert a similar fate.

Jefferson worried that high taxes, standing armies, and public corruption could destroy American liberty by

Man of the People
Foreign diplomats in the United States were often shocked when Jefferson greeted them dressed in every-day working clothes and carpet slippers. But Jefferson thought of himself as a working politician and man of the people, not as an aristocratic figurehead.

Thomas Jefferson's Polygraph, 1806
Jefferson judged this "polygraph" to be the finest invention of his age. He used it to make copies of his letters from 1806 until his death.

turning government into the master rather than servant of the people. To prevent tyranny, he advocated that state governments retain considerable authority. In a vast republic marked by strong local attachments, he reasoned, state governments would be more responsive to the popular will than would the government in Washington.

He also believed that popular liberty required popular virtue. For republican theorists like Jefferson, virtue consisted of a decision to place the public good ahead of one's private interests and to exercise vigilance to keep governments from growing out of control. To Jefferson, the most vigilant and virtuous people were educated farmers, who were accustomed to act and think with sturdy independence. The least vigilant were the inhabitants of cities. Jefferson regarded cities as breeding grounds for mobs and as menaces to liberty. Men who relied on merchants or factory owners for their jobs could have their votes influenced, in contrast to the independence of farmers who worked their own land. When the people "get piled upon one another in large cities, as in Europe," he wrote, "they will become corrupt as in Europe."

Jefferson's "Revolution"

Jefferson described his election as a revolution, but the revolution he sought was to restore the liberty and tranquillity that (he thought) the United States had enjoyed in its early years and to reverse the drift toward despotism that he had seen in Alexander Hamilton's economic program and John Adams's Alien and Sedition Acts (see Chapter 7). One alarming sign of this drift was the growth of the national debt by $10 million under the Federalists. Jefferson and his secretary of the treasury, Albert Gallatin, rejected Hamilton's idea that a national debt would strengthen the government by giving creditors a stake in its health. Paying the interest alone would require taxes, which sucked money from industrious farmers, the backbone of the Republic, and put it into the hands of wealthy creditors, parasites who lived off others' misfortune. Increased tax revenues might also tempt the government to create a standing army, always a threat to liberty.

Jefferson and Gallatin induced Congress to repeal many taxes, and they slashed expenditures by closing some embassies overseas and reducing the army. They

Explosion of the Intrepid

In September 1804 the American fireship *Intrepid*, loaded with powder and intending to penetrate Tripoli harbor and explode enemy ships, blew up before reaching its target, killing Captain Richard Somers and his crew. Seven months earlier, commanded by Lieutenant Stephen Decatur, the *Intrepid* had destroyed the American frigate *Philadelphia*, which had fallen into Tripolitan hands. Britain's Lord Nelson reportedly described Decatur's exploit as "the most bold and daring act of the age."

placed economy ahead of military preparedness. Gallatin calculated that the nation could be freed of debt in sixteen years if administrations held the line on expenditures. In Europe, the Peace of Amiens (1802) brought a temporary halt to the hostilities between Britain and France that had threatened American shipping in the 1790s, which buoyed Jefferson's confidence that minimal military preparedness was a sound policy. The Peace of Amiens, he wrote, "removes the only danger we have to fear. We can now proceed without risks in demolishing useless structures of expense, lightening the burdens of our constituents, and fortifying the principles of free government." This may have been wishful thinking, but it rested on a sound economic calculation, for the vast territory of the United States could not be secured from attack without astronomical expense.

While cutting back expenditures on the army, Jefferson was ready to use the navy to gain respect for the American flag. In 1801 he ordered a naval squadron into action in the Mediterranean against the so-called Tripolitan (or Barbary) pirates of North Africa. For centuries, the Muslim rulers of Tripoli, Morocco, Tunis, and Algiers had solved their budgetary problems by engaging in piracy and extorting tribute in exchange for protection; seamen whom they captured were held for ransom or sold into slavery. Most European powers handed over the fees demanded, but Jefferson calculated that going to war would be cheaper than paying high tribute to maintain peace. Although suffering its share of reverses during the ensuing fighting, the United States did not come away empty-handed. In 1805 it was able to conclude a peace treaty with Tripoli. The war cost roughly half of what the United States had been paying annually for protection.

Jefferson and the Judiciary

Jefferson had hoped to conciliate the moderate Federalists, but conflicts over the judiciary derailed this objective. Because the Washington and Adams administrations had appointed only Federalists, not a single Republican sat on the federal judiciary when Jefferson came to office. Still bitter about the zeal of federal courts in enforcing the Alien and Sedition Acts, Jefferson saw the Federalist-sponsored Judiciary Act of 1801 as the last straw. By reducing the number of Supreme Court justices from six to five, the act threatened to strip him of an early opportunity to appoint a justice. At the same time, the act created sixteen new federal judgeships, which outgoing president John Adams filled by last-minute ("midnight") appointments of Federalists. To Jefferson,

this was proof that the Federalists intended to use the judiciary as a stronghold from which "all the works of Republicanism are to be beaten down and erased." In 1802 he won congressional repeal of the Judiciary Act of 1801.

Jefferson's troubles with the judiciary were not over. On his last day in office, Adams had appointed an obscure Federalist, William Marbury, as justice of the peace in the District of Columbia but failed to deliver Marbury's commission before midnight. When Jefferson's secretary of state, James Madison, refused to release the commission, Marbury petitioned the Supreme Court to issue a writ compelling delivery. In *Marbury* v. *Madison* (1803), Chief Justice John Marshall, an ardent Federalist, wrote the unanimous opinion. Marshall ruled that, although Madison should have delivered Marbury's commission, he was under no legal obligation to do so because part of the Judiciary Act of 1789, which had granted the Court the authority to issue such a writ, was unconstitutional.

For the first time, the Supreme Court had declared its authority to void an act of Congress on the grounds that it was "repugnant" to the Constitution. Jefferson did not reject this principle, known as the doctrine of judicial review and destined to become highly influential, but he was enraged that Marshall had used part of his decision to lecture Madison on his moral duty (as opposed to his legal obligation) to have delivered Marbury's commission. This gratuitous lecture, which was really directed at Jefferson as Madison's superior, struck Jefferson as another example of Federalist partisanship.

While the *Marbury* decision was brewing, the Republicans had already taken the offensive against the judiciary by moving to impeach (charge with wrongdoing) two Federalist judges. One, John Pickering, was an insane alcoholic; the other, Supreme Court justice Samuel Chase, was a partisan Federalist notorious for jailing several Republican editors under the Sedition Act of 1798. These cases raised the same issue: Was impeachment, which the Constitution restricted to cases of treason, bribery, and "high Crimes and Misdemeanors," an appropriate remedy for judges who were insane or excessively partisan? Pickering was removed from office, but the Senate narrowly failed to convict Chase, in part because moderate Republicans were coming to doubt whether impeachment was a solution to judicial partisanship.

Chase's acquittal ended Jefferson's skirmishes with the judiciary. His more radical followers attacked the principle of judicial review and called for an elected rather than appointed judiciary. But Jefferson merely challenged the Federalist use of judicial power for political goals. There was always a gray area between law and

politics. Federalists did not necessarily see a conflict between protecting the Constitution and advancing their party's cause. Nor did they use their control of the federal judiciary to undo Jefferson's "revolution" of 1800. The Marshall court, for example, upheld the constitutionality of the repeal of the Judiciary Act of 1801. For his part, Jefferson never proposed to impeach Marshall. In supporting impeachment of Pickering and Chase, Jefferson was trying to make the judiciary more responsive to the popular will by challenging a pair of judges whose behavior had been outrageous. No other federal judge would be impeached for more than fifty years.

The Louisiana Purchase, 1803

Jefferson's goal of avoiding foreign entanglements would remain beyond reach as long as European powers had large landholdings in North America. In 1800 Spain, a weak and declining power, controlled East and West Florida as well as the vast Louisiana Territory. The latter was equal in size to the United States at that time. In 1800 Spain ceded the Louisiana Territory to France, which was fast emerging under Napoleon Bonaparte as the world's foremost military power. It took six months for news of the treaty to reach Jefferson and Madison but only a few minutes for them to grasp its significance.

Jefferson had long dreamed of an "empire of liberty" extending across North America and even into South America. He saw this empire being gained not by military conquest but by the inevitable expansion of the free and virtuous American people. An enfeebled Spain constituted no real obstacle to this expansion. As long as Louisiana had belonged to Spain, time was on the side of the United States. But Bonaparte's capacity for mischief was boundless. What if Bonaparte and the British reached an agreement that gave England a free hand in the Mediterranean and France a license to expand into North America? The United States would be sandwiched between the British in Canada and the French in Louisiana. What if Britain refused to cooperate with France? In that case, Britain might use its naval power to seize Louisiana before the French took control, thereby trapping the United States between British forces in the South and in the North.

Although Americans feared these two possibilities, Bonaparte actually had a different goal. He dreamed of a new French empire bordering the Caribbean and the Gulf of Mexico, centering on the Caribbean island of Santo Domingo (modern Haiti and the Dominican Republic). He wanted to use Louisiana not as a base from which to threaten the United States but as a breadbasket for an essentially Caribbean empire. His immediate task was to subdue Santo Domingo, where by 1800 a bloody slave revolution had resulted in a takeover of the government by the black statesman Toussaint L'Ouverture (see Chapter 7). Bonaparte dispatched an army to reassert French control and reestablish slavery, but an epidemic of yellow fever combined with fierce resistance by former slaves to destroy the army.

In the short run, Jefferson worried most about New Orleans. Because no rivers, roads, or canals connected the American territories of Ohio, Indiana, and Mississippi with the eastern ports, farmers in the interior had to ship their cash crops, worth $3 million annually, down the Ohio and Mississippi Rivers to New Orleans, a port that did not belong to the United States. The Spanish had temporarily granted Americans the right to park their produce there while awaiting transfer to seagoing vessels. But in 1802, the Spanish colonial administrator in New Orleans issued an order revoking this right. The order had originated in Spain, but most Americans assumed that it had come from Bonaparte, who, although he now owned Louisiana, had yet to take possession of it. An alarmed Jefferson described New Orleans as the "one single spot" on the globe whose possessor "is our natural and habitual enemy." "The day that France takes possession of N. Orleans," he added, "we must marry ourselves to the British fleet and nation."

The combination of France's failure to subdue Santo Domingo and the termination of American rights to deposit produce in New Orleans stimulated two crucial decisions, one by Jefferson and the other by Bonaparte, that ultimately resulted in the purchase of Louisiana by the United States. First, Jefferson nominated James Monroe and Robert R. Livingston to negotiate with France for the purchase of New Orleans and as much of the Floridas as possible. (Because West Florida had repeatedly changed hands among France, Britain, and Spain, no one was sure who owned it.) Meanwhile, Bonaparte, mindful of his military failure in Santo Domingo and of American opposition to French control of Louisiana, had concluded that his projected Caribbean empire was not worth the cost. In addition, he planned to recommence the war in Europe and needed cash. So he decided to sell all of Louisiana. After some haggling between the American commissioners and Bonaparte's minister, Talleyrand, a price of $15 million was settled on. (One-fourth of the total represented an agreement by the United States to pay French debts owed to American citizens.) For this sum, the United

States gained an immense, uncharted territory between the Mississippi River and the Rocky Mountains (see Map 8.1). No one knew its exact size; Talleyrand merely observed that the bargain was noble. But the purchase virtually doubled the area of the United States at a cost, omitting interest, of thirteen and one-half cents an acre.

As a believer in a strict interpretation of the Constitution, the president had doubts about the constitutionality of the purchase. No provision of the Constitution explicitly gave the government authority to acquire new territory. Jefferson therefore drafted a constitutional amendment that authorized the acquisition of territory and prohibited the American settlement of Louisiana for an indefinite period. Fearing that an immediate and headlong rush to settle the area would lead to the destruction of the Native Americans and an orgy of land

speculation, Jefferson wanted to control development so that Americans could advance "compactly as we multiply." Few Republicans shared Jefferson's constitutional reservations. The president himself soon began to worry that ratification of an amendment would take too long and that Bonaparte might in the meantime change his mind about selling Louisiana. He quietly dropped the amendment and submitted the treaty to the Senate, where it was quickly ratified.

It is easy to make too much of Jefferson's dilemma over Louisiana. Believing that the Constitution should be interpreted ("constructed") according to its letter, he was also committed to the principle of establishing an "empire of liberty." Doubling the size of the Republic would guarantee land for American farmers, the backbone of the nation and the true guardians of liberty. Like

MAP 8.1. The Louisiana Purchase and the Exploration of the West
The explorations of Lewis and Clark demonstrated the vast extent of the area purchased from France.

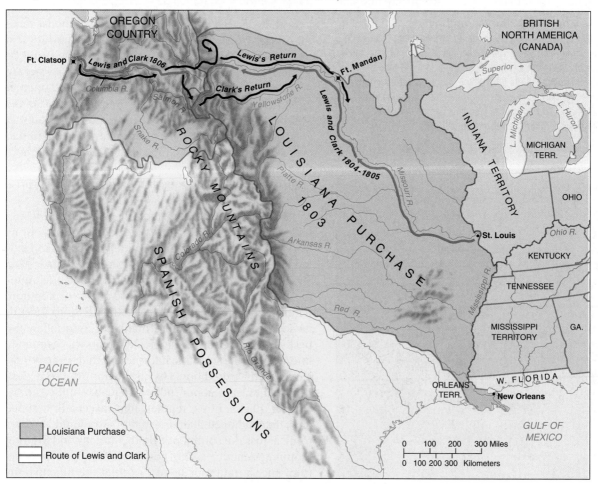

the principle of states' rights to which Jefferson also subscribed, strict construction was not an end in itself but a means to promote republican liberty. If that end could be achieved some way other than by strict construction, so be it. Jefferson was also alert to practical considerations. Most Federalists opposed the Louisiana Purchase on the grounds that it would decrease the relative importance of their strongholds on the eastern seaboard. As the leader of the Republican party, Jefferson saw no reason to hand the Federalists an issue by dallying over ratification of the treaty.

The Election of 1804

Jefferson's acquisition of Louisiana left the Federalists dispirited and without a popular national issue. As the election of 1804 approached, the main threat to Jefferson was not the Federalist party but his own vice president, Aaron Burr. In 1800 Burr had tried to take advantage of a tie in the electoral college to gain the presidency, a betrayal in the eyes of most Republicans, who assumed that he had been nominated for the vice presidency. The

Bull Dance, Mandan Okipa Ceremony

Among the colorful Plains tribes encountered by Lewis and Clark were the Mandans. With the arrival of white men, the Mandans often acted as intermediaries between whites and tribes farther to the west. Their villages became trading centers where hide shirts and buffalo robes were exchanged for European cloth. Unfortunately, the whites also brought smallpox, against which the Mandans had no immunities. By the late 1830s their numbers had dwindled to 125.

adoption in 1804 of the Twelfth Amendment, which required separate and distinct ballots in the electoral college for the presidential and the vice-presidential candidates, put an end to the possibility of an electoral tie for the chief executive. But it did not put an end to Burr. Between 1801 and 1804, Burr entered into enough intrigues with the Federalists to convince the Republicans that it would be unsafe to renominate him for the vice presidency. The Republicans in Congress rudely dumped Burr in favor of George Clinton.

Without a hope of success, the Federalists nominated Charles C. Pinckney and Rufus King, and then watched their candidates go down in complete and crushing defeat in the election. The Federalists carried only two states, failing to hold even Massachusetts. Jefferson's overwhelming victory brought his first term to a fitting close. Between 1801 and 1804, the United States had doubled its territory, taken steps to pay off its debt, and remained at peace.

The Lewis and Clark Expedition

Louisiana dazzled Jefferson. Here was an immense territory about which Americans knew virtually nothing. No one was sure of its western boundary. A case could be made for the Pacific Ocean, but Spain still possessed the American Southwest. Jefferson was content to claim that Louisiana extended at least to the mountains west of the Mississippi. No one, however, was certain of the exact location of these mountains because few Americans had ever seen them. Jefferson himself had never been more than fifty miles west of his home in Virginia. Thus the Louisiana Purchase was both a bargain and a surprise package.

Even before the acquisition of Louisiana, Jefferson had planned an exploratory expedition; picked its leader, his personal secretary and fellow Virginian Lieutenant Meriwether Lewis; and sent him to Philadelphia for a crash course in sciences such as zoology, astronomy, and botany that were relevant to exploration. Jefferson instructed Lewis to trace the Missouri River to its source, cross the western highlands, and follow the best water route to the Pacific. Jefferson was genuinely interested in the scientific information that could be collected on the expedition. His instructions to Lewis cited the need to learn about Indian languages and customs, climate, plants, birds, reptiles, and insects. But, above all, Jefferson hoped that his explorers would find a water route across the continent (see Technology and Culture: Mapping America). The potential economic benefits from such a route included diverting the lucrative fur

trade from Canadian to American hands and boosting trade with China.

Setting forth from St. Louis in May 1804, Lewis, his second-in-command William Clark, and about fifty others followed the Missouri River and then the Snake and Columbia Rivers. In the Dakota country, Lewis and Clark hired a French-Canadian fur trader, Toussaint Charbonneau, as a guide and interpreter. Slow-witted and inclined to panic in crises, Charbonneau proved to be a mixed blessing, but his wife, Sacajawea, who accompanied him on the trip, made up for his failings. A Shoshone and probably no more than sixteen years old in 1804, Sacajawea had been stolen by a rival tribe and then claimed by Charbonneau, perhaps in settlement for a gambling debt. When first encountered by Lewis and Clark, she had just given birth to a son; indeed, the infant's presence helped reassure Native American tribes of the expedition's peaceful intent. Additionally, Sacajawea showed Lewis and Clark how to forage for wild artichokes and other plants, often their only food, by digging into the dens where rodents stored them. Clutching her baby, she rescued most of the expedition's scientific instruments after a boat capsized on the Missouri River.

The group finally reached the Pacific Ocean in November 1805 and then returned to St. Louis, but not before collecting a mass of scientific information, including the disturbing fact that more than three hundred miles of mountains separated the Missouri from the Columbia. The expedition also produced a sprinkling of tall tales, many of which Jefferson believed, about gigantic Indians, soil too rich to grow trees, and a mountain composed of salt. Jefferson's political opponents railed that he would soon be reporting the discovery of a molasses-filled lake. For all the ridicule, the expedition's drawings of the geography of the region led to more accurate maps and heightened interest in the West.

THE GATHERING STORM

In gaining control of Louisiana, the United States had benefited from the preoccupation of European powers with their own struggles. But between 1803 and 1814, the renewal of the Napoleonic Wars in Europe turned the United States into a pawn in a chess game played by others and helped make Jefferson's second term far less successful than his first.

Europe was not Jefferson's only problem. He had to deal with a conspiracy to dismantle the United States, the product of the inventive and perverse mind of Aaron

Plains Pipe Bowl
Instructed by Jefferson to acquaint themselves with the Indians' "ordinary occupations in the arts," Lewis and Clark collected this Lakota sacred pipe, whose red stone symbolized the flesh and blood of all people and whose smoke represented the breath that carries prayers to the Creator. Considering pipes sacred objects, Indians used them to seal contracts and treaties and to perform ceremonial healing.

Burr, and to face down challenges within his own party, led by John Randolph.

Challenges on the Home Front

Aaron Burr suffered a string of reverses in 1804. After being denied renomination as vice president, he entered into a series of intrigues with a faction of despairing and extreme (or "High") Federalists in New England. Led by Senator Timothy Pickering of Massachusetts, these High Federalists plotted to sever the Union by forming a pro-British Northern Confederacy composed of Nova Scotia (part of British-owned Canada), New England, New York, and even Pennsylvania. Although most Federalists disdained the plot, Pickering and others settled on Burr as their leader and helped him gain the Federalist nomination for the governorship of New York. Alexander Hamilton, who had thwarted Burr's plans for the presidency in 1800 by throwing his weight behind Jefferson, now foiled Burr a second time by allowing the publication of his "despicable opinion" of Burr. Defeated in the election for New York's governor, Burr challenged Hamilton to a duel and mortally wounded him at Weehawken, New Jersey, on July 11, 1804.

Under indictment in two states for his murder of Hamilton, Burr, still vice president, now hatched a scheme so bold that it gained initial momentum because his political opponents doubted that even Burr

Mapping America

Writing to Congress in 1777, George Washington had complained that "the want of accurate maps of the Country" placed him at "a great disadvantage." Treating mapmaking as a public expense, the British government staffed its army with surveyors, whose skills were indispensable to making maps. As a result, the British often had a better knowledge of the American countryside than did Washington's army.

Washington himself was a surveyor, but American surveyors had been employed by land-seeking clients, not governments. This approach to mapping yielded local maps, some of which were biased since the clients had an interest in the outcome. Existing maps of entire colonies were compilations of local maps, subject to the all errors that had crept into local surveys and lacking any common geographic frame of reference.

The accurate mapping of large areas that Washington desired required government funding of many survey parties. A typical survey party included several axemen to clear trees, two chain bearers, two or three staff carriers, an instrument carrier, and the surveyor. Surveyors used several basic instruments, including a table

equipped with paper, a compass, a telescope for measuring direction and heights, and an instrument for measuring angles called a theodolite. A surveyor first measured a baseline from one point to another, as marked by the chain bearers. Next he commenced a process known as triangulation by picking a landmark in the distance, like a hilltop, and measuring its angle from the baseline. A staff man might be standing on the hilltop with a flag attached to his staff. Finally, the surveyor employed trigonometry to calculate the length of each side of the triangle, one of which would serve as the next baseline. For every hour spent walking a plot of land, the survey party would spend three hours recording their measurements on paper.

Washington's complaint about inadequate maps led to the appointment of Scottish-born Robert Erskine as surveyor general of the Continental Army and to government funding of his workers. After the war, the Land Ordinance of 1785, which specified that public lands be surveyed and divided into townships six miles square before auction, again led the national government to employ survey parties. The Land Ordinance applied only to

Map of Lewis and Clark Track

Drawn by Meriwether Lewis's traveling mate on the famous expedition and combining Clark's own observations with those of Indians and explorers, this 1814 map gave Americans their first view of the vast territory purchased in 1803. Clark's depiction of the Rockies was substantially accurate, his description of the Southwest less so.

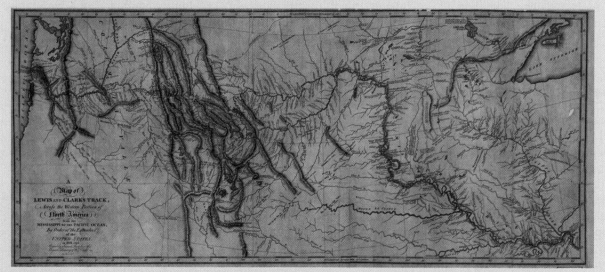

land lying outside any state. The national government did not take responsibility for mapping the states.

Jefferson's purchase of Louisiana in 1803 pricked a new popular interest in geography. Mapping the Purchase presented several obstacles. Early explorers had surveyed small portions of it, but the territory's vastness ruled out surveys of the entire Purchase. Spain discouraged even local surveys, lest information about this valuable possession leak out. Jefferson and others had to rely on maps compiled from the accounts of travelers who relied on a mixture of their own observations, hearsay accounts of fur traders, and wishful thinking.

Wishful thinking took the form of the belief, embraced by Jefferson, that the sources of the major North American rivers were near each other. If this were true, it would be possible to find a great water highway linking the Pacific to American settlements on the Mississippi. Such a highway would turn America into a commercial link between the riches of the East—Persian silks, Arabian perfumes, the wealth of China—and Europe. It would also facilitate the export of American agricultural produce.

Eager to ensure the profitability of agriculture, Jefferson warmed to this idea. He knew more about geography than anyone else in the American government, and he collected maps, most of which supported the water-highway theory. For example, one map published in Britain in 1778 showed the major American rivers—the Mississippi, Missouri, Colorado, and Columbia—all originating in a small pyramid of high land in present-day South Dakota.

By the time Jefferson launched the Lewis and Clark expedition to explore the Louisiana Purchase, better maps were available. Jefferson saw to it that Lewis and Clark carried a recent map by an Englishman, Aaron Arrowsmith. Arrowsmith's map showed the Rocky Mountains, which were often omitted by other maps. But when Lewis and Clark reached the source of the Missouri River in June 1805, they found no sign of the Columbia, whose source the Arrowsmith map portrayed as a stone's throw from the source of the Missouri, just "an immense range of high mountains."

Their expedition established Lewis and Clark as authorities on the West and stimulated the public's and states' interest in geography. During their expedition, Lewis and Clark had benefited from accurate charts of local geography drawn by Indians on the ground with sticks or on hides with charcoal. Settled in St. Louis after the expedition, Clark received a stream of explorers and traders who brought him more information about the geography of the Purchase, enough to enable him to draw a manuscript map of the territory. When finally

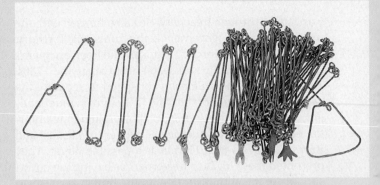

Surveyors chain and pins
The standard surveyor's chain contained 66 links and was 100 feet in length. Eighty lengths of chain equalled one mile, and ten square chains a square mile (640 acres). Surveyors used wooden pins tied at the ends with bright red cloth to mark the chain's position as it was moved.

published in 1814, this map gave ordinary Americans their first picture of what Jefferson had bought in 1803. In 1816 John Melish, drawing on Clark's map and his own travels, published by far the most accurate map yet of the United States.

By enabling ordinary Americans to see the vastness of their nation, Melish's map subtly reinforced their sense that the West rightfully belonged to them, not to the Indians or anyone else. The negotiators of the Transcontinental Treaty of 1819, which gave the United States a claim to part of the Pacific Coast, relied exclusively on the 1818 edition of Melish's map. Melish's example also spurred state legislatures to subsidize the drawing of accurate state maps.

Hiring Melish in 1816, Pennsylvania became the first state to finance construction of a state map based wholly on "actual survey." Melish was delighted. He had been insisting that "every state should have its own map" and that such maps should be state property, "subject to the control of no individual whatever." Taking six years to complete, the project cost Pennsylvania $30,000 and exhausted Melish, who died shortly after the map's publication. But other states were quick to follow Pennsylvania's lead.

Focus Question: We usually think of maps as accurate depictions of land and water, but the early maps contained many inaccuracies. These inaccuracies resulted not just from limits of technology and finance but also from widely held beliefs about what America should look like. Since Americans acted on the basis of their beliefs, how much did maps actually shape events in the age of Jefferson?

was capable of such treachery. He allied himself with the unsavory military governor of the Louisiana Territory, General James Wilkinson. Wilkinson had been on Spain's payroll intermittently as a secret agent since the 1780s. Together, Burr and Wilkinson conspired to separate the western states south of the Ohio River into an independent confederacy. In addition, Wilkinson had long entertained the idea of an American conquest of Mexico, and Burr now added West Florida as a possible target. They presented these ideas to westerners as having the covert support of the administration, to the British as a way to attack Spanish-owned Mexico and West Florida, and to the Spanish (not naming Mexico and West Florida as targets) as a way to divide up the United States.

By fall 1806, Burr and about sixty followers had left their staging ground, an island in the upper Ohio River, and were making their way down the Ohio and Mississippi Rivers to join Wilkinson at Natchez. In October 1806 Jefferson, who described Burr as a crooked gun that never shot straight, denounced the conspiracy. Wilkinson abandoned the conspiracy and proclaimed himself the most loyal of Jefferson's followers. Burr tried to escape to West Florida but was intercepted. Brought back to Richmond, he was put on trial for treason. Chief Justice Marshall presided at the trial and instructed the jury that the prosecution had to prove not merely that Burr had treasonable intentions but also that he had committed treasonable acts, a virtually impossible task inasmuch as the conspiracy had fallen apart before Burr accomplished what he had planned. Jefferson was furious, but Marshall was merely following the clear wording of the Constitution, which deliberately made treason difficult to prove. The jury returned a verdict of not proved, which Marshall entered as "not guilty." Still under indictment for his murder of Hamilton, Burr fled to Europe, where he tried to interest Napoleon in making peace with Britain as a prelude to a proposed Anglo-French invasion of the United States and Mexico. He returned to the United States in 1812. In keeping with his reputation as a womanizer, he fathered two illegitimate children in his seventies and was divorced for adultery at eighty. Perhaps the most puzzling man in American history, Burr died in 1836.

Besides the Burr conspiracy, Jefferson faced a challenge from a group of Republicans known as the Quids (from the Latin *tertium quid* or third thing; roughly, a dissenter). They were led by the president's fellow Virginian, John Randolph, a man of abounding eccentricities and acerbic wit. Randolph still subscribed to the "country" ideology of the 1770s, which celebrated the wisdom of farmers against rulers and warned of government's tendency to encroach on liberty. Jefferson had originally shared these beliefs, but he recognized them as an ideology of opposition, not power; once in office, he compromised. In contrast, Randolph remained frozen in the 1770s, denouncing every change as decline and proclaiming that he would throw all politicians to the dogs if he had less respect for dogs.

Not surprisingly, Randolph turned on Jefferson, most notably for backing a compromise in the Yazoo land scandal. In 1795 the Georgia legislature had sold the huge Yazoo tract (35 million acres comprising most of present-day Alabama and Mississippi) for a fraction of its value to land companies that had bribed virtually the entire legislature. The next legislature canceled the sale, but many investors, knowing nothing of the bribery, had already bought land in good faith. The scandal posed a moral challenge to Jefferson because of these good-faith purchases, and a political dilemma as well, for some purchasers were northerners whom Jefferson hoped to woo to the Republican party. In 1803 a federal commission compromised with an award of 5 million acres to Yazoo investors. For Randolph, the compromise was itself a scandal—further evidence of the decay of republican virtue.

The Suppression of American Trade and Impressment

Burr's acquittal and Randolph's taunts shattered the aura of invincibility that had surrounded Jefferson in the wake of the Louisiana Purchase and the election of 1804. In 1803 the Peace of Amiens collapsed. As Britain and France resumed their war, the United States prospered at Britain's expense by carrying sugar and coffee from the French and Spanish Caribbean colonies to Europe. This trade not only provided Napoleon with supplies but also drove down the price of sugar and coffee from the British colonies by adding to the glut of these commodities on the world market. Understandably, the British concluded that American prosperity was the cause of Britain's economic difficulties.

America's boom was being fueled by the reexport trade. According to the British Rule of 1756, any trade closed in peacetime could not be reopened during war. For example, France usually restricted the sugar trade to French ships during peacetime and thus could not open it to American ships during war. The American response to the Rule of 1756 was the "broken voyage," by which American vessels would carry sugar from the French West Indies to American ports, unload it, pass it through customs, and then reexport it as American produce. Britain tolerated this dodge for nearly a decade but in 1805 initiated a policy of total war against France,

including the strangulation of French trade. In 1805 a British court declared the broken voyage illegal.

In May 1806 the British followed this decision with the first of several regulations known as Orders in Council, which established a blockade of French-controlled ports on the continent of Europe. Napoleon responded with his so-called Continental System, a series of counterproclamations that ships obeying British regulations would be subject to seizure by France. In effect, this Anglo-French war of decrees outlawed virtually all U.S. trade; if an American ship complied with British regulations, it became a French target, and vice versa.

Both Britain and France seized American ships, but British seizures were far more humiliating to Americans. France was a weaker naval power than Britain; much of the French fleet had been destroyed by the British at the Battle of Trafalgar in October 1805. Accordingly, most of France's seizures of American ships occurred in European ports where American ships had been lured by Napoleon's often inconsistent enforcement of his Continental System. In contrast, British warships hovered just beyond the American coast. The Royal Navy stopped and searched virtually every American vessel off New York, for example. At times, U.S. ships had to line up a few miles from the American coast to be searched by the Royal Navy.

To these provocations the British added impressment. For centuries, Royal Navy press gangs had seized British civilians and forced them into service. As war with France intensified Britain's need for sailors, Britain increasingly extended the practice to seizing purported Royal Navy deserters from American merchant ships and forcing them into service. British sailors had good reason to be discontented with their navy. Discipline on the Royal Navy's "floating hells" was often brutal and the pay low; sailors on American ships made up to five times more than those on British ships. Consequently, the Royal Navy suffered a high rate of desertion to American ships. In 1807, for example, 149 of the 419 sailors on the American warship *Constitution* were British subjects.

Impressed sailors led harrowing lives that included frequent escapes and recaptures. One seaman suffered impressment eleven times. Another, facing his third recapture, drowned himself rather than spend an additional day in the Royal Navy. Impressment was, moreover, galling to American pride. Many deserters who had become American citizens were impressed on the principle that once a Briton, always a Briton. The British also impressed U.S.-born seamen, including those who could prove their American birth. Between 1803 and 1812, six thousand Americans were impressed. Although impressment did less damage to the American economy than the seizure of ships, it was more offensive.

Any doubts Americans had about British arrogance evaporated in June 1807. A British warship, HMS *Leopard*, patrolling off Hampton Roads, Virginia, attacked an unsuspecting American naval vessel, USS *Chesapeake*, and forced it to surrender. The British then boarded the vessel and seized four supposed deserters. One, a genuine deserter, was later hanged; the other three were former Britons, now American citizens, who had "deserted" only from impressment. Even the British had never before asserted their right to seize deserters off U.S. navy ships. The so-called Chesapeake Affair enraged the country. Jefferson remarked that he had not seen so belligerent a spirit in America since 1775. Yet while making some preparations for war, the president sought peace, first by conducting fruitless negotiations with Britain to gain redress for the Chesapeake outrage, and second by steering the Embargo Act through Congress in December 1807.

The Embargo Act of 1807

By far the most controversial legislation of either of Jefferson's administrations, the Embargo Act prohibited vessels from leaving American ports for foreign ports. Technically, it prohibited only exports, but its practical effect was to stop imports as well, for few foreign ships would venture into American ports if they had to leave

The Brig *Reaper*, 1809

Although damaged by the Embargo, shipbuilding was among the principal industries of New England. Here the hull of the brig *Reaper* is readied for launch in Medford, Massachusetts. Shipwrights spead tallow on the launching way so that the ship could slide into the water. The small box on the left was used to steam oak panels to make them pliable for installation.

without cargo. Amazed by the boldness of the act, a British newspaper described the embargo as "little short of an absolute secession from the rest of the civilized world."

Jefferson advocated the embargo as a means of "peaceable coercion." By restricting French and especially British trade with the United States, he hoped to pressure both nations into respecting American neutrality. But the embargo did not have the intended effect. Although British sales to the United States dropped 50 percent between 1807 and 1808, the British quickly found new markets in South America, where rebellions against Spanish rule had flared up, and in Spain itself, where a revolt against Napoleon had opened trade to British shipping. Furthermore, the Embargo Act contained some loopholes. For example, it allowed American ships blown off course to put in at European ports if necessary; suddenly, many captains were reporting that adverse winds had forced them across the Atlantic. Treating the embargo as a joke, Napoleon seized any American ships he could lay hands on and then informed the United States that he was only helping to enforce the embargo. The British were less amused, but the embargo confirmed their view that Jefferson was an ineffectual philosopher, an impotent challenger compared with Napoleon.

The harshest effects of the embargo were felt not in Europe but in the United States. Some thirty thousand American seamen found themselves out of work. Hundreds of merchants stumbled into bankruptcy, and jails swelled with debtors. A New York City newspaper noted that the only activity still flourishing in the city was prosecution for debt. Farmers were devastated. Unable to export their produce or sell it at a decent price to hard-pressed urban dwellers, many farmers could not pay their debts. In desperation, one farmer in Schoharie County, New York, sold his cattle, horses, and farm implements, worth eight hundred dollars before the embargo, for fifty-five dollars. Speculators who had purchased land expecting to sell it later at a higher price also took a beating because cash-starved farmers stopped buying land. "I live and that is all," wrote one New York speculator. "I am doing no business, cannot sell anybody property, nor collect any money."

The embargo fell hardest on New England and particularly on Massachusetts, which in 1807 had twice the ship tonnage per capita of any other state and more than a third of the entire nation's ship tonnage in foreign trade. For a state so dependent on foreign trade, the embargo was a calamity. Wits reversed the letters of embargo to form the phrase "O grab me."

The situation was not entirely bleak. The embargo forced a diversion of merchants' capital into manufacturing. In short, unable to export produce, Americans began to make products. Before 1808 the United States had only fifteen mills for fashioning cotton into textiles; by the end of 1809, an additional eighty-seven mills had been constructed (see Chapter 9). But none of this comforted merchants already ruined or mariners driven to soup kitchens. Nor could New Englanders forget that the source of their misery was a policy initiated by one of the "Virginia lordlings," "Mad Tom" Jefferson, who knew little about New England and who had a dogmatic loathing of cities, the very foundations of New England's prosperity. A Massachusetts poet wrote,

Our ships all in motion once whitened the ocean,
They sailed and returned with a cargo;
Now doomed to decay they have fallen a prey
To Jefferson, worms, and embargo.

James Madison and the Failure of Peaceable Coercion

Even before the Embargo Act, Jefferson had announced that he would not be a candidate for reelection. With his blessing, the Republican congressional caucus nominated James Madison and George Clinton for the presidency and vice presidency. The Federalists countered with Charles C. Pinckney and Rufus King, the same ticket that had made a negligible showing in 1804. In 1808 the Federalists staged a modest comeback, gaining twenty-four congressional seats. Still, Madison won 122 of 175 electoral votes for president, and the Republicans retained comfortable majorities in both houses of Congress.

The Federalist revival, modest as it was, rested on two factors. First, the Embargo Act gave the party the national issue it long had lacked. Second, younger Federalists had abandoned their elders' gentlemanly disdain for campaigning and deliberately imitated vote-winning techniques such as barbecues and mass meetings that had worked for the Republicans.

To some contemporaries, the diminutive "Little Jemmy" Madison (he was only five feet, four inches tall) seemed a weak and shadowy figure compared to the commanding presence of Jefferson. But in fact, Madison brought to the presidency an intelligence and a capacity for systematic thought that matched Jefferson's. Like Jefferson, Madison believed that American liberty had to rest on the virtue of the people, which he saw as being critically tied to the growth and prosperity of agriculture.

More clearly than Jefferson, Madison also recognized that agricultural prosperity depended on the vitality of American trade, for Americans would continue to enter farming only if they could get their crops to market. In particular, the British West Indies, dependent on the United States for much of their lumber and grain, struck Madison as a natural trading partner. Britain alone could not fully supply the West Indies. Therefore, if the United States embargoed its own trade with the West Indies, Madison reasoned, the British, who imported sugar from the West Indies, would be forced to their knees before Americans could suffer severe losses from the embargo. Britain, he wrote, was "more vulnerable in her commerce than in her armies."

The American embargo, however, was coercing no one. Increased trade between Canada and the West Indies made a shambles of Madison's plan to pressure Britain. On March 1, 1809, Congress replaced the Embargo Act with the weaker, face-saving Non-Intercourse Act. The act opened trade to all nations except Britain and France and then authorized Congress to restore trade with those nations if they stopped violating neutral rights. But neither complied. In May 1810 Congress substituted a new measure, Macon's Bill No. 2, for the Non-Intercourse Act. This legislation opened trade with Britain and France, and then offered each a clumsy bribe: if either nation repealed its restrictions on neutral shipping, the United States would halt trade with the other.

None of these steps had the desired effect. While Jefferson and Madison lashed out at France and Britain as moral demons ("The one is a den of robbers and the other of pirates," snapped Jefferson), the belligerents saw the world as composed of a few great powers and many weak ones. When great powers went to war, there were no neutrals. Weak nations like the United States should logically seek the protection of a great power and stop babbling about moral ideals and neutral rights. Despite occasional hints to the contrary, neither Napoleon nor the British intended to accommodate the Americans.

As peaceable coercion became a fiasco, Madison came under fire from militant Republicans who demanded more aggressive policies. Coming mainly from the South and West, regions where "honor" was a sacred word, the militants were infuriated by insults to the American flag. In addition, economic recession between 1808 and 1810 had convinced the firebrands that British policies were wrecking their regions' economies. The election of 1810 brought several young malcontents, christened "war hawks," to Congress. Led

by thirty-four-year-old Henry Clay of Kentucky, who preferred war to the "putrescent pool of ignominious peace," the war hawks included John C. Calhoun of South Carolina, Richard M. Johnson of Kentucky, and William King of North Carolina, all future vice presidents. Clay was elected Speaker of the House.

Tecumseh and the Prophet

Voicing a more emotional and pugnacious nationalism than Jefferson and Madison, the war hawks called for the expulsion of the British from Canada and the Spanish from the Floridas. Their demands merged with western settlers' fears that the British in Canada were actively recruiting the Indians to halt the march of American settlement. In reality, American policy, not meddling by the British, was the source of bloodshed on the frontier.

In contrast to his views about blacks, Jefferson believed that Indians and whites could live peacefully together if the Indians abandoned their hunting and nomadic ways for farming. If they farmed, they would

Tecumseh
No fully authenticated portrait of Tecumseh exists, but whites described him as handsome and dominant. Believing that Indian lands were not the possession of individual tribes to negotiate away but collectively belonged to all the Indians, Tecumseh was a formidable opponent of white expansion.

need less land. Jefferson and Madison insisted that the Indians be compensated fairly for ceded land and that only those Indians with a claim to the land they were ceding be allowed to conclude treaties with whites. Reality conflicted with Jefferson's ideals. (See Chapter 7.) The march of white settlement was steadily shrinking Indian hunting grounds, while some Indians themselves were becoming more willing to sign away land in payment to whites for blankets, guns, and the liquor that transported them into a daze even as their culture collapsed.

In 1809 no American was more eager to acquire Indian lands than William Henry Harrison, the governor of the Indiana Territory. The federal government had just divided Indiana, splitting off the present states of Illinois and Wisconsin into a separate Illinois Territory. Harrison recognized that, shorn of Illinois, Indiana would not achieve statehood unless it could attract more settlers and that the territory would not gain such settlers without offering them land currently owned by Indians. Disregarding instructions from Washington to negotiate only with Indians who claimed the land they were ceding, Harrison rounded up a delegation of half-starved Indians, none of whom lived on the rich lands along the Wabash River that he craved. By the Treaty of Fort Wayne in September 1809, these Indians ceded millions of acres along the Wabash at a price of two cents an acre.

This treaty outraged the numerous tribes that had not been party to it, and no one more than Tecumseh, the Shawnee chief, and his brother, Lalawéthica. Late in 1805 Lalawéthica had had a spiritual experience after a frightening dream in which he saw Indians who drank or beat their wives tormented for eternity. Until then, the Shawnees had looked down on Lalawéthica as a drunken misfit, a pale reflection of his handsome brother, Tecumseh. Overnight, Lalawéthica changed. He gave up liquor, began tearful preaching to surrounding tribes to return to their old ways and avoid contact with whites, and quickly became known as The Prophet. Soon, he would take a new name, Tenskwatawa, styling himself the "Open Door" through which all Indians could achieve salvation. Demoralized by the continuing loss of Native American lands to the whites and by the ravages of their society by alcoholism, Shawnees listened to his message. Meanwhile, Tecumseh sought to unite several tribes in Ohio and the Indiana Territory against American settlers.

The Treaty of Fort Wayne infuriated Tecumseh, who insisted that Indian lands belonged collectively to all the tribes and hence could not be sold by needy splinter groups. He held a conference with Harrison that nearly erupted into violence and that led Harrison to conclude that it was time to attack the Indians. His target was a Shawnee encampment called Prophetstown near the mouth of the Tippecanoe River. With Tecumseh away recruiting southern Indians to his cause, Tenskwatawa ordered an attack on Harrison's encampment, a mile from Prophetstown, in the predawn hours of November 7, 1811. Outnumbered two to one and short of ammunition, Tenskwatawa's force was beaten off after inflicting heavy casualties.

Although it was a small engagement, the Battle of Tippecanoe had several large effects. It made Harrison a national hero, and the memory of the battle would contribute to his election as president three decades later. It discredited Tenskwatawa, whose conduct during the battle drew criticism from his followers. It elevated Tecumseh into a position of recognized leadership among the western tribes. Finally, it persuaded Tecumseh, who long had distrusted the British as much as the Americans, that alliance with the British was the only hope to stop the spread of American settlement.

Congress Votes for War

By spring 1812 President Madison had reached the decision that war with Britain was inevitable. On June 1 he sent his war message to Congress. Meanwhile, an economic depression struck Britain, partly because the American policy of restricting trade with that country had finally started to work. Under pressure from its merchants, Britain repealed the Orders in Council on June 23. But Congress, unaware that the British were contemplating repeal of the orders, had already passed the declaration of war.

Neither war hawks nor westerners held the key to the vote in favor of war. The war hawks comprised a minority within the Republican party; the West was still too sparsely settled to have many representatives in Congress. Rather, the votes of Republicans in populous states like Pennsylvania, Maryland, and Virginia were the main force propelling the war declaration through Congress. Opposition to war came mostly from Federalist strongholds in Massachusetts, Connecticut, and New York. Because Federalists were so much stronger in the Northeast than elsewhere, congressional opposition to war revealed a sectional as well as a party split. In general, however, southern Federalists opposed the war declaration, and northern Republicans supported it. In other words, the vote for war followed party lines more closely than sectional lines. Much like James Madison himself, the typical Republican advocate of war had not

wanted war in 1810 or even in 1811, but had been led by the accumulation of grievances to demand it in 1812.

In his war message, Madison had listed impressment, the continued presence of British ships in American waters, and British violations of neutral rights as grievances that justified war. None of these complaints were new. Taken together, they do not fully explain why Americans went to war in 1812 rather than earlier—for example, in 1807 after the Chesapeake Affair. Madison also listed British incitement of the Indians as a stimulus for war. This grievance of recent origin contributed to war feeling in the West. "The War on the Wabash," a Kentucky newspaper proclaimed, "is purely British. The British scalping knife has filled many habitations both in this state as well as in the Indiana Territory with widows and orphans." But the West had too few American inhabitants to drive the nation into war. A more important underlying cause was the economic recession that affected the South and West after 1808, as well as the conviction, held by John C. Calhoun and others, that British policy was damaging America's economy.

Finally, the fact that Madison rather than Jefferson was president in 1812 was of major importance. Jefferson had believed that the only motive behind British seizures of American ships was Britain's desire to block American trade with Napoleon. Hence Jefferson had concluded that time was on America's side; the seizures would stop as soon as the war in Europe ceased. In contrast, Madison had become persuaded that Britain's real motive was to strangle American trade once and for all and thereby eliminate the United States as a trading rival. War or no war in Europe, Madison saw Britain as a menace to America. In his war message, he stated flatly that Britain was meddling with American trade not because that trade interfered with Britain's "belligerent rights" but because it "frustrated the monopoly which she covets for her own commerce and navigation."

THE WAR OF 1812

Maritime issues had dominated Madison's war message, but the United States lacked a navy strong enough to challenge Britain at sea. American cruisers, notably the *Constitution*, would win a few sensational duels with British warships, but the Americans would prove unable to prevent the British from clamping a naval blockade on the American coast. Canada, which Madison viewed as a key prop of the British Empire, became the principal target. With their vastly larger population and resources, few Americans expected a long or difficult struggle. To Jefferson, the conquest of Canada seemed "a mere matter of marching."

The *Constitution* Ranging Alongside the *Guerrière* by Michael Felice Corne, 1812
The *Constitution* won more battles than any other early American frigate. Its most famous victory was over HMS. *Guerrière* in August 1812. Known affectionately as Old Ironsides, it was saved from demolition in 1830 by the poet Oliver Wendell Holmes, became a schoolship for the U.S. Naval Academy, was nearly confiscated by the fledgling Confederate navy in 1861, and today survives as a naval relic in Boston harbor.

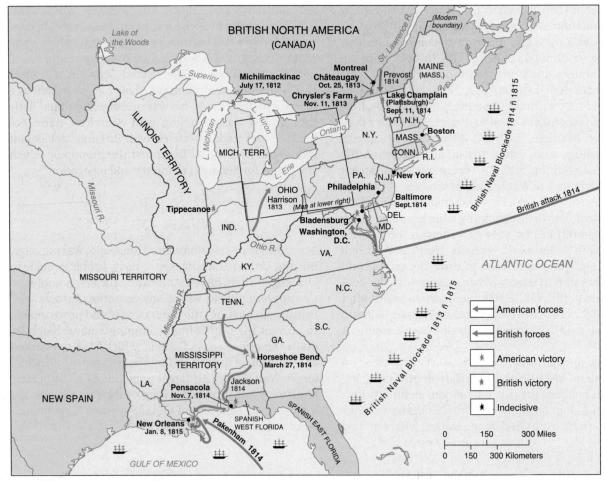

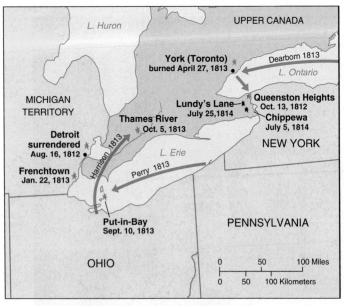

MAP 8.2. Major Battles of the War of 1812
Most of the war's major engagements occurred on or near the northern frontier of the United States; but the Royal Navy blockaded the entire Atlantic coast, and the British army penetrated as far south as Washington and New Orleans.

Little justified this optimism. Although many Canadians were immigrants from the United States, to the Americans' surprise they fought to repel the invaders. Many of the best British troops were in Europe fighting Napoleon, but the British in Canada had an invaluable ally in the Native Americans, who struck fear by dangling scalps from their belts. The British played on this fear, in some cases forcing Americans to surrender by hinting that the Indians might be uncontrollable in battle. Too, the American state militias were filled with Sunday soldiers who "hollered for water half the time, and whiskey the other." Few militiamen understood the goals of the war. In fact, outside Congress there was not much blood lust in 1812. Opposition to the war ran strong in New England; and even in Kentucky, the home

of war hawk Henry Clay, only four hundred answered the first call to arms. For many Americans, local attachments were still stronger than national ones.

On to Canada

From the summer of 1812 to the spring of 1814, the Americans launched a series of unsuccessful attacks on Canada (see Map 8.2). In July 1812 General William Hull led an American army from Detroit into Canada, quickly returned when Tecumseh cut his supply line, and surrendered Detroit and two thousand men to thirteen hundred British and Indian troops. In fall 1812 a force of American regulars was crushed by the British at the Battle of Queenston, near Niagara Falls, while New York militia, contending that they had volunteered only to protect their homes and not to invade Canada, looked on from the New York side of the border. A third American offensive in 1812, a projected attack on Montreal from Plattsburgh, New York, via Lake Champlain, fell apart when the militia again refused to advance into Canada.

The Americans renewed their offensive in 1813 when General William Henry Harrison tried to retake Detroit. A succession of reverses convinced Harrison that offensive operations were futile as long as the British controlled Lake Erie. During the winter of 1812–1813, Captain Oliver H. Perry constructed a little fleet of vessels; on September 10, 1813, he destroyed a British squadron at Put-in-Bay on the western end of the lake. "We have met the enemy, and they are ours," Perry triumphantly reported. Losing control of Lake Erie, the British pulled back from Detroit, but Harrison overtook and defeated a combined British and Indian force at the Battle of the Thames on October 5. Tecumseh died in the battle; Colonel Richard Johnson's claim, never proved, to have killed Tecumseh later contributed to Johnson's election as vice president. These victories by Perry and Harrison cheered Americans, but efforts to invade Canada continued to falter. In June 1814 American troops crossed into Canada on the Niagara front but withdrew after fighting two bloody but inconclusive battles at Chippewa (July 5) and Lundy's Lane (July 25).

The British Offensive

With fresh reinforcements from Europe, where Napoleon had abdicated as emperor after his disastrous invasion of Russia, the British took the offensive in the summer of 1814. General Sir George Prevost led a force of ten thousand British veterans, the largest and best-equipped British force ever sent to North America, in an offensive meant to split the New England states, where opposition to the war was strong, from the rest of the country. The British advanced down Lake Champlain until meeting the well-entrenched American forces at Plattsburgh. Resolving that he had to control the lake before attacking Plattsburgh, Prevost called up his fleet, but an American naval squadron under Captain Thomas Macdonough defeated their British counterparts on September 11. Dispirited, Prevost abandoned the campaign.

Ironically, the British achieved a far more spectacular success in an operation originally designed as a diversion from their main thrust down Lake Champlain. In 1814 a British army sailed from Bermuda for Chesapeake Bay, landed near Washington, and met a larger American force, composed mainly of militia, at Bladensburg, Maryland, on August 24. The Battle of Bladensburg quickly became the "Bladensburg races" as the American militia fled, almost without firing a shot. The British then descended on Washington. Madison, who had witnessed the Bladensburg fiasco, escaped into the Virginia hills. His wife, Dolley, pausing only long

Dolley Madison by Gilbert Stuart, 1804
As the attractive young wife of Secretary of State James Madison, Dolley Madison acted virtually as the nation's First Lady during the administration of Jefferson, a widower. Friendly, tactful, and blessed with an unfailing memory for names and events, she added to her reputation as an elegant hostess after her husband became president.

enough to load her silver, a bed, and a portrait of George Washington onto her carriage, hastened to join her husband, while British troops ate the supper prepared for the Madisons at the presidential mansion. Then they burned the mansion and other public buildings in Washington. A few weeks later, the British attacked Baltimore, but after failing to crack its defenses, they broke off the operation.

The Treaty of Ghent, 1814

In August 1814 negotiations to end the war commenced between British and American commissioners at Ghent, Belgium. The American delegation included Henry Clay, Albert Gallatin, and John Quincy Adams. The son of the last Federalist president, Adams had been the only Federalist in the Senate to support the Louisiana Purchase. He later backed the embargo, joined the Republican party, and served as minister to Russia.

The British appeared to command a strong position. Having frustrated American designs on Canada, they stood poised for their Lake Champlain initiative. Initially, the British demanded territorial concessions from the United States. News of the American naval victory at Plattsburgh and Prevost's retreat to Canada, however, brought home to the British the fact that after two years of fighting, they controlled neither the Great Lakes nor Lake Champlain. Similarly, the spectacular raid on Washington had no strategic significance, so the British gave way on the issue of territorial concessions. The final treaty, signed on Christmas Eve 1814, restored the *status quo ante bellum* (the state of things before the war); the United States neither gained nor lost territory. Several additional issues, including fixing a boundary between the United States and Canada, were referred to joint commissions for future settlement. Nothing was done about impressment, but with Napoleon out of the way, neutral rights became a dead issue. Because there was no longer a war in Europe, there were no longer neutrals.

Ironically, the most dramatic American victory of the war came after the conclusion of the peace negotiations. In December 1814 a British army, composed of veterans of the Napoleonic Wars and commanded by General Sir Edward Pakenham, descended on New Orleans. On January 8, 1815, two weeks after the signing of the Treaty of Ghent but before word reached America, Pakenham's force attacked an American army under General Andrew ("Old Hickory") Jackson. Already a legend for his ferocity as an Indian fighter, Jackson inspired little fear among the British, who advanced into battle far too confidently, but he did strike enough terror in his own men to prevent another American rout. In an hour of gruesome carnage, Jackson's troops shredded the line of advancing redcoats, killing Pakenham and inflicting more than two thousand casualties while losing only thirteen Americans.

The Hartford Convention

Because the Treaty of Ghent had already concluded the war, the Battle of New Orleans had little significance for diplomats. Indirectly, however, it had an effect on domestic politics by eroding Federalist strength.

The Federalist comeback in the election of 1808 had continued into the 1812 campaign. Buoyed by hostility to the war in the Northeast, the Federalists had thrown their support to DeWitt Clinton, an antiwar Republican. Although Madison won the electoral vote 128 to 89, Clinton carried all of New England except Vermont, as well as New York and New Jersey. American military setbacks in the war intensified Federalist disdain for the Madison administration. Federalists saw a nation misruled for over a decade by Republican bunglers. Jefferson's attack on the judiciary had seemed to threaten the rule of law. His purchase of Louisiana, a measure of doubtful constitutionality, had enhanced Republican strength and reduced the relative importance of Federalist New England in the Union. The Embargo Act had severely damaged New England's commerce. Now "Mr. Madison's War" was bringing fresh misery to New England in the form of the British blockade. A few Federalists began to talk of New England's secession from the Union. Most, however, rejected the idea, believing that they would soon benefit from popular exhaustion with the war and spring back into power.

In late 1814 a Federalist convention met in Hartford, Connecticut. Although some advocates of secession were present, moderates took control and passed a series of resolutions summarizing New England's grievances. At the root of these grievances lay the belief that New Englanders were becoming a permanent minority in a nation dominated by southern Republicans who failed to understand New England's commercial interests. The convention proposed to amend the Constitution to abolish the three-fifths clause (which gave the South a disproportionate share of votes in Congress by allowing it to count slaves as a basis of representation), to require a two-thirds vote of Congress to declare war and admit new states into the Union, to limit the president to a single term, to prohibit the election of two successive presidents from the same state, and to bar embargoes lasting more than sixty days.

The timing of these proposals was disastrous for the Federalists. News of the Treaty of Ghent and Jackson's

Two Ottawa Chiefs
These two Ottawa chiefs proudly wear the medals bestowed on them by the British. Expecting British support for their land claims at the war's end, they instead were abandoned by the British.

victory at New Orleans dashed the Federalists' hopes of gaining broad popular support. The goal of the Hartford Convention had been to assert states' rights rather than disunion, but to many the proceedings smelled of a traitorous plot. The restoration of peace, moreover, stripped the Federalists of the primary grievance that had fueled the convention. In the election of 1816, Republican James Monroe, Madison's hand-picked successor and a fellow Virginian, swept the nation over negligible Federalist opposition. He would win reelection in 1820 with only a single dissenting electoral vote. As a force in national politics, the Federalists were finished.

THE AWAKENING OF AMERICAN NATIONALISM

The United States emerged from the War of 1812 bruised but intact. In its first major war since the Revolution, the Republic had demonstrated not only that it could fight on even terms against a major power but also that republics could fight wars without turning to despotism. The war produced more than its share of symbols of American nationalism. Whitewash cleared the smoke damage to the presidential mansion; thereafter, it became known as the White House. The British attack on Fort McHenry, guarding Baltimore, prompted a young

observer, Francis Scott Key, to compose "The Star-Spangled Banner."

The Battle of New Orleans boosted Andrew Jackson onto the stage of national politics and became a source of legends about American military prowess. It appears to most contemporary scholars that the British lost because Pakenham's men, advancing within range of Jackson's riflemen and cannon, unaccountably paused and became sitting ducks. But in the wake of the battle, Americans spun a different tale. The legend arose that Jackson owed his victory not to Pakenham's blundering tactics but to hawk-eyed Kentucky frontiersmen whose rifles picked off the British with unerring accuracy. In fact, many frontiersmen in Jackson's army had not carried rifles; even if they had, gunpowder smoke would have obscured the enemy. But none of this mattered at the time. Just as Americans preferred militia to professional soldiers, they chose to believe that their greatest victory of the war had been the handiwork of amateurs.

Madison's Nationalism and the Era of Good Feelings, 1817–1824

The War of 1812 had three major political consequences. First, it eliminated the Federalists as a national political force. Second, it went a long way toward convincing the Republicans that the nation was strong and resilient,

British Capture of Washington, 1814
Thinking that the British would attack Baltimore, the government failed to provide an adequate defense of Washington. On August 25, 1814, after their victory at Bladensburg, the British entered Washington unopposed, "for the barbarous purpose of destroying the city," confessed a British officer. After setting much of the city ablaze, the British withdrew on August 26 and President Madison returned the following day.

capable of fighting a war while maintaining the liberty of its people. Third, with the Federalists tainted by suspicion of disloyalty and no longer a force, and with fears about the fragility of republics fading, Republicans increasingly embraced doctrines long associated with the Federalists.

In a message to Congress in December 1815, Madison called for federal support for internal improvements, tariff protection for the new industries that had sprung up during the embargo, and the creation of a new national bank. (The charter of the first Bank of the United States had expired in 1811.) In Congress another Republican, Henry Clay of Kentucky, proposed similar measures, which he called the American System, with the aim of making the young nation economically self-sufficient and free from dependence on Europe. In 1816 Congress chartered the Second Bank of the United States and enacted a moderate tariff. Federal support for internal improvements proved to be a thornier problem. Madison favored federal aid in principle but believed that a constitutional amendment was necessary to authorize it. Accordingly, just before leaving office in 1817, he vetoed an internal-improvements bill.

As Republicans adopted positions that they had once disdained, an "Era of Good Feelings" dawned on American politics. A Boston newspaper, impressed by the warm reception accorded President Monroe while touring New England, coined the phrase in 1817. It has stuck as a description of Monroe's two administrations from 1817 to 1825. Compared with Jefferson and Madison, Monroe was not brilliant, polished, or wealthy, but he keenly desired to heal the political divisions that a stronger intellect and personality might have inflamed. The phrase "Era of Good Feelings" reflects not only the war's elimination of some divisive issues but also Monroe's conscious effort to avoid political controversies.

But the good feelings were paper-thin. Madison's 1817 veto of the internal-improvements bill revealed the persistence of disagreements about the role of the federal government under the Constitution. Furthermore, the continuation of slavery was arousing sectional animosities that a journalist's phrase about good feelings could not dispel. Not surprisingly, the postwar consensus began to unravel almost as soon as Americans recognized its existence.

John Marshall and the Supreme Court

In 1819 Jefferson's old antagonist John Marshall, who was still chief justice, issued two opinions that stunned Republicans. The first case, *Dartmouth College* v. *Woodward*, centered on the question of whether New Hampshire could transform a private corporation, Dartmouth College, into a state university. Marshall concluded that the college's original charter, granted to its

John Marshall

In his first three decades as chief justice of the Supreme Court, Marshall greatly strengthened the power of the court and the national government, each of which he thought vital to preserving the intrinsic rights of life, liberty, and property.

trustees by George III in 1769, was a contract. Since the Constitution specifically forbade states to interfere with contracts, New Hampshire's effort to turn Dartmouth into a state university was unconstitutional. The implications of Marshall's ruling were far-reaching. Charters or acts of incorporation provided their beneficiaries with various legal privileges and were sought by businesses as well as by colleges. In effect, Marshall said that once a state had chartered a college or a business, it surrendered both its power to alter the charter and, in large measure, its authority to regulate the beneficiary.

A few weeks later, the chief justice handed down an even more momentous decision in the case of *McCulloch* v. *Maryland*. The issue here was whether the state of Maryland had the power to tax a national corporation, specifically the Baltimore branch of the Second Bank of the United States. Although the bank was a national corporation chartered by Congress, most of the stockholders were private citizens who reaped the profits the bank made. Speaking for a unanimous Court, Marshall ignored these private features of the bank and concentrated instead on two issues. First, did Congress have the power to charter a national bank? Nothing in the Constitution, Marshall conceded, explicitly granted this power. But the Constitution did authorize Congress to lay and collect taxes, to regulate interstate commerce, and to declare war. Surely these enumerated powers, he reasoned, implied a power to charter a bank. Marshall

was clearly engaging in a broad, or "loose," rather than strict, construction (interpretation) of the Constitution. The second issue was whether a state could tax an agency of the federal government that lay within its borders. Marshall argued that any power of the national government, express or implied, was supreme within its sphere. States could not interfere with the exercise of federal powers. A tax by Maryland on the Baltimore branch was such an interference. Since "the power to tax involves the power to destroy," Maryland's tax was plainly unconstitutional.

Marshall's decision in the *McCulloch* case dismayed many Republicans. Although Madison and Monroe had supported the establishment of the Second Bank of the United States, the bank had made itself unpopular by tightening its loan policies during the summer of 1818. This contraction of credit triggered the Panic of 1819, a severe depression that gave rise to considerable distress throughout the country, especially among western farmers. At a time when the bank was widely blamed for the panic, Marshall's ruling stirred controversy by placing the bank beyond the regulatory power of any state government. His decision, indeed, was as much an attack on state sovereignty as it was a defense of the bank. The Constitution, Marshall argued, was the creation not of state governments but of the people of all the states, and thus was more fundamental than state laws. His reasoning assailed the Republican theory, best expressed in the Virginia and Kentucky resolutions of 1798–1799 (see Chapter 7), that the Union was essentially a compact among states. Republicans had continued to view state governments as more immediately responsive to the people's will than the federal government and to regard the compact theory of the Union as a guarantor of popular liberty. As Republicans saw it, Marshall's *McCulloch* decision, along with his decision in the *Dartmouth College* case, stripped state governments of the power to impose the will of their people on corporations.

The Missouri Compromise, 1820–1821

The fragility of the Era of Good Feelings became even more apparent in the two-year-long controversy over statehood for Missouri. Carved from the Louisiana Purchase, Missouri attracted many southerners who, facing declining tobacco profits, expected to employ their slaves in the new territory to grow cotton and hemp. In 1819, 16 percent of its seventy thousand inhabitants were slaves. By the end of 1819, three slave states had been formed out of the Purchase without notable

controversy: Louisiana, Mississippi, and Alabama. Missouri would prove different.

Early in 1819, as the House of Representatives was considering a bill to admit Missouri, a New York Republican offered an amendment that prohibited the further introduction of slaves and provided for the emancipation, at age twenty-five, of all slave offspring born after Missouri's admission as a state. Following rancorous debate, the House accepted the amendment, and the Senate rejected it. Both chambers voted along sectional lines.

Sectional divisions had long troubled American politics, but prior to 1819 slavery had not been the primary source of division. For example, Federalists' opposition to the embargo and the War of 1812 had sprung from their fear that the dominant Republicans were sacrificing New England's commercial interests to those of the South and West, not from hostility to slavery. For various reasons, the Missouri question thrust slavery into the center of sectional conflict. By the end of 1819 the Union had eleven free and eleven slave states. The admission of

Missouri as a slave state would upset this balance to the advantage of the South. Equally important, northerners worried that admitting Missouri as a slave state would set a precedent for the extension of slavery into the northern part of the Purchase, for Missouri was on the same latitude as the free states of Ohio, Indiana, and Illinois. Finally, the disintegration of the Federalists as a national force reduced the need for unity among Republicans, and they increasingly heeded sectional pressures more than calls for party loyalty.

Virtually every issue that was to wrack the Union during the next forty years was present in the controversy over Missouri: southern charges that the North was conspiring to destroy the Union and end slavery; accusations by northerners that southerners were conspiring to extend the institution. Southerners openly proclaimed that antislavery northerners were kindling fires that only "seas of blood" could extinguish. Such threats of civil war persuaded some northern congressmen who had originally supported the restriction of slavery in Missouri to back down. The result was a series

MAP 8.3. The Missouri Compromise, 1820–1821
The Missouri Compromise temporarily quelled controversy over slavery by admitting Maine as a free state and Missouri as a slave state, and by prohibiting slavery in the remainder of the Louisiana Purchase north of 36°30′.

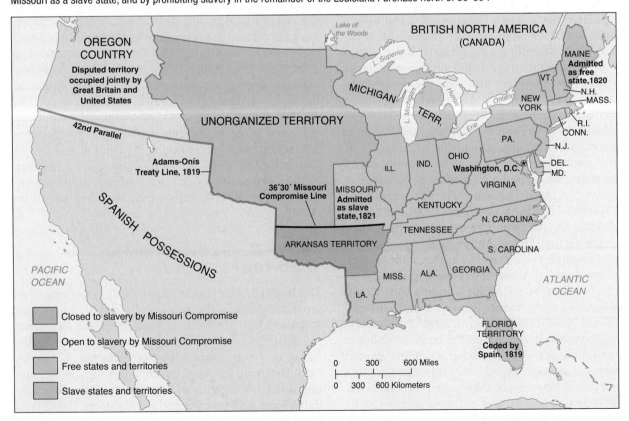

of congressional agreements in 1820 and 1821 known collectively as the Missouri Compromise.

The first of these agreements preserved the balance between slave states and free states. At the same time that Congress was considering statehood for Missouri, Maine was seeking admission as a free state. In 1820 Congress agreed to admit Maine as a free state, to pave the way for Missouri's admission as a slave state, and to prohibit slavery in the remainder of the Louisiana Purchase territory north of 36°30'—the southern boundary of Missouri (see Map 8.3). But compromise did not come easily. The components of the eventual compromise passed by close and ominously sectional votes.

No sooner had the compromise been forged than it nearly fell apart. As a prelude to statehood, Missourians drafted a constitution that prohibited free blacks, whom some eastern states viewed as citizens, from entering their territory. This provision clashed with the federal Constitution's provision that citizens of one state were entitled to the same rights as citizens of other states. Balking at Missourians' exclusion of free blacks, antislavery northerners barred Missouri's admission into the Union until 1821, when Henry Clay engineered a new agreement. This second Missouri Compromise prohibited Missouri from discriminating against citizens of other states but left open the issue of whether free blacks were citizens.

The Missouri Compromise was widely viewed as a southern victory. The South had gained admission of Missouri, whose acceptance of slavery was controversial, while conceding to the North the admission of Maine, whose rejection of slavery inspired no controversy. Yet the South had conceded to freedom a vast block of territory north of 36°30'. Although much of this territory was unorganized Indian country that some viewed as unfit for white habitation, the states of Iowa, Minnesota, Wisconsin, the Dakotas, Nebraska, and Kansas eventually would be formed out of it. Also, the Missouri Compromise reinforced the principle, originally set down by the Northwest Ordinance of 1787, that Congress had the right to prohibit slavery in some territories. Southerners had implicitly accepted the argument that slaves were not like other forms of property that could be moved from place to place at will.

Foreign Policy Under Monroe

American foreign policy between 1816 and 1824 reflected more consensus than conflict. The end of the Napoleonic Wars and the signing of the Treaty of Ghent had removed most of the foreign-policy disagreements between Federalists and Republicans. Moreover, Monroe was fortunate to have as his secretary of state an extraordinary diplomat, John Quincy Adams. An austere and scholarly man whose library equaled his house in monetary value, Adams was a tough negotiator and a fervent nationalist.

As secretary of state, Adams moved quickly to strengthen the peace with Great Britain. During his tenure, the United States and Britain signed the Rush-Bagot Treaty of 1817, which effectively demilitarized the Great Lakes by severely restricting the number of ships that the two powers could maintain there. Next the British-American Convention of 1818 restored to Americans the same fishing rights off Newfoundland that they had enjoyed before the War of 1812 and fixed the boundary between the United States and Canada from the Lake of the Woods west to the Rockies. Beyond the Rockies, the vast country known as Oregon was declared "free and open" to both American and British citizens. As a result of these two agreements, the United States had a secure border with British-controlled Canada for the first time since independence, and a claim to the Pacific.

The nation now turned its attention to dealing with Spain, which still owned East Florida and claimed West Florida. No one was certain whether the Louisiana Purchase included West Florida. Acting as if it did, the United States in 1812 had simply added a slice of West Florida to the state of Louisiana and another slice to the Mississippi Territory. In 1818 Andrew Jackson, the American military commander in the South, seized on the pretext that Florida was both a base for Seminole Indian raids into the United States and a refuge for fugitive slaves. He invaded East Florida, hanged two British subjects, and captured Spanish forts. Jackson had acted without explicit orders, but Adams supported the raid, guessing correctly that it would panic the Spanish into further concessions.

In 1819 Spain agreed to the Adams-Onís (or Transcontinental) Treaty. By its terms, Spain ceded East Florida to the United States, renounced its claims to all of West Florida, and agreed to a southern border of the United States west of the Mississippi that ran north along the Sabine River (separating Texas from Louisiana) and then westward along the Red and Arkansas Rivers to the Rocky Mountains, finally following the forty-second parallel to the Pacific (see Map 8.3). In effect, the United States conceded that Texas was not part of the Louisiana Purchase, while Spain agreed to a northern limit to its claims to the West Coast. It thereby left the United States free to pursue its interests in Oregon.

The Monroe Doctrine, 1823

John Quincy Adams had long believed that God and nature had ordained that the United States would eventually span the entire continent of North America. Throughout his negotiations leading up to the Adams-Onís Treaty, he made it clear to Spain that, if the Spanish did not concede some of their territory in North America, the United States might seize all of it, including Texas and even Mexico. Americans were fast acquiring a reputation as an aggressive people. Yet Spain was concerned with larger issues than American encroachment. Its primary objective was to suppress the revolutions against Spanish rule that had broken out in South America. To accomplish this goal, Spain sought support from the European monarchs who had organized the Holy Alliance in 1815. The brainchild of the tsar of Russia, the Holy Alliance aimed to quash revolutions everywhere in the name of Christian and monarchist principles. By 1822 its members talked of helping Spain suppress the South American revolutions. But Britain refused to join the Holy Alliance; British foreign minister George Canning proposed that the United States and Britain issue a joint statement opposing any European interference in South America while pledging that neither would annex any part of Spain's old empire in the New World.

While sharing Canning's opposition to European intervention in the New World, Adams preferred that the United States make a declaration of policy on its own rather than "come in as a cock-boat in the wake of the British man-of-war." Adams flatly rejected Canning's insistence on a joint Anglo-American pledge never to annex any part of Spain's former territories, for Adams wanted the freedom to annex Texas or Cuba, should their inhabitants one day "solicit a union with us."

This was the background of the Monroe Doctrine, as President Monroe's message to Congress on December 2, 1823, later came to be called. The message, written largely by Adams, announced three key principles: that unless American interests were involved, U.S. policy was to abstain from European wars; that the "American continents" were not "subjects for future colonization by any European power"; and that the United States would construe any attempt at European colonization in the New World as an "unfriendly act."

Europeans widely derided the Monroe Doctrine as an empty pronouncement. Fear of the British navy, not the Monroe Doctrine, prevented the Holy Alliance from intervening in South America. With hindsight, however, the Europeans might have taken the doctrine more seriously, for it had important implications. First, by pledging itself not to interfere in European wars, the United States was excluding the possibility that it would support revolutionary movements in Europe. For example, Adams opposed U.S. recognition of Greek patriots fighting for independence from the Ottoman Turks. Second, by keeping open its options to annex territory in the Americas, the United States was using the Monroe Doctrine to claim a preeminent position in the New World.

CONCLUSION

Jefferson's philosophy left a strong imprint on his age. Seeking to make the federal government more responsive to the people's will, Jefferson moved quickly to slash public expenditures and to contest Federalist control of the judiciary. His purchase of the Louisiana Territory in 1803 reflected his view that American liberty depended on the perpetuation of agriculture, and it would bring new states, dominated by Republicans, into the Union. As the Federalist party waned, Jefferson had to face down challenges from within his own party, notably from the mischief of Aaron Burr and from die-hard old Republicans like John Randolph, who charged that Jefferson was abandoning pure Republican doctrines.

The outbreak of war between Napoleon's France and Britain and the threat it posed to American neutrality preoccupied Jefferson's second term and both terms of his successor, James Madison. The failure of the embargo and peaceable coercion to force Europeans to respect American neutrality led the United States into war with Britain in 1812. The war destroyed the Federalists, who committed political suicide at the Hartford Convention. It also led Madison to jettison part of Jefferson's legacy by calling for a new national bank, federal support for internal improvements, and protective tariffs. The Transcontinental Treaty of 1819 and the Monroe Doctrine's bold pronouncement that European powers must not meddle in the affairs of the Western Hemisphere expressed America's increasingly assertive nationalism.

Conflict was never far below the surface of the apparent consensus of the Era of Good Feelings. In the absence of Federalist opposition, Republicans began to fragment into sectional factions, most notably in the conflict over Missouri's admission to the Union as a slave state.

CHRONOLOGY, 1801–1824

1801	Thomas Jefferson's inauguration.
1802	Repeal of the Judiciary Act of 1801. Yazoo land compromise.
1803	*Marbury* v. *Madison.* Conclusion of the Louisiana Purchase.
1804	Impeachment of Justice Samuel Chase. Aaron Burr kills Alexander Hamilton in a duel. Jefferson elected to a second term.
1804–1806	Lewis and Clark expedition.
1805	British court declares the broken voyage illegal.
1807	Chesapeake Affair. Embargo Act passed.
1808	James Madison elected president.
1809	Non-Intercourse Act passed. Embargo Act repealed.
1810	Macon's Bill No. 2.
1811	Battle of Tippecanoe.
1812	United States declares war on Britain. Madison reelected to a second term. General William Hull surrenders at Detroit. Battle of Queenston.
1813	Battle of the Thames.
1814	British burn Washington, D.C. Hartford Convention. Treaty of Ghent signed.
1815	Battle of New Orleans.
1816	James Monroe elected president. Second Bank of the United States chartered.
1817	Rush-Bagot Treaty.
1818	British-American Convention of 1818 sets U.S.-Canada border in West. Andrew Jackson invades East Florida.
1819	Adams-Onís (Transcontinental) Treaty. *Dartmouth College* v. *Woodward.* *McCulloch* v. *Maryland.*
1820	Monroe elected to a second term.
1820–1821	Missouri Compromise.
1823	Monroe Doctrine.

FOR FURTHER REFERENCE

READINGS

Stephen Ambrose, *Undaunted Courage* (1997). Fine new study of the Lewis and Clark Expedition.

Joseph J. Ellis, *American Sphinx: The Character of Thomas Jefferson* (1997). A prize-winning attempt to unravel Jefferson's complex character.

Jan Ellen Lewis and Peter S. Onuf, eds., *Sally Hemings and Thomas Jefferson* (1999). An excellent compilation of current scholarship on the relationship between Jefferson and Sally Hemings.

Drew R. McCoy, *The Last of the Fathers: James Madison and the Republican Legacy* (1989). The best recent book on Madison.

Merrill Peterson, *Thomas Jefferson and the New Nation: A Biography* (1970). The best one-volume biography of Jefferson.

J. C. A. Stagg, *Mr. Madison's War: Politics, Diplomacy and Warfare in the Early Republic* (1983). An important reinterpretation of the causes of the War of 1812.

John Sugden, *Tecumseh: A Life* (1997). A biography that illuminates the culture of the western Indians as they fought the Americans' advance.

G. Edward White, *The Marshall Court and Cultural Change, 1815–1835* (1991). A seminal reinterpretation of the Supreme Court under John Marshall.

WEBSITES

Monticello: The Home of Thomas Jefferson
http:www:monticello.org/

The American War of 1812
http://www.hillsdale.edu/dept/history/documents/war/FR1812.htm
A website that provides links to many primary sources, including contemporary newspaper articles debating American entry into the war, accounts of naval battles and military campaigns in the East and Northwest, and accounts of the Battle of New Orleans.

Lewis and Clark: The Journey of the Corps of Discovery
http://www.pbs.org/lewisandclark/
This website provides timelines and maps of the historic expedition, along with scholars' assessments of the journey.

CHAPTER 9

The Transformation of American Society

1815–1840

In December 1831 two young French aristocrats, Alexis de Tocqueville and Gustave de Beaumont, arrived in the small town of Memphis, Tennessee, after a harrowing journey from Cincinnati. They had planned to take a steamboat down the Ohio and Mississippi Rivers to New Orleans, but the early freezing of the Ohio had necessitated an overland trip through Kentucky and Tennessee to reach the Mississippi. Now they were exhausted and, worse, faced the prospect of spending the winter in Memphis.

On Christmas Day they saw a puff of smoke on the river, the sign of an approaching steamboat. Unfortunately, the steamboat was bound for Louisville, the wrong direction. The young Frenchmen sought to persuade the captain that ice had made an upriver passage impossible and that the only sensible course was to turn around and head south. The steamboat's passengers pleaded with the captain to keep going north. The captain hesitated.

A large group of Choctaw Indians herded by a federal agent was gathering on the river's bank. Evicted from their homes in Georgia and Alabama, the Choctaws were being resettled on reservations west of the Mississippi. The federal agent accompanying them offered cash to the captain to head south. The captain turned the boat, discharged his passengers, who were forced to wait in Memphis for a thaw, and took on Tocqueville, Beaumont, and the Choctaws.

◀ **Color Panorama of Detroit**
It took only four hours for the small town of Detroit to burn to the ground in 1805. As the Erie Canal enhanced the importance of shipping on the Great Lakes, Detroit was rebuilt with broad avenues carrying the grand names of Washington, Adams, Jefferson, Madison, and Monroe. By the 1830s steamships and sailing vessels crowded its harbor, located on the Detroit River, near the western edge of Lake Erie.

CHAPTER OUTLINE

Westward Expansion

The Growth of the Market Economy

Industrial Beginnings

Equality and Inequality

The Revolution in Social Relationships

Before coming to America, Tocqueville and Beaumont had read James Fenimore Cooper's *The Last of the Mohicans.* These dispirited Choctaws were nothing like the proud Indians of Cooper's fiction. "In this whole scene," Tocqueville wrote, "there was an air of ruin and destruction, something which betrayed a final and irrevocable adieu; one couldn't watch without feeling one's heart wrung." Unlike the Spanish, he wrote, the Americans did not massacre the Indians; instead white Americans believed that "whenever a square mile could nourish ten times as many civilized men as savages," the "savages would have to move away."

The two Frenchmen had arrived in the United States seven months earlier with the stated purpose of reporting on American prisons to the French government, but with the real intent of learning more about the sprawling American republic. Tocqueville eventually would weave his impressions of this "half-civilized, half-wild" nation into his two-volume masterpiece, *Democracy in America* (1835, 1840), still considered the most insightful analysis of the American character by a foreigner. From the start, Tocqueville had been struck by the "restless temper" of the Americans, who appeared to live in the middle of "an always moving stream."

Tocqueville came at a time when everything seemed to be changing: where Americans lived, how they worked, and how they related to each other. Improvements in transportation in the form of new roads, canals, and steamboats were stimulating interregional trade and migration to the trans-Appalachian West, encouraging an unprecedented development of towns and cities, and transforming social relationships. Increasingly, farmers raised crops for sale in distant markets rather than merely for their families' consumption. The new urban dwellers formed a market not only for farm products but also for those of new factories springing up in the industrializing East.

To Tocqueville, Americans seemed to have just one goal: "that of getting rich." In some respects, he admired this attitude. White Americans were an industrious and democratic people with little tolerance for restraints based on tradition or privilege. Yet whites treated nonwhites harshly. In Baltimore, an amazed Beaumont described how, when a black man entered a race track along with whites, "one of them gave him a volley of blows with his cane without this deed appearing to surprise either the crowd or the negro himself." Both Frenchmen recognized slavery as a great blot on the American character. Still, whites treated each other as equals. Indeed, they all seemed alike to Tocqueville, animated by the same passion for getting ahead.

This chapter focuses on five major questions:

- What caused the upsurge of westward migration after the War of 1812?
- What changes were linked to the rise of the market economy?
- How do you account for the vast public investment in canals during this era, and how did the rise of canals affect where Americans lived and how they made their living?
- What caused the rise of industrialization?
- How did the rise of the market economy and industrialization influence relationships within families and communities?

WESTWARD EXPANSION

In 1790 the vast majority of the non-Indian population of the United States lived east of the Appalachian Mountains and within a few hundred miles of the Atlantic Ocean. But by 1840 one-third were living between the Appalachians and the Mississippi River, the area that Americans of the time referred to as the West. Migrants brought old-fashioned values and customs with them, but in adapting to the West they gradually developed new values and customs. In short, they became westerners, men and women with a distinctive culture.

Only a few Americans moved west to seek adventure, and these few usually headed into the half-known region west of the Rocky Mountains, the present Far West. Most migrants desired and expected a better version of the life they had known in the East: more land and more bountiful crops. Several factors nurtured this expectation: the growing power of the federal government; its often ruthless removal of the Indians from the path of white settlement; and a boom in the prices of agricultural commodities after the War of 1812.

The Sweep West

Americans moved west in a series of bursts. The first began even before the 1790s and was reflected in the admission of four new states into the Union between 1791 and 1803: Vermont, Kentucky, Tennessee, and Ohio. Then, after an interlude of over ten years that saw the admission of only one new state, Louisiana, six states entered the Union between 1816 and 1821: Indiana, Mississippi, Illinois, Alabama, Maine, and Missouri. Even as Indiana and Illinois were gaining statehood, set-

tlers were pouring farther west into Michigan. Ohio's population jumped from 45,000 in 1800 to 581,000 by 1820 and 1,519,000 by 1840; Michigan's from 5,000 in 1810 to 212,000 by 1840.

Seeking security, pioneers usually migrated as families rather than as individuals. Because they needed to get their crops to market, most settlers between 1790 and 1820 clustered near the navigable rivers of the West, especially the magnificent water system created by the Ohio and Mississippi Rivers. Only with the spread of canals in the 1820s and 1830s, and later of railroads, did westerners feel free to venture far from rivers. In addition, westerners often clustered with people who hailed from the same region back east. For instance, in 1836 a group of farmers from nearby towns met at Castleton, Vermont, listened to a minister intone from the Bible, "And Moses sent them to spy out the land of Canaan," and soon established the town of Vermontville in Michigan. Other migrants to the West were less organized than these latter-day descendants of the Puritans, but most hoped to settle among familiar faces in the West. When they found that southerners already were well entrenched in Indiana, for example, New Englanders tended to prefer Michigan.

Western Society and Customs

Most westerners craved sociability. Even before there were towns and cities in the West, rural families joined with their neighbors in group sports and festivities. Men met for games that, with a few exceptions like marbles (popular among all ages), were tests of strength or agility. These included wrestling, weightlifting, pole jumping (for distance rather than height), and a variant of the modern hammer toss. Some of these games were brutal. In gander pulling, horseback riders competed to pull the head off a male duck whose neck had been stripped of feathers and greased. Women usually combined work and play in quilting and sewing parties, carpet tackings, and even chicken and goose pluckings. Social activities brought the genders together. Group corn huskings usually ended with dances; and in a variety of "hoedowns" and "frolics," even westerners who in theory might disapprove of dancing promenaded to singing and a fiddler's tune.

Within western families, there was usually a clear division of labor between men and women. Men performed most of the heaviest labor such as cutting down trees and plowing fields. Women usually rose first in the morning because they were responsible for milking the cows and preparing breakfast. As they had always done, women fashioned the coverlets that warmed beds in unheated rooms, and spun yarn and wove the fabrics to make their family's shirts, coats, pants, and dresses. The availability of factory-made clothing in the 1830s lessened this burden for some women. Farm-women often helped butcher hogs. They knew that the best way to bleed a hog was to slit its throat while it was still alive, and after the bleeding, they were adept at scooping out the innards, washing the heart and liver, and hanging them to dry. There was nothing dainty about the work of pioneer women.

Most western sports and customs had been transplanted from the East, but the West developed a character of its own. Before 1840, few westerners could afford elegant living. Arriving on the Michigan frontier from New York City in 1835, the well-bred Caroline Kirkland quickly discovered that her neighbors thought that they had a right to borrow anything she owned with no more

The Mountain Men

Rocky Mountain trappers or "mountain men" were among the most colorful and individualistic of nineteenth-century Americans. Entrepreneurs who trapped beavers for their pelts (which were used until the 1830s to make hats), the mountain men were also hunters, explorers, and adventurers who lived "a wild Robin Hood kind of life" with "little fear of God and none at all of the Devil."

than a blunt declaration that "you've got plenty." "For my own part," Caroline related, "I have lent my broom, my thread, my tape, my spoons, my cat, my thimble, my scissors, my shawl, my shoes, and have been asked for my comb and brushes." Their relative lack of refinement made westerners easy targets for easterners' contemptuous jibes.

Criticisms of the West as a land of half-savage yokels tended, in turn, to give rise to counterassertions by westerners that they lived in a land of honest democracy and that the East was soft and decadent. The exchange of insults fostered a regional identity among westerners that further shaped their behavior. Priding themselves on their simple manners, some westerners were intolerant of other westerners who had pretensions to gentility. On one occasion, a traveler who hung up a blanket in a tavern to shield his bed from public gaze had it promptly ripped down. On another, a woman who improvised a screen behind which to retire in a crowded room was dismissed as "stuck up." A politician who rode to a public meeting in a buggy instead of on horseback lost votes.

The Far West

In contrast to the great majority of pioneers who sought stability and prosperity in the area between the Appalachians and the Mississippi River, the region today known as the Midwest, an adventuring spirit carried a few Americans far beyond the Mississippi. On an exploring expedition in the Southwest in 1806, Zebulon Pike sighted the Colorado peak that was later named after him. The Lewis and Clark expedition whetted interest in the Far West. In 1811 a New York merchant, John Jacob Astor, founded the fur-trading post of Astoria at the mouth of the Columbia River in the Oregon Country. In the 1820s and 1830s, fur traders also operated along the Missouri River from St. Louis to the Rocky Mountains and beyond. At first, whites relied on Native Americans to bring them furs, but during the 1820s white trappers or "mountain men"—among them, Kit Carson, Jedediah Smith, and the mulatto Jim Beckwourth—gathered furs on their own while performing astounding feats of survival in harsh surroundings.

Jedediah Smith was representative of these men. Born in the Susquehanna Valley of New York in 1799, Smith moved west with his family to Pennsylvania and Illinois and signed on with an expedition bound for the upper Missouri River in 1822. In the course of this and subsequent explorations, he was almost killed by a grizzly bear in the Black Hills of South Dakota, learned from the Native Americans to trap beaver and kill buffalo, crossed the Mojave Desert into California, explored California's San Joaquin Valley, and hiked back across the Sierras and the primeval Great Basin to the Great Salt

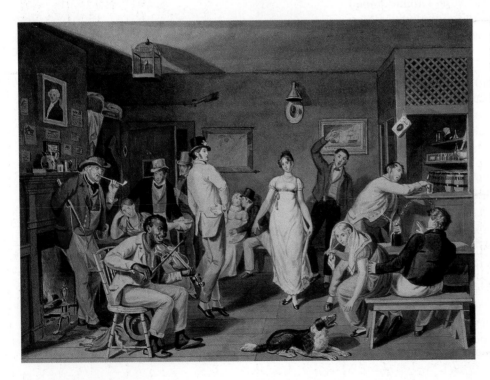

"Barroom Dancing" by John Lewis Krimmel, 1820
We can only guess what George Washington, looking soberly down from the wall, would have thought of these tipsy celebrants at a country tavern.

Lake, a trip so forbidding that even Native Americans avoided it. The exploits of Smith and the other mountain men were popularized in biographies, and they became legends in their own day.

The Federal Government and the West

Of the various causes of expansion to the Mississippi from 1790 to 1840, the one that operated most generally and uniformly throughout the period was the growing strength of the federal government. Even before the Constitution's ratification, several states had ceded their western land claims to the national government, thereby creating the bountiful public domain. The Land Ordinance of 1785 had set forth plans for surveying and selling parcels of this public treasure to settlers. The Northwest Ordinance of 1787 provided for the orderly transformation of western territories into states. The Louisiana Purchase of 1803 brought the entire Mississippi River under American control, and the Transcontinental Treaty of 1819 wiped out the last vestiges of Spanish power east of the Mississippi.

The federal government directly stimulated settlement of the West by promising land to men who enlisted during the War of 1812. With 6 million acres allotted to these so-called military bounties, many former soldiers and their families pulled up roots and settled in the West. To facilitate westward migration, Congress authorized funds in 1816 for the extension of the National Road, a highway begun in 1811 that reached Wheeling, Virginia, on the Ohio River in 1818 and Vandalia, Illinois, by 1838. Soon settlers thronged the road. "Old America seems to be breaking up," a traveler on the National Road wrote in 1817. "We are seldom out of sight, as we travel on this grand track towards the Ohio, of family groups before and behind us."

Although whites gained innumerable advantages from having a more powerful national government behind them, the rising strength of that government brought misery to the Indians. Virtually all the foreign-policy successes during the Jefferson, Madison, and Monroe administrations worked to Native Americans' disadvantage. The Louisiana Purchase and the Transcontinental Treaty stripped them of Spanish protection. In the wake of the Louisiana Purchase, Lewis and Clark bluntly told the Indians that they must "shut their ears to the counsels of bad birds" and listen henceforth only to the "Great Father" in Washington. The outcome of the War of 1812 also worked against the Native Americans; indeed, the Indians were the only real losers of the war.

Early in the negotiations leading to the Treaty of Ghent, the British had insisted on the creation of an Indian buffer state between the United States and Canada in the Old Northwest. But after the American victory at the Battle of Plattsburgh, the British dropped the demand and essentially abandoned the Indians to the Americans.

The Removal of the Indians

Westward-moving white settlers found sizable numbers of Native Americans in their paths, particularly in the South, home to the so-called Five Civilized Tribes: the Cherokees, Choctaws, Creeks, Chickasaws, and Seminoles. Years of commercial dealings and intermarriage with whites had created in these tribes, especially the Cherokees, an influential minority of mixed-bloods who embraced Christianity, practiced agriculture, built gristmills, and even owned slaves. One of their chiefs, Sequoyah, devised a written form of their language; other Cherokees published a bilingual newspaper, the *Cherokee Phoenix*.

The "civilization" of the southern Indians impressed New England missionaries more than southern whites, who viewed the Civilized Tribes with contempt and their land with envy. Presidents James Monroe and John Quincy Adams had concluded several treaties with Indian tribes providing for their voluntary removal to public lands west of the Mississippi River. Although some assimilated mixed-bloods sold their tribal lands to the government, other mixed-bloods, mindful that their prosperity depended on commercial ties with whites, resisted removal. In addition, full-bloods, the majority even in the "civilized" tribes, clung to their land and customs. They wanted to remain near the burial grounds of their ancestors and condemned mixed-bloods who bartered away tribal lands to whites. When the Creek mixed-blood chief William McIntosh sold all Creek lands in Georgia and two-thirds of Creek lands in Alabama to the government in the Treaty of Indian Springs (1825), a Creek tribal council executed him.

During the 1820s, whites in Alabama, Georgia, and Mississippi intensified pressure on the Indians by surveying tribal lands and squatting on them. Southern legislatures, loath to restrain white settlers, passed laws that threatened to expropriate Indian lands unless the Indians moved west. Other laws extended state jurisdiction over the tribes (which effectively outlawed tribal government) and declared that no Indian could be a witness in a court case involving whites (which made it difficult for Indians to collect debts owed them by whites).

Political Cartoon of Jackson and Native Americans
This cartoon, which depicts Native Americans as children or dolls subject to father Andrew Jackson, was intended as a satire on Jackson's policy of forcibly removing the Indians to reservations. The painting in the upper right corner pointedly depicts the goddess Liberty trampling a tyrant.

These measures delighted President Andrew Jackson. Reared on the frontier and sharing its contempt for Indians, Jackson believed that it was ridiculous to treat the Indians as independent nations; rather, they should be subject to the laws of the states where they lived. This position spelled doom for the Indians, who could not vote or hold state office. In 1834 Cherokee Chief John Ross got a taste of what state jurisdiction meant; Georgia, without consulting him, put his house up as a prize in the state lottery.

In 1830 Jackson secured passage of the Indian Removal Act, which authorized him to exchange public lands in the West for Indian territories in the East and appropriated $500,000 to cover the expenses of removal. But the real costs of removal, human and monetary, were vastly greater. During Jackson's eight years in office, the federal government forced Indians to exchange 100 million acres of their lands for 32 million acres of public lands. In the late 1820s and early 1830s the Choctaws, whom Tocqueville had observed near Memphis, Creeks, and Chickasaws started their "voluntary" removal to the West. In 1836 Creeks who clung to their homes were forcibly removed, many in chains. Most Seminoles were removed from Florida, but only after a bitter war between 1835 and 1842 that cost the federal government $20 million.

Ironically, the Cherokees, whose leaders were the most accommodating to American political institutions, suffered the worst fate. In 1827 the Cherokees proclaimed themselves an independent republic within Georgia. When the Georgia legislature subsequently extended the state's jurisdiction over this "nation," the Cherokees petitioned the U.S. Supreme Court for an injunction to halt Georgia's action. In the case of *Cherokee Nation* v. *Georgia* (1831), Chief Justice John Marshall denied the Cherokees' claim to status as a republic within Georgia; rather, they were a "domestic dependent nation," a kind of ward of the United States. Marshall added that prolonged occupancy had given the Cherokees a claim to their lands within Georgia. A year later he clarified the Cherokees' legal position in *Worcester* v. *Georgia* by holding that they were a "distinct" political community entitled to federal protection from tampering by Georgia.

But Marshall's decision had little impact. Jackson ignored it, reportedly sneering, "John Marshall has made his decision; now let him enforce it." Next, federal agents persuaded some minor Cherokee chiefs to sign the Treaty of New Echota (1835), which ceded all Cherokee lands in the United States for $5.6 million and free passage west. Congress ratified this treaty (by one vote), but the vast majority of Cherokees denounced it. In 1839 a Cherokee party took revenge by murdering its three principal signers, including a former editor of the *Cherokee Phoenix*.

The end of the story was simple and tragic. In 1838 the Cherokees were forcibly removed to the new Indian Territory in what is now Oklahoma. They traveled west along what became known as the "Trail of Tears" (see Map 9.1). As a youth, a man who later became a colonel in the Confederate Army had participated in the forced removal of some sixteen thousand Cherokees from their lands east of the Mississippi River where North Carolina, Georgia, Alabama, and Tennessee more or less converge. He recollected: "I fought through the civil war and have seen men shot to pieces and slaughtered by the thousands, but the Cherokees removal was the cruelest work I ever knew." Perhaps as many as eight thousand

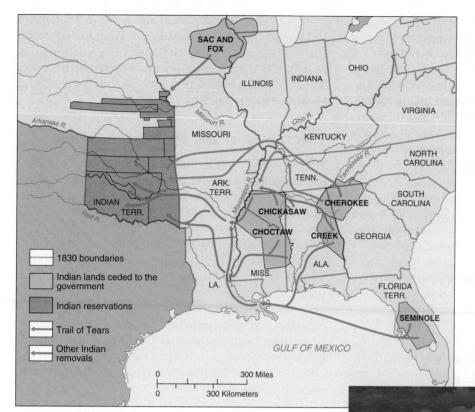

MAP 9.1 The Removal of the Native Americans to the West, 1820-1840
The so-called Trail of Tears, followed by the Cherokees, was one of several routes along which various tribes migrated on their forced removal to reservations west of the Mississippi.

Trail of Tears, by Robert Lindneux

Cherokees, more than one-third of the entire nation, died during and just after the removal.

Indians living in the Northwest Territory fared no better. A series of treaties extinguished their land titles, and most moved west of the Mississippi. The removal of the northwestern Indians was notable for two uprisings. The first, led by Red Bird, a Winnebago chief, began in 1827 but was quickly crushed. The second was led by a Sac and Fox chief, Black Hawk, who resisted removal until 1831 and then moved his people west of the Mississippi, only to return the following year. In June 1832 federal troops and Illinois militia attacked his band and virtually annihilated Black Hawk's followers as they tried to recross the Mississippi into Iowa. Black Hawk's downfall persuaded the other Old Northwest tribes to cede their lands. Between 1832 and 1837, the United States acquired nearly 190 million acres of Indian land in the Northwest for $70 million in gifts and annual payments.

The Agricultural Boom

In pushing Indians from the paths of white settlers, the federal government was responding to whites' demands for land and more land. After the War of 1812, the rising prices of agricultural commodities such as wheat, corn, and cotton drew settlers westward in search of better farmland. Several factors accounted for the skyrocketing farm prices. During the Napoleonic Wars, the United States had quickly captured former British markets in the West Indies and former Spanish markets in South

America. With the conclusion of the wars, American farmers found brisk demand for their wheat and corn in Britain and France, both exhausted by two decades of warfare. In addition, demand within the United States for western farm commodities intensified after 1815 as the quickening pace of industrialization and urbanization in the East spurred a shift of workers toward nonagricultural employment. Finally, the West's splendid river systems made it possible for farmers in Ohio to ship wheat and corn down the Ohio River to the Mississippi and down the Mississippi to New Orleans. There, wheat and corn were either sold or transshipped to the East, the West Indies, South America, or Europe. Just as government policies made farming in the West possible, high prices for foodstuffs made it attractive.

As the prospect of raising wheat and corn pulled farmers toward the Old Northwest, Eli Whitney's invention of the cotton gin in 1793 (see Chapter 7) cleared the path for settlement of the Old Southwest, particularly the states of Alabama and Mississippi. As cotton clothing came into fashion around 1815, the British textile industry provided seemingly bottomless demand for raw cotton. By 1815 Alabama and Mississippi were producing nearly half of the nation's cotton. With its warm climate, wet springs and summers, and relatively dry autumns, the Old Southwest was especially suited to cotton cultivation. The explosive thrust of small farmers and planters from the seaboard South into the Old Southwest resembled a gold rush. By 1817 "Alabama fever" gripped the South; settlers bid the price of good land up to thirty to fifty dollars an acre. Accounting for less than a quarter of all American exports between 1802 and 1807, cotton comprised just over half by 1830, and nearly two-thirds by 1836.

THE GROWTH OF THE MARKET ECONOMY

The high prices of agricultural commodities like wheat and cotton tempted a growing number of farmers who traditionally had grown only enough food to feed their families (called subsistence agriculture) to add a cash crop (called commercial agriculture, or the market economy). In the South, slaves increasingly became a valuable commodity; the sale of slaves from declining agricultural states in the Southeast to planters and farmers migrating to Alabama and Mississippi grew into a huge business after 1815. "Virginia," an observer stated in 1832, "is, in fact, a *negro* raising State for other States; she produces enough for her own supply and six thousand a year for sale."

Farming for markets was not new; many farmers had done so during the colonial era. What was new after 1815 was the extent to which farmers entered the market economy. Buoyed by high prices for their crops, farmers launched into producing for distant markets without always weighing the risks.

The Risks of the Market Economy

While opening new opportunities for whites, commercial agriculture exposed farmers to new risks. Farmers had no control over fluctuating prices in distant markets. Furthermore, there was an interval, often a long one, between harvesting a cash crop and selling it. To sustain themselves during the interval, farmers had to borrow money. Thus, commercial agriculture forced farmers into short-term debt in the hope of long-term profit.

The debt was frequently worse than most had expected. Many western farmers had to borrow money to buy their land. The roots of this indebtedness for land lay in the federal government's inability to devise an effective policy for transferring the public domain directly into the hands of small farmers.

Federal Land Policy

Partisan and sectional pressures buffeted federal land policy like a kite in a March wind. The result was a succession of land laws passed between 1796 and 1820, each of which sought to undo the damage caused by its predecessors.

At the root of early federal land policy lay a preference for the orderly settlement of the public domain. To this end, the Ordinance of 1785 divided public lands into sections of 640 acres (see Chapter 6). The architects of the ordinance did not expect that ordinary farmers could afford such large lots; rather, they assumed that farmers who shared ties based on religion or region of origin would band together to purchase sections. This outcome would ensure that compatible settlers would live on adjoining lots in what amounted to rural neighborhoods, and it would make the task of government much easier than if settlers were to live in isolation on widely scattered homesteads.

Political developments in the 1790s undermined the expectations of the ordinance's framers. Because their political bases lay in the East, the Federalists were reluctant to encourage headlong settlement of the West, but at the same time they were eager to raise revenue for the federal government from land sales. They reconciled the

goals of retarding actual settlement while gaining revenue by encouraging the sale of huge tracts of land to wealthy speculators who had no intention of farming the land themselves. The speculators held onto the land until its value rose and then sold off parcels to farmers. For example, in the 1790s the Holland Land Company, composed mainly of Dutch investors, bought up much of western New York and western Pennsylvania. A federal land law passed in 1796 reflected Federalist aims by maintaining the minimum purchase at 640 acres at a minimum price of two dollars an acre, and by allowing only a year for complete payment. Few small farmers could afford to buy that much land at that price.

Believing that the small farmer was the backbone of the Republic and aware of Republican political strength in the West, Thomas Jefferson and the Republicans took a different tack. Starting in 1800, federal land laws increasingly reflected their desire to ease the transfer of the public domain to farmers. The land law of 1800 dropped the minimum purchase to 320 acres and allowed up to four years for full payment but kept the minimum purchase price at $2 an acre. In 1804 the minimum purchase came down to 160 acres, in 1820 to 80 acres, and in 1832 to 40 acres. The minimum price also declined from $2 an acre in 1800 to $1.64 in 1804 and $1.25 in 1820.

Although Congress steadily liberalized land policy, speculators always remained one step ahead. Long before 1832, speculators were selling 40-acre lots to farmers. Farmers preferred small lots (and rarely bought more than 160 acres) because the farms they purchased typically were forested. A new landowner could clear no more than 10 to 12 acres of trees a year. All land in the public domain was sold at auction, usually for much more than the two-dollar minimum. With agricultural prices soaring, speculators assumed that land would continue to rise in value and accordingly were willing to bid high on new land, which they resold to farmers at hefty prices.

The growing availability of credit after the War of 1812 fed speculation. The chartering of the Second Bank of the United States in 1816 had the dual effect of increasing the amount of money in circulation and stimulating the chartering of private banks within individual states (state banks). The circulation of all banks grew from $45 million in bank notes in 1812 to $100 million in 1817. The stockholders and directors viewed their banks less as a sound investment for their capital (many directors actually had very little capital when they started state banks) than as agencies that could lend them money for land speculation. In other words, banks often were founded so that they could lend their directors money for personal investment in land speculation. The result was an orgy of land speculation between 1815 and 1819. In 1819 the dollar value of sales of public land was over 1,000 percent greater than the average in 1800–1814.

The Speculator and the Squatter

Nevertheless, most of the public domain eventually found its way into the hands of small farmers. Because speculators gained nothing by holding land for prolonged periods, they were only too happy to sell it when the price was right. In addition, a familiar frontier type, the squatter, exerted a restraining influence on the speculator.

Even before the creation of the public domain, squatters had helped themselves to western land. George Washington himself had been unable to drive squatters off lands he owned in the West. Squatters were an independent and proud lot, scornful of their fellow citizens who were "softened by Ease, enervated by Affluence and Luxurious Plenty, & unaccustomed to Fatigues, Hardships, Difficulties or dangers." Disdaining land speculators above all, squatters formed claims associations to police land auctions and prevent speculators from bidding up the price of land. Squatters also pressured Congress to allow them preemption rights—that is, the right to purchase at the minimum price land that they had already settled on and improved. Seeking to undo the damaging effects of its own laws, Congress responded by passing special preemption laws for squatters in specific areas and finally, in 1841, acknowledged a general right of preemption.

Preemption laws were of no use to farmers who arrived after speculators had already bought up land. Having spent their small savings on livestock, seed, and tools, these settlers had to buy land from speculators on credit at interest rates that ranged as high as 40 percent. Hobbled by steep indebtedness, many western farmers had no choice but to skimp on subsistence crops while expanding cash crops in the hope of paying off their creditors. Farmers were not merely entering the market economy; they were lunging into it.

Countless farmers who had carried basically conservative expectations to the West quickly became economic adventurers. Forced to raise cash crops in a hurry, many worked their acreage to exhaustion and thus had to keep moving in search of new land. The phrase "the moving frontier" refers not only to the obvious fact that the line of settlement shifted farther west with each

passing decade, but also to the fact that the same people kept moving. The experience of Abraham Lincoln's parents, who migrated from the East through several farms in Kentucky and then to Indiana, was representative of the westward trek.

The Panic of 1819

In 1819 the land boom collapsed like a house of cards, the victim of a financial panic. The state banks' loose practices contributed mightily to the panic. Like the Bank of the United States, these banks issued their own bank notes. In the absence of any national system of paper money, the notes served as a circulating medium. A bank note was just a piece of paper with a printed promise from the bank's directors to pay the bearer ("redeem") a certain amount of specie (gold or silver coinage) on demand. State banks had long issued far more bank notes than they could redeem, and these notes had fueled the economic boom after 1815. With credit so readily available, farmers borrowed money to buy more land and to plant more crops, confident that they could repay their loans when they sold their crops. After 1817, however, the combination of bumper crops in Europe and a recession in Britain trimmed foreign demand for U.S. wheat, flour, and cotton at the very time American farmers were becoming more dependent on exports to pay their debts.

In the summer of 1818, reacting to the overremission of state bank notes, the Bank of the United States began to insist that state banks redeem in specie their notes that were held by the Bank of the United States. Because the Bank of the United States had more branches than any state bank, notes of state banks were often presented by their holders to branches of the Bank of the United States for redemption. Whenever the Bank of the United States redeemed a state bank note in specie, it became a creditor of the state bank. To pay their debts to the Bank of the United States, the state banks had no choice but to force farmers and land speculators to repay loans. The result was a general curtailment of credit throughout the nation, particularly in the West.

The biggest losers were the land speculators. Land that had once sold for as much as sixty-nine dollars an acre dropped to two dollars an acre. Land prices fell because the credit squeeze drove down the market prices of staples like wheat, corn, cotton, and tobacco. Cotton, which sold for thirty-two cents a pound in 1818, sank as low as seventeen cents a pound in 1820. Since farmers could not get much cash for their crops, they could not pay the debts that they had incurred to buy

land. Since speculators could not collect money owed them by farmers, the value of land that they still held for sale collapsed.

The significance of the Panic lay not only in the economic damage it did but also in the conclusions that many Americans drew from it. First, the Panic left a bitter taste about banks, particularly the Bank of the United States, which was widely blamed for the hard times. Second, plummeting prices for cash crops demonstrated how much farmers were coming to depend on distant markets. In effect, it took a severe business reversal to show farmers the extent to which they had become entrepreneurs. The fall in the prices of cash crops accelerated the search for better forms of transportation to reach those faraway markets. If the cost of transporting crops could be cut, farmers could keep a larger share of the value of their crops and thereby adjust to falling prices.

The Transportation Revolution: Steamboats, Canals, and Railroads

The transportation system linking Americans in 1820 had severe weaknesses. The great rivers west of the Appalachians flowed north to south and hence could not by themselves connect western farmers to eastern markets. Roads were expensive to maintain, and horse-drawn wagons could carry only limited produce. Consequently, after 1820 attention and investment shifted to improving transportation on waterways, thus initiating the transportation revolution.

In 1807 Robert R. Livingston and Robert Fulton introduced the steamboat *Clermont* on the Hudson River. They soon gained a monopoly from the New York legislature to run a New York–New Jersey ferry service. Spectacular profits lured competitors, who secured a license from Congress and then filed suit to break the Livingston-Fulton monopoly. After a long court battle, the Supreme Court decided against the monopoly in 1824 in the famous case of *Gibbons* v. *Ogden*. Speaking for a unanimous court, Chief Justice John Marshall ruled that Congress's constitutional power to regulate interstate commerce applied to navigation and thus had to prevail over New York's power to license the Livingston-Fulton monopoly. In the aftermath of this decision, other state-granted monopolies collapsed, and steamboat traffic increased rapidly. The number of steamboats operating on western rivers jumped from 17 in 1817 to 727 by 1855.

Steamboats assumed a vital role along the Mississippi–Ohio River system. They were vastly superior to

**Steamboat
*Yellowstone***
The first steamboats had open deck space. With its enclosed cabins the *Yellowstone*, shown here passing St. Louis on its way down the Mississippi River in the early 1830s, was typical of the more luxurious second generation of steamboats. As the trans-Mississippi fur trade declined in the 1830s, the *Yellowstone* and similar steamboats plying the Mississippi and Missouri rivers became the key to St. Louis's expansion.

keelboats (covered flatboats pushed by oars or poles). Keelboats could navigate upstream at a snail's pace. It took a keelboat three or four months to complete the 1,350-mile voyage from New Orleans to Louisville; in 1817 a steamboat made the trip in twenty-five days. The development of long, shallow hulls permitted the navigation of the Mississippi-Ohio system even when hot, dry summers lowered the river level. Steamboats became more ornate as well as practical. To compete for passengers, they began to offer luxurious cabins and lounges, called saloons. The saloon of the *Eclipse*, a Mississippi River steamboat, was the length of a football field and featured skylights, chandeliers, a ceiling crisscrossed with Gothic arches, and velvet-upholstered mahogany furniture.

Once steamboats had demonstrated the feasibility of upriver navigation, the interest of farmers, merchants, and their elected representatives shifted away from turnpikes and toward canals. Although the cost of canal construction was mind-boggling—Jefferson dismissed the idea as little short of madness—canals offered the prospect of connecting the Mississippi–Ohio River system with the Great Lakes, and the Great Lakes with eastern markets.

Constructed between 1817 and 1825, New York's Erie Canal, connecting the Hudson River with Lake Erie, enabled produce from Ohio to reach New York City by a continuous stretch of waterways (see Map 9.2; also see Technology and Culture: Building the Erie Canal).

Completion of the Erie Canal started a canal boom during the late 1820s and 1830s. Ohio constructed a network of canals that allowed its farmers to send their wheat by water to Lake Erie. After transport across Lake Erie, the wheat would be milled into flour in Rochester, New York, then shipped on the Erie Canal to Albany and down the Hudson River to New York City. Throughout the nation, canals reduced shipping costs from twenty to thirty cents a ton per mile in 1815 to two to three cents a ton per mile by 1830.

When another economic depression hit in the late 1830s, various states found themselves overcommitted to costly canal projects and ultimately scrapped many. As the canal boom was ending, the railroad, an entirely new form of transportation, was being introduced. In 1825 the world's first commercial railroad began operation in England, and by 1840 some three thousand miles of track had been laid in America, about the same as the total canal mileage in 1840. During the 1830s, investment in American railroads exceeded that in canals. Cities like Baltimore and Boston, which lacked major inland waterway connections, turned to railroads to enlarge their share of the western market. The Baltimore and Ohio Railroad, chartered in 1828, took business away from the Chesapeake and Ohio Canal farther south. Blocked by the Berkshire Mountains from building a canal to the Erie, Massachusetts chartered the Boston and Worcester Railroad in 1831 and the Western Railroad (from Worcester to Albany) in 1833.

TECHNOLOGY AND CULTURE

Building the Erie Canal

The building of canals was the most expensive, difficult, and dramatic feature of the transportation revolution upon which the market economy depended. Water highways that followed the lay of the land, crossing rivers and ascending hills, canals called forth stupendous feats of engineering and numbing labor. Parts of the Erie Canal ran through a virtual wilderness. Trees had to be felled, stumps uprooted, earth excavated to several feet of depth, and solid rock, two miles of it toward the western end of the Erie, blasted through. The builders were aided by a superior type of blasting powder manufactured in Delaware by a French immigrant, E. I. du Pont, and by a clever machine devised in 1819 by one of the canal workers that made it possible to pull down a tree, however tall, by running a cable secured to a screw and crank up the tree and then turning the crank till the tree dropped.

Like other canals, the Erie also required aqueducts, arched causeways whose wooden troughs carried canal boats over natural bodies of water in the path of construction, and locks. The Erie's eighty-three locks were watertight compartments that acted as steps to overcome natural rises and falls in the terrain. At Lockport, side-by-side locks carried traffic up a rise of seventy-three feet. The locks themselves were anywhere from ninety to one hundred feet high by fifteen to eighteen feet wide. Their sides were built of cut stone, with foot-thick timbers as floors and two layers of planks on top of the timber. Huge wooden lock gates were fitted with smaller gates (wickets) for releasing water from a lock while the main gates remained closed.

Although a few short canals had been constructed in the 1790s, nothing on the scale of the Erie had ever been attempted. France and Britain had several canals with locks and aqueducts, but European experience had not been written down and, in any event, the techniques for building canals in Europe were of limited application to New York. The short canals of Europe relied more on

Erie Canal, by John William Hill, 1831
Construction of the Erie Canal was a remarkable feat, all the more so because the United States did not possess a single school of engineering at the time. The project's heroes were lawyers and merchants who taught themselves engineering, and brawny workmen, often Irish immigrants, who hacked a waterway through the forests and valleys of New York.

266

stone than was feasible in New York, where wood was abundant and quarries distant from the canal site. Building a canal 363 miles long required thousands of workers, hundreds of supervisors, and several engineers. When construction of the Erie commenced in 1817, New York had none of these: no public work force, no employees who had ever supervised the building of even a short canal, and virtually no trained engineers. (Aside from the trickle of graduates of the military academy at West Point, the United States had no engineering students and no schools devoted to training them.) By occupation, the prominent engineers on the Erie were judges, merchants, and surveyors; none had formal training in engineering.

Building the canal required endless adaptations to circumstances. Since the state had no public work force, laborers were engaged and paid by private contractors, usually local artisans or farmers, each of whom contracted with the state to build up to a mile of the canal. Engineering problems were solved by trial and error. For example, one of the most difficult tasks in building the Erie was to find a way to seal its banks so that the earth would not absorb the four feet of water that marked the canal's depth and thus leave canal barges stranded on mud. In the 1790s an English immigrant had introduced Americans to a process called "puddling," forming a cement sealant out of soil or rock, but the Erie builders needed to find a form of soil or stone that would make a good sealant and also be abundant in New York. The very length of the canal ruled out transporting substances over long distances. After repeated experiments with different kinds of limestone, in 1818 canal engineer Canvass White discovered a type in Madison County, New York, that, when heated to a high temperature, reduced to a powder and, mixed with water and sand, became a cement with the great virtue of hardening under water. The Erie served as a great school of engineering, educating a generation of Americans in the principles and practices of canal building. After its completion, its "graduates" moved to other states to oversee the construction of new canals.

When the Erie Canal opened in 1825, it was not without defects. Its banks sometimes collapsed. Lines of barges piled up in front of each lock, creating colossal traffic jams. In December, the freezing of the Erie made it unusable until April. But the opening of the canal dazzled

Operation of a Canal Lock

Locks made it possible for canal traffic to follow the rises and falls of the land. To lower a boat, the lock was filled by opening the upper gates (shown on the right, already opened) and letting in water. After the water level had risen, the upper gates were closed, and the lower gates (shown here on the left, still closed), were opened to drain the lock and to allow the water to fall to the level of the canal below. Once the boat had dropped to the lower level, it proceeded on its way, pulled by the two mules shown on the boat's right. These steps were repeated in reverse to raise the boat.

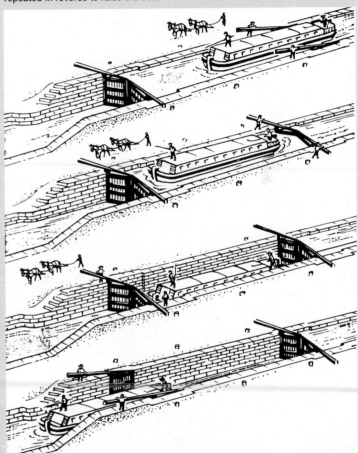

the imaginations of Americans. Not only had technology removed an obstacle placed by nature in the path of progress; it also conveyed small luxuries to unlikely places. Now farmers in the West marveled at the availability of oysters from Long Island.

Focus Question:

- Canals were hugely expensive to build, and railroads were just around the corner. Reviewing the material in this chapter and in Chapter 11, what do you see as the advantages and disadvantages of investment in canals?

Cheaper to build, faster, and able to reach more places, railroads had obvious advantages over canals and also contributed to the growth of communities that were remote from waterways. But railroads' potential was only slowly realized. Most early railroads ran between cities in the East, rather than from east to west,

and carried more passengers than freight. Not until 1849 did freight revenues exceed passenger revenues, and not until 1850 was the East Coast connected by rail to the Great Lakes.

Several factors explain the relatively slow spread of interregional railroads. Unlike canals, which were built

MAP 9.2. Major Rivers, Roads, and Canals, 1825–1860
Railroads and canals increasingly tied the economy of the Midwest to that of the Northeast.

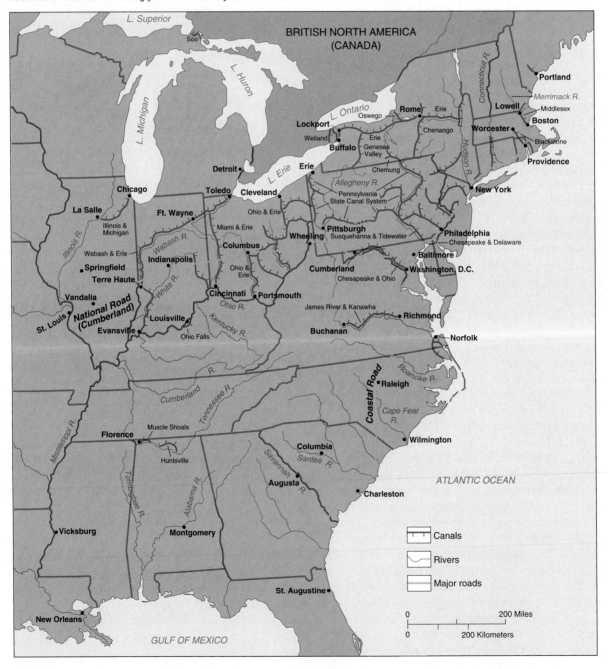

by state governments, most railroads were constructed by private corporations seeking quick profits. To minimize their original investment, railroad companies commonly resorted to cost-cutting measures such as covering wooden rails with iron bars. As a result, although relatively cheap to build, American railroads needed constant repairs. In contrast, although expensive to construct, canals needed relatively little maintenance and were kept in operation for decades after railroads appeared. Moreover, it remained cheaper to ship bulky commodities such as iron ore, coal, and nonperishable agricultural produce by canal.

The Growth of the Cities

The transportation revolution speeded the growth of towns and cities. Canals and railroads vastly increased opportunities for city businesses: banks to lend money, insurers to cover risks of transport, warehouses and brokers to store and sell goods. In relative terms, the most rapid urbanization in American history occurred between 1820 and 1860. New York City's population rose from 124,000 in 1820 to 800,000 by 1860. An even more revealing change was the transformation of sleepy villages of a few hundred people into thriving towns of several thousand. For example, the Erie Canal turned Rochester, New York, from home to a few hundred villagers in 1817 into the Flour City with nine thousand residents by 1830.

City and town growth occurred with dramatic suddenness, especially in the West (see Map 9.3). Pittsburgh, Cincinnati, and St. Louis were little more than hamlets in 1800. The War of 1812 stimulated the growth of Pittsburgh, whose iron forges provided shot and weapons for American soldiers, and Cincinnati, which became a staging ground for attacks on the British in the Old Northwest. Meanwhile, St. Louis acquired some importance as a fur-trading center. Then, between 1815 and 1819, the agricultural boom and the introduction of the steamboat transformed all three places from outposts with transient populations of hunters, traders, and soldiers into bustling cities. Cincinnati's population nearly quadrupled between 1810 and 1820, then doubled in the 1820s.

With the exception of Lexington, Kentucky, whose lack of access to water forced it into relative stagnation after 1820, all the prominent western cities were river ports: Pittsburgh, Cincinnati, and Louisville on the Ohio; St. Louis and New Orleans on the Mississippi (see Map 9.4). Except for Pittsburgh, all were essentially commercial hubs rather than manufacturing centers and were flooded by individuals eager to make money. In 1819 land speculators in St. Louis were bidding as much as a thousand dollars an acre for lots that had sold for thirty dollars an acre in 1815. Waterfronts endowed with natural beauty were swiftly overrun by stores and docks. "Louis Ville, by nature is beautiful," a visitor wrote, "but the handy Work of Man has instead of improving

MAP 9.3 Population Distribution, 1790 and 1850

By 1850 high population density characterized parts of the Midwest as well as the Northeast.
Source: *1900 Census of Population, Statistical Atlas*, plates 2 and 8.

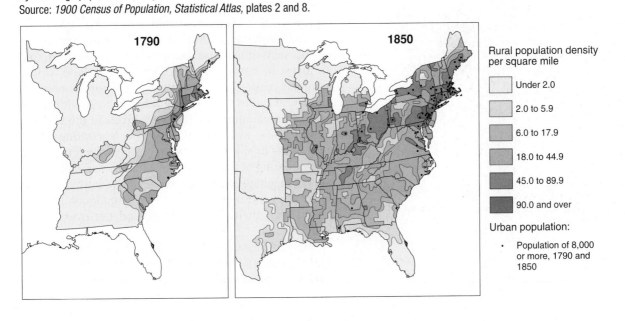

Rural population density per square mile

- Under 2.0
- 2.0 to 5.9
- 6.0 to 17.9
- 18.0 to 44.9
- 45.0 to 89.9
- 90.0 and over

Urban population:

- Population of 8,000 or more, 1790 and 1850

MAP 9.4 American Cities, 1820 and 1860
In 1820 most cities were seaports. By 1860, however, cities dotted the nation's interior and included San Francisco on the West Coast. This change occurred in large measure because of the transportation revolution.
Source: *Statistical Abstract of the United States.*

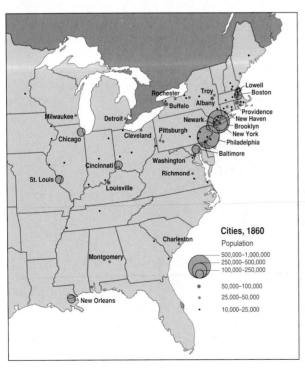

destroy'd the works of Nature and made it a detestable place."

The transportation revolution acted like a fickle god, selecting some cities for growth while sentencing others to relative decline. Just as the steamboat had elevated the river cities over landlocked Lexington, the completion of the Erie Canal shifted the center of western economic activity toward the Great Lakes. The result was a gradual decline in the importance of river cities such as Cincinnati and Louisville and a rise in the importance of lake cities such as Buffalo, Cleveland, Detroit, Chicago, and Milwaukee. In 1830 nearly 75 percent of all western city dwellers lived in the river ports of New Orleans, Louisville, Cincinnati, and Pittsburgh; by 1840 the proportion had dropped to 20 percent.

INDUSTRIAL BEGINNINGS

Spurred initially by the transportation revolution and the development of interregional trade, the growth of cities and towns received an added boost from the development of industrialization. The United States lagged a generation behind Britain in building factories. Eager to keep the lead, Britain banned the emigration of its skilled mechanics. Passing himself off as a farm laborer, one of these mechanics, Samuel Slater, came to the United States in 1789 and helped design and build the first cotton mill in the United States at Pawtucket, Rhode Island, the following year. The mill spun yarn by using Slater's adaptation of the spinning frame invented by Englishman Richard Arkwright. Slater's work force quickly grew from nine to one hundred, and his mills multiplied. From these beginnings, the pace of industrialization quickened in the 1810s and 1820s, especially in the production of cotton textiles and shoes.

Industrialization varied widely from region to region, with little in the South, where planters preferred to invest in slaves, and much in New England, whose poor soil made agriculture an unpromising investment. Industrialization itself was a gradual process with several distinct components. It always involved the subdivision of tasks, with each worker now fabricating only a part of the final product. Often, but not always, it led to the gathering of workers in large factories. Finally, high-speed machines replaced skilled handwork. In some industries, these elements arrived simultaneously, but more often their timing was spread out over several years.

Industrialization changed lives. Most workers in the early factories were recruited from farms. On farms, men and women had worked hard from sunrise to sunset, but

they had set their own pace and taken breaks after completing tasks. Factory workers, operating machines that ran continuously, encountered the new discipline of industrial time, regulated by clocks rather than tasks and signaled by the ringing of bells. Industrialization also changed the lives of those outside of factories. Cheaper to purchase than products made by hand, machine-made products brought luxuries within the reach of working people, but they also undermined skilled artisans. Everywhere, industrialization encouraged specialization. During the colonial era, most farm families had made their own clothes and often their shoes. With industrialization, they concentrated on farming, while purchasing factory-made clothes and shoes.

Causes of Industrialization

A host of factors stimulated industrialization. Some were political. The Embargo Act of 1808 persuaded merchants barred from foreign trade to redirect their capital into factories. The Era of Good Feelings saw general agreement that the United States needed tariffs. Once protected from foreign competition, New England's output of cloth spun from cotton rose from 4 million yards in 1817 to 323 million yards by 1840. America also possessed an environmental advantage in the form of the many cascading rivers that flowed from the Appalachian Mountains to the Atlantic Ocean and that provided abundant waterpower for mills. The transportation revolution also played a key role by bringing eastern manufacturers closer to markets in the South and West.

Industrialization also sprang from tensions in the rural economy, especially in New England, where in the late eighteenth century population grew beyond the available land to support it. Farm families adopted new strategies to survive. For example, a farmer would decide to grow flax, which his wife and daughters would make into linen for sale; or he would choose to plant broomcorn (used for making broom whisks), and he and his sons would spend the winter months making brooms for local sale. In time, he would form a partnership with other broom makers to manufacture brooms on a larger scale and for more-distant markets. At some point, he would cease to be a farmer; instead, he would purchase his broomcorn from farmers and, with hired help, concentrate on manufacturing brooms. By now, his contacts with merchants, who would provide him with broom handles and twine and who would purchase and sell all the brooms he could make, had become extensive.

In contrast to broom making, some industries, like textiles, depended on new technologies. Although Britain had a head start in developing the technology relevant to industrialization, Americans had a strong incentive to close the gap. With a larger population and far less land, Britain contained a class of landless laborers who would work cheaply in factories. In contrast, the comparatively high wages paid unskilled laborers in the United States spurred the search for labor-saving machines. In some instances, Americans simply copied British designs. Ostensibly on vacation, a wealthy Boston merchant, Francis Cabot Lowell, used his visit to England in 1811 to charm information about British textile machinery out of his hosts; later he engaged an American mechanic to construct machines from drawings he had made each night in his hotel room. The United States also benefited from the fact that, unlike Britain, America had no craft organizations (called guilds) that tied artisans to a single trade. As a result, American artisans freely experimented with machines outside their crafts. In the 1790s wagon-maker Oliver Evans of Delaware built an automated flour mill that required only a single supervisor to watch as the grain poured in on one side and was discharged from the other as flour.

Even in the absence of new technology, Americans searched for new methods of production to cut costs. After inventing the cotton gin, Eli Whitney won a government contract in 1798 to produce ten thousand muskets by 1800. Whitney's idea was to meet this seemingly impossible deadline by using unskilled workers to make interchangeable parts that could be used in any of his factory's muskets. Whitney promised much more than he could deliver (see Chapter 11), and he missed his deadline by nearly a decade. But his idea captured the imagination of prominent Americans, including Thomas Jefferson.

Textile Towns in New England

New England became America's first industrial region (see Map 9.5). The trade wars leading up to the War of 1812 had devastated its commercial economy and persuaded its wealthy merchants to invest in manufacturing. The many swift rivers were ideal sources of waterpower for mills. The westward migration of many of New England's young men left a surplus of young women, who supplied cheap industrial labor.

Cotton textiles led the way. In 1813 a group of Boston merchants, known as the Boston Associates and including Francis Cabot Lowell, incorporated the

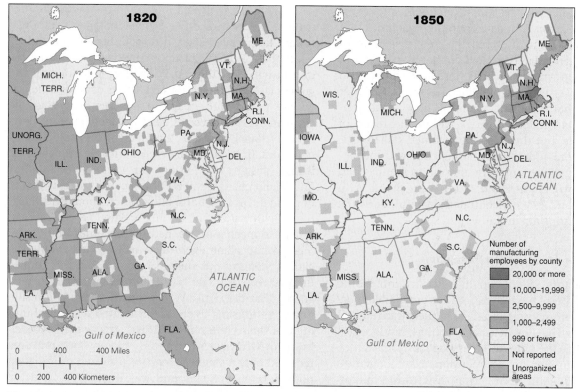

MAP 9.5 U.S. Manufacturing Employment, 1820 and 1850

In 1820 manufacturing employment was concentrated mostly in the Northeast, where the first textile mills appeared. By 1850 the density of manufacturing in the Northeast had increased, but new manufacturing centers arose in Baltimore, Pittsburgh, and Cincinnati.

(Source: *Historical Atlas of the United States, 2nd ed.* (Washington, D.C.: National Geographic Society, 1993), p. 148. Reprinted by permission of National Geographic Maps/National Geographic Society Image Collection.)

Boston Manufacturing Company. With ten times the capital of any previous American cotton mill, this company quickly built textile mills in the Massachusetts towns of Waltham and Lowell. By 1836 the Boston Associates controlled eight companies employing more than six thousand workers.

The Waltham and Lowell mills differed in two ways from the earlier Rhode Island mills established by Samuel Slater. Slater's mills performed only two of the operations needed to turn raw cotton into clothing: carding (separating batches of cotton into fine strands) and spinning these strands into yarn. In what was essentially cottage manufacturing, he contracted the weaving to women working in their homes. Unlike Slater's mills, the Waltham and Lowell mills turned out finished fabrics that required only one additional step, stitching into clothes. In addition, the Waltham and Lowell mills upset the traditional order of New England society to a degree that Slater had never contemplated. Slater had sought to preserve tradition not only by contracting weaving to farm families but also by hiring entire families for carding and spinning in his mill complexes. Men raised

crops on nearby company lands, while women and children tended the machines inside. In contrast, 80 percent of the workers in Waltham and Lowell, places that had not even existed in the eighteenth century, were young unmarried women who had been lured from farms by the promise of wages. Mary Paul, a Vermont teenager, settled her doubts about leaving home for Lowell by concluding that "I . . . must work where I can get more pay."

In place of traditional family discipline, the workers ("operatives") experienced new restraints. They had to live either in company boardinghouses or in licensed private dwellings, attend church on the Sabbath, observe a 10:00 P.M. curfew, and accept the company's "moral police." Regulations were designed to give the mills a good reputation so that New England farm daughters would continue to be attracted to factory work.

Mill conditions were far from attractive. To provide the humidity necessary to keep the threads from snapping, overseers nailed factory windows shut and sprayed the air with water. Operatives also had to contend with

Mill Girls
New England's humming textile mills were a magnet
for untold numbers of independence-seeking young
women in antebellum America.

flying dust and the deafening roar of the machines. Keener competition and a worsening economy in the late 1830s led mill owners to reduce wages and speed up work schedules. The system's impersonality intensified the harshness of the work environment.

Each of the major groups that contributed to the system lived in a self-contained world. The Boston Associates raised capital but rarely visited the factories. Their agents, all men, gave orders to the operatives, mainly women. Some eight hundred Lowell mill women quit work in 1834 to protest a wage reduction. Two years later, there was another "turnout," this time involving fifteen hundred to two thousand women. These were the largest strikes in American history to that date, noteworthy as strikes not only of employees against employers but also of women against men.

The Waltham and Lowell mills were the most conspicuous examples of industrialization before 1840, but they were not typical of industrial development. Outside of textiles, many industries continued to depend on industrial "outwork." In contrast to the farmer who planted flax for fabrication into linen by his wife and daughters, the key movers behind outwork were merchants

who provided households with raw materials and paid wages. For example, more than fifty thousand New England farmwomen, mainly daughters and widows, earned wages in their homes during the 1830s by making hats out of straw and palm leaves. Similarly, before the introduction of the sewing machine led to the concentration of all aspects of shoe manufacture in large factories in the 1850s, women often sewed parts of shoes at home and sent the piecework to factories for finishing.

Artisans and Workers in Mid-Atlantic Cities

Manufacturing in cities like New York and Philadelphia also depended on outwork. These cities lacked the fast-flowing rivers that powered machines in New England, and their high population densities made it unnecessary to gather workers into large factories. Nonetheless, they became industrial centers. Lured by the prospect of distant markets, some urban artisans and merchants started to scour the country for orders for consumer goods. They hired unskilled workers, often women, to work in small shops or homes fashioning parts of shoes or saddles or dresses. A New York reporter wrote,

> We have been in some fifty cellars in different parts of the city, each inhabited by a shoemaker and his family. The floor is made of rough plank laid loosely down, and the ceiling is not quite so high as a tall man. The walls are dark and damp and . . . the miserable room is lighted only by . . . the little light that struggles from the steep and rotting stairs. In this apartment often lives the man and his workbench, the wife, and five or six children of all ages; and perhaps a palsied grandfather or grandmother and often both. . . . Here they work, here they cook, they eat, they sleep, they pray.

New York and Philadelphia were home to artisans with proud craft traditions and independence. Those with highly marketable skills like cutting leather or clothing patterns continued to earn good wages. Others grew rich by turning themselves into businessmen who spent less time making products than making trips to obtain orders. But artisans lacking the capital to become businessmen found themselves on the downslide in the face of competition from cheap, unskilled labor.

In the late 1820s, skilled male artisans in New York, Philadelphia, and other cities began to form trade unions and workingmen's political parties to protect their interests. Disdaining association with unskilled workers, most of these groups initially sought to restore privileges and working conditions that artisans had once enjoyed

Dageurrotype of Skilled Artisan
This photograph of a Pennsylvania tool maker, taken around 1850, omits the furnace in which he heated metal for molding but reveals the pride that he brought to his craft.

that wealth was "universally diffused." Others, like New York merchant Philip Hone, portrayed an unhappy society marked by extremes of "costly luxury" and "squalid misery."

The French visitor Alexis de Tocqueville filled his private journals with references to inequality. But he was sure that the "general equality of condition among the people" was the fundamental shaping force of American society. Inclined to view everything in comparative terms, Tocqueville thought that wealth was more evenly distributed in the United States than in France and that, regardless of an individual's wealth, Americans believed that one person was as good as another. American servants insisted on being called the "help" and being viewed as neighbors invited to assist in running a household rather than as permanent subordinates. Similarly, while in France merchants were disdained by the nobility, in America merchants thought themselves equal to anyone.

Historians continue to argue about the meaning and extent of equality in antebellum America, but by using refined techniques of measurement they have drawn a more detailed portrait of antebellum society than the profile sketched by contemporaries. The following discussion applies mainly to northern society. We examine the South, whose "peculiar institution" of slavery created a distinctive social structure and set of social relationships, in Chapter 12.

rather than to act as leaders of unskilled workers. But the steady deterioration of working conditions in the early 1830s tended to throw skilled and unskilled workers into the same boat. When coal haulers in Philadelphia struck for a ten-hour day in 1835, they were quickly joined by carpenters, cigar makers, shoemakers, leatherworkers, and other artisans in the United States' first general strike.

The emergence of organized worker protest underscored the mixed blessings of economic development. Although some benefited from the new commercial and industrial economy, others found their economic position worsening. By the 1830s, many white Americans wondered whether their nation was truly a land of equality.

EQUALITY AND INEQUALITY

Observers of antebellum (pre-Civil War) America sensed changes sweeping the country but had trouble describing them or agreeing on their direction. Some insisted

Growing Inequality: The Rich and the Poor

The gap between the rich and the poor, which had increased during the late eighteenth century, widened further during the first half of the nineteenth century, especially in the cities. A small fraction of the people owned a huge share of America's urban wealth. In Boston, for example, the richest 10 percent of the population had owned a little over half of the city's real estate and personal property in 1771. By 1833 the richest 4 percent owned 59 percent of the wealth, and by 1848 nearly two-thirds. In New York City, the richest 4 percent owned nearly half the wealth in 1828 and more than two-thirds by 1845. The same was true in all major cities.

Although commentators celebrated the self-made American who rose from poverty to wealth, the vast majority of those who became extremely rich started out with considerable wealth. Fewer than five of every hundred wealthy individuals started poor, and close to ninety of every hundred started rich. The usual way to wealth was to inherit it, marry into more, and then invest wisely.

There were just enough instances of fabulously success-ful poor boys like John Jacob Astor, who built a fur-trad-ing empire, to sustain popular belief in the rags-to-riches myth, but not enough to turn that myth into a reality.

Splendid residences and social clubs set the rich apart. In 1828 over half of the five hundred wealthiest families in New York City lived on only 8 of the city's more than 250 streets. By the late 1820s New York City had a club so exclusive that it was called simply The Club. Elite merchants in western cities copied the lavish living of the eastern upper classes. Tocqueville noted that in America "the wealthiest and most enlightened live among themselves." Yet Tocqueville was also struck by how the rich pretended to respect equality when they moved about in public. They rode in ordinary rather than sumptuous carriages, brushed elbows easily with the less privileged, and avoided the conspicuous display of wealth that marked their private lives.

At the opposite end of the social ladder were the poor. By today's standards, most antebellum Americans were poor. They lived close to the edge of misery, depend-ed heavily on their children's labor to meet expenses, and had little money to spend on medical care or recre-ation. One reason for their poverty was frequent unem-ployment, not just during economic downturns but from month to month, even in prosperous times. Freezing weather, for instance, could temporarily throw workers in factories that depended on water power out of work.

In evaluating economic status, it is important to rec-ognize that statistics on the distribution of wealth to some extent mask the fact that the accumulation of property takes place over a lifetime. With its extraordi-narily high birthrate, antebellum America was over-whelmingly a nation of young people with little proper-ty; not all of them would remain without property as they grew older.

In addition, when antebellum Americans them-selves spoke of poverty, they were not thinking of the condition of hardship that affected most people. Instead, they were referring to a state of dependency, an inability to fend for oneself, that affected some people. They often called this dependency "pauperism." The absence of health insurance and old-age pensions con-demned many infirm and aged people to pauperism. Widows whose children had left home might also have a hard time avoiding pauperism. Contemporaries usu-ally classified all such people as the "deserving" poor and contrasted them with the "undeserving" poor, such as indolent loafers and drunkards whose poverty was seen as being self-willed. Most moralists claimed that

America was happily free of a permanent class of pau-pers. They assumed that since pauperism resulted either from circumstances beyond anyone's control, such as old age and disease, or from voluntary decisions to squander money on liquor, it could not afflict entire groups generation after generation.

This assumption was comforting but also mislead-ing. A class of people who could not escape poverty was emerging in the major cities during the first half of the nineteenth century. One source was immigration. As early as 1801, a New York newspaper called attention to the arrival of boatloads of immigrants with large fami-lies, without money or health, and "expiring from the want of sustenance."

The poorest white immigrants were from Ireland, where English landlords had evicted peasants from the land and converted it to commercial use in the eigh-teenth century. Severed from the land, the Irish increas-ingly became a nation of wanderers, scrounging for wages wherever they could. "The poor Irishman," it was said, "the wheelbarrow is his country." By the early 1830s, the great majority of canal workers in the North were Irish immigrants. Without the backbreaking labor of the Irish, the Erie Canal would never have been built. Other Irish congregated in New York's infamous Five Points district. Starting with the conversion of a brewery into housing for hundreds of people in 1837, Five Points became the worst slum in America.

The Irish were not only poor but were also Catholics, a faith despised by the Protestant majority in the United States. In short, they were different and had little claim on the kindly impulses of most Protestants. But even the Protestant poor came in for rough treatment in the years between 1815 and 1840. The more that Americans con-vinced themselves that success was within everyone's grasp, the less they accepted the traditional doctrine that poverty was ordained by God, and the more they were inclined to hold the poor responsible for their own misery. Ironically, even as many Americans blamed the poor for being poor, they practiced discrimination that kept some groups mired in enduring poverty. Nowhere was this more true than in the case of northern free blacks.

Free Blacks in the North

Prejudice against blacks was deeply ingrained in white society throughout the nation. Although slavery had largely disappeared in the North by 1820, laws penalized blacks in many ways. One form of discrimination was to restrict their right to vote. In New York State, for exam-

ple, a constitutional revision of 1821 eliminated property requirements for white voters but kept them for blacks. Rhode Island banned blacks from voting in 1822; Pennsylvania did the same in 1837. Throughout the half-century after 1800, blacks could vote on equal terms with whites in only one of the nation's major cities, Boston.

Laws frequently barred free blacks from migrating to other states and cities. Missouri's original constitution authorized the state legislature to prevent blacks from entering the state "under any pretext whatsoever." Municipal ordinances often barred free blacks from public conveyances and facilities and either excluded them from public schools or forced them into segregated schools. Segregation was the rule in northern jails, almshouses, and hospitals.

Of all restrictions on free blacks, the most damaging was the social pressure that forced them into the least-skilled and lowest-paying occupations throughout the northern cities. Recollecting his youthful days in Providence, Rhode Island, in the early 1830s, the free black William J. Brown wrote: "To drive carriages, carry a market basket after the boss, and brush his boots, or saw wood and run errands was as high as a colored man could rise." Although a few free blacks became successful entrepreneurs and grew moderately wealthy, urban free blacks were only half as likely as city dwellers in general to own real estate.

One important black response to discrimination was to establish their own churches. White churches confined blacks to separate benches or galleries. When black worshippers mistakenly sat in a gallery designated for whites at a Methodist church in Philadelphia, they were pulled from their knees. Their leader, former slave and future bishop Richard Allen, related, "we all went out of the church in a body, and they were no longer plagued by us." Allen initiated a movement that resulted in the organization of the African Methodist Episcopal Church, the first black-run Protestant denomination, in 1816. By 1822 the A.M.E. Church encompassed a territory bounded by Washington, D.C., Pittsburgh, and New York City. Its members campaigned against slavery, in part by refusing to buy produce grown by slaves, provided education for black children excluded from public school, and formed mutual-aid societies to free blacks from dependence on white charity.

Richard Allen
First bishop of the African Methodist Episcopal Church, Richard Allen spent much of his time traveling, organizing societies of black Methodists, preaching on Sundays, and cutting wood on other days to earn his living.

The "Middling Classes"

The majority of antebellum Americans lived neither in splendid wealth nor in grinding poverty. Most belonged to what men and women of the time called the middling classes. Even though the wealthy owned an increasing proportion of all wealth, most people's standard of living rose between 1800 and 1860, particularly between 1840 and 1860 when per capita income grew at an annual rate of around 1.5 percent.

Americans applied the term *middling classes* to families headed by professionals, small merchants and manufacturers, landowning farmers, and self-employed artisans. Commentators portrayed these people as living stable and secure lives. In reality, life in the middle often was unpredictable. The increasingly commercial economy of antebellum America created greater opportunities for success and for failure. An enterprising import merchant, Alan Melville, the father of novelist Herman Melville, had an abounding faith in his nation, in "our national Eagle, 'with an eye that never winks and a wing that never tires,' " and in the inevitable triumph of honesty and prudence. The Melvilles lived comfortably in

Albany and New York City, but Melville's business sagged in the late 1820s. In 1830 he begged his father for a loan of five hundred dollars, proclaiming that "I am destitute of resources and without a shilling—without immediate assistance I know not what will become of me." He got the five hundred dollars plus an additional three thousand dollars, but the downward spiral continued. In 1832 he died, broken in spirit and nearly insane.

In the emerging market economy, even such seemingly crisp occupational descriptions as farmer and artisan often proved misleading. Asa G. Sheldon, born in Massachusetts in 1788, described himself in his autobiography as a farmer, offered advice on growing corn and cranberries, and gave speeches about the glories of farming. Although Sheldon undoubtedly knew a great deal about farming, he actually spent very little time tilling the soil. In 1812 he began to transport hops from New England to brewers in New York City, and he soon extended this business to Philadelphia and Baltimore. He invested his profits in land, but rather than farm the land, he made money selling its timber. When a business setback forced him to sell his property, he was soon back in operation "through the disinterested kindness of friends" who lent him money with which he purchased carts and oxen. These he used to get contracts for filling in swamps in Boston and for clearing and grading land for railroads. From all this and from the backbreaking labor of the Irish immigrants he hired to do the shoveling, Sheldon the "farmer" grew prosperous.

The emerging market economy also transformed the lives of artisans. During the colonial period, artisans had formed a proud and cohesive group whose members often attained the goal of self-employment. They owned their own tools, made their own products on order from customers, boarded their apprentices and journeymen in their homes, and passed their skills on to their children. By 1840, in contrast, artisans had entered a new world of economic relationships. This was true even of a craft like carpentry that did not experience any industrial or technological change. Town and city growth in the wake of the transportation revolution created a demand for housing. Some carpenters, usually those with access to capital, became contractors. They took orders for more houses than they could build themselves and hired large numbers of journeymen to do the construction work. Likewise, as we have seen, in the early industrialization of shoe manufacturing during the 1820s, some shoemakers spent less time crafting shoes than making trips to obtain orders for their products, then hired workers to fashion parts of shoes. In effect, the old class of artisans was splitting into two new groupings. On one side were artisans who had become entrepreneurs; on the other, journeymen with little prospect of self-employment.

An additional characteristic of the middling classes, one they shared with the poor, was a high degree of transience, or spatial mobility. The transportation revolution made it easier for Americans to purchases services as well as goods and spurred many young men to abandon farming for the professions. For example, the number of medical schools rose from one in 1765 to twenty in 1830 and sixty-five in 1860. Frequently, the new men who crowded into medicine and into the ministry and law were forced into incessant motion. Physicians rode from town to town looking for patients. The itinerant clergyman mounted on an old nag and riding the countryside to visit the faithful or to conduct revivals became a familiar figure in newly settled areas. Even well-established lawyers and judges spent part of each year riding from one county courthouse to another, bunking (usually two to a bed) in rough country inns, to plead and decide cases.

Transience affected the lives of most Americans. Farmers who cultivated land intensively in order to raise a cash crop and so pay their debts exhausted the land quickly and had to move on. For skilled and unskilled workers alike, work often was seasonal; workers had to move from job to job to survive. Canal workers and boatmen had to secure new work when waterways froze. Even city dwellers who shifted jobs often had to change residences, for the cities were spreading out at a much faster rate than was public transportation. Some idea of the degree of transience can be gained from a survey by the Boston police on Saturday, September 6, 1851. At a time when Boston's population was 145,000, the survey showed that from 6:30 A.M. to 7:30 P.M., 41,729 people entered the city and 42,313 left. At a time when there were few suburbs, it is safe to say that these people were not commuters. Most likely, they were moving in search of work, as much a necessity for many in the middling classes as for the poor.

THE REVOLUTION IN SOCIAL RELATIONSHIPS

Following the War of 1812, the growth of interregional trade, commercial agriculture, and manufacturing changed not only the lives of individuals but also the ways in which they related to each other. Two broad generalizations encompass these changes. First, Americans questioned authority to an unprecedented degree. In 1775 they had rebelled against their king. Now, it

seemed, they were rebelling as well against their lawyers, their physicians, their ministers, and even their parents. An attitude of individualism sprouted and took firm root in antebellum America. Once individualism had meant nothing more than selfishness, but now Americans used the word to signify positive qualities: self-reliance and the conviction that each person was the best judge of his or her own true interests. Ordinary Americans might still agree with the opinions of their leaders, but only after they had thought matters through on their own. Those with superior wealth, education, or social position could no longer expect the automatic deference of the common people.

Second, even as Americans widely proclaimed themselves a nation of self-reliant individualists and questioned the traditional basis of authority, they sought to construct new foundations for authority. For example, among middle-class men and women, the idea developed that women possessed a "separate sphere" of authority in the home. In addition, individuals increasingly joined with others in these years to form voluntary associations through which they might influence the direction that their society would take.

The Attack on the Professions

In the swiftly changing antebellum society, claims to social superiority were questioned as never before. As a writer put it in 1836, "Everywhere the disposition is found among those who live in the valleys to ask those who live on the hills, 'How came we here and you there?'"

Intense criticism of lawyers, physicians, and ministers exemplified this assault on authority. As far back as the 1780s, Benjamin Austin, a radical Boston artisan, had complained that lawyers needlessly prolonged and confused court cases so that they could charge high fees. Between 1800 and 1840, a wave of religious revivals known as the Second Great Awakening (see Chapter 10) sparked new attacks on the professions. Some revivalists blasted the clergy for creating complicated theologies that ordinary men and women could not comprehend, for drinking expensive wines, and for fleecing the people. One religious revivalist, Elias Smith, extended the criticism to physicians, whom he accused of inventing Latin and Greek names for diseases in order to disguise their own ignorance of how to cure them.

These jabs at the learned professions peaked between 1820 and 1850. In medicine a movement arose under the leadership of Samuel Thomson, a farmer's son with little formal education, to eliminate all barriers to entry into the medical profession. Thomson believed that

anyone could understand the principles of medicine and become a physician. His crusade was remarkably successful. By 1845 every state had repealed laws that required licenses and education to practice medicine. Meanwhile, attacks on lawyers sharpened, and relations between ministers and their parishioners grew tense and acrimonious. In colonial New England, min-isters had usually served a single parish for life, but by the 1830s a rapid turnover of ministers was becoming the norm as finicky parishioners commonly dismissed clergymen whose theology displeased them. Ministers themselves were becoming more ambitious—more inclined to leave small, poor congregations for large, wealthy ones.

The increasing commercialization of the economy contributed both to the growing number of professionals and to the attacks on them. Like so many other antebellum Americans, freshly minted lawyers and doctors often were transients without deep roots in the towns that they served and without convincing claims to social superiority. Describing lawyers and physicians, a contemporary observer wrote, "Men dropped down into their places as from clouds. Nobody knew who or what they were, except as they claimed, or as a surface view of their character indicated." A horse doctor one day would the next day hang up his sign as "Physician and Surgeon" and "fire at random a box of his pills into your bowels, with a vague chance of hitting some disease unknown to him, but with a better prospect of killing the patient, whom or whose administrator he charged some ten dollars a trial for his marksmanship."

The questioning of authority was particularly sharp on the frontier. Here, to eastern and foreign visitors, it seemed that every man they met was a "judge," "general," "colonel," or "squire." In a society in which everyone was new, such titles were easily adopted and just as easily challenged. Where neither law nor custom sanctioned claims of superiority, would-be gentlemen substituted an exaggerated sense of personal honor. Obsessed with their fragile status, many reacted testily to the slightest insult. Dueling became a widespread frontier practice. At a Kentucky militia parade in 1819, an officer's dog jogged onto the field and sat at his master's knee. Enraged by this breach of military decorum, another officer ran the dog through with his sword. A week later, both officers met with pistols at ten paces. One was killed; the other maimed for life.

The Challenge to Family Authority

In contrast to adults' public philosophical attacks on the learned professions, children engaged in a quiet ques-

tioning of parental authority. Economic change created new opportunities that forced young people to choose between staying at home to help their parents and venturing out on their own. Writing to her parents in Vermont shortly before taking a job in a Lowell textile mill, eighteen-year-old Sally Rice quickly got to the point. "I must of course have something of my own before many more years have passed over my head and where is that something coming from if I go home and earn nothing. You may think me unkind but how can you blame me if I want to stay here. I have but one life to live and I want to enjoy myself as I can while I live."

A similar desire for independence tempted young men to leave home at earlier ages than in the past. Although the great migration to the West was primarily a movement of entire families, movement from farms to towns and cities within regions was frequently spearheaded by restless and single young people. Two young men in Virginia put it succinctly. "All the promise of life seemed to us to be at the other end of the rainbow—somewhere else—anywhere else but on the farm. . . . And so all our youthful plans had as their chief object the getting away from the farm."

Antebellum Americans also widely wished to be free of close parental supervision, and their changing attitudes influenced courtship and marriage. Many young people who no longer depended on their parents for land insisted on privacy in courting and wanted to decide for themselves when and whom to marry. Whereas seventeenth-century Puritans had advised young people to choose marriage partners whom they could learn to love, by the early 1800s young men and women viewed romantic love as indispensable to a successful marriage. "In affairs of love," a young lawyer in Maine wrote, "young people's hearts are generally much wiser than old people's heads."

One sign of young people's growing control over courtship and marriage was the declining likelihood that the young women of a family would marry in their exact birth order. Traditionally, fathers had wanted their daughters to marry in the order of their birth to avoid planting the suspicion that there was something wrong with one or more of them. Toward the end of the eighteenth century, however, daughters were making their own marital decisions, and the practice ceased to be customary. Another mark of the times was the growing number of long engagements. Having made the decision to marry, some young women were reluctant to tie the knot, fearing that marriage would snuff out their independence. For example, New Yorkers Caroline and William Kirkland were engaged for seven years before their marriage in 1828. Equally striking was the increas-

ing number of young women who chose not to marry. Catharine Beecher, the daughter of the prominent minister Lyman Beecher, broke off her engagement to a young man during the 1820s despite her father's pressure to marry him. She later renewed the engagement, but after her fiancé's death in a shipwreck, she remained single for the rest of her life.

Moralists reacted with alarm to signs that young people were living in a world of their own. They flooded the country with books of advice to youth, such as William Alcott's *The Young Man's Guide*, which went through thirty-one editions between 1833 and 1858. The number of such advice books sold in antebellum America was truly vast, but to an amazing extent, they all said the same thing. They did not advise young men and women to return to farms, and they assumed that parents had little control over them. Rather, the authors exhorted youths to develop habitual rectitude, self-control, and "character." It was an age not just of the self-made adult but also of the self-made youth.

Wives and Husbands

Another class of advice books pouring from the antebellum presses counseled wives and husbands on their rights and duties. These were a sign that relations between spouses, too, were changing. Young men and women who had grown accustomed to making decisions on their own as teenagers were more likely than their ancestors to approach wedlock as a compact between equals. Of course, wives remained unequal to their husbands in many ways. Before a reform movement that started in 1839, the law did not allow married women to own property. But relations between wives and husbands were changing during the 1820s and 1830s toward a form of equality.

One source of the change was the rise of a potent ideology known as the doctrine of separate spheres. Traditionally, women had been viewed as subordinate to men in all spheres of life. Now middle-class men and women developed a kind of separate-but-equal doctrine that portrayed men as superior in making money and governing the world and women as superior for their moral influence on family members.

One of the most important duties assigned to the sphere of women was raising children. During the eighteenth century, church sermons reminded fathers of their duty to govern the family; by the 1830s child-rearing manuals were addressed to mothers rather than fathers. "How entire and perfect is this dominion over the unformed character of your infant," the popular writer Lydia Sigourney proclaimed in her *Letters to*

Mothers (1838). Advice books instructed mothers to discipline their children by loving them and withdrawing affection when they misbehaved rather than by using corporal punishment. A whipped child might become more obedient but would remain sullen and bitter; gentler methods would penetrate the child's heart, making the child want to do the right thing.

The idea of a separate women's sphere blended with a related image of the family and home as refuges secluded from a society marked by commotion and disorder. The popular culture of the 1830s and 1840s painted an alluring portrait of the pleasures of home life through songs like "Home, Sweet Home" and poems such as Henry Wadsworth Longfellow's "The Children's Hour" and Clement Moore's "A Visit from St. Nicholas." The publication of Moore's poem coincided with the growing popularity of Christmas as a holiday season in which family members gathered to exchange warm affection. Even the physical appearance of houses changed. The prominent architect Andrew Jackson Downing published plans for peaceful single-family homes that he hoped would offset the "spirit of unrest" and the feverish pace of American life. He wrote of the ideal home, "There should be something to love. There must be nooks about it, where one would love to linger; windows, where one can enjoy the quiet landscape at his leisure; cozy rooms, where all fireside joys are invited to dwell."

As a prophet, Downing deserves high marks because one of the motives that impelled many Americans to flee cities for suburbs in the twentieth century was the desire to own their own homes. In the 1820s and 1830s, this ideal was beyond the reach of most people—not only blacks, immigrants, and sweatshop workers, but also most members of the middle class. In the countryside, although middle-class farmers still managed productive households, these were anything but tranquil; wives milked cows and bled hogs, and children fetched wood, drove cows to pasture, and chased blackbirds from cornfields. In the cities, middle-class families often had to sacrifice their privacy by taking in boarders to supplement family income.

Despite their distortions, the doctrine of separate spheres and the image of the home as a refuge from a harsh world intersected with reality at some points. The rising number of urban families headed by lawyers and merchants (who worked away from home) gave mothers time to spend on child rearing. Above all, even if they

The Country Parson Disturbed at Breakfast
This young couple's decision to wed seems to have been spur-of-the-moment. As young men and women became more independent of parental control, they gave their impulses freer play.

could not afford to live in a Downing-designed house, married women found that they could capitalize on these notions to gain new power within their families. A subtle implication of the doctrine of separate spheres was that women should have control not only over the discipline of children but also over the more fundamental issue of how many children they would bear.

In 1800 the United States had one of the highest birthrates ever recorded. The average American woman bore 7.04 children. It is safe to say that married women had become pregnant as often as possible. In the prevailing farm economy, children carried out essential tasks and, as time passed, took care of their aging parents. Most parents had assumed that the more children, the better. The spread of a commercial economy raised troublesome questions about children's economic value. Unlike a farmer, a merchant or lawyer could not send his children to work at the age of seven or eight. The average woman was bearing only 5.02 children by 1850, and 3.98 by 1900. The birthrate remained high among blacks and many immigrant groups, but it fell drastically among native-born whites, particularly in towns and cities. The birthrate also declined in rural areas, but more sharply in rural villages than on farms, and more sharply in the East, where land was scarce, than in the West, where abundant land created continued incentives for parents to have many children.

For the most part, the decline in the birthrate was accomplished by abstinence from sexual intercourse, by coitus interruptus (withdrawal of the penis before ejaculation), or by abortion. By the 1840s abortionists advertised remedies for "female irregularities," a common euphemism for unwanted pregnancies. There were no foolproof birth-control devices, and as much misinformation as information circulated about techniques of birth control. Nonetheless, interest in birth-control devices was intensifying. In 1832 Charles Knowlton, a Massachusetts physician, described the procedure for vaginal douching in his book *Fruits of Philosophy*. Although Knowlton was frequently prosecuted and once jailed for obscenity, efforts to suppress his ideas publicized them even more. By 1865 popular tracts had familiarized Americans with a wide range of birth-control methods, including the condom and the diaphragm. The decision to limit family size was usually reached jointly by wives and husbands. Economic and ideological considerations blended together. Husbands could note that the economic value of children was declining; wives, that having fewer children would give them more time to nurture each one and thereby carry out domestic duties.

Supporters of the ideal of separate spheres did not advocate full legal equality for women. Indeed, the idea of separate spheres was an explicit alternative to legal equality. But the concept did enhance women's power within marriage by justifying their demands for influence over such vital issues as child rearing and the frequency of pregnancies. In addition, it allowed some women a measure of independence from the home. For example, it sanctioned Catharine Beecher's travels to lecture women on better ways to raise children and manage their households.

Horizontal Allegiances and the Rise of Voluntary Associations

As some forms of authority, such as the authority of parents over their children and husbands over their wives, were weakening, Americans devised new ways for individuals to extend their influence over others. The pre-Civil War period witnessed the widespread substitution of horizontal allegiances for vertical allegiances. The traditional patriarchal family was an example of a vertical allegiance: the wife and children looked up to the father for leadership. Another example occurred in the small eighteenth-century workshop, where apprentices and journeymen took direction from the master craftsman and even lived in the craftsman's house, subject to his authority. In both cases, authority flowed from the top down. In a vertical allegiance, people in a subordinate position identify their best interests with the interests of their superiors rather than with those of other individuals in the same subordinate position.

Although vertical relationships did not disappear, they became less important in people's lives. Increasingly, relationships were more likely to be horizontal, linking those in a similar position. For example, in large textile mills during the 1830s, many operatives discovered that they had more in common with one another than with their managers and overseers. Similarly, married women formed maternal associations to exchange advice about child rearing. Young men formed debating societies to sharpen their wits and to bring themselves to the attention of influential older men. None of these associations was intended to overthrow traditional authority. Many of them, in fact, professed to strengthen the family or community. But all represented the substitution of new allegiances for old ones.

Maternal and debating societies exemplified the American zeal for voluntary associations—associations that arose apart from government and sought to accom-

plish some goal of value to their members. Tocqueville observed that the government stood at the head of every enterprise in France, but that in America "you will be sure to find an association."

Voluntary associations encouraged sociability. As transients and newcomers flocked into towns and cities, they tended to join others with similar characteristics, experiences, or interests. Gender was the basis of many voluntary societies. Of twenty-six religious and charitable associations in Utica, New York, in 1832, for instance, one-third were exclusively for women. Race was still another basis for voluntary associations. Although their names did not indicate it, Boston's Thompson Literary and Debating Society and its Philomathean Adelphic Union for the Promotion of Literature and Science and New York City's Phoenix Society were all organizations for free blacks.

The other key benefit of voluntary associations was that they were vehicles for members to assert their influence. At a time when state legislatures had little interest in regulating the sale of alcoholic beverages, men and women joined in temperance societies to promote voluntary abstinence. To combat prostitution, women formed moral-reform societies, which sought to shame men into chastity by publishing the names of brothel patrons in newspapers. Aiming to suppress an ancient vice, moral-reform societies also tended to enhance women's power over men. Moral reformers attributed the prevalence of prostitution to the lustfulness of men who, unable to control their passions, exploited poor and vulnerable girls. Just as strikes in Lowell in the 1830s were a form of collective action by working women, moral-reform societies represented collective action by middle-class women to increase their influence in society. Here, as elsewhere, the tendency of the times was to forge new forms of horizontal allegiance between like-minded Americans.

CONCLUSION

The flow of population into the area between the Appalachians and the Mississippi River after 1815 set in motion a series of changes that would transform the lives of Americans. European demand for American cotton and other agricultural products, federal policies that eased the sale of public lands and encouraged the removal of Indians from the path of white settlement, and the availability of loose-lending banks and paper money all contributed to the postwar boom. The collapse of the boom in 1819 reminded farmers of how

dependent they had become on distant markets and prompted improvements in transportation during the 1820s and 1830s. The introduction of steamboats, the building of canals, and the gradual spread of railroads—the transportation revolution—encouraged a turn to commercial occupations and the growth of towns and cities. Now able to reach distant consumers, merchants plunged capital into manufacturing enterprises. Ranging from the great textile mills of Lowell and Waltham to rural cottages that performed outwork to urban sweatshops, early industrialization laid the foundations for America's emergence a half-century later as a major industrial power.

CHRONOLOGY, 1815-1840

1790 Samuel Slater opens his first Rhode Island mill for the production of cotton yarn.
1793 Eli Whitney invents the cotton gin.
1807 Robert R. Livingston and Robert Fulton introduce the steamboat *Clermont* on the Hudson River.
1811 Construction of the National Road begins at Cumberland, Maryland.
1813 Incorporation of the Boston Manufacturing Company.
1816 Second Bank of the United States chartered.
1817-1825 Construction of the Erie Canal started. Mississippi enters the Union.
1819 Economic panic, ushering in four-year depression. Alabama enters the Union.
1820-1850 Growth of female moral–reform societies.
1820s Expansion of New England textile mills.
1824 *Gibbons* v. *Ogden*.
1828 Baltimore and Ohio Railroad chartered.
1830 Indian Removal Act passed by Congress.
1831 *Cherokee Nation* v. *Georgia*. Alexis de Tocqueville begins visit to the United States to study American penitentiaries.
1832 *Worcester* v. *Georgia*.
1834 First strike at the Lowell mills.
1835 Treaty of New Echota.
1837 Economic panic begins a depression that lasts until 1843.
1838 The Trail of Tears.
1840 System of production by interchangeable parts perfected.

The changes associated with the market economy and early industrialization carved new avenues to prosperity for some, and to penury for others. They challenged traditional hierarchies and created new forms of social alignment based on voluntary associations. By joining voluntary associations based on shared interests or opinions, footloose Americans forged new identities that paralleled and often supplanted older allegiances to their parents or places of birth.

FOR FURTHER REFERENCE

READINGS

Edward J. Balleisen, *Navigating Failure: Bankruptcy and Commercial Society in Antebellum America* (2001). An important study of the risks spawned by the market economy.

Rowland Berthoff, *An Unsettled People: Social Order and Disorder in American History* (1971). A stimulating interpretation of American social history.

Carl Degler, *At Odds: Women and the Family in America from the Revolution to the Present* (1980). A fine overview of the economic and social experiences of American women.

John Lauritz Larson, *Internal Improvement: National Public Works and the Promise of Popular Government in the Early United States* (2001). An overview of road and canal projects that shows how local and regional rivalries frustrated plans for a nationally integrated system of improvements.

Harry N. Scheiber, *The Ohio Canal Era: A Case Study of Government and the Economy, 1820–1861* (1969). An analysis that speaks volumes about economic growth in the early Republic.

Charles Sellers, *The Market Revolution: Jacksonian America, 1815–1846* (1991). A major, and controversial, reinterpretation of the period.

Alan Taylor, *William Cooper's Town* (1995). A compelling portrait of the New York frontier in the late eighteenth and early nineteenth centuries.

Peter Way, *Common Labour* (1993). Insightful book on the lives of canal workers.

Sean Wilentz, *Chants Democratic: New York City and the Rise of the American Working Class, 1788–1850* (1983). A stimulating synthesis of economic, social, and political history.

WEBSITES

Brotherly Love: The Black Church
http://www.pbs.org/wgbh/aia/part3/3narr3.html
A site that describes the early efforts of such African Americans as Richard Allen and Absalom Jones to form independent black churches. A related site at [http://www.pbs.org/wgbh/aia/part3/3p97.htm] provides extensive information on Richard Allen, the first bishop of the A.M.E. church.

Samuel Slater
http://www.geocities.com/~woon_heritage/slaterhist.htm
This site provides a biography of Samuel Slater, illustrated descriptions of the early Rhode Island textile mill sites, and tours of the Slater Mill Historic Site and the Slatersville Mill Village.

Women in America, 1820–1842
http://xroads.virginia.edu/~HYPER/DETOC/Fem/home.htm
This site portrays the lives of American women through the eyes of eighteen Irish, German, Scottish, English, and French travelers. Topics include courtship and marriage, employment, religion, health, wilderness, education, race, and fashion.

CHAPTER 10

Democratic Politics, Religious Revival, and Reform,

1824–1840

In 1824 the Marquis de Lafayette, former major general in the Continental Army and a Revolutionary War hero, accepted the invitation of President James Monroe and Congress to revisit the United States. For thirteen months as "the Nation's Guest," Lafayette traveled to every state, from Maine to Louisiana, and received a welcome that fluctuated between warm and tumultuous. There seemed no limits to what Americans would do to show their admiration for this "greatest man in the world." "There were," one contemporary wrote, "La Fayette boots—La Fayette hats—La Fayette wine—and La Fayette everything." In New York City some fervid patriots tried to unhitch the horses from Lafayette's carriage and pull it up Broadway themselves.

Lafayette had contributed mightily to the Revolution's success. Americans venerated him as a living embodiment of the entire Revolutionary generation that was fast passing from the scene. The majority of Americans alive in 1824 had been born since George Washington's death in 1799. John Adams and Thomas Jefferson were along in years, and both would die on July 4, 1826, fifty years to the day after the signing of the Declaration of Independence. Seizing on Washington's remark that he loved Lafayette "as my own son," Americans toasted the Frenchman as a cherished member of the family of Revolutionary heroes. In Charleston the toast ran: "WASHINGTON,

CHAPTER OUTLINE

The Rise of Democratic Politics, 1824–1832

The Bank Controversy and the Second Party System, 1833–1840

The Rise of Popular Religion

The Age of Reform

◀ **First State Election in Michigan**
Michigan's early elections were rowdy. Here, Detroit voters cast ballots in Michigan's first state gubernatorial election in 1837. Democrat candidate Stevens Mason, shown on the left soliciting a vote and backed by the "No Monopoly" banner on the right (partial view), defeated the Whig candidate. Mason owed his victory to the Irish-born workers, shown around him, who had come to Michigan to labor on public projects. The sober citizens shown on the right argue their preferences with each other, keeping their distance from the Irish.

285

Lafayette Pitcher
The craze for Lafayette artifacts included tableware.

our Common Father—you his favorite son"; in New Jersey, "LA FAYETTE, a living monument of greatness, virtue, and faithfulness still exists—a second Washington is now among us."

The festive rituals surrounding Lafayette's visit symbolized Americans' conviction that they had remained true to their heritage of republican liberty. The embers of conflict between Federalists and Republicans that once had seemed to threaten the Republic's stability had cooled; the Era of Good Feelings still reigned over American politics in 1824. Yet even as Americans were turning Lafayette's visit into an affirmation of their ties to the Founders, those ties were fraying in the face of new challenges. Westward migration, growing commercial activity, and increasing sectional conflict over slavery shaped politics between 1824 and 1840. The impact of economic and social change shattered old assumptions and contributed to a vigorous new brand of politics.

This transformation led to the birth of a second American party system in which two new parties, the Democrats and the Whigs, replaced the Republicans and the Federalists. More was at work than a change of names. The new parties took advantage of the transportation revolution to spread their messages to the farthest corners of the nation and to arouse voters in all sections. New party leaders were more effective than their predecessors at organizing grass-roots support, more eager to make government responsive to the popular will, and more likely to enjoy politics and welcome conflict as a way to sustain interest in political issues.

Not all Americans looked to politics as the pathway to their goals. Some, in fact, viewed politics as suited only to scoundrels. A Detroit workingman wrote in 1832 that he "did not vote. I'll [have] none of sin." Troubled by the rough-and-tumble of democratic politics and worried by the increasingly unpredictable commercial economy, many Americans sought solace in religion. A wave of religious revivals swept across the United States during the 1820s and 1830s. Religion itself took on some of the features of democratic politics. The most successful leaders of revivals were clergymen who realized that to spread religious fervor they had to speak the language of the common people, not baffle them with the complexities of theology.

Many deeply religious Americans stepped from revivals to reform movements. These movements pursued various goals, among them the abolition of slavery, the suppression of the liquor trade, improved public education, and equality for women. Since politicians usually tried to avoid these causes, most reformers began with a distrust of politics. Yet reformers gradually discovered that the success of their reforms depended on their ability to influence the political process.

During the 1820s and 1830s, the political and reform agendas of Americans diverged increasingly from those of the Founders. The Founders had feared popular participation in politics, enjoyed their wine and rum, left an ambiguous legacy on slavery, and displayed only occasional interest in women's rights. Yet even as Americans shifted their political and social priorities, they continued to venerate the Founders, who were revered in death even more than in life. Histories of the United States, biographies of Revolutionary patriots, and torchlight parades that bore portraits of Washington and Jefferson alongside those of Andrew Jackson all helped reassure the men and women of the young nation that they were remaining loyal to their republican heritage.

This chapter focuses on five major questions:

■ In what ways had American politics become more democratic by 1840 than at the time of Jefferson's election in 1800?

■ What factors explain Andrew Jackson's popularity? How did Jackson's policies contribute to the rise of the rival Whig party?

■ How did the Panic of 1837 and its aftermath solidify the Democratic and Whig parties?

■ What new assumptions about human nature lay behind the religious and reform movements of the period?

■ To what extent did the reform movements aim at extending equality to all Americans? To what extent and how did they attempt to forge a more orderly society?

THE RISE OF DEMOCRATIC POLITICS, 1824–1832

In 1824 Andrew Jackson and Martin Van Buren, who would guide the Democratic party in the 1830s, and Henry Clay and John Quincy Adams, who would become that decade's leading Whigs, all belonged to the Republican party of Thomas Jefferson. Yet by 1824 the Republican party was coming apart under pressures generated by industrialization in New England, the spread of cotton cultivation in the South, and westward expansion. These forces sparked issues that would become the basis for the new political division between Democrats and Whigs. In general, those Republicans (augmented by a few former Federalists) who retained Jefferson's suspicion of a strong federal government and preference for states' rights became Democrats; those Republicans (along with many former Federalists) who believed that the national government should actively encourage economic development became Whigs.

Regardless of which path a politician chose, all leaders in the 1820s and 1830s had to adapt to the rising democratic idea of politics as a forum for the expression of the will of the common people rather than as an activity that gentlemen conducted for the people. Gentlemen could still be elected to office, but their success now depended less on their education and wealth than on their ability to identify and follow the will of the majority. Americans still looked up to their political leaders, but the leaders could no longer look down on the people.

Democratic Ferment

Political democratization took several forms. One of the most common was the substitution of poll taxes for the traditional requirement that voters own property. None of the new western states required property ownership for voting, and eastern states gradually liberalized their laws. Moreover, written ballots replaced the custom of voting aloud (called viva voce or "stand-up" voting), which had enabled superiors to influence, or intimidate, their inferiors at the polls. Too, appointive office increasingly became elective. The electoral college survived, but the choice of presidential electors by state legislatures gave way to their direct election by the voters. In 1800, rather than voting for Thomas Jefferson or John Adams, most Americans could do no more than vote for the men who would vote for the men who would vote for Jefferson or Adams. By 1824, however, legislatures chose electors in only six states, and by 1832 only in South Carolina.

The fierce tug of war between the Republicans and the Federalists in the 1790s and early 1800s chipped away at the old barriers to the people's expression of their will. First the Republicans and then the Federalists learned to woo voters from Massachusetts to Maryland by staging grand barbecues at which men washed down free clams and oysters with free beer and whiskey. Wherever one party was in a minority, it sought to become the majority party by increasing the electorate. Jefferson's followers showed more interest in registering new voters in New England, where they were weak, than in their southern strongholds. Federalists played the same game; the initiator of suffrage reform in Maryland was an aristocratic Federalist.

Political democratization developed at an uneven pace. In 1820 both the Federalists and Republicans were still organized from the top down. To nominate candidates, for example, both parties relied on the caucus (a conference of party members in the legislature) rather than on popularly elected nominating conventions. Nor was political democracy extended to all. Women continued to be excluded from voting. Free blacks in the North found that the same popular conventions that extended voting rights to nearly all whites effectively disfranchised African Americans.

Yet no one could mistake the tendency of the times: to oppose the people or democracy had become a formula for political suicide. The people, a Federalist moaned, "have become too saucy and are really beginning to fancy themselves equal to their betters." Whatever their convictions, politicians learned to adjust.

The Election of 1824

Sectional tensions brought the Era of Good Feelings to an end in 1824 when five candidates, all Republicans, vied for the presidency. John Quincy Adams emerged as New England's favorite. South Carolina's brilliant John C. Calhoun contended with Georgia's William Crawford, an old-school Jeffersonian, for southern support. Out of the West marched Henry Clay of Kentucky, ambitious, crafty, and confident that his American System of protective tariffs and federally supported internal improvements would endear him to manufacturing interests in the East as well as to the West.

TABLE 10.1   The Election of 1824

Candidates	Parties	Electoral Vote	Popular Vote	Percentage of Popular Vote
JOHN QUINCY ADAMS	Democratic-Republican	84	108,740	30.5
Andrew Jackson	Democratic-Republican	99	153,544	43.1
William H. Crawford	Democratic-Republican	41	46,618	13.1
Henry Clay	Democratic-Republican	37	47,136	13.2

Clay's belief that he was holding a solid block of western states was punctured by the rise of a fifth candidate, Andrew Jackson of Tennessee. At first, none of the other candidates took Jackson seriously. But he was popular on the frontier and in the South and stunned his rivals by gaining the support of opponents of the American System from Pennsylvania and other northern states.

Although the Republican congressional caucus chose Crawford as the party's official candidate early in 1824, the caucus could no longer unify the party. Three-fourths of the Republicans in Congress had refused to attend the caucus. Crawford's already diminished prospects evaporated when he suffered a paralyzing stroke. Impressed by Jackson's support, Calhoun withdrew from the race and ran unopposed for the vice presidency.

In the election, Jackson won more popular and electoral votes than any other candidate (Adams, Crawford, and Clay) but failed to gain the majority required by the Constitution (see Table 10.1). Thus the election was thrown into the House of Representatives, whose members had to choose from the three top candidates—Jackson, Adams, and Crawford. Hoping to forge an alliance between the West and Northeast in a future bid for the presidency, Clay gave his support to Adams. Clay's action secured the presidency for Adams, but when Adams promptly appointed Clay his secretary of state, Jackson's supporters raged that a "corrupt bargain" had cheated Jackson of the presidency. Although there is no evidence that Adams had traded Clay's support for an explicit agreement to appoint Clay his secretary of state (an office from which Jefferson, Madison, Monroe, and Adams himself had risen to the presidency), the allegation of a corrupt bargain was widely believed. It formed a cloud that hung over Adams's presidency.

John Quincy Adams as President

Failing to understand the changing political climate, Adams made several other miscalculations that would cloak his presidency in controversy. For example, in 1825 he proposed a program of federal aid for internal improvements. Strict Jeffersonians had always opposed such aid as unconstitutional, but now they were joined by pragmatists like New York's senator Martin Van Buren. Aware that New York had just completed construction of the Erie Canal with its own funds, Van Buren opposed federal aid to improvements on the grounds that it would enable other states to build rival canals. Adams next proposed sending American delegates to a conference of newly independent Latin American nations, a proposal that infuriated southerners because it would imply U.S. recognition of Haiti, the black republic created by slave revolutionaries.

Instead of seeking new bases of support, Adams clung to the increasingly obsolete notion of the president as custodian of the public good, aloof from partisan politics. He alienated his supporters by appointing his opponents to high office and wrote loftily, "I have no wish to fortify myself by the support of any party whatever." Idealistic as his view was, it guaranteed him a single-term presidency.

The Rise of Andrew Jackson

As Adams's popularity declined, Andrew Jackson's rose. Although Jackson's victory over the British in the Battle of New Orleans had made him a hero, veteran politicians distrusted his notoriously hot temper and his penchant for duels. (Jackson had once challenged an opposing lawyer to a duel for ridiculing his legal arguments in a court case.) But as the only presidential candidate in the election of 1824 with no connection to the Monroe administration, Jackson benefited from what Calhoun recognized as "a vague but widespread discontent" in the wake of the Panic of 1819 that left people with "a general mass of disaffection to the Government" and "looking out anywhere for a leader." To many Americans, Jackson, who as a boy had fought in the Revolution, seemed like a living link to a more virtuous past.

Jackson's supporters swiftly established committees throughout the country. Two years before the election of 1828, towns and villages across the United States buzzed

with furious but unfocused political activity. With the exception of the few remaining Federalists, almost everyone called himself a Republican. Some Republicans were "Adams men," others were "Jackson men," and still others styled themselves "friends of Clay." Amid all the confusion, few realized that a new political system was being born. The man most alert to the signs of the times was Martin Van Buren, who was to become vice president during Jackson's second term and president upon Jackson's retirement.

Van Buren exemplified a new breed of politician. A tavernkeeper's son, he had started his political career in county politics and worked his way up to New York's governorship. In Albany he built a powerful political machine, the Albany Regency, composed mainly of men like himself from the lower and middling ranks. His archrival in New York politics, DeWitt Clinton, was all that Van Buren was not—tall, handsome, and aristocratic. But Van Buren had a geniality that made ordinary people feel comfortable and an uncanny ability to sense the direction in which the political winds were about to blow. Van Buren loved politics, which he viewed as a wonderful game. He was one of the first prominent American politicians to make personal friends from among his political enemies.

The election of 1824 convinced Van Buren of the need for renewed two-party competition. Without the discipline imposed by a strong opposition party, the Republicans had splintered into sectional pieces. No candidate had secured an electoral majority, and the House of Representatives had decided the outcome amid charges of intrigue and corruption. It would be better, Van Buren concluded, to let all the shades of opinion in the nation be reduced to two. Then the parties would clash, and a clear popular winner would emerge. Jackson's strong showing in the election persuaded Van Buren that "Old Hickory" could lead a new political party. In the election of 1828, this party, which gradually became known as the Democratic party, put up Jackson for president and Calhoun for vice president. Its opponents, calling themselves the National Republicans, rallied behind Adams and his running mate, treasury secretary Richard Rush. Slowly but surely, the second American party system was taking shape.

The Election of 1828

The 1828 campaign was a vicious, mudslinging affair. The National Republicans attacked Jackson as a drunken gambler, an adulterer, and a murderer. He was directly responsible for several men's deaths in duels and military executions; and in 1791 he had married Rachel

"Cinque" by Nathaniel Joselyn
In 1839, fifty-three Africans who had been illegally transported to Cuba as slaves rose up and seized control of the Cuban schooner Amistad. After an American revenue schooner intercepted the Amistad off Long Island, the slaves were imprisoned in New Haven, Connecticut, while the courts considered the claims of their Cuban owners to restitution. After an impassioned plea for their freedom by former president John Quincy Adams, the U.S. Supreme Court ruled in favor of their leader, Joseph Cinque, and his men and ordered them returned to Africa as free people.

Robards, erroneously believing that her divorce from her first husband had become final. "Ought a convicted adulteress and her paramour husband," the Adams men taunted, "be placed in the highest office of this free and Christian land?" Jackson's supporters replied in kind. They accused Adams of wearing silk underwear, being rich, being in debt, and having gained favor with the tsar of Russia by trying to provide him with a beautiful American prostitute.

Although both sides engaged in tossing barbs, Jackson's men had better aim. Charges by Adams's supporters that Jackson was an illiterate backwoodsman added to Jackson's popular appeal by making him seem like an ordinary citizen. Jackson's supporters portrayed the clash as one between "the democracy of the country, on the one hand, and a lordly purse-proud aristocracy

Andrew Jackson by Ralph Earl
Jackson during the Nullification Crisis, looking serene in the uniform of a major-general and determined to face down the greatest challenge to his presidency.

MAP 10.1
The Election of 1828

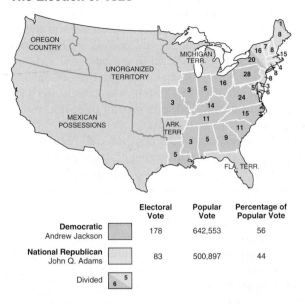

		Electoral Vote	Popular Vote	Percentage of Popular Vote
Democratic Andrew Jackson		178	642,553	56
National Republican John Q. Adams		83	500,897	44
Divided	5 6			

on the other." Jackson, they said, was the common man incarnate, his mind unclouded by learning, his morals simple and true, his will fierce and resolute. In contrast, Jackson's men represented Adams as an aristocrat, a dry scholar whose learning obscured the truth, a man who could write but not fight. Much of this, of course, was wild exaggeration. Jackson was a wealthy planter, not a simple frontiersman. But it was what people wanted to hear. Jackson was presented as the common man's image of his better self as uncorrupt, natural, and plain.

The election swept Jackson into office with more than twice the electoral vote of Adams (see Map 10.1). Yet the popular vote, much closer, made it clear that the people were not simply responding to the personalities or images of the candidates (though these factors dominated the campaign). The vote also reflected the strongly sectional bases of the new parties. The popular vote was close only in the middle states and the Northwest. Adams gained double Jackson's vote in New England; Jackson received double Adams's vote in the South and nearly triple Adams's vote in the Southwest.

Jackson in Office

Jackson rode to the presidency on a wave of opposition to corruption and privilege. As president, his first policy

was to support "rotation in office"—the removal of officeholders of the rival party, which critics called the "spoils system." Jackson did not invent this policy, but his conviction that the federal civil service was riddled with corruption led him to apply it more harshly than his predecessors by firing nearly half of the higher civil servants. So many Washington homes were suddenly put up for sale by ousted officeholders that the real estate market slumped.

Jackson defended rotation on new, democratically flavored grounds: the duties of most officeholders were so simple that as many plain people as possible should be given a chance to work for the government. Jackson never quite grasped the extent to which this elevated principle opened the gates to partisan appointments. Jackson himself was inclined to appoint his loyal friends to office, but the future belonged to Martin Van Buren's view that federal jobs should become rewards for loyalty to the victorious party.

At least to its victims, Jackson's application of rotation seemed arbitrary because he refused to offer any reasons to justify individual removals. His stand on internal improvements and tariffs sparked even more intense controversy. Although not opposed to all federal aid for internal improvements, Jackson was sure that public officials used such aid to woo supporters by handing out favors to special interests. To end this lavish and corrupt giveaway, he flatly rejected federal support for roads within states. Accordingly, in 1830 he vetoed a

bill providing federal money for a road in Kentucky between Maysville and Lexington for its "purely local character."

Jackson's strongest support lay in the South. The Indian Removal Act of 1830 (see Chapter 9) enhanced his popularity there. The tariff issue, however, would test the South's loyalty to Jackson. In 1828, while Adams was still president, some of Jackson's supporters in Congress had contributed to the passage of a high protective tariff that was as favorable to western agriculture and New England manufacturing as it was unfavorable to southerners, who had few industries to protect and who now would have to pay more for manufactured goods. Taking for granted the South's support for Jackson in the coming election, Jackson's supporters had calculated that southerners would blame the Adams administration for this "Tariff of Abominations." In reality, Jackson, not Adams, bore the South's fury over the tariff.

Nullification

The tariff of 1828 laid the basis for a rift between Jackson and his vice president, John C. Calhoun, that was to shake the foundations of the Republic. Early in his career, Calhoun had been an ardent nationalist. He had entered Congress in 1811 as a "war hawk," supported the protectionist tariff of 1816, and dismissed strict construction of the Constitution as refined philosophical nonsense. During the late 1820s, however, Calhoun the nationalist gradually became Calhoun the states' rights sectionalist. The reasons for his shift were complex. He had supported the tariff of 1816 as a measure conducive to national defense in the wake of the War of 1812. By encouraging fledgling industries, he had reasoned, the tariff would free the United States from dependence on Britain and provide revenue for military preparedness. By 1826, however, few Americans perceived national defense as a priority. Furthermore, the infant industries of 1816 had grown into troublesome adolescents that demanded higher and higher tariffs.

Calhoun also burned with ambition to be president. Jackson had stated that he would only serve one term, and Calhoun assumed that he would succeed Jackson. To do so, however, he had to maintain the support of the South, which was increasingly taking an antitariff stance. As the center of cotton production had shifted to Alabama and Mississippi in the Southwest, Calhoun's home state, South Carolina, had suffered an economic decline throughout the 1820s that its voters blamed on high tariffs. Tariffs not only drove up the price of manufactured goods but also threatened to reduce the sale of

***John C. Calhoun,* by Charles Bird King, c. 1825**
Jackson, defeated in the presidential election of 1824, won handily four years later. The magnetic Calhoun, Jackson's vice president, broke with Jackson over nullification and the Peggy Eaton affair and resigned the vice presidency in 1832.

British textile products in the United States. Such a reduction might eventually lower the British demand for southern cotton and cut cotton prices. The more New England industrialized, the clearer it became that tariff laws were pieces of sectional legislation. New Englanders like Massachusetts's eloquent Daniel Webster swung toward protectionism; southerners responded with militant hostility.

Calhoun followed the Virginia and Kentucky resolutions of 1798–1799 in viewing the Union as a compact by which the states had conferred limited and specified powers on the federal government. Although the Constitution did empower Congress to levy tariffs, Calhoun insisted that only tariffs that raised revenue for such common purposes as defense were constitutional. Set so high that it deterred foreign exporters from shipping their products to the United States, the tariff of 1828 could raise little revenue, and hence it failed to meet Calhoun's criterion of constitutionality: that federal laws benefit everyone equally. In 1828 Calhoun anonymously

wrote the widely circulated *South Carolina Exposition and Protest*, in which he spelled out his argument that the tariff of 1828 was unconstitutional and that aggrieved states therefore had the right to nullify, or override, the law within their borders.

Vehement opposition to tariffs in the South, and especially in South Carolina, rested on more than economic considerations, however. Southerners feared that a federal government that passed tariff laws favoring one section over another might also pass laws meddling with slavery. Because Jackson himself was a slaveholder, the fear of federal interference with slavery was perhaps far-fetched. But South Carolinians, long apprehensive of assaults on their crucial institution of slavery, had many reasons for concern. South Carolina was one of only two states in which blacks comprised a majority of the population in 1830. Moreover, in 1831 a bloody slave revolt led by Nat Turner boiled up in Virginia. That same year in Massachusetts, William Lloyd Garrison established *The Liberator*, an abolitionist newspaper. These developments were enough to convince many troubled South Carolinians that a line had to be drawn against tariffs and possible future interference with slavery.

Like Calhoun, Jackson was strong-willed and proud. Unlike Calhoun, he was already president and the leader of a national party that included supporters in protariff states like Pennsylvania (which had gone for Jackson in the election of 1828). Thus to retain key northern support while soothing the South, Jackson devised two policies.

The first was to distribute surplus federal revenue to the states. Tariff schedules kept some goods out of the United States but let many others in for a price. The price, in the form of duties on imports, became federal revenue. In the years before federal income taxes, tariffs were a major source of federal revenue. Jackson hoped that this revenue, fairly distributed among the states, would remove the taint of sectional injustice from the tariff and force the federal government to restrict its own expenditures. All of this was good Jeffersonianism. Second, Jackson hoped to ease tariffs down from the sky-high level of 1828.

Calhoun disliked the idea of distributing federal revenue to the states because he believed that such a policy could become an excuse to maintain tariffs forever. But he was loath to break openly with Jackson. Between 1828 and 1831, Calhoun muffled his protest, hoping that Jackson would lower the tariff and that he, Calhoun, would retain both Jackson's favor and his chances for the presidency. Congress did pass new, slightly reduced tar-

iff rates in 1832, but these did not come close to satisfying South Carolinians.

Before passage of the tariff of 1832, however, two personal issues had ruptured relations between Calhoun and Jackson. In 1829 Jackson's secretary of war, John H. Eaton, married the widowed daughter of a Washington tavernkeeper. By her own account, Peggy O'Neale Timberlake was "frivolous, wayward, [and] passionate." While still married to a naval officer away on duty, Peggy had acquired the reputation of flirting with Eaton, who boarded at her father's tavern. After her husband's death and her marriage to Eaton, she and Eaton were snubbed socially by Calhoun's wife and by his friends in the cabinet. Jackson, who never forgot how his own wife had been wounded by slander during the campaign of 1828, not only befriended the Eatons but concluded that Calhoun had initiated the snubbing to discredit him and to advance Calhoun's own presidential aspirations.

To make matters worse, in 1830 Jackson received convincing documentation of his suspicion that in 1818 Calhoun, as secretary of war under President Monroe, had urged that Jackson be punished for his unauthorized raid into Spanish Florida. The revelation that Calhoun had tried to stab him in the back in 1818, combined with the spurning of the Eatons, convinced Jackson that he had to "destroy [Calhoun] regardless of what injury it might do me or my administration." A symbolic confrontation occurred between Jackson and Calhoun at a Jefferson Day dinner in April 1830. Jackson proposed the toast, "Our Union: It must be preserved." Calhoun responded: "The Union next to Liberty the most dear. May we always remember that it can only be preserved by distributing equally the benefits and burdens of the Union."

The stage was now set for a direct clash between the president and his vice president over nullification. In 1831 Calhoun acknowledged his authorship of the *South Carolina Exposition and Protest*. In November 1832 a South Carolina convention nullified the tariffs of 1828 and 1832 and forbade the collection of customs duties within the state. Jackson reacted quickly. He despised nullification, calling it an "abominable doctrine" that would reduce the government to anarchy, and he berated the South Carolina nullifiers as "unprincipled men who would rather rule in hell, than be subordinate in heaven." Jackson even began to send arms to loyal Unionists in South Carolina. In December 1832 he issued a proclamation that, while promising South Carolinians further tariff reductions, lambasted nullification as itself unconstitutional. The Constitution, he

emphasized, had established "a single nation," not a league of states.

The crisis eased in March 1833 when Jackson signed into law two measures—"the olive branch and the sword," in one historian's words. The olive branch was the tariff of 1833 (also called the Compromise Tariff), which provided for a gradual but significant lowering of duties between 1833 and 1842. The sword was the Force Bill, authorizing the president to use arms to collect customs duties in South Carolina. Although South Carolina did not abandon nullification in principle—in fact, it nullified the Force Bill—it construed the Compromise Tariff as a concession and rescinded its nullification of the tariffs of 1828 and 1832.

Like most of the accommodations by which the Union lurched from one sectional crisis to the next before the Civil War, the Compromise of 1833 grew out of a mixture of partisanship and statesmanship. The moving spirit behind the Compromise Tariff was Kentucky's senator Henry Clay, who had long favored high tariffs. A combination of motives brought Clay and the nullifiers together in favor of tariff reduction. Clay feared that without concessions to South Carolina on tariffs, the Force Bill would produce civil war. Furthermore, he was apprehensive that without compromise, the principle of protective tariffs would disappear under the wave of Jackson's immense popularity. In short, Clay would rather take responsibility for lowering tariffs than allow the initiative on tariff questions to pass to the Jacksonians.

For their part, the nullifiers hated Jackson and defiantly toasted "Andrew Jackson: On the soil of South Carolina he received an humble birthplace. May he not find in it a traitor's grave!" Although recognizing that South Carolina had failed to gain support for nullification from other southern states and that they would have to bow to pressure, the nullifiers preferred that Clay, not Jackson, be the hero of the hour. So they supported Clay's Compromise Tariff. Everywhere Americans now hailed Clay as the Great Compromiser. Even Martin Van Buren frankly stated that Clay had "saved the country."

The Bank Veto and the Election of 1832

Jackson recognized that the gap between the rich and the poor was widening during the 1820s and 1830s (see Chapter 9). He did not object to the rich gaining wealth by hard work. But he believed that the wealthy often grew even richer by securing favors, "privileges," from corrupt legislatures. In addition, his disastrous financial

speculations early in his career led him to suspect all banks, paper money, and monopolies. On each count, the Bank of the United States was guilty.

The Bank of the United States had received a twenty-year charter from Congress in 1816. As a creditor of state banks, the Bank of the United States restrained their printing and lending of money by its ability to demand the redemption of state bank notes in specie (gold or silver coinage). The bank's power enabled it to check the excesses of state banks, but also provoked hostility. In fact, it was widely blamed for precipitating the Panic of 1819. Further, at a time of mounting attacks on privilege, the bank was undeniably privileged. As the official depository for federal revenue, its capacity to lend money vastly exceeded that of any state bank. Its capital of $35 million amounted to more than double the annual expenditures of the federal government. Yet this institution, more powerful than any bank today, was only remotely controlled by the government. Its stockholders were private citizens—a "few monied capitalists" in Jackson's words. Although chartered by Congress, the bank was located in Philadelphia, not Washington, and its directors enjoyed considerable independence. Its president, the aristocratic Nicholas Biddle, viewed himself as a public servant duty-bound to keep the bank above politics.

Urged on by Henry Clay, who hoped to ride a pro-bank bandwagon into the White House in 1832, Biddle secured congressional passage of a bill to recharter the bank. In vetoing the recharter bill, Jackson denounced the bank as a private and privileged monopoly that drained the West of specie, was immune to taxation by the states, and made "the rich richer and the potent more powerful." Failing to persuade Congress to override Jackson's veto, Clay now pinned his hopes on gaining the presidency himself.

By 1832 Jackson had made his views on major issues clear. He was simultaneously a staunch defender of states' rights and a staunch Unionist. Although he cherished the Union, he believed that the states were far too diverse to accept strong direction from Washington. The safest course was to allow the states considerable freedom so that they would remain contentedly within the Union and reject dangerous doctrines like nullification.

Throwing aside earlier promises to retire, Jackson again ran for the presidency in 1832, with Martin Van Buren as his running mate. Henry Clay ran on the National Republican ticket, touting his American System of protective tariffs, national banking, and federal support for internal improvements. Jackson's overwhelming personal popularity swamped Clay. Secure in office for

294 CHAPTER 10 Democratic Politics, Religious Revival, and Reform, 1824–1840

another four years, Jackson was ready to finish dismantling the Bank of the United States.

THE BANK CONTROVERSY AND THE SECOND PARTY SYSTEM, 1833–1840

Jackson's veto of the recharter of the Bank of the United States ignited a searing controversy. Following the veto, Jackson took steps to destroy the Bank of the United States so that it could never be revived. His banking policies spurred the rise of the opposition Whig party, mightily stimulated popular interest in politics, and contributed to the severe economic downturn, known as the Panic of 1837, that greeted his successor, Martin Van Buren. By 1840, the Whig and Democratic parties divided crisply over a fundamental issue: banks or no banks.

In part, tempers flared over banking because the U.S. government did not issue paper currency of its own; there were no "official" dollar bills as we know them today. Paper currency consisted of notes (promises to redeem in specie) dispensed by private banks. These IOUs fueled economic development by making it easier for businesses and farmers to acquire loans to build factories or buy land. But if a note depreciated after its issuance because of public doubts about a bank's solvency, wage earners who had been paid in paper rather than specie would suffer. Further, paper money encouraged a speculative economy, one that raised profits and risks. For example, paper money encouraged farmers to buy land on credit in the expectation that its price would rise, but a sudden drop in agricultural prices would leave them mired in debt. Would the United States embrace swift economic development at the price of allowing some to get rich quickly off investments while others languished? Or would it opt for more modest growth within traditional channels that were based on "honest" manual work and frugality? Between 1833 and 1840 these questions would dominate American politics.

The War on the Bank

Jackson could have allowed the bank to die a natural death when its charter ran out in 1836. But Jackson and several of his rabid followers viewed the bank as a kind of dragon that would grow new limbs as soon as old ones were cut off. When Biddle, anticipating further moves against the bank by Jackson, began to call in the bank's loans and contract credit during the winter of 1832–1833, Jacksonians saw their darkest fears confirmed. The bank, Jackson assured Van Buren, "is trying to kill me, but I will kill it." Accordingly, Jackson embarked on a controversial policy of removing federal deposits from the Bank of the United States and placing them in state banks.

GENERAL JACKSON SLAYING THE MANY HEADED MONSTER.

Jackson Versus the Bank
Andrew Jackson, aided by Martin Van Buren (center), attacks the Bank of the United States, which, like the many-headed serpent Hydra of Greek mythology, keeps sprouting new heads. The largest head belongs to Nicholas Biddle, the bank's president.

The policy of removing deposits from the national bank raised a new and even thornier issue. State banks that became the depositories for federal revenue could use that revenue as the basis for issuing more paper money and for extending more loans. In short, the removal policy enabled state banks to increase their lending capacity. But Jackson hated both paper money and a speculative economy in which capitalists routinely took out large loans. The policy of removal seemed a formula for producing exactly the kind of economy that Jackson wanted to abolish.

Jackson recognized the danger and hoped to sharply limit the number of state banks that would become depositories for federal revenue. But as state banks increasingly clamored for the revenue, the number of state-bank depositories soon multiplied beyond Jackson's expectations. There were twenty-three by the end of 1833. Critics dubbed them "pet banks" because they were usually selected for their loyalty to the Democratic party. During the next few years, fueled by paper money from the pet banks and by an influx of foreign specie to purchase cotton and for investment in canal projects, the economy experienced a heady expansion. Jackson could not stem the tide. In 1836, pressured by Congress, he reluctantly signed into law the Deposit Act, which both increased the number of deposit banks and loosened federal control of them.

Jackson's policy of removing deposits deepened a split within his own Democratic party between advocates of soft money (paper) and those of hard money (specie). Both sides agreed that the Bank of the United States was evil, but for different reasons. Soft-money Democrats resented the bank's role in periodically contracting credit and restricting the lending activities of state banks; their hard-money counterparts disliked the bank because it sanctioned an economy based on paper money. Prior to the Panic of 1837, the soft-money position was more popular among Democrats outside Jackson's inner circle of advisers than within that circle. For example, western Democrats had long viewed the Cincinnati branch of the Bank of the United States as inadequate to supply their need for credit and favored an expansion of banking activity.

Aside from Jackson and a few other figures within the administration, the most articulate support for hard money came from a faction of the Democratic party in New York called the Locofocos. The Locofocos grew out of various "workingmen's" parties that had sprouted during the late 1820s in northern cities and that called for free public education, the abolition of imprisonment for debt, and a ten-hour workday. Most of these parties

had collapsed within a few years, but in New York the "workies" had gradually been absorbed by the Democratic party. Once in the party, they were hard to keep in line. A mixture of intellectuals and small artisans and journeymen threatened by economic change, they worried about inflation, preferred to be paid in specie, and distrusted banks and paper money. In 1835 a faction of workingmen had broken away from Tammany Hall, the main Democratic party organization in New York City, and held a dissident meeting in a hall whose candles were illuminated by a newfangled invention, the "loco foco," or match. Thereafter, these radical workingmen were known as Locofocos.

The Rise of Whig Opposition

During Jackson's second term, the opposition National Republican party gave way to the new Whig party, which developed a broader base in both the South and the North than had the National Republicans. Jackson's magnetic personality had swept him to victory in 1828 and 1832. But as Jackson's vague Jeffersonianism was replaced by suspicion of federal aid for internal improvements and protective tariffs and by hard-and-fast positions against the Bank of the United States and nullification, more of those alienated by Jackson's policies joined the opposition.

Jackson's crushing of nullification, for example, led some of its southern supporters into the Whig party, not because the Whigs favored nullification but because they opposed Jackson. Jackson's war on the Bank of the United States produced the same result. His policy of removing deposits from the bank pleased some southerners but dismayed others who had been satisfied with the bank and who did not share westerners' mania for cheaper and easier credit. Jackson's suspicion of federal aid for internal improvements also alienated some southerners who feared that the South would languish behind the North unless it began to push ahead with improvements. Because so much southern capital was tied up in slavery, pro-improvement southerners looked to the federal government for aid, and when they were met with a cold shoulder, they drifted into the Whig party. None of this added up to an overturning of the Democratic party in the South; the South was still the Democrats' firmest base. But the Whigs were making significant inroads, particularly in southern market towns and among planters who had close ties to southern bankers and merchants.

Meanwhile, social reformers in the North were infusing new vitality into the opposition to Jackson.

These reformers wanted to improve American society by ending slavery and the sale of liquor, bettering public education, and elevating public morality. Most opponents of liquor (temperance reformers) and most public-school reformers gravitated to the Whigs. Whig philosophy was more compatible with their goals than were Democratic ideals. Where Democrats maintained that the government should not impose a uniform standard of conduct on a diverse society, the Whigs' commitment to Clay's American System implied an acceptance of active intervention by the government to change society. Reformers wanted the government to play a positive role by suppressing the liquor trade and by establishing centralized systems of public education. Thus a shared sympathy for active government programs tended to unite Whigs and reformers.

Reformers also indirectly stimulated new support for the Whigs from native-born Protestant workers. The reformers, themselves almost all Protestants, widely distrusted immigrants, especially the Irish, who viewed drinking as a normal recreation and who, as Catholics, suspected (correctly) that the public schools favored by reformers would teach Protestant doctrines. The rise of reform agitation and its frequent association with the Whigs drove the Irish into the arms of the Democrats but, by the same token, gained support for the Whigs from many native-born Protestant workers who were contemptuous of the Irish.

No source of Whig strength, however, was more remarkable than Anti-Masonry, a protest movement against the secrecy and exclusiveness of the Masonic lodges, which had long provided prominent men with fraternal fellowship and exotic rituals. The spark that set off the Anti-Masonic crusade was the abduction and disappearance in 1826 of William Morgan, a stonemason in Genesee County, New York, who had threatened to expose Masonic secrets. Every effort to solve the mystery of Morgan's disappearance ran into a stone wall because local officials were themselves Masons seemingly bent on obstructing the investigation. Throughout the Northeast the public became increasingly aroused against the Masonic order, and rumors spread that Masonry was a powerful conspiracy of the rich to suppress popular liberty, a secret order of men who loathed Christianity, and an exclusive retreat for drunkards.

By 1836 the Whigs had become a national party with widespread appeal. In both the North and South they attracted those with close ties to the market economy—commercial farmers, planters, merchants, and bankers. In the North they also gained support from reformers, evangelical clergymen (especially Presbyterians and Con-

gregationalists), Anti-Masons, and manufacturers. In the South they appealed to some former nullificationists; Calhoun himself briefly became a Whig. Everywhere the Whigs assailed Jackson as an imperious dictator, "King Andrew I"; indeed, they had taken the name "Whigs" to associate their cause with that of the American patriots who had opposed King George III in 1776.

The Election of 1836

When it came to popularity, Jackson was a hard act to follow. In 1836 the Democrats ran Martin Van Buren, whose star had risen as Calhoun's had fallen, for the presidency. Party rhetoric reminded everyone that Van Buren was Jackson's favorite, and then contended that the Democratic party itself, with Van Buren as its mere agent, was the real heir to Jackson, the perfect embodiment of the popular will. Less cohesive than the Democrats, the Whigs could not unite on a single candidate. Rather, four anti–Van Buren candidates emerged in different parts of the country. These included three Whigs—William Henry Harrison of Ohio, Daniel Webster of Massachusetts, and W. P. Mangum of North Carolina—and one Democrat, Hugh Lawson White of Tennessee, who distrusted Van Buren and who would defect to the Whigs after the election.

Democrats accused the Whigs of a plot to so divide the vote that no candidate would receive the required majority of votes in the electoral college. That would throw the election into the House of Representatives, where, as in 1824, deals and bargains would be struck. In reality, the Whigs had no overall strategy, and Van Buren won a clear majority of the electoral votes. But there were signs of trouble ahead for the Democrats. The popular vote was close, notably in the South, where the Democrats had won two-thirds of the votes in 1832 but barely half in 1836.

The Panic of 1837

Jackson left office in a burst of glory and returned to his Nashville home in a triumphal procession. But the public's mood quickly became less festive, for no sooner was Van Buren in office than a severe depression struck.

In the speculative boom of 1835 and 1836 that was born of Jackson's policy of removing federal deposits from the Bank of the United States and placing them in state banks, the total number of banks doubled, the value of bank notes in circulation nearly tripled, and both commodity and land prices soared. Encouraged by easy money and high commodity prices, states made new commitments to build canals. Then in May 1837,

prices began to tumble, and bank after bank suspended specie payments. After a short rally, the economy crashed again in 1839. The Bank of the United States, which had continued to operate as a state bank with a Pennsylvania charter, failed. Nicholas Biddle was charged with fraud and theft. Banks throughout the nation once again suspended specie payments.

The ensuing depression was far more severe and prolonged than the economic downturn of 1819. Those lucky enough to find work saw their wage rates drop by roughly one-third between 1836 and 1842. In despair, many workers turned to the teachings of William Miller, a New England religious enthusiast whose reading of the Bible convinced him that the end of the world was imminent. Dressed in black coats and stovepipe hats, Miller's followers roamed urban sidewalks and rural villages in search of converts. Many Millerites sold their possessions and purchased white robes to ascend into heaven on October 22, 1843, the date on which Millerite leaders calculated the world would end. Ironically, by then the worst of the depression was over; but at its depths in the late 1830s and early 1840s, the economic slump fed the gloom that made poor people receptive to Miller's predictions.

The origins of the depression were both national and international. In July 1836 Jackson had issued a proclamation called the Specie Circular, which provided that only specie was to be accepted in payment for public lands. The Specie Circular was one of Jackson's final affirmations of his belief that paper money encouraged people to embark on speculative, get-rich-quick schemes, sapped "public virtue," and robbed "honest labour of its earnings to make knaves rich, powerful and dangerous." He hoped that the Specie Circular would reverse the damaging effects of the Deposit Act of 1836, which he had signed reluctantly. The Specie Circular took the wind out of the speculative boom by making banks hesitant to issue more of the paper money that was fueling the boom, because western farmers eager to buy public lands would now demand that banks immediately redeem their paper in specie.

Although the Specie Circular chilled bankers' confidence, it was not the sole or even the major reason for the depression. There were international causes as well, most notably the fact that Britain, in an effort to restrain the outflow of British investment, checked the flow of specie from its shores to the United States in 1836.

The Search for Solutions

Called the "sly fox" and the "little magician" for his political craftiness, Van Buren would need these skills to con-

front the depression that was causing misery not only for ordinary citizens but also for the Democratic party. Railing against "Martin Van Ruin," in 1838 the Whigs swept the governorship and most of the legislative seats in Van Buren's own New York.

To seize the initiative, Van Buren called for the creation of an independent Treasury. The idea was simple: instead of depositing its money in banks, which would then use federal funds as the basis for speculative loans, the government would hold its revenues and keep them from the grasp of corporations. When Van Buren finally signed the Independent Treasury Bill into law on July 4, 1840, his supporters hailed it as America's second Declaration of Independence.

The independent Treasury reflected the deep Jacksonian suspicion of an alliance between government and banking. But the Independent Treasury Act failed to address the banking issue on the state level, where newly chartered state banks—of which there were more than nine hundred by 1840—lent money to farmers and businessmen. Blaming the depression on Jackson's Specie Circular rather than on the banks, Whigs continued to encourage the chartering of banks as a way to spur economic development. In contrast, a growing number of Democrats blamed the depression on banks and on paper money and swung toward the hard-money stance long favored by Jackson and his inner circle. In Louisiana and Arkansas, Democrats successfully prohibited banks altogether, and elsewhere they imposed severe restrictions on banks—for example, by banning the issuing of paper money in small denominations. In sum, after 1837 the Democrats became an antibank, hard-money party.

The Election of 1840

Despite the depression, Van Buren gained his party's renomination. Avoiding their mistake of 1836, the Whigs settled on a single candidate, Ohio's William Henry Harrison, and ran former Virginia Senator John Tyler as vice president. Harrison, who was sixty-seven years old and barely eking out a living on a farm, was picked because he had few enemies. Early in the campaign, the Democrats made a fatal mistake by ridiculing Harrison as "Old Granny," a man who desired only to spend his declining years in a log cabin sipping cider. Without knowing it, the Democrats had handed the Whigs the most famous campaign symbol in American history. The Whigs immediately reminded the public that Harrison had been a rugged frontiersman, the hero of the Battle of Tippecanoe, and a defender of all frontier people who lived in log cabins.

Refusing to publish a platform, the Whigs ran a "hurrah" campaign. They used log cabins for headquarters, sang log-cabin songs, gave out log-cabin cider, and called their newspaper *Log Cabin*. For a slogan, they trumpeted "Tippecanoe and Tyler too." When not celebrating log cabins, they attacked Van Buren as a soft aristocrat who lived in "regal splendor." Whereas Harrison was content to drink hard cider from a plain mug, the Whigs observed, Van Buren had turned the White House into a palace fit for an oriental despot and drank fine wines from silver goblets while he watched people go hungry in the streets.

The election results gave Harrison a clear victory (see Map 10.2). Van Buren carried only seven states and even failed to hold his own New York. The depression would have made it difficult, if not impossible, for any Democrat to have triumphed in 1840, but Van Buren had other disabilities besides the economic collapse. Unlike Harrison and Jackson, he had no halo of military glory. Moreover, Van Buren ran a surprisingly sluggish campaign. Prior to 1840 the Whigs had been slower than the Democrats to mobilize voters by new techniques. But in 1840 it was Van Buren who directed his campaign the old-fashioned way by writing encouraging letters to key supporters, whereas Harrison broke with tradition and went around the country (often on railroads) campaigning. Ironically, Van Buren, the master politician, was beaten at his own game.

MAP 10.2
The Election of 1840

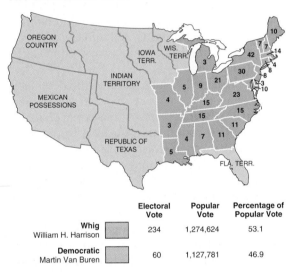

	Electoral Vote	Popular Vote	Percentage of Popular Vote
Whig William H. Harrison	234	1,274,624	53.1
Democratic Martin Van Buren	60	1,127,781	46.9

"The New Era Whig Trap Sprung," New York, 1840.

This Whig cartoon from the election of 1840 shows Democrat Martin Van Buren trapped inside the Whig campaign symbol, a log cabin. Andrew Jackson is desperately tring to pry him out.

THE NEW ERA WHIC TRAP SPRUNG

The Second Party System Matures

In losing the presidency in 1840, Van Buren actually received four hundred thousand more popular votes than any previous presidential candidate. The total number of votes cast in presidential elections had risen from 1.2 million in 1828 to 1.5 million in 1836 to 2.4 million in 1840. The 60 percent leap in the size of the popular vote between 1836 and 1840 is the greatest proportional jump between consecutive elections in American history. Neither lower suffrage requirements nor population growth was the main cause of this increase. Rather, it resulted from a jump in the percentage of eligible voters who chose to vote. In the three elections before 1840, the proportion of white males who voted had fluctuated between 55 percent and 58 percent; in 1840 it rose to 80 percent.

Both the depression and the frenzy of the log-cabin campaign had jolted previously indifferent voters into going to the polls. Yet voter turnout stayed up even after prosperity returned in the 1840s. The second party system, which had been developing slowly since 1828, reached a high plateau in 1840 and remained there for more than a decade. Politicians' appeal to ordinary people resulted not only from their rousing campaign techniques but also from the strong contrasts and simple choices that they could present. The gradual hardening of the line between the two parties stimulated enduring popular interest in politics.

No less than the tariff and banking issues, reform also aroused partisan passions by 1840. Yet the seeds of many of the reform movements that burst upon the national scene in the 1830s were initially sown in the field of religion rather than politics.

THE RISE OF POPULAR RELIGION

In *Democracy in America*, Alexis de Tocqueville pointed out an important difference between France and the United States. "In France I had almost always seen the spirit of religion and the spirit of freedom pursuing courses diametrically opposed to each other; but in America I found that they were intimately united, and that they reigned in common over the same country." From this assertion Tocqueville drew a startling conclusion: religion was "the foremost of the political institutions" of the United States.

In calling religion a political institution, Tocqueville did not mean that Americans gave special political privileges to any particular denomination. Rather, he was referring to the way in which religious impulses reinforced American democracy and liberty. Just as Americans demanded that politics be made accessible to the average person, they insisted that ministers preach doctrines that appealed to ordinary people. The most successful ministers were those who used plain words to move the heart, not those who tried to dazzle their listeners with theological complexities. Increasingly, too, Americans demanded theological doctrines that put individuals in charge of their own religious destiny. They thrust aside the Calvinist creed that God had arbitrarily selected some people for salvation and others for damnation and substituted the belief that anyone could attain heaven.

Thus heaven as well as politics became democratized in these years. The harmony between religious and democratic impulses owed much to a series of religious revivals known as the Second Great Awakening.

The Second Great Awakening

The Second Great Awakening had begun in Connecticut during the 1790s and set ablaze one section of the nation after another during the following half-century. At first, educated Congregationalists and Presbyterians such as Yale University's president Timothy Dwight had dominated the revivals. But as they spread from Connecticut to frontier states like Tennessee and Kentucky, revivals had undergone striking changes that were typified by the rise of camp meetings. Camp meetings were gigantic revivals in which members of several denominations gathered together in sprawling open-air camps for up to a week to hear revivalists proclaim that the Second Coming of Jesus was near and that the time for repentance was now.

The most famous camp meeting occurred at Cane Ridge, Kentucky, in August 1801, when a huge crowd came together on a hillside to listen to thunderous sermons and to sing hymns and experience the influx of divine grace. One eyewitness vividly described the meeting:

> At night, the whole scene was awfully sublime. The ranges of tents, the fires, reflecting light amidst the branches of the towering trees; the candles and lamps illuminating the encampment; hundreds moving to and fro, with lights or torches, like Gideon's army; the preaching, praying, singing, and shouting, all heard at once, rushing from different parts of the ground, like the sound of many waters, was enough to swallow up all the powers of contemplation.

The Cane Ridge revival was an episode of the larger Great Kentucky Revival of 1800–1801. Among the distinguishing features of these frontier revivals was the appearance of "exercises" in which men and women rolled around like logs, jerked their heads furiously (a phenomenon known simply as "the jerks"), and grunted like animals (the "barking exercise"). Observing the apparent pandemonium that had broken loose, critics had blasted the frontier frenzy for encouraging fleshly lust more than spirituality and complained that "more souls were begot than saved" in revivals. In fact, the early frontier revivals had challenged traditional religious customs. The most successful frontier revivalist preachers were not college graduates but ordinary farmers and artisans who had experienced powerful religious conversions and who had contempt for learned ministers with their dry expositions of orthodoxy.

No religious denomination had been more successful on the frontier than Methodists. With fewer than seventy thousand members in 1800, the Methodists had become America's largest Protestant denomination by 1844, claiming a little over a million members. In contrast to New England Congregationalists and Presbyterians, Methodists emphasized that religion was primarily a matter of the heart rather than the head. The frontier Methodists disdained a "settled" ministry in which ministers were tied to fixed parishes. Instead, they preferred itinerant circuit riders—young, unmarried men who moved on horseback from place to place and preached in houses, open fields, or wherever else listeners gathered.

Although the frontier revivals disrupted religious custom, they also worked to promote law, order, and a sense of morality on the frontier. Drunken rowdies who tried to invade camp meetings met their match in brawny itinerants like the Methodist Peter Cartwright. It was not only in camp meetings that Cartwright and his peers sought to raise the moral standard of the frontier. The basic unit of Methodist discipline on the frontier was the "class." When revivals broke up, the converted formed small groups of twelve or so members who met weekly to provide mutual encouragement of both religion and morality. During these class meetings, Methodists chastised one another for drunkenness, fighting, fornication, gossiping, and even slippery business practices.

Charles Finney and Wife

Finney had an active career after his New York revivals. He served as president of Oberlin College from 1851 to 1866. This photograph of Finney and his second wife, Elizabeth Atkinson, was taken while they were on an evangelistic tour of Great Britain in 1850.

Eastern Revivals

By the 1820s the Second Great Awakening had begun to shift back to the East. The hottest revival fires blazed in an area of western New York known as the Burned-Over District. No longer a frontier, western New York teemed with descendants of Puritans who hungered for religious experience and with people drawn by the hope of wealth after the completion of the Erie Canal. It was a fertile field of high expectations and bitter discontent.

The man who harnessed these anxieties to religion was Charles G. Finney. Finney began his career as a lawyer, but after a religious conversion in 1821, which he described as a "retainer from the Lord Jesus Christ to plead his cause," he became a Presbyterian minister and conducted revivals in towns like Rome and Utica along the canal. Although he also found time for trips to New York and Boston, his greatest "harvest" came in the thriving canal city of Rochester in 1830–1831.

The Rochester revival had several features that justify Finney's reputation as the "father of modern revivalism." First, it was a citywide revival in which all denominations participated. Finney was a pioneer of cooperation among Protestant denominations. In addition, in Rochester and elsewhere, Finney introduced devices for speeding conversions. Among these were the

"anxious seat," a bench to which those ready for conversion were led so that they could be made objects of special prayer, and the "protracted meeting," which went on nightly for up to a week.

Finney's emphasis on special revival techniques sharply distinguished him from eighteenth-century revivalists, including Jonathan Edwards. Whereas Edwards had portrayed revivals as the miraculous work of God, Finney made them out to be human creations. The divine spirit flowed in revivals, but humans made them happen. Although a Presbyterian, Finney flatly rejected the Calvinist belief that humans had a natural and nearly irresistible inclination to sin (the doctrine of "human depravity"). Rather, he affirmed, sin was purely a voluntary act; no one had to sin. Men and women could will themselves out of sin just as readily as they had willed themselves into it. Indeed, he declared, it was theoretically possible for men and women to will themselves free of all sin—to live perfectly. Those who heard Finney and similar revivalists came away convinced that they had experienced the washing away of all past guilt and the beginning of a new life. "I have been born again," a young convert wrote. "I am three days old when I write this letter."

The assertions that people could live without sin ("perfectionism") and that revivals were human contrivances made Finney a controversial figure. Yet his ideas came to dominate "evangelical" Protestantism, forms of Protestantism that focused on the need for an emotional religious conversion. He was successful because he told people what they wanted to hear: that their destinies were in their own hands. A society that celebrated the "self-made" individual found plausible Finney's assertion that, even in religion, people could make of themselves what they chose. Moreover, compared to most frontier revivalists, Finney had an unusually dignified style. Taken together, these factors gave him a potent appeal to merchants, lawyers, and small manufacturers in the towns and cities of the North.

More than most revivalists, Finney recognized that few revivals would have gotten off the ground without the mass participation of women. During the Second Great Awakening, female converts outnumbered male converts by about two to one. Finney encouraged women to give public testimonies of their religious experiences in church, and he often converted husbands by first converting their wives and daughters. After a visit by Finney, Melania Smith, the wife of a Rochester physician who had little time for religion, greeted her husband with a reminder of "the woe which is denounced against the families which call not on the Name of the Lord." Soon Dr. Smith heeded his wife's pleading and joined one of Rochester's Presbyterian churches.

Critics of Revivals: The Unitarians

Whereas some praised revivals for saving souls, others doubted that they produced permanent changes in behavior and condemned them for encouraging "such extravagant and incoherent expressions, and such enthusiastic fervor, as puts common sense and modesty to the blush."

One small but influential group of revival critics was the Unitarians. The basic doctrine of Unitarianism—that Jesus Christ was less than fully divine—had gained quiet acceptance among religious liberals during the eighteenth century. However, it was not until the early nineteenth century that Unitarianism emerged as a formal denomination with its own churches, ministry, and national organization. In New England hundreds of Congregational churches were torn apart by the withdrawal of socially prominent families who had embraced Unitarianism and by legal battles over which group—Congregationalists or Unitarians—could occupy church property. Although Unitarians won relatively few converts outside New England, their tendency to attract the wealthy and educated gave them influence beyond their numbers.

Unitarians criticized revivals as uncouth emotional exhibitions and argued that moral goodness should be cultivated by a gradual process of "character building" in which the individual learned to model his or her behavior on that of Jesus rather than by a sudden emotional conversion as in a revival. Yet Unitarians and revivalists shared the belief that human behavior could be changed for the better. Both rejected the Calvinist emphasis on innate human wickedness. William Ellery Channing, a Unitarian leader, claimed that Christianity had but one purpose: "the perfection of human nature, the elevation of men into nobler beings."

The Rise of Mormonism

The Unitarians' assertion that Jesus Christ was more human than divine challenged a basic doctrine of orthodox Christianity. Yet Unitarianism proved far less controversial than another of the new denominations of the 1820s and 1830s, the Church of Jesus Christ of Latter-day Saints, or Mormons. Its founder, Joseph Smith, grew to manhood in one of those families that seemed to be in constant motion to and fro, but never up. After moving

his family nearly twenty times in ten years, Smith's ne'er-do-well father settled in Palmyra, New York, in the heart of the Burned-Over District. As a boy, Smith dreamed of finding buried treasure, while his religious views were convulsed by the conflicting claims of the denominations that thrived in the region. "Some were contending for the Methodist faith, some for the Presbyterian, and some for the Baptists," Smith later wrote. He wondered who was right and who wrong, or whether they were "all wrong together."

The sort of perplexity that Smith experienced was widespread in the Burned-Over District, but his resolution of the confusion was unique. Smith claimed that an angel led him to a buried book of revelation and to special stones for use in translating it. He completed his translation of this Book of Mormon in 1827. The Book of Mormon tells the story of an ancient Hebrew prophet, Lehi, whose descendants came to America and created a prosperous civilization that looked forward to the appearance of Jesus as its savior. Jesus had actually appeared and performed miracles in the New World, the book claimed, but the American descendants of Lehi had departed from the Lord's ways and quarreled among themselves. God had cursed some with dark skin; these were the American Indians, who, when later discovered by Columbus, had forgotten their history.

Despite his astonishing claims, Smith quickly gathered followers. The appeal of Mormonism lay partly in its positioning of America at the center of Christian history and partly in Smith's assertion that he had discovered a new revelation. The idea of an additional revelation beyond the Bible appeared to some to resolve the turmoil created by the Protestant denominations' inability to agree on what the Bible said or meant.

Smith and his followers steadily moved west from New York to Ohio and Missouri. Then they migrated to Illinois, where they built a model city, Nauvoo, and a magnificent temple supported by thirty huge pillars (see Map 10.3). By moving to these areas, the Mormons hoped to draw closer to the Indians, whose conversion was one of their goals, and to escape persecution. Smith's claim to have received a new revelation virtually guaranteed a hostile reception for the Mormons wherever they went because Smith had seemingly undermined the authority of the Bible, one of the two documents (the other being the Constitution) upon which the ideals of the American Republic rested.

Smith added fuel to the fire when he reported in 1843 that he had received still another revelation, this one sanctioning the Mormon practice of having multiple wives, or polygyny. Although Smith did not publicly proclaim polygyny as a doctrine, its practice among

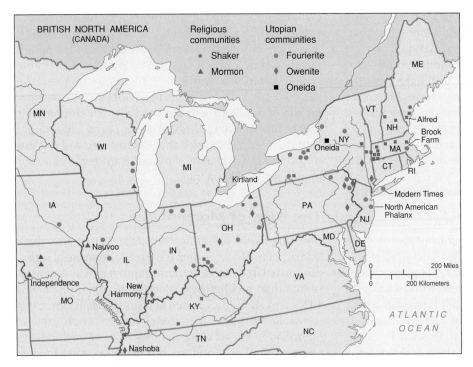

MAP 10.3
Religious and Utopian Communities, 1800–1845
The desire to construct a perfect society influenced the founding of a number of communities, especially in the period from 1800 to 1845. Religious motives dominated the founding of Shaker and Mormon communities. In addition to the ideas of Robert Owen, those of the Frenchman Charles Fourier, who sought to cure the evils of competive society by establishing a harmonious world in which men and women performed on "attractive" labor, influenced the founding of communities like Modern Times on Long Island and the North American Phalanx at Red Bank, New Jersey. Brook Farm was, for a period, a Fourierite community. Noyes's Oneida mingled religious and secular motives in ways hard to disentangle.

Mormons was a poorly kept secret. Smith's self-image also intensified the controversy that boiled around Mormonism. He refused to view himself merely as the founder of another denomination; instead, he saw himself as a prophet of the kingdom of God and was called a "Second Mohammed." Mormonism would be to Christianity what Christianity had been to Judaism: an all-encompassing, higher form of religion. In 1844 Smith announced his candidacy for the presidency of the United States. But the state of Illinois was already moving against him. Charged with treason, he was jailed in Carthage, Illinois, and along with his brother was murdered there by a mob in June 1844.

Mormonism is one of the few religions to have originated in the United States, and Smith initially had hoped that Americans would respond to his call. Some did, especially among the poor and downtrodden, but the hostility of the "Gentiles" (non-Mormons) gradually persuaded Smith that the future of Mormons lay in their separation from society. In this respect, Mormonism mirrored the efforts of several religious communal societies whose members resolutely set themselves apart from society. In general, these religious communitarians were less numerous, controversial, and long-lasting than the Mormons, but one group among them, the Shakers, has continued to fascinate Americans.

The Shakers

The founder and leader of the Shakers was Mother Ann Lee, the illiterate daughter of an English blacksmith. The official name of her group was the United Society of Believers in Christ's Second Appearing, and the name "Shakers" came from a convulsive religious dance that was part of their ceremony. Lee had set sail for America in 1774, and her followers soon organized a tightly knit community in New Lebanon, New York. In this and in other communities, the Shakers proved themselves able artisans (see A Place in Time: The Shaker Village at Alfred, Maine). Shaker furniture became renowned for its beauty and strength, and Shakers invented such conveniences as the clothespin and the circular saw.

For all their achievements as artisans, the Shakers were fundamentally otherworldly and hostile to materialism. Having watched four of her children die in infancy, Mother Lee claimed to have seen a vision in which God expelled Adam and Eve from the Garden of Eden for having engaged in sexual intercourse, and she insisted that her followers abstain from sex. Lee derived many of her doctrines from trances and heavenly visions she said she experienced. Among these was her

conviction that God contained both male and female elements.

Lee's teachings about the evils of sexual relations would quickly have doomed the Shakers to extinction had it not been for the spread of religious revivalism after 1790. Turning up at Cane Ridge and other revival sites, Shaker missionaries made off with converts who had been loosened from their traditional religious moorings by the revivals. In addition, the Shakers adopted orphans, many of whom joined their communities. At their peak during the second quarter of the nineteenth century, the Shakers numbered about six thousand in eight states.

Shakers chose to live apart from society. But the message of most evangelical Protestants, including Charles G. Finney, was that religion and economic individualism—a person's pursuit of wealth—were compatible. Most revivalists told people that getting ahead in the world was acceptable as long as they were honest, temperate, and bound by the dictates of their consciences. By encouraging assimilation into rather than retreat from society, evangelicalism provided a powerful stimulus to the numerous reform movements of the 1820s and 1830s.

THE AGE OF REFORM

Democratic ferment was not confined to politics and religion. During the 1820s and 1830s, unprecedented numbers of men and women joined organizations that aimed to improve society. The abolition of slavery, women's rights, temperance, better treatment of criminals and the insane, public education, and even the establishment of utopian communities were high on various reformers' agendas.

At a time when women were not allowed to vote, free people of color increasingly were excluded from politics, and the major parties usually avoided controversial issues like slavery and women's rights, participation in reform movements offered women and blacks an opportunity to influence public issues. The white males drawn to reform movements viewed politics as a sorry spectacle that allowed a man like Andrew Jackson, a duelist who had married a divorcee, to become president and that routinely rewarded persons who would sacrifice any principle for victory at the polls. Although they occasionally cooperated with political parties, especially the Whigs, reformers gave their loyalty to their causes, not to parties.

Inclined to view all social problems as clashes between good and evil, reformers believed that they

In 1793 Shakers began to construct a village near the bustling town of Alfred in southern Maine (then part of Massachusetts). Smaller than most Shaker villages (it never had more than two hundred members, about two-thirds of whom were women), the community at Alfred lasted until 1931, when dwindling numbers forced the survivors to sell the property.

Like other communities established by the Shakers, the village at Alfred did not resemble other American villages. A strict geometric orderliness marked its built environment. Joshua Bussell, a self-taught artist, (hiring professional artists would have struck Shakers as an example of the sin of pride) painted pictures of the village in 1845. Bussell was a Shaker who had joined the community in 1829 at the age of thirteen and worked in it as a shoemaker. Responsible for about half of the surviving sketches of Shaker villages, Bussell had not mastered perspective. Having reproduced one side of the street, he turned his painting upside down and painted the other. Far from aiming at elegance, he called the painting a "plan" of the village at Alfred to be used to inform or guide other Shaker settlements, and he inserted the exact dimensions of the main buildings. For example, the Nurse House (infirmary) was 34 by 46 feet and the Visiting House 36 by 40 feet.

Other millenarian sects predicted the imminent and catastrophic end of the world followed by a thousand year reign of Christ on earth (the "millennium"). The Shakers believed that the millennium had already started. Their task was to perfect their own lives as a model for others and thereby bring about the redemption of all humankind. Thus they believed that they had to live compactly in order to ensure members' conformity to rules, to control the use of space, and to restrain every sign of pride and individualism.

These values are evident in Bussell's painting. Determined to set themselves apart from the spectacle of larger society, the Shakers avoided ornamentation. In Bussell's painting, there are no porches or window shutters. Reminding us that Shakers rejected the private ownership of land, the farm fields at the Alfred village are not divided by fences or walls. As a sign of the importance of mutual oversight and in contrast to the dispersed dwellings characteristic of other American villages, the buildings at Alfred are close together. Shakers lived in large communal dwellings, called "Families." These Families, each of which might contain from thirty to one hundred Shakers, were not based on kinship but rather on the residents' degree of mastery of Shaker ideals. In a Shaker village there might be one Family for novices and another for seniors.

Following the rules that Shakers sought to impose on all their villages, the Dwelling House and the meeting house (used for religious exercises) at Alfred were painted white, while less important residential buildings were painted red and barns and other utility buildings tan.

In keeping with Mother Ann Lee's belief that God was both male and female, women had considerable influence in Shaker communities. Each Family had an eldress along with an elder to guide spiritual growth, and a deaconess in addition to a deacon to attend to business.

Although Shakers engaged in convulsive religious dances and were given to visions, prophecies, and personal revelations, most of the time they bound themselves by rules that restrained their personal movement in order to attain self-mastery. In Shaker communities, marriage was banned, and men and women were rigidly separated to prevent sexual liaisons. A boundary separated the sleeping quarters of men and women in residential buildings. Even the work activities of men and women were segregated; members could not visit the workplaces of the opposite sex without a specific reason.

Shaker rules governed many other aspects of daily life. As Bussell's painting indicates, there were no diagonal shortcuts in the Alfred village. Paths usually ran at

right angles. Inside Shaker dwellings, even the stovepipes followed right angles on route from stove to vent. At communal tables, printed signs reminded diners to cut their bread and meat into squares. High, stiff-backed Shaker chairs kept Shakers erect when sitting. When Shakers ventured beyond their villages, they were told to walk so closely together that a cat cound not slip between them.

Shakers attached no value to beauty but they made furniture that was beautiful by virtue of its functional simplicity. They did not value wealth, but their villages usually were prosperous, mainly because they cooperated with each other, pooling land and implements, in order to achieve self-sufficiency. Shaker villages usually were mainly devoted to farming, but members also crafted goods for sale to the outside world. The Alfred Shakers made brooms and spinning wheels. But Shakers worked hard to prevent becoming dependent on the world and its evil ways. Journalist Horace Greeley exclaimed that the lawns in Shaker villages would arouse the envy of a monarch. Even their road dust seemed pure, said another observer, while a British visitor concluded that "the earth does not show more flourishing fields, gardens, and orchards, than theirs."

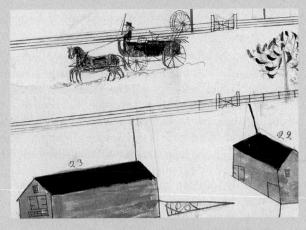

The Shaker Village at Alfred, ca. 1848 (Above) Detail showing a Shaker brother driving a wagon-load of spinning wheels. (Below) Detail showing wagons at the Church Family.

The Shaker Village at Alfred, Maine by Joshua H. Bussell, 1845

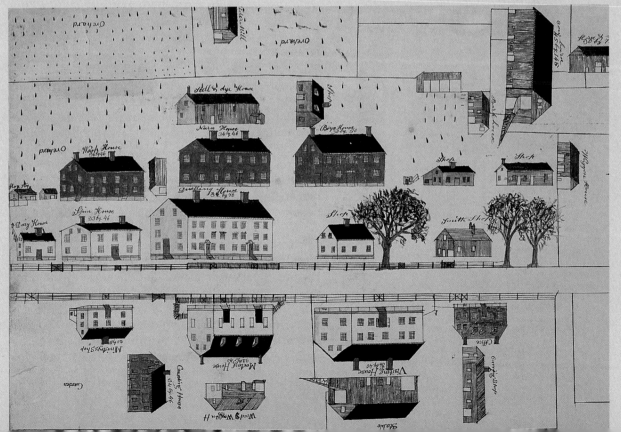

were on God's side on every issue. Religious revivalism contributed to their intense moralism. Virtually all prominent temperance reformers of the 1820s and 1830s, for example, had initially been inspired by revivals. But revivalism and reform were not always intimately linked. Influential school reformers and women's rights advocates were frequently religious liberals either hostile or indifferent to revivals. And although some abolitionists owed their first flush of idealism to revivals, others did not, and almost all came to criticize the churches for condoning slavery. Yet even those reformers opposed to revivalism borrowed the evangelical preachers' language and psychology by portraying drunkenness, ignorance, and inequality as sins that called for immediate repentance.

Although the reform movements appealed to those excluded from or repelled by politics, most lacked the political parties' national organizations. New England and those parts of the Midwest settled by New Englanders were hotbeds of reform. In contrast, southerners actively suppressed abolition, displayed only mild interest in temperance and education reform, ignored women's rights, and saw utopian communities as proof of the mental instability of northern reformers.

The War on Liquor

Agitation for temperance (either total abstinence from alcoholic beverages or moderation in their use) intensified during the second quarter of the nineteenth century. Temperance reformers addressed a growing problem. The spread of the population across the Appalachians stimulated the production and consumption of alcohol. Before the transportation revolution, western farmers, unable to get their grain to markets, commonly distilled it into spirits. Annual per capita consumption of rum, whiskey, gin, and brandy rose until it exceeded seven gallons by 1830, nearly triple today's rate. By the late 1820s, the average adult male drank a half-pint of liquor a day. With some justification, reformers saw alcoholic excess as a male indulgence whose bitter consequences (spending wages on liquor instead of food) fell on women and children.

There had been agitation against intemperance before 1825, but the Connecticut revivalist Lyman Beecher ushered in a new phase that year when, in six widely acclaimed lectures, he thundered against all use of alcohol. A year later, evangelical Protestants created the American Temperance Society, the first national temperance organization. By 1834 some five thousand state and local temperance societies were loosely affiliated with the American Temperance Society. Although these societies were nearly always headed by men, from one-third to one-half of their members were women, who found in temperance agitation a public outlet for their moral energies. Whereas previous temperance supporters had advised moderation in the use of spirits, the American Temperance Society followed Beecher in demanding total abstinence. The society flooded the country with tracts denouncing the "amazing evil" of strong drink and urged churches to expel any members who condoned alcohol.

Among the main targets of the evangelical temperance reformers were moderate drinkers in the laboring classes. In the small shops where a handful of journeymen and apprentices worked informally, passing the jug every few hours was a time-honored way to relieve fatigue and monotony. But with the rise of large factories, there were new demands for a disciplined work

Signing the Pledge, 1840s
Pressured by his determined wife and pleading child, this reluctant tippler is about to submit to "moral suasion" and sign the pledge to abstain from alcohol.

force. Factory owners with precise production schedules to meet needed orderly and steady workers. Thus, evangelical temperance reformers quickly gained manufacturers' support. In East Dudley, Massachusetts, for example, three factory owners refused to sell liquor in factory stores, calculating that any profits from the sale would be more than offset by lost working time and "the scenes of riot and wickedness thus produced."

Workers showed little interest in temperance before the late 1830s. But after the Panic of 1837, a new stage of temperance agitation sprang up in the form of the Washington Temperance Societies. Starting in Baltimore in 1840, the Washingtonians were more likely to be mechanics (workingmen) and laborers than ministers and manufacturers. Many were reformed drunkards, and most had concluded that their survival in the harsh climate of depression depended on their commitment to sobriety and frugality. For example, Charles T. Woodman, a baker, had been forced by the collapse of his business to flee Boston for Philadelphia to escape his creditors. Like most Washingtonians, Woodman blamed his ruin on a relapse into his "old habit" of drink. The forces dislocating workers in the late 1830s were often far beyond their control. Part of the appeal of temperance was that it lay within their control. Take care of temperance, a Washingtonian assured a Baltimore audience, and the Lord would take care of the economy.

For all their differences from earlier temperance associations, the Washingtonians reflected the impact of revivals even more than did the American Temperance Society. Viewing drinking as sinful, they held "experience meetings" in which members described their "salvation" from liquor and their "regeneration" through abstinence or "teetotalism" (an emphatic form of the word *total*). Their wives joined "Martha Washington" societies in which they pledged to smell their husbands' breath each night and paraded with banners that read "Teetotal or No Husband." The Washingtonians spread farther and faster than any other antebellum temperance organization.

As temperance won new supporters, anti-alcohol crusaders gradually shifted from calls for individuals to abstain to demands that cities, towns, and even states ban all traffic in liquor. This shift from moral suasion to legal prohibition was controversial even within the movement. But by the late 1830s, prohibition was scoring victories. In 1838 Massachusetts prohibited the sale of distilled spirits in amounts less than fifteen gallons, thereby restricting small purchases by individual drinkers; in 1851 Maine banned the manufacture and sale of all intoxicating beverages. Controversial though these laws were, the temperance movement won a measure of success. After rising steadily between 1800 and 1830, per capita consumption of distilled spirits began to fall during the 1830s. The rate of consumption during the 1840s was less than half that in the 1820s.

Public-School Reform

No less than temperance reformers, school reformers worked to encourage orderliness and thrift in the common people. Rural America's so-called district schools provided reformers with one of their main targets. One-room log or clapboard cabins containing pupils aged anywhere from three to twenty or more, the district schools taught farmers' children to read and count, but little more. Those who attended the district schools never forgot their primitive conditions and harsh discipline: "the wood-pile in the yard, the open fireplace, the backless benches," and the floggings until "the youngster vomited or wet his breeches."

For all their drawbacks, district schools enjoyed popular and financial support from rural parents. But reformers saw these schools in a different light, insisting that schools had to equip children for the emerging competitive and industrial economy. The most articulate and influential of the reformers, Horace Mann of Massachusetts, became the first secretary of his state's newly created board of education in 1837, and for the next decade he promoted a sweeping transformation of public education. Mann's goals included shifting the burden of financial support for schools from parents to the state, grading the schools (that is, classifying pupils by age and attainment), extending the school term from two or three months to as many as ten months, introducing standardized textbooks, and compelling attendance. In place of loosely structured schools that were mere appendages of the family, Mann and other reformers advocated highly structured institutions that would occupy most of the child's time and energy.

School reformers hoped not only to combat ignorance but also to spread uniform cultural values by exposing all children to identical experiences. Children would arrive at school at the same time and thereby learn punctuality. Graded schools that matched children against their age peers would stimulate the competitiveness needed in a rapidly industrializing society. Children would all read the same books and absorb such common sayings as "Idleness is the nest in which mischief lays its eggs." The McGuffey readers, which sold 50 million copies between 1836 and 1870, created a common curriculum and preached industry, honesty, sobriety, and patriotism.

Although school reform made few gains in the South (see Chapter 12), much of the North remodeled its schools along the lines advocated by Mann, and in 1852 Massachusetts passed the nation's first compulsory school law. Success did not come easily. Educational reformers faced challenges from farmers, who were satisfied with the informality of the district schools, and from urban Catholics led by New York City's Bishop John Hughes, who pointed out that the textbooks used in public schools dispensed anti-Catholic and anti-Irish epithets. And in both rural and urban areas, the laboring poor opposed compulsory education as a menace to parents dependent on their children's wages.

Yet school reformers prevailed, in part because their opponents, rural Protestants and urban Catholics, were incapable of cooperating with each other. In part, too, reformers succeeded by gaining influential allies. For example, their stress on free, tax-supported schools won the backing of the urban workingmen's parties that arose in the late 1820s; and their emphasis on punctuality appealed to manufacturers who needed a disciplined work force. The new ideas also attracted reform-minded women who recognized that the grading of schools would ease women's entry into teaching. People of the times widely believed that a woman could never control the assortment of three- to twenty-year-olds found in a one-room schoolhouse, but managing a class of eight- or nine-year-olds was a different matter. Catharine Beecher accurately predicted that school reform would render teaching a suitable profession for women. Women gradually did take the place of men in the classroom wherever school reform left its mark. By 1900 about 70 percent of the nation's schoolteachers were women.

School reform also appealed to native-born Americans alarmed by the swelling tide of immigration. The public school emerged as the favorite device by which reformers forged a common American culture out of an increasingly diverse society. "We must decompose and cleanse the impurities which rush into our midst" through the "one infallible filter—the SCHOOL."

School reformers were assimilationists in the sense that they hoped to use public education to give children common values through shared experiences. In one respect, however, these reformers wore blinders on the issue of assimilation, for few stressed the integration of black and white children. When black children were fortunate enough to get any schooling, it was usually in segregated schools. Black children who entered integrated public schools met with such virulent prejudice that black leaders in northern cities frequently preferred segregated schools.

Abolition

Antislavery sentiment among whites flourished in the Revolutionary era but declined in the early nineteenth century. The main antislavery organization founded between 1800 and 1830 was the American Colonization Society (1817), which displayed little moral outrage against slavery. The society proposed a plan for gradual emancipation, with compensation to the slave owner, and the shipment of freed blacks to Africa. This proposal attracted support from some slaveholders in the Upper South who would never have dreamed of a general emancipation.

At its core, colonization was hard-hearted and soft-headed. Colonizationists assumed that blacks were a degraded race that did not belong in American society, and they underestimated the growing dependence of the South's economy on slavery. Confronted by a soaring demand for cotton and other commodities, few southerners were willing to free their slaves, even if compensated. In any event, the American Colonization Society never had enough funds to buy freedom for more than a fraction of slaves. Between 1820 and 1830, only 1,400 blacks migrated to Liberia, and most were already free. In striking contrast, the American slave population, fed by natural increase (the excess of births over deaths), rose from 1,191,000 in 1810 to more than 2,000,000 in 1830.

During the 1820s the main source of radical opposition to slavery was blacks themselves. Blacks had little enthusiasm for colonization. Most American blacks were native-born rather than African-born. How, they asked, could they be sent back to a continent that they had never left? "We are natives of this country," a black pastor in New York proclaimed. "We only ask that we be treated as well as foreigners." In opposition to colonization, blacks formed scores of abolition societies. In 1829 a Boston free black, David Walker, published an Appeal for a black rebellion to crush slavery.

Not all whites acquiesced to the continuance of slavery. In 1821 Quaker Benjamin Lundy began a newspaper, the *Genius of Universal Emancipation*, and put forth proposals that no new slave states be admitted to the Union, that the internal slave trade be outlawed, that the three-fifths clause of the Constitution be repealed, and that Congress abolish slavery wherever it had the authority to do so. In 1828 Lundy hired a young New Englander, William Lloyd Garrison, as an assistant editor. Prematurely bald, wearing steel-rimmed glasses, and typically donning a black suit and black cravat, Garrison looked more like a schoolmaster than a rebel. But in 1831, when he launched his own newspaper, *The*

The Antislavery Alphabet
Viewing children as morally pure and hence as natural opponents of slavery, abolitionists produced antislavery toys, games, and, as we see here, alphabet books.

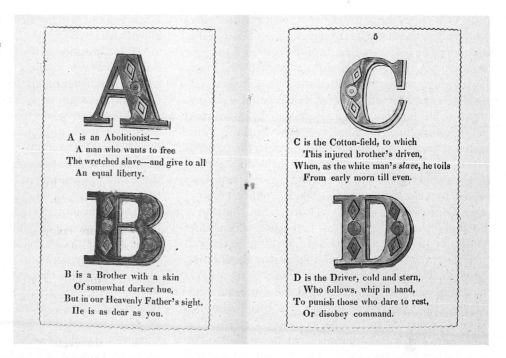

A is an Abolitionist—
A man who wants to free
The wretched slave—and give to all
An equal liberty.

B is a Brother with a skin
Of somewhat darker hue,
But in our Heavenly Father's sight,
He is as dear as you.

C is the Cotton-field, to which
This injured brother's driven,
When, as the white man's *slave,* he toils
From early morn till even.

D is the Driver, cold and stern,
Who follows, whip in hand,
To punish those who dare to rest,
Or disobey command.

Liberator, he quickly established himself as the most famous and controversial white abolitionist. "I am in earnest," Garrison wrote. "I will not equivocate—I will not excuse—I will not retreat a single inch—AND I WILL BE HEARD."

Garrison's battle cry was "immediate emancipation." In place of exiling blacks to Africa, he substituted the truly radical notion that blacks should enjoy civil (or legal) equality with whites. He greeted slaves as "a Man and a Brother," "a Woman and a Sister." Even Garrison, however, did not think that all slaves could be freed overnight. "Immediate emancipation" meant that all people had to realize that slavery was sinful and its continued existence intolerable.

Garrison quickly gained support from the growing number of black abolitionists. A black barber in Pittsburgh sent Garrison sixty dollars to help with *The Liberator.* Black agents sold subscriptions, and three-fourths of *The Liberator's* subscribers in the early years were black.

The escaped slave Frederick Douglass and a remarkable freed slave who named herself Sojourner Truth proved eloquent lecturers against slavery. Douglass could rivet an audience with an opening line. "I appear before the immense assembly this evening as a thief and a robber," he gibed. "I stole this head, these limbs, this body from my master, and ran off with them."

Relations between black and white abolitionists were not always harmonious. White abolitionists called for legal equality for blacks but not necessarily for social

equality. Not without racial prejudice, they preferred light-skinned to dark-skinned Negroes and, Garrison excepted, were hesitant to admit blacks to antislavery societies. Yet the prejudices of white abolitionists were mild compared to those of most whites. A white man or woman could do few things less popular in the 1830s than become an abolitionist. Mobs, often including colonizationists, repeatedly attacked abolitionists. For example, a Boston mob, searching for a British abolitionist in 1835, found Garrison instead and dragged him through town on the end of a rope. An abolitionist editor, Elijah Lovejoy, was murdered by a mob in Alton, Illinois, in 1837.

Abolitionists drew on the language of revivals and described slavery as sin, but the Protestant churches did not rally behind abolition as strongly as they rallied behind temperance. Lyman Beecher roared against the evils of strong drink but whimpered about those of slavery, and in 1834 he tried to suppress abolitionists at Cincinnati's Lane Theological Seminary. In response, Theodore Dwight Weld, an idealistic follower of Charles G. Finney, led a mass withdrawal of students. These "Lane rebels" formed the nucleus of abolitionist activity at antislavery Oberlin College.

As if external hostility were not enough, abolitionists argued continually with each other. The American Anti-Slavery Society, founded in 1833, was the scene of several battles between Garrison and prominent New York and midwestern abolitionists such as the brothers Lewis and Arthur Tappan, Theodore Dwight Weld, and

James G. Birney. One of the issues between the two sides was whether abolitionists should enter politics as a distinct party. In 1840 Garrison's opponents ran Birney for president on the ticket of the newly formed Liberty party. As for Garrison himself, he was increasingly rejecting all laws and governments, as well as political parties, as part of his doctrine of "nonresistance." In 1838 he and his followers had founded the New England Non-Resistance Society. Their starting point was the fact that slavery depended on force. Garrison then added that all governments ultimately rested on force; even laws passed by elected legislatures needed police enforcement. Because Garrison viewed force as the opposite of Christian love, he concluded that Christians should refuse to vote, hold office, or have anything to do with government. It is a small wonder that many abolitionists thought of Garrison as extreme, or "ultra."

The second issue that divided the American Anti-Slavery Society concerned the role of women in the abolitionist movement. In 1837 Angelina and Sarah Grimké, daughters of a South Carolina slaveholder, embarked on an antislavery lecture tour of New England. Women had become deeply involved in antislavery societies during the 1830s, but always in female auxiliaries affiliated with those run by men. What made the Grimké sisters so controversial was that they drew mixed audiences of men and women to their lectures at a time when it was thought indelicate for women to speak before male audiences. Clergymen chastised the Grimké sisters for lecturing men rather than obeying them.

Such criticism backfired, however, because the Grimkés increasingly took up the cause of women's rights. In 1838 each wrote a classic of American feminism. Sarah produced *Letters on the Condition of Women and the Equality of the Sexes*, and Angelina contributed *Letters to Catharine E. Beecher* (Lyman Beecher's daughter, a militant opponent of female equality). Some abolitionists tried to dampen the feminist flames. Abolitionist poet John Greenleaf Whittier dismissed women's grievances as "paltry" compared to the "great and dreadful wrongs of the slave." Even Theodore Dwight Weld, who had married Angelina Grimké, wanted to subordinate women's rights to antislavery. But the fiery passions would not be extinguished. Garrison, welcoming the controversy, promptly espoused women's rights and urged that women be given positions equal to men in the American Anti-Slavery Society. In 1840 the election of a woman, Abby Kelley, to a previously all-male committee split the American Anti-Slavery Society wide open. A substantial minority of profeminist delegates left—some to join the Liberty party, others to follow Lewis Tappan into the new American and Foreign Anti-Slavery Society.

The disruption of the American Anti-Slavery Society did not greatly damage abolitionism. The national society had never had much control over the local societies that had grown swiftly during the mid-1830s. By 1840 there were more than fifteen hundred local societies, principally in Massachusetts, New York, and Ohio. By circulating abolitionist tracts, newspapers, and even chocolates with antislavery messages on their wrappers, these local societies kept the country ablaze with agitation.

One of the most disruptive abolitionist techniques was to flood Congress with petitions calling for an end to slavery in the District of Columbia. Congress had no time to consider all the petitions, but to refuse to address them meant depriving citizens of their right to have petitions heard. In 1836 southerners secured congressional adoption of the "gag rule," which automatically tabled abolitionist petitions and thus prevented discussion of them in Congress. Former president John Quincy Adams, then a representative from Massachusetts, led the struggle against the gag rule and finally secured its repeal in 1845.

The debate over the gag rule subtly shifted the issue from the abolition of slavery to the constitutional rights of free expression and petitioning Congress. Members of Congress with little sympathy for abolitionists found themselves attacking the South for suppressing the right of petition. In a way, the gag-rule episode vindicated Garrison's tactic of stirring up emotions on the slavery issue. By holding passions over slavery at the boiling point, Garrison kept the South on the defensive. The less secure southerners felt, the more they were tempted into clumsy overreactions like the gag rule.

Women's Rights

The position of American women in the 1830s contained many contradictions. Women could not vote. If married, they had no right to own property (even inherited property) or to retain their own earnings. Yet the spread of reform movements provided women with unprecedented opportunities for public activity without challenging the prevailing belief that their proper sphere was the home. By suppressing liquor, for example, women could claim that they were transforming wretched homes into nurseries of happiness.

The argument that women were natural guardians of the family was double-edged. It justified reform activities on behalf of the family, but it undercut women's demands for legal equality. Let women attend to their sphere, the

counterargument ran, and leave politics and finance to men. So deeply ingrained was sexual inequality that most feminists did not start out intending to attack it. Instead, their experiences in other reform movements, notably abolition, led them to the issue of women's rights.

Among the early women's rights advocates who started their reform careers as abolitionists were the Grimké sisters, Philadelphia Quaker Lucretia Mott, Lucy Stone, and Abby Kelley. Like abolition, the cause of women's rights revolved around the conviction that differences of race and gender were unimportant and incidental. "Men and women," Sarah Grimké wrote, "are CREATED EQUAL! They are both moral and accountable beings, and whatever is right for man to do, is right for woman." The most articulate and aggressive advocates of women's rights, moreover, tended to gravitate to William Lloyd Garrison rather than to more moderate abolitionists. Garrison, himself a vigorous feminist, repeatedly stressed the peculiar degradation of women under slavery. The early issues of *The Liberator* contained a "Ladies' Department" headed by a picture of a kneeling slave woman imploring, "Am I Not a Woman and a Sister?" It was common knowledge that slave women were vulnerable to the sexual demands of white masters. Garrison denounced the South as a vast brothel and described slave women as "treated with more indelicacy and cruelty than cattle."

Although their involvement in abolition aroused advocates of women's rights, the discrimination they encountered within the abolition movement infuriated them and impelled them to make women's rights a separate cause. In the 1840s Lucy Stone became the first abolitionist to lecture solely on women's rights. When Lucretia Mott and other American women tried to be seated at the World's Anti-Slavery Convention in London in 1840, they were relegated to a screened-off section. The incident made a sharp impression not only on Mott but also on Elizabeth Cady Stanton, who had elected to accompany her abolitionist husband to the meeting as a honeymoon trip. In 1848 Mott and Stanton organized a women's rights convention at Seneca Falls, New York, that proclaimed a Declaration of Sentiments. Modeled on the Declaration of Independence, the Seneca Falls Declaration began with the assertion that "all men and women are created equal." The convention passed twelve resolutions, and only one, a call for the right of women to vote, failed to pass unanimously; but it did pass. Ironically, after the Civil War, the call for woman suffrage became the main demand of women's rights advocates for the rest of the century.

Although its crusaders were resourceful and energetic, women's rights had less impact than most other reforms. Temperance and school reform were far more

Lucretia Mott, co-organizer of the Seneca Falls convention, recalled growing up "thoroughly imbued with women's rights." The daughter of a sea captain, she was raised in a Quaker family in the whaling community of Nantucket, Massachusetts. With their husbands and fathers often absent on voyages, Nantucket women took over many practical responsibilities. As a Quaker, Mott was taught that men and women had equal spiritual gifts.

popular, and abolitionism created more commotion. Women would not secure the right to vote throughout the nation until 1920, fifty-five years after the Thirteenth Amendment abolished slavery. One reason for the relatively slow advance of women's rights was that piecemeal gains—such as married women's securing the right to own property in several states by the time of the Civil War—satisfied many women. The cause of women's rights also suffered from a close association with abolitionism, which was unpopular. In addition, the advance of feminism was slowed by the competition that it faced from the alternative ideal of domesticity. By sanctioning activities in reforms such as temperance and education, the cult of domesticity provided many women with worthwhile pursuits beyond the family. In this way, it blunted the edge of female demands for full equality.

Penitentiaries and Asylums

Other reform efforts took shape during the 1820s. These included efforts to combat poverty, crime, and insanity by establishing highly regimented institutions, themselves products of striking new assumptions about the

causes of deviancy. As poverty and crime had increased and grown more visible in early-nineteenth-century cities, alarmed investigators concluded that indigence and deviant behavior resulted not from defects in human nature, as colonial Americans had thought, but from drunken fathers and broken homes. The failure of parental discipline, not the will of God or the wickedness of human nature, lay at the root of evil. Both religious revivalists and secular reformers increasingly concluded that human nature could be altered by the right combination of moral influences. Most grasped the optimistic logic voiced by William Ellery Channing: "The study of the causes of crime may lead us to its cure."

To cure crime, reformers created substitutes for parental discipline, most notably the penitentiary. Penitentiaries were prisons marked by an unprecedented degree of order and discipline. Of course, colonial Americans had incarcerated criminal offenders, but jails had been used mainly to hold prisoners awaiting trial or to lock up debtors. For much of the eighteenth century, the threat of the gallows rather than of imprisonment had deterred wrongdoers. In contrast, nineteenth-century reformers believed that, rightly managed, penitentiaries would bring about the sincere reformation of offenders.

To purge offenders' violent habits, reformers usually insisted on solitary confinement. Between 1819 and 1825, New York built penitentiaries at Auburn and Ossining

("Sing Sing") in which prisoners were confined in small, windowless cells at night. By day they could work together but never speak and rarely even look at each other. Some reformers criticized this "Auburn system" for allowing too much contact and preferred the rival "Pennsylvania system," in which each prisoner spent all of his or her time in a single cell with a walled courtyard for exercise and received no news or visits from the outside.

Antebellum America also witnessed a remarkable transformation in the treatment of poor people. The prevailing colonial practice of offering relief to the poor by supporting them in a household ("outdoor relief") gradually gave way to the construction of almshouses for the infirm poor and workhouses for the able-bodied poor ("indoor relief"). The argument for indoor relief was much the same as the rationale for penitentiaries: plucking the poor from their demoralizing surroundings and exposing them to a highly regimented institution could change them into virtuous, productive citizens. However lofty the motives behind workhouses and almshouses, the results were often abysmal. In 1833 a legislative committee found that the inmates of the Boston House of

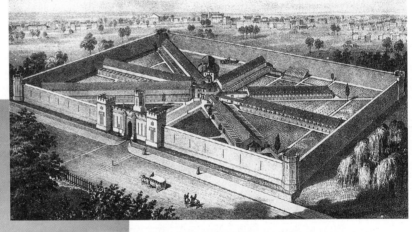

Pennsylvania's Eastern State Penitentiary
Begun in 1822 in Philadelphia, this penitentiary was the showcase of the so-called Pennsylvania or "Separate" system of prison discipline. Each inmate occupied a single cell and at all times was kept from contact with other inmates. This sketch was done by inmate 2954 in 1855.

Industry were packed seven to a room and included unwed mothers, the sick, and the insane as well as the poor.

As for insane people, those living in a workhouse such as the Boston House of Industry were relatively well off, for many experienced even worse treatment by confinement in prisons. In 1841 Dorothea Dix, an idealistic Unitarian schoolteacher, was teaching a Sunday School class in a jail in East Cambridge, Massachusetts, and discovered insane people kept in an unheated room. Dix then investigated jails and almshouses across the state. In 1843 she presented a memorial to the state legislature that described the insane confined "in cages, closets, cellars, stalls, pens! Chained, naked, beaten with rods, and lashed into obedience." With the support of Horace Mann and Boston reformer Samuel G. Howe, she encouraged legislatures to build insane asylums. By the time of the Civil War, twenty-eight states, four cities, and the federal government had constructed public mental institutions.

Penitentiaries, workhouses, and insane asylums all reflected the same optimistic belief that deviancy could be erased by resettling deviants in the right environment. But what was the "right" environment? Part of the answer was clear-cut. Heated rooms were better than frigid ones, and sober parents preferable to drunkards. But reformers demanded much more than warm rooms and responsible parents. They were convinced that the unfettered freedom and individualism of American society were themselves defects in the environment and that the poor, criminal, and insane needed extraordinary regimentation if they were to change. Prison inmates were to march around in lockstep; in workhouses the poor, treated much like prisoners, were often forbidden to leave or receive visitors without permission. The idealism behind such institutions was genuine, but later generations would question reformers' underlying assumptions.

Utopian Communities

The belief that individuals could live perfectly took its most extreme form in the utopian communities that flourished during the reform years. Most of them, founded by intellectuals, were intended as alternatives to the prevailing competitive economy and as models whose success would inspire others.

American interest in utopian communities first surfaced during the 1820s. In 1825 British industrialist and philanthropist Robert Owen founded the New Harmony community in Indiana. Owen had already acquired a formidable reputation (and a fortune) from his management of cotton mills at New Lanark, Scotland. His innovations at New Lanark had substantially improved his workers' educational opportunities and living conditions and left him convinced that similar changes could transform the lives of working people everywhere. He saw the problem of the early industrial age as social rather than political. If social arrangements could be perfected, all vice and misery would disappear; human character was formed, "without exception," by people's surroundings or environment. The key to perfecting social arrangements lay, in turn, in the creation of small, planned communities—"Villages of Unity and Mutual Cooperation" containing a perfect balance of occupational, religious, and political groups.

Lured to the United States by cheap land and by Americans' receptivity to experiments, Owen confidently predicted that by 1827 the northern states would embrace the principles embodied in New Harmony. By 1827 there was little left to embrace, for the community, a magnet for idlers and fanatics, had quickly fallen apart. Owen had clashed with clergymen, who still believed that original sin, not environment, shaped human character. Yet Owenism survived the wreckage of New Harmony. The notions that human character was formed by environment and that cooperation was superior to competition had a potent impact on urban workers for the next half-century. Owen's ideas, for example, impelled workingmen's leaders to support educational reform during the late 1820s.

Experimental communities with names like Hopedale, Fruitlands, and Brook Farm proliferated amid the economic chaos of the late 1830s and 1840s. Brook Farm, near Boston, was the creation of a group of religious philosophers called transcendentalists. Most transcendentalists, including Ralph Waldo Emerson, had started as Unitarians but then sought to revitalize Christianity by proclaiming the infinite spiritual capacities of ordinary men and women. Like other utopias, Brook Farm was both a retreat and a model. Certain that the competitive commercial life of the cities was unnatural, philosophers spent their evenings in lofty musings after a day perspiring in the cabbage patch. Brook Farm attracted several renowned writers, including Emerson and Nathaniel Hawthorne, and its literary magazine, *The Dial*, became a forum for transcendentalist ideas about philosophy, art, and literature (also see Chapter 11).

The most controversial of the antebellum utopian communities, the Oneida community established in 1848 in New York state by John Humphrey Noyes, challenged conventional notions of religion, property, gender

roles, sex, dress, and motherhood. Renouncing private property, Oneidans practiced communism. Noyes insisted that men perform kitchen duties, and allowed women to work in the community's stores and factories. But what most upset outsiders was Noyes's application of communism to marriage. After exchanging wives with one of his followers, Noyes proclaimed that at Oneida all women would be married to all men and all men to all women. A committee of elders headed by "Father" Noyes decided on sexual pairings for procreation.

Contemporaries dismissed Noyes, who was also an abolitionist, as a licentious crackpot. Southerners cited him to prove that antislavery ideals threatened civilization itself. Yet Oneida achieved considerable economic prosperity and attracted new members long after less-radical utopias like Brook Farm had collapsed. By embracing communism in marriage, Oneidans had burned their bridges to society and had little choice but to stay together.

Widely derided as fit only for eccentrics, antebellum utopias nevertheless exemplified in extreme form the idealism and hopefulness that permeated nearly all reform in the Age of Jackson.

CONCLUSION

The voice of the common people resounded through politics during the 1820s and 1830s. As barriers to the direct expression of the popular will such as property requirements for voting and the indirect election of presidential electors collapsed, the gentlemanly leadership and surface harmony of the Era of Good Feelings gave way to the raucous huzzahs of mass political parties. A similar development transformed American religion. Mass revivals swelled the numbers of Methodists and Baptists, denominations that de-emphasized an educated ministry, while Presbyterians and Congregationalists who insisted on an educated clergy declined in relative numbers. Calvinist clergymen found their doctrine of human depravity hammered by popular revivalists' stress on Americans' capacity to remake themselves.

The louder the people spoke, the less unified they became. The cries of "foul" that had enveloped the election of 1824 catapulted Andrew Jackson as the embodiment of the popular will. But Jackson's seemingly dictatorial manner and his stands on internal improvements, tariffs, nullification, and banking divided the electorate and contributed to the emergence of the Whig party. The Panic of 1837 deepened party divisions by shoving wavering Democrats toward a hard-money, antibank position. Similarly, revivals, which aimed to unite Americans in a

CHRONOLOGY, 1824–1840

1824 John Quincy Adams elected president by the House of Representatives.
1826 American Temperance Society organized.
1828 Andrew Jackson elected president.
 "Tariff of Abominations."
 John Calhoun anonymously writes *South Carolina Exposition and Protest.*
1830 Jackson's Maysville Road Bill veto.
 Indian Removal Act.
1830–1831 Charles G. Finney's Rochester revival.
1831 William Lloyd Garrison starts *The Liberator.*
1832 Jackson vetoes recharter of the Bank of the United States.
 Jackson reelected president.
 South Carolina Nullification Proclamation.
1833 Force Bill.
 Compromise Tariff.
 American Anti-Slavery Society founded.
 South Carolina nullifies the Force Bill.
1834 Whig party organized.
1836 Specie Circular.
 Martin Van Buren elected president.
1837 Horace Mann becomes secretary of the Massachusetts Board of Education.
 Elijah Lovejoy murdered by proslavery mob.
 Grimké sisters set out on lecture tour of New England.
1837–1843 Economic Depression
1838 Garrison's New England Non-Resistance Society founded.
 Sarah Grimké's *Letters on the Condition of Women and the Equality of the Sexes* and Angelina Grimké's *Letters to Catharine E. Beecher.*
1840 Independent Treasury Act passed.
 William Henry Harrison elected president.
 First Washington Temperance Society started.
1841 Dorothea Dix begins exposé of prison conditions.
 Brook Farm Community founded.
1848 Seneca Falls Convention.

religion of the heart, spawned critics of religious excess (Unitarians) and indirectly gave rise to hotly controversial religious groups (Mormons).

Seeded in part by religious revivals, a variety of reform movements also sprouted in the 1820s and 1830s. Such causes as women's rights and the abolition of slavery promised legal equality for groups excluded

from participation in politics. The spread of reform movements also underscored the anxieties of Americans faced with the uncertainties of the commercial economy. In an unsettling age, many Americans sought to forge order out of seeming chaos. Reformers did not hesitate to coerce people into change by calling for the legal prohibition of liquor and for compulsory education. For criminals they devised highly repressive institutions designed to bring out the basic goodness of human nature. Both reformers and politicians sought to slay the demons that threatened the Republic. Often disdaining politics as corrupt, reformers blasted liquor, ignorance, and slavery with the same fervor Jacksonians directed at banks and monopolies. Yet reformers who called for the legal prohibition of liquor and the reform of public education or who organized an abolitionist political party were reluctantly acknowledging that in a mass democracy everything sooner or later became political.

FOR FURTHER REFERENCE

READINGS

For additional works, please consult bibliography at the end of the book. Lee Benson, *The Concept of Jacksonian Democracy: New York as a Test Case* (1961). A major revisionist interpretation of the period.

Catherine A. Brekus, *Strangers and Pilgrims: Female Preaching in America, 1740–1845* (1998). An informative overview of how female preachers shaped religious practices in early America.

Donald B. Cole, *The Presidency of Andrew Jackson* (1993). Fine account incorporating the latest scholarship.

William W. Freehling, *Prelude to Civil War* (1966). A major study of the nullification crisis.

Michael F. Holt, *The Rise and Fall of the American Whig Party* (1999). A comprehensive and masterful study.

Richard R. John, *Spreading the News: The American Postal System from Franklin to Morse* (1995). Provides excellent insight into the role of communications in the public life of American democracy.

Paul E. Johnson and Sean Wilentz, *The Kingdom of Matthias* (1994). A significant attempt to illuminate issues of urbanization, gender, and class during the 1820s and 1830s through an investigation of the career of a cult leader, Matthias the Prophet.

Steven Mintz, *Moralists and Modernizers* (1995). A clearly written overview that stresses the modernizing features of antebellum reform movements.

Robert V. Remini, *Henry Clay: Statesman for the Union* (1991). An important biography of the leading Whig statesman of the period.

Arthur M. Schlesinger, Jr., *The Age of Jackson* (1945). A classic study, now dated in some of its interpretations but still highly readable.

Chilton Williamson, *American Suffrage: From Property to Democracy, 1760–1860* (1960). The standard study of changing requirements for voting.

WEBSITES

Andrew Jackson and the Bankwar
http://odur.let.rug.nl/%7Eusa/Ebankwar/bankwarxx.htm
This site introduces the reader to the principal actors and events in Jackson's war against the Bank of the United States

The Reform Impulse
http://www.learner.org/biographyofamerica/prog08/index/html
A valuable guide to several reform movements, including abolition and women's rights.

The Shakers
http://www.shakerworkshops.com/shakers.htm
This site contains information on Shaker history, production, and rules.

Tales of the Early Republic
http://216.202.17.223/
An excellent site for an overview of political and cultural developments in the Jacksonian era.

First State Election in Michigan

CHAPTER 11

Technology, Culture, and Everyday Life, 1840–1860

Isaac M. Singer's life was not going well in 1850. Thirty-nine and often penniless, he had been an unsuccessful actor, stage hand, ticket seller, carpenter, and inventor. His early inventions had been clever, but not much in demand. Having deserted his wife and children, he promised marriage to lure Mary Ann Sponslor into living with him. Mary Ann tried to please him, nursing him when he was sick and even taking up acting, but to no avail. Instead of marrying her, Singer often beat her, and he would have affairs with several other women during the 1850s. But by 1860 Singer had grown fabulously wealthy. In 1850 he had come upon and quickly improved a sewing machine similar to one patented in 1846 by Elias Howe, Jr.

Here was a machine that everyone wanted; sewing-machine designers were practically bumping into each other at the patent office. The rise of the New England textile industry in the 1820s had spurred the development of the ready-made clothing industry, but the textile factories did not stitch pieces of fabric together to make clothes. Rather, factories contracted sewing out to young women who stitched fabric by hand in their homes. Sewing was both a business that employed women and a social activity that women cherished. Even fashionable ladies with no need to earn cash formed sewing circles to finish or mend their families' wardrobes, to make garments for the poor, and to chat.

◀ **Chess Game, mid-1860s**
Elegance and refinement, once reserved for the wealthy, came within the reach of the middle-class Americans in the 1840s and the 1850s, thanks to improvements in the technology of manufacturing.

CHAPTER OUTLINE

Technology and Economic Growth

The Quality of Life

Democratic Pastimes

The Quest for Nationality in Literature and Art

Stitching by hand took as long as three hours for a pair of pants and seven hours for a calico dress. In contrast, a pair of pants could be stitched by machine in thirty-eight minutes, and a calico dress in fifty-seven minutes. But the early sewing machines, themselves hand-made, were expensive; in 1851 the largest sewing machine company could turn out only 700 to 800 sewing machines a year. The number jumped to 21,000 by 1859 and to 174,000 by 1872. What made this huge increase possible was the adaptation to sewing-machine manufacturing of machine tools which had recently been devised for the manufacture of pistols and revolvers (see Culture and Technology: Guns and Gun Culture).

Having adapted machine tools from gun factories in order to speed production, sewing-machine makers then pioneered new ways to market their machines. In 1856 a company formed by Singer initiated installment buying—five dollars down and small monthly payments—to speed the sale of sewing machines.

Contemporaries could not praise sewing machines enough. Most of the machines were sold to factories. By saving time, they made clothing cheaper, and they gave a terrific boost to the ready-made clothing industry. The *New York Tribune* predicted that, with the spread of sewing machines, people "will dress better, change oftener, and altogether grow better looking." This upbeat response to technological change was typical of the 1850s. Many Americans believed that *technology*, a word coined in 1829 to describe the application of science to improving the conveniences of life, was God's chosen instrument of progress. Just as the *Tribune* predicted that sewing machines would create a nation "without spot or blemish," others forecast that the telegraph, another invention of the age, would usher in world peace.

Yet progress had a darker side. Revolvers were useless for hunting and of little value in battle, but excellent for the violent settling of private scores. The farmwomen who had traditionally earned money sewing by hand in their homes gradually gave way to women who sewed by machine in small urban factories that came to be labeled sweatshops for their gruesome conditions. Philosophers and artists began to worry about the despoliation of the landscape by the very factories that made guns and sewing machines, and conservationists launched conscious efforts to preserve enclaves of nature as parks and retreats safe from progress.

This chapter focuses on five major questions:

- What technological improvements increased the productivity of American industry between 1840 and 1860?

- In what ways did technology transform the daily lives of ordinary Americans between 1840 and 1860?

- Technological change contributed to new kinds of national unity and also to new forms of social division. What were the main unifying features of technology? The principal dividing or segmenting features?

- How did the ways in which Americans passed their spare time change between 1840 and 1860?

- What did American writers and artists see as the distinguishing features of their nation? How did their views of American distinctiveness find expression in literature, painting, and landscape architecture?

TECHNOLOGY AND ECONOMIC GROWTH

Widely hailed as democratic, the benefits of technology drew praise from all sides. Conservatives like Daniel Webster praised machines for doing the work of ten people without consuming food or clothing, while Sarah Bagley, a Lowell mill operative and labor organizer, traced the improvement of society to the development of technology.

The technology that transformed life in antebellum America included the steam engine, the cotton gin, the reaper, the sewing machine, and the telegraph. Some of these originated in Europe, but Americans had a flair for investing in others' inventions and perfecting their own. Improvements in Eli Whitney's cotton gin between 1793 and 1860, for example, led to an eightfold increase in the amount of cotton that could be ginned in a day. Of course, technology did not benefit everyone. Improvements in the cotton gin served to rivet slavery more firmly in place by making the South more dependent on cotton. Technology also rendered many traditional skills obsolete and thereby undercut the position of artisans. But technology contributed to improvements in transportation and increases in productivity, which in turn lowered commodity prices and raised the living standards of a sizable body of free Americans between 1840 and 1860.

Agricultural Advancement

Although few settlers ventured onto the treeless, semi-arid Great Plains before the Civil War, settlements edged westward after 1830 from the woodlands of Ohio and Kentucky into parts of Indiana, Michigan, and Illinois, where flat grasslands (prairies) alternated with forests.

The prairie's matted soil was difficult to break for planting, but in 1837 John Deere invented a steel-tipped plow that halved the labor to clear acres to till. Timber for housing and fencing was available in nearby woods, and settlements spread rapidly.

Wheat became to midwestern farmers what cotton was to their southern counterparts. "The wheat crop is the great crop of the North-west, for exchange purposes," an agricultural journal noted in 1850. "It pays debts, buys groceries, clothing and lands, and answers more emphatically the purposes of trade among farmers than any other crop." Technological advances sped the harvesting as well as the planting of wheat on the midwestern prairies. Using the traditional hand sickle consumed huge amounts of time and labor, all the more so because cut wheat had to be picked up and bound. Since the eighteenth century, inventors in Europe had experimented with horse-drawn machines to replace sickles. But until Cyrus McCormick came on the scene, the absence of the right combination of technical skill and business enterprise had relegated mechanical reapers to the realm of tinkerers' dreams.

In 1834 McCormick, a Virginian, patented a mechanical reaper that drew on and improved previous designs. Opening a factory in Chicago in 1847, McCormick mass produced reapers and introduced aggressive marketing techniques such as deferred payments and money-back guarantees. By harvesting grain seven times more rapidly than traditional methods and with half the labor force, the reaper guaranteed the pre-eminence of wheat on the midwestern prairies of Illinois, Indiana, Iowa, and Missouri. McCormick sold 80,000 reapers by 1860, and during the Civil War he made immense profits by selling more than 250,000.

Ironically, just as a Connecticut Yankee, Eli Whitney, had stimulated the foundation of the Old South's economy by his invention of the cotton gin, Cyrus McCormick, a proslavery southern Democrat, would help the North win the Civil War. The North provided the main market for McCormick's reaper and for the models of his many competitors; the South, with its reliance on slave labor, had far less incentive to mechanize agriculture. The reaper would keep northern agricultural production high at a time when labor shortages caused by troop mobilization might otherwise have slashed production.

Although Americans proved resourceful at inventing and marketing machines to speed planting and harvesting, they farmed wastefully. With land abundant, farmers were more inclined to look for virgin soil than to improve "worn out" soil. But a movement for agricultural improvement in the form of more efficient use of the soil did develop before 1860, mainly in the East.

Confronted by the superior fertility of western soil, easterners who did not move west or take jobs in factories increasingly experimented with new agricultural techniques. In Orange County, New York, for example,

"Lagonda Agricultural Workers" by Edwin Forbes, 1859

The manufacture of agricultural implements was becoming a major industry by 1860. Now the farmers shown on the fringe could put down their scythes and let the mechanical reaper do the work.

Guns and Gun Culture

Even in the early 1800s some Americans painted an image of their countrymen as expert marksmen. A popular song attributed the American victory at the Battle of New Orleans in 1815 to the sharpshooting skills of the Kentucky militia. Yet Andrew Jackson, who commanded American forces in the battle, thought otherwise, and historians have agreed with him. Accurate guns were the exception in 1815 and for decades afterward. Balls exited smooth-bore muskets at unpredictable angles and started to tumble after fifty or sixty yards. In 1835 Jackson himself, now president, became a beneficiary of another feature of guns: their unreliability. A would-be assassin fired two single-shot pistols at Jackson at point-blank range. Both misfired.

It was not just the inaccuracy and unreliability of guns that made the sword and bayonet preferred weapons in battle. Guns were expensive. A gunsmith would count himself fortunate if he could turn out twenty a year; at the Battle of New Orleans, less than one-third

Gun Machinery

During the 1850s machinery greatly accelerated the production of guns. Shown here are a machine for making gun stocks and a jigging machine. The jigging machine had a large revolving wheel, to which were attached different cutting tools used to shape the gun lock frames.

of the Kentucky militia had any guns, let alone guns that worked.

Believing that the safety of the republic depended on a well-armed militia, Thomas Jefferson was keenly interested in finding ways to manufacture guns more rapidly. As president-elect in 1801 he witnessed a demonstration by Eli Whitney, the inventor of the cotton gin, of guns manufactured on the new principle of interchangeable parts. If each part of a gun could be machine-made and then fitted smoothly into the final product, there would be no need for the laborious methods of the skilled gunsmith. In Jefferson's presence, Whitney successfully fitted ten different gun locks, one after another, to one musket, using only a screwdriver.

Eager to stave off the impending bankruptcy of his cotton-gin business, Whitney had already accepted a federal contract to manufacture ten thousand muskets by 1800. His demonstration persuaded Jefferson that, although Whitney had yet to deliver any muskets, he could do the job. What Jefferson did not know was that Whitney cheated on the test: he already had hand-filed each lock so that it would fit. It would be another eight years before Whitney finally delivered the muskets.

Whitney's problem was that as late as 1820 no machines existed that could make gun parts with sufficient precision to be interchangeable. During the 1820s and 1830s, however, John Hall, a Maine gunsmith, began to construct such machines at the federal arsenal at Harpers Ferry, Virginia. Hall devised new machines for drilling cast-steel gun barrels, a variety of large and small drop hammers for pounding pieces of metal into shape, and new tools for cutting metal (called milling machines). With improvements by others during the 1840s and 1850s, these machine tools made it possible to achieve near uniformity, and hence interchangeability, in the parts of guns.

At first, Hall's innovations had little effect since the army was scaling back its demand for guns in the 1830s. The outbreak of war with Mexico in 1846 marked a turning point. Ten years earlier, a Connecticut inventor, Samuel

Colt, had secured a patent for a repeating pistol with a rotating chambered-breech, usually called a revolver. At the start of the Mexican-American War, Colt won a federal contract to provide the army with one thousand revolvers. These proved to be of negligible value during the war, but Colt, a masterful publicist, was soon traveling the globe and telling all that his revolvers had won the war.

Eager to heighten the revolver's appeal to Americans, Colt made use of a recent invention, called a gramma-graph, that engraved the same design repeatedly on steel. On the cylinders of his revolvers he impressed images of frontiersmen using their Colt pistols to heroically protect their wives and children from savage Indians.

In contrast to Hall, a man more interested in making than selling guns, Colt had a genius for popularizing gun ownership, not just on the frontier but also among respectable citizens in the East. He gave away scores of specially engraved revolvers to politicians and War Department officials, and he invited western heroes to dine at his Hartford, Connecticut, mansion. New England quickly became the center of a flourishing American gun industry. By 1860 nearly 85 percent of all American guns were manufactured there. By 1859 Colt had cut the price of a new revolver from fifty dollars to nineteen dollars.

As guns became less expensive, they became the weapon of choice for both the military and street toughs. At the Astor Place Riot in 1849 (discussed later), soldiers from New York's Seventh Regiment fired a volley that killed twenty-two people, the first time that militia fired on unarmed citizens. Murderers, who traditionally had gone about their business with knives and clubs, increasingly turned to guns. In the 1850s a surge in urban homicides usually caused by guns led to calls for gun control. In 1857 Baltimore became the first city to allow its police to use firearms. Confronted with an outbreak of gang war-fare the same year, some New York police captains authorized their men to carry guns. No longer a luxury, guns could be purchased by ordinary citizens in new stores that sold only guns and accessories, forerunners of the modern gun supermarket.

Most states had laws barring blacks from owning guns. Women rarely purchased them. But for white American men, owning guns and knowing how to use them increasingly became a mark of manly self-reliance. Samuel Colt did all he could to encourage this attitude. When the home of a Hartford clergyman was burglarized in 1861, Colt promptly sent the clergyman "a copy of my latest work on 'Moral Reform,'" a Colt revolver. Two years earlier Dan Sickles, a New York congressman, had created a sensation by waylaying his wife's lover, Philip Barton Key (the son of the author of the "Star-Spangled Banner"), across the street from the White House. Armed

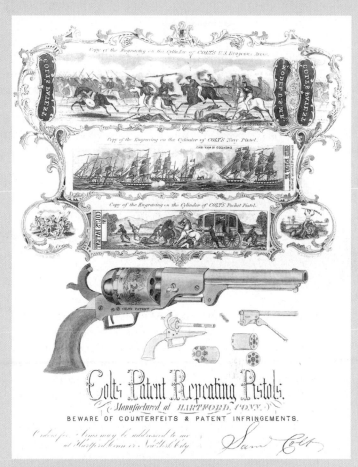

Samuel Colt's Advertising Broadside
A masterful promoter, Samuel Colt saw to it that the cylinders of his revolving pistols were engraved with scenes promoting the use of firearms: the cavalry routing Indians; warships exchanging fire; coach passengers shooting highway robbers.

with two pistols and shouting that Key was a "scoundrel" who had dishonored Sickles's marriage bed, Sickles shot the unarmed Key four times in front of several witnesses, killing him with the final shot. A notorious womanizer, Sickles had repeatedly cheated on his wife, but his behavior struck many men as justifiable. President James Buchanan, a political ally, paid one witness to disappear. Eventually, Sickles was acquitted of murder on the grounds of "temporary insanity." He continued to climb the ladder of politics and in 1863 he led a regiment at the Battle of Gettysburg.

Focus Question:

- Historians of technology remind us that innovations have often been linked, that an invention in one sphere gives rise to inventions in related spheres. How did this principle operate in the history of gun manufacture?

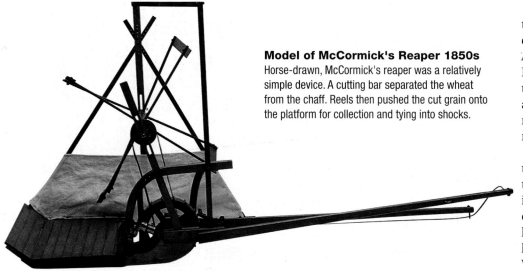

Model of McCormick's Reaper 1850s
Horse-drawn, McCormick's reaper was a relatively simple device. A cutting bar separated the wheat from the chaff. Reels then pushed the cut grain onto the platform for collection and tying into shocks.

farmers fed their cows the best clover and bluegrass and emphasized cleanliness in the processing of dairy products. Through these practices, they produced a superior butter that commanded more than double the price of ordinary butter. Still other eastern farmers turned to the use of fertilizers to keep their wheat production competitive with that of the bountiful midwestern prairies. By fertilizing their fields with plaster left over from the construction of the James River Canal, Virginia wheat growers raised their average yield per acre to fifteen bushels by the 1850s, up from only six bushels in 1800. Similarly, during the 1840s American cotton planters began to import guano, left by the droppings of sea birds on islands off Peru, for use as fertilizer. Fertilizer helped eastern cotton farmers close the gap created by the superior fertility of southwestern soil for cotton.

Technology and Industrial Progress

Industrial advances between 1840 and 1860 owed an immense debt to the nearly simultaneous development of effective machine tools, power-driven machines that cut and shaped metal. In the early 1800s Eli Whitney's plan to manufacture muskets by using interchangeable parts made by unskilled workers was stalled by the absence of machine tools. Such tools were being developed in Britain in Whitney's day, but Americans were near strangers to them until the 1830s. By the 1840s precise machine tools had greatly reduced the need to hand-file parts to make them fit, and they were applied to the manufacture of firearms, clocks, and sewing machines. By 1851 Europeans had started to refer to manufacture by interchangeable parts as the "American System." In 1853 a small-arms factory in England reequipped itself with machine tools manufactured by

two firms in the backwoods of Vermont. After touring American factories in 1854, a British engineer concluded that Americans "universally and willingly" resorted to machines as a substitute for manual labor.

The American manufacturing system had several distinctive advantages. Traditionally, damage to any part of a mechanical contrivance had rendered the whole useless, for no new part would fit. With the perfection of manufacturing by interchangeable parts, however, replacement parts could be obtained. In addition, the improved machine tools upon which the American System depended enabled entrepreneurs to push inventions swiftly into mass production. The likelihood that inventions would quickly enter production attracted investors. By the 1850s Connecticut firms like Smith and Wesson were mass-producing the revolving pistol, which Samuel Colt had invented in 1836. Sophisticated machine tools made it possible, a manufacturer wrote, to increase production "by confining a worker to one particular limb of a pistol until he had made two thousand."

After Samuel F. B. Morse transmitted the first telegraph message from Baltimore to Washington in 1844, Americans also seized enthusiastically on the telegraph's promise to eliminate the constraints of time and space. The speed with which Americans formed telegraph companies and strung lines stunned a British engineer, who noted in 1854 that "no private interests can oppose the passage of a line through any property." Although telegraph lines usually transmitted political and commercial messages, some cities adapted them for reporting fires. By the early 1850s, Boston had an elaborate system of telegraph stations that could alert fire companies throughout the city to a blaze in any neighborhood. By 1852 more than fifteen thousand miles of lines connected cities as distant as Quebec, New Orleans, and St. Louis.

The Railroad Boom

Even more than the telegraph, the railroad dramatized technology's democratic promise. In 1790 even European royalty could travel no faster than fourteen miles an hour and that only with frequent changes of

horses. By 1850 an ordinary American could travel three times as fast on a train, and in considerable comfort. American railroads offered only one class of travel, in contrast to the several classes on European railroads. With the introduction of adjustable upholstered seats that could serve as couches at night, Americans in effect traveled first class except for African-Americans who often were forced to sit separately.

Americans loved railroads "as a lover loves his mistress," one Frenchman wrote, but there was little to love about the earliest railroads. Sparks from locomotives showered passengers riding in open cars, which were common. In the absence of brakes, passengers often had to get out and pull trains to stop them. Lacking lights, trains rarely ran at night. Before the introduction of standard time zones in 1883, scheduling was a nightmare; at noon in Boston it was twelve minutes before noon in New York City. Delays were frequent, for trains on single-track lines had to wait on sidings for oncoming trains to pass. Because a train's location was a mystery once it left the station, these waits could seem endless.

Between 1840 and 1860 the size of the rail network and the power and convenience of trains underwent a stunning transformation. Railroads extended track from three thousand to thirty thousand miles; flat-roofed coaches replaced open cars; kerosene lamps made night travel possible; and increasingly powerful engines let trains climb steep hills. Fifty thousand miles of telegraph wire enabled dispatchers to communicate with trains en route and thus to reduce delays.

Woman at Singer Sewing Machine
Asked to repair a sewing machine that did not do continuous stitching, Isaac M. Singer invented one that did. Patented in 1851, the Singer machine quickly dominated the market. Although most early sewing machines were used in factories, some had made their way into households by 1860.

The First Railroad Train on the Mohawk and Hudson Road
With its small engine and coaches instead of cars to carry passengers, this train was typical of the earliest American railroads.

Nonetheless, problems lingered. Sleeping accommodations remained crude, and schedules erratic. Because individual railroads used different gauge track, frequent changes of train were necessary; eight changes interrupted a journey from Charleston to Philadelphia in the 1850s. Yet nothing slowed the advance of railroads or cured Americans' mania for them. By 1860 the United States had more track than all the rest of the world.

Railroads spearheaded the second phase of the transportation revolution. Canals remained in use; the Erie Canal, for example, did not reach its peak volume until 1880. But railroads, faster and less vulnerable to winter freezes, gradually overtook them, first in passengers and then in freight. By 1860 the value of goods transported by railroads greatly surpassed that carried by canals.

As late as 1860, few rail lines extended west of the Mississippi, but railroads had spread like spider webs east of the great river. The railroads turned southern cities like Atlanta and Chattanooga into thriving commercial hubs. Most important, the railroads linked the East and the Midwest. The New York Central and the Erie Railroads joined New York City to Buffalo; the

MAP 11.1
Railroad Growth, 1850–1860
Rail ties between the East and the Midwest greatly increased during the railroad "boom" of the 1850s.

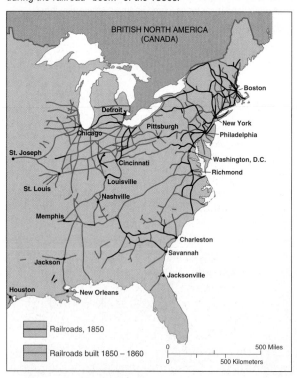

Pennsylvania Railroad connected Philadelphia to Pittsburgh; and the Baltimore and Ohio linked Baltimore to Wheeling, Virginia (now West Virginia). Simultaneously, intense construction in Ohio, Indiana, and Illinois created trunk lines that tied these routes to cities farther west. By 1860 rail lines ran from Buffalo to Cleveland, Toledo, and Chicago; from Pittsburgh to Fort Wayne; and from Wheeling to Cincinnati and St. Louis (see Map 11.1).

Chicago's growth illustrates the impact of these rail links. In 1849 it was a village of a few hundred people with virtually no rail service. By 1860 it had become a city of one hundred thousand served by eleven railroads. Farmers in the Upper Midwest no longer had to ship their grain, livestock, and dairy products down the Mississippi to New Orleans; they could now ship products directly east. Chicago supplanted New Orleans as the interior's main commercial hub.

The east-west rail lines stimulated the settlement and agricultural development of the Midwest. By 1860 Illinois, Indiana, and Wisconsin had replaced Ohio, Pennsylvania, and New York as the leading wheat-growing states. Enabling farmers to speed their products to the East, railroads increased the value of farmland and promoted additional settlement. In turn, population growth triggered industrial development in cities such as Chicago; Davenport, Iowa; and Minneapolis, for the new settlers needed lumber for fences and houses and mills to grind wheat into flour.

Railroads also propelled the growth of small towns along their routes. The Illinois Central Railroad, which had more track than any other railroad in 1855, made money not only from its traffic but also from real estate speculation. Purchasing land for stations along its path, the Illinois Central then laid out towns around the stations. The selection of Manteno, Illinois, as a stop on the Illinois Central, for example, transformed the site from a crossroads without a single house in 1854 into a bustling town of nearly a thousand in 1860, replete with hotels, lumberyards, grain elevators, and gristmills. (The Illinois Central even dictated the naming of streets. Those running east and west were always named after trees, and those running north and south were numbered. Soon one rail town looked much like the next.) By the Civil War, few thought of the railroad-linked Midwest as a frontier region or viewed its inhabitants as pioneers.

As the nation's first big business, the railroads transformed the conduct of business. During the early 1830s, railroads, like canals, depended on financial aid from state governments. With the onset of depression in the late 1830s, however, state governments scrapped overly

ambitious railroad projects. Convinced that railroads burdened them with high taxes and blasted hopes, voters turned against state aid, and in the early 1840s, several states amended their constitutions to bar state funding for railroads and canals. The federal government took up some of the slack, but federal aid did not provide a major stimulus to railroads before 1860. Rather, part of the burden of finance passed to city and county governments in agricultural areas that wanted to attract railroads. Municipal governments, for example, often gave railroads rights-of-way, grants of land for stations, and public funds.

The dramatic expansion of the railroad network in the 1850s, however, strained the financing capacity of local governments and required a turn toward private investment, which had never been absent from the picture. Well aware of the economic benefits of railroads, individuals living near them had long purchased railroad securities issued by governments and had directly bought stock in railroads, often paying by contributing their labor to building the railroads. But the large railroads of the 1850s needed more capital than such small investors could generate.

Gradually, the center of railroad financing shifted to New York City. In fact, it was the railroad boom of the 1850s that helped make Wall Street the nation's greatest capital market. The securities of all the leading railroads were traded on the floor of the New York Stock Exchange during the 1850s. In addition, the growth of railroads turned New York City into the center of modern investment firms. The investment firms evaluated the securities of railroads in Toledo or Davenport or Chattanooga and then found purchasers for these securities in New York, Philadelphia, Paris, London, Amsterdam, and Hamburg. Controlling the flow of funds to railroads, investment bankers began to exert influence over the railroads' internal affairs by supervising administrative reorganizations in times of trouble. A Wall Street analyst noted in 1851 that railroad men seeking financing "must remember that money is power, and that the [financier] can dictate to a great extent his own terms."

Rising Prosperity

Technological advances also improved the lives of consumers by bringing down the prices of many commodities. For example, clocks that cost $50 to fabricate by hand in 1800 could be produced by machine for fifty cents by 1850. In addition, the widening use of steam power contributed to a 25 percent rise in the average worker's real income (actual purchasing power) between 1840 and 1860. Early-nineteenth-century factories, which had depended on water wheels to propel their machines, had to shut down when the rivers or streams that powered the wheels froze. With the spread of steam engines, however, factories could stay open longer, and workers could increase their annual wages by working more hours. Cotton textile workers were among those who benefited: although their hourly wages showed little gain, their average annual wages rose from $163 in 1830 to $176 in 1849 to $201 by 1859.

The growth of towns and cities also contributed to an increase in average annual wages. Farmers experienced the same seasonal fluctuations as laborers in the early factories. In sparsely settled rural areas, the onset of winter traditionally brought hard times; as demand for agricultural labor slumped, few alternatives existed to take up the slack. "A year in some farming states such as Pennsylvania," a traveler commented in 1823, "is only of eight months duration, four months being lost to the laborer, who is turned away as a useless animal." In contrast, densely populated towns and cities offered more opportunities for year-round work. The urban dockworker thrown out of his job as a result of frozen waterways might find work as a hotel porter or an unskilled indoor laborer.

Towns and cities also provided women and children with new opportunities for paid work. (Women and children had long performed many vital tasks on farms, but rarely for pay.) The wages of children between the ages of ten and eighteen came to play an integral role in the nineteenth-century family economy. Family heads who earned more than six hundred dollars a year might have been able to afford the luxury of keeping their children in school, but most breadwinners were fortunate if they made three hundred dollars a year. Although the cost of many basic commodities fell between 1815 and 1860 (another consequence of the transportation revolution), most families lived close to the margin. Budgets of working-class families in New York City and Philadelphia during the early 1850s reveal annual expenditures of five hundred to six hundred dollars, with more than 40 percent spent on food, 25 to 30 percent on rent, and most of the remainder on clothing and fuel. Such a family could not survive on the annual wages of the average male head of the household. It needed the wages of the children and, at times, those of the wife as well.

Life in urban wage-earning families was not necessarily superior to life in farming communities. A farmer who owned land, livestock, and a house did not have to worry about paying rent or buying fuel for cooking and heating, and rarely ran short of food. Many Americans

continued to aspire to farming as the best of all occupations. But to purchase, clear, and stock a farm involved a considerable capital outlay that could easily amount to five hundred dollars, and the effort promised no rewards for a few years. The majority of workers in agricultural areas did not own farms and were exposed to seasonal fluctuations in demand for agricultural labor. In many respects, they were worse off than urban wage earners.

The economic advantages that attended living in cities help explain why so many Americans moved to urban areas during the first half of the nineteenth century. During the 1840s and 1850s cities also provided their residents with an unprecedented range of comforts and conveniences.

THE QUALITY OF LIFE

"Think of the numberless contrivances and inventions for our comfort and luxury," the poet Walt Whitman exclaimed, "and you will bless your star that Fate has cast your lot in the year of Our Lord 1857." Changes in what we now call the standard of living affected housing and such daily activities as eating, drinking, and washing in the 1840s and 1850s. The patent office in Washington was flooded with sketches of reclining seats, beds convertible into chairs, street-sweeping machines, and fly traps. Machine-made furniture began to trans-form the interiors of houses. Stoves revolutionized heating and cooking. Railroads brought fresh vegetables to city dwellers.

Despite all the talk of comfort and progress, however, many Americans experienced little improvement in the quality of their lives. Technological advances made it possible for the middle class to enjoy luxuries formerly reserved for the rich, but often widened the distance between the middle class and the poor. At a time when the interiors of urban, middle-class homes were becoming increasingly lavish, the urban poor congregated in cramped and unsightly tenements. In addition, some aspects of life remained relatively unaffected by scientific and technical advances. Medical science, for example, made a few advances before 1860, but none that rivaled the astonishing changes wrought by the railroad and the telegraph.

The benefits rather than the limitations of progress, however, gripped the popular imagination. Few Americans accepted the possibility that progress could neglect such an important aspect of everyday life as health. Confronted by the failure of the medical profession to rival the achievements of Cyrus McCormick and Samuel F. B. Morse, Americans embraced popular health movements that sprang up outside the medical profession and that promised to conquer disease by the precepts of diet and other health-related regimens.

Family Group
This daguerreotype, taken about 1852, reveals the little things so important to etching a middle-class family's social status: curtains; a wall hanging; a piano with scrolled legs; a small desk with elegantly curved legs; a pet; ladies posed in nonproductive but "improving" activities (music, reading); and a young man seemingly staring into space—and perhaps pondering how to pay for it all.

Dwellings

Whereas most city dwellers in the eighteenth century had lived in unattached frame houses, all of which looked different and faced in different directions, their nineteenth-century counterparts were more likely to inhabit brick row houses. Typically narrow and long, row houses were practical responses to rising urban land values (as much as 750 percent in Manhattan between 1785 and 1815).

Some praised row houses as democratic; others condemned "their extreme uniformity—when you have seen one, you have seen all." But they were not all alike. In the mid-nineteenth century, middle-class row houses were larger (3 to 3 1/2 stories) than working-class row houses (2 to 2 1/2 stories). In addition, soaring land values led to the subdividing of many row houses for occupancy by several families. The worst of these subdivided row houses were called tenements and became the usual habitats of Irish immigrants and free blacks.

The most fashionable urban residences usually surrounded small parks ringed by iron fences, and their addresses contained "Place" or "Square" rather than "Street." The wealthy also had a taste for elegant doors, curved staircases, carved columns, and rooms with fanciful, asymmetrical shapes. All of this was beyond the resources of the urban middle class, but the rise of mass production in such furniture centers as Grand Rapids, Michigan, and Cincinnati between 1840 and 1860 brought the so-called French antique, or rococo, furniture style within the financial reach of the middle class.

Rococo furniture was ornate. Upholstered chairs, for example, displayed intricate scrolls depicting vines, leaves, or flowers and rested on curved legs with ornamental feet (called cabriole legs). The heavily upholstered backs of sofas were often trimmed with floral designs topped by carved medallions. Mirrors with gilded moldings that depicted birds, flowers, and even young women frequently weighed so much that they threatened to tumble from walls. Technological advances in the fabrication of furniture tended to level taste between the middle and upper classes while simultaneously setting off those classes from everyone else.

In rural areas the quality of housing depended as much on the date of settlement as on social class. In recently settled areas, the standard dwelling was a rude one-room log cabin with planked floors, crude clay chimneys, and windows covered by oiled paper or cloth. As rural communities matured, log cabins gave way to frame houses of two or more rooms and better insula-tion. Most of these were balloon-frame houses. In place of foot-thick posts and beams laboriously fitted together, a balloon-frame house had a skeleton of thin-sawn timbers nailed together in such a way that every strain ran against the grain of the wood. The simplicity and cheapness of such houses endeared them to western builders who had neither the time nor the skill to cut and fit heavy beams.

Conveniences and Inconveniences

By today's standards, everyday life in the 1840s and 1850s was primitive, but contemporaries were struck by how much better it was becoming. The transportation and industrial revolutions were affecting heating, cooking, and diet. In urban areas where wood was expensive, coal-burning stoves were rapidly displacing open hearths for heating and cooking. Stoves made it possible to cook several dishes at once and thus contributed to the growing variety of the American diet, while railroads brought in fresh vegetables, which in the eighteenth century had been absent from even lavish banquet tables.

Too, contemporaries were struck by the construction of urban waterworks— systems of pipes and aqueducts that brought fresh water from rivers or reservoirs to street hydrants. In the 1840s New York City completed the Croton aqueduct, which carried water into the city from reservoirs to the north, and by 1860 sixty-eight public water systems operated in the United States.

Despite these improvements, newly acquired elegance still bumped shoulders with squalor. Coal burned longer and hotter than wood, but it left a dirty residue that polluted the air and blackened the snow, and a faulty coal stove could fill the air with poisonous carbon monoxide. Seasonal fluctuations continued to affect diets. Only the rich could afford fruit out of season, since they alone could afford to use sugar to preserve it. Indeed, preserving almost any kind of food presented problems. Home iceboxes were rare before 1860, so salt remained the most widely used preservative. One reason antebellum Americans ate more pork than beef was that salt affected pork's taste less negatively.

Although public waterworks were among the most impressive engineering feats of the age, their impact is easily exaggerated. Since the incoming water usually ended its trip at a street hydrant, and only a fraction of the urban population lived near hydrants, houses rarely had running water. Taking a bath required first heating the water, pot by pot, on a stove. A New

England physician claimed that not one in five of his patients took one bath a year.

Infrequent baths meant pungent body odors, which mingled with a multitude of strong scents. In the absence of municipal sanitation departments, street cleaning was let to private contractors who gained a reputation for slack performance of their duties, so urbanites relied on hogs, which they allowed to roam freely and scavenge. (Hogs that turned down the wrong street often made tasty dinners for the poor.) Stables backed by mounds of manure and outdoor privies added to the stench. Flush toilets were rare outside cities, and within cities sewer systems lagged behind water systems. Boston had only five thousand flush toilets in 1860 for a population of 178,000, a far higher ratio of toilets to people than most cities.

Expensive conveniences like running water and flush toilets became another of the ways in which

Fire Bucket

This ornamental fire bucket reveals the great pride that antebellum fire companies took in their work. They competed with each other to be first on the scene of a fire, so much so that they were accused of sometimes setting fires in order to claim credit for extinguishing them.

progress set the upper and middle classes apart from the poor. Conveniences also sharpened gender differences. In her widely popular *Treatise on Domestic Economy* (1841), Catharine Beecher told women that technological advances made it their duty to make every house a "glorious temple" by utilizing space more efficiently. Women who no longer made articles for home consumption were now expected to achieve fulfillment by obsessively sweeping floors and polishing furniture. Home, a writer proclaimed, had become woman's "royal court," where she "sways her queenly authority." Skeptical of this trend toward fastidiousness, another writer cautioned women in 1857 against "ultra-housewifery."

Disease and Health

Despite the slowly rising standard of living, Americans remained vulnerable to disease. Epidemics swept through antebellum cities and felled thousands. Yellow fever and cholera killed one-fifth of New Orleans's population in 1832–1833, and cholera alone carried off 10 percent of St. Louis's population in 1849.

The transportation revolution increased the peril from epidemics. The cholera epidemic of 1832, the first truly national epidemic, followed shipping routes: one branch of the epidemic ran from New York City up the Hudson River, across the Erie Canal to Ohio, and then down the Ohio River to the Mississippi and south to New Orleans; the other branch followed shipping up and down the East Coast from New York City.

Each major antebellum epidemic of cholera or yellow fever intensified public calls for the establishment of municipal health boards, and by the 1850s most major cities had formed such agencies. However, so few powers did city governments give them that the boards could not even enforce the reporting of diseases. The inability of physicians to find a satisfactory explanation for epidemic diseases led to a general distrust of the medical profession and contributed to making public health a low-priority issue.

Prior to 1860 no one understood that tiny organisms called bacteria caused both cholera and yellow fever. Rather, rival camps of physicians battled furiously and publicly over the merits of the "contagion" theory versus those of the "miasma" theory. Insisting that cholera and yellow fever were transmitted by touch, contagionists called for vigorous measures to quarantine affected areas. In contrast, supporters of the miasma theory argued that poisonous gases (miasmas) emitted by rotting vegetation or dead animals carried disease through

the air. The miasma theory led logically to the conclusion that swamps should be drained and streets cleaned.

Neither theory was consistent with the evidence. Quarantines failed to check cholera and yellow fever (an argument against the contagionist theory), and many residents of filthy slums and stinking, low-lying areas contracted neither of the two diseases (a refutation of the miasma theory). Confronted by this inconclusive debate between medical experts, municipal leaders refused to delegate more than advisory powers to health boards dominated by physicians. After the worst epidemic in the city's history, a New Orleans editor stated in 1853 that it was "much safer to follow the common sense and unbiased opinion of the intelligent mass of the people than the opinions of medical men ... based upon hypothetical theories."

Although most epidemic diseases baffled antebellum physicians, a basis for forward strides in surgery was laid during the 1840s by the discovery of anesthetics. Prior to 1840 young people often entertained themselves at parties by inhaling nitrous oxide, or "laughing gas," which produced sensations of giddiness and painlessness; and semicomical demonstrations of laughing gas became a form of popular entertainment. (Samuel Colt, the inventor of the revolver, had begun his career as a traveling exhibitor of laughing gas.) But nitrous oxide had to be carried around in bladders, which were difficult to handle, and in any case, few recognized its surgical possibilities. Then in 1842 Crawford Long, a Georgia physician who had attended laughing-gas frolics in his youth, employed sulfuric ether (an easily transportable liquid with the same properties as nitrous oxide) during a surgical operation. Long failed to follow up on his discovery, but four years later William T. G. Morton, a dentist, successfully employed sulfuric ether during an operation at Massachusetts General Hospital in Boston. Within a few years, ether came into wide use in American surgery.

The discovery of anesthesia improved the public image of surgeons, long viewed as brutes who hacked away at agonized patients. Furthermore, by making longer operations possible, anesthesia encouraged surgeons to take greater care than previously during surgery. Nevertheless, the failure of most surgeons to recognize the importance of clean hands and sterilized instruments partially offset the benefits of anesthesia before 1860. In 1843 Boston physician and poet Oliver Wendell Holmes, Sr., published an influential paper on how the failure of obstetricians to disinfect their hands often spread a disease called puerperal fever among mothers giving birth in hospitals. Still, the medical profession only gradually accepted the importance of disinfection. Operations remained as dangerous as the diseases or wounds they tried to heal. The mortality rate for amputations hovered around 40 percent. During the Civil War, 87 percent of soldiers who suffered abdominal wounds died from them.

Popular Health Movements

Doubtful of medicine and cynical toward public health, antebellum Americans turned to a variety of therapies and regimens that promised to give them healthier and longer lives. One popular response to disease was hydropathy, or the "water cure," which filtered into the United States from Europe during the 1840s. By the mid-1850s the United States had twenty-seven hydropathic sanatoriums, which used cold baths and wet packs to provide "an abundance of water of dewy softness and crystal transparency, to cleanse, renovate, and rejuvenate the disease-worn and dilapidated system." The water cure held a special attraction for well-off women, partly because hydropathics professed to relieve the pain associated with childbirth and menstruation and partly because hydropathic sanatoriums were congenial gathering places in which middle-class women could relax and exercise in private.

In contrast to the water cure, which necessitated the time and expense of a trip to a sanatorium, a health system that anyone could adopt was propounded by Sylvester Graham, a temperance reformer turned popular health advocate. Alarmed by the 1832 cholera epidemic, Graham counseled changes in diet and regimen as well as total abstinence from alcohol. Contending that Americans ate too much, he urged them to substitute vegetables, fruits, and coarse, whole-grain bread (called Graham bread) for meat and to abstain from spices, coffee, and tea as well as from alcohol. Soon Graham added sexual "excess" (by which he meant most sex) to his list of forbidden indulgences. Vegetables were preferable to meat, according to Graham, because they provoked less hunger. The food cravings of the "flesh-eater" were "greater and more imperious" than those of the vegetarian.

Many of Graham's most enthusiastic disciples were reformers. Grahamites had a special table at the Brook Farm community. Until forced out by indignant parents and hungry students, one of Graham's followers ran the student dining room at reformist Oberlin College. Much like Graham, reformers traced the evils of American society to the unnatural cravings of its people. Abolitionists, for example, contended that slavery inten-

sified white men's lust and contributed to the violent behavior of white southerners. Similarly, Graham believed that eating meat stimulated lust and other aggressive impulses.

Graham's doctrines attracted a broad audience that extended beyond the perimeters of the reform movements. Many towns and cities had boarding houses whose tables were set according to his principles. His books sold well, and his public lectures were thronged. Like hydropathy, Grahamism addressed the popular desire for better health at a time when orthodox medicine seemed to do more damage than good. Graham

"The Illustrated Phrenological Almanac, 1859"

By dividing the brain into a large number of "faculties," phrenologists like Lorenzo Fowler, editor of the Phrenological Almanac for 1859, made the point that each person, regardless of whether born high or low, had an abundance of improvable talents.

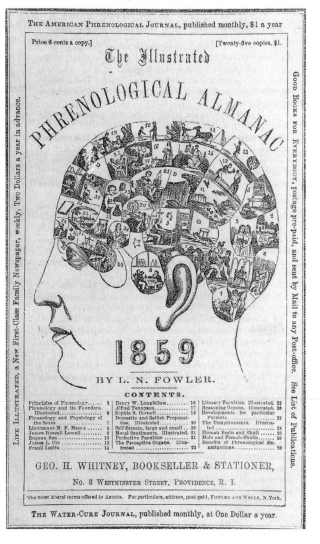

used religious phrases that were familiar to churchgoers and then channeled those concepts toward nonreligious goals. Luxury was "sinful," disease resembled hell, and health was a kind of heaven on earth. In this way, he provided simple and familiar assurances to an audience as ignorant as he was of the true causes of disease.

Phrenology

The belief that each person was master of his or her own destiny underlay not only evangelical religion and popular health movements but also the most popular of the antebellum scientific fads: phrenology. Imported from Europe, phrenology rested on the idea that the human mind comprised thirty-seven distinct faculties, or "organs," each located in a different part of the brain. Phrenologists thought that the degree of each organ's development determined skull shape, so that they could analyze a person's character by examining the bumps and depressions of the skull.

In the United States two brothers, Orson and Lorenzo Fowler, became the chief promoters of phrenology in the 1840s. Originally intending to become a Protestant missionary, Orson Fowler became instead a missionary for phrenology and opened a publishing house in New York City (Fowler and Wells) that mass-marketed books on the subject. The Fowlers' critics were legion, but so were their responses to criticism. Accused of propounding a godless philosophy, they pointed to a part of the brain called "Veneration" to prove that people were naturally religious, and they answered charges that phrenology was pessimistic by claiming that exercise could improve every desirable mental organ. Lorenzo Fowler reported that several of his skull bumps had actually grown. Orson Fowler wrapped it all into a tidy slogan: "Self-Made, or Never-Made."

Phrenology appealed to Americans as a "practical" science. In a mobile, individualistic society, it promised a quick assessment of others. Some merchants used phrenological charts to pick suitable clerks, and some women even induced their fiancés to undergo phrenological analysis before tying the knot.

Phrenologists had close ties to popular health movements. Fowler and Wells published the *Water-Cure Journal* and Sylvester Graham's *Lectures on the Science of Human Life*. Orson Fowler filled his phrenological book with tips on the evils of coffee, tea, meat, spices, and sex that could have been plucked from Graham's writings.

Easily understood and practiced and filled with the promise of universal betterment, phrenology was ideal for antebellum America. Just as Americans had invented

machines to better their lives, so did they invent "sciences" that promised human betterment.

DEMOCRATIC PASTIMES

Between 1830 and 1860 technology increasingly transformed leisure by making Americans more dependent on recreation that could be manufactured and sold. People purchased this commodity in the form of cheap newspapers and novels as well as affordable tickets to plays, museums, and lectures.

Just as the Boston Associates had daringly capitalized on new technology to produce textiles at Lowell and Waltham, imaginative entrepreneurs utilized technology to make and sell entertainment. Men like James Gordon Bennett, one of the founders of the penny press in America, and P. T. Barnum, the greatest showman of the nineteenth century, amassed fortunes by sensing what people wanted and employing available technology to satisfy their desires. Bennett and Barnum thought of themselves as purveyors of democratic entertainment. They would sell their wares cheaply to anyone.

Technology also ignited the process by which individuals became spectators rather than creators of their own amusements. Americans had long found ways to enjoy themselves. Even the gloomiest Puritans had indulged in games and sports. After 1830, however, the burden of providing entertainment began to shift from individuals to entrepreneurs who supplied ways to entertain the public.

Newspapers

In 1830 the typical American newspaper was a mere four pages long, with the front and back pages devoted almost wholly to advertisements. The second and third pages contained editorials, details of ship arrivals and cargoes, reprints of political speeches, and notices of political events. Few papers depended on their circulation for profit; even the most prominent papers had a daily circulation of only one thousand to two thousand. Rather, papers often relied on subsidies from political parties or factions. When a party gained power, it inserted paid political notices only in papers loyal to it. "Journalists," a contemporary wrote, "were usually little more than secretaries dependent upon cliques of politicians, merchants, brokers, and office seekers for their prosperity and bread."

As a result, newspapers could be profitable without being particularly popular. Because of their potential for profit, new papers were constantly being established.

But most had limited appeal. The typical paper sold for six cents an issue at a time when the average daily wage was less than a dollar. Papers often seemed little more than published bulletin boards. They typically lacked the exciting news stories and eye-catching illustrations that later generations would take for granted.

The 1830s witnessed the beginnings of a stunning transformation. Technological changes, most of which originated in Europe, vastly increased both the supply of paper (still made from rags) and the speed of printing presses. The substitution of steam-driven cylindrical presses for flatbed hand presses led to a tenfold increase in the number of printed pages that could be produced in an hour. Enterprising journalists, among them the Scottish-born James Gordon Bennett, grasped the implications of the new technology. Newspapers could now rely on vast circulation rather than on political subsidies to turn a profit. To gain circulation, journalists like Bennett slashed the price of newspapers. In 1833 the *New York Sun* became America's first penny newspaper, and Bennett's *New York Herald* followed in 1835. By June 1835 the combined daily circulation of New York's three penny papers reached 44,000; in contrast, the city's eleven dailies had a combined daily circulation of only 26,500 before the dawn of the penny press in 1833. Spearheaded by the penny papers, the combined daily circulation of newspapers throughout the nation rose from roughly 78,000 in 1830 to 300,000 by 1840. The number of weekly newspapers spurted from 65 in 1830 to 138 in 1840.

Affordability was not the only feature of the penny papers. Dependent on circulation and advertising rather than on subsidies, the penny press revolutionized the marketing and format of papers. Where single copies of the six-cent papers were usually available only at the printer's office, newsboys hawked the penny papers on busy street corners. Moreover, the penny papers subordinated the recording of political and commercial events to human-interest stories of robberies, murders, rapes, and abandoned children. They dispatched reporters to police courts and printed transcripts of trials. As sociologist Michael Schudson observes, "The penny press invented the modern concept of 'news.'" Rather than merely recording events, the penny papers wove events into gripping stories. They invented not only news but also news reporting. Relying on party stalwarts to dispatch copies of speeches and platforms, and reprinting news items from other papers, the older six-cent papers did little, if any, reporting. In contrast, the penny papers employed their own correspondents and were the first papers to use the telegraph to speed news into print.

Some penny papers were little more than scandal sheets, but the best, like Bennett's *New York Herald* and Horace Greeley's *New York Tribune* (1841), pioneered modern financial and political reporting. From its inception, the *Herald* contained a daily "money article" that substituted the analysis and interpretation of financial events for the dull recording of commercial facts. "The spirit, pith, and philosophy of commercial affairs is what men of business want," Bennett wrote. The relentless snooping of the *Tribune's* Washington reporters outraged politicians. In 1848 *Tribune* correspondents were temporarily barred from the House floor for reporting that Representative Sawyer of Ohio ate his lunch (sausage and bread) each day in the House chamber, picked his teeth with a jackknife, and wiped his greasy hands on his pants and coat.

The Theater

Like newspapers, theaters increasingly appealed to a mass audience. Antebellum theaters were large (twenty-five hundred to four thousand seats in some cities) and crowded by all classes. With seats as cheap as twelve cents and rarely more than fifty cents, the typical theater audience included lawyers and merchants and their wives, artisans and clerks, sailors and noisy boys, and a sizable body of prostitutes. Prostitutes usually sat in the top gallery, called the third tier, "that dark, horrible, guilty" place. The presence of prostitutes in theaters was taken for granted; the only annoyance came when they left the third tier to solicit customers in the more expensive seats.

The prostitutes in attendance were not the only factor that made the antebellum theater vaguely disreputable. Theatrical audiences were notoriously rowdy. They showed their feelings by stamping their feet, whistling, hooting at villains, and throwing potatoes or garbage at the stage when they did not like the characters or the acting. Individual actors developed huge followings, and the public displayed at least as much interest in the actors as in the plays. In 1849 a long-running feud between the leading American actor, Edwin Forrest, and popular British actor William Macready ended with a riot at New York City's Astor Place that left twenty-two people dead.

The Astor Place riot demonstrated the broad popularity of the theater. Forrest's supporters included Irish workers who loathed the British and appealed to the "working men" to rally against the "aristocrat" Macready. Macready, who projected a more polished and intellectual image than Forrest, attracted the better-educated classes. Had not all classes patronized the theater, the deadly riot probably would never have occurred.

The plays themselves were as diverse as the audiences. Most often performed were melodramas in which virtue was rewarded, vice punished, and the heroine married the hero. Yet the single most popular dramatist was William Shakespeare. In 1835 audiences in Philadelphia witnessed sixty-five performances of Shakespeare's plays. Americans who may never have read a line of Shakespeare grew familiar with Othello, King Lear, Desdemona, and Shylock. Theatrical managers adapted Shakespeare to a popular audience. They highlighted the sword fights and assassinations, cut some speeches, omitted minor characters, and pruned words or references that might have offended the audience's sense of propriety. For example, they substituted *pottels* for *urinals* and quietly advanced Juliet's age at the time that she falls in love with Romeo from fourteen to eighteen. They occasionally changed sad endings to happy ones.

The producers even arranged for short performances or demonstrations between acts of Shakespeare—and indeed, of every play. During such an interlude, the audience might have observed a brief impersonation of Tecumseh or Aaron Burr, jugglers and acrobats, a drummer beating twelve drums at once, or a three-year-old who weighed a hundred pounds.

Minstrel Shows

The Yankee or "Brother Jonathan" figure who served as a stock character in many antebellum plays helped audiences form an image of the ideal American as rustic, clever, patriotic, and more than a match for city slickers and decadent European blue bloods. In a different way, the minstrel shows that Americans thronged to see in the 1840s and 1850s forged enduring stereotypes that buttressed white Americans' sense of superiority by diminishing black people.

Minstrel shows arose in northern cities in the 1840s when white men in blackface took to the stage to present an evening of songs, dances, and humorous sketches. Minstrelsy borrowed some authentic elements of African-American culture, especially dances characterized by the sliding, shuffling step of southern blacks, but most of the songs had origins in white culture. Such familiar American songs as Stephen Foster's "Camptown Races" and "Massa's in the Cold Ground," which first aired in minstrel shows, reflected white Americans' notions of how blacks sang more than it represented authentic black music.

In addition, the images of blacks projected by minstrelsy both catered to and reinforced the prejudices of the working-class whites who dominated the audience of minstrel shows. Minstrel troupes usually depicted blacks as stupid, clumsy, and obsessively musical and emphasized the Africanness of blacks by giving their characters names like the Ethiopian Serenaders and their acts titles like the Nubian Jungle Dance and the African Fling. At a time of intensifying political conflict over race, minstrel shows planted images and expectations about blacks' behavior through stock characters. These included Uncle Ned, the tattered, humble, and docile slave, and Zip Coon, the arrogant urban free black who paraded around in a high hat, long-tailed coat, and green vest and who lived off his girlfriends' money. Minstrels lampooned blacks who assumed public roles by portraying them as incompetent stump speakers who called Patrick Henry "Henry Patrick," referred to John Hancock as "Boobcock," and confused the word *statute* with *statue*.

By the 1850s major cities from New York to San Francisco had several minstrel theaters. Touring professional troupes and local amateur talent even brought minstrelsy to small towns and villages. Mark Twain recalled how minstrelsy had burst upon Hannibal, Missouri, in the early 1840s as "a glad and stunning surprise." So popular was the craze that minstrels even visited the White House and entertained Presidents John Tyler, James K. Polk, Millard Fillmore, and Franklin Pierce.

Dan Bryant, the Minstrel
Bryant was one of many antebellum popularizers of black minstrelsy. One of the earliest known minstrelsy performances occurred in Boston in 1799, when the white man Gottlieb Graupner, reportedly made up as a black, sang and accompanied himself on the banjo.

P. T. Barnum

P. T. Barnum understood how to turn the antebellum public's craving for entertainment into a profitable business. As a young man in Bethel, Connecticut, he started a newspaper, the *Herald of Freedom*, that assailed wrongdoing in high places. Throughout his life, he thought of himself as a public benefactor and pointed to his profits as proof that he gave people what they wanted. Yet honesty was never his strong suit. As a small-town grocer in Connecticut, he regularly cheated his customers on the principle that they were trying to cheat him. Barnum, in short, was a hustler raised in the land of the Puritans, a cynic and an idealist rolled into one.

After moving to New York City in 1834, Barnum started a new career as an entrepreneur of popular entertainment. His first venture exhibited a black woman, Joice Heth, whom Barnum billed as the 169-year-old former slave nurse of George Washington. Barnum neither knew nor cared how old Joice was (in

fact, she was probably around 80); it was enough that people would pay to see her. Strictly speaking, he cheated the public, but he knew that many of his customers shared his doubts about Joice's age. Determined to expose Barnum's gimmick, some poked her to see whether she was really a machine rather than a person. He was playing a game with the public, and the public with him.

In 1841 Barnum purchased a run-down museum in New York City, rechristened it the American Museum, and opened a new chapter in the history of popular entertainment. The founders of most earlier museums had educational purposes. They exhibited stuffed birds and animals, specimens of rock, and portraits. Most of these museums had languished for want of public interest. Barnum, in contrast, made pricking public curiosity the main goal. To attract people, he added collections of curiosities and faked exhibits. Visitors to the American Museum could see ventriloquists, magicians, albinos, a five-year-old person of short-stature whom Barnum

Tom Thumb
Barnum helped to arrange the 1863 wedding of "General" Tom Thumb and another person of short-stature in his employ, Lavinia Warren. On their wedding tour, Tom and Lavinia visited President Abraham Lincoln in the White House.

named General Tom Thumb and later took on a tour of Europe, and the "Feejee Mermaid," a shrunken oddity that Barnum billed as "positively asserted by its owner to have been taken alive in the Feejee Islands." By 1850 the American Museum had become the best-known museum in the nation and a model for popular museums in other cities.

Blessed with a genius for publicity, Barnum recognized that newspapers could invent as well as report news. One of his favorite tactics was to puff his exhibits by writing letters (under various names) to newspapers in which he would hint that the scientific world was agog over some astonishing curiosity of nature that the public could soon see for itself at the American Museum. But Barnum's success rested on more than publicity. A staunch temperance advocate, he provided regular lectures at the American Museum on the evils of alcohol

and soon gave the place a reputation as a center for safe family amusement. By marketing his museum as family entertainment, Barnum helped break down barriers that had long divided the pastimes of husbands from those of their wives.

Finally, Barnum tapped the public's insatiable curiosity about natural wonders. In 1835 the editor of the *New York Sun* had boosted his circulation by claiming that a famous astronomer had discovered pelicans and winged men on the moon. At a time when each passing year brought new technological wonders, the public was ready to believe in anything, even the Feejee Mermaid.

THE QUEST FOR NATIONALITY IN LITERATURE AND ART

Europeans took little notice of American poetry or fiction before the 1820s. "Who ever reads an American book?" a British literary critic taunted in 1820. Americans responded by pointing to Washington Irving, whose *Sketch Book* (1820) contained two famous stories, "Rip Van Winkle" and "The Legend of Sleepy Hollow." Naming hotels and steamboats after Irving, Americans soaked him in applause, but they had to concede that Irving had done much of his best writing, including the *Sketch Book*, while living in England.

After 1820 the United States experienced a flowering of literature that is sometimes called the "American Renaissance." The leading figures of this Renaissance included James Fenimore Cooper, Ralph Waldo Emerson, Henry David Thoreau, Margaret Fuller, Walt Whitman, Nathaniel Hawthorne, Herman Melville, and Edgar Allan Poe. In 1800 American authors accounted for a negligible proportion of the output of American publishers. By 1830, 40 percent of the books published in the United States were written by Americans; by 1850 this had increased to 75 percent.

Not only were Americans writing more books; increasingly, they sought to depict the features of their nation in literature and art. The quest for a distinctively American literature especially shaped the writings of Cooper, Emerson, and Whitman. It also revealed itself in the majestic paintings of the so-called Hudson River school, the first home-grown American movement in painting, and in the landscape architecture of Frederick Law Olmsted.

Roots of the American Renaissance

Two broad developments, one economic and the other philosophical, contributed to this development. First,

the transportation revolution created a national market for books, especially fiction. Initially, this worked to the advantage of British authors, especially Sir Walter Scott. With the publication of *Waverley* (1814), a historical novel set in Britain of the 1740s, Scott's star began its spectacular ascent on the American horizon. Americans named more than a dozen towns Waverley; advertisements for Scott's subsequent novels bore the simple caption, "By the author of *Waverley*." Scott's success demonstrated that the public wanted to read fiction. Although American publishers continued to pirate British novels (reprinting them without paying copyright fees), Scott's success prompted Americans like James Fenimore Cooper to write fiction for sale.

Second, the American Renaissance reflected the rise of a philosophical movement known as romanticism. By insisting that literature reveal the longings of an individual author's soul, romanticism challenged the eighteenth-century view, known as classicism, that standards of beauty were universal. For the classicist, the ideal author was an educated gentleman who wrote elegant poetry and essays that displayed learning and refinement and that conformed to timeless standards of taste and excellence. In contrast, romantics expected a literary work to be emotionally charged, a unique reflection of its creator's inner feelings.

The emergence of a national market for books and the influence of romanticism combined to democratize literature. The conventions of classicism led writers to view literature as a pastime of gentlemen. They were to write only for one another (and never for profit) and use literature as a vehicle for displaying their learning, especially their knowledge of ancient Greek and Roman civilization. In contrast, the emerging national market for books tended to elevate the importance of fiction, a comparatively democratic form of literature, more than poetry and essays. Writing (and reading) fiction did not require a knowledge of Latin and Greek or a familiarity with ancient history and mythology. Significantly, many of the best-selling novels of the antebellum period—for example, Harriet Beecher Stowe's *Uncle Tom's Cabin*—were written by women, who were still barred from higher education. In addition, fiction had a certain subversive quality that contributed to its popularity. Authors could create unconventional characters, situations, and outcomes. The essay usually had an unmistakable conclusion. In contrast, the novel left more room for interpretation by the reader. A novel might well have a lesson to teach, but the reader's interest was likely to be aroused less by the moral than by the development of characters and plot.

Cooper, Emerson, Thoreau, Fuller, and Whitman

James Fenimore Cooper was the first important figure in this literary upsurge. His most significant innovation was to introduce a distinctively American fictional character, the frontiersman Natty Bumppo ("Leatherstocking"). In *The Pioneers* (1823), Natty appears as an old man settled on the shores of Lake Otsego in upstate New York. A hunter, Natty blames farmers for the wanton destruction of game and for turning the majestic forests into deserts of tree stumps. As a spokesman for nature against the march of civilization, Natty immediately became a popular figure, and in subsequent novels such as *The Last of the Mohicans* (1826), *The Pathfinder* (1840), and *The Deerslayer* (1841), Cooper unfolded Natty's earlier life for an appreciative reading public.

Although he wrote no novels, Ralph Waldo Emerson emerged in the late 1830s as the most influential spokesman for American literary nationalism. As the leading light of the transcendentalist movement, an American offshoot of romanticism, Emerson broke with the traditional view that ideas arise from the toil of human reason, which gathers evidence from the senses. Rather, he contended, our ideas of God and freedom are inborn; knowledge resembles sight—an instantaneous and direct perception of truth. That being so, Emerson concluded, learned people enjoy no special advantage in pursuing truth. All persons can glimpse the truth if only they trust the promptings of their hearts.

Transcendentalist doctrine pointed to the exhilarating conclusion that the United States, a young and democratic society, could produce as noble a literature and art as the more traditional societies of Europe. "Our day of dependence, our long apprenticeship to the learning of other lands draws to a close," Emerson announced in his address "The American Scholar" (1837). The time had come for Americans to trust themselves. Let "the single man plant himself indomitably on his instincts and there abide," he proclaimed, and "the huge world will come around to him."

Emerson admired Cooper's fiction but his own version of American literary nationalism was expressed mainly in his essays, which mixed broad themes—"Beauty," "Wealth," and "Representative Men"—with pungent and vivid language. For example, he wrote in praise of independent thinking that the scholar should not "quit his belief that a popgun is a popgun, though the ancient and honorable of the earth affirm it to be the crack of doom." Equally remarkable was Emerson's way of developing his subjects. A contemporary compared

Margaret Fuller
Disappointed that his first child was a girl, Margaret Fuller's father decided to educate her as if she were a boy. As a child, she wrecked her health studying Latin, English, and French classics. She joined Ralph Waldo Emerson's circle of transcendentalists. In 1846 Horace Greeley sent her to Europe as the *Tribune's* foreign correspondent. There she met artists and writers, observed the Revolutions of 1848, and married an Italian nobleman. On her return to America in 1850, she, her husband, and infant son died in a shipwreck off Long Island.

revenue, he knew, would support the war with Mexico, which he viewed as part of a southern conspiracy to extend slavery. The experience led Thoreau to write "Civil Disobedience" (1849), in which he defended a citizen's right to disobey unjust laws.

In spring 1845 Thoreau moved a few miles from Concord to the woods near Walden Pond. There he constructed a cabin on land owned by Emerson and spent parts of the next two years providing for his wants away from civilization. His stated purpose in retreating to Walden was to write a description (later published) of a canoe trip that he and his brother had taken in 1839. During his stay in the woods, however, he conceived and wrote a much more important book, *Walden* (1854). A contemporary described *Walden* as "the logbook of his woodland cruise," and indeed, Thoreau filled its pages with descriptions of hawks and wild pigeons, his invention of raisin bread, his trapping of the woodchucks that ate his vegetable garden, and his construction of a cabin for exactly $28.50. But true to transcendentalism, Thoreau had a larger message. His rustic retreat taught him that he (and by implication, others) could satisfy material wants with only a few weeks' work each year and thereby leave more time for reexamining life's purpose. The problem with Americans, he said, was that they turned themselves into "mere machines" to acquire wealth without asking why. Thoreau bore the uncomfortable truth that material and moral progress were not as intimately related as Americans liked to think.

Among the most remarkable figures in Emerson's circle, Margaret Fuller's status as an intellectual woman distanced her from conventional society. Disappointed that his first child was not a boy, her Harvard-educated father, a prominent Massachusetts politician, determined to give Margaret the sort of education a male child would have acquired at Harvard. Drilled by her father in Latin and Greek, her reading branched into modern German romantics and the English literary classics. Her exposure to Emerson's ideas during a sojourn in Concord in 1836 pushed her toward transcendentalism, with its vindication of the free life of the spirit over formal doctrines and of the need for each person to discover truth on his or her own.

Ingeniously, Fuller turned transcendentalism into an occupation of sorts. Between 1839 and 1844 she sup-

listening to Emerson to trying to see the sun in a fog; one could see light but never the sun itself. Believing that knowledge reflected God's voice within each person and that truth was intuitive and individual, he never amassed persuasive evidence or presented systematic arguments to prove his point. Rather, he relied on a sequence of vivid if unconnected assertions whose truth the reader would instantly see. (They did not always see it; one reader complained that she might have understood Emerson better if she had stood on her head.)

Emerson had a magnetic attraction for intellectually inclined young men and women who did not fit neatly into American society. In the 1830s several of them gathered in Concord, Massachusetts, to share Emerson's intellectual pursuits. Henry David Thoreau was representative of the younger Emersonians. A crucial difference separated the two men. Adventurous in thought, Emerson was not adventurous in action. Thoreau was more of a doer. At one point he went to jail rather than pay his poll tax. This

ported herself by presiding over "Conversations" for fee-paying participants drawn from Boston's elite men and women. Transcendentalism also influenced her classic of American feminism, *Woman in the Nineteenth Century* (1845). Breaking with the prevailing notion of separate spheres for men and women, Fuller contended that no woman could achieve the kind of personal fulfillment lauded by Emerson unless she developed her intellectual abilities and overcame her fear of being called masculine.

One of Emerson's qualities was an ability to sympathize with such dissimilar people as the reclusive and critical Thoreau, the scholarly and aloof Fuller, and the outgoing and earthy Walt Whitman. Self-taught and in love with virtually everything about America except slavery, Whitman left school at eleven and became a printer's apprentice and later a journalist and editor for various newspapers in Brooklyn, Manhattan, and New Orleans. A familiar figure at Democratic party functions, he marched in party parades and put his pen to the service of its antislavery wing.

Journalism and politics gave Whitman an intimate knowledge of ordinary Americans; the more he knew them, the more he liked them. His reading of Emerson nurtured his belief that America was to be the cradle of a new citizen in whom natural virtue would flourish unimpeded by European corruption, a man like Andrew Jackson, that "massive, yet most sweet and plain character." The threads of Whitman's early career came together in his major work *Leaves of Grass*, a book of poems first published in 1855 and reissued with additions in subsequent years.

Leaves of Grass shattered most existing poetic conventions. Not only did Whitman write in free verse (that is, most of his poems had neither rhyme nor meter), but the poems were also lusty and blunt at a time when delicacy reigned in the literary world. Whitman wrote of "the scent of these armpits finer than prayer" and "winds whose soft-tickling genitals rub against me." No less remarkably, Whitman intruded himself into his poems, one of which he titled "Song of Walt Whitman" (and later retitled "Song of Myself"). Although Whitman thought well of himself, it was not egotism that moved him to sing of himself. Rather, he viewed himself—crude, plain, self-taught, and passionately democratic—as the personification of the American people. He was

Comrade of raftsmen and coalmen, comrade of all who shake hands and welcome to drink and meat,

A learner with the simplest, a teacher of the thoughtfullest.

By 1860 Whitman had acquired a considerable reputation as a poet. Nevertheless, the original edition of *Leaves* (a run of only about eight hundred copies) was ignored or derided as a "heterogeneous mass of bombast, egotism, vulgarity, and nonsense." One reviewer suggested that it was the work of an escaped lunatic. Only Emerson and a few others reacted enthusiastically. Within two weeks of publication, Emerson, never having met Whitman, wrote, "I find it the most extraordinary piece of wit and wisdom that America has yet contributed." Emerson had long called for the appearance of "the poet of America" and knew in a flash that in Whitman was that poet.

Hawthorne, Melville, and Poe

Emerson, Fuller, Thoreau, and Whitman expressed themselves in essays and poetry. In contrast, two major writers of the 1840s and 1850s—Nathaniel Hawthorne and Herman Melville—primarily wrote fiction, and another, Edgar Allan Poe, wrote both fiction and poetry. Although they were major contributors to the American Renaissance, Hawthorne, Melville, and Poe paid little heed to Emerson's call for a literature that would comprehend the everyday experiences of ordinary Americans. Hawthorne, for example, set *The Scarlet Letter* (1850) in New England's Puritan past, *The House of the Seven Gables* (1851) in a mansion haunted not by ghosts but by memories of the past, and *The Marble Faun* (1859) in Rome. Poe set several of his short stories such as "The Murders in the Rue Morgue" (1841), "The Masque of the Red Death" (1842), and "The Cask of Amontillado" (1846) in Europe; as one critic has noted, "His art could have been produced as easily had he been born in Europe." Melville did draw materials and themes from his own experiences as a sailor and from the lore of the New England whaling industry, but for his novels *Typee* (1846), *Omoo* (1847), and *Mardi* (1849) he picked the exotic setting of islands in the South Seas; and for his masterpiece *Moby-Dick* (1851) the ill-fated whaler *Pequod*. If the only surviving documents from the 1840s and 1850s were its major novels, historians would face an impossible task in describing the appearance of antebellum American society.

The unusual settings favored by these three writers partly reflected their view that American life lacked the materials for great fiction. Hawthorne, for example, bemoaned the difficulty of writing about a country "where there is no shadow, no antiquity, no mystery, no picturesque and gloomy wrong, nor anything but a commonplace prosperity in broad and simple daylight, as is

Edgar Allan Poe
Hounded by poverty, Poe scratched out a living as an ill-paid "magazinist." Today, his reputation easily outdistances that of many of his better-paid contemporaries.

happily the case with my dear native land." In addition, psychology rather than society fascinated the three writers; each probed the depths of the human mind rather than the intricacies of social relationships. Their preoccupation with analyzing the mental states of their characters grew out of their underlying pessimism about the human condition. Emerson, Whitman, and (to a degree) Thoreau optimistically believed that human conflicts could be resolved if only individuals followed the promptings of their better selves. In contrast, Hawthorne, Melville, and Poe saw individuals as bundles of conflicting forces that, despite the best intentions, might never be reconciled.

Their pessimism led them to create characters obsessed by pride, guilt, a desire for revenge, or a quest for perfection and then to set their stories along the byways of society, where they would be free to explore the complexities of human motivation without the jarring intrusion of everyday life. For example, in *The Scarlet Letter* Hawthorne turned to the Puritan past in order to examine the psychological and moral consequences of the adultery committed by Hester Prynne and the minister Arthur Dimmesdale. So completely did

Hawthorne focus on the moral dilemmas of his central characters that he conveyed little sense of the social life of the Puritan village in which the novel is set. Melville, who dedicated *Moby-Dick* to Hawthorne, shared the latter's pessimism. In the novel's Captain Ahab, Melville created a frightening character whose relentless and futile pursuit of the white whale fails to fill the chasm in his soul and brings death to all of his mates save the narrator, Ishmael. Poe also channeled his pessimism into creative achievements. In perhaps his finest short story, "The Fall of the House of Usher" (1839), he demonstrated an uncanny ability to weave the symbol of a crumbling mansion with the mental agony of a crumbling family.

Hawthorne, Melville, and Poe ignored Emerson's call to write about the everyday experiences of their fellow Americans. Nor did they follow Cooper's lead by creating distinctively American heroes. Yet each contributed to an indisputably American literature. Ironically, their conviction that the lives of ordinary Americans provided inadequate materials for fiction led them to create a uniquely American fiction marked less by the description of the complex social relationships of ordinary life than by the analysis of moral dilemmas and psychological states. In this way, they unintentionally fulfilled a prediction made by Alexis de Tocqueville that writers in democratic nations, while rejecting many of the traditional sources of fiction, would explore the abstract and universal questions of human nature.

Literature in the Marketplace

No eighteenth-century gentleman-author imagined that he was writing for the public or that he would make money from his literary productions. Such notions were unthinkable. That suspicion that commercialism corrupted art did not disappear during the American Renaissance. The shy and reclusive poet Emily Dickinson, who lived all of her fifty-six years on the same street in Amherst, Massachusetts ("I do not go from home," she wrote with characteristic pithiness) and who wrote exquisite poems that examined, in her words, every splinter in the groove of the brain, refused to publish her work. But in an age lacking university professorships or foundation fellowships for creative writers, authors were both tempted and often compelled to write for profit. For example, Poe, a heavy drinker always pressed for cash, scratched out a meager living writing short stories for popular magazines. Despite his reputation for aloof self-reliance, Thoreau craved recognition by the public and in 1843 tried, unsuccessfully, to market his poems in New York City. Only after meeting disap-

pointment as a poet did he turn to detailed narratives of nature, and these did prove popular.

Emerson, too, wanted to reach a broader public, and after abandoning his first vocation as a Unitarian minister he virtually invented a new one, that of "lyceum" lecturer. Lyceums, local organizations for sponsoring lectures, spread throughout the northern tier of states between the late 1820s and 1860; by 1840 thirty-five hundred towns had lyceums. Most of Emerson's published essays originated as lectures before lyceums in the Northeast and Midwest. He delivered some sixty speeches in Ohio alone between 1850 and 1867, and lecture fees provided him with his main form of income. Thanks to newly built railroads and cheap newspapers that announced their comings and goings, others followed in his path. Thoreau presented a digest of *Walden* as a lyceum lecture before the book itself was published. One stalwart of the lyceum circuit said that he did it for "F-A-M-E—Fifty and My Expenses," and Herman Melville pledged, "If they will pay my expenses and give a reasonable fee, I am ready to lecture in Labrador or on the Isle of Desolation off Patagonia."

The age offered women few opportunities for public speaking, and most lyceum lecturers were men. But women discovered ways to tap into the growing market for literature. Writing fiction was the most lucrative occupation open to women before the Civil War. For example, the popular novelist Susan Warner had been brought up in luxury and then tossed into poverty by the financial ruin of her father in the Panic of 1837. Writing fiction supplied her with cash as well as pleasure.

Warner and others benefited from advances in the technology of printing that brought down the price of books. Before 1830 the novels of Sir Walter Scott had been issued in three-volume sets that retailed for as much as thirty dollars. As canals and railroads opened crossroads stores to the latest fiction, publishers in New York and Philadelphia vied to deliver inexpensive novels to the shelves. By the 1840s cheap paperbacks that sold for as little as seven cents began to flood the market. Those who chose not to purchase books could read fiction in so-called story newspapers such as the *New York Ledger*, which was devoted mainly to serializing novels and which had an astonishing weekly circulation of four hundred thousand by 1860. In addition, the spread of (usually) coeducational public schools and academies contributed to higher literacy and a widening audience, especially among women, for fiction.

The most popular form of fiction in the 1840s and 1850s was the sentimental novel, a kind of women's fiction written by women about women and mainly for women. The tribulations of orphans and the deaths of children filled these tearjerkers. In Susan Warner's *The Wide, Wide World* (1850), the heroine weeps on an average of every other page for two volumes. But women's fiction dealt with more than the flow of tears. It challenged the image of males as trusty providers and of females as delicate dependents by portraying men as dissolute drunkards or vicious misers and women as resourceful and strong-willed. In the typical plot, a female orphan or spoiled rich girl thrown on hard times by a drunken father learned to master every situation. The moral was clear. Women could overcome trials and improve their worlds. Few of the novelists were active feminists, but their writings provide a glimpse into the private feelings of their female readers.

Such authors as Emerson, Hawthorne, Poe, and Melville, who now are recognized as major figures, had to swim in the sea of popular culture represented by the story newspapers and sentimental novels. Emerson, the intellectual, competed on the lecture circuit with P. T. Barnum, the showman. Hawthorne complained about the popularity of the "female scribblers." Poe thought that the public's judgment of a writer's merits was nearly always wrong. Indeed, the public did fail to see Melville's genius; the qualities of *Moby-Dick* were not widely recognized until the twentieth century. By and large, however, the major writers were not ignored by their society. Emerson's lectures made him famous. Hawthorne's *The Scarlet Letter* enjoyed respectable sales. Poe's poem "The Raven" (1844) was so popular that some suggested substituting the raven for the eagle as the national bird. What these writers discovered, sometimes the hard way, was that to make a living as authors they had to meet certain popular expectations. For example, *The Scarlet Letter* had greater popular appeal than *Moby-Dick* in part because the former told a love story while the latter, with its all-male cast and high-seas exploits, was simply not what the public looked for in a novel.

American Landscape Painting

American painters also sought to develop nationality in art between 1820 and 1860. Lacking the mythic past that European artists drew on—the legendary gods and goddesses of ancient Greece and Rome—Americans subordinated history and figure painting to landscape painting. Just as Hawthorne had complained about the flat, dull character of American society, so had the painters of the Hudson River school recognized that the American landscape lacked the European landscape's "poetry of decay" in the form of ruined castles and crumbling temples. Like everything else in the United States, the landscape was fresh, relatively untouched by the human

Cotopaxi
Frederick Church made extended trips in 1853 and 1857 to the Andean Mountains of Colombia and Ecuador. Majesty and tranquility mingle in this painting, considered Church's masterpiece, of smoke pouring from the massive volcano, Cotopaxi, and nearly obliterating the sinking sun.

imprint. This fact posed a challenge to the Hudson River school painters.

The Hudson River school flourished from the 1820s to the 1870s. Numbering more than fifty painters, it was best represented by Thomas Cole, Asher Durand, and Frederick Church. All three men painted scenes of the region around the Hudson River, a waterway that Americans compared in majesty to the Rhine. But none was exclusively a landscapist. Some of Cole's most popular paintings were allegories, including *The Course of Empire*, a sequence of five canvases depicting the rise and fall of an ancient city and clearly implying that luxury doomed republican virtue. Nor did these artists paint only the Hudson. Church, a student of Cole and internationally the best known of the three, painted the Andes Mountains during an extended trip to South America in 1853. After the Civil War, the German-born Albert Bierstedt applied many Hudson River school techniques in his monumental canvases of the Rocky Mountains.

The works of Washington Irving and the opening of the Erie Canal had sparked artistic interest in the Hudson during the 1820s. After 1830 the writings of Emerson and Thoreau popularized a new view of nature. Intent on cultivating land, the pioneers of Kentucky and Ohio had deforested a vast area. One traveler complained that Americans would rather view a wheat field or a cabbage patch than a virgin forest. But Emerson, Thoreau, and landscape architects like Frederick Law Olmsted glorified nature; "in wildness is the preservation of the world," Thoreau wrote. Their outlook blended with growing popular fears that, as one contemporary expressed it in 1847, "The axe of civilization is busy with our old forests." As the "wild and picturesque haunts of the Red Man" became "the abodes of commerce and the seats of civilization," he concluded, "it behooves our artists to rescue from its grasp the little that is left before it is too late."

The Hudson River painters wanted to do more than preserve a passing wilderness. Their special contribution to American art was to emphasize emotional effect over accuracy. Cole's use of rich coloring, billowing clouds, massive gnarled trees, towering peaks, and deep

The Author Painting a Chief at the Base of the Rocky Mountains, 1850

George Catlin's paintings preserved the faces, customs, and habitats of the Indian tribes whose civilization was collapsing in the face of white advance.

Rainmaking Among the Mandan, 1837–1839

Tchow-ee-put-o-kaw, 1834

chasms so heightened the dramatic impact of his paintings that the poet and editor William Cullen Bryant compared them to "acts of religion." Similar motifs marked Church's paintings of the Andes Mountains, which used erupting volcanoes and thunderstorms to evoke dread and a sense of majesty. Lacking the poignant antiquities that dotted European landscapes, the Americans strove to capture the natural grandeur of their own landscape.

Like Cole, the painter George Catlin also tried to preserve a vanishing America. Observing a delegation of Indians passing through Philadelphia in 1824, Catlin resolved on his life's work: to paint as many Native Americans as possible in their pure and "savage" state. Journeying up the Missouri River in 1832, he sketched at a feverish pace, and in 1837 he first exhibited his "Indian gallery" of 437 oil paintings and thousands of sketches of faces and customs from nearly fifty tribes.

Catlin's Indian paintings made him famous, but his romantic view of Indians as noble savages ("the Indian mind is a beautiful blank") was a double-edged sword. Catlin's admirers delighted in his portrayals of dignified Indians but shared his view that such noble creatures were "doomed" to oblivion by the march of progress.

While painters sought to preserve a passing America on canvas, landscape architects aimed at creating little enclaves of nature that might serve as sources of spiritual refreshment to harried city dwellers. Starting with the opening of Mount Auburn Cemetery near Boston in 1831, "rural" cemeteries with pastoral names such as "Harmony Grove" and "Greenwood" sprang up near major cities and quickly became tourist attractions, so much so that one orator described them as designed for the living rather than the dead. In 1858 New York City chose a plan drawn by Frederick Law Olmsted and Calvert Vaux for its proposed Central Park. Olmsted (who became the park's chief architect) and Vaux wanted the park to look as much like the countryside as possible, showing nothing of the surrounding city. A bordering line of trees screened out buildings, drainage pipes were dug to create lakes, and four sunken thoroughfares were cut across the park to carry traffic. The effect was to make Central Park an idealized version of nature, "picturesque" in that it would remind visitors of the landscapes that they had seen in pictures. Thus nature was made to mirror art.

CONCLUSION

Technological advances transformed the lives of millions of Americans between 1840 and 1860. The mechanical reaper increased wheat production and enabled agriculture to keep pace with the growing population. The development of machine tools, first in gun manufacture and next in the manufacturing of sewing machines, helped Americans achieve Eli Whitney's ideal

CHRONOLOGY, 1840–1860

1820 Washington Irving, *The Sketch Book.*
1823 Philadelphia completes the first urban water-supply system.
James Fenimore Cooper, *The Pioneers.*
1826 Cooper, *The Last of the Mohicans.*
1831 Mount Auburn Cemetery opens.
1832 A cholera epidemic strikes the United States.
1833 The *New York Sun*, the first penny newspaper, is established.
1834 Cyrus McCormick patents the mechanical reaper.
1835 James Gordon Bennett establishes the *New York Herald.*
1837 Ralph Waldo Emerson, "The American Scholar."
1841 P. T. Barnum opens the American Museum.
1842 Edgar Allan Poe, "The Murders in the Rue Morgue."
1844 Samuel F. B. Morse patents the telegraph.
Poe, "The Raven."
1846 W. T. G. Morton successfully uses anesthesia.
Elias Howe, Jr., patents the sewing machine.
1849 Second major cholera epidemic.
Astor Place theater riot leaves twenty dead.
1850 Nathaniel Hawthorne, *The Scarlet Letter.*
1851 Hawthorne, *The House of the Seven Gables.*
Herman Melville, *Moby-Dick.*
Erie Railroad completes its line to the West.
1852 Pennsylvania Railroad completes its line between Philadelphia and Pittsburgh.
1853 Ten small railroads are consolidated into the New York Central Railroad.
1854 Henry David Thoreau, *Walden.*
1855 Walt Whitman, *Leaves of Grass.*
1856 Pennsylvania Railroad completes Chicago link.
Illinois Central completed between Chicago and Cairo, Illinois.
1857 Baltimore-St. Louis rail service completed.
1858 Frederick Law Olmsted is appointed architect in chief for Central Park.

of production by interchangeable parts and made a range of luxuries affordable for the middle class. Steam power reduced the vulnerability of factories to the vagaries of the weather, stretched out the employment season, and increased productivity and income. The spread of railroads and the invention of the telegraph shrunk the barriers of space and time.

Many of these developments unified Americans. Railroad tracks threaded the nation together. The telegraph speeded communication and made it possible for Americans to read about the same current events in their newspapers. The advances in printing that gave birth to the penny press and the inexpensive novel contributed to a widening of the reading public. Not only were Americans now more able to read the same news items; increasingly, they read the same best-sellers, just as they flocked to the commercial amusements marketed by P. T. Barnum. Advocates of progress hailed these developments as instruments of ever-rising popular happiness. Even disease came to be seen less as a divine punishment for human depravity than as God's warning to those who ate or drank too much.

Progress carried a price. By bringing commodities once available only to the rich within the financial reach of the middle class, technology narrowed the social distance between these classes. At the same time, though, it set them off more sharply from the poor and intensified the division between the experiences of middle-class men and women. Progress also posed moral and spiritual challenges. The march of progress threatened to devour unspoiled nature. In different ways, writers like James Fenimore Cooper, Ralph Waldo Emerson, and Henry David Thoreau called attention to the conflict between nature and civilization as a distinctive feature of the American experience. Artists of the Hudson River school created majestic paintings of the natural wonders of the New World. For their part, Nathaniel Hawthorne and Herman Melville challenged the easy confidence that technology and democracy could liberate Americans from the dilemmas of the human condition.

FOR FURTHER REFERENCE

READINGS

Lawrence Buell, *New England Literary Culture* (1986). An excellent study of the relationship between writers and their culture.

Mary Kupiec Cayton, *Emerson's Emergence: Self and Society in the Transformation of New England, 1800–1845* (1989). A sensitive interpretation of the major figure in the American Renaissance.

Ruth S. Cowan, *A Social History of American Technology* (1997). An excellent survey.

Ann Douglas, *The Feminization of American Culture* (1977). An analysis of the role of middle-class women and liberal ministers in the cultural sphere during the nineteenth century.

Richard R. John, *Spreading the News: The American Postal System from Franklin to Morse* (1996). A revealing look at the age.

Judith A. McGaw, ed., *Early American Technology* (1994). A collection of fine essays on technology from the colonial era to 1850.

Barbara Novak, *Nature and Culture: American Landscape Painting, 1825–1875* (1982). An insightful study of the relationships between landscape painting and contemporary religious and philosophical currents.

Gwendolyn Wright, *Building the Dream: A Social History of Housing in America* (1981). An exploration of the ideologies and policies that have shaped American housing since Puritan times.

WEBSITES

The Industrial Revolution
http://www.learner.org/biographyofamerica/prog07/feature/index.html
This site contains useful maps of road, canal, and railroad development, 1830–1860.

Labor and Industry in Troy and Cohoes
http://www.albany.edu/history/troy-cohoes
Illuminates manufacturing and working conditions in two industrial centers on the upper Hudson River.

Tales of the Early Republic
http://216.202.17.223/
This site contains links to materials on science, technology, popular culture, and literature in the decades leading up to the Civil War.

For additional works please consult the Bibliography at the end of the book.

CHAPTER 12

The Old South and Slavery, 1830–1860

In the early morning hours of August 22, 1831, Nat Turner and six other slaves slipped into the house of Joseph Travis in Southampton County in Virginia's Southside region. Nat had been preparing for this moment since February, when he had interpreted a solar eclipse as a long-awaited sign from God that the time had come for him to lead his people against slavery by murdering slaveholders. Employing hatchets and axes, Nat and his band quickly slaughtered Travis, his wife Sally (the widow of a former owner of Nat), and two other whites in the house. Later, two of them returned to murder the Travis infant in its cradle. The Turner band then moved through the countryside, picking up muskets, horses, and recruits; shooting, clubbing, and hacking whites to death. Soon "General" Nat had more than forty followers. His hopes ran high. He knew that blacks outnumbered whites in Southampton, and his deeply religious strain, which had led the slaves to acknowledge him as a preacher and prophet, convinced him that God was his greatest ally.

By noon Turner's army, now grown to sixty or seventy followers, had murdered about sixty whites. As word of trouble spread, militia and vigilantes, thousands strong, poured into Southampton from across the border in North Carolina and from other counties in Virginia. Following the path of destruction was easy. One farmstead after another revealed dismembered bodies and fresh blood.

◀ **African American Family Group in Virginia, 1861 or 1862**
This photograph was taken by an antislavery New Englander, Larkin Mead, who went south to assist the slaves after the outbreak of the Civil War.

Now it was the whites' turn for vengeance. Scores of blacks who had no part in the rebellion were killed. Turner's band was overpowered, and those not shot on sight were jailed, to be tried and hanged in due course. Turner himself slipped away and hid in the woods until his capture on October 30. After a trial, he too was hanged.

Revenge was one thing, understanding another. Turner's subsequently published "Confessions" (recorded by his court-appointed lawyer) did not evidence his mistreatment by owners. What they did reveal was an intelligent and deeply religious man who had somehow learned to read and write as a boy and who claimed to have seen heavenly visions of white and black spirits fighting each other. Turner's mystical streak, well known in the neighborhood, had never before seemed dangerous. White Baptist and Methodist preachers had converted innumerable slaves to Christianity at the turn of the century. Christianity was supposed to make slaves more docile, but Nat Turner's ability to read had enabled him to find passages in the Bible that threatened death to him who "stealeth" a man, a fair description of slavery. Asked by his lawyer if he now found himself mistaken, Turner replied, "Was not Christ crucified?" Small wonder that a niece of George Washington concluded that she and all other white Virginians were now living on a "smothered volcano."

Before Turner, white Virginians had worried little about a slave rebellion. There had been a brief scare in 1800 when a plot led by a slave named Gabriel Prosser was discovered and nipped in the bud. Overall, slavery in Virginia seemed mild to whites, a far cry from the harsh regimen of the new cotton-growing areas like Alabama and Mississippi. On hearing of trouble in Southside, many whites had jumped to the conclusion that the British were invading and only gradually absorbed the more menacing thought that the slaves were rebelling.

"What is to be done?" an editorial writer moaned in the *Richmond Enquirer*. "Oh my God, I don't know, but something must be done." In the wake of Turner's insurrection many Virginians, especially nonslaveholding whites in the western part of the state, urged that Virginia follow the lead of northern states and emancipate its slaves. During the winter of 1831–1832, the Virginia legislature wrangled over emancipation proposals. The narrow defeat of these proposals marked a turning point; thereafter, opposition to slavery steadily weakened not only in Virginia but throughout the region known to history as the Old South.

As late as the Revolution, *south* referred more to a direction than to a place. In 1775 slavery had known no

sectional boundaries in America. But as one northern state after another embraced emancipation, slavery became the distinguishing feature, the "peculiar institution," to whose defense the Old South dedicated itself.

A rift of sorts split the Old South into the Upper South (Virginia, North Carolina, Tennessee, and Arkansas) and the Lower, or Deep, South (South Carolina, Georgia, Florida, Alabama, Mississippi, Louisiana, and Texas). With its variegated economy based on raising wheat, tobacco, hemp, vegetables, and livestock, the Upper South relied far less than the Lower South on slavery and cotton, and in 1861 it approached secession more reluctantly than its sister states. Yet in the final analysis slavery forged the Upper South and Lower South into a single Old South where it scarred all social relationships: between blacks and whites, among whites, and even among blacks. Without slavery there never would have been an Old South.

This chapter focuses on four major questions:

- How did the rise of cotton cultivation affect the geographical distribution of population and the economy of the Old South? How did northerners' image of the Old South differ from the way in which southerners saw themselves?

- What major social divisions segmented the white South?

- How did slavery affect social relations in the white South? Why did nonslaveholding whites come to see their futures as bound up with the survival of slavery?

- What conditions in the Old South made it possible for a distinctive culture to develop among the slaves, and what were the predominant features of that culture?

KING COTTON

In 1790 the South was essentially stagnant. Tobacco, its primary cash crop, had lost economic vitality even as it had depleted the once-rich southern soils. The growing of alternative cash crops, rice and cotton, was confined to coastal areas. Three out of four southerners still lived along the Atlantic seaboard, specifically in the Chesapeake and the Carolinas. One of three resided in Virginia alone.

The contrast between that South and the dynamic South of 1850 was stunning. By 1850 southerners had moved south and west. Now only one of every seven southerners lived in Virginia, and cotton reigned as king,

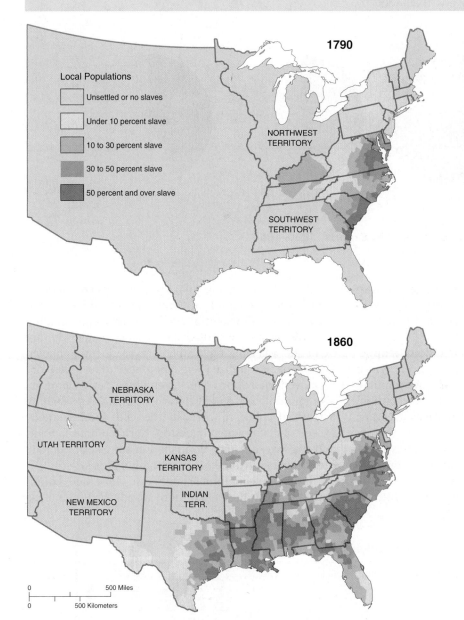

MAP 12.1
Distribution of Slaves, 1790 and 1860
In 1790 the majority of slaves resided along the southeastern seaboard. By 1860, however, slavery had spread throughout the South, and slaves were most heavily concentrated in the Deep South states.

Source: Reprinted with permission of McGraw-Hill, Inc. from *Ordeal by Fire: The Civil War and Reconstruction* by James M. McPherson. Copyright 1982 by Alfred A. Knopf, Inc.

shaping this new South. The growth of the British textile industry had created a huge demand for cotton, while Indian removal (see Chapter 9) had made way for southern expansion into the "Cotton Kingdom," a broad swath of land that stretched from South Carolina, Georgia, and northern Florida in the east through Alabama, Mississippi, central and western Tennessee, and Louisiana, and from there on to Arkansas and Texas (see Map 12.1).

The Lure of Cotton

To British traveler Basil Hall, it seemed that all southerners could talk about was cotton. "Every flow of wind from the shore wafted off the smell of that useful plant; at every dock or wharf we encountered it in huge piles or pyramids of bales, and our decks were soon choked with it. All day, and almost all night long, the captain, pilot, crew, and passengers were talking of nothing else."

With its warm climate, wet springs and summers, and relatively dry autumns, the Lower South was especially suited to the cultivation of cotton. In contrast to the sugar industry, which thrived in southeastern Louisiana, cotton required neither expensive irrigation canals nor costly machinery. Sugar was a rich man's crop that demanded a considerable capital investment to grow and process. But cotton could be grown profitably on any scale. A cotton farmer did not even need to own a gin; commercial gins were available. Nor did a cotton farmer have to own slaves; in 1860, 35 to 50 percent of all

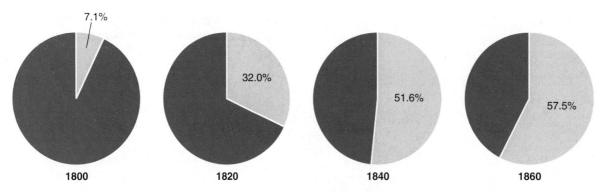

FIGURE 12.1
Value of Cotton Exports as a Percentage of All U.S. Exports, 1800–1860
By 1840 cotton accounted for more than half of all U.S. exports.

farmers in the cotton belt owned no slaves. Cotton was profitable for anyone, even nonslaveholders, to grow; it promised to make poor men prosperous and rich men kings (see Figure 12.1).

Although modest cotton cultivation did not require slaves, large-scale cotton growing and slavery grew together (see Figure 12.2). As the southern slave population nearly doubled between 1810 and 1830, cotton employed three-fourths of all southern slaves. Owning slaves made it possible to harvest vast tracts of cotton speedily, a crucial advantage because a sudden rainstorm at harvest time could pelt cotton to the ground and soil it. Slaveholding also enabled planters to increase their cotton acreage and hence their profits.

An added advantage of cotton lay in its compatibility with the production of corn. Corn could be planted earlier or later than cotton and harvested before or after. Since the cost of owning a slave was the same whether he or she was working or not, corn production enabled slaveholders to utilize slave labor when slaves were not employed on cotton. Nonslaveholding cotton growers also found it convenient to raise corn, and by 1860 the acreage devoted to corn in the Old South actually exceeded that devoted to cotton. Corn fed both families and the livestock that flourished in the South (in 1860 the region had two-thirds of the nation's hogs).

From an economic standpoint, corn and cotton gave the South the best of both worlds. Fed by intense

FIGURE 12.2
Growth of Cotton Production and the Slave Population, 1790–1860
Cotton and slavery rose together in the Old South.

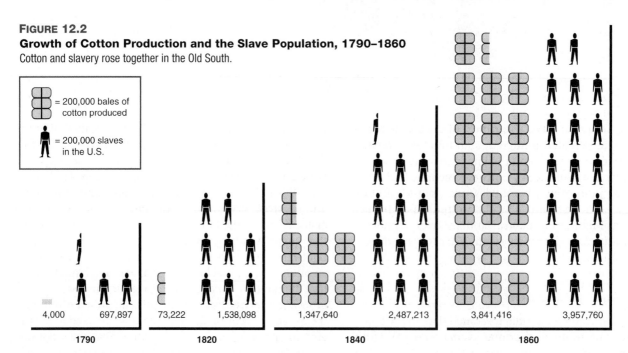

Port and city of New Orleans

In the late 1850s New Orleans was the largest city and port in the South. Cotton bales, sometimes protected by a tarpaulin, awaited loading on sailing ships for transport to Europe or New England. Steamships were used mainly for carrying traffic on the Mississippi River rather than for ocean voyages.

demands in Britain and New England, the price of cotton remained high, with the result that money flowed into the South. Because of southern self-sufficiency in growing corn and in raising hogs that thrived on the corn, money was not drained out of the region to pay for food produced in the North. In 1860 the twelve wealthiest counties in the United States were all in the South.

Ties Between the Lower and Upper South

Two giant cash crops, sugar and cotton, dominated agriculture in the Lower South. The Upper South, a region of tobacco, vegetable, hemp, and wheat growers, depended far less on the great cash crops. Yet the Upper South identified with the Lower South rather than with the agricultural regions of the free states.

A range of social, political, and economic factors promoted this unity. First, many settlers in the Lower South had come from the Upper South. Second, all white southerners benefited from the three-fifths clause of the Constitution, which enabled them to count slaves as a basis for congressional representation. Third, all southerners were stung by abolitionist criticisms of slavery, which drew no distinction between the Upper and Lower South. Economic ties also linked the South. The profitability of cotton and sugar increased the value of slaves throughout the entire region and encouraged the

trading of slaves from the Upper to the Lower South. Without the sale of its slaves to the Lower South, an observer wrote, "Virginia will be a desert" (see Map 12.2).

The North and South Diverge

The changes responsible for the dynamic growth of the South widened the distance between it and the North. At a time when the North was rapidly urbanizing, the South remained predominantly rural. In 1860 the proportion of the South's population living in urban areas was only one-third that of New England and the mid-Atlantic states, down from one-half in 1820.

One reason for the rural character of the South was its lack of industries. Although one-third of the American population lived there in 1850, the South accounted for only 10 percent of the nation's manufacturing. The industrial output of the entire South in 1850 was less than that of New Hampshire and only one-third that of Massachusetts.

Some southerners, including J. D. B. De Bow of New Orleans, advocated factories as a way to revive the economies of older states like Virginia and South Carolina, to reduce the South's dependency on northern manufactured products, and to show that the South was not a backwater. After touring northern textile mills, South Carolina's William Gregg established a company

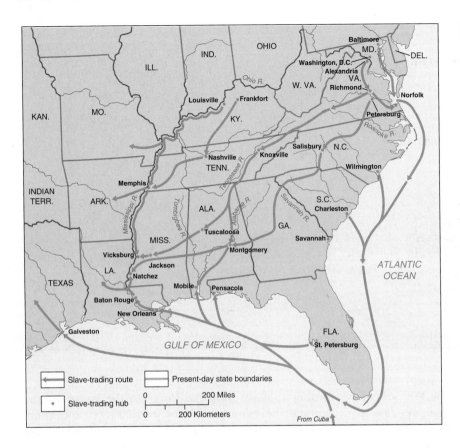

MAP 12.2
The Internal Slave Trade, 1810–1860

An internal slave trade developed after the slave trade with Africa ended in 1808. With the growth of cotton production, farmers in the Upper South found it profitable to sell their slaves to planters in the Lower South.

town for textiles at Graniteville in 1845. By 1860 Richmond boasted the nation's fourth-largest producer of iron products, the Tredegar Iron Works, which contributed greatly to the Confederate cause during the Civil War. But these were exceptions.

Compared to factories in the North, most southern factories were small, produced for nearby markets, and were closely tied to agriculture. The leading northern factories turned hides into tanned leather and leather into shoes, or cotton into threads and threads into suits. In contrast, southern factories, only a step removed from agriculture, turned grain into flour, corn into meal, and logs into lumber.

Slavery posed a major obstacle to southern industrialization, but not because slaves were unfit for factories. The Tredegar Iron Works employed slaves in skilled positions. But industrial slavery troubled southerners. Slaves who were hired out to factory masters sometimes passed themselves off as free and acted as if they were free by negotiating better working conditions. A Virginia planter who rented slaves to an iron manufacturer complained that they "got the habit of roaming about and *taking care of themselves.*"

The chief brake on southern industrialization was money, not labor. To raise the capital needed to build factories, southerners would have to sell slaves. They had little incentive to do so. Cash crops like cotton and sugar were proven winners, whereas the benefits of industrialization were remote and doubtful. Successful industrialization, further, threatened to disrupt southern social relations by attracting antislavery white immigrants from the North. As long as southerners believed that an economy founded on cash crops would remain profitable, they had little reason to leap into the uncertainties of industrialization.

The South also lagged behind the North in provisions for public education. As was true of southern arguments for industrialization, pro-education arguments were bountiful, but these issued from a small segment of the South's leadership and usually fell on deaf ears. Southerners rejected compulsory education and were reluctant to tax property to support schools. They abhorred the thought of educating slaves, so much so that southern lawmakers made it a crime to teach slaves to read. Some public aid flowed to state universities, but for most whites the only available schools were private.

As a result, white illiteracy, which had been declining in the North, remained high in the South. For example, nearly 60 percent of the North Carolinians who enlisted in the U.S. army before the Civil War were illiterate. The comparable proportion for northern enlistees was less than 30 percent.

Agricultural, self-sufficient, and independent, the middling and poor whites of the South remained unconvinced of the need for public education. They had little dependency on the printed word, few complex economic transactions, and infrequent dealings with urban people. Even the large planters, some of whom did support public education, had less commitment to it than did northern manufacturers. Whereas many northern businessmen accepted Horace Mann's argument that public schools would create a more orderly and alert work force, planters had no need for an educated white work force. They already had a black one that they were determined to keep illiterate lest it acquire ideas of freedom.

Because the South diverged so sharply from the North, it is tempting to view the South as backward and lethargic, doomed to be bypassed by the more energetic northern states. Increasingly, northerners associated the spread of cities and factories with progress. Finding few cities and factories in the South, they concluded that the region was a stranger to progress as well. A northern journalist wrote of white southerners in the 1850s that "They work little, and that little, badly; they earn little, they sell little; they buy little, and they have little—very little—of the common comforts and consolations of civilized life." Visitors to the South sometimes thought that they were traveling backward in time. "It seems as if everything had stopped growing, and was growing backwards," novelist Harriet Beecher Stowe wrote of the region.

Yet the white South did not lack progressive features. In 1840 per capita income in the white South was only slightly below the national average, and by 1860 it exceeded the national average. Although it is true that southerners made few contributions to technology to rival those of northerners, many southerners had a progressive zeal for agricultural improvement. Virginian Edmund Ruffin, who allegedly touched off the Civil War by firing the first cannon on Fort Sumter in 1861 and committed suicide in despair at the South's defeat in 1865, was an enthusiastic supporter of crop rotation and of the use of fertilizer and an important figure in the history of scientific agriculture. Like northerners, white southerners were restless, eager to make money, skillful at managing complex commercial enterprises, and, when they chose, capable of becoming successful industrialists.

Rather than viewing the Old South as economically backward, it is more accurate to see it merely as different. Cotton was a wonderful crop, and southerners could hardly be blamed for making it their ruler. "No! You dare not make war upon cotton; no power on earth dares to make war upon it," a senator from South Carolina proclaimed in 1858. "Cotton is king."

THE SOCIAL GROUPS OF THE WHITE SOUTH

Although all agricultural regions of the South contained slaveholders and nonslaveholders, there was considerable diversity within each group. In every southern state some slaveholders owned vast estates, magnificent homes, and hundreds of slaves, but most lived more modestly. In 1860 one-quarter of all white families in the South owned slaves. Of these, nearly half owned fewer than five slaves, and nearly three-quarters had fewer than ten slaves. Only 12 percent owned twenty or more slaves, and only 1 percent had a hundred or more. Large slaveholders clearly were a minority within a minority. Nonslaveholders also formed a diverse group. Most were landowners whose farms drew on the labor of family members, but the South also contained nonslaveholding whites who squatted on land in the so-called pine barrens or piney woods and who scratched out livelihoods by raising livestock, hunting and fishing, and planting a few acres of corn, oats, or sweet potatoes.

Despite the diversity, one might reasonably divide the white South's social structure into four main groups—the planters, the small slaveholders, the yeomen (or family farmers), and the people of the pine barrens. Even this classification is a little arbitrary. Historians usually classify as planters those who owned twenty or more slaves, the minimum number considered necessary for specialized plantation agriculture. Yet in any group of twenty slaves, some were likely to be too old and others too young to work. Arguably, a planter needed more than twenty slaves to run a plantation. Similarly, those with fewer than twenty slaves are usually described as small slaveholders, but an obvious difference separated an individual who owned ten to nineteen slaves and one who owned fewer than five. The former was close to becoming a planter; the latter was only a step removed from a yeoman. A great deal also depended on where one lived. In the low country and delta regions of the South, the planters dominated; most small slaveholders in these areas had dealings with the planters and looked to them for leadership. In the hilly

upland regions, the yeomen were dominant, and small slaveholders tended to acquire their outlook.

Of course, many lawyers, physicians, merchants, and artisans, who did not fall into any of these four main groups, also made the Old South their home. But because the South was fundamentally rural and agricultural, those outside of agriculture usually identified their interests with one or another of the four agricultural groups. Rural artisans and merchants had innumerable dealings with the yeomen. Urban merchants and lawyers depended on the planters and adopted their viewpoint on most issues. Similarly, slave traders relied on the plantation economy for their livelihood. Nathan Bedford Forrest, the uneducated son of a humble Tennessee blacksmith, made a fortune as a slave trader in Natchez, Mississippi. When the Civil War broke out, Forrest enlisted in the Confederate army as a private and rose swiftly to become the South's greatest cavalry general. "That devil Forrest," the Yankees called him. Plantation slavery directed Forrest's allegiances as surely as it did those of planters like Jefferson Davis, the Confederacy's president.

Slave Nurse and Baby Girl
Slavery did not prevent white children and their slave nurses from forming attachments to each other.

Planters and Plantation Mistresses

With porticoed mansion and fields teeming with slaves, the plantation still stands at the center of the popular image of the Old South. This romanticized view, reinforced by novels and motion pictures like *Gone with the Wind*, is not entirely misleading, for the South contained plantations that travelers found "superb beyond description." Whether devoted to cotton, tobacco, rice, or sugar, the plantations were characterized by a high degree of division of labor. In the 1850s Bellmead, a tobacco plantation on Virginia's James River, was virtually an agricultural equivalent of a factory village. Its more than one hundred slaves were classified into the domestic staff (butlers, waiters, seamstresses, laundresses, maids, and gardeners), the pasture staff (shepherds, cowherds, and hog drivers), outdoor artisans (stonemasons and carpenters), indoor artisans (blacksmiths, carpenters, shoemakers, spinners, and weavers), and field hands. Such a division of labor was inconceivable without abundant slaves and land. Wade Hampton's cotton plantation near Columbia, South Carolina, encompassed twenty-four hundred acres. With such resources, it is not surprising that large plantations could generate incomes that contemporaries viewed as immense (twenty to thirty thousand dollars a year).

During the first flush of settlement in the Piedmont and trans-Appalachian South in the eighteenth century, most well-off planters had been content to live in simple log cabins. In contrast, between 1810 and 1860, elite planters often vied with one another to build stately mansions. Some, like Lyman Hardy of Mississippi, hired architects. Hardy's Auburn, built in 1812 near Natchez, featured Ionic columns and a portico thirty-one feet long and twelve feet deep. Others copied designs from books like Andrew Jackson Downing's *The Architecture of Country Houses* (1850), which sold sixteen thousand copies between 1850 and 1865.

However impressive, these were not typical planters. The wealth of most planters, especially in states like Alabama and Mississippi, consisted primarily in the value of their slaves rather than in expensive furniture or silver plate. In monetary terms, slaves were worth a great deal, as much as seventeen hundred dollars for a field hand in the 1850s. Planters could convert their wealth into cash for purchasing luxuries only by selling slaves. A planter who sold his slaves ceased to be a planter and relinquished the South's most prestigious social status. Not surprisingly, most planters clung to large-scale slaveholding even if it meant scrimping on their lifestyles. A northern journalist observed that in the Southwest, men worth millions lived as if they were not worth hundreds.

Planters had to worry constantly about profitability. The fixed costs of operating plantations—including hiring overseers, housing and feeding slaves, and maintaining cotton gins and other equipment—were considerable. Their drive for profits led planters to search constantly for more and better land, to organize their slaves into specialized work gangs for maximum efficiency, and to make their plantations self-sufficient in food. The quest for profits also impelled planters to cultivate far-flung commercial connections. Like any commodity, cotton went up and down in price. Sometimes the fluctuations were long term; more often, the price fluctuated seasonally. In response to these rises and falls, planters assigned their cotton to commercial agents in cities. These agents held the cotton until the price was right and extended credit to enable the planters to pay their bills before the cotton was sold. Thus indebtedness became part of the plantation economy. Persistent debt intensified the planters' quest for more profits to escape from the burden of debt. Planters enjoyed neither repose nor security.

Plantation agriculture placed psychological strains as well as economic burdens on planters and their wives. Frequent moves disrupted circles of friends and relatives, all the more so because migration to the Southwest carried families into progressively less settled, more desolate areas. In 1850 those regions of the South with thriving plantation economies—notably Alabama, Mississippi, and southeastern Louisiana—had only recently emerged from the frontier stage.

For plantation women, migration to the Southwest often amounted to a fall from grace, for many of them had grown up in seaboard elegance, only to find themselves in isolated regions, surrounded by slaves and bereft of the companionship of white social peers. "I am sad tonight, sickness preys on my frame," wrote a bride who moved to Mississippi in 1833. "I am alone and more than 150 miles from any near relative in the wild woods of an Indian nation." At times wives lacked even their husbands' companionship. Plantation agriculture kept men on the road, scouting new land for purchase, supervising outlying holdings, and transacting business in New Orleans or Memphis.

Planters and their wives found various ways to cope with their isolation from civilized society. Many spent long periods of time in cities and left the management of

Colonel and Mrs. James A. Whiteside, Son Charles and Servants, by James A. Cameron, c. 1858–1859
This portrait captures the patriarchy as well as the graciousness that whites associated with the ideal plantation. Not only the slave waiter and nurse but the planter's wife appear overshadowed by the master's presence.

plantations to overseers. In 1850 fully one-half the planters in the Mississippi Delta were absentees living in or near Natchez or New Orleans rather than on their plantations. Yet in 1850 only 30 percent of planters with a hundred or more slaves employed white overseers; the majority managed their own estates. In response, many made plantation life more sociable by engaging in lavish hospitality.

Hospitality imposed enormous burdens on plantation wives, who might have to entertain as many as fifteen people for breakfast and attend to the needs of visitors who stayed for days. Indeed, in the plantation economy, wives had even less leisure than their husbands. Aside from raising their own children and caring for guests, plantation mistresses supervised house slaves, made carpets and clothes, looked after outbuildings such as smokehouses and dairies, and planted garden fruits and vegetables. Plantation women were anything but the delicate idlers of legend. In the absence of their husbands or fathers, they frequently kept the plantation accounts.

Among the greatest sorrows of some plantation mistresses was the presence of mulatto children, who stood as daily reminders of their husbands' infidelity. Mary Boykin Chesnut, an astute Charleston woman and famous diarist, commented, "Any lady is ready to tell you who is the father of all the mulatto children in everybody's household but her own. These, she seems to think, drop from clouds." Insisting on sexual purity for white women, southern men followed a looser standard for themselves. After the death of his wife, the brother of the famous abolitionist sisters Sarah and Angelina Grimké fathered three mulatto children. The gentlemanly code usually tolerated such transgressions as long as they were not paraded in public—and, at times, even if they were. Richard M. Johnson of Kentucky, the man who allegedly killed Tecumseh during the War of 1812, was elected vice president of the United States in 1836 despite having lived openly for years with his black mistress.

The isolation, drudgery, and humiliation that planters' wives experienced turned very few against the system. When the Civil War came, they supported the Confederacy as enthusiastically as any group. However much they might hate living as white islands in a sea of slaves, they recognized no less than their husbands that their wealth and position depended on slavery.

The Small Slaveholders

In 1860, 88 percent of all slaveholders owned fewer than twenty slaves, and most of these possessed fewer than ten slaves. Some slave owners were not even farmers: one out of every five was employed outside of agriculture, usually as a lawyer, physician, merchant, or artisan.

As a large and extremely diverse group, small slaveholders experienced conflicting loyalties and ambitions. In the upland regions, they absorbed the outlook of yeomen (nonslaveholding family farmers), the numerically dominant group. Typically, small upland slaveholders owned only a few slaves and rarely aspired to become large planters. In contrast, in the low country and delta regions, where planters formed the dominant group, small slaveholders often aspired to planter status. In these planter-dominated areas, someone with ten slaves could realistically look forward to the day when he would own thirty. The deltas were thus filled with ambitious and acquisitive individuals who linked success to owning more slaves. Whether one owned ten slaves or fifty, the logic of slaveholding was much the same. The investment in slaves could be justified only by setting them to work on profitable crops. Profitable crops demanded, in turn, more and better land. Much like the planters, the small slaveholders of the low country and delta areas were restless and footloose.

The social structure of the deltas was fluid but not infinitely so. Small slaveholders were usually younger than large slaveholders, and many hoped to become planters in their own right. But as the antebellum period wore on, a clear tendency developed toward the geographical segregation of small slaveholders from planters in the cotton belt.

Small slaveholders led the initial push into the cotton belt in the 1810s and 1820s, whereas the large planters, reluctant to risk transporting their hundreds of slaves into the still turbulent new territory, remained in the seaboard South. Gradually, however, the large planters ventured into Alabama and Mississippi.

Colonel Thomas Dabney, a planter originally from tidewater Virginia, made several scouting tours of the Southwest before moving his family and slaves to the region of Vicksburg, Mississippi, where he started a four-thousand-acre plantation. The small slaveholders already on the scene at first resented Dabney's genteel manners and misguided efforts to win friends. He showed up at house raisings to lend a hand. However, the hands he lent were not his own, which remained gloved, but those of his slaves. The small slaveholders muttered about transplanted Virginia snobs. Dabney responded to complaints by buying up much of the best land in the region. In itself, this was no loss to the small slaveholders. They had been first on the scene, and it was their land that the Dabneys of the South purchased.

Dabney and men like him quickly turned the whole region from Vicksburg to Natchez into large plantations. The small farmers took the proceeds from the sale of their land, bought more slaves, and moved elsewhere to grow cotton. Small slaveholders gradually transformed the region from Vicksburg to Tuscaloosa, Alabama, into a belt of medium-size farms with a dozen or so slaves on each.

The Yeomen

Nonslaveholding family farmers, or yeomen, comprised the largest single group of southern whites. Most were landowners. Landholding yeomen, because they owned no slaves of their own, frequently hired slaves at harvest time to help in the fields. Where the land was poor, as in eastern Tennessee, the landowning yeomen were typically subsistence farmers, but most grew some crops for the market. Whether they engaged in subsistence or commercial agriculture, they controlled landholdings far more modest than those of the planters—more likely in the range of fifty to two hundred acres than five hundred or more acres.

Yeomen could be found anywhere in the South, but they tended to congregate in the upland regions. In the seaboard South, they populated the Piedmont region of Georgia, South Carolina, North Carolina, and Virginia; in the Southwest they usually lived in the hilly upcountry, far from the rich alluvial soil of the deltas. A minority of yeomen did not own land. Typically young, these men resided with and worked for landowners to whom they were related.

The leading characteristic of the yeomen was the value that they attached to self-sufficiency. As nonslaveholders, they were not carried along by the logic that impelled slaveholders to acquire more land and plant more cash crops. Although most yeomen raised cash crops, they devoted a higher proportion of their acreage to subsistence crops like corn, sweet potatoes, and oats than did planters. The ideal of the planters was profit with modest self-sufficiency; that of the yeomen, self-sufficiency with modest profit.

Yeomen dwelling in the low country and delta regions dominated by planters were often dismissed as "poor white trash." But in the upland areas, where they constituted the dominant group, yeomen were highly respectable. There they coexisted peacefully with the slaveholders, who typically owned only a few slaves (large planters were rare in the upland areas). Both the small slaveholders and the yeomen were essentially family farmers. With or without the aid of a few slaves,

fathers and sons cleared the land and plowed, planted, and hoed the fields. Wives and daughters planted and tended vegetable gardens, helped at harvest, occasionally cared for livestock, cooked, and made clothes for the family.

In contrast to the far-flung commercial transactions of the planters, who depended on distant commercial agents to market their crops, the economic transactions of yeomen usually occurred within the neighborhood of their farms. Yeomen often exchanged their cotton, wheat, or tobacco for goods and services from local artisans and merchants. In some areas they sold their surplus corn to the herdsmen and drovers who made a living in the South's upland regions by specializing in raising hogs. Along the French Broad River in eastern Tennessee, some twenty to thirty thousand hogs were fattened for market each year; at peak season a traveler would see a thousand hogs a mile. When driven to market, the hogs were quartered at night in huge stock stands, veritable hog "hotels," and fed with corn supplied by the local yeomen.

The People of the Pine Barrens

One of the most controversial groups in the Old South was the independent whites of the wooded pine barrens. Making up about 10 percent of southern whites, they usually squatted on the land, put up crude cabins, cleared some acreage on which they planted corn between tree stumps, and grazed hogs and cattle in the woods. They neither raised cash crops nor engaged in the daily routine of orderly work that characterized family farmers. With their ramshackle houses and handful of stump-strewn acres, they appeared lazy and shiftless.

Antislavery northerners cited the pine barrens people as proof that slavery degraded poor whites, but southerners shot back that while the pine barrens people were poor, they could at least feed themselves, unlike the paupers of northern cities. In general, the people of the pine barrens were self-reliant and fiercely independent. Pine barrens men were reluctant to hire themselves out as laborers to do "slave" tasks, and the women refused to become servants.

Neither victimized nor oppressed, these people generally lived in the pine barrens by choice. The grandson of a farmer who had migrated from Emanuel County, Georgia, to the Mississippi pine barrens explained his grandfather's decision: "The turpentine smell, the moan of the winds through the pine trees, and nobody within fifty miles of him, [were] too captivating . . . to be resisted, and he rested there."

SOCIAL RELATIONS IN THE WHITE SOUTH

Northerners, even those with little sympathy for slaves, often charged that slavery twisted the entire social structure of the South out of shape. By creating a permanent black underclass of bond servants, they alleged, slavery robbed lower-class whites of the incentive to work, reduced them to shiftless misery, and rendered the South a premodern throwback in an otherwise progressive age. Stung by northern allegations that slavery turned the white South into a region of rich planters and poor common folk, southerners retorted that the real center of white inequality was the North, where merchants and financiers paraded in fine silks and never soiled their hands with manual labor.

In reality, a curious mix of aristocratic and democratic, premodern and modern features marked social relations in the white South. Although it contained considerable class inequality, property ownership was widespread. Rich planters occupied seats in state legislatures out of proportion to their numbers in the population, but they did not necessarily get their way, nor did their political agenda always differ from that of other whites.

Not just its social structure but also the behavior of individual white southerners struck northern observers as running to extremes. One minute southerners were hospitable and gracious; the next, savagely violent. "The Americans of the South," Alexis de Tocqueville asserted, "are brave, comparatively ignorant, hospitable, generous, easy to irritate, violent in their resentments, without industry or the spirit of enterprise." The practice of dueling intensified in the Old South at a time when it was dying in the North. Yet there were voices within the South, especially among the clergy, that urged white southerners to turn the other cheek when faced with insults.

Conflict and Consensus in the White South

Planters tangled with yeomen on several issues in the Old South. With their extensive economic dealings and need for credit, planters and their urban commercial allies inclined toward the Whig party, which was generally more sympathetic to banking and economic development. Cherishing their self-sufficiency and economically independent, the yeomen tended to be Democrats.

The occasions for conflict between these groups were minimal, however, and an underlying political unity reigned. Especially in the Lower South, each of the four main social groups—planters, small slaveholders, yeomen, and pine barrens people—tended to cluster in different regions. The delta areas that planters dominated contained relatively small numbers of yeomen. In other regions small slave-owning families with ten to fifteen slaves predominated. In the upland areas far from the deltas, the yeomen congregated. And the people of the pine barrens lived in a world of their own. There was more geographical intermingling of groups in the Upper South than in the Lower, but throughout the South each group attained a degree of independence from the others. With widespread landownership and relatively few factories, the Old South was not a place where whites worked for other whites, and this tended to minimize friction.

In addition, the white South's political structure was sufficiently democratic to prevent any one social group from gaining exclusive control over politics. It is true that in both the Upper and the Lower South, the majority of state legislators were planters. Large planters with fifty or more slaves were represented in legislatures far out of proportion to their numbers in the population. Yet these same planters owed their election to the popular vote. The white South was affected by the same democratic currents that swept northern politics between 1815 and 1860, and the newer states of the South had usually entered the Union with democratic constitutions that included universal white manhood suffrage—the right of all adult white males to vote.

Although yeomen often voted for planters, the nonslaveholders did not issue their elected representatives a blank check to govern as they pleased. During the 1830s and 1840s Whig planters who favored banks faced intense and often successful opposition from Democratic yeomen. These yeomen blamed banks for the Panic of 1837 and pressured southern legislatures to restrict bank operations. On banking issues, nonslaveholders got their way often enough to nurture their belief that they ultimately controlled politics and that slaveholders could not block their goals.

Conflict over Slavery

Nevertheless, there was considerable potential for conflict between the slaveholders and nonslaveholders. The white carpenter who complained in 1849 that "unjust, oppressive, and degrading" competition from slave labor depressed his wages surely had a point. Between 1830 and 1860 slaveholders gained an increasing proportion of the South's wealth while declining as a proportion of its white population. The size of the slave-

holding class shrank from 36 percent of the white population in 1831 to 31 percent in 1850 and to 25 percent in 1860. A Louisiana editor warned in 1858 that "the present tendency of supply and demand is to concentrate all the slaves in the hands of the few, and thus excite the envy rather than cultivate the sympathy of the people." That same year, the governor of Florida proposed a law guaranteeing to each white person the ownership of at least one slave. Some southerners began to support the idea of Congress's reopening the African slave trade to increase the supply of slaves, bring down their price, and give more whites a stake in the institution.

As the debate over slavery in Virginia in 1831–1832 (see this chapter's introduction) attests, slaveholders had good reasons for uncertainty over the allegiance of nonslaveholders to the "peculiar institution" of slavery. The publication in 1857 of Hinton R. Helper's *The Impending Crisis of the South*, which called upon non-slaveholders to abolish slavery in their own interest, revealed the persistence of a degree of white opposition to slavery. On balance, however, slavery did not create profound and lasting divisions between the South's slaveholders and nonslaveholders. Although antagonism to slavery flourished in parts of Virginia up to 1860, proposals for emancipation dropped from the state's political agenda after 1832. In Kentucky, a state with a history of antislavery activity that dated back to the 1790s, calls for emancipation were revived in 1849 in a popular referendum. But the pro-emancipation forces went down to crushing defeat. Thereafter, the continuation of slavery ceased to be a political issue in Kentucky and elsewhere in the South.

The rise and fall of pro-emancipation sentiment in the South raises a key question. Since the majority of white southerners were not slaveholders, why did they not attack the institution more consistently? To look ahead, why did so many of them fight ferociously and die bravely during the Civil War in defense of an institution in which they appeared not to have had any real stake?

There are various answers to these questions. First, some nonslaveholders hoped to become slaveholders. Second, most simply accepted the racist assumptions upon which slavery rested. Whether slaveholders or nonslaveholders, white southerners dreaded the likelihood that emancipation might encourage "impudent" blacks to entertain ideas of social equality with whites. Blacks might demand the right to sit next to whites in railroad cars and even make advances to white women. "Now suppose they [the slaves] was free," a white southerner told a northern journalist in the 1850s; "you see they'd all think themselves just as good as we; of course

they would if they was free. Now just suppose you had a family of children, how would you like to hev a niggar steppin' up to your darter?" Slavery, in short, appealed to whites as a legal, time-honored, and foolproof way to enforce the social subordination of blacks.

Finally, no one knew where the slaves, if freed, would go or what they would do. After 1830 a dwindling minority of northerners and southerners still dallied with the idea of colonizing freed blacks in Africa, but that alternative seemed increasingly unrealistic in a society where slaves numbered in the millions. Without colonization, southerners concluded, emancipation would produce a race war. In 1860 Georgia's governor sent a blunt message to his constituents, many of them nonslaveholders: "So soon as the slaves were at liberty thousands of them would leave the cotton and rice fields . . . and make their way to the healthier climate of the mountain region [where] we should have them plundering and stealing, robbing and killing." There was no mistaking the conclusion. Emancipation would not merely deprive slaveholders of their property, it would also jeopardize the lives of nonslaveholders.

The Proslavery Argument

Between 1830 and 1860 southern writers constructed a defense of slavery as a positive good rather than a necessary evil. Southerners answered northern attacks on slavery as a backward institution by pointing out that the slave society of ancient Athens had produced Plato and Aristotle and that Roman slaveholders had laid the basis of western civilization. A Virginian, George Fitzhugh, launched another line of attack by contrasting the plight of northern factory workers, "wage slaves" who were callously discarded by their bosses when they were too old or too sick to work, with the southern slaves, who were fed and clothed even when old and ill because they were the property of conscientious masters.

Many proslavery treatises were aimed less at northerners than at skeptics among the South's nonslaveholding yeomanry. Southern clergymen, who wrote roughly half of all proslavery tracts, invoked the Bible, especially St. Paul's order that slaves obey their masters. Too, proslavery writers warned southerners that the real intention of abolitionists, many of whom advocated equal rights for women, was to destroy the family as much as slavery by undermining the "natural" submission of children to parents, wives to husbands, and slaves to masters.

As southerners closed ranks behind slavery, they increasingly suppressed open discussion of the institu-

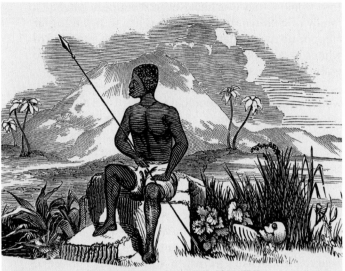

THE NEGRO IN HIS OWN COUNTRY.

THE NEGRO IN AMERICA.

Proslavery propagandists contrasted what they believed to be the black's African savagery with the blessings of civilization on an American plantation.

themselves that slavery was not only compatible with Christianity but also necessary for the proper exercise of the Christian religion. Like the proslavery intellectuals, clergymen contended that slavery provided the opportunity to display Christian responsibility toward one's inferiors, and that it helped blacks develop Christian virtues like humility and self-control.

With this conclusion solidified, southerners increasingly attacked antislavery evangelicals in the North for disrupting the allegedly superior social arrangement of the South. In 1844 the Methodist Episcopal Church split into northern and southern wings. In 1845 Baptists formed a separate Southern Convention. Even earlier, southerners and conservative northerners had combined in 1837 to drive the antislavery New School Presbyterians out of that denomination's main body. All this added up to a profound irony. In 1800 southern evangelicals had been more critical of slavery than southerners as a whole. Yet the evangelicals effectively seceded from national church denominations long before the South seceded from the Union.

Violence in the Old South

However much they agreed on slavery, white southerners' relations with each other were marked by a high degree of violence. No one who lived in a southern community, a northern journalist noted in the 1850s, could fail to be impressed with "the frequency of fighting with deadly weapons." Throughout the colonial and antebellum periods, violence deeply colored the daily lives of white southerners. In the 1760s a minister described backcountry Virginians "biting one anothers Lips and Noses off, and gowging one another—that is, thrusting out anothers Eyes, and kicking one another on the Cods [genitals], to the Great damage of many a Poor Woman." In the 1840s a New York newspaper described a fight between two raftsmen on the Mississippi that started when one accidentally bumped the other into shallow water. When it was over, one raftsman was dead. The other gloated, "I can lick a steamboat. My fingernails is related to a sawmill on my mother's side, . . . and the brass buttons on my coat have all been boiled in poison."

Gouging out eyes became a specialty of sorts among poor whites. On one occasion, a South Carolina judge entered his court to find a plaintiff, a juror, and two witnesses all missing one eye. Stories of eye gouging and ear biting lost nothing in the telling and became part of the folklore of the Old South. Mike Fink, a legendary southern fighter and hunter, boasted that he was so mean

tion within the South. In the 1830s southerners seized and burned abolitionist literature mailed to the South. In Kentucky abolitionist editor Cassius Marcellus Clay positioned two cannons and a powder keg to protect his press, but in 1845 a mob dismantled it anyway. By 1860 any southerner found with a copy of Helper's *The Impending Crisis* had reason to fear for his life.

The rise of the proslavery argument coincided with a shift in the position of the southern churches on slavery. During the 1790s and early 1800s, some Protestant ministers had assailed slavery as immoral. By the 1830s, however, most members of the clergy had convinced

that, in infancy, he refused his mother's milk and cried out for a bottle of whiskey. Yet beneath the folklore lay the reality of violence that gave the Old South a murder rate as much as ten times higher than that of the North.

The Code of Honor and Dueling

At the root of most violence in the white South lay intensified feelings of personal pride that themselves reflected the inescapable presence of slaves. Every day of their lives, white southerners saw slaves who were degraded, insulted, and powerless to resist. This experience had a searing impact on whites, for it encouraged them to react violently to even trivial insults in order to demonstrate that they had nothing in common with the slaves.

Among gentlemen this exaggerated pride took the form of a code of honor. In this context, *honor* can best be defined as an extraordinary sensitivity to one's reputation, a belief that one's self-esteem depends on the judgment of others. In the antebellum North, moralists celebrated a rival ideal, character—the quality that enabled an individual to behave in a steady fashion regardless of how others acted toward him or her. A person possessed of character acted out of the prompting of conscience. In contrast, in the honor culture of the Old South, the slightest insult, as long as it was perceived as intentional, could become the basis for a duel (see A Place in Time: Edgefield District, South Carolina, 1860).

Formalized by British and French officers during the Revolutionary War, dueling gained a secure niche in the Old South as a means by which gentlemen dealt with affronts to their honor. To outsiders, the incidents that sparked duels seemed so trivial as to be scarcely credible: a casual remark accidentally overheard, a harmless brushing against someone at a public event, even a hostile glance. Yet dueling did not necessarily terminate in violence. Dueling constituted part of a complex code of etiquette that governed relations among gentlemen in the Old South and, like all forms of etiquette, called for a curious sort of self-restraint. Gentlemen viewed dueling as a refined alternative to the random violence of lower-class life. The code of dueling did not dictate that the insulted party leap at his antagonist's throat or draw his pistol at the perceived moment of insult. Rather, he was to remain cool, bide his time, settle on a choice of weapons, and agree to a meeting place. In the interval, negotiations between friends of the parties sought to clear up the "misunderstanding" that had evoked the challenge. In this way, most confrontations ended peaceably rather than on the field of honor at dawn.

Although dueling was as much a way of settling disputes peaceably as of ending them violently, the ritual could easily terminate in a death or maiming. Dueling did not allow the resolution of grievances by the courts, a form of redress that would have guaranteed a peaceful outcome. As a way of settling personal disputes that involved honor, recourse to the law struck many southerners as cowardly and shameless. Andrew Jackson's mother told the future president, "The law affords no remedy that can satisfy the feelings of a true man."

In addition, dueling rested on the assumption that a gentleman could recognize another gentleman and hence would know when to respond to a challenge. Nothing in the code of dueling compelled a gentleman to duel someone beneath his status because such a person's opinion of a gentleman hardly mattered. An insolent porter who insulted a gentleman might get a whipping but did not merit a challenge to a duel. Yet it was often difficult to determine who was a gentleman. The Old South teemed with pretentious would-be gentlemen. A clerk in a country store in Arkansas in the 1850s found it remarkable that ordinary farmers who hung around the store talked of their honor and that the store's proprietor, a German Jew, kept a dueling pistol.

The Southern Evangelicals and White Values

With its emphasis on the personal redress of grievances and its inclination toward violence, the ideal of honor potentially conflicted with the values preached by the southern evangelical churches, notably the Baptists, Methodists, and Presbyterians. These evangelical denominations were on the rise even before the Great Kentucky Revival of 1800–1801 and continued to grow in the wake of the revival. For example, the Methodists grew from forty-eight thousand southern members in 1801 to eighty thousand by 1807. All of the evangelical denominations stressed humility and self-restraint, virtues in contrast to the entire culture of show and display that buttressed the extravagance and violence of the Old South.

Evangelicals continued to rail against dueling, but by the 1830s their values had changed in subtle ways. In the late eighteenth century evangelical preachers had reached out to the South's subordinate groups: women, slaves, and the poor. They had frequently allowed women and slaves to exhort in biracial churches. By the 1830s evangelical women were expected to remain silent in church. Pushed to the periphery of white churches,

Located on the western edge of South Carolina near the Georgia border, Edgefield District combined features of the aristocratic low country, to which it was linked by the Savannah River, and the yeoman-dominated upland regions of the Old South. Most Edgefield whites were small farmers or agricultural workers. In 1860 a majority did not own any slaves, and a sizable minority had no land. Yet the invention of the cotton gin had attracted wealthy low-

country planters to Edgefield, and by 1860 the district had become the state's leading cotton producer. These planters formed the nucleus of the district's elite. By 1860 the wealthiest 10 percent of white heads of household in Edgefield controlled 57 percent of the district's real and personal property. Intermarriage strengthened ties within the elite. By the Civil War, the leading families, among them the Butlers, Bonhams, Brookses, Simkinses, and Pickenses, had intermarried.

Black slaves were the basis of upper-crust Edgefield's wealth. By 1860 slaves outnumbered whites by 50 percent in the district. The vast majority of Edgefield's black bond servants were field slaves. Almost all of those dwelling on the great plantations worked under the "gang" system, by which they were divided into a number of groups, each performing a specified amount of work. (The gang system stood in contrast to the "task" system, in which individual slaves carried out designated chores.) The plantations' "plow gangs" comprised strong young men and occasionally some women, whereas "hoe gangs" generally included elderly slaves and women. A small number of Edgefield's slaves were skilled artisans who did black-smithing and carpentry on the district's omnipresent farms. Whether field hands or skilled artisans, most slaves lived with their families in simple, rude one-room cabins in close proximity to the dwellings of other slaves. An Edgefield black born into slavery in 1852 recalled that the slaves "had houses of

Pierce Mason Butler
A leading Edgefield politician, Butler was befriended early in his career by John Calhoun, who secured an army commission for him. Joining Calhoun in the early 1830s in support of nullification, Butler was elected governor of South Carolina in 1836. He led the Palmetto regiment in the Mexican War and was killed in action in 1847.

Francis Wilkinson Pickens
Pickens came to Edgefield to study and practice law. A relative of Calhoun, he favored nullification. Elected governor of South Carolina just before its secession from the Union in 1860, Pickens once said that "before a free people can be dragged into a war, it must be in defense of great national right as well as national honor."

weatherboards, big enough for [a] chicken coop—man, wife, and chillun [live] dere."

Only one-quarter of Edgefield's whites owned twenty or more slaves in 1860. This elite minority accounted for possession of nearly two-thirds of the district's slaves. Using their slaves not only as agrarian workers but also as collateral for loans, the great planters agreed with John C. Calhoun's northern-bred son-in-law Thomas Green Clemson—the owner of the Edgefield plantation called Canebreak—that "slaves are the most valuable property in the South, being the basis of the whole southern fabric."

Despite the yawning gap between the wealth of the planters and the income of most other whites, class conflict did not convulse antebellum Edgefield's white society, which as a whole was tightly unified. Verbal assaults on "aristocrats" did sweep through the district from time to time, but lawyers (whom the people treated with suspicion because they did not work with their hands) rather than planters bore the brunt of these attacks.

Religion contributed mightily to the harmony of Edgefield's white society. Indeed, religion was at the core of both family life and community life in the district and significantly molded the world view of the people. Although many churches dotted the countryside, so dispersed was Edgefield's population—the district contained only two incorporated towns—that ministers were limited. Thus devout Episcopalian planters and zealous Baptist yeomen farmers often found themselves sitting side by side listening to whatever traveling preacher had happened through their neighborhood.

As a further boon to white solidarity, Edgefield's small farmers depended on the plantation lords to gin and market their cotton, and during the harvest they often rented slaves from the great planters. Nonslaveholding yeomen were likelier than small slave owners to be dissatisfied with their lot in life, and many moved west into Georgia, Alabama, Mississippi, and Louisiana rather than stay and complain about the rich. Nearly 60 percent of Edgefield's white heads of household in 1850 no longer resided in the district in 1860.

The code of honor further unified the whites. Like southern gentlemen elsewhere, Edgefield's male elite saw affronts to honor behind every bush. Two military officers fought a duel because one questioned the other's chess moves. Louis Wigfall, an Edgefield planter who later served as a Confederate senator from Texas and who was rumored to be "half drunk all the time," posted signs denouncing as cowards those who refused to accept his innumerable challenges to duels.

However much the code of honor set individual against individual, it could unify the region. For example, in 1856 Preston Brooks, a U.S. congressman from Edgefield, brutally caned Massachusetts Senator Charles Sumner on the Senate floor after Sumner delivered an antislavery oration that dealt roughly with one of Brooks's relatives. As Representative Brooks later wrote to his constituents, it was not just the honor of a relative that he sought to defend. Rather, he had set himself up as a "sentinel" guarding the honor of every white South Carolinian against the slanderous tongues of northerners.

By the mid-1850s attitudes like this were demonstrating that the battle lines had been clearly drawn between southerners and northerners. The time seemed to be fast approaching when, as Edgefield newspaper editor Arthur Simkins observed, southern planters' "rich blessings . . . inherited from a virtuous ancestry" would lead them to band together to strongly oppose "mobocratic tendencies in American society" flourishing in the Northeast's "larger cities and more populous manufacturing towns."

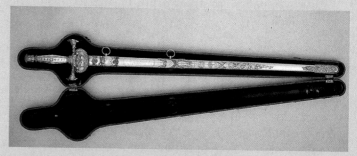

Presentation Sword and Ceramic Jar
Decorative arts in Edgefield ranged from this presentation sword owned by P. M. Butler, which symbolized the valor and military honor associated with the role of the southern planter class, to slave-made pottery such as this jar produced in one of the district's ten or so clayworks. Wheel-thrown and painted with alkaline glazes, the jar gets its distinctive appearance from having been taken from the kiln while red-hot and then thrust into a pit of pine needles.

slaves increasingly conducted their own worship services in black churches. In addition, Methodists and Baptists increasingly attracted well-to-do converts, and they began to open colleges such as Randolph-Macon (Methodist, 1830) and Wake Forest (Baptist, 1838).

With these developments, the once-antagonistic relationship between evangelicals and the gentry became one of cooperation. Evangelical clergymen absorbed some gentry values, including a regard for their honor and reputation that prompted them to throw taunts and threats back at their detractors. In turn, the gentry embraced evangelical virtues. By the 1860s the South contained many Christian gentlemen like the Bible-quoting Presbyterian general Thomas J. "Stonewall" Jackson, fierce in a righteous war but a sworn opponent of strong drink, the gaming table, and the duel.

LIFE UNDER SLAVERY

Slavery, the institution that lay at the root of the code of honor and other distinctive features of the Old South, has long inspired controversy among historians. Some have portrayed slavery as a benevolent institution in which blacks lived contentedly under kind masters; others as a cruel and inhuman system that drove slaves into constant rebellion. Neither view is accurate, but both contain some truth. There were kind masters who accepted the view expressed by a Baptist minister in 1854: "Give your servants that which is just and equal, knowing that you also have a Master in heaven." Moreover, some slaves developed genuine affection for their masters.

Yet slavery was an inherently oppressive institution that forcefully appropriated the life and labor of one race for the material benefit of another. Despite professions to the contrary by apologists for slavery, the vast majority of slaveholders exploited the labor of blacks to earn a profit. Kind masters might complain about cruel overseers, but the masters hired and paid the overseers to get as much work as possible out of blacks. When the master of one plantation chastised his overseer for "barbarity," the latter replied, "Do you not remember what you told me the time you employed me that [if] I failed to make you good crops I would have to leave?" Indeed, kindness was a double-edged sword, for the benevolent master came to expect grateful affection from his slaves and then interpreted that affection as loyalty to the institution of slavery. In fact, blacks felt little, if any, loyalty to slavery. When northern troops descended upon plantations during the Civil War, masters were dismayed to find many of their most trusted slaves deserting to Union lines.

Although the kindness or cruelty of masters made some difference to slaves, the most important determinants of their experiences under slavery depended on such impersonal factors as the kind of agriculture in which they were engaged, whether they resided in rural or urban areas, and whether they lived in the eighteenth or nineteenth century. The experiences of slaves working on cotton plantations in the 1830s differed drastically from those of slaves in 1700 for reasons unrelated to the kindness or brutality of masters.

The Maturing of the Plantation System

Slavery changed significantly between 1700 and 1830. In 1700 the typical slave was a young man in his twenties who had recently arrived aboard a slave ship from Africa or the Caribbean and worked in the company of other recent arrivals on isolated small farms. Drawn from different African regions and cultures, few such slaves spoke the same language. Because commercial slave ships contained twice as many men as women, and because slaves were widely scattered, blacks had difficulty finding sexual partners and creating a semblance of family life. Furthermore, as a result of severe malnutrition, black women who had been brought to North America on slave ships bore relatively few children. Thus the slave trade had a devastating effect on natural increase among blacks. Without importation, the number of slaves in North America would have declined between 1710 and 1730.

In contrast, by 1830 the typical North American slave was as likely to be female as male, had been born in America, spoke a form of English that made communication with other slaves possible, and worked in the company of numerous other slaves on a plantation. The key to the change lay in the rise of plantation agriculture in the Chesapeake and South Carolina during the eighteenth century. Plantation slaves had an easier time finding mates than those on the remote farms of the early 1700s. As the ratio between slave men and women fell into balance, marriages occurred with increasing frequency between slaves on the same or nearby plantations. The native-born slave population rose after 1730 and soared after 1750. Importation of African slaves gradually declined after 1760, and Congress banned it in 1808.

Work and Discipline of Plantation Slaves

In 1850 the typical slave experience was to work on a large farm or plantation with at least ten fellow bond servants. Almost three-quarters of all slaves that year were owned by masters with ten or more slaves, and just over one-half lived in units of twenty or more slaves. To understand the daily existence of the typical antebellum slave, then, requires an examination of the work and discipline routines common on large-scale farming operations.

The day of antebellum plantation slaves usually began an hour before sunrise with the sounding of a horn or bell. After a sparse breakfast, slaves marched to the fields. A traveler in Mississippi described a procession of slaves on their way to work. "First came, led by an old driver carrying a whip, forty of the largest and strongest women I ever saw together; they were all in a simple uniform dress of bluish check stuff, the skirts reaching little below the knee; their legs and feet were bare; they carried themselves loftily, each having a hoe over the shoulder, and walking with a free, powerful swing." Then came the plow hands, "thirty strong, mostly men, but few of them women. . . . A lean and vigilant white overseer, on a brisk pony, brought up the rear."

As this account indicates, slave men and women worked side by side in the fields. Female slaves who did not labor in the fields scarcely idled their hours away. A former slave, John Curry, described how his mother milked cows, cared for the children whose mothers worked in the fields, cooked for field hands, did the ironing and washing for her master's household, and took care of her own seven children. Plantations never lacked tasks for slaves of either gender. As former slave Solomon Northup noted, "ploughing, planting, picking cotton, gathering the corn, and pulling and burning stalks, occupies the whole of the four seasons of the year. Drawing and cutting wood, pressing cotton, fattening and killing hogs, are but incidental labors."

Regardless of the season, the slave's day stretched from dawn to dusk. Touring the South in the 1850s, Frederick Law Olmsted prided himself on rising early and riding late but added, "I always found the negroes in the field when I first looked out, and generally had to wait for the negroes to come from the field to have my horse fed when I stopped for the night." When darkness made fieldwork impossible, slaves toted cotton bales to the gin house, gathered up wood for supper fires, and fed the mules. Weary from their labors, they slept in log cabins on wooden planks. "The softest couches in the world," a former bondsman wryly observed, "are not to be found in the log mansions of a slave."

Although virtually all antebellum Americans worked long hours, no laboring group experienced the same

Black Women and Men on a Trek Home, South Carolina
Much like northern factories, large plantations made it possible to impose discipline and order on their work force. Here black women loaded down with cotton join their men on the march home after a day in the fields.

combination of long hours and harsh discipline as did slave field hands. Northern factory workers did not have to put up with drivers who, like one described by Olmsted, walked among the slaves with a whip, "which he often cracked at them, sometimes allowing the lash to fall lightly upon their shoulders." The lash did not always fall lightly. The annals of American slavery contain stories of repulsive brutality. Pregnant slave women were sometimes forced to lie in depressions in the ground and endure whipping on their backs, a practice that supposedly protected the fetus while abusing the mother.

The disciplining and punishment of slaves was often left to white overseers and black drivers rather than to masters. "Dat was de meanest devil dat ever lived on the Lord's green earth," a former Mississippi slave said of his driver. The barbaric discipline meted out by others pricked the conscience of many a master. But even masters who professed Christianity viewed the disciplining of slaves as a priority—indeed, as a Christian duty to ensure the slaves' proper "submissiveness." The black abolitionist Frederick Douglass, once a slave, recalled that his worst master had been converted at a Methodist camp meeting. "If religion had any effect on his character at all," Douglass related, "it made him more cruel and hateful in all his ways."

Despite the relentless, often vicious discipline, plantation agriculture gave a minority of slaves opportunities for advancement, not from slavery to freedom but from unskilled and exhausting fieldwork to semiskilled or skilled indoor work. Some slaves developed skills like blacksmithing and carpentry and learned to operate cotton gins. Others were trained as cooks, butlers, and dining-room attendants. These house slaves became legendary for their arrogant disdain of field hands and poor whites. The legend often distorted the reality, for house slaves were as subject to discipline as field slaves. "I liked the field work better than I did the house work," a female slave recalled. "We could talk and do anything we wanted to, just so we picked the cotton." Such sentiments were typical, but skilled slave artisans and house servants were greatly valued and treated accordingly; they occupied higher rungs than field hands on the social ladder of slavery.

The Slave Family

Masters thought of slaves as naturally promiscuous and flattered themselves into thinking that they alone held slave marriages together. Masters did have an incentive to encourage slave marriages in order to bring new slaves into the world and to discourage slaves from running away. Some masters baked wedding cakes for slaves and later arbitrated marital disputes. James Henry Hammond, the governor of South Carolina and a large slaveholder, noted in his diary that he "flogged Joe Goodwyn and ordered him to go back to his wife. Ditto Gabriel and Molly and ordered them to come together. Separated Moses and Anny finally."

This picture of benevolent masters holding together naturally promiscuous slaves is misleading. The keenest challenge to the slave family came not from the slaves themselves but from slavery. The law provided neither recognition of nor protection for the slave family. Although some slaveholders were reluctant to break slave marriages by sale, such masters could neither bequeath this reluctance to their heirs nor avoid economic hardships that might force them to sell off slaves. The reality, one historian has calculated, was that in a lifetime, on average, a slave would witness the sale of eleven family members.

Naturally, the commonplace buying and selling of slaves severely disrupted slaves' attempts to create a stable family life. Poignant testimony to the effects of sale on slave families, and to the desire of slaves to remain near their families, was provided by an advertisement for a runaway slave in North Carolina in 1851. The advertisement described the fugitive as presumed to be "lurking in the neighborhood of E. D. Walker's, at Moore's Creek, who owns most of his relatives, or Nathan Bonham's who owns his mother; or, perhaps, near Fletcher Bell's, at Long Creek, who owns his father." Small wonder that a slave preacher pronounced a slave couple married "until death or *distance* do you part."

Aside from disruption by sale, slave families experienced separations and degradations from other sources. The marriage of a slave woman gave her no protection against the sexual demands of a master nor, indeed, of any white. The slave children of white masters became targets of the wrath of white mistresses at times. Sarah Wilson, the daughter of a slave and her white master, remembered that as a child, she was "picked on" by her mistress until the master ordered his wife to let Sarah alone because she "got big, big blood in her." Slave women who worked in the fields were usually separated from their children by day; young sons and daughters often were cared for by the aged or by the mothers of other children. When slave women took husbands from nearby (rather than their own) plantations, the children usually stayed with the mother. Hannah Chapman remembered that her father tried to visit his family under cover of darkness "because he missed us and us longed for him." But if his master found him, "us would track him the nex' day by de blood stains."

Despite enormous obstacles, the relationships within slave families were often intimate and, where possible, long-lasting. In the absence of legal protection, slaves developed their own standards of family morality. A southern white woman observed that slaves "did not consider it wrong for a girl to have a child before she married, but afterwards were extremely severe upon anything like infidelity on her part." When given the opportunity, slaves sought to solemnize their marriages before clergymen. White clergymen who accompanied the Union army into Mississippi and Louisiana in the closing years of the Civil War conducted thousands of marriage rites for slaves who had long viewed themselves as married and desired a formal ceremony and registration.

On balance, slave families differed profoundly from white families. Even on large plantations where roughly equal numbers of black men and women made marriage a theoretical possibility, planters, including George Washington, often divided their holdings into several dispersed farms and distributed their slaves among them without regard to marriage ties. Conditions on small farms and new plantations discouraged the formation of families, and everywhere spouses were vulnerable to being sold as payment for the master's debts. Slave adults were more likely than whites never to marry or to marry late, and slave children were more likely to live with a single parent (usually the mother) or with neither parent.

In white families, the parent-child bond overrode all others; slaves, in contrast, emphasized ties between children and their grandparents, uncles, and aunts as well as their parents. Such broad kinship ties marked the West African cultures from which many slaves had originally been brought to America, and they were reinforced by the separations between children and one or both parents that routinely occurred under slavery. Frederick Douglass never knew his father and saw his mother infrequently, but he vividly remembered his grandmother, "a good nurse, and a capital hand at making nets for catching shad and herring."

In addition, slaves often created "fictive" kin networks; in the absence of uncles and aunts, they simply called friends their uncles, aunts, brothers, or sisters. In effect, slaves invested nonkin relations with symbolic kin functions. In this way, they helped protect themselves against the involuntary disruption of family ties by forced sale and established a broader community of obligation. When plantation slaves greeted each other as "brudder," they were not making a statement about actual kinship but about kindred obligations they felt for each other. Apologists for slavery liked to argue that a "community of interests" bound masters and slaves together. In truth, the real community of interests was the one that slaves developed among themselves in order to survive.

The Longevity, Diet, and Health of Slaves

In general, slaves in the United States reproduced faster and lived longer than slaves elsewhere in the Western Hemisphere. The evidence comes from a compelling statistic. In 1825, 36 percent of all slaves in the Western Hemisphere lived in the United States, whereas Brazil accounted for 31 percent. Yet of the 10 to 12 million African slaves who had been imported to the New World between the fifteenth and nineteenth centuries, only

The Land of the Free and the Home of the Brave, by Henry Byam Martin, 1833
White southerners could not escape the fact that much of the Western world loathed their "peculiar institution." In 1833, when a Canadian sketched this Charleston slave auction, Britain abolished slavery in the West Indies.

some 550,000 (about 5 percent) had come to North America, whereas 3.5 million (nearly 33 percent) had been taken to Brazil. Mortality had depleted the slave populations in Brazil and the Caribbean to a far greater extent than in North America.

Several factors account for the different rates. First, the gender ratio among slaves equalized more rapidly in North America, encouraging earlier and longer marriages and more children. Second, because growing corn and raising livestock were compatible with cotton cultivation, the Old South produced plenty of food. The normal ration for a slave was a peck of cornmeal and three to four pounds of fatty pork a week. Slaves often supplemented this nutritionally unbalanced diet with vegetables grown in small plots that masters allowed them to farm and with catfish and game. In the barren winter months, slaves ate less than in the summer; in this respect, however, they did not differ much from most whites.

As for disease, slaves had greater immunities to both malaria and yellow fever than did whites, but they suffered more from cholera, dysentery, and diarrhea. In the absence of privies, slaves usually relieved themselves behind bushes; urine and feces washed into the sources of drinking water and caused many diseases. Yet slaves developed some remedies that, though commonly ridiculed by whites, were effective against stomach ailments. For example, the slaves' belief that eating white clay would cure dysentery and diarrhea rested on a firm basis; we know now that kaolin, an ingredient of white clay, is a remedy for these ailments.

Although slave remedies were often more effective than those of white physicians, slaves experienced higher mortality rates than whites. At any age, a slave could expect a shorter life than a white, most strikingly in infancy. Rates of infant mortality for slaves were at least twice those of whites. Between 1850 and 1860, fewer than two out of three black children survived to the age of ten. Whereas the worst mortality occurred on plantations in disease-ridden, low-lying areas, pregnant, overworked field hands often miscarried or gave birth to weakened infants even in healthier regions. Masters allowed pregnant women to rest, but rarely enough. "Labor is conducive to health," a Mississippi planter told a northern journalist; "a healthy woman will rear most children."

Slaves Off Plantations

Although plantation agriculture gave some slaves, especially males, opportunities to acquire specialized skills, it imposed a good deal of supervision on them. The greatest opportunities for slaves were reserved for those who worked off plantations and farms, either as laborers in extractive industries like mining and lumbering or as artisans in towns and cities.

Because lucrative cotton growing attracted so many whites onto small farms, a perennial shortage of white labor plagued almost all the nonagricultural sectors of the southern economy. As a consequence, there was a steady demand for slaves to drive wagons, to work as stevedores (ship-cargo handlers) in port cities, to man river barges, and to perform various tasks in mining and lumbering. In 1860 lumbering employed sixteen thousand workers, most of them slaves who cut trees, hauled them to sawmills, and fashioned them into useful lumber. In sawmills black engineers fired and fixed the steam engines that provided power. In iron-ore ranges and ironworks, slaves not only served as laborers but occasionally supervised less-skilled white workers. Just as mill girls comprised the labor force of the booming textile industry in New England, so did slave women and children work in the South's fledgling textile mills.

Slave or free, blacks found it easier to pursue skilled occupations in southern cities than in northern ones, partly because southern cities attracted few immigrants to compete for work, and partly because the profitability of southern cash crops long had pulled white laborers out of towns and cities, and left behind opportunities for blacks, slave or free, to acquire craft skills. Slaves who worked in factories, mining, or lumbering usually were hired rather than owned by their employers. If working conditions deteriorated to the point where slaves fell ill or died, masters would refuse to provide employers with more slaves. Consequently, working conditions for slaves off plantations usually stayed at a tolerable level. Watching workers load cotton onto a steamboat, Frederick Law Olmsted was amazed to see slaves sent to the top of the bank to roll the bales down to Irishmen who stowed them on the ship. Asking the reason for this arrangement, Olmsted was told, "The niggers are worth too much to be risked here; if the Paddies [Irish] are knocked overboard, or get their backs broke, nobody loses anything."

Life on the Margin: Free Blacks in the Old South

Free blacks were more likely than southern blacks in general to live in cities. In 1860 one-third of the free blacks in the Upper South and more than half in the Lower South were urban.

The relatively specialized economies of the cities provided free people of color with opportunities to

A Barber's Shop at Richmond, Virginia, 1861

Free blacks dominated the barber's trade in Richmond on the eve of the Civil War. As meeting places for men, barber shops supplied newspapers and political discussion. Black barbers were politically informed and prosperous. As was the custom at the time, barbers also performed medical procedures like drawing blood.

become carpenters, coopers (barrel makers), barbers, and even small traders. A visitor to an antebellum southern market would find that most of the meat, fish, vegetables, and fruit had been prepared for sale by free blacks. Urban free blacks formed their own fraternal orders and churches; a church run by free blacks was often the largest house of worship in a southern city. In New Orleans free blacks had their own literary journals and opera. In Natchez a free black barber, William Tiler Johnson, invested the profits of his shop in real estate, acquired stores that he rented out, purchased slaves and a plantation, and even hired a white overseer.

As Johnson's career suggests, some free blacks were highly successful. But free blacks were always vulnerable in southern society and became more so as the antebellum period wore on. Although free blacks continued to increase in absolute numbers (a little more than a quarter-million free people of color dwelled in the South in 1860), the rate of growth of the free-black population slowed after 1810. Between 1790 and 1810, this population had more than tripled, to 108,265. The reason for the slowdown after 1810 was that fewer southern whites were setting slaves free. Until 1820 masters with doubts about the rightness of slavery frequently manumitted (freed) their black mistresses and mulatto children, and some set free their entire work forces. In the wake of the Nat Turner rebellion in 1831, laws restricting the liberties of free blacks were tightened. During the mid-1830s, for example, most southern states made it a felony to teach blacks to read and write.

Every southern state forbade free blacks to enter that state, and in 1859 Arkansas ordered all free blacks to leave.

So although a free-black culture flowered in cities like New Orleans and Natchez, that culture did not reflect the conditions under which most free blacks lived. Free blacks were tolerated in New Orleans, in part because there were not too many of them. A much higher percentage of blacks were free in the Upper South than in the Lower South. Furthermore, although a disproportionate number of free blacks lived in cities, the majority lived in rural areas, where whites lumped them together with slaves. Even a successful free black like William Tiler Johnson could never dine or drink with whites. When Johnson attended the theater, he sat in the colored gallery.

The position of free blacks in the Old South contained many contradictions. So did their minds. As the offspring, or the descendants of offspring, of mixed liaisons, a disproportionate number of free blacks had light brown skin. Some of them were as color-conscious as whites and looked down on "darky" field hands and coal-black laborers. Yet as whites' discrimination against free people of color intensified during the late antebellum period, many free blacks realized that whatever future they had was as blacks, not as whites. Feelings of racial solidarity grew stronger among free blacks in the 1850s, and after the Civil War, the leaders of the freed slaves were usually blacks who had been free before the war.

Slave Resistance

The Old South was a seedbed of organized slave insurrections. In the delta areas of the Lower South where blacks outnumbered whites, slaves experienced continuous forced labor on plantations and communicated their bitterness to each other in the slave quarters. Free blacks in the cities could have provided leadership for rebellions. Rumors of slave conspiracies flew around the southern white community, and all whites shuddered over the massive black insurrection that had destroyed French rule in Santo Domingo.

Yet Nat Turner's 1831 insurrection in Virginia was the only slave rebellion that resulted in the deaths of whites. A larger but more obscure uprising occurred in Louisiana in 1811 when some two hundred slaves sought to march on New Orleans. Other, better known, slave insurrections were merely conspiracies that never materialized. In 1800 Virginia slave Gabriel Prosser's planned uprising was betrayed by other slaves, and

Gabriel and his followers were executed. That same year, a South Carolina slave, Denmark Vesey, won fifteen hundred dollars in a lottery and bought his freedom. Purchasing a carpentry shop in Charleston and becoming a preacher at that city's African Methodist Episcopal Church, Vesey built a cadre of black followers, including a slave of the governor of South Carolina and a black conjurer named Gullah Jack. In 1822 they devised a plan to attack Charleston and seize all the city's arms and ammunition, but other slaves informed authorities, and the conspirators were executed.

For several reasons, the Old South experienced far fewer rebellions than the Caribbean region or South America. Although slaves formed a majority in South Carolina and a few other states, they did not constitute a large majority in any state. In contrast to the Caribbean, an area of absentee landlords and sparse white population, the white presence in the Old South was formidable, and the whites had all the guns and soldiers. The rumors of slave conspiracies that periodically swept the

Thomas Noble, *Fugitives in Flight*
Growing up in Kentucky, artist Thomas Noble was probably familiar with scenes of slaves fleeing across the Ohio River to freedom. Although he served in the Confederate army during the Civil War, Noble began to paint antislavery themes after the war.

white South demonstrated to blacks the promptness with which whites could muster forces and mount slave patrols. The development of family ties among slaves made them reluctant to risk death and leave their children parentless. Finally, blacks who ran away or plotted rebellions had no allies. Southern Indians routinely captured runaway slaves and exchanged them for rewards; some Indians even owned slaves.

Short of rebellion, slaves could try to escape to freedom in the North. Perhaps the most ingenious, Henry Brown, induced a friend to ship him from Richmond to Philadelphia in a box and won immediate fame as "Box" Brown. Some light mulattos passed as whites. More often, fugitive slaves borrowed, stole, or forged passes from plantations or obtained papers describing themselves as free. Frederick Douglass borrowed a sailor's papers in making his escape from Baltimore to New York City in 1838. Some former slaves, among them Harriet Tubman and Josiah Henson, made repeated trips back to the South to help other slaves escape. These sundry methods of escape fed the legend of the "Underground Railroad," supposedly an organized network of safe houses owned by white abolitionists who spirited blacks to freedom. In reality, fugitive slaves owed very little to abolitionists. Some white sympathizers in border states did provide safe houses for blacks, but these houses were better known to watchful slave catchers than to most blacks.

Escape to freedom was a dream rather than an alternative for most blacks. Out of millions of slaves, probably fewer than a thousand escaped to the North. Yet slaves often ran away from masters not to escape to freedom but to visit spouses or avoid punishment. Most runaways remained in the South; some returned to kinder former masters. During the eighteenth century, African slaves had often run away in groups to the interior and sought to create self-sufficient colonies or villages of the sort that they had known in Africa. But once the United States acquired Florida, long a haven for runaways, few uninhabited places remained in the South to which slaves could flee.

Despite poor prospects for permanent escape, slaves could disappear for prolonged periods into the free-black communities of southern cities. Because whites in the Old South depended so heavily on black labor, slaves enjoyed a fair degree of practical freedom to drive wagons to market and to come and go when they were off plantations. Slaves hired out or sent to a city might overstay their leave and even pass themselves off as free. The experience of slavery has sometimes been compared to the experience of prisoners in penitentiaries or on chain gangs, but the analogy is misleading.

The supervision that slaves experienced was sometimes intense (for example, when working at harvest time under a driver), but often lax; it was irregular rather than consistent.

The fact that antebellum slaves frequently enjoyed some degree of practical freedom did not change the underlying oppressiveness of slavery. But it did give slaves a sense that they had certain rights on a day-to-day basis, and it helped deflect slave resistance into forms that were essentially furtive rather than open and violent. Theft was so common that planters learned to keep their tools, smokehouses, closets, and trunks under lock and key. Overworked field hands might leave valuable tools out to rust, or feign illness, or simply refuse to work. As an institution, slavery was vulnerable to such tactics; unlike free laborers, slaves could not be fired for negligence or malingering. Frederick Law Olmsted found slaveholders in the 1850s afraid to inflict punishment on slaves "lest the slave should abscond, or take a sulky fit and not work, or poison some of the family, or set fire to the dwelling, or have recourse to any other mode of avenging himself."

Olmsted's reference to arson and poisoning reminds us that not all furtive resistance was peaceful. Arson and poisoning, both common in African culture as forms of vengeance, were widespread in the Old South, and the fear of each was even more so. Masters afflicted by dysentery and similar ailments never knew for sure that they had not been poisoned.

Arson, poisoning, work stoppages, and negligence were alternatives to violent rebellion. Yet these furtive forms of resistance differed from rebellion. The goal of rebellion was freedom from slavery. The goal of furtive resistance was to make slavery bearable. The kind of resistance that slaves usually practiced sought to establish customs and rules that would govern the conduct of masters as well as that of slaves without challenging the institution of slavery as such. Most slaves would have preferred freedom but settled for less. "White folks do as they please," an ex-slave said, "and the darkies do as they can."

THE EMERGENCE OF AFRICAN-AMERICAN CULTURE

A distinctive culture emerged among blacks in the slave quarters of antebellum plantations. This culture drew on both African and American sources, but it was more than a mixture of the two. Enslaved blacks gave a distinctive twist to the American as well as African components of their culture.

The Language of Slaves

Before slaves could develop a common culture, they had to be able to communicate with one another. During the colonial period, verbal communication among slaves had often been difficult, for most slaves had been born in Africa, which contained an abundance of cultures and languages. The captain of a slave ship noted in 1744,

> As for the languages of *Gambia* [in West Africa], they are so many and so different that the Natives on either Side of the River cannot understand each other; which, if rightly consider'd, is no small happiness to the *Europeans* who go thither to trade for slaves.

In the pens into which they were herded before shipment and on the slave ships themselves, however, Africans developed a "pidgin"—a language that has no native speakers in which people with different native languages can communicate. Pidgin is not unique to black people. When Tarzan announced, "Me Tarzan, you Jane," he was speaking pidgin English. Nor is pidgin English the only form of pidgin; slaves who were sent to South America developed Spanish and Portuguese pidgin languages.

Many of the early African-born slaves learned pidgin English poorly or not at all, but as American-born slaves came to comprise an increasingly large proportion of all slaves, pidgin English took root. Indeed, it became the only language most slaves knew. Like all pidgins, it was a simplified language. Slaves usually dropped the verb *to be* (which had no equivalent in African tongues) and either ignored or confused genders. Instead of saying "Mary is in the cabin," they said, "Mary, he in cabin." To negate, they substituted *no* for *not*, saying, "He no wicked." Pidgin English contained several African words. Some, like *banjo*, became part of standard English; others, like *goober* (peanut), became part of southern white slang. Although they picked up pidgin terms, whites ridiculed field hands' speech. Some slaves, particularly house servants and skilled artisans, learned to speak standard English but had no trouble understanding the pidgin of field hands. However strange pidgin sounded to some, it was indispensable for communication among slaves.

African-American Religion

The development of a common language was the first step in forging African-American culture. No less important was the religion of the slaves.

Africa was home to rich and diverse religious customs and beliefs. Some of the early slaves were Muslims; a few had acquired Christian beliefs either in Africa or in the New World. But the majority of the slaves transported from Africa were neither Muslims nor Christians but rather worshipers in one of many native African religions. Most of these religions, which whites lumped together as heathen, drew little distinction between the spiritual and material worlds. Any event or development, from a storm to an earthquake or an illness, was assumed to stem from supernatural forces. These forces were represented by God, by spirits that inhabited the woods and waters, and by the spirits of ancestors. In addition, the religions of West Africa, the region from which most American slaves originally came, attached special significance to water, which symbolized life and hope.

The majority of the slaves brought to America in the seventeenth and eighteenth centuries were young men who may not have absorbed much of this religious heritage before their enslavement. In any case, Africans differed from each other in their specific beliefs and practices. For these reasons, African religions could never have unified blacks in America. Yet some Africans probably clung to their beliefs during the seventeenth and eighteenth centuries, a tendency made easier by the fact that whites undertook few efforts before the 1790s to convert slaves to Christianity.

Dimly remembered African beliefs such as the reverence for water may have predisposed slaves to accept Christianity when they were finally urged to do so, because water has a symbolic significance for Christians, too, in the sacrament of baptism. The Christianity preached to slaves by Methodist and Baptist revivalists during the late eighteenth and nineteenth centuries, moreover, resembled African religions in that it also drew few distinctions between the sacred and the secular. Just as Africans believed that a crop-destroying drought or a plague resulted from supernatural forces, the early revivalists knew in their hearts that every drunkard who fell off his horse and every Sabbath-breaker struck by lightning had experienced a deliberate and direct punishment from God.

By the 1790s blacks formed about a quarter of the membership of the Methodist and Baptist denominations. Masters continued to fear that a Christianized slave would be a rebellious slave. Converted slaves did in fact play a significant role in each of the three major slave rebellions in the Old South. The leaders of Gabriel's rebellion in 1800 used the Bible to prove that slaves, like the ancient Israelites, could prevail against overwhelm-

ing numbers. Denmark Vesey read the Bible, and most of the slaves executed for joining his conspiracy belonged to Charleston's African Methodist Church. Nat Turner was both a preacher and a prophet.

Despite the "subversive" effect of Christianity on some slaves, however, these uprisings, particularly the Nat Turner rebellion, actually stimulated Protestant missionaries to intensify their efforts to convert slaves. Missionaries pointed to the self-taught Turner to prove that slaves would hear about Christianity in any event and that organized efforts to convert blacks were the only way to ensure that slaves learned correct versions of Christianity, which emphasized obedience rather than insurgence. Georgia missionary and slaveholder Charles Colcock Jones reassuringly told white planters of the venerable black preacher who, upon receiving some abolitionist tracts in the mail, promptly turned them over to the white authorities for destruction. A Christian slave, the argument ran, would be a better slave rather than a bitter slave. For whites, the clincher was the split of the Methodists, Baptists, and Presbyterians into northern and southern wings by the mid-1840s. Now, they argued, it had finally become safe to convert slaves, for the churches had rid themselves of their antislavery wings. Between 1845 and 1860 the number of black Baptists doubled.

Princess Feather Quilt
This quilt was woven by Mississippi slaves.

The experiences of Christianized blacks in the Old South illustrate many of the contradictions of life under slavery. Urban blacks often had their own churches, but in the rural South, where the great majority of blacks lived, slaves worshiped in the same churches as whites. Although the slaves sat in segregated sections, they heard the same sermons and sang the same hymns as whites. Some black preachers actually developed followings among whites, and Christian masters were sometimes rebuked by biracial churches for abusing Christian slaves in the same congregation. The churches were, in fact, the most interracial institutions in the Old South. Yet none of this meant that Christianity was an acceptable route to black liberation. Ministers went out of their way to remind slaves that spiritual equality was not the same as civil equality. The effort to convert slaves gained momentum only to the extent that it was certain that

Christianity would not change the basic inequality of southern society.

Although they listened to the same sermons as whites, slaves did not necessarily draw the same conclusions. It was impossible to Christianize the slaves without telling them about the Chosen People, the ancient Jews whom Moses led from captivity in Pharaoh's Egypt into the Promised Land of Israel. Inevitably, slaves drew parallels between their own condition and the Jews' captivity. Like the Jews, blacks concluded, they themselves were "de people of de Lord." If they kept the faith, then, like the Jews, they too would reach the Promised Land. The themes of the Chosen People and the Promised Land ran through the sacred songs, or "spirituals," that blacks sang, to the point where Moses and Jesus almost merged:

Gwine to write to Massa Jesus,
To send some Valiant Soldier
To turn back Pharaoh's army, Hallelu!

Mary Edmonia Lewis and "Forever Free" Named Wildfire by her Chippewa mother and black father, Mary Edmonia Lewis adopted a Christian name upon entering Oberlin College. Later she studied sculpture in Boston and Rome. Her "Forever Free" (1867) commemorated the abolition of slavery.

A listener could interpret a phrase like "the Promised Land" in several ways; it could refer to Israel, to heaven, or to freedom. From the perspective of whites, the only permissible interpretations were Israel and heaven, but some blacks, like Denmark Vesey, thought of freedom as well. The ease with which slaves constructed alternative interpretations of the Bible also reflected the fact that many plantations contained black preachers, slaves trained by white ministers to spread Christianity among blacks. When in the presence of masters or white ministers, these black preachers usually just repeated the familiar biblical command, "Obey your master." Often, however, slaves met for services apart from whites, usually on Sunday evenings but during the week as well. Then the message changed. A black preacher in Texas related how his master would say "tell them niggers iffen they obeys the master they goes to Heaven." The minister quickly added, "I knowed there's something better for them, but I daren't tell them 'cept on the sly. That I done lots. I tells 'em iffen they keep praying, the Lord will set 'em free."

Some slaves privately interpreted Christianity as a religion of liberation from the oppression of slavery, but most recognized that their prospects for freedom were slight. On the whole, Christianity did not turn them into revolutionaries. Neither did it necessarily turn them into model slaves. It did, however, provide slaves with a view of slavery different from their masters' outlook. Where the masters argued that slavery was a benign and divinely ordained institution in blacks' best interests, Christianity told them that slavery was really an affliction, a terrible and unjust institution that God had allowed in order to test their faith. For having endured slavery, he would reward blacks. For having created it, he would punish masters.

Black Music and Dance

Compared to the prevailing cultural patterns among elite whites, the culture of blacks in the Old South was extremely expressive. In religious services, blacks shouted "Amen" and let their bodily movements reflect their

feelings long after white religious observances, some of which had once been similarly expressive, had grown sober and sedate. Frederick Law Olmsted recorded how, during a slave service in New Orleans during the 1850s, parishioners "in indescribable expression of ecstasy" exclaimed every few moments: "Glory! oh yes! yes!—sweet Lord! sweet Lord!"

Slaves also expressed their feelings in music and dance. Drawing on their African musical heritage, which used hand clapping to mark rhythm, American slaves made rhythmical hand clapping—called patting juba—an indispensable accompaniment to dancing because southern law forbade them to own "drums, horns, or other loud instruments, which may call together or give sign or notice to one another of their wicked designs and intentions." Slaves also played an African instrument, the banjo, and beat tin buckets as a substitute for drums. Whatever instrument they played, their music was tied to bodily movement. Sometimes slaves imitated white dances like the minuet, but in a way that ridiculed the high manners of their masters. More often, they expressed themselves in a dance African in origin, emphasizing shuffling steps and bodily contortions rather than the erect precision of whites' dances.

Whether at work or at prayer, slaves liked to sing. Work songs describing slave experiences usually consisted of a leader's chant and a choral response:

> I love old Virginny
> So ho! boys! so ho!
> I love to shuck corn
> So ho! boys! so ho!
> Now's picking cotton time
> So ho! boys! so ho!

Masters encouraged such songs, believing that singing induced the slaves to work harder and that the innocent content of most work songs proved that the slaves were happy. Recalling his own past, Frederick Douglass came closer to the truth when he observed that "slaves sing most when they are most unhappy. The songs of the slave represent the sorrows of his heart; and he is relieved by them, only as an aching heart is relieved by its tears."

Blacks also sang religious songs, later known as spirituals. The origin of spirituals is shrouded in obscurity, but it is clear that by 1820 blacks at camp meetings had improvised what one white described as "short scraps of disjointed affirmations, pledges, or prayers lengthened out with long repetition choruses." As this description suggests, whites usually took a dim view of spirituals and tried to make slaves sing "good psalms and hymns" instead of "the extravagant and nonsensical chants, and catches, and hallelujah songs of their own composing." Indeed, when around whites, blacks often sang hymns like those of Isaac Watts and other white clergymen, but nothing could dampen slaves' enthusiasm for songs of their own making.

Spirituals reflected the potent emphasis that the slaves' religion put on deliverance from earthly travails. To a degree, the same was true of white hymns, but spirituals were more direct and concrete. Slaves sang, for example,

> In that morning, true believers,
>   In that morning,
> We will sit aside of Jesus
>   In that morning,
> If you should go fore I go,
>   In that morning,
> You will sit aside of Jesus
>   In that morning,
> True believers, where your tickets
>   In that morning,
> Master Jesus got your tickets
>   In that morning.

Another spiritual proclaimed, "We will soon be free, when the Lord will call us home."

CONCLUSION

The cotton gin revitalized southern agriculture and spurred a redistribution of the South's population, slave and free, from Virginia and other southeastern states to southwestern states like Alabama and Mississippi. As the Old South became more dependent on cotton, it also became more reliant on slave labor.

Slavery left a deep imprint on social relations among the Old South's major white social groups: the planters, the small slaveholders, the yeomen, and the people of the pine barrens. The presence of slaves fed the exaggerated notions of personal honor that made white southerners so violent. Although there was always potential for conflict between slaveholders and non-slaveholders, slavery gave a distinctive unity to the Old South. Most whites did not own any slaves, but the vast majority concluded that their region's prosperity, their ascendancy over blacks, and perhaps even their safety depended on perpetuating slavery. Slavery also shaped the North's perception of the South. Whether northerners believed that the federal government should tamper

with slavery or not, they grew convinced that slavery had cut the South off from progress and had turned it into a region of "sterile lands and bankrupt estates."

Conversely, to most white southerners, the North, and especially the industrial Northeast, appeared to be the region that deviated from the march of progress. In their eyes, most Americans—indeed, most people throughout the world—practiced agriculture, and agriculture rendered the South a more comfortable place than factories rendered the North. In reaction to northern assaults on slavery, southerners portrayed the institution as a time-honored and benevolent response to the natural inequality of the black and white races. Southerners pointed to the slaves' adequate nutrition, their embrace of Christianity, the affection of some slaves for their masters, and even their work songs as evidence of their contentment.

These white perceptions of the culture that developed in the slave quarters with the maturing of plantation agriculture were misguided. In reality, few if any slaves accepted slavery. Although slaves rebelled infrequently and had little chance for permanent escape, they often engaged in covert resistance to their bondage. They embraced Christianity, but they understood it differently from whites. Whereas whites heard in the Christian gospel the need to make slaves submissive, slaves learned of the gross injustice of human bondage and the promise of eventual deliverance.

FOR FURTHER REFERENCE

READINGS

John Ashworth, *Slavery, Capitalism, and Politics in the Antebellum Republic (1995)*. A reinterpretation of the causes of the Civil War from a Marxist perspective.

Orville Vernon Burton, *In My Father's House Are Many Mansions: Family and Community in Edgefield, South Carolina* (1985). An extremely valuable study of the South Carolina upcountry.

Bruce Collins, *White Society in the Antebellum South* (1985). A very good, brief synthesis of southern white society and culture.

William J. Cooper, *Liberty and Slavery: Southern Politics to 1860* (1983). A valuable synthesis and interpretation of recent scholarship on the antebellum South in national politics.

Clement Eaton, *The Growth of Southern Civilization, 1790–1860* (1961). A fine survey of social, economic, and political change.

Robert W. Fogel, *Without Consent or Contract: The Rise and Fall of American Slavery* (1989). A comprehensive reexamination of the slaves' productivity and welfare.

Robert W. Fogel and Stanley L. Engerman, *Time on the Cross: The Economics of American Negro Slavery* (1974). A controversial book that uses mathematical models to analyze the profitability of slavery.

Eugene D. Genovese, *Roll, Jordan, Roll: The World the Slaves Made* (1974). The most influential work on slavery in the Old South written during the last thirty years; a penetrating analysis of the paternalistic relationship between masters and their slaves.

Christine Leigh Heyrman, *Southern Cross: The Beginnings of the Bible Belt* (1997). An intriguing new account of southern religious culture.

Peter Kolchin, *American Slavery, 1619–1877* (1993). A valuable summary of recent scholarship.

Stephanie McCurry, *Masters of Small Worlds* (1995).

CHRONOLOGY, 1830–1860

1790s Methodists and Baptists start to make major strides in converting slaves to Christianity.

1793 Eli Whitney invents the cotton gin.

1800 Gabriel leads a slave rebellion in Virginia.

1808 Congress prohibits external slave trade.

1812 Louisiana, the first state formed out of the Louisiana Purchase, is admitted to the Union.

1816–1819 Boom in cotton prices stimulates settlement of the Southwest.

1819–1820 Missouri Compromise.

1822 Denmark Vesey's conspiracy is uncovered in South Carolina.

1831 William Lloyd Garrison starts *The Liberator*.
Nat Turner leads a slave rebellion in Virginia.

1832 Virginia legislature narrowly defeats a proposal for gradual emancipation.
Virginia's Thomas R. Dew writes an influential defense of slavery.

1835 Arkansas admitted to the Union.

1837 Economic panic begins, lowering cotton prices.

1844–1845 Methodist Episcopal and Baptist Churches split into northern and southern wings over slavery.

1845 Florida and Texas admitted to the Union.

1849 Sugar production in Louisiana reaches its peak.

1849–1860 Period of high cotton prices.

1857 Hinton R. Helper, *The Impending Crisis of the South*.

1859 John Brown's raid on Harpers Ferry.

1860 South Carolina secedes from the Union.

An illuminating and influential account of race, class, and gender relations in the South Carolina low country.

James Oakes, *The Ruling Race: A History of American Slaveholders* (1982). An important attack on the ideas of Eugene D. Genovese.

U. B. Phillips, *American Negro Slavery* (1918) and *Life and Labor in the Old South* (1929). Works marred by racial prejudice but containing a wealth of information about slavery and the plantation system.

Kenneth M. Stampp, *The Peculiar Institution: Slavery in the Ante-Bellum South* (1956). A standard account of the black experience under slavery.

WEBSITES

American History to 1865
http://www.utep.edu/kc3312/clymer/
Contains useful maps of the distribution of agricultural crops and slaves in the antebellum South.

American Studies at the University of Virginia
http://xroads.virginia.edu
This site contains a link to "regional studies" that introduce a rich variety of sources on the South.

Documenting the American South
http://docsouth.unc.edu/
This site contains links to accounts of life under slavery and the church in a southern black community.

For additional works please consult the Bibliography at the end of the book.

Immigration, Expansion, and Sectional Conflict, 1840–1848

Between 1845 and 1847 fifteen to twenty thousand Mormons undertook one of the most extraordinary treks in American history. After the murder of Joseph Smith, the Mormon Prophet (see Chapter 10), Brigham Young led the main body of Mormons from Illinois to a new homeland in the Great Salt Lake valley. The Mormons labeled this area "Deseret," the "land of the honey bee." In part, Young's aim was to flee persecution by Gentiles (non-Mormons). In 1838 Governor Lilburn Boggs of Missouri had issued an order that Mormons must be "exterminated" if they would not leave Missouri. Smith's murder in 1844 capped a long history of persecution of Mormons.

Young wanted Mormons to do more than flee persecution. They also had to cling together, to retain their distinctive religious beliefs and practices. On route to Deseret Young decreed that Mormons establish permanent camps, each with a garrison of well-armed Mormon militia, wood, blacksmithing tools, and Mormon priests to enforce church discipline and to hold each successive caravan of Mormons to the faith. These camps reinforced the Mormons' tendency to cooperate, to depend on each other for survival, and these attitudes would serve the Mormons again when they finally reached the arid region of Deseret.

Why did the Mormons head for Deseret when so many more fertile regions lay in the West? First, because Deseret lay outside the United States;

CHAPTER OUTLINE

Newcomers and Natives

The West and Beyond

The Politics of Expansion, 1840–1846

The Mexican-American War and its Aftermath, 1846–1848

◀ **Gold Miners**
At first, gold rushers worked individually, each with a shovel and pan. By the 1850s devices like the one shown here, a "long tom," were making mining a cooperative venture. Miners shoveled clay, dirt, and stone into a long and narrow box, hosed in water at one end, stirred the mixture, and waited for the finer gravel, which might include gold, to fall through small holes and lodge under the box.

in 1847 it was part of Mexico. Smith's murder had led Young and most other Mormons to conclude that they could no longer live among the Gentiles. Second, the Gentiles were also on the move west. Before emigrating, Mormons considered and rejected various alternatives: Texas, northern California, and Oregon. The trouble was that the hated Gentiles seemed to be everywhere, tiny, restless dots responding to the spirit that a journalist labeled their "Manifest Destiny" to spread over the whole continent. Texas was in the process of being annexed by the United States. California, still part of Mexico, was starting to fill up with Americans, including the by now former governor of Missouri, Lilburn Boggs. Oregon was even less attractive, for by 1846 it contained ten times more Americans than did Texas. The very remoteness and aridity of Deseret made it unlikely that any permanent settlements of Gentiles would take root there.

This Mormon projection turned out to be accurate. After irrigating the Great Salt Lake valley and building Salt Lake City in present-day Utah, the Mormons were able to earn money trading with Gentile wayfarers, most of whom were heading somewhere else. "Americans regard this continent as their birthright," thundered Sam Houston, the first president of the Republic of Texas, in 1847. Indians and Mexicans had to make way for "our mighty march." This was not idle talk. In less than a thousand fevered days during President James K. Polk's administration (1845–1849), the United States increased its land area by 50 percent. It annexed Texas, negotiated Britain out of half of the vast Oregon territory, and fought a war with Mexico that led to the annexation of California and New Mexico. Meanwhile, immigrants poured into the United States, mainly from Europe. The number of immigrants during the 1840s and 1850s exceeded the nation's entire population in 1790.

Immigration and territorial expansion were linked. Most immigrants gravitated to the expansionist Democratic party, and the immigrant vote helped tip the election of 1844 to Polk, an ardent expansionist. Further, waves of immigrants caused tensions between them and the native-born, which were reflected in ugly outbursts of anti-immigrant feeling. Influential Democrats concluded that the best solution to intensifying class and ethnic conflicts lay in expanding the national boundaries, bringing more land under cultivation, and recapturing the ideal of America as a nation of self-sufficient farmers.

Democrats also saw expansion as a way to reduce strife between the sections. Oregon would gratify the North; Texas, the South; and California, everyone. In reality, expansion brought sectional antagonisms to the boiling point, split the Democratic party in the late 1840s, and set the nation on the path to Civil War.

This chapter focuses on four major issues:

■ How did the massive immigration of the 1840s influence the balance of power between the Whig and Democratic parties?

■ What economic and political forces fed westward expansion during the 1840s?

■ What tactics used by President James K. Polk to unite the Democratic party behind a program of westward expansion threatened war with both Britain and Mexico? How did the Democrats "sell" Texas annexation to the North in the election of 1844?

■ How did the outcome of the Mexican-American War intensify intersectional conflict? Why, specifically, did it split the Democratic party?

NEWCOMERS AND NATIVES

Between 1815 and 1860, 5 million European immigrants landed in the United States (see Figure 13.1). Of these, 4.2 million arrived between 1840 and 1860; 3 million of them came in the single decade from 1845 to 1854. This ten-year period witnessed the largest immigration proportionate to the total population (then around 20 million) in American history. The Irish led the way as the most numerous immigrants between 1840 and 1860, with the Germans running a close second. Smaller contingents continued to immigrate to the United States from England, Scotland, and Wales, and a growing number came from Norway, Sweden, Switzerland, and Holland. But by 1860 three-fourths of the 4.1 million foreign-born Americans were either Irish or German.

Expectations and Realities

A desire for religious freedom drew some immigrants to the United States. For example, when Mormon missionaries actively recruited converts in the slums of English factory towns, a number of English migrated to America. Many emigrants from Norway were Quakers fleeing persecution by the official Lutheran clergy. But a far larger number of Europeans sailed for America to better their economic condition. Their hope was fed by a continuous stream of travelers' accounts and letters from relatives describing America as a utopia for poor people.

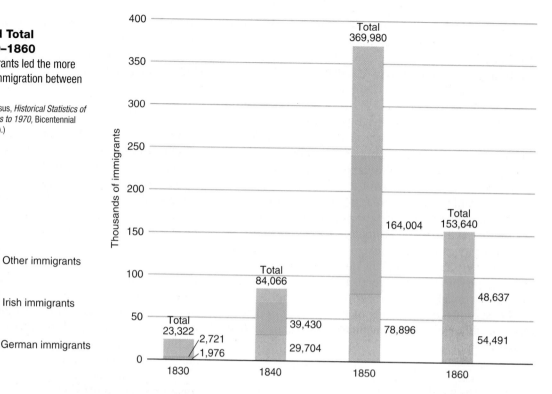

FIGURE 13.1

German, Irish, and Total Immigration, 1830–1860

Irish and German immigrants led the more than tenfold growth of immigration between 1830 and 1860.

(Source: U.S. Bureau of the Census, *Historical Statistics of the United States, Colonial Times to 1970*, Bicentennial Edition (Washington, D.C., 1975).)

German peasants learned that they could purchase a large farm in America for the price of renting a small one in Germany. English men and women were told that enough good peaches and apples were left rotting in the orchards of Ohio to sink the British fleet.

Hoping for the best, emigrants often encountered the worst. Their problems began at ports of embarkation, where hucksters frequently sold them worthless tickets and where ships scheduled to leave in June might not sail until August. Countless emigrants spent precious savings in waterfront slums while awaiting departure. The ocean voyage itself proved terrifying; many emigrants had never set foot on a ship. Most sailed on cargo ships as steerage passengers, where, for six weeks or more, they endured quarters almost as crowded as on slave ships.

For many emigrants, the greatest shock came when they landed. "The folks aboard ship formed great plans for their future, all of which vanished quickly after landing," wrote a young German from Frankfurt in 1840. Immigrants quickly discovered that farming in America was a perilous prospect at best. Not only did immigrants lack the capital to start farms, but farming in the United States also bore little resemblance to farming in Europe. European farmers valued the associations of their communities. Their social and cultural lives revolved around villages that were fringed by the fields that they worked.

In contrast, as many immigrants quickly learned, American farmers lived in relative isolation. They might belong to rural neighborhoods in which farmers on widely scattered plots of land met occasionally at revivals or militia musters. But they lacked the compact village life of European farmers, and they possessed an individualistic psychology that led them to speculate in land and to move frequently.

Despite the shocks and dislocations caused by migration, certain patterns emerged in the distribution of immigrants within the United States. Initially shaped by trade routes, these patterns were then perpetuated by custom. Most of the Irish settlers before 1840 departed from Liverpool on sailing ships that carried English manufactures to eastern Canada and New England in return for timber. On arrival in America, few of these Irish had the capital to become farmers, so they crowded into the urban areas of New England, New York, Pennsylvania, and New Jersey, where they could more easily find jobs. In contrast, German emigrants usually left from continental ports on ships engaged in the cotton trade with New Orleans. Deterred from settling in the South by the presence of slavery, the oppressive climate, and the lack of economic opportunity, the Germans congregated in the upper Mississippi and Ohio valleys, especially in Illinois, Ohio, Wisconsin, and Missouri. Geographical concentration also character-

ized most of the smaller groups of immigrants. More than half of the Norwegian immigrants, for example, settled in Wisconsin, where they typically became farmers.

Immigrants were usually less likely to pursue agriculture in the New World than in Europe. Both the Germans and, to an even greater degree, the Irish tended to concentrate in cities. By 1860 these two groups formed more than 60 percent of the population of St. Louis; nearly half the population of New York City, Chicago, Cincinnati, Milwaukee, Detroit, and San Francisco; and well over a third that of New Orleans, Baltimore, and Boston. These fast-growing cities created an intense demand for the labor of people with strong backs and a willingness to work for low wages. Irish construction gangs built the houses, new streets, and aqueducts that were changing the face of urban America and dug the canals and railroads that threaded together the rapidly developing cities. A popular song recounted the fate of the thousands of Irishmen who died of cholera contracted during the building of a canal in New Orleans:

> Ten thousand Micks, they swung their picks,
> To build the New Canal
> But the choleray was stronger 'n they.
> An' twice it killed them awl.

The cities provided the sort of community life that seemed lacking in farming settlements. Immigrant societies like the Friendly Sons of St. Patrick took root in cities and combined with associations like the Hibernian Society for the Relief of Emigrants from Ireland to welcome the newcomers.

The Germans

In the mid-nineteenth century, the Germans were an extremely diverse group. In 1860 Germany was not a nation-state like France or Britain, but a collection of principalities and small kingdoms. German immigrants thought of themselves as Bavarians, Westphalians, or Saxons rather than as Germans. Moreover, the German immigrants included Catholics, Protestants (usually Lutherans), and Jews as well as a sprinkling of freethinkers who denounced the ritual, clergy, and doctrines of all religions. Although few in number, these critics were vehement in their attacks on the established churches. A pious Milwaukee Lutheran complained in 1860 that he could not drink a glass of beer in a saloon "without being angered by anti-Christian remarks or raillery against preachers."

German immigrants came from a wide range of social classes and occupations. The majority had engaged in farming, but a sizable minority were professionals, artisans, and tradespeople. Heinrich Steinweg, an obscure piano maker from Lower Saxony, arrived in New York City in 1851, anglicized his name to Henry

German Winter Gardens
A well-known beer hall on lower Manhattan's Bowery, the German Winter Gardens were famous for music and sociability.

Steinway, and in 1853 opened the firm of Steinway and Sons, which quickly achieved international acclaim for the quality of its pianos. Levi Strauss, a Jewish tailor from Bavaria, migrated to the United States in 1847. On hearing of the discovery of gold in California in 1848, Strauss gathered rolls of cloth and sailed for San Francisco. When a miner told him of the need for durable work trousers, Strauss fashioned a pair of overalls from canvas. To meet a quickly skyrocketing demand, he opened a factory in San Francisco; his cheap overalls, later known as blue jeans or Levi's, made him rich and famous.

For all their differences, the Germans were bound together by their common language, which strongly induced recent immigrants to the United States to congregate in German neighborhoods. Even prosperous Germans bent on climbing the social ladder usually did so within their ethnic communities. Germans formed their own militia and fire companies, sponsored parochial schools in which German was the language of instruction, started German-language newspapers, and organized their own balls and singing groups. The range of voluntary associations among Germans was almost as broad as among native-born Americans.

Other factors beyond their common language brought unity to the German immigrants. Ironically, the Germans' diversity also promoted their solidarity. For example, because they were able to supply their own doctors, lawyers, teachers, journalists, merchants, artisans, and clergy, the Germans had little need to go outside their own neighborhoods. Moreover, economic self-sufficiency conspired with the strong bonds of their language to encourage a clannish psychology among the German immigrants. Although they admired the Germans' industriousness, native-born Americans resented their economic success and disdained their clannishness. German refugee Moritz Busch complained that "the great mass of Anglo-Americans" held the Germans in contempt. The Germans responded by becoming even more clannish. Their psychological separateness made it difficult for the Germans to be as politically influential as the Irish immigrants.

The Irish

Between 1815 and 1860 Irish immigration to the United States passed through several stages. Irish soldiers who fought against the United States in the War of 1812 had returned to their homeland with reports that America was a paradise filled with fertile land and abundant game, a place where "all a man wanted was a gun and sufficient ammunition to be able to live like a prince."

Among the Irish who subsequently emigrated between 1815 and the mid-1820s, Protestant small landowners and tradespeople in search of better economic opportunity predominated.

From the mid-1820s to the mid-1840s, the character of Irish immigration to the United States gradually changed. Increasingly, the immigrants were Catholics drawn from the poorer classes, many of them tenant farmers whom Protestant landowners had evicted as "superfluous." Protestant or Catholic, rich or poor, eight hundred thousand to a million Irish immigrants entered the United States between 1815 and 1844. Then, between 1845 and the early 1850s, a blight destroyed every harvest of Ireland's potatoes, virtually the only food of the peasantry, and spawned one of the most gruesome famines in history. The Great Famine inflicted indescribable suffering on the Irish peasantry and killed perhaps a million people. One landlord characterized the surviving tenants on his estate as no more than "famished and ghastly skeletons." To escape the ravages of famine, 1.8 million Irish migrated to the United States in the decade after 1845.

Overwhelmingly poor and Catholic, the Irish usually entered the work force at or near the bottom. The popular image of Paddy with his pickax and Bridget the maid contained a good deal of truth. Irish men in the cities dug cellars and often lived in them; outside the cities, they dug canals and railroad beds. Irish women often became domestic servants. Compared to other immigrant women, a high proportion of Irish women entered the work force, if not as maids then often as textile workers. By the 1840s Irish women were displacing native-born women in the textile mills of Lowell and Waltham. Poverty drove Irish women to work at early ages, and the outdoor, all-season work performed by their husbands turned many of them into working widows. Winifred Rooney became a nursemaid at the age of seven and an errand girl at eleven. She then learned needlework, a skill that helped her support her family after her husband's early death. The high proportion of employed Irish women reflected more than their poverty. Compared to the predominantly male German immigrants, more than half of the Irish immigrants were women, most of whom were single adults. In both Ireland and America, the Irish usually married late, and many never married. For Irish women to become self-supporting was only natural.

The lot of most Irish people was harsh. One immigrant described the life of the average Irish laborer in America as "despicable, humiliating, [and] slavish"; there was "no love for him—no protection of life—[he] can be shot down, run through, kicked, cuffed, spat

upon—and no redress, but a response of 'served the damn son of an Irish b____ right, damn him.' " Yet some Irish struggled up the social ladder. In Philadelphia, which had a more varied industrial base than Boston, Irish men made their way into iron foundries, where some became foremen and supervisors. Other Irish rose into the middle class by opening grocery and liquor stores.

The varied occupations pursued by Irish immigrants brought them into conflict with two quite different groups. The poorer Irish who dug canals and cellars, hauled cargo on the docks, washed laundry for others, and served white families competed directly with equally poor free blacks. This competition stirred up Irish animosity toward blacks and a hatred of abolitionists. At the same time, enough Irish men eventually secured skilled or semiskilled jobs that clashes with native-born white workers became unavoidable.

Anti-Catholicism, Nativism, and Labor Protest

The hostility of native-born whites toward the Irish often took the form of anti-Catholicism. Anti-Catholicism had been a strong, if latent, impulse among American Protestants since the early Puritan days. The surge of Irish immigration during the second quarter of the nineteenth century revived anti-Catholic fever. For example, in 1834 rumors circulated among Boston Protestants that a Catholic convent in nearby Charlestown contained dungeons and torture chambers. The mother superior turned away a delegation of officials demanding to inspect the convent. Soon the building lay in ashes, the victim of a Protestant mob. In 1835 Samuel F. B. Morse, the future inventor of the telegraph, warned that the despotic governments of Europe were systematically flooding the United States with Catholic immigrants as part of a conspiracy to destroy republican institutions. "We must first stop this leak in the ship," he wrote, "through which the muddy waters from without threaten to sink us." That same year, the combative evangelical Protestant Lyman Beecher issued *A Plea for the West*, a tract in which he warned faithful Protestants of an alleged Catholic conspiracy to send immigrants to the West in sufficient numbers to dominate the region. A year later, the publication of Maria Monk's best-selling *Awful Disclosures of the Hotel Dieu Nunnery in Montreal* rekindled anti-Catholic hysteria. Although Maria Monk was actually a prostitute who had never lived in a convent, she professed to be a former nun. In her book, she described how the mother superior forced nuns to sub-

mit to the lustful advances of priests who entered the convent by a subterranean passage.

As Catholic immigration swelled in the 1840s, Protestants mounted a political counterattack. It took the form of nativist (anti-immigrant) societies with names like the American Republicans and the United Order of Americans. Although usually started as secret or semisecret fraternal orders, most of these societies developed political offshoots. One, the Order of the Star-Spangled Banner, would evolve by 1854 into the "Know-Nothing," or American, party and would become a major political force in the 1850s.

During the 1840s, however, nativist parties enjoyed only brief moments in the sun. These occurred mainly during flare-ups over local issues, such as whether students in predominantly Catholic neighborhoods should be allowed to use the Catholic Douay rather than Protestant King James version of the Bible for the scriptural readings that began each school day. In 1844, for example, after the American Republican party (which opposed any concessions to Catholics) won some offices in Philadelphia elections, fiery Protestant orators mounted soapboxes to denounce "popery," and Protestant mobs descended on Catholic neighborhoods. Before the militia quelled these "Bible Riots," thirty buildings lay in charred ruins and at least sixteen people had been killed.

Nativism fed on an explosive mixture of fears and discontents. Protestants thought that their doctrine that each individual could interpret the Bible was more democratic than Catholicism, which made doctrine the province of the pope and bishops. In addition, at a time when the wages of native-born artisans and journeymen were depressed by the subdivision of tasks and by the aftermath of the Panic of 1837 (see Chapter 10), many Protestant workers concluded that Catholic immigrants, often desperately poor and willing to work for anything, were threats to their jobs. In reaction, Protestant artisans joined nativist societies.

Nativist outbursts were not labor's only response to the wage cuts that accompanied the depression. Some agitators began to advocate land reform as a solution to workers' economic woes. Americans had long cherished the notion that a nation so blessed by abundant land as the United States would never give rise to a permanent class of factory "wage slaves." In 1844 the English-born radical George Henry Evans organized the National Reform Association and rallied supporters with the slogan "Vote Yourself a Farm." Evans advanced neo-Jeffersonian plans for the establishment of "rural republican townships" composed of 160-acre plots for work-

ers. He quickly gained the backing of artisans who pre-ferred such "agrarian" notions to a further advance of the industrial order that was undermining their position.

Land reformers argued that workers' true interests could never be reconciled with an industrial order in which factory operatives sold their labor for wages. By engaging in wage labor, they said, workers abandoned any hope of achieving economic independence. These reformers most appealed to articulate and self-consciously radical workers, particularly artisans and small masters whose independence was being threatened by factories and who feared that American labor was "fast verging on the servile dependence" common in Europe. But land reform offered little to factory operatives and wage-earning journeymen who completely lacked economic independence. In an age when a horse cost the average worker three months' pay and most factory workers dreaded "the horrors of wilderness life," the idea of solving industrial problems by resettling workers on farms seemed a pipe dream.

Labor unions appealed to workers left cold by the promises of land reformers. For example, desperately poor Irish immigrants, refugees from an agricultural society, believed that they could gain more by unions and strikes than by plowing and planting. Even women workers organized unions in these years. The leader of a seamstresses' union proclaimed, "Too long have we been bound down by tyrant employers."

Probably the most important development for workers in the 1840s was a state court decision. In *Commonwealth* v. *Hunt* (1842), the Massachusetts Supreme Court ruled that labor unions were not illegal monopolies that restrained trade. But because less than 1 percent of the work force belong to labor unions in the 1840s, this decision initially had little impact. Massachusetts employers brushed aside the *Commonwealth* decision, firing union agitators and replacing them with cheap immigrant labor. "Hundreds of honest laborers," a labor paper reported in 1848, "have been dismissed from employment in the manufactories of New England because they have been suspected of knowing their rights and daring to assert them." This repression effectively blunted demands for a ten-hour workday in an era when the twelve- or fourteen-hour day was typical.

Ethnic and religious tensions also split the antebellum working class during the 1830s and 1840s. Friction between native-born and immigrant workers inevitably became intertwined with the political divisions of the second party system.

Labor Protest and Immigrant Politics

Very few immigrants had ever cast a vote in an election prior to their arrival in America, and only a small fraction were refugees from political persecution. Political upheavals had erupted in Austria and several of the German states in the turbulent year of 1848 (the so-called Revolutions of 1848), but among the million German immigrants to the United States, only about ten thousand were political refugees, or "Forty-Eighters."

Once they had settled in the United States, however, many immigrants became politically active. They quickly found that urban political organizations, some of them dominated by earlier immigrants, would help them find lodging and employment, in return for votes. Both the Irish and the Germans identified overwhelmingly with the Democratic party. An obituary of 1837 that described a New Yorker as a "warm-hearted Irishman and an unflinching Democrat" could have been written of millions of other Irish. Similarly, the Germans became stalwart supporters of the Democrats in cities like Milwaukee and St. Louis.

Immigrants' fears about jobs partly explain their widespread support of the Democrats. Former president Andrew Jackson had given the Democratic party an anti-aristocratic coloration, making the Democrats seem more sympathetic than the Whigs to the common people. In addition, antislavery was linked to the Whig party, and the Irish loathed abolitionism because they feared that freed slaves would become economic competitors. Moreover, the Whigs' moral and religious values seemed to threaten those of the Irish and Germans. Hearty-drinking Irish and German immigrants shunned temperance-crusading Whigs, many of whom were also rabid anti-Catholics. Even public-school reform, championed by the Whigs, was seen as a menace to the Catholicism of Irish children and as a threat to German language and culture.

Although liquor regulations and school laws were city or state concerns rather than federal responsibilities, the Democratic party schooled immigrants in broad, national principles. It taught them to venerate George Washington, to revere Thomas Jefferson and Andrew Jackson, and to view "monied capitalists" as parasites who would tremble when the people spoke. It introduced immigrants to Democratic newspapers, Democratic picnics, and Democratic parades. The Democrats, by identifying their party with all that they thought best about the United States, helped give immigrants a sense of themselves as Americans. By the same token, the Democratic party introduced immigrants to

national issues. It redirected political loyalties that often had been forged on local issues into the arena of national politics. During the 1830s the party had persuaded immigrants that national measures like the Bank of the United States and the tariff, seemingly remote from their daily lives, were vital to them. Now, in the 1840s, the Democrats would try to convince immigrants that national expansion likewise advanced their interests.

THE WEST AND BEYOND

As late as 1840, Americans who referred to the West still meant the area between the Appalachian Mountains and the Mississippi River or just beyond, a region that included much of the present-day Midwest. Beyond the states bordering the Mississippi lay an inhospitable region unlike any that the earlier settlers had known. Those who ventured west of Missouri encountered the Great Plains, a semiarid plateau with few trees. Winds sucked the moisture from the soil. Bands of nomadic Indians—including the Pawnees, Kiowas, and Sioux—roamed this territory and gained sustenance mainly from the buffalo. They ate its meat, wore its fur, and covered their dwellings with its hide. Aside from some well-watered sections of northern Missouri and eastern Kansas and Nebraska, the Great Plains presented would-be farmers with massive obstacles.

The formidable barrier of the Great Plains did not stop settlement of the West in the long run. Temporarily, however, it shifted public interest toward the verdant region lying beyond the Rockies, the Far West (see Map 13.1).

MAP 13.1
Trails to the West, 1840
By 1840 several trails carried pioneers from Missouri and Illinois to the West.

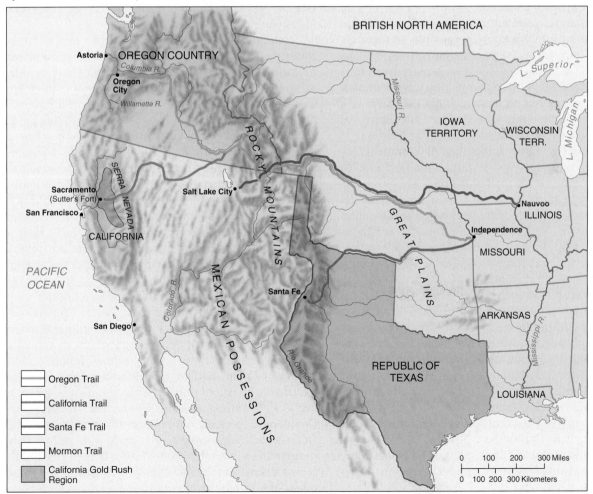

The Far West

With the Transcontinental (or Adams-Onís) Treaty of 1819, the United States had given up its claims to Texas west of the Sabine River. This had left Spain in undisputed possession not only of Texas but also of California and the vast territory of New Mexico. Combined, California and New Mexico included all of present-day California and New Mexico as well as modern Nevada, Utah, and Arizona, and parts of Wyoming and Colorado. Two years later, a series of revolts against Spanish rule had culminated in the independence of Mexico and in Mexico's takeover of all North American territory previously claimed by Spain.

The Transcontinental Treaty also had provided for Spain's ceding to the United States its claims to the country of Oregon north of the forty-second parallel (the northern boundary of California). Then in 1824 and 1825, Russia abandoned its claims to Oregon south of 54°40' (the southern boundary of Alaska). In 1827 the United States and Britain, each of which had claims to Oregon based on discovery and exploration, revived an agreement (originally signed in 1818) for joint occupation of the territory between 42° and 54°40', a colossal area that contemporaries could describe no more precisely than the "North West Coast of America, Westward of the Stony [Rocky] Mountains" and that included all of modern Oregon, Washington, and Idaho as well as parts of present-day Wyoming, Montana, and Canada.

Collectively, Texas, New Mexico, California, and Oregon comprised an area larger than Britain, France, and Germany combined. Such a vast region should have tempted any nation, but during the 1820s Mexico, Britain, and the United States viewed the Far West as a remote and shadowy frontier. By 1820 the American line of settlement had reached only to Missouri, well over two thousand miles (counting detours for mountains) from the West Coast. El Paso on the Rio Grande and Taos

Mission San Gabriel, **by Ferdinand Deppe, 1832**
The San Gabriel Mission was founded in 1771 in southern California, partly with the intent of converting the local Indians, who are shown here settled in a thatched hut, to Catholicism. In 1781 the Spanish governor set out from this mission to found El Pueblo de Nuestra Señora la Reina de Los Angeles' Porciúncula, now usually known simply as Los Angeles.

in New Mexico lay, respectively, twelve hundred and fifteen hundred miles north of Mexico City. Britain, of course, was many thousands of miles from Oregon.

Far Western Trade

The earliest American and British outposts on the West Coast were trading centers established by merchants who had reached California and Oregon by sailing around South America and up the Pacific. Between the late 1790s and the 1820s, for example, Boston merchants had built a thriving exchange of coffee, tea, spices, cutlery, clothes, and hardware—indeed, anything that could be bought or manufactured in the eastern United States—for furs (especially those of sea otters), cattle, hides, and tallow (rendered from cattle fat and used for making soap and candles). Between 1826 and 1828 alone, Boston traders took more than 6 million cattle hides out of California; in the otherwise undeveloped California economy, these hides, called "California banknotes," served as the main medium of exchange. During the 1820s the British Hudson's Bay Company developed a similar trade in Oregon and northern California.

The California trade occasioned little friction with Mexico. Producing virtually no manufactured goods, Hispanic people born in California (called *Californios*) were as eager to buy as the traders were to sell—so eager that they sometimes rowed out to the vessels laden with goods, thus sparing the traders the trip ashore. Many traders who did settle in California quickly learned to speak Spanish and became assimilated into Mexican culture.

Farther south, trading links developed during the 1820s between St. Louis and Santa Fe along the famed Santa Fe Trail. The Panic of 1819 left the American Midwest short of cash and its merchants burdened by unsold goods. Pulling themselves up from adversity, however, plucky midwesterners loaded wagon trains with tools, utensils, clothing, windowpanes, and household sundries each spring and rumbled westward to Santa Fe, where they traded their merchandise for mules and New Mexican silver. To a far greater extent than had Spain, Mexico welcomed this trade. Indeed, by the 1830s more than half the goods entering New Mexico by the Santa Fe Trail trickled into the mineral-rich interior provinces of Mexico such as Chihuahua and Sonora, with the result that the Mexican silver peso, which midwestern traders brought back with them, quickly became the principal medium of exchange in Missouri.

The profitability of the beaver trade also prompted Americans to venture west from St. Louis to trap beaver in what is today western Colorado and eastern Utah. There they competed with agents of the Hudson's Bay Company. In 1825, on the Green River in Mexican territory, the St. Louis-based trader William Ashley inaugurated an annual rendezvous or encampment where traders exchanged beaver pelts for supplies, thereby saving themselves the trip to St. Louis. Although silk hats had become more fashionable than beaver hats by 1854, over a half-million beaver pelts were auctioned off in London alone that year.

For the most part, American traders and trappers operating on the northern Mexican frontier in the 1820s and 1830s posed more of a threat to the beaver than to Mexico's provinces. Not only did the Mexican people of California and New Mexico depend on the American trade for manufactured goods, but Mexican officials in both provinces also relied on customs duties to support their governments. In New Mexico the government often had to await the arrival of the annual caravan of traders from St. Louis before it could pay its officials and soldiers.

Although the relations between Mexicans and Americans were mutually beneficial during the 1820s, the potential for conflict was never absent. Spanish-speaking, Roman Catholic, and accustomed to a more hierarchical society, the Mexicans formed a striking contrast to the largely Protestant, individualistic Americans. And although few American traders themselves became permanent residents of Mexico, many returned with glowing reports of the climate and fertility of Mexico's northern provinces. By the 1820s American settlers were already moving into eastern Texas. At the same time, the ties that bound the central government of Mexico to its northern frontier provinces were starting to fray.

The American Settlement of Texas to 1835

During the 1820s Americans began to settle the eastern part of the Mexican state known as Coahuila-Texas, which lacked the deserts and mountains that formed a natural barrier along the boundaries of New Mexico and California. Initially, Mexico encouraged this migration, partly to gain protection against Indian attacks that had intensified with the erosion of the Spanish-Mexican system of missions.

Spain, and later Mexico, recognized that the key to controlling the frontier provinces lay in promoting their settlement by civilized Hispanic people—that is, by Spaniards and Mexicans, and by Indians who had

embraced Catholicism and agriculture. The key instrument of Spanish expansion on the frontier had long been the mission. Staffed by Franciscan priests, the missions endeavored to convert Native Americans and settle them as farmers on mission lands. To protect the missions, the Spanish often had constructed forts, or presidios, near them. San Francisco was the site of a mission and a presidio founded in 1776, and did not develop as a town until the 1830s.

Dealt a blow by the successful struggle for Mexican independence, Spain's system of missions declined in the late 1820s and 1830s. The Mexican government gradually "secularized" the missions by distributing their lands to ambitious government officials and private ranchers who turned the mission Indians into forced laborers. As many Native Americans fled the missions, returned to their nomadic ways, and joined with Indians who had always resisted the missions, lawlessness surged on the Mexican frontier and few Mexicans ventured into the undeveloped territory.

In 1824 the Mexican government began to encourage American colonization of Texas by bestowing generous land grants on agents known as *empresarios* to recruit peaceful American settlers for Texas. Initially, most Americans, like the *empresario* Stephen F. Austin, were content to live in Texas as naturalized Mexican citizens. But trouble brewed quickly. Most of the American settlers were southern farmers, often slaveholders. Having emancipated its own slaves in 1829, Mexico closed Texas to further American immigration in 1830 and forbade the introduction of more slaves. But the Americans, white and black, kept coming, and in 1834 Austin secured repeal of the 1830 prohibition on American immigration. Two years later, Mexican general Manual Mier y Téran ran a sword through his heart in despair over Mexico's inability to stem and control the American advance. By 1836 Texas contained some thirty thousand white Americans, five thousand black slaves, and four thousand Mexicans.

As American immigration swelled, Mexican politics (which Austin compared to the country's volcanic geology) grew increasingly unstable. In 1834 Mexican president Antonio López de Santa Anna instituted a policy of restricting the powers of the regimes in Coahuila-Texas and other Mexican states. His actions ignited a series of rebellions in those regions, the most important of which became known as the Texas Revolution.

The Texas Revolution, 1836

Santa Anna's brutality in crushing most of the rebellions alarmed Austin, who initially had hoped to secure greater autonomy for Texas within Mexico, not independence. In this, he had the support of the leading *Tejanos* (Mexicans living in Texas). When Santa Anna invaded Texas in the fall of 1835, however, Austin cast his lot with the more radical Americans who wanted independence.

Entirro de un Angel (Funeral of an Angel), by Theodore Gentilz
Protestant Americans who ventured into Texas came upon a Hispanic culture unlike anything they had seen. Here a San Antonio procession follows the coffin of a baptized infant who, in Catholic belief, will become an angel in heaven.

At first, Santa Anna's army met with success. In late February 1836, his force of 4,000 men laid siege to San Antonio, whose 200 Texan defenders retreated into an abandoned mission, the Alamo. After repelling repeated attacks, the remaining 187 Texans, were overwhelmed on March 6. Most were killed in the final assault. A few, including the famed frontiersman Davy Crockett, surrendered. Crockett then was executed on Santa Anna's orders. A few weeks later, Mexican troops massacred some 350 prisoners taken from an American settlement at Goliad.

Even before these events, Texas delegates had met in a windswept shed in the village of Washington, Texas, and declared Texas independent of Mexico. The rebels by then had settled on a military leader, Sam Houston, for their president. A giant man who wore leopard-skin vests, Houston retreated east to pick up recruits (mostly Americans who crossed the border to fight Santa Anna). Once reinforced, Houston turned and surprised Santa Anna on a prairie near the San Jacinto River in April. Shouting "Remember the Alamo," Houston's army of eight hundred tore through the Mexican lines, killing nearly half of Santa Anna's men in fifteen minutes and taking Santa Anna himself prisoner. Houston then forced Santa Anna to sign a treaty (which the Mexican government never ratified) recognizing the independence of Texas (see Map 13.2).

American Settlements in California, New Mexico, and Oregon

California and New Mexico, both less accessible than Texas, exerted no more than a mild attraction for American settlers during the 1820s and 1830s. Only a few hundred Americans resided in New Mexico in 1840. That same year, California contained perhaps four hundred Americans. A contemporary observed that the Americans living in California and New Mexico "are scattered throughout the whole Mexican population, and most of them have Spanish wives. . . . They live in every respect like the Spanish."

Yet the beginnings of change were already evident. California's Hispanic population generally welcomed American immigration as a way to encourage economic development. In addition, some Americans who settled in California before 1840 sent back highly favorable reports of the region to induce immigration. One tongue-in-cheek story told of a 250-year-old man who had to leave the idyllic region in order to die. Such reports produced their intended effect. During the 1840s an ever-widening stream of Americans migrated to the interior Sacramento valley, where they lived geographically and culturally apart from the Mexicans. For these land-hungry settlers, no sacrifice seemed too great if it led to California.

Oregon, with its abundant farmland, beckoned settlers from the Mississippi valley. During the 1830s missionaries like the Methodist Jason Lee moved into Oregon's Willamette valley, and by 1840 the area contained some five hundred Americans. Enthusiastic reports sent back by Lee piqued interest in Oregon. An orator in Missouri described Oregon as a "pioneer's paradise" where "the pigs are running around under the great acorn trees, round and fat and already cooked, with knives and forks sticking in them so that you can cut off a slice whenever you are hungry." Indeed, to some, Oregon seemed even more attractive than California. Oregon was already jointly occupied by Britain and the United States, and its prospects for eventual U.S. annexation appeared better than California's.

The Overland Trails

Whether bound for California or Oregon, the pioneers faced a four-month journey across terrain that was all the more terrifying because little was known about it.

MAP 13.2
Major Battles in the Texas Revolution, 1835–1836
Sam Houston's victory at San Jacinto was the decisive action of the war and avenged the massacres at the Alamo and Goliad.

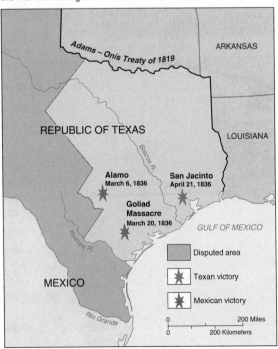

Emigrant Train Bedding Down for the Night
Men, women, and children divided the tasks—caring for oxen, feeding horses, drawing water, preparing supper, washing clothes—on the basis of gender and age.

The eastern press teemed with horror stories, mostly fictitious, of Indian massacres. Assuming that they would have to fight their way across the Plains, settlers prepared for the trip by buying enough guns for an army from merchants in the rival jump-off towns of Independence and St. Joseph, Missouri. In reality, the pioneers were more likely to shoot themselves or each other by accident than to be shot by the usually cooperative Indians, and much more likely to be scalped by the inflated prices charged by merchants in Independence or "St. Joe" than by Native Americans.

Once embarked, the emigrants faced new hardships and hazards: kicks from mules, oxen that collapsed from thirst, overloaded wagons that broke down. Trails were difficult to follow—at least until they became littered by the debris of broken wagons and by the bleached bones of oxen. Guidebooks to help emigrants chart their course were more like guessbooks. The Donner party, which set out from Illinois in 1846, lost so much time following the advice of one such book that its members became snowbound in the High Sierra and reached California only after its survivors had turned to cannibalism.

Emigrants responded to the challenges of the overland trails by cooperating closely with one another. Most set out in huge wagon trains rather than as individuals. Reflecting firmly entrenched traditions, husbands depended on their wives to pack and unpack the wagon each day, to milk the cows brought along to stock the new farms in the West, and to cook. Women, too, assisted with the childbirths that occurred on the trail at about the same frequency as in the nation as a whole. Men yoked and unyoked the oxen, drove the wagons and stock, and formed hunting parties.

Between 1840 and 1848, an estimated 11,500 emigrants followed an overland trail to Oregon, and some 2,700 reached California. These numbers were modest and concentrated in the years from 1844 to 1848. Yet even small numbers could make a huge difference in the Far West, for the British could not effectively settle Oregon at all, and the Mexican population in California was small and scattered. By 1845 California clung to Mexico by the thinnest of threads. The territory's Hispanic population, the *Californios*, felt little allegiance to Mexico, which they contemptuously referred to as the "other shore." Nor did they feel any allegiance to the United States. Some *Californios* wanted independence from Mexico; others looked to the day when California might become a protectorate of Britain or perhaps even France. But these *Californios*, with their shaky allegiances, now faced a growing number of American settlers whose political sympathies were not at all divided.

THE POLITICS OF EXPANSION, 1840–1846

The major issue that arose as a by-product of westward expansion was whether the United States should annex the independent Texas republic. In the mid-1840s the Texas-annexation issue generated the kind of political passions that banking questions had ignited in the

1830s, and became entangled with equally unsettling issues relating to California, New Mexico, and Oregon. Between 1846 and 1848, a war with Mexico and a dramatic confrontation with Britain settled all these questions on terms favorable to the United States.

Yet at the start of the 1840s, western issues occupied no more than a tenuous position on the national political agenda. From 1840 to 1842 questions relating to economic recovery—notably, banking, the tariff, and internal improvements—dominated the attention of political leaders. Only after politicians failed to address the economic issues coherently did opportunistic leaders thrust issues relating to expansion to the top of the political agenda.

The Whig Ascendancy

The election of 1840 brought Whig candidate William Henry Harrison to the presidency and installed Whig majorities in both houses of Congress. The Whigs had raced to power with a program, based on Henry Clay's American System, to stimulate economic recovery, and they had excellent prospects of success. They quickly repealed Van Buren's darling, the Independent Treasury. They then planned to substitute some kind of national "fiscal agent," which, like the defunct Bank of the United States, would be a private corporation chartered by Congress and charged with regulating the currency. The Whigs also favored a tariff, but with a twist. In the past, Whigs had supported a "protective" tariff set high to discourage the importation of goods that would compete with the products of American industries. Now the Whigs proposed a modification in the form of a "revenue" tariff high enough to provide "incidental" protection for American industries but low enough to allow most foreign products to enter the United States. The duties collected on these imports would accrue to the federal government as revenue. The Whigs then planned to distribute this revenue to the states for internal improvements, a measure as popular among southern and western Whigs as the tariff was among northeastern Whigs.

The Whig agenda might have breezed into law had it not been for the untimely death of Harrison after only one month in office. With Harrison's demise, Vice President John Tyler, an upper-crust Virginian who had been put on the ticket in 1840 to strengthen the Whigs' appeal in the South, assumed the presidency. From virtually every angle, the new president proved a disaster for the Whigs.

A former Democrat, Tyler had broken with Jackson over nullification, but he continued to favor the Democratic philosophy of states' rights. As president, he repeatedly used the veto to shred his new party's program. In August 1841 a Whig bill to create a new national bank became the first casualty of Tyler's veto. Stunned, the Whig majority in Congress quickly passed a modified banking bill, only to see Tyler veto it as well.

Congressional Whigs fared little better on the tariff and the distribution of tariff revenues to the states. The Compromise Tariff of 1833 had provided for a gradual scaling down of tariff duties, until none was to exceed 20 percent by 1842. Amid the depression of the early 1840s, however, the provision for a 20 percent maximum tariff appeared too low to generate revenue. Without revenue, the Whigs would have no money to distribute among the states for internal improvements and no program with national appeal. In response, the Whig congressional majority passed two bills in the summer of 1842 that simultaneously postponed the final reduction of tariffs to 20 percent and ordered distribution to the states to proceed. Tyler promptly vetoed both bills. Tyler's mounting vetoes infuriated Whig leadership. "Again has the imbecile, into whose hands accident has placed the power, vetoed a bill passed by a majority of those legally authorized to pass it," screamed the *Daily Richmond Whig*. Some Whigs talked of impeaching Tyler. Finally, in August, needing revenue to run the government, Tyler signed a new bill that maintained some tariffs above 20 percent but abandoned distribution to the states.

Tyler's erratic course confounded and disrupted his party. By maintaining some tariffs above 20 percent, the tariff of 1842 satisfied northern manufacturers, but by abandoning distribution, it infuriated many southerners and westerners. Northern Whigs succeeded in passing the bill with the aid of many northern Democrats, particularly pro-tariff Pennsylvanians, whereas large numbers of Whigs in the Upper South and West opposed the tariff of 1842.

In the congressional elections of 1842, the Whigs paid a heavy price for failing to enact their program. Although retaining a slim majority in the Senate, they lost control of the House to the Democrats. Now the nation had one party in control of the Senate, its rival in control of the House, and a president who appeared to belong to neither party.

Tyler and the Annexation of Texas

Although a political maverick disowned by his party, Tyler ardently desired a second term as president. Domestic issues offered him little hope of building a popular following, but foreign policy was another mat-

ter. In 1842 Tyler's secretary of state, Daniel Webster, concluded a treaty with Great Britain, represented by Lord Ashburton, that settled a long-festering dispute over the boundary between Maine and the Canadian province of New Brunswick. Awarding more than half of the disputed territory to the United States, the Webster-Ashburton Treaty was popular in the North. Tyler reasoned that if he could now arrange for the annexation of Texas, he would build a national following.

The issue of slavery, however, had long clouded every discussion of Texas. By the late 1830s antislavery northerners viewed proposals to annex Texas as part of an elaborate southern conspiracy to extend American territory south into Mexico, Cuba, and Central America, thus allowing for an unlimited number of new slave states, while the British presence in Canada would limit the number of free states. In fact, some southerners talked openly of creating as many as four or five slave states out of the vast territory encompassed by Texas.

Nevertheless, in the summer of 1843, Tyler launched a propaganda campaign for Texas annexation. He justified his crusade by reporting that he had learned of certain British designs on Texas, which Americans, he argued, would be prudent to forestall. Tyler's campaign was fed by reports from his unofficial agent in London, Duff Green, a protégé of John C. Calhoun and a man whom John Quincy Adams contemptuously dismissed as an "ambassador of slavery." Green assured Tyler that, as a prelude to undermining slavery in the United States, the British would pressure Mexico to recognize the independence of Texas in return for the abolition of slavery there. Calhoun, who became Tyler's secretary of state early in 1844, embroidered these reports with fanciful theories about British plans to use abolition as a way to destroy rice, sugar, and cotton production in the United States and gain for itself a monopoly on all three staples.

In spring 1844 Calhoun and Tyler submitted to the Senate for ratification a treaty, secretly drawn up, annexing Texas to the United States. Among the supporting documents accompanying the treaty was a letter from Calhoun to Richard Pakenham, the British foreign minister in Washington, that defended slavery as beneficial to blacks, the only way to protect them from "vice and pauperism." Antislavery northerners no longer had to look under the carpet for evidence that the impulse behind annexation lay in a desire to protect and extend slavery; now they needed only to read Calhoun's words. Both Martin Van Buren, the leading northern Democrat, and Henry Clay, the most powerful Whig, came out against immediate annexation on the grounds that annexation would provoke the kind of sectional conflict

James K. Polk
Lacking charm, Polk bored even his friends, but few presidents could match his record of acquiring land for the United States.

that each had sought to bury. By a vote of 35 to 16, the treaty went down to crushing defeat in the Senate. Decisive as it appeared, however, this vote only postponed the final decision on annexation to the upcoming election of 1844.

The Election of 1844

Tyler's ineptitude turned the presidential campaign into a free-for-all. The president hoped to succeed himself in the White House, but he lacked a base in either party. Testing the waters as an independent, he could not garner adequate support and was forced to drop out of the race.

Henry Clay had a secure grip on the Whig nomination. Martin Van Buren appeared to have an equally firm grasp on the Democratic nomination, but the issue of Texas annexation split his party. Trying to appease all shades of opinion within his party, Van Buren stated that he would abide by whatever Congress might decide on

the annexation issue. Van Buren's attempt to evade the issue succeeded only in alienating the modest number of northern annexationists, led by Michigan's former governor Lewis Cass, and the much larger group of southern annexationists. At the Democratic convention, Van Buren and Cass effectively blocked each other's nomination. The resulting deadlock was broken by the nomination of James K. Polk of Tennessee, the first "dark-horse" presidential nominee in American history and a supporter of immediate annexation.

Jeering "Who is James K. Polk?" the Whigs derided the nomination. Polk was little known outside the South, and he had lost successive elections for the governorship of Tennessee. Yet Polk was a wily campaigner, and he persuaded many northerners that annexation of Texas would benefit them. Conjuring an imaginative scenario, Polk and his supporters argued that if Britain succeeded in abolishing slavery in Texas, slavery would not be able to move westward; racial tensions in existing slave states would intensify; and the chances of a race war, which might spill over into the North, would increase. However far-fetched, this argument played effectively on northern racial fears and helped Polk detach annexation from Calhoun's narrow, prosouthern defense of it.

In contrast to the Democrats who established a clear direction in their arguments, Clay kept muddying the waters. First he told his followers that he had nothing against annexation as long as it would not disrupt sec-

tional harmony. In September 1844 he again came out against annexation. Clay's shifts on annexation alienated his southern supporters and prompted a small but influential body of northern antislavery Whigs to desert to the Liberty party, which had been organized in 1840. Devoted to the abolition of slavery by political action, the Liberty party nominated Ohio's James G. Birney for the presidency.

Annexation was not the sole issue of the campaign. The Whigs infuriated Catholic immigrant voters by nominating Theodore Frelinghuysen as Clay's running mate. A leading Presbyterian layman, Frelinghuysen gave "his head, his hand, and his heart" to temperance and an assortment of other Protestant causes. His presence on their ticket fixed the image of the Whigs as the orthodox Protestant party and roused the largely Catholic foreign-born voters to turn out in large numbers for the Democrats.

On the eve of the election in New York City, so many Irish marched to the courthouse to be qualified for voting that the windows had to be left open for people to get in and out. "Ireland has reconquered the country which England lost," an embittered Whig moaned. Polk won the electoral vote 170 to 105, but his margin in the popular vote was only 38,000 out of 2.6 million votes cast, and he lost his own state of Tennessee by 113 votes (see Map 13.3). In most states the two main parties contended with each other on close terms, a sign of the maturity of the second party system. A shift of 6,000 votes in New York, where the immigrant vote and Whig defections to the Liberty party hurt Clay, would have given Clay both the state and the presidency.

Manifest Destiny, 1845

The election of 1844 demonstrated one incontestable fact: the annexation of Texas had more national support than Clay had realized. The surging popular sentiment for expansion that made the underdog Polk rather than Clay the man of the hour reflected a growing conviction among the people that America's natural destiny was to expand into Texas and all the way to the Pacific Ocean.

Expansionists emphasized extending the "area of freedom" and talked of "repelling the contaminating proximity of monarchies upon the soil that we have consecrated to the rights of man." For contemporary young Americans like Walt Whitman, such restless expansionism knew few limits. "The more we reflect upon annexation as involving a part of Mexico, the more do doubts and obstacles resolve themselves away," Whitman wrote. "Then there is California, on the way to which lovely tract

MAP 13.3
The Election of 1844

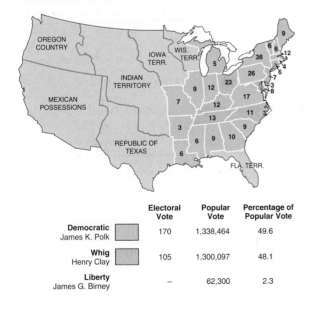

	Electoral Vote	Popular Vote	Percentage of Popular Vote
Democratic James K. Polk	170	1,338,464	49.6
Whig Henry Clay	105	1,300,097	48.1
Liberty James G. Birney	–	62,300	2.3

lies Santa Fe; how long a time will elapse before they shine as two new stars in our mighty firmament?"

Americans awaited only a phrase to capture this ebullient spirit of continentalism. In 1845 John L. O'Sullivan, a New York Democratic journalist, wrote of "our manifest destiny to overspread and to possess the whole of the continent which Providence has given us for the development of the great experiment of liberty and federated self-government entrusted to us."

Advocates of Manifest Destiny used lofty language and routinely invoked God and Nature to sanction expansion. Inasmuch as most proponents of Manifest Destiny were Democrats, many of whom supported the annexation of Texas, northern Whigs frequently dismissed Manifest Destiny as a smoke screen aimed at concealing the evil intent of expanding slavery. In reality, many advocates of Manifest Destiny were neither supporters of slavery nor zealous annexationists. Oregon and California loomed more prominently in their minds than Texas. For despite their flowery phrases, these expansionists rested their case on hard material calculations. Most blamed the post-1837 depression on the failure of the United States to acquire markets for its agricultural surplus and saw the acquisition of Oregon and California as solutions. A Missouri Democrat observed that "the ports of Asia are as convenient to Oregon as the ports of Europe are to the eastern slope of our confederacy, with an infinitely better ocean for navigation." An Alabama Democrat praised California's "safe and capacious harbors," which, he assured, "invite to their bosoms the rich commerce of the East."

Expansionists desired more than profitable trade routes, however. At the heart of their thinking lay an impulse to preserve the predominantly agricultural character of the American people and thereby to safeguard democracy. Most expansionists associated the industrialization that was transforming America with social stratification and class strife, and many saw the concentration of impoverished Irish immigrants in cities and factory towns as evidence of shrinking opportunities for the economic advancement of the common people. After a tour of New England mill towns in 1842, John L. O'Sullivan warned Americans that should they fail to encourage alternatives to factories, the United States would sink to the level of Britain, a nation that the ardent Democratic expansionist James Gordon Bennett described as a land of "bloated wealth" and "terrible misery."

Most Democratic expansionists came to see the acquisition of new territory as a logical complement to their party's policies of low tariffs and decentralized banking. Where tariffs and banks tended to "favor and foster the factory system," expansion would provide farmers with land and with access to foreign markets for their produce. As a consequence, Americans would continue to become farmers, and the foundations of the Republic would remain secure. The acquisition of California and Oregon would provide enough land and harbors to sustain not only the 20 million Americans of 1845 but the 100 million that some expansionists projected for 1900 and the 250 million that O'Sullivan predicted for 1945.

The expansionists' message, especially as delivered by the penny press in such newspapers as Bennett's *New York Herald*, made sense to the laboring poor of America's antebellum cities. The *Herald*, the nation's largest-selling newspaper in the 1840s, played on the anxieties of its working-class readers by arguing relentlessly for the expulsion of the British from Oregon and for thwarting alleged British plans to abolish slavery in the United States. These readers, many of them fiercely antiblack, anti-British Irish immigrants, welcomed any efforts to open up economic opportunities for the common people. Most also favored the perpetuation of slavery, for the freeing of slaves would throw masses of blacks into the already intense competition for jobs.

The expansionists with whom these laboring-class readers sided drew ideas from Thomas Jefferson, John Quincy Adams, and other leaders of the early Republic who had proclaimed the American people's right to displace both "uncivilized" and European people from the path of their westward movement. Early expansionists, however, had feared that overexpansion might create an ungovernable empire. Jefferson, for example, had proposed an indefinite restriction on the settlement of Louisiana. In contrast, the expansionists of the 1840s, citing the virtues of the telegraph and the railroad, believed that the problem of distance had been "literally annihilated." James Gordon Bennett claimed that the telegraph would render the whole nation as compact and homogeneous as New York City. Ironically, although many expansionists pointed with alarm to the negative effects of industrialization on society, their confidence in technology convinced them that the nation could expand with minimal risk to the people.

Polk and Oregon

The most immediate effect of the growing spirit of Manifest Destiny was to escalate the issue of Oregon. To soften northern criticism of the still-pending annexation of Texas, the Democrats had included in their platform

for the election of 1844 the assertion that American title "to the whole of the Territory of Oregon is clear and unquestionable." Taken literally, the platform committed the party to acquire the entire area between California and 54°40', the southern boundary of Alaska. Since Polk had not yet been elected, the British could safely ignore this extraordinary claim for the moment, and in fact the Oregon issue had aroused far less interest during the campaign than had the annexation of Texas. But in his inaugural address, Polk reasserted the "clear and unquestionable" claim to the "country of Oregon." If by this Polk meant all of Oregon, then the United States, which had never before claimed any part of Oregon north of the forty-ninth parallel, had executed an astounding and belligerent reversal of policy.

Polk's objectives in Oregon were more subtle than his language. He knew that the United States could never obtain all of Oregon without a war with Britain, and he wanted to avoid that. He proposed to use the threat of hostilities to persuade the British to accept what they had repeatedly rejected in the past—a division of Oregon at the forty-ninth parallel. Such a division, extending the existing boundary between the United States and Canada from the Rockies to the Pacific, would give the United States both the excellent deep-water harbors of Puget Sound and the southern tip of British-controlled Vancouver Island. For their part, the British had long held out for a division along the Columbia River, which entered the Pacific Ocean far south of the forty-ninth parallel (see Map 13.4).

Polk's comments in his inaugural speech roused among westerners a furious interest in acquiring the whole territory. Mass meetings adopted such resolutions as "We are all for Oregon, and *all* Oregon in the West" and "The Whole or None!" Furthermore, each passing year brought new American settlers into Oregon. Even John Quincy Adams, who advocated neither the annexation of Texas nor the 54°40' boundary for Oregon, believed that the American settlements in Oregon gave the United States a far more reasonable claim to the territory than mere exploration and discovery gave the British. The United States, not Britain, Adams preached, was the nation bound "to make the wilderness blossom as the rose, to establish laws, to increase, multiply, and subdue the earth," all "at the first behest of God Almighty."

In April 1846 Polk secured from Congress the termination of joint British-American occupation of Oregon and promptly gave Britain the required one-year's notice. With joint occupation abrogated, the British could either go to war over American claims to 54°40' or negotiate. They chose to negotiate. Although the British raged against "that ill-regulated, overbearing, and aggressive spirit of American democracy," they had too many domestic and foreign problems to welcome a war over what Lord Aberdeen, the British foreign secretary, dismissed as "a few miles of pine swamp." The ensuing treaty provided for a division at the forty-ninth parallel, with some modifications. Britain retained all of Vancouver Island as well as navigation rights on the Columbia River. The Senate ratified the treaty (with the proviso that Britain's navigation rights on the Columbia were merely temporary) on June 15, 1846.

MAP 13.4
Oregon Boundary Dispute
Although demanding that Britain cede the entire Oregon Territory south of 54°40', the United States settled for a compromise at the forty-ninth parallel.

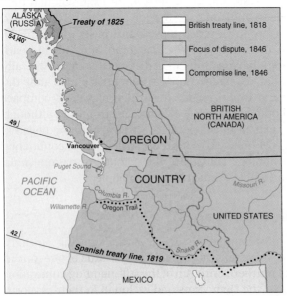

THE MEXICAN-AMERICAN WAR AND ITS AFTERMATH, 1846–1848

Between 1846 and 1848 the United States successfully fought a war with Mexico that led Mexico to renounce all claims to Texas and to cede its provinces of New Mexico and California to the United States. Many Americans rejoiced in the stunning victory. But some recognized that deep divisions over the status of slavery in New Mexico and California boded ill for their nation's future.

The Origins of the Mexican-American War

Even as Polk was challenging Britain over Oregon, the United States and Mexico moved steadily toward war. The impending conflict had both remote and immediate causes. One long-standing grievance lay in the failure of the Mexican government to pay some $2 million in debts owed to American citizens. In addition, bitter memories of the Alamo and of the Goliad massacre continued to arouse in Americans a loathing of Mexicans. Above all, the issue of Texas embroiled relations between the two nations. Mexico still hoped to regain Texas or at least to keep it independent of the United States.

Behind Mexican anxieties about Texas lay a deeper fear. Mexicans viewed the United States with a mixture of awe and aversion. Americans struck them as marked by industriousness and political stability, qualities Mexicans found lacking in themselves (the Mexican presidency changed hands twenty times between 1829 and 1844). But Mexicans also saw this "Colossus of the North" as extremely aggressive, prone to trample on anyone in its path and to disguise its intentions with high-sounding phrases like Manifest Destiny. Once in control of Texas, the Mexicans feared, the United States might seize other provinces, perhaps even Mexico itself, and treat the citizens of Mexico much as it treated its slaves.

Unfortunately for Mexico, Polk's election increased the strength of the pro-annexationists, for his campaign had persuaded many northerners that enfolding Texas would bring national benefits. In February 1845 both houses of Congress responded to popular sentiment by passing a resolution annexing Texas. However, Texans balked, in part because some feared that union with the United States would provoke a Mexican invasion and war on Texas soil.

Confronted by Texan timidity and Mexican belligerence, Polk moved on two fronts. To sweeten the pot for the Texans, he supported their claim to the Rio Grande as the southern boundary of Texas. This claim ran counter to Mexico's view that the Nueces River, a hundred miles northeast of the Rio Grande, bounded Texas. The area between the Nueces and the Rio Grande was largely uninhabited, but the stakes were high. Although only a hundred miles southwest of the Nueces at its mouth on the Gulf of Mexico, the Rio Grande meandered west and then north for nearly two thousand miles and encircled a huge slice of territory, including part of New Mexico. The Texas that Polk proposed to annex thus encompassed far more land than the Texas that had gained

independence from Mexico in 1836. On July 4, 1845, reassured by Polk's largesse, a Texas convention overwhelmingly voted to accept annexation. In response to Mexican war preparations, Polk then made a second move, ordering American troops under General Zachary Taylor to the edge of the disputed territory. Taylor took up a position at Corpus Christi, a tiny Texas outpost situated just south of the Nueces and hence in territory still claimed by Mexico.

Never far from Polk's thoughts in his insistence on the Rio Grande boundary lay his desire for California and for its fine harbors of San Diego and San Francisco. In fact, Polk had entered the White House with the firm intention of extending American control over California. By the summer of 1845, his followers were openly proclaiming that, if Mexico went to war with the United States over Texas, "the road to California will be open to us." Then in October 1845, Polk received a dispatch from Thomas O. Larkin, the American consul at Monterey, California, that warned darkly of British designs on California but ended with the optimistic assurance that the Mexicans in California would prefer American to British rule. Larkin's message gave Polk the idea that California might be acquired by the same methods as Texas: revolution followed by annexation.

With Texans' acceptance of annexation and Taylor's troops at Corpus Christi, the next move belonged to Mexico. In early 1845 a new Mexican government agreed to negotiate with the United States, and Polk, locked into a war of words with Britain over Oregon, decided to give negotiations a chance. In November 1845 he dispatched John Slidell to Mexico City with instructions to gain Mexican recognition of the annexation of Texas with the Rio Grande border. In exchange, the United States government would assume the debt owed by Mexico to American citizens. Polk also authorized Slidell to offer up to $25 million for California and New Mexico. But by the time Slidell reached Mexico City, the government there had become too weak to make concessions to the United States, and its head, General José Herrera, refused to receive Slidell. Polk then ordered Taylor to move southward to the Rio Grande, hoping to provoke a Mexican attack and unite the American people behind war.

The Mexican government dawdled. Polk was about to send a war message to Congress when word finally arrived that Mexican forces had crossed the Rio Grande and ambushed two companies of Taylor's troops. Now the prowar press had its martyrs. "*American blood has been shed on American soil!*" one of Polk's followers proclaimed. On May 11 Polk informed Congress that war

"exists by the act of Mexico herself" and called for a $10 million appropriation to fight the war.

Polk's disarming assertion that the United States was already at war provoked furious opposition in Congress, where John C. Calhoun briefly united with antislavery Whigs to protest the president's high-handedness. Polk's opponents pointed out that the Mexican attack on Taylor's troops had occurred in territory that no previous administration had claimed as part of the United States. By announcing that war already existed, moreover, Polk seemed to be undercutting Congress's power to declare war and using a mere border incident as a pretext for plunging the nation into a general war to acquire more slave territory. The pro-Whig *New York Tribune* warned its readers that Polk was "precipitating you into a fathomless abyss of crime and calamity." Antislavery poet James Russell Lowell of Massachusetts wrote of the Polk Democrats,

> They just want this Californy
> So's to lug new slave-states in
> To abuse ye, an' to scorn ye,
> An' to plunder ye like sin.

But Polk had maneuvered the Whigs into a corner. Few Whigs could forget that the Federalists' opposition to the War of 1812 had wrecked the Federalist party, and few wanted to appear unpatriotic by refusing to support Taylor's beleaguered troops. Swallowing their outrage, most Whigs backed appropriations for war against Mexico.

Throughout the negotiations with Britain over Oregon and with Mexico over Texas, Polk had demonstrated his ability to pursue his goals unflinchingly. A humorless, austere man who banned dancing and liquor at White House receptions, Polk inspired little personal warmth, even among his supporters. But he possessed clear objectives and a single-mindedness in their pursuit. At every point, he had encountered opposition on the home front: from Whigs who saw him as a reckless adventurer; from northerners of both parties opposed to any expansion of slavery; and from John C. Calhoun, who despised Polk for his high-handedness and fretted that a war with Britain would strip the South of its market for cotton. Yet Polk triumphed over all opposition, in part because of his opponents' fragmentation, in part because of expansion's popular appeal, and in part because of the weakness of his foreign antagonists. Reluctant to fight over Oregon, Britain chose to negotiate. Too weak to negotiate, Mexico chose to fight over territory that it had already lost (Texas) and for territories over which its hold was feeble (California and New Mexico).

The Mexican-American War

Most European observers expected Mexico to win the war. With a regular army four times the size of the American forces, Mexico had the added advantage of fighting on home ground. The United States, which had botched its one previous attempt to invade a foreign nation, Canada in 1812, now had to sustain offensive operations in an area remote from American settlements.

In contrast to the Europeans, expansionists in the United States hardly expected the Mexicans to fight at all. A leading Democrat confidently predicted that Mexico would offer only "a slight resistance to the North American race" because its mixed Spanish and Indian population had been degraded by "amalgamation." Newspaper publisher James Gordon Bennett proclaimed that the "imbecile" Mexicans were "as sure to melt away at the approach of [American] energy and enterprise as snow before a southern sun."

In fact, the Mexicans fought bravely and stubbornly, although unsuccessfully. In May 1846 Taylor, "Old Rough and Ready," routed the Mexican army in Texas and pursued it across the Rio Grande, eventually capturing the major city of Monterrey in September. War enthusiasm surged in the United States. Recruiting posters blared, "Here's to old Zach! Glorious Times! Roast Beef, Ice Cream, and Three Months' Advance." Taylor's conspicuously ordinary manner—he went into battle wearing a straw hat and a plain brown coat—endeared him to the public, which kicked up its heels in celebration to the "Rough and Ready Polka" and the "General Taylor Quick Step."

After taking Monterrey, Taylor, starved for supplies, halted and granted Mexico an eight-week armistice. Eager to undercut Taylor's popularity—the Whigs were already touting him as a presidential candidate—Polk stripped him of half his forces and reassigned them to General Winfield Scott. Scott was to mount an amphibious attack on Vera Cruz, far to the south, and proceed to Mexico City, following the path of Cortés and his *conquistadores*. Events outstripped Polk's scheme, however, when Taylor defeated a far larger Mexican army at the Battle of Buena Vista, on February 22–23, 1847.

While Taylor was winning fame in northern Mexico, and before Scott had launched his attack on Vera Cruz, American forces farther north were dealing decisive blows to the remnants of Mexican rule in New Mexico and California. In spring 1846 Colonel Stephen Kearny marched an army from Fort Leavenworth, Kansas, toward Santa Fe. Like the pioneers on the Oregon Trail,

Daguerreotype of Soldiers in the Mexican-American War
This photograph shows General John F. Wool (in the center, wearing a heavy coat) and his staff at Saltillo, the capital of the Mexican state of Coahuila, in 1846 or 1847. Wool respected individual Mexicans as soldiers, but noted Mexico's lack of unity. "Had the nation [Mexico] been united," he wrote, "we could not have gained a single victory."

Patriotism and the Mexican War
U.S. soldiers commonly wore tall hats known as shako caps during the Mexican War. The caps were adorned with decorative plates showing the eagle spreading its wings, the symbol of Manifest Destiny.

Kearny's men faced immense natural obstacles as they marched over barren ground. Finally reaching New Mexico, Kearny took the territory by a combination of bluff, bluster, and perhaps bribery, without firing a shot. The Mexican governor, following his own advice that "it is better to be thought brave than to be so," fled at Kearny's approach. After suppressing a brief rebellion by Mexicans and Indians, Kearny sent a detachment of his army south into Mexico. There, having marched fifteen hundred miles from Fort Leavenworth, these troops joined Taylor in time for the Battle of Buena Vista.

Like New Mexico, California fell easily into American hands. In 1845 Polk had ordered Commodore John D. Sloat and his Pacific Squadron to occupy California's ports in the event of war with Mexico. To ensure victory, Polk also dispatched a courier overland with secret orders for one of the most colorful and important actors in the conquest of California, John C. Frémont. A Georgia-born adventurer, Frémont had married Jessie Benton, the daughter of powerful Senator Thomas Hart Benton of Missouri. Benton used his influence to have accounts of Frémont's explorations in the Northwest (mainly written by Jessie Benton Frémont) published as government documents. All of this earned glory for Frémont as "the Great Pathfinder." Finally over-

taken by Polk's courier in Oregon, Frémont was dispatched to California to "watch over the interests of the United States." In June 1846 a small force of American settlers loyal to Fremont seized the village of Sonoma and proclaimed the independent "Bear Flag Republic." The combined efforts of Frémont, Sloat, his successor David Stockton, and Stephen Kearny (who arrived in California after capturing New Mexico) quickly established American control over California.

The final and most important campaign of the war saw the conquest of Mexico City itself. In March 1847 Winfield Scott landed near Vera Cruz at the head of twelve thousand men and quickly pounded the city into submission. Moving inland, Scott encountered Santa Anna at the seemingly impregnable pass of Cerro Gordo, but a young captain in Scott's command, Robert E. Lee, helped find a trail that led around the Mexican flank to a small peak overlooking the pass. There Scott planted howitzers and, on April 18, stormed the pass and routed the Mexicans. Scott now moved directly on Mexico City. Taking the key fortresses of Churubusco and Chapultepec (where another young captain, Ulysses S.

Grant, was cited for bravery), Scott took the city on September 13, 1847 (see Map 13.5).

In virtually all these encounters on Mexican soil, the Mexicans were numerically superior. In the final assault on Mexico City, Scott commanded eleven thousand troops against Santa Anna's twenty-five thousand. But doom stalked the Mexican army. Hampered by Santa Anna's nearly unbroken string of military miscalculations, the Mexicans fell victim to the vastly superior American artillery and to the ability of the Americans to organize massive military movements. The "barbarians of the North" (as Mexicans called the American soldiers)

died like flies from yellow fever, and they carried into battle the agonies of venereal disease, which they picked up (and left) in many of the Mexican towns they took. But the Americans benefited from the unprecedented quality of their weapons, supplies, and organization.

By the Treaty of Guadalupe Hidalgo (February 2, 1848), Mexico ceded Texas with the Rio Grande boundary, New Mexico, and California to the United States. In return, the United States assumed the claims of American citizens against the Mexican government and paid Mexico $15 million. Although the United States gained the present states of California, Nevada, New

MAP 13.5
Major Battles of the Mexican-American War
The Mexican War's decisive campaign began with General Winfield Scott's capture of Vera Cruz and ended with his conquest of Mexico City.

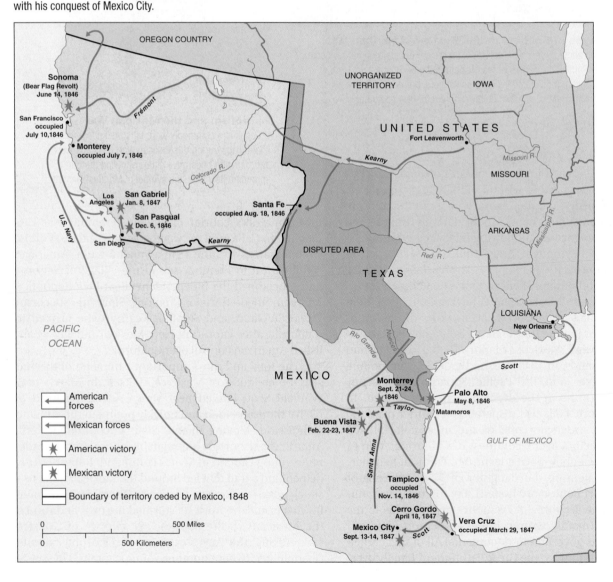

Mexico, Utah, most of Arizona, and parts of Colorado and Wyoming, some rabid expansionists in the Senate denounced the treaty because it failed to include all of Mexico. But the acquisition of California, with its excellent Pacific ports of San Diego and San Francisco, satisfied Polk. Few senators, moreover, wanted to annex the mixed Spanish and Indian population of Mexico. A writer in the *Democratic Review* expressed the prevailing view that "the annexation of the country [Mexico] to the United States would be a calamity," for it would incorporate into the United States "ignorant and indolent half-civilized Indians," not to mention "free negroes and mulattoes" left over from the British slave trade. The virulent racism of American leaders allowed the Mexicans to retain part of their nation. On March 10, 1848, the Senate ratified the treaty by a vote of 38 to 10.

The War's Effects on Sectional Conflict

Wartime patriotic enthusiasm did not stop sectional conflict from sharpening between 1846 and 1848. Questions relating to territorial expansion intensified this conflict, but so too did President Polk's uncompromising and literal Jacksonianism.

Polk had restored the Independent Treasury, to the Whigs' dismay, and had eroded Democratic unity by pursuing Jacksonian policies on tariffs and internal improvements. Despite his campaign promise, applauded by many northern Democrats, to combine a revenue tariff with a measure of protection, his administration's Tariff of 1846 had slashed duties to the minimum necessary for revenue. Polk then disappointed western Democrats, thirsting for federal aid for internal improvements, by vetoing the Rivers and Harbors Bill of 1846.

Important as these issues were, territorial expansion sparked the Polk administration's major battles. To Polk, it mattered little whether new territories were slave or free. Expansion would serve the nation's interests by dispersing population and retaining its agricultural and democratic character. Focusing attention on slavery in the territories struck him as "not only unwise but wicked." The Missouri Compromise, prohibiting slavery north of 36°30', impressed him as a simple and permanent solution to the problem of territorial slavery.

But many northerners were coming to see slavery in the territories as a profoundly disruptive issue that neither could nor should be solved simply by extending the 36°30' line westward. Antislavery Whigs who opposed any extension of slavery on moral grounds were still a minority within their party. They posed a lesser threat to

Polk than did northern Democrats who feared that expansion of slavery into California and New Mexico (parts of each lay south of 36°30') would deter free laborers from settling those territories. These Democrats argued that competition with slaves degraded free labor, that the westward extension of slavery would check the westward migration of free labor, and that such a barrier would aggravate the social problems already beginning to plague the East: class strife, social stratification, and labor protest.

The Wilmot Proviso

A young Democratic congressman from Pennsylvania, David Wilmot, became the spokesman for these disaffected northern Democrats. On a sizzling night in August 1846, he introduced an amendment to an appropriations bill for the upcoming negotiations with Mexico over Texas, New Mexico, and California. This amendment, known as the Wilmot Proviso, stipulated that slavery be prohibited in any territory acquired by the negotiations. Neither an abolitionist nor a critic of Polk on tariff policy, Wilmot spoke for those loyal Democrats who had supported the annexation of Texas on the assumption that Texas would be the last slave state. Wilmot's intention was not to split his party along sectional lines but instead to hold Polk to what Wilmot and other northern Democrats took as an implicit understanding: Texas for the slaveholders, California and New Mexico for free labor.

With strong northern support, the proviso passed in the House but stalled in the Senate. Polk refused to endorse it, and most southern Democrats opposed any barrier to the expansion of slavery south of the Missouri Compromise line. Accepting the view that the westward extension of slavery would reduce the concentration of slaves in the older regions of the South and thus lessen the chances of a slave revolt, southern Democrats tried to put as much distance as possible between themselves and Wilmot.

The proviso raised unsettling constitutional issues. Calhoun and fellow southerners contended that since slaves were property, slaveholders enjoyed the Constitution's protection of property and could carry their slaves wherever they chose. This position led to the conclusion (drawn explicitly by Calhoun) that the Missouri Compromise of 1820, prohibiting slavery in the territories north of 36°30', was unconstitutional. On the other side were many northerners who cited the Northwest Ordinance of 1787, the Missouri Compromise, and the Constitution itself, which gave Congress

the power to "make all needful rules and regulations respecting the territory or other property belonging to the United States," as justification for congressional legislation on slavery in the territories. With the election of 1848 approaching, politicians of both sides, eager to hold their parties together and avert civil war, frantically searched for a middle ground.

The Election of 1848

Having asserted that their policies of national banking and high tariffs alone could pull the nation out of the depression, the Whigs had watched in dismay as prosperity returned under Polk's program of an independent treasury and low tariffs. Never before had Clay's American System seemed so irrelevant. But the Wilmot Proviso gave the Whigs a political windfall; originating in

"Union" Woodcut by Thomas W. Strong, 1848
This 1848 campaign poster for Zachary Taylor reminded Americans of his military victories, unmilitary bearing (note the civilian dress and straw hat), and deliberately vague promises. As president, Taylor finally took a stand on the issue of slavery in the Mexican Cession, but his position angered the South.

the Democratic party, it enabled the Whigs to portray themselves as the South's only dependable friends.

These considerations inclined the majority of Whigs toward Zachary Taylor. As a Louisiana slaveholder, he had obvious appeal to the South. As a political newcomer, he had no loyalty to the discredited American System. As a war hero, he had broad national appeal. Nominating Taylor as their presidential candidate in 1848, the Whigs presented him as an ideal man "without regard to creeds or principles" and ran him without any platform.

The Democrats faced a greater challenge because David Wilmot was one of their own. They could not ignore the issue of slavery in the territories, but if they embraced the position of either Wilmot or Calhoun, the party would split along sectional lines. When Polk declined to run for reelection, the Democrats nominated Lewis Cass of Michigan, who solved their dilemma by announcing the doctrine of "squatter sovereignty," or popular sovereignty as it was later called. Cass argued that Congress should let the question of slavery in the territories be decided by the people who settled there. Squatter sovereignty appealed to many because of its arresting simplicity and vagueness. It neatly dodged the divisive issue of whether Congress had the power to prohibit territorial slavery. In fact, few Democrats wanted a definitive answer to this question. As long as the doctrine remained ambiguous, northern and southern Democrats alike could interpret it to their respective benefit.

In the campaign, both parties tried to ignore the issue of territorial slavery, but neither succeeded. A faction of the Democratic party in New York that favored the Wilmot Proviso, called the Barnburners, broke away from the party, linked up with former Liberty party abolitionists, and courted antislavery "Conscience" Whigs to create the Free-Soil party. Declaring their dedication to "Free Trade, Free Labor, Free Speech, and Free Men," the Free-Soilers nominated Martin Van Buren on a platform opposing any extension of slavery.

Zachary Taylor benefited from the Democrats' alienation of key northern states over the tariff issue, from Democratic disunity over the Wilmot Proviso, and from his war-hero stature. He captured a majority of electoral votes in both North and South. Although failing to carry any state, the Free-Soil party ran well enough in the North to demonstrate the grass-roots popularity of opposition to slavery extension. Defections to the Free-Soilers, for example, probably cost the Whigs Ohio. By showing that opposition to the spread of slavery had far greater appeal than the staunch abolitionism of the old

Liberty party, the Free-Soilers sent the Whigs and Democrats a message that they would be unable to ignore in future elections.

The California Gold Rush

When Wilmot announced his proviso, the issue of slavery in the Far West was more abstract than practical because Mexico had yet to cede any territory and relatively few Americans resided in either California or New Mexico. Nine days before the signing of the Treaty of Guadalupe Hidalgo, however, an American carpenter discovered gold in the foothills of California's Sierra Nevada range. A frantic gold rush began within a few months. A San Francisco newspaper complained that "the whole country from San Francisco to Los Angeles, and from the shore to the base of the Sierra Nevada, resounds with the sordid cry to *gold*, GOLD, GOLD! while the field is left half-planted, the house half-built, and everything neglected but the manufacture of shovels and pickaxes."

Shovels and pickaxes to dig gold from crevices in and around streams were enough for most of the early gold prospectors. But as the most accessible deposits of gold were depleted, individual miners increasingly formed combinations to undertake such costly projects as diverting the course of streams and rivers to uncover gold-laden beds or excavating shafts in the earth. "Hydraulic mining," a development of the mid-1850s, involved channeling water from streams through narrow hoses to blast thousands of cubic yards of earth from hillsides and then sifting the earth through sluices to capture the precious particles of gold.

By December 1848 pamphlets with titles like *The Emigrant's Guide to the Gold Mines* had hit the streets of New York City. Arriving by sea (see Technology and Culture: The Age of the Clipper Ships) and by land, gold-rushers drove up the population of California from around 15,000 in the summer of 1848 to nearly 250,000 by 1852. Miners came from every corner of the world. A female journalist reported walking through a mining camp in the Sierras and hearing English, Italian, French, Spanish, German, and Hawaiian. Conflicts over claims quickly led to violent clashes between Americans and Hispanics (mostly Mexicans, Chileans, and Peruvians). Americans especially resented the Chinese who flooded into California in the 1850s, most as contract laborers for wealthy Chinese merchants, and who struck Americans as slave laborers. Yet rampant prejudice against the Chinese did not stop some American businessmen from hiring them as contract workers for the

American mining combinations that were forming in the 1850s.

Within a decade the gold rush turned the sleepy Hispanic town of Yerba Buena, the population of which was 150 in 1846, into "a pandemonium of a city" of 50,000 known as San Francisco. No other U.S. city contained people from more parts of the world. Many of the immigrants were Irish convicts who arrived by way of Australia, to which they had been exiled for their crimes. All the ethnic and racial tensions of the gold fields were evident in the city. A young clergyman confessed that he carried a harmless-looking cane, which "will be found to contain a sword two-and-a-half feet long." In 1851 San Francisco's merchants organized the first of several Committees of Vigilance, which patrolled the streets, deported undesirables, and tried and hanged alleged thieves and murderers.

With the gold rush, the issue of slavery in the Far West became practical as well as abstract, and immediate rather than remote. The newcomers attracted to

California News

A New York paper reported in 1849 that "gold news has unsettled the minds of even the most cautious and careful among us."

The Age of the Clipper Ship

There was no "first" clipper ship. These legendary "Greyhounds of the Sea," which reached the height of their fame between 1845 and 1859, evolved from the American interest in finding ways to make ships—in fact everything—go faster. Lacking the protection of a great navy, American shipbuilders and sea captains knew that sailing at a fast "clip" was the best way to elude the enemy warships that had threatened American commerce between 1807 and 1815, the era of the Embargo and the War of 1812. The opening of new commercial ports in China in the 1830s and 1840s intensified the quest for speed to overcome both great distances and the tendency of tea leaves to spoil if left in the hold for too long. By the mid-1840s Americans were starting to boast of their "extreme clippers."

Compared to traditional sailing vessels, these extreme clippers—so many were built that before long it became pointless to add "extreme"—carried a lot of sail in relation to their tonnage. In mariners' language, they were heavily "sparred." Spars were wooden masts, yardarms, or booms that supported the rigging and enabled clippers to spread as much canvas as possible in order to take maximum advantage of the wind, their only source of propulsion. The bows of clippers were unusually "sharp," with little buoyancy. While the barrel-chested bows and wide hulls of traditional vessels pushed the water out of the way, the sharp bows and narrow hulls of clippers knifed through it. The clippers' sleekness translated into an average speed of twelve knots an hour (a knot is a nautical mile, about a mile and one-eighth), compared to six to eight knots for traditional vessels.

Had clippers been designed only to carry cargo, their narrow beams would have been a drawback. But in the late 1840s demand for faster passenger ships mounted. British emigrants were heading for Australia, and British shipowners commissioned the building of clippers in American yards. Then the California gold rush sparked

The *Flying Cloud* in Heavy Seas
With its graceful lines and majestic spread of sail, the *Flying Cloud* became a favorite subject for artists.

demand for voyages from eastern ports to San Francisco. Not all of these passengers were headed for the gold fields. In California's dizzy gold-rush economy, cart drivers, carpenters, masons, and cooks could command four to five times the daily wages of workers in the rest of the nation. Paying two hundred dollars, three hundred dollars, or more for sea passage—close to a year's wages—struck many of them as a good investment.

Before the end of February 1849, eleven thousand passengers had left on ships from eastern ports to go to San Francisco and the gold fields, most on slow vessels that averaged 157 days for the sixteen thousand-mile trip from New York to San Francisco around Cape Horn, the southernmost tip of South America. In theory, it was faster to sail from New York to the isthmus of Panama, the narrowest point of North America; cross the sixty-mile isthmus by foot, mule, and boat; and take a steamship north to San Francisco. But dense jungle, snakes, scorpions, armies of mosquitoes, and weeks or months waiting for a steamship limited the appeal of the isthmus route.

By the early 1850s the shipyards of Boston and New York were turning out clippers for the Cape Horn route at astonishing rates. Boston's shipbuilder Donald McKay oversaw the construction of thirty-one clippers between 1850 and 1858. The most famous of these was the *Flying Cloud*, which McKay sold for $60,000 to a Boston ship owner, who almost immediately sold it to a New York owner for $90,000. Guided by its captain, Josiah P. Cressy, and its navigator, Cressy's wife Ellen (a masterful mistress of the sextant and other instruments for locating a ship's position at sea), the *Flying Cloud* made the run from New York to San Francisco around the Horn in eighty-nine days in 1851, a record not broken by any sailing vessel until 1989. At one point on this voyage, the *Flying Cloud* attained the unheard of speed of eighteen knots an hour.

The speed of the *Flying Cloud* and other clippers gripped the public's imagination. A betting industry sprang up around the clippers, with wagers on how many days and hours it would take a ship to reach the equator or to drop anchor at San Francisco. In the early 1850s many shipbuilders were concluding that the newly invented steamship, slow and with boilers prone to explode, had reached its limits and that the future, at least for ocean voyages, belonged to the clipper.

Launching of the *Flying Cloud* at Donald McKay's Shipyard
At its launching in 1851, the *Flying Cloud* was the largest merchant ship in the world. It measured 235 feet from bow to stern and carried ten thousand square yards of canvas.

They were wrong. Like the gold rush itself, the reign of the clipper was brief. The invention in 1836 of the steam-powered screw propeller, which churned off a steamer's stern and eliminated the drag-producing sidewheels of the early steamers, made it possible for steamships to average thirteen knots by the mid-1850s.

However magnificent, clippers were expensive. Managing their immense spreads of sail required relatively large crews of at least sixty, and, running nearly flush to the sea, clippers took a horrific pounding in bad weather. Insurance rates soared by the mid-1850s, less because clippers were sinking than because they needed so much repair after each voyage. As interest in the gold fields waned, most of the clippers were shorn of their masts and miles of rigging and converted to barges. The *Flying Cloud* itself, its masts shortened to make it easier to handle with a smaller crew, met a pitiful end in 1874 when, damaged by a storm while in port, it was deemed not worth repairing. Under orders from the insurance underwriters, a team of workers towed it to sea, doused it with kerosene, set it ablaze, and watched it burn to the water.

Focus Questions

- What were the relative advantages and disadvantages of the Horn and isthmus routes to California? How did each compare with overland travel?
- Why was the reign of the clipper ship so short?

California in 1849 included free blacks and slaves brought by planters from the South. White prospectors loathed the thought of competing with either of these groups and wanted to drive all blacks, along with California's Indians, out of the gold fields. Tensions also intensified between the gold-rushers and the *Californios*, whose extensive (if often vaguely worded) land holdings were protected by the terms of the Treaty of Guadalupe Hidalgo. Spawned by disputed claims and prejudice, violence mounted, and demands grew for a strong civilian government to replace the ineffective military government in place in California since the war. Polk began to fear that without a satisfactory congressional solution to the slavery issue, Californians might organize a government independent of the United States. The gold rush thus guaranteed that the question of slavery in the Mexican cession would be the first item on the agenda for Polk's successor and, indeed, for the nation.

CONCLUSION

The massive immigration of the 1840s changed the face of American politics. Angered by Whig nativism and anti-Catholicism, the new German and Irish immigrants swelled the ranks of the Democratic party. Meanwhile, the Whigs were unraveling. The untimely death of President Harrison brought John Tyler, a Democrat in Whig's clothing, to the White House. Tyler's vetoes of key Whig measures left the Whig party in disarray. In combination, these developments led to the surprise election of James K. Polk, a Democrat and ardent expansionist, in 1844.

Wrapped in the language of Manifest Destiny, westward expansion appealed to Americans for many reasons. It fit their belief that settlers had more right to the American continent than did the Europeans who based their claims on centuries-old explorations, the lethargic and Catholic Mexicans, and the nomadic Indians. Expansion promised trade routes to the Pacific, more land for farming, and, in the case of Texas, more slave states. Polk simultaneously rode the wave of national sentiment for Manifest Destiny and gave it direction by annexing Texas, provoking a crisis with Britain over Oregon, and leading the United States into a war with Mexico. Initially, Polk succeeded in uniting broad swaths of public opinion behind expansion. Polk and his followers ingeniously argued that national expansion was in the interests of northern working-class voters, many of

CHRONOLOGY, 1840–1848

1822	Stephen F. Austin founds the first American community in Texas.
1830	Mexico closes Texas to further American immigration.
1835	Santa Anna invades Texas.
1836	Texas declares its independence from Mexico. Fall of the Alamo. Goliad massacre. Battle of San Jacinto.
1840	William Henry Harrison elected president.
1841	Harrison dies; John Tyler becomes president.
1842	Webster-Ashburton Treaty.
1844	James K. Polk elected president.
1845	Congress votes joint resolution to annex Texas. Mexico rejects Slidell mission.
1846	The United States declares war on Mexico. John C. Frémont proclaims the Bear Flag Republic in California. Congress votes to accept a settlement of the Oregon boundary issue with Britain. Tariff of 1846. Colonel Stephen Kearny occupies Santa Fe. Wilmot Proviso introduced. Taylor takes Monterrey.
1847	Taylor defeats Santa Anna at the Battle of Buena Vista. Vera Cruz falls to Winfield Scott. Mexico City falls to Scott. Lewis Cass's principle of "squatter sovereignty."
1848	Gold discovered in California. Treaty of Guadalupe Hidalgo signed. Taylor elected president.

them immigrants. By encouraging the spread of slavery to the Southwest, the argument went, the annexation of Texas would reduce the chances of a race war in the Southeast that might spill over into the North.

Yet even as war with Mexico was commencing, cracks in Polk's coalition were starting to show. The Wilmot Proviso exposed deep sectional divisions that had only been papered over by the ideal of Manifest Destiny and that would explode in the secession of Free-Soil Democrats in 1848. Victorious over Mexico and enriched by the discovery of gold in California, Americans counted the blessings of expansion but began to fear its costs.

FOR FURTHER REFERENCE

READINGS

Peter J. Blodgett, *Land of Golden Dreams* (1999). A vivid account of California in the gold rush.

William R. Brock, *Parties and Political Conscience: American Dilemmas, 1840–1850* (1979). An excellent interpretive study of the politics of the 1840s.

William H. Goetzmann, *When the Eagle Screamed: The Romantic Horizon in American Diplomacy, 1800–1860* (1966). A lively overview of antebellum expansionism.

Maldwyn A. Jones, *American Immigration* (1960). An excellent brief introduction to immigration.

Michael A. Morrison, *Slavery and the American West: The Eclipse of Manifest Destiny and the Coming of the Civil War* (1997). An important recent study.

Malcolm J. Rorabaugh, *Days of Gold: The California Gold Rush and the American Nation* (1997). Emphasizes how the discovery of gold in California reaffirmed the American belief that, regardless of family name or education, anyone who worked hard in America could grow rich.

Charles G. Sellers, *James K. Polk: Continentalist, 1843–1846* (1966). An outstanding political biography.

Henry Nash Smith, *Virgin Land: The American West as Symbol and Myth* (1950). A classic study of westward expansion in the American mind.

WEBSITES

End of the Oregon Trail Interpretive Center
http://endoftheoregontrail.org/index.html
A valuable site for interpreting the Oregon Trail. In addition to information on wagon travel and communication between whites and Indians, the site includes diaries, narratives, and biographies of pioneer families on the Oregon Trail.

Gold Rush
http://www.museumca.org/goldrush/
This site contains paintings of the gold rush, information on mining, and accounts of the experiences of gold-rushers from many nations and cultures.

The U.S.-Mexican War, 1846–1848
http://www.pbs.org/kera/usmexicanwar/mainframe.html
This site offers valuable chronologies of the war and interpretations of it in English and Spanish from both the American and Mexican perspectives.

For additional works please consult the bibliography at the end of the book.

CHAPTER 14

From Compromise to Secession, 1850–1861

In early July 1859 a man calling himself Isaac Smith and claiming to be a cattle dealer rented a dilapidated farmhouse some seven miles from Harpers Ferry in northern Virginia's Blue Ridge mountains. Neighbors soon noticed that others had joined "Smith," including two young women, and perhaps they observed a wagon loaded with fifteen boxes pull up to the farm one day. But nothing seemed out of the ordinary. True, the men stayed out of sight, but the women chatted amiably with neighbors, and "Smith" referred to the contents of the boxes merely as "hardware."

But in reality, everything was out of the ordinary. "Smith" was John Brown, a brooding abolitionist with a price on his head for the massacre of white southerners in Kansas in 1856 and with a conviction that God had ordained him "to purge this land with blood" of the evil of slavery. One of the women was his daughter, the other his daughter-in-law. The boxes contained rifles and revolvers, with which Brown and his recruits— white idealists (including three of Brown's sons), free blacks, and fugitive slaves— planned to raid Harpers Ferry, the site of a federal arsenal and armory, as a prelude to igniting a slave insurrection throughout the South.

In some respects, Brown was a marginal figure in the abolitionist movement. Unlike better-known abolitionists, he had written no stirring tracts against slavery. But in Kansas, where civil war between free-staters and

◀ **Last Moments of John Brown**
The raid by the abolitionist John Brown on the federal arsenal at Harpers Ferry, Virginia, in 1859 never came close to achieving Brown's goal of starting a slave insurrection. But it did make Brown a hero in the North and brought the Civil War closer.

CHAPTER OUTLINE

slave-staters had broken out in the mid-1850s, Brown had acquired a reputation as someone who could handle the rough stuff. Eastern abolitionists—most of whom were philosophical pacifists, but who were starting to suspect that only violence would end slavery—were fast developing a fascination with Brown. Little suspecting his plans for Harpers Ferry, they accepted his disavowal of a role in the Kansas massacre and endorsed, with contributions, his plans to carry on the fight against those who would forcibly turn Kansas into a slave state.

On the moonless evening of October 16, 1859, Brown and eighteen recruits (three were left behind to guard the farmhouse) entered Harpers Ferry and quickly seized the arsenal and armory. Expecting slaves—half of Harpers Ferry's population was enslaved—to rally at once to his cause, Brown then did nothing, while local whites, jumpy about the possibility of a slave insurrection ever since Nat Turner's 1831 rebellion (see Chapter 12), spread the alarm. Soon armed locals, their courage steeled by liquor, militia from surrounding areas, and U.S. Marines dispatched by President James Buchanan and under the command of Colonel Robert E. Lee, clogged the streets of Harpers Ferry. On October 18 the Marines stormed the armory where Brown and most of his men had taken refuge, severely wounded and captured Brown, and killed or mortally wounded ten others, including two of Brown's sons. Five men, including one of Brown's sons, escaped; the remaining recruits were eventually captured and executed. Brown himself was speedily tried, convicted, and hanged.

In the immediate wake of Brown's capture, prominent northerners distanced themselves from him. His lawyers contended that he was insane and hence not culpable for his deeds. But Brown himself derided the insanity defense. His conduct during his brief imprisonment was serene, his words eloquent. He told his captors that he had rendered to God the "greatest service man can." For their part, white southerners came to reject the notion that Brown's plot was the work of an isolated lunatic. A search of the farmhouse after Brown's capture quickly turned up incriminating correspondence between Brown and leading northern abolitionists. As proslavery southerners saw it, Brown had botched the raid, but his plan to arm nonslaveholding southern whites with guns and disaffected slaves with pikes (Brown had contracted for the manufacture of a thousand pikes) was plausible. In all the southern states slaveholding whites were outnumbered by people who did not own slaves (slaves, free blacks, and nonslaveholding whites) by more than three to one. Northern

opinion increasingly shifted toward sympathy for Brown. Ralph Waldo Emerson exulted that Brown's execution would "make the gallows as glorious as the cross."

This chapter focuses on four major questions:

- To what extent did the Compromise of 1850 represent a genuine meeting of the minds between northerners and southerners? How, specifically, did the controversy over enforcement of the Fugitive Slave Act contribute to the undoing of the Compromise?

- Why did the Whig party collapse in the wake of the Kansas-Nebraska Act? Why did the Democratic party not also collapse?

- How did the outbreak of conflict in Kansas influence the rise of the Republican party? Why was the Republican doctrine of free soil able to unify northerners against the South?

- What led southerners to conclude that the North was bent not merely on restricting territorial slavery but also on extinguishing slavery in southern states?

THE COMPROMISE OF 1850

Ralph Waldo Emerson's grim prediction that an American victory in the Mexican War would be like swallowing arsenic proved disturbingly accurate. When the war ended in 1848, the United States contained an equal number of free and slave states (fifteen each), but the vast territory acquired by the war threatened to upset this balance. Any solution to the question of slavery in the Mexican cession ensured controversy, if not hostility. The doctrine of free soil, which insisted that Congress prohibit slavery in the territories, horrified southerners. The idea of extending the Missouri Compromise line of 36° 30' to the Pacific angered free-soilers because it would allow slavery in New Mexico and southern California, and southern proslavery extremists because it conceded that Congress could bar slavery in some territories. A third solution, popular sovereignty, which promised to ease the slavery extension issue out of national politics by allowing each territory to decide the question for itself, pleased neither free-soilers nor proslavery extremists.

As the rhetoric escalated, events plunged the nation into crisis. Utah and then California, both acquired from Mexico, sought admission to the Union as free states. Texas, admitted as a slave state in 1845, aggravated matters by claiming the eastern half of New Mexico, where

the Mexican government had long since abolished slavery.

By 1850 these territorial issues had become intertwined with two other concerns. Northerners increasingly attacked slavery in the District of Columbia, within the shadow of the Capitol; southerners complained about lax enforcement of the Fugitive Slave Act of 1793. Any broad compromise would have to take both troublesome matters into account.

Zachary Taylor at the Helm

Although elected president in 1848 without a platform, Zachary Taylor came to office with a clear position on the issue of slavery in the Mexican cession. A slaveholder himself, he took for granted the South's need to defend slavery. Taylor insisted that southerners would best protect slavery if they refrained from rekindling the issue of slavery in the territories. He rejected Calhoun's idea that the protection of slavery in the southern states ultimately depended on the expansion of slavery into the western territories. In Taylor's eyes, neither California nor New Mexico was suited to slavery; in 1849 he told a Pennsylvania audience that "the people of the North need have no apprehension of the further extension of slavery."

Although Taylor looked to the exclusion of slavery from California and New Mexico, his position differed from that embodied in the Wilmot Proviso, the free-soil measure proposed in 1846 by a northern Democrat. The proviso had insisted that Congress bar slavery in the territories ceded by Mexico. Taylor's plan, in contrast, left the decision to the states. Recognizing that most Californians opposed slavery in their state, Taylor had prompted California to bypass the territorial stage that normally preceded statehood, to draw up its constitution in 1849, and to apply directly for admission as a free state. The president strongly hinted that he expected New Mexico to do the same.

Taylor's strategy appeared to guarantee a quick, practical solution to the problem of slavery extension. It would give the North two new free states. At the same time, it would acknowledge a position upon which all southerners agreed: a state could bar or permit slavery as it chose. This conviction in fact served as the very foundation of the South's defense of slavery, its armor against all the onslaughts of the abolitionists. Nothing in the Constitution forbade a state to act one way or the other on slavery.

Despite its practical features, Taylor's plan dismayed southerners of both parties. Having gored the Democrats

in 1848 as the party of the Wilmot Proviso, southern Whigs expected more from the president than a proposal that in effect yielded the proviso's goal—the banning of slavery in the Mexican cession. Many southerners, in addition, questioned Taylor's assumption that slavery could never take root in California or New Mexico. To one observer, who declared that the whole controversy over slavery in the Mexican cession "related to an imaginary negro in an impossible place," southerners pointed out that both areas already contained slaves and that slaves could be employed profitably in mining gold and silver. "California is by nature," a southerner proclaimed, "peculiarly a slaveholding State." Calhoun trembled at the thought of adding more free states. "If this scheme excluding slavery from California and New Mexico should be carried out—if we are to be reduced to a mere handful . . . wo, wo, I say to this Union." Disillusioned with Taylor, nine southern states agreed to send delegations to a southern convention that was scheduled to meet in Nashville in June 1850.

Henry Clay Proposes a Compromise

Taylor might have been able to contain mounting southern opposition if he had held a secure position in the Whig party. But the leading Whigs, among them Daniel Webster of Massachusetts and Henry Clay of Kentucky, each of whom had presidential aspirations, never reconciled themselves to Taylor, a political novice. Early in 1850 Clay boldly challenged Taylor's leadership by forging a set of compromise proposals to resolve the range of contentious issues. Clay proposed (1) the admission of California as a free state; (2) the division of the remainder of the Mexican cession into two territories, New Mexico and Utah (formerly Deseret), without federal restrictions on slavery; (3) the settlement of the Texas-New Mexico boundary dispute on terms favorable to New Mexico; (4) as a pot-sweetener for Texas, an agreement that the federal government would assume the considerable public debt of Texas; (5) the continuance of slavery in the District of Columbia but the abolition of the slave trade; and (6) a more effective fugitive slave law.

Clay rolled all of these proposals into a single "omnibus" bill, which he hoped to steer through Congress. The debates over the omnibus during the late winter and early spring of 1850 witnessed the last major appearances on the public stage of Clay, Webster, and Calhoun, the trio of distinguished senators whose lives had mirrored every public event of note since the War of 1812. Clay played the role of the

conciliator, as he had during the controversy over Missouri in 1820 and again during the nullification crisis in the early 1830s. He warned the South against the evils of secession and assured the North that nature would check the spread of slavery more effectively than a thousand Wilmot Provisos. Gaunt and gloomy, a dying Calhoun listened as another senator read his address, in which Calhoun summarized what he had been saying for years: the North's growing power, enhanced by protective tariffs and by the Missouri Compromise's exclusion of slaveholders from the northern part of the Louisiana Purchase, had created an imbalance between the sections. Only a decision by the North to treat the South as an equal could now save the Union. Three days later, Daniel Webster, who believed that slavery, "like the cotton-plant, is confined to certain parallels of climate," delivered his memorable "Seventh of March" speech. Speaking not "as a Massachusetts man, nor as a Northern man, but as an American," Webster chided the North for trying to "reenact the will of God" by legally excluding slavery from the Mexican cession and declared himself a forthright proponent of compromise.

However eloquent, the conciliatory voices of Clay and Webster made few converts. With every call for compromise, some northern or southern speaker would rise and inflame passions. The antislavery New York Whig William Seward, for example, enraged southerners by talking of a "higher law than the Constitution"—namely, the will of God against the extension of slavery. Clay's compromise became tied up in a congressional committee. To worsen matters, Clay, who at first had pretended that his proposals were in the spirit of Taylor's plan, broke openly with the president in May, and Taylor attacked Clay as a glory-hunter.

As the Union faced its worst crisis since 1789, a series of events in the summer of 1850 eased the way toward a resolution. When the Nashville convention assembled in June, extreme advocates of "southern rights," called the fire-eaters because of their recklessness, boldly made their presence felt. But talk of southern rights smelled suspiciously like a plot to disrupt the Union. "I would rather sit in council with the six thousand dead who have died of cholera in St. Louis," Senator Thomas Hart Benton of Missouri declared, "than go into convention with such a gang of scamps." Only nine of the fifteen slave states, most in the Lower South, sent delegates to the convention, where moderates took control and isolated the extremists. Then Zachary Taylor, after eating and drinking too much at an Independence Day celebration, fell ill with gastroenteritis and died on July 9.

His successor, Vice President Millard Fillmore, quickly proved to be more favorable than Taylor to the Senate's compromise measure by appointing Daniel Webster as his secretary of state. After the compromise suffered a devastating series of amendments in late July, Illinois Democrat Stephen A. Douglas took over the floor leadership from the exhausted Clay. Recognizing that Clay's "omnibus" lacked majority support in Congress, Douglas chopped it into a series of separate measures and sought to secure passage of each bill individually. To secure support from Democrats, he included the principle of popular sovereignty in the bills organizing New Mexico and Utah. By summer's end, Congress had passed each component of the Compromise of 1850: statehood for California; territorial status for Utah and New Mexico, allowing popular sovereignty; resolution of the Texas-New Mexico boundary disagreement; federal assumption of the Texas debt; abolition of the slave trade in the District of Columbia; and a new fugitive slave law (see Map 14.1).

MAP 14.1

The Compromise of 1850

The Compromise of 1850 admitted California as a free state. Utah and New Mexico were left open to slavery or freedom on the principle of popular sovereignty.

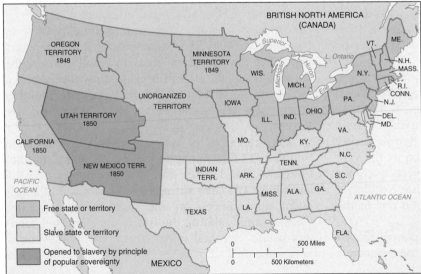

Assessing the Compromise

President Fillmore hailed the compromise as a "final settlement" of sectional divisions, and Clay's reputation for conciliation reached new heights. Yet the compromise did not bridge the underlying differences between the two sections. Far from leaping forward to save the Union, Congress had backed into the Compromise of 1850; the majority of congressmen in one or another section opposed virtually all of the specific bills that made up the compromise. Most southerners, for example, voted against the admission of California and the abolition of the slave trade in the District of Columbia; the majority of northerners opposed the Fugitive Slave Act and the organization of New Mexico and Utah without a forthright congressional prohibition of slavery. These measures passed only because the minority of congressmen who genuinely desired compromise combined with the majority in either the North or the South who favored each specific bill.

Each section both gained and lost from the Compromise of 1850. The North won California as a free state, New Mexico and Utah as likely future free states, a favorable settlement of the Texas-New Mexico boundary (most of the disputed area was awarded to New Mexico, a probable free state), and the abolition of the slave trade in the District of Columbia. The South's benefits were cloudier. By stipulating popular sovereignty for New Mexico and Utah, the compromise, to most southerners' relief, had buried the Wilmot Proviso's insistence that Congress formally prohibit slavery in these territories. But to southerners' dismay, the position of the free-soilers remained viable, for the compromise left open the question of whether Congress could prohibit slavery in territories outside of the Mexican cession.

Not surprisingly, southerners reacted ambivalently to the Compromise of 1850. In southern state elections during the fall of 1850 and in 1851, procompromise, or Unionist, candidates thrashed anticompromise candidates who talked of southern rights and secession. But even southern Unionists did not dismiss the possibility of secession. Unionists in Georgia, for example, forged the celebrated Georgia platform, which threatened secession if Congress either prohibited slavery in New Mexico or Utah or repealed the Fugitive Slave Act.

The one clear advantage gained by the South, a more stringent fugitive slave law, quickly proved a mixed blessing. Because few slaves had been taken into the Mexican cession, the question of slavery there had a hypothetical quality. However, the issues raised by the new fugitive slave law were far from hypothetical; the law authorized real southerners to pursue real fugitives on northern soil. Here was a concrete issue to which the average northerner, who may never have seen a slave and who cared little about slavery a thousand miles away, would respond with fury.

Enforcement of the Fugitive Slave Act

Northern moderates accepted the Fugitive Slave Act as the price the North had to pay to save the Union. But the law contained a string of features distasteful to moderates and outrageous to staunchly antislavery northerners. It denied alleged fugitives the right of trial by jury, did not allow them to testify in their own behalf, permitted their return to slavery merely on the testimony of the claimant, and enabled court-appointed commissioners to collect ten dollars if they ruled for the slaveholder but only five dollars if they ruled for the fugitive. In authorizing federal marshals to raise posses to pursue fugitives on northern soil, the law threatened to turn the North into "one vast hunting ground." In addition, the law targeted not only recent runaways but also those who had fled the South decades earlier. For example, it allowed slave-catchers to wrench a former slave from his family in Indiana in 1851 and return him to the master from whom he had fled in 1832. Above all, the law brought home to northerners the uncomfortable truth that the continuation of slavery depended on their complicity. By legalizing the activities of slave-catchers on northern soil, the law reminded northerners that slavery was a national problem, not merely a peculiar southern institution.

Antislavery northerners assailed the law as the "vilest monument of infamy of the nineteenth century." "Let the President . . . drench our land of freedom in blood," proclaimed Ohio Whig Congressman Joshua Giddings, "but he will never make us obey that law." His support for the law turned Senator Daniel Webster of Massachusetts into a villain in the eyes of the very people who for years had revered him as the "godlike Daniel." The abolitionist poet John Greenleaf Whittier wrote of his fallen idol,

> All else is gone; from those giant eyes
> The soul has fled:
> When faith is lost, when honor dies,
> The man is dead.

Efforts to catch and return fugitive slaves inflamed feelings in both the North and the South. In 1854 a Boston mob, aroused by antislavery speeches, broke into a courthouse and killed a guard in an abortive effort to rescue the fugitive slave Anthony Burns. Determined to prove that the law could be enforced "even in Boston," President Franklin Pierce sent a detachment of federal

troops to escort Burns to the harbor, where a ship carried him back to slavery. No witness would ever forget the scene. As five platoons of troops marched with Burns to the ship, some fifty thousand people lined the streets. As the procession passed, one Bostonian hung from his window a black coffin bearing the words "THE FUNERAL OF LIBERTY." Another draped an American flag upside down as a symbol that "my country is eternally disgraced by this day's proceedings." The Burns incident shattered the complacency of conservative supporters of the Compromise of 1850. "We went to bed one night old fashioned conservative Compromise Union Whigs," the textile manufacturer Amos A. Lawrence wrote, "and waked up stark mad Abolitionists." A Boston committee later successfully purchased Burns's freedom, but the fate of many fugitives was far less happy. One such unfortunate was Margaret Garner, who, about to be captured and sent back to Kentucky as a slave, slit her daughter's throat and tried to kill her other children rather than witness their return to slavery.

In response to the Fugitive Slave Act, vigilance committees sprang up in many northern communities to spirit endangered blacks to safety in Canada. As another ploy, lawyers used obstructive tactics to drag out legal proceedings and thus raise the slave-catchers' expenses. Then, during the 1850s, nine northern states passed "personal-liberty laws." By such techniques as forbidding the use of state jails to incarcerate alleged fugitives, these laws aimed to preclude state officials from enforcing the law.

The frequent cold stares, obstructive legal tactics, and occasional violence encountered by slaveholders who ventured north to capture runaway slaves helped demonstrate to southerners that opposition to slavery boiled just beneath the surface of northern opinion. In the eyes of most southerners, the South had gained little more from the Compromise of 1850 than the Fugitive Slave Act, and now even that northern concession seemed to be a phantom. After witnessing riots against the Fugitive Slave Act in Boston in 1854, a young Georgian studying law at Harvard wrote to his mother, "Do not be surprised if when I return home you find me a confirmed disunionist."

Uncle Tom's Cabin

The publication in 1852 of Harriet Beecher Stowe's novel *Uncle Tom's Cabin* aroused wide northern sympathy for fugitive slaves. Stowe, the daughter of the famed evangelical Lyman Beecher and the younger sister of Catharine Beecher, the stalwart advocate of domesticity for women, greeted the Fugitive Slave Act with horror and outrage. In a memorable scene from the novel, she depicted the slave Eliza escaping to freedom, clutching her infant son while bounding across ice floes on the Ohio River.

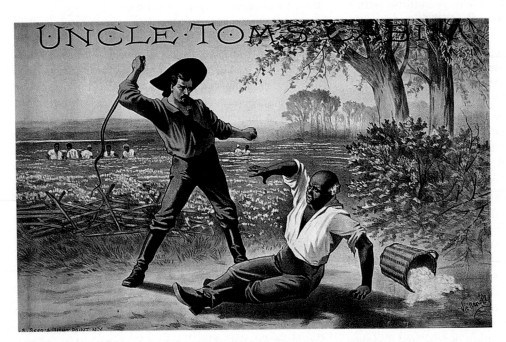

***Uncle Tom's Cabin* Theater Poster**
With its vivid word pictures of slavery, Harriet Beecher Stowe's *Uncle Tom's Cabin* translated well to the stage. Stowe herself was among the many who wrote dramatizations of the novel. Scenes of Eliza crossing the ice of the Ohio River with bloodhounds in pursuit and the evil Simon Legree whipping Uncle Tom outraged northern audiences and turned many against slavery. Southerners damned Mrs. Stowe as a "vile wretch in petticoats."

Yet Stowe targeted slavery itself more than merely the slave-catchers who served the institution. Much of her novel's power derives from its intimation that even good intentions cannot prevail against so evil an institution. Torn from his wife and children by sale and shipped on a steamer for the Lower South, the black slave Uncle Tom rescues little Eva, the daughter of kindly Augustine St. Clare, from drowning. In gratitude, St. Clare purchases Tom from a slave trader and takes him into his home in New Orleans. But after St. Clare dies, his cruel widow sells Tom to the vicious (and northern-born) Simon Legree, who whips Tom to death. Stowe played effectively on the emotions of her audience by demonstrating to an age that revered family life how slavery tore the family apart.

Three hundred thousand copies of *Uncle Tom's Cabin* were sold in 1852, and 1.2 million by the summer of 1853. Dramatized versions, which added dogs to chase Eliza across the ice, eventually reached perhaps fifty times the number of people as the novel itself. As a play, *Uncle Tom's Cabin* enthralled working-class audiences normally indifferent, if not hostile, to abolitionism. During one stage performance, a reviewer for a New York newspaper observed that the gallery was filled with men "in red woollen shirts, with countenances as hardy and rugged as the implements of industry employed by them in the pursuit of their vocations." Astonished by the silence that fell over these men at the point when Eliza escapes across the river, the reviewer turned to discover that many of them were in tears.

The impact of *Uncle Tom's Cabin* cannot be precisely measured. Although the novel stirred deep feelings, it reflected the prevailing stereotypes of blacks far more than it overturned commonly held views. Stowe portrayed only light-skinned blacks as aggressive and intelligent; she depicted dark-skinned blacks such as Uncle Tom as docile and submissive. In addition, some of the stage dramatizations softened the novel's antislavery message. In one version, which P. T. Barnum produced, Tom was rescued from Legree and happily returned as a slave to his original plantation.

Surgery on the plot, however, could not fully excise the antislavery message of *Uncle Tom's Cabin*. Though the novel hardly lived up to the prediction of a proslavery lawyer that it would convert 2 million people to abolitionism, it did push many waverers toward a more aggressively antisouthern and antislavery stance. Indeed, fear of its effect inspired a host of southerners to pen anti-Uncle Tom novels. As historian David Potter concluded, the northern attitude toward slavery "was never quite the same after *Uncle Tom's Cabin*."

Frederick Douglass
Born into slavery, Frederick Douglass became a commanding orator and writer in the 1840s and 1850s. He bitterly attacked the Fugitive Slave Act. The only way to make the law a "dead letter," he vowed, was to make "half a dozen or more dead kidnappers." In an Independence Day speech in 1852, he reminded white Americans that "This Fourth of July is yours, not mine."

The Election of 1852

The Fugitive Slave Act fragmented the Whig party. By masterminding defiance of the law, northern Whigs put southern Whigs, who long had come before the southern electorate as the party best able to defend slavery within the Union, on the spot.

In 1852 the Whigs' nomination of Mexican War hero Winfield Scott as their presidential candidate widened the sectional split within the party. Although a Virginian, Scott owed his nomination to the northern free-soil Whigs. His single feeble statement endorsing the Compromise of 1850 undercut southern Whigs trying to portray the Democrats as the party of disunion and themselves as the party of both slavery and the Union.

The Democrats bridged their own sectional division by nominating Franklin Pierce of New Hampshire, a dark-horse candidate whose chief attraction was that no faction of the party strongly opposed him. The "ultra men of the South," a friend of Pierce noted, "say they

can cheerfully go for him, and none, none, say they cannot." North and South, the Democrats rallied behind both the Compromise and the idea of applying popular sovereignty to all the territories. In the most one-sided election since 1820, Pierce swept to victory. Defeat was especially galling for southern Whigs. In 1848 Zachary Taylor had won 49.8 percent of the South's popular vote; Scott, by comparison, limped home with only 35 percent. In state elections during 1852 and 1853, moreover, the Whigs were devastated in the South; one Whig stalwart lamented "the decisive breaking-up of our party."

THE COLLAPSE OF THE SECOND PARTY SYSTEM, 1853–1856

Franklin Pierce had the dubious distinction of being the last presidential candidate for eighty years to win the popular and electoral vote in both the North and the South. Not until 1932 did another president, Franklin D. Roosevelt, repeat this accomplishment. Pierce was also the last president to hold office under the second party system—Whigs against Democrats. For two decades the Whigs and the Democrats had battled, often on even terms. Then, within the four years of Pierce's administration, the Whig party disintegrated. In its place two new parties, first the American (Know-Nothing) party, then the Republican party, arose.

Unlike the Whig party, the Republican party was a purely sectional, northern party. Its support came from former northern Whigs and discontented northern Democrats. The Democrats survived as a national party, but with a base so shrunken in the North that the Republican party, although scarcely a year old, swept two-thirds of the free states in 1856.

For decades the second party system had kept the conflict over slavery in check by giving Americans other issues—banking, internal improvements, tariffs, and temperance—to argue about. By the 1850s the debate over slavery extension was pushing such issues into the background and exposing raw divisions in each party. Of the two parties, Whig and Democratic, the Whigs had the larger, more aggressive free-soil wing, and hence they were more vulnerable than the Democrats to disruption. When Stephen A. Douglas put forth a proposal in 1854 to organize the vast Nebraska territory without restrictions on slavery, he ignited a firestorm that consumed the Whig party.

The Kansas-Nebraska Act

Signed by President Pierce at the end of May 1854, the Kansas-Nebraska Act dealt a shattering blow to the already weakened second party system. Moreover, the law triggered a renewal of the sectional strife that many Americans believed the Compromise of 1850 had satisfactorily silenced. The origins of the act lay in the seemingly uncontroversial advance of midwestern settlement. Farm families in Iowa and Missouri had long dreamed of establishing homesteads in the vast prairies to their west, and their congressional representatives had repeatedly introduced bills to organize the territory west of these states so that Native American land titles could be extinguished and a basis for government provided. Too, since the mid-1840s, advocates of national expansion had looked to the day when a railroad would link the Midwest to the Pacific; and St. Louis, Milwaukee, and Chicago had vied to become the eastern end of the projected Pacific railroad.

In January 1854 Senator Stephen A. Douglas of Illinois proposed a bill to organize Nebraska as a territory. An ardent expansionist, Douglas had formed his political ideology in the heady atmosphere of Manifest Destiny during the 1840s. As early as the mid-1840s, he had embraced the ideas of a Pacific railroad and the organization of Nebraska as ways to promote a continuous line of settlement between the Midwest and the Pacific. Although he preferred a railroad from his hometown of Chicago to San Francisco, Douglas dwelled on the national benefits that would attend construction of a railroad from anywhere in the Midwest to the Pacific. Such a railroad would enhance the importance of the Midwest, which could then hold the balance of power between the older sections of the North and South and guide the nation toward unity rather than disruption. In addition, westward expansion through Nebraska with the aid of a railroad struck Douglas as an issue, comparable to Manifest Destiny, around which the contending factions of the Democratic party would unite.

Douglas recognized two sources of potential conflict over his Nebraska bill. First, some southerners advocated a rival route for the Pacific railroad that would start at either New Orleans or Memphis. Second, Nebraska lay within the Louisiana Purchase and north of the Missouri Compromise line of 36°30', a region closed to slavery (see Map 14.2). Unless Douglas made some concessions, southerners would have little incentive to vote for his bill; after all, the organization of Nebraska would simultaneously create a potential free state and

MAP 14.2

The Kansas-Nebraska Act, 1854

Kansas and Nebraska lay within the Louisiana Purchase, north of 36°30′, and hence were closed to slavery until Stephen A. Douglas introduced his bills in 1854.

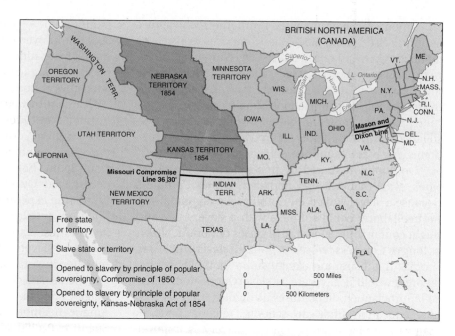

increase the chances for a northern, rather than a southern, railroad to the Pacific.

As the floor manager of the Compromise of 1850 in the Senate, Douglas thought that he had an ideal concession to offer to the South. The Compromise of 1850 had applied the principle of popular sovereignty to New Mexico and Utah, territories outside of the Louisiana Purchase and hence unaffected by the Missouri Compromise. Why not assume, Douglas reasoned, that the Compromise of 1850 had taken the place of the Missouri Compromise everywhere? Believing that expansion rather than slavery was uppermost in the public's mind, Douglas hoped to avoid controversy over slavery by ignoring the Missouri Compromise. But he quickly came under pressure from southern congressmen, who wanted an explicit repudiation of the Missouri Compromise. Soon they forced Douglas to state publicly that the Nebraska bill "superseded" the Missouri Compromise and rendered it "void." Still under pressure, Douglas next agreed to a division of Nebraska into two territories: Nebraska to the west of Iowa, and Kansas to the west of Missouri. Because Missouri was a slave state, most congressmen assumed that the division aimed to secure Kansas for slavery and Nebraska for free soil.

The modifications of Douglas's original bill set off a storm of protest. Congress quickly tabled the Pacific railroad (which, in the turn of events, would not be built until after the Civil War) and focused on the issue of slavery extension. A group of "Independent Democratic" northern congressmen, composed of antislavery Whigs and free-soil Democrats, assailed the bill as "part and parcel of an atrocious plot" to violate the "sacred pledge" of the Missouri Compromise and to turn Kansas into a "dreary region of despotism, inhabited by masters and slaves." Their rage electrified southerners, many of whom initially had reacted indifferently to the Nebraska bill. Some southerners had opposed an explicit repeal of the Missouri Compromise from fear of stimulating sectional discord; others doubted that Kansas would attract many slaveholders. But the furious assault of antislavery northerners united the South behind the Kansas-Nebraska bill by turning the issue into one of sectional pride as much as slavery extension.

Despite the uproar, Douglas successfully guided the Kansas-Nebraska bill through the Senate, where it passed by a vote of 37 to 14. In the House of Representatives, where the bill passed by little more than a whisker, 113 to 100, the true dimensions of the conflict became apparent. Not a single northern Whig representative in the House voted for the bill, whereas the northern Democrats divided evenly, 44 to 44.

The Surge of Free Soil

Amid the clamor over his bill, Douglas ruefully observed that he could now travel to Chicago by the light of his own burning effigies. Neither a fool nor a political novice, he was the victim of a political bombshell that exploded under his feet.

Support for free soil united northerners who agreed on little else. Some free-soilers opposed slavery on moral grounds and rejected racist legislation, but others were racists who opposed allowing any African-Americans, slave or free, into the West. An abolitionist traced the free-soil convictions of many westerners to a "perfect, if not supreme" hatred of blacks. Racist free-soilers in Iowa and Illinois secured laws prohibiting settlement by black people.

One opinion shared by free-soilers of all persuasions was that slavery impeded whites' progress. Because a slave worked for nothing, the argument ran, no free laborer could compete with a slave. A territory might contain only a handful of slaves or none at all, but as long as Congress refused to prohibit slavery in the territories, the institution would gain a foothold and free laborers would flee. Wherever slavery appeared, a free-soiler proclaimed, "labor loses its dignity; industry sickens; education finds no schools; religion finds no churches; and the whole land of slavery is impoverished." Free-soilers also blasted the idea that slavery had natural limits. One warned that "slavery is as certain to invade New Mexico and Utah as the sun is to rise"; others predicted that if slavery gained a toehold in Kansas, it would soon invade Minnesota.

To free-soilers, the Kansas-Nebraska Act, with its erasure of the Missouri Compromise, was the last straw, for it revealed, one wrote, "a continuous movement by slaveholders to spread slavery over the entire North." For a Massachusetts Whig congressman who had voted for the Compromise of 1850 and opposed abolitionists, the Kansas-Nebraska Act, "that most wanton and wicked act, so obviously designed to promote the extension of slavery," was too much to bear. "I now advocate the freedom of Kansas under all circumstances, and the prohibition of slavery in all territories now free."

The Ebbing of Manifest Destiny

The uproar over the Kansas-Nebraska Act embarrassed the Pierce administration. It also doomed Manifest Destiny, the one issue that had held the Democrats together in the 1840s.

Franklin Pierce had come to office championing Manifest Destiny, but increasing sectional rivalries sidetracked his efforts. In 1853 his emissary James Gadsden negotiated the purchase from Mexico of a strip of land south of the Gila River (now southern Arizona and part of southern New Mexico), an acquisition favored by advocates of a southern railroad route to the Pacific. Fierce opposition to the Gadsden Purchase revealed mounting free-soilers' suspicion of expansion, and the Senate approved the treaty only after slashing nine thousand square miles from the parcel. The sectional rivalries beginning to engulf the Nebraska bill clearly threatened any proposal to gain new territory.

Cuba provided even more vivid proof of the change in public attitudes about expansion. In 1854 a former Mississippi governor, John A. Quitman, planned a filibuster (an unofficial military expedition) to seize Cuba from Spain. Eager to acquire Cuba, Pierce may have encouraged Quitman, but Pierce forced Quitman to scuttle the expedition when faced with intense opposition from antislavery northerners who saw filibusters as just another manifestation of the Slave Power; the conspiracy of slaveholders and their northern dupes to grab more territory for slavery.

Pierce still hoped to purchase Cuba, but events quickly slipped out of his control. In October 1854 the American ambassadors to Great Britain, France, and Spain, two of them southerners, met in Belgium and issued the unofficial Ostend Manifesto, calling on the United States to acquire Cuba by any means, including force. Beset by the storm over the Kansas-Nebraska Act and the furor over Quitman's proposed filibuster, Pierce rejected the mandate.

Despite Pierce's disavowal of the Ostend Manifesto, the idea of expansion into the Caribbean continued to attract southerners, including the Tennessee-born adventurer William Walker. Slightly built and so unassuming that he usually spoke with his hands in his pockets, Walker seemed an unlikely soldier of fortune. Yet between 1853 and 1860, the year a firing squad in Honduras executed him, Walker led a succession of filibustering expeditions into Central America. Taking advantage of civil chaos in Nicaragua, he made himself the chief political force there, reinstituted slavery, and talked of making Nicaragua a U.S. colony.

For all the proclamations and intrigues that surrounded the movement for southern expansion, its strength and goals remained open to question. With few exceptions, the adventurers were shady characters whom southern politicians might admire but on whom they could never depend. Some southerners, among them Louisiana sugar planters who opposed acquiring Cuba because Cuban sugar would compete with their product, were against expansion. But expansionists stirred enough commotion to worry antislavery northerners that the South conspired to establish a Caribbean slave empire. Like a card in a poker game, the threat of expansion southward was all the more menacing for not being played. As long as the debate on

the extension of slavery focused on the continental United States, prospects for expansion were limited. However, adding Caribbean territory to the pot changed all calculations.

The Whigs Disintegrate, 1854–1855

While straining Democratic unity, the Kansas-Nebraska Act wrecked the Whig party. In the law's immediate aftermath, most northern Whigs hoped to blame the Democrats for the act and to entice free-soil Democrats to their side. In the state and congressional elections of 1854, the Democrats were decisively defeated. But the Whig party failed to benefit from the backlash against the Democrats. However furious they felt at Douglas for initiating the act, free-soil Democrats could not forget that the southern Whigs had supported Douglas. In addition, the northern Whigs themselves were deeply divided between antislavery "Conscience" Whigs, led by Senator William Seward of New York, and conservatives, led by former President Millard Fillmore, who were convinced that the Whig party had to adhere at all costs to the Compromise of 1850 to maintain itself as a national party.

Divisions within the Whig party not only repelled antislavery Democrats from affiliating with it but also prompted many antislavery Whigs to look for an alternative party. By 1856 the new Republican party would become the home for most of these northern refugees from the traditional parties; but in 1854 and 1855, when the Republican party was only starting to organize, the American, or Know-Nothing, party emerged as the principal alternative.

The Rise and Fall of the Know-Nothings, 1853–1856

The Know-Nothings evolved out of a secret nativist organization, the Order of the Star-Spangled Banner, founded in 1850. (The party's popular name, Know-Nothing, derived from the standard response of its members to inquiries about its activities: "I know nothing.") One of many such societies that mushroomed in response to the unprecedented immigration of the 1840s, the Order of the Star-Spangled Banner had sought to rid the United States of immigrant and Catholic political influence by pressuring the existing parties to nominate and appoint only native-born Protestants to office, and by advocating an extension of the naturalization period before immigrants could vote.

Throughout the 1840s nativists usually voted Whig, but their allegiance to the Whigs started to buckle during Winfield Scott's campaign for the presidency in 1852. In an attempt to revitalize his party, which was badly split over slavery, Scott had courted the traditionally Democratic Catholic vote. But Scott's tactic backfired. Most Catholics voted for Franklin Pierce. Nativists, meanwhile, felt betrayed by their party, and after Scott's defeat, many gravitated toward the Know-Nothings. The Kansas-Nebraska Act cemented their allegiance to the Know-Nothings, who in the North opposed both the extension of slavery and Catholicism. Indeed, an obsessive fear of conspiracies unified the Know-Nothings. Just as they denounced the pope for allegedly conspiring to subvert the American Republic, they saw the evil influence of Slave Power everywhere.

The Know-Nothings' surge was truly stunning. In 1854 they captured the governorship, all the congressional seats, and almost all the seats in the state legislature in Massachusetts. Know-Nothings were sufficiently strong in the West to retard the emergence of the Republican party, and so strong in the East that they exploded any hopes that the Whigs had of capitalizing on hostility to the Kansas-Nebraska Act.

After rising spectacularly between 1853 and 1855, the star of Know-Nothingism nevertheless plummeted and gradually disappeared below the horizon after 1856. The Know-Nothings proved as vulnerable as the Whigs to sectional conflicts over slavery. Although primarily a force in the North, the Know-Nothings had a southern wing, composed mainly of former Whigs who loathed both the antislavery northerners who were abandoning the Whig party and the southern Democrats, whom they viewed as disunionist firebrands. In 1855 these southern Know-Nothings combined with northern conservatives to make acceptance of the Kansas-Nebraska Act part of the Know-Nothing platform, and thus they blurred the attraction of Know-Nothingism to those northern voters who were more antislavery than anti-Catholic.

One such Whig refugee, Illinois Congressman Abraham Lincoln, asked pointedly: "How can anyone who abhors the oppression of negroes be in favor of degrading classes of white people?" "We began by declaring," Lincoln continued, "that 'all men are created equal.' We now practically read it 'all men are created equal except negroes.' When the Know-Nothings get control, it will read 'all men are created equal, except Negroes and foreigners and Catholics.'" Finally, even most Know-Nothings eventually came to conclude that, as one observer put it, "neither the Pope nor the foreigners ever can govern the country or endanger its liberties,

but the slavebreeders and slavetraders do govern it, and threaten to put an end to all government but theirs." Consequently, the Know-Nothings proved vulnerable to the challenge posed by the emerging Republican party, which did not officially embrace nativism and which had no southern wing to blunt its antislavery message.

The Republican Party and the Crisis in Kansas, 1855–1856

Born in the chaotic aftermath of the Kansas-Nebraska Act, the Republican party sprang up in several northern states in 1854 and 1855. With the Know-Nothings' demise after 1856, the Republicans would become the main opposition to the Democratic party, and they would win each presidential election from 1860 through 1880; but in 1855 it was unclear whether the Republicans had any future. While united by opposition to the Kansas-Nebraska Act, the party held various shades of opinion in uneasy balance. At one extreme were conservatives who merely wanted to restore the Missouri Compromise; at the other was a small faction of former Liberty party abolitionists; and the middle held a sizable body of free-soilers.

In addition to bridging these divisions, the Republicans confronted the task of building organizations on the state level, where the Know-Nothings were already well established. Politicians of the day knew that the voters' allegiances were often shaped by state issues, including temperance. Maine's passage of the nation's first statewide prohibition law in 1851 spurred calls elsewhere for liquor regulation. Linking support for temperance with anti-Catholicism and antislavery, the Know-Nothings were well positioned to answer these calls.

Frequently, the same voters who were antislavery were also protemperance and anti-Catholic. The common thread was the belief that addiction to alcohol and submission to the pope were forms of enslavement that had to be eradicated. Intensely moralistic, such voters viewed the traditional parties as controlled by unprincipled hacks, and they began to search for a new party. In competing with the Know-Nothings on the state level, the Republicans faced a dilemma, stemming from the fact that both parties were targeting many of the same voters. The Republican leadership had clearer antislavery credentials than did the Know-Nothing leadership, but this fact alone did not guarantee that voters would respond more to antislavery than to anti-Catholicism or temperance. Thus, if the Republicans attacked the Know-Nothings for stressing anti-Catholicism over antislavery, they ran the risk of alienating the very vot-

ers whom they had to attract. If they conciliated the Know-Nothings, they might lose their own identity as a party.

Sometimes attacking, sometimes conciliating, the Republicans had some successes in state elections in 1855; but as popular ire against the Kansas-Nebraska Act cooled, they also suffered setbacks. Even at the start of 1856, they were organized in only half the northern states and lacked any national organization. The Republicans desperately needed a development that would make voters worry more about the Slave Power than about rum or Catholicism. No single occurrence did more to unite the party around its free-soil center, to galvanize voters' antislavery feelings, and, consequently, to boost the Republicans' fortunes than the outbreak of violence in Kansas, which quickly gained for the territory the name Bleeding Kansas.

In the wake of the Kansas-Nebraska Act, Boston-based abolitionists had organized the New England Emigrant Aid Company to send antislavery settlers into Kansas. The abolitionists' aim was to stifle escalating efforts to turn Kansas into a slave state. But antislavery New Englanders arrived slowly in Kansas; the bulk of the territory's early settlers came from Missouri or elsewhere in the Midwest. Very few of these early settlers opposed slavery on moral grounds. Some, in fact, favored slavery; others wanted to keep all blacks, whether slave or free, out of Kansas. "I kem to Kansas to live in a free state," exclaimed a clergyman, "and I don't want niggers a-trampin' over my grave."

Despite most settlers' racist leanings and utter hatred of abolitionists, Kansas became a battleground between proslavery and antislavery forces. In March 1855 thousands of proslavery Missourian "border ruffians," led by Senator David R. Atchison, crossed into Kansas to vote illegally in the first election for a territorial legislature. Drawing and cocking their revolvers, they quickly silenced any judges who questioned their right to vote in Kansas. These proslavery advocates probably would have won an honest election because they would have been supported by the votes both of slaveholders and of nonslaveholders horrified at rumors that abolitionists planned to use Kansas as a colony for fugitive slaves. But by stealing the election, the proslavery forces committed a grave tactical blunder. A cloud of fraudulence thereafter hung over the proslavery legislature subsequently established at Lecompton, Kansas. "There is not a proslavery man of my acquaintance in Kansas," wrote the wife of an antislavery farmer, "who does not acknowledge that the Bogus Legislature was the result of a gigantic and well planned fraud, that the elections

"Liberty, the Fair Maid of Kansas in the Hands of the 'Border Ruffians'"
This cartoon savagely attacks leading northern Democrats for their acquiescence in the murderous actions of proslavery mobs in Kansas. On the left, James Buchanan steals a watch from a corpse. In the center, a tipsy President Franklin Pierce and Lewis Cass leer at the fair maid of Kansas, while on the right Stephen Douglas scalps a victim.

LIBERTY, THE FAIR MAID OF KANSAS_IN THE HANDS OF THE "BORDER RUFFIANS".

were carried by an invading mob from Missouri." This legislature then further darkened its image by expelling several antislavery legislators and passing a succession of outrageous acts. These laws limited officeholding to individuals who would swear allegiance to slavery, punished the harboring of fugitive slaves by ten years' imprisonment, and made the circulation of abolitionist literature a capital offense.

The territorial legislature's actions set off a chain reaction. Free-staters, including a small number of abolitionists and a much larger number of settlers enraged by the proceedings at Lecompton, organized a rival government at Topeka, Kansas, in the summer and fall of 1855. In response, the Lecompton government in May 1856 dispatched a posse to Lawrence, where free-staters, heeding the advice of antislavery minister Henry Ward Beecher that rifles would do more than Bibles to enforce morality in Kansas, had taken up arms and dubbed their guns "Beecher's Bibles." Riding under flags emblazoned "southern rights" and "let yankees tremble and abolitionists fall," the proslavery posse tore through the town like a hell-bent mob. Although the intruders did not kill anyone, they burned several buildings and destroyed two free-state printing presses—enough for the Republican press to label their actions "the sack of lawrence."

The next move was made by John Brown. The sack of Lawrence convinced Brown that God now beckoned him, in the words of a neighbor, "to break the jaws of the wicked." In late May Brown led seven men, including his four sons and his son-in-law, toward the Pottawatomie

Creek near Lawrence. Setting upon five men associated with the Lecompton government, they shot one to death and hacked the others to pieces with broadswords. Brown's "Pottawatomie massacre" struck terror into the hearts of southerners and completed the transformation of Bleeding Kansas into a battleground between the South and the North (see Map 14.3). A month after the massacre, a South Carolinian living in Kansas wrote to his sister,

> I never lie down without taking the precaution to fasten my door and fix it in such a way that if it is forced open, it can be opened only wide enough for one person to come in at a time. I have my rifle, revolver, and old home-stocked pistol where I can lay my hand on them in an instant, besides a hatchet and an axe. I take this precaution to guard against the midnight attacks of the Abolitionists, who never make an attack in open daylight, and no Proslavery man knows when he is safe in this Ter[ritory.]

In Kansas popular sovereignty flunked its major test. Instead of quickly resolving the issue of slavery extension, popular sovereignty merely institutionalized the division over slavery by creating rival governments in Lecompton and Topeka. The Pierce administration then shot itself in the foot by denouncing the Topeka government and recognizing only its Lecompton rival. Pierce had forced northern Democrats into the awkward position of appearing to ally with the South in support of the fraudulently elected legislature at Lecompton.

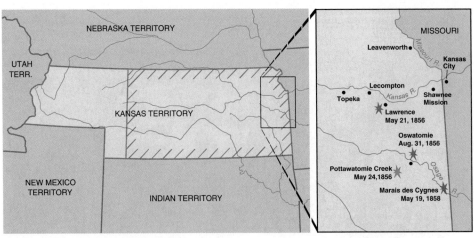

MAP 14.3
Bleeding Kansas
Kansas became a battleground between free-state and slave-state factions in the 1850s.

Nor did popular sovereignty keep the slavery issue out of national politics. On the day before the sack of Lawrence, Republican Senator Charles Sumner of Massachusetts delivered a bombastic and wrathful speech, "The Crime Against Kansas," in which he verbally whipped most of the U.S. Senate for complicity in slavery. Sumner singled out Senator Andrew Butler of South Carolina for his choice of "the harlot, slavery" as his mistress and for the "loose expectoration" of his speech (a nasty reference to the aging Butler's tendency to drool). Sumner's oration stunned most senators. Douglas wondered aloud whether Sumner's real aim was "to provoke some of us to kick him as we would a dog in the street." Two days later a relative of Butler,

Democratic Representative Preston Brooks of South Carolina, strode into the Senate chamber, found Sumner at his desk, and struck him repeatedly with a cane. The hollow cane broke after five or six blows, but Sumner required stitches, experienced shock, and did not return to the Senate for three years. Brooks became an instant hero in the South, and the fragments of his weapon were "begged as sacred relics." A new cane, presented to Brooks by the city of Charleston, bore the inscription "Hit him again."

Now Bleeding Kansas and Bleeding Sumner united the North. The sack of Lawrence, Pierce's recognition of the proslavery Lecompton government, and Brooks's actions seemed to clinch the Republican argument that

SOUTHERN CHIVALRY — ARGUMENT versus CLUB'S.

"Southern Chivalry"
Cartoons like this one, showing the beating of antislavery Senator Charles Sumner by Preston "Bully" Brooks, confirmed northern images of white southerners as people who prided themselves on their genteel manners but who behaved like street toughs.

an aggressive "slaveocracy" held white northerners in contempt. Abolitionists remained unpopular in northern opinion, but southerners were becoming even less popular. Northern migrants to Kansas coined a name reflecting their feelings about southerners: "the pukes." Other northerners attacked the slaveholding migrants to Kansas as the "Missouri savages." By denouncing Slave Power more than slavery itself, Republican propagandists sidestepped the issue of slavery's morality, which divided their followers, and focused on portraying southern planters as arrogant aristocrats and the natural enemies of the laboring people of the North.

The Election of 1856

The election of 1856 revealed the scope of the political realignments of the preceding few years. In this, its first presidential contest, the Republican party nominated John C. Frémont, the famed "pathfinder" who had played a key role in the conquest of California during the Mexican War. The Republicans then maneuvered the northern Know-Nothings into endorsing Frémont. The southern Know-Nothings picked the last Whig president, Millard Fillmore, as their candidate, and the Democrats dumped Pierce for the seasoned James Buchanan of Pennsylvania. A four-term congressman and long an aspirant to the presidency, Buchanan finally secured his party's nomination because he had the good luck to be out of the country (as minister to Great Britain) during the furor over the Kansas-Nebraska Act. As a signer of the Ostend Manifesto, he was popular in the South: virtually all of his close friends in Washington were southerners.

The campaign quickly turned into two separate races—Frémont versus Buchanan in the free states and Fillmore versus Buchanan in the slave states. In the North the candidates divided clearly over slavery extension; Frémont's platform called for congressional prohibition of slavery in the territories, whereas Buchanan pledged congressional "non-interference." In the South Fillmore appealed to traditionally Whig voters and called for moderation in the face of secessionist threats. But by nominating a well-known moderate in Buchanan, the Democrats undercut some of Fillmore's appeal. Although Fillmore garnered more than 40 percent of the popular vote in ten of the slave states, he carried only Maryland. In the North Frémont outpolled Buchanan in the popular vote and won eleven of the sixteen free states; if Frémont had carried Pennsylvania and either Illinois, Indiana, or New Jersey, he would have won the election. As it turned out, Buchanan, the only truly national candidate in the race, secured the presidency.

The election yielded three clear conclusions. First, the American party was finished as a major national force. Having worked for the Republican Frémont, most northern Know-Nothings now joined that party, and in the wake of Fillmore's dismal showing in the South, southern Know-Nothings gave up on their party and sought new political affiliations. Second, although in existence scarcely more than a year, lacking any base in the South, and running a political novice, the Republican party did very well. A purely sectional party had come within reach of capturing the presidency. Finally, as long as the Democrats could unite behind a single national candidate, they would be hard to defeat. To achieve such unity, however, the Democrats would have to find more James Buchanans—"doughface" moderates who would be acceptable to southerners and who would not drive even more northerners into Republican arms.

THE CRISIS OF THE UNION, 1857–1860

No one ever accused James Buchanan of impulsiveness or fanaticism. Although he disapproved of slavery, he believed that his administration could neither restrict nor end the institution. In 1860 he would pronounce secession a grave wrong, but would affirm that his administration could not stop it. Understandably, contemporaries hailed his election as a victory for moderation. Yet his administration encountered a succession of controversies, first over the famed *Dred Scott* decision of the Supreme Court, then over the proslavery Lecompton constitution in Kansas, next following the raid by John Brown on Harpers Ferry, and finally concerning secession itself. Ironically, a man who sought to avoid controversy presided over one of the most controversy-ridden administrations in American history.

Buchanan's problems arose less from his own actions than from the fact that the forces driving the nation apart were already spinning out of control by 1856. By the time of Buchanan's inauguration, southerners who looked north saw creeping abolitionism in the guise of free soil, whereas northerners who looked south saw an insatiable Slave Power. Once these images had taken hold in the minds of the American people, politicians like James Buchanan had little room to maneuver.

The Dred Scott Case, 1857

Pledged to congressional "non-interference" with slavery in the territories, Buchanan had long looked to the courts for a nonpartisan resolution of the vexatious

issue of slavery extension. A case that appeared to promise such a solution had been wending its way through the courts for years; and on March 6, 1857, two days after Buchanan's inauguration, the Supreme Court handed down its decision in *Dred Scott* v. *Sandford*.

During the 1830s Dred Scott, a slave, had been taken by his master from the slave state of Missouri into Illinois and the Wisconsin Territory, areas respectively closed to slavery by the Northwest Ordinance of 1787 and the Missouri Compromise. After his master's death, Scott sued for his freedom on the grounds of his residence in free territory. In 1856 the case finally reached the Supreme Court.

The Court faced two key issues. First, did Scott's residence in free territory during the 1830s make him free? Second, regardless of the answer to this question, did Scott, again enslaved in Missouri, have a right to sue in the federal courts? The Court could have resolved the case on narrow grounds by answering the second question in the negative, but Buchanan wanted a far-reaching decision that would deal with the broad issue of slavery in the territories.

In the end, Buchanan got the broad ruling that he sought, but one so controversial that it settled little. In the most important of six separate majority opinions, Chief Justice Roger B. Taney, a seventy-nine-year-old Marylander whom Andrew Jackson had appointed to succeed John Marshall in 1835, began with the narrow conclusion that Scott, a slave, could not sue for his freedom. Then the thunder started. No black, whether a slave or a free person descended from a slave, could become a citizen of the United States, Taney continued. Next Taney whipped the thunderheads into a tornado. Even if Scott had been a legal plaintiff, Taney ruled, his residence in free territory years earlier did not make him free, because the Missouri Compromise, whose provisions prohibited slavery in the Wisconsin Territory, was itself unconstitutional. The compromise, declared Taney, violated the Fifth Amendment's protection of property (including slaves).

Contrary to Buchanan's hopes, the decision touched off a new blast of controversy over slavery in the territories. The antislavery press flayed it as a "willful perversion" filled with "gross historical falsehoods." Taney's ruling gave Republicans more evidence that a fiendish Slave Power conspiracy gripped the nation. Although the Kansas-Nebraska Act had effectively repealed the Missouri Compromise, the Court's majority now rejected even the principle behind the compromise, the idea that Congress could prohibit slavery in the territories. Five of the six justices who rejected this principle were

from slave states. The Slave Power, a northern paper bellowed, "has marched over and annihilated the boundaries of the states. We are now one great homogenous slaveholding community."

Like Stephen Douglas after the Kansas-Nebraska Act, President Buchanan now appeared as a northern dupe of the "slaveocracy." Republicans restrained themselves from open defiance of the decision only by insisting that it did not bind the nation; Taney's comments on the constitutionality of the Missouri Compromise, they contended, amounted merely to *obiter dicta*, opinions superfluous to settling the case.

Reactions to the decision underscored the fact that by 1857 no "judicious" or nonpartisan solution to slavery extension was possible. Anyone who still doubted this needed only to read the fast-breaking news from Kansas.

The Lecompton Constitution, 1857

While the Supreme Court wrestled with the abstract issues raised by the expansion of slavery, Buchanan sought a concrete solution to the gnawing problem of Kansas, where the free-state government at Topeka and the officially recognized proslavery government at Lecompton viewed each other with profound distrust. Buchanan's plan for Kansas looked simple: an elected territorial convention would draw up a constitution that would either permit or prohibit slavery; Buchanan would submit the constitution to Congress; Congress would then admit Kansas as a state.

Unfortunately, no sooner had Buchanan devised his plan than it began to explode in his face. Popular sovereignty, the essence of Buchanan's plan, demanded fair play, a scarce quality in Kansas. The territory's history of fraudulent elections left both sides reluctant to commit their fortunes to the polls. An election for a constitutional convention took place in June 1857, but free-staters, by now a majority in Kansas, boycotted the election on the grounds that the proslavery side would rig it. Dominated by proslavery delegates, a constitutional convention then met and drew up a frame of government, the Lecompton constitution, that protected the rights of those slaveholders already living in Kansas to their slave property and provided for a referendum in which voters could decide whether to allow in more slaves.

The Lecompton constitution created a dilemma for Buchanan. A supporter of popular sovereignty, he had gone on record in favor of letting the voters in Kansas decide the slavery issue. Now he was confronted by a constitution drawn up by a convention that had been

elected by less than 10 percent of the eligible voters, by plans for a referendum that would not allow voters to remove slaves already in Kansas, and by the prospect that the proslavery side would conduct the referendum no more honestly than it had other ballots. Yet Buchanan had compelling reasons to accept the Lecompton constitution as the basis for the admission of Kansas as a state. The South, which had provided him with 112 of his 174 electoral votes in 1856, supported the constitution. Buchanan knew, moreover, that only about two hundred slaves resided in Kansas, and he believed that the prospects for slavery in the remaining territories were slight. The contention over slavery in Kansas struck him as another example of how extremists could turn minor issues into major ones. To accept the constitution and speed the admission of Kansas as either a free state or a slave state seemed the best way to pull the rug from beneath the extremists and quiet the ruckus in Kansas. Accordingly, in December 1857 Buchanan formally endorsed the Lecompton constitution.

Buchanan's decision provoked a bitter attack from Senator Stephen A. Douglas. What rankled Douglas and many others was that the Lecompton convention, having drawn up a constitution, then allowed voters to decide only whether more slaves could be brought into the territory. "I care not whether [slavery] is voted down or voted up," Douglas declared. But to refuse to allow a vote on the constitution itself, with its protection of existing slave property, smacked of a "system of trickery and jugglery to defeat the fair expression of the will of the people."

Even as Douglas broke with Buchanan, events in Kansas took a new turn. A few months after electing delegates to the convention that drew up the Lecompton constitution, Kansans had gone to the polls to elect a territorial legislature. So flagrant was the fraud in this election—one village with thirty eligible voters returned more than sixteen hundred proslavery votes—that the governor disallowed enough proslavery returns to give free-staters a majority in the legislature. After the drafting of the Lecompton constitution, this territorial legislature called for a referendum on the entire document. Whereas the Kansas constitutional convention's goal had been to restrict the choice of voters to the narrow issue of the future introduction of slaves, the territorial legislature sought a referendum that would allow Kansans to vote against the protection of existing slave property as well.

In December 1857 the referendum called earlier by the constitutional convention was held. Boycotted by free-staters, the constitution with slavery passed over-whelmingly. Two weeks later, in the election called by the territorial legislature, the proslavery side abstained, and the constitution went down to crushing defeat. Having already cast his lot with the Lecompton convention's election, Buchanan simply ignored this second election. But he could not ignore the obstacles that the division in Kansas created for his plan to bring Kansas into the Union under the Lecompton constitution. When he submitted the plan to Congress, a deadlock in the House forced him to accept a proposal for still another referendum. This time, Kansans were given the choice between accepting or rejecting the entire constitution, with the proviso that rejection would delay statehood. Despite the proviso, Kansans overwhelmingly voted down the constitution.

Not only had Buchanan failed to tranquilize Kansas, but he had alienated northerners in his own party. His support for the Lecompton constitution confirmed the suspicion of northern Democrats that the southern Slave Power pulled all the important strings in their party. Douglas became the hero of the hour for northern Democrats and even for some Republicans. "The bone and sinew of the Northern Democracy are with you," a New Yorker wrote to Douglas. Yet Douglas himself could take little comfort from the Lecompton fiasco, as his cherished formula of popular sovereignty increasingly looked like a prescription for civil strife rather than harmony.

The Lincoln-Douglas Debates, 1858

Despite the acclaim he gained in the North for his stand against the Lecompton constitution, Douglas faced a stiff challenge in Illinois for reelection to the United States Senate. Of his Republican opponent, Abraham Lincoln, Douglas said: "I shall have my hands full. He is the strong man of his party—full of wit, facts, dates—and the best stump speaker with his droll ways and dry jokes, in the West."

Physically as well as ideologically, the two men formed a striking contrast. Tall (6′4″) and gangling, Lincoln once described himself as "a piece of floating driftwood." Energy, ambition, and a passion for self-education had carried him from the Kentucky log cabin in which he was born in 1809 through a youth filled with odd occupations (farm laborer, surveyor, rail-splitter, flatboatman, and storekeeper) into law and politics in his adopted Illinois. There he had capitalized on westerners' support for internal improvements to gain election to Congress in 1846 as a Whig. Having opposed the

Mexican-American War and the Kansas-Nebraska Act, he joined the Republican party in 1856.

Douglas was fully a foot shorter than the towering Lincoln. But his compact frame contained astonishing energy. Born in New England, Douglas appealed primarily to the small farmers of southern origin who populated the Illinois flatlands. To these and others, he was the "little giant," the personification of the Democratic party in the West. The campaign quickly became more than just another Senate race, for it pitted the Republican party's rising star against the Senate's leading Democrat and, thanks to the railroad and the telegraph, received unprecedented national attention.

Although some Republicans extolled Douglas's stand against the Lecompton constitution, to Lincoln nothing had changed. Douglas was still Douglas, the author of the infamous Kansas-Nebraska Act and a man who cared not whether slavery was voted up or down as long as the vote was honest. Opening his campaign with the "House Divided" speech ("this nation cannot exist

Stephen A. Douglas

Douglas's politics were founded on his unflinching conviction that most Americans favored national expansion and would support popular sovereignty as the fastest and least controversial way to achieve it. Douglas's self-assurance blinded him to rising northern sentiment for free soil.

Abraham Lincoln

Clean-shaven at the time of his famous debates with Douglas, Lincoln would soon grow a beard to give himself a more distinguished appearance.

permanently half slave and half free"), Lincoln reminded his Republican followers of the gulf that still separated his doctrine of free soil from Douglas's popular sovereignty. Douglas dismissed the house-divided doctrine as an invitation to secession. What mattered to him was not slavery, which he viewed as merely an extreme way to subordinate an allegedly inferior race, but the continued expansion of white settlement. Like Lincoln, he wanted to keep slavery out of the path of white settlement. But unlike his rival, Douglas believed that popular sovereignty was the surest way to attain this goal without disrupting the Union.

The high point of the campaign came in a series of seven debates held from August to October 1858. The Lincoln-Douglas debates mixed political drama with the atmosphere of a festival. At the debate in Galesburg, for example, dozens of horse-drawn floats descended on the town from nearby farming communities. One bore thirty-two girls dressed in white, one for each state, and a thirty-third who dressed in black with the label "Kansas" and carried a banner proclaiming "they won't let me in."

Douglas used the debates to portray Lincoln as a virtual abolitionist and advocate of racial equality. Both charges were calculated to doom Lincoln in the eyes of the intensely racist Illinois voters. In response, Lincoln affirmed that Congress had no constitutional authority to abolish slavery in the South, and in one debate he asserted bluntly that "I am not, nor ever have been in favor of bringing about the social and political equality of the white, and black man." However, fending off charges of extremism was getting Lincoln nowhere; so in order to seize the initiative, he tried to maneuver Douglas into a corner.

In view of the *Dred Scott* decision, Lincoln asked in the debate at Freeport, could the people of a territory lawfully exclude slavery? In essence, Lincoln was asking Douglas to reconcile popular sovereignty with the *Dred Scott* decision. Lincoln had long contended that the Court's decision rendered popular sovereignty as thin as soup boiled from the shadow of a pigeon that had starved to death. If, as the Supreme Court's ruling affirmed, Congress had no authority to exclude slavery from a territory, then it seemingly followed that a territorial legislature created by Congress also lacked power to do so. To no one's surprise, Douglas replied that notwithstanding the *Dred Scott* decision, the voters of a territory could effectively exclude slavery simply by refusing to enact laws that gave legal protection to slave property.

Douglas's "Freeport doctrine" salvaged popular sovereignty but did nothing for his reputation among southerners, who preferred the guarantees of the *Dred Scott* ruling to the uncertainties of popular sovereignty. Whereas Douglas's stand against the Lecompton constitution had already tattered his reputation in the South ("he is already dead there," Lincoln affirmed), his Freeport doctrine stiffened southern opposition to his presidential ambitions.

Lincoln faced the problem throughout the debates that free soil and popular sovereignty, although distinguishable in theory, had much the same practical effect. Neither Lincoln nor Douglas doubted that popular sovereignty, if fairly applied, would keep slavery out of the territories. In the closing debates, in order to keep the initiative and sharpen their differences, Lincoln shifted toward attacks on slavery as "a moral, social, and political evil." He argued that Douglas's view of slavery as merely an eccentric and unsavory southern custom would dull the nation's conscience and facilitate the legalization of slavery everywhere. But Lincoln compromised his own position by rejecting both abolition and equality for blacks.

Neither man scored a clear victory in argument, and the senatorial election itself settled no major issues. Douglas's supporters captured a majority of the seats in the state legislature, which at the time was responsible for electing U.S. senators. But despite the racist leanings of most Illinois voters, Republican candidates for the state legislature won a slightly larger share of the popular vote than did their Democratic rivals. Moreover, in its larger significance, the contest solidified the sectional split in the national Democratic party and made Lincoln famous in the North and infamous in the South.

The Legacy of Harpers Ferry

Although Lincoln rejected abolitionism, he called free soil a step toward the "ultimate extinction" of slavery. Similarly, New York Republican Senator William H. Seward spoke of an "irrepressible conflict" between slavery and freedom. Predictably, many southerners ignored the distinction between free soil and abolition and concluded that Republicans and abolitionists were joined in an unholy alliance against slavery. To many in the South, the North seemed to be controlled by demented leaders bent on civil war. One southern defender of slavery equated the doctrines of the abolitionists with those of "Socialists, of Free Love and Free Lands, Free Churches, Free Women and Free Negroes-of No-Marriage, No-Religion, No-Private Property, No-Law and No-Government."

Nothing did more to freeze this southern image of the North than the evidence of northern complicity in John Brown's raid on Harpers Ferry and northern sermons that turned Brown into a martyr. In Philadelphia, some 250 outraged southern students seceded from the city's medical schools to enroll in southern schools. True, Lincoln and Seward condemned the raid, but southerners suspected that they regretted the conspiracy's failure more than the attempt itself.

Brown's abortive raid also rekindled southern fears of a slave insurrection. Rumors flew around the South, and vigilantes turned out to battle conspiracies that existed only in their minds. Volunteers, for example,

mobilized to defend northeastern Texas against thousands of abolitionists supposedly on their way to pillage Dallas and its environs. In other incidents, vigilantes rounded up thousands of slaves, tortured some into confessing to nonexistent plots, and then lynched them. The hysteria fed by such rumors played into the hands of the extremists known as fire-eaters, who encouraged the witch hunt by spreading tales of slave conspiracies in the press so that southern voters would turn to them as alone able to "stem the current of Abolition."

More and more southerners concluded that the Republican party itself directed abolitionism and deserved blame for Brown's raid. After all, had not influ-

Illustrations from the American Anti-Slavery Almanac

Northern antislavery propagandists indicted the southern way of life, not just slavery. These illustrations depict the South as a region of lynchings, duels, cockfights, and everyday brawls. Even northerners who opposed the abolition of slavery resolved to keep slaveholders out of the western territories.

ential Republicans assailed slavery, unconstitutionally tried to ban it, and spoken of an "irrepressible conflict" between slavery and freedom? The Tennessee legislature reflected southern views when it passed resolutions declaring that the Harpers Ferry raid was "the natural fruit of this treasonable 'irrepressible conflict' doctrine put forth by the great head of the Black Republican party and echoed by his subordinates."

The South Contemplates Secession

A pamphlet published in 1860 embodied in its title the growing conviction of southerners that *The South Alone Should Govern the South*. Southerners reached this conclusion gradually and often reluctantly. In 1850 few southerners could have conceived of transferring their allegiance from the United States to some new nation. Relatively insulated from the main tide of immigration, southerners thought of themselves as the most American of Americans. But the events of the 1850s persuaded many southerners that the North had deserted the true principles of the Union. Southerners interpreted northern resistance to the Fugitive Slave Act and to slavery in Kansas as either illegal or unconstitutional, and they viewed headline-grabbing phrases such as "irrepressible conflict" and "a higher law" as virtual declarations of war on the South. To southerners, it was the North, not the South, that had grown peculiar.

This sense of the North's deviance tinged reports sent home by southern visitors to the North in the 1850s. A Mississippi planter, for example, could scarcely believe his eyes when he witnessed a group of northern free blacks refusing to surrender their seats to white women. When assured by northern friends of their support for the South, southerners could only wonder why northerners kept electing Republicans to office. Southerners increasingly described their visits to the North as forays into "enemy territory." More and more they agreed with a South Carolinian's insistence that the South had to sever itself "from the rotten Northern element."

Viewed as a practical tactic to secure concrete goals, secession did not make a great deal of sense. Some southerners contended that secession would make it easier for the South to acquire more territory for slavery in the Caribbean; yet the South was scarcely united in desiring additional slave territory in Mexico, Cuba, or Central America. States like Alabama, Mississippi, and Texas contained vast tracts of unsettled land that could be converted to cotton cultivation far more easily than

the Caribbean. Other southerners continued to complain that the North blocked the access of slaveholders to territories in the continental United States. But it is unclear how secession would solve this problem. If the South were to secede, the remaining continental territories would belong exclusively to the North, which could then legislate for them as it chose. Nor would secession stop future John Browns from infiltrating the South to provoke slave insurrections.

Yet to dwell on the impracticality of secession as a choice for the South is to miss the point. Talk of secession was less a tactic with clear goals than an expression of the South's outrage at what southerners viewed as the irresponsible and unconstitutional course that the Republicans were taking in the North. It was not merely that Republican attacks on slavery sowed the seeds of slave uprisings. More fundamentally, southerners believed that the North was treating the South as its inferior—indeed, as no more than a slave. "Talk of Negro slavery," exclaimed southern proslavery philosopher George Fitzhugh, "is not half so humiliating and disgraceful as the slavery of the South to the North." Having persuaded themselves that slavery made it possible for them to enjoy unprecedented freedom and equality, white southerners took great pride in their homeland. They bitterly dismissed Republican portrayals of the South as a region of arrogant planters and degraded white common folk. Submission to the Republicans, declared Democratic Senator Jefferson Davis of Mississippi, "would be intolerable to a proud people."

THE COLLAPSE OF THE UNION, 1860–1861

As long as the pliant James Buchanan occupied the White House, southerners did no more than talk about secession. Once aware that Buchanan had declined to seek reelection, however, they approached the election of 1860 with anxiety. Although not all voters realized it, when they cast their ballots in 1860 they were deciding not just the outcome of an election but the fate of the Union. Lincoln's election initiated the process by which the southern states abandoned the United States for a new nation, the Confederate States of America. Initially, the Confederacy consisted only of states in the Lower South. As the Upper South hesitated to embrace secession, moderates searched frantically for a compromise that would save the Union. But they searched in vain. The time for compromise had passed.

The Election of 1860

As a single-issue, free-soil party, the Republicans had done well in the election of 1856. To win in 1860, however, they would have to broaden their appeal in the North, particularly in states like Pennsylvania and Illinois, which they had lost in 1856. To do so, Republican leaders had concluded, they needed to forge an economic program to complement their advocacy of free soil.

A severe economic slump following the so-called Panic of 1857 furnished the Republicans with a fitting opening. The depression shattered more than a decade of American prosperity and thrust economic concerns to the fore. In response, in the late 1850s, the Republicans developed an economic program based on support for a protective tariff (popular in Pennsylvania) and on two issues favored in the Midwest, federal aid for internal improvements and the granting to settlers of free 160-acre homesteads out of publicly owned land. By proposing to make these homesteads available to immigrants who were not yet citizens, the Republicans went far in shedding the nativist image that lingered from their early association with the Know-Nothings. Carl Schurz, an 1848 German political refugee who had campaigned for Lincoln against Douglas in 1858, now labored mightily to bring his antislavery countrymen over to the Republican party.

The Republicans' desire to broaden their appeal also influenced their choice of a candidate. At their convention in Chicago, they nominated Abraham Lincoln over the early front-runner, William H. Seward of New York. Although better known than Lincoln, Seward failed to convince his party that he could carry the key states of Pennsylvania, Illinois, Indiana, and New Jersey. (Rueful Republicans remembered that their presidential candidate John C. Frémont would have won in 1856 if he had carried Pennsylvania and one of the other three states.) Lincoln held the advantage not only of hailing from Illinois but also of projecting a more moderate image than Seward on the slavery issue. Seward's penchant for controversial phrases like "irrepressible conflict" and "higher law" had given him a radical image. Lincoln, in contrast, had repeatedly affirmed that Congress had no constitutional right to interfere with slavery in the South and had explicitly rejected the "higher law" doctrine. The Republicans now needed only to widen their northern appeal.

The Democrats, still claiming to be a national party, had to bridge their own sectional differences. The *Dred Scott* decision and the conflict over the Lecompton constitution had weakened the northern Democrats and strengthened southern Democrats. While Douglas still desperately defended popular sovereignty, southern Democrats stretched *Dred Scott* to conclude that Congress now had to protect slavery in the territories.

The Democratic party's internal turmoil boiled over at its Charleston convention in the spring of 1860. Failing to force acceptance of a platform guaranteeing federal protection of slavery in the territories, the delegates from the Lower South stalked out. The convention adjourned to Baltimore, where a new fight broke out over the question of seating hastily elected pro-Douglas slates of delegates from the Lower South states that had seceded from the Charleston convention. The decision to seat these pro-Douglas slates led to a walkout by delegates from Virginia and other states in the Upper South. The remaining delegates nominated Douglas; the seceders marched off to another hall in Baltimore and nominated Buchanan's vice president, John C. Breckinridge of Kentucky, on a platform calling for the congressional protection of slavery in the territories. Unable to rally behind a single nominee, the divided Democrats thus ran two candidates, Douglas and Breckinridge. The disruption of the Democratic party was now complete.

The South still contained an appreciable number of moderates, often former Whigs who had joined with the Know-Nothings behind Fillmore in 1856. In 1860 these moderates, aided by former northern Whigs who opposed both Lincoln and Douglas, forged the new Constitutional Union party and nominated John Bell, a Tennessee slaveholder who had opposed both the Kansas-Nebraska Act and the Lecompton constitution. Calling for the preservation of the Union, the new party took no stand on the divisive issue of slavery extension.

With four candidates in the field, voters faced a relatively clear choice. Lincoln conceded that the South had a constitutional right to preserve slavery but demanded that Congress prohibit its extension. At the other extreme, Breckinridge insisted that Congress had to protect slavery in any territory that contained slaves. This left the middle ground to Bell and Douglas, the latter still committed to popular sovereignty but in search of a verbal formula that might reconcile it with the *Dred Scott* decision. Lincoln won a clear majority of the electoral vote, 180 to 123 for his three opponents combined. Although Lincoln gained only 39 percent of the popular vote, his popular votes were concentrated in the North, the majority section, and were sufficient to carry every free state. Douglas ran a respectable second to Lincoln in the popular vote but a dismal last in the electoral vote.

As the only candidate to campaign in both sections, Douglas suffered from the scattered nature of his votes and carried only Missouri. Bell won Virginia, Kentucky, and Tennessee, and Breckinridge captured Maryland and the Lower South (see Map 14.4).

The Movement for Secession

As the dust from the election settled, southerners faced a disconcerting fact: a man so unpopular among southerners that his name had not even appeared on the ballot in much of their section was now president. Lincoln's election struck most of the white South as a calculated northern insult. The North, a South Carolina planter told a visitor from England, "has got so far toward being abolitionized as to elect a man avowedly hostile to our institutions."

Few southerners believed that Lincoln would fulfill his promise to protect slavery in the South, and most feared that he would act as a mere front man for more John Browns. "Now that the black radical Republicans have the power I suppose they will Brown us all," a South Carolinian lamented. An uneducated Mississippian residing in Illinois expressed his reaction to the election more bluntly:

> It seems the north wants the south to raise cotton and sugar rice tobacco for the northern states, also to pay taxes and fight her battles and get territory for the purpose of the north to send her greasy Dutch and free niggers into the territory to get rid of them. At any rate that was what elected old Abe President. Some professed conservative Republicans Think and say that Lincoln will be conservative also but sir my opinion is that Lincoln will deceive them. [He] will undoubtedly please the abolitionists for at his election they nearly all went into fits with Joy.

Some southerners had threatened secession at the prospect of Lincoln's election. Now the moment of choice had arrived. On December 20, 1860, a South Carolina convention voted unanimously for secession; and by February 1, 1861, Alabama, Mississippi, Florida, Georgia, Louisiana, and Texas had followed South Carolina's lead (see A Place in Time: Charleston, South Carolina, 1860–1861). On February 4 delegates from these seven states met in Montgomery, Alabama, and established the Confederate States of America.

Despite the abruptness of southern withdrawal from the Union, the movement for secession had been,

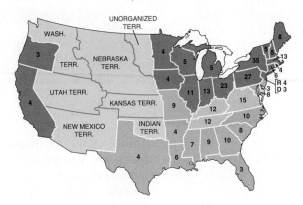

MAP 14.4
The Election of 1860

	Electoral Vote	Popular Vote	Percentage of Popular Vote
Republican Abraham Lincoln	180	1,865,593	39.8
Democratic, Southern John C. Breckinridge	72	848,356	18.1
Democratic, Northern Stephen A. Douglas	12	1,382,713	29.5
Constitutional Union John Bell	39	592,906	12.6
Divided			

and continued to be, laced with uncertainty. Many southerners had resisted calls for immediate secession. Even after Lincoln's election, fire-eating secessionists had met fierce opposition in the Lower South from so-called cooperationists, who called upon the South to act in unison or not at all. Many cooperationists had hoped to delay secession in order to wring concessions from the North that might remove the need for secession. Jefferson Davis, who was inaugurated in February 1861 as the first president of the Confederacy, was a most reluctant secessionist, and he remained in the United States Senate for two weeks after his own state of Mississippi had seceded. Even zealous advocates of secession had a hard time reconciling themselves to secession and believing that they were no longer citizens of the United States. "How do you feel now, dear Mother," a Georgian wrote, "that *we* are in a foreign land?"

In the month after the establishment of the Confederate States of America, moreover, secessionists suffered stinging disappointments in the Upper South. Virginia, North Carolina, Tennessee, Arkansas, and the border slave states of Maryland, Kentucky, Delaware, and Missouri all rejected calls for secession

After securing the nomination of Pennsylvania's James Buchanan for the presidency in 1856, northern Democrats made a conciliatory gesture to the South. They agreed to hold their party's 1860 convention in Charleston, South Carolina. Time would give northerners many opportunities to regret that gesture. Long in decline, with only a few overpriced hotels, Charleston offered little as a convention city. The supporters of Stephen A. Douglas had to convert the second floor of a meeting hall into a giant dormitory, where they slept in rows of beds and baked in one-hundred-degree heat. Even more troubling to the delegates who descended on the city in April 1860 was the hysteria that consumed Charleston in reaction to John Brown's raid on Harpers Ferry in Virginia six months earlier. Mounted police, armed with swords and muskets, patrolled the streets, and vigilantes combed the byways in search of abolitionists. Panicked Charlestonians viewed every northerner in the city—whether a politician, a traveling salesman, or a schoolteacher—as "necessarily imbued with doctrines hostile to our institutions."

Suspicion and harassment greeted northern sojourners, but Charleston's blacks endured a virtual reign of terror after "the late outrage at Harpers Ferry." A little under half the city's population in 1860 was black, and 81 percent of the blacks were slaves. White southerners distrusted urban slaves, most of whom lived apart from their rural masters and were hired out to city employers. Indeed, some slaves took advantage of the distance from their masters to hire themselves out for wages, a practice that whites feared would infect slaves with the notion that they were free. In addition, white workingmen resented competition from urban slaves in the skilled trades, and they used the furor over John Brown's raid to pressure the city's mayor into enforcing an old and long-neglected ordinance that slaves working away from their masters wear badges. Those without badges were rounded up and jailed, and their masters fined.

Charleston's enslaved blacks were not the sole targets of the city's increasingly repressive mood. Few southern cities had more visible or well-organized communities of free blacks than Charleston. Composed mainly of mulattos who took pride in their light skin and assembled in the Brown Fellowship Society, Charleston's free people of color formed a brown aristocracy of skilled tailors, carpenters, and small tradesmen. Free blacks like John Marsh Johnson worshiped in the same Episcopal church as such elite whites as Christopher G. Memminger, a prominent lawyer and politician who would soon become the Confederacy's secretary of the treasury. The financial prosperity of these free blacks depended on the white aristocrats who frequented their stores, admired their thrift and sobriety, and took comfort in their apparent loyalty. When a bill calling for the enslavement or expulsion of South Carolina's free blacks came before the state legislature in 1859, Memminger reminded the legislators that a free black had helped expose Denmark Vesey's planned uprising of slaves back in 1822. Heartened by the support of Memminger and others, John Marsh Johnson congratulated himself for predicting "from the onset that nothing would be done affecting our position."

Johnson little realized the extent to which the world of Charleston's free blacks was in danger of falling apart. The city had been a center of southern-rights radicalism

Slave Badge
The badges that they were forced to wear constantly reminded Charleston's slaves of their bondage.

since the days of the nullification crisis. Charleston was the home of the fire-eater Robert Barnwell Rhett, and it always rolled out the welcome carpet for Edmund Ruffin, a Virginia drumbeater for slavery. Furthermore, after John Brown's raid, even moderate citizens, including former Unionists, were embracing secession. The cause of secession demanded, in turn, that elite whites unite with working-class whites in a common front against the North. During the 1850s Charleston's working-class whites had grown increasingly powerful and aggressive; the increase in their numbers gave the city its first white majority in 1860. Working-class whites feared competition from any blacks but had a special loathing for free blacks, who on Sundays dared "to draw up in fine clothes" and "wear a silk hat and gloves" and who celebrated weddings by drinking champagne and riding to the church in elegant carriages.

Soon free blacks became the victims of the growing cooperation between elite and working-class whites. Indeed, by August 1860 Charleston was in the grip of an "enslavement crisis." The same police dragnets that had snared urban slaves without badges now trapped innumerable free blacks as well. Blacks who were not enslaved suddenly had to prove that they were free, a tall order inasmuch as South Carolina had long prohibited the freeing of slaves. For decades white masters who wanted to free favored slaves had resorted to complicated legal ruses, with the result that many blacks who had lived for years as free people could not prove that they were free and were forced back into slavery. Abandoning his initial optimism, John Marsh Johnson wrote nervously to his brother-in-law to report "cases of persons who for 30 yrs. have been paying capitation Tax [as free persons of color] & one of 35 yrs. that have to go back to bondage & take out their Badges." Many other free African-Americans fled to the North.

A religious man, Johnson believed that God helped those who helped themselves. Rather than "supinely wait for the working of a miracle by having a Chariot let down to convey us away," he resolved in late August 1860 to stay and endure the "present calamity." By then, however, the Democratic party had snapped apart under the pressure of southern demands for the congressional recognition of slavery in all the territories. "The last party pretending to be a national party, is broken up," the secessionist Charleston Mercury exulted, "and the antagonism of the sections of the Union has nothing to arrest its fierce collision." In December 1860 another convention meeting in Charleston proclaimed South Carolina's secession from the United States. In April 1861, only a year after the Democratic delegates had assembled in Charleston for their party's convention, shore batteries along Charleston's harbor opened fire on Fort Sumter. This action set in motion a train of events leading to the extinction of slavery itself. After the Civil War, the free blacks who had weathered the enslavement crisis of 1860 would emerge as the leaders of the city's black people, all of them now free.

First Shots of the Civil War
Stunned Charleston residents crowded the city's rooftops to view the firing on Fort Sumter—a siege that lasted thirty-four hours.

Saluda Sentinels, Always Ready
Secessionist sentiment also flared in interior areas of South Carolina such as Saluda. This militia flag of the Saluda Sentinels, featuring an officer in Revolutionary War garb, shows how secessionists invoked memories of the American struggle for independence.

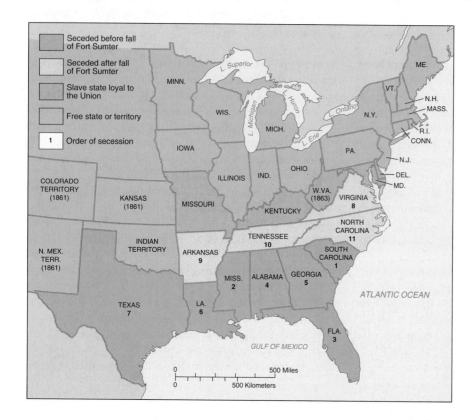

MAP 14.5
Secession
Four key states—Virginia, Arkansas, Tennessee, and North Carolina—did not secede until after the fall of Fort Sumter. The border slave states of Maryland, Delaware, Kentucky, and Missouri stayed in the Union.

(see Map 14.5). Various factors account for the Upper South's unwillingness to embrace the movement. In contrast to the Lower South, which had a guaranteed export market for its cotton, the Upper South depended heavily on economic ties to the North that would be severed by secession. Furthermore, with proportionately far fewer slaves than the Lower South, the states of the Upper South and the border states doubted the loyalty of their sizable nonslaveholding populations to the idea of secession. Virginia, for example, had every reason to question the allegiance to secession of its nonslaveholding western counties, which would soon break away to form Unionist West Virginia. Few in the Upper South could forget the raw nerve touched by the publication in 1857 of Hinton R. Helper's *The Impending Crisis of the South*. A nonslaveholding North Carolinian, Helper had described slavery as a curse upon poor white southerners and thereby questioned one of the most sacred southern doctrines, the idea that slavery rendered all whites equal. If secession were to spark a war between the states, moreover, the Upper South appeared to be the likeliest battleground. Whatever the exact weight assignable to each of these factors, one point is clear: the secession movement that South

Carolina so boldly started in December 1860 seemed to be falling apart by March 1861.

The Search for Compromise

The lack of southern unity confirmed the view of most Republicans that the secessionists were more bluster than substance. Seward described secession as the work of "a relatively few hotheads," and Lincoln believed that the loyal majority of southerners would soon wrest control from the fire-eating minority.

This perception stiffened Republican resolve to resist compromise. Moderate John J. Crittenden of Kentucky proposed compensation for owners of runaway slaves, repeal of northern personal-liberty laws, a constitutional amendment to prohibit the federal government from interfering with slavery in the southern states, and another amendment to restore the Missouri Compromise line for the remaining territories and protect slavery below it. But in the face of steadfast Republican opposition, the Crittenden plan collapsed.

Lincoln's faith in a "loyal majority" of southerners exaggerated both their numbers and their devotion to the Union. Many southern opponents of the fire-eating

secessionists were sitting on the fence and hoping for major concessions from the North; their allegiance to the Union thus was conditional. Lincoln can be faulted for misreading southern opinion, but even if his assessment had been accurate, it is unlikely that he would have accepted the Crittenden plan. The sticking point was the proposed extension of the Missouri Compromise line. To Republicans this was a surrender, not a compromise, because it hinged on the abandonment of free soil, the founding principle of their party. In addition, Lincoln well knew that some southerners still talked of seizing more territory for slavery in the Caribbean. In proposing to extend the 36°30' line, the Crittenden plan specifically referred to territories "hereafter acquired." Lincoln feared that it would be only a matter of time "till we shall have to take Cuba as a condition upon which they [the seceding states] will stay in the Union."

Beyond these considerations, the precipitous secession of the Lower South subtly changed the question that Lincoln faced. The issue was no longer slavery extension but secession. The Lower South had left the Union in the face of losing a fair election. For Lincoln to have caved in to such pressure would have violated majority rule, the principle upon which the nation, not just his party, had been founded.

The Coming of War

By the time Lincoln took office in March 1861, little more than a spark was needed to ignite a war. Lincoln pledged in his inaugural address to "hold, occupy, and possess" federal property in the seven states that had seceded, an assertion that committed him to the defense of Fort Pickens in Florida and Fort Sumter in the harbor of Charleston, South Carolina. William Seward, whom Lincoln had appointed secretary of state, now became obsessed with the idea of conciliating the Lower South in order to hold the Upper South in the Union. In addition to advising the evacuation of federal forces from Fort Sumter, Seward proposed a scheme to reunify the nation by provoking a war with France and Spain. But Lincoln brushed aside Seward's advice. Instead, the president informed the governor of South Carolina of his intention to supply Fort Sumter with much-needed provisions, but not with men and ammunition. To gain the dubious military advantage of attacking Fort Sumter before the arrival of relief ships, Confederate batteries began to bombard the fort shortly before dawn on April 12. The next day, the fort's garrison surrendered.

Proclaiming an insurrection in the Lower South, Lincoln now appealed for seventy-five thousand militiamen from the loyal states to suppress the rebellion. His proclamation pushed citizens of the Upper South off the fence upon which they had perched for three months. "I am a Union man," one southerner wrote, "but when they [the Lincoln administration] send men south it will change my notions. I can do nothing against my own people." In quick succession, Virginia, North Carolina, Arkansas, and Tennessee leagued with the Confederacy. After acknowledging that "I am one of those dull creatures that cannot see the good of secession," Robert E. Lee resigned from the army rather than lead federal troops against his native Virginia.

The North, too, was ready for a fight, less to abolish slavery than to punish secession. Worn out from his efforts to find a peaceable solution to the issue of slavery extension, and with only a short time to live, Stephen Douglas assaulted "the new system of resistance by the sword and bayonet to the results of the ballot-box" and affirmed: "I deprecate war, but if it must come I am with my country, under all circumstances, and in every contingency."

CONCLUSION

The expectation of most American political leaders that the Compromise of 1850 would finally resolve the vexing issue of slavery extension had a surface plausibility. In neither 1850 nor 1860 did the great majority of Americans favor the abolition of slavery in the southern states. Rather, they divided over slavery in the territories, an issue seemingly settled by the Compromise. Stephen A. Douglas, its leading architect and a man who assumed that he always had his finger on the popular pulse, was sure that slavery had reached its natural limits, that popular sovereignty would keep it out of the territories, and that the furor over slavery extension would die down.

Douglas believed that only a few hotheads had kept the slavery extension issue alive. He was wrong. The differences between northerners and southerners over slavery extension were grounded on different understandings of liberty, which to northerners meant their freedom to pursue self-interest without competition from slaves, and to southerners their freedom to dispose of their legally acquired property, slaves, as they chose. The Compromise, which had barely scraped through Congress, soon unraveled. Enforcement of the Fugitive Slave Act brought to the surface widespread northern

resentment of slaveholders, people who seemingly lived off the work of others, and a determination to exclude the possibility of slavery in the territories. Southern support for Douglas's Kansas-Nebraska bill, with its repeal of the Missouri Compromise and its apparent invitation to southerners to bring slaves into Kansas, persuaded many northerners that the South harbored the design of extending slavery. For their part, southerners, already angered by northern defiance of the Fugitive Slave Act, interpreted northern outrage against Douglas's bill as further evidence of the North's disrespect for the rule of law.

By the mid-1850s the sectional division was spinning out of the control of politicians. Deep divisions between the Whigs' free-soil northern wing and pro-slavery southern wing led to the party's collapse in the wake of the Kansas-Nebraska Act. Divisions between northern and southern Democrats would be papered over as long as the Democratic party could unite behind Douglas's formula of popular sovereignty. But popular sovereignty failed its test in Kansas. The outbreak of civil strife in Kansas pushed former northern Whigs and many northern Democrats toward the new, purely sectional, Republicans, a party whose very existence southerners interpreted as a mark of northern contempt for them.

The South was not yet ready for secession. Before it took that drastic step, it had to convince itself that the North's real design was not merely to restrict slavery extension but to destroy slavery and, with it, the South itself. Northern hostility to the *Dred Scott* decision and sympathy for John Brown struck southerners as proof of just such an intent.

As an expression of principled outrage, secession capped a decade in which each side had clothed itself in principles that were deeply embedded in the nation's political heritage. Both sides subscribed to the rule of law, which each accused the other of deserting. In the end, war broke out between siblings who, although they claimed the same heritage and inheritance, had become virtual strangers to each other.

CHRONOLOGY, 1850–1861

1846 Wilmot Proviso.

1848 Treaty of Guadalupe Hidalgo ends Mexican War.
Free-Soil party formed.
Zachary Taylor elected president.

1849 California seeks admission to the Union as a free state.

1850 Nashville convention assembles to discuss the South's grievances.
Compromise of 1850.

1852 Harriet Beecher Stowe, *Uncle Tom's Cabin*.
Franklin Pierce elected president.

1853 Gadsden Purchase.

1854 Ostend Manifesto.
Kansas-Nebraska Act.
William Walker leads a filibustering expedition into Nicaragua.

1854–1855 Know-Nothing and Republican parties emerge.

1855 Proslavery forces steal the election for a territorial legislature in Kansas.
Proslavery Kansans establish a government in Lecompton.
Free-soil government established in Topeka, Kansas.

1856 "The Sack of Lawrence."
John Brown's Pottawatomie massacre.
James Buchanan elected president.

1857 *Dred Scott* decision.
President Buchanan endorses the Lecompton constitution in Kansas.
Panic of 1857.

1858 Congress refuses to admit Kansas to the Union under the Lecompton constitution.
Lincoln-Douglas debates.

1859 John Brown's raid on Harpers Ferry.

1860 Abraham Lincoln elected president.
South Carolina secedes from the Union.

1861 The remaining Lower South states secede.
Confederate States of America established.
Crittenden compromise plan collapses.
Lincoln takes office.
Firing on Fort Sumter; Civil War begins.
Upper South secedes.

FOR FURTHER REFERENCE

READINGS

William W. Freehling, *The Road to Disunion: Secessionists at Bay, 1776–1854* (1990). A major study that traces the roots of secession.

Eric Foner, *Free Soil, Free Labor, Free Men: The Ideology of the Republican Party Before the Civil War* (1970). An outstanding analysis of the thought, values, and components of the Republican party.

William E. Gienapp, *The Origins of the Republican Party, 1852–1856* (1987). A comprehensive account of the birth of a major party.

Michael F. Holt, *The Political Crisis of the 1850s* (1978). A lively reinterpretation of the politics of the 1850s.

Allan Nevins, *The Ordeal of the Union* (vols. 1 and 2, 1947). A detailed, highly regarded account of the coming of the Civil War.

David Potter, *The Impending Crisis, 1848–1861* (1976). The best one-volume overview of the events leading to the Civil War.

Mark Stegmaier, *Texas, New Mexico, and the Compromise of 1850* (1996). A good study of the significance of the Texas-New Mexico boundary dispute for the sectional crisis.

WEBSITES

American History to 1865
http://www.utep.edu/kc3312/clymer/lectures/
Contains useful lecture outlines and political maps of the sectional crisis of the 1850s.

Uncle Tom's Cabin and American Culture
http://www.iath.virginia.edu/utc
This site recreates the story of the writing and reception of Harriet Beecher Stowe's famous novel. It includes contemporary reviews, African-American responses to the novel, and proslavery responses.

The Valley of the Shadow
http://jefferson.village.edu/vshadow2/contents.html
An award-winning site that investigates the experiences of two communities—Augusta County, Virginia, and Franklin County, Pennsylvania—before, during, and after the Civil War. Sources include newspapers, letters, diaries, photographs, maps, church records, population and agricultural censuses, and military records.

For additional works please consult the bibliography at the end of the book

CHAPTER 15

Crucible of Freedom: Civil War, 1861–1865

"Events transcending in importance anything that has ever happened within the recollection of any living person in *our* country, have occurred since I have written last in my journal," wrote Georgia matron Gertrude Clanton Thomas in July 1861. "*War* has been declared." Fort Sumter in South Carolina had surrendered; Lincoln had called for 75,000 troops; four more southern states—Virginia, North Carolina, Arkansas, and Tennessee—had left the Union; the newly formed Confederate government had moved from Montgomery, Alabama, to Richmond, Virginia; and thousands of troops had passed through Augusta, Georgia, on their way to the front. "So much has taken place," Gertrude Thomas declared, that "I appear to be endeavoring to recall incidents which have occurred many years instead of months ago."

At her marriage in 1852, Gertrude Thomas had become mistress of a small estate, Belmont, about six miles south of Augusta, in Richmond County, Georgia. The estate and thirty thousand dollars worth of slaves had been part of her dowry. While her husband, Jefferson Thomas, farmed plantation land he had inherited in nearby Burke County, Gertrude Thomas supervised the work force at Belmont and wrestled with her position on slavery. "I will stand to the opinion that the institution of slavery degrades the white man more than the Negro," she had declared in 1858; "all southern women are abolitionists at heart." After secession, her doubts about slavery

◀ **Soldiers' Photographs, 1861–1865**
These photos of Civil War soldiers, made by unknown photographers, ended up at the Dead Letter Office, an agency of the U.S. Postal Service.

CHAPTER OUTLINE

Mobilizing for War

In Battle, 1861–1862

Emancipation Transforms the War, 1863

War and Society, North and South

The Union Victorious, 1864–1865

persisted. "[T]he view has gradually become fixed in my mind that the institution of slavery is not right," she confided to her journal during the war. "I can but think that to hold men and women in *perpetual* bondage is wrong." On other occasions, more practical concerns about slaves emerged. "I do think that if we had the same [amount] invested in something else as a means of support," Gertrude Thomas wrote, "I would willingly, nay gladly, have the responsibility of them taken off my shoulders."

But slavery was the basis of Gertrude Thomas's wealth and social position; she disliked it not because it oppressed the enslaved but because of the problems it posed for the slave-owning elite. When war began, Gertrude and Jefferson Thomas fervently supported the newborn Confederacy. Jefferson Thomas enlisted in the Richmond Hussars, a cavalry company, and served until 1862, when, passed over for promotion, he hired a substitute. During the months that he spent with his company in Virginia, Jefferson Thomas longed for swift triumph. "Today I feel as if I wished this war was over and that I was home and that every Yankee engaged in it was at the bottom of the ocean," he wrote to his wife as 1861 came to a close. Sharing his militance and hatred of Yankees, Gertrude Thomas loyally boosted the Confederate cause. "Our country is invaded—our homes are in danger—We are deprived or they are attempting to deprive us of that glorious liberty for which our Fathers fought and bled and shall we finally submit to this? Never!" she declared. "We are only asking for self-government and freedom to decide our own destinies. We claim nothing of the North but—*to be let alone.*"

During the Civil War, Gertrude Thomas pondered the conflict's potential benefits. "One great advantage which will be gained by the war is the distinction which will be made between the Northerner and the Southerner," she wrote in her journal on New Year's Day 1862. "God speed the day when our independence shall be achieved, our southern confederacy acknowledged, and peace be with us again." But peace came at a price. In the last year of war, Union invasions damaged the Thomas plantations in Burke County and threatened the property near Augusta as well. The Civil War's end brought further hardship to the Thomas family, which lost a small fortune of fifteen thousand dollars in Confederate bonds and ninety slaves. One by one, the former slaves left the Belmont estate, never to return. "As to the emancipated Negroes," Gertrude Thomas told her journal in May 1865, "while there is of course a natural dislike to the loss of so much property, in my inmost soul, I cannot regret it."

In their idealism, belligerence, and rage at the enemy, the Thomases were not alone. After Fort Sumter fell, Union and Confederate volunteers like Jefferson Thomas responded to the rush to arms that engulfed both regions. Partisans on both sides, like Gertrude Thomas, claimed the ideals of liberty, loyalty, and patriotism as their own. Like the Thomas family, most Americans of 1861 harbored what turned out to be false expectations.

Few volunteers or even politicians anticipated a protracted war. Most northern estimates ranged from one month to a year; rebels, too, counted on a speedy victory. Neither northerners nor southerners anticipated the carnage that the war would bring; one out of every five soldiers who fought in the Civil War died in it. Once it became clear that the war would not end with a few battles, leaders on both sides considered strategies once unpalatable or even unthinkable. The South, where the hand of government had always fallen lightly on the citizenry, found that it had to impose a draft and virtually extort supplies from its civilian population. By the war's end, the Confederacy was even ready to arm its slaves in an ironically desperate effort to save a society founded on slavery. The North, which began the war with the limited objective of overcoming secession and explicitly disclaimed any intention of interfering with slavery, found that in order to win it had to shred the fabric of southern society by destroying slavery. For politicians as well as soldiers, the war defied expectations and turned into a series of surprises. The inseparable connection of Union war goals and the emancipation of slaves was perhaps the most momentous surprise.

This chapter focuses on five major questions:

■ What major advantages did each of the combatants, Union and Confederacy, possess at the start of the Civil War?

■ How successfully did the governments and economies of the North and South respond to the pressures of war?

■ How did the issues of slavery and emancipation transform the war?

■ What factors determined the military outcome of the war?

■ In what lasting ways did the Civil War change the United States as a nation?

MOBILIZING FOR WAR

North and South alike were unprepared for war. In April 1861 the Union had only a small army of sixteen thousand men scattered all over the country, mostly in the West. One-third of the officers of the Union army had resigned to join the Confederacy. The nation had not had a strong president since James K. Polk in the 1840s. Its new president, Abraham Lincoln, struck many observers as a yokel. That such a government could marshal its people for war seemed a doubtful proposition. The federal government had levied no direct taxes for decades, and it had never imposed a draft. The Confederacy was even less prepared, for it had no tax structure, no navy, only two tiny gunpowder factories, and poorly equipped, unconnected railroad lines.

During the first two years of the war, both sides would have to overcome these deficiencies, raise and supply large armies, and finance the heavy costs of war. In each region mobilization for war expanded the powers of the central government to an extent that few had anticipated.

Recruitment and Conscription

The Civil War armies were the largest organizations ever created in America; by the end of the war, over 2 million men would serve in the Union army and 800,000 in the Confederate army (see Figure 15.1). In the first flush of enthusiasm for war, volunteers rushed to the colors. "I go for wiping them out," a Virginian wrote to his governor. "War! and volunteers are the only topics of conversation or thought," an Oberlin College student told his brother in April 1861. "I cannot study. I cannot sleep. I cannot work, and I don't know as I can write."

At first, the raising of armies depended on local efforts rather than on national or even state direction.

FIGURE 15.1

Opposing Armies of the Civil War

"They sing and whoop, they laugh: they holler to de people on de ground and sing out 'Good-bye,' " remarked a slave watching rebel troops depart. "All going down to die." As this graph shows (see also Figure 15.3), the Civil War had profound human costs. North and South, hardly a family did not grieve for a lost relative or friend. Injured veterans became a common sight in cities, towns, and rural districts well into the twentieth century.

	Union Forces	Confederate Forces
Total size	2,100,000	800,000
Draftees	46,000	120,000
Substitutes	118,000	70,000
Desertions	200,000	104,000
Desertees caught and returned	80,000	21,000
Deaths from battle wounds	110,070	94,000
Deaths from disease	249,930	166,000

Citizens opened recruiting offices in their hometowns, held rallies, and signed up volunteers; regiments were usually composed of soldiers from the same locale. Southern cavalrymen provided their own horses, and uniforms everywhere were left mainly to local option. In both armies, officers up to the rank of colonel were elected by other officers and enlisted men.

This informal and democratic way of raising and organizing soldiers could not long withstand the stress of war. As early as July 1861, the Union instituted examinations for officers. Also, as casualties mounted, military demand soon exceeded the supply of volunteers. The Confederacy felt the pinch first and in April 1862 enacted the first conscription law in American history. All able-bodied white men aged eighteen to thirty-five were required to serve in the military for three years. Subsequent amendments raised the age limit to forty-five and then to fifty, and lowered it to seventeen.

The Confederacy's Conscription Act antagonized southerners. Opponents charged that the draft was an assault on state sovereignty by a despotic regime and that the law would "do away with all the patriotism we have." Exemptions that applied to many occupations, from religious ministry to shoemaking, angered the nonexempt. So did a loophole, closed in 1863, that allowed the well-off to hire substitutes. One amendment, the so-called 20-Negro law, exempted an owner or overseer of twenty or more slaves from service. Although southerners widely feared that the slave population could not be controlled if all able-bodied white men were away in the army, the 20-Negro law led to complaints about "a rich man's war but a poor man's fight."

Despite opposition, the Confederate draft became increasingly hard to evade, and this fact stimulated volunteering. Only one soldier in five was a draftee, but 70 to 80 percent of eligible white southerners served in the Confederate army. A new conscription law of 1864, which required all soldiers then in the army to stay in for the duration of the war, ensured that a high proportion of Confederate soldiers would be battle-hardened veterans.

Once the army was raised, the Confederacy had to supply it. At first, the South relied on arms and ammunition imported from Europe, weapons confiscated from federal arsenals, and guns captured on the battlefield. These stopgap measures bought time until an industrial base was established. By 1862 southerners had a competent head of ordnance (weaponry), Josiah Gorgas. The Confederacy assigned ordnance contracts to privately owned factories like the Tredegar Iron Works in Richmond, provided loans to establish new factories, and created government-owned industries like the giant Augusta Powder Works in Georgia. The South lost few, if any, battles for want of munitions.

Supplying troops with clothing and food proved more difficult. Southern soldiers frequently went without shoes; during the South's invasion of Maryland in 1862, thousands of Confederate soldiers had to be left behind because they could not march barefoot on Maryland's gravel-surfaced roads. Late in the war, Robert E. Lee's Army of Northern Virginia ran out of food but never out of ammunition. Southern supply problems had several sources: railroads that fell into disrepair or were captured, an economy that relied more heavily on producing tobacco and cotton than growing food, and Union invasions early in the war that overran the livestock and grain-raising districts of central Tennessee and Virginia. Close to desperation, the Confederate Congress in 1863 passed the Impressment Act, which authorized army officers to take food from reluctant farmers at prescribed prices. This unpopular law also empowered agents to impress slaves into labor for the army, a provision that provoked yet more resentment.

The industrial North had fewer problems supplying its troops with arms, clothes, and food. However, recruiting troops was another matter. When the initial tide of enthusiasm for enlistment ebbed, Congress followed the Confederacy's example and turned to conscription. The Enrollment Act of March 1863 made every able-bodied white male citizen aged twenty to forty-five eligible for draft into the Union army.

Like the Confederate conscription law of 1862, the Enrollment Act granted exemptions, although only to high government officials, ministers, and men who were the sole support of widows, orphans, or indigent parents. It also offered two means of escaping the draft: substitution, or paying another man who would serve instead; and commutation, paying a $300 fee to the government. Enrollment districts often competed for volunteers by offering cash payments (bounties); dishonest "bounty jumpers" repeatedly registered and deserted after collecting their payment. Democrats denounced conscription as a violation of individual liberties and states' rights. Ordinary citizens of little means resented the commutation and substitution provision and leveled their own "poor man's fight" charges. Still, as in the Confederacy, the law stimulated volunteering. Only 8 percent of Union soldiers were draftees or substitutes.

Financing the War

The recruitment and supply of huge armies lay far beyond the capacity of American public finance at the

start of the war. In the 1840s and 1850s, annual federal spending had averaged only 2 percent of the gross national product. With such meager expenditures, the federal government met its revenue needs from tariff duties and income from the sale of public lands. During the war, however, annual federal expenditures gradually rose to 15 percent of the gross national product, and the need for new sources of revenue became urgent. Yet neither the Union nor the Confederacy initially wished to impose taxes, to which Americans were unaccustomed. In August 1861 the Confederacy enacted a small property tax and the Union an income tax, but neither raised much revenue.

Both sides therefore turned to war bonds; that is, to loans from citizens to be repaid by future generations. Patriotic southerners quickly bought up the Confederacy's first bond issue ($15 million) in 1861. That same year, a financial wizard, Philadelphia banker Jay Cooke, induced the northern public to subscribe to a much larger bond issue ($150 million). But bonds had to be paid for in gold or silver coin (specie), which was in short supply. Soaking up most of its available specie, the South's first bond issue threatened to be its last. In the North many hoarded their gold rather than spend it on bonds.

Recognizing the limitations of taxation and of bond issues, both sides began to print paper money. Early in 1862 Lincoln signed into law the Legal Tender Act, which authorized the issue of $150 million of the so-called greenbacks. Christopher Memminger, the Confederacy's treasury secretary, and Salmon P. Chase, his Union counterpart, shared a distrust of paper money, but as funds dwindled each came around to the idea. The availability of paper money would make it easier to pay soldiers, to levy and raise taxes, and to sell war bonds. Yet doubts about paper money lingered. Unlike gold and silver, which had established market values, the value of paper money depended mainly on the public's confidence in the government that issued it. To bolster that confidence, Union officials made the greenbacks legal tender (that is, acceptable in payment of most public and private debts).

In contrast, the Confederacy never made its paper money legal tender, and suspicions arose that the southern government lacked confidence in its own paper issues. To compound the problem, the Confederacy raised less than 5 percent of its wartime revenue from taxes. (The comparable figure for the North was 21 percent.) The Confederacy did enact a comprehensive tax measure in 1863, but Union invasions and the South's relatively undeveloped system of internal transportation made tax collection a hit-or-miss proposition.

Confidence in the South's paper money quickly evaporated, and the value of Confederate paper in relation to gold plunged. The Confederacy responded by printing more paper money, a billion dollars by 1865, but this action merely accelerated southern inflation. Whereas prices in the North rose about 80 percent during the war, the Confederacy suffered an inflation rate of over 9,000 percent. What cost a southerner one dollar in 1861 cost forty-six dollars by 1864.

By raising taxes, floating bonds, and printing paper money, both the Union and the Confederacy broke with the hard-money, minimal-government traditions of American public finance. For the most part, these changes were unanticipated and often reluctant adaptations to wartime conditions. But in the North, the Republicans took advantage of the departure of the southern Democrats from Congress to push through one measure that they and their Whig predecessors had long advocated, a system of national banking. Passed in February 1863 over the opposition of northern Democrats, the National Bank Act established criteria by which a bank could obtain a federal charter and issue national bank notes (notes backed by the federal government). It also gave private bankers an incentive to purchase war bonds. The North's ability to revolutionize its system of public finance reflected not only its longer experience with complex financial transactions but its greater political cohesion during the war.

Political Leadership in Wartime

The Civil War pitted rival political systems as well as armies and economies against each other. The South entered the war with several apparent political advantages. Lincoln's call for militiamen to suppress the rebellion had transformed hesitators in the South into tenacious secessionists. "Never was a people more united or more determined," a New Orleans resident wrote in the spring of 1861. "There is but one mind, one heart, one action." Southerners also claimed a strong leader. A former secretary of war and U.S. senator from Mississippi, President Jefferson Davis of the Confederacy possessed experience, honesty, courage, and what one officer described as "a jaw sawed in *steel*."

In contrast, the Union's list of political liabilities appeared lengthy. Loyal but contentious, northern Democrats wanted to prosecute the war without conscription, without the National Bank Act, and without the abolition of slavery. Within his own rival Republican party, Lincoln had trouble commanding respect. Unlike Davis, he had served in neither the cabinet nor the Senate, and his informal western manners dismayed

eastern Republicans. Northern setbacks early in the war convinced most Republicans in Congress that Lincoln was an ineffectual leader. Criticism of Lincoln sprang from a group of Republicans who became known as the Radicals and who included Secretary of the Treasury Salmon P. Chase, Senator Charles Sumner of Massachusetts, and Representative Thaddeus Stevens of Pennsylvania. The Radicals never formed a tightly knit group; on some issues they cooperated with Lincoln. But they did berate him early in the war for failing to make emancipation a war goal and later for being too eager to readmit the conquered rebel states into the Union.

Lincoln's distinctive style of leadership at once encouraged and disarmed opposition within the Republican party. Keeping his counsel to himself until ready to act, he met complaints with homespun anecdotes that caught his opponents off guard. The Radicals

Abraham Lincoln
When Lincoln became president in March 1861, he faced more severe problems than any predecessor. Photographer Mathew Brady captured this image of the solemn president-elect on February 23, 1861, a few weeks after the formation of the Confederacy and shortly before Lincoln's inauguration.

frequently concluded that Lincoln was a prisoner of the conservative wing of the party, whereas conservatives complained that Lincoln was too close to the Radicals. But Lincoln's cautious reserve had the dual benefit of leaving open his lines of communication with both wings of the party and fragmenting his opposition. He also co-opted some of his critics, including Chase, by bringing them into his cabinet.

In contrast, Jefferson Davis had a knack for making enemies. A West Pointer, he would rather have led the army than the government. His cabinet suffered from frequent resignations; the Confederacy had five secretaries of war in four years, for example. Davis's relations with his vice president, Alexander Stephens of Georgia, bordered on disastrous. A wisp of a man, Stephens weighed less than a hundred pounds and looked like a boy with a withered face. But he compensated for his slight physique with a tongue as acidic as Davis's. Leaving Richmond, the Confederate capital, in 1862, Stephens spent most of the war in Georgia, where he sniped at Davis as "weak and vacillating, timid, petulant, peevish, obstinate."

The clash between Davis and Stephens involved not just personalities but also an ideological division, a rift, in fact, like that at the heart of the Confederacy. The Confederate Constitution, drafted in February 1861, explicitly guaranteed the sovereignty of the Confederate states and prohibited the Confederate Congress from enacting protective tariffs and from supporting internal improvements (measures long opposed by southern voters). For Stephens and other influential Confederate leaders—among them the governors of Georgia and North Carolina—the Confederacy existed not only to protect slavery but, equally important, to enshrine the doctrine of states' rights. In contrast, Davis's main objective was to secure the independence of the South from the North, a goal that often led him to override the wishes of state governors for the good of the Confederacy as a whole.

This difference between Davis and Stephens bore some resemblance to the discord between Lincoln and the northern Democrats. Like Davis, Lincoln believed that winning the war demanded a boost in the central government's power; like Stephens, northern Democrats resisted governmental centralization. But Lincoln could control his foes more skillfully than Davis because, by temperament, he was more suited to conciliation and also because the nature of party politics in the two sections differed.

In the South the Democrats and the remaining Whigs agreed to suspend party rivalries for the duration of the war. Although intended to promote southern

unity, this decision actually encouraged disunity. Without the institutionalization of conflict that party rivalry provided, southern politics disintegrated along personal and factional lines. Lacking a party organization to back him, Davis could not mobilize votes to pass measures that he favored, nor could he depend on the support of party loyalists.

In contrast, in the Union, northern Democrats' organized opposition to Lincoln tended to unify the Republicans. In the 1862 elections, which occurred at a low ebb of Union military fortunes, the Democrats won control of five large states, including Lincoln's own Illinois. Republican leaders learned a lesson: no matter how much they disdained Lincoln, they had to rally behind him or risk losing office. Ultimately, the Union would develop more political cohesion than the Confederacy, not because it had fewer divisions but because it managed its divisions more effectively.

Securing the Union's Borders

Even before large-scale fighting began, Lincoln moved to safeguard Washington, which was bordered by two slave states (Virginia and Maryland) and filled with Confederate sympathizers. A week after Fort Sumter, a Baltimore mob attacked a Massachusetts regiment bound for Washington, but enough troops slipped through to protect the capital. Lincoln then dispatched federal troops to Maryland, where he suspended the writ of habeas corpus (a court order requiring that the detainer of a prisoner bring that person to court and show cause for his or her detention); federal troops could now arrest prosecession Marylanders without formally charging them with specific offenses. Cowed by Lincoln's bold moves, the Maryland legislature rejected secession. Delaware, another border slave state, followed suit.

Next Lincoln authorized the arming of Union sympathizers in Kentucky, a slave state with a Unionist legislature, a secessionist governor, and a thin chance of staying neutral. Lincoln also stationed troops under General Ulysses S. Grant just across the Ohio River from Kentucky, in Illinois. When a Confederate army invaded Kentucky early in 1862, the state's legislature turned to Grant to drive it out. Officially, at least, Kentucky became the third slave state to declare for the Union. The fourth, Missouri, was ravaged by four years of fighting between Union and Confederate troops and between bands of guerrillas and bushwhackers, a name for Confederate guerrillas who lurked in the underbrush. These included William Quantrill, a rebel desperado, and his murderous apprentices, Frank and Jesse James. Despite savage fighting and the divided loyalties of its people, Mis-

souri never left the Union. West Virginia, admitted to the Union in 1863, would become the fifth border state. (This state originated in the refusal of thirty-five counties in the mainly nonslaveholding region of Virginia west of the Shenandoah Valley to follow the state's leaders into secession in 1861.)

By holding the first four border slave states—Maryland, Delaware, Kentucky, and Missouri—in the Union, Lincoln kept open his routes to the free states and gained access to the river systems in Kentucky and Missouri that led into the heart of the Confederacy. Lincoln's firmness, particularly in Maryland, scotched charges that he was weak-willed. The crisis also forced the president to exercise long-dormant powers. In the case *Ex parte* Merryman (1861), Chief Justice Roger B. Taney ruled that Lincoln had exceeded his authority in suspending the writ of habeas corpus in Maryland. The president, citing the Constitution's authorization of the writ's suspension in "Cases of Rebellion" (Article I, Section 9), insisted that he, rather than Congress, would determine whether a rebellion existed; and he ignored Taney's ruling.

IN BATTLE, 1861–1862

The Civil War was the first war to rely extensively on railroads, the telegraph, mass-produced weapons, joint army-navy tactics, iron-plated warships, rifled guns and artillery, and trench warfare. All of this lends some justification to its description as the first modern war. But to the participants, slogging through muddy swamps and weighed down with equipment, the war hardly seemed modern. In many ways, the soldiers had the more accurate perspective, for the new weapons did not always work, and both sides employed tactics that were more traditional than modern.

Armies, Weapons, and Strategies

Compared to the Confederacy's 9 million people, one-third of them slaves, the Union had 22 million people in 1861 (see Figure 15.2). The North also had 3.5 times as many white men of military age, 90 percent of all U.S. industrial capacity, and two-thirds of its railroad track. Yet the Union faced a daunting challenge. Its goal was to force the South back into the Union, whereas the South was fighting merely for its independence. To subdue the Confederacy, the North would have to sustain offensive operations over a vast area.

Measured against this challenge, the Union's advantages in population and technology shrank. The North

FIGURE 15.2

Comparative Population and Economic Resources of the Union and the Confederacy, 1861

At the start of the war, the Union enjoyed huge advantages in population, industry, railroad mileage, and wealth, and, as it would soon prove, a superior ability to mobilize its vast resources. The Confederacy, however, enjoyed the many advantages of fighting a defensive war.

 Union   Confederacy

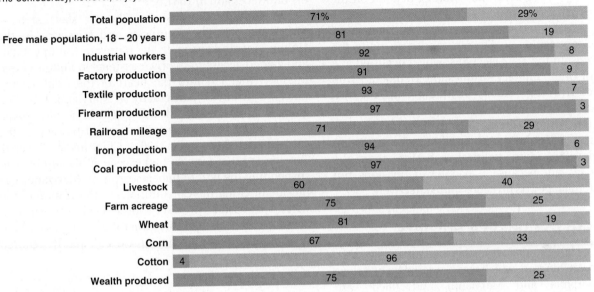

	Union	Confederacy
Total population	71%	29%
Free male population, 18 – 20 years	81	19
Industrial workers	92	8
Factory production	91	9
Textile production	93	7
Firearm production	97	3
Railroad mileage	71	29
Iron production	94	6
Coal production	97	3
Livestock	60	40
Farm acreage	75	25
Wheat	81	19
Corn	67	33
Cotton	4	96
Wealth produced	75	25

had more men, but needing to defend long supply lines and occupy captured areas, it could commit a smaller proportion of them to frontline duty. The South, which relied on slaves for labor, could assign a higher proportion of its white male population to combat. As for technology, the North required, and possessed, superior railroads. Fighting defensively on so-called interior lines, the South could shift its troops relatively short distances within its defensive arc without using railroads, whereas the North had to move its troops and supplies huge distances around the exterior of the arc. Not only could guerrillas easily sabotage northern railroads, but once Union troops moved away from their railroad bases, their supply wagons often bogged down on wretched southern roads that became watery ditches in bad weather. Even on good roads, horses and mules, which themselves consumed supplies, were needed to pull wagons; an invading army of 100,000 men required 35,000 horses or mules. Finally, southerners had an edge in soldiers' morale, for Confederate troops battled on home ground. "No people ever warred for independence," a southern general acknowledged, "with more relative advantages than the Confederates."

The Civil War witnessed experiments with a variety of newly developed weapons, including the submarine, the repeating rifle, and the multibarreled Gatling gun,

the forerunner of the machine gun. Yet these futuristic innovations had less impact on the war than did the perfection in the 1850s of a bullet whose powder would not clog a rifle's spiraled internal grooves after a few shots. Like the smoothbore muskets that both armies had employed at the start of the war, most improved rifles had to be reloaded after each shot. But where the smoothbore musket had an effective range of only eighty yards, the Springfield or Enfield rifles widely employed by 1863 could hit targets accurately at four hundred yards.

The development of the rifle posed a challenge to long-accepted military tactics. Manuals used at West Point in the 1840s and 1850s had identified the mass infantry charge against an opponent's weakest point as the key to victory. These manuals assumed that defenders armed with muskets would be able to fire only a round or two before being overwhelmed. Armed with rifles, however, a defending force could fire several rounds before closing with the enemy. Attackers would now have far greater difficulty getting close enough to thrust bayonets; fewer than 1 percent of the casualties in the Civil War resulted from bayonet wounds.

Thus the rifle produced some changes in tactics during the war. Both sides gradually came to understand the value of trenches, which provided defenders

protection against withering rifle fire. By 1865 trenches pockmarked the landscape in Virginia and Georgia. In addition, growing use of the rifle forced generals to rely less on cavalry. Traditionally, the cavalry had ranked among the most prestigious components of an army, in part because cavalry charges were often devastatingly effective and in part because the cavalry helped maintain class distinctions within the army. But rifles reduced the effectiveness of cavalry by increasing the firepower of foot soldiers. Bullets that might miss the rider would at least hit the horse. Thus as cavalry charges against infantry became more difficult, both sides relegated cavalry to reconnaissance missions and raids on supply trains.

Although the rifle exposed traditional tactics to new hazards, it by no means invalidated those tactics. On the contrary, historians now contend, high casualties reflected the long duration of battles rather than the new efficacy of rifles. The attacking army still stood an excellent chance of success if it achieved surprise. The South's lush forests provided abundant opportunities for an army to sneak up on its opponent. For example, at the Battle of Shiloh in 1862, Confederate attackers surprised and almost defeated a larger Union army despite the rumpus created by green rebel troops en route to the battle, many of whom fired their rifles into the air to see if they would work.

Achieving such complete surprise normally lay beyond the skill or luck of generals. In the absence of any element of surprise, an attacking army might invite disaster. At the Battle of Fredericksburg in December 1862, Confederate troops inflicted appalling casualties on Union forces attacking uphill over open terrain, and at Gettysburg in July 1863, Union riflemen and artillery shredded charging southerners. But generals might still achieve partial surprise by hitting an enemy before it had concentrated its troops; in fact, this is what the North tried to do at Fredericksburg. Because surprise often proved effective, most generals continued to believe that their best chance of success lay in striking an unwary or weakened enemy with all the troops they could muster rather than in relying on guerrilla or trench warfare.

Much like previous wars, the Civil War was fought basically in a succession of battles during which exposed infantry traded volleys, charged, and countercharged. Whichever side withdrew from the field usually was

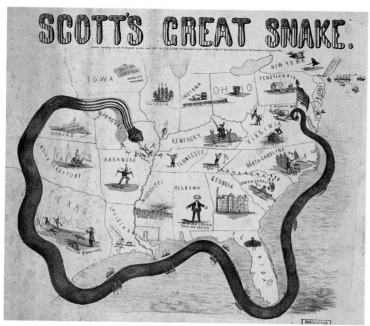

"Scott's Great Snake," 1861
General Winfield Scott's scheme to surround the South and await a seizure of power by southern Unionists drew scorn from critics who called it the Anaconda plan. In this lithograph, the "great snake" prepares to thrust down the Mississippi, seal off the Confederacy, and crush it.

thought to have lost the battle, but the losing side frequently sustained lighter casualties than the supposed victor. Both sides had trouble exploiting their victories. As a rule, the beaten army moved back a few miles from the field to lick its wounds; the winners stayed in place to lick theirs. Politicians on both sides raged at generals for not pursuing a beaten foe, but it was difficult for a mangled victor to gather horses, mules, supply trains, and exhausted soldiers for a new attack. Not surprisingly, for much of the war, generals on both sides concluded that the best defense was a good offense.

To the extent that the North had a long-range strategy in 1861, it lay in the so-called Anaconda plan. Devised by the Mexican War hero General Winfield Scott, the plan called for the Union to blockade the southern coastline and to thrust, like a huge snake, down the Mississippi River. Scott expected that sealing off and severing the Confederacy would make the South recognize the futility of secession and bring southern Unionists to power. But Scott, a southern Unionist, overestimated the strength of Unionist spirit in the South. Furthermore, although Lincoln quickly ordered a blockade of the southern coast, the North hardly had the troops and naval flotillas to seize the Mississippi in 1861. So while the Mississippi remained an objective, north-

ern strategy did not unfold according to any blueprint like the Anaconda plan.

Early in the war, the pressing need to secure the border slave states, particularly Kentucky and Missouri, dictated Union strategy west of the Appalachian Mountains. Once in control of Kentucky, northern troops plunged southward into Tennessee. The Appalachians tended to seal this western theater off from the eastern theater, where major clashes of 1861 occurred.

Stalemate in the East

The Confederacy's decision in May 1861 to move its capital from Montgomery, Alabama, to Richmond, Virginia,

shaped Union strategy. "Forward to Richmond" became the Union's first war cry. Before they could reach Richmond, one hundred miles southwest of Washington, Union troops had to dislodge a Confederate army brazenly encamped at Manassas Junction, only twenty-five miles from the Union capital (see Map 15.1). Lincoln ordered General Irvin McDowell to attack his former West Point classmate, Confederate general P. G. T. Beauregard. "You are green, it is true," Lincoln told McDowell, "but they are green also; you are all green alike." In the resulting First Battle of Bull Run (or First Manassas), amateur armies clashed in bloody chaos under a blistering July sun. Well-dressed, picnicking Washington dignitaries gathered to view the action. Aided by last-minute reinforcements and by the disor-

MAP 15.1
The War in the East, 1861–1862
Union advances on Richmond were turned back at Fredericksburg and the Seven Days' Battles, and the Confederacy's invasion of Union territory was stopped at Antietam.

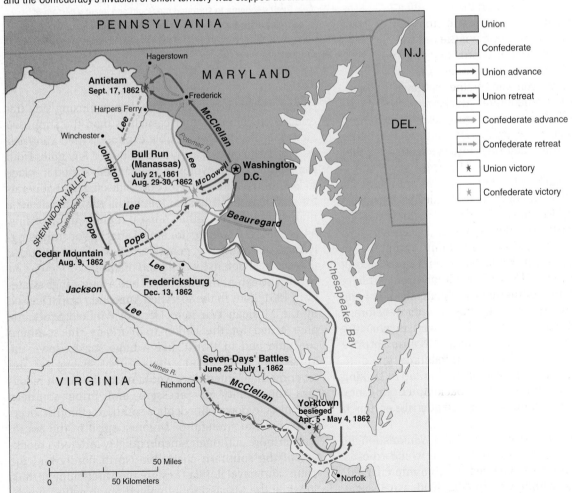

ganization of the attacking federals, Beauregard routed the larger Union army.

After Bull Run, Lincoln replaced McDowell with General George B. McClellan as commander of the Army of the Potomac, the Union's main fighting force in the East. Another West Pointer, McClellan had served with distinction in the Mexican War and mastered the art of administration by managing midwestern railroads in the 1850s. Few generals could match his ability to turn a ragtag mob into a disciplined fighting force. His soldiers adored him, but Lincoln quickly became disenchanted. Lincoln believed that the key to a Union victory lay in simultaneous, coordinated attacks on several fronts so that the North could exploit its advantage in manpower and resources. McClellan, a proslavery Democrat, hoped to maneuver the South into a relatively bloodless defeat and then negotiate a peace that would readmit the Confederate states with slavery intact.

McClellan soon got a chance to implement his strategy. After Bull Run, the Confederates had pulled back to await the Union onslaught against Richmond. Rather than directly attack the Confederate army, McClellan formulated a plan in spring 1862 to move the Army of the Potomac by water to the tip of the peninsula formed by the York and James Rivers and then move northwestward up the peninsula to Richmond. McClellan's plan had several advantages. Depending on water transport rather than on railroads (which Confederate cavalry could cut), the McClellan strategy reduced the vulnerability of northern supply lines. By dictating an approach to Richmond from the southeast, it threatened the South's supply lines. By aiming for the capital of the Confederacy rather than for the Confederate army stationed northeast of Richmond, McClellan hoped to maneuver the southern troops into a futile attack on his army in order to avert a destructive siege of Richmond.

By far the most massive military campaign in American history to that date, the Peninsula Campaign unfolded smoothly at first. Three hundred ships transported seventy thousand men and huge stores of supplies to the tip of the peninsula. Reinforcements swelled McClellan's army to one hundred thousand. By late May McClellan was within five miles of Richmond. But then he hesitated. Overestimating the Confederates' strength, he refused to launch a final attack without further reinforcements, which were turned back by Confederate general Thomas "Stonewall" Jackson in the Shenandoah Valley.

While McClellan delayed, General Robert E. Lee took command of the Confederacy's Army of Northern Virginia. A foe of secession and so courteous that at times he seemed too gentle, Lee possessed the qualities

that McClellan most lacked, boldness and a willingness to accept casualties. Seizing the initiative, Lee attacked McClellan in late June 1862. The ensuing Seven Days' Battles, fought in the forests east of Richmond, cost the South nearly twice as many men as the North and ended in a virtual slaughter of Confederates at Malvern Hill. Unnerved by his own casualties, McClellan sent increasingly panicky reports to Washington. Lincoln, who cared little for McClellan's peninsula strategy, ordered McClellan to call off the campaign and return to Washington.

With McClellan out of the picture, Lee and his lieutenant, Stonewall Jackson, boldly struck north and, at the Second Battle of Bull Run (Second Manassas), routed a Union army under General John Pope. Lee's next stroke was even bolder. Crossing the Potomac River in early September 1862, he invaded western Maryland, where the forthcoming harvest could provide him with desperately needed supplies. By seizing western Maryland, moreover, Lee could threaten Washington, indirectly relieve pressure on Richmond, improve the prospects of peace candidates in the North's upcoming fall elections, and possibly induce Britain and France to recognize the Confederacy as an independent nation. But McClellan met Lee at the Battle of Antietam (or Sharpsburg) on September 17. Although a tactical draw, Antietam proved a strategic victory for the North, for Lee subsequently called off his invasion and retreated south of the Potomac.

Heartened by the apparent success of northern arms, Lincoln then issued the Emancipation Proclamation, a war measure that freed all slaves under rebel control. The toll of 24,000 casualties at Antietam, however, made it the bloodiest day of the entire war. A Union veteran recollected that one part of the battlefield contained so many bodies that a man could have walked through it without stepping on the ground.

Complaining that McClellan had "the slows," Lincoln faulted his commander for not pursuing Lee after the battle. McClellan's replacement, General Ambrose Burnside, thought himself and soon proved himself unfit for high command. In December 1862 Burnside led 122,000 federal troops against 78,500 Confederates at the Battle of Fredericksburg. Burnside captured the town of Fredericksburg, northeast of Richmond, but then sacrificed his army in futile charges up the heights west of the town. Even Lee was shaken by the northern casualties. "It is well that war is so terrible, or we should grow too fond of it," he told an aide during the battle. Richmond remained, in the words of a southern song, "a hard road to travel." The war in the East had become a stalemate.

A painting of the Antietam battlefield by James Hope, a Union soldier of the Second Vermont Infantry, shows three brigades of Union troops advancing under Confederate fire. In the photograph of Antietam, dead rebel gunners lie next to the wreckage of their battery at Antietam. The building in both painting and photograph, a Dunker church, was the scene of furious fighting.

The War in the West

The Union fared better in the West. There, the war ranged over a vast and crucial terrain that provided access to rivers leading directly into the South. The West also spawned new leadership. During the first year of war, an obscure Union general, Ulysses S. Grant, proved his competence. A West Point graduate, Grant had fought in the Mexican War and retired from the army in 1854 with a reputation for heavy drinking. He then failed at ventures in farming and in business. When the Civil War began, he gained an army commission through political pressure.

In 1861–1862 Grant retained control of two border states, Missouri and Kentucky. Moving into Tennessee, he captured two strategic forts, Fort Henry on the Tennessee River and Fort Donelson on the Cumberland. Grant then headed south to attack Corinth, Mississippi, a major railroad junction (see Map 15.2).

In early April 1862, Confederate forces under generals Albert Sidney Johnston and P. G. T. Beauregard tried to relieve the Union pressure on Corinth by a surprise attack on Grant's army, encamped twenty miles north of the town, in southern Tennessee near a church named Shiloh. Hoping to whip Grant before Union reinforcements arrived, the Confederates exploded from the woods near Shiloh before breakfast and almost drove the federals into the Tennessee River. Beauregard cabled Richmond with news of a splendid Confederate victory. But Grant and his lieutenant, William T. Sherman, steadied the Union line. Union reinforcements arrived in the

night, and federal counterattack drove the Confederates from the field the next day. Although Antietam would soon erase the distinction, the Battle of Shiloh was the bloodiest in American history to that date. Of the seventy-seven thousand men engaged, twenty-three thousand were killed or wounded, including Confederate general Albert Sidney Johnston, who bled to death from a leg wound. Defeated at Shiloh, the Confederates soon evacuated Corinth.

To attack Grant at Shiloh, the Confederacy had stripped the defenses of New Orleans, leaving only three thousand militia to guard its largest city. A combined Union land-sea force under General Benjamin Butler, a Massachusetts politician, and Admiral David G. Farragut, a Tennessean loyal to the Union, capitalized on the opportunity. Farragut took the city in late April and soon added Baton Rouge and Natchez to his list of conquests. Meanwhile, another Union flotilla moved down the Mississippi and captured Memphis in June. Now the North controlled the entire river, except for a two-hundred-mile stretch between Port Hudson, Louisiana, and Vicksburg, Mississippi.

Union and Confederate forces also clashed in 1862 in the trans-Mississippi West. On the banks of the Rio Grande, Union volunteers, joined by Mexican-American companies, drove a Confederate army from Texas out of New Mexico. A thousand miles to the east, in northern Arkansas and western Missouri, armies vied to secure the Missouri River, a crucial waterway that flowed into the Mississippi. In Pea Ridge, Arkansas, in March 1862, forewarned northern troops scattered a Confederate force of sixteen thousand that included three Cherokee regiments. (Indian units fought on both sides in Missouri, where guerrilla combat raged until the war's end.)

These Union victories changed the nature of the trans-Mississippi war. As the rebel threat faded, regiments of western volunteers that had mobilized to crush Confederates turned to fighting Indians. Conflict between the Dakota Sioux and Minnesota volunteers in the fall of 1862 spread to the north and west. Indian wars erupted in Arizona, Nevada, Colorado, and New Mexico, where California volunteers and the New Mexico cavalry, led by Colonel Kit Carson, overwhelmed the Apaches and Navajos. After 1865 federal troops moved west to complete the rout of the Indians that had begun in the Civil War.

The Soldiers' War

Civil War soldiers were typically volunteers who left farms and small towns to join companies of recruits from their locales. Many men who enrolled in 1861 and

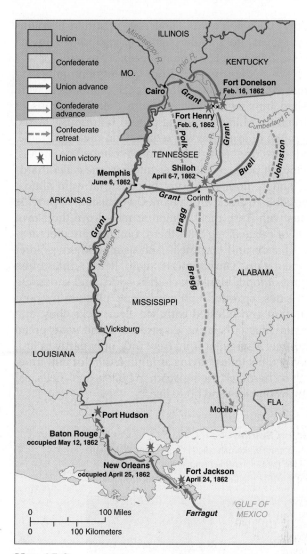

MAP 15.2
The War in the West, 1861–1862
By the end of 1862, the North held New Orleans and the entire Mississippi River except for the stretch between Vicksburg and Port Hudson.

1862—those who served at Shiloh and Antietam—reenlisted when their terms expired; these hardy survivors became the backbones of their respective armies. Local loyalties spurred enrollment, especially in the South; so did ideals of honor and valor. Soldiers on both sides shared a vision of military life as a transforming experience in which citizens became warriors and boys became men. To serve in combat was to achieve "manhood." One New York father who sent two young sons to enlist marveled at how the war provided "so much manhood suddenly achieved." Exultant after a victory, an Alabama volunteer told his father, "With your first shot

you become a new man." Thousands of underage volunteers, that is, boys under eighteen, also served in the war; so did at least 250 women disguised as men.

New soldiers moved from recruitment rallies to camps of rendezvous, where local companies were meshed into regiments, and from there to camps of instruction. Military training proved notoriously weak, and much of army life was tedious and uncomfortable. Food was one complaint. Union troops ate beans, bacon, salt pork, pickled beef, and a staple called hardtack, square flour-and-water biscuits that were almost impossible to crack with a blow. On occasion, to provide troops with fresh meat, Union armies drove their own herds of cattle along with them. Confederate diets featured bacon and cornmeal, and as a southern soldier summed it up, "Our rations is small." Rebel armies often ran out of food, blankets, clothes, socks, and shoes. On both sides, crowded military camps, plagued by poor sanitation and infested with lice, fleas, ticks, flies, and rodents, insured soaring disease rates and widespread grievance. A sergeant from New York, only partly in jest, described his lot as "laying around in the dirt and mud, living on hardtack, facing death in bullets and shells, eat up by wood-ticks and body-lice."

A Union Soldier

Sarah Rosetta Wakeman, alias Private Lyons Wakeman, served in the Union Army disguised as a man. She joined the 153rd Regiment, New York State Volunteers.

Expectations of military glory swiftly faded. For most soldiers, Civil War battles meant inuring themselves to the stench of death. "We don't mind the sight of dead men no more than if they were dead hogs," a Union soldier claimed. Soldiers rapidly grasped the value of caution in combat. You learned, a southerner wrote, "to become cool and deliberate." According to a northern volunteer, "The consuming passion is to get out of the way." Others described the zeal aroused by combat. "[I]t is a terrible sight to see a line of men, two deep, coming up within 300 or 400 yards of you, with bayonets flashing and waving their colors," a New Jersey artilleryman recalled. "[Y]ou know that every shot you fire into them sends some one to eternity, but still you are a prompted by a terrible desire to kill all you can." The deadly cost of battle fell most heavily on the infantry, in which at least three out of four soldiers served. Although repeating rifles were superior weapons, with three or four times the range of the old smoothbore muskets, a combination of inexperience, inadequate training, and barriers of terrain curbed the impact of the new weapons in practice. Instead, large masses of soldiers faced one another at close range for long periods of time, exchanging fire until one side or the other gave up and fell back. The high casualty figures at Shiloh and Antietam reflected not advanced technology but the armies' inability to use it effectively. "Our victories . . . seem to settle nothing; to bring us no nearer to the end of the war," a southern officer wrote in 1862. "It is only so many killed or wounded, leaving the war of blood to go on." Armies gained efficiency in battle through experience, and only late in the war.

In their voluminous letters home (Civil War armies were the most literate armies that had ever existed), volunteers often discussed their motives as soldiers. Some Confederates enlisted to defend slavery, which they paired with liberty. "I choose to fight for southern rights and southern liberty" against the "vandals of the North" who were "determined to destroy slavery," a Kentucky Confederate announced. "A stand must be made for African slavery or it is forever lost," wrote a South Carolinian. A small minority of northern soldiers voiced antislavery sentiments early in the war: "I have no heart in this war if the slaves cannot go free," a soldier from Wisconsin declared. Few Union recruits, however, initially shared this antipathy to slavery, and some voiced the opposite view. "I don't want to fire another shot for the negroes and I wish all the abolitionists were in hell," a New York soldier declared. But as the war went on, northern soldiers accepted the need to free the slaves, sometimes for humanitarian reasons. "Since I am down here I have learned and seen more of what the horrors of

slavery was than I ever knew before," wrote an Ohio officer from Louisiana. Others had more practical goals. By the summer of 1862, Union soldiers in the South had become agents of liberation; they harbored fugitives who fled behind federal lines. Many who once had damned the "abolitionist war" now endorsed emancipation as part of the Union war effort. As a soldier from Indiana declared, "Every negro we get strengthens us and weakens the rebels."

Ironclads and Cruisers: The Naval War

By plunging its navy into the Confederacy like a dagger, the Union exploited one of its clearest advantages. The North began the war with over forty active warships against none for the South, and by 1865 the United States had the largest navy in the world. Steam-driven ships could penetrate the South's excellent river system from any direction. For example, the Confederacy had stripped New Orleans's defenses in the belief that the real threat to the city would come from the north, only to find Farragut slipping in from the south.

Despite its size, the Union navy faced an extraordinary challenge in its efforts to blockade the South's 3,500 miles of coast. Early in the war, small, sleek Confederate blockade-runners darted in and out of southern harbors and inlets with little chance of cap-ture. The North gradually tightened the blockade by outfitting tugs, whalers, excursion steamers, and ferries as well as frigates to patrol southern coasts. The proportion of Confederate blockade-runners that made it through dropped from 90 percent early in the war to 50 percent by 1865. Northern seizure of rebel ports and coastal areas shrank the South's foreign trade even more. In daring amphibious assaults during 1861 and 1862, the Union captured the excellent harbor of Port Royal, South Carolina, the coastal islands off South Carolina, and most of North Carolina's river outlets. Naval patrols and amphibious operations shrank the South's ocean trade to one-third its prewar level.

Despite meager resources, the South strove to offset the North's naval advantage. Early in the war, the Confederacy raised the scuttled Union frigate *Merrimac*, sheathed its sides with an armor of iron plate, rechristened it *Virginia*, and dispatched it to attack wooden Union ships in Hampton Roads, Virginia. The *Merrimac* destroyed two northern warships but met its match in the hastily built Union ironclad the *Monitor*. In the first engagement of ironclads in history, the two ships fought an indecisive battle on March 9, 1862. The South constructed other ironclads and even the first submarine, which dragged a mine through the water to sink a Union ship off Charleston in 1864. Unfortunately, the "fish" failed to resurface and went down with its victim.

The *Merrimac* versus the *Monitor*
The huge Confederate ironclad, the *Virginia* (formerly the *Merrimac*), clashes with the smaller Union vessel, the *Monitor*, in the first battle of ironclads on March 9, 1862. The engagement ended in a draw.

But the South could never build enough ironclads to overcome the North's supremacy in home waters. The Confederacy had more success on the high seas, where wooden, steam-driven commerce raiders like the *Alabama* and the *Florida* (both built in England) wreaked havoc on the Union's merchant marine. Commerce raiding, however, would not tip the balance of the war in the South's favor because the North, unlike its foe, did not depend on imports for war materials. The South would lose the naval war.

The Diplomatic War

While armies and navies clashed in 1861–1862, conflict developed on a third front, diplomacy. At the outbreak of the war, the Confederacy began a campaign to gain European recognition of its independence. Southern confidence in a swift diplomatic victory ran high. Planning to establish a colonial empire in Mexico, Napoleon III of France had grounds to welcome the permanent division of the United States. Moreover, the upper classes in France and Britain seemed sympathetic to the aristocratic South and eager for the downfall of the brash Yankee republic. Furthermore, influential southerners had long contended that an embargo of cotton exports would bring Britain to its knees. These southerners reasoned that Britain, dependent on the South for four-fifths of its cotton, would break the Union blockade and provoke a war with the North rather than watch its textile workers sink into revolutionary discontent under the weight of an embargo.

Leaving nothing to chance, the Confederacy in 1861 dispatched emissaries James Mason to Britain and John Slidell to France to lobby for recognition of the South as an independent nation. When a Union ship captain, acting without orders, boarded the British vessel the *Trent,* which was carrying Mason and Slidell, and brought the two men to Boston as prisoners, British tempers exploded. Considering one war at a time enough, President Lincoln released Mason and Slidell. But settling the *Trent* affair did not eliminate friction between the United States and Britain. The construction in British shipyards of two Confederate commerce raiders, the *Florida* and the *Alabama,* led to protests from Union diplomats. In 1863 the U.S. minister to London, Charles Francis Adams (the son of former president John Quincy Adams), threatened war if two British-built ironclads commissioned by the Confederacy, the so-called Laird rams, were turned over to the South. Britain capitulated to Adams's protests and purchased the rams for its own navy.

On balance, the South fell far short of its diplomatic objectives. Although recognizing the Confederacy as a belligerent, neither Britain nor France ever recognized it as a nation. Basically, the Confederacy overestimated the power of its vaunted "cotton diplomacy." The Confederate government talked of embargoing cotton exports in order to bring the British to their knees, but could never do so. Planters conducted business as usual by raising cotton and trying to slip it through the blockade. Still, the South's share of the British cotton market slumped from 77 percent in 1860 to only 10 percent in 1865. This loss resulted from forces beyond southern control. Bumper cotton crops in the late 1850s had glutted the British market by the start of the war and weakened British demand for cotton. In addition, Britain had found new suppliers in Egypt and India, thereby buffering itself from southern pressure. Gradually, too, the North's tightened blockade restricted southern exports.

The South also exaggerated Britain's stake in helping the Confederacy. As a naval power that had frequently blockaded its own enemies, Britain's diplomatic interest lay in supporting the Union blockade in principle; from Britain's standpoint, to help the South break the blockade would set a precedent that could easily boomerang. Finally, although France and Britain often considered recognizing the Confederacy, the timing never seemed quite right. The Union's success at Antietam in 1862 and Lincoln's subsequent issuance of the Emancipation Proclamation dampened Europe's enthusiasm for recognition at a crucial juncture. By transforming the war into a struggle to end slavery, the Emancipation Proclamation produced an upsurge of pro-Union feeling in antislavery Britain, particularly among liberals and the working class. Workingmen in Manchester, England, wrote Lincoln to praise his resolve to free the slaves. The proclamation, declared Henry Adams (diplomat Charles Francis Adams's son) from London, "has done more for us here than all of our former victories and all our diplomacy."

EMANCIPATION TRANSFORMS THE WAR, 1863

"I hear old John Brown knocking on the lid of his coffin and shouting 'Let me out! Let me out!' " abolitionist Henry Stanton wrote to his wife after the fall of Fort Sumter. "The Doom of Slavery is at hand." In 1861 this prediction seemed wildly premature. In his inaugural that year, Lincoln had stated bluntly, "I have no purpose, directly or indirectly, to interfere with the institution of slavery in the states where it exists." Yet in two years, the

North's priorities underwent a decisive transformation. A mix of practical necessity and ideological conviction thrust the emancipation of the slaves to the forefront of northern war goals.

The rise of emancipation as a Union war goal reflected the changing character of the war itself. As late as July 1862, General George McClellan had restated to Lincoln his conviction that "neither confiscation of property . . . or forcible abolition of slavery should be contemplated for a moment." As the struggle dragged on, however, demands for the prosecution of "total war" intensified in the North. Even northerners who saw no moral value in abolishing slavery started to recognize the military value of emancipation as a tactic to cripple the South.

From Confiscation to Emancipation

Union policy on emancipation developed in stages. As soon as northern troops began to invade the South, questions arose about the disposition of captured rebel property, including slaves. Slaves who fled behind the Union lines were sometimes considered "contraband"— enemy property liable to seizure—and were put to work for the Union army. Some northern commanders viewed this practice as a useful tool of war, others did not, and the Lincoln administration was evasive. To establish an official policy, Congress in August 1861 passed the first Confiscation Act, which authorized the seizure of all property used in military aid of the rebellion, including slaves. Under this act, slaves who had been employed directly by the armed rebel forces and who later fled to freedom became "captives of war." But nothing in the act actually freed these contrabands, nor did the law apply to contrabands who had not worked for the Confederate military.

Several factors underlay the Union's cautious approach to the confiscation of rebel property. Officially maintaining that the South's rebellion lacked any legal basis, Lincoln argued that southerners were still entitled to the Constitution's protection of property. The president also had practical reasons to walk softly. The Union not only contained four slave states but also held a sizable body of proslavery Democrats who strongly opposed turning the war into a crusade against slavery. If the North in any way tampered with slavery, these Democrats feared, "two or three million semi-savages" might come north and compete with white workers. Aware of such fears, Lincoln assured Congress in December 1861 that the war would not become a "remorseless revolutionary struggle."

From the start of the war, however, Lincoln faced pressure from the loosely knit but determined Radical Republicans to adopt a policy of emancipation. Pennsylvanian Thaddeus Stevens urged the Union to "free every slave—slay every traitor—burn every Rebel mansion, if these things be necessary to preserve this temple of freedom." Radicals agreed with black abolitionist Frederick Douglass that "to fight against slaveholders without fighting against slavery, is but a half-hearted business." With every new northern setback, support for the Radicals' stance grew. Each Union defeat reminded northerners that the Confederacy, with a slave labor force in place, could commit a higher proportion of its white men to battle. The idea of emancipation as a military measure thus gained increasing favor in the North, and in July 1862 Congress passed the second Confiscation Act. This law authorized the seizure of the property of all persons in rebellion and stipulated that slaves who came within Union lines "shall be forever free." The law also authorized the president to employ blacks as soldiers.

Nevertheless, Lincoln continued to stall, even in the face of rising pressure for emancipation. "My paramount object in this struggle is to save the Union, and is not either to save or destroy slavery," Lincoln told antislavery journalist Horace Greeley. "If I could save the Union without freeing *any* slave, I would do it; and if I could save it by freeing *all* the slaves, I would do it; and if I could do it by freeing some and leaving others alone, I would also do that." Yet Lincoln had always loathed slavery, and by the spring of 1862, he had come around to the Radical position that the war must lead to its abolition. He hesitated principally because he did not want to be stampeded by Congress into a measure that might disrupt northern unity. He also feared that a public commitment to emancipation in the summer of 1862, on the heels of the northern defeat at Second Manassas and the collapse of the Peninsula Campaign, might be interpreted as an act of desperation. After failing to persuade the Union slave states to emancipate slaves in return for federal compensation, he drafted a proclamation of emancipation, circulated it within his cabinet, and waited for a right moment to issue it. Finally, after the Union victory in September 1862 at Antietam, Lincoln issued the preliminary Emancipation Proclamation, which declared all slaves under rebel control free as of January 1, 1863. Announcing the plan in advance softened the surprise, tested public opinion, and gave the states still in rebellion an opportunity to preserve slavery by returning to the Union—an opportunity that none, however, took. The final Emancipation Proclamation, issued

on January 1, 1863, declared "forever free" all slaves in areas in rebellion.

The proclamation had limited practical impact. Applying only to rebellious areas where the Union had no authority, it exempted the Union slave states and those parts of the Confederacy then under Union control (Tennessee, West Virginia, southern Louisiana, and sections of Virginia). Moreover, it mainly restated what the second Confiscation Act had already stipulated: if rebels' slaves fell into Union hands, those slaves would be free. Yet the proclamation was a brilliant political stroke. By issuing it as a military measure in his role as commander-in-chief, Lincoln pacified northern conservatives. Its aim, he stressed, was to injure the Confederacy, threaten its property, heighten its dread, sap its morale, and hasten its demise. By issuing the proclamation himself, Lincoln stole the initiative from the Radicals in Congress and mobilized support for the Union among European liberals far more dramatically than could any act of Congress. Furthermore, the declaration pushed the border states toward emancipation: by the end of the war, Maryland and Missouri would abolish slavery. Finally, it increased slaves' incentives to escape as northern troops approached. Fulfilling the worst of Confederate fears, it enabled blacks to join the Union army.

The Emancipation Proclamation did not end slavery everywhere or free "*all* the slaves." But it changed the war. From 1863 on, the war for the Union would also be a war against slavery.

Crossing Union Lines

The attacks and counterattacks of the opposing armies turned many slaves into pawns of war. Some slaves became free when Union troops overran their areas. Others fled their plantations at the approach of federal troops to take refuge behind Union lines. A few were freed by northern assaults, only to be reenslaved by Confederate counterthrusts. One North Carolina slave celebrated liberation on twelve occasions, as many times as Union soldiers marched through his area. By 1865 about half a million slaves were in Union hands.

In the first year of the war, when the Union had not yet established a policy toward contrabands (fugitive slaves), masters were able to retrieve them from the Union army. After 1862, however, the thousands of slaves who crossed Union lines were considered free. Many freedmen served in army camps as cooks, teamsters, and laborers. Some worked for pay on abandoned plantations or were leased out to planters who swore allegiance to the Union. In camps or outside them, freedmen had reason to question the value of their liberation. Deductions for clothing, rations, and medicine ate up most, if not all, of their earnings. Labor contracts frequently tied them to their employers for prolonged periods. Moreover, freedmen encountered fierce prejudice among Yankee soldiers, many of whom feared that emancipation would propel blacks north after the war. The best solution to the "question of what to do with the darkies," wrote one northern soldier, "would be to shoot them."

Fording the Rappahannock River
When federal troops came within reach, those slaves who could do so liberated themselves by fleeing behind Union lines. These Virginia fugitives, lugging all their possessions, move toward freedom in the summer of 1862, after the Second Battle of Bull Run.

But this was not the whole story. Contrabands who aided the Union army as spies and scouts helped to break down ingrained bigotry. "The sooner we get rid of our foolish prejudice the better for us," a Massachusetts soldier wrote home. Before the end of the war, northern missionary groups and freedmen's aid societies sent agents into the South to work among the freed slaves, distribute relief, and organize schools. In March 1865, just before the hostilities ceased, Congress created the Freedmen's Bureau, which had responsibility for the relief, education, and employment of former slaves. The Freedmen's Bureau law also stipulated that forty acres of abandoned or confiscated land could be leased to each freedman or southern Unionist, with an option to buy after three years. This was the first and only time that Congress provided for the redistribution of confiscated Confederate property.

Black Soldiers in the Union Army

During the first year of war, the Union had rejected African-American soldiers. Northern recruiting offices sent black applicants home, and black companies that had been formed in the occupied South were disbanded. After the second Confiscation Act, Union generals formed black regiments in occupied New Orleans and on the Sea Islands off the coasts of South Carolina and Georgia. Only after the Emancipation Proclamation did large-scale enlistment begin. Leading African-Americans such as Frederick Douglass and Harvard-educated physician Martin Delany worked as recruiting agents in northern cities. Douglass linked black military service to black claims as citizens. "Once let the black man get upon his person the brass letters, U.S.; let him get an eagle on his button, and a musket on his shoulder and bullets in his pocket, and there is no power on earth which can deny that he has earned the right to citizenship." Union drafts now included blacks, recruiting offices appeared in the loyal border states, and freedmen in refugee camps throughout the occupied South were enlisted. By the end of the war, 186,000 African-Americans had served in the Union army, one-tenth of all Union soldiers. Fully half came from the Confederate states.

White Union soldiers commonly objected to the new recruits on racial grounds. But some, including Colonel Thomas Wentworth Higginson, a liberal minister and former John Brown supporter who led a black regiment, welcomed the black soldiers. "Nobody knows anything about these men who has not seen them in battle," Higginson exulted after a successful raid in

Florida in 1863. "There is a fierce energy about them beyond anything of which I have ever read, except it be the French Zouaves [French troops in North Africa]." Even Union soldiers who held blacks in contempt came to approve of "anything that will kill a rebel." Furthermore, black recruitment offered new opportunities for whites to secure commissions, for blacks served in separate regiments under white officers. Colonel Robert Gould Shaw of the 54th Massachusetts Infantry, an elite black regiment, died in combat—as did half his troops—in an attack on Fort Wagner in Charleston harbor in July 1863.

Black soldiers suffered a far higher mortality rate than white troops. Typically assigned to labor detachments or garrison duty, blacks were less likely than whites to be killed in action but more likely to die of illness in the disease-ridden garrisons. In addition, the Confederacy refused to treat captured black soldiers as prisoners of war, a policy that prevented their exchange for Confederate prisoners. Instead, Jefferson Davis ordered all blacks taken in battle to be sent back to the states from which they came, where they were re-enslaved or executed. In an especially gruesome incident, when Confederate troops under General Nathan Bedford Forrest captured Fort Pillow, Tennessee, in 1864,

Come and Join
A recruitment poster urges black men to enlist in the Union Army. African-American volunteers served in black regiments led by white officers.

COME AND JOIN US BROTHERS.

PUBLISHED BY THE SUPERVISORY COMMITTEE FOR RECRUITING COLORED REGIMENTS
1210 CHESTNUT ST. PHILADELPHIA.

they massacred many blacks—an action that provoked outcries but no retaliation from the North.

Well into the war, African-American soldiers faced inequities in their pay. White soldiers earned $13 a month plus a $3.50 clothing allowance; black privates received only $10 a month, with clothing deducted. "We have come out like men and we Expected to be Treated as men but we have bin Treated more Like Dogs then men," a black soldier complained to Secretary of War Edwin Stanton. In June 1864 Congress belatedly equalized the pay of black and white soldiers.

Although fraught with hardships and inequities, military service became a symbol of citizenship for blacks. It proved that "black men can give blows as well as take them," Frederick Douglass declared. "Liberty won by white men would lose half its lustre." Above all, the use of black soldiers, especially former slaves, was seen by northern generals as a major strike at the Confederacy. "They will make good soldiers," General Grant wrote to Lincoln in 1863, "and taking them from the enemy weakens him in the same proportion they strengthen us."

Slavery in Wartime

Anxious white southerners on the home front felt as if they were perched on a volcano. "We should be practically helpless should the negroes rise," declared a Louisiana planter's daughter, "since there are so few men left at home." When Mary Boykin Chesnut of South Carolina learned of her cousin's murder in bed by two trusted house slaves, she became almost frantic. "The murder," Chesnut wrote, "has clearly driven us all wild." To control 3 million slaves, white southerners resorted to a variety of measures. They tightened slave patrols, at times moved entire plantations to relative safety in Texas or in the upland regions of the coastal South, and spread scare stories among the slaves. "The whites would tell the colored people not to go to the Yankees, for they would harness them to carts . . . in place of horses," reported Susie King Taylor, a black fugitive from Savannah.

Wartime developments had a significant effect on the slaves. Some remained faithful to their owners and helped hide family treasures from marauding Union soldiers. Others were torn between loyalty and lust for freedom: one slave accompanied his master to war, rescued him when he was wounded, and then escaped on his master's horse. Given a viable choice between freedom and bondage, slaves usually chose freedom. Few slaves helped the North as dramatically as Robert Smalls, a

hired-out slave boatman who turned over a Confederate steamer to the Union navy, but most who had a chance to flee to Union lines did so. The idea of freedom held irresistible appeal. Upon learning from a Union soldier that he was free, a Virginia coachman dressed in his master's clothes, "put on his best watch and chain, took his stick, and . . . told him [the master] that he might for the future drive his own coach."

The arrival of the Union navy on the Sea Islands off the coast of Georgia and South Carolina in November 1861 liberated some ten thousand slaves, the first large group of enslaved people to be emancipated by the Civil War (see Map 15.3). Northern teachers and missionaries arrived to run schools, and northern managers to run cotton plantations. A small number of former slaves received land; many worked for wages on the plantations; and some served as members of a black Union army regiment. By the last year of the war, the Sea Islands had become a haven for African American refugees from all over the South.

The majority of slaves, however, had no escape and remained under the nominal control of their owners. Despite the fears of southern whites, no general uprising of slaves occurred; and the Confederacy continued to impress thousands of slaves to toil in war plants, army camps, and field hospitals. But even slaves with no chance of flight were alert to the opportunity that war provided and swiftly tested the limits of enforced labor. As a Savannah mistress noted as early as 1861, the slaves "show a very different face from what they have had heretofore." Moreover, wartime conditions reduced the slaves' productivity. With most of the white men off at war, the master-slave relationship weakened. The women and boys who remained on plantations complained of their difficulty in controlling slaves, who commonly refused to work, performed their labors inefficiently, or even destroyed property. A Texas wife contended that her slaves were "trying all they can, it seems to me, to aggravate me" by neglecting the stock, breaking plows, and tearing down fences. "You may give your Negroes away," she finally wrote despairingly to her husband in 1864.

Whether southern slaves fled to freedom or merely stopped working, they acted effectively to defy slavery, to liberate themselves from its regulations, and to undermine the plantation system. Thus southern slavery disintegrated even as the Confederacy fought to preserve it. Hard-pressed by Union armies, short of manpower, and unsettled by the erosion of plantation slavery, the Confederate Congress in 1864 considered the drastic step of impressing slaves into its army as soldiers in exchange

MAP 15.3
The Sea Islands
The island chain was the site of unique wartime experiments in new social policies.

Sea Island Wage Labor/Sea Island Teachers

The arrival of the Union navy on the Sea Islands off the coast of Georgia and South Carolina in November 1861 liberated some ten thousand slaves, the first large group of enslaved people to be freed by the Civil War. The site of pioneer ventures in freedmen's education, black wage labor, and land redistribution, the Sea Islands served as a wartime testing ground for new social policies. Here, teachers and missionaries who worked among ex-slaves gather in front of a stately home in Port Royal (top); free blacks sort cotton on an Edisto Island plantation (bottom).

for their freedom at the war's end. Robert E. Lee favored the use of slaves as soldiers on the grounds that if the Confederacy did not arm its slaves, the Union would. Others were adamantly opposed. "If slaves will make good soldiers," a Georgia general argued, "our whole theory of slavery is wrong." Originally against arming slaves, Jefferson Davis changed his mind in 1865. In March 1865

the Confederate Congress narrowly passed a bill to arm three hundred thousand slave soldiers, although it omitted any mention of emancipation. As the war ended a few weeks later, however, the plan was never put into effect.

Although the Confederacy's decision to arm the slaves came too late to affect the war, the debate over

arming them damaged southern morale. By then, the South's military position had started to deteriorate.

The Turning Point of 1863

In the summer and fall of 1863, Union fortunes dramatically improved in every theater of the war. Yet the year began badly for the North. The slide, which had started with Burnside's defeat at Fredericksburg, Virginia, in December 1862, continued into the spring of 1863. Burnside's successor, General Joseph "Fighting Joe" Hooker, a windbag fond of issuing pompous proclamations to his troops, devised a plan to dislodge the Confederates from Fredericksburg by crossing the Rappahannock River north of the town and descending on the rebel rear. But Lee and Stonewall Jackson routed Hooker at Chancellorsville, Virginia, early in May 1863 (see Map 15.4). The battle proved costly for the South because Jackson was accidentally shot by Confederate sentries and died a few days later. Still, Hooker had twice as many men as Lee, so the Union defeat at Chancellorsville humiliated the North. Reports from the West brought no better news. Although repulsed at Shiloh in western Tennessee, the Confederates still had a powerful army in central Tennessee under General Braxton Bragg. Furthermore, despite repeated efforts, Grant was unable to take Vicksburg; the two-hundred-mile stretch of the Mississippi between Vicksburg and Port Hudson remained in rebel hands.

The upswing in Union fortunes began with Lee's decision after Chancellorsville to invade the North. Lee needed supplies that war-wracked Virginia could no longer provide. He also hoped to panic Lincoln into moving troops from besieged Vicksburg to the eastern theater. Lee envisioned a major Confederate victory on northern soil that would tip the balance in northern politics to the pro-peace Democrats and gain European recognition of the Confederacy. Moving his seventy-five thousand men down the Shenandoah Valley, Lee crossed the Potomac into Maryland and pressed forward into southern Pennsylvania. At this point, with Lee's army far to the west of Richmond, Hooker recommended a Union stab at the Confederate capital. But Lincoln brushed aside the advice. "Lee's *army,* and not *Richmond,* is your true objective," Lincoln shot back, and he replaced Hooker with the more reliable George G. Meade.

Early in July 1863, Lee's offensive ground to a halt at a Pennsylvania road junction, Gettysburg, (see Map 15.5). Confederates foraging for shoes in the town encountered some Union cavalry. Soon both sides called for reinforcements, and the war's greatest battle commenced. On July 1 Meade's troops installed themselves in hills south of town along a line that resembled a fishhook: the shank ran along Cemetery Ridge and a northern hook encircled Culp's Hill. By the end of the first day of fighting, most of the troops on both sides had arrived: Meade's army outnumbered the Confederates ninety thousand to seventy-five thousand. On July 2 Lee rejected advice to plant the Confederate army in a defensive position between Meade's forces and Washington and instead attacked the Union flanks, with some success. But because the Confederate assaults were uncoordinated, and some southern generals disregarded orders and struck where they chose, the Union was able to move in reinforcements and regain its earlier losses.

By the afternoon of July 3, believing that the Union flanks had been weakened, Lee attacked Cemetery Ridge in the center of the North's defensive line. After southern cannon shelled the line, a massive infantry force of fifteen thousand Confederates, Pickett's charge, moved in. But as the Confederate cannon sank into the ground and fired a shade too high, and as Union fire wiped out the rebel charge, rifled weapons proved their deadly effectiveness. At the end of the day, Confederate bodies lit-

MAP 15.4

The War in the East, 1863

Victorious at Chancellorsville in May 1863, Lee again invaded Union territory but was decisively stopped at Gettysburg.

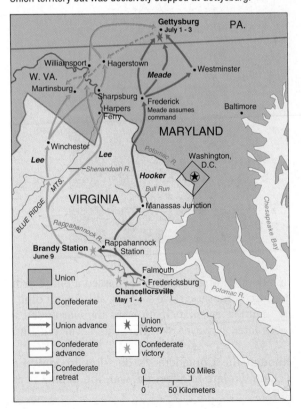

Gettysburg, 1863
At the end of the three-day Battle of Gettysburg, Lee's army had suffered over 25,000 casualties. These uninjured Confederate captives, who refused to face the camera and stare off in different directions, may have spent the rest of the war in northern prison camps.

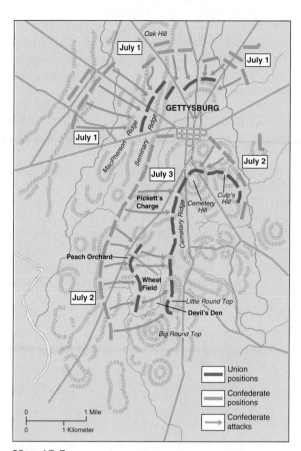

MAP 15.5
Gettysburg, 1863
The failure of Pickett's charge against the Union center on July 3 was the decisive action in the war's greatest battle.

tered the field. "The dead and the dying were lying by the thousands between the two lines," a dazed Louisiana soldier wrote. A little more than half of Pickett's troops were dead, wounded, or captured in the horrible encounter. When Lee withdrew to Virginia on July 4, he had lost seventeen generals and over one-third of his army. Total Union and Confederate casualties numbered almost fifty thousand. Although Meade failed to pursue and destroy the retreating rebels, he had halted Lee's foray into the North, and the Union rejoiced.

Almost simultaneously, the North won a less bloody but more strategic victory in the West, where Grant finally pierced Vicksburg's defenses (see Map 15.6). Situated on a bluff on the east bank of the Mississippi, Vicksburg was protected on the west by the river and on the north by hills, forests, and swamps. It could be attacked only over a thin strip of dry land to its east and south. Positioned to the north of Vicksburg, Grant had to find a way to get his army south of the city and onto the Mississippi's east bank. His solution lay in moving his troops far to the west of the city and down to a point on the river south of Vicksburg. Meanwhile, Union gunboats and supply ships ran past the Confederate batteries overlooking the river at Vicksburg (not without sustaining considerable damage) to rendezvous with Grant's army and transport it across to the east bank. Grant then swung in a large semicircle, first northeastward to capture Jackson, the capital of Mississippi, and then westward back to Vicksburg. After a six-week siege, during which famished soldiers and civilians in Vicksburg were reduced to eating mules and even rats, General John C. Pemberton surrendered his thirty-thousand-man garrison to Grant on July 4, the day after Pickett's charge at Gettysburg. Port Hudson, the last Confederate holdout on the Mississippi, soon surrendered to another Union army. "The Father of Waters flows unvexed to the sea," Lincoln declared.

Before the year was out, the Union won another crucial victory in the West. General William S. Rosecrans fought and maneuvered Braxton Bragg's Confederate army out of central Tennessee and into Chattanooga, in the southeastern tip of the state, and then forced Bragg to evacuate Chattanooga. Bragg defeated the pursuing Rosecrans at the Battle of Chickamauga (September 19–20, 1863), one of the bloodiest of the war, and drove

him back into Chattanooga. But the arrival of Grant and reinforcements from the Army of the Potomac enabled the North to break Bragg's siege of Chattanooga in November. With Chattanooga secure, the way lay open for a Union strike into Georgia.

Union successes in the second half of 1863 stiffened the North's will to keep fighting and plunged some rebel leaders into despair. Hearing of the fall of Vicksburg, Confederate ordnance chief Josiah Gorgas wrote, "Yesterday we rode the pinnacle of success—today absolute ruin seems our portion. The Confederacy totters to its destruction."

Totter it might, but the South was far from beaten. Although the outcome at Gettysburg quashed southerners' hopes for victory on northern soil, it did not significantly impair Lee's ability to defend Virginia. The loss of Vicksburg and the Mississippi cut off the Confederate

states west of the river—Arkansas, Louisiana, and Texas—from those to the east; but these western states could still provide soldiers. Even with the loss of Chattanooga, the Confederacy continued to hold most of the Carolinas, Georgia, Florida, and Mississippi. Few contemporaries thought that the fate of the Confederacy had been sealed.

WAR AND SOCIETY, NORTH AND SOUTH

Extending beyond the battlefields, the Civil War engulfed two economies and societies. By 1863 stark contrasts emerged: with its superior resources, the Union could meet wartime demands as the imperiled Confederacy could not. But both regions experienced labor shortages and inflation. As the conflict dragged on, both societies confronted problems of disunity and dissent, for war issues opened fissures between social classes. In both regions war encroached on everyday life. Families were disrupted and dislocated, especially in the

MAP 15.6
The War in the West, 1863: Vicksburg
Grant first moved his army west of Vicksburg to a point on the Mississippi south of the town. Then he marched northeast, taking Jackson, and finally west to Vicksburg.

Union Infantry at Vicksburg
Veterans of the six-week siege of Vicksburg, the 17th Illinois Infantry remained to garrison the Mississippi town. Posing for the camera in 1864, these battle-hardened troops suggest the determination of the Union Army.

South. Women on both sides took on new roles at home, in the workplace, and in relief efforts.

The War's Economic Impact: The North

The war affected the Union's economy unevenly. Some industries fared poorly. For instance, the loss of southern markets damaged the shoe industry in Massachusetts, and a shortage of raw cotton sent the cotton-textile industry into a tailspin. On the other hand, industries directly related to the war effort, such as the manufacture of arms and clothing, benefited from huge government contracts. By 1865, for example, the ready-made clothing industry received orders for more than a million uniforms a year. Military demand also meant abundant business for the railroads. Some privately owned lines, which had overbuilt before the war, doubled their volume of traffic. In 1862 the federal government itself went into the railroad business by establishing the United States Military Railroads (USMRR) to carry troops and supplies to the front. By 1865 the USMRR was the largest railroad in the world.

The Republicans in Congress actively promoted business growth during the war. Holding 102 of 146 House seats and 29 of 36 Senate seats in 1861, they overrode Democratic foes and hiked the tariff in 1862 and again in 1864 to protect domestic industries. The Republican-sponsored Pacific Railroad Act of 1862 provided for the development of a transcontinental railroad, an idea that had foundered before the war on feuds over which route such a railroad should follow. With the South out of the picture and no longer able to demand a southern route from New Orleans across the Southwest, Congress chose a northern route from Omaha to San Francisco. Chartering the Union Pacific and Central Railroad corporations, Congress then gave to each large land grants and generous loans. These two corporations combined received more than 60 million acres in land grants and $20 million in government loans. The issuance of greenbacks and the creation of a national banking system, meanwhile, brought a measure of uniformity to the nation's financial system.

The Republicans designed these measures to benefit a variety of social classes, and to a degree, they succeeded. The Homestead Act, passed in 1862, embodied the party's ideal of "free soil, free labor, free men" by granting 160 acres of public land to settlers after five years of residence on the land. By 1865 twenty thousand homesteaders occupied new land in the West under the Homestead Act. The Republicans also secured passage

in 1862 of the Morrill Land Grant Act, which gave to the states proceeds of public lands to fund the establishment of universities emphasizing "such branches of learning as are related to agriculture and mechanic arts." The Morrill Act spurred the growth of large state universities, mainly in the Midwest and West. Michigan State, Iowa State, and Purdue universities, among many others, profited from the law.

In general, however, the war benefited the wealthy more than the average citizen. Corrupt contractors grew fat by selling the government substandard merchandise such as the notorious "shoddy" clothing made from compressed rags, which quickly fell apart. Speculators who locked their patriotism in the closet made millions in the gold market. Because the price of gold in relation to greenbacks rose whenever public confidence in the government fell, those who bought gold in the hope that its price would rise gained from Union defeats, and even more from Union disasters. Businessmen with access to scarce commodities also reaped astounding profits. For example, manpower shortages stimulated wartime demand for the mechanical reaper that Cyrus McCormick had patented in 1834. When paid for reapers in greenbacks, which he distrusted, McCormick immediately reinvested them in pig iron and then watched in glee as wartime demand drove its price from twenty-three dollars to forty dollars a ton.

The war had a far less happy impact on ordinary Americans. Protected from foreign competition by higher tariffs, northern manufacturers hoisted the prices of finished goods. Wartime excise taxes and inflation combined to push prices still higher. At the same time, wages lagged 20 percent or more behind cost increases for most of the war. Common in most periods of rapid inflation, lagging wages became especially severe during the war because boys and women poured into government offices and factories to replace adult male workers who had joined the army. For women employees, entry into government jobs—even at half the pay of male clerks—represented a major advance. Still, employers' mere threats of hiring more low-paid youths and females undercut the bargaining power of the men who remained in the work force.

Some workers decried their low wages. "We are unable to sustain life for the price offered by contractors who fatten on their contracts," Cincinnati seamstresses declared in a petition to President Lincoln. Cigar makers and locomotive engineers formed national unions, a process that would accelerate after the war. But protests had little impact on wages; employers often denounced worker complaints as unpatriotic hindrances to the war

effort. In 1864 army troops were diverted from combat to put down protests in war industries from New York to the Midwest.

The War's Economic Impact: The South

The war shattered the South's economy. Indeed, if both regions are considered together, the war retarded *American* economic growth. For example, the commodity output of the American economy, which had registered huge increases of 51 percent and 62 percent in the 1840s and 1850s respectively, rose only 22 percent during the 1860s. This modest gain depended wholly on the North, for in the 1860s commodity output in the South actually *declined* 39 percent.

Multiple factors offset the South's substantial wartime industrial growth. For example, the war wrecked the South's railroads; invading Union troops tore up tracks, twisted rails, and burned railroad cars. Cotton production, once the foundation of the South's prosperity, sank from more than 4 million bales in 1861 to three hundred thousand bales in 1865 as Union invasions took their toll on production, particularly in Tennessee and Louisiana.

Invading Union troops also occupied the South's food-growing regions. Moreover, in areas under Confederate control, the drain of manpower into the army decreased the yields per acre of crops like wheat and corn. Food shortages abounded late in the war. "The

A Confederate Family

An unknown photographer made this ambrotype of Walter Bryan, a Confederate private, with his sisters Ann and Dora in 1861 before he left for war. He was killed on January 15, 1865.

people are subsisting on the ungathered crops and nine families out of ten are left without meat," a Mississippi citizen lamented in 1864. Agricultural shortages worsened the South's already severe inflation. By 1863 salt selling for $1.25 a sack in New York City cost $60 in the Confederacy. Food riots erupted in 1863 in Mobile, Atlanta, and Richmond; in Richmond the wives of ironworkers paraded to demand lower food prices.

Part of the blame for the South's food shortages rested with the planter class. Despite government pleas to grow more food, many planters continued to raise cotton, with far-reaching consequences. Slave labor, which could have been diverted to army camps, remained essential on cotton plantations. This increased the Confederacy's reliance on its unpopular conscription laws. Moreover, to feed its hungry armies, the Confederacy had to impress food from civilians. This policy not only led to resentment but also contributed to the South's mounting military desertions. Food-impressment agents usually concentrated on the easiest targets—farms run by the wives of active soldiers, who found it hard to resist desperate pleas to return home. "I don't want you to stop fighting them Yankees," wrote the wife of an Alabama soldier, "but try and get off and come home and fix us all up some and then you can go back." By the end of 1864, half of the Confederacy's soldiers were absent from their units.

The manpower drain that hampered food production reshaped the lives of southern white women. With the enlistment of about three out of four men of military age over the course of the war, Confederate women found their locales "thinned out of men," as a South Carolina woman described her town in 1862. "There is a vacant chair in every house," mourned a Kentucky Confederate girl. Often left in charge of farms and plantations, women faced new challenges and chronic shortages. As factory-made goods became scarce, the southern press urged the revival of home production; one Arkansas woman, a newspaper reported with admiration, not only wove eight yards of cloth a day but had also built her own loom. More commonly, southern homemakers concocted replacements for goods no longer attainable, including inks, dyes, coffee, shoes, and wax candles. "I find myself, every day, doing something I never did before," a Virginia woman declared in 1863. The proximity of war forced many Confederate women into lives as refugees. Property destruction or even the threat of Union invasions drove women and families away from their homes; those with slave property to preserve, in particular, sought to flee before Union forces arrived. Areas remote from military action, especially Texas, were favored destinations. Disorienting

and disheartening, the refugee experience sapped morale. "I will never feel like myself again," a Georgia woman who had escaped from the path of Union troops wrote to her husband in 1864.

In one respect, the persistence of cotton growing did aid the South because cotton became the basis for the Confederacy's flourishing trade with the enemy. The U.S. Congress virtually legalized this trade in July 1861 by allowing northern commerce with southerners loyal to the Union. In practice, of course, it proved impossible to tell loyalists from disloyalists. As long as Union textile mills stood idle for lack of cotton, northern traders happily swapped bacon, salt, blankets, and other necessaries for southern cotton. The Union's penetration of the Confederate heartland eased business dealings between the two sides. By 1864 traffic through the lines provided enough food to feed Lee's Army of Northern Virginia. To a northern congressman, it seemed that the Union's policy was "to feed an army and fight it at the same time."

Trading with the enemy alleviated the South's food shortages but intensified its morale problems. The prospect of traffic with the Yankees gave planters an incentive to keep growing cotton, and it fattened merchants and middlemen. "Oh! the extortioners," complained a Confederate war-office clerk in Richmond. "Our patriotism is mainly in the army and among the ladies of the South. The avarice and cupidity of men at home could only be exceeded by ravenous wolves."

Dealing with Dissent

Both wartime governments faced mounting dissent and disloyalty. Within the Confederacy, dissent took two basic forms. First, a vocal group of states' rights activists, notably Vice President Alexander Stephens and governors Zebulon Vance of North Carolina and Joseph Brown of Georgia, spent much of the war attacking Jefferson Davis's government as a despotism. Second, loyalty to the Union flourished among a segment of the Confederacy's common people, particularly those living in the Appalachian Mountain region that ran from western North Carolina through eastern Tennessee and into northern Georgia and Alabama. The nonslaveholding small farmers who predominated here saw the Confederate rebellion as a slaveowners' conspiracy. Resentful of such measures as the 20-Negro exemption from conscription, they were reluctant to fight for what a North Carolinian defined as "an adored trinity, cotton, niggers, and chivalry." "All they want," an Alabama farmer complained of the planters, "is to get you pupt up and to fight for their infurnal negroes and after you do

there fighting you may kiss there hine parts for o they care."

On the whole, the Confederate government responded mildly to popular disaffection. In 1862 the Confederate Congress gave Jefferson Davis the power to suspend the writ of habeas corpus, but Davis used his power only sparingly, by occasionally and briefly putting areas under martial law, mainly to aid tax collectors.

Lincoln faced similar challenges in the North, where the Democratic minority opposed both emancipation and the wartime growth of centralized power. Although "War Democrats" conceded that war was necessary to preserve the Union, "Peace Democrats" (called Copperheads by their opponents, to suggest a resemblance to a species of easily concealed poisonous snakes) demanded a truce and a peace conference. They charged that administration war policy was intended to "exterminate the South," make reconciliation impossible, and spark "terrible social change and revolution" nationwide.

Strongest in the border states, the Midwest, and the northeastern cities, the Democrats mobilized the support of farmers of southern background in the Ohio Valley and of members of the urban working class, especially recent immigrants, who feared losing their jobs to an influx of free blacks. In 1863 this volatile brew of political, ethnic, racial, and class antagonisms in northern society exploded into antidraft protests in several cities. By far the most violent eruption occurred in July in New York City. Enraged by the first drawing of names under the Enrollment Act and by a longshoremen's strike in which blacks had been used as strikebreakers, mobs of Irish working-class men and women roamed the streets for four days until suppressed by federal troops. The city's Irish loathed the idea of being drafted to fight a war on behalf of the slaves who, once emancipated, might migrate north to compete with them for low-paying jobs. They also resented the provision of the draft law that allowed the rich to purchase substitutes. The rioters lynched at least a dozen blacks, injured hundreds more, and burned draft offices, the homes of wealthy Republicans, and the Colored Orphan Asylum.

President Lincoln's dispatch of federal troops to quash these riots typified his forceful response to dissent. Lincoln imposed martial law with far less hesitancy than Davis. After suspending the writ of habeas corpus in Maryland in 1861, he barred it nationwide in 1863 and authorized the arrest of rebels, draft resisters, and those engaged in "any disloyal practice." The contrasting responses of Davis and Lincoln to dissent underscored the differences between the two regions'

The Camera and the Civil War

In October 1862, crowds gathered at photographer Mathew Brady's New York studio to gaze at images of the Civil War, especially at gruesome views of corpses on the battlefield. "Mr. Brady has done something to bring home to us the terrible reality and earnestness of war," declared the *New York Times*. "You will see hushed, reverent groups standing around these weird copies of carnage, bending down to look at the dead. . . . These pictures have a terrible distinctness." Entrepreneurs like Brady and his staff of photographers played an innovative role in the Civil War. Just as new technologies reshaped military strategy, so did the camera transform the image of war. Some fifteen hundred wartime photographers, who took tens of thousands of photos in makeshift studios, in army camps, and in the field, brought visions of military life to people at home. The Civil War became the first heavily photographed war in history.

Invented in 1839, the camera had played a small part in the Mexican-American War (1846–1848) and the Crimean War (1854–1855), but the still-unsophisticated nature of photography limited its influence. Photographs of the 1840s and 1850s were mainly daguerreotypes, reversed images (mirror images) on silver-coated surfaces of copper plates. The daguerreotype process required between fifteen and thirty minutes of exposure and produced only one image. Most daguerreotypes were stiff-looking portraits made in studios. Cheaper versions of daguerreotypes, ambrotypes (negatives on glass) and tintypes (negatives on iron), remained popular for years to come. In the 1850s, a new era of photography opened, with the development of the wet-plate or collodion process and the printing of photographs on paper. In the wet-plate process, the photographer coated a glass plate, or negative, with a chemical solution; exposed the negative (took the photo); and developed it at once in a darkroom. The new process required a short exposure time—a few second outdoors and up to a minute indoors—and lent itself to landscapes as well as portraits. Most important, the wet-plate process enabled photographers to generate multiple prints from a single negative. Professional photographers could now mass-produce prints of photos for a wide audience; the wet-plate process made photography not just a craft but a profitable enterprise.

Using new methods and older ones, Civil War photographers churned out many portraits of individual soldiers, often made in temporary tents in army camps; some were ambrotypes or tintypes, and others were cartes-de-visite, or mass-produced portraits mounted on cards (see the first page of this chapter). They disseminated images of political leaders and battle sites; some were stereographs, or two images, each made from the position of one eye, which, fused together, created a sense of spatial depth. Lugging their heavy equipment with them, including portable dark-boxes for developing images, wartime photographers competed both with one another and with sketch artists who also sought to record the war. Wood engravings derived from photographs appeared alongside lithographs in popular magazines such as *Harpers Weekly* and *Frank Leslie's Illustrated Weekly.* Finally, the Union army

An etching of Mathew Brady's Photographic Gallery in New York City. Visitors crowded the staircase in the rear, left, to reach an upstairs gallery where Brady exhibited war photos in the fall of 1862.

used photography for military purposes. Photographers in the army's employ took photos of maps, battle terrain, bridges, armaments, and even medical procedures. The Union army's Surgeon General commissioned and collected hundreds of photos to illustrate case studies and surgical techniques.

Several factors limited the scope of Civil War photography. First, most camera work of the war years was northern; the Union blockade of the South, dwindling photographic supplies, and the sinking Confederate economy curbed southern photography. Photos of the South became part of the record mainly as Union forces invaded the Confederacy. Second, no Civil War photos showed battles in progress; action photos were not yet possible. Instead, photographers rushed to arrive right after battles had ended, perhaps with cannon and smoke in the distance, to photograph casualties before bodies were removed. But limitations aside, the camera now served, in Mathew Brady's words, as "the eye of history." Americans of the Civil War era appreciated the minute detail of photographs and the apparent truthfulness of the camera. They also responded with emotion to the content of photographs—to the courage of soldiers, to the massive might of the Union army, and to the deathly toll of war.

Two postwar publications by photographers George N. Barnard and Alexander Gardner, Brady's large collection of glass negatives, a huge military archive, and thousands of soldiers' portraits remain part of the Civil War's photographic legacy. Only in 1888, when inventor George Eastman introduced roll film (made of celluloid, a synthetic plastic) and a simple box camera, the Kodak, did members of the general public, until then primarily viewers of photography, become photographers themselves.

Focus Question:

How do photographs affect people's perceptions of the past? In what ways does the camera change the historical record?

Two photographers attached to the Army of the Potomac pose in front of their makeshift studio.

Northern photographers who traveled south with the Union army were the first to take photos of African American communities during the Civil War. Photographer Timothy O'Sullivan portrayed these former slaves on a plantation near Beaufort, South Carolina in January 1863 as they celebrated the first "Emancipation Day," the day that Lincoln issued the Emancipation Proclamation.

wartime political systems. As we have seen, Davis lacked the institutionalization of dissent provided by party conflict and thus had to tread warily, lest his opponents brand him a despot. In contrast, Lincoln and other Republicans used dissent to rally patriotic fervor against the Democrats. After the New York City draft riots, the Republicans blamed the violence on New York's antidraft Democratic governor, Horatio Seymour.

Forceful as he was, Lincoln did not unleash a reign of terror against dissent. In general, the North preserved freedom of the press, speech, and assembly. Although some fifteen thousand civilians were arrested during the war, most were quickly released. A few cases, however, aroused widespread concern. In 1864 a military commission sentenced an Indiana man to be hanged for an alleged plot to free Confederate prisoners. The Supreme Court reversed his conviction two years later when it ruled that civilians could not be tried by military courts when the civil courts were open (*Ex parte Milligan*, 1866). Of more concern were the arrests of politicians, notably Clement L. Vallandigham, an Ohio Peace Democrat. Courting arrest, Vallandigham challenged the administration, denounced the suspension of habeas corpus, proposed an armistice, and in 1863 was sentenced to jail for the rest of the war by a military commission. When Ohio Democrats then nominated him for governor, Lincoln changed the sentence to banishment. Escorted to enemy lines in Tennessee,

Vallandigham was left in the hands of bewildered Confederates and eventually escaped to Canada. The Supreme Court refused to review his case.

The Medical War

Despite the discontent and disloyalty of some citizens, both the Union and the Confederacy witnessed a remarkable wartime patriotism that impelled civilians, especially women, to work tirelessly to alleviate soldiers' suffering. The United States Sanitary Commission, organized early in the war by civilians to assist the Union's medical bureau, depended on women volunteers. Described by one woman functionary as a "great artery that bears the people's love to the army," the commission raised funds at "sanitary fairs," bought and distributed supplies, ran special kitchens to supplement army rations, tracked down the missing, and inspected army camps. The volunteers' exploits became legendary. One poor window, Mary Ann "Mother" Bickerdyke, served sick and wounded Union soldiers as both nurse and surrogate mother. When asked by a doctor by what authority she demanded supplies for the wounded, she shot back, "From the Lord God Almighty. Do you have anything that ranks higher than that?"

Women also reached out to aid the battlefront through the nursing corps. Some 3,200 women served the Union and the Confederacy as nurses. Already

Carver Hospital in Washington, D.C.
Clean and gaily decorated, this Union hospital was a vast improvement over unsanitary field hospitals.

famed for her tireless campaigns on behalf of the insane, Dorothea Dix became the head of the Union's nursing corps. Clara Barton began the war as a clerk in the U.S. Patent Office, but she, too, greatly aided the medical effort, finding ingenious ways of channeling medicine to the sick and wounded. Catching wind of Union movements before Antietam, Barton showed up at the battlefield on the eve of the clash with a wagonload of supplies. When army surgeons ran out of bandages and started to dress wounds with corn husks, she raced forward with lint and bandages. "With what joy," she wrote, "I laid my precious burden down among them." After the war, in 1881, she would found the American Red Cross.

The Confederacy, too, had extraordinary nurses. One, Sally Tompkins, was commissioned a captain for her hospital work; another, Belle Boyd, served the Confederacy as both a nurse and a spy and once dashed through a field, waving her bonnet, to give Stonewall Jackson information. Danger stalked nurses even in hospitals far from the front. Author Louisa May Alcott, a nurse at the Union Hotel Hospital in Washington, D.C., contracted typhoid. Wherever they worked, nurses witnessed haunting, unforgettable sights. "About the amputating table," one reported, "lay large piles of human flesh—legs, arms, feet, and hands . . . the stiffened membranes seemed to be clutching oftentimes at our clothing."

Pioneered by British reformer Florence Nightingale in the 1850s, nursing was a new vocation for women and, in the eyes of many, a brazen departure from women's proper sphere. Male doctors were unsure about how to react to women in the wards. Some saw the potential for mischief, but others viewed nursing and sanitary work as potentially useful. The miasm theory of disease (see Chapter 11) won wide respect among physicians and stimulated some valuable sanitary measures, particularly in hospitals behind the lines. In partial consequence, the ratio of disease to battle deaths was much lower in the Civil War than in the Mexican War. Still, for every soldier killed during the Civil War, two died of disease. "These Big Battles is not as Bad as the fever," a North Carolina soldier wrote. The scientific investigations that would lead to the germ theory of disease were only commencing during the 1860s. Arm and leg wounds frequently led to gangrene or tetanus, and typhoid, malaria, diarrhea, and dysentery raged through army camps.

Prison camps posed a special problem. Prisoner exchanges between the North and the South, common early in the war, collapsed by midwar, partly because the

South refused to exchange black prisoners and partly because the North gradually concluded that exchanges benefited the manpower-short Confederacy more than the Union. As a result, the two sides had far more prisoners than either could handle. Prisoners on both sides suffered gravely from camp environments, but the worst conditions plagued southern camps. Squalor and insufficient rations turned the Confederate prison camp at Andersonville, Georgia, into a virtual death camp; three thousand prisoners a month (out of a total of thirty-two thousand) were dying there by August 1864. After the war an outraged northern public secured the execution of Andersonville's commandant. Although the commandant was partly to blame, the deterioration of the southern economy had contributed massively to the wretched state of southern prison camps. The Union camps were not much better, but the fatality rate among northerners held by the South exceeded that of southerners imprisoned by the North.

The War and Women's Rights

Female nurses and Sanitary Commission workers were not the only women to serve society in wartime. In both northern and southern government offices and mills, thousands of women took over jobs vacated by men. Moreover, home industry revived at all levels of society. In rural areas, where manpower shortages were most acute, women often did the plowing, planting, and harvesting.

Few women worked more effectively for their region's cause than Philadelphia-born Anna E. Dickinson. After losing her job in the federal mint (for denouncing General George McClellan as a traitor), Dickinson threw herself into hospital volunteer work and public lecturing. Her lecture "Hospital Life," recounting the soldiers' sufferings, won the attention of Republican politicians. In 1863, hard-pressed by the Democrats, these politicians invited Dickinson, then scarcely twenty-one, to campaign for Republicans in New Hampshire and Connecticut. This decision paid handsome dividends for the party. Articulate and poised, Dickinson captivated her listeners. Soon Republican candidates who had dismissed the offer of aid from a woman begged her to campaign for them.

Northern women's rights advocates hoped that the war would yield equality for women as well as freedom for slaves. Not only should a grateful North reward women for their wartime services, these women reasoned, but it should recognize the link between black rights and women's rights. In 1863 Elizabeth Cady

Andersonville Prison
Started in early 1864, the overcrowded Andersonville prison in southwest Georgia provided no shelter for its inmates, who built tentlike structures out of blankets, sticks, or whatever they could find. Exposure, disease, and poor sanitation contributed to a mortality rate almost double that in other Confederate prison camps and made Andersonville a scandal that outlived the war.

Stanton and Susan B. Anthony organized the Woman's National Loyal League. The league's main activity was to gather four hundred thousand signatures on a petition calling for a constitutional amendment to abolish slavery, but Stanton and Anthony used the organization to promote woman suffrage as well.

Despite high expectations, the war did not bring women significantly closer to economic or political equality. Women in government offices and factories continued to be paid less than men. Sanitary Commission workers and most wartime nurses, as volunteers, earned nothing. Nor did the war alter the prevailing definition of woman's sphere. In 1860 that sphere already included charitable and benevolent activities; during the war the scope of benevolence grew to embrace organized care for the wounded. Yet men continued to dominate the medical profession, and for the rest of the nineteenth century, nurses would be classified in the census as domestic help.

The keenest disappointment of women's rights advocates lay in their failure to capitalize on rising sentiment for the abolition of slavery to secure the vote for women. Northern politicians could see little value in woman suffrage. The *New York Herald*, which supported the Loyal League's attack on slavery, dismissed its call for woman suffrage as "nonsense and tomfoolery." Stanton wrote bitterly, "So long as woman labors to second man's endeavors and exalt his sex above her own, her virtues pass unquestioned; but when she dares to demand rights and privileges for herself, her motives, manners, dress, personal appearance, and character are subjects for ridicule and detraction."

THE UNION VICTORIOUS, 1864–1865

Despite successes at Gettysburg and Vicksburg in 1863, the Union stood no closer to taking Richmond at the start of 1864 than in 1861, and most of the Lower South still remained under Confederate control. The Union invasion had taken its toll on the South's home front, but the North's inability to destroy the main Confederate armies had eroded the Union's will to keep attacking. Northern war weariness strengthened the Democrats and jeopardized Lincoln's prospects for reelection in 1864.

The year 1864 proved crucial for the North. While Grant dueled with Lee in the East, a Union army under William T. Sherman attacked from Tennessee into northwestern Georgia and took Atlanta in early September.

Atlanta's fall boosted northern morale and helped to reelect Lincoln. Now the curtain rose on the last act of the war. After taking Atlanta, Sherman marched across Georgia to Savannah, devastated the state's resources, and cracked its morale. Pivoting north from Savannah, Sherman moved into South Carolina. Meanwhile, having backed Lee into trenches around Petersburg and Richmond, Grant forced the evacuation of both cities and brought on the Confederacy's collapse.

The Eastern Theater in 1864

Early in 1864 Lincoln made Grant commander of all Union armies and promoted him to lieutenant general. At first glance, the stony-faced Grant seemed an unlikely candidate for so exalted a rank, held previously only by George Washington. Grant's only distinguishing characteristics were his ever-present cigars and a penchant for whittling sticks into chips. "There is no glitter, no parade about him," a contemporary noted. But Grant's success in the West had made him the Union's most popular general. With his promotion, Grant moved his headquarters to the Army of the Potomac in the East and mapped a strategy for final victory.

Like Lincoln, Grant believed that the Union had to coordinate its attacks on all fronts in order to exploit its numerical advantage and prevent the South from shifting troops back and forth between the eastern and western theaters. (The South's victory at Chickamauga in September 1863, for example, had rested in part on reinforcements sent by Lee to Braxton Bragg in the West.) Accordingly, Grant planned a sustained offensive against Lee in the East while ordering William T. Sherman to attack the rebel army in Georgia commanded by Bragg's replacement, General Joseph Johnston. Sherman's mission was to break up the Confederate army and "to get into the interior of the enemy's country . . . inflicting all the damage you can."

In early May 1864, Grant led 118,000 men against Lee's 64,000 in a forested area near Fredericksburg, Virginia, called the Wilderness. Checked by Lee in a series of bloody engagements (the Battle of the Wilderness, May 5–7), Grant then tried to swing around Lee's right flank, only to suffer new reverses at Spotsylvania on May 12 and Cold Harbor on June 3. These engagements were among the war's fiercest; at Cold Harbor, Grant lost 7,000 men in a single hour. Oliver Wendell Holmes, Jr., a Union lieutenant and later a Supreme Court justice, wrote home how "immense the butcher's bill has been." But Grant refused to interpret repulses as defeats. Rather, he viewed the engagements at the Wilderness, Spotsylvania, and Cold Harbor as less-

than-complete victories. Pressing on, he forced Lee to pull back to the trenches guarding Petersburg and Richmond.

Grant had accomplished a major objective, because once entrenched, Lee could no longer swing around to the Union rear, cut Yankee supply lines, or as at Chancellorsville, surprise the Union's main force. Lee did dispatch General Jubal A. Early on raids down the Shenandoah Valley, which the Confederacy had long used both as a granary and as an indirect way to menace Washington. But Grant countered by ordering General Philip Sheridan to march up the valley from the north and so devastate it that a crow flying over would have to carry its own provisions. The time had come, a Union chaplain wrote, "to peel this land." After defeating Early at Winchester, Virginia, in September 1864, Sheridan controlled the valley.

While Grant and Lee grappled in the Wilderness, Sherman advanced into Georgia at the head of 98,000 men. Opposing him with 53,000 Confederate troops (soon reinforced to 65,000), General Joseph Johnston retreated toward Atlanta. Johnston's plan was to conserve strength for a final defense of Atlanta while forcing Sherman to extend his supply lines. But Jefferson Davis, dismayed by Johnston's defensive strategy, replaced him with the adventurous John B. Hood. Hood, who had lost the use of an arm at Gettysburg and a leg at Chickamauga, had to be strapped to his saddle; but for all his disabilities, he liked to take risks. In a prewar poker game, he had bet $2,500 with "nary a pair in his hand." Hood gave Davis what he wanted, a series of attacks on Sherman's army. The forays, however, failed to dislodge Sherman and severely depleted Hood's army. No longer able to defend Atlanta's supply lines, Hood evacuated the city, which Sherman took on September 2, 1864.

The Election of 1864

Atlanta's fall came at a timely moment for Lincoln, who faced a tough reelection campaign. Lincoln had secured the Republican renomination with difficulty. The Radicals, who had flayed Lincoln for delay in adopting emancipation as a war goal, now dismissed his plans to restore the occupied parts of Tennessee, Louisiana, and Arkansas to the Union. The Radicals insisted that only Congress, not the president, could set the requirements for readmission of conquered states and criticized Lincoln's reconstruction standards as too lenient. The Radicals endorsed Secretary of the Treasury Salmon P. Chase for the nomination. The Democrats, meanwhile, had never forgiven Lincoln for making emancipation a war goal, and now the Copperheads, or Peace

Democrats, demanded an immediate armistice, followed by negotiations between the North and the South to settle outstanding issues.

Facing formidable challenges, Lincoln benefited from both his own resourcefulness and his foes' problems. Chase's challenge failed, and by the time of the Republican convention in July, Lincoln's managers were firmly in control. To isolate the Peace Democrats and attract prowar Democrats, the Republicans formed a temporary organization, the National Union party, and replaced Lincoln's vice president, Hannibal Hamlin, with a prowar southern Unionist, Democratic Senator Andrew Johnson of Tennessee. This tactic helped exploit the widening division among the Democrats, who nominated George B. McClellan, the former commander of the Army of the Potomac and an advocate of continuing the war until the Confederacy's collapse. But McClellan, saddled with a platform written by the Peace Democrats, spent much of his campaign distancing himself from his party's peace-without-victory plank.

Despite the Democrats' disarray, as late as August 1864, Lincoln seriously doubted that he would be reelected. Leaving little to chance, he arranged for furloughs so that Union soldiers, most of whom supported him, could vote in states lacking absentee ballots. But the timely fall of Atlanta aided him even more. The Confederate defeat punctured the northern antiwar movement and saved Lincoln's presidency. With 55 percent of the popular vote and 212 out of 233 electoral votes, Lincoln swept to victory.

The convention that nominated Lincoln had endorsed a constitutional amendment to abolish slavery, which Congress passed early in 1865. The Thirteenth Amendment would be ratified by the end of the year (see Table 15.1).

Sherman's March Through Georgia

Meanwhile, Sherman gave the South a new lesson in total war. After evacuating Atlanta, Hood led his Confederate army north toward Tennessee in the hope of luring Sherman out of Georgia. But Sherman refused to chase Hood around Tennessee and stretch his own supply lines to the breaking point. Rather, Sherman proposed to abandon his supply lines altogether, march his army across Georgia to Savannah, and live off the countryside as he moved along. He would break the South's will to fight, terrify its people, and "make war so terrible . . . that generations would pass before they could appeal again to it."

Sherman began by burning much of Atlanta and forcing the evacuation of most of its civilian population. This harsh measure relieved him of the need to feed and garrison the city. Then, sending enough troops north to ensure the futility of Hood's campaign in Tennessee, he led the bulk of his army, sixty-two thousand men, on a 285-mile trek to Savannah (see Map 15.7). Soon thousands of slaves were following the army. "Dar's de man dat rules the world," a slave cried on seeing Sherman.

TABLE 15.1 Emancipation of Slaves in the Atlantic World: A Selective List

HAITI	1794	A series of slave revolts began in St. Domingue in 1791 and 1792, and spread under the leadership of Toussaint L'Ouverture. In 1794 the French Republic abolished slavery in all French colonies. In 1804 St. Domingue became the independent republic of Haiti.
BRITISH WEST INDIES	1834	Parliament in 1833 abolished slavery gradually in all lands under British control, usually with compensation for slave owners. The law affected the entire British Empire, including British colonies in the West Indies such as Barbados and Jamaica. It took effect in 1834.
MARTINIQUE AND GUADELOUPE	1848	Napoleon had restored slavery to these French colonies in 1800; the Second French Republic abolished it in 1848.
UNITED STATES	1865	The Thirteenth Amendment, passed by Congress in January 1865 and ratified in December 1865, freed all slaves in the United States. Prior to that, the Second Confiscation Act of 1862 liberated those slaves who came within Union lines, and the Emancipation Proclamation of January 1, 1863, declared free all slaves in areas under Confederate control.
CUBA	1886	In the early 1880s, the Spanish Parliament passed a plan of gradual abolition, which provided an intermediate period of "apprenticeship." In 1886 Spain abolished slavery completely. Cuba remained under Spanish control until the end of the Spanish-American War in 1898.
BRAZIL	1888	Brazil, which had declared its independence from Portugal in 1822, passed a law to effect gradual emancipation in 1871, and in 1888, under the "Golden Law," abolished slavery completely.

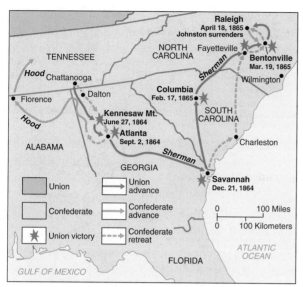

MAP 15.7
Sherman's March Through the South, 1864–1865

New Hope Church, Georgia
General Sherman's campaign through Georgia and South Carolina in 1864 turned parts of the landscape into rubble. This scene of devastation in Georgia, captured by northern photographer George N. Barnard in 1866, suggests the impact of war on the southern environment.

Sherman's four columns of infantry, augmented by cavalry screens, moved on a front sixty miles wide and at a pace of ten miles a day. They destroyed everything that could aid southern resistance—arsenals, railroads, munitions plants, cotton gins, cotton stores, crops, and livestock. Railroad destruction was especially thorough; ripping up tracks, Union soldiers heated rails in giant fires and twisted them into "Sherman neckties." Although Sherman's troops were told not to destroy civilian property, foragers carried out their own version of total war, ransacking and sometimes demolishing homes. Indeed, the havoc seemed a vital part of Sherman's strategy. By the time he occupied Savannah, he estimated that his army had destroyed about a hundred million dollars' worth of property.

After taking Savannah in December 1864, Sherman's army wheeled north toward South Carolina, the first state to secede and, in the general's view, one "that deserves all that seems in store for her." Sherman's columns advanced unimpeded to Columbia, South Carolina's capital. After fires set by looters, slaves, soldiers of both sides, and liberated Union prisoners gutted much of the city, Sherman headed for North Carolina. By the spring of 1865, his army had left in its wake over four hundred miles of ruin. Other Union armies moved into Alabama and Georgia and took thousands of prisoners. Northern forces had penetrated the entire Confederacy, except for Texas and Florida, and crushed its wealth. "War is cruelty and you cannot refine it," Sherman wrote. "Those who brought war into our country deserve all the curses and maledictions a people can pour out."

Toward Appomattox

While Sherman headed north, Grant renewed his assault on the entrenched Army of Northern Virginia. His objective was Petersburg, a railroad hub south of Richmond (see Map 15.8). Although Grant had failed on several occasions to overwhelm the Confederate defenses in front of Petersburg, the devastation wrought by Sherman's army had taken its toll on Confederate morale. Rebel desertions reached epidemic proportions. Reinforced by Sheridan's army, triumphant from its campaign in the Shenandoah Valley, Grant late in March 1865 swung his forces around the western flank of Petersburg's defenders. Lee could not stop him. On April 2 Sheridan smashed the rebel flank at the Battle of Five Forks. A courier bore the grim news to Jefferson Davis, attending church in Richmond: "General Lee telegraphs that he can hold his position no longer."

Davis left his pew, gathered his government, and fled the city. In the morning of April 3, Union troops entered Richmond, pulled down the Confederate flag, and ran up the Stars and Stripes over the capitol. As white and black regiments entered in triumph, explosions set by retreating Confederates left the city "a sea of flames." "Over all," wrote a Union officer, "hung a canopy of dense smoke lighted up now and then by the bursting shells from the numerous arsenals throughout the city." Fires damaged the Tredegar Iron Works. Union troops liberated the town jail, which housed slaves awaiting sale, and its rejoicing inmates poured into the streets. On April 4 Lincoln toured the city and, for a few

MAP 15.8
The Final Virginia Campaign, 1864–1865

Refusing to abandon his campaign in the face of enormous casualties, Grant finally pushed Lee (below) into defensive fortifications around Petersburg, whose fall doomed Richmond. When Lee tried to escape to the west, Grant cut him off and forced his surrender.

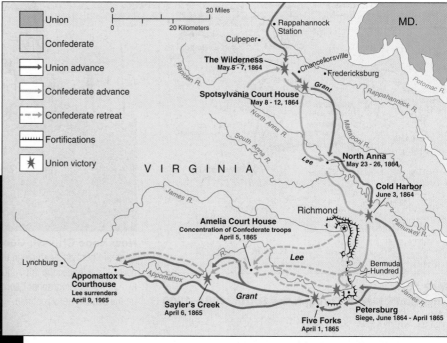

Grant in 1864
Exuding determination and competence, General Ulysses S. Grant posed in front of his tent in 1864. Within a year, Grant's final assault on Petersburg and the Union army's triumphant march into Richmond would bring the war to an end.

minutes, sat at Jefferson Davis's desk with a dreamy expression on his face.

Lee made a last-ditch effort to escape from Grant and reach Lynchburg, sixty miles west of Petersburg. He planned to use the rail connections at Lynchburg to join General Joseph Johnston's army, which Sherman had pushed into North Carolina. But Grant and Sheridan swiftly choked off Lee's escape route, and on April 9 Lee bowed to the inevitable. He asked for terms of surrender and met Grant in a private home in the village of Appomattox Courthouse, Virginia, east of Lynchburg. While stunned troops gathered outside, Lee appeared in full dress uniform, with a sword. Grant entered in his customary disarray, smoking a cigar. When Union troops began to fire celebratory salutes, Grant put a stop to it. The final surrender of Lee's army occurred four days later. Lee's troops laid down their arms between federal ranks. "On our part," wrote a Union officer, "not a sound of trumpet . . . nor roll of drum; not a cheer . . . but an awed stillness rather." Grant paroled Lee's twenty-six thousand men and sent them home with their horses and mules "to work their little farms." The remnants of Confederate resistance collapsed within a month of Appomattox. Johnston surrendered to Sherman on April 18, and Davis was captured in Georgia on May 10.

Grant returned to a jubilant Washington, and on April 14 he turned down a theater date with the Lincolns. That night at Ford's Theater, an unemployed pro-Confederate actor, John Wilkes Booth, entered Lincoln's box and shot him in the head. Waving a knife, Booth

FIGURE 15.3
Civil War Deaths Compared to U.S. Deaths in Other Wars

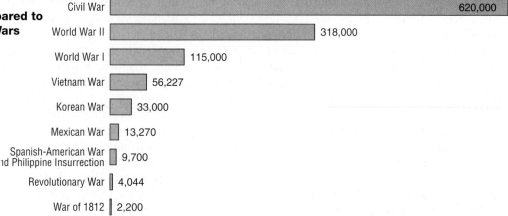

leaped onstage shouting the Virginia state motto, "*Sic semper tyrannis*" ("Such is always the fate of tyrants") and then escaped, despite having broken his leg. That same night, a Booth accomplice stabbed Secretary of State Seward, who later recovered, while a third conspirator, assigned to Vice President Johnson, failed to attack. Union troops hunted down Booth and shot him within two weeks, or else he shot himself. Of eight accused accomplices, including a woman boardinghouse keeper, four were hanged and the rest imprisoned. On April 15, when Lincoln died, Andrew Johnson became president. Six days later Lincoln's funeral train departed on a mournful journey from Washington to Springfield, Illinois, with crowds of thousands gathering at stations to weep as it passed.

The Impact of the War

The Civil War took a larger human toll than any other war in American history. The 620,000 soldiers who lost their lives nearly equaled the number of American soldiers killed in all the nation's earlier and later wars combined (see Figure 15.3). The death count stood at 360,000 Union soldiers and 260,000 Confederates. Most families in the nation suffered losses. Vivid reminders of the price of Union remained beyond the end of the century. For many years armless and legless veterans gathered at regimental reunions. Citizens erected monuments to the dead in front of town halls and on village greens. Soldiers' widows collected pensions well into the twentieth century.

The economic costs were staggering, but the war did not ruin the national economy, only the southern part of it. The vast Confederate losses, about 60 percent of southern wealth, were offset by northern advances. At the war's end, the North had almost all of the nation's wealth and capacity for production. Spurring economic moderniza-

tion, the war provided a hospitable climate for industrial development and capital investment. No longer the largest slaveowning power in the world, the United States would now become a major industrial nation.

The war had political as well as economic ramifications. It created a "more perfect Union" in place of the prewar federation of states. The doctrine of states' rights did not disappear, but it was shorn of its extreme features. Talk of secession ended; states would never again exercise their antebellum range of powers. The national banking system, created in 1863, gradually supplanted state banks. The greenbacks provided a national currency. The federal government had exercised powers that many in 1860 doubted it possessed. By abolishing slavery and imposing an income tax, it asserted power over kinds of private property once thought untouchable. The war also promoted large-scale organization in both the business world and public life. The giant railroad corporation, with its thousands of employees, and the huge Sanitary Commission, with its thousands of auxiliaries and volunteers, pointed out the road that the nation would take.

Finally, the Civil War fulfilled abolitionist prophecies as well as Unionist goals. Liberating 3.5 million slaves, the war produced the very sort of radical upheaval within southern society that Lincoln had originally said that would not induce.

CONCLUSION

When war began in April 1861, both sides were unprepared, but each had distinct strengths. The Union held vast advantages of manpower and resources, including most of the nation's industrial strength and two-thirds of its railroads. The North, however, faced a stiff challenge. To achieve its goal of forcing the rebel states back into the Union, it had to conquer large pieces of southern

territory, cripple the South's resources, and destroy its armies. The Union's challenge was the Confederacy's strength. To sustain Confederate independence, the South had to fight a defensive war, far less costly in men and material. It had to prevent Union conquest of its territory, preserve its armies from annihilation, and hold out long enough to convince the North that further effort would be pointless. Moreover, southerners expected to be fighting on home ground and to enjoy an advantage in morale. Thus, though its resources were fewer, the Confederacy's task was less daunting.

The start of war challenged governments, North and South, in similar ways: both sides had to raise armies and funds. Within two years, both the Union and the Confederacy had drafted troops, imposed taxes, and printed paper money. As war dragged on, both regions faced political and economic problems. Leaders on each side confronted disunity and dissent. Northern Democrats assailed President Lincoln; in the South, states-rights supporters defied the authority of the Confederate government. The North's two-party system and the skills of its political leaders proved to be assets that the Confederacy lacked. Economically, too, the North held an edge. Both regions endured labor shortages and inflation. But the Union with its far greater resources more handily met the demands of war. In the North, Republicans in Congress enacted innovative laws

that enhanced federal might, such as the National Banking Act, the Pacific Railroad Act, and the Homestead Act. The beleaguered South, in contrast, had to cope with food shortages and economic dislocation. Loss of southern manpower to the army took a toll as well; slavery began to disintegrate as a labor system during the war. By 1864 even the Confederate Congress considered measures to free at least some slaves.

Significantly, war itself pressed the North to bring slavery to an end. To deprive the South of resources, the Union began to seize rebel property, including slaves, in 1861. Step by step, Union policy shifted toward emancipation. The Second Confiscation Act in 1862 freed slaves who fled behind Union lines. Finally, seizing the initiative from Radical Republicans, Lincoln announced a crucial change in policy. A war measure, the Emancipation Proclamation of January 1, 1863, served many purposes. The edict freed only slaves behind Confederate lines, those beyond the reach of the Union army. But it won foreign support, outflanked the Radicals, and confounded the Confederates. It also gave Union soldiers the power to liberate slaves, enabled former slaves to serve in the Union army, and vastly strengthened the Union's hand. "Crippling the institution of slavery," as a Union officer declared, meant "striking a blow at the heart of the rebellion." Most important, the proclamation changed the nature of the war. After January 1, 1863, the war to save the Union was also a war to

CHRONOLOGY, 1861–1865

1861 President Abraham Lincoln calls for volunteers to suppress the rebellion (April).
Virginia, Arkansas, Tennessee, and North Carolina join the Confederacy (April–May).
Lincoln imposes a naval blockade on the South (April).
U.S. Sanitary Commission formed (June).
First Battle of Bull Run (July).
First Confiscation Act (August).

1862 Legal Tender Act (February).
George B. McClellan's Peninsula Campaign (March–July).
Battle of Shiloh (April).
Confederate Congress passes the Conscription Act (April).
David G. Farragut captures New Orleans (April).
Homestead Act (May).
Seven Days' Battles (June–July).
Pacific Railroad Act (July).
Morrill Land Grant Act (July).
Second Confiscation Act (July).
Second Battle of Bull Run (August).
Battle of Antietam (September).
Preliminary Emancipation Proclamation (September).
Battle of Fredericksburg (December).

1863 Emancipation Proclamation issued (January).
Lincoln suspends writ of habeas corpus nationwide (January).
National Bank Act (February).
Congress passes the Enrollment Act (March).
Battle of Chancellorsville (May).
Woman's National Loyal League formed (May).
Battle of Gettysburg (July).
Surrender of Vicksburg (July).
New York City draft riots (July).
Battle of Chickamauga (September).

1864 Ulysses S. Grant given command of all Union armies (March).
Battle of the Wilderness (May).
Battle of Spotsylvania (May).
Battle of Cold Harbor (June).
Surrender of Atlanta (September).
Lincoln reelected (November).
William T. Sherman's march to the sea (November–December).

1865 Congress passes the Thirteenth Amendment (January).
Sherman moves through South Carolina (January–March).
Grant takes Richmond (April).
Robert E. Lee surrenders at Appomattox (April).
Lincoln dies (April).
Joseph Johnston surrenders to Sherman (April).

end slavery. Emancipation took effect mainly at the war's end and became permanent with the ratification of the Thirteenth Amendment in 1865. The proclamation of 1863 was a pivotal turning point in the war.

Historians have long debated the causes of the Union victory. They have weighed many factors, including the North's imposing strengths, or what Robert E. Lee called its "overwhelming numbers and resources." Recently, two competing interpretations have held sway. One focuses on southern shortcomings. Did the South, in the end, lose the will to win? Did the economic dislocations of war undercut southern morale? Were there defects of Confederate nationalism that could not be overcome? Some historians point to internal weaknesses in the Confederacy as a major cause of Union triumph. Other historians stress the utterly unpredictable nature of the conflict. In their view, the two sides were fairly equally matched, and the war was a cliffhanger; that is, the North might have crushed the South much earlier or, alternatively, not at all. The North won the war, these historians contend, because it won a series of crucial contests on the battlefield, including the battles of Antietam, Vicksburg, Gettysburg, and Atlanta, any one of which could have gone the other way. The factors that determined the military outcome of the war continue to be a source of contention.

The impact of the Civil War is more clear-cut than the precise cause of Union triumph. The war gave a massive boost to the northern economy. It left in its wake a stronger national government, with a national banking system, a national currency, and an enfeebled version of states rights. It confirmed the triumph of the Republican party, with its commitment to competition, free labor, and industry. Finally, it left a nation of free people, including the millions of African-Americans who had once been slaves. Emancipation and a new sense of nationalism were the war's major legacies. The nation now turned its attention to the restoration of the conquered South to the Union and to deciding the future of the former slaves.

FOR FURTHER REFERENCE

READINGS

David Herbert Donald, *Lincoln* (1995). A compelling biography that reveals connections between Lincoln's private and public lives.

Drew Gilpin Faust, *Mothers of Invention: Women of the Slaveholding South in the American Civil War* (1996). Discusses elite women's relation to slavery, southern culture, and the deprivations of war.

Gary W. Gallagher, *The Confederate War* (1997). Shows how Confederate leaders pursued promising strategies; explores links between morale and the battlefield.

Leon Litwack, *Been in the Storm So Long: The Aftermath of Slavery* (1979). A prizewinning examination of slaves' responses to the process of emancipation.

James M. McPherson, *Battle Cry of Freedom: The Civil War Era* (1988). An award-winning study of the war years, skillfully integrating political, military, and social history.

James M. McPherson, *For Cause and Comrades: Why Men Fought in the Civil War* (1997). Uses soldiers' letters to explore motivation and responses to combat.

George C. Rable, *The Confederate Republic: A Revolt Against Politics* (1994). Discusses the tension between nationalism and individualism in the Confederacy.

Charles Royster, *The Destructive War: William Tecumseh Sherman, Stonewall Jackson, and the Americans* (1991). An exploration of the meaning of violence and nationality in the Civil War era.

Lyde Cullen Sizer, *The Political Work of Northern Women Writers and The Civil War, 1850–1872* (2000). Shows how northern women responded to national issues of the Civil War era, including slavery and emancipation.

Michael Vorenberg, *Final Freedom: The Civil War, the Abolition of Slavery, and the Thirteenth Amendment* (2001). Considers the framing and ratification of the Thirteenth Amendment and the political context in which emancipation became law.

WEBSITES

Abraham Lincoln Online.org
http://showcase.netins.net/web/creative/lincoln.html
Provides links to hundreds of websites and resources, including Lincoln's presidential papers.

The American Civil War Homepage
http://sunsite.utk.edu/civil-war/warweb.html
A guide to hundreds of resources, continually updated, including battles, state and local histories, regimental histories, images, and more.

Civil War Women: Primary Sources on the Internet
http://scriptorium.lib.duke.edu/women/cwdocs.html
Primary sources from Duke University's manuscript collection include diaries, letters, and photographs.

Freedmen and Southern Society Project
http://www.inform.umd.edu/EdRes/colleges/ARHU/Depts/History/fssphome.htm
Resources from the University of Maryland include a chronology of emancipation and sample documents.

Mathew Brady's National Portrait Gallery: A Virtual Tour
http://www.npg.si.edu/exh/brady/gallery/gallery.html
Offers a range of photographs taken by Brady and his corps of photographers, plus background material.

The Valley of the Shadow: Two Communities in the American Civil War
http://www.iath.virginia.edu/vshadow2
Presents extensive source materials on Augusta County in Virginia and Franklin County in Pennsylvania before, during, and after the Civil War.

CHAPTER 16

The Crises of Reconstruction, 1865–1877

"The war weren't so great as folks suppose," declared former slave Felix Heywood. "It was the endin' of it that made the difference. That's when we all wakes up that somethin' had happened." To Heywood, who was twenty years old at the Civil War's end, emancipation was breathtaking. "We was all walkin' on golden clouds," he recalled. "We all felt like heroes and nobody made us that way but ourselves. We was free! Just like that, we was free!"

Heywood's parents had been purchased in Mississippi by William Gudlow and brought to southern Texas, where the Gudlows ran a ranch. There, Heywood and his five brothers and sisters were born. As a teenager, Felix Heywood had been a sheepherder and cowpuncher, and the war, he claimed, left his routine intact. "The ranch went on just like it always had. . . . Church went on," he observed. But after the war, Heywood noticed an important change in the African-American community: the impulse among newly freed people to move somewhere else. "Nobody took our homes away," Heywood recalled. "But right off colored folks started on the move. They seemed to want to get closer to freedom so they'd know what it was—like it was a place or a city."

Felix Heywood did not change place at once. Instead, he "stuck close as a lean tick to a sick chicken." At the outset, the Gudlows provided Heywood and his father with ranch land, where they rounded up cattle that had wandered astray. Then local ranchers gave the two Heywoods a herd of seventy

◀ **Former Slaves** A group of former slaves in Jacksonville, Florida, pose for a photograph.

477

The Devastated South
After the Civil War, parts of the defeated Confederacy resembled a wasteland. Homes, crops, and railroads had been destroyed; farming and business had come to a standstill; and uprooted southerners wandered about. Here, ruins of homes in Baton Rouge, Louisiana.

cattle, and they ran their own ranch. Eventually, however, like many other former slaves, Felix Heywood migrated to the nearest city. He moved to San Antonio, a booming cattle town, where he found a job with the waterworks.

In old age, after raising a family, Felix Heywood still lived in San Antonio, now with his youngest sister. Looking back on his long life, he dwelled on the era right after the war and on the instant that emancipation arrived. "We know'd freedom was on us, but we didn't know what was to come with it," he recalled. "We thought we was goin' to be richer and better off than the white folks; cose we was stronger and knowed how to work, and the whites didn't and they didn't have us to work for them anymore. Hallelujah! But it didn't turn out like that. We soon found out that freedom could make folks proud but it didn't make 'em rich."

For the nation, as for Felix Heywood, the end of the Civil War was a turning point and a moment of uncharted possibilities. It was also a time of unresolved conflicts. While former slaves exulted over freedom, the postwar mood of ex-Confederates was often as grim as the wasted southern landscape. Unable to face "southern Yankeedom," some planters considered emigrating to the American West or to Europe, Mexico, or Brazil, and a

few thousand did. The morale of the vanquished rarely concerns the victors, but the Civil War was a special case, for the Union had sought not merely military triumph but the return of national unity. The questions that the federal government faced in 1865 were therefore unprecedented.

First, how could the Union be restored and the defeated South reintegrated into the nation? Would the Confederate states be treated as conquered territories, or would they quickly rejoin the Union with the same rights as other states? Who would set the standards for readmission—Congress or the president? Would Confederate leaders be punished for treason? Would their property be confiscated and their political rights curtailed? Most important, what would happen to the more than 3.5 million former slaves? The future of the freedmen constituted the crucial issue of the postwar era, for emancipation had set in motion the most profound upheaval in the nation's history. Before the war slavery had determined the South's social, economic, and political structure. What would replace it in the postwar South? The end of the Civil War, in short, posed two problems that had to be solved simultaneously: how to readmit the South to the Union and how to define the status of free blacks in American society.

Between 1865 and 1877, the nation met these challenges, but not without discord and turmoil. Conflict prevailed in the halls of Congress as legislators debated plans to readmit the South to the Union; in the former Confederacy where defeated southerners and newly freed former slaves faced an era of turbulence; and in the postwar North where economic and political clashes arose. Indeed, the crises of Reconstruction—the restoration of the former Confederate states to the Union—reshaped the legacy of the Civil War.

This chapter focuses on five major questions:

■ How did Radical Republicans gain control of Reconstruction politics?

■ What impact did federal Reconstruction policy have on the former Confederacy, and on ex-Confederates?

■ In what ways did newly freed southern slaves reshape their lives after emancipation?

■ What factors contributed to the end of Reconstruction in the 1870s, and which was most significant?

■ To what extent should Reconstruction be considered a failure?

RECONSTRUCTION POLITICS, 1865–1868

At the end of the Civil War, President Johnson might have exiled, imprisoned, or executed Confederate leaders and imposed martial law indefinitely. Demobilized Confederate soldiers might have continued armed resistance to federal occupation forces. Freed slaves might have taken revenge on former owners and the rest of the white community. But none of these drastic possibilities occurred. Instead, intense *political* conflict dominated the immediate postwar years. In national politics, unparalleled disputes produced new constitutional amendments, a presidential impeachment, and some of the most ambitious domestic legislation ever enacted by Congress, the Reconstruction Acts of 1867–1868. The major outcome of Reconstruction politics was the enfranchisement of black men, a development that few—black or white—had expected when Lee surrendered.

In 1865 only a small group of politicians supported black suffrage. All were Radical Republicans, a minority faction that had emerged during the war. Led by Senator Charles Sumner of Massachusetts and Congressman Thaddeus Stevens of Pennsylvania, the Radicals had clamored for the abolition of slavery and a demanding reconstruction policy. Any plan to restore the Union, Stevens contended, must "revolutionize Southern institutions, habits, and manners . . . or all our blood and treasure have been spent in vain." But the Radicals, outnumbered in Congress by other Republicans and opposed by the Democratic minority, faced long odds. Still, they managed to win broad Republican support for parts of their Reconstruction program, including black male enfranchisement. Just as civil war had led to emancipation, a goal once supported by only a minority of Americans, so Reconstruction policy became bound to black suffrage, a momentous change that originally had only narrow political backing.

Lincoln's Plan

Conflict over Reconstruction began even before the war ended. In December 1863 President Lincoln issued the Proclamation of Amnesty and Reconstruction, which outlined a path by which each southern state could rejoin the Union. Under Lincoln's plan a minority of voters (equal to at least 10 percent of those who had cast ballots in the election of 1860) would have to take an oath of allegiance to the Union and accept emancipation. This minority could then create a loyal state government. Lincoln's plan excluded some southerners from taking the oath: Confederate government officials, army and naval officers, as well as those military or civil officers who had resigned from Congress or from U.S. commissions in 1861. All such persons would have to apply for presidential pardons. Also excluded, of course, were blacks, who had not been voters in 1860. Lincoln hoped that his "10 percent plan" would undermine the Confederacy by establishing pro-Union governments

Radical Republican Leaders

Charles Sumner, left, Senator from Massachusetts, and Thaddeus Stevens, Congressman from Pennsylvania, led the Radical Republican faction in Congress.

within it. Characteristically, Lincoln had partisan goals, too. He wanted to win the allegiance of southern Unionists (those who had opposed secession), especially former Whigs, and to build a southern Republican party.

Radical Republicans in Congress, however, envisioned a slower readmission process that would bar even more ex-Confederates from political life. Most Republicans agreed that Lincoln's program was too weak. Thus, in July 1864 Congress passed the Wade-Davis bill, which provided that each former Confederate state would be ruled by a military governor. Under the Wade-Davis plan, after at least half the eligible voters took an oath of allegiance to the Union, delegates could be elected to a state convention that would repeal secession and abolish slavery. To qualify as a voter or delegate, a southerner would have to take a second, "ironclad" oath, swearing that he had never voluntarily supported the Confederacy. Like the 10 percent plan, the congressional plan did not provide for black suffrage, a measure then supported by only some Radicals. Unlike Lincoln's plan, however, the Wade-Davis scheme would have delayed the readmission process almost indefinitely.

Claiming that he did not want to bind himself to any single restoration policy, Lincoln pocket-vetoed the Wade-Davis bill (that is, he failed to sign the bill within ten days of the adjournment of Congress). The bill's sponsors, Senator Benjamin Wade of Ohio and Congressman Henry Winter Davis of Maryland, blasted Lincoln's act as an outrage. By the war's end, the president and Congress had reached an impasse. Arkansas, Louisiana, Tennessee, and parts of Virginia under Union army control moved toward readmission under variants of Lincoln's plan. But Congress refused to seat their delegates, as it had a right to do. Lincoln, meanwhile, hinted that a more rigorous Reconstruction policy might be in store. What Lincoln's ultimate policy would have been remains unknown. But after his assassination, on April 14, 1865, Radical Republicans turned with hope toward his successor, Andrew Johnson of Tennessee, in whom they felt they had an ally.

Presidential Reconstruction Under Johnson

The only southern senator to remain in Congress when his state seceded, Andrew Johnson had served as military governor of Tennessee from 1862 to 1864. He had taken a strong anti-Confederate stand, declaring that "treason is a crime and must be made odious." Above all, Johnson had long sought the destruction of the planter aristocracy. A self-educated man of humble North Carolina origins, Johnson had moved to Greenville, Tennessee, in 1826 and became a tailor. His wife, Eliza McCardle, had taught him how to write. He had entered politics in the 1830s as a spokesman for nonslaveowning whites and rose rapidly from local official to congressman to governor to senator. Once the owner of eight slaves, Johnson reversed his position on slavery during the war. When emancipation became Union policy, he supported it. But Johnson neither adopted abolitionist ideals nor challenged racist sentiments. He hoped mainly that the fall of slavery would injure southern aristocrats. Andrew Johnson, in short, had his own political agenda, which, as Republicans would soon learn, did not coincide with theirs. Moreover, he was a lifelong Democrat who had been added to the Republican, or National Union, ticket in 1864 to broaden its appeal and who had become president by accident.

Many Republicans voiced shock when Johnson announced a new plan for the restoration of the South in May 1865—with Congress out of session and not due to convene until December. In two proclamations, the president explained how the seven southern states still without reconstruction governments—Alabama, Florida, Georgia, Mississippi, North Carolina, South Carolina, and Texas—could return to the Union. Almost all southerners who took an oath of allegiance would receive a pardon and amnesty, and all their property except slaves would be restored. Oath takers could elect delegates to state conventions, which would provide for regular elections. Each state convention, Johnson later added, would have to proclaim the illegality of secession, repudiate state debts incurred when the state belonged to the Confederacy, and ratify the Thirteenth Amendment, which abolished slavery. (Proposed by an enthusiastic wartime Congress early in 1865, the amendment would be ratified in December of that year.) As under Lincoln's plan, Confederate civil and military officers could not take the oath needed to vote. Johnson also disqualified all well-off ex-Confederates—those with taxable property worth $20,000 or more. This purge of the plantation aristocracy, he said, would benefit "humble men, the peasantry and yeomen of the South, who have been decoyed . . . into rebellion." Poorer whites would now be in control.

Presidential Reconstruction took effect in the summer of 1865, but with unforeseen consequences. Southerners disqualified on the basis of wealth or high Confederate position applied for pardons in droves, and Johnson handed out pardons liberally—some thirteen thousand of them. He also dropped plans for the pun-

ishment of treason. By the end of 1865, all seven states had created new civil governments that in effect restored the status quo from before the war. Confederate army officers and large planters assumed state offices. Former Confederate congressmen, state officials, and generals were elected to Congress. Georgia sent Alexander Stephens, the former Confederate vice president, back to Washington as a senator. Some states refused to ratify the Thirteenth Amendment or to repudiate their Confederate debts.

Most infuriating to Radical Republicans, all seven states took steps to ensure a landless, dependent black labor force: they passed "black codes" to replace the slave codes, state laws that had regulated slavery. Because the ratification of the Thirteenth Amendment was assured by the terms of Johnson's Reconstruction plan, all states guaranteed the freedmen some basic rights. They could marry, own property, make contracts, and testify in court against other blacks. But the codes harshly restricted freedmen's behavior. Some established racial segregation in public places; most prohibited racial intermarriage, jury service by blacks, and court testimony by blacks against whites. All codes included provisions that effectively barred former slaves from leaving the plantations. South Carolina required special licenses for blacks who wished to enter nonagricultural employment. Mississippi prohibited blacks from buying and selling farmland. Most states required annual contracts between landowners and black agricultural workers and provided that blacks without lawful employment would be arrested as vagrants and their labor auctioned off to employers who would pay their fines.

The black codes left freedmen no longer slaves but not really liberated either. Although "free" to sign labor contracts, for instance, those who failed to sign them would be considered in violation of the law and swept back into involuntary servitude. In practice, many clauses in the codes never took effect: the Union army and the Freedmen's Bureau (a federal agency that assisted former slaves) swiftly suspended the enforcement of racially discriminatory provisions of the new laws. But the black codes revealed white southern intentions. They showed what "home rule" would have been like without federal interference.

Many northerners denounced what they saw as southern defiance. "What can be hatched from such an egg but another rebellion?" asked a Boston newspaper. Republicans in Congress agreed. When Congress convened in December 1865, it refused to seat the delegates of the ex-Confederate states. Establishing the Joint (House-Senate) Committee on Reconstruction, Republicans prepared to dismantle the black codes and lock ex-Confederates out of power.

Congress Versus Johnson

The status of the southern blacks now became the major issue in Congress. Radical Republicans like congressman Thaddeus Stevens—who hoped to impose black suffrage on the former Confederacy and delay the readmission of the southern states into the Union—were still a minority in Congress. Conservative Republicans, who tended to favor the Johnson plan, formed a minority too, as did the Democrats, who also supported the president. Moderate Republicans, the largest congressional bloc, agreed with the Radicals that Johnson's plan was too feeble. But they thought that northern voters would oppose black suffrage, and they wanted to avoid a dispute with the president. Since none of the four congressional blocs could claim the two-thirds majority required to overturn a presidential veto, Johnson's program would prevail unless the moderates and the Radicals joined forces. Ineptly, Johnson alienated a majority of moderates and pushed them into the Radicals' arms.

The moderate Republicans supported two proposals drafted by one of their own, Senator Lyman Trumbull of Illinois, to invalidate the black codes. These measures won wide Republican support. In the first, Congress voted to continue the Freedmen's Bureau, established in 1865, whose term was ending. This federal agency, headed by former Union general O. O. Howard and staffed mainly by army officers, provided relief, rations, and medical care. It also built schools for the freed blacks, put them to work on abandoned or confiscated lands, and tried to protect their rights as laborers. Congress extended the bureau's life for three years and gave it new power: it could run special military courts to settle labor disputes and could invalidate labor contracts forced on freedmen by the black codes. In February 1866 Johnson vetoed the Freedmen's Bureau bill. The Constitution, he declared, did not sanction military trials of civilians in peacetime, nor did it support a system to care for "indigent persons."

In March 1866 Congress passed a second measure proposed by Trumbull, a bill that made blacks U.S. citizens with the same civil rights as other citizens and authorized federal intervention in the states to ensure black rights in court. Johnson vetoed the civil rights bill also. He argued that it would "operate in favor of the colored and against the white race." In April Congress overrode his veto; the Civil Rights Act of 1866 was the first

major law ever passed over a presidential veto. In July Congress enacted the Supplementary Freedmen's Bureau Act over Johnson's veto as well. Johnson's vetoes puzzled many Republicans because the new laws did not undercut presidential Reconstruction. The president insisted, however, that both bills were illegitimate because southerners had been shut out of the Congress that passed them. His stance won support in the South and from northern Democrats. But the president had alienated the moderate Republicans, who began to work with the Radicals against him. Johnson had lost "every friend he has," one moderate declared.

Some historians view Andrew Johnson as a political incompetent who, at this crucial turning point, bungled both his readmission scheme and his political future. Others contend that he was merely trying to forge a coalition of the center, made up of Democrats and non-Radical Republicans. In either case, Johnson underestimated the possibility of Republican unity. Once united, the Republicans moved on to a third step: the passage of

a constitutional amendment that would prevent the Supreme Court from invalidating the new Civil Rights Act and would block Democrats in Congress from repealing it.

The Fourteenth Amendment, 1866

In April 1866 Congress adopted the Fourteenth Amendment, which had been proposed by the Joint Committee on Reconstruction. To protect blacks' rights, the amendment declared in its first clause that all persons born or naturalized in the United States were citizens of the nation and citizens of their states and that no state could abridge their rights without due process of law or deny them equal protection of the law. This section nullified the *Dred Scott* decision of 1857, which had declared that blacks were not citizens. Second, the amendment guaranteed that if a state denied suffrage to any of its male citizens, its representation in Congress would be proportionally reduced. This clause did not

King Andrew

This Thomas Nast cartoon, published in *Harper's Weekly* just before the 1866 congressional elections, conveyed Republican antipathy to Andrew Johnson. The president is depicted as an autocratic tyrant. Radical Republican Thaddeus Stevens, upper right, has his head on the block and is about to lose it. The Republic sits in chains.

guarantee black suffrage, but it threatened to deprive southern states of some legislators if black men were denied the vote. This was the first time that the word *male* was written into the Constitution. To the dismay of women's rights advocates, woman suffrage seemed a yet more distant prospect. Third, the amendment disqualified from state and national office *all* prewar officeholders—civil and military, state and federal—who had supported the Confederacy, unless Congress removed their disqualifications by a two-thirds vote. In so providing, Congress intended to invalidate Johnson's wholesale distribution of amnesties and pardons. Finally, the amendment repudiated the Confederate debt and maintained the validity of the federal debt.

The Fourteenth Amendment was the most ambitious step that Congress had yet taken. It revealed Republican legislators' growing receptivity to the Radicals' demands, including black male enfranchisement. Republicans now realized that southern states would not deal fairly with blacks unless forced to do so. The Fourteenth Amendment was the first national effort to limit state control of civil and political rights. Its passage created a firestorm. Abolitionists decried the second clause as a "swindle" because it did not explicitly ensure black suffrage. Southerners and northern Democrats condemned the third clause as vengeful. Southern legislatures, except for Tennessee's, refused to ratify the amendment, and President Johnson denounced it. His defiance solidified the new alliance between moderate and Radical Republicans, and turned the congressional elections of 1866 into a referendum on the Fourteenth Amendment.

Over the summer Johnson set off on a whistle-stop train tour from Washington to St. Louis and Chicago and back. But this innovative campaign tactic—the "swing around the circle," as Johnson called it—failed. Humorless and defensive, the president made fresh enemies and doomed his hope of creating a new National Union party that would sink the Fourteenth Amendment. Moderate and Radical Republicans defended the amendment, condemned the president, and branded the Democratic party "a common sewer . . . into which is emptied every element of treason, North and South."

Republicans carried the congressional elections of 1866 in a landslide, winning almost two-thirds of the House and almost four-fifths of the Senate. They had secured a mandate to overcome southern resistance to the Fourteenth Amendment and to enact their own Reconstruction program, even if the president vetoed every part of it.

Congressional Reconstruction, 1866–1867

The congressional debate over reconstructing the South began in December 1866 and lasted three months. Radical Republican leaders called for black suffrage, federal support for public schools, confiscation of Confederate estates, and an extended period of military occupation in the South. Moderate Republicans, who once would have found such a plan too extreme, now accepted parts of it. In February 1867, after complex legislative maneuvers and many late-night sessions, Congress passed the Reconstruction Act of 1867. Johnson vetoed the law, and on March 2 Congress passed it over his veto. Later that year and in 1868, Congress passed three further Reconstruction acts, all enacted over presidential vetoes, to refine and enforce the first (see Table 16.1).

The Reconstruction Act of 1867 invalidated the state governments formed under the Lincoln and Johnson plans. Only Tennessee, which had ratified the Fourteenth Amendment and had been readmitted to the Union, escaped further reconstruction. The new law divided the other ten former Confederate states into five temporary military districts, each run by a Union general (see Map 16.1). Voters—all black men, plus those white men who had not been disqualified by the Fourteenth Amendment—could elect delegates to a state convention that would write a new state constitution granting black suffrage. When eligible voters ratified the new constitution, elections could be held for state officers. Once Congress approved the state constitution, once the state legislature ratified the Fourteenth Amendment, and once the amendment became part of the federal Constitution, Congress would readmit the state into the Union—and Reconstruction, in a constitutional sense, would be complete.

The Reconstruction Act of 1867 was far more radical than the Johnson program because it enfranchised blacks and disfranchised many ex-Confederates. It fulfilled a central goal of the Radical Republicans: to delay the readmission of former Confederate states until Republican governments could be established and thereby prevent an immediate rebel resurgence. But the new law was not as harsh toward ex-Confederates as it might have been. It provided for only temporary military rule. It did not prosecute Confederate leaders for treason or permanently exclude them from politics. Finally, it made no provision for the confiscation or redistribution of property.

During the congressional debates, Radical Republican congressman Thaddeus Stevens had argued for the

TABLE 16.1   Major Reconstruction Legislation

Law and Date of Congressional Passage	Provisions	Purpose
Civil Rights Act of 1866 (April 1866)*	Declared blacks citizens and guaranteed them equal protection of the laws.	To invalidate the black codes.
Supplementary Freedmen's Bureau Act (July 1866)*	Extended the life of the Freedmen's Aid Bureau and expanded its powers.	To invalidate the black codes.
Reconstruction Act of 1867 March 1867)*	Invalidated state governments formed under Lincoln and Johnson.	To replace presidential Reconstruction with a more stringent plan.
	Divided the former Confederacy into five military districts.	
	Set forth requirements for readmission of ex-Confederate states to the Union.	
Supplementary Reconstruction Acts		To enforce the First Reconstruction Act.
Second Reconstruction Act (March 1867)*	Required military commanders to initiate voter enrollment.	
Third Reconstruction Act (July 1867)*	Expanded military commanders' powers.	
Fourth Reconstruction Act (March 1868)*	Provided that a majority of voters, however few, could put a new state constitution into force.	
Army Appropriations Act (March 1867)*	Declared in a rider that only the general of the army could issue military orders.	To prevent President Johnson from obstructing Reconstruction.
Tenure of Office Act (March 1867)*	Prohibited the president from removing any federal official without the Senate's consent.	To prevent President Johnson from obstructing Reconstruction.
Omnibus Act (June 1868)†	Readmitted seven ex-Confederate states to the Union.	To restore the Union, under the term of the First Reconstruction Act.
Enforcement Act of 1870 (May 1870)‡	Provided for the protection of black voters.	To enforce the Fifteenth Amendment.
Second Enforcement Act (February 1871)	Provided for federal supervision of southern elections.	To enforce the Fifteenth Amendment.
Third Enforcement Act (Ku Klux Klan Act) (April 1871)	Strengthened sanctions against those who impeded black suffrage.	To combat the Ku Klux Klan and enforce the Fourteenth Amendment.
Amnesty Act (May 1872)	Restored the franchise to almost all ex-Confederates.	Effort by Grant Republicans to deprive Liberal Republicans of a campaign issue.
Civil Rights Act of 1875 (March 1875)§	Outlawed racial segregation in transportation and public accommodations and prevented exclusion of blacks from jury service.	To honor the late senator Charles Sumner.

*Passed over Johnson's veto.   ‡Sections of the law declared unconstitutional in 1876.

†Georgia was soon returned to military rule.
The last four states were readmitted in 1870.   §Invalidated by the Supreme Court in 1883.

confiscation of large Confederate estates to "humble the proud traitors" and to provide for the former slaves. He had proposed subdividing such confiscated property into forty-acre tracts to be distributed among the freedmen and selling the rest, some 90 percent of it, to pay off war debts. Stevens wanted to crush the planter aristocracy and create a new class of self-sufficient black yeoman farmers. His land-reform bill won the support of other Radicals, but it never made progress, for most Republicans held property rights sacred. Tampering

MAP 16.1
The Reconstruction of the South
The Reconstruction Act of 1867 divided the former Confederate states, except Tennessee, into five military districts and set forth the steps by which new state governments could be created.

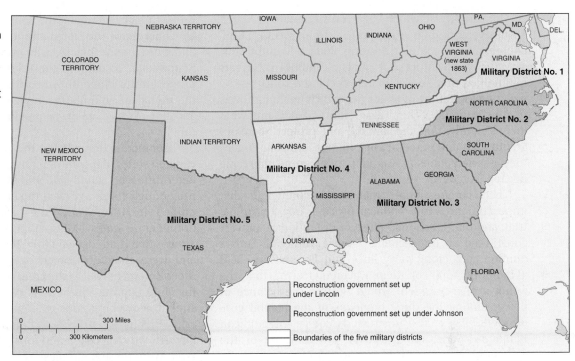

with such rights in the South, they feared, would jeopardize those rights in the North. Moreover, Stevens's proposal would alienate southern ex-Whigs from the Republican cause, antagonize other white southerners, and thereby endanger the rest of Reconstruction. Thus land reform never came about. The "radical" Reconstruction acts were a compromise.

Congressional Reconstruction took effect in the spring of 1867, but it could not be enforced without military power. Johnson, as commander-in-chief, impeded the congressional plan by replacing military officers sympathetic to the Radical cause with conservative ones. Republicans seethed. More suspicious than ever of the president, congressional moderates and Radicals once again joined forces to block Johnson from obstructing Reconstruction.

The Impeachment Crisis, 1867–1868

In March 1867 Republicans in Congress passed two laws to limit presidential power. The Tenure of Office Act prohibited the president from removing civil officers without Senate consent. Cabinet members, the law stated, were to hold office "during the term of the president by whom they may have been appointed" and could be fired only with the Senate's approval. The goal was to bar Johnson from dismissing Secretary of War Henry Stanton, the Radicals' ally, whose support Congress needed to

enforce the Reconstruction acts. The other law, a rider to an army appropriations bill, barred the president from issuing military orders except through the commanding general, Ulysses S. Grant, who could not be removed without the Senate's consent.

The Radicals' enmity toward Johnson, however, would not die until he was out of office. They began to seek grounds on which to impeach him. The House Judiciary Committee, aided by private detectives, could at first uncover no valid charges against Johnson. But Johnson again rescued his foes by providing the charges they needed.

In August 1867, with Congress out of session, Johnson suspended Secretary of War Stanton and replaced him with General Grant. In early 1868 the reconvened Senate refused to approve Stanton's suspension, and Grant, sensing the Republican mood, vacated the office. Johnson then removed Stanton and replaced him with an aged general, Lorenzo Thomas. Johnson's defiance forced Republican moderates, who had at first resisted impeachment, into yet another alliance with the Radicals: the president had "thrown down the gauntlet," a moderate charged. The House approved eleven charges of impeachment, nine of them based on violation of the Tenure of Office Act. The other charges accused Johnson of being "unmindful of the high duties of office," of seeking to disgrace Congress, and of not enforcing the Reconstruction acts.

Johnson's trial, which began in the Senate in March 1868, riveted public attention for eleven weeks. Seven congressmen, including leading Radical Republicans, served as prosecutors or "managers." Johnson's lawyers maintained that he was merely seeking a court test by violating the Tenure of Office Act, which he thought was unconstitutional. They also contended, somewhat inconsistently, that the law did not protect Secretary Stanton, an appointee of Lincoln, not Johnson. Finally, they asserted, Johnson was guilty of no crime indictable in a regular court.

The congressional "managers" countered that impeachment was a political process, not a criminal trial, and that Johnson's "abuse of discretionary power" constituted an impeachable offense. Although Senate opinion split along party lines and Republicans held a majority, some of them wavered, fearing that the removal of a president would destroy the balance of power among the three branches of the federal government. They also distrusted Radical Republican Benjamin Wade, the president pro tempore of the Senate, who, because there was no vice president, would become president if Johnson were thrown out.

Intense pressure weighed on the wavering Republicans. Late in May 1868, the Senate voted against Johnson 35 to 19, one vote short of the two-thirds majority needed for conviction. Seven Republicans had risked political suicide and sided with the twelve Senate Democrats in voting against removal. In so doing, they set a precedent. Their vote discouraged impeachment on political grounds for decades to come. But the anti-Johnson forces had also achieved their goal: Andrew Johnson's career as a national leader would soon end. After serving out the rest of his term, Johnson returned to Tennessee, where he was reelected to the Senate five years later. Republicans in Congress, meanwhile, pursued their last major Reconstruction objective: to guarantee black male suffrage.

The Fifteenth Amendment and the Question of Woman Suffrage, 1869–1870

Black suffrage was the linchpin of congressional Reconstruction. Only with the support of black voters could Republicans secure control of the ex-Confederate states. The Reconstruction Act of 1867 had forced every southern state legislature to enfranchise black men as a prerequisite for readmission to the Union. But though black voting had begun in the South, much of the North rejected black suffrage at home. Congressional Republicans therefore had two aims. They sought to

protect black suffrage in the South against future repeal by Congress or the states and to enfranchise northern and border-state blacks, who would presumably vote Republican. To achieve these goals, Congress in 1869 proposed the Fifteenth Amendment, which prohibited the denial of suffrage by the states to any citizen on account of "race, color, or previous condition of servitude."

Democrats argued that the proposed amendment violated states' rights by denying each state the power to determine who would vote. But Democrats did not control enough states to defeat the amendment, and it was ratified in 1870. Four votes came from those ex-Confederate states—Mississippi, Virginia, Georgia, and Texas—that had delayed the Reconstruction process and were therefore forced to approve the Fifteenth Amendment, as well as the Fourteenth, in order to rejoin the Union. Some southerners contended that the new amendment's omissions made it acceptable, for it had, as a Richmond newspaper pointed out, "loopholes through which a coach and four horses can be driven." What were these loopholes? The Fifteenth Amendment did not guarantee black officeholding, nor did it prohibit voting restrictions such as property requirements and literacy tests. Such restrictions might be used to deny blacks the vote, and indeed, ultimately they were so used.

The debate over black suffrage drew new participants into the political fray. Since the end of the war, a small group of abolitionists, men and women, had sought to revive the cause of women's rights. In 1866, when Congress debated the Fourteenth Amendment, women's rights advocates tried to join forces with their old abolitionist allies to promote both black suffrage and woman suffrage. Most Radical Republicans, however, did not want to be saddled with the woman-suffrage plank; they feared it would impede their primary goal, black enfranchisement.

This defection provoked disputes among women's rights advocates. Some argued that black suffrage would pave the way for the women's vote and that black men deserved priority. "If the elective franchise is not extended to the Negro, he is dead," explained Frederick Douglass, a longtime women's rights supporter. "Woman has a thousand ways by which she can attach herself to the ruling power of the land that we have not." But the women's rights leaders Elizabeth Cady Stanton and Susan B. Anthony disagreed. In their view, the Fourteenth Amendment had disabled women by including the word *male* and the Fifteenth Amendment compounded the injury by failing to prohibit the denial of suffrage on account of sex. Instead, Stanton contended,

the Fifteenth Amendment established an "aristocracy of sex" and increased women's disadvantages.

The battle over black suffrage and the Fifteenth Amendment split women's rights advocates into two rival suffrage associations, both formed in 1869. The Boston-based American Woman Suffrage Association, endorsed by reformers such as Julia Ward Howe and Lucy Stone, retained an alliance with male abolitionists and campaigned for woman suffrage in the states. The New York-based and more radical National Woman Suffrage Association, led by Stanton and Anthony, condemned its leaders' one-time male allies and promoted a federal woman suffrage amendment.

For the rest of the 1870s, the rival woman suffrage associations vied for constituents. In 1869 and 1870, independent of the suffrage movement, two territories, Wyoming and Utah, enfranchised women. But lacking support, suffragists failed to sway legislators elsewhere. In 1872 Susan B. Anthony mobilized about seventy women to vote nationwide and, as a result, was indicted, convicted, and fined. One of the women who tried to vote in 1872, Missouri suffragist Virginia Minor, brought suit with her husband against the registrar who had excluded her. The Minors based their case on the Fourteenth Amendment, which, they claimed, enfranchised women. In *Minor* v. *Happersett* (1875), however, the Supreme Court declared that a state could constitutionally deny women the vote. Divided and rebuffed, woman suffrage advocates braced for a long struggle.

By the time the Fifteenth Amendment was ratified in 1870, Congress could look back on five years of momentous achievement. Since the start of 1865, federal legisla-

Stanton and Anthony, c. 1870
Women's rights advocates Susan B. Anthony and Elizabeth Cady Stanton began to promote woman suffrage in 1866 when the issue of black suffrage arose, and subsequently assailed the proposed Fifteenth Amendment for excluding women. By the end of the 1860s, activists had formed two competing suffragist organizations.

tors had broadened the scope of American democracy by passing three constitutional amendments. The Thirteenth Amendment abolished slavery, the Fourteenth expanded civil rights, and the Fifteenth prohibited the denial of suffrage on the basis of race (see Table 16.2). Congress had also readmitted the former Confederate states into the Union. But after 1868 congressional momentum slowed, and in 1869, when

TABLE 16.2 The Reconstruction Amendments

Amendment and Date of Congressional Passage	Provisions	Ratification
Thirteenth (January 1865)	Prohibited slavery in the United States.	December 1865.
Fourteenth (June 1866)	Defined citizenship to include all persons born or naturalized in the United States.	July 1868, after Congress made ratification a prerequisite for readmission of ex-Confederate states to the Union.
	Provided proportional loss of congressional representation for any state that denied suffrage to any of its male citizens.	
	Disqualified prewar officeholders who supported the Confederacy from state or national office.	
	Repudiated the Confederate debt.	
Fifteenth (February 1869)	Prohibited the denial of suffrage because of race, color, or previous condition of servitude.	March 1870; ratification required of Virginia, Texas, Mississippi, and Georgia for readmission to the Union.

Ulysses S. Grant became president, enmity between Congress and the chief executive ceased. The theater of action now shifted to the South, where an era of tumultuous change was under way.

RECONSTRUCTION GOVERNMENTS

During the unstable years of presidential Reconstruction, 1865–1867, the southern states had to create new governments, revive the war-torn economy, and face the impact of emancipation. Social and economic crises abounded. War costs had cut into southern wealth, cities and factories lay in rubble, plantation-labor systems distintegrated, and racial tensions flared. Beginning in 1865, freedmen organized black conventions, politi-

The Carpetbaggers

Southern Democrats disparaged carpetbaggers as interlopers who hoped to "fatten on our misfortunes." In reality, most were Union army officers, businessmen, and professionals with capital and energy to invest in the South. This 1869 sheet-music cover caricatures the carpetbaggers by depicting a predatory northern migrant casting a greedy eye upon the defeated Confederacy.

cal meetings at which they protested ill treatment and demanded equal rights. These meetings occurred in a climate of violence. Race riots erupted in major southern cities, such as Memphis in May 1866 and in New Orleans two months later. Even when Congress imposed military rule, ex-Confederates did not feel defeated. "Having reached bottom, there is hope now that we may rise again," a South Carolina planter wrote in his diary.

Congressional Reconstruction, supervised by federal troops, took effect in the spring of 1867. The Johnson regimes were dismantled, state constitutional conventions met, and voters elected new state governments, which Republicans dominated. In 1868 a majority of the former Confederate states rejoined the Union, and two years later, the last four states—Virginia, Mississippi, Georgia, and Texas—followed.

Readmission to the Union did not end the process of Reconstruction, for Republicans still held power in the South. But Republican rule was very brief, lasting less than a decade in all southern states, far less in most of them, and on average under five years. Opposition from southern Democrats, the landowning elite, thousands of vigilantes, and indeed, most white voters proved insurmountable. Still, the governments formed under congressional Reconstruction were unique, because black men, including ex-slaves, participated in them. In no other society where slaves had been liberated—neither Haiti, where slaves had revolted in the 1790s, nor the British Caribbean islands, where Parliament had ended slavery in 1833—had freedmen gained democratic political rights.

A New Electorate

The Reconstruction laws of 1867–1868 transformed the southern electorate by temporarily disfranchising 10 to 15 percent of potential white voters and by enfranchising more than seven hundred thousand freedmen. Outnumbering white voters in the South by one hundred thousand, blacks held voting majorities in five states.

The new electorate provided a base for the Republican party, which had never existed in the South. In the eyes of the Democrats, southern Republicans comprised three types of scoundrels: northern "carpetbaggers," who had allegedly come south seeking wealth and power (with so few possessions that they could be stuffed into traveling bags made of carpet material); southern "scalawags," predominantly poor and ignorant whites, who sought to profit from Republican rule; and

hordes of uneducated freedmen, who were ready prey for Republican manipulators. Although the "carpetbag" and "scalawag" labels were derogatory and the stereotypes that they conveyed inaccurate, they remain in use as a form of shorthand. Crossing class and racial lines, the hastily established Republican party was in fact a loose coalition of diverse factions with often contradictory goals.

To northerners who moved south after the Civil War, the former Confederacy was an undeveloped region, ripe with possibility. The carpetbaggers' ranks included many former Union soldiers who hoped to buy land, open factories, build railroads, or simply enjoy the warmer climate. Albion Tourgee, a young lawyer who had served with the New York and Ohio volunteers, for example, relocated in North Carolina after the war to improve his health. There he worked as a journalist, politician, and Republican judge. Perhaps no more than twenty thousand northern migrants like Tourgee—including veterans, missionaries, teachers, and Freedmen's Bureau agents—headed south immediately after the war, and many returned north by 1867. But those who remained played a disproportionate part in Reconstruction politics, for they held almost one out of three state offices.

Scalawags, white southerners who supported the Republicans, included some entrepreneurs who applauded party policies such as the national banking system and high protective tariffs as well as some prosperous planters, former Whigs who had opposed secession. Their numbers included a few prominent politicians, among them James Orr of South Carolina and Mississippi's governor James Alcorn, who became Republicans in order to retain influence and limit Republican radicalism. Most scalawags, however, were small farmers from the mountain regions of North Carolina, Georgia, Alabama, and Arkansas. Former Unionists who had owned no slaves and had no allegiance to the landowning elite, they sought to improve their economic position. Unlike carpetbaggers, they were not committed to black rights or black suffrage; most came from regions with small black populations and cared little whether blacks voted or not. Scalawags held the most political offices during Reconstruction, but they proved the least stable element of the southern Republican coalition: eventually, many drifted back to the Democratic fold.

Freedmen, the backbone of southern Republicanism, provided eight out of ten Republican votes. Republican rule lasted longest in states with the largest black populations—South Carolina, Mississippi, Alabama, and

Louisiana. Introduced to politics in the black conventions of 1865–1867, the freedmen sought land, education, civil rights, and political equality and remained loyal Republicans. As an elderly freedman announced at a Georgia political convention in 1867, "We know our friends." Although Reconstruction governments would have collapsed without black votes, freedmen held at most one in five political offices. Blacks served in all southern legislatures and filled many high posts in Louisiana, Mississippi, and South Carolina. They constituted a majority, however, only in the legislature of South Carolina, whose population was more than 60 percent black. No blacks became governor, and only two served in the U.S. Senate, Hiram Revels and Blanche K. Bruce, both of Mississippi. In the House of Representatives, a mere 6 percent of southern members were black, and almost half of these came from South Carolina.

Republicans in the South Carolina Legislature, c. 1868

Only in South Carolina did blacks comprise a majority in the legislature and dominate the legislative process during Reconstruction. This photographic collage of "Radical" legislators, black and white, suggests the extent of black representation. In 1874, blacks won the majority of seats in South Carolina's state senate as well.

RADICAL MEMBERS
OF THE SO. CA. LEGISLATURE.

Black officeholders on the state level formed a political elite. They often differed from black voters in background, education, wealth, and complexion. A disproportionate number were literate blacks who had been free before the Civil War. (More former slaves held office on the local level than on the state level.) South Carolina's roster of elected officials illustrates some distinctions between high-level black officeholders and the freedmen who voted for them. Among those sent to Congress, almost all claimed some secondary education; some held advanced degrees. In the state legislature, most black members, unlike their constituents, came from large towns and cities; many had spent time in the North; and some were well-off property owners or even former slaveowners. Color differences were evident, too: 43 percent of South Carolina's black state legislators were mulattos (mixed race), compared to only 7 percent of the state's black population.

Black officials and black voters often had different priorities. Most freedmen cared mainly about their economic future, especially about acquiring land, whereas black officeholders cared most about attaining equal rights. Still, both groups shared high expectations and prized enfranchisement. "We'd walk fifteen miles in wartime to find out about the battle," a Georgia freedman declared. "We can walk fifteen miles and more to find how to vote."

Republican Rule

Large numbers of blacks participated in American government for the first time in the state constitutional conventions of 1867–1868. The South Carolina convention had a black majority, and in Louisiana half the delegates were freedmen. The conventions forged democratic changes in their state constitutions. Delegates abolished property qualifications for officeholding, made many appointive offices elective, and redistricted state legislatures more equitably. All states established universal manhood suffrage, and Louisiana and South Carolina opened public schools to both races. These provisions integrated the New Orleans public schools as well as the University of South Carolina, from which whites withdrew.

But no state instituted land reform. When proposals for land confiscation and redistribution arose at the state conventions, they fell to defeat, as they had in Congress. Hoping to attract northern investment to the reconstructed South, southern Republicans hesitated to threaten property rights or to adopt land-reform measures that northern Republicans had rejected. South Carolina did set up a commission to buy land and make it available to freedmen, and several states changed their tax structures to force uncultivated land onto the market, but in no case was ex-Confederate land confiscated.

Once civil power shifted from the federal army to the new state governments, Republican administrations began ambitious programs of public works. They built roads, bridges, and public buildings; approved railroad bonds; and funded institutions to care for orphans, the insane, and the disabled. Republican regimes also expanded state bureaucracies, raised salaries for government employees, and formed state militia, in which blacks were often heavily represented. Finally, they created public-school systems, almost nonexistent in the South until then.

Because rebuilding the devastated South and expanding state government cost millions of dollars, state debts and taxes skyrocketed. State legislatures increased poll taxes or "head" taxes (levies on individuals); enacted luxury, sales, and occupation taxes; and imposed new property taxes. Before the war southern states had taxed property in slaves but had barely taxed landed property. Now state governments assessed even small farmers' holdings, and propertied planters paid what they considered an excessive burden. Although northern tax rates still exceeded southern rates, southern landowners resented the new levies. In their view, Reconstruction was punishing the propertied, already beset by labor problems and falling land values, in order to finance the vast expenditures of Republican legislators.

To Reconstruction's foes, Republican rule was wasteful and corrupt, the "most stupendous system of organized robbery in history." A state like Mississippi, which had an honest government, provided little basis for such charges. But critics could justifiably point to Louisiana, where the governor pocketed thousands of dollars of state funds and corruption permeated all government transactions (as indeed it had before the war). Or they could cite South Carolina, where bribery ran rampant. Besides government officials who took bribes, the main postwar profiteers were the railroad promoters who doled them out. Not all were Republicans. Nor did the Republican regimes in the South hold a monopoly on corruption. After the war bribery pervaded government transactions North and South, and far more money changed hands in the North. But critics assailed Republican rule for additional reasons.

Counterattacks

Ex-Confederates chafed at black enfranchisement and spoke with dread about the "horror of Negro domination." As soon as congressional Reconstruction took

effect, former Confederates began a clamorous campaign to undermine it. Democratic newspapers assailed delegates to North Carolina's constitutional convention as an "Ethiopian minstrelsy . . . baboons, monkeys, mules . . . and other jackasses," and demeaned Louisiana's constitution as "the work of ignorant Negroes cooperating with a gang of white adventurers."

The Democrats did not mobilize until the southern states were readmitted to the Union. Then they swung into action, calling themselves Conservatives in order to attract former Whigs. At first they sought to win the votes of blacks; but when that effort failed, they tried other tactics. In 1868–1869 Georgia Democrats challenged the eligibility of black legislators and expelled them from office. In response, the federal government reestablished military rule in Georgia, but determined Democrats still undercut Republican power. In every southern state, they contested elections, backed dissident Republican factions, elected some Democratic legislators, and made inroads among scalawags, siphoning some of their votes from the Republicans.

Vigilante efforts to reduce black votes bolstered the Democrats' campaigns to win white ones. Antagonism toward free blacks, long a motif in southern life, had resurged after the war. In 1865 Freedmen's Bureau agents itemized outrages against blacks, including shooting, murder, rape, arson, roasting, and "severe and inhuman beating." Vigilante groups sprang up spontaneously in all parts of the former Confederacy under names like moderators, regulators, and in Louisiana, Knights of the White Camelia. One group rose to dominance. In the spring of 1866, when the Johnson governments were still in power, six young Confederate war veterans in Tennessee formed a social club, the Ku Klux Klan, distinguished by elaborate rituals, hooded costumes, and secret passwords. New Klan dens spread through the state; within a year Democratic politicians and former Confederate officers took control of them. By the election of 1868, when black suffrage took effect, Klan dens existed in all the southern states. Klansmen embarked on night raids to intimidate black voters. No longer a social club, the Ku Klux Klan was now a widespread terrorist movement and a violent arm of the Democratic party.

The Klan sought to suppress black voting, reestablish white supremacy, and topple the Reconstruction governments. Its members attacked Freedmen's Bureau officials, white Republicans, black militia units, economically successful blacks, and black voters. Concentrated in areas where the black and white populations were most evenly balanced and racial tensions greatest, Klan dens adapted their tactics and timing to local

The Ku Klux Klan

The menacing disguise characterized the Ku Klux Klan's campaign of intimidation during Reconstruction. This Mississippi Klansman, black-hooded and carrying a pistol, displays the regalia he used to threaten African Americans. Captured by federal authorities in 1871, he turned state's witness and revealed to his captors the Klan's secret passwords, signals, and rituals.

conditions. In Mississippi the Klan targeted black schools; in Alabama it concentrated on Republican officeholders. In Arkansas terror reigned in 1868; in Georgia and Florida Klan strength surged in 1870. Some Democrats denounced Klan members as "cut-throats and riff-raff." But prominent ex-Confederates were also known to be active Klansmen, among them General Nathan Bedford Forrest, the leader of the 1864 Fort Pillow massacre, in which Confederate troops who captured a Union garrison in Tennessee murdered black soldiers after they had surrendered. Vigilantism united southern whites of different social classes and drew on the energy of many Confederate veterans. In areas where the Klan was inactive, other vigilante groups took its place.

Republican legislatures outlawed vigilantism through laws providing for fines and imprisonment of offenders. But the state militia could not enforce the laws, and state officials turned to the federal government for help. In May 1870 Congress passed the Enforcement Act to protect black voters, but witnesses to violations were afraid to testify against vigilantes, and local juries refused to convict them. The Second Enforcement Act, which provided for federal supervision of southern elections, followed in February 1871. Two months later Congress passed the Third Enforcement Act, or Ku Klux Klan Act, which strengthened punishments for those who prevented blacks from voting. It also empowered the president to use federal troops to enforce the law and to suspend the writ of habeas corpus in areas that he declared in insurrection. (The writ of habeas corpus is a court order requiring that the detainer of a prisoner bring that person to court and show cause for his or her detention.) President Grant, elected in 1868, suspended the writ in nine South Carolina counties that had been devastated by Klan attacks. The Ku Klux Klan Act generated thousands of arrests; most terrorists, however, escaped conviction.

By 1872 the federal government had effectively suppressed the Klan, but vigilantism had served its purpose. Only a large military presence in the South could have protected black rights, and the government in Washington never provided it. Instead, federal power in the former Confederacy diminished. President Grant steadily reduced troop levels in the South; Congress allowed the Freedmen's Bureau to die in 1869; and the Enforcement acts became dead letters. White southerners, a Georgia politician told congressional investigators in 1871, could not discard "a feeling of bitterness, a feeling that the Negro is a sort of instinctual enemy of ours." The battle over Reconstruction was in essence a battle over the implications of emancipation, and it had begun as soon as the war ended.

THE IMPACT OF EMANCIPATION

"The master he says we are all free," a South Carolina slave declared in 1865. "But it don't mean we is white. And it don't mean we is equal." Emancipated slaves faced extreme handicaps. They had no property, tools, or capital and usually possessed meager skills. Only a minority had been trained as artisans, and more than 95 percent were illiterate. Still, the exhilaration of freedom was overwhelming, as slaves realized, "Now I am

for myself" and "All that I make is my own." At emancipation they gained the right to their own labor and a new sense of autonomy. Under Reconstruction the freed blacks asserted their independence by seeking to cast off white control and shed the vestiges of slavery.

Confronting Freedom

For the former slaves, liberty meant they could move where they pleased. Some moved out of the slave quarters and set up dwellings elsewhere on their plantations; others left their plantations entirely. Landowners found that one freed slave after another vanished, with house servants and artisans leading the way. "I have never in my life met with such ingratitude," one South Carolina mistress exclaimed when a former slave ran off. Field workers, who had less contact with whites, were more likely to stay behind or more reluctant to leave. Still, flight remained tempting. "The moment they see an opportunity to improve themselves, they will move on," diarist Mary Chesnut observed.

Emancipation stirred waves of migration within the former Confederacy. Some freed slaves left the Upper South for the Deep South and the Southwest—Florida, Mississippi, Arkansas, and Texas—where planters desperately needed labor and paid higher wages. Even more left the countryside for towns and cities, traditional havens of independence for blacks. Urban black populations sometimes doubled or tripled after emancipation (see A Place in Time: Atlanta Reconstructed). Overall during the 1860s, the urban black population rose by 75 percent, and the number of blacks in small rural towns grew as well. Many migrants eventually returned to their old locales, but they tended to settle on neighboring plantations rather than with their former owners. Freedom was the major goal. "I's wants to be a free man, cum when I please, and nobody say nuffin to me, nor order me roun'," an Alabama freedman told a northern journalist.

Freed blacks' yearnings to find lost family members prompted much movement. "They had a passion, not so much for wandering as for getting together," a Freedmen's Bureau official commented. Parents sought children who had been sold; husbands and wives who had been separated by sale, or who lived on different plantations, reunited; and families reclaimed youngsters from masters' homes. The Freedmen's Bureau helped former slaves get information about missing relatives and travel to find them. Bureau agents also tried to resolve entanglements over the multiple alliances of spouses who had been separated under slavery.

Reunification efforts often failed. Some fugitive slaves had died during the war or were untraceable. Other ex-slaves had formed new partnerships and could not revive old ones. "I am married," one husband wrote to a former wife (probably in a dictated letter), "and my wife [and I] have two children, and if you and I meet it would make a very dissatisfied family." But there were success stories, too. "I's hunted an' hunted till I track you up here," one freedman told his wife, whom he found in a refugee camp twenty years after their separation by sale.

Once reunited, freed blacks quickly legalized unions formed under slavery, sometimes in mass ceremonies of up to seventy couples. Legal marriage affected family life. Men asserted themselves as household heads; wives and children of able-bodied men often withdrew from the labor force. "When I married my wife, I married her to wait on me and she has got all she can do right here for me and the children," a Tennessee freedman explained.

Black women's desire to secure the privileges of domestic life caused planters severe labor shortages. Before the war at least half of field workers had been women; in 1866, a southern journal claimed, men performed almost all the field labor. Still, by the end of Reconstruction, many black women had returned to agricultural work as part of sharecropper families. Others took paid work in cities, as laundresses, cooks, and domestic servants. (White women often sought employment as well, for the war had incapacitated many white breadwinners, reduced the supply of future husbands, and left families destitute or in diminished circumstances.) However, former slaves continued to view stable, independent domestic life, especially the right to bring up their own children, as a major blessing of freedom. In 1870 eight out of ten black families in the cotton-producing South were two-parent families, about the same proportion as among whites.

Black Institutions

The freed blacks' desire for independence also led to the postwar growth of black churches. In the late 1860s, some freedmen congregated at churches operated by northern missionaries; others withdrew from white-run churches and formed their own. The African Methodist Episcopal church, founded by Philadelphia blacks in the 1790s, gained thousands of new southern members. Negro Baptist churches sprouted everywhere, often growing out of plantation "praise meetings," religious gatherings organized by slaves.

The black churches offered a fervent, participatory experience. They also provided relief, raised funds for schools, and supported Republican policies. From the outset black ministers assumed leading political roles, first in the black conventions of 1865–1866 and later in the Reconstruction governments. After southern Democrats excluded most freedmen from political life at

The Freedmen's School

Supported by the Freedmen's Bureau, northern freedmen's aid societies, and black denominations, freedmen's schools reached about 12 percent of school-age black children in the South by 1870. Here, a northern teacher poses with her students at a school in rural North Carolina.

At the Civil War's end, Atlanta presented "a scene of charred and desolate ruins." Before abandoning the city in September 1864, General John Bell Hood and his Confederate army had destroyed its railroads, locomotives, depots, ammunition, and any other property that could help the enemy. Arriving amid smoke and flames after a six-week siege, General William T. Sherman and the Union Army finished the fiery job that Hood had begun. When Sherman moved on, about four hundred buildings remained standing amid burned-out ruins and twisted rails. One 1865 visitor found "a wilderness of mud, with a confused jumble of railroad sheds" and the bones and skulls of animals lying in the street.

Perched at the southern edge of the Appalachian mountains in the wooded hills of upland Georgia, Atlanta had long been known for enterprise. A railroad center since the 1840s, with rail lines that extended to the west and to the sea, Atlanta was a portal for freight en route between the South and other regions. During the war, the city had grown rapidly especially as a center for the manufacture and distribution of war supplies. When peace came in 1865, Atlanta swiftly leapt back to life.

"From all this ruin and devastation, a new city is springing up with marvelous rapidity," wrote the young northern journalist Sidney Andrews during his visit in the fall of 1865. Its narrow streets, he reported, were "alive from morning till night with drays and carts and hand-barrows and wagons . . . with a never-ending throng of pushing and crowding and scrambling and eager and enterprising men, all bent on building and trading and swift-fortune-making." Other observers confirmed this view. "Busy life is resuming its sway," wrote merchant Samuel Richards in July 1865. All kinds of stores had appeared, he noted, "as if by magic." As a new Atlanta arose from the ruins, commerce flourished. "The one sole idea first in everyone's mind is to make money," Andrews declared.

Atlanta's phenomenal postwar growth depended on railroads. Four rail lines converged at the very center of the city, in a thriving commercial district near the most prosperous residential area, and made Atlanta the trading hub of the postwar South. The volume of cotton shipped out of the city leapt from 17,000 bales in 1867 to 76,000 in 1876. The Georgia convention of 1868, moreover, voted to move the state capital from the small town of Milledgeville to Atlanta. Legislators and lobbyists arrived, and real estate values rose. "Our friends in Atlanta are a fast people," a Milledgeville newspaper sniffed in 1867. "They make money fast and they spend it fast. . . . To a stranger the whole city seems to be running on wheels."

Atlanta's vibrant economy boasted diversity. Local manufacturers produced food products, such as flour, cornmeal, meat, candy, coffee, beer, and whiskey, and consumer goods, such as tobacco, dry goods, clothing, boots, shoes, furniture, books, and hardware. Armies of "drummers," or traveling sales agents, who dealt directly with store owners in small towns, canvassed the South. Banks and financial institutions arose, city boosters planned extravagant expositions, and newspapers touted the city's success. Henry W. Grady, editor of the *Atlanta Constitution*, celebrated the "sturdy genius of Atlanta's self-made men," such as cotton magnate S. M. Inman and

Atlanta's depot in ruin after Sherman's siege of the city, 1864.

druggist Asa Griggs Candler, who had bought some formulas for patent medicines. One of these, a headache remedy, earned him a fortune. Selling Coca-Cola out of his drugstore, Candler reached an expanding market.

As the economy boomed, Atlanta's population surged, leaping from 9,500 in 1860 to 22,000 in 1870 to 37,000 in 1880 and 65,000 in 1890. A high proportion of newcomers were African-American. One-fifth of the city's residents in 1860, blacks accounted for 46 percent in 1870 (see Table 16.3). Like freed people elsewhere, many in Georgia moved to cities. Settling first in tents and shanties, postwar black migrants faced food shortages, unpaved streets, and poor sanitation. Employment was limited. Men found jobs as servants, porters, and laborers, and some worked in industry. Black women, the majority of African-American migrants to Atlanta, labored as cooks, laundresses, nurses, and maids. Still, urban life represented liberty, opportunity, and even a measure of refuge from harassment. "The military is here and nobody interferes with us," declared a black Republican legislator in 1866. "We cannot stop anywhere else so safely."

By 1870 groups of blacks lived in every ward. But trends toward residential segregation were under way. African-Americans moved away from the central city, with its business district and elite residential area, to lower elevations on the perimeter. By the 1880s over a third of Atlanta's blacks lived in a handful of areas, such as Sumner Hill, a tract of land in the southeast—including an area once used as the city dump—that had been plundered by Sherman's troops. They also lived in Shermantown to its north, in Diamond Hill on the west side of town, or in smaller clusters in Merchanicsville and Pittsburg in the southeast. In all these areas, schools and churches arose. In Sumner Hill, in 1867, the African Methodist Episcopal denomination started a chapel and the American Missionary Association built a school. Northern Methodists founded Clarke University (1869). Diamond Hill welcomed the Atlanta Baptist Seminary, which later became Morehouse College (1879), the Atlanta Baptist Female Seminary (1881), which later became Spelman College, and Atlanta University, which acquired land in 1879. Within black communities, too, African-Americans built enterprises to serve a black clientele—grocery stores, barber shops, funeral parlors, and other small businesses. Atlanta's black enclaves created an economic base for the growth of an African-American business class.

Atlanta's new black voters boosted the fortunes of the Republican party, but the Republicans never won control of city government. Reconstruction in fact was brief. By 1871 Democratic power was secure and the spirit of reconciliation firmly in place. City business leaders welcomed northern capital and championed reunion. They embraced the conquering federal troops in the late 1860s, and in 1879 hosted the triumphant Union war hero, General Sherman. By the 1880s dynamic Atlanta symbolized the enterprise and energy of the "New South." Meanwhile, in Shermantown and Sumner Hill, Atlanta's large black population lived a life apart. "[B]y far the largest proportion of Negroes are never really known to us," a reporter observed in 1881. "They . . . drift off to themselves and are almost as far from the white people . . . as if the two races never met."

TABLE 16.3 **Atlanta's Population**

	1860	1870	1880	1890
White	7,615	11,860	21,079	39,416
Black	1.939	9,929	16,330	28,098
% Black	20	46	44	43

Source: Howard N. Rabinowitz, *Race Relations in the Urban South, 1865–1890* (1978), p. 19.

Bustling Whitehall Street, a center of commerce, 1882.

Domestic workers with tools of their trades—bridle, pot, broom, duster, wheelbarrow, and wagon—pose in front of their employer's home.

Reconstruction's end, ministers remained the main pillars of authority within black communities.

Black schools played a crucial role for freedmen as well. The ex-slaves eagerly sought literacy for themselves and even more for their children. At emancipation blacks organized their own schools, which the Freedmen's Bureau soon supervised. Northern philanthropic societies paid the wages of instructors, about half of them women. In 1869 the bureau reported that there were more than four thousand black schools in the former Confederacy. Within three years each southern state had a public-school system, at least in principle, generally with separate schools for blacks and whites. Advanced schools for blacks opened as well, to train tradespeople, teachers, and ministers. The Freedmen's Bureau and northern organizations like the American Missionary Association helped found Howard, Atlanta, and Fisk universities (all started in 1866–1867) and Hampton Institute (1868).

Despite these advances, black education remained limited. Few rural blacks could reach the freedmen's schools located in towns. Underfunded black public schools, similarly inaccessible to most rural black children, held classes only for very short seasons and were sometimes the targets of vigilante attacks. At the end of Reconstruction, more than 80 percent of the black population was still illiterate. Still, the proportion of youngsters who could not read and write had declined and would continue to fall (see Table 16.4).

School segregation and other forms of racial separation were taken for granted. Some black codes of 1865–1866 had segregated public-transit conveyances and public accommodations. Even after the invalidation of the codes, the custom of segregation continued on streetcars, steamboats, and trains as well as in churches, theaters, inns, and restaurants. On railroads, for example, whites could ride in the "ladies' car" or first-class car, whereas blacks had to stay in smoking cars or boxcars with benches. In 1870 Senator Charles Sumner of Massachusetts began promoting a bill to desegregate schools, transportation facilities, juries, and public accommodations. After Sumner's death in 1874, Congress honored him by enacting a new law, the Civil Rights Act of 1875, which encompassed many of his proposals, except for the controversial school-integration provision. But the law was rarely enforced, and in 1883, in the *Civil Rights Cases,* the Supreme Court invalidated it. The Fourteenth Amendment did not prohibit discrimination by individuals, the Court ruled, only that perpetrated by the state.

White southerners rejected the prospect of racial integration, which they insisted would lead to racial mixing. "If we have social equality, we shall have intermarriage," one white southerner contended, "and if we have intermarriage, we shall degenerate." Urban blacks sometimes challenged segregation practices, and black legislators promoted bills to desegregate public transit. Some black officeholders decried all forms of racial separatism. "The sooner we as a people forget our sable complexion," said a Mobile official, "the better it will be for us as a race." But most freed blacks were less interested in "social equality," in the sense of interracial mingling, than in black liberty and community. The newly formed postwar elite—teachers, ministers, and politicians—served black constituencies and therefore had a vested interest in separate black institutions. Rural blacks, too, widely preferred all-black institutions. They had little desire to mix with whites. On the contrary, they sought freedom from white control. Above all else, they wanted to secure personal independence by acquiring land.

TABLE 16.4 **Percentage of Persons Unable to Write, by Age Group, 1870–1890, in South Carolina, Georgia, Alabama, Mississippi, and Louisiana**

Age Group	1870	1880	1890
10–14			
Black	78.9	74.1	49.2
White	33.2	34.5	18.7
15–20			
Black	85.3	73.0	54.1
White	24.2	21.0	14.3
Over 20			
Black	90.4	82.3	75.5
White	19.8	17.9	17.1

Source: Roger Ransom and Richard Sutch, *One Kind of Freedom* (Cambridge: Cambridge University Press, 1978), 30.

Land, Labor, and Sharecropping

"The sole ambition of the freedman," a New Englander wrote from South Carolina in 1865, "appears to be to become the owner of a little piece of land, there to erect a humble home, and to dwell in peace and security, at his own free will and pleasure." Indeed, to freed blacks everywhere, "forty acres and a mule" (a phrase that originated in 1864 when Union General William T. Sherman set aside land on the South Carolina Sea Islands for black settlement) promised emancipation from plantation labor, from white domination, and from cotton, the

"slave crop." Just as garden plots had provided a measure of autonomy under slavery, so did landownership signify economic independence afterward. "We want to be placed on land until we are able to buy it and make it our own," a black minister had told General Sherman in Georgia during the war. Some freedmen defended their right to the land they lived on by pointing out that they and their forebears had worked on it for decades without pay.

But freedmen's visions of landownership failed to materialize, for, as we have seen, neither Congress nor the southern states imposed large-scale land reform. Some freedmen did obtain land with the help of the Union army or the Freedmen's Bureau, and black soldiers sometimes pooled resources to buy land, as on the Sea Islands of South Carolina and Georgia. The federal government also attempted to provide ex-slaves with land. In 1866 Congress passed the Southern Homestead Act, which set aside 44 million acres of public land in five southern states for freedmen and loyal whites. This acreage contained poor soil, and few former slaves had the resources to survive even until their first harvest. About four thousand blacks resettled on homesteads under the law, but most were unable to establish farms. (White southern homesteaders fared little better.) By the end of Reconstruction, only a small minority of former slaves in each state owned working farms. In Georgia in 1876, for instance, blacks controlled a mere 1.3 percent of total acreage. Without large-scale land reform, the obstacles to black landownership remained overwhelming.

What were these obstacles? First, most freedmen lacked the capital to buy land and the equipment needed to work it. Furthermore, white southerners on the whole opposed selling land to blacks. Most important, planters sought to preserve a black labor force. They insisted that freedmen would work only under coercion, and not at all if the possibility of landownership arose. As soon as the war ended, the white South took steps to make sure that black labor would remain available where it was needed, on the plantations.

During presidential Reconstruction, southern state legislatures tried to limit black mobility and to preserve a captive labor force through the black codes. Under labor contracts in effect in 1865–1866, freedmen received wages, housing, food, and clothing in exchange for fieldwork. With cash scarce, wages usually took the form of a very small share of the crop, often one-eighth or less, divided among the entire plantation work force. Freedmen's Bureau agents promoted the new labor system; they urged freedmen to sign labor contracts and tried to ensure adequate wages. Imbued with the north-ern free-labor ideology, which held that wage workers could rise to the status of self-supporting tradesmen and property owners, bureau officials endorsed black wage labor as an interim arrangement that would lead to economic independence. "You must begin at the bottom of the ladder and climb up," Freedmen's Bureau head O. O. Howard exhorted a group of Louisiana freedmen in 1865.

But the freedmen disliked the new wage system, especially the use of gang labor, which resembled the work pattern under slavery. Planters had complaints, too. In some regions the black labor force had shrunk to half its prewar size or less, due to the migration of freedmen and to black women's withdrawal from fieldwork. Once united in defense of slavery, planters now competed for black workers. But the freedmen, whom planters often scorned as lazy and incorrigible, did not intend to work as long or as hard as they had labored under slavery. One planter estimated that workers accomplished only "two-fifths of what they did under the old system." As productivity fell, so did land values. Some planters considered importing white immigrant labor, but they doubted that whites would perform black fieldwork for long. To top off the planters' woes, cotton prices plummeted, for during the war northern and foreign buyers had found new sources of cotton in Egypt and India, and the world supply had vastly increased. Finally, the harvests of 1866 and 1867 were extremely poor. By then an agricultural impasse had been reached: landowners lacked labor and freedmen lacked land. But free blacks, unlike slaves, had the right to enter into contracts—or to refuse to do so—and thereby gained some leverage.

Planters and freedmen began experimenting with new labor schemes, including the division of plantations into small tenancies (see Map 16.2). Sharecropping, the most widespread arrangement, evolved as a compromise. Under the sharecropping system, landowners subdivided large plantations into farms of thirty to fifty acres, which they rented to freedmen under annual leases for a share of the crop, usually half. Freedmen preferred this system to wage labor because it represented a step toward independence. Heads of households could use the labor of family members. Moreover, a half-share of the crop far exceeded the fraction that freedmen had received as wages under the black codes. Planters often spoke of sharecropping as a concession to freedmen, but they gained as well. Landowners retained power over tenants, because annual leases did not have to be renewed; they could expel undesirable tenants at the end of the year. Planters also shared the risk of planting with tenants: if a crop failed, both suffered the loss. Most

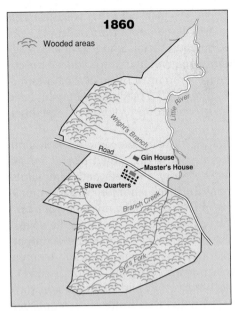
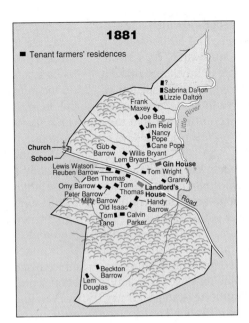

MAP 16.2

The Barrow Plantation, 1860 and 1881

The transformation of the Barrow plantation in Oglethorpe County, Georgia, illustrates the striking changes in southern agriculture during Reconstruction. Before the Civil War, about 135 slaves worked on the plantation, supervised by an overseer and a slave foreman. After the war, the former slaves who remained on the plantation signed labor contracts with owner David Crenshaw Barrow. Supervised by a hired foreman, the freedmen grew cotton for wages in competing squads, but they disliked the new arrangement. In the late 1860s, Barrow subdivided his land into tenant farms of twenty-five to thirty acres, and freedmen moved their households from the old slave quarters to their own farms. By 1881, 161 tenants lived on the Barrow plantation, at least half of them children. One out of four families was named Barrow.

important, planters retained control of their land and in some cases extended their holdings. The most productive land, therefore, remained in the hands of a small group of owners, as before the war. Sharecropping forced planters to relinquish daily control over the labor of freedmen but helped to preserve the planter elite.

Sharecropping arrangements varied widely. On sugar and rice plantations, the wage system continued; strong markets for sugar and rice meant that planters of those crops could pay their workers in cash—cash that cotton planters lacked. Some freedmen remained independent renters. Some landowners leased areas to white tenants, who then subcontracted with black labor. But by the end of the 1860s, sharecropping prevailed in the cotton South, and the new system continued to expand. A severe depression in 1873 drove many black renters into sharecropping. By then thousands of independent white farmers had become sharecroppers as well. Stung by wartime losses and by the dismal postwar economy, they sank into debt and lost their land to creditors. Many backcountry residents, no longer able to get by on subsistence farming, shifted to cash crops like cotton and

suffered the same fate. At the end of Reconstruction, one-third of the white farmers in Mississippi, for instance, were sharecroppers.

By 1880, 80 percent of the land in the cotton-producing states had been subdivided into tenancies, most of it farmed by sharecroppers, white and black (see Map 16.3). Indeed, white sharecroppers now outnumbered black ones, although a higher proportion of southern blacks, about 75 percent, were involved in the system. Changes in marketing and finance, meanwhile, made the sharecroppers' lot increasingly precarious.

Toward a Crop-Lien Economy

Before the Civil War, planters had depended on factors, or middlemen, who sold them supplies, extended credit, and marketed their crops through urban merchants. These long-distance credit arrangements were backed by the high value and liquidity of slave property. When slavery ended, the factorage system collapsed. The postwar South, with hundreds of thousands of tenants and sharecroppers, needed a far more localized network of credit.

MAP 16.3
Southern Sharecropping, 1880

The depressed economy of the late 1870s caused poverty and debt, increased tenancy among white farmers, and forced many renters, black and white, into sharecropping. By 1880 the sharecropping system pervaded most southern counties, with the highest concentrations in the cotton belt from South Carolina to eastern Texas.

(Source: U.S. Census Office, Tenth Census, 1880, *Report of the Production of Agriculture* (Washington, D.C.: Government Printing Office, 1883), Table 5.)

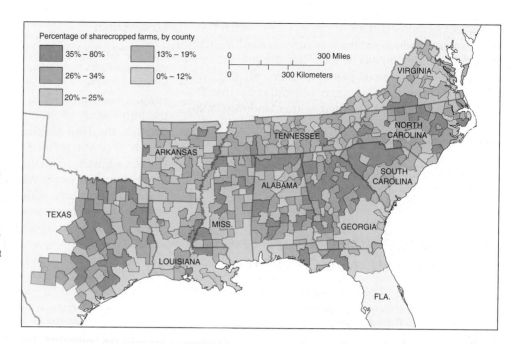

Percentage of sharecropped farms, by county

35% – 80% · 26% – 34% · 20% – 25% · 13% – 19% · 0% – 12%

Into the gap stepped the rural merchants (often themselves planters), who advanced supplies to tenants and sharecroppers on credit and sold their crops to wholesalers or textile manufacturers. Because renters had no property to use as collateral, the merchants secured their loans with a lien, or claim, on each farmer's next crop. Exorbitant interest rates of 50 percent or more quickly forced many tenants and sharecroppers into a cycle of indebtedness. Owing part of the crop to a landowner for rent, a sharecropper also owed a rural merchant a large sum (perhaps amounting to the rest of his crop, or more) for supplies. Illiterate tenants who could not keep track of their financial arrangements often fell prey to unscrupulous merchants. "A man that didn't know how to count would always lose," an Arkansas freedman later explained. Once a tenant's debts or alleged debts exceeded the value of his crop, he was tied to the land, to cotton, and to sharecropping.

By the end of Reconstruction, sharecropping and crop liens had transformed southern agriculture. They bound the region to staple production and prevented crop diversification. Despite plunging cotton prices, creditors—landowners and merchants—insisted that tenants raise only easily marketable cash crops. Short of capital, planters could no longer invest in new equipment or improve their land by such techniques as crop rotation and contour plowing. Soil depletion, land erosion, and agricultural backwardness soon locked much of the South into a cycle of poverty.

Trapped in perpetual debt, tenant farmers became the chief victims of the new agricultural order. Raising

Sharecroppers during Reconstruction
By the end of the 1870s, about three out of four African-Americans in the cotton-producing states had become sharecroppers. Below, sharecroppers pick cotton in Aiken, South Carolina.

cotton for distant markets, for prices over which they had no control, remained the only survival route open to poor farmers, regardless of race. But the low income thus derived often forced them into sharecropping and crop liens, from which escape was difficult. African-American tenants, who attained neither landownership nor economic independence, saw their political rights dwindle, too. As one southern regime after another returned to Democratic control, freedmen could no longer look to the state governments for protection. Nor could they turn to the federal government, for northern politicians were preoccupied with their own problems.

NEW CONCERNS IN THE NORTH, 1868–1876

The nomination of Ulysses S. Grant for president in 1868 launched an era of crises in national politics. Grant's two terms in office featured political scandals, a party revolt, a massive depression, and a steady retreat from Reconstruction policies. By the mid-1870s, northern voters cared more about the economic climate, unemployment, labor unrest, and currency problems than about the "southern question." Responsive to the shift in popular mood, Republicans became eager to end sectional conflict and turned their backs on the freedmen of the South.

Grantism

Republicans had good reason to pass over party leaders and nominate the popular Grant to succeed Andrew Johnson. A war hero, Grant was endorsed by Union veterans, widely admired in the North, and unscathed by the bitter feuds of Reconstruction politics. To oppose Grant in the 1868 election, the Democrats nominated New York governor Horatio Seymour, arch-critic of the Lincoln administration during the war and now a foe of Reconstruction. Grant ran on his personal popularity more than on issues. Although he carried all but eight states, the popular vote was very close; in the South, newly enfranchised freedmen provided Grant's margin of victory.

A strong leader in war, Grant proved a passive president. Although he lacked Johnson's instinct for disaster, he had little skill at politics. Many of his cabinet appointees—business executives, army men, and family friends—were mediocre if not unscrupulous; scandals plagued his administration. In 1869 financier Jay Gould and his partner Jim Fisk attempted to corner the gold market with the help of Grant's brother-in-law, a New York speculator. When gold prices tumbled, Gould salvaged his own fortune, but investors were ruined and Grant's reputation was tarnished. Then before the president's first term ended, his vice president, Schuyler Colfax, was found to be linked to the Crédit Mobilier, a fraudulent construction company created to skim off the profits of the Union Pacific Railroad. Using government funds granted to the railroad, the Union Pacific directors awarded padded construction contracts to the Crédit Mobilier, of which they were also the directors. Discredited, Colfax was dropped from the Grant ticket in 1872.

More trouble lay ahead. Grant's private secretary, Orville Babcock, was unmasked in 1875 after taking money from the "whiskey ring," a group of distillers who bribed federal agents to avoid paying millions of dollars in whiskey taxes. And in 1876 voters learned that

Boss Tweed

Thomas Nast's cartoons in *Harper's Weekly* helped topple New York Democratic boss William M. Tweed, who, with his associates, embodied corruption on a large scale. The Tweed Ring had granted lucrative franchises to companies they controlled, padded construction bills, practiced graft and extortion, and exploited every opportunity to plunder the city's funds.

Grant's secretary of war, William E. Belknap, had taken bribes to sell lucrative Indian trading posts in Oklahoma. Impeached and disgraced, Belknap resigned.

Although uninvolved in the scandals, Grant loyally defended his subordinates. To his critics, "Grantism" came to stand for fraud, bribery, and political corruption, evils that spread far beyond Washington. In Pennsylvania, for example, the Standard Oil Company and the Pennsylvania Railroad controlled the legislature. Urban politics also provided rich opportunities for graft and swindles. The New York City press revealed in 1872 that Democratic boss William M. Tweed, the leader of Tammany Hall, led a ring that had looted the city treasury and collected an estimated $200 million in kickbacks and payoffs. When Mark Twain and coauthor Charles Dudley Warner published their satiric novel *The Gilded Age* (1873), readers recognized the book's speculators, self-promoters, and opportunists as familiar types in public life. (The term "Gilded Age" was subsequently used to refer to the decades from the 1870s to the 1890s.)

Grant had some success in foreign policy. In 1872 his competent secretary of state, Hamilton Fish, engineered the settlement of the *Alabama* claims with England. To compensate for damage done by British-built raiders sold to the Confederacy during the war, an international tribunal awarded the United States $15.5 million. But the Grant administration faltered when it tried to add nonadjacent territory to the United States, as the Johnson administration had done. In 1867 Johnson's secretary of state, William H. Seward, had negotiated a treaty in which the United States bought Alaska from Russia at the bargain price of $7.2 million. Although the press mocked "Seward's Ice Box," the purchase kindled expansionists' hopes. In 1870 Grant decided to annex the eastern half of the Caribbean island of Santo Domingo. Today called the Dominican Republic, the territory had been passed back and forth since the late eighteenth century among France, Spain, and Haiti. Annexation, Grant believed, would promote Caribbean trade and provide a haven for persecuted southern blacks. American speculators anticipated windfalls from land sales, commerce, and mining. But Congress disliked Grant's plan. Senator Charles Sumner denounced it as an imperialist "dance of blood." The Senate rejected the annexation treaty and further diminished Grant's reputation.

As the election of 1872 approached, dissident Republicans expressed fears that "Grantism" at home and abroad would ruin the party. Even Grant's new running mate, Henry Wilson, referred to the president privately as a burden on his fellow Republicans. The dissi-

dents took action. Led by a combination of former Radicals and other Republicans left out of Grant's "Great Barbecue" (a disparaging reference to profiteers who feasted at the public trough), the president's critics formed their own party, the Liberal Republicans.

The Liberals' Revolt

The Liberal Republican revolt marked a turning point in Reconstruction history. By splitting the Republican party, the Liberals undermined support for Republican southern policy. (The label "liberal" at the time referred to those who endorsed economic doctrines such as free trade, the gold standard, and the law of supply and demand). The Liberals attacked the "regular" Republicans on several key issues. Denouncing "Grantism" and "spoilsmen" (political hacks who gained party office), they demanded civil-service reform to bring the "best men" into government. Rejecting the usual Republican high-tariff policy, they espoused free trade. Most important, the Liberals condemned "bayonet rule" in the South. Even some Republicans once known for radicalism now claimed that Reconstruction had achieved its goal: blacks had been enfranchised and could manage for themselves from now on. Corruption in government, North and South, they asserted, posed a greater danger than Confederate resurgence. In the South, indeed, corrupt Republican regimes were *kept* in power, the Liberals said, because the "best men"—the most capable politicians—were ex-Confederates who had been barred from officeholding.

For president the new party nominated *New York Tribune* editor Horace Greeley, who had inconsistently supported both a stringent reconstruction policy and leniency toward former rebels. The Democrats endorsed Greeley as well, despite his long-time condemnation of them. Their campaign slogan explained their support: "Anything to Beat Grant." Horace Greeley proved so diligent a campaigner that he worked himself to death making speeches from the back of a campaign train. He died a few weeks after the election.

Grant, who won 56 percent of the popular vote, carried all the northern states and most of the sixteen southern and border states. But the division among Republicans affected Reconstruction. To deprive the Liberals of a campaign issue, Grant Republicans in Congress, the "regulars," passed the Amnesty Act, which allowed all but a few hundred ex-Confederate officials to hold office. The flood of private amnesty acts that followed convinced white southerners that any ex-Confederate save Jefferson Davis could rise to power.

During Grant's second term, Republican desires to discard the "southern question" mounted as a depression of unprecedented scope gripped the whole nation.

The Panic of 1873

The postwar years brought accelerated industrialization, rapid economic expansion, and frantic speculation. Investors rushed to profit from rising prices, new markets, high tariffs, and seemingly boundless opportunities. Railroads provided the biggest lure. In May 1869 railroad executives drove a golden spike into the ground at Promontory Point, Utah, joining the Union Pacific and Central Pacific lines. The first transcontinental railroad heralded a new era. By 1873 almost four hundred railroad corporations crisscrossed the Northeast, consuming tons of coal and miles of steel rail from the mines and mills of Pennsylvania and neighboring states. Transforming the economy, the railroad boom led entrepreneurs to overspeculate, with drastic results.

Philadelphia banker Jay Cooke, who had helped finance the Union effort with his wartime bond campaign, had taken over a new transcontinental line, the Northern Pacific, in 1869. Northern Pacific securities sold briskly for several years, but in 1873 the line's construction costs outran new investments. In September of that year, his vaults full of bonds he could no longer sell, Cooke failed to meet his obligations, and his bank, the largest in the nation, shut down. A financial panic began; other firms collapsed, as did the stock market. The Panic of 1873 triggered a five-year depression. Banks closed, farm prices plummeted, steel furnaces stood idle, and one out of four railroads failed. Within two years, eighteen thousand businesses went bankrupt, and 3 million employees were out of jobs by 1878. Those still at work suffered repeated wage cuts; labor protests mounted; and industrial violence spread. The depression of the 1870s revealed that conflicts born of industrialization had replaced sectional divisions.

The depression also fed a dispute over currency that had begun in 1865. The Civil War had created fiscal chaos. During the war, Americans had used both national bank notes, yellow in color, which would eventually be converted into gold, and greenbacks, a paper currency not "backed" by a particular weight in gold. To stabilize the postwar currency, greenbacks would have to be withdrawn from circulation. This "sound-money" policy, favored by investors, was implemented by Treasury Secretary Hugh McCulloch with the backing of Congress. But those who depended on easy credit, both indebted farmers and manufacturers, wanted an expanding currency; that is, more greenbacks. Once the depression began, demands for such "easy money" rose. The issue divided both major parties and was compounded by another one: how to repay the federal debt.

During the war the Union government had borrowed what were then astronomical sums, on whatever terms it could get, mainly through the sale of war bonds—in effect, short-term federal IOUs—to private citizens. By 1869 the issue of war-debt repayment afflicted the Republican party, whose support came from voters with diverse financial interests. To pacify bondholders, Senator John Sherman of Ohio and other Republican leaders obtained passage of the Public Credit Act of 1869, which promised to pay the war debt in "coin," a term that meant either gold or silver. Holders of war bonds expected no less, although many had bought their bonds with greenbacks!

With investors reassured by the Public Credit Act, Sherman guided legislation through Congress that swapped the old short-term bonds for new ones payable over the next generation. In 1872 another bill in effect defined "coin" as "gold coin" by dropping the traditional silver dollar from the official coinage. Through a feat of ingenious compromise, which placated investors and debtors, Sherman preserved the public credit, the currency, and Republican unity. In 1875 he engineered the Specie Resumption Act, which promised to put the nation on the gold standard in 1879, while tossing a few more immediate but less important bones to Republican voters who wanted "easy money."

Republican leaders had acted not a moment too soon because when the Democrats gained control of the House in 1875, with the depression in full force, a verbal storm broke out. Many Democrats and some Republicans demanded that the silver dollar be restored in order to expand the currency and relieve the depression. These "free-silver" advocates secured passage of the Bland-Allison Act of 1878, which partially restored silver coinage. The law required the Treasury to buy $2–4 million worth of silver each month and turn it into coin but did not revive the silver standard. In 1876 other expansionists formed the Greenback party, which adopted the debtors' cause and fought to keep greenbacks in circulation. But despite the election of fourteen Greenback congressmen, they did not get even as far as the free-silver people had. As the nation emerged from depression in 1879, the clamor for "easy money" subsided, only to resurge in the 1890s. The controversial "money question" of the 1870s, never resolved, gave politicians and voters another reason to forget about the South.

Reconstruction and the Constitution

The Supreme Court of the 1870s also played a role in weakening northern support for Reconstruction. During the war, few cases of note had come before the Court. After the war, however, constitutional questions surged into prominence.

First, would the Court support congressional laws to protect freedmen's rights? The decision in *Ex parte Milligan* (1866) suggested not. In this case, the Court declared that a military commission established by the president or Congress could not try civilians in areas remote from war where the civil courts were functioning. Thus special military courts to enforce the Supplementary Freedmen's Bureau Act were doomed. Second, would the Court sabotage the congressional Reconstruction plan, as Republicans feared? Their qualms were valid, for if the Union was indissoluble, as the North had claimed during the war, then the concept of *restoring* states to the Union would be meaningless. In *Texas* v. *White* (1869), the Court ruled that although the Union was indissoluble and secession was legally impossible, the process of Reconstruction was still constitutional. It was grounded in Congress's power to ensure each state a republican form of government and to recognize the legitimate government in any state.

The 1869 decision protected the Republicans' Reconstruction plan. But in the 1870s, when cases arose involving the Fourteenth and Fifteenth amendments, the Court backed away from Reconstruction policy. In the *Slaughterhouse* cases of 1873, the Supreme Court began to chip away at the Fourteenth Amendment. The cases involved a business monopoly rather than freedmen's rights, but they provided an opportunity to interpret the amendment narrowly. In 1869 the Louisiana legislature had granted a monopoly over the New Orleans slaughterhouse business to one firm and closed down all other slaughterhouses in the interest of public health. The excluded butchers brought suit. The state had deprived them of their lawful occupation without due process of law, they claimed, and such action violated the Fourteenth Amendment, which guaranteed that no state could "abridge the privileges or immunities" of U.S. citizens. The Supreme Court upheld the Louisiana legislature by issuing a doctrine of "dual citizenship." The Fourteenth Amendment, declared the Court, protected only the rights of *national* citizenship, such as the right of interstate travel or the right to federal protection on the high seas. It did not protect those basic civil rights that fell to citizens by virtue of their *state* citizenship. Therefore, the federal government was not obliged to protect such rights against violation by the states. The *Slaughterhouse* decision came close to nullifying the intent of the Fourteenth Amendment—to secure freedmen's rights against state encroachment.

The Supreme Court again backed away from Reconstruction in two cases in 1876 involving the Enforcement Act of 1870, which had been enacted to protect black suffrage. In *U.S.* v. *Reese* and *U.S.* v. *Cruikshank*, the Supreme Court undercut the effectiveness of the act. Continuing its retreat from Reconstruction, the Supreme Court in 1883 invalidated both the Civil Rights Act of 1875 and the Ku Klux Klan Act of 1871. These decisions cumulatively dismantled the Reconstruction policies that Republicans had sponsored after the war and confirmed rising northern sentiment that Reconstruction's egalitarian goals could not be enforced.

Republicans in Retreat

The Republicans did not reject Reconstruction suddenly but rather disengaged from it gradually. The withdrawal process began with Grant's election to the presidency in 1868. Although not one of the architects of Reconstruction policy, Grant defended it. But he shared with most Americans a belief in decentralized government and a reluctance to assert federal authority in local and state affairs.

In the 1870s, as the northern military presence shrank in the South, Republican idealism waned in the North. The Liberal Republican revolt of 1872 eroded what remained of radicalism. Although the "regular" Republicans, who backed Grant, continued to defend Reconstruction in the 1872 election, many held ambivalent views. Commercial and industrial interests now dominated both wings of the party, and Grant supporters had greater zeal for doing business in and with the South than for rekindling sectional strife. After the Democrats won control of the House in the 1874 elections, support for Reconstruction became a political liability.

By 1875 the Radical Republicans, so prominent in the 1860s, had vanished from the political scene. Chase, Stevens, and Sumner were dead. Other Radicals had lost office or abandoned their former convictions. "Waving the Bloody Shirt"—defaming Democratic opponents by reviving wartime animosity—now struck many Republicans, including former Radicals, as counterproductive. Party leaders reported that voters were "sick of carpet-bag government" and tiring of both the "southern question" and the "Negro question." It seemed

pointless to continue the unpopular and expensive policy of military intervention in the South to prop up Republican regimes that even President Grant found corrupt. Finally, few Republicans shared the egalitarian spirit that had animated Stevens and Sumner. Politics aside, Republican leaders and voters generally agreed with southern Democrats that blacks, although worthy of freedom, were inferior to whites. To insist on black equality would be a thankless, divisive, and politically suicidal undertaking. Moreover, it would quash any hope of reunion between the regions. The Republicans' retreat from Reconstruction set the stage for its demise in 1877.

RECONSTRUCTION ABANDONED, 1876–1877

"We are in a very hot political contest just now," a Mississippi planter wrote to his daughter in 1875, "with a good prospect of turning out the carpetbag thieves by whom we have been robbed for the past six to ten years." Similar contests raged through the South in the 1870s, as the resentment of white majorities grew and Democratic influence surged. By the end of 1872, the Democrats had regained power in Tennessee, Virginia, Georgia, and North Carolina. Within three years they won control in Texas, Alabama, Arkansas, and Mississippi (see Table 16.5). As the 1876 elections approached, Republican rule survived in only three states—South Carolina, Florida, and Louisiana. Democratic victories in the state elections of 1876 and political bargaining in Washington

in 1877 abruptly ended what little remained of Reconstruction.

Redeeming the South

The Republicans' collapse in the South accelerated after 1872. Congressional amnesty enabled ex-Confederate officials to regain office; divisions among the Republicans loosened their party's weak grip on the southern electorate; and attrition diminished Republican ranks. Some carpetbaggers gave up and returned North; others shifted to the Democratic party. Scalawags deserted in even larger numbers. Southerners who had joined the Republicans to moderate rampant radicalism tired of northern interference; once "home rule" by Democrats became a possibility, staying Republican meant going down with a sinking ship. Scalawag defections ruined Republican prospects. Unable to win new white votes or retain the old ones, the always-precarious Republican coalition crumbled.

Meanwhile, the Democrats mobilized formerly apathetic white voters. The resurrected southern Democratic party was divided: businessmen who envisioned an industrialized "New South" opposed an agrarian faction called the Bourbons, the old planter elite. But all Democrats shared one goal: to oust Republicans from office. Their tactics varied from state to state. Alabama Democrats won by promising to cut taxes and by getting out the white vote. In Louisiana the "White League," a vigilante organization formed in 1874, undermined the Republicans' hold. Intimidation also proved effective in

TABLE 16.5　The Duration of Republican Rule in the Ex-Confederate States

Former Confederate States	Readmission to the Union Under Congressional Reconstruction	Democrats (Conservatives) Gain Control	Duration of Republican Rule
Alabama	June 25, 1868	November 14, 1874	6½ years
Arkansas	June 22, 1868	November 10, 1874	6½ years
Florida	June 25, 1868	January 2, 1877	8½ years
Georgia	July 15, 1870	November 1, 1871	1 year
Louisiana	June 25, 1868	January 2, 1877	8½ years
Mississippi	February 23, 1870	November 3, 1875	5½ years
North Carolina	June 25, 1868	November 3, 1870	2 years
South Carolina	June 25, 1868	November 12, 1876	8 years
Tennessee	July 24, 1866*	October 4, 1869	3 years
Texas	March 30, 1870	January 14, 1873	3 years
Virginia	January 26, 1870	October 5, 1869†	0 years

*Admitted before start of congressional Reconstruction.　†Democrats gained control before readmission.

Source: John Hope Franklin, *Reconstruction After the Civil War* (Chicago: University of Chicago Press, 1962), 231.

Mississippi, where violent incidents—like the 1874 slaughter in Vicksburg of about three hundred blacks by rampaging whites—terrorized black voters. In 1875 the "Mississippi plan" took effect: local Democratic clubs armed their members, who dispersed Republican meetings, patrolled voter-registration places, and marched through black areas. "The Republicans are paralyzed through fear and will not act," the anguished carpetbag governor of Mississippi wrote to his wife. "Why should I fight a hopeless battle?" In 1876 South Carolina's "Rifle Clubs" and "Red Shirts," armed groups that threatened Republicans, continued the scare tactics that had worked so well in Mississippi.

New outbursts of intimidation did not completely squelch black voting, but the Democrats deprived the Republicans of enough black votes to win state elections. In some counties they encouraged freedmen to vote Democratic at supervised polls where voters publicly placed a card with a party label in a box. In other instances employers and landowners impeded black suffrage. Labor contracts included clauses barring attendance at political meetings; planters used the threat of eviction to keep sharecroppers in line. Since the Enforcement acts could not be enforced, intimidation and economic pressure succeeded.

Redemption, the word Democrats used to describe their return to power, introduced sweeping changes. Some states called constitutional conventions to reverse Republican policies. All cut back expenses, wiped out social programs, lowered taxes, and revised their tax systems to relieve landowners of large burdens. State courts limited the rights of tenants and sharecroppers. Most important, the Democrats, or "redeemers," used the law to ensure a stable black labor force. Legislatures restored vagrancy laws, revised crop-lien statutes to make landowners' claims superior to those of merchants, and rewrote criminal law. Local ordinances in heavily black counties often restricted hunting, fishing, gun carrying, and ownership of dogs and thereby curtailed the everyday activities of freedmen who lived off the land. States passed severe laws against trespassing and theft; stealing livestock or wrongly taking part of a crop became grand larceny with a penalty of up to five years at hard labor. By the end of Reconstruction, a large black convict work force had been leased out to private contractors at low rates.

For the freedmen, whose aspirations had been raised by Republican rule, redemption was devastating. The new laws, Tennessee blacks contended at an 1875 convention, would impose "a condition of servitude scarcely less degrading than that endured before the late

The White League

Alabama's White League, formed in 1874, strove to oust Republicans from office by intimidating black voters. To political cartoonist Thomas Nast, such vigilante tactics suggested an alliance between the White League and the outlawed Ku Klux Klan.

civil war." In the late 1870s, as the political climate grew more oppressive, an "exodus" movement spread through Mississippi, Tennessee, Texas, and Louisiana. Some African-Americans decided to become homesteaders in Kansas. After a major outbreak of "Kansas fever" in 1879, four thousand "exodusters" from Mississippi and Louisiana joined about ten thousand who had reached Kansas earlier in the decade. But the vast majority of freedmen, devoid of resources, had no migration options or escape route. Mass movement of southern blacks to the North and Midwest would not gain momentum until the twentieth century.

The Election of 1876

By the autumn of 1876, with redemption almost complete, both parties moved to discard the heritage of animosity left by the war and Reconstruction. The Republicans nominated Rutherford B. Hayes, three times Ohio's governor, for president. Untainted by the scandals of the Grant years and popular with all factions in his party, Hayes presented himself as a "moderate" on southern policy. He favored "home rule" in the South and a guarantee of civil and political rights for all—two planks that were clearly contradictory. The Democrats nominated Governor Samuel J. Tilden of New York, a

The Exodus to Kansas

Benjamin "Pap" Singleton, a one-time fugitive slave from Tennessee, returned there to promote the "exodus" movement of the late 1870s. Forming a real estate company, Singleton traveled the South recruiting parties of freedmen who were disillusioned with the outcome of Reconstruction. These emigrants, awaiting a Mississippi River boat, looked forward to political equality, freedom from violence, and homesteads in Kansas.

Ho for Kansas!

Brethren, Friends, & Fellow Citizens:

I feel thankful to inform you that the

REAL ESTATE

AND

Homestead   Association,

Will Leave Here the

15th of April, 1878,

In pursuit of Homes in the Southwestern Lands of America, at Transportation Rates, cheaper than ever was known before.

For full information inquire of

Benj. Singleton, better known as old Pap,

NO. 5 NORTH FRONT STREET.

Beware of Speculators and Adventurers, as it is a dangerous thing to fall in their hands,

Nashville, Tenn., March 18, 1878.

millionaire corporate lawyer and political reformer. Known for his assaults on the Tweed Ring that had plundered New York City's treasury, Tilden campaigned against fraud and waste. Both candidates were fiscal conservatives, favored sound money, endorsed civil-service reform, and decried corruption, an irony since the 1876 election would be extremely corrupt.

Tilden won the popular vote by a 3 percent margin and seemed destined to capture the 185 electoral votes needed for victory (see Map 16.4). But the Republicans challenged the pro-Tilden returns from South Carolina, Florida, and Louisiana. If they could deprive the Democrats of these nineteen electoral votes, Hayes would triumph. The Democrats, who needed only one of the disputed electoral votes for victory, challenged the validity of Oregon's single electoral vote, which the Republicans had won, on a technicality. Twenty electoral votes, therefore, were in contention. But Republicans still controlled the electoral machinery in the three unredeemed southern states, where they threw out enough Democratic ballots to declare Hayes the winner.

The nation now faced an unprecedented dilemma. Each party claimed victory in the contested states, and each accused the other of fraud. In fact, both sets of southern results involved fraud: the Republicans had discarded legitimate Democratic ballots, and the Democrats had illegally prevented freedmen from voting. To resolve the conflict, Congress in January 1877 created a special electoral commission to decide which party would get the contested electoral votes. Made up of senators, representatives, and Supreme Court justices, the commission included seven Democrats, seven Republicans, and one independent, Justice David Davis of Illinois. When Davis resigned to run for the Senate, Congress replaced him with a Republican, and the commission gave Hayes the election by an 8 to 7 vote.

Congress now had to certify the new electoral vote. But since the Democrats controlled the House, a new problem loomed. Some Democrats threatened to obstruct debate and delay approval of the electoral vote. Had they carried out their scheme, the nation would have been without a president on inauguration day, March 4. There remained room for compromise, for many southern Democrats accepted Hayes's election. Among them were former scalawags with commercial interests to protect, who still favored Republican financial policies, and railroad investors, who hoped that a Republican administration would help them build a southern transcontinental line. Other southerners cared mainly about Democratic state victories and did not mind conceding the presidency as long as the new Republican administration would leave the South alone.

MAP 16.4
The Disputed Election of 1876

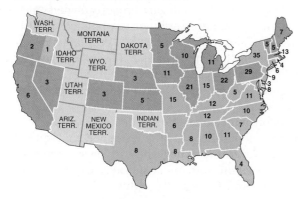

	Uncontested Electoral Vote	Electoral Vote	Popular Vote	Percentage of Popular Vote
Republican Rutherford B. Hayes	165	185	4,034,311	48.0
Democratic Samuel J. Tilden	184	184	4,288,546	51.0
Greenback Peter Cooper	–	–	75,973	1.0

Disputed

Republican leaders, although sure of eventual triumph, were willing to bargain as well, for candidate Hayes desired not merely victory but southern approval.

A series of informal negotiations ensued, at which politicians exchanged promises. Ohio Republicans and southern Democrats, who met at a Washington hotel, reached an agreement that if Hayes won the election, he would remove federal troops from South Carolina and Louisiana, and Democrats could gain control of those states. In other bargaining sessions, southern politicians asked for federal patronage, federal aid to railroads, and federal support for internal improvements. In return, they promised to drop the filibuster, to accept Hayes as president, and to treat freedmen fairly.

With the threatened filibuster broken, Congress ratified Hayes's election. Once in office, Hayes fulfilled some of the promises his Republican colleagues had made. He appointed a former Confederate as postmaster general and ordered federal troops who guarded the South Carolina and Louisiana statehouses back to their barracks. Although federal soldiers remained in the South after 1877, they no longer served a political function. The Democrats, meanwhile, took control of state governments in Louisiana, South Carolina, and Florida. When Republican rule toppled in these states, the era of Reconstruction finally ended, though more with a whimper than with a resounding crash.

But some of the bargains struck in the Compromise of 1877, such as Democratic promises to treat southern blacks fairly, were forgotten, as were Hayes's pledges to ensure freedmen's rights. "When you turned us loose, you turned us loose to the sky, to the storm, to the whirlwind, and worst of all . . . to the wrath of our infuriated masters," Frederick Douglass had charged at the Republican convention in 1876. "The question now is, do you mean to make good to us the promises in your Constitution?" The answer provided by the 1876 election and the 1877 compromises was "No."

CONCLUSION

Between 1865 and 1877, the nation experienced a series of crises. In Washington conflict between President Johnson and Congress led to a stringent Republican plan for restoring the South, a plan that included the radical provision of black male enfranchisement. President Johnson ineptly abetted the triumph of the radical plan by his defiant stance, which drove moderate Republicans into an alliance against him with Radical Republicans. In the ex-Confederate states, governments were reorganized, Republicans took over, and far-reaching changes occurred. Emancipation reshaped black communities where former slaves sought new identities as free people, and transformed the southern economy as a new labor system replaced slavery. The North, meanwhile, hurtled headlong into an era of industrial growth, labor unrest, and financial crises. By the mid-1870s, northern politicians were ready to discard the Reconstruction policies that Congress had imposed a decade before. Simultaneously, the southern states returned to Democratic control, as Republican regimes toppled one by one. Reconstruction's final collapse in 1877 reflected not only a waning of northern resolve but a successful ex-Confederate campaign of violence, intimidation, and protest that had started in the 1860s.

The end of Reconstruction gratified both political parties. Although unable to retain a southern constituency, the Republican party was no longer burdened by the unpopular "southern question." The Democrats, who had regained power in the former Confederacy, would remain entrenched there for over a century. To be sure, the South was tied to sharecropping and economic backwardness as securely as it had once been tied to slavery. But "home rule" was firmly in place. Reconstruction's end also signified a triumph for nationalism and the spirit of reunion. In the fall of 1877, President Hayes toured the South to champion reconciliation, and similar celebrations continued for decades. When former President Grant died in 1885, veterans of

both Civil War armies served as pallbearers. Jefferson Davis, imprisoned for two years after the war but never brought to trial, urged young men to "lay aside all rancor, all bitter sectional feeling."

As the nation applauded reunion, Reconstruction's reputation sank. Looking back on the 1860s and 1870s, most late-nineteenth-century Americans dismissed the congressional effort to reconstruct the South as a fiasco—a tragic interlude of "radical rule" or "black reconstruction" fashioned by carpetbaggers, scalawags, and Radical Republicans. With the hindsight of a century, historians continued to regard Reconstruction as a failure, though of a different kind.

No longer viewed as a misguided scheme that collapsed because of radical excess, Reconstruction is now widely seen as a democratic experiment that did not go far enough. Historians cite two main causes. First, Congress did not promote freedmen's independence through land reform; without property of their own, southern blacks lacked the economic power to defend their interests as free citizens. Property ownership, however, does not necessarily ensure political rights, nor does it invariably provide economic security. Considering the depressed state of southern agriculture in the postwar decades, the freedmen's fate as independent farmers would likely have been perilous. Thus the land-reform question, like much else about Reconstruction, remains a subject of debate. A second cause of Reconstruction's collapse is less open to dispute: the federal government neglected to back congressional Reconstruction with military force. Given the choice between protecting blacks' rights at whatever cost and promoting reunion, the government opted for reunion. Reconstruction's failure, therefore, was the federal government's failure to fulfill its own goals and create a biracial democracy in the South. As a result, the nation's

CHRONOLOGY, 1865–1877

1863 President Abraham Lincoln issues Proclamation of Amnesty and Reconstruction.

1864 Wade-Davis bill passed by Congress and pocket-vetoed by Lincoln.

1865 Freedmen's Bureau established.
Civil War ends.
Lincoln assassinated.
Andrew Johnson becomes president.
Johnson issues Proclamation of Amnesty and Reconstruction.
Ex-Confederate states hold constitutional conventions (May–December).
Black conventions begin in the ex-Confederate states.
Thirteenth Amendment added to the Constitution.
Presidential Reconstruction completed.

1866 Congress enacts the Civil Rights Act of 1866 and the Supplementary Freedmen's Bureau Act over Johnson's vetoes.
Ku Klux Klan founded in Tennessee.
Tennessee readmitted to the Union.
Race riots in southern cities.
Republicans win congressional elections.

1867 Reconstruction Act of 1867.
William Seward negotiates the purchase of Alaska.
Constitutional conventions meet in the ex-Confederate states.
Howard University founded.

1868 President Johnson is impeached, tried, and acquitted.
Omnibus Act.
Fourteenth Amendment added to the Constitution.
Ulysses S. Grant elected president.

1869 Transcontinental railroad completed.

1870 Congress readmits the four remaining southern states to the Union.
Fifteenth Amendment added to the Constitution.
Enforcement Act of 1870.

1871 Second Enforcement Act.
Ku Klux Klan Act.

1872 Liberal Republican party formed.
Amnesty Act.
Alabama claims settled.
Grant reelected president.

1873 Panic of 1873 begins (September–October), setting off a five-year depression.

1874 Democrats gain control of the House of Representatives.

1875 Civil Rights Act of 1875.
Specie Resumption Act.

1876 Disputed presidential election: Rutherford B. Hayes versus Samuel J. Tilden.

1877 Electoral commission decides election in favor of Hayes.
The last Republican-controlled governments overthrown in Florida, Louisiana, and South Carolina.

1879 "Exodus" movement spreads through several southern states.

adjustment to the consequences of emancipation would continue into the twentieth century.

The Reconstruction era left some significant legacies, including the Fourteenth and Fifteenth amendments. Although neither amendment would be used to protect minority rights for almost a century, they remain monuments to the democratic zeal that swept Congress in the 1860s. The Reconstruction years also hold a significant place in African-American history. During this brief respite between slavery and repression, southern blacks reconstituted their families, created new institutions, took part in the transformation of southern agriculture, and participated in government, for the first time in American history. The aspirations and achievements of the Reconstruction era left an indelible mark on black citizens. Consigning Reconstruction to history, other Americans turned to their economic futures—to railroads, factories, and mills, and to the exploitation of the country's bountiful natural resources.

FOR FURTHER REFERENCE

READINGS

David W. Blight, *Race and Reunion: The Civil War in American Memory* (2001).
Explores competing views on the significance of the Civil War in the Reconstruction era and the decades that followed.

Ellen Carol DuBois, *Feminism and Suffrage: The Emergence of an Independent Women's Movement in America, 1848–1869* (1978).
Shows how the woman suffrage movement developed in the context of Reconstruction politics.

Eric Foner, *Reconstruction: America's Unfinished Revolution, 1863–1877* (1988).
A thorough exploration of Reconstruction that draws on recent scholarship and stresses the centrality of the black experience.

Tera W. Hunter, *To 'Joy My Freedom: Southern Black Women's Lives and Labors After the Civil War* (1997).
Explores the experience of women workers in Atlanta from Reconstruction into the twentieth century.

Leon Litwack, *Been in the Storm So Long: The Aftermath of Slavery* (1979).
A comprehensive study of the black response to emancipation in 1865–1866.

Michael Perman, *The Road to Redemption: Southern Politics, 1869–1879* (1984). Examines the impact of Reconstruction on party politics in the post-Civil War South and explains how Reconstruction governments in the southern states collapsed.

Roger L. Ransom and Richard Sutch, *One Kind of Freedom: The Economic Consequences of Emancipation* (1977).
Two economists' assessment of the impact of free black labor on the South and explanation of the development of sharecropping and the crop-lien system.

Heather Cox Richardson, *The Death of Reconstruction: Race, Labor, and Politics in the Post-Civil War North, 1865–1901* (2001).
Explores northern disenchantment with Reconstruction policies and the dwindling of northern support for freed blacks in the South.

Kenneth M. Stampp, *The Era of Reconstruction, 1865–1877* (1965).
A classic revisionist interpretation of Reconstruction, focusing on the establishment and fall of Republican governments.

Joel Williamson, *The Negro in South Carolina During Reconstruction, 1861–1877* (1965).
A pioneer study of black life and institutions after emancipation.

WEBSITES

American Slave Narratives: An Online Anthology
http://xroads.virginia.edu/~HYPER/wpa/wpahome.html
A sample of the interviews with over 2300 former slaves made by employees of the Works Progress Administration in the 1930s. Typically, the narratives discuss emancipation and its aftermath.

Freedmen's Bureau Online
http://freedmensbureau.com
A small but growing collection of transcriptions of the records and reports of the federal Freedmen's Bureau; includes labor records, marriage records, and state-by-state reports on local conditions.

Hayes vs. Tilden: The Electoral College Controversy of 1876–1877
http://elections.harpweek.com/controversy.htm
Offers an overview, a day-by-day account, biographies of major figures, and cartoons and illustrations from *Harper's Weekly.*

The Impeachment of Andrew Johnson
http://www.impeach-andrewjohnson.com
Provides access to *Harper's Weekly* coverage of President Andrew Johnson's impeachment in 1868 plus much additional information, including arguments for and against impeachment.

The Valley of the Shadow: Two Communities in the American Civil War
http://www.iath.virginia.edu/vshadow2
Presents extensive sources materials on Augusta County in Virginia and Franklin County in Pennsylvania before, during, and after the Civil War. For the Reconstruction era, see "Aftermath."

CHAPTER 17

The Transformation of the Trans-Mississippi West, 1860–1900

In spring 1871 fifteen-year-old Luna Warner began a diary as she ventured west with her family to a new homestead claim near the Solomon River in western Kansas. In it she carefully recorded her impressions of the vast western landscape that seemed so different from the countryside near her Massachusetts home. She was delighted by the rugged beauty of the local river and gathered wildflowers everywhere, but she was most impressed by the large numbers of birds and animals she saw: great shaggy bison, wild turkeys and ducks, antelope, and prairie chickens.

In her diary, which chronicled her family's struggle to build a cabin, break the sod, and plant crops, Luna singled out for special attention the bison hunt that her uncle participated in the following winter. She noted that her uncle, who eventually brought back six bison, initially lost his way, but was helped by an Indian who led him back to camp. The following summer Luna was out riding with her father and two younger cousins when they, too, encountered a bison. She vividly described what happened.

"Pa got off. He handed me the bridle while he went for the buffalo, revolver in hand. . . . He fired and then they [the buffalo] came right toward us. The horse sprang and snorted and whirled around me, but I kept fast hold and talked to her and she arched her neck. . . . Then he [the buffalo] fell dead in the ravine. [We] hitched the oxen to the buffalo and dragged him up where

◀ **Red Cloud's Delegation to Washington, c. 1870**
Red Cloud (seated, second from left), an Oglala Sioux, visited President Grant at the White House to argue for his people's right to trade at Fort Laramie, Wyoming. His clothing, unlike the traditional Native American dress of the other chiefs, reflected his desire to negotiate with whites on equal terms.

CHAPTER OUTLINE

511

Luna Warner's Family Homestead, c. 1880
Overlooking the Solomon River in Kansas, Luna wrote in her diary on May 17, 1871, "I am 16 years old today. I do not feel so old. Mama and I went across the river and went all over our claim. It is splendid."

Luna Warner, Age 16

they could skin him . . . [and] they all went to skinning the buffalo with pocket knives."

Luna Warner and her family were part of one of the great human migrations in modern history. Lured by tales of the West as a region of free land and rare minerals, miners, farmers, land speculators, and railroad developers flooded onto the fertile prairies of Iowa, Minnesota, and Kansas, carving the land into farms and communities. Then, tempted by the discovery of gold in the Rocky Mountains, these same settlers, aided by the U.S. army, pushed aside the Indian inhabitants who lived there and swarmed onto the Great Plains and the semiarid regions beyond them. Scarcely a decade later, when Luna married and settled on her own farm, the trans-Mississippi West had been transformed into a contested terrain as Native peoples fought to preserve their homeland from being broken up into new settlements, reservations, mines, ranches, farmland, and national parks.

The transformation of the West left a mixed legacy. Although many white families like the Warners prospered on the High Plains, the heedless pursuit of land and profit proved destructive to the Native Americans, to the environment, and often to the settlers themselves. Under the banner of civilization and progress, industrious western entrepreneurs exploited white, Native American, Chinese, and Mexican laborers alike. They slaughtered millions of bison for their hides, skinned the

mountainsides in search of minerals, and tore up the prairie sod to build farms even in areas west of the ninety-eighth meridian, where limited rainfall made farming problematic.

Although entrepreneurs attributed their economic achievements to American individualism and self-reliance, the West's development depended heavily on the federal government. The government sent troops to pacify the Indians, promoted the acquisition of farm land through the Homestead Act (1862), and subsidized the construction of the transcontinental railroad. Eastern banks and foreign capitalists provided investment capital and eased access to international markets. Yet westerners clung to their ideal of the self-reliant individual who could handle any obstacle. That ideal, though often sorely tested, survived to form the bedrock of western Americans' outlook even today.

This chapter will focus on five major questions:

- How was Indian life on the Great Plains transformed in the second half of the nineteenth century?

- What roles did the army and the railroads play in the settlement of the West?

- To what extent did the Homestead Act succeed in making free land available to those who settled in the West?

- How was the Wild West image of cowboys and Indians created? Why has it remained so popular?

- How did some Americans become more aware of the need to conserve natural resources by setting them aside in national parks?

NATIVE AMERICANS AND THE TRANS-MISSISSIPPI WEST

No aspect of the transformation of the West was more visible and dramatic than the destruction of the traditional Indian way of life. Even before settlers, ranchers, and miners poured onto the Great Plains at midcentury, Indian life in the trans-Mississippi West was changing. In the southwest earlier in the century, the Spanish had forcibly incorporated pueblo peoples such as the Hopis and Zuñis into their Mexican trading networks. Other tribes, such as the Navajos, had gradually given up migratory life in favor of settled agriculture. To the North, the Cheyenne and the Lakota Sioux, already expelled from the Great Lakes region by the expansion of white settlement, had moved onto the grasslands of the Great Plains and had seized hunting grounds from their enemies, the Pawnees and the Crows. These and other nomadic warrior tribes, dispersed in small bands and moving from place to place to follow the bison herds, had developed a resilient culture adapted to the harsh environment.

When white pioneers invaded their territory at midcentury, it was the resistance of these nomadic Indians that most captured the public's attention and spurred debate. Caught between a stampede of miners and settlers who took their land and depleted their natural resources and the federal government that sought to force them onto reservations, Native Americans desperately fought back. By the 1890s relocation to distant, often inferior lands had become the fate of almost every Indian nation. Beaten and victimized, resilient Native Americans struggled to preserve their traditions and rebuild their numbers.

The Plains Indians

The Indians of the Great Plains inhabited three major subregions. The northern Plains, from the Dakotas and Montana southward to Nebraska, were dominated by several large tribes such as the Lakota who spoke Siouan languages, as well as by the Flatheads, Blackfeet, Assiniboins, northern Cheyennes, Arapahos, and Crows. Some of these were allies, but others were bitter enemies perpetually at war. In the central region the so-called

Five Civilized Tribes, who had been driven there from the Southeast in the 1830s, pursued an agricultural life in the Indian Territory (present-day Oklahoma). The Pawnees in Nebraska maintained the older, more settled tradition characteristic of Plains river valley culture before the introduction of horses, spending at least half the year in villages of earthen lodges along watercourses. Surrounding these to the South were the migratory tribes of western Kansas, Colorado, eastern New Mexico, and Texas—the Comanches, Kiowas, southern Arapahos, and Kiowa Apaches.

Considerable diversity flourished among the Plains peoples, and customs varied even within subdivisions of the same tribe. For example, the easternmost branch of the great Sioux Nation, the Dakota Sioux of Minnesota who inhabited the wooded edge of the prairie, led a semisedentary life based on small-scale agriculture, deer and bison hunting, wild-rice harvesting, and maple-sugar production. In contrast, many Plains tribes—not only the Lakota Sioux, but also the Blackfeet, Crows, and Cheyennes—using horses obtained from the Spanish and guns obtained from traders, roamed the High Plains to the west, and followed the bison migrations.

For all the Plains Indians, life revolved around extended family ties and tribal cooperation. Within the various Sioux-speaking tribes, for example, children were raised without physical punishment and were taught to treat each adult clan member with the respect accorded to relatives. Families and clans joined forces to hunt and farm and reached decisions by consensus.

For the various Sioux bands, religious and harvest celebrations provided the cement for village and camp life. Sioux religion was complex and entirely different from the Judeo-Christian tradition. The Lakota Sioux thought of life as a series of circles. Living within the daily cycles of the sun and moon, Lakotas were born into a circle of relatives, which broadened to the band, the tribe, and the Sioux Nation. The Lakotas also believed in a hierarchy of plant and animal spirits whose help could be invoked in the Sun Dance. To gain access to spiritual power and to benefit the weaker members of the community, young men would "sacrifice" themselves by suffering self-torture. For example, some fastened skewers to their chest from which they dragged buffalo skulls; others suspended themselves from poles or cut pieces of their flesh and placed them at the foot of the Sun Dance pole. Painter George Catlin, who recorded Great Plains Indian life before the Civil War, described such a ceremony. "Several of them, seeing me making sketches, beckoned me to look at their faces, which I watched through all this horrid operation, without being able to detect anything but the pleasantest smiles as they

looked me in the eye, while I could hear the knife rip through the flesh, and feel enough of it myself, to start involuntary and uncontrollable tears over my cheeks."

On the semiarid High Plains where rainfall averaged less than twenty inches a year, both the bison and the Native peoples adapted to the environment. The huge herds, which at their peak contained an estimated 30 million animals, broke into small groups in the winter and dispersed into river valleys where they sought protection from harsh storms and bone-numbing cold. In the summer, they returned to the High Plains in vast herds to feed on the nutritious short grasses and mate. Like the bison, the Indians dispersed across the landscape to minimize their impact on any one place, wintering in the river valleys and returning to the High Plains in summer. When their herds of horses consumed the grasses near their camps, they moved. Hunting the bison not only supplied the Native peoples with food, clothing, and teepee covers, but also created a valuable trading commodity, buffalo robes. To benefit from this trade, Indians themselves, as the nineteenth century progressed, dramatically increased their harvest of animals.

The movement of miners and settlers onto the eastern High Plains in the 1850s began to erode the bison's habitat and threaten the Native American way of life. As the pioneers trekked westward, they occupied the river valley sites where the buffalo had wintered and exhausted the tall grasses upon which the animals depended. In the 1860s whites began systematically to hunt the animals, often with Indian help, to supply the eastern market with carriage robes and industrial belting. William F. "Buffalo Bill" Cody, a famous scout, Indian fighter, and organizer of Wild West shows, killed nearly forty-three hundred bison in 1867–1868 to feed construction crews building the Union Pacific Railroad. Army commanders also encouraged the slaughter of buffalo to undermine Indian resistance to the encroachment of miners and settlers. The carnage that resulted was almost inconceivable in its scale. Between 1872 and 1875, hunters killed 9 million buffalo, taking only the skin and leaving the carcasses to rot. By the 1880s the once-thundering herds had been reduced to a few thousand animals, and the Native American way of life dependent on the buffalo had been ruined.

The Destruction of Nomadic Indian Life

As early as the 1850s, the seeds of the impending crisis were apparent. The Indians who felt pressure from the declining bison herds and deteriorating grasslands now faced the onslaught of thousands of pioneers lured by

George Catlin, *Buffalo Hunt Surround*
Surrounding a herd of buffalo, as this painting depicts, required the careful organization and coordination of all involved. One false move by an errant brave and the buffalo would scatter and escape.

the discovery of gold and silver in the Rocky Mountains. The federal government's response was to reexamine its Indian policies. Abandoning the previous position that treated much of the West as a vast Indian reserve, the federal government sought to introduce a system of smaller, separate, bounded areas—tribal reservations— where the Indians were to be concentrated, by force if necessary, and where they were expected to exchange their nomadic ways for a settled agricultural life. To achieve this goal, the army established outposts along well-traveled trails and stationed troops that could be mobilized at a moment's notice.

Some Native Americans, like the Pueblos of the Southwest, the Crows of Montana, and the Hidatsas of North Dakota, peacefully accepted their fate. Others, among them the Navajos of Arizona and New Mexico and the Dakota Sioux, opposed the new policy to no avail. By 1860 eight western reservations had been established.

Significant segments of the remaining tribes on the Great Plains, more than a hundred thousand people, fought against removal for decades. From the 1860s through the 1890s, many bands from these tribes—the

Buffalo Skulls at the Michigan Carbon Works, 1895
Once the vast herds of bison had been decimated, resourceful entrepreneurs, such as those pictured here, collected the skulls and sold them for industrial use. In all, nearly two million tons of bones were processed.

western Sioux, Cheyennes, Arapahos, Kiowas, and Comanches on the Great Plains; the Nez Perces and Bannocks in the northern Rockies; and the Apaches in the Southwest—faced the U.S. army in a series of final battles for the West (see Map 17.1).

Misunderstandings, unfulfilled promises, brutality, and butchery marked the conflict. Nowhere was this more evident than in the eroding relationship between the Cheyennes and Arapahos and the settlers near Sand Creek, Colorado, in 1864. During the gold rush six years earlier, more than a hundred thousand people (more than twice the number who went to California in 1849) had stampeded into the area. The Indians, facing starvation because of unfulfilled treaties that had promised food, support, and farm equipment, slipped away from the reservation areas to hunt bison and steal livestock from nearby settlers.

In the spring of the year, local militia troops (replacements for soldiers fighting in the Civil War) attacked Cheyenne and Arapaho camps. The Indians retaliated with a flurry of attacks on travelers. The governor, in a panic, issued an extraordinary proclamation, authorizing Colorado's white citizenry to seek out and kill all hostile Indians on sight. He then activated a regiment of troops under Colonel John M. Chivington, a Methodist minister. At dawn on November 29, under orders to "remember the murdered women and children on the Platte [River]," Chivington's troops massacred a peaceful band of Indians, including terrified women and children, camped at Sand Creek who believed that they would be protected by the nearby fort.

This massacre and others that followed rekindled public debate over federal Indian policy. In response, in 1867 Congress sent a peace commission to end the fighting, and set aside two large districts, one north of Nebraska, the other south of Kansas. There, it was hoped, the tribes would take up farming and convert to Christianity. Behind the federal government's persuasion lay the threat of force. Any Native Americans who refused to "locate in [the] permanent abodes provided for them," warned Commissioner of Indian Affairs Ely S. Parker, himself a Seneca Indian, "would be subject wholly to the control and supervision of military authorities, [and] . . . treated as friendly or hostile as circumstances might justify."

At first the plan appeared to work. Representatives of sixty-eight thousand southern Kiowas, Comanches, Cheyennes, and Arapahos signed the Medicine Lodge Treaty of 1867 and pledged to live on land in present-day Oklahoma. The following year, scattered bands of Sioux, representing nearly fifty-four thousand northern Plains Indians, signed the Fort Laramie Treaty and agreed to

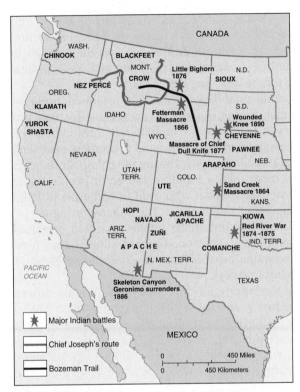

MAP 17.1

Major Indian-White Clashes in the West

Although they were never recognized as such in the popular press, the battles between Native Americans and the U.S. Army on the Great Plains amounted to a major undeclared war.

move to reservations on the so-called Great Sioux Reserve in the western part of what is now South Dakota in return for money and provisions.

But Indian dissatisfaction with the treaties ran deep. As a Sioux chief, Spotted Tail, told the commissioners, "We do not want to live like the white man. . . . The Great Spirit gave us hunting grounds, gave us the buffalo, the elk, the deer, and the antelope. Our fathers have taught us to hunt and live on the Plains, and we are contented." Rejecting the new system, many bands of Indians refused to move to the reservations or to remain on them once there.

In August 1868 war parties of defiant Cheyennes, Arapahos, and Sioux raided settlements in Kansas and Colorado, burning homes and killing whites. In retaliation, army troops attacked Indians, even peaceful ones, who refused confinement. That autumn Lieutenant Colonel George Armstrong Custer's raiding party struck a sleeping Cheyenne village, killing more than a hundred warriors, shooting more than eight hundred horses, and taking fifty-three women and children prisoner.

Other hostile Cheyennes and Arapahos were pursued, captured, and returned to the reservations.

In 1869, spurred on by Christian reformers, Congress established a Board of Indian Commissioners drawn from the major Protestant denominations to reform the reservation system. But the new and inexperienced church-appointed Indian agents quickly encountered obstacles in trying to implement the board's policies. The pacifist Quaker agent Lawrie Tatum, a big-boned Iowa farmer, for example, failed to persuade the Comanches and Kiowas to stay on their reservations in Oklahoma rather than raid Texas settlements. Two Kiowa chiefs, Satanta and Big Tree, insisted that they could be at peace with the federal government while remaining at war with Texans. Other agents were unable to restrain scheming whites who fraudulently purchased reservation lands from the Indians. By the 1880s the federal government, frustrated with the churches, ignored their nominations for Indian agents and made its own appointments.

Caught in the sticky web of an ambiguous and deceptive federal policy, and enraged by continuing non-Indian settlement of the Plains, defiant Native Americans struck back in the 1870s. On the southern Plains, Kiowa, Comanche, and Cheyenne raids in the Texas panhandle in 1874 set off the so-called Red River War. In a fierce winter campaign, regular army troops destroyed Indian supplies and slaughtered a hundred Cheyenne fugitives near the Sappa River in Kansas. With the exile of seventy-four "ringleaders" to reservations in Florida, Native American independence on the southern Plains came to an end. In the Southwest, in present-day Arizona and New Mexico, the Apaches fought an intermittent guerrilla war until their leader, Geronimo, surrendered in 1886.

Custer's Last Stand, 1876

Of all the acts of Indian resistance against the new reservation policy, none aroused more passion or caused more bloodshed than the battles waged by the western Sioux tribes in the Dakotas, Montana, and Wyoming. The 1868 Treaty of Fort Laramie had set aside the Great Sioux Reserve "in perpetuity." But not all the Sioux bands had fought in the war or signed the treaty.

In 1873, skillfully playing local officials against the federal government, Chief Red Cloud's Oglala band and Chief Spotted Tail's Brulé band won the concession of staying on their traditional lands. To protect their hunting grounds, they raided encroaching non-Indian settlements in Nebraska and Wyoming, intimidated federal

Indian Chiefs

Early photographs of the Indian leaders Chief Joseph *(left)* and Sitting Bull *(right)* captured both their pride and the frustration they felt after years of alternately negotiating and battling with the U.S. Army. "I don't want a white man over me," Sitting Bull insisted. "I want to have the white man with me, but not to be my chief. I ask this because I want to do right by my people. . . ."

agents, and harassed miners, railroad surveyors, and any others who ventured onto their lands.

Non-treaty Sioux found a powerful leader in the Hunkpapa Lakota Sioux chief and holy man Sitting Bull. Broad-shouldered and powerfully built, Sitting Bull led by example and had considerable fighting experience. "You are fools," he told the reservation Indians, "to make yourselves slaves to a piece of fat bacon, some hardtack, and little sugar and coffee."

Pressured by would-be settlers and developers and distressed by the Indian agents' inability to prevent the Sioux from entering and leaving the reservations at will, the federal government took action. In 1874 General William Tecumseh Sherman sent a force under Colonel George Armstrong Custer into the Black Hills of South Dakota, near the western edge of the Great Sioux Reserve. Lean and mustachioed, with shoulder-length reddish-blond hair, the thirty-four-year-old Custer had been a celebrity since his days as an impetuous young Civil War officer, when he was known for the black velvet uniform embellished with gold braid he wore on the battlefield. Now he had switched to a fringed buckskin uniform set off by a crimson scarf.

Custer's ostensible purpose was to find a location for a new fort and to keep an eye on renegade Indians. But his real objective was to confirm rumors about the existence of gold in the Black Hills. In this he was spurred on by the Northern Pacific Railroad, which wanted to attract settlers to the area. While Custer's troops mapped the lush meadows and chose a site for the fort, two "practical miners" panned the streams for gold. In a report that he telegraphed to the *New York World*, Custer described the region as excellent farm country and casually mentioned finding "gold among the roots of the grass." The gold stampede that predictably followed gave the army a new justification for interceding against the Indians.

Custer had in fact become part of a deliberate army plan to force concessions from the Sioux. In November 1875 negotiations to buy the Black Hills broke down because the Indians' asking price was deemed too high. President Grant and his generals then decided to remove all roadblocks to the entry of miners. Indians still outside the reservations after January 31, 1876, the government announced, would be hunted down by the army and taken in by force.

The army mobilized for an assault. In June 1876, leading 600 troops of the Seventh Cavalry, Custer proceeded to the Little Bighorn River area of present-day Montana, a hub of Indian resistance. On the morning of June 25, underestimating the Indian enemy and unwisely dividing his force, Custer, with 209 men, recklessly advanced against a large company of Cheyenne and Sioux warriors led by Chief Sitting Bull who had encamped along the Little Bighorn. Custer and his outnumbered troops were wiped out. Two days later, another company of cavalry came upon the carnage and buried the bodies where they lay. A single creature was found alive: a horse that had belonged to one of Custer's captains.

Americans reeled from this unexpected Indian victory. Newspaper columnists groped to assess the meaning of "Custer's last stand." Some went beyond criticism of Custer's leadership to question the wisdom of current federal policy toward the Indians. Others worried that an outraged public would demand retaliation and the extermination of the Sioux. Most, however, endorsed the federal government's determination to quash the Native American rebellion. "It is inconsistent with our civilization and with common sense," trumpeted a writer in the *New York Herald*, "to allow the Indian to roam over a country as fine as that around the Black Hills, preventing its development in order that he may shoot game and scalp his neighbors. That can never be. This region must be taken from the Indian."

Defeat at Little Bighorn made the army more determined. In Montana troops harassed various Sioux bands for more than five years, attacking Indian camps in the dead of winter and destroying all supplies. Even Sitting Bull, who had led his band to Canada to escape the army, surrendered in 1881 for lack of provisions: the slaughter of the buffalo had wiped out his tribe's major food supply. Ever resourceful, Sitting Bull joined Buffalo Bill's Wild West show for a time after his surrender and earned enough money to bring additional supplies to his people.

Similar measures were used elsewhere in the West against Chief Joseph and his Nez Percés of Oregon and against the Northern Cheyennes, who had been forcibly transported to Oklahoma after the Battle of Little Bighorn. Chief Dull Knife led some 150 survivors, including men, women, and children, north in September 1878 to join the Sioux. But the army chased them down and imprisoned them in Fort Robinson, Nebraska. When the army denied their request to stay nearer to their traditional northern lands, tribal leaders refused to cooperate. The post commander then withheld all food, water, and fuel. On a frigid night in January 1879, a desperate Dull Knife and his followers, in a suicidal escape attempt, shot the guards and broke for freedom. Members of the startled garrison chased the Indians and gunned down half of them in the snow, including women and children as well as Dull Knife himself. The Atlanta *Constitution* condemned the incident as "a dastardly outrage upon humanity and a lasting disgrace to our boasted civilization." But although sporadic Indian resistance continued until the end of the century, these brutal tactics had sapped the Indians' will to resist.

"Saving" the Indians

A growing number of Americans were outraged not only by bloody atrocities like the Fort Robinson massacre but also by the federal government's flagrant violation of its Indian treaties. The Women's National Indian Rights Association, founded in 1883, and other groups took up the cause. Helen Hunt Jackson, a Massachusetts writer who had recently moved to Colorado, published *A Century of Dishonor* in 1881 to rally public opinion against the government's record of broken treaty obligations. "It makes little difference . . . where one opens the record of the history of the Indians;" she wrote, "every page and every year has its dark stain."

Well-intentioned humanitarians concluded that the Indians' interests would be best served by breaking up the reservations, ending all recognition of the tribes, and propelling individual Native Americans into mainstream society. In short, they proposed to eliminate the "Indian problem" by eliminating the Indians as a culturally distinct entity. Inspired by this vision, they threw their support behind a plan that resulted in the passage in 1887 of the Dawes Severalty Act (see Map 17.2).

The Dawes Act was designed to reform what well-meaning whites perceived to be the weaknesses of Indian life—the absence of private property and the Native peoples' nomadic tradition—by turning Indians into landowners and farmers. The law emphasized severalty, or the treatment of Indians as individuals rather than as members of tribes, and called for the distribution of 160 acres of reservation land for farming, or 320 acres for grazing, to each head of an Indian family who accepted the law's provisions. The remaining reservation lands (often the richest) were to be sold to speculators and settlers, and the income thus obtained would go toward purchase of farm tools. To prevent unscrupulous people from gaining control of the lands granted to individual Indians, the government would hold the property of each tribal member in trust for twenty-five years. Those Indians who at that point had accepted allotments would also be declared citizens of the United States.

Speculators who coveted reservation lands, as well as military authorities who wanted to break up the reservations for security reasons, had lobbied heavily for the Dawes Act. But the bill's strongest support had come from the "friends of the Indian" like Helen Hunt Jackson. Convinced that citizenship would best protect the Indians and that full assimilation into society would enable them to get ahead, the reformers systematically tried to "civilize" the Indian peoples and wean them from their traditional culture (see A Place in Time: The Phoenix Indian School).

The Dawes Act did not specify a timetable for the breakup of the reservations. Few allotments were made to the Indians until the 1890s. The act eventually proved

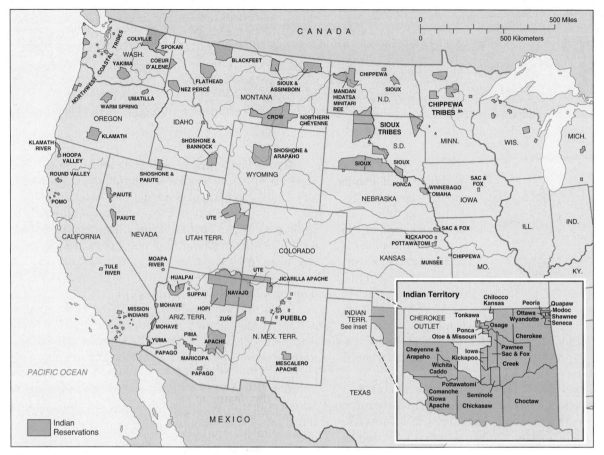

MAP 17.2
Western Indian Reservations, 1890
Native-American reservations were almost invariably located on poor-quality lands. Consequently, when the Dawes Severalty Act broke up the reservations into 160-acre farming tracts, many of the semiarid divisions would not support cultivation.

to be a boon to speculators, who commonly evaded its safeguards and obtained the Indians' most arable tracts. By 1934 the act had slashed the total Indian acreage by 65 percent. Much of what remained in Indian hands was too dry and gravelly for farming. In the twentieth century, ironically, periodic droughts and the fragile, arid High Plains landscape would push many white farmers back off the land.

Although some Native Americans who received land under the Dawes Act prospered enough to expand their holdings and go into large-scale farming or ranching, countless others struggled just to survive. Hunting restrictions on the former reservation lands prevented many Indians from supplementing their limited farm yields. Alcoholism, a continuing problem exacerbated by the prevalence of whiskey as a trade item (and by the boredom that resulted from the disruption of hunting and other traditional pursuits), became more prevalent

as Native Americans strove to adapt to the constraints of reservation life.

The Ghost Dance and the End of Indian Resistance on the Great Plains, 1890

Living conditions for the Sioux worsened in the late 1880s. The federal government reduced their meat rations and imposed more and more restrictions. When disease killed a third of their cattle, they became desperate. The Sioux, who still numbered almost twenty-five thousand, turned to Wovoka, a new prophet popular among the Great Basin Indians in Nevada. Wovoka promised to restore the Sioux to their original dominance on the Plains if they performed the Ghost Dance.

Wearing sacred Ghost Shirts—cotton or leather vestments decorated to ward off evil—the dancers

Ten-year old Chehia Red Arrow was scared when she left her home on the Gila River Reservation in 1908 for the Phoenix Indian School. Raised in a traditional Pima Indian family, Chehia, or Anna Moore Shaw, as she would later be called, had heard rumors that children at the school were whipped when they disobeyed. Would that happen to her? Would she have any friends? How would she be treated?

Chehia had good cause for concern. Founded in 1891, the Phoenix Indian School had been modeled after Richard Henry Pratt's famous military-style, off-reservation boarding school in Carlisle, Pennsylvania, which was designed to "Americanize" and "uplift" the Indian. Pratt believed that the Indians' culture, customs, and languages had halted their progress toward white civilization. His motto therefore became "Kill the Indian in him and save the man."

Opening in a converted hotel and nearby farm in 1891, the Phoenix Indian School was a joint product of local boosters and the federal Indian Office. Nestled between mountain ranges in the Salt River Valley, the city of Phoenix had been founded in 1868. The early settlers had restored the ancient Hohokam Indian irrigation system and had begun to create a bustling desert oasis. Although Phoenix in 1890 had a population of only three thousand, local promoters had also persuaded the legislature to place the territorial capital there. They now campaigned for an industrial training school that might provide "cheap and efficient" labor for local families and for the production of fruit and cotton. The city's citizens joined with the federal government to purchase 160 acres of land located three miles north of the city for a school farm. In support of the school, federal Indian Commissioner Thomas Morgan visited Phoenix and delivered a speech entitled "Cheaper to Educate Indians Than to Kill Them."

The school, which enrolled both Indian and Mexican-American students, was run along strict military lines. Upon arrival, students were washed, given a haircut, and issued a military uniform. Forbidden to speak their native languages, they were assigned "civilized" Christian names. Often lonely or homesick, some ran away. Twelve-year-old James McCarthy, a Papago Indian, surprised his mother when he showed up at her doorstep after walking 115 miles.

Other runaways were caught. Helen Sekaquaptewa, a Hopi student, noted that boys who returned were placed in detention, or had their heads shaved and were forced to march in the schoolyard wearing girl's clothing. Girls might have to cut grass with scissors or wear a sign saying "I ran away." Although many school superintendents avoided physical punishment, some of their subordinates beat the students. Occasionally, measles, influenza, and mumps swept through the school and students died.

Anna Moore Shaw, *A Pima Past*, U. Arizona Press, Tucson, AZ

The academic program at the Phoenix Indian School, like that at Booker T. Washington's Tuskegee Institute, focused primarily on vocational training that was designed to change traditional Indian gender roles. Boys, who were traditionally hunters, could learn carpentry, blacksmithing, tailoring, shoemaking, harness making, and farming; girls, who in Indian society did the farming, were now viewed as "the uplifter of the home." They studied home economics, dressmaking, and nursing. The

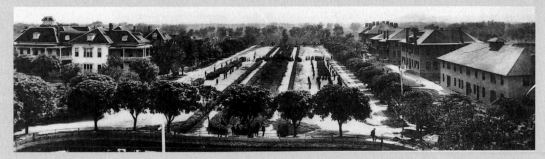

At boarding school, Indians and nature were made to conform with white concepts of order, space, and beauty as evidenced in this scene at Phoenix Indian School, ca. 1900.

students kept the school solvent. The boys ran the school farm; the girls sewed, washed, and ironed their own clothes, cleaned the buildings, and cooked and served the food.

To gain additional practical experience, students participated in the "outing" system that sent them into the community to work for local farmers or to serve as domestic help for families. As long as they behaved properly, students experienced little discrimination and were often pleased by the income made possible by their jobs. Eventually, however, the "outing" system, originally designed to promote assimilation, primarily became a method of supplying cheap labor to white employers.

Despite the strict discipline of school life, many students enjoyed their life there. Music was particularly popular. As Chehia remembered, "They had a boys' and a girls battalion . . . . The students were taught to keep in step to the music of the school band. . . . A snare drummer always beat his rhythms in front of the academic building, and we had to keep in step." Like other off-reservation boarding schools, the Phoenix Indian School was well known for its marching band, which was often invited to play for civic occasions in town. Tourists and townspeople frequently visited the school, and the Christmas pageant became an annual city event.

Sports, particularly football and baseball, were also popular. At the turn of the century, teams at Carlisle and other Indian schools competed against Harvard, Notre Dame, and Michigan State. The most famous Indian athlete, Jim Thorpe, captained the football and basketball teams at Carlisle and won gold medals at the 1912 Olympic games in Stockholm.

By the mid-1890s many Native American families acknowledged the value of boarding school education, and Phoenix and other schools were overwhelmed with requests for admission. By 1899 more than seven hundred Indians were attending the Phoenix school, making it second only to Carlisle. In 1900 the federal government was operating 153 boarding schools attended by more than seventeen thousand pupils.

Ironically, although many students valued the discipline and education of boarding school life, the attempt to stamp out Indian identity often resulted in resistance.

Forming friendships with Indians from many different tribes, boarding school students forged their own sense of Indian identity. As Mitch Walking Elk, a Cheyenne-Arapaho-Hopi singer put it, "They put me in the boarding school and they cut off all my hair, gave me an education, but the Apache's still in there."

After graduating, Chehia Red Arrow moved back to the reservation and married Ross Shaw, a classmate. One month later, "with mixed emotions," they returned to Phoenix. "Our hearts ached for them [Shaw's parents] in their difficult existence," she admitted, "but both Ross and I knew that laboring beside his parents in the fields each day was not the best way to help. The educations they had strived so hard to give us had prepared us to bring in money from the white man's world: it would be wrong to waste all those years on a life of primitive farming. . . .

True," she admitted, "we had been educated in the white man's ways, but we were still traditional Pimas with strong feelings of duty to our families and an intense love of our land." Decades later, after raising a family, she helped establish a Pima Indian museum, edited the tribal newsletter, and, to reaffirm and preserve her Indian identity, published her own book, *Pima Indian Legends*.

Prayers before bedtime, Phoenix Indian School, 1900.

moved in a circle, accelerating until they reached a trancelike state and experienced visions of the future. Many believed that the Ghost Shirts would protect them from harm.

In the fall of 1890, as the Ghost Dance movement spread among the Sioux in the Dakota Territory, Indian officials and military authorities grew alarmed. The local reservation agent, Major James McLaughlin, decided that Chief Sitting Bull, whose cabin on the reservation had become a rallying point for the Ghost Dance movement, must be arrested. On a freezing, drizzly December morning, McLaughlin dispatched a company of forty-two Indian policemen from the agency to take Sitting Bull into custody. When two policemen pulled the chief from his cabin, his bodyguard Catch-the-Bear shot one of them. As the policeman fell, he in turn shot Sitting Bull at point-blank range. Bloody hand-to-hand fighting immediately broke out. As bullets whizzed by, Sitting Bull's horse began to perform the tricks it remembered from its days in the Wild West show. Some observers were terrified, convinced that the spirit of the dead chief had entered his horse.

Two weeks later, one of the bloodiest episodes of Indian-white strife on the Plains occurred. On December 29, the Seventh Cavalry was rounding up 340 starving and freezing Sioux at Wounded Knee, South Dakota, when an excited Indian fired a gun hidden under a blanket. The soldiers retaliated with cannon fire. Within minutes 300 Indians, including 7 infants, were slaughtered. Three days later, a baby who had miraculously survived was found wrapped in a blanket under the snow. She wore a buckskin cap on which a beadwork American flag had been embroidered. Brigadier General L. W. Colby, who adopted the baby, named her Marguerite, but the Indians called her Lost Bird.

As the frozen corpses at Wounded Knee were dumped into mass graves, a generation of Indian-white conflict on the Great Plains shuddered to a close. Lost Bird, with her poignantly patriotic beadwork cap, highlights the irony of the Plains Indians' response to white expansion. Many did try to adapt to non-Indian ways, but few succeeded fully, and many others were devastated at being forced to abandon deeply held religious beliefs and a way of life rooted in hunting, cooperative

Wounded Knee
Piled up like cordwood, the frozen bodies of the Sioux slaughtered at Wounded Knee were a grim reminder that the U.S. Army would brook no opposition to its control of Indian reservation life.

living, and nomadism. Driven onto reservations, the Plains Indians were reduced to almost complete dependency. By 1900 the Plains Indian population had shrunk from nearly a quarter-million to just over a hundred thousand. Nevertheless, the population began to increase slowly after 1900. Against overwhelming odds, the pride, group memory, and cultural identity of the Plains Indians survived all efforts at eradication.

Unlike the nomadic western Sioux, the more settled Navajos of the Southwest adjusted more successfully to the reservation system, preserving traditional ways while incorporating elements of the new order in a complex process of cultural adaptation. By 1900 the Navajos had tripled their reservation land, dramatically increased their numbers and their herds, and carved out for themselves a distinct place in Arizona and New Mexico.

These extraordinary changes were forced on the Indian population by the advance of non-Indian settlement. In the name of civilization and progress, non-Indians in the generation after the Civil War pursued a course that involved a mixture of sincere (if misguided) benevolence, coercion wrapped in an aura of legality,

and outbursts of naked violence. Many white Americans felt toward the Indians only contempt, hatred, and greed for their land. Others viewed themselves as divinely chosen instruments for uplifting and Christianizing the Indians. Both groups, however, were blind to the value of Native American life and traditions. And both played their part in shattering a proud people and an ancient culture. The Indians' fate would weigh on the American conscience for generations.

SETTLING THE WEST

The successive defeats of the Native Americans transformed the western landscape by opening up for settlement a vast territory that reached from the Great Plains to the Sierra Nevada and Cascade Mountains. In the 1840s, when nearly a quarter-million Americans had trudged overland to Oregon and California, they had typically endured a six- to eight-month trip in ox-drawn wagons. After 1870 railroad expansion made the trip faster and considerably easier. In the next three decades, more land was parceled out into farms than in the previous 250 years of American history combined, and agricultural production doubled.

The First Transcontinental Railroad

Passed in 1862, the Pacific Railroad Act authorized the construction of a new transcontinental link. The act provided grants of land and other subsidies to the railroads for each mile of track laid, which made them the largest landholders in the West. Over the next half-century, nine major routes, which ran from the South or Midwest to the West, were built. More than any other factor, the expansion of these railroads accelerated the transformation of everyday life west of the Mississippi.

Building the railroad took backbreaking work. Searching for inexpensive labor, the railroads turned to immigrants. The Central Pacific employed Chinese workers to chip and blast rail bed out of solid rock in the Sierra Nevada. The railroad preferred the Chinese laborers because they worked hard for low wages, did not drink, and furnished their own food and tents. Nearly twelve thousand Chinese graded the roadbed while Irish, Mexican-American, and black workers put down the track.

On May 10, 1869, Americans celebrated the completion of the first railroad spanning North America. As the two sets of tracks—the Union Pacific's, stretching westward from Omaha, Nebraska, and the Central Pacific's, reaching eastward from Sacramento, California—met at Promontory Point, Utah, beaming officials drove in a

General Colby and Child
In keeping with his missionary vision, Brigadier General L. W. Colby, commander of the Nebraska National Guard, proudly holds his adopted Indian daughter whose parents had been killed in the bloody massacre.

Immigrants Looking for Homesteads, Kansas Garden City Square & Land Company, 1910
Railroads often joined forces with land companies to settle foreign immigrants on their holdings. Posed in their Sunday clothes against a background of a productive farm, this picture was meant to suggest the endless acres of land available for those willing to move west.

final ceremonial golden spike. The nation's vast midsection was now far more accessible than it had ever been.

The railroads quickly proved their usefulness. In the battles against Native Americans, the army shipped horses and men west in the dead of winter to attack the Indians when they were most vulnerable. From the same trains, hunters gained quick access to the bison ranges and increased their harvest of the animals. Once Indian resistance had been broken, the railroads not only expedited the shipment of new settlers and their supplies; they also provided fast access for the shipment of cattle and grain to eastern urban markets. In short, the railroads influenced much of the development of the West.

Settlers and the Railroad

During the decade after the passage of the Pacific Railroad Act, Congress awarded the railroads 170 million acres, worth over half a billion dollars. By 1893 the states of Minnesota and Washington had also deeded to railroad companies a quarter of their state lands; Wisconsin, Iowa, Kansas, North Dakota, and Montana had turned over a fifth of their acreage. As mighty landowners, the railroads had a unique opportunity to shape settlement in the region—and to reap enormous profits (see Map 17.3).

The railroads used several different tactics to attract inhabitants. They created land sales offices and sent agents to the East Coast and Europe to recruit settlers. While the agents glorified the West as a new Garden of Eden, the land bureaus offered prospective buyers long-term loans and free transportation. Acknowledging that life on the Great Plains could be lonely, the promoters advised young men to bring their wives (because "maidens are scarce") and to emigrate as entire families and with friends.

One unintended consequence of these land promotions was to make land available to single women, or "girl homesteaders" as they were known at the time, to establish farms near other family members. In Wyoming single women made up more than 18 percent of the claimants.

In addition to the millions of Americans who migrated from nearby states, the railroads helped bring nearly 2.2 million foreign-born settlers to the trans-Mississippi West between 1870 and 1900. Some agents recruited whole villages of Germans and eastern Europeans to relocate to the North Dakota plains. Irish laborers hired to lay track could be found in every town

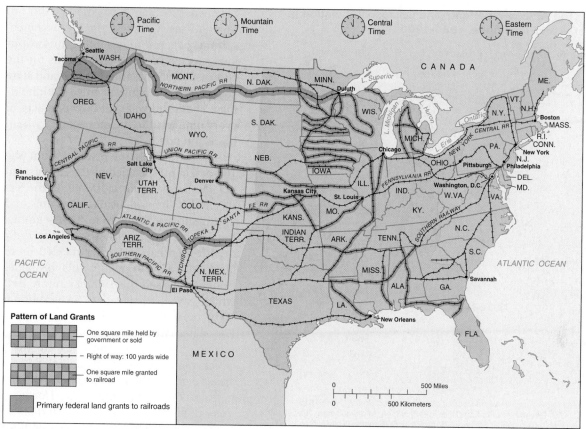

MAP 17.3

Transcontinental Railroads and Federal Land Grants, 1850–1900

Despite the laissez-faire ideology that argued against government interference in business, Congress heavily subsidized American railroads and gave them millions of acres of land. As illustrated in the box, belts of land were reserved on either side of a railroad's right of way. Until the railroad claimed the exact one-mile-square sections it chose to possess, all such sections within the belt remained closed to settlement.

along the rail lines. By 1905 the Santa Fe Railroad alone had transported sixty thousand Russian Mennonites to the fertile Kansas plains where black pioneers called exodusters had preceded them in the 1870s (see Table 17.1 as well as Chapter 16).

The railroads influenced agriculture as well. To ensure quick repayment of the money owed to them, the railroads urged new immigrants to specialize in cash crops—wheat on the northern Plains, corn in Iowa and Kansas, cotton and tobacco in Texas. Although these crops initially brought in high revenues, many farmers grew dependent on income from a single crop and became vulnerable to fluctuating market forces.

An African-American Homestead Near Guthrie, Oklahoma Territory, 1889

Seated proudly in front of their sod house and barn, the two generations of this black family were part of the more than 56,000 blacks who had moved to Oklahoma by 1900.

TABLE 17.1   The African-American and Chinese Population in Western States and Territories, 1880–1900

State or Territory	Blacks		Chinese	
	1880	1900	1880	1900
Arizona Ter.	155	1,846	1,630	1,419
California	6,018	11,045	75,132	45,753
Colorado	2,435	8,570	612	599
Idaho	53	293	3,379	1,467
Kansas	43,107	52,003	19	39
Montana	346	1,523	1,765	1,739
Nebraska	2,385	6,269	18	180
Nevada	488	134	5,416	1,352
New Mexico Ter.	1,015	1,610	57	341
North Dakota	113	286	NA	32
Oklahoma Indian Ter.	NA	56,684*	NA	31
Oregon	487	1,105	9,510	10,397
South Dakota	288	465	NA	165
Texas	393,384	620,722	136	836
Utah	232	672	510	572
Washington	325	2,514	3,186	3,629

NA—not available.

*Combined total for Indian and Oklahoma territories.

Source: *U.S. Bureau of the Census, Negro Population in the United States, 1790–1915* (Washington, D.C.: U.S. Government Printing Office, 1918), 43, 44; Michael Doran, "Population Statistics of Nineteenth Century Indian Territory," *Chronicles of Oklahoma* 53:4 (Winter 1975), 501; and *The Tenth Census, 1880, Population*, and *Twelfth Census, 1900, Population*, (Washington, D.C.: U.S. Government Printing Office, 1883 &1901).

Homesteading on the Great Plains

Liberalized land laws were another powerful magnet pulling settlers westward. The Homestead Act passed in 1862 reflected the Republican party's belief that free land would enable the poor to achieve economic independence. It offered 160 acres of land to any individual who would pay a ten-dollar registration fee, live on the land for five years, and cultivate and improve it. Because getting to the Great Plains was costly, most settlers migrated from nearby states.

The Homestead Act also proved attractive to immigrants from the British Isles as well as from Scandinavia and other regions of Europe where good-quality land was prohibitively expensive. Urged on by land promoters, waves of English, Irish, Germans, Swedes, Danes, Norwegians, and Czechs immigrated to the United States in the 1870s and 1880s and formed their own communities.

Although nearly four hundred thousand families claimed land under the provisions of the Homestead Act

between 1860 and 1900, the law did not function as Congress had envisioned. Advance agents representing unscrupulous speculators filed false claims for the choicest locations, and railroads and state governments acquired huge landholdings. The result was that only one acre in every nine went to the pioneers for whom it was intended.

A second problem resulted from the 160-acre limit specified by the Homestead Act. On the rich soils of Iowa or in the fertile lands in California, Oregon, and Washington, a 160-acre farm was ample, but in the drier areas west of the hundredth meridian, a farmer needed more land. In 1873, to rectify this problem, Congress passed the Timber Culture Act, which gave homesteaders an additional 160 acres if they planted trees on 40 acres. For states with little rainfall, Congress enacted the Desert Land Act in 1877, which made 640 acres available at $1.25 an acre on condition that the owner irrigate part of it within three years. However, this act, along with the Timber and Stone Act of 1878, which permitted the purchase of up to 160 acres of forest land for $2.50 an acre, was abused by grasping speculators, lumber-company representatives, and cattle ranchers seeking to expand their holdings. Yet, even though families did not receive as much land as Congress had intended, federal laws kept alive the dream of the West as a place for new beginnings.

In addition to problems faced by those who bought from unscrupulous speculators or chose property in areas that lacked sufficient rainfall to grow crops, almost all settlers faced difficult psychological adjustments to frontier life. The first years of settlement were the most difficult. Toiling to build a house, plow the fields, plant the first crop, and drill a well, the pioneers put in an average of sixty-eight hours of tedious, backbreaking work a week in isolated surroundings. Howard Ruede, a Pennsylvania printer who migrated to Kansas to farm, wrote home in 1877 complaining about the mosquitoes and bedbugs infesting his house, which was cut out of thick grass sod and dug into the ground. He and countless others coping with the severe Plains conditions saw their shining vision of Edenic farm life quickly dim. For blacks who emigrated from the South to Kansas and

other parts of the Plains after the Civil War, prejudice compounded the burdens of adjusting to a different life (see Chapter 16).

Many middle-class women, swept up in the romantic conventions of the day, found adaptation to Plains frontier life especially difficult. At least initially, some were enchanted by the haunting landscape, and in letters they described the open Plains as arrestingly beautiful. But far more were struck by the "horrible tribes of Mosquitoes"; the violent weather-drenching summer thunderstorms with hailstones as "big as hen's eggs" and blinding winter blizzards; and the crude sod huts that served as their early homes because of the scarcity of timber. One woman burst into tears upon first seeing her new sod house. The young bride angrily informed her husband that her father had built a better house for his hogs.

The high transience rate on the frontier in these years reflected the difficulty that newcomers faced in adjusting to life on the Great Plains. Nearly half of those who staked homestead claims in Kansas between 1862 and 1890 relinquished their rights to the land and moved on. However, in places like Minnesota and the Pacific Northwest that were populated largely by Germans, Norwegians, and other immigrants with a tradition of family prosperity tied to continuous landownership, the persistence rate (or percentage of people staying for a decade or more) could be considerably higher.

Many who weathered the lean early years eventually came to identify deeply with the land. Within a decade, the typical Plains family that had "stuck it out" had moved into a new wood-framed house and had fixed up the front parlor. Women worked particularly hard on these farms and took pride in their accomplishments. "Just done the chores," wrote one woman to a friend. "I went fence mending and getting out cattle . . . and came in after sundown. I fed my White Leghorns [chickens] and then sat on the step to read over your letter. I forgot my wet feet and shoes full of gravel and giggled joyously."

New Farms, New Markets

Farmers on the Plains took advantage of advances in farm mechanization and the development of improved strains of wheat and corn to boost production dramatically. Efficient steel plows; spring-tooth harrows that broke up the dense prairie soil more effectively than earlier models; specially designed wheat planters; and improved grain binders, threshers, and windmills all allowed the typical Great Plains farmer of the late nineteenth century to increase the land's yield tenfold.

Barbed wire, patented in 1874, was another crucial invention that permitted farmers who lived where few trees grew to keep roving livestock out of their crops. But fencing the land touched off violent clashes between farmers and cattle ranchers, who demanded the right to let their herds roam freely until the roundup. Generally the farmers won.

The invention of labor-saving machinery together with increased demand for wheat, milk, and other farm products created the impression that farming was entering a period of unparalleled prosperity. But few fully understood the perils of pursuing agriculture as a livelihood. The cost of the land, horses, machinery, and seed needed to start up a farm could exceed twelve hundred dollars, far more than the annual earnings of the average industrial worker. Faced with substantial mortgage payments, many farmers had to specialize in a crop such as wheat or corn that would fetch high prices. This specialization made them dependent on the railroads for shipping and put them at the mercy of the international grain market's shifting prices.

Far from being an independent producer, the western grain grower was a player in a complex world market economy. Railroad and steamship transport enabled the American farmer to compete in the international market. High demand could bring prosperity, but when world overproduction forced grain prices down, the heavily indebted grower faced ruin. Confronted with these realities, many Plains farmers quickly abandoned the illusion of frontier independence and easy wealth.

Unpredictable rainfall and weather conditions further exacerbated homesteaders' difficulties west of the hundredth meridian, where rainfall averaged less than twenty inches a year. Farmers compensated through "dry farming"—plowing deeply to stimulate the capillary action of the soils and harrowing lightly to raise a covering of dirt that would retain precious moisture after a rainfall. They also built windmills and diverted creeks for irrigation. But the onset of unusually dry years in the 1870s, together with grasshopper infestations and the major economic depression that struck the United States between 1873 and 1878 (see Chapter 16), made the plight of some midwesterners desperate.

Building a Society and Achieving Statehood

Despite the hardships, many remote farm settlements often blossomed into thriving communities. Churches and Sunday schools among the first institutions to appear became humming centers of social activity as

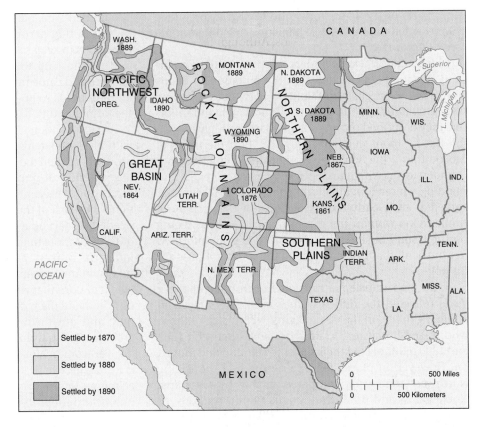

MAP 17.4
The Settlement of the Trans-Mississippi West, 1860–1890
The West was not settled by a movement of peoples gradually creeping westward from the East. Rather, settlers first occupied California and the Midwest and then filled up the nation's vast interior.

well as of worship. Farmers gathered for barn raisings and group threshings, and families pooled their energies in quilting and husking bees. Neighbors readily lent a hand to the farmer whose barn had burned or whose family was sick. Cooperation was a practical necessity and a form of insurance in a rugged environment where everyone was vulnerable to instant misfortune or even disaster.

As settlements grew into small towns, their inhabitants labored to reverse easterners' images of rural life as unrefined and backward. They eagerly established lyceums and libraries to uplift local residents. Masonic lodges, temperance clubs, and a wide variety of social associations followed. Larger communities established fashionable hotels, the symbol of sophistication and culture, and brought in entertainers to perform at their new "opera houses."

When the population increased, local boosters lobbied to turn the territory into a state. Achieving statehood required the residents of the territory to petition Congress to pass an enabling act establishing the territory's boundaries and authorizing an election to select delegates for a state constitutional convention. Once the state constitution had been drawn up and ratified by popular vote, the territory applied to Congress for admission as a state.

Under these procedures, Kansas entered the Union in 1861, followed by Nevada in 1864 and Nebraska in 1867. Colorado joined in 1876. Not until 1889 did North Dakota, South Dakota, Montana, and Washington gain statehood. Wyoming and Idaho came into the Union the following year. Utah, long prevented from joining because of the Mormon practice of polygamy, finally declared plural marriages illegal and entered in 1896. With Oklahoma's admission in 1907 and Arizona's and New Mexico's in 1912, the process of creating permanent political institutions in the trans-Mississippi West was complete (see Map 17.4).

Although generally socially conservative, the new state governments supported woman suffrage. As territories became states, pioneer women, encouraged by women's rights activists like Susan B. Anthony and Elizabeth Cady Stanton, battled for the vote. Seven western states held referenda on this issue between 1870 and 1910. Success came first in the Wyoming Territory, where the tiny legislature enfranchised women in 1869 in the belief that the vote would give women equal political rights and would make them more effective moral caretakers on the rowdy frontier. The Utah Territory followed in 1870 and reaffirmed its

support for woman suffrage when it became a state. Nebraska in 1867 and Colorado in 1876 permitted women to vote in school elections. Although these successes were significant, by 1910 only four states—Idaho, Wyoming, Utah, and Colorado—had granted women full voting rights. The very newness of their place in the Union may have sensitized legislators in these states to women's important contributions to settlement and made them open to experimentation, but by and large, familiar practices persisted.

THE SOUTHWESTERN FRONTIER

In 1848 the Treaty of Guadalupe Hildalgo that had ended the Mexican War ceded to the United States an immense territory, part of which became California, Arizona, and New Mexico. At the time, Mexicans had controlled vast expanses of the Southwest. They had built their own churches, maintained large ranching operations, and had traded with the Indians. Although the United States had pledged to protect the liberty and property of Mexicans who remained on American soil, in the next three decades, American ranchers and settlers took control of the territorial governments and forced the Spanish-speaking population off much of the land. Mexicans who stayed behind adapted to the new Anglo society with varying degrees of success.

In Texas the struggle for independence from Mexico had left a legacy of bitterness and misunderstanding.

After 1848 Texas cotton planters confiscated Mexican lands and began a racist campaign to label Mexicans as nonwhite. Only white people, the Texans assumed, deserved economic and legal rights. Angered by their loss of land and discriminatory treatment, Mexican bandits retaliated by raiding American communities. Tensions peaked in 1859 when Juan Cortina, a Mexican rancher, attacked the Anglo border community of Brownsville, Texas, and freed all the prisoners in jail. Pursued by the U.S. army, Cortina battled the Americans for years until the Mexican government, fearing a U.S. invasion, imprisoned him in 1875.

Mexican-Americans in California in the 1850s and 1860s faced similar exclusionary pressures. A cycle of flood and drought, together with a slumping cattle industry at midcentury, had ruined many of the large southern California ranches owned by the *californios*, the Spanish-speaking descendants of the original Spanish settlers. The collapse of the ranch economy forced many of these Mexican-Americans to retreat into socially segregated urban neighborhoods called barrios. Spanish-surnamed citizens made up nearly half the 2,640 residents of Santa Barbara, California, in 1870; they comprised barely a quarter of the population ten years later. Maintaining a tenacious hold on their traditions, Spanish-speaking people in Santa Barbara and other towns survived by working as low-paid day laborers.

In California, the pattern of racial discrimination, manipulation, and exclusion was similar for Mexicans,

Santa Fe Plaza, New Mexico, in the 1880s, by Francis X. Grosshenney
After the railroad went through in 1878, Santa Fe became a popular tourist attraction known for its historic adobe buildings. Although the town retained a large Spanish-speaking population with their own newspaper, by the 1880s American and German immigrants monopolized most positions in business, government, the professions, and the skilled trades.

Native Americans, and Chinese. As the number of Anglo newcomers increased, they identified minority racial, cultural, and language differences as marks of inferiority. White state legislators passed laws that made ownership of property difficult for non-Anglos. Relegated to a migratory labor force, non-Anglos were tagged as shiftless and irresponsible. Yet their labor made possible increased prosperity for the farmers, railroads, and households that hired them.

The cultural adaptation of Spanish-speaking Americans to Anglo society unfolded more smoothly in Arizona and New Mexico, where initial Spanish settlement had been sparse and a small class of wealthy Mexican landowners had long dominated a poor, illiterate peasantry. Moreover, beginning in the 1820s, well-to-do Mexicans in Tucson, Arizona, had educated their children in the United States and formed trading partnerships and business alliances with Americans. One of the most successful was Estevan Ochoa, who began a long-distance freighting business in 1859 with a U.S. partner and then expanded it into a lucrative merchandising, mining, and sheep-raising operation.

The success of hard-working businessmen such as Ochoa, who became mayor of Tucson, helped moderate American settlers' antagonistic attitudes toward the indigenous Mexican-American population. So, too, did the work of popular writers like Bret Harte and Helen Hunt Jackson. By sentimentalizing an older, gracious Spanish-Mexican past, these authors increased public sympathy for Spanish-speaking Americans. Jackson's 1884 romance *Romona*, a tale of doomed love set on a California Spanish-Mexican ranch overwhelmed by the onrushing tide of Anglo civilization, was enormously popular. Moreover, over time, Mexican and Spanish revival architecture, with its white adobe-style walls and red-clay tile roofs, which was associated with this romantic past, fused with Anglo building traditions to create a distinctive Southwest regional building style.

Even in Arizona and New Mexico, not all interactions between Mexican-Americans and Anglos were harmonious. In the 1880s, Mexican-American and Anglo ranchers became embroiled in fiery land disputes. Organizing themselves as Las Gorras Blancas (the White Caps) in 1888, Mexican-American ranchers tore up railroad tracks and intimidated and attacked both Anglo newcomers and those Hispanics who had fenced acreage in northern New Mexico previously considered public grazing land. But this vigilante action gained them little, as Anglo-dominated corporate ranching steadily reduced their resources. Relations changed in the urban centers as well, as Mexican-American businessmen increasingly restricted their business dealings to their own people, and the Spanish-speaking population as a whole became more impoverished. Even in Tucson, where the Mexican-American elite enjoyed considerable economic and political success, 80 percent of the Mexican-Americans in the work force were laborers in 1880, taking jobs as butchers, barbers, cowboys, and railroad workers.

As increasing numbers of Mexican-American men lost title to their lands and were forced to search for seasonal migrant work, Mexican-American women took responsibility for holding families and communities together. Women managed the households when their husbands were away, and fostered group identification through their emphasis on traditional customs, kinship, and allegiance to the Catholic Church. They served as *madrinas*, or godmothers, for one another's children; tended garden plots; and traded food, soap, and produce with other women. This economy, invisible to those outside the village, stabilized the community in times of drought or persecution by Anglos.

Violence and discrimination against Spanish-speaking citizens of the Southwest escalated in the 1890s, a time of rising racism in the United States. Riots against Mexican-Americans broke out in the Texas communities of Beeville and Laredo in 1894 and 1899. Expressions of anti-Catholicism, as well as verbal attacks on Mexican-Americans as violent and lazy, increased among hostile Anglos. For Spanish-speaking citizens, the battle for fair treatment and cultural respect would continue into the twentieth century.

EXPLOITING THE WESTERN LANDSCAPE

The domination of Mexican-Americans and the removal of Native peoples opened the way for the transformation and exploitation of the natural environment in the trans-Mississippi West. White publicists, developers, and boosters had long promoted the region as a land of boundless opportunity. Between 1860 and 1900, a generation of Americans sought to strike it rich by joining the ranks of miners, ranchers, and farmers intent on making a fortune. Although the mining, ranching, and farming "bonanzas" promised unheard of wealth, in reality they set in motion a boom-and-bust economy in which many people went bankrupt or barely survived and others were bought out by large-scale enterprises that have continued to dominate production until today. Of all the groups that surged into the nation's mid-continent in the late nineteenth century, none had to revise

their expectations more radically than the speculators and adventurers thirsting for quick fortunes.

The Mining Frontier

In the half-century that began with the California gold rush in 1849, a series of mining booms swept from the Southwest northward into Canada and Alaska. Sensational discoveries in California's Sierra Nevada produced more than $81 million worth of gold bullion in 1852. The following year, Henry Comstock, an illiterate prospector, stumbled on the rich Comstock Lode along Nevada's Carson River. Months later, feverishly pursuing rumors of new strikes, prospectors swarmed into the Rocky Mountains and uncovered deep veins of gold and silver near present-day Denver. Over the next five decades, gold was discovered in Idaho, Montana, Wyoming, South Dakota, and, in 1896, in the Canadian Klondike. Although the popular press clearly exaggerated reports of miners scooping up gold by the panful, by 1900 more than a billion dollars worth of gold had been mined in California alone.

The early discoveries of "placer" gold, panned from streams, attracted a young male population thirsting for wealth and reinforced the myth of mining country as "a poor man's paradise" (see Map 17.5). In contrast to the Great Plains, where ethnic groups recreated their own ethnic enclaves, western mining camps became ethnic melting pots. In the California census of 1860, more than thirty-three thousand Irish and thirty-four thousand Chinese had staked out early claims (see Table 17.1).

Although a few prospectors became fabulously wealthy, the experience of Henry Comstock, who sold out one claim for eleven thousand dollars and another

MAP 17.5
The Mining and Cattle Frontiers, 1860–1890
The western mining and ranching bonanzas lured thousands of Americans hoping to get rich quick.

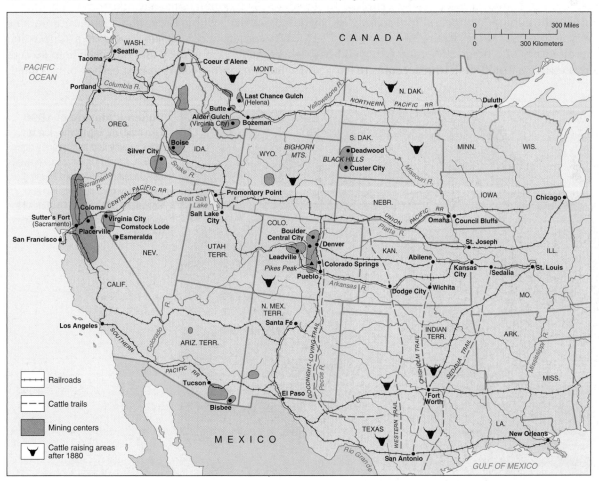

for two mules, was more typical. Because the larger gold and silver deposits lay embedded in veins of quartz deep within the earth, extracting them required huge investments in workers and expensive equipment. Deep shafts had to be blasted into the rock. Once lifted to the surface, the rock had to be crushed, flushed with mercury or cyanide to collect the silver, and smelted into ingots. No sooner had the major discoveries been made, therefore, than large mining companies backed by eastern or British capital bought them out and took them over.

Life in the new mining towns was vibrant but unpredictable. During the heyday of the Comstock Lode in the 1860s and 1870s, Virginia City, Nevada, erupted in an orgy of speculation and building. Started as a shanty-town in 1859, it swelled by 1873 into a thriving metropolis of twenty thousand people complete with elaborate mansions, a six-story hotel, an opera house, 131 saloons, 4 banks, and uncounted brothels. Men outnumbered women three to one. Money quickly earned was even more rapidly lost.

The boom-and-bust cycle evident in Virginia City was repeated in towns across the west. Mark Twain captured the thrill of the mining "stampedes" in *Roughing It* (1872). "Every few days," wrote Twain, "news would come of the discovery of a brand-new mining region: immediately the papers would teem with accounts of its

richness, and away the surplus population would scamper to take possession. By the time I was fairly inoculated with the disease, 'Esmeralda' had just had a run and 'Humboldt' was beginning to shriek for attention. 'Humboldt! Humboldt!' was the new cry, and straightway Humboldt, the newest of the new, the richest of the rich, the most marvelous of the marvelous discoveries in silver-land, was occupying two columns of the public prints to 'Esmeralda's' one."

One unintended consequence of the gold rush mania was the growth of settlement in Alaska (see Map 17.5). Small strikes were made there in 1869, two years after the United States had purchased the territory from Russia. More miners arrived in the 1880s after prospector Joe Juneau, for whom the town of Juneau was named, and others developed the Treadwell Mine. But it was the discovery of gold in the Canadian Klondike in 1897 that brought thousands of prospectors into the area and eventually enabled Alaska to establish its own territorial government in 1912.

Word of new ore deposits like the ones in Alaska lured transient populations salivating to get rich. Miners who worked deep within the earth for large corporations typically earned about $2,000 a year at a time when teachers made $450 to $650 and domestic help $250 to $350. But most prospectors at best earned only enough

Juneau, Alaska, c. 1896
Like other mining towns, Juneau grew rapidly and haphazardly after Kowee, a local Tlingit man, showed Joe Juneau and Richard Harris the location of gold nuggets in 1880. Between 1881 and 1944 Juneau's mines produced 6.7 million ounces of gold.

to go elsewhere, perhaps buy some land, and try again. Nevertheless, the production of millions of ounces of gold and silver stimulated the economy, lured new foreign investors, and helped usher the United States into the mainstream of the world economy.

Progress came at a price. The long-term cost to the environment to extract these metals was high. Hydraulic mining, which used water cannons to dislodge minerals, polluted rivers, turned creeks brown, and flushed millions of tons of silt into valleys. The scarred landscape that remained was littered with rock and gravel filled with traces of mercury and cyanide, and nothing would grow on it. Smelters spewed dense smoke containing lead, arsenic, and other carcinogenic chemicals on those who lived nearby and often made them sick. The destruction to the environment is still evident today.

Cowboys and the Cattle Frontier

As Mark Twain so colorfully related, accounts of gold strikes in the popular press had helped fuel the feverish expansion of the mining frontier during the 1860s and 1870s. Similar stories romanticizing the life of the hardy cowboy, driving dusty herds of longhorns northward from Texas through Oklahoma to markets in Dodge City and Abilene, Kansas, sparked the transformation of the cattle industry in these same decades. In this case, astute businessmen and railroad entrepreneurs, eager to fund their new investments in miles of track, promoted cattle herding as the new route to fame and fortune, and the eastern press took up the theme. The cowboy, once scorned as a ne'er-do-well and drifter, was now glorified as a man of rough-hewn integrity and self-reliant strength.

In 1868 Joseph G. McCoy, a young cattle dealer from Springfield, Illinois, shrewdly combined organizational and promotional skills to turn the cattle industry into a new money-maker. With the relocation of the Plains Indians onto reservations and the extension of the railroads into Kansas in the post–Civil War period, McCoy realized that cattle dealers could now amass enormous fortunes by raising steers cheaply in Texas and bringing them north for shipment to eastern urban markets (see Map 17.5).

Forming a partnership with his brothers, McCoy built a new stockyard in Abilene, Kansas. By guaranteeing to transport his steers in railcars to hungry eastern markets, he obtained a five-dollar kickback from the railroads on each cattle car shipped. To make the overland cattle drives from Texas to Abilene easier, McCoy also helped survey and shorten the Chisholm Trail in

Kansas. Finally, in a clever feat of showmanship, he organized the first Wild West show, sending four Texas cowboys to St. Louis and Chicago, where they staged roping and riding exhibitions that attracted exuberant crowds. At the end of his first year in business, thirty-five thousand steers were sold in Abilene; the following year the number more than doubled.

The great cattle drives of the 1860s and 1870s turned into a bonanza for herd owners. Steers purchased in Texas at nine dollars a head could be sold in Abilene, after deducting four dollars in trail expenses, for twenty-eight dollars. A herd of two thousand head could thus bring a tidy thirty-thousand-dollar profit. But the cattlemen, like the grain growers farther north on the Great Plains, lived at the mercy of high interest rates and an unstable market. During the financial panic of 1873, cattle drovers, unable to get extensions on their loans, fell into bankruptcy by the hundreds.

Little of the money made by the large-scale cattle ranchers found its way into the pockets of the cowboys themselves. The typical cowpunchers who drove herds through the dirt and dust from southern Texas to Abilene earned a mere thirty dollars a month, about the same as common laborers. They also braved the gangs of cattle thieves that operated along the trails. The most notorious of the cattle rustlers, William H. Bonney, better known as Billy the Kid, may have murdered as many as eleven men before he was killed by a sheriff in 1881 at the age of twenty-one. The long hours, low pay, and hazardous work discouraged older ranch hands from applying. Most cowboys were men in their teens and twenties who worked for a year or two and then pursued different livelihoods.

Of the estimated 35,000 to 55,000 men who rode the trails in these years, nearly one-fifth were black or Mexican. Barred by discrimination from many other trades, blacks enjoyed the freedom of life on the trail. Although they were excluded from the position of trail boss, they distinguished themselves as resourceful and shrewd cowpunchers. Nat Love, the son of Tennessee slaves, left for Kansas after the Civil War to work for Texas cattle companies. As chief brander, he moved through Texas and Arizona "dancing, drinking, and shooting up the town." By his own account, he was "wild, reckless, free," and "afraid of nothing." On July 4, 1876, when the Black Hills gold rush was in full swing, Love delivered three thousand head of cattle to a point near the hills and rode into Deadwood to celebrate. Local miners and gamblers had raised prize money for roping and shooting contests, and Nat Love won both, as well as a new title, Deadwood Dick.

Ned Huddleston, Alias Isom Dart
Outlaws and gunfighters, although small in number, created an image of the trans-Mississippi West as lawless and dangerous. Isom Dart, a member of Brown's Park outlaw faction in Colorado and Wyoming, here poses with his six-shooters.

Close relationships sometimes developed between black and white cowboys. Shortly before Charles Goodnight, a white pioneer trailblazer, died in 1929, he recalled of the black cowboy Bose Ikard, a former slave, that "he was my detective, banker, and everything else in Colorado, New Mexico, and the other wild country I was in. The nearest and only bank was at Denver, and when we carried money I gave it to Bose." Goodnight revealed much about the economic situation of blacks on the Plains, however, when he added that "a thief would never think of robbing him [Ikard]—never think of looking in a Negro's bed for money."

Although the typical cowboy led a lonely, dirty, and often boring existence, a mythic version of the frontier cowboy who might with equal ease become a gunslinging marshal or a dastardly villain was glamorized in the eastern press as early as the 1870s. The image of the West

as a wild and lawless land fired easterners' imaginations. In 1877 Edward L. Wheeler, a writer for the publishing house of Beadle and Adams, penned his first dime novel, *Deadwood Dick, The Prince of the Road: or, the Black Rider of the Black Hills.* Over the next eight years, Wheeler turned out thirty-three Deadwood Dick novels relating the adventures of the muscular young hero who wore black clothes and rode a black horse. Cast alternately as outlaw, miner, gang leader, and cowboy, Deadwood Dick turned his blazing six-shooters on ruthless ruffians and dishonest desperadoes. He had much in common with the real-life Deadwood Dick except that Wheeler, to please his white readership, made him a white man.

The reality was a good deal less picturesque. Although Abilene, for example, went through an early period of violence that saw cowboys pulling down the walls of the jail as it was being built, the town quickly established a police force to maintain law and order. City ordinances forbade carrying firearms and regulated saloons, gambling, and prostitution. James B. ("Wild Bill") Hickok served as town marshal in 1871, but his tenure was less eventful than legend had it. Dime novelists described him as "a veritable terror to bad men on the border," but during his term as Abilene's lawman, Hickok killed just two men, one of them by mistake. Transient, unruly types certainly gave a distinctive flavor to cattle towns like Abilene, Wichita, and Dodge City, but the overall homicide rates there were not unusually high.

More typical of western conflicts were the range wars that pitted "cattle kings" (who thought that the open range existed for them alone to exploit) against farmers. Gaining the upper hand in state legislatures, farming interests sought to cripple the freewheeling cattlemen with quarantine laws and inspection regulations. Ranchers retaliated against the spread of barbed-wire farm fencing, first by cutting the settlers' fences and then by buying up and enclosing thousands of acres of their own. Meanwhile, dozens of small-scale shooting incidents broke out between inhabitants of isolated farms and livestock drovers, as well as between rival cattlemen and sheep ranchers.

Despite these range wars, the cattle bonanza, which peaked between 1880 and 1885, produced more than 4.5 million head of cattle for eastern markets. Prices began to sag as early as 1882, however, and many ranchers, having expanded too rapidly, plunged heavily into debt. When President Grover Cleveland, trying to improve federal observance of Indian treaties, ordered cattlemen to remove their stock from the Cheyenne-Arapaho reser-

vation in 1885, two hundred thousand more cattle were crowded onto already overgrazed ranges. That same year and the following, two of the coldest and snowiest winters on record combined with summer droughts and Texas fever destroyed nearly 90 percent of the cattle in some regions, pushing thousands of ranchers into bankruptcy. The cattle industry lived on, but railroad expansion, which enabled ranchers to ship their steers north, brought the days of the open range and the great cattle drives to an end. As had the mining frontier, the cattle frontier left behind memories of individual daring, towering fortunes for some, and hard times for many.

Bonanza Farms

The enthusiasm that permeated mining and ranching in the 1870s and 1880s also percolated into agriculture. Like the gold rushes and cattle bonanzas, the wheat boom in the Dakota Territory started small but rapidly attracted large capital investments that produced the nation's first agribusinesses.

The boom began during the Panic of 1873, when the failure of numerous banks caused the price of Northern Pacific Railroad bonds to plummet. The railroad responded by exchanging land for its depreciated bonds. Speculators, including the railroad's own president, George W. Cass, jumped at the opportunity and purchased more than three hundred thousand acres in the fertile Red River valley of North Dakota for between fifty cents and a dollar an acre.

Operating singly or in groups, the speculators established factorylike ten-thousand-acre farms, each run by a hired manager, and invested heavily in labor and equipment. On the Cass-Cheney-Dalrymple farm near Fargo, North Dakota, which covered an area six miles long by four miles wide, fifty or sixty plows rumbled across the flat landscape on a typical spring day. The New York *Tribune* reported that Cass, who had invested fifty thousand dollars for land and equipment, paid all his expenses plus the cost of the ten thousand acres with his first harvest alone.

The publicity generated by the tremendous success of a few large investors like Cass and Oliver Dalrymple led to an unprecedented wheat boom in the Red River valley in 1880. Eastern banking syndicates and small farmers alike rushed to buy land. North Dakota's population tripled in the 1880s. Wheat production skyrocketed to almost 29 million bushels by the end of the decade. But the profits so loudly celebrated in the eastern press soon evaporated. By 1890 some Red River valley farmers were destitute.

The wheat boom collapsed for a variety of reasons. Overproduction, high investment costs, too little or too much rain, excessive reliance on one crop, and depressed grain prices on the international market all undercut farmers' earnings. Large-scale farmers who had invested in hopes of getting rich felt lucky just to survive. Oliver Dalrymple lamented in 1889 that "it seems as if the time has come when there is no money in wheat raising."

Large-scale farms proved most successful in California's Central Valley. Using canals and other irrigation systems to water their crops, farmers were growing higher-priced specialty crops and had created new cooperative marketing associations for cherries, apricots, grapes, and oranges by the mid-1880s. Led by the California Citrus Growers' Association, which used the "Sunkist" trademark for their oranges, large-scale agribusinesses in California were shipping a variety of fruits and vegetables in refrigerated train cars to midwestern and eastern markets by 1900.

The Oklahoma Land Rush, 1889

As farmers in the Dakotas and Minnesota were enduring poor harvests and falling prices, hard-pressed would-be homesteaders greedily eyed the enormous Indian Territory, as present-day Oklahoma was then known. The federal government, considering much of the land in this area virtually worthless, had reserved it for the Five Civilized Tribes since the 1830s. Because these tribes (except for some Cherokees) had sided with the Confederacy during the Civil War, Washington had punished them by settling thousands of Indians from other tribes on lands in the western part of the territory. By the 1880s, land-hungry non-Indians argued that the Civilized Tribes' betrayal of the Union justified further confiscation of their land.

In 1889, over the Native Americans' protests, Congress transferred to the federally owned public domain nearly 2 million acres in the central part of the Oklahoma Territory that had not been specifically assigned to any Indian tribe. At noon on April 22, 1889, thousands of men, women, and children in buggies and wagons stampeded into the new lands to stake out homesteads. (Other settlers, the so-called Sooners, had illegally arrived earlier and were already plowing the fields.) Before nightfall tent communities had risen at Oklahoma City and Guthrie near stations on the Santa Fe Railroad. Nine weeks later, six thousand homestead claims had been filed. The next decade, the Dawes Severalty Act broke up the Indian reservations into

MAP 17.6
**The Oklahoma Land Rush,
1889–1906**

Lands in Oklahoma not settled by "Sooners" were sold by lotteries, allotments, and sealed-bid auctions. By 1907 the major reservations had been broken up, and each Native American family had been given a small farm.

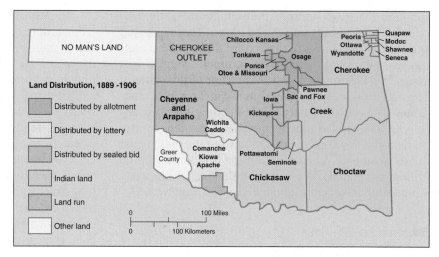

individual allotments and opened the surplus to non-Indian settlement (see Map 17.6).

The Oklahoma land rush demonstrated the continuing power of the frontier myth, which tied "free" land to the ideal of economic opportunity. Despite early obstacles—the 1889 rush occurred too late in the season for most settlers to plant a full crop, and a drought parched the land the following year—Oklahoma farmers remained optimistic about their chances of making it on the last frontier. Most survived because they were fortunate enough to have obtained fertile land in an area where the normal rainfall was thirty inches, ten inches more than in the semiarid regions farther west. Still, within two generations a combination of exploitative farming, poor land management, and sporadic drought would place Oklahoma at the desolate center of what in the 1930s would be called the dust bowl (see Chapter 24).

THE WEST OF LIFE AND LEGEND

In 1893, four years after the last major tract of western Indian land, the Oklahoma Territory, was opened to non-Indian settlement, a young Wisconsin historian, Frederick Jackson Turner, delivered a lecture entitled "The Significance of the Frontier in American History." "[T]he frontier has gone," declared Turner, "and with its going has closed the first period of American history." Although Turner's assertion that the frontier was closed was based on a Census Bureau announcement, it was inaccurate (more western land would be settled in the twentieth century than in the nineteenth). But his linking of economic opportunity with the transformation of the trans-Mississippi West caught the popular imagination and launched a new school of historical inquiry into the effects of the frontier on U.S. history.

Scholars now recognize that many parts of Turner's "frontier thesis," particularly its ethnocentric omission of Native Americans' claims to the land, were inaccurate. Yet his idealized view of the West did reflect ideas popular among his contemporaries in the 1890s. As farmers, miners, ranchers, Indian agents, and prostitutes had pursued their varied activities in the real West, a parallel legendary West had taken deep root in the American imagination. In the nineteenth century, this mythic West was a product of novels, songs, and paintings. In the twentieth century, it would be perpetuated by movies, radio programs, and television shows. The legend merits attention, for its evolution is fascinating and its influence has been far-reaching.

The American Adam and the Dime-Novel Hero

In the early biographies of frontiersmen like Daniel Boone and in the wilderness novels of James Fenimore Cooper, the western hero's personal development sometimes parallels, but more often runs counter to, the interests of society. Mid-nineteenth-century writers, extending the theme of the western wilderness as an alternative to society, presented the frontiersman as a kind of mythic American Adam—simple, virtuous, and innocent, untainted by a corrupt social order. For example, an early biographer of Kit Carson, the Kentucky-born guide who made one of the first recorded crossings of California's Mojave Desert in 1830, depicted him as a perfect antidote to the evils of refined society, an indi-

vidual of "genuine simplicity, . . . truthfulness . . .[and] bravery." At the end of Mark Twain's *Huckleberry Finn*, Huck rejects the constraints of settled society as represented by Aunt Sally and heads west with the declaration, "I reckon I got to light out for the territory ahead of the rest, because Aunt Sally she's going to adopt me and sivilize me, and I can't stand it. I been there before." In this version of the legend, the West is a place of adventure, romance, or contemplation where one can escape from society and its pressures.

But even as this conception of the myth was being popularized, another powerful theme had emerged as well. The authors of the dime novels of the 1860s and 1870s offered the image of the western frontiersman as a new masculine ideal, the tough guy who fights for truth and honor. In *Buffalo Bill: King of the Border Men* (1869), a dime novel loosely based on real-life William F. ("Buffalo Bill") Cody, Edward Judson (who published under the name Ned Buntline) created an idealized hero who is a powerful moral force as he drives off treacherous Indians and rounds up villainous cattle rustlers.

So enthusiastically did the public welcome this new fictional frontiersman that Cody was inspired in 1883 to start his Wild West show. A former army scout and buffalo hunter, Cody was a natural showman, and his exhibitions proved immensely popular. Cody presented mock battles between army scouts and Indians that were, in effect, morality dramas of good versus evil. Along with entertainment, in short, the Wild West show reinforced the dime-novel image of the West as an arena of moral encounter where virtue always triumphed.

Revitalizing the Frontier Legend

Eastern writers and artists eagerly embraced both versions of the myth—the West as a place of escape from society and the West as a stage on which the moral conflicts confronting society were played out. Three young members of the eastern establishment, Theodore Roosevelt, Frederic Remington, and Owen Wister, spent much time in the West in the 1880s, and each was intensely affected by the adventure.

Each man found precisely what he was looking for in the West. The frontier that Roosevelt glorified in such books as *The Winning of the West* (four volumes, 1889–1896), and that Remington portrayed in his work, was a stark physical and moral environment that stripped away all social artifice and tested each individual's character. Drawing on a popular version of English scientist Charles Darwin's evolutionary theory, which characterized life as a struggle in which only the fittest

survived, Roosevelt and Remington exalted the disappearing frontier as the proving ground for a new kind of virile manhood and the last outpost of an honest and true social order.

This version of the frontier myth reached its apogee in Owen Wister's enormously popular novel *The Virginian* (1902), later reincarnated as a 1929 Gary Cooper movie and a 1960s television series. In Wister's tale, the elemental physical and social environment of the Great Plains produces individuals like his unnamed cowboy hero, "the Virginian," an honest, strong, and compassionate man, quick to help the weak and fight the wicked. The Virginian is one of nature's aristocrats— ill-educated and unsophisticated but tough, steady, and deeply moral. The Virginian sums up his own moral code in describing his view of God's justice: "He plays a square game with us." For Wister, as for Roosevelt and Remington, the cowboy was the Christian knight on the Plains, indifferent to material gain as he upheld virtue, pursued justice, and attacked evil.

Needless to say, the western myth was far removed from the reality of the West. Critics delighted in pointing out that not one scene in *The Virginian* showed the hard physical labor of the cattle range. The idealized version of the West also glossed over the darker underside of frontier expansion—the brutalities of Indian warfare, the forced removal of the Indians to reservations, the racist discrimination against Mexican-Americans and blacks, the risks and perils of commercial agriculture and cattle growing, and the boom-and-bust mentality rooted in the selfish exploitation of natural resources.

Further, the myth obscured the complex links between the settlement of the frontier and the emergence of the United States as a major industrialized nation increasingly tied to a global economy. Eastern and foreign capitalists controlled large-scale mining, cattle, and agricultural operations in the West. The technical know-how of industrial America underlay the marvels of western agricultural productivity. Without the railroad, that quintessential symbol of the new industrial order, the transformation of the West would have been far slower.

Beginning a Conservation Movement

Despite its one-sided and idealized vision, Owen Wister's celebration of the western experience reinforced a growing recognition that many unique features of the western landscape were being threatened by overeager entrepreneurs. One important by-product of

The Grand Canyon of the Yellowstone, by Thomas Moran, 1872
Dazzled by the monumental beauty of the scene, painters strove to portray the western landscape as one of God's wonders. In the process, they stimulated a new popular interest in preserving the spectacular features of the land.

the western legend was a surge of public support for creating national parks and the beginning of an organized conservation movement.

Those who went west in the 1860s and 1870s to map the rugged terrain of the High Plains and the Rocky Mountains were often awed by the natural beauty of the landscape. Major John Wesley Powell, the one-armed veteran of the Civil War who charted the Colorado River through the Grand Canyon in 1869, waxed euphoric about its towering rock formations and powerful cataracts. "A beautiful view is presented. The river turns sharply to the east, and seems enclosed by a wall, set with a million brilliant gems. . . . On coming nearer, we find fountains bursting from the rock, high overhead, and the spray in the sunshine forms the gems which bedeck the way. "

In his important study, *Report on the Lands of the Arid Regions of the United States* (1878), Powell argued that settlers needed to change their pattern of settlement and readjust their expectations about the use of water in the dry terrain west of the hundredth meridian. Recognizing that incoming farmers had often mistaken-

ly believed that rain would miraculously follow the plow, Powell called for public ownership and governmental control of watersheds, irrigation, and public lands, a request that went largely unheeded.

Around the time Powell was educating Congress about the arid nature of the far West, a group of adventurers led by General Henry D. Washburn visited the hot springs and geysers near the Yellowstone River in northwestern Wyoming and eastern Montana. They were stunned by what they saw. "You can stand in the valley of the Yosemite," [The California park land protected by Congress in 1864] wrote one of the party, "and look up its mile of vertical granite, and distinctly recall its minutest feature; but amid the canyon and falls, the boiling springs and sulphur mountain, and, above all, the mud volcano and the geysers of the Yellowstone, your memory becomes filled and clogged with objects new in experience, wonderful in extent, and possessing unlimited grandeur and beauty." Overwhelmed by the view, the Washburn explorers abandoned their plan to claim the area for the Northern Pacific Railroad and instead petitioned Congress to protect it from settlement, occupan-

cy, and sale. Congress responded in 1872 by creating Yellowstone National Park to "provide for the preservation . . . for all time, [of] mineral deposits, natural curiosities, or wonders within said park . . . in their natural condition." In doing so, they excluded the Native Americans who had long considered the area a prime hunting range.

These first steps to conserve a few of the West's unique natural sites reflected the beginning of a changed awareness of the environment. In his influential study *Man and Nature* in 1864, George Perkins Marsh, an architect and politician from Vermont, had attacked the view that nature existed to be tamed and conquered. Cautioning Americans to curb their destructive use of the landscape, he warned the public to change its ways. "Man," he wrote, "is everywhere a disturbing agent. Wherever he plants his foot, the harmonies of nature are turned to discords."

Marsh's plea for conservation found its most eloquent support in the work of John Muir, a Scottish immigrant who had grown up in Wisconsin. Temporarily blinded by an accident, Muir left for San Francisco in 1869 and quickly fell in love with the redwood forests. For the next forty years he tramped the rugged mountains of the West and campaigned for their preservation. A romantic at heart, he struggled to experience the wilderness at its most elemental level. Once trekking high in the Rockies during a summer storm, he climbed the tallest pine he could find and swayed back and forth in the raging wind.

Muir became the late nineteenth century's most articulate publicist for wilderness protection. "Climb the mountains and get their good tidings," he advised city dwellers. "Nature's peace will flow into you as the sunshine into the trees. The winds will blow their freshness into you, and the storms their energy, while cares will drop off like autumn leaves." Muir's spirited campaign to protect the wilderness contributed strongly to the establishment of Yosemite National Park in 1890. Two years later, the Sierra Club, an organization created to encourage the enjoyment and protection of the wilderness in the mountain regions of the Pacific Coast, made Muir its first president.

The precedent established by the creation of Yellowstone National Park remained ambiguous well into the twentieth century. Other parks that preserved the high rugged landforms of the West were often chosen because Congress viewed the sites as worthless for other purposes (see Map 30.2). Awareness of the need for the biological conservation would not emerge until later in the twentieth century (see Chapter 21).

Ironically, despite the crusades of Muir, Powell, and Marsh to educate the public about conservation, the campaign for wilderness preservation reaffirmed the image of the West as a unique region whose magnificent landscape produced tough individuals of superior ability. Overlooking the senseless violence and ruthless exploitation of the land, contemporary writers, historians, and publicists proclaimed that the settlement of the final frontier marked a new stage in the history of civilization, and they kept alive the legend of the western frontier as a seedbed of American virtues.

CONCLUSION

The image of the mythic West has long obscured the transformation of people and landscape that took place there in the second half of the nineteenth century. Precisely because industrialization, urbanization, and immigration were altering the rest of the nation in unsettling ways (see Chapters 18 and 19), many Americans embraced the legend of the West as a visionary, uncomplicated, untainted Eden of social simplicity and moral clarity. The mythic West represented what the entire society had once been like (or so Americans chose to believe), before the advent of cities, factories, and masses of immigrants.

But the reality of westward expansion was more complex than the mythmakers acknowledged. Under the banner of economic opportunity and individual achievement, nineteenth-century Americans used the army to drive out the Indians and ruthlessly exploited the region's vast natural resources. In less than three decades, they killed off the enormous buffalo herds, destroyed Native peoples' traditional way of life, and drove them onto reservations.

Thus the mythic view of the frontier West as the arena for society building and economic opportunity obscured the dark side of the expansion onto the Great Plains and beyond. Despite the promise of the Homestead Act, which offered 160 acres of free land to those who would settle on it for five years, much of the best land had been given to railroads to encourage their expansion. Speculators had grabbed other prime locations. Homesteaders were often forced to settle on poorer quality tracts in areas where rainfall was marginal. In many places, large business enterprises in mining, ranching, and agribusiness, financed by eastern and European bankers, shoved aside the small entrepreneur and took control of the choicest natural resources.

Nevertheless, the settlement of the vast internal continental land did reinforce the popular image of the

CHRONOLOGY, 1860–1900

1858 Henry Comstock strikes gold on the Carson River in Nevada.
Gold discovered at Clear Creek, Colorado.

1862 Homestead Act.
Pacific Railroad Act.

1864 Nevada admitted to the Union.
Massacre of Cheyennes at Sand Creek, Colorado.
George Perkins Marsh, *Man and Nature.*

1867 Joseph McCoy organizes cattle drives to Abilene, Kansas.
New Indian policy of smaller reservations adopted.
Medicine Lodge Treaty.
The purchase of Alaska.

1868 Fort Laramie Treaty.

1869 Board of Indian Commissioners established to reform Indian reservation life.
Wyoming gives women the vote.

1872 Mark Twain, *Roughing It.*
Yellowstone National Park established.

1873 Panic allows speculators to purchase thousands of acres in the Red River valley of North Dakota cheaply.
Timber Culture Act.
Biggest strike on Nevada's Comstock Lode.

1874 Invention of barbed wire.
Gold discovered in the Black Hills of South Dakota.
Red River War pits the Kiowas, Comanches, and Cheyennes against the United States Army.

1875 John Wesley Powell, *The Exploration of the Colorado River.*

1876 Colorado admitted to the Union, gives women the right to vote in school elections.
Massacre of Colonel George Armstrong Custer and his troops at Little Bighorn.

1877 *Munn* v. *Illinois.*
Desert Land Act.

1878 Timber and Stone Act.
John Wesley Powell, *Report on the Lands of the Arid Regions of the United States.*

1879 Massacre of northern Cheyennes at Fort Robinson, Nebraska.

1881 Helen Hunt Jackson, *A Century of Dishonor.*

1883 William ("Buffalo Bill") Cody organizes Wild West show.

1886 Severe drought on the Plains destroys cattle and grain.
Wabash v. *Illinois.*

1887 Dawes Severalty Act.

1888 Las Gorras Blancas (the White Caps) raid ranchers in northern New Mexico.

1889 Oklahoma Territory opened for settlement.

1889–1896 Theodore Roosevelt, *The Winning of the West.*

1890 Ghost Dance movement spreads to the Black Hills.
Massacre of Teton Sioux at Wounded Knee, South Dakota.
Yosemite National Park established.

1892 John Muir organizes the Sierra Club.

1893 Frederick Jackson Turner, "The Significance of the Frontier in American History."

United States as a land of unprecedented economic opportunity and as a seedbed for democracy. Although the exclusion of blacks, Indians, and Spanish-speaking Americans belied the voiced commitment to an open society, the founding of new towns, the creation of new territorial and state governments, and the interaction of peoples of different races and ethnicities tested these ideas and, with time, forced their rethinking. The increasing willingness to give women the vote in many of the new western states would spread within the next two decades.

Although the persistence of the mythic view of the West served to hide the more ruthless and destructive features of western expansionism, the experiences gained from settling the interior territories and the utilization of the region's extensive physical resources led to the beginnings of the conservation movement and a reassessment of traditional American views of the envi-ronment. By the turn of the century, the thriving farms, ranches, mines, and cities of that region would help make the United States into one of the world's most prosperous nations.

FOR FURTHER REFERENCE

READINGS

Robert V. Hine and John M. Faragher, *The American West: A New Interpretative History* (2000). An updated and comprehensive summary of the American West's history using the new and provocative scholarship of the last decade.

Andrew Isenberg, *The Destruction of the Bison: An Environmental History, 1750–1900* (2000). A skillful analysis of the grassland environment of the Great Plains and its effect on the bison, Indian life, and the European settlers and the plants, animals, and insects they brought with them.

Peter Iverson, *When Indians Became Cowboys: Native Peoples and Cattle Ranching in the American West* (1994). A useful and important study of the ways in which Native peoples were able to adapt to reservation policies by raising cattle and, at the same time, preserve many of their traditional cultural practices.

Joy S. Kasson, *Buffalo Bill's Wild West: Celebrity, Memory, and Popular History* (2000). An innovative study of Buffalo Bill's Wild West show and its contribution to the mythology of the American West.

Glenda Riley and Richard W. Etulain, eds., *By Grit and Grace: Eleven Women Who Shaped the American West* (1997). Essays on Calamity Jane, Annie Oakley, and other forceful and accomplished western women.

Elliott West, *The Contested Plains: Indians, Goldseekers, and the Rush to Colorado* (1998). The story, with a keen eye for its environmental setting, of the competition among Indians, miners, army volunteers, and settlers on the central Great Plains.

WEBSITES

The American Indians of the Pacific Northwest
http://memory.loc.gov/ammem/award98/wauhtml/aipnhome.html
This Library of Congress site contains useful material from the Annual Reports of the Commissioners of Indian Affairs

The Evolution of the Conservation Movement, 1860–1920
http://memory.loc.gov/ammem/amrvhtml/conshome.html
This Library of Congress site makes available hundreds of pamphlets, government documents and motion picture footage that documents the movement to conserve and protect America's natural environment.

History of the American West
http://memory.loc.gov/ammem/award97/codhtml/
A collection of photographs and documents at the Denver Public Library that provides excellent examples of town life, landscape transformations, and mining in Colorado.

CHAPTER 18

The Rise of Industrial America, 1865–1900

On October 21, 1892, before a crowd of more than two hundred thousand onlookers, presidential candidate Grover Cleveland proudly opened the World's Columbian Exposition in Chicago. Grasping a small electric key connected to a two-thousand-horsepower engine, he proclaimed, "As by a touch the machinery that gives life to this vast Exposition is now set in motion, so in the same instant let our hopes and aspirations awaken forces which in all time to come shall influence the welfare, the dignity, and the freedom of mankind." A moment later, electric fountains shot streams of water high into the air, officially marking the exposition's start.

The Chicago world's fair represented the triumph of fifty years of industrial development. The country's largest corporations displayed their newest products: Westinghouse Company's dynamos mysteriously lit a tower of incandescent light bulbs; American Bell Telephone offered the first long-distance telephone calls to the East Coast; and inventor Thomas A. Edison exhibited his latest phonograph. The fair dazzled its more than 25 million visitors. But Isabelle Garland, mother of writer Hamlin Garland, who visited the fair from a small midwestern farm community, was simply stunned. "[M]y mother sat in her chair, visioning it all yet comprehending little of its meaning," Garland later observed. "Her life had been spent among homely small things, and these gorgeous scenes dazzled her, . . . letting in upon her

◀ **Night Pagent, the Grand Columbian Carnival**
As this flyer for the World's Fair attests, the Chicago World's Fair was intended to be "the most significant and grandest spectacle of modern times." The monumental lagoons and neo-classical buildings announced that the United States, like Greece and Rome before it, had become the world's most powerful economy.

543

in one mighty flood a thousand stupefying suggestions of art and history and poetry of the world. . . . At last utterly overcome, she leaned her head against my arm, closed her eyes and said, 'Take me home, I can't stand any more of it.' "

Isabelle Garland's emotional reaction captured the ambivalence of many late-nineteenth-century Americans who found themselves both unsettled and exhilarated as the nation was transformed by industrialization. At midcentury, the United States had played a minor role in world economy. Five decades later, innovations in management, technology, production, and transportation had expanded manufacturing output fivefold. The United States now produced 35 percent of the world's manufactured goods—more than England, Germany, and France combined. It had become the world's greatest industrial power.

Although the hallmark of this prodigious growth had been the rise of giant corporations that brought mass production and national distribution of oil, steel, and a variety of other products, important though less visible strides forward were made in numerous other areas of the economy. In countless small industries, new technologies were developed, manufacturing output soared, and innovative advertising and marketing techniques were created. By 1900 new enterprises both large and small, supported by investment bankers and using a nationwide railroad distribution system, offered a dazzling array of goods for national and international markets.

This stunning industrial growth came at a high cost to all involved. New manufacturing processes transformed the nature of work, undercutting skilled labor and creating mind-numbing assembly-line routines. Large-scale manufacturing companies often polluted their immediate environment, spewing noxious smoke into the air and dumping toxic waste into nearby streams and rivers. The challenges of new business practices made the American economy difficult to control. Rather than smoothly rolling forward, it lurched between booms and busts in business cycles that produced labor unrest and crippling depressions in 1873–1879 and 1893–1897.

This chapter will focus on five major questions:

■ What innovations in technology and business practices helped launch vast increases in industrial production in the post-Civil War period?

■ How were Andrew Carnegie, John D. Rockefeller, and other corporate leaders able to dominate their rivals and consolidate control over their industries?

■ Why did the South's experience with industrialization differ from that of the North and the Midwest?

■ How did workers respond to the changing nature of work and the growth of national corporations?

■ In the clash between industry and labor, what tactics enabled corporate executives in the 1890s to undercut labor's bargaining power?

THE RISE OF CORPORATE AMERICA

In the early nineteenth century, the corporate form of business organization had been used to raise large amounts of start-up capital for transportation enterprises such as turnpikes and canals. By selling stocks and bonds to raise money, the corporation separated the company's managers, who guided its day-to-day operation, from the owners—those who had purchased the stocks and bonds as investments. After the Civil War, American business leaders pioneered new forms of corporate organization that combined innovative technologies, creative management structures, and limited liability should the enterprise fail. The rise of corporate America in this period is a story of risk-taking and innovation as well as of rapacity and ruthlessness.

The Character of Industrial Change

Six features dominated the world of large-scale manufacturing after the Civil War: first, the exploitation of immense coal deposits as a source of cheap energy; second, the rapid spread of technological innovation in transportation, communication, and factory systems; third, the need for enormous numbers of new workers who could be carefully controlled; fourth, the constant pressure on firms to compete tooth-and-nail by cutting costs and prices, as well as the impulse to eliminate rivals and create monopolies; fifth, the relentless drop in price levels (a stark contrast to the inflation of other eras); and finally, the failure of the money supply to keep pace with productivity, a development that drove up interest rates and restricted the availability of credit.

All six factors were closely related. The great coal deposits in Pennsylvania, West Virginia, and Kentucky provided the cheap energy that fueled the railroads, the factories, and explosive urban growth. Exploiting these inexpensive energy sources, new technologies stimulated productivity and catalyzed breathtaking industrial expansion. Technology also enabled manufacturers to cut costs and hire cheap unskilled or semiskilled labor. This cost cutting enabled firms to undersell one another,

destroying weaker competitors and prompting stronger, more efficient, and more ruthless firms to consolidate. At least until the mid-1890s, cost reduction, new technology, and fierce competition forced down overall price levels.

But almost everyone suffered terribly during the depression years, when the government debated whether it should get involved but did nothing to relieve distress. "The sufferings of the working classes are daily increasing," wrote a Philadelphia worker in 1874. "Famine has broken into the home of many of us, and is at the door of all." Above all, business leaders' unflagging drive to maximize efficiency both created colossal fortunes at the top of the economic ladder and forced millions of wage earners to live near the subsistence level.

Out of the new industrial system poured dismal clouds of haze and soot, as well as the first tantalizing trickle of what would become an avalanche of consumer goods. In turn, mounting demands for consumer goods stimulated heavy industry's production of capital goods—machines to boost farm and factory output even further. Together with the railroads, the corporations that manufactured capital goods, refined petroleum, and made steel became driving forces in the nation's economic growth.

Railroad Innovations

Competition among the aggressive and innovative capitalists who headed American heavy industry was intense. As the post-Civil War era opened, nowhere was it more intense than among the nation's railroads, which to many Americans most symbolized industrial progress. By 1900, 193,000 miles of railroad track crisscrossed the United States—more than in all of Europe including Russia. These rail lines connected every state in the Union and opened up an immense new internal market. Most important, railroad companies pioneered crucial aspects of large-scale corporate enterprise. These included the issuance of stock to meet their huge capital needs, the separation of ownership from management, the creation of national distribution and marketing systems, and the formation of new organizational and management structures.

Railroad entrepreneurs such as Collis P. Huntington of the Central Pacific Railroad, Jay Gould of the Union Pacific, and James J. Hill of the Northern Pacific faced enormous financial and organizational problems. To raise the staggering sums necessary for laying track, building engines, and buying out competitors, railroads at first appealed for generous land and loan subsidies from federal, state, and local governments (see Chapter 17). Even so, the larger lines had to borrow heavily by selling stocks and bonds to the public. Bond holders earned a fixed rate of interest; stockholders received dividends only when the company earned a profit. By 1900 the yearly interest repayments required by the combined debt of all U.S. railroads (which stood at an astounding $5.1 billion—nearly five times that of the federal government) cut heavily into their earnings.

In the shop of the Baldwin Locomotive Works, small teams of skilled workers custom built each engine to the specifications of the purchaser.

Abusive Monopoly Power
This Puck cartoon depicts financiers Jay Gould (left) and Cornelius Vanderbilt (right) and suggests that their manipulation of markets and their ownership of railroads, telegraph companies, and newspapers is powerful enough to strangle Uncle Sam.

In addition to developing ways to raise large amounts of capital, the railroads created new systems for collecting and using information. To coordinate the complex flow of cars across the country, railroads relied heavily on the magnetic telegraph, invented in 1837. To improve efficiency, the railroads set up clearly defined, hierarchical organizational structures and divided their lines into separate geographic units, each with its own superintendent. Elaborate accounting systems documented the cost of every operation for each division, from coal consumption to the repair of engines and cars. Using these reports, railroad officials could set rates and accurately predict profits as early as the 1860s, a time

when most businesses had no idea of their total profit until they closed their books at year's end. Railroad management innovations thus became a model for many other businesses seeking a national market.

Consolidating the Railroad Industry

The expansion and consolidation of railroading reflected both the ingenuity and the dishonesty flourishing on the corporate management scene. Although by the 1870s railroads had replaced the patchwork of canal and stagecoach operations that dominated domestic transportation before the Civil War, the industry itself was in a state of chaos. Hundreds of small companies used widely different standards for car couplers, rails, track width, and engine size. Financed by large eastern and British banks, Huntington, Gould, and others devoured these smaller lines to create large, integrated track networks. In the Northeast four major trunk lines were completed. West of the Mississippi five great lines—the Union Pacific (1869); the Northern Pacific (1883); the Atchison, Topeka, and Santa Fe (1883); the Southern Pacific (1883); and the Great Northern (1893)—controlled most of the track by 1893.

Huntington, Gould, and the other larger-than-life figures who reorganized and expanded the railroad industry in the 1870s and 1880s were often depicted by their contemporaries as villains and robber barons who manipulated stock markets and company policies to line their own pockets. For example, newspaper publisher Joseph Pulitzer called Jay Gould, the short, secretive president of the Union Pacific, "one of the most sinister figures that have ever flitted batlike across the vision of the American people." Recent historians, however, have pointed out that the great industrialists were a diverse group. Although some were ironfisted pirates who engaged in fraudulent practices, others were upstanding businessmen who managed their companies with sophistication and innovation. Indeed, some of their ideas were startling in their originality and inventiveness.

The massive trunk systems created by these entrepreneurs became the largest business enterprises in the world, towering over state and federal governments in the size and scale of their operations. As they consolidated a hodgepodge of small railroads into a few interlocking systems, these masterminds pioneered the most advanced methods of accounting and large-scale organization. They also standardized all basic equipment and facilities, from engines and cars to automatic couplers, air brakes, signal systems, and outhouses (now provided in standard one-, two-, and three-hole sizes). In 1883,

independently of the federal government, the railroads corrected scheduling problems by dividing the country into four time zones. In May 1886 all railroads shifted simultaneously to the new standard 4′8 1/2″-gauge track. Finally, cooperative billing arrangements enabled the railroads to ship cars from other roads, including dining and sleeping cars owned by the Pullman Palace Car Company, at uniform rates nationwide.

But the systemization and consolidation of the railroads had its costs. Heavy indebtedness, overextended systems, and crooked business practices forced the railroads to compete recklessly with each other for traffic. They cut rates for large shippers, offered special arrangements for handling bulk goods, showered free passes on politicians who supported their operations, and granted substantial rebates and kickbacks to favored clients. None of these tactics, however, shored up the railroads' precarious financial position. And the continuous push to expand drove some overbuilt lines into bankruptcy.

Caught in the middle of the railroads' tug-of-war and stung by exorbitant rates and secret kickbacks, farmers and small business owners turned to state governments for help. In the 1870s many midwestern state legislatures responded by outlawing rate discrimination. Initially upheld by the Supreme Court, these and other decisions were negated in the 1880s when the Court ruled that states could not regulate interstate commerce. In response in 1887, Congress, persuaded by Illinois Senator Shelby M. Cullom's detailed study of devious railroad practices, passed the Interstate Commerce Act. A five-member Interstate Commerce Commission (ICC) was established to oversee the practices of interstate railroads. The law banned monopolistic activity like pooling, rebates, and discriminatory short-distance rates.

The railroads challenged the commission's rulings in the federal courts. Of the sixteen cases brought to the Supreme Court before 1905, the justices found in favor of the railroads in all but one, essentially nullifying the ICC's regulatory clout. The Hepburn Act (see Chapter 21), passed in 1906, strengthened the ICC by finally empowering it to set rates.

The railroads' vicious competition did not abate until a national depression that began in 1893 forced a number of roads into the hands of J. Pierpont Morgan and other investment bankers. Morgan, a massively built man with piercing eyes and a commanding presence, took over the weakened systems, reorganized their administration, refinanced their debts, and built intersystem alliances. By 1906, thanks to the bankers' central-

ized management, seven giant networks controlled two-thirds of the nation's rail mileage.

Applying the Lessons of the Railroads to Steel

The close connections between railroad expansion, which absorbed millions of tons of steel for tracks, and the growth of corporate organization and management are well illustrated in the career of Andrew Carnegie. A diminutive dynamo of a man, only 5′3″ tall, Carnegie was born in Scotland and immigrated to America in 1848 at the age of twelve, in the company of his father, a skilled handloom weaver who never found steady employment once the industry mechanized.

Ambitious and hard-working, Carnegie took a job at $1.20 a week as a bobbin boy in a Pittsburgh textile mill. Although he worked a sixty-hour week, the aspiring youngster also enrolled in a night course to learn bookkeeping. The following year, Carnegie became a Western Union messenger boy. Taking over when the telegraph operators wanted a break, he soon became the city's fastest telegraph operator. Because he had to decode the messages for every major business in Pittsburgh, Carnegie gained an insider's view of their operations.

Carnegie's big break came in 1852 when Tom Scott, superintendent of the Pennsylvania Railroad's western division, hired him as his secretary and personal telegrapher. When Scott became vice president of the Pennsylvania Railroad seven years later, the twenty-four-year-old Carnegie took over as head of the line's western division. A daring innovator, Carnegie, in his six years as division chief, used the complex cost-analysis techniques developed by Scott to more than double the road's mileage and quadruple its traffic. He slashed commuter fares to keep ridership at capacity and developed various cost-cutting techniques. Having invested his earnings in the railroads, by 1868 Carnegie was earning more than $56,000 a year from his investments, a substantial fortune in that era.

In the early 1870s Carnegie decided to build his own steel mill. His connections within the railroad industry, the country's largest purchaser of steel, made this a logical choice. Starting with his first mill, he introduced a production technology named after its English inventor, Henry Bessemer, which shot a blast of air through an enormous crucible of molten iron to burn off carbon and impurities. Combining this new technology with the cost-analysis approach learned from his railroad experience, Carnegie became the first steelmaker to know the actual production cost of each ton of steel.

Andrew Carnegie
Although his contemporaries called him "the world's richest man," Andrew Carnegie was careful to deflect criticism by focusing on his philanthropic and educational activities.

Andrew Carnegie Sums Up the Cost Savings of Vertical Integration*

The eighth wonder of the world is this:
two pounds of iron-stone purchased on
the shores of lake Superior and
    transported to Pittsburgh;
two pounds of coal mined in Connellsville
and manufactured into coke and
    brought to Pittsburgh;
one half pound of limestone mined
east of the Alleghenies and
    brought to Pittsburgh;
a little manganese ore,
mined in Virginia and
    brought to Pittsburgh.
And these four and one half pounds of
material manufactured into one pound of
solid steel and sold for one cent.
That's all that need be said
    about the steel business.

*Vertical integration: The control of all aspects of production from the mining of raw materials to the selling of the final product.
Source: Harold C. Livesay, *Andrew Carnegie and the Rise of Big Business* (Boston: Little, Brown, 1975), 189.

Carnegie's philosophy was deceptively simple: "Watch the costs, and the profits will take care of themselves." From the start he priced his rails below the competition. Then, through rigorous cost accounting and by limiting wage increases to his workers, he lowered his production costs even further. Moreover, he was not above asking for favors from his railroad-president friends or giving "commissions" to railroad purchasing agents.

As output climbed, Carnegie discovered the benefits of vertical integration—that is, controlling all aspects of manufacturing from extracting raw materials to selling the finished product. In Carnegie's case, this control embraced every stage from the mining and smelting of ore to the selling of steel rails. Carnegie Steel thus became the classic example of how sophisticated new technology might be combined with innovative management (and brutally low wages) to create a mass-production system that could slash consumer prices (see Figure 18.1).

The management of daily operations by his close associates left Carnegie free to pursue philanthropic activities. While still in his early thirties, Carnegie resolved to donate his money to charitable projects. (He knew full well that such actions would buttress his popularity.) Carnegie set up foundations and eventually gave more than $300 million to libraries, universities, and international-peace causes.

By 1900 Carnegie Steel, employing twenty thousand people, had become the world's largest industrial corporation. Carnegie's competitors, worried about the wily Scot's domination of the market, decided to buy him out. In 1901 J. Pierpont Morgan, who controlled Federal Steel, asked Charles Schwab, Carnegie Steel's president, to inquire what Carnegie wanted for his share of Carnegie Steel. The next day Carnegie gave Schwab a penciled note asking for nearly half a billion dollars. Morgan's response was simple: "Tell Carnegie I accept his price." Combining Carnegie's companies with Federal Steel, Morgan set up the United States Steel Corporation, the first business capitalized at more than $1 billion. The corporation, made up of two hundred member companies employing 168,000 people, marked a new scale in industrial enterprise.

FIGURE 18.1
Iron and Steel Production, 1875–1915
New technologies, improved plant organization, economies of scale, and the vertical integration of production brought a dramatic spurt in iron and steel production.

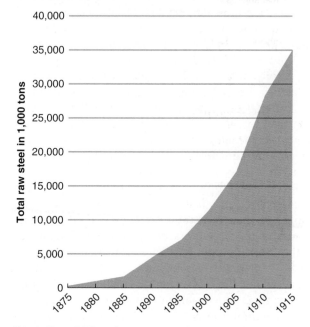

Note: short ton = 2,000 pounds.

Source: Historical Statistics of the United States.

Throughout his chain of corporate-world triumphs, Carnegie consistently portrayed his success as the result of self-discipline and hard work. The full story was more complex. Carnegie did not mention his uncanny ability to see the larger picture, his cleverness in hiring talented associates who would drive themselves (and the company's factory workers) mercilessly, his ingenuity in transferring organizational systems and cost-accounting methods from railroads to steel, and his callousness in keeping wages as low as possible. To a public unaware of corporate management techniques, however, Carnegie's success reaffirmed the openness of the American economic system. For the new immigrants flooding the nation's shores, Carnegie's career gave credence to the idea that anyone might rise from rags to riches.

The Trust: Creating New Forms of Corporate Organization

Between 1870 and 1900, the same fierce competition that had stimulated consolidation in the railroad and steel industries (see Table 18.1) also swept the oil, salt,

sugar, tobacco, and meatpacking industries. Like steel, these highly competitive businesses required large capital investments. Entrepreneurs in each industry therefore raced to reduce costs, lower prices, and drive their rivals out of the market. Chicago meatpackers Philip Armour and Gustavus Swift, for example, raised the process of making bacon, pork chops, and steak from hogs and cattle to a high level of efficiency by using every part of the animal. Hides were tanned into leather, bones became fertilizer, and hooves were turned into gelatin. When lowering costs failed to drive out rivals, new organizational methods were pioneered to control competition and preserve market share.

The evolution of the oil industry illustrates the process by which new corporate structures evolved. After Edwin L. Drake drilled the first successful petroleum (or "crude-oil") well in 1859 near Titusville in northwestern Pennsylvania, competitors rushed into the business, sinking wells and erecting small refineries nearby. Petroleum was distilled into oil, which soon replaced animal tallow as the major lubricant, and into kerosene, which became the leading fuel for household and public lighting. By the 1870s the landscape near Pittsburgh and Cleveland, the sites of the first discoveries, was littered with rickety drilling rigs, assorted collection tanks, and ramshackle refineries. Oil spills were a constant problem. "So much oil is produced," reported one Pennsylvania newspaper in 1861, "that it is impossible to care for it, and thousands of barrels are running into the creek; the surface of the river is covered with oil for miles. "

In this rush for riches, John D. Rockefeller, a young Cleveland merchant, gradually achieved dominance. Although he did not share Andrew Carnegie's outgoing personality, the solemn Rockefeller resembled the opportunistic steelmaker in other respects. Having gotten his start as a bookkeeper and opened his first refinery in 1863, Rockefeller, like Carnegie, had a passion for cost cutting and efficiency. When he became the head of

TABLE 18.1 **Industrial Consolidation: Iron and Steel Firms, 1870 and 1900**

	1870	1900
No. of firms	808	669
No. of employees	78,000	272,000
Output (tons)	3,200,000	29,500,000
Capital invested	$121,000,000	$590,000,000

Source: Robert L. Heilbroner and Aaron Singer, The Economic Transformation of America: 1600 to Present, 2d ed. (San Diego: Harcourt Brace Jovanovich, 1984), 92.

the Standard Oil Company in 1873, he scrutinized every aspect of its operation. In one case he insisted that a manager find 750 missing barrel stoppers. He realized that in a mass production enterprise, small changes could save thousands of dollars.

Rockefeller resembled Carnegie, too, in his ability to understand the inner workings of an entire industry and the benefits of vertical integration. The firm that controlled the shipment of oil between the well and the refinery and between the refinery and the retailers, he realized, could dominate the industry. In 1872 he purchased his own tanker cars and obtained not only a 10 percent rebate from the railroads for hauling his oil shipments but also a kickback on his competitors' shipments. When new pipeline technology became available, Rockefeller set up his own massive interregional pipeline network.

Like Carnegie, Rockefeller aggressively forced out his competitors. When local refineries rejected his offers to buy them out, he priced his products below cost and strangled their businesses. When rival firms teamed up against him, Rockefeller set up a pool—an agreement among several companies—that established production quotas and fixed prices. By 1879 Rockefeller had seized control of 90 percent of the country's oil-refining capacity.

Worried about competition, Rockefeller in 1882 decided to eliminate it by establishing a new form of corporate organization, the Standard Oil Trust. In place of the "pool" or verbal agreement among companies to control prices and markets, which lacked legal status, the trust created an umbrella corporation that ran them all. To implement his trust, Rockefeller and his associates persuaded the stockholders of forty companies to exchange their stock for trust certificates. Under this arrangement, stockholders retained their share of the trust's profits while enabling the trust to control production. Within three years the Standard Oil Trust had consolidated crude-oil buying throughout its member firms and slashed the number of refineries in half. In this way Rockefeller integrated the petroleum industry both vertically, by controlling every function from production to local retailing, and horizontally, by merging the competing oil companies into one giant system.

Taking a leaf from Rockefeller's book, companies in the copper, sugar, whiskey, lead, and other industries established their own trust arrangements. By limiting the number of competitors, the trusts created an oligopoly, the market condition that exists when the limited number of sellers can greatly influence price and other market factors. But their rapacious tactics, semimonopolistic control, and sky-high earnings provoked a public outcry. Beginning in New York State in 1879 and progressing to the federal level, legislative committees exposed the unscrupulous practices of the trusts, and

FIGURE 18.2

Mergers in Mining and Manufacturing, 1895–1910

A wave of business mergers occurred after the Supreme Court's 1897 and 1898 rulings that any firms concluding price-fixing or market-allocating agreements violated the Sherman Anti-Trust Act. But the merger mania died down when business leaders quickly discovered that companies could remain profitable only through vertical integration.

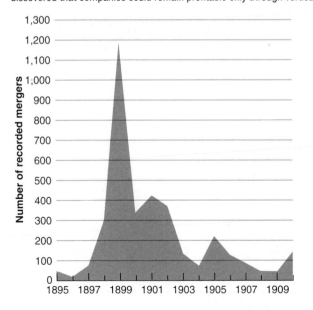
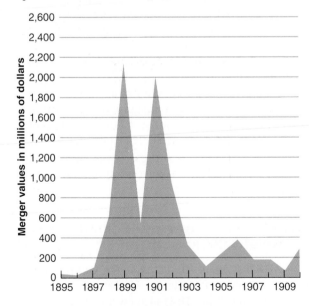

both parties denounced them in the presidential election of 1888.

Fearful that the trusts would stamp out all competition, Congress, under the leadership of Senator John Sherman of Ohio, passed the Sherman Anti-Trust Act in 1890. The Sherman Act outlawed trusts and any other monopolies that fixed prices in restraint of trade and slapped violators with fines of up to five thousand dollars and a year in jail. But the act failed to define clearly either *trust* or *restraint of trade*. The government prosecuted only eighteen antitrust suits between 1890 and 1904. When Standard Oil's structure was challenged in 1892, its lawyers simply reorganized the trust as an enormous holding company. Unlike a trust, which literally owned other businesses, a holding company simply owned a controlling share of the stock of one or more firms. The new board of directors for Standard Oil (New Jersey), the new holding company, made more money than ever.

The Supreme Court further hamstrung congressional antitrust efforts by interpreting the Sherman Act in ways sympathetic to big business. In 1895, for example, the federal government brought suit against the sugar trust in *United States* v. *E. C. Knight Company*. It argued that the Knight firm, which controlled more than 90 percent of all U.S. sugar refining, operated in illegal restraint of trade. Asserting that manufacturing was not interstate commerce and ignoring the company's vast distribution network that enabled it to dominate the market, the Court threw out the suit. Thus vindicated, corporate mergers and consolidations surged ahead at the turn of the century. By 1900 these mammoth firms accounted for nearly two-fifths of the capital invested in the nation's manufacturing sector (see Figure 18.2).

STIMULATING ECONOMIC GROWTH

Although large-scale corporate enterprise significantly increased the volume of manufactured goods in the late nineteenth century, it alone did not account for the colossal growth of the U.S. economy in this period. Other factors proved equally important, including new inventions, specialty production, and innovations in advertising and marketing. In fact, the resourcefulness of small enterprises, which combined innovative technology with new methods of advertising and merchandising, enabled many sectors of the economy to grow dramatically by adapting quickly to changing fashions and consumer preferences.

The Triumph of Technology

New inventions not only streamlined the manufacture of traditional products but also frequently stimulated consumer demand by creating entirely new product lines. The development of a safe, practical way to generate electricity, for example, made possible a vast number of electrical motors, household appliances, and lighting systems.

Many of the major inventions that stimulated industrial output and underlay mass production in these years were largely hidden from public view. Few Americans had heard of the Bessemer process for manufacturing steel or of the improved technologies that facilitated bottle making and glassmaking, canning, flour milling, match production, and petroleum refining. Fewer still knew much about the refrigerated railcars that enabled Gustavus Swift's company to slaughter beef in Chicago and ship it east or about the Bonsack cigarette-making machine that could roll 120,000 cigarettes a day, replacing sixty skilled handworkers.

Singer Sewing Machines
The Singer Company's success was built not only on its innovative use of interchangeable parts but also on advertising campaigns that stressed how easy its machines were to use.

The inventions that people did see were ones that changed the patterns of everyday life and encouraged consumer demand. Inventions like the sewing machine, mass-produced by the Singer Sewing Machine Company beginning in the 1860s; the telephone, developed by Alexander Graham Bell in 1876; and the light bulb, perfected by Thomas A. Edison in 1879 eased household drudgery and, in some cases, reshaped social interactions. With the advent of the sewing machine, many women were relieved of the tedium of sewing the family's apparel by hand; inexpensive mass-produced clothing thus led to a considerable expansion in personal wardrobes. The spread of telephones—by 1900 the Bell Telephone Company had installed almost eight hundred thousand in the United States—not only transformed communication but also undermined social conventions for polite behavior that had been premised on face-to-face or written exchanges. The light bulb, by further freeing people from dependence on daylight, made it possible to shop after work.

In the eyes of many, Thomas A. Edison epitomized the inventive impulse and the capacity for the creation of new consumer products. Born in 1847 in Milan, Ohio, Edison, like Andrew Carnegie, had little formal education and got his start in the telegraphic industry. Also like the shrewd Scot, Edison was a born salesman and self-promoter. When he modestly said that "genius is one percent inspiration and ninety-nine percent perspiration," he tacitly accepted the popular identification of himself as an inventing "wizard." Edison moreover shared Carnegie's vision of a large, interconnected industrial system resting on a foundation of technological innovation.

In his early work, Edison concentrated on the telegraph. His experimentation led to his first major invention, a stock-quotation printer, in 1868. The money earned from the patents on this machine enabled Edison to set up his first "invention factory" in Newark, New Jersey, a research facility that he moved to nearby Menlo Park in 1876. Assembling a staff that included university-trained scientists, Edison boastfully predicted "a minor invention every ten days, and a big one every six months."

Buoyed by the success and popularity of his invention in 1877 of a phonograph, or "sound writer" (*phono*: "sound"; *graph*: "writer"), Edison set out to develop a new filament for incandescent light bulbs. Characteristically, he announced his plans for an electricity-generation process before he perfected his inventions and then worked feverishly, testing hundreds of materials before he found a carbon filament that would glow dependably in a vacuum.

Edison realized that practical electrical lighting had to be part of a complete system containing generators,

Thomas Edison's Laboratories in Menlo Park, New Jersey, c. 1881
Always a self-promoter, Edison used this depiction of his "invention factory" to suggest that his development of a durable light bulb in 1879 would have an impact on life around the globe.

voltage regulators, electric meters, and insulated wiring and that the system needed to be easy to install and repair. It also had to be cheaper and more convenient than kerosene or natural gas lighting, its main competitors. In 1882, having built this system with the support of banker J. Pierpont Morgan, the Edison Illuminating Company opened a power plant in the heart of New York City's financial district, furnishing lighting for eighty-five buildings.

On the heels of Edison's achievement, other inventors rushed into the electrical field. Edison angrily sued many of his competitors for patent violations. Embittered by the legal battles that cost him more than $2 million, Edison relinquished control of his enterprises in the late 1880s. In 1892, with Morgan's help, Edison's company merged with a major competitor to form the General Electric Company (GE). Four years later, GE and Westinghouse agreed to exchange patents under a joint Board of Patent Control. Such corporate patent-pooling agreements became yet another mechanism of market domination.

In the following years, Edison and his researchers pumped out invention after invention, including the mimeograph machine, the microphone, the motion-picture camera and film, and the storage battery. By the time of his death in 1931, he had patented 1,093 inventions and amassed an estate worth more than $6 million. Yet Edison's greatest achievement remained his laboratory at Menlo Park. A model for the industrial research labs later established by Kodak, General Electric, and Du Pont, Edison's laboratory demonstrated that the systematic use of science in support of industrial technology paid large dividends. Invention had become big business.

Custom-Made Products

Along with inventors, manufacturers of custom and specialized products such as machinery, jewelry, furniture, and women's clothes dramatically expanded economic output. Using skilled labor, these companies crafted one-of-a-kind or small batches of articles that ranged in size from large steam engines and machine tools to silverware, furniture, and custom-made dresses. Keenly attuned to innovations in technology and design, they constantly created new products tailored to the needs of individual buyers.

Although they were vastly different in terms of size and number of employees, Philadelphia's Baldwin Locomotive Works and small dressmaking shops were typical of flexible specialization displayed by small batch processors. Both faced sharp fluctuations in the demand for their products as well as the necessity of employing skilled workers to make small numbers of specialized items. Founded before the Civil War, by the 1890s the Baldwin Locomotive Works employed two thousand workers and produced about nine hundred engines a year. Each machine was custom designed to meet the needs of its purchaser. Construction was systematized through precision plans for every part of an engine, but standardization was not possible since no single engine could meet the needs of every railroad.

Until the turn of the twentieth century, when ready-to-wear clothes came to dominate the market, most women's apparel was custom produced in small shops run by women proprietors. Unlike the tenement sweatshops that produced men's shirts and pants, dressmakers and milliners (a term derived from fancy goods vendors in sixteenth- and seventeenth-century Milan, Italy) paid good wages to highly skilled seamstresses. The small size of the shops together with the skill of the workers enabled them to shift styles quickly to follow the latest fashions.

Thus, alongside of the increasingly rationalized and bureaucratic big businesses like steel and oil in the late nineteenth-century, American productivity was also stimulated by custom and batch producers who provided a variety of goods that supplemented the bulk-manufactured staples of everyday life.

Advertising and Marketing

As small and large factories alike spewed out a dazzling array of new products, business leaders often discovered that their output exceeded what the market could absorb. This was particularly true in two kinds of businesses—those that manufactured devices for individual use such as sewing machines and farm implements, and those that mass-produced consumer goods such as matches, flour, soap, canned foods, and processed meats. Not surprisingly, these industries were trailblazers in developing advertising and marketing techniques. Strategies for whetting consumer demand and for differentiating one product from another represented a critical component of industrial expansion in the post-Civil War era.

The growth of the flour industry illustrates both the spread of mass production and the emergence of new marketing concepts. In the 1870s the nation's flour mills adopted the most advanced European manufacturing technologies and installed continuous-process machines that graded, cleaned, hulled, ground, and packaged the product in one rapid operation. These

Flush Toilets and the Invention of the Nineteenth-Century Bathroom

The development of a system of indoor plumbing was typical of the technological breakthroughs that simplified everyday life in the late nineteenth century. In the 1860s only about 5 percent of American houses had running water. Most Americans used chamber pots or outhouses that emptied into slimy, smelly cesspools. Two decades later, indoor plumbing standards had been established in most major U.S. cities, and wealthier urban Americans used flush toilets connected to municipal sewer systems.

The driving force for change came from outbreaks of cholera, typhoid, and yellow fever, diseases spread by polluted water, that periodically terrorized American cities. Building upon the discovery of germs by Louis Pasteur and Robert Koch, sanitary reformers established stringent metropolitan health laws, created state boards of health, and mandated the licensing of plumbers and the inspection of their work. By the turn of the century, George E. Waring, Jr., a prominent sanitary engineer,

could confidently declare that "Plumbing, as we know it, is essentially and almost exclusively an American Institution."

The decision to adopt a water-based system for the removal of human wastes depended on a series of inventions. First, municipal water systems had to be built with reservoirs, pumps, and water towers to provide water to the pipes that supplied buildings. A sewage system of interconnected pipes was also necessary to remove and process wastes. Machines to manufacture lead, cast-iron, and glazed stoneware pipes had to be created, as did a uniform system of pipe threads and melted lead joints to create a reliable standardized system for connecting them. Finally, a porcelain toilet with a built-in gas trap was needed because the bacteria in feces produce methane or sewer gas. (A trap is a U-shaped joint that uses the water at the low part of the U to prevent gas from seeping back into the bathroom. The gas is then vented through a pipe in the roof.)

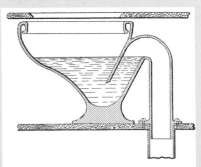

A deluxe bathroom as depicted in the J. L. Mott Iron Works Catalogue of 1888
The fixtures inside of the wooden cabinetry were made of cast-iron and were porcelain enameled. The style shown here is "Eastlake."

Toilet
Porcelain toilets were designed for easy cleaning. They contained a trap which sealed the connection to the sewer with a u-shaped drain that prevented sewer gas from seeping back into the house.

Despite its usefulness, the new technology was adopted only slowly by Americans. In 1890 only 24 percent of American dwellings had running water. As late as 1897, over 90 percent of the families in tenements had no baths and had to wash in hallway sinks or courtyard hydrants. By 1920, 80 percent of American houses, particularly those in rural areas, still lacked indoor flush toilets. The reason was simple: indoor plumbing was expensive and depended on the availability of water and sewer systems. Adding indoor plumbing increased the price of a new house by 20 percent.

Advertisers did their best to increase demand. They skillfully used the findings of science to advocate new standards of cleanliness or "hygiene," as it was called, which they associated with upper-class principles of respectability and decorum. Bathing and washing one's hands were touted as symbols of upper-class refinement.

Indoor plumbing not only reinforced higher standards for personal hygiene; it also enmeshed the homeowner in a web of local and state regulations. As sewage and water systems expanded to cover larger constituencies, political control moved from local to state and sometimes national arenas. Once largely independent, the homeowner now had to deal with water and power companies that often functioned regionally.

The adoption of strict sanitation systems and the use of indoor plumbing did achieve their intended result: they dramatically reduced the spread of disease. But the advances had unintended consequences. Indoor plumbing encouraged the phenomenal waste of water. A single faulty toilet could easily leak a hundred gallons of water a day. Not until the 1990s with the development of new low-water-usage toilets, which could save between 18,000 and 26,400 gallons of water a year, would new standards be established to reduce the use of water, an increasingly precious natural resource.

Focus Question:

- Why does the successful introduction of new technologies often involve a system of inventions rather than a single invention?

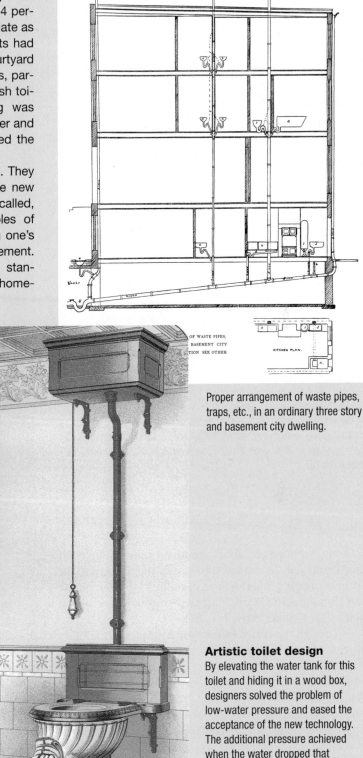

Proper arrangement of waste pipes, traps, etc., in an ordinary three story and basement city dwelling.

Artistic toilet design

By elevating the water tank for this toilet and hiding it in a wood box, designers solved the problem of low-water pressure and eased the acceptance of the new technology. The additional pressure achieved when the water dropped that distance ensured that the contents of the toilet bowl would be effectively flushed.

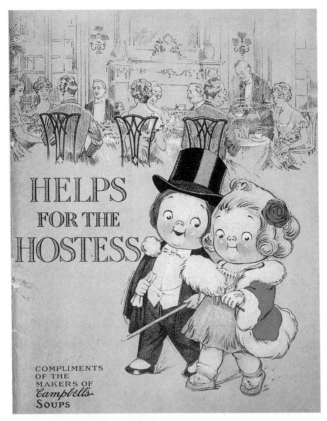

Campbell Soup (c. 1890)
By cleverly suggesting that Campbells Soups might be served at this elegant upper-class dinner party, the Campbell Soup Company implied that its soups were so good that they were indistinguishable from gourmet food.

Duluth Imperial Flour Company
This advertisement for bread flour implies, both through the label "imperial" and the image of the hot air balloon, that this product is internationally famous for its dough rising qualities. The image of numerous smokestacks in the background also suggests that Duluth, Minnesota, is a booming commercial city.

companies, however, soon produced more flour than they could sell. To unload this excess, the mills thought up new product lines such as cake flours and breakfast cereals and sold them using easy-to-remember brand names like Quaker Oats.

Through the use of brand names, trademarks, guarantees, slogans, endorsements, and other gimmicks, manufacturers built demand for their products and won enduring consumer loyalty. Americans bought Ivory Soap, first made in 1879 by Procter and Gamble of Cincinnati, because of the absurdly overprecise but impressive pledge that it was "99 and 44/100ths percent pure." James B. ("Buck") Duke's American Tobacco Company used trading cards, circulars, box-top premiums, prizes, testimonials, and scientific endorsements to convert Americans to cigarette smoking.

In the 1880s in the photographic field, George Eastman developed a paper-based photographic film as an alternative to the bulky, fragile glass plates then in use. Manufacturing a cheap camera for the masses, the Kodak, and devising a catchy slogan ("You press the button, we do the rest"), Eastman introduced a system whereby customers returned the one-hundred-exposure film and the camera to his Rochester factory. There, for a charge of ten dollars, the film was developed and printed, the camera reloaded, and everything shipped back. In marketing a new technology, Eastman had revolutionized an industry and democratized a visual medium previously confined to a few.

Economic Growth: Costs and Benefits

By 1900 the chaos of early industrial competition, when thousands of companies had struggled to enter a national market, had given way to the most productive economy in the world, supported by a legion of small, specialized companies and dominated by a few enormous ones. An industrial transformation that had originated in railroading and expanded to steel and petroleum had spread to every nook and cranny of American business and raised the United States to a position of world leadership.

For those who fell by the wayside in this era of spectacular economic growth, the cost could be measured in bankrupted companies and shattered dreams. John D. Rockefeller put things with characteristic bluntness when he said he wanted "only the big ones, only those who have already proved they can do a big business" in the Standard Oil Trust. "As for the others, unfortunately they will have to die."

The cost was high, too, for millions of American workers, immigrant and native-born alike. The vast expansion of new products was built on the backs of an army of laborers who were paid subsistence wages and who could be fired on a moment's notice when hard times or new technologies made them expendable.

Industrial growth often devastated the environment as well. Rivers fouled by oil or chemical waste, skies filled with clouds of soot, and a landscape littered with reeking garbage and toxic materials bore mute witness to the relentless drive for efficiency and profit.

To be sure, the vast expansion of economic output brought social benefits as well, in the form of labor-saving products, lower prices, and advances in transportation and communications. The benefits and liabilities sometimes seemed inextricably interconnected. The sewing machine, for example, created thousands of new factory jobs, made available a wider variety of clothing, and eased the lives of millions of housewives. At the same time, it encouraged avaricious entrepreneurs to operate sweatshops in which the immigrant poor—often vulnerable young women—toiled long hours for pitifully low wages (see Chapter 21).

Whatever the final balance sheet of social gains and costs, one thing was clear: the United States had muscled its way onto the world stage as an industrial titan. The ambition and drive of countless inventors, financiers, managerial innovators, and marketing wizards had combined to lay the groundwork for a new social and economic order in the twentieth century.

Industrial Boston
For many Americans, the price of progress was often pollution. Lacking the technology to filter carbon and gases from smoke, factory owners had no choice but to fill the skies with soot.

THE NEW SOUTH

The South entered the industrial era far more slowly than the Northeast. As late as 1900, total southern cotton-mill output, for example, remained little more than half that of the mills within a thirty-mile radius of Providence, Rhode Island. Moreover, the South's $509 average per capita income was less than half that of northerners.

The reasons for the South's late economic blossoming are not hard to discern. The Civil War's physical devastation, the scarcity of southern towns and cities, lack of capital, illiteracy, northern control of financial markets and patents, and a low rate of technological innovation crippled efforts by southern business leaders to promote industrialization. Economic progress was also impeded by the myth of the Lost Cause, which, through its nostalgic portrayal of pre-Civil War society, perpetuated an image of the South as traditional and unchanging. As a result, southern industrialization inched forward haltingly and was shaped in distinctive ways.

Obstacles to Economic Development

Much of the South's difficulty in industrializing arose from its lack of capital and the devastation of the Civil War. So many southern banks failed during the Civil War that by 1865 the South, with more than a quarter of the nation's population, possessed just 2 percent of its banks.

Federal government policies adopted during the war further restricted the expansion of the southern banking system. The Republican-dominated wartime Congress, which had created a national currency and banking structure, required anyone wishing to start a bank to have fifty thousand dollars in capital. Few southerners could meet this standard.

With banks in short supply, country merchants and storekeepers became bankers by default, lending supplies rather than cash to local farmers in return for a lien, or mortgage, on their crops (see Chapter 16). As farmers sank in debt, they increased their production of cotton and tobacco in an effort to stay afloat, and became trapped on the land. As a result, the labor needed for industrial expansion remained in short supply.

The shift from planting corn to specializing in either cotton or tobacco made small southern farmers particularly vulnerable to the fluctuations of commercial agriculture. When the price of cotton tumbled in national and international markets from eleven cents per pound in 1875 to less than five cents in 1894, well under the cost of production, many southern farmers grew desperate.

The South also continued to be the victim of federal policies designed to aid northern industry. High protective tariffs raised the price of machine technology imported from abroad; the demonetization of silver (see Chapter 20) further limited capital availability; and discriminatory railroad freight rates hiked the expense of shipping finished goods and raw materials.

The South's chronic shortage of funds affected the economy in indirect ways as well, by limiting the resources available for education. During Reconstruction northern philanthropists together with the Freedmen's Bureau, the American Missionary Association, and other relief agencies had begun a modest expansion of public schooling for both blacks and whites. But Georgia and many other southern states operated segregated schools and refused to tax property for school support until 1889. As a result, school attendance remained low, severely limiting the number of educated people able to staff technical and managerial positions in business and industry.

Southern states, like those in the North, often contributed the modest funds they had to war veterans' pensions. In this way, southern state governments built a white patronage system for Confederate veterans and helped reinforce southerners' idealization of the old Confederacy—the South's Lost Cause. As late as 1911, veterans' pensions in Georgia ate up 22 percent of the state's entire budget, leaving little for economic or educational development.

The New South Creed and Southern Industrialization

Despite the limited availability of private capital for investment in industrialization, energetic southern newspaper editors such as Henry W. Grady of the Atlanta *Constitution* and Henry Watterson of the Louisville *Courier Journal* championed the doctrine that became known as the New South creed. The South's rich coal and timber resources and cheap labor, they proclaimed in their papers, made it a natural site for industrial development. As one editor declared, "The El Dorado [the fabled land of riches] of the next half century is the South. The wise recognize it; the dull and the timid will ere long regret their sloth or their hesitancy."

The movement to industrialize the South gained momentum in the 1880s. To attract northern capital, southern states offered tax exemptions for new businesses, set up industrial and agricultural expositions, and leased prison convicts to serve as cheap labor. Florida, Texas, and other states gave huge tracts of lands to railroads, which expanded dramatically throughout the South and in turn stimulated the birth of new towns and villages. Other states sold forest and mineral rights on nearly 6 million acres of federal lands to speculators, mostly from the North, who significantly expanded the production of iron, sulfur, coal, and lumber.

Following the lead of their northern counterparts, the southern iron and steel industries expanded as well. Birmingham, Alabama, founded in 1871 in the heart of a region blessed with rich deposits of coal, limestone, and iron ore, grew in less than three decades to a bustling city with noisy railroad yards and roaring blast furnaces. By 1900 it was the nation's largest pig-iron shipper. In these same years, Chattanooga, Tennessee, housed nine furnaces, seventeen foundries, and numerous machine shops.

As large-scale recruiters of black workers, the southern iron and steel mills contributed to the migration of blacks to the cities. By 1900, 20 percent of the southern black population was urban. Many urban blacks toiled as domestics or in similar menial capacities, but others entered the industrial work force. Southern industry reflected the patterns of racial segregation in southern

life. Tobacco companies used black workers, particularly women, to clean the tobacco leaves while white women, at a different location, ran the machines that made cigarettes. The burgeoning textile mills were lily-white. In the iron and steel industry, blacks, who comprised 60 percent of the unskilled work force by 1900, had practically no chance of advancement. Nevertheless, in a rare reversal of the usual pattern, southern blacks in the iron and steel industry on average earned more than did southern white textile workers.

The Southern Mill Economy

Unlike the urban-based southern iron and steel industry, the textile mills that mushroomed in the southern countryside in the 1880s often became catalysts for the formation of new towns and villages. (This same pattern had occurred in rural New England in the 1820s.) In those southern districts that underwent the gradual transition from an agricultural to a mill economy, country ways and values suffused the new industrial workplace.

The cotton-mill economy grew largely in the Piedmont, a beautiful highland country of rolling hills and rushing rivers stretching from central Virginia to northern Georgia and Alabama. The Piedmont had long been the South's backcountry, a land of subsistence farming and limited roads. But postwar railroad construction opened the region to outside markets and sparked a period of intense town building and textile-mill expansion. Between 1880 and 1900 track mileage in North Carolina grew dramatically; the number of towns and villages jumped, quickening the pulse of commerce; and the construction of textile mills accelerated. Between 1860 and 1900 cotton-mill capacity shot up 1,400 percent, and by 1920 the South was the nation's leading textile-mill center. Augusta, Georgia, with 2,800 mill workers, became known as the Lowell of the South, named after the mill town in Massachusetts where industrialization had flourished since the 1820s. The expansion of the textile industry nurtured promoters' visions of a new, more prosperous, industrialized South.

Even sharecroppers and tenant farmers at first hailed the new cotton mills as a way out of rural poverty. But appearances were deceptive. The chief cotton-mill promoters were drawn from the same ranks of merchants, lawyers, doctors, and bankers who had profited from the commercialization of southern agriculture (and from the misfortunes of poor black and white tenant farmers and sharecroppers enmeshed in the new system). R. R. Haynes, a planter and merchant from North Carolina's Rutherford County, was typical of the new entrepreneurs. Starting out as a storekeeper, he purchased land and water rights on Second Broad Creek in 1884 and formed a company to finance construction of the Henrietta Mills. By 1913 Haynes owned not only one of the South's largest gingham-producing operations but also banks, railroads, lumber businesses, and general stores.

To run the mills, mill superintendents commonly hired poor whites from impoverished nearby farms. They promised that textile work would free these farming families from poverty and instill in them the virtues of punctuality and industrial discipline. The reality was different. Cotton-mill entrepreneurs shamelessly exploited their workers, paying just seven to eleven cents an hour, 30 percent to 50 percent less than what comparable mill workers in New England were paid.

The mills dominated most Piedmont textile communities. The mill operator not only built and owned the workers' housing and the company store but also supported the village church, financed the local elementary school, and pried into the morals and behavior of the mill hands. To prevent workers from moving from one mill to another seeking better opportunities, the mill owner usually paid them just once a month, often in scrip—a certificate redeemable only in goods from the company store. Since few families had enough money to get through a month, they usually overspent and fell behind in their payments. The charges were deducted from workers' wages the following month. In this way, the mill drew workers and their families into a cycle of indebtedness very much like that faced by sharecroppers and tenant farmers.

Since farm families had shared farm responsibilities together, Southern mill superintendents accommodated themselves to local customs and hired whole families, including the children. Mothers commonly brought babies into the mills and kept them in baskets nearby while tending their machines. Little children who were visiting older siblings in the mills sometimes learned to operate the machines themselves. Laboring a twelve-hour day, the mill hands relieved their tedium by stationing themselves near friends so that they might talk as they worked. Ties among the workers were strong. One employee put it simply, "The mill community was a close bunch of people . . . like one big family. We just loved one another."

To help make ends meet, mill workers kept their own garden patches and raised chickens, cows, and pigs. Southern mill hands thus brought communal farm values, nurtured through cooperative planting and harvesting, into the mills and mill villages. Although they had to adapt to machine-paced work and received barely

enough pay to live on, the working poor in the mill districts, like their prewar counterparts in the North, eased the shift from rural to village-industrial life by clinging to a cooperative country ethic.

As northern cotton mills did before the Civil War, southern textile companies exploited the cheap rural labor around them, settling transplanted farm people in paternalistic company-run villages. Using these tactics, the industry underwent a period of steady growth.

The Southern Industrial Lag

Industrialization occurred on a smaller scale and at a slower rate in the South than in the North and also depended far more on outside financing, technology, and expertise. The late-nineteenth-century southern economy remained essentially in a colonial status, subject to control by northern industries and financial syndicates. U.S. Steel, for example, controlled the foundries in Birmingham, and in 1900 its executives began to price

**"Pig Iron Scene, Birmingham, Alabama,"
by Charles Graham, 1886**
Although Birmingham, Alabama's, extensive foundries turned out inexpensive iron ingots, the northern owners forced factory operators to price their products at the same rate as ingots produced in Pittsburgh.

Birmingham steel according to the "Pittsburgh plus" formula based on the price of Pittsburgh steel, plus the freight costs of shipping from Pittsburgh. As a result, southerners paid higher prices for steel than did northerners, despite the cheaper production costs.

An array of factors thus combined to retard industrialization in the South. Banking regulations requiring large reserves, scarce capital, absentee ownership, unfavorable railroad rates, cautious state governments, wartime debts, lack of industrial experience, and control by profit-hungry northern enterprises all hampered the region's economic development. Dragged down by a poorly educated white population unskilled in modern technology and by an equally poorly trained, indigent black population excluded from skilled jobs, southern industry languished. Not until after the turn of the century did southern industry undergo the restructuring and consolidation that had occurred in northern business enterprise two decades earlier.

As in the North, industrialization brought significant environmental damage, including polluted rivers and streams, decimated forests, grimy coal-mining towns, and soot-infested steel-making cities. Although Henry Grady's vision of a New South may have inspired many southerners to work toward industrialization, economic growth in the South, limited as it was by outside forces, progressed in its own distinctly regional way.

FACTORIES AND THE WORK FORCE

Industrialization proceeded unevenly nationwide, and most late-nineteenth-century Americans still worked in small shops. But as the century unfolded, large factories with armies of workers sprang onto the industrial scene in more and more locales. The pattern of change was evident. Between 1860 and 1900, the number of industrial workers jumped from 885,000 to 3.2 million, and the trend toward large-scale production became unmistakable.

From Workshop to Factory

The transition to a factory economy came not as a major earthquake but rather as a series of jolts varying in strength and duration. Whether they occurred quickly or slowly, the changes in factory production had a profound impact on artisans and unskilled laborers alike, for they involved a fundamental restructuring of work habits and a new emphasis on workplace discipline. The impact of these changes can be seen by examining the

boot and shoe industry. As late as the 1840s, almost every shoe was custom-made by a skilled artisan who worked in a small, independent shop. Shoemakers were aristocrats in the world of labor. Taught in an apprentice system, they took pride in their work and controlled the quality of their products. In some cases they hired and paid their own helpers.

A distinctive working-class culture subdivided along ethnic lines evolved among these shoemakers. Foreign-born English, German, and Irish workers set up ethnic trade organizations and joined affiliated benevolent associations. Bound together by their potent religious and ethnic ties, they observed weddings and funerals according to old-country traditions and relaxed together at the local saloon after work. Living in tenements and boardinghouses within the same tight-knit ethnic neighborhood, they developed a strong ethnic and community pride and helped one another weather accidents or sicknesses.

As early as the 1850s, even before the widespread use of machinery, changes in the ready-made shoe trade had eroded the status of skilled labor. The manufacturing process was broken down into a sequence of repetitive, easily mastered tasks. Skilled shoe artisans now worked in "teams" of four men, each responsible for one function: putting the shoe on the last (a form shaped like a person's foot), attaching the heel, trimming the sole, "finishing" the leather with stain and polish, and so forth. Thus instead of crafting a pair of shoes from start to finish, each team member specialized in only one part of the process.

Under the new factory system of shoe manufacture, workers also lost the freedom to drink on the job and to take time off for special occasions. A working-class culture that had reinforced group solidarity was now dismissed by owners and shop foremen as wasteful and inefficient.

In the 1880s, shoe factories became larger and more mechanized, and traditional skills largely vanished. Sophisticated sewing and buffing machines allowed shoe companies to replace skilled operatives with lower-paid, less-skilled women and children. By 1890 women made up more than 35 percent of the work force in an industry once dominated by men. In many other industries, skilled artisans found their responsibilities and relation to the production process changing. With the exception of some skilled construction crafts such as carpentry and bricklaying, artisans no longer participated in the production process as a whole. Like the laborer whose machine nailed heels on 4,800 shoes a day, even "skilled" workers in the new factories specializing in consumer goods found themselves performing numbingly repetitive tasks.

The Hardships of Industrial Labor

The expansion of the factory system spawned an unprecedented demand for unskilled labor. By the 1880s nearly one-third of the 750,000 workers employed in the railroad and steel industries, for example, were common laborers.

In the construction trades, the machine and tool industries, and garment making, the services of unskilled laborers were procured under the so-called contract system. To avoid the problems of hiring, managing, and firing their own workers, large companies negotiated an agreement with a subcontractor who took responsibility for employee relations. A foreman or boss employed by the subcontractor supervised gangs of unskilled day laborers. These common workers were seasonal help, hired in times of need and laid off in slack periods. The steel industry employed them to shovel ore in the yards and to move ingots inside the mills. The foremen drove the gangs hard; in the Pittsburgh area, the workers called the foremen "pushers."

Notoriously transient, unskilled laborers drifted from city to city and from industry to industry. In the late 1870s unskilled laborers earned $1.30 a day, while bricklayers and blacksmiths earned more than $3. Only unskilled southern mill workers, whose wages averaged a meager eighty-four cents a day, earned less.

Unskilled and skilled workers alike not only worked up to twelve-hour shifts but also faced grave hazards to their health and safety. The alarming incidence of industrial accidents stemmed from a variety of circumstances, including dangerous factory conditions, workers' inexperience, and the rapid pace of the production process. Author Hamlin Garland described the perilous environment of a steel-rail mill at Carnegie's Homestead Steel Works in Pittsburgh. One steelworker recalled that on his first day at the mill, "I looked up and a big train carrying a big vessel with fire was making towards me. I stood numb, afraid to move, until a man came to me and led me out of the mill." Under such conditions the accident rate in the steel mills was extremely high.

In the coal mines and cotton mills, child laborers typically entered the work force at age eight or nine. These youngsters not only faced the same environmental hazards as adults but were especially prone to injury because of the pranks and play that they engaged in on the job. When supervision was lax in the cotton mills, for example, child workers would grab the belts that

powered the machines and see who could ride them farthest up toward the drive shaft in the ceiling before letting go and falling to the floor. In the coal industry, children were commonly employed as slate pickers. Sitting at a chute beneath the breakers that crushed the coal, they removed pieces of slate and other impurities. The cloud of coal dust that swirled around them made them vulnerable to black lung disease—a disorder that could progress into emphysema and tuberculosis. Children and others who toiled in the cotton mills, constantly breathing in cotton dust, fell ill with brown lung, another crippling disease.

For adult workers, the railroad industry was one of the most perilous. In 1889, the first year that the Interstate Commerce Commission compiled reliable statistics, almost two thousand rail workers were killed on the job and more than twenty thousand were injured.

Disabled workers and widows received only minimal financial aid from employers. Until the 1890s the courts considered employer negligence to be one of the normal risks borne by employees. Railroad and factory owners regularly fought against the adoption of state safety and health standards on the grounds that the economic costs would be excessive. For sickness and accident benefits, workers joined fraternal organizations and ethnic clubs, part of whose monthly dues benefited

those in need. But in most cases, the amounts set aside were too low to be of much help. When a worker was killed or maimed in an accident, the family became dependent on relatives or kindly neighbors for assistance and support.

Immigrant Labor

In their search for cheap labor, factory owners turned to unskilled immigrant workers for the muscle needed in the booming factories, mills, and railroads and in heavy-construction industries. In Philadelphia, where native-born Americans and recent German immigrants dominated the highly skilled metalworking trades, Irish newcomers remained mired in unskilled horse-carting and construction occupations until the 1890s, when the "new immigrants" from southern and eastern Europe replaced them (see Chapter 19). Poverty-stricken French Canadians filled the most menial positions in the textile mills of the Northeast. On the West Coast, Chinese immigrants performed the dirtiest and most physically demanding jobs in mining, canning, and railroad construction.

Writing home in the 1890s, eastern European immigrants described the hazardous and draining work in the steel mills. "Wherever the heat is most insupportable, the flames most scorching, the smoke and soot most choking, there we are certain to find compatriots bent and wasted in toil," reported one Hungarian. Yet those immigrants disposed to live frugally in a boardinghouse and to work an eighty-four-hour week could save fifteen dollars a month, far more than they could have earned in their homeland.

Although most immigrants worked hard, few adjusted easily to the frantic pace of the factory. Rural peasants from southern and eastern Europe who immigrated after 1890 found it especially difficult to abandon their irregular work habits for the unrelenting factory schedules. Where farm routines had followed a seasonal pace, slowing in the winter, factory operations were relentless, dictated by the invariable speed of the machines. A brochure that the International Harvester Corporation used to teach English to its Polish

Textile Workers
Young children like this one were often used in the textile mills because their small fingers could tie together broken threads more easily than those of adults.

workers attempted to instill the "proper" values. Lesson 1 read:

> I hear the whistle. I must hurry.
> I hear the five minute whistle.
> It is time to go into the shop.
> I take my check from the gate board and hang it on the department board.
> I change my clothes and get ready to work.
> The starting whistle blows.
> I eat my lunch.
> It is forbidden to eat until then.
> The whistle blows at five minutes of starting time.
> I get ready to go to work.
> I work until the whistle blows to quit.
> I leave my place nice and clean.
> I put all my clothes in the locker.
> I must go home.

As this "lesson" reveals, factory work tied the immigrants to a rigid timetable very different from the pace of farm life.

When immigrant workers resisted the tempo of factory work, drank on the job, or took unexcused absences, employers used a variety of tactics to enforce discipline. Some sponsored temperance societies and Sunday schools to teach punctuality and sobriety. Others cut wages and put workers on the piecework system, paying them only for the items produced. Employers sometimes also provided low-cost housing to gain leverage against work stoppages; if workers went on strike, the boss could simply evict them.

In the case of immigrants from southern Europe whose skin colors were often darker than northern Europeans, employers asserted that the workers were nonwhite and thus did not deserve the same compensation as native-born Americans. Because the concept of "whiteness" in the United States bestowed a sense of privilege and the automatic extension of the rights of citizenship, Irish, Greek, Italian, Jewish, and a host of other immigrants, although of the Caucasian race, were also considered nonwhite. Rather than being a fixed category based on biological differences, the concept of race was thus used to justify the harsh treatment of foreign-born labor.

Women and Work in Industrial America

Women's work experiences, like those of men, were shaped by marital status, social class, and race. White married women in all classes widely accepted an ideology of "separate spheres" (see Chapter 19) and remained at home, raised children, and looked after the household. The well-to-do hired maids and cooks to ease their burdens. Working-class married women, in contrast, not only lacked such assistance but also often had the added

Shoeworkers
Shoeworkers pose near their machines in Haverhill, Massachusetts, c. 1880. For them as well as for others, work became increasingly repetitive and routinized.

responsibility of earning money at home to make ends meet.

For working-class married women, working for wages at home by sewing, button-making, taking in boarders, or doing laundry had predated industrialization. In the late nineteenth century, urbanization and economic expansion enabled unscrupulous entrepreneurs to exploit this captive work force. Cigar manufacturers would buy or lease a tenement and require their twenty families to live and work there. In the clothing industry, manufacturers hired out finishing tasks to lower-class married women and their children, who labored long hours in crowded apartments.

Young, working-class single women often viewed factory work as an opportunity. In 1870, 13 percent of all women worked outside the home, the majority as cooks, maids, cleaning ladies, and laundresses. But most working women intensely disliked the long hours, dismally low pay, and social stigma of being a "servant." When jobs in industry expanded in the last quarter of the century, growing numbers of single white women abandoned domestic employment for better-paying work in the textile, food-processing, and garment industries. Discrimination barred black working women from fol-

lowing this path. Between 1870 and 1900, the number of women of all races working outside the home nearly tripled, and by the turn of the century, women made up 17 percent of the country's labor force.

A variety of factors propelled the rise in the employment of single women. Changes in agriculture prompted many young farm women to seek employment in the industrial sector (see Chapter 19), and immigrant parents often sent their daughters to the factories to supplement meager family incomes. Plant managers welcomed young immigrant women as a ready source of inexpensive unskilled labor. But factory owners assumed that many of these women would marry within a short time and thus treated them as temporary help and kept their wages low. Late in the century, young women in the clothing industry were earning as little as five dollars for seventy hours of work.

Despite their paltry wages, long hours, and often unpleasant working conditions, many young women relished earning their own income and joined the work force in increasing numbers. Although the financial support that these working women contributed to their families was significant, few working women were paid enough to provide homes for themselves. Rather than fostering their independence, industrial work enmeshed them more deeply in a family economy that depended on their earnings.

When the typewriter and the telephone came into general use in the 1890s, office work provided new employment opportunities, and women with a high school education moved into clerical and secretarial jobs earlier filled primarily by men. They were attracted by the clean, safe working conditions and relatively good pay. First-rate typists could earn six to eight dollars a week, which compared favorably with factory wages. Even though women were excluded from managerial positions, office work carried higher prestige and was generally steadier than work in the factory or shop.

Despite the growing number of women workers, the late-nineteenth-century popular press portrayed women's work outside the home as temporary. Few people even considered the possibility that a woman could attain local or even national prominence in the emerging corporate order.

Women in the Workplace

As this telephone office in Roanoke, Virginia, reveals, women office employees usually worked under the direct supervision of male managers.

Hard Work and the Gospel of Success

Although women were generally excluded from the equation, influential opinion molders in these years preached that any man could achieve success in the new industrial era. In *Ragged Dick* (1867) and scores of later

tales, Horatio Alger, a Unitarian minister turned dime novelist, recounted the adventures of poor but honest lads who rose through ambition, initiative, and self-discipline. In his stories shoeshine boys stopped runaway horses and were rewarded by rich benefactors who gave them a start in business. The career of Andrew Carnegie was often offered as proof that the United States remained the land of opportunity and "rags to riches."

Not everyone embraced this belief. In an 1871 essay, Mark Twain chided the public for its naïveté and suggested that business success was more likely to come to those who lied and cheated. In testimony given in 1883 before a Senate committee investigating labor conditions, a New Yorker named Thomas B. McGuire dolefully recounted how he had been forced out of the horse-cart business by larger, better-financed concerns. Declared McGuire, "I live in a tenement house, three stories up, where the water comes in through the roof, and I cannot better myself. My children will have to go to work before they are able to work. Why? Simply because this present system . . . is all for the privileged classes, nothing for the man who produces the wealth." Only with starting capital of ten thousand dollars—then a large sum—said McGuire, could the independent entrepreneur hope to compete with the large companies.

What are the facts? Certainly Carnegie's rise from abject poverty to colossal wealth was the rare exception, as studies of nearly two hundred of the largest corporations reveal. Ninety-five percent of the industrial leaders came from middle- and upper-class backgrounds. However, even if skilled immigrants and native-born working-class Americans had little chance to move into management in the largest corporations, they did have considerable opportunity to rise to the top in small companies. Although few of them reaped immense fortunes, many attained substantial incomes.

The different fates of immigrant workers in San Francisco show the possibilities and perils of moving up within the working class. In the 1860s the Irish-born Donahue brothers grew wealthy from the Union Iron Works they had founded, where six hundred men built heavy equipment for the mining industry. In contrast, the nearly fifteen thousand Chinese workers who returned to the city after the Central Pacific's rail line was completed in 1869 were consigned by prejudice to work in cigar, textile, and other light-industry factories. Even successful Chinese entrepreneurs faced discrimination. When a Chinese merchant, Mr. Yung, refused to sell out to the wealthy Charles Crocker, a dry-goods merchant turned railroad entrepreneur who was building a mansion on Nob Hill, Crocker built a thirty-foot-high "spite fence" around Yung's house so that it would be completely sealed from view.

Thus, while some skilled workers became owners of their own companies, the opportunities for advancement for unskilled immigrant workers were considerably more limited. Some did move to semiskilled or skilled positions. Yet most immigrants, particularly the Irish, Italians, and Chinese, moved far more slowly than the sons of middle- and upper-class Americans who began with greater educational advantages and family financial backing. The upward mobility possible for such unskilled workers was generally mobility within the working class. Immigrants who got ahead in the late nineteenth century went from rags to respectability, not rags to riches.

One positive economic trend in these years was the rise in real wages, representing gains in actual buying power. Average real wages climbed 31 percent for unskilled workers and 74 percent for skilled workers between 1860 and 1900. Overall gains in purchasing power, however, were often undercut by injuries and unemployment during slack times or economic slumps. The position of unskilled immigrant laborers was particularly shaky. Even during a prosperous year like 1890, one out of every five nonagricultural workers was unemployed at least one month of the year. During the depressions of the 1870s and 1890s, wage cuts, extended layoffs, and irregular employment pushed those at the bottom of the industrial work force to the brink of starvation.

Thus the overall picture of late-nineteenth-century economic mobility is complex. At the top of the scale, a mere 10 percent of American families owned 73 percent of the nation's wealth in 1890, while less than half of industrial laborers earned more than the five-hundred-dollar poverty line annually. In between the very rich and the very poor, skilled immigrants and small shopkeepers swelled the ranks of the middle class. So although the standard of living for millions of Americans rose, the gap between the poor and the well-off remained a yawning abyss.

LABOR UNIONS AND INDUSTRIAL CONFLICT

The rapid growth of large corporations in the late nineteenth century transformed the working conditions for millions of Americans and drove them to seek new forms of organization and support. Aware that the expansion of regional markets and their integration into national and world markets gave industrial leaders

unprecedented power to control the workplace, labor leaders searched for ways to create broad-based, national organizations that could protect their members and resist corporate power.

From the outset, the drive to create a nationwide labor movement faced many problems. Ethnic and racial divisions within the work force, including competition between immigrant groups, hampered unionizing efforts. Skilled craftsworkers, moreover, felt little kinship with low-paid common laborers. Divided into different trades, they often saw little reason to work together. Thus, unionization efforts moved forward slowly and experienced many setbacks.

Two groups, the National Labor Union and the Knights of Labor, struggled to build a mass labor movement that would unite skilled and unskilled workers regardless of their specialties. After impressive initial growth, however, both efforts collapsed. Far more effective was the American Federation of Labor (AFL), which represented an amalgamation of powerful independent craft unions. The AFL survived and grew, but it still represented only a small portion of the total labor force.

With unions so weak, labor unrest reached crisis proportions. When working conditions became intolerable, laborers walked off the job. These actions, born of desperation, often exploded into violence. The labor crisis of the 1890s, with its strikes and bloodshed, would reshape the legal environment, increase the demand for state regulation, and eventually contribute to a movement for progressive reform.

Organizing the Workers

The Civil War marked a watershed in the development of labor organizations. From the eighteenth century on, skilled workers had organized local trade unions to fight wage reductions and provide benefits for their members in times of illness or accident. By the 1850s some tradesmen had even organized national associations along craft lines. But the effectiveness of these organizations was limited. The main challenge that labor leaders faced in the postwar period was how to boost the unions' clout. Some believed that this goal could be achieved by forming one big association that would transcend craft lines and pull in a mass membership.

One person inspired by this vision was Philadelphian William H. Sylvis, who in 1863 was elected president of the Iron Molders' International Union, an organization of iron-foundry workers. Strongly built and bearded, with a "face and eyes beaming with intelligence," Sylvis traveled the country exhorting iron mold-

ers to organize. Within a few years, Sylvis had built his union from "a mere pygmy" to a membership of eighty-five hundred.

In 1866, acting on his dream of a nationwide association to represent all workers, Sylvis called a convention in Baltimore that formed a new organization, the National Labor Union (NLU). Reflecting the lingering aura of pre-Civil War utopianism, the NLU endorsed the eight-hour-day movement, which insisted that labor deserved eight hours for work, eight hours for sleep, and eight hours for personal affairs. Leaders also called for an end to convict labor, for the establishment of a federal department of labor, and for currency and banking reform. To push wage scales higher, they endorsed restriction on immigration, especially of Chinese migrants, whom native-born workers blamed for undercutting prevailing wage levels. The NLU under Sylvis's leadership supported the cause of working women and elected a woman as one of its national officers. It urged black workers to organize as well, though in racially separate unions.

In the winter of 1866–1867, Sylvis's own union became locked in a harrowing strike against the nation's foundry owners. When the strike failed miserably, Sylvis turned to national political reform. He invited a number of reformers to the 1868 NLU convention, including woman suffrage advocates Susan B. Anthony and Elizabeth Cady Stanton who, according to a reporter, made "no mean impression on the bearded delegates." But the NLU suffered a shattering blow when Sylvis suddenly died in 1869. Despite a claim of three hundred thousand members, it faded quickly. After a brief incarnation in 1872 as the National Labor Reform party, it vanished from the scene.

The dream of a national labor movement lived on in a new organization, the Noble and Holy Order of the Knights of Labor, founded in 1869 by nine Philadelphia tailors led by Uriah H. Stephens, head of the Garment Cutters of Philadelphia. A secret society modeled on the Masonic order, the Knights welcomed all wage earners or former wage earners; they excluded only bankers, doctors, lawyers, stockbrokers, professional gamblers, and liquor dealers. Calling for a great association of all workers, the Knights demanded equal pay for women, an end to child labor and convict labor, and the cooperative employer-employee ownership of factories, mines, and other businesses. At a time when no federal income tax existed, they called for a tax on all earnings, graduated so that higher income earners would pay more.

The Knights grew slowly at first. But membership rocketed in the 1880s after Terence V. Powderly replaced

Stephens as the organization's head. A young Pennsylvania machinist of Irish-Catholic immigrant origins, Powderly was an unlikely labor leader. He was short and slight, with a blond drooping mustache, elegant attire, and a fastidious, somewhat aloof manner. One journalist expressed surprise at finding such a fashionable man as the leader of "the horny-fisted sons of toil." But Powderly's eloquence, coupled with a series of successes in labor clashes, brought in thousands of new members.

During its growth years in the early 1880s, the Knights of Labor reflected both its idealistic origins and Powderly's collaborative vision. Powderly opposed strikes, which he considered "a relic of barbarism," and organized producer and consumer cooperatives. A teetotaler, he also urged temperance upon the membership. Powderly advocated the admission of blacks into local Knights of Labor assemblies, although he recognized the strength of racism and allowed local assemblies to be segregated in the South. Under his leadership the Knights welcomed women members; by 1886 women organizers such as the feisty Irish-born Mary Harris Jones, known as Mother Jones, had recruited thousands of workers, and women made up an estimated 10 percent of the union's membership.

Powderly supported restrictions on immigration and a total ban on Chinese immigration. Union members feared that immigrants would work so cheaply that they would steal their jobs. In the West such fears were directed particularly against the Chinese, and they were heightened when California railroad magnate Leland

Stanford declared, "[O]pen the door and let everybody come who wants to come . . . until you get enough [immigrants] here to reduce the price of labor to such a point that its cheapness will stop their coming." In 1877 San Francisco workers demonstrating for an eight-hour workday destroyed twenty-five Chinese-run laundries and terrorized the local Chinese population. In 1880 both major party platforms included anti-Chinese immigration plans. Two years later, Congress passed the Chinese Exclusion Act, placing a ten-year moratorium on Chinese immigration. The ban was made permanent in 1902.

Although inspired by Powderly's vision of a harmonious and cooperative future, most rank-and-file Knights of Labor strongly disagreed with Powderly's antistrike position. In 1883–1884 local branches of the Knights led a series of spontaneous strikes that elicited only reluctant support from the national leadership. In 1885, however, when Jay Gould tried to eradicate the Knights of Labor from his Wabash railroad by firing active union members, Powderly and his executive board instructed all Knights employed by the Wabash line to walk off the job and those working for other lines to refuse to handle Wabash cars. This highly effective action crippled the Wabash's operations. To the nation's amazement, the arrogant Jay Gould met with Powderly and cancelled his campaign against the Knights of Labor. "The Wabash victory is with the Knights," declared a St. Louis newspaper; "no such victory has ever before been secured in this or any other country."

The Eight-Hour-Day Movement
Striking artisans from more than three hundred companies filled New York streets for weeks in 1872 in a campaign to reduce the workday from ten hours to eight hours. As is evident in this illustration, the eight-hour movement gained additional support from local saloons catering to German immigrants.

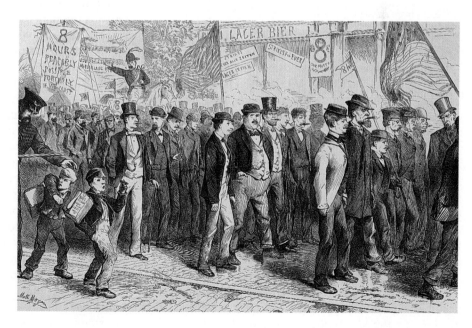

Ethnic and Racial Hatred
Conservative business owners used racist advertising such as this trade card stigmatizing Chinese laundry workers to promote their own products and to associate their company with patriotism.

shadow of its former self. Nevertheless, the organization had served as a major impetus to the labor movement and had awakened in thousands of workers a sense of group solidarity and potential strength. Powderly, who survived to 1924, always remained proud of his role "in forcing to the forefront the cause of misunderstood and downtrodden humanity."

As the Knights of Labor weakened, another national labor organization, pursuing more immediate and practical goals, was gaining strength. The skilled craft unions had long been uncomfortable with labor organizations like the Knights that welcomed skilled and unskilled alike. They were also concerned that the Knights' emphasis on broad reform goals would undercut their own commitment to better wages and protecting the interests of their particular crafts. The break came in May 1886 when the craft unions left the Knights of Labor to form the American Federation of Labor (AFL).

The AFL replaced the Knights' grand visions with practical tactics aimed at bread-and-butter issues. This philosophy was vigorously pursued by Samuel Gompers, the immigrant cigar maker who became head of the AFL in 1886 and led it until his death in 1924. Gompers believed in "trade unionism, pure and simple." For Gompers, higher wages were not simply an end in themselves but were rather the necessary base to enable working-class families to exist decently, with respect and dignity. The stocky, mustachioed labor leader had lost faith in utopian social reforms and recognized that "the poor, the hungry, have not the strength to engage in a conflict even when life is at stake." To stand up to the corporations, Gompers asserted, labor would have to harness the bargaining power of skilled workers, whom employers could not easily replace, and concentrate on the practical goals of raising wages and reducing hours.

A master tactician, Gompers believed that the trend toward large-scale industrial organization necessitated a comparable degree of organization by labor. He also recognized, however, that the skilled craft unions that made up the AFL retained a strong sense of independence. He knew that he had to persuade craftsworkers from the various trades to join forces without violating their sense of craft autonomy. Gompers's solution was to organize the AFL as a federation of trade unions, each retaining control of its own members but all linked by an executive council that coordinated strategy during boycotts and strike actions. "We want to make the trade union movement under the AFL as distinct as the billows, yet one as the sea," he told a national convention.

Focusing the federation's efforts on short-term improvements in wages and hours, Gompers at first sidestepped divisive political issues. The new organiza-

With this apparent triumph, membership in the Knights of Labor soared. By 1886 more than seven hundred thousand workers were organized in nearly six thousand locals. Turning to political action that fall, the Knights mounted campaigns in nearly two hundred towns and cities nationwide, electing several mayors and judges (Powderly himself had served as mayor of Scranton since 1878) and claimed a role in electing a dozen congressmen. In state legislatures they secured passage of laws banning convict labor, and at the national level they lobbied successfully for a law against the importation of foreign contract labor. Business executives warned darkly that the Knights could cripple the economy and take over the country if they chose.

But the organization's strength soon waned. Workers became disillusioned when a series of unauthorized strikes failed in 1886. The national reaction to the Haymarket riot (see below) also contributed to the decline. By the late 1880s, the Knights of Labor was a

the giant corporations had been achieved through savage competition, exploited workers, shady business practices, polluted factory sites, and the collapse of an economic order built on craft skills. In the South in particular, the devastation of the Civil War and the control of banking and raw materials by northern capitalists encouraged industrialists to adopt a paternalistic, family-oriented approach in the cotton mills and to pay exceedingly low wages.

Outbursts of labor violence and the ominous phenomenon of urban slums and grinding poverty showed starkly that all was not well in industrial America. Although the Knights of Labor and the American Federation of Labor attempted to organize workers nationally, the labor movement could not control spontaneous wildcat strikes and violence. In response, government authorities sided with company owners, arrested strikers, obtained court injunctions, and crippled the ability of labor leaders to expand their organizations.

As a result, Americans remained profoundly ambivalent about the new industrial order. Caught between their desire for the higher standard of living that industrialization made possible and their fears of capitalist power and social chaos, Americans of the 1880s and 1890s sought strategies that would preserve the benefits while alleviating the undesirable social by-products. Efforts to regulate railroads at the state level and such national measures as the Interstate Commerce Act and the Sherman Anti-Trust Act, as well as the fervor with which the ideas of a utopian theorist like Edward Bellamy were embraced, represented early manifestations of this impulse. In the Progressive Era of the early twentieth century, Americans would redouble their efforts to formulate political and social responses to the nation's economic transformation after the Civil War.

FOR FURTHER REFERENCE

READINGS

Edward L. Ayers, *The Promise of the New South: Life After Reconstruction* (1992). A comprehensive overview of economic and social change in the post-Civil War South.

David Bain, *Empire Express: Building the First Transcontinental Railroad* (1999). An important study of the early leaders of the railroad industry.

Ron Chernow, *Titan: The Life of John D. Rockefeller, Sr.* (1998). A balanced, insightful examination of the character and business practices of one of the most successful captains of industry.

Wendy Gamber, *The Female Economy: The Millinery and Dressmaking Trades, 1860–1930* (1997). An important study of ways in which women's custom dressmaking businesses provided important entrepreneurial opportunities for women in the late nineteenth century.

Matthew F. Jacobson, *Whiteness of a Different Color: European Immigrants and the Alchemy of Race* (1998). A study how the concept of race was defined and applied to immigrants in the nineteenth century.

Richard Schneirov, Shelton Stromquist, and Nick Salvatore, eds., *The Pullman Strike and the Crisis of the 1890s: Essays on Labor and Politics* (1999). An important survey of the impact of the Pullman Strike on politics, the role of the state, and the public controversy over governmental regulation of corporate activity.

Philip Scranton, *Endless Novelty: Specialty Production and American Industrialization, 1865–1925* (1997). A useful corrective to the argument that large corporations alone account for American economic growth in the post-Civil War period.

Joel A. Tarr, *The Search for the Ultimate Sink: Urban Pollution in Historical Perspective* (1996). An important study of the environmental problems created by industrialization.

Kim Voss, *The Making of American Exceptionalism: The Knights of Labor and Class Formation in the Nineteenth Century* (1993). A comparative analysis of American labor's attempts to mobilize workers in the face of business opposition.

WEBSITES

The Alexander Graham Bell Family Papers at the Library of Congress, 1862–1969
http://memory.loc.gov/ammem/bellhtml/bellhome.html
Part of the Library of Congress American Memory Series, this site contains correspondence, notebooks, and articles about the famous scientist and inventor.

America at Work, America at Leisure: Motion Pictures from 1894–1915
http://memory.loc.gov/ammem/awlhtml/awlwork.html
Part of the Library of Congress American Memory Series, this site provides information about cattle breeding, coal mining, and a variety of manufacturing companies.

The Emergence of Advertising in America, 1850–1920
http://memory.loc.gov/ammem/award98/ncdhtml/eaahome.html
Part of the Library of Congress American Memory Series, this site has a useful timeline organized by decade.

The Haymarket Riot
http://www.chipublib.org/004chicago/timeline/haymarket.html
Information about the Haymarket riot of 1886 from the Chicago Public Library.

CHAPTER 19

Immigration, Urbanization, and Everyday Life, 1860–1900

On a sweltering day in August 1899, Scott Joplin, a young, black pianist and composer, signed an unusual contract with his music publisher in Sedalia, Missouri. Instead of receiving an outright payment for his new sheet music composition, "Maple Leaf Rag," Joplin would earn one cent for every copy sold. At a time when most composers were paid a small fixed fee per composition, the contract signaled a new era in the popular-music industry. Over the next two decades, "Maple Leaf Rag" would sell more than half a million copies a year and make Joplin the king of ragtime, the popular, syncopated dance music that had become a national sensation.

Scott Joplin's transformation from unknown saloon piano player to renowned composer sheds light not only on the extraordinary expansion and commercialization of the entertainment industry at the turn of the nineteenth century but also on the class and racial tensions that pervaded popular culture. Although Joplin would publish more than seventy-five songs or piano rags in the next decade and a half, his success was undercut by white competitors who stereotyped his compositions as "Negro music" and "Coon songs." Joplin, who dreamed of gaining national recognition as an opera composer, remained frustrated by publishers' refusal to accept his classical compositions. Opera was considered serious music, a high art form controlled by the upper classes; blacks, even those with Joplin's talent, could not

CHAPTER OUTLINE

◀ **Backyard Baseball, Boston, 1906, by Lewis Hine**
Often idealized as a rural pastime, baseball at the turn of the century became immensely popular in cities where professional teams turned the sport into entertainment for the masses.

575

enter the field. Scott Joplin died in 1917, an admired leader in the entertainment industry whose genius for serious music would not be recognized for another half century. As Joplin's experience revealed, racial discrimination could reinforce the barriers of social class.

Scott Joplin's struggle to be accepted was not unusual. Countless others faced similar difficulties in moving up the economic ladder and adjusting to the changes taking place at the turn of the century. American society was slowly shifting from a rural producer economy that stressed work and thrift to an urban consumer economy in which new forms of entertainment, leisure activities, and material possessions were becoming the hallmarks of personal identity.

Nevertheless, Joplin's success as a ragtime composer mirrored the upward mobility of many Americans who could now enjoy unheard of levels of comfort and convenience. Industrialization had opened up new jobs and destroyed older ones, rearranging the occupational structure, altering the distribution of income within society, and sharpening class divisions. These changes, together with the expansion of white-collar occupations, created new expectations for family life and fostered a growing class awareness.

While the middle and upper classes prospered, immigrants, farmers, and the urban working classes—the overwhelming majority of the population—improved their families' economic position only slowly and slightly. The growth of consumer products and leisure activities actually widened the gulf between the haves and the have-nots and intensified the sense of class consciousness among rich and poor. Nowhere were these divisions more visible than in the cities teeming with immigrants.

While the very rich lived in a world apart and the middle class embraced its particular behavior code and cultural pursuits, the working class to whom Joplin had first appealed created its own vigorous culture of dance halls, saloons, vaudeville theaters, social clubs, and amusement parks in the bustling cities. Middle-class reformers who strove to remake this working-class culture into their own image of propriety were soon frustrated. In the long run, the culture of the masses would prove more influential in shaping modern America.

This chapter will focus on five major questions:

■ How did the growth of cities and the influx of immigrants create a new awareness of ethnic and class differences? How were racial stereotypes used to reinforce these distinctions?

■ What was Victorian morality, and in what ways did it influence social conventions and patterns of everyday life?

■ How did women's educational opportunities change in this period, and why did women pioneer new approaches to social welfare?

■ How did the conflict between the working classes and those above them help reshape attitudes toward leisure and recreation at the turn of the century?

■ Why did Americans of different social classes grow disenchanted with Victorian social and intellectual ideals?

EVERYDAY LIFE IN FLUX: THE NEW AMERICAN CITY

Nowhere were the changes in everyday life more visible than in cities. During the late nineteenth century, American cities grew spectacularly (see Table 19.1). Not only on the East Coast but also in the South, cities swelled at an astonishing pace. Between 1870 and 1900 New Orleans's population nearly doubled, Buffalo's tripled, and Chicago's increased more than fivefold. By the start of the new century, Philadelphia, New York, and Chicago all had more than a million residents, and 40 percent of all Americans lived in cities. (In the census, cities were defined as having more than twenty-five hundred inhabitants). In 1900 New York's 3.4 million inhabitants almost equaled the nation's entire 1850 urban population.

This spectacular urban growth, fueled by migration from the countryside and the arrival of nearly 11 million foreign immigrants between 1870 and 1900, created a dynamic new environment for economic development. Mushrooming cities created new jobs and markets that in turn dramatically stimulated national economic expansion. Like the frontier, the city symbolized opportunity for all comers.

The city's unprecedented scale and diversity threatened traditional expectations about community life and social stability. Rural America had been a place of face-to-face personal relations where most people shared the same likes and dislikes. In contrast, the city was a seething caldron where a medley of immigrant groups contended with one another and with native-born Americans for jobs, power, and influence. Moreover, the same rapid growth that energized manufacturing and production strained city services, generated terrible housing and sanitation problems, and accentuated class differences.

TABLE. 19-1 Urban Growth: 1870-1900

City	1870 Population	1900 Population	Percent Increase
Boston	250,525	560,892	123.88
Chicago	298,977	1,698,575	468.12
Cincinnati	216,239	325,902	50.71
Los Angeles	5,728	102,479	1,689.08
Milwaukee	74,440	285,315	299.37
New Orleans	191,418	287,104	49.98
New York	1,478,103	3,437,202	132.54
Philadelphia	1,293,697	647,022	99.94
Pittsburgh	321,616	86,075	273.64
Portland	90,426	8,293	990.38
Richmond	51,038	85,050	66.64
San Francisco	149,473	342,782	129.32
Seattle	1,107	237,194	21,326.73

Source: *Thirteenth Census of the United States* (Washington, D.C.: U.S. Government Printing Office, 1913).

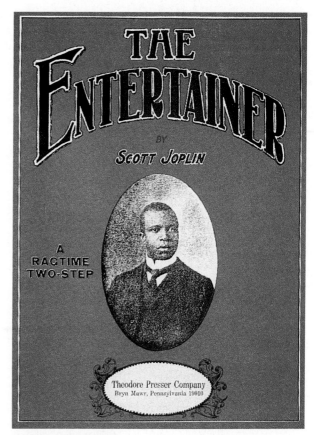

Scott Joplin Music
Despite Scott Joplin's desire to be recognized for his talent as an opera composer, publishers of his music preferred his popular ragtime compositions, such as his 1902 piano rag, "The Entertainer."

Native-born city-dwellers complained about the noise, stench, and congestion of this transformed cityscape. They fretted about the newcomers' squalid tenements, fondness for drink, and strange social customs. When native-born reformers set about cleaning up the city, they sought not only to improve the physical environment but also to destroy the distinctive customs that made immigrant culture different from their own. The late nineteenth century thus witnessed an intense struggle to control the city and benefit from its economic and cultural potential. The stakes were high, for America was increasingly becoming an urban nation.

Migrants and Immigrants

The growing concentration of industries in urban settings produced demands for thousands of new workers. The promise of good wages and a broad range of jobs (labeled by historians as "pull factors") drew men and women from the countryside and small towns. So great was the migration from rural areas, especially New England, that some farm communities vanished from the map.

Young farm women led the exodus to the cities. With the growing mechanization of farming in the late nineteenth century, farming was increasingly male work. At the same time, rising sales of factory-produced goods through mail-order catalogs serving country areas reduced rural needs for women's labor on subsistence tasks. So young farmwomen flocked to the cities, where they competed for jobs with immigrant, black, and city-born white women.

From 1860 to 1890, the prospect of a better life also attracted nearly 10 million northern European immigrants to East Coast and midwestern cities, where they joined the more than 4 million who had settled there in the 1840s and 1850s. Germans made up the largest group, numbering close to 3 million, followed by nearly 2 million English, Scottish, and Welsh immigrants and almost 1.5 million Irish. Moreover, by 1900 more than eight hundred thousand French-Canadians had migrated south to work in the New England mills, and close to a million Scandinavian newcomers had put down roots in the rich farmlands of Wisconsin and Minnesota. On the West Coast, despite the Chinese Exclusion Act of 1882 (see Chapter 18), more than eighty-one thousand Chinese remained in California and nearby states in 1900.

FIGURE 19.1

The Changing Face of U.S. Immigration, 1865–1920

Between 1865 and 1895, the majority of newcomers to America hailed from northern and western Europe. But the early twentieth century witnessed a surge of immigration from southern and eastern Europe.

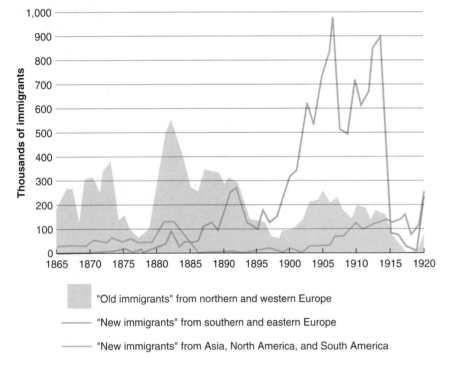

"Old immigrants" from northern and western Europe

"New immigrants" from southern and eastern Europe

"New immigrants" from Asia, North America, and South America

In the 1890s these "old immigrants" from northern and western Europe were joined by swelling numbers of "new immigrants"—Italians, Slavs, Greeks, and Jews from southern and eastern Europe, Armenians from the Middle East, and, in Hawaii, Japanese from Asia (see Figure 19.1). In the next three decades, these new immigrants, many from peasant backgrounds, would boost America's foreign-born population by more than 18 million (see Map 19.1).

The overwhelming majority of immigrants settled in cities in the northeastern and north-central states, with the Irish predominating in New England and the Germans in the Midwest. The effect of their numbers was staggering. In 1890 New York City (including Brooklyn, still a legally separate municipality) contained twice as many Irish as Dublin, as many Germans as Hamburg, half as many Italians as Naples, and 2 1/2 times the Jewish population of Warsaw. That same year four out of five people living in New York had been born abroad or were children of foreign-born parents.

Some recent immigrants had been forced out of their home countries by overpopulation, crop failure,

famine, religious persecution, violence, or industrial depression. (Historians call these reasons for immigration "push factors," since they drove immigrants out of their homelands.) Emigration from England, for example, spurted during economic downturns in 1873 and 1883. German peasants, squeezed by overpopulation and threatened by church reorganizations that they opposed, left in large numbers in the 1880s.

Many others came voluntarily in search of better opportunities. More than one hundred thousand Japanese laborers, for example, were lured to Hawaii in the 1890s to work on the lucrative sugar plantations by promises of high wages.

A large number of immigrants were single young men. Birger Osland, an eighteen-year-old Norwegian, explained his reasons for leaving to a friend, "as I now probably have a foundation upon which I can build my own further education, I have come to feel that the most sensible thing I can do is to emigrate to America." Although significant numbers of young men remained in the United States after they had become successful, large numbers, especially Italians and Chinese, returned home as well.

Although single women were less likely to come on their own, Irish women often did so and sent their earnings back home. Most commonly, wives and children waited in the old country until the family breadwinner had secured a job and saved enough money to pay for their passage to America.

Would-be immigrants first had to travel to a port—Hamburg was a major embarkation point—where they boarded a crowded steamship. The cramped ocean journey was noted for its poor food, lack of privacy, and rudimentary sanitary facilities. Immigrants arrived tired, fearful, and in some cases very sick.

Further complications awaited the travelers when they reached their destination, most often New York City or San Francisco. Customs officials inspected the newcomers for physical handicaps and contagious diseases. After 1892 those with "loathsome" infections such as leprosy, trachoma (a contagious viral disease of the eye),

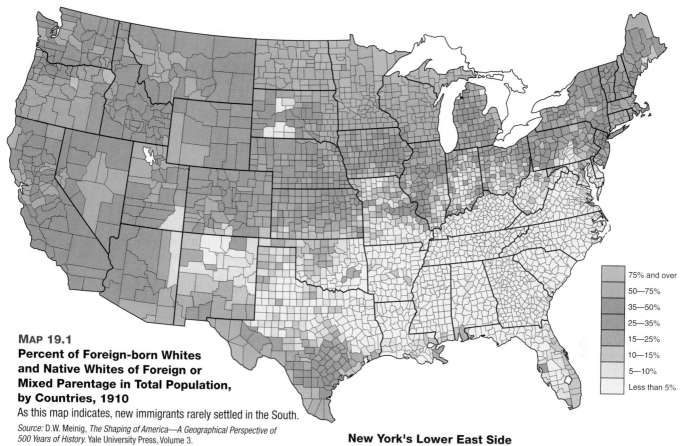

MAP 19.1

Percent of Foreign-born Whites and Native Whites of Foreign or Mixed Parentage in Total Population, by Countries, 1910

As this map indicates, new immigrants rarely settled in the South.

Source: D.W. Meinig, *The Shaping of America—A Geographical Perspective of 500 Years of History.* Yale University Press, Volume 3.

	75% and over
	50—75%
	35—50%
	25—35%
	15—25%
	10—15%
	5—10%
	Less than 5%

or sexually transmitted diseases were refused admittance and deported. Immigrants who passed the physical examination then had their names recorded. If a customs inspector had difficulty pronouncing a foreign name, he often Anglicized it. One German Jew became flustered when asked for his name and mumbled, "Schon vergessen [already forgotten]," meaning that he could not recall it. The inspector, who did not understand Yiddish, wrote "Sean Ferguson" on the man's roster. In this manner, many immigrants ended up with Americanized names.

In 1855 New York State had established a special facility for admitting immigrants at Castle Garden on the tip of Manhattan Island. Later, when the numbers swelled, the federal government took control and built a new station on Ellis Island in New York harbor in 1892. Angel Island in San Francisco Bay on the West Coast served a similar purpose after 1910. At the immigrant processing centers, America's newest residents exchanged foreign currency for U.S. dollars, purchased railroad tickets, and arranged lodgings. In other cities immigrants were hounded by tavernkeepers, peddlers,

New York's Lower East Side

In the era before automobiles, the streets pulsed with life as shops, vendors, and shoppers spilled out on the streets.

and porters who tried to exploit their ignorance of the English language and American ways. "When you land in America," wrote one Swedish resident to friends back home, "you will find many who will offer their services, but beware of them because there are so many rascals who make it their business to cheat the immigrants."

Those who arrived with sufficient cash, including many German artisans and Scandinavian farmers, commonly traveled west to Chicago, Milwaukee, and the rolling prairies beyond. Most of the Irish, and later the Italians, who hailed largely from poor peasant backgrounds, remained in eastern cities like Boston, New York, and Philadelphia. The Irish and Italians who did go west typically made the trip in stages, moving from job to job on the railroad and canal systems.

Adjusting to an Urban Society

For many immigrants the stress of adjusting to a new life was eased by the fact that they could settle among compatriots who had preceded them. (Historians call this tendency to relocate near friends or relatives from one's original town "chain migration.") If a map of New York City's streets and neighborhoods were colored in by nationality, Jacob Riis observed in 1890, it "would show more stripes than on the skin of a zebra, and more colors than any rainbow." The streets of Manhattan between the West Side Irish neighborhoods and the East Side German neighborhoods teemed with Poles, Hungarians, Russians, Italians, and Chinese.

Late-nineteenth-century social commentators often assumed that each nationality clumped together for reasons of national clannishness. But settlement patterns were far more complex. Most immigrants preferred to live near others not merely from their own country but also from their own village or region. On New York's Lower East Side, for example, Italians divided into many different subgroups: Neapolitans and Calabrians at Mulberry Bend, Genoese on Baxter Street, northern Italians west of Broadway, and Tyrolese Italians on Sixty-ninth Street near the Hudson River.

In the competition to get ahead, some immigrant groups adjusted more easily than others. Those with a background in the skilled trades and a familiarity with

Jakob Mithelstadt and Family, 1905
The Mithelstadts were Russian Germans who arrived in New York City on the *S.S. Pretoria*. The poorest immigrants traveled in steerage, below-deck cargo areas that lacked portholes and originally housed the cables to the ship's rudders.

Anglo-American customs had relatively few problems. English-speaking immigrants from the British Isles, particularly those from mill, mining, and manufacturing districts, found comparable work and encountered relatively little discrimination. Ethnic groups that formed a substantial percentage of a city's population also had a major advantage. The Irish, for example, who by the 1880s made up nearly 16 percent of New York's population, 8 percent of Chicago's, and 17 percent of Boston's, facilitated Irish immigrants' entry into the American mainstream by dominating Democratic party politics and controlling the hierarchy of the Catholic church in all three cities.

Ironically, domination of urban institutions by members of the larger immigrant groups often made adjustment to American society more difficult for members of smaller groups. Germans and other well-organized and skilled immigrants tended to exclude less-skilled newcomers from desirable jobs. English and German dominance of the building trades, for example, enabled those nationalities to limit the numbers of Italians hired.

The diversity of immigrants, even those from the same country, was remarkable. Nevertheless, the experience of being labeled a foreigner and of being discriminated against helped create a new common ethnic identity for many groups. Immigrants from the same home country forged a new sense of ethnic distinctiveness as Irish-American, German-American, or Jewish-American that helped them downplay internal divisions, compete for political power, and eventually assimilate into mainstream society.

Not all immigrants were interested in assimilation or intended to remain permanently in the United States. Young Chinese and Italian men often journeyed to American shores to earn enough money to return home and buy land or set themselves up in business. Expecting only a brief stay, they made little effort to learn English or understand American customs. Of the Italians who immigrated to New York before 1914, nearly 50 percent went back to Italy. Although the rate of return migration was greatest among Chinese and Italians, significant numbers of immigrants of other nationalities eventually returned to their homelands as well.

Various factors thus influenced the ability of immigrants to adapt to urban society in America. Nevertheless, as the number of foreigners in U.S. cities ballooned toward the turn of the century, all immigrant groups faced increasing hostility from white native-born Americans who not only disliked the newcomers' social customs but also feared their growing influence. Fearing

Chinatown
As is evident in this photograph of San Francisco at the turn of the century, Chinese immigrant workers often retained their traditional ways of dress and lived in the most congested part of town.

the loss of the privileges and status that were associated with their white skin color, native-born whites began to stigmatize immigrants as racially different and inferior, even when they were of the same race. Only gradually, and with much effort, did Irish, Jews, Slavs, and Mediterranean people, although they were biologically Caucasian, come to be considered "white."

Slums and Ghettos

Every major city had its share of rundown, overcrowded slum neighborhoods. Generally clustered within walking distance of manufacturing districts, slums developed when landlords subdivided old buildings and packed in too many residents. The poorer the renters, the worse the slum. Slums became ghettos when laws, prejudice, and community pressure prevented the tene-

ment inhabitants from renting elsewhere. During the 1890s Italians in New York, blacks in Philadelphia and Chicago, Mexican-Americans in Los Angeles, and Chinese in San Francisco increasingly became locked in segregated ghettos.

Life in the slums was particularly difficult for children. Juvenile diseases such as whooping cough (pertussis), measles, and scarlet fever took a fearful toll, and infant mortality was high. In one immigrant ward in Chicago in 1900, 20 percent of infants died in their first year of life.

Since tenements often bordered industrial districts, residents had to put up with the noise, pollution, and foul odors of tanneries, foundries, factories, and packing houses. Because most factories used coal-fired steam engines as their energy source, and because coal was also the preferred fuel for heating most apartment houses and businesses, vast quantities of soot and coal dust drifted skyward daily.

Most immigrants stayed in the shabbiest tenements only until they could afford better housing. Blacks, in contrast, were trapped in segregated districts. Driven out of the skilled trades and excluded from most factory work, blacks took menial jobs whose low pay left them little income for housing (see Chapter 18). Racist city-dwellers used high rents, real-estate covenants (agreements not to rent or sell to blacks), and neighborhood pressure to exclude them from areas inhabited by whites. Because the numbers of northern urban blacks in 1890 remained relatively small—for example, they composed only 1.2 percent of Cleveland's population and 1.3 percent of Chicago's—they could not overcome whites' concerted campaigns to shut them out. Nevertheless, as W. E. B. DuBois, a black sociologist, pointed out in *The Philadelphia Negro* (1899), wealthy black entrepreneurs within these neighborhoods built their own churches, ran successful businesses, and established charitable organizations to help their people.

Fashionable Avenues and Suburbs

As remains true today, the same cities that harbored slums, suffering, and violence also boasted neighborhoods of dazzling opulence. Wealthy Americans such as John D. Rockefeller and Jay Gould built monumental residences near exclusive streets just outside the downtown area. Rockefeller and Gould lived near Fifth Avenue in New York; others lived on Commonwealth Avenue in Boston, Euclid Avenue in Cleveland, and Summit Avenue in St. Paul. In the 1870s and 1880s wealthy city-dwellers began moving to new suburbs to distance themselves farther from the crowded tenement districts. Promoters of the suburban ideal, playing on the romantic rural nostalgia popular at the time, contrasted the rolling lawns and stately houses on the city's periphery with the teeming streets, noisy saloons, and mounds of garbage and horse excrement downtown. Soon many major cities could boast of their own stylish suburbs: Haverford, Ardmore, and Bryn Mawr outside Philadelphia; Brookline near Boston; and Shaker Heights near Cleveland.

Middle-class city-dwellers followed the precedents set by the wealthy. Skilled artisans, shopkeepers, clerks, accountants, and sales personnel moved either to new developments at the city's edge or to outlying suburban communities (although those at the lower fringe of the middle class typically rented apartments in neighborhoods closer to the city center). Lawyers, doctors, small businessmen, and other professionals moved farther out along the main thoroughfares served by the street railway, where they purchased homes on large lots. By the twentieth century, this process would result in suburban sprawl.

In time, a pattern of informal residential segregation by income took shape in the cities and suburbs. Built up for families of a particular income level, certain neighborhoods and suburbs developed remarkably similar standards for lot size and house design. (Two-story houses with front porches, set back thirty feet from the sidewalk, became the norm in many neighborhoods.) Commuters who rode the new street railways out from the city center could identify the social class of the suburban dwellers along the way as readily as a geologist might distinguish different strata on a washed-out riverbank.

By 1900 whirring trolley cars and hissing steam-powered trains had burst the boundaries of the compact midcentury city. As they expanded, cities often annexed the contingent suburbs. Within this enlarged city, sharp dissimilarities in building height and neighborhood quality set off business sectors from fashionable residential avenues and differentiated squalid manufacturing districts from parklike suburban subdivisions. Musing about urban America in 1902, James F. Muirhead, a popular Scottish guidebook author, wrote that New York and other U.S. cities reminded him of "a lady in a ball costume, with diamonds in her ears, and her toes out at her boots." To Muirhead, urban America had become a "land of contrasts" in which the spatial separations of various social groups and the increasingly dissimilar living conditions for rich and poor had

heightened ethnic, racial, and class divisions. Along with the physical change in American cities, in short, had come a new awareness of class and cultural disparities.

MIDDLE-CLASS SOCIETY AND CULTURE

Spared the struggle for survival that confronted most Americans after the Civil War, society's middle and upper ranks faced a different challenge: how to rationalize their enjoyment of the products of the emerging consumer society. To justify the position of society's wealthier members, ministers such as Brooklyn preacher Henry Ward Beecher and advice-book writers appealed to Victorian morality, a set of social ideas embraced by the privileged classes of England and America during the long reign (1837–1901) of Britain's Queen Victoria.

E. L. Godkin, the editor of *The Nation*, Phillips Brooks, minister to Boston's Trinity Church, and other proponents of Victorian morality argued that the financial success of the middle and upper classes was linked to their superior talent, intelligence, morality, and self-control. They also extended the antebellum ideal of separate spheres by arguing that women were the driving force for moral improvement. While men were expected to engage in self-disciplined, "manly" dedication to the new industrial order, women would provide the gentle, elevating influence that would lead society in its upward march. While Beecher, Godkin, and others defended the superiority of America's middle and upper classes, a network of institutions, from elegant department stores and hotels to elite colleges and universities, reinforced the privileged position of these groups.

Manners and Morals

The Victorian world view, which first emerged in the 1830s and 1840s, rested on a number of assumptions. One was that human nature was malleable: people could improve themselves. Hence, Victorian Americans were intensely moralistic and eager to reform practices they considered evil or undesirable. A second assumption emphasized the social value of work. Proponents of Victorian morality believed that a commitment to working hard not only developed personal self-discipline and self-control, but also helped advance the progress of the nation. Finally, Victorian Americans stressed the importance of good manners and the value of literature and the fine arts as marks of a truly civilized society. Although this genteel outlook set a standard that was often violated in practice, particularly by the middle classes and the rich, it remained an ideal that was widely preached as the norm for all society.

Before the Civil War, reformers such as Henry Ward Beecher had energized the crusades to abolish slavery and alcoholism by appealing to the ethical standards of Victorian morality. (Both slavery and intemperance threatened feminine virtue and family life.) After the war, Beecher and other preachers became less interested in social reform and more preoccupied with the importance of manners and social protocol. Following their advice, middle- and upper-class families in the 1870s and 1880s increasingly defined their own social standing in terms not only of income but also of behavior. Good manners, especially a knowledge of dining and entertaining etiquette, and good posture became important badges of status.

In her popular advice book *The American Woman's Home* (1869), Catharine Beecher (the sister of Henry Ward Beecher) reflected typical Victorian self-consciousness about proper manners. The following list of dinner-table behaviors, she said, should be avoided by those of "good breeding":

> Reaching over another person's plate; standing up to reach distant articles, instead of asking to have them passed; . . . using the table-cloth instead of napkins; eating fast, and in a noisy manner; putting large pieces in the mouth; . . . [and] picking the teeth at the table.

For Beecher and other molders of manners, meals became important rituals that differentiated the social classes. Not only were they occasions for displaying the elaborate china and silver that wealthy families exclusively possessed, but they also provided telltale clues to a family's level of refinement and sophistication.

The Victorian code—with its emphasis on morals, manners, and proper behavior—thus served to heighten the sense of class differences for the post-Civil War generation. Prominent middle- and upper-class Americans made bold claims about their interest in helping others improve themselves. More often than not, however, their self-righteous, intensely moralistic outlook simply widened the gap that income disparities had already opened.

The Cult of Domesticity

Victorian views on morality and culture, coupled with rising pressures on consumers to make decisions about a mountain of domestic products, had a subtle but important effect on middle-class expectations about

women's role within the home. From the 1840s on, many architects, clergymen, and other promoters of the so-called cult of domesticity had idealized the home as "the woman's sphere." They praised the home as a protected retreat where females could express their special maternal gifts, including sensitivity toward children and an aptitude for religion. "The home is the wife's province," asserted one writer; "it is her natural field of labor . . . to govern and direct its interior management."

During the 1880s and 1890s a new obligation was added to the traditional woman's role as director of the household: to foster an artistic environment that would nurture her family's cultural improvement. For many Victorian Americans of the comfortable classes, houses became statements of cultural aspiration. Excluded from the world of business and commerce, many mid-dle- and upper-class women devoted considerable time and energy to decorating their homes, seeking to make the home, as one advice book suggested, "a place of repose, a refuge from the excitement and distractions of outside . . . , provided with every attainable means of rest and recreation."

Not all middle-class women pursued this domestic ideal. For some, housework and family responsibilities overwhelmed the concern for artistic accomplishment. For others the artistic ideal was not to their taste. Sixteen-year-old Mary Putnam complained privately to a friend that she played the piano because of "an abstract general idea . . . of a father coming home regularly tired at night (from the plow, I believe the usual legend runs), and being solaced by the brilliant yet touching performance of a sweet only daughter upon the piano." She then confessed that she detested the piano. Increasingly, middle- and upper-class women in the 1880s and 1890s sought other outlets for their creative energies in settlement house work and social reform.

Department Stores

Although Victorian social thought justified the privileged status of the well-to-do, many thrifty people who had grown up in the early nineteenth century found it difficult to accept the new preoccupation with accumulation and display. To dull their pangs of guilt, merchandisers in the 1880s stressed the high quality and low cost of the objects they sold, encouraging Americans to loosen their purse strings and enjoy prosperity without reservations.

A key agent in modifying attitudes about consumption was the department store. In the final quarter of the nineteenth century, innovative entrepreneurs led by Rowland H. Macy in New York, John Wanamaker in Philadelphia, and Marshall Field in Chicago built giant department stores that became urban institutions and transformed the shopping experience for the millions of middle- and upper-class consumers who were their greatest patrons.

Merchants like Wanamaker and Macy helped overcome the middle and upper classes' reluctance to spend by advertising their products at "rock-bottom" prices and engaging in price wars. To avoid keeping their stock too long, they held giant end-of-the-season sales at drastically marked-down prices.

The major department stores tried to make shopping an exciting activity. Not only did rapid turnover of merchandise create a sense of constant novelty, but the mammoth stores themselves were designed as imitation

Trade Card, c. 1880
For middle and upper-class Victorian families, the front parlor with its elaborate curtains and artwork reflected the domestic ideal. Like the sleeping dog in the picture, pets were seen appropriate means for teaching children kindness, compassion, and discipline.

Department Store

Department stores used periodic sales to lure shoppers into their stores. At the special bargain counter at the Siegel Cooper store in New York in 1897, young women mobbed the attendants to purchase inexpensive new products.

palaces, complete with stained-glass skylights, marble staircases, brilliant chandeliers, and plush carpets. The large urban department store functioned as a kind of social club and home away from home for comfortably fixed women. Shopping became an adventure, a form of entertainment, and a way to affirm their place in society.

The Transformation of Higher Education

At a time when relatively few Americans had even a high school education, U.S. colleges and universities represented another institutional stronghold of the business and professional elite and the moderately well-to-do middle class. In 1900, despite enrollment increases in the preceding decades, only 4 percent of the nation's eighteen- to twenty-one-year-olds were enrolled in institutions of higher learning.

Wealthy capitalists gained status and a measure of immortality by endowing colleges and universities. Leland Stanford and his wife, Jane Lathrop Stanford, launched Stanford University in 1885 with a bequest of $24 million in memory of their dead son; John D. Rockefeller donated $34 million to the University of Chicago in 1891. Industrialists and businessmen domi-

nated the boards of trustees of many educational institutions and forced their probusiness views on administrators. Sardonic economist Thorstein Veblen called these business-oriented academic managers "Captains of Erudition."

Not only the classroom experience but also social contacts and athletic activities—especially football—prepared affluent young men for later responsibilities in business and the professions. Adapted by American college students in 1869 from English rugby, football was largely an elite sport. But the game, initially played without pads or helmets, was marred by violence. In 1905 eighteen students died of playing-field injuries. Many college presidents dismissed football as a dangerous waste of time and money. In 1873, when the University of Michigan challenged Cornell to a game in Ann Arbor, Cornell's president Andrew D. White huffily telegraphed back, "I will not permit thirty men to travel four hundred miles merely to agitate a bag of wind."

But eager alumni and coaches strongly defended the new sport. Some—among them Henry Lee Higginson, the Civil War veteran and Boston banker who gave Harvard "Soldiers' Field" stadium as a memorial to those who had died in battle—praised football as a character-building sport. Others, including famed Yale

Cigar-Box Label, c. 1910
Vassar College promoted the new image of womanhood by stressing the interconnections among education, athletics, and ethics.

coach Walter Camp, insisted that football could function as a surrogate frontier experience in an increasingly urbanized society. By 1900 collegiate football had become a popular fall ritual, and team captains were campus heroes.

Although postsecondary education remained confined to a small minority, more than 150 new colleges and universities were founded between 1880 and 1900, and enrollments more than doubled. While wealthy capitalists endowed some institutions, others, such as the state universities of the Midwest, were financed largely through public funds generated from state sales of public lands under the Morrill Land Grant Act (1862). Many colleges were also founded and funded by religious denominations.

On the university level, innovative presidents such as Cornell's Andrew D. White and Harvard's Charles W. Eliot sought to change the focus of higher education. New discoveries in science and medicine sparked the reform. In the 1850s most physicians had attended medical school for only two sixteen-week terms. They typically received their degrees without ever having visited a hospital ward or examined a patient. The Civil War exposed the abysmal state of American medical education. Twice as many soldiers died from infections as from wounds. Doctors were so poorly trained and ignorant about sanitation that they often infected soldiers' injuries when they probed wounds with hands wiped on

pus-stained aprons. "The ignorance and general incompetency of the average graduate of American medical schools, at the time when he receives the degree which turns him loose upon the community," wrote Eliot in 1870, "is something horrible to contemplate."

In the 1880s and 1890s the public's well-justified skepticism about doctors encouraged leading medical professors, many of whom had studied in France and Germany, to begin restructuring American medical education. Using the experimental method developed by German scientists, they insisted that all medical students be trained in biology, chemistry, and physics, including laboratory experience. By 1900 graduate medical education had been placed on a firm professional foundation. Similar reforms took place in undergraduate and graduate programs in architecture, engineering, and law.

These changes were part of a larger transformation in higher education after the Civil War that gave rise to a new institution, the research university. Unlike the best of the mid-nineteenth-century colleges, whose narrow, unvarying curriculum focused on teaching Latin and Greek, theology, logic, and mathematics, the new research universities offered courses in a wide variety of subject areas, established professional schools, and encouraged faculty members to pursue basic research. For President Andrew D. White of Cornell University, the objective was to create an environment "where any person can find instruction in any study." At Cornell, the University of Wisconsin at Madison, Johns Hopkins, Harvard, and other institutions, this new conception of higher education laid the groundwork for the central role that America's universities would play in the intellectual, cultural, and scientific life of the twentieth century.

Despite these significant changes, higher education remained largely the privilege of a few as the nineteenth century ended. The era when college attendance would become the norm rather than the rare exception lay many years ahead.

WORKING-CLASS POLITICS AND REFORM

The contrast between the affluent world of the college-educated middle and upper classes and the gritty lives of the working class was most graphically displayed in the nation's growing urban centers, where immigrant newcomers reshaped political and social institutions to meet their own needs. If fancy department stores and elegant hotels furnished new social spaces for the middle and upper classes, saloons became the poor man's

club, and dance halls became single women's home away from home. While the rich and the wellborn looked askance at lower-class recreational activities and sought to force the poor to change their ways, working-class Americans, the immigrant newcomers in particular, fought to preserve their own distinctive way of life. Indeed, the late nineteenth century witnessed an ongoing battle to eradicate social drinking, reform "boss" politics, and curb lower-class recreational activities.

Political Bosses and Machine Politics

Earlier in the century the swelling numbers of urban poor had given rise to a new kind of politician, the "boss," who listened to his urban constituents and lobbied to improve their lot. The boss presided over the city's "machine"—an unofficial political organization designed to keep a particular party or faction in office. Whether officially serving as mayor or not, the boss, assisted by local ward or precinct captains, wielded enormous influence in city government. Often a former saloonkeeper or labor leader, the boss knew his constituents well.

For better or worse, the political machine was America's unique contribution to municipal government in an era of pell-mell urban growth. Typified by Tammany Hall, the Democratic organization that dominated New York City politics from the 1830s to the 1930s, machines emerged in Baltimore, Philadelphia, Atlanta, San Francisco, and a host of other cities during the Gilded Age.

By the turn of the century, many cities had experienced machine rule. Working through the local ward captains to turn out unusually high numbers of voters (see Chapter 20), the machine rode herd on the tangle of municipal bureaucracies, controlling who was hired for the police and fire departments. It rewarded its friends and punished its enemies through its control of taxes, licenses, and inspections. The machine gave tax breaks to favored contractors in return for large payoffs and slipped them insider information about upcoming street and sewer projects. (On water service in the city, see Technology and Culture, Flush Toilets and the Invention of the Nineteenth-Century Bathroom, in Chapter 18).

At the neighborhood level, the ward boss often acted as a welfare agent, helping the needy and protecting the troubled. It was important to the boss that he be viewed as generous to his constituents. To spend three dollars to pay a fine for a juvenile offense meant a lot to the poor, but it was small change to a boss who raked in

millions from public-utility contracts and land deals. While the machine helped alleviate some suffering, it entangled urban social services with corrupt politics and often prevented city government from responding to the real problems of the city's neediest inhabitants.

Under New York City's boss William Marcy Tweed, the Tammany Hall machine revealed the slimy depths to which extortion and contract padding could sink. Between 1869 and 1871, Tweed gave $50,000 to the poor and $2,250,000 to schools, orphanages, and hospitals. In these same years, his machine dispensed sixty thousand patronage positions and pumped up the city's debt by $70 million through graft and inflated contracts. The details of the Tweed ring's massive fraud and corruption were brilliantly satirized in *Harper's Weekly* by German immigrant cartoonist Thomas Nast. In one cartoon Nast portrayed Tweed and his cronies as vultures picking at

"Let Us Prey," 1871

Cartoonist Thomas Nast hated William Marcy Tweed's ostentatious style. Pictured here as the chief vulture standing over the body of New York City, Boss Tweed wears an enormous diamond, a symbol of his insatiable greed.

the city's bones. Tweed bellowed in fury. "I don't care a straw for your newspaper articles—my constituents don't know how to read," he told *Harper's*, "but they can't help seeing them damned pictures." Convicted of fraud and extortion, Tweed was sentenced to jail in 1873, served two years, escaped to Spain, was reapprehended and reincarcerated, and died in jail in 1878.

By the turn of the century the bosses were facing well-organized assaults on their power, led by an urban elite whose members sought to restore "good government" (see Chapter 21). In this atmosphere the bosses increasingly forged alliances with civic organizations and reform leagues. The results, although never entirely satisfactory to any of the parties involved, paved the way for new sewer and transportation systems, expanded parklands, and improved public services—a record of considerable accomplishment, given the magnitude of the problems created by urban growth.

Battling Poverty

Impatient with the political bosses' piecemeal attempts to help the urban poor, middle-class city leaders sought comprehensive solutions for relieving poverty. Jacob Riis and the first generation of reformers believed that the basic cause of urban distress was the immigrants' lack of self-discipline and self-control. Consequently, Riis and

his peers focused on moral improvement. Only later would Jane Addams, Florence Kelley, and other settlement house workers examine the crippling impact of low wages and dangerous working conditions. Although many reformers genuinely sympathized with the suffering of the lower classes, the humanitarians often turned their campaigns to help the destitute into missions to Americanize the immigrants and eliminate customs that they perceived as offensive and self-destructive.

Poverty-relief workers first targeted their efforts at the young, who were thought to be most impressionable. Energized by the religious revivals of the 1830s and 1840s, Protestant reformers started charitable societies to help transient youths and abandoned street children. In 1843 Robert M. Hartley, a former employee of the New York Temperance Society, organized the New York Association for Improving the Condition of the Poor to urge poor families to change their ways.

Hartley's voluntaristic approach was supplemented by the more coercive tactics of Charles Loring Brace, who founded the New York Children's Aid Society in 1853. Brace admired "these little traders of the city . . . battling for a hard living in the snow and mud of the street" but worried that they might join the city's "dangerous classes." Brace established dormitories, reading rooms, and workshops where the boys could learn practical skills; he also swept orphaned children

Orphan train on the Atchison, Topeka & Santa Fe Railroad line, c.1900
From the 1850s to the 1920s, the Children's Aid Society placed more than two hundred and fifty thousand orphans such as these with foster families in the western United States. Families who wished to adopt an orphan needed recommendations from their pastor and a justice of the peace.

off the streets, shipped them to the country, and placed them with families to work as farm hands.

Where Brace's Children's Aid Society gave adolescents an alternative to living in the slums, the Young Men's Christian Association (YMCA), founded in England in 1841 and exported to America ten years later, provided housing and wholesome recreation for country boys who had migrated to the city. The Young Women's Christian Association (YWCA) similarly provided housing and a day nursery for young women and their children. In the Protestant tradition of moral improvement, both organizations subjected their members to curfews and expelled them for drinking and other forbidden behavior.

By 1900 more than fifteen hundred YMCAs and YWCAs served as havens for nearly a quarter-million young men and women. But YMCA and YWCA leaders reached only a small portion of the young adult population. Some whom they sought to help were put off by the organizations' close supervision and moralistic stance. Others, eager to assert their independence, preferred not to ask for help. Although charity workers made some progress in their efforts to aid youth, the strategy was too narrowly focused to stem the rising tide of urban problems.

New Approaches to Social Work

The inability of the Children's Aid Society, YMCA, YWCA, and other relief organizations to cope with the explosive growth of the urban poor in the 1870s and 1880s convinced some reformers to search for other ways to fight poverty. One of the earliest and most effective agencies was the Salvation Army. A church established along pseudomilitary lines in England in 1865 by Methodist minister "General" William Booth, the Salvation Army sent its uniformed volunteers to the United States in 1880 to provide food, shelter, and temporary employment for families. Known for its rousing music and attention-getting street meetings, the group ran soup kitchens and day nurseries and dispatched its "slum brigades" to carry the message of morality to the immigrant poor. The army's strategy was simple. Attract the poor with marching bands and lively preaching; follow up with offers of food, assistance, and employment; and then teach them the solid middle-class virtues of temperance, hard work, and self-discipline.

A similar approach to poor relief was implemented by the New York Charity Organization Society (COS), founded in 1882 by Josephine Shaw Lowell. Of a prominent Boston family, the strong-willed Lowell had been widowed when her husband of a few months was killed during the Civil War, and she wore black for the rest of her life. Adopting what they considered a scientific approach to make aid to the poor more efficient, Lowell and the COS leaders divided New York City into districts, compiled files on all aid recipients, and sent "friendly visitors" into the tenements to counsel families on how to improve their lives. Convinced that moral deficiencies lay at the root of poverty and that the "promiscuous charity" of overlapping church welfare agencies undermined the desire to work, the COS tried to foster self-sufficiency in its charges. In 1891, Lowell helped found the Consumers' League of New York.

Although the COS did serve as a useful coordinator for relief efforts and developed helpful statistics on the extent of poverty, critics justly accused the society of being more interested in controlling the poor than in alleviating their suffering. One of the manuals, for example, stressed the importance of introducing "messy housekeepers" to the "pleasures of a cheery, well-ordered home." Unable to see slum problems from the vantage point of the poor, they failed, for the most part, in their underlying objective: to convert the poor to their own standards of morality and decorum.

The Moral-Purity Campaign

The failure of Josephine Shaw Lowell and other like-minded social disciplinarians to eradicate urban poverty prompted other reformers to push for even tougher measures against sin and immorality. In 1872 Anthony Comstock, a pious young dry-goods clerk, founded the New York Society for the Suppression of Vice. The organization demanded that municipal authorities close down gambling and lottery operations and censor obscene publications.

Nothing symbolized the contested terrain between middle- and lower-class culture better than the fight over prostitution. Considered socially degenerate by some and a source of recreation by others, prostitution both exploited women and offered them a steady income and a measure of personal freedom. After the Civil War, the number of brothels—specialized houses controlled by women known as madams where prostitutes plied their trade—expanded rapidly. In the 1880s saloons, tenements, and cabarets, often controlled by political machines, hired prostitutes of their own. Even though immigrant women do not appear to have made up the majority of big-city prostitutes, reformers often labeled them as the major source of the problem.

In 1892 brothels, along with gambling dens and saloons, became targets for the reform efforts of New

York Presbyterian minister Charles Parkhurst. Blaming the "slimy, oozy soil of Tammany Hall" and the New York City police—"the dirtiest, crookedest, and ugliest lot of men ever combined in semi-military array outside of Japan and Turkey"—for the city's rampant evils, he organized the City Vigilance League to clean up the city. Two years later a nonpartisan Committee of Seventy elected a new mayor who pressured city officials to enforce the laws against prostitution, gambling, and Sunday liquor sales.

The purity campaign lasted scarcely three years. The reform coalition quickly fell apart. New York City's population was too large, and its ethnic constituencies too diverse, for middle- and upper-class reformers to curb all the illegal activities flourishing within the sprawling metropolis.

The Social Gospel

In the 1870s and 1880s a handful of Protestant ministers began to explore several radical alternatives for aiding the poor. Instead of focusing on their alleged moral flaws and character defects, these ministers argued that the rich and the wellborn deserved part of the blame for urban poverty and thus had a responsibility to do something about it.

William S. Rainsford, the Irish-born minister of New York City's Saint George's Episcopal Church, pioneered the development of the so-called institutional church movement. Large downtown churches in once-elite districts that had been overrun by immigrants would provide their new neighbors with social services as well as a place to worship. With the financial help of J. Pierpont Morgan, a warden of his church, Rainsford organized a boys' club, built church recreational facilities for the destitute on the Lower East Side, and established an industrial training program.

Another effort within Protestantism to right contemporary social wrongs was the Social Gospel movement launched in the 1870s by Washington Gladden, a Congregational minister in Columbus, Ohio. Gladden insisted that true Christianity commits men and women to fight social injustice wherever it exists. Thus, in response to the wave of violent strikes in 1877, he urged church leaders to mediate the conflict between business and labor. Their attempt to do so was unsuccessful.

If Gladden set the tone for the Social Gospel, Walter Rauschenbusch, a minister at a German Baptist church in New York's notorious "Hell's Kitchen" neighborhood, articulated the movement's central philosophy. Educated in Germany, Rauschenbusch argued that a truly Christian society would unite all churches, reorganize the industrial system, and work for international peace. Rauschenbusch's appeal for Christian unity led to the formation of the Federal Council of Churches in 1908, but his other goals were never achieved. The Social Gospel's attack on what its leaders blasted as the complacent Christian support of the status quo attracted only a handful of Protestants. Nevertheless, their earnest voices blended with a growing chorus of critics bemoaning the nation's urban woes.

The Settlement-House Movement

By the 1880s many thoughtful Americans had become convinced that reform pressures applied from the top by the Charity Organization Society and the purity crusaders, however well intentioned, were not only ineffective but were also wrongheaded. A new approach to social work was needed. Relief workers would have to take up residence in poor neighborhoods where, in the words of Jane Addams, an early advocate of the movement, they could see firsthand "the struggle for existence, which is so much harsher among people near the edge of pauperism." A new institution—the settlement house—was born.

The youngest daughter of a successful Illinois businessman, Jane Addams purchased a dilapidated mansion on Chicago's South Halsted Street in 1889. After overseeing extensive repairs, she and her coworkers opened it as Hull House, the first experiment in the settlement house approach. Drawing on the middle-class domestic ideal of true womanhood as supportive and self-sacrificing, the indefatigable Addams turned Hull House into a social center for recent immigrants. She and her coworkers invited them to plays; sponsored art projects; held classes in English, civics, cooking, and dressmaking; and encouraged them to preserve their traditional crafts. She set up a kindergarten, a laundry, an employment bureau, and a day nursery for working mothers. Hull House also sponsored recreational and athletic programs and dispensed legal aid and health care.

In the hope of upgrading the filthy and overcrowded housing in its environs, Addams and her coworkers made studies of city housing conditions and pressured politicians to enforce sanitation regulations. For a time, demonstrating her principle of direct engagement with the lives of the poor, Addams even served as garbage inspector for her local ward.

By 1895 at least fifty settlement houses had opened in cities around the nation. Settlement house leaders trained a generation of young college students, mostly

Garbage Box, First Ward, Chicago, c, 1900
Lacking space for recreation, immigrant children played atop garbage boxes in crowded alleys. Concerned for their health, Jane Addams wrote that "this slaughter of the innocents, this infliction of suffering on the newborn, is so gratuitous and so unfair, that it is only a question of time until an outraged sense of justice shall be aroused on behalf of these children."

women, many of whom would later serve as state and local government officials. Florence Kelley, for example, who had worked at Hull House, became the chief factory inspector for Illinois in 1893. For Kelley as for other young female settlement workers, settlement houses functioned as a supportive sisterhood of reform through which they developed skills in working with municipal governments. Many settlement house veterans would later draw on their experience to play an influential role in the regulatory movements of the Progressive Era (see Chapter 21). Through their sympathetic attitudes toward the immigrants and their systematic publication of data about slum conditions, settlement house workers gave turn-of-the-century Americans new hope that the city's problems could be overcome.

But in their attempt to promote class cooperation and social harmony, settlement houses had mixed success. Although many immigrants appreciated the settlement houses' resources and activities, they felt that the reformers were uninterested in increasing their political power. Settlement house workers did tend to overlook immigrant organizations and their leaders. In 1894 Hull House attracted two thousand visitors per week, but this was only a fraction of the more than seventy thousand people who lived within six blocks of the building. "They're like the rest," complained one immigrant, "a bunch of people planning for us and deciding what is good for us without consulting us or taking us into their confidence."

WORKING-CLASS LEISURE IN THE IMMIGRANT CITY

In colonial America preachers had linked leisure time to "idleness," a dangerous step on the road to sin and wickedness. In the overwhelmingly rural culture of the early nineteenth century, the unremitting routines of farm labor left little time for relaxation. Family picnics, horse races, county fairs, revival meetings, and Fourth of July and Christmas celebrations had provided occasional permissible diversions. But most Americans continued to view leisure activities skeptically. Henry Clay Work's popular song "My Grandfather's Clock" (1876), which praised the ancient timepiece for "wasting no time" and working "ninety years, without slumbering," bore witness to the tenacity of this deep-seated reverence for work and suspicion of leisure.

After the Civil War, as immigration soared, urban populations shot up, and a new class of wealthy entrepreneurs arose, striking new patterns of leisure and amusement emerged, most notably among the urban working class. Middle-class educators and moralists continued to ponder the distinction between "wholesome" and "unwholesome" recreation, but they were little heeded by immigrants in the throbbing cities. After spending long hours in factories, in mills, behind department-store counters, or working as domestic servants in the homes of the wealthy, working-class Americans sought relaxation and diversion. Scorning

the museums and concert halls favored by the wealthy, they thronged the streets, patronized saloons and dance halls, cheered at boxing matches and baseball games, and organized group picnics and holiday celebrations. As amusement parks, vaudeville theaters, sporting clubs, and racetracks provided further outlets for workers' need for entertainment, leisure became a big business catering to a mass public rather than to a wealthy elite.

For millions of working-class Americans, leisure time took on increasing importance as factory work became ever more routinized and impersonal. Although many recreational activities involved both men and women, others attracted one gender in particular. Saloons offered an intensely male environment where patrons could share good stories, discuss and bet on sporting events, and momentarily put aside pressures of job and family. Young working women preferred to share confidences with friends in informal social clubs, tried out new fashions in street promenading, and found excitement in neighborhood dance halls and amusement parks.

Streets, Saloons, and Boxing Matches

No segment of the population had a greater need for amusement and recreation than the urban working class. Hours of tedious, highly disciplined, and physically exhausting labor left workers tired and thirsting for excitement and escape at the end of the day. A banner carried by the Worcester, Massachusetts, carpenters' union in an 1889 demonstration for the eight-hour workday summed up the importance of workers' leisure hours: "EIGHT HOURS FOR WORK, EIGHT HOURS FOR REST, AND EIGHT HOURS FOR WHAT WE WILL."

City streets provided recreation that anyone could afford. Relaxing after a day's work, shop girls and laborers clustered on busy corners, watching shouting pushcart peddlers and listening to organ grinders and buskers (street musicians) play familiar melodies. For a penny or a nickel, they could buy bagels, baked potatoes, soda, and other foods and drinks. In the summer, when the heat and humidity in tenement apartments reached unbearable levels, the streets became a hive of neighborhood social life. One immigrant fondly recalled

***McSorley's Bar*, by John Sloan, 1912**
Neighborhood saloons were places where friends could get together. In his novel Sister Carrie, *Theodore Dreiser* admiringly described "the long bar . . . [with its] blaze of lights, polished woodwork, colored and cut glassware and many fancy bottles."

his boyhood on the streets of New York's Lower East Side, "Something was always happening, and our attention was continually being shifted from one excitement to another."

The streets were open to all, but other leisure institutions drew mainly a male clientele. For example, in cities with a strong German immigrant presence like Baltimore, Milwaukee, and Cincinnati, gymnastic clubs (called *Turnverein*) and singing societies (*Gesangverein*) provided both companionship and the opportunity to perpetuate old-world cultural traditions.

For workmen of all ethnic backgrounds, saloons offered companionship, conviviality, and five-cent beer, often with a free lunch thrown in. New York City had an estimated ten thousand saloons by 1900 and Denver nearly five hundred. As neighborhood gathering places, saloons reinforced group identity and became centers for immigrant politics. Saloonkeepers, who often doubled as local ward bosses, performed small services for their patrons, including finding jobs and writing letters for illiterate immigrants. Sports memorabilia and pictures of prominent prizefighters adorned saloon walls. With their rich mahogany bars, etched glass, shiny brass rails, and elegant mirrors, saloons provided patrons with a taste of high-toned luxury. Although working-class women rarely joined their husbands at the saloon, they might send a son or daughter to the corner pub to fetch a "growler"—a large tin pail of beer.

The conventions of saloon culture thus stood in marked contrast to both the socially isolating routines of factory labor and the increasingly private and family-centered social life of the middle class. Nevertheless, it would be a mistake to view the old-time saloon through a haze of sentimental nostalgia. Prostitution and crime flourished in the rougher saloons. Moreover, drunken husbands sometimes beat their wives and children, squandered their limited income, and lost their jobs. The pervasiveness of alcoholism was devastating. Temperance reformers, in their attack on saloons, targeted a widespread social problem.

For working-class men, bare-knuckled prizefighting became one of the most popular amusements. Drawing its heroes from the poorer ranks of society, the ring became an arena where lower-class men could assert their individuality and physical prowess. In East Coast cities, blacks, Irish, and Germans formed their own "sporting clubs" and used athletics to bolster their self-confidence and reaffirm their racial or ethnic identity.

The Rise of Professional Sports

Contrary to the prevailing myth, schoolboy Abner Doubleday did not invent baseball in Cooperstown, New York, in 1839. As an English game called rounders, the pastime had existed in one form or another since the seventeenth century. But if Americans did not create

Baltimore, 1897
An overflow crowd watches the Baltimore Orioles play the Boston Beaneaters. Nestled in among the row houses, urban stadiums like this one drew huge crowds.

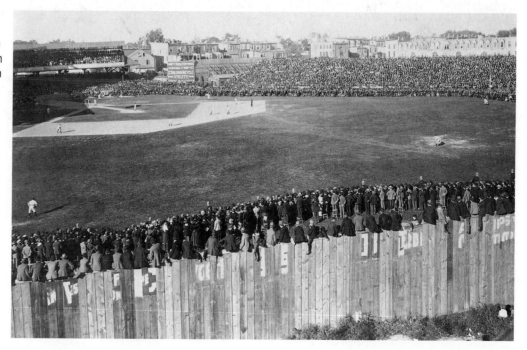

baseball, they unquestionably took this informal children's game and turned it into a major professional sport. The first organized baseball team, the New York Knickerbockers, was formed in 1845. In the 1860s the rules were codified, and the sport assumed its modern form. Overhand pitches replaced underhand tosses. Fielders, who now wore gloves, had to catch the ball on the fly to make an out instead of fielding it on one bounce. Games were standardized at nine innings, and bases were spaced ninety feet apart, as they are today.

In that same decade, promoters organized professional clubs and began to charge admission and compete for players. The Cincinnati Red Stockings, the first team to put its players under contract for the whole season, gained fame in 1869 by touring the country and ending the season with fifty-seven wins and no losses. Team owners organized the National League in 1876, took control from the players by requiring them to sign contracts that barred them from playing for rival organizations, and limited each city to one professional team. Soon the owners were filling baseball parks with crowds of ten to twelve thousand fans and earning enormous profits. By the 1890s baseball had become big business.

Although baseball attracted a national following from all social levels, the working class particularly took the sport to heart. The most profitable teams were those in major industrial cities with a large working-class population. Workers attended the games when they could and avidly followed their team's progress when they could not. Some saloons reported scores on blackboards. In Cleveland just after the turn of the century, Mayor Tom Johnson erected a bulletin board downtown that recorded game results.

Newspapers thrived on baseball. Joseph Pulitzer introduced the first separate sports page when he bought the *New York World* in 1883, and much of the sporting news in the *World* and other papers was devoted to baseball. For the benefit of German immigrants, the New York *Staats Zeitung* published a glossary of German equivalents of baseball terms; for example, *umpire* was *Unparteiischer*. Baseball, declared novelist Mark Twain in a burst of hyperbole, had become "the very symbol . . . and visible expression of the drive and push and rush and struggle of the raging, tearing, booming nineteenth century."

Although no organized sport attracted as large a following as baseball, horse racing and boxing contests were also widely covered in the popular press and drew big crowds of spectators and bettors. Whereas races like Louisville's Kentucky Derby became important social

Published by Arthur T. Lumley, New York Illustrated News.

FOR THE HEAVY-WEIGHT CHAMPIONSHIP OF THE WORLD.

John Lawrence Sullivan, the Champion, and James J. Corbett, the Adonis of the Fistic Arena, Who Are to Battle September 7th Next For a Purse and Stakes of $25,000 and the Big Fellow's Title.

World's Heavyweight Boxing Championship, 1892

In dethroning ring champion John L. Sullivan, "Gentleman Jim" Corbett demonstrated that speed and finesse were more than a match for brute strength.

events for the rich, professional boxing aroused more passionate devotion among the working class. By far the most popular sports hero of the nineteenth century was heavyweight fighter John L. Sullivan, "the Boston Strong Boy." Of Irish immigrant stock, Sullivan began boxing in 1877 at the age of nineteen. His first professional fight came in 1880 when he knocked out John Donaldson, "the Champion of the West," in a Cincinnati beer hall. With his massive physique, handlebar mustache, and arrogant swagger, Sullivan was enormously popular among immigrants. Barnstorming across the country, he vanquished a succession of local strong men, invariably wearing his trademark green tights with an American flag wrapped around his middle. Cleverly, Sullivan also refused to fight blacks, in deference, he said, to the wishes of his fans. This policy conveniently allowed him to avoid facing the finest boxer of the 1880s, the Australian black, Peter Jackson.

Sullivan loved drink and high living, and by the end of the eighties he was sadly out of shape. But when the editor of the *Police Gazette*, a sensational tabloid, designed a new heavyweight championship belt— allegedly containing two hundred ounces of silver and encrusted with diamonds and pure gold—and awarded it to Sullivan's rival Jake Kilrain, the champion had to defend himself. The two met on a sweltering, hundred-degree day in New Orleans in July 1889 for the last bare-knuckles championship match. After seventy-five short but grueling rounds, Kilrain's managers threw in the towel. Newspapers around the nation banner-headlined the story. Contemptuously returning the championship belt to the *Police Gazette* after having had it appraised at $175, Sullivan went on the road to star in a melodrama written specifically for him. Playing the role of a blacksmith, he (in the words of a recent historian of bare-knuckles boxing) "pounded an anvil, beat a bully, and mutilated his lines." But his fans did not care; he was one of them, and they adored him. As one admirer wrote,

His colors are the Stars and Stripes,
He also wears the green,
And he's the grandest slugger that
The ring has ever seen.

Vaudeville, Amusement Parks, and Dance Halls

In contrast to the male preserve of saloons and prize-fights, the world of vaudeville, amusement parks, and neighborhood dance pavilions welcomed all comers regardless of gender. Some of them proved particularly congenial to working-class women.

Vaudeville evolved out of the pre-Civil War minstrel shows in which white comedians made up as blacks had performed songs and comic sketches. Vaudeville performances offered a succession of acts, all designed for mass appeal. The shows typically opened with a trained animal routine or a dance number. This were followed by a musical interlude featuring sentimental favorites such as "On the Banks of the Wabash Far Away" or new hits such as "Meet Me in St. Louis, Louis," a jaunty spoof of a young wife's frustration with her stick-in-the-mud husband. Comic skits followed, ridiculing the trials of urban life, satirizing the ineptitude of the police and municipal officials, poking fun at the babel of accents in the immigrant city, and mining a rich vein of broad ethnic humor and stereotypes. After more musical numbers and acts by ventriloquists, pantomimes, and magicians, the program ended with a "flash" finale such as flying-trapeze artists swinging against a black background.

By the 1880s vaudeville was drawing larger crowds than any other form of theater. Not only did it provide an inexpensive evening of lighthearted entertainment, but in the comic sketches, immigrant audiences could also laugh at their own experience as they saw it translated into slapstick and caricature.

The white working class's fascination with vaudeville's blackface acts has been the subject of considerable recent scrutiny by historians. Some have interpreted it as a way for the white working class to mock middle-class ideals. By pretending to act like the popular stereotypes of blacks, white working-class youths could challenge traditional family structures, the virtue of sexual self-denial, and adult expectations about working hard. In this view popular culture was making fun of the ideals of thrift and propriety being promoted in marketplace and domestic ideology. Other historians have argued that blackface buffoonery, with its grotesque, demeaning caricatures of African-Americans, reinforced prejudice against blacks and restricted their escape from lower-class status. Paradoxically, therefore, the popularity of blackface vaudeville acts reinforced white racial solidarity and strengthened the expanding wall separating whites and African-Americans.

Where vaudeville offered psychological escape from the stresses of working-class life by exploiting its comic potential, amusement parks provided physical escape, at least for a day. The prototype of the sprawling urban amusement park was New York's Coney Island, a section of Brooklyn's oceanfront that evolved into a resort for the masses in the 1870s. At Coney Island young couples went dancing, rode through the dark Tunnel of Love, sped down the dizzying roller coaster in Steeplechase

Park, or watched belly dancers in the carnival atmosphere of the sideshows. Customers were encouraged to surrender to the spirit of play, forget the demands of the industrial world, and lose themselves in fantasy.

By the end of the nineteenth century, New York City had well over three hundred thousand female wage earners, most of them young, unmarried women working as seamstresses, laundresses, typists, domestic servants, and department store clerks. For this army of low-paid young working women and their counterparts in other cities, amusement parks exerted a powerful lure. Here they could meet friends, spend time with young men beyond the watchful eyes of their parents, show off their new dresses, and try out the latest dance steps. As a twenty-year-old German immigrant woman who worked as a servant in a wealthy household observed,

> I have heard some of the high people with whom I have been living say that Coney Island is not tony. The trouble is that these high people don't know how to dance. I have to laugh when I see them at their balls and parties. If only I could get out on the floor and show them how—they would be astonished.

For such women, the brightly decorated dance pavilion, the exciting music, and the spell of a warm summer night could seem a magical release from the drudgery of daily life.

Ragtime

Since the days of slavery, black Americans had developed a strong, creative musical culture, and thus it is not surprising that blacks made a major contribution to the popular music of the late nineteenth century in the form of ragtime. Nothing could illustrate more sharply the differences between middle- and working-class culture than the contrasting styles of popular music they favored. The middle class preferred hymns or songs that conveyed a moral lesson. The working class delighted in ragtime, which originated in the 1880s with black musicians in the saloons and brothels of the South and Midwest and was played strictly for entertainment (see A Place in Time: New Orleans, Louisiana, 1890s).

Ragtime developed out of the rich tradition of sacred and secular songs through which African-Americans had long eased the burdens of their lives. Like spirituals, ragtime used syncopated rhythms and complex harmonies, but it blended these with marching-band musical structures to create a distinctive style. A favorite of "honky-tonk" piano players, ragtime was

introduced to the broader public in the 1890s and became a national sensation.

The reasons for the sudden ragtime craze were complex. Inventive, playful, with catchy syncopations and an infectious rhythm in the bass clef, the music displayed an originality that had an appeal all its own. Part of ragtime's popularity also came from its origin in brothels and its association with blacks, who were widely stereotyped in the 1890s as sexual, sensual, and uninhibited by the rigid Victorian social conventions that restricted whites. The "wild" and complex rhythms of ragtime were widely interpreted to be a freer and more "natural" expression of elemental feelings about love and sex.

Ragtime's great popularity proved a mixed blessing for blacks. It testified to the achievements of brilliant composers like Scott Joplin, helped break down the barriers faced by blacks in the music industry, and contributed to a spreading rebellion against the repressiveness of Victorian standards. But ragtime simply confirmed some whites' stereotype of blacks as primitive and sensual, a bias that underlay the racism of the period and helped justify segregation and discrimination.

CULTURES IN CONFLICT

In the late nineteenth century the United States was embroiled in class conflict and cultural unrest. Part of this turmoil raged within the middle class itself. Victorian morality and genteel cultural standards were never totally accepted even within the elite and middle classes; and as the century ended, ethical questionings and new cultural stirrings intensified. Women stood at the center of the era's cultural turbulence. Thwarted by a restrictive code of feminine propriety, middle-class women made their dissatisfactions heard. Developments as diverse as the rise of women's clubs, the growth of women's colleges, and an 1890s bicycle fad contributed to the emergence of what some began to call the "new woman."

Although Victorian culture was challenged from within the middle class, a widening chasm divided the well-to-do from urban working-class immigrants. In no period of American history have class conflicts—cultural as well as economic—been more open and raw. As middle-class leaders nervously eyed the rambunctious and sometimes disorderly culture of city streets, saloons, boxing clubs, dance halls, and amusement parks, they saw a massive if unconscious challenge to their own cultural and social standing. Some middle-class reformers promoted the public school as a way to impose middle-class

values on the urban masses. Others battled the hydra-headed manifestations of urban "vice" and "immorality." But ultimately it was the polite mores of the middle class, not urban working-class culture, that proved more vulnerable. By 1900 the Victorian social and moral ethos was crumbling on every front.

The Genteel Tradition and Its Critics

What was this genteel culture that aroused such opposition? In the 1870s and 1880s a group of upper-class writers and magazine editors, led by Harvard art history professor Charles Eliot Norton and New York editors Richard Watson Gilder of *The Century* magazine and E. L. Godkin of *The Nation,* codified Victorian standards for literature and the fine arts. They joined forces with artistic allies in Boston and New York in a campaign to improve American taste in interior furnishings, textiles, ceramics, wallpaper, and books. By fashioning rigorous

criteria for excellence in writing and design, they hoped to create a coherent national artistic culture.

In the 1880s Norton, Godkin, and Gilder, joined by the editors of other highbrow periodicals such as the *Atlantic Monthly* and *North American Review,* set up new guidelines for serious literature. They lectured the middle class about the value of high culture and the insights to be gained from the fine arts. They censored their own publications to remove all sexual allusions, vulgar slang, disrespectful treatments of Christianity, and unhappy endings. Expanding their combined circulation to nearly two hundred thousand copies and opening their magazines to a variety of new authors, Godkin and the other editors of "quality" periodicals created an important forum for serious writing. Novelists Henry James, who published virtually all of his work in the *Atlantic,* and William Dean Howells, who served as editor of the same magazine, helped lead this elite literary establishment. James believed that "it is art that makes

Sarah Orne Jewett and Mark Twain
Jewett and Twain not only broke from highbred literary standards but also created unique personal styles through their studied poses and distinctive attire.

New Orleans was a unique city in the 1890s. Its popular culture fused elements from the culinary and musical traditions of the varied groups in its population, especially its free blacks and Creoles of color. The latter were the offspring of Africans and eighteenth-century Spanish and French immigrants who had settled along the swampy bayous of the Mississippi Delta south of the city. During the early nineteenth century, New Orleans's large free-black and "colored" Creole population had enjoyed a degree of independence people of color found nowhere else in the South. Free blacks had established their own churches and fraternal societies, formed their own militia, and borne arms. Both wealthy and poor free blacks had created a distinctive culture melding African and French customs. In the Vieux Carré, the old French part of the city, slaves and free blacks joined together on Sunday afternoons to play drums, banjos, and violins. Young people danced and sang, mingling African voodoo rhythms with Roman Catholic liturgical melodies.

During the Civil War and Reconstruction, however, the humiliating occupation of New Orleans by federal troops had left a legacy of southern white bitterness against the black population. Then in the 1880s and 1890s, when Italian immigrants swelled the city's population, racial tensions were rekindled. Despite the discord, festivals like Mardi Gras, with its riotous parades and boisterous balls, continued. The city won notoriety for racetrack betting, gambling, and prostitution. Sightseers flocked to New Orleans to savor spicy Creole food, drink in smoky bars, and visit seedy bordellos and raunchy dance halls. The sidewalks thronged with commercial travelers, longshoremen, country folk in the city for a day, and racetrack bettors. "One is apt to see here at some hour of the day anybody from a St. Louis capitalist to the man who came the night before with no change of linen, and seven dollars sewn in his waistcoat," wrote a visiting journalist. Appropriately, promoters chose New Orleans as the site of the September 1892 championship boxing match in which "Gentleman Jim" Corbett defeated John L. Sullivan.

Among the city's liveliest traditions was the marching band. A product of the eighteenth-century military whose drummers and fifers helped identify regiments' locations amidst battlefield chaos, by the mid-nineteenth century the marching band had become a fixture in cities and towns

The Queen City Band of Sedalia, Missouri

Marching bands helped popularize ragtime music. When he lived in Sedalia, Missouri, Scott Joplin often allowed the Queen City Band, pictured here in the 1890s, to give the first performance of his new compositions.

across America, and prominently so in New Orleans. On Saturday nights, young and old alike ambled to the city-park bandstand to hear local groups belt out the stirring marches of John Philip Sousa and other composers.

New Orleans's black brass bands pioneered new playing styles that captured national attention. Having snapped up the affordable used musical instruments piled high in pawn shops after the Civil War, blacks in New Orleans—unfettered by written scores and formal music lessons—developed innovative styles for bugles, trombones, and the newly invented piston-valve trumpets. Every black social organization, club, fire station, and lodge boasted its own twelve-member brass marching band. The bands played at picnics, parades, dances, church socials, circuses, minstrel shows, athletic contests, and holiday gatherings. By the 1880s many brass bands gained fame for playing in the new "ratty," "raggy," unscored, syncopated style, with its echoes of the older call-and-response African-American singing in which one person shouted a phrase and was answered by the group. Brass bands were also known for playing religious hymns "straight" on the way to the cemetery and "jazzing them up" on the way home. Within the bands, which often played in bars and brothels, individual soloists such as coronetist Charles "Buddy" Bolden became famous for improvisational blues solos. These soulful performances were the forerunners of a new musical style, "jazz," that emerged in the 1890s and became a national rage after the turn of the century.

Although the popularity of these musicians—who were later immortalized in Irving Berlin's song "Alexander's Ragtime Band"—increasingly attracted middle-class white audiences and seemed to imply a growing general acceptance of black musicians, racial prejudice continued to shape local practices. If a black band marched into a white neighborhood, the residents commonly pelted the musicians with rocks.

In 1897, seeking to isolate and regulate prostitution, city administrators created a special district, named Storyville after Sydney Story, the councilman who proposed the new quarter. Storyville's glittering saloons and ubiquitous houses of prostitution hired some of the best black ragtime piano players. Other black musicians, excluded from some white establishments, could find jobs only in the racially segregated bars and cabarets of the two-block "Tango Belt" surrounding Storyville. Musically talented Creoles of color—the proud descendants of free-black mulattos whose musical training had assured them positions in local orchestras and opera houses—could secure employment only in these districts, where they worked alongside criminals and prostitutes.

For all its uniqueness, New Orleans typified larger strands in the turn-of-the-century American fabric. (The city's cultural diversity also anticipated trends that in the twentieth century would make the United States a truly multicultural society.) And the complex history of early jazz in New Orleans paralleled the ironic relationship of popular culture and racism in the larger society. White middle-class America, like the middle class in New Orleans, would soon embrace this African-American musical contribution. Captivated by New Orleans "Dixieland" jazz, they would idolize its best practitioners, including the great trumpeter Louis Armstrong, a veteran of the New Orleans brass marching bands. Yet these middle-class Americans, like their counterparts in New Orleans, would see no contradiction in harboring deep prejudices against the very people from whose culture this vital new music had emerged.

Valve Trombone
Members of New Orlean's Reliance Brass Band played this pre-World War I vintage trombone. The band's founder, "Papa" Jack Laine, was known as the father of white jazz.

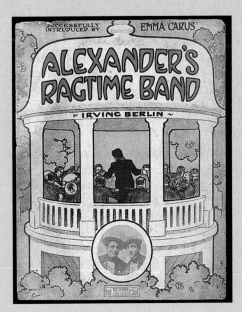

Ragtime Sheet Music
The nearly universal popularity of ragtime music was confirmed when sheetmusic publishers on New York's 28th Street, an area nicknamed Tin Pan Alley, brought out Irving Berlin's "Alexander's Ragtime Band." Although Berlin was a Russian Jewish immigrant and the song had hardly a trace of ragtime in it, the connection with the New Orleans ragtime tradition made the tune an instant hit.

life, . . . [There is] no substitute whatever for [its] force and beauty. . . ."

This interest in art for art's sake paralleled a broader crusade called the "aesthetic movement," led in England by William Morris, Oscar Wilde, and other art critics, who sought to bring art into every facet of life. In America, Candace Wheeler and other reformers made its influence felt through the work of architects, jewelers, and interior decorators.

Although the magazines initially provided an important forum for new writers, their editors' elitism and desire to control the nation's literary standards soon aroused opposition. Samuel Langhorne Clemens, better known as Mark Twain, spoke for many young writers when he declared that he was through with "literature and all that bosh." Attacking aristocratic literary conventions, Twain and other authors who shared his concerns explored new forms of fiction and worked to broaden its appeal to the general public.

These efforts to chart new directions for American literature rested on fundamental changes taking place in the publishing industry. To compete with elite periodicals costing twenty-five to thirty-five cents, new magazines like *Ladies' Home Journal, Cosmopolitan,* and *McClure's* lowered their prices to a dime or fifteen cents and tripled or quadrupled their circulation. Supporting themselves through advertising, these magazines encouraged new trends in fiction while mass-marketing new products. Their editors sought writers who could provide accurate depictions of the "whirlpool of real life" and create a new civic consciousness to heal the class divisions of American society.

Some of these authors have been called regionalists because they captured the distinctive dialect and details of local life in their environs. In *The Country of the Pointed Firs* (1896), for example, Sarah Orne Jewett wrote of the New England village life that she knew in South Berwick, Maine. Others, most notably William Dean Howells, have been called realists because of their focus on the truthful depiction of the commonplace and the everyday, especially in urban areas. Still others have been categorized as naturalists because their novels and stories deny free will and stress the ways in which life's outcomes are determined by economic and psychological forces. Stephen Crane's *Maggie: A Girl of the Streets* (1892), a bleak story of an innocent girl's exploitation and ultimate suicide in an urban slum, is generally considered the first naturalistic American novel. Yet in practice, these categories are imprecise and often overlap. What many of these writers shared was a skepticism about lit-

erary conventions and an intense desire to understand the society around them and portray it in words.

The careers of Mark Twain and Theodore Dreiser highlight the changes in the publishing industry and the evolution of new forms of writing. Both authors grew up in the Midwest, outside the East Coast literary establishment. Twain was born near Hannibal, Missouri, in 1835, and Dreiser in Terre Haute, Indiana, in 1871. As young men both worked as newspaper reporters and traveled widely. Both learned from direct and sometimes bitter experience about the greed, speculation, and fraud that figured centrally in Gilded Age life.

Of the two, Twain more incessantly sought a mass-market audience. With his drooping mustache, white hair, and white suits, Twain turned himself into a media personality, lecturing from coast to coast, founding his own publishing house, and using door-to-door salesmen to sell his books. The name Mark Twain became his trademark, identifying him to readers as a literary celebrity much as the labels Coca-Cola and Ivory Soap won instant consumer recognition. Although Dreiser possessed neither Twain's flamboyant personality nor his instinct for salesmanship, he, too, learned to crank out articles.

Drawing on their own experiences, Twain and Dreiser wrote about the human impact of the wrenching social changes taking place around them: the flow of people to the cities and the relentless scramble for power, wealth, and fame. In the *Adventures of Huckleberry Finn* (1884), Twain presents a classic narrative of two runaways, the rebellious Huck and the slave Jim, drifting down the Mississippi in search of freedom. Their physical journey, which contrasts idyllic life on the raft with the tawdry, fraudulent world of small riverfront towns, is a journey of identity that brings with it a deeper understanding of contemporary American society.

Dreiser's *Sister Carrie* (1900) also tells of a journey. In this case, the main character, Carrie Meeber, an innocent girl on her way from her Wisconsin farm home to Chicago, is first seduced by a traveling salesman and then moves in with the married proprietor of a fancy saloon. Driven by her desire for expensive department-store clothes and lavish entertainment, Carrie is an opportunist incapable of feeling guilt. She follows her married lover to New York, knowing that he has stolen the receipts from his saloon, abandons him when his money runs out, and pursues her own career in the theater.

Twain and Dreiser broke decisively with the genteel tradition's emphasis on manners and decorum. *Century*

magazine readers complained that *Huckleberry Finn* was coarse and "destitute of a single redeeming quality." The publisher of *Sister Carrie* was so repelled by Dreiser's novel that he printed only a thousand copies (to fulfill the legal terms of his contract) and then stored them in a warehouse, refusing to promote them.

Growing numbers of scholars and critics similarly challenged the self-serving certitudes of Victorian mores, including assumptions that moral worth and economic standing were closely linked and that the status quo of the 1870s and 1880s represented a social order decreed by God and nature alike. Whereas Henry George, Lester Ward, and Edward Bellamy elaborated their visions of a cooperative and harmonious society (see Chapter 18), economist Thorstein Veblen in *The Theory of the Leisure Class* (1899) offered a caustic critique of the lifestyles of the new capitalist elite. Raised in a Norwegian farm community in Minnesota, Veblen looked at the captains of industry and their families with a jaundiced eye, mercilessly documenting their "conspicuous consumption" and lamenting the widening economic gap between "those who worked without profit" and "those who profited without working."

Within the new discipline of sociology, Annie MacLean exposed the exploitation of department store clerks, Walter Wyckoff uncovered the hand-to-mouth existence of unskilled laborers, and W. E. B. DuBois documented the suffering and hardships faced by blacks in Philadelphia. The publication of these social scientists' writings, coupled with the economic depression and seething labor agitation of the 1890s, made it increasingly difficult for turn-of-the-century middle-class Americans to accept the smug, self-satisfied belief in progress and gentility that had been a hallmark of the Victorian outlook.

Modernism in Architecture and Painting

The challenge to the genteel tradition also found strong support among architects and painters. By the 1890s Chicago architects William Holabird, John Wellborn Root, and others had tired of copying European designs. Breaking with established architects such as Richard Morris Hunt, the designer of French chateaux for New York's Fifth Avenue, these Chicago architects followed the lead of Louis Sullivan, who argued that a building's form should follow its function. In their view, banks should look like the financial institutions they were, not like Greek temples. Striving to evolve functional

American design standards, the Chicago architects looked for inspiration to the future—to modernism—not to the past.

Frank Lloyd Wright's "prairie-school" houses, first built in the Chicago suburb of Oak Park in the 1890s, represented a typical modernist break with past styles. Wright scorned the bulky Victorian house with its large attic and basement. His designs, which featured broad, sheltering roofs and low silhouettes, used interconnecting rooms to create a sense of spaciousness.

The call of modernism, with its rejection of Victorian refinement, influenced late-nineteenth-century American painting as well. The watercolors of Winslow Homer, a magazine illustrator during the Civil War, revealed nature as brutally tough and unsentimental. In Homer's grim, elemental seascapes, lone men struggle against massive waves that constantly threaten to overwhelm them. Thomas Eakins's canvases of swimmers, boxers, and rowers (such as his well-known *Champion Single Sculls*, painted in 1871) similarly captured moments of vigorous physical exertion in everyday life.

The revolt by architects and painters against Victorian standards was symptomatic of a larger shift in middle-class thought. This shift resulted from fundamental economic changes that had spawned a far more complex social environment than that of the past. As Protestant minister Josiah Strong perceptively observed in 1898, the transition from muscle to mechanical power had "separated, as by an impassable gulf, the simple, homespun, individualistic world of the . . . past, from the complex, closely associated life of the present." The increasingly evident gap between rural or small-town life—a world of quiet parlors and flickering kerosene lamps—and life in the big, glittering, electrified cities of iron and glass made nineteenth-century Americans acutely aware of differences in upbringing and wealth. Given the disparities between rich and poor, between rural and urban, and between native-born Americans and recent immigrants, it is no wonder that pious Victorian platitudes about proper manners and graceful arts seemed out of touch with the new social realities.

Distrusting the idealistic Victorian assumptions about social progress, middle-class journalists, novelists, artists, and politicians nevertheless remained divided over how to replace them. Not until the Progressive Era would social reformers draw on a new expertise in social research and an enlarged conception of the federal government's regulatory power to break sharply with their Victorian predecessors' social outlook.

From Victorian Lady to New Woman

Although middle-class women figured importantly in the revolt against Victorian refinement, their role was complex and ambiguous. Dissatisfaction with the cult of domesticity did not necessarily lead to open rebellion. Many women, although chafing against the constraints of deference and the assumption that they should limit their activities to the home, remained committed to playing a nurturing and supportive role within the family. In fact, early advocates of a "widened sphere" for women often fused the traditional Victorian ideal of womanhood with a firm commitment to political action.

The career of temperance leader Frances Willard illustrates how the cult of domesticity, with its celebration of special female virtues, could evolve into a broader view of women's social and political responsibilities. Like many of her contemporaries, Willard believed that women were compassionate and nurturing by nature. She was also convinced that drinking encouraged thriftlessness and profoundly threatened family life. Resigning as dean of women and professor of English at Northwestern University in 1874, Willard devoted her energies full-time to the temperance cause. Five years later she was elected president of the newly formed Woman's Christian Temperance Union (WCTU).

Willard took the traditional belief that women had unique moral virtues and transformed it into a rationale for political action. The domestication of politics, she asserted, would protect the family and improve public morality. Choosing as the union's badge a bow of white ribbon, symbolizing the purity of the home, she launched a crusade in 1880 to win the franchise for women so that they could vote to outlaw liquor. Willard soon expanded WCTU activities to include welfare work, prison reform, labor arbitration, and public health. Under her leadership the WCTU, with a membership of nearly 150,000 by 1890, became the nation's first mass organization of women. Through it, women gained experience as lobbyists, organizers, and lecturers, in the process undercutting the assumption of "separate spheres."

An expanding network of women's clubs offered another means by which middle- and upper-class women could hone their skills in civic affairs, public speaking, and intellectual analysis. In the 1870s many well-to-do women met weekly to study topics of mutual interest. These clubwomen soon became involved in social-welfare projects, public library expansion, and tenement reform. By 1892 the General Federation of Women's Clubs, an umbrella organization established that year, boasted 495 affiliates and a hundred thousand members.

Another major impetus to an expanded role for women came from a younger generation of college women. Following the precedent set by Oberlin College in 1836, coeducational private colleges and public universities in the Midwest enrolled increasing numbers of women. Columbia, Brown, and Harvard universities in the East admitted women to the affiliated but separate institutions of Barnard (1889), Pembroke (1891), and Radcliffe (1894), respectively. Nationally, the percentage of colleges admitting women jumped from 30 percent to 71 percent between 1880 and 1900. By the turn of the century, women made up more than one-third of the total college-student population.

Initially, female collegiate education reinforced the prevailing concepts of femininity. The earliest women's colleges—Mount Holyoke (1837), Vassar (1865), Wellesley and Smith (1875), and Bryn Mawr (1884)—were founded to prepare women for marriage, motherhood, and Christian service. But participation in college organizations, athletics, and dramatics enabled female students to learn traditionally "masculine" strategies for gaining power. The generation of women educated at female institutions in the late nineteenth century developed the self-confidence to break with the Victorian ideal of passive womanhood and to compete on an equal basis with men by displaying the strength, aggressiveness, and intelligence popularly considered male attributes. By 1897 the U.S. commissioner of education noted, "[I]t has become an historical fact that women have made rapid strides, and captured a greater number of honors in proportion to their numbers than men."

Victorian constraints on women were further loosened at the end of the century when a bicycling vogue swept urban America. Fearful of waning vitality, middle- and upper-class Americans explored various ways to improve their vigor. Some used health products such as cod liver oil and sarsaparilla for "weak blood." Others played basketball, invented in 1891 by a physical education instructor at Springfield College in Massachusetts to keep students in shape during the winter months. But bicycling, which could be done individually or in groups, quickly became the most popular sport for those who wished to combine exercise with recreation.

Bicycles of various designs had been manufactured since the 1870s, but bicycling did not become a national craze until the invention in the 1880s of the so-called safety bicycle, with smaller wheels, ball-bearing axles,

and air-filled tires. By the 1890s over a million Americans owned bicycles.

Bicycling especially appealed to young women who had chafed under the restrictive Victorian attitudes about female exercise, which held that proper young ladies must never sweat and that the female body must be fully covered at all times. Pedaling along in a shirt-waist or "split" skirt, a woman bicyclist made an implicit feminist statement suggesting that she had broken with genteel conventions and wanted to explore new activities beyond the traditional sphere.

Changing attitudes about femininity and women's proper role also found expression in gradually shifting ideas about marriage. Charlotte Perkins Gilman, a suffrage advocate and speaker for women's rights, asserted that women would make an effective contribution to society only when they won economic independence from men through work outside the home (see Chapter 21). One very tangible indicator of women's changing relationship to men was the substantial rise in the divorce rate between 1880 and 1900. In 1880 one in every twenty-one marriages ended in divorce. By 1900 the rate had climbed to one in twelve. Women who brought suit for divorce increasingly cited their husbands' failure to act responsibly and to respect their autonomy. Accepting such arguments, courts frequently awarded the wife alimony, a monetary settlement payable by the ex-husband to support her and their children.

Women writers generally welcomed the new female commitment to independence and self-sufficiency. In the short stories of Mary Wilkins Freeman, for example, women's expanding role is implicitly compared to the frontier ideal of freedom. Feminist Kate Chopin pushed the debate to the extreme by having Edna Pontellier, the married heroine of her 1899 novel *The Awakening*, violate social conventions. First Edna falls in love with another man; then she takes her own life when his ideas about women prove as narrow and traditional as those of her husband.

Despite the efforts of these and other champions of the new woman, attitudes changed slowly. The enlarged conception of women's role in society exerted its greatest influence on college-educated, middle-class women who had leisure time and could reasonably hope for success in journalism, social work, and nursing. For female immigrant factory workers and for shop girls who worked sixty hours a week to try to make ends meet, however, the ideal remained a more distant goal. Although many women were seeking more independence and control over their lives, most still viewed the home as their primary responsibility.

Public Education as an Arena of Class Conflict

While the debate over women's proper role remained largely confined to the middle class, a very different controversy, over the scope and function of public education, engaged Americans of all socioeconomic levels. This debate starkly highlighted the class and cultural divisions in late-nineteenth-century society. From the 1870s on, viewing the public schools as an instrument for indoctrinating and controlling the lower ranks of society, middle-class educators and civic leaders campaigned to expand public schooling and bring it under centralized control. Not surprisingly, the reformers' efforts aroused considerable opposition from ethnic and religious groups whose outlook and interests differed sharply from theirs.

Thanks to the crusade for universal public education started by Horace Mann and other antebellum educational reformers, most states had public school systems by the Civil War, and more than half the nation's children were receiving some formal education. But most attended school for only three or four years, and few went on to high school.

Concerned that many Americans lacked sufficient knowledge to participate wisely in public affairs or function effectively in the labor force, reformers such as William Torrey Harris worked to increase the number of years that children spent in school. First as superintendent of the St. Louis public schools in the 1870s and later as the federal commissioner of education, Harris urged teachers to instill in their students a sense of order, decorum, self-discipline, and civic loyalty. Believing that modern industrial society depended on citizens' conforming to the timetables of the factory and the train, he envisioned the schools as models of punctuality and precise scheduling: "The pupil must have his lessons ready at the appointed time, must rise at the tap of the bell, move to the line, return; in short, go through all the evolutions with equal precision."

To achieve these goals and to wrest control of the schools from neighborhood leaders and ward politicians, reform-minded educators like Harris elaborated a philosophy of public education stressing punctuality, centralized administration, compulsory-attendance laws, and a tenure system to insulate teachers from political favoritism and parental pressure. By 1900 thirty-one states required school attendance of all children from eight to fourteen years of age.

The steamroller methods used by Harris and like-minded administrators to systematize public education

Interior Urban School
Photographers were careful to picture public elementary schools, such as this one on New York's Lower East Side
in 1886, as models of immigrant children's decorum and good behavior.

quickly prompted protests. New York pediatrician Joseph Mayer Rice, who toured thirty-six cities and interviewed twelve hundred teachers in 1892, scornfully criticized an educational establishment that stressed singsong memorization and prisonlike discipline.

Rice's biting attack on public education overlooked the real advances in reading and computation made in the previous two decades. Nationally, despite the influx of immigrants, the illiteracy rate for individuals ten years and older dropped from 17 percent in 1880 to 13 percent in 1890, largely because of the expansion of urban educational facilities. American high schools were also coeducational, and girls made up the majority of the students by 1900. But Rice was on target in assailing many teachers' rigid emphasis on silence, docility, and unquestioning obedience to the rules. When a Chicago school inspector found a thirteen-year-old boy huddled in the basement of a stockyard building and ordered him back to school, the weeping boy blurted out, "[T]hey hits ye if yer don't learn, and they hits ye if ye whisper, and

they hits ye if ye have string in yer pocket, and they hits ye if yer seat squeaks, and they hits ye if ye don't stan' up in time, and they hits ye if yer late, and they hits ye if ye ferget the page."

By the 1880s several different groups found themselves in opposition to centralized urban public school bureaucracies. Although many working-class families valued education, those who depended on their children's meager wages for survival resisted the attempt to force their sons and daughters to attend school past the elementary grades. Although some immigrant families made great sacrifices to enable their children to get an education, many withdrew their offspring from school as soon as they had learned the rudiments of reading and writing, and sent them to work.

Furthermore, Catholic immigrants objected to the overwhelmingly Protestant orientation of the public schools. Distressed by the use of the King James translation of the Bible and by the schools' failure to observe saints' days, Catholics set up separate parochial school

systems. In response, Republican politicians, resentful of the Catholic immigrants' overwhelming preference for the Democratic party, tried unsuccessfully to pass a constitutional amendment cutting off all public aid to church-related schools in 1875. Catholics in turn denounced federal aid to public schools as intended "to suppress Catholic education, gradually extinguish Catholicity in this country, and to form one homogeneous American people after the New England Evangelical type."

At the other end of the social scale, upper-class parents who did not wish to send their children to immigrant-thronged public schools enrolled their daughters in female seminaries such as Emma Willard's in Troy, New York, and their sons in private academies and boarding schools like St. Paul's in Concord, New Hampshire. The proliferation of private and parochial schools, together with the controversies over compulsory education, school funding, and classroom decorum, reveal the extent to which public education had become entangled in ethnic and class differences. Unlike Germany and Japan, which standardized and centralized their national education systems in the late nineteenth century, the United States, reflecting its social heterogeneity, created a diverse system of locally run public and private institutions that allowed each segment of society to retain some influence over the schools attended by its own children. Amid the disputes, school enrollments dramatically expanded. In 1870 fewer than seventy-two thousand students attended the nation's 1,026 high schools. By 1900 the number of high schools had jumped to more than 5,000 and the number of students to more than half a million.

CONCLUSION

By the 1890s class conflict was evident in practically every area of city life from mealtime manners to popular entertainment and recreation. As new immigrants flooded the tenements and spilled out onto neighborhood streets, it became impossible for native-born Americans to ignore their strange religions and social customs. Ethnic differences were compounded by class differences. Often poor and from peasant or working-class backgrounds, the immigrants took unskilled jobs and worked for subsistence-level wages. Middle- and upper-class Americans often responded by stigmatizing them as nonwhite and racially inferior.

To raise their own standards and to distinguish themselves from these newcomers, native-born Americans adopted a Victorian code of morality that emphasized good manners, decorum, and self-control. Although never fully accepted even among the well-to-do, these Victorian moral ideals were meant to apply a new standard for civilization and refinement.

These moral standards were further reinforced by an expanded educational system that featured high school and university education as the path to becoming educators, lawyers, doctors, and other professionals. As defenders of the new Victorian morality, middle- and upper-class women, educated in the expanding college and university system, were expected to become the protectors of the home. Discontented with this new role, Jane Addams and other social workers developed the settlement house movement and campaigned for legislation to curb the evils of boss politics and urban blight.

Nowhere was the conflict between the social classes more evident than in the controversy over leisure entertainment. Caught up in the material benefits of a prospering industrial society, middle- and upper-class Americans battled against what they deemed "indecent" lower-class behavior in all its forms, from dancing to ragtime, gambling, and prizefighting to playing baseball on Sunday and visiting bawdy boardwalk sideshows. Even public parks became arenas of class conflict. Whereas the elite favored large, impeccably groomed urban parks that would serve as models of orderliness and propriety, working people fought for parks where they could picnic, play ball, drink beer, and escape the stifling heat of tenement apartments.

Although the well-to-do classes often appeared to have the upper hand in these clashes, significant disagreements about moral standards surfaced early within their own ranks. The aged poet Walt Whitman was not alone in his sentiments when he lamented in the essay "Democratic Vistas" (1881) that "certain portions of the people" were trying to force their cultural standards and moral values on the great mass of the population, who were thereby made to feel "degraded, humiliated, [and] of no account." Other critics, among them Charlotte Perkins Gilman, faulted middle-class society for its obsession with polite manners, empty social rituals, and restrictions on the occupations open to women.

By the end of the century, the contest for power between the elite classes and the largely immigrant working class headed toward a partial resolution in a series of compromises that neither side had anticipated. As Victorian morality eroded, undermined by dissension from within and opposition from without, new standards emerged that blended elements of earlier positions. For example, new rules regulated behavior in the boxing ring and on the baseball field. Still, it was immi-

CHRONOLOGY, 1860–1900

1843	Robert M. Hartley founds the New York Association for Improving the Condition of the Poor.
1851	The American branch of the Young Men's Christian Association (YMCA) opens.
1852	Charles Loring Brace Founds the New York Children's Aid Society
1855	New York opens its Castle Garden immigrant center.
1865	Vasser College founded.
1869	Boss William Marcy Tweed gains control of New York's Tammany Hall political machine. First intercollegiate football game.
1871	Thomas Eakins, *The Champion Single Sculls*.
1872	Anthony Comstock founds the New York Society for the Suppression of Vice and leads a "purity" campaign.
1873	John Wanamaker opens his Philadelphia department store.
1874	Smith College founded. Frances Willard joins the Woman's Christian Temperance Union. Henry Clay Work, "My Grandfather's Clock."
1876	National League of baseball players organized.
1880	William Booth's followers establish an American branch of the Salvation Army.

1881	Josephine Shaw Lowell founds the New York Charity Organization Society (COS).
1884	Mark Twain, *Huckleberry Finn*. Bryn Mawr College founded.
1889	Jane Addams and Ellen Gates Starr open Hull House.
1891	Stanford University founded. University of Chicago founded. Columbia University adds Barnard College as a coordinate institution for women. Basketball invented at Springfield College in Massachusetts.
1892	Joseph Mayer Rice writes his expose of public education in *Forum* magazine. General Federation of Women's Clubs organized.
1895	Coney Island amusement parks open in Brooklyn.
1899	Scott Joplin, "Maple Leaf Rag." Kate Chopin, *The Awakening*. Thorstein Veblen, *The Theory of the Leisure Class*. W. E. B. DuBois, *The Philadelphia Negro*.
1900	Theodore Dreiser, *Sister Carrie*.
1910	Angel Island Immigration Center opens in San Francisco

grant heroes who captured the popular imagination. The elite vision of sport as a vehicle for instilling self-discipline and self-control was transformed into a new commitment to sports as spectacle and entertainment. Like it or not, sports had become big business and an important part of the new consumerism.

Similar patterns of compromise and change took place in other arenas. Vaudeville houses, attacked by the affluent for their risqué performances, evolved into the nation's first movie theaters. Ragtime music, with its syncopated rhythms, gave rise to jazz. In short, the raffish, disreputable, raucous, and frequently denounced working-class culture of the late-nineteenth-century city can be seen as the seedbed of twentieth-century mass culture. And everywhere popular culture became increasingly dominated by commercial interests that capitalized on the disposable income created by the nation's explosive industrial growth and encouraged the popular fondness for material goods, leisure, sports, and other entertainments.

FOR FURTHER REFERENCE

READINGS

William L. Barney, ed., *A Companion to 19ᵗʰ-Century America* (2001). A useful survey of urbanization, ethnicity, class difference, and other topics in the late nineteenth century.

Martin J. Burke, *The Conundrum of Class: Public Discourse on the Social Order in America* (1995). A pioneering study into the ways in which nineteenth-century Americans tried to understand class difference.

Ruth H. Crocker, *Social Work and Social Order: The Settlement Movement in Two Industrial Cities, 1889–1930* (1992). An important, balanced assessment of the settlement house movement.

William Cronon, *Nature's Metropolis: Chicago and the Great West* (1991). An innovative study of the link between urban growth and regional economic prosperity in the Midwest.

Elliot Gorn and Warren Goldstein, *A Brief History of American Sports* (1993). A skillful analysis of the effect of urbanization, industrialization, and commercialization on American sports.

Hadassa Kosak, *Cultures of Opposition: Jewish Immigrant Workers, New York City, 1881–1905* (2000). A careful examination of the tensions within an ethnic community and the ways in which a distinctive working-class political culture emerged on New York's Lower East Side.

Martin Melosi, ed., *Pollution and Reform in American Cities, 1870–1930* (1980). A pioneering examination of the environmental impact of U.S. industrial and urban growth.

Carl Smith, *Urban Disorder and the Shape of Belief: The Great Chicago Fire, the Haymarket Bomb, and the Model Town of Pullman* (1995). An innovative study of the ways in which the nineteenth-century responses to urban disorders shaped contemporary perceptions about city life.

Peter Stearns, *Schools and Students in Industrial Society: Japan and the West, 1870–1940* (1998). Stearns's comparative examination of high school education in Europe, the United States, and Japan highlights the distinctive features of American education.

Virginia Yans-McLaughlin and Marjorie Lightman, *Ellis Island and the Peopling of America* (1997). A broad overview of the process of migration, with useful documents.

Olivier Zunz, *Making America Corporate, 1879–1920* (1990) A pioneering exploration of corporate capitalism's effect on the creation of a consumer culture.

WEBSITES

The American Variety Stage: Vaudeville and Popular Entertainment, 1870–1920
http://memory.loc.gov/ammem/vshtml/vshome.html
Contains theater playbills and programs and sound recordings.

America at Work, School, and Leisure: Motion Pictures from 1894–1915
http://memory.loc.gov/ammem/awlhtml/awlhome.html
A Library of Congress collection that contains video clips.

Forms of Variety Theater
http://lcweb2.loc.gov/ammem/vshtml/vsforms.html#ms
Covers vaudeville, variety, and minstrel shows and contains playbills, programs, and sound recordings.

Mark Twain in His Times
http://etext.lib.virginia.edu/railton/index2.html
By Stephen Railton at the University of Virginia, this site uses texts, images, and interactive exhibits to examine how "Mark Twain" and his works were created, marketed, and performed.

Selected Images of Ellis Island and Immigration, ca. 1880–1920
http://lcweb.loc.gov/rr/print/070_immi.html
From the Prints and Photographs Division of the Library of Congress.

For additional works please consult the bibliography at the end of the book.

CHAPTER 20

Politics and Expansion in an Industrializing Age, 1877–1900

J uly 2, 1881, was a muggy summer day in Washington, D.C., and President James A. Garfield was leaving town for a visit to western Massachusetts. At 9:30 A.M., as he strolled through the railroad station, shots rang out. Garfield fell, a bullet in his back. The shooter, Charles Guiteau, immediately surrendered.

At first, doctors thought the president would recover. But Garfield, a veteran who had seen the long-term effects of gunshot wounds, knew better. "I am a dead man," he told them. His doctors tried everything. But as the doctors probed the wound with bare hands and unsterilized instruments, blood poisoning set in. On September 19, Garfield died.

The nation mourned. An Ohio farm boy, Will Boyer, was shocked to hear the news from another farmer as he walked along a country road. Garfield embodied the American dream of the self-made man. Born in a log cabin in Ohio (he was the last log-cabin president), he had worked his way through Williams College, preached in the Disciples of Christ Church, taught at Hiram College, practiced law, and won election to the Ohio senate. He fought in the Civil War, went to Congress in 1863, and was elected president in 1880—thereby sealing his death warrant. As for Guiteau, the jury rejected his insanity plea, and in June 1882 he was hanged.

CHAPTER OUTLINE

◄ **The politics of Industrialization**
As this cartoon in *Puck* attests, most Americans in the late nineteenth century believed that decisions about levying tariffs on imported goods could fundamentally alter the American economy and way of life.

A decent, well-meaning man, Garfield also embodied a political generation that seemed more preoccupied with the spoils of office than with the problems of ordinary people. In Congress Garfield had been tainted by the 1873 Crédit Mobilier scandal and other corruption charges. His presidential nomination in 1880 had resulted from a split in the Republican party between two rival factions, the Stalwarts and the Half-Breeds, that vied with each other over the distribution of patronage jobs.

The obscure Guiteau, a Stalwart who had supported Garfield, expected to be rewarded with a high diplomatic post. When this failed to materialize, his delusionary mental state worsened. Viewing Garfield's death as "a political necessity," he believed that the Stalwarts would hail him as a hero. (Indeed, he had selected as his gun a .44-caliber "British Bulldog" pistol because it would look good in a museum.)

While contemporary critics like Henry Adams viewed Garfield's assassination as an example of the absurdity of late-nineteenth century politics—a time, Adams sneered, of "little but damaged reputations"—historians today see it as a sign of how closely contested and highly emotional political battles were. The phenomenal expansion of large corporations, the settlement of the trans-Mississippi West, and the surge in urban growth put intense pressure on the political process. At stake was not only the government's proper role in the stimulation and regulation of America's explosive industrial growth, but also the thorny issues of how to assimilate the new immigrants, control chaotic urban life, gain access to new markets, and encourage territorial expansion.

These intense debates over economic and social policy involved nothing less than contending visions of how industrial growth should or should not be regulated and who should benefit financially. The struggle to control economic expansion reached its peak in the 1890s when a new third party, the Populists, joined with the Democrats to challenge corporate control of the economy. The Populist campaign for "free silver," a monetary policy that would back currency with silver reserves instead of gold, implied strong support for reforms that would have relieved the exploitation of labor and the abysmal working conditions that accompanied the surging industrialization of this period. Representing the opposite position, the Republican party's support for high tariffs and the gold standard represented a commitment to encouraging the growth of large corporations, to freeing industry to expand without regulation, and to developing new markets.

From the mid-1870s to the mid-1890s, power seesawed back and forth between the political parties. No

party was able to control the political process. But in 1896, the election of President William F. McKinley, who would also die from an assassin's bullet, brought the bitter battle over economic standards to an end and ushered in a generation of Republican domination of national politics. Having been elected in a campaign focused on the restoration of prosperity, McKinley stumbled into war with Spain, substantially increased U.S. territorial holdings, and established new outposts from which American corporations could gain access to overseas markets. Why it took twenty years to resolve the debate over economic policy and achieve a realignment in national politics, how the Republicans triumphed over the protests of farmers and laborers, and what effect the Republican vision had on territorial expansion are the subjects of this chapter.

This chapter focuses on four major questions:

- How did the Democratic and Republican parties build coalitions of loyal followers out of their diverse ethnic and regional constituencies?

- How did environmental factors influence the rise of the Grange and the Farmers' Alliance movements?

- Why was the election of 1896 a watershed event? Why did William Jennings Bryan fail to win the presidency?

- Why did the United States go to war with Spain and become an imperial power?

PARTY POLITICS IN AN ERA OF SOCIAL AND ECONOMIC UPHEAVAL, 1877–1884

Between 1877 and 1894 four presidents squeezed into office by the narrowest of margins; control of the House of Representatives changed hands five times; and seven new western states were admitted into the Union. Competition between political parties was intense. No one party could muster a working majority.

To meet these challenges, Republicans, Democrats, and third-party leaders sought desperately to reshape their political organizations to win over and cement the loyalty of their followers. While the Democrats rebuilt their strength in the South and mounted new challenges, Republicans struggled to maintain the loyalties of the working class, to strengthen their support from business, and to fight off the threat of new third parties. Not until 1896, in the aftermath of a massive depression that hit when the Democrats and a new third party, the

Populists, were in office, did the Republicans consolidate their power and build a coalition that would control Congress and the presidency for the next fifteen years.

Between 1876 and 1896, the intense competition between parties produced an incredible turnout of voters. Although most women did not yet have the vote and blacks were increasingly being disenfranchised, more than 80 percent of eligible white males often voted, and in particularly hard-fought state and local elections, the percentage could rise to 95 percent. Voter participation a century later would equal scarcely half that level.

Higher voter turnout resulted in part from the attempts of the major parties to navigate the stormy economy created by postwar industrial and geographic expansion, the influx of millions of immigrants, and the pell-mell growth of cities (see Chapters 18 and 19). At the same time that voter turnout shot up, however, political parties sidestepped many of the issues created by industrialization such as taxation of corporations, support for those injured in factory accidents, and poverty relief. Nor was the American labor movement, unlike its counterparts in Europe, able to organize itself effectively as a political force (see Chapter 18). Except for the Interstate Commerce Act of 1887 and the largely symbolic Sherman Anti-Trust Act of 1890, Washington generally ignored the social consequences of industrialization and focused instead on encouraging economic growth.

How can we explain this refusal and, at the same time, account for the enormous popular support for parties? The answer lies in the political ideology of the period and the two major symbolic and economic issues that preoccupied lawmakers nationally. The first involved the economic issues of the tariff and the money supply. The second issue focused on civil-service reform, aimed at awarding government jobs on the basis of merit rather than political connections.

Contested Political Visions

Political parties in the late nineteenth century energized voters not only by appealing to economic self-interest, as was evident in support for industrialization and pensions for Civil War veterans and their widows, but also by linking their programs to deeply held beliefs about the nature of the family and the proper role of government. In its prewar years, the Republican party had enhanced economic opportunities for common people by using governmental authority to expand railroads, increase tariff protection for industry, and provide land subsidies to farmers. With encouragement from evangelical ministers, it had also espoused a belief in female moral superiority and a willingness to use government as an instrument to protect family life. Hostility to slavery was based in part on the assumption that slaveholding corroded family values. The Democrats, in contrast, had viewed emancipation as a threat to patriarchal order and racial control.

After the Civil War, these positions hardened into political ideologies. Republicans justified their support for the tariff and defended their commitment to Union widow's pensions as a protection for the family home and female wage earners. Men, in particular, associated loyalty to party with a sense of masculinity. Democrats countered, using metaphors of the seduction and rape of white women by external forces and labeling Republican programs as classic examples of the perils of using excessive government force. High tariffs imperiled the family and threatened economic disaster.

Despite their differences over the tariff and monetary policy, neither Republicans nor Democrats believed that the national government had any right to regulate corporations or to protect the social welfare of workers. Many members of the dominant parties, particularly among the middle and upper classes, embraced the doctrine of laissez-faire—the belief that unregulated competition represented the best path to progress. According to this view, the federal government should promote economic development but not regulate the industries that it subsidized.

Rather than looking to Washington, people turned to local or state authorities. On the Great Plains, angry farmers demanded that their state legislatures regulate railroad rates. In the cities, immigrant groups competed for political power while native-born reformers periodically attempted to oust the political machines.

Moreover, city and state governments vied with each other for control. Cities often could not change their system of government, alter their tax structure, or regulate municipal utilities without state approval. When Chicago wanted to issue permits to street popcorn vendors, for example, the Illinois legislature had to pass a special act.

Party loyalty for both Republicans and Democrats was reinforced by a sense of personal grievance that resulted from the belief, often true, that the other party had engaged in election fraud to steal elections. Although both parties, in both the North and the South, practiced fraud by rigging elections, throwing out opposition votes, and paying for "floaters" who moved from precinct to precinct to vote, each developed a sense of moral outrage at the other's behavior that invigorated party spirit.

By linking economic policy to family values, both national parties reinforced the appeal of their platforms

and, in the process, encouraged the participation of women in the political process. Although most women could not vote, they played an active role in politics in this period. Francis Willard and her followers in the Woman's Christian Temperance Union (WCTU), for example, helped create a Prohibition and Home Protection Party in the 1880s. A decade later western women Populists won full suffrage in Colorado, Idaho, and Utah.

Patterns of Party Strength

In the 1870s and 1880s each party had its own ideological appeal and centers of regional strength. The Democrats ruled the South; southern sections of border states like

**Poster Announcing GAR
Encampment, Chicago, 1900**
In addition to their nostalgic annual reunions, Union army veterans, organized as the Grand Army of the Republic, were a potent force in Republican party politics, lobbying for pensions and other benefits.

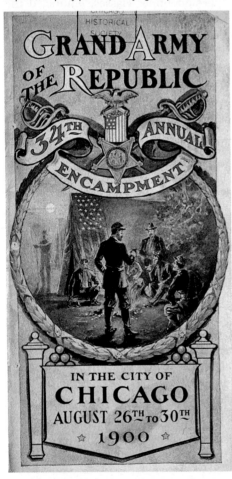

Ohio; and northern cities with large immigrant populations. In the South the white Democratic party elite viewed Republicans as villains who had devastated their lands and set up fraudulent carpetbag governments in the defeated Confederacy. The Democrats campaigned for minimal government expenditures, opposed tariff increases, and generally attacked what they considered to be "governmental interference in the economy."

In addition to resisting government support for the economy, Democrats staunchly defended their immigrant followers. On the state and local levels, they fiercely opposed prohibition and other attempts to limit alcohol use and license saloons. They also advocated support for parochial schools and opposed attempts to require immigrant children to attend only those schools that taught in English.

The Republicans, who reigned in rural and small-town New England, Pennsylvania, and the upper Midwest and who drew support from the Grand Army of the Republic (GAR), a social and political lobbying organization of northern Civil War veterans, often "waved the bloody shirt," reminding voters that their party had led the nation during the Civil War. "The Democratic Party," wrote one Republican, "may be described as a common sewer and loathsome receptacle, into which is emptied every element of treason North and South." To solidify their followers, the Republicans ran a series of former Union army generals for president and voted generous veterans' benefits.

State and local party leaders managed campaigns. They chose the candidates, raised money, organized rallies, and—if their candidate won—distributed public jobs to party workers. Chieftains like the former saloon-keepers "Big Jim" Pendergast of Kansas City, a Democrat, and George B. Cox of Cincinnati, a Republican, turned out the vote by taking care of constituents, handing out municipal jobs, and financing campaigns with "contributions" extracted from city employees.

Although the struggle to define the legitimate use of governmental authority shaped the general debate between the two major parties on the federal level, family tradition, ethnic ties, religious affiliation, and local issues often determined an individual's vote. Outside the South, ethnicity and religion were the most reliable predictors of party affiliation. Catholics, especially Irish Catholics, and Americans of German ancestry tended to vote Democratic. Old-stock northerners, in contrast, including 75 percent of Methodists and Congregationalists, 65 percent of Baptists, and 60 percent of Presbyterians voted Republican. Among immigrant groups, most British-born Protestants and 80 percent of

Swedish and Norwegian Lutherans voted Republican, as did African Americans, North and South. Although intolerant of racial differences, the Democrats were generally more accepting of religious diversity than were the Republicans.

As a result of the effect of ethnicity on politics, electoral skirmishes between groups often centered on cultural differences, as native-born Protestants tried to force on the immigrants their own views on gambling, prostitution, temperance, and Sabbath observance. No issue on the local level aroused more conflict than prohibition. Irish whiskey drinkers, German beer drinkers, and Italian wine drinkers were equally outraged by antiliquor legislation. State and local prohibition proposals always aroused passionate voter interest.

The Hayes White House: Virtue Restored

In this era of locally based politics and a diminished presidency, the state leaders who ran party politics tended to favor appealing but pliable presidential candidates. Rutherford B. Hayes fit the mold perfectly. A lawyer and Civil War general wounded in action, Hayes had won admiration as an honest governor of Ohio. His major presidential achievement was to restore respect for the office after the Grant scandals. With his flowing beard, the benevolent Hayes brought dignity and decorum to the White House. In part, this reflected the influence of his wife, Lucy, an intelligent, college-educated woman of great moral earnestness. The Hayeses and their five children often gathered after dinner for hymns and family prayers.

In contrast to the bibulous Grant, Hayes drank only moderately. He also recognized the political strength of the temperance movement. "Lemonade Lucy" Hayes supported the Woman's Christian Temperance Union. After one White House dinner, Hayes's secretary of state grumbled, "It was a brilliant affair. The water flowed like champagne."

Regulating the Money Supply

In the 1870s politicians confronted a tough problem of economic policy: how to create a money supply adequate for a growing economy without producing inflation. Americans' almost superstitious reverence for gold and silver added to the difficulty of establishing a coherent monetary policy. The only trustworthy money, many believed, was gold or silver, or certificates exchangeable for these precious metals. Reflecting this notion, all the federally issued currency in circulation in 1860 consisted

of gold or silver coins or U.S. Treasury notes redeemable for gold or silver. (Currency from some sixteen hundred state banks was also in circulation, worsening a chaotic monetary situation.)

To complicate matters, opposing groups clashed over the money question. Bankers and creditors, most business leaders, economists, and politicians believed that economic stability required a strictly limited currency supply. Debtors, especially southern and western farmers, favored expanding the money supply to make it easier for them to pay off their debts. The monetary debate focused on a specific question: should the Civil War paper "greenbacks" that were still in circulation be retained and even expanded, or phased out, leaving only a currency backed by gold (see Chapter 15). The hard times associated with the Panic of 1873 sharpened this dispute.

The Greenback party (founded 1877) advocated an expanded money supply, health and safety regulations for the workplace, and other measures to benefit workers and farmers. In the 1878 midterm elections, with the support of labor organizations angered by the government's hostility in the labor unrest of 1877, Greenback candidates won fourteen seats in Congress.

As prosperity returned, the Greenback party faded, but the money issue did not. The debate now focused on the coinage of silver. In 1873, with little silver being mined, Congress instructed the U.S. mint to stop making silver coins. Silver had been "demonetized." But new discoveries in Nevada (see Chapter 17) soon increased the silver supply, and debtor groups now demanded that the government resume the coinage of silver.

Enthusiastically backed by the silver-mine owners, silver forces won a partial victory in 1878, when Congress required the Treasury to buy up to $4 million worth of silver each month and mint it into silver dollars. But the Treasury, dominated by monetary conservatives, sabotaged the law's intent by refusing to circulate the silver dollars that it minted.

Frustrated silver advocates tried a new approach in the Sherman Silver Purchase Act of 1890. This measure instructed the Treasury to buy, at current market prices, 4.5 million ounces of silver monthly—almost precisely the output of the nation's silver mines. The act further required the government to issue Treasury notes, redeemable in gold or silver, equivalent to the cost of these purchases. This law did slightly increase the money supply; but as silver prices fell in 1893 and after, the government paid far less for its monthly purchases and therefore issued fewer Treasury notes. The controversy over silver dragged on.

The Spoils System

For decades successful candidates in national, state, and local elections had rewarded supporters and contributors with jobs ranging from cabinet seats and ambassadorships to lowly municipal posts. To its defenders, this system, originally called rotation in office, seemed the most democratic means of filling government positions, and it provided upward mobility for lucky appointees. But unqualified and incompetent applicants often got jobs simply because of their party loyalty. Once in office, these appointees had to contribute to the reelection campaigns of their political patrons. Because of such abuses, this mode of filling public jobs came to be called the spoils system after the old expression, "To the victor belong the spoils."

For years, a small but influential group of upper-class reformers, including Missouri Senator Carl Schurz and editor E. L. Godkin of the *Nation*, had campaigned for a professional civil service based on merit. Well bred, well educated, and well heeled, these reformers favored a civil service staffed by "gentlemen." Whatever their class biases, the reformers had a point. A professional civil service was needed as government grew more complex.

Cautiously embracing the civil-service cause, President Hayes launched an investigation of the corruption-riddled New York City customs office in 1877 and ordered the resignation of two high officials. Both men had ties to Conkling, the leader of the Stalwart faction; one, Chester A. Arthur, was Conkling's top lieutenant in passing out jobs. When the two ignored Hayes's order, the president suspended them. Hayes's action won praise from civil-service reformers, but Conkling simply ridiculed "snivel service" and "Rutherfraud B. Hayes."

Civil-Service Reform Succeeds

When Congressman James A. Garfield, who had ties to the Half-Breed faction, won the 1880 Republican presidential nomination, the delegates, to soften the blow to Conkling, chose Chester A. Arthur, the Conkling loyalist Hayes had recently fired, as Garfield's running mate. Since Garfield enjoyed excellent health, the choice of the totally unqualified Arthur seemed safe.

The Democrats nominated a career army officer from Pennsylvania, Winfield Scott Hancock, and the Greenbackers gave the nod to Congressman James B. Weaver of Iowa. Garfield's managers stressed his Civil War record and his log-cabin birth. By a razor-thin margin of under forty thousand votes (of 9.2 million cast), Garfield edged out Hancock; Weaver trailed far behind.

When Garfield chose Blaine as secretary of state and named a Conkling opponent as the New York City customs collector, Conkling, in a political maneuver,

"Where Is the Difference?" 1894
By equating criminal pay-offs to the police to corporate contributions to senators, this cartoon suggests that corruption pervades society and needs to be stopped.

resigned from the Senate. He hoped that the New York legislature would reelect him and thereby strengthen his political power. But Conkling miscalculated. The legislature chose another senator and ended Conkling's career.

Garfield's assassination in 1881, which brought to the White House Vice President Arthur, the very symbol of patronage corruption, gave a powerful emotional thrust to the cause, as civil-service reformers portrayed the fallen president as a spoils-system martyr. In 1883 Congress enacted a civil-service law introduced by Senator George Pendleton of Ohio (Garfield's home state) and drafted by the Civil Service Reform League that had been created two years earlier. The Pendleton Civil Service Act set up a commission to prepare competitive examinations and establish standards of merit for a variety of federal jobs; it also forbade political candidates from soliciting contributions from government workers. The Pendleton Act initially covered only about 12 percent of federal employees but was gradually expanded. The creation of a professional civil service helped bring the federal government in step with the modernizing trends transforming society.

As for Chester A. Arthur, the fact that he proved to be a mediocre president pleasantly surprised those who had expected him to be an utter disaster. Some feared that Roscoe Conkling would be "the power behind the throne," but Arthur supported civil-service reform and proved quite independent. Fed up with the feuding Republicans, in 1882 the voters gave the Democrats a strong majority in the House of Representatives. In 1884, for the first time since the 1850s, they would put a Democrat in the White House: Grover Cleveland.

POLITICS OF PRIVILEGE, POLITICS OF EXCLUSION, 1884–1892

The stalemate between the two major parties in their battle to establish the standards for economic growth continued under President Cleveland. Although no radical, Cleveland challenged powerful interests by calling for cuts in the tariff and in veterans' pensions. In 1888 aroused business groups and the veterans' lobby rallied to defeat Cleveland and elect Benjamin Harrison of Indiana, a former Civil War general, in one of the most corrupt campaigns in American history. Harrison further alienated voters by passing a high tariff and an expanded pension law that increased the number of pensioners by 43 percent.

Fed up with both the Democrats' and Republicans' fraud and inattention to the needs of rural Americans, debt-ridden, drought-stricken farmers mounted a spirited protest. While the Grange and Farmers' Alliance movements condemned the monopolistic practices of grain and cotton buyers, in the post-Reconstruction South the white majority took steps to consolidate their political power by denying the region's black citizens their most basic rights.

1884: Cleveland Victorious

At a tumultuous Chicago convention in 1884, the Republicans nominated their best-known leader, James G. Blaine. A gifted orator with a keen memory for names and faces, Blaine spoke for the younger, more dynamic wing of the Republican party eager to shed the taint of "Grantism," promote economic development, and take a greater interest in foreign policy.

But Blaine's name had been smirched in the tawdry politics of the Gilded Age. In Blaine's 1876 senatorial campaign, his opponents had published letters in which Blaine, as Speaker of the House, offered political favors to a railroad company in exchange for stock. For civil-service reformers, Blaine epitomized the hated patronage system. To E. L. Godkin, he "wallowed in spoils like a rhinoceros in an African pool."

Sensing Blaine's vulnerability, the Democrats chose a sharply contrasting nominee, Grover Cleveland of New York. In a meteoric political rise from reform mayor of Buffalo to governor, Cleveland had fought the bosses and spoilsmen. Short, rotund, and resembling a bulldog, Cleveland was his own man.

The shrewdness of the Democrats' choice became apparent when Godkin, Carl Schurz, and other Republican reformers bolted to Cleveland. They were promptly nicknamed Mugwumps, an Algonquian term for a renegade chief.

But Cleveland had liabilities, including the fact that as a young man he had fathered an illegitimate child. Cleveland admitted the indiscretion, but the Republicans still jeered at rallies: "Ma, Ma, where's my pa?" Cleveland also faced opposition from Tammany Hall, the New York City Democratic machine that he had fought as governor. If Tammany's immigrant voters stayed home on election day, Cleveland could lose his own state. But in October a New York City clergyman denounced the Democrats as the party of "Rum, Romanism, and Rebellion." Blaine failed to immediately repudiate the remark. The Cleveland campaign managers widely publicized this triple insult to Catholics, to

patriotic Democrats tired of the "bloody shirt," and to drinkers. This blunder and the Mugwumps' defection allowed Cleveland to carry New York State by twelve hundred votes, and with it the election.

Tariffs and Pensions

In some respects, Cleveland fits the passive image of Gilded Age presidents. He had early embraced the belief that government must not meddle in the economy. In Andrew Jackson's day, laissez-faire had been a radical idea endorsed by ambitious small entrepreneurs who wanted business conditions favorable to competition; by the 1880s it had become the rallying cry of a corporate elite opposed to any public regulation or oversight. Sharing this outlook, Cleveland asserted the power of the presidency mostly through his vetoes and displayed a limited grasp of industrialization's impact. Vetoing a bill that would have provided seeds to drought-stricken farmers in Texas, he warned that people should not expect the government to solve their problems.

One public matter did arouse Cleveland's energies: the tariff, an issue involving a tangle of conflicting economic and political interests. Tariff duties were a major source of revenue in the era before a federal income tax, so the tariff was really a form of taxation. But which imported goods should be subject to duties, and how much? Opinions differed radically.

The producers of such commodities as coal, hides, timber, and wool demanded tariff protection against foreign competition, and industries that had prospered behind tariff walls—iron and steel, textiles, machine tools—wanted protection to continue. Many workers in these industries agreed, convinced that high tariffs meant higher wages. Other manufacturers, however, while seeking protection for their finished products, wanted low tariffs on the raw materials they required. Massachusetts shoe manufacturers, for example, urged high duties on imported shoes but low duties on imported hides. Most farmers, by contrast, hated the protective tariff, charging that it inflated farm-equipment prices and, by impeding trade, made it hard to sell American farm products abroad.

Cleveland's call for lower tariffs arose initially from the fact that in the 1880s the high tariff, generating millions of dollars in federal revenue, was feeding a growing budget surplus. This surplus tempted legislators to distribute the money in the form of veterans' pensions or expensive public-works programs, commonly called pork-barrel projects, in their home districts. With his horror of paternalistic government, Cleveland viewed

the budget surplus as a corrupting influence. In his annual message to Congress in 1887, Cleveland argued that lower tariffs would not only cut the federal surplus but would also reduce prices and slow the development of trusts. Although the Democratic campaign of 1888 gave little attention to the issue, Cleveland's talk of lowering the tariff struck many corporate leaders as highly threatening.

Cleveland stirred up another hornet's nest when he took on the Grand Army of the Republic. Veterans' disability pensions cost the government millions of dollars annually. No one opposed pensions for the deserving, but by the 1880s fraudulent claims had become a public scandal. Unlike his predecessors, Cleveland investigated these claims and rejected many of them. In 1887 he vetoed a bill that would have pensioned all disabled veterans (even if their disability had nothing to do with military service) and their dependents. The pension list should be an honor roll, he declared, not a refuge for frauds.

1888: Big Business and the GAR Strike Back

By 1888 some influential interest groups had concluded that Cleveland must go. When Blaine decided not to challenge him, the Republicans turned to Benjamin Harrison of Indiana, the grandson of William Henry Harrison. A corporation lawyer and former senator, Harrison was so aloof that some ridiculed him as the human iceberg. His campaign managers learned to whisk him away after speeches before anyone could talk with him or experience his flabby handshake.

Harrison's managers also developed a new style of electioneering. They brought delegations to Indianapolis and hammered at the tariff issue. Falsely portraying Cleveland as an advocate of "free trade"—the elimination of all tariffs—they warned of the bad effects of such a step. The high protective tariff, they argued, ensured prosperity, decent wages for industrial workers, and a healthy home market for farmers.

The Republicans amassed a $4 million campaign fund from worried business leaders. (Because the Pendleton Civil Service Act had outlawed campaign contributions by government workers, political parties depended more than ever on corporate donors.) This war chest purchased not only posters and buttons but also votes.

Despite such chicanery, Cleveland got almost a hundred thousand more votes than Harrison. But Harrison carried the key states of Indiana and New York

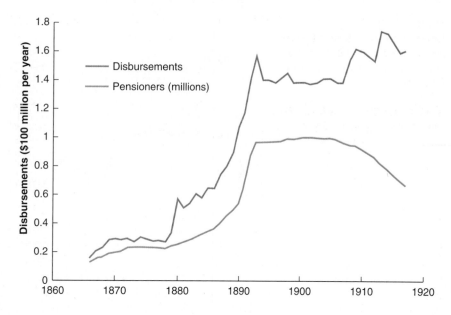

FIGURE 20.1

Civil War Pensions and Pensioners, 1866–1917

The pension system for Union army veterans represented a major federal welfare program in the late nineteenth and early twentieth centuries.

Source: William H. Glasson, *Federal Military Pensions in the United States* (New York: Oxford University Press, 1918), p. 273.

and won in the electoral college. The Republicans held the Senate and regained the House. When Harrison piously observed that Providence had aided the Republican cause, his campaign chairman snorted, "Providence hadn't a damn thing to do with it. . . . [A] number of men . . . approach[ed] the gates of the penitentiary to make him president."

Harrison swiftly rewarded his supporters. He appointed as commissioner of pensions a GAR official who, on taking office, declared "God help the surplus!" The pension rolls soon ballooned from 676,000 to nearly a million (see Figure 20.1). This massive pension system (which was coupled with medical care in a network of veterans' hospitals) became America's first large-scale public-welfare program. In 1890 the triumphant Republicans also enacted the McKinley Tariff, which pushed rates to an all-time high.

Rarely has the federal government been so subservient to entrenched economic interests and so out of touch with the plight of the disadvantaged as during the 1880s. But discontent was rising. The midterm election of 1890, when the Democrats gained sixty-six congressional seats to win control of the House of Representatives, awakened the nation to a tide of political activism engulfing the agrarian South and West. This activism, spawned by chronic problems in rural America, had a long history.

The Grange Movement

As discussed in Chapter 17, Great Plains farming proved far riskier than many had anticipated. Terrible grasshop-

per infestations consumed nearly half the midwestern wheat crop between 1873 and 1877. Although overall production surged after 1870, the abundant harvests undercut prices. Wheat tumbled from $2.95 a bushel in 1866 to $1.06 in 1880 (see Figure 20.2). Countless farmers who had borrowed heavily to finance homesteads and expensive new machinery went bankrupt or barely survived. One struggling Minnesota farmer wrote the governor in 1874, "[W]e can see nothing but starvation in the future if relief does not come."

When relief did not come, the farmers responded by setting up cooperative ventures. In 1867, under the leadership of Oliver H. Kelley, a Department of Agriculture clerk, midwestern farmers formed the Grange, or "Patrons of Husbandry," as it was officially called. Membership climbed to more than 1.5 million in the trying years of the early 1870s. Patterned after the Masonic Order, the Grange offered information, emotional support, and fellowship. For the inexperienced homesteader, it made available a library of the latest findings on planting and livestock raising. For the lonely farm family, the Grange organized biweekly social gatherings, including cooperative meals and lively songfests.

But the Grange's central concern was farmers' economic plight. An 1874 circular announced the organization's primary purpose: to help farmers "buy less and produce more, in order to make our farms more self-sustaining." Grangers embraced the Jacksonian belief that the products of the soil were the basis of all honorable wealth and that the producer classes—people who worked with their hands—formed the true backbone of society. Members sought to restore self-sufficiency to

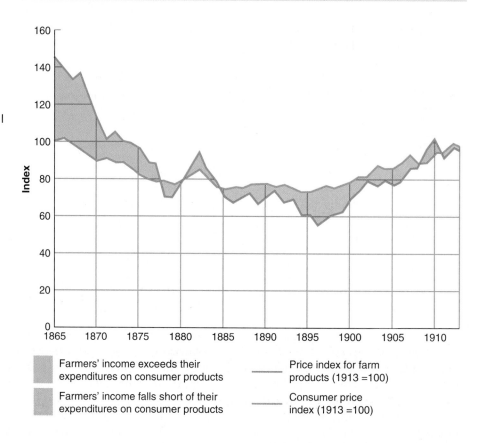

FIGURE 20.2

Consumer Prices and Farm-Product Prices, 1865–1913

As cycles of drought and debt battered Great Plains wheat growers, a Kansas farmer wrote, "At the age of 52, after a long life of toil, economy, and self-denial, I find myself and family virtually paupers."

Farmers' income exceeds their expenditures on consumer products

Farmers' income falls short of their expenditures on consumer products

Price index for farm products (1913 =100)

Consumer price index (1913 =100)

the family farm. Ignoring the contradiction in farmers' banding together to help individuals become more independent, they negotiated special discounts with farm-machinery dealers and set up "cash-only" cooperative stores and grain-storage elevators to cut out the "middlemen"—the bankers, grain brokers, and merchants who made money at their expense.

Grangers vehemently attacked the railroads, which routinely gave discounts to large shippers, bribed state legislators, and charged higher rates for short runs than for long hauls. These practices stung hard-pressed farmers. Although professing to be nonpolitical, Grangers in Illinois, Wisconsin, Minnesota, and Iowa lobbied state legislatures in 1874 to pass laws fixing maximum rates for freight shipments.

The railroads appealed to the Supreme Court to declare these "Granger laws" unconstitutional. But in *Munn* v. *Illinois* (1877) the Court not only rejected the railroads' appeal but also upheld an Illinois law setting a maximum rate for the storage of grain. The regulation of grain elevators, declared the Court's majority, was legitimate under the federal Constitution's grant of police powers to states. When the Court in *Wabash* v. *Illinois* (1886) modified this position by prohibiting states from

regulating interstate railroad rates, Congress passed the Interstate Commerce Act (1887), reaffirming the federal government's power to investigate and oversee railroad activities and establishing a new agency, the Interstate Commerce Commission (ICC), to do just that. Although the commission failed to curb the railroads' monopolistic practices, it did establish the principle of federal regulation of interstate transportation.

Despite promising beginnings, the Grange movement soon faltered. The railroads, having lost their battle on the national level, lobbied state legislatures and won repeal of most of the rate-regulation laws by 1878. Moreover, the Grange system of cash-only cooperative stores failed because few farmers had ample cash. Ultimately, the Grange ideal of complete financial independence proved unrealistic. Under the conditions that prevailed on the Plains, it was impossible to farm without borrowing money.

How valid was the Grangers' analysis of the farmers' problems? The Grangers blamed greedy railroads and middlemen for their difficulties, but the situation was not that simple. The years 1873–1878 saw the entire economy in a depression; railroad operators and merchant middlemen, no less than farmers, had to scramble

to survive. Farm commodity prices did fall between 1865 and 1900, but so, too, did the wholesale prices of manufactured goods, including items needed on the farm. Even the railroads' stiff freight charges could be justified in part by the scarcity of western settlement and the seasonality of grain shipments.

Still, the farmers and the Grange leaders who voiced their grievances had reason to complain. Farmers who had no control over the prices of their crops were at the mercy of local merchants and farm-equipment dealers who exercised monopolistic control over the prices that they could charge. Similarly, railroads sometimes would transport wheat to only one mill. Some even refused to stop at small towns to pick up local wheat shipments. Policies like these struck the farmers as completely arbitrary and made them feel powerless. Hamlin Garland captured farmers' despair in his *Main-Travelled Roads* (1891) and *Son of the Middle Border* (1917), describing barely surviving families who "rose early and toiled without intermission, till the darkness fell on the plain, then tumbled into bed, every bone and muscle aching with fatigue."

When the prices of corn, wheat, and cotton briefly revived after 1878, many farmers deserted the Grange. Although the Grange lived on as a social and educational institution, it lost its economic clout because it was ultimately unable to improve its members' financial position. For all its weaknesses, the Grange movement did lay the groundwork for an even more powerful wave of agrarian protest.

The Alliance Movement

While the Grange was centered in the Midwest and the Great Plains, the Farmers' Alliance movement first arose in the South and West, where farmers grappled with many of the same problems. In the cotton South, small planters found themselves trapped by the crop-lien system, mortgaging future harvests to cover current expenses. Mired in debt, many gave up their land and became tenants or sharecroppers. About a third of southern farmers were tenants by 1900. One historian has aptly called the South in these years "a giant pawn-shop."

Black Farmers Bring Cotton to the County Gin, Georgia, c. 1890
In areas of Georgia and Alabama where Blacks outnumbered whites, black businessmen were able to flourish despite segregation and discrimination.

The Farmers' Alliance movement began in Texas in the late 1870s as poor farmers gathered to discuss their hardships. Soon an organization took shape, promoted by activists who organized hundreds of local alliances. The alliance idea advanced eastward across the lower South, especially after Texan Charles W. Macune, a self-trained lawyer and a physician, assumed leadership in 1887. By 1889 Macune had merged several regional organizations into the National Farmers' Alliance and Industrial Union, or Southern Alliance. A parallel black organization, the National Colored Farmers' Alliance, had meanwhile emerged in Arkansas and spread to other southern states.

Like the Grange, the Farmers' Alliance initially advocated farmers' cooperatives to purchase equipment and supplies and to market their cotton. These cooperatives mostly failed, however, because farmers lacked the capital to finance them. Still, by 1890 the Southern Alliance boasted 3 million members, with an additional 1.2 million claimed by the National Colored Farmers' Alliance. Alliance members generally comprised not only the poorest farmers but also those most dependent on a single crop and most geographically isolated. As they

attended alliance rallies and picnics, read the alliance newspaper, and listened to alliance speakers, hard-hit farm families felt less cut off and increasingly aware of their political potential. An Arkansas member wrote in 1889, "Reform never begins with the leaders, it comes from the people."

Meanwhile, alliance fever hit the Great Plains as well. In the drought-plagued years of 1880 and 1881, alliances sprang up in Kansas, Nebraska, Iowa, and Minnesota. But the protest spirit faded as renewed rainfall revived confidence and lured thousands of settlers to the northern plains. The boom triggered frenzied land speculation. Kansas farms that had sold for $6.25 an acre in the 1860s went for $270 an acre in 1887. Railroads promoting settlement along their routes fed the boom mentality.

In 1886–1887, however, drought returned. From 1887 to 1897, only two Great Plains wheat crops were worth harvesting. Searing winds shriveled the half-ripe grain as locusts and chinch bugs gnawed away the rest. To make matters worse, wheat prices fell as world production increased.

Many settlers returned East. "In God we trusted, in Kansas we busted," some scrawled on their wagons. Western Kansas lost 50 percent of its population between 1888 and 1892. But others hung on, and the Northwestern Alliance grew rapidly. By 1890 the Kansas Alliance claimed 130,000 members, followed closely by alliances in Nebraska, the Dakotas, and Minnesota. Like the Southern Alliance, the Northwestern Alliance first experimented with cooperatives and gradually turned to politics.

Southern Alliance leaders Tom Watson of Georgia and Leonidas Polk of North Carolina urged southern farmers, black and white, to act together. For a time, this message of racial cooperation in the interest of reform offered promise. In Kansas, meanwhile, Jerry Simpson, a rancher who lost his stock in the hard winter of 1886–1887, became a major alliance leader. Mary E. Lease, a Wichita lawyer, burst on the scene in 1890 as a fiery alliance orator.

Other women, veterans of the Granger or prohibition cause, also rallied to the new movement, founding the National Women's Alliance (NWA) in 1891. Declared the NWA, "Put 1,000 women lecturers in the field and revolution is here." By no coincidence, a strong feminist strain pervades Ignatius Donnelly's *The Golden Bottle* (1892), a novel portraying the agrarian reformers' social vision.

As the movement swelled, the opposition turned nasty. When Jerry Simpson mentioned the silk stockings

of a conservative politician in his district and noted that he had no such finery, a hostile newspaper editor labeled him "Sockless Jerry" Simpson, the nickname he carried to his grave. When Mary Lease advised Kansas to "raise less corn and more hell," another editor sneered: "[Kansas] has started to raise hell, as Mrs. Lease advised, and [the state] seems to have an overproduction. But that doesn't matter. Kansas never did believe in diversified crops."

From all this activity, a political agenda took form. In 1889 the Southern and Northwestern Alliances loosely merged and adopted a political litmus test for candidates in the 1890 midterm elections. Their overall goal was to reform the American economic system. Their objectives, which focused on increasing government action on behalf of farmers and workers, included tariff reduction, a graduated income tax, public ownership of the railroads, federal funding for irrigation research, a ban on landownership by aliens, and "the free and unlimited coinage of silver."

The 1890 elections revealed the depth of agrarian disaffection. Southern Democrats who endorsed alliance goals won four governorships and control of eight state legislatures. On the Great Plains, alliance-endorsed candidates secured control of the Nebraska legislature and gained the balance of power in Minnesota and South Dakota. In Kansas the candidates of the alliance-sponsored People's party demolished all opposition. Three alliance-backed senators, together with some fifty congressmen (including Watson and Simpson), went to Washington as angry winds from the hinterlands buffeted the political system.

But differences soon surfaced. Whereas Northwestern Alliance leaders favored a third party, the Southern Alliance, despite Watson's and Polk's advice, rejected such a move, fearing it would weaken the southern Democratic party, the bastion of white supremacy. By 1892, however, some Southern Alliance leaders had reluctantly adopted the third-party idea, since many Democrats whom they had backed in 1890 had ignored the alliance agenda once in office. In February 1892 alliance leaders organized the People's Party of the United States, generally called the Populist party. At the party convention that August, cheering delegates nominated for president the former Civil War general and Greenback nominee James B. Weaver of Iowa. Courting the South, they chose as Weaver's running mate the Virginian James Field, who had lost a leg fighting for the Confederacy.

The Populist platform restated the alliance goals while adding a call for the direct popular election of sen-

ators and other electoral reforms. It also endorsed a plan devised by alliance leader Charles Macune by which farmers could store their nonperishable commodities in government warehouses, receive low-interest loans using the crops as collateral, and then sell the stored commodities when market prices rose. Ignatius Donnelly's ringing preamble pronounced the nation on "the verge of moral, political, and material ruin" and called for a return of the government "to the hands of 'the plain people' with which class it originated."

African-Americans After Reconstruction

As the Populists geared up for the 1892 campaign, another group of citizens with far more profound grievances found themselves pushed even farther to the margins of American public life. The end of Reconstruction in 1877 and the restoration of power to the southern white elites, the so-called redeemers (see Chapter 16), spelled bad news for southern blacks. The redeemer coalition of large landowners, merchants, and "New South" industrialists had little interest in the former

slaves except as a docile labor force or as political pawns. However, southern white opinion demanded an end to the hated "Negro rule," and local Democratic party officials pursued this objective. Suppressing the black vote was a major goal. At first, black disfranchisement was achieved by intimidation, terror, and vote fraud, as blacks were either kept from the polls or forced to vote Democratic. Then in 1890 Mississippi amended its state constitution in ways that effectively excluded most black voters, and other southern states soon followed suit.

Because the Fifteenth Amendment (1870) guaranteed all male citizens' right to vote, disfranchisement had to be accomplished indirectly by such means as literacy tests, poll taxes, and property requirements. The racist intent of these devices became obvious when procedures were introduced to ensure that they affected only black voters. One stratagem, the so-called grandfather clause, exempted from these electoral requirements anyone whose ancestor had voted in 1860. Black disfranchisement proceeded erratically over the South, but by the early twentieth century, it was essentially complete.

Disfranchisement was only one part of the system of white supremacy laboriously erected in the South. In a

Southern Prison Chain Gang, 1898
The southern chain gang and convict-lease system gave rise to appalling abuses in the late nineteenth century, reducing thousands of African-American men and youths to slavery-like conditions.

parallel development that culminated in the early twentieth century, state after state passed laws imposing strict racial segregation in many realms of life (see Chapter 21).

Black caterers, barbers, bricklayers, carpenters, and other artisans lost their white clientele. Blacks who went to prison—sometimes for minor offenses—faced the convict-lease system, by which cotton planters, railroad builders, coal-mine operators, and other employers "leased" prison gangs and forced them to work under slave-labor conditions.

The convict-lease system not only enforced the racial hierarchy but also played an important economic role as industrialization and agricultural change came to the South. The system brought income to hard-pressed state governments and provided factories, railroads, mines, and large-scale farms with a predictable, controllable, and cheap labor supply. The system also intimidated free laborers. One observer commented, "[O]n account of the convict employment, strikes are of rare occurrence." Recognizing this danger, free miners in Tennessee successfully agitated against the employment of convict labor in their state in the 1890s. Thousands died under the brutal convict-labor system. It survived into the early decades of the twentieth century, ultimately succumbing to humanitarian protest and to economic changes that made it unprofitable.

The ultimate enforcer of southern white supremacy was the lynch rope. Through the 1880s and 1890s, about a hundred blacks were lynched annually in the United States, mainly in the South. The stated reasons, often the rape of a white woman, frequently arose from rumor and unsubstantiated accusations. (The charge of "attempted rape" could cover a wide range of behaviors unacceptable to whites.)

The lynch mob demonstrated whites' absolute power. In *Festival of Violence*, their 1995 computer-assisted study of 2,805 Southern lynchings, Stewart E. Tolnay and E. M. Beck found that more than 80 percent involved black victims. Lynchings most commonly occurred in the Cotton Belt, and they tended to peak at times of economic distress when cotton prices were falling and job competition between poor whites and poor blacks was most intense. By no coincidence, lynching peaked in 1892 as many poor blacks embraced the Farmers' Alliance movement and rallied to the Populist party banner. Fifteen black Populists were killed in Georgia alone, it has been estimated, during that year's acrimonious campaign.

The relationship between southern agrarian protest and white racism was complex. Some Populists, like Georgia's Tom Watson, sought to build an interracial movement. Watson denounced lynching and the convict-lease system. When a black Populist leader pursued by a lynch mob took refuge in his house during the 1892 campaign, Watson summoned two thousand armed white Populists to defend him. But most white Populists, abetted by rabble-rousers like "Pitchfork Ben" Tillman of South Carolina, clung to racism. Watson complained that most poor whites "would joyously hug the chains of . . . wretchedness rather than do any experimenting on [the race] question."

The white elite, eager to drive a wedge in the protest movement, inflamed lower-class white racism. The agricultural crisis of the period, which included a precipitous decline in cotton prices, had driven poor white tenant farmers in the South to the brink of despair. Those who lost control of their farms felt that they not only faced economic ruin, but that they also risked loss of their manhood. Conscious of themselves as a racial group, they feared that if they fell further down the economic ladder they would lose the racial privileges that came from their "whiteness" and be treated like blacks, Mexicans, and the foreign born. Hence, they were swayed by conservative Atlanta editor Henry W. Grady when he warned against division among white southerners: the region's only hope, he said, was "the clear and unmistakable domination of the white race."

Even as they raised the bugaboo of "Negro rule," the white elite manipulated the urban black vote as a weapon against agrarian radicalism, driving Tom Watson to despair. On balance, the rise of southern agrarian protest deepened racial hatred and ultimately worsened blacks' situation.

While southern blacks suffered racist oppression, the federal government stood aside. A generation of northern politicians paid lip service to egalitarian principles but failed to apply them to blacks.

The Supreme Court similarly abandoned blacks. The Fourteenth Amendment (1868) had granted blacks citizenship and the equal protection of the laws, and the Civil Rights Act of 1875 outlawed racial discrimination on juries, in public places such as hotels and theaters, and on railroads, streetcars, and other such conveyances. But the Supreme Court soon ripped gaping holes in these protective laws.

In the *Civil Rights Cases* (1883), the Court declared the Civil Rights Act of 1875 unconstitutional. The Fourteenth Amendment protected citizens only from governmental infringement of their civil rights, the justices ruled, not from acts by private citizens such as railroad conductors. In *Plessy* v. *Ferguson* (1896), the justices

upheld a Louisiana law requiring segregated railroad cars. Racial segregation was constitutional, the Court held, if equal facilities were made available to each race. (In a prophetic dissent, Associate Justice John Marshall Harlan observed, "Our Constitution is color blind." Segregation, he added, violated the constitutional principle of equality before the law.) With the Supreme Court's blessing, the South segregated its public school system, ignoring the caveat that such separate facilities must be equal. White children studied in nicer buildings, used newer equipment, and were taught by better-paid teachers. Not until 1954 did the Court abandon the "separate but equal" doctrine. Rounding out their dismal record, in 1898 the justices upheld the poll tax and literacy tests by which southern states had disfranchised blacks.

Few northerners protested the South's white-supremacist society. Until the North condemned lynching outright, declared the aged abolitionist Frederick Douglass in 1892, "it will remain equally involved with the South in this common crime." The restoration of sectional harmony, in short, came at a high price: acquiescence by the North in the utter debasement of the South's African-American citizenry. Further, the separatist principle endorsed in *Plessy* had a pervasive impact, affecting blacks nationwide, Mexicans in Texas, Asians in California, and other groups.

Blacks responded to their plight in various ways. The nation's foremost black leader from the 1890s to his death in 1915 was Booker T. Washington. Born in slavery in Virginia in 1856, the son of a slave woman and her white master, Washington attended a freedman's school in Hampton, Virginia, and in 1881 organized a black state vocational school in Alabama that eventually became Tuskegee University. Although Washington secretly contributed to lawyers who challenged segregation, his public message was accommodation to a racist society. In a widely publicized address in Atlanta in 1895, he insisted that the first task of America's blacks must be to acquire useful skills such a farming and carpentry. Once blacks proved their economic value, he predicted, racism would fade; meanwhile, they must patiently accept their lot. Washington lectured widely, and his autobiography, *Up From Slavery* (1901), recounted his rise from poverty thanks to honesty, hard work, and kindly patrons—themes familiar to a generation reared on Horatio Alger's self-help books.

Other blacks responded resourcefully to the racist society. Black churches provided emotional support, as did black fraternal lodges like the Knights of Pythias. Some African-Americans started businesses to serve their community. Two black-owned banks, in Richmond and Washington, D.C., were chartered in 1888. The North Carolina Mutual Insurance Company, organized in 1898 by John Merrick, a prosperous Durham barber, evolved into a major enterprise. Bishop Henry M. Turner of the African Methodist Episcopal church urged blacks to return to Africa and build a great Christian nation. Turner made several trips to Africa in pursuit of his proposal.

African-American protest never wholly died out. Frederick Douglass urged that blacks press for full equality. "Who would be free, themselves must strike the first blow," he proclaimed in 1883. Blacks should meet violence with violence, insisted militant New York black leader T. Thomas Fortune.

Other blacks answered southern racism by leaving the region. In 1879 several thousand moved to Kansas (see Chapter 16). Some ten thousand migrated to Chicago between 1870 and 1890. Blacks who moved north soon found, however, that although white supremacy was not official policy, public opinion

The Knights of Labor

Black delegate Frank J. Farrell introduces Terence V. Powderly, head of the Knights of Labor, at the organization's 1886 convention. The Knights were unusual in accepting both black and female workers.

sanctioned many forms of de facto discrimination. Northern black laborers, for example, encountered widespread prejudice. The Knights of Labor welcomed blacks and by the mid-1880s had an estimated sixty thousand black members. Its successor, the American Federation of Labor, officially forbade racial discrimination, but in practice many of its member unions excluded blacks.

The rise of the so-called solid South, firmly established on racist foundations, had important political implications. For one thing, it made a mockery of the two-party system in the South. For years, the only meaningful election south of the Potomac was the Democratic primary. Only in the 1960s, in the wake of sweeping social and economic changes, would a genuine two-party system emerge there. The large bloc of southern Democrats elected to Congress each year, accumulating seniority and power, exerted a great and often reactionary influence on public policy. Above all, they mobilized instantly to quash any threat to southern white supremacy. Finally, southern Democrats wielded enormous clout in the national party. No Democratic contender for national office who was unacceptable to them stood a chance.

Above all, the caste system that evolved in the post-Reconstruction South shaped the consciousness of those caught up in it, white and black alike. White novelist Lillian Smith described her girlhood in turn-of-the-century Florida and Georgia, "From the day I was born, I began to learn my lessons. . . . I learned it is possible to be a Christian and a white southerner simultaneously; to be a gentlewoman and an arrogant callous creature at the same moment; to pray at night and ride a Jim Crow car the next morning; . . . to glow when the word democracy was used, and to practice slavery from morning to night."

THE 1890S: POLITICS IN A DEPRESSION DECADE

Discontent with the major parties and their commitment to supporting unrestricted business enterprise, which had smoldered during the 1870s and 1880s, burst into flames in the 1890s. As banks failed and railroads went bankrupt, the nation slid into a grinding depression. The crises of the 1890s laid bare the paralysis of the federal government—dominated by a business elite—when confronted by the new social realities of factories, urban slums, immigrant workers, and desperate farmers. In response, irate farmers, laborers, and their supporters created a new party, the Populists, to change the system.

1892: Populists Challenge the Status Quo

The Populist party platform adopted in July 1892 offered an angry catalog of agrarian demands. That same month, thirteen people died in a gun battle between strikers and strikebreakers at the Homestead steel plant near Pittsburgh, and President Harrison sent federal troops to Coeur d'Alene, Idaho, where a silver-mine strike had turned violent. Events seemed to justify the Populists' warnings of chaos ahead.

Faced with domestic turmoil and fearful that the powerful European socialist movement would spread to the United States, both major parties acted cautiously. The Republicans renominated Harrison and adopted a platform that ignored escalating unrest. The Democrats turned again to Grover Cleveland, who in four years out of office had made clear his growing conservatism and his opposition to the Populists. Cleveland won by more than 360,000 votes, a decisive margin in this era of close elections. A public reaction against labor violence and the McKinley Tariff hurt Harrison, while Cleveland's support for the gold standard won conservative business support.

Populist strength proved spotty. James B. Weaver got just over a million votes—8.5 percent of the total—and the Populists elected five senators, ten congressmen, and three governors. The new party carried Kansas and registered some appeal in the West and in Georgia, Alabama, and Texas, where the alliance movement had taken deep root. But it made no dent in New England, the urban East, or the traditionally Republican farm regions of the Midwest. It even failed to show broad strength in the upper Great Plains. "Beaten! Whipped! Smashed!" moaned Minnesota Populist Ignatius Donnelly in his diary.

Throughout most of the South, racism, ingrained Democratic loyalty, distaste for a ticket headed by a former Union general, and widespread intimidation and vote fraud kept the Populist vote under 25 percent. This failure killed the prospects for interracial agrarian reform in the region. After 1892, as Populism began to revive in the South and Midwest, many southern politicians seeking to appeal to poor whites—including a disillusioned Tom Watson—stayed within the Democratic fold and laced their populism with racism.

The Panic of 1893: Capitalism in Crisis

Cleveland soon confronted a major crisis, an economic collapse in the railroad industry that quickly spread. In

the economic boom of the 1880s, railroads had led the way, triggering speculation among investors. Some railroads had fed the speculative mania by issuing more stock (and enticing investors with higher dividends) than their business prospects warranted. Weakened by agricultural stagnation, railroad growth slowed in the early 1890s, affecting many related industries, including iron and steel. The first hint of trouble ahead came in February 1893 with the failure of the Philadelphia and Reading Railroad.

This bankruptcy came at a time of weakened confidence in the gold standard, the government's pledge to redeem paper money for gold on demand. This diminished confidence had several sources. First, when a leading London investment bank collapsed in 1890, hard-pressed British investors sold millions of dollars worth of stock in American railroads and other corporations and converted their dollars to gold, draining U.S. gold reserves. Second, Congress's lavish veterans' benefits and pork-barrel appropriations during the Harrison administration drained government resources just as tariff revenues were dropping because of the high McKinley Tariff. Third, the 1890 Sherman Silver Purchase Act further strained the gold reserve. This measure required the government to pay for its monthly silver purchases with treasury certificates redeemable for either silver or gold, and many certificate holders chose to convert them to gold. Finally, the election of Grover Cleveland in 1892 further eroded confidence in the dollar. Although Cleveland endorsed the gold standard, his party harbored many advocates of inflationary policies.

Between January 1892 and March 1893, when Cleveland took office, the gold reserve had fallen sharply to around $100 million, the minimum considered necessary to support the dollar. This decline alarmed those who viewed the gold standard as the only sure evidence of the government's financial stability.

The collapse of a railroad early in 1893 thus triggered an economic crisis whose preconditions already existed. Fear fed on itself as panicky investors converted their stock holdings to gold. Stock prices plunged in May and June; gold reserves sank; by the end of the year, seventy-four railroads and more than fifteen thousand commercial institutions, including six hundred banks, had failed. After the Panic of 1893 came four years of hard times.

The Depression of 1893–1897

By 1897 about a third of the nation's railroad mileage was in bankruptcy. Just as the railroad boom had spurred the industrial prosperity of the 1880s, so had the railroad

crisis of the early 1890s battered the entire economy as banks and other businesses failed. A full-scale depression gripped the nation.

The crisis took a heavy human toll. Industrial unemployment soared into the 20 to 25 percent range, leaving millions of factory workers with no money to feed their families and heat their homes. Recent immigrants faced disaster. Jobless men tramped the streets and rode freight trains from city to city seeking work.

The unusually harsh winters of 1893 and 1894 made matters worse. In New York City, where the crisis quickly swamped local relief agencies, a minister reported actual starvation. Amid the suffering, a rich New Yorker named Bradley Martin threw a lavish costume ball costing several hundred thousand dollars. Popular outrage over this flaunting of wealth in a prostrate city forced Martin and his family to move abroad.

Rural America, already hard-hit by declining agricultural prices, faced ruin. Farm prices dropped by more than 20 percent between 1890 and 1896. Corn plummeted from fifty cents to twenty-one cents a bushel; wheat, from eighty-four cents to fifty-one cents. Cotton sold for five cents a pound in 1894.

Some desperate Americans turned to protest. In Chicago workers at the Pullman factory reacted to successive wage cuts by walking off the job in June 1894 (see Chapter 18). In Massillon, Ohio, self-taught monetary expert Jacob Coxey proposed as a solution to unemployment a $500 million public-works program funded with paper money not backed by gold but simply designated "legal tender" (just as it is today). A man of action as well as ideas, Coxey organized a march on Washington to lobby for his scheme. Thousands joined him en route, and several hundred actually reached Washington in late April 1894. Police arrested Coxey and other leaders when they attempted to enter the Capitol grounds, and his "army" broke up. Although some considered Coxey eccentric, his proposal closely resembled programs that the government would adopt during the depression of the 1930s.

As unrest intensified, fear clutched middle-class Americans. A church magazine demanded that troops put "a pitiless stop" to outbreaks of unrest. To some observers, a bloody upheaval seemed imminent.

Business Leaders Hunker Down

In the face of suffering and turmoil, Cleveland retreated into a laissez-faire fortress. Boom-and-bust economic cycles were inevitable, he insisted, echoing the conventional wisdom of the day; the government could do

Coxey's Army
Jacob Coxey's "army" of the unemployed reaches the outskirts of Washington, D.C., in 1894. Note the new electrical or telephone poles.

nothing. Failing to grasp the larger picture, Cleveland focused on a single peripheral issue: defending the gold standard. As the gold reserve dwindled, he blamed the Sherman Silver Purchase Act, and in August 1893 he called on Congress to repeal it. Silver advocates protested, but Congress followed Cleveland's wishes.

Nevertheless, the gold drain continued. In early 1895, with the gold reserve down to $41 million, Cleveland turned to Wall Street. Bankers J. P. Morgan and August Belmont agreed to lend the government $62 million in exchange for U.S. bonds at a special discount. With this loan, the government purchased gold to replenish its reserve. Meanwhile, Morgan and Belmont resold the bonds for a substantial profit. This complicated deal did help restore confidence in the government's economic stability. The gold drain stopped, and when the Treasury offered $100 million in bonds early in 1896, they sold quickly.

Cleveland saved the gold standard, but at a high price. His dealings with Morgan and Belmont, and the bankers' handsome profits on the deal, confirmed radicals' suspicions of an unholy alliance between Washington and Wall Street. Cleveland's readiness to use force against the Pullman strikers and against Jacob Coxey's peaceful marchers deepened such suspicions.

In the ongoing maneuverings of competing interest groups, corporate interests held the whip hand, as a battle over the tariff made clear. Although Cleveland favored tariff reform, the Congress of 1893–1895—despite its Democratic majorities—generally yielded to high-tariff lobbyists. The Wilson-Gorman Tariff of 1894 lowered duties somewhat, but made so many concessions to protectionist interests that Cleveland disgustedly allowed it to become law without his signature.

Hinting at changes ahead, the Wilson-Gorman Tariff imposed a modest income tax of 2 percent on all income over $4,000 (about $40,000 in purchasing power today). But in *Pollock* v. *Farmers' Loan & Trust Co.* (1895), the Supreme Court narrowly held the law unconstitutional, ruling that the federal government could impose such a direct tax on personal property only if it were apportioned according to the population of each state. Whether one looked at the executive, the legislature, or the judiciary, Washington's subordination to a single interest group, the moneyed class, seemed absolute.

Cleveland's policies split the Democratic party. Farm leaders and silver Democrats condemned his opposition to the Sherman Silver Purchase Act. South Carolina's Ben Tillman, running for the Senate in 1894, proclaimed, "[T]his scoundrel Cleveland . . . is an old bag of beef and I am going to Washington with a pitchfork and prod him in his fat old ribs." This split in the Democratic ranks affected the elections of 1894 and 1896 and reshaped politics as the century ended.

The depression also helped reorient social thought. Middle-class charitable workers, long convinced that individual character flaws caused poverty, now realized—as socialists proclaimed and as the poor well knew—that even sober and hardworking people could succumb to economic forces beyond their control. As the social work profession took form in the early twentieth century, its members spent less time preaching to the poor and more time investigating the social sources of poverty.

Laissez-faire ideology weakened in the 1890s as many depression-worn Americans adopted a broadened view of the government's role in dealing with the social consequences of industrialization. In the early twentieth century, this new view would activate powerful political energies. The depression, in short, not only brought suffering; it also taught lessons.

THE WATERSHED ELECTION OF 1896

Republican gains in the 1894 midterm election revealed the depths of revulsion against Cleveland and the Democrats, who were blamed for the hard times. As 1896 approached, the monetary question became the overriding symbolic issue. Conservatives clung to the gold standard; agrarian radicals rallied to the banner of "free silver." At the 1896 Democratic convention, the nomination went to a young champion of the silver cause, William Jennings Bryan. Despite Bryan's eloquence, Republican William McKinley emerged victorious (see Map 20.1). His triumph laid the groundwork for a major political realignment that would influence American politics for a generation.

1894: Protest Grows Louder

With the depression at its worst and President Grover Cleveland deeply unpopular, the midterm election of 1894 spelled Democratic disaster. The Republicans, gaining 5 seats in the Senate and 117 in the House, won both houses of Congress. They also secured control of several key states—including New York, Illinois, and Wisconsin—as immigrant workers, battered by the depression, abandoned their traditional Democratic allegiance.

Populist candidates garnered nearly 1.5 million votes in 1894, an increase of more than 40 percent over their 1892 total. Populism's most impressive gains occurred in the South. Although several western states that had voted Populist in 1892 returned to their traditional Republican allegiance in 1894, the overall results heartened Populist leaders.

The serious economic divisions that split Americans in the mid-1890s focused especially on a symbolic issue: free silver. Cleveland's rigid defense of the gold standard forced his opponents into an equally exaggerated obsession with silver, obscuring the genuine issues that divided rich and poor, creditor and debtor, and farmer and city-dweller. Whereas conservatives tirelessly upheld the gold standard, agrarian radicals extolled silver as a universal panacea. They were urged on and sometimes financed by western silver-mine owners who stood to profit if silver again became a monetary metal.

Each side had a point. Gold advocates recognized that a nation's paper money must be based on more than a government's ability to run printing presses and that uncontrolled inflation could be catastrophic. The silver advocates knew from experience how tight-money

MAP 20.1
The Election of 1896

	Electoral Vote	Popular Vote	Percentage of Popular Vote
Republican William McKinley	271	7,102,246	51.1
Democratic William J. Bryan	176	6,492,559	47.7
Minor parties	–	–	315,398	1.2

policies depressed prices and devastated farmers. Unfortunately, these underlying realities were rarely expressed clearly. The silverites' most influential propaganda, William H. Harvey's widely distributed *Coin's Financial School* (1894), explained the monetary issue in simplified partisan terms, denounced "the conspiracy of Goldbugs," and insisted that the free coinage of silver would banish debt and end the depression.

Silver Advocates Capture the Democratic Party

At the 1896 Democratic convention in Chicago, western and southern delegates adopted a platform— including a demand for the free and unlimited coinage of silver at the ratio to gold of sixteen to one—that in effect repudiated the Cleveland administration. The front-running candidate was Congressman Richard Bland of Missouri, a silverite. But behind the scenes, the groundwork was being laid for the nomination of a dark horse, William Jennings Bryan, a thirty-six-year-old Nebraska lawyer and politician. During two terms in Congress (1891–1895), he championed western agrarian interests.

Joining Christian imagery with economic analysis, Bryan delivered his major convention speech in the debate over the platform. In an era before electronic amplification, his booming voice easily reached the upper gallery of the cavernous hall. Bryan praised western farmers and scorned advocates of the gold standard.

Populist Jerry Simpson addresses the crowd, Kansas
Despite the fact that women could not vote in most western states, women, as the two on the platform in the center of this picture indicate, were actively involved in political campaigning.

By the time he reached his rousing conclusion—"You shall not press down upon the brow of labor this crown of thorns, you shall not crucify mankind upon a cross of gold"—the wildly cheering delegates had identified their candidate.

The silverites' capture of the Democratic party presented a dilemma to the Populists. They, too, advocated free silver, but only as one reform among many. To back Bryan would be to abandon the broad Populist program. Furthermore, fusion with the Democrats could destroy their influence as a third party. Yet the Populist leaders recognized that a separate Populist ticket would likely siphon votes from Bryan and ensure a Republican victory. Reluctantly, the Populists endorsed Bryan, while preserving a shred of independence (and confusing voters) by naming their own vice-presidential candidate, Tom Watson of Georgia. The Populists were learning the difficulty of organizing an independent political movement in a nation wedded to the two-party system.

The Republicans, meanwhile, had nominated former governor William McKinley, who as an Ohio congressman had given his name to the McKinley Tariff of 1890. The Republican platform embraced the high protective tariff and endorsed the gold standard.

1896: Republicans Triumphant

Bryan tried to sustain the momentum of the Chicago convention. Crisscrossing the nation by train, he delivered his free-silver campaign speech to hundreds of audiences in twenty-nine states. One skeptical editor compared him to Nebraska's notoriously shallow Platte River: six inches deep and a mile wide at the mouth.

McKinley's campaign was shrewdly managed by Mark Hanna, a Cleveland industrialist. Dignified and aloof, McKinley could not match Bryan's popular touch. Accordingly, Hanna built the campaign not around the candidate but around posters, pamphlets, and newspaper editorials that warned of the dangers of free silver, caricatured Bryan as a rabid radical, and portrayed McKinley and the gold standard as twin pillars of prosperity.

Drawing on a war chest possibly as large as $7 million, Hanna spent lavishly. J. P. Morgan and John D. Rockefeller together contributed half a million dollars, far more than Bryan's total campaign contributions. Like Benjamin Harrison in 1888, McKinley stayed home in Canton, Ohio, emerging from time to time to read speeches to visiting delegations. Carefully orchestrated by Hanna, McKinley's deceptively bucolic "front-porch" campaign involved elaborate organization. All told, some 750,000 people trekked to Canton that summer.

On election day, McKinley beat Bryan by over six hundred thousand votes (see Map 6.1). He swept the Northeast and the Midwest and even carried three farm states beyond the Mississippi—Iowa, Minnesota, and North Dakota—as well as California and Oregon. Bryan's strength was limited to the South and the sparsely settled Great Plains and mountain states. The Republicans retained control of Congress.

Why did Bryan lose despite the depression and the protest spirit abroad in the land? Certainly, Republican scare tactics played a role. But Bryan's candidacy carried its own liabilities. His core constituency, while passionately loyal, was limited. Seduced by free silver and Bryan's oratory, the Democrats had upheld a platform and a candidate with little appeal for factory workers, the urban middle class, or the settled family farmers of the midwestern corn belt. Urban voters, realizing that higher farm prices, a major free-silver goal, also meant higher food prices, went heavily for McKinley. Bryan's weakness in urban America reflected cultural differences as well. To urban Catholics and Jews, this moralistic, teetotaling Nebraskan thundering like a Protestant revival preacher seemed utterly alien.

Finally, despite their telling critique of laissez-faire capitalism, the Populists' effort to define a humane and democratic alternative relied heavily on visions of a premodern economic order of independent farmers and entrepreneurs. Although appealing, this vision bore little relationship to the new corporate order taking shape in America.

The McKinley administration quickly translated its conservative platform into law. The Dingley Tariff (1897) pushed rates to all-time high levels, and the Currency Act of 1900 officially committed the United States to the gold standard. With returning prosperity, rising farm prices after 1897, and the discovery of gold in Alaska and elsewhere, these measures aroused little protest. Bryan won renomination in 1900, but the fervor of 1896 was missing. The Republican campaign theme of prosperity easily won McKinley a second term.

The elections of 1894 and 1896 produced a Republican majority that, except for Woodrow Wilson's two presidential terms (1913–1921), would dominate national politics until the election of Franklin D. Roosevelt in 1932. Bryan's defeat and the Republicans' emergence as the party of prosperity and the sound dollar killed the Populist party and drove the Democrats back to their regional base in the South. But although populism collapsed, a new reform movement called progressivism was emerging. Many of the Populists' reform proposals would be enacted into law in the progressive years.

EXPANSIONIST STIRRINGS AND WAR WITH SPAIN, 1878–1901

The same corporate elite that dominated late-nineteenth-century domestic politics influenced U.S. foreign policy as well, contributing to surging expansionist pressures. Not only business leaders but also politicians, statesmen, and editorial writers insisted that national greatness required America to match Europe's imperial

William McKinley's "Front-Porch" Campaign, 1896
McKinley (front row, fifth from left) poses with an Italian-American brass band from Buffalo, New York, in front of his home in Canton, Ohio.

expansion. Fanned by sensationalistic newspaper coverage of a Cuban struggle for independence and by elite calls for greater American international assertiveness, war between the United States and Spain broke out in 1898.

Roots of Expansionist Sentiment

Since the first European settlers colonized North America's Atlantic coast, the newcomers had been an expansionist people. By the 1840s the push westward had acquired a name: Manifest Destiny. The expansionist impulse had faded as the Civil War and then industrialization absorbed American energies, but it revived strongly after 1880 as politicians and opinion molders proclaimed America's global destiny.

The example set by other nations encouraged this expansionist sentiment. By the 1890s Great Britain, France, Belgium, Italy, Germany, and Japan were busily collecting colonies from North Africa to the Pacific islands. National greatness, it appeared, demanded an empire.

In corporate circles, meanwhile, the opinion spread that continued prosperity required overseas markets. With industrial capacity expanding and the labor force growing, foreign markets offered a "safety valve" for potentially explosive pressures in the U.S. economy. Secretary of State James Blaine warned in 1890 that U.S. productivity was outrunning "the demands of the home market" and insisted that American business must look abroad.

Advocates of a stronger navy further fueled the expansionist mood. In *The Influence of Sea Power upon History* (1890), Alfred T. Mahan equated sea power with national greatness and urged a U.S. naval buildup. Since a strong navy required bases abroad, Mahan and other naval advocates supported the movement to acquire foreign territories, especially Pacific islands with good harbors. Military strategy, in this case and others, often masked the desire for access to new markets.

Religious leaders proclaimed America's mission to spread Christianity. This expansionist argument sometimes took on a racist tinge. As Josiah Strong put it in his 1885 work *Our Country*, "God is training the Anglo-Saxon race for its mission"—a mission of Christianizing and civilizing the world's "weaker races."

A group of Republican expansionists, led by Senator Henry Cabot Lodge of Massachusetts, diplomat John Hay, and Theodore Roosevelt of New York, preached imperial greatness and military might. "I should welcome almost any war," declared Roosevelt in 1897, ". . . this country needs one." Advocates of expansionism,

like Roosevelt and Lodge, built upon the social Darwinist rhetoric of the day and argued that war, as a vehicle for natural selection, would test and refurbish American manhood, restore chivalry and honor, and create a new generation of civic-minded Americans. This gendered appeal to renew American masculinity both counterbalanced concerns about women's political activism and helped forge the disparate arguments for expansionism into a simpler, more visceral plea for international engagement that had a broad appeal.

A series of diplomatic skirmishes between 1885 and 1895 revealed the newly assertive American mood and paved the way for the war that Roosevelt desired. In the mid-1880s, quarrels between the United States and Great Britain over fishing rights in the North Atlantic and in the Bering Sea off Alaska reawakened Americans' latent anti-British feelings as well as the old dream of acquiring Canada. A poem published in the *Detroit News* (adapted from an English music-hall song) supplied the nickname that critics would apply to the promoters of expansion—jingoists:

> We do not want to fight,
> But, by jingo, if we do,
> We'll scoop in all the fishing grounds
> And the whole dominion too!

The fishing-rights dispute was resolved in 1898, but by then attention had shifted to Latin America. In 1891, as civil war raged in Chile, U.S. officials seized a Chilean vessel that was attempting to buy guns in San Diego. Soon after, a mob in Valparaiso, Chile, killed two unarmed sailors on shore leave. President Harrison practically called for war. Only when Chile apologized and paid an indemnity was the incident closed.

Another Latin American conflict arose from a boundary dispute between Venezuela and British Guiana in 1895 (see Map 20.2). The disagreement worsened after gold was discovered in the contested territory. When the British rejected a U.S. arbitration offer and condescendingly insisted that America's revered Monroe Doctrine had no standing in international law, a livid Grover Cleveland asked Congress to set up a commission to settle the disputed boundary even without Britain's approval. As patriotic fervor pulsed through the nation, the British in 1897 accepted the commission's findings.

Pacific Expansion

Meanwhile, the U.S. navy focused on the Samoan Islands in the South Pacific, where it sought access to the port of Pago Pago as a refueling station. Britain and

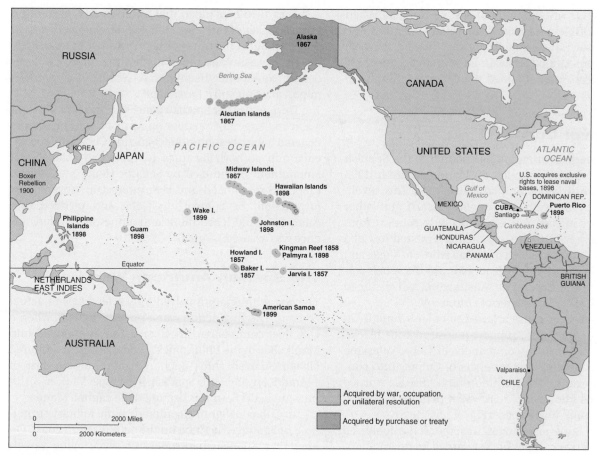

MAP 20.2
U.S. Territorial Expansion in the Late Nineteenth Century
The major period of U.S. territorial expansion abroad came in a short burst of activity in the late 1890s, when newspapers and some politicians beat the drums for empire.

Germany had ambitions in Samoa as well, and in March 1889 the United States and Germany narrowly avoided a naval clash when a hurricane wrecked both fleets. Secretary of State Blaine's wife wrote to one of their children, "Your father is now looking up Samoa on the map." Once he found it, negotiations began, and the United States, Great Britain, and Germany established a three-way "protectorate" over the islands.

Attention had by that time shifted to the Hawaiian Islands, which had both strategic and economic significance for the United States (see Map 20.2). New England trading vessels had visited Hawaii as early as the 1790s, and Yankee missionaries had come in the 1820s. By the 1860s American-owned sugar plantations worked by Chinese and Japanese laborers dotted the islands. Under an 1887 treaty (negotiated after the planters had forcibly imposed a new constitution on Hawaii's native ruler, Kalākaua), the United States built a naval base at Pearl Harbor, near Honolulu. American economic dominance and the influx of foreigners angered Hawaiians. In 1891 they welcomed Liliuokalani, a strong-willed woman hostile to Americans, to the Hawaiian throne.

Meanwhile, in 1890, the framers of the McKinley Tariff, pressured by domestic sugar growers, eliminated the duty-free status enjoyed by Hawaiian sugar. In January 1893, facing ruin as Hawaii's wholesale sugar prices plunged 40 percent, the planters deposed Queen Liliuokalani, proclaimed the independent Republic of Hawaii, and requested U.S. annexation. The U.S. State Department's representative in Hawaii cabled Washington, "The Hawaiian pear is now fully ripe, and this is the golden hour for the United States to pluck it." But the grab for Hawaii troubled Grover Cleveland, who sent a representative to investigate the situation. This representative's report questioned whether the Hawaiian people actually desired annexation.

Cleveland's scruples infuriated expansionists. When William McKinley succeeded Cleveland in 1897, the acquisition of Hawaii rapidly moved forward. In 1898 Congress proclaimed Hawaii an American territory. Sixty-one years later, it joined the Union as the fiftieth state.

Crisis over Cuba

By 1898 American attention had shifted to the Spanish colony of Cuba, ninety miles off Florida, where in 1895 an anti-Spanish rebellion had broken out. This revolt, organized by the Cuban writer José Martí and other Cuban exiles in New York City, won little support from U.S. business, which had $50 million invested in Cuba and annually imported $100 million worth of sugar and other products from the island. Nor did the rebels initially secure the backing of Washington, which urged Spain to grant Cuba a degree of autonomy.

But the rebels' cause aroused popular sympathy in the United States. This support increased with revelations that the Spanish commander in Cuba, Valeriano Weyler, was herding vast numbers of Cubans into concentration camps. Malnutrition and disease turned these camps into hellholes in which perhaps two hundred thousand Cubans died.

Fueling American anger was the sensationalized reporting of two competing New York City newspapers, William Randolph Hearst's *Journal* and Joseph Pulitzer's *World*. The *Journal's* color comic strip, "The Yellow Kid," provided a name for Hearst's debased editorial approach: yellow journalism. The Hungarian immigrant Pulitzer normally had higher standards, but in the cutthroat battle for readers, Pulitzer's *World* matched the *Journal's* sensationalism. Both editors exploited the Cuban crisis. Headlines turned rumor into fact, and feature stories detailed "Butcher" Weyler's atrocities. When a young Cuban woman was jailed for resisting a rape attempt by a Spanish officer, a Hearst reporter helped the woman escape and brought her triumphantly to New York.

In 1897 a new, more liberal Spanish government sought a peaceful resolution of the Cuban crisis. But Hearst and Pulitzer continued to inflame the public. On February 8, 1898, Hearst's *Journal* published a private letter by Spain's minister to the United States that described McKinley as "weak" and "a bidder for the admiration of the crowd." Irritation over this incident turned to outrage when on February 15 an explosion rocked the U.S. battleship *Maine* in Havana harbor and killed 266 crewmen. A painstaking review of the evidence in 1976 concluded that a shipboard ammunition explosion, set off by a fire in a coal bunker, had caused the blast. But at the time neither Washington nor the yellow press was in any mood to view the tragedy as accidental. Newspaper headlines screamed of a "Spanish mine," and war spirit flared high.

Despite further Spanish concessions, McKinley sent a war message to Congress on April 11, and legislators enacted a joint resolution recognizing Cuba's independence and authorizing force to expel the Spanish. An amendment introduced by Senator Henry M. Teller of Colorado renounced any U.S. interest in "sovereignty, jurisdiction, or control" in Cuba and pledged that America would leave the island alone once independence was assured.

The Spanish-American War, 1898

The war with Spain involved only a few days of actual combat. The first action came on May 1, 1898, when a U.S. fleet commanded by George Dewey steamed into Manila Bay in the Philippines and destroyed or captured all ten Spanish ships anchored there, at the cost of 1 American and 381 Spanish lives (see Map 20.3). In mid-August U.S. troops occupied the capital, Manila.

In Cuba the fighting centered on the military stronghold of Santiago de Cuba on the southeastern coast. On May 19 a Spanish battle fleet of seven aging vessels sailed into the Santiago de Cuba harbor, where five U.S. battleships and two cruisers blockaded them (see Map 20.4). On July 1, in the war's only significant land action, American troops seized two strongly defended Spanish garrisons on El Caney Hill and San Juan Hill overlooking Santiago de Cuba. Leading the volunteer "Rough Riders" unit in the capture of San Juan Hill was Theodore Roosevelt, who at last got his taste of war.

On July 3 the Spanish attempted to pierce through the American blockade to the open sea. U.S. naval fire raked and sank their archaic vessels. Spain lost 474 men in this gallant but doomed show of the flag. Americans might have found a cautionary lesson in this sorry end to four hundred years of Spanish rule in the New World, but few had time for somber musings. The *Washington Post* observed, "A new consciousness seems to have come upon us—the consciousness of strength—and with it a new appetite, the yearning to show our strength . . . , [t]he taste of empire. . . ." John Hay was more succinct. It had been, he wrote Roosevelt, "a splendid little war."

Many who served in Cuba found the war far from splendid. Ill trained and poorly equipped, the troops

MAP 20.3
Dewey's Route in the Philippines, 1898

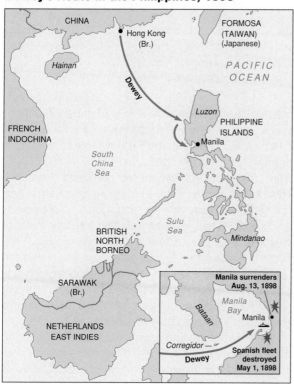

MAP 20.4
The Cuban Campaign, 1898

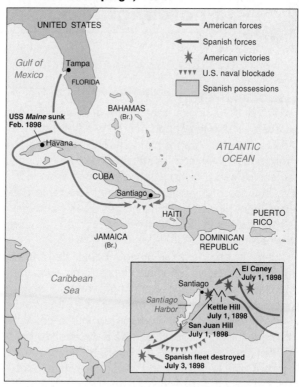

went into summer combat in the tropics wearing heavy woolen uniforms. While 379 American soldiers died in combat, more than 5,000 succumbed to food poisoning, yellow fever, malaria, and other diseases during and after the war.

Several thousand black troops fought in Cuba. Some, such as the twenty-fourth infantry and tenth cavalry, were seasoned regular-army veterans transferred from bases in the West. Others were volunteers from various states. At assembly points in Georgia, and then at the embarkation port of Tampa, Florida, these troops encountered the racism of a Jim Crow society. Tampa restaurants and bars refused them service; Tampa whites disparaged them. On June 6, after weeks of racist treatment, some black troops exploded in riotous rage, storming into restaurants, bars, and other establishments that had barred them. White troops from Georgia restored order. Although white and black troops sailed to Cuba on the same transport ships (actually, hastily converted freighters), the ships themselves were segregated, with black troops often confined to the lowest quarters in the stifling heat, denied permission to mingle on deck with the other units, and in other ways discriminated against.

Despite the racism, African-Americans served with distinction once they reached Cuba. Black troops played key roles in the taking of both San Juan Hill and El Caney Hill. Of the total U.S. troops involved in the latter action, some 15 percent were black.

The Spanish sought an armistice on July 17. In the peace treaty signed that December in Paris, Spain recognized Cuba's independence and, after a U.S. payment of $20 million, ceded the Philippines, Puerto Rico, and the Pacific island of Guam to the United States. Americans now possessed an island empire stretching from the Caribbean to the Pacific.

From 1898 to 1902 the U.S. army governed Cuba under the command of General Leonard Wood. Wood's administration improved public health, education, and sanitation but nevertheless violated the spirit of the 1898 Teller Amendment. The troops eventually withdrew, though under conditions that limited Cuban sovereignty. The 1901 Platt Amendment, attached to an army appropriations bill offered by a Connecticut senator at the request of the War Department, authorized American withdrawal only after Cuba agreed not to make any treaty with a foreign power limiting its independence and not to borrow beyond its means. The

Photoengraving

Before 1890 books, magazines, and newspapers were unable to print photographs. Publishers who wanted to use photographs had to turn to engravers and illustrators to redraw them as lithographs or block prints, an expensive and time-consuming process. Then in the 1890s, a series of inventions combined to enable publishers to print black-and-white images quickly and inexpensively. The result revolutionized the process of reporting the news.

Before a photographic image could be printed, inventors had to solve a number of problems. First, they had to develop a system for printing a range of shades between white and black. A method also had to be devised for breaking a photograph up into a series of dots. The resulting images had to be transferred to printing plates that could work on large, continuous feed, rotary presses. In all, printing black-and-white photographs required the redesign of high-speed rotary printing presses, the creation of new rolls of paper of uniform thickness, the development of new inks, and, most important of all, the creation of a new way to transfer a photograph to a printing plate.

The solutions to all these problems gradually emerged in the 1880s. First, printers invented a method to print shades of gray by exposing a bichromated gelatin film to light. When washed in water, a gelatin relief of the negative was created which, under pressure, produced an impression on a lead plate. The hollows in the lead plate could then contain varying amounts of ink and thus print different shades of gray. But printing these plates required paper of higher quality and more uniform thickness than that used previously.

To turn the picture into a series of lines and dots, the image was "screened." A finely ruled glass screen was created by etching a piece of glass with thousands of lines running in the vertical direction, blackening the

Interior of the Manufactures and Liberal Arts Building at the Chicago World's Fair, 1893
The new photogravure process allowed publishers to capture the scale and grandeur of the monumental buildings at the World's Fair.

depressions, and gluing the glass to a second piece of glass whose etched lines ran in a horizontal direction. When a photograph was exposed through this screen, the picture was broken up into thousands of dots. The density of dots in a particular area of the photographic plate determined the blackness of that area. The new halftone photographic film was printed on a sensitized metallic surface that was then etched to produce the desired printing plate. Any blurred areas on the halftone plate could be retouched by engravers to improve the quality of the image. Photoengraving, which was often called halftone printing, allowed pictures to be printed directly from photographs and cut the cost from $300 a picture to less than $20 without sacrificing quality.

In the 1890s magazines such as *McClure's, Cosmopolitan, Munsey's,* and *Ladies Home Journal* quickly exploited the new process. Newspapers, once they had discovered how to transfer this process to the softer, more porous newsprint, quickly followed suit. Adolph Och's *New York Times*, and William Randolph Hearst's *New York Journal* published Sunday news-magazines heavily illustrated with photographs of sports celebrities and socialites, reduced the price of their papers, and vastly expanded circulation.

The publication of halftone photographs gave magazines and newspapers a contemporary, journalistic look, which created a sense of immediacy—of being "inside" and behind the scenes. Pictures, short articles, and sensational language introduced immigrant and middle-class readers alike to the accidents, crimes, and murders that made up what one magazine editor called the "whirlpool of real life." In the process the media helped create cultural communities that were connected not by shared interaction but by shared information. Some pictures took armchair travelers to exotic overseas destinations; others gave ordinary Americans a peek into the private lives of celebrities, as when Theodore Roosevelt invited cameras into the family quarters of the White House. The vast increase in published photographs also spurred public action to tackle child labor, slum housing, and industrial safety.

Advertisers were quick to take advantage of the new technology to spur interest in bicycles, cereals, and other consumer items. *Cosmopolitan* magazine ran an article on "bicycling for women" that featured the latest attire.

Critics protested that photographs reinforced the tendency to react without thinking. A picture might be worth a thousand words, but its value would be far lower, they asserted, if it replaced published articles that analyzed society's problems. Finally, the halftone photograph, with its low cost and accessibility, rendered obso-

Street Arabs in Sleeping Quarters
Jacob Riis, the Danish immigrant reporter, published one of the first books of photographs using the new photogravure process in 1890 entitled *How the Other Half Lives.* This picture of homeless children, though obviously posed, elicited great sympathy.

lete the artists that magazines and newspapers had previously relied on for wood engravings, pen drawings, and etchings. While the photographs might seem more "real," they, too, were subject to cropping and distortion.

Nevertheless, publishers now recognized that published photographs possessed the power to persuade and inspire. In the political realm, parties moved from mobilizing voters to advertising charismatic candidates, like Theodore Roosevelt, whose colorful lives could be endlessly photographed. Like it or not, photographs would become an increasingly important force in the public's understanding of politics and world events.

Focus Questions

- Under William Randolph Hearst and Joseph Pulitzer, large urban newspapers at the turn of the century became more sensationalistic and greatly expanded their circulation. How did photoengraving affect the kinds of stories that could be covered?
- What impact did photoengraving have on the conception of what "art" is?

one of them wrote, "Dewey took Manila with the loss of one man—and all our institutions." The military fever that accompanied expansionism also dismayed the anti-imperialists. Some labor leaders feared that imperial expansion would lead to competition from cheap foreign labor and products.

In February 1899 the anti-imperialists failed by one vote to prevent Senate ratification of the expansionist peace treaty with Spain. McKinley's overwhelming reelection victory in 1900 and the defeat of expansionist critic William Jennings Bryan eroded the anti-imperialists' cause. Nevertheless, at a time of jingoistic rhetoric and militaristic posturing, they had upheld an older and finer vision of America.

African-American Soldiers of the Tenth U.S. Cavalry in Cuba, July 1898
These men posed shortly after the capture of San Juan Hill. Black troops played an important role in the Spanish-American War, but they were also subject to harassment and discrimination.

United States also reserved the right to intervene in Cuba when it saw fit and to maintain a naval base there. With U.S. troops still occupying the island, the Cuban constitutional convention of 1901 accepted the Platt Amendment, which remained in force until 1934. Under its terms the United States established a naval base at Guantánamo Bay, near Santiago de Cuba, which it still maintains. U.S. investments in Cuba, some $50 million in 1898, soared to half a billion dollars by 1920.

Critics of Empire

The victories of the expansionists in Cuba and the Philippines did not bring universal praise. Some Americans, who had opposed imperialism for more than a decade, were dismayed by the results. Although few in number, the critics, like the Mugwumps who had challenged the spoils system, were influential. Indeed, some of them, like Carl Schurz and E. L. Godkin, were former Mugwumps. Other anti-imperialists included William Jennings Bryan, settlement house founder Jane Addams, novelist Mark Twain, and Harvard philosopher William James. Steel king Andrew Carnegie gave thousands of dollars to the cause. In 1898 these critics of empire had formed the Anti-Imperialist League.

For the United States to rule other peoples, the anti-imperialists believed, was to violate the principles of the Declaration of Independence and the Constitution. As

Guerrilla War in the Philippines, 1898–1902

The worst fears of the anti-imperialists were subsequently borne out by events in the Philippines. When the Spanish-American War ended, President McKinley was faced with the urgent problem of what to do about this group of Pacific islands that had a population of more than 5 million people. At the war's outset, few Americans knew that the Philippines belonged to Spain or even where they were. Without a map, McKinley later confessed, "I could not have told where those darn islands were within two thousand miles."

But the victory over Spain whetted the appetite for expansion. To the U.S. business community, the Philippines offered a stepping-stone to the China market. McKinley, reflecting the prevailing mood as always, reasoned that the Filipinos were unready for self-government and would be gobbled up if set adrift in a world of imperial rivalries. McKinley further persuaded himself that American rule would enormously benefit the Filipinos, whom he called "our little brown brothers." A devout Methodist, he explained that America's mission was "to educate the Filipinos, and to uplift and civilize and Christianize them, and by God's grace do the very best we could by them." (In fact, most Filipinos were already Christian, a legacy of centuries of Spanish rule.) Having prayerfully reached his decision, McKinley

instructed the American peace negotiators in Paris to insist on U.S. acquisition of the Philippines.

Uplifting the Filipinos required a struggle. In 1896 young Emilio Aguinaldo had organized a Filipino independence movement to drive out Spain. In 1898, with arms supplied by George Dewey, Aguinaldo's forces had captured most of Luzon, the Philippines' main island. When the Spanish surrendered, Aguinaldo proclaimed Filipino independence and drafted a democratic constitution. Feeling betrayed when the peace treaty ceded his country to the United States, Aguinaldo ordered his rebel force to attack Manila, the American base of operations. Seventy thousand more U.S. troops were shipped to the Philippines, and by the end of 1899 this initial Filipino resistance had been crushed.

These hostilities became the opening phase of a long guerrilla conflict. Before it ended, over 125,000 American men had served in the Philippines, and 4,000 had been killed. As many as 20,000 Filipino independence fighters died. As in the later Vietnam War, casualties and suffering ravaged the civilian population as well. Aguinaldo was captured in March 1901, but large-scale guerrilla fighting went on through the summer of 1902.

In 1902 a special Senate committee heard testimony from veterans of the Philippines war about the execution of prisoners, the torture of suspects, and the burning of villages. The humanitarian mood of 1898, when Americans had rushed to save Cuba from the cruel Spaniards, seemed remote indeed. In retrospect, the American troops' ambivalent attitudes about the peoples of the Philippines, while deplorable, are not hard to understand. Despite America's self-image as a beacon of liberty and a savior of the world's peoples, many Americans in the 1880s and 1890s had been deeply troubled by the new immigrants from southern and eastern Europe and had expressed concerns over "backward" and "useless" races. As American nationalism was reformulated in this cauldron of immigration, imperialism, and the "winning of the West," racist attitudes about Native peoples and foreigners intermixed with rhetorical pleas for supervision and stewardship. In the process, as was evident in the treatment of American Indians (see Chapter 17), well-meaning paternalism often degenerated into deadly domination.

The subjugation of the Philippines followed years of expansionism that proclaimed America's debut on the world stage and underscored the global reach of U.S. capitalism. Nevertheless, most Americans remained ambivalent about the acquisition of territory. While anti-imperialist Mark Twain could acidly condemn "the Blessings of Civilization Trust," labor leader Samuel Gompers warned that "an inundation of Mongolians"

The Philippines Quagmire
Anticipating the Vietnam War, the U.S. suppression of the Philippines' independence struggle involved American troops in a long and nasty guerrilla campaign. One of the men in this 1900 photograph scrawled on the back: "27 hours on march, mud and rain, 24 hours without food."

might steal jobs from white labor. From the debate over the annexation of Hawaii in 1898 to the end of the war against Philippine independence in 1902, white Americans recoiled from making these "barbarian peoples" a part of the United States. Not fit to manage their own affairs, Cuban, Puerto Rican, Hawaiian and Filipino peoples were placed in a protective status that denied their independence but kept them under U.S. control

To stabilize relations in the Philippines, Congress passed the Philippine Government Act in 1902, which vested authority in a governor general to be appointed by the president. The act also provided for an elected Filipino assembly and promised eventual self-government. Progress toward this goal inched forward, with intervals of semimilitary rule. In 1946, nearly half a century after Admiral Dewey's guns had boomed in Manila Bay, independence finally came to the Philippines.

CONCLUSION

By 1900 immigration, the settlement of the frontier West, and rapid industrial expansion had pushed America to the forefront of the world economy and had sparked a major realignment in American politics. After nearly two

decades of hard-fought elections in which political control had seesawed back and forth between the major parties, the Republicans now held power.

It had been difficult to achieve dominance. The dynamic growth of the American economy together with rapid urbanization and a massive influx of immigrants had initially strained the political process. As the parties struggled to define their vision of the proper role of government in stimulating economic development, they were forced to deal with ethnic, cultural, and racial issues that included prohibition, church schools, and segregation. All this was further complicated by the Democratic party's attempt to throw off the limits imposed by Reconstruction and gain political control of the South.

On the national level, both parties built a loyal following by linking their positions to deeply held beliefs about the family and the proper role of government. Republicans justified their support for the tariff and soldiers' pensions in terms of patriotic protection of the family. Democrats countered that a high-tariff policy was indicative of precisely the kind of excessive governmental force that would destroy family life. On the local level, both parties secured loyal voters by stressing ethnic and cultural issues. Democrats courted the new immigrants, while Republicans catered to rural and small-town native-born Americans in the Northeast and Midwest.

In the competition for new voters, the needs of rural Americans were often overlooked. Caught between declining prices for grain and cotton, and high railroad and bank rates, farmers struggled to make ends meet. Their precarious position was further strained by years of drought, insect infestation, and overspecialization in one crop. In desperation, farmers turned first to the Grange and Farmers' Alliance movements and then to the Populist party for help. In the South, after first courting black farmers, members of the Farmers' Alliance and later the Populists joined with Democrats to disenfranchise black voters. Using lynching and intimidation, Democrats seized control of southern politics.

In the face of these threats, the Republican party in 1896 raised huge sums from big business to turn back the Populist challenge and take control of national politics. The fusion of the Populists and Democrats behind William Jennings Bryan and the silver issue created problems of its own. Although he carried the South and almost all the Midwest, the teetotaling Bryan had little appeal for urban workers and the middle class who believed that a monetary policy based on free silver promised only inflation and higher prices. McKinley

won by playing down moral reforms such as prohibition and emphasizing patriotism and fiscal responsibility instead. When the dust settled, Republicans had won over the urban-industrial core of the nation—the Northeast and much of the Midwest. They would control the House of Representatives for twenty-eight out of the thirty-six years following 1894. The South, in contrast, had now become a Democratic stronghold.

Once elected, McKinley's administration was drawn by events in Cuba and jingoistic advocates within his

CHRONOLOGY, 1877–1900

1878 Congress requires U.S. Treasury to purchase silver.

1880 James Garfield elected president.

1881 Assassination of Garfield; Chester A. Arthur becomes president.

1883 Pendleton Civil Service Act.

1884 Grover Cleveland elected president.
Wabash v. *Illinois*

1887 Interstate Commerce Act.

1888 Benjamin Harrison elected president.

1889 National Farmers' Alliance formed.

1890 Sherman Silver Purchase Act.
Sherman Anti-Trust Act.
McKinley Tariff pushes tariffs to all-time high.

1893 Panic of 1893; depression of 1893–1897 begins.
Drain of Treasury's gold reserve.
Repeal of the Sherman Silver Purchase Act.
Overthrow of Queen Liliuokalani of Hawaii.
Chicago World's Fair.

1894 "Coxey's Army" marches on Washington.
Pullman strike.
Wilson-Gorman Tariff.

1895 Supreme Court declares federal income tax unconstitutional.
Banker's loans end drain on gold reserves.
United States intervenes in Venezuela-British Guiana boundary dispute.

1896 Free-silver forces capture Democratic party and nominate William Jennings Bryan.
William McKinley elected president.

1898 Spanish-American War.

1898–1902 Guerilla uprising in Philippines.

1900 Currency Act officially places United States on gold standard.

1901 Platt Amendment retains U.S. role in Cuba.
Assassination of McKinley; Theodore Roosevelt becomes president.

1902 Philippines Government Act.

own party into the Spanish-American War and the subsequent acquisition of Hawaii, Samoa, Guam, the Philippines, and Cuba. Although the Republicans preferred the term "expansionism" to "imperialism," the move to acquire new bases for the access to global markets fit the party's probusiness stance. But expansion into the Pacific created its own obstacles when the U.S. became involved in a guerilla war with Philippine nationalists. Facing mounting criticism at home, the expansionists adopted the Teller and Platt Amendments, which foreshadowed eventual disengagement from the acquisition of foreign territory.

Notwithstanding these foreign interventions, the fundamental question of late nineteenth-century American politics persisted: could a government designed for the needs of a small agrarian society serve an industrialized nation of factories and immigrant-crowded cities? The answer was by no means clear. Although issues such as patronage, the tariff, veteran's benefits, and monetary policy had enabled the industrial system to grow dramatically, the needs of farmers, workers, and immigrant Americans had largely been ignored. The Republicans successfully carried the field in 1896, but the insistence of Populists and other critics that government play an assertive role in solving social and economic problems would form the political environment of the progressive movement.

FOR FURTHER REFERENCE

READINGS

Cesar J. Ayala, *American Sugar Kingdom: The Plantation Economy of the Spanish Caribbean, 1898–1934* (1999). A careful analysis of the consolidation of the sugar industry and its effect on U.S. foreign policy and on the people living in Cuba, Puerto Rico, and the Dominican Republic.

Edward L. Ayers, *The Promise of the New South: Life After Reconstruction* (1992). A richly textured work that explores the complexity of the topic and pays close attention to nonelite men and women.

Richard F. Bensel, *The Political Economy of American Industrialization, 1877–1900* (2000). An astute analysis, based on a close reading of party platforms, of the connections between the tariff, monetary policy, veterans benefits, and industrial expansion.

Robert Cherny, *American Politics in the Gilded Age* (1997). A careful overview of the ethnic and institutional basis of the late nineteenth-century political process.

Rebecca Edwards, *Angels in the Machinery: Gender in American Party Politics from the Civil War to the Progressive Era* (1997). An innovative exploration of women's role in the political process and in the formation of political ideology.

William F. Holmes, ed., *American Populism* (1994). A well-selected set of nineteen scholarly essays interpreting the agrarian reform movement and surveying its varied aspects.

Ari Hoogenboom, *Rutherford B. Hayes: Warrior and President* (1995). A detailed, sympathetic, and balanced assessment of an able and decent public figure constrained by the political realities of his time; a good introduction to the political and economic issues of post-Reconstruction America.

Matthew F. Jacobson, *Barbarian Virtues: The United States Encounters Foreign Peoples at Home and Abroad, 1877–1900* (2000). An innovative study of the interconnections between politics, racism, and American economic development.

Michael Perman, *Struggle for Mastery: Disfranchisement in the South, 1888–1908* (2001). An important examination of the Democratic party's systematic disfranchisement of black voters.

David M. Pletcher, *The Diplomacy of Trade and Investment: American Economic Expansion in the Hemisphere, 1865–1900* (1998). An astute analysis of the direct and indirect governmental support for trade expansionism in the late nineteenth century.

WEBSITES

The Last Days of a President: Films of McKinley and the Pan-American Exposition, 1901, in Buffalo, New York
Library of Congress, American Memory Series
http://memory.loc.gov/ammem/papr/mckhome.html
This site provides a view of America's self-image as a world power.

The Spanish-American War in Motion Pictures, 1898–1901
Library of Congress, American Memory Series
http://memory.loc.gov/ammem/papr/mckhome.html
Contains helpful background essays for Edison films of the conflict.

Theodore Roosevelt, His Life and Times in Film, 1898–1919
Library of Congress, American Memory Series
http://memory.loc.gov/ammem/trfhtml/trfhome.html
Includes an introductory essay and a contemporary assessment of Roosevelt as a media personality.

For additional readings please consult the bibliography at the end of the book.

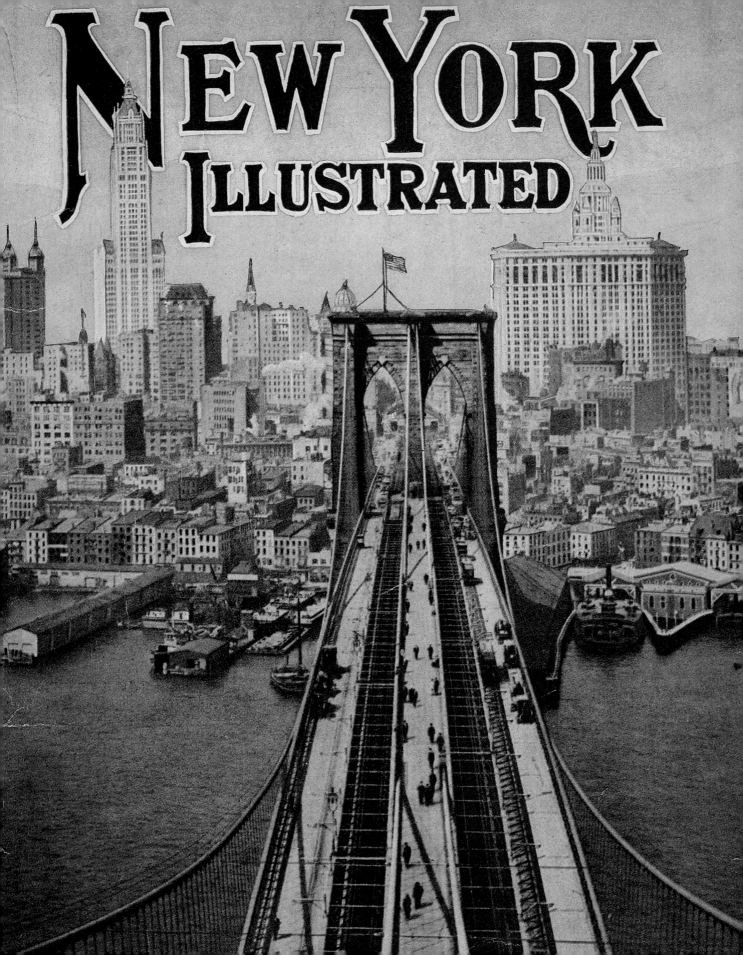

NEW YORK
ILLUSTRATED

The Progressive Era, 1900–1917

It was late Saturday afternoon on March 25, 1911, but at the Triangle Shirtwaist factory in New York City, hundreds of young women and a few men were still at work. In the eighth- and ninth-floor workrooms, the clatter of sewing machines filled the air. Suddenly fire broke out. Feeding on bolts of cloth, the fire soon turned the upper floors into an inferno. Panicked workers rushed for the doors, only to find some of them locked. Other doors opened inward (a fire-law violation) and were jammed shut by the crush of people trying to get out.

There were a few miraculous escapes. Young Pauline Grossman crawled to safety across a narrow alleyway when three male employees formed a human bridge. As others tried to cross, however, the weight became too great, and the three men fell to their deaths. Dozens of workers leaped from the windows to certain death on the sidewalk below.

Immigrant parents searched all night for their daughters; newspaper reporters could hear "a dozen pet names in Italian and Yiddish rising in shrill agony above the deeper moan of the throng." Sunday's headlines summed up the grim count: 141 dead.

The Triangle fire offered particularly horrifying evidence of what many citizens had recognized for years. Industrialization, for all its benefits, had taken a heavy toll on American life. For immigrants in unsafe factories and unhealthy slums, life often meant a desperate cycle of poverty, exhausting

◀ **The Brooklyn Bridge (opened May 24, 1883)**
This illustration from around 1900 evokes the magnetic attraction of America's expanding cities at the turn of the last century.

The Triangle Fire
The bodies of young women workers lie on the sidewalk after they jumped from the burning building.

labor, and early death. In the aftermath of the Triangle Shirtwaist factory tragedy, New York passed a series of laws regulating factories and protecting workers.

Industrialization, urban growth, and the rise of great corporations affected all Americans. A new middle class of white-collar workers and urban professionals gained political influence. As middle-class women joined clubs and reform organizations, they became powerful voices in addressing the social issues of the day.

From this volatile social stew erupted a wave of reformist energy that came to be called the progressive movement. Historians once portrayed this movement rather simplistically as a triumph of "the people" over evil corporations. More recent historians have complicated this picture, noting the role of special-interest groups (including big business) in promoting specific reforms, as well as the movement's darker side; its failures, and, above all, its rich diversity.

The progressive movement was a response to vast changes after the Civil War that had obliterated the familiar contours of an older, simpler America. Whatever their specific agendas, all progressives grappled with the new world of corporations, factories, cities, and immigrants. In contrast to the agrarian-based populists (see Chapter 20), progressives concentrated on the social effects of the new urban-industrial order.

Emerging in the 1890s at the city and state levels, a dizzying array of organizations, many led by women, pursued varied reform objectives. Under the influence of journalists, novelists, religious leaders, social thinkers, and politicians, these grass-roots efforts evolved into a powerful national movement. At the federal level, the reform spirit gripped Congress and the White House. By 1917, when reform gave way to war, America's political and social landscape had been transformed. New organization, new laws, and new regulatory agencies had arisen to grapple with the consequences of helter-skelter urbanization, industrial expansion, and corporate growth. The progressives could be maddeningly moralistic. They had their blind spots (especially on such subjects as immigration and race), and their reforms didn't always work out as planned. But, on balance, their imposing record of achievement left a powerful legacy for future generations to build upon.

This chapter focuses on five major questions:

■ How did intellectuals, novelists, and journalists help lay the groundwork for the progressive movement?

■ What problems of the new urban-industrial order particularly disturbed progressives, and how did they address these problems?

■ How did progressive reform affect ordinary Americans, including workers, women, immigrants, city dwellers, and African Americans?

■ As progressivism emerged as a national movement, which politicians and issues proved most important?

■ How did progressivism change Americans' view of the proper role of government?

PROGRESSIVES AND THEIR IDEAS

As the twentieth century dawned, local groups across the nation grappled with the problems of the new urban-industrial order. Workers protested unsafe and exhausting jobs. Expert commissions investigated social and economic conditions. Women's clubs turned from cultural uplift to reform. Intellectuals challenged the ideological foundations of a business-dominated social order, and journalists publicized municipal corruption and industrialism's human toll. Reform gained momentum as activists tried to make government more democratic, eradicate dangerous conditions in cities and factories, and curb corporate power.

Looking back on all these efforts, historians grouped them under a single label: "the progressive movement." In fact, "progressivism" was never a single movement. It is perhaps best understood as a widespread yearning for reform and an exciting sense of new social possibilities. This yearning found many outlets and focused on a wide array of issues.

The Many Faces of Progressivism

Who were the progressives, and what reforms did they pursue? To answer these questions, we need to look at the pattern of urban growth in the early twentieth century. Along with immigration, a rapidly growing middle class transformed U.S. cities . From the men and women of this class—most of whom were native-born, white, and Protestant—came many of the leaders and foot soldiers of the progressive movement.

From 1900 to 1920, the white-collar work force jumped from 5.1 million to 10.5 million—more than double the growth rate of the labor force as a whole. As industry grew, the number of secretaries, civil engineers, and people in advertising increased phenomenally. This white-collar class included corporate technicians and desk workers; the owners and managers of local businesses; and professionals such as lawyers, physicians, and teachers. Existing professional societies such as the American Bar Association grew rapidly. Scores of new professional groups arose, from the American Association of Advertising Agencies (1917) to the American Association of University Professors (1915). The age of organization had dawned, bringing new professional allegiances, a new emphasis on certification and licensing, and in general a more standardized, routinized society. For many middle-class Americans, membership in a national professional society provided a sense of identity that might earlier have come from neighborhood, church, or political party affiliations. Ambitious, well educated, and valuing social stability, the members of this new middle class were eager to make their influence felt.

For middle-class women, the city offered both opportunities and frustrations. Young unmarried women often became schoolteachers, secretaries, typists, clerks, and telephone operators. The number of women in such white-collar jobs surged from 949,000 in 1900 to 3.4 million in 1920. The ranks of college-educated women, although still small, more than tripled in this twenty-year period.

But for middle-class married women caring for homes and children, city life could mean isolation and frustration. The divorce rate crept up from one in twelve marriages in 1900 to one in nine by 1916. As we shall see, many middle-class women joined female white-collar workers and college graduates in leading a resurgent women's movement. Cultural commentators wrote nervously of the "New Woman."

The progressive reform impulse drew on the energies of men and women of this new urban middle class. The initial reform impetus came not from political parties but from women's clubs, settlement houses, and private groups with names like the Playground Association of America, the National Child Labor Committee, the National Consumers' League, and the American League for Civic Improvement. In this era of organizations, the reform movement, too, drew strength from organized interest groups.

Important as it was, the native-born middle class was not the only force behind progressivism. On issues affecting factory workers and slum dwellers, the urban-immigrant political machines—and workers themselves — provided critical support and often took the initiative. Some corporate leaders helped shape regulatory measures in ways to serve their interests.

What, then, was progressivism? At the most basic level, it was a series of political and cultural responses to industrialization and its by-products: immigration, urban growth, the rise of corporate power, and widening class divisions. In contrast to populism, progressivism's strength lay in the cities, and it enlisted many more journalists, academics, social theorists, and urban dwellers generally. Finally, most progressives were reformers, not radicals. They wished to remedy the social ills of industrial capitalism, not uproot the system itself.

But which parts of the urban-industrial order most needed attention, and what remedies were required? These key questions stirred deep disagreements, and the progressive impulse spawned an array of activities that sometimes overlapped and sometimes diverged. Many reformers wanted stricter regulation of business, from local transit companies to the almighty trusts. Others focused on protecting workers and the urban poor. Still others tried to reform the structure of government, especially at the municipal level. Finally, some reformers, viewing immigration, urban immorality, and social disorder as the central problems, fought for immigration restriction or various social-control strategies. All this contributed to the mosaic of progressive reform.

Central to progressivism was the confidence that all social problems could be solved through careful study and organized effort. Progressives had a high regard for

The Gendering of Labor in Corporate America
Male bookkeepers and female "type-writers" at the headquarters of the Metropolitan Life Insurance Company in New York City.

science and expert knowledge. Scientific and technological expertise had produced the new industrial order, and progressives tended to believe that such expertise would also solve the social problems spawned by industrialism. Progressives marshaled research data, expert opinion, and statistics to support their various causes.

Some historians have portrayed progressivism as an organizational stage that all modernizing societies pass through. This is a useful perspective, provided we remember that it was not an automatic process unfolding independently of human will. Eloquent leaders, gifted journalists, activist workers, and passionate reformers all played a role. Human emotion—whether indignation over child labor, intense moralism, fear of the alien, hatred of unbridled corporate power, or raw political ambition—drove the movement forward.

Intellectuals Offer New Social Views

A group of early-twentieth-century thinkers helped build progressivism's ideological scaffolding. As we have seen, some Gilded Age intellectuals had argued that Charles Darwin's theory of evolution justified brutal, unrestrained economic competition. In the 1880s and 1890s, sociologist Lester Ward, utopian novelist Edward Bellamy, and leaders of the settlement-house and Social Gospel movements had all attacked this harsh version of Social Darwinism (see Chapters 18 and 19). This attack intensified as the twentieth century opened.

One of the sharpest critics of the new business order was economist Thorstein Veblen, who was reared by frugal Norwegian-American parents on a farm in Minnesota. In *The Theory of the Leisure Class* (1899), Veblen mercilessly satirized the lifestyle of the newly rich captains of industry. Dissecting their habits the way an anthropologist might study the customs of an exotic tribal people, he argued that they built showy mansions, threw elaborate parties, and otherwise engaged in "conspicuous consumption" to flaunt their wealth and assert their claims to superiority.

While Veblen scorned the "wastemanship" of the business class, he shared the era's admiration for efficiency, science, and technical expertise. In later works, he argued that workers and engineers, shaped by the discipline of the machine, were better fitted to lead society than the nation's corporate leaders.

Other intellectuals built a case for reform. Harvard philosopher William James, in an influential 1907 essay called "Pragmatism," argued that truth emerges not from abstract theorizing but from the experience of coping with life's realities. James emphasized the fluidity of knowledge and the importance of practical action. In this way, he contributed to the progressives' skepticism toward the conventional wisdom of conservatives, and to their confidence that social conditions could be bettered through intelligent and purposeful action.

No thinker better captured this faith in the power of new ideas to transform society than Herbert Croly. The

son of New York journalists and reformers, Croly grew up in a cosmopolitan world where social issues were hotly debated. In *The Promise of American Life* (1909), he called for an activist government of the kind advocated by Alexander Hamilton, the first secretary of the Treasury, in the 1790s. But rather than serving only the interests of the business class, as Hamilton had proposed, Croly argued that this activist government should promote the welfare of all citizens.

To build support for this enlarged view of government, Croly argued, intellectuals must play a key role. In 1914 he founded the *New Republic* magazine to promote progressive ideas.

Few intellectuals argued more effectively for organized efforts to address the social by-products of industrialization than the settlement-house leader Jane Addams. In her books *Democracy and Social Ethics* (1902) and *Twenty Years at Hull House* (1910), Addams rejected the idea that unrestrained competition offered the best path to social progress. Instead, she argued, in a complex, modern industrial society, each individual's well-being depends on the well-being of all. Addams urged privileged middle-class men and women to recognize their common interests with the laboring masses, and to take the lead in demanding better conditions in factories and immigrants slums. Teaching by example, Addams made her Chicago social settlement, Hull House, a center of social activism and legislative-reform initiatives.

For philosopher John Dewey, the key social institution that could bring about a more humane and cooperative social order was the public school. With public-school enrollment growing from about 7 million in 1870 to more than 23 million in 1920, Dewey saw schools as potent engines of social change. Banishing bolted-down chairs and desks from his model school at the University of Chicago, he encouraged pupils to interact with one another. The ideal school, he said in *Democracy and Education* (1916), would be an "embryonic community" where children would learn to live as members of a social group.

For other thinkers, the key to social change lay in transforming the nation's courts. Conservative judges citing ancient precedents had upheld corporate interests and struck down reform legislation for decades. A few jurists, however, had argued for a more flexible view. In *The Common Law* (1881), law professor Oliver Wendell Holmes, Jr., had insisted that law must evolve as society changes. In a phrase much quoted by progressives, he had declared, "The life of the law has not been logic; it has been experience." Appointed to the Supreme Court

in 1902, Holmes wrote a series of eloquent opinions dissenting from the conservative Court majority. Under the influence of the new social thinking, the courts slowly became more receptive to reform legislation.

Novelists, Journalists, and Artists Spotlight Social Problems

While intellectuals and social thinkers reoriented American social thought, novelists and journalists roused the reform spirit by chronicling corporate wrongdoing, municipal corruption, slum conditions, and industrial abuses. Advances in printing and photo reproduction ensured a mass audience and sharpened the emotional impact of their message.

In his popular novel *The Octopus* (1901), the young San Francisco writer Frank Norris portrayed the epic struggle between California railroad owners and the state's wheat growers. Basing his fiction on the actual practices of Gilded Age railroad barons, Norris described the bribery, intimidation, rate manipulation, and other means they used to promote their interests.

Theodore Dreiser's novel *The Financier* (1912) featured a hard-driving business tycoon utterly lacking a social conscience. Like Norris, Dreiser modeled his story on the career of an actual tycoon, Charles Yerkes, a railway financier with a reputation for underhanded practices. Like Veblen's *Theory of the Leisure Class,* such works undermined the reputation of the industrial elite and stimulated pressures for tougher regulation of business.

Also influential in forging the progressive spirit were articles exposing urban political corruption and corporate wrongdoing published in mass magazines such as *McClure's* and *Collier's*. President Theodore Roosevelt criticized the authors as "muckrakers" obsessed with the seamier side of American life, but the name became a badge of honor. Journalist Lincoln Steffens began the exposé vogue in October 1902 with a *McClure's* article documenting municipal corruption in St. Louis and the efforts of a crusading district attorney to fight it.

The muckrakers emphasized facts rather than abstractions. To gather material, some worked as factory laborers or lived in slum tenements. In a 1903 series, journalist Maria Van Vorst described her experiences working in a Massachusetts shoe factory where women's fingernails rotted away from repeated immersion in caustic dyes.

The muckrakers awakened middle-class readers to conditions in industrial America. The circulation of *McClure's* and *Collier's* soared. Some magazine exposés later appeared in book form, including Lincoln Steffens's

Lincoln Steffens (1866–1936)
Steffens, the quintessential muckraker, targeted urban political corruption in *The Shame of the Cities* (1904). Visiting revolutionary Russia in 1919, he declared: "I have seen the future, and it works."

The Shame of the Cities (1904), Ida Tarbell's damning *History of the Standard Oil Company* (1904), and David Graham Phillips's *Treason of the Senate* (1906).

Artists and photographers played a role as well. A group of New York painters dubbed the Ashcan School portrayed the harshness of life in the city's crowded slums. The Wisconsin-born photographer Lewis Hine captured images of immigrants and factory laborers. As official photographer for the National Child Labor Committee from 1911 to 1916, Hine took photographs of child workers with stunted bodies and worn expressions that helped build support for national legislation outlawing child labor.

STATE AND LOCAL PROGRESSIVISM

While they read novels, magazine articles, and works of social analysis on the problems besetting urban-industrial America, middle-class citizens also observed these problems firsthand in their own communities. In fact, the progressive movement began with grass-roots campaigns from New York to San Francisco to end urban political corruption, regulate corporate behavior, and improve conditions in factories and city slums. Eventually, these state and local movements came together in a powerful national surge of reform.

Reforming the Political Process

In a series of grass-roots campaigns beginning in the 1890s, native-born elites and middle-class reformers battled corrupt city governments. New York City experienced a succession of reform spasms in which Protestant clergy rallied the forces of righteousness against Tammany Hall, the city's entrenched Democratic organization. In Detroit the reform mayor Hazen Pingree (served 1890–1897) brought honesty to city hall, lowered transit fares, adopted a fairer tax structure, and provided public baths and other services for the poor. Pingree once slapped a health quarantine on a brothel, holding a prominent business leader hostage until he promised to back Pingree's reforms.

In San Francisco, a courageous newspaper editor led a 1907 crusade against the city's corrupt boss, Abe Reuf. Thanks to attorney Hiram Johnson, who took over the case when the original prosecutor was gunned down in court, Reuf and his cronies were convicted. Sternly self-righteous and full of reform zeal—one observer called him "a volcano in perpetual eruption"—Johnson rode his newly won fame to the California governorship and the U.S. Senate.

In Toledo, Ohio, a colorful eccentric named Samuel M. ("Golden Rule") Jones led the reform crusade. A self-made businessman converted to the Social Gospel (see Chapter 19), Jones introduced profit sharing in his factory, and as mayor he established playgrounds, free kindergartens, and lodging houses for homeless transients.

The political reform movement soon moved beyond simply "throwing the rascals out" to probing the roots of urban misgovernment, including the private monopolies that ran municipal water, gas, electricity, and transit systems. Reformers passed laws regulating the rates these utilities could charge, raising their taxes, and curbing their political influence. (Some even advocated public ownership of these companies.) This new regulatory structure would remain the rule for a century, until an equally strong deregulatory movement swept the nation in the 1990s.

Reflecting the Progressive Era vogue of expertise and efficiency, some municipal reformers advocated substituting professional managers and administrators, chosen in citywide elections, for mayors and aldermen elected on a ward-by-ward basis. Natural disasters

sometimes gave a boost to this particular reform. Dayton, Ohio, went to a city-manager system after a ruinous flood in 1913. Supposedly above politics, these experts were expected to run the city like an efficient business.

Municipal reform attracted different groups depending on the issue. The native-born middle class, led by clergymen, editors, and other opinion molders, provided the initial impetus and core support. Business interests often pushed for citywide elections and the city-manager system, since these changes tended to reduce immigrants' political clout and increase the influence of the corporate elite. Reforms that addressed the immediate needs of ordinary city dwellers, such as improved city services, won support from immigrants and even from political bosses who realized that explosive urban growth was swamping the old, informal system of meeting constituents' needs.

The electoral-reform movement soon expanded to the state level. By 1910, for example, all states had replaced the old system of voting, which involved preprinted ballots bearing the names of specific candidates, with the secret ballot, which made it harder to rig elections. An electoral reform introduced in Wisconsin in 1903, the direct primary, enabled rank-and-file voters rather than party bosses to select the candidates who would run in the general election.

To restore government by the people rather than by moneyed interests, some western states inaugurated electoral reforms known as the *initiative, referendum, and recall.* By an initiative, voters can instruct the legislature to consider a specific bill. In a referendum, they can actually enact a law or (in a nonbinding referendum) express their views on a proposed measure. By a recall petition, voters can remove a public official from office if they muster enough signatures.

While these reforms aimed to democratize voting, party leaders and interest groups soon learned to manipulate the new electoral machinery. Ironically, the new procedures may have weakened party loyalty and reduced voter interest. Voter-participation rates dropped steeply in these years, while political activity by organized interest groups increased.

The Dayton Flood, 1913
This devastating flood, which claimed over 300 lives and left large areas of the city in ruin, led this Ohio city to adopt the city-manager system of municipal government, an important Progressive-era reform.

Regulating Business, Protecting Workers

The late-nineteenth-century corporate consolidation that produced giants like Carnegie Steel and Standard Oil (see Chapter 18) continued after 1900. The United States Steel Company created by J. P. Morgan in 1901 controlled 80 percent of all U.S. steel production. A year later Morgan combined six competing companies into the International Harvester Company, which dominated the farm-implement business. The General Motors Company, formed in 1908 by William C. Durant with backing from the Du Pont Corporation, bought various independent automobile manufacturers, from the inexpensive Chevrolet to the luxury Cadillac, and consolidated their operations under one corporate umbrella.

Many workers benefited from this corporate growth. Industrial workers' average annual real wages (defined, that is, in terms of actual purchasing power) rose from $532 in the late nineteenth century to $687 by 1915. In railroading and other unionized industries, wages climbed still higher. But even though the cost of living was far lower than today, such wages could barely sup-

port a family and provided little cushion for emergencies.

To survive, entire families went to work. Two-thirds of young immigrant women entered the labor force in the early 1900s, working as factory help or domestics or in small establishments like laundries and bakeries. Even children worked. In 1910 the nonfarm labor force probably included at least 1.6 million children aged ten to fifteen who were working in factories, mills, tenement sweatshops, and street trades such as shoe shining and newspaper vending (see Table 21.1). The total may have been higher, since many "women workers" listed in the census were in fact young girls. One investigator found a girl of five working at night in a South Carolina textile mill.

Most laborers faced long hours and great hazards. Despite the eight-hour movement of the 1880s, in 1900 the average worker still toiled 9 1/2 hours a day. Some southern textile mills required workdays of 12 or 13 hours. In one typical year (1907), 4,534 railroad workers and more than 3,000 miners were killed on the job. Few employers accepted responsibility for work-related acci-

Child Worker

A young girl sells newspapers near an elevated train station in New York City, 1896.

dents and illnesses. Vacations and retirement benefits were practically unheard of.

New industrial workers accustomed to the rhythms of farm labor faced the discipline of the time clock and the machine. Efficiency experts used time-and-motion studies to increase production and make human workers as predictable as machines. In *Principles of Scientific Management* (1911), Frederick W. Taylor explained how to increase output by standardizing job routines and rewarding the fastest workers. "Efficiency" became a popular catchword, but most workers deeply resented the pressures to speed up output.

For Americans troubled by the social implications of industrialization, the expansion of corporate power and the hazards of the workplace stirred urgent concern. The drive to regulate big business, inherited from the populists, thus became a vitally important impetus for progressivism. Since corporations had benefited from the government's economic policies, such as high protective tariffs, reformers reasoned, they should also be subject to government supervision.

Of the many states that passed laws regulating railroads, mines, and other businesses, none did so more avidly than Wisconsin under Governor Robert ("Fighting Bob") La Follette. As a Republican congressman, La Follette had feuded with the state's conservative party leadership, and in 1900 he won the governorship as an independent. Challenging the state's long-dominant business interests, La Follette and his administration adopted the direct-primary system, set up a railroad regulatory commission, increased corporate taxes, and limited campaign spending. Reflecting progressivism's faith in experts, La Follette met regularly with reform-minded professors at the University of Wisconsin. He also set up a legislative reference library so lawmakers would not be solely dependent on corporate lobbyists for factual information. La Follette's reforms gained national attention as the "Wisconsin Idea."

If electoral reform and corporate regulation represented the brain of progressivism, the impulse to improve conditions in factories and mills represented its heart. This movement, too, began at the local and state level. By 1907, for example, some thirty states had outlawed child labor. A 1903 Oregon law limited women in industry to a ten-hour workday.

Campaigns to improve industrial safety and otherwise better conditions for the laboring masses won support from political bosses in cities with large immigrant populations, such as New York, Cleveland, and Chicago. New York state senator Robert F. Wagner, a leader of Tammany Hall, headed the investigating committee set

TABLE 21.1 Children in the Labor Force, * 1880–1930

	1880	1890	1900	1910	1920	1930
Total number of children aged 10–15 (in millions)	6.6	8.3	9.6	10.8	12.5	14.3
Total number of children employed (in millions)	1.1	1.5	1.7	1.6	1.4	0.7
Percentage of children employed	16.8	18.1	18.2	15.0	11.3	4.7

*Nonagricultural workers.

Source: *The Statistical History of the United States from Colonial Times to the Present* (Stamford, Conn.: Fairfield Publishers, 1965).

up after the 1911 Triangle fire. Thanks to the committee's efforts, New York legislators passed fifty-six worker-protection laws, including required fire-safety inspections of factories. By 1914, spurred by the Triangle disaster, twenty-five states had passed laws making employers liable for job-related injuries or deaths.

Florence Kelley was a leader in the drive to remedy industrial abuses. The daughter of a conservative Republican congressman, Kelley became a Hull House resident in 1891. Investigating conditions in factories and sweatshops, in 1893 she helped secure passage of an Illinois law prohibiting child labor and limiting working hours for women. In 1899 she became general secretary of the National Consumers' League, which mobilized consumer pressure for improved factory conditions. Campaigning for a federal child-labor law, Kelley pointedly asked, "Why are seals, bears, reindeer, fish, wild game in the national parks, buffalo, [and] migratory birds all found suitable for federal protection, but not children?"

Like many progressive reforms, the crusade for workplace safety relied on expert research. Alice Hamilton, for example, a pioneer in the new field of "industrial hygiene," taught bacteriology at Northwestern University while also working with Jane Addams at Hull House. In 1910, fusing her scientific training and her reformist impulses, she conducted a major study of lead poisoning among industrial workers. Appointed as an investigator by the U.S. Bureau of Labor in 1911, Hamilton became an expert on—and public campaigner against—work-related medical hazards.

Workers, who understood the hazards of their jobs better than anyone, provided further pressure for reform. For example, when the granite industry introduced new power drills that created a fine dust that workers inhaled, the *Granite Cutters' Journal* warned of "stone cutters' consumption" and called the new drills "widow makers." Sure enough, investigators soon linked the dust to a deadly respiratory disease, silicosis. This, too, became another industrial hazard that worker-safety advocates sought to remedy.

Making Cities More Livable

In the early twentieth century, America became an urban nation. By 1920 the urban population passed the 50 percent mark, and sixty-eight U.S. cities boasted more than a hundred thousand inhabitants. New York City grew by 2.2 million from 1900 to 1920, and Chicago by 1 million.

Political corruption was only one of many problems plaguing these burgeoning urban centers. As manufacturing and businesses grew, a surging tide of immigrants and native-born newcomers engulfed the cities. Overwhelmed by this rapid growth, many cities became dreary, sprawling human warehouses. They lacked adequate parks, municipal services, public-health resources, recreational facilities, and other basic civic amenities. Unsurprisingly, as the progressive movement took shape, this worrisome tangle of urban problems loomed large.

Drawing on the efforts of Frederick Law Olmsted and others (see Chapter 19), reform-minded men and women campaigned for parks, boulevards, and street lights and proposed laws against billboards and unsightly overhead electrical wires. An influential voice for city planning and beautification was Daniel Burnham, chief architect of the 1893 Chicago world's fair. Burnham led a successful 1906 effort to revive a plan for Washington, D.C., first proposed by Charles L'Enfant in 1791. He also developed city plans for Cleveland, San Francisco, and other cities.

Burnham's 1909 plan for Chicago offered a seductive vision of a city both more efficient and more beautiful. He recommended lakefront parks and museums, wide boulevards to improve traffic flow, and a redesign of Chicago's congested major thoroughfare, Michigan Avenue. The focal point of Burnham's dream city was a majestic domed city hall and vast civic plaza. Although not all of Burnham's plan was adopted, Chicago spent more than $300 million on projects reflecting his ideas. Many Progressive Era urban planners shared Burnham's faith that more beautiful cities and imposing public

A Poor Neighborhood in Philadelphia, c. 1915
Scenes like this in the immigrant wards of America's great cities stirred middle-class reformers to action at the turn of the century.

buildings would ensure a law-abiding and civic-minded urban populace.

Beyond urban beautification, the municipal reform impulse also included such practical goals as decent housing and better garbage collection and street cleaning. Providing a model for other cities and states, the New York legislature passed laws imposing strict health and safety regulations on tenements in 1911.

Public health loomed large as well. With the discovery in the 1880s that germs cause diseases such as cholera and typhoid fever, municipal hygiene and sanitation became high priorities. Progressive reformers called for improved water and sewer systems, regulation of milk suppliers and food handlers, school medical examinations and vaccination programs, and informational campaigns to spread public-health information to the urban masses.

All these efforts bore fruit. From 1900 to 1920, infant mortality (defined as death in the first year of life) dropped from 165 per 1,000 population to around 75, and the tuberculosis death rate fell by nearly half. The municipal health crusades had a social-class dimension. Middle-class reformers set the "sanitary agenda," and the campaigns often targeted immigrants and the poor as the sources of contagion. When Mary Mallon, an Irish-immigrant cook in New York, was found to be a healthy carrier of the typhoid bacillus in 1907, she was confined for years by the city health authorities and demonized in the press as "Typhoid Mary."

Urban reformers also shared the heightened environmental consciousness of these years (see Chapter 17). The battle against air pollution illustrates both the promise and the frustrations of municipal environmentalism. Coal-fueled steam boilers, the major energy source for factories, produced massive amounts of soot and smoke. Factory chimneys belching smoke had once inspired pride, but by the early 1900s physicians had linked factory smoke to respiratory problems, and civic reformers were deploring the resulting air pollution.

As with other progressive reforms, the antismoke campaign combined expertise with activism. Civil engineers formed the Smoke Prevention Association in 1906, and researchers at the University of Pittsburgh—one of the nation's smokiest cities with its nearby steel mills—documented the hazards and costs of air pollution. Chicago merchant Marshall Field declared that the "soot tax" he paid to clean his stores was larger than his real-estate taxes. As women's clubs and other civic groups embraced the cause, many cities passed smoke-abatement laws.

Success proved elusive. Railroads and corporations fought back in the courts and often won. With coal still

Proposed Chicago Civic Center, 1910
In their ambitious plan for the rapidly growing immigrant city on Lake Michigan, Daniel Burnham and Edward H. Bennett envisioned a soaring new civic center "to be seen and felt by the people as the symbol of civic order and unity."

providing 70 percent of the nation's energy as late as 1920, cities remained smoky. Not until years later, with the shift from coal to other energy sources, did the battle against municipal air pollution make significant headway.

Progressivism and Social Control

Progressives' belief that they could improve society through research, legislation, and aroused public opinion sprang from their confidence that they knew what was best for other people. While municipal corruption, unsafe factories, and corporate abuses captured their attention, so, too, did issues of personal behavior, particularly the behavior of immigrants. The problems they addressed deserved attention, but their self-righteous

rhetoric and the remedies they proposed also betrayed an impulse to impose their own moral standards by force of law.

Moral Control in the Cities

Early twentieth-century urban life was more than crowded slums and exhausting labor. For all their problems, cities also offered fun and diversion. Department stores, vaudeville, music halls, and amusement parks (see Chapter 19) continued to flourish. While some vaudeville owners strove for respectability, raucous and bawdy routines full of sexual innuendo, including those of the comedienne Mae West, were popular with working-class audiences. New York City's amusement park, Coney Island, drew more patrons than ever. A subway ride from the city, it attracted as many as a million visitors a day by 1914.

For families, amusement parks provided escape from tenements. For female garment workers or department-store clerks, they provided an opportunity to spend time with friends, meet young men, and show off new outfits. With electrification, simply riding the streetcars or taking an evening stroll on well-lit downtown streets became leisure activities in themselves News of Orville and Wilbur Wright's successful airplane flight in 1903, and the introduction of Henry Ford's Model T in 1908, which transformed the automobile from a toy of the rich to a vehicle for the masses, heightened the sense of exciting changes ahead, with cities at the heart of the action.

Jaunty popular songs, introduced in the music halls and produced in a district of lower Manhattan called Tin Pan Alley, added to the vibrancy of city life. The blues, rooted in the chants of southern black sharecroppers, reached a broader public with such songs as W. C. Handy's classic "St. Louis Blues" (1914). Ragtime, another import from the black South (see Chapter 19), enjoyed great popularity in early-twentieth-century urban America. Both the black composer Scott Joplin, with such works as "Maple Leaf Rag" (1899), and the white composer Irving Berlin, with his hit tune "Alexander's Rag-Time Band" (1911), contributed to this vogue.

These years also brought a new medium of mass entertainment—the movies. Initially a part of vaudeville shows, movies soon migrated to five-cent halls called "nickelodeons" in immigrant neighborhoods. At first featuring brief comic sequences like *The Sneeze* or *The Kiss*, the movies began to tell stories with *The Great Train Robbery* (1903). *A Fool There Was* (1914), with its famous line, "Kiss me, my fool!", made Theda Bara (really

Coney Island, Luna Park Entrance, 1912
Electric street lights, illuminated buildings, and the headlights of automobiles and streetcars added to the excitement of early 20th-century urban nightlife.

Theodosia Goodman of Cincinnati) the first female movie star. The British music-hall performer Charlie Chaplin emigrated to America in 1913 and appeared in some sixty short two-reel comedies between 1914 and 1917. Like amusement parks, the movies allowed immigrant youth to briefly escape parental supervision. As a New York garment worker recalled, "The one place I was allowed to go by myself was the movies. My parents wouldn't let me go anywhere else."

Ironically, the diversions that made city life more bearable for the poor struck some middle-class reformers as moral traps no less dangerous than the physical hazards of the factory or the slum tenement. Fearful of immorality and social disorder, reformers campaigned to regulate amusement parks, dance halls, and the movies. The early movies, in particular, struck many middle-class men and women as degenerate, and the darkened nickelodeons were seen as potential dens of vice. Warning of "nickel madness," reformers demanded film censorship. Several states and cities set up censorship boards, and the Supreme Court upheld such measures in 1915.

Building on the moral-purity crusade of the Woman's Christian Temperance Union (WCTU) and other groups in the 1890s (see Chapter 19), reformers also targeted prostitution, a major urban problem. Male

procurers lured young women into the business and then took a share of their income. The paltry wages paid women for factory work or domestic service attracted many to this more-lucrative occupation. One prostitute wrote that she was unwilling "to get up at 6:30 . . . and work in a close stuffy room . . . until dark for $6 or $7 a week" when an afternoon with a man could bring in more.

Addressing the issue in the usual progressive fashion, investigators gathered statistics on what they called "the social evil." The American Social Hygiene Association (1914), financed by John D. Rockefeller, Jr., sponsored medical research on sexually transmitted diseases, paid for "vice investigations" in various cities, and drafted model municipal statutes against prostitution.

As prostitution came to symbolize the larger moral dangers of cities, a "white slave" hysteria gripped the nation. Novels, films, and muckraking articles warned of farm girls' being kidnapped and forced into urban brothels. The Mann Act (1910) made it illegal to transport a woman across a state line "for immoral purposes." Amid much fanfare, reformers shut down the red-light districts of New Orleans, Chicago, and other cities.

Racism, anti-immigrant prejudice, fear of the city, and anxieties about changing sexual mores all fueled the antiprostitution crusade. Tipped off by neighbors and angry spouses, authorities employed the new legislation to pry into private sexual behavior. Scam artists entrapped men into Mann Act violations and blackmailed them. In 1913 the African-American boxer Jack Johnson, who had won the heavyweight championship five years earlier, was convicted under the Mann Act for traveling with a (white) woman across state lines for "immoral purposes." Johnson went abroad to escape imprisonment.

Battling Alcohol and Drugs

Temperance had long been part of the American reform agenda, but reformers' tactics and objectives changed in the Progressive Era. Most earlier campaigns had urged individuals to give up drink. The powerful Anti-Saloon League (ASL), founded in 1895, shifted the emphasis to

Patent Medicines

Progressive-era reformers targeted unregulated and often dangerous nostrums. Hamlin's Wizard Oil, a pain remedy marketed by traveling shows and musical groups, contained alcohol, ammonia, chloroform, and turpentine, among other ingredients.

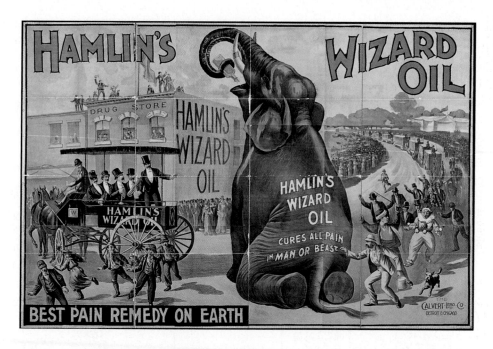

legislating a ban on the sale of alcoholic beverages. The ASL was a typical progressive organization. Full-time professionals ran the national office, while Protestant ministers staffed a network of state committees. The ASL presses in Westerville, Ohio, produced propaganda documenting alcohol's role in many social problems and touting prohibition as the answer. As the ASL added its efforts to those of the WCTU and various church bodies, many localities banned the sale of alcoholic beverages and the campaign for national prohibition gained strength.

This was a heavy-drinking era, and alcohol abuse did indeed contribute to domestic abuse, health problems, and work injuries. But like the antiprostitution crusade, the prohibition campaign became a symbolic battleground pitting native-born citizens against the new immigrants. The ASL, while it raised legitimate issues, also embodied Protestant America's impulse to control the immigrant city.

These years also saw the first sustained campaign against drug abuse—and for good reason. Physicians, patent-medicine peddlers, and legitimate drug companies freely prescribed or sold opium (derived from poppies) and its derivatives morphine and heroin. Cocaine, extracted from coca leaves, was widely used as well. Coca-Cola contained cocaine until about 1900.

As reformers focused on the problem, the federal government backed a 1912 treaty aimed at halting the international opium trade. The Narcotics Act of 1914, also known as the Harrison Act, banned the distribution of heroin, morphine, cocaine, and other addictive drugs except by licensed physicians or pharmacists. In their battle against drugs, as in their environmental concerns, the progressives anticipated an issue that would remain important into the twenty-first century. But this reform, too, had racist undertones. Antidrug crusaders luridly described Chinese "opium dens" and warned that "drug-crazed Negroes" imperiled white womanhood.

Immigration Restriction and Eugenics

While many of the new city dwellers came from farms and small towns, the main source of urban growth continued to be immigration. More than 17 million newcomers arrived from 1900 to 1917 (many passing through New York's immigration center, Ellis Island), and most settled in cities (see Figure 21.1). As in the 1890s (see Chapter 19), the influx came mainly from southern and eastern Europe, but more than two hundred thousand Japanese and forty thousand Chinese also arrived between 1900 and 1920, as well as thousands of Mexicans seeking railroad work. Some immigrants prospered, but many sank into poverty or survived precariously on the economic margins.

The dismay that middle-class Americans felt about appalling conditions in the urban slums stimulated support not only for protective legislation, but also for immigration restriction. If the immigrant city was a morass of social problems, some concluded, then immi-

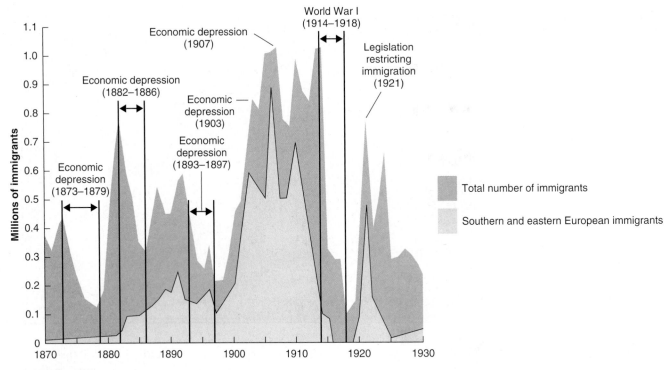

FIGURE 21.1

Immigration to the United States, 1870–1930

With the end of the depression of the 1890s, immigrants from southern and eastern Europe poured into American cities, spurring an immigration-restriction movement, urban moral-purity campaigns, and efforts to improve the physical and social conditions of immigrant life.

Sources: Statistical History of the United States from Colonial Times to the Present (Stamford, Conn.: Fairfield Publishers, 1965); and report presented by Senator William P. Dillingham, Senate document 742, 61st Congress, 3rd session, December 5, 1910: Abstracts of Reports to the Immigration Commission.

grants should be excluded. Prominent Bostonians formed the Immigration Restriction League in 1894. The American Federation of Labor, fearing job competition, also endorsed restriction.

Progressives who supported this reform characteristically documented their case with claims of scientific expertise. In 1911 a congressional commission produced a massive statistical study allegedly proving the new immigrants' innate degeneracy. Sociologist Edward A. Ross, a prominent progressive, described the recent immigrants as "low-browed, big-faced persons of obviously low mentality."

Led by Massachusetts senator Henry Cabot Lodge, Congress passed literacy-test bills in 1896, 1913, and 1915, only to see them vetoed. These measures would have excluded would-be immigrants over sixteen years old who were unable to read, either in English or in some other language, thus discriminating against persons lacking formal education. In 1917 one such bill became law over President Woodrow Wilson's veto. Immigrants also faced physical examinations and tests in which

legitimate public-health concerns became mixed up with stereotypes of entire ethnic groups as mental or physical defectives. This, too, was part of progressivism's mixed legacy.

Anti-immigrant fears helped fuel the eugenics movement. Eugenics is the control of reproduction to alter a plant or animal species, and some U.S. eugenicists believed that human society could be improved by this means. A leading eugenicist, the zoologist Charles B. Davenport, urged immigration restriction to keep America from pollution by "inferior" genetic stock.

In *The Passing of the Great Race* (1916), Madison Grant, a prominent progressive and eugenics advocate, used bogus data to denounce immigrants from southern and eastern Europe, especially Jews. He also viewed African Americans as inferior. Anticipating the program of Adolf Hitler in the 1930s (see Chapter 25), Grant called for racial segregation, immigration restriction, and the forced sterilization of the "unfit," including "worthless race types." The vogue of eugenics gave "scientific" respectability to anti-immigrant sentiment, as well as

Ellis Island, 1920

Early-twentieth-century immigrants faced rigorous tests that reflected not only public-health concerns but also a rising exclusionary sentiment that culminated in the restrictive Immigration Act of 1924.

the racism, that pervaded white America in these years. Inspired by eugenics, many states legalized the sterilization of criminals, sex offenders, and persons adjudged mentally deficient. In the 1927 case *Buck* v. *Bell*, the Supreme Court upheld such laws.

Racism and Progressivism

Progressivism arose at a time of significant changes in African-American life, and also of intense racism in white America. These racial realities are crucial to a full understanding of the movement.

Most of the nation's 10 million blacks lived in the South as sharecroppers and tenant farmers in 1900. As devastating floods and the cotton boll weevil, which spread from Mexico in the 1890s, worsened their lot, many southern blacks left the land. By 1910 over 20 percent of the black population lived in cities, mostly in the South, but many in the North as well. Black men in the cities took jobs in factories, mines, docks, and railroads or became carpenters, plasterers, or bricklayers. Many black women became domestic servants, seamstresses,

or workers in laundries and tobacco factories. By 1910, 54 percent of America's black women held jobs.

Across the South, legally enforced racism peaked in the early twentieth century. Local "Jim Crow" laws segregated streetcars, schools, parks, and even cemeteries. The facilities for blacks, including the schools, were invariably inferior. Many southern cities imposed residential segregation by law until the Supreme Court restricted it in 1917. Most labor unions excluded black workers. Disfranchised and trapped in a cycle of poverty, poor education, and discrimination, southern blacks faced bleak prospects.

Fleeing poverty and racism and drawn by job opportunities, two hundred thousand blacks migrated North between 1890 and 1910. Wartime opportunities drew still more in 1917–1918 (see Chapter 22), and by 1920, 1.4 million African Americans lived in the North. They found conditions only slightly better than in the South. In northern cities, too, racism worsened after 1890 as hard times and immigration heightened social tensions. (Immigrants, competing with blacks for jobs and housing, sometimes exhibited the most intense racial preju-

dice.) Segregation, though not imposed by law, was enforced by custom and sometimes by violence. Blacks lived in run-down "colored districts," attended dilapidated schools, and worked at the lowest-paying jobs.

Their ballots—usually cast for the party of Lincoln—brought little political influence. The only black politicians tolerated by Republican politicians were those willing to distribute low-level patronage jobs and otherwise keep silent. African Americans in the segregated army faced hostility not only from white soldiers and officers, but also from civilians near the bases. Even the movies preached racism. D. W. Griffith's *The Birth of a Nation* (1915) disparaged blacks and glorified the Ku Klux Klan.

Smoldering racism sometimes exploded in violence. Antiblack rioters in Atlanta in 1906 murdered twenty-five blacks and burned many black homes. From 1900 to 1920 an average of about seventy-five lynchings occurred yearly. Some lynch mobs used trumped-up charges to justify the murder of blacks whose assertive behavior or economic aspirations angered whites. Some

lynchings involved incredible sadism: with large crowds on hand, the victim's body was mutilated, and graphic postcards were sold later. Authorities rarely intervened. At a 1916 lynching in Texas, the mayor warned the mob not to damage the hanging tree, since it was on city property.

In the face of such hostility, blacks developed strong social institutions and a vigorous culture. Black religious life, centered in the African Methodist Episcopal church, proved a bulwark of support. Working African-American women, drawing on strategies dating to slavery days, relied on relatives and neighbors to provide child care. Dedicated teachers and administrators at a handful of black higher-education institutions such as Fisk in Nashville and Howard in Washington, D.C., carried on against heavy odds. John Hope, a university-trained classics scholar who became president of Atlanta's Morehouse College in 1906, assembled a distinguished faculty, championed African-American education, and fought racial segregation. His sister Jane (Hope) Lyons was dean of women at Spelman College, another black institution in Atlanta.

The urban black community included several black-owned insurance companies and banks, a small elite of entrepreneurs, teachers, ministers, and sports figures like Jack Johnson. Although major-league baseball excluded blacks, a thriving Negro League attracted many black fans.

In this racist age, progressives compiled a mixed record on racial issues. Lillian Wald, director of New York's Henry Street Settlement, protested racial injustice. Muckraker Ray Stannard Baker documented racism in his 1908 book, *Following the Color Line*. Settlement-house worker Mary White Ovington helped found the National Association for the Advancement of Colored People (see below) and wrote *Half a Man* (1911) about the emotional scars of racism.

But most progressive kept silent as blacks were lynched, disfranchised, and discriminated against. Many saw African Americans, like immigrants, not as potential allies but as part of the problem. Viewing blacks as inferior and prone to immorality and social disorder, white progressives generally supported or tolerated segregated schools and housing, restrictions on black voting rights, the strict moral oversight of African-American communities, and, at best, paternalistic efforts to "uplift" this supposedly backward and childlike people. Viciously racist southern politicians like Governor James K. Vardaman of Mississippi and Senator Ben Tillman of South Carolina also supported progressive reforms. Southern woman-suffrage leaders argued that granting women the vote would strengthen white supremacy.

The Birth of a Nation (1912)

D. W. Griffith's epic film glorified the racist Ku Klux Klan. President Woodrow Wilson called it "history written with lightning."

BLACKS, WOMEN, AND WORKERS ORGANIZE

The organizational impulse so important to progressivism generally also proved a useful strategy for groups that found themselves discriminated against or exploited. African Americans, middle-class women, and wage workers all had ample reason for dissatisfaction in these years, and all three groups organized to address those grievances.

African-American Leaders Organize Against Racism

With racism on the rise, Booker T. Washington's accommodationist message (see Chapter 20) seemed increasingly unrealistic, particularly to educated northern blacks. In 1902 William Monroe Trotter, the editor of the *Boston Guardian*, a black newspaper, called Washington's go-slow policies "a fatal blow . . . to the Negro's political rights and liberty." Another opponent was black journalist Ida Wells-Barnett. Moving to Chicago from Memphis in 1892 after a white mob destroyed her offices, she mounted a national antilynching campaign, in contrast to Booker T. Washington's public silence on the subject. Washington's self-help theme would appeal to later generations of African Americans, but in the early twentieth century, many blacks confronting lynching, blatant racism, and rising segregationist pressures tired of his cautious approach.

Washington's most potent challenger was W. E. B. Du Bois (1868–1963). After earning a Ph.D. in history from Harvard in 1895, Du Bois taught at Atlanta University. Openly criticizing Washington in *The Souls of Black Folk* (1903), he rejected Washington's call for patience and his exclusive emphasis on manual skills. Instead, Du Bois demanded full racial equality, including the same educational opportunities open to whites, and called on blacks to resist all forms of racism.

Du Bois's militancy signaled a new era of African-American activism. In 1905, under his leadership, blacks who favored vigorous, sustained resistance to racism held a conference at Niagara Falls. For the next few years, participants in the "Niagara Movement" met annually. Meanwhile, a group of white reformers had also grown dissatisfied with Washington's cautiousness. Their leader was newspaper publisher Oswald Garrison Villard, grandson of abolitionist William Lloyd Garrison. In 1909 Villard and his allies, Du Bois, and other blacks from the Niagara Movement formed the National Association for the Advancement of Colored People (NAACP). This new organization called for vigorous activism, including legal challenges, to achieve political equality for blacks and full integration into American life. Attracting the urban black middle class, by 1914 the NAACP had six thousand members in fifty branches.

Revival of the Woman-Suffrage Movement

As late as 1910, women could vote in only four thinly populated western states: Wyoming, Utah, Colorado, and Idaho. Woman suffrage failed in six state referenda after 1896. But the progressive reform movement, in

A New Black Leadership
Ida Wells-Barnett, crusader against lynching, and W. E. B. Du Bois, outspoken critic of Booker T. Washington and author of the classic, *The Souls of Black Folk*. The challenge, wrote Du Bois, was to find a way "to be both a Negro and an American."

which women played a leading role, gave the cause fresh vitality. Middle-class women found disfranchisement especially galling when recently arrived immigrant men could vote. A vigorous suffrage movement in Great Britain reverberated in America as well. Like progressivism itself, this revived campaign started at the grass roots. A suffrage campaign in New York State in 1915, though unsuccessful, underscored the movement's new momentum.

So, too, did events in California. Indeed, the California campaign, as recounted by historian Gayle Gullett, illustrates both the strengths and the limitations of the revived movement. In the 1880s California's women's clubs focused mainly on cultural and domestic themes. By the early 1900s they had evolved into a potent statewide organization actively pursuing municipal reforms and public-school issues. This evolution convinced many members that full citizenship meant the right to vote. A state woman-suffrage referendum lost in 1896, but the leaders bounced back to form alliances with labor leaders and male progressives, built on a shared commitment to "good government" and

Election Day

Critics of the woman-suffrage movement, including this cartoonist, believed that women's place was in the home, not in the public sphere.

opposition to municipal corruption. But while joining forces with male reformers, these woman-suffrage strategists always insisted on the unique role of "organized womanhood" in building a better society. Success came in 1911 when California voters approved woman suffrage.

"Organized womanhood" had its limits. The California campaign was led by elite and middle-class women, mainly based in Los Angeles and San Francisco. Working-class women and farm women played little role in this campaign, while African-American, Mexican-American, and Asian-American women were almost totally excluded.

New leaders translated the momentum in California and other states into a revitalized national movement. When Susan B. Anthony retired from the presidency of the National American Woman Suffrage Association (NAWSA) in 1900, Carrie Chapman Catt of Iowa succeeded her. Under Catt's shrewd direction, NAWSA adopted the so-called Winning Plan: grass-roots organization with tight central coordination.

Suffragists shrewdly deployed techniques drawn from the new urban consumer culture. They not only lobbied legislators, but also organized parades in open cars; devised catchy slogans; ran newspaper ads; put up posters; waved eye-catching banners; held fundraisers; arranged photo opportunities for the media; and distributed fans, playing cards, and other items emblazoned with the suffrage message. Gradually, state after state fell into the suffrage column (see Map 21.1). A key victory came in 1917 when New York voters approved a woman-suffrage referendum.

As in California (and like progressive organizations generally), NAWSA's membership remained largely white, native born, and middle class. Few black, immigrant, or working-class women joined. Some upper-class women opposed the reform. The leader of the "Antis," the wealthy Josephine Dodge of New York, argued that women already had behind-the-scenes influence, and that to invade the male realm of electoral politics would tarnish their moral and spiritual role.

Not all suffragists accepted Catt's strategy. Alice Paul, who had observed the British suffragists' militant tactics while studying in England, grew impatient with NAWSA's state-by-state approach. In 1913 Paul founded the Congressional Union, later renamed the Woman's party, to pressure Congress to enact a woman-suffrage amendment. Targeting the "the party in power"—in this case, the Democrats—Paul and her followers picketed the White House round the clock in the war year of 1917 and posted large signs accusing President Wilson of

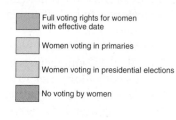

MAP 21.1
Woman Suffrage Before the Nineteenth Amendment
Beginning with Wyoming in 1869, woman suffrage made steady gains in western states before 1920. Farther east, key victories came in New York (1917) and Michigan (1918). But much of the East remained an anti-woman-suffrage bastion throughout the period.

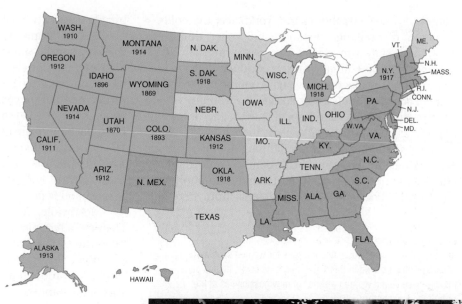

Full voting rights for women with effective date

Women voting in primaries

Women voting in presidential elections

No voting by women

hypocrisy in championing democracy abroad while opposing woman suffrage at home. Several protesters were jailed and, when they went on a hunger strike, force-fed. At both the state and federal level, the momentum of the organized woman-suffrage movement had become well-nigh irresistible.

Enlarging "Woman's Sphere"

As the careers of such women as Florence Kelley, Alice Hamilton, and Ida Wells-Barnett make clear, the suffrage cause did not exhaust women's energies in the Progressive era. Women's clubs, settlement-house residents, and individual female activists joined a wide range of reform efforts. These included the campaigns to bring playgrounds and day nurseries to the slums, abolish child labor, help women workers, and ban unsafe foods and quack remedies. As Jane Addams observed, the nurturing that women gave their own children could also draw them into broader political activism in an industrial age when hazards came from outside the home as well as inside.

Cultural assumptions about "woman's sphere" weakened as women became active on many fronts. Penologist Katherine Bement Davis served as the innovative superintendent of a woman's reformatory and then as New York City's commissioner of corrections. Anarchist Emma Goldman crisscrossed the country lecturing on politics, feminism, and modern drama while coediting a radical monthly, *Mother Earth*. A vanguard of pioneering women in higher education included Marion

Parading for Woman Suffrage
Suffrage leaders built support for the cause by using modern advertising and publicity techniques, including automobiles festooned with flags, bunting, banners, posters, and—in this case—smiling little girls.

Talbot, first dean of women at the University of Chicago.

In *Women and Economics* (1898) and other works, feminist intellectual Charlotte Perkins Gilman explored the historical and cultural roots of female subordination and gender stereotyping; and linked women's inferior status to their economic dependence on men. Confining women to the domestic sphere, Gilman argued, was an evolutionary throwback that had become outdated and inefficient. She advocated economic independence for

women through equality in the workplace; the collectivization of cooking, cleaning, and other domestic tasks; and state-run day-care centers. In the novel *Herland* (1915), Gilman wittily critiqued patriarchal assumptions by injecting three naïve young males into a utopian society populated exclusively by women.

No Progressive Era reform raised the issue of women's rights more directly than the campaign challenging federal and state laws banning the distribution of contraceptives and birth-control information. Although countless women, particularly the poor, suffered exhaustion and health problems from frequent

College Women

Athletics, the bicycle vogue, and colleges for women such as Wellesley, all portrayed in this 1898 magazine cover, helped give middle-class young women a sense of new possibilities at the turn of the last century.

pregnancies, artificial contraception was widely denounced as immoral. In 1914 Margaret Sanger of New York, a practical nurse and socialist whose mother had died after bearing eleven children, began her crusade for birth control, a term she coined. When the authorities prosecuted her journal *The Woman Rebel* on obscenity charges, Sanger fled to England. She returned in 1916 to open the nation's first birth-control clinic in Brooklyn. In 1918 she founded a new journal, the *Birth Control Review*, and three years later she founded the American Birth Control League, the ancestor of today's Planned Parenthood Federation.

Meanwhile, another New Yorker, Mary Ware Dennett, a feminist and activist, had also emerged as an advocate of birth control and sex education. (Her 1919 pamphlet for youth, *The Sex Side of Life*, discussing human reproduction in clear, straightforward terms, was long banned as obscene.) Dennett founded the National Birth Control League (later the Voluntary Parenthood League) in 1915. While Sanger championed direct action, Dennett urged lobbying efforts to amend obscenity laws. More importantly, while Sanger insisted that contraceptives should be supplied only by physicians, Dennett argued that they should be freely available. Sanger's inability to tolerate any other leaders in the movement made for bad relations between the two women.

In retrospect, the emergence of the birth-control movement stands as one of progressivism's most important and little-recognized legacies. At the time, however, it stirred bitter resistance among conservatives and many religious leaders. Indeed, not until 1965 did the Supreme Court fully legalize the dissemination of contraceptive materials and information.

Workers Organize; Socialism Advances

In this age of organization, labor unions continued to expand. The American Federation of Labor (AFL) grew from fewer than half a million members in 1897 to some 4 million by 1920. This was still only about 20 percent of the industrial work force. With recent immigrants hungry for jobs, union activities could be risky. The boss could always fire an "agitator" and hire a docile newcomer. Judicial hostility also plagued the movement. In the 1908 *Danbury Hatters* case, for example, the Supreme Court forbade unions from organizing boycotts in support of strikes. Such boycotts were a "conspiracy in restraint of trade," said the high court, and thus a violation of the Sherman Anti-Trust Act. The AFL's

strength remained in the skilled trades, not in the factories and mills where most immigrants and women worked.

A few unions did try to reach these laborers. The International Ladies' Garment Workers' Union (ILGWU), founded in 1900 by immigrants working in New York City's needle trades, conducted a successful strike in 1909 and another after the 1911 Triangle fire. The women on the picket lines found these strikes both exhilarating and frightening. Some were beaten by police; others fired. The 1909 strike began when young Clara Lemlich jumped up as speechmaking droned on at a protest rally and passionately called for a strike. Thousands of women garment workers stayed off the job the next day. Through such strikes, workers gained better wages and improved working conditions.

Another union that targeted the most exploited workers was the Industrial Workers of the World (IWW), nicknamed the Wobblies, founded in Chicago in 1905. The IWW's colorful leader was William "Big Bill" Haywood, a compelling orator. Utah-born Haywood became a miner as a boy and joined the militant Western Federation of Miners in 1896. In 1905 he was acquitted of complicity in the assassination of an antilabor former governor of Idaho. IWW membership peaked at around thirty thousand, and most members were western miners, lumbermen, fruit pickers, and itinerant laborers. But it captured the imagination of young cultural rebels in New York City's Greenwich Village, where Haywood often visited.

The IWW led mass strikes of Nevada gold miners; Minnesota iron miners; and timber workers in Louisiana, Texas, and the Northwest. Its greatest success came in 1912 when it won a bitter textile strike in Massachusetts. This victory owed much to two women: the birth-control reformer Margaret Sanger, and Elizabeth Gurley Flynn, a fiery Irish-American orator who publicized the cause by sending strikers' children to sympathizers in New York City for temporary care. Although the IWW's reputation for violence was much exaggerated, it faced government harassment, especially during World War I, and by 1920 its strength was broken.

Other workers, as well as some middle-class Americans, turned to socialism. All socialists advocated an end to capitalism and backed public ownership of factories, utilities, railroads, and communications systems, but they differed on how to achieve these goals. The revolutionary ideology of German social theorist Karl Marx won a few converts, but the vision of democratic socialism achieved at the ballot box proved more appealing. In 1900 democratic socialists formed the Socialist Party of America (SPA). Members included Morris Hillquit, a New York City labor organizer; Victor Berger, the leader of Milwaukee's German socialists; and Eugene V. Debs, the Indiana labor leader. Debs, a popular orator, was the SPA's presidential candidate five times

IWW Journalism
On April 28, 1917, three weeks after the United States entered World War I, the IWW periodical *Solidarity* pictured a heroic IWW worker battling against an array of evils, including "militarism."

Eugene V. Debs (1855–1926)
The much-beloved, much-reviled Socialist leader speaks in Canton, Ohio, in 1918, shortly before he was jailed for his opposition to U.S. intervention in World War I.

***The Masses*, 1912**
This socialist publication edited in New York's Greenwich Village denounced the abuses of capitalism, including child labor.

between 1900 and 1920. Many cultural radicals of New York's Greenwich Village embraced socialism as well and supported the radical magazine *The Masses*, founded in 1911.

Socialism's high-water mark came around 1912 when SPA membership stood at 118,000. Debs won more than 900,000 votes for president that year (about 6 percent of the total), and the Socialists elected a congressman (Berger) and hundreds of municipal officials. The Intercollegiate Socialist Society carried the message to college campuses. The party published over three hundred daily and weekly newspapers, many in foreign languages for immigrant members.

NATIONAL PROGRESSIVISM PHASE I: ROOSEVELT AND TAFT, 1901–1913

By around 1905 local and state reform activities were coalescing into a national movement. Symbolically, in 1906 Wisconsin governor Robert La Follette went to Washington as a U.S. senator. Five years earlier, progressivism had found its first national leader, Theodore Roosevelt, nicknamed "TR".

Bombastic, self-righteous, and jingoistic—but also brilliant, politically savvy, and endlessly interesting—Roosevelt became president in 1901 and at once made the White House a cauldron of activism. Skillfully orchestrating public opinion, the popular young president pursued his goals—labor mediation, consumer protection, conservation, business virtue, and engage-

ment abroad (see Chapter 20)—while embracing and publicizing progressives' ideas and objectives.

Roosevelt's activist approach to the presidency permanently enlarged the powers of the office. TR's handpicked successor, William Howard Taft, lacked the master's political genius, however, and his administration floundered amid sniping among former allies.

In the exciting election of 1912, voters faced a choice among four major presidential candidates: the conservative Taft; the socialist Eugene V. Debs; Theodore Roosevelt; and political newcomer Woodrow Wilson, who offered differing visions of progressive reform.

Roosevelt's Path to the White House

On September 6, 1901, in Buffalo, anarchist Leon Czolgosz shot William McKinley. At first the president seemed likely to recover, and Vice President Theodore Roosevelt proceeded with a hiking trip in New York's Adirondack Mountains. But on September 14, McKinley died. At age forty-two, Theodore Roosevelt became president of the United States.

Many politicians shuddered at the thought of the impetuous Roosevelt as president. Republican kingmaker Mark Hanna exclaimed, "My God, that damned cowboy in the White House!" Roosevelt did, indeed, display many traits associated with the West. The son of an aristocratic New York family of Dutch origins, he was sickly as a child. But a bodybuilding program and summers in Wyoming transformed him into a model of physical fitness. When his young wife died in 1884, he stoically carried on. Two years on a Dakota ranch (1884–1886) further toughened him and deepened his enthusiasm for what he termed "the strenuous life."

Plunging into politics at a time when his social peers considered it unfit for gentlemen, he served as a state assemblyman, New York City police commissioner, and a U.S. civil-service commissioner. In 1898, fresh from his Cuban exploits (see Chapter 20), he was elected New York's governor. Two years later, the state's Republican boss, eager to be rid of him, arranged for Roosevelt's nomination as vice president.

As was the case with everything he did, TR found the presidency energizing. "I have been President emphatically . . . ," he boasted; "I believe in a strong executive." He enjoyed public life and loved the limelight. "When Theodore attends a wedding he wants to be the bride," his daughter observed, "and when he attends a funeral he wants to be the corpse." With his toothy grin, machine-gun speech, and amazing energy, he dominat-

ed the political landscape. When he refused to shoot a bear cub on a hunting trip, a shrewd toy maker marketed a cuddly new product, the Teddy Bear.

Labor Disputes, Trustbusting, Railroad Regulation

The new president's political skills were quickly tested. In May 1902 the United Mine Workers Union (UMW) called a strike to gain not only higher wages and shorter hours but also recognition as a union. The mine owners refused even to talk with the UMW leaders. After five months, with winter looming, TR acted. Summoning the two sides to the White House and threatening to take over the mines, he won their reluctant acceptance of an arbitration commission to settle the dispute. The commission granted the miners a 10 percent wage increase and reduced their working day from ten to nine hours.

TR's approach to labor disputes differed from that of his predecessors, who typically sided with management, sometimes using troops as strikebreakers. Though not consistently prolabor, he defended workers' right to organize. When a mine owner insisted that the miners' welfare be left to those "to whom God in his infinite wisdom has given control of the property interests of the country," Roosevelt derided such "arrogant stupidity."

With his elite background, TR neither feared nor much liked business tycoons. The prospect of spending time with "big-money men," he once wrote a friend, "fills me with frank horror." While he believed that big corporations contributed to national greatness, he also embraced the progressive conviction that business behavior must be regulated. A strict moralist, he held corporations, like individuals, to a high standard.

At the same time, Roosevelt the political realist also understood that many Washington politicians abhorred his views—among them Senator Nelson Aldrich of Rhode Island, a wily defender of business interests. Roosevelt's progressive impulses and his grasp of power realities in capitalist America remained in continuing tension.

Another test of Roosevelt's political skill came in 1901 when J. P. Morgan formed the United States Steel Company, the nation's first billion-dollar corporation. As public distrust of big corporations deepened, TR dashed to the head of the parade. His 1902 State of the Union message gave high priority to breaking up business monopolies, or "trustbusting." Roosevelt's attorney general soon filed suit against the Northern Securities Company, a giant holding company that had recently

been formed to control railroading in the Northwest, for violating the Sherman Anti-Trust Act of 1890—a law that hitherto had seemed pathetically ineffective. On a speaking tour that summer, TR called for a "square deal" for all Americans and denounced special treatment for capitalists. "We don't wish to destroy corporations," he said, "but we do wish to make them . . . serve the public good." In 1904, on a 5 to 4 vote, the Supreme Court ordered the Northern Securities Company dissolved.

The Roosevelt administration filed forty-three other antitrust lawsuits. In two key cases decided in 1911, the Supreme Court ordered the breakup of the Standard Oil Company and the reorganization of the American Tobacco Company to make it less monopolistic.

As the 1904 election neared, Roosevelt made peace with his party's business wing, writing cordial letters to J. P. Morgan and other magnates. When the convention that unanimously nominated Roosevelt in Chicago adopted a probusiness platform, $2 million in corporate contributions poured in. The Democrats, meanwhile, eager to erase the taint of radicalism, embraced the gold standard and nominated a conservative New York judge, Alton B. Parker.

Winning easily, Roosevelt turned to one of his major goals: railroad regulation. He now saw corporate regulation as a more promising long-term strategy than antitrust lawsuits. This shift underlay his central role in the passage of the Hepburn Act of 1906. This measure empowered the Interstate Commerce Commission to set maximum railroad rates and to examine railroads' financial records. It also curtailed the railroads' practice of distributing free passes to ministers and other influential shapers of public opinion.

The Hepburn Act displayed TR's knack for political bargaining, as he skillfully fenced with Senator Aldrich and other conservatives. In one key compromise, he agreed to delay tariff reform in return for railroad regulations. Although the Hepburn Act did not fully satisfy reformers, it did significantly increase the government's regulatory powers.

Consumer Protection and Racial Issues

No progressive reform proved more popular than the campaign against unsafe and falsely labeled food, drugs, and medicine. Upton Sinclair's *The Jungle* (1906) graphically described the foul conditions in some meatpacking plants. Wrote Sinclair in one vivid passage, "[A] man could run his hand over these piles of meat and sweep off handfuls of dried dung of rats. These rats were nui-

sances, and the packers would put poisoned bread out for them, they would die, and then rats, bread, and meat would go into the hoppers together." (The socialist Sinclair also detailed the exploitation of immigrant workers, but this message proved less potent. "I aimed at the nation's heart, but hit it in the stomach," he later lamented.) Women's organizations and consumer groups rallied public opinion on this issue, and an Agriculture Department chemist, Harvey W. Wiley, helped shape the proposed legislation. Other muckrakers exposed useless or dangerous patent medicines, many laced with cocaine, opium, or alcohol. One tonic "for treatment of the alcohol habit" contained 26.5 percent alcohol. Peddlers of these nostrums freely claimed that they could cure cancer, grow hair, and restore sexual vigor.

Sensing the public mood, Roosevelt supported the Pure Food and Drug Act and the Meat Inspection Act, both passed in 1906. The former outlawed the sale of adulterated foods or drugs and required accurate ingredient labels; the latter imposed strict sanitary rules on meatpackers and set up a federal meat-inspection system. The more reputable food-processing, meatpacking, and medicinal companies, eager to regain public confidence, supported these regulatory measures.

On racial matters, Roosevelt's record was marginally better than that of other politicians in this dismally racist age. He appointed a black to head the Charleston customhouse despite white opposition, and closed a Mississippi post office rather than yield to demands that he dismiss the black postmistress. In a symbolically important gesture, he dined with Booker T. Washington at the White House. The worst blot on his record came in 1906 when he approved the dishonorable discharge of an entire regiment of black soldiers, including Congressional Medal of Honor winners, in Brownsville, Texas, because some members of the unit, goaded by racist taunts, had killed a local civilian. The "Brownsville Incident" incensed black Americans. (In 1972, when most of the men were long dead, Congress removed the dishonorable discharges from their records.)

Environmentalism Progressive-Style

With Theodore Roosevelt in the White House, environmental concerns ranked high on the national agenda. Singling out conservation in his first State of the Union message as "the most vital internal question" facing America, he highlighted an issue that still reverberates.

By 1900 decades of urban-industrial growth and western expansion had taken a heavy toll on the land. In

the West, land-use disputes raged as mining and timber interests, farmers, ranchers, sheep growers, and preservationists advanced competing claims.

While business interests and boosters preached exploitation of the West's resources and agricultural groups sought government aid for irrigation projects, organizations such as the Sierra Club battled to preserve the unspoiled beauty of wilderness areas. Socially prominent easterners also embraced the wilderness cause. Under an act passed by Congress in 1891, Presidents Harrison and Cleveland had set aside some 35 million acres of public lands as national forests.

In the early twentieth century, a wilderness vogue swept America. Amid cities and factories, the wilderness promised tranquillity and solace. As Sierra Club president John Muir observed, "I never saw a discontented tree." Popular writers evoked the tang of the campfire and the lure of the primitive. Summer camps, which began in the 1890s, as well as the Boy Scouts (founded in 1910) and Girl Scouts (1912), gave city children a taste of wilderness living.

Between the wilderness enthusiasts and the developers stood government professionals like Gifford Pinchot who saw the public domain as a resource to be managed wisely. Appointed by President Roosevelt in 1905 to head the new U.S. Forest Service, Pinchot stressed not preservation but conservation—the planned, regulated use of forest lands for public and commercial purposes.

Wilderness advocates viewed Pinchot's Forest Service warily. They welcomed his opposition to mindless exploitation but worried that the multiple-use approach would despoil wilderness areas. As a Sierra Club member wrote, "It is true that trees are for human use. But there are . . . uses for the spiritual wealth of us all, as well as for the material wealth of some." Conservationists, in turn, dismissed the wilderness advocates as hopeless romantics.

By temperament Theodore Roosevelt was a preservationist. In 1903 he spent a blissful few days camping in Yosemite National Park with John Muir. He once compared "the destruction of a species" to the loss of "all the works of some great writer." But TR the politician backed the conservationists' call for planned development. He supported the National Reclamation Act of 1902 that designated the money from public-land sales for water management in arid western regions, and set up the Reclamation Service to plan and construct dams and irrigation projects.

As historian William Cronon notes, this measure (also known as the Newlands Act for its sponsor, a Nevada congressman) ranks in importance with the Northwest Ordinance of 1787 for promoting the development of a vast continental region. Under director Frederick Newell, the Reclamation Service undertook projects that sped settlement and productivity between the Rockies and the Pacific. The Roosevelt Dam in Arizona spurred the growth of Phoenix, and a complex of dams and waterways in the Snake River valley watered thousands of barren acres in Idaho, stimulating the production of potatoes and other commodities. The law required farmers who benefited from these projects to repay the construction costs, creating a revolving federal fund for further projects. The Newlands Act and other measures of these years helped transform the West from a series of isolated "island settlements" into a thriving, interconnected region.

TR and Gifford Pinchot
The two friends and allies in the conservation cause aboard the steamboat *Mississippi* on a 1907 tour with the Inland Waterways Commission.

The competition for scarce water resources in the West sometimes led to bitter political battles. The Los Angeles basin, for example, with 40 percent of California's population in 1900, found itself with only 2 percent of the state's available surface water. In 1907 the city derailed a Reclamation Service project intended for the farmers of California's Owens Valley, more than 230 miles to the north, and diverted the precious water to Los Angeles.

Meanwhile, President Roosevelt, embracing Pinchot's multiple-use land-management program, set aside 200 million acres of public land (85 million of them in Alaska) as national forests, mineral reserves, and water-power sites. But this, too, provoked opposition in the West, and in 1907 Congress revoked the president's authority to create national forests in six timber-rich western states. Roosevelt signed the bill, but only after he had designated 16 million acres in the six states as national forests.

With Roosevelt's blessing, Pinchot organized a White House conservation conference for the nation's governors in 1908. There experts discussed the utilitarian benefits of resource management. John Muir and other wilderness preservationists were not invited. But the struggle between wilderness purists and multiple-use advocates went on (see A Place in Time: Hetch Hetchy Valley, California). Rallying support through magazine articles, preservationists won key victories. For example, campaigns by private groups, including women's organizations, saved a large grove of California's giant redwoods and a lovely stretch of the Maine coastline from logging.

While expanding the national forests, TR also created fifty-three wildlife reserves, sixteen national monuments, and five new national parks. As the parks drew more visitors, Congress created the National Park Service in 1916 to manage them. Earlier, the Antiquities Act (1906) had protected archaeological sites, especially in the Southwest, some of which eventually became national parks.

Taft in the White House, 1909–1913

Roosevelt had pledged not to run for a third term, and to the sorrow of millions, he kept his promise as the 1908 election approached. The Republican party's most conservative elements easily regained party control. They nominated TR's choice, Secretary of War William Howard Taft, for president but chose a conservative vice-presidential nominee. The party platform, influenced by the National Association of Manufacturers, was deeply conservative. The Democrats, meanwhile, nominated William Jennings Bryan for a third and final time. The Democratic platform called for a lower tariff, denounced the trusts, and embraced the cause of labor.

With Roosevelt's endorsement, Taft coasted to victory. But the Democrats made gains—Bryan bested Alton B. Parker's 1904 vote total by 1.3 million—and progressive Republican state candidates outran the national ticket. Overall, the outcome suggested a lull in the reform movement, not its end.

Republican conservatives, increasingly unhappy with Roosevelt's policies, were delighted when he departed to hunt big game in Africa. Quipped Senator Aldrich, "Let every lion do its duty." But even with TR an ocean away, his presence remained vivid. "When I am addressed as 'Mr. President,' " Taft wrote him, "I turn to see whether you are not at my elbow."

Taft, from an old political family in Cincinnati, was no Roosevelt. Whereas TR kept in fighting trim, the sedentary Taft was obese. Roosevelt had set up a boxing ring in the White House; Taft preferred golf. TR loved speechmaking and battling the forces of evil; Taft disliked controversy. His happiest days would come later, as chief justice of the United States.

Pledged to carry on TR's program, Taft supported the Mann-Elkins Act (1910), which beefed up the Interstate Commerce Commission's rate-setting powers and extended its regulatory authority to telephone and telegraph companies. The Taft administration actually prosecuted more antitrust cases than had Roosevelt. But Taft characteristically proceeded without much publicity; and to the public TR remained the mighty trustbuster.

The reform spotlight, meanwhile, shifted from the White House to Congress. During the Roosevelt administration, a small group of reform-minded Republicans nicknamed the Insurgents, who included Senators La Follette and Albert Beveridge of Indiana and Congressman George Norris of Nebraska, had challenged their party's conservative congressional leadership. In 1909 the Insurgents turned against President Taft after a bruising battle over the tariff.

Taft at first backed the Insurgents' call for a lower tariff. But in 1909, when high-tariff advocates in Congress pushed through the Payne-Aldrich Tariff, raising duties on hundreds of items, Taft not only signed it but praised it extravagantly. The battle between conservative and progressive Republicans was on.

A major Insurgent target was Speaker of the House Joseph G. Cannon of Illinois. Wielding near-absolute power, the arch-conservative Cannon kept most reform bills from even reaching a vote. In March 1910 the Insurgents joined with the Democrats to remove Cannon from the pivotal Rules Committee. This was a direct slap at Taft, who supported Cannon.

The so-called Ballinger-Pinchot affair widened the rift between Taft and the progressive Republicans. Taft's interior secretary, Richard Ballinger, was a Seattle lawyer who disliked federal controls and favored the private development of natural resources. In one of several decisions galling to conservationists, Ballinger approved the sale of several million acres of public lands in Alaska containing coal deposits to a group of Seattle businessmen in 1909. They in turn sold the land to a consortium of New York bankers including J. P. Morgan. When a Department of the Interior official protested, he was fired. In true muckraking style, he immediately published an article in *Collier's* blasting Ballinger's actions. When Gifford Pinchot of the Forestry Service publicly criticized Ballinger, he too got the ax. TR's supporters seethed.

Upon Roosevelt's return to America in June 1910, Pinchot met the boat. In the 1910 midterm election, Roosevelt campaigned for Insurgent candidates. In a speech that alarmed conservatives, he attacked judges who struck down progressive laws and endorsed the radical idea of reversing judicial rulings by popular vote. Borrowing a term from Herbert Croly's *The Promise of American Life*, TR proposed a "New Nationalism" that would powerfully engage the federal government in reform.

The Democrats captured the House in 1910, and a coalition of Democrats and Insurgent Republicans controlled the Senate. As the reform tide rose, TR sounded more and more like a presidential candidate.

The Four-Way Election of 1912

In February 1912 Roosevelt announced his candidacy for the Republican nomination, openly opposing Taft. But Taft wanted a second term, and a Republican battle loomed. For a time, Senator Robert La Follette's candidacy attracted reform-minded Republicans, but when TR entered the race, La Follette's support collapsed.

In a series of Republican state primaries and conventions, Roosevelt generally walloped Taft. But Taft controlled the party machinery, and the Republican convention in Chicago disqualified many of Roosevelt's hard-won delegates. Outraged, TR's backers bolted the

convention and reassembled to form the Progressive party. What had been a general term for a broad reform movement became the official name of a political organization.

"I feel fit as a bull moose," Roosevelt trumpeted, thereby giving his organization its nickname, the Bull Moose party. Riding an emotional high, the cheering delegates nominated their hero and designated California senator Hiram Johnson as his running mate. The convention platform endorsed practically every reform cause of the day, including tariff reduction, woman suffrage, business regulation, the abolition of child labor, the eight-hour workday, workers' compensation, the direct primary, and the popular election of senators. The new party attracted a highly diverse following, united in admiration for the charismatic Roosevelt.

Meanwhile, the reform spirit had also infused the Democratic party at the local and state levels. In New Jersey in 1910, voters had elected a political novice, Woodrow Wilson, as governor. A "Wilson for President" boom soon arose, and when the Democrats assembled in Baltimore in June 1912, Wilson won the nomination, defeating several established party leaders

In the campaign, Taft more or less gave up, happy to have kept his party safe for conservatism. The Socialist party candidate Eugene Debs proposed an end to

Woodrow Wilson and William Howard Taft
Having just squared off in the 1912 election campaign, the two politicians share a light moment before Wilson's inauguration on March 4, 1913.

In 1900 one of the loveliest spots in California was Hetch Hetchy Valley, where glaciers and the Tuolumne River had carved deep, sharp-edged gorges of spectacular beauty. The Indian name referred to the Valley's grassy meadows. But when officials of San Francisco, 150 miles away, visited Hetch Hetchy, they saw a solution to their city's water problems. A dam at the valley's mouth would create a vast reservoir that could supply water for San Francisco and pay for itself as a hydroelectric power source.

Because Hetch Hetchy was in Yosemite National Park, the secretary of the interior at first rejected San Francisco's application to dam the Tuolumne. But the city applied again in 1908, two years after an earthquake and fire had devastated San Francisco, and this time the secretary approved. The application needed congressional approval as well, and opponents of the plan confidently geared up to defeat it.

The Sierra Club and its president, John Muir, led the opposition. Muir and his associates alerted wilderness groups across the nation and published magazine articles describing the beauty of the valley that would be forever hidden under the waters of the reservoir.

Muir compared flooding Hetch Hetchy to the willful destruction of a great cathedral. Amid rampant urban growth, he argued, Americans needed wilderness for their spiritual well-being. He wrote bitterly, "These temple destroyers, devotees of ravaging commercialism, seem to have a perfect contempt for Nature, and instead of lifting their eyes to the God of the Mountains, lift them to the Almighty Dollar."

But the project had attracted powerful backers, including Gifford Pinchot, head of the U.S. Forest Service, who advocated a multiple-use approach to national forests and wilderness areas. San Francisco

authorities also pushed hard for the plan. The reservoir, they argued, could support a variety of recreational activities. The *San Francisco Chronicle* called the dam's critics "hoggish and mushy esthetes." San Francisco's chief engineer ridiculed them as "short-haired women and long-haired men."

At first President Theodore Roosevelt endorsed the plan. As opposition grew he vacillated. In the national parks, he said in 1908, "all wild things should be protected and the scenery kept wholly unmarred."

The battle culminated in 1913 with hearings before the Public Lands Committee of the U.S. House of Representatives. Opponents rallied public opinion through more magazine articles; backers lobbied members of Congress. Pinchot, testifying in support of the application, offered his own utilitarian definition of conservation: "The fundamental principle . . . is that of use,

John Muir in Hetch Hetchy Valley, 1895

by Gilbert Dellinger, 1963. This painting based on a photograph, portrays the influential mature writer and Sierra Club president in the valley he loved and fought unsuccessfully to save.

to take every part of the land and its resources and put it to that use . . . which . . . will serve the most people." A California congressman pointed out that the "old barren rocks" of Hetch Hetchy Valley had a market value of only about three hundred thousand dollars, whereas the proposed dam would be worth many times that amount. Another legislator posed the issue in dramatic terms, "We all love the sound of whispering winds amid the trees," he said, but "the wail of a hungry baby will make us forget it."

Late in 1913, both houses of Congress passed the Hetch Hetchy dam bill by large margins. Within a year John Muir was dead of pneumonia. Some said he had died of a broken heart.

The dam project proceeded slowly, at twice the estimated cost. The first water reached San Francisco in 1934. The vision of Hetch Hetchy reservoir as a vacation paradise remained unfulfilled. Writes environmental historian Stephen Fox, "As the water level rose and fell with the changing seasons the shoreline was marred by slimy mud and decaying vegetation. Nothing could grow at the edge of the artificial lake. Under moonlight, with tree trunks scattered around like so many bodies, it resembled a battlefield one day after the fight: a wasteland bearing stark testimony to man's befuddled ingenuity."

Although the dam's opponents lost this battle, historians point out that the struggle had a larger meaning. For the first time, over a five-year period, the American public debated the aesthetic implications of a major public-works project. In the nineteenth century such a debate would have been unthinkable. Hetch Hetchy helped put wilderness preservation on the public agenda.

The battle also underscored tensions in Progressive Era environmental thought. Both sides considered themselves progressives, but while one group fought for wilderness preservation, the other advocated the "wise use" of natural resources for human purposes.

Hetch Hetchy retains its power to stir emotions. In 1987 Secretary of the Interior Donald Hodel proposed draining the reservoir and restoring the valley to its natural state. This, Hodel said, would relieve overcrowding in nearby Yosemite Valley. While environmentalists expressed interest, San Francisco officials reacted with the same outrage their predecessors had shown seventy-five years before. Meanwhile, Hetch Hetchy Valley lies under three hundred feet of water, submerged but not forgotten.

Hetch Hetchy: From the Sublime to the Utilitarian

California's lovely Hetch Hetchy Valley was a favorite subject of nineteenth-century artists, as this romantic painting by Albert Bierstadt, dating from the 1870s, reveals. When the Tuolumne River was dammed to create a reservoir for San Francisco, only the mountainous peaks above the waterline stood, silent reminders of the wild grandeur that had been sacrificed.

MAP 21.2
The Election of 1912

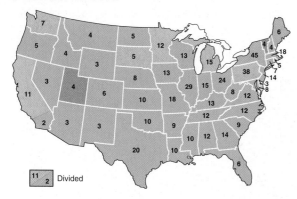

		Electoral Vote	Popular Vote	Percentage of Popular Vote
Democratic Woodrow Wilson		435	6,296,547	41.9
Progressive (Bull Moose) Theodore Roosevelt		88	4,118,571	27.4
Republican William H. Taft		8	3,486,720	23.2
Socialist Eugene V. Debs		–	900,672	6.1

capitalism and a socialized economic order. Roosevelt and Wilson offered less radical prescriptions. TR preached his New Nationalism. The new corporate order was here to stay, he acknowledged, but big business must be strictly regulated in the public interest. The welfare of workers and consumers should be safeguarded, and the environment protected.

Wilson, by contrast, called his political vision the "New Freedom." Warning that the new corporate order was choking off opportunity for ordinary Americans, he nostalgically evoked an era of small government, small businesses, and free competition. "The history of liberty," he said, "is the history of the limitation of governmental power, not the increase of it."

Roosevelt garnered 630,000 more votes than Taft, but the divided Republicans proved no match for the united Democrats (see Map 21.2). Wilson won the presidency, and the Democrats also took both houses of Congress. More than 900,000 voters opted for Debs and socialism.

The 1912 election linked the Democrats firmly with reform (except on the issue of race)—a link on which Franklin D. Roosevelt would build in the 1930s. The breakaway Progressive party demonstrated the strength of the reform impulse among grass-roots Republicans while leaving the national party itself in the grip of conservatives.

NATIONAL PROGRESSIVISM PHASE II: WOODROW WILSON, 1913–1917

The son and grandson of Presbyterian ministers, Wilson grew up in southern towns in a churchly atmosphere that shaped his oratorical style and moral outlook. Although slow in school (probably because of the learning disorder dyslexia), Wilson graduated from Princeton and earned a Ph.D. in political science from Johns Hopkins. He taught at Princeton and became its president in 1902. He lost support because of an unwillingness to compromise, and in 1910 left the academic world to enter politics. Three years later he was president of the United States.

Impressive in bearing, with piercing gray eyes, Wilson was an eloquent orator. But the idealism that inspired people could also alienate them. At his best, he excelled at political dealmaking. "He can walk on dead leaves and make no more noise than a tiger," declared one awed politician. But he could also retreat into a fortress of absolute certitude that tolerated no opposition. During his years as president, all these facets of his personality would come into play.

In his first term, Wilson played a key leadership role as Congress enacted an array of reform measures. Despite the nostalgia for simpler times evoked in some of his campaign speeches, he proved ready to use government to address the problems of the new corporate order. Under Wilson, the national progressive movement gained powerful new momentum (see Table 21.2).

Tariff and Banking Reform

Tariff reform—long a goal of southern and agrarian Democrats—headed Wilson's agenda. Breaking a precedent dating from Thomas Jefferson's presidency, on April 8, 1913, Wilson appeared before Congress in person to read his tariff message. A low-tariff bill quickly passed the House but bogged down in the Senate. Showing his flair for drama, Wilson denounced the tariff lobbyists flooding into Washington. His censure led to a Senate investigation of lobbyists and of senators who profited from high tariffs. Stung by the publicity, the Senate slashed tariff rates even more than the House had done. The Underwood-Simmons Tariff reduced rates an average of 15 percent.

In June 1913 Wilson addressed Congress again, this time to call for banking and currency reform. The

TABLE 21.2   **Progressive Era Legislation, Court Rulings, and Constitutional Amendments**

Legislation

	Act	Provisions
1902	National Reclamation Act	Funded dams and irrigation projects in the West.
1906	Hepburn Act	Regulates railroad rates and other practices.
	Pure Food and Drug Act	Imposes strict labeling requirements for food processors and pharmaceutical companies.
	Meat Inspection Act	Requires federal inspection of packinghouses.
	Antiquities Act	Protects archeological sites in Southwest.
1909	Payne-Aldrich Tariff	Raises tariffs, deepens Republican split.
1910	Mann Act	Antiprostitution measure; prohibits transporting a woman across state lines for "immoral purposes."
	Mann-Elkins Act	Strengthens powers of Interstate Commerce Commission.
1913	Underwood-Simmons Tariff	Lowers tariff rates; Wilson plays key role.
	Federal Reserve Act	Restructures U.S. money and banking system.
1914	Federal Trade Commission Act	Creates FTC as federal watchdog agency over corporations.
	Clayton Antitrust Act	Specifies illegal business practices.
	Narcotics Act	Forbids distribution of addictive drugs except by physicians and pharmacists.
1916	Federal Farm Loan Act	Enables farmers to secure low-interest federal loans.
	Keating-Owen Act	Bans products manufactured by child labor from interstate commerce.
	Adamson Act	Establishes eight-hour workday for interstate railway workers.
	Workmen's Compensation Act	Provides accident and injury projection for federal workers.

Court Rulings

	Court Case	Significance
1904	*Northern Securities* case	Supreme Court upholds antitrust suit against Northern Securities Company, a railroad conglomerate.
1906	*Lochner* v. *New York*	Supreme Court overturns New York law setting maximum working hours for bakery workers.
1908	*Muller* v. *Oregon*	Supreme Court upholds Oregon law setting maximum working hours for female laundry workers.
1911	*Standard Oil Co.* v. *U.S.*	Supreme Court orders dissolution of Standard Oil.
1927	*Buck* v. *Bell*	Supreme Court upholds Virginia sterilization law.

Constitutional Amendments

	Amendment	Provisions
1913	Sixteenth Amendment	Gives Congress authority to impose income tax.
	Seventeenth Amendment	Requires the direct election of U.S. senators by voters.
1919	Eighteenth Amendment	Prohibits the manufacture and sale of intoxicating liquors.
1920	Nineteenth Amendment	Grants women the vote.

nation's banking system clearly needed overhauling. Totally decentralized, it lacked a strong central institution, a "lender of last resort" to help banks survive fiscal crises. The Panic of 1907, when many banks had failed, remained a vivid memory.

But no consensus existed on specifics. Many reformers wanted a publicly controlled central banking system. But the nation's bankers, whose Senate spokesman was Nelson Aldrich, favored a privately controlled central bank similar to the Bank of England. The large banks of New York City advocated a strong central bank, preferably privately owned, so they could better compete with London banks in international finance. Others, including influential Virginia congressman Carter Glass, opposed any central banking authority, public or private.

No banking expert, Wilson listened to all sides. He did insist that the monetary system ultimately be publicly controlled. As the bargaining went on, Wilson played a crucial behind-the-scenes role. The result was the Federal Reserve Act of December 1913. A compromise measure, this law created twelve regional Federal Reserve banks under mixed public and private control. Each regional bank could issue U.S. dollars, called Federal Reserve notes, to the banks in its district to make loans to corporations and individual borrowers. Overall control of the system was assigned to the heads of the twelve regional banks and a Washington-based Federal Reserve Board (FRB), whose members were appointed by the president for fourteen-year-terms. (The secretary of the Treasury and the comptroller of the currency were made ex officio members.)

The Federal Reserve Act stands as Wilson's greatest legislative achievement. Initially, the Federal Reserve's authority was diffuse, but eventually the FRB, nicknamed "the Fed," grew into the strong central monetary institution it remains today, adopting fiscal policies to prevent financial panics, promote economic growth, and dampen inflationary pressures.

Regulating Business; Aiding Workers and Farmers

In 1914 Wilson and Congress turned to that perennial progressive cause, business regulation. Two key laws were the result: the Federal Trade Commission Act and the Clayton Antitrust Act. Though both sought a common goal, they embodied significantly different approaches.

The Federal Trade Commission Act took an administrative approach. This law created a new "watchdog" agency, the Federal Trade Commission (FTC), with power to investigate suspected violations of federal regulations, require regular reports from corporations, and issue cease-and-desist orders (subject to judicial review) when it found unfair methods of competition.

The Clayton Antitrust Act, by contrast, took a legal approach. It listed specific corporate activities that could lead to federal lawsuits. The Sherman Act of 1890, although outlawing business practices in restraint of trade, had been vague about details. The Clayton Act spelled out a series of illegal practices, such as selling at a loss to undercut competitors.

Because some of the watchdogs Wilson appointed to the FTC were conservatives with big-business links, this agency proved ineffective. But under the Clayton Act, the Wilson administration filed antitrust suits against nearly a hundred corporations.

Leading a party historically identified with workers, Wilson supported the American Federation of Labor and defended workers' right to organize. He also endorsed a Clayton Act clause exempting strikes, boycotts, and picketing from the antitrust laws' prohibition of actions in restraint of trade.

In 1916 (a campaign year) Wilson and congressional Democrats enacted three important worker-protection laws. The Keating-Owen Act barred from interstate commerce products manufactured by child labor. (This law was declared unconstitutional in 1918, as was a similar law enacted in 1919.) The Adamson Act established an eight-hour day for interstate railway workers. The Workmen's Compensation Act provided accident and injury protection to federal workers.

Other 1916 laws helped farmers. The Federal Farm Loan Act and the Federal Warehouse Act enabled farmers, using land or crops as security, to get low-interest federal loans. The Federal Highway Act, providing matching funds for state highway programs, benefited not only the new automobile industry but also farmers plagued by bad roads.

Like many progressives, Wilson's sympathies for the underdog stopped at the color line. A Virginia native reared in Georgia, he displayed a patronizing attitude toward blacks, praised the racist movie *The Birth of a Nation*, and allowed southerners in his cabinet and in Congress (some of them powerful committee chairmen) to impose rigid segregation on all levels of the government.

Progressivism and the Constitution

The probusiness bias of the courts in the late nineteenth century softened a bit in the Progressive Era. Evidence of the changing judicial climate came in *Muller* v. *Oregon* (1908), in which the Supreme Court upheld an Oregon ten-hour law for women laundry workers. Defending the constitutionality of the Oregon law was Boston attorney Louis Brandeis, who offered economic, medical, and sociological evidence of how long hours harmed women workers. Rejecting a legal claim long made by business, the high court held that such worker-protection laws did not violate employers' rights under the due-process clause of the Fourteenth Amendment. *Muller* v. *Oregon* marked a breakthrough in making the legal system more responsive to new social realities.

In 1916 Woodrow Wilson nominated Brandeis to the Supreme Court. Disapproving of Brandeis's innovative

approach to the law, the conservative American Bar Association protested, as did the *New York Times*, the president of Harvard, and Republican leaders in Congress. Anti-Semites opposed Brandeis because he was a Jew. But Wilson stood by his nominee, and after a fierce battle, the Senate confirmed him.

These years also produced four amendments to the Constitution, the first since 1870. The Sixteenth (ratified in 1913) granted Congress the authority to tax income, thus ending a long legal battle. A Civil War income tax had been phased out in 1872. Congress had authorized an income tax in an 1894 tariff act, but in *Pollock* v. *Farmers' Loan and Trust* (1895) the Supreme Court had not only ruled this measure unconstitutional, but also blasted it as "communistic." This ruling, denounced by populists and then by progressives, had spurred the campaign for a constitutional amendment. Quickly exercising its new authority, in 1913 Congress imposed a graduated federal income tax with a maximum rate of 7 percent on incomes in excess of five hundred thousand dollars. Income-tax revenues helped the government pay for the expanded regulatory activities assigned to it by various progressive reform measures.

The Seventeenth Amendment (1913) mandated the direct election of U.S. senators by the voters, rather than their selection by state legislatures as provided by Article I of the Constitution. This amendment brought to fruition a reform first advocated by the Populists as a way of making the Senate less subject to corporate influence and more responsive to the popular will.

The next two amendments, although coming after World War I, culminated reform campaigns that we have already examined. The Eighteenth (1919) established nationwide prohibition of the manufacture, sale, or importation of "intoxicating liquors." The Nineteenth (1920) granted women the vote. This remarkable wave of amendments underscored how profoundly the progressive impulse had transformed the political landscape.

1916: Wilson Edges Out Hughes

Wilson easily won renomination in 1916. The Republicans turned to Charles Evans Hughes, a Supreme Court justice and former New York governor. The Progressive party again courted Theodore Roosevelt, but TR's reform interests had given way to an obsession with drawing the United States into the war that had broken out in Europe in 1914 (see Chapter 22). At his urging, the Progressives endorsed Hughes and effectively committed political suicide.

With the Republicans now more or less reunited, the election was extremely close. War-related issues loomed large. Wilson won the popular vote, but the electoral college outcome remained in doubt for several weeks as the California tally seesawed back and forth. Ultimately, Wilson carried the state by fewer than four thousand votes and, with it, the election.

Following the flurry of worker-protection laws in 1916, the progressive movement lost momentum as the nation's attention turned from reform to war. A few reform measures enacted in the 1920s and a 1924 presidential campaign by an aging Senator La Follette under a revived Progressive party banner offered reminders of the progressive agenda. But the movement's zest and drive clearly waned with the coming of World War I.

CONCLUSION

Progressivism in its many facets left a remarkable legacy not only in specific laws but also in a changed view of government. To be sure, this altered perspective had ideological roots in the American past, including Jeffersonian optimism about human perfectibility, Jacksonian opposition to special privilege, and the rising status of science and social research that had come with advances in higher education and in such academic disciplines as economics, sociology, and statistics.

But the progressives combined these diverse ingredients in creative new ways. By 1916 the consensus was that government should properly play a central social and economic role. The progressive movement expanded the meaning of democracy and challenged the cynical view that government was nothing but a tool of the rich. Theodore Roosevelt and Woodrow Wilson, together with governors like Robert La Follette, mayors like Tom Johnson, and scores of organizations pursuing many different reform agendas, vastly enlarged the role of government in American life.

Progressives did not seek "big government" for its own sake. Rather, they recognized that in an era of gargantuan industries, sprawling cities, and concentrated corporate power, government's role had to grow correspondingly to serve the public interest, ensure a decent common life, and protect society's more vulnerable members.

Unquestionably, this ideal often faltered in practice. Reform laws and regulatory agencies inspired by moral indignation and a vision of social justice often fell short of their purpose as emotional fervor gave way to bureaucratic routine. Indeed, reforms that the progressives

envisioned as serving the larger society sometimes mainly benefited special interests. Corporations that initially fought regulation proved remarkably adept at manipulating the new regulatory state to their own advantage. Unquestionably, too, progressivism had its illiberal and coercive dimensions; on the issue of racial justice, its record was generally dismal.

After all this has been acknowledged, however, the Progressive Era stands as a time when American politics seriously confronted the social upheavals wrought by industrialization. It was also a time when Americans learned to think of their government neither as remote and irrelevant nor as a plaything of the powerful, but rather as an arena of possibility where public issues and social problems could be thrashed out. Twenty years later, another great reform movement, the New Deal, would draw heavily on progressivism's legacy.

FOR FURTHER REFERENCE

READINGS

Alan Dawley, *Struggles for Justice: Social Responsibility and the Liberal State* (1991). A thoughtful study placing the progressive movement in a larger historical and ideological context.

Steven J. Diner, *A Very Different Age: Americans of the Progressive Era* (1998). A readable overview stressing the diversity of Progressives and their reforms.

Nan Enstad, *Ladies of Labor, Girls of Adventure: Working Women, Popular Culture, and Labor Politics at the Turn of the Twentieth Century* (1999). An innovative blending of labor history and popular-culture history.

Mark Fiege, *Irrigated Eden: The Making of an Agricultural Landscape in the American West* (1999). A valuable case study of land reclamation in Idaho, with especially good coverage of the Progressive era.

CHRONOLOGY; 1900–1917

1895 Anti-Saloon League founded.

1898 Charlotte Perkins Gilman, *Women and Economics.*

1899 Thorstein Veblen, *The Theory of the Leisure Class.*

1900 International Ladies' Garment Workers' Union (ILGWU) founded.
Socialist Party of America organized.
Theodore Dreiser, *Sister Carrie.*
Carrie Chapman Catt becomes president of the National American Woman Suffrage Association (NAWSA).

1901 Assassination of McKinley; Theodore Roosevelt becomes president.
J. P. Morgan forms United States Steel Company.
Frank Norris, *The Octopus.*

1902 Roosevelt mediates coal strike.
Jane Addams, *Democracy and Social Ethics.*

1903 W. E. B. Du Bois, *The Souls of Black Folk.*
The Great Train Robbery (movie).
Wright Brothers' flight.

1904 Roosevelt elected president.
Lincoln Steffens, *The Shame of the Cities.*
Ida Tarbell, *History of the Standard Oil Company.*

1905 Industrial Workers of the World (IWW) organized.
Niagara Movement established by W. E. B. Du Bois and others.
Gifford Pinchot appointed head of U.S. Forest Service.

1906 Upton Sinclair, *The Jungle*

1907 William James, *Pragmatism.*

1908 William Howard Taft elected president.
Model T Ford introduced.

1909 Ballinger-Pinchot controversy.
National Association for the Advancement of Colored People (NAACP) founded.
Herbert Croly, *The Promise of American Life.*
Daniel Burnham, *Plan of Chicago.*

1910 Jane Addams, *Twenty Years at Hull House.*
Insurgents curb power of House Speaker Joseph Cannon.

1911 Triangle Shirtwaist Company fire.
Frederick W. Taylor, *Scientific Management.*

1912 Republican party split; Progressive (Bull Moose) party founded.
Woodrow Wilson elected president.
International Opium Treaty.
Theodore Dreiser, *The Financier.*

1913 Thirty thousand march for woman suffrage in New York.

1914 American Social Hygiene Association founded.

1915 D. W. Griffith, *The Birth of a Nation.*
Mary Ware Dennett founds National Birth Control League.

1916 Wilson reelected.
John Dewey, *Democracy and Education.*
Margaret Sanger opens nation's first birth-control clinic in Brooklyn, New York.
National Park Service created.
Louis Brandeis appointed to Supreme Court.
Madison Grant, *The Passing of the Great Race.*

Leon Fink, *Progressive Intellectuals and the Dilemmas of Democratic Commitment* (1997). Insightful exploration of the tensions between democratic theory and the Progressive Era focus on expertise and specialized knowledge.

Leon Fink, ed., *Major Problems in the Gilded Age and Progressive Era* (1993). Useful, well-chosen collection of primary sources and interpretive essays.

Noralee Frankel and Nancy S. Dye, eds., *Gender, Class, Race, and Reform in the Progressive Era* (1991). Selected essays exploring progressivism from various social perspectives.

Gayle Gullett, *Becoming Citizens: The Emergence and Development of the California Woman's Movement, 1880–1911* (2000). Illuminating case study of the movement in a key Western state.

Christine Stansell, *American Moderns: Bohemian New York and the Creation of a New Century* (2000). A fresh treatment of pre-World War I Greenwich Village, stressing the linkages between cultural and political radicalism.

David Stradling, *Smokestacks and Progressives: Environmentalists, Engineers, and Air Quality in America, 1881–1951* (1999). Well-researched account of the mixed record of the Progressive Era campaign for cleaner air, with attention to the role of civil engineers.

WEBSITES

Muckrakers
http://www.acusd.edu/~freeman/
A brief history, with links to writings by Ida Tarbell, Upton Sinclair, and other Progressive Era journalists.

The 1912 Election
http://1912.history.ohio-state.edu/
A well-designed site including details of the campaign, the candidates, and the issues.

The Triangle Shirtwaist Factory Fire, March 25, 1911
http://www.ilr.cornell.edu/trianglefire/
Extensive collection of primary documents, including newspaper stories and firsthand accounts.

Woman Suffrage and the 19th Amendment: Primary Sources, Activities, and Links to Related Web Sites for Educators and Students
National Archives and Records Administration
http://www.nara.gov/education/teaching/woman/home.html
Rich array of sources and useful links.

For additional works, please consult the Bibliography at the end of the book.

CHAPTER 22

Global Involvements and World War I, 1902–1920

It was April 6, 1917, and Jane Addams was troubled. By overwhelming margins, Congress had just supported President Woodrow Wilson's call for a declaration of war on Germany. Addams belonged to the Daughters of the American Revolution (DAR); her father had served in the Illinois legislature with future President Abraham Lincoln. But she believed in peace and deplored her nation's decision to go to war. As the founder of Hull House, a Chicago settlement house, Addams had worked to overcome tensions among different ethnic groups. In *Newer Ideals of Peace* (1907), she had insisted that the multiethnic "internationalism" of America's immigrant neighborhoods proved that national and ethnic hostilities could be overcome. Addams had also observed how war spirit can inflame a people. During the Spanish-American War, she had watched Chicago street urchins playing at killing "Spaniards."

When war broke out in Europe in 1914, Addams worked to end the conflict and to keep America out of the fray. A founder of the Woman's Peace party in January 1915, she attended an International Congress of Women in April that called on the warring nations to submit their differences to arbitration. Addams personally met with President Wilson to enlist his support for arbitration, but with no success.

Now America had entered the war, and Addams had to take a stand. Deepening her dilemma, many of her friends, including philosopher and

◀ **New York City, 1917**
Bidding farewell to U.S. troops about to embark for France.

677

educator John Dewey, were lining up behind Wilson. Theodore Roosevelt, whose 1912 Progressive party presidential campaign Addams had enthusiastically supported, was beating the drums for war.

Despite the pressures, Addams concluded that she must remain faithful to her conscience and oppose the war. The reaction was swift. Editorial writers who had earlier praised her settlement house work now criticized her. The DAR expelled her. For years after, the DAR, the American Legion, and other patriotic organizations attacked Addams for her "disloyalty" in 1917.

Addams did not sit out the war on the sidelines. She traveled across America, giving speeches urging increased food production to aid refugees and other war victims. Once the war ended, she resumed her work for peace. In 1919 she was elected first president of the Women's International League for Peace and Freedom. She described her wartime isolation in a moving book, *Peace and Bread in Time of War* (1922). In 1931 she won the Nobel Peace Prize. During the 1960s, some opponents of the Vietnam War found inspiration in her earlier example.

Addams's experience underscores how deeply World War I affected American life. Whether they donned uniforms, worked on farms or in factories, or simply experienced U.S. life in wartime, all Americans were touched by the war. Beyond its immediate effects, the war had long-lasting social, economic, and political ramifications.

Well before 1917, however, events abroad gripped the attention of government officials, the media, and ordinary Americans. From this perspective, World War I was one episode in a larger process of deepening U.S. involvement overseas. In the late nineteenth century, America had become an industrial and economic powerhouse seeking markets and raw materials worldwide. In the early twentieth century, these broadening economic interests helped give rise to a new international role for the nation. This expanded role profoundly influenced developments at home as well as U.S. actions abroad, and has continued to shape American history to the present. These broader global realities, culminating in World War I, are the focus of this chapter.

This chapter will focus on five major questions:

■ What general motivations or objectives underlay America's involvement in Asia and Latin America in the early twentieth century?

■ Considering both immediate provocations and broader factors, why did the United States enter the European war in April 1917?

■ How did America's participation in the war affect the home front and the reform spirit of the prewar Progressive Era?

■ How did the role of the federal government in the U.S. economy, and in American life generally, change in 1917–1918?

■ What was President Woodrow Wilson's role in the creation of the League of Nations and in the Senate's rejection of U.S. membership in the League?

DEFINING AMERICA'S WORLD ROLE, 1902–1914

As we saw in Chapter 20, the annexation of Hawaii, the Spanish-American War, the occupation of the Philippines, and other developments in the 1890s signaled an era of intensified U.S. involvement abroad, especially in Asia and Latin America. These foreign engagements reflected a growing determination to assert American might in an age of imperial expansion by European powers, to protect and extend U.S. business investments abroad, and to impose American stan-

World War I Sheet Music
Tin Pan Alley helps whip up the war spirit.

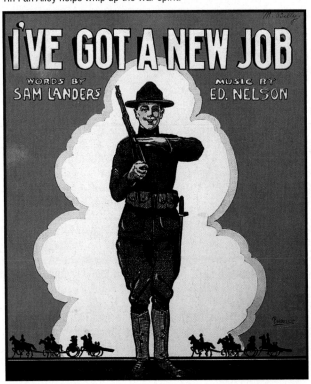

dards of good government beyond the nation's borders. This process of foreign engagement continued under presidents Theodore Roosevelt, William Howard Taft, and Woodrow Wilson. The strongly moralistic tone of the progressive movement, whose domestic manifestations we examined in Chapter 21, emerged in America's dealings with other nations as well.

The "Open Door": Competing for the China Market

As the campaign to suppress the Philippines insurrection dragged on (see Chapter 20), American policy makers turned their attention farther west, to China. Their aim was not territorial expansion but rather protection of U.S. commercial opportunities. Proclaimed Indiana Senator Albert J. Beveridge in 1898, "American factories are making more than the American people can use; American soil is producing more than they can consume. . . . [T]he trade of the world must and shall be ours."

The China market beckoned. Textile producers dreamed of clothing China's millions of people; investors envisioned Chinese railroad construction. As China's 250-year-old Manchu Ch'ing empire grew weaker, U.S. businesspeople watched carefully. In 1896 a consortium of New York capitalists formed a company to promote trade and railroad investment in China.

But other nations were also eyeing the China market. Some pressured the weak Manchu rulers to designate certain ports and regions as "spheres of influence" where they would enjoy exclusive trading and development rights. In 1896 Russia won both the right to build a railway across Manchuria and a twenty-five-year lease on much of the region. In 1897 Germany forcibly secured a ninety-nine-year lease on a Chinese port as well as mining and railroad rights in the adjacent province. The British won various concessions, too.

In September 1899 U.S. Secretary of State John Hay asked the major European powers with economic interests in China not to interfere with American trading rights in China. Specifically, he requested them to open the ports in their spheres of influence to all countries. The six nations gave noncommittal answers, but Hay blithely announced that they had accepted the principle of an "Open Door" to American business in China.

Hay's Open Door note showed how commercial considerations were increasingly influencing American foreign policy. It reflected a form of economic expansionism that has been called "informal empire." The U.S. government had no desire to occupy Chinese territory,

Woodrow Wilson, Schoolteacher
This 1914 political cartoon captures the patronizing self-righteousness of Wilson's approach to Latin America that planted the seeds of long-term resentments.

but it did want to keep Chinese markets open to American businesses.

As Hay pursued this effort, a more urgent threat emerged in China. For years, antiforeign feeling had simmered in China, fanned by the aged Ch'ing empress who was disgusted by the growth of Western influence. In 1899 a fanatical antiforeign secret society known as the Harmonious Righteous Fists (called "Boxers" by Western journalists) killed thousands of foreigners and Chinese Christians. In June 1900 the Boxers occupied Beijing (Peking), the Chinese capital, and besieged the district housing the foreign legations. The United States contributed twenty-five hundred soldiers to an international army that marched on Beijing, drove back the Boxers, and rescued the occupants of the threatened legations.

The defeat of the Boxer uprising further weakened China's government. Fearing that the regime's collapse would allow European powers to carve up China, John Hay issued a second, more important, series of Open Door notes in 1900. He reaffirmed the principle of open

U.S. Troops in China, 1900
On a dirt road flanked by stone elephants, mounted American troops sent by President McKinley prepare to march on Beijing as part of an international force assembled to suppress the Boxer Rebellion. This intervention signaled a deepening U.S. involvement in Asia.

trade in China for all nations and announced America's determination to preserve China's territorial and administrative integrity. In general, China remained open to U.S. business interests as well as to Christian missionary effort. In the 1930s, when Japanese expansionism menaced China's survival, Hay's policy helped shape the American response.

The Panama Canal: Hardball Diplomacy

Traders had long dreamed of a canal across the forty-mile-wide ribbon of land joining North and South America to eliminate the hazardous voyage around South America. In 1879 a French company secured permission from Colombia to build a canal across Panama, then part of Colombia (see Map 22.1). But mismanagement and yellow fever doomed the project, and ten years and $400 million later, with the canal half completed, it went bankrupt. Seeking to recoup its losses, the French company offered its assets, including the still-valid concession from Colombia, to the United States for $109 million.

America was in an expansionist mood. In 1902, after the French lowered their price to $40 million, Congress authorized President Theodore Roosevelt to accept the offer. The following year, Secretary of State Hay signed an agreement with the Colombian representative, Tomás Herrán, granting the United States a ninety-nine-year lease on the proposed canal for a down payment of $10 million and an annual fee of $250,000. But the Colombian senate, seeking a better deal, rejected the agreement. An outraged Roosevelt, using the racist lan-

guage of the day, privately denounced the Colombians as "greedy little anthropoids."

Determined to have his canal, Roosevelt found a willing collaborator in Philippe Bunau-Varilla, an official of the bankrupt French company. Dismayed that his company might lose its $40 million, Bunau-Varilla organized a "revolution" in Panama from a New York hotel room. While his wife stitched a flag, he wrote a declaration of independence and a constitution for the new nation. When the "revolution" occurred as scheduled on November 3, 1903, a U.S. warship hovered offshore. Proclaiming Panama's independence, Bunau-Varilla appointed himself its first ambassador to the United States. John Hay quickly recognized the newly hatched nation and signed a treaty with Bunau-Varilla granting the United States a ten-mile-wide strip of land across Panama "in perpetuity" (that is, forever) on the same terms earlier rejected by Colombia. Theodore Roosevelt later summed up the episode, "I took the Canal Zone, and let Congress debate, and while the debate goes on, the canal does also."

The U.S. canal builders' first challenge was to overcome the yellow fever that had haunted the French. Leading this effort was Dr. Walter Reed of the Army Medical Corps. Earlier, in a brilliant research project in Cuba, Reed and his associates had used themselves and army volunteers as experimental subjects to prove that the yellow-fever virus was spread by female mosquitoes that bred in stagnant water. In Panama Reed organized a large-scale drainage project that eradicated the disease-bearing mosquito—a remarkable public-health achievement. Construction began in 1906, and in August 1914 the first ship sailed through the canal. In 1921, implicitly conceding the dubious methods used to acquire the Canal Zone, the U.S. Senate voted a payment of $25 million to Colombia. But the ill feeling generated by Theodore Roosevelt's high-handed actions, combined with other instances of U.S. interventionism, would long shadow U.S.-Latin American relations.

Roosevelt and Taft Assert U.S. Power in Latin America and Asia

While the Panama Canal remains the best-known foreign-policy achievement of these years, other actions by Presidents Theodore Roosevelt and William Howard Taft

MAP 22.1

U.S. Hegemony in the Caribbean and Latin America

Through many interventions, territorial acquisitions, and robust economic expansion, the United States became the predominant power in Latin America in the early twentieth century. Acting on Theodore Roosevelt's assertion of a U.S. right to combat "wrongdoing" in Latin America and the Caribbean, the United States dispatched troops to the region where they met nationalist opposition.

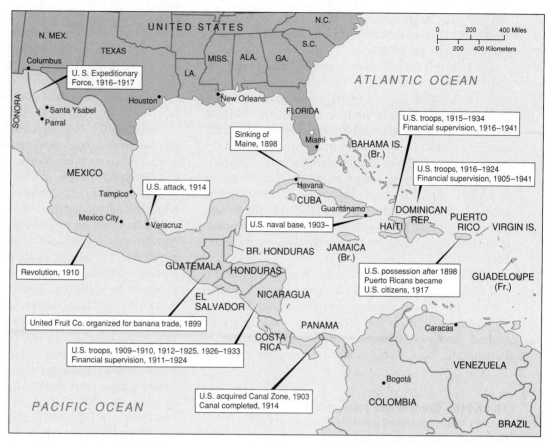

underscored their belief that Washington had to assert U.S. power and protect U.S. business interests in Latin America (see Map 22.1) and Asia. Two crises early in Roosevelt's presidency arose as a result of European powers' intervention in Latin America. In 1902 German, British, and Italian warships blockaded and bombarded the ports of Venezuela, which had defaulted on its debts to European investors. The standoff ended when all sides agreed to Roosevelt's proposal of arbitration.

The second crisis flared in 1904 when several European nations threatened to invade the Dominican Republic, a Caribbean island nation that had also defaulted on its debts to them. Roosevelt reacted swiftly. If anyone were to intervene, he believed, it should be the United States. While denying any territorial ambitions in Latin America, Roosevelt in December 1904 declared that "chronic wrongdoing" by any Latin American nation would justify U.S. intervention.

This pronouncement has been called "the Roosevelt Corollary" to the Monroe Doctrine of 1823, which had warned European powers against intervening in Latin America. Now Roosevelt asserted that in cases of

"wrongdoing" (a word he left undefined), the United States had the right to precisely such intervention. Suiting actions to words, the Roosevelt administration ended the threat of European intervention by taking over the Dominican Republic's customs service for two years and managing its foreign debt. Roosevelt summed up his foreign-policy approach in a 1901 speech quoting what he said was an old African proverb, "Speak softly and carry a big stick." (He followed the second part of this rule more consistently than the first.)

The foreign policy of the Taft administration (1909–1913) focused on advancing American commercial interests abroad, a policy some called "dollar diplomacy." A U.S.-backed revolution in Nicaragua in 1911 brought to power Adolfo Díaz, an officer of an American-owned mine. Washington feared growing British influence in Nicaragua's affairs, and also that a foreign power might build a canal across Nicaragua to rival the Panama Canal. In exchange for control of Nicaragua's national bank, customs service, and railroad, American bankers lent Diaz's government $1.5 million. When a revolt against Díaz broke out in 1912,

Taft ordered in the marines to protect the bankers' investment. Except for one brief interval, marines occupied Nicaragua until 1933.

In Asia, too, both Roosevelt and Taft sought to project U.S. power and advance the interests of American business. In 1900, exploiting the turmoil caused by the Boxer uprising, Russian troops occupied the Chinese province of Manchuria, and Russia promoted its commercial interests by building railroads. This alarmed the Japanese, who also had designs on Manchuria and nearby Korea. In February 1904 a surprise Japanese attack destroyed Russian ships anchored at Port Arthur, Manchuria. Japan completely dominated in the Russo-Japanese War that followed. For the first time, European imperialist expansion had been checked by an Asian power.

Roosevelt, while pleased to see Russian expansionism challenged, believed that a Japanese victory would disrupt the Asian balance of power and threaten America's position in the Philippines. Accordingly, he invited Japan and Russia to a peace conference at Portsmouth, New Hampshire. In September 1905 the

TR and the Great White Fleet, 1909
President Theodore Roosevelt greets the crew of the *U.S.S. Constitution* as the fleet returns from a world cruise designed to impress other nations with America's emergence as a world power.

two rivals signed a peace treaty. Russia recognized Japan's rule in Korea and made other territorial concessions. After this outcome, curbing Japanese expansionism—peacefully, if possible—became America's major objective in Asia. For his role in ending the war, Roosevelt, in the unaccustomed role of peacemaker, received the Nobel Peace Prize.

Meanwhile, U.S.-Japanese relations soured when the San Francisco school board, reflecting West Coast hostility to Asian immigrants, assigned all Asian children to segregated schools in 1906. Japan angrily protested this insult. Summoning the school board to Washington, Roosevelt persuaded them to reverse this discriminatory policy. In return, in 1908 the administration negotiated a "gentlemen's agreement" with Japan by which Tokyo pledged to halt Japanese emigration to America. Racist attitudes continued to poison U.S.-Japanese relations, however. In 1913, the California legislature prohibited Japanese aliens from owning land.

While Californians warned of the "yellow peril," Japanese journalists, eyeing America's military strength and involvement in Asia, spoke of a "white peril." In 1907 Roosevelt ordered sixteen gleaming U.S. battleships on a "training operation" to Japan. Although officially treated as friendly, this "Great White Fleet" underscored America's growing naval might.

Under President Taft, U.S. foreign policy in Asia continued to focus on dollar diplomacy, which in this case meant promoting U.S. commercial interests in China—the same goal Secretary of State John Hay had sought with his Open Door notes. As it happened, however, a plan for a U.S.-financed railroad in Manchuria did not work out. Not only did U.S. bankers find the project too risky, but Russia and Japan signed a treaty carving up Manchuria for commercial purposes, freezing out the Americans.

Wilson and Latin America

Upon entering the White House in 1913 as the first Democratic president in sixteen years, Woodrow Wilson criticized his Republican predecessors' expansionist policies. The United States, he pledged, would "never again seek one additional foot of territory by conquest." But he, too, soon intervened in Latin America. In 1915, after upheavals in Haiti and the Dominican Republic (two nations sharing the Caribbean island of Santo Domingo), Wilson sent in the marines (see Map 22.1). A Haitian constitution favorable to U.S. commercial interests was overwhelmingly ratified in 1918 in a vote supervised by the marines. Under Major General Smedley ("Old Gimlet Eye") Butler, marines brutally suppressed

Haitian resistance to U.S. rule. The marines remained in the Dominican Republic until 1924 and in Haiti until 1934.

The most serious crisis Wilson faced in Latin America was the Mexican Revolution. Mexico had won independence from Spain in 1820, but the nation remained divided between a small landowning elite and an impoverished peasantry. In 1911 rebels led by the democratic reformer Francisco Madero had ended the thirty-year rule of President Porfirio Díaz, who had defended the interests of the wealthy elite. Early in 1913, just as Wilson took office, Mexican troops loyal to General Victoriano Huerta, a full-blooded Indian, overthrew and murdered Madero.

In this turbulent era, Wilson tried to promote good government, protect U.S. investments, and safeguard U.S. citizens living in Mexico or along its border. Forty thousand Americans had settled in Mexico under Díaz's regime, and U.S. investors had poured some $2 billion into Mexican oil wells and other ventures. Reversing the long-standing U.S. policy of recognizing all governments, Wilson refused to recognize Huerta's regime, which he called "a government of butchers." Authorizing arms sales to General Venustiano Carranza, Huerta's rival, Wilson also ordered the port of Veracruz blockaded to prevent a shipment of German arms from reaching Huerta (see Map 22.1). Announced Wilson, "I am going to teach the South American republics to elect good men." In April 1914 seven thousand U.S. troops occupied Veracruz and engaged Huerta's forces. Sixty-five Americans and approximately five hundred Mexicans were killed or wounded. Bowing to U.S. might, Huerta abdicated; Carranza took power; and the U.S. troops withdrew.

But the turmoil continued. In January 1916 a bandit chieftain in northern Mexico, Pancho Villa, murdered sixteen U.S. mining engineers. Soon after, Villa's gang burned the town of Columbus, New Mexico, and killed nineteen inhabitants. Enraged Americans demanded action. Wilson dispatched a punitive expedition into Mexico under General John J. Pershing. When Pancho Villa not only eluded Pershing but also brazenly staged another cross-border raid into Texas, Wilson ordered 150,000 National Guardsmen to the Mexican border—a heavy-handed response that embittered U.S.-Mexican relations for years after.

Although soon overshadowed by World War I, these involvements in Asia and Latin America illuminate the U.S. foreign-policy goal, which was, essentially, to achieve an international system based on democratic values and capitalist enterprise. Washington planners envisioned a harmonious, stable global order that would welcome both American political values and American business. President Wilson summed up this view in a speech to corporate leaders: "[Y]ou are Americans and are meant to carry liberty and justice and the principles of humanity wherever you go. . . . [G]o out and sell goods that will make the world more comfortable and more happy, and convert them to the principles of America." Wilson's vision of an American-based world order shaped his response to a crisis unfolding in Europe.

WAR IN EUROPE, 1914–1917

When war engulfed Europe in 1914, most Americans wished only to remain aloof. For nearly three years, the United States stayed neutral. But by April 1917 cultural ties to England and France, economic considerations, visions of a world remade in America's image, and German violations of Wilson's definition of neutral rights all combined to draw the United States into the maelstrom.

The Coming of War

Europe was at peace through much of the nineteenth century, and some people concluded that war was a thing of the past. Beneath the surface, however, ominous developments, including a complex web of alliances, belied such hopes. Germany, Austria, and Italy signed a mutual-defense treaty in 1882. In turn, France concluded military treaties with Russia and Great Britain.

Beyond the treaties imperial ambitions and nationalistic passions stirred. The once-powerful Ottoman Empire, centered in Turkey, grew weaker in the 1870s, leaving in its wake such newly independent nations as Romania, Bulgaria, and Serbia.

Serbian patriots dreamed of creating a greater Serbia that would include Serbs living in Bosnia-Herzegovina, Serbia's neighbor to the west. Russia, home to millions of Slavs, the same ethnic group as the Serbian population, supported Serbia's expansionist ambitions. Meanwhile, the Austro-Hungarian Empire, with its capital in Vienna, also saw opportunities for expansion as the Ottoman Empire faded. In 1908 Austria-Hungary annexed (took over) Bosnia-Herzegovina, alarming Russia and Serbia.

Germany, ruled by Kaiser Wilhelm II, also displayed expansionist impulses. Many Germans believed that their nation had lagged in the race for empire. Expansion, modernization, and military power became the goal in Berlin.

Such was the context when Archduke Franz Ferdinand of Austria made a state visit to Bosnia in June

1914. As he and his wife rode in an open car through Sarajevo, the Bosnian capital, a young Bosnian Serb nationalist gunned them down. In response, Austria declared war on Serbia on July 28. Russia, which had a secret treaty with Serbia, mobilized for war. Germany declared war on Russia and Russia's ally France. Great Britain, linked by treaty to France, declared war on Germany. An assassin's bullet had plunged Europe into war.

This was the start of the conflict that we today know as World War I. Until the outbreak of World War II in 1939, however, it was simply called The Great War. On one side were Great Britain, Russia, and France, called the Allies. On the other side were the Central Powers: Germany and Austria-Hungary. Italy, although bound by treaty to the Central Powers, switched sides and joined the Allies in 1915.

The Perils of Neutrality

Proclaiming U.S. neutrality, President Wilson urged the nation to be neutral "in thought as well as in action." Most Americans, grateful that an ocean lay between

Opposing War

This popular song of 1915 conveys the antiwar sentiment that swept America after the European war began in 1914.

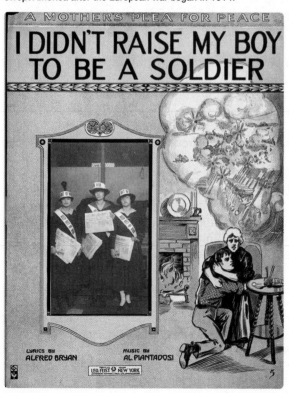

them and the war, fervently agreed. A popular song summed up the mood: "I Didn't Raise My Boy to Be a Soldier."

Neutrality proved difficult, however. Wilson privately dreaded a victory by militaristic Germany. Strong economic interests bound the United States and Britain. Many Americans, including Wilson himself, had ancestral ties to England. Well-to-do Americans routinely traveled in England. Schoolbooks stressed the English origins of American institutions. The English language itself—the language of Shakespeare, Dickens, and the King James Bible—deepened the bond. British propaganda subtly stressed the British-American link.

But not all Americans felt emotional ties to England. Many German-Americans sympathized with Germany's cause. Irish-Americans speculated that a German victory might free Ireland from British rule. Some Scandinavian immigrants identified more with Germany than with England. But these cultural and ethnic crosscurrents did not at first override Wilson's commitment to neutrality. For most Americans, staying out of the conflict became the chief goal.

Neutral in 1914, America went to war in 1917. What caused this turnabout? Fundamentally, Wilson's vision of a world order in America's image conflicted with his neutrality. An international system based on democracy and capitalism would be impossible, he believed, in a world dominated by imperial Germany. Even an Allied victory would not ensure a transformed world order, Wilson gradually became convinced, without a U.S. role in the postwar settlement. To shape the peace, America would have to fight the war.

These underlying ideas influenced Wilson's handling of the immediate issue that dragged the United States into the conflict: neutral nations' rights on the high seas. When the war began, Britain started intercepting U.S. merchant ships bound for Germany, insisting that their cargo could aid Germany's war effort. Wilson's protests intensified in late 1914 and early 1915 when Britain declared the North Sea a war zone; planted it with explosive mines; and blockaded all German ports, choking off Germany's imports, including food. Britain was determined to exploit its naval advantage, even if it meant alienating American public opinion.

But Germany, not England, ultimately pushed the United States into war. If Britannia ruled the waves, Germany controlled the ocean depths with its torpedo-equipped submarines, or U-boats. In February 1915 Berlin proclaimed the waters around Great Britain a war zone and warned off all ships. Wilson quickly responded: Germany would be held to "strict accountability" for any loss of U.S. ships or lives.

On May 1, 1915, in a small ad in U.S. newspapers, the German embassy cautioned Americans against travel on British or French vessels. Six days later, a U-boat sank the British liner *Lusitania* off the Irish coast, with the loss of 1,198 lives, including 128 Americans. As headlines screamed the news, U.S. public opinion turned sharply anti-German. (The *Lusitania*, historians later discovered, had carried munitions destined for England.)

Wilson demanded that Germany stop unrestricted submarine warfare. He insisted that America could persuade the belligerents to recognize the principle of neutral rights without going to war. "There is such a thing as a man being too proud to fight," he said.

The *Lusitania* disaster exposed deep divisions in U.S. public opinion. Many Americans, now ready for war, ridiculed Wilson's "too proud to fight" speech. Theodore Roosevelt denounced the president's "abject cowardice." The National Security League, a lobby of bankers and industrialists, promoted a U.S. arms buildup and universal military training and organized "preparedness" parades in major cities. By late 1915 Wilson himself called for a military buildup.

Other citizens had taken Wilson's neutrality speeches seriously and deplored the drift toward war. Some feminists and reformers warned that war fever was eroding support for progressive reforms. Jane Addams lamented that the international movements to reduce infant mortality and improve care for the aged had been "scattered to the winds by the war."

As early as August 1914, fifteen hundred women marched down New York's Fifth Avenue protesting the war. Carrie Chapman Catt and other feminists joined Jane Addams in forming the Woman's Peace party. Late in 1915 automaker Henry Ford chartered a vessel to take a group of pacifists to Scandinavia to persuade the belligerents to accept neutral mediation and fulfill his dream of ending the war by Christmas.

Divisions surfaced even within the Wilson administration. Secretary of State William Jennings Bryan, believing that Wilson's *Lusitania* notes were too hostile to Germany, resigned in June 1915. His successor, Robert Lansing, let Wilson act as his own secretary of state.

Some neutrality advocates concluded that incidents like the *Lusitania* crisis were inevitable if Americans persisted in sailing on belligerent ships. Early in 1916, Congress considered a bill to ban such travel, but President Wilson successfully opposed it, insisting that the principle of neutral rights must be upheld.

For a time, Wilson's approach seemed to work. Germany ordered U-boat captains to spare passenger ships, and agreed to pay compensation for the

American lives lost in the *Lusitania* sinking. In March 1916, however, a German submarine sank a French passenger ship, the *Sussex*, in the English Channel, injuring several Americans. Wilson threatened to break diplomatic relations—a step toward war. In response, Berlin pledged not to attack merchant vessels without warning, provided that Great Britain, too, observe "the rules of international law." Ignoring this qualification, Wilson announced Germany's acceptance of American demands. For the rest of 1916, the crisis over neutral rights eased.

U.S. bankers' financial support to the warring nations also undermined the principle of neutrality. Early in the war, Secretary of State Bryan had rejected banker J. P. Morgan's request to extend loans to France. Such loans, said Bryan, would be "inconsistent with the true spirit of neutrality." But economic considerations, combined with outrage over the *Lusitania* sinking, undermined this policy. In August 1915 Treasury Secretary William G. McAdoo warned Wilson of dire economic consequences if U.S. neutrality policy forced cuts in Allied purchases of American munitions and farm products. "To maintain our prosperity, we must finance it," McAdoo insisted. Only substantial loans to England, agreed Secretary of State Lansing, could prevent serious financial problems in the United States, including "unrest and suffering among the laboring classes." The neutrality principle must not "stand in the way of our national interests," warned Lansing.

Swayed by such arguments and personally sympathetic to the Allies, Wilson permitted Morgan's bank to lend $500 million to the British and French governments. By April 1917 U.S. banks had lent $2.3 billion to the Allies, in contrast to $27 million to Germany.

While Americans concentrated on neutral rights, the land war settled into a grim stalemate. An autumn 1914 German drive into France bogged down along the Marne River. The two sides then dug in, in trenches across France from the English Channel to the Swiss border. For more than three years, this line scarcely changed. Occasional offensives took a terrible toll. A German attack in February 1916 began with the capture of two forts near the town of Verdun and ended that June with the French recapture of the same two forts, now nothing but rubble, at a horrendous cost in human life. Trench warfare was a nightmare of mud, lice, rats, artillery bursts, poison gas, and random death.

British propaganda focused on the atrocities committed by "the Huns" (a derogatory term for the Germans), such as impaling babies on bayonets. After the war, much of this propaganda was exposed as false. Documents seized in 1915 revealing German espionage

in U.S. war plants, however, further discredited the German cause.

The war dominated the 1916 presidential election. Woodrow Wilson faced Republican Charles Evans Hughes, a former governor of New York (and future chief justice of the U.S. Supreme Court). The Democrats' campaign theme emerged when a convention speaker, praising Wilson's foreign policy, aroused wild applause as he ended each episode with the refrain "We didn't go to war."

Hughes criticized Wilson's lack of aggressiveness while rebuking him for policies that risked war. Theodore Roosevelt, still influential in public life, campaigned more for war than for the Republican ticket. The only difference between Wilson and the bearded Hughes, he jeered, was a shave. While Hughes did well among Irish-Americans and German-Americans who considered Wilson too pro-British, Wilson held the Democratic base and won support from women voters in western states that had adopted woman suffrage. Wilson's victory, although extremely close, revealed the strength of the popular longing for peace as late as November 1916.

The United States Enters the War

In January 1917, facing stalemate on the ground, Germany resumed unrestricted submarine warfare. Germany's military leaders believed that even if the United States declared war as a result, full-scale U-boat warfare could bring victory before American troops reached the front.

Events now rushed forward with grave inevitability. Wilson broke diplomatic relations on February 3. During February and March, U-boats sank five American ships. A coded telegram from the German foreign secretary, Arthur Zimmermann, to Germany's ambassador to Mexico promised that if Mexico would declare war on the United States, Germany would help restore Mexico's "lost territories" of Texas, Arizona, and New Mexico. Intercepted and decoded by the British and passed along to Washington, the "Zimmermann telegram" further inflamed the war spirit in America.

Events in distant Russia also helped create favorable conditions for America's entry into the war. In March 1917 Russian peasants, industrial workers, intellectuals inspired by Western liberal values, and revolutionaries who embraced the communist ideology of Karl Marx all joined in a revolutionary uprising that overthrew the repressive government of Tsar Nicholas II. A provisional government under the liberal Alexander Kerensky

briefly seemed to promise that Russia would take a democratic path, making it easier for President Wilson to portray the war as a battle for democracy.

On April 2 Wilson appeared before a joint session of Congress and solemnly called for a declaration of war. Applause and shouts rang out as Wilson eloquently described his vision of America's role in creating a post-war international order to make the world "safe for democracy." As the speech ended amid a final burst of cheers, Republican Senator Henry Cabot Lodge of Massachusetts, one of Wilson's staunchest political foes, rushed forward to shake his hand.

After a short but bitter debate, the Senate voted 82 to 6 for war. The House agreed, 373 to 50. Three key factors—German attacks on American shipping, U.S. economic investment in the Allied cause, and American cultural links to the Allies, especially England—had propelled the United States into the war.

MOBILIZING AT HOME, FIGHTING IN FRANCE, 1917–1918

America's entry into World War I underscored a deepening international involvement that had been underway for several decades. Yet compared to its effects on Europe, the war only grazed the United States. Russia, ill-prepared for war and geographically isolated from its allies, suffered very heavily. France, Great Britain, and Germany fought for more than four years; the United States, for nineteen months. Their armies suffered casualties of 70 percent or more; the U.S. casualty rate was 8 percent. The fighting left parts of France and Belgium brutally scarred; North America was physically untouched. Nevertheless, the war profoundly affected America. It changed not only those who participated directly in it, but also the American home front and the nation's government and economy.

Raising, Training, and Testing an Army

April 1917 found America's military woefully unprepared. The regular army consisted of 120,000 men, few with combat experience, plus 80,000 National Guard members. An aging officer corps dozed away the years until retirement. Ammunition reserves were paltry. The War Department was a snake pit of jealous bureaucrats, one of whom hoarded thousands of typewriters as the war approached.

While army chief-of-staff Peyton C. Marsh brought order to the military bureaucracy, Wilson's secretary of war, Newton D. Baker, concentrated on raising an army. Formerly the reform mayor of Cleveland, Baker lacked administrative talent but was a public-relations genius. The Selective Service Act of May 1917 required all men between twenty-one and thirty (later expanded to eighteen through forty-five) to register with local draft boards. Mindful of the Civil War draft riots, Baker planned the first official draft-registration day, June 5, 1917, as a "festival and patriotic occasion."

By the time the war ended in November 1918, more than 24 million men had registered, of whom nearly 3 million were drafted. Volunteers and National Guardsmen swelled the total to 4.3 million. Recruits got their first taste of army life in home front training camps. Along with military discipline and combat instruction, the camps built morale through shows, games, and recreation provided by volunteer organizations. The American Library Association contributed books. YMCA volunteers staffed base clubs and offered classes in literacy, French slang, and Bible study. In Plattsburgh, New York, local women opened a "Hostess House" to provide a touch of domesticity for homesick recruits at the nearby training camp. The idea soon spread to other communities near military camps.

The War Department monitored the off-duty behavior of young men cut off from the watchful eye of family and community. The Commission on Training Camp Activities presented films, lectures, and posters on the dangers of alcohol and prostitution. Any soldier disabled by venereal (that is, sexually transmitted) disease, one poster warned, "is a Traitor!" Camp commanders confined trainees to the base until nearby towns closed all brothels and saloons. The army's antiliquor, antiprostitution policies strengthened the moral-reform campaigns of the Progressive Era (see Chapter 21).

Beginning in December 1917, all recruits also underwent intelligence testing. Psychologists were eager to demonstrate the usefulness of their new field of expertise and claimed that tests measuring recruits' "intelligence quotient" (IQ) could help in assigning their duties and showing who had officer potential. Intelligence testing, declared Robert M. Yerkes, presi-

War Enthusiasm in the Heartland
In Denver, automobiles carrying young army recruits parade through the city.

dent of the American Psychological Association, would "help win the war."

When the psychologists announced that a high percentage of recruits were "morons," editorial writers bemoaned the wave of imbecility supposedly sweeping the nation. In fact, the tests mostly revealed that many recruits lacked formal education and cultural sophistication. One question asked whether *mauve* was a drink, a color, a fabric, or a food. Another—at a time when automobiles were rare in rural America—asked in which city a particular car, the Overland, was built. The testing also confirmed racial and ethnic stereotypes: native-born recruits of northern European origins scored highest; African Americans and recent immigrants lowest.

In short, the World War I training camps not only turned civilians into soldiers, they also reinforced the prewar moral-control reforms, and signaled changes ahead, including the national infatuation with standardized testing.

Some twelve thousand Native Americans served in the American Expeditionary Force (AEF). While some reformers eager to preserve Indian culture argued for all-Indian units, the army took a different view and integrated Native Americans into the general army. Some

Battling Prostitution on the Homefront
In this scene from "Fit to Fight," a 1917 War Department training film, Kid McCarthy tempts the hero, Hank, into a house of prostitution.

observers predicted that the wartime experience would hasten the assimilation of Indians into mainstream American life, considered by many a desirable goal at the time.

In April 1917 the African-American leader W. E. B. DuBois urged African Americans to "close ranks" and support the war. While some blacks resisted the draft, especially in the South (discussed later in "Opponents of the War"), others followed DuBois's advice. More than 260,000 blacks volunteered or were drafted, and 50,000 went to France. Racism pervaded the military, as it did American society. The navy assigned blacks only to menial positions, and the marines excluded them altogether.

One racist senator from Mississippi warned that the sight of "arrogant, strutting" black soldiers would trigger race riots. Blacks in training camps experienced crude racial abuse. Tensions exploded in Houston in August 1917 when some black soldiers, endlessly goaded by local whites, seized weapons from the armory and killed seventeen white civilians. After a hasty trial with no

appeal process, thirteen black soldiers were hanged and forty-one imprisoned for life. Not since the 1906 Brownsville incident (see Chapter 21) had black confidence in military justice been so shaken.

Organizing the Economy for War

The war years of 1917–1918 helped shape modern America. As historian Ellis Hawley has shown, the war's administrative innovations sped up longer-term processes of social reorganization. Many key developments of the 1920s and beyond—including the spread of mass production; the collaboration between government, business, and labor; and the continued growth of new professional and managerial elites—were furthered by the war.

The war led to unprecedented government oversight of the economy. Populists and progressives had long urged more public control of corporations. Wartime brought an elaborate supervisory apparatus. In 1916 Congress had created an advisory body, the Council of National Defense, to oversee the government's preparedness program. After war was declared, this council set up the War Industries Board (WIB) to coordinate military purchasing; ensure production efficiency; and provide weapons, equipment, and supplies to the military. Wilson reorganized the WIB in March 1918 and put Bernard Baruch in charge. A South Carolinian of German-Jewish origin, Baruch had made a fortune on Wall Street. Awed by his range of knowledge, Wilson called him Dr. Facts. Under Baruch, the WIB controlled the industrial sector. It allocated raw materials, established production priorities, and induced competing companies to standardize and coordinate their products and processes to save scarce commodities. The standardization of bicycle manufacturing, for example, saved tons of steel.

Acting under the authority of a law passed in August 1917, Wilson set up two more new agencies, the Fuel Administration and the Food Administration. The Fuel Administration controlled coal output, regulated fuel prices and consumption, and introduced daylight-saving time—an idea first proposed by Benjamin Franklin in the 1770s. The Food Administration, headed by Herbert Hoover, oversaw the production and allocation of wheat, meat, and sugar to ensure adequate supplies for the army as well as for the desperately food-short Allies. Born in poverty in Iowa, Hoover had prospered as a mining engineer in Asia. He was organizing food relief in Belgium when Wilson brought him back to Washington.

These regulatory agencies relied on voluntary cooperation reinforced by official pressure. For example, a barrage of Food Administration posters and magazine ads urged Americans to conserve food. Housewives signed pledges to observe "meatless" and "wheatless" days. President Wilson pitched in by pasturing a flock of sheep on the White House lawn. Slogans such as "Serve Beans by All Means" promoted substitutes for scarce commodities.

Harriot Stanton Blatch, daughter of woman's-rights pioneer Elizabeth Cady Stanton, headed the Food Administration's Speakers' Bureau, which spread the administration's conservation message. Blatch also organized the Woman's Land Army, which recruited women to replace male farm workers.

These agencies were the tip of the regulatory iceberg. Nearly five thousand government boards supervised home-front activities. These included the Shipping Board, which oversaw the transport of goods by water; the National War Labor Board, which resolved labor-management disputes that jeopardized production; and the Railroad Administration, headed by Treasury Secretary William McAdoo. When a railroad tie-up during the winter of 1917–1918 threatened the flow of supplies to Europe, the Railroad Administration stepped in and soon transformed the thousands of miles of track owned by many competing companies into an efficient national rail system.

American business, much criticized by progressive reformers, utilized the war emergency to improve its image. Corporate executives ran regulatory agencies. Factory owners distributed prowar propaganda to workers. Trade associations coordinated war production.

The war sped up the ongoing process of corporate consolidation and economic integration. In place of trustbusting, the government now encouraged cooperation among businesses, and corporate mergers jumped sharply. Commenting on the epidemic of "mergeritis," one magazine observed, "The war has accelerated . . . a tendency that was already irresistible. . . . Instead of punishing companies for acting in concert, the government is now in some cases forcing them to unite."

Overall, the war was good for business. Despite added business taxes imposed by Congress, wartime profits soared. After-tax profits in the copper industry, for example, jumped from 12 percent in 1913 to 24 percent in 1917.

This colossal regulatory apparatus was quickly dismantled after the war, but its influence lingered. The wartime mergers, coordination, and business-government cooperation affected the evolution of American business. The old laissez-faire suspicion of government, already weakened, eroded further in 1917–1918. In the 1930s, when the nation faced a different crisis, the government activism of World War I would be remembered (see Chapter 24).

With the American Expeditionary Force in France

When the United States entered the conflict, Allied prospects looked bleak. Germany's resumption of unrestricted U-boat warfare was taking a horrendous toll on Allied shipping: 1.5 million tons in March and April 1917. A failed French offensive on the Marne that spring caused such losses that French troops mutinied. A British offensive along the French-Belgian border in November 1917 gained four miles at a cost of more than four hundred thousand killed and wounded. That same month, the Italian army suffered a disastrous defeat at Caporetto near the Austrian border.

Worsening the Allies' situation, Russia left the war late in 1917, after the communist faction of the revolutionary movement, the Bolsheviks (Russian for "majority"), won control. The Bolsheviks had gained the initiative in April when its top leaders, including Vladimir Lenin, returned from exile in Switzerland. On November 6, 1917 (October 24 by the Russian calendar), a Bolshevik coup led by Lenin and Leon Trotsky, another exile recently arrived from New York City, overthrew Alexander Kerensky and seized power. Early in 1918 the Bolsheviks signed an armistice with Germany, the Treaty of Brest-Litovsk, freeing thousands of German troops on the Russian front for fighting in France.

The stalemate in the trenches continued, broken by periodic battles. In November 1917, in an important breakthrough in the technology of war, the British mobilized three hundred tanks along a six-mile section of the front near Cambrai, France, shattering the German defenses.

Initially, U.S. assistance to the Allies consisted of supplying munitions and organizing a convoy system that safeguarded Allied ships crossing the dangerous Atlantic. The first U.S. troops arrived in France in October 1917. Eventually about 2 million American soldiers served in France as members of the AEF under General John J. Pershing. Ironically, Pershing was of German origin; his family name had been Pfoersching. A West Point graduate and commander of the 1916 expedition against Pancho Villa in Mexico, Pershing was an iron-willed officer with a ramrod bearing, steely eyes, and trim mustache. The death of his wife and

three of their children in a fire in 1915 had further hardened him.

Most men of the AEF at first found the war a great adventure. Plucked from towns and farms, they sailed for Europe on crowded freighters; a lucky few traveled on captured German passenger liners. Once in France, railroad freight cars marked "HOMMES 40, CHEVAUX 8" (forty men, eight horses) took them to the front. Then began the routine of marching, training—and waiting.

The African Americans in the AEF who reached France worked mainly as mess-boys (mealtime aides), laborers, and stevedores (ship-cargo handlers). Although discriminatory, the latter assignments vitally aided the war effort. Sometimes working twenty-four hours nonstop, black stevedores unloaded supply ships with impressive efficiency. Some whites of the AEF pressed

The Faces of War
A wounded U.S. marine receives first aid in a trench near Toulon, France, in March 1918.

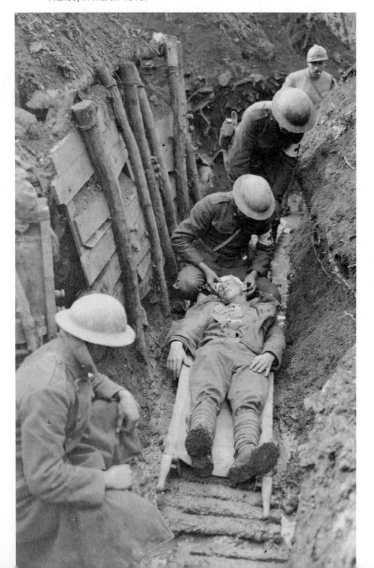

the French to treat African Americans as inferiors, but most ignored this advice and related to blacks without prejudice. This eye-opening experience would remain with blacks in the AEF after the war.

For the troops at the front, aerial dogfights between German and Allied reconnaissance planes offered spectacular sideshows. Germany's legendary "Red Baron," Manfred von Richthofen, shot down eighty British and French planes before his luck ran out in April 1918. In 1916 a group of American volunteers had joined the French air corps as the Lafayette Escadrille. Secretary of War Baker, grasping the military importance of air power, pushed a plane-construction program. Few planes were actually built, however—a rare failure of the U.S. war-production program.

France offered other diversions as well, and the U.S. military mobilized to warn young male recruits of the danger of venereal disease. One poster declared, "A German bullet is cleaner than a whore." When the French premier, Georges Clemenceau, offered to provide prostitutes for the American troops (as was the custom for French soldiers), Secretary of War Baker exclaimed, "For God's sake, don't show this to the President, or he'll stop the war."

The YMCA, Red Cross, and Salvation Army, including many young American women volunteers, provided a touch of home. Some 16,500 U.S. women served directly in the AEF in the United States and in France as nurses, telephone operators, canteen workers, and secretaries.

President Wilson, eager to underscore the distinctiveness of the U.S. role in the war, and to ensure a strong voice for America at the peace table, insisted that the United States be described as an "Associate Power" of the Allies. The French and British generals, however, facing desperate circumstances, wanted to absorb the Americans into existing units. But for both military and political reasons, Pershing and his superiors in Washington insisted that the AEF be "distinct and separate." A believer in aggressive combat, Pershing abhorred the defensive mentality ingrained by three years of trench warfare.

In March 1918, however, when Germany launched a major offensive along the Somme, the Allies created a unified command under Marshal Ferdinand Foch, chief of the French general staff. Some Americans participated in the fighting around Amiens and Armentières that stemmed the German advance.

The second phase of the Germans' spring 1918 offensive came in May along the Aisne River, where they broke through to the Marne and faced a nearly open

route to Paris, fifty miles away. On June 4, as the French government prepared for evacuation, American forces arrived in strength. Parts of three U.S. divisions and a marine brigade helped stop the Germans at the town of Château-Thierry and nearby Belleau Wood, a huge German machine-gun nest. (An AEF division at full strength consisted of twenty-seven thousand men and one thousand officers, plus twelve thousand support troops.)

These two German offensives had punched deep holes (or salients) in the Allied line. A German drive aimed at the cathedral city of Rheims between these two salients was stopped with the help of some eighty-five thousand American troops (see Map 22.2). This was the war's turning point. At enormous cost, the German offensive had been defeated. Contributing to this defeat was the fact that many German soldiers, already weakened by battle fatigue and poor diet, fell victim to influenza, an infectious disease that would soon emerge as a deadly worldwide epidemic (see the section "Public Health Crisis: The 1918 Influenza Epidemic").

Turning the Tide

The final Allied offensive began on July 18, 1918. Some 270,000 American soldiers fought in the Allied drive to push the Germans back from the Marne. Rain pelted down as the Americans moved into position on the night of July 17. One wrote in his diary, "Trucks, artillery, infantry columns, cavalry, wagons, caissons, mud, MUD, utter confusion." Meanwhile, another 100,000 AEF troops joined a parallel British offensive north of the Somme to expel the Germans from that area.

Pershing's first fully independent command came in September, when Foch authorized an AEF campaign to close a German salient around the town of St. Mihiel on the Meuse River, about 150 miles east of Paris. Eager to test his offensive strategy, Pershing assembled nearly five hundred thousand American and one hundred thousand French soldiers. Shelling of German positions began at 1:00 A.M. on September 11. Recorded an American in his diary, "[I]n one instant the entire front . . . was a sheet of flame, while the heavy artillery

MAP 22.2

The United States on the Western Front, 1918

American troops first saw action in the campaign to throw back Germany's spring 1918 offensive in the Somme and Aisne-Marne sectors. The next heavy American engagement came that autumn as part of the Allies' Meuse-Argonne offensive that ended the war.

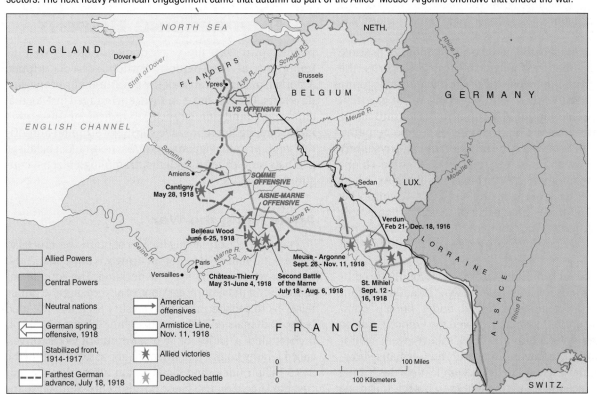

African-Americans at the Front
Black troops of the 369th Infantry Regiment in the trenches near Maffrecourt, France, in 1918. Most African-American soldiers were assigned to noncombat duty, such as unloading supplies and equipment.

made the earth quake." Within four days the salient was closed, in part because some German units had already withdrawn. Even so, St. Mihiel cost seven thousand U.S. casualties.

The war's last battle began on September 26 as some 1.2 million Americans joined the struggle to drive the Germans from the Meuse River and the dense Argonne Forest north of Verdun. The stench of poison gas (first used by the Germans in 1915) hung in the air, and bloated rats scurried in the mud, gorging on human remains. Americans now endured the filth, vermin, and dysentery familiar to veterans of the trenches. Frontline troops would never forget the terror of combat. As shells streaked overhead at night, one recalled, "We simply lay and trembled from sheer nervous tension." Some welcomed injuries as a ticket out of the battle zone. Others collapsed emotionally and were hospitalized for "shell shock."

One all-black division, the ninety-second, saw combat in the Meuse-Argonne campaign. In addition, four black infantry regiments served under French command. One entire regiment received the French Croix de Guerre, and several hundred black soldiers were awarded French decorations for bravery. The Germans showered the ninety-second division with leaflets describing American racism and urging blacks to defect, but none did.

The AEF's assignment was to cut the Sedan-Mezières Railroad, a major German supply route. In the way lay three long, heavily fortified German trenches, called Stellungen. "We are not men anymore, just savage beasts," wrote a young American. Death came in many forms, and without ceremony. Bodies, packs, rifles, photos of loved ones, and letters from home sank indiscriminately into the all-consuming mud. Influenza struck on both sides of the line, killing thousands of AEF members at the front and in training camps back home. One day as General Pershing rode in his staff car, he buried his head in his hands and moaned his dead wife's name: "Frankie, Frankie, my God, sometimes I don't know how I can go on."

Religious and ethical principles faded as men struggled to survive. "Love of thy neighbor is forgotten," recalled one, with "all the falsities of a sheltered civilization." The war's brutality would shape the literature of the 1920s as writers such as Ernest Hemingway stripped away the illusions obscuring the reality of mass slaughter.

But the AEF at last overran the dreaded German trenches, and the survivors slogged northward. In early November the Sedan-Mezières railroad was cut. The AEF had fulfilled its assignment, at a cost of 26,277 dead.

PROMOTING THE WAR AND SUPPRESSING DISSENT

In their own way, the war's domestic effects were as important as its battles. Patriotic fervor gripped America, in part because of the government's propaganda efforts. The war fever, in turn, encouraged intellectual conformity and intolerance of radical or dissenting ideas. Fueling the repressive spirit, government authorities and private vigilante groups hounded socialists, pacifists, and other dissidents, trampling citizens' constitutional rights.

Advertising the War

To President Wilson, selling the war at home was crucial to success in France. "It is not an army we must shape and train for war, it is a nation," he declared. The administration drew on the new professions of advertising and public relations to pursue this goal. Treasury Secretary McAdoo (who had married Wilson's daughter Eleanor in 1914) orchestrated a series of five government bond drives, called Liberty Loans, that financed about two-thirds of the $35.5 billion (including loans to the Allies) that the war cost the United States. These bonds were essentially loans to the government to cover war expenses.

Mobilizing the Home Front; Financing the War
Movie star Douglas Fairbanks at a New York City war-bond rally; a patriotic war-time poster.

Posters exhorted citizens to "Fight or Buy Bonds." Liberty Loan parades featured flags, banners, and marching bands. Movie stars like Mary Pickford and Charlie Chaplin worked for the cause. Schoolchildren purchased "thrift stamps" convertible into war bonds. Patriotic war songs reached a large public through phonograph recordings (see the Culture and Technology feature). Beneath the ballyhoo ran a note of coercion. Only "a friend of Germany," McAdoo warned, would refuse to buy bonds.

The balance of the government's war costs came from taxes. Using the power granted it by the Sixteenth Amendment, Congress imposed wartime income taxes that reached 70 percent at the top levels. War-profits taxes, excise taxes on liquor and luxuries, and increased estate taxes also helped finance the war.

Journalist George Creel headed the key wartime propaganda agency, the Committee on Public Information (CPI). While claiming merely to combat rumors with facts, the Creel committee in reality publicized the government's version of events and discredited all who questioned that version. One of CPI's twenty-one divisions distributed posters drawn by leading illustrators. Another wrote propaganda releases that appeared in the press as "news" with no indication of their source. The *Saturday Evening Post* and other popular magazines published CPI ads that warned against spies, saboteurs,

and anyone who "spreads pessimistic stories" or "cries for peace." Theaters screened CPI films bearing such titles as *The Kaiser: The Beast of Berlin*.

The CPI poured foreign-language pamphlets into immigrant neighborhoods and supplied prowar editorials to the foreign-language press. At a CPI media event at George Washington's Mount Vernon home on July 4, 1918, an Irish-born tenor sang "The Battle Hymn of the Republic" while immigrants from thirty-three nations filed reverently past Washington's tomb. The CPI also targeted workers. Factory posters attacked the charge by some socialists that this was a capitalists' war. Samuel Gompers of the American Federation of Labor headed a prowar "American Alliance for Labor and Democracy" funded by the CPI. An army of seventy-five thousand CPI volunteers gave short prowar talks to movie audiences and other gatherings. Creel later calculated that these "Four-Minute Men" delivered 7.5 million speeches.

Teachers, writers, religious leaders, and magazine editors overwhelmingly supported the war. These custodians of culture saw the conflict as a struggle to defend threatened values. Historians wrote essays contrasting German brutality with the Allies' lofty ideals. In *The Marne* (1918), expatriate American writer Edith Wharton expressed her love for France. The war poems of Alan Seeger enjoyed great popularity. A Harvard graduate who volunteered to fight for France and died in action in

The Phonograph, Popular Music, and Home-Front Morale in World War I

Today's compact disks, MTV videos, and Internet music websites all trace their ancestry to technologies developed in the late nineteenth century. Along with the movies and nationally distributed magazines, recorded music laid the groundwork for an American mass culture in the early twentieth century, and helped build support for the U.S. war effort in 1917–1918.

Thomas Edison first recorded the human voice in 1877. (Historians differ over whether the first recorded words were "Halloo," in July or "Mary had a little lamb" in December.) The following year, Edison patented a "phonograph" utilizing cylinders wrapped in tin foil. Other inventors patented recording machinery involving wax-coated cylinders, which proved superior to tin foil. The first known recorded musical performance was by an eleven-year-old pianist, Josef Hoffmann, in Edison's laboratory in New Jersey in 1887.

Emile Berliner patented a new technique of recording on disks in 1887, and disks quickly proved superior

Thomas A. Edison contemplates an early cylinder phonograph.

to cylinders. In a critical breakthrough, Berliner also developed a technique for mass producing hard-rubber records from a zinc master disk.

In sound reproduction by means of a phonograph, the sound being recorded is converted to electrical impulses, which in turn create slight mechanical variations in circular grooves on a rotating master disk. When a record manufactured from the master disk is played, a stylus, or needle, attached to a tone arm tracks the circular grooves, converting the variations back into electrical signals that are amplified and converted into sound by a loudspeaker.

The new technology became commercially available in 1890 when the Columbia Phonograph Company published a catalog of cylinder recordings. By 1894 Emile Berliner's U.S. Gramophone Company was selling around a thousand phonographs and some twenty-five thousand records a year, including hymns, classical works, and popular songs. The United States Marine Band conducted by John Philip Sousa was an early favorite. The first commercial jazz record, "Livery Stable Blues," appeared in 1917, recorded by a white New Orleans group called the Original Dixieland Jass [sic] Band. The Sears Roebuck catalog, widely distributed in rural and small-town America in the early twentieth century, devoted several pages to "talking machines" on which buyers could play commercially produced records or make their own recordings.

In 1900 Eldridge Johnson bought Emile Berliner's company and formed what soon became the industry leader, the Victor Talking Machine Company. Six years later Victor marketed the Victrola, a handsome cabinet-style phonograph that proved so popular that "Victrola" became a generic name for all record players. The earliest phonographs had amplified the sound by a large and rather unsightly external speaker horn. The Victrola concealed the horn inside the cabinet, making the unit more attractive for the living room or parlor. The "volume control" had two settings: open the cabinet doors to increase the volume, close them to reduce it.

Early Victrolas were expensive, ranging from $75 for the cheapest table model to far more luxurious models

featuring exotic woods, lacquer finishes, and painted decorations. Despite the prices, annual sales reached 573,000 by 1917. Although electric-powered Victrolas became available in 1913, most buyers preferred the hand-cranked model well into the 1920s.

Records made of laminated shellac with a paper core (1906) and then of Condensite, an early form of plastic, introduced in 1913, proved more durable than the older hard-rubber disks, with less surface noise. The first vinyl records did not appear until 1929.

The American home front during World War I resonated to the sound of patriotic music blaring from thousands of Victrolas and phonographs produced by rival companies. War songs ranged from the sentimental, such as the waltz "Till We Meet Again," to novelty numbers, including "Oo-La-La Wee, Wee"; the tongue-twister "Sister Susie's Sewing Shirts for Soldiers," and Irving Berlin's comic soldier's lament "Oh! How I Hate to Get Up in the Morning."

Other songs were rousingly patriotic, such as "America, I Love You" and George M. Cohan's 1917 hit "Over There." Born in Rhode Island in 1878, Cohan appeared in vaudeville as a child with his parents and sister in "The Four Cohans" and went on to became a successful producer of Broadway musicals.

"Over There," pledging America to fight to the end, became the unofficial anthem of the war. With many Americans opposed to U.S. intervention, prowar songs played an important propaganda role, and Cohan received a Congressional citation for his song. In September 1918 the great Italian tenor Enrico Caruso sang "Over There," popularized by his earlier recording of the song, before a huge audience in New York's Central Park.

In the nineteenth century, new songs had been introduced by music-hall performers and then sold in sheet-music form, allowing families and social groups to sing them at home around the piano. Sheet music remained popular, but by 1917–1918 the recording industry was firmly established, and many thousands of phonograph owners purchased recordings of popular wartime songs for repeated listening at home.

By the war's end, American popular music was firmly linked to the recording technology pioneered by Edison, Berliner, Johnson, and others. Early records were played mainly in the home, but with the coming of radio in the 1920s, recordings of classical music and popular songs could reach a mass audience simultaneously.

By the middle of the twentieth century, phonographs and phonograph records, incorporating many technological advances, played a huge role in American popular culture, accounting for millions of dollars in annual sales and spreading the fame of recording artists from Ella Fitzgerald and Bing Crosby to Elvis Presley, Bob Dylan, and the Beatles.

Focus Questions

- What key technical developments made it possible for the phonograph to evolve from a laboratory novelty into a major commercial product?

- How did popular songs spread by phonograph recordings help build support for American participation in World War I?

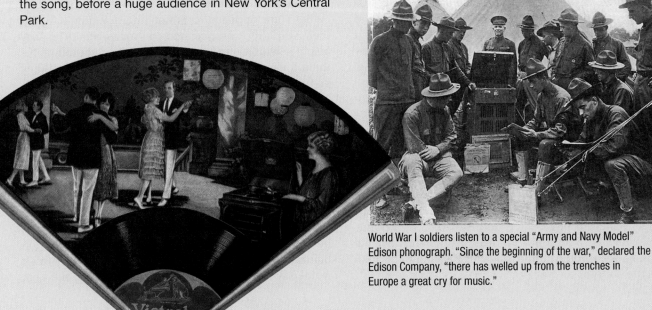

World War I soldiers listen to a special "Army and Navy Model" Edison phonograph. "Since the beginning of the war," declared the Edison Company, "there has welled up from the trenches in Europe a great cry for music."

A fan advertising Victrola records and phonographs.

1916, Seeger held a romantic vision of the conflict as a noble crusade. An artillery barrage was for him "the magnificent orchestra of war."

Many progressive reformers who had applauded Wilson's domestic program now cheered his war. Herbert Croly, Walter Lippmann, and other progressive intellectuals associated with the *New Republic* magazine zealously backed the war. In gratitude, Wilson administration officials regularly briefed the editors on the government's policies.

The Progressive educator John Dewey supported the war and condemned its opponents in a series of *New Republic* essays. Socially engaged intellectuals must accept reality and shape it toward positive social goals, he wrote, not stand aside in self-righteous isolation. The war, he went on, presented exciting "social possibilities." Domestically, government activism stimulated by the war could be channeled to reform purposes when peace returned. Internationally, America's entry into the war could transform an imperialistic struggle into a global democratic crusade.

Wartime Intolerance and Dissent

Responding to the propaganda, some Americans became almost hysterical in their strident patriotism, their hatred of all things German, and their hostility to aliens and dissenters. Isolated acts of sabotage by German sympathizers, including the blowing up of a New Jersey munitions dump, fanned the flames. Persons believed to harbor pro-German sentiments were forced to kiss the flag or recite the Pledge of Allegiance. An Ohio woman suspected of disloyalty was wrapped in a flag, marched to a bank, and ordered to buy a war bond. In Collinsville, Illinois, a mob lynched German-born Robert Prager in April 1918. When a jury freed the mob leaders, a jury member shouted, "Nobody can say we aren't loyal now." The *Washington Post*, although deploring the lynching, saw it as evidence of "a healthful and wholesome awakening in the interior of the country."

An Iowa politician charged that "90 percent of all the men and women who teach the German language are traitors." German books vanished from libraries, towns with German names changed them, and on some restaurant menus "liberty sandwich" and "liberty cabbage" replaced "hamburger" and "sauerkraut." A popular evangelist, Billy Sunday, proclaimed, "If you turn hell upside down you will find 'Made in Germany' stamped on the bottom."

Even the music world suffered. The Boston Symphony Orchestra dismissed its conductor, Karl Muck, for having accepted a decoration from Kaiser Wilhelm. Except for Bach, Beethoven, Mozart, and Brahms, the Philadelphia Orchestra banned all German music.

The zealots also targeted war critics and radicals. A Cincinnati mob horsewhipped a pacifist minister. Theodore Roosevelt branded antiwar Senator Robert La Follette "an unhung traitor." Columbia University fired two antiwar professors. In Bisbee, Arizona, vigilantes forced twelve hundred miners who belonged to the Industrial Workers of the World onto a freight train and shipped them into the New Mexico desert without food or water. The IWW opposed the war, and its members were accused of aiding the German cause.

Despite the climate of intolerance, many Americans persisted in opposing the war. Some were immigrants with ancestral ties to Germany. Others were religious pacifists, including Quakers, Mennonites, and Jehovah's Witnesses. Congresswoman Jeannette Rankin of Montana, a pacifist and the first woman elected to Congress, voted against the declaration of war. "I want to stand by my country," she told the House of Representatives, "but I cannot vote for war."

Of some sixty-five thousand men who registered as conscientious objectors (COs), twenty-one thousand were drafted. Assigned to noncombat duty on military bases, such as cleaning latrines, these COs sometimes experienced considerable abuse. When two Hutterite brothers who had refused to wear military uniforms died in prison, their bodies were dressed in uniforms before they were shipped home.

Woodrow Wilson heaped scorn on the pacifists. "What I am opposed to is not [their] feeling . . . , but their stupidity," he declared in November 1917; "my heart is with them, but my mind has contempt for them. I want peace, but I know how to get it, and they do not."

Socialist leaders such as Eugene Debs and Victor Berger viewed the war as a capitalist contest for markets, with the soldiers as cannon fodder. The U.S. declaration of war, they insisted, mainly reflected Wall Street's desire to protect its loans to England and France. Other socialists supported the war, however, dividing the party.

The war split the women's movement as well. While some leaders joined Jane Addams in opposition, others endorsed the war while keeping their own goals in view. In *Mobilizing Woman-Power* (1918), Harriot Stanton Blatch offered a variant of Woodrow Wilson's theme: women who wished to help shape the peace, she said,

must support the war. Anna Howard Shaw, a former president of the National American Woman Suffrage Association (NAWSA), accepted an appointment to chair the Woman's Committee of the Council of National Defense, a largely symbolic post.

Carrie Chapman Catt, Shaw's successor as president of NAWSA, had helped start the Woman's Peace party in 1915. But she supported U.S. entry into the war in 1917, sharing to some extent Wilson's vision of a more liberal postwar world order. Catt continued to focus mainly on woman suffrage, however, insisting that this was NAWSA's "number one war job." For this, some superpatriots accused her of disloyalty.

Draft resistance extended beyond the ranks of conscientious objectors. An estimated 2.4 to 3.6 million young men failed to register at all, and of those who did, about 12 percent either did not appear when drafted or deserted from training camp. Historian Jeanette Keith has documented high levels of draft resistance in the rural South. The urban elites who ran the draft boards were more inclined to defer young men of their own class than poor farmers, white or black, fueling class resentment. In June 1918 a truck loaded with U.S. soldiers seeking draft evaders in rural Georgia crashed when a wooden bridge collapsed, killing three soldiers and injuring others. Investigators found that the bridge timbers has been deliberately sawed nearly through.

Southern critics of the war included the one-time populist Tom Watson of Georgia. (Watson was also notoriously racist and anti-Semitic.) The war was a rich-man's plot, Watson charged in his paper *The Jeffersonian*, adding that draft boards discriminated against the poor.

Blacks had added reasons to oppose the draft. Of southern blacks who registered, one-third were drafted, in contrast to only one-quarter of whites. White draft boards justified this by arguing that low-income black families could more easily spare a male breadwinner. As an Alabama board observed: "[I]t is a matter of common knowledge that it requires more for a white man and his wife to live than it does a negro man and his wife, due to their respective stations in life." But the dynamics of race worked in complex ways: some southern whites, fearful of arming black men even for military service, favored drafting only whites.

The war's most incisive critic was Randolph Bourne, a young journalist. Although Bourne admired John Dewey, he rejected Dewey's prowar position and dissected his arguments in several penetrating essays. He dismissed the belief that reformers could direct the war to their own purposes. "If the war is too strong for you to prevent," he asked, "how is it going to be weak enough for you to control and mould to your liberal purposes?"

Eventually, many prowar intellectuals came to agree. By 1919 Dewey conceded that the war, far from promoting reform, had encouraged reaction and intolerance. Bourne did not live to see his vindication, however. He died in 1918, at the age of thirty-two, of influenza.

Suppressing Dissent by Law

Wartime intolerance also surfaced in federal laws and official actions. The Espionage Act of June 1917 set stiff fines and prison sentences for a variety of loosely defined antiwar activities. The Sedition Amendment (May 1918) imposed heavy penalties on anyone convicted of using "disloyal, profane . . . or abusive language" about the government, the Constitution, the flag, or the military.

Wilson's attorney general, Thomas W. Gregory, used these laws to stamp out dissent. Opponents of the war, proclaimed Gregory, should expect no mercy "from an outraged people and an avenging government." Under the federal legislation and similar state laws, some fifteen hundred pacifists, socialists, IWW leaders, and other war critics were arrested. One socialist, Rose Pastor Stokes, received a ten-year prison sentence (later commuted) for telling an audience, "I am for the people, and the government is for the profiteers." Kate Richards O'Hare, a midwestern socialist organizer, spent over a year in jail for declaring, "The women of the United States are nothing more than brood sows, to raise children to get into the army and be made into fertilizer." Eugene Debs was imprisoned in 1918 for a speech discussing the economic causes of the war, and served for three years until his sentence was commuted by President Warren Harding.

Under the authority of the Espionage Act, Postmaster General Albert S. Burleson, a reactionary superpatriot, suppressed socialist periodicals, including *The Masses*, published by radicals in New York City's Greenwich Village, and Tom Watson's *Jeffersonian*. Burleson "didn't know socialism from rheumatism," according to socialist Norman Thomas, but he pursued his repressive crusade. In January 1919 Congressman-elect Victor Berger was convicted under the Espionage Act for publishing antiwar articles in his socialist newspaper, the *Milwaukee Leader*. (The Supreme Court reversed Berger's conviction in 1921.) Upton Sinclair protested to President Wilson that a man of Burleson's

"childish ignorance" should wield such power; but Wilson did little to restrain Burleson's excesses.

A patriotic group called the American Protective League and local "Councils of Defense" operating with vague governmental authority further enforced ideological conformity. The 1917 Bolshevik takeover in Russia sharpened the wartime attacks on domestic radicals. As communists, the Bolsheviks believed in a one-party state and anticipated the violent overthrow of the capitalist system. Some Americans feared that the United States could fall to communism as well.

In three 1919 decisions, the U.S. Supreme Court upheld the Espionage Act convictions of war critics. In *Schenck* v. *United States*, Justice Oliver Wendell Holmes, Jr., writing for a unanimous court, justified such repression in cases where a person's exercise of the First Amendment right of free speech posed a "clear and present danger" to the nation.

The early wartime mood of idealism had degenerated into suspicion, narrow conformity, and persecution of all who failed to meet the zealots' notions of "100 percent Americanism." The effects of this wartime climate would linger long after the armistice was signed.

ECONOMIC AND SOCIAL TRENDS IN WARTIME AMERICA

The war affected the lives of millions of ordinary Americans, including industrial workers, farmers, women, and blacks. The moral-control aspects of progressivism gained momentum in 1917–1918, but for the most part progressive reform energies faded amid the distractions of war. Amid these social changes, a deadly influenza epidemic in 1918 took a grievous toll.

Boom Times in Industry and Agriculture

World War I benefited the U.S. economy. From 1914 to 1918 factory output grew by more than one-third. Even with several million men in the military, the civilian work force expanded by 1.3 million between 1916 and 1918, thanks largely to new jobs in war-related industries such as shipbuilding, munitions, steel, and textiles. Prices rose, but so did wages. Even unskilled workers enjoyed wartime wage increases averaging nearly 20 percent. Samuel Gompers urged workers not to strike during the war. Some IWW workers and maverick AFL locals went on strike anyway, but with the economy

booming, most workers observed the no-strike request.

The war's social impact took many forms. The stream of job seekers pouring into industrial centers strained housing, schools, and municipal services. The consumption of cigarettes, which soldiers and workers could carry in their shirt pockets more conveniently than pipes or cigars, soared from 14 billion in 1914 to 48 billion in 1918. Reflecting wartime prosperity, automobile production quadrupled, from 460,000 in 1914 to 1.8 million in 1917, then dipped briefly in 1918 as steel went for military production.

Farmers profited, too. With European farm production disrupted, U.S. agricultural prices more than doubled between 1913 and 1918, and farmers' real income rose significantly. Cotton prices rose from twelve cents a pound in 1913 to twenty-nine cents a pound by 1918, and corn prices surged upward as well.

This agricultural boom proved a mixed blessing. Farmers who borrowed heavily to expand production faced a credit squeeze when farm prices fell after the war. In the 1920s and 1930s, hard-pressed farmers would look back to the war years as a golden age of prosperity.

Blacks Migrate Northward

The war speeded up the exodus of southern blacks. An estimated half-million African Americans moved north during the war, and most settled in cities. Each day fresh arrivals trudged through the railroad stations of Philadelphia, New York, Detroit, and Pittsburgh. Chicago's black population grew from 44,000 in 1910 to 110,000 in 1920, Cleveland's from 8,000 to 34,000.

Economic opportunity beckoned. The war nearly halted immigration from Europe, so booming industries hired black workers to help take up the slack. African-American newspapers like the *Chicago Defender* spread the word of job opportunities. Some companies sent labor agents south to recruit black workers. Letters and word-of-mouth reports swelled the ranks of blacks heading north. One southern black, newly settled near Chicago, wrote home, "Nothing here but money, and it is not hard to get." A Pittsburgh newcomer presented a more balanced picture: "They give you big money for what you do, but they charge you big things for what you get."

To the southern black sharecropper, the prospect of earning three dollars a day or more in a region where racism seemed less intense appeared a heaven-sent opportunity. By 1920, 1.5 million African Americans were working in northern factories and other urban-based jobs.

Migration of the Negro Series: No. 1, *During the World War,* **by Jacob Lawrence, 1940–1941**

These newcomers brought with them their social institutions—above all, the church. Large churches and storefront missions met the spiritual and social needs of deeply religious migrants from the South. The concentration of blacks in New York City laid the groundwork for the Harlem Renaissance, a cultural flowering of the 1920s (see "A Place in Time: Harlem in the Twenties" in Chapter 23). This migration also strengthened black organizations. The National Association for the Advancement of Colored People (NAACP) doubled its membership during the war.

Once the initial elation faded, newly arrived African Americans often found that they had exchanged one set of problems for another. White workers resented the labor competition, and white homeowners lashed out as jammed black neighborhoods spilled over into surrounding areas. A bloody outbreak occurred on July 2, 1917, in East St. Louis, Illinois, home to thousands of recently arrived southern blacks. In a coordinated attack, a white mob torched black homes and shot the residents as they fled for their lives. At least thirty-nine blacks died, including a two-year-old who was shot and then thrown into a burning house.

A few weeks later, a silent march down New York's Fifth Avenue organized by the NAACP protested racist violence. One banner bore a slogan that echoed Wilson's phrase justifying U.S. involvement in the war: "Mr. President, Why Not Make AMERICA Safe for Democracy?" Like other wartime social trends, growing racial tensions did not end with the return of peace.

Women in Wartime

From one perspective, World War I seems a uniquely male experience. Male politicians and statesmen led their nations into war. Male generals sent other men into battle. Yet war touches all of society, not just half of it. The war affected women differently, but it affected them profoundly.

Feminist leaders like Carrie Chapman Catt and Anna Howard Shaw hoped that the war would lead to full equality and greater opportunity for women. For a time, these goals seemed attainable. In addition to the women who served with the AEF and in wartime volunteer agencies, about 1 million women worked in industry. Thousands more held other jobs, from streetcar conductors to bricklayers. "Out of . . . repression into opportunity is the meaning of the war to thousands of women," wrote Florence Thorne of the American Federation of Labor in 1917.

Hope glowed brightly as the woman suffrage movement sped toward victory on a tide of wartime enthusiasm. Through their war service, President Wilson wrote Catt, women had earned the right to vote. As we saw in Chapter 21, New York passed a state woman-suffrage referendum in 1917. In 1919, barraged by prosuffrage

petitions, the House and Senate overwhelmingly passed the Nineteenth Amendment granting women the vote. Ratification followed in 1920.

Beyond this victory, hopes that the war would permanently better women's status proved unfounded. Relatively few women actually entered the work force for the first time in 1917–1918; most simply moved to more highly paid jobs. Despite women's protests and War Labor Board rulings, even in these better-paying jobs most earned less than the men they replaced. As for the women in the AEF, the War Department refused their requests for military rank and benefits.

At the end of the war, many women lost their jobs to returning veterans. The New York labor federation advised, "The same patriotism which induced women to enter industry during the war should induce them to vacate their positions after the war." Male streetcar workers in Cleveland went on strike to force women conductors off the job. By 1920 the percentage of all U.S. women who were in the work force was actually slightly lower than it had been in 1910. As industrial researcher Mary Van Kleeck wrote in 1921, when the war emergency ended, traditional male attitudes toward women "came to life once more."

Public Health Crisis: The 1918 Influenza Epidemic

Amid battlefield casualties and home-front social changes, the nation also coped with influenza, a highly contagious viral infection often complicated by pneumonia. The 1918 epidemic, spread by a particularly deadly strain of the virus, killed as many as 30 million people worldwide. Despite medical and public-health advances, doctors had few weapons against the flu in 1918 (see Figure 22.1).

Moving northward from its origins in southern Africa, the epidemic spread from the war zone in France to U.S. military camps, striking Fort Riley, Kansas, in March and quickly advancing to other bases and the urban population. In September an army health official visiting Camp Devens in Massachusetts wrote, "I saw hundreds of young stalwart men in uniform coming into . . . the hospital. . . . The faces wore a bluish cast, a cough brought up blood-stained sputum. In the morning, the dead bodies are stacked about the morgue like cordwood."

The flu hit the cities hard. In Philadelphia on September 19, the day after 200,000 people had turned out for a Liberty Loan rally, 635 new influenza cases were reported. Many cities forbade all public gatherings. The worst came in October, when the flu killed 195,000

FIGURE 22.1
Death Rate from Influenza and Pneumonia, 1900–1960
This chart shows the devastating toll of the 1918 influenza epidemic, as well as the gradual decline of influenza mortality thanks to the discovery of antibiotics that combat the secondary infections that are often fatal.

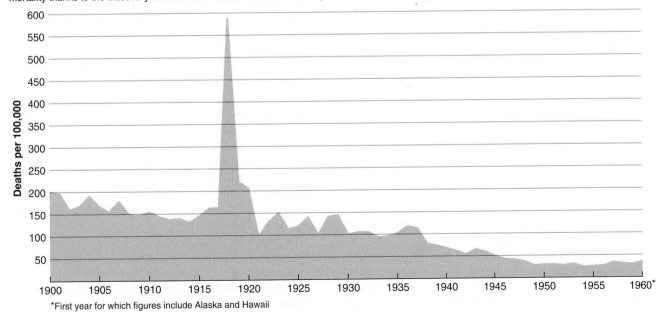

*First year for which figures include Alaska and Hawaii

Source: Historical Statistics of the United States: Colonial Times to 1970 (1975) vol. I, p. 58   *Note:* Number of deaths per 100,000 population

Battling Influenza, 1918
Red Cross workers like these in Philadelphia and other public-health professionals mobilized to combat a deadly epidemic that claimed over half a million American lives.

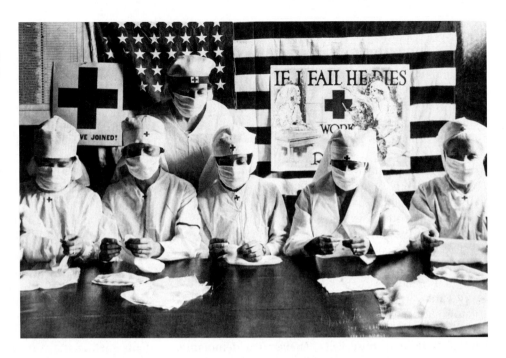

Americans. The total U.S. death toll was about 550,000, over six times the total of AEF battle deaths in France. The epidemic stimulated research, partially funded by a $1 million congressional appropriation to the U.S. Public Health Service, that eventually isolated the virus and produced vaccines and antibiotics that made future flu outbreaks less lethal.

The War and Progressivism

In assessing the war's effects on Progressive Era reform movements, historians paint a mixed picture.

The war strengthened the coercive, moral-control aspect of progressivism, including the drive for the prohibition of alcohol. Exploiting anti-German sentiment, prohibitionists pointed out that the nation's biggest breweries bore such German names as Pabst, Schlitz, and Anheuser-Busch. Beer, they hinted, was part of a German plot to undermine Americans' fitness for combat. With Herbert Hoover preaching food conservation, they stressed the wastefulness of using grain to make liquor. When the Eighteenth Amendment establishing national prohibition passed Congress in December 1917, it was widely seen as a war measure. Ratified in 1919, it went into effect on January 1, 1920.

As we have seen, the War Department reinforced the Progressive Era antiprostitution campaign by closing brothels near military bases, including New Orleans's famed Storyville. (As Storyville's jazz musicians moved north to Memphis, St. Louis, Kansas City, and Chicago, jazz reached a national audience.) The Commission on Training Camp Activities hired sixty female lecturers to tour the nation urging women to uphold standards of sexual morality. "Do Your Bit to Keep Him Fit" one wartime pamphlet advised women.

Congress contributed to the antiprostitution campaign by appropriating $4 million to combat venereal disease, especially among war workers. In San Antonio, a major military hub, an antiprostitution leader reflected the war mood when he declared, "We propose to fight vice . . . with the cold steel of the law, and to drive in the steel from the point to the hilt until the law's supremacy is acknowledged."

The surge of wartime moral-reform activity convinced some that traditional codes of behavior, weakening before the war, had been restored. One antiprostitution crusader exulted, "Young men of today . . . are nearer perfection in conduct, morals, and ideals than any similar generation of young men in the history of the world. Their minds have been raised to ideals that would never have been attained save by the heroism of . . . the World War."

Other reform causes gained momentum as well. The woman-suffrage movement finally achieved success. And the proworker side of progressivism made some gains. The War Labor Board (WLB), spurred by progressives interested in the cause of labor, encouraged workers to join unions and guaranteed unions' right to bar-

gain collectively with management. The WLB also pressured factory owners to introduce the eight-hour workday, end child labor, provide worker-compensation benefits, and open their plants to safety and sanitation inspectors. William McAdoo's Railroad Administration also recognized railway workers' right to unionize. Under these favorable conditions, union membership rose from 2.7 million in 1916 to more than 5 million by 1920.

Another wartime agency, the United States Housing Corporation, built housing projects for workers, including some that encompassed schools, playgrounds, and recreational centers. Several state legislatures, concluding that worker-protection laws would help the war effort, passed wage-and-hour laws and other measures benefiting factory laborers.

The Bureau of War Risk Insurance (BWRI), created by Congress in October 1917 to aid soldiers' families, established an important precedent of government help for families at risk. As Julia Lathrop, head of the Federal Children's Bureau, observed, "The least a democratic nation can do, which sends men into war, is to give a solemn assurance that the families will be cared for." By the war's end, the BWRI was sending regular checks to 2.1 million families.

The Bureaucracy of War
Employees of the federal Bureau of War Risk Insurance, which provided support to families of World War I servicemen, operate a machine that automatically signs ten checks at one time.

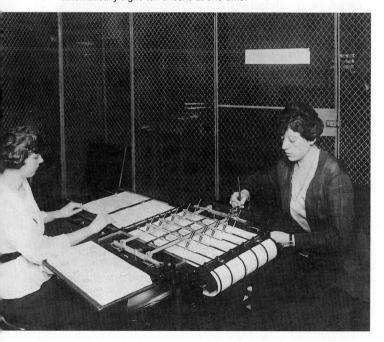

Despite some gains, however, the war's long-term effect was to weaken the progressive social-justice impulse. While the years 1917–1918 brought increased corporate regulation—a major progressive goal—the regulatory agencies were often dominated by the very business interests supposedly being supervised, and they were quickly dismantled when the war ended.

The government's repression of radicals and antiwar dissenters fractured the fragile coalition of left-leaning progressives, women's groups, trade unionists, and some socialists that had provided the momentum for prewar worker-protection laws, and ushered in a decade of reaction. The 1918 midterm election signaled the shift: the Democrats lost both houses of Congress to a deeply conservative Republican party.

Nevertheless, taking a still longer view, the Progressive Era reform coalition would reemerge in the depression decade of the 1930s. And as Franklin D. Roosevelt's New Deal took shape in 1933 (see Chapter 24), ideas and inspiration came from World War I precedents such as the War Labor Board, the United States Housing Corporation, and the Bureau of War Risk Insurance.

JOYOUS ARMISTICE, BITTER AFTERMATH, 1918–1920

In November 1918 the war finally ended. The peace conference that followed stands as a high point of America's growing internationalist involvement, but it also triggered a sharp domestic reaction against that involvement. Woodrow Wilson dominated the peace conference but failed in his most cherished objective—American membership in the League of Nations. At home, as racism and intolerance worsened, the electorate repudiated Wilsonianism and in 1920 sent a conservative Republican to the White House.

Wilson's Fourteen Points; The Armistice

From the moment the United States entered the war, President Wilson planned to put a "Made in America" stamp on the peace. U.S. involvement, he and his reform-minded supporters believed, could transform a sordid power conflict into a crusade for a more democratic world order. As the nation mobilized in 1917, Wilson recruited a group of advisers called The Inquiry to translate his vision into specific war aims. The need for a clear statement of U.S. war objectives grew urgent

after the Bolsheviks, having seized power in Russia, published many of the self-serving secret treaties signed by European powers prior to 1914.

In a speech to Congress in January 1918, Wilson summed up U.S. war aims in fourteen points. Eight of these goals dealt with territorial settlements in postwar Europe; Wilson stated that the subject peoples of the Austro-Hungarian and Ottoman empires should have the right to determine their own political futures (self-determination). A ninth point insisted that colonial disputes take into account the interests of the colonized peoples. The remaining five points offered Wilson's larger postwar vision: a world of free navigation, free trade, reduced armaments, openly negotiated treaties, and "a general association of nations" to resolve conflicts peacefully. The Fourteen Points helped solidify American support for the war, especially among liberals. The high-minded objectives seemed proof that the United States had entered the war not for selfish reasons but out of noble motives.

In early October 1918, with the Allies advancing on several fronts, the German high command proposed an armistice based on Wilson's Fourteen Points. The British and French hesitated, but when Wilson threatened to negotiate a separate peace with Germany, they agreed. Meanwhile, in Berlin, Kaiser Wilhelm II had abdicated and a German republic had been proclaimed.

As dawn broke over the forest of Compiègne some fifty miles north of Paris on November 11, 1918, Marshal Foch and his German counterparts, seated in Foch's private railway car, signed an armistice ending hostilities at 11:00 A.M. An American air ace, Captain Edward Rickenbacker, flew over the lines and watched as the booming guns fell silent. Rockets burst over the front that night not in anger but in relief and celebration. Back home, cheering throngs (some wearing face masks against the influenza epidemic) filled the streets. "Everything for which America has fought has been accomplished," Wilson proclaimed.

Troop transports soon ferried the soldiers home. One returnee, artillery captain Harry Truman of Missouri, described his feelings in a letter to his fiancée, Bess Wallace:

> I've never seen anything that looks so good as the Liberty Lady in New York Harbor. . . . [T[he men have seen so much and have been in so many hard places that it takes something real to give them a thrill, but when the band . . . played "Home Sweet Home" there were not many dry eyes. The hardest of hard-boiled cookies even had to blow his nose a time or two.

The Versailles Peace Conference, 1919

Eager to play a central role in forging the peace, Wilson made a crucial decision to lead the U.S. delegation to the peace conference. This was probably a mistake. The strain of long bargaining sessions soon took its toll on his frail nerves and slim reserve of energy.

Wilson compounded his mistake by his choices of his fellow negotiators. All but one were Democrats, and the sole Republican was an elderly diplomat with little influence in the party. Selecting one or two prominent Republicans might have spared Wilson future grief. The Democrats' loss of Congress in the 1918 midterm election was a further ill-omen.

Nevertheless, spirits soared on December 4, 1918, as the *George Washington*, a converted German liner, steamed out of New York bearing Wilson —the first president to cross the Atlantic while in office—to Europe. Ships' whistles blared as Wilson waved to the crowd on the docks. The giddy mood continued when Wilson reached France. In Paris, shouts of "Voodrow Veelson" rang out as he rode up the Champs-Élysées, the city's ceremonial boulevard. When Wilson visited England, children at the dock in Dover spread flowers in his path. In Italy an exuberant local official compared him to Jesus Christ.

The euphoria faded once the peace conference began at the palace of Versailles near Paris, where the treaty ending the Revolutionary War and granting American independence had been signed 136 years before. Joining Wilson were the other Allied heads of state: Italy's Vittorio Orlando; the aged and cynical Georges Clemenceau of France; and England's David Lloyd George, of whom Wilson said, "He is slippery as an eel, and I never know when to count on him." Japan participated in the conference as well.

The European statesmen at Versailles represented nations that had suffered greatly and were determined to avenge their losses. Their goals bore little relation to Wilson's liberal vision. As Clemenceau remarked, "God gave us the Ten Commandments and we broke them. Mr. Wilson has given us the Fourteen Points. We shall see."

Differences surfaced quickly. Orlando demanded a port for Italy on the eastern Adriatic Sea. Japan insisted on keeping the trading rights that it had seized from Germany in the Chinese province of Shandong (Shantung). Clemenceau was obsessed with revenge. At one point, an appalled Wilson threatened to leave the conference.

Reflecting this poisonous climate, the peace treaty forced upon a sullen German delegation on June 28, 1919, was harshly punitive. Germany was disarmed, stripped of its colonies, forced to admit sole blame for the war, and saddled with whopping reparation payments of $56 billion. France regained the provinces of Alsace and Lorraine lost to Germany in 1871 and took control for fifteen years of Germany's coal-rich Saar Basin. The treaty demilitarized a zone of Germany thirty miles east of the Rhine and transferred a slice of eastern Germany to Poland. All told, Germany lost one-tenth of its population and one-eighth of its territory. The treaty granted Japan's Shandong claims and gave Italy a slice of Austria where two hundred thousand German-speaking inhabitants were then living. These harsh terms stirred bitter resentment in Germany, planting the seeds of a future, even more devastating, world war.

Wilson's theme of self-determination and democracy did influence some of the treaty's provisions. Germany's former colonies went to the various Allies under a "mandate" or trusteeship system that in theory would lead to eventual independence. The treaty also recognized the independence of Poland and the Baltic states of Estonia, Latvia, and Lithuania (territories that Germany had seized in its peace treaty with Bolshevik Russia in 1918). Separate treaties provided for the independence of two new nations carved from the old Austro-Hungarian and Ottoman empires: Czechoslovakia and Yugoslavia.

Palestine, a part of Turkey's collapsed Ottoman empire, went to Great Britain under a mandate arrangement. In 1917, after gaining military control of Palestine, the British had issued the Balfour Declaration supporting a Jewish "national home" in the region and also acknowledging the rights of the non-Jewish Palestinians.

But the treaty makers rejected the efforts of colonized peoples in Asia and Africa to throw off European rule. For example, Ho Chi Minh, a young Vietnamese nationalist who would later become head of his nation, visited Versailles in an unsuccessful effort to secure Vietnamese independence from France.

The framers of the Versailles Treaty and the other treaties shaping the postwar world made little effort to come to terms with revolutionary Russia. Indeed, in August 1918 a fourteen-nation Allied army, including some seven thousand U.S. troops, had landed at various Russian ports, ostensibly to protect Allied war materiel and secure the ports from German attack, but in fact to assist in efforts to overthrow the new Bolshevik regime, whose communist ideology and practice stirred deep fear in the capitals of Europe and America. Wilson, having welcomed the liberal Russian revolution of March 1917, viewed Lenin's coup that autumn and Russia's withdrawal from the war as a betrayal of the Allied cause and of his hopes for a democratic Russian future. The Versailles treaty reflected this hostility. Its territorial settlements in eastern Europe were designed to weaken Russia. Before leaving Versailles, Wilson and the other Allied leaders agreed to support a Russian military leader who was still fighting the Bolsheviks. Not until 1933 did the United States recognize the Soviet Union.

The Fight over the League of Nations

Dismayed by the treaty's vindictive features, Wilson focused on his one shining achievement at Versailles— the creation of a new international organization, the League of Nations. The agreement or "covenant" to establish the League, written into the peace treaty itself, embodied Wilson's vision of a liberal, harmonious, and peaceful world order.

But Wilson's dream would soon lie in ruins. A warning sign had come in February 1919 when thirty-nine Republican senators and senators-elect, including Henry Cabot Lodge, signed a letter rejecting the League in its present form. Wilson had retorted defiantly, "You cannot dissect the Covenant from the treaty without destroying the whole vital structure."

When Wilson sent the treaty to the Senate for ratification in July 1919, Lodge bottled it up in the Foreign Relations Committee. Furious at Lodge's tactics and convinced that he could rally popular opinion to his cause, Wilson left Washington on September 3 for a western speaking tour. Covering more than nine thousand miles by train, Wilson defended the League in thirty-seven speeches in twenty-two days. Crowds were large and friendly. People wept as Wilson described his visits to American war cemeteries in France and cheered his vision of a new world order.

But the grueling trip left Wilson exhausted. On September 25, he collapsed in Colorado. The train sped back to Washington, where Wilson suffered a devastating stroke on October 2. For a time, he lay near death. Despite a partial recovery, Wilson spent the rest of his term mostly in bed or in a wheelchair, a reclusive invalid, his mind clouded, his fragile emotions betraying him into vindictive actions and tearful outbursts. He broke with close advisers, refused to see the British ambassador, and dismissed Secretary of State Lansing, accusing him of disloyalty. In January 1920 his physician advised him to resign, but Wilson refused.

Wilson's first wife, Ellen, had died in 1914. His strong-willed second wife, Edith Galt, played a crucial

behind-the-scenes role during these months. Fiercely guarding her incapacitated husband, she hid his condition from the public, controlled his access to information, and decided who could see him. Cabinet members, diplomats, and congressional leaders, even Vice President Thomas R. Marshall, were barred from the White House. When one political leader seeking a meeting urged Mrs. Wilson to consider "the welfare of the country," she snapped, "I am not thinking of the country now, I am thinking of my husband." Since Wilson remained alive and the twenty-fifth amendment, dealing with issues of presidential disability, was not adopted until 1967, the impasse continued.

Under these trying circumstances, the League drama unfolded. On September 10, 1919, the Foreign Relations Committee at last sent the treaty to the Senate, but with a series of amendments. The Senate split into three groups: Democrats who supported the League covenant without changes; Republican "Irreconcilables," led by Hiram Johnson of California , Wisconsin's Robert La Follette, and Idaho's William Borah, who opposed the League absolutely; and Republican "Reservationists" led by Lodge, who demanded amendments to the League covenant as a condition of their support. The Reservationists especially objected to Article 10 of the covenant, which pledged each member nation to preserve the political independence and territorial integrity of all other members. This blank-check provision, the Reservationists believed, limited America's freedom of action in foreign affairs and infringed on Congress's constitutional right to declare war.

Had Wilson accepted compromise, the Senate would probably have ratified the Versailles Treaty, bringing the United States into the League of Nations. But Wilson's illness aggravated his tendency toward rigidity. From his isolation in the White House, he instructed Senate Democrats to vote against the treaty with Lodge's reservations. Although international-law specialists believed that these reservations would not significantly weaken U.S. participation in the League, Wilson rejected them as "a knife thrust at the heart of the treaty."

Despite the positive responses to Wilson's speaking tour, the American people did not rally behind the League. The reactionary political mood that Wilson's own administration had helped create was not conducive to a grand gesture of political idealism. As the editor of *The Nation* magazine observed, "If [Wilson] loses his great fight for humanity, it will be because he was deliberately silent when freedom of speech and the right of conscience were struck down in America."

"Seein' Things" (*Brooklyn Eagle,* 1919)
Supporters of the League of Nations believed that the opponents exaggerated the threat to U.S. sovereignty that League membership represented.

On November 19, 1919, pro-League Democrats obeying Wilson's instructions and anti-League Irreconcilables joined forces to defeat the Versailles treaty with Lodge's reservations. A second vote the following March produced the same result. The United States would not join the League. A president elected amid high hopes in 1912, applauded when he called for war in 1917, and adulated when he arrived in Europe in 1918 lay isolated and sick, his leadership repudiated. What might have been Wilson's crowning triumph had turned to ashes.

Racism and Red Scare, 1919–1920

The wartime spirit of "100 percent Americanism" left a bitter aftertaste. The years 1919–1920 saw new racial violence and fresh antiradical hysteria. Mobs in various parts of the country lynched seventy-six blacks in 1919, the worst toll in fifteen years. The victims included ten veterans, several still in uniform. Some lynchings involved incredible brutality. In Omaha, Nebraska, a mob shot a black prisoner more than a thousand times, mutilated him, and hung his body in a busy intersection.

The bloodiest violence exploded in 1919 in Chicago, where the influx of southern blacks had pushed racial tension to a high level. On a hot July afternoon, whites at a Lake Michigan beach threw stones at a black youth

swimming offshore. When he sank and drowned, black neighborhoods erupted in fury. A thirteen-day reign of terror followed as white and black marauders engaged in random attacks and arson. Black gangs stabbed an Italian peddler; white gangs pulled blacks from streetcars and shot or whipped them. Before an uneasy calm returned, the outbreak left fifteen whites and twenty-three blacks dead, over five hundred injured, and more than a thousand families, mostly black, homeless.

The wartime antiradical panic crested in a postwar Red Scare. (Communists were called "reds" because of the red flag favored by radical and revolutionary organizations, including the new Bolshevik regime in Russia.) Fears of "bolshevism" deepened when a rash of strikes broke out in 1919. When the IWW and other Seattle labor unions organized a general strike early that year, the mayor accused the strikers of seeking to "duplicate the anarchy of Russia" and called for federal troops to maintain public order. Anxiety crackled again in April, when various public officials received packages containing bombs. One blew off the hands of a senator's maid; another damaged the home of Attorney General A. Mitchell Palmer. When 350,000 steelworkers went on

J. Edgar Hoover, Newly Appointed Director of the Federal Bureau of Investigation, 1924

Earlier, during the postwar "Red Scare" of 1919–1920, Hoover headed the Justice Department's General Intelligence Division that investigated radicals and alleged subversives.

strike in September, mill owners broke the strike in part through newspaper ads describing the walkout as a Bolshevik plot engineered by "Red agitators."

The antiradical paranoia soon took political form. In November 1919 the House of Representatives refused to seat Milwaukee socialist Victor Berger because of his indictment under the Espionage Act. Milwaukee voters promptly reelected him, but the House stood firm. The New York legislature expelled several socialist members. The Justice Department set up a countersubversion division under young J. Edgar Hoover, future head of the Federal Bureau of Investigation, who ordered the arrest of hundreds of suspected communists and radicals. In December 1919 the government deported 249 Russian-born aliens, including radical Emma Goldman, a leader of the birth-control movement. The government's antiradical crusade won applause from the American Legion, a newly founded veterans' association, as well as the National Association of Manufacturers.

On January 2, 1920, in a dragnet coordinated by the Justice Department, federal marshals and local police raided the homes of suspected radicals and the headquarters of radical organizations in thirty-two cities. Without search warrants or arrest warrants, they took more than 4,000 persons into custody (some 550 were eventually deported) and seized papers and records. In Lynn, Massachusetts, police arrested a group of men and women meeting to plan a cooperative bakery. In Boston, police paraded arrested persons through the streets in handcuffs and chains and then confined them in crowded and unsanitary cells without formal charges or the right to post bail.

Attorney General Palmer, ambitious for higher office, coordinated these "Red raids." A Quaker who had compiled a reform record as a congressman, Palmer succumbed to the anticommunist hysteria. Defending his actions, Palmer later described the menace he believed the nation faced in 1919:

> The blaze of revolution was sweeping over every American institution of law and order . . . eating its way into the homes of the American workman, its sharp tongues of revolutionary heat . . . licking at the altars of the churches, leaping into the belfry of the school bell, crawling into the sacred corners of American homes, . . . burning up the foundations of society.

The Red Scare subsided as Palmer's lurid predictions failed to materialize. When a bomb exploded in New York City's financial district in September 1920,

killing thirty-eight people, most Americans saw the deed as the work of an isolated fanatic, not evidence of approaching revolution.

The Election of 1920

In this unsettled climate, the election of 1920 approached. Wilson, out of touch with political reality, considered seeking a third term, but was persuaded otherwise. Treasury Secretary McAdoo and Attorney General Palmer harbored presidential hopes. But when the Democrats convened in San Francisco, the delegates sang "How Dry I Am" (prohibition had just taken effect), tepidly backed Wilson's League position, and nominated James M. Cox, the mildly progressive governor of Ohio. As Cox's running mate they chose the young assistant secretary of the navy, Franklin D. Roosevelt, who possessed a potent political name.

The confident Republicans, meeting in Chicago, nominated Senator Warren G. Harding of Ohio, an amiable politician whose principal qualification was his availability. As one Republican leader observed, "There ain't any first raters this year. . . . We got a lot of second raters, and Harding is the best of the second raters." For vice president, they chose Massachusetts governor Calvin Coolidge, who had won attention in 1919 with his denunciation of a Boston policemen's strike.

Wilson proclaimed the election a "solemn referendum" on the League, but a nation psychologically drained by the war and the emotional roller-coaster ride of the Wilson presidency ignored him. "The bitterness toward Wilson is everywhere . . .," wrote a Democratic campaign worker; "he hasn't a friend."

Harding, promising a return to "normalcy," delivered campaign speeches empty of content but vaguely reassuring. One critic described them as "an army of pompous phrases moving over the landscape in search of an idea." Whatever the shortcomings of his campaign, Harding piled up a landslide victory—16 million votes

"Convict No. 9653 for President"
Although socialist Eugene V. Debs was in prison in 1920, he still received over 900,000 votes for president.

against 9 million for Cox. Nearly a million citizens defiantly voted for socialist Eugene Debs, who was behind bars in an Atlanta penitentiary (see Table 22.1).

The election dashed all hope for American entry into the League of Nations. During the campaign Harding had spoken vaguely of some form of "international organization," but once elected he bluntly declared the League question "dead." Senator Lodge, who had praised Wilson's idealistic war message so highly in 1917, now expressed grim pleasure that the voters had ripped "Wilsonism" up by the roots. The sense of national destiny and high purpose that Woodrow Wilson had evoked so eloquently in April 1917 survived only as an ironic memory as Americans impatiently turned to a new president and a new era.

TABLE 22.1 The Election of 1920

Candidates	Parties	Electoral Vote	Popular Vote	Percentage Popular Vote
WARREN G. HARDING	Republican	404	16,143,407	60.4
James M. Cox	Democrat	127	9,130,328	34.2
Eugene V. Debs	Socialist		919,799	3.4
P. P. Christensen	Farmer-Labor		265,411	1.0

CONCLUSION

The early twentieth century, an era of reform at home, also saw intensifying U.S. involvement abroad. Focused initially on Latin America and Asia, this new globalism arose from a desire to promote U.S. business interests internationally; export American values to other societies; and extend the power of a newly confident, industrialized United States as a counterweight to the expansive ambitions of Great Britain, Germany, and other imperial nations.

After 1914 this new internationalism focused on the European war, which in 1917 became an American war as well. Like many Americans, President Wilson felt deep cultural ties to the Allies. He took the nation into the conflict in defense of his understanding of neutral rights and,

in a larger sense, to further his vision of a transformed world order that would emerge from the struggle.

By conservative estimate, World War I cost 10 million dead and 20 million wounded. Included in this toll were 112,000 deaths in the American military—49,000 in battle and 63,000 from diseases, mostly influenza. The conflict brought marked advances in the technology of slaughter, from U-boat torpedoes and primitive aerial bombs to tanks, toxic gases, and more efficient machine guns.

The social, political, and economic effects of the war extended far beyond the battlefield. The war furthered the goals of some reformers, particularly the advocates of woman suffrage and prohibition. As a result of war mobilization, the federal government expanded its regulatory power over corporations and took steps to ensure

CHRONOLOGY, 1902–1920

1899 First U.S. Open Door note seeking access to China market.
Boxer Rebellion erupts in China.

1900 Second U.S. Open Door note.

1904 President Theodore Roosevelt proclaims "Roosevelt Corollary" to Monroe Doctrine.

1905 Roosevelt mediates the end of the Russo-Japanese War.

1906 At the request of Roosevelt, San Francisco ends segregation of Asian schoolchildren.
Panama Canal construction begins.

1911 U.S.-backed revolution in Nicaragua.

1912 U.S. Marines occupy Nicaragua.

1914 U.S. troops occupy Veracruz, Mexico.
Panama Canal opens.
World War I begins; President Wilson proclaims American neutrality.

1915 U.S. Marines occupy Haiti and the Dominican Republic.
Woman's Peace party organized.
British liner *Lusitania* sunk by German U-boat.
Wilson permits U.S. bank loans to Allies.

1916 U.S. punitive expedition invades Mexico, seeking Pancho Villa.
Germany pledges not to attack merchant ships without warning.
Wilson reelected.

1917 U.S. troops withdraw from Mexico.
Germany resumes unrestricted U-boat warfare; United States declares war.
Selective Service Act sets up national draft.
War Industries Board, Committee on Public Information, and Food Administration created.

Espionage Act passed.
War Risk Insurance Act authorizes payments to servicemen's dependents.
NAACP march in New York City protests upsurge in lynchings.
Bolsheviks seize power in Russia; Russia leaves the war.
New York State passes woman-suffrage referendum.
U.S. government operates the nation's railroads.

1918 Wilson outlines Fourteen Points.
Sedition Amendment passed.
Influenza epidemic sweeps nation.
National War Labor Board created.
American forces see action at Château-Thierry, Belleau Wood, St. Mihiel, and Meuse-Argonne campaign.
Republicans win control of both houses of Congress (November 5).
Armistice signed (November 11).

1919 Eighteenth Amendment added to the Constitution (prohibition).
Peace treaty, including League of Nations covenant, signed at Versailles.
Supreme Court upholds silencing of war critics in *Schenck* v. *U.S.*
Racial violence in Chicago.
Wilson suffers paralyzing stroke.
Versailles treaty, with League covenant, rejected by Senate.

1920 "Red raids" organized by Justice Department.
Nineteenth Amendment added to the Constitution (woman suffrage).
Warren G. Harding elected president.

workers' well-being and efficiency. Wartime regulatory agencies and social programs offered models that would prove influential in the future.

But the war also undermined the best aspects of progressivism—its openness to new ideas, its commitment to social justice, and its humanitarian concern for the underdog. As government war propaganda encouraged intolerance of dissent, ideological conformity and fear of radicalism smothered the prewar reform impulse. The climate of reaction intensified in 1919–1920, as the nation repudiated Wilsonian idealism.

The war at least temporarily improved the economic lot of many workers, farmers, blacks, and women, and enhanced the standing of the corporate executives, psychologists, public-relations specialists, and other professionals who contributed their expertise to the cause. Internationally, despite the wrangles that kept America out of the League of Nations, the conflict propelled the United States to the center of world politics and left the nation's businesses and financial institutions poised for global expansion.

Some of these changes endured; others proved fleeting. Cumulatively, however, their effect was profound. The nation that celebrated the armistice in November 1918 was very different from the one that Woodrow Wilson had solemnly taken into battle only nineteen months earlier.

FOR FURTHER REFERENCE

READINGS

Nancy K. Bristow, *Making Men Moral: Social Engineering During the Great War* (1996). Perceptive study of the Commission on Training Camp Activities.

Robert H. Ferrell, *Woodrow Wilson and World War I, 1917–1921* (1985). A vigorously written critical synthesis; especially good on the peace negotiations.

Mark T. Gilderhus, *Pan American Visions: Woodrow Wilson in the Western Hemisphere* (1986). Examines Wilson's approach to U.S.-Latin American relations.

Meiron and Susie Harries, *The Last Days of Innocence: America at War, 1917–1918* (1997). Readable and well-researched overview history of both the military and the home-front aspects of the war.

Michael H. Hunt, *The Making of a Special Relationship: The United States and China to 1914* (1983). Valuable study of the Open Door notes and the larger context of U.S. policy toward China.

John Keegan, *The First World War* (1999). A military historian's comprehensive account of the advance plans, battles, and campaigns of the conflict.

David M. Kennedy, *Over Here: The First World War and American Society* (1980). Deeply researched interpretive study of the home front during the war.

Thomas J. Knock, *To End All Wars: World War I and the Quest for a New World Order* (1992). A compelling study of the origins of Wilson's internationalism and the links between domestic reform and foreign policy.

Gina Bari Kolata, *Flu: The Story of the Great Influenza Pandemic of 1918 and the Search for the Virus that Caused It* (1999). Fascinating account by a *New York Times* science writer.

Ronald Schaffer, *America in the Great War: The Rise of the War Welfare State* (1991). Explores the war's effect on corporate organization and business-government links, as well as wartime initiatives to benefit industrial workers.

WEBSITES

Influenza 1918
http://www.pbs.org/wgbh/amex/influenza/timeline/index.html
The American Experience
A wealth of information on the deadliest epidemic in American history.

The Unkindest Cut: The Down and Dirty Story of the Panama Canal
http://www.discovery.com/stories/history/panana/1907.html
by Patrick J. Kiger, The Discovery Channel
Text, sound, video, a slide show, statistics, and maps covering the historical background and the building of the canal.

World War I: Trenches on the Web: An Internet History of the Great War
http://www.WorldWar1.com.
The History Channel
A rich resource, including documents, song clips, the soldiers' experience, the home front, specific battles, and much more.

For additional works, please consult the Bibliography at the end of the book.

CHAPTER 23

The 1920s: Coping with Change, 1920–1929

Sam Groipen of Medford, Massachusetts, was washing the windows of his grocery store, the Cooperative Cash Market, in June 1928 when a meat truck pulled up in front of the A&P supermarket next door. Sam knew the meaning of this seemingly ordinary event: his days as an independent grocer were numbered. A Russian-Jewish immigrant, Sam had opened his market in 1923, the year that he married. At first Sam and his wife did well. Sam served the customers; his wife kept the books. They knew their patrons by name and extended credit to neighbors short on cash.

In 1925, however, the chain stores came. A&P moved in next door, then First National and Stop & Shop across the street. Small by today's standards, the chain stores at first carried only brand-name groceries, not meat or fish. But the A&P added meat and fish in 1928. Sam watched as former customers who still owed him money walked past his door on their way to a supermarket. "I felt like I was being strangled," he later recalled; "those bastard chains were destroying me."

In 1935 Sam Groipen sold out. Abandoning his dream of prospering as an independent businessman, he joined the giant Prudential Life Insurance Company. Eventually, Sam's bitterness toward the chains softened. "I have been mellowed by the system," he reflected.

◀ **A Pleasure-Mad Decade**
A 1925 railroad poster advertises the Lake Michigan beaches near Chicago.

Groipen's experience paralleled that of many independent entrepreneurs in the 1920s, as corporate consolidation, new techniques of mass marketing, and rising consumer expectations transformed American society. In the 1920s, too, the nation's vast industrial capacity produced a tidal wave of automobiles, radios, electrical appliances, and other consumer goods. This stimulated the economy and transformed the lives of ordinary Americans. Ingrained patterns of diet, dress, travel, entertainment, and even thought changed rapidly as the economic order evolved.

These technological changes, following decades of immigration and urban growth, spawned social tensions. While Republican presidents espoused conservative political and cultural values, conflicts ripped at the social fabric. But this same ferment also stimulated creativity in literature and the arts.

In the 1920s many features of contemporary American life first became clearly evident. Indeed, in some ways the decade marks the dawn of the modern era. This chapter explores how different groups of Americans responded to technological, social, and cultural changes that could be both intensely exciting and deeply threatening.

This chapter focuses on five major questions:

■ What economic developments underlay American prosperity of the 1920s, and how did those developments affect different social groups?

■ What political values shaped public life in this era of Republican ascendancy? How did Herbert Hoover's social and political thought differ from that of presidents Harding and Coolidge?

■ How did the Republican administrations of the 1920s promote U.S. economic interests abroad?

■ What is meant by "mass culture"? What forces helped create a mass culture in the 1920s, and how thoroughly did it penetrate U.S. society?

■ The 1920s saw both cultural creativity and social tensions. What developments in American society in these years contributed to both the creativity and the tensions?

A New Economic Order

Fueled by new consumer products, innovative corporate structures, and new methods of producing and selling goods, the economy surged in the 1920s. Not everyone benefited, and farmers in particular suffered chronic economic woes. Still, the overall picture seemed rosy. As we shall see in later sections, these economic changes influenced the political, social, and cultural climate of the decade, as Americans struggled to cope with a society that was changing with breathtaking rapidity.

Booming Business, Ailing Agriculture

A sharp recession struck in 1920 after the government canceled wartime defense contracts and returning veterans reentered the job market. Recovery came in 1922, however, and for the next few years the industrial sector of the economy hummed (see Figure 23.1). Unemployment fell to as low as 3 percent, prices held steady, and the gross national product (GNP) grew by 43 percent from 1922 to 1929.

New consumer goods, including home electrical products, contributed to the prosperity. Many factories were already electrified, but now the age of electricity dawned for urban households as well. By the mid-1920s, with more than 60 percent of the nation's homes electrified, a parade of appliances, from refrigerators, washing machines, and vacuum cleaners to fans, razors, and mixers, crowded the stores. The manufacture of such appliances, as well as of hydroelectric generating plants and equipment for the electrical industry itself, provided a massive economic stimulus.

The 1920s business boom rested, too, on the automobile. Already well established before World War I (see Chapter 21), the automobile in the 1920s fully came into its own. Registrations jumped from about 8 million in 1920 to more than 23 million in 1930, by which time some 60 percent of U.S. families owned cars (see Figure 23.2). The Ford Motor Company led the market until mid-decade, when General Motors (GM) spurted ahead by touting a range of colors (Ford's Model T came only in black) and greater comfort. GM's lowest-priced car, named for French automotive designer Louis Chevrolet, proved especially popular. Meeting the challenge, in 1927 Ford introduced the stylish Model A in various colors. By the end of the decade, the automobile industry accounted for about 9 percent of all wages in manufacturing and had stimulated such related industries as rubber, gasoline and motor oil, advertising, and highway construction.

Rising stock-market prices reflected the prevailing prosperity. As the stock market surged ever higher, a speculative frenzy gripped Wall Street. By 1929 the market had reached wholly unrealistic levels, creating conditions for a catastrophic collapse (see Chapter 24).

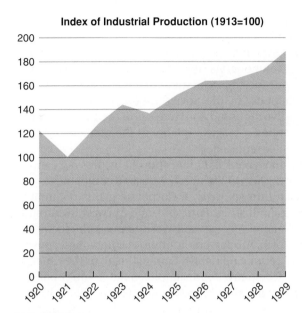

FIGURE 23.1
Economic Expansion, 1920–1929
After a brief postwar downturn, the American economy surged
in the 1920s.

Source: U.S. Department of Commerce, *Long-Term Economic Growth* (Washington,
D.C.: U.S. Government Printing Office, October 1966), 169.

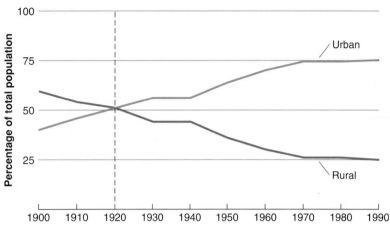

FIGURE 23.2
**The Urban and Rural Population of the United States,
1900–2000**
The urbanization of America in the twentieth century had profound political,
economic, and social consequences.

Source: Theodore Caplow, Louis Hicks, Ben J. Wattenburg, *The First Measured Century: An
Illustrated Guide to Trends in America, 1900–2000.* Reprinted with permission of the American
Enterprise Institute for Public Policy Research, Washington, D.C.

The business boom also stimulated capitalist expansion abroad. To supply overseas markets, Ford, GM, and other big corporations built production facilities abroad. Other U.S. firms acquired foreign factories or sources of raw materials. U.S. meatpackers built plants in Argentina; Anaconda Copper acquired Chile's biggest copper mine; and the mammoth United Fruit Company established processing plants across Latin America. Capital also flowed to Europe, especially Germany, as U.S. investors loaned European nations money to repay war debts and modernize their economies. U.S. private investment abroad increased nearly fivefold between 1914 and 1930.

But the era of a truly global economy still lay far in the future. Economic nationalism prevailed in the 1920s, as the industrialized nations, including the United States, erected high tariff barriers. The Fordney-McCumber Tariff (1922) and Smoot-Hawley Tariff (1930) pushed U.S. import duties to all-time highs, benefiting domestic manufacturers but stifling foreign trade. As a percentage of the GNP, U.S. exports actually fell between 1913 and 1929. Yet change was underway as U.S. industry retooled for mass production. Manufactured goods, less than half the value of total U.S. exports in 1913, rose to 61 percent of the total by the end of the 1920s.

"Honey, Where Did You Park the Car?"
Hundreds of identical Fords jam Nantasket Beach near Boston on a
Fourth of July in the early 1920s.

While overall wage rates rose amid the general prosperity of the 1920s, workers benefited unequally, reflecting regional variations as well as discriminatory patterns rooted in stereotypes and prejudices. Of the regional variations, the one between North and South loomed largest. In 1928 the average unskilled laborer in New England earned forty-seven cents an hour, in contrast to twenty-eight cents in the South. Many textile corporations moved south in search of lower wage rates, devastating New England mill towns. Women workers, blacks, Mexican-Americans, and recent immigrants clustered at the bottom of the wage scale. African-American workers, many of them recent migrants from the rural South, faced special difficulties. "Last hired and first fired," they generally performed the most menial unskilled jobs.

Farmers did not share in the boom; for them, wartime prosperity gave way to hard times. Grain prices plummeted when government purchases for the army dwindled, European agriculture revived, and America's high protective tariff depressed agricultural exports. From 1919 to 1921, farm income fell by some 60 percent, and, unlike the industrial sector, it did not bounce back. When farmers compensated by increasing production, the result was large surpluses and still weaker prices. Farmers who had borrowed heavily to buy land and equipment during the war now felt the squeeze as payments came due.

New Modes of Producing, Managing, and Selling

Building on the industrial feats of the war years, the 1920s saw striking increases in productivity. New assembly-line techniques boosted the per capita output of industrial workers by some 40 percent during this decade. At the sprawling Ford plants near Detroit, workers stood in one place and performed repetitive tasks as chains conveyed the partly assembled vehicles past them.

Assembly-line production influenced industrial employees' view of their work and themselves. Managers discouraged expressions of individuality; even talking or laughter could divert workers from their repetitive task. Ford employees learned to speak without moving their lips and adopted an expressionless mask that some called "Fordization of the face." As work became more routine, its psychic rewards diminished. The assembly line did not foster pride in the skills that came from years of farming or mastering a craft. Nor did assembly-line labor offer much prospect of advancement. In Muncie, Indiana, factories employing over four thousand workers announced only ten openings for foremen in 1924 and 1925.

Nevertheless, the new mass-production methods had a revolutionary impact. *Fordism* became a synonym worldwide for American industrial might and assembly-line methods. In the Soviet Union, which purchased twenty-five thousand Ford tractors in the 1920s, the people "ascribed a magical quality to the name of Ford," a 1927 visitor reported.

Business consolidation, spurred by the war, continued. By the late 1920s, over a thousand companies a year vanished through merger. Corporate giants dominated the major industries: Ford, GM, and Chrysler in automobiles; General Electric and Westinghouse in electricity; and so forth. Among public-utilities companies, consolidation became epidemic. Samuel Insull of the Chicago Edison Company, for example, built a multi-billion-dollar empire of local power companies. By 1930 one hundred corporations controlled nearly half the nation's business. Without actually merging, companies that made the same product often cooperated through trade associations on such matters as pricing, product specifications, and division of markets.

As U.S. capitalism matured, more elaborate management structures arose. Giant corporations set up separate divisions for product development, market research, economic forecasting, employee relations, and so forth. Day-to-day oversight of these highly complex corporate operations increasingly fell to professional managers.

The modernization of business affected wage policies. Rejecting the old view that employers should pay the lowest wages possible, business leaders now concluded that higher wages would improve productivity and increase consumer buying power. Henry Ford had led the way in 1914 by paying his workers five dollars a day, well above the average for factory workers. Other companies soon followed his lead.

New systems for distributing goods emerged as well. Automobiles reached consumers through vast dealer networks. By 1926 the number of Ford dealerships approached ten thousand. Chain stores accounted for about a quarter of all retail sales by 1930. The A&P grocery chain, which caused Sam Groipen such grief in Medford, Massachusetts, boasted 17,500 stores by 1928. Department stores grew more inviting, with attractive display windows, remodeled interiors, and a larger array of goods. Air conditioning, an invention of the early twentieth century, made departments stores (as well as movie theaters and restaurants) welcome havens on hot summer days.

Above all, the 1920s business boom bobbed along on a frothy sea of advertising. In 1929 corporations spent nearly two billion dollars promoting their wares via radio, billboards, newspapers, and magazines, and the advertising business employed some six hundred thousand people. Advertising barons ranked among the corporate elite. Chicago ad man Albert Lasker owned the Chicago Cubs baseball team and his own golf course. As they still do, the advertisers in the twenties used celebrity endorsements ("Nine out of ten screen stars care for their skin with Lux toilet soap"), promises of social success, and threats of social embarrassment. Beneath a picture of a sad young woman, for example, a Listerine mouthwash ad proclaimed: "She was a beautiful girl and talented too . . . . Yet in the one pursuit that stands foremost in the mind of every girl and woman—marriage— she was a failure." The young woman's problem was "halitosis," or bad breath. The remedy, of course, was Listerine, and lots of it.

Advertisers offered a seductive vision of the new era of abundance. Portraying a fantasy world of elegance, grace, and boundless pleasure, ads aroused desires that the new consumer-oriented capitalist system happily fulfilled. As one critic wrote in 1925,

[W]hen all is said and done, advertising . . . creates a dream world: smiling faces, shining teeth, schoolgirl complexions, cornless feet, perfect fitting [underwear], distinguished collars, wrinkleless pants, odorless breath, regularized bowels, . . . charging motors, punctureless tires, perfect busts, shimmering shanks, self-washing dishes, backs behind which the moon was meant to rise.

Americans of the 1920s increasingly bought major purchases on credit. In earlier days credit had typically involved pawnbrokers, personal loans, or informal arrangements between buyers and sellers. Now consumer credit was rationalized as retailers offered installment plans with fixed payment schedules. But while today's consumers use credit cards for all kinds of purchases, from restaurant meals to video rentals, credit buying in the 1920s involved mostly big-ticket items such as automobiles, furniture, and refrigerators. By 1929 credit purchases accounted for 75 percent of automobile sales.

Business values saturated the culture. As the *Independent* magazine put it in 1921: "America stands for one idea: Business . . . Thru business, properly conceived, managed, and conducted, the human race is finally to be redeemed." Presidents Harding and Coolidge praised American business and hobnobbed with businessmen. Magazines profiled corporate leaders. A 1923 opinion poll ranked Henry Ford as a leading presidential prospect. In *The Man Nobody Knows* (1925), ad man Bruce Barton described Jesus Christ as a managerial genius who "picked up twelve men from the bottom ranks of business and forged them into an organization that conquered the world." In *Middletown* (1929), a study of Muncie, Indiana, sociologists Robert and Helen Lynd observed, "More and more of the activities of life are coming to be strained through the bars of the dollar sign."

Women in the New Economic Era

In the decade's advertising, glamorous women smiled behind the steering wheel, operated their new appliances, and smoked cigarettes in romantic settings. (One ad man promoted cigarettes for women as "torches of freedom.") The cosmetics industry flourished, offering women (in the words of historian Kathy Peiss) "hope in a jar." In the advertisers' dream world, housework became an exciting challenge. As one ad put it, "Men are judged . . . according to their power to delegate work. Similarly the wise woman delegates to electricity all that electricity can do."

As for women in the workplace, the assembly line, involving physically less-demanding work, theoretically should have increased job opportunities. In fact, however, male workers dominated the auto plants and other assembly-line factories. Although the ranks of working women increased by more than 2 million in the 1920s, their number as a proportion of the total female population hardly changed, hovering at about 24 percent.

Women workers faced wage discrimination. In 1929, for example, a male trimmer in the meatpacking industry received fifty-two cents an hour, a female trimmer, thirty-seven cents. The weakening of the union movement in the 1920s (next page) hit women workers hard. By 1929 the proportion of women workers belonging to unions fell to a miniscule 3 percent.

Many women found work in corporate offices. By 1930 some 2 million women were working as secretaries, typists, or filing clerks. Few women entered the managerial ranks, however. Indeed, office space was arranged to draw clear gender distinctions between male managers and female clerks. Nor did the professions welcome women. With medical schools imposing a 5 percent quota on female admissions, the number of women physicians actually declined from 1910 to 1930.

The proportion of female high-school graduates going on to college edged upward, however, reaching 12 percent by 1930. Nearly fifty thousand women received college degrees that year, almost triple the 1920 figure. Despite the hurdles, more college women combined marriage and career. Most took clerical jobs or entered traditional "women's professions" such as nursing, library work, social work, and teaching. A handful, however, followed the lead of Progressive Era feminist trailblazers to become faculty members in colleges and universities.

Struggling Labor Unions in a Business Age

Organized labor faced tough sledding in the 1920s. Union membership fell from 5 million in 1920 to 3.4 million in 1929. Several factors underlay this decline. For one thing, despite various inequities and regional variations, overall wage rates climbed steadily in the decade, reducing the incentive to join a union. Industrial

Gastonia, North Carolina, 1929
Two women textile workers confront an armed guard in a bitter strike that took several lives.

changes played a role as well. The trade unions' strength lay in established industries like printing, railroading, coal mining, and construction. These older craft-based unions were ill suited to the new mass-production factories.

Management hostility further weakened organized labor. Henry Ford hired thugs to intimidate union organizers. In Marion, North Carolina, deputy sheriffs shot and killed six striking textile workers. Violence also marked a 1929 strike in Gastonia, North Carolina, by the communist-led National Textile Workers Union. When armed thugs in league with the mill owners invaded union headquarters, the police chief was shot. Strike leader Ella May Wiggins was killed by a bullet fired at a truck on the way to a union rally.

The anti-union campaign took subtler forms as well. Manufacturers' associations renamed the nonunion shop the "open shop" and dubbed it the "American Plan" of labor relations. Some firms set up employee associations and provided cafeterias and recreational facilities for workers. A few big corporations such as U.S. Steel sold company stock to their workers at bargain prices. Some publicists praised "welfare capitalism" (the term for this new approach to labor relations) as evidence of corporations' heightened ethical awareness. In reality, it mainly reflected management's desire to kill off independent unions.

By 1929 black membership in labor unions stood at only about eighty-two thousand, most of whom were longshoremen, miners, and railroad porters. The American Federation of Labor officially prohibited racial discrimination, but most AFL unions in fact barred African-Americans. Corporations often hired blacks as strikebreakers, increasing organized labor's hostility toward them. Black strikebreakers, denounced as "scabs," took such work only because they had to. As a jobless black character says in Claude McKay's 1929 novel *Home to Harlem*, "I got to live, and I'll scab through hell to live."

THE HARDING AND COOLIDGE ADMINISTRATIONS

With Republicans in control of Congress and the White House, politics in the 1920s reflected the decade's business orientation. Reacting to the unsettling pace of social change, many voters turned to conservative candidates who seemed to represent stability and traditional values. In this climate, former progressives, would-be reformers, and groups excluded from the prevailing prosperity had few political options.

Stand Pat Politics in a Decade of Change

In the 1920s the Republican party continued to attract northern farmers, corporate leaders, businesspeople, native-born white-collar workers and professionals, and some skilled blue-collar workers. The Democrats' base remained the white South and the immigrant cities.

With Republican progressives having bolted to Theodore Roosevelt in 1912, GOP conservatives controlled the 1920 convention and nominated Senator Warren G. Harding of Marion, Ohio, for president. A struggling newspaper editor, Harding had married the local banker's daughter, who helped manage his election to the Senate in 1915. A genial backslapper, he enjoyed good liquor, a good poker game, and occasional trysts with his mistress, Nan Britton. This amiable mediocrity overwhelmed his Democratic opponent James M. Cox. After the stresses of war and Wilson's lofty moralizing, Harding's blandness and empty oratory had a soothing appeal.

Harding made some notable cabinet selections: Henry C. Wallace, the editor of an Iowa farm periodical, as secretary of agriculture; Charles Evans Hughes, former New York governor and 1916 presidential candidate, secretary of state; and Andrew W. Mellon, a Pittsburgh financier, treasury secretary. Herbert Hoover, the wartime food czar, dominated the cabinet as secretary of commerce.

Harding also made some disastrous appointments: his political manager, Harry Daugherty, as attorney general; a Senate pal, Albert Fall of New Mexico, as secretary of the interior; a wartime draft dodger, Charles Forbes, as Veterans' Bureau head. These men set the sleazy and corrupt tone of the Harding presidency. By 1922 Washington rumor hinted at criminal activity in high places, and Harding confessed to a friend, "I have no trouble with my enemies. . . . But . . . my goddamn friends . . . keep me walking the floor nights." In July 1923, vacationing in the West, Harding suffered a heart attack; on August 2 he died in a San Francisco hotel.

In 1924 a Senate investigation pushed by Democratic Senator Thomas J. Walsh of Montana exposed the full scope of the scandals. Charles Forbes, convicted of stealing Veterans' Bureau funds, evaded prison by fleeing abroad. The bureau's general counsel committed suicide, as did an aide to Attorney General Daugherty accused of influence peddling. Daugherty himself narrowly escaped conviction in two criminal trials. Interior Secretary Fall went to jail for leasing government oil reserves, one in Teapot Dome, Wyoming, to two oilmen

President Harding with Laddie, June 1922
As politicians learned the arts of publicity, posed scenes like this became more common.

in return for a $400,000 bribe. Like "Watergate" in the 1970s, "Teapot Dome" became a shorthand label for a tangle of presidential scandals.

With Harding's death, Vice President Calvin Coolidge, on a family visit in Vermont, took the presidential oath by lantern light from his father, a local magistrate. A painfully shy youth, Coolidge had attended Amherst College in Massachusetts, where he struggled to eliminate all rural traces from his speech. Whereas Harding was outgoing and talkative, Coolidge's taciturnity became legendary. As he left California after a visit, a radio reporter asked for a parting message to the state. "Good-bye," Coolidge responded. Coolidge's appeal for old-stock Americans in an era of rapid social change has been summed up by historian John D. Hicks, "They understood his small-town cracker-barrel philosophy, they believed in his honesty, and they tended to have the same respect he had for the big business leaders who had known how to get on in the world."

Republican Policymaking in a Probusiness Era

The moral tone of the White House improved under Coolidge, but the probusiness climate, symbolized by the high tariffs of these years, persisted. Prodded by

Treasury Secretary Andrew Mellon, Congress lowered income taxes and inheritance taxes for the wealthy. Mellon embraced what later came to be called the "trickle down" theory, which held that tax cuts for the wealthy would promote business investment, stimulate the economy, and thus benefit everyone. (Mellon did, however, resist pressure from rich Americans eager to abolish the income tax altogether. Such a step, he warned, would build support for socialists and other left-wing radicals.) In the same probusiness spirit, the Supreme Court under Chief Justice William Howard Taft, who was appointed by Harding in 1921, overturned several reform measures opposed by business, including a federal anti-child-labor law passed in 1919.

While eager to promote corporate interests, Coolidge opposed government assistance for other groups. His position faced a severe test in 1927 when torrential spring rains throughout the Mississippi River watershed sent a massive wall of water crashing downstream. Soil erosion caused by decades of poor farming practices worsened the flood conditions, as did ill-planned engineering projects aimed at holding the river within bounds and reclaiming its natural floodplain for development purposes. One official described the river as "writh[ing] like an imprisoned snake" within its artificial confines. From Cairo, Illinois, to the Gulf, the water poured over towns and farms, inundating twenty-seven thousand square miles in Illinois, Tennessee, Arkansas, Mississippi, and Louisiana. It is estimated that more than a thousand people died, and the refugee toll, including many African-Americans, reached several hundred thousand. Disease spread in makeshift refugee camps.

Despite the scope of the catastrophe, Coolidge rejected calls for government aid to the flood victims, and even ignored pleas from local officials to visit the flooded regions. The government had no duty to protect citizens "against the hazards of the elements," he declared primly. (Coolidge did, however, reluctantly sign the Flood Control Act of 1928 and appropriate $325 million for a ten-year program to construct levees along the Mississippi.)

Further evidence of Coolidge's views came when hard-pressed farmers rallied behind the McNary-Haugen bill, a price-support plan under which the government would annually purchase the surplus of six basic farm commodities—cotton, corn, rice, hogs, tobacco, and wheat—at their average price in 1909–1914 (when farm prices were high). The government would then sell these surpluses abroad at prevailing prices and make up any resulting losses through a tax on domestic sales of these commodities. Congress passed the McNary-Haugen bill in 1927 and 1928, but Coolidge vetoed it both times, warning of "the tyranny of bureaucratic regulation and control." The measure would help farmers at the expense of the general public, he went on, ignoring the fact that business had long benefited from high tariffs and other special-interest measures. These vetoes led many angry farmers to abandon their traditional Republican ties and vote Democratic in 1928.

Independent Internationalism

Although U.S. officials participated informally in some League of Nations activities in the 1920s, the United States refused to join the League or its International Court of Justice (the World Court) in the Netherlands. Despite isolationist tendencies, however, the United States remained a world power, and the Republican administrations of these years pursued global policies that they believed to be in America's national interest— an approach historians have called independent internationalism.

President Harding's most notable achievement was the Washington Naval Arms Conference. After the war ended in 1918, the United States, Great Britain, and Japan edged toward a dangerous (and costly) naval-arms race. In 1921 Harding called for a conference to address the problem. When the delegates gathered in Washington, Secretary of State Hughes startled them by proposing a specific ratio of ships among the world's naval powers. In February 1922 the three nations, together with Italy and France, pledged to reduce their battleship tonnage by specified amounts and to halt all battleship construction for ten years. The United States and Japan also agreed to respect each other's territorial holdings in the Pacific. Although this treaty ultimately failed to prevent war, it did represent an early arms-control effort.

Another U.S. peace initiative was mainly symbolic and accomplished little. In 1928 the United States and France, eventually joined by sixty other nations, signed the Kellogg-Briand Pact renouncing aggression and calling for the outlawing of war. Lacking any enforcement mechanism, this high-sounding document did nothing to prevent World War II.

The Republican administrations of these years actively used international diplomacy to promote U.S. economic interests. The government, for example, vigorously sought repayment of the $22 billion it claimed the Allies owed in war debts and Germany owed in reparation payments. A joint study commission in 1924

sharply reduced these claims, but high U.S. tariffs and economic problems in Europe, including runaway inflation in Germany, made repayment of even the reduced claims unrealistic. When Adolph Hitler rose to power in Germany in 1933 (see Chapter 25), he repudiated all reparations payments.

With U.S. foreign investments expanding, the government worked to advance American business interests abroad. For example, the Harding and Coolidge administrations opposed the Mexican government's efforts to reclaim title to oilfields earlier granted to U.S. companies. In 1927 Coolidge appointed Dwight Morrow, a New York banker, to negotiate the issue with Mexico, but the talks collapsed in 1928 when Mexico's president was assassinated. Complicating U.S.-Mexican relations was Washington's fear that Mexico, gripped by revolutionary upheaval, might go communist. These fears deepened in 1924 when Mexico recognized the Soviet Union, nine years before the United States took the same step.

Progressive Stirrings, Democratic Party Divisions

The reform spirit survived feebly in the legislative branch. Congress staved off Andrew Mellon's proposals for even deeper tax cuts for the rich. Senator George Norris of Nebraska prevented the Coolidge administration from selling a federal hydroelectric facility at Muscle Shoals, Alabama, to automaker Henry Ford at bargain prices. And in 1927 Congress created the Federal Radio Commission, extending the regulatory principle to this new industry.

In 1922, a midterm election year, labor and farm groups formed the Conference for Progressive Political Action (CPPA), which helped defeat some conservative Republicans. In 1924 CPPA delegates revived the Progressive party and nominated Senator Robert La Follette for president. The Socialist party and the American Federation of Labor endorsed La Follette.

The Democrats, split between urban and rural wings, met in New York City for their 1924 convention. By one vote, the delegates defeated a resolution condemning the Ku Klux Klan (see below). While the party's rural, Protestant, southern wing favored former Treasury Secretary William G. McAdoo for president, the big-city delegates rallied behind Governor Alfred E. Smith of New York, a Roman Catholic of Irish, German, and Italian immigrant origins. The split in the Democratic party mirrored deep divisions in the nation. After 102 ballots, the exhausted delegates gave up and nominated an obscure New York corporation lawyer, John W. Davis.

Calvin Coolidge easily won the Republican nomination. The Republican platform praised the high Fordney-McCumber Tariff and urged tax and spending cuts. With the economy humming, Coolidge polled nearly 16 million votes, about twice Davis's total. La Follette's 4.8 million votes on the Progressive party ticket cut into the Democratic total, contributing to the Coolidge landslide.

Women and Politics in the 1920s: A Dream Deferred

Suffragists' hope that votes for women would transform politics survived briefly after the war. The 1920 major-party platforms endorsed several measures proposed by the League of Women Voters. Polling places shifted from saloons to schools and churches as politics ceased to be an exclusively male pursuit. A coalition of women's groups called the Women's Joint Congressional Committee lobbied for child-labor laws, protection of women workers, and federal support for education. It also backed the Sheppard-Towner Act (1921), which funded rural prenatal and baby-care centers staffed by public-health nurses. Overall, however, the Nineteenth Amendment had little political effect. Women who had joined forces to work for suffrage now scattered across the political spectrum or withdrew from politics altogether.

As the women's movement splintered, it lost focus. The League of Women Voters, drawing middle-class and professional women, abandoned activism for "non-partisan" studies of civic issues. Alice Paul's National Woman's party proposed an equal-rights amendment to the Constitution, but other reformers argued that such an amendment could jeopardize gender-based laws protecting women workers. The reactionary and materialistic climate of the 1920s underlay this disarray. Jane Addams and other women's-rights leaders faced accusations of communist sympathies. Women of the younger generation, bombarded by ads that defined liberation in terms of consumption, rejected the prewar feminists' civic idealism. One young woman in 1927 ridiculed "the old school of fighting feminists" for their lack of "feminine charm" and their "constant clamor about equal rights."

The few reforms achieved by women's groups often proved short-lived. The Supreme Court struck down child-labor laws in 1922 and women's protective laws in 1923. A 1924 child-labor constitutional amendment

passed Congress after heavy lobbying by women's organizations, but few states ratified it. The Sheppard-Towner rural-health-care act, denounced by the American Medical Association as a threat to physicians' monopoly of the health business, expired in 1929.

MASS SOCIETY, MASS CULTURE

The torrent of new consumer products, together with the growth of advertising, innovations in corporate organization, assembly-line manufacturing, and new modes of mass entertainment, signaled profound changes in American life. Taken together, these changes infused the decade with an aura of modernity that some found tremendously exciting and others deeply disorienting.

Cities, Cars, Consumer Goods

In the 1920 census, for the first time, the urban population (defined as persons living in communities of twenty-five hundred or more) surpassed the rural (see Figure 23.3). The United States had become an urban nation.

Urbanization affected different groups of Americans in different ways. African-Americans, for example, migrated cityward in massive numbers, especially after the terrible 1927 Mississippi River floods. By 1930 more than 40 percent of the nation's 12 million blacks lived in cities, 2 million of them in Chicago, Detroit, New York, and other metropolitan centers of the North and West (see Figure 23.4). The first black congressman since Reconstruction, Oscar De Priest, won election in 1928 from Chicago's South Side.

For women, city life meant electric and gas appliances that reduced household labor. When the Lynds interviewed working-class women in Muncie in 1925, nearly 75 percent reported spending less time on housework than had their mothers. Vacuum cleaners supplanted brooms and dustpans. Wood-burning kitchen stoves became a memory. Store-bought clothes replaced homemade apparel. Electric refrigerators replaced labor-intensive iceboxes. The electric washing machine and electric iron lightened wash-day labor.

Food preparation and diet shifted in response to urbanization and technological changes. The availability of canned fruit and vegetables undermined the annual ritual of canning. Home baking declined with the rise of commercial bakeries. With refrigeration, supermarkets, and motor transport, fresh fruits, vegetables, and salads became available year-round.

FIGURE 23.3

The Automobile Age: Passenger Cars Registered in the United States, 1900–1992

From a plaything for the rich, the automobile emerged after 1920 as the basic mode of transportation for the masses, in the process transforming American life in countless ways.

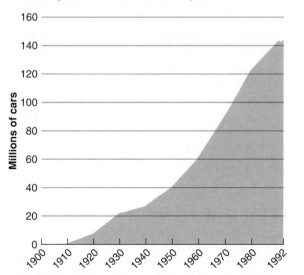

Sources: Historical Statistics of the United States, Colonial Times to 1970 (Washington, D.C.: U.S. Government Printing Office, 1975), 716; *Statistical Abstract of the United States, 1994* (Washington, D.C.: U.S. Government Printing Office.

FIGURE 23.4

The African-American Urban Population, 1880–1960 (in millions)

The increase in America's urban black population from under one million in 1880 to nearly fourteen million by 1960 represents one of the great rural-urban migrations of modern history.

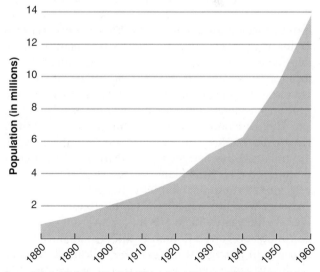

Source: Historical Statistics of the United States, Colonial Times to 1970 (Washington, D.C. Bureau of the Census, 1975) vol. I p. 12.

***East River from the 30th Story of the Sheridan Hotel,* by Georgia O'Keeffe, 1928**
Better known for her later paintings inspired by the New Mexico desert, O'Keeffe in this painting of a New York City scene incidentally recorded the atmospheric pollution issuing from factory smoke stacks, one of many warnings of environmental problems ahead.

For social impact, however, nothing matched the automobile. A Muncie resident challenged the Lynds, "Why . . . do you need to study what's changing this country? I can tell you . . . in just four letters: A-U-T-O."

Any effort to assess the A-U-T-O's social impact produces a decidedly mixed balance sheet. With increased mobility came new headaches. Traffic jams, parking problems, and highway fatalities (more than twenty-six thousand in 1924) attracted worried comment. In some ways, the automobile brought families together. Family vacations, rare a generation earlier, became more common. Tourist cabins and roadside restaurants served vacationing families. But in other respects, the automobile eroded family cohesion and parental authority. Young people could borrow the car to go to the movies, attend a dance miles from home, or simply park in a secluded "lover's lane."

Women of the middle and upper classes welcomed the automobile enthusiastically. They used the car to drive to work; run errands; attend meetings; visit friends; and, in the words of historian Virginia Scharff, simply to get out of the house and explore "new possibilities for excitement, for leisure and for sociability."

Stereotypes of feminine delicacy and timidity faded as women demonstrated confident mastery of this new technology. As the editor of an automotive magazine wrote in 1927, "[E]very time a woman learns to drive—and thousands do every year—it is a threat at yesterday's order of things."

For farm families, the automobile offered easier access to neighbors and to the city, lessening the isolation of rural life. The automobile's country cousin, the tractor, proved instantly popular, with nearly a million in use in America by 1930, increasing productivity and reducing the heavy physical demands of farm labor. As farmers bought automobiles, tractors, and other mechanized equipment on credit, however, the rural debt crisis worsened.

Automobile ads celebrated the freedom of the open road, and indeed car owners, unlike train or streetcar passengers, could travel when and where they wished. Yet the automobile and other forms of motor transport in many ways further standardized American life. One-room schoolhouses stood empty as buses carried children to consolidated schools. Neighborhood grocery stores declined as people drove to supermarkets. With

Three Young Mexican-American Women of Tucson, Arizona
The spread of automobile culture in the early twentieth century gave a new freedom and mobility to many women, particularly the young and urban.

the automobile came the first suburban department stores, the first shopping center (in Kansas City), and the first fast-food chain (A & W Root Beer).

Even at $300 or $400, however, and despite a thriving used-car market, the automobile remained too expensive for many. The "automobile suburbs" that sprang up beyond the streetcar lines attracted mainly the prosperous. The urban poor remained behind, widening class divisions in American society. However one assessed the automobile's social effects, one thing was certain: American life would never be the same.

Soaring Energy Consumption and a Threatened Environment

Electrification and the spread of motorized vehicles had implications for the nation's natural resources and for the environment. As electrical use more than tripled in the 1920s, generating plants consumed growing quantities of coal, oil, and natural gas. In 1929, with 20 million cars on the road, U.S. refineries used over a billion barrels of crude oil to meet the demand for gasoline.

Rising gasoline consumption underlay Washington's efforts to ensure U.S. access to Mexican oil; played a role in the Teapot Dome scandal; and triggered fevered activity in the oilfields of Texas and Oklahoma. As wildcatters made and lost fortunes, corporate giants like Standard, Texaco, and Gulf solidified their dominance of the industry. The natural gas found with petroleum seemed so abundant that much of it was simply burned off. In short, the profligate consumption of fossil fuels, though small by later standards and not yet recognized as a problem, already characterized American society by the 1920s.

The wilderness that had inspired nineteenth-century Americans became more accessible as the automobile, improved roads, and tourist facilities opened the national parks and once-pristine regions to easy access. Vacationing city dwellers—along with thousands of other motorized tourists—rediscovered the land. For the first time, millions of Americans came to view natural settings as places of recreation and leisure rather than of labor.

As with other technological and social changes of the time, this development had mixed effects. On the one hand, easier access to the wilderness democratized the environmental movement, creating a broad constituency for the cause of preservation. On the other hand, it subjected the areas to heavy pressures as more tourists arrived, expecting good highways, service stations, restaurants, and hotels. The problem of heavy auto tourism in the nation's parks and wilderness areas would grow more urgent in future decades.

These developments worried Secretary of Commerce Herbert Hoover. Hoover believed that urban dwellers benefited from periodically escaping the city, but the effects of tourism on parks and wilderness areas concerned him. Hoover created a National Conference on Outdoor Recreation to set national recreation policies and try to balance the Progressive Era conservationist ethic and the vacation-minded leisure culture of the 1920s.

The Sierra Club, the Audubon Society, and other groups worked to protect wilderness and wildlife. In 1923 the Izaak Walton League, devoted to recreational fishing, persuaded Congress to halt a private-development scheme to drain a vast stretch of wetlands on the upper Mississippi and instead declare the beautiful expanse of river a wildlife preserve. Aldo Leopold of the U.S. Forest Service warned of the dangers of unchecked technology. For too long, he wrote in 1925, "a stump was our symbol

Mass Society, Mass Culture

of progress." Few listened, however. The expansive, confident generation of the 1920s had little time for the environmental issues that would occupy future generations.

Mass-Produced Entertainment

The routinization of work and the increase in disposable income contributed to the rising interest in leisure-time activities in the 1920s. In their free hours workers sought the fulfillment many found missing in the workplace.

For some, light reading provided diversion. Mass-circulation magazines flourished. By 1922 ten American magazines boasted circulation of more than 2.5 million. The venerable *Saturday Evening Post*, with its Norman Rockwell covers and fiction featuring small-town life, specialized in prepackaged nostalgia. *Reader's Digest*, founded in 1921 by DeWitt and Lila Wallace, offered condensed versions of articles originally published elsewhere. A kind of journalistic equivalent of the Model T or the A&P, the *Digest* offered familiar fare for mass consumption. Book publishers sold popular novels and other works not only through traditional bookstores, but also through department stores or directly to the public via the Book-of-the-Month Club and the Literary Guild, both launched in 1926. While these mass-market ventures were often accused of debasing literary taste, they did help sustain a common national culture in an increasingly diverse society.

Just as corporations standardized the production and marketing of consumer goods, the two fastest-growing media of the 1920s, radio and the movies, offered stan-

Christmas in Consumerland
Giving a modern twist to an ancient symbol, this advertising catalog of the 1920s offered an enticing array of new electric products for the home.

dardized cultural fare. Mass-produced culture was hardly new, but the process accelerated in the 1920s.

The radio era began on November 2, 1920, when Pittsburgh station KDKA reported Warren Harding's election. The following year New York's WEAF began a regular news program, and a Newark station broadcast the World Series (the New York Giants beat the New York Yankees). In 1922 five hundred new stations began operations, and radio quickly became a national obsession.

Radio: the Early Years
In 1925, to promote the Ringling Brothers Barnum & Bailey Circus, radio station WJZ in New York City offered an hour-long broadcast of circus sounds, including the bellowing of Dolly, a two-year-old elephant.

At first these new stations were independent ventures, but in 1926 three big corporations—General Electric, Westinghouse, and the Radio Corporation of America—formed the first radio network, the National Broadcasting Company (NBC). The Columbia Broadcasting System (CBS) followed in 1927. Testing popular taste through market research, the networks soon ruled radio broadcasting. Americans everywhere laughed at the same jokes, hummed the same tunes, and absorbed the same commercials.

WEAF broadcast the first sponsored program in 1922, and commercial sponsorship soon became the rule. The first network comedy show, the popular *Amos 'n' Andy* (1928), brought prosperity to its sponsor, Pepsodent toothpaste. White actors played the black characters on *Amos 'n' Andy,* which offered stereotyped caricatures of African-American life, softening the realities of a racist society.

The movies reached all social classes as they expanded from the rowdy nickelodeons of the immigrant wards into elegant uptown theaters with names like Majestic, Ritz, and Palace. Charlie Chaplin, who had played anarchic, anti-authority figures in his prewar comedies, now started his own production studio and softened his character in such feature-length films as *The Gold Rush* (1925). Rudolph Valentino, an uneducated Italian immigrant, offered female moviegoers fantasies of romance in exotic settings in *The Sheik* (1921) and other films. At a time when many young women were transgressing traditional behavior codes, "America's sweetheart" Mary Pickford, with her golden curls and look of frail vulnerability, played innocent girls in need of protection, reinforcing traditional gender stereotypes. (In fact, Pickford was a shrewd businesswoman who became enormously wealthy.) Director Cecil B. De Mille, the son of an Episcopal clergyman, pioneered lavish biblical spectacles with *The Ten Commandments* (1923). In this decade of rapid cultural change, De Mille's epic sternly warned of the consequences of breaking the moral law.

After Al Jolson's *The Jazz Singer* (1927) introduced sound to the movies, a new generation of screen idols arose, including the Western hero Gary Cooper and the aloof Scandinavian beauty Greta Garbo. Walt Disney's Mickey Mouse debuted in a 1928 animated cartoon, *Steamboat Willy.*

Like radio, movies became more standardized. By 1930, with weekly attendance approaching 80 million, the corporate giants Metro-Goldwyn-Mayer, Warner Brothers, and Columbia relying on predictable plots and typecast stars, produced most movies. In a cultural parallel to the overseas expansion of U.S. business, Hollywood increasingly sought foreign as well as domestic markets for its films.

Moviegoers entered a world far removed from reality. One ad promised "all the adventure, all the romance, all the excitement you lack in your daily life." These mass-produced fantasies shaped behavior and values, especially of the young. Hollywood, observed novelist John Dos Passos, offered a "great bargain sale of five-

Moviemaking at Warner Brothers Hollywood Studio
Pioneering in sound films in a movie-mad decade, Warner Brothers Pictures earned profits of more than $17 million in 1929.

and-ten-cent lusts and dreams." The film industry also stimulated consumption with alluring images of the good life. Romantic comedies such as DeMille's lavish *Road to Yesterday* (1925) joined department stores, mass magazines, and advertisers in opening new vistas of consumer abundance.

This spread of mass culture was a byproduct of urbanization, a social process that involves not only the physical movement of people, but also changing patterns of culture. Even when the radio networks, the movie industry, the advertisers, and the popular magazines nostalgically evoked rural or small-town life, they did so from big-city offices and studios.

For all its influence, however, the new mass culture penetrated society unevenly. It had less impact in rural America, and met strong resistance among evangelical Christians suspicious of modernity. Mexican-Americans preserved traditional festivals and leisure activities despite the "Americanization" efforts of non-Hispanic priests and well-intentioned outsiders. In big-city black neighborhoods, uninhibited rent parties featured dancing to local musicians or to blues and jazz phonograph records targeted to this market. Along with the network radio shows, local stations also broadcast farm reports, ethnic music, local news, and community announcements. Country music enlivened radio programming in the South. Despite a craze for professional sports, local athletic leagues flourished as well.

Similarly, along with the great downtown movie palaces, small neighborhood theaters provided opportunities for conversation, socializing, and sometimes jeering catcalls at the film being shown. The *Chicago Defender*, the voice of the city's black middle class, deplored the raucousness of movie theaters in poor black neighborhoods, where "during a death scene . . . you are likely to hear the orchestra jazzing away." In short, despite the power of the new mass media, the American cultural scene still had room for diversity in the 1920s.

Celebrity Culture

Professional sports and media-promoted spectacles provided entertainment as well. In 1921 Atlantic City business promoters launched a bathing-beauty competition they grandly called the Miss America Pageant. Larger-than-life celebrities dominated professional sports: Babe Ruth of the New York Yankees, who hit sixty home runs in 1927; Ty Cobb, the Detroit Tigers' manager, whose earlier record of 4,191 hits still inspired awe; prizefighters Jack Dempsey and Gene Tunney, whose two heavyweight fights drew thousands of fans and mas-

sive radio audiences. Ruth was a coarse, heavy-drinking womanizer; Cobb, an ill-tempered racist. Yet the alchemy of publicity transformed them into heroes with contrived nicknames: "the Sultan of Swat" (Ruth) and "the Georgia Peach" (Cobb).

This celebrity culture illuminates the anxieties and aspirations of ordinary Americans in these years of social change. For young women uncertain about society's shifting expectations, the beauty pageants offered one ideal to which they could aspire. For men whose sense of mastery had been shaken by unsettling developments from feminism to Fordism, the exploits of sports heroes like Dempsey or Ruth could momentarily restore confidence and self-esteem.

The psychological meaning of celebrity worship emerged most clearly in the response to Charles Lindbergh, a young pilot who flew solo across the Atlantic in his small biplane, *The Spirit of St. Louis,* on May 20–21, 1927. A Minnesotan of Swedish ancestry, Lindbergh was a daredevil stunt pilot who decided on impulse to enter a $25,000 prize competition offered by a New York hotel

Charles A. Lindbergh and the *Spirit of St. Louis*
In a celebrity-obsessed decade, Lindbergh rocketed to instant fame after his 1927 solo transatlantic flight.

for the first nonstop New York to Paris flight. The flight captured the public's imagination. In New York, thousands turned out for a ticker-tape parade. Radio, newspapers, magazines, and movie newsreels provided saturation coverage.

Caught up in the celebrity culture, Lindbergh became a kind of blank screen onto which people projected their own hopes, fears, and ideologies. President Coolidge, who had no time for Mississippi flood victims, received him at the White House, praising the flight as a triumph of American business and corporate technology. Many editorial writers, on the other hand, saw Lindbergh as proof that even in an era of standardization and mechanization, the individual still counted. Others praised this native-born midwesterner of northern European origins as a more authentic American than the more recent immigrants crowding the cities.

Overall, the new mass media had mixed social effects. Certainly they promoted cultural standardization and uniformity of thought. But radio, movies, and mass-circulation magazines also helped forge a national culture and introduced new viewpoints and ways of behaving. Implicitly they conveyed a potent message: a person's horizons need not be limited by his or her immediate surroundings. They opened a larger world for ordinary Americans. If that world was often superficial and tawdry, it could also be exciting and liberating.

CULTURAL FERMENT AND CREATIVITY

American life in the 1920s involved more than political scandals, assembly lines, and media-created celebrities. College-age youth explored the possibilities of a postwar moment when familiar pieties and traditional ways came under challenge. A new generation of writers, artists, musicians, and scientists contributed to the modernist spirit of cultural innovation and intellectual achievement. African Americans asserted a new pride and self-confidence through a cultural flowering known as the Harlem Renaissance.

The Jazz Age and the Postwar Crisis of Values

The war and its aftermath of disillusionment sharpened the cultural restlessness already evident in the prewar years. The year 1918, wrote Randolph Bourne, marked "a sudden, short stop at the end of an intellectual era." Poet Ezra Pound made the same point more brutally in 1920. America had gone to war, he wrote, to save "a botched civilization; . . . an old bitch gone in the teeth."

The bubbling postwar cultural ferment took many forms. Some young people—especially affluent college students—boisterously assailed their elders' notion of proper behavior. Taking advantage of the era's prosperity and the freedom offered by the automobile, they threw parties, drank bootleg liquor, flocked to jazz clubs, and danced the Charleston. When asked about her favorite activity, a California college student replied, "I adore dancing; who doesn't?"

Young people also discussed—and sometimes indulged in—sex more freely than their parents. Wrote novelist F. Scott Fitzgerald, "None of the Victorian mothers had any idea how casually their daughters were accustomed to be kissed." Sigmund Freud, the Viennese founder of psychoanalysis who explored the role of sexuality in human psychological development, enjoyed a popular vogue in America in the 1920s.

For all the talk about sex, the 1920s' "sexual revolution" is known largely from anecdotes and journalistic accounts. Premarital intercourse may have increased, but it remained exceptional and widely disapproved. What *can* be documented are changing courtship patterns. "Courting" had once been a prelude to marriage. The 1920s brought the more informal ritual of "dating." Through casual dating, young people gained social confidence without necessarily contemplating marriage. The twenties brought greater erotic freedom, but within bounds. Despite moralists' charges of immorality, most 1920s youth drew a clear line between permissible and taboo behavior.

The double standard, which held women to a stricter code of conduct, remained in force. Young men could boast of their sexual adventures, but young women reputed to be "fast" risked a smirched reputation. Still, the postwar changes in behavior had a liberating effect on women. Female sexuality was more openly acknowledged. Skirt lengths crept up; wearing makeup became more acceptable; and the elaborate armor of petticoats and corsets fell away. The awesome matronly bosom mysteriously deflated as a more boyish figure became the fashion ideal. Unaware of the medical risks of tobacco, many young women took up cigarettes, especially college students and urban workers. For some, smoking became a feminist issue. As one woman college student put it, "[W]hy [should] men . . . be permitted to smoke while girls are expelled for doing it?"

Moral guardians protested the behavior of the young. A Methodist bishop denounced new dances that brought "the bodies of men and women in unusual relation to each other." When Bryn Mawr, a Pennsylvania woman's college, permitted students to smoke in 1925, denunciations erupted.

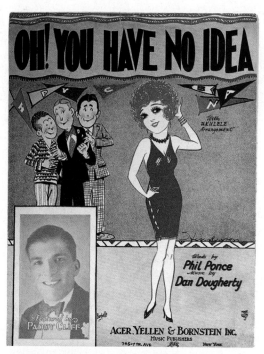

The New Woman, 1920s Model
This 1928 novelty song, arranged for the newly popular
Hawaiian ukulele, included the lyrics: "Has she the lips
the boys adore? Does she know what she's got'm for?
Oh! you have no idea."

F. Scott Fitzgerald and His Wife Zelda
While Fitzgerald chronicled the 1920s in his fiction, he and Zelda lived the high
life in New York and in Europe.

Around 1922, according to F. Scott Fitzgerald, adults embraced the rebelliousness of
the young. Middle-aged Americans "discovered that young liquor will take the place of
young blood," he wrote, "and with a whoop the
orgy began." But sweeping cultural generalizations can be misleading. During the years of
Fitzgerald's alleged national orgy, the U.S. divorce rate
remained constant, and millions of Americans firmly
rejected alcohol and wild parties.

The most enduring twenties stereotype is the flapper, the sophisticated, pleasure-mad young woman. The
term originated with a drawing by a magazine illustrator
depicting a fashionable young woman whose rubber
boots were open and flapping. Although the flapper
stereotype was created by journalists, fashion designers,
and advertisers, it played a significant cultural role. In
the nineteenth century, the idealized woman on her
moral pedestal had symbolized an elaborate complex of
cultural ideals. The flapper, with her bobbed hair, defiant cigarette, lipstick, and short skirt, similarly epitomized youthful rejection of the older stereotype of womanhood.

The entire Jazz Age was partially a media and novel-
istic creation. Fitzgerald's romanticized novel about the
affluent postwar young, *This Side of Paradise* (1920),
spawned many imitators. With his movie-idol good
looks, the youthful Fitzgerald not only wrote about the
Jazz Age but lived it. He and his wife Zelda partied away
the early twenties in New York, Paris, and the French
Riviera. A moralist at heart, Fitzgerald both admired and
deplored the behavior he chronicled. His *The Great
Gatsby* (1925) captured not only the glamorous, party-
filled lives of the moneyed class of the 1920s, but also
their materialism, self-absorption, and casual disregard
of those below them on the social scale.

Old values persisted, of course. Millions of Americans adhered to traditional ways and standards. Most
farmers, blacks, industrial workers, and recent immigrants

Braving chilly breezes, New Yorkers cheered warmly on February 17, 1919, as the all-black fifteenth infantry regiment, back from France, paraded up Fifth Avenue. Led by Lieutenant James Europe's band, thousands of black troops marched in formation. Banners blazed: "our heroes—welcome home." When the parade reached Harlem north of Central Park, discipline collapsed amid joyous reunions. A new day seemed at hand for black America, and Harlem stood at its center.

The part of Manhattan Island that the early Dutch settlers had called Nieuw Haarlem was in transition by 1920. An elite suburb in the late nineteenth century, Harlem evolved rapidly during the First World War as its black population swelled. Some 400,000 southern blacks in search of wartime work migrated northward from 1914 to 1918, and the influx continued in the 1920s. Blacks also poured in from Jamaica and other Caribbean islands. New York City's black community surged from 152,000 to 327,000. Most of the newcomers settled in Harlem, where handsome old brownstone apartments were subdivided to house them.

Racism and lack of education took their toll. Black Harlem had a small middle class of entrepreneurs, ministers, real-estate agents, and funeral directors, but most Harlemites held low-paying, unskilled jobs. Many found no work at all. Overcrowding and the population spurt gave rise to social problems and high rates of tuberculosis, infant mortality, and venereal disease.

Harlem also became a vibrant center of black culture in the twenties. The Mississippi-born classical composer William Grant Still moved to Harlem in 1922, pursuing his composition studies and completing his best-known work, *Afro American Symphony* (1931). On the musical-comedy stage, the 1921 hit *Shuffle Along* launched a series of popular all-black reviews. The 1923 show *Runnin' Wild* sparked the Charleston dance craze.

The Cotton Club and other Harlem cabarets featured such jazz geniuses as Duke Ellington, Fletcher Henderson, and Jelly Roll Morton. Muralist Aaron Douglas, concert tenor Roland Hayes, and singer-actor Paul Robeson contributed to the cultural ferment.

Above all, the Harlem Renaissance was a literary movement. Poet Langston Hughes drew upon the oral traditions of transplanted southern blacks in *The Weary Blues* (1926). The Jamaican writer Claude McKay evoked Harlem's throbbing, sometimes sinister nightlife in *Home to Harlem* (1928). In his avant-garde work *Cane* (1923), Jean Toomer used poems, drama, and short stories to convey the thwarted efforts of a young northern mulatto to penetrate the mysterious, sensual world of the black South. In her novel *Quicksand* (1928), Nella

Jazz Pianist, Composer, and Band Leader Ferdinand (Jelly Roll) Morton
Rooted in the rich musical traditions of African-Americans, jazz shaped the rhythm and beat of the Harlem Renaissance.

Larsen, a native of the Danish West Indies, told of a mulatto woman's struggle with her own sexuality and her mixed ethnic background.

In essays and conversations at late-night parties, talented young blacks explored the challenge of finding a distinct cultural voice in white America. The gentle philosopher Alain Locke, a former Rhodes scholar who taught at Howard University in Washington, D.C., assembled essays, poems, and short stories in *The New Negro* (1925), a landmark work that hailed the Harlem Renaissance as black America's "spiritual coming of age." Wrote Locke, "Harlem, I grant you, isn't typical, but it is significant. It is prophetic."

White America quickly took notice. Book publishers courted black authors. Charlotte Mason, a wealthy Park Avenue matron, funded the aspiring writers Langston Hughes and Zora Neale Hurston. Novelist and photographer Carl Van Vechten introduced black artists and writers to editors, publishers, and producers. White writers discovered and sometimes distorted black life. Eugene O'Neill's play *The Emperor Jones*, produced in 1921, starred Charles Gilpin as a fear-crazed West Indian tyrant. King Vidor's 1929 movie *Hallelujah*, featuring an all-black cast, romanticized plantation life and warned of the city's dangers. The 1925 novel *Porgy*, by Dubose and Dorothy Heyward, offered a sympathetic but sentimentalized picture of Charleston's black community. George Gershwin's musical adaptation, *Porgy and Bess*, appeared in 1935.

In a decade of prohibition and shifting sexual mores, Harlem seemed to offer sensuality, eroticism, and escape from taboos. Prostitutes, speakeasies, and cocaine were readily available. The whites who packed the late-night jazz clubs and the pulsating dance reviews and who patronized black writers and artists widely praised black culture for its "spontaneous," "primitive," or "spiritual" qualities. Few whites bothered to examine the more prosaic realities of Harlem life. The Cotton Club, controlled by gangsters, featured black performers but barred most blacks from the audience.

And with patronage came subtle attempts at control. When Langston Hughes began to write about urban poverty rather than Africa or black spirituality in the 1930s, Charlotte Mason angrily withdrew her support. Wrote Hughes later, "Concerning Negroes, she felt that they were America's great link with the primitive. . . . But unfortunately I did not feel the rhythms of the primitive surging through me . . . I was only an American Negro. I was not Africa. I was Chicago and Kansas City and Broadway and Harlem."

The Harlem Renaissance lacked a political framework or organic ties to the larger African-American

Poet and Novelist Langston Hughes, by Winold Reiss

experience. Indeed, in *The New Negro* Alain Locke urged talented blacks to shift from "the arid fields of controversy and debate to the productive fields of creative expression." The writers and artists of the Renaissance mostly ignored the racism, discrimination, and economic troubles faced by African Americans in the 1920s. They reacted with hostility to Marcus Garvey and his efforts to mobilize the urban black masses.

With the stock market crash in 1929 and the onset of the Great Depression, the Harlem Renaissance ended. In the 1930s a new generation of writers led by Richard Wright would launch a more politically engaged black cultural movement. Looking back in 1935, Alain Locke wrote sadly, "The rosy enthusiasm and hopes of 1925 were cruelly deceptive mirages. [The Depression] revealed a Harlem that the social worker knew all along, but had not been able to dramatize. There is no cure or saving magic in poetry and art for precarious marginal employment, high mortality rates, and civic neglect." Langston Hughes tersely assessed the movement in his 1940 autobiography, "The ordinary Negroes hadn't heard of the Negro Renaissance. And if they had, it hadn't raised their wages any."

But for all its naïveté, the Harlem Renaissance left an important legacy. The post-World War II literary flowering that began with Ralph Ellison's *Invisible Man* (1952) and continued with the works of James Baldwin, Toni Morrison, Alice Walker, and others owed a substantial debt to the Harlem Renaissance. For black writers in the West Indies and in French West Africa, "Harlem" would become a symbol of racial achievement. A fragile flower battered by the cold winds of the depression, the Harlem Renaissance nevertheless stands as a monument to African-American cultural creativity even under difficult circumstances.

found economic survival more pressing than the latest fads and fashions. But like the flapper, the Jazz Age stereotype captured a part of the postwar scene, especially the brassy, urban mass culture and the hedonism so different from the high-minded reformism of the Progressive Era.

Alienated Writers

Like Fitzgerald, many young writers found the cultural turbulence of the 1920s a creative stimulus. The decade's most talented writers equally disliked the moralistic pieties of the old order and the business pieties of the new. Novelist Sinclair Lewis took a sharply critical view of postwar America. In *Main Street* (1920) Lewis satirized the smugness and cultural barrenness of a fictional midwestern farm town, Gopher Prairie, based on his native Sauk Centre, Minnesota. In *Babbitt* (1922) he skewered a mythic larger city, Zenith, in the character of George F. Babbitt, a real estate agent trapped in middle-class conformity.

Lewis' journalistic counterpart was Henry L. Mencken, a Baltimore newspaperman who in 1924 launched *The American Mercury* magazine, the bible of the decade's alienated intellectuals. Mencken championed writers like Lewis and Theodore Dreiser while ridiculing small-town America, Protestant fundamentalism, the middle class "Booboisie," and all politicians. His devastating essays on Wilson, Harding, Coolidge, and Bryan are classics of political satire. Asked why he remained in America, Mencken replied, "Why do people visit zoos?"

For this generation of writers, World War I was a watershed experience. This was particularly true of Ernest Hemingway, who was seriously wounded in July 1918 while serving in northern Italy as a youthful Red Cross volunteer. In 1921, at twenty-two, he became an expatriate in Paris. In *The Sun Also Rises* (1926) Hemingway portrayed a group of American and English young people, variously damaged by the war, as they drift around Spain. His *A Farewell to Arms* (1929), loosely based on his own experiences, depicts the war's futility and politicians' empty rhetoric. In one passage, the narrator says,

> I was always embarrassed by the words sacred, glorious, and sacrifice and the expression in vain. We . . . had read them, on proclamations that were slapped up . . . over other proclamations, now for a long time, and I had seen nothing sacred, and the things that were glorious had no glory and the sacrifices were like the stockyards at Chicago if nothing was done with the meat except to bury it.

Although writers like Lewis and Hemingway felt contempt for the inflated rhetoric of the war years and the materialistic culture of the postwar years, and even though some became expatriates, they remained American at heart. The desire to create a vital national culture inspired their literary efforts, as it had inspired the likes of Nathaniel Hawthorne, Herman Melville, and Walt Whitman in the nineteenth century.

The social changes of these years energized African-American cultural life as well. The growth of New York City's black population underlay the Harlem Renaissance. The artistic creativity of the Renaissance took many forms, from all-black Broadway musical reviews to poems and novels (see A Place in Time: Harlem in the Twenties). The Harlem Renaissance was important to different groups for different reasons. Black women writers and performers gained a welcome career boost. Young whites in rebellion against Victorian propriety romanticized black life, as expressed in the Harlem Renaissance, as freer and less inhibited. Cultural nationalists both black and white welcomed the Renaissance as a promising step toward an authentically American modernist culture.

Architects, Painters, and Musicians Celebrate Modern America

A burst of architectural activity transformed the urban skyline in the 1920s. By 1930 the United States boasted 377 buildings over seventy stories tall. The skyscraper, proclaimed one writer, "epitomizes American life and American civilization." Not everyone was thrilled. Cultural critic Lewis Mumford denounced crowded, impersonal cities, with their "audacious towers, [and] . . . endless miles of asphalted pavements." Mumford preferred a network of regional cultures and smaller communities on a more human scale.

For inspiration, artists turned to America—either the real nation around them or an imagined one. While muralist Thomas Hart Benton evoked a half-mythic past of cowboys, pioneers, and riverboat gamblers, Edward Hopper portrayed faded towns and lonely cities of the present. Hopper's painting *Sunday* (1926), picturing a man slumped on the curb of an empty street of abandoned stores, conveyed both the bleakness and the potential beauty of urban America.

Other 1920s artists offered more upbeat images. Charles Sheeler painted and photographed giant factory complexes, including Henry Ford's plant near Detroit. The Italian immigrant Joseph Stella captured the excite-

***The Great White Way,*
by Howard Thain, 1925**
This painting radiates the vibrancy, bright lights, and raucous commercialism of New York City, the nation's premier metropolis in the booming 1920s.

ment and energy of New York in such paintings as *The Bridge* (1926), an abstract representation of the Brooklyn Bridge. Wisconsin's Georgia O'Keeffe moved to New York City in 1918 when the photographer Alfred Stieglitz (whom she later married) mounted a show of her work. O'Keeffe's 1920s paintings evoked both the congestion and the allure of the city.

The ferment of the 1920s reached the musical world as well. The composer Aaron Copland later recalled, "The conviction grew inside me that the two things that seemed always to have been so separate in America— music and the life about me—must be made to touch." While Copland drew upon folk traditions, others evoked the new urban-industrial America. Composer Frederick Converse's 1927 tone poem about the automobile, "Flivver Ten Million," for example, featured such episodes as "May Night by the Roadside" and "The Collision."

Of all the musical innovations, jazz best captured the modernist spirit. The Original Dixieland Jazz Band— white musicians imitating the black jazz bands of New Orleans—had debuted in New York City in 1917, launch-ing a jazz vogue that spread by live performances, radio, and phonograph records (see Technology and Culture: The Phonograph, Popular Music, and Home-Front Morale in World War I in Chapter 22). Popular white bandleader Paul Whiteman offered watered-down "jazz" versions of standard tunes. Of the white composers who embraced jazz, George Gershwin, with his *Rhapsody in Blue* (1924) and *An American in Paris* (1928), was the most gifted.

Meanwhile, black musicians preserved authentic jazz and explored its potential. Guitar picker Hudie Ledbetter (nicknamed Leadbelly) performed his blues and work songs before appreciative black audiences. Bessie Smith and Gertrude ("Ma") Rainey packed auditoriums on Chicago's South Side and recorded on black-oriented labels. Trumpeter and singer Louis Armstrong did his most creative work in the 1920s. The recordings by Armstrong's "Hot Five" and "Hot Seven" groups in the late 1920s decisively influenced the future of jazz. While the composer and band leader Duke Ellington performed to sell-out audiences at Harlem's Cotton Club, Fats Waller and Ferdinand (Jelly Roll) Morton

demonstrated the piano's jazz potential. Although much of 1920s popular culture faded quickly, jazz survived and flourished.

Advances in Science and Medicine

The creativity of the 1920s also found expression in science and medicine. Nuclear physicist Arthur H. Compton of the University of Chicago won the Nobel Prize in 1927 for his work on x-rays. In this decade, too, Ernest O. Lawrence of the University of California did the basic research that led to the cyclotron, or particle accelerator, an apparatus that enables scientists to study the atomic nucleus. These research findings would have profound implications for the future.

In medicine, Harvey Cushing of Harvard Medical School made dramatic advances in neurosurgery, while University of Wisconsin chemist Harry Steenbock created vitamin D in milk using ultraviolet rays. Other researches made key discoveries that helped conquer such killers as diphtheria, whooping cough, measles, and influenza, which had struck with devastating impact in 1918 (see Chapter 22).

In 1919 Robert Goddard, a physicist at Clark University in Massachusetts, published a little-noticed article entitled "A Method of Reaching Extreme Altitudes." In 1926 Goddard launched a small liquid-fuel rocket. Although Goddard was ridiculed at the time, his predictions of lunar landings and space exploration proved prophetic.

Of the many changes affecting American life in the 1920s, the achievements and rising cultural prestige of science loom large. In *Science and the Modern World* (1925), philosopher Alfred North Whitehead underscored science's growing role. Although "individually powerless," Whitehead concluded, scientists were "ultimately the rulers of the world." While some welcomed this prospect, others saw it as another of the decade's deeply disturbing developments.

A SOCIETY IN CONFLICT

Rapid social change often produces a backlash, and this proved especially true in 1920s' America as a series of highly charged episodes and social movements highlighted the era's tensions. While Congress restricted immigration from southern and eastern Europe and Asia, highly publicized court cases in Massachusetts and Tennessee spotlighted other sources of fear and uneasiness. Millions of whites embraced the racist bigotry and moralistic rhetoric of a revived Ku Klux Klan, and many newly urbanized African-Americans rallied to a magnetic black leader with a riveting message of racial pride. Prohibition, widely supported in the Progressive Era, proved another source of controversy in this conflict-ridden decade.

Immigration Restriction

Fed by the effort in 1917–1918 to enforce unquestioning support for the war, the old impulse to remake America into a nation of like-minded, culturally homogenous people revived in the 1920s. In a study of the decade's immigration legislation and court decisions, historian Mae M. Ngai has shown how thoroughly they were shaped by eugenicist and racist thinking, and how systematically they sought to preserve America as a "white" nation.

The National Origins Act of 1924, a revision of the immigration law, restricted annual immigration from any foreign country to 2 percent of the total number of persons of that "national origin" in the United States in 1890. Since the great influx of southern and eastern Europeans had come after 1890, the intent of this provision was clear: to reduce the immigration of these nationalities. As Calvin Coolidge observed on signing the law, "America must be kept American."

In 1929 Congress changed the base year for determining "national origins" to 1920, but even under this formula, the annual quota for Poland stood at a mere 6,524; for Italy, 5,802; for Russia, 2,784; and for Hungary, 869. This quota system, which survived to 1965, represented a strong counterattack by native-born Protestant America against the immigrant cities. Total immigration fell from 1.2 million in 1914 to 280,000 in 1929. The law excluded Asians and South Asians entirely as "persons ineligible to citizenship."

Court rulings underscored the nativist message. In *Ozawa v. U.S.* (1922), the U.S. Supreme Court rejected a citizenship request by a Japanese-born student at the University of California–Berkeley. In 1923 the Supreme Court upheld a California law limiting the right of Japanese immigrants to own or lease farmland. That same year, the Supreme Court rejected an immigration application by a man from India who claimed that he was "Caucasian" and thus eligible for entry under the Nationality Act of 1790, which had limited naturalized citizenship to "free white persons." In framing this law, the court ruled, the founders had intended "to include only the type of man whom they knew as white . . . [those] from the British Isles and northwestern Europe."

Needed Workers/Unwelcome Aliens: Hispanic Newcomers

While the 1924 law excluded Asians and restricted immigration from southern and eastern Europe, it placed no restraints on immigrants from the Western Hemisphere. Accordingly, immigration from Latin America (as well as from French Canada) soared in the 1920s. Poverty and domestic political turmoil propelled thousands of Mexicans northward. By 1930 at least 2 million Mexican-born people lived in the United States, mostly in the Southwest. California's Mexican-American population mushroomed from 90,000 in 1920 to nearly 360,000 in 1930.

Many of the immigrants were low-paid migratory workers in the region's large-scale agribusinesses. Mexican labor sustained California's citrus industry. Cooperatives such as the Southern California Fruit Growers Exchange (Sunkist) hired itinerant workers on a seasonal basis, provided substandard housing in isolated settlements the workers called *colonias*, and fought the migrants' attempts to form labor unions.

Not all Mexican immigrants were migratory workers; many settled into U.S. communities. Mexican-Americans in the Midwest worked not only in agriculture, for example, but also in the automobile, steel, and railroad industries. While still emotionally linked to "México Lindo" (Beautiful Mexico), they formed local support networks and cultural institutions. Mexican-Americans were split, however, between recent arrivals and earlier immigrants who had become U.S. citizens. The strongest Mexican-American organization in the 1920s, the Texas-based League of United Latin-American Citizens, ignored the migrant laborers of the Southwest.

Though deeply religious, Mexican-Americans found little support from the U.S. Catholic Church. Earlier, European Catholic immigrants had attended ethnic parishes and worshiped in their own languages, but church policy had changed by the 1920s. In "Anglo" parishes with non-Hispanic priests, Spanish-speaking Mexican newcomers faced discrimination and pressure to abandon their language, traditions, and folk beliefs.

Attitudes toward Mexican immigrants were deeply ambivalent. Their labor was needed, but their presence disturbed nativists eager to preserve a "white" and Protestant nation. While not formally excluded, would-be Mexican immigrants faced strict literacy and means tests. The Border Patrol was created in 1925; deportations increased; and in 1929 Congress made illegal entry a criminal offense. While these measures sharply reduced legal immigration from Mexico, the flow of illegal migration continued, as an estimated one hundred thousand Mexican newcomers arrived annually to fill pressing demands in the U.S. labor market.

Nativism, Anti-Radicalism, and the Sacco-Vanzetti Case

The xenophobic, antiradical sentiments underlying the postwar Red Scare (see Chapter 22) and the immigration-restriction movement emerged starkly in a Massachusetts murder case that became a cause célèbre. On April 15, 1920, robbers shot and killed the paymaster and guard of a shoe factory in South Braintree, Massachusetts, and stole two cash boxes. The police charged two Italian immigrants, Nicola Sacco and Bartolomeo Vanzetti, and a jury found them guilty in 1921. After many appeals and a review of the case by a commission of notable citizens, they were electrocuted on August 23, 1927.

These bare facts hardly convey the passions the case aroused, mirroring fault lines in the larger society. Sacco and Vanzetti were anarchists, and the prosecution harped on their radicalism. The judge barely concealed his hostility to the defendants, whom he privately called "those anarchist bastards." While many conservatives insisted that these alien anarchists must die, liberals and socialists rallied to their defense. As the two went to the chair, the writer John Dos Passos summed up his bitterness in a poem that ended:

> All right you have won you will kill the brave men our friends tonight
> . . . all right we are two nations.

While the case against Sacco and Vanzetti was circumstantial and far from airtight, later research on Boston's anarchist community and ballistics tests on Sacco's gun pointed to their guilt. But the prejudices that tainted the trial remain indisputable, as does the case's symbolic importance in exposing the deep divisions in American society of the 1920s.

Fundamentalism and the Scopes Trial

Meanwhile, in Tennessee, an equally celebrated case cast a spotlight on another front in the cultural wars of the decade. Post-Civil War American Protestantism faced not only an expanding Catholic and Jewish population, but also the growing prestige of science, challenging reli-

gion's cultural standing. Scholars subjected the Bible to critical scrutiny, psychologists and sociologists studied supernatural belief systems as human social constructs and expressions of emotional needs, and biologists generally accepted the naturalistic explanation for the variety of life forms on Earth advanced in Charles Darwin's *Origin of Species* (1859).

Liberal Protestants accepted the findings of science and espoused the reform-minded Social Gospel. But a reaction was building, and it came to be called fundamentalism, after *The Fundamentals*, a series of essays published in 1909–1914. Fundamentalists insisted on the literal truth of the Bible, including the Genesis account of Creation. Religious "modernists," they charged, had abandoned the truths revealed in God's Word.

In the early 1920s fundamentalists especially targeted Darwin's theory of evolution as a threat to their faith. Legislators in many states introduced bills to bar the teaching of evolution in public schools, and several southern states enacted such laws. Texas governor Miriam ("Ma") Ferguson personally censored textbooks that discussed evolution. "I am a Christian mother," she declared, "and I am not going to let that kind of rot go into Texas textbooks." Fundamentalism's best-known champion, the former Democratic presidential candidate and secretary of state William Jennings Bryan, endorsed the anti-evolution cause.

When the Tennessee legislature barred the theory of evolution from the state's public schools in 1925, the American Civil Liberties Union (ACLU) offered to defend any teacher willing to challenge this law. A high-school teacher in Dayton, Tennessee, John T. Scopes, accepted the offer. He was encouraged by local businessmen who saw an opportunity to promote their town. Scopes summarized Darwin's theory to a science class and was arrested. Famed criminal lawyer Clarence Darrow headed the defense team, and Bryan assisted the prosecution. Journalists poured into Dayton; a Chicago radio station broadcast the proceedings live; and the Scopes trial became a media sensation.

Cross-examined by Darrow, Bryan insisted on the literal veracity of every Bible story and dismissed evolutionary theory. Although the jury found Scopes guilty, the Dayton trial exposed fundamentalism to ridicule. When Bryan died of a heart attack soon after, H. L. Mencken wrote a column mercilessly deriding him and the "gaping primates" who idolized him.

In fact, the Scopes trial was only one skirmish in a long battle. Numerous southern and western states passed anti-evolution laws after 1925, and textbook publishers deleted or modified their treatment of evolution to avoid offending local school boards. Fundamentalism weakened in mainstream Protestantism, but many local congregations, radio preachers, and newly formed conservative denominations upheld the traditional faith. So, too, did the flamboyant evangelist Billy Sunday, who denounced the loose living and modernism of the 1920s.

In Los Angeles, the charismatic Aimee Semple McPherson, anticipating later TV evangelists, regularly filled her cavernous Angelus Temple and reached thousands more by radio. The beautiful, white-gowned McPherson entranced audiences with theatrical sermons. She once used a gigantic electric scoreboard to illustrate the triumph of good over evil. Her followers, mainly transplanted midwesterners, embraced her fundamentalist theology while reveling in her mass-entertainment techniques. When she died in 1944, her International Church of the Foursquare Gospel had more than six hundred branches in the United States and abroad.

The Ku Klux Klan and the Garvey Movement

The tensions and hostilities tearing at the American social fabric also emerged in a resurrected Ku Klux Klan (KKK) movement. The original Klan of the Reconstruction era had faded by the 1870s, but in November 1915 it was revived by hooded men gathered at Stone Mountain, Georgia. D. W. Griffith's glorification of the Klan in *The Birth of a Nation* (1915) provided further inspiration.

The movement remained obscure until 1920, when two Atlanta entrepreneurs organized a national membership drive. Sensing the appeal of the Klan's ritual and its nativist, white-supremacist ideology, they devised a recruitment scheme involving a ten-dollar membership fee divided among the salesman (called the Kleagle), the local sales manager (King Kleagle), the district sales manager (Grand Goblin), the state leader (Grand Dragon), and the national leader (Imperial Wizard)—with a rake-off to themselves. They also sold Klan robes and masks, the horse robe that every member had to buy, and the Chattahoochee River water used in initiation rites (ten dollars a bottle). This elaborate scam succeeded beyond their wildest dreams.

The Klan demonized a variety of targets, and won a vast following. Under the umbrella term "100 percent Americanism," it attacked not only African-Americans but also Catholics, Jews, and aliens. Some Klan groups

The Ku Klux Klan in Washington, D.C.
In a brazen display of power, the Ku Klux Klan organized a march in the nation's capital in 1926. By this time, the Klan was already in decline.

carried out vigilante attacks on whites suspected of sexual immorality or prohibition-law violations. Estimates of membership in the KKK and its women's auxiliary in the early 1920s range as high as 5 million. From its southern base, the Klan spread through the Midwest and across the country from Long Island to the West Coast, especially among the working class and lower middle class in cities with native-born Protestant majorities. In 1922 Imperial Wizard Hiram Wesley Evans admitted the Klan's image as a haven of "hicks" and "rubes" and urged college graduates to support the great cause.

The Klan filled emotional needs for its members. Although corrupt at the top, it was not a haven for criminals or fanatics; observers commented on members' ordinariness. (Evans, a Texas dentist, called himself "the most average man in America.") The Klan's promise to restore the nation's lost purity—racial, ethnic, religious, and moral—appealed to many old-stock Protestants disoriented by social change. For some small businessmen caught between organized labor and the new corporate order, the Klan's litany of menace offered a vocabulary for articulating economic anxieties. Some citizens upset by changing sexual mores welcomed the Klan's defense of "the purity of white womanhood." Klan membership, in short, gave a sense of empowerment and group cohesion to people who felt marginalized by the

new social order of immigrants, big cities, great corporations, mass culture, and racial and religious diversity. The rituals, parades, and cross burnings added drama to unfulfilling lives.

But if individual Klan members seemed more needy than sinister, the Klan's menacing potential as a mass movement was real. Some KKK groups resorted to intimidation, threats, beatings, and lynching in their quest for a purified America. In several states, the Klan won political power. Oklahoma's Klan-controlled legislature impeached and removed an anti-Klan governor. In Oregon the Klan elected a governor and pushed through legislation requiring all children to attend public school, a slap at the state's Catholic schools.

The Klan collapsed with shocking suddenness. In March 1925 Indiana's politically powerful Grand Dragon, David Stephenson, raped his young secretary. When she swallowed poison the next day, Stephenson panicked and refused to call a physician. The woman died several weeks later, and Stephenson went to jail. From prison he revealed details of political corruption in Indiana. Its moral pretensions in shreds, the KKK faded.

Among African-Americans who had escaped southern rural poverty and racism only to find continued poverty and more racism in the urban North, the decade's social strains produced a different kind of mass

Marcus Garvey (1887–1945)
Jamaican-born Garvey, shown here in New York City in 1922, attracted many poor and working-class urban African-Americans with the parades and regalia of his Universal Negro Improvement Association and its message of black pride, self help, and African nationalism.

movement led by the spellbinding Marcus Garvey and his Universal Negro Improvement Association (UNIA). Born in Jamaica in 1887, Garvey founded UNIA in 1914 and two years later moved to New York City's Harlem, which became the movement's headquarters. In a white-dominated society, Garvey glorified all things black. Urging black economic solidarity, he founded a chain of UNIA grocery stores and other businesses. He summoned blacks to return to "Motherland Africa" and establish there a great nation.

An estimated eighty thousand blacks joined the UNIA, and thousands more felt the lure of Garvey's oratory; the uplift of UNIA parades, uniforms, and flags; and the seduction of Garvey's dream of a glorious future in Africa. Garvey's popularity unsettled not only white America but also the middle-class leaders of the NAACP and the black churches. W .E. B. Du Bois was one of Garvey's sharpest critics. The movement also highlighted social tensions in Harlem, where two long-separated streams of the African diaspora, one from the Caribbean, the other from the American South, came together in the 1920s. This convergence provoked rivalry for limited economic opportunities and political power. Garvey himself was Jamaican, and critics charged that Caribbean immigrants controlled UNIA.

In 1923 a federal court convicted Garvey of fraud in one of his business ventures, the Black Star Steamship Line. In 1927, after two years' imprisonment, he was deported to Jamaica, and the UNIA collapsed. But as the first mass movement in black America, it revealed both the seething discontent and the activist potential among African-Americans in the urban North. "In a world where black is despised," commented an African-American newspaper after Garvey's fall, "he taught his followers that black is beautiful."

Prohibition: Cultures in Conflict

The deep fissures in American society also surfaced in the controversy over alcohol. As we discussed in Chapter 21, many Progressive Era reformers supported prohibition as a legitimate response to the social problems associated with alcohol abuse. But the issue also had symbolic overtones, as native-born Americans struggled to maintain cultural and political dominance over the immigrant cities. When the Eighteenth Amendment took effect in January 1920, prohibitionists rejoiced. Billy Sunday proclaimed,

> The reign of tears is over. The slums will soon be only a memory. We will turn our prisons into factories and our jails into storehouses and corncribs. Men will walk upright now. Women will smile and children will laugh.

Sunday's dream seemed attainable as saloons closed, liquor advertising vanished, and arrests for drunkenness declined. In 1921 alcohol consumption stood at about one-third the prewar level. Yet prohibition gradually lost support, and in 1933 it ended.

What went wrong? Essentially, prohibition's failure illustrates the virtual impossibility of enforcing a widely opposed law in a democracy. From the beginning, the Volstead Act, the 1919 prohibition law, was underfunded and weakly enforced, especially in antiprohibition areas. New York, for example, repealed its prohibition-enforcement law as early as 1923. Would-be drinkers grew bolder as enforcement faltered. For rebellious young people, alcohol's illegality increased its appeal. "[P]rohibition has been an incentive for young folks to learn to drink," declared once college student. "It is the natural reaction of youth to rules and regulations."

Prohibition Alley Scene, by Ben Shahn, c. 1934 In this fanciful painting, incorporating a portrait of gangster Al Capone, Shahn linked the crime and violence of bootlegging with the respectable citizenry who patronized speakeasies that sold illicit liquor.

Every city boasted speakeasies where customers could buy drinks, and rumrunners routinely smuggled liquor from Canada and the West Indies. Shady entrepreneurs sold flavored industrial-grade alcohol. People concocted their own home brew, and the demand for sacramental wine soared. By 1929 alcohol consumption was about 70 percent of the prewar level.

Organized crime helped circumvent the law. In Chicago rival gangs battled to control the liquor business. The city witnessed 550 gangland killings in the 1920s. Chicago gangster Al Capone controlled a network of speakeasies that generated annual profits of $60 million. Although not typical, Chicago's crime wave underscored prohibition's failure. A reform designed to produce a more orderly and virtuous America was turning citizens into lawbreakers and mobsters into celebrities.

Thus prohibition, too, became a battleground in the decade's cultural wars. The "drys"—usually native-born Protestants—praised it as a necessary social reform. The "wets"—liberals, alienated intellectuals, Jazz Age rebels, big-city immigrants—condemned it as moralistic meddling. At one college, the student newspaper suggested a campus distillery as the senior class gift, "with the proceeds going to the college."

Prohibition influenced the 1928 presidential campaign. While Democratic candidate Al Smith advocated repeal of the Eighteenth Amendment, Republican Herbert Hoover praised it as "a great social and economic experiment, noble in motive and far-reaching in purpose." Once elected, Hoover appointed a commission to study the matter. In a confusing 1931 report, the commission conceded prohibition's failure, but urged its retention. A New York journalist parodied the findings:

Prohibition is an awful flop.
    We like it.
It can't stop what it's meant to stop.
    We like it.
It's left a trail of graft and slime,
It's filled our land with vice and crime,
It don't prohibit worth a dime,
    Nevertheless we're for it.

By the time the Eighteenth Amendment was finally repealed in 1933, prohibition was thoroughly discredited and seemed little more than a relic of another age.

HOOVER AT THE HELM

Herbert Hoover, elected president in 1928, appeared well fitted to sustain the nation's prosperity. No standpat conservative like Harding and Coolidge, Hoover espoused a distinctive social and political philosophy that

reflected his engineering background. In some ways, he seemed the ideal president for the new technological age.

The Election of 1928

A Hollywood casting agent could not have chosen two individuals who better personified the nation's social and cultural schisms than the 1928 presidential candidates. Al Smith, the governor of New York, easily won the Democratic nomination. The party's urban-immigrant wing had gained strength since the deadlocked 1924 convention. A Catholic and a wet, Smith exuded the flavor of immigrant New York City. Originally a machine politician and basically conservative, he had won the support of progressive reformers by backing social-welfare measures. His inner circle included several reform-minded women, notably Frances Perkins, the head of the state industrial board, and Belle Moskowitz, a key adviser.

Secretary of Commerce Herbert Hoover won the Republican nomination after Calvin Coolidge chose not to run. Some conservative party leaders, however, mistrusted the brilliant but aloof Hoover, who had never held elective office and indeed had spent much of his adult life abroad. Born in Iowa and orphaned at an early age, Hoover had put himself through Stanford University

and made a fortune as a mining engineer in China and Australia. His service as wartime food administrator had won him a place in the Harding and Coolidge cabinets.

Hoover disdained handshaking and baby kissing. Instead, he issued "tons of reports on dull subjects" (in Mencken's jaundiced view) and read radio speeches in a droning monotone. His boring campaign style obscured the originality of his ideas. Smith, by contrast, campaigned spiritedly across the nation. This may actually have hurt him, however, because his big-city wisecracking and New York accent grated on many voters in the heartland.

Whether Smith's Catholicism helped or hurt his candidacy remains debatable. Hoover urged tolerance, and Smith denied any conflict between his faith and the duties of the presidency, but anti-Catholic prejudice unquestionably played a role. Rumors circulated that the Vatican would relocate to the United States if Smith won. (A postelection joke had Smith sending the pope a one-word telegram, "Unpack.") The decisive campaign issue was probably not popery but prosperity. Republican orators pointed to the booming economy and warned that a Smith victory would mean "soup kitchens instead of busy factories." In his nomination-acceptance speech, Hoover foresaw "the final triumph over poverty."

Al Smith on the Campaign Trail
With his trademark derby hat in hand, Smith greets Denver politicians in his unsuccessful 1928 race for the presidency.

MAP 23.1
The Election of 1928

	Electoral Vote	Popular Vote	Percentage of Popular Vote
Republican Herbert C. Hoover	444	21,391,993	58.2
Democratic Alfred E. Smith	87	15,016,169	40.9
Minor parties	–	–	330,725	0.9

TABLE 23.1   Presidential Voting by Selected Ethnic Groups in Chicago, 1924, 1928, and 1932

	Percent Democratic		
	1924	1928	1932
Blacks	10	23	21
Czechoslovaks	40	73	83
Germans	14	58	69
Italians	31	63	64
Jews	19	60	77
Lithuanians	48	77	84
Poles	35	71	80
Swedes	15	34	51
Yugoslavs	20	54	67

Source: John M. Allswang, *A House for All Peoples: Ethnic Politics in Chicago, 1890–1936* (Lexington: University Press of Kentucky, 1971).

Hoover won in a landslide, grabbing 58 percent of the vote and even making deep inroads in the Democratic "solid South" (see Map 23.1). Socialist Norman Thomas received only 267,000 votes, less than a third of Eugene V. Debs's 1920 total. However, the election also offered evidence of an emerging political realignment (see Table 23.1). Smith did well in the rural Midwest, where hard-pressed farmers, angered by Coolidge's insensitivity to their plight, abandoned their normal Republican allegiance. In northern cities, Catholic and Jewish immigrant wards voted heavily Democratic. In 1924 the nation's twelve largest cities had all gone Republican; in 1928 Smith carried all twelve. Should prosperity end, these portents suggested, the Republican party faced trouble.

Herbert Hoover's Social Thought

Americans looked hopefully to their new president, whom admirers dubbed the Great Engineer. Hoover had described his social creed in a 1922 book *American Individualism.* Although a self-made man himself, he did not uncritically praise big business. His Quakerism, humanitarian activities, engineering experience, and Republican loyalties combined to produce a unique social outlook.

Like Theodore Roosevelt (whom he had supported in 1912), Hoover disapproved of cutthroat capitalist competition. Rational economic development, he insisted, demanded corporate cooperation in market-ing, wage policy, raw-material allocation, and product standardization. The economy, in short, should operate like an efficient machine. Believing that business had social obligations, Hoover welcomed the growth of welfare capitalism. But above all, he believed in voluntarism. The cooperative, socially responsible economic order that he envisioned must arise from the voluntary action of capitalist leaders, not government coercion or labor-management power struggles.

Hoover had put his philosophy into practice as secretary of commerce. To encourage corporate consolidation and cooperation, he had convened more than 250 conferences in which business leaders discussed such issues as unemployment, pricing policies, and labor-management relations. He urged higher wages to increase consumer purchasing power, and in 1923 he persuaded the steel industry to adopt an eight-hour workday as an efficiency measure. During the disastrous 1927 Mississippi River floods, as President Coolidge remained in Washington, Hoover had rushed to the stricken area and helped mobilize relief efforts.

Hoover's ideology had its limitations. He showed more interest in cooperation among capitalists than among consumers or workers. His belief that capitalists would voluntarily embrace enlightened labor policies and an ethic of social responsibility overestimated the role of altruism in business decisionmaking. And his opposition to government economic intervention brought him grief when such intervention became urgently necessary.

Hoover's early months as president seemed promising. He set up a President's Council on Recent Social Trends and other commissions to study public issues and gather data to guide policy makers. Responding to the farm problem, he secured passage of legislation creating a Federal Farm Board (1929) to promote cooperative commodity marketing. This, he hoped, would raise farm prices while preserving the voluntarist principle.

By late summer 1929, the Hoover administration appeared to be off to a good start. But while Hoover applied his engineering skills to the machinery of government, a crisis was approaching that would overwhelm and ultimately destroy his presidency.

CONCLUSION

Reacting against the exalted idealism of the war, America pursued a nationalistic foreign policy in the 1920s. Although the nation rejected Wilson's vision of global leadership, the myth of U.S. "isolationism" is belied by corporate expansion abroad, U.S. involvement in Latin America, and Washington's pursuit of reparations payments.

On the domestic front, the era remains memorable as a time when new consumer products, new modes of mass production, and new methods of marketing and advertising gave the economy a glow of prosperity. The 1920s is also remembered as a decade when an entire people grappled with massive technological and social change. Like world travelers groggy from jet lag, Americans of the twenties sought to adapt to the rise of a new mass-culture, mass-production, urban world. Skyscrapers, radio, the automobile, the movies, electrical appliances—all familiar today—were exciting novelties in 1920s America.

Republican-dominated Washington generally celebrated the new corporate, consumerist culture ("The business of America is business" said Calvin Coolidge) and pursued probusiness policies. While politicians fell back on time-worn ideologies, the larger society seethed in ferment. Ironically, the same stresses that sparked angry social conflict and confrontations also stimulated a rich cultural flowering. The native-born advocates of prohibition and fundamentalism; the embittered white Protestants who joined the Klan; the uprooted urban blacks who rallied to Marcus Garvey; the artists and

CHRONOLOGY, 1920–1929

1915 Modern Ku Klux Klan founded.
1916 Marcus Garvey moves to New York City.
1919 Volstead Act (Prohibition).
1920–1921 Sharp postwar recession.
1920 Warren G. Harding elected president.
Radio station KDKA, Pittsburgh, broadcasts election returns.
Sinclair Lewis, *Main Street*
1921 Economic boom begins; agriculture remains depressed.
Sheppard-Towner Act.
Shuffle Along, all-black musical review.
1921–1922 Washington Naval Arms Conference.
1922 Supreme Court declares child-labor law unconstitutional.
Fordney-McCumber Tariff restores high rates.
Herbert Hoover, *American Individualism*.
Sinclair Lewis, *Babbitt*.
1923 Harding dies; Calvin Coolidge becomes president.
Supreme Court strikes down minimum-wage law for women.
1924 Teapot Dome scandals investigated.
National Origins Act.
Calvin Coolidge elected president.
McNary-Haugen farm bill introduced.

1925 Scopes trial
Ku Klux Klan scandal in Indiana.
Alain Locke, *The New Negro*.
Dorothy and DuBose Heyward, *Porgy*.
F. Scott Fitzgerald, *The Great Gatsby*.
1926 Book-of-the-Month Club founded.
National Broadcasting Company founded.
Langston Hughes, *The Weary Blues*.
1927 *The Jazz Singer*, first sound movie.
Coolidge vetoes the McNary-Haugen bill.
Henry Ford introduces the Model A.
Execution of Sacco and Vanzetti.
Charles A. Lindbergh's transatlantic flight.
Marcus Garvey deported.
Mississippi River flood.
1928 Herbert Hoover elected president.
1929 Federal Farm Board created.
Sheppard-Towner program terminated.
Hallelujah, first all-black movie.
Ernest Hemingway, *A Farewell to Arms*.
Stock market speculative frenzy.

writers of the Harlem Renaissance; the young novelists and poets who revitalized American literature; and the decade's innovative architects, composers, painters, and photographers were all, in their different ways, responding to the promise, perils, and uncertainties of a new and modern age.

FOR FURTHER REFERENCE

READINGS

Charles C. Alexander, *Here the Country Lies: Nationalism and the Arts in Twentieth Century America* (1980). A valuable study stressing the positive achievements of 1920s' cultural creators.

Scott Berg, *Lindbergh* (1998). Excellent study of the life and personality of an American hero.

Lendol Calder, *Financing the American Dream: A Cultural History of Consumer Credit* (1999). Explores the rise of new mechanisms of consumer credit and changing cultural attitudes about borrowing.

Paul Carter, *The Twenties in America* (1968) and *Another Part of the Twenties* (1977). Two short books offering refreshingly personal interpretive judgments.

Juan R. Garcia, *Mexicans in the Midwest, 1900–1932* (1996). Comprehensive, well-researched history of a little-studied aspect of the Mexican-American experience.

Ellis W. Hawley, *The Great War and the Search for a Modern Order* (1979). An economic study that traces the emergence (and collapse in 1929) of the first mass-consumption society.

John D. Hicks, *Republican Ascendancy, 1921–1933* (1960). Somewhat dated but still-valuable study of politics and politicians in the 1920s.

George Hutchinson, *The Harlem Renaissance in Black and White* (1995). Original study linking the Harlem Renaissance to larger cultural and intellectual movements.

Joan Shelley Rubin, The Making of Middle-Brow Culture (1992). An interpretive study of the Book-of-the-Month Club and other 1920s institutions that mediated high culture and popular culture.

Virginia Scharff, *Taking the Wheel: Women and the Coming of the Motor Age* (1991). Well-researched and readable study of the gender aspects of early automobile culture.

WEBSITES

Famous Trials in American History: *Tennessee* vs. *John Scopes.* The Monkey Trial
http://www.umkc.edu/faculty/projects/ftrials/scopes.htm
Excellent collection of primary sources including trial excerpts, observers' accounts, biographies of key participants, photographs, and newspaper cartoons.

Fatal Flood
http://www.pbs.org/wgbh/amex/flood
Excellent *American Experience* website treating the catastrophic 1927 Mississippi River flood, including film clips, reminiscences and songs, maps, and a timeline.

A History of Mexican Americans in California
http://www.cr.nps.gov/history/online_books/5views/5views5c.htm
This National Park Service online book covers the subject comprehensively, with photographs of historic sites, selected references, and speculation on future trends.

Lindbergh
http://www.pbs.org/wgbh/pages/amex/lindbergh
Comprehensive web page of a PBS *American Experience* program, including details of Lindbergh's flight and features on his eventful and sometimes controversial later life.

Senate Investigates the "Teapot Dome" Scandal
http://www.senate.gov/learning/min-5c.html
This U.S. Senate web page includes a brief narrative of the scandal and the Senate's investigative role, with links to key figures and suggestions for further reading.

For additional works, please consult the bibliography at the end of the book.

The Great Depression and the New Deal, 1929–1939

Rugged Campobello Island lying off Eastport, Maine, was sunlit that August afternoon in 1921. A small sailboat bobbed in the waters off the island. At the helm, with several of his children, was thirty-nine-year-old Franklin D. Roosevelt. Assistant secretary of the navy during World War I, Roosevelt had been the Democratic party's vice-presidential candidate in 1920. But all this was far from his mind now. He loved sailing, and he loved Campobello Island.

The idyllic afternoon suddenly took an ominous turn when Roosevelt spotted a fire. Beaching the boat, he and the children frantically beat back the spreading flames. The exertion left Roosevelt unusually fatigued. The next morning his left leg dragged when he tried to walk. Soon all sensation disappeared in both legs. He had suffered an attack of poliomyelitis (infantile paralysis), a viral infection that most often struck children but sometimes struck adults as well. Except for a cumbersome shuffle with crutches and heavy metal braces, he would never walk again.

This illness changed the lives of both Franklin Roosevelt and his wife Eleanor. To Franklin, it seemed the end of his career. But he endured endless therapy and gradually reentered politics. In 1928, laboriously mounting the podium at the Democratic National Convention, he nominated his friend Al Smith for president. That fall, he himself was elected governor of New York.

◀ **A young farm worker in western Pennsylvania in the 1930s, photographed by Walker Evans.**

Somewhat superficial and even arrogant before 1921, this privileged only child became, through his ordeal, more understanding of the disadvantaged and far more determined. "If you had spent two years in bed trying to wiggle your big toe," he once said, "after that everything else would seem easy!"

Eleanor Roosevelt at first devoted herself to her husband's care and to the child-rearing duties that now fell to her. But she also encouraged his return to politics, resisting his domineering mother's efforts to turn him into an invalid at the family home at Hyde Park, New York. Eleanor became her husband's eyes and ears. Already involved with social issues, she now became active in the New York Democratic party and edited its newsletter for women. Painfully shy, she forced herself to make public speeches.

The Roosevelts would soon need the qualities of character they had acquired. Elected president in 1932 amidst the worst depression in American history, Franklin Roosevelt dominated U.S. politics until his death in 1945. Roosevelt's presidency, the so-called New Deal, spawned an array of laws, agencies, and programs that historians ever since have tried to whip into coherent form. And, indeed, certain patterns do emerge. In what some label the First New Deal (1933–1935), the dual themes were relief and recovery through a united national effort. In 1935, facing political challenges on the left and right, Roosevelt charted a more radical course. In the so-called Second New Deal (1935–1936), the administration placed less emphasis on unity and more on business regulation and on policies benefiting workers, small farmers, sharecroppers, migrant laborers, and others at the lower end of the scale.

The New Deal involved myriad programs, political infighting, and countless officials and bureaucrats. But in the public mind, it meant Roosevelt. Loved by some almost like a family member and reviled by others as a demagogue or would-be dictator, Roosevelt was a consummate politician whose administration set the national political agenda for a generation.

This chapter develops two interconnected themes. The first is the New Deal's profound effect on ideas about government, as it defined a more expansive view of the role of the state in promoting economic and social welfare. The second theme is the response of the American people to the Great Depression. From assembly-line workers, urban blacks, and migrant laborers to moviemakers, artists, writers, and photographers, diverse groups met the crisis with resourcefulness, social activism, and creative expression.

The chapter focuses on five major questions:

■ What were the main causes of the Great Depression?

■ What depression-fighting strategy underlay the so-called First New Deal, and why did the Roosevelt administration change course in 1935, giving rise to the so-called Second New Deal?

■ Which New Deal programs have had the greatest long-term effect, and how did ideas about the role of government change as a result of the New Deal?

■ How did the depression and the New Deal affect specific groups in the United States? (Consider, for example, small farmers and sharecroppers, Native Americans, industrial workers, women, African-Americans, and Mexican-Americans.)

■ How did American culture—including both the mass-entertainment industries and the efforts of novelists, artists, photographers, and composers—respond to the events of the 1930s?

CRASH AND DEPRESSION, 1929–1932

The prosperity of the 1920s came to a jolting end in October 1929 with the collapse of the stock market. The Wall Street crash, and the deeper economic problems that underlay it, launched a depression that reached every household. President Hoover struggled with the crisis, but his ideological commitment to private initiative and his horror of governmental coercion limited his effectiveness. In November 1932 voters turned to the Democratic party and its new leader, Franklin Roosevelt. This pivotal election set the stage for a vast expansion in the role of the federal government in addressing social and economic issues.

Black Thursday and the Onset of the Depression

Stock prices had risen steadily through much of the 1920s, but 1928–1929 brought a frenzied upsurge as speculators plunged into the market. In 1925 the market value of all stocks had stood at about $27 billion; by October 1929, with some 9 million Americans playing the market, it hit $87 billion (see Figure 24.1A,B). With stockbrokers lending speculators up to 75 percent of a stock's cost, credit or "margin" buying spread. The income-tax cuts promoted by Treasury Secretary

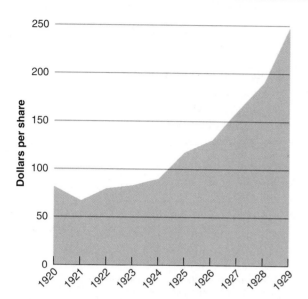

FIGURE 24.1A
Stock Market Prices in the 1920s
After rising moderately in the early 1920s, stock market prices shot up later in the decade. Looking at such statistics, Herbert Hoover declared in 1929, "I have no fears for the future of our country. It is bright with hope."

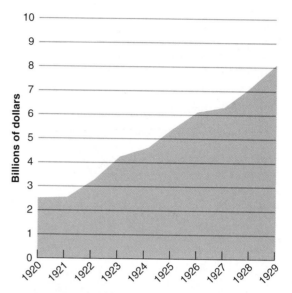

FIGURE 24.1B
Consumer Borrowing in the 1920s
Americans plunged heavily into debt in the 1920s to play the stock market and to buy their new Fords, Chevrolets, and other consumer products. By 1929 their total debt stood at about $8 billion.

Andrew Mellon had increased the volume of money available for speculation. Optimistic pronouncements also fed the speculative boom. In March 1929 former president Calvin Coolidge declared stocks "cheap at current prices." "Investment trusts," akin to today's mutual funds, but totally unregulated, lured novices into the market. The construction industry declined sharply in 1928–1929—an omen few heeded.

In 1928, and again in September 1929, the Federal Reserve Board tried to dampen speculation by raising the interest rate on federal reserve notes. Early in 1929 the Fed warned member banks to tighten their lending policies. But with speculators willing to pay up to 20 percent interest for money to buy more stock, lending institutions continued to loan money freely—an act akin to dumping gasoline on a raging fire. Stock prices zoomed ever higher.

The collapse came on October 24, 1929—"Black Thursday." As prices fell, some stocks found no buyers at all: they had literally become worthless. On Tuesday, October 29, a record 16 million stocks changed hands in frantic trading. In the ensuing weeks, feeble upswings alternated with further plunges.

President Hoover, in the first of many optimistic statements, pronounced the economy "sound and prosperous." But few listened. By mid-November the loss in

the value of stocks stood at $30 billion. A weak upswing early in 1930 suggested that the worst might be over. However, instead of recovering, as many analysts predicted, the economy went into a long tailspin, producing a full-scale depression.

What were the underlying causes of this depression? Many economists focus on structural problem that made 1920s' prosperity so unstable. The agricultural sector remained depressed throughout the decade. In the industrial sector, increased productivity did not generate fully equivalent wage increases, but rather took the form of higher corporate profits. In 1929 the 40 percent of Americans who were lowest on the economic scale received only about 12 percent of the total national income. This reduced consumer purchasing power. At the same time, assembly-line methods encouraged overproduction. By summer 1929 the automobile, housing, textile, tire, and other durable-goods industries were seriously overextended. Further, important sectors of industry–including railroads, steel, textiles, and mining—lagged technologically in the 1930s and could not attract the investment needed to stimulate recovery.

Some economists, the so-called monetarist school, also focus on the banking system's collapse in the early 1930s, which they blame on Federal Reserve System's

FIGURE 24.2
The Statistics of Hard Times

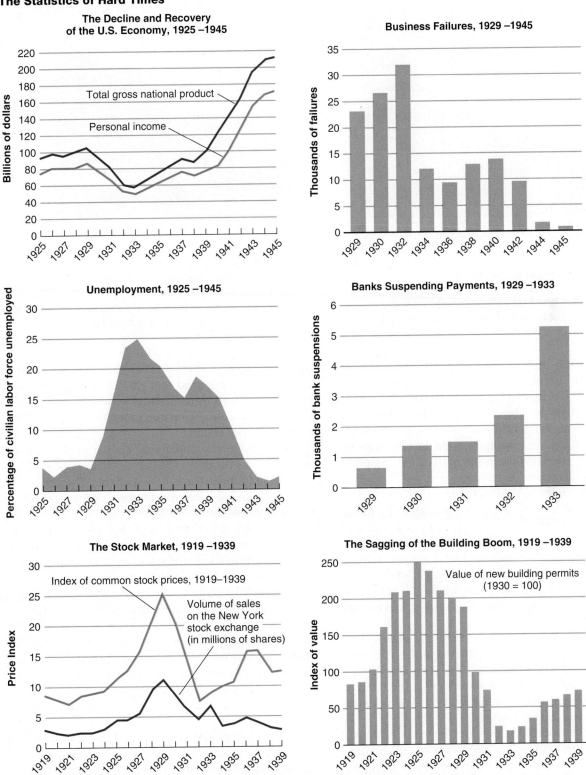

Sources: C. D. Bremmer, *American Bank Failures* (New York: Columbia University Press, 1935), 42; Thomas C. Cochran, *The Great Depression and World War II: 1929–1945* (Glenview, Illinois: Scott, Foresman, 1968); *Historical Statistics of the United States, Colonial Times to 1970* (Washington, D.C.: U.S. Government Printing Office, 1975).

tight-money policies. This policy, they charge, strangled any hope of economic recovery by reducing the amount of money available to businesses for investment and growth.

All analysts link the U.S. depression to a global economic crisis. European economies, already enfeebled by war debt payments and a severe trade imbalance with the United States, collapsed in 1931. This larger crisis depressed U.S. exports and fed the fear gripping the nation.

Whatever the causes, the depression had a chilling impact on the U.S. economy. From 1929 to 1932, the gross national product dropped from $104 billion to $59 billion. Farm prices, already low, fell by nearly 60 percent. By early 1933 more than fifty-five hundred banks had closed, and unemployment stood at 25 percent, or nearly 13 million workers (see Figure 24.2). In some cities the jobless rate far exceeded the national average. In Toledo in 1932, for example, it stood at 80 percent. Many who still had jobs faced cuts in pay and hours.

Hoover's Response

Historically, Americans had viewed depressions as acts of nature: little could be done other than ride out the storm. President Hoover, an intelligent moderate with activist impulses, disagreed. Drawing upon the legacy of progressive reform and his service as U.S. food administrator in World War I, Hoover initially confronted the crisis boldly. But his approach also reflected his belief in localism and private initiative.

Acting on his convictions, Hoover urged business leaders to maintain wages and employment. Viewing unemployment as a local issue, he advised municipal and state governments to create public-works projects. In October 1930 he set up an Emergency Committee for Employment to coordinate voluntary relief efforts. In 1931 he persuaded the nation's largest banks to set up a private lending agency, the National Credit Corporation, to help hard-pressed smaller banks make business loans.

These antidepression measures did little good. As the crisis worsened and joblessness increased, public opinion turned against Hoover. In the 1930 midterm election, the Republicans lost the House of Representatives and gave up eight Senate seats. In 1931, dreading a budget deficit, Hoover called for a tax increase, further angering hard-pressed Americans. That same year, despite their pledges to Hoover, U.S. Steel, General Motors, and other big corporations announced major wage cuts. The crisis quickly swamped private

charities and local welfare agencies. Philadelphia, with more than three hundred thousand jobless by 1932, cut weekly relief payments to $4.23 per family and then suspended them entirely.

In 1932, a presidential election year, Hoover swallowed his principles and launched a bold federal response to the crisis. In January, at Hoover's recommendation, Congress set up a new agency, the Reconstruction Finance Corporation (RFC), to make loans to major economic institutions such as banks and insurance companies. By July the RFC had pumped $1.2 billion into the economy. Congress also authorized the RFC to grant $2 billion to state and local governments for job-creating public-works programs, and allocated $750 million for loans to businesses struggling to survive.

Hoover approved all these measures, but he reaped little political benefit from them. He supported them reluctantly, warning that they could open the door to "socialism and collectivism." Blaming global forces for the depression, he argued that only international measures would help. Some of his proposals, such as a moratorium on war-debt and reparations payments by European nations, made sense, but seemed irrelevant to the plight of ordinary Americans.

As Hoover issued press releases urging self-help and local initiative and endlessly saw prosperity "just around the corner," his relations with the news media soured. When he appointed a new press secretary disliked by the White House journalists, one reporter called it the first instance of a rat boarding a sinking ship. An administration launched so hopefully in 1929 by a widely admired president was ending in bitterness and failure.

Mounting Discontent and Protest

An ominous mood spread over the nation as hordes of the jobless waited in breadlines, slept on park benches, trudged the streets, and rode freight trains from city to city seeking work. Americans reared on the ethic of hard work and self-support experienced chronic unemployment as a shattering psychic blow. Because most of the jobless had families, the unemployment figures must be multiplied several times over to reflect the full impact of the crisis. Family savings vanished as banks failed.

Newspapers humanized the crisis. The *New York Times* described "Hoover Valley"—a section of Central Park where jobless men lived in boxes and packing crates. In winter they wrapped themselves in layers of newspapers they called Hoover blankets. The suicide rate climbed nearly 30 percent between 1928 and 1932.

In Youngstown, Ohio, a fifty-seven-year-old jobless father of ten whose family faced eviction jumped to his death from a bridge. Violence threatened in some cities when people unable to pay their rent were evicted from homes and apartments.

Hard times battered the nation's farms. Many underwent mortgage foreclosures or forced sales because of tax delinquency, with Iowa and the Dakotas especially hard hit. Driving through the midwestern farm belt early in 1931, writer Malcolm Cowley found much of it untended and empty. "I wondered," Cowley wrote in the *New Republic*, "how much more of it will be abandoned next spring, after the milch cows have been sold for beef, the tractors and combine harvesters seized by finance corporations, the notes and mortgages allowed to go unpaid." At some forced farm auctions, neighbors bought the foreclosed farm for a trivial sum, and returned it to the evicted family.

In 1931 midwestern farmers organized a boycott movement called the Farmers' Holiday Association to force prices up by withholding grain and livestock from the market. Dairy farmers angered by low prices dumped milk in Iowa and Wisconsin.

The most alarming protest came from World War I veterans. In 1924 Congress had voted veterans a bonus stretched over a twenty-year period. In June 1932 some ten thousand veterans, many jobless, descended on Washington to lobby for immediate payment of these bonuses. When Congress refused, most of the "bonus marchers" went home, but about two thousand stayed on, building makeshift shelters on the outskirts of Washington. President Hoover called in the army.

On July 28 a thousand troops commanded by General Douglas MacArthur armed with tear gas, tanks, and machine guns drove the veterans from their encampment and burned their shelters. A journalist described the scene:

> [The veterans and their families] wandered from street to street or sat in ragged groups, the men exhausted, the women with wet handkerchiefs laid over their smarting eyes, the children waking from sleep to cough and whimper from the tear gas in their lungs. The flames behind them were climbing into the night sky . . . . Their shanties and tents had been burned, their personal property destroyed, except for the few belongings they could carry on their backs.

To many Americans, this action symbolized the administration's utter bankruptcy.

Matching the mood of discontent, American fiction of the early depression exuded disillusionment and despair. In *The 42nd Parallel* (1930), the first volume of a trilogy, John Dos Passos drew a dark panorama of twentieth-century America as money-mad, exploitive, and lacking spiritual meaning. As one character says, "Everything you've wanted crumbles in your fingers as you grasp it." In *Young Lonigan* (1932), which also launched a trilogy, James T. Farrell portrayed the empty existence of Studs Lonigan, a working-class Irish-immigrant youth in Chicago. Unable to find work and feeling betrayed by the American dream, Studs wanders the streets, trying to piece together a coherent worldview from the bits of mass culture that drift his way.

Some radical novelists of the early thirties attacked the capitalist system even more explicitly. The Communist party encouraged such fiction through writers' clubs and contests for working-class writers. Jack Conroy's *The Disinherited* (1933), dealing with life in the

Unrest in the Heartland
Protesting Minnesota farmers demand relief in a 1933 march on the state capital.

Missouri coal fields, gained force from the fact that Conroy's father and brother had died in a mine disaster.

The Election of 1932

Gloom pervaded the 1932 Republican convention that renominated Hoover. The Democrats who gathered in Chicago, by contrast, scented victory. Their platform, crafted to erase the party divisions of the 1920s, appealed to urban voters with a call for repeal of prohibition, to farmers with support for aid programs, and to fiscal conservatives with demands for a balanced budget and cuts in federal spending. Rejecting Al Smith, the party's 1928 standard-bearer, the delegates nominated Franklin D. Roosevelt, governor of New York, for president.

Breaking precedent, FDR flew to Chicago to accept the nomination in person with a rousing speech pledging "a new deal for the American people." Despite this ringing phrase, Roosevelt's campaign offered no clear program. He called for "bold persistent experimentation" and compassion for "the forgotten man at the bottom of the economic pyramid," yet he also attacked Hoover's "reckless" spending and insisted that "only as a last resort" should the federal government play a larger depression-fighting role.

But Roosevelt exuded confidence, and above all he was not Hoover. On November 8, FDR and his running mate, Texas congressman John Nance Garner, received nearly 23 million votes, compared to fewer than 16 million for Hoover (see Map 24.1). Both houses of Congress went heavily Democratic. What did this landslide mean in terms of public policies? The nation waited.

THE NEW DEAL TAKES SHAPE, 1933–1935

The Roosevelt years began on a note of feverish activity. Enjoying strong majorities in Congress, FDR proposed an array of emergency measures that passed by large margins. These measures reflected differing and sometimes contradictory approaches, but they involved three basic goals: industrial recovery through business-government cooperation and pump-priming federal spending; agricultural recovery through crop reduction; and short-term emergency relief funneled through state and local agencies when possible, but directly by the federal government if necessary. Taken together, these programs expressed the vision of an activist government addressing urgent national problems. Hovering over the bustle loomed a confident Franklin Roosevelt, cigarette

MAP 24.1
The Election of 1932

	Electoral Vote	Popular Vote	Percentage of Popular Vote
Democratic Franklin D. Roosevelt	472	22,809,638	57.4
Republican Herbert C. Hoover	59	15,758,901	39.7
Minor parties	–	–	1,153,306	2.9

holder jauntily tilted upward, a symbol of hope. By 1935, however, some early New Deal programs were in trouble, and opposition was building.

Roosevelt and His Circle

FDR's inaugural address dedicated his administration to helping a people in crisis. "The only thing we have to fear," he intoned, "is fear itself." In an outpouring of support, half a million approving letters deluged the White House.

Roosevelt seemed an unlikely figure to become a popular hero. Like his distant cousin Theodore, FDR was of the social elite, with merchants and landowners among his Dutch-immigrant ancestors. He attended Harvard College and Columbia Law School. But as a state senator and governor of New York, he had allied with the Democratic party's urban-immigrant wing. When the depression struck, he had introduced innovative measures in New York, including unemployment insurance and a public-works program. Intent on reviving the economy while preserving capitalism and democracy, Roosevelt had no detailed agenda. He encouraged competing proposals, compromised (or papered over) differences, and then backed the measures he sensed could be sold to Congress and the public.

Roosevelt brought to Washington a circle of advisers nicknamed the brain trust. It included Columbia University professor Rexford G. Tugwell and lawyer

The Old Order and the New
With little in common but their top hats, Herbert Hoover and Franklin D. Roosevelt ride to Roosevelt's inauguration on March 4, 1933

Eleanor Roosevelt Visits a West Virginia Coal Mine, 1933
A *New Yorker* cartoon of 1933 portrayed one coal miner exclaiming to another: "Oh migosh, here comes Mrs. Roosevelt." But reality soon caught up with humor, as the First Lady immersed herself in the plight of the poor and the exploited.

Adolph A. Berle. Shaped by the progressive reform tradition, Tugwell and Berle rejected laissez-faire ideas and advocated federal economic planning and corporate regulation. But no single ideology or set of advisers controlled the New Deal, for FDR sought a broad range of opinions.

Eleanor Roosevelt played a key role. A niece of Theodore Roosevelt, she had a keen social conscience expressed in settlement-house work and Florence Kelley's National Consumers' League. Through her, FDR met reformers, social workers, and advocates of minority rights. Recalled Rexford Tugwell: "No one who ever saw Eleanor Roosevelt sit down facing her husband, and holding his eyes firmly, say to him 'Franklin, I think you should. . . ,' or 'Franklin, surely you will not . . .' will ever forget the experience." Mrs. Roosevelt traveled ceaselessly and served as an astute observer for her wheelchair-bound husband. (A Washington newspaper once headlined "MRS. ROOSEVELT SPENDS NIGHT AT WHITE HOUSE.") In 1935 she began writing a syndicated newspaper column, "My Day."

Roosevelt's cabinet reflected the New Deal's diversity. Postmaster General James Farley, FDR's top political adviser, distributed patronage jobs, managed the 1932 and 1936 campaigns, and dealt with state and local Democratic leaders. Secretary of Labor Frances Perkins, the first woman cabinet member, had served as industrial commissioner of New York. Interior Secretary Harold Ickes had organized liberal Republicans for Roosevelt in 1932. Secretary of Agriculture Henry A. Wallace of Iowa held the same post his father had occupied in the 1920s. Treasury Secretary Henry Morgenthau, Jr., FDR's Hudson valley neighbor and political ally, though a fiscal conservative, tolerated the unbalanced budgets necessary to finance New Deal antidepression programs.

A host of newcomers poured into Washington in 1933—former progressives, liberal-minded professors, bright young lawyers. Joining the administration, they drafted bills, competed for influence, and debated recovery strategies. From this pressure-cooker environment

emerged the laws, programs, and agencies gathered under a catch-all label: the New Deal.

The Hundred Days

Between March 9 and its adjournment on June 16, 1933, a period labeled the "Hundred Days," Congress enacted more than a dozen important measures (see Table 24.1). Rooted in the experience of the Progressive Era, World War I, and the Hoover presidency, these measures expanded the federal government's involvement in the nation's economic life.

FDR first addressed the banking crisis. As borrowers defaulted, panicky depositors withdrew savings, and homeowners missed mortgage payments, thousands of banks had failed, undermining confidence in the entire system. On March 5 Roosevelt ordered all banks to close for four days. At the end of this so-called bank holiday, he proposed an Emergency Banking Act. This law, supplemented by a later one, permitted healthy banks to reopen, set up procedures for managing failed banks, increased government oversight of banking, and required banks to separate their savings deposits from their investment funds. Congress also created the Federal Deposit Insurance Corporation (FDIC) to insure all bank deposits up to five thousand dollars. In the first of a series of radio talks dubbed "fireside chats," the president assured Americans that they could again trust their banks.

Other measures of the Hundred Days addressed the problem of relief—the urgent plight of Americans strug-

TABLE 24.1

Major Measures Enacted During the "Hundred Days"
(March 9–June 16, 1933)

March 9	Emergency Banking Act
20	Economy Act
31	Unemployment Relief Act (Civilian Conservation Corps)
May 12	Agricultural Adjustment Act
12	Federal Emergency Relief Act
18	Tennessee :Valley Authority
27	Federal Securities Act
June 13	Home Owners' Refinancing Act
16	Farm Credit Act
16	Banking Act of 1933 (Federal Deposit Insurance Corporation)
16	National Industrial Recovery Act (National Recovery Administration; Public Works Administration)

gling to survive. Two new agencies assisted those who were losing their homes. The Home Owners Loan Corporation (HOLC) helped city-dwellers refinance their mortgages. The Farm Credit Administration provided loans to rural Americans to meet their farm payments (see Figure 24.3).

Another early New Deal relief program, the Civilian Conservation Corps (CCC), employed jobless youths in such government projects as reforestation, park maintenance, and erosion control. The CCC thus combined

FIGURE 24.3
Agriculture During the Great Depression

The depression hit rural America with brutal ferocity, as the statistics on commodity prices and farm mortgages show.

*The graph shows the price per pound for cotton and the price per bushel for corn and wheat.
Source: Historical Statistics of the United States, Colonial Times to 1970 (Washington, D.C., Government Printing Office, 1975), 511, 517.

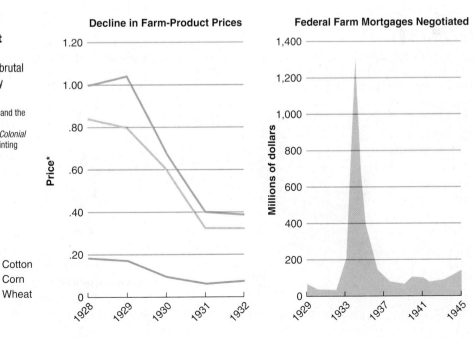

work relief with environmental programs. By 1935 half a million young men were earning thirty-five dollars a month in CCC camps—a godsend to families with no income at all.

The principal relief measure of the Hundred Days, the Federal Emergency Relief Act, appropriated $500 million for state and local relief agencies that had exhausted their funds. To head this program, FDR chose Harry Hopkins, the relief administrator in New York State. A gaunt chain smoker who enjoyed parties and the racetrack, Hopkins soon emerged as a powerful New Deal figure.

While supplying money for immediate relief of the needy, the early New Deal also faced the longer-term challenge of promoting recovery in the agricultural and industrial sectors of the economy. In confronting the chronic problem of low farm prices, New Dealers held different opinions. Some favored the approach of the 1920s McNary-Haugen bill (see Chapter 23) by which the government would buy agricultural surpluses and sell them abroad. Others, however, advocated reduced production as a means of raising farm income, and this approach won the day.

As a first step to cutting production, the government paid southern cotton planters to plow under much of their crop and midwestern farmers to slaughter some 6 million piglets and pregnant sows. This proved a public-relations nightmare, as Americans criticized the killing of pigs amid widespread hunger. Pursuing the same goal more systematically, Congress passed the Agricultural Adjustment Act in May 1933. This law set up a program

by which producers of the major agricultural commodities—including hogs, wheat, corn, cotton, and dairy products—received payments, called subsidies, in return for cutting production. A tax on grain mills and other food processors (a tax ultimately passed along to consumers) financed these subsidies. A new agency, the Agricultural Adjustment Administration (AAA), supervised the program.

The other key recovery measure of the Hundred Days, the National Industrial Recovery Act, appropriated $3.3 billion for heavy-duty government public-works programs to provide jobs and stimulate the economy. Interior Secretary Harold Ickes headed the agency that ran this program, the Public Works Administration (PWA).

This law also set up another new agency, the National Recovery Administration (NRA). The NRA brought together business leaders to draft codes of "fair competition" for their industries. These codes set production limits, prescribed wages and working conditions, and forbade price cutting and unfair competitive practices. The aim was to promote recovery by breaking the cycle of wage cuts, falling prices, and layoffs. This approach revived the trade associations that Washington had encouraged during World War I (see Chapter 22). Indeed, the NRA's head, Hugh Johnson, had served with the War Industries Board of 1917–1918. The NRA also echoed the theme of business-government cooperation that Herbert Hoover had promoted as secretary of commerce in the 1920s.

The NRA's success depended on voluntary support by both business and the public. Johnson, a flamboyant showman, used parades, billboards, magazine ads, and celebrity events to persuade people to buy only from companies that subscribed to an NRA code and that displayed the NRA symbol, a blue eagle, and its slogan, "We Do Our Part."

While the NRA's purpose was to promote economic recovery, some New Dealers saw its reform potential as well. Under pressure from Labor Secretary Frances Perkins, the NRA's textile-industry code banned child labor. And thanks to Senator Robert Wagner of New York, Section 7a of the National Industrial Recovery Act affirmed workers' right to organize unions and to bargain collectively.

The Reconstruction Finance Corporation, dating from the Hoover years, remained active in the New Deal era. Under its chairman Jesse H. Jones, a Houston banker, the RFC lent billions of dollars to banks, insurance companies, and even new business ventures, making the RFC a potent financial resource for corporate

"We Do Our Part"
Companies that cooperated with the National Recovery Administration displayed this poster. The NRA, a centerpiece of the early New Deal, soon ran into difficulties.

America. The early New Deal thus had a strong probusiness flavor. In his speeches of 1933–1935, FDR always included business as a key player in the "all-American team" fighting the depression.

A few measures adopted during the Hundred Days, however, took a more regulatory approach to business. The stock-market crash had produced a strong antibusiness reaction and led to a Senate investigation of Wall Street. This probe revealed that not one of the twenty partners of the Morgan Bank had paid any income tax in 1931 or 1932. People jeered when the president of the New York Stock Exchange told a Senate committee considering regulatory legislation, "You gentlemen are making a big mistake. The Exchange is a perfect institution."

Reflecting the antibusiness mood, the early New Deal legislation also included a key regulatory measure, the Federal Securities Act. This law required corporations to inform the Federal Trade Commission fully on all stock offerings, and made executives personally liable for any misrepresentation of securities their companies issued. (In 1934 Congress curbed the purchase of stock on credit—a practice that had contributed to the crash of 1929—and created the Securities and Exchange Commission [SEC], to enforce the new regulations.)

The most innovative long-range recovery program of the Hundred Days was the Tennessee Valley Authority (TVA). This program had its origins in World War I, when the government had built a hydroelectric station on the Tennessee River in Alabama to power a nearby nitrate plant run by the War Department. In the 1920s Senator George Norris of Nebraska had urged the use of this facility to supply electricity to nearby farmers. Expanding Norris's idea, TVA advanced the economic and social development of the entire Tennessee River valley, one of the nation's most poverty-stricken regions.

A European visitor in the 1930s described the region's farms:

[A] very large percentage of them had kitchens with ovens burning wood. . . . They were lighted by dim, smoking, smelly oil lamps . . . . [T]he washing of clothes was done by hand in antiquated tubs . . . . [T]he water was brought into the house by women and children, from wells invariably situated at inconvenient and tiring distances. . . . Ordinarily there is no icebox, so many products that might be grown to vary the horribly monotonous diet are out of the question; they could not be stored.

Such conditions stunted the lives of the region's inhabitants. Wrote a Tennessee school administrator of the children in her schools, "Due to insufficient clothing

and food, many are unable to attend school. . . . It is not uncommon for a child to have but one dress or one shirt. They have to stay at home the day the mother launders them."

TVA's ambitious goal was to remedy such conditions. A series of TVA dams supplied cheap hydroelectric power, bringing electricity to the region. TVA also promoted flood control, water recreation, and erosion prevention. Under director David Lilienthal, TVA proved one of the New Deal's most popular and enduring achievements.

For many Americans, the mind-boggling burst of laws and the "alphabet-soup" of new agencies during the Hundred Days symbolized both the dynamism and the confusion of the New Deal. How these new programs and agencies would work in practice remained to be seen.

Failures and Controversies Plague the Early New Deal

As the depression persisted, several early New Deal programs, including the NRA, the AAA, and the various relief agencies, faced difficulties. The NRA's problems related partly to the personality of the hard-driving, hard-drinking Hugh Johnson. But the trouble went deeper. As the unity spirit of the Hundred Days faded, corporate America chafed under NRA regulation. Code violations increased. Small businesses complained that the codes favored big corporations. The agency itself, meanwhile, became bogged down in drafting trivial codes. The shoulder-pad industry, for example, had its own code. Corporate trade associations used the codes to restrict competition and maintain prices, not to stimulate recovery.

Gradually, the NRA sank of its own weight. Johnson left in 1934, and in May 1935 the Supreme Court unanimously ruled the NRA unconstitutional. The Court cited two reasons: first, the law gave the president regulatory powers that constitutionally belonged to Congress; second, the NRA regulated commerce within states, violating the constitutional provision limiting federal regulation to interstate commerce. Few mourned the NRA. As a recovery measure, it had failed.

The AAA fared better, but it too proved controversial. Farm prices did rise as production declined, fulfilling the planners' hopes. In 1933–1937, overall farm income increased by 50 percent. But the AAA did not help farm laborers or migrant workers; indeed, its crop-reduction payments actually hurt southern tenants and sharecroppers when cotton growers removed acreage

MAP 24.2
The Dust Bowl
From the Dakotas southward to the Mexican border, farmers in the Great Plains suffered from a lack of rainfall and severe soil erosion in the 1930s, worsening the hardships of the Great Depression.

Harry Hopkins (1890–1946)
A former administrator of New York State charitable organizations, Hopkins emerged as one of the most powerful figures in the New Deal.

from production, banked the subsidy checks, and evicted the sharecroppers. One Georgia sharecropper wrote Harry Hopkins, "I have Bin farming all my life But the man I live with Has Turned me loose . . . I can't get a Job."

Some victims of this process resisted. In 1934 the interracial Southern Tenant Farmers' Union, led by the Socialist party, emerged in Arkansas. Declared one black sharecropper at the organizing meeting, "The same chain that holds my people holds your people too. . . . [We should] get together and stay together." The landowners struck back, harassing union organizers.

Debate raged between New Dealers intent on raising total agricultural income and others who urged special attention to the poorest farmers. FDR at first backed the former group, but the advocates of a more class-based farm policy soon gained influence. Their cause was strengthened as a parching drought turned the Great Plains into a dust bowl (see Map 24.2). The rains failed in 1930, devastating wheat and livestock on the southern plains. In 1934 dust clouds spread across the nation, darkening cities from Chicago to Boston and Savannah before blowing out to sea. Through 1939, each summer brought a new scourge of dust. The worst year was 1937, with the dust storms centered in Kansas, Oklahoma, Texas, Colorado, and New Mexico.

Survivors never forgot the experience. Even night brought no relief. Recalled a Kansas woman, "A trip for water to rinse the grit from our lips, and then back to bed with washcloths over our noses. We try to lie still, because every turn stirs the dust on the blankets." Folk singer Woody Guthrie recalled his 1930s' boyhood in Oklahoma and Texas in his song "The Great Dust Storm." It began:

> It fell across our city like a curtain of black rolled down. We thought it was our judgment, we thought it was our doom.

Battered by debt and drought alike, many families gave up, leaving behind abandoned houses and farms. Nearly 3.5 million people left the Great Plains in the 1930s; the population of Cimarron County, Oklahoma, fell by 40 percent. Some migrated to nearby cities, further swamping relief rolls. Others packed their meager belongings into old cars and headed west. Though coming from various states, they all bore a derisive nickname, Okies. The plight of dust-bowl migrants further complicated New Deal agricultural planning.

Rivalries and policy differences also plagued the New Deal relief program. As unemployment continued, Harry Hopkins convinced Roosevelt to support direct federal relief programs, rather than channeling funds through state and local agencies. Late in 1933 FDR named Hopkins to head a temporary public works agency, the Civil Works Administration (CWA). Through

the winter the CWA expended nearly a billion dollars on short-term work projects for the jobless. When warm weather returned, FDR abolished the CWA. Like his conservative critics, FDR feared creating a permanent underclass living on welfare payments. But persistent unemployment swamping local relief agencies made further federal programs inevitable.

Hopkins and Harold Ickes, head of the Public Works Administration, competed to control federal relief policy. The cautious Ickes examined every PWA proposal with a fine-tooth comb. Large-scale PWA public-works projects did promote economic recovery, but "Honest Harold's" deliberate approach left billions in relief funds stalled in the pipeline. Hopkins, by contrast, wanted to put people to work and get money circulating. Even make-work projects like raking leaves and collecting litter had merit, he argued, if they achieved these goals. Given the urgency of the crisis, Hopkins's approach proved more influential in shaping federal relief policy.

1934–1935: Challenges from Right and Left

Despite the New Deal's brave beginnings, the depression persisted. In 1934 national income rose about 25 percent above 1933 levels, but remained far below that of 1929. Millions had been jobless for three or four years. The rising frustration found expression in 1934 in nearly two thousand strikes, some of them communist-led, from New York taxi drivers to San Francisco dockworkers. With the NRA under attack, conflict flaring over farm policy, and relief spending growing rather than declining, criticism mounted. Conservatives attacked the New Deal as socialistic. In 1934 several business leaders, joined by an embittered Al Smith, formed the anti-New Deal American Liberty League. The U.S. Chamber of Commerce blasted the New Deal. Anti-Roosevelt jokes circulated among the rich, many of whom denounced him as a traitor to his class.

But the New Deal remained popular, reflecting both its achievements and FDR's political skills. Assisted by speechwriters and publicists, Roosevelt commanded the political stage. Pursuing his "national unity" theme, Roosevelt exhorted everyone to join the battle for economic recovery just as Americans had united in 1917 against a foreign foe. Although Republican newspaper publishers remained hostile, FDR enjoyed good relations with the working press. He loved bantering with reporters, and they responded by portraying his administration favorably.

In contrast to Hoover, Roosevelt loved public appearances and took naturally to radio. Frances Perkins described his radio talks, "His head would nod and his hands would move in simple, natural, comfortable gestures. His face would smile and light up as though he were actually sitting on the front porch or in the parlor with [his listeners]." Roosevelt's mastery of radio provided a model for his successors in the era of television.

The 1934 midterm election ratified the New Deal's popularity. Reversing the usual pattern, the Democrats increased their congressional majorities. As for FDR, Kansas journalist William Allen White observed, "He's been all but crowned by the people." As the returns rolled in, Harry Hopkins exulted to a group of New Deal friends, "Boys, this is our hour!"

Despite this seeming vote of confidence, the political scene was highly unstable in 1934–1935. While conservatives criticized the New Deal for going too far, critics on the left attacked it for not going far enough. Socialists and communists ridiculed Roosevelt's efforts to include big business in his "all-American team." Clifford Odets' 1935 play *Waiting for Lefty* portrayed noble workers battling evil bosses and ended by inciting the audience to chant "Strike! Strike! Strike!".

Pushing the New Deal's experimental spirit still further, demagogues peddled more radical social and economic programs. The Detroit Catholic priest and radio spellbinder Charles Coughlin attacked FDR as a "great betrayer and liar," made anti-Semitic allusions, and called for nationalization of the banks. For a time, Coughlin's followers, organized as the National Union of Social Justice and drawn mainly from the lower middle class, seemed a potent force.

Meanwhile, California physician Francis Townsend proposed that the government pay two hundred dollars a month to all retired citizens, requiring them to spend the money within thirty days. This plan, Townsend insisted, would help the elderly, stimulate the economy, and open up jobs by encouraging retirement. The scheme would have bankrupted the nation, but many older citizens, especially in California, rallied to Townsend's banner.

FDR's wiliest rival was flamboyant Huey Long of Louisiana. A country lawyer elected governor of Louisiana in 1928, Long built highways, schools, and public housing. He roared into Washington as a senator in 1933, preaching his "Share Our Wealth" program: a 100 percent tax on all incomes over $1 million and appropriation of all fortunes in excess of $5 million. With this money, Long promised, every family could enjoy a comfortable income, a house, a car, old-age benefits, and free college education. "Every man a king," Long proclaimed, and millions responded. By 1935 he boast-

ed 7.5 million supporters. The title of his 1935 book, *My First Days in the White House,* made clear his ultimate goal. An assassin's bullet killed Long that September, but his organization survived.

Responding vigorously to these challenges, Roosevelt regained the political high ground in 1935 with a bold series of legislative initiatives. The result was a fresh surge of social legislation that rivaled that of the Hundred Days.

THE NEW DEAL CHANGES COURSE, 1935–1936

As the spirit of national unity faded and Roosevelt faced criticism from the left and right, he abandoned the unity theme and veered leftward. In 1935–1936, Roosevelt pushed through a bundle of reform measures so impressive that some call this phase the Second New Deal (see Table 24.2). His commitment to fighting the depression and to an activist role for government continued. But while he had initially tried to win the support of all

TABLE 24.2
Major Later New Deal Legislation (November 1933–1938)

Nov. 1933	Civilian Works Administration
1934	Civil Works Emergency Relief Act
	Home Owners' Loan Act
	Securities Exchange Act (Securities and Exchange Commission)
	Communications Act (Federal Communications Commission)
	Federal Farm Bancruptcy Act
	National Housing Act (Federal Housing Administration)
	Taylor Grazing Act
1935	Emergency Relief Appropriations Act (Works Progress Administration)
	National Youth Administration
	National Labor Relations Act (Wagner Act)
	Revenue Act of 1935
	Social Security Act
	Public Utilities Holding Company Act
	Banking Act of 1935
	Resettlement Administration
	Rural Electrification Act
1936	Soil Conservation and Domestic Allotment Act
1937	National Housing Act
	Bankhead-Jones Farm Tenancy Act (Farm Security Administration)
1938	Fair Labor Standards Act
	Agricultural Adjustmnet Act of 1938

Americans including big business, from 1935 on FDR increasingly criticized the wealthy and the business class, and focused on aiding the most disadvantaged Americans.

In his January 1935 State of the Union address, Roosevelt offered six initiatives reflecting his new priorities: an expanded public-works program, assistance to the rural poor, support for organized labor, benefits for retired workers and other needy groups, tougher business regulation, and heavier taxes on the well-to-do. These goals shaped his program thereafter.

Expanding Federal Relief

With unemployment still high, Congress passed the $5 billion Emergency Relief Appropriation Act in April 1935. Roosevelt swiftly set up the Works Progress Administration (WPA) and put Harry Hopkins in charge. Like the Civil Works Administration of 1933–1934, the WPA funneled assistance directly to individuals. Roosevelt insisted that the WPA provide work, not handouts, for the jobless. Over its eight-year life, the WPA employed more than 8 million Americans; pumped $11 billion into the economy; constructed or improved 650,000 miles of roads; built or repaired 124,000 bridges; and erected 125,000 schools, hospitals, post offices, and other public buildings.

The WPA also assisted writers, performers, and artists. In the South, WPA workers collected the reminiscences of former slaves. The Federal Writers' Project employed jobless authors to produce state guides and histories of ethnic and immigrant groups. Under the Federal Music Project, unemployed musicians gave free concerts, often featuring American composers. By 1938 more than 30 million Americans had attended an FMP concert.

The Federal Theatre Project (FTP) employed actors. One FTP project, the Living Newspaper, which dramatized contemporary social issues, was criticized as New Deal propaganda. Marc Blitzstein's radical musical *The Cradle Will Rock* (1937), which had FTP funding, was cancelled by nervous WPA officials before the opening-night performance. The cast and audience defiantly walked to another theater, and the show went on. FTP drama companies touring small-town America gave many their first taste of theater. Artists working for the Federal Arts Project

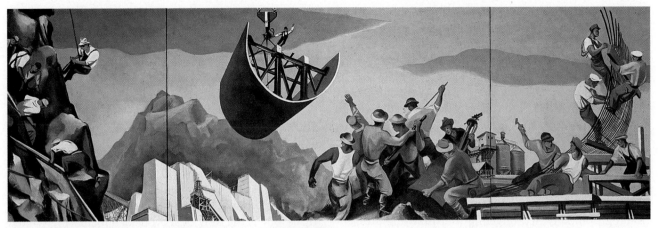

Construction of a Dam, **by William Gropper (1897–1977)**
The New Deal's Federal Arts Project commissioned murals for post offices and other public buildings. Gropper, whose work often exposed social injustice and class inequalities, painted this upbeat mural for the Department of the Interior building in Washington, D.C.

designed posters, offered school courses, and decorated post offices and courthouses with murals.

Harold Ickes' Public Works Administration, after a slow start, now picked up steam, expending more than $4 billion over its life span. PWA workers completed some thirty-four thousand construction projects, including dams, bridges, and public buildings. Among the PWA's undertakings were New York City's Triborough Bridge and Lincoln Tunnel, and the awesome Grand Coulee Dam on the Columbia River.

With heavy relief spending came large federal budget deficits, cresting at $4.4 billion in 1936. These deficits were covered by government borrowing. According to British economist John Maynard Keynes, governments should deliberately use deficit spending during depressions to fund public-works programs, thereby increasing purchasing power and stimulating recovery. The New Deal approach, however, was not Keynesian. Because all the dollars spent on relief and recovery programs were withdrawn from the economy through taxation or government borrowing, the stimulus effect was nil. FDR saw deficits as an unwelcome necessity, not a positive good.

Aiding Migrants, Supporting Unions, Regulating Business, Taxing the Wealthy

The second phase of the New Deal was more frankly geared to the interests of workers, the poor, and the disadvantaged. Social-justice advocates like Frances Perkins and Eleanor Roosevelt helped shape this program, but so did hard-headed politics. Looking to 1936,

FDR's political advisers feared that the followers of Coughlin, Townsend, and Long could siphon off enough votes to cost him the election. This worry underlay FDR's 1935 political agenda.

The Second New Deal's agricultural policy addressed the plight of sharecroppers (a plight the AAA had helped create) and other poor farmers. The Resettlement Administration (1935), directed by Rexford Tugwell, made loans to help tenant farmers buy their own farms and to enable displaced sharecroppers, tenants, and dust-bowl migrants move to more productive areas. The Rural Electrification Administration, also started in 1935, made low-interest loans to utility companies and farmers' cooperatives to extend electricity to the 90 percent of rural America that still lacked it. By 1941, 40 percent of U.S. farms enjoyed electric power.

The agricultural-recovery program suffered a setback in January 1936 when the Supreme Court declared the Agricultural Adjustment Act unconstitutional. The processing tax that funded the AAA's subsidies, the court held, was an illegal use of the government's tax power. To replace the AAA, Congress passed a soil-conservation act that paid farmers to plant grasses and legumes instead of soil-depleting crops such as wheat and cotton (which also happened to be the major surplus commodities).

Organized labor won a key victory in 1935, again thanks to Senator Robert Wagner. During the New Deal's national-unity phase, FDR had criticized Wagner's campaign for a prolabor law as "special interest" legislation. But Wagner persisted, and in 1935, when the Supreme Court ruled the NIRA, including Section 7a protecting union members' rights, unconstitutional, FDR called for

a labor law that would survive constitutional scrutiny. The National Labor Relations Act of July 1935 guaranteed collective-bargaining rights, permitted closed shops (in which all employees must join a union), and outlawed such management tactics as blacklisting union organizers. The law created the National Labor Relations Board (NLRB) to supervise shop elections and deal with labor-law violations. The Wagner Act, as it was called, stimulated a wave of unionization (see below).

The Second New Deal's more class-conscious thrust shaped other 1935 measures as well. The Banking Act strengthened the Federal Reserve Board's control over the nation's financial system. The Public Utilities Holding Company Act, targeting the sprawling public-utility empires of the 1920s, restricted gas and electric companies to one geographic region.

In 1935, too, Roosevelt called for steeper taxes on the rich to combat the "unjust concentration of wealth and economic power." Congress responded with a revenue act, also called the Wealth Tax Act, that raised taxes on corporations and on the well-to-do to a maximum of 75 percent on incomes above $5 million. Though this law had many loopholes and was not quite the "soak the rich" measure some believed, it did express the Second New Deal's more radical spirit.

The Social Security Act of 1935; End of the Second New Deal

The Social Security Act of 1935, perhaps the most important of all New Deal laws, stands out for its long-range significance. Drafted by a committee chaired by Frances Perkins, this measure had complex sources, including Progressive Era ideas and the social-welfare programs of England and Germany. It established a mixed federal-state system of workers' pensions; unemployment insurance; survivors' benefits for victims of industrial accidents; and aid for disabled persons and dependent mothers with children.

Taxes paid partly by employers and partly by workers (in the form of amounts withheld from their paychecks) funded the pension and survivors' benefit features. This payroll-withholding provision helped bring on a recession in 1937. But it made sense politically because workers would fight any effort to end a pension plan they had contributed to. As Roosevelt put it, "With those taxes in there, no damned politician can ever scrap my social security program."

The initial Social Security Act paid low benefits and bypassed farmers, domestic workers, and the self-employed. But it established the principle of federal responsibility for social welfare and laid the foundation for a vastly expanded welfare system in the future.

By September 1935, when Congress adjourned, the Second New Deal, with its historic record of legislative accomplishment, was complete. Without embracing the panaceas preached by Coughlin, Townsend, or Long, FDR had addressed the grievances they had exploited. Although conservatives called this phase of the New Deal "antibusiness," FDR always insisted that he had saved capitalism by addressing the social problems it spawned. During much of the post-Civil War era the business class had dominated government, marginalizing other groups. Business remained influential in the 1930s, but as the New Deal evolved, it increasingly acted as a broker for all organized interest groups, including organized labor, not just corporate America. And in 1935, with an election looming, New Deal strategists reached farther still, to address the situation of sharecroppers and migrant workers, the disabled, the elderly, needy mothers with dependent children, and others whose plight had rarely concerned politicians of the past.

In the process, the New Deal vastly expanded the role of the federal government in American life, as well as the power of the presidency. Building on precedents set by Theodore Roosevelt a generation earlier, FDR so dominated the politics of the 1930s that Americans began to expect presidents to offer "programs," address national issues, and shape the terms of public debate. This decisively altered the balance of power between the White House and Congress. The New Deal's importance thus lies not only in specific laws, but also in the way it redefined the scope of the executive branch and, more broadly still, the social role of the state.

The 1936 Roosevelt Landslide and the New Democratic Coalition

With the Second New Deal in place, FDR faced the 1936 campaign with confidence. "There's one issue . . . ," he told an aide; "it's myself, and people must be either for me or against me."

The Republican candidate, Governor Alfred Landon of Kansas, was a fiscal conservative who nevertheless believed that government must address social issues. Landon proved to be an earnest if inept campaigner. ("Wherever I have gone in this country, I have found Americans," he revealed in one speech.) When Republicans lambasted FDR's alleged dictatorial ambitions and charged that the social security law would require all workers to wear metal dog tags, he struck

TABLE 24.3   The Election of 1936

Candidates	Parties	Electoral Vote	Popular Vote	Percentage of Popular Vote
Franklin D. Roosevelt	Democratic	523	27,752,869	60.8
Alfred M. Landon	Republican	8	16,674,665	36.5
William Lemke	Union	–	882,479	1.9

back with his usual zest. Only the forces of "selfishness and greed" opposed him, he declared at an enthusiastic election-eve rally in New York City, adding, "They are united in their hatred for me—and I welcome their hatred."

In the most crushing electoral victory since 1820, FDR carried every state but Maine and Vermont (see Table 24.3). Landon even lost Kansas. Pennsylvania went Democratic for the first time since 1856. The Democrats increased their already top-heavy majorities in Congress. Roosevelt buried his minor-party opponents as well. Socialist Norman Thomas received under 200,000 votes, the Communist party's presidential candidate only about 80,000. The Union party, a coalition of the Coughlinites, Townsendites, and Huey Long supporters who had appeared so formidable in 1935, polled only 892,000 votes.

FDR's 1936 landslide victory announced the emergence of a potent new Democratic coalition. Since Reconstruction, the Democrats had counted on three bases of support: the white South, parts of the West, and urban white ethnic voters mobilized by big-city Democratic machines. FDR retained and solidified these centers of strength. He rarely challenged state or local party leaders who produced the votes, whether they supported the New Deal or not. In Virginia he even withdrew support from a pro-New Deal governor who clashed with the state's conservative but powerful Democratic senators. When the Democratic boss of Jersey City, Frank Hague, faced mail tampering charges, FDR said to Jim Farley, "Tell Frank to knock it off . . . , but keep this thing quiet because we need Hague's support if we want New Jersey."

Building on Al Smith's urban breakthrough in 1928, FDR carried the nation's twelve largest cities. Not only did New Deal relief programs aid city-dwellers, but Roosevelt wooed them persuasively. When the presidential entourage swept through cities like New York and Boston, cheering crowds lined the route. FDR also appointed many representatives of the newer urban-immigrant groups, including Catholics and Jews, to New Deal positions.

Expanding the Democratic base, FDR reached out to four partially overlapping groups: farmers, union members, northern blacks, and women. Midwestern farmers, long rock-ribbed Republicans, liked the New Deal's agricultural program and switched to Roosevelt. In Iowa, where Democrats had garnered scarcely 20 percent of the vote in the 1920s, FDR won decisively in 1936. Organized labor also joined the New Deal coalition. The unions pumped money into Roosevelt's campaigns (although far less than business gave the Republicans), and union members voted overwhelmingly for Roosevelt. Despite his early foot dragging on the Wagner bill, FDR's reputation as a "friend of labor" proved unassailable.

Although most southern blacks remained disfranchised, northern blacks voted in growing numbers, and as late as 1932 two-thirds of them went for Hoover, leading one exasperated African-American editor to advise: "[T]urn Lincoln's picture to the wall. That debt has been paid in full." The New Deal era saw a historic shift. In 1934 Chicago's black voters replaced Republican Congressman Oscar DePriest with a Democrat. In 1936, 76 percent of black voters supported FDR.

In economic terms, this shift made sense. Owing mainly to racial discrimination, blacks' unemployment rates in the 1930s surpassed those of the work force as a whole. Thus, jobless blacks benefited heavily from New Deal relief programs.

On issues of racial justice, however, the New Deal's record was mixed at best. Some NRA codes contained racially discriminatory clauses, leading black activists to dismiss the agency as "Negroes Ruined Again." TVA and other New Deal agencies tolerated racial bias. Lynchings increased in the 1930s as some whites translated economic worries into racial aggression, but Roosevelt kept aloof from the NAACP's campaign to make lynching a federal crime. An antilynching bill passed the House of Representatives in 1935, but southern Democratic senators killed it with a filibuster. To protect his legislative program and retain southern white voters, FDR did little. Blacks must realize, the NAACP concluded bitterly, "that . . . the Roosevelt administration [has] nothing for them."

In limited ways, however, FDR did address racial issues. Assuring an audience at Howard University, a black institution in Washington, D.C., that there would be "no . . . forgotten races" in his administration, Roosevelt cautiously worked to rid New Deal agencies of blatant racism. He appointed more than a hundred blacks to policy-level and judicial positions, including Mary McLeod Bethune as director of minority affairs in the National Youth Administration. Bethune, a Florida educator, head of the National Council of Negro Women, and a friend of Eleanor Roosevelt, led the so-called black cabinet that linked the administration and black organizations. The "Roosevelt Supreme Court" that took shape after 1936 issued antidiscrimination rulings in cases involving housing, voting rights, wage inequity, and jury selection.

The New Deal also supported racial justice in symbolic ways. In 1938, when a meeting of the interracial Southern Conference for Human Welfare in Birmingham, Alabama, was segregated in compliance with local statutes, Mrs. Roosevelt pointedly placed her chair halfway between the white and black delegates. In 1939, when the Daughters of the American Revolution barred black contralto Marian Anderson from performing in Washington's Constitution Hall, Mrs. Roosevelt resigned from the organization, and Harold Ickes arranged an Easter concert by Anderson at the Lincoln Memorial. Even symbolic gestures outraged many southern whites. When a black minister delivered the invocation at the 1936 Democratic convention, Senator Ed Smith of South Carolina noisily stalked out.

The Roosevelt administration courted women voters. The head of the Democratic party's women's division, Molly Dewson, a friend of the Roosevelts, led this effort. In the 1936 campaign Dewson mobilized fifteen thousand women who went door to door distributing flyers describing New Deal programs. "[W]e did not make the old-fashioned plea that our nominee was charming," she later recalled; " . . . we appealed to [women's] intelligence."

Unlike earlier feminists, Dewson did not promote a specifically feminist agenda. New Deal efforts for economic recovery and social welfare, she argued, served the best interests of both sexes. She did, however, push for more women in federal policy-level positions. FDR appointed not only the first woman cabinet member but also the first woman ambassador and unprecedented numbers of female federal judges. Through Dewson's efforts, the 1936 Democratic platform committee reflected a fifty-fifty gender balance.

Symbolic gestures and the appointment of a few blacks and women ought not be overemphasized. Racism and sexism pervaded American society in the 1930s, and Roosevelt, preoccupied with the economic crisis, did relatively little to change things. That challenge would await a later generation.

The Environment, the West, and Indian Policy

Environmental issues loomed large in the 1930s, reflecting FDR's own priorities. As early as 1910, in the New York Senate, he had sought to regulate logging that threatened wildlife. As president, he prodded the Civilian Conservation Corps to plant trees, thin forests, and build hiking trails.

Soil conservation emerged as a major priority. The Great Plains dust storms of the 1930s resulted not only from drought but also from years of overgrazing and unwise farming practices. Throughout history, periodic drought had struck the Great Plains beyond the hundredth meridian, which bisects central Kansas. But the dust storms were not inevitable. For decades settlers had used ever more powerful tractors and combines to cultivate more land. In the process they had plowed up the grama-buffalo grass and other native grasses that anchored the soil, leaving the topsoil exposed to parching winds when the rains failed. By the 1930s, 9 million acres of farmland had been lost to erosion in the Great Plains, the South, and elsewhere, with more in jeopardy.

The Department of Agriculture's Soil Conservation Service set up projects to demonstrate the value of contour plowing, crop rotation, and soil-strengthening grasses. The Taylor Grazing Act of 1934—enacted as dust clouds darkened the skies over Washington, D.C.—restricted the grazing on public lands that had contributed to the problem. The TVA helped control the floods that worsened erosion in the Tennessee valley.

New Deal planners avidly promoted the national-park movement. Olympic National Park in Washington, Virginia's Shenandoah National Park, and Kings Canyon National Park in California all date from the 1930s. The administration also established some 160 new national wildlife refuges. Roosevelt even closed a Utah artillery range that threatened a nesting site of the endangered trumpeter swan.

The wilderness movement won powerful new adherents. In 1935 Robert Marshall of the U.S. Forest Service and environmentalist Aldo Leopold helped found the Wilderness Society to lobby for the cause. Under pressure from wilderness advocates, Congress set aside a large portion of Kings Canyon National Park as a wilderness area. These movements sometimes created unusual alliances. For example, the National Wildlife

Federation (1936) was funded by the firearms industry, which had an economic interest in preserving wilderness areas and wild game for hunters.

To be sure, today's environmental issues—pollution, pesticides, dwindling fossil fuels, and so forth—received little attention in the 1930s. Most New Dealers welcomed ever-rising levels of energy consumption. The decade's hydroelectric projects, while necessary at a time when most farmers still lacked electricity, nevertheless fed an ideology of boundless consumption that in retrospect seems heedless and wasteful. Nor did the ecological effects of these projects attract much attention. The Grand Coulee Dam, for example, destroyed salmon spawning on much of the Columbia River's tributary system. As Joseph E. Taylor shows in *Making Salmon: An Environmental History of the Northwest Fisheries* (1999), not only Grand Coulee but also other New Deal dams disrupted fragile ecosystems and adversely affected local residents, particularly Native American communities, that depended on them for their livelihood.

Still, when viewed in context, the New Deal's environmental record remains impressive. While coping with a grave economic crisis, the Roosevelt administration focused a level of attention on environmental issues that had not been seen since the Progressive Era, and would not be seen again for a generation.

The depression profoundly affected the American West, particularly as hordes of hard-hit citizens, including dust-bowl refugees, sought a fresh start in the region, especially in California. Continuing a long-term demographic trend, the West Coast's share of the population spiked upward in the 1930s, and Los Angeles jumped from tenth to fifth among U.S. cities.

The New Deal had a big impact on the West as well, especially because the federal government owned a third or more of the land in eleven western states. New Deal agencies and laws such as the AAA, the Soil Conservation Service, the Taylor Grazing Act, and the Farm Security Administration (see below) set new rules for western agriculture from the grain and cattle of the Great Plains to the Pacific Coast citrus groves and truck farms dependent on migrant labor.

Some of the largest PWA and WPA projects were built in the West, including thousands of public buildings (246 in Washington State alone) from courthouses and post offices to tourist facilities such as Timberline Lodge on Oregon's Mount Hood. The highways linking the West to the rest of America, such as the Lincoln Highway from Philadelphia to San Francisco, Yellowstone Trail from Chicago to Seattle, and Route 66 from Chicago to Los Angeles, were upgraded in the 1930s with

federal assistance.

Above all, the PWA in the West built dams—not only Grand Coulee, but also Shasta on the Sacramento River, Bonneville on the Columbia, Glen Canyon on the Colorado, and others. Boulder (later Hoover) Dam on the Colorado, authorized by Congress in 1928, was completed by the PWA. Despite their ecological effect, these great undertakings—among the largest engineering projects in human history—supplied hydroelectric power to vast regions while also contributing to flood control, irrigation, and soil conservation.

A New Deal initiative with special importance for the West was Harold Ickes' National Planning Board of 1934, later renamed the National Resources Planning Board. This agency facilitated state and regional management of natural resources, including water, soil,

Power to the People
The New Deal's massive hydroelectric power projects were celebrated in this 1937 "Living Newspaper" production by the WPA's Federal Theatre Project.

timber, and minerals. Despite the West's celebrated "rugged individualism," the New Deal's emphasis on planning, in tandem with the PWA's dams and infrastructure development, reshaped the public life of the region.

The 1930s also revived attention to the nation's 330,000 Native Americans, most of whom endured poverty, scant education, poor health care, and bleak prospects. The Dawes Severalty Act of 1887 (see Chapter 17) had dissolved the tribes as legal entities, allocated some tribal lands to individual Indians, and offered the rest for sale. By the 1930s whites held about two-thirds of the land that Indians had possessed in 1887, including much of the most valuable acreage. Indians had been granted full citizenship and voting rights in 1924, but this did little to improve their lot.

In the 1920s a reform movement arose to reverse the Dawes Act approach. One reformer, John Collier, who had lived among the Pueblo Indians of New Mexico, founded the American Indian Defense Association in 1923 to preserve what he saw as the spiritual beauty and harmony of traditional Indian life. Gertrude Bonnin, a Yankton Dakota Sioux and president of the National Council of American Indians, while not sharing all of Collier's goals, also pressed for reform.

Appointed commissioner of Indian affairs in 1933, Collier cadged funds from New Deal agencies to construct schools, hospitals, and irrigation systems on reservations, and to preserve sites of cultural importance. The Civilian Conservation Corps employed twelve thousand Indian youths to work on projects on Indian lands.

Pursuing his vision of renewed tribal life, Collier drafted a bill to halt the sale of tribal land, restore the remaining unallocated lands to tribal control, create new reservations, and expand existing ones. It also envisioned tribal councils with broad governing powers and required Indian schools to teach Native American history and handicrafts. Collier's bill sparked opposition in western states. Some Indian leaders criticized it as a plan to transform the reservations into living museums and to treat Native Americans as an exotic people cut off from modern life. Indians who had succeeded as individual property owners or entrepreneurs rejected the bill's tribalist assumptions. The bill did, indeed, reflect the idealism of well-meaning outsiders rather than the views of the nation's diverse Native American groups.

The Indian Reorganization Act of 1934, a compromise measure, halted the sale of tribal lands and enabled tribes to regain title to unallocated lands. But Congress scaled back Collier's proposals for tribal self-government and dropped his calls for renewal of traditional tribal culture.

A majority of tribes approved the law (a requirement for it to go into effect), but opinion was divided. Of the tribes that voted, 181, representing 130,000 Indians, approved, while 77, comprising 86,000 persons, did not. America's largest tribal group, the 40,000-strong Navajo, voted no, largely because the law, to promote soil conservation, restricted grazing rights.

Indian policy clearly remained contentious. But the law did reflect greater recognition of Indian interests and a greater acceptance of cultural diversity. The restoration of tribes as legal entities laid the groundwork for later tribal business ventures as well as tribal lawsuits seeking to enforce long-violated treaty rights (see Chapters 30 and 31).

THE NEW DEAL'S END STAGE, 1937–1939

Buoyed by his landslide victory in 1936, Roosevelt launched an abortive attack on the Supreme Court. Bloodied by this divisive fight, an embattled FDR confronted both a stubborn recession and newly energized conservative opposition. With a few final measures in 1937–1938, the New Deal came to a close.

FDR and the Supreme Court

In 1937 the Supreme Court was made up of nine elderly justices, four of whom were archconservatives who abhorred the New Deal. Joined by others of more moderate views, these conservatives had invalidated the NRA, the AAA, and progressive state laws. With good reason, Roosevelt feared that key measures of the Second New Deal, including the Social Security Act and the Wagner Act, would meet a similar fate. Indeed, some corporate lawyers were so sure that the Social Security Act would be found unconstitutional that they advised their clients to ignore it.

In February 1937 FDR proposed a court-reform bill that would have allowed him to appoint an additional Supreme Court member for each justice over age seventy, up to a total of six. Roosevelt blandly insisted that he was concerned about the heavy workload of aging justices, but his political motivation was obvious.

FDR hoped that his personal popularity would assure support for his Court plan, but in fact the congressional and public reaction was sharply hostile. The Supreme Court's size (unspecified in the Constitution) had fluctuated several times in the early Republic, but the membership of nine, dating to 1869, had become almost sacrosanct. Conservatives blasted the "court-

packing" scheme. Some feared a power grab by FDR in the wake of his electoral triumph; others resented the devious way FDR presented the plan. Even some New Dealers disapproved. When the Senate voted down the scheme in July, FDR quietly gave up the fight.

But was it a defeat? One conservative justice retired in May 1937; others announced retirement plans. In April and May the Court upheld several key New Deal measures, including the Wagner Act, as well as a state minimum-wage law. This outcome may have been Roosevelt's objective all along. His challenge to the Court, plus his 1936 victory, sent powerful political signals that the justices heeded. From 1937 to 1939 FDR appointed four new members to the Supreme Court, laying the groundwork for a liberal majority that would long outlive Roosevelt and his New Deal.

The Roosevelt Recession

After improving in 1936 and early 1937, the economy again plunged ominously in August 1937. Industrial production slumped. Steel output sank to 19 percent of capacity. Jobless rates of more than 20 percent again dominated the headlines. This short but severe "Roosevelt recession" resulted in part from federal policies that reduced consumer income. Social-security payroll taxes withdrew some $2 billion from circulation. A drastic contraction of the money supply undertaken by the Federal Reserve Board to forestall inflation contributed to the recession. Furthermore, concerned about mounting deficits, FDR had seized on the signs of recovery to end or cut back the various New Deal relief programs.

Echoing Hoover, FDR assured his cabinet, "Everything will work out all right if we just sit tight and keep quiet." Meanwhile, however, some New Dealers had been persuaded by the Keynesian view that deficit spending was the key to recovery. Aware that FDR would have to be persuaded by political rather than economic arguments, they warned the president of a political backlash if breadlines and soup kitchens returned. Convinced, in April 1938 FDR authorized new relief spending. WPA work-relief checks soon rained down on the parched economy, and the PWA received a new lease on life. By late 1938 unemployment declined and industrial output increased.

Final Measures; Growing Opposition

Preoccupied by the Supreme Court fight, the 1937–1938 recession, and a menacing world situation (see Chapter 25), FDR offered few domestic initiatives in his second term. Congress, however, enacted several significant measures.

The Farm Tenancy Act of 1937 created the Farm Security Administration (FSA), replacing Rexford Tugwell's Resettlement Administration. The FSA made low-interest loans enabling tenant farmers and sharecroppers to buy family-size farms. Although the FSA generally bypassed the poorest farmers, considering them a bad credit risk, it did lend more than $1 billion through 1941, easing the plight of many rural folk battered by hard times.

The FSA operated camps offering clean, sanitary shelter and medical services to migrant farm workers living in wretched conditions. The FSA also commissioned some of the nation's most gifted photographers to record the lives of tenants, migrants, and uprooted dust-bowl families. These FSA photographs helped shape a starkly realistic documentary style that pervaded 1930s' popular culture, including Hollywood movies and Henry Luce's photo magazine *Life*, launched in

A Camera's-Eye View of Depression-Era America
This 1937 image by Dorothea Lange, a photographer with the Farm Security Administration, pictures migrants from the Texas Dust Bowl gathered at a roadside camp near Calipatria in southern California.

1936. Today they comprise a haunting album of depression-era images.

Other late New Deal measures set important precedents for the future. The Housing Act of 1937 appropriated $500 million for urban slum clearance and public housing, projects that would loom large in the 1950s. The Fair Labor Standards Act of 1938 banned child labor and set a national minimum wage (initially forty cents an hour) and a maximum workweek of forty hours. This measure reflected not only humanitarianism but also some northern legislators' desire to undermine the competitive edge of the South, with its low wage scales. Despite many loopholes, the law improved conditions for some of the nation's most exploited workers, and underscored the government's role in regulating abuses by employers.

In a final stab at dealing with farm surpluses and low farm prices, the Agricultural Adjustment Act of 1938 set up new procedures for limiting production of basic commodities. It also created a mechanism by which the government, in years of big harvests and low prices, would make loans to farmers and warehouse their surplus crops. When prices rose, farmers could repay their loans and market their commodities. This complicated system of price supports set the basic framework of federal agricultural policy for decades to come.

Overall, however, the New Deal's pace clearly slowed after 1935. This reflected in part the rise of an anti-New Deal congressional coalition of Republicans and conservative southern Democrats. In 1937 this coalition teamed up to torpedo FDR's proposal for a major reorganization of the executive branch. The plan made administrative sense, but critics warned darkly of a White House dictatorship.

The conservative coalition also slashed relief appropriations; cut corporate taxes in 1938; and in 1939 killed the WPA's Federal Theatre Project, long a conservative target for its alleged radicalism. The 1939 Hatch Act, forbidding federal employees from participating in electoral campaigns, reflected conservatives' suspicions that FDR was using WPA staff for campaign purposes. The Fair Labor Standards Act became law only after intense White House lobbying and watering down by conservatives. Congress and the public, lamented Harry Hopkins, had become "bored with the poor, the unemployed, the insecure."

Although FDR campaigned actively in the midterm election of 1938, the Republicans gained heavily in the House and Senate and won a net of thirteen governorships. Roosevelt also tried to purge several prominent anti-New Deal Democratic senators, but his major tar-

gets all won reelection. Focusing on foreign affairs in his January 1939 State of the Union message, FDR proposed no new domestic measures and merely noted the need to "preserve our reforms." The New Deal was over.

SOCIAL CHANGE AND SOCIAL ACTION IN THE 1930S

For a fuller picture of American life in the 1930s, we must look beyond the New Deal and take a broader view of society and culture. The depression's effects were psychological and social as well as economic and political. The crisis was traumatic for the jobless and their families; it had significant implications for working women; and it affected all age groups. For industrial workers, African Americans, and migrant laborers, the activist climate of the New Deal stimulated movements to resist exploitation and discrimination.

The Depression's Psychological and Social Impact

This decade of hard times brought untold human suffering and marked all who lived through it. Despite the New Deal, unemployment never fell below about 14 percent in the 1930s, and for much of the decade it was considerably higher. Even those who remained employed were often forced to take jobs below their level of training: college alumni pumped gas; business-school graduates sold furniture; a retired navy captain became an usher in a movie theater. With rural America the scene of bankruptcies, foreclosures, and abandoned farms, a quarter of all farm families had to accept public or private assistance during the 1930s.

Psychologists described "unemployment shock": jobless persons who walked the streets seeking work and then lay awake at night worrying. When shoe soles wore out, cardboard or folded newspapers had to serve. Tacks pierced worn shoe heels, cutting the skin. "You pass . . . shoe-shops where a tack might be bent down," one young man recalled, "but you can't pull off a shoe and ask to have that done—for nothing."

In the face of adversity, some people went to great lengths to maintain appearances. Advertisements for mouthwashes, deodorants, and correspondence courses exploited feelings of shame and failure. Women's magazines described low-cost meals and other budget-trimming strategies. Habits of scrimping and saving acquired in the 1930s often survived into more affluent times. As Caroline Bird wrote in *The Invisible Scar*, a

social history of the 1930s, the depression for many boiled down to "a dull misery in the bones."

New York Senator Robert Wagner called the working woman in the depression "the first orphan in the storm." Indeed, for the 25 percent of American women employed in 1930, the depression brought difficult times. The female jobless rate stood at more than 20 percent through much of the decade. Women desperate to continue working often did so only by taking lower-paying jobs. A laid-off factory worker might become a waitress. Many young women new to the job market had to settle for temporary or part-time work. Competition from displaced male workers reduced the proportion of women even in such traditional "women's professions" as library work, social work, and school teaching.

Married women workers faced harsh criticism. Although most worked because of economic necessity, they were accused of stealing jobs from unemployed men. Even Secretary of Labor Frances Perkins joined in the criticism, urging married women to stay out of the labor market so more jobless men could be hired. Many cities refused to employ married women as teachers and even fired women teachers who married.

Women workers also faced wage discrimination. In 1939, for example, the average woman teacher earned nearly 20 percent less than the average male with comparable experience. Female office workers generally earned far less than male factory workers. A number of the NRA codes authorized lower pay for women workers. The minimum-wage clause of the Fair Labor Standards Act helped some women workers, but did not cover many, including the more than 2 million women who worked for wages in private households.

A unionization campaign of the later 1930s (see below) had mixed effect on women workers. Some who were employed in the mass-production industries benefited, but the most heavily female sectors of the labor force—textile, clerical, service, and sales work—proved resistant to unionization. A 1937 campaign to unionize mostly female clerical workers was opposed by male bosses and many male union leaders, and made little progress.

Despite the roadblocks, the proportion of women working for wages crept up in the 1930s. In the face of criticism, the percentage of wage-earning married women increased from under 12 percent to nearly 16 percent. The crisis may actually have accelerated the long-term movement of women into the workplace as married women took jobs to augment the family income. One working wife explained, "One day in '32 [my husband] just went fishing . . . and he fished for the

rest of the bad times. . . . So at twenty-eight, with two little girls, . . . I took a job as a salesclerk in the J.C. Penney, and worked through the Depression."

As this woman's account suggests, the depression had a profound effect on families, old and young alike. Bank failures wiped out the savings of many older Americans. By 1935 a million Americans over sixty-five were on relief. The birthrates fell in the early thirties as married couples postponed a family or limited its size. Family planning became easier with the spread of birth-control devices such as condoms and diaphragms. A declining birthrate plus reduced immigration held population growth in the 1930s to a scant 7 percent, in contrast to an average of 20 percent per decade between 1900 and 1930.

For parents, running a household in the 1930s often meant a struggle to make ends meet and hold the family together. They patched clothes, stretched food resources, and turned to public assistance when necessary. In homes with a tradition of strong male authority, the husband's loss of a job and consequent erosion of self-esteem often had a devastating psychological impact. "I would rather turn on the gas and put an end to the whole family than let my wife support me," one man told a social investigator. Desertions increased, and the divorce rate, after a dip in the early- and mid-1930s, edged upward, hitting a then all-time high by 1940.

As for young people, one observer compared them to a team of runners waiting for a starting gun that never sounded. High-school enrollment increased sharply, since many youths, seeing no jobs in view, simply stayed in school. The marriage rate declined as young people facing bleak prospects postponed this step. Commented Eleanor Roosevelt in 1934, "I have moments of real terror when I think we might be losing this generation. We have got to bring these young people into the active life of the community and make them feel that they are necessary."

Children found vacation plans canceled, birthdays with few presents, and mealtimes tense with anxious discussions. Maria Tighe of Long Island, who was seven years old when the stock market crashed, recalled sneaking to 6 A.M. mass so her friends would not see her shoes, which were provided by the welfare bureau. Many children of the depression wrote sad letters to Eleanor Roosevelt. A Michigan high-school senior described her shame at not having a graduation dress. "I give all I earn for food for the family," she explained. A thirteen-year-old Arkansas girl wrote, "I have to stay out of school because I have no books or clothes to ware."

Out of necessity, many depression-era families also rediscovered traditional skills. They painted their own houses and repaired their own cars. Domestic skills such as baking and canning revived. Many who lived through the 1930s would later recall it as a time when adversity encouraged cooperation, savoring simple pleasures, and sharing scant resources.

For the neediest families, among them blacks, Hispanics, and southern sharecroppers, the depression imposed added misery on poverty-blighted lives. In his novel *Native Son* (1940), Richard Wright vividly portrayed the desperate conditions of depression-era family life in Chicago's black slums. Yet not all was bleak. Emotional resilience, long-standing patterns of mutual aid, and survival skills developed through years of oppression helped many black families cope with the depression. In New York's Harlem a charismatic black religious leader calling himself Father Divine institutionalized this cooperative spirit by organizing kitchens that distributed thousands of free meals daily.

Industrial Workers Unionize

Between 1900 and 1930, the ranks of factory workers had soared from 3.7 million to 7.7 million. Yet most of these workers remained unorganized. Major industries such as steel, automobiles, and textiles had resisted attempts to unionize their workers. The prosperity and probusiness mood of the 1920s had further weakened the labor movement.

But in the 1930s hard times and a favorable government climate bred a new labor militancy. When the Wagner Act of 1935 guaranteed labor's right to bargain collectively, tremors of activism shook the American Federation of Labor. In November 1935 John L. Lewis of the United Mine Workers (UMW) and Sidney Hillman of the Amalgamated Clothing Workers, frustrated by the AFL's slowness in organizing factory workers, started the Committee for Industrial Organization (CIO) within the AFL. Young CIO activists preached unionization in Pittsburgh steel mills, Detroit auto plants, Akron rubber factories, and southern textile mills. Unlike the craft-based and racially exclusive AFL unions, CIO unions welcomed all workers in a particular industry, regardless of race, gender, or degree of skill.

In 1936 a CIO-sponsored organizing committee geared up for a major strike to win union recognition by the steel industry. (In fact, John L. Lewis had already secretly worked out a settlement with the head of U.S. Steel.) In March 1937 U.S. Steel recognized the steelworkers' union, granted a wage increase, and accepted a forty-hour workweek. Other big steel companies followed suit, and soon four hundred thousand steelworkers had signed union cards (see Figure 24.4).

Meanwhile, organizers had mapped a campaign to unionize General Motors, an antiunion stronghold. Their leader was a redheaded young autoworker and labor activist, Walter Reuther. Reuther's father, of German-immigrant stock, was a socialist who idolized Eugene V. Debs. When the depression hit, Reuther and his brother Victor rediscovered their socialist roots. In December 1936 employees at GM's two body plants in Flint stopped work and peacefully occupied the factories, carefully protecting the equipment and the cars on the assembly lines. This "sit-down strike" paralyzed GM's production.

Although women workers did not participate in the plant occupation (to avoid gossip that might discredit the strike), they picketed on the outside. A Women's Auxiliary organized by strikers' wives, sisters, and daughters fed the striking workers, set up a speakers' bureau, and marched through downtown Flint.

GM's management responded by calling in local police to harass the sit-down strikers, sending spies to union meetings, and threatening to fire strikers. A January 1937 showdown with the police at one of the body plants led to the formation of the Women's Emergency Brigade, on twenty-four-hour alert for picket

FIGURE 24.4
The Growth of Labor Union Membership, 1933–1946

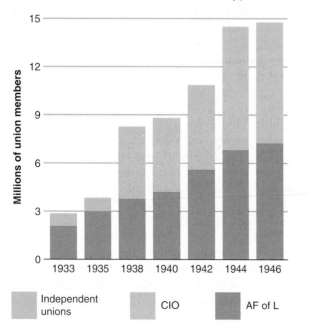

duty. With red berets and armbands, Emergency Brigade members played a key role during the rest of the strike.

Perhaps recalling the army's eviction of protesting veterans from Washington in 1932, GM asked the Roosevelt administration and the governor of Michigan to send troops to expel the strikers by force. Both officials declined, however. Although FDR disapproved of the sit-down tactic, he refused to intervene with troops.

On February 11 GM signed a contract recognizing the United Automobile Workers (UAW). Bearded workers who had vowed not to shave until victory was won streamed out of the plants. As Chrysler fell into line also, the UAW soon boasted more than four hundred thousand members. Unionization of the electrical and rubber industries moved forward as well.

In 1938 the Committee for Industrial Organization broke with the AFL to become the Congress of Industrial Organizations, a 2-million-member association of industrial unions including the autoworkers. In response to the CIO challenge, the AFL began to adapt to the changed nature of the labor force. Overall, union membership in the United States shot from under 3 million in 1933 to over 8 million in 1941.

Some big corporations fought on. Henry Ford hated unions, and his tough lieutenant Harry Bennett organized a squad of union-busting thugs to fight the UAW. In 1937 Bennett's men viciously beat Walter Reuther and other UAW officials outside Ford's plant near Detroit. Not until 1941 did Ford yield to the union's pressure.

The Republic Steel Company, headed by a union hater named Tom Girdler, dug in as well. Even after U.S. Steel and other major steelmakers signed with the CIO, Republic and a group of smaller companies known collectively as "Little Steel" resisted. In May 1937 workers in twenty-seven Little Steel plants, including Republic's factory in South Chicago, walked off the job. Anticipating the strike, Girdler had assembled an arsenal of riot guns and tear gas. On May 30, Memorial Day, a mass of strikers approached over 250 police guarding the factory. When someone threw a large stick at the police, they responded with a hail of gunfire that left four strikers dead and scores wounded. A blue-ribbon investigative committee found that the killings had been "clearly avoidable by the police." In 1941, under growing pressure, the Little Steel companies, including Republic, finally accepted the CIO union.

Another holdout was the textile industry, with over six hundred thousand workers, mostly in the South and 40 percent female. Most textile workers earned very low wages and had no recourse against autocratic bosses. The AFL's United Textile Workers had made little head-way in the 1920s owing to a series of failed strikes, a lack of support from AFL officials, and a policy of admitting only skilled workers. In 1934 the CIO launched its own drive to organize textile workers. Some four hundred thousand workers went on strike, but the mill owners viciously fought back. Southern governors mobilized the National Guard to fight the strike. Several strikers were killed, many wounded, and thousands arrested. The strike failed, and the 1930s ended with most textile workers still unorganized.

Also left behind by this unionizing wave was a large pool of low-paid workers—domestics, agricultural laborers, department-store clerks, and restaurant and laundry workers, for example—who tended to be women, blacks, or recent immigrants. Overall, more than three-quarters of nonfarm workers remained unorganized in 1940. Nevertheless, the unionization of key sectors of America's industrial work force ranks as one of the decade's most memorable developments.

Why did powerful corporations finally yield to unionization after resisting for so long? Certainly workers' militancy and the tactical skill of labor leaders like Reuther were crucial. But labor's successes also reflected a changed government climate. Historically, corporations had routinely called on the government to help

Labor Organizing, 1930s-Style
Walter Reuther (left) and Richard Frankensteen of the United Auto Workers, after their beating by Ford Motor Company security guards, Detroit, May 1937.

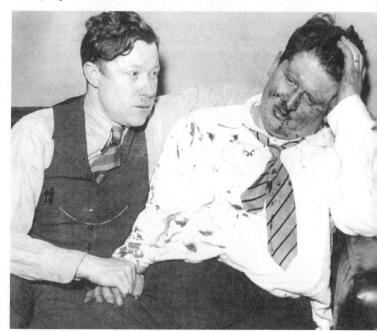

break strikes. Although this still occasionally happened in the 1930s, as in the failed textile-industry strike, in general the Roosevelt administration and key state officials refused to intervene on the side of management. The Wagner Act, the Fair Labor Standards Act, and the oversight role of the National Labor Relations Board made clear that Washington would no longer automatically back management in labor disputes. Once corporate managers realized this, unionization soon followed.

Organized labor's apparent unity by the end of the 1930s concealed some complex tensions. A hard core of activists, many of them advocates of radical social change, had led the unionizing drive. But most rank-and-file factory workers had no desire to overthrow the capitalist system. Indeed, many initially held back from striking, fearful for their jobs. But once the CIO's militant minority showed that picket lines and sit-down strikes could win union contracts and tangible gains, workers signed up by the thousands. As they did, the radical organizers lost influence, and the unions became more conservative.

Reuther himself, despite his socialist roots, reflected the shift and tried to rein in the more radical spirits in the CIO unions. After World War II, in a different political climate, Reuther purged from the CIO some of the same leftists and communists who had led the organizational battles of the 1930s.

Blacks and Hispanic Americans Resist Racism and Exploitation

The depression also brought social changes to and stirred activism within the African-American and Hispanic communities. Black migration to northern cities continued in the 1930s, though at a slower rate than in the 1920s. Four hundred thousand southern blacks moved to northern cities in the 1930s, and by 1940 23 percent of the nation's 12 million blacks lived in the urban North.

Rural or urban, life was hard. Black tenant farmers and sharecroppers often faced eviction. Among black industrial workers, the depression-era jobless rate far outran the rate for whites, largely because of racism and discriminatory hiring policies. Although black workers in some industries benefited from the CIO's nondiscriminatory policy, workplace racism remained a fact of life.

Lynching and miscarriage of justice continued, especially in the South. Twenty-four blacks died by lynching in 1933. In 1931 an all-white jury in Scottsboro, Alabama, sentenced eight black youths to death on highly suspect charges of rape. In 1935, after heavy publicity and an aggressive defense, the Supreme Court ordered a new trial for the "Scottsboro Boys" because they had been denied legal counsel and blacks had been excluded from the jury. Five of the group were again convicted, however, and served long prison terms.

But a rising tempo of activism signaled changes ahead. The NAACP battled in courts and legislatures against lynching, segregation, and the denial of voting rights. The Urban League campaigned against businesses in black neighborhoods that employed only whites. Under the banner "don't shop where you can't work," black protesters picketed and boycotted businesses that refused to hire blacks. In March 1935 hostility toward white-owned businesses in Harlem, fueled by more diffuse anger over racism and joblessness, ignited a riot that caused an estimated $200 million in damage and left three blacks dead.

The Communist party publicized lynchings and racial discrimination as part of a depression-era recruitment effort in the black community. A defense committee formed by the Communist party supplied lawyers for the "Scottsboro Boys". But despite a few notable recruits (including the young novelist Richard Wright), few blacks joined the party.

1934: Protesting Lynching
This young Howard University student demonstrates with a rope around her neck to protest the lack of federal action against the lynching of African-Americans. The year 1933 saw twenty-eight lynchings in the United States.

Other minority groups also faced discrimination. California continued its efforts to prevent Japanese-Americans from owning land. In 1934 Congress set an annual quota of fifty for immigrants from the newly created Commonwealth of the Philippines, still a U.S. colony—lower than that for any other nation. Congress also offered free travel "home" for Filipinos long settled in the United States.

The more than 2 million Hispanic-Americans faced trying times as well. Some were citizens with ancestral roots in the Southwest, but most were recent arrivals from Mexico or Caribbean islands such as Cuba and Puerto Rico (a U.S. holding whose residents were and are American citizens). While the Caribbean immigrants (including those from Jamaica, a British colony) settled in East Coast cities, most Mexican newcomers worked as migratory agricultural laborers in the Southwest and elsewhere, or in midwestern steel or meatpacking plants.

As the depression deepened, Mexican-born residents endured rising hostility. The western trek of thousands of "Okies" fleeing the dust bowl worsened the job crisis for local Hispanic farm workers. By 1937 more than half of Arizona's cotton workers were out-of-staters who had supplanted Mexican-born laborers. With their traditional patterns of migratory work disrupted, Mexican-Americans poured into the barrios (Hispanic neighborhoods) of southwestern cities. Some later recalled signs warning "NO NIGGERS, MEXICANS, OR DOGS ALLOWED."

Lacking work, half a million Mexicans returned to their native land in the 1930s. Many did so voluntarily; others were repatriated by immigration officials and local authorities. Los Angeles welfare officials announced free one-way transportation to Mexico. The annual savings in relief payments, they calculated, would more than offset the cost of sending a full train-load of *repatriados* to Mexico. Though the plan was "voluntary," those who remained were denied relief payments or jobs with the various New Deal work programs. Under combined federal and local pressure, an estimated seventy thousand Mexicans left Los Angeles in 1931 alone.

Mexican-American farm workers who remained endured appalling conditions and near-starvation wages. A wave of protests and strikes (some led by Communist party organizers) swept California. A labor organization called the Confederación de Uniones de Campesinos y Obreros Mexicanos (Confederation of Unions of Mexican Workers and Farm Laborers) emerged from a 1933 strike of grape workers in El

Young Mexican Cotton Picker in the 1930s
Whether in agricultural labor or urban barrios, Mexican-Americans endured harsh conditions during the depression.

Monte, California. More strikes erupted in 1935–1936 from the celery fields and citrus groves around Los Angeles to the lettuce fields of the Salinas Valley.

Organizations like the Associated Farmers of California and the California Fruit Growers Exchange (which marketed its citrus under the brand name Sunkist) fought the unions, sometimes with violence. In October 1933 bullets presumably fired by someone hostile to the strikers ripped into a cotton pickers' union hall in Pixley, California, killing two men and wounding others. Undeterred, the strikers won a 20 percent increase in pay. Other Mexican-American farm workers gained a few hard-fought victories. Striking cotton pickers, for example, increased the rate for a hundred pounds of cotton from sixty cents to seventy-five cents. These strikes awakened at least some Americans to the plight of one of the nation's most exploited groups.

THE AMERICAN CULTURAL SCENE IN THE 1930s

Hard times and the New Deal shaped American cultural life in the 1930s. While radio and the movies offered escapist fare, novelists, artists, playwrights, and photographers responded to the crisis as well. When the depression first struck, as we have seen, their view of U.S. society and of the capitalist system tended to be highly critical. As the decade wore on, however, a more positive and affirmative view emerged, reflecting both the renewed hope stimulated by the New Deal and apprehensions stirred by a deepening threat of war.

Avenues of Escape: Radio and the Movies

The standardization of mass culture continued in the 1930s. Each evening, millions of Americans gathered around their radios to listen to network news, musical programs, and comedy shows. Radio humor flourished as hard times battered the real world. Comedians like Jack Benny and the husband-and-wife team George Burns and Gracie Allen attracted millions.

So, too, did the fifteen-minute afternoon domestic dramas known as soap operas (for the soap companies that sponsored them). Despite their assembly-line quality, these daily dollops of romance and melodrama won a devoted audience, consisting mostly of housewives. Some wrote letters advising the characters how to handle their problems. Identifying with the ordeals of the radio heroines, female listeners gained at least temporary escape from their own difficulties. As one put it, "I can get through the day better when I hear they have sorrows, too."

The movies were also extremely popular in depression America, when most people could still afford the twenty-five-cent admission. In 1939, 65 percent of Americans went to the movies at least once a week. The motion picture, declared one Hollywood executive, had become "as necessary as any other daily commodity."

A few movies dealt realistically with such social issues as labor unrest and the sharecroppers' plight. Two New Deal documentaries, *The Plow That Broke the Plains*, on the origins of the dust bowl, and *The River*, dealing with soil erosion and floods in the Mississippi valley, evoked the human and environmental toll of westward expansion.

Warner Brothers studio (which had close ties with the Roosevelt administration) made a series of movies in 1934–1936 celebrating the New Deal. And in *Mr. Deeds Goes to Town* (1936) and *Mr. Smith Goes to Washington* (1939), director Frank Capra, the son of Italian immigrants, offered the idealistic message that "the people" would ultimately triumph over entrenched interests.

The gangster movies of the early thirties, drawing inspiration from real-life criminals like Al Capone and John Dillinger, served up a different style of film realism. Films like *Little Caesar* (1930) and *The Public Enemy* (1931) offered gritty images of urban America: looming skyscrapers; menacing, rain-swept streets; lonely bus depots and all-night diners; the rat-tat-tat of machine guns as rival gangs battled. When civic groups protested the glorification of crime, Hollywood simply made the police and "G-men" (FBI agents) the heroes, while retaining the violence. The movie gangsters played by Edward G. Robinson and James Cagney represented variants of the Horatio Alger hero struggling upward against adversity. Their portrayals appealed to depression-era moviegoers facing equally heavy odds.

Above all, Hollywood offered escape—the chance briefly to forget the depression. The publicist who claimed that the movies "literally laughed the big bad wolf of the depression out of the public mind" exaggerated, but cinema's escapist function in the 1930s is clear. Musicals such as *Gold Diggers of 1933* (with its theme song, "We're in the Money") offered dancing, music, and cheerful plots involving the triumph of pluck over all obstacles. When color movies arrived in the late 1930s (see Technology and Culture: Sound, Color, and Animation Come to the Movies), they seemed an omen of better times ahead.

The Marx Brothers provided the depression decade's zaniest movie moments. In comedies like *Animal Crackers* and *Duck Soup*, these vaudeville troupers of German-Jewish immigrant origins created an anarchic world that satirized authority, fractured the English language, and defied logic. Amid widespread cynicism about the economic and social order that had collapsed so spectacularly in 1929, the Marx Brothers' mockery matched the American mood.

Thirties' movies dealt with African Americans, if at all, largely in stereotypes. Hollywood confined black performers to such roles as the scatterbrained maid played by Butterfly McQueen in *Gone with the Wind* and the indulgent house servant played by tap dancer Bill Robinson and patronized by child star Shirley Temple in *The Little Colonel* (1935). Under the denigrating screen name Stepin Fetchit, black actor Lincoln Perry played the slow-witted butt of humor in many movies.

In representing women, Hollywood offered mixed messages. While many 1930s' movie heroines found fulfillment in traditional marriage and subordination to a man, a few films chipped away at the stereotype. Joan Bennett played a strong-willed professional in *The Wedding Present* (1936) and Carol Lombard emerged as a brilliant comedienne in *My Man Godfrey* (1936). Mae West, brassy, openly sexual, and fiercely independent, mocked conventional stereotypes in *I'm No Angel* and other 1930s hits. Toying with would-be lovers and tossing off double entendres, West made clear that she was her own woman.

The Later 1930s: Opposing Fascism; Reaffirming Traditional Values

As the 1930s drew to a close, many Americans viewed the nation with a newly appreciative eye. It had survived the economic crisis. The social fabric remained whole; revolution had not come. As other societies collapsed into dictatorships, American democracy endured. Writers, composers, and other cultural creators reflected the changed climate, as despair and pessimism gave way to a more upbeat and patriotic outlook.

International developments and a domestic political movement known as the Popular Front influenced this shift. In the early 1930s, as we have seen, the U.S. Communist party attacked Roosevelt and the New Deal. But in 1935 Russian dictator Joseph Stalin, fearing attack by Nazi Germany, called for a worldwide alliance, or Popular Front, against Adolf Hitler and his Italian fascist counterpart, Benito Mussolini. (Fascism is a form of government involving one-party rule, extreme nationalism, hostility to minority groups, and the forcible suppression of dissent.) Parroting the new Soviet line, U.S. communists now praised Roosevelt and summoned writers and intellectuals to the antifascist cause. Many noncommunists, alarmed by developments in Europe, responded to the call.

The high-water mark of the Popular Front came during the Spanish Civil War of 1936–1939. In July 1936 Spanish fascist general Francisco Franco launched a revolt against Spain's legally elected government, a coalition of left-wing parties. With military aid from Hitler and Mussolini, Franco won backing from Spanish monarchists, landowners, industrialists, and the Roman Catholic hierarchy.

In America, the cause of the anti-Franco Spanish Loyalists (that is, those loyal to the elected government) rallied support from writers, artists, and intellectuals who backed the Popular Front. The novelist Ernest Hemingway, who visited Spain in 1936–1937, was among the writers who support the Loyalists. In contrast to his disillusioned novels of the 1920s (see Chapter 23), Hemingway's *For Whom the Bell Tolls* (1940) told of a young American volunteer who dies while fighting with a Loyalist guerrilla band. Looking back on these years, Hemingway recalled, "The Spanish Civil War offered something which you could believe in wholly and completely, and in which you felt an absolute brotherhood with the others who were engaged in it."

The Popular Front collapsed in August 1939 when the Soviet Union and Nazi Germany signed a nonaggression pact and divided Poland between them. Overnight, enthusiasm for working with the communists under the banner of "antifascism" faded. But while it lasted, the Popular Front helped shape U.S. culture and alerted Americans to threatening developments abroad.

The New Deal's programs for writers, artists, and musicians, as well as its turn leftward in 1935–1936, contributed mightily to the cultural shift of the later 1930s as well. The satirical and cynical tone of the 1920s and early 1930s now gave way to a more hopeful view of grass-roots America. In John Steinbeck's best-selling novel *The Grapes of Wrath* (1939), an uprooted dustbowl family, the Joads, make their difficult way from

Let Us Now Praise Famous Men (1941)
Journalist James Agee and photographer Walker Evans created a memorable record of a month spent with Alabama sharecoppers in 1936.

Sound, Color, and Animation Come to the Movies

Movies were a familiar part of the U.S. cultural landscape by the 1930s, but this decade brought technological advances that vastly increased their popularity. In 1920 movies were silent and black-and-white. By 1940 they had been transformed by sound, color, and animation.

From the earliest days of motion pictures, filmmakers had struggled to bring sound to the medium. Thomas Edison experimented with synchronizing phonograph recordings with the action on the screen. Warner Brothers, a new film studio in the 1920s, explored the commercial possibilities of this technology through a subsidiary company called Vitaphone. This method was complicated, and coordinating sound with the moving image proved difficult. Nevertheless, the most-famous

early "sound" movie, Warner Brothers' *The Jazz Singer* (1927) starring Al Jolson, used the Vitaphone technology. *The Jazz Singer* was actually a silent film with a few recorded songs and snatches of dialogue. But audiences sensed an important breakthrough and cheered when Jolson suddenly and prophetically declared,: "Wait a minute, wait a minute. You ain't heard nothin' yet." The first film featuring sound from beginning to end, Warner Brothers' *Lights of New York* (1928), also used Vitaphone recordings.

Meanwhile, as early as 1900 an inventor had secured a patent for a different technology that involved adding a soundtrack to the film itself by means of a photoelectric cell. Development lagged until 1923, when radio pioneer Lee DeForest invented a technique he called Phonofilm.

Fox film studio acquired Phonofilm, rechristened it "Movietone," and introduced sound films far superior to those using Warner Brothers' Vitaphone system.

Movies of the 1930s were a cacophony of sound: spoken dialogue, orchestras in musical extravaganzas, and squealing tires and explosive gunfire in gangster films. The Wurlitzer theater organs that had accompanied the silent movies gathered dust; stars of the silent era whose voices did not match their appearance faded. The coming of sound initially made movies more stilted and artificial by forcing actors to stand motionless near microphones hidden in trees, lamps, and flower pots, but this problem was soon solved. Another unanticipated consequence was to slow the export of U.S. films to non-English-speaking countries.

Color came more slowly, even though experiments with tinting motion-picture film dated to the 1890s. In 1915 two Americans, Herbert Kalmus and Daniel Comstock, developed a more advanced system, which they called Technicolor. It involved a camera with two film tracks and two apertures, one with a red filter and the other with a blue filter. The two films were then bonded

Technicians test the Vitaphone, an early machine for adding sound to movies by synchronizing disk recordings with filmed images.

together in the production process. The first film made by this method was *Toll of the Sea* (1922).

This primitive technology was not very satisfactory, but the Technicolor company made improvements, notably a movie camera that could film the same scene simultaneously in the three primary colors, red, blue, and green, with the three films later combined into one. Two hit movies of 1939, *Gone With the Wind* and *The Wizard of Oz,* introduced color to the masses. The latter had a particularly powerful effect because the opening scenes, set in Kansas, were black-and-white. When Dorothy awakens in Oz, the movie bursts into color.

Film animation, too, has a long history. *Gertie the Dinosaur,* an animated cartoon by Winsor McCay, a New York newspaper cartoonist, appeared in 1908. In the 1920s movie bills included simple cartoons featuring comic-strip characters such as Felix the Cat. The animation process was slow and labor-intensive, involving individual photographs of hundreds of drawings. A key breakthrough was "cel" animation, by which the moving parts could be sketched on celluloid sheets without redrawing the entire character.

By the late 1920s animation technology became more sophisticated, and theaters presented more and more cartoons. Walt Disney (1901–1966), a Chicago art student, moved to Los Angeles in 1923 to make animated cartoons. His most famous character, Mickey Mouse, first appeared in *Plane Crazy* in May 1928 and made his sound debut later that year in *Steamboat Willie*. *Three Little Pigs*, an all-color animated cartoon, delighted audiences in 1933. Donald Duck made his debut in *Orphan's Benefit* (1936). Along with his technical genius, Disney rationalized the animation process and, like Henry Ford, put it on a mass-production basis. With *Snow White and the Seven Dwarfs* (1937), he moved from short cartoons to feature-length films. His *Fantasia* (1940), featuring imaginative and colorful visual sequences accompanying well-known musical works, was a watershed in animation history.

The cultural (and economic) impact of these technological developments was great. Thanks to sound, color, and animation—along with marketing innovations such as double features (1931) and drive-in theaters (1933)—the movie industry not only survived but prospered in the hard times of the 1930s. Movies provided cheap entertainment, and the technical innovations of these years added to their appeal and novelty.

The addition of sound, bringing spoken dialogue, music, and sound effects to the screen, was especially important. A series of musicals with elaborate dance routines choreographed by Busby Berkeley, such as *Footlight Parade* (1933), proved highly popular. Dancers

Gone With the Wind (1939), an early triumph of the new technology of color film.

Fred Astaire and Ginger Rogers wove together music and dance in *Flying Down to Rio* (1933) and other films. Disney integrated music in many of his animated films.

The added realism that sound brought to films added to the alarm of the Catholic Legion of Decency and other conservative groups concerned about the moral effect on the young of sexual suggestiveness in romantic movies and brutal violence in gangster films. To forestall a movement to boycott or censor objectionable movies, Hollywood in 1934 adopted a production code that imposed strict rules on what could be shown on the screen.

The new technologies also affected the fortunes of the film industry. The high costs involved in converting to sound and color encouraged consolidation and mergers, reducing the number of smaller producers. As the studios borrowed heavily to acquire the new technologies, Wall Street gained an increasingly important behind-the-scenes role in the industry. The rise of corporate economic power in Hollywood had a subtle but distinct effect on film content, encouraging escapist, predictable formula films most likely to turn a profit, and discouraging riskier work and critical explorations of the darker corners of American society.

Focus Questions

- In what specific ways did the coming of sound, color, and animation increase the box-office appeal and entertainment value of movies in the depression decade of the 1930s?
- How did these new technologies affect the economics of the film industry itself?

Jazz at Carnegie Hall
Percussionist Gene Krupa played in the Benny Goodman Orchestra that presented a history-making jazz concert at Carnegie Hall in 1938.

Oklahoma to California along Route 66. Steinbeck stressed not only the strength and endurance of ordinary Americans in depression America, but also their social cooperation and mutual support. As Ma Joad tells her son Tom, "They ain't gonna wipe us out. Why, we're the people—we go on." Made into a movie by John Ford, and starring Henry Fonda, *The Grapes of Wrath* stands as one of the most memorable cultural products of the 1930s.

In 1936 journalist James Agee and photographer Walker Evans spent several weeks living with Alabama sharecropper families while researching a magazine article. From this experience came Agee's masterpiece, *Let Us Now Praise Famous Men* (1941). Enhanced by Walker Evans's unforgettable photographs, Agee's intensely personal work evoked the strength and decency of Americans living on society's margins.

The new cultural mood also found expression on the stage. Thornton Wilder's play *Our Town* (1938) portrayed a New England town in which everyday events become, in memory, infinitely precious. William Saroyan's *The Time of Your Life* (1939) affectionately celebrated the foibles and virtues of a colorful collection of American "types" gathered in a San Francisco waterfront bar.

Composers, too, caught the spirit of cultural nationalism. In such works as *Billy the Kid* (1938), Aaron Copland drew upon American legends and folk melodies. George Gershwin's 1935 opera *Porgy and Bess*, adapted from a play by Dubose and Dorothy Heyward, portrayed black street life in Charleston, South Carolina.

Jazz surged in popularity thanks to swing, a flowing, danceable style originated by the pianist Fletcher Henderson and popularized by the big bands of Count Basie, Benny Goodman, Duke Ellington, and others. The Basie band started at Kansas City's Reno Club, where, as Basie later recalled, "We played from nine o'clock in the evening to five or six the next morning, . . . and the boys in the band got eighteen dollars a week and I got twenty one." Moving to New York in 1936, Basie helped launch the swing era.

Benny Goodman, of a Chicago immigrant family, had played the clarinet as a boy at Jane Addams's Hull House. Challenging the color line in jazz, Goodman included black musicians like pianist Teddy Wilson and vibraphonist Lionel Hampton along with white performers in his orchestra. A turning point in the acceptance of jazz as a serious musical form came in 1938, when Goodman's band performed at New York's Carnegie Hall, a citadel of high culture.

Bringing in the Maple Sugar, **by Anna "Grandma" Moses, c. 1939**
A mood of patriotism and nostalgia for simpler times contributed to the popularity of folk artists in the later 1930s.

In *Swingin' the Dream: Big Band Jazz and the Rebirth of American Culture* (1998), historian Lewis Erenberg links swing to the politics of the later 1930s. In its optimism, innovativeness, and "democratic ethos," he argues, swing "expressed in cultural form many of the themes of . . . the New Deal."

The later 1930s also saw a heightened interest in regional literature, painting, and folk art. Zora Neale Hurston's novel *Their Eyes Were Watching God* (1937), exploring a black woman's search for fulfillment, was set in rural Florida. In *Absalom, Absalom!* (1936) William Faulkner continued the saga of his mythic Yoknapatawpha County in Mississippi. Painters Thomas Hart Benton of Missouri (a descendant of the nineteenth-century senator of the same name), John Steuart Curry of Kansas, and Grant Wood of Iowa struck strongly regional notes in their work.

Galleries displayed Amish quilts, New England weather vanes, and paintings by colonial folk artists. A 1938 show at New York's Museum of Modern Art introduced Horace Pippin, a black Philadelphia laborer whose right arm had been shattered in World War I. In such paintings as *John Brown Going to His Hanging,* Pippin revealed a genuine, if untutored, talent. In 1939 the same museum featured seventy-nine-year-old Anna "Grandma" Moses of Hoosick Falls, New York, whose memory paintings of her farm girlhood enjoyed great popularity.

The surge of cultural nationalism heightened interest in the nation's past. Americans flocked to historical re-creations such as Henry Ford's Greenfield Village near Detroit and Colonial Williamsburg in Virginia, restored by the Rockefeller Foundation. In 1936–1939 Texans restored the Alamo in San Antonio, the "Cradle of Texas Liberty." Historical novels like Margaret Mitchell's epic of the Old South, *Gone with the Wind* (1936), became best-sellers. These recreations and fictions often presented a distorted view of history. Slavery was blurred or sentimentalized at Colonial Williamsburg and in Mitchell's novel. "Texas Liberty" had a different meaning for the state's African American, Indian, and Hispanic populations than it did for the patriotic organizations that turned the Alamo into a tourist shrine.

Streamlining and a World's Fair: Corporate America's Utopian Vision

The visual cultural of late 1930s' America was also shaped by a design style called streamlining. This innovation originated in the 1920s when a group of industrial

designers, inspired by the romance of flight, introduced rounded edges and smoothly flowing curves into the design of commercial products. Streamlining appealed to American business in the 1930s. It made products more attractive to consumers—a vital consideration during the depression. When Raymond Loewy streamlined Sears Roebuck's Coldspot refrigerators, sales surged. Streamlined products also helped corporate America rebuild its tarnished image and present itself as the benevolent shaper of a better future. Products ranging from house trailers to cigarette lighters emerged in sleek new forms. Pencil sharpeners evolved into gleaming, aerodynamic works of art poised for takeoff. The streamlined service stations that Norman Bel Geddes designed for Texaco, he boasted, would make oil changes "a stimulating experience" rather than a boring necessity.

Under the theme "The World of Tomorrow," the 1939 New York World's Fair represented the high point of the streamlining vogue and of corporate America's public-relations blitz. The fair's instantly famous logo was the Trylon and Perisphere: a seven-hundred-foot needle and a globe that seemed to float on a circular pool of water. Inside the Perisphere, visitors found "Democracity," a revolving diorama portraying a thriving, harmonious city of the future.

The hit of the fair was Futurama, the General Motors exhibit designed by Norman Bel Geddes. Visitors entered a darkened circular auditorium where, amid piped-in music and a resonant recorded narration, a vision of America in the distant year of 1960 majestically unfolded. A multilane highway network complete with cloverleaf exits and stacked interchanges dominated the imagined landscape. A brilliant public-relations investment by GM, Futurama built support for the interstate highway system that would soon become a reality.

Also featuring such wonders as television and automatic dishwashers, the World's Fair did, indeed, offer a glimpse of "The World of Tomorrow" as a smoothly functioning technological utopia made possible by the nation's great corporations. A business magazine editorialized, "If there are any doubters left, a visit to the New York World's Fair should convince them that American business has been the vehicle which carried the discoveries of science and the benefits of machine production to the doorstep of American consumers." The fair epitomized corporate capitalism's version of the patriotism and hopefulness that pervaded American culture as the 1930s ended.

The hopefulness was mixed with muted fear. The nation had survived the worst of the depression, but danger loomed beyond the seas. The anxiety triggered

New York World's Fair, 1939
Despite the fair's dreamy vision of a future made bright by technology, world events looked grim as the 1930s ended.

by the menacing world situation surfaced on October 31, 1938, when CBS radio aired an adaptation of H. G. Wells's science-fiction story *War of the Worlds* directed by Orson Welles. In realistic detail, the broadcast reported the landing of a spaceship in New Jersey, the emergence of aliens with ray guns, and their advance toward New York City. The show sparked a panic as horrified listeners concluded that the end was at hand. Some jumped in their cars and sped off into the night. Others prayed. A few attempted suicide. Beneath the terror lay a more well-founded fear: of approaching war. For a decade, as Americans had coped with the depression, the international situation had steadily worsened. By October 1938 radio news bulletins warned of impending war between Germany and England.

The panic triggered by Orson Welles's Halloween prank quickly changed to sheepish embarrassment, but the fear aroused by the real dangers looming on the horizon only escalated. By the time the New York World's Fair offered its vision of "The World of Tomorrow," the actual world of 1939 had become very scary indeed.

CONCLUSION

Economists trace the Great Depression to weaknesses in the U.S. and world economies of the 1920s. These weaknesses, masked by the glow of prosperity, ranged from low farm prices and uneven income distribution to trade barriers, a glut of consumer goods, and problems in the money supply. The depression affected all facets of American life, from individual families to movies and radio programs that entertained millions. It also shaped the outlook of writers and other culture creators. From an initial mood of despair, the cultural climate by the end of the 1930s had become far more hopeful and affirmative.

The depression and the New Deal affected different groups in different ways. For residents of the Tennessee Valley and across the West, hydroelectric projects and other public works brought electric power and other major changes. For Native Americans, the era brought legislation restoring the legal status of tribes, laying the groundwork for economic revitalization and treaty claims in the future. For Mexican farm laborers, these years brought both the threat of deportation and strikes for better wages and working conditions. Women in the 1930s faced pressure to stay out of the workplace, so that men could find jobs. Many resisted these pressures, however, and the female labor force continued to grow.

The New Deal that so dominates the 1930s was hardly an unqualified success. Some New Deal programs failed, and full recovery proved elusive. As late as 1939 more than 17 percent of the labor force remained jobless. Only in 1943, as war plants boomed, was full employment finally achieved. And the New Deal had its blind spots. Apart from symbolic gestures, it only hesitantly addressed the issue of racism. While African Americans benefited economically from New Deal programs, black leaders sharply criticized the administration's failure to address lynching and racial discrimination.

The New Deal shifted course over time. Initially Roosevelt focused on relief and economic recovery and welcomed big business in his depression-fighting coalition. In 1935, however, the New Deal adopted a more class-based approach. This "Second New Deal" addressed the plight of the poorest Americans, including sharecroppers and migrants; pursued tougher business regulation and higher taxes for the wealthy; and championed such fundamental and long-lasting legislative reforms as the Social Security Act, laying the groundwork of the welfare state, and the Wagner Act, guaranteeing workers' right to unionize.

As the New Deal moved from fighting the depression to shifting the balance of power in American politics and advancing the well-being of those whom Roosevelt once called the "forgotten" Americans—a commitment that involved an unprecedented level of governmental involvement with social and economic issues—it set a new standard of what citizens could expect of their government. In its five-year span, the New Deal radically redefined the nation's political agenda, the role of the federal government, and the nature of the presidency. For decades after, national political campaigns and public-policy debates would be shaped by differing opinions about the New Deal's legacy.

Any evaluation of the New Deal must confront Franklin D. Roosevelt. Neither saint nor superman, he could be calculating and devious, superficially genial, and breezily casual about details. But for most Americans of the 1930s—and most historians since—his strengths outweighed his liabilities. His open, experimental approach served the nation well in a time of crisis. He once compared himself to a football quarterback, deciding which play to call after seeing how the last one worked out.

Above all, Roosevelt's optimism inspired a demoralized people. "We Americans of today . . . ," he observed to an audience of young people in 1939, "are characters in the living book of democracy. But we are also its

CHRONOLOGY, 1929–1939

1929 Stock Market crash; onset of depression.

1932 Reconstruction Finance Corporation.
Veterans' bonus march.
Franklin D. Roosevelt elected president.

1933 Repeal of Eighteenth Amendment.
Civilian Conservation Corps (CCC).
Federal Emergency Relief Act (FERA).
Tennessee Valley Authority (TVA).
Agricultural Adjustment Administration (AAA).
National Recovery Administration (NRA).
Public Works Administration (PWA).

1934 Securities and Exchange Commission (SEC).
Taylor Grazing Act.
Indian Reorganization Act.

1934–1936 Strikes by Mexican-American agricultural workers in the West.

1935 Supreme Court declares NRA unconstitutional.
Works Progress Administration (WPA).
Resettlement Administration.
National Labor Relations Act (Wagner Act).
Social Security Act.
NAACP campaign for federal antilynching law.
Huey Long assassinated.
Revenue Act raises taxes on corporations and the wealthy.
Supreme Court reverses conviction of the "Scottsboro Boys."
Harlem riot.

1935–1939 Era of the Popular Front.

1936 Supreme Court declares AAA unconstitutional.
Roosevelt wins landslide reelection victory.
Autoworkers' sit-down strike against General Motors begins (December).

1937 Roosevelt's "court packing" plan defeated.
Farm Security Administration.
GM, U.S. Steel, and Chrysler sign union contracts.

1937–1938 The "Roosevelt Recession."

1938 Fair Labor Standards Act.
Republicans gain heavily in midterm elections.
Congress of Industrial Organizations (CIO) formed.
Carnegie Hall concert by Benny Goodman orchestra.

1939 Hatch Act.
Marian Anderson concert at Lincoln Memorial.
John Steinbeck, *The Grapes of Wrath.*

1940 Ernest Hemingway, *For Whom the Bell Tolls.*

author. It falls upon us now to say whether the chapters that are to come will tell a story of retreat or a story of continued advance."

FOR FURTHER REFERENCE

READINGS

Caroline Bird, *The Invisible Scar* (1966). Moving look at the depression's human and psychological toll.

Lizabeth Cohen, *Making a New Deal: Industrial Workers in Chicago, 1919–1939* (1990). Influential, well-researched study of working-class and union culture.

Blanche D. Coll, *Safety Net: Welfare and Social Security, 1929–1979* (1995). Balanced, well-written history of the sources of the Social Security Act and its aftermath.

Lewis Erenberg, *Swingin' the Dream: Big Band Jazz and the Rebirth of American Culture* (1998). Stimulating interpretive study linking New Deal politics and popular music in the later 1930s.

Steve Fraser and Gary Gerstle, eds., *The Rise and Fall of the New Deal Order, 1930–1980* (1989). Incisive critical essays on the New Deal's long-term legacy.

David M. Kennedy, *Freedom from Fear: The American People in Depression and War* (1998). A sweeping synthesis, especially good on Washington politics and the Social Security Act.

William E. Leuchtenberg, *Franklin D. Roosevelt and the New Deal* (1983). A comprehensive, readable overview, rich in illuminating detail.

Albert U. Romasco, *The Politics of Recovery: Roosevelt's New Deal* (1983). A study particularly useful on the New Deal's business policies.

Harvard Sitkoff, *A New Deal for Blacks* (1978). An exploration of the Roosevelt administration's policies toward black Americans.

Robert H. Zieger, *The CIO, 1935–1955* (1995). Valuable on organized labor in the later New Deal, and on tensions between the leadership and the rank-and-file.

WEBSITES

America from the Great Depression to World War II: Photographs from the FSA-OWI, 1935–1945
Library of Congress, American Memory
http://memory.loc.gov/ammem/fsowhome.html
This massive archive of over 160,000 photographs from the files of the Farm Security Administration and the Office of War Information is searchable by subject matter, photographer, and geographic location.

America in the 1930s
University of Virginia American Studies Program
http://xroads.virginia.edu/~1930s/home-1.html
This website includes a wealth of primary-source materials from the 1930s relating to "film, radio programs, literature, journalism, museums, exhibitions, architecture, art, and other forms of cultural expression."

Franklin D. Roosevelt Library and Digital Archives
http://www.fdrlibrary.marist.edu/
This site contains thirteen thousand digitized "documents, photographs, sound and video recordings, finding aids, and other primary source materials" held by the FDR Library at Hyde Park, New York.

New Deal Network
The Franklin and Eleanor Roosevelt Institute and the Institute for Learning Technologies, Teachers College, Columbia University
http://newdeal.feri.org/
A rich resource featuring primary articles, speeches, poems, photos, songs, oral-history interviews, and much more on the New Deal era.

Surviving the Dust Bowl
The American Experienc
http://www.pbs.org/wgbh/amex/dustbowl/
Includes the PBS *American Experience* film on the Dust Bowl, plus bibliography, maps, and other supplementary materials.

For additional works please consult the bibliography at the end of the book.

CHAPTER 25

Americans and a World in Crisis, 1933–1945

Most Americans have agreed that the United States fought a just war to meet the crisis of military aggression by Nazi Germany and Japan. As the years passed, particularly after the traumas of the Vietnam War and the economic setbacks of the 1970s, that necessary war—a complex, uncertain, chaotic event—became remembered as a golden age, as the "Good War" fought by the "Greatest Generation." Nostalgic myths abounded of a nation fully united and sure of its cause, of Americans of every race, religion, and ethnicity working together in the foxhole as well as the factory, of courageous U.S. soldiers—who never committed atrocities—quickly and easily returning to civilian life after clear-cut victories.

Such myths have little to do with the war experienced by E. B. Sledge. Born in 1923, Sledge enjoyed a carefree boyhood of fishing, hunting, and riding in Mobile, Alabama, until the United States entered the Second World War. Filled with idealism and patriotism, he dropped out of school to join the marines and defend his country. His harrowing experiences drove him to write a wartime memoir, *With the Old Breed*, of unrelenting horror. Describing the battles of Peleliu and Okinawa, Sledge depicts a brutal landscape of war without mercy, of kill or be killed, of prisoners tortured and the dead mutilated, of the most savage violence coupled with the most lethal technology of modern warfare.

◀ **Okinawa, 1945**
Wounded in the head, his hands clasped as if in prayer, a GI from the Seventh Infantry Division awaits evacuation from Rocky Crags in southern Okinawa.

On Peleliu, where Sledge's Company K reported 64 percent casualties in an island campaign later deemed unnecessary, he witnessed helpless comrades being slaughtered. Because the closeness of the enemy made it too dangerous to try to reclaim the dead, he watched as buddies oozed into a wasteland of mud and excreta, land crabs feeding on them. He saw a fellow marine use a knife to try to extract the gold teeth of a wounded Japanese soldier. Frustrated in the attempt, the marine sliced open the prisoner's cheeks and continued to gouge and pry, unfazed by the man's thrashing and gurgling. On Okinawa's Half Moon Hill he dreamed that the decomposed bodies of marines sprawled about him slowly rose, unblinkingly stared at him, and said, "It is over for us who are dead, but you must struggle, and will carry the memories all your life. People back home will wonder why you can't forget."

The wartime experiences of few Americans matched those of Sledge. Yet World War II fundamentally changed national institutions and behavior, immensely affecting most Americans. History's greatest armed conflict proved as much a turning point in personal lives as in world affairs. Amidst strikes and overcrowding, profiteering and black markets, the war lifted the nation out of the depression, redistributed income, and transformed the United States into a middle-class society. Despite continuing discrimination and prejudice, it gave millions of women and minorities an opportunity to savor independence and prosperity. As it destroyed certain traditional American ways and communities, it created a new world order that left the United States at the pinnacle of its power and sowed the seeds of a postwar crisis. It was indeed, in Eleanor Roosevelt's words, "no ordinary time."

This chapter focuses on five major questions:

■ How did the Roosevelt administration and the American people respond to the international crises of the 1930s?

■ How did war mobilization transform the American economy and government?

■ What were the major aspects of Allied military strategy in Europe and Asia?

■ What were the major effects of World War II on American society, including minorities and women?

■ What were the arguments for and against the use of the atomic bomb to end the war with Japan?

THE UNITED STATES IN A MENACING WORLD, 1933–1939

Apart from improving relations with Latin America, the early administration of President Franklin D. Roosevelt (FDR) remained largely aloof from the crises in the world. Americans reacted ambivalently as Italy, Germany, and Japan grew more aggressive. Millions of Americans, determined not to stumble into war again, supported neutrality. Others insisted that the United States help embattled democracies abroad. All the while, the world slid toward the precipice.

Nationalism and the Good Neighbor

During the Great Depression, Roosevelt put U.S. economic interests above all else. He showed little interest in pursuing his secretary of state's hopes for free trade and international economic cooperation.

He did, however, adopt an internationalist approach in Latin America, where bitterness over decades of "Yankee imperialism" ran high. He announced a "Good Neighbor" policy, and in late 1933 the United States signed a formal convention that "No state has the right to intervene in the internal or external affairs of another." To support this policy, FDR withdrew the last U.S. troops from Haiti and the Dominican Republic, persuaded American bankers to loosen their grip on Haiti's central banking system, renounced the Platt Amendment that had given the United States control over the Cuban government since 1901, and reduced the U.S. role in Panamanian affairs.

The key tests of the Good Neighbor policy came in Cuba and Mexico. In Cuba, an economic crisis in 1933 brought to power a leftist regime that the United States opposed. Instead of sending in the marines, as earlier administrations might have done, the United States provided indirect aid to a conservative revolt led by Fulgencio Batista in 1934 that overthrew the radical government. To shore up the Batista regime, Washington lowered the tariff on Cuban sugar cane. American economic assistance allowed Batista to retain power, for the most part, until he was overthrown by Fidel Castro in 1959.

In Mexico, a reform government came to power in 1936 and promptly nationalized several oil companies owned by U.S. and British corporations. While insisting on fair compensation, the United States refrained from military intervention and conceded Mexico's right to

MAP 25.1
European Aggression Before World War II

Less than twenty years after the end of World War I, war again loomed in Europe as Hitler launched Germany on a course of military and territorial expansion.

nationalize the companies. After lengthy negotiations, Mexico and the oil companies reached a compromise compensation agreement.

The Good Neighbor policy thus neither ended U.S. interference in Latin American affairs nor stemmed the increasing envy of "rich Uncle Sam" by his southern neighbors. But it did substitute economic leverage for heavy-handed intervention, particularly military occupation. The better relations fostered by FDR would become important when the United States sought hemispheric solidarity in World War II, and later in the Cold War.

The Rise of Aggressive States in Europe and Asia

As early as 1922, economic and social unrest in Italy enabled Benito Mussolini and his Fascist party to seize power. The regime suppressed dissent, imposed one-party rule, and, hoping to recreate a Roman empire, invaded Ethiopia in October 1935.

The rise of Adolf Hitler in Germany proved more menacing. Hitler's National Socialist (Nazi) party, capi-

talizing on Germany's hard times and resentment of the harsh Versailles Treaty, gained strength. In January 1933, five weeks before the inauguration of Franklin Roosevelt, Hitler became Germany's chancellor. (The two men's lives would fatefully intertwine for the next twelve years until they died within two weeks of each other in April 1945.) Crushing opponents and potential rivals, Hitler imposed a brutal dictatorship on Germany and began a program to purify it of Jews—whom he considered an "inferior race" responsible for Germany's defeat in World War I.

Violating the Versailles treaty, Hitler began a military buildup in 1935. A year later German troops reoccupied the Rhineland, the demilitarized region west of the Rhine River that had been controlled by France since the end of World War I. In 1938, as German tanks rolled into Vienna, Hitler proclaimed an *Anschluss* (union) between Austria and Germany. London, Paris, and Washington murmured their disapproval but took no action (see Map 25.1).

An emboldened Hitler then turned to the Sudetenland, a part of neighboring Czechoslovakia containing 3 million ethnic Germans. Insisting that the area

must be part of Germany, Hitler thundered his determination to take it. British prime minister Neville Chamberlain and his French counterpart, eager to avoid hostilities, appeased Hitler and at a conference in Munich in September 1938 agreed to turn the Sudetenland over to Germany. Believing in Chamberlain's claim to have achieved "peace in our time," FDR and most Americans applauded the Munich Pact for having avoided war.

In Japan, meanwhile, militarists had gained control of the government. To gain the raw materials needed for heavy industry, especially coal, metals, petroleum, and timber, they launched a fateful course of expansion. In 1931 Japan sent troops into the northern Chinese province of Manchuria, and within two years took total control of the province. Then, having signed treaties of political alliance and mutual defense with Germany and Italy, Japan began a full-scale war against China in July 1937; within a year Japan controlled most of that vast nation (see Map 25.2). Weak protests by Washington did little to deter Japan's plans for further aggression in Asia and the Pacific.

MAP 25.2

Japanese Expansion Before World War II

Dominated by militarists, Japan pursued an expansionist policy in Asia in the 1930s, extending its sphere of economic and political influence. In July 1937, having already occupied the Chinese province of Manchuria, Japan attacked China proper.

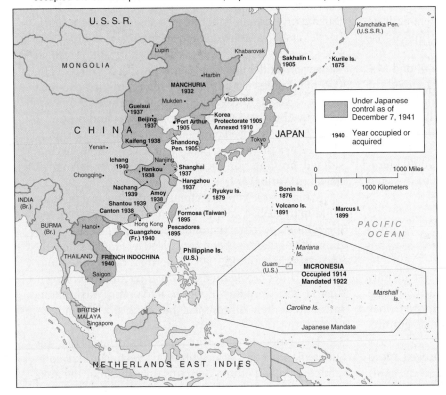

The American Mood: No More War

The feeble responses to aggression by the Roosevelt administration reflected the American people's belief that the decision to go to war in April 1917 had been a mistake. This conviction was rooted in the nation's isolationist tradition—its wish to avoid military and political entanglements in Old World quarrels—as well as in its desire to have the government focus on economic matters, not foreign affairs, in the midst of the Great Depression. A series of books and films stressing American disillusionment with World War I 's failure to make the world safe for democracy strengthened isolationist sentiment. So did a 1934–1936 Senate investigation headed by Republican Gerald P. Nye of North Dakota, which concluded that banking and munitions interests, whom it called "merchants of death," had tricked the United States into war to protect loans and weapon sales to England and France.

By the mid-1930s an overwhelming majority of Americans thought that the United States should have stayed out of World War I and that the "mistake" of intervention should never be repeated. Congress responded by passing a series of Neutrality Acts in 1935–1937. To prevent a repetition of 1917, these measures outlawed arms sales and loans to nations at war and barred Americans from traveling on the ships of belligerent powers. Considering even these laws an insufficient safeguard against war, in 1938 Indiana congressman Louis Ludlow proposed a constitutional amendment requiring a national referendum on any U.S. declaration of war except in cases of direct attack. Only a direct appeal from FDR steeled Congress to reject the Ludlow Amendment by the narrowest of margins.

With American companies like IBM heavily invested in Nazi Germany, the sole confrontation with the fascist onslaught in the thirties came in the sports arena. At the 1936 Olympics in Berlin, African-American track star Jesse Owens made a mockery of Nazi theories of racial superiority by winning four gold medals and breaking or tying three world records. In 1938, in a boxing match laden with symbolism,

the black American Joe Louis knocked out German fighter Max Schmeling in the first round of their world heavyweight championship fight. Although Americans cheered Lewis, they still opposed any policies that might involve them in war.

The Gathering Storm: 1938–1939

The reduced tension that followed the Munich Pact proved tragically brief. "Peace in our time" lasted a mere 5 1/2 months. On March 15, 1939, Nazi troops occupied what remained of Czechoslovakia, violating the Munich accords. Five months later, Hitler reached an agreement with Stalin in the German-Soviet Nonaggression Pact that their nations would not fight one another and that they would divide Poland after Germany invaded it. No longer worried about a Soviet reaction, Hitler took aim on Poland despite claims by Britain and France that they would come to an invaded Poland's assistance.

Such actions intensified the debate over America's role abroad. Some warned that American involvement in war would destroy the reform impulse and spawn reaction, as it had a generation earlier. "The place to save democracy is at home," argued historian Carl Becker. But pacifist and neutralist opinion was weakening. Warning of the "cancerous spread" of fascism, critic Lewis Mumford issued "A Call to Arms" in the *New Republic*, exhorting Americans to mobilize against fascism.

President Roosevelt began to do so. After the fall of Czechoslovakia, he called for actions "short of war" to demonstrate America's will to check fascism, and he asked Hitler and Mussolini to pledge not to invade thirty-one listed nations. A jeering Hitler read FDR's message to an amused German Reichstag (legislative assembly), while in Rome Mussolini mocked Roosevelt's physical disability, joking that the president's paralysis must have reached his brain.

Roosevelt, however, did more than send messages. In October 1938 he asked Congress for a $300 million military appropriation; in November he instructed the Army Air Corps to plan for an annual production of twenty thousand planes; and in January 1939 he submitted a $1.3 billion defense budget. Hitler and Mussolini, the now-aroused president proclaimed, were "two madmen" who "respect force and force alone."

America and the Jewish Refugees

Hitler and the Nazis had used the power of the state and their own paramilitary organizations to assault German Jews, confiscate their property, and force them to emi-

Isolationism vs. Interventionism
In front of the White House in 1941, an American soldier grabs a sign from an isolationist picketing against the United States entering the war in Europe. A diverse group, isolationists ran the gamut from pacifists who opposed all wars, to progressives who feared the growth of business and centralized power that a war would bring, to ultra-rightists who sympathized with fascism and/or shared Hitler's anti-Semitism.

grate. The Nuremberg Laws of 1935 outlawed marriage and sexual intercourse between Jews and non-Jews, stripped Jews of the rights of German citizenship, and increased restrictions on Jews in all spheres of German educational, social, and economic life. This campaign of hatred reached a violent crescendo on November 9–10, 1938, when the Nazis unleashed *Kristallnacht* (Night of the Broken Glass), a frenzy of arson, destruction, and looting against Jews throughout Germany.

No longer could anyone mistake the perilous situation of German Jews or misunderstand Hitler's evil intent. Jews left Germany by the tens of thousands. Among those coming to the United States were hundreds of distinguished scholars, artists, and scientists including pianist Rudolph Serkin, architect Walter Gropius, political theorist Hannah Arendt, and future secretary of state Henry Kissinger. Among the many gifted physicists were Leo Szilard, James Franck, and Enrico Fermi, who would play key roles in building the atomic bomb. It is hard to imagine what the cultural, intellectual, and scientific achievements of the United States in the second half of the twentieth century would have been without the contributions of these refugees.

But the United States of the 1930s, in the grip of the depression and imbued with its own anti-Semitism, proved reluctant to grant sanctuary to the mass of Nazism's Jewish victims. Roosevelt did little other than deplore Hitler's persecution of the Jews, and Congress consistently rejected efforts to liberalize the immigration law or abolish its discriminatory quotas (see Chapter 23). Few Americans seemed bothered that the sixty thousand Jews admitted to the United States by the end of 1938 constituted just a tiny ripple of the refugee tide. When asked by pollsters that year whether the immigration law should be changed to admit "a larger number of Jewish refugees from Germany," 75 percent said no.

The consequences of such attitudes became clear in June 1939 when the *St. Louis*, a vessel jammed with nine hundred Jewish refugees, asked permission to put its passengers ashore at Fort Lauderdale, Florida. Immigration officials refused the request and, according to the *New York Times*, had a Coast Guard ship deployed "to prevent possible attempts by refugees to jump off and swim ashore." The *St. Louis* turned slowly away from the lights of America and sailed back to Germany, where the majority of its passengers would die at the hands of the Nazis.

INTO THE STORM, 1939–1941

After a decade of crises—worldwide depression and regional conflicts—war erupted in Europe in 1939. While initially relying on neutrality to keep America out of the war, President Roosevelt switched to economic intervention following the lightning German victories in western Europe in spring 1940. He knew that extending increasing amounts of aid to those resisting aggression by the so-called Rome-Berlin-Tokyo Axis, as well as his toughening conduct toward Germany and Japan, could, as he said, "push" the U.S. into the crisis of worldwide war. Japan's attack on the U.S. fleet at Pearl Harbor would provide the push.

The European War

Hitler began the war by demanding that Poland return the city of Danzig (Gdansk), taken from Germany after World War I. When Poland refused, Nazi troops poured into Poland on September 1, 1939. Two days later, Britain and France, honoring commitments to Poland, declared war on Germany. Although FDR invoked the Neutrality Acts, he would not ask Americans to be impartial in thought and deed (as had President Wilson in 1914).

Tailoring his actions to the public mood, which favored both preventing a Nazi victory and staying out of war, FDR persuaded Congress in November to amend the Neutrality Acts to allow the belligerents to purchase weapons from the United States if they paid cash and carried the arms away in their own ships. He assumed that "cash-and-carry" would mainly aid the Allies, given their control of the seas.

"Cash-and-carry" did not stop the Nazis. In spring 1940, after a winter lull that followed the defeat of Poland, Hitler's armies taught the world the meaning of *Blitzkrieg* (lightning war) as they quickly overwhelmed Denmark, Norway, Belgium, Holland, Luxembourg, and France and pinned the British army against the sea at Dunkirk. Narrowly escaping disaster, the British used every possible craft to evacuate their army and some French troops across the English Channel. By then, however, Hitler virtually controlled western Europe, and on June 22 he dictated France's surrender in the same spot and the same railway car in which Germany had surrendered in 1918.

Hitler now took aim at Great Britain. The *Luftwaffe* (German air force) intended to terror-bomb Britain into submission, or at least prepare the ground for a German invasion. Round-the-clock aerial assaults killed or wounded thousands of civilians, destroyed the city of Coventry, and reduced parts of London to rubble. Britain's new Prime Minister Winston Churchill, who replaced Chamberlain in May 1940, pleaded for more U.S. aid. Most Americans, shocked at the use of German air power against British civilians, wanted to give it to him. But a large and vocal minority opposed it as wasteful of materials needed for U.S. defenses or as a ruse to draw Americans into a war not vital to their interests.

From Isolation to Intervention

In the United States in 1940, news of the "battle of Britain" competed with speculation about whether FDR would break with tradition and run for an unprecedented third term. Not until the eve of the Democrats' July convention did he reveal that, given the world crisis, he would consent to being drafted by his party. The sense of being at a critical moment in world affairs clinched his renomination and forced conservative Democrats to accept the very liberal Henry Wallace, FDR's former secretary of agriculture, as his running mate. Republicans bowed to the public mood by nominating an all-out internationalist who championed greater aid to Britain, Wendell Willkie of Indiana.

With the GOP uncertain how to oppose Roosevelt effectively, FDR played the role of the crisis leader too

busy to engage in politics. He appointed Republicans Henry Stimson and Frank Knox as secretaries of war and the navy. He signed the Selective Service and Training Act, the first peacetime draft in U.S. history, and approved an enormous increase in spending for rearmament. With Willkie's support, FDR engineered a "destroyers-for-bases" swap with England, sending fifty vintage ships to Britain in exchange for leases on British naval and air bases in the Western Hemisphere. Although FDR pictured the agreement as a way to keep the country out of war, it infuriated isolationists.

In the 1930s the isolationist camp had included prominent figures from both major parties and both the Right and Left. But in 1940 the arch-conservative America First Committee was isolationism's dominant voice. Largely financed by Henry Ford, the committee featured pacifist Charles Lindbergh as its most popular speaker. It insisted that "Fortress America" could stand alone. But a majority of Americans supported Roosevelt's effort to assist Great Britain while staying out of war. Reassured by the president's promise never to "send an American boy to fight in a European war," 55 percent of the voters chose to give Roosevelt a third term.

Calling on the United States to be the "great arsenal of democracy," Roosevelt now proposed a "lend-lease" program to supply war materiel to cash-strapped Britain. While Roosevelt likened the plan to loaning a garden hose to a neighbor whose house was on fire, isolationist Senator Robert Taft compared it to chewing gum: after a neighbor uses it, "you don't want it back." A large majority of Americans supported lend-lease, however, and Congress approved the bill in March 1941, abolishing the "cash" provision of the Neutrality Acts and allowing the president to lend or lease supplies to any nation deemed "vital to the defense of the United States." Shipments to England began at once, and after Hitler invaded the USSR in June, U.S. war supplies flowed to the Soviet Union as well, despite American hostility toward communism. To defeat Hitler, FDR confided, "I would hold hands with the Devil."

In April 1941, to counter the menace of German submarines to the transatlantic supply line, Roosevelt authorized the U.S. navy to help the British track U-boats. In mid-summer the navy began convoying British ships carrying lend-lease supplies, with orders to destroy enemy vessels if necessary to protect the shipments. U.S. forces also occupied Greenland and Iceland to keep those strategic Danish islands out of Nazi hands.

In August Roosevelt met with Churchill aboard a warship off the coast of Newfoundland to map strategy. They issued a document, the Atlantic Charter, that condemned international aggression, affirmed the right of national self-determination, and endorsed the principles of free trade, disarmament, and collective security. Providing the ideological foundation of the anti-Axis cause, the Charter envisioned a postwar world in which the peoples of "all the lands may live out their lives in freedom from fear and want."

After a U-boat torpedoed and sank the *Reuben James*, killing 115 American sailors, Roosevelt persuaded Congress in November to permit the arming of merchant ships and their entry into belligerent ports in war zones. Virtually nothing now remained of the Neutrality Acts. Unprepared for a major war, America was already fighting a limited one, and full-scale war seemed imminent.

Pearl Harbor and the Coming of War

Hitler's triumphs in western Europe encouraged Japan to expand farther into Asia. Seeing Germany as its primary danger, the Roosevelt administration tried to apply just enough pressure to frighten off the Japanese without provoking Tokyo to war before the United States had built the "two-ocean navy" authorized by Congress in 1940. "It is terribly important for the control of the Atlantic for us to keep peace in the Pacific," Roosevelt told Harold Ickes in mid-1941. "I simply have not got enough navy to go around—and every episode in the Pacific means fewer ships in the Atlantic."

Both Japan and the United States hoped to avoid war, but neither would compromise. Japan's desire to create a Greater East Asia Co-Prosperity Sphere (an empire embracing much of China, Southeast Asia, and the western Pacific) matched America's insistence on the Open Door in China and status quo in the rest of Asia. Japan saw the U.S. stand as a ploy to block its rise to world power; and the United States viewed Japan's talk of legitimate national aspirations as a smoke screen to hide aggression. Decades of "yellow peril" propaganda had hardened American attitudes toward Japan. Widely depicted in American media as bowlegged little people with buck teeth and thick spectacles, the Japanese appeared pushovers for the American navy. With isolationists as virulently anti-Japanese as internationalists, no significant groups organized to prevent a war with Japan.

The two nations became locked in a deadly dance. In 1940, believing that economic coercion would force the Japanese out of China, the United States ended a long-standing trade treaty with Japan and banned the sale of aviation fuel and scrap metal to it. Tokyo responded by occupying northern Indochina, a French colony, and signing the Tripartite Pact with Germany and Italy in September, creating a military alliance, the

Berlin-Rome-Tokyo Axis, that required each government to help the others in the event of a U.S. attack.

With the French and Dutch defeated by Germany, and Britain with its back to the wall, Japan gambled on a war for hegemony in the western Pacific. It chose to conquer new lands to obtain the resources it needed rather than retreat from China to gain a resumption of trade with the United States. Fatefully, Japan overran the rest of Indochina in July 1941. In turn, expecting that firmness would more likely deter Japan than provoke her to war, FDR froze all Japanese assets in the United States, imposed a new fuel embargo, and clamped a total ban on trade with Japan. But as Japan's fuel meters dropped toward empty, the expansionist General Hideki Tojo replaced a more conciliatory prime minister in October. Tojo set the first week in December as a deadline for a preemptive attack if the United States did not yield.

By late November U.S. intelligence's deciphering of Japan's top diplomatic code alerted the Roosevelt administration that war was imminent. Negotiators made no concessions, however, during the eleventh-hour talks under way in Washington. "I have washed my hands of it," Secretary of State Hull told Secretary of War Stimson on November 27, "and it is now in the hands of you and Knox—the Army and the Navy." War warnings went out to all commanders in the Pacific, advising that negotiations were deadlocked and that a Japanese attack was expected. But where? U.S. officials assumed that the Japanese offensive would continue southward, striking Malaya or the Philippines. The Japanese banked on a knockout punch; they believed that a surprise raid on Pearl Harbor would destroy America's Pacific fleet and compel a Roosevelt preoccupied with Germany to seek accommodation with Japan.

On Sunday morning, December 7, 1941, Japanese dive-bombers and torpedo planes attacked the U.S. fleet at anchor in Pearl Harbor on the Hawaiian island of Oahu. Pounding the harbor and nearby airfields, the Japanese sank or crippled nearly a score of warships, destroyed or damaged some 350 aircraft, killed more than 2,400 Americans, and wounded another 1,200. American forces suffered their most devastating loss in history, and simultaneous attacks by Japan on the Philippines, Malaya, and Hong Kong opened the way for Japan's advance on Australia.

Some critics later charged that Roosevelt knew the attack on Pearl Harbor was coming and deliberately left the fleet exposed in order to bring the United States into the war against Germany. There is no conclusive evidence to support this accusation. Roosevelt and his advisers knew that war was close but did not expect an assault on Pearl Harbor. Neither did the U.S. military officials at Pearl Harbor, who took precautions only against possible sabotage by the Japanese in Hawaii. In part because of their own prejudices, Americans underestimated the resourcefulness, skill, and daring of the Japanese. They simply did not believe that Japan would attack an American stronghold nearly five thousand miles from its home base. At the same time, Japanese leaders counted on a paralyzing blow to compel the soft, weak-willed Americans, unready for a two-ocean war, to compromise rather than fight. That miscalculation ensured Roosevelt an aroused and united nation determined to avenge the attack that, he said, "will live in infamy."

On December 8 Congress approved a declaration of war against Japan. (The only dissenter was Montana's Jeannette Rankin, who had also cast a nay vote against U.S. entry into World War I.) Three days later, honoring Germany's treaty obligation to Japan, Hitler declared war on the "half Judaized and the other half Negrified" American people; Mussolini followed suit. Congress immediately reciprocated without a dissenting vote. The United States faced a global war that it was not ready to fight.

After Pearl Harbor, U-boats wreaked havoc in the North Atlantic and prowled the Caribbean and the East Coast of the United States. Every twenty-four hours, five more Allied vessels went to the bottom. German submarines even bottled up the Chesapeake Bay for nearly six weeks. By the end of 1942, U-boat "wolf packs" had sunk more than a thousand Allied ships, offsetting the pace of American ship production. The United States was losing the Battle of the Atlantic.

The war news from Europe and Africa, as Roosevelt admitted, was also "all bad." Hitler had painted the swastika across an enormous swath of territory, from the outskirts of Moscow and Leningrad—a thousand miles deep into Russia—to the Pyrenees on the Spanish-French border, and from northern Norway to the Libyan desert. In North Africa the German Afrika Korps swept toward Cairo and the Suez Canal, the British oil lifeline. It seemed as if the Mediterranean would become an Axis sea and that Hitler would be in India to greet Tojo marching across Asia before the United States was ready to fight.

Japan followed its attack on Pearl Harbor by seizing Guam, Wake Island, Singapore, Burma, and the Dutch East Indies. Having pushed the U.S. garrison on the Philippines first onto the Bataan peninsula and then onto the tiny island of Corregidor, Japan took more than eleven thousand American soldiers prisoner early in

Remember Pearl Harbor

At Minneapolis's Northern Pump Co., nightshift workers heralded the new year 1942 with a demonstration of national unity and determination. Rather than resorting to drafting workers or compelling them to work in certain areas, the government relied primarily on what FDR called "voluntary cooperation" to fill the labor shortages in war-related jobs.

May 1942. Japan's Rising Sun blazed over hundreds of islands in the Pacific and over the entire eastern perimeter of the Asian mainland from the border of Siberia to the border of India.

AMERICA MOBILIZES FOR WAR

In December 1941 American armed forces numbered just 1.6 million, and only 15 percent of industrial output was going to war production. Finally committed to full involvement in the world crisis, the United States now had to harness all the strengths and resources of the nation and the American people. Congress passed a War Powers Act granting the president unprecedented authority over all aspects of the conduct of the war. Volunteers and draftees swelled the armed forces; by war's end more than 15 million men and nearly 350,000 women would serve. More would work in defense industries. Mobilization required unprecedented coordination of the American government, economy, and military. In 1942 those responsible for managing America's growing war machine moved into the world's largest building, the newly constructed Pentagon. Like the Pentagon, which was intended to house civilian agencies after the war, American attitudes, behavior, and institutions would also be significantly altered by far-reaching wartime domestic changes.

Organizing for Victory

To direct the military engine, Roosevelt formed the Joint Chiefs of Staff, made up of representatives of the army, navy, and army air force. (Only a minor "corps" within the army as late as June 1941, the air force would grow more dramatically than any other branch of the service, achieve virtual autonomy, and play a vital role in combat strategy.) The changing nature of modern warfare also led to the creation of the Office of Strategic Services (OSS), forerunner of the Central Intelligence Agency, to conduct the espionage required for strategic planning.

To organize the conversion of American industry to war production, Roosevelt established a host of new government agencies. The War Production Board (WPB) allocated materials, limited the production of civilian goods, and distributed contracts among manufacturers. The War Manpower Commission (WMC) supervised the mobilization of men and women for the military, agriculture, and industry, while the National War Labor Board (NWLB) mediated disputes between management and labor. Finally, the Office of Price Administration (OPA) rationed scarce products and imposed price controls to check inflation. Late in 1942 FDR persuaded Justice James F. Byrnes to leave the Supreme Court to become his "assistant president" in charge of the domestic war effort, and in May 1943 he formally appointed him to head the new Office of War

Mobilization (OWM), which coordinated the production, procurement, transportation, and distribution of civilian and military supplies. "If you want something done, go see Jimmie Byrnes," understood those in the know.

"The Americans can't build planes," a Nazi commander had jeered, "only electric iceboxes and razor blades." But soon after February 1942, when the last civilian car came off an assembly line, the United States achieved a miracle of war production. Auto makers retooled to produce planes and tanks; a merry-go-round factory switched to fashioning gun mounts; a pinball-machine maker converted to armor-piercing shells. By late 1942 a third of the economy was committed to war production, equaling the military output of Germany, Italy, and Japan combined. Whole new industries appeared virtually overnight. With almost all of the nation's crude-rubber supply now in Japanese-controlled territory, the government built some fifty new synthetic-rubber plants. By the end of the war, the United States, once the world's largest importer of crude rubber, had become the world's largest exporter of synthetic rubber.

America also became the world's greatest weapons' manufacturer, producing twice as much war material than all its Axis enemies by 1944. "To American production," Stalin would toast FDR and Churchill, "without which the war would have been lost." Indeed, the three hundred thousand military aircraft, 2.6 million machine guns, 6 million tons of bombs, and more than five thousand cargo ships and eighty-six thousand warships assembled by Americans did essentially win the war for the United States and its allies. Henry J. Kaiser, who had supervised the construction of Boulder Dam, introduced prefabrication to cut the time needed to produce a Liberty-class merchant ship from six months in 1941 to less than two weeks in 1943, and then just ten days. In 1945 Kaiser, dubbed "Sir Launchalot," and other shipbuilders were completing a cargo ship a day.

Such breakneck production had its costs. The size and powers of the government swelled as defense spending zoomed from 9 percent of the GNP in 1940 to 46 percent in 1945 and the budget soared from $9 billion to $98 billion. The number of federal civilian employees mushroomed from 1.1 million to 3.8 million. The executive branch, directing the war effort, grew the most; and an alliance formed between the defense industry and the military. (A generation later, Americans would call these concentrations of power the "imperial presidency" and the "military-industrial complex.") Because the government sought the greatest volume of war production in the shortest possible time, it encouraged corporate profits. "If you are going to try to go to war in a capitalist country," Secretary of War Stimson pointed out, "you have to let business make money out of the process or business won't work."

"Dr. New Deal," in FDR's words, gave way to "Dr. Win the War." To encourage business to convert to war production and expand its capacity, the government guaranteed profits, provided generous tax write-offs and subsidies, and suspended antitrust prosecutions. America's ten biggest corporations got a third of the war contracts, and two-thirds of all war-production spending went to the hundred largest firms, greatly accelerating trends toward economic concentration.

The War Economy

The United States spent more than $320 billion ($250 million a day) to defeat the Axis—ten times more than the cost of World War I in real dollars and nearly twice the amount that had been spent by the government since its founding. This massive expenditure ended the depression and stimulated an industrial boom that brought prosperity to most American workers. It doubled U.S. industrial output and the per capita GNP, created 17 million new jobs, increased corporate after-tax profits by 70 percent, and raised the real wages or purchasing power of industrial workers by 50 percent (see Figure 25.1).

The government poured nearly $40 billion into the West, more than any other region, and four times as much as it had in the preceding decade, making the West an economic powerhouse. California alone secured more than 10 percent of all federal funds, and by 1945 nearly half the personal income in the state came from expenditures by the federal government.

A newly prospering South also contributed to the emergence of a dynamic Sunbelt. In an arc stretching from the Southeast to the Southwest, the billions spent by Uncle Sam meant millions of jobs in the textile, oil and natural gas, chemical, and aluminum industries, as well as in the shipyards of Norfolk, Mobile, and New Orleans, and the aircraft plants in Dallas-Fort Worth and Marietta, Georgia. The South's industrial capacity increased by 40 percent, and per capita income tripled. Boom times enabled hundreds of thousands of sharecroppers and farm tenants to leave the land for better-paying industrial jobs. While the South's farm population decreased by 20 percent in the 1940s, its urban population grew 36 percent.

Full employment, longer workweeks, larger paychecks, and the increased hiring of minorities, women, the elderly, and teenagers made the United States a truly

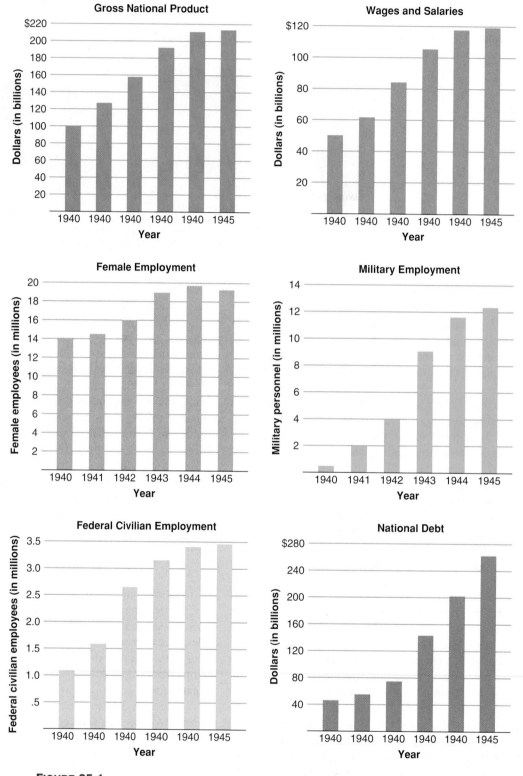

FIGURE 25.1
U.S. Wartime Production
Between 1941 and 1945, the economy grew at a remarkable pace.

Producing for Victory
The 1942 dual launching of warships at Charleston, South Carolina, Navy Yard. By war's end the United States had built almost 100,000 new ships of one kind or another.

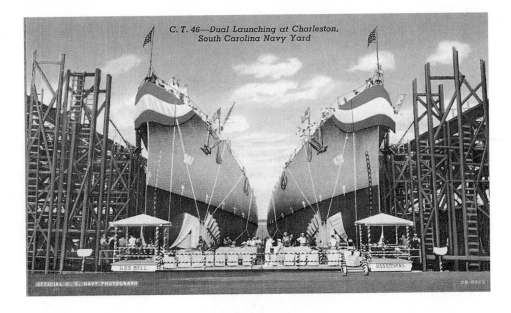

C. T. 46—Dual Launching at Charleston, South Carolina Navy Yard

U.S.S BELL   U.S.S STEVENS.

OFFICIAL U. S. NAVY PHOTOGRAPH   2R-R853

middle-class nation. In California the demand for workers in the shipyards and aircraft factories opened opportunities for thousands of Chinese-Americans previously confined to menial jobs in their own communities. In San Diego 40 percent of retirees returned to work. Deafening factories hired the hearing-impaired, and aircraft plants employed dwarfs as inspectors because of their ability to crawl inside small spaces. The war years produced the only significant twentieth-century shift in the distribution of income toward greater equality. The earnings of the bottom fifth of all workers rose 68 percent, and those of the middle class doubled. The richest 5 percent, conversely, saw their share of total disposable income drop from 23 to 17 percent.

Large-scale commercial farmers prospered as a result of higher consumer prices and increased productivity, thanks to improved fertilizers and more mechanization. As the consolidation of small farms into fewer large ones proceeded, commercial farming became dominated by corporations. Organized agriculture (later called agribusiness) took its seat in the council of power, alongside big government, big business, and organized labor.

Labor-union membership leaped from 9 million in 1940 to 14.8 million in 1945 (35 percent of nonagricultural employment). This growth resulted from the huge increase in the work force and the NWLB's "maintenance-of-membership" rule, which automatically enrolled new workers in unions and required workers to retain their union membership through the life of a contract. In return, unions agreed not to strike and to limit wage increases to 15 percent. In lieu of higher pay, they negotiated unprecedented fringe benefits for their members, including paid vacation time, health insurance, and pension plans.

Only a tiny minority of unionists broke the no-strike pledge. Most were "wildcat strikes," not authorized by union officials, and of brief duration. All told, strikes amounted to less than one-tenth of 1 percent of wartime working hours, barely affecting war production. In the most glaring exception, John L. Lewis, the iron-willed head of the United Mine Workers (UMW), led more than half a million coal-field workers out of the pits three times in 1943. Although the miners won wage concessions, their victory cost the union movement dearly. Many states passed laws to limit union power and, over Roosevelt's veto, Congress passed the Smith-Connally War Labor Disputes Act of 1943, which empowered the president to take over any facility where strikes interrupted war production.

Far more than strikes, inflation threatened the wartime economy. Throughout 1942 prices climbed by 2 percent a month as a result of the combination of increased spending power and a scarcity of consumer goods. At the end of the year, Congress gave the president authority to control wages, prices, and rents, and as the OPA clamped down, inflation slowed dramatically. Consumer prices rose just 8 percent during the last two years of war.

The OPA also instituted rationing to combat inflation and conserve scarce materials,. Under the slogan "Use it up, wear it out, make it do or do without," the OPA rationed gasoline, coffee, sugar, butter, cheese, and meat. Americans endured "meatless Tuesdays" and cuffless trousers, ate sherbet instead of ice cream, and put up with imitation chocolate that tasted like soap and

imitation soap that did not lather. American men and women planted 20 million victory gardens, served as air-raid wardens, and organized collection drives to recycle cooking grease and used paper and tires, while their children, known as "Uncle Sam's Scrappers" and "Tin-Can Colonels," scoured their neighborhoods for scrap metal and other valuable trash.

Buying war bonds further curtailed inflation by decreasing consumer purchasing power, while giving civilians a sense of involvement in the distant war. The sale of bonds—"bullets in the bellies of Hitler's hordes!" claimed the Treasury department—to schoolchildren, small investors, and corporations raised almost half the money needed to finance the war. Roosevelt sought to raise the rest by drastically increasing taxes. Congress refused the president much of what he sought. Still, the Revenue Act of 1942 raised the top income-tax rate from 60 percent to 94 percent and imposed income taxes on middle-and lower-income Americans for the first time, quadrupling the number of people who paid taxes. Beginning in 1943, the payroll-deduction system automatically withheld income taxes from wages and salaries. By 1945 the federal government was taking in nearly twenty times the tax revenue that it had in 1940.

"A Wizard War"

Winston Churchill labeled the conflict "a wizard war" in tribute to the importance of wartime scientific and technological developments. As never before, the major combatants mobilized scientists into virtually armies of invention. Their labors brought forth both miracles in healing and advances in the technology of killing, as well as a new faith that the minds of engineers and scientists, plus enough money, could overcome any obstacles.

In early 1941 Roosevelt had formed a committee to organize scientists for a weapons race against the Axis, and created the Office of Scientific Research and Development (OSRD) for the development of new ordnance. OSRD spent more than $1 billion to generate radar and sonar devices, rocket weapons, and bomb fuses. It advanced the development of jet aircraft and high-altitude bombsights, and its employment of scientists to devise methods for utilizing new weapons resulted in a brand-new field called operational analysis. The need to improve military radar spurred the development of the laser, while research in quantum physics to build atomic bombs later became the basis for transistors and semiconductors. The need to supply rapidly advancing troops with unspoiled food resulted in the instant mashed potatoes we eat today.

The quest for greater accuracy in ordnance, moreover, required the kind of rapid, detailed calculations that only computing machines could supply. So a half-dozen teams of scientists went to work in 1942 to develop what would become the earliest computers. By mid-1944 navy personnel in the basement of Harvard's physics laboratory were operating IBM's Automatic Sequence Controlled Calculator, known as Mark I—a cumbersome device 51 feet long and 8 feet high that weighed five tons, used 530 miles of wire, and contained 760,000 parts. ENIAC, developed to improve artillery accuracy for the army, reduced the time required to multiply two tenth-place numbers from Mark I's three seconds to less than three-thousandths of a second.

Military needs also hastened improvements in blood-transfusion and blood-banking techniques, heart and lung surgery, and the use of synthetic drugs to substitute for scarce quinine and toxoid vaccine to prevent tetanus. So-called miracle drugs, antibiotics to combat infections, a rarity on the eve of war, would be copiously produced. The military, which had only enough penicillin for about a hundred patients at the Battle of Midway in June 1942, had enough for all major casualties by D-Day in June 1944, and far more than it could use by V-J Day in August 1945, allowing the beginning of the sale of penicillin for civilian use.

Insecticides initially seemed as much a miracle. The use of DDT cleared many islands of malaria-carrying mosquitoes, like those that in 1942 had infected more than half the men of the First Marine Division, forcing it to be withdrawn from the Pacific war. DDT also stopped an incipient typhus epidemic in Naples in January 1944. Along with innovations like the Mobile Auxiliary Surgical Hospital (MASH), science helped save tens of thousands of lives, halving the World War I death rate of wounded soldiers who reached medical installations. It improved the health of the nation as well. Life expectancy rose by three years during the war, and infant mortality fell by more than a third.

No scientific endeavor had a higher priority than the Manhattan Project to develop the atomic bomb. In August 1939 physicist Albert Einstein, a Jewish refugee, warned Roosevelt that German scientists were seeking to construct a weapon of extraordinary destructiveness. The president promptly established an advisory committee and in late 1941 launched an Anglo-American secret program—the Soviets were excluded—to produce atomic bombs. In 1942 the participating physicists, both Americans and Europeans, achieved a controlled atomic reaction under the University of Chicago football stadium, the first step toward developing the bomb. In

1943–1944 the Manhattan Engineer District—the code name for the atomic project—stockpiled uranium-235 at Oak Ridge, Tennessee, and plutonium at Hanford, Washington. In 1945 engineers and scientists headquartered in Los Alamos, New Mexico, assembled two bombs utilizing those fissionable materials. By then the Manhattan Project had employed more than 120,000 people and spent nearly $2 billion.

Just before dawn on July 16, 1945, a blinding fireball with "the brightness of several suns at midday" rose over the Alamogordo, New Mexico, desert at a test site named Trinity. A huge, billowing mushroom cloud soon towered 40,000 feet above the ground. With a force of twenty thousand tons of TNT, the blast shattered windows more than 120 miles away. "A few people laughed, a few people cried," recalled J. Robert Oppenheimer, the Manhattan Project's scientific director. "Most people were silent. I remembered the line from the Hindu scripture, the Bhagavad-Gita: 'Now I am become Death, the destroyer of worlds.' " A new era had dawned.

Propaganda and Politics

People as well as science and machinery had to be mobilized for the global conflict. To sustain a spirit of unity and fan the fires of patriotism, the Roosevelt administration managed public opinion. The Office of Censorship examined letters going overseas and worked with publishers and broadcasters to suppress information that might hinder the war effort. A year passed before casualty and damage figures from Pearl Harbor were disclosed. Fearful of demoralizing the public, the government banned the publication of photographs of American war dead until 1943. Then, concerned that the public had become overconfident, the media was prompted to display pictures of American servicemen killed by the enemy and to emphasize accounts of Japan's atrocities against American prisoners.

To shape public opinion and sell the faraway war to the American people, Roosevelt created the Office of War Information (OWI) in June 1942. The OWI employed more than four thousand artists, writers, and advertising specialists to explain the war and counter enemy propaganda. The OWI depicted the war as a mortal struggle between good and evil and harped on the necessity of totally destroying, not merely defeating, the enemy.

Hollywood answered the OWI directive—"Will this help win the war?"—by highlighting the heroism and unity of the American forces, while inciting hatred of the enemy. Films about the war portrayed the Japanese, in particular, as treacherous and cruel, as beasts in the jungle, as "slant-eyed rats." Jukeboxes blared songs like "We're Gonna Have to Slap the Dirty Little Jap." U.S. propaganda also presented the war as a struggle to preserve the "American way of life," usually depicted in images of small-town, middle-class, white Americans enjoying a bountiful consumer society.

While the Roosevelt administration concentrated on the war, Republican critics seized the initiative in domestic politics. Full employment and higher wages undercut the appeal of the New Deal, and resentment over wartime shortages and dismay over Axis victories further weakened the Democrats. With voter turnout low because many soldiers and defense workers were far from the hometowns where they had registered and were thus unable to vote, the Republicans gained forty-four seats in the House and nine in the Senate in 1942.

All Have a Role to Play

This poster by the famous artist Thomas Hart Benton emphasized the need for all Americans to do their part in winning the war—by buying was bonds and laboring in factories and fields, as well as by fighting in the armed forces and, not incidently, contributing their artistic talents.

Politics shifted to the Right. The conservative coalition of Republicans and southern Democrats abolished some New Deal agencies, such as the WPA and CCC, drastically curtailed others, and rebuffed the adoption of new liberal programs. But the dynamics of the war enormously expanded governmental power, especially the power of the executive branch. As never before, the federal government managed the economy, molded public opinion, funded scientific research, and influenced people's daily lives.

THE BATTLEFRONT, 1942–1944

Following the Japanese attack on Pearl Harbor, the outlook for the Allies appeared critical. Then America's industrial might and Soviet manpower turned the tides of war. Diplomacy followed the tides of war in its wake. Allied unity dwindled as Germany and Japan weakened. As the United States, Soviet Union, and Great Britain each sought wartime strategies and postwar arrangements best suited to its own interests, the Allies sowed the seeds of a postwar crisis.

Liberating Europe

Although British and American officials agreed to concentrate on defeating Germany first and then smashing Japan, they differed on where to attack. While German U-boats sank Allied ships at an appalling rate in early 1942, Hitler's forces advanced toward the Suez Canal in Egypt and penetrated deeper into the Soviet Union. Roosevelt sought to placate Stalin, who demanded a second front in western Europe to relieve the pressure on the Soviet Union, which faced the full fury of two hundred German divisions. But Churchill, fearing a repeat of the World War I slaughter in the trenches of France and wanting American assistance in maintaining British control of the vital Suez Canal, persuaded FDR to postpone the "second front" in Europe and invade North Africa instead. In Operation Torch, begun in November 1942, American forces under U.S. General Dwight D. Eisenhower pressed eastward from Morocco and Algeria. General Bernard Montgomery's British troops, which had stopped the Germans at El Alamein in Egypt and then advanced westward toward Tunisia, caught the retreating army of Field Marshall Erwin Rommel in a vise and forced some 260,000 German and Italian troops to surrender, despite Hitler's orders to fight to the death (see Map 25.3).

The Soviet Union proved to be the graveyard of the Wehrmacht (German army). In the turning point of the European war, the Russians defeated the Germans in the protracted Battle of Stalingrad (August 1942–January 1943; see Map 25.3). As the Russian snow turned red with blood (costing each side more battle deaths in half a year than the United States suffered in the entire war), and its hills strewn with human bones became "white fields," Soviet forces saved Stalingrad, defended Moscow, and relieved besieged Leningrad.

Stalin pleaded again for a second front; Churchill objected again; and again Roosevelt gave in to Churchill, agreeing to invade Sicily. In summer 1943, after a month of fighting, the Allies seized Sicily and landed in southern Italy. Italian military officials deposed Mussolini and surrendered to the Allies in early September. But as Allied forces moved up the Italian peninsula, German troops poured into Italy. Facing elite Nazi divisions in strong defensive positions, the Allies spent eight months inching their way 150 miles to Rome. They were still battling through the mud and snow of northern Italy when the war in Europe ended in 1945.

In 1943–1944 the Allies turned the tide in the Atlantic and instituted round-the-clock bombardment of Germany. American science and industry developed sophisticated radar and sonar systems and better torpedoes and depth charges, and produced ever-increasing quantities of destroyers and aircraft. Britain's Royal Air Force by night and the U.S. army air force by day rained thousands of tons of bombs on German cities. In raids on Hamburg in July 1943 Allied planes dropped incendiary bombs mixed with high explosives, killing nearly a hundred thousand people and leveling the city, much as they had earlier done to Cologne and would do to Dresden in February 1945, where an estimated sixty thousand people died and another thirty-seven thousand were injured.

Meanwhile, in July 1943 German and Soviet divisions fought the largest tank battle in history near the city of Kursk in the Ukraine, and the victorious Red Army began an offensive that rid the Soviet Union of Germans by mid-1944. It then plunged into Poland and established a puppet government, took control of Romania and Bulgaria, and assisted communist guerrillas led by Josip Broz Tito in liberating Yugoslavia.

As the Soviets swept across eastern Europe, Allied forces finally opened the long-delayed second front. Early on the morning of June 6, 1944—D-Day—nearly two hundred thousand American, British, and Canadian troops, accompanied by six hundred warships and more than ten thousand planes, stormed a sixty-mile stretch

"Full Victory— Nothing Else!" Commander-in-Chief of the Allied Expeditionary Force General Dwight D. ("Ike") Eisenhower gives the order of the day to U.S. paratroopers in England on the eve of D-Day.

of the Normandy coast in the largest amphibious invasion in history. Led by General Eisenhower, now Supreme Commander of the Allied Expeditionary Force in Western Europe, Operation Overlord gradually pushed inland, securing the low countries, liberating Paris, and approaching the border of Germany. There, in the face of supply problems and stiffened German resistance, the Allied offensive ground to a halt. In mid-December, as the Allies prepared for a full-scale assault on Germany, Hitler threw his last reserves against Americans in the forest of Ardennes. The Battle of the Bulge—named for the eighty-mile-long and fifty-mile-wide "bulge" that the German troops drove inside the American lines—raged for nearly a month, and ended

MAP 25.3
World War II in Europe and Africa
The momentous German defeats at Stalingrad and in Tunisia early in 1943 marked the turning point in the war against the Axis. By 1945 Allied conquest of Hitler's "thousand-year" Reich was imminent.

with American forces on the banks of the Rhine, the German Army depleted, and the end of the European war in sight.

War in the Pacific

The day after the Philippines fell to Japan in mid-May 1942, the U.S. and Japanese fleets clashed in the Coral Sea off northeastern Australia in the first battle in history fought entirely by planes from aircraft carriers (see Map 25.4). Each lost a carrier, but the battle stymied the Japanese advance on Australia.

Less than a month later, a Japanese armada, eager to knock the Americans out of the war, headed toward Midway Island, a crucial American outpost between Hawaii and Japan. The U.S. Signal Corps, however, had broken the Japanese naval code. Knowing the plans and locations of Japan's ships, the U.S. carriers and planes won a decisive victory, sinking four Japanese carriers and destroying hundreds of planes. Suddenly on the defensive, the stunned Japanese could now only try to hold what they had already won.

On the offensive, U.S. marines waded ashore at Guadalcanal in the Solomon Islands in August 1942. Facing fierce resistance as well such tropical diseases as malaria, the Americans needed six months to take the island, a bitter preview of the battles to come. As the British moved from India to retake Burma, the United States began a two-pronged advance toward Japan in 1943. The army, under General Douglas MacArthur, advanced north on the islands between Australia and the Philippines, and the navy and marines, under

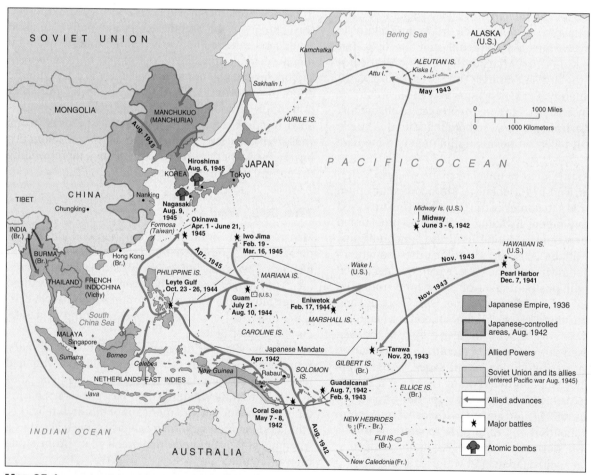

MAP 25.4
World War II in the Pacific
American ships and planes stemmed the Japanese offensive at the Battles of the Coral Sea and Midway Island. Thereafter, the Japanese were on the defensive against American amphibious assaults and air strikes.

Admiral Chester Nimitz, "island-hopped" across the central Pacific to seize strategic bases and put Tokyo in range of American bombers. In fall 1944 the navy annihilated what remained of the Japanese fleet at the battles of the Philippine Sea and Leyte Gulf, giving the United States control of Japan's air and shipping lanes and leaving the Japanese home islands open to invasion.

The Grand Alliance

President Roosevelt had two main goals for the war: the total defeat of the Axis at the least possible cost in American lives, and the establishment of a world order strong enough to preserve peace, open trade, and ensure national self-determination in the postwar era. Aware that only a common enemy fused the Grand Alliance together, Roosevelt tried to promote harmony by concentrating on military victory and postponing divisive postwar matters.

Churchill and Stalin had other goals. Britain wanted to create a balance of power in Europe and retain its imperial possessions. As Churchill said, he had "not become the King's First Minister to preside over the liquidation of the British Empire." The Soviet Union wanted a permanently weakened Germany and a sphere of influence in eastern Europe to protect itself against future attacks from the West. To hold together this fragile alliance, FDR relied on personal diplomacy to mediate conflicts.

The first president to travel by plane while in office, Roosevelt arrived in Casablanca, Morocco's main port, in January 1943 to confer with Churchill. They resolved to attack Italy before invading France and proclaimed that the war would continue until the "unconditional surrender" of the Axis. By so doing, they sought to reduce Soviet mistrust of the West, which had deepened because of the postponement of the second front. Ten months later, in Cairo, Roosevelt met with Churchill and Jiang Jieshi (Chiang Kai-shek), the anticommunist head of the Chinese government. To keep China in the war, FDR promised the return of Manchuria and Taiwan to China and a "free and independent Korea." From Cairo, FDR and Churchill continued on to Tehran, Iran's capital, to meet with Stalin. Here they set the invasion of France for June 1944, and agreed to divide Germany into zones of occupation and to impose reparations on the Reich. Most importantly to Roosevelt, Stalin pledged to enter the war against Japan after Hitler's defeat.

Roosevelt then turned his attention to domestic politics. Increasing conservative sentiment in the nation led him to drop the liberal Henry A. Wallace from the ticket and accept Harry S. Truman as his vice-presidential candidate. A moderate senator from Missouri now dubbed "the new Missouri Compromise," Truman restored a semblance of unity to the Democrats for the 1944 campaign. To compete, the Republicans nominated moderate and noncontroversial New York governor Thomas E. Dewey. The campaign focused more on personalities than on issues, and the still-popular FDR defeated his dull GOP opponent, but with the narrowest margin since 1916—winning just 53 percent of the popular vote. A weary Roosevelt, secretly suffering from hypertension and heart disease, now directed his waning energies toward defeating the Axis and constructing an international peacekeeping system.

WAR AND AMERICAN SOCIETY

The crisis of war altered the most basic patterns of American life, powerfully affecting those on the home front as well as those who served in the armed forces. Few families were untouched: more than 15 million Americans went to the war, an equal number were on the move, and unprecedented numbers of women went to work outside the home. As well, the war opened some doors of opportunity for African Americans and other minorities, although most remained closed. It heightened minority aspirations and widened cracks in the wall of white racist attitudes and policy, while maintaining much of America's racial caste system, thereby tilling the ground for future crises.

The GIs' War

Most Americans in the armed forces griped about regimentation and were more interested in dry socks than in ideology. They knew little of the big strategies, and cared less. They fought because they were told to and wanted to stay alive. Reluctant recruits rather than heroic warriors, most had few aims beyond returning to a safe, familiar United States.

But the GIs' war dragged on for almost four years, transforming them in the process. Millions who had never been far from home traveled to unfamiliar cities and remote lands, shedding their parochialism. Sharing tents and foxholes with Americans of different religions, ethnicities, and classes, their military service acted as a "melting pot" experience that freed them from some prewar prejudices.

In countless ways, the war modified how GIs saw themselves and others. Besides serving with people they had never previously encountered, over a million mar-

ried overseas, broadening personal horizons and sowing the seeds of a more tolerant and diverse national culture that placed far less emphasis on divisions of class, national origin, region, and religion. At the same time many GIs became evermore distrustful of foreigners and outsiders, and returned home obsessed with the flag as a symbol of patriotism.

Physical misery, chronic exhaustion, and, especially, intense combat took a heavy toll, leaving lasting psychological as well as physical wounds. Both American and Japanese troops saw the other in racist images, as animals to be exterminated, and brutality became as much the rule as the exception in "a war without mercy." Both sides machine-gunned hostile flyers in parachutes; both tortured and killed prisoners in cold blood; both mutilated enemy dead for souvenirs. In the fight against Germany, cruelties and atrocities also occurred, although on a lesser scale. A battalion of the second armored division calling itself "Roosevelt's Butchers" boasted that it shot all the German soldiers it captured. Some U.S. pilots laughed at the lifeboats they strafed and the bodies they exploded out of trucks. Some became cynical about human life. Some still languish in veterans' hospitals, having nightmares about the war.

The Home Front

Nothing transformed the social topography more than the vast internal migration of an already mobile people. About 15 million men moved because of military service, often accompanied by family members. Many other Americans moved to secure new economic opportunities, especially in the Pacific Coast states. Nearly a quarter of a million found jobs in the shipyards of the Bay area and at least as many in the aircraft industry that arose in the orange groves of southern California. More than one hundred thousand worked in the Puget Sound shipyards of Washington State and half as many in the nearby Boeing airplane plants. Others flocked to the world's largest magnesium plant in Henderson, Nevada, to the huge Geneva Steel Works near Provo, Utah, and to the Rocky Mountain Arsenal and Remington Rand arms plant outside Denver (see Map 25.5).

At least 6 million people left farms to work in urban areas, including several million southern blacks and whites. They doubled Albuquerque's population and increased San Diego's some 90 percent. This mass uprooting of people from familiar settings made Americans both more cosmopolitan and more lonely, alienated, and frustrated. Lifestyles became freewheeling as Americans left their hometowns and ignored traditional

values. Housing shortages left millions living in converted garages and trailer camps, and even in their own cars. Some workers in Seattle lived in chicken coops. The swarms of migrants to Mobile, Alabama, attracted by a new aluminum plant, two massive shipyards, an air base, and an army supply depot, transformed a sleepy fishing village into a symbol of urban disorder.

There and elsewhere, overcrowding along with wartime separations strained family and community life. High rates of divorce, mental illness, family violence, and juvenile delinquency reflected the disruptions caused in part by the lack of privacy, the sense of impermanence, the absence of familiar settings, and the competition for scarce facilities. Few boom communities had the resources to supply their suddenly swollen populations with transportation, recreation, and social services. Urban blight and conflicts between newcomers and old-timers accelerated.

While military culture fostered a sexist mentality toward women, emphasizing the differences between "femininity" and "masculinity," millions of American women donned pants, put their hair in bandannas, and went to work in defense plants. Reversing a decade of efforts to exclude women from the labor force, the federal government urged women into war production in 1942. Songs like "We're the Janes Who Make the Planes" appealed to women to take up war work, and propaganda called upon them to "help save lives" and "release able-bodied men for fighting." More than 6 million women entered the labor force during the war, increasing the number of employed women to 19 million. Less than a quarter of the labor force in 1940, women constituted well over a third of all workers in 1945.

Before the war most female wage earners had been young and single. By contrast, 75 percent of the new women workers were married, 60 percent were over thirty-five, and more than 33 percent had children under the age of fourteen. They tended blast furnaces, operated cranes, greased locomotives, drove taxis, welded hulls, loaded shells, and worked in coke plants and rolling mills. On the Pacific Coast, more than one-third of all workers in aircraft and shipbuilding were women. "Rosie the Riveter," holding a pneumatic gun in arms bulging with muscles, became the symbol of the woman war worker; she was, in the words of a popular song, "making history working for victory."

Yet wartime also strengthened traditional convictions, and gender discrimination flourished throughout the war. Women earned only about 65 percent of what men earned for the same work. Government propaganda

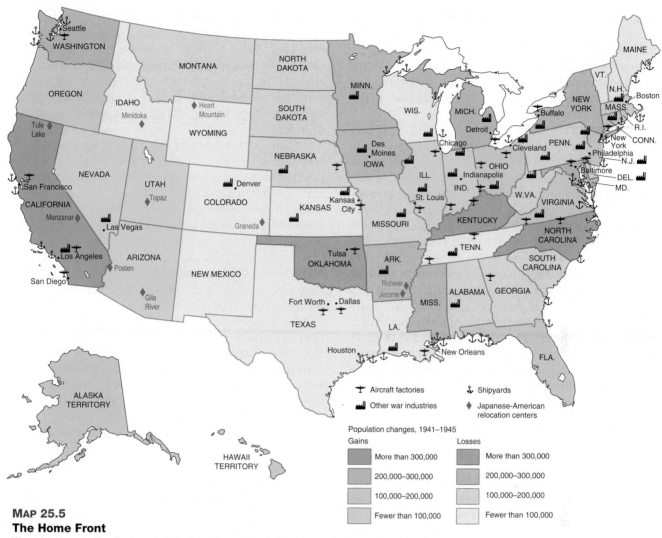

Map 25.5
The Home Front
War-related production finally ended the Great Depression, but it also required many Americans to move, especially to western states where the jobs were. This map shows major war-related industries and the states that gained and lost populations. For Japanese Americans, relocation did not mean new jobs, but a loss of freedom as they were assigned to one of ten relocation centers across the country.

portrayed women's war work as a temporary response to an emergency. "A woman is a substitute," claimed a War Department brochure, "like plastic instead of metal." Work was pictured as an extension of women's roles as wives and mothers. A newspaperwoman wrote of the "deep satisfaction which a woman of today knows who has made a rubber boat which may save the life of her aviator husband, or helped fashion a bullet which may avenge her son!" As a result, the public attitude about women's employment changed little in World War II. In 1945 only 18 percent of the respondents in a poll approved of married women working.

Traditional notions of a woman's place and the stigma attached to working mothers also shaped govern-

ment resistance to establishing child-care centers for women employed in defense. "A mother's primary duty is to her home and children," the Labor Department's Children's Bureau stated. "This duty is one she cannot lay aside, no matter what the emergency." New York Mayor Fiorello LaGuardia proclaimed that the worst mother was better than the best nursery. Funds for federal child-care centers covered fewer than 10 percent of defense workers' children, and the young suffered. Terms like "eight-hour orphans" and "latch-key children" were coined to describe unsupervised children forced to fend for themselves. Fueling the fears of those who believed that the employment of women outside the home would cause the family to disintegrate, juve-

Rosie the Riveter
Memorialized in song and story, "Rosie the Riveter" symbolized the woman war workers who assumed jobs in heavy industry to take up the slack for the absent 15 million men in the armed services. Here a very real Rosie the Riveter is doing her job in April 1943 at the Baltimore manufacturing plant for Martin PMB mariners. Although sometimes scorned by male workers, the dedication and efficiency of most female workers won them the praise of male plant supervisors.

nile delinquency increased fivefold and the divorce rate zoomed from 16 per 100 marriages in 1940 to 27 per 100 in 1944.

The impact of war on women and the family proved multifaceted and even contradictory. As the divorce rate soared, so did marriage rates and birthrates. Although some women remained content to roll bandages for the Red Cross, more than three hundred thousand joined the armed forces and, for the first time in American history, were given regular military status and served in positions other than that of nurse. As members of the Women's Army Corps (WACs) and the Navy's Women Appointed for Volunteer Emergency Service (WAVES) they replaced men in such noncombat jobs as mechanics and radio operators. About a thousand women served as civilian pilots with the WASPs (Women's

Airforce Service Pilots). When they left the service, moreover, they had the same rights and privileges as the male veterans.

Despite lingering notions of separate spheres, female workers gained unprecedented employment opportunities and public recognition. Although some eagerly gave up their jobs at the end of the war, others did not relish losing the income and self-esteem they had gained in contributing to the war effort. As Inez Sauer, who went to work for Boeing in Seattle, recalled,

> My mother warned me when I took the job that I would never be the same. She said, "You will never want to go back to being a housewife." She was right, it definitely did. At Boeing I found a freedom and an independence I had never known. After the war I could never go back to playing bridge again, being a clubwoman and listening to a lot of inanities when I knew there were things you could use your mind for. The war changed my life completely.

Overall, women gained a new sense of their potential. The war proved their capabilities and widened their world. Recalled one war wife whose returning husband did not like her independence, "He had left a shrinking violet and come home to a very strong oak tree." Wartime experiences markedly affected a generation of women and the sons and daughters they later raised.

Some of these women were among the 350,000 teachers who took better-paying war work or joined the armed services, leaving schools badly understaffed. Students, too, abandoned school in record numbers. High school enrollments sank as the full-time employment of teenagers rose from 900,000 in 1940 to 3 million in 1944.

The loss of students to war production and the armed services forced colleges to admit large numbers of women and to contract themselves out to the armed forces. Nearly a million servicemen took college classes in science, engineering, and foreign languages. The military presence was all-pervasive. Harvard University awarded four military-training certificates for every academic degree it conferred. The chancellor of one branch of the University of California announced that his school was "no longer an academic tent with military sideshows. It is a military tent with academic sideshows." Higher education became more dependent on the federal government, and most universities sought increased federal contracts and subsidies, despite their having to submit to greater government interference and regulation. The universities in the West received some $100 billion from the Office of Scientific Research

and Development, more money than had been spent on scientific research by all the western universities since their founding.

The war profoundly affected American popular culture as well. The media, emphasizing mass production and targeting mass audiences as never before, emerged from the war more highly organized and with greater concentrations of power. Expenditures on books and theater entertainment doubled between 1941 and 1945. Between 60 million and 100 million Americans a week (in a population of 135 million) went to the movies, and the film industry reached its zenith in 1945–1946. But as the war dragged on, people tired of patriotic war films, and Hollywood reemphasized romance and nostalgia with such stars as Katharine Hepburn and Judy Garland.

Similarly, popular music early in the war featured patriotic themes. "Goodbye, Mama, I'm Off to Yokohama" became the first hit of 1942. As the war continued, themes of lost love and loneliness dominated lyrics. Numbers like "They're Either Too Young or Too Old" expressed the laments of women separated from the men they loved. So, too, did the dozens of "dream songs" in which love denied by the real world could be achieved only in a dream. By 1945 bitterness rather than melancholy pervaded the lyrics of best-selling records, and songs like "Saturday Night Is the Loneliest Night of the Week" revealed impatience for the war's end.

In bookstores, nonfiction ruled the roost and every newsmagazine increased its circulation. Wendell Willkie's *One World* (1943) became the fastest-selling title in publishing history to that time, with 1 million copies snapped up in two months. A euphoric vision of a world without military alliances and spheres of influence, this brief volume expressed hope that an international organization would extend peace and democracy through the postwar world. The Government Printing Office published Armed Services Editions, paperback reprints of classics and new releases; and the nearly 350 million copies distributed free to soldiers sped up the American acceptance of quality paperbacks, which were introduced in 1939 by the Pocket Book Company.

An avid interest in wartime news also spurred the major radio networks to increase their news programs from 4 percent to nearly 30 percent of broadcasting time, and enticed Americans to listen to the radio an average of 4 1/2 hours a day. Daytime radio serials, like those featuring Dick Tracy tracking down Axis spies, reached the height of their popularity, as did juvenile comic books in which a platoon of new superheroes, including Captain America and Captain Marvel, saw action on the battlefield. Even Bugs Bunny donned a uniform to combat America's foes.

Racism and New Opportunities

Recognizing that the government needed the loyalty and labor of a united people, black leaders entered World War II determined to secure equal rights. In 1942 civil-rights spokesmen insisted that African-American support of the war hinged on America's commitment to racial justice. They called for a "Double V" campaign—victory over racial discrimination as well as over the Axis.

Membership in the NAACP multiplied nearly ten times, reaching half a million in 1945. The association pressed for legislation outlawing the poll tax and lynching, decried discrimination in defense industries and the armed services, and sought to end black disfranchisement. The campaign for voting rights gained momentum when the Supreme Court, in *Smith* v. *Allwright* (1944), ruled the Texas all-white primary unconstitutional. The decision eliminated a bar that had existed in eight southern states, although these states promptly resorted to other devices to minimize voting by blacks.

A new civil-rights organization, the Congress of Racial Equality (CORE), was founded in 1942. Employing the same forms of nonviolent direct action that Mohandas Gandhi used in his campaign for India's independence, CORE sought to desegregate public facilities in northern cities.

Also proposing nonviolent direct action, A. Philip Randolph, president of the Brotherhood of Sleeping Car Porters, in 1941 called for a "thundering march" of one hundred thousand blacks on Washington "to wake up and shock white America as it has never been shocked before." He warned Roosevelt that if the president did not end discrimination in the armed services and the defense industry, African Americans would besiege Washington. FDR agreed to compromise.

In June 1941 Roosevelt issued Executive Order 8802, the first presidential directive on race since Reconstruction. It prohibited discriminatory employment practices by federal agencies and all unions and companies engaged in war-related work, and established the Fair Employment Practices Commission (FEPC) to enforce this policy. Although the FEPC lacked effective enforcement powers, booming war production and a labor supply depleted by military service resulted in the employment of some 2 million African Americans in industry and two hundred thousand in the federal civil service. Between 1942 and 1945 the proportion of

blacks in war-production work rose from 3 to 9 percent. Black membership in labor unions doubled to 1.25 million, and the number of skilled and semiskilled black workers tripled. Formerly mired in low-paying domestic and farm jobs, some three hundred thousand black women found work in factories and the civil service. "Hitler was the one that got us out of the white folks' kitchen," recalled one black women who went to work for Boeing in Seattle, a city whose black population rose from four thousand to forty thousand during the war. Overall, the average wage for African Americans increased from $457 to $1,976 a year, compared with a gain from $1,064 to $2,600 for whites.

About 1 million African Americans served in the armed forces. Wartime needs forced the military to end policies of excluding blacks from the marines and coast guard, restricting them to jobs as mess boys in the navy, and confining them to noncombatant units in the army. From just five in 1940, the number of black officers grew to over seven thousand in 1945. The all-black 761st tank battalion gained distinction fighting in Germany, and the 99th pursuit squadron won eighty Distinguished Flying Crosses for its combat against the *Luftwaffe* in Europe. In 1944 both the army and navy began token integration in some training facilities, ships, and battlefield platoons.

The great majority of blacks, however, served throughout the war in segregated service units commanded by white officers. This indignity, made worse by the failure of military authorities to protect black servicemen off the post and by the use of white military police to keep blacks "in their place," sparked rioting on army bases. At least fifty black soldiers died in racial conflicts during the war. "I used to sing gospel songs until I joined the Army," recalled blues-guitar great B. B. King, "then I sang the blues."

Violence within the military mirrored growing racial tensions on the home front. As blacks protested against discrimination, many whites stiffened their resistance to racial equality. Numerous clashes occurred. Scores of cities reported pitched battles between blacks and whites. Race riots erupted in 1943 in Harlem, Mobile, and Beaumont, Texas. The bloodiest melee exploded in Detroit that year when white mobs assaulted blacks caught riding on trolleys or sitting in movie theaters and blacks smashed and looted white-owned stores and shops. After thirty hours of racial beatings, shootings, and burning, twenty-five African Americans and nine whites lay dead, more than seven hundred had been injured, and over $2 million of property had been destroyed. The fear of continued violence led to a greater emphasis on racial tolerance by liberal whites and to a reduction in the militancy of African-American leaders.

Yet the war brought significant changes that would eventually result in a successful drive for black civil rights. The migration of over seven hundred thousand blacks from the South turned a southern problem into a national concern. It created a new attitude of independence in African Americans freed from the stifling constraints of caste. Despite the continuation of racial prejudice and discrimination, most who left the rural South found a more abundant and hopeful life than the one they had left behind. As the growing numbers of blacks in the industrial cities of the North began to vote, moreover, the bloc of African-American voters could tip the victory to either Democrats or Republicans in close elections. This prompted politicians in both major parties to extend greater recognition to blacks and to pay more attention to civil-rights issues.

African-American expectations of greater government concern for their rights also resulted from the new prominence of the United States as a major power in a predominantly nonwhite world. As Japanese propaganda appeals to the peoples of Asia and Latin America emphasized lynchings and race riots in the United

A "Double V" Protest

As the mobilization for war lifted the pall of the Depression for white workers, management and labor joined together to exclude African-Americans from the benefits of the war boom. To protest, picketers rallied for defense jobs outside the Glenn Martin aircraft plant in Omaha, Nebraska.

States, Americans had to confront the peril that white racism posed to their national security. In addition, the horrors of Nazi racism made Americans more sensitive to the harm caused by their own white-supremacist attitudes and practices. As a former governor of Alabama complained, Nazism has "wrecked the theories of the master race with which we were so contented so long." Swedish economist Gunnar Myrdal, in his massive study of race problems, *An American Dilemma* (1944), concluded that "not since Reconstruction had there been more reason to anticipate fundamental changes in American race relations."

Black veterans, with a new sense of self-esteem gained from participating in the war effort, returned to civilian life with high expectations. Like the athlete Jackie Robinson, who as a young lieutenant had refused to take a seat at the rear of a segregated bus and had fought and won his subsequent court martial, African Americans faced the postwar era resolved to gain all the rights enjoyed by whites.

War and Diversity

Wartime winds of change also brought new opportunities and difficulties to other minorities. More than twenty-five thousand Native Americans served in the armed forces during the war. Navajo "code talkers" confounded the Japanese by using the Navajo language to relay messages between U.S. command centers. "Were it not for the Navajos, the Marines would never have taken Iwo Jima," one Signal Corps officer declared.

Another fifty thousand Indians left the reservation to work in defense industries, mainly on the West Coast. The Rosebud Reservation in South Dakota lost more than a quarter of its population to migration during the war. It was the first time most had lived in a non-Indian world, and the average income of Native American households tripled during the war. Such economic improvement encouraged many Indians to remain outside the reservation and to try to assimilate into mainstream life. But anti-Indian discrimination, particularly in smaller towns near reservations such as Gallup, New Mexico, and Billings, Montana, forced many Native Americans back to their reservations, which had suffered severely from budget cuts during the war. Prodded by those who coveted Indian lands, lawmakers demanded that Indians be taken off the backs of the taxpayers and "freed from the reservations" to fend for themselves." To mobilize against the campaign to end all reservations and trust protections, Native Americans organized the National Congress of American Indians in 1944.

To relieve labor shortages in agriculture, caused by conscription and the movement of rural workers to city factories, the U.S. government negotiated an agreement with Mexico in July 1942 to import *braceros*, or temporary workers. Classified as foreign laborers rather than as immigrants, an estimated two hundred thousand *braceros*, half of them in California, received short-term contracts guaranteeing adequate wages, medical care, and decent living conditions. But farm owners frequently violated the terms of these contracts and also encouraged an influx of illegal migrants from Mexico desperate for employment. Unable to complain about their working conditions without risking arrest and deportation, hundreds of thousands of Mexicans were exploited by agribusinesses in Arizona, California, and Texas. At the same time, tens of thousands of Chicanos left agricultural work for jobs in factories, shipbuilding yards, and steel mills. By 1943 about half a million Chicanos were living in Los Angeles County, 10 percent of the total population. In New Mexico nearly 20 percent of Mexican American farm laborers escaped from rural poverty to urban jobs. Even as their occupational status and material conditions improved, most Mexican Americans remained in communities called *colonias*, segregated from the larger society and frequently harassed by the police.

Much of the hostility toward Mexican Americans focused on young gang members who wore "zoot suits"—a fashion that originated in Harlem and emphasized long, broad-shouldered jackets and pleated trousers tightly pegged at the ankles. Known as *pachucos*, zoot-suited Mexican Americans aroused the ire of servicemen stationed or on leave in Los Angeles who saw them as delinquents and draft dodgers. After a series of minor clashes, bands of sailors from nearby bases and soldiers on leave in Los Angeles rampaged through the city in early June 1943, stripping *pachucos*, cutting their long hair, and beating them. Military authorities looked the other way. City police intervened only to arrest Mexican Americans. *Time* magazine described the violence as "the ugliest brand of mob action since the coolie race riots of the 1870s"; yet Los Angeles officials praised the servicemen's actions, and the city council made the wearing of a zoot suit a misdemeanor. Nothing was done about the substandard housing, disease, and racism Hispanics had to endure.

Unlike African Americans, however, more than 350,000 Mexican Americans served in the armed forces without segregation, and in all combat units. They volunteered in much higher numbers than warranted by their percentage of the population and earned a disproportionate number of citations for distinguished service

as well as seventeen Medals of Honor. Air corps hero Jose Holguin from Los Angeles won the Distinguished Flying Cross, the Air Medal, and the Silver Star. Returning Mexican-American GIs joined long-standing antidiscrimination groups, like the League of United Latin American Citizens (LULAC) and organized their own associations, like the American GI Forum, to press for veterans' interests and equal rights.

Thousands of gay men and lesbians who served in the armed forces also found new wartime opportunities. Although the military officially barred those they defined as "sexual perverts," the urgency of building a massive armed forces led to just four to five thousand men out of eighteen million examined for induction to be excluded because of homosexuality. For the vast majority of gays not excluded, being emancipated from traditional expectations and the close scrutiny of family and neighbors, and living in overwhelmingly all-male or all-female environments, brought freedom to meet like-minded gay men and women and to express their sexual orientation. Like other minorities, many gays saw the war as a chance to prove their worth under fire. Some were ideologically committed because the Nazis had targeted European homosexuals for liquidation. On one American warship, the most highly regarded officer was "a notorious Queen" who wore a hair net. Yet others suspected of being gay were dishonorably discharged, sent to psychiatric hospitals, or imprisoned in so-called queer stockades, where some were mentally and physically abused by military police. The anger of gays at having fought against oppression while remaining oppressed themselves led them to think far more than ever before about their right to equal treatment and opportunity. In 1945 gay veterans established the Veteran's Benevolent Association, the first major gay organization in the United States to combat discrimination.

The Internment of Japanese-Americans

Far more than any other minority in the United States, Japanese Americans suffered grievously during the war. The internment of about thirty-seven thousand first-generation Japanese immigrants (Issei) and nearly seventy-five thousand native-born Japanese-American citizens of the United States (Nisei) in "relocation centers" guarded by military police was a tragic reminder of the fragility of civil liberties in wartime.

The internment reflected forty years of anti-Japanese sentiment on the West Coast, rooted in racial prejudice and economic rivalry. Nativist politicians and farmers who wanted Japanese-American land had long

decried the "yellow peril." Following the attack on Pearl Harbor they whipped up the rage of white Californians, aided by a government report falsely blaming Japanese Americans in Hawaii for aiding the Japanese naval force. One barber advertised "free shave for Japs," but "not responsible for accidents." Patriotic associations and many newspapers clamored for evacuating the Japanese Americans, as did local politicians, West Coast congressional delegations, and the army general in charge of the Western Defense Command, who proclaimed, "A Jap is a Jap. It makes no difference whether he is an American citizen or not. . . . I don't want any of them."

In February 1942 President Roosevelt gave in to the pressure and issued Executive Order 9066, authorizing the removal from military areas of anyone deemed a threat. Although not a single Japanese American was apprehended for espionage or sedition and neither the FBI nor military intelligence uncovered any evidence of disloyal behavior by Japanese Americans, the military ordered the eviction of all Nisei and Issei from the West Coast. Only Hawaii was excepted. Despite the far larger number of Hawaiians of Japanese ancestry, as well as of

A Japanese-American child being evacuated from Los Angeles in April 1942. It did not matter that she, along with some 80,000 other Niesi, were American citizens. "A Jap's a Jap," said General John De Witt, commander of West Coast defenses.

Japanese living in Hawaii, no internment policy was implemented there, and no sabotage occurred (see A Place in Time: Honolulu, Hawaii, 1941–1945).

Forced to sell their lands and homes quickly at whatever prices they could obtain, Japanese Americans lost an estimated $2 billion in property and possessions. Tagged with numbers rather than names, they were herded into barbed-wire-encircled detention camps in the most remote and desolate parts of the West and Great Plains—places, wrote one historian, "where nobody had lived before and no one has lived since." Few other Americans protested the incarceration. Stating that it would not question government claims of military necessity during time of war, the Supreme Court upheld the constitutionality of the evacuation in the *Korematsu* case (1944). By then the hysteria had subsided, and the government had begun a program of gradual release, allowing some Nisei to attend college or take factory jobs (but not on the West Coast); about eighteen thousand served in the military. The 442nd regimental combat team, entirely Japanese American, became the most decorated unit in the military.

In 1982 a special government commission concluded in its report, *Personal Justice Denied*, that internment "was not justified by military necessity." It blamed the Roosevelt administration's action on "race prejudice, war hysteria, and a failure of political leadership" and apologized to Japanese Americans for "a grave injustice." In 1988 Congress voted to pay twenty thousand dollars in compensation to each of the nearly sixty-two thousand surviving internees; and in 1998 President Bill Clinton further apologized for the injustice by giving the nation's highest civilian honor, the Presidential Medal of Freedom, to Fred Korematsu, who had protested the evacuation decree all the way to the Supreme Court.

TRIUMPH AND TRAGEDY, 1945

Spring and summer 1945 brought stunning changes and new crises. In Europe a new balance of power emerged after the collapse of the Third Reich. In Asia continued Japanese reluctance to surrender led to the use of atomic bombs. And in the United States a new president, Harry Truman, presided over both the end of World War II and the beginning of the Cold War and the nuclear age.

The Yalta Conference

By the time Roosevelt, Churchill, and Stalin met in the Soviet city of Yalta in February 1945, the military situation favored the Soviet Union. The Red Army had over-

run Poland, Romania, and Bulgaria; driven the Nazis out of Yugoslavia; penetrated Austria, Hungary, and Czechoslovakia; and was massed just fifty miles from Berlin. American forces, in contrast, were still recovering from the Battle of the Bulge and facing stiff resistance on the route to Japan. The Joint Chiefs of Staff, contemplating the awesome cost in American casualties of an invasion of Japan, insisted that Stalin's help was worth almost any price. And Stalin was in a position to make demands. The Soviet Union had suffered most in the war against Germany, it already dominated eastern Europe, and, knowing that the United States did not want to fight a prolonged war against Japan, Stalin had the luxury of deciding whether and when to enter the Pacific war.

The Yalta accords reflected these realities. Stalin again vowed to declare war on Japan "two or three months" after Germany's surrender, and in return Churchill and Roosevelt reneged on their arrangement with Jiang Jieshi (made in Cairo) and promised the Soviet Union concessions in Manchuria and the territories it had lost in the Russo-Japanese War (1904). Unable to reach agreement about the future of Germany, the Big Three delegated a final settlement of the reparations issue to a postwar commission, and left vague the matter of partitioning Germany and its eventual reunification. Similarly without specific provisions or timetables, the conference called for interim governments in eastern Europe "broadly representative of all democratic elements" and, ultimately, for freely elected permanent governments. On the matter dearest to FDR's heart, the negotiators accepted a plan for a new international organization and agreed to convene a founding conference of the new United Nations in San Francisco in April 1945.

Stalin proved adamant about the nature of the postwar Polish government. Twice in the twentieth century German troops had used Poland as a springboard for invading Russia. Stalin would not expose his land again, and after the Red Army had captured Warsaw in January 1945 he installed a procommunist regime and brutally subdued the anticommunist Poles. Refusing to recognize the communist government, Roosevelt and Churchill called for free, democratic elections. But at Yalta they sidestepped this crucial issue by accepting Stalin's vague pledge to include some prowesterners in the new Polish government and to allow elections "as soon as possible." Conservative critics would later charge that FDR "gave away" eastern Europe. Actually, the Soviet Union gained little it did not already control, and short of going to war against the Soviet Union while still battling Germany and Japan, FDR could only hope that Stalin would keep his word.

Victory in Europe

As the Soviets prepared for their assault on Berlin, American troops crossed the Rhine at Remagen in March 1945 and encircled the Ruhr Valley, Germany's industrial heartland. Churchill now proposed a rapid thrust to Berlin. But Eisenhower, with Roosevelt's backing, overruled Churchill. They saw no point in risking high casualties to rush to an area of Germany that had already been designated as the Soviet occupation zone. So Eisenhower advanced methodically along a broad front until the Americans met the Russians at the Elbe River on April 25. By then the Red Army had taken Vienna and reached the suburbs of Berlin. On April 30, as Soviet troops approached his headquarters, Hitler committed suicide. Berlin fell to the Soviets on May 2, and on May 8 a new German government surrendered unconditionally.

Jubilant Americans celebrated Victory in Europe (V-E) Day less than a month after they had mourned the death of their president. On April 12 an exhausted President Roosevelt had abruptly clutched his head, moaned that he had a "terrific headache," and fell unconscious. A cerebral hemorrhage ended his life. As the nation grieved, Roosevelt's unprepared successor assumed the burden of ending the war and dealing with the Soviet Union.

"I don't know whether you fellows ever had a load of hay or a bull fall on you," Harry S. Truman told reporters on his first full day in office, "but last night the moon, the stars, and all the planets fell on me." An unpretentious politician awed by his new responsibilities, Truman struggled to continue FDR's policies. But Roosevelt had made no effort to familiarize his vice president with world affairs. Perhaps sensing his own inadequacies, Truman adopted a tough pose toward adversaries. In office less than two weeks, he lashed out at Soviet ambassador V. M. Molotov that the United States was tired of waiting for the Russians to allow free elections in Poland, and he threatened to cut off lend-lease aid if the Soviet Union did not cooperate. The Truman administration then reduced U.S. economic assistance to the Soviets and stalled on their request for a $1 billion reconstruction loan. Simultaneously, Stalin strengthened his grip on eastern Europe, ignoring the promises he had made at Yalta.

The United States would neither concede the Soviet sphere of influence in eastern Europe nor take steps to terminate it. Although Truman still sought Stalin's cooperation in establishing the United Nations and in defeating Japan, Soviet-American relations deteriorated. By June 1945, when the Allied countries succeeded in

Yalta Conference, 1945
The palaces where Roosevelt, Churchill, Stalin, and their advisers gathered were still standing, but the rest of Yalta had been reduced to ruin during the German occupation.

framing the United Nations Charter, hopes for a new international order had dimmed, and the United Nations emerged as a diplomatic battleground. Truman, Churchill, and Stalin met at Potsdam, Germany, from July 16 to August 2 to complete the postwar arrangements begun at Yalta. But the Allied leaders could barely agree to demilitarize Germany and to punish Nazi war criminals. All the major divisive issues were postponed and left to the Council of Foreign Ministers to resolve later. Given the diplomatic impasse, only military power remained to determine the contours of the postwar world.

The Holocaust

When news of the Holocaust—the term later given to the Nazis' extermination of European Jewry—first leaked out in early 1942, many Americans discounted the reports. Not until November did the State Department admit knowledge of the massacres. A month later the American broadcaster Edward R. Murrow, listened to nationwide, reported on the systematic killing of millions of Jews, "It is a picture of mass murder and moral depravity unequalled in the history of the world. It is a horror beyond what imagination can grasp. . . . There are no longer 'concentration camps'—we must speak now only of 'extermination camps.' "

Much as the war came to the United States initially and most dramatically at Pearl Harbor, the outlines of an increasingly multicultural United States emerging from the Second World War could be seen first and most clearly in Hawaii. The nearly one million soldiers, sailors, and marines stopping in Hawaii on their way to the battlefront, as well as the more than one hundred thousand men and women who left the mainland to find war work on the islands, expected the Hollywood image of a simple Pacific paradise: blue sky, green sea, white sand, palm trees, tropical sunsets, and exotic women with flowers in their hair. They found instead a complex multiracial and multiethnic society. The experience would change them, as they in turn would change the islands.

Before December 7, 1941, few Americans knew where Hawaii was or that it was part of their country, a colonial possession annexed by the U.S. government in 1898. Few realized that Honolulu, a tiny fishing village when Captain James Cook sailed by its harbor in 1778, had become a gritty port city that would serve as the major staging ground for the war to be waged in the Pacific. And few knew that, as a result of successive waves of immigration by Chinese, Portuguese, Japanese, and Filipinos, this American outpost had a population in which native Hawaiians and white Americans (called *haoles*, which in Hawaiian means "strangers") each constituted only 15 percent of the islands' inhabitants.

The approximately 160,000 Hawaiians of Japanese ancestry—including some 100,000 second-generation Japanese, or Nisei, who had been born in Hawaii and were therefore U.S. citizens—made up Hawaii's largest ethnic group, more than a third of the population. Japan's attack on Pearl Harbor immediately raised fears of sabotage or espionage by them. Rumors flew of arrow-shaped signs cut in the sugar-cane fields to direct Japanese planes to military targets and of Nisei women waving kimonos to signal Japanese pilots. But in stark contrast to the internment of Japanese Americans in the Pacific coast states, military policy in the islands was to maintain traditional interracial harmony throughout the war, and to treat all law-abiding inhabitants of Japanese ancestry justly and humanely. "This is America and we must do things the American way," announced Hawaii's military governor. "We must distinguish between loyalty and disloyalty among our people." There was no mass internment of the Nisei and Issei (those who emigrated from Japan) and there were no acts of sabotage.

For many Issei, loyalty to the United States had become an obligation, a matter of honor. To eliminate potential associations with the enemy, they destroyed old books, photographs of relatives, and brocaded *obi* (kimono sashes) and replaced portraits of the Japanese emperor with pictures of President Roosevelt. A burning desire to prove that they were true Americans prompted many of their Hawaiian-born children, often referred to as AJAs (Americans of Japanese ancestry), to become superpatriots. AJAs contributed heavily to war-bond drives and sponsored their own "Bombs on Tokyo" campaign. They converted the halls of Buddhist temples, Shinto shrines, and Japanese-language schools (all closed for the duration and reopened after the war) into manufactories of bandages and hospital gowns. Their newly expanded contact with other Hawaiians, including *haoles*, hastened their assimilation into the larger Hawaiian society. In addition, AJAs served in the military campaigns in the Pacific as interpreters—translating, interrogating, intercepting transmissions, and cracking enemy codes—and they fought in Europe with the all-Nisei 442d regimental combat team, the most highly decorated organization in the U.S. Army.

These contributions gave the Japanese in Hawaii, as it did other ethnic groups in the United States, a new sense of their worth and dignity. The war experience aroused expectations of equal opportunity and equal treatment, of full participation in island politics, of no longer accepting a subordinate status to *haoles*.

The attitudes of many Hawaiians toward *haoles* changed as native islanders witnessed large numbers of whites doing manual labor for the first time. Their view that whites would always hold superior positions in society—as bosses, plantation owners, and politicians—was turned topsy-turvy by the flood of Caucasian mainland war workers, mostly from the fringes of respectability, and easily stereotyped as drunks and troublemakers. The hordes of white servicemen crowding into Honolulu's Hotel Street vice district for liquor, for posed pictures with hula girls in grass skirts, for three-dollar sex at the many brothels, and then for treatment at prophylaxis stations to ward off venereal diseases also tarnished traditional notions of white superiority. White prostitutes who brazenly operated in Honolulu further mocked the belief that those with white skin had a "natural" right to rule those of a darker hue.

The Hawaiian experience, in turn, changed the outlooks of many of the servicemen and war workers stationed there. In Honolulu they grew accustomed to women holding full-time jobs, as a far higher percentage of women worked outside the home than was the case on the mainland. Given the scarcity of "available" white women, the men gradually became less uneasy about interracial dating, joking that "the longer you were on the island, the lighter [skinned] the girls became." Not a few GIs ultimately married women of Chinese, Filipino, or Hawaiian ancestry.

Most of the whites who had come to Hawaii had never lived where whites did not constitute a majority and where they were the ones who were different. Most had never before encountered or conversed with people of African or Asian ancestry. Suddenly, they were in the midst of a mixture of ethnic and racial groups unmatched anywhere in the United States, in a diverse society where people of different backgrounds worked together for a common cause. This example of multicultural harmony was especially an eye-opener for the nearly thirty thousand African-American servicemen and workers who came to Honolulu before the war's end. In the fluid and relaxed racial relations of Hawaiian society, blacks discovered an alternative to the racist America they knew. "I thank God often," wrote a black shipyard worker, "for letting me experience the occasion to spend a part of my life in a part of the world where one can be respected and live as a free man should." Some chose never to go back to the mainland. Others returned home to press for the rights and freedoms they had first tasted in Hawaii. In so many ways, wartime Hawaii, termed "the first strange place" by historians Beth Bailey and David Farber, would anticipate the "strangeness" of U.S. society today.

As if to emphasize the "strangeness" of the Hawaiian experience for many whites from the mainland, the sign at KauKau corner in downtown Hawaii points to places both faraway and unfamiliar to most Americans.

A spontaneous victory celebration on Hotel Street, Honolulu, August 14, 1945. For many servicemen in Hawaii, Emperor Hirohito's surrender meant they would not have to take part in an invasion of Japan. "We are going to live," exulted one soldier. "We are going to grow up to adulthood after all."

Bergen Belsen Concentration Camp
Entering Germany in 1945, American troops discovered the horrors that the Nazis had perpetrated on European Jews and others. Here, General Eisenhower and U.S. soldiers view the bodies of victims at Bergen-Belsen. One GI wrote of the ghastly concentration camp scene: "I've seen what wasn't ever meant for human eyes to see."

Nazis' "final solution" to the "Jewish question." Its feeble response was due to its overwhelming focus on winning the war as quickly as possible, congressional and public fears of an influx of destitute Jews into the United States, Britain's wish to placate the Arabs by keeping Jewish settlers out of Palestine, and the fear of some Jewish-American leaders that pressing the issue would increase anti-Semitism at home. The War Refugee Board managed to save the lives of just two hundred thousand Jews and twenty thousand non-Jews. Six million other Jews, about 75 percent of the European Jewish population, were gassed, shot, and incinerated, as were several million gypsies, communists, homosexuals, Polish Catholics, and others deemed unfit to live in the Third Reich.

"The things I saw beggar description," wrote General Eisenhower after visiting the first death camp liberated by the U.S. army. He sent immediately for a delegation of congressional leaders and newspaper editors to make sure Americans would never forget the gas chambers and human ovens. Only after viewing the photographs and newsreels of corpses stacked like cordwood, boxcars heaped with the bones of dead prisoners, bulldozers shoving emaciated bodies into hastily dug ditches, and liberated, barely-alive living skeletons lying in their own filth, their vacant, sunken eyes staring through barbed wire, did most Americans see that the Holocaust was no myth.

Most Americans considered the annihilation of Europe's 6 million Jews beyond belief. There were no photographs to prove it, and, some argued, the atrocities attributed to the Germans in World War I had turned out to be false. So few took issue with the military's view that the way to liberate those enslaved by Hitler was by speedily winning the war. Pleas by American Jews for the Allies to bomb the death camps and the railroad tracks leading to them fell on deaf ears. In fall 1944 U.S. planes flying over Auschwitz in southern Poland bombed nearby factories but left the gas chambers and crematoria intact, in order, American officials explained, not to divert air power from more vital raids elsewhere. "How could it be," historian David Wyman has asked, "that Government officials knew that a place existed where 2,000 helpless human beings could be killed in less than an hour, knew that this occurred over and over again, and yet did not feel driven to search for some way to wipe such a scourge from the earth?"

How much could have been done remains uncertain. Still, the U.S. government never seriously considered rescue schemes or searched for a way to curtail the

The Atomic Bombs

Meanwhile, the war with Japan ground on. Early in 1945 an assault force of marines invaded Iwo Jima, 700 miles from Japan. In places termed the "Meat Grinder" and "Bloody Gorge," the marines savagely battled thousands of Japanese soldiers hidden in tunnels and behind concrete bunkers and pillboxes. Securing the five-square-mile island would cost the marines nearly twenty-seven thousand casualties, and one-third of all the marines killed in the Pacific. In June American troops waded ashore on Okinawa, 350 miles from Japan and a key staging area for the planned U.S. invasion of the Japanese home islands. Death and destruction engulfed Okinawa as waves of Americans attacked nearly impregnable

Japanese defenses head-on, repeating the bloody strategy of World War I. After eighty-three days of fighting on land and sea, twelve thousand Americans lay dead and three times as many wounded, a 35 percent casualty rate, higher than at Normandy.

The appalling rate of loss on Iwo Jima and Okinawa weighed on the minds of American strategists as they thought about an invasion of the Japanese home islands. The Japanese Cabinet showed no willingness to give up the war despite Japan's being blockaded and bombed daily (on March 9–10 a fleet of B-29s dropped napalm-and-magnesium-bombs on Tokyo, burning sixteen square miles of the city to the ground and killing some eighty-four thousand). Its military leaders insisted on fighting to the bitter end; surrender was unthinkable. Japan possessed an army of over two million, plus up to four million reservists and five thousand kamikaze aircraft, and the U.S. Joint Chiefs estimated that American casualties in invasions of Kyushu and Honshu (the main island of Japan) might exceed 1 million.

The successful detonation of history's first nuclear explosion at Alamagordo in mid-July gave Truman an alternative. On July 25, while meeting with Stalin and Churchill in Potsdam, Truman ordered the use of an atomic bomb if Japan did not surrender before August 3. The next day he warned Japan to surrender unconditionally or face "prompt and utter destruction." Japan rejected the Potsdam Declaration on July 28. On August 6 a B-29 bomber named *Enola Gay* took off from the Marianas island of Tinian and dropped a uranium bomb on Hiroshima, plunging the city into what Japanese novelist Masuji Ibuse termed "a hell of unspeakable torments." The 300,000 degree centigrade fireball incinerated houses and pulverized people. More than sixty thousand died in the initial searing blast of heat, and many of the seventy thousand injured died later from burns and radiation poisoning. On August 8 Stalin declared war on Japan, and U.S. planes dropped leaflets on Japan warning that another bomb would be dropped if it did not surrender. The next day, at high noon, the *Bock's Car* flattened Nagasaki with a plutonium bomb, killing thirty-five thousand and injuring more than sixty thousand. On August 14 Japan accepted the American terms of surrender, which implicitly permitted the emperor to retain his throne but subordinated him to the U.S. commander of the occupation forces.

The Aftermath of the Atomic Bombs
The atomic bombs dropped on Hiroshima and Nagasaki on August 6 and 9, 1945 instantly incinerated some 140,000 Japanese and left many slowly dying of radiation disease. On September 8, Dr. Nagai was photographed in front of what remained of the Nagasaki hospital he had worked in. A few days later he died from atomic radiation.

General MacArthur received Japan's surrender on the battleship *Missouri* on September 2, 1945. The war was over.

Some historians have subsequently questioned whether the United States needed to resort to atomic weapons to end the war promptly. They believe that racist American attitudes toward the Japanese motivated the decision to drop the bombs. As war correspondent Ernie Pyle wrote, "The Japanese are looked upon as something inhuman and squirmy—like some people feel about cockroaches or mice." While racial hatred undoubtedly stirred exterminationist sentiment, those involved in the Manhattan Project had regarded Germany as the target; and considering the ferocity of the Allied bombings of Hamburg and Dresden, there is little reason to assume that the Allies would not have dropped atomic bombs on Germany had they been available. By 1945 the Allies as well as the Axis had abandoned restraints on attacking civilians.

Other historians contend that demonstrating the bomb's terrible destructiveness on an uninhabited island would have moved Japan to surrender. We will never know for sure. American policy makers had rejected a demonstration bombing because the United States

had an atomic arsenal of only two bombs, and they did not know whether the mechanism for detonating them in the air would work. Still others argue that Japan was ready to surrender and that an invasion of the home islands was unnecessary. Again, we cannot know for sure. All that is certain is that as late as July 28, 1945, Japan refused a demand for surrender, and not until after the bombs were used did Japan capitulate.

The largest number of historians critical of Truman's decision believe that the president, aware of worsening relations between the United States and the USSR, ordered the atomic attack primarily to end the Pacific war before Stalin could enter it and also to intimidate Stalin into making concessions in eastern Europe. Referring to the Soviets, President Truman noted just before the atomic test at Alamogordo, "If it explodes, as I think it will, I'll certainly have a hammer on those boys." Truman's new secretary of state, James Byrnes, thought that the bomb would "make Russia more manageable" and would "put us in a position to dictate our own terms at the end of the war."

Although the president and his advisers believed that the atomic bombs would strengthen their hand against the Soviets, that was not the foremost reason the bombs were dropped. As throughout the war, American leaders in August 1945 relied on production and technology to win the war with the minimum loss of American life. Every new weapon was put to use; the concept of "total war" easily accommodated the bombing of civilians; and the atomic bomb was one more item in an arsenal that had already wreaked enormous destruction on the Axis. The rules of war that had once stayed the use of weapons of mass destruction against enemy civilians no longer prevailed. No responsible official counseled that the United States should sacrifice American servicemen to lessen death and destruction in Japan, or not use a weapon developed with 2 billion tax-payer dollars. To the vast majority of Americans, the atomic bomb was, in Churchill's words, "a miracle of deliverance" that saved Allied lives. So E. B. Sledge and his comrades in the First Marine Division, slated to take part in the first wave of the invasion of Japan's home islands, breathed "an indescribable sense of relief." Hearing the news of the atomic bombs and Japan's surrender, Sledge wrote, they sat in stunned silence:

> We remembered our dead. So many dead. So many maimed. So many bright futures consigned to the ashes of the past. So many dreams lost in the madness that engulfed us. Except for a few widely scattered shouts of joy, the survivors of the abyss sat hollow-eyed and silent, trying to comprehend a world without war.

CONCLUSION

The atomic bombs ended the deadliest war in history. More than 20 million men and women under arms, including more than three hundred thousand Americans, had died. Another 25 million civilians had perished. Much of Asia and Europe was rubble. Although physically unscathed, the United States was profoundly changed by the crisis of world war—for better and worse. Mobilizing for war transformed the scope and authority of the federal government, vastly expanding presidential powers. It ended the unemployment of the depression and stimulated an unprecedented economic boom that would enable millions of Americans to become middle-class citizens. It tilted the national economic balance toward the South Atlantic, Gulf, and Pacific coasts. It accelerated trends toward bigness in business, agriculture, and labor. It involved the military in the economy and education as never before. The war also catalyzed vital changes in racial and social relations, sometimes intensifying prejudices against minorities and women, but also broadening educational and employment opportunities that widened their public spheres and heightened their expectations. Fighting and winning the greatest war in history, moreover, was a vital coming-of-age experience for an entire generation that did much to give postwar American society a "can-do" spirit.

The United States, Britain, and the Soviet Union each met the crisis of war in a manner best suited to enlarge or preserve its sphere of influence in the world. To keep the Allies united and force the unconditional surrender of the Nazis and the Japanese, Roosevelt gave in to Churchill's pleas to delay a second front in Europe until 1944 and reluctantly accepted Soviet dominance in eastern Europe. To end the war in the Pacific as rapidly as possible, to minimize American losses, and to gain leverage over the Soviet Union, Truman ordered the dropping of atomic bombs on Japan. The United States became the world's superpower; and the mass destruction of the war and total defeat of the Axis created new crises and a Cold War that would see the United States play a role in global affairs that would have seemed inconceivable to most Americans just five years before.

FOF FURTHER REFERENCE

READINGS

Michael C. C. Adams, *The Best War Ever* (1994). A critical interpretation of the experience of war on the homefront and abroad.

CHRONOLOGY, 1933–1945

1931–1932 Japan invades Manchuria and creates a puppet government.

1933 Adolf Hitler becomes chancellor of Germany and assumes dictatorial powers.

1934–1936 Nye Committee investigations.

1935–1937 Neutrality Acts.

1937 Japan invades China.

1938 Germany annexes Austria; Munich Pact gives Sudetenland to Germany.
Kristallnacht, night of Nazi terror against German and Austrian Jews.

1939 Nazi-Soviet Pact.
Germany invades Poland; War II begins.

1940 Germany conquers the Netherlands, Belgium, France, Denmark, Norway, and Luxembourg.
Germany, Italy, and Japan sign the Tripartite Pact.
Selective Service Act.
Franklin Roosevelt elected to an unprecedented third term.

1941 Lend-Lease Act.
Roosevelt establishes the Fair Employment Practices Commission (FEPC).
Germany invades the Soviet Union.
Japan attacks Pearl Harbor; the United States enters World War II.
War Powers Act.

1942 Battles of Coral Sea and Midway halt Japanese offensive.
Internment of Japanese-Americans.
Revenue Act expands graduated income-tax system.
Allies invade North Africa (Operation Torch).
First successful atomic chain reaction.
CORE founded.

1943 Soviet victory in Battle of Stalingrad.
Coal miners strike; Smith-Connally War Labor Disputes Act.

1943 Detroit and Los Angeles race riots.
Allied invasion of Italy.
Big Three meet in Tehran.

1944 Allied invasion of France (Operation Overlord).
U.S. forces invade the Philippines
Roosevelt wins fourth term.
Battle of the Bulge.

1945 Big Three meet in Yalta.
Battles of Iwo Jima and Okinawa.
Roosevelt dies; Harry S. Truman becomes president.
Germany surrenders.
Truman, Churchill, and Stalin meet in Potsdam.
United States drops atomic bombs on Hiroshima and Nagasaki; Japan surrenders.

Beth Bailey and David Farber, *The First Strange Place: The Alchemy of Race and Sex in World War II Hawaii* (1992). A wide-ranging survey of the war's impact on Hawaiian society.

John Dower, *War Without Mercy* (1986). An insightful look at racism among the Americans and the Japanese.

John Keegan, *The Second World War* (1990). This is the standard account of the military aspects of the war.

Warren Kimball, *The Juggler: Franklin Roosevelt as Wartime Statesman* (1991). A study of the president's war aims and postwar vision.

Neil McMillen, ed., *Remaking Dixie: The Impact of World War II on the American South* (1997). Ten essays assess the war as a watershed in southern history.

Gerald D. Nash, *The American West Transformed: The Impact of the Second World War* (1985) and *World War II and the West: Reshaping the Economy* (1990). Two in-depth examinations of the changes in the West wrought by the war.

Holly Cowan Shulman, *The Voice of America* (1991). An in-depth account of America's wartime propaganda policies and programs.

E. B. Sledge, *With the Old Breed at Peleliu and Okinawa* (1990). A candid memoir of a marine's war in the Pacific.

David Wyman, *The Abandonment of the Jews* (1985). A critical assessment of the United States' role in the Holocaust.

WEBSITES

A People at War
http://www.nara.gov/exhall/people/people.html
A National Archives exhibit on American contributions to the war effort.

Photographs from the FSA and OWI
http://memory.loc.gov/ammem/fsowhome.html
Photographs of the American people, 1935–1945, from the Farm Security Administration and Office of War Information.

Resource Listing for WWII
http://www.sunsite.unc.edu/pha/index.html
A good introductory site to primary documents on all aspects of World War II.

The Atomic Bomb Controversy
http://www.glue.umd.edu/~enola/
A comprehensive site on the atomic bomb and the controversy surrounding its use.

The United States Holocost Memorial Museum
http://ushmm.org/index.html
The official website of the Holocaust Museum in Washington, D.C.

World War II Links
http://wrightmuseum.org/links.html
The Wright Museum's link to diverse information about the World War II era.

For additional works, please consult the Bibliography at the end of the book.

The Cold War Abroad and at Home, 1945–1952

Dan Collins grew up in Boston's South End community. Like most other Irish-American Catholic teenagers from families that had a hard time during the Great Depression, Dan could not wait to enlist once the Second World War began. He served with the U.S. First Army in North Africa and the Tenth Army in Okinawa, witnessing, as he put it, "more than I care to talk about." His body intact, although he suffered recurring nightmares, Dan returned to Boston in 1946 and stashed his uniform in the attic, "hoping to relax, get rich, and enjoy a bit of the good life."

Qualifying under the GI Bill of Rights for a small business loan, Collins started a Massachusetts construction company. He married, had a family, and, like many veterans, fretted about his wife's working outside the home, consulted Dr. Benjamin Spock's child-care manual, took his children's pictures with the first Polaroid camera, bought a Ford with automatic transmission, and moved to a split-level house in the suburbs. Dan earned more money in construction during the postwar housing boom than he had ever dreamed possible, and gained reassurance by attending church regularly and unfurling his flag on holidays. But he couldn't shake the nightmares, and peace of mind seemed as elusive as peace in the world. The decisive changes at home and abroad brought about by the Second World War intruded on and disturbed Dan Collins and most other Americans.

◀ **McCarthyism and the Hollywood Witch Hunts (detail)**
by Thomas Maitland Cleland

CHAPTER OUTLINE

815

Disagreement over the postwar fate of Eastern Europe had sparked a confrontation in which the Soviet Union and the United States each sought to reshape the postwar world to serve its own national interests. An uncompromising Truman squared off against an obsessive Stalin, each intensifying the insecurities of the other. A new form of international conflict emerged—a Cold War, or state of mutual hostility short of direct armed confrontation—in which the two powers did all they could to thwart the other's objectives.

Abandoning its historic aloofness from events outside the Western Hemisphere, the United States plunged into a global struggle to contain the Soviet Union and stop communism. In 1940 the United States had no military alliances, a small defense budget, and limited troops. By 1952 it had built a massive military establishment, signed mutual-defense pacts with some forty countries, directly intervened in the affairs of allies and enemies alike, erected military bases on every continent, and embarked on a seemingly unending nuclear-arms race.

Containing communism abroad also profoundly affected American thoughts and actions at home. It directly affected the economy, minority rights, and domestic politics. The anxieties provoked by fears of communist aggression and domestic subversion, moreover, spawned a second "Red Scare" reminiscent of the first one in 1919, with witch hunts undermining civil liberties. The reckless hurling of unfounded charges of disloyalty added "McCarthyism" to the American vocabulary. McCarthyism destroyed careers, silenced criticism, fueled intolerance, and discredited both the American Left and the Truman administration.

Dan Collins and many Americans thought McCarthyism made sense. The presence of communist spies at home and American setbacks abroad convinced him that "McCarthy must be on target in attacking those liberals in Washington." In 1952, believing the Truman administration to be "riddled with Reds and corruption," Collins, whose family had been staunch Democrats, decided that "it was time to give the other guys a chance." He turned to his hero, Dwight D. Eisenhower, the favorite general of most of his GI buddies, as the man needed in dangerous times.

This chapter focuses on five major questions:

■ How did the postwar policies of the United States and the Soviet Union contribute to the beginnings of the Cold War?

■ What was the doctrine of containment, and how was it implemented from 1947 to 1952?

■ What accounts for the decline of the New Deal spirit after World War II, and what effect did this have on Truman's domestic program?

■ How did the Cold War affect the rights of African-Americans?

■ What were the main domestic and international factors leading to the postwar Red Scare, and why did Americans react to it as they did?

THE POSTWAR POLITICAL SETTING, 1945–1946

After going without during the Great Depression and World War II, Americans like Dan Collins looked forward to the postwar era. The emerging Cold War, however, profoundly changed the United States for better and for worse. It spurred a quarter of a century of economic growth and prosperity, the longest such period in American history. It propelled research in medicine and science that, for the most part, made lives longer and better. And it contributed to a vast expansion of higher education that enabled many Americans to become middle class.

Demobilization and Reconversion

As soon as the war ended, GIs and civilians alike wanted those who had served in the military "home alive in '45." Troops demanding transport ships barraged Congress with threats of "no boats, no votes." On a single day in December 1945, sixty thousand postcards arrived at the White House with the message "Bring the Boys Home by Christmas." Truman bowed to popular demand. American military strength dropped from 12 million men at war's end to just 1.5 million by 1948.

The psychological problems of readjustment faced by veterans were intensified by a drastic housing shortage and soaring divorce rate. By 1950 more than a million couples who had married during the war had gotten divorced. Some veterans could not reestablish prewar ties with family and friends or adjust to the greater independence of once-submissive wives. Some experienced profound loneliness, missing the companionship and community of their wartime buddies. Others worried that automation—machines performing industrial operations faster and more accurately than human workers—would displace them, or that the stalled unionization drive, especially in the South and West, would depress wages. As war plants closed, reviving memories of the hard times immediately after World War I (see Chapter 22), many feared unemployment and economic

depression. Defense spending dropped from $76 billion in 1945 to under $20 billion in 1946, and more than a million defense jobs vanished.

"What's Become of Rosie the Riveter?" asked the *New York Times Magazine* in May 1946. She had probably lost her job in war industry, married that year, and had a child and/or had gone back to work. By the end of the decade more women were working outside the home than during World War II. Most women did not enter heavy industry, as they had during the war, or surge into the professions. Rather, they took jobs in traditional women's fields, especially office work and sales, to pay for family needs. Although the postwar economy created new openings for women in the labor market, many public figures urged women to seek fulfillment at home. With feminist ideology and organizations at low ebb, popular culture romanticized married bliss and demonized career women as a threat to social stability. Having endured depression and war, many women looked forward to traditional roles in a secure, prosperous America, and few answered negatively when popular magazines asked, "Isn't a Woman's Place in the Home?"

The G.I. Bill of Rights

In 1944 Congress had enacted the Servicemen's Readjustment Act. Commonly called the GI Bill of Rights or GI Bill, it was designed to forestall the expected recession by easing veterans back into the work force, as well as to reward the "soldier boys" and reduce their fears of female competition. The GI Bill gave veterans priority for many jobs, occupational guidance, and, if need be, fifty-two weeks of unemployment benefits. It also established veterans' hospitals and provided low-interest loans to returning GIs who were starting businesses or buying homes or farms. Almost four million veterans bought homes with government loans, fueling a baby boom, suburbanization, and a record demand for new goods and services.

Most vitally in the long run, the government promised to pay Dan Collins and millions of others who had served in the armed forces for up to four years of further education or job training. Not all Americans approved. Some opposed it as opening the door to socialism or to demands by minorities to special entitlements. Many university administrators, fearing that riffraff would sully their bastions of privilege, echoed the complaint of the University of Chicago president that their hallowed halls of learning would become "educational hobo jungles."

In 1946, flush with stipends of sixty-five dollars a month—ninety dollars for those with dependents—and up to five hundred dollars a year for tuition and books, 1.5 million veterans were attending college, spurring a huge increase in higher education and the creation of many new state and community colleges. Almost immediately, California State University established additional campuses in Fullerton, Hayward, Long Beach, Los Angeles, Northridge, Sacramento, and San Bernardino. Various "normal schools" for the training of teachers were upgraded into full-fledged colleges to create the State University of New York in 1948. Veterans made up over half of all college students in 1947. Often married and the fathers of young children, they were less interested in knowledge (frequently asking "what good will it do me?") than in a degree and a higher-paying job. To accommodate them, colleges converted old military barracks and Quonset huts into so-called Veterans' Village housing units and featured accelerated programs and more vocational or career-oriented courses. Campus life, at least for a time, became less social and less fun, as the survivors of Normandy spurned fraternity high-jinks in favor of "learning and earning," getting on with life.

Veteran Go to College

So many World War II veterans wanted to use their GI benefits for higher education that colleges were overwhelmed; many had to turn away students. In 1946, registration of new students was done at temporary desks set up in Wildermuth Field House at Indiana University.

To make room for the millions of GIs pursuing higher education after the war, many colleges limited the percentage of women admitted or barred students from out of state. The percentage of college graduates who were women dropped from 40 percent in 1949 to 25 percent in 1950. By then most women students were the working wives of the eight million veterans who were taking advantage of the GI Bill to go college.

The GI Bill democratized higher education. It allowed many more Americans (most the first in their families to attend) to go to college. Later they expected their children to follow suit, and higher education became an accepted part of the American Dream. Speaking for many other veterans, the president of a Midwest publishing firm would later say that "the GI Bill made all the difference in the world" to him; otherwise he "could never have afforded college." No longer a citadel of privilege, universities awarded almost half-million degrees in 1950, more than twice as many as in 1940.

FIGURE 26.1
Gross National Product, 1929–1990
Following World War II, the United States achieved the highest living standard in world history. Between 1950 and 1970, the real GNP, which factors out inflation and reveals the actual amount of goods and services produced, steadily increased. However, in 1972, 1974–1975, 1980, and 1982 the real GNP declined.

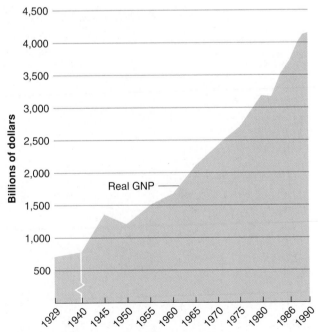

Source: Economic Report of the President, 1991. *Note:* Data shown in 1982 dollars.

The cost was huge. Between 1945 and 1956, when the education benefits ended, the government spent $14.5 billion to send 2.2 million veterans to colleges, 3.5 million to technical schools, and seven hundred thousand to agricultural instruction on farms. The money was well spent. The GI Bill fueled the upward mobility of veterans, enabling them to return in income taxes the money advanced to them by the government. It propelled millions of veterans into middle-class status in employment, education, and residence—the dream of Dan Collins and his buddies in the trenches—accelerating the postwar demand for goods and services.

The Economic Boom Begins

In addition to the assistance given returning servicemen, a 1945 tax cut of $6 billion spurred corporate investment in new factories and equipment and helped produce an economic boom that began in late 1946 (see Figure 26.1). Boosting postwar growth and prosperity, Americans spent much of the $135 billion they had saved from wartime work and service pay to satisfy their desire for consumer goods formerly beyond their means or not produced during the war. As advertisements promising "a Ford in your future" and an "all-electric kitchen of the future" furthered the rage to consume, sales of homes, cars, and appliances skyrocketed. Scores of new products—televisions, high-fidelity phonographs, filter cigarettes, automatic transmissions, freezers, and air conditioners—soon defined the middle-class lifestyle.

In 1944 representatives of the wartime Allies had met in Bretton Woods, New Hampshire, to hammer out a framework for the global economy in the postwar world. The Bretton Woods Agreement created the International Monetary Fund (IMF) to stabilize exchange rates by valuing ("pegging") other currencies in relation to the U.S. dollar. The agreement established the International Bank for Reconstruction and Development (World Bank) to help rebuild war-battered Asia and Europe. It also laid the groundwork for the 1947 General Agreement on Tariffs and Trade (GATT) to break up closed trading blocs and expand international trade. Since the United States largely controlled and funded these powerful economic institutions, they further aided the speedy reconversion of the American economy and gave the United States an especially favorable position in international trade and finance.

With many nations temporarily in ruins, American firms could import raw materials cheaply; with little competition from other industrial countries, they could

increase exports to record levels. U.S. economic dominance also resulted from the 35 percent increase in the productivity of American workers in the decade following the war. Wartime advances in science and technology, which led to revolutionary developments in such industries as electronics and plastics, further bolstered the notion of the postwar years as the dawn of "the American century."

Truman's Domestic Program

The hunger to enjoy the fruits of affluence left Americans with little appetite for more New Deal reforms, and Truman agreed. "I don't want any experiments," he confided to an aide. "The American people have been through a lot of experiments and they want a rest." Accordingly, the only major domestic accomplishment of the Seventy-ninth Congress was the Employment Act of 1946. The act committed the federal government to ensuring economic growth and established the Council of Economic Advisers to confer with the president and formulate policies for maintaining employment, production, and purchasing power. Congress gutted both the goal of full employment and the enhanced executive powers to achieve that objective, blocking Truman's main effort to advance beyond the New Deal.

Congressional eagerness to dismantle wartime controls worsened the nation's chief economic problem: inflation. Consumer demand outran the supply of goods, intensifying the pressure on prices. The Office of Price Administration (OPA) sought to hold the line by enforcing price controls, but food producers, manufacturers, and retailers opposed continuing wartime controls. While some consumers favored the OPA, others deplored it as an irksome relic of the war. In June 1946 Truman vetoed a bill that would have extended the OPA's life, but deprived it of power, effectively ending all price controls. Within a week food costs rose 16 percent and the price of beef doubled. "PRICES SOAR, BUYERS SORE, STEERS JUMP OVER THE MOON," headlined the *New York Daily News*.

Congress then passed, and Truman signed, a second bill extending price controls in weakened form. Protesting any price controls, farmers and meat producers threatened to withhold food from the market. Knowing that "meatless voters are opposition voters," "Horsemeat Harry," as some now referred to Truman, lifted controls on food prices just before the 1946 midterm elections. When Democrats fared poorly anyway, Truman ended all price controls. By then the con-

President Truman with Union Supporters
Following his veto of the Taft-Hartley bill and 1948 election victory, won, in large part, by the strong backing of organized labor, a smiling Truman dons a hard hat with copper miners in Butte, Montana.

sumer price index had jumped nearly 25 percent since the end of the war.

This staggering increase in the cost of living, coming on top of the end of wartime bonuses and overtime, intensified organized labor's demand for the higher wages that had been disallowed during the war. More than 4.5 million workers went on strike in 1946. When a United Mine Workers walkout paralyzed the economy for forty days, Truman ordered the army to seize the mines. A week later, after Truman had pressured owners to grant most of the union's demands, the miners returned to work, only to walk out again six months later. Meanwhile, on the heels of the first mine workers settlement, railway engineers and trainmen announced that they would shut down the nation's railroad system for the first time in history. "If you think I'm going to sit here and let you tie up this whole country," Truman shouted at the heads of the two unions, "you're crazy as hell." In May he asked Congress for authority to draft workers who struck vital industries. Before he could finish his speech, the unions gave in. Still, Truman's threat alienated most labor leaders.

By fall 1946, Truman had angered virtually every major interest group. Less than a third of the Americans polled approved of his performance. "To err is Truman," some gibed. One commentator suggested that the Democrats nominate Hollywood humorist W. C. Fields

for president: "If we're going to have a comedian in the White House, let's have a good one." Summing up the public discontent Republicans asked, "Had enough?" In the 1946 elections they captured twenty-five governorships and, for the first time since 1928, won control of both houses of Congress.

The public mood reflected more than just economic discontent. Under the surface laughter at stores advertising atomic sales or bartenders mixing atomic cocktails ran a new, deep current of fear, symbolized by the rash of "flying saucer" sightings that had begun after the war. An NBC radio program depicted a nuclear attack on Chicago in which most people died instantly. "Those few who escaped the blast, but not the gamma rays, died slowly after they had left the ruined city," intoned the narrator. "No attempt at identification of the bodies or burial ever took place. Chicago was simply closed." There was much talk of urban dispersal—resettling people in small communities in the country's vast open spaces—and of how to protect oneself in a nuclear attack. Some schoolchildren wore dog tags in order to be identified after an atomic attack, while also practicing crawling under their desks and putting their hands over their heads—"Duck and Cover"—to protect themselves from the bomb. The end of World War II had brought an uneasy peace.

ANTICOMMUNISM AND CONTAINMENT, 1946–1952

By late 1946 the simmering antagonisms between Moscow and Washington had come to a boil. With the Nazis defeated, the "shotgun wedding" between the United States and the U.S.S.R. dissolved into a struggle to fill the power vacuums left by the defeat of Germany and Japan, the exhaustion of Western Europe, and the crumbling of colonial empires in Asia and Africa. Misperception and misunderstanding mounted as the two powers sought greater security, each feeding the other's fears. The Cold War was the result.

Polarization and Cold War

The destiny of Eastern Europe, especially Poland, stood at the heart of the strife between the United States and the U.S.S.R. Wanting to end the Soviet Union's vulnerability to invasions from the West, Stalin insisted on a buffer zone of nations friendly to Russia along its western flank, and sought a demilitarized and deindustrialized Germany. He considered a Soviet sphere of influ-

ence in Eastern Europe essential to Russian security, a just reward for bearing the brunt of the war against Germany, and no different than the American spheres of influence in Western Europe, Japan, and Latin America. Stalin also believed that Roosevelt and Churchill had implicitly accepted a Soviet zone in Eastern Europe at the Yalta Conference (see Chapter 25).

With the 10-million-strong Red Army occupying most of Eastern Europe at war's end, Stalin had installed pro-Soviet puppet governments in Bulgaria and Romania by the time of the Potsdam Conference in July 1945, and supported the establishment of communist regimes in nominally independent Albania and Yugoslavia. Ignoring the Yalta Declaration of Liberated Europe, Stalin barred free elections in Poland and brutally suppressed Polish democratic parties. Poland, he said, was "not only a question of honor for Russia, but one of life and death."

Stalin's insistence on dominance in Eastern Europe collided with Truman's unwillingness to concede Soviet supremacy beyond Russia's borders. What Stalin saw as critical to Russian security, Truman viewed as a violation of national self-determination, a betrayal of democracy, and a cover for communist aggression. Truman and his advisers believed, that the appeasement of dictators fed their appetites for expansion. They thought that traditional balance-of-power politics and spheres of influence had precipitated both world wars, and that only a new world order maintained by the United Nations could guarantee peace.

Truman also thought that accepting the "enforced sovietization" of Eastern Europe would betray American war aims and condemn nations rescued from Hitler's tyranny to another totalitarian dictatorship. He worried, too, that a Soviet stranglehold on Eastern Europe would hurt American businesses dependent on exports and on access to raw materials. Truman understood that the Democratic party would invite political disaster if he reneged on the Yalta agreements. The Democrats counted on winning most of the votes of the 6 million Polish-Americans and millions of other Americans of Eastern European origin, who remained keenly interested in the fates of their homelands. Not appearing "soft on communism" was a political necessity.

Combativeness fit the temperament of the feisty Truman. Eager to prove he was in command, the president matched Stalin's intransigence on Polish elections with his own demands for Polish democracy. Encouraged by America's monopoly of atomic weapons and its position as the world's economic superpower, the new president hoped that the United States could, in the

words of a November 1945 State Department document, "establish the kind of world we want to live in."

The Iron Curtain Descends

As Stalin's and Truman's mistrust of one another grew, Stalin tightened his grip on Eastern Europe, stepping up his confiscation of materials and factories from occupied territories and forcing his satellite nations (countries under Soviet control) to close their doors to American trade and influence. In a February 1946 speech that the White House considered a "declaration of World War III," Stalin asserted that there could be no lasting peace with capitalism and vowed to overcome the American lead in weaponry no matter what the cost.

Two weeks later, George F. Kennan, an American diplomat in Moscow, wired a long telegram to his superiors at the State Department. A leading student of Russian affairs, Kennan described Soviet expansionism as moving "inexorably along a prescribed path, like a toy automobile wound up and headed in a given direction, stopping only when it meets some unanswerable force." Therefore, he concluded, U.S. policy must be the "long-term, patient but firm and vigilant containment of Russian expansive tendencies." The idea that only strong, sustained U.S. resistance could "contain" Soviet expansionism suited the mood of Truman, who a month earlier had insisted that the time had come "to stop babying the Soviets" and "to get tough with Russia." If they did not like it, the president added, they could "go to hell." "Containment"—a doctrine uniting military, economic, and diplomatic strategies to prevent communism from spreading and to enhance America's security and influence abroad—became Washington gospel.

In early March 1946 Truman accompanied former British Prime Minister Winston Churchill to Fulton, Missouri. In an address at Westminister College, Churchill warned of a new threat to Western democracies, this time from Moscow. Stalin, he said, had drawn an iron curtain across the eastern half of Europe. The threat of further Soviet aggression required an alliance of the English-speaking peoples and an Anglo-American monopoly of atomic weapons: "There is nothing the Communists admire so much as strength and nothing for which they have less respect than for military weakness."

Truman agreed. In spring 1946 he threatened to send in American combat troops unless the Soviets withdrew from oil-rich Iran. In June he submitted an atomic-energy control plan to the United Nations requiring the Soviet Union to stop all work on nuclear weapons and to submit to U.N. inspections before the United States would destroy its own atomic arsenal. As expected, the Soviets rejected the proposal and offered an alternative plan equally unacceptable to the United States. With mutual hostility escalating, the Soviets and Americans rushed to develop their own doomsday weapons. In 1946 Congress established the Atomic Energy Commission (AEC) to develop nuclear energy and nuclear weaponry. The AEC devoted more than 90 percent of its effort to atomic weapon development. By 1950, one AEC adviser reckoned, the United States "had a stockpile capable of somewhat more than reproducing World War II in a single day."

Thus, less than a year after American and Soviet soldiers had jubilantly met at the Elbe River to celebrate Hitler's defeat, the Cold War had begun. It would be waged by economic pressure, nuclear intimidation, propaganda, proxy wars, and subversion rather than by direct U.S.-Soviet military confrontation. It would be viewed by many Americans as an ideological conflict pitting democracy against dictatorship, freedom against totalitarianism, religion against atheism, and capitalism against socialism. It would affect American life as decisively as any military engagement that the nation had fought.

Containing Communism

On February 21, 1947, the British informed the United States that they could no longer afford to assist Greece and Turkey in their struggles against communist-supported insurgents and Soviet pressure for access to the Mediterranean. A stricken Britain asked the United States to bear the costs of thwarting communism in the eastern Mediterranean. The harsh European winter, the most severe in memory, intensified the sense of urgency in Washington. The economies of Western Europe had come to a near-halt. Famine and tuberculosis plagued the Continent. European colonies in Africa and Asia had risen in revolt. Cigarettes and candy bars circulated as currency in Germany, and the communist parties in France and Italy appeared ready to topple democratic coalition governments. Truman resolved to meet the challenge.

Truman first had to mobilize support for a radical departure from the American tradition of avoiding entangling alliances. In a tense White House on February 27, the new secretary of state, former army chief of staff George C. Marshall, presented the case for aid to Greece and Turkey to key congressional leaders. They balked, more concerned about inflation at home than civil war in Greece. But Dean Acheson, the newly appointed undersecretary of state, seized the moment.

The issue, he said, was not one of assisting the Greek oligarchy and Turkey's military dictatorship, but rather a universal struggle of freedom against tyranny. "Like apples in a barrel infected by the corruption of one rotten one," he warned, the fall of Greece or Turkey would open Asia, Western Europe, and the oil fields of the Middle East to the Red menace. "The Soviet Union [is] playing one of the greatest gambles in history," Acheson concluded. "We and we alone are in a position to break up this play." Shaken, the congressional leaders agreed to support the administration's request if Truman could "scare hell out of the country."

Truman did. On March 12, 1947, addressing a joint session of Congress, he asked for $400 million in military assistance to Greece and Turkey. In a world endangered by communism, Truman said, the United States must support free peoples everywhere "resisting attempted subjugation by armed minorities or by outside pressures." If we fail to act now, the president concluded, "we may endanger the peace of the world—and we shall surely endanger the welfare of our own nation." His rhetoric worked. Congress appropriated funds that helped the Greek monarchy defeat the rebel movement and helped Turkey stay out of the Soviet orbit.

Truman's statement of a new policy of active U.S. engagement to contain communism, soon known as the Truman Doctrine, persisted long after the crisis in the Mediterranean. It became as comprehensive as the Monroe Doctrine's "Keep Out" sign posted on the Western Hemisphere. It laid the foundation for American Cold War policy for much of the next four decades.

To back up the new international initiative, Congress passed the National Security Act of 1947. It created the National Security Council (NSC) to advise the president on strategic matters. It established the Central Intelligence Agency (CIA) to gather information abroad and to engage in covert activities in support of the nation's security. And it began the processes of transforming the old War and Navy Departments into a new Department of Defense and combining the leadership of the army, navy, and air force (now a separate and equal military service) under the Joint Chiefs of Staff.

Congress also approved the administration's proposal for massive U.S. assistance for European recovery in 1947. Advocated by the secretary of state, and thus called the Marshall Plan, it was to be another weapon in the arsenal against the spread of communism. With Europe, in Churchill's words, "a rubble heap . . . a breeding ground of pestilence and hate," Truman wanted to end the economic devastation believed to spawn communism. Truman correctly guessed that the Soviet Union and its satellites would refuse to take part in the plan, because of the controls linked to it, and accurately foresaw that Western European economic recovery would expand sales of American goods abroad and promote prosperity in the United States.

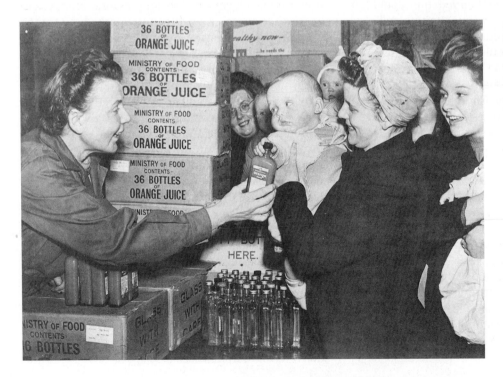

American Food for a Hungry Europe
Grateful English mothers line up for orange juice sent by the United States to assist Europeans devastated by the Second World War.

The Berlin Airlift, 1948
German children watching an American plane in "Operation Vittles" bring food and supplies to their beleaguered city. The airlift kept a city of 2 million people alive for nearly a year and made West Berlin a symbol of the West's resolve to contain the spread of Soviet communism.

Although denounced by the Left as a "Martial Plan" and by isolationist voices on the Right as a "Share-the-American-Wealth Plan," the Marshall Plan more than fulfilled its sponsors' hopes. By 1952 the economic and social chaos that communists had exploited had been overcome in the sixteen nations that shared the $17 billion in aid provided by the plan. Industrial production had risen 200 percent in Western Europe between 1947 and 1952, and that region had became a major center of American trade and investment.

Confrontation in Germany

Reacting to the Truman Doctrine and the Marshall Plan, the Soviet Union tightened its grip on Eastern Europe. Communist takeovers added Hungary and Czechoslovakia to the Soviet sphere in 1947 and 1948. Stalin then turned his sights on Germany. The 1945 Potsdam Agreement had divided Germany into four separate zones (administered by France, Great Britain, the Soviet Union, and the United States) and created a joint four-power administration for Germany's capital, Berlin, lying 110 miles within the Soviet-occupied eastern zone. As the Cold War intensified, the Western powers moved toward uniting their zones into an anti-Soviet West German state to help contain communism. Stalin viewed that with alarm. Demanding a powerless Germany that could never attack the Soviet Union again, he responded in June 1948 by blocking all rail and highway routes through the Soviet zone into Berlin. He calculated that the Western powers would be unable to provision the 2 million Berliners under their control and would either have to abandon plans to create a West German nation or accept a communist Berlin.

Truman resolved neither to abandon Berlin nor to shoot his way into the city and possibly trigger World War III. Instead he ordered a massive airlift to provide Berliners with the food and fuel necessary for survival. American cargo planes landed at West Berlin's Tempelhof Airport every three minutes around the clock, bringing a mountain of supplies. To prevent the Soviets from shooting down the U.S. planes, Truman ordered a fleet of B-29s, the only planes capable of delivering atomic bombs, to bases in England in July 1948. Truman hinted that he would use "the bomb" if necessary. Tensions rose. The president confided to his diary that "we are very close to war." Meanwhile, for nearly a year, "Operation Vittles" provided the blockaded city with a precarious lifeline.

In May 1949 the Soviets ended the blockade. Stalin's gambit had failed. The airlift highlighted American determination and technological prowess, revealed Stalin's readiness to starve innocent people to achieve his ends, and dramatically heightened anti-Soviet feeling in the West. U.S. public opinion polls in late 1948 revealed an overwhelming demand for "firmness and increased 'toughness' in relations with Russia."

Continuing fears of a Soviet attack on Western Europe fostered support for a rearmed West German state and for an Atlantic collective security alliance. In

May 1949 the United States, Britain, and France ended their occupation of Germany and approved the creation of the Federal Republic of Germany (West Germany). A month earlier, ten nations of Western Europe had adopted the North Atlantic Treaty, establishing a mutual defense pact with the United States and Canada in which "an armed attack against one or more of them . . . shall be considered an attack against them all." For the first time in its history, the United States entered into a peacetime military alliance. In effect, Western Europe now lay under the American "nuclear umbrella," protected from Soviet invasion by the U.S. threat of nuclear retaliation. Senator Robert Taft of Ohio, speaking for a small band of Republican senators, warned that this agreement would provoke the Soviets to respond in kind, stimulate a massive arms race, and open the floodgates of American military aid to Europe. But the Senate overwhelmingly approved the treaty, and in July the United States officially joined the North Atlantic Treaty

Organization (NATO), marking the formal end of U.S. isolationism.

Truman ranked the Marshall Plan and NATO as his proudest achievements, convinced that if the latter had been in existence in 1914 and 1939 that the world would have been spared two disastrous wars. Accordingly, he spurred Congress to authorize $1.3 billion for military assistance to NATO nations, persuaded General Dwight D. Eisenhower to become supreme commander of NATO forces, and authorized the stationing of four American army divisions in Europe as the nucleus of the NATO armed force. As Taft had predicted, the Soviet Union responded in kind to what it saw as a series of anti-Soviet provocations. It created the German Democratic Republic (East Germany) in 1949, and exploded its own atomic bomb that same year. Finally, in 1955, it set up a rival Eastern bloc military alliance, the Warsaw Pact (see Map 26.1). The United States and Soviet Union had divided Europe into two armed camps.

MAP 26.1

The Postwar Division of Europe

The wartime dispute between the Soviet Union and the Western Allies over Poland's future hardened after World War II into a Cold War that split Europe into competing American and Russian spheres of influence. Across an "iron curtain," NATO countries faced the Warsaw Pact nations.

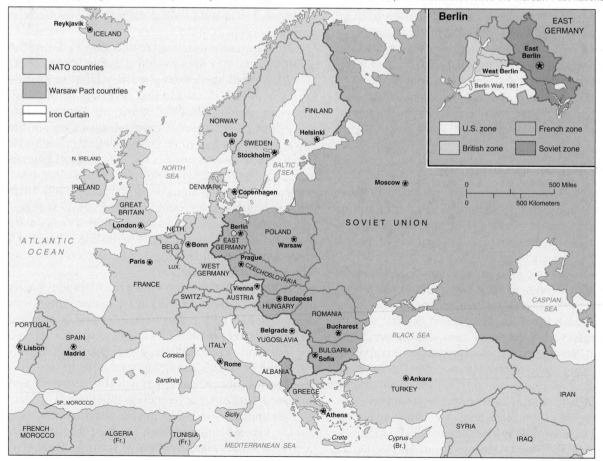

The Cold War in Asia

Moscow-Washington hostility also carved Asia into contending camps. The Russians created a sphere of influence in Manchuria; the Americans occupied and imposed a U.S.-written democratic constitution on Japan; and both partitioned a helpless Korea.

As head of the U.S. occupation forces in Japan, General Douglas MacArthur oversaw that nation's transformation from an empire in ruins into a prosperous democracy. By 1948 the Cold War had caused American policy to shift from keeping Japan's economy and government weak, thereby preventing it from threatening peace again, to making it as strong as possible an ally in a vital part of the world. The Japanese economy flourished, and, although the official occupation ended in 1952, a military security treaty allowed the U.S. to retain its Japanese bases and brought Japan under the American "nuclear umbrella." In further pursuit of containment, the United States helped crush procommunist insurgency in the Philippines and aided the efforts of France to reestablish its colonial rule in Indochina (Vietnam, Laos, and Cambodia), despite American declarations in favor of national self-determination and against imperialism.

In China, however, U.S. efforts to block communism failed. The Truman administration first tried to mediate the civil war between the Nationalist government of Jiang Jieshi (Chiang Kai-shek) and the communist forces of Mao Zedong (Mao Tse-tung). It also sent nearly $3 billion in aid to the Nationalists between 1945 and 1949. American dollars, however, could not force Jiang's corrupt government to reform itself and win the support of the Chinese people, whom it had widely alienated. As Mao's well-disciplined and motivated troops marched south, Jiang's soldiers mutinied or surrendered without fighting. Unable to stem revolutionary sentiment or to hold the countryside—where the communists, in Mao's words, "swam like fishes in the peasant sea"—Jiang's regime collapsed, and he fled to exile on the island of Taiwan (Formosa), off the coast of southeast China.

Mao's establishment of the communist People's Republic of China (PRC) shocked Americans. The most populous nation in the world, imagined by Washington as a counterforce to Asian communism and a market for American exports, had become "Red China." Although the Truman administration explained that it could have done nothing to alter the outcome and placed the blame for Jiang's defeat on his failure to reform China, most Americans were unconvinced. China's "fall" especially embittered conservatives who believed that America's power in the world rested on Asia, not Europe. The pres-

sure from the China lobby, which included congressional Republicans, conservative business leaders, and religious groups, influenced the administration's refusal to recognize the PRC, block its admission to the United Nations, and proclaim Jiang's Nationalist government in Taiwan as the legitimate government of China.

In September 1949, as the "Who lost China" debate raged, the president announced that the Soviet Union had exploded an atomic bomb, ending the American monopoly on nuclear weapons.. Suddenly the world had changed, shattering illusions of American invincibility. While military leaders and politicians pressed Truman to develop an even more powerful weapon, ordinary Americans sought safety in civil defense. Public schools held air-raid drills. "We took the drills seriously," recalled novelist Annie Dillard; "surely Pittsburgh, which had the nation's steel, coke, and aluminum, would be the enemy's first target." Four million Americans volunteered to be Sky Watchers, looking for Soviet planes. More than a million purchased or constructed their own family bomb shelters. Those who could not afford a bomb shelter were advised by the Federal Civil Defense Administration to "jump in any handy ditch or gutter . . . bury your face in your arms . . . never lose your head."

On January 31, 1950, stung by charges that he was "soft on communism," Truman ordered the development of a fusion-based hydrogen bomb (H-bomb). In November 1952 the United States exploded its first thermonuclear bomb, nicknamed Mike, containing ten times more power than the Hiroshima atomic bomb. The blast, equal to more than 10 million tons of TNT, completely vaporized one of the Marshall Islands in the Pacific, carved a mile-long crater in the ocean floor, and spilled radioactive dust over thousands of square miles. Nine months later the Soviets detonated their own H-bomb. The danger of thermonuclear terror escalated.

Truman also called for a top-secret review of defense policy by the National Security Council in early 1950. Completed in April, its secret report, NSC-68, emphasized the Soviet Union's military strength and aggressive intentions. To counter what the NSC saw as the U.S.S.R.'s "design for world domination"—the mortal challenge posed by the Soviet Union "not only to this Republic but to civilization itself"—NSC-68 urged a militarized anticommunist offensive, not merely containment. It endorsed massive increases in America's nuclear arsenal, a large standing army, vigorous covert actions by the CIA, and a quadrupling of the defense budget. Truman hesitated. An aide to Secretary of State Acheson recalled, "We were sweating over it, and then, with regard to NSC-68, thank God Korea came along." By

Late in 1942, looking for an isolated site that could be easily guarded and that had some buildings for temporary use, General Leslie Groves and Robert Oppenheimer found the Los Alamos Ranch School atop a circular mesa on the Pajarito ("Little Bird") Plateau, twenty miles northwest of Santa Fe, New Mexico. Only a poor jagged road led to the financially troubled school, which was secluded by the ponderosa pine-covered Jemez Range to the west and the Sangre de Cristo Mountains to the east.

The army quickly took possession of the school and the surrounding fifty-four thousand acres, supposedly for a "demolition range." Using the code name Project Y, it transformed "the Hill" into a temporary town of army-style barracks, old log cabins, adobe buildings, crude laboratories, and unpaved roads without street names. On that windswept outpost, patrolled by armed MPs and surrounded by high barbed wire fence, some five thousand scientists and engineers—called "longhairs" and "plumbers" by the soldiers enforcing the regimen and regimentation dictated by rigid security requirements—developed the atomic bombs that left Hiroshima and Nagasaki in ashes.

With the war over, most of the scientists at Los Alamos considered their job to be done. Almost all hoped to replace military control over the site with democratic decision making and to convert weapons of war into tools of peace. Fed up with wood-burning kitchen stoves, irregular food supplies, and being closely monitored by the army, they sought to return to pure science and teaching careers. Some, as Oppenheimer noted, had "learned sin" and felt guilty for what they had accomplished. By September 1945 State Highway 4, the rutted road connecting Los Alamos to Santa Fe, was blocked daily by a stream of departing trailers. By then, however, an atomic arms race with the Soviet Union had already begun, and Washington had decided to retain Los Alamos as a weapons research center to improve and stockpile atomic bombs. To do otherwise, said Norris Bradbury, who succeeded Openheimer as director of the Los Alamos National Laboratory in October, would "weaken the nation's bargaining power" and ultimately prove suicidal.

There would be no return to a pre-atomic America. Science and national security had become inseparable. In Los Alamos canteens gave way to restaurants, bathless cabins to comfortable homes, and dirt tracks to gracefully curved streets laid out according to the most up-to-date standards of urban design. Modern office and administrative complexes sprang up to serve the needs of a rapidly growing scientific community, and permanent concrete laboratories replaced wooden structures. But the wartime patterns of cooperation between the military, corporations, and university science remained, as did an atomic culture emphasizing rigid compartmentalization and classification of work, censorship, and secrecy. Not until the late 1950s did the gates that had kept Los Alamos a closed city come down.

The behaviors and beliefs that had guided the Manhattan Project spread to the West beyond New Mexico. Because of the cheap electricity generated by the Bonneville and Grand Coulee Dams, the Hanford Engineer Works in Washington continued to produce plutonium for atomic bombs, and Seattle's Boeing Airplane Company to manufacture the planes that could deliver them. With the postwar slogan "Air power is peace power," Boeing employed more Washingtonians than did the logging and lumbering industries.

Immediately after the war, moreover, proponents of air power established the Rand Corporation (a contraction of "r and d," research and development) as a branch of the Douglas Aircraft Corporation in Los Angeles to retain the services of scientists and engineers returning to civilian life. It became an independent unit in 1948, mainly supported by the Air Force, and moved to Santa

Monica, where it devised nuclear strategies. Californians also prospered from the defense expenditures going to Lockheed as well as from atomic research at the Lawrence Radiation Laboratory of the University of California, Berkeley, rocketry work at the California Institute of Technology's Jet Propulsion Laboratory in Pasadena, and nuclear weaponry developments at the Lawrence Livermore National Laboratory established by Edward Teller in 1952.

Although the Cold War and atomic arms race had furthered the modernization, prosperity, and urbanization of the West, there were serious environmental costs. The Atomic Energy Commission knew of the pathological and genetic dangers of nuclear particles as early as 1950, yet kept its medical studies hidden from the public. The race for nuclear superiority against the Soviets took precedence over the safety of Americans. While workers at Hanford sang of glowing in the dark in a ghoulish ditty they called "Plutonium Blues," radioactive liquids continued to be dumped into leaky tanks and trenches near the Columbia River. Nothing about health hazards was said to workers in the uranium processing plants of Colorado and Utah. Nor were the dangers of radioactivity conveyed to people who lived downwind of the nuclear test site near Las Vegas. There, more than a hundred atmospheric detonations of atomic devices in the 1950s sent pink-orange clouds of ash, dust, and gases over towns in Arizona, Nevada, and Utah, causing a sudden spurt of acute leukemia deaths and abnormally high cancer rates in the region. Soil in the Los Alamos area is still contaminated with plutonium residue from the Second World War, and the only movement at the Trinity Site of the original atomic explosion comes from wind-whipped sands in the desert called Jornado del Muerto— Journey of Death.

Soldiers of the 11th Airborn Division watch as an atomic explosion mushrooms into the sky during 1951 testing maneuvers in Nevada.

AEC Chairman Gordon Dean (3rd from right in front row) and other officials, scientists, and news photographers view a 1952 atomic bomb test.

FIGURE 26.2
National Defense Spending, 1941–1960

In 1950 the defense budget was $13 billion, less than a third of the total federal outlay. In 1961 defense spending reached $47 billion, fully half of the federal budget and almost 10 percent of the gross national product.

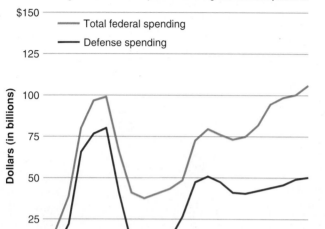

Source: From *American Promise*, Vol. 2, 4th ed., by James A. Henretta et al. Reprinted with permission of Bedford/St. Martin's.

the end of 1950 NSC-68 had become official U.S. policy (see Figure 26.2).

The Korean War, 1950–1953

After World War II the United States and Soviet Union temporarily divided Korea, which had been controlled by Japan since the Russo-Japanese War of 1904, at the thirty-eighth parallel for purposes of military occupation. This line then solidified into a political frontier between the American-supported Republic of Korea, or South Korea, and the Soviet-backed Democratic People's Republic of Korea in the north, each claiming the sole right to rule all of Korea.

On June 24, 1950, North Korean troops swept across the thirty-eighth parallel to attack South Korea (see Map 26.2). Truman decided to fight back, viewing the assault as a Soviet test of U.S. will and containment. "Korea is the Greece of the Far East," Truman maintained. "If we are tough enough now, if we stand up to them like we did in Greece . . . they won't take any next steps." Mindful of the failure of appeasement at Munich in 1938, he believed that the communists were doing in Korea exactly what Hitler and the Japanese had done in the 1930s: "Nobody had stood up to them. And that is what led to the Second World War." Having been accused of

"selling out" eastern Europe and "losing" China, Truman needed to prove he could stand up to "the Reds."

Without consulting Congress, Truman ordered air and naval forces to Korea from their bases in Japan on June 27. That same day he asked the United Nations to authorize action to repel the North Korean attack. Fortunately for Truman, the Soviet delegate was boycotting the Security Council to protest the U.N.'s unwillingness to seat a representative from Mao's China, and Truman gained approval for a U.N. "police action" to restore South Korea's border. He appointed General Douglas MacArthur to command the U.N. effort and ordered American ground troops into the fray. The Cold War had turned hot.

North Korean forces initially routed the disorganized American and South Korean troops. "All day and night we ran like antelopes," recalled Sergeant Raymond Remp. "We didn't know our officers. They didn't know us. We lost everything we had." Then, in mid-September, with U.N. forces cornered on the tip of the peninsula around Pusan, struggling to avoid being pushed into the sea, MacArthur's troops landed at Inchon in a brilliant amphibious maneuver. Within two weeks, U.S. and South Korean forces drove the North Koreans back across the thirty-eighth parallel. Seeking an all-out victory, MacArthur persuaded Truman to let him cross the border to liberate all of Korea from communism.

As U.N. troops swept across the thirty-eighth parallel and neared the Yalu River—the boundary between Korea and China—the Chinese warned that they would not "sit back with folded hands and let the Americans come to the border." Dismissing the threat as "hot air," an overconfident MacArthur deployed his forces in a thin line south of the river. On November 25 thirty-three Chinese divisions (about three hundred thousand men) counterattacked. Within two weeks they had driven the U.N. forces south of the thirty-eighth parallel. By winter's end the contending forces were deadlocked at roughly the original dividing line between the two Koreas. "We were eyeball to eyeball," recalled Bev Scott, one of the first black lieutenants to head a racially integrated infantry squad.

Just 20 meters of no man's land between us. We couldn't move at all in the daytime without getting shot at . . . It was like World War I. We lived in a maze of bunkers and deep trenches. . . . There were bodies strewn all over the place. Hundreds of bodies frozen in the snow. We could see the arms and legs sticking up. Nobody could get their dead out of there.

U.S. Marines Battling for Seoul, September 1950
From the start Truman believed that the Soviet Union had orchestrated the North Korean invasion of South Korea. He steadfastly maintained that "if the Russian totalitarian state was intending to follow in the path of the dictatorship of Hitler and Mussolini, they [had to] be met head on in Korea."

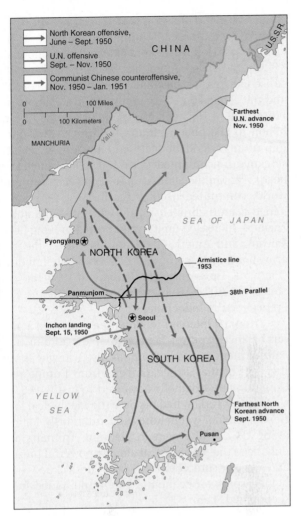

MAP 26.2
The Korean War, 1950–1953
The experience of fighting an undeclared and limited war for the limited objective of containing communism confused the generation of Americans who had just fought an all-out war for the total defeat of the Axis. General MacArthur spoke for the many who were frustrated by the Korean conflict's mounting costs in blood and dollars: "There is no substitute for victory."

Stalemated, Truman reversed course. In spring 1951 he sought a negotiated peace based on the original objective of restoring the integrity of South Korea. MacArthur rocked the boat, however, pressing for authority to blockade and bomb Mao's China and to "unleash" Jiang Jieshi's forces to invade the mainland. "In war" MacArthur insisted "there is no substitute for victory." But Truman, fearing such actions would bring the Soviet Union into the conflict, shot back, "We are trying to prevent a world war—not start one."

When MacArthur continued to criticize Truman's limited war—publicly blasting his decision to keep the fight confined to one area and not use nuclear weapons—the president fired the general on April 10, 1951. The Joint Chiefs endorsed Truman's decision, but public opinion backed the general. The very idea of limited war, of containing rather than defeating the enemy, baffled many Americans; and the mounting toll of American casualties in pursuit of a stalemate angered them. It seemed senseless. Despite the warning by General Omar Bradley, Chairman of the Joint Chiefs of Staff, that MacArthur's proposals "would involve us in

the wrong war at the wrong place in the wrong time and with the wrong enemy," a growing number of Americans listened sympathetically to Republican charges that communist agents were in control of American policy.

After two more years of fighting, the two sides reached an armistice in July 1953 that left Korea as divided as it had been at the start of the war. The "limited" conflict cost the United States 54,246 lives, another 103,284 wounded, and some $54 billion. The Chinese lost about 900,000 men, and both Korean armies lost

about 800,000. Following the pattern of World War II, massive U.S. "carpet bombing" killed over 2 million civilians, and left North Korea looking like a moonscape.

The so-called forgotten war also had significant consequences. It accelerated implementation of NSC-68 and the expansion of containment into a global policy. From 1950 to 1953 defense spending zoomed from $13 billion to $60 billion—from one-third to two-thirds of the entire federal budget—and the American atomic stockpile mushroomed from 150 to 750 nuclear warheads. The United States acquired new bases around the world, committed itself to rearm West Germany, and joined a mutual-defense pact with Australia and New Zealand. Increased military aid flowed to Jiang Jieshi on Taiwan, and American dollars supported the French army fighting the communist Ho Chi Minh in Indochina (Vietnam, Laos, and Cambodia). By 1954 the United States would be paying three-quarters of the cost of France's war in Indochina.

Truman's intervention in Korea preserved a precarious balance of power. It stepped up the administration's commitment to the anticommunist struggle as well as the shift of that struggle's focus from Europe to Asia. Containment, originally advanced to justify U.S. aid to Greece and Turkey, had become the ideological foundation for a major war in Korea and, ominously, for a deepening U.S. involvement in Vietnam. Truman's actions enhanced the powers of an already powerful presidency and set the precedent for later undeclared wars. It helped spark an economic boom and added fuel to a second Red Scare.

THE TRUMAN ADMINISTRATION AT HOME, 1945–1952

Since 1929 most Americans had known little but the sufferings and shortages of depression and war. They wanted to enjoy life. The Cold War both hindered that and helped create a postwar affluence that changed dreams into reality. Americans flocked to the suburbs, launched a huge baby boom, and rushed to buy refrigerators and new cars. Sales of TV sets soared from fewer than seven thousand in 1946 to more than 7 million by 1949, and by 1953 half of all U.S. homes had at least one television. Not all Americans shared these good times. Poverty remained a stark fact of life for millions. Minorities experienced the grim reality of racism. Yet a major movement by African-Americans for equality emerged from these Cold War years.

Family and career, not public issues, interested most Americans. The New Deal's reform energies subsided into complacency. Although Truman occasionally sought liberal measures, the mood of the times was against him. An increasingly conservative political order wanted to reduce taxes, not raise them, and to contract, not expand, the power of government and organized labor. Anticommunism bred repression, stifled dissent, and rewarded conformity, further undercutting efforts for progressive change.

The Eightieth Congress, 1947–1948

The Republicans of the Eightieth Congress interpreted the 1946 elections as a mandate to reverse the New Deal. As "Mr. Republican," Senator Robert A. Taft of Ohio, declared, "We have got to break with the corrupting idea that we can legislate prosperity, legislate equality, legislate opportunity." Congress defeated Democratic bills to raise the minimum wage and to provide federal funds for education and housing.

Truman and the GOP waged their major battle over the pro-union Wagner Act of 1935 (see Chapter 24). The massive postwar strikes by miners and railway workers had created a consensus for curbing union power. In 1947 more than twenty states passed laws to restrict union activities. Most important, Congress passed the Taft-Hartley Act (officially the Labor-Management Relations Act), which barred the closed shop, outlawed secondary boycotts, required union officials to sign loyalty oaths, and permitted the president to call a cooling-off period to delay any strike that might endanger national safety or health. Although hardly the "slave labor bill" that unions characterized it, the Taft-Hartley Act weakened organizing drives in the nonunion South and West, hastening the relocation of labor-intensive industries, such as textiles, from the Northeast and Midwest to the Sunbelt. It also helped drive communists and other leftists out of CIO leadership positions, making organized labor less of a social justice movement and more of a special-interest group.

Eager for labor's support in the upcoming presidential election, Truman vetoed the bill. Congress overrode the veto. But Truman had taken a major step toward reforging FDR's majority coalition. He played the role of a staunch New Dealer to the hilt, urging Congress to repeal Taft-Hartley; raise the minimum wage, social-security benefits, and price supports for farmers; enact federal aid to education and housing; and adopt a federal health insurance program. To woo ethnic voters of Eastern European descent, Truman stressed his opposi-

The Good Life, Forties-style
After the war, Americans grabbed for the good life, whether that meant jiving to a jukebox, trying some fast food at the first McDonald's in San Bernadino, California, or celebrating Thanksgiving—as this couple in Joliet, Illinois, does with their sixteen children.

tion to the Iron Curtain. To court Jewish-American voters as well as express his deep sympathy toward Holocaust survivors, he overrode the objections of the State Department, which feared alienating the oil-rich Arab world, and extended diplomatic recognition to the new state of Israel immediately after it proclaimed independence on May 14, 1948.

The Politics of Civil Rights and the Election of 1948

In 1947 Jackie Robinson, the grandson of a slave, joined the Brooklyn Dodgers, breaking major-league baseball's color barrier. It would not be an easy trip around the bases to interracial harmony. Unhappy fans insulted Robinson and mailed death threats. Opposition pitchers tried to bean him and runners to spike him. The humiliations and stress injured him physically and psychologically. But Robinson endured and triumphed,

winning Rookie of the Year and then going on to win Most Valuable Player in the National League, inducted into the Baseball Hall of Fame, and see every major-league team integrated by the late 1950s. Robinson's example also led to the start of integration by the Cleveland and Los Angeles franchises of the All-American Football Conference and the Boston Celtics of the National Basketball Association. African-Americans took heart and pressed assertively for an end to racial discrimination.

In 1945 Walter White, the head of the NAACP had noted, "World War II has immeasurably magnified the

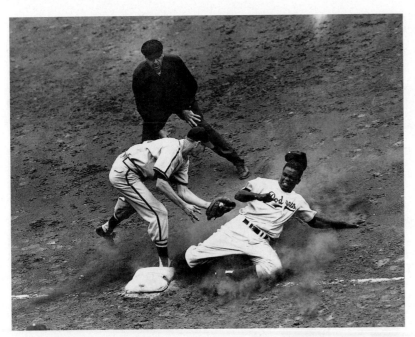

Jackie Robinson, 1947
Before he became the first African-American to play major league baseball, Robinson had excelled at track as well as baseball at UCLA and had been an army officer in World War II. Even his brilliant play for the Brooklyn Dodgers did not save him from racial taunts of fans and players or exclusion from restaurants and hotels that catered to his white teammates.

the political importance of the growing black vote, particularly in northern cities, he promised action. Truman realized, too, that white racism damaged U.S. relations with much of the world. The U.S.S.R. highlighted the mistreatment of African-Americans, both to undercut U.S. appeals to the nonwhites of Africa, Asia, and Latin America, and to counter criticism of its own repression behind the Iron Curtain. Accordingly, Truman established the first President's Committee on Civil Right. Its 1947 report, *To Secure These Rights*, dramatized the inequities of life in Jim Crow America and emphasized all the compelling moral, economic, and international reasons for the government to enact federal legislation outlawing lynching and the poll tax, establish a permanent FEPC, desegregate the armed forces, and support a legal assault on segregation in education, housing, and interstate transportation.

Southern segregationists reacted immediately, accusing Truman of "stabbing the South in the back" and warning of a Dixie boycott of the national Democratic ticket. Truman backtracked. Cowed by the prospect of losing the Solid South, he dropped plans to submit civil-rights bills to Congress and endorsed a weak civil-rights plank for the Democratic platform. But liberals and urban politicians who needed the votes of African-Americans rejected the president's feeble civil-rights plank at the Democratic convention in July 1948 and committed the party to act on Truman's original proposals. Thirty-five delegates from Alabama and Mississippi stalked out, joining other southern segregationists to form the States' Rights Democratic party, which nominated Governor Strom Thurmond of South Carolina for the presidency. The "Dixiecrats" hoped to win enough electoral votes to deny Truman reelection, restore their dominance in the Democratic party, and preserve the segregationist "southern way of life." They placed their electors on the ballot as the regular Democratic ticket in several states, posing a major roadblock to Truman's chances of victory.

Negro's awareness of the disparity between the American profession and practice of democracy." The war had heightened African-American expectations for racial equality, and numerous blacks, especially veterans, were actively demanding a permanent Fair Employment Practices Commission (FEPC), the outlawing of lynching, and the end of the poll tax. Voter-registration drives raised the percentage of southern blacks registered to vote from 2 percent in 1940 to 12 percent in 1947.

Fearful of further gains as well as of a bold new spirit among African-Americans, some southern whites turned to violence. In 1946 whites killed several black war veterans who had voted that year in rural Georgia, flogged to death an "uppity" black tenant farmer in Mississippi, blowtorched a young black in Louisiana for daring to enter a white woman's house, and blinded a black soldier for failing to sit in the rear of a bus in South Carolina. In Columbia, Tennessee, in 1946 whites rioted against blacks who insisted on their rights. The police then arrested seventy blacks and did nothing as a white mob broke into the jail to murder two black prisoners.

In September 1946 Truman met with a delegation of civil-rights leaders. Believing that every American should enjoy the full rights of citizenship and knowing

Truman's electoral hopes faded further when left-wing Democrats joined with communists to launch a new Progressive party, which nominated former Vice President Henry A. Wallace for president and called for

friendly relations with the Soviet Union. The Wallace candidacy threatened Truman's chances in key northern states, where many urban Democrats saw Wallace as the true heir of New Deal liberalism. The divisions in the Democratic party heartened Republicans. To play it safe they bypassed conservative, controversial senator Robert A. Taft and nominated moderate, bland governor Thomas E. Dewey of New York. Confident of victory, Dewey ran a complacent campaign designed to offend the fewest people. Truman, in contrast, campaigned tirelessly, blasting the "no-good, do-nothing" Republican-controlled Eightieth Congress. To shouts of "Give 'em hell, Harry," the president crisscrossed the country hammering away at the GOP as the party of "privilege, pride, and plunder." Political pundits applauded Truman's spunk, but all fifty of the experts polled by *Newsweek* predicted a sure Dewey victory.

A surprised nation awoke the day after the election to learn that the president had won the biggest upset in electoral history and that his party had regained control of both houses of Congress (see Map 26.3). Ironically, the Progressives and Dixiecrats had helped Truman. Their radicalism had kept moderate Democrats safely in the fold. The Berlin crisis, a coup in Czechoslovakia, and Wallace's failure to repudiate communist support forced most liberals away from the Progressives. Although the support for Thurmond signaled the first cracks in the solid South, few southern Democrats felt sufficiently threatened by Truman's civil-rights stand to desert the party in 1948. "The only sane and constructive course to follow is to remain in the house of our fathers—even though the roof leaks, and there be bats in the belfry, rats in the pantry, a cockroach in the kitchen and skunks in the parlor," explained a southern officeholder. Moreover, Dixiecrat defections had freed Truman to campaign as a champion of civil rights. In July 1948 he had issued executive orders barring discrimination in federal employment and requiring "equality of treatment and opportunity for all persons in the armed services without regard to race, color, religion or national origin." Truman had also benefited from Supreme Court decisions declaring segregation in interstate bus transportation unconstitutional (*Morgan v. Virginia*) and outlawing restrictive housing covenants that forbade the sale or rental of property to minorities (*Shelley v. Kraemer*).

Truman's unexpected victory proved his skills as a campaigner and, even more, the political power of the New Deal coalition of workers, farmers, and ethnic and racial minorities. "In a sense," wrote one journalist, "Roosevelt won his greatest victory after his death."

MAP 26.3
The Election of 1948

	Electoral Vote	Popular Vote	Percentage of Popular Vote
Democratic Harry S Truman	303	24,105,812	49.5
Republican Thomas E. Dewey	189	21,970,065	45.1
States' Rights Strom Thurmond	39	1,169,063	2.4
Minor parties	–	1,442,667	3.0

A. Philip Randolph
Leading a group of protesters at the 1948 Democratic national convention, Randolph vowed: "I am prepared to oppose a Jim Crow army till I rot in jail." Soon after, however, President Truman issued Executive Order 9981, asserting equality of treatment and opportunity for all members of the armed services, and a pleased Randolph called off his protest.

The Fair Deal

Proclaiming in his inaugural address of 1949 that "every segment of our population . . . has a right to expect from our government a fair deal," Truman proposed a domestic agenda that included civil rights, national health care legislation, and federal aid to education, among many other measures. Unlike the New Deal, the Fair Deal was based on the belief in continual economic growth: the constantly expanding economic pie would mean a progressively bigger piece for most Americans (so they would not resent helping those left behind) and for the government (so it would have the revenue to pay for social welfare programs.

The Eighty-first Congress complied with Truman's requests to extend existing programs but rejected new Fair Deal measures. It raised the minimum wage; increased social-security benefits and coverage; expanded appropriations for public power, conservation, and slum clearance; and authorized the construction of nearly a million low-income housing units. It also enacted the Displaced Persons Act, which allowed entry to 205,000 survivors of the Nazi forced-labor and death camps. But Congress rejected federal aid to education, national health insurance, civil-rights legislation, larger farm subsidies, and repeal of the Taft-Hartley Act.

Congress's rejection of most Fair Deal proposals stemmed from Truman's own lessening commitment to domestic reform in favor of foreign and military affairs, as well as from the power of the coalition of Republicans and conservative Democrats that held sway in Congress. Widening prosperity sapped public enthusiasm for reform. In 1949, according to the Hickock Manufacturing Company, the belt size of the average American man had expanded to thirty-four inches, up from the depression years' average of thirty-one inches. The full-belly sense of well-being and popular fears of communism doomed hopes for expanded liberal reform.

THE POLITICS OF ANTICOMMUNISM

As the Cold War worsened, many Americans came to believe that communist spies and traitors at home were the cause of setbacks for the United States abroad. How else could the communists have defeated Jiang in China and built an atomic bomb? Millions of fearful Americans enlisted in a crusade that equated dissent with disloyalty and sought scapegoats to blame for the nation's problems.

Similar intolerance had prevailed in the Red Scare of 1919–1920 (see Chapter 22). Since its establishment in 1938, the House Committee on Un-American Activities (later called the House Un-American Activities Committee, or HUAC) had served as a platform for right-wing denunciations of the New Deal as a communist plot. Only the extreme Right initially took such charges seriously. But after World War II mounting numbers of Democrats as well as Republicans climbed aboard the anti-Red bandwagon.

The Great Fear affected both governmental and personal actions. Millions of Americans were subjected to security investigations and loyalty oaths. Anticommunist extremism destroyed the Left, undermined labor militancy, spawned a "silent generation" of college students, and ensured foreign-policy rigidity and the defeat of liberal reforms.

Loyalty and Security

American fear of a war with the Soviet Union and of other countries' going communist raised legitimate concerns about security in the United States. The Communist party had claimed eighty thousand members in the United States during the Second World War, and far more sympathizers. No one knew how many party members occupied sensitive government and military positions. In mid-1945 a raid on the offices of a procommunist magazine, *Amerasia*, revealed that classified documents had been given to the periodical by two State Department employees and a naval intelligence officer. Then the Canadian government exposed a major spy network that had passed American atomic secrets to the Soviets during the war. Republicans accused the Democratic administration of being "soft on communism."

A week after his Truman Doctrine speech of March 1947, the president issued Executive Order 9835, establishing the Federal Employee Loyalty Program to root out subversives in the government. The first such peacetime program, it barred members of the Communist party and anyone guilty of "sympathetic association" with it from federal employment. "Reasonable grounds for belief that the person is disloyal," such as being homosexual, led to dismissal. Those suspected were allowed neither to face their accusers nor to require investigators to reveal sources. Instead of focusing on potential subversives in high-risk areas, review boards extended the probe to the associations and beliefs of every government worker.

Mere criticism of American foreign policy could result in an accusation of disloyalty. Clouds of suspicion

The Red Menace, 1949

Although Hollywood generally avoided overtly political films, it released a few dozen explicitly anticommunist films in the postwar era. Depicting American communists as vicious hypocrites, if not hardened criminals, Hollywood's Cold War movies, like its blacklist, were an effort to protect its imperiled public image after HUAC's widely publicized investigation of the movie industry.

hovered over those who liked foreign films and favored the unionization of federal workers or civil rights for blacks. "Of course the fact that a person believes in racial equality doesn't prove he's a communist," mused an Interior Department Loyalty Board chairman, "but it certainly makes you look twice, doesn't it?" Some people lost jobs because they had friends who were radicals or had once belonged to organizations now declared disloyal. People's reading became fair game. An employee was asked if he read the *New Republic.* Another was asked, "What do you think of female chastity?" Tastes in music might trigger concern.

Of the 4.7 million jobholders and applicants who underwent loyalty checks by 1952, 560 were fired or denied jobs on security grounds, several thousand resigned or withdrew their applications, and countless were intimidated. Although Loyalty Board probes uncovered no proof of espionage or subversion, they heightened people's fears of what Truman called "the enemy within," adding credibility to the Red Scare. "Why lead with your chin?" became a dominant reflex. "If communists like apple pie and I do," claimed one federal worker, "I see no reason why I should stop eating it. But I would."

The Anticommunist Crusade

The fear of disloyalty generated by Truman's inquest fed mounting anticommunist hysteria. It promoted fears of

communist infiltrators and legitimated a witch hunt for subversives. FBI chief J. Edgar Hoover claimed that colleges were centers of "red propaganda," and a senator, decrying "communist-line textbooks" and professors, accused colleges of admitting "good Americans" and returning them "four years later as wild-eyed radicals." At Yale the FBI, with the consent of the college administration, spied on students and faculty, screening candidates for jobs and fellowships. Many universities banned controversial speakers, and Truman's Office of Education introduced a "Zeal for Democracy" campaign, providing local school boards with curriculum materials to combat "communist subversion." New York State's Department of Education added a new unit on "How Can We Fight Communism?" to its *Teaching American History* curriculum. Popular magazines featured articles like "Reds Are After Your Child." Comics joined the fray: "Beware, commies, spies, traitors, and foreign agents! Captain America, with all loyal, free men behind him, is looking for you, ready to fight until the last one of you is exposed for the yellow scum you are." The Ford Motor Company put FBI agents on its payroll to look for communists on the assembly line.

By the end of Truman's term, thirty-nine states had created loyalty programs, most with virtually no procedural safeguards. Schoolteachers, college professors, and state and city employees throughout the nation had to sign loyalty oaths or lose their jobs. No one knows for sure how many were dismissed, denied tenure, or

quietly drifted away, leaving behind colleagues too frightened to speak out.

In 1947 the House Un-American Activities Committee began hearings to expose communist influence in American life. HUAC's probes blurred distinctions between dissent and disloyalty, between radicalism and subversion. Those called to testify were in a bind. When asked whether they had ever been members of the Communist party, witnesses could say yes and be forced to reveal the names of others; say no and be vulnerable to charges of perjury; or refuse to answer, pleading the First or Fifth Amendments, and risk being viewed by the public as a communist. In Washington, D.C., a man who invoked the Fifth Amendment lost his license to sell secondhand furniture, and his livelihood. A woman who did the same suffered a boycott that destroyed her once-thriving drugstore. A Stanford University biochemist poisoned himself rather than respond to HUAC's questions. In a suicide note he blasted the committee for wrecking careers and lives: "The scientific mind cannot flourish in an atmosphere of fear, timidity, and imposed conformity."

To gain publicity for itself and to influence the content of movies, HUAC also probed Hollywood. In its hearings on "Communist infiltration of the motion picture industry," HUAC listened to testimony by "friendly witnesses," such as conservative novelist Ayn Rand, film producer Walt Disney, and Screen Actors Guild president Ronald Reagan. They saw as proof of communist activity wartime films about the Soviet Union showing Russians smiling, or movies featuring the line "share and share alike, that's democracy." In 1947, HUAC cited for contempt of Congress a group of prominent film directors and screenwriters who, claiming the freedom of speech and assembly guaranteed by the First Amendment, refused to say whether they had been members of the Communist party. The so-called Hollywood Ten—some of them Communists, all of them leftists—were convicted of contempt and sent to prison. The threat of further investigations prompted the movie colony, financially dependent on favorable press and public opinion, to deny work to them as well as to other "unfriendly witnesses," such as directors Orson Welles and Charlie Chaplin. Soon the studios established a blacklist barring the employment of anyone suspected of communism.

Between 1947 and 1952 Hollywood brought out almost fifty anticommunist movies. One studio canceled a film on Longfellow, explaining that Hiawatha had tried to stop wars between Indian tribes and that some might see the effort as communist propaganda for peace.

Another withdrew plans to film the story of Robin Hood because he took from the rich and gave to the poor.

HUAC also frightened the labor movement into expelling communists and avoiding progressive causes. Fearful of appearing "red," or even "pink," most unions focused on securing better pay and benefits for their members.

The 1948 presidential election campaign also fed national anxieties. Truman lambasted Henry Wallace as a Stalinist dupe and accused the Republicans of being "unwittingly the ally of the communists." In turn, the GOP dubbed the Democrats "the party of treason." Republican Congressman Richard Nixon of California charged that Democrats bore responsibility for "the unimpeded growth of the communist conspiracy in the United States."

To blunt such accusations, Truman's Justice department prosecuted eleven top leaders of the American Communist party under the Smith Act of 1940, which outlawed any conspiracy advocating the overthrow of the government. In 1951, in *Dennis* v. *United States*, the Supreme Court affirmed the conviction and jailing of the communists, despite the absence of any acts of violence or espionage, declaring that Congress could curtail freedom of speech if national security required such restriction.

Ironically, the Communist party was fading into obscurity at the very time when politicians magnified its threat. By 1950 its membership had shrunk to fewer than thirty thousand. Yet Truman's attorney general warned that American Reds "are everywhere—in factories, offices, butcher stores, on street corners, in private businesses—and each carries in himself the germ of death for society."

Alger Hiss and the Rosenbergs

Nothing set off more alarms of a Red conspiracy in Washington than the case of Alger Hiss. Amid the 1948 political campaign, HUAC conducted a hearing in which Whittaker Chambers, a *Time* editor and former Soviet agent who had broken with the communists in 1938, identified Hiss as belonging to a secret communist cell in the 1930s.

A rumpled, repentant, former communist and college dropout, Chambers appeared to be a tortured soul crusading to save the West from the Red peril. The elegant Hiss, in contrast, seemed the very symbol of the liberal establishment. He was a Harvard-trained lawyer who had clerked for Supreme Court Justice Oliver Wendell Holmes, served FDR in the New Deal and later

Left and Right in Cold War America
Arrested in 1950 and charged with being members of a Soviet atomic spy ring during World War II,
American communists Julius and Ethel Rosenberg were found guilty of conspiring to commit
espionage and were executed in 1953. Although they and their defenders protested their innocence,
Soviet documents made public in the 1990s identified Julius Rosenberg as a secret communist agent.

as a State Department official, and presided over the inaugural meeting of the United Nations. For conservative Republicans, a better villain could not have been invented. Hiss denied any communist affiliation or even knowing Chambers, and most liberals believed him. They saw him as a victim of conservatives bent on tarnishing New Deal liberalism. Truman denounced Chambers's allegation as a "red herring" being used to deflect attention from the failures of the Eightieth Congress.

To those suspicious of the Roosevelt liberal tradition, Chambers's persistence and Hiss's bizarre notions—"Until the day I die, I shall wonder how Whitakker Chambers got into my house to use my typewriter"— intensified fears that the Democratic administration teemed with communists. Under relentless questioning by Congressman Richard Nixon, Hiss finally admitted that he had known Chambers and had even let Chambers have his car and live in his apartment. But he still denied ever having been a communist. Chambers then broadened his accusation, claiming that Hiss had committed espionage in the 1930s by giving him secret State Department documents to be sent to the Soviet Union. To prove his charge, Chambers led federal agents to his farm in Maryland where, in a hollowed-out pumpkin, he had microfilm copies of confidential government papers that had been copied on a typewriter traced to Hiss. A grand jury then indicted Hiss for perjury. (The

statute of limitations for espionage prevented a charge of treason.) After one trial ended in a hung jury, a second resulted in a conviction and a five-year prison sentence for Hiss. While prominent Democrats continued to defend Hiss, Republican conservatives were emboldened. Who knew how many other bright young New Dealers had betrayed the country?

Hard on the heels of the Hiss conviction, another spy case shocked Americans. In February 1950 the British arrested Klaus Fuchs, a German-born scientist involved in the Manhattan Project, for passing atomic secrets to the Soviets during the Second World War. Fuchs's confession led to the arrest of his American accomplice, Harry Gold, who then implicated David Greenglass, a machinist who had worked at Los Alamos. Greenglass named his sister and brother-in-law, Ethel and Julius Rosenberg, as co-conspirators in the wartime

spy network. The children of Jewish immigrants, the Rosenbergs insisted that they were victims of anti-Semitism and were being persecuted for their leftist beliefs. In March 1951 a jury found both of them guilty of conspiring to commit espionage. The trial judge, declaring their crime "worse than murder," sentenced them to die in the electric chair. Offered clemency if they named other spies, neither Rosenberg would confess. On June 19, 1953, they were executed—the first American civilians to lose their lives for espionage.

Both the Rosenbergs and Alger Hiss protested their innocence to their end, and their defenders continued to do so for decades. Soviet secret documents released by the National Security Agency in the 1990s—called the Venona Intercepts— lent weight to Chamber's charges against Hiss and confirmed Julius Rosenberg's guilt. (Ethel's role in her husband's spying remained uncertain.)

McCarthyism

A term invented by cartoonist Herblock, McCarthyism to most liberals and Democrats meant the use of lies, slander, and innuendo to attack and discredit the Democratic party for "twenty years of treason."

HERBLOCK
©1954 THE WASHINGTON POST

McCarthyism

At the time, when few Americans could separate fact from fantasy, the Hiss and Rosenberg cases tarnished liberalism and fueled other loyalty investigations. Only a conspiracy, it seemed, could explain U.S. weakness and Soviet might. Frustrated by their unexpected failure to win the White House in 1948, Republicans eagerly exploited the fearful mood and abandoned restraint in accusing the "Commiecrats" of selling out America.

No individual would inflict as many wounds on the Democrats as Republican Senator Joseph R. McCarthy of Wisconsin. Falsely claiming to be a wounded war hero, "Tail-Gunner Joe" won a Senate seat in the 1946 Republican landslide, and promptly gained a reputation for lying and heavy drinking. His political future in jeopardy, McCarthy decided to imitate Republicans like Richard Nixon who had gained popularity by accusing Democrats of being "soft on communism." In February 1950 McCarthy told an audience in Wheeling, West Virginia, that the United States found itself in a "position of impotency" because of "the traitorous actions" of high officials in the Truman administration. "I have here in my hands a list of 205," McCarthy claimed as he waved a laundry ticket, "a list of names known to the Secretary of State as being members of the Communist party and who nevertheless are still working and shaping policy." Although McCarthy offered no evidence, the newspapers printed his charges, giving him a national forum. McCarthy soon repeated his accusations, reducing his numbers to 81, to 57, and to "a lot," and toning down his rhetoric from "card-carrying communists" to "subversives" to "bad risks." A Senate committee found

McCarthy's charges "a fraud and a hoax," but he persisted.

Buoyed by the partisan usefulness of Senator McCarthy's onslaught, Republicans encouraged even more accusations. "Joe, you're a dirty s.o.b.," declared Ohio Senator John Bricker, "but there are times when you've got to have an s.o.b. around, and this is one of them." Even the normally fair-minded Robert Taft, who privately dismissed McCarthy's charges as "nonsense," urged him "to keep talking, and if one case doesn't work, try another." He did just that, and "McCarthyism" became a synonym for personal attacks on individuals by means of indiscriminate allegations, especially unsubstantiated charges.

As the Korean War dragged on, McCarthy's efforts to "root out the skunks" escalated. He ridiculed Secretary of State Dean Acheson as the "Red Dean," termed Truman's dismissal of MacArthur "the greatest victory the communists have ever won," and charged George Marshall with having "aided and abetted a communist conspiracy so immense as to dwarf any previous such venture in the history of man."

Such attacks appealed most to Republicans indignant about the Europe-first emphasis of Truman's foreign policy and eager to turn the public's fears into votes for the GOP. For many in the American Legion and the Chambers of Commerce, anticommunism was a weapon of revenge against liberals and internationalists, as well as a means to regain the controlling position that conservative forces had once held. McCarthy also won a devoted following among blue-collar workers who identified with his charge that a person was either a true American who detested "communists and queers" or an "egg sucking phony liberal." Laborers praised his demand that the war against communism be fought with brass knuckles, not kid gloves, while both small and big businessmen sniffed an opportunity to destroy the power of organized labor. McCarthy's flag-waving appeals held a special attraction for traditionally Democratic Catholic ethnics, who sought to gain acceptance as "100 percent Americans" by their anticommunist zeal, especially after such tactics had won the blessings of New York's Cardinal Francis Spellman and television personality Bishop Fulton J. Sheen. Countless Americans also shared McCarthy's scorn for privilege and gentility, for the "bright young men who are born with silver spoons in their mouths," for the "striped-pants boys in the State Department."

While McCarthy's conspiratorial explanation offered the public an appealingly simple answer to the perplexing questions of the Cold War, his political power rested on the support of the Republican establishment and on Democrats' fears of antagonizing him. McCarthy appeared invincible after he helped GOP candidates in the 1950 congressional elections unseat Democrats who had denounced him. "Look out for McCarthy" became the Senate watchword. "Joe will go that extra mile to destroy you," warned the new majority leader, Democrat Lyndon B. Johnson of Texas. Few dared incur McCarthy's wrath.

In 1950, over Truman's veto, federal lawmakers adopted the McCarran Internal Security Act, which required organizations deemed communist by the attorney general to register with the Department of Justice. It also authorized the arrest and detention during a national emergency of "any person as to whom there is reason to believe might engage in acts of espionage or sabotage." As part of this effort, a Senate committee sought to root out homosexuals holding government jobs. The linking of disloyalty with homosexuality in turn legitimated the armed forces' effort to dismiss "queers" and the raiding of gay bars by city police. The McCarran-Walter Immigration and Nationality Act of 1952, also enacted over Truman's veto, maintained the quota system that severely restricted immigration from southern and eastern Europe, increased the attorney general's authority to prevent homosexuals from entering the country, and gave the Justice Department the power to exclude or deport aliens suspected of sympathy for communism.

The Election of 1952

In 1952 public apprehension about the loyalty of government employees combined with frustration over the Korean stalemate to sink Democratic electoral prospects to their lowest level since the 1920s. Both business and labor also resented Truman's decision to freeze wages and prices during the Korean conflict. Revelations of bribery and influence peddling by some of Truman's old political associates gave Republicans ammunition for charging the Democrats with "plunder at home, and blunder abroad."

With Truman too unpopular to run for reelection, dispirited Democrats drafted Governor Adlai Stevenson of Illinois. But Stevenson could not separate himself politically from Truman, and his lofty speeches failed to stir most voters. An intellectual out of touch with the common people, he was jokingly referred to as an "egghead," someone with more brains than hair. Above all, Stevenson could not overcome the widespread sentiment that twenty years of Democratic rule was enough.

Compounding Democratic woes, the GOP nominated popular war hero Dwight D. Eisenhower. In 1948 Eisenhower had rejected Democratic pleas that he head their ticket, insisting that "lifelong professional soldiers should abstain from seeking higher political office." But in 1952 he answered the call of the moderate wing of the Republican party and accepted the nomination. As a concession to the hard-line anticommunists in the party, "Ike" chose as his running mate Richard Nixon, who had won a seat in the Senate in 1950 by red-baiting his opponent, Helen Gahagan Douglas, as "pink right down to her underwear."

Eisenhower and Nixon proved unbeatable. With his captivating grin and unimpeachable record of public service, Eisenhower projected both personal warmth and the vigorous authority associated with military command. His smile, wrote one commentator, was one "of infinite reassurance." At the same time, Nixon kept public apprehensions at the boiling point. Accusing the Democrats of treason, he charged that the election of "Adlai the appeaser . . . who got a Ph.D. from Dean Acheson's College of Cowardly Communist Containment" would bring "more Alger Hisses, more atomic spies."

The GOP ticket stumbled when newspapers revealed the existence of a "slush fund" that California businessmen created to keep Nixon in "financial comfort." But Nixon saved himself with a heart-tugging speech on the new medium of television. Less than two weeks before the election, Eisenhower dramatically pledged to "go to Korea" to end the stalemated war. It worked, and 62.7 percent of those eligible to vote (compared to just 51.5 percent in 1948) turned out in 1952 and gave the Republican ticket 55 percent of the ballots. Ike cracked the Solid South, carrying thirty-nine states. Enough Republicans rode his coattails to give the GOP narrow control of both houses of Congress.

CONCLUSION

The 1952 election ended two decades of Democratic control of the White House. It also closed the first phase of the Cold War, in which an assertive United States, eager to protect and expand its influence and power in the world, sought to contain a Soviet Union obsessed with its own security and self-interest. In the name of containment—the policy to prevent further Soviet, and eventually Chinese, communist advances in the world—the United States aided Greece and Turkey, established

CHRONOLOGY, 1945–1952

1944 Servicemen's Readjustment Act (GI Bill).

1945 Postwar strike wave begins.

1946 Employment Act.
George Kennan's "long telegram."
Winston Churchill's "iron curtain" speech.
Coal miners' strike.
More than a million GIs attend college.
Inflation soars to more than 18 percent.
Republicans win control of Congress.

1947 Truman Doctrine.
Federal Employee Loyalty Program.
Jackie Robinson breaks major league baseball's color line.
Taft-Hartley Act.
National Security Act
Marshall Plan to aid Europe proposed.
President's Committee on Civil Rights issues *To Secure These Rights*.
HUAC holds hearings on Hollywood.

1948 Communist coup in Czechoslovakia.
State of Israel founded.
Soviet Union begins blockade of Berlin; United States begins airlift.
Congress approves Marshall Plan.
Truman orders an end to segregation in the armed forces.
Communist leaders put on trial under the Smith Act.
Truman elected president.

1949 North Atlantic Treaty Organization (NATO) established.
East and West Germany founded as separate nations.
Communist victory in China; People's Republic of China established.
Soviet Union detonates an atomic bomb.

1950 Truman authorizes building a hydrogen bomb.
Soviet spy ring at Los Alamos uncovered.
Alger Hiss convicted of perjury.
Joseph McCarthy launches anticommunist crusade.
Korean War begins.
Julius and Ethel Rosenberg arrested as atomic spies.
McCarran Internal Security Act.
Truman accepts NSC-68.
China enters the Korean War.

1951 Douglas MacArthur dismissed from his Korean command.
Supreme Court upholds Smith Act.
Rosenbergs convicted of espionage.

1952 First hydrogen bomb exploded.
Dwight D. Eisenhower elected president; Republicans win control of Congress.

the Marshall Plan, airlifted supplies into Berlin for a year, approved the creation of the Federal Republic of Germany (West Germany), established NATO, and went to war in Korea.

American fear of global communism spawned anxieties at home as well. Truman's Cold War rhetoric and loyalty probe encouraged others to seek scapegoats and legitimated conservative accusations that equated dissent with disloyalty. The postwar Red Scare, combined with economic prosperity and pent-up demand for consumer goods, weakened the appeal of liberal reform. New Deal measures stood, but Truman's Fair Deal initiatives in education, health insurance, and civil rights failed. Although bold proposals to end racial discrimination and segregation had little chance in the midst of the Great Fear, the need of the United States to appeal to the nonwhites of the world during the Cold War brought racial issues to the fore in American politics. They would remain there as a Republican assumed the presidency.

FOR FURTHER REFERENCE

READINGS

Gary Donaldson, *Truman Defeats Dewey* (1999). An interpretation of Truman's political fortunes.

Mary L. Dudziak, *Cold War Civil Rights: Race and the Image of American Democracy* (2000). A key study of the effect of the Cold War on civil rights.

Elizabeth Fones-Wolf, *Selling Free Enterprise: The Business Assault on Labor and Liberalism, 1945–1960* (1994). An important examination of the postwar relationship between government and business.

Richard M. Fried, *The Russians Are Coming! The Russians Are Coming! Pageantry and Patriotism in Cold-War America* (1999). A balanced introduction to some of the social consequences of the Cold War.

John Earl Haynes and Harvey Klehr, *Venona: Recoding Soviet Espionage in America* (1999). Soviet spying in the United States, as disclosed by recently declassified yet sometimes ambiguous evidence,

Michael Hogan, *A Cross of Iron: Harry S Truman and the Origins of the National Security State* (1998). A vital analysis of postwar national defense policies.

Robbie Lieberman, *The Strangest Dream: Communism, Anticommunism, and the U.S. Peace Movement, 1945–1963* (2000). A wide-ranging assessment of the Great Fear's effect on antiwar activism.

Stanley Sandler, *The Korean War: No Victors, No Vanquished* (1999). An indispensable account of the war.

Sean Savage, *Truman and the Democratic Party* (1998). Another interpretation of Truman's political fortunes.

William Stueck, *The Korean War* (1995). Another indispensable account of the war.

Allen Weinstein and Alexander Vassiliev, *The Haunted Wood: Soviet Espionage in America—The Stalin Era* (1999). More on Soviet spying in the United States.

WEBSITES

Cold War International History Project of the Woodrow Wilson International Center for Scholars
http://cwihp.si.edu/default.htm

National Archives and Records Administration (NARA)
http://www.nara.gov/publications/rip/rip107/rip107.html
Two sites rich in documents of the Cold War.

Jackie Robinson
http://www.nara.gov/education/teaching/robinson/robmain.html
A website on Jackie Robinson's quest for racial justice.

McCarthyism
http://expert.cc.purdue.edu/~phealy/mccarthy.html
A good site on the rise and fall of McCarthyism, with many links.

For additional works please consult bibliography at the end of the book.

POST

June 6, 1959 · 15¢

AUTO INSURANCE: WHY SO COSTLY?

Faubus and Little Rock

State Officials to Seek US Help for Job Woes

Remedies Better Than Relief, House Group Told

By Jackson F. Mormann   Special to the Chronicle

Tax Hike Passed By Legisl...

KHRUSHCHEV WARN WEST OF WAR DANG

Threatens Use Atomic Weapo

War Would Be Short

UN ATOM-STUDY PANEL SEES FALL-OUT PERIL

Many Food Items Held Radioactiv Fall-out Cited in Mental Diseas

5000 At Jobless Rally

nd China Agree nd Denounce US

Advocates Broa

Senate Passes Draft Extension

Need for Trained Manpower Will Continue to Grow in Missile Era, According to Top Defense Expert

National Safet Council Predicts 250 Traffic Deaths Over Week End

Rail Unions Asked To Take Wage Cuts

Doctors May Forecast Potential Coronaries Within Next Decade

INFLATION NUMBER-PROBLEM, SAYS LAN

Heads Unite to Fight Price

By James Becotte

Thugs Beat Two Men Due to Testify Today Against Union Pickets

Norman Rockwell

Billion

The Weat

CHAPTER 27

America at Midcentury, 1952–1960

"It starts with these giant ants that crawl out of the ground from that place in New Mexico where they tested the atomic bomb—Alamogordo. They're desperate for sugar, and they rip apart anybody who gets in their way. It ends in the sewers of Los Angeles—and it's really scary!"

The year was 1954, and moviegoers shivered in terror at *Them!* the giant-ant film that was part of a wave of mutant movies pouring out of Hollywood. In *The Incredible Shrinking Man*, the unlucky hero is accidentally exposed to "atomic dust" and begins to shrink. In *The Attack of the Fifty-Foot Women*, the process is reversed. Nuclear radiation spawned a giant octopus in *It Came from Beneath the Sea*, unleashed *The Attack of the Crab Monsters*, and was responsible for the *Invasion of the Body Snatchers* by pods from outer space.

The popularity of science fiction movies reflected both the amusing and fearful aspects of the 1950s. It was a happy, confident decade for some, a troubled time for others, and a mix of both for the majority of Americans. The Cold War and expanding economic prosperity dominated the 1950s, deeply and widely shaping life in the United States. Despite President Eisenhower's calm assurances, and beneath the placid surface of a supposedly complacent people, many Americans worried about the spread of communism, juvenile delinquency, and homosexuality (usually depicted as an "alien" lifestyle, and associated with blackmail by Soviet agents). Parents particularly worried about the arms race. *Them!* and other films highlighted the

The 1950s College Graduate
by Norman Rockwell

fears of atmospheric nuclear testing that pumped stron-tium 90, a cancer-causing chemical that accumulates in the teeth and bone marrow of children, into the world's environment.

As such fears dimmed, later decades plagued by tur-moil looked back with nostalgia at the seemingly tran-quil "nifty fifties." In the distorting lens of memory, the decade came to seem a time of pervasive affluence and consumerism, of cheap gasoline and big cars, of new suburban homes and family togetherness, of conser-vatism and conformity. The mass media portrayed the 1950s as a sunny time when almost everybody liked Ike and loved Lucy, except teenagers who idolized Elvis Presley.

Like many historical generalizations, "the Fifties," now a singular noun, substituted sweeping, simplistic images for analysis. Many Americans did enjoy the fruits of the decade's consumer culture. Having endured the hard times of the depression and war years, they reveled in prosperity guided by a popular president. They trust-ed Dwight Eisenhower and welcomed the thaw in the Cold War that came after the Korean War. Some high-school students did lead the carefree, fun-filled exis-tence captured in later media images.

Widespread poverty also existed in the 1950s, as did racial discrimination and Americans who railed against mainstream values. A complex era, the decade saw sci-entists end the scourge of polio, unravel the structure of DNA, invent the maser that then became the laser, and send satellites into space. It was a time of hydrogen bombs as well as of Women Strike for Peace, an organi-zation of mostly middle-class housewives concerned about radioactivity in the atmosphere and the possibili-ty of nuclear war. It was a period of intense political pas-sions, kindled by Senator Joseph McCarthy, the Warren Court, and civil-rights leader Martin Luther King, Jr. A time of fundamental changes and of portents of yet greater change, the 1950s brought the advent of an auto-mated and computerized postindustrial society, televi-sion's growing power, and the baby boom, as well as mass suburbanization and a remarkable internal migra-tion. Midcentury America encompassed peace and a widening Cold War, prosperity and persistent poverty, civil-rights triumphs and rampant racism, consensus and alienation. Although the 1950s were good years for many Americans, they were hardly placid, and they sowed the seeds of future crises.

This chapter focuses on five major questions:

■ What domestic policies support the notion of Eisenhower as a centrist or moderate politician?

■ In what ways did Eisenhower continue Truman's for-eign policy, and in what ways did he change it? How successfully did Eisenhower accomplish his foreign policy goals?

■ What were the main sources, and consequences, of economic prosperity in the 1950s?

■ How accurate is the image of the 1950s as a period of conservatism and conformity?

■ What strategies did minorities adopt in order to gain greater equality in the 1950s, and how successful were they?

THE EISENHOWER PRESIDENCY

Rarely in U.S. history has a president better fit the national mood than did Dwight David Eisenhower. Exhausted by a quarter-century of upheaval—the depression, World War II, the Cold War—Americans craved peace and stability. Eisenhower delivered. He gave a nation weary of partisanship a sense of unity; he inspired confidence; and his moderate politics pleased most Americans.

President Eisenhower steered a middle course between Democratic liberalism and traditional Republican conservatism. In the main, he neither expanded nor dismantled New Deal and Fair Deal poli-cies and programs. He did little publicly to challenge Joseph McCarthy or to support the desegregation of public education, until events forced his hand.

"Dynamic Conservatism"

The most distinguished general of the Second World War, Eisenhower projected the image of a plain but good man. He expressed complicated issues in simple terms, yet governed a complex, urban, technological society. The hero who had vanquished Hitler, a grandfatherly figure with twinkling blue eyes, Ike comforted an anx-ious people.

Born in Denison, Texas, on October 14, 1890, Dwight Eisenhower grew up in Abilene, Kansas, in a poor, strongly religious family. More athletic than studious, he graduated from the U.S. Military Academy at West Point in 1915. In directing the Allied invasion of North Africa in 1943 and of Western Europe in 1944, he proved himself a brilliant war planner and organizer, widely lauded for his managerial ability and skill at conciliation.

Eisenhower's approach to the presidency reflected his wartime leadership style. He concentrated on "the

big picture," delegating authority while reconciling contending factions. His restrained view of presidential powers stemmed from his respect for the constitutional balance of power as well as his sense of the dignity of the Oval Office. He rarely intervened publicly in the legislative process. He shunned using his office as a "bully pulpit." He promised his cabinet that he would "stay out of its hair." This low-key style led Democrats to scoff at Eisenhower as a bumbler who preferred golf to government, who "reigned but did not rule."

The image of passivity actually masked an active and occasionally ruthless politician. Determined to govern the nation on business principles, Eisenhower staffed his administration with corporate executives. "Eight millionaires and a plumber," jested one journalist about the cabinet. (The "plumber" was union leader Martin Durkin, who headed the Labor Department, and soon resigned.) The president initially worked with the Republican-controlled Congress to reduce the size of government and to slash the federal budget. He promoted the private development of hydroelectric and nuclear power, and persuaded Congress to turn over to coastal states the oil-rich "tidelands" that the Supreme Court had previously awarded to the federal government.

For the most part, however, the Eisenhower administration followed a centrist course. More pragmatic than ideological, he wished to reduce taxes, contain inflation, and govern efficiently. Summing up the president's views, his brother and adviser Milton Eisenhower declared, "We should keep what we have, catch our breath for a while, and improve administration; it does not mean moving backward."

Eager to avoid a depression, Eisenhower relied heavily on the Council of Economic Advisers (CEA) despite conservative calls for its abolition. He followed the advice of CEA head Arthur Burns (the only government official other than the secretary of state who had a weekly appointment with Ike) to act positively to fine-tune the economy. When recessions struck in 1953 and 1957, Eisenhower abandoned his balanced budgets and increased government spending in order to restore prosperity.

The president labeled his ideas "dynamic conservatism" and "modern Republicanism." Whatever the slogan, Eisenhower went along with Congress when it extended social-security benefits to more than 10 million Americans. He approved raising the minimum wage from seventy-five cents to a dollar an hour, making 4 million more workers eligible for unemployment benefits, and increasing federally financed public housing for low-income families. He also approved establishing a Department of Health, Education and Welfare. He sup-

Ike in the White House
Like a benign grandfather, Dwight D. Eisenhower provided a reassuring presence in the White House in the 1950s. His moderation, balanced judgment, and apparent aloofness from partisanship appealed to as many as did his fondness for bridge and poker, bourbon, fishing and hunting, and golf.

ported constructing the St. Lawrence Seaway, linking the Great Lakes and the Atlantic Ocean, and he proposed that the federal government take the lead in building forty thousand miles of freeways to replace old, unsafe roads (see Technology and Culture: The Interstate Highway System).

Republicans renominated Ike by acclamation in 1956, and voters gave him a landslide victory over Democrat Adlai Stevenson. With the GOP crowing "Everything's booming but the guns," Eisenhower won by the greatest popular majority since FDR's in 1936 and carried all but seven states.

The Downfall of Joseph McCarthy

Although he despised McCarthy—and called him a "pimple on the path to progress," Eisenhower considered it beneath his dignity to "get into the gutter with that guy." Fearing a direct confrontation with the senator, he tried to steal McCarthy's thunder by tightening security requirements for government employees. When that failed, he allowed McCarthy to grab plenty of rope in the hope that the demagogue would hang himself.

The Interstate Highway System

As a young lieutenant after World War I, Dwight Eisenhower had been given the task of accompanying a convoy of army trucks across the country. The woefully inadequate state of the roads for military transport dismayed him then as much as he would later be impressed by the German autobahns that allowed Hitler to deploy troops around Germany with incredible speed. Not surprisingly, when he became president he sought a transportation system that would facilitate the rapid movement of the military, as well as increase road safety and aid commerce. The arms race with the Soviet Union, moreover, necessitated a network of highways for evacuating cities in case of a nuclear attack—a change, according to the *Bulletin of the Atomic Scientists*, from "Duck and Cover" to "Run Like Hell."

In 1954 Eisenhower set up a high-powered commission to recommend a highway program that would cost as much as a war. He appointed an army general to head it to emphasize the connection between highways, national defense, and the concerns Americans had about their security. The next year, with the entire federal budget at $71 billion, Eisenhower asked Congress for a $40 billion, forty-one-thousand-mile construction project, to be financed by government bonds. Conservative Republicans, fearful of increasing the federal debt,

balked. So Ike switched to a financing plan based on new gasoline, tire, bus, and trucking taxes. The federal government would use the taxes to pay 90 percent of the construction costs in any state willing to come up with the other 10 percent.

Millions of suburbanites commuting to central cities loved the idea of new multilane highways. So did motorists dreaming of summer travel; the powerful coalition of automobile manufacturers, oil companies, asphalt firms, and truckers, who stood to benefit financially the most; and the many special interests in virtually every congressional district, including real estate developers, shopping mall entrepreneurs, engineers, and construction industries. Indeed, the interstate highway bill promised something to almost everybody except the inner-city poor. It sailed through Congress in 1956, winning by voice vote in the House and by an 89 to 1 margin in the Senate.

The largest and most expensive public works scheme in American history, the interstate highway system was designed and built as a single project for the entire country, unlike the haphazard development of the canal and railroad networks. It required taking more land by eminent domain than had been taken in the entire history of road building in the United States. Expected

Projected Interstate Highway System, 1957

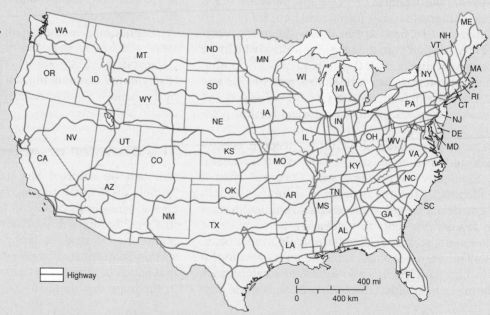

Highway

0   400 mi

0   400 km

increases in highway use, speed of travel, and weight of loads necessitated drastic changes in road engineering and materials. Utilizing the technological advances that had produced high-quality concrete and asphalt, diesel-powered roadbed graders, reinforced steel, and safely controlled explosives, construction crews built superhighways with standardized twelve-foot-wide lanes, ten-foot shoulders, and median strips of at least thirty-six feet in rural areas. Terrain in which a dirt trail was difficult to blaze was laced with cloverleaf intersections and some sixteen thousand exits and entrances. More than fifty thousand bridges, tunnels, and overpasses traversed swamps, rivers, and mountains. Road curves were banked for speeds of seventy miles per hour, with grades no greater than 3 percent and minimum sight distances of six hundred feet. The massive amounts of concrete poured, Ike later boasted, could have made "six sidewalks to the moon" or sixty Panama Canals.

The network of four-to-eight-lane roads linking cities and suburbs made it possible to drive from New York to San Francisco without encountering a stoplight. It more than fulfilled the initial hopes of most of its backers, enormously speeding the movement of goods and people across the country, invigorating the tourist industry, providing steady work for construction firms, enriching those who lived near the interstates and sold their lands to developers, and hastening suburban development.

The freeways that helped unify Americans by increasing the accessibility of once-distant regions also helped homogenize the nation with interchangeable shopping malls, motels, and fast-food chains. In 1955 Ray Kroc, who supplied the Multimixers for milk shakes to the original McDonald's drive-in in San Bernardino, California, began to franchise similar family restaurants beside highways, each serving the same standardized foods under the instantly recognizable logo of the golden arches. By century's end McDonald's would be the world's largest private real-estate enterprise, as well as the largest food provider, serving more than forty million meals daily in some hundred countries.

Moreover, the expressways boosting the interstate trucking business hastened the decline of the nation's railroad lines and urban mass-transportation systems. The highways built to speed commuters into the central cities—"white men's roads through black men's bedrooms" said the National Urban League—often bulldozed minority neighborhoods out of existence or served

Breaking Ground for I-70 in Missouri

Better Roads, But More Cars

as barriers between black and white neighborhoods. The beltways that lured increasingly more residents and businesses to suburbia eroded city tax bases, which, in turn, accelerated urban decay, triggering the urban crisis that then furthered suburban sprawl. The interstates had locked the United States into an ever-increasing reliance on cars and trucks, drastically increasing air pollution and American dependence on a constant supply of cheap and plentiful gasoline.

Focus Questions

- Why did Congress authorize the construction of an interstate highway system?
- Describe some of the unintended consequences of the new highway system.

McCarthy did so in 1954. Angry that one of his aides had not received a draft deferment, the senator accused the army of harboring communist spies. The army then charged McCarthy with using his influence to gain preferential treatment for the aide who had been drafted.

The resulting nationally televised Senate investigation, begun in April 1954, brought McCarthy down. A national audience witnessed McCarthy's boorish behavior firsthand on television. His dark scowl, raspy voice, endless interruptions ("point of order, Mr. Chairman, point of order"), and disregard for the rights of others repelled many viewers. He behaved like the bad guy in a TV western, observed novelist John Steinbeck: "He had a stubble of a beard, he leered, he sneered, he had a nasty laugh. He bullied and shouted. He looked evil." In June McCarthy slurred the reputation of a young lawyer assisting Joseph Welch, the army counsel. Suddenly the mild-mannered Welch turned his wrath on McCarthy, "Until this moment, Senator, I think I really never gauged your cruelty or your recklessness. . . . Have you no sense of decency?" The gallery burst into applause.

McCarthy's popularity ratings plummeted. The GOP no longer needed him to drive the "Commiecrats" from power. The Democrats eagerly sought to be rid of their scourge. The Senate, with Eisenhower applying pressure behind the scenes, voted in December 1954 to censure McCarthy for contemptuous behavior. This powerful rebuke—only the third in the Senate's history—demolished McCarthy as a political force. McCarthyism, Ike gloated, had become "McCarthywasism."

In 1957 McCarthy died a broken man, suffering from the effects of alcoholism. But the fears he exploited lingered. Congress established Loyalty Day in 1955 and annually funded the House Un-American Activities Committee's search for suspected radicals. State and local governments continued to require teachers to take loyalty oaths.

McCarthyism also remained a rallying call of conservatives disenchanted with the postwar consensus. Young conservatives like William F. Buckley, Jr. (a recent Yale graduate who founded the *National Review* in 1955), and the Christian Anti-Communist Crusade continued to claim that domestic communism was a major subversive threat. None did so more than the John Birch Society, which denounced Eisenhower as a conscious agent of the communist conspiracy, and equated liberalism with treason. Its grass-roots network of as many as a hundred thousand activists promoted like-minded political candidates, while waging local struggles against taxes, gun control, and sex education in the schools. Although few saw all the dangers lurking in every shadow that the John Birch Society did, Barry Goldwater,

George Wallace, and Ronald Reagan, among others, used its anticommunist, antigovernment rhetoric to advantage. Stressing victory over communism, rather than its containment, the self-proclaimed "new conservatives" (or radical right, as their opponents called them) criticized the "creeping socialism" of Eisenhower, advocated a return to traditional moral standards, and condemned the liberal rulings of the Supreme Court.

Jim Crow in Court

Led by a new chief justice, Earl Warren (1953), the Supreme Court incurred conservatives' wrath for defending the rights of persons accused of subversive beliefs. In *Jencks* v. *United States* (1957) the Court held that the accused had the right to inspect government files used by the prosecution. In *Yates* v. *United States* (1957) the justices overturned the convictions of Communist party officials under the Smith Act (see Chapter 26), emphasizing the distinction between unlawful concrete acts and the teaching of revolutionary ideology. *Yates* essentially ended further prosecutions of communists, and right-wing opponents of the decision demanded limitations on the Court's powers and plastered "Impeach Earl Warren" posters on highway billboards.

These condemnations paled beside those of segregationists following *Brown* v. *Board of Education of Topeka* (May 17, 1954). Argued by the NAACP's Thurgood Marshall, *Brown* combined lawsuits from four states and the District of Columbia in which black plaintiffs claimed that segregated public education was unconstitutional. It built on an earlier federal court ruling that had prohibited the segregation of Mexican-American children in California schools, as well as on cases in 1950 in which the Supreme Court had significantly narrowed the possibility of separate education being in fact equal education, and thus constitutional. Chief Justice Warren, speaking for a unanimous Court, reversed *Plessy* v. *Ferguson* (see Chapter 20). The high court held that separating schoolchildren "solely because of their race generates a feeling of inferiority as to their status in the community that may affect their hearts and minds in a way unlikely ever to be undone," thereby violating the equal protection clause of the Fourteenth Amendment. "In the field of public education," the Court concluded, "the doctrine of 'separate but equal' has no place. Separate educational facilities are inherently unequal." A year later, the Court ordered federal district judges to monitor compliance with *Brown*, requiring only that desegregation proceed "with all deliberate speed"—an oxymoron that implied the

necessity for gradualism—the price Warren paid to gain a unanimous decision.

The border states complied, and in such cities as Baltimore, St. Louis, and Washington, D.C., African-American and white students sat side by side for the first time in history. But in the South, where segregation was deeply entrenched in law and social custom, politicians vowed resistance, and Eisenhower refused to press them to comply. "The fellow who tries to tell me that you can do these things by force is just plain nuts," he stated. "I don't believe you can change the hearts of men with laws or decisions." Although not personally a racist, Ike never publicly endorsed the *Brown* decision and privately called his appointment of Earl Warren "the biggest damn fool mistake I ever made."

Public-opinion polls in 1954 indicated that some 80 percent of white southerners opposed the *Brown* decision. Encouraged by the president's silence, white resistance stiffened. White Citizens Councils sprang up, and the Ku Klux Klan revived. Declaring Brown "null, void, and of no effect," southern legislatures claimed the right to "interpose" themselves against the federal government and adopted a strategy of "massive resistance" to thwart compliance with the law. They denied state aid to local school systems that desegregated and even closed public schools ordered to desegregate. Most effectively, the states enacted pupil-placement laws that permitted school boards to assign black and white children to different schools.

In 1956 more than a hundred members of Congress signed the Southern Manifesto, denouncing *Brown* as "a clear abuse of judicial power." White southern politicians competed to "outnigger" each other in opposition to desegregation. When a gubernatorial candidate in Alabama promised to go to jail to defend segregation, his opponent swore that he would die for it. Segregationists also resorted to violence and economic reprisals against blacks to maintain all-white schools. At the end of 1956, not a single African-American attended school with whites in the Deep South, and few did so in the Upper South.

The Laws of the Land

Southern resistance reached a climax in September 1957. Although the Little Rock school board had accepted a federal court order to desegregate Central High School, Arkansas Governor Orval E. Faubus mobilized the state's National Guard to bar nine African-American students from entering the school. After another court order forced Faubus to withdraw the guardsmen, an angry mob of whites blocked the black students' entry.

Although Eisenhower sought to avoid the divisive issue of civil rights, he believed he had to uphold federal law. He also worried that the Soviets were "gloating over this incident and using it everywhere to misrepresent our whole nation." The Cold War had made segregation in the United States a national security liability.

Little Rock, 1957
Elizabeth Eckford, age fifteen, one of the nine black students to desegregate Central High School, endures abuse on her way to school, September 4, 1957. Forty years later, the young white woman shouting insults asked for forgiveness.

Understanding that racism at home hampered American efforts to gain the support of nonwhite Third World nations, the president federalized the Arkansas National Guard and, for the first time since Reconstruction, dispatched federal troops to protect blacks' rights. To ensure the safety of the black students, soldiers patrolled Central High for the rest of the year. Rather than accept integration, however, Faubus shut down Little Rock's public high schools for two years. At the end of the decade, fewer than 1 percent of African-American students in the Deep South attended desegregated schools.

Nevertheless, Little Rock strengthened the determination of African-Americans for desegregation. The crisis also foreshadowed television's vital role in the demise of Jim Crow. The contrast between the images of howling white racists and those of resolute black students projected on the TV screen immensely aided the civil-rights cause. According to a 1957 public-opinion poll, fully 90 percent of whites outside the South approved the use of federal troops in Little Rock.

Most northern whites also favored legislation to enfranchise southern blacks, and during the 1956 campaign Eisenhower proposed a voting rights bill. The Civil Rights Act of 1957, the first since Reconstruction, established a permanent commission on civil rights with broad investigatory powers, but did little to guarantee the ballot to blacks. The Civil Rights Act of 1960 only slightly strengthened the first measure's enforcement provisions. Neither act empowered federal officials to register African-Americans to vote. Like the *Brown* decision, however, these laws implied a changing view of race relations by the federal government, and that further encouraged blacks to fight for their rights.

THE COLD WAR CONTINUES

Eisenhower continued Truman's containment policy. Stalin's death in 1953 and Eisenhower's resolve to reduce the risk of nuclear war did bring a thaw in the Cold War, but the United States and the USSR remained deadlocked. Neither the Cold War nor American determination to check communism ceased. Fears at home and abroad of a nuclear holocaust mounted as both the United States and Soviet Union stockpiled increasingly destructive weapons.

Honoring his campaign pledge, Eisenhower visited Korea in December 1952, but did not bring home a settlement. The fate of thousands of prisoners of war (POWs) who did not want to return to communist rule remained the sticking point. The uncertainty in the communist world after Stalin's death and Eisenhower's veiled threat to use nuclear weapons broke the stalemate. The armistice signed in July 1953 established a panel of representatives from neutral nations to oversee the return of POWs and set the boundary between North and South Korea once again at the thirty-eighth parallel. Some Americans claimed that communist aggression had been thwarted and containment vindicated; others condemned the truce as peace without honor.

Ike and Dulles

Eager to ease Cold War tensions, Eisenhower first sought to quiet the GOP right-wing clamoring to roll back the Red tide. To do so he chose as his secretary of state, John Foster Dulles. A rigid Presbyterian whose humorlessness led some to dub him "Dull, Duller, Dulles," the secretary of state talked of a holy war against "atheistic communism," "liberating" the captive peoples of Eastern Europe, and unleashing Jiang Jieshi against Communist China. Believing that the Soviet Union understood only force, Dulles threatened "instant, massive retaliation" with nuclear weapons in response to Soviet aggression. He insisted on the necessity of "brinksmanship," the art of never backing down in a crisis, even if it meant risking war.

Such saber-rattling pleased the Right, but Eisenhower preferred conciliation. Partly because he feared a nuclear war with the Soviet Union, which had tested its own H-bomb in 1953, Eisenhower refused to translate Dulles's rhetoric into action. Aware of the limits of American power, the United States did nothing to check the Soviet interventions that crushed uprisings in East Germany (1953) and Hungary (1956).

As Hiroshima-size atomic bombs gave way to multimegaton thermonuclear weapons in the American and Soviet arsenals, Eisenhower tried to reduce the probability of mutual annihilation. He proposed an "atoms for peace" plan, whereby both superpowers would contribute fissionable materials to a new U.N. agency for use in industrial projects. In the absence of a positive Soviet response, the government began construction of the Distant Early Warning Line across the Aleutians and arctic Alaska, providing a twenty-four-hour-a-day electronic air defense system that would alert the United States to an invasion by the "over-the-pole" route. The government then built the Cheyenne Mountain Operations Center, a Rocky Mountain fortress where, behind twenty-five-ton blast doors, military crews scanned radar and satellite signals for signs of a Soviet attack.

Work also began on commercial nuclear plants in the mid-1950s, promising electricity "too cheap to meter." However, the lion's share of the money for nuclear research continued to be military-related, like that going to naval captain Hyman Rickover's development of nuclear-powered submarines. Mounting fears over radioactive fallout from atmospheric atomic tests, especially the 1954 U.S. test series in the Pacific that spread strontium 90 over a wide area, heightened world concern about the nuclear-arms race.

In 1955 Eisenhower and the Soviet leaders met in Geneva for the first East-West summit conference since World War II. Mutual talk of "peaceful coexistence" led reporters to hail the "spirit of Geneva." The two nations could not agree on a specific plan for nuclear-arms control, but Moscow suspended further atmospheric tests of nuclear weapons in March 1958, and the United States followed suit.

Still, the Cold War continued. Dulles negotiated mutual-defense pacts with any nation that would join the United States in opposing communism. His "pacto-mania" committed the United States to the defense of forty-three nations. The administration relied primarily on the U.S. nuclear arsenal to deter the Soviets. Tailored to suit fiscally conservative Republicans, the "New Look" defense program promised "more bang for the buck" by emphasizing nuclear weapons and reducing conventional forces. It spurred the Soviets to seek "more rubble for the ruble" by expanding their nuclear stockpile. In anticipation of nuclear war, Congress built a 112,000-square-foot bunker for itself 700 feet below the grounds of the elegant Greenbrier resort in West Virginia. It featured dormitories, a restaurant, an operating clinic, decontamination showers, and chambers in which the legislators would meet.

Meanwhile, the focus of the Cold War shifted from Europe to the Third World, the largely nonwhite developing nations. There the two superpowers waged war by proxy, using local guerrillas and military juntas to battle in isolated deserts and steamy jungles. There, too, the Central Intelligence Agency (CIA) fought covert wars against those deemed to imperil American interests.

CIA Covert Actions

To command the CIA, Eisenhower chose Allen Dulles, a veteran of wartime OSS cloak-and-dagger operations and the brother of the secretary of state. Established in 1947 to conduct foreign intelligence gathering, the CIA became increasingly involved in secret operations to topple regimes friendly to communism. By 1957 half its

Man (and Machine) of the Year
The launching of Sputnik, the first man-made satellite to orbit Earth, in October 1957, and Sputnik II, several weeks later, with a dog inside to test the effects of space travel on a living creature, made Soviet Premier Nikita Khrushchev *Time's* 1957 Man of the Year.

personnel and 80 percent of its budget were devoted to "covert action"—subverting governments, putting foreign leaders (like King Hussein of Jordan) on its payroll, supporting foreign political parties (such as the Liberal Democratic Party of Japan), and subsidizing foreign newspapers and labor unions that hewed to a pro-American line.

To woo influential foreign thinkers away from communism, the CIA also sponsored intellectual conferences and jazz concerts. It bankrolled exhibitions of abstract expressionist paintings to counter Soviet socialist realism art. It purchased the film rights to George Orwell's *Animal Farm* and *1984* to make their messages more overtly anticommunist. It subsidized magazines like *Encounter* to publish articles supporting Washington's foreign policy. College students and businessmen traveling abroad were recruited as "fronts" in clandestine CIA activities.

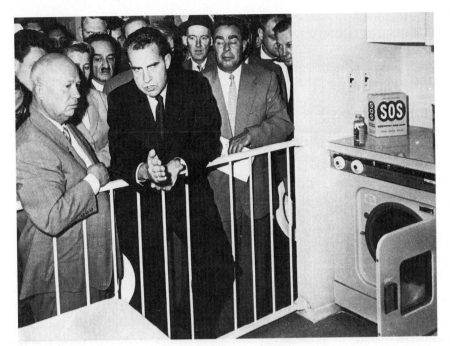

The Great Debate, July 24, 1959
At the opening of the American National Exhibit in Moscow, Vice President Richard Nixon and Soviet Premier Nikita Khrushchev engaged in a "kitchen debate," arguing not about the strength of their rockets or bombs but about the relative merits of American and Soviet washing machines and television sets.

Led by a grandson of Teddy Roosevelt, the CIA's "Operation Ajax" orchestrated a coup to overthrow the government of Iran in 1953. Fearing that the prime minister who had nationalized oil fields might open oil-rich Iran to the Soviet Union, the CIA replaced him with the pro-American Shah Reza Pahlavi. The United States thus gained a loyal ally on the Soviet border, and American oil companies prospered when the Shah made low-priced oil available to them. But the seeds of Iranian hatred of America had been sown—an enmity that would haunt the United States a quarter-century later.

To ensure another pro-American government in 1953, the CIA helped the anticommunist Ramon Magaysay become president of the Philippines. The next year, in "Operation Pbsuccess," a CIA-trained and financed band of mercenaries overthrew Jacobo Arbenz Guzman's elected government in Guatemala. Strongly influenced by the Guatemalan Communist party, Guzman had nationalized and redistributed tracts of land owned by the United Fruit Company. The new pro-American regime restored United Fruit's lands and trampled all political opposition.

The Vietnam Domino

The most extensive CIA covert operations during the 1950s took place in Indochina. As a result of Mao Zedong's victory in China and the outbreak of war in Korea, the United States viewed Indochina as a key battleground in the Cold War. The Truman administration had provided France with large-scale military assistance to fight the Vietminh, a broad-based Vietnamese nationalist coalition led by the communist Ho Chi Minh (see Chapter 26). By 1954 American aid accounted for three-quarters of French expenditures. Nevertheless, France tottered near defeat. In early 1954 the Vietminh trapped twelve thousand French troops in the northern valley of Dienbienphu, near the border with Laos.

France appealed for U.S. intervention, and some American officials toyed with the idea of launching a ground invasion or nuclear strike. "You boys must be crazy," the president replied. "We can't use those awful things against Asians for the second time in ten years. My God." When the Democratic majority leader, Senator Lyndon Johnson of Texas, opposed "sending American GIs into the mud and muck of Indochina on a blood-letting spree to perpetuate colonialism and white man's exploitation in Asia," Ike refused to commit U.S. troops. In May the French surrendered at Dienbienphu and gave up the effort to retake Vietnam. An international conference in Geneva arranged a cease-fire and temporarily divided Vietnam at the seventeenth parallel, pending elections in 1956 to choose the government of a unified nation.

Although Eisenhower would not take the United States into an Asian land war, he also would not permit a communist takeover of all of Vietnam. In what became known as the "domino theory," Eisenhower warned that

if Vietnam fell to the communists, then Thailand, Burma, Indonesia, and ultimately all of Asia would fall like dominos. Accordingly, the United States refused to sign the Geneva Peace Accords, and in late 1954 created the Southeast Asia Treaty Organization (SEATO), a military alliance patterned on NATO.

The CIA installed Ngo Dinh Diem, a fiercely anticommunist Catholic, as premier and then president of an independent South Vietnam. It helped Diem train his armed forces and secret police, eliminate political opposition, and block the 1956 election to reunify Vietnam specified by the Geneva agreement. As Eisenhower admitted, "possibly 80 percent of the population would have voted for the communist Ho Chi Minh as their leader." "Because we know of no one better," said John Foster Dulles, Washington pinned its hopes on Diem, and Vietnam became a test of its ability to defeat communism in Asia with American dollars rather than American lives.

The autocratic Diem, who saw himself as "the mediator between the people and heaven," never rallied public support. His Catholicism alienated the predominantly Buddhist population, and his refusal to institute land reform and to end corruption spurred opposition. In 1957 former Vietminh guerrillas began sporadic antigovernment attacks, and in December 1960 opposition to Diem coalesced in the National Front for the Liberation of Vietnam (NLF). Backed by North Vietnam, the insurgency attracted broad support and soon controlled half of South Vietnam. Although few Americans were aware of what was happening, the administration's commitment to "sink or swim with Ngo Dinh Diem" had cost over $1 billion, and Diem was sinking.

Troubles in the Third World

Eisenhower faced his greatest crisis in the Middle East. In 1954 Gamal Abdel Nasser came to power in Egypt, determined to modernize his nation. To woo him, the United States offered to finance a dam at Aswan to harness the Nile River. When Nasser purchased arms from Czechoslovakia and officially recognized the People's Republic of China, Dulles cancelled the loan. Nasser then nationalized the British-owned Suez Canal.

Viewing the canal as the lifeline of its empire, Britain planned to take it back by force. The British were supported by France, which feared Arab nationalism in their Algerian colony, and by Israel, which feared the Egyptian arms buildup. The three countries, America's closest allies, coordinated an attack on Egypt in October 1956 without consulting Eisenhower. Ike fumed that the military action would drive the Arab world and its precious oil to the Russians. When Moscow threatened to intervene, Eisenhower forced his allies to withdraw their troops.

The Suez crisis had major consequences. It swelled antiwestern sentiment in the Third World; and the United States replaced Britain and France as the protector of western interests in the Middle East. Determined to keep Arab oil flowing to the West, the president announced the Eisenhower Doctrine, a proclamation that the United States would send military aid and, if necessary, troops to any Middle Eastern nation threatened by "Communist aggression." To back up his words, Eisenhower ordered fourteen thousand marines into Lebanon in July 1958 to quell a threatened Muslim revolt against the Christian-dominated, prowestern regime.

Such interventions intensified anti-American feelings in the Third World. Shouting "yanqui imperialism," angry crowds in Peru and Venezuela spat at Vice President Nixon and stoned his car in 1958. The next year Fidel Castro overturned a dictatorial regime in Cuba, confiscating American properties without compensation. In 1960 anti-American riots forced Eisenhower to cancel his visit to Japan.

An even tougher blow came on May 1, 1960. Two weeks before a scheduled summit conference with Soviet premier Nikita Khrushchev, the Soviets shot down a U.S. spy plane far inside their border. Khrushchev displayed to the world the captured CIA pilot and the photos he had taken of Soviet missile sites. Eisenhower refused to apologize to the Soviet Union. The summit to limit nuclear testing collapsed, and both sides resumed atmospheric tests in 1961.

The Eisenhower Legacy

Just before leaving office, Eisenhower offered Americans a farewell and warning. The demands of national security, he stated, had produced the "conjunction of an immense military establishment and a large arms industry that is new in the American experience." Swollen defense budgets had yoked American economic well-being to military expenditures. Military contracts had become the staff of life for research scholars, politicians, and the nation's largest corporations. This combination of interests, Eisenhower believed, exerted enormous leverage and threatened the traditional subordination of the military in American life. "We must guard against the acquisition of unwarranted influence . . . by the military-industrial complex. The potential for the disastrous rise of misplaced power exists and will persist."

The president concluded that he had avoided war but that lasting peace was not in sight. Most scholars agreed. Eisenhower had ended the Korean War, avoided direct intervention in Vietnam, begun relaxing tensions with the Soviet Union, and suspended atmospheric nuclear testing. He had also presided over an accelerating nuclear-arms race and a widening Cold War, and had given the CIA a green light to intervene in local conflicts around the globe.

The moderate, centrist Eisenhower had pleased neither the Left nor the Right. His acceptance of New Deal social-welfare measures angered conservative Republicans, and liberal Democrats grumbled about his passivity in the face of McCarthyism and racism. Yet Ike had given most Americans what they most wanted—prosperity, reassurance, and a breathing spell in which to relish the comforts of life.

THE AFFLUENT SOCIETY

In 1958 economist John Kenneth Galbraith published *The Affluent Society*, a study of postwar America whose title reflected the broad-based prosperity that made the 1950s seem the fulfillment of the American dream. By the end of the decade, about 60 percent of American families owned homes; 75 percent, cars; and 87 percent, at least one TV. The gross national product (GNP) increased 50 percent in the 1950s as a consequence of heavy government spending, a huge upsurge in productivity, and a steadily increasing demand for consumer goods and services.

Three brief recessions and a rising national debt, almost $290 billion by 1961, evoked concern but did little to halt economic growth or stifle optimism. The United States had achieved the world's highest living standard ever. Historian David Potter labeled Americans a "people of plenty" in 1954; and by 1960 the average worker's income, adjusted for inflation, was 35 percent higher than in 1945. With just 6 percent of the world's population, the United States produced and consumed nearly half of everything made and sold on Earth.

The New Industrial Society

Federal spending constituted a major source of economic growth. It nearly doubled in the 1950s to $180 billion, as did the outlays of state and local governments. Federal expenditures (accounting for 17 percent of the GNP in the mid-1950s, compared to just 1 percent in 1929) built roads and airports, financed home mortgages, supported farm prices, and provided stipends for education. More than half the federal budget—about 10 percent of the GNP—went to defense industries, a development highlighted by Eisenhower's choice of Charles Wilson of General Motors and then Neil McElroy of Procter and Gamble to head the Department of Defense. Continued superpower rivalry in atomic munitions, missile-delivery systems, and the space race kept the federal government the nation's main financier of scientific and technological research and development (R&D).

For the West, especially, it was as if World War II never ended, as the new Air Force Academy in Colorado Springs signified. Politicians from both parties labored to keep defense spending flowing westward. Liberal and conservative members of Congress from California sought contracts for Lockheed. So did those from Texas for General Dynamics and those from Washington State for Boeing. In the late 1950s California alone received half the space budget and a quarter of all major military contracts. By then, as well, Denver had the largest number of federal employees outside Washington, D.C.; Albuquerque boasted more Ph.D. degrees per capita than any other U.S. city; and over a third of those employed in Los Angeles depended on defense industries. The Mormon dream of an agricultural utopia gave way to a Utah that led the nation in receiving expenditures per capita on space and defense research. Government spending transformed the mythic West of individualistic cowboys, miners, and farmers into a West of bureaucrats, manufacturers, and scientists dependent on federal funds.

Science became a ward of the state, with government funding and control transforming both the U.S. military and industry. Financed by the Atomic Energy Commission (AEC) and utilizing navy scientists, the Duquesne Light Company began construction in Shippingport, Pennsylvania, of the nation's first nuclear-power plant in 1954. Chemicals surged from the fiftieth-largest industry before the war to the nation's fourth-largest in the 1960s. As chemical fertilizers and pesticides contaminated groundwater supplies, and as the use of plastics for consumer products reduced landfill space, Americans—unaware of the hidden perils—marveled at fruits and vegetables covered with Saran Wrap and delighted in their Dacron suits, Orlon shirts, Acrilan socks, and Teflon-coated pots and pans.

Electronics became the fifth-largest American industry, providing industrial equipment and consumer appliances. Electricity consumption tripled in the 1950s as industry automated and consumers, "to live better electrically," as commercials urged, purchased electric

The New West

Symbolic of the defense spending and investment that helped the West's economy flourish, Seattle's Boeing plant in 1951 began production of the first of the B-52 Stratofortress heavy bombers. They would continue rolling off the Boeing assembly line until the end of the decade.

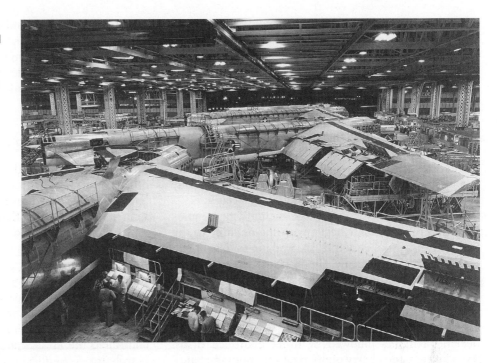

washers and dryers, freezers, blenders, television sets, and stereos. Essential to the expansion of both the chemical and the electronics industries was inexpensive petroleum. With domestic crude-oil production increasing close to 50 percent and petroleum imports rising from 74 million to 371 million barrels between 1945 and 1960, oil replaced coal as the nation's main energy source. Hardly anyone paid attention when a physicist warned in 1953 that "adding 6 billion tons of carbon dioxide to the atmosphere each year is warming up the Earth."

Plentiful, cheap gasoline fed the growth of the automobile and aircraft industries. The nation's third-largest industry in the 1950s, aerospace depended heavily on defense spending and on federally funded research. In Washington State, the manufacturers of jet aircraft, ballistic missiles, and space equipment employed more people than did logging and timbering firms. The four metropolitan areas of Seattle, Dallas-Fort Worth, San Diego, and Los Angeles accounted for nearly all of the nation's aircraft production. The automobile industry, still the titan of the American economy, also utilized technological R&D. Where it had once partially replaced human labor with machinery, it now used automation to control the machines. Between 1945 and 1960 the industry halved the number of hours and of workers required to produce a car. Other manufacturers followed suit, investing $10 billion a year throughout the fifties on labor-saving machinery.

The Age of Computers

The computer was a major key to the technological revolution. In 1944 International Business Machines (IBM), cooperating with Harvard scientists, had produced the Mark I calculator to decipher secret Axis codes. It was a slow, cumbersome device of five hundred miles of wiring and three thousand electromechanical relays. Two years later, to improve artillery accuracy, the U.S. army developed ENIAC, the first electronic computer. Still unwieldly, and having to be "debugged" of the insects attracted to its heat and light (giving rise to the term still used for solving computer glitches), ENIAC reduced the time required to multiply two tenth-place numbers from Mark I's three seconds to less than three-thousandths of a second. Then came the development of operating instructions, or programs, that could be stored inside the computer's memory; the substitution of printed circuits for wired ones; and in 1948, at Bell Labs, the invention of tiny solid-state transistors that ended reliance on radio tubes.

The computer changed the American economy and society as fundamentally as the steam engine in the First Industrial Revolution and the electric motor and internal combustion engine in the Second. Sales of electronic computers to industry rose from twenty in 1954 to more than a thousand in 1957 and more than two thousand in 1960. Major manufacturers used them to monitor production lines, track inventory, and

ensure quality control. The government, which used three machines in computing the 1950 census returns, employed several hundred on the 1960 census. They became as indispensable to Pentagon strategists playing war games as to the Internal Revenue Service, as integral to meteorologists as to scientists "flying" rockets on the drawing board. By the mid-1960s more than thirty thousand mainframe computers were used by banks, hospitals, and universities. Further developments led to the first integrated circuits and to what would ultimately become the Internet, fundamentally changing the nature of work as well as its landscape.

The development of the high-technology complex known as Silicon Valley began with the opening of the Stanford Industrial Park in 1951. Seeking to develop its landholdings around Palo Alto and to attract financial aid from business and the military, Stanford University utilized its science and engineering faculties to design and produce products for the Fairchild Semiconductor and Hewlett-Packard companies. This relationship became a model followed by other high-tech firms. Soon apricot and cherry orchards throughout the Santa Clara valley gave way to industrial parks filled with computer firms and pharmaceutical laboratories. Initially a far cry from dirty eastern factories, these cam-

pus-like facilities would eventually choke the valley with traffic congestion, housing developments, and smog. Similar developments would follow the military-fueled research complexes along Boston's Route 128, near Austin, Texas, and in North Carolina's Research Triangle.

The Costs of Bigness

Rapid technological advances accelerated the growth and power of big business. In 1950 twenty-two U.S. firms had assets of more than $1 billion; ten years later more than fifty did. By 1960 one-half of 1 percent of all companies earned more than half the total corporate income in the United States. The wealthiest, which could afford huge R&D outlays, became oligopolies, swallowing up weak competitors. Three television networks monopolized the nation's airwaves; three automobile and three aluminum companies produced more than 90 percent of America's cars and aluminum; and a handful of firms controlled the lion's share of assets and sales in steel, petroleum, chemicals, and electrical machinery. Corporations also acquired overseas facilities to become "multinational" enterprises, and formed "conglomerates" by merging companies in unrelated industries:

Scientific Agriculture, 1955
A Pennsylvania farmer surveying the array of synthetic fertilizers, insecticides, and chemicals he annually uses on his 78-acre farm.

International Telephone and Telegraph (ITT) owned hotel chains, insurance businesses, and car-rental companies. Despite talk of "people's capitalism," the oil-rich Rockefeller family alone owned more corporate stock than all the nation's wage earners combined.

Growth and consolidation brought further bureaucratization. "Executives" replaced "capitalists." Rewarded in their own careers for "fitting in" rather than sticking out, they knew not to rock the corporate boat. Success required conformity not creativity, teamwork not individuality. According to sociologist David Riesman's *The Lonely Crowd* (1950), the new "company people" were "other-directed," eager to follow the cues from their peers and not think innovatively or act independently. In the old nursery rhyme "This Little Pig Went to Market," Riesman noted, each pig went his own way. "Today, however, all little pigs go to market; none stay home; all have roast beef, if any do; and all say 'we-we.' "

Changes in American agriculture paralleled those in industry. Farming grew increasingly scientific and mechanized. Technology cut the work hours necessary to grow crops by half between 1945 and 1960. In 1956 alone, one-eleventh of the farm population left the land (see Figure 27.1). Meanwhile, well-capitalized farm businesses, running "factories in the field," prospered by using more and more machines and chemicals.

FIGURE 27.1

The American Farmer, 1940–1993

The postwar years saw a fundamental transformation of American agriculture. While the small family farmer joined the rural exodus to the cities, large farms prospered.

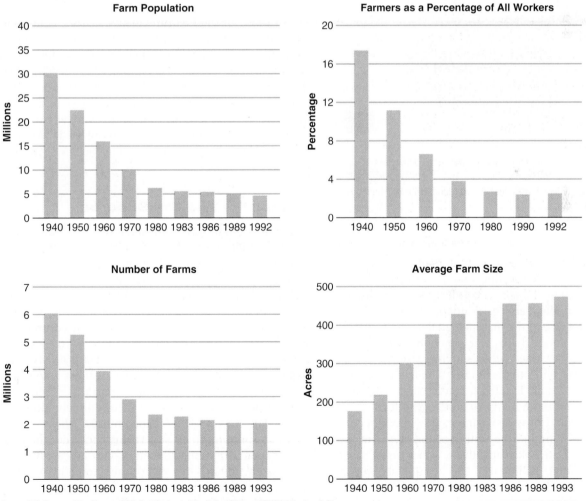

Source: U.S. Bureau of the Census. *Statistical Abstract of the United States,* 1993 (Washington, D.C.).

Rachel Carson
The mother of modern ecology, Carson exposed the dangers of pesticides to animal and human life in her 1962 bestseller *Silent Spring*, an enormously influential work that helped redefine the way humans look at their place in nature.

Until the publication of Rachel Carson's *Silent Spring* in 1962, few Americans understood the extent to which fertilizers, herbicides, and pesticides poisoned the environment. Carson, a former researcher for the Fish and Wildlife Service, dramatized the problems caused by the use of the insecticide DDT and its spread through the food chain. Her depiction of a "silent spring" caused by the death of songbirds from DDT toxicity led many states to ban its use. The federal government followed suit. But the incentives for cultivating more land, and more marginal land, led to further ravages. The Army Corps of Engineers and the Bureau of Reclamation dammed the waters of the West, turning the Columbia and Missouri Rivers into rows of slackwater reservoirs, killing fish and wildlife as well as immersing hundreds of square miles of Indian tribal lands.

Blue-Collar Blues

Consolidation also transformed the labor movement. In 1955 the merger of the AFL and CIO brought 85 percent of union members into a single federation. AFL-CIO leadership promised aggressive unionism, but organized labor fell victim to its own success. The benefits earned at the bargaining table bred complacency. Higher wages, shorter workweeks, paid vacations, health-care coverage, and automatic wage hikes tied to the cost of living led union leaders to view themselves as middle class rather than as a militant proletariat. The 1950s saw far fewer strikes than the 1930s.

A decrease in the number of blue-collar workers further sapped organized labor. Automation reduced membership in the once-mighty coal, auto, and steelworkers' unions by more than half. Most of the new jobs in the 1950s were in the service sector and in public employment, which banned collective bargaining by labor unions.

In 1956, for the first time in U.S. history, white-collar workers outnumbered blue-collar workers, leading some to believe that the United States had become a "postindustrial" society. This notion minimized the fact that more service jobs involved manual labor than intellect. Most office work was as routinized as any factory job. Yet few unions sought to woo white-collar workers. The percentage of the unionized labor force dropped from a high of 36 percent in 1953 to 31 percent in 1960.

Prosperity and the Suburbs

As real income (adjusted for inflation) rose, Americans spent a smaller percentage of their income on necessities and more on powered lawnmowers and air conditioners. After the deprivations of the 1930s and the scarcities of the war years, they heaped their shopping carts with frozen, dehydrated, and fortified foods. When they lacked cash, they signed installment contracts at the appliance store and charged the new furniture on department-store credit cards. In 1950 Diner's Club issued the first credit card; American Express followed in 1958. Installment buying, home mortgages, and auto loans tripled Americans' total private indebtedness in the 1950s. Advertising expenditures also tripled. Business spent more on advertising each year than the nation spent on public education. Virtually everywhere one looked, advertisements appealed to people's desire for status and glamor to convince them to buy what they did not need.

FIGURE 27.2
Urban, Suburban, and Rural Americans, 1940–1960
In the fifteen years following World War II, more than 40 million Americans migrated to the suburbs, where, as one father put it, "a kid could grow up with grass stains on his pants." Over the same period, fourteen of the fifteen largest U.S. cities lost population.

Source: Adapted from U.S. Bureau of the Census, *Current Censuses*, 1930–1970 (Washington, D.C.: U.S. Government Printing Office).

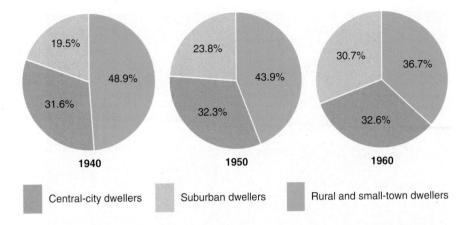

1940	**1950**	**1960**

■ Central-city dwellers   ■ Suburban dwellers   ■ Rural and small-town dwellers

Responding to the slogan "You auto buy now," Americans purchased 58 million new cars during the 1950s. Manufacturers enticed people to trade up by offering flashier models. One could now purchase two-tone colors, extra-powerful engines—like Pontiac's 1955 "Sensational Strato-Streak V-8," that could propel riders more than twice as fast as any speed limit—and tail fins inspired by the silhouette of the Lockheed P-38 fighter plane. Seat belts remained an unadvertised extra-cost option. The consequences were increases in highway deaths, air pollution, oil consumption, and "autosclerosis"—clogged urban arteries.

Government policy as well as "auto mania" spurred white Americans' exodus to the suburbs (see Figure 27.2). Federal spending on highways skyrocketed from $79 million in 1946 to $2.6 billion in 1960, putting once-remote areas within "commuting distance" for city workers (see Technology and Culture: The Interstate Highway System). The income tax code stimulated home sales by allowing deductions for home-mortgage interest payments and for property taxes. Both the Federal Housing Administration (FHA) and Veterans Administration (VA) offered low-interest loans; and neither promoted housing desegregation, despite the Supreme Court's 1948 ruling that state courts could not enforce restrictive covenants (see Chapter 23). In 1960 suburbia was 98 percent white.

Eighty-five percent of the 13 million new homes built in the 1950s were in the suburbs. While social critics lampooned the "ticky-tacky" houses in "disturbia," many families considered them the embodiment of the American Dream. They longed for single-family homes of their own, good schools, a safe environment for the children, fresh air, and friendly neighbors just like themselves.

Park Forest, Illinois, was carefully planned to be a "complete community for middle-income families with children." While wives stayed home to raise the kids and shop at the Plaza, husbands commuted the thirty miles to Chicago on the Illinois Central Railroad or drove into the city on Western Avenue. On Long Island, some thirty miles from midtown Manhattan, Alfred and William Levitt used the mass production construction techniques they perfected building housing for wartime navy workers in Norfolk, Virginia, to construct thousands of standardized 720-square-foot houses as quickly as possible. All looked alike. Deeds to the property required door chimes, not buzzers, prohibited picket fences, mandated regular lawn mowing, and even specified when the wash could be hung to dry in the backyard. All the town streets curved at the same angle. A tree was planted every twenty-eight feet. The Levitts then built a second, larger Levittown in Bucks County, Pennsylvania, and a third in Willingboro, New Jersey.

In the greatest internal migration in its history, some 20 million Americans moved to the suburbs in the 1950s—doubling the numbers and making the suburban population equal to that of the central cities. Contractors built 2 million new homes a year, 85 percent of them in the suburbs. By 1960 over 60 percent of American families owned their homes—the symbol of the affluent society.

Many former servicemen who had first glimpsed the Sunbelt in military camps returned to take up residence, as did others lured by job opportunities, the climate, and the pace of life. California's population went from 9 to 19 million between 1945 and 1964, supplanting New York as the most populous state. Los Angeles epitomized the enormous expansion of the suburbs as well as the rapid growth of the Sunbelt. It boasted the highest per capita ownership of private homes and automobiles of any city, as well as 250 miles of freeways by 1960. Bulldozers ripped out three thousand acres of orange groves a day in Los Angeles County to make way for new housing developments. Orange County, bordering Los Angeles,

Made for Each Other
The two-tone 1955 Chevy Bel Air convertible and a California suburban drive-in. As Americans flocked to the new suburban communities the number of cars in the country increased by 133 percent between 1945 and 1960; and as Americans raced to buy the latest, flashiest model, almost as many cars were junked each year in the mid-1950s as were manufactured.

doubled its population in the 1940s and then tripled it in the 1950s.

Industry also headed South and West. Drawn by low taxes, low energy costs, and anti-union right-to-work laws, industrialists transferred their conservative politics along with their plants and corporate headquarters. Senior citizens, attracted to places like Sun City, Arizona, "a complete community geared to older Americans," brought a more conservative outlook to the Sunbelt as well. By 1980 the population of the Sunbelt, which stretched from the Old Confederacy across Texas to southern California, exceeded that of the North and East. The political power of the Republican party rose accordingly.

CONSENSUS AND CONSERVATISM

Not everyone embraced the conformity of 1950s consumer culture. Intellectuals found a wide audience for their attack on "an America of mass housing, mass markets, massive corporations, massive government, mass media, and massive boredom." These critics targeted "organization men" bent on getting ahead by going along and "status seekers" pursuing external rewards to compensate for inner insecurities. Others took aim at the consumerist middle-class: "all items in a national supermarket—categorized, processed, labeled, priced, and readied for merchandising."

This social criticism oversimplified reality. It ignored ethnic and class diversity. It overlooked the acquisitiveness and conformity of earlier generations—the peer-group pressures in small-town America. It failed to gauge the currents of dissent swirling beneath the surface. It caricatured rather than characterized American society. But the critique rightly spotlighted the elevation of comfort over challenge, and of private pleasures over public affairs. It was, in the main, a time of political passivity and preoccupation with personal gain. Americans, indeed, sought refuge in "the good life." Voices of protest were muted, and a large majority shared aspirations and agreed on values, rejecting radicalism at home and opposing the spread of communism abroad.

Togetherness and the Baby Boom

In 1954 *McCall's* magazine coined the term "togetherness" to celebrate the "ideal" couple: the man and woman who married young and centered their lives around home and children. Americans in the 1950s wed at an earlier age than had their parents (one woman in three married by age nineteen). Confident in continued economic prosperity and influenced by the popular culture, they had more babies sooner. The fertility rate (the number of births per thousand women), 80 in 1940, peaked at 123 in 1957, when an American baby was born every seven seconds.

New antibiotics subdued such diseases as diphtheria and whooping cough, and the Salk and Sabin vaccines ended the dread of poliomyelitis (polio). Prior to the April 1955 announcement by Dr. Jonas Salk of an effective vaccine, fear of a child being paralyzed or killed by polio haunted American families. Most knew of a stricken child wearing metal leg braces or confined to an iron lung. Millions contributed to the March of Dimes to fund research; and the number of American children afflicted dropped from fifty-eight thousand in 1952 to fifty-seven hundred in 1958. The decline in childhood mortality helped raise American life expectancy from 65.9 years in 1945 to 70.9 years in 1970. Coupled with the "baby boom," it brought a 19 percent increase in the U.S. population during the 1950s—a larger jump than in any previous decade. By 1960 children under fourteen made up one-third of the population.

The immense size of the baby-boom generation (the 76 million Americans born between 1946 and 1964) guaranteed its historical importance. Its movement through each stage of life would be as contorting as the digestion of a pig by a boa constrictor. First came the bulge in baby carriages in the late 1940s. In the 1950s school construction boomed, as did college enrollments in the 1960s. Then in the 1970s—as the baby boomers had families—home construction and sales peaked. The 1980s and 1990s brought a surge in retirement investments that sent the stock market soaring. In the 1950s the baby boom also made child rearing a huge concern, reinforcing the idea that women's place was in the home. With Americans convinced of the psychological importance of early childhood experiences, motherhood became an increasingly vital, time-consuming calling.

No one did more to emphasize children's need for the love and care of full-time mothers than Dr. Benjamin Spock. Only the Bible outsold his *Common Sense Book of Baby and Child Care* (1946) in the 1950s. Spock urged mothers not to work outside the home, in order to create the atmosphere of warmth and intimacy necessary for their children to mature into well-adjusted adults. Crying babies were to be comforted so that they would not feel rejected. Breast-feeding came back into vogue. Spock's advice also led to less scolding and spanking and to more "democratic" family discussions. In some homes his "permissive" approach produced a "filiarchy" in which kids ruled the roost; in many it unduly burdened mothers.

Domesticity

Popular culture in the 1950s glorified marriage and parenthood more than ever before. Bolstered by "experts,"

often cloaked in psychological garb, and drawing support from such developments as prosperity, suburban growth, and the baby boom, domesticity emphasized women's role as a helpmate to her husband and a full-time mother to her children. Smiling movie stars like Doris Day showed how to win a man, the assumed goal of every woman; and as actress Debbie Reynolds declared in *The Tender Trap* (1955), "A woman isn't a woman until she's been married and had children."

Television invariably pictured women as at-home mothers. Women's magazines featured articles with titles like "Cooking to Me Is Poetry." While *Esquire* magazine called working wives a "menace," *Life* lauded Marjorie Sutton for marrying at sixteen, cooking and sewing for the family, raising four children, being a pillar of the PTA and Campfire Girls, and working out on a trampoline "to keep her size 12 figure." Millions of teenage girls swooned when Paul Anka sang "You're Having My Baby" and read *Seventeen* magazine's advice to them in 1957:

> In dealing with a male, the art of saving face is essential. Traditionally he is the head of the family, the dominant partner, the man in the situation. Even on those occasions when you both know his decision is wrong, more often than not you will be wise to go along with his decision.

According to a Gallup public-opinion poll in 1962, 96 percent of the women surveyed declared themselves extremely, or very, happy. "Being subordinate to men is part of being feminine," an Arizona mother told the pollster. "Women who ask for equality fight nature," added one from New Jersey.

Education reinforced these notions. While girls learned typing and cooking, boys were channeled into carpentry and courses leading to professional careers. Guidance counselors cautioned young women not to "miss the boat" of marriage by pursuing higher education. "Men are not interested in college degrees but in the warmth and humanness of the girls they marry," stressed a textbook on the family. While a higher percentage of women than men graduated from high school in the 1950s, more men than women went to college. Almost two-thirds of college women failed to complete a degree. They dropped out, people joked, to get their M.R.S. degree and a Ph.T.—"Putting Hubbie Through." The laughter sometimes hid dissatisfaction: cooking the perfect dinner could still leave a woman starved for fulfillment in her own life.

From 1947 on, despite domesticity's holding sway, increasing numbers of women entered the work force. By 1952, 2 million more women worked outside the home than had during the war; and by 1960, twice as

many did as in 1940. In 1960 one-third of the labor force was female, and one out of three married women worked outside the home. Of all women workers that year, 60 percent were married, while 40 percent had school-age children.

Forced back into low-paying, gender-segregated jobs, most women worked to add to the family income, not to fulfill personal aspirations or challenge stereotypes. White women mostly filled clerical positions, while African-Americans held service jobs in private households and restaurants. Some, as during World War II, developed a heightened sense of expectations and empowerment as a result of employment. Transmitted to their daughters, their experience would lead to a feminist resurgence in the late 1960s.

Religion and Education

"Today in the U.S.," *Time* claimed in 1954, "the Christian faith is back in the center of things." Domestic anxieties and Cold War fears catalyzed a surge of religious activity. Evangelist Billy Graham, Roman Catholic Bishop Fulton J. Sheen, and Protestant minister Norman Vincent Peale all had syndicated newspaper columns, best-selling books, and radio and television programs. None was more influential than Graham. Backed to the hilt by the Hearst press and Luce publications, Graham peddled a potent mixture of religious salvation and aggressive anticommunism. In what he pictured as a duel to the death against the atheistic Kremlin, Graham supported McCarthyism and backed GOP demands to "unleash" Jiang's troops against mainland China. He termed communism "a great sinister anti-Christian movement masterminded by Satan" and echoed Billy Sunday's emphasis on the traditional morality of the nineteenth-century American village, lashing out at homosexuals and working wives.

The turn to religion found expression in Hollywood religious extravaganzas, such as *Ben Hur* and *The Ten Commandments,* and in popular songs like "I Believe" and "The Man Upstairs." Sales of Bibles reached an all-time high. Television proclaimed that "the family that prays together stays together." Dial-a-Prayer offered telephone solutions for spiritual problems. Congress added "under God" to the Pledge of Allegiance and required "IN GOD WE TRUST" to be put on all U.S. currency.

"Everybody should have a religious faith," President Eisenhower declared, "and I don't care what it is." Most Americans agreed. Church attendance swelled, and the percentage of people who said they belonged to a church or synagogue increased from 49 percent in 1940

to 55 percent in 1950, and to a record-high 69 percent in 1959. It had become "un-American to be unreligious" noted *The Christian Century* in 1954. Professions of faith became a way to affirm "the American way of life" and to relieve anxieties.

While increasing numbers of Americans identified with some denomination, the intensity of religious faith diminished for many. Religious belief was intermixed with patriotism, family togetherness, and Thursday night bingo. Mainstream Protestant churches downplayed sin and evil and emphasized fellowship, offering a sense of belonging in a rapidly changing society. Many Jews spurned the orthodoxy of their parents for the easier-to-follow practices of Reform or Conservative Judaism. Catholicism broadened its appeal as a new pope, John XXIII, charmed the world with ecumenical reforms.

Similarly, education flourished in the 1950s yet seemed shallower than in earlier decades. Swelled by the baby boom, primary school enrollment rose by 10 million in the 1950s (compared with 1 million in the 1940s). California opened a new school every week throughout the decade and still faced a classroom shortage. The proportion of college-age Americans in higher education climbed from 15 percent in 1940 to more than 40 percent by the early 1960s. "Progressive" educators promoted sociability and self-expression over science, math, and history. The "well-rounded" student became more prized than one who was highly skilled or knowledgeable. Surveys of college students found them conservative, conformist, and careerist, a "silent generation" seeking security above all.

While administrators ran universities like businesses, faculty focused on the cultural and psychological aspects of American society. Few challenged the economic structure or ideology of the United States, or addressed the problems of minorities and the poor. Many historians downplayed past class conflicts. Instead, they highlighted the pragmatic ideas and values shared by most Americans, differentiating the American experience from that of Europe. It became commonplace to assert that America's unique national character had been shaped primarily by economic abundance.

The Culture of the Fifties

American culture reflected the expansive spirit of prosperity as well as Cold War anxieties. With increasing leisure and fatter paychecks, Americans spent one-seventh of the 1950s GNP on entertainment. Yellowstone National Park lured four times as many people through

its gates each summer as lived in Wyoming; Glacier National Park attracted more visitors than lived in Montana. Spectator sports boomed; new symphony halls opened; and book sales doubled.

With the opening of a major exhibit of abstract expressionists by the Museum of Modern Art in 1951, New York replaced Paris as the capital of the art world. Like the immense canvases of Jackson Pollock and the cool jazz of trumpeter Miles Davis, introspection and improvisation characterized the major novels of the era. Their personal yearnings sharply contrasted with the political engagement and social realism of literature in the 1930s. Novels such as John Cheever's *The Wapshot Chronicles* (1957) and John Updike's *Rabbit Run* (1960) presented characters dissatisfied with jobs and home, longing for a more vital and authentic existence, yet incapable of decisive action.

Southern, African-American, and Jewish-American writers turned out the decade's most vital fiction. William Faulkner continued his dense saga of Yoknapatawpha County, Mississippi, in *The Town* (1957) and *The Mansion* (1960), while Eudora Welty evoked southern small-town life in *The Ponder Heart* (1954). The black experience found memorable expression in James Baldwin's *Go Tell It on the Mountain* (1953) and Ralph Ellison's *Invisible Man* (1951). Bernard Malamud's *The Assistant* (1957) explored the Jewish immigrant world of New York's Lower East Side, and Philip Roth's *Goodbye Columbus* (1959) dissected the very different world of upwardly mobile Jews.

The many westerns, musicals, and costume spectacles churned out by Hollywood further reflected the diminished interest in political issues. Most films about contemporary life portrayed Americans as one happy white, middle-class family. Minorities and the poor remained invisible, and the independent career women of films of the 1940s were replaced by "dumb blondes" and cute helpmates. Movie attendance dropped 50 percent as TV viewing soared, and a fifth of the nation's theaters became bowling alleys and supermarkets by 1960. Hollywood tried to recoup by developing three-dimensionality and wide-screen processes that accentuated the difference from television's small black-and-white image. No technological wizardry, however—not even Smell-O-Vision and its rival Aroma-Rama—could stem TV's astounding growth.

The Message of the Medium

No cultural medium ever became as popular and as powerful as quickly, or so reinforced the public mood, as television. Ownership of a TV set soared from one of every eighteen thousand households in 1946 to nine of ten American homes by 1960 (see Figure 27.3). By then, more Americans had televisions than had bathrooms.

FIGURE 27.3
The Television Revolution, 1950–1994
As televisions became commonplace in the 1950s, TV viewing altered the nature of American culture and politics.

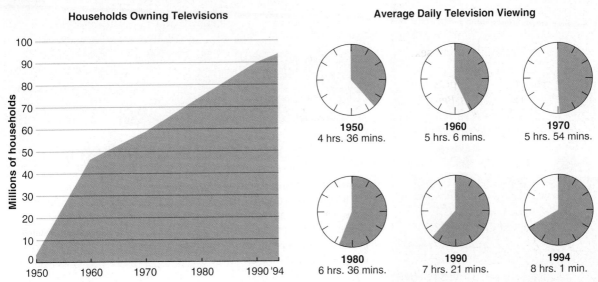

Households Owning Televisions

Average Daily Television Viewing

1950 — 4 hrs. 36 mins.
1960 — 5 hrs. 6 mins.
1970 — 5 hrs. 54 mins.
1980 — 6 hrs. 36 mins.
1990 — 7 hrs. 21 mins.
1994 — 8 hrs. 1 min.

Source: Statistical Abstracts of the United States.

Business capitalized on the phenomenon. The three main radio networks—ABC, CBS, and NBC—gobbled up virtually every TV station in the country, and, just as in radio, they profited by selling time to advertisers who wanted to reach the largest possible audiences. By the mid-fifties, the three networks each had larger advertising revenues than any other communications medium in the world. Whereas advertisers had spent some $50 million on TV in 1949, they would be spending more than $1.5 billion a decade later.

Introduced in 1952, *TV Guide* outsold every other periodical and was being published in fifty-three separate regional editions by 1960. The TV dinner, first marketed in 1954, altered the nation's eating habits. Television, it seemed, could sell almost anything. When Walt Disney produced a show on Davy Crockett in 1955, stores could not keep up with the massive demand for "King of the Wild Frontier" coonskin caps. Television quickly became the vital center of the consumer culture. Corporations spent fortunes on TV ads creating needs and wants for the consumer. "The message of the media," a critic noted, "is the commercial."

The TV Culture

Geared to its initial small audiences, TV showcased talent and creativity. Opera performances appeared in prime time, as did sophisticated comedies and political dramas, and documentaries like Edward R. Murrow's *See It Now*. Early situation comedies such as *The Life of Riley* and *The Goldbergs* featured ethnic working-class families. As the price of TV sets came down and program producers felt the chill of McCarthyism, the networks' appetite for a mass audience transformed TV into a cautious celebration of conformity and consumerism. Controversy went off the air, and conflict disappeared from the screen. Only a few situation comedies, like Jackie Gleason's *The Honeymooners*, set in Brooklyn, did not feature suburban, consumer-oriented, upper-middle-class families. Most, like *Leave It to Beaver* and *The Adventures of Ozzie and Harriet*, portrayed perfectly coiffed moms who loved to vacuum in high heels, frisky yet ultimately obedient kids, and all-knowing dads who never lost their tempers. Even Lucille Ball and Desi Arnaz in *I Love Lucy*—which no network initially wanted

The Mickey Mouse Club
Popular daily TV children's programs, such as "The Mickey Mouse Club" and the "Howdy Doody Show," attracted loyal fans who shared a common experience and badgered their parents to buy coonskin caps, Hula-Hoops, Silly Putty, and wiffle balls.

TV adds so much to family happiness

Motorola TV and Family Happiness
The television set, so grandly advertised and displayed, itself was a symbol of postwar affluence, and both advertising and programming, which featured largely middle-class, consumption-oriented suburban families, stimulated the consumer culture. Overall, TV powerfully reinforced the conservative, celebratory values of everyday American life in the 1950s.

because an all-American redhead was married to a Cuban—had a baby and left New York for suburbia.

Decrying TV's mediocrity in 1961, the head of the Federal Communications Commission dared broadcasters to watch their own shows for a day: "I can assure you that you will observe a vast wasteland." A steady parade of soaps, unsophisticated comedies, and violent westerns led others to call TV the "idiot box."

Measuring television's impact is difficult. Depending on the many factors that differentiate individuals, people read the "texts" of TV (or of movies or books) their own way and so receive their own messages or signals from the media. While TV bound some to the status quo, it brought others glimpses of unaccustomed possibilities that raised expectations. It functioned simultaneously as conservator and spur to change. In the main, television reflected existing values and institutions. It stimulated the desire to be included in American society, not to transform it. It spawned mass fads for Barbie dolls and hula hoops, spread the message of consumerism, and made Americans ever more name-brand conscious. It reinforced gender and racial stereotypes. TV rarely showed African Americans and Latinos—except in servile roles or prison scenes. It extolled male violence in fighting evil; and it portrayed women as either zany madcaps ("My Friend Irma") or self-effacing moms ("The Donna Reed Show"). It virtually ended network radio, returning local stations to a music-based format, especially "Top-40" programs geared to youth. While promoting professional baseball and football into truly national phenomena, TV decreased the audience of motion picture theaters and of general interest magazines such as *Look* and *Life*.

Television also changed the political life of the nation. Politicians could effectively appeal to the voters over the heads of party leaders, and appearance mattered more than content. Millions watched Senator Estes Kefauver grill mobsters about their ties to city governments, instantly transforming the Tennessean into a serious contender for the presidency. At least 20 million observed the combative Senator Joseph McCarthy bully and slander witnesses during the hearings on disloyalty in the army. The 58 million who witnessed Richard Nixon's appeal for support in the "Checkers" speech helped save his place on the GOP ticket. And Eisenhower's pioneering use of brief "spot advertisements" combined with Stevenson's avoidance of televised appearances clinched Ike's smashing presidential victories. In 1960 John F. Kennedy's "telegenic" image would play a significant role in his winning the presidency.

Television vastly increased the cost of political campaigning while decreasing the content level of political

discussion. It helped produce a more-national culture, diminishing provincialism and regional differences. Its overwhelming portrayal of a contented citizenry reinforced complacency and hid the reality of "the other America."

THE OTHER AMERICA

"I am an invisible man," declared the African-American narrator of Ralph Ellison's *Invisible Man*; "I am invisible, understand, simply because people refuse to see me." Indeed, few middle-class white Americans perceived the extent of social injustice in the United States. "White flight" from cities to suburbs produced physical separation of the races and classes. New expressways walled off ghettos and rural poverty from middle-class motorists speeding by. Popular culture focused on affluent Americans enjoying the "good life." In the consensus of the Eisenhower era, deprivation had supposedly disappeared. In reality, poverty and racial discrimination were rife and dire, and the struggles for social justice intensified.

Poverty and Urban Blight

Although the percentage of poor families (defined as a family of four with a yearly income of less than three thousand dollars) declined from 34 percent in 1947 to 22 percent in 1960, 35 million Americans remained below the "poverty line." Eight million senior citizens existed on annual incomes below one thousand dollars. A third of the poor lived in depressed rural areas, where 2 million migrant farm workers experienced the most abject poverty. Observing a Texas migratory-labor camp in 1955, a journalist reported that 96 percent of the children had consumed no milk in the previous six months; eight out of ten adults had eaten no meat; and most slept "on the ground, in a cave, under a tree, or in a chicken house." In California's Imperial Valley, the infant death rate among migrant workers was more than seven times the statewide average.

The bulk of the poor huddled in decaying inner-city slums. Displaced southern blacks and Appalachian whites, Native Americans forced off reservations, and newly arrived Hispanics strained cities' inadequate facilities. Nearly two hundred thousand Mexican-Americans were herded into San Antonio's Westside barrio. A local newspaper described them as living like cattle in a stockyard, "with roofed-over corrals for homes and chutes for streets." A visitor to New York City's slums in 1950 found "25 human beings living in a dark and airless coal cellar ten feet below the street level. . . . No animal could live there long, yet here were 17 children, the

youngest having been born here two weeks before." The " 'promised land' that Mammy had been singing about in the cotton fields for many years," observed Claude Brown, had become a slum, "a dirty, stinky, uncared-for closet-size section of a great city."

As described by Michael Harrington in *The Other America: Poverty in the United States* (1962), the poor were trapped in a vicious cycle of want and a culture of deprivation. Because they could not afford good housing, a nutritious diet, and doctors, the poor got sick more often and for longer than more affluent Americans. Losing wages and finding it hard to hold steady jobs, they could not pay for decent housing, good food, or doctors— that would keep them from getting and staying sick. The children of the poor started school disadvantaged, quickly fell behind, and, lacking encouragement and expectation of success, dropped out. Living with neither hope nor the necessary skills to enter the mainstream of American life, the poor bequeathed a similar legacy to their children.

The pressing need for low-cost housing went unanswered. In 1955 fewer than 200,000 of the 810,000 public-housing units called for in the Housing Act of 1949 had been built. A decade later only 320,000 had

been constructed. "Slum clearance" generally meant "Negro clearance," and "urban renewal" meant "poor removal," as developers razed low-income neighborhoods to put up parking garages and expensive housing. The Los Angeles barrio of Chavez Ravine was bulldozed to construct Dodger Stadium.

At the same time, landlords, realtors, and bankers deliberately excluded nonwhites from decent housing. Half of the housing in New York's Harlem predated 1900. A dozen people might share a tiny apartment with broken windows, faulty plumbing, and gaping holes in the walls. Harlem's rates of illegitimate births, infant deaths, narcotics use, and crime soared above the averages for the city and the nation. "Where flies and maggots breed, where the plumbing is stopped up and not repaired, where rats bite helpless infants," black social psychologist Kenneth Clark observed, "the conditions of life are brutal and inhuman."

Blacks' Struggle for Justice

The collision between the hopes raised by the 1954 *Brown* decision and the indignities of persistent discrimination and segregation sparked a new phase in the

North Chicago Slum
Life was not the "nifty fifties" for all Americans. Nearly one in four lived below the poverty line, which was calculated by the federal government to be $2,973 for a family of four in 1959.

civil-rights movement. To sweep away the separate but rarely equal Jim Crow facilities in the South, African Americans turned to new tactics, organizations, and leaders. They utilized nonviolent direct-action protest to engage large numbers of blacks in their own freedom struggle and to arouse white America's conscience.

In the 1950s racism still touched even the smallest details of daily life. In Montgomery, Alabama, black bus riders had to surrender their seats so that no white rider would stand. Although they were more than three-quarters of all passengers, the African-Americans had to pay their fares at the front of the bus, leave, and reenter through the back door, sit only in the rear, and then give up their seats to any standing white passengers.

On December 1, 1955, Rosa Parks refused to get up so that a white man could sit. Parks, an officer of the Montgomery NAACP who would not drink from fountains labeled "Colored Only" and who climbed stairs rather than use a segregated elevator, was arrested. Montgomery's black leaders organized a boycott of the buses to protest. "There comes a time when people get tired," declared Martin Luther King, Jr., a twenty-seven-year-old African-American minister who articulated the anger of Montgomery blacks, "tired of being segregated and humiliated; tired of being kicked about by the brutal feet of oppression." The time had come, King continued, to cease being patient "with anything less than freedom and justice." This speech marked the beginning of what would become a year-long bus boycott by fifty thousand black citizens of Montgomery. "My soul has been tired for a long time," an old woman told a minister who had stopped his car to offer her a ride; "now my feet are tired, and my soul is resting." When the city leaders would not budge, the blacks challenged the constitutionality of bus segregation. In November 1956 the U.S. Supreme Court affirmed a lower-court decision outlawing segregation on the buses.

The Montgomery bus boycott demonstrated African-American strength and determination. It shattered the myth that blacks favored segregation and that only outside agitators fought Jim Crow. It affirmed the possibility of social change. It vaulted Dr. King, whose oratory simultaneously inspired black activism and touched white consciences, into the national spotlight.

King's philosophy of civil disobedience fused the spirit of Christianity with the strategy of nonviolent resistance. His emphasis on direct action gave every African American an opportunity to demonstrate the moral evil of racial discrimination; and his insistence on nonviolence diminished the likelihood of bloodshed. Preaching that blacks must lay their bodies on the line to

Rosa Parks

A member of the Montgomery chapter of the NAACP since 1943, and the organization's secretary, Rosa Parks had protested segregation by refusing to drink from fountains labeled "Colored Only" and by climbing stairs rather than using segregated elevators. Her act of protest against bus segregation inspired a whole black community to join her cause and sparked the massive nonviolent civil disobedience phase of the struggle against white supremacy.

provoke crises that would force whites to confront their racism, King urged his followers to love their enemies. By so doing, he believed, blacks would convert their oppressors and bring "redemption and reconciliation." In 1957 King and a group of black ministers formed the Southern Christian Leadership Conference (SCLC) "to carry on nonviolent crusades against the evils of second-class citizenship." Yet more than on leaders, the movement's triumphs would depend on the domestic servants who walked instead of riding the buses, the children on the front lines of the battle for school desegregation, and the tens of thousands of ordinary people who marched, rallied, and demonstrated.

Latinos and Latinas

Hispanic-Americans initially made less headway in ending discrimination. High unemployment on the Caribbean island and cheap airfares to New York City

brought a steady stream of Puerto Ricans, who as U.S. citizens could enter the mainland without restriction. From seventy thousand in 1940 to a quarter of a million in 1950 and then nearly a million in 1960, El Barrio in New York City's East Harlem had a larger Puerto Rican population and more bodegas than San Juan by the late 1960s.

In New York they suffered from inadequate schools and police harassment, and were denied decent jobs and political recognition. More than half lived in inadequate housing. Like countless earlier immigrants, Puerto Ricans gained greater personal freedom in the United States while losing the security of a strong cultural tradition. Family frictions flared in the transition to unaccustomed ways. Parents felt upstaged by children who learned English and obtained jobs that were closed to them. The relationship between husbands and wives changed as women found readier access to jobs than did men. One migrant explained, "Whether I have a husband or not I work . . . and if my husband dare to complain, I throw him out. That is the difference; in Puerto Rico I should have to stand for anything a man asks me to do because he pays the rent. Here I belong to myself." Others hoped to earn money in the United States and then return home. Most stayed. Yet however much they tried to embrace American ways, many could not enjoy the promise of the American Dream because of their skin color and Spanish language.

Mexican-Americans suffered the same indignities. Most were underpaid, overcharged, and segregated from mainstream American life. The presence of countless "undocumented aliens" compounded their woes.

After World War II, new irrigation systems added 7.5 million acres to the agricultural lands of the Southwest, stimulating farm owners' desire for cheap Mexican labor. In 1951, to stem the resulting tide of illegal Mexican immigrants, Congress reintroduced the wartime "temporary worker" program that brought in seasonal farm laborers called *braceros*. The workers were supposed to return to Mexico at the end of their labor contract, but many stayed without authorization, joining a growing number of Latinos who entered the country illegally.

During the 1953–1955 recession, the Eisenhower administration's "Operation Wetback" (*wetback* was a term of derision for illegal Mexican immigrants who supposedly swam across the Rio Grande to enter the United States) deported some 3 million allegedly undocumented entrants. Periodic roundups, however, did not substitute for a sound labor policy or an effective enforcement strategy, and millions of Mexicans continued to cross the poorly guarded two-thousand-mile border. The *bracero* program itself peaked in 1959, admitting 450,000 workers. Neither the *Asociación Nacional México-Americana* (founded in 1950) nor the League of United Latin American Citizens (LULAC) could stop their exploitation or the widespread violations of the rights of Mexican-American citizens.

The Mexican-American population of Los Angeles County doubled to more than six hundred thousand,

A Periodic Roundup
Los Angeles police remove a group of undocumented Mexican immigrants from a freight train and prepare to send them back across the border.

and the *colonias* of Denver, El Paso, Phoenix, and San Antonio grew proportionately as large. The most rural of all major ethnic groups in 1940, the percentage of Mexican-Americans living in urban areas rose to 65 percent in 1950 and to 85 percent by 1970. As service in World War II gave Hispanics an increased sense of their own American identity and a claim on the rights supposedly available to all American citizens, urbanization gave them better educational and employment opportunities. Unions like the United Cannery, Agricultural, Packing and Allied Workers of America sought higher wages and better working conditions for their Mexican-American members, and such middle-class organizations as LULAC, the GI Forum, and the Unity League campaigned to desegregate schools and public facilities.

In 1954 the Supreme Court banned the exclusion of Mexican-Americans from Texas jury lists. The mobilization of Hispanic voters led to the election of the first Mexican-American mayor, in El Paso in 1958. Latinos also took pride in baseball star Roberto Clemente and their growing numbers in the major leagues, in Nobel Prize winners like biologist Severo Ochoa, and in such Hollywood stars as Ricardo Montalban and Anthony Quinn. But the existence of millions of undocumented aliens and the continuation of the *bracero* program stigmatized all people of Spanish descent and depressed their wages. The median income of Hispanics was less than two-thirds that of Anglos. At least a third lived in poverty.

Native Americans

Native Americans remained the poorest minority, with a death rate three times the national average. Unemployment rates on reservations during the 1950s reached 70 percent for the Blackfeet of Montana and the Hopi of New Mexico, and a staggering 86 percent for the Choctaw of Mississippi. After World War II Congress veered away from John Collier's efforts to reassert Indian sovereignty and cultural autonomy and had moved toward the goal of assimilation. This meant terminating treaty relationships with tribes, ending the federal trusteeship of Indians. Some favored it as a move toward Indian self-sufficiency; others desired an end to the communal culture of Indians; and still others wanted access to Indian lands and mineral resources. Between 1954 and 1962 Congress passed a dozen termination bills, withdrawing financial support from sixty-one reservations.

First applied to Menominees of Wisconsin and Klamaths of Oregon, who owned valuable timberlands, the termination policy proved disastrous. Further impoverishing the Indians whom it affected, the law transferred more than five hundred thousand acres of Native American lands to non-Indians. To lure Indians off the reservations and into urban areas, and to speed the sale of Indian lands to developers, the government established the Voluntary Relocation Program. It provided Native Americans with moving costs, assistance in finding housing and jobs, and living expenses until they obtained work. "We're like wheat," said one Hopi woman who went to the city. "The wind blows, we bend over. . . . You can't stand up when there's wind."

By the end of the decade about sixty thousand reservation Indians had been relocated to cities. Some became assimilated into middle-class America. Most could not find work and ended up on state welfare rolls living in rundown shantytowns. A third returned to the reservations. Not surprisingly, the National Congress of American Indians vigorously opposed termination, and most tribal politicians advocated Indian sovereignty, treaty rights, federal trusteeship, and the special status of Indians.

SEEDS OF DISQUIET

Late in the 1950s apprehension ruffled the calm surface of American life. Academics spotlighted shortcomings and questioned the nation's values. Periodic recessions, rising unemployment, and the growing national debt made Khrushchev's 1959 threat to bury the United States economically, and his boast that "your grandchildren will live under communism," ring in American ears. Third World anticolonialism, especially in Cuba, diminished Americans' sense of national pride, adding to their discontent. So did the growing alienation of American youth and a technological breakthrough by the Soviet Union.

Sputnik

On October 4, 1957, the Soviet Union launched the first artificial satellite, *Sputnik* ("Little Traveler"). Weighing 184 pounds and a mere twenty-two inches in diameter, it circled Earth at eighteen thousand miles per hour. *Sputnik* dashed the American myth of unquestioned technological superiority; and when *Sputnik II*, carrying a dog, went into a more distant orbit on November 3, critics charged that Eisenhower had allowed a "technological Pearl Harbor." Democrats warned of a "missile gap" between the United States and the Soviet Union.

The Eisenhower administration publicly disparaged the Soviet achievement. Behind the scenes it hurried to

"Flopnik," "Stayputnik"
The Soviet launching of Sputnik into orbit around Earth jolted Americans. To reassure a jittery public, Eisenhower advanced the date for the launching of an American satellite. In December 1957, the hastily prepared Vanguard rocket exploded seconds after takeoff.

have the American Vanguard missile launch a satellite. On December 6, with millions watching on TV, the Vanguard rose six feet in the air and exploded. Newspapers rechristened the missile "Flopnik."

Eisenhower did not find it a laughing matter. He doubled the funds for missile development to $4.3 billion in 1958 and raised the amount to $5.3 billion in 1959. He also established the Science Advisory Committee, whose recommendations led to the creation of the National Aeronautics and Space Administration (NASA) in July 1958. By the end of the decade, the United States had launched several space probes and successfully tested the Atlas intercontinental ballistic missile (ICBM).

Critics had long complained that Americans honored football stars more than brainy students. To no avail they warned that the Soviet Union was producing twice as many scientists and engineers as the United States. *Sputnik* suddenly provided the impetus for a crash program to improve American education. Political

barriers to federal aid for education crumbled. Funds from Washington built new classrooms and laboratories, raised teachers' salaries, and installed instructional television systems in schools. In 1958 Congress passed the National Defense Education Act, providing loans to students, funds for teacher training, and money to develop instructional materials in the sciences, mathematics, and foreign languages.

Americans now banked on higher education to ensure national security. The number of college students, 1.5 million in 1940 and 2.5 million in 1955, skyrocketed to 3.6 million in 1960. That year the U.S. government funneled $1.5 billion to universities, a hundred-fold increase over 1940. Linked directly to the Cold War, federal aid to education raised unsettling questions. By 1960 nearly a third of scientists and engineers on university faculties worked full-time on government research, primarily defense projects. Some would dub it the "military-industrial-educational complex."

A Different Beat

Few adults considered the social implications of their affluence on the young, or the consequences of having a generation of teenagers who could stay in school instead of working. Few thought about the effects of growing up in an age when traditional values like thrift and self-denial had declining relevance, or of maturing at a time when young people had the leisure and money to shape their own subculture. Little attention was paid to the decline in the age of menarche (first menstruation), or the ways that the relatively new institution of the junior high school affected the behavior of youth. Despite talk of family togetherness, fathers were often too busy to pay much attention to their children, and mothers sometimes spent more time chauffeuring their young than listening to them. Indeed, much of what adults knew about teenagers (a noun that first appeared in the 1940s and was not commonly used until the 1950s) they learned from the mass media, which focused on the sensational and the superficial.

Accounts of juvenile delinquency abounded. News stories portrayed high schools as war zones, city streets as jungles, and teenagers as zip-gun-armed hoodlums. Highly publicized hearings by a Senate subcommittee on juvenile delinquency stoked the fears. Teenage crime, in fact, had barely increased. Male teenagers aroused alarm by sporting black leather motorcycle jackets and slicking their hair back in a "ducktail".

As dismaying to parents, young Americans embraced rock-and-roll. In 1951 Alan Freed, the host of

a classical music program on Cleveland radio, had observed white teenagers dancing to rhythm-and-blues records by such black performers as Chuck Berry, Bo Diddley, and Little Richard. In 1952 Freed started a new radio program, "Moondog's Rock and Roll Party," to play "race music." It was popular, and in 1954 Freed took the program to New York, creating a national craze for rock-and-roll.

Just as white musicians in the 1920s and 1930s had adapted black jazz for white audiences, white performers in the 1950s transformed rhythm-and-blues into "Top Ten" rock-and-roll. In 1954 Bill Haley and the Comets dropped the sexual allusions from Joe Turner's "Shake, Rattle, and Roll," added country-and-western guitar riffs, and had the first major white rock-and-roll hit. When Haley performed "Rock Around the Clock" in *The Blackboard Jungle*, a 1955 film about juvenile delinquency, many parents linked rock-and-roll with disobedience and crime. Red-hunters saw it as a communist plot to corrupt youth. Segregationists claimed it was a ploy "to mix the races." Psychiatrists feared it was "a communicable disease." Some churches condemned it as the "devil's music."

Nothing confirmed their dismay as much as swaggering Elvis Presley. Born in Tupelo, Mississippi, Elvis was a nineteen-year-old truck driver in 1954 when he paid four dollars to record two songs at a Memphis studio. He melded the Pentecostal music of his boyhood with the powerful beat and sexual energy of the rhythm-and-blues music he heard on Memphis' Beale Street, and his songs like "Hound Dog" and "All Shook Up" transformed the cloying pop music that youth found wanting into a proclamation of teenage "separateness." Presley's smirking lips and bucking hips shocked white middle-class adults. The more adults condemned rock-and-roll, the more teenagers loved it. Record sales tripled between 1954 and 1960, and Dick Clark's *American Bandstand* became the decade's biggest TV hit. As teens listened to 45-rpm records in their own rooms and to radios in their own cars, the music directed to them by such "outsiders" as Buddy Holly from West Texas, Richie Valens (Valenzuela) from East Los Angeles, and Frankie Lymon from Spanish Harlem, nourished the roots of the coming youth revolt.

Portents of Change

Teens cherished rock-and-roll for its frankness and exuberance. They elevated the characters played by Marlon Brando in *The Wild One* (1954) and James Dean in *Rebel Without a Cause* (1955) to cult status for their overturn-

ing of respectable society's mores. They delighted in *Mad* magazine's ridiculing of the phony and pretentious in middle-class America. They customized their cars to reject Detroit's standards. All were signs of their variance from the adult world, of their distinct community.

Nonconformist writers known as the Beats expressed a more fundamental revolt against middle-class society. In Allen Ginsberg's *Howl* (1956) and Jack Kerouac's *On the Road* (1957), the Beats scorned conformity and materialism as much as they did conventional punctuation. They scoffed at the "square" America described by Kerouac as "rows of well-to-do houses with lawns and television sets in each living room with everybody looking at the same thing and thinking the same thing at the same time." They romanticized society's outcasts—the mad ones, wrote Kerouac, "the ones who never yawn or say a commonplace thing, but burn,

"Elvis the Pelvis"
In 1956 Elvis Presley skyrocketed to rock-'n'-roll stardom. His wild, rebellious style captivated young audiences. Girls screamed and fainted, and boys tried to imitate his gyrating hips and ducktail haircut.

burn, burn like fabulous yellow roman candles exploding like spiders across the stars." Outraging respectability, they glorified uninhibited sexuality and spontaneity in the search for "It," the ultimate authentic experience, foreshadowing the counterculture to come.

The mass media scorned the Beats, as they did all dissenters. *Look* magazine derided them as Americans "turned inside out. The goals of the Beats are *not* watching TV, *not* wearing gray flannel, *not* owning a home in the suburbs, and especially—*not* working." But some college youth admired their rejection of conformity and complacency. Students protested capital punishment and demonstrated against the continuing investigations of the House Un-American Activities Committee. Others decried the nuclear-arms race. In 1958 and 1959 thousands participated in Youth Marches for Integrated Schools in Washington. Together with the Beats and rock music, this vocal minority of the "silent generation" heralded a youth movement that would explode in the 1960s.

CONCLUSION

A far more complex era than that implied in the stereotype of the "nifty fifties," the decade encompassed contradictions. Although mightier than any nation in history and basking in prosperity, many Americans felt uneasiness as the Cold War continued and boom times brought unsettling changes. Most were pleased that continuity rather than change characterized the switch from a Democratic to a Republican administration. Differing from Truman's policies more in degree than in kind, Eisenhower pursued a centrist course in domestic affairs. While tilting to the right in favoring private corporations, the Eisenhower administration left New Deal reforms in place, expanded existing social welfare benefits, employed Keynesian deficit spending to curtail economic recessions, made no effort to hamper labor unionization, and proposed construction of a vast interstate highway system—the largest domestic spending program in the nation's history. The size and scope of the federal government continued to expand.

So did its involvement throughout the world. The Eisenhower administration followed that of Truman's in its determination to contain communism while putting new emphasis on the need to avoid nuclear war and to fight communism in the Third World. Although generally successful in all three endeavors, Eisenhower and Dulles often gained short-term victories in local conflicts by clandestine means, ignoring the nationalistic yearnings and socioeconomic deprivations of the local peoples, and increasingly allying the United States with reactionary, repressive regimes.

The postwar era was one of unparalleled, sustained material prosperity for most Americans. Building on the accumulated savings and pent-up demand for consumerism from the Second World War, continuing high levels of government spending and new technologies

---

CHRONOLOGY, 1952–1960

1946 ENIAC, the first electronic computer, begins operation.

1947 Levittown, New York, development started.

1948 Bell Labs develops the transistor.

1950 Asosiacion Nacional Mexico-Americana established.

1952 Dwight D. Eisenhower elected president.

1953 Korean War truce signed.
Earl Warren appointed chief justice.
Operation Wetback begins.

1954 Army-McCarthy hearings.
Brown v. *Board of Education of Topeka.*
Fall of Dienbienphu; Geneva Conference.
Father Knows Best begins on TV.

1955 Salk polio vaccine developed.
AFL-CIO merger.
First postwar U.S.-Soviet summit meeting.
James Dean stars in *Rebel Without a Cause.*
Montgomery bus boycott begins.

1956 Interstate Highway Act.
Suez crisis.
Soviet intervention in Poland and Hungary.

1957 Eisenhower Doctrine announced.
Civil Rights Act (first since Reconstruction).
Little Rock school-desegregation crisis.
Soviet Union launches *Sputnik.*
Peak of baby boom (4.3 million births).
Southern Christian Leadership Conference founded.

1958 National Defense Education Act.
United States and Soviet Union halt atomic tests.
National Aeronautics and Space Administration (NASA) founded.

1959 Fidel Castro comes to power in Cuba.
Khrushchev and Eisenhower meet at Camp David.

1960 U-2 incident.
Second Civil Rights Act.
Suburban population almost equals that of central city.

that increased productivity drove the GNP ever upward. The economic boom further enriched the rich, transformed the working class into the middle-class, and left the poor isolated on a remote island of deprivation and powerlessness.

Overall, the United States in the 1950s seemed the very model of a contented, complacent society. There was, indeed, much conservatism and conformity. But there were also cracks in the picture of a placid, harmonious people. Unrest coexisted with consensus. Along with bland, shallow TV programs, Americans saw a renaissance of creativity and energy in the arts and literature. Beat writers as well as social scientists criticized the hypocrisies and evasions of postwar America. Many young people, alienated from the status quo that their parents embraced and inspired by their own subculture, entered a period of ferment, of rebellion.

Likewise, the African-American struggle to end white supremacy, to arouse the nation's conscience, quickened its pace. In the courts, the NAACP ceased demanding that separate facilities really be equal and instead insisted that true equality could be achieved only through racial integration. In the streets, Martin Luther King, Jr., and the Southern Christian Leadership Conference employed the techniques of nonviolent civil disobedience to mobilize the black masses to attack Jim Crow. The passage of the first civil rights acts since Reconstruction and Supreme Court decisions that nullified the legal foundations of segregation brought some gains. More vitally, they stimulated the hopefulness that spurred further protest.

Most middle-class whites, however, ignored the inequities in American society and tuned out the voices of discontent. Preoccupied with their own pursuit of private pleasures, they rejected radicalism, extolled religion, and idealized traditional gender roles, domesticity, and togetherness. Busy working and spending, those able to do so left for a future decade the festering problems of poverty, urban decay, and racial injustice, and the explosive consequences of a younger generation rejecting their parent's conformity and conservatism.

FOR FURTHER REFERENCE

READINGS

David Anderson, *Trapped by Success: The Eisenhower Administration and Vietnam, 1953–1961* (1993). An analysis of America's policy of supporting South Vietnam.

Robert Bowie and Richard Immerman, *Waging Peace: How Eisenhower Shaped an Enduring Cold War Strategy* (2000). A thoughtful and provocative account.

Mary Dudziak, *Cold War Civil Rights: Race and the Image of American Democracy* (2000). An important analysis of how the Cold War furthered and constrained the civil-rights movement.

William Graebner, *Coming of Age in Buffalo* (1990). An excellent autobiographical study of teenage life.

Julia Grant, *Raising Baby by the Book: The Education of American Mothers* (1998). The influence of pediatrician Benjamin Spock is assessed.

Margot Henriksen, *Dr. Strangelove's America: Society and Culture in the Atomic Age* (1997). An imaginative look at the impact of the Cold War on popular culture.

Joanne Meyerowitz, ed., *Not June Cleaver: Women and Gender in Postwar America, 1945–1960* (1994). A wide-ranging collection of essays examining American women from diverse perspectives.

Thomas Sugrue, *The Origins of the Urban Crisis: Race and Inequality in Postwar Detroit* (1996). An award-winning account of racial and economic inequality.

Jessica Weiss, *To Have and To Hold: Marriage, the Baby Boom, and Social Change* (2000). An incisive study that places the family patterns of the 1950s in historical perspective.

Stephen J. Whitfield, *The Culture of the Cold War* (1991). A keen-sighted meditation on postwar cultural phenomena.

WEBSITES

Readings in the 1950s
http://www.english.upenn.edu/~afilreis/50s
Many good articles and links to information on life in the 1950s.

Martin Luther King, Jr., and Civil Rights
http://www.umich.edu/politics/mlk
An informative website on the *Brown* decision and the Montgomery bus boycott.

National Archives and Records Administration
http://www.nara.gov
Click on "Presidential Libraries" for historical materials from the Eisenhower and other presidential libraries.

"Nifty Fifties"
http://www.fiftiesweb.com
A fun site on music and television in the 1950s.

For additional readings please consult the bibliography at the end of the book.

CHAPTER 28

The Liberal Era, 1960–1968

On the afternoon of February 1, 1960, four students at North Carolina Agricultural and Technical (A&T) College in Greensboro—Ezell Blair, Jr., Franklin McCain, Joseph McNeil, and David Richmond—entered the local Woolworth's and sat down at the whites-only lunch counter. "We don't serve colored here," the waitress replied when the freshmen asked for coffee and doughnuts. The black students remained seated. They would not be moved. Middle class in aspirations, the children of urban civil servants and industrial workers, they believed that the Supreme Court's *Brown* decision of 1954 should have ended the indignities of racial discrimination and segregation. But the promise of change had outrun reality. Massive resistance to racial equality still proved the rule throughout Dixie. In 1960 most southern blacks could neither vote nor attend integrated schools. They could not enjoy a cup of coffee alongside whites in a public restaurant.

Impatient yet hopeful, the A&T students could not accept the inequality their parents had endured. They had been inspired by the Montgomery bus boycott led by Martin Luther King, Jr., as well as by successful African independence movements in the late 1950s. They vowed to sit in until the store closed and to repeat their request the next day and beyond, until they were served.

On February 2 more than twenty A&T students joined them in their protest. The following day, over sixty sat in. By the end of the week, the students overflowed Woolworth's and sat in at the lunch counter in the nearby

Selma to Montgomery
March, 1965

CHAPTER OUTLINE

S. H. Kress store. Six months later, after prolonged sit-ins, boycotts, and demonstrations, and violent white resistance, Greensboro's white civic leaders grudgingly allowed blacks to sit down at restaurants and be served.

Meanwhile, the example of the Greensboro "coffee party" had inspired similar sit-ins throughout North Carolina and in neighboring states. By April 1960 sit-ins had disrupted seventy-eight southern communities. The black students endured beatings, tear-gassing, and jailing. Yet by September 1961 some seventy thousand students had sat in to desegregate eating facilities, as well as "kneeled in" in churches, "slept in" in motel lobbies, "waded in" on restricted beaches, "read in" at public libraries, "played in" at city parks, and "watched in" at segregated movie theaters.

The determination of the students transformed the struggle for racial equality. Their activism emboldened black adults to voice their dissatisfaction; their courage inspired other youths to act. Stokely Carmichael, a student at Howard University initially indifferent to the civil-rights movement, saw "those young kids on TV, getting back up on the lunch counter stools after being knocked off them, sugar in their eyes, ketchup in their hair—well, something happened to me. Suddenly I was burning." Their assertiveness both desegregated facilities and generated a new sense of self-esteem and strength. "I possibly felt better on that day than I've ever felt in my life," remembered Franklin McCain. "I myself desegregated a lunch counter, not somebody else, not some big man, some powerful man, but little me," claimed another student. "I walked the picket line and I sat-in and the walls of segregation toppled." Each new victory convinced thousands more that "nothing can stop us now."

As well as beginning the 1960's stage of the freedom movement, the sit-ins helped redefine liberalism. In the liberal's management of the economy, greater emphasis was now placed on equalizing the possibilities of opportunity and targeting benefits to those who had earlier been ignored. In their concern for civil liberties and civil rights, liberals sought to expand individual freedoms and to free African Americans from the shackles of racial discrimination and segregation. Liberalism was also redefined by others, including Ralph Nader sounding the consumer alarm that many automobiles were "unsafe at any speed," Betty Friedan writing *The Feminine Mystique* to denounce "the housewife trap" that caused educated women to subordinate their own aspirations to the needs of men, and students protesting against what they saw as an immoral war in Vietnam.

These endeavors symbolized a spirit of new beginnings. The impatience and idealism of the young would lead many to embrace John Kennedy's New Frontier and to rally behind Lyndon Johnson's Great Society. Both liberal administrations advocated an active federal government, particularly an activist presidency, to attack domestic and international problems and to achieve economic and social justice. Both relied on expanding economic growth to increase the social-welfare responsibilities of the government and give greater government benefits to the disadvantaged. Both also pursued an assertive foreign policy, boldly intervening abroad in Cuba and Vietnam. The new era of liberal activism thus generated fervent hopes and lofty expectations for diverse Americans, and an intensification of Cold War conflicts that triggered a militant antiwar movement. Assassinations of cherished leaders, increasing racial strife, and a frustrating war in Vietnam would dampen optimism, and a reaction by the majority who opposed radical change would curtail reform. The liberal era that began with bright promise would end in discord and disillusionment.

This chapter focuses on five major questions:

■ How liberal was the New Frontier in civil rights and economic matters?

■ What was the new liberalism of the 1960s, and how did Lyndon Johnson's Great Society exemplify it?

■ What were the major successes and failures of the black movements for civil rights and socioeconomic progress from 1964 to 1968?

■ In what ways did 1960's liberalism affect other minorities and women, and how did minorities and women affect liberalism?

■ How did the United States get involved in Vietnam, and to what extent was President Johnson responsible for the tragedy of Vietnam?

THE KENNEDY PRESIDENCY, 1960–1963

Projecting an image of vigor and proposing new approaches to old problems, John F. Kennedy personified the self-confident liberal who believed that an activist state could improve life at home and confront the Communist challenge abroad. His wealthy father, Joseph P. Kennedy, had held appointive office under

Franklin D. Roosevelt until his outspoken isolationism ended his public career. Seething with ambition, he raised his sons to attain the political power that had eluded him. He instilled in each a passion to excel and to rule. Despite a severe back injury, John Kennedy served in the navy in World War II, and the elder Kennedy persuaded a popular novelist to write articles lauding John's heroism in rescuing his crew after their PT boat had been sunk in the South Pacific.

Esteemed as a war hero, John Kennedy used his charm and his father's connections to win election to the House of Representatives in 1946 from a Boston district in which he had never lived. Kennedy earned little distinction in Congress, but the voters of Massachusetts, captivated by his personality, sent him to the Senate in 1952 and overwhelmingly reelected him in 1958. By then he had a beautiful wife, Jacqueline, and a Pulitzer Prize for *Profiles in Courage* (1956), written largely by a staff member.

Despite the obstacle of his Roman Catholic faith, the popular Kennedy won a first-ballot victory at the 1960 Democratic convention. Just forty-two years old, he sounded the theme of a "New Frontier" to "get America moving again" by liberal activism at home and abroad.

The Sit-Ins

The sit-ins of 1960 initiated the student phase of the civil-rights movement. Across the South, young black activists challenged segregation by staging nonviolent demonstrations to demand access to public facilities. Their courage and commitment reinvigorated the movement, leading to still greater grass-roots activism.

A New Beginning

"All at once you had something exciting," recalled Don Ferguson, a University of Nebraska student. "You had a guy who had little kids and who liked to play football on his front lawn. Kennedy was talking about pumping new life into the nation and steering it in new directions." But most voters, middle aged and middle class, wanted the stability and continuation of Eisenhower's "middle way" promised by the Republican candidate, Vice President Richard M. Nixon. Although scorned by liberals for his McCarthyism, Nixon was better known and more experienced than Kennedy, a Protestant, and identified with the still-popular Ike.

Nixon fumbled his opportunity, agreeing to meet his challenger in televised debates. More than 70 million tuned in to the first televised debate between presidential candidates, a broadcast that secured the dominance of television in American politics. The tanned,

dynamic Kennedy contrasted strikingly with his pale, haggard opponent. The telegenic Democrat radiated confidence; Nixon, sweating visibly, appeared insecure. Radio listeners judged the debate a draw, but the far more numerous television viewers declared Kennedy the victor. He shot up in the polls, and Nixon never regained the lead.

Kennedy also benefited from an economic recession in 1960, as well as from his choice of a southern Protestant, Senate Majority Leader Lyndon B. Johnson, as his running mate. Still, the election was the closest since 1884. Only 120,000 votes separated the two candidates. Kennedy's religion cost him millions of popular votes, but his capture of 80 percent of the Catholic vote in the closely contested midwestern and northeastern states delivered crucial electoral college votes, enabling him to squeak to victory (see Map 28.1).

Kennedy's inauguration set the tone of a new era: "the torch has been passed to a new generation of Americans." In sharp contrast to Eisenhower's "eight millionaires and a plumber" (see Chapter 27), Kennedy surrounded himself with liberal intellectuals—the "best

MAP 28.1
The Election of 1960

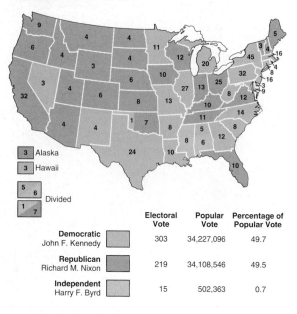

	Alaska 3
	Hawaii 3
	Divided 5 6
	1 7

		Electoral Vote	Popular Vote	Percentage of Popular Vote
Democratic John F. Kennedy		303	34,227,096	49.7
Republican Richard M. Nixon		219	34,108,546	49.5
Independent Harry F. Byrd		15	502,363	0.7

"America's leading man," novelist Norman Mailer called him. Kennedy seemed more a celebrity than a politician, and his dash played well on TV, highlighting his charisma and determination "to get America moving again." Aided by his wife, he adorned his presidency with the trappings of culture and excellence, inviting distinguished artists to perform at the White House and studding his speeches with quotations from Emerson. Awed by his grace and taste, as well as by his wit and wealth, the media extolled him as a vibrant leader and adoring husband. The public knew nothing of his fragile health, frequent use of mood-altering drugs to alleviate pain, and extramarital affairs.

Kennedy's Domestic Record

Media images obscured Kennedy's lackluster domestic record. The Kennedy years saw little significant social legislation. His narrow victory, and the conservative coalition of Republicans and southern Democrats that had stifled Truman's Fair Deal, doomed the New Frontier. Lacking the necessary votes, JFK rarely pressed Congress, maintaining that "there is no sense in raising hell, and then not being successful."

JFK made economic growth the key to his liberal agenda. To stimulate the economy, he combined higher defense expenditures with investment incentives for private enterprise. In 1961 he persuaded Congress to

and brightest," in author David Halberstam's wry phrase. For attorney general he selected his brother Robert Kennedy. "I see nothing wrong with giving Robert some legal experience before he goes out to practice law," JFK joked.

Inspiring Idealism
An excited Bill Clinton, almost 17, meets President John Kennedy at the White House. Many young Americans, like the future 42nd president of the United States, were captivated by the Kennedy aura and responded to his call to action: "Ask not what your country can do for you—ask what you can do for your country."

boost the defense budget by 20 percent. He vastly increased America's nuclear stockpile, strengthened the military's conventional forces, and established the Special Forces ("Green Berets") to engage in guerrilla warfare. By 1963 the defense budget reached its highest level as a percentage of total federal expenditures in the entire Cold War era. To further boost the economy as well as avoid "another *Sputnik*," Kennedy also persuaded Congress to finance a "race to the moon." The effort to land astronauts Neil Armstrong and Buzz Aldrin on the lunar surface in 1969 would cost more than $25 billion. Most importantly, to pay for the federal aid to education, medical care for the elderly, and urban renewal that he proposed, Kennedy accepted his liberal advisers' Keynesian approach to economic growth. He called for a huge cut in corporate taxes that would greatly increase the deficit but would presumably provide capital for business to invest in ways that would stimulate the economy and thus increase tax revenues. Economic growth, accordingly, was the way for the government to create a better life for all Americans.

When the Kennedy presidency ended suddenly in November 1963, the proposed tax cut was bottled up in Congress (symbolic of JFK's overall failure in domestic legislation). Military spending, continued technological innovation, heightened productivity, and low-cost energy, however, had already doubled the 1960 rate of economic growth, decreased unemployment, and held increases in inflation to 1.3 percent a year. The United States was in the midst of its longest uninterrupted boom ever. The boom would both cause further ecological damage and provide the affluence that enabled Americans to care about the environment.

Environmentalism had its roots in both the older conservation movement, emphasizing the efficient use of resources, and the preservation movement, focusing on preserving "wilderness." The fallout scare of the 1950s raised questions about the biological well-being of the planet. The publication in 1962 of Rachel Carson's *Silent Spring* (see Chapter 27), which described the devastating effects of pesticides on the environment, particularly birds, intensified concern. Additionally, postwar prosperity made large numbers of Americans less concerned with increased production and more concerned with the quality of life. Responding to the furor set off by Carson's documentation of the hazards of DDT, Kennedy appointed an advisory committee that warned against widespread pesticide use. In 1963 Congress passed a Clean Air Act, regulating automotive and industrial emissions. After decades of heedless pollution, hardly helped by the introduction of aluminum pop-top cans

Birmingham, 1963
The ferocious attempts by local authorities, led by Eugene "Bull" Connor, to repel nonviolent black protesters with fire hoses (capable of 100 pounds of water pressure per square inch), electrically charged cattle prods, and snarling, biting police dogs—shown nightly on TV—made white supremacy an object of revulsion throughout most of the country and forced the Kennedy administration to intervene to end the crisis.

in 1963, Washington hesitatingly began to deal with environmental problems.

Cold War Activism

In his inaugural address Kennedy proclaimed, "we shall pay any price, bear any burden, meet any hardship, support any friend, oppose any foe to assure the survival and success of liberty." To back up that pledge he launched a major buildup of the military arsenal, made foreign policy his top priority, and surrounded himself with Cold Warriors who shared his belief that American security depended on superior force and the willingness to use it. At the same time, he gained congressional backing for liberal programs of economic assistance to Third World countries to counter the appeal of communism. The Peace Corps, created in 1961, exemplified the New Frontier's liberal anticommunism. By 1963 five thousand Peace Corps volunteers were serving two-year stints as teachers, sanitation engineers, crop specialists, and health workers in more than forty Third World nations. They were, according to liberal historian and Kennedy aide Arthur Schlesinger, Jr., "reform-minded

missionaries of democracy who mixed with the people, spoke the native dialects, ate the food, and involved themselves in local struggles against ignorance and want."

In early 1961 a crisis flared in Laos, a tiny, land-locked nation created by the Geneva agreement in 1954 (see Chapter 27). There a civil war between American-supported forces and Pathet Lao rebels seemed headed toward a communist triumph. Considering Laos strate-gically insignificant, in July 1962 Kennedy agreed to a face-saving compromise that restored a neutralist gov-ernment but left communist forces dominant in the countryside. The accord stiffened Kennedy's resolve not to allow further communist gains.

Spring 1961 brought Kennedy's first major foreign-policy crisis. To eliminate a communist outpost on America's doorstep, he approved a CIA plan, drawn up in the Eisenhower administration, for anti-Castro exiles, "La Brigada," to invade Cuba. In mid-April fifteen hun-dred exiles stormed Cuba's Bay of Pigs, assuming that their arrival would trigger a general uprising to over-throw Fidel Castro. It was a fiasco. Deprived of air cover by Kennedy's desire to conceal U.S. involvement, the invaders had no chance against Castro's superior forces. Although Kennedy accepted blame for the failure, he neither apologized nor ceased attempting to topple Castro.

In July 1961, on the heels of the Bay of Pigs failure, Kennedy met Soviet premier Nikita Khrushchev in Vienna to try to resolve a peace treaty with Germany (see Chapter 26). Comparing the American troops in the divided city of Berlin to "a bone stuck in the throat," Khrushchev threatened war unless the West retreated. A shaken Kennedy returned to the United States and declared the defense of West Berlin essential to the Free World. He doubled draft calls, mobilized 150,000 reserv-ists, and requested an additional $3 billion defense ap-propriation. The threat of nuclear war escalated until mid-August, when the Soviets constructed a wall to seal off East Berlin and end the exodus of brains and talent to the West. The Berlin Wall became a concrete symbol of communism's denial of personal freedom until it fell in 1989.

To the Brink of Nuclear War

In mid-October 1962 aerial photographs revealed that the Soviet Union had built bases for intermediate-range ballistic missiles (IRBMs) in Cuba, which could reach U.S. targets as far as twenty-two hundred miles away. Kennedy responded forcefully, fearing unchecked Soviet interference in the Western Hemisphere, still smarting from the Bay of Pigs disaster, and believing that his cred-ibility was at stake. In a somber televised address he

Anti-Diem Buddhist Protests
After Diem's troops fired on Buddhists attempting to celebrate Buddha's 2,587th birthday, Buddhist monk Thich Quang Duc burned himself to death in downtown Saigon in June 1963. It was the first of several self-immolations in South Vietnam. Photographs and videotapes of these horrific protests, shown around the world, helped convince the Kennedy administration that Diem's leadership of South Vietnam could no longer be supported.

denounced the Soviet "provocative threat to world peace" and demanded that the missiles be removed. The United States, he asserted, would "quarantine" Cuba—impose a naval blockade—to prevent delivery of more missiles and would dismantle by force the missiles already in Cuba if the Soviets did not do so.

Kennedy's ultimatum, and Khrushchev's defiant response that the quarantine was "outright banditry," rocked the world. More than ever before, the two superpowers appeared on a collision course toward nuclear war. Apprehension mounted as the Soviet technicians worked feverishly to complete missile launch pads and as Soviet missile-carrying ships steamed toward the blockade. Americans stayed glued to their radios and television sets as 180 U.S. naval ships in the Caribbean prepared to confront the Soviet freighters; B-52s armed with nuclear bombs took to the air; and nearly a quarter-million troops assembled in Florida to invade Cuba. Secretary of State Dean Rusk reported, "We're eyeball to eyeball."

"I think the other fellow just blinked," a relieved Rusk announced on October 25. The Cuba-bound Soviet ships stopped dead in the water, and Kennedy received a message from Khrushchev promising to remove the missiles if the U.S. pledged never to invade Cuba. As Kennedy prepared to respond positively, a second, more belligerent, message arrived from Khrushchev insisting that American missiles be withdrawn from Turkey as part of the deal. Hours later an American U-2 reconnaissance plane was shot down over Cuba. It was "the blackest hour of the crisis," recalled a Kennedy aide. Various presidential advisers urged an immediate invasion, but the president, heeding Robert Kennedy's advice, decided to ignore the second Soviet message and accept the original offer. That night, October 27, the president's brother met secretly with the Soviet ambassador to inform him that this was the only way to avoid nuclear war. The next morning Khrushchev pledged to remove the missiles in return for Kennedy's noninvasion promise. Less publicly, Kennedy subsequently removed U.S. missiles from Turkey.

The full dimensions of the crisis became known only after the end of the Cold War, when the Russian military disclosed that Soviet forces in Cuba had possessed thirty-six nuclear warheads as well as nine tactical nuclear weapons for battlefield use. Soviet field commanders had independent authority to use these weapons. Worst of all, Kennedy had not known that the Soviets already had the capability to launch a nuclear strike from Cuba. "We do not need to speculate," said a shaken McNamara in 1992, "about what would have happened had the U.S. attack been launched, as many in the U.S. government—military and civilian alike—were recommending to the President on October 27th and 28th. We can predict the results with certainty. . . . No one should believe that U.S. troops could have been attacked by tactical nuclear warheads without the U.S.'s responding with nuclear warheads. . . . And where would it have ended? In utter disaster."

Staring over the brink of nuclear war chastened both Kennedy and Khrushchev. "Having come so close to the edge," JFK's national security adviser said, "the leaders of the two governments have since taken care to keep away from the cliff." They agreed to install a Kremlin-White House "hot line" so that the two sides could communicate instantly in future crises. In June 1963 JFK advocated a relaxation of superpower tensions, and two months later the two nations agreed to a treaty outlawing atmospheric and undersea nuclear testing. These efforts signaled a new phase of the Cold War, later called détente, in which the superpowers moved from confrontation to negotiation. Ironically, the Cuban missile crisis also had the unintended consequence of accelerating the arms race for another twenty-five years. It confirmed American belief in the need for nuclear superiority to prevent war while convincing Russian leaders that they must overtake the American lead in nuclear missiles to avoid future humiliation.

The Thousand-Day Presidency

On November 22, 1963, during a trip to Texas to improve his chances for victory in the 1964 presidential election, John and Jackie Kennedy rode in an open car along Dallas streets, smiling at the cheering crowds. As the motorcade slowed to turn, shots rang out. The president slumped, his skull and throat shattered. While the driver sped the mortally wounded president to a nearby hospital, where the doctors pronounced Kennedy dead, Secret Service agents rushed Lyndon Johnson to Air Force One to be sworn in as president.

Grief and disbelief numbed the nation. Millions of Americans sat stunned in front of TV sets during the next four days, staring at the steady stream of mourners filing by the slain president's coffin in the Capitol rotunda; at the countless replays of the murder of Kennedy's accused assassin, Lee Harvey Oswald, in the Dallas city jail by a nightclub owner; at the somber state funeral, with the small boy saluting his father's casket; at the grieving family lighting an eternal flame at Arlington National Cemetery. Few who watched would ever forget. Kennedy had helped make television central to

The Kennedy Assassination
As Jacqueline Kennedy reacts to her husband being fatally shot in the head, their open-air limousine races to nearby Parkland Hospital. The President died less than an hour later. CBS television news anchor Walter Cronkite cried as he told the nation the news.

American politics, and now television, which made Kennedy a celebrity in life, made him, in death, the heroic king of Camelot.

The assassination made a martyr of JFK. More admired by the public in death than in life, he was now ranked with Washington, Lincoln, and Roosevelt as a "great" president. For decades after, despite revelations of character blemishes, JFK would loom large in the American imagination, his romantic aura a reminder of what seemed a better time. Emphasizing "might have beens," Kennedy loyalists have stressed his intelligence, his ability to change and grow. His detractors, however, point to the gap between rhetoric and substance, the discrepancy between his public image and his compulsive, even reckless, private sexual behavior. Some deplore his aggressive Cold War tactics; others condemn him for raising unrealistic expectations and expanding presidential powers.

Kennedy's rhetoric expressed the new liberalism, but he rarely made liberal ideas a reality. Economic expansion came from spending on missiles and the space race, not on social welfare and human needs. Constrained by the lack of a liberal majority, Kennedy frequently compromised with conservative and segregationist congressional leaders. Partly because his own personal behavior made him beholden to J. Edgar Hoover, JFK allowed the FBI unprecedented authority to infringe on civil liberties, even as the CIA was conniving with the Mafia to assassinate Fidel Castro. (The tangled web of plots and policies that enmeshed John and Robert Kennedy, FBI Director J. Edgar Hoover, organized

crime, and the national security agencies remains to be sorted out by scholars.) The New Frontier barely existed for environmental protection, for slowing corporate consolidation, or for women. (JFK appointed fewer women to high-level federal posts than had his predecessors and was the first president since Herbert Hoover not to have a woman in the cabinet.)

Internationally, Kennedy left a mixed record. He signed the world's first nuclear-test-ban treaty, yet also initiated a massive nuclear-arms buildup. He compromised on Laos but deepened U.S. involvement in Vietnam. Despite gradually changing from a Cold Warrior to a leader who questioned the necessity of conflict with the Soviets, JFK nevertheless insisted on maintaining U.S. global superiority and halting the spread of international communism. He did so, moreover, by increasing the powers of the executive branch, particularly his own White House staff. As never before, a small group of aides, personally loyal to the president, secretly dominated policy making.

Yet JFK had fired the energies and imaginations of millions of Americans. He gave liberals new hope, aroused the poor and the powerless, and challenged the young, stimulating a flowering of social criticism and political activism. Like other heroes, Kennedy left the stage before his glory tarnished. He would leave his successor a liberal agenda as well as soaring expectations at home and a deteriorating entanglement in Vietnam. That legacy, as well as his assassination, would shatter illusions, leading an increasing number of Americans to lose confidence in their government and their future.

"The Whole World Is Watching"
Photographs and televised pictures of Chicago police beating and gassing antiwar protesters and innocent bystanders at the Democratic convention in 1968 linked Democrats in the public mind with violence and mayhem. The scenes made Republican Richard Nixon a reassuring presence to those he would term "the silent majority."

MAP 29.2
The Election of 1968

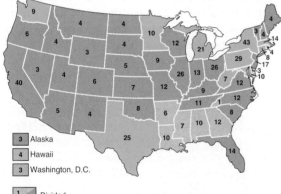

	Electoral Vote	Popular Vote	Percentage of Popular Vote
Republican Richard M. Nixon	301	31,770,237	43.4
Democratic Hubert H. Humphrey	191	31,270,533	42.7
American Independent George C. Wallace	46	9,906,141	13.5
Minor parties	–	239,908	0.4

dominant New Deal coalition was shattered. The 1968 election brought both the inauguration of a new president and the end of the liberal era.

The 57 percent of the electorate who chose Nixon or Wallace would dominate American politics for the rest of the century. While the Democratic party fractured into a welter of contending groups, the Republicans attracted a new majority who lived in the suburbs, the West, and the Sunbelt. The GOP appealed to those most concerned with traditional values, most upset by high taxes, and most opposed to racial integration and special efforts to assist minorities and people on welfare. Of all the states in the South and West, the Democrats would carry only Texas and Washington in 1968, and not a single one four years later. The new conservative coalition looked hopefully to the Republican president to end the Vietnam War and restore social harmony.

NIXON AND WORLD POLITICS

A Californian of Quaker origins, Richard Milhous Nixon had worked with the wartime Office of Price Administration before joining the navy. Elected to Congress in 1946, he won prominence for his role in the House Un-Americans Committee investigation of Alger Hiss (see Chapter 26) and advanced to the Senate in 1950 by accusing his Democratic opponent of disloyalty. After two terms as Eisenhower's vice president, Nixon lost to Kennedy in 1960 and made an unsuccessful 1962 bid for the California governorship, which seemingly ended his political career. But Nixon persevered, campaigned vigorously for GOP candidates in 1966, and won

his party's nomination and the presidency in 1968 by promising to restore domestic tranquillity.

Nixon focused mainly on foreign affairs. Considering himself a master of realpolitik—a pragmatic approach stressing national interest rather than ethical goals—he sought to check Soviet expansionism and to reduce superpower conflict, to limit the nuclear-arms race and to enhance America's economic well-being. He planned to get the United States out of Vietnam and into a new era of détente—an easing of tensions—with the communist world. To manage diplomacy, Nixon chose Henry Kissinger, a refugee from Hitler's Germany and professor of international relations, who shared Nixon's penchant for secrecy and for the concentration of decision-making power in the White House.

Vietnamization

Nixon's grand design hinged on ending the Vietnam War. It was sapping American military strength, worsening inflation, and thwarting détente. Announcing the Nixon Doctrine in August 1969, the president redefined America's role in the Third World as that of a helpful partner rather than a military protector. Nations facing communist subversion could count on U.S. support, but

they would have to defend themselves. Sales of American military supplies abroad jumped from $1.8 billion to $15.2 billion in the next six years.

The Nixon Doctrine reflected the president's understanding of the war weariness of both the electorate and the U.S. troops in Vietnam. Johnson's decision to negotiate rather than escalate had left American troops with the sense that little mattered except survival. Morale plummeted. Discipline collapsed. Army desertions rocketed from twenty-seven thousand in 1967 to seventy-six thousand in 1970, and absent-without-leave (AWOL) rates rose even higher. Racial conflict became commonplace. Drug use soared; the Pentagon estimated that two out of three soldiers in Vietnam were smoking marijuana and that one in three had tried heroin. The army reported hundreds of cases of "fragging," the assassination of officers and noncommissioned officers by their own troops.

The toll of atrocities against the Vietnamese also mounted. Increasing instances of Americans' dismembering enemy bodies, torturing captives, and murdering civilians came to light. In March 1968, in the hamlet of My Lai, an army unit led by Lieutenant William Calley massacred several hundred South Vietnamese. The soldiers gang-raped girls, lined up women and children

The My Lai Massacre
Under the command of First Lieutenant William Calley, the men of Charlie Company attacked the hamlet of My Lai in March 1968. Believing it to be a Viet Cong stronghold, they massacred some five hundred unarmed villagers, mostly women and children. The military kept the incident secret for a year, but it then became a symbol of the war's brutality and immorality.

in ditches and shot them, and burned the village. Revelations of such incidents, and the increasing number of returning soldiers who joined Vietnam Veterans Against the War, undercut the already-diminished support for the war.

Despite pressure to end the war, Nixon claimed that he would not sacrifice U.S. prestige. Seeking "peace with honor," he acted on three fronts. First was "Vietnamization," replacing American troops with South Vietnamese. It was hardly a new idea; the French had tried *jaunissement* or "yellowing" in 1951, and it had not worked. By 1972 the U.S. forces in Vietnam had been reduced to thirty thousand, down from more than half a million when Nixon took office in 1969, and the policy still had not worked. Second, bypassing South Vietnamese leaders who feared that any accord with the communists would doom them, Nixon sent Kissinger to secretly negotiate with North Vietnam's foreign minister, Le Duc Tho. Third, to force the communists to compromise despite the withdrawal of U.S. combat troops, Nixon escalated the bombing of North Vietnam and secretly ordered air strikes on their supply routes in Cambodia and Laos. He told an aide,

> I want the North Vietnamese to believe I've reached the point where I might do *anything* to stop the war. We'll just slip the word to them that "for God's sake, you know Nixon is obsessed about communism. We can't restrain him when he's angry—and he has his hand on the nuclear button"—and Ho Chi Minh himself will be in Paris in two days begging for peace.

LBJ's War Becomes Nixon's War

The secret B-52 raids against Cambodia neither made Hanoi beg for peace nor disrupted communist supply bases. They did, however, undermine the stability of that tiny republic and precipitated a civil war between pro-American and communist factions. In early 1970 North Vietnam increased its infiltration of troops into Cambodia both to aid the Khmer Rouge (Cambodian communists) and to escalate its war in South Vietnam. Nixon ordered a joint U.S.-South Vietnamese incursion into Cambodia at the end of April 1970. The invaders seized large caches of arms and bought time for Vietnamization. But the costs were high. The invasion ended Cambodia's neutrality, widened the war throughout Indochina, and provoked massive American protests against the war, culminating in the student deaths at Kent State and Jackson State Universities.

In 1971 Nixon combined Vietnamization with renewed blows against the enemy. In February he had South Vietnamese troops invade Laos to destroy communist bases there and to restrict the flow of supplies and men southward from North Vietnam. The South Vietnamese were routed. Emboldened by its success, North Vietnam mounted a major campaign in April 1972—the Easter Offensive—their largest since 1968. Nixon retaliated by mining North Vietnam's harbors and unleashing B-52s on its major cities. "The bastards have never been bombed like they are going to be bombed this time," he vowed.

America's Longest War Ends

The 1972 bombing helped break the impasse in the Paris peace talks, stalemated since 1968. In late October, just days before the 1972 presidential election, Kissinger announced that "peace is at hand." The cease-fire agreement he had secretly negotiated with Le Duc Tho required the withdrawal of all U.S. troops, provided for the return of American prisoners of war, and allowed North Vietnamese troops to remain in South Vietnam.

Kissinger's negotiation sealed Nixon's reelection, but South Vietnam's President Thieu refused to sign a cease-fire permitting North Vietnamese troops to remain in the South. An angry Le Duc Tho then pressed Kissinger for additional concessions. Nixon again resorted to massive B-52 raids. The 1972 Christmas bombing of Hanoi and Haiphong, the most destructive of the war, roused fierce opposition in Congress and the United Nations, but broke the deadlock. Nixon's secret reassurance to Thieu that the United States would "respond with full force should the settlement be violated by North Vietnam" ended Saigon's recalcitrance.

The Paris Accords, signed in late January 1973, essentially restated the terms of the October truce. Nixon and Kissinger knew well that it would not end the war or bring an honorable peace. At best they hoped that the war would remain stalemated until Nixon was safely out of office. The agreement ended hostilities between the United States and North Vietnam, but left unresolved the differences between North and South Vietnam, guaranteeing that Vietnam's future would yet be settled on the battlefield. Even before the ink on the treaty had dried, both North and South Vietnam, seeking military advantage, began to violate its terms (see Table 29.1).

The war in Vietnam would continue despite fifty-eight thousand American dead, three hundred thousand wounded, and an expenditure of at least $150 billion.

TABLE 29.1   The Vietnam War: A Chronology

1945   Ho Chi Minh announces Declaration of Independence from France.

1950   French-controlled Vietnam receives U.S. financial aid and military advisers.

1954   Dienbienphu falls to Ho's Vietminh.
Geneva Accords end Indochina War and temporarily divide Vietnam at the seventeenth parallel.
Ngo Dinh Diem becomes South Vietnam's premier.

1955   Diem establishes the Republic of Vietnam.
U.S. advisers take over training of South Vietnamese army (ARVN).

1960   National Liberation Front (Vietcong) formed.

1961   President John Kennedy markedly increases military aid to South Vietnam.

1962   Strategic-hamlet program put in operation.

1963   Buddhist protests commence.
ARVN coup overthrows and assassinates Diem.
16,000 U.S. military personnel in Vietnam.

1964   General William Westmoreland takes charge of U.S. Military Assistance Command in South Vietnam.
Gulf of Tonkin incident and subsequent U.S. congressional resolution.
United States bombs North Vietnam.
23,300 U.S. military personnel in Vietnam.

1965   First American combat troops arrive in South Vietnam, at Danang.
184,000 U.S. military personnel in Vietnam.

1966   B-52s attack North Vietnam for first time.
Senate Foreign Relations Committee opens hearings on U.S. in Vietnam.
385,000 U.S. military personnel in Vietnam.

1967   Major antiwar demonstrations in New York and San Francisco; protest march on the Pentagon.
485,600 U.S. military personnel in Vietnam.

1968   North Vietnamese forces surround Khesanh.
Tet offensive.
My Lai massacre.
President Lyndon Johnson announces partial bombing halt and decision not to run for reelection.
Peace talks begin in Paris.
General Creighton Abrams replaces Westmoreland as commander of American troops in Vietnam.
536,000 U.S. military personnel in Vietnam.

1969   United States begins bombing North Vietnamese bases in Cambodia.
Provisional Revolutionary Government (PRG) formed by Vietcong.

First U.S. troop withdrawal announced after American military personnel in Vietnam reach peak strength of 543,400 in April.
Ho Chi Minh dies.
Nationwide antiwar protests in October.
475,200 U.S. military personnel in Vietnam.

1970   United States and South Vietnamese forces join in Cambodian incursion.
Student protests force some four hundred colleges and universities to close following Kent State killings.
Cooper-Church amendment limits U.S. role in Cambodia.
Senate repeals Gulf of Tonkin Resolution.
334,600 U.S. military personnel in Vietnam.

1971   United States provides air support for South Vietnamese invasion of Laos.
Antiwar rally of 400,000 in Washington.
Daniel Ellsberg releases Pentagon Papers to the *New York Times*.

1972   North Vietnam launches first ground offensive since 1968.
U.S. bombing and mining of North Vietnamese ports.
Last U.S. ground troops leave South Vietnam.
Preliminary peace agreement reached; National Security Adviser Henry Kissinger announces that "peace is at hand."
South Vietnam rejects peace treaty.
United States bombs Hanoi and Haiphong.
24,200 U.S. military personnel in Vietnam.

1973   Peace agreement signed in Paris by North and South Vietnam, the Vietcong, and the United States.
End of U.S. draft.
Congress passes War Powers Act.
First American POWs released in Hanoi.
U.S. bombing in Southeast Asia ends.
Fewer than 250 U.S. military personnel in Vietnam.

1974   South Vietnam announces new outbreak of war.

1975   North Vietnamese offensive captures Danang.
Senate rejects President Gerald Ford's request for emergency aid for South Vietnam.
South Vietnam surrenders following North Vietnam's capture of Saigon.
Khmer Rouge takes control in Cambodia.
Pro-Hanoi People's Democratic Republic established in Laos.

Twenty percent of the Americans who served in Vietnam, nearly five hundred thousand, received less-than-honorable discharges—a measure of the desertion rate, drug usage, antiwar sentiment in the military, and immaturity of the troops (the average U.S. soldier in Vietnam was just nineteen years old, seven years younger than the average American GI in World War II).

Virtually all who survived, wrote one marine, returned "as immigrants to a new world. For the culture we had known dissolved while we were in Vietnam, and the culture of combat we lived in so intensely . . . made us aliens when we returned." Reminders of a war that Americans wished to forget, most veterans were ignored. Other than media attention to their psychological difficulties in readjusting to civilian life, which principally fostered an image of them as disturbed and dangerous, the nation paid little heed to its Vietnam veterans.

Relieved that the long nightmare had ended, most Americans wanted "to put Vietnam behind us" and just forget. The bitterness of many veterans, as of embattled hawks and doves, moderated with time. Few gave much thought to the 2 million casualties and the devastation in Vietnam, or to the suffering in Laos, or the price paid by Cambodia. After the war had spread there, the fanatical Khmer Rouge took power and killed 3 million Cambodians, 40 percent of the population.

"We've adjusted too well," complained Tim O'Brien, a veteran and novelist of the war, in 1980. "Too many of us have lost touch with the horror of war. . . . It would seem that the memories of soldiers should serve, at least in a modest way, as a restraint on national bellicosity. But time and distance erode memory. We adjust, we lose the intensity. I fear that we are back where we started. I wish we were more troubled."

Détente

Disengagement from Vietnam helped Nixon achieve a turnabout in Chinese-American relations and détente with the communist powers. These developments, the most significant shift in U.S. foreign policy since the start of the Cold War, created a new relationship among the United States, the Soviet Union, and China.

Presidents from Truman to Johnson had refused to recognize the People's Republic of China, allow its admission to the United Nations, or permit American allies to trade with it. But by 1969 a widening Sino-Soviet split made the prospect of improved relations attractive to both Mao Zedong and Nixon. China wanted to end its isolation; the United States wanted to play one communist power off against the other; and both wanted to thwart USSR expansionism in Asia.

In fall 1970 Nixon opened what Kissinger called "the three-dimensional game" by calling China "the People's Republic" rather than "Red China." Kissinger began secret negotiations with Beijing, and in mid-1971 Nixon announced that he would go to the People's Republic "to seek the normalization of relations." In February 1972

Nixon in China
One of the great triumphs of his administration was the rapprochment with the People's Republic of China. Planned in total secrecy. Nixon's trip to China in February 1972 stunned the world and gave the president the aura of a bold, imaginative statesman.

Air Force One landed in China, the first visit ever by a sitting American president to the largest nation in the world. Although differences between the two powers delayed official diplomatic relations until 1979, Nixon's trip, the Chinese foreign minister said, bridged "the vastest ocean in the world, twenty-five years of no communication."

Equally significant, Nixon went to Moscow in May 1972 to sign agreements with the Soviets on trade, technological cooperation, and the limitation of nuclear weapons. The Strategic Arms Limitation Talks (SALT I), ratified by the Senate in October 1972, limited each nation to two antiballistic missile systems, froze each side's offensive nuclear missiles for five years, and committed both countries to strategic equality rather than nuclear superiority. SALT I reflected the belief that the fear of destruction offered the surest guarantee against nuclear war and that mutual fear could be maintained only if neither side built nationwide missile-defense systems. Although it did not end the arms race, SALT I reduced Soviet-American tensions and, in an election year, enhanced Nixon's stature.

Shuttle Diplomacy

Not even rapproachment with China and détente with the Soviet Union could ensure global stability. The Middle East, in particular, remained an arena of conflict. After the Six-Day War of 1967 in which Israeli forces routed the forces of Egypt, Jordan, and Syria and seized strategic territories from the three nations, the Arab states continued to refuse to negotiate with Israel or to recognize its right to exist. Palestinians, many of them refugees since the creation of Israel in 1948, turned increasingly to the militant Palestinian Liberation Organization (PLO), which demanded Israel's destruction.

War exploded again in October 1973 when Egypt and Syria launched surprise attacks against Israel on Yom Kippur, the most sacred Jewish holy day. Only massive shipments of military supplies from the United States enabled a reeling Israel to stop the assault and counterattack. In retaliation, the Arab states launched their biggest weapon, cutting off oil shipments to the United States and its allies. The five-month embargo dramatized U.S. dependence on foreign energy sources. It spawned acute fuel shortages, which spurred coal production in Montana and Wyoming, triggered an oil boom on Alaska's North Slope, and provided the impetus for constructing more nuclear-power plants. Most immediately, the hike in the price of crude oil from three dollars to more than twelve dollars a barrel sharply intensified inflation.

The dual shocks of the energy crisis and rising Soviet influence in the Arab world spurred Kissinger to engage in "shuttle diplomacy." Flying from one Middle East capital to another for two years, he negotiated a cease-fire, pressed Israel to cede captured Arab territory, and persuaded the Arabs to end the oil embargo. Although Kissinger's diplomacy left the Palestinian issue festering, it successfully excluded the Soviets from a major role in Middle Eastern affairs.

To counter Soviet influence, the Nixon administration also supplied arms and assistance to the shah of Iran, the white supremacist regime of South Africa, and President Ferdinand Marcos in the Philippines. Nixon-Kissinger realpolitik based American aid on a nation's willingness to oppose the Soviet Union, not on the nature of its government. Thus, the administration gave aid to antidemocratic regimes in Argentina, Brazil, Nigeria, and South Korea, as well as to Portuguese colonial authorities in Angola.

When Chileans elected a Marxist, Salvador Allende, president in 1970, Nixon secretly funneled $10 million to the CIA to fund opponents of the leftist regime. The United States also cut off economic aid to Chile, blocked banks from granting loans, and pressed the World Bank to lower Chile's credit rating. In September 1973 a military junta overthrew the Chilean government and killed Allende. Nixon quickly recognized the dictatorship, and economic aid and investment again flowed to Chile.

The administration's active opposition to Allende reflected the extent to which American policy remained committed to containing communist influence. At the same time, Nixon understood the limits of U.S. power and the changed realities of world affairs. Discarding the model of a bipolar conflict that had shaped American foreign policy since 1945, Nixon took advantage of the Chinese-Soviet rift to improve American relations with both nations. His administration also improved the U.S. position in the Middle East and ended American involvement in Vietnam. The politician who had built his reputation as a hard-line Cold Warrior had initiated a new era of détente.

DOMESTIC PROBLEMS AND DIVISIONS

Richard Nixon yearned to be remembered as an international statesman, but domestic affairs kept intruding. He displayed creativity in seeking to reform the welfare sys-

tem and in grappling with complex economic problems. But the underside of Nixon's personality appealed to the darker recesses of national character and intensified the fears and divisions among Americans.

Richard Nixon: Man and Politician

Close observers of Nixon noted the multiple levels of his character. Beneath the calculated public persona hid a shadowy man who rarely revealed himself. Nixon the politician was highly intelligent, yet also displayed the rigid self-control of a man monitoring his own every move. Largely hidden was the insecure Nixon, suspicious and filled with anger. Seething with resentments, he saw life as a series of crises to be met and surmounted. His conviction that enemies lurked everywhere, waiting to destroy him, verged on paranoia. Accordingly, he sought to annihilate, not merely defeat, his partisan enemies, particularly the "eastern liberal establishment" that had long opposed him.

Probing the source of his furies, some viewed him as the classic outsider: reared in pinched surroundings, physically awkward, unable to relate easily to others.

Even at the height of national power, Nixon remained fearful that he would never be accepted. At the beginning of his administration, his strengths stood out. He spoke of national reconciliation, took bold initiatives internationally, and dealt with domestic problems responsibly. But the darker side ultimately prevailed and drove him from office in disgrace.

The Nixon Presidency

Nixon began his presidency in a moderate manner reminiscent of Eisenhower. Symbolic of this harmonious start, a united nation joined the president in celebrating the first successful manned mission to the moon. On July 21, 1969, the Apollo 11 lunar module, named *Eagle*, descended to the Sea of Tranquillity. As millions watched on television, astronaut Neil Armstrong, the first human to set foot on another celestial body, walked on the moon's surface and proclaimed, "That's one small step for man, one giant leap for mankind." Americans were proud that the United States had come from behind to win the space race. They thrilled as Armstrong and Buzz Aldrin planted an American flag, collected rock and soil

A Walk on the Moon, 1969
Ten years after John F. Kennedy challenged America to put a person on the moon, astronaut Neil Armstrong stepped down from his lunar module onto the surface of the moon. From the White House, President Nixon told the astronauts and the nation, "this has to be the proudest day of our lives."

samples, and left a plaque reading, "Here men from planet earth first set foot on the moon, July 1969 A.D. We came in peace for all mankind." By 1973 five more American missions visited the lunar surface; and in 1975, when U.S. and Soviet spacecraft met in space, docked, and conducted joint research and shared information for nine days, the space race essentially ended, superceded by cooperative international efforts to explore the rest of the universe.

The first newly elected president since 1849 whose party controlled neither house of Congress, Nixon could not pursue a consistently conservative course. He instituted wage and price controls, inaugurated affirmative action policies, and approved the vote for eighteen-year-olds. More grudgingly, he responded to an energized environmental movement. It had been aroused by the horrible sights in 1969, televised throughout the nation, of the polluted Cuyahoga River near Cleveland bursting into flames and of two oil spills off the coast of California soiling both birds and beaches with globs of gooey, black oil. It had been informed by Barry Commoner's warnings on the hazards of nuclear wastes and chemical pollution in *Science and Survival* (1966) and by Paul Ehrlich's *The Population Bomb* (1968) on the dangers of overpopulation. Its fury would help bring new laws limiting pesticide use, further protecting endangered species and marine mammals, safeguarding coastal lands, and controlling strip-mining. Further legislation regulated consumer-product safety and the transportation of hazardous materials, established maximum levels for the emissions of pollutants into the air, created the Occupational Safety and Health Administration (OSHA) to enforce health and safety standards in the workplace, and required federal agencies to prepare an environmental-impact analysis of all proposed projects. Overseeing all these regulations and restrictions was the newly established Environmental Protection Agency (EPA).

Growing environmental awareness culminated in 20 million Americans celebrating the first Earth Day in April 1970. Speeches and demonstrations spotlighted such problems as thermal pollution, dying lakes, oil spills, and dwindling resources, introducing Americans to the idea of "living lightly on the earth." Organic gardening, vegetarianism, solar power, recycling, composting, and preventive health care came into vogue, as did zero population growth—the birthrate should not exceed the death rate.

Conservatives grumbled as government grew larger and more intrusive; under Nixon, the number of pages in the Federal Register detailing federal regulations tripled. Race-conscious employment regulations for all federal contractors (including quotas to increase minority access to skilled jobs) displeased them even more. Conservatives grew still angrier when Nixon unveiled the Family Assistance Plan (FAP) in 1969. A bold effort to overhaul the welfare system, FAP proposed a guaranteed minimum annual income for all Americans. Caught between liberals who thought the income inadequate and conservatives who disliked both the cost and the principle of the program, FAP died in the Senate.

A Troubled Economy

Nixon inherited the fiscal consequences of President Johnson's effort to wage the Vietnam War and finance the Great Society—to have both "guns and butter"—by deficit financing. He faced a "whopping" budget deficit of $25 billion in 1969 and an inflation rate of 5 percent (see Figure 29.1). As mounting energy prices threatened worse inflation, Nixon cut government spending and encouraged the Federal Reserve Board to raise interest rates. The result was the first recession since Eisenhower plus inflation, a combination economists called "stagflation" and Democrats termed "Nixonomics."

Accelerating inflation wiped out some families' savings and lowered the standard of living of many more. It sparked a wave of strikes as workers sought wage hikes to keep up with the cost of living. It encouraged the wealthy to invest in art and real estate rather than technology and factories. That meant more plant shutdowns, fewer industrial jobs, and millions of displaced workers whose savings were depleted, mortgages foreclosed, and health and pension benefits lost.

Throughout 1971 Nixon lurched from policy to policy in an effort to curb inflation and cure the recession. Early in the year, declaring "I am now a Keynesian," Nixon increased deficit spending to stimulate the private sector. That resulted in the largest budget deficit since World War II, yet economic decline continued. Then, in mid-1971, Nixon changed course, devaluing the dollar to correct the balance-of-payment deficit and imposing a ninety-day freeze on wages, prices, and rents. This "Band-Aid" gave the economy a shot in the arm that worked until after the 1972 election.

In January 1973, safely reelected, Nixon again reversed course, replacing wage-and-price ceilings with "voluntary restraints" and "guidelines." Inflation zoomed to 9 percent, then to 12 percent in 1974 as the

"Earth Day," May 4, 1970
Designed to alert people about the threats to the air, land, and water, the first Earth Day signaled the emergence of the modern environmental movement. It would put pressure on the federal government to take major steps in cleaning up the nation's environment and educate a generation of Americans to understand the ecology of the planet as a delicate, interconnected series of elements, in which damage to any single element damages many others.

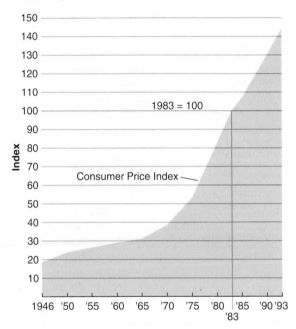

FIGURE 29.1
Inflation, 1946–1993

Inflation, which had been moderate during the two decades following the Second World War, began to soar with the escalation of the war in Vietnam in the mid-1960s. In 1979 and 1980 the nation experienced double-digit inflation in two consecutive years for the first time since World War I.

1983 = 100

Consumer Price Index

Organization of Petroleum Exporting Countries (OPEC) boycott quadrupled the price of crude oil (see Figure 29.2). Inflation and sluggish growth would dog the U.S. economy throughout the decade.

Law and Order

Despite his public appeals for unity, Nixon hoped to divide the American people in ways that would make him unbeatable in the 1972 election. He understood the appeal of Merle Haggard's "Okie from Muskogee," ridiculing "the hippies up in San Francisco" and bragging of drinking "white lightning" instead of doing drugs. He knew that circulation of the *NationalReview* had more than doubled in the 1960s, and that editor William

Buckley's once-fringe denunciations of the welfare state, campus unrest, black violence, and the radical Left had become mainstream. To outflank George Wallace and win the support of blue-collar workers, southern segregationists, and northern ethnics—voters whom political strategist Kevin Phillips described as "in motion between a Democratic past and a Republican future"—Nixon opposed court-ordered busing and took a tough stand against criminals, drug users, and radicals.

The president used the full resources of the government against militants. The IRS audited their tax returns; the Small Business Administration denied them loans; and the National Security Agency illegally wiretapped them and intercepted their communications. While the FBI worked with local law officials to disrupt and immo-

FIGURE 29.2

The Energy Crisis: Crude-Oil Imports and Gasoline Prices

Not until the 1980s, through the combination of a deep recession and fuel conservation, did U.S. petroleum imports finally begin dropping off (top). OPEC's ability to act as a supercartel in setting oil prices sent the cost of filling a car's gas tank skyrocketing in the 1970s (bottom).

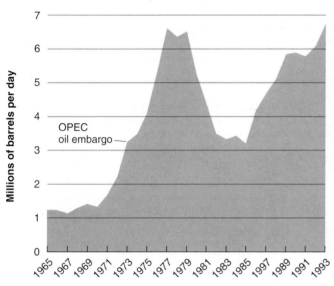

Imports of Crude Oil

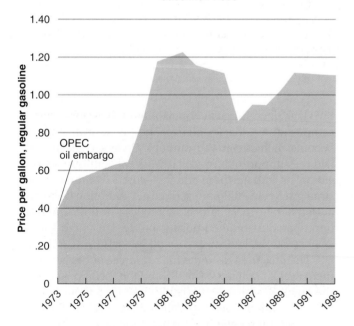

Gasoline Prices

Source: Energy Information Administration, Annual Energy Review, 1993.

bilize the Black Panthers, the CIA illegally investigated and compiled dossiers on thousands of American citizens, and the Justice Department prosecuted antiwar activists and black radicals in highly publicized trials. Nixon himself drew up an "enemies list" of adversaries to be harassed by the government. "Anyone who opposes us, we'll destroy," warned a top White House official. "As a matter of fact, anyone who doesn't support us, we'll destroy."

In 1970 Nixon widened his offensive against the antiwar movement by approving the Huston Plan. It called for extensive wiretapping and infiltrating of radical organizations by White House operatives, as well as their breaking into the homes and offices of militants to gather or plant evidence. FBI chief J. Edgar Hoover opposed the Huston Plan as a threat to the bureau's power. Blocked, Nixon secretly created his own operation to discredit his opposition and to ensure executive secrecy. Nicknamed "the plumbers" because of their assignment to plug government leaks, the team was head by former FBI agent G. Gordon Liddy and former CIA operative E. Howard Hunt.

The plumbers first targeted Daniel Ellsberg, a former Defense Department analyst who had given the press the Pentagon Papers, a secret documentary history of U.S. involvement in Vietnam. On June 13 the *New York Times* began publishing the Pentagon Papers, revealing a long history of White House lies to Congress, foreign leaders, and the American people. Although the papers contained nothing damaging about his administration, Nixon, fearing that they would undermine trust in government and establish a precedent for publishing classified material, sought to bar their publication. The Supreme Court, however, ruled that their publication was protected by the First Amendment. Livid, Nixon directed the Justice Department to indict Ellsberg for theft and ordered the plumbers to break into the office of Ellsberg's psychiatrist in search of information to discredit the man who had become a hero to the antiwar movement.

The Southern Strategy

Nixon especially courted whites who were upset by the drive for racial equality. The administration opposed extension of the Voting Rights Act of 1965, sought to cripple enforcement of the Fair Housing Act of 1968, pleaded for the postponement of desegregation in Mississippi's schools, and filed suits to prohibit busing schoolchildren in order to desegregate public schools.

In 1971, when the Supreme Court upheld busing as a constitutional and necessary tactic in *Swann* v. *Charlotte-Mecklenburg Board of Education*, Nixon condemned the ruling and asked Congress to enact a moratorium on busing. That pleased white parents who disliked the inconvenience of having their children transported to schools farther from home, feared for the children's safety in strange schools, and opposed the integration of black and white schoolchildren for racist reasons. Busing to desegregate education, combined with conflicts between whites and African Americans over jobs and housing, had made working-class ethnic white voters in metropolitan areas an inviting target for the GOP.

The strategy of wooing white southerners also dictated Nixon's Supreme Court nominations. To reverse the Warren court's liberalism, he sought strict constructionists, judges who would not "meddle" in social issues or be "soft" on criminals. In 1969 he appointed Warren Burger as chief justice. Although the Senate then twice rejected southern conservatives nominated by Nixon, by 1973 the president had appointed three additional justices to the Supreme Court. Harry Blackmun of Minnesota, Lewis Powell of Virginia, and William Rehnquist of Arizona, along with Burger, steered the Court in a decidedly more moderate direction. Although ruling liberally in cases involving abortion, desegregation, and the death penalty, the Burger court shifted to the right on civil liberties, community censorship, and police power.

As the 1970 congressional elections neared, Nixon encouraged his vice president, Spiro T. Agnew, to step up attacks on "hooligans, hippies, and radical liberals." Agnew assailed the Democrats as "sniveling handwringers," intellectuals as "an effete corps of impudent snobs," and the news media as "nattering nabobs of negativism." Liberals deplored Agnew's alarming alliterative allegations, but conservatives found them on target. The 1970 elections ended in a draw, with the GOP losing nine House seats and winning two Senate seats.

THE CRISIS OF THE PRESIDENCY

President Nixon won a resounding reelection in 1972 and pledged, in his second inaugural, "to make these four years the best four years in America's history." Ironically, they would rank among its sorriest. His vice president would resign in disgrace; his closest aides would go to jail; and he would serve barely a year and a

Driving Southward and Backward
To outflank George Wallace and win the votes of both southern whites and urban blue-collar workers in the North, Nixon's "southern strategy" included delaying school desegregation plans and strong opposition to busing children to achieve racial balance in the schools.

half of his second term before resigning to avoid impeachment.

The Election of 1972

Nixon's reelection appeared certain. He faced a deeply divided Democratic party. His diplomatic successes and the winding down of the Vietnam War appealed to moderate voters. The southern strategy and law-and-order posture attracted Democrats who had voted for George Wallace in 1968. Nixon's only possible worry, another third-party candidacy by Wallace, vanished on May 15, 1972. During a campaign stop in Maryland, Wallace was shot and paralyzed from the waist down. He withdrew from the race, leaving Nixon a monopoly on the white backlash.

Capitalizing on the support of antiwar activists, the Senate's most outspoken dove, George McGovern of South Dakota, blitzed the Democratic primaries. He gained additional support from new party rules requiring state delegations to include minority, female, and youthful delegates in approximate proportion to their numbers. Actress Shirley MacLaine approvingly described California's delegation as "looking like a couple of high schools, a grape boycott, a Black Panther rally, and four or five politicians who walked in the wrong door." A disapproving labor leader grumbled about "too much hair and not enough cigars at this convention." McGovern won the nomination on the first ballot.

Perceptions of McGovern as inept and radical drove away all but the most committed supporters. After pledging to stand behind his vice presidential running mate Thomas Eagleton "1,000 percent" when it became known that Eagleton had received electric-shock therapy for depression, McGovern dumped him and suffered the embarrassment of having several prominent Democrats publicly decline to run with him. McGovern's endorsement of income redistribution, decriminalization of marijuana, immediate withdrawal from Vietnam, a $30 billion defense-budget cut, and pardons for those who had fled the United States to avoid the draft exposed him to GOP ridicule as the candidate of the radical fringe.

Remembering his narrow loss to Kennedy in 1960 and too-slim victory in 1968, Nixon left no stone unturned. To do whatever was necessary to win, he appointed his attorney general, John Mitchell, to head the Committee to Re-Elect the President (CREEP). Millions of dollars in campaign contributions financed "dirty tricks" to create dissension in Democratic ranks and an espionage unit to spy on the opposition. Led by Liddy and Hunt of the White House plumbers, the Republican undercover team received Mitchell's approval to wiretap telephones at the Democratic National Committee headquarters in the Watergate apartment and office complex in Washington. Early one morning in June 1972, a security guard foiled the break-in to install the bugs. Arrested were James McCord, the security coordinator of CREEP, and several other Liddy and Hunt associates.

A White House cover-up began immediately. Nixon claimed that "no one in the White House staff, no one in this administration, presently employed, was involved in this bizarre incident." He then ordered staff members to expunge Hunt's name from the White House telephone directory. To buy the silence of those arrested, he approved $400,000 in hush money and hints of a presidential pardon. On the pretext that an inquiry would damage national security, the President directed the CIA to halt the FBI's investigation of the Watergate break-in. With the McGovern campaign a shambles and Watergate seemingly contained, Nixon won overwhelmingly, amassing nearly 61 percent of the popular vote and 520 electoral votes. The southern strategy had worked to perfection. Strongly supported only by minorities and low-income voters, McGovern carried only Massachusetts and the District of Columbia. The election solidified the 1968 realignment.

The GOP, however, gained only twelve seats in the House and lost two in the Senate, demonstrating the growing difficulty of unseating incumbents, the rise in ticket-splitting, and the decline of both party loyalty and voter turnout. Only 55.7 percent of eligible voters went to the polls (down from 63.8 percent in 1960). Whether indifferent to politics or disenchanted with the choices offered, a growing number of citizens no longer bothered to participate in the electoral process.

The Watergate Upheaval

The scheme to conceal links between the White House and the accused Watergate burglars had succeeded during the 1972 campaign. But after the election, federal judge "Maximum John" Sirica, known for his tough treatment of criminals, refused to accept the defendants' claim that they had acted on their own. Threatening severe prison sentences, Sirica coerced James McCord of CREEP into confessing that White House aides had known in advance of the break-in and that the defendants had committed perjury during the trial. Two *Washington Post* reporters, Carl Bernstein and Bob Woodward, following clues furnished by an secret informant named "Deep Throat"(the title of a notorious pornographic film of the time), wrote a succession of front-page stories tying the break-in to illegal contributions and "dirty tricks" by CREEP.

In February 1973 the Senate established the Special Committee on Presidential Campaign Activities to investigate. As the trail of revelations led closer to the Oval Office, Nixon fired his special counsel, John Dean, who refused to be a scapegoat, and announced the resignations of his two principal aides, H. R. Haldeman and John Ehrlichman. Pledging to get to the bottom of the scandal, the president appointed Secretary of Defense Elliot Richardson, a Boston patrician of unassailable integrity, as his new attorney general, and instructed Richardson to appoint a special Watergate prosecutor with broad powers of investigation and subpoena. Richardson selected Archibald Cox, a Harvard law professor and a Democrat.

In May the special Senate committee began a televised investigation. Chaired by Sam Ervin of North Carolina, the hearings revealed the existence of a White House "enemies list," the president's use of government agencies to harass opponents, and administration favoritism in return for illegal campaign donations. Most damaging to Nixon, the hearings exposed the White House's active involvement in the Watergate cover-up. But the Senate still lacked concrete evidence of the president's criminality, the "smoking gun" that would prove Nixon's guilt. Because it was his word against that of John Dean, who testified that the presi-

dent directed the cover-up, Nixon expected to survive the crisis.

Then another presidential aide dropped a bomb-shell by revealing that Nixon had installed a secret taping system that recorded all conversations in the Oval Office. The Ervin committee and Cox insisted on access to the tapes, but Nixon refused, claiming executive privilege. In October, when Cox sought a court order to obtain the tapes, Nixon ordered Richardson to fire him. Richardson instead resigned in protest, as did the deputy attorney general, leaving it to the third-ranking official in the Department of Justice, Solicitor General Robert Bork, to dump Cox. The furor stirred by this "Saturday Night Massacre" sent Nixon's public-approval rating rapidly downward. Even as Nixon named a new special prosecutor, Leon Jaworski, the House Judiciary Committee began impeachment proceedings.

A President Disgraced

Adding to Nixon's woes that October, Vice President Agnew, charged with income-tax evasion and accepting bribes, pleaded no contest—"the full equivalent to a plea of guilty," according to the trial judge. Dishonored, Agnew left office with a three-year suspended sentence, a $10,000 fine, and a letter from Nixon expressing "a great sense of personal loss." Popular House Minority Leader Gerald R. Ford of Michigan replaced Agnew.

In March 1974 Jaworski and the House Judiciary Committee subpoenaed the president for the tape recordings of Oval Office conversations after the Watergate break-in. Nixon released edited transcripts of the tapes, filled with gaps and the phrase "expletive deleted." Despite the excisions, the president emerged as petty and vindictive. "We have seen the private man and we are appalled," declared the staunchly Republican *Chicago Tribune*.

Nixon's sanitized version of the tapes satisfied neither Jaworski nor the House Judiciary Committee. Both pressed for unedited tapes. In late July the Supreme Court rebuffed the president's claim to executive privilege. Citing the president's obligation to provide evidence necessary for the due process of law, Chief Justice Burger ordered Nixon to release the unexpurgated tapes.

In late July the House Judiciary Committee adopted three articles of impeachment, accusing President Nixon of obstruction of justice for impeding the Watergate investigation, abuse of power for his partisan use of the FBI and IRS, and contempt of Congress for refusing to obey a congressional subpoena for the tapes. Checkmated, Nixon conceded in a televised address on

The Cover-up Unravels
James McCord's revelation of White House involvement in the Watergate burglary led President Nixon to dismiss White House counsel John Dean, announce the resignations of Ehrlichman and Haldeman, and promise "There can be no whitewash at the White House." Nevertheless, a special committee of the Senate, chaired by Sam Ervin of North Carolina, began its own investigation of Watergate in May 1973.

August 5 that he had withheld relevant evidence. He then surrendered the subpoenaed tapes, which contained the "smoking gun" proving that the president had ordered the cover-up, obstructed justice, subverted one government agency to prevent another from investigating a crime, and lied about his role for more than two years. Impeachment and conviction were now certain. On August 9, 1974, Richard Nixon became the first president to resign, and Gerald Ford took office as the nation's first chief executive who had not been elected either president or vice president.

CONCLUSION

Unlike the generations that preceded and succeeded them, baby boomers took material comfort and their own importance for granted. Many came from affluent, liberal, and indulgent households. They longed for

meaning in their lives, as well as personal liberty. They sought a more humane democracy and a less racist and materialist society. Above all, as the war in Vietnam escalated, a growing number of students took to the streets in protest. Unable to force a quick end to the war, some became increasingly radical and violent. Most of the young, however, were more interested in enjoying "sex, drugs, and rock-and-roll." Ultimately, the youth movement helped prod the United States into becoming a more tolerant, diverse, and open society, and end America's longest war, which had cost the nation dearly in lives and dollars, in turning Americans against one another, and in diverting the society from its pressing needs.

The behavior of the young, along with increasing frustration with the war in Vietnam, brought politics to a boil in 1968. The result was a narrow victory for Richard Nixon in 1968 and a major political realignment that gave him a landslide reelection victory in 1972. Pursuing the national interest by realpolitik, he had withdrawn most American troops from Vietnam and lessened hostilities with China and the Soviet Union. Most vital to his political success, Nixon had pursued a "southern strategy" that appealed to whites upset by black militancy and radicalism, and emphasized law-and-order to attract those concerned with the upsurge of criminality and breakdown of traditional values.

In 1972 the secret schemes Nixon had put in place to spy upon and destroy those who opposed his Vietnam policies began to unravel. His obsession for secrecy and paranoia about those who opposed him brought his downfall. The arrest of the Watergate burglars and the subsequent attempted cover-up of White House involvement led to revelations of a host of "dirty

CHRONOLOGY, 1968–1974

1960 Birth-control pill marketed.
1963 Bob Dylan releases "Blowin' in the Wind."
1964 Berkeley Free Speech Movement (FSM).
The Beatles arrive in the United States, and "I Want to Hold Your Hand" tops the charts.
1965 Ken Kesey and Merry Pranksters stage first "acid test."
1966 Abolition of automatic student deferments from the draft.
1967 March on the Pentagon.
Israeli-Arab Six-Day War.
1968 Tet offensive.
President Lyndon Johnson announces that he will not seek reelection.
Martin Luther King, Jr., assassinated; race riots sweep nation.
Students take over buildings and strike at Columbia University.
Robert F. Kennedy assassinated.
Violence mars Democratic convention in Chicago.
Vietnam peace talks open in Paris.
Richard Nixon elected president.
1969 Appollo 11 lands first Americans on the moon.
Nixon begins withdrawal of U.S. troops.
Woodstock festival.
March Against Death in Washington, D.C.
Lieutenant William Calley charged with murder of civilians at My Lai.
1970 United States invades Cambodia.
Students killed at Kent State and Jackson State Universities.
Nixon proposes Huston Plan.
Environmental Protection Agency established.
OSHA created.
Earth Day first celebrated.
The Beatles disband; Janis Joplin and Jimi Hendrix die of drug overdoses.
1971 United States invades Laos.
Swann v. Charlotte-Mecklenburg Board of Education.
New York Times pulishes Pentagon Papers.
Nixon institutes wage-and-price freeze.
South Vietnam invades Laos with the help of U.S. air support.
1972 Nixon visits China and the Soviet Union.
SALT I agreement approved.
Break-in at Democratic National Committee headquarters in Watergate complex.
Nixon reelected in landslide victory.
Christmas bombing of North Vietnam.
1973 Vietnam cease-fire agreement signed.
Trial of Watergate burglars.
Senate establishes Special Committee on Presidential Campaign Activities to investigate Watergate.
President Salvador Allende ousted and murdered in Chile.
Vice President Spiro Agnew resigns; Gerald Ford appointed vice president.
Row v. Wade.
Yom Kippur War; OPEC begins embargo of oil to the West.
Saturday Night Massacre.
1974 Supreme court orders Nixon to release Watergate tapes.
House Judiciary Committee votes to impeach Nixon.
Nixon resigns; Ford becomes president.

tricks" and criminal acts. These resulted in the indictment of nearly fifty Nixon administration officials, and the jailing of a score of the president's associates, including his attorney general. Nixon's actions also led to a House Judiciary Committee vote to impeach him. To avoid certain conviction, Nixon resigned.

When his successor, Gerald Ford, took the oath of office, many Americans took pride in the smooth continuity of the political system and in its ability to curb excesses and abuses. Others worried that so many Americans had for so long just shrugged off Watergate as politics as usual, and that the Nixon scandals might never have come to light if not for coercion by a federal judge and the president's desire to tape and preserve his conversations. The consequent public distrust of politicians and disillusionment with government would last into the next century.

FOR FURTHER REFERENCE

READINGS

David Allyn, *Make Love, Not War; The Sexual Revolution, An Unfettered History* (2000). A well-written and illuminating narrative.

Howard Brick, *Age of Contradiction: American Thought and Culture in the 1960s* (2000). An excellent, insightful survey.

Alice Echols, *Scars of Sweet Paradise: The Life and Times of Janis Joplin* (1999). A fascinating biography that sheds much light on the history of the counterculture.

Ignacio Garcia, *Chicanismo: The Forging of a Militant Ethos Among Mexican Americans* (2000). A balanced assessment of this vital development.

Paul Lyons, *New Left, New Right, and the Legacy of the Sixties* (1996). A fair overview filled with acute observations and interpretations.

Melvin Small, *The Presidency of Richard Nixon* (1999). The best overview to date.

David Szatmary, *Rockin in Time: A Social History of Rock-and-Roll* (1997). A fresh, and refreshing, account.

James E. Westheider, *Fighting on Two Fonts: African Americans and the Vietnam War* (1997). A comprehensive and engaging analysis.

WEBSITES

The Free Speech Movement
http://www.lib.berkeley.edu/BANC/FSM
The best site for materials on and links to the Free Speech Movement.

The Sixties Project
http://lists.village.virginia.edu/sixties
"The Sixties Project" is a wide-ranging site hosted by the University of Virginia, especially rich on the counterculture

The Vietnam War
http://servercc.oakton.edu/~wittman
A good source for research materials and resources on the Vietnam War, and links to other valuable Vietnam sites.

Watergate
Two comprehensive sites for the Watergate scandal are **http://www.washingtonpost.com/wp-srv/national/longterm/watergate/front.htm.** and **http://vcepolitics.com/watergate**

For additional readings, please consult the bibliography at the end of the book.

CHAPTER 30

Society, Politics, and World Events from Ford to Reagan, 1974–1989

In October 1985 *Forbes* business magazine hailed "the richest man in America," Sam Walton of Arkansas, founder of the Wal-Mart Corporation, one of the discount chains that transformed U.S. mass marketing after 1960. Estimating his wealth at "$20 or $25 billion," he lived modestly, sported a Wal-Mart baseball cap, and got his haircuts at the local barbershop.

Born in Oklahoma in 1918, Walton grew up in Missouri. While his father, a mortgage agent, repossessed farms during the Great Depression, young Sam sold magazine subscriptions door-to-door. In 1945, after serving in World War II and marrying Helen Robson, he became the manager of a Ben Franklin variety store in Newport, Arkansas. Sam and Helen opened their own Walton's Five and Dime in Bentonville, Arkansas, in 1950 and a second one in nearby Fayetteville two years later. Walton tirelessly searched out bargain-priced merchandise that he sold at a small markup. As the Fayetteville store manager recalled, "Sam used to come down . . . driving an old fifty-three Plymouth. He had that car so loaded up he barely had room to drive. And would you like to guess what he had in it? Ladies' panties. Three for $1.00 and four for $1.00 and nylon hose."

By the later 1960s Wal-Mart stores dotted Arkansas, Oklahoma, Missouri, and beyond. "We just started repeating what worked, stamping out stores cookie-cutter style," Walton recalled. Together with other chains, including Target, Woolco, and K-Mart, Walton pioneered discount selling. As inflation

◀ **Jesse Treviño,** *Progreso* **(1977)**

CHAPTER OUTLINE

The Long Shadow of the 1960s: Cultural Changes and Continuities

Patterns of Social Change in Post-1960s America

Years of Malaise: Post-Watergate Politics and Diplomacy, 1974–1980

The Reagan Revolution, 1981–1984

A Sea of Problems in Reagan's Second Term, 1985–1989

Sam Walton
Founder of the Wal-Mart chain and an entrepreneurial genius.

eroded consumer buying power in the 1970s, Wal-Mart with its rock-bottom prices prospered. Walton also created a unique corporate culture that included promotional gimmicks such as "shopping cart bingo" and employee rallies punctuated by cheers and company songs. Thanks to successive stock splits, one hundred shares of Wal-Mart stock purchased for $1,650 in 1970 were worth about $11.5 million by 2002.

Walton had critics. Labor organizers attacked his anti-union policies. Small-town merchants battered by Wal-Mart's price-slashing complained bitterly. Responded Walton, "[Their] customers were the ones who shut [them] down. They voted with their feet. . . . Wal-Mart has actually [saved] quite a number of small towns . . . by offering low prices [and] . . . by creating hundreds of thousands of jobs."

On March 17, 1992, shortly before Walton's death of bone cancer, President George Bush awarded him the Medal of Freedom. Said Bush, "Sam Walton embodies the entrepreneurial spirit and epitomizes the American dream." By 2002, with 1.3 million employees and nearly six thousand Wal-Marts, Sam's Clubs, and Super Centers worldwide, Wal-Mart Corporation boasted annual sales of more than $220 billion and was the world's largest retailer of general merchandise.

Wal-Mart extended trends that had long been underway: the rise of great corporations; marketing innovations from department stores to shopping malls; the spread of a national consumer culture through the mass distribution of standardized goods. Wal-Mart also contributed to changes that transformed the U.S. economy in the 1970s and 1980s. The service sector grew rapidly as discount stores, fast-food outlets, and high-tech industries expanded and prospered. Other sectors of the economy, including family farms, the inner cities, and the fac-

tories of the old industrial heartland, did not fare as well. Sam Walton may have lived the American Dream, but that dream proved elusive for many Americans.

This chapter, covering the years from Nixon's resignation in 1974 to the end of Ronald Reagan's presidency in 1989, is structured around two key themes. The first is the sustained impact of the 1960s on U.S. culture and politics. On one hand, the activist, radical spirit of the sixties continued to influence the environmental movement, the women's movement, and changing sexual norms. On the other hand, these years also saw a reaction against the 1960s, expressed both in a retreat from public concerns to private pursuits and in a sharp conservative backlash.

These years also brought important social changes affecting middle-class women, farmers, African Americans, Native Americans, and the growing ranks of Hispanic and Asian immigrants. All Americans coped with an unsettled economy marked by inflation, recessions, boom times, and soaring budget deficits.

The second theme, which emerges as the chapter progresses, is the continuing importance of events abroad. Although many citizens turned inward after Vietnam, the outside world remained inescapable. As Americans of the 1970s faced rising gasoline prices, long lines at gas stations, and soaring inflation—all linked to economic decisions made in distant capitals—they realized that however much they might wish otherwise, they could not turn their backs on the world. Worsening Cold War tensions in the late 1970s and early 1980s, Middle East crises, and deadly terrorist attacks underscored the fact that America's future could not be separated from unfolding world events.

This chapter focuses on five major questions:

■ How were the cultural climate and social activism of 1974–1989 influenced by the 1960s?

■ What social developments most affected farmers, middle-class women, African Americans, and Native Americans in these years, and how did patterns of immigration change?

■ What core beliefs shaped Ronald Reagan's political ideology, and what steps did his administration take to translate this ideology into practice?

■ How did U.S.-Soviet relations evolve from the late 1970s through 1988?

■ In what respects did the international situation improve during these years, from the U.S. perspective, and in what ways did it grow more threatening?

THE LONG SHADOW OF THE 1960S: CULTURAL CHANGES AND CONTINUITIES

Social and cultural trends of the 1970s and 1980s reflected both the afterglow of 1960s activism and a reaction against that decade. While many young people turned away from public issues to pursue personal goals, some social trends and causes rooted in the 1960s survived and even gained momentum. A backlash against the sixties, as well as the sobering effects of the AIDS epidemic, also shaped the culture of these years. Radicals of the 1960s had celebrated sexual freedom and alternative lifestyles, and feminists had demanded reproductive choice, but the years after 1970 brought a conservative reaction and fierce debates over abortion, homosexuality, and other issues. The pace of change also led to a quest for moral certitude and a revival of religion.

The Post-1960s Mood: Personal Preoccupations; New Activist Energies

The Vietnam War shattered the liberal consensus, and the New Left coalition that protested the war soon fragmented as well, creating a vacuum of political leadership on the Left. The Watergate crisis, in turn, temporarily disoriented conservatives. With politics in disarray, personal preoccupations beckoned. To replace the long-haired, pot-smoking "campus radical" of the 1960s, journalists created a new stereotype, the "Yuppie" (young urban professional), preoccupied with physical fitness and consumer goods.

The stereotype had a basis in fact. Physical well-being became a middle-class obsession. Yuppies jogged and exercised, ate natural foods free of pesticides and additives, and stopped smoking when medical evidence linked cigarettes to lung cancer and heart disease. Meditation techniques won devoted followers. Reversing the middle-class flight to the suburbs, yuppies purchased and restored rundown inner-city apartments. This process, known as gentrification, often had the effect of pushing out poorer and elderly residents.

Self-improvement could easily turn selfish. Historian Christopher Lasch summed up his view of the era in the title of his 1978 book, *The Culture of Narcissism*. Novelist Tom Wolfe satirized the "Me Generation." *Newsweek* magazine, proclaiming "the Year of the Yuppie" in 1984, commented, "[T]hey're making lots of money, spending it conspicuously, and switching political candidates like they test cuisines."

TV viewing time increased. Prime-time soap operas like *Dallas*, chronicling the steamy affairs of a Texas oil family, captivated millions. *The Brady Bunch*, with its family of teenagers, recalled the insipid TV sit-coms of the 1950s. The Disney Corporation launched its Florida theme park Disney World in 1982. Blockbuster movies like *Jaws* (1975), *Star Wars* (1977), and *E.T.* (1982) offered escapist fare. Baseball's World Series, football's Super Bowl, and the National Basketball Association playoffs attracted vast TV audiences.

The politically engaged songs of the 1960s gave way to bland disco tunes, suitable for dancing but carrying little cultural weight. In *Saturday Night Fever* (1977), with a soundtrack by a disco group called the Bee Gees, John Travolta plays a self-absorbed working-class Brooklyn youth whose life revolves around dance contests but who readily abandoned his friends to pursue a career in Manhattan. A fitting symbol for this aspect of the 1970s, suggests historian Bruce Schulman, was the brief fad of pet rocks, "which just sat there doing nothing."

The Rise of the Yuppie
In 1984, *Newsweek* Magazine proclaimed "the Year of the Yuppie," or young urban professional, a rapidly growing group in the 1980s.

Innovations in consumer electronics shaped the era as well. By the early 1990s, 70 percent of U.S. households had VCRs (videocassette recorders), enabling users to tape TV shows for later viewing and to rent movies on cassette. As entertainment became privatized, families stayed home with the VCR instead of going to the movies. In the music field, the compact disc (CD), in which laser beams "read" millions of dots molded into concentric circles on the disk, offered remarkably high-quality sound. In a development of great future significance, the late 1970s also saw the advent of the personal computer (see Technology and Culture: The Personal Computer).

American life in these years was not all escapism and technological novelties. The protest mood of the 1960s survived. In sharp contrast to disco were the raw working-class songs of Bruce Springsteen of Asbury Park, New Jersey. His *Darkness at the Edge of Town* (1978) and *Born in the USA* (1984) evoked the stresses of blue-collar life and offered a bleak view of widening class divisions in post-Vietnam, post-Watergate America. *Born in the USA* tells of a young man "sent . . . off to a foreign land to go and kill the yellow man" who now finds himself "in the shadow of the penitentiary" with "[n]owhere to run . . . nowhere to go." Bob Dylan, best-known for his 1960s protest songs, produced some of his best work in the 1970s. His 1974 album *Blood on the Tracks* expressed distrust of authority and the difficulty of personal relationships while celebrating outlaws and outsiders who defied the established order.

Along with escapist fare, directors also produced some brilliant films exploring the darker side of American life in the 1970s. Robert Altman's *Nashville* (1975) offered a disturbing vision of cynical mass-culture producers, manipulative politicians, and lonely, alienated drifters. Roman Polanski's *Chinatown* (1974) probed the personal and political corruption beneath the sunny surface of Southern California life. Such work, too, is part of the cultural legacy of the decade.

The Environmental Movement Gains Support

A legacy of the 1960s that grew stronger in the 1970s was the movement to protect the environment against the effects of heedless exploitation. This movement built upon a decade of activism triggered by Rachel Carson's *Silent Spring* of 1962 and including the environmental laws of the 1960s and the inauguration of Earth Day in 1970 (see Chapters 27 and 29).

The heightened environmental consciousness found many outlets. Established groups such as the Sierra Club

as well as new organizations won fresh recruits. One of the new organizations, Greenpeace, was founded in 1971 when Canadian activists protested a planned U.S. nuclear test at Amchitka Island in the Bering Sea. The U.S. branch, established soon after, addressed a range of environmental issues, including the preservation of old-growth forests and protection of the world's oceans. By 2000 Greenpeace had 250,000 U.S. members and 2.5 million members worldwide. The Save the Whales campaign, launched by the Animal Welfare Institute in 1971, mobilized opposition to the killing of the world's largest mammals by fleets of floating processing factories to provide dog and cat food for pet owners.

In the later 1970s environmentalists targeted the nuclear-power industry. Reviving protest techniques first used in the civil-rights and antiwar campaigns, activists across America staged rallies at planned nuclear-power plants. The movement crested in 1979 when a partial meltdown crippled the Three Mile Island nuclear-power plant in Pennsylvania. A movie released at the same time, *China Syndrome*, graphically portrayed a fictitious but plausible nuclear-power disaster caused by a California earthquake. *China Syndrome* starred Jane Fonda, an antiwar leader of the 1960s, underscoring both the continuities and the changes of focus in the activism of the two decades.

The Women's Movement: Gains and Uncertainties

Of the many legacies of the 1960s, the revitalized women's movement (see Chapter 28) had a particularly lasting effect. As middle-class young women had found themselves marginalized in the civil-rights and antiwar movements, many had begun to examine their own status in society. The National Organization for Women (NOW), founded in 1966, boasted nearly fifty thousand members by 1975. Feminist support groups and Gloria Steinem's *Ms.* magazine (launched in 1972) spread the message. The movement, however, remained mainly white and middle class.

With the movement's growth came political clout. The National Women's Political Caucus (1971) promoted a feminist agenda. By 1972 many states had liberalized their abortion laws and outlawed gender discrimination in hiring. That same year Congress passed an equal rights amendment (ERA) to the Constitution barring discrimination on the basis of sex. When twenty-eight states quickly ratified it, ultimate adoption seemed assured.

In the landmark case *Roe* v. *Wade* (1973), the Supreme Court proclaimed women's constitutional right to abor-

tion by a 7 to 2 vote. The decision gave women broad abortion rights in the first trimester of pregnancy, in consultation with a physician, while granting states more regulatory authority as the pregnancy progressed. The majority decision, written by Justice Harry Blackmun, relied heavily on the right to privacy grounded in the Fourteenth Amendment's due-process clause. In the wake of *Roe* v. *Wade*, the number of abortions rose from about 750,000 in 1973 to more than 1.5 million in 1980 and then leveled off.

The women's movement splintered in the late 1970s, as Betty Friedan and other moderates opposed the lesbians who were becoming increasingly assertive (see below). The moderates also deplored the strident rhetoric of some radical feminists and criticized their tendency to downgrade the family while celebrating female autonomy and careerist goals. In *The Second Stage* (1981), Friedan urged feminists to add family-protection issues to their agenda.

While feminist leaders struggled to define the movement, the realities of many women's lives changed dramatically. The proportion of women working outside the home leaped from 35 percent in 1960 to nearly 60 percent in 1992 (see Figure 30.1). Not only feminist ideology but also the soaring cost of living encouraged this trend, as many families found they could not manage on a single income.

Despite the gains, working women's earnings still lagged behind those of men, and the workplace remained largely gender segregated. Women were still concentrated in such fields as nursing, teaching, sales, and secretarial work, while men dominated management positions and the professions. But even this was changing as more women entered the ranks of manage-

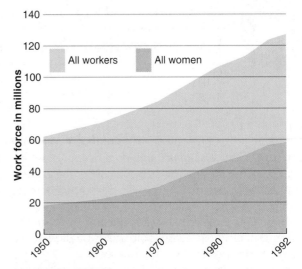

FIGURE 30.1
Women in the Work Force, 1950–1992
After 1960 the proportion of American women who were gainfully employed surged upward. As a result, young women coming of age in the 1990s had far different expectations about their lives than had their grandmothers or even their mothers.

Sources: Statistical Abstract of the United States, 1988 (Washington, D.C.: U.S. Government Printing Office, 1987), 373; *World Almanac and Book of Facts, 1989* (New York: Pharos Books, 1988), 152; *Statistical Abstract of the United States, 1993* (Washington, D.C., U.S. Government Printing Office, 1993), 400, 401.

ment. (Top management remained a male preserve, however, a phenomenon known as the "glass ceiling.") Even in medicine and the law, change was in the air. By the early 1990s the legal and medical professions were nearly 20 percent female, while the growing ranks of female medical students and law students promised even more dramatic changes in the future.

Breaking the Gender Barrier
Martha Fransson, the sole female member of the Class of 1970 at the Tuck School of Business at Dartmouth College, poses with her classmates.

The Personal Computer

Computer technology dated from World War II; by 1970 giant IBM mainframe computers were well-known (see Chapter 27). The size and cost of these computers made them practical only for big corporations or government agencies such as the Pentagon and the Census Bureau. Even the smaller minicomputers built by Seattle's Digital Equipment Corporation (DEC) were far too bulky and expensive for individual use.

An exciting new entrant, the personal computer, loomed on the horizon. With the development of silicon-chip transistors and integrated circuits in the late 1950s, the data that could be implanted in a single chip increased enormously. "Moore's Law," proclaimed in 1965 by Gordon Moore, founder of Intel, a computer-chip manufacturer, held that silicon chips' capacity would double every eighteen months. The prediction proved remarkably accurate. With silicon chips, computers could be miniaturized and still match the mainframes' capacity.

Unlike the inventions that had once emerged from Thomas Edison's New Jersey laboratory, the personal computer did not spring from a single research project, but rather from many young hobbyists working at home and hovering around the margins of the industry. In the late 1960s, for example, Seattle high-school students Bill Gates and Paul Allen biked daily to the offices of DEC, where company officials let them tinker with computers in exchange for finding flaws (or "bugs") in the instructional programs (called software) that enabled DEC's computers to perform useful functions. "We were called computer nerds," Gates recalled. "Anyone who spends their life on a computer is pretty unusual." In 1972 Gates and Allen, still teenagers, formed Traf-O-Data, a programming company.

Meanwhile, the actual machinery, or hardware, of small computers evolved rapidly. In 1974 a struggling Albuquerque electronics company, Micro Instrumentation Telemetry Systems (MITS), developed a $397 do-it-yourself Altair computer kit using Intel chips. (The name Altair came from the TV show *Star Trek*.) When *Popular Electronics* magazine featured the Altair on its January 1975 cover, orders poured in.

The Altair appealed mainly to hobbyists. It had limited memory and primitive programming, and it was awkward to use, with levers rather than a keyboard. For home computers to be practical, better software was essential. Paul Allen, now working in Massachusetts, and Bill Gates, a Harvard freshman, volunteered to solve that problem. The *Popular Electronics* article caught their notice, and they offered to provide an operating system for the Altair by modifying BASIC, a program developed at Dartmouth College in 1964. MITS accepted, and Allen and Gates, changing their company name to Microsoft, moved to Albuquerque. MITS soon collapsed, and the Altair vanished, but the personal-computer era was underway.

Early home-computer enthusiasts valued cooperation and a casual, counterculture lifestyle. As one later recalled, "[We had our] genetic coding in the 60s, in the anti-establishment, anti-war, pro-freedom, anti-discipline attitudes." Groups of hobbyists such as the Homebrew Computer Club of San Francisco and New Jersey's Amateur Computer Group freely shared ideas, hardware, and software. In Cupertino, California, working in a garage, young Stephen Wozniak and Steven Jobs assembled a prototype small computer and soon began selling handmade models to friends.

As the personal computer's commercial potential became clear, this laid-back, cooperative attitude gave way to a competitive, proprietary business ethic. As early as 1976 Bill Gates, having reached the ripe old age of twenty-one, published "An Open Letter to Hobbyists," criticizing the free sharing (or "piracy") of software.

In 1976 Wozniak and Jobs began to sell their computers, called the Apple I, through the Byte Shop, a Bay Area computer store. The Apple II followed in 1977. The initial price of $666.66 soon dropped to $475. By 1980 sales hit $118 million. New marketing outlets quickly sprang up. The first ComputerShack opened in New Jersey in 1977. Radio Shack, Computerland, and other chains soon followed.

In the late 1970s IBM engineers working in Boca Raton, Florida, developed IBM's version of a personal computer. The IBM-PC hit the market in 1981. Priced at $1,565 it was far more expensive than the Apple II, but it bore the prestigious IBM name and boasted state-of-the-art hardware and Microsoft software.

Whether users chose Apple or IBM-PC, personal computers had an enormous cultural and economic impact. The sizzling industry fueled an economic boom that began in the mid-1980s and roared on into the 1990s. Youthful founders of start-up companies in "Silicon Valley" (a region south of San Francisco) amassed fortunes as investors bid up the prices of new stock offerings. (When recession hit in 2000, some of those fortunes evaporated.)

Bulky calculators, adding machines, and typewriters—the cutting-edge information technologies of earlier eras—gathered dust as people shifted to computer-based systems of data management, record-keeping, and word-processing. Popular in the home, personal computers also transformed office routines in businesses, hospitals, churches, and educational institutions. Secretaries who had spent their time filing, typing letters, and entering payroll and account records in ledger books now learned new computer-based skills. School typing classes gave way to computer instruction; library card catalogs to computerized databases. Library patrons were as likely to sit at a computer as to browse bookshelves. Computer games transformed juvenile leisure-time activities.

The possibilities seemed endless. "[I]f you're . . . thinking of buying [a personal computer]," proclaimed an industry publication in 1985, "you are only a few steps away from entering an expanding universe of incredible size and power." Further innovations came in the late 1980s and the 1990s: vastly enhanced memory capacity; ever-smaller laptop and hand-held models; microcomputers to control operating systems in automobiles and appliances; e-mail; and the Internet. The explosive growth of the Internet and the World Wide Web revolutionized the retrieval and transmission of information.

By 2000, 60 percent of U.S. homes had personal computers. Some cultural commentators worried about this fast-growing new technology. Would hours on the Internet cut users off from human contact? Would video games isolate the young from social interaction and blur the distinction between the real and the virtual? Others noted class differences in access to personal computers, as ownership spread much more slowly among blue-collar families and inner-city minorities than among the more educated and well-to-do.

The young Bill Gates

The prototype personal computer, the Altair 8800, introduced in 1975

Nevertheless, the personal computer was clearly here to stay. Only the future would reveal the full dimensions of the technological revolution launched in the 1970s by a handful of teenaged "computer nerds."

Focus Questions

- What key technological developments made the personal computer possible?
- What were the most important cultural and social effects of the spread of personal computers?

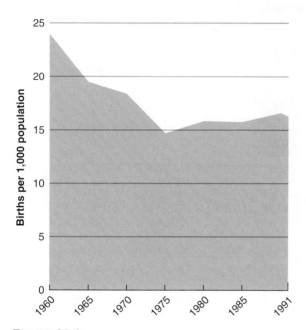

FIGURE 30.2
The American Birthrate, 1960–1991
Families of four or five children or even more were once common in the United States. But from 1960 to the mid-1970s, the U.S. birthrate fell by nearly half.

Source: Statistical Abstract of the United States, 1994 (Washington, D.C.: U.S. Government Printing Office, 1994), 76.

These changes had broad social effects. As women delayed marriage to pursue higher education or careers, their median age at first marriage rose from twenty in 1960 to twenty-four in 1990. The birthrate fell as well (see Figure 30.2). By 1980 the statistically average U.S. family had 1.6 children, far below the figure in earlier times. Conservatives worried that women's changing roles would weaken the family. Working women themselves conceded the stresses of balancing career and family, but few were prepared to return to the era when "women's sphere" had consisted exclusively of child care, housework, and good works. As the 1980s ended, feminists could take satisfaction in many gains achieved. But major challenges still loomed and complex issues remained unresolved.

Changing Patterns of Sexual Behavior; the Looming Specter of AIDS

The long shadow of the 1960s was evident, too, in the realm of sexual behavior. The 1960s counterculture had challenged the prevailing sexual code, and the loosening of old taboos that resulted had long-lasting effects. In 1960 about 30 percent of unwed nineteen-year-old U.S. women had sexual experience. By 1980 more than half did, and the figure soared still higher by 2000. The number of unmarried couples living together jumped from 523,000 in 1970 to 3.5 million by 1993. This trend, too, accelerated as the twentieth century wore on.

Many gay men and lesbians "came out of the closet" in the 1970s and openly avowed their sexual preference. As we saw in Chapter 29, the 1969 Stonewall riot, when patrons at a gay club in Greenwich Village fought back against a police raid, launched an era in which homosexuals became more vocal in asserting their presence and demanding equal rights. This movement continued in the later 1970s and beyond, in a wave of rallies, parades, and protests against job discrimination and harassment. In 1977 "Gay Pride" parades drew seventy-five thousand marchers in New York City and three hundred thousand in San Francisco, a center of gay activism. Two years later the first national gay and lesbian civil-rights parade attracted one hundred thousand to Washington, D.C. Exclaimed one participant later, "It was such a feeling of power, like the storming of the Bastille."

In 1974 Elaine Noble, an avowed lesbian, won a seat in the Massachusetts legislature. Harvey Milk, a proudly gay candidate, was elected to the San Francisco board of supervisors in 1977. In 1987 Massachusetts Congressman Barney Frank acknowledged his homosexuality.

Organizations like the National Gay Task Force, founded in 1973 and later renamed the National Gay and Lesbian Task Force, and a militant New York group called ACT-UP (1987) demanded the repeal of anti-gay laws and passage of legislation protecting the civil rights of homosexuals. Responding to the pressure, many states and cities repealed laws against same-sex relations between consenting adults. Like other reforms of these years, this movement was mainly white and middle class, though black gay and lesbian organizations emerged as well.

The freer attitude toward sex received a setback with the spread of sexually transmitted diseases (STDs), especially the deadly viral infection AIDS (acquired immune deficiency syndrome), first diagnosed in 1981. At first, AIDS spread mainly among sexually active homosexuals and bisexuals, intravenous drug users sharing needles, and persons having sexual intercourse with members of these high-risk groups. (Early in the epidemic some persons, including tennis star Arthur Ashe, contracted AIDS through blood transfusions.) Though the worst of the epidemic still lay ahead, more than thirty-one thousand Americans had died of AIDS by the end of the 1980s.

Medical authorities warned against unprotected sex. The message was driven home when basketball super-

Gays and Lesbians Organize
The director of the National Gay and Lesbian Task Force, Urvashi Vaid, speaks outside the Supreme Court building in Washington, D.C., in October 1987.

star Earvin ("Magic") Johnson and Olympic diver Greg Louganis announced that they carried the HIV virus, a precursor of AIDS. While the AIDS epidemic emboldened some Americans to express their hatred of homosexuality (see below), it also stimulated medical research and an outpouring of concern. Hospices cared for sufferers, and a large AIDS quilt honoring victims toured the nation. Under the shadow of AIDS and other STDs, many Americans grew more cautious in their sexual behavior. The exuberant slogan of the 1960s, "Make Love, Not War," gave way to the more somber message of "Safer Sex."

Conservative Backlash and Evangelical Renaissance

As we saw in Chapter 29, another legacy of the 1960s was a conservative reaction. An early target was *Roe* v. *Wade*. In the wake of the Supreme Court's legalization of abortion, a "Right to Life" movement led by Roman Catholic and conservative Protestant groups pressed for a constitutional amendment outlawing abortion. This practice, they charged, undermined respect for human life; it was "the murder of the unborn." "Pro-life" advocates held rallies, signed petitions, and picketed abortion clinics and pregnancy-counseling centers.

Responding to the pressure, Congress in 1976 cut off Medicaid funding for most abortions, in effect denying this procedure to the poor. Most feminists adopted a "pro-choice" stance, arguing that reproductive decisions should be made by women and their physicians, not by the government. Opinion polls reflected deep divisions, although a majority favored the "pro-choice" position.

The women's movement, too, faced an antifeminist backlash. In 1972 President Nixon vetoed a bill setting up a national network of day-care centers, criticizing its "communal approach to child-rearing." The ERA amendment died in 1982, three states short of the three-fourths required for ratification.

The gay and lesbian movement particularly inflamed conservatives, who saw it as evidence of society's moral collapse. TV evangelist Jerry Falwell thundered, "God . . . destroyed the cities of Sodom and Gomorrah because of this terrible sin." In 1977 singer Anita Bryant led a campaign against a recently passed Miami ordinance protecting the civil rights of homosexuals. "God created Adam and Eve, not Adam and Bruce," she pointed out. Thanks in large part to Bryant's efforts, Miami voters repealed the ordinance by a two-to-one margin. Soon after, readers of *Good Housekeeping* magazine voted Bryant "the most admired woman in America." Other cities, too, reversed earlier measures in favor of gay rights.

In 1978, as the backlash intensified, a conservative member of the San Francisco board of supervisors, Dan White, fatally shot gay board-member Harvey Milk and Milk's ally, Mayor George Moscone. "the city weeps"

headlined the *San Francisco Examiner*. When White got off with a light sentence (after claiming that junk food had affected his judgment), riots erupted in the city. In 1980 disco singer Donna Summer, highly popular in the gay community, announced that she had been become a born-again Christian and speculated that AIDS had been "sent by God to punish homosexuals."

Another manifestation of the conservative turn was a revival of religion and spiritual questing. Some young people joined the Reverend Sun Myung Moon's Unification church or the International Society for Krishna Consciousness, whose shaved-head, saffron-robed followers added an exotic note in airports, city streets, and college campuses. More long-lasting was the rapid growth of evangelical Protestant denominations such as the Assemblies of God and the Southern Baptist Convention, which espoused strict morality, the Bible's verbatim truth, and a "born-again" religious conversion.

Evangelical Christians had pursued social reform before the Civil War, including the abolition of slavery, and their modern-day successors also preached reform, but of a conservative variety. As one evangelical observed in 1985, "I always thought that churches should stay out of politics. Now it seems almost a sin not to get involved." Jerry Falwell's Moral Majority, founded in 1979 as a "pro-life, pro-family, pro-moral, and pro-America" crusade, channeled this activism into support for conservative candidates. While battling domestic evils such as abortion, homosexuality, and pornography, many evangelicals also embraced a fiercely militant anticommunism.

A network of Christian bookstores, radio stations, and TV evangelists fueled the revival. Along with Falwell's *Old Time Gospel Hour*, popular broadcasts included Pat Robertson's *700 Club*, Jim and Tammy Bakker's *PTL* (Praise the Lord) program, and Jimmy Swaggart's telecasts from Louisiana. Many of these shows aired on Robertson's CBN (Christian Broadcasting Network). With their constant pleas for money, the televangelists repelled many Americans, but millions embraced their spiritual message. The so-called electronic church suffered after 1987 amid sexual and financial scandals, but the influence of evangelicalism continued. In *The Culture of Disbelief* (1993), law professor Stephen J. Carter called on politicians and the media to cease "trivializing" religion and to recognize its importance for many Americans. In a world of change, evangelicals found certitude, reassurance, and a sense of community in their shared faith. In the process, they profoundly influenced late-twentieth-century American life.

PATTERNS OF SOCIAL CHANGE IN POST-1960s AMERICA

While white, urban, middle-class Americans pursued the good life or embraced various reform causes, other groups grappled with urgent economic worries and struggled to move up the ladder. Family farmers became an endangered species amid the proliferation of giant agribusinesses. Although many African-Americans successfully pursued the academic and professional avenues opened by the civil-rights movement, others remained trapped in poverty. While Native Americans continued to face many hurdles, the 1970s brought brighter economic prospects and a new assertiveness in pursuing long-ignored treaty rights. New patterns of immigration, meanwhile, changed the nation's ethnic and demographic profile, with profound implications for the future.

Decline of the Family Farm

The family farm, historically revered as the backbone of America, continued its long decline in these years. In 1960 about 6 percent of the U.S. labor force worked on farms; by 1994 the figure was 2.5 percent. The farm population was aging, as young people sought opportunities in the cities. The small-farm operators who still hung on often held second jobs to make ends meet.

Total farm production increased, however, thanks to factory farms and agribusinesses. The acreage of the average farm grew from 375 to 430 between 1970 and 1990, and farms of several thousand acres were not unusual. Big operators bought up failing farms, demolished the homes that had sheltered successive generations, and consolidated them into large-scale operations involving major capital investment and heavy-duty equipment. Mass-production factory farms dominated poultry and hog production. Although politicians paid lip service to the family farm, federal crop subsidy programs accelerated the process of consolidation, as they had since the 1930s.

While the family farm disappeared, movies, novels, and songs kept it vivid in the nation's collective memory. In the 1985 film *The Trip to Bountiful*, an aging Texas woman, movingly played by Geraldine Page, living in a cramped city house with her son and his wife, pays a nostalgic final visit to her girlhood farm home, only to find it abandoned and falling to ruin. In that same year, country singer Willie Nelson, combining nostalgia and show-

business savvy with a genuine desire to help small farmers, began a popular series of annual concerts he called "Farm Aid." The first, in Champaign, Illinois, featured Nelson, Bob Dylan, Billy Joel, Roy Orbison, and other stars. By 1999 Farm Aid had contributed nearly $15 million to programs designed to help small farmers survive.

Like much else in the 1970s, the movement to recapture a vanishing rural past owed a debt to the 1960s. As the sixties ended, many members of the counterculture formed rural communes to escape the urban-corporate world and live in harmony with nature. As one commented, "We're learning self-sufficiency and rediscovering old technologies . . . and we're doing this, as much as possible, outside the existing structures." Several thousand rural communes soon arose across America. Periodicals like *The Whole Earth Catalog* and *The Mother Earth News* provided guidance on organic farming and sold simple, hand-operated products for rural living.

The Two Worlds of Black America

The story of black America in these years is really two very different stories. On one hand, millions of blacks experienced significant upward mobility thanks to the doors opened by the civil-rights movement. In 1965 black students accounted for under 5 percent of college enrollments; by 1990 the figure had risen to 12 percent, as the proportion of black high-school graduates going on to college nearly matched that of whites. By 1990 some 46 percent of black workers held white-collar jobs. TV's *Cosby Show*, a comedy of the later 1980s in which Bill Cosby played a doctor married to a lawyer, portrayed this upwardly mobile world.

Outside this world lay the inner-city slums, inhabited by perhaps a third of the black population. Here, up to half the young people never finished high school, and the jobless rate soared as high as 60 percent. Inflation, periodic recessions, growing demands for specialized skills, and economic changes that eliminated many of the unskilled jobs once held by the urban poor all wreaked havoc with the black underclass. Black factory workers suffered from job cuts in steel, automaking, and other industries.

Cocaine and other drugs pervaded the inner cities. Some black children recruited as lookouts for drug dealers became dealers themselves when they reached their early teens. With drugs came violence. In the 1980s a young black male was six times as likely to be murdered as a young white male. In Los Angeles two rival gangs, the Bloods and the Crips, accounted for more than four hundred killings in 1987. Warned Jewelle Taylor Gibbs of

The Endangered Family Farm
West Virginia farmer Bob Daniels visits the graves of ancestors who farmed the land before him.

the University of California at Berkeley, "Young black males in America's inner cities are an endangered species. . . . , [the] rejects of our affluent society."

In truth, drug abuse affected all social levels, including yuppies, sports and show-business celebrities, and young corporate executives. Despite the tough Comprehensive Drug Abuse Act of 1970, illegal-substance abuse was widespread and was even glorified in movies, songs, and rock concerts. But the devastating impact of drug use and drug trafficking on entire communities fell most heavily on the inner cities.

Unmarried women—mostly young and poor—accounted for nearly 60 percent of all black births in 1980, and the figure rose still higher thereafter. Scarcely beyond childhood themselves, many of these single mothers depended on welfare payments for survival. Buffeted by complex social and economic forces, the predominantly nonwhite inner-city populations posed a major social challenge. Caught in a cycle of dependence, they were at risk of becoming a permanent underclass, cut off from all hope of bettering their lot.

In one effort to improve conditions, governments extended "affirmative action" programs to groups previously discriminated against. Cities set aside a percentage of building contracts for minority businesses, for example. Some educational institutions reserved a certain number of slots for minority applicants. Such programs faced court challenges, however. In *Bakke* v. *U.S.*

(1978) the Supreme Court overthrew the affirmative-action plan of a California medical school. In 1989 the High Court invalidated a Richmond, Virginia, requirement that 30 percent of building contracts be awarded to minority businesses.

The conservative backlash affected African-Americans. The Reagan administration, distrusting government, opposed federal action to remedy past injustices. Reagan's appointees to the U.S. Civil Rights Commission, charged with enforcing civil-rights laws, shared his suspicion of federal activism. This governmental foot dragging complicated efforts to address the urgent problems of inner-city joblessness and social disorganization.

Brightening Prospects for Native Americans

Like other developments discussed in this chapter, the Native American experience in these years was shaped by events of the 1960s. Influenced by the decade's protest climate, members of the militant American Indian Movement (AIM) had occupied Alcatraz Island in San Francisco Bay; the Bureau of Indian Affairs in Washington; and, in 1973, a trading post at Wounded Knee, South Dakota, site of the 1890 Indian massacre by the U.S. Army. This militancy spurred yet another shift in federal policy. The Indian Self-Determination Act of 1974 granted tribes control of federal aid programs on the reservations and oversight of their own schools.

In the 1990 census, more than 1.7 million persons identified themselves as American Indians, in contrast to fewer than eight hundred thousand in 1970. This upsurge reflected not only natural increase and ethnic pride, but also economic advantages associated with tribal membership. Under a 1961 law permitting them to buy or develop land for commercial and industrial projects, tribes launched business ventures ranging from resorts to mining and logging operations. They licensed food-processing plants, electronics firms, and manufacturing enterprises on tribal lands, providing jobs and income. Tribes also opened gambling casinos, although some Native American leaders deplored the casinos as a threat to traditional Indian values.

Indian tribes also reasserted rights granted them in treaties that had long gathered dust in government archives. The Indian Claims Commission, a federal agency set up in 1946, worked overtime after 1970. In 1971 the Native peoples of Alaska won 40 million acres of land and nearly $1 billion in settlement of long-standing treaty claims. In 1980 the Sioux were awarded $107 million for South Dakota lands taken from them in violation of treaty agreements. The Penobscot Indians in Maine won claims based on a 1790 federal law. In 1988 the tiny Puyallup tribe of Washington State received $162 million in settlement of their claim that the city of Tacoma occupied land granted them by treaty in the 1850s. Among other projects, the Puyallups laid plans to restore salmon runs on the Puyallup River.

High jobless rates, alcoholism, and disease persisted on the reservations and among urbanized Indians. But the renewal of tribal life, new federal policies, and the courts' willingness to honor legally binding treaties clearly represented an advance. In the popular culture, movies such as *Little Big Man* (1970) and *Dances with Wolves* (1990), while idealizing Indians, represented an improvement over the grotesque stereotypes of earlier cowboy-and-Indian films.

New Patterns of Immigration

America's growth from 204 million people in 1970 to 275 million in 2000 reflected a steady influx of immigrants, both legal and illegal. Whereas most immigrants once came from Europe, some 45 percent of the late-twentieth-arrivals came from the Western Hemisphere and 30 percent from Asia. As in the past, economic need drew these newcomers. In oil-rich Mexico, for example, an oil price collapse in the 1980s worsened the nation's chronic poverty, spurring many to seek jobs in the north. But these immigrants, like their predecessors, faced continued hardships. In 1990 nearly 20 percent of Mexican-Americans and 30 percent of Puerto Ricans lived below the poverty line.

Despite adversity, Hispanic newcomers preserved their language and traditions, influencing U.S. culture in the process. In Los Angeles, with nearly a million Mexican-Americans, Spanish-language businesses, churches, newspapers, and radio stations proliferated. Large parts of Miami seemed wholly Hispanic (see Chapter 31, A Place in Time: Miami, Florida).

Estimates of the number of illegal aliens in the United States ranged as high as 12 million by the early 1990s. Working long hours with few legal protections, these migrants, mostly Mexicans and Haitians (as well as Puerto Ricans, who are U.S. citizens), sweated in the garment trades, cleaned houses, changed diapers, and labored in agricultural fields. Addressing the problem, the Immigration Reform and Control Act of 1986 outlawed the hiring of illegal aliens, strengthened border controls, and offered legal status to aliens who had lived in the United States for five years.

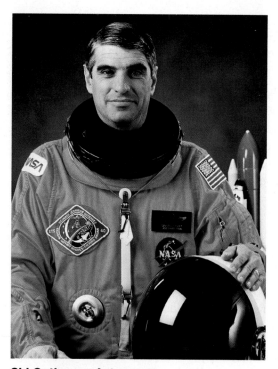

Sid Gutierrez, Astronaut
Hispanics entered all arenas of American life in the late twentieth century. Gutierrez, a native of Albuquerque, New Mexico, piloted space shuttle *Columbia* on a 1991 NASA mission.

New Americans, 1994
Beneath the political icons and popular-culture imagery of their adopted nation, children of Hmong (Laotian) immigrants study at Lincoln Elementary School, Wausau, Wisconsin.

Immigration from Asia climbed as newcomers arrived from Korea, Vietnam, and the Philippines. Prizing education, many Asian immigrants moved up rapidly. The younger generation, torn between the new and the old, generally retained strong group loyalties while exploring larger opportunities. All these ethnic trends made contemporary America of the 1970s and 1980s a more diverse and vibrant place than it had been a generation earlier.

YEARS OF MALAISE: POST-WATERGATE POLITICS AND DIPLOMACY, 1974–1980

The Vietnam debacle and the disastrous end of Richard Nixon's presidency had a dispiriting effect on the nation's political culture, as Gerald Ford and Jimmy Carter grappled with a tangle of domestic and foreign problems. As soaring oil prices led to inflation, unemployment, and recession, a sense of the limits of economic growth gripped many Americans. Globally, the later 1970s brought mostly humiliations, from the sorry end of the Vietnam War to Iran's seizure of U.S. hostages. The stark polarities of the Cold War blurred as complex problems in Asia, the Middle East, Latin America, and Africa hinted at the kinds of issues the United States would face in the future.

The confident days of the 1950s and early 1960s, when a prosperous America had savored its role as the Free World's leader, equal to any challenge, now seemed remote. A nation long convinced that it was immune to the historical forces that hedged in other societies seemed buffeted by forces beyond its control. Although the Vietnam failure encouraged isolationist tendencies, the events of the post-1970 era made it clear that America could not evade global involvement. By 1980 the accumulating frustration had generated a strong political revolt.

The Caretaker Presidency of Gerald Ford, 1974–1976

Gerald Ford took the presidential oath on August 9, 1974, following Richard Nixon's forced resignation. A Michigan congressman who had been House minority leader before becoming vice president, Ford conveyed a

likeable decency, if little evidence of brilliance. After the trauma of Watergate, he inspired cautious hope. "Our long national nightmare is over," he declared.

Ford's period of grace soon ended, however, when he pardoned Richard Nixon for "any and all crimes" committed while in office, thus shielding him from prosecution for his Watergate role. Ford said he wanted to help heal the body politic, but many Americans reacted with outrage.

On domestic issues Ford proved more conservative than Nixon, vetoing a series of environmental, social-welfare, and public-interest measures, among them a 1974 freedom of information bill granting citizens greater access to government records. The Democratic Congress overrode most of these vetoes.

Economic problems triggered by events abroad occupied Ford's attention. Beginning in 1973, oil prices shot up as a result of an Arab oil embargo (see Chapter 29) and price hikes by the Organization of Petroleum Exporting Countries (OPEC), a thirteen-nation consortium formed in 1960. The effect on the United States, heavily dependent on imported oil, was severe. The soaring cost of gasoline, heating oil, and other petroleum-based products worsened already-serious inflation. Consumer prices rose by 23 percent in 1974–1975. In October 1974 Ford unveiled a program of voluntary restraint dubbed "Whip Inflation Now" (WIN), but prices continued to zoom. When the Federal Reserve Board tried to cool the economy by raising interest rates, a severe recession resulted. Unemployment approached 11 percent by 1975. As tax receipts dropped, the federal deficit increased.

In a dramatic turnaround, Americans seriously tried to curb their energy consumption for the first time since World War II. As they stopped buying Detroit's gas guzzlers, GM, Ford, and Chrysler laid off more than 225,000 workers. Smaller, fuel-efficient imports increased their market share from 17 to 33 percent in the 1970s. Congress set fuel-efficiency standards for automobiles in 1975 and imposed a national speed limit of fifty-five miles per hour.

The national morale suffered another blow in April 1975 when the South Vietnamese government fell, ending two decades of U.S. effort in Vietnam. The TV networks chronicled desperate helicopter evacuations from the roof of the U.S. embassy in Saigon (soon renamed Ho Chi Minh City) as North Vietnamese troops closed in. A few weeks later, when Cambodia seized a U.S. merchant ship, the *Mayagüez*, a frustrated Ford ordered a military rescue. This hasty show of force freed the thirty-nine *Mayagüez* crew members but cost the lives of forty-one U.S. servicemen.

As the nation entered the election year 1976—also the bicentennial of the Declaration of Independence—Americans found little reason for optimism.

The Outsider as Insider: President Jimmy Carter, 1977–1980

Gerald Ford won the Republican nomination in 1976 despite a challenge from former California Governor Ronald Reagan. On the Democratic side, Jimmy Carter, a Georgia peanut grower and former governor, swept the primaries by stressing themes that appealed to post-Vietnam, post-Watergate America. He emphasized his status as a Washington outsider, pledged never to lie to the American people, and avowed his religious faith as a "born-again" Christian. As his running mate Carter chose Minnesota Senator Walter Mondale, a liberal Democrat.

Carter's early lead eroded as voters sensed a certain vagueness in his program, but he won by a narrow margin. The vote broke sharply along class lines: the well-to-do went for Ford; the poor, overwhelmingly for Carter. The Georgian swept the South and received 90 percent of the black vote. While in the long run the conservative backlash against 1960s radicalism would help the Republicans, popular revulsion against Nixon and Watergate temporarily interrupted the Republican advance, providing an opening for the Carter-Mondale ticket.

Underscoring his outsider image, Carter rejected the trappings of what some in Nixon's day had labeled "the imperial presidency." On inauguration day, with his wife and daughter, he walked from the Capitol to the White House. In an echo of Franklin Roosevelt's radio chats, he delivered some of his TV speeches wearing a sweater and seated by a fireplace. To broad public approval, he appointed a number of women and members of minority groups to federal judgeships.

Despite the populist symbolism and gestures of inclusiveness, Carter never framed a clear political philosophy. Liberals and conservatives both claimed him. Intensely private, he relied on young staff members from Georgia and avoided socializing with politicians. "Carter couldn't get the Pledge of Allegiance through Congress," groused one legislator. An intellectual who had worked as a nuclear-submarine engineer after graduating from the U.S. Naval Academy, Carter was at his best when focused on specific problems. His larger political vision, if any, remained unclear. He fought the recession with a tax cut and a modest public-works program, and the unemployment rate dropped to around 5 percent by late 1978. But he sensed the nation's lack of sympathy for

large-scale government initiatives, and offered few proposals to deal with inner-city poverty, the family-farm crisis, the plight of unemployed industrial workers, and other major social problems.

Environmental issues did loom large for Carter, however, just as they did for many Americans. In 1980, in a major victory for environmentalists and for the administration, Congress passed the Alaska Lands Act, which set aside more than 100 million acres of public land in Alaska for parks, wildlife refuges, recreational areas, and national forests, and added twenty-six rivers to the nation's Wild and Scenic River System. Energy companies eager to exploit Alaska's oilfields were deeply unhappy, and laid plans to renew the battle at a later time.

A major environmental crisis during Carter's presidency erupted in Niagara Falls, New York, where for years the Hooker Chemical and Plastics Corporation had dumped tons of waste products in a district known as the Love Canal. In 1953, as the landfill reached capacity, Hooker had covered the site with earth and sold it to the city. Schools, single-family houses, and low-income apartments soon sprang up, but residents complained of odors and strange substances oozing from the ground. In the later 1970s tests confirmed that toxic chemicals, including deadly dioxin, were seeping into basements, polluting the air, and discharging into the Niagara River. Medical researchers found elevated levels of cancer, miscarriages, and birth defects among Love Canal inhabitants.

In 1978 New York's health commissioner declared a medical emergency and closed a school directly over the landfill. A few days later, President Carter authorized federal funds to relocate the families most at risk. In 1980 Carter declared the Love Canal a national emergency, freeing more federal money for relocation and clean-up. The fact that Love Canal lay a few miles from Niagara Falls, once a symbol of America's sublime and unspoiled wilderness, added a level of tragic irony to the situation. Viewed together, the Alaska Lands Act, involving long-term wilderness preservation, and the urgent Love Canal crisis illustrate the complexity of the effort to confront the environmental implications of decades of industrialization and corporate pressures for further development.

Overall, Carter's domestic record proved thin. Congress ignored his proposals for administrative reforms in the civil service and the executive branch of government. His calls for a national health-insurance program, an overhaul of the welfare system, and reform of the income tax laws fell flat. His problems arose from his own political clumsiness, but perhaps even more from the limitations imposed by a conservative electorate in no mood for bold initiatives.

Carter's foreign-policy record was similarly mixed. As a candidate he had urged increased attention to human rights. His secretary of state, Cyrus Vance, worked to combat abuses in Chile, Argentina, Ethiopia, South Africa, and elsewhere. (Human-rights problems in countries allied with the United States, such as South Korea and the Philippines, received less attention.)

In Latin America Carter sought improved relations with Panama. Since 1964, when anti-American riots had rocked Panama, successive administrations had been negotiating a new Panama Canal treaty that would address Panama's grievances. The Carter administration

Abandoned Homes in Love Canal
The Love Canal neighborhood, near Niagara Falls, was evacuated in 1978 as experts found dangerous levels of toxic industrial chemicals in the soil.

completed negotiations on treaties transferring the Panama Canal and the Canal Zone to Panama by 1999. Although these agreements protected U.S. security interests, conservatives attacked them as proof of America's post-Vietnam loss of nerve, and recalled Teddy Roosevelt's bold maneuvers that had brought the canal into existence. But in a rare congressional success, Carter won Senate ratification of the treaties.

In dealing with America's Cold War adversaries China and the Soviet Union, Carter pursued the Nixon-Kissinger strategy of seeking to normalize relations. After China's long-time leader Mao Zedong died in 1976, his successor, Deng Xiaoping, expressed interest in closer links with the United States. Carter responded by restoring full diplomatic relations with Beijing in 1979, thus opening the door to scientific, cultural, and commercial exchanges. Relations with China remained rocky because of that nation's human-rights abuses, but the era of total hostility and diplomatic isolation had ended.

Toward the Soviet Union Carter showed both conciliation and toughness, with toughness ultimately winning out. In a 1979 meeting in Vienna, Carter and the Soviet leader Leonid Brezhnev signed the SALT II treaty, limiting each side's nuclear-weapons arsenals. When Carter sent the treaty to the Senate for ratification, however, advocates of a strong military attacked it for favoring the Soviets. Support for SALT II dissolved entirely in

January 1980 when Russia invaded Afghanistan. The reasons for the invasion were complex, but many Americans viewed it as proof of Moscow's expansionist designs. As U.S.-Soviet relations soured, Carter withdrew SALT II from the Senate and adopted a series of anti-Soviet measures, including a boycott of the 1980 Summer Olympics in Moscow. This hard-line Soviet policy reflected the growing influence of Carter's national security adviser, Polish-born Zbigniew Brzezinski, who advocated a tough stance toward Moscow.

The Middle East: Peace Accords and Hostages

Carter's proudest achievement and his bitterest setbacks came in the Middle East. Despite Henry Kissinger's efforts, a state of war still prevailed between Israel and Egypt. When Egyptian leader Anwar el-Sadat unexpectedly flew to Israel in 1977 to negotiate with Israeli prime minister Menachem Begin, Carter saw an opening. In September 1978 Carter hosted Sadat and Begin at Camp David, the presidential retreat in Maryland. The Camp David Accords that resulted set a timetable for granting greater autonomy to the Palestinians living in the West Bank and Gaza Strip, occupied by Israel since the 1967 war. In March 1979 the two leaders signed a formal peace treaty at the White House.

Carter's hopes for a comprehensive Middle Eastern settlement came to nothing. Despite the Camp David Accords, Israel continued to build Jewish settlements in the occupied territories. The other Arab states rejected the accords, and in 1981 Islamic fundamentalists assassinated Sadat. Tension in the region remained high, and peace seemed as elusive as ever.

A new Middle Eastern crisis erupted in 1979. For years, Iran had been ruled by Shah Mohammed Reza Pahlavi, who headed a harshly repressive but pro-U.S. regime. Iran's Shiite Muslims, inspired by their exiled spiritual head, Ayatollah Ruhollah Khomeini, bitterly opposed the shah's rule. In January 1979, amid rising Shiite unrest, the shah fled Iran. Khomeini returned in triumph, imposed strict Islamic rule, and preached hatred of the United States.

In November, after Carter admitted the shah to the United States for cancer treatment, Khomeini supporters stormed the U.S. embassy in Tehran and seized more than fifty American hostages. Thus began a 444-day ordeal that nearly paralyzed the Carter administration. TV images of blindfolded hostages, anti-American mobs, and U.S. flags being used as garbage bags rubbed American nerves raw. A botched rescue attempt in April 1980 left eight GIs dead. Secretary of State Vance, who

President Jimmy Carter with Egypt's Anwar Sadat at Camp David, 1978

Carter's role in brokering a peace accord between Israel and Egypt was the high point of his presidency. This event was cited as one of the reasons that Carter received the Nobel Peace Prize in 2002.

Iran Hostage Crisis, 1979
As the Iranians staged scenes like this at the U.S. embassy in Tehran for the TV cameras, American frustration soared and President Carter's political fortunes plunged.

had opposed the rescue effort, resigned. Not until January 20, 1981, the day Carter left office, did the Iranian authorities release the hostages.

Troubles and Frustration at the End of Carter's Term

The decade's second oil crisis hit in 1979. When OPEC again boosted oil prices, U.S. gasoline prices edged toward the then-unheard-of level of $1 a gallon. Tempers flared as long lines formed at gas stations. Driven by repeated oil-price hikes, inflation worsened. Prices rose by more than 13 percent in both 1979 and 1980. In 1979 alone, U.S. consumers paid $16.4 billion in added costs related to the oil-price increases. As the Federal Reserve Board battled inflation by raising interest rates, mortgages and business loans became prohibitively expensive. Economic activity stalled, producing "stagflation"—a combination of business stagnation and price inflation. Once again, events abroad directly affected the American home front.

Pondering the crisis, Carter drew a larger lesson: the nation's wasteful energy consumption must give way to a new ethic of conservation. He recognized that two key factors that had buttressed U.S. economic growth—cheap, unlimited energy and the lack of foreign competition—could no longer be counted on. The era of endless expansion was over, he concluded, and the nation must adopt a philosophy of restraint. In 1977 Carter had created a new Department of Energy and proposed an energy bill involving higher oil and gasoline taxes, tax credits for conservation measures, and research on alternative energy resources. Congress had passed a watered-down version of his plan in 1978, and Carter

now decided that tougher energy legislation was needed. But he failed to convince either Congress or the public that he could provide the leadership to resolve either the hostage crisis abroad or the energy crisis at home.

As with Herbert Hoover in the early 1930s, Americans turned against the remote figure in the White House. When Carter's approval rating sagged to 26 percent in the summer of 1979 (lower than Nixon's at the depths of Watergate), he isolated himself at Camp David and then emerged to deliver a TV address that seemed to shift the blame to the American people for their collective "malaise" and "crisis of confidence." A cabinet reshuffle followed, but the whole exercise deepened suspicions that Carter himself was a big part of the problem. In mid-1980, an election year, Carter's approval rating fell to an appalling 23 percent. The Democrats glumly renominated him, but defeat in November loomed.

Carter's sudden emergence in 1976 illustrated how, in the TV era, a relative unknown could bypass party power brokers and win a national following almost overnight. At a moment when Americans longed to see integrity restored to the presidency, he seemed a godsend. Keenly analytical, Carter identified many emerging issues, including the need for environmental protection; energy conservation; and reform of the nation's tax, welfare, and health-care structures.

But in contrast to Franklin Roosevelt and Lyndon Johnson, he lacked the political skills to build a consensus around the solutions he believed necessary. A post-presidential career devoted to humanitarian service and international conflict-resolution restored Carter's reputation, and brought him the Nobel Peace Prize in 2002. But when he left office in January 1981, few expressed regrets.

THE REAGAN REVOLUTION, 1981–1984

In 1980, with the conservative backlash against the 1960s in full swing, voters turned to a candidate who promised to break with the recent past: Ronald Reagan. His unabashed patriotism appealed to a nation still traumatized by Vietnam. His promise to reverse the Democrats' "tax and spend" policies and his attacks on the social-welfare ideology of the New Deal, the Fair Deal, and the Great Society resonated with millions of white middle-class and blue-collar Americans.

As president, Reagan called for a renewal of patriotism. His economic policies at first brought on a recession, but eventually lowered inflation and triggered consumer buying and a stock-market boom. These same policies caused economic difficulties after his departure. In his first term Reagan unleashed blasts of belligerent Cold War rhetoric, pursued the arms race with the Soviets, and financed guerrilla forces in Latin America seeking to overthrow leftist regimes. He also confronted crises in the Middle East and elsewhere that did not readily fit into his Cold War world view.

Background of the Reagan Revolution

What underlay Reagan's appeal? First, voters frightened by the prospect of chronic stagflation were drawn to his seemingly painless panacea: a big tax cut that would stimulate the economy. This in turn would boost tax revenues so the budget could be balanced, reducing inflationary pressures. George Bush, Reagan's rival for the Republican nomination, ridiculed this plan as "voodoo economics," but it impressed many voters. Moreover, Reagan's tributes to self-help and private enterprise appealed to many as an alternative to the New Deal-Great Society ideology of government activism. His uncomplicated patriotism, calls for military strength, and praise of America's greatness soothed the battered national psyche.

Reagan also embraced the cultural conservatism of the so-called New Right, which included millions of religious evangelicals. The social unrest and sexual revolution of the 1960s; the women's movement; rising abortion and divorce rates; the open celebration of homosexuality; the pervasiveness of sex and violence in the media; court rulings against prayer in the classroom; and "secular humanism" in school textbooks all upset Americans who longed for clear-cut moral standards and a return to "traditional values."

Jerry Falwell and others eagerly translated such concerns into political action. Falwell's pro-Reagan Moral Majority registered an estimated 2 million new voters in 1980 and 1984. The organization disbanded after 1984, but Pat Robertson's Christian Coalition took its place, mobilizing conservative Christians to elect candidates to town councils and school boards as a prelude to expanded national influence. Reagan also benefited from the erosion of Democratic strength in the South fostered earlier by George Wallace and Richard Nixon.

Demographics contributed to Reagan's success. While New York City, Chicago, Detroit, and other Democratic strongholds in the Northeast and Midwest lost population in the 1970s, Texas, California, Florida, and other historically conservative Sunbelt states gained population. In 1978 Californians passed Proposition 13, a referendum calling for deep tax cuts. Elsewhere in the West, ranchers and developers demanded a return of federal lands to state control.

Reagan, a skillful actor and seasoned public speaker, combined these themes into a potent message. Belying his sixty-nine years, he conveyed a youthful vigor. At a time of national malaise, he seemed to offer confident, assured leadership. Critics found him superficial and his ideology selfish and mean-spirited, and time would reveal gaps between substance and image in Reagan's appeal, but in 1980 a majority of voters found him irresistible.

Reagan grew up in Dixon, Illinois, the son of an alcoholic father and a pious mother active in a fundamentalist church. After finishing college he announced sports events for a Des Moines radio station and in 1937 moved to Hollywood. His fifty-four films proved forgettable, but he gained political experience as president of the Screen Actors' Guild. A New Dealer in the 1930s, Reagan had moved to the right in the 1950s, and in 1954 he became a corporate spokesman for the General Electric Company. In a 1964 TV speech for presidential candidate Barry Goldwater, he passionately praised American individualism and the free-enterprise system.

Elected governor of California in 1966 with the help of a group of California millionaires, Reagan continued to popularize conservative ideas while taking a tough line against campus demonstrators. He nearly won the Republican presidential nomination in 1976, and in 1980 he easily disposed of his principal opponent, George Bush, whom he then chose as his running mate. Like his one-time political hero Franklin Roosevelt, Reagan promised the American people a new deal. But unlike FDR, Reagan's new deal meant smaller govern-

The Rev. Pat Robertson
Head of the Christian Broadcasting Network
(CBN) and founder of the Christian Coalition, Robertson helped mobilize
evangelical Christians politically in the 1980s and beyond.

MAP 30.1
The Election of 1980
Jimmy Carter's unpopularity and Ronald Reagan's telegenic
appeal combined to give Reagan a crushing electoral victory.

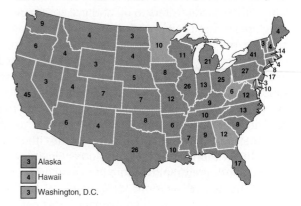

		Electoral Vote	Popular Vote	Percentage of Popular Vote
Republican Ronald Reagan		489	43,899,248	50.8
Democratic Jimmy Carter		49	35,481,435	41.0
Independent John B. Anderson		–	5,719,437	6.6
Minor parties		–	1,395,558	1.6

ment, reduced taxes and spending, and untrammeled free enterprise.

Hammering at the question "Are you better off now than you were four years ago?" Reagan garnered 51 percent of the popular vote to Carter's 41 percent (see Map 30.1). (An independent candidate, liberal Republican John Anderson, collected most of the balance.) Republicans gained eleven Senate seats, and with them, for the first time since 1955, a majority. These Senate victories revealed the power of conservative political action committees (PACs), which used computerized mass mailings focusing on emotional issues like abortion and gun control. (PACs were not confined to conservatives; organizations of all ideological stripes used them.)

Reaping the benefits of Nixon's southern strategy, Reagan carried every southern state except Carter's own Georgia as well as every state west of the Mississippi except Minnesota and Hawaii. Over half the nation's blue-collar workers voted Republican. Of FDR's New Deal political alliance, only black voters remained firmly Democratic.

Reaganomics

The new president's economic program, called Reaganomics by the media, boiled down to the belief that U.S. capitalism, if freed from heavy taxes and government regulation, would achieve wonders of productivity. Reagan's first budget message proposed a 30 per-

cent reduction in federal income taxes over three years. Trimming this proposal slightly, Congress voted a 25 percent income tax cut: 5 percent in 1981 and 10 percent in 1982 and 1983.

To make up the lost revenues, Reagan proposed massive cuts in such programs as school lunches, student loans, job training, and urban mass transit. Congress cut less than Reagan wanted, but it did slash more than $40 billion from domestic spending. Conservative southern Democrats, nicknamed boll weevils, joined Republicans in voting these cuts. Journalists harked back to FDR's Hundred Days of 1933 to find a time when government had shifted gears so dramatically. Economists warned that the tax cut would produce huge federal deficits, but Reagan insisted that lower tax rates would stimulate business growth and thereby push up total tax revenues.

Reaganomics also involved drastic cutbacks in federal regulation of business. Deregulation had begun under Carter, but Reagan extended it into new areas such as banking, the savings-and-loan industry, transportation, and communications. The head of the Federal Communications Commission hacked away at federal rules governing the broadcast industry. The secretary of transportation cut back on regulations Congress had

passed in the 1970s to reduce air pollution and improve vehicle efficiency and safety.

Secretary of the Interior James Watt of Wyoming worked tirelessly to open federal wilderness areas, forest lands, and coastal waters to oil and gas companies and developers; undermine endangered-species programs; and cut programs to protect environmentally threatened regions. Before coming to Washington, Watt had headed the Mountain States Legal Foundation which spearheaded the so-called Sagebrush Rebellion of western conservatives seeking to open public lands to private development (see Map 30.2). In response to Watt's extreme anti-environmentalist positions, the Sierra Club, the Wilderness Society, and other environmental organizations grew rapidly. More than a million environmentalists signed petitions demanding Watt's ouster. After a series of public-relations gaffes and comments offensive to various groups, Watt resigned in 1983.

Although the Reagan administration's attack on "big government" affected certain federal functions, particularly in the regulatory and environmental realm, it had little overall effect. The century-long growth of the federal government's budget and bureaucracy continued in the 1980s.

While implementing Reaganomics, the administration also faced the immediate problem of inflation. The Federal Reserve Board led the charge, pushing interest rates ever higher. This harsh medicine, coupled with a drop in oil prices, did its job. Inflation fell to around 4 percent in 1983 and held steady thereafter.

Recession and Boom Times

The high interest rates necessary to curb inflation soon brought on a recession. By late 1982 unemployment stood at 10 percent. As funding for social programs dried up, the plight of the poor worsened. Inner-city blacks and Hispanics suffered severely. The Reagan recession also contributed to falling exports. As foreign investors bought dollars to earn high U.S. interest rates, the dollar rose in value vis-à-vis foreign currencies, making U.S. goods more expensive abroad. With exports declining and U.S. consumers buying TVs, stereos, and automobiles made in Japan and other countries, the U.S. trade deficit (the gap between exports and imports) more than tripled in the early 1980s, reaching a whopping $111 billion in 1984.

The industrial heartland reeled under the triple blows of slumping exports, foreign competition, and technological obsolescence. The hard-hit auto plants, aging steel mills, and other industries of the Midwest laid off hordes of workers, and many plants closed. In 1979–1983, 11.5 million U.S. workers lost jobs as a result of plant closings and slack work. Farmers suffered as well. Wheat exports fell 38 percent from 1980 to 1985, and corn exports by 49 percent. In foreclosure sales evocative of the 1930s, still more family farms vanished.

Soaring federal deficits added to the economic muddle. Reagan's tax cuts reduced federal revenues without immediately producing the predicted business boom, while soaring military appropriations far exceeded domestic spending cuts. With the economy sputtering, budget deficits mounting, and critics denouncing him as callous toward the poor, Reagan in 1982–1983 accepted a reduced rate of military spending, a slowing of funding cuts in social programs, new emergency job programs, and various tax increases disguised as "revenue-enhancement measures."

Despite a stock-market upturn, the economy remained worrisome through 1982. In the elections that fall, the Democrats gained twenty-six House seats. Like other recent presidents, Reagan appeared headed for failure. But 1983 brought an economic rebound. Encouraged by tax cuts, falling interest rates, and evidence that inflation had been tamed at last, consumers went on a buying binge; unemployment dropped; and Reagan's popularity revived.

With better times came a wave of stock-market speculation reminiscent of the 1920s. The bull market began in August 1982, and it lasted for five years. Entrepreneurs like Donald Trump, a Manhattan real-estate tycoon, and Ivan Boesky, an apparent genius at stock transactions, became celebrities. E. F. Hutton and other brokerage firms advertised heavily to lure new investors. Corporate mergers proliferated. Chevron bought Gulf for $13 billion in 1984; GE acquired RCA (and its NBC subsidiary) for $6.3 billion in 1986. The stock market roared on. Banks and savings-and-loan companies, newly deregulated and flush with the deposits of eager investors, ladled out billions to developers planning shopping malls, luxury apartments, condominiums, retirement villages, and office buildings.

The Wall Street frenzy had a downside. In 1985 E. F. Hutton officials pled guilty to the illegal manipulation of funds. Ivan Boesky went to prison after a 1986 conviction for insider trading (profiting through advance knowledge of corporate actions). On October 19, 1987, the stock market crashed. The Dow Jones Industrial Average, a leading indicator of stock prices, plunged 508 points as one-fifth of the paper value of the nation's stocks evaporated. Thanks to prompt government action to ease credit, the market soon recovered, but the collapse reminded giddy investors that stocks can go down as well as up.

MAP 30.2 Land Ownership in the West

From national parks and forests to hydroelectric facilities and military test sites, the federal government's vast holdings in the West helped shape the politics of the region. *Source:* Time, Inc. Copyright © 2001. Reprinted with permission.

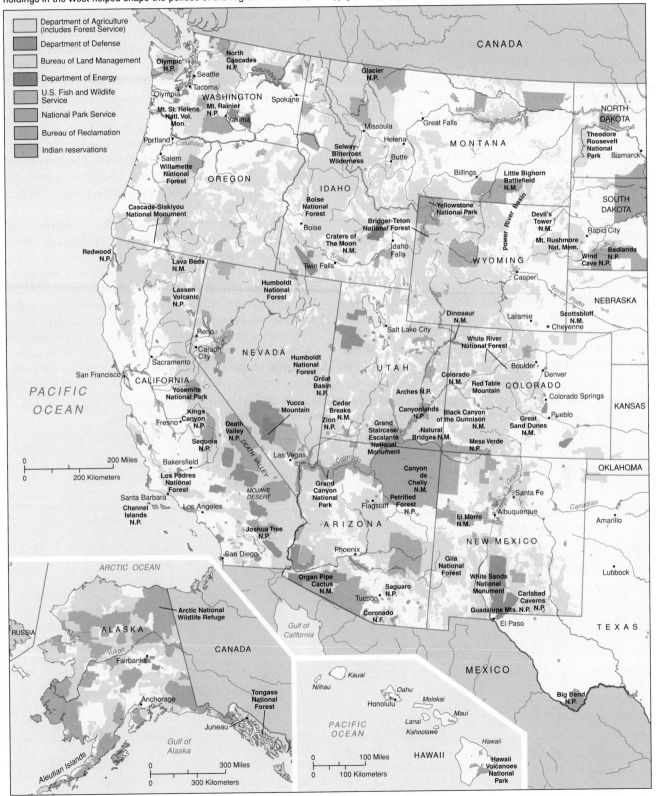

Even during the great bull market, economic problems persisted. The trade gap widened; the deficit passed $200 billion in 1986; and many farmers, inner-city poor, recent immigrants, and displaced industrial workers suffered through the boom times. But by 1988—just in time for Reagan's reelection campaign—the overall economic picture looked brighter than it had in years.

Reagan Confronts the "Evil Empire" and Crises in the Middle East

The anti-Soviet rhetoric of the late 1970s intensified during Reagan's first term. Addressing a convention of Protestant evangelicals, the president demonized the Soviet Union as "the focus of evil in the modern world." Anti-Soviet fury exploded in September 1983 when the Russians shot down a Korean passenger plane that had strayed into their airspace, killing all 269 aboard. Moscow claimed that the plane had been spying, but later abandoned this excuse.

The administration's anti-Soviet obsession influenced its policy toward El Salvador and Nicaragua, two desperately poor Central American nations caught up in revolutionary turmoil (see Map 30.3). The Reagan White House backed the Salvadoran military junta in its brutal suppression of a leftist insurgency supported by Fidel Castro's Cuba. A U.S.-backed moderate won the 1984 presidential election in El Salvador, but the killing of the regime's opponents went on.

In Nicaragua, the Carter administration had initially granted aid to the Sandinista revolutionaries who overthrew dictator Anastasio Somoza in 1979. Reagan reversed this policy, claiming that the leftist Sandinistas were turning Nicaragua into a procommunist state like Castro's Cuba. In 1982 the CIA organized and financed a ten-thousand-man anti-Sandinista guerrilla army, called the contras, based in neighboring Honduras and Costa Rica. The contras, many of whom were linked to the hated Somoza regime, conducted raids, planted mines, and carried out sabotage inside Nicaragua. This U.S.-financed guerrilla campaign took a heavy toll of civilian lives.

For Reagan, the campaign to overthrow the Sandinistas and to control events in Latin America became an obsession. "The national security of all the Americas is at stake," he somberly told a joint session of Congress in May 1983; "... if we cannot defend ourselves there, we cannot expect to prevail elsewhere. . . and the safety of our homeland would be put at jeopardy."

Fearing another Vietnam, Americans grew alarmed as details of this U.S.-run "covert" war leaked out. Congress voted a yearlong halt in U.S. military aid to the

MAP 30.3   The United States in Latin America and the Caribbean   Plagued by poverty, population pressures, repressive regimes, and drug trafficking, Latin America saw turmoil and conflict—but also some hopeful developments—in the 1980s and 1990s.

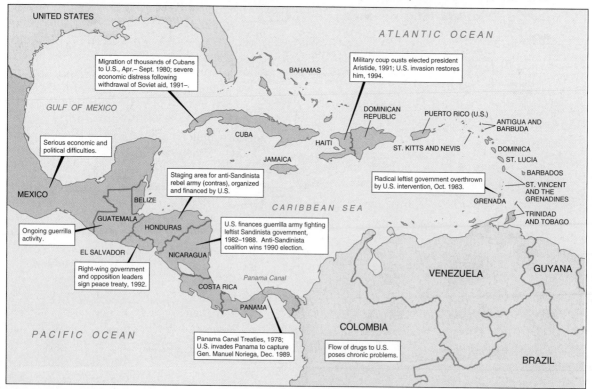

contras in December 1982 and imposed a two-year ban in 1984. Reagan's enthusiasm for the contras held steady. Despite congressional prohibitions, the White House continued to funnel money contributed by foreign governments and right-wing groups in the United States to the contras. Reagan grudgingly backed a 1988 truce between the Sandinistas and the contras arranged by Central American leaders, but he still hoped for a contra victory.

Reagan's militarization of U.S. foreign policy fell heavily on the tiny West Indian island of Grenada, where a 1983 coup had installed a radical leftist government. In October 1983 two thousand U.S. marines invaded Grenada and set up a pro-U.S. government. Democrats voiced sharp criticism, but most Grenadians, as well as other West Indian governments, approved.

The continuing turmoil and conflict in the Middle East that had so frustrated President Carter also preoccupied the Reagan administration. Hoping to slow the spread of Islamic fundamentalism, the United States tilted toward Saddam Hussein's Iraq in its eight-year war with Iran (1980–1988), which resulted in an estimated 1.5 million casualties, devastated both nations' economies, and created millions of refugees.

Meanwhile, the conflict among Israel, the Palestinians, and Israel's Arab foes dragged on. The United States had vital interests in the region. Many Americans felt a deep emotional bond with Israel, and each year the United States gave Israel large grants in military aid and other assistance. At the same time, the United States also gave extensive aid to Egypt and relied heavily on oil from Saudi Arabia and other Arab states, some of which were violently anti-Israel. Despite or because of these conflicting pressures, successive U.S. administrations proved unable to achieve peace in the region, and the Reagan administration was no more successful than the others.

In 1981 Israel and the Palestine Liberation Organization (PLO) concluded a cease-fire. But the PLO continued building up forces at its base in southern Lebanon. In June 1982, when an extremist faction within the PLO shot and critically wounded Israel's ambassador to Great Britain, Israeli troops under General Ariel Sharon, Israel's defense minister, invaded Lebanon, defeated the PLO, and forced its leaders, including chairman Yasir Arafat, to evacuate Lebanon. The invasion intensified conflicts among Lebanon's various Christian and Muslim factions. With Sharon's approval, a Lebanese Christian militia force entered two Palestinian refugee camps near Beirut to root out armed gunmen. Instead, in revenge for the assassinatin of Lebanon's Christian president a few days earlier, they massacred as many as 700-800 camp residents, including women and children. An Israeli commission of inquiry found Sharon negligent for permitting the militiamen to enter the camp and recommended his dismissal, but found no evidence that Sharon knew of the planned massacre in advance. Sharon resigned as defense minister, but remained in the government.

After the Beirut massacre, President Reagan ordered two thousand marines to Lebanon as part of a multinational peacekeeping force. The Muslim militias saw the Americans as favoring Israel and the Christian side, and in October 1983 a Shiite Muslim on a suicide mission crashed an explosive-laden truck into a poorly guarded U.S. barracks, killing 239 marines. Reagan had never clearly explained how the deployment served U.S. interests, and the disaster further discredited his policy. In early 1984 he withdrew the surviving marines.

Reagan's efforts to promote a wider Middle East peace settlement proved equally ineffective. In September 1982 he tried to use the Lebanese crisis to jump-start Arab-Israeli peace talks based on the 1978 Camp David Accords. This effort failed, like others before it.

Military Buildup and Antinuclear Protest

Insisting that the United States had grown dangerously weak since the end of the war in Vietnam, Reagan launched a massive military expansion. The Pentagon's budget nearly doubled, reaching more than $300 billion by 1985. Later, after the Cold War ended, Reagan's supporters would claim that Moscow's efforts to match Reagan's military buildup was the final blow to an already faltering Soviet economy. Others, however, traced the Soviet collapse primarily to structural weaknesses within the USSR itself.

The military buildup included nuclear weapons. Secretary of State Alexander Haig spoke of the utility of "nuclear warning shots" in a conventional war, and other administration officials mused about the "winnability" of nuclear war. Despite popular protests across Europe, the administration deployed 572 nuclear-armed missiles in Western Europe in 1983, fulfilling a NATO decision to counterbalance Soviet missiles in Eastern Europe. The Federal Emergency Management Agency issued a nuclear-war defense plan whereby city residents would flee to nearby small towns. A Defense Department official argued that backyard shelters would provide protection in a nuclear war. "With enough shovels," he asserted, "everybody's going to make it."

Such talk, coupled with the military buildup and Reagan's anti-Soviet rhetoric, convinced many Americans that a serious threat of nuclear war existed. A campaign for a freeze on the manufacture and deployment of nuclear weapons won strong support. Antinuclear protesters packed New York's Central Park in June 1982. That November, voters in nine states, including California and Wisconsin, approved nuclear-freeze resolutions.

To counter the freeze campaign, Reagan in March 1983 proposed the Strategic Defense Initiative (SDI), a system of space-based lasers and other high-tech defenses against nuclear missiles that critics quickly dubbed Star Wars. Even though skeptics warned of the project's monumental technical hurdles and the danger that it would further escalate the nuclear-arms race, the Pentagon launched a costly SDI research program.

Reagan Reelected

As the 1984 election neared, liberal Democrats and many independents criticized the Reagan presidency for runaway military spending, Cold War belligerence, massive budget deficits, cuts in social programs, and assaults on the government's regulatory powers. To critics, jingoism abroad and selfishness at home summed up the meaning of *Reaganism*.

But many Americans applauded Reagan's attacks on big government and his tough policy toward the Soviets. Rhetoric aside, the administration had some solid achievements to its credit, a booming economy and notably an end to rampant inflation. Reagan's personal popularity remained high. Some dubbed him the Teflon president—nothing seemed to stick to him. Feminists welcomed his 1981 nomination of Sandra Day O'Connor as the first woman justice on the U.S. Supreme Court. Americans admired his jaunty response when a ricocheting bullet fired by a deranged young man struck him in the chest as he left a Washington hotel in March 1981. Rushed to the hospital, Reagan walked in under his own steam, quipping to the physicians, "Please tell me you're all Republicans." (The attack disabled Reagan's press secretary, James Brady, who with his wife Sarah later became leaders of the campaign for stricter gun-control laws.) By 1984 many citizens believed that Reagan had fulfilled his promise to revitalize the free-enterprise system, rebuild U.S. military might, and make America again "stand tall" in the world. The 1984 Republican convention, staged for TV, accented themes of patriotism, prosperity, and the personality of Ronald Reagan.

The Democratic hopefuls included Gary Hart, a former Colorado senator, and Jesse Jackson, a Chicago black leader who proposed a "rainbow coalition" of African-Americans, Hispanics, displaced workers, and other outsiders. But former vice president Walter Mondale won the nomination with backing from labor unions, party bigwigs, and various interest groups. His vice-presidential choice, New York congresswoman Geraldine Ferraro, became the first woman to run on a major-party presidential ticket.

Reagan and Bush won 59 percent of the popular vote and carried every state but Mondale's Minnesota and the District of Columbia. Many traditionally Democratic voters, especially blue-collar workers, again defected to Reagan. Despite Ferraro's presence on the Democratic ticket, a higher percentage of women voted Republican in 1984 than in 1980. Reagan's ideological appeal and his mastery of TV, combined with prosperity, had carried the day. Though the Democrats retained control of Congress and remained strong at the state and local levels, the Republicans' post-1968 dominance of the White House—interrupted only by Jimmy Carter's single term—continued.

Some frustrated Democrats sought to reverse their image as a "big government" and "tax-and-spend" party dominated by special-interest groups. In 1985 Arkansas governor Bill Clinton and Senators Al Gore of Tennessee, Joseph Lieberman of Connecticut, and John Breaux of Louisiana, along with others, formed the Democratic Leadership Council (DLC) to stake out a more centrist party position. In the early 1990s Clinton would use his chairmanship of the DLC as a springboard for a presidential bid.

A SEA OF PROBLEMS IN REAGAN'S SECOND TERM, 1985–1989

In his first term, Ronald Reagan had set the political agenda: tax cuts, deregulation, and more military spending. His second term, by contrast, was dominated by economic problems and by events linked to foreign affairs. In 1986 the so-called Iran-contra scandal erupted, caused by Reagan's stubborn determination to pursue his objectives in Latin America by secret means despite congressional prohibitions. Reagan's historic trip to Moscow in 1988 marked a dramatic easing of Cold War tensions, but continued conflict in the Middle East and a wave of terrorist bombings made clear that even if the Cold War ended, the world would remain a dangerous place.

Budget Deficits and Trade Gaps

Reagan's second term brought some legislative achievements, including the Immigration Reform and Control Act of 1986, discussed earlier, and a tax-reform law that made the system fairer by eliminating many deductions and establishing uniform rates for taxpayers at comparable income levels. The law removed some 6 million low-income Americans from the income-tax rolls as well. Reagan also reshaped the Supreme Court and the federal judiciary in his own conservative image.

But sky-high federal deficits—the legacy of Reaganomics—grew worse. The deficit surged to over $200 billion in 1985 and 1986, and hovered at about $150 billion for the next two years. This, coupled with the yawning trade gap, were Reagan's principal economic legacies to his successor.

Issues related to foreign policy dominated Reagan's second term. His domestic record would rest on the tax cuts, deregulation, and other legislative initiatives of his first term.

The Iran-Contra Affair and Other Scandals

The worst scandal to hit the Reagan presidency arose from the administration's efforts to control events in Latin America, a perennial temptation for U.S. presidents. Late in 1986 a Beirut newspaper reported the shocking news that in 1985 the United States had shipped, via Israel, 508 antitank missiles to the anti-American government of Iran. Admitting the sale, Reagan claimed that the goal had been to encourage "moderate elements" in Tehran and to gain the release of U.S. hostages held in Lebanon by pro-Iranian groups. In February 1987 a presidentially appointed investigative panel placed heavy blame on Reagan's chief of staff, Donald Regan, who resigned.

More details soon spilled out, including the explosive revelation that Lieutenant Colonel Oliver North, a National Security Council aide in the White House, had secretly diverted the profits from the Iran arms sales to the Nicaraguan contras at a time when Congress had forbidden such aid. In November 1986, a step ahead of FBI agents, North and his secretary had altered and deleted sensitive computer files and destroyed incriminating documents. North implicated CIA Director William Casey in illegalities, but Casey's death thwarted this line of investigation.

In May 1987 a joint House-Senate investigative committee opened televised hearings on the scandal.

The nation watched in fascination as "Ollie" North, resplendent in his marine uniform, boasted of his patriotism, and as Reagan's national security adviser, Admiral John Poindexter, testified that he had deliberately concealed the fund-diversion scheme from the president.

In some ways the scandal seemed a sickening replay of the Watergate crisis of 1974. The committee found no positive proof of Reagan's knowledge of illegalities, but roundly criticized the lax management style and contempt for the law that had pervaded the Reagan White House. In 1989, after his indictment by a special prosecutor, North was convicted of obstructing a congressional inquiry and destroying and falsifying official documents. (The conviction was later reversed on the technicality that some testimony used against North had been given under a promise of immunity.) Although less damaging than Watergate, the Iran-contra scandal dogged the Reagan administration's final years as a gross abuse of executive power in a zealous campaign to overthrow a Latin American government the administration found objectionable.

Other unsavory revelations plagued Reagan's second term, including allegations of bribery and conspiracy in military-procurement contracts. Reagan's California friend Edwin Meese resigned as attorney general in 1988 amid charges that he had used his influence to promote ventures in which he had a financial interest. In 1989 came revelations that former Interior Secretary James Watt and other prominent Republicans had been paid hundreds of thousands of dollars for using their influence on behalf of housing developers seeking federal subsidies.

Reagan's personal popularity seemed unaffected by all this dirty linen. Drawing on his training as an actor, he possessed an uncanny ability to communicate warmth and sincerity and to shrug off damaging revelations with a disarming joke. Moreover, Reagan benefited from an unanticipated turn of events abroad that would end his presidency on a note of triumph.

Reagan's Mission to Moscow

A dramatic warming of Soviet-American relations began early in Reagan's second term. At meetings in Switzerland and Iceland in 1985 and 1986, Reagan and Soviet leader Mikhail Gorbachev revived the stalled arms-control process. Beset by economic problems, Gorbachev pursued an easing of superpower tensions to gain breathing space for domestic reform.

In 1987 the two leaders signed the Intermediate-range Nuclear Forces (INF) Treaty, providing for the

President Reagan Visits Red Square
As the Cold War crumbled, President Reagan flew to Moscow in 1988 to sign a nuclear-arms reduction treaty with Soviet premier Mikhail Gorbachev.

removal of twenty-five hundred U.S. and Soviet missiles from Europe (see Table 30.1). This treaty, for the first time, eliminated an entire class of existing nuclear weapons rather than merely limiting the number of future weapons as SALT I had done. It, in turn, led to Reagan's historic visit to Moscow in May 1988, where the two leaders strolled and chatted in Red Square, in front of the Kremlin.

Some of Reagan's supporters were dismayed as their hero, having denounced the Soviet Union as an "evil empire" five years before, now cozied up to the world's top communist. One conservative paper, *The Manchester* [New Hampshire] *Union-Leader*, called Reagan's trip "a sad week for the free world." Reagan himself, with his usual breezy good humor, pointed to changes in Soviet policy and argued that "the evil empire" was becoming more benign. Most Americans welcomed improved relations with the long-time Cold War enemy.

Historic in themselves, the INF treaty and Reagan's trip to Moscow proved a mere prelude to more dramatic events. They marked, in fact, nothing less than the beginning of the end of the Cold War. That one of America's most dedicated Cold Warriors should be the president to preside over its final phase remains one of the great ironies of recent U.S. history.

TABLE 30.1   Milestones in Nuclear-Arms Control

Year	Event	Provisions
1963	Limited Test Ban Treaty	Prohibits atmospheric, underwater, and outer-space nuclear testing.
1967	Outer Space Treaty	Prohibits weapons of mass destruction and arms testing in space.
1968	Non-Proliferation Treaty	Promotes peaceful international uses of nuclear energy; aims to stop the global proliferation of nuclear weaponry.
1972	Strategic Arms Limitation Treaty (SALT I)	Limits for five years U.S. and Soviet deployment of strategic weapons systems.
	Anti-Ballistic Missile (ABM) Treaty	Restricts U.S. and Soviet testing and deployment of defensive systems. (Allowed to expire, 2002.)
1974	Threshold Test Ban Treaty	Establishes limits on size of underground tests.
1979	Strategic Arms Limitation Treaty (SALT II)	Limits strategic launch vehicles and delivery craft and restricts the development of new missiles. (The treaty was never ratified, but the United States and the Soviet Union observed its terms.)
1982	Strategic Arms Reduction Talks (START)	Sought a 50 percent reduction in U.S. and Soviet strategic nuclear weapons.
1988	Intermediate-range Nuclear Forces (INF) Treaty	Commits the United States and the Soviet Union to withdraw their intermediate-range nuclear missiles from Eastern and Western Europe and to destroy them.
1991	START Treaty	Provides for a 25 percent cut in U.S. and Soviet strategic nuclear weapons.
2002	Treaty on Strategic Offensive Reduction.	Requires deep cuts in number of U.S. and Soviet nuclear warheads by 2012.

The Dangerous Middle East: Continued Tension and Terrorism

As relations with Moscow improved in Reagan's second term, the situation in the Middle East worsened. In 1987 Palestinians in Gaza and the West Bank rose up against Israeli occupation. In response, Secretary of State George Shultz tried to start talks among Israel, the Palestinians, and Jordan on a plan for Palestinian autonomy. Israel refused to negotiate until the uprising ended, and the Palestinians rejected Shultz's proposals as not going far enough toward creating a Palestinian state. Despite U.S. opposition, Israel continued to build settlements in the disputed West Bank region.

A deadly by-product of the Middle East conflict was a series of bombings, kidnappings, assassinations, airplane hijackings, and other attacks linked to Palestinian terrorists (or "freedom fighters," as the Palestinians called them) and their backers in the Arab world. In 1985 terrorists set off deadly bombs in the Vienna and Rome airports and hijacked a TWA flight en route to Rome from Athens, holding the crew and 145 passengers hostage for seventeen days and murdering a U.S. sailor among the passengers. That same year, four heavily armed PLO members demanding the release of Palestinian prisoners held by Israel hijacked an Italian cruise ship, the *Achille Lauro*, dumping a wheelchair-bound Jewish-American tourist into the sea. In 1986 two GIs died and many were injured in the bombing of a Berlin disco club popular with U.S. troops.

Accusing Libyan strongman Muammar el-Qadaffi of masterminding the Berlin bombing and other terrorist attacks, Reagan ordered U.S. bombers to hit Libyan military sites in 1986. But the cycle of large-scale and small-scale terrorist attacks continued, reaching more than one thousand in 1988. In the worst attack, Pan Am flight 103 from London to New York crashed in December 1988 near Lockerbie, Scotland, killing all 259 aboard, including many Americans. Experts quickly identified a concealed bomb as the cause. In 1991 the United States and Great Britain brought formal charges against Libya for the attack. After years of stalling, Qaddafi allowed two accused Libyan officials to be extradited and face trial in 1999. In 2001 a special Scottish court sitting in the Netherlands acquitted one of the men but found the other guilty of murder and imposed a life sentence.

This cycle of terrorism, which would continue well beyond the 1980s, was a by-product of festering tensions in the Middle East. Hatred of Israel, and even the belief that the Jewish state had no right to exist, gripped parts of the Arab world, particularly the Islamic fundamentalists who appeared to be growing in numbers and influ-

Pan Am Flight 103 Ends in Tragedy
The destruction of this plane by a concealed bomb over Scotland in 1988, with a heavy loss of life, was one of a wave of terrorist incidents in these years.

ence as the century ended. The Palestinian leader Yasir Arafat bore responsibility as well, for repeated failures of leadership and missed opportunities. The continued building of Israeli settlements in the Palestinian territories also contributed to the climate of hopelessness and resentment that helped spawn terrorist attacks.

In a global context, then, Reagan's term ended on a note of deep uncertainty. The easing of Cold War tensions offered hope of a more peaceful and secure future. Yet the rising tempo of surprise attacks by shadowy terrorist groups pointed to a future that, in its way, threatened to be as dangerous and unsettling as the Cold War itself.

Assessing the Reagan Years

After Nixon's disgrace, Ford's caretaker presidency, and Carter's rocky tenure, Ronald Reagan's two full terms helped restore a sense of stability and continuity to U.S. politics. Domestically Reagan compiled a mixed record. Inflation was tamed, and the economy turned upward after 1983. But the federal deficit soared, and the administration largely ignored festering social issues, environmental concerns, and long-term economic problems.

Reagan's critics, stressing the Hollywood aspects of his presidency, dismissed his two terms as more an interlude of nostalgia and drift than of positive achievement—a time when self-interest trumped the public good. Critics pointed out how readily Reagan's celebration of individual freedom translated into self-centered

materialism and a callousness disregard of social injustice. Apart from anticommunism, a military buildup, and flag waving, they contended, Reagan offered few goals around which the nation as a whole could rally.

The critics gained an unexpected ally from the Reagan inner circle in 1988 when former Chief of Staff Donald Regan, still smarting over his forced resignation during the Iran-contra scandal, published a memoir of his White House years that portrayed the president as little more than an automaton: "Every moment of every public appearance was scheduled, every word was scripted, every place where Reagan was expected to stand was chalked with toe marks."

To his admirers, such criticism was beside the point. They felt that Reagan deserved high marks for reasserting traditional values of self-reliance and free enterprise; contributing to America's Cold War victory through his military buildup; and, with his infectious optimism and patriotism, helping restore national pride.

On the international front, Reagan's aggressive anti-communism dragged his administration into the swamp of the Iran-contra scandal. But he had the good fortune to hold office as the Cold War thawed and the Soviet menace eased. By the end of his term, détente, derailed in the late 1970s, was barreling ahead. The shadow world of international terrorism, however, which announced itself with assassinations, exploding bombs, and crashing airplanes, signaled new global challenges ahead. In his post-presidential years, as Reagan himself lived on in a twilight realm darkened by Alzheimer's disease, "the Reagan revolution" continued in some ways to define the terms of contemporary American politics.

CONCLUSION

U.S. culture in the 1970s and 1980s revealed contradictory tendencies. On one hand, in reaction against the turmoil of the 1960s, movies, TV, and popular music provided escapism; and many middle-class citizens turned to personal pursuits and careerist goals. But at the same time, activist energies rooted in the 1960s found expression in a revived women's movement, a gay-rights campaign, and support for environmental causes. As a conservative backlash gained momentum, this activism also stirred vigorous opposition. Amid a resurgence of evangelical religion, conservatives organized politically to achieve their vision of a better America.

On the social and economic fronts, these years saw equally divergent tendencies. In the 1970s rising oil prices brought simultaneous stagnation and inflation that soured the national mood and shadowed the presidencies of Gerald Ford and Jimmy Carter. The 1980s, though bracketed by recessions (see Chapter 31), brought a boom that suffused parts of Reagan's America with a glow of prosperity. Millions of Americans, however, mostly in the inner cities and mostly darker-skinned minorities, seemed permanently frozen out of a high-tech economy that increasingly demanded education and specialized skills. Family farms proved unable to compete with large agribusinesses. Many African Americans entered the ranks of the middle class and the professions, but a large minority remained trapped in poverty. Native Americans faced continuing deprivation but also new economic opportunities and the prospect of benefiting from long-ignored treaty rights. Throughout the era growing immigration from Latin America and Asia reshaped the nation's ethnic and demographic profile.

Internationally, Ford, Carter, and Reagan all grappled with a rapidly changing world in which solutions seemed maddeningly elusive. U.S.-Soviet relations worsened in the late 1970s and early 1980s, but improved dramatically in Reagan's second term. Economic and social problems in the Soviet Union—perhaps hastened by Reagan's heavy defense spending—signaled nothing less than the end of the Cold War, an amazing and largely unanticipated development that would fully unfold during the presidency of Reagan's successor, George Bush.

Brightening prospects on one front were matched by heightened menace elsewhere. The Middle East, in particular, riven by ancient conflicts, brought moments of illusory hope interspersed with frustration and tragedy. As the 1980s ended, a rising tempo of terrorist attacks suggested that the nation was entering a period no less dangerous, in its own way, than that which Americans had faced during the darkest days of the Cold War.

FOR FURTHER REFERENCE

READINGS

Robert Bellah et al., *Habits of the Heart* (1985). Reflections on the discontents of the American middle class in the early 1980s, drawn from extensive interviews.

Paul Boyer, ed., *Reagan as President* (1990). Contemporary speeches, articles, and editorials commenting on Reagan and his program, with an introduction by the editor.

Peter Carroll, *It Seemed Like Nothing Happened* (1983). A perceptive overview history of the 1970s.

Thomas Byrne Edsall with Mary D. Edsall, *Chain Reaction: The Impact of Race, Rights, and Taxes on American Politics* (1992). Insightful analysis of the social and economic sources of the rise of a conservative voting majority.

CHRONOLOGY, 1974–1989

1970	Comprehensive Drug Abuse Act.
1972	Equal Rights Amendment passed by Congress.
1973	Major rise in OPEC prices; Arab oil boycott. *Roe* v. *Wade*.
1974	Richard Nixon resigns presidency; Gerald Ford sworn in. Indian Self-Determination Act.
1975	South Vietnamese government falls. *Mayagüez* incident.
1976	Jimmy Carter elected president.
1977	Panama Canal treaties ratified. Introduction of Apple II computer. Gay Pride parades in New York and San Francisco.
1978	Carter authorized federal funds to relocate Love Canal residents.
1979	Menachem Begin and Anwar el-Sadat sign peace treaty at White House. Second round of OPEC price increases. Accident at Three Mile Island nuclear plant. Carter restores full diplomatic relations with the People's Republic of China.
1980	Alaska Lands Act. Soviet invasion of Afghanistan.

	Iran hostage crisis preoccupies nation. Ronald Reagan elected president.
1981	Major cuts in taxes and domestic spending, coupled with large increases in military budget. AIDS first diagnosed.
1982	Equal Rights Amendment dies. CIA funds contra war against Nicaragua's Sandinistas. Central Park rally for nuclear-weapons freeze.
1983	239 U.S. Marines die in Beirut terrorist attack. U.S. deploys Pershing II and cruise missiles in Europe. Reagan proposes Strategic Defense Initiative (Star Wars).
1984	Reagan defeats Walter Mondale in landslide.
1984–1986	Congress bars military aid to contras.
1985	Rash of airline hijackings and other terrorist acts. First Farm Aid concert.
1986	Congress passes South African sanctions. Immigration Reform and Control Act.
1987	Congressional hearings on Iran-contra scandal. Stock market crash.
1988	Reagan trip to Moscow.

Haynes Johnson, *Sleepwalking Through History: America in the Reagan Years* (1991). An account of U.S. politics and culture in the 1980s by a seasoned journalist.

Joane Nagel, *American Indian Ethnic Renewal: Red Power and the Resurgence of Identity and Culture* (1996). Interpretive study of recent Indian history and culture.

Carl H. Nightingale, *On the Edge: A History of Poor Black Children and Their American Dreams* (1993). Moving presentation of the effect of inner-city poverty.

Bruce J. Schulman, *The Seventies: The Great Shift in American Culture, Society, and Politics* (2001). An engaging history stressing the rise of a "populist conservatism" featuring religious revival and suspicion of authority.

John W. Sloan, *The Reagan Effect: Economics and Presidential Leadership* (1999). A generally positive revisionist study arguing that Reagan, for all his antigovernment rhetoric, used government effectively.

Robert A. Strong, *Working in the World: Jimmy Carter and the Making of American Foreign Policy* (2000). Presenting nine case studies, the author argues that Carter's foreign-policy record is impressive.

WEBSITES

Defining Evangelicalism
http://www.wheaton.edu/isae/defining_evangelicalism.html
An informative introduction to an important movement in American Protestantism that profoundly influenced U.S. culture and politics in the 1970s and 1980s.

Greatest Films of the 1970s
http://www.filmsite.org/70sintro.html
Includes plot summaries and background on the movies that helped shape the popular culture of the 1970s.

Internet Public Library, POTUS, Presidents of the United States Series: Jimmy Carter
http://www.ipl.org/ref/POTUS/jecarter.html
Basic facts about the Carter presidency and cabinet members, with links to specific events, biographies, historical documents, audio sources, etc.

National Organization for Women Website
http://www.now.org/history/history.html
This website includes extensive information on the modern women's movement, the Equal Rights Amendment, abortion rights, and other topics.

State University of New York-Buffalo, Love Canal Website
http://ubib.buffalo.edu/libraries/projects/love canal/
History and chronology of the toxic pollution of the Love Canal site and the public and governmental response, primary documents, maps, visual materials. etc.

Time **magazine, Newsfile: Ronald Reagan**
http://www.time.com/newsfiles/reagan
Cover stories, articles, essays, and photographs from *Time* documenting all stages of Reagan's political career.

For additional readings please consult the bibliography at the end of the book.

CHAPTER 31

Beyond the Cold War:

Charting a New Course, 1988–1995

Tension gripped the gray streets of East Berlin late in 1989, amid rumors that "Die Mauer," the wall that divided the city, might soon be opened. In May Soviet Premier Mikhail Gorbachev had announced that Moscow would no longer use its power to uphold the pro-Soviet governments of Eastern Europe. One by one, these governments fell. On October 18, the East German communist regime run by Erich Honecker collapsed, and a new, more liberal government took its place.

One of the most detested features of the old regimes had been their restrictions on travel, and as these governments disintegrated, travel barriers fell. Thousands of people poured westward in early September, for example, when Hungary opened its border with Austria. Of all the physical barriers preventing free travel, the most notorious was the Berlin Wall. The Russians had built it in 1961, at a time of bitter East-West conflict. Snaking ninety-six miles around the city and ramming through its heart, this concrete and barbed-wire barrier with 302 watchtowers and armed guards had stood for nearly thirty years as a stark emblem of Cold War oppression and divisions.

Passage was permitted only at three closely guarded checkpoints, nick-named Alpha, Bravo, and Charlie by the U.S. military. Checkpoint Charlie, the most famous of the three, was the scene of several Cold War spy exchanges between the United States and the Soviet Union. Nearly two hundred people had been shot trying to escape across the Wall, and more than

◀ **Massachusetts High School Students Admire Their Computer Web Page**

End of the Berlin Wall, November 1989
As East German border guards watch passively, a West Berliner pounds away at the hated symbol of a divided city.

three thousand arrested. (An estimated five thousand had succeeded.) On the West Berlin side, the Wall was covered with colorful graffiti that defied its grim expanse.

In 1963 President Kennedy had visited the Wall and uttered his memorable proclamation, "Ich bin ein Berliner" ("I am a Berliner"). In 1987 President Reagan had made the pilgrimage, demanding, "Mr. Gorbachev, tear down this wall!"

Now the end had come. One of the first acts of the new East German government was to remove the restrictions on free movement within Berlin. At a press conference on November 9, 1989, a government official was asked when the travel ban would be lifted. He replied (in German), "Well, as far as I can see . . . , immediately."

This was the news East Berliners had been waiting for. Thousands rushed to the Wall and demanded that the crossing points be opened. At 10:30 P.M. the guards flung

open the gates. Pandemonium resulted. As East Berliners joyously poured through, West Berliners greeted them with flowers, tears, and shouts of welcome. Declared one old woman, "Ick glob es erst, wenn icke drüben bin" ("I won't believe it until I'm on the other side.") A blind man made the crossing simply to breath the air of freedom, he said. Giddy young people danced on the Wall itself. Families divided for years were reunited.

The glare of TV lights, beaming the event worldwide via communications satellites, added a surreal quality to the scene. This was not only a watershed moment in world affairs, but also one of the first truly real-time global media events. Americans sat glued to their sets as CNN and other networks carried the story live.

The celebrations went on for days. Famed Russian cellist Mstislav Rostropovitch gave an impromptu concert at the Wall. East Berliners who visited West Berlin's giant Ka De We department store were given one hundred deutsche marks (the West German currency) as a welcoming gift. Hundreds of Berliners whom the newspapers dubbed "woodpeckers" attacked the Wall with picks, chisels, and hammers to gather chunks of concrete as souvenirs or simply to share in its destruction.

The official demolition began in June 1990. Workers mobilizing bulldozers, cranes, and other heavy equipment worked through the summer and fall. By November, the wall had disappeared, except for a few sections left for commemorative purposes. A hated Cold War symbol had faded into history.

The end of the Cold War and the global events of the immediate post-Cold War era provide the framework of the early parts of this chapter. At first, the Soviet Union's shocking collapse brought an enormous sigh of relief in the United States. An era of great danger was over; surely the future would be safer and more tranquil. As the initial euphoria faded, however, Americans realized that the world remained a threatening and unsettled place. While U.S. leaders struggled to come to terms with the new post-Cold War world order, an immediate crisis arose in the Middle East as Saddam Hussein's Iraq invaded oil-rich Kuwait, forcing Reagan's successor, President George Bush, to respond.

Changes were underway at home as well as abroad. When Bill Clinton replaced George Bush in the White House in 1993, domestic policy moved front and center. This chapter also discusses home-front politics and culture in the 1990s, as well as long-term social and economic trends, the effect of which became particularly visible in this eventful decade. U.S. history has always been a story of change, and the changes came at a dizzying pace as the twentieth century ended.

This chapter focuses on five major questions:

■ What major events marked the end of the Cold War, and why did the long conflict between the United States and the Soviet Union end so suddenly?

■ How effectively did George Bush, President Reagan's successor, cope with the "new world order" that emerged with the end of the Cold War?

■ What key themes dominated Bill Clinton's 1992 presidential campaign and the early years of his presidency?

■ What long-term social and economic trends had the greatest effect on the United States at the end of the twentieth century?

■ How did U.S. popular culture reflect the prosperity of the 1990s, and what issues divided Americans in the "culture wars" of these years?

THE BUSH YEARS: GLOBAL RESOLVE, DOMESTIC DRIFT, 1988–1993

Ronald Reagan's vice president, George Bush, elected president in his own right in 1988, was a patrician in politics. The son of a Connecticut senator, he had attended Yale and fought in World War II before entering the Texas oil business. He had served in Congress, lost a Senate race, been U.S. ambassador to the United Nations, and directed the CIA before being tapped as Ronald Reagan's running mate in 1980.

As president, Bush compiled an uneven record. Internationally, his administration responded cautiously but positively to upheavals in the Soviet Union that signaled the end of the Cold War. Bush also reacted decisively when Iraq invaded Kuwait, took positive steps in Latin America, and worked to ease Israeli-Palestinian tensions. Bush's domestic record was thin, however, as he typically substituted platitudes for policy.

The Election of 1988

As the 1988 election approached, Vice President Bush easily won the Republican presidential nomination. A large group of Democratic contenders eventually narrowed to two: Jesse Jackson and Massachusetts Governor Michael Dukakis. Jackson, preaching concern for the poor and urging a full-scale war on drugs, ran well in the primaries. But Dukakis's victories in major primary states like New York and California proved decisive. As

his running mate, Dukakis chose Texas Senator Lloyd Bentsen.

Accepting the Republican nomination, Bush called for a "kinder, gentler America" and pledged, "Read my lips: no new taxes." As his running mate he selected Senator Dan Quayle of Indiana, the son of a wealthy newspaper publisher. In the campaign Bush stressed Reagan's achievements while distancing himself from the Iran-contra scandal. Emphasizing peace and prosperity, he pointed to better Soviet relations, low inflation, and the 14 million new jobs created during the 1980s—an achievement unmatched by any other industrial nation.

A TV commercial aired by Bush supporters, playing on racist stereotypes, featured a black man who committed rape and murder after his release under a Massachusetts prisoner-furlough program. Bush assailed Dukakis's veto of a bill requiring Massachusetts schoolchildren to recite the Pledge of Allegiance, even though the Supreme Court had found such laws unconstitutional. In response, Dukakis emphasized his accomplishments as governor. "This election is not about ideology, it's about competence," he insisted. He hammered at the failures of the "Swiss-cheese" Reagan economy and urged "Reagan Democrats" to return to the fold. But Dukakis seemed edgy and defensive, and his dismissal of ideology made it difficult for him to define his vision of America. Even Dukakis supporters wearied of his stock phrases and his repeated boasts of his managerial skills.

Both candidates avoided serious issues in favor of TV-oriented "photo opportunities" and "sound bites." Bush visited flag factories and military plants. Dukakis proved his toughness on defense by posing in a tank. Editorial writers grumbled about the "junk-food" campaign, but fleeting visual images, catchy phrases, and twenty-second spots on the evening news had seemingly become the essence of presidential politics.

On November 8 Bush carried forty states and garnered 54 percent of the vote. Dukakis prevailed in only ten states plus the District of Columbia. The Democrats, however, retained control of both houses of Congress and most state legislatures.

The Cold War Ends

The collapse of Soviet power symbolized by the opening of the Berlin Wall proceeded with breathtaking rapidity. Germany reunited for the first time since 1945. Estonia, Latvia, and Lithuania, the Baltic republics forcibly annexed by the Soviet Union on the eve of World War II,

declared independence. Calls for autonomy resounded within the other Soviet republics as well.

The Cold War was over. In August 1991 President Bush and Mikhail Gorbachev signed a treaty in Moscow reducing their strategic nuclear arsenals by 25 percent. The nuclear-arms race seemed to be over as well. Secretary of Defense Dick Cheney proposed a 25 percent reduction in U.S. military forces over five years. With the Soviet-sponsored Warsaw Pact ended, NATO announced plans for a 50 percent troop reduction.

As the Soviet Communist party's centralized control collapsed, the nation's economy sank into crisis. Soviet reformers called for a market economy on the Western model. In August 1991 hard-line Communist leaders in Moscow tried to overthrow Gorbachev, but thousands of Muscovites, rallied by Boris Yeltsin, president of the Russian Republic, protectively surrounded the Russian

General Manuel Noriega
The Panamanian strongman, once on the payroll of the Central Intelligence Agency, was overthrown by U.S. forces in 1989 and eventually imprisoned for drug trafficking

parliament, and the coup failed. Yeltsin increasingly assumed a dominant role.

Exuberant crowds toppled statues of Lenin and other communist leaders across the Soviet Union. Leningrad resumed its tsarist name, St. Petersburg. As the various Soviet republics rushed to independence, Gorbachev was overwhelmed by forces he himself had unleashed. The coup attempt thoroughly discredited the Soviet Communist party. Late in 1991 most of the Soviet republics proclaimed the end of the USSR. Bowing to the inevitable, Gorbachev resigned.

Secretary of State James Baker, a long-time Bush ally who had been chief of staff and Treasury secretary under Reagan, proceeded cautiously as the Soviet empire disintegrated. U.S. influence was limited, in any event, as long-suppressed forces of nationalism and ethnicity burst forth in Eastern Europe and in the former Soviet Union.

One issue of vital concern was the future of the Soviet arsenal of twenty-seven thousand nuclear weapons, based not only in Russia but in newly independent Ukraine, Belarus, and Kazakhstan. Baker worked to ensure the security of these weapons and to prevent nuclear know-how from leaking out to other nations or terrorist groups. As strategic talks with Yeltsin and other leaders went forward, Bush announced further major reductions in the U.S. nuclear arsenal.

For decades the superpowers had backed their client states and rebel insurgencies throughout the Third World. As the Cold War faded, the prospect for resolving some local disputes brightened. In Nicaragua, for example, Bush abandoned Reagan's failed policy of financing the contra's war against the leftist Sandinista government. Instead, Bush and Congress worked out a program aimed at reintegrating the contras into Nicaraguan life and politics. In the 1990 elections in Nicaragua, a multiparty anti-Sandinista coalition emerged victorious.

Poverty, ignorance, and economic exploitation still plagued Latin America, however, and open guerrilla war continued in Peru. The flow of cocaine and heroin to U.S. cities from the region posed a serious problem as well. In December 1989 concern over the drug traffic led to a U.S. invasion of Panama to capture the nation's strongman ruler, General Manuel Noriega. Formerly on the CIA payroll, Noriega had accepted bribes to permit drugs to pass through Panama on their way north. Convicted of drug trafficking, Noriega received a life prison term.

America's relations with the Philippines, a former colony and long-time U.S. ally, shifted as well. In 1991

the Philippines legislature ended the agreement by which the United States had maintained two naval bases in the islands. With the Cold War over, the Bush administration accepted this decision and closed the bases.

In a key development, U.S. policy helped bring an end to South Africa's policy of racial segregation, called apartheid. In 1986, over a Reagan veto, Congress had imposed economic sanctions against white-ruled South Africa, including a ban on U.S. corporate investment. This action, strongly endorsed by U.S. black leaders, reflected an anti-apartheid campaign led by South African Anglican Bishop Desmond Tutu. Economic sanctions by America and other nations hastened change in South Africa. In 1990 the government released black leader Nelson Mandela after long imprisonment and opened negotiations with Mandela's African National Congress. When South Africa scrapped much of its apartheid policy in 1991, President Bush lifted the economic sanctions.

China proved an exception to the world trend toward greater freedom. Improved relations with China suffered a grievous setback in 1989, when the Chinese army crushed a prodemocracy demonstration by masses of unarmed students in Beijing's Tiananmen Square, killing several hundred young men and women. A wave of repression, arrests, and public executions followed. The Bush administration protested, curtailed diplomatic contacts, and urged international financial institutions to postpone loans to China. But Bush, strongly committed to U.S. trade expansion, did not break diplomatic relations or cancel trade agreements with China.

As the Cold War faded, trade issues loomed large. The U.S. trade deficit with Japan stirred special concern. Although this gap dropped from its 1987 high, it still hovered at $43 billion in 1991. Early in 1992, facing a recession and rising unemployment in an election year, President Bush turned a planned Asian trip into a trade mission. He took along a team of business leaders, including the heads of the "big three" U.S. auto companies, who tried, with little success, to persuade the Japanese to buy more U.S. products. When Bush collapsed and vomited from a sudden attack of flu at a state dinner in Tokyo, some found the mishap unhappily symbolic.

Operation Desert Storm

As the Bush administration cautiously charted a course in the post-Cold War world, one unexpected crisis brought a clear-cut, forceful response. On August 2, 1990, Iraq invaded the neighboring nation of Kuwait.

Iraq's dictator, Saddam Hussein, had long dismissed Kuwait's ruling sheiks as puppets of Western imperialists and asserted Iraq's historic claims to Kuwait's vast oilfields.

Under Saddam, Iraq for years had threatened not only Kuwait but also other Arab nations as well as Israel. Iraq's military program, including both chemical- and nuclear-weapons projects, had worried many governments. During the Iran-Iraq war, however, the United States had favored Iraq over Iran, and even assisted Iraq's military buildup (see Chapter 30). But Iran's anti-Americanism eased after the death of Ayatollah Khomeini in 1989, removing this incentive for the United States to tilt toward Iraq. When Iraq invaded Kuwait, Washington reacted quickly.

Avoiding Lyndon Johnson's mistakes in the Vietnam era, Bush built a consensus for a clear military objective—Iraq's withdrawal from Kuwait—in Congress, at the United Nations, and among the American people. He deployed more than four hundred thousand troops in Saudi Arabia to achieve that goal. The U.N. imposed economic sanctions against Iraq and insisted that Saddam withdraw by January 15, 1991. On January 12, on divided votes, the Senate and the House endorsed military action against Iraq. Most Democrats voted against war, favoring continued economic sanctions instead.

The air war began on January 16. For six weeks B-52 and F-16 bombers pounded Iraqi troops, supply depots, and command targets in Iraq's capital, Baghdad. The air forces of other nations participated as well. In retaliation, Saddam fired Soviet-made Scud missiles against Tel Aviv and other Israeli cities, as well as against the Saudi capital, Riyadh. Americans watched transfixed as CNN showed U.S. Patriot missiles streaking off to intercept incoming Scuds. As portrayed on TV, the war seemed a glorified video game. The reality of many thousands of Iraqi deaths, military and civilian, hardly impinged on the national consciousness.

On February 23 two hundred thousand U.S. troops under General H. Norman Schwarzkopf moved across the desert toward Kuwait (see Map 31.1). Although rain turned the roadless sands to soup, the army pushed on. Iraqi soldiers either fled or surrendered en masse. U.S. forces destroyed thirty-seven hundred Iraqi tanks while losing only three. With Iraqi resistance crushed, President Bush declared a cease-fire, and Kuwait's ruling family returned from various safe havens where they had sat out the war. U.S. casualties numbered 148 dead—including 35 killed inadvertently by U.S. firepower—and 467 wounded.

MAP 31.1

Operation Desert Storm: The Ground War

Preceding the ground operations that ended the war was a massive air assault. Iraq's Scud missile attacks on Israel and Saudi Arabia provided TV drama but had little effect on the war's outcome.

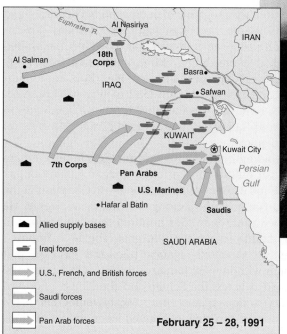

February 25 – 28, 1991

Kuwait, 1991

Burning oilfields, set ablaze by retreating Iraqis, provide an eerie backdrop to motorized U.S. troops participating in Operation Desert Storm, the high point of the Bush presidency.

Despite some campus protests, the war enjoyed broad public support. After the victory celebrations, however, the outcome seemed less than decisive. Saddam still held power. His army brutally suppressed uprisings by Shiite Muslims in the south and ethnic Kurds in the north. Saddam agreed to grant U.N. inspection teams access to his weapons-production facilities, but reneged on this agreement within a few years. Despite the stunning military success of 1991, Iraq remained a thorn in the flesh for the United States and its U.N. allies.

Home-Front Discontents: Economic, Racial, and Environmental Problems

In the early 1990s some of the longer-term effects of the Reagan-era tax cuts, Pentagon spending, and deregulatory fervor began to be felt. As the economy soured, the go-go climate of the 1980s seemed remote, and discontent increased, especially among the middle class.

First came the collapse of the savings-and-loan (S&L) industry, which had long provided home loans to borrowers and a modest but secure return to depositors.

As interest rates rose in the late 1970s because of inflation, the S&Ls had been forced to pay high interest to attract deposits, even though most of their assets were in long-term, fixed-rate mortgages. In the early 1980s money freed up by the Reagan tax cuts flowed into S&Ls that were offering high rates of return. In the fever to deregulate, the rules governing S&Ls were eased. Caught up in the high-flying mood of the decade, S&Ls nationwide made risky loans on speculative real-estate ventures. As the economy cooled, many of these investments went bad. In 1988–1990, nearly six hundred S&Ls failed, especially in the Southwest, wiping out many depositors' savings.

Because the government insures savings-and-loan deposits, the Bush administration in 1989 set up a program to repay depositors and sell hundreds of foreclosed office towers and apartment buildings in a depressed real-estate market. Estimates of the bailout's cost topped $400 billion. " 'Savings and loan,' " wrote a journalist, "had become synonymous with 'bottomless pit.' "

The federal deficit, another problem linked to the Reagan tax cuts and military spending, continued to mount. In 1990 Congress and Bush agreed on a five-year

deficit-reduction plan involving spending cuts and tax increases. Bush would pay a high political price for this retreat from his 1988 campaign pledge, "Read my lips: no new taxes." Despite the agreement, the red ink flowed on. The deficit reached $290 billion in 1992. The Gulf War, the S&L bailout, and soaring welfare and Medicare/Medicaid payments combined to undercut the budget-balancing effort.

To make matters worse, recession struck in 1990. Retail sales slumped; housing starts declined. The U.S. auto industry, battered by Japanese imports, fared disastrously. GM cut its work force by more than seventy thousand. Hard times hung on into 1992, with a jobless rate of more than 7 percent. As the states' tax revenues fell, they slashed social-welfare funding. The number of Americans below the poverty line rose by 2.1 million in 1990, to about 34 million. As the economy stumbled, the plight of the poor roused resentment rather than sympathy. Political strategists diagnosed a middle-class phenomenon they called "compassion fatigue." Declared Ohio's governor, "Most Ohioans have had enough welfare, enough poverty, enough drugs, enough crime."

In this bleaker economic climate, many Americans took a second look at Reaganism. If 1984 was "morning in America," wrote a columnist, quoting a Reagan campaign slogan, this was "the morning after."

For middle-class Americans the recession was more anxiety-producing than desperate. For the poor it could be disastrous. In April 1992 an outbreak of arson and looting erupted in a poor black district of Los Angeles. The immediate cause was black rage and incredulity (shared by many others) over a jury's acquittal of four white Los Angeles police officers whose beating of a black motorist, Rodney King, had been filmed on videotape. For several days the explosion of anger and pent-up frustration raged, leaving some forty persons dead and millions in property damage, and again reminding the nation of the desperate conditions in its inner cities.

The Bush administration did little to address these issues. In 1990, when Congress passed a bill broadening federal protection against job discrimination, Bush vetoed it, claiming that it encouraged racial quotas in hiring. (In 1991, announcing that his concerns had been met, Bush signed a similar bill.) When Bush came to Atlanta in 1992 to observe Martin Luther King Day, King's daughter, a minister, asked bitterly, "How dare we celebrate in the midst of a recession, when nobody is sure whether their jobs are secure?"

The recession also stung public school budgets. Bush proclaimed himself the "education president" but addressed the issue only fitfully. He called for national testing of schoolchildren, supported a voucher system by which parents could enroll their children in private schools at public expense, and urged corporate America to fund experimental schools. Such proposals hardly matched the magnitude of the problems facing the public-school system.

One measure supported by Bush, the Americans with Disabilities Act of 1990, did have significant educational implications. This law, barring discrimination against disabled persons, improved job and educational opportunities for the handicapped. Thanks in part to the measure, the number of physically or cognitively impaired children attending public schools rose from 4.4 million to 5.6 million in the 1990s.

Environmental concerns surged in March 1989 when a giant oil tanker, the *Exxon Valdez*, ran aground in Alaska's Prince William Sound and spilled more than 10 million gallons of crude oil. The accident fouled coastal and marine habitats, killed thousands of sea otters and shore birds, and jeopardized Alaska's herring and salmon industries. That summer the Environmental Protection Agency (EPA) reported that air pollution in more than one hundred U.S. cities exceeded federal

Disabled Citizens Occupy a San Francisco Federal Building in 1977

This protest was part of a wave of demonstrations by handicapped persons seeking laws protecting their rights and guaranteeing access to public facilities. Two demonstrators sleep on foam mattresses supplied by the mayor.

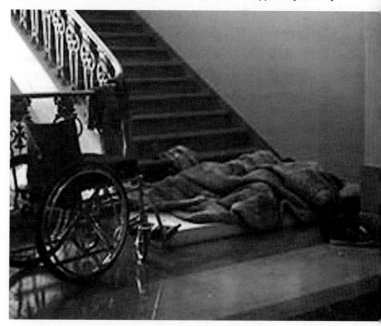

Aftermath of the *Exxon Valdez* Disaster
Fisherman John Thomas rescues an oil-soaked cormorant after the massive oil spill in Alaska's Prince William Sound in March 1989.

standards. A 1991 EPA study found that pollutants were depleting the ozone shield—the layer of the atmosphere that protects human life from cancer-causing solar radiation—at twice the rate scientists had predicted.

Squeezed between public worries and corporate calls for a go-slow policy, Bush compiled a mixed environmental record. He deplored the *Exxon Valdez* spill but defended oil exploration and drilling. In a bipartisan effort, the White House and the Democratic Congress passed a toughened Federal Clean Air Act in 1990. (California and other states enacted even stricter laws, tightening auto-emission standards, for example.) In addition, the government began the costly task of disposing of radioactive wastes and cleaning up nuclear facilities that in some cases had been contaminating the soil and ground water for years.

The Bush administration more often downgraded environmental concerns. It scuttled treaties on global warming and mining in Antarctica, backed oil exploration in Alaskan wilderness preserves, and proposed to open vast tracts of protected wetlands to developers. Vice President Quayle openly ridiculed environmental-

ists. Bush's defensive, self-serving speech to a U.N.-sponsored environmental conference in Rio de Janeiro in 1992 further alienated environmentalists.

The Supreme Court Moves Right

Like all presidents, Reagan and Bush sought to perpetuate their political ideology through their Supreme Court choices. In addition to the Sandra Day O'Connor appointment (see Chapter 30), Reagan named William Rehnquist as chief justice, replacing Warren Burger, and chose another conservative, Antonin Scalia, to fill the Burger vacancy. When another vacancy opened in 1987, Reagan nominated Robert Bork, a judge and legal scholar whose rigidity and doctrinaire opposition to judicial activism led the Senate to reject him. Reagan's next nominee withdrew after admitting that he had smoked marijuana. Reagan's third choice, Anthony Kennedy, a conservative California jurist, won quick confirmation.

President Bush made two Court nominations: David Souter in 1990 and Clarence Thomas in 1991. Souter, a New Hampshire judge, won easy confirmation, but Thomas proved controversial. Bush nominated him to replace Thurgood Marshall, a black who had fought segregation as an NAACP lawyer. Thomas, also an African American, was notable mainly for supporting conservative causes and opposing affirmative-action programs. Having risen from poverty to attend Yale Law School and to head the Equal Employment Opportunity Commission (EEOC), Thomas viewed individual effort, not government programs, as the avenue of black progress. Noting his lack of qualifications, critics charged Bush with playing racial politics.

The nomination became even more contentious when a former Thomas associate at EEOC, Anita Hill, accused him of sexual harassment. As the Senate Judiciary Committee probed Hill's accusations, the face-off dominated the nation's TV screens and heightened awareness of the harassment issue. In the end, Thomas narrowly won confirmation and joined the court.

These conservative appointments blunted the liberal social-activist thrust of the Court that began in the 1930s and continued in the 1950s and 1960s under Chief Justice Earl Warren and others. In 1990–1991 the Court narrowed the rights of arrested persons and upheld federal regulations barring physicians in federally funded clinics from discussing abortion with their clients. In a 5-to-4 decision in 1992, the Supreme Court upheld a Pennsylvania law further restricting abortion rights. The majority, however, did affirm *Roe* v. *Wade*, the 1973 decision upholding women's constitutional right to an abortion.

The Politics of Frustration

In the afterglow of Operation Desert Storm, George Bush's approval ratings hit an amazing 88 percent, only to fall below 50 percent as the recession hit home. In 1991 the *New York Times* damningly described him as "shrewd and energetic in foreign policy . . . , clumsy and irresolute at home. . . . The domestic Bush flops like a fish, leaving the impression that he doesn't know what he thinks or doesn't much care, apart from the political gains to be extracted from an issue." In January 1992 Bush offered various recession-fighting proposals, including tax breaks for home buyers, lower taxes on capital gains, and tax incentives for business investment. Democrats dismissed this initiative as politically motivated and inadequate to the problem.

Intimidated by Bush's post-Desert Storm popularity, top Democrats had stayed out of the 1992 presidential race. But Governor Bill Clinton of Arkansas took the plunge and, despite rumors of his marital infidelity, defeated other hopefuls in the primaries and won the nomination. As his running mate, Clinton chose Senator Al Gore of Tennessee. In his acceptance speech at the Democratic convention, Clinton pledged an activist government addressing the environment, health care, and the economy. On abortion, he was strongly pro-choice. As he oriented the party toward the middle class and muted its concern with the poor, traditional liberals and black leaders expressed uneasiness.

President Bush easily quashed a primary challenge by conservative columnist Pat Buchanan, but the Republican right dominated the party convention. Buchanan and evangelist Pat Robertson gave divisive speeches urging a GOP crusade for "family values" and denouncing abortion, sexual permissiveness, radical feminism, and gay rights. Delegates who belonged to Robertson's Christian Coalition cheered, but moderate Republicans deplored this rightward turn.

One gauge of voter discontent was the presidential race of political outsider H. Ross Perot. At the peak of "Perotmania," nearly 40 percent of the voters supported the Texan, who had grown rich as founder of a data-processing firm. The nation's economic problems were simple, Perot insisted on TV talk shows; only party politics stood in the way of solving them. As president he would conduct electronic "town meetings" by which voters would judge his proposals. Perot's eccentricities and thin-skinned response to critics turned off many potential supporters, but he remained an unpredictable wild card in the election.

Bush attacked Clinton's character and charged that he had evaded the draft during the Vietnam War.

Addressing public concerns about the recession, Bush promised to put James A. Baker in charge of domestic affairs in a second term. Clinton, meanwhile, focused on the stagnant economy and the problems of the middle class. He pledged to work for a national health-care system, welfare reform, and a national industrial policy to promote economic recovery and new technologies.

In the election, 43 percent of the voters chose Clinton. Bush trailed with 38 percent, and Perot amassed 19 percent—the largest share for a third-party candidate since Teddy Roosevelt's Bull Moose campaign in 1912. Clinton, carrying such key states as California, Ohio, and New Jersey, lured back many blue-collar and suburban "Reagan Democrats" and partially reclaimed the South for the Democrats. Younger voters, who had tilted Republican in the 1980s, went for Clinton in 1992.

Most incumbents in Congress won reelection. In Pennsylvania, Republican Senator Arlen Specter, a Judiciary Committee member who had angered women by his harsh questioning of Anita Hill in the Clarence Thomas hearings, narrowly beat back a woman challenger. Congress was becoming less of a white male club. Thirty-eight African Americans and seventeen Hispanics won election. Colorado elected American Indian Ben Nighthorse Campbell to the Senate, and a California congressional district sent the first Korean-American to Washington.

California became the first state to elect two women senators, Barbara Boxer and Diane Feinstein. Illinois sent the first African-American woman to the Senate, Carol Moseley Braun. Overall, the new Congress included fifty-three women: six in the Senate and forty-seven in the House. This outcome encouraged feminists who had proclaimed 1992 the "Year of the Woman."

The 1992 election marked a shift of voter attention to domestic issues as the Cold War faded. With Democrats in control of both the legislative and executive branches, the end of the much-deplored Washington "gridlock" seemed possible. In the hopeful beginnings of his term, President Bill Clinton eagerly engaged the formidable challenges facing the nation.

THE CLINTON ERA I: DEBATING DOMESTIC POLICY, 1993–1997

George Bush was of the generation shaped by World War II. William Jefferson Clinton—or Bill, as he preferred—was a baby boomer formed by Vietnam, JFK, and the Beatles. Born in Arkansas in 1946, he admired Elvis Presley, played the saxophone, and thought of becoming

a pop musician. Graduation from Georgetown University and Yale Law School, and a stint at Oxford University as a Rhodes scholar, roused an interest in politics. After marrying his law-school classmate Hillary Rodham, he won the Arkansas governorship in 1979, at age thirty-two.

Clinton began his presidency with high energy. But his administration soon encountered rough waters, and the 1994 midterm election produced a Republican landslide. The newly energized congressional Republicans pursued their conservative agenda, including—with Clinton's cooperation—a sweeping welfare-reform law.

Shaping a Domestic Agenda

In contrast to Republican predecessors like Nixon and Bush, Clinton preferred domestic issues to foreign policy. Of course, no modern president can wholly neglect world issues, and Clinton and his first secretary of state, Warren Christopher, confronted an array of diplomatic challenges: ethnic conflict in Bosnia and Somalia, trade negotiations with China, an evolving new framework of world trade, and the Israeli-Palestinian conflict. (For a full discussion of Clinton-era foreign-policy issues, see Chapter 32.) For the most part, however, global issues took a back seat to domestic policy in the Clinton era.

Clinton and Vice President Al Gore were leaders of the New Democratic Coalition, the group of moderates who sought to shed the party's reputation for high taxes and heavy spending. Trying to win back middle-class and blue-collar voters, Clinton's campaign stressed Middle America's concerns: the recession, health care, and runaway welfare costs. Clinton also embraced causes that had inspired activists of his generation, including abortion rights, environmental concerns, and feminism.

Clinton named women to head the Departments of Justice, Energy, and Health and Human Services; the Council of Economic Advisers; the Environmental Protection Agency; the United Nations delegation; and (in 1994) the Bureau of the Budget. To fill a Supreme Court vacancy in 1993, he nominated Judge Ruth Bader Ginsberg. (To fill a second vacancy in 1994, Clinton nominated moderate liberal Stephen G. Breyer, a federal judge in Boston.) Clinton appointed his wife Hillary Rodham to head the Task Force on National Health-Care Reform.

Clinton's early weeks in office proved rocky. His effort to fulfill a campaign pledge to end the exclusion of homosexuals from military service provoked much controversy. A study commission eventually crafted a compromise summed up in the phrase "Don't ask, don't tell."

Amid a recession and high budget deficits, Clinton promised to focus "like a laser beam" on the economy. His economic program, offered in February 1993, proposed spending cuts (especially in military appropriations) and tax increases to ease the budget deficit. Clinton also proposed new spending to stimulate job creation and economic growth. In August Congress passed an economic plan that incorporated Clinton's spending cuts and tax increases but not his economic-stimulus package. Enactment of even a modified budget plan spared Clinton a major early embarrassment.

Clinton also endorsed the North American Free Trade Agreement (NAFTA) negotiated by the Bush administration. This pact admitted Mexico to the free-trade zone earlier created by the United States and Canada. While critics warned that low-wage jobs would flee to Mexico, NAFTA backers, including most economists, predicted a net gain in jobs as Mexican markets opened to U.S. products. The House passed NAFTA by a comfortable margin in 1993, handing Clinton another welcome victory.

An improving economy eased pressures on Clinton to devise an economic-stimulus program. By 1994 the unemployment rate fell to the lowest point in more than four years. Inflation remained under control as well, owing to interest-rate increases by the Federal Reserve Board and a weakening of the OPEC oil cartel. In constant dollars, crude oil cost about the same in 1993 as it had in 1973, before the cycle of OPEC price increases. The 1994 federal deficit dropped as well, with further decline expected.

Meanwhile, Hillary Rodham Clinton's health-care task force, working mainly in secret, devised a sweeping reform plan. Providing universal coverage, the plan mandated that employers pay 80 percent of workers' health-insurance costs. To cover start-up expenses, the plan proposed new taxes on tobacco. The proposal also addressed the serious problem of spiraling health-care costs. From 1980 to 1992 government Medicare and Medicaid payments ballooned from 8 percent to 14 percent of the federal budget. Without controls, analysts calculated, total U.S. health spending would soon consume 20 percent of the Gross Domestic Product. The plan's cost-containment provisions included regional health-care purchasing cooperatives, caps on health-insurance premiums and on Medicare and Medicaid payments, and a national health board to monitor costs.

Lobbyists for doctors, the insurance industry, tobacco companies, retired persons, and hospital associations all worked to defeat the plan. Critics also attacked the secretive way the plan had been formulated. By fall 1994

health-care reform was stalled, at a heavy cost to the Clinton presidency. The administration had misread public complaints about medical costs and about bureaucratic red tape as support for a radical overhaul of the system. But the problems that had triggered the administration's reform effort persisted, and health care remained on the political agenda.

As the economy improved, crime and welfare reform topped voter concerns. In response, Clinton in 1994 proposed an anticrime bill to fund drug treatment, more prisons and police officers, boot camps for first-time offenders, and a ban on assault weapons. After much partisan maneuvering, Congress enacted a crime bill similar to Clinton's proposal.

Clinton's 1994 welfare-reform bill fulfilled a campaign pledge to "end welfare as we know it." Under Clinton's bill, all able-bodied recipients of payments from the government's major welfare program, Aid to Families with Dependent Children (AFDC), would have to go to work after two years, in a public-service job if necessary. The bill included job training and child-care provisions, as well as measures to force absent fathers ("deadbeat dads") to support their offspring. It also permitted states to deny additional payments to welfare mothers who bore more children. Congress took no action on Clinton's bill, but this issue, too, remained high on the public agenda.

By mid-1994 Clinton's approval ratings had dropped to 42 percent. Many found him too ready to compromise and too inclined to flit from issue to issue. Exploiting the "character issue," critics publicized various questionable dealings from the Clintons' Arkansas days, including their involvement in a shady real estate speculation, the Whitewater Development Company. The 1993 suicide of assistant White House counsel Vincent Foster, the Clintons' close friend, whetted the interest of conspiracy theorists. Charges of sexual harassment, first aired during the campaign, resurfaced in 1994 when Paula Jones, an Arkansas state employee, alleged in a lawsuit that Clinton had solicited sexual favors when he was governor.

As Clinton proved vulnerable, the political climate turned nasty. Radio commentator Rush Limbaugh won celebrity with his jeering attacks on liberals. Televangelist Jerry Falwell offered a videotape suggesting that Clinton had arranged the murder of political enemies. Pat Robertson's Christian Coalition mobilized voters at the local level. By 1994, with some nine hundred chapters nationwide, the Christian Coalition controlled several state Republican parties. With its passion and organizational energy, the religious Right represented a potent force in American politics of the 1990s.

Rush Limbaugh at Las Vegas Motor Speedway, October 2001
The conservative radio talk-show host enjoyed a loyal following in the 1990s and after, and helped produce a Republican landslide in the 1994 midterm election.

1994: A Sharp Right Turn

Bill Clinton had won in 1992 as a "new Democrat" offering fresh ideas, but by 1994 many voters saw him as simply an old Democrat of the big-government, "tax-and-spend" variety. His early call for an end to the ban on homosexuals in the military convinced some that special-interest groups controlled the White House agenda. To his critics, Clinton's failed health-care plan epitomized the dead end of a New Deal/Great Society style of top-down reform. The "character issue" further undermined Clinton's standing, as did his reputation as hopelessly indecisive. Commented Jesse Jackson, "When the president comes to a fork in the road, he chooses the fork."

Meanwhile, a movement to downsize government, reform welfare, slash taxes and spending, and shift power to the states gained momentum among the middle class. A bubbling brew of cultural and social issues added to the disaffection. These included such emotional topics as abortion, pornography, school prayer, "radical feminism," affirmative action, and an alleged collapse of "family values."

A network of conservative organizations orchestrated the rightward swing. As the Christian Coalition mobilized evangelicals, the National Rifle Association (NRA) contributed to candidates who opposed restrictions on firearms. Conservative think tanks such as the Heritage Foundation funded studies critiquing liberal policies. Limbaugh and other conservative radio commentators continued to denounce the "liberal elite."

Normally, prosperity helps the party in power, but not in 1994, in part because the recovery did little for ordinary Americans. Adjusted for inflation, the actual buying power of the average worker's paycheck fell from 1986 to 1990, and remained flat through the 1990s. Automation, foreign competition, an influx of immigrants into the labor market, and the weakness of organized labor all combined to keep average wages down. In October 1994 an ominous 58 percent of Americans told pollsters that they felt no better off despite the economic upturn.

Republican Congressman Newt Gingrich of Georgia shrewdly translated the disgruntled mood into Republican votes. In a photogenic ceremony on the Capitol steps, some three hundred Republican candidates signed Gingrich's "Contract with America" pledging tax cuts, congressional term limits, tougher crime laws, a balanced-budget amendment, and other popular reforms.

In a Republican landslide that November, voters gave the GOP control of both houses of Congress for the first time since 1954; increased the number of Republican governors to thirty-one; and cut down such Democratic giants as New York Governor Mario Cuomo and Texas Governor Ann Richards. Only 38 percent of eligible voters went to the polls, so the great shift rightward was actually achieved by about one-fifth of the total electorate. Still, a significant ideological change seemed under way.

Evangelical Christians flocked to the polls, mostly to vote for GOP candidates. Republican strategists hailed the election as the death knell of the activist, big-government tradition, and a further step in a conservative resurgence launched by Barry Goldwater in 1964. Republican governors like Wisconsin's Tommy Thompson, a champion of welfare reform, insisted that the states, not Washington, were now the best source of policy ideas. In the Senate, Republican Robert Dole of Kansas became majority leader; the reactionary Jesse Helms of North Carolina ascended to the chairmanship of the Foreign Relations Committee; and ninety-two-year-old Strom Thurmond of South Carolina, presidential candidate of the States Rights (Dixiecrat) party in 1948, headed the Armed Services Committee.

In the House of Representatives, a jubilant horde of 230 Republicans, 73 of them newly elected, chose Newt Gingrich as Speaker by acclamation, made Rush Limbaugh an "honorary member," and set about enacting the "Contract with America." One early bill forbade unfunded mandates, by which Washington had imposed regulations on the states without providing money to cover the costs. A constitutional amendment requiring a balanced federal budget passed by the House was narrowly rejected by the Senate.

On the cultural front, House Republicans targeted such "liberal elite" institutions as the Public Broadcasting Corporation and the National Endowments for the Arts. Fulfilling pledges to restore morality and uphold family values, Congress passed legislation to increase the government's power to combat obscenity in the mass media and curb pornography on the Internet. Other "Contract with America" issues, including repeal of a 1993 ban on assault weapons (the NRA's top priority), awaited their turn.

GOP leaders also promised tax credits and benefits for the middle class and the wealthy that, if enacted, would have gutted the Tax Reform Act of 1986, which had been designed to eliminate tax breaks and loopholes. As in the Reagan years, the promise of tax cuts coupled with increased defense spending threatened worse budget deficits, but Republican leaders insisted that large savings could be achieved in other parts of the budget. Where these savings would come from was unclear, since the biggest budget items apart from defense were mandatory interest payments on the national debt and two programs sacred to the middle class, social security and Medicare.

The torrent of bills, hearings, and press releases of early 1995 recalled the heady days of Lyndon Johnson's Great Society and even the early years of FDR's New Deal. Now, however, the activist energy came from conservatives, not from liberals.

For a time, House Speaker Newt Gingrich displayed a cockiness that struck many as arrogance. He stumbled early in 1995, however, when he first accepted, and then turned down, a $4.5 million book-royalty advance from a publishing house owned by Rupert Murdoch, a publishing tycoon with vital interests in federal legislation. Journalists also focused on Gingrich's network of political action groups, dubbed "Newt, Inc.," funded by corporate money and conservative foundations. Attacking "left-wing elitists," the Georgia firebrand praised laissez-faire sink-or-swim individualism and challenged the entire structure of social programs and federal-state relations that had evolved since the New Deal.

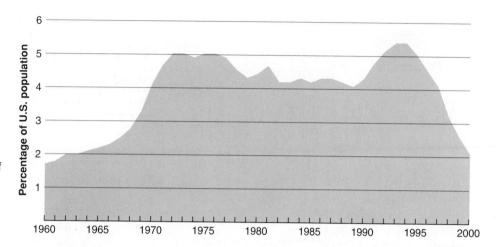

FIGURE 31.1

Percentage of U.S. Population on Welfare, 1960–2000

From just 1.7 percent in 1960, the percentage of Americans on welfare crept steadily upward until 1994, when it peaked at 5.5 percent, representing more than 14 million people. The percentage declined sharply thereafter, reflecting both the booming economy of the later 1990s and the impact of the Welfare Reform Act of 1996.

Source: Administration for Children and Families, Department of Health and Human Services. http://www.acf.dhss.gov/news/stats/6097rf.htm.

On the foreign-relations front, the 1994 Republican landslide signaled a turn inward. Newt Gingrich's "Contract with America" largely ignored foreign policy, and key Republican legislators pushed isolationist views. Jesse Helms denounced the United Nations, criticized environmental treaties, and saw little good in U.N. peacekeeping efforts or America's $14 billion foreign-aid program. Congressional Republicans refused to pay America's $1 billion in past U.N. dues. Even the Clinton administration felt the pressure. Yielding to Pentagon objections, Clinton rejected a multinational treaty banning land mines. The isolationist upsurge dismayed those who saw an intimate link between America's long-term well-being and the fate of the world.

Welfare Reform

In the aftermath of the Republican sweep in 1994, welfare reform took on fresh urgency. Newly confident conservatives challenged the underlying premises of the welfare system, whose origins stretched back to the New Deal of the 1930s. The critics offered two principal arguments. The first was cost. AFDC, with 14.2 million women and children on its rolls, cost about $125 billion in 1994, including direct payments, food stamps, and Medicaid benefits, a sharp jump since 1989 (see Figure 31.1). Though dwarfed by the benefits that flowed to the middle class through social security, Medicare, farm subsidies, and various tax deductions, this was still a heavy drain on the budget. The second argument for welfare reform was ideological—the belief that the system undermined the work ethic and trapped the poor in a cycle of dependence.

The debate raised serious policy issues and ethical questions. Would cutting welfare penalize children for their parents' actions? Would the government provide public employment to individuals dropped from the welfare rolls if no private-sector jobs were available? In *The Poverty of Welfare Reform* (1995), historian Joel Handler took a skeptical view. Dismissing the welfare-reform campaign as largely symbolic, he argued that without fundamental changes in the labor market and the political and social climate, changes in welfare policies would mean little: "[F]or the vast majority of mothers and their families, life will go on much as before."

Nevertheless, politicians of both parties jumped aboard the welfare-reform bandwagon. A broad con-

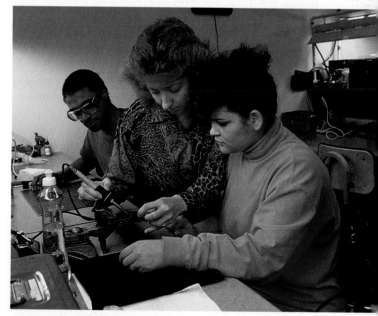

Welfare to Work
A former welfare recipient in Georgia receives training for a new job.

Criticizing the NRA
Amid a wave of school shootings, a political cartoonist offered a sardonic comment on the National Rifle Association's enthusiastic defense of the right to gun ownership.

sensus held that the present system had failed and that welfare should be a short-term bridge to gainful employment, not a lifelong entitlement. Many observers also saw a link between a system that paid higher benefits for each child and the soaring rate of out-of-wedlock births. The debate, therefore, was not over whether change was needed, but what changes. While Clinton favored federally funded child-care, job-training, and work programs to ease the transition from welfare to employment, conservative Republicans believed that the labor market and state and local agencies could best handle these problems. Clinton vetoed two welfare bills that lacked the safeguards he thought essential.

At last, in August 1996, Clinton signed a landmark welfare reform bill. Reversing sixty years of federal welfare policy, the law ended the largest federal program, AFDC. Instead, states were free to develop their own welfare programs with federal block grants while following tough federal rules limiting most welfare recipients to two years of continuous coverage, with a lifetime total of five years. The law also granted states authority to withdraw Medicaid coverage once welfare benefits had been terminated.

Supporters argued that ending welfare as a lifetime entitlement would encourage initiative and personal responsibility. Critics warned of the effects on poor children and on ill-educated welfare mothers in inner cities lacking jobs and social services, and cautioned that the real test of the reform would come in times of recession and high unemployment.

Clinton's approval of a Republican welfare bill disappointed liberals, including Senator Edward Kennedy, and such mainstays of the Democratic coalition as women's groups, minority organizations, and advocacy groups for children and the poor. In the election summer of 1996, still smarting from the repudiation of 1994, Clinton had adjusted to the shifting political winds and moved to the right.

In the short run, the law seemed a success. By December 1998 the welfare rolls had dropped by 38 percent to a thirty-year low of 7.6 million people. The reductions came at a time of economic expansion. How the new system would work when the boom ended, as it did in 2000–2001, remained to be seen.

SOCIAL AND CULTURAL TRENDS IN 1990S AMERICA

As the economy expanded through most of the 1990s (see Chapter 32), Americans continued to move to the thriving South and West, and immigrants poured in from Asia and Latin America. Not all Americans prospered. Minorities in the inner cities, including recent immigrants, struggled under harsh conditions to make ends meet. Long-term changes in the economy affected the lives of millions of citizens, benefiting some and creating serious difficulties for others.

U.S. culture of the 1990s reflected the general prosperity, with a heavy emphasis on consumerism, leisure pursuits, and mass-media diversions. But uneasiness

stirred beneath the surface, and the good times did not prevent bitter conflicts over issues of morality and belief.

America in the 1990s: A People in Transition

Historically, U.S. society has been marked by rapid growth, geographic mobility, and ethnic diversity, and—as the 2000 census revealed—this remained true as a new century began. The total population in 2000 stood at more than 281 million, some 33 million more than in 1990, the largest ten-year increase ever. The historic shift of population to the South and West continued, reflecting both internal migration and immigration patterns. The West added 10.4 million residents in the 1990s, with California alone increasing by more than 4 million. Maricopa County, Arizona (which includes Phoenix), grew by nearly 1 million. The South expanded by nearly 15 million people in the decade. Georgia, which outpaced Florida as the most rapidly expanding southern state, grew by more than 26 percent.

The graying of the baby-boom generation (those born between 1946 and 1964) pushed the median age from around 33 in 1990 to 35.3 in 2000, the highest since census records began. The 45 to 54 age group (including most baby boomers), grew by nearly 50 percent in the decade. Government planners braced for pressures on the social-security system and old-age facilities as the baby boomers reached retirement age.

The census also revealed changing living arrangements and family patterns. The proportion of "traditional" nuclear-family households headed by a married couple fell from 74 percent in 1960 to 52 percent in 2000. People living alone made up more than one-quarter of all households, while the proportion of households maintained by unmarried partners continued to increase, reaching 5 percent in 2000. Commenting on the census data, the *New York Times* observed, "[T]he nuclear family is not the only kind of family or even the only healthy kind of family. In modern America no type of family can really be recognized to the exclusion of all others."

The overall crime rate fell nearly 20 percent between 1992 and 2000. Experts attributed the decline to a variety of factors, including the decade's prosperity, stricter gun-control laws, a drop in the young male population, the waning crack-cocaine epidemic, and tougher law enforcement and sentencing rules. The U.S. prison population increased sharply throughout the decade, approaching 2 million by 2000.

Aftermath of a School Shooting
Students express their shock and grief after a deadly shooting spree by two students at Columbine High School in Littleton, Colorado, in April 1999.

Despite the falling crime rate, public fears of crime and violence remained high, fed in part by the appalling annual toll of gun deaths, which exceeded thirty thousand in 1998. Multiple shootings drew special notice. In 1999 an Atlanta man distraught by investment losses shot and killed nine employees at a financial firm. A rash of school shootings proved particularly unsettling. In a particularly horrendous 1999 event, two students at Columbine High School near Denver shot and killed twelve students and a teacher before committing suicide. These episodes produced anxious discussions of America's obsession with firearms, of a breakdown of parental authority, and of the influence of mass-media violence. In the aftermath of the school massacre in Colorado, President Clinton intensified his campaign for tougher gun-control laws.

Public-health statistics, by contrast, brought encouraging news. Average life expectancy at birth rose from seventy-four to seventy-seven between 1980 and 1999. (Life expectancy differed by gender, race, and other variables, however.) Total health expenditures hit $1.2 trillion in 2000, up 17 percent from 1990. The decline in cigarette smoking by Americans continued, falling to under 25 percent of the population in 2000.

The U.S. AIDS epidemic peaked at last, thanks to safer-sex practices and advances in drug therapies. After cresting in 1995 AIDS deaths and new HIV/AIDS cases both declined thereafter. Health officials warned against complacency: AIDS remained deadly, producing some forty-one thousand new cases in 2000, with African

Americans and Hispanics especially at risk. New (and expensive) drugs slowed the progression from HIV to full-blown AIDS, but no cure had been found. Wrote a gay journalist in 2001, "[Public-health warnings] may have to start anew with gay America as a whole, since some of us weren't around the first time HIV started killing us."

Globally, the AIDS epidemic raged on, with 22 million deaths and an estimated 36 million HIV/AIDS cases worldwide by 2001. Sub-Saharan Africa, with 25 million cases, was devastated by the disease, and many women and children were among the victims.

The 2000 census underscored the nation's growing racial and ethnic diversity. The U.S. population at century's end was about 13 percent Hispanic, 12 percent African American, 4 percent Asian, and 1 percent American Indian (see Figure 31.2). Each of these broad categories, of course, included many subgroups. The Asian category included persons whose origins lay in the Phil-

ippines, China and Hong Kong, Vietnam, India, Korea, and elsewhere. The Hispanics (who may be of any race, and are linked by a shared language, Spanish) were nearly 60 percent of Mexican origin, with Puerto Ricans, Cubans, and Salvadorans comprising most of the balance. The number of persons with ancestral roots in Haiti (where the languages are Creole and French) increased as well, reaching 385,000 by 2000.

While many Mexicans entered the country legally, others bypassed immigration checkpoints, making dangerous treks across the desert led by guides called "coyotes." In May 2001 fourteen young Mexicans died of dehydration and exposure when their "coyote" abandoned them in the Arizona desert.

Growing immigration from Asia and Latin America reversed a long decline in the proportion of foreign-born persons in the population. From a low of about 5 percent in 1970, the figure rose steadily, reaching more than 10 percent in 2000. As in earlier immigration cycles, the

FIGURE 31.2

U.S. Population by Race and Hispanic Origin, 2000 and 2050 (Projected)

By 2050, the Census Bureau projects, the Asian-American population will total some 40 million persons, and the number of Hispanics, at around 90 million, will surpass the number of African-Americans. According to these projections, non-Hispanic whites will constitute less than half the total U.S. population at midcentury.

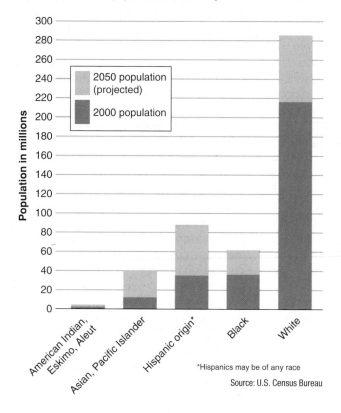

*Hispanics may be of any race

Source: U.S. Census Bureau

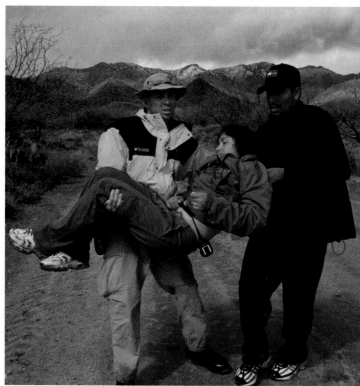

The Hazards of Illegal Immigration
A Mexican woman suffering from hypothermia following a night in the Arizona desert after sneaking across the U.S. border is carried to a rescue helicopter. In 2000, nearly 400 persons died as they tried to enter the United States illegally.

new immigrants mostly settled in cities from Los Angeles, San Francisco, Houston, and Seattle on the West Coast to New York City and Miami in the East. In New York, Catholic priests regularly said mass in thirty-five different languages!

Challenges and Opportunities in a Multiethnic Society

At century's end the African-American community continued to present diverse social, educational, and economic characteristics. In a decade of prosperity, many African Americans made significant advances. The black unemployment rate fell from more than 11 percent in 1990 to 6.7 percent in 2000, and the proportion of blacks below the government's poverty line dropped from 32 percent to under 24 percent.

By 2000, black families' median income stood at nearly $28,000, a record high, close to that of non-Hispanic white families. The earnings of college-educated blacks was significantly higher, while the number of black-owned businesses, including such giants as TLC Beatrice International, a food company, reached six hundred thousand by mid-decade. Reversing a long trend, some 370,000 blacks moved from North to South in 1990–1995, strengthening the thriving black middle-class and professional communities in Atlanta and other cities. (When recession hit in 2001, some of these encouraging trends slowed or reversed, at least temporarily; see Chapter 32.)

In the inner cities, chronic problems persisted. Movies such as *Boyz 'N the Hood* (1991), set in Los Angeles, portrayed the grim inner-city reality. Drug-related carnage, peaking in the early 1990s, took a fearful toll. In April 1994 James Darby, a black third-grader in New Orleans, wrote to President Clinton as a school assignment, expressing his fear of violence. A week later, walking home from a Mother's Day picnic, James was shot dead. While the crack-cocaine epidemic diminished, another dangerous hallucinogenic drug called Ecstacy, sold in tablet form at rave clubs and house parties, gained popularity.

In the battle against urban violence, several big cities sued the major gun manufacturers in cases of injury or death caused by unregistered firearms. The manufacturers deliberately overproduced guns, the suits alleged, knowing that many of them would enter the illegal market. In one such suit in 1999, a Brooklyn, New York, jury awarded a victim nearly $4 million.

African Americans, mostly young males convicted of drug-related crimes, comprised 41 percent of prison inmates in 2000. Although the rapid expansion of the prison population slowed as the decade ended, young black males continued to be incarcerated at nearly ten times the rate of young white males. By 2000, one study found, a third of all black men in their twenties were either in prison, on probation, or on parole. Such statistics highlighted the continuing heavy odds facing this vulnerable sector of the African-American community.

Inner-city black women faced risks as well, particularly drug use and out-of-wedlock pregnancy. In 1970 unmarried women had accounted for some 37 percent of all black births; by the 1990s the figure hovered at around 70 percent. Some 30 percent of these births were to teenagers, reducing the young mothers' opportunities for education and employment and narrowing their children's prospects. (The out-of-wedlock childbirth rate for white women, while far lower, rose as well.) Whether eliminating automatic benefit increases for each new baby would reduce teen pregnancy in the inner cities, as welfare reformers predicted, remained to be seen, particularly as recession hit and job opportunities diminished.

Among Native Americans, the reassertion of tribal pride and activism continued in the 1990s. Citing Article VI of the U.S. Constitution, which describes all treaties approved by Congress as "the supreme law of the land," and assisted by groups like the Indian Law Resource Center of Helena, Montana, tribes pursued the enforcement of the 331 Indian treaties ratified between 1778 and 1871. This movement roused antagonism, as non-Indians, including some Western politicians, complained that the treaty-rights movement was going too far.

The growth of Indian-run businesses produced further controversy. In Utah, the tiny Skull Valley Band of Goshute Indians, proclaiming themselves an independent nation, offered to lease the valley for nuclear-waste disposal, alarming environmentalists. The Omaha Indians of Nebraska opened a cigarette factory, dismaying public-health advocates.

Indian gambling casinos, approved by Congress in 1988, stirred intense debate. The giant Foxwoods Casino run by the Mashantucket Pequots in Connecticut earned $6 billion annually. As they competed for casino licenses, Indian tribes became major political contributors, pouring $7 million into the 1996 campaign. While the casinos brought needed capital into Indian communities, many citizens deplored the spread of gambling; states battled to extract more tax revenues from the casinos; and some Indians lamented the internal conflicts and erosion of traditional values the casinos brought in their wake.

Despite new sources of income, alcoholism, joblessness, and poor education persisted in Indian communities. The tribes fought back, supporting tribal colleges

and community centers, and using casino earnings to fund alcohol-treatment centers that drew upon such Native American traditions as the sweat lodge and respect for the wisdom of elders.

The Hispanic population, fueled by immigration and high natural increase, grew rapidly in the 1990s. The name most frequently given to male babies in California and Texas in 1999, reported the Social Security Administration, was José. Given a birthrate notably higher than that of either non-Hispanic whites or African Americans, demographers predicted, Hispanics would comprise 25 percent of the population by 2050.

The diverse Hispanic population, too, resisted easy generalizations. While Mexican-Americans concentrated in the Southwest and West Coast, many lived in other regions as well. Cubans, Puerto Ricans, and other Hispanic groups, as well as Haitians, resided mainly in Florida, New York, New Jersey, and Illinois. Many Hispanics were well educated, prosperous, and upwardly mobile. The median income of Hispanic households rose to more than $30,000 by 2000, and the poverty rate fell. Unemployment among Hispanics dropped from more than 8 percent in 1990 to 5.7 percent in 2000. In the five-year interval between 1993 and 1998, Hispanic-owned business nearly doubled in number, with more than two hundred thousand in Los Angeles County alone. Miami's Cuban émigré community, with many professionals and

benefiting from government aid programs for refugees from communism, was especially prosperous (see A Place in Time: Miami, Florida, 1990s).

As was the case with African-Americans, however, perhaps a quarter of Hispanics lived in inner-city neighborhoods plagued by gangs, addiction, failing schools, and teen pregnancy. Despite the importance of religion and family in Hispanic culture, 25 percent of Hispanic children lived in households with only the mother present in 2000. Ill-educated and unskilled Hispanic newcomers settled in decaying neighborhoods and took the lowest-paid jobs as gardeners, maids, day laborers, and migrant farm workers. Despite the low status of such work, however, the economy depended on it. The British journal *The Economist* wrote in 1998, "Wherever the booming [U.S.] economy cries out for workers, or a place needs regenerating, the ever-arriving and ever-progressing Latinos will move in. Nothing daunts them."

Hispanics, like other immigrant groups, mobilized to address problems, lobby politically, and campaign for community betterment. The largest advocacy group, La Raza, worked to promote Hispanic interests. By the early 1990s, in California alone, more than four thousand Hispanics held public office.

One thing was clear: the burgeoning Hispanic population was changing America. In June 2001 *Time* magazine devoted a special issue to what it called "Amexica," a Southwestern border region of 24 million people, growing at double the national rate. "The border is vanishing before our eyes," declared *Time*, creating a new nation within a nation "where hearts and minds and money and culture merge." *Time* focused on the paired U.S. and Mexican cities dotting this border: from Brownsville, Texas, and Matamoros, Mexico, near the Gulf of Mexico, westward to San Diego and Tijuana on the Pacific. This vast region, the magazine argued, was spawning a vibrant new borderlands culture; new trade and economic ties; and also social problems, including communicable diseases such as tuberculosis, illegal immigration, and drug trafficking.

Asian newcomers also presented a highly variegated picture. Prizing education, supported by

Americanization, Twenty-first-Century Style
Recent immigrants from Afghanistan join a fitness class in Fremont, California, in 2001.

close family networks, and often possessing needed skills and entrepreneurial talent, many Asian immigrants moved rapidly up the economic ladder. After passage of the Immigration Reform Act of 1965, for example, Indian doctors, engineers, and academics emigrated to America in large numbers, often joined later by aging parents and other family members, for a total of some 1.7 million by 2000.

Chinese and other Asian immigrant groups often followed a similar pattern of assimilation and upward mobility. In Fremont, California, near San Francisco, the Asian population increased from 19 percent in 1990 to 37 percent in 2000. Many of the newcomers worked as engineers and businesspeople in nearby Silicon Valley. At Fremont's Mission San José High School, the enrollment was 61 percent Asian; a visitor in 2001 found walls plastered with such signs as "Amanda Chan for Class Treasurer" and "Sadaf Gowani for Secretary." The Hmong, a Laotian mountain people who had supported the United States in the Vietnam War, formed a distinct Asian immigrant group. Settling mainly in Wisconsin and Minnesota, their numbers reached about one hundred thousand by 2000. On campuses and in city neighborhoods, Asian-Americans organized to promote their interests, sometimes acting collectively and sometimes in specific national groups.

Rethinking Citizenship in an Era of Diversity

By 2050, demographers calculate, no single racial or ethnic group will be a majority in America. Non-Hispanic whites, in other words, while still a plurality, will simply be another ingredient in the ethnic mix. In a parallel development, many Americans of mixed racial and ethnic origins, like the golfer Tiger Woods, resisted being pigeonholed. The number of interracial married couples in the United States rose tenfold in the years 1960–2000, from 149,000 to 1.5 million. Recognizing these realities, in 2000 the Census Bureau permitted citizens to check more than one racial category.

Many Americans found the new diversity exhilarating and full of promise, but others did not, and the phenomenon of "white flight" continued. As immigrants arrived in the cities, native-born whites tended to move out. Between 1990 and 1995 both Los Angeles and New York lost more than 1 million native-born inhabitants, approximately equal to the new arrivals from Asia and Latin America. Cities such as Las Vegas, Phoenix, Portland, Denver, and Austin attracted non-Hispanic whites departing from larger metropolitan centers with growing immigrant populations.

Amid these swirling demographic changes, what did it mean to be an "American" in a multiethnic, multicultural society? What would bind together such a diverse population? Some observers feared that Americans, at least emotionally and psychologically, would divide into separate camps based on ethnicity, religion, national origin, or skin color. The pressures in this direction seemed strong. At the UCLA law school, for example, blacks, Latinos, and Asians had their own student associations and their own law reviews. Newt Gingrich in 1995 gloomily foresaw "a civilization in danger of simply falling apart."

While countertrends toward a more cosmopolitan culture could be seen, particularly among the professional classes, racial and ethnic loyalties remained strong. This was hardly surprising as long as income and opportunity remained linked to race and ethnicity. Nor was it surprising that Americans disturbed by the anonymity of modern mass society should seek the reassurance of a clear-cut group identity, whether of blood, geography, ancestry, or faith.

Language became a major battleground. While some Anglo politicians campaigned to make English America's "official language," advocates for various immigrant groups called for school instruction in children's native tongue, or at least bilingual classes. However, a 1998 study of immigrant children found that they overwhelmingly wished to learn and speak English in school.

In his 1908 play *The Melting Pot*, Israel Zangwill, a Jewish immigrant from England, foresaw the blending of different immigrant groups into a common national identity. By the century's end, the "melting pot" metaphor had faded, in part because its advocates had usually assumed that as immigrants entered the "melting pot" they would abandon their ethnic roots and cultural traditions and conform to a standard "American" model.

If there was to be no "melting pot," what would unite this diverse society? Americans shared a common identity as consumers of goods and as participants in the mass culture of movies, TV, theme parks, and professional sports. Was this enough? Could the nation's civic culture match its commercial and leisure culture? This question, first posed by social thinkers of the 1920s, remained unresolved at the dawning of a new century.

The "New Economy"

In 1973 sociologist Daniel Bell published a book called *The Coming of Post-Industrial Society: A Venture in Social*

A PLACE IN TIME
Miami, Florida,
1990s

In the 1990s America's changing ethnic profile was nowhere better illustrated than in Miami, whose sun-drenched beaches, flamboyant skyscrapers, and pastel-tinted Art Deco buildings all proclaim its status as the nation's southernmost major city. Spain, having subdued the local Calusas Indians, claimed the region until 1819, when the Adams-Onís Treaty ceded title to the United States. Florida entered the Union in 1845, but sporadic Indian resistance—the so-called Seminole Wars—persisted into the 1850s. (A small tribe of Native Americans, the Miccosukee, lives on a nearby reservation.)

A 1920s land boom collapsed in the wake of a killer hurricane, but Miami burgeoned after World War II as GIs who had trained in the area returned. Miami Beach proved especially popular with Jewish retirees from New York. The novelist I. B. Singer, recalling his first visit in 1948, wrote, "Miami Beach resembled a small Israel. . . . Yiddish resounded around us in accents as thick as those you would hear in Tel Aviv."

Today's Miami is more Havana than Tel Aviv. In 2000, 57 percent of the 2.3 million residents of Miami-Dade County were Hispanic, and most of them were Cuban-Americans. Cubans fled their island country en masse after Fidel Castro seized power in 1959; by 1973 three hundred thousand had settled in Greater Miami. Thousands more, the so-called Mariel boat people who left with Castro's approval, arrived in 1980.

Far from being a struggling minority, Cuban-Americans compose a confident, fully developed ethnic community. They influence not only Miami's cultural ambience but also its political and economic agenda. Cuban-born Xavier Saurez became mayor in 1985. "Little Havana," the sprawling downtown district centered on Calle Ocho (Eighth Street), boasts not only churches, restaurants, and shops but also banks, medical centers, law offices, insurance companies, and construction firms employing professionals of all kinds.

This community's political clout was displayed in November 1999 when two fishermen rescued six-year-old Elian Gonzales, who was floating in an inner tube off Key Biscayne, Florida. Elian was one of three survivors of a boatload of Cubans, including his mother, who were lost at sea when attempting to reach Florida. Miami's Cuban-Americans rallied around the boy, and for months the story dominated the media. Parades, demonstrations, banners, and Elian T-shirts were mobilized in a campaign to keep him in the United States. (One person wearied by the media saturation launched an Internet website called "The Elian Gonzales Channel—All Elian all the Time," with parody headlines such as "Elian Gains One Pound. Experts Blame McDonalds.") Stories circulated of dolphins that had miraculously watched over the boy during his watery ordeal. Finally, in June 2000, federal officers, enforcing a court order, removed Elian from his Miami relatives and returned him to his father in Cuba.

A mother and her daughter's in Miami's Little Haiti District.

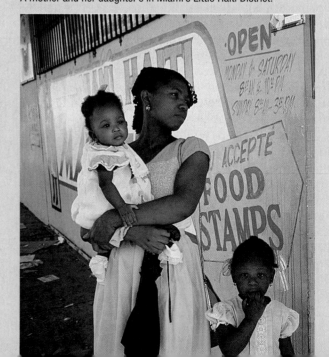

984

Jamaicans and other Hispanic groups also call Miami home. The 1980s brought emigrants from troubled Nicaragua, El Salvador, and especially Haiti. Although U.S. immigration officials intercept and repatriate Haitian refugees arriving by sea, this community continues to grow.

Miami's black community, making up some 20 percent of the population, is centered in Liberty City, Richmond Heights, and other enclaves. While Richmond Heights is middle class and well-to-do, overall the black population ranks among the city's poorest. Relations between African Americans and Hispanics are strained. While many native-born blacks feel alienated and exploited, Hispanic newcomers tend to view the United States more positively. African Americans generally vote Democratic, the Cuban-Americans are mostly conservative Republicans.

Ethnic diversity generates a distinctive Miami style. Jewish delis coexist with Hispanic restaurants. Snapper, paella, conch fritters, stone crabs, Haitian curried goat, potent Cuban coffee, and an array of salsas tempt local palates. In prosperous times, ethnic lines blur in a shared pursuit of the good life. A recession in the 1970s drove the jobless rate to 13 percent, but the economy bounced back in the 1980s and 1990s. The city's love of sports finds many outlets: sailing, windsurfing, sports car rallies, horseracing at Hialeah, and avid support for the Miami Dolphins football team, the Miami Heat basketball team, and the University of Miami Hurricanes.

With its round of parades, fairs, and festivals, the city seems dedicated to the pleasure principle. Casual dress and gold jewelry set the tone for both sexes. The beaches encourage what some call Miami's "body culture." Fashion photography is big business. Journalist Patrick May sums up the city this way: "Non-stop entertainment. Over a stage backdropped by fruit salad sunsets and palm tree props, the curtain for 100 years has risen faithfully each dawn. And there it stands, tongue firmly in cheek, hogging the spotlight. The show-off of American cities admiring itself in a full-length mirror."

Behind the façade lie problems. Racial tensions simmer near the surface. Black neighborhoods erupted in violence in 1968 and again in 1980 when a jury acquitted a white police officer in a black man's death. As the Hispanic population has grown, non-Hispanic whites have moved out. Civic leaders bemoan "Anglo flight," and some non-Hispanics flaunt hostile bumper stickers that proclaim, "Will the last American leaving Miami please bring the flag?"

With Spanish the predominant native tongue, language is contested terrain. In many neighborhoods English is rarely heard or seen. Other languages thrive as well. In 1994 a reporter observed a Vietnamese, a

The Café Cubano in Miami's "Little Havana."

Spanish-speaking Colombian, and a French-speaking Haitian vainly trying to communicate at an auto-repair shop. (They eventually diagnosed the problem: a faulty distributor.) In 1980 the Miami-Dade County commissioners proclaimed English the official language for government business. But many Miamians continue to conduct their daily lives without resort to English.

Miami's links with organized crime go far back. Rum-running and gambling proliferated in the 1920s. Mobster Al Capone retired here in the 1930s. Today, a thriving wholesale drug traffic drives up the crime statistics. Fast boats smuggle in cocaine from "mother ships" hovering offshore; commercial aircraft arriving from South America unwittingly transmit drugs. Miami-Dade County's 1981 homicide toll of 621 earned it the dubious title "Murder Capital USA." A popular TV show of 1984–1989, *Miami Vice*, glamorized the city's underside along with its tropical setting, laid-back fashions, and stage-set architecture. While drug wars and domestic disputes account for most of the bloodshed, the killing of several tourists during robbery attempts tarnished the city's appeal in the early 1990s. "Miami wears its crime like cheap perfume," observes a guidebook half boastfully; "it's hard to ignore."

Decades of development have taken a heavy toll on fragile wetlands and unspoiled wilderness areas. The nearby Everglades, once spread over 4 million acres, has dwindled to one-tenth its former size. Of the exotic wildlife that formerly inhabited this fragile ecosystem, only a fraction survives.

Crime, ethnic tensions, environmental degradation, cultural diversity, hedonistic pleasure seeking—for better or worse, Miami has it all. In this vibrant, garish, future-oriented city, the demographic changes as well as the social problems that characterize contemporary America emerge in particularly stark fashion.

FIGURE 31.3
Changing Patterns of Work, 1900–2000

This chart illustrates the sweeping changes in the male U.S. labor force in the twentieth century. The share of the male work force engaged in farming, fishing, forestry, and mining fell dramatically. The percentage of workers in industry and related occupations climbed until about 1960, and then began to decline. The service, technical, managerial, sales, clerical, and professional categories rose steadily throughout the century.

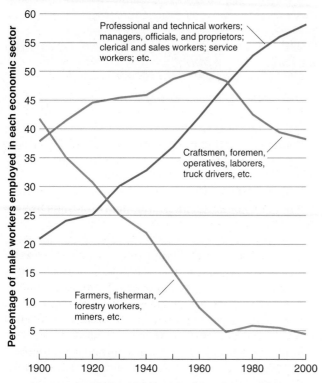

Source: *Historical Statistics of the United States, Colonial Times to 1970* (1975); *Statistical Abstract of the United States, 2002*; Caplow, Hicks, and Wattenberg, *The First Measured Century: An Illustrated Guide to Trends in America* (Washington, D.C.: The AEI Press, 2001).

A young college student studies on his laptop and listens to a CD while awaiting a train on his way to classes.

Forecasting. Unlike many such works, Bell's proved remarkably accurate. In the late nineteenth and early twentieth centuries, America's farm-based economy had given way to an economy based on factory production and manual labor in cities. As the twentieth century ended, a second major transformation was again reshaping the U.S. economy: the decline of the industrial sector and the rise of a service-based economy (see Figure 31.3). Manufacturing continued, of course, but it faded as a major source of employment. In 1960 about half of the male labor force worked in industry or in related jobs such as truck driving. By the late 1990s this figure had fallen to under 40 percent.

In the same period, the percentage of professional, technical, and service workers continued its century-long upward trend. In 1960 such workers had comprised about 42 percent of the male labor force; by 1998 the fig-ure was 58 percent. The percentage of women workers in the service sector was even higher.

The service economy was highly segmented. At one end were low-paying jobs in fast-food outlets, video rental stores, nursing homes, and chain stores such as Wal-Mart. At the other end were lawyers and physicians; money managers and accountants; and workers in the entertainment and telecommunications fields. The latter category expanded rapidly with the growth of high-speed telecommunications systems and the rise of the personal computer with its Internet-based spinoffs (see Technology and Culture: The Personal Computer in Chapter 30).

This sector of the service economy helped give the economic boom of the later 1990s its aura of sizzle and excitement (see below). As the Web-based *Encyclopedia of the New Economy* proclaimed somewhat breathlessly,

> When we talk about the new economy, we're talking about a world in which people work with their brains instead of their hands. . . . A world in which innovation is more important than mass production. A world in which investment buys new concepts . . . rather than new machines. A world in which rapid change is a constant.

The decline of the industrial economy and the rise of the service economy had different meanings for different groups. Young people with the education, skills, and contacts to enter the new high-tech industries often found exciting challenges and substantial economic rewards. For less-privileged youths, supermarkets, fast-food outlets, or discount superstores could provide entry-level work, but doubtful job security and long-term career prospects. For older workers displaced from industrial jobs, the impact could be devastating both economically and emotionally. Whatever their position in society, few Americans were unaffected by the rise of the new economy with all its implications for social change.

Affluence, Conspicuous Consumption, a Search for Heroes

The economic boom that began in 1992 and roared through the Clinton years produced instant fortunes for some and an orgy of consumption that set the tone of the decade. Wall Street and Silicon Valley spawned thousands of twenty-something millionaires. In 1997, surveying the ostentatious lifestyles of young investment geniuses, most of whom had never experienced anything but rising stock prices, *Vanity Fair* magazine described New York as "the champagne city, making the brash consumption of the 1980s look like the depression." Tales circulated of elegant restaurants offering obscenely expensive cigars and rare wines, and exclusive shops selling $13,000 handbags. In 1999, as the good times rolled on, the nation's top one hundred advertisers spent $43 billion promoting their goods.

The economic boom also encouraged what some considered a smug, hard-edged "winner take all" mentality like that of the Gilded Age, when those at the top turned their backs on the larger society. In *Bowling Alone: The Collapse and Revival of American Community* (2000), political scientist Robert Putnam sharply criticized American public life. Putnam found diminished civic engagement and weakened interest in public issues, as evidenced by declines in voter participation, political activism, and participation in civic organizations. He even found less informal socializing, from dinner with friends to card parties and bowling leagues, as Americans pursued purely personal goals. While some saw the Internet as a new form of community, Putnam viewed it as further evidence of the privatization of life and the erosion of the public sphere.

Anecdotal evidence supported Putnam's conclusions. A 1997 survey of college students found that 77 percent expected to become millionaires. A motivation-

al book called *The Prayer of Jabez*, which became a best-seller in 2000, cited a biblical prayer by a shepherd recorded in I Chronicles ("Bless me indeed, and enlarge my territory") as a key to success. Wrote the author, the Reverend Bruce Wilkinson, "If Jabez had worked on Wall Street, he might have prayed 'Lord, increase the value of my investment portfolio.'"

With the stock market surging, the Cold War over, and other threats only beginning to come into focus, many Americans set out to enjoy themselves. Attendance at the Disney theme parks in Florida and California neared 30 million in 2000. The sales of massive sport-utility vehicles (SUVs) soared, despite environmentalists' laments about their fuel inefficiency. When a White House press secretary was asked in the summer of 2001 if Americans should change their consumption patterns to conserve energy, he replied, "[I]t should be the goal of policy makers to protect the American way of life—the American way of life is a blesséd one."

As in the 1980s, the media offered escapist fare. Popular movies included historical extravaganzas like *Braveheart* (1995) and *Gladiator* (2000). The 1997 blockbuster film *Titanic*, with spectacular special effects, grossed $600 million. In the 1994 hit movie *Forest Gump*, Tom Hanks played a kindly but simple-minded young man who becomes a wealthy business tycoon by chance. The top-rated TV show of 1999–2000, *Who Wants to Be a Millionaire?*, unabashedly celebrated greed. So-called "reality" TV shows like *Survivor*, popular as the decade ended, offered viewers a risk-free taste of the hazards that American life itself (at least for the affluent) conspicuously lacked.

Millions avidly followed TV coverage of the 1995 trial of O. J. Simpson, a former football star accused of murdering his estranged wife and her friend. The 1996 murder of a six-year-old Colorado girl whose parents had pushed her into child beauty pageants similarly mesmerized the public. So did the 2001 disappearance of a young federal-government intern from California after an alleged affair with her congressman. (In 2002 the congressman was defeated for reelection, and the young woman's body was found in a remote section of a Washington park.) The sex scandals that swirled around President Clinton and ultimately led to his impeachment (see Chapter 32) often seemed to be no more than another media diversion in a sensation-hungry decade.

Again, as was true of the 1980s, other evidence from the popular culture suggests a more complex picture. Some critics interpreted *Titanic*, which sided with its working-class hero in steerage against the rich snobs in first class, as a subtle comment on a decade when class differences in America were blatantly on display. One

even called the movie "an exercise in class hatred." *American Beauty* (1999) explored dark and murderous currents beneath the façade of a comfortable suburban family.

The Clint Eastwood western *Unforgiven*, winner of the 1992 Academy Award for best picture, seemed to express nostalgia for an earlier era when life presented rugged challenges and hard moral choices. The same longings, some suggested, underlay the outpouring of admiring biographies of larger-than-life heroes from the past, such as Stephen Ambrose's *Eisenhower* (1991), A. Scott Berg's *Lindbergh* (1999), and David McCullough's *Truman* (1993) and *John Adams* (2001).

The decade also reveled in the heroic era of World War II, featuring it in a series of TV specials, books such as Ambrose's *Citizen Soldiers* (1997) and Tom Brokaw's *The Greatest Generation* (1998), and movies like *Saving Private Ryan* (1998) and *Pearl Harbor* (2001). Commenting on the latter film, *New York Times* columnist Frank Rich observed,

> *Pearl Harbor* is more about the present than the past. . . . The motivation, in part, is overcompensation . . . for what is missing in our national life: some cause larger than ourselves, whatever it might be. . . . Even those Americans who are . . . foggy about World War II . . . know intuitively that it was fought over something more blessed than the right to guzzle gas.

Matthew Shepherd

The brutal murder of Shepherd in Laramie, Wyoming, by two homophobic youths in October 1998 stirred nationwide protests by gay-rights activists and many others.

A Truce in the Culture Wars?

Elsewhere on the cultural landscape, the 1990s also saw a continuation of the moralistic battles that had begun in the 1970s, which some viewed as nothing less than a struggle for the nation's soul. The Christian Coalition's attempted takeover of the Republican party was only part of a larger campaign to reverse what conservatives saw as America's moral decay. In earlier times, the culture wars had raged along sectarian lines, with native-born Protestants battling Catholic and Jewish immigrants. During the Cold War, the source of evil had been clear: the global communist conspiracy, centered in Moscow. Now many Americans translated the same apocalyptic world view to the home front, and searched for the enemy within.

Some viewed the sexual revolution as the great threat. As gays and lesbians grew more vocal politically (and increasingly visible in the popular culture and in TV programming), a rash of state-level efforts sought to counter their demands for equality. In 1998, amid this climate of reaction, a gay student at the University of Wyoming, Matthew Shepard, was tortured and murdered by two local youths because of his sexual orientation.

As the abortion controversy continued, a small number of "pro-life" advocates turned from peaceful protest to violence. In 1995 an anti-abortion activist fatally shot a physician and his bodyguard outside a Florida abortion clinic, and an unstable young man murdered two people and wounded five others at a clinic near Boston. In 1997 bombers struck abortion clinics in Tulsa and Atlanta. The following year, a Buffalo, New York, physician who performed abortions was shot dead. (In part because of such terror tactics, the abortion rate dropped by some 12 percent between 1992 and 1996.)

On April 19, 1995, in the worst outburst of domestic terrorism up to that time, a bomb demolished an Oklahoma City federal building, killing 168 people. The bomber struck precisely two years after a government raid on the Waco, Texas, compound of the Branch Davidians, an apocalyptic religious sect charged with firearms violations. The 1993 Waco raid ended tragically when fires burst out inside the main building as federal tanks moved in, leaving some eighty Branch Davidians dead. After the Oklahoma City blast, the authorities soon arrested Timothy McVeigh, a Gulf War veteran outraged by the Waco incident. McVeigh and his co-conspirator, Terry Nichols, had vague links to the secretive right-wing militia movement that sprang up in the 1990s. These organizations were often obsessed with conspiracy theories and deeply suspicious of the gov-

ernment. McVeigh, convicted of murder, was executed by lethal injection in June 2001. Nichols received a life sentence.

Adding to the national jitters over violence-prone loners and shadowy antigovernment groups was a series of bombs mailed between 1978 and 1995 to individuals whose business or professional activities could be interpreted as anti-environmental. The bombs killed three people and injured twenty-eight others. In 1996 authorities arrested Theodore Kaczynski, a Harvard-trained mathematician and obsessive opponent of modern technology, in his remote Montana cabin. Kaczynski was convicted but escaped the death penalty by reason of mental incapacity.

The culture wars were fought mainly with words and symbolic gestures, not bullets and bombs. In 1995 the Smithsonian Institution cancelled an exhibit marking the fiftieth anniversary of the atomic bombing of Japan when veterans' organizations and some politicians attacked it for allegedly overemphasizing the bombs' human toll and for presenting historians' differing views of Truman's decision.

The struggle unfolded on many fronts, from televangelists' programs and radio talk shows to school-board protests and boycotts of TV shows deemed morally offensive. Conservatives attacked history textbooks for promoting "multiculturalism," for being insufficiently patriotic, and for pandering to the forces of "political correctness." The cultural measures undertaken by Congress after the 1994 Republican landslide, discussed earlier, were a part of this larger drive to purge American life of the evils that religious and cultural conservatives saw on every hand.

Religious conservatives proposed a constitutional amendment permitting prayer in classrooms and called for a renewal of traditional morality and "family values." The rapidly growing evangelical and charismatic churches continued to denounce society's wickedness and the government's role in the moral decline. In October 1997 some seven hundred thousand men belonging to a conservative Protestant religious movement called Promise Keepers rallied in Washington, D.C., for a day of prayer, hymn singing, and pledges to reclaim the moral and spiritual leadership of their households.

Pat Robertson's *The New World Order* (1991) saw much of U.S. and indeed world history as a vast conspiracy that would soon end in the rule of the Antichrist. As the year 2000 neared, popularizers of Bible prophecy intensified their warnings that history's final crisis was at hand. (Widespread fears of massive computer failures associated with "Y2K," the shorthand term for the com-

Remembering Oklahoma City
Matt Story and Dawn Mahan, whose mother died in the 1995 bombing of the Murrah federal building in Oklahoma City, pause at her memorial in the commemorative park honoring the 168 victims.

ing of the year 2000, added to the apprehension.) The charges of infidelity levied against President Clinton underscored for conservatives the moral rot they saw eating away at America.

As the 1990s ended, the cultural wars seemed to diminish. The Christian Coalition lost momentum when its politically savvy director, Ralph Reed, resigned in 1997. By 1998 leaders of the Christian Coalition and other groups were expressing open frustration with Republican politicians who courted conservative Christians' votes but failed to fight for their cultural agenda once in power. In *One Nation After All* (1998), sociologist Alan Wolfe reported on his interviews with middle-class Americans, whom he found suspicious of extremist positions and broadly accepting of diversity. The virtues of tolerance and live-and-let-live, Wolfe suggested, were thriving in middle America. One of Wolfe's interviewees reflected, "I wish more people would recognize [that] we can't just stand back and whine about the ways things are and . . . about how terrible the changes will be. We've got to move forward and trust that we can . . . get to a solution eventually." In its optimism and moderate tone, such a perspective captured a deep-seated American pragmatic approach to social problems, and struck an encouraging note as a new century dawned.

CONCLUSION

Both America and the world changed profoundly in the 1990s. The sudden collapse of the Soviet Union radically upset the familiar world order, posing major challenges for Reagan's successor, George Bush. Bush successfully met the first post-Cold War international crisis, mobilizing an international coalition to repel Iraq's invasion of Kuwait, but his domestic record proved less impressive. In 1992, having broken a promise not to raise taxes, and with America in recession, Bush lost to the Democratic presidential candidate Bill Clinton, who heavily emphasized the theme of economic recovery in his campaign.

In choosing Clinton, the nation elected a highly intelligent politician with a mastery of policy issues and an easy empathy ("I feel your pain" was a phrase he liked to use), but with character flaws that continually threatened to overshadow his strengths. Clinton's ambitious plan for a major restructuring of the health-care system became bogged down in Congress and ultimately died. This failure, coupled with other missteps, laid the groundwork for a Republican landslide in the 1994 midterm election.

A rebounding economy erased the federal budget deficits and gave the 1990s a glow of prosperity. The good times were unevenly distributed, however, and left the problems of the inner cities unresolved. Along with day-to-day events, the history of the period was also shaped by long-term social and economic trends. A continuing population shift southward and westward, coupled with high levels of immigration from Latin America and Asia, affected the politics of the decade and gave the nation an ever more multiethnic and multicultural flavor. At the same time, new information technologies, including the rise of the personal computer, contributed to a fundamental economic restructuring marked by the decline of the old factory-based economy and the growth of a new knowledge-based service economy.

Culturally, Americans who prospered in these boom years continued their 1980s' preoccupation with consumer goods and escapist diversions. Cultural conservatives, however, grew increasingly vocal, hammering on such emotional issues as abortion, homosexuality, and the nation's alleged moral decay. The culture wars seemed to ease as the decade ended, and Americans looked to the new century with confidence.

CHRONOLOGY, 1988–1995

1986 William Rehnquist becomes chief justice of the United States.
Antonin Scalia joins Supreme Court.

1988 George Bush elected president.
Anthony Kennedy joins Supreme Court.

1989 Massive Alaskan oil spill by *Exxon Valdez*.
Supreme Court, in several 5 to 4 decisions, restricts civil-rights laws.
U.S. invasion of Panama; Manuel Noriega overthrown.
China's rulers crush prodemocracy movement.
Berlin Wall is opened.

1990 Federal Clean Air Act strengthened.
Americans with Disabilities Act passed.
President Bush and Congress agree on five-year budget-deficit reduction package.
Iraq invades Kuwait.
Recession begins.
Germany reunified; Soviet troops start withdrawal from Eastern Europe.
David H. Souter joins Supreme Court.

1991 Gulf War (Operation Desert Storm).
Clarence Thomas seated on Supreme Court.

1992 Supreme Court approves Pennsylvania restriction on abortion but upholds *Roe* v. *Wade*.
Arkansas Governor Bill Clinton elected president.

1993 Congress enacts modified version of Clinton economic plan.
Congress approves NAFTA treaty.
Recovery begins; economy expands, stock-market surges (1993–2000).
Congress debates health-care reform (1993–1994).
Ruth Bader Ginsberg joins Supreme Court.
Federal forces raid Branch Davidian compound in Waco, Texas.

1994 Christian Coalition gains control of Republican party in several states.
Stephen G. Breyer joins Supreme Court.
Republican candidates proclaim "Contract with America."
Republican victory in 1994 elections; Newt Gingrich becomes Speaker of the House.

1995 AIDS epidemic peaks in the United States; continues worldwide.
Oklahoma City federal building bombed.

1996 Welfare Reform Act passed.

1999 Columbine High School shootings

2000 Federal census finds population surge in West and South, sharp increases in Hispanic and Asian population, and changing family patterns.

On the political front, despite the rocky start of the Clinton presidency, the sustained economic boom worked in the Democrats' favor, and Clinton easily won a second term in 1996. The years beyond 1996, however, would severely test the mood of confidence, bringing political scandal; recession; and, early in the new century, the most horrendous act of terrorism the nation had ever experienced.

FOR FURTHER REFERENCE

READINGS

Discussions of trends in contemporary America may be found in such journals as *The American Prospect, The Atlantic Monthly, Business Week, Christianity Today, Commentary, The Economist* (London*), Fortune, Harper's Magazine, Monthly Labor Review* (U.S. Department of Labor*), The New Republic, National Review, The Nation, Nation's Business, New York Times Magazine, The Progressive, Scientific American,* and *U.S. News and World Report.*

Mary Jo Bane and David T. Ellwood, *Welfare Realities: From Rhetoric to Reform* (1994). Ellwood, assistant secretary of health and human services in the Clinton administration, and his coauthor explore the complexities of welfare reform.

Michael R. Beschloss and Strobe Talbott, *At the Highest Levels: The Inside Story of the End of the Cold War* (1994). A historian and a journalist-turned-diplomat collaborate on an early but valuable account of the Cold War's demise.

Haynes Johnson, *The Best of Times: America in the Clinton Years* (2001). A Washington journalist offers an informed, critical view of Clinton and his era.

David Maraniss *First in His Class: A Biography of Bill Clinton* (1995) Explores the sources of Clinton's political drive and his almost desperate need to be liked.

Gwendolyn Mink, ed., *Whose Welfare?* (1999) Essays on welfare policy and the effects of the 1996 welfare-reform act.

Richard J. Payne, *Getting Beyond Race: The Changing American Culture* (1998). An argument for moving beyond the emphasis on division and difference.

Robert D. Putnam, *Bowling Alone: The Collapse and Revival of American Community* (2000). A well-researched and carefully argued assessment of the decline of civic engagement and human connectedness in late-twentieth century America.

Rickie Solinger, ed., *Abortion Wars: A Half Century of Struggle* (1998). Scholars offer historical perspectives on a contentious issue.

Roberto Suro, *Strangers Among Us: How Latino Immigration Is Transforming America* (1998). A rich and perceptive assessment, based on careful research and firsthand interviews, of sweeping demographic trends that are changing the United States in profound ways.

U.S. Bureau of the Census, *Statistical Abstract of the United States, 2002. The National Data Book* (2002). An annual treasure trove of information on economic and social trends, from the federal budget to college enrollments.

Alan Wolfe, *One Nation After All: What Middle Class Americans Really Think . . .* (1998). A sociologist reports on his extensive firsthand interviews, and finds reason for optimism about middle-class attitudes on a variety of issues.

WEBSITES

The Berlin Wall
http://userpage.chemie.fu-berlin.de/BIW/wall.html
This extensive website, by a Berliner, includes a historical narrative; firsthand accounts; stories, photographs and art relating to the Wall; and links to many specific topics.

Hmong Home Page
http://hmongnet.org/
Interesting home page maintained by Hmong immigrants, with history, news, and current events.

The Internet Public Library, POTUS, Presidents of the United States, George Herbert Walker Bush
http://www.ipl.org/ref/POTUS/ghwbush.html
Factual information about Bush and his administration, with links to election results, specific events, historical documents, and audio sites.

The Internet Public Library, POTUS, Presidents of the United States, William Jefferson Clinton
http://www.ipl.org/ref/POTUS/wjclinton.html
Basic biographical information, with many links to election results, cabinet members, historical documents, notable events, and audio sources.

PBS *Frontline* **Program, The Gulf War**
http://www.pbs.org/wgbh/pages/frontline/gulf/
Maps, chronology, tapes and transcripts of oral-history interviews with participants. Also includes a four-hour BBC-Radio special on the Gulf War.

Time **Magazine Webpage on the U.S.-Mexican Border Region**
http://www.aola.com/newfrontier
This site, based the *Time* special issue of June 11, 2001, includes an interactive map of the U.S.-Mexican border region, video and audio clips, and other resources.

U.S. Bureau of the Census Home Page
http://www.census.gov
This site includes a wealth of information about the U.S. population..

Wired Digital, Inc., a Lycos Network site, Encyclopedia of the New Economy
http://hotwired.lycos.com/special/ene/
This fascinating website contains dozens of short, readable essays on a wide range of topics relating to the economic changes of the 1990s and beyond.

For additional readings please consult the bibliography at the end of the book.

CHAPTER 32

New Century, New Challenges,

1996 to the Present

Friday, February 26, 1993, began like most other business days at New York's World Trade Center, two 110-story towers soaring over lower Manhattan. But suddenly, at 12:18 P.M., a bomb containing over one thousand pounds of explosives ripped through Level B2 of the parking garage under the north tower. The blast cut off electricity, plunging the building into darkness. Fifty thousand workers hastily evacuated, and hundreds were trapped in stalled elevators. Six persons died in the blast, and more than one thousand were injured.

The first investigators found an eerie scene: a giant hole extending five stories underground, fires from ruptured automobile gasoline tanks, 124 cars destroyed and others heavily damaged, water and sewage cascading from broken pipes, car alarms wailing in the darkness. The FBI quickly identified the vehicle that had carried the bomb into the garage: a Ford Econoline van rented in Jersey City. Five Islamic militants, including a blind Egyptian sheik, Omar Abdel Rahman, the alleged mastermind, were arrested and convicted of conspiracy and other crimes. Three, including Sheik Omar, were found guilty of murder and received life sentences.

Shocking as it was, the attack could have been far worse: at least the tower had survived, and comparatively few lives had been lost. In reality, this event was one of a nightmarish series of attacks that would take a heavy toll in life and property, as the upsurge of terrorist attacks in the 1980s (see Chapter 31) continued. In November 1995 a bomb shattered a U.S. military

◀ A candlelight vigil in Grayslake, Illinois, after the terrorist attacks of September 11, 2001.

CHAPTER OUTLINE

The Clinton Era II: Domestic Politics, Scandals, Impeachment, 1996–2000

Clinton's Foreign Policy: Defining America's Role in the Post-Cold War World

The Economic Boom of the 1990s

Disputed Election; Conservative Administration, 2000–2002

Recession Woes; Environmental Debates; Campaign Finance Battles

September 11 and Beyond

training center in Riyadh, Saudi Arabia, killing seven, including five Americans. In June 1996 another bomb ripped through a U.S. military barracks in Saudi Arabia, leaving nineteen U.S. airmen dead. Further deadly attacks in East Africa and the Middle East killed more Americans.

Like distant thunder signaling an approaching storm, the attacks were ominous warnings of worse ahead. On September 11, 2001, terrorists again struck the World Trade Center, as well as the Pentagon, this time with horrendous consequences.

Much of this chapter focuses on the impact of escalating terrorist attacks, particularly the aftermath of September 11, at home and abroad. As Americans faced these dangers, they also coped with domestic political battles and economic turmoil. Amid calls for unity, deep divisions remained. A White House scandal in Clinton's second term, a disputed presidential election in 2000, and the policies of Clinton's successor, George W. Bush, who seemed to favor the privileged and powerful, all proved highly divisive. As prosperity gave way to recession, bankruptcies and charges of fraud hit some of the nation's largest companies, undermining investors' confidence and tarnishing the reputation of the corporate world.

This chapter focuses on five key questions:

■ What domestic initiatives marked Clinton's second term, and how did the scandals that swirled around him in 1998–1999 affect his ability to govern?

■ On balance, was President Clinton's foreign-policy record a success?

■ What factors fueled the economic boom of the 1990s, and why did it end?

■ What key domestic policies did George W. Bush propose early in his presidency?

■ How did the government respond to the terrorist attacks of September 2001, domestically and internationally? Was the response appropriate? Was it effective?

THE CLINTON ERA II: DOMESTIC POLITICS, SCANDALS, IMPEACHMENT, 1996–2000

Moving to the political center, Bill Clinton won a second term in 1996. Apart from his support for tough regulation of the tobacco industry, Clinton's second term is remembered mainly for a sex scandal that led to an impeach-

ment effort by his Republican foes. This effort further poisoned an already highly partisan political climate.

Campaign 1996 and After; The Battle to Regulate Big Tobacco

After the Republican landslide in 1994, Clinton's prospects looked bleak. But he had won the nickname "the Comeback Kid" after a long-shot victory in the 1992 New Hampshire presidential primary, and he again hit the comeback trail. Despite the missteps of 1993, he had won good marks for signing the budget-balancing and welfare-reform bills (see Chapter 31). The Republicans suffered a black eye in 1995 when House Speaker Newt Gingrich, battling Clinton over the budget, twice allowed a partial government shutdown.

Clinton got another lucky break: a weak Republican opponent in 1996. When General Colin Powell, the popular former chairman of the Joint Chiefs of Staff, declined to run, Kansas Senator and Majority Leader Bob Dole, a partially disabled World War II hero, won the nomination. A seventy-three-year-old party stalwart, Dole ran a lackluster campaign, delivering wooden speeches.

Clinton won with just under 50 percent of the vote, to Dole's 41 percent. (The Texas maverick H. Ross Perot garnered 8 percent.) The Republicans held control of Congress, though Gingrich and other GOP legislators proved less combative than after their 1994 triumph.

The cost of television advertising continued to drive up campaign expenses, and fundraising scandals marked the 1996 contest. One Democratic fundraiser with links to Indonesian and possibly Chinese corporate interests raised $3.4 million, of which nearly half was eventually returned. After an event at a Los Angeles Buddhist temple attended by Vice President Al Gore, priests and nuns sworn to poverty contributed over a hundred thousand dollars to the Democratic cause. The money apparently came from Asian business tycoons eager to curry favor with the administration.

Launching his second term, Clinton proceeded cautiously, further distancing himself from his party's New Deal-Great Society past. In 1997 he signed a Republican bill providing some tax cuts and setting a timetable for a balanced budget by 2002. (In fact, as prosperity continued, Clinton beat that deadline by three years.) Many Clinton proposals involved no legislation or spending. He urged parents to read to their children, and set up a citizens' commission to lead a national dialogue on race.

Clinton cautiously defended affirmative action, but support for such programs was weakening, especially among non-Hispanic whites. The Supreme Court re-

stricted the awarding of federal contracts on the basis of race in 1995, and in 1996 California voters barred racial or ethnic preferences in state agencies, including the universities.

Clinton did act forcefully on one issue: tobacco regulation. In 1997, facing lawsuits by former smokers and by states hit with heavy medical costs related to smoking-related diseases, the tobacco industry agreed to pay some $368 billion in settlement. The agreement limited tobacco advertising, especially when directed at young people.

Since the agreement required government approval, the debate now shifted to Washington. Southern legislators close to the tobacco companies defended the industry, but the Clinton administration supported a bill that would have imposed tougher penalties, higher cigarette taxes, and stronger antismoking measures. Supporters of the administration's bill documented the industry's manipulation of nicotine levels and deliberate targeting of children. The industry struck back with a $40 million lobbying campaign and heavy contributions to key legislators, killing the bill. Commented John McCain, Arizona's maverick Republican senator, "Some Republicans might be vulnerable to the charge that their party is in the pocket of the tobacco companies."

In 1998, facing a wave of private lawsuits, the tobacco industry reached a new settlement, scaled back to some $200 billion, with forty-six states. Clinton, however, continued to push for tougher federal regulation and for legal action to recover Medicare costs arising from smoking-related illnesses.

In his January 1998 State of the Union address, Clinton boasted that his 1999 budget would include a modest surplus, the first in thirty years. Most of the surplus, he argued, should go to reduce the national debt and strengthen the social-security system, which faced eventual bankruptcy as the baby boomers retired. Clinton's call to "Save social security first" not only made fiscal sense but also painted Republican tax cutters as irresponsible.

This speech defined Clinton's second-term agenda. After the health care fiasco, he had abandoned large-scale programs in favor of modest proposals that appealed to progressives without alienating moderates. He offered some initiatives to help the poor, such as enrolling the nation's 3 million uninsured low-income

"I Solemnly Swear . . ."
Tobacco-industry executives prepare to testify before the House Commerce Committee in January 1998. Political and legal issues related to smoking loomed large in the 1990s, as cigarettes' deadly effects became more widely understood.

children in Medicaid. But he also introduced proposals attractive to the middle class (college-tuition tax credits; extending Medicare to early retirees) and to fiscal conservatives (reducing the national debt; shoring up social security). Some liberals dismissed Clinton's program as "Progressivism Lite," but it was politically shrewd. Under normal conditions, the speech would have certified Clinton's political comeback.

Scandal Grips the White House

But conditions were not normal. Even as Clinton spoke, scandal enveloped the White House. Adultery charges had long clung to Clinton, and now he faced the Paula Jones sexual-harassment suit, dating from his days as the governor of Arkansas (see Chapter 31). The Supreme Court had helped Jones's case by permitting lawsuits against sitting presidents.

Seeking to show a pattern of sexual harassment, Jones's lawyers subpoenaed Clinton and quizzed him about reports linking him to a young White House intern, Monica Lewinsky. The president denied the story, as did Lewinsky in an affidavit. As the rumors became public (via an Internet website devoted to political gossip), Clinton denounced them as false. Hillary Clinton blamed "a vast right-wing conspiracy." In fact, political conservatives *were* digging for damaging information on Clinton's personal life, and he helpfully provided them with ample material.

Ken Starr Meets the Press, January 1998
Independent Counsel Starr's dogged investigations into legal issues arising from President Clinton's affair with a White House intern set off a media frenzy, which in turn set off a round of hand-wringing about the state of American journalism.

Clinton settled the Paula Jones suit by paying her $850,000, but more problems awaited. In telephone conversations secretly and illegally taped by Monica Lewinsky's "friend" Linda Tripp, Lewinsky had graphically described an affair with Clinton starting in 1995, when she was twenty-one, and continuing through early 1997. On January 12, 1998, Tripp passed the tapes to Kenneth Starr, an independent counsel appointed by a three-judge panel to investigate the Whitewater matter. At Starr's request, FBI agents fitted Tripp with a recording device and secured further Lewinsky evidence.

Starr now focused on whether Clinton had committed perjury in his testimony and whether he had persuaded Lewinsky to lie as well. In August, after jail threats and a promise of immunity, Lewinsky admitted the affair in testimony before Starr's grand jury. Soon after, in testimony videotaped at the White House, Clinton admitted "conduct that was wrong" with Lewinsky but denied a "sexual relationship" under his rather narrow definition of the term. In a brief TV address, Clinton admitted to an inappropriate relationship with Lewinsky, but called his testimony in the Jones case "legally accurate" and attacked Starr as politically motivated. The scandal provided grist for late-night television, Internet humor, and conservative radio talk-shows.

Other presidents had pursued extramarital affairs, but by the 1990s the women's movement and sexual-harassment laws had made such behavior increasingly objectionable. In a media-saturated age, politicians lived in the constant glare of public scrutiny. Indeed, politicians themselves had paraded intimate personal details for political advantage. Unsurprisingly, then, the Clinton scandal unfolded on TV and in tabloid headlines.

Impeachment

In a September 1998 report to the House Judiciary Committee, Kenneth Starr narrated the Clinton-Lewinsky affair in lurid detail and found "substantial and credible" grounds for impeachment. The president, Starr charged, had committed perjury and influenced others to do the same, and had obstructed justice by retrieving gifts he had given Lewinsky and coaching his secretary on his version of events.

The Judiciary Committee, on a straight party-line vote, forwarded four articles of impeachment to the House of Representatives. In a similarly partisan vote, the House approved and sent to the Senate two articles of impeachment charging Clinton with perjury in his grand-jury testimony and with obstructing justice. For the first time since Andrew Johnson's day, a president of the United States had been impeached.

Opinion polls sent the Republicans an ominous message: most Americans opposed impeachment. In the 1998 midterm elections, as the House impeachment process went forward, the Democrats gained five House seats. Soon after, Speaker Newt Gingrich abruptly resigned both the speakership and his House seat.

Since removing a president requires a two-thirds Senate vote, and since the Republicans held only a fifty-five to forty-five Senate majority, the impeachment campaign seemed foredoomed to failure. Nevertheless, early in 1999 the new Senate conducted a trial. As Chief Justice William Rehnquist presided, Republican members of the House Judiciary Committee, acting as the impeachment managers, presented their case. White House lawyers challenged what one called a "witches' brew of speculation."

Paradoxically, as these events unfolded, Clinton's approval ratings soared. While the public clearly deplored Clinton's personal behavior, few believed that it met the "high crimes and misdemeanors" standard set by the Constitution for removal from office. With the economy booming and Clinton adopting popular posi-

tions on most issues, the public appeared willing to tolerate his personal flaws. Further, many people concluded that whatever Clinton's misdeeds, he was also the target of Republican zealots determined to drive him from office at a time of deep polarization in American public life.

On February 12, 1999, the Senate rejected the impeachment charges and ended the trial. In a brief statement President Clinton again apologized and urged the nation to move on. While some Republicans warned darkly of a double standard of justice, most Americans felt relief that the ordeal was over.

On his last day in office, admitting that he had lied in sworn testimony, Clinton agreed to a $25,000 fine and a five-year suspension of his law license. In March 2002 the special counsel who had succeeded Kenneth Starr in the original Whitewater inquiry found insufficient evidence to convict the Clintons of criminal behavior. The *New York Times* offered a final assessment:

> The nation may never again see a president with Bill Clinton's natural political talents, his instinctive grasp of policy and his breadth of understanding of government issues. He was capable of being an extraordinary leader. The fact that he turned out to be so much less is a tragedy, and the tragedy's first act was Whitewater.

While escaping removal, Clinton had suffered grievous damage, mostly self-inflicted. His character flaws, whose consequences he had managed to avoid in a charmed political life, had overtaken him at last, eroding his leadership and tarnishing his historical standing. The Republican party suffered as well, as some of its most extreme and moralistic members took center stage, rubbing raw the partisan differences that threatened to fragment American public life.

CLINTON'S FOREIGN POLICY: DEFINING AMERICA'S ROLE IN A POST-COLD WAR WORLD

Bill Clinton preferred domestic issues to foreign policy. Yet the United States, as the world's only remaining superpower, could not escape its global role. Confronting scandal and partisan sniping a home, Clinton turned his attention abroad. He faced two key challenges: using American power wisely in the post-Cold War era and responding to terrorist acts against the United States and the threat of further attacks.

The Comeback Kid Comes Back
Political cartoonists enjoyed a field day with the impeachment of Bill Clinton, which, in the short run at least, did more damage to the Republicans than it did to Clinton, whose approval ratings remained high.

The Balkans, Russia, and Eastern Europe in the Post-Soviet Era

In the region of southeastern Europe known as the Balkans, the Soviet collapse unleashed bitter ethnic conflicts. As Yugoslavia broke apart in 1991, Serbian forces launched a campaign of "ethnic cleansing" in neighboring Bosnia, which meant supporting Bosnia's ethnic Serbs while slaughtering or driving out Muslims and Croats. Incited by Serbia's president Slobodan Milosevic, Serbian troops overran U.N.-designated "safe havens" and committed brutal atrocities against Muslims.

To stop the slaughter, the United Nations introduced a peacekeeping force. When this effort failed, the NATO command in Europe, in its first joint military operation, launched air strikes against Bosnian Serb targets in August 1995. The Clinton administration reluctantly joined this operation.

Later in 1995 the administration flew the leaders of Bosnia's warring factions to Dayton, Ohio, for talks. The resulting Dayton Accords imposed a cease-fire and created a framework for governing the region. Clinton committed twenty thousand U.S. troops to a NATO force in Bosnia to enforce the cease-fire.

In 1998, Slobodan Milosevic launched a campaign against Muslims in Serbia's southern province Kosovo. In March 1999, as the bloodshed continued, NATO, under U.S. leadership, bombed Serbian facilities in Kosovo and

in Serbia itself, including Belgrade, the capital. This reliance on air power, with minimal risk of U.S. casualties, soon emerged as America's preferred form of military engagement.

President Clinton, eager to avoid U.S. losses and haunted by memories of Vietnam, held back from committing ground forces. American public opinion wavered as well, appalled by the suffering and a growing refugee crisis, but wary of expanding U.S. involvement. In June 1999, however, U.S. troops joined a NATO force that occupied Kosovo. With the Serbian army under control, the refugees trickled back. Slobodan Milosevic was overthrown in 2001, and a more democratic Yugoslav government, eager for Western aid, delivered him for trial before a war-crimes tribunal at the Hague.

These developments affected U.S. relations with its former Cold War opponent, Russia. Although Russia protested the air attacks on its traditional ally, Serbia, Russian forces joined in NATO's occupation of Kosovo. Facing unrest among its own Muslim population, Russia in 1995–1996 waged war against the breakaway Muslim republic of Chechnya. Some called this unpopular and inconclusive conflict Russia's Vietnam.

Amid these troubles, Russia's hasty conversion to a free-market economy caused a severe economic crisis that threatened to topple President Boris Yeltsin. Having put together a multi-billion-dollar loan package for Russia, the Clinton administration watched anxiously as chaos threatened. Despite U.S. disapproval of the Chechnya war, and despite Yeltsin's growing unpopularity and periodic alcoholic binges, Clinton continued to support him as Russia's best hope. In 1999 the adminis-

tration backed Russia's admission to the Group of Seven (G-7), the world's leading industrial nations, and the G-7 became the G-8. In the same year, over Russia's protests, NATO admitted three new members from the former Soviet bloc—Hungary, Poland, and the Czech Republic. Yeltsin resigned in December 1999, transferring power to Vladimir Putin, a former agent of the KGB, the Soviet secret police.

Symbolic Gestures in Africa; a Modest Success in Haiti

Clinton was stirred by conditions in Africa, a continent wracked by poverty, AIDS (see Chapter 31), tribal conflict, and authoritarian regimes. His engagement, however, proved mainly symbolic.

In 1992 in the East African nation of Somalia, afflicted by civil war and famine, President Bush had committed some twenty-six thousand U.S. troops to a U.N. mission to provide humanitarian aid and end the fighting. As the warring factions battled, forty-four Americans were killed and many injured. President Clinton withdrew the U.S. force in 1994, and the U.N. mission ended a year later. Traumatized by this fiasco, Clinton failed to intervene in other African conflicts, including an appalling human tragedy in Rwanda, where as many as half a million people died and thousands more became refugees in intertribal massacres.

During Clinton's presidency South Africa ended apartheid and became a multiracial democracy—a transformation hastened by U.S. and other nations' economic sanctions. In 1994 Nelson Mandela, long impris-

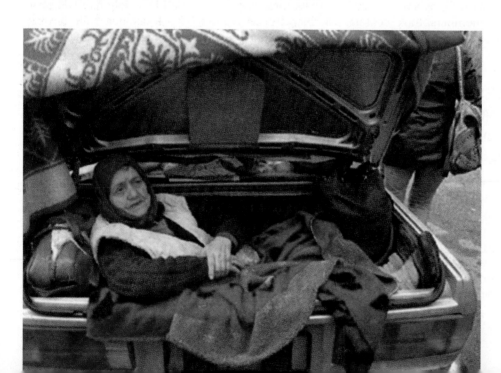

Kosovo, 1999
As the 1990s ended, NATO and the United States launched a bombing campaign again Serbia in an effort to halt President Slobodan Milosevic's "ethnic cleansing" campaign against Kosovo's ethnic Albanians. Here, an elderly ethnic Albanian peers from the trunk of a car filled with refugees fleeing Kosovo.

oned by South Africa's white government, was elected president. On a whirlwind tour of Africa in 1998, President Clinton visited South Africa and greeted Mandela. Calling upon six nations in eleven days, he offered modest aid assistance.

Closer to home, in Haiti, a 1991 military junta overthrew President Jean-Bertrand Aristide and terrorized his supporters. Thousands of Haitians fleeing poverty and repression set out for Florida in small, leaky boats. African-American leaders demanded U.S. action, as did Haitian's born in the United States. To dislodge the junta, Clinton assembled an invasion flotilla off Haiti's coast in 1994, and former president Jimmy Carter persuaded the junta's leaders to accept voluntary exile. Backed by a U.S. occupation force, Aristide resumed the presidency, giving Clinton a modest diplomatic success.

The Middle East: Seeking an Elusive Peace, Combating a Wily Foe

After hopeful beginnings, Clinton's pursuit of peace in the Middle East failed. The 1987 Palestinian uprising, or Intifada, against Israel's military occupation of the West Bank and Gaza (see Chapter 30) continued into the 1990s. Prospects for peace brightened in 1993, after Israeli and Palestinian negotiators meeting in Norway agreed on a six-year timetable for peace.

The so-called Oslo Accords provided for the creation of a Palestinian state, the return of most Israeli-held land in the West Bank and Gaza to the Palestinians, and further talks on the claims of Palestinian refugees and the final status of Jerusalem (see Map 32.1). In 1994 President Clinton presided as Israeli prime minister Yitzhak Rabin and Yasir Arafat, head of the Palestine Liberation Organization, signed the agreement at the White House.

The bloodshed continued, however, and in 1995 Rabin was assassinated by a young Israeli opposed to the Oslo Accords. Israel's next election brought Benjamin Netanyahu of the hard-line Likud party to power. Suicide bombings by Palestinian extremists in 1996–1997 killed some eighty Israelis, triggering retaliatory attacks. Under U.S. pressure Netanyahu in 1998

MAP 32.1
The Mideast Crisis, 1980-Present
With terrorist attacks, the Iran-Iraq War, the Persian Gulf War, Iraq's secretive weapons program, and the ongoing struggle between Israel and the Palestinians, the Middle East was the site of almost unending violence, conflict, and tension in these years.

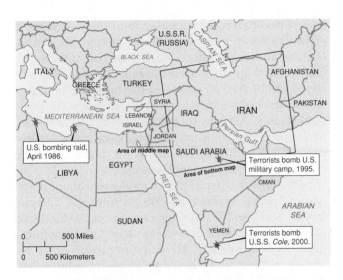

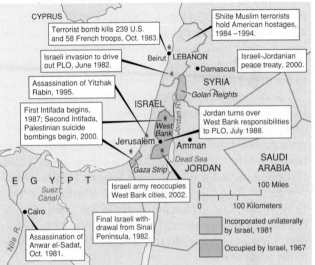

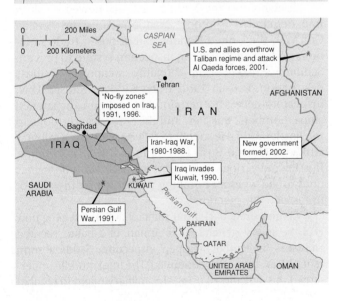

agreed to withdraw Israeli forces from some West Bank areas in 1998 in return for security guarantees. But as terrorist attacks continued, Netanyahu halted the withdrawal. More Jewish housing was built in Palestinian territory, and by 2000 an estimated two hundred thousand Israeli settlers were living there. Secretary of State Madeleine K. Albright struggled to bring the two sides back to the negotiating table. (Albright was named to the post in 1997, thereby becoming the highest-ranking woman in U.S. government history.)

Ehud Barak of Israel's more moderate Labour party became prime minister in 1999. In July 2000 Clinton invited Barak and Arafat to meet at Camp David. Barak made unprecedented concessions based on the principle of "land for peace." According to press reports, he agreed to Israeli withdrawal from 95 percent of the West Bank and all of Gaza; the creation of a Palestinian state; Palestinian control of East Jerusalem; and the transfer of control over Jerusalem's Temple Mount, sacred to both Muslims and Jews, from Israel to a vaguely defined "religious authority." In return, Arafat would declare an end to hostilities and give up further claims on Israel.

Arafat refused Barak's offer, and the summit failed. In September the Likud leader Ariel Sharon—with nearly one thousand Israeli soldiers and police—made a provocative visit to the site of Al-Asqa Mosque, an Islamic shrine on Temple Mount. Soon after, Palestinians launched a new Intifada against Israel. Clinton continued last-ditch peacemaking efforts, but they came to nothing. In elections early in 2001, Ariel Sharon became prime minister. Like other presidents before him, Clinton bequeathed the Israeli-Palestinian conflict to his successor.

Elsewhere in the Middle East, a renewed crisis in Iraq demanded Clinton's attention. After the Persian Gulf War, the United Nations had imposed trade sanctions on Iraq and set up an inspection system to prevent Saddam Hussein from building weapons of mass destruction. Late in 1997, when Saddam refused U.N. inspectors access to certain sites, Clinton dispatched ships, bombers, missiles, and thirty thousand troops to the Persian Gulf. He sought to rally support for a military strike, as George Bush had done in 1991, but France, Russia, and various Arab states resisted. At home, critics questioned whether bombing would further the goal of unrestricted inspections.

Clinton drew back from military action after the new U.N. secretary general, Kofi Annan of Ghana, secured Saddam's agreement to open inspection. Saddam soon reneged, and the crisis continued. The Iraqi muddle underscored the difficulty of using U.S. military might to combat potential terrorist threats, and of rallying post-Vietnam U.S. public opinion behind a military course whose long-term outcome seemed murky.

Nuclear Proliferation and Terrorism: Confronting Global Security Challenges

Under the Nuclear Nonproliferation Treaty of 1970, sixty-two nations agreed to ban the spread of nuclear weapons beyond countries that already possessed them. Despite this treaty, the proliferation threat continued. In May 1998 a long-simmering dispute between India and Pakistan over Kashmir escalated sharply when India tested a nuclear bomb. Despite urgent pleas from the United States and other powers, Pakistan followed suit, and fears of nuclear conflict rose.

Proliferation fears also focused on communist North Korea, which, in violation of the 1970 treaty, began a program of nuclear-weapons development and missile testing. In 1994, facing U.N. economic sanctions and the loss of $9 billion in international assistance (and following a visit by Jimmy Carter), North Korea pledged to halt this program. In 1999, confronting famine and economic crisis, North Korea agreed to suspend long-range missile testing in return for an easing of U.S. trade and travel restrictions. In 2002, triggering fresh tensions, North Korea admitted to continued nuclear weapons research.

Nuclear dangers also arose in the former Soviet Union. In the 1993 Strategic Arms Reduction Treaty (START II), the United States and Russia agreed to cut their long-range nuclear arsenals by half. This left many nuclear weapons in Russia and in three newly independent nations that had once been part of the Soviet Union: Ukraine, Kazakstan, and Belarus. With social unrest and economic crisis in the region, Washington feared that foreign powers or terrorist groups might acquire nuclear weapons or know-how through clandestine operations or bribery. The Bush and Clinton administrations expended much money and diplomatic effort to speed the "denuclearization" of Ukraine, Kazakstan, and Belarus, and the safe dismantling of nuclear weapons within Russia itself.

The cycle of terrorism continued in the Clinton years. On August 7, 1998, powerful bombs exploded almost simultaneously outside the U.S. embassies in Nairobi, Kenya, and Dar-es-Salaam, Tanzania, killing 220 people, including Americans and many Kenyans and Tanzanians. U.S. antiterrorism specialists pinpointed a shadowy and wealthy Saudi Arabian, Osama bin Laden, who in 1982 had moved to Afghanistan, where he

established and financed terrorist training camps. In the 1990s he had spent time in Sudan.

Two weeks after the embassy bombings, Clinton ordered cruise missile strikes on a suspected chemical-weapons factory in Sudan allegedly financed by bin Laden and on a training camp in Afghanistan. In November 1998 a U.S. grand jury indicted bin Laden on charges of planning the embassy attacks and also of inciting the killing of GIs in Somalia in 1993.

In 1999 Clinton called for increased spending and new measures to cope with rogue states and terrorist groups that might acquire nuclear, chemical, or biological weapons. "[W]e are involved here in a long-term struggle . . . ," declared Secretary of State Albright; "This is, unfortunately, the war of the future."

Underscoring Albright's grim assessment, on October 12, 2000, a bomb aboard a small boat in the harbor of Aden, Yemen, ripped a gaping hole in the U.S. destroyer *Cole*, killing seventeen sailors. At a memorial service, President Clinton told the grieving families, "[Terrorists] . . . can never heal, or build harmony, or bring people together. That is work only free, law-abiding people can do. People like the sailors of the USS *Cole*." The peaceful post-Cold War era that many had anticipated seemed an ever-receding mirage.

A New World Order?

As we saw in Chapter 31, the end of the Cold War initially brought a wave of joy and relief. But as time passed, it became clear that world conditions remained dangerous and posed challenges as daunting as those of the Cold War itself. The Soviet empire had collapsed, and the threat of global nuclear war had subsided, but trouble spots around the world still clamored for attention. Like firefighters battling many small blazes rather than a single conflagration, policymakers now wrestled with a tangle of seemingly unrelated issues. Somalia, Bosnia, Iraq, Kosovo, North Korea, Pakistan, Afghanistan, Israel and the Palestinians, and terrorists who ignored national boundaries all claimed Washington's attention.

At the same time, many citizens turned away from world affairs. In a 1997 poll only 20 percent of Americans said that they followed foreign news, a sharp decline from the 1980s, with the biggest drop among young people. TV coverage of world news fell by more than 50 percent from 1989 to 1995. Post-Cold War America, commented one observer in 1998, "has no mission other than to keep itself entertained."

Taking a broad view, four large-scale developments helped define America's post-Cold War global role. The first was the growing centrality of economic and trade issues. Commercial considerations, multinational corporations, and global systems of communications, finance, and marketing increasingly defined international relations and America's foreign-policy interests.

Second, in contrast to economic globalization, the world saw a turning inward toward various forms of religious fundamentalism. Muslim fundamentalists, reacting against Western secularism, searched for Islamic purity, in some cases concluding that terrorist attacks on America, which they viewed as demonic and threatening, represented a religious duty. In Israel, some Orthodox Jews claimed Palestinian lands on the basis of biblical prophecies. In India, a fundamentalist Hindu party gained power in 1998, replacing the secularist Congress party. America harbored Christian fundamentalists suspicious of international organizations and of the U.S. government itself and dismayed by an array of social and cultural trends. The struggle between fundamentalist and inward-turning impulses, on the one hand, and the globalizing economy and communications system, on the other, posed a major challenge for diplomats.

Third, a growing gulf divided the world between prosperous, industrialized societies with high living standards and stable birthrates, and regions scourged by poverty, disease, illiteracy, explosive population growth, and a dangerous gap between the masses and privileged elites. This vast disparity created conditions ripe for conflict and unrest, including the spreading menace of terrorism.

Finally, the role of international organizations was uncertain. With the Cold War's end, some Americans either turned to isolationism or favored unilateralist, go-it-alone approaches. Some Americans even demanded U.S. withdrawal from the United Nations and other world organizations.

Others, however, continued to hope that the United Nations, long a pawn of the superpowers' conflict, could at last function as its more idealistic supporters had envisioned in 1945. Indeed, in 2002 some forty-four thousand U.N. peacekeeping forces and civilian personal were serving in fifteen trouble spots around the world. U.N. agencies also addressed global environmental and public-health issues.

Post-Cold War opinion polls indicated that most Americans supported internationalist approaches to world problems and viewed the United Nations favorably. Despite flagging attention to foreign affairs, Americans could become engaged when they understood an issue in human terms, or grasped how events abroad affected U.S. interests. Clearly, however, Amer-

icans of the 1990s were still adjusting to a new era of complex international issues that could not be reduced to simple Cold War slogans.

THE ECONOMIC BOOM OF THE 1990s

The 1990s saw one of the longest periods of sustained economic growth in U.S. history. Productivity increased, unemployment fell, and inflation remained under control. Prosperity helped bring crime rates down and reduce welfare rolls. Federal deficits gave way to surpluses as tax revenues increased.

For some, the surging stock market stimulated the urge to get rich quick, acquire more possessions, and enjoy the good times. But real wages did not keep pace with the stock market, and many workers who lacked the specialized skills required by the new economy remained stuck in dead-end jobs. America's participation in an increasingly global economy fueled economic growth, but when foreign economies faltered, the U.S. economy felt the effects as well.

New York Stock Exchange, August 1998
Despite economic crises elsewhere, U.S. stock prices soared as the 1990s wore on, fueled especially by computer and information-technology stocks.

Economic Upturn; Surging Stock Market

Although Bill Clinton targeted the sluggish economy in the 1992 campaign, a turnaround had already begun. Economists differ over the sources of the prosperity of the 1990s, but the new products, efficiencies, and business opportunities associated with the personal computer and the information revolution were certainly crucial (see Chapter 31). Rising international trade and high consumer confidence helped sustain the boom, as did low inflation, the Federal Reserve Board's low interest rates, and a steady flow of immigrants eager to work.

Whatever its sources, the fact of the boom is clear. Unemployment, which stood at 7.5 percent in 1992, fell to 4 percent by 2000. Corporate earnings soared. Wal-Mart racked up revenues of $193 billion in 2000; General Motors, $185 billion; and on down the list. The Houston-based Enron Corporation, an energy broker, vaulted into the ranks of corporate giants, reporting revenues of $101 billion. The gross domestic product, a key economic indicator, rose nearly 80 percent in the decade (see Figure 32.1).

The stock market reflected and then outran the economic upturn as the stock of many companies soared far beyond their actual value or earnings prospects. From under 3,000 in 1991, the Dow Jones Industrial Average edged toward 12,000 by early 2001. New investors flocked into the market. By 1998 nearly 50 percent of American families owned stock directly or through their pension plans.

Information-technology stocks proved especially popular. The NASDAQ composite index, loaded with technology stocks, soared from under 500 in 1991 to over 5,000 by early 2000. Some new stock offerings by Silicon Valley start-up companies surged to fantastic levels, turning young entrepreneurs into paper millionaires. The brokers who managed these offerings (and profited from the rising stock prices) fueled the speculation with glowing assessments of new companies' earning prospects. As early as 1996 Alan Greenspan, chairman of the Federal Reserve Board, warned of "irrational exuberance" in the stock market, but it only surged higher.

Corporate mergers proliferated as companies sought to improve their profitability. In 2000 the communications giant Viacom swallowed CBS for $41 billion, and the pharmaceutical company Pfizer acquired rival Warner-Lambert for $90 billion. In the biggest merger of all, the Internet company America Online (AOL) acquired Time-Warner (itself the product of earlier mergers) for $182 billion.

FIGURE 32.1

The U.S. Economy, 1990–2002

The unemployment rate fell and the gross domestic product (GDP) rose during the boom years of the 1990s. As recession hit in 2001, however, the jobless rate increased.

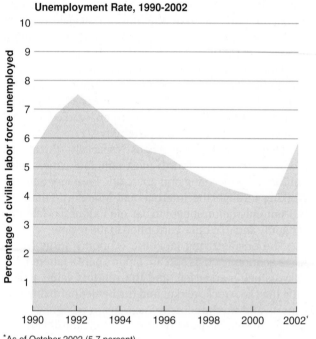

Unemployment Rate, 1990-2002

*As of October 2002 (5.7 percent)

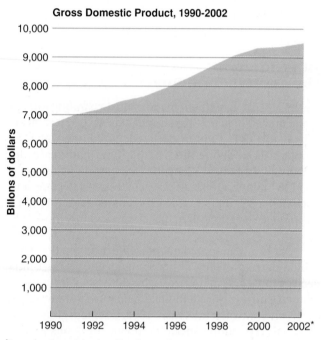

Gross Domestic Product, 1990-2002

*Annual estimate based on First Quarter figures

The rising stock market made many Americans wealthy, at least on paper, stimulating the quest for luxury possessions and leisure pursuits that helped shape the cultural climate of the decade (see Chapter 31). In 2000 Americans spent $105 billion on new cars; $107 billion on video, audio, and computer equipment; and $81 billion on foreign travel. The so-called dot-com millionaires of Silicon Valley and Wall Street seemed living proof that the new economy was the wave of the future. Some economists waved caution flags. With so many Americans speculating in stocks rather than putting money in more secure forms of savings, they warned, the inevitable downturn could have severe consequences.

An Uneven Prosperity

The benefits of the boom were unevenly distributed. From 1979 to 1996 the portion of total income going to the wealthiest 20 percent of the population increased by 13 percent, while the share going to the poorest 20 percent dropped by 22 percent. Commented Harvard economist Richard Freeman in 1998, "The U.S. has the most unequal distribution of income among advanced countries—and the degree of inequality has increased more

here than in any comparable country." While stockholding was widely diffused by the later 1990s, the top 5 percent of the owners held 80 percent of all stock.

As corporations maintained profits through "downsizing" and cost cutting, job worries gnawed at many Americans. Adjusted for inflation, the real wages of industrial workers rose only slightly in the 1990s. The rapidly growing service sector included not only high-income positions but also low-paying, low-skilled jobs in sales, fast-food outlets, custodial work, telemarketing, and so forth (see Chapter 31). While many service workers as well as teachers and other white-collar groups were unionized, overall union membership stood at only 13.5 percent of the labor force by 2000, weakening this means by which workers had historically organized to improve their wages and job conditions. Unions' political clout weakened as well. Congress ratified the 1993 NAFTA treaty, for example, despite protests from organized labor (see Chapter 31).

Job-market success increasingly required advanced training and special skills, posing problems for young people, displaced industrial workers, and welfare recipients thrown into the labor force. Overall employment statistics also concealed racial and ethnic variables. In

2000 the jobless rate for blacks and Hispanics, despite having dropped, remained significantly higher than the rate for whites. In short, while the economic boom brought real benefits to many, a wide gap existed between those who prospered dramatically, and those who experienced only modest gains, or none at all.

America and the Global Economy

As the NAFTA agreement made plain, expanding foreign trade ranked high on Clinton's agenda. At the 1994 meeting of the G-7, Clinton declared, "Trade as much as troops will . . . define the ties that bind nations in the twenty-first century." When the U.S. trade deficit shot up to $133 billion in 1993, after several years of decline, and included a $59 billion trade gap with Japan, Clinton like his predecessor pressured the Japanese to buy more U.S. goods.

Clinton also opted to preserve trading ties with China despite Beijing's human-rights abuses. Brushing aside protests from human-rights activists, Clinton welcomed Chinese president Jiang Zemin for a state visit in 1997, and returned the visit in 1998. Congress grew skeptical of the administration's policy of "constructive engagement" with China as Beijing continued perpetrating human-rights abuses, pursuing restrictive trade practices, threatening Taiwan, and pirating U.S. movies, CDs, and computer software.

Clinton's China policy reflected hard economic realities: China had become America's fourth largest trading partner, after Canada, Mexico, and Japan. In 2000 Congress passed legislation that permanently granted China the same trading status as America's other trading partners, rather than making trade agreements with China dependent on year-by-year congressional action, as in the past. That year U.S. imports from China surpassed $100 billion.

Economic calculations also increasingly defined U.S. relations with Europe, which became a powerful trading competitor in 1993 when fifteen nations created the European Union (EU), pledged to coordinating their economic policies. Furthering this policy of economic cooperation, in 2001 the EU nations adopted a common currency, the Euro.

The growing importance of world trade was underscored in 1994 when the Senate ratified a new global trading agreement that created the World Trade Organization (WTO) replacing the old General Agreement on Tariffs and Trade (GATT) established in 1947 (see Chapter 26). The WTO agreement provided for a gradual lowering of trade barriers worldwide and set up mechanisms for resolving trade disputes.

The interconnectedness of the global economy became evident in the 1990s. When the Mexican peso collapsed in 1995, jeopardizing U.S.-Mexican trade and threatening to increase the flow of illegal migrants northward, Clinton quickly granted Mexico $40 billion in loan guarantees. In 1997–1998 the economies of Thailand, South Korea, Indonesia, and other Asian nations weakened as a result of corruption, excessive debt, and other factors. Viewing the crisis as a danger to the United States, the State Department worked to avoid political chaos and regional instability.

Political and social chaos especially threatened Indonesia, the world's fourth-most-populous nation, ruled until 1998 by the aging and autocratic President Suharto. Working through the International Monetary Fund, the U.S. administration sought to bail out Indonesia's faltering economy and to reduce corruption in the regime.

The once-sizzling Japanese economy stumbled as Asia's economic crisis spread. Japan's banks faltered; the Tokyo stock market fell; and the yen lost value, unsettling the U.S. stock market and further jeopardizing U.S. exports and investments in Asia. Again recognizing the threat to U.S. prosperity, the Clinton administration urged Japan to undertake needed economic reforms. By 1999, as the economies of Brazil, Argentina, and other South American nations sank into recession as well, analysts questioned how long the American boom could continue.

In the new global economy, European and other investors flocked into the American market. By 2000 foreign investment in the United States totaled a staggering $1.24 trillion. Australian-born tycoon Rupert Murdoch snapped up U.S. entertainment and communications companies. Investment flowed the other way as well. As American fast-food chains, soft drinks, movies, pop music, and TV programs spread globally, other nations fretted about being swamped by U.S. mass culture.

Globalization aroused opposition in other quarters as well. Union leaders and environmentalists warned that multinational corporations could bypass national environmental-protection laws and exploit unprotected workers in poor nations. Activists pressured companies selling clothing, footwear, and other consumer goods made in poor nations to upgrade labor conditions in their factories. At a 1999 WTO conference in Seattle, opposition exploded in the streets. For several days, demonstrators representing a variety of causes nearly shut down the city.

DISPUTED ELECTION; CONSERVATIVE ADMINISTRATION, 2000–2002

The 2000 election highlighted the acrimony pervading U.S. politics. The disputed election ended the Democrats' hold on the White House, but only after the Supreme Court intervened on behalf of the Republican candidate, George W. Bush. Pursuing his father's unfulfilled agenda, Bush advocated policies supported by corporate America and by religious conservatives. On the military front, Bush pursued a missile-defense system first proposed by Ronald Reagan. In its approach to the world, the administration initially followed a go-it-alone policy, arousing widespread criticism abroad.

Election 2000: Bush Versus Gore

The 2000 campaign shaped up as a contest of personalities more than issues. The Democrats, bouncing back from the impeachment crisis, confidently nominated Al Gore for president. As his running mate, Gore chose Connecticut Senator Joseph Lieberman, making him the first Jewish-American candidate on a major party ticket. The fact that Lieberman had denounced Clinton's extramarital affair and his efforts to cover up the scandal helped insulate Gore from the "sleaze factor" in the Clinton legacy.

The Republican contest narrowed down to Senator John McCain of Arizona, a former prisoner of war in Vietnam, and Texas Governor George W. Bush, son of the former president. The maverick McCain, a champion of campaign-finance reform and a critic of corporate influences in his party, made a strong bid. Bush, however, with powerful backers and a folksy manner, won the nomination. His running mate Dick Cheney had been defense secretary in the first Bush administration and then head of the Halliburton Corporation, a Dallas-based energy company. Conservative columnist Pat Buchanan won the nomination of Ross Perot's Reform party. The Green party nominated consumer advocate and environmentalist Ralph Nader.

Both Gore and Bush courted the center while trying to hold their bases. For Bush, this meant corporate interests, religious conservatives, and the so-called Reagan Democrats in the white middle and working classes. Gore's base, by contrast, consisted of liberals, academics and professionals, union members, African-Americans, and many Hispanics.

Al and Tipper Gore
Accused of being aloof and overly intellectual, Gore demonstrated his amorous technique at the 2000 Democratic convention.

With the economy still healthy (despite signs of weakening), Gore's prospects looked good. He pointed to the nation's prosperity and pledged to extend health care coverage and protect social security. In televised debates Gore displayed greater mastery of detail than his opponent.

Bush, by contrast, while projecting a likeable manner, had little national or foreign-policy experience. Many saw him as a lightweight who owed his political success to family influence. As one Texas Democrat quipped, "George Bush was born on third base and thought he had hit a home run." But he campaigned hard, pledging tax cuts, education reform, and a missile-defense system. Calling himself a "compassionate conservative," Bush subtly reminded voters of Clinton's misdeeds by promising to restore dignity to the White House.

Gore had image problems. He had been tainted by fund-raising scandals in the 1996 campaign, and many voters found him pompous. The factual mastery he flaunted in the debates struck many as arrogant. Eager to prove his political independence after eight years as vice president, Gore distanced himself from Clinton, despite the president's high approval ratings. Peeved, Clinton played little role in the campaign.

Polls showed that most voters agreed with Gore on the issues, approved the Democrats' economic policies,

and conceded Gore's intellectual edge. Ominously for Gore, however, they preferred Bush as a person. The election seemed a toss-up.

Feuding in Florida

The intensely partisan politics of these years, so vividly on display in the impeachment crisis, was further symbolized by a bitter dispute over the election outcome (see Map 32.2). When the polls closed on November 7, Gore had won the popular vote by a narrow but clear margin of more than 500,000. The electoral college, however, remained up for grabs. Soon the struggle narrowed to Florida, whose 25 electoral votes would give either candidate the presidency.

Flaws in Florida's electoral process quickly became apparent. In Palm Beach County, a poorly designed ballot led several thousand Gore supporters to vote for Buchanan by mistake. In other counties, particularly those with a high proportion of poor and African-American voters, antiquated vote-counting machines threw out thousands of ballots in which the paper tabs, called "chads," were not fully punched out. Gore supporters demanded a hand count of these rejected bal-

lots, confident that they would carry their man to victory. Bush's lawyers filed suit to halt the recounts.

Florida secretary of state Katherine Harris refused to extend the deadline for certifying the Florida vote to allow for a hand recount. Democrats questioned Harris's impartiality, since she had cochaired Bush's Florida campaign and was an ally of Florida Governor Jeb Bush, the candidate's brother.

As various counties conducted hand counts, election officials scrutinized ballots to see whether the chads were detached, dangling, or "pregnant" (partially pushed out). On November 21 the Florida Supreme Court, with a preponderance of Democrats, unanimously held that the hand count should constitute the official results. Bush's legal team appealed to the U.S. Supreme Court, which, despite a well-established precedent of letting state courts decide electoral disputes, accepted the case. Overturning the Florida justices' ruling, the U.S. Supreme Court on December 4 sent the case back to Tallahassee for clarification. The seemingly endless dispute dominated the media.

Meanwhile, on November 26, Secretary of State Harris had formally certified the Florida vote, awarding Bush the state. But on December 8, ten days before the

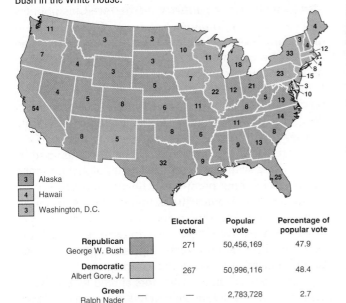

MAP 32.2
The Election of 2000.
For the first time since 1888, the winner of the popular vote, Al Gore, failed to win the presidency. The electoral-college system and the Supreme Court's intervention in the disputed Florida vote put George W. Bush in the White House.

3	Alaska
4	Hawaii
3	Washington, D.C.

	Electoral vote	Popular vote	Percentage of popular vote
Republican George W. Bush	271	50,456,169	47.9
Democratic Albert Gore, Jr.	267	50,996,116	48.4
Green Ralph Nader	—	2,783,728	2.7

The Florida Election Dispute
A Fort Lauderdale judge scrutinizes a partially punched-out ballot in late November 2000.

electoral college was to convene, the Florida Supreme Court ordered an immediate recount of all ballots thrown out by voting machines. "At this rate," mused a radio commentator, "the Inaugural Ball will be a surprise party." The U.S. Supreme Court again heard an appeal, and on December 12, in a 5 to 4 vote, ordered an end to the recount. Republican appointees to the court generally supported Bush. Gore conceded the next day. Five Supreme Court justices had, in effect, made George W. Bush president.

Ralph Nader who, though winning only 3 percent of the vote, also helped put Bush in the White House. Had it not been for the 97,488 Floridian's who voted for Nader, Gore would doubtless have won the state.

The election produced an evenly divided Senate. Each party had fifty senators, giving Vice President Cheney the deciding vote. (The Republicans narrowly held the House of Representative.) Hillary Rodham Clinton won election as senator from New York, becoming the first presidential wife to pursue a political career. Overall, the new Senate included thirteen women, a record number.

To the end, President Clinton maintained the same balance of statesmanlike and shady behavior that bedeviled his entire presidency. In January 2001, as his term ended, Clinton issued tougher worker-safety regulations, particularly relating to repetitive-motion injuries common among computer workers. He also issued an executive order protecting nearly 67 million acres of federal forest land from logging and road building.

On his last day in office, however, he issued federal pardons to 167 people, including his half-brother, in trouble with the law on drug charges; persons caught up in Clinton-era scandals; and white-collar offenders who had White House influence or were major Democratic contributors, including a commodities trader who had fled to Switzerland to avoid trial for tax evasion and other crimes. Despite Clinton's political skills and good intentions, few Americans expressed regret as he left Washington.

The George W. Bush Administration: A Conservative Turn in Domestic Politics

As the election crisis ended, Americans focused on the incoming president, fifty-four-year-old George W. Bush. After graduating from Yale, serving in the Texas Air National Guard during the Vietnam War, and earning an MBA from Harvard Business School, Bush returned to Texas and entered the oil business. Known for partying

and heavy drinking since his college days, he was convicted of drunk driving in 1976, but then experienced a religious conversion and married a schoolteacher, Laura Welch, who helped bring stability to his life. Bush's business ventures did not thrive, but in 1989 he joined a consortium that bought the Texas Rangers baseball team. Frequently appearing at games, he used this visibility, plus his family connections, to win the Texas governorship in 1994.

Attention soon focused on the team Bush assembled. Colin Powell, former head of the Joint Chiefs of Staff, became secretary of state, and the highest ranking African-American ever to serve in a presidential administration. As national security adviser Bush named Condoleezza Rice of Stanford University, also an African-American.

Other Bush appointees were, like Vice President Cheney, veterans of earlier Republican administrations with strong corporate ties. Secretary of Defense Donald Rumsfeld had held the same post under President Ford and later headed a large pharmaceutical company. Treasury Secretary Paul O'Neill had been CEO of Alcoa Corporation. Army Secretary Thomas E. White came from Houston's Enron Corporation. To appease the Republican right wing, Bush named ultra-conservative John Ashcroft, who had just lost a bid for reelection to the Senate, as attorney general. After a stiff grilling, Ashcroft won confirmation on a 58 to 42 Senate vote.

Despite his razor-thin victory, Bush did not move to the center, as many had expected. Rather he tailored his domestic policies to reflect the interests of the wealthy, corporate leaders, and the religious right. His own conservative outlook and business background, combined with the influence of businesspeople in his inner circle and a desire to win favor with religious conservatives (whose alienation had helped defeat his father's reelection bid in 1992), shaped his administration.

On education, Bush proposed standardized national tests from grades three through eight, to make sure children were learning basic skills, with penalties on schools that failed to measure up. He also called for a voucher system by which children could attend private or religious schools at taxpayers' expense. In December 2001 Congress mandated annual testing and provided funds for tutors in poorly performing schools, but rejected the controversial voucher provision.

In February 2001, fulfilling a campaign promise, Bush proposed a bill to cut taxes by $1.6 trillion over a ten-year period. Though the measure reduced rates in most tax brackets, the wealthiest taxpayers benefited most. Proponents argued that the tax cuts would stimulate

investment as the economy went into recession (see below). Democrats attacked the bill for favoring the rich. Recalling the huge deficits that followed the Reagan tax cut of 1981, they also charged that Bush's plan reflected overly optimistic economic projections. In May Congress passed a $1.35 trillion tax cut—lower than Bush's proposal and somewhat less tilted toward the rich. As the economy worsened and budget surpluses vanished, second thoughts about Bush's tax cut increased. The *New York Times,* estimating the lost federal revenue over a twenty-year period at a staggering $4 trillion, warned that the shortfall could be covered only by dipping into social security and Medicare trust funds.

Bush's energy program reflected the industry's influence in Republican circles. Kenneth Lay, for example, head of Houston's Enron Corporation and a major GOP contributor, enjoyed access to top Bush administration officials and the heads of federal regulatory agencies.

Warning of America's dependence on imported oil, Bush proposed two thousand new electric power plants, including more nuclear power plants, and vastly expanded coal, oil, and natural-gas production, including mining and drilling in environmentally fragile regions such as the Alaska National Wildlife Refuge. Conservation and research on renewable energy barely figured in the program. Critics attacked the administration's ties to the energy industry and the fact that the plan had been drafted in closed meetings between Dick Cheney and energy-company executives.

The Republican House passed a bill favored by the White House. It provided $27 billion in incentives for the domestic oil, gas, and coal industries and permitted drilling in Alaska's Arctic National Wildlife Refuge. In April 2002 the Democratic Senate passed a very different bill featuring tax breaks and other incentives to promote energy conservation and the use of renewable fuels, and forbidding Alaska drilling. The two bills went to a joint House-Senate conference committee, with the final outcome uncertain. The process illustrated the difficulties of governing in a climate of sharp partisan divisions, with each side holding sharply, opposed ideological positions.

As Bush's conservative program unfolded, moderate Republicans grew restive. In May 2001, Vermont Senator James Jeffords announced his departure from the Republican party to become an independent. With Jeffords' vote, the Democrats regained the chairmanship of all Senate committees and the opportunity to shape the Senate agenda. The four-month interval when the White House and both houses of Congress were controlled by the same party came to an end, suggesting still more divisive political battles ahead.

Jeffords' action, observed political commentator Flora Lewis, offered "a sharp reminder that the voters did not choose the clear swing to the right that George W. Bush seems to assume."

The Democrats' Senate takeover added momentum to a bill, opposed by the administration, to regulate

Musk Oxen in Alaska's Arctic National Wildlife Refuge
Proposals by the George W. Bush administration to permit oil drilling in the refuge stirred bitter controversy.

health maintenance organizations (HMOs) and broaden patients' right to choose specialists and to sue their HMOs. With 80 percent of U.S. workers in HMOs, and with rising complaints about paperwork, unpaid claims, and HMO decisions driven by cost rather than by patients' well-being, such legislation enjoyed broad support. In August 2001 both houses passed so-called patients' bill of rights bills, though they differed on the permissible size of lawsuits and other provisions.

The battle illustrated the power of pressure groups and soft money. In what one Washington observer called "a lobbying war of near-epic proportions," the HMO industry, health insurers, and business associations fought the bill, while consumer groups and the trial-lawyers association supported it. Whether such a law, if finally enacted, would actually improve health care or reduce public frustration with an increasingly bureaucratic and cost-conscious system remained unclear.

Bush's attempt to placate the religious right without alienating less-conservative voters was illustrated by his effort to find a middle way on the emotional issue of research on stem cells, which are produced during an early stage of human embryo development (see Technology and Culture: The Promise and Dilemma of Genetic Research). Biomedical specialists and many bioethicists argued that the potential medical benefits justified stem-cell research. Some religious organizations as well as anti-abortion groups strongly protested, arguing that such research could lead down a slippery slope of subordinating potential human life to scientific projects. Bush's compromise ruling, announced in August 2001, permitted federal funding of research on stem-cell lines already held by laboratories, but barring funding for research on stem cells taken from embryos in the future.

A Go-it-Alone Foreign Policy; Pursuing Missile Defense

The administration of George W. Bush at first proceeded with scant regard for other nations' views. This contrasted with his father's approach, which had been quite internationalist in outlook. On military matters, the younger Bush pursued programs initiated by his Republican predecessors.

Both these generalizations are illustrated by the administration's determination to build the antimissile system first proposed by President Reagan in 1983 (see Chapter 30). Reagan's "Star Wars" initiative had been criticized as a technological fantasy, and its strategic rationale seemingly evaporated with the Cold War's end.

Clinton had downgraded antimissile research, but George W. Bush gave it high priority. True believers and military contractors eager to promote the project argued that the technical problems could be solved. As for its strategic rationale, they now focused on possible missile attacks from "rogue states" such as Iraq and North Korea.

Bush's enthusiasm for missile defense had diplomatic implications, because such a system would violate the 1972 Anti-Ballistic Missile (ABM) Treaty. Russian president Vladimir Putin, eager for U.S. investment and a greater role in NATO, agreed to discuss dropping the ABM Treaty if both sides agreed to reduce their remaining arsenals of some six to seven thousand nuclear weapons. The Bush administration valued Russia as an ally in the war against terrorism (see below) and as a potential supplier of oil should imports from the Middle East be disrupted, and accepted Putin's terms. In 2002 the United States withdrew from the ABM Treaty and it officially lapsed. Soon after, Bush and Putin signed a treaty pledging to cut their nuclear arsenals by two-thirds within ten years. Fulfilling another of Moscow's objectives, NATO granted Russia a close consultative relationship, though not full membership.

In June 2002 work began at Fort Greely, Alaska, on a facility for developing and testing a missile defense system, which planners hoped would be operational by 2004. Alaskans who were worried about the state's economy welcomed the infusion of jobs and federal dollars the project promised.

Other U.S. actions underscored the administration's go-it-alone approach. At a 178-nation conference on global warming in Bonn, Germany, in 2001, the U.S. delegation refused to participate in or sign the resulting agreement. When most other nations, including the European Union and Japan, agreed to strengthen a 1972 treaty banning biological weapons, the United States refused to accept the plan. The administration also rejected a U.N. agreement to regulate the global trade in handguns, as well as a treaty banning discrimination against women ratified by 169 other nations.

The United Nations had long been a target of conservatives skeptical of international commitments. Beginning in 1994, conservatives in Congress led by Republican Jesse Helms of North Carolina had withheld payment of America's U.N. dues. By 2001 the back debt totaled $2.3 billion. Early in 2001 the Senate Foreign Relations Committee agreed to pay part of this sum and to resume payment of future dues at a reduced percentage rate. Even this agreement was jeopardized in 2002, however, when the Bush administration opposed the creation of an International Criminal Court

The Promise and Dilemma of Genetic Research

Quantum physics was the most exciting scientific and technological frontier in the early twentieth century, as researchers made theoretical discoveries that ultimately gave rise to the atomic bomb, the nuclear-power industry, radiation therapy in cancer treatment, and the use of radioactive isotopes in medical diagnosis. After 1950, the biological sciences, especially molecular biology and genetics, produced the most stunning breakthroughs. But the same discoveries that deepened understanding of life also raised complex social and ethical issues.

For centuries, farmers had understood genetic principles in practical terms as a way to increase crop yield and breed fatter hogs and cows that produced more milk. Modern genetics dates back to the 1860s, when Austrian monk Gregor Mendel experimented with hybridizing pea plants.

The field of molecular biology arose in the 1950s. In 1953 Max Perutz of Cambridge University showed how x-rays could be used to establish the structure of protein molecules, the basic working elements of all living organisms. Modern genetics leapt forward in 1953–1954 when a young American scientist, James D. Watson, working with Francis Crick of Cambridge University and using data from Maurice Wilkins and Rosalind Franklin of King's College, London, established the double-helix structure of DNA (deoxyribonucleic acid), a mega-molecule essential in the transmission of genetic information. For their achievements, Perutz, Kendrew, Watson, Wilkins, and Crick all received Nobel prizes in 1962. (Franklin had died in 1958.)

By the end of the twentieth century, geneticists and molecular biologists were achieving breakthroughs on many fronts and applying their findings in unexpected ways. For example, DNA testing resulted in freeing a number of prisoners wrongly convicted of murder, including some on death row.

In 1986, with funds appropriated by Congress, the U.S. Department of Energy and the National Institutes of Health launched the Human Genome Project to determine the precise DNA sequence of all the genetic material in the forty-six human chromosomes. Establishing a significant precedent, Congress set aside 5 percent of the budget for studies of ethical and social questions raised by the project.

The task involved the computer analysis of massive quantities of biostatistical data. A private biotech company, the Celera Genomics Corporation, soon joined the race. In June 2000 the heads of the Celera and Human Genome Project teams jointly made a "working draft" of the human genome available to researchers. Some compared the achievement to the mapping of the vast North American interior in the nineteenth century.

In 1997 in Scotland, meanwhile, veterinary researchers successfully cloned a sheep, producing a lamb named Dolly. In other words, they created a precise genetic replica of a sheep by transferring the nuclei of its cells into an unfertilized egg from a female sheep, and then implanting the egg into the donor female, where it grew the way an egg fertilized by normal breeding would have. This soon lead to excited speculation about cloning human beings—a scary prospect that some scientists dismissed as science-fiction. Nevertheless, President Bill Clinton banned the use of federal funds for human-cloning research, and urged a "voluntary moratorium" on all such efforts.

Developmental biologist James Thomson, researcher on human stem cells, in his laboratory at the University of Wisconsin-Madison.

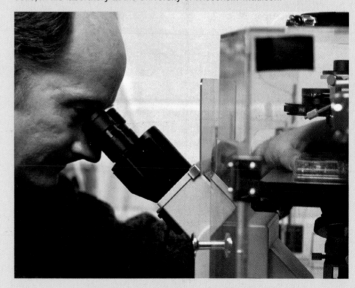

More immediate concern focused on the medical applications of genetic research. By 2000 medical investigators had isolated defective genes that created a higher than normal probability that individuals would develop breast cancer, ovarian cancer, cardiovascular disease, dementia, cystic fibrosis, Huntington's disease (the neurological disorder that killed folksinger Woody Guthrie), and other ailments. In 2001 physicians began offering tests to expectant Caucasian parents to see if both carried the genetic defect linked to cystic fibrosis. (This disease most commonly strikes Caucasians, with some thirty-thousand sufferers in America.)

The development of genetic-screening technologies to identify persons at risk for specific diseases offered the promise of early medical intervention, but also raised ethical dilemmas. While some individuals sought out such information so they could take precautionary measures, others preferred not to know. The danger that genetic information could fall into the hands of potential employers, insurance companies, and government agencies threatened patients' right of confidentiality.

Another troubling moral issue arose when James A. Thomson at the University of Wisconsin-Madison, along with scientists at other institutions, developed techniques for harvesting human stem cells from blastocysts (an early stage of embryo development) that had been frozen for the use of couples experiencing fertility problems. Typically, when a fertilized blastocyst is implanted in a woman's body and she successfully gives birth, any leftover blastocysts are discarded. Scientists proposed to use these "surplus" embryonic stem cells for research on diabetes, heart disease, and other illnesses. Stem cells are especially useful because they can develop into many different specialized human cells. But stem-cell research stirred controversy because it involved the destruction of early-stage human embryos, which some religious groups consider to be human life. Said one American Catholic leader, "We are talking about not only the direction of genetic science, but also [about] . . . questions of human dignity." In August 2001 President George W. Bush issued a compromise ruling allowing federal funding of research using existing stem-cell lines, but forbidding government support for research using human embryos dating from the period after his ruling.

In 2001 researchers converted cow skin cells into cow heart cells. If the same technique could be made to work with human cells, it would be unnecessary to use stem cells, and science would have resolved—or bypassed—this particular ethical dilemma.

These breakthroughs in human genetics opened new scientific horizons while raising profound ethical

Dolly, the sheep cloned in 1997 by researchers in Scotland.

issues. Politicians debated; medical ethicists offered advice; and the American Medical Association set up websites to help physicians deal with the ethical dilemmas they faced as genetics increasingly affected medical practice.

As we have seen throughout *The Enduring Vision*, scientific discoveries and new technologies have vastly benefited Americans. But they have also had unanticipated cultural implications and posed troubling public-policy issues. As the twenty-first century unfolded, both the technological advances and their unexpected social consequences and ethical dilemmas seemed certain to continue.

Focus Questions

- What have been the key achievements in molecular biology since 1950?

- What promise did these achievements hold, and what ethical issues did they raise?

at the Hague. In 2001, in a symbolic action underscoring the growing resentment of America's strong-arm tactics at the United Nations, the United States was voted off the U.N. Human Rights Commission, on which it had served since 1947.

The Bush administration did actively promote U.S. trade interests, a fact underscored by its relations with China. In April 2001 a U.S. spy plane off China's coast collided with a Chinese aircraft monitoring it. The Chinese plane crashed, killing the pilot, and the damaged U.S. plane landed in China. Angry words followed, but $120 billion in annual trade spoke more loudly, and after negotiations China released the U.S. crew. Six months later President Bush attended an Asia-Pacific economic cooperation conference hosted by Beijing, and in November 2001 China formally entered the World Trade Organization.

The global economy remained a focus of protest, however. When the G-8 met at Genoa, Italy, in July 2001, violent street protests resulted in one death, many arrests, and over two hundred injuries. The 2002 G-8 meeting was held in Calgary in the Canadian Rockies, which planners hoped would be remote enough to discourage protesters.

Despite Bush's commitment to foreign trade, domestic pressures influenced him as well. In 2002, responding to demands from U.S. steel producers and the steelworkers' union, Bush slapped tariffs of up to 30 percent on imported steel products for a three-year period. While the tariffs did not apply to Canada, Mexico, or certain developing nations, they did hit China, Japan, Russia, South Korea, and the EU, which protested this violation of free-trade principles. Whether the U.S. steel industry, with its steadily shrinking labor force and high production costs, could long survive even with tariff protection remained an open question.

RECESSION WOES; CAMPAIGN FINANCE BATTLES; ENVIRONMENTAL DEBATES

A sharp recession abruptly ended the prosperity of the 1990s and raised questions about the wisdom of the tax cut. Disagreements over economic policy, combined with criticism of Bush's environmental record and a long-running battle over campaign-finance reform, helped perpetuate the climate of intense political partisanship that pervaded the early Bush years.

End of the Economic Boom

The good times and stock-market boom of the 1990s barely outlasted the decade. As Asian and Latin American economies faltered, the U.S. economy suffered as well. In March 2001, when according to economists the recession officially began, the stock market recorded its worst week since 1989, falling by 6 percent. Millions of stockholders felt the pain. Consumer confidence fell to the lowest level in years. As corporate profits plunged, businesses announced layoffs. Ford fired five thousand managers and engineers. The unemployment rate rose from under 4 percent in 2000 to nearly 6 percent by November 2001. In that month alone, three hundred thousand workers lost their jobs.

The bursting of the Internet bubble worsened the downturn. By one calculation, nearly 250 dot-com businesses collapsed in a few months' time. The market value of the companies that did survive fell sharply. Instant millionaires watched their portfolios melt away.

To stimulate the economy, the Federal Reserve Board cut interest rates eleven times in 2001, to a forty-year low. The Bush administration, having based its tax-cut plan on the assumption of continued budget surpluses, now projected years of deficits. Democrats stepped up their attacks on the administration's overly optimistic economic projections and warned about threats to social security and Medicare funds. As an anti-recession stimulus package, the administration proposed generous new tax breaks for corporations and the wealthy, and a speeding up of tax cuts that were already approved.

Few shed tears when casinos, luxury boutiques, overpriced restaurants, and dealers in vintage wines and expensive cigars reported declining income. But retirees with pensions plans invested in the stock market and low-paid workers lacking job security typically suffer most in hard times, and the recession that began in Silicon Valley and Wall Street soon spread ominously. Industrial production was shrinking, and every state was losing jobs. Service-sector employment fell faster in the last quarter of 2001 than in any three-month period since World War II. Unskilled workers and former welfare recipients seeking entry-level jobs faced problems. Openings for temporary workers dropped precipitously. The longest economic boom in American history had ended with a thud, and the impact spread through society. An anemic recovery began in 2002, but it was slowed by a series of business scandals that eroded investor confidence (see below).

The Rocky Path of Campaign Finance Reform

In Congress, meanwhile, two senators—Arizona Republican John McCain and, Wisconsin Democrat Russ Feingold—carried on the battle for campaign-finance reform. They targeted so-called soft money contributions made to political parties (rather than to specific candidates) by individuals, corporations, unions, and lobbying organizations seeking to influence legislation. Such lobbies ranged from (mostly pro-Republican) business associations, tobacco companies, anti-abortion groups, and the National Rifle Association to the (mostly pro-Democratic) National Education Association, trial lawyers association, and labor unions. Given the soaring cost of TV advertising, soft money loomed increasingly large in electoral campaigns. In the 1997–1998 electoral cycle the national parties raised more than $190 million in soft money; Wall Street investment companies alone contributed $9 million to the Republican party and $6.2 million to the Democratic party.

President Clinton had paid lip service to reform while endlessly appearing at fundraising events, and as scandal gripped the White House, the campaign-finance issue had faded. In the 2000 election soft-money contributions reached $400 million.

McCain and Feingold persevered, and in April 2001 the Senate passed a version of their bill. In the Republican-controlled House, campaign-finance reform was championed by Christopher Shays, a Connecticut Republican, and Massachusetts Democrat Martin Meehan. The Shays-Meehan bill passed in 2002. A committee reconciled the House and Senate versions, and Bush signed the bill. It banned soft-money contributions to national parties and phony TV "issue ads" that were really aimed at influencing elections, and included other measures seeking to reduce the torrent of money sloshing through the election system.

Whether the new law would achieve its purpose remained unclear. Opponents vowed a court challenge on free-speech grounds, and some observers predicted that interest groups would find ways to bypass the bill. In June 2002 the Federal Election Commission, a bipartisan regulatory body charged with administering and enforcing election laws, issued a ruling that undermined key provision of the law. As the battle went on, skeptics compared politicians of both parties, whose careers depended on an endless flow of campaign money, to drug addicts facing the agonies of withdrawal.

Environmental Issues Persist

The Three Mile Island and *Exxon Valdez* incidents (see Chapters 30 and 31) forcibly reminded Americans of modern technology's environmental risks, and a 1984 disaster in Bhopal, India, in which deadly gases from a U.S.-owned chemical plant killed seventeen hundred people underscored the international scope of these risks. Beyond specific incidents, long-term environmental changes had grave implications for human well-being. The late twentieth and early twenty-first centuries brought growing environmental awareness, but a mixed record of environmental action.

With the Cold War over, Americans faced the estimated $150-billion cost of cleaning up nuclear-weapons facilities, including disposing of tons of weapons-grade uranium and plutonium. The Hanford Nuclear Reservation in Washington State was a vast dump of radioactive waste (see Chapter 26, A Place in Time: The Atomic West). The disposal of this material, as well as of radioactive plutonium from dismantled nuclear weapons and fuel rods from aging nuclear-power plants, stirred political disputes and grass-roots protest. In 1997 scientists reported water seepage into the vast cave intended for nuclear-waste storage at Nevada's Yucca Mountain. In 2002, over objections from environmentalists, Nevada politicians, and Las Vegas gambling casinos, the Senate

Documenting Global Warming
As Alaska's average temperatures rose, melting permafrost caused highways to buckle.

approved the Yucca Mountain site. In 2002 further controversy erupted over a Department of Energy (DOE) plan to transfer six tons of plutonium from a former nuclear weapons plant in Rocky Flats, Colorado to the DOE's Savannah River facility in South Carolina for reprocessing into fuel for nuclear power plants.

Other environmental and health risks arose from atmospheric changes linked to industrial processes. Acid rain carrying sulfur dioxide and other pollutants from U.S. factories and auto exhaust threatened Appalachian forests and Canadian lakes. Fluorocarbons from spray cans, refrigeration equipment, and other sources depleted the upper-atmosphere ozone layer, allowing increased solar radiation to reach Earth's surface, increasing skin-cancer risks and other health hazards.

The threat of global warming seemed especially urgent. Carbon dioxide and other gases produced by fossil-fuel emissions and deforestation (as well as naturally occurring sources) were accumulating in the lower atmosphere, and the resulting "greenhouse effect" prevented Earth's heat from escaping. Projecting current world trends, scientists predicted a 40 percent increase in carbon dioxide emissions by 2020. Atmospheric scientists warned of long-term global warming that could disrupt agricultural production and plant and animal ecosystems. In the most dire scenario, melting polar ice could cause rising sea levels, flooding low-lying coastal regions.

Heightening global-warming fears, meteorologists reported that the ten hottest years of the twentieth century all occurred after 1985. In Alaska, where the average annual temperature rose seven degrees from 1972 to 2002, rising water levels in the Chukchi Sea threatened coastal villages, and a new species of beetle that arrived with the warmer weather devastated a four-million-acre spruce forest. Highways buckled as the permafrost melted, and engineers warned that the Alaska pipeline stretching from Prudhoe Bay to Valdez could be destabilized.

Some environmental gains were recorded. According to the Environmental Protection Agency (EPA), U.S. emissions of the principal air pollutants fell more than 60 percent from 1970 to 1999. In 1996–1997, President Clinton secured passage of a bill strengthening pesticide regulation and announced new air-quality standards to reduce soot and ground-level ozone. In 1997 the EPA created an environmental "superfund" to clean up hazardous-waste sites. By 2001 more than thirteen hundred such sites had been designated, though the pace of cleanup proved slow.

Despite growing opposition to government regulations, support for environmental protection remained strong. Environmental groups that had long focused on wilderness preservation now addressed urban issues as well. When Republican legislators in 1995–1996 attacked the EPA, they faced a sharp public backlash. In 2001 the Supreme Court unanimously upheld EPA's right to establish national air-quality standards.

The first two years of the George W. Bush administration dismayed environmentalists. On taking office, Bush announced that he would not implement proposed EPA measures to reduce carbon dioxide emissions from power plants. As noted above, the administration's energy program stressed "energy abundance" through increased production and less regulation, with little attention to environmental concerns. Conservation might be a "sign of personal virtue," Vice President Cheney suggested, but was no basis for "a sound, comprehensive energy policy." Some of Bush's environmental actions roused particular opposition. An order permitting higher levels of arsenic in drinking water proved a public-relations nightmare. The proposed oil drilling in the Arctic National Wildlife Reserve and other public lands stirred intense resistance.

On the international front, Bush repudiated the protocol produced at a 1997 U.N.-sponsored international environmental conference in Kyoto, Japan, that set strict emission standards for industrialized nations, charging that it would jeopardize America's economic growth and standard of living. The administration, alone among 178 nations, including 38 industrialized states, also refused to sign a 2001 Bonn treaty specifically designed to meet Bush's objections to the Kyoto protocol. The Bonn treaty was "not in [America's] interests," declared national security advisor Condoleezza Rice tersely, offering no alternative proposals for cutting industrial emissions.

These actions came at a time when the United States, with under 5 percent of the world's population, accounted for 25 percent of global energy consumption. In 2001 passenger-vehicle fuel economy (including the popular light trucks and sport-utility vehicles) fell to the lowest level in a decade. Yet the Bush administration appeared to envision no slacking in this rate of consumption.

The administration's environmental insensitivity flew in the face of mounting scientific evidence. A National Science Foundation (NSF) report in 2001 concluded that global warming was real, and likely to become more serious.

Thanks in part to his approach to energy and environmental issues, Bush's approval rating stood at only about 50 percent midway through his first year. But suddenly, politics as usual went out the window, and not only President Bush but the entire nation faced a crisis that would test them to the limit.

SEPTEMBER 11 AND BEYOND

The course of American history changed profoundly in September 2001, when a terrorist attack left thousands dead and the nation in shock. The nation's priorities shifted at home and abroad. President Bush summoned the country to a war on terrorism that soon led to Afghanistan and beyond. At home, the administration took far-reaching measures to enhance security and prevent future attacks. While all Americans agreed on the objective of these actions, some saw a potential threat to civil liberties in the vast strengthening of governmental powers of surveillance and detention.

Having shown little concern for world opinion earlier, Bush now called upon all nations to join the United States in a war on terrorism. Despite the administration's single-minded focus on the antiterrorism campaign, other world issues demanded attention, particularly the Israeli-Palestinian conflict. As that struggle threatened to spiral out of control, the administration at last became involved in the elusive quest for peace.

Domestically, despite the post-September 11 unity impulse, political partisanship soon revived. The freedom to disagree was, after all, what made America worth defending. Contentiousness deepened as Americans reacted in disbelief and anger to revelations of greed, deception, and fraud in some of the nation's largest corporations during the boom years of the 1990s.

America Under Attack

Throughout American history, watershed events have marked historic turning points. The clash between Massachusetts farmers and British redcoats on April 19, 1775, hastened the Revolutionary War. The Confederates' attack on Fort Sumter in Charleston harbor on April 12, 1861, began the Civil War.

Another such pivotal moment came on the morning of September 11, 2001. As Americans watched their televisions in horror, the blazing twin towers of New York's World Trade Center crashed to the earth, carrying more than 2,800 men and women to their deaths. A simultaneous attack on the Pentagon left 245 dead on the ground, and a plane crash in western Pennsylvania directly related to these events killed still more innocent people. Only the Civil War battle of Antietam, in which 3,650 soldiers died, brought a higher single-day toll of American dead.

At the World Trade Center, nearly 350 firefighters and 23 police officers perished. Many people trapped by the flames leapt to their death. Father Mychal Judge, a fire department chaplain, suffered a fatal heart attack while administering last rites to victims. Firemen placed his body on the altar of nearby St. Peter's Catholic church. Businesses with offices in the Twin Towers suffered catastrophic losses. One brokerage firm lost 600 workers.

New York City essentially shut down. Bridges were closed; subway trains stopped running. Commercial

America Under Attack
Rescuers remove a flag-draped body from the ruins of the World Trade Center.

aircraft were grounded; incoming flights from abroad were ordered to return or diverted to Canada. Only military fighters patrolled the skies over New York and Washington. President Bush put the military on high alert and mobilized the national guard.

The World Trade Center towers and the Pentagon had been struck by three commercial aircraft piloted by hijackers in a carefully planned assault on these highly visible symbols of U.S. economic and military power. The Pennsylvania crash occurred when heroic passengers prevented terrorists from diverting the plane to another target, possibly the White House.

The destruction of the World Trade Center that terrorists had failed to accomplish eight years before (see chapter introduction) had now tragically been achieved. Along with the dead on the ground, 246 passengers and crew, plus 19 hijackers, died in the four planes. The government soon identified the hijackers, all foreigners from the Middle East, and traced their actions before September 11, including enrollment in Florida flight-training schools.

In a few hours of terror, a new and menacing era began. Terrorism—whether assassinations or bombed buildings, buses, ships, and planes—was familiar elsewhere, of course, and many U.S. citizens, civilian and military, had died in earlier terrorist attacks in the 1980s and 1990s. The lethal career of the letter bomber Ted Kaczynski and the 1995 bombing of the Oklahoma City federal building had made clear that America was not immune to such attacks. But now terrorism had erupted on U.S. soil on a far vaster and more horrifying scale. For the first time since the War of 1812, a foreign enemy had attacked the American homeland.

A wave of patriotism gripped the nation. The political divisions that had grown so intense were temporarily put aside. Flags flew from homes, public buildings, and automobile antennas. Irving Berlin's "God Bless America," often heard during World War II, became the anthem of the moment. "United We Stand" proclaimed banners, billboards, and bumper stickers. President Bush visited a mosque to urge Americans to distinguish between a handful of terrorists claiming to act in the name of Allah and the world's 1.2 billion Muslims, including as many as 6 million in the United States. Nevertheless, many Middle Easterners in America faced hostility and even violence in the post-attack period.

The damaged New York Stock Exchange closed for six days. When it reopened, stock prices plunged. Even after stocks slowly edged upward, retail sales declined and consumer confidence remained fragile amid anxiety about the future. The airline and travel industries reeled as jittery travelers canceled trips or chose ground transportation. A $15 billion bailout of the airlines by Congress helped, but the industry's problems remained. New York's tourist and entertainment industries suffered severely. "Vacant Rooms, Empty Tables, and Scared Tourists," headlined one New York newspaper.

Post-September 11 anxieties deepened in early October when an editor at the Florida offices of the *National Enquirer*, a tabloid newspaper that had attacked Osama bin Laden, died of anthrax, a rare and deadly bacterial disease. He had contracted it, investigators claimed, from anthrax spores sent in a letter. Letters containing high-grade anthrax spores next appeared in the office of NBC news anchor Tom Brokaw and Senators Tom Daschle and Patrick Leahy. The Senate Office Building was closed for decontamination. Four other persons, two of them postal workers, died from anthrax-tainted pieces of mail, evidently contaminated by contact with the original letters.

Panic spread, and people feared opening their mail. Analysis of the anthrax spores indicated that they had probably been made in a U.S. research laboratory, and investigators focused on finding a domestic source of the deadly mailings.

Battling Terrorist Networks Abroad

President Bush, speaking briefly from the White House on September 12, declared the attacks an "act of war." On September 15, the Senate unanimously authorized Bush to use "all necessary and appropriate force" to respond.

On September 20, as had other presidents in times of crisis, a somber Bush addressed a joint session of Congress. He blamed the attack on the Al Qaeda terrorist network headed by Osama bin Laden from headquarters in Afghanistan. Bin Laden, already under indictment for the 1998 attack on U.S. embassies in Africa, had long denounced America for supporting Saudi Arabia's corrupt regime, stationing "infidel" troops on Saudi soil, backing Israel, and spreading wickedness through its sinful mass culture. (Ironically, the United States and bin Laden had been uneasy allies in the 1980s, when he was fighting Russian forces in Afghanistan.) A videotape of bin Laden describing how he planned the attack and even laughing about the massive damage, discovered in Afghanistan and released by the Bush administration in December, helped convince any remaining doubters of his guilt. Though bin Laden claimed to have acted on behalf of Islam and endlessly invoked the name of Allah,

most Islamic leaders repudiated him and condemned attacks on innocent civilians.

Bush announced a military campaign to uproot Al Qaeda and its protectors, the Pakistan-trained Islamicist group called the Taliban, which had seized power in Afghanistan in 1996. As part of a program to disrupt the terrorists' money supply, Bush froze the assets of organizations with possible links to the terrorists.

Despite the pro-Taliban sympathies of Muslim fundamentalists in Pakistan, Bush enlisted the cooperation of Pakistan's military government. Complicating U.S. military planning was Afghanistan's forbidding terrain and patchwork of ethnic and tribal groups. The major anti-Taliban force, the Northern Alliance, was an uneasy coalition of rival warlords.

The military phase of the antiterrorist operation, launched on October 7, achieved impressive success. Battered by U.S. bombing and an offensive by Northern Alliance forces, the Taliban soon surrendered Kabul (the Afghan capital) and other strongholds. British, Canadian, Pakistani, and other forces played an important role in this campaign. By mid-December, despite sporadic resistance, the United States claimed victory. As more U.S. special forces arrived, a remnant of Al Qaeda fighters retreated to fortified caves in the rugged mountains of eastern Afghanistan, between Kabul and the Khyber Pass, pursued by local Afghan fighters backed by U.S. and British commandos and American bombing raids. The whereabouts of Osama bin Laden remained unknown, however.

The fighting was brutal. Northern Alliance fighters killed some Taliban even after they had surrendered. In late November, Taliban prisoners, mostly Pakistanis, among hundreds held at a fortress near Kunduz, seized weapons from their guards. In a wild night of fighting and bombing, most of the prisoners were killed. The civilian population, already devastated by drought and years of civil war, suffered terribly. Despite U.S. and international relief efforts, including food drops, the refugee situation—worsened by winter weather—remained desperate. Military operations unquestionably disrupted the Al Qaeda forces, but many retreated into remote parts of Afghanistan and Pakistan, suggesting that a long struggle lay ahead. More than three hundred captured Al Qaeda fighters were transferred to prison facilities at the U.S. base in Guantanamo, Cuba.

The diplomatic challenge of welding rival factions into a workable post-Taliban government proved difficult as well. As a first step, a British-led international force was mobilized to maintain law and order in Kabul. In June 2002, with U.S. support, an assembly of Afghan tribal leaders called a loya jirga established a new government and chose an interim prime minister, Hamid Karzai. The nation-building effort had the blessing of Afghanistan's eighty-nine-year-old former king, who returned to Kabul after years in exile.

International support for the initial phase of America's antiterrorist campaign remained strong. British Prime Minister Tony Blair proved a pillar of strength. For the first time, NATO forces fought in defense of a member nation.

The administration sought to broaden the struggle beyond Afghanistan and Al Qaeda. In his January 2002 State of the Union address, President Bush identified Iran, Iraq, and North Korea as an "axis of evil" hostile to America and intent on developing weapons of mass destruction, including chemical and biological weapons. In May the president added Cuba, Libya, and Syria to the list. Most of these nations denied the charges.

Shadowing the post-September 11 strategic debate was a troubling question: would eliminating Al Qaeda and bin Laden end the terrorist threat? While most Arab leaders repudiated bin Laden, many among the impoverished, ill-educated Arab masses were receptive to his anti-American harangues. Ending terrorism, clearly, involved not only military operations, but also long-term diplomatic, political, and ideological efforts as well.

High-Tech Warfare
A U.S. soldier uses a laptop computer in a training exercise at Fort Irwin, California. Such technology loomed large in the post-September 11 U.S. campaign in Afghanistan.

Tightening Home-Front Security

Thanks to the post-September 11 spirit of unity and Americans' strong support for the military campaign in Afghanistan, Bush's approval ratings soared. The administration's domestic antiterrorism campaign proved more controversial, however. Despite Republicans' traditional hostility to big government, the administration significantly expanded the federal government's role in many aspects of American life.

The initial response was somewhat confused. No clear lines of authority emerged among various government agencies. Bush appointed former Pennsylvania governor Tom Ridge to head a new White House office of homeland security, but his duties remained vague.

Political divisions emerged over the newly urgent issue of aviation security. While some legislators and others urged that the nation's 28,000 airport security workers become federal employees, others opposed this expansion of the federal labor force. Late in 2001, Congress required all security personnel to be U.S. citizens and to meet rigorous job criteria and performance requirements set by a newly created Transportation Security Administration.

After September 11, the Justice Department detained more than one thousand Middle Easterners living in the United States, some for visa violations, and held them for questioning without filing charges or, in most cases, revealing their names. In an Orwellian touch, Attorney General Ashcroft claimed that to identify the detainees would violate their civil rights. These arrests raised serious civil-liberties issues. Some local police officials refused to cooperate in the wholesale roundup of persons not accused of crimes simply on the basis of their ethnicity or national origin.

The treatment of the prisoners at Guantanamo raised questions as well. Human-rights advocates urged according them the rights of prisoners of war under the Geneva conventions. U.S. officials insisted that the men were being treated humanely, but took the position that they could be held indefinitely as a matter of national security.

The USA-Patriot Act, a sweeping antiterrorist law proposed by the administration and overwhelmingly passed by Congress in October 2001, extended the government's powers to monitor telephone and e-mail communications, including conversations between prisoners and their lawyers. This, too, stirred apprehension in civil-liberties circles. Conservatives suspicious of big government, who had applauded John Ashcroft's appointment as attorney general, were troubled by his calls for vastly expanded federal powers after September 11.

In November, without consulting Congress, Bush signed an executive order empowering the government to try noncitizens accused of fomenting terrorism in secret military tribunals rather than in the civilian justice system. While precedent existed for such tribunals in wartime, this proposal roused opposition from civil libertarians and others. Opinion polls found Americans to be divided evenly on the use of military tribunals, but strongly at odds with Bush's failure to consult Congress in the matter.

In May 2002 news media reported disturbing evidence of missed clues before the terrorist attack. In August 2001, for example, a flight school in Minnesota warned the FBI of a suspicious person named Zacarias Moussaoui who had tried to enroll. Moussaoui had been arrested on immigration charges, but the Justice Department had denied a request by the Minneapolis FBI office for permission to check his computer. (After September 11 Moussaoui's link to bin Laden was discovered, and in 2002 he went on trial in Virginia.) In June Congress launched an investigation of these intelligence breakdowns, as well as of the poor relations between the FBI and the CIA that prevented the two agencies from cooperating.

Diverting attention from these potentially damaging inquiries, President Bush seized the moment to propose a new cabinet-level Department of Homeland Security to coordinate the domestic antiterrorism effort. Having earlier rejected calls for such an agency, Bush now shifted ground abruptly. The new department, approved by Congress in November, 2002 absorbed many government agencies, including the Coast Guard, the Customs Service, the Immigration and Naturalization Service, the Federal Emergency Management Agency, and even a plant inspection agency in the Department of Agriculture. It would not, however, include the FBI or the CIA. As Congress debated the proposal, some Americans questioned whether a reshuffling of existing agencies made America more secure.

Deepening Crisis in the Middle East

With Yasir Arafat's rejection of Israel's peace plan at Camp David and the launching of a second Intifada in September 2000, violence in the region exploded. Suicide bombings took many Israeli lives. The bombers deliberately chose crowded targets such as buses and restaurants. An Israeli cabinet minister was assassinated.

Asserting its right of self-defense, Israel retaliated, using U.S.-supplied tanks and military aircraft to attack Palestinian targets in the West Bank, and assassinated leaders of Hamas, a violently anti-Israel organization

The Israeli-Palestinian Struggle
Wreckage of an Israeli bus after a suicide-bomber attack near Netanya, September 2001. The Palestinian refugee camp at Jenin after an Israeli attack, April 2002.

responsible for many of the bombings. The Israelis periodically closed border crossings for security reasons, keeping Palestinian laborers from jobs in Israel and deepening Palestinian anger. None of these measures stopped the suicide attacks; indeed, the number of attacks increased in the spring and summer of 2002.

Prime Minister Ariel Sharon, backed by Israeli public opinion, demanded an end to violence before peace talks could resume, and dismissed Arafat as too weak and devious to stop the terrorists or end corruption in the Palestinian Authority. Arafat, in turn, insisted that as long as Israel fostered Jewish settlements in the West Bank and Gaza; dominated the region militarily; controlled water rights and highway access; and in other ways behaved as a colonial power, the anger that fueled the violence would continue. A fact-finding mission headed by former Senator George Mitchell concluded that peace prospects were dim unless Israel halted construction of new West Bank settlements.

Since Israel depended upon economic and military aid from the United States, America was deeply implicated in the events in the region. Nevertheless, the Bush administration initially stood apart from the worsening conflict. A U.S.-brokered truce in June 2001 collapsed amid continued attacks and counterattacks.

In March 2002, after a particularly devastating round of suicide bombings, including a deadly attack on a Passover seder at a restaurant, Israel launched a major assault in the West Bank. Parts of the city of Jenin, a cen-

ter of terrorist activity, were reduced to rubble. A standoff between armed Palestinians and Israeli troops unfolded around Bethlehem's Church of the Nativity. The Israelis besieged Arafat's compound in Ramallah, confining him in a single building for days. Eventually the Israelis withdrew, but conditions remained tense, and violence continued on both sides.

In a June 2002 speech, President Bush called for creation of a Palestinian state and the resolution of other disputed issues. But he spoke only in generalities, offering no plan. He also demanded an end to terrorism and embraced the Israeli position that Arafat must go. While many Palestinians and Arab leaders privately agreed that Arafat had outlived his day, they resented outside attempts to push him aside. Experts on the region warned that Arafat's successor might be even less acceptable.

Since 1948 the United States, as Israel's principal ally, had tried without success to broker an enduring peace in the region. The familiar pattern of fresh initiatives by each new administration followed by frustration and defeat appeared to be repeating itself. Yet optimists pointed to other long-running conflicts, such as the one in Northern Ireland, where progress toward a resolution had been achieved. Despite the frustration, they insisted, the effort for peace must continue.

As the war on terrorism and the Israeli-Palestinian conflict continued in the fall of 2002, the Bush administration focused increasingly on Iraq. Iraq's president

Saddam Hussein had been a thorn in America's flesh since the Persian Gulf War, which had left him weakened but still in power. In a barrage of speeches, Bush, Cheney, and Defense secretary Rumsfeld warned of Saddam's hatred of the United States and Israel; his record of aggression; and his efforts to develop weapons of mass destruction. U.S. security, they argued, demanded a preemptive war to overthrow the Iraqi dictator.

Initially opposing the administration position were some prominent Democrats and even a few Republican leaders, as well as religious groups and organizations committed to international cooperation and conflict-resolution through diplomacy. Charging that a preemptive war would violate U.S. principles, the critics challenged the administration to produce firm evidence that Saddam posed an immediate threat to the United States, and warned that such a war could unleash turmoil across the Arab world and bog down U.S. forces for years. Some even accused the administration of using Iraq to divert attention from the worsening economy. Critics also cautioned that the preoccupation with Saddam could undermine the larger anti-terrorist campaign. While British Prime Minister Tony Blair backed the administration, France, Germany, other European nations, and most Arab leaders objected. To counter the rush to war, they called for a UN resolution demanding that Iraq grant complete and unrestricted access to UN weapons inspectors, who had departed in 1998 when the Iraqis denied them full access to all sites.

Under pressure to secure UN backing, President Bush in October 2002 presented the case against Saddam in a UN address. Despite deep divisions in U.S. public opinion, the House and Senate passed resolutions authorizing U.S. military action against Iraq. Republican lawmakers embraced the resolutions while Democrats divided, fearful of opposing Bush as an election neared but concerned about what some saw as a rush to war with no clear plan for dealing with a post-Saddam Iraq. On November 8, the UN Security Council unanimously adopted a resolution imposing tough new weapons inspections on Iraq. Baghdad sullenly agreed and UN inspectors returned, but a U.S.-led war remained a real possibility if Iraq violated the resolution's strict terms.

Bankruptcies and Scandals in Corporate America

The recession soon led to a series of high-profile bankruptcies among energy and telecommunications companies that had thrived in the high-flying 1990s. With the bankruptcies came accusations of criminal behavior and false accounting reports that produced a crisis of confidence in the integrity of corporate America.

The first casualty was Houston's Enron Corporation, with close ties to the Bush-Cheney administration. Selling electric power in advance at guaranteed rates, Enron flourished in the freewheeling climate of the 1990s and branched out into utilities and telecommunications. Celebrated as a model of the new economy, the company charmed investors. In 2000, claiming assets of $62 billion, it ranked seventh in *Fortune* magazine's list of the top five hundred U.S. corporations.

Suddenly the house of cards collapsed. Late in 2001, with its stock selling for sixty-one cents a share, Enron filed for bankruptcy and admitted to vastly overstating profits. Thousands of Enron workers lost not only their jobs but also their retirement funds, which consisted mostly of Enron stock. Like the collapse of the savings and loan boom and the disgrace of traders like Michael Milkin and Ivan Boesky in the 1980s (see Chapter 30), Enron's demise highlighted the risks of obsession with soaring profits, fat bonuses, and ever-rising stock prices.

Enron was only the beginning. The overbuilt fiber-optics industry, having laid 100 million miles of optical fiber worldwide in 1999–2001, suffered staggering blows. Lucent Technologies, a telecommunications giant, cut nearly one hundred thousand jobs in 2001. Global

Scandal in Corporate America
Jeffrey Skilling, former CEO of Houston's collapsed Enron Corporation, testifies before a Congressional committee in February 2002. A cascade of other corporate scandals soon followed.

Crossing, a high-speed voice and data carrier, declared bankruptcy in 2002, the fourth largest in U.S. history. In June 2002 WorldCom, America's second-largest telecommunications company and owner of long-distance company MCI, announced that its chief financial officer had overstated profits by $3.8 billion. As WorldCom stock dropped to nine cents a share, the company fired seventeen thousand employees and filed for bankruptcy. The Securities and Exchange Commission launched criminal proceedings; congressional committees held hearings; and President Bush called the WorldCom deception "outrageous."

Charges of fraud and deception spread throughout the business world. In 2002 the Justice Department brought criminal charges against Arthur Andersen, a giant Chicago accounting firm that had certified the accuracy of the financial reports of Enron, WorldCom, and other troubled companies. As Enron's problems had become public, officials at Arthur Andersen's Houston office destroyed potentially incriminating files and e-mail communications. A grand jury found the firm guilty, and it faced dissolution. The integrity of the accounting industry as a whole, so crucial to investor confidence, fell under suspicion.

Investment companies faced scrutiny as well, amid evidence that to generate business and keep profits high during the boom years, analysts at Merrill Lynch and other Wall Street firms had advised investors to buy stocks at inflated prices. Under pressure from the New York State attorney general, Merrill Lynch agreed to pay $100 million in fines.

Public outrage deepened amid reports of corporate executives who sold their own stock holdings for millions of dollars just before their companies' troubles became public. Attention focused, too, on the stratospheric salaries and stock benefits these CEO's had earned. In his 2002 book *Wealth and Democracy*, Kevin Phillips reported that America's top ten CEO's earned an average of $154 million each in 2000. The greed prevailing at the upper levels of capitalist America seemed boundless.

The wave of bankruptcies of seemingly healthy companies and the disclosures of deception and shady practices in corporate America slowed the economic recovery. Despite positive economic news, the stock market sank through much of 2002, as distrustful investors stayed away.

At a deeper level, the escalating scandals seriously eroded the standing of corporate America. Executives who had been celebrities in the 1990s now faced deep public skepticism if not criminal investigation. The University of Maryland business school took its students on field trips to penitentiaries where white-collar criminals warned them to be honest. Declared the chairman of Goldman Sachs, a major Wall Street investment bank, "I cannot think of a time when business . . . has been held in less repute."

In the summer of 2002, as the stock-market sank to five-year lows and more corporate scandals erupted, politicians and government agencies scrambled to respond to mounting public anger. President Bush delivered a stern speech about the need for business morality. The head of the understaffed and quiescent Securities and Exchange Commission, the watchdog agency created in the 1930s, declared that the SEC would vigorously pursue wrongdoers. In late July, in the first of what promised to be a series of criminal prosecutions, John J. Rigas and two of his sons, who had allegedly looted the family-owned TV-cable business, bankrupt Adelphia Communications, of $1 billion, were arrested and held for trial. At the same time, Congress passed by overwhelming margins and President Bush signed a new regulatory law designed to reassure investors. It imposed stricter accounting rules, tightened regulations for corporate financial reporting, and toughened criminal penalties for business fraud. The widespread disgust with big business evoked memories of the Progressive Era, when reformers and muckraking journalists had denounced corporate greed and ruthlessness. It also recalled the early 1930s, when business leaders who had been admired in the prosperous 1920s faced public hostility as hard times sank in. The pendulum would no doubt swing again, but for the moment the status of corporate America could hardly have been lower.

Election 2002

The corporate scandals posed dangers for the Bush administration, with its close ties to big business. The Halliburton Company, formerly headed by Vice President Cheney, was one of the firms whose financial reporting practices came under scrutiny. Bush's energy program had been crafted by leaders of the industry, and his proposed "economic stimulus package" would have given lucrative tax breaks to America's biggest corporations, including a $254 million windfall to Enron. Bush's own highly profitable 1990 sale of his stock in a failing Texas energy company of which he was a director came up for fresh examination.

As the business scandals unfolded, the 2002 election approached. Midterm elections often serve as referenda on the president's performance, as Bill Clinton learned in 1992. How would voters assess President Bush, and how would their assessment affect the election out-

come? Would Bush be seen as the bold leader of a united people waging a just war on terrorism? Or would he be viewed as a president who did the bidding of a powerful and socially irresponsible corporate elite whose reputation lay in tatters?

November 5, 2002, brought the answer, as Republicans regained control of the Senate and increased their House majority. The outcome reversed the usual mid-term election pattern, when the president's party typically loses ground. President Bush, enjoying popularity ratings close to 70 percent, had campaigned tirelessly, stressing the war on terrorism and the threat of Saddam Hussein. The Democrats proved unable to shift focus to the economy and corporate scandals. Said Senator Tom Daschle of South Dakota, the out-going majority leader: "The president made [Iraq and the war on terrorism] his drumbeat. It resonated." A Colorado voter commented: "[R]ight now in our country we need protection and I don't want to see President Bush get stalemated by another party's views as far as protecting our country." In the wake of the defeat, Representative Richard Gephardt of Missouri resigned as House Democratic leader. He was replaced by Nancy Pelosi of California, who became the first woman of either party to hold such a major leadership position in Congress. As Bush laid plans to push his agenda abroad and at home, including further tax cuts, an aggressive energy policy, and congressional confirmation of conservative judicial nominees, Republicans looked forward eagerly to 2004.

CONCLUSION

The years spanning Bill Clinton's second term and the onset of George W. Bush's presidency also marked the transition from one century to another. Brief as it was, this eventful interval brought many changes. The Republican administration that emerged from the disputed 2000 election pursued a conservative, probusiness domestic agenda and a more-independent, go-it-alone approach to foreign policy. The humming economy of the 1990s stalled in 2000–2001, affecting American life in many ways. And, as we saw in Chapter 31, America's social and demographic profile continued to change as the surging growth of the Sunbelt continued and the Hispanic and Asian populations grew at a rapid pace.

On September 11, 2001, a shocking act of terrorism transformed America. Sixty years earlier, President Franklin D. Roosevelt had called December 7, 1941, "a day that will live in infamy." The same could be said of September 11. The shattering events of that day opened a new chapter in U.S. history—a chapter that would

challenge the endurance, tolerance, and wisdom of all Americans. Coping with the threat of terrorism required not only military and security measures, but also a renewed commitment to fair play, respect for civil rights, and concern for the oppressed of the world, whatever their ethnicity, religion, or skin color—the values that make America worth preserving.

CHRONOLOGY, 1996 TO THE PRESENT

1994 Oslo Accords establish framework for peace between Israel and Palestinians.

1995 World Trade Organization (WTO) replaces GATT as regulator of world trade.

Dayton Accords establish cease-fire in Bosnia.

1996 Clinton reelected.

1997 Kyoto Accords on emissions standards.

1998 Terrorists bombings of U.S. embassies in Kenya and Tanzania.

House of Representatives impeaches Clinton.

1999 NATO offensive drives Yugoslav forces out of Kosovo.

Senate trial acquits Clinton.

2000 Congress normalizes trade relations with China.

End of economic boom.

Yasir Arafat rejects Israeli peace plan; second Intifada begins.

USS. *Cole* bombed in Aden harbor, Yemen.

Presidential election: Al Gore wins popular vote; George W. Bush chosen by electoral college after Supreme Court intervenes to resolve disputed Florida vote.

Republicans retain slim majorities in both houses of Congress.

2001 Bush administration repudiates Kyoto protocol on emission standards.

Congress passes $1.35 trillion tax cut bill.

Senator Jeffords becomes an independent; Democrats regain control of Senate.

September 11 terrorist attacks on World Trade Center, Pentagon.

U.S. and allied forces defeat Taliban regime in Afghanistan and attack Al Qaeda terrorist network.

U.S. withdraws from ABM (Anti-Ballistic Missile) Treaty and begins construction of missile defense system.

Collapse of Enron Corporation leads to wave of corporate bankruptcies and accounting scandals.

2002 Bipartisan Campaign Reform Act.

Department of Homeland Security approved.

Palestinian suicide bombings; Israeli invasion of West Bank.

As 2001 ended, Norway awarded the Nobel Peace Prize to Kofi Annan, secretary general of the United Nations. Accepting the award in Oslo, Annan acknowledged the irony of celebrating peace amidst rampant war and terrorism. "We have entered the third millennium through a gate of fire," he said. Annan went on to call for a rededication to the vision that had inspired the U.N.'s founders fifty-six years earlier. Despite the hatred and vast inequalities dividing nations and peoples, he insisted, the fate of all Earth's inhabitants was interconnected. "In the 21ˢᵗ century," he said, "I believe the mission of the United Nations will be defined by a new, more profound awareness of the sanctity and dignity of every human life, regardless of race or religion. . . . Humanity is indivisible."

FOR FURTHER REFERENCE

READINGS

The journals of political and cultural commentary listed in the "For Further Reference" section of Chapter 31 are relevant to this chapter as well, as is the annual government publication *Statistical Abstract of the United States,* with its wealth of economic, social, and demographic information.

David Barney, *Prometheus Wired: The Hope for Democracy in the Age of Network Technology* (2000). Reflections on the civic and political implications of the new information technologies.

David Brooks, *Bobos in Paradise: The New Upper Class and How They Got There* (2000). Witty and shrewd cultural profile of the baby-boom generation in the affluent 1990s.

James W. Caesar and Andrew E. Busch, *The Perfect Tie: The True Story of the 2000 Presidential Election* (2001). A thoughtful and readable account of the Bush-Gore campaign.

Fred Halliday, *Two Hours that Shook the World: September 11, 2001: Causes and Consequences* (2001). A British international-affairs specialist views terrorism in the context of political and ideological struggles within the Arab world.

Chalmers Johnson, *Blowback: The Costs and Consequences of American Empire* (2001). A diplomatic historian examines the domestic and international consequences of America's global economic expansion.

Haynes Johnson, *The Best of Times: America in the Clinton Years* (2001). Thoughtful reflections on American culture in the 1990s.

Anthony Lake, *Six Nightmares: Real Threats in a Dangerous World and How America Can Meet Them* (2001). A foreign-affairs specialist explores a variety of terrorist threats and offers recommendations for responding to them.

Kevin Phillips, *Wealth and Democracy* (2002). Critical analysis of the corporate practices of the 1990s and their implications for American democracy.

Paul Pillar, *Terrorism and U.S. Foreign Policy* (2001). A counterterrorism specialist argues that effective intelligence work and cooperation with other nations offer the best hope.

Cass R. Sunstein and Richard A. Epstein, eds., *The Vote: Bush, Gore, and the Supreme Court* (2001). Scholars representing a broad spectrum of viewpoints analyze the legal struggle to resolve the 2000 election controversy.

Peter Trubowitz, *Defining the National Interest: Conflict and Change in American Foreign Policy* (1998). Explores the domestic economic and political calculations that help shape U.S. diplomacy.

William Julius Wilson, *When Work Disappears: The World of the New Urban Poor* (1996). A sociologist looks at those left behind by the high-tech, high-skilled economy.

WEBSITES

Bureau of Labor Statistics
http://www.bls.gov/home.htm
The home page of this government agency includes a wealth of data about the U.S. economy and labor force.

CNN, Election 2000
http://www.cnn.com/ELECTION 2000
Everything you wanted to know about the 2000 election, including the disputed Florida outcome.

National Institutes of Health, Stem Cells, A Primer
http://www.nih.gov/news/stemcell/primer.htm
Basic scientific information about human stem cells, the subject of public-policy debate in 2001.

PBS, The Impeachment Trial
http://www.pbs.org/newshour/impeachment
Extensive information on the impeachment of President Bill Clinton based on PBS *News Hour* broadcasts, including a complete transcript of the Senate trial, statements by key figures, historical background on impeachment, and historians' commentary.

Research and Reference Resources. Events of September 11, 2001.
http://www.freepint.com/gary/91101.html
This website, maintained by a librarian and information consultant in Washington, D.C., offers documents, speeches, journalistic accounts, editorials, articles, and videos relating to the attack of September 11, 2001; the anthrax scare; the U.S. military action in Afghanistan, and the domestic antiterrorism campaign.

The White House: President George W. Bush
http://www.whitehouse.gov/president/gwbbio.html
This White House website includes a biography of President George W. Bush in English and Spanish.

For additional works please consult the bibliography at the end of the book.

Appendix

DOCUMENTS

Declaration of Independence

IN CONGRESS, JULY 4, 1776

THE UNANIMOUS DECLARATION OF THE THIRTEEN UNITED STATES OF AMERICA

When, in the course of human events, it becomes necessary for one people to dissolve the political bands which have connected them with another, and to assume, among the powers of the earth, the separate and equal station to which the laws of nature and of nature's God entitle them, a decent respect to the opinions of mankind requires that they should declare the causes which impel them to the separation.

We hold these truths to be self-evident: That all men are created equal; that they are endowed by their Creator with certain unalienable rights; that among these are life, liberty, and the pursuit of happiness; that, to secure these rights, governments are instituted among men, deriving their just powers from the consent of the governed; that whenever any form of government becomes destructive of these ends, it is the right of the people to alter or to abolish it, and to institute new government, laying its foundation on such principles, and organizing its powers in such form, as to them shall seem most likely to effect their safety and happiness. Prudence, indeed, will dictate that governments long established should not be changed for light and transient causes; and accordingly all experience hath shown that mankind are more disposed to suffer, while evils are sufferable, than to right themselves by abolishing the forms to which they are accustomed. But when a long train of abuses and usurpations, pursuing invariably the same object, evinces a design to reduce them under absolute despotism, it is their right, it is their duty, to throw off such government, and to provide new guards for their future security. Such has been the patient sufferance of these colonies; and such is now the necessity which constrains them to alter their former systems of government. The history of the present King of Great Britain is a history of repeated injuries and usurpations, all having in direct object the establishment of an absolute tyranny over these states. To prove this, let facts be submitted to a candid world.

He has refused his assent to laws, the most wholesome and necessary for the public good.

He has forbidden his governors to pass laws of immediate and pressing importance, unless suspended in their operation till his assent should be obtained; and, when so suspended, he has utterly neglected to attend to them.

He has refused to pass other laws for the accommodation of large districts of people, unless those people would relinquish the right of representation in the legislature, a right inestimable to them, and formidable to tyrants only.

He has called together legislative bodies at places unusual, uncomfortable, and distant from the depository of their public records, for the sole purpose of fatiguing them into compliance with his measures.

He has dissolved representative houses repeatedly, for opposing, with manly firmness, his invasions on the rights of the people.

He has refused for a long time, after such dissolutions, to cause others to be elected; whereby the legislative powers, incapable of annihilation, have returned to the people at large for their exercise; the state remaining, in the mean time, exposed to all the dangers of invasions from without and convulsions within.

He has endeavored to prevent the population of these states; for that purpose obstructing the laws of naturalization of foreigners; refusing to pass others to encourage their migration hither, and raising the conditions of new appropriation of lands.

He has obstructed the administration of justice, by refusing his assent to laws for establishing judiciary powers.

He has made judges dependent on his will alone, for the tenure of their offices, and the amount and payment of their salaries.

He has erected a multitude of new offices, and sent hither swarms of officers to harass our people and eat out their substance.

He has kept among us, in times of peace, standing armies, without the consent of our legislatures.

He has affected to render the military independent of, and superior to, the civil power.

He has combined with others to subject us to a jurisdiction foreign to our constitution, and unacknowledged by our laws, giving his assent to their acts of pretended legislation:

For quartering large bodies of armed troops among us;

For protecting them, by a mock trial, from punishment for any murders which they should commit on the inhabitants of these states;

For cutting off our trade with all parts of the world;

For imposing taxes on us without our consent;

For depriving us, in many cases, of the benefits of trial by jury;

For transporting us beyond seas, to be tried for pretended offenses;

For abolishing the free system of English laws in a neighboring province, establishing therein an arbitrary government, and enlarging its boundaries, so as to render it at once an example and fit instrument for introducing the same absolute rule into these colonies;

For taking away our charters, abolishing our most valuable laws, and altering fundamentally the forms of our governments;

For suspending our own legislatures, and declaring themselves invested with power to legislate for us in all cases whatsoever.

He has abdicated government here, by declaring us out of his protection and waging war against us.

He has plundered our seas, ravaged our coasts, burned our towns, and destroyed the lives of our people.

He is at this time transporting large armies of foreign mercenaries to complete the works of death, desolation, and tyranny already begun with circumstances of cruelty and perfidy scarcely paralleled in the most barbarous ages, and totally unworthy of the head of a civilized nation.

He has constrained our fellow-citizens, taken captive on the high seas, to bear arms against their country, to become the executioners of their friends and brethren, or to fall themselves by their hands.

He has excited domestic insurrection among us, and has endeavored to bring on the inhabitants of our frontiers the merciless Indian savages, whose known rule of warfare is an undistinguished destruction of all ages, sexes, and conditions.

In every stage of these oppressions we have petitioned for redress in the most humble terms; our repeated petitions have been answered only by repeated injury. A prince, whose character is thus marked by every act which may define a tyrant, is unfit to be the ruler of a free people.

Nor have we been wanting in our attentions to our British brethren. We have warned them, from time to time, of attempts by their legislature to extend an unwarrantable jurisdiction over us. We have reminded them of the circumstances of our emigration and settlement here. We have appealed to their native justice and magnanimity; and we have conjured them by the ties of our common kindred, to disavow these usurpations, which would inevitably interrupt our connections and correspondence. They, too, have been deaf to the voice of justice and of consanguinity. We must, therefore, acquiesce in the necessity which denounces our separation, and hold them, as we hold the rest of mankind, enemies in war, in peace friends.

We, therefore, the representatives of the United States of America, in General Congress assembled, appealing to the Supreme Judge of the world for the rectitude of our intentions, do, in the name and by the authority of the good people of these colonies, solemnly publish and declare, that these United Colonies are, and of right ought to be, FREE AND INDEPENDENT STATES; that they are absolved from all allegiance to the British crown, and that all political connection between them and the state of Great Britain is, and ought to be, totally dissolved; and that, as free and independent states, they have full power to levy war, conclude peace, contract alliances, establish commerce, and do all other acts and things which independent states may of right do. And for the support of this declaration, with a firm reliance on the protection of Divine Providence, we mutually pledge to each other our lives, our fortunes, and our sacred honor.

JOHN HANCOCK [*President*]
[*and fifty-five others*]

The Articles of Confederation and Perpetual Union

BETWEEN THE STATES OF NEW HAMPSHIRE, MASSACHUSETTS BAY, RHODE ISLAND AND PROVIDENCE PLANTATIONS, CONNECTICUT, NEW YORK, NEW JERSEY, PENNSYLVANIA, DELAWARE, MARYLAND, VIRGINIA, NORTH CAROLINA, SOUTH CAROLINA, GEORGIA.*

Article 1.

The stile of this confederacy shall be "The United States of America."

Article 2.

Each State retains its sovereignty, freedom and independence, and every power, jurisdiction, and right, which is not by this confederation expressly delegated to the United States, in Congress assembled.

Article 3.

The said states hereby severally enter into a firm league of friendship with each other for their common defence, the security of their liberties and their mutual and general welfare; binding themselves to assist each other against all force offered to, or attacks made upon them, or any of them, on account of religion, sovereignty, trade, or any other pretence whatever.

Article 4.

The better to secure and perpetuate mutual friendship and intercourse among the people of the different states in this union, the free inhabitants of each of these states, paupers, vagabonds, and fugitives from justice excepted, shall be entitled to all privileges and immunities of free citizens in the several states; and the people of each State shall have free ingress and regress to and from any other State, and shall enjoy therein all the privileges of trade and commerce, subject to the same duties, impositions, and restrictions, as the inhabitants thereof respectively; provided, that such restrictions shall not extend so far as to prevent the removal of property, imported into any State, to any other State of which the owner is an inhabitant; provided also, that no imposition, duties, or restric-

tion, shall be laid by any State on the property of the United States, or either of them.

If any person guilty of, or charged with treason, felony, or other high misdemeanor in any State, shall flee from justice and be found in any of the United States, he shall, upon demand of the governor or executive power of the State from which he fled, be delivered up and removed to the State having jurisdiction of his offence.

Full faith and credit shall be given in each of these states to the records, acts, and judicial proceedings of the courts and magistrates of every other State.

Article 5.

For the more convenient management of the general interests of the United States, delegates shall be annually appointed, in such manner as the legislature of each State shall direct, to meet in Congress, on the 1st Monday in November in every year, with a power reserved to each State to recall its delegates, or any of them, at any time within the year, and to send others in their stead for the remainder of the year.

No State shall be represented in Congress by less than two, nor by more than seven members; and no person shall be capable of being a delegate for more than three years in any term of six years; nor shall any person, being a delegate, be capable of holding any office under the United States, for which he, or any other for his benefit, receives any salary, fees, or emolument of any kind.

Each State shall maintain its own delegates in a meeting of the states, and while they act as members of the committee of the states.

In determining questions in the United States, in Congress assembled, each State shall have one vote.

Freedom of speech and debate in Congress shall not be impeached or questioned in any court or place out of Congress: and the members of Congress shall be protected in their persons from arrests and imprisonments, during the time of their going to and from, and attendance on Congress, *except for treason,* felony, or breach of the peace.

---

*This copy of the final draft of the Articles of Confederation is taken from the *Journals,* 9:907–925, November 15, 1777.

Article 6.

No State, without the consent of the United States, in Congress assembled, shall send any embassy to, or receive any embassy from, or enter into any conference, agreement, alliance, or treaty with any king, prince, or state; nor shall any person, holding any office of profit or trust under the United States, or any of them, accept of any present, emolument, office or title, of any kind whatever, from any king, prince, or foreign state; nor shall the United States, in Congress assembled, or any of them, grant any title of nobility.

No two or more states shall enter into any treaty, confederation, or alliance, whatever, between them, without the consent of the United States, in Congress assembled, specifying accurately the purposes for which the same is to be entered into, and how long it shall continue.

No State shall lay any imposts or duties which may interfere with any stipulations in treaties entered into by the United States, in Congress assembled, with any king, prince, or state, in pursuance of any treaties already proposed by Congress to the courts of France and Spain.

No vessels of war shall be kept up in time of peace by any State, except such number only as shall be deemed necessary by the United States, in Congress assembled, for the defence of such State or its trade; nor shall any body of forces be kept up by any State, in time of peace, except such number only as, in the judgment of the United States, in Congress assembled, shall be deemed requisite to garrison the forts necessary for the defence of such State; but every State shall always keep up a well regulated and disciplined militia, sufficiently armed and accoutred, and shall provide, and constantly have ready for use, in public stores, a due number of field pieces and tents, and a proper quantity of arms, ammunition and camp equipage.

No State shall engage in any war without the consent of the United States, in Congress assembled, unless such State be actually invaded by enemies, or shall have received certain advice of a resolution being formed by some nation of Indians to invade such State, and the danger is so imminent as not to admit of a delay till the United States, in Congress assembled, can be consulted; nor shall any State grant commissions to any ships or vessels of war, nor letters of marque or reprisal, except it be after a declaration of war by the United States, in Congress assembled, and then only against the kingdom or state, and the subjects thereof, against which war has been so declared, and under such regulations as shall be established by the United States, in Congress assembled, unless such States be infested by pirates, in which case vessels of war may be fitted out for that occasion, and kept so long as the danger shall continue, or until the United States, in Congress assembled, shall determine otherwise.

Article 7.

When land forces are raised by any State for the common defence, all officers of or under the rank of colonel, shall be appointed by the legislature of each State respectively, by whom such forces shall be raised, or in such manner as such State shall direct; and all vacancies shall be filled up by the State which first made the appointment.

Article 8.

All charges of war and all other expences, that shall be incurred for the common defence or general welfare, and allowed by the United States, in Congress assembled, shall be defrayed out of a common treasury, which shall be supplied by the several states, in proportion to the value of all land within each State, granted to or surveyed for any person, as such land and the buildings and improvements thereon shall be estimated according to such mode as the United States, in Congress assembled, shall, from time to time, direct and appoint.

The taxes for paying that proportion shall be laid and levied by the authority and direction of the legislatures of the several states, within the time agreed upon by the United States, in Congress assembled.

Article 9.

The United States, in Congress assembled, shall have the sole and exclusive right and power of determining on peace and war, except in the cases mentioned in the 6th article; of sending and receiving ambassadors; entering into treaties and alliances, provided that no treaty of commerce shall be made, whereby the legislative power of the respective states shall be restrained from imposing such imposts and duties on foreigners as their own people are subjected to, or from prohibiting the exportation or importation of any species of goods or commodities whatsoever; of establishing rules for deciding, in all cases, what captures on land or water shall be legal, and in what manner prizes, taken by land or naval forces in the service of the United States, shall be divided or appropriated; of granting letters of marque and reprisal in times of peace; appointing courts for the trial of piracies

and felonies committed on the high seas, and establishing courts for receiving and determining, finally, appeals in all cases of captures; provided, that no member of Congress shall be appointed a judge of any of the said courts.

The United States, in Congress assembled, shall also be the last resort on appeal in all disputes and differences now subsisting, or that hereafter may arise between two or more states concerning boundary, jurisdiction or any other cause whatever; which authority shall always be exercised in the manner following: whenever the legislative or executive authority, or lawful agent of any State, in controversy with another, shall present a petition to Congress, stating the matter in question, and praying for a hearing, notice thereof shall be given, by order of Congress, to the legislative or executive authority of the other State in controversy, and a day assigned for the appearance of the parties by their lawful agents, who shall then be directed to appoint, by joint consent, commissioners or judges to constitute a court for hearing and determining the matter in question; but, if they cannot agree, Congress shall name three persons out of each of the United States, and from the list of such persons each party shall alternately strike out one, in the petitioners beginning, until the number shall be reduced to thirteen; and from that number not less than seven, nor more than nine names, as Congress shall direct, shall, in the presence of Congress, be drawn out by lot; and the persons whose names shall be drawn, or any five of them, shall be commissioners or judges to hear and finally determine the controversy, so always as a major part of the judges who shall hear the cause shall agree in the determination; and if either party shall neglect to attend at the day appointed, without shewing reasons which Congress shall judge sufficient, or, being present, shall refuse to strike, the Congress shall proceed to nominate three persons out of each State, and the secretary of Congress shall strike in behalf of such party absent or refusing; and the judgment and sentence of the court to be appointed, in the manner before prescribed, shall be final and conclusive; and if any of the parties shall refuse to submit to the authority of such court, or to appear or defend their claim or cause, the court shall nevertheless proceed to pronounce sentence or judgment, which shall, in like manner, be final and decisive, the judgment or sentence and other proceedings being, in either case, transmitted to Congress, and lodged among the acts of Congress for the security of the parties concerned: provided, that every commissioner, before he sits in judgment, shall take an oath, to be administered by one of the judges of the supreme or superior court of the State

where the cause shall be tried, "well and truly to hear and determine the matter in question, according to the best of his judgment, without favour, affection, or hope of reward": provided, also, that no State shall be deprived of territory for the benefit of the United States.

All controversies concerning the private right of soil, claimed under different grants of two or more states, whose jurisdictions, as they may respect such lands and the states which passed such grants, are adjusted, the said grants, or either of them, being at the same time claimed to have originated antecedent to such settlement of jurisdiction, shall, on the petition of either party to the Congress of the United States, be finally determined, as near as may be, in the same manner as is before prescribed for deciding disputes respecting territorial jurisdiction between different states.

The United States, in Congress assembled, shall also have the sole and exclusive right and power of regulating the alloy and value of coin struck by their own authority, or by that of the respective states; fixing the standard of weights and measures throughout the United States; regulating the trade and managing all affairs with the Indians not members of any of the states; provided that the legislative right of any State within its own limits be not infringed or violated; establishing and regulating post offices from one State to another throughout all the United States, and exacting such postage on the papers passing through the same as may be requisite to defray the expences of the said office; appointing all officers of the land forces in the service of the United States, excepting regimental officers; appointing all the officers of the naval forces, and commissioning all officers whatever in the service of the United States; making rules for the government and regulation of the said land and naval forces, and directing their operations.

The United States, in Congress assembled, shall have authority to appoint a committee to sit in the recess of Congress, to be denominated "a Committee of the States," and to consist of one delegate from each State, and to appoint such other committees and civil officers as may be necessary for managing the general affairs of the United States, under their direction; to appoint one of their number to preside; provided that no person be allowed to serve in the office of president more than one year in any term of three years; to ascertain the necessary sums of money to be raised for the service of the United States, and to appropriate and apply the same for defraying the public expences; to borrow money or emit bills on the credit of the United States, transmitting, every half year, to the respective states, an account of the sums of money so borrowed or emitted; to build and

equip a navy; to agree upon the number of land forces, and to make requisitions from each State for its quota, in proportion to the number of white inhabitants in such State; which requisitions shall be binding; and, thereupon, the legislature of each State shall appoint the regimental officers, raise the men, and cloathe, arm, and equip them in a soldier-like manner, at the expence of the United States; and the officers and men so cloathed, armed, and equipped, shall march to the place appointed and within the time agreed on by the United States, in Congress assembled; but if the United States, in Congress assembled, shall, on consideration of circumstances, judge proper that any State should not raise men, or should raise a smaller number than its quota, and that any other State should raise a greater number of men than the quota thereof, such extra number shall be raised, officered, cloathed, armed, and equipped in the same manner as the quota of such State, unless the legislature of such State shall judge that such extra number cannot be safely spared out of the same, in which case they shall raise, officer, cloathe, arm, and equip as many of such extra number as they judge can be safely spared. And the officers and men so cloathed, armed, and equipped, shall march to the place appointed and within the time agreed on by the United States, in Congress assembled.

The United States, in Congress assembled, shall never engage in a war, nor grant letters of marque and reprisal in time of peace, nor enter into any treaties or alliances, nor coin money, nor regulate the value thereof, nor ascertain the sums and expences necessary for the defence and welfare of the United States, or any of them: nor emit bills, nor borrow money on the credit of the United States, nor appropriate money, nor agree upon the number of vessels of war to be built or purchased, or the number of land or sea forces to be raised, nor appoint a commander in chief of the army or navy, unless nine states assent to the same; nor shall a question on any other point, except for adjourning from day to day, be determined, unless by the votes of a majority of the United States, in Congress assembled.

The Congress of the United States shall have power to adjourn to any time within the year, and to any place within the United States, so that no period of adjournment be for a longer duration than the space of six months, and shall publish the journal of their proceedings monthly, except such parts thereof, relating to treaties, alliances or military operations, as, in their judgment, require secrecy; and the yeas and nays of the delegates of each State on any question shall be entered on the journal, when it is desired by any delegate; and

the delegates of a State, or any of them, at his, or their request, shall be furnished with a transcript of the said journal, except such parts as are above excepted, to lay before the legislatures of the several states.

Article 10.

The committee of the states, or any nine of them, shall be authorized to execute, in the recess of Congress, such of the powers of Congress as the United States, in Congress assembled, by the consent of nine states, shall, from time to time, think expedient to vest them with; provided, that no power be delegated to the said committee for the exercise of which, by the articles of confederation, the voice of nine states, in the Congress of the United States assembled, is requisite.

Article 11.

Canada acceding to this confederation, and joining in the measures of the United States, shall be admitted into and entitled to all the advantages of this union; but no other colony shall be admitted into the same, unless such admission be agreed to by nine states.

Article 12.

All bills of credit emitted, monies borrowed and debts contracted by, or under the authority of Congress before the assembling of the United States, in pursuance of the present confederation, shall be deemed and considered as a charge against the United States, for payment and satisfaction whereof the said United States and the public faith are hereby solemnly pledged.

Article 13.

Every State shall abide by the determinations of the United States, in Congress assembled, on all questions which, by this confederation, are submitted to them. And the articles of this confederation shall be inviolably observed by every State, and the union shall be perpetual; nor shall any alteration at any time hereafter be made in any of them, unless such alteration be agreed to in a Congress of the United States, and be afterwards confirmed by the legislatures of every State.

These articles shall be proposed to the legislatures of all the United States, to be considered, and if approved of by them, they are advised to authorize their delegates to ratify the same in the Congress of the United States; which being done, the same shall become conclusive.

Constitution of the United States of America

PREAMBLE

We the people of the United States, in order to form a more perfect union, establish justice, insure domestic tranquillity, provide for the common defense, promote the general welfare, and secure the blessings of liberty to ourselves and our posterity, do ordain and establish this CONSTITUTION for the United States of America.

Article I

Section 1. All legislative powers herein granted shall be vested in a Congress of the United States, which shall consist of a Senate and a House of Representatives.

Section 2. The House of Representatives shall be composed of members chosen every second year by the people of the several States, and the electors in each State shall have the qualifications requisite for electors of the most numerous branch of the State Legislature.

No person shall be a Representative who shall not have attained to the age of twenty-five years, and been seven years a citizen of the United States, and who shall not, when elected, be an inhabitant of that State in which he shall be chosen.

Representatives and direct taxes shall be apportioned among the several States which may be included within this Union, according to their respective numbers, *which shall be determined by adding to the whole number of free persons, including those bound to service for a term of years and excluding Indians not taxed, three-fifths of all other persons.* The actual enumeration shall be made within three years after the first meeting of the Congress of the United States, and within every subsequent term of ten years, in such manner as they shall by law direct. The number of Representatives shall not exceed one for every thirty thousand, but each State shall have at least one Representative; *and until such enumeration shall be made, the State of New Hampshire shall be entitled to choose three, Massachusetts eight, Rhode Island and Providence Plantations one, Connecticut five, New York six, New Jersey four, Pennsylvania eight, Delaware one, Maryland six, Virginia ten, North Carolina five, South Carolina five, and Georgia three.*

Note: Passages that are no longer in effect are printed in italic type.

When vacancies happen in the representation from any State, the Executive authority thereof shall issue writs of election to fill such vacancies.

The House of Representatives shall choose their Speaker and other officers; and shall have the sole power of impeachment.

Section 3. The Senate of the United States shall be composed of two Senators from each State, *chosen by the legislature thereof,* for six years; and each Senator shall have one vote.

Immediately after they shall be assembled in consequence of the first election, they shall be divided as equally as may be into three classes. The seats of the Senators of the first class shall be vacated at the expiration of the second year, of the second class at the expiration of the fourth year, and of the third class at the expiration of the sixth year, so that one-third may be chosen every second year; and if vacancies happen by resignation or otherwise, during the recess of the legislature of any State, the Executive thereof may make temporary appointments until the next meeting of the legislature, which shall then fill such vacancies.

No person shall be a Senator who shall not have attained to the age of thirty years, and been nine years a citizen of the United States, and who shall not, when elected, be an inhabitant of that State for which he shall be chosen.

The Vice President of the United States shall be President of the Senate, but shall have no vote, unless they be equally divided.

The Senate shall choose their other officers, and also a President *pro tempore,* in the absence of the Vice President, or when he shall exercise the office of the President of the United States.

The Senate shall have the sole power to try all impeachments. When sitting for that purpose, they shall be on oath or affirmation. When the President of the United States is tried, the Chief Justice shall preside: and no person shall be convicted without the concurrence of two-thirds of the members present.

Judgment in cases of impeachment shall not extend further than to removal from the office, and disqualification to hold and enjoy any office of honor, trust or profit under the United States; but the party convicted shall nevertheless be liable and subject to indictment, trial, judgment and punishment, according to law.

Section 4. The times, places and manner of holding elections for Senators and Representatives shall be prescribed in each State by the legislature thereof; but the Congress may at any time by law make or alter such regulations, except as to the places of choosing Senators.

The Congress shall assemble at least once in every year, and such meeting *shall be on the first Monday in December, unless they shall by law appoint a different day.*

Section 5. Each house shall be the judge of the elections, returns and qualifications of its own members, and a majority of each shall constitute a quorum to do business; but a smaller number may adjourn from day to day, and may be authorized to compel the attendance of absent members, in such manner, and under such penalties, as each house may provide.

Each house may determine the rules of its proceedings, punish its members for disorderly behavior, and with the concurrence of two-thirds, expel a member.

Each house shall keep a journal of its proceedings, and from time to time publish the same, excepting such parts as may in their judgment require secrecy; and the yeas and nays of the members of either house on any question shall, at the desire of one-fifth of those present, be entered on the journal.

Neither house, during the session of Congress, shall, without the consent of the other, adjourn for more than three days, nor to any other place than that in which the two houses shall be sitting.

Section 6. The Senators and Representatives shall receive a compensation for their services, to be ascertained by law and paid out of the treasury of the United States. They shall in all cases except treason, felony and breach of the peace, be privileged from arrest during their attendance at the session of their respective houses, and in going to and returning from the same; and for any speech or debate in either house, they shall not be questioned in any other place.

No Senator or Representative shall, during the time for which he was elected, be appointed to any civil office under the authority of the United States, which shall have been created, or the emoluments whereof shall have been increased, during such time; and no person holding any office under the United States shall be a member of either house during his continuance in office.

Section 7. All bills for raising revenue shall originate in the House of Representatives; but the Senate may propose or concur with amendments as on other bills.

Every bill which shall have passed the House of Representatives and the Senate, shall, before it become a law, be presented to the President of the United States; if he approve he shall sign it, but if not he shall return it with objections to that house in which it originated, who shall enter the objections at large on their journal, and proceed to reconsider it. If after such reconsideration two-thirds of that house shall agree to pass the bill, it shall be sent, together with the objections, to the other house, by which it shall likewise be reconsidered, and, if approved by two-thirds of that house, it shall become a law. But in all such cases the votes of both houses shall be determined by yeas and nays, and the names of the persons voting for and against the bill shall be entered on the journal of each house respectively. If any bill shall not be returned by the President within ten days (Sundays excepted) after it shall have been presented to him, the same shall be a law, in like manner as if he had signed it, unless the Congress by their adjournment prevent its return, in which case it shall not be a law.

Every order, resolution, or vote to which the concurrence of the Senate and House of Representatives may be necessary (except on a question of adjournment) shall be presented to the President of the United States; and before the same shall take effect, shall be approved by him, or being disapproved by him, shall be repassed by two-thirds of the Senate and House of Representatives, according to the rules and limitations prescribed in the case of a bill.

Section 8. The Congress shall have power

To lay and collect taxes, duties, imposts, and excises, to pay the debts and provide for the common defense and general welfare of the United States; but all duties, imposts and excises shall be uniform throughout the United States;

To borrow money on the credit of the United States;

To regulate commerce with foreign nations, and among the several States, and with the Indian tribes;

To establish an uniform rule of naturalization, and uniform laws on the subject of bankruptcies throughout the United States;

To coin money, regulate the value thereof, and of foreign coin, and fix the standard of weights and measures;

To provide for the punishment of counterfeiting the securities and current coin of the United States;

To establish post offices and post roads;

To promote the progress of science and useful arts by securing for limited times to authors and inventors the exclusive right to their respective writings and discoveries;

To constitute tribunals inferior to the Supreme Court;

To define and punish piracies and felonies committed on the high seas and offenses against the law of nations;

To declare war, grant letters of marque and reprisal, and make rules concerning captures on land and water;

To raise and support armies, but no appropriation of money to that use shall be for a longer term than two years;

To provide and maintain a navy;

To make rules for the government and regulation of the land and naval forces;

To provide for calling forth the militia to execute the laws of the Union, suppress insurrections, and repel invasions;

To provide for organizing, arming, and disciplining the militia, and for governing such part of them as may be employed in the service of the United States, reserving to the States respectively the appointment of the officers, and the authority of training the militia according to the discipline prescribed by Congress;

To exercise exclusive legislation in all cases whatsoever, over such district (not exceeding ten miles square) as may, by cession of particular States, and the acceptance of Congress, become the seat of government of the United States, and to exercise like authority over all places purchased by the consent of the legislature of the State, in which the same shall be, for erection of forts, magazines, arsenals, dock-yards, and other needful buildings;—and

To make all laws which shall be necessary and proper for carrying into execution the foregoing powers, and all other powers vested by this Constitution in the government of the United States, or in any department or officer thereof.

Section 9.   *The migration or importation of such persons as any of the States now existing shall think proper to admit shall not be prohibited by the Congress prior to the year 1808; but a tax or duty may be imposed on such importation, not exceeding $10 for each person.*

The privilege of the writ of habeas corpus shall not be suspended, unless when in cases of rebellion or invasion the public safety may require it.

No bill of attainder or ex post facto law shall be passed.

No capitation, or other direct, tax shall be laid, unless in proportion to the census or enumeration herein before directed to be taken.

No tax or duty shall be laid on articles exported from any State.

No preference shall be given by any regulation of commerce or revenue to the ports of one State over those of another; nor shall vessels bound to, or from, one State, be obliged to enter, clear, or pay duties in another.

No money shall be drawn from the treasury, but in consequence of appropriations made by law; and a regular statement and account of the receipts and expenditures of all public money shall be published from time to time.

No title of nobility shall be granted by the United States: and no person holding any office of profit or trust under them, shall, without the consent of the Congress, accept of any present, emolument, office, or title, of any kind whatever, from any king, prince, or foreign state.

Section 10.   No State shall enter into any treaty, alliance, or confederation; grant letters of marque and reprisal; coin money; emit bills of credit; make anything but gold and silver coin a tender in payment of debts; pass any bill of attainder, ex post facto law, or law impairing the obligation of contracts, or grant any title of nobility.

No State shall, without the consent of Congress, lay any imposts or duties on imports or exports, except what may be absolutely necessary for executing its inspection laws: and the net produce of all duties and imposts, laid by any State on imports or exports, shall be for the use of the treasury of the United States; and all such laws shall be subject to the revision and control of the Congress.

No State shall, without the consent of Congress, lay any duty of tonnage, keep troops or ships of war in time of peace, enter into any agreement or compact with another State, or with a foreign power, or engage in war, unless actually invaded, or in such imminent danger as will not admit of delay.

Article II

Section 1. The executive power shall be vested in a President of the United States of America. He shall hold his office during the term of four years, and, together with the Vice President, chosen for the same term, be elected as follows:

Each state shall appoint, in such manner as the legislature thereof may direct, a number of electors, equal to the whole number of Senators and Representatives to which the State may be entitled in the Congress; but no Senator or Representative, or person holding an office of trust or profit under the United States, shall be appointed an elector.

The electors shall meet in their respective States, and vote by ballot for two persons, of whom one at least shall not be an inhabitant of the same State with themselves. And they shall make a list of all the persons voted for, and of the number of votes for each; which list they shall sign and certify, and transmit sealed to the seat of government of the United States, directed to the President of the Senate. The President of the Senate shall, in the presence of the Senate and the House of Representatives, open all the certificates, and the votes shall then be counted. The person having the greatest number of votes shall be the President, if such number be a majority of the whole number of electors appointed; and if there be more than one who have such majority, and have an equal number of votes, then the House of Representatives shall immediately choose by ballot one of them for President; and if no person have a majority, then from the five highest on the list said house shall in like manner choose the President. But in choosing the President the votes shall be taken by States, the representation from each State having one vote; a quorum for this purpose shall consist of a member or members from two-thirds of the States, and a majority of all the States shall be necessary to a choice. In every case, after the choice of the President, the person having the greatest number of votes of the electors shall be the Vice President. But if there should remain two or more who have equal votes, the Senate shall choose from them by ballot the Vice President.

The Congress may determine the time of choosing the electors and the day on which they shall give their votes; which day shall be the same throughout the United States.

No person except a natural-born citizen, *or a citizen of the United States at the time of the adoption of this Constitution,* shall be eligible to the office of President; neither shall any person be eligible to that office who shall not have attained to the age of thirty-five years, and been fourteen years a resident within the United States.

In case of the removal of the President from office or of his death, resignation, or inability to discharge the powers and duties of the said office, the same shall devolve on the Vice President, and the Congress may by law provide for the case of removal, death, resignation, or inability, both of the President and Vice President, declaring what officer shall then act as President, and such officer shall act accordingly, until the disability be removed, or a President shall be elected.

The President shall, at stated times, receive for his services a compensation, which shall neither be increased nor diminished during the period for which he shall have been elected, and he shall not receive within that period any other emolument from the United States, or any of them.

Before he enter on the execution of his office, he shall take the following oath or affirmation:—"I do solemnly swear (or affirm) that I will faithfully execute the office of the President of the United States, and will to the best of my ability preserve, protect and defend the Constitution of the United States."

Section 2. The President shall be commander in chief of the army and navy of the United States, and of the militia of the several States, when called into the actual service of the United States; he may require the opinion, in writing, of the principal officer in each of the executive departments, upon any subject relating to the duties of their respective offices, and he shall have power to grant reprieves and pardons for offenses against the United States, except in cases of impeachment.

He shall have power, by and with the advice and consent of the Senate, to make treaties, provided two-thirds of the Senators present concur; and he shall nominate, and by and with the advice and consent of the Senate, shall appoint ambassadors, other public ministers and consuls, judges of the Supreme Court, and all other officers of the United States, whose appointments are not herein otherwise provided for, and which shall be established by law: but Congress may by law vest the appointment of such inferior officers, as they think proper, in the President alone, in the courts of law, or in the heads of departments.

The President shall have power to fill up all vacancies that may happen during the recess of the Senate, by granting commissions which shall expire at the end of their next session.

Section 3. He shall from time to time give to the Congress information of the state of the Union, and recommend to their consideration such measures as he shall

judge necessary and expedient; he may, on extraordinary occasions, convene both houses, or either of them, and in case of disagreement between them, with respect to the time of adjournment, he may adjourn them to such time as he shall think proper; he shall receive ambassadors and other public ministers; he shall take care that the laws be faithfully executed, and shall commission all the officers of the United States.

Section 4. The President, Vice President and all civil officers of the United States shall be removed from office on impeachment for, and on conviction of, treason, bribery, or other high crimes and misdemeanors.

Article III

Section 1. The judicial power of the United States shall be vested in one Supreme Court, and in such inferior courts as the Congress may from time to time ordain and establish. The judges, both of the Supreme and inferior courts, shall hold their offices during good behavior, and shall, at stated times, receive for their services a compensation which shall not be diminished during their continuance in office.

Section 2. The judicial power shall extend to all cases, in law and equity, arising under this Constitution, the laws of the United States, and treaties made, or which shall be made, under their authority;—to all cases affecting ambassadors, other public ministers and consuls;—to all cases of admiralty and maritime jurisdiction;—to controversies to which the United States shall be a party;—to controversies between two or more States;—*between a State and citizens of another State;*—between citizens of different States;—between citizens of the same State claiming lands under grants of different States, and between a State, or the citizens thereof, and foreign states, citizens or subjects.

In all cases affecting ambassadors, other public ministers and consuls, and those in which a State shall be party, the Supreme Court shall have original jurisdiction. In all the other cases before mentioned, the Supreme Court shall have appellate jurisdiction, both as to law and fact, with such exceptions, and under such regulations, as the Congress shall make.

The trial of all crimes, except in cases of impeachment, shall be by jury; and such trial shall be held in the State where said crimes shall have been committed; but when not committed within any State, the trial shall be at such place or places as the Congress may by law have directed.

Section 3. Treason against the United States shall consist only in levying war against them, or in adhering to their enemies, giving them aid and comfort. No person shall be convicted of treason unless on the testimony of two witnesses to the same overt act, or on confession in open court.

The Congress shall have power to declare the punishment of treason, but no attainder of treason shall work corruption of blood, or forfeiture except during the life of the person attainted.

Article IV

Section 1. Full faith and credit shall be given in each State to the public acts, records, and judicial proceedings of every other State. And the Congress may by general laws prescribe the manner in which such acts, records, and proceedings shall be proved, and the effect thereof.

Section 2. The citizens of each State shall be entitled to all privileges and immunities of citizens in the several States.

A person charged in any State with treason, felony, or other crime, who shall flee from justice, and be found in another State, shall on demand of the executive authority of the State from which he fled, be delivered up, to be removed to the State having jurisdiction of the crime.

No person held to service or labor in one State, under the laws thereof, escaping into another, shall, in consequence of any law or regulation therein, be discharged from such service or labor, but shall be delivered up on claim of the party to whom such service or labor may be due.

Section 3. New States may be admitted by the Congress into this Union; but no new State shall be formed or erected within the jurisdiction of any other State; nor any State be formed by the junction of two or more States, or parts of States, without the consent of the legislatures of the States concerned as well as of the Congress.

The Congress shall have power to dispose of and make all needful rules and regulations respecting the territory or other property belonging to the United States; and nothing in this Constitution shall be so construed as to prejudice any claims of the United States, or of any particular State.

Section 4. The United States shall guarantee to every State in this Union a republican form of government,

and shall protect each of them against invasion; and on application of the legislature, or of the executive (when the legislature cannot be convened), against domestic violence.

Article V

The Congress, whenever two-thirds of both houses shall deem it necessary, shall propose amendments to this Constitution, or, on the application of the legislatures of two-thirds of the several States, shall call a convention for proposing amendments, which, in either case, shall be valid to all intents and purposes, as part of this Constitution, when ratified by the legislatures of three-fourths of the several States, or by conventions in three-fourths thereof, as the one or the other mode of ratification may be proposed by the Congress; provided *that no amendments which may be made prior to the year one thousand eight hundred and eight shall in any manner affect the first and fourth clauses in the ninth section of the first article;* and that no State, without its consent, shall be deprived of its equal suffrage in the Senate.

Article VI

All debts contracted and engagements entered into, before the adoption of this Constitution, shall be as valid against the United States under this Constitution, as under the Confederation.

This Constitution, and the laws of the United States which shall be made in pursuance thereof; and all treaties made, or which shall be made, under the authority of the United States, shall be the supreme law of the land; and the judges in every State shall be bound thereby, anything in the Constitution or laws of any State to the contrary notwithstanding.

The Senators and Representatives before mentioned, and the members of the several State legislatures, and all executive and judicial officers, both of the United States and of the several States, shall be bound by oath or affirmation to support this Constitution; but no religious test shall ever be required as a qualification to any office or public trust under the United States.

Article VII

The ratification of the conventions of nine States shall be sufficient for the establishment of this Constitution between the States so ratifying the same.

Done in Convention by the unanimous consent of the States present, the seventeenth day of September in the year of our Lord one thousand seven hundred and eighty-seven and of the Independence of the United States of America the twelfth. In witness whereof we have hereunto subscribed our names.

[Signed by]
Gº WASHINGTON
Presidt and Deputy from Virginia
[*and thirty-eight others*]

AMENDMENTS TO THE CONSTITUTION

Amendment I*

Congress shall make no law respecting an establishment of religion, or prohibiting the free exercise thereof; or abridging the freedom of speech, or of the press; or the right of the people peaceably to assemble, and to petition the government for a redress of grievances.

Amendment II

A well-regulated militia being necessary to the security of a free State, the right of the people to keep and bear arms shall not be infringed.

Amendment III

No soldier shall, in time of peace, be quartered in any house without the consent of the owner, nor in time of war, but in a manner to be prescribed by law.

Amendment IV

The right of the people to be secure in their persons, houses, papers, and effects, against unreasonable searches and seizures, shall not be violated, and no warrants shall issue but upon probable cause, supported by oath or affirmation, and particularly describing the place to be searched, and the persons or things to be seized.

Amendment V

No person shall be held to answer for a capital, or otherwise infamous crime, unless on a presentment or indict-

---

*The first ten Amendments (Bill of Rights) were adopted in 1791.

ment of a grand jury, except in cases arising in the land or naval forces, or in the militia, when in actual service in time of war or public danger; nor shall any person be subject for the same offense to be twice put in jeopardy of life or limb; nor shall be compelled in any criminal case to be a witness against himself, nor be deprived of life, liberty, or property, without due process of law; nor shall private property be taken for public use without just compensation.

Amendment VI

In all criminal prosecutions, the accused shall enjoy the right to a speedy and public trial, by an impartial jury of the State and district wherein the crime shall have been committed, which district shall have been previously ascertained by law, and to be informed of the nature and cause of the accusation; to be confronted with the witnesses against him; to have compulsory process for obtaining witnesses in his favor, and to have the assistance of counsel for his defense.

Amendment VII

In suits at common law, where the value in controversy shall exceed twenty dollars, the right of trial by jury shall be preserved, and no fact tried by a jury shall be otherwise reexamined in any court of the United States, than according to the rules of the common law.

Amendment VIII

Excessive bail shall not be required, nor excessive fines imposed, nor cruel and unusual punishments inflicted.

Amendment IX

The enumeration in the Constitution, of certain rights, shall not be construed to deny or disparage others retained by the people.

Amendment X

The powers not delegated to the United States by the Constitution, nor prohibited by it to the States, are reserved to the States respectively, or to the people.

Amendment XI
[Adopted 1798]

The judicial power of the United States shall not be construed to extend to any suit in law or equity, commenced or prosecuted against one of the United States by citizens of another State, or by citizens or subjects of any foreign state.

Amendment XII
[Adopted 1804]

The electors shall meet in their respective States, and vote by ballot for President and Vice President, one of whom, at least, shall not be an inhabitant of the same State with themselves; they shall name in their ballots the person voted for as President, and in distinct ballots the person voted for as Vice President, and they shall make distinct lists of all persons voted for as President, and of all persons voted for as Vice President, and of the number of votes for each, which lists they shall sign and certify, and transmit sealed to the seat of government of the United States, directed to the President of the Senate;—the President of the Senate shall, in the presence of the Senate and House of Representatives, open all the certificates and the votes shall then be counted;—the person having the greatest number of votes for President shall be the President, if such number be a majority of the whole number of electors appointed; and if no person have such majority, then from the persons having the highest numbers not exceeding three on the list of those voted for as President, the House of Representatives shall choose immediately, by ballot, the President. But in choosing the President, the votes shall be taken by States, the representation from each State having one vote; a quorum for this purpose shall consist of a member or members from two-thirds of the States, and a majority of all the States shall be necessary to a choice. And if the House of Representatives shall not choose a President whenever the right of choice shall devolve upon them, before *the fourth day of March* next following, then the Vice President shall act as President, as in the case of the death or other constitutional disability of the President.

The person having the greatest number of votes as Vice President shall be the Vice President, if such a number be a majority of the whole number of electors appointed; and if no person have a majority, then from the two highest numbers on the list the Senate shall choose the Vice President; a quorum for the purpose shall consist of two-thirds of the whole number of Senators, and a majority of the whole number shall be necessary to a choice. But no person constitutionally ineligible to the office of President shall be eligible to that of Vice President of the United States.

Amendment XIII
[*Adopted 1865*]

Section 1. Neither slavery nor involuntary servitude, except as a punishment for crime whereof the party shall have been duly convicted, shall exist within the United States, or any place subject to their jurisdiction.

Section 2. Congress shall have power to enforce this article by appropriate legislation.

Amendment XIV
[*Adopted 1868*]

Section 1. All persons born or naturalized in the United States, and subject to the jurisdiction thereof, are citizens of the United States and of the State wherein they reside. No State shall make or enforce any law which shall abridge the privileges or immunities of citizens of the United States; nor shall any State deprive any person of life, liberty, or property, without due process of law; nor deny to any person within its jurisdiction the equal protection of the laws.

Section 2. Representatives shall be apportioned among the several States according to their respective numbers, counting the whole number of persons in each State, excluding Indians not taxed. But when the right to vote at any election for the choice of Electors for President and Vice President of the United States, Representatives in Congress, the executive and judicial officers of a State, or the members of the legislature thereof, is denied to any of the male inhabitants of such State, being twenty-one years of age and citizens of the United States, or in any way abridged, except for participation in rebellion, or other crime, the basis of representation therein shall be reduced in the proportion which the number of such male citizens shall bear to the whole number of male citizens twenty-one years of age in such State.

Section 3. No person shall be a Senator or Representative in Congress or Elector of President and Vice President, or hold any office, civil or military, under the United States, or under any State, who, having previously taken an oath, as a member of Congress, or as an officer of the United States, or as a member of any State legislature, or as an executive or judicial officer of any State, to support the Constitution of the United States, shall have engaged in insurrection or rebellion against the same, or given aid and comfort to the enemies thereof. Congress may, by a vote of two-thirds of each house, remove such disability.

Section 4. The validity of the public debt of the United States, authorized by law, including debts incurred for payment of pensions and bounties for services in suppressing insurrection or rebellion, shall not be questioned. But neither the United States nor any State shall assume or pay any debt or obligation incurred in aid of insurrection or rebellion against the United States, or any claim for the loss or emancipation of any slave; but all such debts, obligations, and claims shall be held illegal and void.

Section 5. The Congress shall have the power to enforce, by appropriate legislation, the provisions of this article.

Amendment XV
[*Adopted 1870*]

Section 1. The right of citizens of the United States to vote shall not be denied or abridged by the United States or by any State on account of race, color, or previous condition of servitude.

Section 2. The Congress shall have power to enforce this article by appropriate legislation.

Amendment XVI
[*Adopted 1913*]

The Congress shall have power to lay and collect taxes on incomes, from whatever source derived, without apportionment among the several States, and without regard to any census or enumeration.

Amendment XVII
[*Adopted 1913*]

Section 1. The Senate of the United States shall be composed of two Senators from each State, elected by the people thereof, for six years; and each Senator shall have one vote. The electors in each State shall have the qualifications requisite for electors of [voters for] the most numerous branch of the State legislatures.

Section 2. When vacancies happen in the representation of any State in the Senate, the executive authority of such State shall issue writs of election to fill such vacancies: Provided, that the Legislature of any State may empower the executive thereof to make temporary appointments until the people fill the vacancies by election as the Legislature may direct.

Section 3. This amendment shall not be so construed as to affect the election or term of any Senator chosen before it becomes valid as part of the Constitution.

Amendment XVIII
[*Adopted 1919; repealed 1933*]

Section 1. *After one year from the ratification of this article the manufacture, sale, or transportation of intoxicating liquors within, the importation thereof into, or the exportation thereof from the United States and all territory subject to the jurisdiction thereof, for beverage purposes, is hereby prohibited.*

Section 2. *The Congress and the several States shall have concurrent power to enforce this article by appropriate legislation.*

Section 3. *This article shall be inoperative unless it shall have been ratified as an amendment to the Constitution by the legislatures of the several States, as provided by the Constitution, within seven years from the date of the submission thereof to the States by the Congress.*

Amendment XIX
[*Adopted 1920*]

Section 1. The right of citizens of the United States to vote shall not be denied or abridged by the United States or by any State on account of sex.

Section 2. The Congress shall have the power to enforce this article by appropriate legislation.

Amendment XX
[*Adopted 1933*]

Section 1. The terms of the President and Vice President shall end at noon on the 20th day of January, and the terms of Senators and Representatives at noon on the 3d day of January, of the years in which such terms would have ended if this article had not been ratified; and the terms of their successors shall then begin.

Section 2. The Congress shall assemble at least once in every year, and such meeting shall begin at noon on the 3d of January, unless they shall by law appoint a different day.

Section 3. If, at the time fixed for the beginning of the term of the President, the President-elect shall have

died, the Vice President-elect shall become President. If a President shall not have been chosen before the time fixed for the beginning of his term, or if the President-elect shall have failed to qualify, then the Vice President-elect shall act as President until a President shall have qualified; and the Congress may by law provide for the case wherein neither a President-elect nor a Vice President-elect shall have qualified, declaring who shall then act as President, or the manner in which one who is to act shall be selected, and such persons shall act accordingly until a President or Vice President shall have qualified.

Section 4. The Congress may by law provide for the case of the death of any of the persons from whom the House of Representatives may choose a President whenever the right of choice shall have devolved upon them, and for the case of the death of any of the persons from whom the Senate may choose a Vice President whenever the right of choice shall have devolved upon them.

Section 5. Sections 1 and 2 shall take effect on the 15th day of October following the ratification of this article.

Section 6. This article shall be inoperative unless it shall have been ratified as an amendment to the Constitution by the Legislatures of three-fourths of the several States within seven years from the date of its submission.

Amendment XXI
[*Adopted 1933*]

Section 1. The eighteenth article of amendment to the Constitution of the United States is hereby repealed.

Section 2. The transportation or importation into any State, Territory, or Possession of the United States for delivery or use therein of intoxicating liquors, in violation of the laws thereof, is hereby prohibited.

Section 3. This article shall be inoperative unless it shall have been ratified as an amendment to the Constitution by conventions in the several States, as provided in the Constitution, within seven years from the date of submission thereof to the States by the Congress.

Amendment XXII
[*Adopted 1951*]

Section 1. No person shall be elected to the office of President more than twice, and no person who has held

the office of President, or acted as President, for more than two years of a term to which some other person was elected President shall be elected to the office of President more than once. But this article shall not apply to any person holding the office of President when this article was proposed by the Congress, and shall not prevent any person who may be holding the office of President, or acting as President, during the term within which this article becomes operative from holding the office of President or acting as President during the remainder of such term.

Section 2.   This article shall be inoperative unless it shall have been ratified as an amendment to the Constitution by the legislatures of three-fourths of the several States within seven years from the date of its submission to the States by the Congress.

Amendment XXIII
[*Adopted 1961*]

Section 1.   The District constituting the seat of Government of the United States shall appoint in such manner as the Congress may direct:

A number of electors of President and Vice President equal to the whole number of Senators and Representatives in Congress to which the District would be entitled if it were a State, but in no event more than the least populous State; they shall be in addition to those appointed by the States, but they shall be considered for the purposes of the election of President and Vice President, to be electors appointed by a State; and they shall meet in the District and perform such duties as provided by the twelfth article of amendment.

Section 2.   The Congress shall have the power to enforce this article by appropriate legislation.

Amendment XXIV
[*Adopted 1964*]

Section 1.   The right of citizens of the United States to vote in any primary or other election for President or Vice President, for electors for President or Vice President, or for Senator or Representative in Congress, shall not be denied or abridged by the United States or any State by reason of failure to pay any poll tax or other tax.

Section 2.   The Congress shall have the power to enforce this article by appropriate legislation.

Amendment XXV
[*Adopted 1967*]

Section 1.   In case of the removal of the President from office or of his death or resignation, the Vice President shall become President.

Section 2.   Whenever there is a vacancy in the office of the Vice President, the President shall nominate a Vice President who shall take office upon confirmation by a majority vote of both Houses of Congress.

Section 3.   Whenever the President transmits to the President pro tempore of the Senate and the Speaker of the House of Representatives his written declaration that he is unable to discharge the powers and duties of his office, and until he transmits to them a written declaration to the contrary, such powers and duties shall be discharged by the Vice President as Acting President.

Section 4.   Whenever the Vice President and a majority of either the principal officers of the executive departments or of such other body as Congress may by law provide, transmit to the President pro tempore of the Senate and the Speaker of the House of Representatives their written declaration that the President is unable to discharge the powers and duties of his office, the Vice President shall immediately assume the powers and duties of the office as Acting President.

Thereafter, when the President transmits to the President pro tempore of the Senate and the Speaker of the House of Representatives his written declaration that no inability exists, he shall resume the powers and duties of his office unless the Vice President and a majority of either the principal officers of the executive department[s] or of such other body as Congress may by law provide, transmit within four days to the President pro tempore of the Senate and the Speaker of the House of Representatives their written declaration that the President is unable to discharge the powers and duties of his office. Thereupon Congress shall decide the issue, assembling within forty-eight hours for that purpose if not in session. If the Congress, within twenty-one days after receipt of the latter written declaration, or, if Congress is not in session, within twenty-one days after Congress is required to assemble, determines by two-thirds vote of both Houses that the President is unable to discharge the powers and duties of his office, the Vice President shall continue to discharge the same as Acting President; otherwise, the President shall resume the powers and duties of his office.

Amendment XXVI
[Adopted 1971]

Section 1. The right of citizens of the United States, who are eighteen years of age or older, to vote shall not be denied or abridged by the United States or by any State on account of age.

Section 2. The Congress shall have power to enforce this article by appropriate legislation.

Amendment XXVII*
[Adopted 1992]

No law, varying the compensation for services of the Senators and Representatives, shall take effect, until an election of Representatives shall have intervened.

*Originally proposed in 1789 by James Madison, this amendment failed to win ratification along with the other parts of what became the Bill of Rights. However, the proposed amendment contained no deadline for ratification, and over the years other state legislatures voted to add it to the Constitution; many such ratifications occurred during the 1980s and early 1990s as public frustration with Congress's performance mounted. In May 1992 the Archivist of the United States certified that, with the Michigan legislature's ratification, the article had been approved by three-fourths of the states and thus automatically became part of the Constitution.

THE AMERICAN LAND

Admission of States into the Union

State	Date of Admission	State	Date of Admission
1. Delaware	December 7, 1787	26. Michigan	January 26, 1837
2. Pennsylvania	December 12, 1787	27. Florida	March 3, 1845
3. New Jersey	December 18, 1787	28. Texas	December 29, 1845
4. Georgia	January 2, 1788	29. Iowa	December 28, 1846
5. Connecticut	January 9, 1788	30. Wisconsin	May 29, 1848
6. Massachusetts	February 6, 1788	31. California	September 9, 1850
7. Maryland	April 28, 1788	32. Minnesota	May 11, 1858
8. South Carolina	May 23, 1788	33. Oregon	February 14, 1859
9. New Hampshire	June 21, 1788	34. Kansas	January 29, 1861
10. Virginia	June 25, 1788	35. West Virginia	June 20, 1863
11. New York	July 26, 1788	36. Nevada	October 31, 1864
12. North Carolina	November 21, 1789	37. Nebraska	March 1, 1867
13. Rhode Island	May 29, 1790	38. Colorado	August 1, 1876
14. Vermont	March 4, 1791	39. North Dakota	November 2, 1889
15. Kentucky	June 1, 1792	40. South Dakota	November 2, 1889
16. Tennessee	June 1, 1796	41. Montana	November 8, 1889
17. Ohio	March 1, 1803	42. Washington	November 11, 1889
18. Louisiana	April 30, 1812	43. Idaho	July 3, 1890
19. Indiana	December 11, 1816	44. Wyoming	July 10, 1890
20. Mississippi	December 10, 1817	45. Utah	January 4, 1896
21. Illinois	December 3, 1818	46. Oklahoma	November 16, 1907
22. Alabama	December 14, 1819	47. New Mexico	January 6, 1912
23. Maine	March 15, 1820	48. Arizona	February 14, 1912
24. Missouri	August 10, 1821	49. Alaska	January 3, 1959
25. Arkansas	June 15, 1836	50. Hawaii	August 21, 1959

Territorial Expansion

Territory	Date Acquired	Square Miles	How Acquired
Original states and territories	1783	888,685	Treaty of Paris
Louisiana Purchase	1803	827,192	Purchased from France
Florida	1819	72,003	Adams-Onís Treaty
Texas	1845	390,143	Annexation of independent country
Oregon	1846	285,580	Oregon Boundary Treaty
Mexican cession	1848	529,017	Treaty of Guadalupe Hidalgo
Gadsden Purchase	1853	29,640	Purchased from Mexico
Midway Islands	1867	2	Annexation of uninhabited islands
Alaska	1867	589,757	Purchased from Russia
Hawaii	1898	6,450	Annexation of independent country
Wake Island	1898	3	Annexation of uninhabited island
Puerto Rico	1899	3,435	Treaty of Paris
Guam	1899	212	Treaty of Paris
The Philippines	1899–1946	115,600	Treaty of Paris; granted independence
American Samoa	1900	76	Treaty with Germany and Great Britain
Panama Canal Zone	1904–1978	553	Hay-Bunau-Varilla Treaty
U.S. Virgin Islands	1917	133	Purchased from Denmark
Trust Territory of the Pacific Islands*	1947	717	United Nations Trusteeship

*A number of these islands have been granted independence: Federated States of Micronesia, 1990; Marshall Islands, 1991; Palau, 1994.

THE AMERICAN PEOPLE

Population, Percentage Change, and Racial Composition for the United States, 1790–2000

Census	Population of United States	Increase over Preceding Census		Racial Composition, Percent Distribution*			
		Number	Percentage	White	Black	Latino	Asian
1790	3,929,214			80.7	19.3	NA	NA
1800	5,308,483	1,379,269	35.1	81.1	18.9	NA	NA
1810	7,239,881	1,931,398	36.4	81.0	19.0	NA	NA
1820	9,638,453	2,398,572	33.1	81.6	18.4	NA	NA
1830	12,866,020	3,227,567	33.5	81.9	18.1	NA	NA
1840	17,069,453	4,203,433	32.7	83.2	16.8	NA	NA
1850	23,191,876	6,122,423	35.9	84.3	15.7	NA	NA
1860	31,433,321	8,251,445	35.6	85.6	14.1	NA	NA
1870	39,818,449	8,375,128	26.6	86.2	13.5	NA	NA
1880	50,155,783	10,337,334	26.0	86.5	13.1	NA	NA
1890	62,947,714	12,791,931	25.5	87.5	11.9	NA	NA
1900	75,994,575	13,046,861	20.7	87.9	11.6	NA	0.3
1910	91,972,266	15,997,691	21.0	88.9	10.7	NA	0.3
1920	105,710,620	13,738,354	14.9	89.7	9.9	NA	0.3
1930	122,775,046	17,064,426	16.1	89.8	9.7	NA	0.4
1940	131,669,275	8,894,229	7.2	89.8	9.8	NA	0.4
1950	150,697,361	19,028,086	14.5	89.5	10.0	NA	0.4
1960†	179,323,175	28,625,814	19.0	88.6	10.5	NA	0.5
1970	203,235,298	23,912,123	13.3	87.6	11.1	NA	0.7
1980	226,504,825	23,269,527	11.4	85.9	11.8	6.4	1.5
1990	248,709,873	22,205,048	9.8	83.9	12.3	9.0	2.9
2000	281,421,906	32,712,033	13.2	82.2	12.2	11.7	3.8

*Not every racial group included (e.g., no Native Americans). Persons of Latino origin may be of any race. Data for 1980, 1990, 2000 add up to more than 100% because those who identify themselves as "Latino" could still be counted as "White."
†First year for which figures include Alaska and Hawaii.
(*Source:* Census Bureau, *Historical Statistics of the United States,* updated by relevant *Statistical Abstract of the United States.*)

Population Density and Distribution, 1790–2000

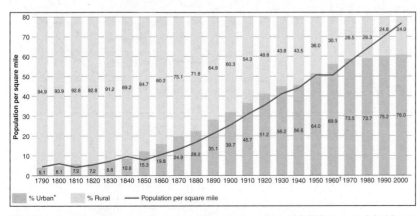

*The Bureau of the Census defines "urban" as communities of 2,500 or more inhabitants.
†First year for which figures include Alaska and Hawaii.
(*Source:* Census Bureau, *Historical Statistics of the United States,* updated by relevant *Statistical Abstract of the United States.*)

Changing Characteristics of the U.S. Population

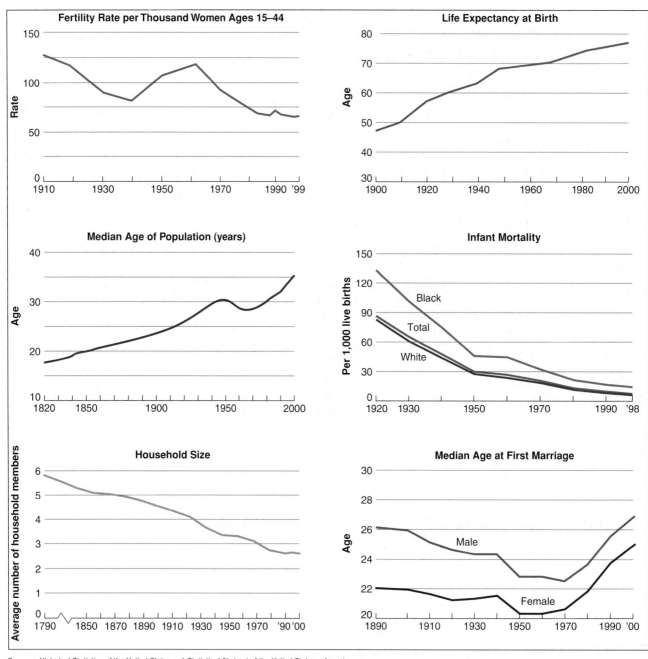

Sources: *Historical Statistics of the United States* and *Statistical Abstract of the United States,* relevant years.

Immigrants to the United States

Immigration Totals by Decade			
Years	Number	Years	Number
1820–1830	151,824	1911–1920	5,735,811
1831–1840	599,125	1921–1930	4,107,209
1841–1850	1,713,251	1931–1940	528,431
1851–1860	2,598,214	1941–1950	1,035,039
1861–1870	2,314,824	1951–1960	2,515,479
1871–1880	2,812,191	1961–1970	3,321,677
1881–1890	5,246,613	1971–1980	4,493,314
1891–1900	3,687,546	1981–1990	7,338,062
1901–1910	8,795,386	1991–2000	9,095,417
		Total	66,089,431

Major Sources of Immigration, 1820–1998

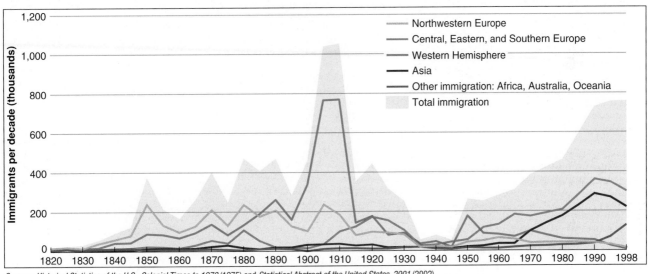

Sources: *Historical Statistics of the U.S., Colonial Times to 1970* (1975) and *Statistical Abstract of the United States, 2001* (2002).

The American Worker

Year	Total Number of Workers	Males as Percent of Total Workers	Females as Percent of Total Workers	Married Women as Percent of Female Workers	Female Workers as Percent of Female Population	Percent of Labor Force Unemployed
1870	12,506,000	85	15	NA	NA	NA
1880	17,392,000	85	15	NA	NA	NA
1890	23,318,000	83	17	14	19	4 (1894 = 18)
1900	29,073,000	82	18	15	21	5
1910	38,167,000	79	21	25	25	6
1920	41,614,000	79	21	23	24	5 (1921 = 12)
1930	48,830,000	78	22	29	25	9 (1933 = 25)
1940	53,011,000	76	24	36	27	15 (1944 = 1)
1950	62,208,000	72	28	52	31	5.3
1960	69,628,000	67	33	55	38	5.5
1970	82,771,000	62	38	59	43	4.9
1980	106,940,000	58	42	55	52	7.1
1990	125,840,000	55	45	54	58	5.6
2000	135,208,000	53	47	55	60	4.0

NA = Not available.

THE AMERICAN GOVERNMENT

Presidential Elections, 1789–2000

Year	States in the Union	Candidates	Parties	Electoral Vote	Popular Vote	Percentage of Popular Vote
1789	11	GEORGE WASHINGTON	No party designations	69		
		John Adams		34		
		Minor candidates		35		
1792	15	GEORGE WASHINGTON	No party designations	132		
		John Adams		77		
		George Clinton		50		
		Minor candidates		5		
1796	16	JOHN ADAMS	Federalist	71		
		Thomas Jefferson	Democratic-Republican	68		
		Thomas Pinckney	Federalist	59		
		Aaron Burr	Democratic-Republican	30		
		Minor candidates		48		
1800	16	THOMAS JEFFERSON	Democratic-Republican	73		
		Aaron Burr	Democratic-Republican	73		
		John Adams	Federalist	65		
		Charles C. Pinckney	Federalist	64		
		John Jay	Federalist	1		
1804	17	THOMAS JEFFERSON	Democratic-Republican	162		
		Charles C. Pinckney	Federalist	14		
1808	17	JAMES MADISON	Democratic-Republican	122		
		Charles C. Pinckney	Federalist	47		
		George Clinton	Democratic-Republican	6		
1812	18	JAMES MADISON	Democratic-Republican	128		
		DeWitt Clinton	Federalist	89		
1816	19	JAMES MONROE	Democratic-Republican	183		
		Rufus King	Federalist	34		
1820	24	JAMES MONROE	Democratic-Republican	231		
		John Quincy Adams	Independent Republican	1		
1824	24	JOHN QUINCY ADAMS	Democratic-Republican	84	108,740	30.5
		Andrew Jackson	Democratic-Republican	99	153,544	43.1
		William H. Crawford	Democratic-Republican	41	46,618	13.1
		Henry Clay	Democratic-Republican	37	47,136	13.2
1828	24	ANDREW JACKSON	Democratic	178	642,553	56.0
		John Quincy Adams	National Republican	83	500,897	44.0
1832	24	ANDREW JACKSON	Democratic	219	687,502	55.0
		Henry Clay	National Republican	49	530,189	42.4
		William Wirt	Anti-Masonic	7 }		
		John Floyd	National Republican	11 }	33,108	2.6

Because candidates receiving less than 1 percent of the popular vote are omitted, the percentage of popular vote may not total 100 percent. Before the Twelfth Amendment was passed in 1804, the electoral college voted for two presidential candidates; the runner-up became vice president.

Presidential Elections, 1789–2000 *(continued)*

Year	States in the Union	Candidates	Parties	Electoral Vote	Popular Vote	Percentage of Popular Vote
1836	26	MARTIN VAN BUREN	Democratic	170	765,483	50.9
		William H. Harrison	Whig	73		
		Hugh L. White	Whig	26		
		Daniel Webster	Whig	14	739,795	49.1
		W. P. Mangum	Whig	11		
1840	26	WILLIAM H. HARRISON	Whig	234	1,274,624	53.1
		Martin Van Buren	Democratic	60	1,127,781	46.9
1844	26	JAMES K. POLK	Democratic	170	1,338,464	49.6
		Henry Clay	Whig	105	1,300,097	48.1
		James G. Birney	Liberty	0	62,300	2.3
1848	30	ZACHARY TAYLOR	Whig	163	1,360,967	47.4
		Lewis Cass	Democratic	127	1,222,342	42.5
		Martin Van Buren	Free Soil	0	291,263	10.1
1852	31	FRANKLIN PIERCE	Democratic	254	1,601,117	50.9
		Winfield Scott	Whig	42	1,385,453	44.1
		John P. Hale	Free Soil	0	155,825	5.0
1856	31	JAMES BUCHANAN	Democratic	174	1,832,955	45.3
		John C. Frémont	Republican	114	1,339,932	33.1
		Millard Fillmore	American	8	871,731	21.6
1860	33	ABRAHAM LINCOLN	Republican	180	1,865,593	39.8
		Stephen A. Douglas	Democratic	12	1,382,713	29.5
		John C. Breckinridge	Democratic	72	848,356	18.1
		John Bell	Constitutional Union	39	592,906	12.6
1864	36	ABRAHAM LINCOLN	Republican	212	2,206,938	55.0
		George B. McClellan	Democratic	21	1,803,787	45.0
1868	37	ULYSSES S. GRANT	Republican	214	3,013,421	52.7
		Horatio Seymour	Democratic	80	2,706,829	47.3
1872	37	ULYSSES S. GRANT	Republican	286	3,596,745	55.6
		Horace Greeley	Democratic	*	2,843,446	43.9
1876	38	RUTHERFORD B. HAYES	Republican	185	4,034,311	48.0
		Samuel J. Tilden	Democratic	184	4,288,546	51.0
		Peter Cooper	Greenback	0	75,973	1.0
1880	38	JAMES A. GARFIELD	Republican	214	4,453,295	48.5
		Winfield S. Hancock	Democratic	155	4,414,082	48.1
		James B. Weaver	Greenback-Labor	0	308,578	3.4
1884	38	GROVER CLEVELAND	Democratic	219	4,879,507	48.5
		James G. Blaine	Republican	182	4,850,293	48.2
		Benjamin F. Butler	Greenback-Labor	0	175,370	1.8
		John P. St. John	Prohibition	0	150,369	1.5
1888	38	BENJAMIN HARRISON	Republican	233	5,477,129	47.9
		Grover Cleveland	Democratic	168	5,537,857	48.6
		Clinton B. Fisk	Prohibition	0	249,506	2.2
		Anson J. Streeter	Union Labor	0	146,935	1.3

*When Greeley died shortly after the election, his supporters divided their votes among the minor candidates.

Because candidates receiving less than 1 percent of the popular vote are omitted, the percentage of popular vote may not total 100 percent.

Presidential Elections, 1789–2000 *(continued)*

Year	States in the Union	Candidates	Parties	Electoral Vote	Popular Vote	Percentage of Popular Vote
1892	44	GROVER CLEVELAND	Democratic	277	5,555,426	46.1
		Benjamin Harrison	Republican	145	5,182,690	43.0
		James B. Weaver	People's	22	1,029,846	8.5
		John Bidwell	Prohibition	0	264,133	2.2
1896	45	WILLIAM McKINLEY	Republican	271	7,102,246	51.1
		William J. Bryan	Democratic	176	6,492,559	47.7
1900	45	WILLIAM McKINLEY	Republican	292	7,218,491	51.7
		William J. Bryan	Democratic; Populist	155	6,356,734	45.5
		John C. Wooley	Prohibition	0	208,914	1.5
1904	45	THEODORE ROOSEVELT	Republican	336	7,628,461	57.4
		Alton B. Parker	Democratic	140	5,084,223	37.6
		Eugene V. Debs	Socialist	0	402,283	3.0
		Silas C. Swallow	Prohibition	0	258,536	1.9
1908	46	WILLIAM H. TAFT	Republican	321	7,675,320	51.6
		William J. Bryan	Democratic	162	6,412,294	43.1
		Eugene V. Debs	Socialist	0	420,793	2.8
		Eugene W. Chafin	Prohibition	0	253,840	1.7
1912	48	WOODROW WILSON	Democratic	435	6,296,547	41.9
		Theodore Roosevelt	Progressive	88	4,118,571	27.4
		William H. Taft	Republican	8	3,486,720	23.2
		Eugene V. Debs	Socialist	0	900,672	6.0
		Eugene W. Chafin	Prohibition	0	206,275	1.4
1916	48	WOODROW WILSON	Democratic	277	9,127,695	49.4
		Charles E. Hughes	Republican	254	8,533,507	46.2
		A. L. Benson	Socialist	0	585,113	3.2
		J. Frank Hanly	Prohibition	0	220,506	1.2
1920	48	WARREN G. HARDING	Republican	404	16,143,407	60.4
		James N. Cox	Democratic	127	9,130,328	34.2
		Eugene V. Debs	Socialist	0	919,799	3.4
		P. P. Christensen	Farmer-Labor	0	265,411	1.0
1924	48	CALVIN COOLIDGE	Republican	382	15,718,211	54.0
		John W. Davis	Democratic	136	8,385,283	28.8
		Robert M. La Follette	Progressive	13	4,831,289	16.6
1928	48	HERBERT C. HOOVER	Republican	444	21,391,993	58.2
		Alfred E. Smith	Democratic	87	15,016,169	40.9
1932	48	FRANKLIN D. ROOSEVELT	Democratic	472	22,809,638	57.4
		Herbert C. Hoover	Republican	59	15,758,901	39.7
		Norman Thomas	Socialist	0	881,951	2.2
1936	48	FRANKLIN D. ROOSEVELT	Democratic	523	27,752,869	60.8
		Alfred M. Landon	Republican	8	16,674,665	36.5
		William Lemke	Union	0	882,479	1.9

Because candidates receiving less than 1 percent of the popular vote are omitted, the percentage of popular vote may not total 100 percent.

Presidential Elections, 1789–2000 *(continued)*

Year	States in the Union	Candidates	Parties	Electoral Vote	Popular Vote	Percentage of Popular Vote
1940	48	FRANKLIN D. ROOSEVELT	Democratic	449	27,307,819	54.8
		Wendell L. Willkie	Republican	82	22,321,018	44.8
1944	48	FRANKLIN D. ROOSEVELT	Democratic	432	25,606,585	53.5
		Thomas E. Dewey	Republican	99	22,014,745	46.0
1948	48	HARRY S TRUMAN	Democratic	303	24,105,812	49.5
		Thomas E. Dewey	Republican	189	21,970,065	45.1
		Strom Thurmond	States' Rights	39	1,169,063	2.4
		Henry A. Wallace	Progressive	0	1,157,172	2.4
1952	48	DWIGHT D. EISENHOWER	Republican	442	33,936,234	55.1
		Adlai E. Stevenson	Democratic	89	27,314,992	44.4
1956	48	DWIGHT D. EISENHOWER	Republican	457	35,590,472	57.6
		Adlai E. Stevenson	Democratic	73	26,022,752	42.1
1960	50	JOHN F. KENNEDY	Democratic	303	34,227,096	49.7
		Richard M. Nixon	Republican	219	34,108,546	49.5
		Harry F. Byrd	Independent	15	502,363	.7
1964	50	LYNDON B. JOHNSON	Democratic	486	43,126,506	61.1
		Barry M. Goldwater	Republican	52	27,176,799	38.5
1968	50	RICHARD M. NIXON	Republican	301	31,770,237	43.4
		Hubert H. Humphrey	Democratic	191	31,270,533	42.7
		George C. Wallace	American Independent	46	9,906,141	13.5
1972	50	RICHARD M. NIXON	Republican	520	47,169,911	60.7
		George S. McGovern	Democratic	17	29,170,383	37.5
1976	50	JIMMY CARTER	Democratic	297	40,827,394	49.9
		Gerald R. Ford	Republican	240	39,145,977	47.9
1980	50	RONALD W. REAGAN	Republican	489	43,899,248	50.8
		Jimmy Carter	Democratic	49	35,481,435	41.0
		John B. Anderson	Independent	0	5,719,437	6.6
		Ed Clark	Libertarian	0	920,859	1.0
1984	50	RONALD W. REAGAN	Republican	525	54,451,521	58.8
		Walter F. Mondale	Democratic	13	37,565,334	40.5
1988	50	GEORGE H. W. BUSH	Republican	426	47,946,422	54.0
		Michael S. Dukakis	Democratic	112	41,016,429	46.0
1992	50	WILLIAM J. CLINTON	Democratic	370	43,728,275	43.2
		George H. W. Bush	Republican	168	38,167,416	37.7
		H. Ross Perot	Independent	0	19,237,247	19.0
1996	50	WILLIAM J. CLINTON	Democratic	379	47,401,185	49.0
		Robert Dole	Republican	159	39,197,469	41.0
		H. Ross Perot	Independent	0	8,085,295	8.0
2000	50	GEORGE W. BUSH	Republican	271	50,456,169	47.9
		Albert Gore, Jr.	Democratic	267	50,996,116	48.4
		Ralph Nader	Green	0	2,783,728	2.7

Because candidates receiving less than 1 percent of the popular vote are omitted, the percentage of popular vote may not total 100 percent.

Supreme Court Justices

Name	Term of Service	Appointed By
JOHN JAY	1789–1795	Washington
James Wilson	1789–1798	Washington
John Rutledge	1790–1791	Washington
William Cushing	1790–1810	Washington
John Blair	1790–1796	Washington
James Iredell	1790–1799	Washington
Thomas Johnson	1792–1793	Washington
William Paterson	1793–1806	Washington
JOHN RUTLEDGE*	1795	Washington
Samuel Chase	1796–1811	Washington
OLIVER ELLSWORTH	1796–1800	Washington
Bushrod Washington	1799–1829	J. Adams
Alfred Moore	1800–1804	J. Adams
JOHN MARSHALL	1801–1835	J. Adams
William Johnson	1804–1834	Jefferson
Brockholst Livingston	1807–1823	Jefferson
Thomas Todd	1807–1826	Jefferson
Gabriel Duvall	1811–1835	Madison
Joseph Story	1812–1845	Madison
Smith Thompson	1823–1843	Monroe
Robert Trimble	1826–1828	J. Q. Adams
John McLean	1830–1861	Jackson
Henry Baldwin	1830–1844	Jackson
James M. Wayne	1835–1867	Jackson
ROGER B. TANEY	1836–1864	Jackson
Philip P. Barbour	1836–1841	Jackson
John Cartron	1837–1865	Van Buren
John McKinley	1838–1852	Van Buren
Peter V. Daniel	1842–1860	Van Buren
Samuel Nelson	1845–1872	Tyler
Levi Woodbury	1845–1851	Polk
Robert C. Grier	1846–1870	Polk
Benjamin R. Curtis	1851–1857	Fillmore
John A. Campbell	1853–1861	Pierce
Nathan Clifford	1858–1881	Buchanan
Noah H. Swayne	1862–1881	Lincoln
Samuel F. Miller	1862–1890	Lincoln
David Davis	1862–1877	Lincoln

Note: The names of Chief Justices are printed in capital letters.
*Although Rutledge acted as Chief Justice, the Senate refused to confirm his appointment.

Supreme Court Justices *(continued)*

Name	Term of Service	Appointed By
Stephen J. Field	1863–1897	Lincoln
SALMON P. CHASE	1864–1873	Lincoln
William Strong	1870–1880	Grant
Joseph P. Bradley	1870–1892	Grant
Ward Hunt	1873–1882	Grant
MORRISON R. WAITE	1874–1888	Grant
John M. Harlan	1877–1911	Hayes
William B. Woods	1881–1887	Hayes
Stanley Matthews	1881–1889	Garfield
Horace Gray	1882–1902	Arthur
Samuel Blatchford	1882–1893	Arthur
Lucious Q. C. Lamar	1888–1893	Cleveland
MELVILLE W. FULLER	1888–1910	Cleveland
David J. Brewer	1890–1910	B. Harrison
Henry B. Brown	1891–1906	B. Harrison
George Shiras, Jr.	1892–1903	B. Harrison
Howell E. Jackson	1893–1895	B. Harrison
Edward D. White	1894–1910	Cleveland
Rufus W. Peckham	1896–1909	Cleveland
Joseph McKenna	1898–1925	McKinley
Oliver W. Holmes	1902–1932	T. Roosevelt
William R. Day	1903–1922	T. Roosevelt
William H. Moody	1906–1910	T. Roosevelt
Horace H. Lurton	1910–1914	Taft
Charles E. Hughes	1910–1916	Taft
EDWARD D. WHITE	1910–1921	Taft
Willis Van Devanter	1911–1937	Taft
Joseph R. Lamar	1911–1916	Taft
Mahlon Pitney	1912–1922	Taft
James C. McReynolds	1914–1941	Wilson
Louis D. Brandeis	1916–1939	Wilson
John H. Clarke	1916–1922	Wilson
WILLIAM H. TAFT	1921–1930	Harding
George Sutherland	1922–1938	Harding
Pierce Butler	1923–1939	Harding
Edward T. Sanford	1923–1930	Harding
Harlan F. Stone	1925–1941	Coolidge
CHARLES E. HUGHES	1930–1941	Hoover
Owen J. Roberts	1930–1945	Hoover
Benjamin N. Cardozo	1932–1938	Hoover

Supreme Court Justices *(continued)*

Name	Term of Service	Appointed By
Hugo L. Black	1937–1971	F. Roosevelt
Stanley F. Reed	1938–1957	F. Roosevelt
Felix Frankfurter	1939–1962	F. Roosevelt
William O. Douglas	1939–1975	F. Roosevelt
Frank Murphy	1940–1949	F. Roosevelt
HARLAN F. STONE	1941–1946	F. Roosevelt
James F. Byrnes	1941–1942	F. Roosevelt
Robert H. Jackson	1941–1954	F. Roosevelt
Wiley B. Rutledge	1943–1949	F. Roosevelt
Harold H. Burton	1945–1958	Truman
FREDERICK M. VINSON	1946–1953	Truman
Tom C. Clark	1949–1967	Truman
Sherman Minton	1949–1956	Truman
EARL WARREN	1953–1969	Eisenhower
John Marshall Harlan	1955–1971	Eisenhower
William J. Brennan, Jr.	1956–1990	Eisenhower
Charles E. Whittaker	1957–1962	Eisenhower
Potter Stewart	1958–1981	Eisenhower
Byron R. White	1962–1993	Kennedy
Arthur J. Goldberg	1962–1965	Kennedy
Abe Fortas	1965–1970	L. Johnson
Thurgood Marshall	1967–1991	L. Johnson
WARREN E. BURGER	1969–1986	Nixon
Harry A. Blackmun	1970–1994	Nixon
Lewis F. Powell, Jr.	1971–1987	Nixon
William H. Rehnquist	1971–1986	Nixon
John Paul Stevens	1975–	Ford
Sandra Day O'Connor	1981–	Reagan
WILLIAM H. REHNQUIST	1986–	Reagan
Antonin Scalia	1986–	Reagan
Anthony Kennedy	1988–	Reagan
David Souter	1990–	Bush
Clarence Thomas	1991–	Bush
Ruth Bader Ginsburg	1993–	Clinton
Stephen Breyer	1994–	Clinton

THE AMERICAN ECONOMY

Key Economic Indicators

Year	Gross National Product (GNP) and Gross Domestic Product (GDP)[a] (in $ billions)	Steel Production (in tons)	Corn Production (millions of bushels)	Automobiles Registered	New Housing Starts	Foreign Trade (in $ millions) Exports	Foreign Trade (in $ millions) Imports
1790	NA	NA	NA	NA	NA	20	23
1800	NA	NA	NA	NA	NA	71	91
1810	NA	NA	NA	NA	NA	67	85
1820	NA	NA	NA	NA	NA	70	74
1830	NA	NA	NA	NA	NA	74	71
1840	NA	NA	NA	NA	NA	132	107
1850	NA	NA	592[d]	NA	NA	152	178
1860	NA	13,000	839[e]	NA	NA	400	362
1870	7.4[b]	77,000	1,125	NA	NA	451	462
1880	11.2[c]	1,397,000	1,707	NA	NA	853	761
1890	13.1	4,779,000	1,650	NA	NA	910	823
1900	18.7	11,227,000	2,662	8,000	328,000	1,499	930
1910	35.3	28,330,000	2,853	458,300	189,000	1,919	1,646
1920	91.5	46,183,000	3,071	8,131,500	387,000 (1918 = 118,000)	8,664	5,784
1930	90.7	44,591,000	2,080	23,034,700	247,000 (1925 = 937,000)	4,013	3,500
1940	100.0	66,983,000	2,457	27,465,800	330,000 (1933 = 93,000)	4,030	7,433
1950	286.5	96,836,000	3,075	40,339,000	603,000 (1944 = 142,000)	9,997	8,954
1960	506.5	99,282,000	4,314	61,682,300	1,952,000	19,659	15,093
1970	1,016.0	131,514,000	4,200	89,279,800	1,365,000	42,681	40,356
1980	2,819.5	111,835,000	6,600	121,601,000	1,434,000	220,626	244,871
1990	5,764.9	98,906,000	7,933	133,700,000	1,292,000	394,030	485,453
2000	9,963.1	112,242,000	9,968	133,600,000[g]	1,569,000	781,918	1,218,022

[a]In December 1991 the Bureau of Economic Analysis of the U.S. government began using Gross Domestic Product rather than Gross National Product as the primary measure of U.S. production.

[b]Figure is average for 1869–1878.

[c]Figure is average for 1879–1888.

[d]Figure for 1849.

[e]Figure for 1859.

[f]Figure for 1997.

[g]Does not include sports utility vehicles (SUVs) and light trucks.

NA = Not available.

Federal Budget Outlays and Debt

Year	Defense[a]	Veterans Benefits[a]	Income Security[a]	Social Security[a]	Health and Medicare[a]	Education[a,d]	Net Interest Payments[a]	Federal Debt (dollars)
1790	14.9	4.1[b]	NA	NA	NA	NA	55.0	75,463,000[c]
1800	55.7	.6	NA	NA	NA	NA	31.3	82,976,000
1810	48.4 (1814: 79.7)	1.0	NA	NA	NA	NA	34.9	53,173,000
1820	38.4	17.6	NA	NA	NA	NA	28.1	91,016,000
1830	52.9	9.0	NA	NA	NA	NA	12.6	48,565,000
1840	54.3 (1847: 80.7)	10.7	NA	NA	NA	NA	.7	3,573,000
1850	43.8	4.7	NA	NA	NA	NA	1.0	63,453,000
1860	44.2 (1865: 88.9)	1.7	NA	NA	NA	NA	5.0	64,844,000
1870	25.7	9.2	NA	NA	NA	NA	41.7	2,436,453,000
1880	19.3	21.2	NA	NA	NA	NA	35.8	2,090,909,000
1890	20.9 (1899: 48.6)	33.6	NA	NA	NA	NA	11.4	1,222,397,000
1900	36.6	27.0	NA	NA	NA	NA	7.7	1,263,417,000
1910	45.1 (1919: 59.5)	23.2	NA	NA	NA	NA	3.1	1,146,940,000
1920	37.1	3.4	NA	NA	NA	NA	16.0	24,299,321,000
1930	25.3	6.6	NA	NA	NA	NA	19.9	16,185,310,000
1940	17.5 (1945: 89.4)	6.0	16.0	.3	.5	20.8	9.4	42,967,531,000
1950	32.2	20.3	9.6	1.8	.6	.6	11.3	256,853,000,000
1960	52.2	5.9	8.0	12.6	.9	1.0	7.5	290,525,000,000
1970	41.8	4.4	8.0	15.5	6.2	4.4	7.3	308,921,000,000
1980	22.7	3.6	14.6	20.1	9.4	5.4	8.9	909,050,000,000
1990	23.9	2.3	11.7	19.8	12.4	3.1	14.7	3,266,073,000,000
2000	16.2	2.6	14.1	22.7	19.9	3.5	12.3	5,629,000,000,000

[a]Figures represent percentage of total federal spending for each category. Not included are transportation, commerce, housing, and various other categories.

[b]1789–1791 figure.

[c]1791 figure.

[d]Includes training, employment, and social services.

NA = Not available.

Additional Bibliography

Chapter 1

History and Archaeology

Sally A. Kitt Chappell, *Cahokia: Mirror of the Cosmos* (2002); Inga Clendinnen, *Aztecs: An Interpretation* (1991); Michael Coe et al., *Atlas of Ancient America* (1986); Geoffrey W. Conrad and Arthur A. Demarest, *Religion and Empire: The Dynamics of Aztec and Inca Expansionism* (1984); Linda S. Cordell, *Prehistory of the Southwest* (1984); Philip J. Deloria and Neal Salisbury, eds., *A Companion to American Indian History* (2002); E. James Dixon, *Bones, Boats, and Bison: Archeology and the First Civilizations of Western North America* (1999); Patricia Galloway, ed., *The Southeastern Ceremonial Complex: Artifacts and Analysis* (1989); Stephen H. Lekson, *The Chaco Meridian: Centers of Political Power in the Ancient Southwest* (1999); Timothy R. Pauketat and Thomas E. Emerson, eds., *Cahokia: Domination and Ideology in the Mississippian World* (1997); Carroll L. Riley, *Rio del Norte: People of the Upper Rio Grande from Earliest Times to the Pueblo Revolt* (1995); Karl Schleiser, ed., *Plains Indians, A.D. 500–1500* (1994); Bruce D. Smith, ed., *The Mississippian Emergence* (1990) and *Rivers of Change: Essays on Early Agriculture in Eastern North America* (1992); David Hurst Thomas, *Skull Wars: Kennewick Man, Archaeology, and the Battle for Native American Identity* (2000); Russell Thornton, *American Indian Holocaust and Survival: A Population History Since 1492* (1987); Stephen E. Williams, *Towns and Temples Along the Mississippi* (1990).

Spirituality and Culture

Donald Bahr et al., *The Short, Swift Time of Gods on Earth: The Hohokam Chronicles* (1994); John Bierhorst, *The Mythology of North America* (1985); Robert L. Hall, *An Archaeology of the Soul: North American Indian Belief and Ritual* (1997); Åke Hultkrantz, *The Religions of the American Indians* (1979); Lee Irwin, *The Dream Seekers: Native American Visionary Traditions of the Great Plains* (1994); Peter Nabokov, *A Forest of Time: American Indian Ways of History* (2002); Peter Nabokov and Robert Easton, *Native American Architecture* (1989); Paul Radin, *The Trickster: A Study in American Indian Mythology* (1972); Elisabeth Tooker, ed., *Native North American Spirituality of the Eastern Woodlands* (1979); Christopher Vecsey, *Imagine Ourselves Richly: Mythic Narratives of North American Indians* (1988); Ray A. Williamson, *Living the Sky: The Cosmos of the American Indian* (1987); Paul Zolbrod, *Diné bahané: The Navajo Creation Story* (1984).

Chapter 2

Africa and Slavery

Robin Blackburn, *The Making of New World Slavery: From the Baroque to the Modern, 1492–1800* (1997); Adu Boahen, *Topics in West African History*, 2d ed. (1986); Philip D. Curtin, *Economic Change in Precolonial Africa: Senegambia in the Era of the Slave Trade* (1975) and *The Rise and Fall of the Plantation Complex: Essays in Atlantic History* (1990); David Eltis, *The Rise of African Slavery in the Americas* (2000); Robin Law, *The Slave Coast of West Africa, 1550–1750: The Impact of the Atlantic Slave Trade on an African Society* (1991); Paul E. Lovejoy, *Transformations in Slavery: A History of Slavery in Africa* (1983); Patrick Manning, *Slavery and African Life: Occidental, Oriental, and African Slave Trades* (1990); Hugh Thomas, *The Slave Trade: The Story of the Atlantic Slave Trade* (1997).

Europe

William J. Bouwsma, *The Waning of the Renaissance, 1540–1640* (2000); Robin Briggs, *Witches and Neighbours: The Social and Cultural Context of European Witchcraft* (1996); Peter Burke, *Popular Culture in Early Modern Europe* (1978); Natalie Z. Davis, *Society and Culture in Early Modern France* (1975) and *Women on the Margins: Three Seventeenth-Century Lives* (1995); Ralph Davis, *Rise of the Atlantic Economies* (1973); Christopher Dunston and Jacqueline Eales, eds., *The Culture of English Puritanism* (1996); Anthony Fletcher, *Gender, Sex, and Subordination in England, 1500–1800* (1995); J. R. Hale, *War and Society in Renaissance Europe, 1450–1620* (1985); George Huppert, *After the Black Death: A Social History of Early Modern Europe* (1986); Lisa Jardine, *Worldly Goods: A New History of the Renaissance* (1996); David I. Kertzer and Marzio Barbagli, eds., *The History of the European Family*, vol. 1: *Family Life in Early Modern Times, 1500–1789* (2001); Sherrin Marshall, ed., *Women in Reformation and Counter-Reformation Europe: Public and Private Worlds* (1989); Stephen Ozment, *The Age of Reform, 1250–1550* (1980); Simon Schama, *An Embarrassment of Riches: Dutch Culture in the Golden Age* (1987); Keith Wrightson, *English Society, 1580–1680* (1982).

European Expansion and Colonization

W. J. Eccles, *France in America*, rev. ed. (1990); J. H. Elliott, *The Old World and the New, 1492–1650* (1970); Stephen J. Greenblatt, *Marvelous Possessions: The Wonder of the New World* (1991); Karen Ordahl Kupperman, *Roanoke: The Abandoned Colony* (1984); James Lockhart and Stuart B. Schwartz, *Early Latin America: A History of Colonial Spanish America and Brazil* (1983); William Roger Louis, gen. ed., *Oxford History of the British Empire*, vol. 1: *Origins of Empire*, ed. Nicholas Canny (1998); Anthony Pagden, *European Encounters with the New World: From Renaissance to Romanticism* (1993); J. H. Parry, *The Establishment of the European Hegemony: Trade and Expansion in the Age of Renaissance* (1966); William D. Phillips, Jr., and Carla Rahn Phillips, *The Worlds of Christopher Columbus* (1992); Oliver Rink, *Holland on the Hudson: An Economic and Social History of Dutch New York* (1986); Gordon Sayre, *Les Sauvages Americains: Representations of Native Americans in French and English Colonial Literature* (1997); Patricia Seed, *Ceremonies of Possession in Europe's Conquest of the New World, 1492–1640* (1995); David J. Weber, *The Spanish Frontier in North America* (1992); Eric Wolf, *Europe and the People Without History* (1982).

Native Americans

James Axtell, *After Columbus: Essays in the Ethnohistory of Colonial North America* (1988); Noble D. Cook, *Born to Die: Disease and the New World Conquest, 1492–1650* (1998); Charles Hudson and Carmen C. Tesser, eds., *The Forgotten Centuries: Indians and Europeans in the American South, 1521–1704* (1994); Francis Jennings, *The Invasion of America: Indians, Colonialism, and the Cant of Conquest* (1975); Calvin Martin, *Keepers of the Game: Indian-Animal Relationships and the Fur Trade* (1978); Daniel K. Richter, *The Ordeal of the Longhouse: The Peoples of the Iroquois League in the Era of European Colonization* (1992); Helen C. Rountree, *Pocahontas's People: The Powhatan Indians of Virginia Through Four Centuries* (1990); Neal Salisbury, *Manitou and Providence: Indians, Europeans, and the Making of New England, 1500–1643* (1982); David Hurst Thomas, *Columbian Consequences* (3 vols., 1989–1991); Russell Thornton, *American Indian Holocaust and Survival: A Population History Since 1492* (1987); Bruce G. Trigger, *Natives and Newcomers: Canada's "Heroic Age" Reconsidered* (1985); John W. Verano and Douglas H. Ubelaker, eds., *Disease and Demography in the Americas* (1992).

Chapter 3
New England

Virginia DeJohn Anderson, *New England's Generation: The Great Migration and the Formation of Society and Culture in the Seventeenth Century* (1991); Richard Archer, *Fissures in the Rock: New England in the Seventeenth Century* (2001); Cornelia Hughes Dayton, *Women Before the Bar: Gender, Law, and Society in Connecticut, 1639–1789* (1995); John Demos, *Entertaining Satan: Witchcraft and the Culture of Early New England* (1982); Richard Godbeer, *The Devil's Dominion: Magic and Religion in Early New England* (1992); Philip F. Gura, *A Glimpse of Sion's Glory: Puritan Radicalism in New England, 1620–1660* (1984); David D. Hall, *Worlds of Wonder, Days of Judgment: Popular Religious Belief in Early New England* (1990); Carol F. Karlsen, *The Devil in the Shape of a Woman: Witchcraft in Colonial New England* (1987); David Thomas Konig, *Law and Society in Puritan Massachusetts, 1629–1692* (1979); Mary Beth Norton, *In the Devil's Snare : The Salem Witchcraft Crisis of 1692* (2002); Carla Gardina Pestana, *Quakers and Baptists in Colonial Massachusetts* (1991); Robert Blair St. George, *Conversing by Signs: Poetics of Implication in Colonial New England Culture* (1998); Laurel Thatcher Ulrich, *Good Wives: Image and Reality in the Lives of Women in Northern New England, 1650–1763* (1982) and *Age of Homespun: Objects and Stories in the Creation of an American Myth* (2001); Daniel Vickers, *Farmers and Fishermen: Two Centuries of Work in Essex County, Massachusetts, 1630–1850* (1994).

The Southern Colonies and the West Indies

Hilary M. Beckles, *White Servitude and Black Slavery in Barbados, 1627–1715* (1989); Timothy H. Breen and Stephen Innes, *"Myne Own Ground": Race and Freedom on Virginia's Eastern Shore, 1640–1676* (1980); Kathleen M. Brown, *Good Wives, Nasty Wenches, and Anxious Patriarchs: Gender, Race, and Power in Colonial Virginia* (1996); Lois Green Carr et al., *Colonial Chesapeake Society* (1988); Judith A. Carney, *Black Rice: The African Origins of Rice Cultivation in the Americas* (2001); Richard S. Dunn, *Sugar and Slaves: The Rise of the Planter Class in the English West Indies, 1624–1713* (1972); James Horn, *Adapting to a New World: English Society in the Seventeenth-Century Chesapeake* (1994); Darret B. Rutman and Anita S. Rutman, *A Place in Time: Middlesex County, Virginia, 1650–1750* (1984); Betty Wood, *The Origins of American Slavery: Freedom and Bondage in the English Colonies* (1997); Peter H. Wood, *Black Majority: Negroes in Colonial South Carolina from 1670 Through the Stono Rebellion* (1974).

The Middle Colonies

Thomas J. Archdeacon, *New York City, 1664–1710: Conquest and Change* (1976); Richard S. Dunn and Mary Maples Dunn, eds., *The World of William Penn* (1986); Joyce D. Goodfriend, *Before the Melting Pot: Society and Culture in Colonial New York City, 1664–1730* (1991); Barry Levy, *Quakers and the American Family: British Settlement in the Delaware Valley* (1988); Donna Merwick, *Possessing Albany, 1630–1710: The Dutch and English Experiences* (1990); Gary B. Nash, *Quakers and Politics: Pennsylvania, 1681–1726* (1968); Robert C. Ritchie, *The Duke's Province: A Study of New York Politics and Society, 1664–1691* (1977); Oliver A. Rink, *Holland on the Hudson: An Economic and Social History of Dutch New York* (1986).

French and Spanish Colonies

Amy Turner Bushnell, *Situado and Sabana: Spain's Support System for the Presidio and Mission Provinces of Florida* (1994); Donald E. Chipman, *Spanish Texas, 1519–1821* (1992); Leslie Choquette, *Frenchmen into Peasants: Modernity and Tradition in the Peopling of French Canada* (1997); Louise Dechêne, *Habitants and Merchants in Seventeenth-Century Montreal* (1992); W. J. Eccles, *France in America*, rev. ed. (1990); Ramón A. Gutiérrez, *When Jesus Came, the Corn Mothers Went Away: Marriage, Sexuality, and Power in New Mexico, 1500–1846* (1991); Richard Colebrook Harris, *The Seigneurial System in Early Canada* (1966); Peter N. Moogk, *La Nouvelle France: The Making of French Canada, A Cultural History* (2000); David J. Weber, *The Spanish Frontier in North America* (1992).

Indian-European Relations

James Axtell, *The Invasion Within: The Contest of Cultures in Colonial North America* (1985); Colin G. Calloway, *New Worlds for All: Indians, Europeans, and the Remaking of Early America* (1997); Alfred A. Cave, *The Pequot War* (1996); James D. Drake, *King Philip's War: Civil War in New England, 1675–1676* (1999); Robert S. Grumet, ed., *Northeastern Indian Lives, 1632–1816* (1996); Andrew L. Knaut, *The Pueblo Revolt of 1680: Conquest and Resistance in Seventeenth-Century New Mexico* (1995); Karen Ordahl Kupperman, *Indians and English: Facing Off in Early America* (2000); Jill Lepore, *The Name of War: King Philip's War and the Origins of American Identity* (1998); James H. Merrell, *The Indians' New World: Catawbas and Their Neighbors from European Contact Through the Era of Removal* (1989); Ann Marie Plane, *Colonial Intimacies: Indian Marriage in Early New England* (2000); Daniel K. Richter, *The Ordeal of the Longhouse: The Peoples of the Iroquois League in the Era of European Colonization* (1992) and *Facing East from Indian Country: A Native History of Early America* (2001); Neal Salisbury, *Manitou and Providence: Indians, Europeans, and the Making of New England, 1500–1643* (1982); Ian K. Steele, *Warpaths: Invasions*

of North America (1994); Richard White, *The Middle Ground: Indians, Empires, and Republics in the Great Lakes Region, 1650–1815* (1991).

Chapter 4

The Glorious Revolution and the British Empire

Richard R. Johnson, *Adjustment to Empire: The New England Colonies, 1675–1715* (1981); David S. Lovejoy, *The Glorious Revolution in America, 1660–1692* (1972); William Roger Louis, gen. ed., *Oxford History of the British Empire*, vol. 1: *Origins of Empire*, ed. Nicholas Canny; vol. 2: *The Eighteenth Century*, ed. P. J. Marshall (1998).

Anglo-American Society and Economy

Kathleen M. Brown, *Good Wives, Nasty Wenches, and Anxious Patriarchs: Gender, Race, and Power in Colonial Virginia* (1996); Richard L. Bushman, *The Refinement of America: People, Houses, Cities* (1992); Kirsten Fischer, *Suspect Relations: Sex, Race, and Resistance in Colonial North America* (2002); Stephen Innes, ed., *Work and Labor in Early America* (1988); Rhys Isaac, *The Transformation of Virginia, 1740–1790* (1982); Barry Levy, *Quakers and the American Family: British Settlement in the Delaware Valley* (1988); Judith A. McGaw, ed., *Early American Technology: Making and Doing Things from the Colonial Era to 1850* (1994); Donna Merwick, *Death of a Notary: Conquest and Change in Colonial New York* (1999); Gary B. Nash, *The Urban Crucible: Social Change, Political Consciousness, and the Origins of the American Revolution* (1979); A. G. Roeber, *Palatines, Liberty, and Property: German Lutherans in Colonial British America* (1993); Sharon V. Salinger, *Taverns and Drinking in Early America* (2002); Marylynn Salmon, *Women and the Law of Property in Early America* (1986); Timothy Silver, *A New Face on the Countryside: Indians, Colonists, and Slaves in South Atlantic Forests, 1500–1800* (1990); Karin Wulf, *Not All Wives: Women of Colonial Philadelphia* (2000).

Blacks and Slavery

Ira Berlin, *Many Thousands Gone: The First Two Centuries of Slavery in North America* (1998); Jeffrey Bolster, *Black Jacks: African American Seamen in the Age of Sail* (1997); Sylvia R. Frey and Betty Wood, *Come Shouting to Zion: African Protestantism in the American South and British Caribbean to 1830* (1998); Graham Russell Hodges, *Root and Branch: African Americans in New York and East New Jersey, 1613–1863* (1999); Jane Landers, *Black Society in Spanish Florida* (1999); Gwendolyn Midlo Hall, *Africans in Colonial Louisiana: The Development of Afro-Creole Culture in the Eighteenth Century* (1992); Edmund S. Morgan, *American Slavery, American Freedom: The Ordeal of Colonial Virginia* (1975); William D. Piersen, *Black Yankees: The Development of an Afro-American Subculture in Eighteenth-Century New England* (1988); Peter H. Wood, *Black Majority: Negroes in Colonial South Carolina from 1670 Through the Stono Rebellion* (1974).

Indian-European Relations

James F. Brooks, *Captives and Cousins: Slavery, Kinship, and Community in the Southwest Borderlands* (2002); Colin G. Calloway, ed., *After King Philip's War: Presence and Persistence in Indian New England* (1997) and *New Worlds for All: Indians, Europeans, and the Remaking of Early America* (1997); John Demos, *The Unredeemed Captive: A Family Story from Early America* (1994); Gregory Evans Dowd, *A Spirited Resistance: The North American Indian Struggle for Unity, 1745–1815* (1992); Elizabeth A. H. John, *Storms Brewed in Other Men's Worlds: The Confrontations of Indians, Spanish, and French in the Southwest, 1540–1795* (1975); Joel W. Martin, *Sacred Revolt: The Muskogees' Struggle for a New World* (1991); James H. Merrell, *The Indians' New World: Catawbas and Their Neighbors from European Contact Through the Era of Removal* (1989); Daniel K. Richter, *The Ordeal of the Longhouse: The Peoples of the Iroquois League in the Era of European Colonization* (1992); Ian Steele, *Warpaths: Invasions of North America* (1994); Daniel H. Usner, Jr., *Indians, Settlers, and Slaves in a Frontier Exchange Economy: The Lower Mississippi Valley Before 1783* (1992); Richard White, *The Middle Ground: Indians, Empires and Republics in the Great Lakes Region, 1650–1815* (1991).

French and Spanish Colonies

J. M. Bumsted, *The Peoples of Canada: A Pre-Confederation History* (1992); Donald E. Chipman, *Spanish Texas, 1519–1821* (1992); Leslie Choquette, *Frenchmen into Peasants: Modernity and Tradition in the Peopling of French Canada* (1997); Allan Greer, *People of New France* (1997); Naomi Griffiths, *The Contexts of Acadian History, 1686–1784* (1992); Ramón A. Gutiérrez, *When Jesus Came, the Corn Mothers Went Away: Marriage, Sexuality, and Power in New Mexico, 1500–1846* (1991); Peter N. Moogk, *La Nouvelle France: The Making of French Canada, A Cultural History* (2000); Jesús de la Teja, *San Antonio de Béxar: A Community on New Spain's Northern Frontier* (1995); David J. Weber, *The Spanish Frontier in North America* (1992).

The Enlightenment, Religion, and Politics

Bernard Bailyn, *The Origins of American Politics* (1968); Patricia Bonomi, *Under the Cope of Heaven: Religion, Society, and Politics in Colonial America* (1986); Richard D. Brown, *Knowledge Is Power: The Diffusion of Information in Early America, 1700–1865* (1991); Jon Butler, *Awash in a Sea of Faith: Christianizing the American People* (1990); Christopher Grasso, *A Speaking Aristocracy: Transforming Public Discourse in Eighteenth-Century Connecticut* (1999); Susan Juster, *Disorderly Women: Sexual Politics and Evangelicalism in Revolutionary New England* (1994); Frank Lambert, *"Pedlar in Divinity": George Whitefield and the Transatlantic Revivals* (1994) and *Inventing the "Great Awakening"* (1999); Harry S. Stout, *The New England Soul: Preaching and Religious Culture in Colonial New England* (1988); Michael Warner, *The Letters of the Republic: Publication and the Public Sphere in Eighteenth-Century America* (1990).

Chapter 5

The Military Background

Fred Anderson, *A People's Army: Massachusetts Soldiers and Society in the Seven Years' War* (1984); Sylvia R. Frey, *The British Soldier in America: A Social History of Military Life in the Colonial Period* (1981); John Shy, *Toward Lexington: The Role of the British Army in the Coming of the American Revolution* (1965); Ian K. Steele, *Betrayals: Fort William Henry and the "Massacre"* (1990).

Native Americans and the Backcountry

Gregory Evans Dowd, *A Spirited Resistance: The North American Indian Struggle for Unity, 1745–1815* (1992); Tom Hatley, *The Dividing Paths: Cherokees and South Carolinians Through the Era of Revolution* (1993); Francis Jennings, *Empire of Fortune: Crowns, Colonies and Tribes in the Seven Years' War in America* (1988); Marjoleine Kars, *Breaking Loose Together: The Regulator Rebellion in Pre-Revolutionary North Carolina* (2002); Michael N. McConnell, *A Country Between: The Upper Ohio Valley and Its Peoples, 1724–1774* (1992); Geoffrey Plank, *An Unsettled Conquest: The British Campaign Against the Peoples of Acadia* (2001); Timothy J. Shannon, *Indians and Colonists at the Crossroads of Empire: The Albany Congress of 1754* (2000); Richard White, *The Middle Ground: Indians, Empires, and Republics in the Great Lakes Region, 1650–1815* (1991).

Constitutional Issues

Richard L. Bushman, *King and People in Provincial Massachusetts* (1985); Jack P. Greene, *Peripheries and Center: Constitutional Development in the Extended Politics of the British Empire and the United States, 1607–1788* (1987); Jerrilyn G. Marston, *King and Congress: The Transfer of Political Legitimacy, 1774–1776* (1987); Edmund S. Morgan, *Inventing the People: The Rise of Popular Sovereignty in England and America* (1988); J. G. A. Pocock, ed., *Three British Revolutions: 1641, 1688, 1776* (1980); J. R. Pole, *Political Representation in England and the Origins of the American Republic* (1966); John Philip Reid, *Constitutional History of the American Revolution* (4 vols., 1986–1993).

Religious and Intellectual Dimensions

Ruth H. Bloch, *Visionary Republic: Millennial Themes in American Thought, 1756–1800* (1985); Jay Fleigelman, *Prodigals and Pilgrims: The American Revolution Against Patriarchal Authority, 1750–1800* (1982) and *Declaring Independence: Jefferson, Natural Language, and the Culture of Performance* (1993); Jack P. Greene and William G. McLoughlin, *Preachers and Politicians: Two Essays on the Origin of the American Revolution* (1977); Nathan O. Hatch, *The Sacred Cause of Liberty: Republican Thought and the Millennium in Revolutionary New England* (1977); Rhys Isaac, *The Transformation of Virginia, 1740–1790* (1982); Susan Juster, *Disorderly Women: Sexual Politics and Evangelicalism in Revolutionary New England* (1994); Linda K. Kerber, *Women of the Republic: Intellect and Ideology in Revolutionary America* (1980); Garry Wills, *Inventing America: Jefferson's Declaration of Independence* (1978).

Politics and Resistance

John L. Brooke, *The Heart of the Commonwealth: Society and Political Culture in Worcester County, Massachusetts, 1713–1861* (1989); David W. Conroy, *In Public Houses: Drink and the Revolution of Authority in Colonial Massachusetts* (1995); Marc Egnal, *A Mighty Empire: The Origins of the American Revolution* (1988); David Hackett Fischer, *Paul Revere's Ride* (1994); Eric Foner, *Tom Paine and Revolutionary America* (1976); Sylvia R. Frey, *Water from the Rock: Black Resistance in a Revolutionary Age* (1991); Eliga H. Gould, *The Persistence of Empire: British Political Culture in the Age of the American Revolution* (2000); Robert A. Gross, *The Minutemen and Their World* (1976); Jesse

Lemisch, *Jack Tar vs. John Bull: The Role of New York's Seamen in Precipitating the Revolution* (1997); Pauline Maier, *From Resistance to Revolution: Colonial Radicals and the Development of American Opposition to Britain, 1765–1776* (1972); Robert Middlekauff, *The Glorious Cause: The American Revolution, 1763–1789* (1982); Gary B. Nash, *The Urban Crucible: Social Change, Political Consciousness, and the Origins of The American Revolution,* (1979); John Sainsbury, *Disaffected Patriots: London Supporters of Revolutionary America, 1769–1782* (1987); Ann Fairfax Withington, *Toward a More Perfect Union: Virtue and the Formation of American Republics* (1991); Gordon S. Wood, *The Radicalism of the American Revolution* (1991); Rosemarie Zagarri, *A Woman's Dilemma: Mercy Otis Warren and the American Revolution* (1995).

Chapter 6
The Military Struggle

Robert M. Calhoon, *The Loyalists in Revolutionary America, 1760–1781* (1973); E. Wayne Carp, *To Starve the Army at Pleasure: Continental Army Administration and American Political Culture, 1775–1783* (1984); Thomas E. Chavez, *Spain and the Independence of the United States: An Intrinsic Gift* (2002); John Mack Faragher, *Daniel Boone: The Life and Legend of an American Pioneer* (1992); Barbara Graymont, *The Iroquois in the American Revolution* (1972); Christopher Hibbert, *Redcoats and Rebels: The American Revolution Through British Eyes* (1990); Don Higginbotham, *The War of American Independence: Military Attitudes, Policies, and Practice, 1763–1789* (1983); Isabel Thompson Kelsay, *Joseph Brant, 1743–1807: Man of Two Worlds* (1984); Mark V. Kwansey, *Washington's Partisan War, 1775–1783* (1997); William Roger Louis, gen. ed., *Oxford History of the British Empire,* vol. 2: *The Eighteenth Century,* ed. P. J. Marshall (1998); Holly A. Mayer, *Belonging to the Army: Camp Followers and Community During the American Revolution* (1996); Andrew Jackson O'Shaughnessy, *An Empire Divided: The American Revolution and the British Caribbean* (2000); Elizabeth A. Perkins, *Border Life: Experience and Memory in the Revolutionary Ohio Valley* (1998); Ray Raphael, *A People's History of the American Revolution: How Common People Shaped the Fight for Independence* (2001); Charles Royster, *A Revolutionary People at War: The Continental Army and American Character* (1980).

Society and Economy

Dee Andrews, *The Methodists and Revolutionary America, 1760–1800* (2000); Ira Berlin and Ronald Hoffman, eds., *Slavery and Freedom in the Age of the American Revolution* (1983); Joy Day Buel and Richard Buel, Jr., *The Way of Duty: A Woman and Her Family in Revolutionary America* (1984); Sylvia R. Frey, *Water from the Rock: Black Resistance in a Revolutionary Age* (1991); Ronald Hoffman et al., eds., *The Economy of Early America: The Revolutionary Period, 1763–1790* (1988); Rhys Isaac, *The Transformation of Virginia, 1740–1790* (1982); Michael Kammen, *A Season of Youth: The American Revolution and the Historical Imagination* (1978); Susan Juster, *Disorderly Women: Sexual Politics and Evangelicalism in Revolutionary New England* (1994); Duncan J. MacLeod, *Slavery, Race, and the American Revolution* (1974); Gary B. Nash, *Race and Revolution* (1990); Gary B. Nash and Jean R. Soderlund, *Freedom by*

Degrees: Emancipation in Pennsylvania and Its Aftermath (1991); Mary Beth Norton, *Liberty's Daughters: The Revolutionary Experience of American Women, 1750–1800* (1980); Anthony F. C. Wallace, *The Death and Rebirth of the Seneca* (1969).

Politics and Constitutionalism

Lance Banning, *The Sacred Fire of Liberty: James Madison and the Founding of the Federal Republic* (1995); Richard Beeman et al., eds., *Beyond Confederation: Origins of the Constitution and American National Identity* (1987); Michael A. Bellesiles, *Revolutionary Outlaws: Ethan Allen and the Struggle for Independence* (1993); Herman Belz et al., eds., *To Form a More Perfect Union: The Critical Ideas of the Constitution* (1992); John L. Brooke, *The Heart of the Commonwealth: Society and Political Culture in Worcester County, Massachusetts, 1713–1861* (1989); Francis D. Cogliano, *Revolutionary America, 1763–1815* (2000); Robert A. Gross, ed., *In Debt to Shays: The Bicentennial of an Agrarian Rebellion* (1993); Owen S. Ireland, *Religion, Ethnicity, and Politics: Ratifying the Constitution in Pennsylvania* (1995); Marc W. Kruman, *State Constitution Making in Revolutionary America* (1997); Donald S. Lutz, *Origins of American Constitutionalism* (1988); Cathy D. Matson and Peter S. Onuf, *Union of Interests: Political and Economic Thought in Revolutionary America* (1990); William Pencak, *War, Politics, and Revolution in Provincial Massachusetts* (1981); Jack N. Rakove, *The Beginnings of National Politics: An Interpretive History of the Continental Congress* (1979); Leonard L. Richards, *Shays's Rebellion: The American Revolution's Final Battle* (2002); Gordon S. Wood, *The Creation of the American Republic, 1776–1787* (1969); Rosemarie Zagarri, *A Woman's Dilemma: Mercy Otis Warren and the American Revolution* (1995).

Chapter 7
Early National Society

Ira Berlin, *Slaves Without Masters: The Free Negro in the Antebellum South* (1974); Jeanne Boydston, *Home and Work: Housework, Wages, and the Ideology of Labor in the Early Republic* (1990); James Essig, *Bonds of Wickedness: American Evangelicals Against Slavery, 1770–1808* (1982); Sylvia R. Frey, *Water from the Rock: Black Resistance in a Revolutionary Age* (1991); Paul A. Gilje, ed., *Wages of Independence: Capitalism in the Early American Republic* (1997); Ruth Wallis Herndon, *Unwelcome Americans: Living on the Margins in Early New England* (2001); Alfred N. Hunt, *Haiti's Influence on Antebellum America* (1989); Jan Lewis, *The Pursuit of Happiness: Family and Values in Jefferson's Virginia* (1983); Billy G. Smith, *The "Lower Sort": Philadelphia's Laboring People, 1750–1800* (1990); Merril D. Smith, *Breaking the Bonds: Marital Discord in Pennsylvania, 1730–1830* (1991); Charles G. Steffen, *The Mechanics of Baltimore: Workers and Politics in the Age of Revolution, 1763–1812* (1984); Alan Taylor, *Liberty Men and Great Proprietors: The Revolutionary Settlement on the Maine Frontier, 1760–1820* (1990); Anthony F. C. Wallace, *The Death and Rebirth of the Seneca* (1969); Shane White, *Somewhat More Independent: The End of Slavery in New York City, 1770–1810* (1991); T. Stephen Whitman, *The Price of Freedom: Slavery and Manumission in Baltimore and Early National Maryland* (1997); Betty Wood, *Women's Work, Men's Work: The Informal Slave Economies of Lowcountry Georgia* (1995).

Diplomatic, Military, and Western Affairs

Stephen Aron, *How the West Was Lost: Kentucky from Daniel Boone to Henry Clay* (1996); Colin G. Calloway, *Crown and Calumet: British-Indian Relations, 1783–1815* (1987); Andrew R. L. Cayton and Frederika J. Teute, eds., *Contact Points: American Frontiers from the Mohawk Valley to the Mississippi, 1750–1830* (1998); Gregory Evans Dowd, *A Spirited Resistance: The North American Indian Struggle for Unity, 1745–1815* (1992); John Mack Faragher, *Daniel Boone: The Life and Legend of an American Pioneer* (1992); Reginald Horsman, *The Frontier in the Formative Years, 1783–1815* (1970); Richard H. Kohn, *Eagle and Sword: The Federalists and the Creation of the Military Establishment in America, 1783–1802* (1975); Daniel G. Lang, *Foreign Policy in the Early Republic: The Law of Nations and the Balance of Power* (1985); Peter Onuf and Nicholas Onuf, *Federal Union, Modern World: The Law of Nations in an Age of Revolutions, 1776–1814* (1993); Thomas P. Slaughter, *The Whiskey Rebellion: Frontier Epilogue to the American Revolution* (1986); John Sugden, *Blue Jacket: Warrior of the Shawnees* (2000); Richard White, *The Middle Ground: Indians, Empires, and Republics in the Great Lakes Region, 1650–1815* (1991); J. Leitch Wright, *Britain and the American Frontier, 1783–1815* (1975).

Political and Economic Affairs

Joyce Appleby, *Capitalism and a New Social Order: The Republican Vision of the 1790s* (1984); Lance Banning, *The Jeffersonian Persuasion: Evolution of a Party Ideology* (1978); John E. Crowley, *The Privileges of Independence: Neomercantilism and the American Revolution* (1993); Jacob E. Cooke, *Alexander Hamilton* (1982); Michael Durey, *Transatlantic Radicals and the Early American Republic* (1997); Joseph J. Ellis, *American Sphinx: The Character of Thomas Jefferson* (1996) and *Passionate Sage: The Character and Legacy of John Adams* (1993); Paul Finkleman, *Slavery and the Founders: Race and Liberty in the Age of Jefferson* (1996); Joyce Lee Malcolm, *To Keep and Bear Arms: The Origins of an Anglo-American Right* (1994); Drew R. McCoy, *The Elusive Republic: Political Economy in Jeffersonian America* (1980); Conor Cruise O'Brien, *The Long Affair: Thomas Jefferson and the French Revolution, 1785–1800* (1996); Peter S. Onuf, ed., *Jeffersonian Legacies* (1993); Thomas L. Pangle, *The Spirit of Modern Republicanism: The Moral Vision of the American Founders and the Followers of Locke* (1988); James Roger Sharp, *American Politics in the Early Republic: The New Nation in Crisis* (1993); Herbert E. Sloan, *Thomas Jefferson and the Problem of Debt* (1995); David Waldstreicher, *In the Midst of Perpetual Fetes: The Making of American Nationalism, 1776–1820* (1997); Alfred F. Young, *The Democratic Republicans of New York: The Origins, 1763–1797* (1967).

Chapter 8
The Age of Jefferson

Joyce Appleby, *Capitalism and a New Social Order: The Republican Vision of the 1790s* (1984); Leonard Baker, *John Marshall* (1974); Lance Banning, *The Jeffersonian Persuasion: Evolution of a Party Ideology* (1978); Andrew Burstein, *The Inner Jefferson* (1995); Noble Cunningham, *The Jeffersonian Republicans and Power: Party Operations, 1801–1809* (1963); Richard E. Ellis, *The Jeffersonian Crisis: Courts and Politics in the Young Republic* (1971); Ronald P. Formisano, *The*

Transformation of Political Culture: Massachusetts Parties, 1790s–1840s (1983); Annette Gordon-Reed, Thomas Jefferson and Sally Hemings (1997); Peter C. Hofer and N. E. H. Hull, Impeachment in America, 1635–1805 (1984); Morton Horwitz, The Transformation of American Law, 1780–1860 (1977); Linda K. Kerber, Federalists in Dissent: Image and Ideology in Jeffersonian America (1970); Drew McCoy, The Elusive Republic: Political Economy in Jeffersonian America (1980); Herbert Sloan, Principle and Interest: Thomas Jefferson and the Problem of Debt (1995); Alan Taylor, Liberty Men and Great Proprietors: The Revolutionary Settlement on the Maine Frontier (1990); Steven Watts, The Republic Reborn (1987); James S. Young, The Washington Community: 1800–1828 (1966).

The Gathering Storm

Thomas P. Abernethy, The Burr Conspiracy (1954); Maurice G. Baxter, Henry Clay and the American System (1995); Robert Dawidoff, The Education of John Randolph (1979); David Hackett Fisher, The Revolution of American Conservatism: The Federalist Party in the Era of Jeffersonian Democracy (1965); Milton Lomask, Aaron Burr (2 vols.,1979, 1982); Samuel Eliot Morison, Harrison Gray Otis, 1765–1848: The Urbane Federalist (1962); Robert Shalhope, John Taylor of Caroline: Pastoral Republican (1978).

The War of 1812

Lance Banning, To the Hartford Convention: The Federalists and the Origins of Party Politics in the Early Republic, 1789–1815 (1967); Pierre Berton, The Invasion of Canada (1980); Roger H. Brown, The Republic in Peril (1964); A. L. Burtt, The United States, Great Britain, and British North America (1940); Harry L. Coles, The War of 1812 (1965); Donald R. Hickey, The War of 1812: A Forgotten Conflict (1989); Reginald Horsman, The Causes of the War of 1812 (1962); Shaw Livermore, The Twilight of Federalism (1962); Bradford Perkins, Prologue to War: England and the United States, 1805–1812 (1961); Julius W. Pratt, Expansionists of 1812 (1925); John Sugden, Tecumseh: A Life (1997).

The Awakening of American Nationalism

Harry Ammon, Jr., James Monroe: The Quest for National Identity (1971); George Dangerfield, The Awakening of American Nationalism, 1815–1828 (1965) and The Era of Good Feelings (1952); Don E. Fehrenbacher, The South and Three Sectional Crises (1980); James E. Lewis, Jr., The American Union and the Problem of Neighborhood (1998); Ernest May, The Making of the Monroe Doctrine (1975); Glover Moore, The Missouri Compromise, 1819–1821 (1953); Frank Owsley, Jr., and Gene Smith, Filibusters and Expansionists (1997); Donald L. Robinson, Slavery in the Structure of American Politics, 1765–1820 (1971); Fred Russell, John Quincy Adams and the Public Virtues of Diplomacy (1995).

Chapter 9

Westward Expansion and the Growth of the Market Economy

Jeffrey S. Adler, Merchants and the Making of the Urban West (1991); Stephen Aron, How the West Was Lost: The Transformation of Kentucky from Daniel Boone to Henry Clay

(1996); Robert F. Berkhofer, Jr., The White Man's Indian: Images of the American Indian from Columbus to the Present (1979); Stuart Blumin, The Urban Threshold: Growth and Change in a Nineteenth-Century American Community (1976); Charles Danhof, Change in Agriculture: The Northern United States, 1820–1870 (1969); Don H. Doyle, The Social Order of a Frontier Community: Jacksonville, Illinois, 1825–1870 (1978); Robert Feller, The Public Lands in Jacksonian Politics (1984); John R. Finger, The Eastern Band of Cherokees, 1819–1900 (1984); Albert Fishlow, American Railroads and the Transformation of the Ante-Bellum Economy (1965); Robert W. Fogel, Railroads and Economic Growth (1964); Paul W. Gates, The Farmer's Age: Agriculture, 1815–1860 (1960); William H. Goetzmann, Explorations and Empire: The Explorer and the Scientist in the Winning of the American West (1966); Michael D. Green, The Politics of Indian Removal (1982); Eric F. Haites, James Mak, and Gary M. Walton, Western River Transportation: The Era of Early Internal Development, 1800–1860 (1975); Hildegard B. Johnson, Order Upon the Land (1976); Paul Johnson, A Shopkeeper's Millennium: Society and Revivals in Rochester, New York, 1815–1837 (1978); William G. McLoughlin, Cherokee Renascence in the New Republic (1978); Malcolm J. Rohrbough, The Land Office Business: The Settlement and Administration of American Public Lands, 1789–1837 (1968); Steven J. Ross, Workers on the Edge: Work, Leisure, and Politics in Industrializing Cincinnati, 1788–1890 (1985); R.E. Shaw, Erie Water West (1966); Carol Sheriff, The Artificial River (1996); Richard Slotkin, Regeneration Through Violence: The Mythology of the American Frontier, 1600–1860 (1973); George R. Taylor, The Transportation Revolution, 1815–1860 (1951); Anthony Wallace, Rockdale: The Growth of an American Village in the Early Industrial Revolution (1977); Michael Williams, Americans and Their Forests (1989); J. Leitch Wright, Jr., Creeks and Seminoles (1986).

Industrial Beginnings

W. Elliot Brownlee, Dynamics of Ascent (1974); Stuart Bruchey, The Roots of American Economic Growth, 1607–1861 (1965); Christopher Clark, The Roots of Rural Capitalism: Western Massachusetts, 1780–1860 (1990); Thomas C. Cochran, Frontiers of Change: Early Industrialism in America (1981); Alan Dawley, Class and Community: The Industrial Revolution in Lynn (1976); Thomas Dublin, Women at Work: The Transformation of Work and Community in Lowell, Massachusetts, 1826–1860 (1979) and Transforming Women's Work (1994); Siegfried Giedion, Mechanization Takes Command (1948); H. J. Habakkuk, American and British Technology in the Nineteenth Century (1962); Bruce Laurie, Working People of Philadelphia, 1800–1850 (1980); Otto Mayr and Robert C. Post, eds., Yankee Enterprise: The Rise of the American System of Manufactures (1981); Judith A. McGaw, ed., Early American Technology (1999) and Most Wonderful Machine: Mechanization and Social Change in Berkshire Paper Making, 1815–1885 (1987); Douglass North, The Economic Growth of the United States, 1790–1860 (1961); Ronald Schultz, The Republic of Labor: Philadelphia Artisans and the Politics of Class, 1720–1830 (1993); Philip Scranton, Proprietary Capitalism (1983); Merritt R. Smith, Harpers Ferry Armory and the New Technology (1977); Theodore Steinberg, Nature Incorporated: Industrialization and the Waters of New England (1991); Peter Temin, The Jacksonian Economy (1969); Barbara

Tucker, *Samuel Slater and the Origins of the American Textile Industry, 1790–1860* (1984).

Equality and Inequality

Elizabeth Blackmar, *Manhattan for Rent, 1785–1850* (1989); Martin Burke, *The Conundrum of Class* (1995); Leonard P. Curry, *The Free Black in Urban America, 1800–1850* (1981); Jay P. Dolan, *The Immigrant Church: New York's Irish and German Catholics, 1815–1860* (1975); Paul A. Gilje, *The Road to Mobocracy: Popular Disorder in New York City, 1763–1834* (1987); James Oliver Horton and Lois E. Horton, *In Hope of Liberty: Culture, Community and, and Protest Among Northern Blacks, 1700–1860* (1997); Peter Knights, *The Plain People of Boston, 1830–1860* (1971); Edward Pessen, *Riches, Class, and Power Before the Civil War* (1973); Harry Reed, *Platform for Change: The Foundations of Freedom in the Northern Free Black Community, 1775–1865* (1994); Stephan Thernstrom, *Poverty and Progress* (1964); Peter Way, *Common Labour: Workers and the Digging of the North American Canals, 1780–1860* (1994).

The Revolution in Social Relationships

Jeanne Boydston, *Home and Work* (1990); Daniel H. Calhoun, *Professional Lives in America: Structure and Aspiration, 1750–1850* (1965); Nancy Cott, *The Bonds of Womanhood: "Woman's Sphere" in New England, 1780–1835* (1977); Suzanne Lebsock, *The Free Women of Petersburg,: Status and Culture in a Southern Town, 1784–1860* (1984); James C. Mohr, *Abortion in America* (1978); Mary Ryan, *Cradle of the Middle Class: The Family in Oneida County, New York, 1790–1865* (1981); Donald M. Scott, *From Office to Profession: The New England Ministry, 1750–1850* (1978); Richard Shryock, *Medical Licensing in America, 1650–1965* (1967); William B. Skelton, *An American Profession of Arms: The Army Officer Corps, 1784–1861* (1993); Kathryn Sklar, *Catharine Beecher* (1973); Christine Stansell, *City of Women: Sex and Class in New York, 1789–1860* (1986).

Chapter 10
The Rise of Democratic Politics, 1824–1832

Jean H. Baker, *Affairs of Party: The Political Culture of Northern Democrats in the Mid-Nineteenth Century* (1983); Steven C. Bullock, *Revolutionary Brotherhood: Freemasonry and the Transformation of the American Social Order, 1730–1840* (1996); Donald B. Cole, *Martin Van Buren and the American Political System* (1984); Ronald P. Formisano, *The Birth of Mass Political Parties, 1827–1861* (1971) and *The Transformation of American Political Culture: Massachusetts Parties, 1790s–1840s* (1983); Paul Goodman, *Towards a Christian Republic: Antimasonry and the Great Tradition in New England, 1826–1836* (1988); Daniel W. Howe, *The Political Culture of the American Whigs* (1980); Richard Latner, *The Presidency of Andrew Jackson* (1979); Merrill D. Peterson, *The Great Triumvirate: Webster, Clay, and Calhoun* (1987); Robert V. Remini, *The Election of Andrew Jackson* (1963) and *Andrew Jackson and the Course of American Empire* (1977); Leonard L. Richards, *The Life and Times of Congressman John Quincy Adams* (1986); Harry L. Watson, *Jacksonian Politics and Community Conflict: The Emergence of the Second American Party System in Cumberland County, North Carolina* (1981); Sean Wilentz, *Chants Democratic: New York City and the Rise of the American Working Class, 1788–1850* (1983); Major Wilson, *The Presidency of Martin Van Buren* (1984).

The Bank Controversy and the Second Party System

Bray Hammond, *Banks and Politics in America from the Revolution to the Civil War* (1957); John M. McFaul, *The Politics of Jacksonian Finance* (1972); William G. Shade, *Banks or No Banks: The Money Question in Western Politics* (1972); James Roger Sharp, *The Jacksonians Versus the Banks: Politics in the United States After the Panic of 1837* (1970); Peter Temin, *The Jacksonian Economy* (1965).

The Rise of Popular Religion

Sydney E. Ahlstrom, *A Religious History of the American People* (2 vols., 1975); Leonard J. Arrington, *The Mormon Experience* (1979) and *Brigham Young: American Moses* (1985); John Boles, *The Great Revival, 1787–1805* (1972); Richard Cawardine, *Evangelicals and Politics in Antebellum America* (1993); Paul Conkin, *The Uneasy Center* (1995); Whitney Cross, *The Burned-Over District* (1950); Nathan O. Hatch, *The Democratization of American Christianity* (1989); Donald G. Mathews, *Religion in the Old South* (1977); Stephen J. Stein, *The Shaker Experience in America* (1992).

The Age of Reform

Robert Abzug, *Passionate Liberator: Theodore Dwight Weld and the Dilemma of Reform* (1980); Gilbert Barnes, *The Anti-Slavery Impulse* (1933); Thomas J. Brown, *Dorothea Dix* (1998); Jed Dannenbaum, *Drink and Disorder* (1984); Michael Barkun, *Crucible of the Millennium* (1986); William Cheek and Aimee Lee Cheek, *John Mercer Langston and the Fight for Black Freedom, 1829–1865* (1989); Louis Gerteis, *Morality and Utility in American Antislavery Reform* (1987); Lori D. Ginzberg, *Women and the Work of Benevolence* (1990); Paul Goodman, *Of One Blood: Abolitionism and the Origins of Racial Equality* (1998); Clifford S. Griffin, *Their Brothers' Keepers: Moral Stewardship in the United States* (1960); Elisabeth Griffith, *In Her Own Right: The Life of Elizabeth Cady Stanton* (1984); Carl Guarneri, *Utopian Alternative: Fourierism in Nineteenth-Century America* (1991); Carl F. Kaestle, *Pillars of the Republic: Common Schools and American Society, 1780–1860* (1983); Carl F. Kaestle and Maris Vinovskis, *Education and Social Change in Nineteenth-Century Massachusetts* (1980); Carol Kolmerten, *Women in Utopia* (1990); Gerda Lerner, *The Grimké Sisters from South Carolina* (1967); W. David Lewis, *From Newgate to Dannemora: The Rise of the Penetentiary* (1965); William McFeely, *Frederick Douglass* (1991); William Lee Miller, *Arguing Against Slavery* (1996); Mary Ryan, *Cradle of the Middle Class: The Family in Oneida County, New York, 1790–1865* (1981); Stanley K. Schultz, *The Culture Factory: Boston Public Schools, 1789–1860* (1973); Timothy L. Smith, *Revivalism and Social Reform* (1957); Anna Speicher, *The Religius Ideals of Antislavery Women* (2000); Ian Tyrrell, *Sobering Up: From Temperance to Prohibition in Antebellum America* (1979).

Chapter 11
Technology and Economic Growth

Eugene Alvarez, *Travel on Southern Antebellum Railroads, 1818–1860* (1974); Alfred D. Chandler, *The Visible Hand: The Managerial Revolution in American Business* (1977); Ruth S.

Cowan, *A Social History of American Technology* (1997); H. J. Habakkuk, *American and British Technology in the Nineteenth Century* (1962); William Hosley, *Colt: The Making of an American Legend* (1996); David A. Hounshell, *From the American System to Mass Production, 1800–1932* (1984); John F. Kasson, *Civilizing the Machine: Technology and Republican Values in America, 1776–1900* (1976); Edward C. Kirkland, *Men, Cities, and Transportation* (1948); Robert J. Parks, *Democracy's Railroads: Public Enterprise in Michigan* (1972); Wolfgang Schivelbusch, *The Railway Journey* (1986); David W. Shaw, *Flying Cloud* (2000).

The Quality of Life

Ruth Schwartz Cowan, *More Work for Mother: The Ironies of Household Technology from the Open Hearth to the Microwave* (1983); John D. Davies, *Phrenology: Fad and Science* (1955); John S. Haller, Jr., *American Medicine in Transition, 1840–1910* (1981); Dolores Hayden, *The Grand Domestic Revolution: A History of Feminist Designs for American Homes, Neighborhoods, and Cities* (1981); Jack Larkin, *Reshaping Everyday Life, 1790–1849* (1988); Stephen Nissenbaum, *Sex, Diet, and Debility in Jacksonian America: Sylvester Graham and Health Reform* (1980); Martin S. Pernick, *A Calculus of Suffering: Pain, Professionalism, and Anesthesia in Nineteenth-Century America* (1985); Charles Rosenberg, *The Cholera Years: The United States in 1832, 1849, and 1866* (1962); Paul Starr, *The Social Transformation of American Medicine* (1982); Susan Strasser, *Never Done: A History of American Housework* (1983).

Democratic Pastimes

Richard D. Brown, *Knowledge Is Power: The Diffusion of Information in Early America, 1700–1865* (1989); Daniel A. Cohen, *Pillars of Salt, Monuments of Grace: New England Crime Literature and the Origins of American Popular Culture, 1674–1860* (1993); Ann Fabian, *Card Sharps, Dream Books, and Bucket Shops: Gambling in 19th-Century America* (1990); David Grimsted, *Melodrama Unveiled: American Theater and Culture, 1800–1850* (1968); Karen Halttunen, *Confidence Men and Painted Women: A Study in Middle-Class Culture in America, 1830–1870* (1982); Neil Harris, *Humbug: The Art of P. T. Barnum* (1973); Dan Schiller, *Objectivity and the News: The Public and the Rise of Commercial Journalism* (1981); Michael Schudson, *Discovering the News: A Social History of American Newspapers* (1978); Robert C. Toll, *Blacking Up: The Minstrel Show in Nineteenth-Century America* (1974); Ronald J. Zboray, *A Fictive People: Antebellum Economic Development and the American Reading Public* (1993).

The Quest for Nationality in Literature and Art

Elizabeth Barlow, *Frederick Law Olmsted's New York* (1972); Nina Baym, *Woman's Fiction: A Guide to Novels by and About Women in America, 1820–1870* (1978); Thomas Bender, *Towards an Urban Vision* (1975); Vincent Buranelli, *Edgar Allan Poe* (1977); Charles Capper, *Margaret Fuller* (1992); William Charvat, *The Profession of Authorship in America, 1800–1870* (ed. Matthew J. Bruccoli, 1968); Cathy Davidson, *Revolution and the Word* (1986); Steven Fink, *Prophet in the Marketplace: Thoreau's Development as a Professional Writer* (1992); Francis R. Kowsky, *Country, Park and City: The Architecture and Life of Calvert Vaux* (1998); David Levin, *History as Romantic Art:*

Bancroft, Prescott, Motley, and Parkman (1963); Lucy Maddox, *Removals: Nineteenth-Century American Literature and the Politics of Indian Affairs* (1991); James Mellow, *Nathaniel Hawthorne in His Time* (1980); Nancy Rash, *The Painting and Politics of George Caleb Bingham* (1991); David S. Reynolds, *Walt Whitman's America* (1995); David Schuyler, *Apostle of Taste: Andrew Jackson Downing, 1815–1852* (1996); Benjamin T. Spencer, *The Quest for Nationality: An American Literary Campaign* (1957); Tony Tanner, *The Reign of Wonder: Naiveté and Reality in American Literature* (1965); Bryan J. Wolf, *Romantic Re-Vision: Culture and Consciousness in Nineteenth-Century American Painting and Literature* (1982); Larzer Ziff, *Literary Democracy: The Declaration of Cultural Independence in America* (1981).

Chapter 12
King Cotton

Fred Bateman and Thomas Weiss, *A Deplorable Scarcity: The Failure of Industrialism in the Slave Economy* (1972); Charles B. Dew, *Ironmaker to the Confederacy* (1966); Eugene D. Genovese, *The Political Economy of Slavery* (1965); Gavin Wright, *The Political Economy of the Cotton South* (1978).

The Social Groups of the White South

Orville V. Burton, *In My Father's House Are Many Mansions: Family and Community in Edgefield, South Carolina* (1985); Mary B. Chesnut, *A Diary from Dixie* (ed. Ben Ames Williams, 1949); Blanche Henry Clark, *The Tennessee Yeoman, 1840–1860* (1942); Catherine G. Clinton, *The Plantation Mistress: Women's World in the Old South* (1982); Barbara J. Fields, *Slavery and Freedom on the Middle Ground: Maryland During the Nineteenth Century* (1985); Elizabeth Fox-Genovese, *Within the Plantation Household: Black and White Women of the Old South* (1988); Steven Hahn, *The Roots of Southern Populism: Yeomen Farmers and the Transformation of the Georgia Upcountry, 1850–1890* (1983); Suzanne Lebsock, *The Free Women of Petersburg: Status Culture in a Southern Town, 1784–1860* (1984); Stephanie McCurry, *Masters of Small Worlds* (1995); Frank L. Owsley, *Plain Folk of the Old South* (1949); Anne F. Scott, *The Southern Lady: From Pedestal to Politics, 1830–1930* (1970); Herbert Weaver, *Mississippi Farmers, 1850–1860* (1945); Ralph A. Wooster, *Politicians, Planters, and Plain Folk* (1975).

Social Relations in the White South

David F. Allmendinger, Jr., *Ruffin: Family and Reform in the Old South* (1990); Edward L. Ayers, *Vengeance and Justice: Crime and Punishment in the Nineteenth-Century American South* (1984); David T. Bailey, *Shadow on the Church: Southwestern Evangelical Religion and the Issue of Slavery, 1783–1860* (1985); Dickson D. Bruce, *Violence and Culture in the Antebellum South* (1979); William J. Cooper, *The South and the Politics of Slavery, 1829–1856* (1978); Daniel W. Crofts, *Old Southampton: Politics and Society in a Virginia County, 1834–1869* (1992); James D. Essig, *The Bonds of Wickedness: American Evangelicals Against Slavery, 1770–1808* (1982); Drew G. Faust, *A Sacred Circle: The Dilemma of the Intellectual in the Old South, 1840–1860* (1977) and *James Henry Hammond and the Old South: A Design for Mastery* (1982); John Hope Franklin, *The Militant South* (1966); George M. Fredrickson, *The Black Image in the White Mind: The Debate on Afro-American Character and*

Destiny, 1817–1914 (1971) and *White Supremacy: A Comparative Study in American and South African History* (1981); Alison G. Freehling, *Drift Toward Dissolution: The Virginia Slavery Debate of 1831–1832* (1982); Elliott J. Gorn, "'Gouge and Bite, Pull Hair and Scratch': The Social Significance of Fighting in the Southern Backcountry," *American Historical Review* 90 (February 1985): 18–43; Michael Hindus, *Prison and Plantation: Crime, Justice, and Authority in Massachusetts and South Carolina, 1767–1878* (1980); John McCardell, *The Idea of a Southern Nation: Southern Nationalists and Southern Nationalism* (1979); Donald G. Mathews, *Religion in the Old South* (1977); Mitchell Snay, *Gospel of Disunion: Religion and Separatism in the Antebellum South* (1993); J. Mills Thornton, *Politics and Power in a Slave Society: Alabama, 1800–1860* (1978); Larry E. Tise, *Proslavery: A History of the Defense of Slavery in America, 1701–1840* (1987); Bertram Wyatt-Brown, *Southern Honor: Ethics and Behavior in the Old South* (1982).

The Emergence of African American Culture

Ira Berlin, *Slaves Without Masters: The Free Negro in the Antebellum South* (1974); John Blassingame, *The Slave Community* (1972); Leonard P. Curry, *The Free Black in Urban America, 1800–1850: The Shadow of the Dream* (1981); Carl N. Degler, *Neither Black Nor White: Slavery and Race Relations in Brazil and the United States* (1971); Dena J. Epstein, *Sinful Tunes and Spirituals: Black Folk Music to the Civil War* (1977); Claudia D. Goldin, *Urban Slavery in the American South, 1820–1860* (1976); Herbert G. Gutman, *The Black Familiy in Slavery and Freedom, 1759–1925* (1976); Martha Hodes, *White Women, Black Men: Illicit Sex in the Nineteenth Century South* (1997); Walter Johnson, *Soul by Soul: Life Inside the Antebellum Slave Market* (1999); Jacqueline Jones, *Labor of Love, Labor of Sorrow: Black Women, Work, and the Family from Slavery to the Present* (1985); Mark Kruman, *Parties and Politics in North Carolina, 1836–1865* (1983); Lawrence W. Levine, *Black Culture and Black Consciousness: Afro-American Folk Thought from Slavery to Freedom* (1977); Ann P. Malone, *Sweet Chariot: Slave Family and Household Structure in Nineteenth-Century Louisiana* (1992); Thomas D. Morris, *Southern Slavery and the Law* (1996); Stephen B. Oates, *The Fires of Jubilee* (1975); Leslie H. Owens, *This Species of Property: Slave Life and Slave Culture in the Old South* (1976); Albert J. Raboteau, *Slave Religion* (1978); George P. Rawick, *From Sundown to Sunup: The Making of a Black Community* (1972); David Robinson, *Denmark Vesey* (1999); Jon Michael Spencer, *Black Hymnody* (1992); Robert S. Starobin, *Industrial Slavery in the Old South* (1970); Brenda R. Stevenson, *Life in Black and White: Family and Community in the Slave South* (1996); Michael Tadman, *Speculators and Slaves: Traders and Slaves in the Old South* (1989).

Chapter 13
Newcomers and Natives

Lee Benson, *The Concept of Jacksonian Democracy: New York as a Test Case* (1961); Ray A. Billington, *The Protestant Crusade, 1800–1860: A Study of the Origins of Nativism* (1938); R. A. Burchell, *The San Francisco Irish, 1848–1880* (1980); Kathleen Conzen, *Immigrant Milwaukee, 1836–1860* (1976); Hasia R. Diner, *Erin's Daughters in America* (1983); Oscar Handlin,

Boston's Immigrants, rev. ed. (1969); Bruce Laurie, *Working People of Philadelphia, 1800–1850* (1980); Bruce Levine, *The Spirit of 1848: German Immigrants, Labor Conflict, and the Coming of the Civil War* (1992); Lawrence J. McCaffrey, *The Irish Diaspora in America* (1984); Kerby A. Miller, *Emigrants and Exiles: Ireland and the Irish Exodus to North America* (1985); Norman Ware, *The Industrial Worker, 1840–1860* (1964); Carl Wittke, *The Irish in America* (1956).

The West and Beyond

Malcolm Clark, Jr., *Eden Seekers: The Settlement of Oregon, 1818–1862* (1981); Douglas H. Daniels, *Pioneer Urbanities: A Social and Cultural History of Black San Francisco* (1980); Arnoldo De Leon, *They Called Them Greasers: Anglo Attitudes Toward Mexicans in Texas, 1821–1900* (1983); John Mack Faragher, *Women and Men on the Overland Trail* (1979); William H. Goetzmann, *Exploration and Empire: The Explorer and the Scientist in the Winning of the American West* (1966); Albert Hurtado, *Intimate Friendship: Sex, Gender, and Culture in Old California* (1999); Theodore J. Karaminski, *Fur Trade and Exploration: Opening of the Far Northwest, 1821–1852* (1983); Frederick Merk, *History of the Westward Movement* (1978); John I. Unruh, Jr., *The Plains Across: Overland Emigrants and the Trans-Mississippi West, 1840–1860* (1979); David J. Weber, *The Mexican Frontier, 1821–1846: The American Southwest Under Mexico* (1982) and *The Spanish Frontier in North America* (1992); Kenneth H. Winn, *Exiles in a Land of Liberty: Mormons in America, 1830–1860* (1989).

The Politics of Expansion, 1840–1846

Paul H. Bergeron, *The Presidency of James K. Polk* (1987); William C. Binkley, *The Texas Revolution* (1952); Gene M. Brack, *Mexico Views Manifest Destiny* (1976); William J. Cooper, *Liberty and Slavery: Southern Politics to 1860* (1983); Bernard DeVoto, *The Year of Decision, 1846* (1943); Norman A. Graebner, *Empire on the Pacific: A Study in American Continental Expansion* (1955); Thomas R. Hietala, *Manifest Design: Anxious Aggrandizement in Late Jacksonian America* (1985); Reginald Horsman, *Race and Manifest Destiny: The Origins of American Racial Anglo-Saxonism* (1981); Robert W. Johannsen, *To the Halls of the Montezumas: The Mexican War in the American Imagination* (1985); Ernest McPherson Lander, Jr., *Reluctant Imperialist: Calhoun, the South Carolinian, and the Mexican War* (1980); Frederick Merk, *Slavery and the Annexation of Texas* (1972); David M. Pletcher, *The Diplomacy of Annexation: Texas, Oregon, and the Mexican War* (1973); Joseph G. Raybeck, *Free Soil: The Election of 1848* (1970); Charles G. Sellers, *James K. Polk: Jacksonian, 1795–1843* (1957); Joel H. Silbey, *The Shrine of Party: Congressional Voting Behaviour, 1841–1852* (1967).

The Mexican-American War and its Aftermath, 1846–1848

K. Jack Bauer, *The Mexican War, 1846–1848* (1974); John W. Caughey, *The California Gold Rush* (1975); Seymour Connor and Odie Faulk, *North America Divided: The Mexican War, 1846–1848* (1971); Neal Harlow, *California Conquered: War and Peace on the Pacific, 1846–1850* (1982); Susan Lee Johnson, *Roaring Camp: The Social World of the California Gold Rush* (2000); Leonard Pitt, *The Decline of the Californios : A Social History of the Spanish-Speaking Californians, 1846–1890*

(1966); John H. Schroeder, *Mr. Polk's War: American Opposition and Dissent, 1846–1848* (1971); Otis A. Singletary, *The Mexican War* (1960).

Chapter 14
The Compromise of 1850
Thomas F. Gossett, *Uncle Tom's Cabin and American Culture* (1985); Holman Hamilton, *Prologue to Conflict: The Crisis and Compromise of 1850* (1964); Peter Knupfer, *The Union as It Is: Constitutional Unionism and Sectional Compromise, 1787–1861* (1991); Thomas D. Morris, *Free Men All: The Personal Liberty Laws of the North, 1780–1861* (1974); Chaplain W. Morrison, *Democratic Politics and Sectionalism: The Wilmot Proviso Controversy* (1967); Mark Stegmaier, *Texas, New Mexico, and the Compromise of 1850* (1996); Albert J. Von Frank, *The Trials of Anthony Burns* (1998).

The Collapse of the Second Party System, 1853–1856
Tyler Anbinder, *Nativism and Slavery: The Northern Know Nothings and the Politics of the 1850s* (1992); Eugene Berwanger, *The Frontier Against Slavery: Western Anti-Negro Prejudice in the Slavery Extension Controversy* (1967); Charles H. Brown, *Agents of Manifest Destiny: The Lives of the Filibusters* (1978); Michael F. Holt, *Political Parties and American Political Development from the Age of Jackson to the Age of Lincoln* (1992); Geoffrey W. Wolff, *The Kansas-Nebraska Bill* (1977).

The Crisis of the Union, 1857–1860
Robert Dykstra, *Bright Radical Star: Black Freedom and White Supremacy on the Hawkeye Frontier* (1993); John Hope Franklin, *The Militant South, 1800–1861* (1970) and *A Southern Odyssey: Travelers in the Antebellum North* (1976); Michael P. Johnson and James L. Roark, eds., *No Chariot Let Down: Charleston's Free People of Color on the Eve of the Civil War* (1984); Robert E. May, *The Southern Dream of a Caribbean Empire, 1854–1861* (1973); John McCardell, *The Idea of a Southern Nation: Southern Nationalists and Southern Nationalism, 1830–1861* (1979); Rollin G. Osterweiss, *Romanticism and Nationalism in the Old South* (1949); James A. Rawley, *Race and Politics: Bleeding Kansas and the Coming of the Civil War* (1969); Ronald L. Takaki, *A Proslavery Crusade: The Agitation to Reopen the African Slave Trade* (1971); J. Mills Thornton, *Politics and Power in a Slave Society* (1978).

The Collapse of the Union, 1860–1861
William L. Barney, *The Road to Secession* (1972); Steven A. Channing, *Crisis of Fear: Secession in South Carolina* (1970); David Donald, *Charles Sumner and the Coming of the Civil War* (1960); Don E. Fehrenbacher, *The Dred Scott Case* (1978) and *Prelude to Greatness: Lincoln in the 1850s* (1962); Paul W. Finkelman, ed., *His Soul Goes Marching On: Responses to John Brown and the Harpers Ferry Raid* (1995); George B. Forgie, *Patricide in the House Divided: A Psychological Interpretation of Lincoln and His Age* (1979); Henry V. Jaffa, *Crisis of the House Divided: An Interpretation of the Lincoln-Douglas Debates* (1959); Robert W. Johannsen, *Stephen A. Douglas* (1973); Michael Johnson, *Secession and Conservatism in the Lower South: The Social and Ideological Bases of Secession in Georgia, 1860–1861* (1983); Albert J. Kirwan, *John J. Crittenden: The Struggle for the Union* (1962); Milton Klein, *President James Buchanan: A Biography* (1962); Michael Morison, *Slavery and the American West* (1997); Paul C. Nagel, *One Nation Indivisible: The Union in American Thought* (1964); Allan Nevins, *The Emergence of Lincoln* (2 vols., 1950); Roy F. Nichols, *The Disruption of American Democracy* (1948); Stephen B. Oates, *To Purge This Land with Blood: A Biography of John Brown* (1970); David Potter, *Lincoln and His Party in the Secession Crisis* (1942); Kenneth Stampp, *And the War Came: The North and the Secession Crisis, 1860–1861* (1970).

Chapter 15
General
Daniel Aaron, *The Unwritten War* (1973); William L. Barney, *Flawed Victory* (1975); David P. Crook, *Diplomacy During the Civil War* (1975); Keith F. Davis, "A Terrible Distinctiveness: Photography of the Civil War Era" in Martha M. Sandweiss, ed., *Photography in Nineteenth Century America* (1991), 130–179; William C. Davis, *Fighting for Time: Volume Four of the Image of War, 1861–1865* (1983); Brian R. Dirck, *Lincoln and Davis: Imagining America, 1809–1865* (2001); David Donald, ed., *Why the North Won the Civil War* (1960); Alice Fahs, *The Imagined Civil War: Popular Literature of the North and South, 1861–1865* (2001); Eric Foner, *Politics and Ideology in the Age of the Civil War* (1980); Paul G. Gates, *Agriculture and the Civil War* (1965); Allen C. Guelzo, *The Crisis of the American Republic: A History of the Civil War and Reconstruction Era* (1995); Harold Hyman, *A More Perfect Union* (1975); James M. McPherson, *Ordeal by Fire* (1982); Allan Nevins, *The War for the Union*, 4 vols. (1959–1971); Anne C. Rose, *Victorian America and the Civil War* (1992); Lewis P. Simpson, *Mind and the American Civil War* (1989); Maris A. Vinovskis, *Toward a Social History of the American Civil War: Exploratory Essays* (1990); Edmund Wilson, *Patriotic Gore* (1961); Jay Winik, *April, 1865: The Month That Saved America* (2001).

Lincoln
LaWanda Cox, *Lincoln and Black Freedom* (1981); David Donald, *Lincoln Reconsidered: Essays on the Civil War Era*, 2d ed. (1956); Allen C. Guelzo, *Abraham Lincoln: Redeemer President* (1999); William K. Klingaman, *Abraham Lincoln and the Road to Emancipation, 1861–1865* (2002); James M. McPherson, *Abraham Lincoln and the Second American Revolution* (1990); William Lee Miller, *Lincoln's Virtues: An Ethical Biography* (2002); Mark E. Neely, Jr., *The Last Best Hope on Earth: Abraham Lincoln and the Promise of America* (1993); Stephen B. Oates, *With Malice Toward None: The Life of Abraham Lincoln* (1979); Phillip Shaw Paludan, *The Presidency of Abraham Lincoln* (1994); James R. Randall, *Lincoln the President*, 4 vols. (1944–1955); Edward Steers, Jr., *Blood on the Moon: The Assassination of Abraham Lincoln* (2002); Benjamin Thomas, *Abraham Lincoln* (1952); T. Harry Williams, *Lincoln and the Radicals* (1941) and *Lincoln and His Generals* (1952); Garry Wills, *Lincoln at Gettysburg: The Words That Remade America* (1992); Douglas L. Wilson, *Honor's Voice: The Transformation of Abraham Lincoln* (1998).

The Military Experience

Michael Barton, *Good Men: The Character of Civil War Soldiers* (1981); Richard G. Beringer et al., *Why the South Lost the Civil War* (1986); Bruce Catton, *Mr. Lincoln's Army* (1951), *Glory Road* (1952) and *A Stillness at Appomattox* (1953); Shelby Foote, *The Civil War: A Narrative*, 3 vols. (1958–1974); Joseph T. Glatthaar, *The March to the Sea and Beyond* (1985) and *Partners in Command: The Relationships Between Leaders in the Civil War* (1994); Paddy Griffith, *Rally Once Again: Battle Tactics of the Civil War* (1989); Edward Hagerman, *The American Civil War and the Origins of Modern Warfare* (1988); Herman Hattaway, *Shades of Blue and Gray* (1997); Herman Hattaway and Archer Jones, *How the North Won: A Military History of the Civil War* (1984); Earl J. Hess, *Pickett's Charge: The Last Attack at Gettysburg* (2001); Alvin M. Josephy, Jr., *The Civil War in the American West* (1991); Maury Klein, *Days of Defiance: Sumter, Secession, and the Coming of the Civil War* (1997); Gerald F. Linderman, *Embattled Courage: The Experience of Combat in the American Civil War* (1987); James M. McPherson, *What They Fought for, 1861–1865* (1994); Carol Reardon, *Pickett's Charge in History and Memory* (1997).

The African-American Experience

Ira Berlin et al., eds., *Freedom, A Documentary History of Emancipation, 1861–1867* (1982–1993); Dudley Cornish, *The Sable Arm: Negro Troops in the Union Army* (1956); John Hope Franklin, *The Emancipation Proclamation* (1963); Louis S. Gerteis, *From Contraband to Freeman: Federal Policy Toward Southern Blacks, 1861–1865* (1973); Joseph T. Glatthaar, *Forged in Battle: The Civil War Alliance of Black Soldiers and White Officers* (1990); James M. McPherson, ed., *The Negro's Civil War* (1965); Benjamin Quarles, *The Negro in the Civil War* (1953); Willie Lee Rose, *Rehearsal for Reconstruction: The Port Royal Experiment* (1964).

The Southern Experience

Thomas B. Alexander and Richard E. Beringer, *The Anatomy of the Confederate Congress* (1972); William C. Davis, *An Honorable Defeat: The Last Days of Confederate Government* (2001) and *The Union That Shaped the Confederacy:* Robert Toombs and Alexander Stephens (2001); Paul D. Escott, *After Secession: Jefferson Davis and the Failure of Southern Nationalism* (1978); Eli N. Evans, *Judah P. Benjamin* (1987); Drew Gilpin Faust, *The Creation of Confederate Nationalism* (1988) and *Southern Stories: Slaveholders in Peace and War* (1992); William H. Freehling, *The South vs. the South: How Anti-Confederate Southerners Shaped the Course of the Civil War* (2001); Douglas Southall Freeman, *R. E. Lee: A Biography*, 4 vols. (1934–1935); Gary W. Gallagher, *The Confederate War* (1997); Mark Grimsley, *The Hard Hand of War: Union Military Policy Toward Southern Civilians, 1861–1865* (1995); Clarence Mohr, *On the Threshold of Freedom: Masters and Slaves in Civil War Georgia* (1986); Robert M. Myers, ed., *The Children of Pride: A True Story of Georgia and the Civil War* (1972); Alan T. Nolan, *Lee Considered: General Robert E. Lee and Civil War History* (1991); George C. Rable, *Civil Wars: Women and the Crisis of Southern Nationalism* (1989); James L. Roark, *Masters Without Slaves: Southern Planters in the Civil War and Reconstruction* (1978); Emory M. Thomas, *The Confederate Nation, 1861–1865* (1979); Bell I. Wiley, *The Plain People of the Confederacy* (1943) and *Road to Appomattox* (1956).

The Northern Experience

Iver Bernstein, *The New York Draft Riots: The Significance for American Society and Politics in the Age of the Civil War* (1990); Adrian Cook, *Armies of the Streets: The New York City Draft Riots of 1863* (1974); George M. Fredrickson, *The Inner Civil War: Northern Intellectuals and the Crisis of the Union* (1965); David Gilchrist and W. David Lewis, eds., *Economic Change in the Civil War Era* (1965); Frank L. Klement, *The Copperheads of the Middle West* (1960) and *Dark Lanterns: Secret Political Socieities, Conspiracies, and Treason Trials in the Civil War* (1984); William S. McFeely, *Grant: A Biography* (1981); Reid Mitchell, *The Vacant Chair: The Northern Soldier Leaves Home* (1993); Phillip Shaw Paludan, *"A People's Contest": The Union and the Civil War, 1861–1865* (1988); Joel Silbey, *A Respectable Minority: The Democratic Party in the Civil War Era, 1860–1868* (1977); George W. Smith and Charles Judah, eds., *Life in the North During the Civil War* (1968); Hans L. Trefousse, *The Radical Republicans* (1968).

Women in the Civil War Era

Jeanie Attie, *Patriotic Toil: Northern Women and the American Civil War* (1998); Carol K. Bleser and Lesley J. Gordon, eds. *Intimate Strategies of the Civil War: Military Commanders and Their Wives* (2001); Thomas J. Brown, *Dorothea Dix: New England Reformer* (1995); Edward D. C. Campbell, Jr., and Kim S. Rice, eds., *A Woman's War: Southern Women, Civil War, and the Confederate Legacy* (1996); Catherine Clinton, *Tara Revisited: Women, War, and the Plantation Legend* (1995); Catherine Clinton and Nina Silber, eds., *Divided Houses: Gender and the Civil War* (1992); Lauren M. Cook, *They Fought Like Demons: Women Soldiers in the American Civil War* (2002); Laura F. Edwards, *Scarlett Doesn't Live Here Anymore: Southern Women in the Civil War Era* (2000); Ella Forbes, *African-American Women During the Civil War* (1998); Judith Ann Giesberg, *Civil War Sisterhood: African-American Women During the Civil War* (2000); Elizabeth D. Leonard, *Yankee Women: Gender Battles in the Civil War* (1994) and *All the Daring of the Soldier: Women of the Civil War Armies* (1999); Mary Elizabeth Massey, *Bonnet Brigades: American Women and the Civil War* (1966); Stephen B. Oates, *A Woman of Valor: Clara Barton and the Civil War* (1994); George C. Rable, *Civil Wars: Women and the Crisis of Southern Nationalism* (1989); Wendy Hamand Venet, *Neither Ballots nor Bullets: Women Abolitionists and the Civil War* (1991); Lee Ann Whites, *The Civil War as a Crisis in Gender: Augusta, Georgia, 1860–1890* (1995); Elizabeth Young, *Disarming the Nation: Women's Writing and the American Civil War* (1999).

Personal Narratives

Eliza Frances Andrews, *Wartime Journal of a Georgia Girl* (1908); Virginia Ingraham Burr, ed., *The Secret Eye: The Journal of Ella Clanton Thomas, 1848–1889* (1990); David Donald, ed., *Inside Lincoln's Cabinet: The Civil War Diaries of Salmon P. Chase* (1959); Ulysses S. Grant, *Memoirs and Selected Letters* (1990); Rupert S. Hallard, ed., *The Letters and Diaries of Laura M. Towne* (1970); T. W. Higginson, *Army Life in a Black Regiment*

(1867); Mary Ashton Livermore, *My Story of the War* (1881); W. T. Sherman, *Memoirs* (1990); C. Vann Woodward, ed., *Mary Chesnut's Civil War* (1982).

Chapter 16
Reconstruction Politics
Richard H. Abbott, *The Republican Party and the South, 1855–1877* (1986); Herman Belz, *Emancipation and Equal Rights: Politics and Constitutionalism in the Civil War Era* (1978); Michael Les Benedict, *A Compromise of Principle: Congressional Republicans and Reconstruction, 1863–1869* (1974) and *The Impeachment and Trial of Andrew Johnson* (1973); W. R. Brock, *An American Crisis: Congress and Reconstruction, 1865–1867* (1963); Fawn Brodie, *Thaddeus Stevens: Scourge of the South* (1959); Richard O. Curry, ed., *Radicalism, Racism, and Party Realignment: The Border States During Reconstruction* (1969); David Donald, *Charles Sumner and the Rights of Man* (1970) and *The Politics of Reconstruction, 1863–1867* (1965); William Gillette, *The Right to Vote: Politics and Passage of the Fifteenth Amendment* (1969); William C. Harris, *With Charity for All: Lincoln and the Reconstruction of the Union* (1997); Harold Hyman, *A More Perfect Union: The Impact of the Civil War and Reconstruction on the Constitution* (1973); Stanley I. Kutler, *Judicial Power and Reconstruction* (1968); Eric McKitrick, *Andrew Johnson and Reconstruction* (1960); James C. Mohr, *Radical Republicans in the North: State Politics During Reconstruction* (1976); William E. Nelson, *The Fourteenth Amendment* (1988); Hans Trefousse, *Andrew Johnson: A Biography* (1989) and *Thaddeus Stevens: Nineteenth-Century Egalitarian* (1997).

The South
Dan C. Carter, *When the War Was Over: Self-Reconstruction in the South, 1865–1867* (1985); William Cohen, *At Freedom's Edge: Black Mobility and the Southern White Quest for Racial Control, 1861–1915* (1991); Frederick Cooper, Thomas C. Holt, and Rebecca J. Scott, *Beyond Slavery: Explorations of Race, Labor, and Citizenship in Postemancipation Societies* (2000); Richard Nelson Current, *Those Terrible Carpetbaggers* (1988); Don H. Doyle, *New Men, New Cities, New South: Atlanta, Nashville, Charleston, Mobile, 1860–1910* (1990); Laura F. Edwards, *Gendered Strife and Confusion: The Political Culture of Reconstruction* (1997); John Hope Franklin, *Reconstruction After the Civil War* (1961); Stephen Hahn, *The Roots of Southern Populism* (1983); William C. Harris, *The Day of the Carpetbagger: Republican Reconstruction in Mississippi* (1979); James C. Hollandsworth, Jr., *An Absolute Massacre: The New Orleans Race Riot of July 30, 1866* (2001); Otto Olsen, ed., *Reconstruction and Redemption in the South* (1980); Michael Perman, *Reunion Without Compromise: The South and Reconstruction, 1865–1868* (1973) and *The Road to Redemption: Southern Politics, 1869–1879* (1984); Howard N. Rabinowitz, *Race Relations in the Urban South, 1865–1890* (1978); George C. Rable, *But There Was No Peace: The Role of Violence in the Politics of Reconstruction* (1984); Mark W. Summers, *Railroads, Reconstruction, and the Gospel of Prosperity* (1984); Allen W. Trelease, *White Terror: The Ku Klux Klan Conspiracy and Southern Reconstruction* (1971); Ted Tunnell, *Crucible of Reconstruction: War, Radicalism, and Race in Louisiana, 1862–1877* (1984); Jonathan M. Wiener, *Social Origins of the New South: Alabama, 1860–1885* (1978); Gavin Wright, *Old South, New South: Revolutions in the Southern Economy Since the Civil War* (1986).

Emancipation and the Freedmen
Ira Berlin et al., eds., *Freedom, A Documentary History of Emancipation, 1861–1867* (1982–1993); Carol Rothrock Bleser, *The Promised Land: The History of the South Carolina Land Commission, 1869–1890* (1969); Jane Dailey, *Before Jim Crow: The Politics of Race in Postemancipation Virginia* (2000); W. E. B. Du Bois, *Black Reconstruction in America, 1860–1880* (1935); Barbara Jeanne Fields, *Slavery and Freedom on the Middle Ground: Maryland During the Nineteenth Century* (1985); Eric Foner, *Nothing but Freedom: Emancipation and Its Legacies* (1983) and *Politics and Ideology in the Age of the Civil War* (1980), Chapters 6–7; Norale Frankel, *Freedom's Women: Black Women and Families in Civil War Mississippi* (1999); Herbert G. Gutman, *The Black Family in Slavery and Freedom, 1750–1925* (1976); Robert Higgs, *Competition and Coercion: Blacks in the American Economy, 1865–1914* (1977); Thomas Holt, *Black over White: Negro Political Leadership in South Carolina During Reconstruction* (1977); Gerald Jaynes, *Branches Without Roots: Genesis of the Black Working Class in the American South, 1862–1882* (1986); Jacqueline Jones, *Soldiers of Light and Love: Northern Teachers and Georgia Blacks, 1865–1873* (1980) and *Labor of Love, Labor of Sorrow: Black Women, Work, and the Family from Slavery to the Present* (1985), Chapter 2; Peter Kolchin, *First Freedom: The Responses of Alabama's Blacks to Emancipation and Reconstruction* (1972); Lawrence W. Levine, *Black Culture and Black Consciousness: Afro-American Folk Thought from Slavery to Freedom* (1977); William S. McFeely, *Yankee Stepfather: General O. O. Howard and the Freedmen* (1966); Nell Irvin Painter, *Exodusters* (1977); Elizabeth Regosin, *Freedom's Promise: Ex-Slave Families and Citizenship in the Age of Emancipation* (2002); James Roark, *Masters Without Slaves: Southern Planters in the Civil War and Reconstruction* (1978); Leslie A. Schwalm, *A Hard Fight for We: Women's Transition from Slavery to Freedom in South Carolina* (1997); William Preston Vaughan, *Schools for All: The Blacks and Public Education in the South, 1865–1877* (1974); Joel Williamson, *The Crucible of Race: Black-White Relations in the American South Since Emancipation* (1984).

National Trends
Paul H. Buck, *The Road to Reunion, 1865–1900* (1937); Adrian Cook, *The Alabama Claims* (1975); William Gillette, *Retreat from Reconstruction, 1869–1879* (1979); Ari M. Hoogenboom, *Outlawing the Spoils: A History of the Civil Service Reform Movement* (1961); William S. McFeely, *Grant: A Biography* (1981); David Montgomery, *Beyond Equality: Labor and the Radical Republicans, 1862–1872* (1967); Walter T. K. Nugent, *The Money Question During Reconstruction* (1967) and *Money and American Society, 1865–1880* (1968); Keith I. Polakoff, *The Politics of Inertia: The Election of 1876 and the End of Reconstruction* (1973); John C. Sproat, *"The Best Men": Liberal Reformers in the Gilded Age* (1968); Mark W. Summers, *The Era of Good Stealings* (1993); Irwin Unger, *The Greenback Era: A Social and Political History of American Finance* (1964); Allen Weinstein, *Prelude to Populism: Origins of the Silver Issue, 1867–1878* (1970); C. Vann Woodward, *Reunion and Reaction: The Compromise of 1877 and the End of Reconstruction* (rev. ed., 1956).

Chapter 17

The Western Mystique

William Cronon, George Miles, and Jay Gitlin, eds., *Under the Open Sky: Rethinking America's Western Past* (1992); Patricia N. Limerick, *The Legacy of Conquest: The Unbroken Past of the American West* (1987) and *Something in the Soil: Legacies and Reckonings in the New West* (2000); Valerie J. Matsumoto and Blake Allmendinger, *Over the Edge: Remapping the American West* (1999); Clyde A. Milner II, *A New Significance: Re-envisioning the History of the American West* (1996); Walter Nugent, *Into the West: The Story of Its People* (1999); Quintard Taylor, *In Search of the Racial Frontier: African Americans in the American West, 1528–1990* (1998); David M. Wrobel and Michael C. Steiner, *Many Wests: Place, Culture, and Regional Identity* (1997); Patricia Trenton, ed., *Independent Spirits: Women Painters of the American West, 1890–1945* (1995); Richard White, *"Its Your Misfortune and None of My Own": A History of the American West* (1991); Donald Worster, *An Unsettled Country: Changing Landscapes of the American West* (1994).

Native Americans

David W. Adams, *Education for Extinction: American Indians and the Boarding School Experience, 1875–1928* (1995); Gary C. Anderson, *Sitting Bull and the Paradox of Lakota Nationhood* (1996); Brenda J. Child, *Boarding School Seasons: American Indian Families, 1900–1940* (1998); Michael C. Coleman, *American Indian Children at School, 1850–1930* (1993); Lisbeth Haas, *Conquests and Historical Identities in California, 1769–1936* (1995); Fred Hoxie, *Parading Through History: The Making of the Crow Nation in America, 1805–1935* (1995); Shari M. Huhndorf, *Going Native: Indians in the American Cultural Imagination* (2001); David R. Lewis, *Neither Wolf nor Dog: American Indians, Environment, and Agrarian Change* (1994); Janet A. McDonnell, *The Dispossession of the American Indian, 1887–1934* (1991); Theda Perdue, *The Cherokee* (1989); Catherine Price, *The Oglala People, 1841–1879* (1996); Francis Paul Prucha, *The Great Father: The United States Government and the American Indians*, (2 vols., 1984); Glenda Riley, *Women and Indians on the Frontier, 1825–1915* (1984); Robert A. Trennert, Jr., *The Phoenix Indian School: Forced Assimilation in Arizona, 1891–1935* (1988); Scott Riney, *The Rapid City Indian School, 1898–1933* (1999); Anna Moore Shaw, *A Pima Past* (1974); Sherry L. Smith, *Reimagining Indians: Native Americans Through Anglo Eyes, 1880–1940* (2000); Robert M. Utley, *The Indian Frontier of the American West, 1846–1890* (1984) and *The Lance and the Shield: The Life and Times of Sitting Bull* (1993); Richard White, *The Roots of Dependency: Subsistence, Environment, and Social Change Among the Choctaws, Pawnees, and Navajos* (1983).

Settling the West

Richard Griswold del Castillo, *La Familia: Chicano Families in the Urban Southeast, 1848 to the Present* (1984); Sarah Deutsch, *No Separate Refuge: Culture, Class, and Gender on the Anglo-Hispanic Frontier in the Early Southwest, 1880–1940* (1987); Neil Foley, *The White Scourge; Mexicans, Blacks, and Poor Whites in Texas Cotton Culture* (1997); Paul W. Gates, *Jeffersonian Dream: Studies in the History of American Land Policy and Development* (1996); Jon Gjerde, *The Minds of the West: Ethnocultural Evolution in the Rural Middle West, 1830–1917* (1997); Lisbeth Haas, *Conquests and Historical Identities in California, 1769–1936* (1995); Katherine Harris, *Long Vistas: Women and Families on the Colorado Homesteads* (1993); John C. Hudson, *Making the Corn Belt: A Geographical History of Middle-Western Agriculture* (1994); Maury Klein, *Union Pacific: Birth of a Railroad, 1862–1893* (1987); Bradford Luckingham, *Minorities in Phoenix: A Profile of Mexican American, Chinese American, and African American Communities, 1860–1992* (1994); Dean L. May, *Three Frontiers: Family, Land, and Society in the American West, 1850–1994* (1994); Timothy Mahoney, *River Towns in the Great West* (1990); Lucy E. Murphy and Wendy H. Venet, eds., *Midwestern Women: Work, Community, and Leadership at the Crossroads* (1997); Glenda Riley, *The Female Frontier* (1988) and *Building and Breaking Families in the American West* (1996); Thomas E. Sheridan, *Los Tuconenses: The Mexican Community in Tucson, 1854–1941* (1986); Kenneth L. Steward and Arnold De Leon, *Not Room Enough: Mexicans, Anglos, and Socioeconomic Change in Texas, 1850–1900* (1993); Elliott West, *Growing Up with the Country: Childhood on the Far Western Frontier* (1989) and *The Way to the West* (1995).

The Bonanza West

Susan Armitage and Elizabeth Jameson, eds., *The Woman's West* (1987) and *Writing the Range* (1997); Anne M. Butler, *Daughters of Joy, Sisters of Misery* (1985); William Cronon, *Nature's Metropolis: Chicago and the Great West* (1991); Paul H. Carlson, ed., *The Cowboy Way: An Exploration of History and Culture* (2000); Christopher M. Klyza, *Who Controls Public Lands?; Mining, Forestry, and Grazing Policies, 1870–1990* (1996); Rodman Paul and Elliott West, *Mining Frontiers of the Far West, 1848–1880* (2001); Sally Zanjani, *A Mine of Her Own: Women Prospectors in the American West, 1850–1950* (1997).

The Frontier Legend

Richard Aquila, ed., *Wanted Dead or Alive: The American West in Popular Culture* (1996); Christine Bold, *Selling the West: Popular Western Fiction, 1860–1960* (1987); John M. Faragher, ed., *Rereading Frederick Jackson Turner: "The Significance of the Frontier in American History" and Other Essays* (1994); Alexander Nemertov, *Frederic Remington and Turn-of-the-Century America* (1995); L. G. Moses, *Wild West Shows and Images of American Indians, 1883–1933* (1996); Joseph G. Rosa, *Wild Bill Hickok: The Man and His Myth* (1996); Richard Slotkin, *Gunfighter Nation: The Myth of the Frontier in 20th-Century America* (1992); R. L. Wilson with Greg Martin, *Buffalo Bill's Wild West: An American Legend* (1998).

Beginning a Conservation Movement

Karl Jacoby, *Crimes Against Nature: Squatters, Poachers, Thieves, and the Hidden History of Conservation* (2001); Roderick Nash, *The Rights of Nature: A History of Environmental Ethics* (1989); Richard Orsi, Alfred Runte, and Marlene Smith-Barazini, eds., *Yosemite and Sequoia: A Century of California National Parks* (1993); Donald J. Pisani, *To Reclaim a Divided West: Water, Law, and Public Policy, 1848–1901* (1993); Albert Runte, *Yosemite: The Embattled Wilderness* (1990); Ian Tyrrell, *True Gardens of the Gods: Californian-Australian Environmental Reform, 1860–1930*

(1999); Thurman Wilkins, *John Muir: Apostle of Nature* (1995); Donald Worster, *Rivers of Empire: Water, Aridity, and the Growth of the American West* (1985) and *A River Running West: The Life of John Wesley Powell* (2001).

Chapter 18

The Character of Industrial Change

Stephen Ambrose, *Nothing Like It in the World: The Men Who Built the Transcontinental Railroad, 1863–1869* (2000); William L. Barney, ed., *A Companion to 19th-Century America* (2001); Charles W. Calhoun, ed., *The Gilded Age: Essays in Modern America* (1995); Alfred D. Chandler, Jr., *The Visible Hand: The Managerial Revolution in American Business* (1977); Ruth S. Cowan, *A Social History of American Technology* (1997); Lawrence B. Glickman, *A Living Wage: American Workers and the Making of Consumer Society* (1997); Victoria C. Hattam, *Labor Visions and State Power: The Origins of Business Unionism in the United States* (1993); Maury Klein, *The Flowering of the Third America: The Making of an Organizational Society, 1850–1920* (1993); Naomi R. Lamoreaux, *The Great Merger Movement in American Business* (1985); Walter Licht, *Industrializing America: The Nineteenth Century* (1995); Nelson Lichtenstein, ed., *Who Built America? Working People and the Nation's Economy, Politics, Culture, and Society*, 2d ed. (2000); Harold Livesay, *Andrew Carnegie and the Rise of Big Business* (1975); Albro Martin, *Railroads Triumphant: The Growth, Rejection, and Rebirth of a Vital American Force* (1994); Martin V. Melosi, *Coping with Abundance: Energy and Environment in Industrial America* (1985); Andre Millard, *Edison and the Business of Innovation* (1990); David E. Nye, *Electrifying America* (1990), *American Technological Sublime* (1994), and *Consuming Power: A Social History of American Energies* (1998); David Stradling, *Smokestacks and Progressives: Environmentalist, Engineers, and Air Quality in America, 1881–1951* (1999); Oliver Zunz, *Making America Corporate, 1870–1920* (1990).

The New South

Eric Arnesen, *Waterfront Workers of New Orleans: Race Class, and Politics, 1863–1923* (1991); James C. Cobb, *Industrialization and Southern Society, 1877–1984* (1984) and *The Most Southern Place on Earth: The Mississippi Delta and the Roots of Regional Identity* (1992); Don Doyle, *New Men, New Cities, New South* (1990); Paul M. Gaston, *The New South Creed: A Study in Southern Mythmaking* (1970); Dewey W. Grantham, *The South in Modern America: A Region at Odds* (1995); Steven Hahn and Jonathan Prude, eds., *The Countryside in the Age of Capitalist Transformation: Essays in the Social History of Rural America* (1985); Jacquelyn D. Hall et al., *Like a Family: The Making of a Southern Cotton Mill World* (1987); James L. Leloudis, *Schooling in the New South* (1996); Michael Shirley, *From Congregation Town to Industrial City: Culture and Social Change in a Southern Community* (1994); Gavin Wright, *Old South, New South: Revolutions in the Southern Economy Since the Civil War* (1986).

Industrial Work and the Labor Force

Eric Arnesen, Julie Greene, and Bruce Laurie, eds., *Labor Histories: Class, Politics, and the Working Class Experience* (1998); Ava Baron, *Work Engendered: Toward a New History of American Labor* (1991); David Brody, *In Labor's Cause: Main Themes on the History of the American Worker* (1993); Wendy Gamber, *The Female Economy: The Millinery and Dressmaking Trades, 1860–1930* (1997); William Hartford, *Working People of Holyoke: Class and Ethnicity in a Massachusetts Mill Town, 1850–1960* ((1990); Jacqueline Jones, *A Social History of the Laboring Classes* (1999); Alice Kessler-Harris, *Out to Work: A History of Wage-Earning Women in the United States,* (1982); Hadassa Kosak, *Cultures of Opposition: Jewish Immigrant Workers, New York City, 1881–1905* (2000); Angel Kwolek-Folland, *Engendering Business: Men and Women in the Corporate Office, 1870–1930* (1994); Susan Levine, *Labor's True Woman: Carpet Weavers, Industrialization, and Labor Reform in the Gilded Age* (1984); David Montgomery, *The Fall of the House of Labor: The Workplace, the State, and American Labor Activism, 1865–1925* (1987); J. Carroll Moody and Alice Kessler-Harris, eds., *Perspectives on American Labor History: The Problems of Synthesis* (1989); Peter Rachleff, *Black Labor in Richmond, 1865–1890* (1984); Stephen J. Ross, *Workers on the Edge: Work, Leisure, and Politics in Industrializing Cincinnati, 1788–1890* (1985).

Industrial Conflict

Paul Avrich, *The Haymarket Tragedy* (1984); Robert C. Bannister, *Social Darwinism: Science and Myth in Anglo-America Social Thought* (1879); Mari Jo Buhle, *Women and American Socialism, 1870–1920* (1983); David P. Demerest, Jr., ed., *"The River Ran Red": Homestead 1892* (1992); David Montgomery, *Worker's Control in America: Studies in the History of Work, Technology, and Labor Struggles* (1979); Richard J. Oestreicher, *Solidarity and Fragmentation: Working People and Class Consciousness in Detroit* (1986); William Serrin, *Homestead: The Glory and the Tragedy of an American Steel Town* (1992); Shelton Stromquist, *A Generation of Boomers: The Pattern of Railroad Labor Conflict in Nineteenth-Century America* (1993); John L. Thomas, *Alternative America: Henry George, Edward Bellamy, Henry Demarest Lloyd, and the Adversary Tradition* (1987); Daniel J. Walkowitz, *Worker City, Company Town: Iron and Cotton-Workers Protest in Troy and Cohoes, New York, 1855–1884* (1978).

Chapter 19

The Growth of Urban America

Thomas J. Archdeacon, *Becoming American: An Ethnic History* (1983); Ronald H. Bayor and Timothy J. Meagher, eds., *The New York Irish* (1996); Selma Berrol, *East Side/East End: Eastern European Jews in London and New York, 1870–1920* (1994); John E. Bodnar, *The Transplanted: A History of Immigrants in Urban America* (1985); Roger Daniels, *Coming to America: A History of Immigration and Ethnicity in American Life* (1990); Kathie Friedman-Kasaba, *Memories of Migration: Gender, Ethnicity and Work in the Lives of Jewish and Italian Women in New York, 1870–1924* (1996); Lawrence H. Fuchs, *The American Kaleidoscope: Race, Ethnicity, and the Civic Culture* (1990); Susan A. Glenn, *Daughters of the Shtetl: Life and Labor in the Immigrant Generation* (1990); Kenneth L. Kusmer, *A Ghetto Takes Shape: Black Cleveland, 1870–1930* (1976); Mario Maffi, *Gateway to the Promised Land: Ethnic Cultures in New York's Lower East Side* (1995); Eric H. Monkkonen, *Police in Urban America, 1860–1920* (1981) and *America Becomes Urban: The*

Development of U.S. Cities and Towns, 1780–1980 (1988); Lucy E. Salyer, *Laws Harsh as Tigers: Chinese Immigrants and the Shaping of Modern Immigration Law* (1995); Henry L. Taylor, Jr., ed., *Race and the City: Work, Community, and Protest in Cincinnati, 1820–1970* (1993).

Middle-Class Society and Culture

Stuart Blumin, *The Emergence of the Middle Class: Social Experience in the American City, 1760–1900* (1989); Clifford E. Clark, Jr., *The American Family Home, 1800–1960* (1986); Judy Hilkey, *Character Is Capital: Success Manuals and Manhood in Gilded Age America* (1997); Helen L. Horowitz, *Alma Mater: Design and Experience in Women's Colleges from Their Nineteenth-Century Beginnings to the 1930s* (1984); John F. Kasson, *Rudeness and Civility: Manners in Nineteenth-Century Urban America* (1990); Alan M. Kraut, *Silent Travelers: Germs, Genes, and the "Immigrant Menace"* (1994); Angel Kwolek-Foland, *Engendering Business: Men and Women in the Corporate Office, 1870–1930* (1994); Steven Mintz and Susan Kellogg, *Domestic Revolutions: A Social History of American Family Life* (1988); Michael Oriard, *Reading Football* (1993); Thomas Schlereth, ed., *Victorian America: Transformations in Everyday Life* (1991); Barbara M. Solomon, *In the Company of Educated Women: A History of Women and Higher Education in America* (1985); Louise L. Stevenson, *The Victorian Homefront: American Thought and Culture, 1860–1880* (1991); Susan Strasser, *Satisfaction Guaranteed: The Making of the American Mass Market* (1989); David Tyack and Elisabeth Hansot, *Learning Together: A History of Coeducation in American Schools* (1990); Laurence R. Veysey, *The Emergence of the American University* (1965).

Working Class Politics and Reform

Jane Addams, *Twenty Years at Hull House* (1910); Allen F. Davis, *Spearheads for Reform: The Social Settlements and the Progressive Movement, 1890–1914* (1967); John Duffy, *The Sanitarians: A History of American Public Health* (1990); Timothy J. Gilfoyle, *City of Eros: New York City, Prostitution, and the Commercialization of Sex, 1790–1920* (1992); Lori Ginzberg, *Women and the Work of Benevolence: Morality, Politics, and Class in the Nineteenth-Century United States* (1990); Eric Homberger, *Scenes from the Life of a City: Corruption and Conscience in Old New York* (1994); Elisabeth Lasch-Quinn, *Black Neighbors: Race and the Limits of Reform in the American Settlement House Movement, 1890–1945* (1993); Henry F. May, *Protestant Churches and Industrial America* (1963); Peter McCaffery, *When Bosses Ruled Philadelphia: The Emergence of the Republican Machine, 1867–1933* (1993); William L. Riordan, ed., *Plunkitt of Tammany Hall* (1994); Shelia Rothman, *Living in the Shadow of Death: Tuberculosis and the Social Experience of Illness in American History* (1994).

Working-Class Leisure in the Immigrant City

Robert C. Allen, *Horrible Prettiness: Burlesque and American Culture* (1991); John C. Burnham, *Bad Habits: Drinking, Smoking, Taking Drugs, Gambling, Sexual Misbehavior, and Swearing in American History* (1993); Thomas Dublin, *Transforming Women's Work: New England Lives in the Industrial Revolution* (1994); Perry Duis, *The Saloon: Public Drinking in Chicago and Boston, 1880–1920* (1983); Elliot J.

Gorn, *The Manly Art: Bare-Knuckle Prize Fighting in America* (1986); Karen Halttunen, *Confidence Men and Painted Women: A Study of Middle-Class Culture in America, 1830–1870* (1982); Neil Harris, *Cultural Excursions: Marketing Appetites and Cultural Tastes in Modern America* (1990); John F. Kasson, *Amusing the Millions: Coney Island at the Turn of the Century* (1978); Peter Levine, *A. G. Spalding and the Rise of Baseball: The Promise of American Sport* (1985); Mary E. Odem, *Delinquent Daughters: Protecting and Policing Adolescent Female Sexuality in the United States, 1885–1920* (1995); Steven A. Riess, *City Games: The Evolution of American Urban Society and the Rise of Sports* (1995) and *Sport in Industrial America, 1850–1920* (1995); Roy Rosenzweig, *Eight Hours for What We Will: Workers and Leisure in an Industrial City, 1870–1920* (1983); Robert W. Snyder, *The Voice of the City: Vaudeville and Popular Culture in New York* (1989); James C. Whorton, *Crusaders for Fitness: The History of Health Reformers* (1984).

Cultures in Conflict

Edward A. Berlin, *King of Ragtime: Scott Joplin and His Era* (1993); Burton J. Bledstein, *The Culture of Professionalism: The Middle Class and the Development of Higher Education in America* (1976); Ruth Borodin, *Francis Willard: A Biography* (1986); Lawrence A. Cremin, *American Education: The Metropolitan Experience, 1876–1980* (1988); Robert Crunden, *American Salons: Encounters with European Modernism, 1885–1917* (1993); Helen Damon-Moore, *Magazines for the Millions: Gender and Commerce in the "Ladies Home Journal" and the "Saturday Evening Post," 1880–1910* (1994); Emory Elliott, ed., *Columbia Literary History of the United States* (1988); Jessica Foy and Thomas J. Schlereth, eds., *American Home Life, 1876–1915* (1992); Lori Ginsberg, *Women and the Work of Benevolence: Morality, Politics, and Class in the Nineteenth-Century United States* (1990); William F. Hartford, *Working People of Holyoke: Class and Ethnicity in a Massachusetts Mill Town, 1850–1960* (1990); Jacqueline Jones, *Labor of Love, Labor of Sorrow: Black Women, Work, and the Family from Slavery to the Present* (1985) and *The Dispossessed: America's Underclasses from the Civil War to the Present* (1992); S. J. Kleinberg, *The Shadow of the Mills: Working-Class Families in Pittsburgh, 1870–1907* (1989); T. J. Jackson Lears, *No Place of Grace: Antimodernism and the Transformation of American Culture, 1880–1920* (1981); Matthew Schneirov, *The Dream of a New Social Order: Popular Magazines in America, 1893–1914* (1994); Michael Shirley, *From Congregation Town to Industrial City: Culture and Social Change in a Southern Community* (1994); Olivier Zunz, *The Changing Face of Inequality: Urbanization, Industrial Development, and Immigrants in Detroit, 1880–1920* (1982).

Chapter 20
Party Politics in an Era of Social and Economic Upheaval

Peter H. Argersinger, "The Value of the Vote: Political Representation in the Gilded Age," *Journal of American History* 76 (June 1989): 59–90; Paula Baker *The Moral Framework of Public Life: Gender, Politics and the State in Rural New York, 1870–1930* (1991); Richard F. Hamm, *Shaping the Eighteenth Amendment: Temperance Reform, Legal Culture, and the Polity, 1880–1920* (1995); Richard J. Jensen, *The Winning of the*

Midwest: Social and Political Conflict, 1888–1896 (1971); David J. Rothman, *Politics and Power: The United States Senate, 1869–1901* (1966).

Politics of Privilege, Politics of Exclusion

Jane Dailey, Glenda E. Gilmore, and Bryant Simon, eds., *Jumpin' Jim Crow: Southern Politics from Civil War to Civil Rights* (2000); Louis R. Harlan, *Booker T. Washington: The Making of a Black Leader, 1865–1901* (1972) and *Booker T. Washington : The Wizard of Tuskegee, 1901–1915* (1983); Ari A. Hoogenboom, *Outlawing the Spoils: The Civil Service Movement* (1961); J. Morgan Kousser, *The Shaping of Southern Politics: Suffrage Restriction and the Establishment of the One-Party South* (1974); Alex Lichtenstein, *Twice the Work of Free Labor: The Political Economy of Convict Labor in the South* (1996); Matthew J. Mancini, *One Dies, Get Another: Convict Leasing in the American South, 1866–1928* (1996); Gerald W. McFarland, *Mugwumps, Morals, and Politics, 1884–1920* (1975); Neil R. McMillan, *Dark Journey: Black Mississippians in the Age of Jim Crow* (1989); John Sproat, *"The Best Men": Liberal Reformers in the Gilded Age* (1968); Howard N. Rabinowitz, *Race Relations in the Urban South* (1978); Allen Weinstein, *Prelude to Populism: Origins of the Silver Issue* (1970); C. Vann Woodward, *The Origins of the New South, 1877–1913* (1951).

The 1890s: Politics in a Depression Decade

Peter H. Argersinger, *The Limits of Agrarian Radicalism: Western Populism and American Politics* (1995); Gene Clanton, *Populism: The Humane Preference in America, 1890–1900* (1991); Stephen Cresswell, *Multiparty Politics in Mississippi, 1877–1902* (1995); Lawrence Goodwyn, *The Populist Moment: A Short History of the Agrarian Revolt in America* (1978); Steven Hahn, *The Roots of Southern Populism: Yeoman Farmers and the Transformation of the Georgia Upcountry, 1850–1890* (1983); Stephen Kantrowitz, *Ben Tillman and the Reconstruction of White Supremacy* (2000); Donald B. Marti, *Women of the Grange: Mutuality and Sisterhood in Rural America, 1866–1920* (1991); Megan J. McClintock, "Civil War Pensions and the Reconstruction of Union Families," *Journal of American History* 83 (September 1996): 456–480; Joanne Reitano, *The Tariff Question in the Gilded Age: The Great Debate of 1888* (1994); Richard Schneirov, *Labor and Urban Politics: Class Conflict and the Origins of Modern Liberalism in Chicago, 1864–97* (1998); Theda Skocpol, *Protecting Soldiers and Mothers: The Political Origins of Social Policy in the United States* (1992); Tom E. Terrill, *The Tariff, Politics, and American Foreign Policy, 1874–1901* (1973).

The Watershed Election of 1896

Peter H. Argersinger, " 'A Place on the Ballot': Fusion Politics and Antifusion Laws," *American Historical Review* 85 (April 1980): 287–306; Paolo E. Coletta, *William Jennings Bryan* (3 vols., 1964–1969); Robert F. Durden, *The Climax of Populism: The Election of 1896* (1965); Lewis L. Gould, *The Presidency of William McKinley* (1980); Elizabeth Sanders, *Roots of Reform: Farmers, Workers, and the American State, 1877–1917* (1999).

Expansionist Stirrings and War with Spain, 1878–1901

Robert L. Beisner, *Twelve Against Empire: The Anti-Imperialists, 1898–1900* (1968); H. W. Brands, *Bound to Empire: The United States and the Philippines* (1992); H. Paul Jeffers, *Colonel Roosevelt: Theodore Roosevelt Goes to War, 1897–1898* (1996); Walter LeFeber, *New Empire: American Expansionism, 1860–1898* (1963); Gerald F. Linderman, *The Mirror of War: American Society and the Spanish-American War* (1974); Ernest R. May, *American Imperialism* (1968); Glenn A. May, *Social Engineering in the Philippines: The Aims, Execution, and Impact of American Colonial Policy, 1900–1913* (1980); Stuart Creighton Miller, *"Benevolent Assimilation": The American Conquest of the Philippines, 1899–1903* (1982); Ian Mugridge, *The View from Xanadu: William Randolph Hearst and United States Foreign Policy* (1995); David Nasaw, *The Chief: The Life of William Randolph Hearst* (2000); Thomas J. Osborne, *"Empire Can Wait": American Opposition to Hawaiian Annexation, 1893–1898* (1981); Emily S. Rosenberg, *Spreading the American Dream: American Economic and Cultural Expansion, 1890–1945* (1982); Edward Van Zile Scott, *The Unwept: Black American Soldiers and the Spanish-American War* (1996): Mark Russell Shulman, *Navalism and the Emergence of American Sea Power, 1882–1893* (1995); John Edward Weems, *The Fate of the* Maine (1992); Richard E. Welch, *Response to Imperialism: The United States and the Philippine-American War* (1979).

Chapter 21

Society, Workers, Popular Culture

David Brody, *Workers in Industrial America: Essays on the Twentieth-Century Struggle*, 2d ed. (1985); Ardis Cameron, *Radicals of the Worst Sort: Laboring Women in Lawrence, Massachusetts, 1860–1912* (1993); John Whiteclay Chambers II, *The Tyranny of Change: America in the Progressive Era, 1890–1920* (1992); George Chauncey, *Gay New York: Gender, Urban Culture, and the Making of the Gay Male World, 1890–1940* (1994); Susan A. Glenn, *Daughters of the Shtetl: Life and Labor in the Immigrant Generation* (1990); Rick Halpern, *Down on the Killing Floor: Black and White Workers in Chicago's Packinghouses, 1904–1954* (1997); M. Alison Kihler, *Rank Ladies: Gender and Cultural Hierarchy in American Vaudeville* (1999); Gerald W. McFarland, *Inside Greenwich Village: A New York Neighborhood, 1898–1918* (2001); Kathy Peiss, *Cheap Amusements: Working Women and Leisure in Turn of the Century New York* (1986); Lauren Rabinovitz, *For the Love of Pleasure: Women, Movies, and Culture in Turn-of-the-Century Chicago* (1998); Christine Stansell, *American Moderns: Bohemian New York and the Creation of a New Century* (2000); Leon Stein, *The Triangle Fire* (1962; paperback, 2002).

The Progressive Impulse

Lawrence A. Cremin, *The Transformation of the Schools: Progressivism in American Education, 1876–1957* (1971); Allen F. Davis, *Spearheads for Reform: The Social Settlements and the Progressive Movement, 1890–1914*, 2d ed. (1984); Jacob H. Dorn, ed., *Socialism and Christianity in Early Twentieth Century America* (1998); Arthur S. Link and Richard L. McCormick, *Progressivism* (1983); Judith Ann Trolander, *Professionalism and Social Change: From the Settlement House Movement to Neighborhood Centers* (1987); Robert B. Westbrook, *John Dewey and American Democracy* (1991); Clarence E. Wunderlin, Jr., *Visions of a New Industrial Order: Social Science and Labor Theory in America's Progressive Era* (1992).

Urban Progressivism

John D. Buenker, *Urban Liberalism and Progressive Reform* (1973); James S. Connolly, *The Triumph of Ethnic Progressivism: Urban Political Culture in Boston, 1900–1925* (1998); Ruth H. Crocker, *Social Work and Social Order: The Settlement Movement in Two Industrial Cities, 1889–1930* (1992); Melvin G. Holli, *Reform in Detroit: Hazen S. Pingree and Urban Politics* (1969); Martin Paulson, *The Social Anxieties of Progressive Reform: Atlantic City, 1854–1920* (1994); Steven L. Piott, *Holy Joe: Joseph W. Folk and the Missouri Idea* (1997); Bradley R. Rice, *Progressive Cities: The Commission Government Movement in America, 1901–1920* (1977).

Moral Reform, Labor Relations, and Social Control

Paul Boyer, *Urban Masses and Moral Order in America, 1820–1920* (1978); Mark T. Connelly, *The Response to Prostitution in the Progressive Era* (1980); Mark H. Haller, *Eugenics: Hereditarian Attitudes in American Thought* (1963); Richard F. Hamm, *Shaping the Eighteenth Amendment: Temperance Reform, Legal Culture, and the Polity, 1880–1920* (1995); Alan M. Kraut, *Silent Travelers: Germs, Genes, and the "Immigrant Menace"* (1994); David Langum, *Crossing Over the Line: Legislating Morality and the Mann Act* (1994); Joseph A. McCartin, *Labor's Great War: The Struggle for Industrial Democracy and the Origins of Modern American Labor Relations, 1912–1921* (1997); John F. McClymer, *War and Welfare: Social Engineering in America, 1890–1925* (1980); Ruth Rosen, *The Lost Sisterhood: Prostitution in America, 1900–1918* (1982); Joseph F. Spillane, *Cocaine: From Medical Marvel to Modern Menace in the United States, 1884–1920* (2000); Peter Temin, *Taking Your Medicine: Drug Regulation in the United States* (1980).

Women in the Progressive Movement

Constance M. Chen, *"The Sex Side of Life": Mary Ware Dennett's Pioneering Battle for Birth Control and Sex Education* (1996); Ellen Chesler, *Woman of Valor: Margaret Sanger and the Birth Control Movement in America* (1992); Nancy F. Cott, *A Woman Making History: Mary Ritter Beard Through Her Letters* (1991); Ellen Carol DuBois, *Harriot Stanton Blatch and the Winning of Woman Suffrage* (1997); Margaret Finnegan, *Selling Suffrage: Consumer Culture and Votes for Women* (1999); Ellen Fitzpatrick, *Endless Crusade: Women Social Scientists and Progressive Reform* (1990); Sandra Haarsager, *Organized Womanhood: Cultural Politics in the Pacific Northwest, 1840–1920* (1997); Patricia Greenwood Harrison, *Connecting Links: The British and American Woman Suffrage Movements, 1900–1914* (2000); Ann J. Lane, *To Herland and Beyond: The Life and Work of Charlotte Perkins Gilman* (1990); Marian J. Morton, *Emma Goldman and the American Left* (1992); Robyn Muncy, *Creating a Female Dominion in American Reform, 1890–1935* (1991).

African-American Life and Thought

Garna L. Christian, *Black Soldiers in Jim Crow Texas, 1899–1917* (1995); Louis R. Harlan, *Booker T. Washington: Wizard of Tuskegee, 1901–1915* (1983); Charles F. Kellogg, *NAACP: The History of the National Association for the Advancement of Colored People, 1909–1920* (1967); David Levering Lewis, *W. E. B. DuBois: Biography of a Race* (1994); Joe W. Trotter, Jr., ed., *The Great Migration in Historical Perspective: New Dimensions of Race, Class, and Gender* (1991).

Progressivism in National Politics

Kendrick A. Clements, *The Presidency of Woodrow Wilson* (1992); Paola E. Coletta, *The Presidency of William Howard Taft* (1973); Lewis L. Gould, *The Presidency of Theodore Roosevelt* (1991); Nick Salvatore, *Eugene V. Debs* (1982); David Steigerwald, *Wilsonian Idealism in America* (1994); Melvin I. Urofsky, *Louis D. Brandeis and the Progressive Tradition* (1981); Bernard A. Weisberger, *The LaFollettes of Wisconsin: Love and Politics in Progressive America* (1994).

Progressives, Public Health, and the Environment

Stephen R. Fox, *The American Conservation Movement: John Muir and His Legacy* (1981); Lorine Swainston Goodwin, *The Pure Food, Drink, and Drug Crusaders, 1879–1914* (1999); Judith Walzer Leavitt, *Typhoid Mary: Captive to the Public Health* (1996); Carolyn Merchant, "Women of the Progressive Conservation Movement, 1900–1916," *Environmental Review* 8 (Spring 1984): 57–85; Elmo R. Richardson, "The Struggle for the Valley: California's Hetch Hetchy Controversy, 1905–1913," *California Historical Society Quarterly* 38 (1959): 249–258; Christopher C. Sellers, *Hazards of the Job: From Industrial Disease to Environmental Health Science* (1997); Nancy Tomes, *The Gospel of Germs: Men, Women, and the Microbe in American Life* (1998); Thurman Wilkins, *John Muir: Apostle of Nature* (1995).

Chapter 22

The United States in Latin America and Asia

Michael L. Coniff, *Panama and the United States: The Forced Alliance* (1992); Linda B. Hall, *Oil, Banks, and Politics: The United States and Post–Revolutionary Mexico, 1917–1923* (1995); Michael Hunt, *The Making of a Special Relationship: The United States and China to 1914* (1983); Friedrich Katz, *The Secret War in Mexico: Europe, the United States, and the Mexican Revolution* (1981); Walter LaFeber, *The Clash: A History of U.S.-Japanese Relations* (1997) and *The Panama Canal* (1979); Lester E. Langley, *The Banana Wars: An Inner History of American Empire, 1900–1934* (1983); David McCullough, *The Path Between the Seas: The Creation of the Panama Canal, 1870–1914* (1977); Nancy Mitchell, *The Danger of Dreams: German and American Imperialism in Latin America* (1999); Frank Ninkovich, *The Wilsonian Century: U.S. Foreign Policy Since 1900* (1999); James Reed, *The Missionary Mind and America's East Asian Policy, 1911–1915* (1983); Thomas Schoonover, *The United States in Central America, 1860–1911* (1991).

The Road to War, Wartime Diplomacy, and the Russian Revolution

Lloyd E. Ambrosius, *Woodrow Wilson and the American Diplomatic Tradition* (1987); Leo J. Bacino, *Reconstructing Russia: U.S. Policy in Revolutionary Russia, 1917–1922* (1999); David S. Fogelsong, *America's Secret War Against Bolshevism: U.S. Intervention and the Russian Civil War, 1917–1920* (1995); Lloyd C. Gardner, *Safe for Democracy: The Anglo American Response to Revolution, 1913–1923* (1984).

The Battlefield Experience

Thomas A. Britten, *American Indians in World War I: At Home and at War* (1997); John Whiteclay Chambers II, *To Raise an Army: The Draft in Modern America* (1987); Paul Fussell, *The Great War and Modern Memory* (1975); Martin Gilbert, *The First World War* (1994); Bernard Nalty, *Strength for the Fight: A History of Black Americans in the Military* (1986); Frank E. Vandiver, *Black Jack: The Life and Times of John J. Pershing* (1977).

The Government Mobilizes for War

Kathleen Burk, *Britain, America and the Sinews of War* (1985); Robert D. Cuff, *The War Industries Board* (1973); Ellis W. Hawley, *The Great War and the Search for a Modern Order*, 2d ed. (1992); K. Walter Hickel, "War, Region, and Social Welfare: Federal Aid to Servicemen's Dependents in the South, 1917–1921," *Journal of American History* (March 2001); Herbert A. Johnson, *Wingless Eagle: U.S. Army Aviation Through World War I* (2002); Jordan A. Schwartz, *The Speculator: Bernard M. Baruch in Washington, 1917–1965* (1981); Leila Zenderland, *Measuring Minds: Henry Herbert Goddard and the Origins of American Intelligence Testing* (1998).

American Society and Culture in World War I

Maurine W. Greenwald, *Women, War and Work* (1980); Jeffrey Haydu, *Making American Industry Safe for Democracy: Comparative Perspectives on the State and Employee Representation in the Era of World War I* (1967); Florette Henri, *Black Migration: Movement Northward, 1900–1920* (1975); John F. McClymer, *War and Welfare: Social Engineering in America, 1890–1925* (1980); Barbara J. Steinson, *American Women's Activism in World War I* (1982); Jacqueline van Voris, *Carrie Chapman Catt: A Public Life* (1987); Susan Zeiger, *In Uncle Sam's Service: Women Workers with the American Expeditionary Force, 1917–1919* (1999).

Patriotism, Dissent, and Repression

Ray H. Abrams, *Preachers Present Arms: The Role of the American Churches and Clergy in World Wars I and II* (1969); Bruce Clayton, *Forgotten Prophet: The Life of Randolph Bourne* (1984); Alfred E. Cornebise, *War as Advertised: The Four Minute Men and America's Crusade, 1917–1918* (1984); Leslie Midkiff DeBauche, *Reel Patriotism: The Movies and World War I* (1997); Christopher Gibbs, *The Great Silent Majority: Missouri's Resistance to World War I* (1988); Carol S. Gruber, *Mars and Minerva: World War I and the Uses of Higher Learning in America* (1975); Jeanette Keith, "The Politics of Southern Draft Resistance, 1917–1918: Class, Race, and Conscription in the Rural South," *Journal of American History* (March 2001); Michael Pearlman, *To Make Democracy Safe for America: Patricians and Preparedness in the Progressive Era* (1984); Harold C. Peterson and Gilbert Fite, *Opponents of War, 1917–1918* (1968); William Preston, Jr., *Aliens and Dissenters: Federal Suppression of Radicals, 1903–1933* (1966); Stephen Vaughn, *Holding Fast the Inner Lines: Democracy, Nationalism, and the Committee on Public Information* (1980).

Aftermath: Red Scare, Failed Peace, and Disillusionment

David Brody, *Labor in Crisis: The Steel Strike of 1919* (1965); Stanley A. Coben, *A. Mitchell Palmer: Politician* (1963); Arno Mayer, *Politics and Diplomacy of Peacemaking* (1967); Robert K. Murray, *Red Scare: A Study in National Hysteria, 1919–1920* (1955); Stewart I. Rochester, *American Liberal Disillusionment in the Wake of World War I* (1977); Klaus Schwabe, *Woodrow Wilson, Revolutionary Germany, and Peacemaking, 1918–1919* (1985); Ralph Stone, *The Irreconcilables: The Fight Against the League of Nations* (1970); William M. Tuttle, Jr., *Race Riot: Chicago in the Red Summer of 1919* (1970); Arthur J. Walworth, *Wilson and His Peacemakers* (1986); William C. Widenor, *Henry Cabot Lodge and the Search for an American Foreign Policy* (1980).

Chapter 23

Economic Trends, Labor Unions, the Environment

Guy Alchon, *The Invisible Hand of Planning: Capitalism, Social Science, and the State in the 1920s* (1985); John M. Barry, *Rising Tide: The Great Mississippi Flood of 1927 and How It Changed America* (1997); Irving Bernstein, *The Lean Years: A History of the American Worker, 1920–1933* (1966); Lizbeth Cohen, *Making a New Deal: Industrial Workers in Chicago, 1919–1939* (1990); Lynn Dumenil, *The Modern Temper: America in the 1920s* (1995); Gilbert C. Fite, *American Farmers: The New Minority* (1981); Jacqueline Dowd Hall, *Like a Family: The Making of a Southern Cotton Mill World* (1987); Angel Kwolek-Folland, *Engendering Business: Men and Women in the Corporate Office, 1870–1930* (1994); Roland Marchand, *Advertising the American Dream: Making Way for Modernity, 1920–1940* (1985); John A. Salmond, *Gastonia 1929: The Story of the Loray Mill Strike* (1995); Susan Strasser, *Satisfaction Guaranteed: The Making of the American Mass Market* (1989).

Politics, International Relations, Immigration Restriction

J. Leonard Bates, *Senator Thomas J. Walsh of Montana: Law and Public Affairs from TR to FDR* (1999); Thomas Buckley, *The United States and the Washington Conference, 1921–1922* (1970); Douglas B. Craig, *After Wilson: The Struggle for the Democratic Party, 1920–1934* (1992); L. Ethan Ellis, *Republican Foreign Policy, 1921–1933* (1968); John Earl Haynes, ed., *Calvin Coolidge and the Coolidge Era: Essays on the History of the 1920s* (1998); Donald R. McCoy, *Calvin Coolidge: The Quiet President* (1967); Charles L. Mee, *The Ohio Gang: The World of Warren G. Harding* (1981); Mae M. Ngai, "The Architecture of Race in American Immigration Law: A Reexamination of the Immigration Act of 1924," *Journal of American History* (June 1999); Daniela Spenser, *The Impossible Triangle: Mexico, Soviet Russia, and the United States in the 1920s* (1999).

Mass Culture

James J. Flink, *The Car Culture* (1975); Sumiko Higashi, *Cecil B. DeMille and American Culture: The Silent Era* (1994); Gwenyth L. Jackaway, *Media at War: Radio's Challenge to the Newspapers, 1924–1939* (1995); Lary May, *Screening Out the Past: The Birth of Mass Culture and the Motion Picture Industry* (1980); Susan Smulyan, *Selling Radio: The Commercialization of American Broadcasting, 1920–1934* (1994); Ruth Vasey, *The World According to Hollywood, 1918–1939* (1997).

Youth, Dissident Writers, Artists, and Intellectuals

Beth A. Bailey, *From Front Porch to Back Seat: Courtship in Twentieth-Century America* (1988); George Chauncey, *Gay New York: Gender, Urban Culture, and the Making of the Gay

Male World, 1890–1940 (1994); Douglas Clayton, *Floyd Dell: The Life and Times of an American Rebel* (1994); Stanley Coben, *Rebellion Against Victorianism: The Impetus for Cultural Change in 1920s America* (1991); Wanda M. Corn, *The Great American Thing: Modern Art and National Identity, 1915–1935* (2000); Paula Fass, *The Damned and the Beautiful: American Youth in the 1920s* (1977); Fred Hobson, *Mencken: A Life* 1994).

Women in the 1920s

Kristi Anderson, *After Suffrage: Women in Partisan and Electoral Politics Before the New Deal* (1996); Kathleen M. Blee, *Women and the Klan: Racism and Gender in the 1920s* (1991); Dorothy M. Brown, *Setting a Course: American Women in the 1920s* (1987); Nancy Cott, *The Grounding of Modern Feminism* (1987); Stanley Lemons, *The Woman Citizen: Social Feminism in the 1920s* (1973); Kathy Peiss, *Hope in a Jar: The Making of America's Beauty Culture* (1998); Leslie Woodcock Tentler, *Wage-Earning Women: Industrial Work and Family in the United States, 1900–1930* (1979).

African Americans, Jazz, the Harlem Renaissance

Ted Gioia, *The History of Jazz* (1997); David L. Lewis, *When Harlem Was in Vogue* (1981); Kathy H. Ogren, *The Jazz Revolution: Twenties America and the Meaning of Jazz* (1989); Gilbert Osofsky, *Harlem: The Making of a Ghetto* (1968); Burton W. Peretti, *The Creation of Jazz: Race and Culture in Urban America* (1992); Arnold Rampersand, *The Life of Langston Hughes* (2 vols., 1986–1988); Judith Stein, *The World of Marcus Garvey: Race and Class in Modern Society* (1985); Tyrone Tillery, *Claude McKay* (1992); Cheryl A. Wall, *Women of the Harlem Renaissance* (1995); Irma Watkins-Owens, *Blood Relations: Caribbean Immigrants and the Harlem Community, 1900–1930* (1996).

Hispanic Life and Culture

Jay P. Dolan et al., eds., *Mexican Americans and the Catholic Church, 1900–1965* (1994); Camille Guerin-Gonzales, *Mexican Workers and American Dreams: Immigration, Repatriation, and California Farm Labor, 1900–1939* (1994); David G. Gutiérrez, *Walls and Mirrors: Mexican Americans, Mexican Immigrants, and the Politics of Ethnicity* (1995); Martha Menchaca, *The Mexican Outsider: A Community History of Marginalization and Discrimination in California* (1995); F. Arturo Roasales, *¡Pobre Raza! Violence, Justice, and Mobilization among México Lindo Immigrants, 1900–1936* (1999).

Religious Trends

Edith L. Blumhofer, *Aimee Semple McPherson* (1993); Lyle W. Dorsett, *Billy Sunday and the Redemption of Urban America* (1991); Henry L. Feingold, *A Time for Searching: Entering the Mainstream, 1920–1945* [The Jewish People in America, Vol. 3] (1992); George M. Marsden, *Fundamentalism and American Culture* (1980); Martin E. Marty, *The Noise of Conflict, 1919–1941* [Modern American Religion, Vol. 2] (1991).

The Klan, Prohibition, Symbolic Events

Paul Avrich, *Sacco and Vanzetti: The Anarchist Background* (1991); Norman H. Clark, *Deliver Us From Evil: An Interpretation of American Prohibition* (1976); Robert A. Hohner, *Prohibition and Politics: The Life of Bishop James Cannon, Jr.* (1999); Kenneth T. Jackson, *The Ku Klux Klan in the City, 1915–1930* (1967); Edward J. Larson, *Summer for the Gods* [The Scopes Trial] (1997); Shawn Lay, ed., *The Invisible Empire in the West: Toward a New Historical Appraisal of the Ku Klux Klan in the 1920s* (1992); Leonard J. Moore, *Citizen Klansman: The Ku Klux Klan in Indiana, 1921–1928* (1991); Francis Russell, *Tragedy in Dedham: The Story of the Sacco-Vanzetti Case* (1971).

Herbert Hoover and the 1928 Election

David Burner, *Herbert Hoover: The Public Life* (1979); Kendrick A. Clements, *Hoover, Conservation, and Consumerism: Engineering the Good Life* (2000); E. Paula Elder, *Governor Alfred E. Smith: The Politician as Reformer* (1983); Ellis W. Hawley, ed., *Herbert Hoover as Secretary of Commerce* (1981); Allan J. Lichtman, *Prejudice and the Old Politics: The Presidential Election of 1928* (1979); George H. Nash, *The Life of Herbert Hoover* (3 vols., 1983–1996).

Chapter 24
Onset of the Depression, Hoover's Response

John A. Clausen, *American Lives: Looking Back at the Children of the Great Depression* (1993); John Kenneth Galbraith, *The Great Crash, 1929* (1961); John A. Garraty, *The Great Depression* (1986); Joan Hoff, *Herbert Hoover: Forgotten Progressive* (1975); Robert S. McElvaine, ed., *Down and Out in the Great Depression* (1983); George H. Nash, *Life of Herbert Hoover*, vol. 3 (1996); John Shover, *Cornbelt Rebellion: The Farmers' Holiday Association* (1965); Peter Temin, *Did Monetary Forces Cause the Great Depression?* (1976) and *Lessons from the Great Depression* (1989); Studs Terkel, *Hard Times* (1970).

The New Deal Era: Biographical Studies

Jeanne Nienaber Clarke, *Roosevelt's Warrior: Harold L. Ickes and the New Deal* (1996); Blanche Wiesen Cook, *Eleanor Roosevelt*, vol. 2, 1933–1938 (1999); William Ivy Hair, *The Kingfish and His Realm: The Life and Times of Huey P. Long* (1991); J. Joseph Huchmacher, *Robert F. Wagner and the Rise of Urban Liberalism* (1968); Sean J. Savage, *Roosevelt: The Party Leader, 1932–1945* (1991); Jordan Schwarz, *The New Dealers: Power Politics in the Age of Roosevelt* (1993); Geoffrey C. Ward, *Before the Trumpet: The Young Franklin D. Roosevelt* (1985) and *A First-Class Temperament: The Emergence of Franklin Roosevelt* (1989).

The New Deal: General Studies and Assessments

Edwin Amenta, *Bold Relief: Institutional Politics and the Origins of Modern Social Policy* (1998); Anthony J. Badger, *The New Deal* (1989); William J. Barber, *Designs Within Disorder: Franklin D. Roosevelt, the Economists, and the Shaping of American Economic Policy, 1933–1945* (1996); Matthew J. Dickinson, *Bitter Harvest: FDR, Presidential Power, and the Growth of the Presidential Branch* (1997); Gerald H. Gamm, *The Making of New Deal Democrats: Voting Behavior and Realignment in Boston, 1920–1940* (1989); Mark Leff, *The Limits of Symbolic Reform: The New Deal and Taxation, 1933–1939* (1984); David Plotke, *Building a Democratic Political Order: Reshaping American Liberalism in the 1930s and 1940s* (1996); Theodore Rosenof, *Economics in the Long Run: New Deal Theorists and Their Legacies* (1997); G. Edward White, *The Constitution and the New Deal* (2000).

The Early New Deal

Bernard Bellush, *The Failure of NRA* (1975); Walter L. Creese, *TVA's Public Planning: The Vision, the Reality* (1990); Otis L. Graham, Jr., *Toward a Planned Society: From Roosevelt to Nixon* (1976); Nancy L. Grant, *TVA and Black Americans: Planning for the Status Quo* (1990); Peter H. Irons, *The New Deal Lawyers* (1982); Van L. Perkins, *Crisis in Agriculture: The AAA and the New Deal* (1969).

The Later New Deal

Kenneth J. Bindas, *All of This Music Belongs to the Nation: The WPA's Federal Music Project and American Society* (1995); Alan Brinkley, *Voices of Protest: Huey Long, Father Coughlin, and the Great Depression* (1982); Michael R. Grey, *New Deal Medicine: The Rural Health Programs of the Farm Security Administration* (1999); William F. MacDonald, *Federal Relief Administration and the Arts* (1969); Marlene Park and Gerald Markowitz, *Democratic Vistas: Post Offices and Public Art in the New Deal* (1984); Charles McKinley and Robert W. Frase, *Launching Social Security* (1970); Nancy J. Weiss, *Farewell to the Party of Lincoln: Black Politics in the Age of FDR* (1983).

The Dust Bowl, the West, Environmental Issues

Carl Abbott, "The Federal Presence," in Clyde A. Milner II et al., eds., *The Oxford History of the American West* (1994); Stephen Fox, *The American Conservation Movement*, ch. 6, "Franklin D. Roosevelt and New Deal Conservation" (1985); James N. Gregory, *American Exodus: The Dust Bowl Migration and Okie Culture in California* (1989); Richard Lowitt, *The New Deal and the West* (1984); Pamela Riney-Kehrberg, *Rooted in Dust: Surviving Drought and Depression in Southwestern Kansas* (1994); Joseph E. Taylor, *Making Salmon: An Environmental History of the Northwest Fisheries* (1999); Donald Worster, *Dust Bowl* (1979) and *Rivers of Empire: Water, Aridity, and the Growth of the American West* (1985).

Conservative Opposition, the End of the New Deal

Alan Brinkley, *The End of Reform: New Deal Liberalism in Recession and War* (1995); Dewey W. Grantham, *The Democratic South* (1963); James T. Patterson, *Congressional Conservatives and the New Deal* (1967); Milton Plesur, "The Republican Congressional Comeback of 1938," *Review of Politics* 24 (1962): 525–562; Clyde P. Weed, *The Nemesis of Reform: The Republican Party During the New Deal* (1984).

Social Trends and Labor Acitivism in the 1930s

Sidney Fine, *Sitdown: The General Motors Strike of 1936–1937* (1969); Gary Gerstle, *Working-Class Americanism: The Politics of Labor in a Textile City, 1914–1960* (1989); Cheryl Lynn Greenberg, *"Or Does It Explode?": Black Harlem in the Great Depression* (1991); David G. Gutiérrez, *Walls and Mirrors: Mexican Americans, Mexican Immigrants, and the Politics of Ethnicity* (1995); Janet Irons, *Testing the New Deal: The General Textile Strike of 1934 in the American South* (2000); Nelson Lichtenstein, *The Most Dangerous Man in Detroit: Walter Reuther and the Fate of American Labor* (1995); Paul K. Longmore and David Goldberger, "The League of the Physically Handicapped and the Great Depression: A Case Study of the New Disability History," *Journal of American History* (December 2000); Timothy P. Lynch, *Strike Songs of the Depression* (2001); Richard A. Reiman, *The New Deal and American Youth* (1992); Lois Scharf, *To Work and to Wed: Female Employment, Feminism, and the Great Depression* (1980); Catherine McNichol Stock, *Main Street in Crisis: The Great Depression and the Old Middle Class on the Northern Plains* (1992); Susan Ware, *Beyond Suffrage: Women and the New Deal* (1981) and *Holding Their Own: American Women in the 1930s* (1982); Jill Watts, *God, Harlem U.S.A.: The Father Divine Story* (1992); Devra Weber, *Dark Sweat, White Gold: California Farm Workers, Cotton, and the New Deal* (1994); Marsha L. Weisiger, *Land of Plenty: Oklahomans in the Cotton Fields of Arizona, 1933–1942* (1995).

Cultural Trends in the Great Depression and New Deal Era

Matthew Baigell, *The American Scene: Painting in the 1930s* (1974); Lili Corbus Bezner, *Photography and Politics in America: From the New Deal into the Cold War* (1999); Laura Browder, *Rousing the Nation: Radical Culture in Depression America* (1998); Terry A. Cooney, *Balancing Acts: American Thought and Culture in the 1930s* (1995); Malcolm Goldstein, *The Political State: American Drama and Theatre of the Great Depression* (1974); Harvey Klehr, *The Heyday of American Communism: The Depression Decade* (1984); Jeffrey Meikle, *Twentieth-Century Limited: Industrial Design in America, 1925–1939* (1979); Guiliana Muscio, *Hollywood's New Deal* (1997); Richard H. Pells, *Radical Visions and American Dreams: Culture and Social Thought in the Depression Years* (1973); William Stott, *Documentary Expression and Thirties America* (1973); Douglas Wixon, *Worker-Writer in America: Jack Conroy and the Tradition of Midwestern Literary Radicalism, 1898–1990* (1994).

Chapter 25
The Coming of War

Joanna Bourke, *The Second World War: A People's History* (2002); Steven Casey, *Cautious Crusade: Franklin D. Roosevelt, American Public Opinion, and the War Against Nazi Germany* (2001); Patricia Clavin, *The Failure of Economic Diplomacy: Britain, Germany, France, and the United States, 1931–1936* (1996); Robert Cohen, *When the Old Left Was Young: America's First Mass Student Movement, 1929–1941* (1993); Wayne S. Cole, *Roosevelt and the Isolationists, 1932–1945* (1983); Robert A. Divine, *The Reluctant Belligerent* (1979); Thomas N. Guinsburg, *The Pursuit of Isolation in the United States Senate from Versailles to Pearl Harbor* (1982); Fredrick B. Pike, *FDR's Good Neighbor Policy* (1995); David S. Wyman, *Paper Walls: America and the Refugee Crisis, 1938–1941* (1985).

The Battlefront

Joseph Bendersky, *The "Jewish Threat": Anti-Semitic Politics of the U.S. Army* (2000); Ed Cray, *General of the Army: George C. Marshall, Soldier and Statesman* (1990); Michael Doubler, *Closing with the Enemy: How GIs Fought the War in Europe* (1994); John Ellis, *Brute Force: Allied Strategy and Tactics in the Second World War* (1990); Lee Kennett, *G.I.: The American Soldier in World War II* (1987); Gerald F. Linderman, *The World Within War: America's Combat Experience in World War II* (1997); Peter Schrijvers, *The Crash of Ruin: American Combat Soldiers in Europe* (1998); Michael Sherry, *The Rise of American Air Power* (1987); Ronald H. Spector, *Eagle Against the Sun: The American War with Japan* (1984); Mark Stoler, *Allies and*

Adversaries: The Joint Chiefs of Staff, the Grand Alliance, and U.S. Strategy in World War II (2000).

America Mobilizes for War

Stephen Adams, *Mr. Kaiser Goes to War* (1998); Amy Bentley, *Eating for Victory: Food Rationing and the Politics of Domesticity* (1998); Keith Eiler, *Mobilizing America: Robert P. Patterson and the War Effort, 1940–1945* (1997); George Q. Flynn, *The Draft, 1940–1973* (1993); Mark S. Foster, *Henry J. Kaiser: Builder in the Modern American West* (1989); Gerd Horten, *Radio Goes to War: The Cultural Politics of Propaganda During World War II* (2001); John W. Jeffries, *Wartime America: The World War II Home Front* (1996); Paul A. C. Koistinen, *The Military-Industrial Complex: A Historical Perspective* (1980); Nelson Lichtenstein, *Labor's War at Home: The CIO in World War II* (1983); David R. Segal, *Recruiting for Uncle Sam: Citizenship and Military Manpower Policy* (1989); Bradley F. Smith, *The Shadow Warriors: The OSS and the Origins of the CIA* (1983); B. H. Sparrow, *From the Outside In: World War II and the American State* (1996); Michael Sweeney, *Secrets of Victory: The Office of Censorship and the American Press and Radio in World War II* (2001).

War and American Society

Alison R. Bernstein, *American Indians and World War II* (1991); Allan Berube, *Coming Out Under Fire: The History of Gay Men and Women in World War II* (1990); Dominic Capeci and Martha Wilkerson, *Layered Violence: The Detroit Rioters of 1943* (1991); Roger Daniels, *Prisoners Without Trial* (1993); John D'Emilio, *Sexual Politics, Sexual Communities: The Making of a Homosexual Minority in the United States* (1983); Jere Bishop Franco, *Crossing the Pond: The Native American Effort in World War II* (1999); Frank Furedi, *The Silent War: Imperialism and the Changing Perception of Race* (1998); Mario T. Garcia, *Mexican-Americans: Leadership, Ideology, and Identity, 1930–1960* (1989); Maureen Honey, *Creating Rosie the Riveter: Class, Gender, and Propaganda During World War II* (1984); Walter Jackson, *Gunnar Myrdal and America's Conscience* (1990); Andrew Edmund Kerston, *Race, Jobs, and the War: The FEPC in the Midwest, 1941–1946* (2000); Amy Kesselman, *Fleeting Opportunities: Women Shipyard Workers in Portland and Vancouver During World War II and Reconversion* (1990); Daniel Kryder, *Divided Arsenal: Race and the American State During World War II* (2000); Deborah E. Lipstadt, *Beyond Belief: The American Press and the Coming of the Holocaust* (1993); Ruth Milkman, *Gender at Work: The Dynamics of Job Discrimination by Sex During World War II* (1987); Merl Reed, *Seedtime for the Modern Civil Rights Movement* (1991); George H. Roeder, Jr., *The Censored War: American Visual Experience During World War II* (1993); Viki Ruiz, *Cannery Women, Cannery Lives: Mexican Women, Unionization, and the California Food Processing Industry* (1987); Page Smith, *Democracy on Trial: The Japanese American Evacuation and Relocation in World War II* (1995); Kevin Starr, *Embattled Dreams: California in War and Peace, 1940–1950* (2002); Ronald Takaki, *Double Victory: A Multicultural History of America in World War II* (2000); Frank Warren, *Noble Extractions: American Liberal Intellectuals and World War II* (1999).

Triumph and Tragedy

Gar Alperovitz, *Atomic Diplomacy: Hiroshima and Potsdam*, rev. ed. (1995); Russell D. Buhite, *Decision at Yalta* (1986); John Chappell, *Before the Bomb: How America Approached the End of the Pacific War* (1997); Wayne S. Cole, *Roosevelt and the Isolationists, 1932–1945* (1983); Waldo Heinrichs, Jr., *Threshold of War* (1988); Gregg Herken, *The Winning Weapon: The Atomic Bomb in the Cold War, 1945–1950* (1980); Michael J. Hogan, ed., *Hiroshima in History and Memory* (1996); James H. Madison, ed., *Wendell Wilkie: Hoosier Internationalist* (1992); Verne Newton, ed., *FDR and the Holocaust* (1996); Keith Sainsbury, *Churchill and Roosevelt at War* (1994); Leon Sigal, *Fighting to a Finish* (1995); John Ray Skates, *The Invasion of Japan, Alternative to the Bomb* (1994); J. Samuel Walker, *Prompt and Utter Destruction: Truman and the Use of Atomic Bombs Against Japan* (1997); Donald Watt, *How War Came* (1989).

Chapter 26

The Postwar Political Setting

Len Ackland, *Making a Real Killing: Rocky Flats and the Nuclear West* (1999); John Culver and John Hyde, *American Dreamer: The Life and Times of Henry A. Wallace* (2000); Kari Frederickson, *The Dixiecrat Revolt and the End of the Solid South, 1932–1968* (2001); Michele Stenehjem Gerber, *On the Home Front: The Cold War Legacy of the Hanford Nuclear Site* (1992); William Graebner, *The Age of Doubt: American Thought and Culture in the 1940s* (1991); Sean Savage, *Truman and the Democratic Party* (1998).

Anticommunism and Containment

H. W. Brands, *The Devil We Knew: Americans and the Cold War* (1993); Gregory Fossedal, *Our Finest Hour: Will Clayton, The Marshall Plan and the Triumph of Democracy* (1993); Michael Hogan, *The Marshall Plan* (1987); Robert H. Johnson, *Improbable Dangers: U.S. Perceptions of Threat in the Cold War and After* (1994); Deborah Welch Larson, *Anatomy of Mistrust: U.S.-Soviet Relations During the Cold War* (1997); I. J. McCormick, *America's Half Century: United States Foreign Policy in the Cold War* (1992); Wilson Miscamble, *George F. Kennan and the Making of American Foreign Policy* (1992); David Painter, *Oil and the American Century* (1986); Ronald Powaksi, *The Cold War: The United States and the Soviet Union, 1917–1991* (1998); Arch Puddington, *Broadcasting Freedom: The Cold War Triumph of Radio Free Europe and Radio Liberty* (2000); David Rudgers, *Creating the Secret State: The Origins of the Central Intelligence Agency, 1943–1947* (2000); H. Schaffer, *Chester Bowles: New Dealer in the Cold War* (1993).

The Cold War in Asia

Roy Appleman, *Disaster in Korea* (1992); Thomas Christensen, *Useful Adversaries* (1996); June Grasso, *Harry Truman's Two-China Policy* (1987); John Halliday and Bruce Cumings, *Korea: The Unknown War* (1989); Andrew Rotter, *The Path to Vietnam* (1987); Stanley Sandler, *The Korean War: No Victors, No Vanquished* (1999); Howard Schonberger, *Aftermath of War: Americans and the Remaking of Japan* (1989); William Stueck, *The Korean War: An International History* (1995); Stanley Weintraub, *MacArthur's War: Korea and the Undoing of an American Hero* (2000); Shu Guang Zhang, *Deterrence and Strategic Culture: Chinese-American Confrontations* (1993).

The Politics of Anticommunism

Paul Boyer, *By the Bomb's Early Light* (1985); Nadine Cohodas, *Strom Thurmond and the Politics of Southern Change* (1993); Marjorie Garber and Rebecca Walkowitz, eds., *Secret Agents: The Rosenberg Case, McCarthyism, and Fifties America* (1995);

Harvey Klehr and Ronald Radosh, *The Amerasia Spy Case* (1996); Joel Kovel, *Red Hunting in the Promised Land* (1994); David Krugler, *The Voice of America and the Domestic Propaganda Battle, 1945–1953* (2000); Robbie Lieberman, *The Strangest Dream: Communism, Anticommunism, and the U.S. Peace Movement, 1945–1963* (2000); Greg Mitchell, *Tricky Dick and the Pink Lady: Richard Nixon vs. Helen Gahagan Douglas—Sexual Politics and the Red Scare, 1950* (1998); Ronald Radosh and Joyce Milton, *The Rosenberg File* (1983); Raye C. Ringholz, *Uranium Frenzy: Boom and Bust on the Colorado Plateau* (1989); Hal Rothman, *On Rims and Ridges: The Los Alamos Area Since 1880* (1992); Arthur Sabin, *In Calmer Times: The Supreme Court and Red Monday* (1999); Ellen Schrecker, *Many Are the Crimes: McCarthyism in America* (1998); Jessica Wang, *American Scientists in an Age of Anxiety: Scientists, Anticommunism, and the Cold War* (1999); Stephen Whitfield, *The Culture of the Cold War,* rev. ed. (1996).

Chapter 27

The Eisenhower Administration

Elizabeth Huckaby, *Crisis at Central High: Little Rock, 1957–1958* (1980); Tom Lewis, *Divided Highways: Building the Interstate Highways, Transforming American Life* (1997); Richard Melanson and David Mayers, eds., *Reevaluating Eisenhower* (1986); Nicol Rae, *The Decline and Fall of the Liberal Republicans* (1989); David W. Reinhard, *The Republican Right Since 1945* (1983); Mark Rose, *Interstate: Express Highway Politics, 1941–1956* (1979).

Foreign Affairs

David Anderson, *Trapped by Success: The Eisenhower Administration and Vietnam* (1991); Howard Ball, *Justice Downwind: America's Nuclear Testing Program in the 1950s* (1986); John Fousek, *The Leader of the Free World: American Nationalism and the Cultural Roots of the Cold War* (2000); John Gaddis, *We Now Know: Rethinking Cold War History* (1997); Walter L. Hixson, *Parting the Curtain: Propaganda, Culture, and the Cold War, 1945–1961* (1997); Richard Immerman, *John Foster Dulles: Piety, Pragmatism, and Power in U.S. Foreign Policy* (1999); Burton Kaufman, *The Arab Middle East and the United States* (1996); Gabriel Kolko, *Confronting the Third World* (1988); Andrew Rotter, *The Path to Vietnam* (1987); Frances Stonor Saunders, *The Cultural Cold War: The CIA and the World of Arts and Letters* (1999).

The Affluent Society

Len Ackland, *Making a Real Killing: Rocky Flats and the Nuclear West* (1999); David P. Calleo, *The Imperious Economy* (1982); Daniel Clark, *Like Night and Day: Unionization in a Southern Mill Town* (1997); Joshua B. Freeman, *Working-Class New York: Life and Labor Since World War II* (2000); Owen D. Gutfreund, *20th Century Sprawl: Accommodating the Automobile and the Decentralization of the United States* (2002); Donald Katz, *Home Fires: An Intimate Portrait of One Middle-Class Family in Postwar America* (1992); Linda Lear, *Rachel Carson: Witness for Nature* (1997); Thomas Maier, *Dr. Spock* (1998); J. R. Oakley, *God's Country: America in the Fifties* (1986); Gregory Randall, *America's Original GI Town: Park Forest, Illinois* (2000); Jon C. Teaford, *Post-Suburbia: Government and Politics in the Edge Cities* (1997).

Culture and Conservatism

Craig Allen, *Eisenhower and the Mass Media: Peace, Prosperity, and Prime-Time TV* (1993); James Baughman, *The Republic of Mass Culture: Journalism, Filmmaking, and Broadcasting Since 1941* (1992); Daniel Belgrad, *The Culture of Spontaneity: Improvisation and the Arts in Cold War America* (1998); William Boddy, *Fifties Television: The Industry and Its Critics* (1994); Joel Carpenter, *Revive Us Again: The Reawakening of American Fundamentalism* (1997); Michael Coyne, *The Crowded Prairie: American National Identity in the Hollywood Western* (1997); Paul N. Edwards, *The Closed World: Computers and the Politics of Discourse in Cold War America* (1996); Joel Foreman, ed., *The Other Fifties: Interrogating Midcentury American Icons* (1997); Owen Lynch, *Selling Catholicism: Bishop Sheen and the Power of Television* (1998); Lynn Spigel, *Make Room for TV* (1992); Ella Taylor, *Prime-Time Families: Television Culture in Postwar America* (1989); Alan M. Wald, *The New York Intellectuals* (1987).

Women's History

S. Paige Baty, *American Monroe: The Making of a Body Politic* (1995); Wini Breines, *Young, White, and Miserable: Growing Up Female in the Fifties* (1992); Stephanie Coontz, *The Way We Never Were* (1992); Eugenia Kaledin, *Mothers and More: American Women in the 1950s* (1984); Leila Rupp and Verta Taylor, *Survival in the Doldrums* (1987); Rickie Solinger, *Wake Up Little Susie: Single Pregnancy and Race Before Roe v. Wade* (1992).

The Other America

Bruce Adelson, *Brushing Back Jim Crow: The Integration of Minor League Baseball in the American South* (1999); Michael Bertrand, *Race, Rock, and Elvis* (2000); Thomas Cripps, *Making Movies Black: The Hollywood Message Movie from World War II to the Civil Rights Era* (1993); Donald Fixico, *Termination and Relocation: Federal Indian Policy, 1945–1970* (1986); Maria Cristina Garcia, *Havana USA: Cuban Exiles and Cuban Americans in South Florida, 1959–1994* (1996); Mario Garcia, *Mexican Americans: Leadership, Ideology, and Identity, 1930–1960* (1989); James Miller, *Flowers in the Dustbin: The Rise of Rock and Roll, 1947–1977* (1999); Grace Palladino, *Teenagers* (1996); Linda Reed, *Simple Decency and Common Sense* (1992); James Salem, *The Late Great Johnny Ace and the Transition from R&B to Rock'n'Roll* (1999); Thomas J. Sugrue, *The Origins of the Urban Crisis* (1996); Stuart Svonkin, *Jews Against Prejudice* (1997); Brian Ward, *Just My Soul Responding: Rhythm and Blues, Black Consciousness, and Race Relations* (1998); Steven Watson, *The Birth of the Beat Generation* (1995).

Chapter 28

The Kennedy Presidency

Thomas Brown, *JFK: History of an Image* (1988); James Giglio, *The Presidency of John F. Kennedy* (1991); Jim F. Heath, *Decade of Disillusionment: The Kennedy-Johnson Years* (1975); Seymour Hersh, *The Dark Side of Camelot* (1997); Bruce Miroff, *Pragmatic Illusions: The Presidential Politics of JFK* (1976); Herbert Parmet, *Jack* (1980) and *JFK* (1983); Mark White, ed., *Kennedy: The New Frontier Revisited* (1998).

Foreign Affairs

James Arnold, *The First Domino* (1991); Bernard Firestone, *The Quest for Nuclear Stability* (1982); Lawrence Freedman, *Kennedy's Wars: Berlin, Cuba, Laos, and Vietnam* (2000); Aleksandr Fursenko and Timothy Naftali, *'One Hell of a Gamble': Khrushchev, Castro, and Kennedy, 1958–1964* (1998); John Girling, *America and the Third World* (1980); Michael Latham, *Modernization as Ideology: American Social Science and "Nation Building" in the Kennedy Era* (2000); Richard Mahoney, *JFK: Ordeal in Africa* (1983); Ernest R. May and Philip D. Zelikow, eds., *The Kennedy Tapes: Inside the White House During the Cuban Missile Crisis* (1997); Philip Nash, *The Other Missiles of October: Eisenhower, Kennedy, and the Jupiters, 1957–1963* (1998); Deborah Shapley, *Promises and Power: The Life and Times of Robert McNamara* (1993); Mark White, *Missiles in Cuba: Kennedy, Khrushchev, Castro and the 1962 Crisis* (1997).

Liberalism Ascendant

E. Berkowitz and Kim McQuaid, *Creating the Welfare State* (1992); Irving Bernstein, *Guns or Butter: The Presidency of Lyndon Johnson* (1996); Michael R. Beschloss, *Taking Charge: The Johnson White House Tapes, 1963–1964* (1997); Michael Katz, *The Undeserving Poor: From the War on Poverty to the War on Welfare* (1989); Robert Mann, *The Walls of Jericho: Lyndon Johnson, Hubert Humphrey, Richard Russell, and the Struggle for Civil Rights* (1996); Charles Morris, *A Time of Passion* (1984); Charles Murray, *Losing Ground: American Social Policy, 1950–1980* (1984); Nicol Rae, *The Decline and Fall of the Liberal Republicans* (1989); Gregory Schneider, *Cadres for Conservatism: Young Americans for Freedom and the Rise of the Contemporary Right* (1999); Kent Schuparra, *Triumph of the Right: The Rise of the California Conservative Movement, 1945–1966* (1998); Jeff Shesol, *Mutual Contempt: Lyndon Johnson, Robert Kennedy, and the Feud that Defined the Decade* (1997); D. Zarefsky, *President Johnson's War on Poverty: Rhetoric and History* (1986).

The Struggle for Black Equality

Taylor Branch, *Parting the Waters: America in the King Years* (1988); Elaine Brown, *A Taste of Power: A Black Woman's Story* (1992); Michael K. Brown, *Race, Money, and the American Welfare State* (1999); Eric Burner, *And Gently He Shall Lead Them: Robert Parris Moses and Civil Rights in Mississippi* (1994); Clayborne Carson, *In Struggle: SNCC and the Black Awakening of the 1960s* (1981); David Chappell, *Inside Agitators: White Southerners in the Civil Rights Movement* (1994); E. C. Clark, *The Schoolhouse Door: Segregation's Last Stand at the University of Alabama* (1993); W. M. Dulaney and Kathleen Underwood, eds., *Essays on the American Civil Rights Movement* (1993); James Gwynne, ed., *Malcolm X—Justice Seeker* (1993); James C. Hall, *Mercy, Mercy Me: African-American Culture and the American Sixties* (2001); Robert Lieberman, *Shifting the Color Line: Race and the American Welfare State* (1998); K. Mills, *This Little Light of Mine: The Life of Fannie Lou Hamer* (1993); James Ralph, Jr., *Northern Protest: Martin Luther King, Jr., Chicago, and the Civil Rights Movement* (1993); Mark Stern, *Calculating Visions: Kennedy, Johnson and Civil Rights* (1992); Frederick Wirt, *"We Ain't What We Was": Civil Rights in the New South* (1997); Joe Wood, ed., *Malcolm X: In Our Own Image* (1992).

Voices of Protest

Dennis Deslippe, *"Rights, Not Roses": Unions and the Rise of Working-Class Feminism, 1945–80* (2000); Juan Gonzalez, *Harvest of Empire: A History of Latinos in America* (2000); Michael Jones-Correa, *Between Two Nations: The Political Predicament of Latinos in New York City* (1998); Carlos Munoz, Jr., *Youth, Identity, Power: Chicano Movement* (1989); Joanne Nagel, *American Indian Ethnic Renewal: Red Power and the Resurgence of Identity and Culture* (1996); Juan Gomez Quinones, *Chicano Politics: Reality and Promise, 1940–1990* (1990); Ruth Rosen, *The World Split Open: How the Modern Women's Movement Changed America* (2000); Douglas Rossinow, *The Politics of Authenticity: Liberalism, Christianity, and the New Left in America* (1998); Vicki L. Ruiz, *From Out of the Shadows: Mexican Women in Twentieth-Century America* (1998); Paul Chaat Smith and Robert Allen Warrior, *Like a Hurricane: The Indian Movement from Alcatraz to Wounded Knee* (1996); Benson Tong, *The Chinese Americans* (2000); Kate Weigand, *Red Feminism: American Communism and the Making of Women's Liberation* (2001).

The Vietnam War

David Anderson, *Trapped by Success* (1991); C. Appey, *Working Class War* (1992); Eric Bergerud, *The Dynamics of Defeat* (1991); Robert Buzzanco, *Masters of War: Military Dissent and Politics in the Vietnam Era* (1996); Phillip Davidson, *Vietnam at War* (1991); Lloyd Gardner, *Pay Any Price: Lyndon Johnson and the Wars for Vietnam* (1995); George Herring, *LBJ and Vietnam* (1995); Gary Hess, *Vietnam and the United States* (1990); David Levy, *The Debate over Vietnam* (1990); Robert J. McMahon, *The Limits of Empire: The United States and Southeast Asia Since World War II* (1999); Joseph G. Morgan, *The Vietnam Lobby: The American Friends of Vietnam, 1955–1975* (1997); Jeffrey Record, *The Wrong War: Why We Lost in Vietnam* (1998); Orrin Schwab, *Defending the Free World: John F. Kennedy, Lyndon Johnson, and the Vietnam War, 1961–1965* (1998); Robert Tomes, *Apocalypse Then: American Intellectuals and the Vietnam War, 1954–1975* (1998); Fred Turner, *Echoes of Combat: The Vietnam War in American Memory* (1996); Marilyn Young, *The Vietnam Wars* (1991).

Chapter 29
The Youth Movement and the Counterculture

Beth Bailey, *Sex in the Heartland* (1999); Wini Breines, *Community and Organization in the New Left* (1989); Paul Buhle, ed., *History and the New Left: Madison, Wisconsin, 1950–1970* (1989); Peter Collier and David Horowitz, *Destructive Generation: Second Thoughts About the Sixties* (1989); C. DeBenedetti and C. Chatfield, *An American Ordeal: The Antiwar Movement of the Vietnam Era* (1990); John D'Emilio, William Turner, and Urvashi Vaid, eds., *Creating Change: Sexuality, Public Policy, and Civil Rights* (2000); Donald A. Downs, *Cornell '69: Liberalism and the Crisis of the American University* (1999); David Farber, *Chicago '68* (1988) and *The Age of Great Dreams: America in the 1960s* (1994); Lewis Gann and Peter Duignan, *The New Left and the Cultural Revolution of the 1960s: A Reevaluation* (1995); Todd Gitlin, *The Sixties: Years of Hope, Days of Rage* (1987); David L. Goines, *The Free Speech Movement: Coming of Age in the 1960s* (1993); Kenneth Heineman, *Campus Wars* (1992); Maurice Isserman, *If I Had a Hammer: The Death of*

the Old Left—and the Birth of the New Left (1989); Ron Jacobs, The Way the Wind Blew: A History of the Weather Underground (1997); Joseph Keiner and James Munves, The Kent State Coverup (1980); Peter Levy, The New Left and Labor in the 1960s (1994); C. Manes, Green Rage: Radical Environmentalism (1990); Gerald McKnight, The Last Crusade: Martin Luther King, Jr., the FBI, and the Poor People's Campaign (1998); James Miller, Democracy Is in the Streets (1987); Theodore Roszak, The Making of a Counterculture (1969); Marc Stein, City of Sisterly and Brotherly Loves: Lesbian and Gay Philadelphia, 1945–1972 (2000); Alan Wald, Writing from the Left: New Essays on Radical Culture and Politics (1994); Jon Wiener, Come Together (1991).

The Politics of 1968

Paul Berman, A Tale of Two Utopias: The Political Journey of the Generation of 1968 (1996); Mary C. Brennan, Turning Right in the Sixties: The Conservative Capture of the GOP (1995); Dan Carter, The Politics of Rage (1995); Marshall Frady, Wallace (1970); Louis Gould, 1968: The Election That Changed America (1993); Joe McGinniss, The Selling of the President, 1968 (1969); Kevin Phillips, The Emerging Republican Majority (1969); Richard Scammon and Ben Wattenberg, The Real Majority (1970); Herbert Schandler, The Unmaking of a President (1977); Jeff Shesol, Mutual Contempt: Lyndon Johnson, Robert Kennedy, and the Feud That Defined a Decade (1997); Irwin Unger and Debi Unger, Turning Point: 1968 (1988); Jules Witcover, The Year the Dream Died: Revisiting 1968 in America (1997).

Nixon and World Politics

Lloyd Gardner, A Covenant with Power (1984); Stephen Green, Living by the Sword: America and Israel in the Middle East, 1968–1987 (1988); Andrew Hunt, The Turning: A History of Vietnam Veterans Against the War (1999); Arnold R. Isaac, Vietnam Shadows: The War, Its Ghosts, and Its Legacy (1997); Jeffrey Kimball, Nixon's Vietnam War (1998); Henry Kissinger, White House Years (1979) and Years of Upheaval (1982); Walter LaFeber, Inevitable Revolutions (1993); Robert Litwack, Détente and the Nixon Doctrine (1984); Robert McMahon, The Cold War on the Periphery (1994); Charles E. Neu, ed., After Vietnam: Legacies of a Lost War (2000); Stephen Rabe, The Road to OPEC (1982); Stuart Rochester and Frederick Kiley, Honor Bound: The History of American Prisoners of War in Southeast Asia, 1961–1973 (1998); Franz Schurmann, The Foreign Policies of Richard Nixon (1987); William Shawcross, Side-Show: Kissinger, Nixon, and the Destruction of Cambodia (1979); Melvin Small, Johnson, Nixon, and the Doves (1988); William Slater, Chile and the United States (1990); Lewis Sorley, The Better War: The Unexamined Victories and the Final Tragedy of America's Last Years in Vietnam (1999).

The Nixon Administration

Jonathan Aitken, Nixon: A Life (1994); Stephen Ambrose, The Triumph of a Politician (1989); Fawn Brodie, Richard Nixon: The Shaping of His Character (1981); Vincent Burke, Nixon's Good Deed: Welfare Reform (1974); David Calleo, The Imperious Economy (1982); Jody Carleson, George Wallace and the Politics of Powerlessness (1981); J. Brooks Flippen, Nixon and the Environment (2000); Ronald Formisano, Boston Against Busing: Race, Class, and Ethnicity in the 1960s and 1970s (1991); J. Greene, The Limits of Power: The Nixon and Ford Administrations (1992); Roger Morris, Richard Milhous Nixon (1990); James Reichley, Conservatives in an Age of Change: The Nixon and Ford Administrations (1981); Anthony Summers, The Arrogance of Power: The Secret World of Richard Nixon (2000).

The Crisis of the Presidency

John Dean, Blind Ambition (1976); James Doyle, Not Above the Law (1977); John Ehrlichman, Witness to Power (1982); Jim Houghan, Secret Agenda: Watergate, Deep Throat and the CIA (1984); J. Anthony Lukas, Nightmare: The Underside of the Nixon Years (1976); Kim McQuaid, The Anxious Years: America in the Vietnam-Watergate Era (1989); Michael Schudson, Watergate in American Memory: How We Remember, Forget, and Reconstruct the Past (1992); John Sirica, To Set the Record Straight (1979); Maurice Stans, The Terrors of Justice (1984); Athan Theoharis, Spying on Americans (1978).

Chapter 30
The Ford and Carter Presidencies

Patrick Anderson, Electing Jimmy Carter: The Campaign of 1976 (1994); William C. Berman, America's Right Turn: From Nixon to Bush (1994); Douglas Brinkley, The Unfinished Presidency: Jimmy Carter's Journey Beyond the White House (1998); John Robert Greene, The Presidency of Gerald R. Ford (1995); Steven B. Hunt, The Energy Crisis (1978); Burton I. Kaufman, The Presidency of James Earl Carter Jr. (1993); A. James Riechley, Conservatives in an Age of Change (1980).

The Reagan Presidency

S. Baer, Reinventing Democrats: The Politics of Liberalism from Reagan to Clinton (2000); William J. Broad, Teller's War: The Top Secret Story Behind the Star Wars Deception (1992); Paul S. Dempsey, The Social and Economic Consequences of Deregulation (1988); Jane Feuer, Seeing Through the Eighties: Television and Reaganism (1995); Benjamin Friedman, Day of Reckoning: The Consequences of American Economic Policy Under Reagan and After (1988); Jack W. Germond and Jules Witcover, Blue Smoke and Mirrors: How Reagan Won and Why Carter Lost the Election of 1980 (1981); Lisa McGirr, Suburban Warriors: The Origins of the New American Right (2001); Frances Fox Piven and Richard A. Cloward, The New Class War: Reagan's Attack on the Welfare State and Its Consequences (1982); Michael Schaller, Reckoning with Reagan: America and Its President in the 1980s (1992); Garry Wills, Reagan's America: Innocents at Home (1987).

U.S. Foreign Relations, 1974–1989

James Bill, The Eagle and the Lion: . . . American-Iranian Relations (1987); Thomas Carothers, In the Name of Democracy: U.S. Policy Toward Latin America in the Reagan Years (1991); Raymond L. Garthoff, Détente and Confrontation: American-Soviet Relations from Nixon to Reagan (1987); David E. Kyvig, ed., Reagan and the World (1990); William M. LeoGrande, Our Own Backyard: The United States in Central America, 1977–1992 (1998); John D. Martz, United States Policy in Latin America (1995); George D. Moffett III, The Limits of Victory: . . . The Panama Canal Treaties (1983); Morris H. Morley, Washington, Somoza, and the Sandinistas (1994); Peter R. Odell, Oil and World Power, 5th ed. (1979); William B. Quandt, Camp David (1987); David Schoenbaum, The United States and the State of Israel (1993); Lars Shoultz, Human Rights

and U.S. Policy Toward Latin America (1981); Charles D. Smith, *Palestine and the Arab-Israeli Conflict*, 2d ed. (1992); Gaddis Smith, *Morality, Reason, and Power* (1986) [Carter's foreign policy]; Strobe Talbott, *Endgame* (1979) [SALT II].

Social, Economic, and Immigration Trends in the 1970s and 1980s

Frank D. Bean et al., *Mexican and Central American Population and U.S. Immigration Policy* (1989); Bongyoun Choy, *Koreans in America* (1979); John Crewden, *The Tarnished Door: The New Immigrants and the Transformation of America* (1983); Kathryn Marie Dudley, *Debt and Dispossession: Farm Loss in America's Heartland* (2000); Paul Freiberger and Michael Swaine, *Fire in the Valley: The Making of the Personal Computer* (2d ed., 1999); Douglas Glasgow, *The Black Underclass* (1980); Andrew Hacker, *Two Nations: Black and White, Separate, Hostile, Unequal* (1992); Sylvia Ann Hewlett, *When the Bow Breaks: The Cost of Neglecting Our Children* (1991); Denis Heyck, ed., *Barrios and Borderlands: Cultures of Latinos and Latinas in the U.S.* (1993); Lloyd D. Johnson et al., *Trends in Drug Use. . . 1975–1989* (National Institute on Drug Abuse, 1991); J. Anthony Lucas, *Common Ground: A Turbulent Decade in the Lives of Three American Families* (1986); Michael Moritz, *The Little Kingdom: The Private Story of Apple Computer* (1984); James B. Stewart, *Den of Thieves* [business scandals of the 1980s] (1991); Catherine McNicol Stock and Robert D. Johnston, eds., *The Countryside in the Age of the Modern State* (2001); Vance Trimble, *Sam Walton: The Inside Story of America's Richest Man* (1990); Reed Ueda, *Postwar Immigrant America* (1994); Sam Walton, *Made in America* (1992); William Julius Wilson, *The Truly Disadvantaged: The Inner City, the Underclass, and Public Policy* (1987).

Women's Issues, Gay and Lesbian History, Sexuality

Dudley Clendinen and Adam Nagourney, *Out for Good: The Struggle to Build a Gay Rights Movement in America* (1999); Barbara Hinkson Craig and David M. O'Brien, *Abortion and American Politics* (1993); Sara Evans, *Personal Politics: The Roots of Women's Liberation in the Civil Rights Movement and the New Left* (1979); David J. Garrow, *Liberty and Sexuality: The Right to Privacy and the Making of* Roe v. Wade (1994); Roger Rosenblatt, *Life Itself* [the abortion debate] (1992); Leigh W. Rutledge, *The Gay Decades: From Stonewall to the Present* (1992); Barry D. Schoub, *AIDS and HIV in Perspective* (1994); Suzanne Staggenborg, *The Pro-Choice Movement* (1991); Winifred D. Wandersee, *On the Move: American Women in the 1970s* (1988).

Cultural and Religious Trends in the 1970s and 1980s

Randall Balmer, *Mine Eyes Have Seen the Glory: A Journey Through the Evangelical Subculture in America*, 3d ed. (2000); Paul Boyer, *When Time Shall Be No More: Prophecy Belief in Modern American Culture* (1992); Joel A. Carpenter, *Revive Us Again: The Reawakening of American Fundamentalism* (1997); Jim Cullen, *Born in the U.S.A.: Bruce Springsteen and the American Tradition* (1997); Donald W. Dayton and Robert K. Johnston, eds., *The Variety of American Evangelicalism* (1991); Ethics and Public Policy Center, *No Longer Exiles: The Religious New Right in American Politics* (1993); Christopher Lasch, *The Culture of Narcissism* (1978); Michael Lienesch, *Redeeming

America: Piety and Politics in the New Christian Right* (1993); Nicholas Mills, ed., *Culture in the Age of Money* (1991); Mark Noll, *One Nation Under God: Christian Faith and Political Action in America* (1988); Edwin Shur, *The Awareness Trap: Self-Absorption Instead of Social Change* (1976); Garry Wills, *Under God: Religion and American Politics* (1990); Robert Wuthnow, *The Restructuring of American Religion: Society and Faith Since World War II* (1988).

Environmental, Western, and Sunbelt History

Carl Abbott, *The New Urban America: Growth and Politics in the Sunbelt Cities* (1981); Michael Bennett and David W. Teague, eds., *The Nature of Cities: Ecocriticism and Urban Environments* (1999); Craig E. Colten and Peter N. Skinner, *The Road to Love Canal: Managing Industrial Waste Before EPA* (1996); Joel Gareau, *Edge City: Life at the New Frontier* (1991); Samuel P. Hays, *Beauty, Health, and Permanence: Environmental Politics in the United States, 1955–1985* (1987); James Howard Kunstler, *Geography of Nowhere: The Rise and Decline of America's Man-Made Landscape* (1994); Jonathan Lash, *A Season of Spoils: The Story of the Reagan Administration's Attack on the Environment* (1984); Clyde A. Milner II, *A New Significance: Re-Envisioning the History of the American West* (1996); Gregg Mitman, *Reel Nature: America's Romance with Wildlife on Film* (1999); Gerald D. Nash, *The Federal Landscape: An Economic History of the Twentieth-Century West* (1999); Stephanie S. Pincetl, *Transforming California: A Political History of Land Use and Development* (1999); Hal Rothman, *Greening of a Nation? Environmentalism in the United States Since 1945* (1989); C. Brant Short, *Ronald Reagan and the Public Lands: America's Conservation Debates, 1979–1984* (1989).

Chapter 31
The Bush Presidency, End of the Cold War, Persian Gulf War

Rick Arkinson, *Crusade: The Untold Story of the Persian Gulf War* (1993); Michael Duffy, *Marching in Place: The Status Quo Presidency of George Bush* (1992); Alan Friedman, *Spider's Web: The Secret History of How the White House Illegally Armed Iraq* (1993); John Lewis Gaddis, *The United States and the End of the Cold War* (1992); Raymond L. Garthoff, *The Great Transition: American-Soviet Relations and the End of the Cold War* (1994); Ken Gross, *Ross Perot: The Man Behind the Myth* (1992); Roger Hilsman, *George Bush vs. Saddam Hussein* (1992); Michael J. Hogan, ed., *The End of the Cold War: Its Meaning and Implications* (1992); Martin Lowy, *High Rollers: Inside the Savings and Loan Debacle* (1991); John R. MacArthur, *Second Front: Censorship and Propaganda in the Gulf War* (1992); Richard Rose, *The Post-Modern Presidency: George Bush Meets the World* (1991); U.S. News & World Report, *Triumph Without Victory* [the Persian Gulf War] (1992).

Domestic Politics in the Early Clinton Years

E. J. Dionne, *They Only Look Dead: Why Progressives Will Dominate the Next Political Era* (1996); Elizabeth Drew, *Whatever It Takes: The Real Struggle for Political Power in America* (1997); Jacob S. Hacker, *The Road to Nowhere: The Genesis of President Clinton's Plan for Health Security* (1997); Roderick P. Hart, *Seducing America: How Television Charms the

Modern Voter (1994); Kathleen Hall Jamieson, *Packaging the Presidency*, 3d ed. [campaign advertising] (1996); Michael B. Katz, *The Price of Citizenship: Redefining the American Welfare State* (2001); Linda Killian, *The Freshmen: What Happened to the Republican Revolution?* (1998); Charles Noble, *Welfare as We Knew It: A Political History of the American Welfare State* (1997); Paul Starr, *The Logic of Health Care Reform* (1992); Bob Woodward, *The Agenda: Inside the Clinton White House* (1994) and *The Choice: How Clinton Won* (1996).

Hispanic Americans, Asian Americans, Native Americans

Fergus M. Bordewich, *Killing the White Man's Indian: Reinventing Native Americans at the End of the Twentieth Century* (1996); Jorge Durand, Douglas S. Massey, and Emilio A. Parrado, "The New Era of Mexican Migration to the United States," *Journal of American History* (September 1999); Geoffrey Fox, *Hispanic Nation: Culture, Politics, and the Constructing of Identity* (1996); Bill Ong Hing, *Making and Remaking Asian America Through Immigration Policy, 1950–1990* (1993); Michael Jones-Correa, *Between Two Nations: The Political Predicament of Latinos in New York City* (1998); Jong-deuk Jung, *A Study of Korean Immigration in America* (1991); Jo Ann Koltyk, *New Pioneers in the Heartland: Hmong Life in Wisconsin* (1998); Joel Millman, *The Other Americans: How Immigrants Renew Our Country, Our Economy, and Our Values* (1997); Padma Rangaswamy, *Namasté America: Indian Immigrants in an American Metropolis* (2000); Peter Skerry, *Mexican Americans: The Ambivalent Minority* (1993); Alex Stepick, *Pride Against Prejudice: Haitians in the United States* (1998); Robert Suro, *Strangers Among Us: How Latino Immigration Is Transforming America* (1998); William Wei, *The Asian American Movement* (1993); Bernard Wong, *Ethnicity and Entrepreneurship: The New Chinese Immigrants in the San Francisco Bay Area* (1998).

African-American Issues, the Inner Cities, Economic Trends

Thomas D. Boston and Catherine L. Ross, eds., *The Inner City: Urban Poverty and Economic Development in the Next Century* (1997); Ellis Cose, *The Rage of a Privileged Class: Why Are Middle-Class Blacks Angry?* (1993); Susan D. Holloway et al., *Through My Own Eyes: Single Mothers and the Cultures of Poverty* (1997); Todd E. Jones, ed., *Affirmative Action: Social Justice or Reverse Discrimination* (1997); Jonathan Kozol, *Amazing Grace: The Lives of Children and the Conscience of a Nation* (1995); Paul Osterman et al., *Working in America: A Blueprint for the New Labor Market* (2001); Orlando Patterson, *The Ordeal of Integration: Progress and Resentment in America's "Racial" Crisis* (1997).

Cultural Trends and Commentary in the 1990s

William J. Bennett, *The Devaluing of America: How to Win the Fight for Our Culture and Our Children* (1992); Stephen L. Carter, *The Culture of Disbelief: How American Law and Politics Trivialize Religious Devotion* (1993); Tyler Cowan, *In Praise of Commercial Culture* (1998); Cynthia Gorney, *Articles of Faith: A Frontline History of the Abortion Wars* (1998); James L. Guth et al., *The Bully Pulpit: The Politics of Protestant Clergy* (1997); Robert Hughes, *Culture of Complaint: The Fraying of America* (1993); David Hollinger, *Post-Ethnic America: Beyond Multiculturalism* (1995); Robert Kuttner, *Everything for Sale: The Virtues and Limits of Markets* (1996); George Lakoff, *Moral Politics: What Conservatives Know That Liberals Don't* (1997); Christopher Lasch, *The Revolt of the Elites and the Betrayal of Democracy* (1995); Edward T. Linenthal, *The Unfinished Bombing: Oklahoma City in American Memory* (2001); Edward T. Linenthal and Tom Engelhardt, eds., *History Wars: The Enola Gay and Other Battles for the American Past* (1996); Edward N. Luttwack, *The Endangered American Dream* (1993); William Martin, *With God on Our Side: The Rise of the Religious Right in America* (1996); Walter Benn Michaels, *Our America: Nativism, Modernism, and Pluralism* (1995); Joseph S. Nye et al., eds., *Why People Don't Trust Government* (1997); Michael J. Sandel, *Democracy's Discontents: America in Search of a Public Philosophy* (1996); Jean Stefancic and Richard Delgado, *No Mercy: How Conservative Think Tanks and Foundations Changed America's Social Agenda* (1996); James D. Tabor and Eugene V. Gallagher, *Why Waco? Cults and the Battle for Religious Freedom in America* (1995); Justin Watson, *The Christian Coalition: Dreams of Restoration, Demands for Recognition* (1997).

Chapter 32

Clinton's Second Term, Conservative Activism, Political Thought

David Brock, *Blinded by the Right: The Conscience of an Ex-Conservative* (2002); Sue E. S. Crawford and Laura R. Olson, eds., *Christian Clergy and American Politics* (2001); Bonnie Hong, *Democracy and the Foreigner* (2001); James T. Kloppenberg, *The Virtues of Liberalism* (1998); Richard Kluger, *Ashes to Ashes* [tobacco and public health] (1996); Carrick Mollenkamp et al., *The People v. Big Tobacco* (1998); Kenneth Starr, *The Starr Report: The Official Report of the Independent Counsel's Investigation of the President* (1998); James B. Stewart, *Blood Sport: The President and His Adversaries* (1996).

The 2000 Election, George W. Bush

Frank Bruni, *Ambling into History: The Unlikely Odyssey of George W. Bush* (2002); Correspondents of *The New York Times*, *Thirty-Six Days: The Complete Chronicle of the 2000 Presidential Election Crisis* (2001); Alan M. Dershowitz, *Supreme Injustice: How the High Court Hijacked Election 2000* (2001); Howard Gillman, *The Votes That Counted: How the Court Decided the 2000 Election* (2001); Richard A. Posner, *Breaking the Deadlock: The 2000 Election, the Constitution, and the Courts* (2001); Jack N. Rakove, ed., *The Unfinished Election of 2000* (2001).

Biotechnology, the Internet, the Environment

Walter Truett Anderson, *All Connected Now: Life in the First Global Civilization* (2001); Francis Cairncross, *The Death of Distance: How the Communications Revolution Will Change Our Lives* (1997); Arthur L. Caplan, *Am I My Brother's Keeper? The Ethical Frontiers of Biomedicine* (1997); Al Gore, *Earth in the Balance: Ecology and the Human Spirit* (1992); Gina Kolata, *Clone: The Road to Dolly and the Path Ahead* (1997); J. R. McNeill, *Something New Under the Sun: An Environmental History of the Twentieth-Century World* (2000); Philip Shabecoff, *A Fierce Green Fire: The American Environmental Movement* (1994); Mark Sloutka, *War of the Worlds: Cyberspace*

and the High-Tech Assault on Reality (1995); M. L. Tina Stevens, *Bioethics in America* (2000); Don Tapscott, *Growing Up Digital: The Rise of the Net Generation* (1998); Sherry Turkle, *Life on the Screen: Identity in the Age of the Internet* (1995).

Recession, Economic Trends, Globalization, Trade

John Cassidy, *Dot.con: The Greatest Story Ever Sold* (2002); Kenneth W. Dam, *The Rules of the Global Game* (2001); Peter C. Fusaro and Ross M. Miller, *What Went Wrong at Enron: Everyone's Guide to the Largest Bankruptcy in U.S. History* (2002); Ruth Milkman, *Farewell to the Factory: Auto Workers in the Late Twentieth Century* (1998); Michael Rowbotham, *Goodbye America: Globalization, Debt, and the Dollar Empire* (2001); James Shoch, *Trading Blows: Party Competition and U.S. Trade Policy in a Globalizing Era* (2001); Richard J. Schroth and A. Larry Elliott, *How Companies Lie: Why Enron Is Just the Tip of the Iceberg* (2002); U.S. Bureau of the Census, *Statistical Abstract of the United States, The National Databook, 2002* (2003).

American Foreign Relations in the Post-Cold War Era

Timothy Garton Ash, *History of the Present: Essays, Sketches, and Dispatches from Europe in the 1990s* (2000); Andrew J. Bacevich and Eliot A. Cohen, eds., *War Over Kosovo: Politics and Strategy in a Global Age* (2001); Gary Jonathan Bass, *Stay the Hand of Vengeance: The Politics of War Crimes Tribunals* (2001); Wayne Bert, *The Reluctant Superpower: United States Policy in Bosnia, 1991–1995* (1997); Slavoljub Djukic, *Milosevic and Markovic: A Lust for Power* (2001); Michael McFaul, *Russia's Unfinished Revolution: Political Change from Gorbachev to Putin* (2001); Ronald E. Powaski, *Return to Armageddon: The United States and the Nuclear Arms Race, 1981–1999* (2000); Michael Schaller, *The United States and China* (2002); Louis Sell, *Slobodan Milosevic and the Destruction of Yugoslavia* (2002); Strobe Talbott, *The Russia Hand: A Memoir of Presidential Diplomacy* (2002); Daniel Yergin and Thane Gustafson, *Russia 2010* (1993).

Terrorism, Counterterrorism, Biological Weapons

Peter L. Bergen, *Holy War, Inc.: Inside the Secret World of Osama bin Laden* (2001); Martin Ewans, *Afghanistan: A New History* (2001); M. J. Gohari, *The Taliban: Ascent to Power (2000)*; Gilles Kepel, *Jihad: The Trail of Political Islam* (2002); Elaine Landau, *Osama bin Ladin: A War Against the West* (2001); Walter Laqueur, *The New Terrorism: Fanaticism and the Arms of Mass Destruction* (2000); Kamal Matinuddin, *The Taliban Phenomenon* (2000); Matthew Meselson, "Bioterror: What Can Be Done?" *New York Review of Books* (December 20, 2001): 38–41; Judith Miller, Steven Engelberg, and William Broad, *Germs: Biological Weapons and America's Secret War* (2001); Ahmed Rashid, *Taliban: Islam, Oil, and the New Great Game in Central Asia* (2000) and *Jihad: The Rise of Militant Islam in Central Asia* (2002); Gregory F. Treverton, *Reshaping National Intelligence for an Age of Information* (2001); Stansfield Turner, *Caging the Nuclear Genie* (1997).

Islam, the Middle East, and the West

Abraham Ben-Zvi, *The United States and Israel: The Limits of the Special Relationship* (1993); John E. Esposito, *Islam*, rev. ed. (1992); Thomas L. Friedman, *From Beirut to Jerusalem* (updated ed., 1990); Fawaz A. Gerges, *America and Political Islam: Clash of Cultures or Clash of Interests* (2001); Fred Halliday, *Nation and Religion in the Middle East* (2000); Asma Gull Hasan, *American Muslims: The New Generation* (2001); Bernard Lewis, *Islam and the West* (1993), *Islam in History: Ideas, People, and Events in the Middle East* (1993), and *The Shaping of the Modern Middle East* (1994); Annemarie Schimmel, *Islam* (1992); David Schoenbaum, *The United States and the State of Israel* (1993); Bernard Wasserstein, *Divided Jerusalem: The Struggle for the Holy City* (2001).

America's Global Role in the Twenty-First Century

David Callahan, *Unwinnable Wars: American Power and Ethnic Conflict* (1997); Jeanne Chase, "Porous Boundaries and Shifting Borderlands: The American Experience in a New World Order," *Reviews in American History* 26 (March 1998): 54–69; *Foreign Affairs* magazine, special issue on "The World Ahead" (September/October 1997); Richard Sobel, *The Impact of Public Opinion on U.S. Foreign Policy Since Vietnam* (2001); Robert W. Tucker and David C. Hendrickson, *The Imperial Temptation: The New World Order and America's Purposes* (1992).

Photograph Credits

Prologue *p. xxxiv:* "Great West" poster, Granger Collection; *p. xxxvi:* Map of Piscataqua River, courtesy of the Trustees of the British Library; *p. xxxvii:* White Salmon Trout from the Clark Journals, Missouri Historical Society; *p. xxxix: View of the Mountain Pass Called the Notch of the White Mountains,* by Thomas Cole, Andrew W. Mellon Fund © 1995 Board of Trustees, National Gallery of Art, Washington, D.C.; *p. xl:* John Muir *Wilderness* poster, © by Carr Clift, published by Roberts Rinehart Publishers with The Wilderness Society.

Chapter 16 *p. 476,* William Gladstone; *p. 478,* Civil War Photographic Album, Louisiana and Lower Mississippi Valley Collection, LSU Libraries, Louisiana State University; *p. 479 (left),* Library of Congress; *p. 479 (right),* Library of Congress; *p. 482,* Harper's Weekly, 1866; *p. 487,* Schlesinger Library; *p. 488,* Granger Collection; *p. 489,* Museum of the Confederacy; *p. 491 (left),* Private Collection; *p. 491 (top right),* Chicago Historical Society; *p. 493,* William Gladstone; *p. 494,* Library of Congress; *p. 495 (bottom),* Atlanta History Center; *p. 495 (top),* Atlanta History Center; *p. 499,* © Collection of the New York Historical Society; *p. 500 (left),* Brown Brothers; *p. 500 (right),* Harper's Weekly, 1871; *p. 505 (top),* Harper's Weekly, October 24, 1874; *p. 506 (left),* Library of Congress; *p. 506 (right),* Kansas State Historical Society.

Chapter 17 *p. 510,* National Anthropological Archives, Smithsonian Institution, Washington, D.C.; *p. 512 (left),* Kansas State Historical Society; *p. 512 (right),* Kansas State Historical Society; *p. 514,* Smithsonian American Art Museum, Washington, D.C./Art Resource, NY; *p. 515,* Detroit Public Library, Burton Historical Collection; *p. 517 (left),* National Anthropological Archives, Smithsonian Institution, Washington, D.C.; *p. 517 (right),* Library of Congress; *p. 520,* From *A Pima Past* by Anna Moore Shaw, University of Arizona Press, Tuson, Arizona; *p. 521 (top),* National Archives; *p. 521 (bottom),* National Archives; *p. 522,* The Huntington Library & Art Collections, San Marino, California; *p. 523,* National Museum of Natural History, Smithsonian Institution, Washington, D.C.; *p. 524 (top),* Kansas Collection, University of Kansas Libraries; *p. 524 (right),* Library of Congress; *p. 525,* Denver Public Library, Western History Division; *p. 529,* Museum of New Mexico; *p. 532,* Alaska and Polar Regions Archive, Elmer E. Rasmunson Library University of Alaska; *p. 534,* Denver Public Library, Western History Division; *p. 538,* Lent by the Department of the Interior Museum, National Museum of American Art, Smithsonian Institution, Washington, D.C./Art Resource, NY.

Chapter 18 *p. 542,* Chicago Historical Society; *p. 545,* Hagley Museum & Library; *p. 546,* Frank & Marie-Therese Wood Print Collections, Alexandria, VA; *p. 548,* National Portrait Gallery, Smithsonian Institution/Art Resource, NY; *p. 552,* Departrment of the Interior, National Park Service, Edison National Historic Site; *p. 556 (left),* William L. Clements Library; *p. 556 (right),* Library of Congress; *p. 557,* Trustees of the Boston Public Library Print department; *p. 560,* Harper's Weekly, March 26, 1877; *p. 562,* Library of Congress; *p. 563,* Courtesy of the Trustees of the Haverhill Public Library, Special Collections Department; *p. 564,* Library of Congress; *p. 567,* Museum of American Political Life; *p. 568,* Library of Congress; *p. 570,* Chicago Historical Society; *p. 554 (left), House Drainage and Sanitary Plumbing* by William Paul Gerhard, 1882. Miriam and Ira D. Wallach Division of Art, Prints and Photographs, The New York Public Library. Astor, Lenox and Tilden Foundations; *p. 554 (right), House Drainage and Sanitary Plumbing* by William Paul Gerhard, 1882. Miriam and Ira D. Wallach Division

of Art, Prints and Photographs, The New York Public Library. Astor, Lenox and Tilden Foundations; *p. 555 (top),* Avery Architectural and Fine Arts Library, Columbia University; *p. 555 (bottom), House Drainage and Sanitary Plumbing* by William Paul Gerhard, 1882. Miriam and Ira D. Wallach Division of Art, Prints and Photographs, The New York Public Library. Astor, Lenox and Tilden Foundations;

Chapter 19 *p. 574,* George Eastman House; *p. 577,* Granger Collection; *p. 579,* Library of Congress; *p. 580,* Ellis Island Immigration Museum; *p. 581,* California Historical Society; *p. 584,* Picture Research Consultants & Archives; *p. 585,* Museum of the City of New York; *p. 586,* The Gifted Line, John Grossman; *p. 587, Harper's Weekly* 1871; *p. 588,* Santa Fee Collection, Kansas State Historical Society; *p. 591,* Chicago Historical Society; *p. 592,* Detroit Institute of Arts, Founders Society Purchase; *p. 593,* Library of Congress; *p. 594,* Henry Ford Museum and Greenfield Village; *p. 597 (left),* Granger Collection; *p. 597 (right),* North Wind Picture Archives; *p. 598,* Fisk University Special Collections; *p. 599 (left),* Courtesy New Orleans Jazz Club Collection, Louisiana State Museum Jan White Brantley; *p. 599 (right),* Courtesy New Orleans Jazz Club Collection, Louisiana State Museum Jan White Brantley; *p. 604,* © Bettmann/Corbis.

Chapter 20 *p. 608,* Frank & Marie-Therese Wood Print Collections, Alexandria, VA; *p. 612,* Chicago Historical Society; *p. 614,* Granger Collection; *p. 619,* Hargrett Rare Book & Manuscript Library, University of Georgia Libraries; *p. 621,* © Bettmann/Corbis; *p. 623,* Library of Congress; *p. 625,* Library of Congress; *p. 628,* Kansas State Historical Society; *p. 629,* Smithsonian Institution, Washington, D.C.; *p. 634,* Rare Book Department, The Free Library of Philadelphia; *p. 635,* The Jacob A. Riis Collection, #123, Museum of the City of New York; *p. 636,* National Archives; *p. 637,* National Archives.

Chapter 21 *p. 640,* Picture Research Consultants & Archives; *p. 642,* Brown Brothers; *p. 644,* Metlife Archives; *p. 646,* © Bettmann/Corbis; *p. 647,* Ohio Historical Society; *p. 648,* Staten Island Historical Society; *p. 650,* Philadelphia City Archives; *p. 651,* Chicago Historical Society; *p. 652,* Picture Research Consultants & Archives; *p. 653,* Chicago Historical Society; *p. 655,* © Bettmann/Corbis; *p. 656,* Picture Research Consultants & Archives; *p. 657 (left),* Schomburg Center for Research in Black Culture, New York Public Library; *p. 657 (right),* Archives of the University of Massachusetts at Amherst; *p. 658,* Library of Congress; *p. 659,* Library of Congress; *p. 660,* Courtesy, Wellesley College Archives; *p. 661,* © Bettmann/Corbis; *p. 662 (top right),* © Bettmann/Corbis; *p. 662 (bottom left),* Library of Congress; *p. 665,* Library of Congress; *p. 667,* Library of Congress; *p. 668,* University of the Pacific; *p. 669 (top right),* The Wadsworth Atheneum, Bequest of Mrs. Theodore Lyman in memory of her husband; *p. 669 (bottom right),* © Bettmann/Corbis.

Chapter 22 *p. 676,* © Bettmann/Corbis; *p. 678,* Picture Research Consultants & Archives; *p. 679,* Granger Collection; *p. 680,* National Archives; *p. 682,* Naval Historical Foundation; *p. 684,* © Bettmann/Corbis; *p. 687,* Denver Public Library, Western History Division; *p. 688,* Social Hygiene, 4 April 1918; *p. 690,* National Archives; *p. 692,* U.S. Army Military History Institute; *p. 693 (left),* Brown Brothers; *p. 693 (right),* Picture Research Consultants & Archives; *p. 694,* U.S. Department of the Interior, National Park Service, Edison National Historic Site; *p. 695 (left),* Collection of Paul Boyer; *p. 695 (right),* Library of Congress; *p. 699,* The Phillips Collection, © Gwendolyn Knight

Lawrence, courtesy of the Jacob and Gwendolyn Lawrence Foundation; *p. 701,* Courtesy American Red Cross; *p. 702,* Library of Congress; *p. 705,* Brooklyn Eagle, 1919; *p. 706,* Library of Congress; *p. 707,* Collection of Janice L. and David J. Frent.

Chapter 23 *p. 710,* Chicago Historical Society; *p. 713,* Archive Photos; *p. 716,* Walter P. Reuther Library/Wayne State University; *p. 717,* Library of Congress; *p. 721,* New Britain Museum of American Art Stephen Lawrence Fund, Photograph by E. Irving Blomstrann; *p. 722,* Courtesy of the Arizona Historical Society/Tuscon AHS #62669; *p. 723 (top),* Strong Museum; *p. 723 (bottom),* Library of Congress; *p. 724,* Warner Brother's Archives; *p. 725,* National Archives; *p. 727 (left),* Picture Research Consultants & Archives; *p. 727 (right),* Stock Montage; *p. 728,* Archive Photos; *p. 729,* National Portrait Gallery, Smithsonian Institution, Washington, D.C./Art Resource, NY; *p. 731,* © Collection of the New York Historical Society; *p. 735,* Library of Congress; *p. 736,* © Bettmann/Corbis; *p. 737,* Museum of the City of New York; *p. 738,* Denver Public Library, Western History Division.

Chapter 24 *p. 742,* Library of Congress; *p. 748,* Minnesota Historical Society; *p. 750 (top),* Library of Congress; *p. 750 (bottom),* © Bettmann/Corbis; *p. 752,* Collection of Janice L. and David J. Frent; *p. 754,* Culver Pictures; *p. 757,* Smithsonian American Art Museum, Washington, D.C./Art Resource, NY; *p. 761,* Library of Congress; *p. 763,* Library of Congress; *p. 767,* Archives of Labor and Urban Affairs/Wayne State University; *p. 768,* © Bettmann/Corbis; *p. 769,* Library of Congress; *p. 771,* Photography Collection, Harry Ransom Humanities Research Center, The University of Texas at Austin General Libraries; *p. 772,* Courtesy AT&T Archives; *p. 773,* Christies Images, Inc.; *p. 774,* Photofest; *p. 775,* © 1989, Grandma Moses Properties Co, NY; *p. 776,* Archive Photos.

Chapter 25 *p. 780,* W. Eugene Smith/Timepix; *p. 785,* Thomas McAvoyTimepix; *p. 789,* Myron H. Davis/Timepix; *p. 792,* © Curt Teich Postcard Archives, Lake County (IL) Museum; *p. 794,* Library of Congress; *p. 796,* National Archives; *p. 801,* National Archives; *p. 803,* Scurlock Studio Collection Archives Center, National Museum of American History and the Schomburg Center for Research in Black Culture, New York Public Library; *p. 805,* Library of Congress; *p. 807,* US Army/Franklin D. Roosevelt Library; *p. 809 (left),* National Archives; *p. 809 (right),* National Archives; *p. 810,* Yivo Institute for Jewish Research; *p. 811,* National Archives.

Chapter 26 *p. 814,* Courtesy Edenhurst Gallery, Los Angeles, Daniel Nicodemo, Thomas Gianetto and Donald Merrill; *p. 817,* Indiana University; *p. 819,* Corbis-Bettmann; *p. 822,* National Archives; *p. 823,* Corbis-Bettmann; *p. 827 (top),* © Bettmann/Corbis; *p. 827 (bottom),* J.R. Eyerman/LIFE Magazine © Time, Inc.; *p. 829,* Corbis-Bettmann 4E P.799; *p. 831 (top right),* Wide World Photos, Inc.; *p. 831 (left middle),* © Bettmann/Corbis; *p. 831 (bottom right),* Wide World ; *p. 832,* Hy Peskin/Timepix; *p. 833,* Corbis-Bettmann; *p. 835,* The Michael Barson Collection/Past Perfect; *p. 837 (left),* © Elliot Erwitt/ Magnum Photos, Inc.; *p. 837 (right),* © Elliot Erwitt/Magnum Photos, Inc.; *p. 838,* "I Have Here in My Hand..." from *HERBLOCK : A Cartoonist's Life* (Macmillian Publishing Company, 1993).

Chapter 27 *p. 842,* © The Curtis Publishing Company; *p. 845,* Courtesy Dwight D. Eisenhower Library; *p. 847 (top),* Missouri State Archives; *p. 847 (bottom),* Original Artwork by Anatole Kovarsky. Copyright © 1959 The New Yorker Magazine, Inc. Reprinted by permission. All Rights Reserved; *p. 849,* Wide World Photos, Inc.; *p. 851,* TIME Magazine © Time, Inc.; *p. 852,* Wide World Photos, Inc.; *p. 855,* Courtesy Boeing Defense & Space Group; *p. 856,* Corbis-Bettmann; *p. 858,* Alfred

Eisenstaedt/LIFE Magazine © Time, Inc.; *p. 860,* © 1992 Cindy Lewis; *p. 864 (left),* Photofest; *p. 864 (right),* Gaslight Advertising Archives; *p. 866,* Chicago Historical Society; *p. 867,* Corbis-Bettmann; *p. 868,* Corbis-Bettmann; *p. 870,* NASA/ Johnson Space Center; *p. 871,* © Bettmann/Corbis; *p. 874,* Dan Budnick/Woodfin Camp & Associates.

Chapter 28 *p. 877,* Wide World Photos, Inc.; *p. 878,* © Bettmann/Corbis; *p. 879,* Wide World; *p. 880,* Wide World Photos, Inc.; *p. 882,* National Archives; *p. 883,* Lyndon B. Johnson Presidential Library; *p. 891,* Corbis-Bettmann; *p. 893,* James Prigoff; *p. 896,* Wyeth-Ayerst Laboratories; *p. 897,* Timepix; *p. 899,* Robert J. Ellison/Black Star/Stockphoto.com; *p. 901 (top),* Corbis-Bettmann; *p. 901 (bottom right),* Cartoon by Paul Szep © *The Boston Globe.*

Chapter 29 *p. 904,* Wide World/AP photo /Henri Huet; *p. 907,* University of California at Berkeley, Bancroft Library; *p. 908,* Corbis-Bettmann; *p. 909,* John Filo; *p. 910,* © Bettmann/Corbis; *p. 911,* John and Leni SInclair Collection, Bentley Historical Library, University of Michigan; *p. 914 (left),* Gene Anthony/ Black Star; *p. 914 (right),* Elliot Landy/ Magnum Photos, Inc.; *p. 915 (left),* Gene Anthony/Black Star; *p. 915 (right),* M.L. Carlebach/Black Star; *p. 916 (top left),* Wide World; *p. 916 (bottom right),* Wide World; *p. 919,* © Bettmann/Corbis; *p. 920,* Ron Haeberle/ Timepix; *p. 923,* Wally McNamee/ Woodfin Camp & Associates; *p. 925,* NASA/Johnson Space Center; *p. 927,* Flip Schulke/Black Star/Stock Photo; *p. 929,* Cartoon News International; *p. 931,* Illustration by Jack Davis for *Time* cover, April 30, 1973/Timepix.

Chapter 30 *p. 934,* (detail) Collection of Katherine Sosa; *p. 936,* Rob Nelson/Black Star; *p. 937,* © 1984 Newsweek, Inc. All rights reserved. Reprinted by permission; *p. 939,* Courtesy Tuck School of Business Archives, Dartmouth College, Hanover, N.H.; *p. 941 (top left),* © Bettmann/Corbis; *p. 941 (bottom right),* Reproduced from *Popular Mechanics,* January 1975, by permission of Gernsback Publications, Inc.; *p. 943,* © 2002 JEB (Joan E. Biren); *p. 945,* American Folklife Collection/Library of Congress; *p. 947 (left),* NASA/Johnson Space Center; *p. 947 (right),* Leonard Freed/Magnum Photos, Inc.; *p. 949,* © Galen Rowell/ Bettmann/ Corbis; *p. 950,* Jimmy Carter Presidential Library; *p. 951,* Sipa Press; *p. 953,* © Wally McNamee/ Bettmann/Corbis; *p. 960,* Wide World; *p. 961,* © Bettmann/ Corbis.

Chapter 31 *p. 964,* Seth Resnick/Stock Boston; *p. 966,* © Bettmann/Corbis/Seth Resnick/Stock Boston; *p. 968,* © Bettmann/Corbis; *p. 970,* Bruno Barbey/Magnum Photos, Inc.; *p. 971,* HolLynn D'Lil; *p. 972,* © Bettmann/Corbis; *p. 975,* Photo Courtesy Richard Petty Driving Experience; *p. 977,* Brooks Kraft/Corbis/Sygma; *p. 978,* CartoonStock Ltd.; *p. 979,* © Bettmann/Corbis; *p. 980,* J. Nachtwey/Cosmos/VII Photo Agency; *p. 982,* M. Almeida/*The New York Times*; *p. 984,* Alex Webb/Magnum Photos, Inc.; *p. 985,* Susan Greenwood/ Gamma Liaison/Getty Images; *p. 986,* Dorothy Littel Greco/ Stock Boston; *p. 988,* © Corbis /Sygma; *p. 989,* R. Fremson/The New York Times.

Chapter 32 *p. 992,* Steve Liss/Timepix; *p. 995,* Agence France Presse© Bettmann/Corbis; *p. 996,* Richard Ellis/Sygma/Corbis; *p. 997,* Tribune Media Services, Inc. All rights reserved. Reprinted with permission; *p. 998,* AFP/Corbis; *p. 1002,* Richard Ellis/ Sygma/Corbis; *p. 1005,* Mark Peterson/SABA/Corbis; *p. 1006,* Reuters/Corbis; *p. 1008,* John Domines Timepix; *p. 1011,* © Reuters/Corbis; *p. 1010,* Photo by Jeff Miller/University of Wisconsin; *p. 1013,* Eric Engman for *The New York Times*; *p. 1015,* Don Tellock/Gamma Press USA, Inc.; *p. 1017,* © Sygma /Corbis; *p. 1019 (left),* Michael Kaemer/AFP /Corbis; *p. 1019 (right),* Luc Delahaye/Magnum Photos for *Newsweek; p. 1020,* Wide World.

Chapter 16 *p. 476*, William Gladstone; *p. 478*, Civil War Photographic Album, Louisiana and Lower Mississippi Valley Collection, LSU Libraries, Louisiana State University; *p. 479 (left)*, Library of Congress; *p. 479 (right)*, Library of Congress; *p. 482*, Harper's Weekly, 1866; *p. 487*, Schlesinger Library; *p. 488*, Granger Collection; *p. 489*, Museum of the Confederacy; *p. 491 (left)*, Private Collection; *p. 491 (top right)*, Chicago Historical Society; *p. 493*, William Gladstone; *p. 494*, Library of Congress; *p. 495 (bottom)*, Atlanta History Center; *p. 495 (top)*, Atlanta History Center; *p. 499*, © Collection of the New York Historical Society; *p. 500 (left)*, Brown Brothers; *p. 500 (right)*, Harper's Weekly, 1871; *p. 505 (top)*, Harper's Weekly, October 24, 1874; *p. 506 (left)*, Library of Congress; *p. 506 (right)*, Kansas State Historical Society.

Chapter 17 *p. 510*, National Anthropological Archives, Smithsonian Institution, Washington, D.C.; *p. 512 (left)*, Kansas State Historical Society; *p. 512 (right)*, Kansas State Historical Society; *p. 514*, Smithsonian American Art Museum, Washington, D.C./Art Resource, NY; *p. 515*, Detroit Public Library, Burton Historical Collection; *p. 517 (left)*, National Anthropological Archives, Smithsonian Institution, Washington, D.C.; *p. 517 (right)*, Library of Congress; *p. 520*, From *A Pima Past* by Anna Moore Shaw, University of Arizona Press, Tuson, Arizona; *p. 521 (top)*, National Archives; *p. 521 (bottom)*, National Archives; *p. 522*, The Huntington Library & Art Collections, San Marino, California; *p. 523*, National Museum of Natural History, Smithsonian Institution, Washington, D.C.; *p. 524 (top)*, Kansas Collection, University of Kansas Libraries; *p. 524 (right)*, Library of Congress; *p. 525*, Denver Public Library, Western History Division; *p. 529*, Museum of New Mexico; *p. 532*, Alaska and Polar Regions Archive, Elmer E. Rasmunson Library University of Alaska; *p. 534*, Denver Public Library, Western History Division; *p. 538*, Lent by the Department of the Interior Museum, National Museum of American Art, Smithsonian Institution, Washington, D.C./Art Resource, NY.

Chapter 18 *p. 542*, Chicago Historical Society; *p. 545*, Hagley Museum & Library; *p. 546*, Frank & Marie-Therese Wood Print Collections, Alexandria, VA; *p. 548*, National Portrait Gallery, Smithsonian Institution/Art Resource, NY; *p. 552*, Departrment of the Interior, National Park Service, Edison National Historic Site; *p. 556 (left)*, William L. Clements Library; *p. 556 (right)*, Library of Congress; *p. 557*, Trustees of the Boston Public Library Print department; *p. 560*, *Harper's Weekly*, March 26, 1877; *p. 562*, Library of Congress; *p. 563*, Courtesy of the Trustees of the Haverhill Public Library, Special Collections Department; *p. 564*, Library of Congress; *p. 567*, Museum of American Political Life; *p. 568*, Library of Congress; *p. 570*, Chicago Historical Society; *p. 554 (left)*, *House Drainage and Sanitary Plumbing* by William Paul Gerhard, 1882. Miriam and Ira D. Wallach Division of Art, Prints and Photographs, The New York Public Library. Astor, Lenox and Tilden Foundations; *p. 554 (right)*, *House Drainage and Sanitary Plumbing* by William Paul Gerhard, 1882. Miriam and Ira D. Wallach Division of Art, Prints and Photographs, The New York Public Library. Astor, Lenox and Tilden Foundations; *p. 555 (top)*, Avery Architectural and Fine Arts Library, Columbia University; *p. 555 (bottom)*, *House Drainage and Sanitary Plumbing* by William Paul Gerhard, 1882. Miriam and Ira D. Wallach Division of Art, Prints and Photographs, The New York Public Library. Astor, Lenox and Tilden Foundations;

Chapter 19 *p. 574*, George Eastman House; *p. 577*, Granger Collection; *p. 579*, Library of Congress; *p. 580*, Ellis Island Immigration Museum; *p. 581*, California Historical Society; *p. 584*, Picture Research Consultants & Archives; *p. 585*, Museum of the City of New York; *p. 586*, The Gifted Line, John Grossman; *p. 587*, *Harper's Weekly* 1871; *p. 588*, Santa Fee

Collection, Kansas State Historical Society; *p. 591*, Chicago Historical Society; *p. 592*, Detroit Institute of Arts, Founders Society Purchase; *p. 593*, Library of Congress; *p. 594*, Henry Ford Museum and Greenfield Village; *p. 597 (left)*, Granger Collection; *p. 597 (right)*, North Wind Picture Archives; *p. 598*, Fisk University Special Collections; *p. 599 (left)*, Courtesy New Orleans Jazz Club Collection, Louisiana State Museum Jan White Brantley; *p. 599 (right)*, Courtesy New Orleans Jazz Club Collection, Louisiana State Museum Jan White Brantley; *p. 604*, © Bettmann/Corbis.

Chapter 20 *p. 608*, Frank & Marie-Therese Wood Print Collections, Alexandria, VA; *p. 612*, Chicago Historical Society; *p. 614*, Granger Collection; *p. 619*, Hargrett Rare Book & Manuscript Library, University of Georgia Libraries; *p. 621*, © Bettmann/Corbis; *p. 623*, Library of Congress; *p. 625*, Library of Congress; *p. 628*, Kansas State Historical Society; *p. 629*, Smithsonian Institution, Washington, D.C.; *p. 634*, Rare Book Department, The Free Library of Philadelphia; *p. 635*, The Jacob A. Riis Collection, #123, Museum of the City of New York; *p. 636*, National Archives; *p. 637*, National Archives.

Chapter 21 *p. 640*, Picture Research Consultants & Archives; *p. 642*, Brown Brothers; *p. 644*, Metlife Archives; *p. 646*, © Bettmann/Corbis; *p. 647*, Ohio Historical Society; *p. 648*, Staten Island Historical Society; *p. 650*, Philadelphia City Archives; *p. 651*, Chicago Historical Society; *p. 652*, Picture Research Consultants & Archives; *p. 653*, Chicago Historical Society; *p. 655*, © Bettmann/Corbis; *p. 656*, Picture Research Consultants & Archives; *p. 657 (left)*, Schomburg Center for Research in Black Culture, New York Public Library; *p. 657 (right)*, Archives of the University of Massachusetts at Amherst; *p. 658*, Library of Congress; *p. 659*, Library of Congress; *p. 660*, Courtesy, Wellesley College Archives; *p. 661*, © Bettmann/Corbis; *p. 662 (top right)*, © Bettmann/Corbis; *p. 662 (bottom left)*, Library of Congress; *p. 665*, Library of Congress; *p. 667*, Library of Congress; *p. 668*, University of the Pacific; *p. 669 (top right)*, The Wadsworth Atheneum, Bequest of Mrs. Theodore Lyman in memory of her husband; *p. 669 (bottom right)*, © Bettmann/Corbis.

Chapter 22 *p. 676*, © Bettmann/Corbis; *p. 678*, Picture Research Consultants & Archives; *p. 679*, Granger Collection; *p. 680*, National Archives; *p. 682*, Naval Historical Foundation; *p. 684*, © Bettmann/Corbis; *p. 687*, Denver Public Library, Western History Division; *p. 688*, Social Hygiene, 4 April 1918; *p. 690*, National Archives; *p. 692*, U.S. Army Military History Institute; *p. 693 (left)*, Brown Brothers; *p. 693 (right)*, Picture Research Consultants & Archives; *p. 694*, U.S. Department of the Interior, National Park Service, Edison National Historic Site; *p. 695 (left)*, Collection of Paul Boyer; *p. 695 (right)*, Library of Congress; *p. 699*, The Phillips Collection, © Gwendolyn Knight Lawrence, courtesy of the Jacob and Gwendolyn Lawrence Foundation; *p. 701*, Courtesy American Red Cross; *p. 702*, Library of Congress; *p. 705*, Brooklyn Eagle, 1919; *p. 706*, Library of Congress; *p. 707*, Collection of Janice L. and David J. Frent.

Chapter 23 *p. 710*, Chicago Historical Society; *p. 713*, Archive Photos; *p. 716*, Walter P. Reuther Library/Wayne State University; *p. 717*, Library of Congress; *p. 721*, New Britain Museum of American Art Stephen Lawrence Fund, Photograph by E. Irving Blomstrann; *p. 722*, Courtesy of the Arizona Historical Society/Tuscon AHS #62669; *p. 723 (top)*, Strong Museum; *p. 723 (bottom)*, Library of Congress; *p. 724*, Warner Brother's Archives; *p. 725*, National Archives; *p. 727 (left)*, Picture Research Consultants & Archives; *p. 727 (right)*, Stock Montage; *p. 728*, Archive Photos; *p. 729*, National Portrait Gallery, Smithsonian Institution, Washington, D.C./Art Resource, NY; *p. 731*, © Collection of the New York Historical

Society; *p. 735*, Library of Congress; *p. 736*, © Bettmann/Corbis; *p. 737*, Museum of the City of New York; *p. 738*, Denver Public Library, Western History Division.

Chapter 24   *p. 742*, Library of Congress; *p. 748*, Minnesota Historical Society; *p. 750 (top)*, Library of Congress; *p. 750 (bottom)*, © Bettmann/Corbis; *p. 752*, Collection of Janice L. and David J. Frent; *p. 754*, Culver Pictures; *p. 757*, Smithsonian American Art Museum, Washington, D.C./Art Resource, NY; *p. 761*, Library of Congress; *p. 763*, Library of Congress; *p. 767*, Archives of Labor and Urban Affairs/Wayne State University; *p. 768*, © Bettmann/Corbis; *p. 769*, Library of Congress; *p. 771*, Photography Collection, Harry Ransom Humanities Research Center, The University of Texas at Austin General Libraries; *p. 772*, Courtesy AT&T Archives; *p. 773*, Christies Images, Inc.; *p. 774*, Photofest; *p. 775*, © 1989, Grandma Moses Properties Co, NY; *p. 776*, Archive Photos.

Chapter 25   *p. 780*, W. Eugene Smith/Timepix; *p. 785*, Thomas McAvoyTimepix; *p. 789*, Myron H. Davis/Timepix; *p. 792*, © Curt Teich Postcard Archives, Lake County (IL) Museum; *p. 794*, Library of Congress; *p. 796*, National Archives; *p. 801*, National Archives; *p. 803*, Scurlock Studio Collection Archives Center, National Museum of American History and the Schomburg Center for Research in Black Culture, New York Public Library; *p. 805*, Library of Congress; *p. 807*, US Army/Franklin D. Roosevelt Library; *p. 809 (left)*, National Archives; *p. 809 (right)*, National Archives; *p. 810*, Yivo Institute for Jewish Research; *p. 811*, National Archives.

Chapter 26   *p. 814*, Courtesy Edenhurst Gallery, Los Angeles, Daniel Nicodemo, Thomas Gianetto and Donald Merrill; *p. 817*, Indiana University; *p. 819*, Corbis-Bettmann; *p. 822*, National Archives; *p. 823*, Corbis-Bettmann; *p. 827 (top)*, © Bettmann/Corbis; *p. 827 (bottom)*, J.R. Eyerman/LIFE Magazine © Time, Inc.; *p. 829*, Corbis-Bettmann 4E P.799; *p. 831 (top right)*, Wide World Photos, Inc.; *p. 831 (left middle)*, © Bettmann/Corbis; *p. 831 (bottom right)*, Wide World ; *p. 832*, Hy Peskin/Timepix; *p. 833*, Corbis-Bettmann; *p. 835*, The Michael Barson Collection/Past Perfect; *p. 837 (left)*, © Elliot Erwitt/ Magnum Photos, Inc.; *p. 837 (right)*, © Elliot Erwitt/Magnum Photos, Inc.; *p. 838*, "I Have Here in My Hand..." from *HERBLOCK : A Cartoonist's Life* (Macmillian Publishing Company, 1993).

Chapter 27   *p. 842*, © The Curtis Publishing Company; *p. 845*, Courtesy Dwight D. Eisenhower Library; *p. 847 (top)*, Missouri State Archives; *p. 847 (bottom)*, Original Artwork by Anatole Kovarsky. Copyright © 1959 The New Yorker Magazine, Inc. Reprinted by permission. All Rights Reserved; *p. 849*, Wide World Photos, Inc.; *p. 851*, *TIME* Magazine © Time, Inc.; *p. 852*, Wide World Photos, Inc.; *p. 855*, Courtesy Boeing Defense & Space Group; *p. 856*, Corbis-Bettmann; *p. 858*, Alfred Eisenstaedt/ *LIFE* Magazine © Time, Inc.; *p. 860*, © 1992 Cindy Lewis; *p. 864 (left)*, Photofest; *p. 864 (right)*, Gaslight Advertising Archives; *p. 866*, Chicago Historical Society; *p. 867*, Corbis-Bettmann; *p. 868*, Corbis-Bettmann; *p. 870*, NASA/Johnson Space Center; *p. 871*, © Bettmann/Corbis; *p. 874*, Dan Budnick/Woodfin Camp & Associates.

Chapter 28   *p. 877*, Wide World Photos, Inc.; *p. 878*, © Bettmann/Corbis; *p. 879*, Wide World; *p. 880*, Wide World Photos, Inc.; *p. 882*, National Archives; *p. 883*, Lyndon B. Johnson Presidential Library; *p. 891*, Corbis-Bettmann; *p. 893*, James Prigoff; *p. 896*, Wyeth-Ayerst Laboratories; *p. 897*, Timepix; *p. 899*, Robert J. Ellison/Black Star/Stockphoto.com; *p. 901 (top)*, Corbis-Bettmann; *p. 901 (bottom right)*, Cartoon by Paul Szep © *The Boston Globe*.

Chapter 29   *p. 904*, Wide World/AP photo /Henri Huet; *p. 907*, University of California at Berkeley, Bancroft Library; *p. 908*, Corbis-Bettmann; *p. 909*, John Filo; *p. 910*, © Bettmann/Corbis; *p. 911*, John and Leni SInclair Collection, Bentley Historical Library, University of Michigan; *p. 914 (left)*, Gene Anthony/Black Star; *p. 914 (right)*, Elliot Landy/ Magnum Photos, Inc.; *p. 915 (left)*, Gene Anthony/Black Star; *p. 915 (right)*, M.L. Carlebach/Black Star; *p. 916 (top left)*, Wide World; *p. 916 (bottom right)*, Wide World; *p. 919*, © Bettmann/Corbis; *p. 920*, Ron Haeberle/ Timepix; *p. 923*, Wally McNamee/ Woodfin Camp & Associates; *p. 925*, NASA/Johnson Space Center; *p. 927*, Flip Schulke/Black Star/Stock Photo; *p. 929*, Cartoon News International; *p. 931*, Illustration by Jack Davis for *Time* cover, April 30, 1973/Timepix.

Chapter 30   *p. 934*, (detail) Collection of Katherine Sosa; *p. 936*, Rob Nelson/Black Star; *p. 937*, © 1984 Newsweek, Inc. All rights reserved. Reprinted by permission; *p. 939*, Courtesy Tuck School of Business Archives, Dartmouth College, Hanover, N.H.; *p. 941 (top left)*, © Bettmann/Corbis; *p. 941 (bottom right)*, Reproduced from *Popular Mechanics*, January 1975, by permission of Gernsback Publications, Inc.; *p. 943*, © 2002 JEB (Joan E. Biren); *p. 945*, American Folklife Collection/Library of Congress; *p. 947 (left)*, NASA/Johnson Space Center; *p. 947 (right)*, Leonard Freed/Magnum Photos, Inc.; *p. 949*, © Galen Rowell/Bettmann/Corbis; *p. 950*, Jimmy Carter Presidential Library; *p. 951*, Sipa Press; *p. 953*, © Wally McNamee/ Bettmann/Corbis; *p. 960*, Wide World; *p. 961*, © Bettmann/ Corbis.

Chapter 31   *p. 964*, Seth Resnick/Stock Boston; *p. 966*, © Bettmann/Corbis/Seth Resnick/Stock Boston; *p. 968*, © Bettmann/Corbis; *p. 970*, Bruno Barbey/Magnum Photos, Inc.; *p. 971*, HolLynn D'Lil; *p. 972*, © Bettmann/Corbis; *p. 975*, Photo Courtesy Richard Petty Driving Experience; *p. 977*, Brooks Kraft/Corbis/Sygma; *p. 978*, CartoonStock Ltd.; *p. 979*, © Bettmann/Corbis; *p. 980*, J. Nachtwey/Cosmos/VII Photo Agency; *p. 982*, M. Almeida/*The New York Times*; *p. 984*, Alex Webb/Magnum Photos, Inc.; *p. 985*, Susan Greenwood/Gamma Liaison/Getty Images; *p. 986*, Dorothy Littel Greco/Stock Boston; *p. 988*, © Corbis /Sygma; *p. 989*, R. Fremson/The New York Times.

Chapter 32   *p. 992*, Steve Liss/Timepix; *p. 995*, Agence France Presse© Bettmann/Corbis; *p. 996*, Richard Ellis/Sygma/Corbis; *p. 997*, Tribune Media Services, Inc. All rights reserved. Reprinted with permission; *p. 998*, AFP/Corbis; *p. 1002*, Richard Ellis/Sygma/Corbis; *p. 1005*, Mark Peterson/SABA/Corbis; *p. 1006*, Reuters/Corbis; *p. 1008*, John Domines Timepix; *p. 1011*, © Reuters/Corbis; *p. 1010*, Photo by Jeff Miller/University of Wisconsin; *p. 1013*, Eric Engman for *The New York Times*; *p. 1015*, Don Tellock/Gamma Press USA, Inc.; *p. 1017*, © Sygma /Corbis; *p. 1019 (left)*, Michael Kaemer/AFP /Corbis; *p. 1019 (right)*, Luc Delahaye/Magnum Photos for *Newsweek*; *p. 1020*, Wide World.

Index

Auburn system, 312
Audiotapes: Nixon and, 931
Audubon Society, 722
Augusta Powder Works, 440
Austin, Stephen F., 387
Australia, 788
Austria, 704, 783, 965
Austria-Hungary: World War I and, 683, 703, 704
Authority: under Constitution (U.S.), 187–188; of family, 278–279; horizontal and vertical allegiances, 281; questioning of, 277–278
Author Painting a Chief at the Base of the Rocky Mountains, The (Catlin), 341
Authors, *see* Literature; specific authors
Autobiography of Malcolm X, The (Malcolm X), 891
Automation, 816, 858
Automobiles and automobile industry, 651, 712, 713 (illus.), 722 (illus.), 855; corporate dominance in, 714; cultural impact of, 721; environment and, 722; fuel-efficient, 948; Japanese cars and, 968; labor unions and, 766; Nader and, 886; in 1950s, 859, 860 (illus.); registered cars (1900–1992), 720; teens and, 871; women workers and, 715; in World War I, 698
Awakening, The (Chopin), 603
Awful Disclosures of the Hotel Dieu Nunnery in Montreal (Monk), 382
Axis, 798, 811
Aztec empire, 7, 41

Babbitt (Lewis), 730
Babcock, Orville, 500
Baby boom, 860–861, 979; youth movement and, 906–910
Backcountry, 146–148
Bacon, Nathaniel, 73
Bacon's Rebellion, 72–74
Bagley, Sarah, 318
Baker, James A., 968, 973
Baker, Newton D., 687, 690
Baker, Ray Stannard, 656
Baker v. *Carr*, 886–887
Bakker, Jim and Tammy, 944
Bakke v. *U.S.*, 945–946
Balanced budget bill, 994
Balance of power: after Korean War, 830; World War II and, 798, 820

Balboa, Vasco Núñez de, 39
Baldwin, James, 729, 863
Baldwin Locomotive Works, 545 (illus.), 553
Balfour Declaration, 704
Balkan region: conflicts in, 997–998
Ball courts: Hohokam, 9
Ballinger, Richard, 667
Ballinger-Pinchot affair, 667
Balloon-frame houses, 327
Baltic states, 704, 967
Baltimore, Lord, *see* Calvert family
Baltimore and Ohio Railroad, 265, 324
Baltimore Orioles, 593 (illus.)
Bank holiday, 751
Bank of England, 96
Bank of the United States, 294 (illus.), 294–295; charter of (1816), 293; First, 200–201; Marshall on, 249; Panic of 1819 and, 264; Second, 248
Bankruptcies: corporate, 1020–1021; economic growth and, 557; railroad, 625
Banks and banking: expansionism and, 393; Federal Reserve banks, 672; in Great Depression, 745–746; growth of, 217; land speculation and, 263; national system of, 441; in New Deal, 751; Panic of 1819 and, 264; payments suspended by, 746; reform of, 670–672; in South, 558; in states, 295; Whigs and, 390; World War I loans and, 685. *See also* Bank of the United States
Banneker, Benjamin, 176
Bannocks, 515
Baptism: Half-Way Covenant and, 61–62
Baptists, 119, 359; blacks as, 370–371, 493; colleges founded by, 362; northern and southern wings of, 371; women's church role and, 120
Barak, Ehud, 1000
Barbados, 37, 76, 76 (illus.)
Barbary pirates, *see* Tripolitan pirates
Barbed wire, 527
Barlowe, Arthur, 46
Barnard, George N., 465, 471 (illus.)
Barnard, Hannah, 101 (illus.)
Barnard College, 602
Barnum, P. T., 331, 333–334
Barriers to trade, 1004
Barrios, 529, 769
"Barroom Dancing" (Krimmel), 258 (illus.)
Barrow, David Crenshaw, 498 (map)

Barrow plantation, 498 (map)
Barter: in rural communities, 101
Bartholomew Gosnold Trading with Wampanoag Indians at Martha's Vineyard (de Bry), 22 (illus.)
Barton, Bruce, 715
Barton, Clara, 467
Bartram, John, 102
Baruch, Bernard, 688
Baseball, 574 (illus.), 593 (illus.), 593–594; integration of, 831, 832 (illus.)
BASIC program, 940
Basie, Count, 774
Basketball, 602
Bataan peninsula, 788
Batch producers, 553
Bathroom: flush toilets and, 554 (illus.), 554–555, 555 (illus.)
Batista, Fulgencio, 782
Baton Rouge, 449
Battle of Britain, 786
Battles: in War of 1812, 244 (map). *See also* specific battles and wars
Bay of Pigs fiasco, 880
"Bayonet rule," 501
Beatles, 912
Beats, 871–872
Beaumont, Gustave de, 255–256
Beauregard, P. G. T., 446, 447, 448
Beautification movement, 649–650
Beaver pelts, 45, 45 (illus.), 65. *See also* Fur trade
Beaver wars, 78, 83
Beck, E. M., 622
Becker, Carl, 785
Beckwourth, Jim, 258
Beecher family: Catharine, 279, 308, 328, 583; Henry Ward, 419, 583; Lyman, 279, 306, 309, 382. *See also* Stowe, Harriet Beecher
Begin, Menachem, 950
Beijing: Boxers in, 679. *See also* China
Beirut: massacre in, 957
Belarus, 968, 1000
Bel Geddes, Norman, 776
Belgium, 786
Belknap, William E., 501
Bell, Alexander Graham, 552
Bell, Daniel, 983
Bell, John, 428, 429 (map)
Bellamy, Edward, 571, 601, 644
Belleau Wood, battle at, 691
Bell Labs, 855
Bell Telephone Company, 552
Belmont, August, 626

Caribbean region: colonies in (1660), 75 (map); Europeans in, 42; expansion into, 416, 417; France and, 232; immigrants from, 769; slavery in, 75–76; trade with, 181; United States and, 681 (map), 956 (map). *See also* specific locations
Carlisle Indian school, 520, 521
Carmichael, Stokely, 876
Carnegie, Andrew, 547–549, 548 (illus.), 565, 571, 636
Carnegie Steel Company, 548, 569–570, 647
Carolinas: Florida and, 106; immigration to, 100; Indians in, 77–78, 110; racism in, 104; slaves and, 77, 86; Spanish invasion of, 93. *See also* North Carolina; South Carolina
Carpetbaggers, 488 (illus.), 488–489, 504
Carpet bombing, 830
Carranza, Venustiano, 683
Cars, *see* Automobiles and automobile industry
Carson, Kit, 258, 449, 536–537
Carson, Rachel, 858, 858 (illus.), 879, 938
Carter, Jimmy, 948–950; Camp David Accords and, 950; election of 1976 and, 948, 951; Haiti and, 999; Nobel Prize and, 950 (illus.); North Korea and, 1000
Carter, Stephen J., 944
Carteret, Philip, 80
Cartier, Jacques, 40, 45
Cartography, 34
Cartoon movies, 773
Cartwright, Peter, 300
Carver Hospital (Washington, D.C.), 466 (illus.)
Casablanca, 798
Casey, William, 959
Cash-and-carry policy, 786
Cash crops, 262, 263–264, 349. *See also* Crops; specific crops
"Cash-only" cooperative stores, 618
Casinos, *see* Gambling
Cass, George W., 535
Cass, Lewis, 392, 400, 419 (illus.)
Caste system: in South, 624
Castile, 25, 28
Castle Garden immigrant center, 579
Castro, Fidel, 782, 853, 880, 882
Casualties: of Civil War, 438, 439, 445, 448, 449, 459; of Korean War,

829–830; in Persian Gulf War, 969; in Revolution, 152, 173; in Tet Offensive, 913–914; in Vietnam War, 921–922; in World War I, 708; of World War II, 812
Catawba Indians, 110
Catch-the-Bear, 522
Catherine of Aragón, 32
Catholicism: anti-Catholicism and, 382; birth control and, 913; in England, 32–33; of Irish immigrants, 381; of James II, 91; Klan and, 734; in Maryland, 69, 92; of Mexican-Americans, 733; in New France, 83; in New York, 91; in 1950s, 862; non-slave immigration and, 96; public education and, 604–605; of Pueblo Indians, 112; Quebec Act and, 151; reform of, 32; school reform and, 308; in 16th century, 31; in Spanish colonies, 84; of workers, 296. *See also* Protestantism
Catholic Legion of Decency, 773
Catlin, George, 341 (illus.), 342, 513–514, 514 (illus.)
Catt, Carrie Chapman, 658, 685, 697, 699
Cattle industry, 529; drives and, 533; trails and, 531 (map); in West, 531 (map), 533–535
Cattle kings, 534
Cavalry: Civil War and, 445; in Spanish-American War, 636 (illus.)
Cayuga Iroquois Indians: King William's War and, 93
CBS, *see* Columbia Broadcasting System (CBS)
CCC, *see* Civilian Conservation Corps (CCC)
CD (compact disk), 937
Celebrities, *see* Movies and movie stars
Celebrity culture, 725–726
Celera Genomics Corporation, 1010
Cemeteries: landscaping of, 342
Censorship: of movies, 652, 773; in World War II, 794
Census: of 1920, 720; of 2000, 978
Central America: agriculture in, 5
Central High School: desegregation of, 849 (illus.), 849–850
Central Intelligence Agency (CIA), 789, 822; Americans investigated by, 928; Bay of Pigs and, 880; covert operations of, 825, 851–852, 924; Iran-contra and, 959; Sandinistas

and, 956
Centralization: royal, 90–91
Central Pacific Railroad, 502, 523–524
Central Park (New York), 342
Central Valley: farming in, 535
Century, The, magazine, 597
Century of Dishonor, A (Jackson), 518
Ceremonies: of Indians, 14, 513–514. *See also* specific ceremonies
Cession of land, *see* Land
Chaco Canyon, 9, 9 (illus.)
Chain gang, 621 (illus.), 622
Chain migration, 580
Chain stores, 714
Chamberlain, Mary Brown, 220
Chamberlain, Neville, 784
Chambers, Whittaker, 836–838
Champion Single Sculls (Eakins), 601
Champlain, Samuel de, 45–46
Chancellorsville, Battle of, 458, 458 (map), 469
Channing, William Ellery, 301, 312
Chaplin, Charlie, 652, 836
Chapman, Hannah, 364
Charbonneau, Toussaint, 235
Charity Organization Society (COS), 589, 590
Charles I (England), 55, 68, 69, 90
Charles II (England), 61, 77, 79, 80, 90
Charles V (Holy Roman Empire), 31
Charleston (Charles Town), 77, 103, 105, 360–361, 430–431; blacks in, 430–431; immigration to, 100; as port, 94; in Revolutionary War, 171 (map)
Charleston (dance), 728
Charter: for Bank of the United States, 201, 293; in Massachusetts, 91, 150; for Raleigh's colony, 46; Supreme Court on, 249; to Virginia, 47
Chase, Salmon P., 441, 442, 469, 470, 503
Chase, Samuel, 231, 232
Château-Thierry, battle at, 691
Chattanooga: siege of, 459–460
Chauncy, Charles, 104
Chávez, César, 893
Chavín de Huántar, 6
Chechnya, 998
"Checkers" speech (Nixon), 864
Checks and balances, 188
Cheever, John, 863
Chemical industry, 854
Chemical weapons, 1001
Cheney, Dick, 968, 1005, 1007, 1008, 1014, 1021

Denmark, 786
Dennett, Mary Ware, 660
Dennison, Patience, 59–60
Dennis v. *United States,* 836
Departments of government, *see* specific departments
Department stores, 584–585, 585 (illus.), 651
Deposit Act (1836), 295, 297
Deppe, Ferdinand, 385 (illus.)
Depressions: of 1830s, 324–325; of 1840s, 390; of 1873, 498, 502, 527, 618–619; of 1893-1897, 624, 625–626; in Chesapeake, 72; in New England, 185; Panic of 1837 and, 297; after Revolution, 181. *See also* Great Depression; Panics
De Priest, Oscar, 720
Deregulation, 953–954
Desegregation, 849 (illus.), 867; of buses, 867; Nixon and, 928–929; in Reconstruction South, 496; of schools, 848–850. *See also* Civil rights movement
Deseret, 377–378. *See also* Utah
Desert: cultures of, 14–15
Desert Land Act (1877), 526
Desert Storm, *see* Operation Desert Storm
De Soto, Hernando, 43, 44
Despotism: Jefferson and, 230
Destroyers-for-bases swap, 787
Détente policy, 881, 923–924, 962
Detroit, 109, 132, 254 (illus.); Brant at, 184; growth of city, 270; racial protests in, 803, 890–891; in War of 1812, 245
Dewey, George, 632, 633 (map), 637
Dewey, John, 645, 678, 696, 697
Dewey, Thomas E., 798, 833
De Witt, John, 805 (illus.)
Dewson, Molly, 760
Dial, The (magazine), 313
Días, Bartolomeu, 34
Díaz, Adolfo, 681–682
Díaz, Porfirio, 683
Dickinson, Anna E., 467
Dickinson, Emily, 338
Dickinson, John, 137, 139, 141, 151, 180
Dictatorship: in Germany, 783
Diem, Ngo Dinh, 853, 880 (illus.), 898–899
Dienbienphu, 852
Diet: antebellum, 327; in Civil War, 450; health and, 329; of slaves, 366. *See also* Food(s); Nutrition

Diggers, 915
Digital Equipment Corporation (DEC), 940
Dillard, Annie, 825
Dillinger, John, 770
Dime novels, 534, 537
Dingley Tariff (1897), 629
Diphtheria: epidemic of, 118
Diplomacy: Adams, John, and, 215–216; Bush, George W., and, 1009; in Civil War ("cotton diplomacy"), 452; Indian-British (1764), 132 (illus.); in 1920s, 718–719; Nixon and, 923–924; Washington and, 205. *See also* Foreign policy
Direct election: of presidential electors, 287; of senators, 673
Direct primary, 647, 648
Disabled persons, 971, 971 (illus.)
Discount chains, 935–936
Discrimination: against African-Americans, 275–276; against Asian children, 682; by gender, 894; industrialization and, 565; job, 971; resistance to, 768–769; in Southwest, 529–530; wage, 715
Disease: AIDS and, 942–943; antebellum, 328–329; in Carolina, 77; in Chesapeake, 70; in cities, 102; in Civil War, 467; diphtheria epidemic and, 118; genetic research and, 1011; health movements and, 326; among Indians, 54, 62, 946; indoor plumbing and, 555; in New England, 60; in Philadelphia, 130; among slaves, 366; smallpox as, 234; in Spanish-American War, 633; Spanish introduction of, 41–42, 204; theories of, 328–329; treatments for, 861; in urban slums, 582; in World War I, 691. *See also* Epidemics
Disestablishment, 180
Disfranchisement: of black voters, 621; of middle-class women, 658
Disinherited, The (Conroy), 748–749
Disney, Walt, 773, 836; theme parks of, 937, 987
Displaced Persons Act, 834
Dissent: in Civil War, 463–466; legal suppression of, 697–698; in New England, 56–58; in Plymouth, 49; in World War I, 696–697. *See also* Protest(s); Puritans and Puritanism; Separatists
Distant Early Warning Line, 850

Distribution of income: in 1990s, 1003–1004
Distribution of wealth: in New England, 63; single tax and, 571
Distribution systems: in 1920s, 714; of railroads, 545
District of Columbia: slavery in, 409, 410
District schools, 307
Diversification: economic, 95
Diversity, *see* Cultural diversity
Division of labor: on southern plantations, 352
Divorce, 220, 603, 643, 801, 816; in New England, 60; sexual revolution and, 912–913
Dix, Dorothea, 313, 467
Dixiecrats, 832, 833
Dixieland jazz, 599, 731
Djerassi, Carl, 896
DNA: genetics research and, 1010
Doctors, *see* Medicine; Physicians
Doctrine of separate spheres, *see* Separate spheres doctrine
Documentaries: in 1930s, 770
Dodge, Josephine, 658
Doeg Indians, 73
Dole, Robert, 976, 994
Dollar diplomacy, 681, 682
Domesticity, 311; in 1950s, 861–862; women's movement and, 894
Domestic policy, *see* specific presidents
Domestic sphere, 659
Dominican Republic, 38, 232, 782; intervention in, 681, 682, 683
Dominion of New England, 91, 93
Domino theory, 852–853
Donahue brothers, 565
Donaldson, John, 595
Donelson, Fort, 448
Donnelly, Ignatius, 620, 621, 624
Donner party, 389
Dos Passos, John, 724, 748
Dot-coms, 1003; recession and, 1012
Doubleday, Abner, 593
"Double V" campaign, 802, 803 (illus.)
Douglas, Helen Gahagan, 840
Douglas, Stephen A., 414–415, 422, 424 (illus.); Compromise of 1850 and, 410; election of 1860 and, 428–429; Lincoln debates with, 423–425
Douglas Aircraft Corporation, 826
Douglass, Frederick, 309, 365, 413 (illus.), 453, 455, 456, 486, 507, 623; freedom of, 369; on slavedriver, 364

Declaration of Independence and, 154; Enlightenment and, 116, 117; on Irish immigrants, 100; on labor, 102; and Peace of Paris, 172; Philadelphia sanitation and, 130; social class and, 174; will of, 117–118
Franklin, Rosalind, 1010
Fransson, Martha, 939 (illus.)
Franz Ferdinand (Austria), 683–684
Fraternal orders: anti-Catholicism and, 382; black, 623
Fredericksburg, Battle of, 445, 448, 458, 469
Free African Society of Philadelphia, 223
Free blacks, 74, 222; in Charleston, 431; in Missouri, 251; in Mose, 107; in North, 275–276; occupations of, 276; Revolution and, 175; in South, 175, 366–367; by state (1800), 223; status of, 224; voluntary associations for, 282. See also African-Americans
Freed, Alan, 870–871
Freedmen, 478; black codes and, 481; in Civil War, 454–455; election of 1868 and, 500; land for, 494, 496–497; political rights of, 488; in Reconstruction governments, 488–490; redemption and, 505; southern counterattacks against, 491
Freedmen's Bureau, 455, 481, 491, 492, 496, 497
Freedmen's schools, 493 (illus.)
Freedom(s): in Bill of Rights, 198; of press, 116; of religion, 162; of speech, 214, 310, 836; after World War I, 698. See also African-Americans; Slaves and slavery; specific rights and freedoms
Freedom movement, see Civil rights movement
Freedom rides, 887
Freedom Schools, 889
Freeman, Mary Wilkins, 603
Freeman, Richard, 1003
Free-market economy: in Russia, 998
Free persons of color, 175–176
"Freeport doctrine": of Douglas, 425
Free-silver monetary policy, 502, 610, 627
Free-soilers, 400–401; Kansas-Nebraska Act and, 415–416, 417
Free Speech Movement, 907, 907 (illus.)
Free-staters: Kansas and, 418–423

Free states: Compromise of 1850 and, 408–414; election of 1856 and, 421; Maine as, 250, 251; Missouri Compromise and, 251
Free trade, 501
Freeways, see Interstate highway system
Frelinghuysen, Theodore, 118, 392
Frémont, John C., 397, 421, 428
French and Indian War, see Seven Years' War
French Canada: Quebec Act and, 151
French-Canadians: in cities, 577; as industrial labor, 562
French Revolution (1789), 124, 203, 206–207
Frick, Henry Clay, 572
Friedan, Betty, 876, 894, 939
Fries Rebellion, 215
Frobisher, Martin, 46
Frontier: authority questioned on, 278; "moving," 263–264; myths and legends of, 536–537; revivalism along, 300; settlers, railroads, and homesteading and, 524–527
Frontiersmen, 247
Frontier thesis (Turner), 536
"Front-porch" campaign, 628, 629 (illus.)
Fruitlands community, 313
Fruits of Philosophy (Knowlton), 281
FSA, see Farm Security Administration (FSA)
FTP, see Federal Theatre Project (FTP)
Fuchs, Klaus, 838
Fuel Administration, 688
Fugitive Slave Act (1850), 411–412
Fugitive Slave Law (1793), 223, 409
Fugitive slaves, 364, 369
Fulbright, William, 891, 901
Fuller, Margaret, 334, 336 (illus.), 336–337
Fulton, Robert, 264
Fundamental Constitutions of Carolina, 77
Fundamentalism: Christian, 1001; Islamic, 957, 961, 1001; Scopes trial and, 733–734; vs. secularism, 1001. See also Christianity; Islam; Terrorism
Fundamentals, The, 734
Funerals, see Burials
Furniture: production of, 327
Fur trade, 45 (illus.), 49, 62, 257 (illus.); Astor and, 258, 275; beaver pelts and, 65; "beaver wars" and, 78–79;

in Far West, 386; French and, 45, 110; furs as export, 95, 96; in New England, 61; in New France, 83; New Netherland and, 50, 78–79
Futurama: at New York World's Fair, 776

Gabriel's Rebellion, 223
Gadsden, Christopher, 135
Gadsden Purchase, 416
Gage, Thomas, 151, 152
Gag rule: in Congress, 310
Gallatin, Albert, 230, 246
Galloway, Joseph: at Continental Congress, 151–152
Gálvez, Bernardo de, 204
Gama, Vasco da, 34
Gambia, 97
Gambling: Indians and, 981
Gandhi, Mohandas, 802
Gang labor, 497
Gangs, see Organized crime; Street gangs
Gangster movies, 770
Gang system: of slave labor, 104
Garden, Alexander, 89, 119, 120
Gardner, Alexander, 465
Garfield, James A.: assassination of, 609, 610, 615; election of 1880 and, 614; life of, 609–610
Garland, Hamlin, 543–544, 561, 619
Garland, Isabelle, 543–544
Garment Cutters of Philadelphia, 566
Garner, John Nance, 749
Garner, Margaret, 412
Garrison, William Lloyd, 292, 308–309, 657; women's rights and, 310, 311
Garvey, Marcus, 729, 735–736, 736 (illus.)
Gasoline, 855. See also Oil and oil industry
Gates, Bill, 940, 941 (illus.)
Gates, Horatio, 166, 172
Gatling gun, 444
GATT, see General Agreement on Tariffs and Trade (GATT)
Gay Liberation Front, 913
Gay Pride parades, 942
Gays and lesbians, 943 (illus.); AIDS and, 942–943; conservatives and, 943; gay liberation and, 913; immigration restrictions on, 839; McCarthyism and, 839; in military, 974; reaction against, 988, 988 (illus.); women's movement and, 939; in World War II, 805

Income tax, 626, 673, 793. *See also* Taxation

Indentured servants: in Carolina, 77; in Chesapeake, 70–71; contracts for, 70 (illus.); costs of, 104; in New France, 84; slaves and, 74; in Virginia, 48

Independence: of Mexico, 387

Independence (American colonies), 149–156; after Peace of Paris, 173. *See also* American Revolution

Independence Hall, 186

Independent internationalism, 718–719

Independent Treasury, 390, 399

India: commerce with, 210; immigrants from, 732, 983; Pakistan and, 1000; routes to, 26 (map), 38

Indiana, 209, 250, 256

Indiana Territory: Indians and, 242

Indiana University, 817 (illus.)

"Indian fashion," 65

Indian Knoll, Kentucky, 5

Indian Law Resource Center, 981

Indian Non-Intercourse Act (1790), 206, 221

Indian Ocean, 34

Indian policy: in New Deal, 762; reservation system, 515–516, 519 (map); of Washington, 206; in World War II, 804

Indian Removal Act (1830), 260, 291

Indian Reorganization Act (1934), 762

Indians, *see* Native Americans

Indians Claims Commission, 946

Indian Self-Determination Act (1974), 946

Indian Springs, Treaty of, 259

Indian Territory, 513. *See also* Oklahoma Territory

Indian wars: in Civil War, 449

Indigo: as export, 95

Individualism, 278, 512

Indochina, 787, 788, 825, 830, 852–853. *See also* Cambodia; Laos; Vietnam

Indonesia, 1004

Indoor plumbing, 554–555

Indulgences, 31

Industrial accidents, 561

Industrial design, 776

Industrial hygiene, 649

Industrialization, 217, 270–274, 542–572; Civil War and, 473; politics of, 608 (illus.); progressivism and, 643–644; in South, 350; toll from, 641–642. *See also* Manufacturing; specific industries

Industrial safety: progressivism and, 648–649

Industrial Workers of the World (IWW, Wobblies), 661, 661 (illus.), 696, 698

Industry, 216–217; in 1920s, 714–715; in 1950s, 854–855; Embargo Act and, 240; high-tech, 987; in New Deal, 763; in New England, 61; outworkers in, 273; after September 11, 2001, 1016; in South, 349, 462; 558–559; technology and, 322; in World War I, 688, 698; World War II and, 789–793, 792 (illus.), 818–819. *See also* Labor unions; specific industries

Infant mortality, 650; in Chesapeake, 70; decline in, 886; in New England, 60; in urban slums, 582

Inflation: in Civil War, 461, 462; in 1970s, 948, 951; Nixon and, 926–927; World War II and, 792, 819

Influence of Sea Power upon History, The (Mahan), 630

Influenza epidemic, 691, 700–701, 701 (illus.)

Inheritance, 96

Initiative (electoral reform), 647

Injunction: Pullman strike and, 570

Inman, S. M., 495

Inner cities, 981; blacks in, 945; Hispanics in, 982; in 1990s, 978; slums in, 865–866

Inner Light: of Quakers, 80–81

In re Debs, 570

Insane asylums: reform of, 312

Insecticides, 793, 858

Insider trading, 954

Installment buying, 318, 858

Institutional church movement, 590

Insull, Samuel, 714

Insurgents, 666–667

Integration: in armed forces, 803; in public schools, 308; of sports, 831, 832 (illus.). *See also* Desegregation; Segregation

Intel, 940

Intellectual thought: Enlightenment and, 90, 116–117; Harlem Renaissance and, 728–729; Jefferson and, 228–229; Marxist, 571–572; in 1920s, 726–732; political writing and, 137–139; progressives and, 644–646; in Renaissance, 28; social, 571, 626; transcendentalists and, 313; utopian, 571; Victorian, 584; on

World War I, 697. *See also* Enlightenment; specific people and movements

Intelligence gathering, 851

Intelligence testing, *see* IQ tests

Interchangeable parts, 271, 320, 322

Intercollegiate Socialist Society, 662

Intercontinental ballistic missile (ICBM), 870

Interest rates, 951, 1012

Intermediate-range Nuclear Forces (INF) Treaty, 959–960

Internal improvements: Jackson and, 295; Madison and, 248

International Bank for Reconstruction and Development, *see* World Bank

International Business Machines (IBM), 784, 855, 896, 940–941

International Congress of Women, 677

International Court of Justice, 718

International Criminal Court, 1009–1012

International Harvester, 562–563, 647

Internationalism, *see* Globalism

International Ladies' Garment Workers' Union (ILGWU), 661

International Monetary Fund, 818, 1004

International organizations, 1001. *See also* specific organizations

International Telephone and Telegraph (ITT), 857

Internet, 986

Interracial relationships, 42, 809, 983

Interstate commerce, 264, 547

Interstate Commerce Act (1887), 547, 611, 618

Interstate Commerce Commission (ICC), 547, 562, 618, 664, 666

Interstate highway system, 845, 846 (illus.), 846–847, 847 (illus.)

Intervention: in Dominican Republic, 681, 682, 683; in Grenada, 957; in Haiti, 682–683, 999; vs. isolationism, 785 (illus.); in Lebanon, 853, 957; in Nicaragua, 681–682; in Somalia, 998; in Vietnam, 852–853. *See also* Latin America

Intolerable Acts, 150–151

Intrepid (ship), 230 (illus.)

Inuits, *see* Eskimos (Inuits)

Inventions: at Chicago World's Fair, 543; farm machinery, 527; by Jefferson, 228–229; in late 19th century, 551–553. *See also* specific inventors and inventions

Newfoundland, 16, 39, 40, 45, 93, 127, 787
New France, 45, 83–84, 93, 97, 162
New Freedom, 670
New Frontier, 877, 878
New Hampshire, 58, 147
New Harmony community, 313
New Haven Colony, 57 (illus.)
New immigrants, 578
New Jersey, 78, 79–80; Revolutionary War in, 164; women's political rights in, 217
New Jersey Plan, 187
New Lanark, Scotland: Owen and, 313
Newlands Act (1902), 665
New Left, 906–907, 910, 937
New Lights, 119
New Mexico, 398–399, 528, 529; American settlements in, 388; annexation of, 378; atomic bomb and, 826; boundary of, 410, 411; Indians of, 44–45; Mexican-American War and, 396–397; popular sovereignty and, 410; Pueblo Bonito in, 9, 9 (illus.); slave-raiding expedition in, 112 (illus.); slavery and, 399, 409; Spain and, 43, 84–86, 112, 385; Spanish-speaking Americans in, 530; Texas and, 408–409
New Nationalism, 667, 670
New Negro, The (Locke), 729
New Netherland, 50, 78; as New York, 79
New Orleans, 195, 205 (illus.), 269, 270, 349 (illus.), 449, 451; American commerce and, 184–185; Battle of, 246, 247; in 1890s, 598 (illus.), 598–599, 599 (illus.); jazz in, 731; Jefferson and, 232; Spain and, 205; War of 1812 and, 246
New Republic magazine, 645, 696
New Right, 952
"New slavery," 34–35. See also Slaves and slavery; Slave trade
New South, 504, 557–560; Atlanta and, 495; creed, 558
New Spain, 41
Newspapers: ads in, 103 (illus.); African-American, 698; penny press and, 331–332; photoengraving and, 635; politics and, 116; readership of, 212; Socialist, 662, 662 (illus.); sports in, 594; yellow journalism and, 632. See also Media
New Sweden, 78

Newton, Huey P., 892
Newton, Isaac, 116
New Woman, 602–603, 643
New World, see Americas; specific regions
New world order, 1001–1002
New World Order, The (Robertson), 989
New York (city), 699; antidraft riots in, 463; artisans and workers in, 273–274; Five Points district in, 275; Harlem Renaissance and, 728–729; immigrants in, 578; landscape architects in, 342; lower East Side, 579 (illus.); O'Keefe painting of, 721 (illus.); poor relief in, 589; Puerto Ricans in, 868; purity campaign in, 589–590; railroads and, 325; September 11 and, 1014–1015; slaves in, 105; World's Fair of 1939 in, 776, 776 (illus.)
New York (colony), 78, 79–80; Catholics in, 91; Leisler's Rebellion in, 92; politics in, 116; population of, 103; Quartering Act and, 140; Revolutionary War in, 164, 165 (map), 166
New York (state): backcountry and, 147; Erie Canal and, 265; inequality of wealth in, 274; as port, 94
New York, Treaty of, 205–206
New York Association for Improving the Condition of the Poor, 588
New York Central Railroad, 324
New York Herald, 331, 332, 393
New York Journal, 632, 635
New York Knickerbockers, 594
New York Ledger, 339
New York Society for the Suppression of Vice, 589
New York Stock Exchange, 217, 325
New York Sun, 331
New York Suspending Act, 140
New York Times, 635
New York Times Co. v. Sullivan, 886
New York Tribune, 332, 396
New-York Weekly Journal, 116
New York World, 594
Nez Percés, 515, 518
Ngai, Mae M., 732
Niagara Movement, 657
Nicaragua, 681–682, 956, 968, 985; Iran-contra scandal and, 959; Walker in, 416
Nichols, Terry, 988
Nicholson, Francis, 91
Nickelodeons, 651, 652, 724

Nightingale, Florence, 467
Nimitz, Chester, 798
Nineteenth Amendment, 659 (map), 671, 673, 700
Ninigret (sachem), 65 (illus.)
Ninth Amendment, 198
Nisei, 805, 810
Nixon, Richard M., 836, 838; Cambodia and, 908; character of, 925; "Checkers" speech of, 864; China and, 923 (illus.), 923–924; domestic policy of, 924–929; election of 1952 and, 840; election of 1960 and, 877; election of 1968 and, 906, 918–919, 919 (map); election of 1972 and, 906, 929–930; Hiss and, 837; impeachment and, 931; Khrushchev and, 852 (illus.); in Latin America, 853; law and order theme of, 887, 927–928; pardon of, 948; resignation of, 931; Soviet Union and, 924; world affairs and, 919–924
Nixon Doctrine, 920
Nixonomics, 926
Nobel Prize winners: Addams as, 678; Annan as, 1023; Carter as, 950 (illus.); Compton as, 732; Ochoa as, 869; Roosevelt, Theodore, as, 682
Noble, Elaine, 942
Noble, Thomas, 368 (illus.)
"Noble savages": Indians as, 342
Nonconsumption agreements: women and, 143
Nonfarming societies, 14–16
Nonfiction, 802
Nonimportation, 146, 151–152
Non-Intercourse Act (1809), 241
Nonslaveholders, 351, 463
Nonviolence, 802, 887
Nonwhites: equality and, 174; limitations on, 222–224; as loyalists, 162; voting rights of, 115. See also specific groups
Noriega, Manuel, 968, 968 (illus.)
Normalcy: Harding and, 707
Norris, Frank, 645
Norris, George, 666, 719, 753
Norse, 15–16, 38, 38 (map)
North: black migration to, 623–624, 655–656, 698–699, 768, 803; Civil War and, 433, 439–443, 460–468; draft in, 440; finances of, 441; free blacks in, 275–276; French Revolution and, 207; McCormick reaper and, 319; public school

Profit sharing, 646

Progreso (Treviño), 935 (illus.)

Progress and Poverty (George), 571

Progressive education, 862

Progressive Era, 591, 640–673

Progressive party: of 1912, 667, 673; of 1948, 832–833; La Follette and (1924), 719

Progressivism, 642–646; African-Americans and, 657; labor and, 660–662; moral reform and, 651–652; racism and, 655–656; Roosevelt, Theodore, and, 662–666; state and local, 646–656; Taft and, 666–670; Wilson and, 670–673; women and, 657–660; World War I and, 701–702

Prohibition, 701, 736–737, 737 (illus.); campaign, 652–653

Prohibition and Home Protection Party, 612

Project Head Start, *see* Head Start

"Pro-life" advocates, 943, 988

Promise Keepers, 989

Promise of American Life, The (Croly), 645, 667

Promontory Point, Utah, 502, 523

Propaganda: red, 835; in World War II, 794, 794 (illus.), 799–800; yellow peril and, 787

Property, 115; rights to, 145, 490; slaves as, 35; for voting, 178, 276, 287, 621; wealth and, 275; women and, 60

Prophet, The, *see* Tenskwatawa

Prophetstown, 242

Proportional representation, 187

Proposition 13 (California), 952

Proprietary colonies: Maryland as, 69; in New York and New Jersey, 79–80

Proslavery argument, 357–358, 358 (illus.)

Prosperity, 1003–1004; furniture ownership and, 101 (illus.); technology and, 325–326; in World War I, 698

Prosser, Gabriel, 346, 368

Prostitution, 589–590, 652; in antebellum theaters, 332; in New Orleans, 599; in World War I, 687, 688 (illus.), 690, 701; in World War II, 809

Protective tariffs, 287, 291, 293, 390

Protest(s): antinuclear, 958; antiwar, 900–901, 901 (illus.), 906–910; by blacks after Reconstruction, 623;

against British, 123–124, 128–129; against customs agents, 145; in depression of 1893-1897, 625, 626 (illus.); against globalization, 1004; by Hispanics, 893–894; by Indians, 892–893; by labor, 273–274, 383–384; by merchants and artisans, 141–142; in 1970s, 937–942; against Quartering Act, 139–140; against racial violence, 699; by slaves, 105; against Stamp Act, 134 (illus.), 135–137; student, 871; youth movement and, 907–908. *See also* Abolitionism; Anti-draft riots; Civil rights movement

Protestantism: in 1950s, 862; in 1970s, 944; black, 119; evangelical, 301; Great Awakening and, 118–120; institutional church movement in, 590; Luther and, 31; in Maryland, 69; in Massachusetts, 91; Methodists and, 300; Social Gospel and, 590. *See also* Religion; specific denominations

Providence: settlements near, 57

Provincial congresses, 152

Psychedelics, 911

Psychology: problems after World War II, 816; testing in World War I, 687

Ptolemy, 34

Public Credit Act (1869), 502

Public domain, 259, 263

Public education, *see* Education

Public Friends, 82

Public health, 650–651; AIDS and, 942–943; immigrants and, 654; influenza epidemic and, 700–701, 701 (illus.); movements and, 329; in 1990s, 979; urban reform and, 650–651; in World War I, 691; yellow fever and, 680. *See also* Health; Medicine; Sanitation

Public land: Homestead Act and, 461; Morrill Land Grant Act and, 461; Ordinance of 1785 and, 262. *See also* Land

Public Lands Committee: Hetch Hetchy Valley plan and, 668–669

Public opinion, 212; clergy political protests and, 139; on women's role, 861

Public schools: prayer in, 886; progressive thought and, 645; in recession of 1990s, 971; reform of, 307–308; segregation in, 623. *See also* Education; Schools

Public transportation: desegregation of, 833; segregation of, 496; suburbs and, 582

Public utilities, 714

Public virtue, 138, 230

Public works: debate over, 668–669; in South, 490; WPA and, 756

Public Works Administration (PWA), 755, 757

Publishing industry, 597–600, 634–635

Puddling, 267

Pueblo Bonito, Chaco Canyon (New Mexico), 9, 9 (illus.)

Pueblo Indians, 44–45, 84–85, 112, 515

Pueblo Revolt, 84–85, 112

Puerperal fever, 329

Puerto Rico and Puerto Ricans, 43, 633, 946, 982; immigrants and, 769, 868; militance and, 894; slaves in, 40–41

Pulitzer, Joseph, 546, 594, 632

Pullman, George, 570

Pullman Palace Car Company, 547, 570

Pullman strike, 570, 625, 626

Purchasing power, 565

Pure Food and Drug Act (1906), 664, 671

Puritans and Puritanism: Church of England and, 58; commerce and, 86; education and, 56–57; Elizabeth I and, 33; in England, 32–33, 55; Half-Way Covenant and, 61–62; Indians and, 55–56; market economy and, 58; on marriage partners, 279; Massachusetts Bay and, 55; in New England, 49; in New Jersey, 80. *See also* Separatists

Purity campaign, 589–590

Purvis, James, 174

Push factors: for immigration, 578

Putin, Vladimir, 1009

Put-in-Bay, battle at, 245

Putnam, Israel, 174

Putnam, Mary, 584

Putnam, Robert, 987

Puyallup Indians, 892, 946

Pyle, Ernie, 811

Pynchon, John, 62

Pyramids, 6–7, 7 (illus.)

El-Qadaffi, Muammar, 961

Quaeda, Al, *see* Al Quaeda

Quaker Oats, 556

Quakers: antislavery attitudes of, 175; Great Awakening and, 119; in New Jersey, 80; in Pennsylvania, 80–82

Quality of life, *see* Lifestyle

612; Insurgents of, 666–667; Kansas-Nebraska Act and, 418; McCarthyism and, 838–839; in 1920s, 717–719; Reconstruction and, 488–490, 489 (illus.), 503–504; regional strength of, 612; in World War II, 794–795. *See also* Liberal Republicans; Radical Republicans; specific presidents

Republicans, 138; after Revolution, 174; revolutionary leaders as, 179

Republicans (Jeffersonian), 211–212

Republic of Hawaii, 631

Republic of Korea, *see* South Korea

Republic of Texas, 378

Republic Steel Company: strike at, 767

Research and development (R&D): genetic research and, 1010–1011; in 1950s, 854, 855

Research university, 586

"Reservationists," 705

Reservations (Indian), 515, 946; Dawes Severalty Act and, 518–519, 519 (map); in New Deal, 762; for New England Indians, 63; resettlement on, 255; termination of, 869

Resettlement Administration, 757, 763

Residential segregation, 582

Resistance: to Coercive Acts, 152; to discrimination, 768–769; to Quartering Act, 139–140; religion, ideology, and, 137–138; by slaves, 368–369; women and, 142–143; youth movement and, 907–908. *See also* Protest(s); Rebellions; Revolts; specific acts

Resources: New Deal planning for, 761–762

Restoration (England, 1660), 61, 90

Restoration colonies, 77, 79

Restraint of trade: trusts and, 551

Retailing: chain stores in, 711–712; department stores and, 584–585, 585 (illus.), 652; discount stores and, 935–936

Retirees: recession and, 1012

Reuben James (ship), 787

Reuf, Abe, 646

Reuther, Walter, 766, 767, 767 (illus.), 768

Revels, Hiram, 489

Revenue acts, 128–129; of 1767, 140–141; of 1942, 793. *See also* Wealth Tax Act; specific acts

Revenue tariff, 390

Revere, Paul, 122 (illus.), 152

Revivalism: in East, 300–301; First Great Awakening and, 118–120; New Lights and, 119; Second Great Awakening and, 278, 299–300

Revolts: peasant, 28; Pueblo, 84–85; in Richmond, Virginia, 223; on Saint Domingue, 223; by Toussaint L'Ouverture, 232. *See also* Protest(s); Rebellions

Revolution(s): African-American, 887–888; of 1848, 383; in Mexico, 683; in Russia, 704. *See also* American Revolution; specific countries

Revolving pistol, 321, 321 (illus.), 322

Reynolds v. *Sims,* 886

Rheims: in World War I, 691

Rhett, Robert Barnwell, 431

Rhineland, 783

Rhode Island, 57, 58, 91, 154

Rhodes, James, 909 (illus.)

Rhythm-and-blues, 871

Rice, Condoleezza, 1007

Rice, Joseph Mayer, 604

Rice, Sally, 279

Rice industry, 77–78, 95

Rich, *see* Wealth

Rich, Frank, 988

Richards, Ann, 976

Richards, Samuel, 494

Richardson, Elliot, 930, 931

Richmond, 350, 367 (illus.), 442, 446; fall of, 471–472

Richmond, David, 875

Richthofen, Manfred von ("Red Baron"), 690

Rickenbacker, Edward, 703

Rickover, Hyman, 851

Ridge, Tom, 1018

Riesman, David, 857

Rifle, 444–445

"Rifle Clubs," 505

Rigas, John J., 1021

Right, the, *see* Conservatives and conservatism; Right wing

Rights: of African-Americans, 223; of enemy citizens, 213–214; of Englishmen, 133; of Indians, 946; of preemption, 263; in state constitutions, 178; Warren Court and, 886. *See also* Reform and reform movements; specific rights

"Right to Life" movement, 943

Right wing: Dulles and, 850; Goldwater and, 884; in Great Depression, 755–756; militant blacks and, 891

Right-wing militia, 988–989

Riis, Jacob, 580, 588, 635 (illus.)

Rimmer, Robert, 915

Rio de Janeiro environmental conference, 972

Rio Grande River, 112, 395, 398

Riots: in Alton, Illinois, 309; antidraft, 463; Astor Place, 321, 332; for food in South, 462; in Harlem, 768; after King's death, 917; in Los Angeles, 971. *See also* Race riots

Rivers, 262, 264–265, 268 (map), 269. *See also* specific river regions

Riyadh, Saudi Arabia: terrorist bombing in, 994

Roads and highways, 268 (map); of Inca, 8; interstate highway system and, 845, 846–847; legislation for, 672; National Road and, 259; in 1950s, 859

Roanoke colony, 45, 46–47

Robards, Rachel, 289

Robber barons, 546

Robertson, Pat, 944, 952, 973, 975, 989

Robinson, Christopher, 70

Robinson, Jackie, 804, 831, 832 (illus.)

Rochester, New York: revivalism in, 300–301

Rock, John, 896

Rock-and-roll, 870–871

Rockefeller, John D., 549–550, 557, 582, 585, 628

Rockefeller, John D., Jr., 652

Rockets: Goddard and, 732. *See also* Space exploration

Rockingham, Marquis de, 137, 139

Rockwell, Norman, 723, 842 (illus.)

Rocky Mountains, 15, 237

Rococo furniture, 327

Roe v. *Wade,* 912, 938–939, 943, 972

Roghman, Geertruyd, 28 (illus.)

Rolfe, Mary, 59

Rolling Stones, 912

Roman Catholic Church, *see* Catholicism

Romania, 795, 820

Romanticism, 335

Romantic love, 279

Rome-Berlin-Tokyo Axis, 786

Rommel, Erwin, 795

Romona (Jackson), 530

Roosevelt, Eleanor, 743, 744, 750, 750 (illus.), 757, 759, 765

Roosevelt, Franklin D., 670, 743, 750 (illus.), 782; African-Americans and, 802–803; criticism of, 755–756; death